WHO WAS WHO

VOLUME XII

2006–2010

WHO'S WHO

An annual biographical dictionary
first published in 1849

WHO WAS WHO

WHO WAS WHO VOLUME XII

WHO WAS WHO

2006–2010

A COMPANION TO

WHO'S WHO

CONTAINING THE BIOGRAPHIES
OF THOSE WHO DIED DURING
THE PERIOD 2006–2010

A & C BLACK
LONDON

FIRST PUBLISHED 2011
BY A&C BLACK PUBLISHERS LTD
36 SOHO SQUARE, LONDON W1D 3QY

COPYRIGHT © 2011 A&C BLACK PUBLISHERS LTD

ISBN 978-1-408-14658-3

Printed in the UK by
MPG Books Ltd, Bodmin

PREFACE

This, the twelfth volume of biographies removed from *Who's Who* on account of death, contains the entries of those who died between 2006 and 2010. Those whose deaths occurred before the end of 2005, but were not reported until after the volume of *Who Was Who* covering the years 2001–2005 had been published, are listed as Addenda at the beginning of the biographical section.

The entries are as they last appeared in *Who's Who*, with the date of death added and in some cases further information, such as posthumous publications. It has not always been possible to ascertain the exact date of death, and the editors will welcome such information for inclusion in the next edition of this volume.

CONTENTS

ABBREVIATIONS USED IN THIS BOOK

Some of the designatory letters in this list are used merely for economy of space and do not necessarily imply any professional or other qualification.

A

AA	Anti-aircraft; Automobile Association; Architectural Association; Augustinians of the Assumption; Associate in Arts
AAA	Amateur Athletic Association; American Accounting Association; Abdominal Aortic Aneurysm
AAAL	American Academy of Arts and Letters
AA&QMG	Assistant Adjutant and Quartermaster-General
AAAS	American Association for the Advancement of Science
AABC	(Register of) Architects Accredited in Building Conservation
AAG	Assistant Adjutant-General
AAMC	Australian Army Medical Corps (now see RAAMC)
A&AEE	Aeroplane and Armament Experimental Establishment
A&E	Accident and Emergency
A and SH	Argyll and Sutherland Highlanders
AAS	American Astronomical Society
AASA	Associate, Australian Society of Accountants (now see FCPA)
AB	Bachelor of Arts (US); able-bodied seaman; airborne; Alberta (postal)
ABC	Australian Broadcasting Commission; American Broadcasting Companies; Amateur Boxing Club; Associate, Birmingham Conservatoire
ABI	Association of British Insurers
ABM	Advisory Board of Ministry
ABP	Associated British Ports
ABRC	Advisory Board for the Research Councils
ABSA	Association for Business Sponsorship of the Arts
ABTA	Association of British Travel Agents
AC	Companion, Order of Australia; Ante Christum (before Christ)
ACA	Associate, Institute of Chartered Accountants
Acad.	Academy
ACARD	Advisory Council for Applied Research and Development
ACAS	Advisory, Conciliation and Arbitration Service; Assistant Chief of the Air Staff
ACC	Association of County Councils; Anglican Consultative Council
ACCM	Advisory Council for the Church's Ministry (now see ABM)
ACDS	Assistant Chief of Defence Staff
ACF	Army Cadet Force
ACGI	Associate, City and Guilds of London Institute
ACI	Airports Council International (Europe)
ACIB	Associate, Chartered Institute of Bankers
ACII	Associate, Chartered Insurance Institute
ACIS	Associate, Institute of Chartered Secretaries and Administrators (formerly Chartered Institute of Secretaries)
ACM	Association of Computing Machinery
ACMA	Associate, Chartered Institute of Management Accountants (formerly Institute of Cost and Management Accountants)
ACNS	Assistant Chief of Naval Staff
ACOS	Assistant Chief of Staff
ACOST	Advisory Council on Science and Technology
ACPO	Association of Chief Police Officers
ACS	American Chemical Society; Additional Curates Society
acsc	passed Advanced Command and Staff Course
AcSS	Member, Academy of Learned Societies for the Social Sciences
ACT	Australian Capital Territory; Australian College of Theology; Associate, College of Technology; Association of Corporate Treasurers
ACU	Association of Commonwealth Universities
ACWA	Associate, Institute of Cost and Works Accountants (now see ACMA)
AD	Dame of the Order of Australia; Anno Domini (in the year of the Lord); Air Defence
ADAS	Agricultural Development and Advisory Service
ADC	Aide-de-camp; Association of District Councils
Adjt	Adjutant
Adm.	Admiral
ADMS	Assistant Director of Medical Services
ADP	Automatic Data Processing
Adv.	Advisory; Advocate
AE	Air Efficiency Award
AEA	Atomic Energy Authority; Air Efficiency Award (now see AE); American Economic Association
AEC	Agriculture Executive Council; Army Educational Corps (now see RAEC); Atomic Energy Commission
AEEU	Amalgamated Engineering and Electrical Union
AEI	Associated Electrical Industries
AER	Army Emergency Reserve
AERE	Atomic Energy Research Establishment (Harwell)
AEU	Amalgamated Engineering Union (later AEEU)
AFASIC	Association for All Speech Impaired Children
AFC	Air Force Cross; Association Football Club
AFCEA	Armed Forces Communications and Electronics Association
AFCENT	Allied Forces in Central Europe
AFD	Doctor of Fine Arts (US)
AFHQ	Allied Force Headquarters
AFIAP	Artiste, Fédération Internationale de l'Art Photographique
AFNORTH	Allied Forces in Northern Europe
AFOM	Associate, Faculty of Occupational Medicine
AFRAeS	Associate Fellow, Royal Aeronautical Society (now see MRAeS)
AFRC	Agricultural and Food Research Council (now see BBSRC)
AG	Attorney-General
AGC	Adjutant General's Corps

AGR	Advanced Gas-cooled Reactor
AHA	Area Health Authority; American Hospitals Association; Associate, Institute of Health Service Administrators (later AHSM)
AHA(T)	Area Health Authority (Teaching)
AHQ	Army Headquarters
ai	*ad interim*
AIA	Associate, Institute of Actuaries; American Institute of Architects; Association of International Artists
AIAA	American Institute of Aeronautics and Astronautics
AID	Artificial Insemination by Donor
AIDS	Acquired Immunity Deficiency Syndrome
AIE	Associate, Institute of Education
AIF	Australian Imperial Forces
AIFireE	Associate, Institution of Fire Engineers
AIG	Adjutant-Inspector-General
AIIRA	Associate, International Industrial Relations Association
AIMarE	Associate, Institute of Marine Engineers
AIMBE	American Institute for Medical and Biological Engineering
AIME	American Institute of Mechanical Engineers
AJAG	Assistant Judge Advocate General
AK	Knight, Order of Australia; Alaska (postal)
AKC	Associate, King's College London
Ala	Alabama
ALCD	Associate, London College of Divinity
ALFSEA	Allied Land Forces South-East Asia
ALI	Argyll Light Infantry; Associate, Landscape Institute (*now see* MLI)
Alta	Alberta
AM	Albert Medal; Member, Order of Australia; Master of Arts (US); Alpes Maritimes
AMA	Association of Metropolitan Authorities; Assistant Masters Association (later AMMA, *now see* ATL); Associate, Museums Association; Australian Medical Association
AMARC	Associated Marine and Related Charities
Amb.	Ambulance; Ambassador
AMCT	Associate, Manchester College of Technology
AMF	Australian Military Forces
AMICE	Associate Member, Institution of Civil Engineers (*now see* MICE)
AMIMechE	Associate Member, Institution of Mechanical Engineers (*now see* MIMechE)
AMP	Advanced Management Program; Air Member for Personnel
AMRC	Association of Medical Research Charities
AMS	Assistant Military Secretary; Army Medical Services
Anat.	Anatomy; Anatomical
ANU	Australian National University
ANZAAS	Australian and New Zealand Association for the Advancement of Science
Anzac	Australian and New Zealand Army Corps
AO	Officer, Order of Australia; Air Officer
AOA	Air Officer in charge of Administration
AOC	Air Officer Commanding
AOC-in-C	Air Officer Commanding-in-Chief
APEX	Association of Professional, Executive, Clerical and Computer Staff
APHA	American Public Health Association
APS	Aborigines Protection Society; American Physical Society
AQ	Administration and Quartering
AQMG	Assistant Quartermaster-General
ARA	Associate, Royal Academy; Armada de la República Argentina
ARAD	Associate, Royal Academy of Dancing

ARAgS	Associate, Royal Agricultural Societies (*ie* of England, Scotland and Wales)
ARAM	Associate, Royal Academy of Music
ARAS	Associate, Royal Astronomical Society
ARBS	Associate, Royal Society of British Sculptors
ARC	Architects' Registration Council (*now see* ARB); Agricultural Research Council (later AFRC); Aeronautical Research Council; Arthritis and Rheumatism Council
ARCA	Associate, Royal College of Art; Associate, Royal Canadian Academy
ARCM	Associate, Royal College of Music
ARCO	Associate, Royal College of Organists
ARCS	Associate, Royal College of Science; Accreditation Review and Consulting Service (*now see* ISI)
ARCVS	Associate, Royal College of Veterinary Surgeons
ARE	Associate, Royal Society of Painter-Printmakers (*formerly* of Painter-Etchers and Engravers); Arab Republic of Egypt; Admiralty Research Establishment
ARIAS	Associate, Royal Incorporation of Architects in Scotland
ARIBA	Associate, Royal Institute of British Architects (*now see* RIBA)
ARIC	Associate, Royal Institute of Chemistry (later MRIC; *now see* MRSC)
ARPS	Associate, Royal Photographic Society
ARSM	Associate, Royal School of Mines
AS	Anglo-Saxon
ASA	Associate Member, Society of Actuaries; Associate of Society of Actuaries (US); Australian Society of Accountants; Army Sailing Association; Advertising Standards Authority; Alment Aksjeselskap
ASC	Administrative Staff College, Henley
ASCE	American Society of Civil Engineers
ASCL	Association of School and College Leaders
ASD	Armament Supply Department
ASH	Action on Smoking and Health
ASLIB or Aslib	Association for Information Management (*formerly* Association of Special Libraries and Information Bureaux)
ASM	Association of Senior Members; Australian Service Medal
ASME	American Society of Mechanical Engineers; Association for the Study of Medical Education
Asst	Assistant
ASTMS	Association of Scientific, Technical and Managerial Staffs (subsequently part of MSF)
ASWE	Admiralty Surface Weapons Establishment
ATC	Air Training Corps; Art Teacher's Certificate
ATD	Art Teacher's Diploma
ATI	Associate, Textile Institute
ato	Ammunition Technical Officer
ATP	Association of Tennis Players
ATV	Associated Television (*formerly* Association TeleVision)
AUEW	Amalgamated Union of Engineering Workers (later AEU, then AEEU)
AUS	Army of the United States
AWA	Anglian Water Authority
AWRE	Atomic Weapons Research Establishment
aws	Graduate of Air Warfare Course
AZ	Arizona (postal)

B

b	born; brother
BA	Bachelor of Arts
BAA	British Airports Authority; British Accounting Association
BAAB	British Amateur Athletic Board
BAAL	British Association for Applied Linguistics
BAAS	British Association for the Advancement of Science
BAC	British Aircraft Corporation
BAe	British Aerospace
BAFTA	British Academy of Film and Television Arts
BALPA	British Air Line Pilots' Association
BAO	Bachelor of Art of Obstetrics
BAOR	British Army of the Rhine (*formerly* on the Rhine)
BAppSc(MT)	Bachelor of Applied Science (Medical Technology)
BAPS	British Association of Plastic Surgeons
BArch	Bachelor of Architecture
Bart	Baronet
BASCA	British Academy of Songwriters, Composers and Authors
Batt.	Battery
BBA	British Bankers' Association; Bachelor of Business Administration
BBC	British Broadcasting Corporation
BBSRC	Biotechnology and Biological Sciences Research Council
BC	Before Christ; British Columbia; Borough Council
BCAR	British Civil Airworthiness Requirements
BCC	British Council of Churches (later CCBI)
BCh or **BChir**	Bachelor of Surgery
BChD	Bachelor of Dental Surgery
BCIA	British Clothing Industries Association
BCL	Bachelor of Civil Law
BCOF	British Commonwealth Occupation Force
BCom or **BComm**	Bachelor of Commerce
BCPC	British Crop Protection Council
BCS	Bengal Civil Service; British Computer Society; Bachelor of Combined Studies
Bd	Board
BD	Bachelor of Divinity
BDA	British Dental Association; British Deaf Association; British Dyslexia Association
Bde	Brigade
BDS	Bachelor of Dental Surgery
BE	Bachelor of Engineering; British Element
BEA	British East Africa; British European Airways; British Epilepsy Association
BEC	Business Education Council (*now see* BTEC)
BEd	Bachelor of Education
Beds	Bedfordshire
BEF	British Expeditionary Force; British Equestrian Federation
BEM	British Empire Medal
BEMAS	British Educational Management and Administration Society
BEME	Brigade Electrical and Mechanical Engineer
BEng	Bachelor of Engineering
Berks	Berkshire
BESO	British Executive Service Overseas
BFI	British Film Institute
BFSS	British Field Sports Society
BGCStJ	Bailiff Grand Cross, Most Venerable Order of the Hospital of St John of Jerusalem
BGS	Brigadier General Staff
Bhd	Berhad
BHF	British Heart Foundation
BHRA	British Hydromechanics Research Association
BHRCA	British Hotels, Restaurants and Caterers' Association (*now see* BHA)
BHS	British Horse Society
BICC	British Insulated Callender's Cables
BIM	British Institute of Management
BIR	British Institute of Radiology
BIS	Bank for International Settlements; British Interplanetary Society; Department for Business, Innovation and Skills
BISPA	British Independent Steel Producers Association
BISRA	British Iron and Steel Research Association
BITC	Business in the Community
BJSM	British Joint Services Mission
BL	Bachelor of Law; British Library
BLA	British Liberation Army
BLitt	Bachelor of Letters
BM	British Museum; Bachelor of Medicine; Brigade Major; British Monomark
BMA	British Medical Association
BMG	British Military Government
BMJ	British Medical Journal
BMRA	Brigade Major Royal Artillery
Bn	Battalion
BNEC	British National Export Council
BNOC	British National Oil Corporation; British National Opera Company
BNP	Banque Nationale de Paris; British National Party
BOAC	British Overseas Airways Corporation
BoT	Board of Trade
BOTB	British Overseas Trade Board
Bp	Bishop
BPA	British Paediatric Association (later CPCH; *now see* RCPCH); Bachelor of Performing Arts
BPG	Broadcasting Press Guild
BPharm	Bachelor of Pharmacy
BPMF	British Postgraduate Medical Federation
BR	British Rail
Br.	Branch
BRA	Brigadier Royal Artillery; British Rheumatism & Arthritis Association
BRB	British Railways Board
BRCS	British Red Cross Society
Brig.	Brigadier
BRIT	British Recording Industry Trust
BRNC	Britannia Royal Naval College
BS	Bachelor of Surgery; Bachelor of Science; British Standard
BSA	Bachelor of Scientific Agriculture; Birmingham Small Arms; Building Societies' Association
BSc	Bachelor of Science
BSC	British Steel Corporation; Bengal Staff Corps
BScEcon	Bachelor of Science in Economics
BScEng	Bachelor of Science in Engineering
BSI	British Standards Institution
BSJA	British Show Jumping Association
Bt	Baronet; Brevet
BT	Bachelor of Teaching; British Telecommunications
BTA	British Tourist Authority (*formerly* British Travel Association)
BTDB	British Transport Docks Board (*now see* ABP)
BTEC	Business and Technology (*formerly* Technician) Education Council
BTS	Bachelor of Theological Studies

Bucks	Buckinghamshire
BUPA	British United Provident Association
BV	Besloten Vennootschap
BVA	British Veterinary Association; British Video Association

C

C	Conservative; 100
c	child; cousin; *circa* (about)
CA	Central America; County Alderman; Chartered Accountant (Scotland and Canada); California (postal)
CAA	Civil Aviation Authority
CAAV	(Member of) Central Association of Agricultural Valuers
CAB	Citizens' Advice Bureau; Centre for Agricultural and Biosciences (*formerly* Commonwealth Agricultural Bureau)
CABE	Commission for Architecture and the Built Environment
CACTM	Central Advisory Council of Training for the Ministry (later ACCM; *now see* ABM)
Calif	California
CAM	Communications, Advertising and Marketing
Cambs	Cambridgeshire
C&G	City and Guilds of London Institute
Cantab	*Cantabrigiensis* (of Cambridge)
CAP	Common Agricultural Policy
Capt.	Captain
CARE	Cottage and Rural Enterprises
CAS	Chief of the Air Staff
CB	Companion, Order of the Bath; County Borough
CBC	County Borough Council
CBE	Commander, Order of the British Empire
CBI	Confederation of British Industry
CBIM	Companion, British Institute of Management (later CIMgt)
CBiol	Chartered Biologist
CC	Companion, Order of Canada; City Council; County Council; Cricket Club; Cycling Club; County Court
CCAB	Consultative Committee of Accountancy Bodies
CCBE	Commission Consultative des Barreaux de la Communauté Européenne
CCBI	Council of Churches for Britain and Ireland
CCC	Corpus Christi College; Central Criminal Court; County Cricket Club
CCF	Combined Cadet Force
CCG	Control Commission Germany
CCH	Cacique's Crown of Honour, Order of Service of Guyana
CChem	Chartered Chemist
CCJ	Council of Christians and Jews
CCMI	Companion, Chartered Management Institute
CCPR	Central Council of Physical Recreation
CD	Canadian Forces Decoration; Commander, Order of Distinction (Jamaica); Civil Defence; Compact Disc
Cdo	Commando
Cdre	Commodore
CDS	Chief of the Defence Staff
CDU	Christlich-Demokratische Union
CE	Civil Engineer
CEC	Commission of the European Communities
CECD	Confédération Européenne du Commerce de Détail
CEDR	Centre for Effective Dispute Resolution

CEED	Centre for Economic and Environmental Development
CEGB	Central Electricity Generating Board
CEIR	Corporation for Economic and Industrial Research
CEMA	Council for the Encouragement of Music and Arts
CEng	Chartered Engineer
Cento	Central Treaty Organisation
CEnv	Chartered Environmentalist
CEO	Chief Executive Officer
CERN	Organisation (*formerly* Centre) Européenne pour la Recherche Nucléaire
CF	Chaplain to the Forces; Companion, Order of Fiji; Corporate Finance
CFE	Central Fighter Establishment
CFS	Central Flying School; Chronic Fatigue Syndrome
CGA	Community of the Glorious Ascension; Country Gentlemen's Association
CGeol	Chartered Geologist
CGIA	Insignia Award of City and Guilds of London Institute (*now see* FCGI)
CGLI	City and Guilds of London Institute (*now see* C&G)
CGRM	Commandant-General Royal Marines
CGS	Chief of the General Staff
CH	Companion of Honour
Chap.	Chaplain
ChB	Bachelor of Surgery
CHB	Companion of Honour of Barbados
CHC	Community Health Council
ChM	Master of Surgery
Chm.	Chairman or Chairwoman
ChStJ	Chaplain, Most Venerable Order of the Hospital of St John of Jerusalem
CI	Imperial Order of the Crown of India; Channel Islands
CIArb	Chartered Institute of Arbitrators
CIB	Chartered Institute of Bankers
CID	Criminal Investigation Department
CIE	Companion, Order of the Indian Empire; Confédération Internationale des Etudiants
CIEx	Companion, Institute of Export
CIGEM	Companion, Institution of Gas Engineers and Managers
CIGS	Chief of the Imperial General Staff (*now see* CGS)
CIIA	Canadian Institute of International Affairs
CILT	Chartered Institute of Logistics and Transport
CIMA	Chartered Institute of Management Accountants
CIMarE	Companion, Institute of Marine Engineers
CIMgt	Companion, Institute of Management (*now see* CCMI)
C-in-C	Commander-in-Chief
CIPFA	Chartered Institute of Public Finance and Accountancy
CIPM	Companion, Institute of Personnel Management (later CIPD)
CIS	Institute of Chartered Secretaries and Administrators (*formerly* Chartered Institute of Secretaries); Command Control Communications and Information Systems; Commonwealth of Independent States
CIT	Chartered Institute of Transport; California Institute of Technology
CITP	Chartered Information Technology Professional
cl	*cum laude*

Cl.	Class
CLA	Country Land & Business Association (*formerly* Country Landowners' Association)
CLIC	Cancer and Leukemia in Childhood
CLit	Companion of Literature (Royal Society of Literature Award)
CLP	Constituency Labour Party
CM	Member, Order of Canada; Congregation of the Mission (Vincentians); Master in Surgery; Certificated Master; Canadian Militia
CMA	Canadian Medical Association; Cost and Management Accountant (NZ)
CMAC	Catholic Marriage Advisory Council
CMath	Chartered Mathematician
CMB	Central Midwives' Board
CMF	Commonwealth Military Forces; Central Mediterranean Force
CMG	Companion, Order of St Michael and St George
CMILT	Chartered Member, Chartered Institute of Logistics and Transport
CMM	Commander, Order of Military Merit (Canada)
CMO	Chief Medical Officer
CMP	Corps of Military Police
CMS	Church Mission (*formerly* Church Missionary) Society; Certificate in Management Studies
CNAA	Council for National Academic Awards
CND	Campaign for Nuclear Disarmament
CNRS	Centre National de la Recherche Scientifique
CNZM	Companion, New Zealand Order of Merit
CO	Commanding Officer; Commonwealth Office (after Aug. 1966) (*now see* FCO); Colonial Office (before Aug. 1966); Conscientious Objector; Colorado (postal)
Co.	County; Company
C of E	Church of England
C of I	Church of Ireland
C of S	Chief of Staff; Church of Scotland
COI	Central Office of Information
Col	Colonel
Coll.	College; Collegiate
Colo	Colorado
Comd	Command
Comdg	Commanding
Comdr	Commander
Comdt	Commandant
COMEC	Council of the Military Education Committees of the Universities of the UK
Commn	Commission
Commnd	Commissioned
CompICE	Companion, Institution of Civil Engineers
CompIERE	Companion, Institution of Electronic and Radio Engineers
CompIMechE	Companion, Institution of Mechanical Engineers
CompOR	Companion, Operational Research Society
CompTI	Companion of the Textile Institute
Comr	Commissioner
Conn	Connecticut
Const.	Constitutional
Co-op.	Co-operative
COPUS	Committee on the Public Understanding of Science
Corp.	Corporation; Corporal
Corresp. Mem.	Corresponding Member
COS	Chief of Staff; Charity Organization Society
COSPAR	Committee on Space Research

CP	Central Provinces; Cape Province; Congregation of the Passion
CPA	Commonwealth Parliamentary Association; Chartered Patent Agent; Certified Public Accountant (USA)
CPAG	Child Poverty Action Group
CPC	Conservative Political Centre
CPEng	Chartered Professional Engineer (of Institution of Engineers of Australia)
CPFA	Member or Associate, Chartered Institute of Public Finance and Accountancy
CPHVA	Community Practitioners & Health Visitors' Association
CPhys	Chartered Physicist
CPRE	Campaign to Protect Rural England (*formerly* Council for the Protection of Rural England)
CPRW	Campaign for the Protection of Rural Wales
CPS	Crown Prosecution Service; Certificate in Pastoral Studies
CPSA	Civil and Public Services Association; Church of the Province of South Africa
CPSU	Communist Party of the Soviet Union
CQSW	Certificate of Qualification in Social Work
cr	created or creation
CR	Community of the Resurrection
CRA	Commander, Royal Artillery
CRAeS	Companion, Royal Aeronautical Society
CRC	Cancer Research Campaign; Community Relations Council
CRE	Commander, Royal Engineers; Commission for Racial Equality; Commercial Relations and Exports; Conference of Rectors of European Universities (*formerly* Association of European Universities)
Cres.	Crescent
CRO	Commonwealth Relations Office (*now see* FCO)
CS	Civil Service; Clerk to the Signet; Companion, Order of Samoa
CSAB	Civil Service Appeal Board
CSCE	Conference on Security and Co-operation in Europe
CSci	Chartered Scientist
CSD	Civil Service Department; Co-operative Secretaries Diploma; Chartered Society of Designers
CSEU	Confederation of Shipbuilding and Engineering Unions
CSI	Companion, Order of the Star of India; Cross, Order of Solomon Islands
CSIR	Commonwealth Council for Scientific and Industrial Research (*now see* CSIRO); Council of Scientific and Industrial Research, India
CSIRO	Commonwealth Scientific and Industrial Research Organization (Australia)
CSO	Chief Scientific Officer; Chief Signal Officer; Chief Staff Officer; Central Statistical Office
CSP	Chartered Society of Physiotherapists; Civil Service of Pakistan
CSSB	Civil Service Selection Board
CSTI	Council of Science and Technology Institutes
CStJ	Commander, Most Venerable Order of the Hospital of St John of Jerusalem
CSU	Christlich-Soziale Union in Bayern
CSV	Community Service Volunteers
CT	Connecticut (postal)
CTC	Cyclists' Touring Club; Commando Training Centre; City Technology College

CText	Chartered Textile Technologist
CU	Cambridge University
CUAC	Cambridge University Athletic Club; Colleges and Universities of the Anglican Communion
CUF	Common University Fund
CUNY	City University of New York
CVCP	Committee of Vice-Chancellors and Principals of the Universities of the United Kingdom (*now see* UUK)
CVO	Commander, Royal Victorian Order
CVS	Council for Voluntary Service
CVSNA	Council of Voluntary Service National Association
CWA	Crime Writers Association
CWS	Co-operative Wholesale Society

D

D	Duke
d	died; daughter
DA	Dame of St Andrew, Order of Barbados; Diploma in Anaesthesia; Diploma in Art; Doctor of Arts
DAA	Diploma in Archive Administration
DAA&QMG	Deputy Assistant Adjutant and Quartermaster-General
DA&QMG	Deputy Adjutant and Quartermaster-General
DAAG	Deputy Assistant Adjutant-General
DAC	Development Assistance Committee; Diocesan Advisory Committee
DACG	Deputy Assistant Chaplain-General
DAdmin	Doctor of Administration
DAG	Deputy Adjutant-General
DAgr	Doctor of Agriculture
DAMS	Deputy Assistant Military Secretary
DAppSc	Doctor of Applied Science
DAQMG	Deputy Assistant Quartermaster-General
DArt	Doctor of Art
DArts	Doctor of Arts
DATA	Draughtsmen's and Allied Technicians' Association (later AUEW(TASS))
DAvMed	Diploma in Aviation Medicine, Royal College of Physicians
DBA	Doctor of Business Administration
DBE	Dame Commander, Order of the British Empire
DC	District Council; District of Columbia
DCB	Dame Commander, Order of the Bath
DCDS	Deputy Chief of Defence Staff
DCGS	Deputy Chief of the General Staff
DCh	Doctor of Surgery
DCH	Diploma in Child Health
DCHS	Dame Commander, Order of the Holy Sepulchre
DCL	Doctor of Civil Law; Dr of Canon Law
DCLI	Duke of Cornwall's Light Infantry
DCM	Distinguished Conduct Medal
DCMG	Dame Commander, Order of St Michael and St George
DCMS	Department for Culture, Media and Sport
DCnL	Doctor of Canon Law
DCNZM	Distinguished Companion, New Zealand Order of Merit
DCO	Duke of Cambridge's Own
DCom or DComm	Doctor of Commerce
DCSO	Deputy Chief Scientific Officer
DCVO	Dame Commander, Royal Victorian Order
DD	Doctor of Divinity
DDes	Doctor of Design

DDME	Deputy Director of Mechanical Engineering
DDMS	Deputy Director of Medical Services
DDra	Doctor of Drama
DDS	Doctor of Dental Surgery; Director of Dental Services
DDSM	Defense Distinguished Service Medal
DE	Doctor of Engineering; Delaware (postal)
DEA	Department of Economic Affairs
decd	deceased
DEd	Doctor of Education
Deleg.	Delegate
DenD	Docteur en Droit
DEng	Doctor of Engineering
Dep.	Deputy
DERA	Defence Evaluation and Research Agency
DES	Department of Education and Science (later DFE); Dr in Environmental Studies
DesRCA	Designer of the Royal College of Art
DFA	Doctor of Fine Arts
DFC	Distinguished Flying Cross
DFE	Department for Education (later DFEE)
DFEE or DfEE	Department for Education and Employment (later DFES)
DFH	Diploma of Faraday House
DFID	Department for International Development
DG	Director General; Directorate General; Dragoon Guards
DGAMS	Director-General Army Medical Services
DGCHS	Dame Grand Cross, Order of the Holy Sepulchre
DGMS	Director-General of Medical Services
DH	Doctor of Humanities
DHA	District Health Authority
Dhc	Doctor *honoris causa*
DHEW	Department of Health Education and Welfare (US)
DHL	Doctor of Humane Letters; Doctor of Hebrew Literature
DHM	Dean Hole Medal
DHMSA	Diploma in the History of Medicine (Society of Apothecaries)
DHS	Dame, Order of the Holy Sepulchre
DHSS	Department of Health and Social Security
DHum	Doctor of Humanities
DHumLit	Doctor of Humane Letters
DIAS	Dublin Institute of Advanced Sciences
DIC	Diploma of the Imperial College
DIH	Diploma in Industrial Health
Dio.	Diocese
DipArch	Diploma in Architecture
DipCE	Diploma in Civil Engineering; Diploma of a College of Education (Scotland)
DipEcon	Diploma in Economics
DipEd	Diploma in Education
DipFE	Diploma in Further Education
DipSocSc	Diploma in Social Science
DipT&CP	Diploma in Town and Country Planning
DipTh	Diploma in Theology
DistTP	Distinction in Town Planning
Div.	Division; Divorced
DJAG	Deputy Judge Advocate General
DJur	*Doctor Juris* (Doctor of Law)
DL	Deputy Lieutenant; Democratie Libérale
DLC	Diploma of Loughborough College
DLI	Durham Light Infantry
DLit or DLitt	Doctor of Literature; Doctor of Letters
DLJ	Dame of Grace, Order of St Lazarus of Jerusalem
DLO	Diploma in Laryngology and Otology
DLP	Diploma in Legal Practice; Democratic Labour Party

DM	Doctor of Medicine
DMD	Doctor of Medical Dentistry (Australia)
DMet	Doctor of Metallurgy
DMO	Director of Military Operations
DMRD	Diploma in Medical Radiological Diagnosis
DMRT	Diploma in Medical Radio-Therapy
DMS	Director of Medical Services; Decoration for Meritorious Service (South Africa); Diploma in Management Studies
DMus	Doctor of Music
DNB	Dictionary of National Biography
DNI	Director of Naval Intelligence
DO	Diploma in Ophthalmology
DOAE	Defence Operational Analysis Establishment
DObstRCOG	Diploma of Royal College of Obstetricians and Gynaecologists (now see DRCOG)
DoE	Department of the Environment
DoH	Department of Health
DoI	Department of Industry
DOMS	Diploma in Ophthalmic Medicine and Surgery
DOS	Director of Ordnance Services; Doctor of Ocular Science
DPA	Diploma in Public Administration; Discharged Prisoners' Aid; Doctor of Public Administration
DPH	Diploma in Public Health
DPh or DPhil	Doctor of Philosophy
DPM	Diploma in Psychological Medicine; Diploma in Personnel Management
DPP	Director of Public Prosecutions
DPR	Director of Public Relations
DQMG	Deputy Quartermaster-General
Dr	Doctor
Dr jur	Doctor of Laws
Dr phil	Doctor of Philosophy
Dr rer. nat.	Doctor of Natural Science
DRCOG	Diploma of Royal College of Obstetricians and Gynaecologists
DS	Directing Staff; Doctor of Science
DSAC	Defence Scientific Advisory Council
DSAO	Diplomatic Service Administration Office
DSc	Doctor of Science
DSC	Distinguished Service Cross
DSc (SocSci)	Doctor of Science in Social Science
DSc(Eng)	Doctor of Engineering Science
DSIR	Department of Scientific and Industrial Research (later SRC; then SERC)
DSL	Doctor of Sacred Letters
DSM	Distinguished Service Medal
DSO	Companion of the Distinguished Service Order
DSocSc	Doctor of Social Science
DSP	Director of Selection of Personnel; Docteur en sciences politiques (Montreal)
DSS	Department of Social Security; Doctor of Sacred Scripture
DSSc	Doctor of Social Science
DStJ	Dame of Grace, Most Venerable Order of the Hospital of St John of Jerusalem; Dame of Justice, Most Venerable Order of the Hospital of St John of Jerusalem
DTech	Doctor of Technology
DTh or DTheol	Doctor of Theology
DTI	Department of Trade and Industry
DTM&H	Diploma in Tropical Medicine and Hygiene
DU or DUniv	Honorary Doctor of the University
Dunelm	Dunelmensis (of Durham)
DUP	Democratic Unionist Party; Docteur de l'Université de Paris
DVSc	Doctor of Veterinary Science
DVSM	Diploma in Veterinary State Medicine
DWP	Department for Work and Pensions

E

E	East; Earl; England
e	eldest
EAF	East African Forces
EBC	English Benedictine Congregation
EBU	European Broadcasting Union
EC	Etoile du Courage (Canada); European Community; European Commission; Emergency Commission
ECA	Economic Co-operation Administration; Economic Commission for Africa
ECAFE	Economic Commission for Asia and the Far East
ECE	Economic Commission for Europe
ECGD	Export Credits Guarantee Department
ECLAC	United Nations Economic Commission for Latin America and the Caribbean
ECSC	European Coal and Steel Community
ed	edited
ED	Efficiency Decoration; Doctor of Engineering (US); European Democrat
EDC	Economic Development Committee
EdD	Doctor of Education
EDG	European Democratic Group; Employment Department Group
Edin.	Edinburgh
Edn	Edition
Educ	Educated
Educn	Education
EEA	European Environment Agency
EEC	European Economic Community (now see EC); Commission of the European Communities
EEF	Engineering Employers' Federation; Egyptian Expeditionary Force
EETPU	Electrical Electronic Telecommunication & Plumbing Union (later AEEU)
EFTA	European Free Trade Association
EIB	European Investment Bank
E-in-C	Engineer-in-Chief
ELT	English Language Teaching
EMBO	European Molecular Biology Organisation
EMEA	European Medicines Agency (formerly European Agency for the Evaluation of Medical Products); Europe, Middle East and Africa
EMI	European Monetary Institute
EMS	Emergency Medical Service
Eng.	England
Engr	Engineer
ENO	English National Opera
ENSA	Entertainments National Service Association
ENT	Ear Nose and Throat
EP	European Parliament
EPP	European People's Party
EPSRC	Engineering and Physical Sciences Research Council
er	elder
ER	Eastern Region (BR); East Riding
ERA	Electrical Research Association
ERD	Emergency Reserve Decoration (Army)
ESA	European Space Agency
ESF	European Science Foundation
ESRC	Economic and Social Research Council; Electricity Supply Research Council
ESU	English-Speaking Union

ETH	Eidgenössische Technische Hochschule
ETU	Electrical Trades Union
EU	European Union
Eur Ing	European Engineer
Euratom	European Atomic Energy Community
EurBiol	European Biologist
EurChem	European Chemist
EUW	European Union of Women
Ext	Extinct; external

F

FA	Football Association
FAA	Fellow, Australian Academy of Science; Fleet Air Arm
FAAAS	Fellow, American Association for the Advancement of Science
FAAV	Fellow, Central Association of Agricultural Valuers
FACC	Fellow, American College of Cardiology
FACD	Fellow, American College of Dentistry
FACE	Fellow, Australian College of Educators (*formerly* of Education)
FAChPM	Fellow, Australasian Chapter of Palliative Medicine, Royal Australian College of Physicians
FACMA	Fellow, Australian College of Medical Administrators
FACOG	Fellow, American College of Obstetricians and Gynæcologists
FACP	Fellow, American College of Physicians
FACR	Fellow, American College of Radiology
FACS	Fellow, American College of Surgeons
FAGS	Fellow, American Geographical Society
FAHA	Fellow, Australian Academy of the Humanities; Fellow, American Heart Association
FAI	Fellow, Chartered Auctioneers' and Estate Agents' Institute (*now* (after amalgamation) *see* FRICS); Fédération Aéronautique Internationale
FAIA	Fellow, American Institute of Architects; Fellow, Association of International Accountants
FAIAA	Fellow, American Institute of Aeronautics and Astronautics
FAICD	Fellow, Australian Institute of Company Directors
FAIFST	Fellow, Australian Institute of Food Science and Technology
FAIM	Fellow, Australian Institute of Management
FAIP	Fellow, Australian Institute of Physics
FAMS	Fellow, Ancient Monuments Society; Fellow, Academy of Medicine, Singapore
F and GP	Finance and General Purposes
FANY	First Aid Nursing Yeomanry
FANZCA	Fellow, Australian and New Zealand College of Anaesthetists
FAO	Food and Agriculture Organization of the United Nations
FAPA	Fellow, American Psychiatric Association
FARELF	Far East Land Forces
FASA	Fellow, Australian Society of Accountants (*now see* FCPA)
FASCE	Fellow, American Society of Civil Engineers
FASI	Fellow, Architects' and Surveyors' Institute
FASME	Fellow, American Society of Mechanical Engineers
FASSA	Fellow, Academy of the Social Sciences in Australia

FBA	Fellow, British Academy; Federation of British Artists
FBC	Fellow, Birmingham Conservatoire
FBCartS	Fellow, British Cartographic Society
FBCS	Fellow, British Computer Society
FBHI	Fellow, British Horological Institute
FBI	Federation of British Industries (*now see* CBI); Federal Bureau of Investigation
FBIM	Fellow, British Institute of Management (later FIMgt)
FBIS	Fellow, British Interplanetary Society
FBKSTS	Fellow, British Kinematograph, Sound and Television Society
FBOA	Fellow, British Optical Association
FBPsS	Fellow, British Psychological Society
FC	Football Club
FCA	Fellow, Institute of Chartered Accountants; Fellow, Institute of Chartered Accountants in Australia; Fellow, New Zealand Society of Accountants; Federation of Canadian Artists
FCAM	Fellow, CAM Foundation
FCASI	Fellow, Canadian Aeronautics and Space Institute
FCCA	Fellow, Chartered Association of Certified Accountants
FCCS	Fellow, Corporation of Secretaries (*formerly* of Certified Secretaries)
FCEM	Fellow, College of Emergency Medicine
FCFI	Fellow, Clothing and Footwear Institute
FCGI	Fellow, City and Guilds of London Institute
FCIArb	Fellow, Chartered Institute of Arbitrators
FCIB	Fellow, Corporation of Insurance Brokers; Fellow, Chartered Institute of Bankers
FCIBS	Fellow, Chartered Institution of Building Services; Fellow, Chartered Institute of Bankers in Scotland
FCIC	Fellow, Chemical Institute of Canada (*formerly* Canadian Institute of Chemistry)
FCIHT	Fellow, Chartered Institution of Highways & Transportation
FCII	Fellow, Chartered Insurance Institute
FCIL	Fellow, Chartered Institute of Linguists
FCILT	Chartered Fellow, Chartered Institute of Logistics and Transport
FCIM	Fellow, Chartered Institute of Marketing; Fellow, Institute of Corporate Managers (Australia)
FCIOB	Fellow, Chartered Institute of Building
FCIPD	Fellow, Chartered Institute of Personnel and Development
FCIPR	Fellow, Chartered Institute of Public Relations
FCIPS	Fellow, Chartered Institute of Purchasing and Supply
FCIS	Fellow, Institute of Chartered Secretaries and Administrators (*formerly* Chartered Institute of Secretaries)
FCIT	Fellow, Chartered Institute of Transport (*now see* FCILT)
FCIWEM	Fellow, Chartered Institution of Water and Environmental Management
FCLIP	Fellow, Chartered Institute of Library and Information Professionals
FCM	Faculty of Community Medicine
FCMA	Fellow, Chartered Institute of Management Accountants (*formerly* Institute of Cost and Management Accountants); Fellow, Communications Management Association
FCMC	Fellow grade, Certified Management Consultant
FCMI	Fellow, Chartered Management Institute
FCMSA	Fellow, College of Medicine of South Africa

FCO	Foreign and Commonwealth Office
FCollP	Fellow, College of Preceptors
FCOphth	Fellow, College of Ophthalmologists (now see FRCOphth)
FCOptom	Fellow, College of Optometrists
FCP	Fellow, College of Preceptors
FCP(SoAf)	Fellow, College of Physicians, South Africa
FCPA	Fellow, Australian Society of Certified Practising Accountants
FCPS	Fellow, College of Physicians and Surgeons
FCPS (Pak)	Fellow, College of Physicians and Surgeons of Pakistan
FCS	Federation of Conservative Students
FCSD	Fellow, Chartered Society of Designers
FCSHK	Fellow, College of Surgeons of Hong Kong
FCSP	Fellow, Chartered Society of Physiotherapy
FCSSL	Fellow, College of Surgeons of Sri Lanka
FCST	Fellow, College of Speech Therapists
FCT	Federal Capital Territory (now see ACT); Fellow, Association of Corporate Treasurers; Fellow, College of Teachers
FDI	Fédération Dentaire Internationale
FDS	Fellow in Dental Surgery
FDSRCPSGlas	Fellow in Dental Surgery, Royal College of Physicians and Surgeons of Glasgow
FDSRCS or FDS RCS	Fellow in Dental Surgery, Royal College of Surgeons of England
FDSRCSE	Fellow in Dental Surgery, Royal College of Surgeons of Edinburgh
FE	Far East
FEAF	Far East Air Force
FEANI	Fédération Européenne d'Associations Nationales d'Ingénieurs
FEBS	Federation of European Biochemical Societies
FEI	Fédération Equestre Internationale; Fellow, Energy Institute
FEIS	Fellow, Educational Institute of Scotland
FEng	Fellow, Royal Academy (formerly Fellowship) of Engineering (now see FREng)
FF	Fianna Fáil; Field Force
FFA	Fellow, Faculty of Actuaries (in Scotland); Fellow, Institute of Financial Accountants
FFAEM	Fellow, Faculty of Accident and Emergency Medicine (now see FCEM)
FFARACS	Fellow, Faculty of Anaesthetists, Royal Australasian College of Surgeons (now see FANZCA)
FFARCS	Fellow, Faculty of Anaesthetists, Royal College of Surgeons of England (now see FRCA)
FFARCSI	Fellow, Faculty of Anaesthetists, Royal College of Surgeons in Ireland
FFAS	Fellow, Faculty of Architects and Surveyors, London (now see FASI)
FFB	Fellow, Faculty of Building
FFCM	Fellow, Faculty of Community Medicine (now see FFPH); Fellow, Faculty of Church Music
FFDRCSI	Fellow, Faculty of Dentistry, Royal College of Surgeons in Ireland
FFFP	Fellow, Faculty of Family Planning & Reproductive Health Care of the Royal College of Obstetricians and Gynaecologists
FFGDP(UK)	Fellow, Faculty of General Dental Practitioners of the Royal College of Surgeons
FFHom	Fellow, Faculty of Homoeopathy
FFI	Finance for Industry; Fauna & Flora International
FFOM	Fellow, Faculty of Occupational Medicine

FFPath, RCPI	Fellow, Faculty of Pathologists of the Royal College of Physicians of Ireland
FFPH	Fellow, Faculty of Public Health
FFPHM	Fellow, Faculty of Public Health Medicine (now see FFPH)
FFPM	Fellow, Faculty of Pharmaceutical Medicine
FFSSoc	Fellow, Forensic Science Society
FGCM	Fellow, Guild of Church Musicians
FGS	Fellow, Geological Society
FGSM	Fellow, Guildhall School of Music and Drama
FHA	Fellow, Institute of Health Service Administrators (formerly Hospital Administrators) (later FHSM); Fellow, Historical Association
FHSA	Family Health Services Authority
FHSM	Fellow, Institute of Health Services Management (later FIHM)
FIA	Fellow, Institute of Actuaries
FIAgrM	Fellow, Institute of Agricultural Management
FIAM	Fellow, International Academy of Management
FIB	Fellow, Institute of Bankers (now see FCIB)
FIBiol	Fellow, Institute of Biology (now see FSB)
FIBMS	Fellow, Institute of Biomedical Sciences
FIC	Fellow, Institute of Chemistry (then FRIC; now see FRSC); Fellow, Imperial College, London
FICE	Fellow, Institution of Civil Engineers
FICFor	Fellow, Institute of Chartered Foresters
FIChemE	Fellow, Institution of Chemical Engineers
FICPD	Fellow, Institute of Continuing Professional Development
FICS	Fellow, Institute of Chartered Shipbrokers; Fellow, International College of Surgeons
FIDE	Fédération Internationale des Echecs; Fellow, Institute of Design Engineers; Fédération Internationale pour le Droit Européen
FIEAust	Fellow, Institution of Engineers, Australia
FIEE	Fellow, Institution of Electrical Engineers (now see FIET)
FIEEE	Fellow, Institute of Electrical and Electronics Engineers (NY)
FIEEIE	Fellow, Institution of Electronics and Electrical Incorporated Engineers (later FIIE)
FIEEM	Fellow, Institute of Ecology and Environmental Management
FIET	Fédération Internationale des Employés, Techniciens et Cadres; Fellow, Institution of Engineering and Technology
FIEx	Fellow, Institute of Export
FIFA	Fédération Internationale de Football Association
FIFireE	Fellow, Institution of Fire Engineers
FIFM	Fellow, Institute of Fisheries Management
FIFST	Fellow, Institute of Food Science and Technology
FIH	Fellow, Institute of Housing; Fellow, Institute of the Horse; Fellow, Institute of Hospitality
FIHE	Fellow, Institute of Health Education
FIHort	Fellow, Institute of Horticulture
FIHT	Fellow, Institution of Highways & Transportation (now see FCIHT)
FIIC	Fellow, International Institute for Conservation of Historic and Artistic Works
FIIM	Fellow, Institution of Industrial Managers
FIInfSc	Fellow, Institute of Information Scientists (now see FCLIP)

FIIPC	Fellow, India International Photographic Council
FIIPE	Fellow, Indian Institution of Production Engineers
FIL	Fellow, Institute of Linguists (*now see* FCIL)
Fil.Hed.	Filosofie Hedersdoktor
FILT	Fellow, Institute of Logistics and Transport (*now see* FCILT)
FIM	Fellow, Institute of Materials (*formerly* Institution of Metallurgists, then Institute of Metals) (*now see* FIMMM)
FIMA	Fellow, Institute of Mathematics and its Applications
FIMarEST	Fellow, Institute of Marine Engineering, Science and Technology
FIMBRA	Financial Intermediaries, Managers and Brokers Regulatory Association
FIMechE	Fellow, Institution of Mechanical Engineers
FIMfgE	Fellow, Institution of Manufacturing Engineers (later FIEE)
FIMgt	Fellow, Institute of Management (*now see* FCMI)
FIMH	Fellow, Institute of Materials Handling (later FIMatM); Fellow, Institute of Military History
FIMI	Fellow, Institute of the Motor Industry
FIMinE	Fellow, Institution of Mining Engineers (later FIMM)
FIMM	Fellow, Institution of Mining and Metallurgy (*now see* FIMMM)
FIMMM	Fellow, Institute of Materials, Minerals and Mining
FIMunE	Fellow, Institution of Municipal Engineers (now amalgamated with Institution of Civil Engineers)
FINRA	Financial Industry Regulatory Authority
FInstD	Fellow, Institute of Directors
FInstE	Fellow, Institute of Energy (*now see* FEI)
FInstF	Fellow, Institute of Fuel (later FInstE); Fellow, Institute of Fundraising
FInstHE	Fellow, Institute of Highways Engineers (later FIHT, *now see* FCIHT)
FInstM	Fellow, Institute of Meat; Fellow, Institute of Marketing (*now see* FCIM)
FInstMC	Fellow, Institute of Measurement and Control
FInstP	Fellow, Institute of Physics
FInstPet	Fellow, Institute of Petroleum (*now see* FEI)
FInstR	Fellow, Institute of Refrigeration
FINucE	Fellow, Institution of Nuclear Engineers
FIOB	Fellow, Institute of Building (*now see* FCIOB)
FIP3	Fellow, Institute of Paper, Printing and Publishing
FIPA	Fellow, Institute of Practitioners in Advertising
FIPD	Fellow, Institute of Personnel and Development (*now see* FCIPD)
FIPHE	Fellow, Institution of Public Health Engineers (later FIWEM)
FIPM	Fellow, Institute of Personnel Management (later FIPD)
FIProdE	Fellow, Institution of Production Engineers (later FIMfgE)
FIQA	Fellow, Institute of Quality Assurance
FIRA	Furniture Industry Research Association
FIRTE	Fellow, Institute of Road Transport Engineers
FIStructE	Fellow, Institution of Structural Engineers
FITD	Fellow, Institute of Training and Development (later FIPD)
FIWEM	Fellow, Institution of Water and Environmental Management (*now see* FCIWEM)

FIWES	Fellow, Institution of Water Engineers and Scientists (later FIWEM)
FIWM	Fellow, Institution of Works Managers (*now see* FIIM); Fellow, Institute of Wastes Management
FIWPC	Fellow, Institute of Water Pollution Control (later FIWEM)
FIWSP	Fellow, Institute of Work Study Practitioners
FKC	Fellow, King's College London
FL	Florida (postal)
Fla	Florida
FLA	Fellow, Library Association (*now see* FCLIP)
FLAS	Fellow, Chartered Land Agents' Society (*now* (after amalgamation) *see* FRICS)
FLCM	Fellow, London College of Music
FLS	Fellow, Linnean Society
Flt	Flight
FM	Field-Marshal
FMA	Fellow, Museums Association
FMedSci	Fellow, Academy of Medical Sciences
FMES	Fellow, Minerals Engineering Society
FMI	Foundation for Manufacturing and Industry
FMSA	Fellow, Mineralogical Society of America
FNA	Fellow, Indian National Science Academy
FNAEA	Fellow, National Association of Estate Agents
FNI	Fellow, Nautical Institute; Fellow, National Institute of Sciences in India (*now see* FNA)
FNZIC	Fellow, New Zealand Institute of Chemistry
FNZIM	Fellow, New Zealand Institute of Management
FNZPsS	Fellow, New Zealand Psychological Society
FO	Foreign Office (*now see* FCO); Field Officer; Flag Officer; Flying Officer
FOR	Fellowship of Operational Research
For.	Foreign
FOREST	Freedom Organisation for the Right to Enjoy Smoking Tobacco
FPA	Family Planning Association
FPC	Family Practitioner Committee (later FHSA); Financial Planning Certificate
FPHM	Faculty of Public Health Medicine (*see now* FPH)
FPIA	Fellow, Plastics Institute of Australia; Fellow, Planning Institute of Australia
FPMI	Fellow, Pensions Management Institute
FPRI	Fellow, Plastics and Rubber Institute (later FIM)
FPS	Fellow, Pharmaceutical Society (*now also* FRPharmS); Fauna Preservation Society (later FFPS)
FRAC	Fellow, Royal Agricultural College
FRACI	Fellow, Royal Australian Chemical Institute
FRACOG	Fellow, Royal Australian College of Obstetricians and Gynaecologists
FRACP	Fellow, Royal Australasian College of Physicians
FRACS	Fellow, Royal Australasian College of Surgeons
FRAeS	Fellow, Royal Aeronautical Society
FRAgS	Fellow, Royal Agricultural Societies (*ie* of England, Scotland and Wales)
FRAI	Fellow, Royal Anthropological Institute of Great Britain & Ireland
FRAM	Fellow, Royal Academy of Music
FRAS	Fellow, Royal Astronomical Society; Fellow, Royal Asiatic Society
FRASE	Fellow, Royal Agricultural Society of England
FRBS	Fellow, Royal Society of British Sculptors; Fellow, Royal Botanic Society

FRCA	Fellow, Royal College of Art; Fellow, Royal College of Anaesthetists
FRCD(Can.)	Fellow, Royal College of Dentists of Canada
FRCGP	Fellow, Royal College of General Practitioners
FRCM	Fellow, Royal College of Music
FRCN	Fellow, Royal College of Nursing
FRCO	Fellow, Royal College of Organists
FRCO(CHM)	Fellow, Royal College of Organists with Diploma in Choir Training
FRCOG	Fellow, Royal College of Obstetricians and Gynaecologists
FRCOphth	Fellow, Royal College of Ophthalmologists
FRCP	Fellow, Royal College of Physicians, London
FRCP&S (Canada)	Fellow, Royal College of Physicians and Surgeons of Canada
FRCPath	Fellow, Royal College of Pathologists
FRCPCH	Fellow, Royal College of Paediatrics and Child Health
FRCPE or FRCPEd	Fellow, Royal College of Physicians, Edinburgh
FRCPGlas	Fellow, Royal College of Physicians and Surgeons of Glasgow
FRCPI	Fellow, Royal College of Physicians of Ireland
FRCPSGlas	Hon. Fellow, Royal College of Physicians and Surgeons of Glasgow
FRCPsych	Fellow, Royal College of Psychiatrists
FRCR	Fellow, Royal College of Radiologists
FRCS	Fellow, Royal College of Surgeons of England
FRCSE or FRCSEd	Fellow, Royal College of Surgeons of Edinburgh
FRCSGlas	Fellow, Royal College of Physicians and Surgeons of Glasgow
FRCSI	Fellow, Royal College of Surgeons in Ireland
FRCVS	Fellow, Royal College of Veterinary Surgeons
FREconS	Fellow, Royal Economic Society
FREng	Fellow, Royal Academy of Engineering
FRES	Fellow, Royal Entomological Society of London
FRG	Federal Republic of Germany
FRGS	Fellow, Royal Geographical Society
FRHistS	Fellow, Royal Historical Society
FRHS	Fellow, Royal Horticultural Society
FRIAS	Fellow, Royal Incorporation of Architects of Scotland; Royal Institute for the Advancement of Science
FRIBA	Fellow, Royal Institute of British Architects (and see RIBA)
FRIC	Fellow, Royal Institute of Chemistry (now see FRSC)
FRICS	Fellow, Royal Institution of Chartered Surveyors
FRIN	Fellow, Royal Institute of Navigation
FRINA	Fellow, Royal Institution of Naval Architects
FRIPH	Fellow, Royal Institute of Public Health (now see FRSPH)
FRMetS	Fellow, Royal Meteorological Society
FRMS	Fellow, Royal Microscopical Society
FRNCM	Fellow, Royal Northern College of Music
FRPharmS	Fellow, Royal Pharmaceutical Society
FRPS	Fellow, Royal Photographic Society
FRPSL	Fellow, Royal Philatelic Society, London
FRS	Fellow, Royal Society
FRS(Can)	Fellow, Royal Society of Canada (used when a person is also a Fellow of the Royal Society of Chemistry)

FRSA	Fellow, Royal Society of Arts
FRSAI	Fellow, Royal Society of Antiquaries of Ireland
FRSAMD	Fellow, Royal Scottish Academy of Music and Drama
FRSC	Fellow, Royal Society of Canada; Fellow, Royal Society of Chemistry
FRSE	Fellow, Royal Society of Edinburgh
FRSGS	Fellow, Royal Scottish Geographical Society
FRSH	Fellow, Royal Society for the Promotion of Health (now see FRSPH)
FRSL	Fellow, Royal Society of Literature
FRSN	Fellow, Royal Society of New South Wales
FRSNZ	Fellow, Royal Society of New Zealand
FRSocMed	Fellow, Royal Society of Medicine
FRSPH	Fellow, Royal Society for Public Health
FRSSAf	Fellow, Royal Society of South Africa
FRSTM&H	Fellow, Royal Society of Tropical Medicine and Hygiene
FRSV	Fellow, Royal Society of Victoria
FRTPI	Fellow, Royal Town Planning Institute
FRTS	Fellow, Royal Television Society
FRUSI	Fellow, Royal United Services Institute
FRVA	Fellow, Rating and Valuation Association (now see IRRV)
FRVC	Fellow, Royal Veterinary College
FRWCMD	Fellow, Royal Welsh College of Music and Drama
FS	Field Security
FSA	Fellow, Society of Antiquaries; Financial Services Authority
FSAE	Fellow, Society of Automotive Engineers; Fellow, Society of Art Education
FSAScot	Fellow, Society of Antiquaries of Scotland
FSB	Fellow, Society of Biology
fsc	Foreign Staff College
FSCA	Fellow, Society of Company and Commercial Accountants
FScotvec	Fellow, Scottish Vocational Education Council
FSE	Fellow, Society of Engineers
FSIA	Fellow, Securities Institute of Australia
FSIAD	Fellow, Society of Industrial Artists and Designers (now see FCSD)
FSLTC	Fellow, Society of Leather Technologists and Chemists
FSME	Fellow, Society of Manufacturing Engineers
FSRP	Fellow, Society for Radiological Protection
FSS	Fellow, Royal Statistical Society
FTCL	Fellow, Trinity College of Music, London
FTS	Fellow, Australian Academy of Technological Sciences and Engineering (now see FTSE); Flying Training School; Fellow, Tourism Society
FTSE	Fellow, Australian Academy of Technological Sciences and Engineering
FUMIST	Fellow, University of Manchester Institute of Science and Technology
FWeldI	Fellow, Welding Institute
FZS	Fellow, Zoological Society

G

g s	grandson
GA	Geologists' Association; Gaelic Athletic (Club); Georgia (postal)
Ga	Georgia
GAP	Gap Activity Projects
GAPAN	Guild of Air Pilots and Air Navigators
GATT	General Agreement on Tariffs and Trade (now World Trade Organisation)

GB	Great Britain
GBA	Governing Bodies Association
GBE	Knight or Dame Grand Cross, Order of the British Empire
GBGSA	Governing Bodies of Girls' Schools Association (formerly Association of Governing Bodies of Girls' Public Schools)
GBM	Grand Bauhinia Medal (Hong Kong)
GBS	Gold Bauhinia Star (Hong Kong)
GC	George Cross
GCB	Knight or Dame Grand Cross, Order of the Bath
GCCS	Government Code and Cipher School
GCIE	Knight Grand Commander, Order of the Indian Empire
GCLM	Grand Commander, Order of the Legion of Merit of Rhodesia
GCM	Gold Crown of Merit (Barbados)
GCMG	Knight or Dame Grand Cross, Order of St Michael and St George
GCSE	General Certificate of Secondary Education
GCSG	Knight Grand Cross, Order of St Gregory the Great
GCSI	Knight Grand Commander, Order of the Star of India
GCSK	Grand Commander, Order of the Star and Key of the Indian Ocean (Mauritius)
GCSL	Grand Cross, Order of St Lucia
GCStJ	Bailiff or Dame Grand Cross, Most Venerable Order of the Hospital of St John of Jerusalem
GCVO	Knight or Dame Grand Cross, Royal Victorian Order
GDC	General Dental Council
Gdns	Gardens
GDR	German Democratic Republic
GDST	Girls' Day School Trust
Gen.	General
Ges.	Gesellschaft
GHQ	General Headquarters
GLA	Greater London Authority
GLC	Greater London Council
Glos	Gloucestershire
GM	George Medal; Grand Medal (Ghana); genetically modified
GMB	(Union for) General, Municipal, Boilermakers
GMBATU	General, Municipal, Boilermakers and Allied Trades Union (now see GMB)
GmbH	Gesellschaft mit beschränkter Haftung
GMC	General Medical Council; Guild of Memorial Craftsmen; General Management Course (Henley)
GNC	General Nursing Council
GOC	General Officer Commanding
GOC-in-C	General Officer Commanding-in-Chief
GOE	General Ordination Examination
GOQ	Grand Officer, National Order of Quebec
Gov.	Governor
Govt	Government
GP	General Practitioner; Grand Prix
Gp	Group
GPDST	Girls' Public Day School Trust (now see GDST)
GPO	General Post Office
Gr.	Greek
GRSM	Graduate of the Royal Schools of Music
GS	General Staff; Grammar School
GSA	Girls' Schools Association
GSM	General Service Medal; (Member of) Guildhall School of Music and Drama

GSMD	Guildhall School of Music and Drama
GSO	General Staff Officer
GWR	Great Western Railway

H

HA	Historical Association; Health Authority
HAA	Heavy Anti-Aircraft
HAC	Honourable Artillery Company
Hants	Hampshire
HBM	His (or Her) Britannic Majesty (Majesty's); Humming Bird Gold Medal (Trinidad)
hc	honoris causa (honorary)
HCSC	Higher Command and Staff Course
HE	His (or Her) Excellency; His Eminence
HEA	Health Education Authority (later HDA)
HEC	Ecole des Hautes Etudes Commerciales; Higher Education Corporation
HEFCE	Higher Education Funding Council for England
HEFCW	Higher Education Funding Council for Wales
Heir-pres.	Heir-presumptive
Herts	Hertfordshire
HFEA	Human Fertilisation and Embryology Authority
HG	Home Guard
HH	His (or Her) Highness; His Holiness; Member, Hesketh Hubbard Art Society
HHA	Historic Houses Association
HKSAR	Hong Kong Special Administrative Region
HLI	Highland Light Infantry
HM	His (or Her) Majesty, or Majesty's
HMA	Head Masters' Association
HMAS	His (or Her) Majesty's Australian Ship
HMC	Headmasters' and Headmistresses' (formerly Headmasters') Conference; Hospital Management Committee
HMCIC	His (or Her) Majesty's Chief Inspector of Constabulary
HMI	His (or Her) Majesty's Inspector
HMNZS	His (or Her) Majesty's New Zealand Ship
HMOCS	His (or Her) Majesty's Overseas Civil Service
HMS	His (or Her) Majesty's Ship
HMSO	His (or Her) Majesty's Stationery Office
HND	Higher National Diploma
H of C	House of Commons
H of L	House of Lords
Hon.	Honourable; Honorary
HQ	Headquarters
HRH	His (or Her) Royal Highness
HRSA	Honorary Member, Royal Scottish Academy
HSC	Health and Safety Commission
HSE	Health and Safety Executive
Hum.	Humanity, Humanities (Classics)

I

I	Island; Ireland
IA	Indian Army; Iowa (postal)
IAAF	International Association of Athletics Federations (formerly International Amateur Athletic Federation)
IACP	International Association of Chiefs of Police
IADB	Inter American Development Bank
IADR	International Association for Dental Research
IAEA	International Atomic Energy Agency

IAM	Institute of Advanced Motorists; Institute of Aviation Medicine	**IFBWW**	International Federation of Building Woodworkers
IAOC	Indian Army Ordnance Corps	**IFIP**	International Federation for Information Processing
IAS	Indian Administrative Service; Institute for Advanced Studies; International Academy of Science	**IFLA**	International Federation of Library Associations
IATA	International Air Transport Association	**IFRA**	World Press Research Association
IAU	International Astronomical Union	**IFS**	Irish Free State; Indian Forest Service; Institute for Fiscal Studies
IAWPRC	International Association on Water Pollution Research and Control	**IG**	Instructor in Gunnery
IBA	Independent Broadcasting Authority; International Bar Association	**IGasE**	Institution of Gas Engineers
		IILS	International Institute for Labour Studies
IBCA	International Braille Chess Association	**IInfSc**	Institute of Information Scientists
IBRD	International Bank for Reconstruction and Development (World Bank)	**IISS**	International Institute of Strategic Studies
		IL	Illinois (postal)
i/c	in charge; in command	**ILEA**	Inner London Education Authority
ICA	Institute of Contemporary Arts; Institute of Chartered Accountants in England and Wales (*now see* ICAEW)	**Ill**	Illinois
		ILO	International Labour Office; International Labour Organisation
ICAC	Independent Commission Against Corruption, Hong Kong	**IMA**	International Music Association; Institute of Mathematics and its Applications
ICAEW	Institute of Chartered Accountants in England and Wales	**IMechE**	Institution of Mechanical Engineers
		IMF	International Monetary Fund
ICAO	International Civil Aviation Organization	**IMinE**	Institution of Mining Engineers
ICC	International Chamber of Commerce; International Cricket Council (*formerly* International Cricket Conference)	**IMM**	Institution of Mining and Metallurgy (*now see* IMMM)
		IMMM	Institute of Materials, Minerals and Mining
ICE	Institution of Civil Engineers	**Imp.**	Imperial
IChemE	Institution of Chemical Engineers	**IMRO**	Investment Management Regulatory Organisation
ICI	Imperial Chemical Industries		
ICJ	International Commission of Jurists	**IMS**	Indian Medical Service; Institute of Management Services; International Military Staff
ICL	International Computers Ltd		
ICMA	Institute of Cost and Management Accountants (*now see* CIMA)	**IMU**	International Mathematical Union
ICOM	International Council of Museums	**IN**	Indian Navy; Indiana (postal)
ICOMOS	International Council on Monuments and Sites	**Inc.**	Incorporated
		Ind.	Independent
ICPO	International Criminal Police Organization (Interpol)	**Inf.**	Infantry
		INFORM	Information Network Focus on New Religious Movements
ICREA	Institució Catalana de Recerca i Estudis Avançats	**Insp.**	Inspector
ICRF	Imperial Cancer Research Fund	**Inst.**	Institute
ICS	Indian Civil Service	**Instn**	Institution
ICSC	International Council of Shopping Centres	**IoD**	Institute of Directors
ICSID	International Council of Societies of Industrial Design; International Centre for Settlement of Investment Disputes	**IODE**	Imperial Order of the Daughters of the Empire
		I of M	Isle of Man
ICSM	Imperial College School of Medicine	**IOM**	Isle of Man; Indian Order of Merit
ICSU	International Council for Science (*formerly* International Council of Scientific Unions)	**IOSCO**	International Organisation of Securities Commissions
		IoW	Isle of Wight
ICT	International Computers and Tabulators Ltd (later ICL); Information and Communications Technology	**IPA**	International Publishers' Association
		IPC	International Property Corporation
		IPFA	Member or Associate, Chartered Institute of Public Finance and Accountancy (*now see* CPFA)
ID	Independence Decoration (Rhodesia); Idaho (postal)		
IDB	Internal Drainage Board; Industrial Development Board	**IPPR**	Institute for Public Policy Research
		IPPS	Institute of Physics and The Physical Society
IDC	Imperial Defence College (*now see* RCDS); Inter-Diocesan Certificate	**IProdE**	Institution of Production Engineers (later Institution of Manufacturing Engineering)
idc	completed a course at, or served for a year on the Staff of, the Imperial Defence College (*now see* rcds)	**IPS**	Indian Police Service; Indian Political Service; Institute of Purchasing and Supply
IDS	Institute of Development Studies; Industry Department for Scotland	**IPU**	Inter-Parliamentary Union
		IRC	Industrial Reorganization Corporation; Interdisciplinary Research Centre
IEA	Institute of Economic Affairs		
IEE	Institution of Electrical Engineers	**IRRV**	(Fellow/Member of) Institute of Revenues, Rating and Valuation
IEEE	Institution of Electrical and Electronics Engineers (NY)		
		IRTE	Institute of Road Transport Engineers
IEETE	Institution of Electrical and Electronics Technician Engineers (later IIE)	**Is**	Island(s)
		ISC	Imperial Service College, Haileybury; Indian Staff Corps; Independent Schools Council
IERE	Institution of Electronic and Radio Engineers		

ISCis	Independent Schools Council Information Service
ISCO	Independent Schools Careers Organisation
ISIS	Independent Schools Information Service (*see now* ISCis)
ISJC	Independent Schools Joint Council (*now see* ISC)
ISM	Incorporated Society of Musicians
ISMAR	International Society of Magnetic Resonance
ISO	Imperial Service Order; International Organization for Standardization
IStructE	Institution of Structural Engineers
IT	Information Technology; Indian Territory (US)
ITA	Independent Television Authority (later IBA)
ITB	Industry Training Board
ITC	International Trade Centre; Independent Television Commission
ITCA	Independent Television Association (*formerly* Independent Television Companies Association Ltd)
ITDG	Intermediate Technology Development Group
ITF	International Transport Workers' Federation; International Tennis Federation
ITN	Independent Television News
ITU	International Telecommunication Union
ITV	Independent Television
IUPAC	International Union of Pure and Applied Chemistry
IUPAP	International Union of Pure and Applied Physics
IUPC	Inter-University and Polytechnic Council for Higher Education Overseas
IVF	In-vitro Fertilisation
IVS	International Voluntary Service
IZ	I Zingari

J

JA	Judge Advocate
JAG	Judge Advocate General
JCD	*Juris Canonici* (or *Civilis*) *Doctor* (Doctor of Canon (or Civil) Law)
JCO	Joint Consultative Organisation (of AFRC, MAFF, and Department of Agriculture and Fisheries for Scotland)
JD	Doctor of Jurisprudence
JDipMA	Joint Diploma in Management Accounting Services
JMN	Johan Mangku Negara (Malaysia)
JP	Justice of the Peace
Jr	Junior
JSCSC	Joint Services Command and Staff College
JSM	Johan Setia Mahkota (Malaysia); Master of the Science of Jurisprudence
jssc	completed a course at Joint Services Staff College
JSSC	Joint Services Staff College
jt, jtly	joint, jointly
Jun.	Junior

K

KA	Knight of St Andrew, Order of Barbados
KAR	King's African Rifles
KBE	Knight Commander, Order of the British Empire

KC	King's Counsel
KCB	Knight Commander, Order of the Bath
KCGSJ	Knight Commander of Magisterial Grace, Order of St John of Jerusalem (Knights Hospitaller)
KCH	King's College Hospital; Knight Commander, Hanoverian Order
KCHS	Knight Commander, Order of the Holy Sepulchre
KCIE	Knight Commander, Order of the Indian Empire
KCL	King's College London
KCMG	Knight Commander, Order of St Michael and St George
KCSG	Knight Commander, Order of St Gregory the Great
KCSI	Knight Commander, Order of the Star of India
KCSJ	Knight Commander, Sovereign Order of St John of Jerusalem (Knights Hospitaller)
KCVO	Knight Commander, Royal Victorian Order
KG	Knight, Order of the Garter
KHP	Hon. Physician to the King
KHS	Hon. Surgeon to the King; Knight, Order of the Holy Sepulchre
K-i-H	Kaisar-i-Hind
KLJ	Knight, Order of St Lazarus of Jerusalem
KM	Knight of Malta
KOM	Companion, National Order of Merit (Malta)
KORR	King's Own Royal Regiment
KOSB	King's Own Scottish Borderers
KOYLI	King's Own Yorkshire Light Infantry
KPM	King's Police Medal
KRRC	King's Royal Rifle Corps
KSC	Knight of St Columba
KSG	Knight, Order of St Gregory the Great
KSLI	King's Shropshire Light Infantry
KStJ	Knight, Most Venerable Order of the Hospital of St John of Jerusalem
Kt	Knight
KT	Knight, Order of the Thistle
Ky	Kentucky

L

L	Liberal
L of C	Library of Congress; Lines of Communication
LA	Los Angeles; Library Association; Liverpool Academy; Louisiana (postal)
La	Louisiana
LAA	Light Anti-Aircraft
Lab	Labour
LAMDA	London Academy of Music and Dramatic Art
Lancs	Lancashire
Lautro	Life Assurance and Unit Trust Regulatory Organisation
LBC	London Broadcasting Company; London Borough Council
LCC	London County Council (later GLC)
LCCI	London Chamber of Commerce and Industry
LCSP	London and Counties Society of Physiologists
LDP	Liberal Democratic Party (Japan)
Ldr	Leader
LDS	Licentiate in Dental Surgery
LEA	Local Education Authority

LEAD	Leadership in Environment and Development
LEP	Local Ecumenical Project
LEPRA	British Leprosy Relief Association
LGA	Local Government Association
LHD	*Literarum Humaniorum Doctor* (Doctor of Literature)
LI	Light Infantry; Long Island
Lib Dem	Liberal Democrat
Lieut	Lieutenant
LIFFE	London International Financial Futures and Options Exchange
LIMA	Licentiate, Institute of Mathematics and its Applications; International Licensing Industry Merchandisers' Association
Lincs	Lincolnshire
LIOB	Licentiate, Institute of Building
Lit.	Literature; Literary
Lit.Hum.	*Literae Humaniores* (Classics)
LitD	Doctor of Literature; Doctor of Letters
LittD	Doctor of Literature; Doctor of Letters
LLB	Bachelor of Laws
LLC	Limited Liability Company
LLD	Doctor of Laws
LLM	Master of Laws
LLP	Limited Liability Partnership
LMC	Local Medical Committee
LMRTPI	Legal Member, Royal Town Planning Institute
LMS	London, Midland and Scottish Railway; London Missionary Society; London Mathematical Society
LMSSA	Licentiate in Medicine and Surgery, Society of Apothecaries
LNER	London and North Eastern Railway
LOB	Location of Offices Bureau
LPO	London Philharmonic Orchestra
LRAM	Licentiate, Royal Academy of Music
LRCP	Licentiate, Royal College of Physicians, London
LRCPE	Licentiate, Royal College of Physicians, Edinburgh
LRCSE	Licentiate, Royal College of Surgeons, Edinburgh
LRFPS(G)	Licentiate, Royal Faculty of Physicians and Surgeons, Glasgow
LRIBA	Licentiate, Royal Institute of British Architects (*now see* RIBA)
LRPS	Licentiate, Royal Photographic Society
LRT	London Regional Transport
LSA	Licentiate, Society of Apothecaries; Licence in Agricultural Sciences
LSE	London School of Economics and Political Science
LSHTM	London School of Hygiene and Tropical Medicine
LSO	London Symphony Orchestra
Lt	Lieutenant; Light
LT	Lady, Order of the Thistle; London Transport (later LRT); Licentiate in Teaching
Lt Col	Lieutenant Colonel
LTA	Lawn Tennis Association
LTCL	Licentiate of Trinity College of Music, London
LTE	London Transport Executive (later LRT)
LTh	Licentiate in Theology
LVO	Lieutenant, Royal Victorian Order (*formerly* MVO (Fourth Class))
LWT	London Weekend Television

M

M	Marquess; Member; Monsieur
m	married
MA	Master of Arts; Military Assistant; Massachusetts (postal)
MACE	Member, Australian College of Education; Member, Association of Conference Executives
MAE	Member, Academia Europaea
MAFF	Ministry of Agriculture, Fisheries and Food
MAI	*Magister in Arte Ingeniaria* (Master of Engineering)
MAIBC	Member, Architectural Institute of British Columbia
Maj. Gen.	Major General
Man	Manitoba
MAP	Ministry of Aircraft Production
MARIS	Multi-State Aquatic Resources Information System
MASME	Member, American Society of Mechanical Engineers
Mass	Massachusetts
MAT	Master of Arts and Teaching (US)
Math.	Mathematics; Mathematical
MB	Medal of Bravery (Canada); Bachelor of Medicine; Manitoba (postal)
MBA	Master of Business Administration
MBC	Metropolitan/Municipal Borough Council
MBCS	Member, British Computer Society
MBE	Member, Order of the British Empire
MBFR	Mutual and Balanced Force Reductions (negotiations)
MBIM	Member, British Institute of Management (later MIMgt)
MC	Military Cross; Missionaries of Charity
MCC	Marylebone Cricket Club; Metropolitan County Council
MCD	Master of Civic Design
MCFP	Member, College of Family Physicians (Canada)
MCh *or* MChir	Master in Surgery
MCIJ	Member, Chartered Institute of Journalists
MCIPR	Member, Chartered Institute of Public Relations
MCLIP	Member, Chartered Institute of Library and Information Professionals
MCMI	Member, Chartered Management Institute
MCom	Master of Commerce
MCSP	Member, Chartered Society of Physiotherapy
MCST	Member, College of Speech Therapists
Md	Maryland
MD	Doctor of Medicine; Military District; Maryland (postal)
MDC	Metropolitan District Council
MDS	Master of Dental Surgery
ME	Mining Engineer; Middle East; Master of Engineering; Maine (postal); Myalgic Encephalomyelitis
MEAF	Middle East Air Force
MEC	Member of Executive Council; Middle East Command
MECAS	Middle East Centre for Arab Studies
Mech.	Mechanics; Mechanical
MEd	Master of Education
Med.	Medical
MEF	Middle East Force
MELF	Middle East Land Forces
Mencap	Royal Society for Mentally Handicapped Children and Adults
MEng	Master of Engineering

MEO	Marine Engineering Officer
MEP	Member of the European Parliament
MFA	Master of Fine Arts
MFCM	Member, Faculty of Community Medicine (later MFPHM)
MFH	Master of Foxhounds
MFOM	Member, Faculty of Occupational Medicine
MFPHM	Member, Faculty of Public Health Medicine
MGA	Major General in charge of Administration
MGDSRCS	Member in General Dental Surgery, Royal College of Surgeons
MGO	Master General of the Ordnance; Master of Gynaecology and Obstetrics
Mgr	Monsignor
MHA	Member of House of Assembly
MHR	Member of the House of Representatives
MHRA	Modern Humanities Research Association
MHSM	Member, Institute of Health Services Management
MI	Military Intelligence; Michigan (postal)
MICE	Member, Institution of Civil Engineers
Mich	Michigan
MIChemE	Member, Institution of Chemical Engineers
MICS	Member, Institute of Chartered Shipbrokers
MIEE	Member, Institution of Electrical Engineers (*now see* MIET)
MIEEM	Member, Institute of Ecology and Environmental Management
MIET	Member, Institution of Engineering and Technology (*formerly* Member, Institute of Engineers and Technicians)
MIEx	Member, Institute of Export
MIFA	Member, Institute of Field Archaeologists
MIFM	Member, Institute of Fisheries Management
Mil.	Military
MILT	Member, Chartered Institute of Logistics and Transport
MIM	Member, Institute of Materials (*formerly* Institution of Metallurgists, then Institute of Metals) (*now see* MIMMM)
MIMechE	Member, Institution of Mechanical Engineers
MIMMM	Member, Institute of Materials, Minerals and Mining
MIMunE	Member, Institution of Municipal Engineers (now amalgamated with Institution of Civil Engineers)
Min.	Ministry
Minn	Minnesota
MInstD	Member, Institute of Directors
MInstMC	Member, Institute of Measurement and Control
MInstP	Member, Institute of Physics
MInstPet	Member, Institute of Petroleum
MIPD	Member, Institute of Personnel and Development
MIProdE	Member, Institution of Production Engineers (later MIEE)
MIRTE	Member, Institute of Road Transport Engineers
MIS	Member, Institute of Statisticians
Miss	Mississippi
MIT	Massachusetts Institute of Technology
MJA	Medical Journalists Association
ML	Licentiate in Medicine; Master of Laws
MLA	Member of Legislative Assembly; Modern Language Association; Master in Landscape Architecture; Museums, Libraries and Archives Council
MLC	Member of Legislative Council; Meat and Livestock Commission
MLitt	Master of Letters
MM	Military Medal; Merchant Marine

MMB	Milk Marketing Board
Mme	Madame
MN	Merchant Navy; Minnesota (postal)
MNAS	Member, National Academy of Sciences (US)
MND	Motor Neurone Disease
Mo	Missouri
MO	Medical Officer; Military Operations; Missouri (postal)
MoD	Ministry of Defence
Mods	Moderations (Oxford)
MOH	Medical Officer(s) of Health
MOI	Ministry of Information
MOMA	Museum of Modern Art
MOMI	Museum of the Moving Image
Mon	Monmouthshire
Mont	Montgomeryshire
Most Rev.	Most Reverend
MoT	Ministry of Transport
MP	Member of Parliament
MPBW	Ministry of Public Building and Works
MPhil	Master of Philosophy
MRAC	Member, Royal Agricultural College
MRAeS	Member, Royal Aeronautical Society
MRAIC	Member, Royal Architectural Institute of Canada
MRC	Medical Research Council
MRCGP	Member, Royal College of General Practitioners
MRCOG	Member, Royal College of Obstetricians and Gynaecologists
MRCP	Member, Royal College of Physicians, London; Member, Royal College of Physicians, United Kingdom
MRCPath	Member, Royal College of Pathologists
MRCPE	Member, Royal College of Physicians, Edinburgh
MRCPGlas	Member, Royal College of Physicians and Surgeons of Glasgow
MRCPsych	Member, Royal College of Psychiatrists
MRCS	Member, Royal College of Surgeons of England
MRCVS	Member, Royal College of Veterinary Surgeons
MRI	Magnetic Resonance Imaging; Member, Royal Institution
MRIA	Member, Royal Irish Academy
MRICS	Member, Royal Institution of Chartered Surveyors
MRINA	Member, Royal Institution of Naval Architects
MRSH	Member, Royal Society for the Promotion of Health
MRSocMed	Member, Royal Society of Medicine
MRTPI	Member, Royal Town Planning Institute
MS	Master of Surgery; Master of Science (US); Mississippi (postal); Multiple Sclerosis; Motor Ship
MS, MSS	Manuscript, Manuscripts
MSAE	Member, Society of Automotive Engineeers (US)
MSc	Master of Science
MSC	Manpower Services Commission; Missionaries of the Sacred Heart
MSF	(Union for) Manufacturing, Science, Finance
MSI	Member, Securities Institute (later Securities & Investment Institute)
MSIA	Member, Society of Industrial Artists
MSTD	Member, Society of Typographic Designers
MStJ	Member, Most Venerable Order of the Hospital of St John of Jerusalem
Mt	Mount, Mountain

MTD	Midwife Teachers' Diploma
MTech	Master of Technology
MUniv	Honorary Master of the University
MusB	Bachelor of Music
MusD	Doctor of Music
MVO	Member, Royal Victorian Order
MVSc	Master of Veterinary Science

N

N	Nationalist; Navigating Duties; North
NAAS	National Agricultural Advisory Service
NABC	National Association of Boys' Clubs (later NABC-CYP)
NACF	National Art-Collections Fund
NACRO	National Association for the Care and Resettlement of Offenders
NADFAS	National Association of Decorative and Fine Arts Societies
NAE	National Academy of Engineering
NAMMA	NATO MRCA Management Agency
NAS	National Academy of Sciences
NASA	National Aeronautics and Space Administration (US)
NASD	National Association of Securities Dealers
NAS/UWT	National Association of Schoolmasters/ Union of Women Teachers
NATO	North Atlantic Treaty Organisation
NATS	National Air Traffic Services
Nat. Sci.	Natural Sciences
NAYC	Youth Clubs UK (formerly National Association of Youth Clubs)
NB	New Brunswick; Nebraska (postal)
NBL	National Book League
NBPI	National Board for Prices and Incomes
NC	National Certificate; North Carolina
NCB	National Coal Board
NCC	National Computing Centre; Nature Conservancy Council (later NCCE); National Consumer Council
NCCI	National Committee for Commonwealth Immigrants
NCCL	National Council for Civil Liberties
NCD	National Capital District, Papua New Guinea
NCET	National Council for Educational Technology
NCVO	National Council for Voluntary Organisations
NCVQ	National Council for Vocational Qualifications
NDA	National Diploma in Agriculture
NDC	National Defence College; NATO Defence College
NDD	National Diploma in Dairying; National Diploma in Design
NDH	National Diploma in Horticulture
NDP	New Democratic Party
NE	North-east
NEAC	New English Art Club
NEAF	Near East Air Force
NEB	National Enterprise Board
NEC	National Executive Committee
NECInst	North East Coast Institution of Engineers and Shipbuilders
NEDC	National Economic Development Council; North East Development Council
NEDO	National Economic Development Office
NERC	Natural Environment Research Council
NFC	National Freight Consortium (formerly Corporation, then Company)

NFER	National Foundation for Educational Research
NFT	National Film Theatre
NFU	National Farmers' Union
NH	New Hampshire
NHBC	National House-Building Council
NHS	National Health Service
NI	Northern Ireland; Native Infantry
NIAB	National Institute of Agricultural Botany
NICG	Nationalised Industries Chairmen's Group
NICS	Northern Ireland Civil Service
NIESR	National Institute of Economic and Social Research
NIH	National Institutes of Health (US)
NJ	New Jersey
NL	National Liberal; No Liability
NM	New Mexico (postal)
NMR	Nuclear Magnetic Resonance
Northants	Northamptonshire
Notts	Nottinghamshire
NP	Notary Public
NPA	Newspaper Publishers' Association
NPFA	National Playing Fields Association
NPG	National Portrait Gallery
NPL	National Physical Laboratory
NRA	National Rifle Association; National Recovery Administration (US); National Rivers Authority
NRCC	National Research Council of Canada
NRDC	National Research Development Corporation
NRPB	National Radiological Protection Board
NS	Nova Scotia; New Style in the Calendar (in Great Britain since 1752); National Society; National Service
NSF	National Science Foundation (US)
NSPCC	National Society for Prevention of Cruelty to Children
NSRA	National Small-bore Rifle Association
NSW	New South Wales
NT	New Testament; Northern Territory (Australia); Northwest Territories (Canada); National Theatre; National Trust
NUI	National University of Ireland
NUJ	National Union of Journalists
NUM	National Union of Mineworkers
NUPE	National Union of Public Employees
NUS	National Union of Students; National University of Singapore
NUT	National Union of Teachers
NUU	New University of Ulster
NV	Nevada (postal)
NW	North-west
NWFP	North-West Frontier Province
NY	New York
NYC	New York City
NYO	National Youth Orchestra
NZ	New Zealand
NZEF	New Zealand Expeditionary Force

O

o	only
OAM	Medal of the Order of Australia
O&M	organisation and method
OAS	Organisation of American States; On Active Service
OASC	Officer Aircrew Selection Centre
OBC	Order of British Columbia
OBE	Officer, Order of the British Empire

OC	Officer, Order of Canada (equivalent to former award SM)
OCC	Order of the Caribbean Community
OCS	Officer Candidates School
OCTU	Officer Cadet Training Unit
OCU	Operational Conversion Unit
ODA	Overseas Development Administration
ODI	Overseas Development Institute
ODM	Ministry of Overseas Development
OE	Order of Excellence (Guyana)
OECD	Organization for Economic Co-operation and Development
OEEC	Organization for European Economic Co-operation (*now see* OECD)
OF	Order of the Founder, Salvation Army
OFM	Order of Friars Minor (Franciscans)
OFR	Order of the Federal Republic of Nigeria
OGC	Office of Government Commerce
OGS	Oratory of the Good Shepherd
OH	Ohio (postal)
OJ	Order of Jamaica
OM	Order of Merit; Order of Manitoba
ON	Order of the Nation (Jamaica); Ontario (postal)
Ont	Ontario
ONZ	Order of New Zealand
OOnt	Order of Ontario
OP	*Ordinis Praedicatorum* (of the Order of Preachers (Dominican)); Observation Post
OPCS	Office of Population Censuses and Surveys
OQ	Officer, National Order of Quebec
ORT	Organization for Rehabilitation through Training
o s	only son
OSCE	Organisation for Security and Co-operation in Europe
OStJ	Officer, Most Venerable Order of the Hospital of St John of Jerusalem
OSUK	Ophthalmological Society of the United Kingdom
OTC	Officers' Training Corps
OTS	Office of the Third Sector
OU	Oxford University; Open University
OUAFC	Oxford University Association Football Club
OUDS	Oxford University Dramatic Society
OUP	Oxford University Press; Official Unionist Party
Oxon	Oxfordshire; *Oxoniensis* (of Oxford)

P

PA	Pakistan Army; Personal Assistant; Pennsylvania (postal)
P&O	Peninsular and Oriental Steamship Co.
P&OSNCo.	Peninsular and Oriental Steam Navigation Co.
PAO	Prince Albert's Own
PBS	Public Broadcasting Service
PC	Privy Counsellor; Police Constable; Perpetual Curate; Peace Commissioner (Ireland); Progressive Conservative (Canada)
PCC	Parochial Church Council; Protected Cell Company (Guernsey); Private Cell Company
PCFC	Polytechnics and Colleges Funding Council
PCNZM	Principal Companion, New Zealand Order of Merit
PCT	Primary Care Trust
PE	Procurement Executive; Prince Edward Island (postal)

PEN	Poets, Playwrights, Editors, Essayists, Novelists (Club)
Penn	Pennsylvania
PFA	Professional Footballers' Association
PGA	Professional Golfers' Association
PGCE	Post Graduate Certificate of Education
PHAB	Physically Handicapped & Able-bodied
PhD	Doctor of Philosophy
Phil.	Philology, Philological; Philosophy, Philosophical
PhL	Licentiate in Philosophy
PHLS	Public Health Laboratory Service
Phys.	Physical
PIA	Personal Investment Authority
PIARC	Permanent International Association of Road Congresses
PIRA	Paper Industries Research Association
PLA	Port of London Authority
PLC or plc	public limited company
PLP	Parliamentary Labour Party; Progressive Liberal Party (Bahamas)
PLR	Public Lending Right
PMG	Postmaster-General
PMO	Principal Medical Officer; Princess Mary's Own
PMRAFNS	Princess Mary's Royal Air Force Nursing Service
PNG	Papua New Guinea
PO	Post Office
POB	Presidential Order of Botswana
POMEF	Political Office Middle East Force
POST	Parliamentary Office of Science and Technology
POW	Prisoner of War; Prince of Wales's
PP	Parish Priest; Past President
PPA	Periodical Publishers Association
PPE	Philosophy, Politics and Economics
PPITB	Printing and Publishing Industry Training Board
PPP	Private Patients Plan
PPRA	Past President, Royal Academy
PPRE	Past President, Royal Society of Painter-Printmakers (*formerly* of Painter-Etchers and Engravers)
PPRTPI	Past President, Royal Town Planning Institute
PPS	Parliamentary Private Secretary
PQ	Province of Quebec
PR	Public Relations; Parti républicain
Preb.	Prebendary
Prep.	Preparatory
Pres.	President
Prin.	Principal
PRO	Public Relations Officer; Public Records Office
PRO NED	Promotion of Non-Executive Directors
Proc.	Proctor; Proceedings
Prof.	Professor; Professional
Prov.	Provost; Provincial
PRS	President, Royal Society; Performing Right Society Ltd
PSA	Property Services Agency; Petty Sessions Area
psa	Graduate of RAF Staff College
psc	Graduate of Staff College († indicates Graduate of Senior Wing Staff College)
PSD	Petty Sessional Division; Social Democratic Party (Portugal)
PSI	Policy Studies Institute
PSO	Principal Scientific Officer; Personal Staff Officer

PTA	Passenger Transport Authority; Parent-Teacher Association
ptsc	passed Technical Staff College
Pty	Proprietary
PWD	Public Works Department
PWE	Political Welfare Executive
PWO	Prince of Wales's Own
PWR	Pressurized Water Reactor

Q

Q	Queen
QAA	Quality Assurance Agency for Higher Education
QARANC	Queen Alexandra's Royal Army Nursing Corps
QARNNS	Queen Alexandra's Royal Naval Nursing Service
QBD	Queen's Bench Division
QC	Queen's Counsel; Quebec (postal)
QCA	Qualifications and Curriculum Authority
QCVSA	Queen's Commendation for Valuable Service in the Air
QEH	Queen Elizabeth Hall
QFSM	Queen's Fire Service Medal for Distinguished Service
QHC	Honorary Chaplain to the Queen
QHDS	Honorary Dental Surgeon to the Queen
QHNS	Honorary Nursing Sister to the Queen
QHP	Honorary Physician to the Queen
QHS	Honorary Surgeon to the Queen
Qld	Queensland
Qly	Quarterly
QMC	Queen Mary College, London
QMG	Quartermaster-General
QMW	Queen Mary and Westfield College, London
QO	Qualified Officer
QOY	Queen's Own Yeomanry
QPM	Queen's Police Medal
QS	Quarter Sessions; Quantity Surveying
qs	RAF graduates of the Military or Naval Staff College
QSM	Queen's Service Medal (NZ)
QSO	Queen's Service Order (NZ)
QUB	Queen's University, Belfast
qv	*quod vide* (which see)
qwi	Qualified Weapons Instructor

R

RA	Royal Academician; Royal Academy; Royal (Regiment of) Artillery
RAA	Regional Arts Association; Royal Australian Artillery
RAAF	Royal Australian Air Force
RAAMC	Royal Australian Army Medical Corps
RAC	Royal Automobile Club; Royal Agricultural College; Royal Armoured Corps
RAChD	Royal Army Chaplains' Department
RACI	Royal Australian Chemical Institute
RACP	Royal Australasian College of Physicians
RACS	Royal Australasian College of Surgeons; Royal Arsenal Co-operative Society
RADA	Royal Academy of Dramatic Art
RADAR	Royal Association for Disability Rights (*formerly* Royal Association for Disability and Rehabilitation)
RADC	Royal Army Dental Corps

RADIUS	Religious Drama Society of Great Britain
RAE	Royal Australian Engineers; Royal Aerospace Establishment (*formerly* Royal Aircraft Establishment); Research Assessment Exercise
RAEC	Royal Army Educational Corps
RAEng	Royal Academy of Engineering
RAeS	Royal Aeronautical Society
RAF	Royal Air Force
RAFA	Royal Air Forces Association
RAFO	Reserve of Air Force Officers
RAFVR	Royal Air Force Volunteer Reserve
RAI	Royal Anthropological Institute of Great Britain & Ireland; Radio Audizioni Italiane
RAIA	Royal Australian Institute of Architects
RAM	(Member of) Royal Academy of Music
RAMC	Royal Army Medical Corps
RAN	Royal Australian Navy
R&D	Research and Development
RANR	Royal Australian Naval Reserve
RANVR	Royal Australian Naval Volunteer Reserve
RAOC	Royal Army Ordnance Corps
RAPC	Royal Army Pay Corps
RARDE	Royal Armament Research and Development Establishment
RARO	Regular Army Reserve of Officers
RAS	Royal Astronomical Society; Royal Asiatic Society; Recruitment and Assessment Services
RASC	Royal Army Service Corps (*now see* RCT)
RASE	Royal Agricultural Society of England
RAuxAF	Royal Auxiliary Air Force
RAVC	Royal Army Veterinary Corps
RB	Rifle Brigade
RBA	Member, Royal Society of British Artists
RBK&C	Royal Borough of Kensington and Chelsea
RBL	Royal British Legion
RBSA	(Member of) Royal Birmingham Society of Artists
RC	Roman Catholic
RCA	Member, Royal Canadian Academy of Arts; Royal College of Art; (Member of) Royal Cambrian Academy
RCAF	Royal Canadian Air Force
RCamA	Member, Royal Cambrian Academy
RCAnaes	Royal College of Anaesthetists
RCDS	Royal College of Defence Studies
rcds	completed a course at, or served for a year on the Staff of, the Royal College of Defence Studies
RCGP	Royal College of General Practitioners
RCHME	Royal Commission on Historical Monuments of England
RCM	(Member of) Royal College of Music
RCN	Royal Canadian Navy; Royal College of Nursing
RCNC	Royal Corps of Naval Constructors
RCO	Royal College of Organists
RCOG	Royal College of Obstetricians and Gynaecologists
RCP	Royal College of Physicians, London
RCPath	Royal College of Pathologists
RCPCH	Royal College of Paediatrics and Child Health
RCPI	Royal College of Physicians of Ireland
RCPSG	Royal College of Physicians and Surgeons of Glasgow
RCPsych	Royal College of Psychiatrists
RCR	Royal College of Radiologists

RCS	Royal College of Surgeons of England; Royal Corps of Signals; Royal College of Science
RCSI	Royal College of Surgeons in Ireland
RCT	Royal Corps of Transport
RCVS	Royal College of Veterinary Surgeons
Rd	Road
RD	Rural Dean; Royal Naval and Royal Marine Forces Reserve Decoration
RDC	Rural District Council
RDF	Royal Dublin Fusiliers
RDI	Royal Designer for Industry (Royal Society of Arts)
RE	Royal Engineers; Fellow, Royal Society of Painter-Printmakers (formerly of Painter-Etchers and Engravers); Religious Education
Rear Adm.	Rear Admiral
Regt	Regiment
REME	Royal Electrical and Mechanical Engineers
REPC	Regional Economic Planning Council
Res.	Resigned; Reserve; Resident; Research
RETI	Association of Traditional Industrial Regions
Rev.	Reverend; Review
RFC	Royal Flying Corps (now RAF); Rugby Football Club
RFH	Royal Festival Hall
RFU	Rugby Football Union
RGI	Royal Glasgow Institute of the Fine Arts
RGJ	Royal Green Jackets
RGN	Registered General Nurse
RGS	Royal Geographical Society
RHA	Royal Hibernian Academy; Royal Horse Artillery; Regional Health Authority
RHB	Regional Hospital Board
RHBNC	Royal Holloway and Bedford New College, London
RHG	Royal Horse Guards
RHistS	Royal Historical Society
RHQ	Regional Headquarters
RHS	Royal Horticultural Society; Royal Humane Society
RI	(Member of) Royal Institute of Painters in Water Colours; Rhode Island
RIA	Royal Irish Academy
RIAS	Royal Incorporation of Architects in Scotland
RIASC	Royal Indian Army Service Corps
RIBA	(Member of) Royal Institute of British Architects
RIC	Royal Irish Constabulary; Royal Institute of Chemistry (now see RSC)
RICS	(Member of) Royal Institution of Chartered Surveyors
RIIA	Royal Institute of International Affairs
RILEM	Réunion internationale des laboratoires d'essais et de recherches sur les matériaux et les constructions
RINA	Royal Institution of Naval Architects
RINVR	Royal Indian Naval Volunteer Reserve
RIPA	Royal Institute of Public Administration
RIPH&H	Royal Institute of Public Health and Hygiene (later RIPH)
RLC	Royal Logistic Corps
RLSS	Royal Life Saving Society
RM	Royal Marines; Resident Magistrate; Registered Midwife
RMA	Royal Marine Artillery; Royal Military Academy Sandhurst (now incorporating Royal Military Academy, Woolwich)
RMC	Royal Military College Sandhurst (now see RMA)

RMCS	Royal Military College of Science
RMetS	Royal Meteorological Society
RMIT	Royal Melbourne Institute of Technology
RMLI	Royal Marine Light Infantry
RMO	Resident Medical Officer(s)
RMP	Royal Military Police
RMT	National Union of Rail, Maritime and Transport Workers; Registered Massage Therapist
RN	Royal Navy; Royal Naval; Registered Nurse
RNAS	Royal Naval Air Service
RNC	Royal Naval College
RNCM	(Member of) Royal Northern College of Music
RNEC	Royal Naval Engineering College
RNIB	Royal National Institute of Blind People (formerly Royal National Institute for the Blind, then Royal National Institute of the Blind)
RNID	Royal National Institute for Deaf People (formerly Royal National Institute for the Deaf)
RNLI	Royal National Life-boat Institution
RNLO	Royal Naval Liaison Officer
RNR	Royal Naval Reserve
RNSC	Royal Naval Staff College
RNT	Registered Nurse Tutor; Royal National Theatre
RNVR	Royal Naval Volunteer Reserve
RNZAC	Royal New Zealand Armoured Corps
RNZAF	Royal New Zealand Air Force
RNZN	Royal New Zealand Navy
RNZNVR	Royal New Zealand Naval Volunteer Reserve
RoSPA	Royal Society for the Prevention of Accidents
RP	(Member of) Royal Society of Portrait Painters
RPC	Royal Pioneer Corps
RPMS	Royal Postgraduate Medical School
RPO	Royal Philharmonic Orchestra
RPR	Rassemblement pour la République
RPS	Royal Photographic Society
RRC	Royal Red Cross; Rapid Reaction Corps
RRE	Royal Radar Establishment (later RSRE)
RSA	Royal Scottish Academician; Royal Society of Arts; Republic of South Africa
RSAF	Royal Small Arms Factory
RSAMD	Royal Scottish Academy of Music and Drama
RSAS	Royal Surgical Aid Society
RSC	Royal Society of Canada; Royal Society of Chemistry; Royal Shakespeare Company
RSCM	(Member of) Royal School of Church Music
RSE	Royal Society of Edinburgh
RSF	Royal Scots Fusiliers
RSFSR	Russian Soviet Federated Socialist Republic
RSGS	Royal Scottish Geographical Society
RSL	Royal Society of Literature; Returned Services League of Australia
RSM	Royal School of Mines
RSM or RSocMed	Royal Society of Medicine
RSMHCA	Royal Society for Mentally Handicapped Children and Adults (see Mencap)
RSNC	Royal Society for Nature Conservation
RSO	Rural Sub-Office; Railway Sub-Office; Resident Surgical Officer
RSPB	Royal Society for Protection of Birds
RSPCA	Royal Society for Prevention of Cruelty to Animals

RSSAf	Royal Society of South Africa
RSSPCC	Royal Scottish Society for Prevention of Cruelty to Children
RSTM&H	Royal Society of Tropical Medicine and Hygiene
RSV	Revised Standard Version
RSW	Member, Royal Scottish Society of Painters in Water Colours
Rt Hon.	Right Honourable
Rt Rev.	Right Reverend
RTE	Radio Telefis Eireann
RTL	Radio-Télévision Luxembourg
RTPI	Royal Town Planning Institute
RTR	Royal Tank Regiment
RTS	Religious Tract Society; Royal Toxophilite Society; Royal Television Society
RU	Rugby Union
RUC	Royal Ulster Constabulary
RURAL	Society for the Responsible Use of Resources in Agriculture & on the Land
RUSI	Royal United Services Institute for Defence and Security Studies (formerly Royal United Service Institution)
RVC	Royal Veterinary College
RWA	(Member of) Royal West of England Academy
RWF	Royal Welch Fusiliers
RWS	(Member of) Royal Society of Painters in Water Colours
RYA	Royal Yachting Association

S

(S)	(in Navy) Paymaster; Scotland
S	Succeeded; South; Saint
s	son
SA	South Australia; South Africa; Société Anonyme; Society of the Atonement
SAAF	South African Air Force
SABC	South African Broadcasting Corporation
SACEUR	Supreme Allied Commander Europe
SACLANT	Supreme Allied Commander Atlantic
SADG	Société des Architectes Diplômés par le Gouvernement
SAE	Society of Automobile Engineers (US)
SAMC	South African Medical Corps
SARL	Société à Responsabilité Limitée
Sarum	Salisbury
SAS	Special Air Service
Sask	Saskatchewan
SASO	Senior Air Staff Officer
SBAC	Society of British Aerospace Companies (formerly Society of British Aircraft Constructors)
SBS	Special Boat Service; Silver Bauhinia Star (Hong Kong)
SBStJ	Serving Brother, Most Venerable Order of the Hospital of St John of Jerusalem
SC	Star of Courage (Canada); Senior Counsel; South Carolina
sc	student at the Staff College
SCAA	School Curriculum and Assessment Authority
ScD	Doctor of Science
SCF	Senior Chaplain to the Forces; Save the Children Fund
Sch.	School
SCI	Society of Chemical Industry
SCM	State Certified Midwife; Student Christian Movement
SCONUL	Standing Conference of National and University Libraries

Scot.	Scotland
SCOTVEC	Scottish Vocational Education Council
SD	Staff Duties; South Dakota (postal)
SDA	Social Democratic Alliance; Scottish Diploma in Agriculture; Scottish Development Agency
SDP	Social Democratic Party
SE	South-east
SEAC	South-East Asia Command
SEATO	South-East Asia Treaty Organization
Sec.	Secretary
SEFI	European Society for Engineering Education
SEPM	Society of Economic Palaeontologists and Mineralogists
SERC	Science and Engineering Research Council
SESO	Senior Equipment Staff Officer
SF	Sinn Féin
SFA	Securities and Futures Authority
Sgt	Sergeant
SHA	Secondary Heads Association (now see ASCL); Special Health Authority
SHAEF	Supreme Headquarters, Allied Expeditionary Force
SHAPE	Supreme Headquarters, Allied Powers, Europe
SHHD	Scottish Home and Health Department
SIAD	Society of Industrial Artists and Designers (now see CSD)
SIB	Shipbuilding Industry Board; Securities and Investments Board (now see FSA)
SICOT	Société Internationale de Chirurgie Orthopédique et de Traumatologie
SIESO	Society of Industrial and Emergency Services Officers
SIME	Security Intelligence Middle East
SITPRO	Simpler Trade Procedures Board (formerly Simplification of International Trade Procedures)
SJ	Society of Jesus (Jesuits)
SJAB	St John Ambulance Brigade
SK	Saskatchewan (postal)
SLD	Social and Liberal Democrats
SME	School of Military Engineering
SMMT	Society of Motor Manufacturers and Traders Ltd
SMO	Senior Medical Officer; Sovereign Military Order
SMPTE	Society of Motion Picture and Television Engineers (US)
SNP	Scottish National Party
SNTS	Society for New Testament Studies
SO	Staff Officer; Scientific Officer; Symphony Orchestra
SOAS	School of Oriental and African Studies
Soc.	Society; Socialist (France)
SOE	Special Operations Executive; Society of Operations Engineers
SOLT	Society of London Theatre
SOSc	Society of Ordained Scientists
SOTS	Society for Old Testament Study
sowc	Senior Officers' War Course
SpA	Società per Azioni
SPAB	Society for the Protection of Ancient Buildings
SPCK	Society for Promoting Christian Knowledge
SPD	Salisbury Plain District; Sozialdemokratische Partei Deutschlands
SPG	Society for the Propagation of the Gospel (now see USPG)
SPk	Sitara-e-Pakistan
SPMO	Senior Principal Medical Officer

SPSO	Senior Principal Scientific Officer
SPTL	Society of Public Teachers of Law
sq	staff qualified
Sq.	Square
Sqdn or Sqn	Squadron
SR	Special Reserve; Southern Railway; Southern Region (BR)
SRA	Solicitors Regulation Authority
SRC	Science Research Council (later SERC); Students' Representative Council
SRN	State Registered Nurse
SRO	Supplementary Reserve of Officers; Self-Regulatory Organisation
SS	Saints; Straits Settlements; Steamship
SSA	Society of Scottish Artists; Side Saddle Association
SSAFA	Soldiers, Sailors, Airmens and Families Association-Forces Help (formerly Soldiers', Sailors', and Airmen's Families Association)
SSC	Solicitor before Supreme Court (Scotland); Sculptors Society of Canada; *Societas Sanctae Crucis* (Society of the Holy Cross); Short Service Commission
SSEB	South of Scotland Electricity Board
SSEES	School of Slavonic and East European Studies
SSO	Senior Supply Officer; Senior Scientific Officer
SSR	Soviet Socialist Republic
SSRC	Social Science Research Council (*now see* ESRC)
St	Street; Saint
STA	Sail Training Association
STC	Senior Training Corps
STD	*Sacrae Theologiae Doctor* (Doctor of Sacred Theology)
STL	*Sacrae Theologiae Lector* (Reader or a Professor of Sacred Theology)
STM	*Sacrae Theologiae Magister* (Master of Sacred Theology)
STSO	Senior Technical Staff Officer
SUNY	State University of New York
Supt	Superintendent
Surg.	Surgeon
SW	South-west
SWET	Society of West End Theatre

T

T	Telephone; Territorial
TA	Telegraphic Address; Territorial Army
TAA	Territorial Army Association
TAF	Tactical Air Force
T&AFA	Territorial and Auxiliary Forces Association
T&AVR	Territorial and Army Volunteer Reserve
TARO	Territorial Army Reserve of Officers
TAS	Torpedo and Anti Submarine Course
TASS	Technical, Administrative and Supervisory Section of AUEW (now part of MSF)
TAVRA or TA&VRA	Territorial Auxiliary and Volunteer Reserve Association
TC	Order of the Trinity Cross (Trinidad and Tobago)
TCCB	Test and County Cricket Board
TCD	Trinity College, Dublin (University of Dublin, Trinity College)
TCPA	Town and Country Planning Association
TD	Territorial Efficiency Decoration; Efficiency Decoration (T&AVR) (since April 1967); Teachta Dala (Member of the Dáil, Eire)

TEC	Technician Education Council (later BTEC); Training and Enterprise Council
Temp.	Temperature; Temporary
Tenn	Tennessee
TES	Times Educational Supplement
TESOL	Teaching English to Speakers of other Languages
TET	Teacher of Electrotherapy
Tex	Texas
TGWU	Transport and General Workers' Union
ThD	Doctor of Theology
THES	Times Higher Education Supplement
ThL	Theological Licentiate
ThM	Master of Theology
TLS	Times Literary Supplement
TMMG	Teacher of Massage and Medical Gymnastics
TN	Tennessee (postal)
TPI	Town Planning Institute (*now see* RTPI)
Trans.	Translation; Translated
TRE	Telecommunications Research Establishment (later RRE)
TRH	Their Royal Highnesses
TRIC	Television and Radio Industries Club
Trin.	Trinity
TSB	Trustee Savings Bank
tsc	passed a Territorial Army Course in Staff Duties
TUC	Trades Union Congress
TV	Television
TX	Texas (postal)

U

U	Unionist
UAE	United Arab Emirates
UAR	United Arab Republic
UBC	University of British Columbia
UC	University College
UCCA	Universities Central Council on Admissions
UCE	University of Central England
UCEA	Universities and Colleges Employers Association
UCH	University College Hospital (London)
UCL	University College London
UCLA	University of California at Los Angeles
UCMSM	University College and Middlesex School of Medicine
UCNW	University College of North Wales
UCSB	University of California at Santa Barbara
UCSD	University of California at San Diego
UCW	University College of Wales; Union of Communication Workers
UDC	Urban District Council; Urban Development Corporation
UEA	University of East Anglia
UEFA	Union of European Football Associations
UEL	University of East London
UFC	Universities' Funding Council
UGC	University Grants Committee (later UFC)
UHI	University of Highlands & Islands Millennium Institute
UICC	Union Internationale contre le Cancer
UK	United Kingdom
UKAEA	United Kingdom Atomic Energy Authority
UKERNA	United Kingdom Education and Research Networking Association
UKIP	United Kingdom Independence Party
UKLF	United Kingdom Land Forces
UKMIS	United Kingdom Mission
ULPS	Union of Liberal and Progressive Synagogues

UMDS	United Medical and Dental Schools
UMIST	University of Manchester Institute of Science and Technology
UN	United Nations
UNA	United Nations Association
UNDP	United Nations Development Programme
UNEP	United Nations Environment Programme
UNESCO or **Unesco**	United Nations Educational, Scientific and Cultural Organisation
UNIDO	United Nations Industrial Development Organisation
UNITAR	United Nations Institute of Training and Research
Univ.	University
UNRRA	United Nations Relief and Rehabilitation Administration
UNRWA	United Nations Relief and Works Agency
UP	United Provinces; Uttar Pradesh; United Presbyterian
URC	United Reformed Church; Urban Regeneration Company
URSI	Union Radio-Scientifique Internationale
US	United States
USA	United States of America
USAAF	United States Army Air Force
USAF	United States Air Force
USC	University of Southern California
USDAW	Union of Shop Distributive and Allied Workers
USMC	United States Marine Corps
USN	United States Navy
USNR	United States Naval Reserve
USPG	United Society for the Propagation of the Gospel
USPHS	United States Public Health Service
USSR	Union of Soviet Socialist Republics
UUK	Universities UK
UWCC	University of Wales College of Cardiff
UWCM	University of Wales College of Medicine
UWE	University of the West of England
UWIST	University of Wales Institute of Science and Technology

V

V	Five (Roman numerals); Version; Vicar; Viscount; Vice
v	*versus* (against)
Va	Virginia
VA	Virginia (postal)
V&A	Victoria and Albert
VAT	Value Added Tax
VC	Victoria Cross; Voluntary Controlled
VCGS	Vice Chief of the General Staff
VD	Royal Naval Volunteer Reserve Officers' Decoration (*now* VRD); Volunteer Officers' Decoration; Victorian Decoration
VDC	Volunteer Defence Corps
Ven.	Venerable
Vet.	Veterinary

VG	Vicar-General
Vic	Victoria
Vice Adm.	Vice Admiral
VMA	Fixed Wing Marine Attack
VMH	Victoria Medal of Honour (Royal Horticultural Society)
Vol.	Volume; Voluntary; Volunteers
VQMG	Vice-Quartermaster-General
VRD	Royal Naval Volunteer Reserve Officers' Decoration
VSO	Voluntary Service Overseas
VT	Vermont (postal)

W

W	West
W/Cdr	Wing Commander
WA	Western Australia; Washington (postal)
WAAF	Women's Auxiliary Air Force (later WRAF)
Wash	Washington State
WCC	World Council of Churches
WCMD	Welsh College of Music and Drama
WEA	Workers' Educational Association; Royal West of England Academy
WEU	Western European Union
WHO	World Health Organization
WI	West Indies; Women's Institute; Wisconsin (postal)
Wilts	Wiltshire
Wis	Wisconsin
WLA	Women's Land Army
Wm	William
WMO	World Meteorological Organization
WNO	Welsh National Opera
WO	War Office; Warrant Officer
Worcs	Worcestershire
WR	West Riding; Western Region (BR)
WRNS	Women's Royal Naval Service
WRVS	Women's Royal Voluntary Service
WS	Writer to the Signet
WVS	Women's Voluntary Services (*now see* WRVS)
WWF	World Wide Fund for Nature (*formerly* World Wildlife Fund)

XYZ

X	Ten (Roman numerals)
y	youngest
Yeo.	Yeomanry
YHA	Youth Hostels Association
YMCA	Young Men's Christian Association
Yorks	Yorkshire
yr	younger
yrs	years
YT	Yukon Territory (postal)
ZANU PF	Zimbabwe African National Union Patriotic Front
ZAPU	Zimbabwe African People's Union
ZIPRA	Zimbabwe People's Revolutionary Army

ADDENDA

The following biographies are of those whose deaths occurred before 31 December 2005, but were not reported until after the volume of *Who Was Who* covering the years 2000–2005 had been published.

ASTON, Sir Harold (George), Kt 1983; CBE 1976; Chairman and Chief Executive, Bonds Coats Patons Ltd, 1981–87 (Deputy Chairman, 1970–80); Director, Central Sydney Area Health Service, 1988–92; *b* Sydney, 13 March 1923; *s* of Harold John Aston and Annie Dorothea McKeown; *m* 1947, Joyce Thelma Smith (decd); one *s* one *d. Educ:* Crown Street Boys' Sch., Sydney, Australia. Manager, Buckinghams Ltd, Sydney, 1948–55; Bonds Industries Ltd: Merchandising Manager, 1955–63; Gen. Man., 1963–67; Man. Dir, 1967–70; Director: Bonds Coats Patons Ltd (formerly Bonds Industries Ltd); Manufacturers Mutual Insurance, 1982– (Vice Chm., 1987–); Downard-Pickfords Pty Ltd, 1983–89 (Chm.); Australian Guarantee Corp. Ltd, 1983–88; Australian Manufacturing Life Assce Ltd, 1984–88; Rothmans Hldgs Ltd, 1986– (Dep. Chm., 1989–); Westpac Banking Corp., 1988–92; Chm., Television and Telecasters Ltd, 1991–92; Consultant, Pacific Dunlop Ltd, 1987–. President: Textile Council of Australia, 1973–80 (Life Mem., 1984); Confedn of Aust. Industry, 1980 82; Hon. Trustee, Cttee for Econ. Develt of Australia, 1988–; Governor: Aesop Foundn, 1988–; (Founding), Heart Inst. of Australia, 1986–93. CompTI 1984; FCFI 1986; CStJ 1993 (Dep. Receiver-Gen., Finance Cttee, 1985–). *Recreations:* walking, gardening, travelling. *Address:* 58/129 Surf Parade, Broadbeach, Qld 4218, Australia. *Clubs:* American, Australian, Royal Sydney Yacht Squadron (Sydney); Concord Golf. *Died 15 May 2005.*

BELL, James Steven, CMG 1989; CBE 1964; DFC 1946; QPM 1956; CPM 1950; Director General, Ministry of the Interior, Bahrain, retired; *b* 30 Sept. 1914; *s* of Lachlan Steven Bell and Mary (*née* Bertram). *Educ:* Whitehaven School. Grenadier Guards A Cadet, 1933–35; Kent County Constabulary, 1935–41; RAF, 1941–46; Nigeria Police, 1946–64; Bahrain Public Security, Ministry of the Interior, 1966–93. Nigerian Police Medal, 1960; Order of Bahrain 1st Cl., 1983; Bahrain Public Security Medal for Distinguished Service, 1988. *Recreations:* walking, reading, travel. *Address:* c/o Barclays Bank, Strand Street, Whitehaven, Cumbria CA28 7DL. *Died 20 Nov. 2000.*

BESLEY, Christopher; a Metropolitan Magistrate, 1964–88; *b* 18 April 1916; *s* of late C. A. Besley, Tiverton; *m* 1947, Pamela, *d* of Dr W. E. David, Sydney, Australia; four *s* two *d. Educ:* King's Coll., Wimbledon; King's Coll., London. Called to the Bar, Gray's Inn, 1938; practised Western Circuit. Served War of 1939–45, Devon Regt (wounded, N Africa). *Address:* Queen Elizabeth Building, Temple, EC4Y 9BS; 15 Belvedere Avenue, SW19 7PP. *Club:* Lansdowne. *Died 26 June 2004.*

BLAND, Louise Sarah, (Mrs S. Bland); *see* Godfrey, L. S.

BONELLI, Pierre Sauveur Ernest; Chairman and Chief Executive Officer, Bull Group, since 2001; *b* 28 May 1939; *s* of Pierre Bonelli and Victoria Bonelli (*née* Seren); *m* 1962, Harriet Becker; three *s. Educ:* Ecole Polytechnique, Paris; Harvard Business Sch. (MBA 1965). Joined Texas Instruments, Dallas, 1966: engr, 1966–68; Financial Manager, 1968–75; Vice-Pres. i/c US Digital Circuits Div., 1975; Gen. Manager, 1971, then Pres.-Gen. Manager, 1971–76, Texas Instruments France; Sema-Metra, Paris: Dir Gen., 1976–82; CEO, 1982–88; Sema-Metra merged with CAP Gp, UK, 1988 to form Sema Gp;

CEO, Sema Gp plc, 1988–2001. Mem., Adv. Bd and Technol. Regulatory Bd, Bank of France. Mem. Adv. Council, LSO. Légion d'Honneur (France), 1993. *Died 1 April 2004.*

BOOTH, Brian George, OBE 2004; JP; DL; Chairman, Lancashire Teaching Hospitals (formerly Preston Acute Hospitals) NHS Trust, 1997 2004; Vice Chancellor, University of Central Lancashire (formerly Rector and Chief Executive, Lancashire Polytechnic), 1989–98; *b* 6 Sept. 1942; *s* of George and Ada Booth; *m* 1965, Barbara Ann (*née* Wright); two *d. Educ:* Univ. of Manchester (BA Econ 1964); Brunel Univ. (MTech 1972). FSS 1968–2000. Asst Lectr in Statistics, High Wycombe Coll. of Technology, 1965–68; Lectr, Sen. Lectr, and Principal Lectr, Kingston Polytechnic, 1968–73; Hd, Dept of Business and Admin, 1974–78, Dean, Faculty of Business and Management, 1978–82, Preston Polytechnic; Dep. Dir, Preston Polytechnic, later Lancashire Polytechnic, 1982–89. Chair of Bd, Preston Business Venture, 1983–92; Chair of Trustees, Preston Postgrad. Med. Centre, 1990–96; Director: Lancs Partnership Against Crime, 1997–; Central Lancs Develt Agency, 1998–2000; (non-exec.), Student Loans Co. Ltd, 1998–. Trustee, Nat. Football Museum, 1996– (Chm., 2001–). JP Preston, 1987; DL Lancs, 2002. CCMI (CIMgt 1992). DUniv Central Lancashire, 1998. *Recreations:* golf, watching Preston North End. *Address:* 9 Moorfield Close, Fulwood, Preston, Lancs PR2 9SW. *T:* (01772) 864243, *Fax:* (01772) 865636. *Died 24 Oct. 2004.*

BROINOWSKI, John Herbert, CMG 1969; FCA; finance and investment consultant; Senior Partner, J. H. Broinowski & Storey, Chartered Accountants, 1944–54; Founder/Chairman and Managing Director, Consolidated Metal Products Ltd, 1954–70; Chairman, Vielun Poll Hereford Stud, since 1955; *b* 19 May 1911; *s* of late Dr G. H. Broinowski and Mrs Ethel Broinowski (*née* Hungerford); *m* 1939, Jean Gaerloch Broinowski, *d* of Sir Norman and Lady Kater; one *s* one step *s. Educ:* Sydney Church of England Grammar Sch. Served Australian Imperial Forces (Captain), 1940–44, New Guinea. Chief Exec. and Dep. Chm., Schroder Darling and Co. Ltd, 1963–73; Exec. Chm., Sims Consolidated Ltd, 1970–83; Chairman: Zip Heaters Ltd, 1987–93; Utilux Ltd, 1977–93; Allied Lyons Australia, 1982–92; Director: Electrical Equipment Ltd, 1954–77; Readers Digest Aust., 1955–77; Mount Morgan Ltd, 1962–67 (Chm.); Peko-Wallsend Ltd, 1962–83; South British United Insurance Gp, 1965–73; Hoyts Theatres Ltd, 1968–79 (Chm.); Compunet Ltd, 1969–77 (Chm.); Orient Lloyd Gp, Singapore, 1970–87 (Chm.); Doulton Aust. Ltd, 1972–77; Robe River Ltd, 1972–73; Aquila Steel Co. Ltd, 1973–81 (Chm.); Formfit Ltd, 1974–79 (Chm.); John Sands Ltd, 1974–77; Clive Hall Ltd, 1974–84 (Chm.); Castlemaine Tooheys Ltd, 1977–83 (Dep. Chm.); Hin Kong Ltd, 1977–86 (Chm.); Judson Steel Corp., San Francisco, 1979–83 (Chm.). Chm., Photographic Index of Australian Wildlife, 1980–93. Hon. Life Member: Aust. Council for Rehabilitation of the Disabled (Pres., 1964–68); Northcott Soc. (formerly NSW Soc. for Crippled Children) (Pres., 1970–77); Vice-Pres., Internat. Soc. for Rehabilitation of the Disabled, 1966–72. *Publications:* A Family Memoir, 1993. *Address:* 7 South Avenue, Double Bay, Sydney, NSW 2028, Australia. *T:* (2) 93287534. *Clubs:* Australian (Sydney); Royal Sydney Golf. *Died 16 April 2005.*

BROWN, David John Bowes, CBE 1982; FCSD; Chairman, Multidrive Ltd, since 1996; *b* 2 Aug. 1925; *s* of Matthew and Helene Brown; *m* 1st, 1954, Patricia Robson (marr. diss. 1982); two *s* two *d*; 2nd, 1986, Eve Watkinson (marr. diss. 1998). *Educ:* King James Grammar Sch., Knaresborough; Leeds College of Technology. Logging Contractor, UK and W Africa, 1946–60; joined Hunslet Engine Co. as Designer/Draughtsman, 1960–62; designed and patented transmission and exhaust gas conditioning systems for underground mines tractors; joined Chaseside as Chief Designer, 1962–65; designed and patented 4 wheel drive loading shovels; became Director and Chief Executive; joined Muir-Hill Ltd as Man. Dir, 1965–73; designed and patented 4 wheel drive tractors, cranes, steering systems, transmissions, axles; started DJB Engineering Ltd, 1973 (which became Artix Ltd, 1985); designed, manufactured and sold a range of off-highway articulated dump trucks in Peterlee, Co. Durham; the company gained 4 Queen's Awards and 1 Design Council Award; formed Brown Design Engineering Ltd, 1987 for design and building of Telescopic Handlers and the patented Multidrive system; both cos sold to Caterpillar Inc., 1996; founded Multidrive Ltd, 1996, for design and manuf. of tractors, construction trucks and military vehicles. FRSA. *Address:* Ravensthorpe Manor, Boltby, Thirsk, N Yorks YO7 2DX. *Died 28 Jan. 2004.*

CAMPBELL, Robert, FICE; management consultant; Chairman and Chief Executive, Rem Campbell Management Ltd, 1987–2000; *b* 18 May 1929; *s* of Robert Stewart Campbell and Isobella Frances Campbell; *m* 1950, Edna Maud Evans. *Educ:* Emmanuel IGS; Loughborough Univ. (DLC (Hons), MSc). MIWES. Member of Gray's Inn, 1960. Contracts Engineer, Wyatts, Contractors, 1954–56; Chief Asst Engr, Stirlingshire and Falkirk Water Board, 1956–59; Water Engr, Camborne, 1959–60; Chief Asst City Water Engr, Plymouth, 1960–65; Civil Engr, Colne Valley Water Co., 1965–69; Engrg Inspector, Min. of Housing and Local Govt/DoE, 1969–74; Asst Dir, Resources, Planning, Anglian Water Authority, 1974–77; Chief Executive, Epping Forest Dist Council, 1977–79; Sec., ICE, 1979–81, and Man. Dir, Thomas Telford Ltd, Dir, Watt Cttee on Energy, and Hon. Sec., ICE Benevolent Fund, 1979–81; Chm., Rem Campbell Internat., 1981–87. Freeman of City of London, 1977; Liveryman of Horners' Co., 1977–. *Publications:* The Pricing of Water, 1973. *Recreations:* golf, music, caravanning, cricket. *Address:* Bronafon, Pen-y-Banc, Llechryd, near Cardigan, Dyfed SA43 2NR. *Club:* MCC. *Died May 2003.*

CARR, Glyn; see Styles, F. S.

CHARLES, Sir George (Frederick Lawrence), KCMG 1998; CBE 1972; JP; Chief Minister, St Lucia, 1960–64; *b* 7 June 1916; *s* of James Luke Charles and Marie Philomene Jean Baptiste; *m* 1942, Amelia Charles (*née* Francois); two *s* three *d*. *Educ:* Soufriere RC Boys' Sch.; Dennery RC Boys' Sch.; St Mary's Coll. Secondary Sch. Mem., St Lucia Volunteer Force, 1940–43. Trade unionist, 1946–79: Sec., 1949–54, Pres., 1954–68, St Lucia Workers' Union; Pres., St Lucia Agriculture and General Workers' Union, 1968–79. Mem. (Lab), Castries CC, 1949–52, 1954–57. MHA (Lab) S Castries, St Lucia, 1951–74; Minister of Social Services, 1956–60; Leader of the Opposition, 1964–69. Labour Advr to govt, 1979–82. Editor, St Lucia Workers' Clarion, 1950–57. JP St Lucia, 1950. St Lucia Cross, 1986. *Publications:* History of the Labour Movement in Saint Lucia (1946–1974), 1995. *Recreations:* reading, bridge, games, TV, conversationalist. *Address:* Summersdale, Castries, St Lucia. *T:* 4527265. *Died 26 June 2004.*

CHINO, Yoshitoki, Hon. KBE 1992; Hon. Chairman, Daiwa Securities Co. Ltd, since 1991; *b* 18 March 1923; *s* of Hisakichi Chino and Tokiyo Chino; *m* 1950, Sachiko Kawabata; one *s* one *d*. *Educ:* Keio Univ. (BA Law 1946). Joined Daiwa Securities Co. Ltd, 1946: Gen. Manager, Sales and Foreign Depts, 1959–61; Dir, 1961–65; Man.

Dir, 1966–70; Sen. Man Dir, 1970–72; Exec. Vice-Pres., 1972–81; Vice-Chm., 1981–82; Chm., 1982–91. Commendatore dell'Ordine al Merito (Italy), 1994. *Publications:* Internationalization by Feel, 1988. *Recreations:* personal computer, reading books, fishing. *Address:* Daiwa Securities Co. Ltd, 6–4 Otemachi 2-chome, Chiyoda-ku, Tokyo 100, Japan. *Died 2004.*

CHRISTIANSON, Alan, CBE 1971; MC 1945; Deputy Chairman, South of Scotland Electricity Board, 1967–72; *b* 14 March 1909; *s* of Carl Robert Christianson; *m* 1936, Gladys Muriel Lewin, *d* of William Barker; two *d*. *Educ:* Royal Grammar Sch., Newcastle upon Tyne. FCA, FIEE. Served as Major, RA, 1939–45: comd Field Battery, 1943–45. Central Electricity Bd, 1934–48; Divisional Sec., British Electricity Authority, SW Scotland Div., 1948–55; Dep. Sec., S of Scotland Electricity Bd, 1955–62; Chief Financial Officer, 1962–65; Gen. Man., Finance and Administration, 1965–67. *Recreation:* golf. *Address:* Tynedale, Lennox Drive East, Helensburgh, Argyll and Bute G84 9JD. *T:* (01436) 674503. *Deceased.*

COOK, George David, CEng, FIEE; Consultant, Quantel Ltd, 1985–93, retired; *b* 23 Sept. 1925; *s* of late John and Jean C. Cook; *m* 1954, Sylvia Ann Sampson; two *d*. *Educ:* Hendon College of Technology. BBC Planning and Installation Dept, 1947; Asst to Supt Engineer, Television Outside Broadcasts, 1955; Head of Engineering, Wales, 1963; Asst Chief Engr, Television, 1967; Chief Engr Transmitters, 1974; Asst Dir of Engrg, 1978; Dep. Dir of Engrg, 1984–85. *Recreations:* golf, theatre. *Address:* 26 Ridge Lane, Watford, Herts WD1 3TA. *T:* (01923) 229638. *Died 16 Dec. 2005.*

CORCORAN, Hon. (James) Desmond, AO 1982; Chairman, South Australia Greyhound Racing Board, 1983–95; Member, South Australia Totalisator Board, 1982–95; *b* 8 Nov. 1928; *s* of James and Catherine Corcoran; *m* 1957, Carmel Mary Campbell; four *s* four *d*. *Educ:* Tantanoola Public School. Enlisted Australian Regular Army, 1950; served Korea, Japan, Malaya and New Guinea (despatches twice); discharged, rank of Captain, 1962. Entered politics, contested and won House of Assembly seat of Millicent, SA Parliament, 1962, Member for Coles, 1975; MP (Lab) Hartley, 1977–82; held portfolios of Minister of Lands, Irrigation, Repatriation, Immigration and Tourism, in Labor Govt, 1965–68; Dep. Leader of Opposition, 1968–70; Dep. Premier, Minister of Works and Minister of Marine, 1970–77, additionally Minister of Environment, 1977–79; Premier, Treasurer, and Minister of Ethnic Affairs, of S Australia, Feb.–Sept. 1979. *Address:* 44/ Stamford Grand Apts, Moseley Square, Glenelg, SA 5045, Australia. *Died 3 Jan. 2004.*

D'ARCY, Most Rev. (Joseph) Eric; Archbishop (RC) of Hobart (Australia), 1988–99, then Emeritus; *b* 25 April 1924; *s* of late Joseph D'Arcy, MM and Eileen (*née* McCoy). *Educ:* De La Salle Coll. and Corpus Christi Coll., Melbourne; Univs of Melbourne (BA Hons; MA). Oxford (DPhil), and Gregoriana (PhD). Asst priest, Melbourne, 1949–55; Chaplain, Nat. Civic Council, 1955–59; Lectr, 1962, Sen. Lectr, 1966, Reader in Philosophy, 1975–81, Univ. of Melbourne; Bishop of Sale, 1981–88. Danforth Prof of Philosophy, Univ. of Minnesota, 1968. Member: Pontifical Commn for Culture, 1982–92; Vatican Pontifical Congregation for Bishops, 1993–98; Pontifical Congregation for Catholic Educn, 1989–94. *Publications:* Conscience, Right to Freedom, 1961 (trans. Spanish 1964, French 1965); Human Acts, 1963; (ed and trans.) St Thomas Aquinas, Pleasure, 1967, The Emotions, 1975. *Recreations:* walking, reading. *Address:* PO Box 146, East Melbourne, Vic 3002, Australia. *Clubs:* Oxford and Cambridge; University House (Melbourne). *Died 12 Dec. 2005.*

DAVIS, Nathanael Vining; Chairman, 1947–86, and Chief Executive Officer, 1947–79, Alcan Aluminium Limited; *b* 26 June 1915; *s* of Edward Kirk Davis and Rhea Reineman Davis; *m* 1941, Lois Howard

Thompson; one *s* one *d*. *Educ*: Harvard Coll.; London Sch. of Economics. With Alcan group, 1939–79, with exception of 3 years on active duty with US Navy. Director: Bank of Montreal, 1961–86; Canada Life Assurance Co., Toronto, 1961–86. *Address*: 50 Fox Island Road, Box 309, Osterville, MA 02655, USA. *Club*: University (New York).   *Died 22 March 2005.*

de FARIA, Antonio Leite, Hon. GCVO 1973; Grand Cross of Christ (Portugal), 1949; Portuguese Ambassador to the Court of St James's, 1968–73; retired; *b* 23 March 1904; *s* of Dr Antonio B. Leite de Faria and Dona Lucia P. de Sequeira Braga Leite de Faria; *m* 1926, Dona Herminia Cantilo de Faria; two *s*. *Educ*: Lisbon University (Faculty of Law). Attaché to Min. of Foreign Affairs, 1926; Sec. to Portuguese Delegn, League of Nations, 1929–30; 2nd Sec., Rio de Janeiro, 1931, Paris, 1933, Brussels, 1934; 1st Sec., London, 1936; Counsellor, London, 1939; Minister to Exiled Allied Govts, London, 1944; Minister to The Hague, 1945; Dir Gen., Political Affairs, and Actng Sec. Gen., Min. of Foreign Affairs, 1947; Ambassador: Rio de Janeiro, 1950; NATO, 1958; Paris, 1959; Rome (Holy See), 1961. Holds many foreign decorations. *Address*: Rua da Horta Seca 11, 1200 Lisboa, Portugal. *T*: (1) 3422538.   *Died 16 Nov. 2000.*

DOIG, Ralph Herbert, CMG 1974; CVO 1954; *b* 24 Feb. 1909; *s* of late William and Rose Doig; *m* 1937, Barbara Crock; two *s* four *d*. *Educ*: Guildford Grammar Sch.; University of Western Australia (BA, DipCom). Entered Public Service of WA, 1926; Private Sec. to various Premiers, 1929–41; Asst Under-Sec., Premier's Dept, 1941, Under-Sec., Premier's Dept, and Clerk of Executive Council, Perth, Western Australia, 1945–65; Public Service Comr, W Australia, 1965–71; Chm., Public Service Board, WA, 1971–74. State Director: visit to Western Australia of the Queen and the Duke of Edinburgh, 1954; visit of the Duke of Edinburgh for British Empire and Commonwealth Games, 1962; visit of the Queen and the Duke of Edinburgh, 1963. *Recreation*: bowls. *Address*: 12B Corbett Street, Scarborough, WA 6019, Australia. *T*: (8) 93411701.   *Died 15 March 2005.*

DONDELINGER, Jean; Ambassador of Luxembourg to Greece, 1993–95; *b* Luxembourg, 4 July 1930; *m*; one *s*. *Educ*: Nancy Univ.; Paris Univ.; St Antony's Coll., Oxford. Barrister, Luxembourg, 1954–58; Asst to Head, Internat. Economic Relations Service, Dept of Foreign Affairs, 1958–61; Dep. Permanent Rep. of Luxembourg to EEC, 1961–70, Ambassador and Permanent Rep., 1970–84; Sec.-Gen., Min. of Foreign Affairs, 1984; Mem., EEC, 1989–92. Rep. of Pres. of Govt, Cttee on Institutional Affairs (Dooge Cttee), 1984–85; Chm., Negotiating Gp on Single Act, 1986; Vice-Pres., ITU World Conf. on Fixing of Orbital Frequencies of Satellites, 1988. *Address*: 12 Chaussée St Martin, 6989 Hostert, Niederanven, Luxembourg.   *Died 21 Oct. 2004.*

EALES, Victor Henry James, CEng, MIMechE; Director of Weapons Production and Quality (Naval), 1980–81, and Head of Naval Weapons Professional and Technical Group, 1979–81, Ministry of Defence; *b* 11 Dec. 1922; *s* of William Henry and Frances Jean Eales; *m* 1949, Elizabeth Gabrielle Irene James; two *s* one *d*. *Educ*: Wimbledon Central Sch.; Guildford Technical Coll.; Portsmouth Polytechnic. Ministry of Defence: Asst Director, Weapons Production (Naval), 1970; Dep. Director, Surface Weapons Projects (Naval), 1975; Director, Weapons Production (Naval), 1979. *Recreation*: golf. *Address*: 11 Penrhyn Avenue, East Cosham, Portsmouth, Hants PO6 2AX.   *Died 30 Dec. 2004.*

FORD, George Johnson; DL; Member, Cheshire County Council, 1962–87 (Chairman, 1976–82); *b* 13 March 1916; *s* of James and Esther Ford; *m* 1941, Nora Helen Brocklehurst; three *s* one *d*. *Educ*: Chester Coll. Qualified estate agent, 1938. FAI 1938. Member, Runcorn RDC, 1953 (Chm., 1962); Mem. Bd, Warrington and Runcorn Develt Corp., 1981–87

(Runcorn Develt Corp., 1964–81). Mem., West Mercia Cttee, Nat. Trust, 1982. Pres., Frodsham Conservative Assoc., 1962–; Vice Pres., Eddisbury Parly Div., 1984. DL Cheshire, 1979. *Recreations*: horse racing, music and drama. *Address*: Windmill Bank, Manley, Warrington, Cheshire WA6 9DZ. *T*: (01928) 740447. *Club*: City (Chester).   *Died 17 July 2005.*

FOSTER, Peter Martin, CMG 1975; HM Diplomatic Service, retired; *b* 25 May 1924; *s* of Capt. Frederick Arthur Pearce Foster, RN and Marjorie Kathleen Sandford; *m* 1947, Angela Hope Cross; one *s* one *d*. *Educ*: Sherborne; Corpus Christi Coll., Cambridge. Army (Horse Guards), 1943–47; joined Foreign (later Diplomatic) Service, 1948; served in Vienna, Warsaw, Pretoria/Cape Town, Bonn, Kampala, Tel Aviv; Head of Central and Southern Africa Dept, FCO, 1972–74; Ambassador and UK Rep. to Council of Europe, 1974–78; Ambassador to German Democratic Republic, 1978–81. Dir, Council for Arms Control, 1984–86; Chm., Internat. Social Service of GB, 1985–90. *Address*: Rew Cottage, Abinger Lane, Abinger Common, Surrey RH5 6ZH.   *Died April 2004.*

FROST, Dame Phyllis Irene, AC 1992; DBE 1974 (CBE 1963); Patron, Victorian Relief Committee, since 2001 (Member since 1964; Chairman, 1973–2001); *b* 14 Sept. 1917; *née* Turner; *m* 1941, Glenn Neville Frost (*d* 1987), LDS, BDSc, JP; three *d*. *Educ*: Croydon Coll., Vic.; St Duthus Coll.; Presbyterian Ladies' Coll.; Univ. of Melbourne. Dip. of Physiotherapy, 1939; studied Criminology, 1955–56. Chairman: Victorian (formerly Fairlea) Women's Prison Council, 1953–99; Aust. Contact Emergency Service, 1984–; Vice Chairman: Victorian Assoc. for Care and Resettlement of Offenders, 1977–; Clean World Internat., 1980–92; Mem., State Disaster Welfare Cttees, Vic, 1983–; Exec. Mem., Aust. Football League Foundn, 1997–. Hon. Life Member: Aust. Crime Prevention Council, 1972; Aust. Freedom from Hunger Campaign, 1977; Nat. Council of Women of Victoria, 1979; Keep Australia Beautiful Nat. Council (former Chm.); Trustee, patron, hon. life mem., hon. convener, and life governor of many community service, health and welfare orgns. Attended several internat. confs as Aust. delegate or representative, including: Internat. Council of Women; FAO; FFHC (Chm., 4th Session in Rome, 1969; Chm., 3rd Regional Congress for Asia and the Far East, at Canberra, 1970, and Rome, 1971). Fellow, Melvin Jones Internat. Foundn, 1991. Chm., Bd of Dirs, Brain Behaviour Res. Inst., La Trobe Univ., 1984–91. JP, Vic, 1957–84. Freedom: City of Croydon, 1989; City of Maroondah, 1997. DSocSc *hc*, Univ. of Technol., Melb., 1993. Woman of the Year, Sun News Pictorial, 1970; Humanitarian Award, Rosicrucian Order, USA, 1971; Community Service Award, Victorian Employers' Fedn, 1978, Distinguished Service to Children Award, Aust. Parents without Partners, Vic, 1984; Community Service Award, Seventh Day Adventists, 1985; Australian Achiever, Australia Day, 1998. *Address*: Llanberis, 4 Jackson Street, Croydon, Vic 3136, Australia. *T*: (3) 97232382. *Clubs*: Royal Automobile (Vic); War Widows Guild.   *Died 31 Oct. 2004.*

GARDINER, Dame Helen (Louisa), DBE 1961 (CBE 1952); MVO 1937; *b* 24 April 1901; *y d* of late Henry Gardiner, Bristol. *Educ*: Clifton High School. Formerly in Private Secretary's Office, Buckingham Palace; Chief Clerk, 1946–61. *Recreations*: reading, gardening.   *Died 21 July 2001.*

GETHING, Air Commodore Richard Templeton, CB 1960; OBE 1945; AFC 1939; *b* 11 Aug. 1911; *s* of George A. Gething, Wilmslow, Cheshire; *m* 1940, Margaret Helen, *d* of late Sir Herbert Gepp, Melbourne, Australia; one *s* one *d*. *Educ*: Malvern; Sydney Sussex Coll., Cambridge. Joined RAF, 1933; navigator and co-pilot of Vickers Wellesley aircraft which set world record for distance in straight line (flying Ismailia, Egypt to Darwin, Australia non-stop), 1938. Served War of 1939–45: Canada; UK; India; Burma. Actg Group

Capt., 1943; Group Capt., 1950; Actg Air Commodore, 1956; Dir Operations, Maritime Navigation and Air Traffic, Air Ministry, 1956–60, retired. FRIN (FIN 1956). *Recreation:* gliding. *Address:* Garden Hill, Kangaroo Ground, Vic 3097, Australia. *Club:* Royal Air Force.
Died 15 May 2004.

GODFREY, Louise Sarah, (Mrs Stanley Bland); QC 1991; a Recorder of the Crown Court, since 1989; a Deputy High Court Judge, since 1994; *b* 17 April 1950; *d* of Philip Godfrey and Pearl (*née* Goodman); *m* 1977, Stanley Leslie Bland; two *d. Educ:* Tadcaster Grammar Sch.; St Hugh's Coll., Oxford (MA Jurisprudence). Called to the Bar, Middle Temple, 1972, Bencher 1998. Part-time Chm., Police Disciplinary Tribunal, 1997–; Member: Mental Health Review Tribunal, 2000–; Criminal Injuries Compensation Appeals Panel, 2000–. Leader, NE Circuit, 2001–02. *Recreations:* cooking, reading. *Address:* Park Court Chambers, 16 Park Place, Leeds LS1 2SJ. *T:* (0113) 243 3277. *Died 12 June 2002.*

GODSELL, Stanley Harry; Regional Director (South West), Departments of Environment and Transport, 1978–80; retired; *b* 19 March 1920; *s* of Thomas Harry Godsell and Gladys Godsell; *m* 1946, Rosemary Blackburn (*d* 1990); one *s* (and one *s* decd). *Educ:* Alsop High Sch., Liverpool. Civil Service: PO, 1937–48; Min. of Town and Country Planning, 1948; Asst Sec., Min. of Housing and Local Govt, 1965. *Recreations:* bridge, swimming, croquet, photography. *Address:* 6 Pitch and Pay Park, Sneyd Park, Bristol BS9 1NJ. *T:* (0117) 968 3791. *Died 8 Aug. 2004.*

GOOD, Sir John K.; *see* Kennedy-Good.

HART, Frank Thomas; JP; *b* London, 9 Nov. 1911; *s* of late Samuel Black and Ada Frances Laura Hart; *m* 1938, Eveline Brenda Deakin (*d* 1993), Leek, Staffs; three *s. Educ:* Gravesend and Sheerness Jun. Technical Schs; DPA (London); Dip. of Econs (London); BA Open, 1982. Asst Sec., 1931–34, Sec., 1934–42, Buchanan Hosp., St Leonards-on-Sea; Sec., Central London Eye Hosp., 1942–44; Sec.-Superintendent, Princess Louise Hosp., 1944–48; Superintendent, Royal Infirmary, Sheffield, 1948–52; House Governor and Sec. to the Bd, Charing Cross Hosp., 1952–73; Hosp. Manager, Zambia Medical Aid Soc., 1973–75. Mem. Tribunal set up by President of Zambia to hear applications for release from political detainees. Life Pres., League of Friends, Charing Cross Hosp., 1985–; Past President: Assoc. of Hosp. Secretaries; Hosp. Officers' Club. JP: Co. Middx, 1955–65; Co. Surrey, 1965–77; East Sussex, 1978–81. Freeman, City of London, 1959; Liveryman, Worshipful Soc. of Apothecaries. *Publications:* (jointly) A Study of Hospital Administration, 1948; Roots of Service (A History of Charing Cross Hospital), 1985. *Recreations:* all games, walking, reading. *Address:* 124 Marine Court, St Leonards on Sea, E Sussex TN38 0DY. *Died 21 April 2001.*

HASSETT, Maj.-Gen. Ronald Douglas Patrick, CB 1978; CBE 1975; Executive Director, Orient New Zealand Trading Co. Ltd, 1979–85; *b* 27 May 1923; *s* of Edmond Hassett and Elinor Douglas; *m* 1953, Lilian Ivy Gilmore; two *s* one *d. Educ:* St Patrick's Coll., Wellington; RMC Duntroon; psc, G, rcds. 2nd NZ Expeditionary Force, Italy, 1944–46; NZ Army Liaison Staff, London, 1948–50; served Korea, NZ and Malaya, 1952–62; NZ Instructor, Australian Staff Coll., 1963–65; Dir of Equipment, NZ Army, 1966–67; DQMG, 1967–69; Comdr NZ Inf. Brigade Group, 1969; DCGS, 1970; RCDS, 1971; ACDS (Policy), 1972–74; Dep. Chief of Defence Staff, 1974–76; Chief of General Staff, NZ Army, 1976–78. *Recreation:* gardening. *Address:* 5A Ventnor Road, Remuera, Auckland, New Zealand.
Died 13 Aug. 2004.

HATCHARD, Frederick Henry; Stipendiary Magistrate for Metropolitan County of West Midlands (Birmingham), 1981–91, retired; *b* 22 April 1923; *s* of Francis and May Hatchard; *m* 1955, Patricia Egerton; two *s. Educ:* Yardley Grammar Sch., Birmingham. Justices Clerk: Sutton Coldfield and Coleshill, 1963–67; Walsall, 1967–81. *Recreations:* walking, gardening. *Address:* 3(B) Manor Road, Streetly, Sutton Coldfield B74 3NQ.
Died 30 Nov. 2005.

HEATHCOTE-SMITH, Clifford Bertram Bruce, CBE 1963; HM Diplomatic Service, 1936–72; acting Senior Clerk, Department of Clerk of House of Commons, 1973–77; *b* 2 Sept. 1912; *s* of late Sir Clifford E. Heathcote-Smith, KBE, CMG; *m* 1940, Thelma Joyce Engström; two *s. Educ:* Malvern; Pembroke Coll., Cambridge. Entered Consular Service, 1936; served in China, 1937–44; Foreign Office, 1944–47; Political Adviser, Hong-Kong, 1947–50, Montevideo, 1951–56; Commercial Counsellor: Ankara, 1956–60; Copenhagen, 1960–64; Washington, 1964–65; Dep. High Comr, Madras, 1965–68; a Diplomatic Service Inspector, 1969–72. *Address:* 4 Britts Farm Road, Buxted, E Sussex TN22 4LZ. *T:* (01825) 733635.
Died 31 Aug. 2003.

HENREY, Madeleine, (Mrs Robert Henrey); authoress; *b* Paris, 13 Aug. 1906; *née* Madeleine Gal; *m* 1928, Robert Selby Henrey (*d* 1982), *o s* of Rev. Thomas Selby Henrey, Vicar of Old Brentford, Mddx, and Euphemia, *d* of Sir Coutts and Lady Lindsay of Balcarres; one *s. Educ:* Protestant Girls' Sch., Clichy, Convent of The Holy Family, Tooting, SW. *Publications:* autobiographical sequence in the following chronological order: The Little Madeleine, 1951, NY 1953; An Exile in Soho, 1952; Julia, 1971; A Girl at Twenty, 1974; Madeleine Grown Up, 1952, NY 1953; Green Leaves, 1976; Madeleine Young Wife, NY 1954, London 1960; London under Fire 1940–45, 1969; A Month in Paris, 1954; Milou's Daughter, 1955, NY 1956; Her April Days, 1963; Wednesday at Four, 1964; Winter Wild, 1966; She Who Pays, 1969; The Golden Visit, 1979 (read in the above order these volumes make one consecutive narrative); *other books:* A Farm in Normandy, 1941; A Village in Piccadilly, 1943; The Incredible City, 1944; The Foolish Decade, 1945; The King of Brentford, 1946; The Siege of London, 1946; The Return to the Farm, 1947; London (illustrations by Phyllis Ginger, RWS) 1948, New York, 1949; A Film Star in Belgrave Square, 1948; A Journey to Vienna, 1950; Matilda and the Chickens, 1950; Paloma, 1951, NY 1955; A Farm in Normandy and the Return, 1952; Madeleine's Journal, 1953; This Feminine World, 1956; A Daughter for a Fortnight, 1957; The Virgin of Aldermanbury (illustrations by Phyllis Ginger), 1958; Mistress of Myself, 1959; The Dream Makers, 1961; Spring in a Soho Street, 1962. *Recreations:* most feminine occupations: sewing, knitting, ironing, gardening. *Address:* c/o J. M. Dent & Sons, Orion House, 5 Upper St Martin's Lane, WC2H 9EA; Ferme Robert Henrey, 14640 Villers-sur-Mer, Calvados, France. *T:* (2) 31870388. *Died 25 April 2004.*

HERBERT, Alfred James; British Council Representative, Portugal, 1980–84; *b* 16 Oct. 1924; *s* of Allen Corbyn Herbert and Betty Herbert; *m* 1st, 1958, Helga Elberling (*d* 1981); two *s*; 2nd, 1982, Dr Wanda Wolska. *Educ:* Royal Masonic Schs; University Coll. London (BA 1950, MA 1952). Guest Prof. of English Lit., Univs of Yokohama and Tokyo, 1958–60; Lectr, English Dept, Birmingham Univ., 1960–62; joined British Council, 1962: Sierra Leone, 1962–65; Brazil, 1965–68; Representative: Somalia, 1968–70; Pakistan, 1974–77; Poland, 1977–80. *Publications:* Modern English Novelists, (Japan), 1960; Structure of Technical English, 1965. *Recreations:* travelling, reading. *Address:* Quinta do Val do Riso, São Simão, Azeitão, 2900 Setubal, Portugal.
Died 7 May 2003.

HEWITT, Stephen Geoffrey, CB 2003; Director of Product and Business Design, Jobcentre Plus, Department for Work and Pensions, since 2001; *b* 9 March 1950; *s* of late Geoffrey Gordon Hewitt and Doreen Brinsdon Hewitt; *m* 1992, Jill Elizabeth Harris; one *s. Educ:* Weymouth Grammar Sch.; Dulwich Coll.; Sussex Univ.

(BSc Chem. 1971; MSc Hist. of Science 1972). Admin trainee, N Ireland Office, 1975; Private Sec. to Ray Carter, MP, 1977–78; transf. to Dept of Social Security, 1990; Dir of Personnel, 1993–98; Dir for People of Working Age, subseq. Dir of Working Age Change, 1998–2001. *Address:* Jobcentre Plus, Caxton House, Tothill Street, SW1H 9NA. *Died 8 Dec. 2005.*

HITCHEN, John David; a Recorder of the Crown Court, 1978–2001; *b* 18 July 1935; *s* of late Harold Samuel and Frances Mary Hitchen; *m* 1966, Pamela Ann Cellan-Jones (*d* 2002). *Educ:* Woodhouse Grove Sch., nr Bradford; Pembroke Coll., Oxford (BA(Hons)). Called to Bar, Lincoln's Inn, 1961. *Recreations:* music, reading. *Address:* 39 Rutland Drive, Harrogate, Yorks HG1 2NX. *T:* (01423) 566236. *Died 23 Dec. 2004.*

HUTCHINSON, Prof. George William, PhD; Professor of Physics, Southampton University, 1960–85, then Emeritus; *b* Feb. 1921; *s* of George Hutchinson, farmer, and Louisa Ethel (*née* Saul), Farnsfield, Notts; *m* 1943, Christine Anne (marr. diss. 1970), *d* of Matthew Rymer and Mary (*née* Proctor), York; two *s. Educ:* Abergele Grammar Sch.; St John's Coll., Cambridge (State Schol. and Schol., 1939–42; MA 1946; PhD 1952). Research worker and factory manager in cotton textile industry, 1942–47; Cavendish Lab., Cambridge, 1947–52; Clerk-Maxwell Schol. of Cambridge Univ., 1949–52; Nuffield Fellow, 1952–53, and Lecturer, 1953–55, in Natural Philosophy, University of Glasgow; Research Assoc. of Stanford Univ., Calif, 1954; Lecturer, 1955, Sen. Lectr, 1957, in Physics, University of Birmingham. Member: Nat. Exec. Cttee, AUT, 1978–84; Nat. Council, CND, 1981–84, Internat. Sec., Scientists Against Nuclear Arms, 1985–90; Exec. Cttee, British Peace Assembly, 1988–92 (Acting Chm., 1990–92; Chm., 1992); Exec. Cttee, World Disarmament Campaign UK, 1988– (Jt Chm., 1999–; Chm., 2003–04). Exec. Cttee, Labour Action for Peace, 1990– (Membership Sec., 1992–97). Duddell Medal, Physical Soc., 1959. FRAS; FRSA. *Publications:* papers on nuclear and elementary particle physics, nuclear instrumentation and cosmic rays, and disarmament and peace. *Recreations:* music, travel. *Address:* Physical Laboratory, University of Southampton, Southampton SO9 5NH. *T:* (023) 8059 5000. *Died 22 Oct. 2004.*

HUTCHINSON, Hon. Sir Ross, Kt 1977; DFC 1944; Speaker, Legislative Assembly, Western Australia, 1974–77, retired; MLA (L) Cottesloe, 1950–77; *b* 10 Sept. 1914; *s* of Albert H. Hutchinson and Agnes L. M. Hutchinson; *m* 1939, Amy Goodall Strang; one *s* one *d. Educ:* Wesley Coll., Perth. RAAF, 1942–45. School teacher, 1935–49. Chief Sec., Minister for Health and Fisheries, 1959–65; Minister for Works and Water Supplies, 1965–71. Australian Rules Football, former Captain Coach; East Fremantle, West Perth and South Fremantle; Captain Coach, WA, 1939. *Recreations:* tennis, reading. *Address:* 42 Griver Street, Cottesloe, WA 6011, Australia. *T:* (8) 93842680. *Club:* Royal King's Park Tennis (Perth, WA). *Died 19 Dec. 1999.*

HUYDECOPER, Jonkheer (Jan Louis) Reinier, Hon. GCVO 1982 (Hon. KCVO 1972); Commander, Order of Orange Nassau, 1986 (Officer, 1966); Chevalier, Order of Netherlands Lion, 1980; Ambassador of the Netherlands to the Court of St James's, and concurrently to Iceland, 1982–86; *b* 23 Feb. 1922; *s* of Jonkheer Louis Huydecoper and Jonkvrouwe Laurence B. W. Ram; *m* 1944, Baroness Constance C. van Wassenaer; one *s* two *d. Educ:* Univ. of Utrecht (LLM). Banking, 1942–44; Legal Dept, Min. of Finance, The Hague, 1945–46; entered Min. of For. Affairs, 1946; UN, NY, 1946; Ottawa, 1947–48; Mil. Mission, Berlin, 1949–50; Bonn, 1950–52; London, 1952–56; Djakarta, 1956–59; Washington, 1959–62; Rome, 1962–66; Min. of For. Affairs, 1966–70; London, 1970–73; Ambassador, Hd of Delegn to Conf. on Security and Co-operation in

Europe, Helsinki and Geneva, 1973–74; Ambassador: Moscow, 1974–77; Lisbon, 1978–80; Inspector of For. Service, Min. of For. Affairs, 1981–82. Holds various foreign orders. *Died 19 Oct. 2005.*

JACK, Sir David (Emmanuel), GCMG 1991; MBE 1975; Governor General, St Vincent and The Grenadines, 1989–96; *b* 16 July 1918; *s* of John Fitzroy Jack and Margaret Lewis Jack; *m* 1946, Esther Veronica McKay; two *s* two *d* (and one *s* decd). *Educ:* Stubbs Govt School; La Salle Extension Univ., Chicago (Dip. Higher Accountancy). Teacher's Cert., St Vincent Educn Dept. School Teacher, 1934–43; Engine Operator, Shell Oil Refinery, 1943–45; Commercial Accounting, 1945–69; Gen. Manager, A'Root Ind., 1969–79; in business and politics, 1979–84; MP for N Windward, 1984–89; Minister of Labour and Community Develt, and of Health, 1984–89. Methodist local preacher, 1940–96. *Recreations:* carpentry, music. *Address:* PO Box 381, New Montrose, St Vincent and The Grenadines. *T:* 4561270. *Died 18 July 1998.*

JAHN, Dr Wolfgang; Managing Director, Commerzbank AG, Düsseldorf, 1969–84; *b* 27 Sept. 1918; *s* of Dr Georg Jahn and Ella (*née* Schick); *m* 1949, Gabriele (*née* Beck); two *s* one *d. Educ:* Zürich Univ.; Berlin Univ.; Heidelberg Univ. (DrEcon). Industrial Credit Bank, Düsseldorf, 1949–54; IBRD, Washington, 1954–57; Commerzbank AG, Düsseldorf, 1957–84. *Address:* c/o Commerzbank AG, PO Box 101137, 40002 Düsseldorf, Germany. *Died 24 June 2005.*

JAYAWARDENA, Dr Lal; Chairman, World Bank-sponsored Global Development Network of Development Research Institutions, Washington, 2000–02; Senior Fellow, Social Scientists Association, Colombo, 2000–02; *b* 27 May 1934; *s* of late Neville Ubesinghe Jayawardena and Gertrude Mildred Jayawardena; *m* 1958, Kumari de Zoysa; one *s. Educ:* Royal Coll., Colombo; King's Coll., Cambridge (BA 1956; MA, PhD 1963; Hon. Fellow, 1989). Econs Affairs Officer, UN, 1963–66; Econ. Advr and Dir, Perspective Planning Div., Min. of Planning and Econ. Affairs, Colombo, 1963–71; Additional Sec., 1971–75, Sec. to Treasury, and Sec., 1975–78, Min. of Finance and Planning; Ambassador to Belgium, The Netherlands, Luxembourg and EC, 1978–82; Dir-Gen., Econ. Affairs, Min. of Foreign Affairs, 1982–85; Asst Sec.-Gen., UN, and Dir, World Inst. for Develt Econs Res., Helsinki, 1985–93; Econ. Advr to Pres. of Sri Lanka, 1994–99; Dep. Chm., Nat. Develt Council, 1996–99; High Comr for Sri Lanka in UK and concurrently to Republic of Ireland, 1999–2000. Rapporteur, Vice-Chm., then Chm., 1972–74, Second Vice-Chm., then First Vice-Chm., 1997–99, Deputies of Gp of Twenty-Four (G-24); Dep., Cttee of Twenty on Reform of Internat. Monetary System, 1972–74; Mem., Gp of Eminent Persons advising Brandt Commn on Internat. Develt Issues, 1978–80. *Publications:* (contrib.) The International Monetary and Financial System, ed G. K. Helleiner, 1996; contrib. and contrib. jtly numerous monographs in World Inst. for Develt Econs Res. Study Gp series; contrib. numerous articles on develt econs. *Recreations:* reading, music. *Address:* No 69 Gregory's Road, Colombo 7, Sri Lanka. *T:* (1) 692656, *Fax:* (1) 697792. *Died 8 April 2004.*

JENKINS, Hon. Dr Henry Alfred, AM 1991; retired; *b* 24 Sept. 1925; *s* of Henry Alfred Jenkins and Eileen Clare Jenkins (*née* McCormack); *m* 1951, Hazel Eileen Winter; three *s* one *d. Educ:* Ormond, Eltham and Heidelberg State Schools; Ivanhoe Grammar Sch.; Univ. of Melbourne (MSc, MB BS); Deakin Univ. (BA). Tutor, Univ. of Melbourne, 1946–52; RMO Alfred Hosp., 1953; Medical Practitioner, 1953–61; MLA (Lab) Reservoir, Parliament of Victoria, 1961–69; MP (Lab) Scullin, Federal Parliament of Australia, 1969–85; Chm. of Committees and Dep. Speaker, House of Representatives, 1975–76, Speaker, 1983–85; Aust.

Ambassador to Spain, 1986–88. *Recreations:* reading, hobby farming, community service. *Address:* 61 Mill Park Drive, Mill Park, Vic 3082, Australia. *Club:* Royal Automobile of Victoria. *Died 27 July 2004.*

JOHNSON, (Robert) Brian, CBE 1990; QPM 1981; DL; Chief Constable, Lancashire Constabulary, 1983–95; *b* 28 July 1932; *s* of Robert and Hilda Johnson; *m* 1954, Jean Thew; two *d. Educ:* Stephenson Memorial Boys' Sch.; College of Commerce, Newcastle. Newcastle City Police: Police Cadet, 1948; Police Constable, 1952; Detective Constable, 1955; Detective Sergeant, 1962; Detective Inspector, 1966; Detective Chief Inspector, 1969; Detective Supt, Northumbria Police, 1971; Chief Supt, Northumbria Police, Home Office, 1976; Asst Chief Constable, Northumbria, 1977; Dep. Chief Constable, Lancashire, 1981. President: ACPO, 1991–92; Lancs Assoc. of Boys Clubs, 1983–95; Lancs Outward Bound Assoc., 1983–95; Vice-Pres., Lancs Council for Voluntary Youth Services, 1985–. DL Lancs, 1989. *Recreations:* reading, golf. *Died 23 April 2005.*

JOHNSTON, James Campbell, CBE 1972; Chairman: Capel Court Corporation Ltd, 1969–84; Australian Foundation Investment Co., 1967–84; Director, National Mutual T&G Life Association of Australasia Ltd (formerly of T&G Mutual Life Society), 1976–84; *b* 7 July 1912; *s* of late Edwin and Estelle Johnston; *m* 1938, Agnes Emily, *yr d* of late Richard Thomas; two *s* one *d. Educ:* Prince Alfred Coll., Adelaide; Scotch Coll., Melbourne; University of Melbourne. Admitted to Inst. Chartered Accountants, Australia, 1933; joined J. B. Were & Son, Stock and Share Brokers, 1935, Sen. Partner, 1967–78; Stock Exchange of Melbourne: Mem., 1947; Chm., 1972–77; Hon. Fellow, Australian Stock Exchange, 1991. Comr. State Electricity Commn of Victoria, 1978–83. Chartered Accountant of the Year, 1984. *Address:* 2/714 Orrong Road, Toorak, Vic 3142, Australia. *Clubs:* Melbourne, Royal Melbourne Golf (Melbourne). *Died 14 Aug. 2003.*

KATENGA-KAUNDA, Reid Willie; Malaŵi Independence Medal, 1964; Malaŵi Republic Medal, 1966; Political Adviser to State President, Malaŵi, since 1994; *b* 20 Aug. 1929; *s* of Gibson Amon Katenga Kaunda and Maggie Talengeske Nyabanda; *m* 1951, Elsie Nyabanda; one *s* three *d* (and one *s* one *d* decd). *Educ:* Ndola Govt Sch., Zambia; Inst. of Public Administration, Malaŵi; Trinity Coll., Oxford Univ.; Administrative Staff Coll., Henley; LSE. Sec., Nkhota Kota Rice Co-op. Soc. Ltd, 1952–62; Dist Comr, Karonga, Malaŵi, 1964–65; Sen. Asst Sec., Min. of External Affairs, Zomba, Malaŵi, 1966; MP and Parly Sec., Office of the President and Cabinet, Malaŵi, 1966–68; Dep. Regional Chm., MCP, Northern Region, 1967–68; Under Sec., Office of the President and Cabinet, 1968–69; High Comr in London, 1969–70; Perm. Sec., Min. of Trade, Industry and Tourism, 1971–72; High Comr in London, 1972–73, and concurrently to the Holy See, Portugal, Belgium, Holland and France; business exec., 1975–94. Dep. Sec. Gen., 1992–99, Sec. Gen., 1999–, United Democratic Front, Malaŵi. Chm., Interparty Technical Cttee on Peace and Unity, 1999–. Dep. Chm., Ncheu and Mchinji Inquiry Commn, 1967. *Recreations:* reading, walking, cinema, Association football. *Address:* c/o PO Box 511, Blantyre, Malaŵi. *Died 21 April 2004.*

KENNEDY-GOOD, Sir John, KBE 1983; QSO 1977; JP; Mayor of Lower Hutt, 1970–86; *b* Goulburn, NSW, 8 Aug. 1915; *s* of Charles Kennedy-Good; *m* 1940, June, *d* of Charles Mackay; four *s* three *d. Educ:* Southland Boys' High Sch.; Otago Univ. (BDS). Practised as dentist, 1942–72. Mem., Lower Hutt City Council, 1962–87. Dir, Hutt Milk Corp., 1970–71, 1974–87; Chairman: Hutt Valley Underground Water Authy, 1970–72 (Mem., 1962–72); Wellington Regl Council, 1980–87 (Dep. Chm., 1980–83); NZ Council of Social Services, 1975–82; Member: Wellington Harbour Bd, 1971–80; Hutt Valley Energy Bd, 1970–87. Past Mem., NZ Catchment Authorities' Exec. Pres., NZ Sister Cities Inc. Chm., Dowse Art Mus. Bd, 1971–87; Dep. Chm., Nat.

Art Gall. and Mus. Trust Bd (Mem., 1971). Mem., NZ Acad. Fine Arts, 1948. Founder Chm., John Kennedy-Good Human Resources Centre; Chm., Wellington Paraplegic Trust Bd (Vice-Pres., NZ Fed.); past Chm., Council for Dental Health, and past Pres., Wellington Br., NZ Dental Assoc.; Life Patron and Mem. Bd, Hutt Valley Disabled Resources Trust; Pres., Wellington Div., Order of St John; Patron, Wellington Reg. Centre, NZ Red Cross Soc.; patron, pres. or vice-pres. of numerous charity, cultural and sporting orgns. Trustee, Waiwhetu Marae, 1970–; Hon. Elder, Te Atiawa Tribe. JP Lower Hutt, 1970. *Address:* 129 Peninsula Club Resort, 441 Whangaparaoa Road, Hybiscus Coast, Auckland, New Zealand. *Clubs:* Hutt, Hutt Rotary (past Pres.), Hutt Golf. *Died 11 July 2005.*

KEPA, Sailosi Wai; a Judge of the High Court, Fiji, 1992–2003; Ombudsman, Fiji, 1996–2002 (on secondment); *b* 4 Nov. 1938; *m* Adi Teimumu Tuisawau; four *c. Educ:* Draiba Fijian Sch.; Lelean Memorial Sch.; Nasinu Training Coll.; Sydney Univ. (Dip. in Teaching of English, 1966). Called to the Bar, Middle Temple, 1972; Barrister and Solicitor, Fiji, 1974. Joined Judicial Dept, as Magistrate, 1969; served Suva, Northern Div., Sigatoka, Nadi; Chief Magistrate, July 1980; Dir of Public Prosecutions, Nov. 1980; High Comr for Fiji in London, 1985–88; Attorney-Gen. and Minister for Justice, Fiji, 1988–92. Chairman: Bd of Legal Educn, Fiji, 1997–; Fiji Human Rights Commn, 1998–. Rugby player (rep. Fiji, Australia 1961), coach, manager, administrator; Life Mem., Fiji Rugby Football Union (Chm., 1983–85); Pres., Suva Rugby Union, 1989–92. *Address:* GPO Box 982, Suva, Fiji. *T:* (office) 211652, (home) 313416, *Fax:* 314756. *Clubs:* Suva Bowling, United Improvement (Suva). *Died 1 March 2004.*

KOTSOKOANE, Hon. Joseph Riffat Larry; Commander, Order of Ramatseatsana, 1982; development consultant (agriculture and rural development, formerly human and natural resources), since 1986; Minister of Education, Sports and Culture, Lesotho, 1984–86; *b* 19 Oct. 1922; *s* of Basotho parents, living in Johannesburg, South Africa; *m* 1947, Elizabeth (*née* Molise); two *s* three *d. Educ:* BSc (SA); BSc Hons (Witwatersrand); Cert. Agric. (London). Development Officer, Dept of Agric., Basutoland, 1951–54; Agric. Educn Officer i/c of Agric. Sch. for junior field staff, 1955–62; Agric. Extension Officer i/c of all field staff of Min. of Agric., 1962–63; Prin. Agric. Off. (Dep. Dir), Min. of Agric., 1964–66; High Comr for Lesotho, in London, 1966–69; Ambassador to Germany, Holy See, Rome, France, and Austria, 1968–69; Permanent Sec. and Hd of Diplomatic Service, Lesotho, 1969–70; Permanent Sec. for Health, Educn and Social Welfare, Lesotho, 1970–71; High Comr for Lesotho in East Africa, Nigeria and Ghana, 1972–74; Minister: of Foreign Affairs, Lesotho, 1974–75; of Education, 1975–76; of Agriculture, 1976–78; Perm. Rep. to UN, 1978; Sec. to the Cabinet and Head of CS (Sen. Perm. Sec.), 1978–84. Guest of Min. of Agric., Netherlands, 1955; studied agric. educn, USA (financed by Carnegie Corp. of NY and Ford Foundn), 1960–61; FAO confs in Tunisia, Tanganyika and Uganda, 1962 and 1963; Mem. Lesotho delegn to 24th World Health Assembly, 1971; travelled extensively to study and observe methods of agric. administration, 1964; meetings on nutrition, Berlin and Hamburg, 1966; diplomatic trainee, Brit. Embassy, Bonn, 1966. Hon. PhD Fort Hare, S Africa, 2001. Gold Medal, Fertilizer Soc. of SA, 1998; Merit Award, Nat. African Farmers' Union of SA, 1998; Medal, ARC of SA, 1999. *Recreations:* swimming, amateur dramatics, photography, debating, reading, travelling. *Address:* PO Box 1015, Maseru 100, Lesotho, Southern Africa. *T:* 22312913, *Fax:* 22311769. *Died 25 July 2004.*

KRISTIANSEN, Erling (Engelbrecht), Grand Cross, Order of Dannebrog; Hon. GCVO 1974; Director, East Asiatic Co., 1978–90, and other companies; *b* 31 Dec. 1912; *s* of Kristian Engelbrecht Kristiansen, Chartered Surveyor, and Andrea Kirstine (*née* Madsen); *m* 1st, 1938,

Annemarie Selinko (*d* 1986), novelist; 2nd, 1996, Harriet Thrige Laursen (*née* Lund Jensen). *Educ:* Herning Gymnasium; University of Copenhagen (degree awarded equiv. of MA Econ). Postgraduate Studies, Economics and Internat. Relations, Geneva, Paris, London, 1935–37. Sec.-Gen., 1935, Pres. 1936, of the Fédération Universitaire Internationale pour la Société des Nations. Danish Civil Servant, 1941; served with: Free Danish Missions, Stockholm, 1943; Washington, 1944; London, 1945; joined Danish Diplomatic Service and stayed in London until 1947; Danish Foreign Ministry, 1947–48; Head of Denmark's Mission to OEEC, Paris, 1948–50; Sec. to Economic Cttee of Cabinet, 1950–51; Asst Under-Sec. of State, 1951; Dep. Under-Sec. of State (Economic Affairs), Danish For. Min., 1954–64; Ambassador to UK, 1964–77 (concurrently accredited to Republic of Ireland, 1964–73); Doyen of the Diplomatic Corps, 1973–77; retd 1977. Dir, S. G. Warburg & Co. International Holdings Ltd, 1980–84; Mem., Internat. Adv. Bd, S. G. Warburg & Co., 1984–86, Mercury Internat. Gp, 1986–90; Nordic Investment Bank: Dir, 1977–86; Vice-Chm., 1977–78; Chm., 1978–80. Co-founder and Bd Mem., CARE, Denmark, 1987–91. Grand Officier, Légion d'Honneur; Kt Comdr: Order of St Olav; Order of White Rose of Finland; Star of Ethiopia; Knight Grand Cross, Icelandic Falcon; Comdr, Order of Northern Star of Sweden. *Publications:* Folkeforbundet (The League of Nations), 1938. *Recreations:* ski-ing, fishing and other out-door sports, modern languages. *Address:* Kratkrogen 8, 2920, Charlottenlund, Denmark. *Clubs:* MCC; Special Forces *et al.* *Died 21 May 2005.*

LAMBERT, Harold George; *b* 8 April 1910; *s* of late Rev. David Lambert; *m* 1934, Winifred Marthe, *d* of late Rev. H. E. Anderson, Farnham, Surrey; two *s. Educ:* King Edward's Sch., Birmingham; Corpus Christi Coll., Cambridge (MA); Imperial College of Science, London. Entered Ministry of Agriculture and Fisheries, 1933; Private Secretary to Parliamentary Secretary, 1938–39; Sec., Agricultural Machinery Develt Bd, 1942–45; Assistant Secretary, 1948; Under-Sec., MAFF, 1964–70, retired. Mem., panel of indep. inspectors for local enquiries, DoE and DoT, 1971–80. *Recreations:* music, art. *Address:* 74 Chichester Drive West, Saltdean, Brighton BN2 8SF. *Died 19 Feb. 2005.*

LAMBO, Prof. Thomas Adeoye, NNOM 1979; CON 1979; OBE 1962; MD, DPM; FRCP; JP; Deputy Director-General, World Health Organization, 1973–88 (Assistant Director-General, 1971–73); Executive Director, Lambo Foundation, since 1988; *b* 29 March 1923; *s* of Chief D. B. Lambo, The Otunbade of Igbore, Abeokuta, and Madam F. B. Lambo, The Iyalode of Egba Christians; *m* 1945, Dinah Violet Adams; three *s. Educ:* Baptist Boys' High Sch., Abeokuta; Univs of Birmingham and London. From 1949, served as House Surg. and House Phys., Birmingham, England; Med. Officer, Lagos, Zaria and Gusau; Specialist, Western Region Min. of Health, 1957–60; Consultant Psychiatrist, UCH Ibadan, 1956–63; Sen. Specialist, Western Region Min. of Health, Neuro-Psychiatric Centre, 1960–63; Prof. of Psychiatry and Head of Dept of Psychiatry and Neurology, Univ. of Ibadan, 1963–71; Dean, Medical Faculty, Univ. of Ibadan, 1966–68; Vice-Chancellor, Univ. of Ibadan, 1968–71. Member: Scientific Council for Africa (Chm., 1965–70); Expert Adv. Panel on Mental Health, WHO, 1959–71; UN Perm. Adv. Cttee on Prevention of Crime and the Treatment of Offenders (Chm. 1968–71); Exec. Cttee, World Fedn for Mental Health, 1964–; Scientific Adv. Panel, Ciba Foundn, 1966–; WHO Adv. Cttee on Med. Research, 1970–71; Scientific Cttee on Advanced Study in Developmental Sciences, 1967–; Nigeria Medical Council, 1969–; Scientific Council of the World Future Studies Fedn, 1975–; World Soc. for Ekistics (Pres., 1979–81); Adv. Bd, Earthscan, 1975–; Bd of Dirs, Internat. Inst. for Envmt and Develt, 1986–; Vice-Chm., UN Adv. Cttee on Application of Science and Technology to Development, 1970–71; Co-Chm.,

Internat. Soc. for Study of Human Development, 1968–; Chairman: West African Examinations Council, 1969–71, co-ordinating Bd, African Chairs of Technology in Food Processing, Biotechnologies and Nutrition and Health, 1986–, etc. Founding Member: Third World Acad. of Scis, 1986–; African Acad. of Scis, 1986–. Member: Pontifical Acad. of Sciences, 1974– (first African Life Mem., 1982); Internat. Inst. for World Resources, Washington. Patron, Nigerian Assoc. of Gen. and Pvte Med. Practitioners, 1999. Hon. Fellow: RCPsych, 1970 (Founding Fellow); Royal Australian and NZ Coll. of Psychiatrists. JP Western State, 1968. Hon. LLD: Kent State, Ohio, 1969; Birmingham 1971; Pennsylvania, Philadelphia; Hon. DSc: Ahmadu Bello, Nigeria; Long Island, NY, 1975; McGill, Canada, 1978; Jos, Nigeria, 1979; Nigeria, Nsukka, 1979; Hacettepe, Ankara, 1980; Hahnemann, Philadelphia, 1984; Dr *hc*: Benin, 1973; Aix-Marseille, France, 1974; Louvain, Belgium, 1976. Haile Selassie African Res. Award, 1970; Leader of Psychiatry Award, World Psychiatric Assoc., 1999. *Publications:* (jtly) Psychiatric Disorders Among the Yorubas, 1963; monographs, and contribs to medical and other scientific jls. *Recreation:* tennis. *Address:* Lambo Foundation, 15 Olatunbosun Street, Shonibare Estate, Maryland, Ikeja, Lagos State, Nigeria. *T:* (1) 4976110, *T:* and *Fax:* (home) (1) 4976110; *e-mail:* talambo@ beta.linkserve.com. *Died 16 March 2004.*

LLEWELLYN, Sir Donald Rees, (Sir Don), KNZM 1999; CBE 1992; JP; Foundation Vice-Chancellor, University of Waikato, 1964 85; *b* 20 Nov. 1919; *s* of late R. G. Llewellyn, Dursley; *m* 1943, Ruth Marian, *d* of late G. E. Blandford, Dursley; one *s* one *d. Educ:* Dursley Grammar Sch.; Univ. of Birmingham (BSc 1st cl. hons Chem. 1941; DSc 1957); DPhil Oxon 1943. Research Fellow, Cambridge Univ., 1944 46; Lectr in Chemistry, UC of N Wales, 1946–49; ICI Research Fellow, UCL, 1949–52; Lectr in Chemistry, UCL, 1952–57; Prof. of Chemistry and Dir of Labs, Univ. of Auckland, 1957–64; Asst Vice-Chancellor, Univ. of Auckland, 1962–64. Mem., NZ Atomic Energy Cttee, 1958–85. Pres., NZ Inst. Chemistry, 1967 and 1988 (Vice-Pres., 1965–67, 1986–88). Member: Council, Hamilton Teachers Coll., 1965–85; Council, Waikato Tech. Inst., 1968–85; Pres., NZ Nat. Fieldays Soc., 1969–75 and 1978–81 (Life Mem., 1981); Patron, Waikato Med. Res. Foundn, 1990–99. Hon. Mem., Golden Key Internat. Honor Soc., 2001. JP Waikato, 1971. Freeman, City of Hamilton, 1985. CChem, FRSC (FRIC 1952); FNZIC 1957 (Hon. FNZIC 1985); FRSA 1960. Hon. Dr Waikato, 1985. Paul Harris Fellow, Rotary Foundn; Waikato Business Pioneer, 1990; Thomson Medal, Royal Soc. of NZ, 1994. *Publications:* numerous papers on application of stable isotopes in Jl Chem. Soc. and others. *Recreations:* showjumping (FEI Judge), photography, travel. *Address:* RD4, Hamilton, New Zealand. *T:* (7) 8569172. *Club:* Hamilton (NZ). *Died 4 Aug. 2004.*

MACARA, Sir Hugh Kenneth, 4th Bt *cr* 1911, of Ardmore, St Anne-on-the-Sea, Co. Lancaster; *b* 17 Jan. 1913; 4th *s* of Sir William Cowper Macara, 2nd Bt and Lilian Mary (*d* 1971), *d* of John Chapman; *S* brother, 1982, but his name does not appear on the Official Roll of the Baronetage. *Heir:* none. *Died April 1986 (ext).*

MACARTNEY, Sir John Barrington, 6th Bt *cr* 1799, of Lish, Co. Armagh; dairy farmer, retired; *b* 21 Jan. 1917; *s* of John Barrington Macartney (*d* 1951) (3rd *s* of Sir John Macartney, 3rd Bt) and Selina Koch, Hampden, Mackay, Qld, Australia; *S* uncle, Sir Alexander Miller Macartney, 5th Bt, 1960; *m* 1944, Amy Isobel Reinke (*d* 1978); one *s. Heir: s* John Ralph Macartney [*b* 24 July 1945; *m* 1966, Suzanne Marie Fowler; four *d*]. *Address:* 37 Meadow Street, North Mackay, Qld 4740, Australia. *Died 1 Sept. 1999.*

McBURNEY, Air Vice-Marshal Ralph Edward, CBE 1945; CD; RCAF, retired; *b* Montreal, Quebec, 17 Aug. 1906; *s* of Irville Albert and Lilian McBurney, Saskatoon, Sask.; *m* 1931, Gertrude Elizabeth Bate, Saskatoon; two *s*

(one *d* decd). *Educ:* Univs of Saskatchewan (BSc (EE)) and Manitoba. Commenced flying training as a cadet in RCAF, 1924; Pilot Officer, 1926; employed on Forest Fire Patrols and photographic mapping; Course in RAF School of Army Co-operation and tour as Instructor in RCAF School of Army Co-operation, 1931; Course at RAF Wireless School, Cranwell, and tour as Signals Adviser at Air Force HQ, Ottawa, 1935–36; RAF Staff Coll., Andover, 1939; Dir of Signals, AFHQ, Ottawa, 1939–42; CO, RCAF Station, Trenton, Ont., 1943; CO, RCAF Station, Dishforth, Yorks, 1943; Air Cdre 1944; Base Comdr of 61 Training Base, and later, 64 Operational Base in No 6 (RCAF) Bomber Group of Bomber Comd; SASO of the Group, Dec. 1944; AOC RCAF Maintenance Comd, 1945–46; Senior Canadian Air Force Liaison Officer, London, 1946–48; AOC Air Materiel Comd, RCAF, Ottawa, 1948–52. Business Consultant, 1952–60; Chief, Technical Information Service, Nat. Research Council, Ottawa, 1960–72. Pres., Internat. Fedn for Documentation, 1968–72. *Address:* 302–2604 Draper Avenue, Ottawa, ON K2H 9BI, Canada. *Died 25 Oct. 2004.*

McCORMICK, John Ormsby, CMG 1965; MC 1943; HM Diplomatic Service, retired; *b* Dublin, 7 Feb. 1916; *s* of Albert Victor McCormick and Sarah Beatty de Courcy; *m* 1955, Francine Guieu (*née* Pâris); one *d*, and one step *s*. *Educ:* The Leys Sch., Cambridge; New Coll., Oxford (BA Hon. Mods and Greats 1938). Passed Competitive Exam. for Consular Service, 1939, and appointed Asst Officer, Dept of Overseas Trade. Served War of 1939–45, in Royal Corps of Signals, Africa, Sicily, Germany, 1940–45. 2nd Sec. (Commercial), British Embassy, Athens, 1945–47; FO, London, 1948–50; 1st Sec., UK High Commn, Karachi, 1950–52; Consul, New York, 1952–54; transferred to Washington, 1954–55; NATO Defence Coll., 1955; Asst Head, SE Asia Dept, FO, 1956–59; Foreign Service Officer, Grade 6, 1959; Counsellor (Commercial), British Embassy, Djakarta, 1959–62; Corps of Inspectors, FO, 1962–64; Counsellor (Commercial), British Embassy, Ankara, 1965–67; Consul-General, Lyons, 1967–72. *Publications:* The Higher Lakes of Wicklow, 1994. *Address:* Oldfort, Newcastle, Co. Wicklow, Ireland. *Died 2003.*

MACKAY, Maj.-Gen. Kenneth, CB 1969; MBE 1943; idc, psc; GOC, Field Force Command Australia, Nov. 1973–Feb. 1974, retired; *b* 17 Feb. 1917; *m* 1943, Judith, *d* of F. Littler; two *s* one *d*. *Educ:* University High Sch., Melbourne; RMC Duntroon. Served War of 1939–45: Artillery, and Liaison Officer HQ 9th Australian Division, Middle East, 1940–41; ME Staff Sch., 1942; Bde Maj. 26 Bde, 1942–44; MO 12, War Office, 1944–45; Joint Sec., JCOSA, 1945–48; CO, 67 Inf. Bn, 1948; CO, 3 Bn Royal Aust. Regt, 1949; AHQ, 1949–52; Chief Instructor, Sch. of Tactics and Admin. 1952–55; Asst Aust. Defence Rep. UK, 1955–57; successively Dir of Maintenance, Personnel Admin., Quartering and Military Training, 1957–61; IDC, 1962; Dir Military Operations and Plans, Army HQ, Canberra, 1962–66; Comdr Aust. Force Vietnam, 1966; Commander 1st Division Australian Army, 1967–68; QMG AHQ, 1968–71; GOC Eastern Comd, 1971–73. *Recreations:* fishing, golf. *Address:* Unit 31, Glenaeon, Glenaeon Avenue, Belrose, NSW 2085, Australia. *Clubs:* Australian (Sydney); Gordon Golf, New South Wales Golf. *Died 18 May 2004.*

McLOUGHLIN, Most Rev. James; Bishop (RC) of Galway and Kilmacduagh, since 1993; *b* 9 April 1929; *s* of Patrick McLoughlin and Winifred (*née* McDermott). *Educ:* St Patrick's Coll., Maynooth (BA, HDipEd). Ordained priest, 1954; Professor, St Mary's Coll., Galway, 1954–65; Diocesan Secretary, 1965–83; Parish Priest, Galway Cathedral, 1983–93. *Address:* Diocesan Office, The Cathedral, Galway, Ireland. *T:* (91) 563566. *Died 25 Nov. 2005.*

MACMILLAN, Alexander Ross, FCIBS; Director, 1974–87, Chief General Manager, 1971–82, Clydesdale Bank PLC; *b* 25 March 1922; *s* of Donald and Johanna Macmillan; *m* 1961, Ursula Miriam Grayson; two *s* one *d*. *Educ:* Tain Royal Acad. FCIBS (FIBScot 1942). Served War, RAF, 1942–46 (despatches, King's Birthday Honours, 1945). Entered service of N of Scotland Bank Ltd, Tain, 1938; after War, returned to Tain, 1946; transf. to Supt's Dept, Aberdeen, and thereafter to Chief Accountant's Dept, Clydesdale Bank, Glasgow, 1950, on amalgamation with N of Scotland Bank; Chief London Office, 1952; Gen. Manager's Confidential Clerk, 1955; Manager, Piccadilly Circus Br., 1958; Supt of Branches, 1965; Gen. Manager's Asst, 1967; Asst Gen. Man., 1968. Director: The High Sch. of Glasgow Ltd, 1979–92; Caledonian Applied Technology Ltd, 1982–87; Highland-North Sea Ltd, 1982–2000 (Chm., 1982–); John Laing plc, 1982–86; Martin-Black PLC, 1982–85; Radio Clyde Ltd, 1982–93; Scottish Develt Finance Ltd, 1982–92; Kelvin Technology Develts Ltd, 1982–96; Compugraphics Internat. Ltd, 1982–87; Highland Deephaven Ltd, 1983–2000; TEG Products Ltd, 1986–87; New Generation Housing Soc. Ltd, 1986–95; Castle Wynd Housing Soc. Ltd, 1987–89; Wilsons Garage (Argyll) Ltd, 1987–94; Wilsons Fuels Ltd, 1987–94; EFT Gp (formerly Edinburgh Financial Trust) plc, 1987–93; Balmoral Gp Ltd, 1988–93; North of Scotland Radio Ltd, 1989–93; Radio Clyde Holdings plc, 1991–93; Gilmorhill Power Management Ltd, 1994–96; Nemoquest Ltd, 1994–96; Dumwilco Ltd, 1995–96; Chm., First Northern Corporate Finance Ltd, 1983–87. Chm., Nat. House Bldg Council (Scotland), 1982–88. Mem. Court, Univ. of Glasgow, 1981–96. Freeman, Royal Burgh of Tain, 1975. CCMI (CBIM 1980). DUniv Glasgow, 1989. *Recreation:* golf. *Address:* 4 Cochrane Court, Fairways, Milngavie, Glasgow G62 6QT. *Died 20 Nov. 2004.*

MAIR, John Magnus; Director of Social Work, Edinburgh, 1969–75; Lecturer in Social Medicine, University of Edinburgh, 1959–75; *b* 29 Dec. 1912; *s* of Joseph Alexander Mair and Jane Anderson; *m* 1940, Isobelle Margaret Williamson (*d* 1969); three *s*. *Educ:* Anderson Inst., Lerwick; Univs of Aberdeen (MB, ChB) and Edinburgh (DPH). MFCM. Asst GP, Highlands and Islands Medical Service, 1937–40; RAMC, 1940–45; Edinburgh Public Health Dept (latterly Sen. Depute Medical Officer of Health), 1945–69. *Recreation:* golf. *Club:* Grampian (Corby). *Died 31 May 2002.*

MANSAGER, Felix Norman, Hon. KBE 1976 (Hon. CBE 1973); Honorary Director, Hoover Co. USA (President-Chairman, Hoover Co. and Hoover Worldwide Corporation, 1966–75); Director, Hoover Ltd UK (Chairman, 1966–75); *b* 30 Jan. 1911; *s* of Hoff Mansager and Alice (*née* Qualseth); *m* Geraldine (*née* Larson); one *s* two *d*. *Educ:* South Dakota High Sch., Colton. Joined Hoover Co. as Salesman, 1929; Vice-Pres., Sales, 1959; Exec. Vice-Pres. and Dir, 1961. Dir, Belden and Blake Energy Co. Member: Council on Foreign Relations; Newcomen Soc. in N America; Trustee, Graduate Theological Union (Calif); The Pilgrims of the US; Assoc. of Ohio Commodores; Masonic Shrine (32nd degree Mason); Mem. and Governor, Ditchley Foundn; Member Board of Trustees: Ohio Foundn of Ind. Colls; Ind. Coll. Funds of America. Hon. Mem., World League of Norsemen. Marketing Award, British Inst. of Marketing, 1971. Executive Prof. of Business (Goodyear Chair), Univ. of Akron (Mem. Delta Sigma Pi; Hon. Mem., Beta Sigma Gamma). Hon. Fellow, UC Cardiff, 1973. Hon. Dr of Laws Capital Univ., 1967; Hon. LLD Strathclyde, 1970; Hon. DHL Malone Coll., Canton, Ohio, 1972; Hon. PhD Walsh Coll., Canton, 1974; Hon. Dr Humanities Wartburg Coll., Waverly, Iowa, 1976; Medal of Honor, Vassa Univ., Finland, 1975; Person of Year, Capital Univ. Chapter of Tau Pi Phi, 1981. Grand Officer, Dukes of Burgundy, 1968; Chevalier: Order of Leopold, 1969; Order of St Olav, Norway, 1971; Legion of Honour, France, 1973; Grande Officiale, Order Al

Merito della Republica Italiana, 1975. *Recreation:* golf. *Address:* 3421 Lindel Court NW, Canton, OH 44718, USA. *Clubs:* Metropolitan (NYC); Congress Lake Country (Hartville, Ohio); Torske (Hon.) (Minneapolis).
Died 10 Feb. 1998.

MATTHEWS, Henry Melvin; Managing Director, Texaco Ltd, 1982–88; *b* 26 Feb. 1926; *s* of Phillip Lawrence and Agnes K. Matthews; *m* 1947, Margaret Goodridge; one *s* two *d. Educ:* Columbia University; Tufts Univ. (BSNS, BSME). Commnd Ensign, 1945, USNR; retired 1986. General Manager, Texaco Europe, USA, 1976; Vice Pres. Manufacture and Marketing, Texaco Europe, USA, 1980. Mem., US Navy League, London. *Recreations:* tennis, golf, swimming, gardening, music (choir), YMCA, Congregational Church. *Address:* (winter) 6280 Winged Foot Drive, Stuart, FL 34997, USA; (summer) Three Winds, 338 West Beach Road, Charlestown, RI 02813, USA. *Club:* Mariner Sands CC (Stuart, Fla).
Died 17 March 2005.

MIDDLETON, Francis; Advocate; Sheriff of Glasgow and Strathkelvin (formerly of Lanarkshire) at Glasgow, 1956–78, retired; Temporary Sheriff, 1979; *b* 21 Nov. 1913; Scottish; *m* 1942, Edith Muir, two *s* one *d. Educ:* Rutherglen Academy; Glasgow Univ. MA, LLB 1937. Practising as Solicitor, 1937–39; volunteered Sept. 1939; Cameronian Scottish Rifles; commissioned to 6th Battn 11th Sikh Regt, Indian Army, 1940; Captain 1940; Major 1942, injured; Interpreter 1st Class in Hindustani, 1943; posted to Judge Advocate's Branch, 1944; released Dec. 1945. Admitted Faculty of Advocates in Scotland, 1946. Sheriff Substitute of Inverness, Moray, Nairn and Ross and Cromarty, 1949–52, Fife and Kinross, 1952–56. Mem., Rotary Club. *Recreations:* reading, gardening. *Address:* c/o Buchanan House, 5 Grampian Way, Bearsden G61 4SP.
Died 15 Nov. 2002.

MITCHELL, Alec Burton, MA; CEng, MIMechE, FRINA; Director, Admiralty Marine Technology Establishment, 1977–84; Scientific Adviser to Director General Ships, Ministry of Defence, 1981–84; *b* 27 Aug. 1924; *er s* of Ronald Johnson Mitchell and Millicent Annie Mitchell; *m* 1952, Barbara, *d* of Arthur Edward and Katie Florence Jane Archer; three *s. Educ:* Purley County Sch.; St John's Coll., Cambridge (MA). Mechanical Sciences Tripos, Cambridge, 1944. Aeronautical Engineer with Rolls Royce Ltd, Hucknall, 1944–46; Grad. apprentice and gas turbine design engr with English Electric Co. Ltd, Rugby, 1946–48. Joined RN Scientific Service, 1948; Dep. Head of Hydrodynamic Research Div., Admty Research Lab., 1961; promoted Dep. CSO, 1966; Dep. Dir, Admty Research Laboratory, 1973, Dir, 1974–77. *Publications:* numerous scientific papers on hydrodynamics and under-water propulsion systems. *Recreations:* golf, horology, wood-work. *Address:* 32 Ormond Crescent, Hampton, Middx TW12 2TH.
Died 21 Oct. 2005.

MONTLAKE, Henry Joseph; solicitor; Senior Partner, H. Montlake & Co., 1954–2000; a Recorder of the Crown Court, 1983–98; *b* 22 Aug. 1930; *s* of Alfred and Hetty Montlake; *m* 1952, Ruth Rochelle Allen; four *s. Educ:* Ludlow Grammar Sch., Ludlow; London Univ. (LLB 1951). Law Soc.'s final exam., 1951; admitted Solicitor, 1952. National Service, commnd RASC, 1953. Dep. Registrar of County Courts, 1970–78; Dep. Circuit Judge and Asst Recorder, 1978–83. Pres., West Essex Law Soc., 1977–78. Mem. Ethics Cttee, BUPA Roding Hosp. IVF Unit, 1991–2000. Chm., Ilford Round Table, 1962–63; Pres., Assoc. of Jewish Golf Clubs and Socs, 1984–94 (Sec.), 1977–84). Gov., Redbridge Coll. of Further Educn, 1991–92. *Recreations:* golf, The Times crossword, people, travel. *Address:* Chelston, 5 St Mary's Avenue, Wanstead, E11 2NR. *T:* (020) 8989 7228, *Fax:* (020) 8989 5173; *e-mail:* henry@chelston.org. *Clubs:* Dyrham Park Golf; Abridge Golf (Chm. 1964, Captain 1965).
Died 8 Oct. 2004.

MOORE, Prof. Leslie Rowsell, PhD, DSc; CEng, FIMinE, FGS; Consultant Geologist; Sorby Professor of Geology, University of Sheffield, 1949–77, then Emeritus Professor; *b* 23 June 1912; *m* 1946, Margaret Wilson MacRae (*d* 1985); one *s. Educ:* Midsomer Norton Grammar Sch.; Bristol Univ. Univ. of Bristol, 1930–37; Lecturer and Senior Lecturer, Cardiff, 1939–46; Research Dir, Univ. of Glasgow, 1946–48; Reader in Geology, Univ. of Bristol, 1948–49. *Publications:* contributions to: Quarterly Journal Geol Soc., London; Geological Magazine; S Wales Inst. Engineers. *Recreations:* soccer, cricket, golf. *Address:* c/o 107 Wentworth Road, Harborne, Birmingham B17 9SU.
Died 13 Nov. 2003.

MUGNOZZA, Carlo S.; *see* Scarascia-Mugnozza.

NEWSOME, William Antony; Director-General, Association of British Chambers of Commerce, 1974–84; *b* 8 Nov. 1919; *s* of William F. Newsome and Elizabeth (*née* Thompson); *m* 1951, Estella Ann (*née* Cope); one *s. Educ:* King Henry VIII Sch., Coventry; Bedford Modern Sch. Student Engineer, W. H. Allen, Sons & Co. Ltd, Bedford, 1937–40. Served War, Royal Engineers: N Africa, Sicily, Italy campaigns, 1940–47. Engrg Dept, Crown Agents for Oversea Governments and Administrations, 1949–61; Principal: Home Office, 1961–64; Min. of Technology, 1964–70; Dept of Trade and Industry, 1970–71; Asst Sec., Dept of Trade, 1971–74. Member: SITPRO, 1972–84; Production Statistics Adv. Cttee, 1975–84; Home Office Standing Cttee on Crime Prevention, 1978–84. *Recreations:* photography, swimming, golf. *Address:* Bourdon Lacey, Old Woking Road, Woking, Surrey GU22 8HR. *T:* (01483) 762237.
Deceased.

NICHOLAS, William Ford, OBE 1954; Director, London Chamber of Commerce and Industry, 1974–84; *b* 17 March 1923; *s* of William and Emma Nicholas; *m* 1954, Isobel Sybil Kennedy; two *s. Educ:* Stockport Grammar School. Called to Bar, Middle Temple, 1965. Joined S Rhodesia Civil Service, 1947; Private Sec. to Prime Minister, S Rhodesia, 1950; Private Sec. to Prime Minister, Fedn of Rhodesia and Nyasaland, 1953; Counsellor, High Comr's Office, London, 1960; retd 1963. Dir, UK Cttee, Fedn of Commonwealth Chambers of Commerce, 1964; Dep. Dir, London Chamber of Commerce, 1966. *Address:* 2 Lime Close, Frant, Tunbridge Wells, Kent TN3 9DP. *T:* (01892) 750428.
Died 2 June 2005.

NICHOLS, John Winfrith de Lisle, BSc (Eng); CEng; FIET; Director: National Maritime Institute, 1976–79; Computer Aided Design Centre, Cambridge, 1977–79; *b* 7 June 1919; *er s* of late John F. Nichols, MC, PhD, FRHistS, FSA, Godalming; *m* 1942, Catherine Lilian (*d* 1984), *er d* of Capt. A. V. Grantham, RNR, Essex; two *s* two *d. Educ:* Sir Walter St John's Sch., Battersea; London Univ. Royal Navy, 1940–46; GPO, Dollis Hill, 1946–47; RN Scientific Service, 1947–55; Chief Research Officer, Corp. of Trinity House, 1955–59; UKAEA, 1959–65; Min. of Technology, later DTI and Dept of Industry, 1965–76; Under-Sec., and Chm., Requirement Bd for Computers, Systems and Electronics, 1972–74; Under Sec., Research Contractors Div., DoI, 1974–76. *Recreations:* gardening, sailing, caravanning.
Died 26 April 2003.

OAKLEY, John Davidson, CBE 1981; DFC 1944; Chairman: Grosvenor Development Capital, 1981–92; Grosvenor Technology Ltd, 1986–91; Gardners Transformers Ltd, 1986–91 (Deputy Chairman, 1984–86; Director, 1982–91); Third Grosvenor Ltd, 1987–91); *b* 15 June 1921; *s* of Richard Oakley and Nancy Davidson; *m* 1943, Georgina Mary Hare; two *s. Educ:* Green Lane Sch. Joined Briggs Motor Bodies Ltd, 1937. Served War in RAF, 1941–46: commissioned 1942; Flt Lt 1943; actg Sqdn Leader 1944; apptd to Air Min. Directorate Staff, 1945. Engrg Buyer, Briggs Motor Bodies Ltd, 1946–53; Dep. Purchase Manager, Body Div., Ford Motor Co. Ltd, 1953–56; Production Dir/General Manager, Standard

Triumph (Liverpool) Ltd, until 1962; Managing Director: Copeland & Jenkins Ltd, 1963–71; R. Woolf & Co. Ltd, 1964–67; Gp Man. Dir, L. Sterne & Co., 1967–69; Chairman: General Electric & Mechanical Systems Ltd, 1970–73; Berwick Timpo Ltd, 1970–82; Edgar Allen Balfour Ltd, 1974–79; Australian British Trade Assoc., 1977–81 (Vice-Pres., British Council, 1981); BOTB Adv. Gp Australia and NZ, 1977–81; Mem., British Overseas Trade Adv. Council, 1977–83. Director: Blairs Ltd, 1976–82; Eagle & Globe Steel Ltd, NSW, 1978–79; Ionian Securities Ltd, 1978–88; Nexos Office Systems Ltd, 1981–82; Isis Gp PLC (formerly Industrial Services plc), 1982; Beau Brummel Ltd, 1972–85; Robert Jenkins (Hldgs) Ltd, 1976–92 (Dep. Chm., 1978–83, Chm., 1983–90). Oxford Univ. Business Summer School: Dir for 1978; Mem., Steering Cttee, 1981, Chm., 1984–87. Cons. Mem., Essex CC, 1982–85. Member: Glovers' Co.; Cutlers' Co. in Hallamshire; Inst. of British Carriage & Automobile Manufacturers. CCMI; FIPS. FRSA. *Recreations:* golf, tennis, walking, bridge. *Address:* 25 Manor Links, Bishop's Stortford, Herts CM23 5RA. *T:* (01279) 507552. *Clubs:* Reform, Royal Air Force; Bishop's Stortford Golf (Bishop's Stortford, Herts).
Died 9 Oct. 2000.

OWEN, Idris Wyn; a director of a company in the construction industry; *b* Feb. 1912; *m*; two *c. Educ:* Stockport Sch. and Coll. of Technology; Manchester Sch. of Commerce. Contested (C): Manchester Exchange, 1951; Stalybridge and Hyde, 1955; Stockport North 1966; MP (C) Stockport North, 1970–Feb. 1974; contested (C) Stockport North, Oct. 1974. Member, Stockport Borough Council, 1946; Mayor, 1962–63. Vice-Pres., Nat. Fedn of Building Trades Employers, 1965. FCIOB. *Address:* 3 Prestbury Court, Castle Rise, Prestbury, Macclesfield, Cheshire SK10 4UR. *Died 21 Dec. 2003.*

PALETTE, John, OBE 1986; Director of Personnel, British Rail, 1982–86; *b* 19 May 1928; *s* of Arthur and Beatrice Palette; *m* 1950, Pamela Mabel Palmer; three *s. Educ:* Alexandra Sch., Hampstead. MCIT. Gen. Railway Admin, 1942–69; Divl Manager, Bristol, 1969–72; Asst Gen. Manager, Western Region, 1972–74; Divl Manager, Manchester, 1974–76; Gen. Manager, Scottish Region, 1976–77, Southern Region, 1977–82, British Railways. Chm., British Transport Ship Management (Scotland) Ltd, 1976. *Recreations:* walking, reading, gardening, watching sport. *Address:* 90 Wargrave Road, Twyford, Reading, Berks RG10 9PJ. *T:* (0118) 934 0965. *Died 28 May 2005.*

PARTON, Prof. John Edwin; Professor of Electrical Engineering, University of Nottingham, 1954–78, then Emeritus; *b* Kingswinford, Staffordshire, 26 Dec. 1912; *s* of Edwin and Elizabeth Parton; *m* 1940, Gertrude Brown (*d* 1998); one *s* one *d. Educ:* Huntington Church of England Sch.; Cannock Chase Mining Coll.; University of Birmingham. BSc (1st Class Hons), 1936, PhD, 1938, Birmingham; DSc Glasgow, 1971. Training: Littleton Collieries, 1934; Electrical Construction Co., 1935; Asst Engineer, PO Engineering Dept, Dollis Hill Research Station, 1938–39; Part-time Lecturer: Cannock Chase Mining Coll., 1931–38; Northampton Polytechnic, 1938–39. Served RNVR Electrical Branch, Sub-Lt, 1939, to Lt-Comdr, 1943–45. Sen. Sci. Officer, British Iron and Steel Research Assoc., 1946; Lecturer, 1946–54, Senior Lecturer, 1954, University of Glasgow. Sen. Vis. Scientist, Nat. Sci. Foundn at Univ. of Tennessee, 1965–66; Vis. Prof., Univ. of W Indies, Trinidad, 1979, 1980. Chairman, East Midland Centre Institution of Electrical Engineers, 1961–62. FIET (FIEE 1966); Life MIEEE 1990; FIMechE 1967. *Publications:* Applied Electromagnetics (jtly), 1975; papers in Proc. IEE, Trans. IEEE, Trans. IES, Instrument Practice, International Journal of Electrical Engineering Education, etc. *Recreations:* golf, gardening, bowls, bridge. *Address:* Bramcote House Nursing Home, Town Street, Bramcote, Nottingham NG9 3DP. *T:* (0115) 922 7877. *Died 31 Oct. 2002.*

PECKOVER, Dr Richard Stuart; Chief Safety Adviser, UK Atomic Energy Authority, 2000–02, Consultant, since 2002; *b* 5 May 1942; *s* of Rev. Cecil Raymond Peckover and Grace Lucy (*née* Curtis); *m* 1st, 1971, Carole Jordan, FRS (marr. diss. 1983); 2nd, 1996, Elizabeth Griffiths (*née* Richardson); two step *s. Educ:* King Edward VII Sch., King's Lynn; Wadham Coll., Oxford (MA); Corpus Christi Coll., Cambridge (PhD). FInstP, FIMA, FRMetS, FRAS, FSaRS. United Kingdom Atomic Energy Authority, 1969–2002: Res. Scientist, Culham Lab., 1969–81; Res. Associate, MIT, 1973–74; Safety and Reliability Directorate, 1982, Br. Head, 1983–87; Asst Dir, AEE Winfrith, 1987, Dep. Dir, 1989, Sites Dir, 1990; Corporate Dir of Safety, subseq. Corporate Dir of Safety and Envmt, 1992–2000. Mem., Purbeck Standards Cttee, 2001–. Member: Amer. Nucl. Soc.; Soc. for Radiol. Protection. FCMI. DUniv Middlesex, 2002. *Recreations:* talking, listening to music. *Address:* The Barn, Pallington, Dorchester, Dorset DT2 8QU. *T:* (01305) 848712. *Died 15 Aug. 2005.*

PENNY, (Francis) David, CBE 1982; FRSE; FREng; consulting engineer; *b* 20 May 1918; *s* of late David Penny and Esther Colley; *m* 1949, Betty E. Smith, *d* of late Oswald C. Smith. *Educ:* Bromsgrove County High School; University Coll., London (BSc; Fellow 1973). Engineering Apprenticeship, Cadbury Bros Ltd, 1934–39; Armament Design Establishment, Ministry of Supply, 1939–53; Chief Development Engineer, Fuel Research Station, 1954–58; Dep. Dir, Nat. Engineering Laboratory, 1959–66, Dir, 1967–69; Managing Director: YARD Ltd, 1969–79; Yarrow Public Ltd Co., 1979–83. Chairman: Control Systems Ltd, 1979–83; Automatic Revenue Controls Ltd, 1979–83. Mem. Bd, BSI, 1982–91. FIMarEST; FIMechE (Mem. Council, 1964–85; a Vice-Pres., 1977–81; Pres., 1981–82); FREng (FEng 1980); Pres., Smeatonian Soc. of Civil Engrs, 1991–92. *Publications:* various technical papers. *Recreations:* gardening, walking. *Address:* The Park, Dundrennan, Kirkcudbright DG6 4QH. *T:* (01557) 500244. *Died 24 Sept. 2005.*

POLAK, Cornelia Julia, OBE 1964 (MBE 1956); HM Diplomatic Service, retired; *b* 2 Dec. 1908; *d* of late Solomon Polak and Georgina Polak (*née* Pozner). Foreign Office, 1925–38; Asst Archivist, British Embassy, Paris, 1938–40; Foreign Office, 1940–47; Vice-Consul, Bergen, 1947–49; Consul, Washington, 1949–51; Foreign Office, 1951–55; Consul, Paris, 1955–57; Consul, Brussels, 1957–60; Foreign Office, 1960–63; Head of Treaty and Nationality Department, Foreign Office, 1963–67; Consul General, Geneva, 1967–69, retired; re-employed at FCO, 1969–70. *Address:* Sunridge Court, 76 The Ridgeway, NW11 8PT. *Died 30 Oct. 2005.*

RAWSON, Christopher Selwyn Priestley; JP; *b* 25 March 1928; *e s* of late Comdr Selwyn Gerald Caygill Rawson, OBE, RN (retd) and late Dr Doris Rawson, MB, ChB (*née* Brown); *m* 1959, Rosemary Ann Focke; two *d. Educ:* The Elms Sch., Colwall, near Malvern, Worcs; The Nautical College, Pangbourne, Berks. Navigating Apprentice, Merchant Service, T. & J. Brocklebank Ltd, 1945–48. Sheriff of the City of London, 1961–62; Member of Court of Common Council (Ward of Bread Street), 1963–72; Alderman, City of London, (Ward of Lime Street), 1972–83; one of HM Lieutenants of City of London, 1980–83. A Younger Brother of Trinity House, 1988–. Chairman: Governors, The Elms Sch., Colwall, near Malvern, Worcs, 1965–84; Port and City of London Health Cttee, 1967–70; Billingsgate and Leadenhall Mkt Cttee, 1972–75. Silver Medal for Woollen and Worsted Raw Materials, City and Guilds of London Institute, 1951; Livery of Clothworkers' Co., 1952 (Mem. Court of Assistants, 1977; Master, 1988–89); Freeman, Co. of Watermen and Lightermen, 1966 (Mem. Ct of Assts, 1974, Master, 1982–84; secured warrant for Company to fly defaced Red Ensign, 2003). Hon. Mem., London Metal Exchange, 1979. JP City of London, 1967. ATI 1953; AIMarE 1962. CStJ

1985. Commander: National Order of Senegal, 1961; Order of the Ivory Coast, 1962; Star of Africa, Liberia, 1962. *Recreations:* shooting, sailing. *Address:* 23 Cristowe Road, SW6 3QF. *Clubs:* Garrick, Royal London Yacht (Cdre, 1990–91), City Livery Yacht (Cdre, 1987–90).
Died 24 Dec. 2005.

SALCEDO-BASTARDO, José Luis; writer and diplomat; *b* Carúpano, Venezuela, 15 March 1926; *s* of Joaquin Salcedo-Arocha and Catalina Salcedo-Arocha (*née* Bastardo); *m* 1968, María Cecilia Avila Prieto; four *s*. *Educ:* Central Univ. of Venezuela; Univ. of Paris; London Sch. of Economics. Teacher of social sciences, 1945; Chief Editor, Nat. Magazine of Culture, 1948–50; Asst Lectr, Central Univ., 1949; Founder Rector, Univ. of Santa Maria, Caracas, 1953; Senator for State of Sucre, 1958; Mem., Senate Foreign Relations Cttee; Ambassador to Ecuador, 1959–61; to Brazil, 1961–63; Prof. of Sociology, Central Univ., 1964; Pres., Nat. Inst. of Culture and Fine Arts, 1965–67; Vice-Pres., Supreme Electoral Council, 1970–74; Ambassador to France, 1974–76; Minister, Secretariat of the Presidency, 1976–77; Minister of State for Sci., Tech. and Culture, 1977–79; Ambassador to UK, 1984–87, to GDR, 1987–90. Dir, Nat. Acad. for Lang., 1997–2003. Member, councils and commns, S America and Europe. *Publications:* Through the Sociological World of Cecilio Acosta, 1945; In Pursuit of Glory, 1947; Vision and Revision of Bolívar, 1957; Biography of Don Egidio Montesinos, 1957; Thesis for Union, 1963; Basis for Cultural Action, 1965; Fundamental History of Venezuela, 1970; Conscience of the Present, 1971; Carabobo: nationality and history, 1972; Bolívar: a continent and its destiny, 1972 (26 edns, trans into 12 langs); The First Duty, 1973; To Make History Unpolitical, 1973; Of History and Duties, 1975; Bolívar and San Martín, 1975; A Transparent Man, 1976; Crucible of Americanism, 1979; Ideological and Literary Concordances in Bolívar, 1981; Andrés Bello: an American, 1982; Bolivarian Repetition, 1983; Andrés Eloy Blanco For the Young, 1983; Simón Bolívar, 1983; Bolívar, Ideas and People, 1994; Man and Men, 1994. *Recreation:* travelling abroad. *Address:* PO Box 2777, Caracas 1010, Venezuela. *Died 16 Feb. 2005.*

SANDERS, Raymond Adrian; Social Security Commissioner, 1986–99; a Child Support Commissioner, 1993–99; *b* 13 May 1932; *s* of Leslie Harry Sanders and Beatrice Sanders; *m* 1st, 1961, Anna Margaret Burton (marr. diss.); one *s*; 2nd, 1985, Virginia Varnell Dunn; three *d. Educ:* Auckland Univ. (LLB); London School of Economics (LLB). Barrister and Solicitor, New Zealand, 1956–66; Partner in Jackson, Russell and Co., Barristers and Solicitors, Auckland, NZ, 1962–66; part-time Lectr 1960–66 and Examiner 1961–66, Auckland Univ.; Solicitor, Allen and Overy, London, 1967–71; practising barrister, 1971–73; DHSS, 1973–74, 1975–84; Law Officers' Dept, 1974–75. Legal Advr to Warnock Inquiry (Human Fertilisation and Embryology), 1982–84; Regional Chm., Social Security and Medical Appeal Tribunals, 1984–86. *Publications:* Credit Management (jtly) 1966; Building Contracts and Practice, 1967. *Recreations:* theatre, music, cycling, tennis. *Address:* 7 Melville Road, Barnes, SW13 9RH.
Died 2 March 2002.

SCARASCIA-MUGNOZZA, Carlo; Hon. President: International Centre for Advanced Mediterranean Agronomic Studies, Paris, since 1988 (President, 1983–87); Council of State, Italy, since 1990 (Member, 1977–90); President, Accademia Nazionale di Danza, Rome, since 1968; *b* Rome, 19 Jan. 1920. Mem., Italian Chamber of Deputies, for Lecce-Brindisi-Taranto, 1953–72; Vice-Pres., Christian Democrat Party Gp, 1958–62; Leader, Italian Delegn to UNESCO, 1962; Secretary of State: for Educn, 1962–63; for Justice, June 1963–Dec. 1963; Mem., European Parliament, 1961–72,

Chm., Political Cttee, 1969–72; a Vice-Pres., EEC, 1972–77. Mem., Accademia Agricoltura di Francia. *Address:* Via Timavo 32, 00195 Rome, Italy. *T:* (6) 37351379. *Died 13 May 2004.*

SMITH, Clifford Bertram Bruce H.; *see* Heathcote-Smith.

SOROKOS, Lt-Gen. John A.; Greek Gold Medal for Gallantry (3 times); Greek Military Cross (twice); Medal for Distinguished Services (3 times); Silver and Gold Cross (with swords) of Order of George I; Comdr, Order of George I and Order of Phoenix; Military Medal of Merit (1st Class); Ambassador of Greece to the United States of America, 1972–74; *b* 1917; *s* of A. and P. Sorokos; *m* 1954, Pia Madaros; one *s. Educ:* Mil. Acad. of Greece; Staff and Nat. Defence Colls, Greece; British Staff Coll., Camberley; US Mil. Schools. Company Comdr: in Second World War in Greece, 1940–41; in El Alamein Campaign, N Africa, 1942–43; Div. Staff Officer and Bn Comdr, 1947–49; served as Staff Officer: in Mil. Units in Army HQ and Armed Forces HQ, 1952–63; in NATO Allied Forces Southern Europe, 1957–59; Instructor, Nat. Defence Coll., Greece, 1963–64; Regt Comdr, 1965; Mil. Attaché to Greek Embassies in Washington and Ottawa, 1966–68; Div. Comdr, 1968–69; Dep. Comdr, Greek Armed Forces, 1969; Ambassador to UK, 1969–72. Officer, Legion of Merit (US). *Recreations:* horses, boating, fishing. *Address:* Mimnermou 2, Athens 10674, Greece. *Died 1999.*

SOULBURY, 2nd Viscount *cr* 1954, of Soulbury; **James Herwald Ramsbotham;** Baron 1941; *b* 21 March 1915; *s* of 1st Viscount Soulbury, PC, GCMG, GCVO, OBE, MC, and Doris Violet (*d* 1954), *d* of late S. de Stein; *S* father, 1971; *m* 1949, Anthea Margaret (*d* 1950), *d* of late David Wilton. *Educ:* Eton; Magdalen College, Oxford. *Heir: b* Hon. Sir Peter Edward Ramsbotham, *b* 8 Oct. 1919. *Died 12 Dec. 2004.*

SOUYAVE, Sir (Louis) Georges, Kt 1971; District Judge, Hong Kong, 1980–89; *b* 29 May 1926; *m* 1953, Mona de Chermont; two *s* four *d. Educ:* St Louis Coll., Seychelles; Gray's Inn, London. Barrister-at-Law, Gray's Inn, 1949. In private practice, Seychelles, 1949–56; Asst Attorney-Gen., Seychelles, 1956–62; Supreme Court, Seychelles: Additional Judge, 1962–64; Puisne Judge, 1964–70; Chief Justice, 1970–76; New Hebrides: Resident Judge of the High Court (British jurisdiction) and British Judge of the Supreme Ct of the Condominium, 1976–80. *Recreations:* walking, swimming. *Address:* 1 Flinders Court, Mount Ommaney, Brisbane, Qld 4074, Australia. *Died 24 Aug. 2004.*

STEPHENSON, Prof. Patrick Hay, MA, CEng, FIMechE; consultant Mechanical Engineer, retired; *b* 31 March 1916; *e s* of late Stanley George Stephenson and Florence (*née* Atkinson); *m* 1947, Pauline Roberts (*d* 2000); two *s* one *d. Educ:* Wyggeston Sch., Leicester; Cambridge Univ. (MA). Apprenticeship and Research Engr, Brit. United Shoe Machinery Co., 1932–39. War Service as Ordnance Mechanical Engr and REME, India and Far East, 1939–45; held as POW by Japanese, 1942–45. Chief Mechanical Engr, Pye Ltd, 1949–67; Prof. of Mech. Engrg, Univ. of Strathclyde, 1967–79; Dir, Inst. of Advanced Machine Tool and Control Technology, Min. of Technology, 1967–70; Dir, Birniehill Inst. and Manufacturing Systems Group, DTI, 1970–72; Head of Research Requirements Branch 2, DoI, 1972–77. Research advisor to Institution of Mechanical Engineers; senior industrial advisor to the Design Council. Mem. Council, IMechE, 1960–68; Member: Bd, UKAC, 1964–73; Engrg Bd, SRC, 1973. *Publications:* papers and articles in technical press. *Recreations:* music, vintage motoring. *Address:* Toft Lane, Great Wilbraham, Cambridge CB1 5JH. *T:* (01223) 880405. *Died 24 June 2005.*

STEWART, Roger Black Dow; Head of Education, Fife Council, since 2002; *b* 21 Oct. 1945; *s* of Joseph and Jane Stewart; *m* 2002, Margaret Brunton; one step *s*, and three *d* by a previous marriage. *Educ:* Dundee Univ. (MA Hons; DipEd); Open Univ. (MA Educn). Electrician, 1963–71. Teacher, subseq. Principal Teacher, History, Dingwall and Alness Acads, 1976–85; Divisional Educn Officer, Highland Region, 1985–90; Headteacher, Inveralmond Community High Sch., Livingston, 1990–95; Corporate Manager, Educn Services, W Lothian Council, 1995–2002. *Recreations:* hill-walking, wine drinking. *Address:* 13 Hermand Gardens, West Calder, West Lothian EH55 8BT. *T:* (01506) 873083. *Died 17 Sept. 2005.*

STÜCKLEN, Richard; Grosskreuz des Verdienstordens der Bundesrepublik Deutschland, 1963; Bayerischer Verdienstorden; President of the Bundestag, Federal Republic of Germany, 1979–83 (Vice-President, 1976–79 and 1983–90); *b* 20 Aug. 1916; *s* of Georg Stücklen and Mathilde (*née* Bach); *m* 1943, Ruth Stücklen (*née* Geissler); one *s* one *d*. *Educ:* primary sch.; technical sch.; engineering sch. Industrial Dept Manager and Manager in family business, 1945–49. Mem. of Bundestag, 1949–90; Dep. Chm., CDU/ Christian Social Union and Party Leader, Christian Social Union, 1953–57 and 1967–76; Federal Minister of Posts and Telegraphs, 1957–66. *Publications:* Bundestagsreden und Zeitdokumente, 1979; and others. *Recreations:* skating, chess, soccer. *Address:* Eichstätter Strasse 27, 91781 Weissenburg, Germany. *Club:* Lions. *Died 2 May 2002.*

STYLES, (Frank) Showell, FRGS; author; *b* 14 March 1908; *s* of Frank Styles and Edith (*née* Showell); *m* 1954, Kathleen Jane Humphreys; one *s* two *d*. *Educ:* Bishop Vesey's Grammar Sch., Sutton Coldfield. Served Royal Navy, 1939; retd (Comdr), 1946. Professional author, 1946–76, retd. Led two private Arctic expedns, 1952–53; led private Himalayan expedn, 1954. FRGS 1954. *Publications:* 130 books: *travel,* incl. Mountains of the Midnight Sun, 1954; Blue Remembered Hills, 1965; *biography,* incl. Mr Nelson's Ladies, 1954; Mallory of Everest, 1967; *mountain guidebooks,* incl. The Mountains of North Wales, 1973; The Glyder Range, 1973; *instructional books,* incl. Modern Mountaineering, 1964; Introduction to Mountaineering, 1955; *naval historical fiction,* incl. Stella and the Fireships, 1985; The Lee Shore, 1986; Gun-brig Captain, 1987; HMS Cracker, 1988; Nelson's Midshipman, 1990; *children's fiction,* incl. Kami the Sherpa, 1957; The Shop in the Mountain, 1961; *detective fiction* (under *pen-name,* Glyn Carr), incl. Death under Snowdon, 1954; The Corpse in the Crevasse, 1957. *Recreations:* mountaineering, gardening, music. *Address:* Trwyn Cae Iago, Borth-y-Gest, Porthmadog, Gwynedd LL49 9TW. *T:* (01766) 2849. *Club:* Midland Association of Mountaineers (Birmingham). *Died 19 Feb. 2005.*

SUNDERLAND, (Arthur) John; Commissioner-in-Chief, St John Ambulance Brigade, 1986–90; *b* 24 Feb. 1932; *s* of George Frederick Irvon Sunderland and Mary Katharine Sunderland; *m* 1st, 1958, Audrey Ann Thompson (*d* 1992); three *s*; 2nd, 1994, Penelope Hall (*née* Wood). *Educ:* Marlborough Coll. Served Army, RE, 1953–55 (2nd Lieut). Director: James Upton Ltd, 1963–69; Surrey Fine Art Press Ltd, 1963–69; Sunderland Print Ltd, 1969–84; Randall Bros Ltd, 1970–84; Alday Green & Welburn, 1978–84; Foxplan Ltd, 1984–; Rapidflow Ltd, 1985–91; SADC Ltd, 1986–. Chm., Adventure Service Challenge Scheme, 2000–. Dep. County Comr, 1976–78; County Comr, 1978–86, St John Ambulance Bde, W Midlands; KStJ 1986 (CStJ 1982; OStJ 1978). Chm., Ladypool Road Neighbourhood Centre, Balsall Heath, 1970–76. Governor, West House Sch., Birmingham, 1973–91. *Recreations:* walking, sport generally. *Address:* Rowans, Grafton Flyford, Worcs WR7 4PJ. *T:* (01905) 391281. *Died 23 Oct. 2005.*

SUTTON, Sir Frederick (Walter), Kt 1974; OBE 1971; Founder and Chairman of Directors of the Sutton Group of Companies; *b* 1 Feb. 1915; *s* of late William W. Sutton and Daisy Sutton; *m* 1934; three *s*; *m* 1977, Morna Patricia Smyth. *Educ:* Sydney Technical College. Motor Engineer. *Recreations:* flying, going fishing, boating. *Address:* (office) Level 1, 134 William Street, Potts Point, Sydney, NSW 2011, Australia. *T:* (2) 93571777. *Clubs:* Royal Automobile of Victoria; American (Sydney). *Died 7 Dec. 2004.*

SYMES, (Lilian) Mary; Clerk to Justices, 6 Divisions in Suffolk, 1943–74; Chairman, Norfolk and Suffolk Rent Tribunal, 1974–83; *b* 18 Oct. 1912; *d* of Walter Ernest and Lilian May Hollowell; *m* 1953, Thomas Alban Symes (*d* 1984); one *s*. *Educ:* St Mary's Convent, Lowestoft; Great Yarmouth High School. Articled in Solicitor's Office; qualified as Solicitor, 1936. Became first woman Clerk to Justices (Stowmarket), 1942; first woman Deputy Coroner, 1945; Clerk to the Justices, Woodbridge, 1946, Bosmere and Claydon, 1951; first woman Coroner, 1951; Deputy Coroner, Northern District, Suffolk, 1956–82. *Recreations:* Worcester porcelain, gardening. *Address:* Leiston Old Abbey, Leiston, Suffolk IP16 4RF. *Died 28 July 2005.*

THOMPSON, Dennis Cameron; Founder, Journal of World Trade (formerly Journal of World Trade Law), 1967 (Editor, 1977–86); *b* 25 Oct. 1914; *s* of late Edward Vincent Thompson, CB, and Jessie Forbes; *m* 1959, Maria von Skramlik; one *d*. *Educ:* Oundle; King's Coll., Cambridge. Nat. Sci. Tripos Pt I, Law Pt II; MA 1949. RAF, 1940–45: Sqdn-Ldr, personnel staff, Desert Air Force, and Germany. Called to Bar, Inner Temple, 1939; practised London and Midland Circuit, 1946–63; Asst Dir (European Law), British Inst. of Internat. and Comparative Law, 1963–66; Legal Adviser, Secretariat of EFTA, Geneva, 1967–73; participated in negotiations for European Patent Convention, 1969–73; Dir, Restrictive Practices and Dominant Positions, EEC, 1973–76; Consultant to UNCTAD on Restrictive Business Practices and Transfer of Technol., 1977–82. Convenor, Geneva Conf., Antarctica, the Environment and the Future, 1992; Pres., Internat. Cttee for Cryosphere Ecosystems, Geneva, 1993–. Vis. Prof., Georgia Univ. Sch. of Law, Athens, GA, 1978. Trustee, Federal Trust, 1962–71. *Publications:* (ed) Kennedy, CIF Contracts, 3rd edn 1959; (with Alan Campbell) Common Market Law, 1962; The Proposal for a European Company, 1969; articles in Internat. and Compar. Law Quarterly; (ed jtly) Common Market Law Review, 1963–67. *Recreations:* walking, Antarctic studies. *Address:* 8 rue des Belles Filles, 1299 Crans, Switzerland. *T:* (22) 7761687, *Fax:* (22) 7767303. *Club:* Oxford and Cambridge. *Died 7 June 2005.*

TOGANIVALU, Ratu Josua Brown, CBE 1980; JP; Chairman, Fiji Meat Industry Board, since 1997; *b* Fiji, 2 May 1930; *m*; two *s* one *d*. *Educ:* Levuka Public Sch.; Marist Brothers Sch., Suva; Queensland Agricultural Coll.; Royal Agricultural Coll., Cirencester. With Native Lands Trust Board, 1953–71; MP Fiji, 1966–77: Minister for Lands, Mines and Mineral Resources, 1972–73; Minister for Agriculture, Fisheries and Forests, 1974–77; High Commissioner for Fiji: to New Zealand, 1978–81; in London, 1981–85. Chairman: Fiji Public Service Commn, 1989–92; Fiji Broadcasting Commn, 1988–94; Mem., Fiji Electoral Commn, 1997–. Represented Fiji at ACP Meeting, Guyana, 1975, ACP Meeting, Malawi, 1976, ACP/EEC Sugar Meetings, Brussels, 1976. Chm., Fiji Care Insurance Ltd, 1995–99; Director: Hunts Travel Service, 1994–; Hunts Investment, 1994–; Treasure Island Resort Ltd, 1996–. JP (Fiji) 1968. *Recreations:* cricket, Rugby, boxing. *Address:* Box 13326, Suva, Fiji. *Clubs:* United, Defence (Fiji). *Died Aug. 2002.*

TUCKER, Brian George, CB 1976; OBE 1963; Deputy Secretary, Department of Energy, 1974–81; Member, UKAEA, 1976–81; *b* 6 May 1922; *s* of late Frank Ernest Tucker and May Tucker; *m* 1948, Marion Pollitt; three *d*. *Educ:* Christ's Hospital. Entered Home Civil Service,

1939, as Clerical Officer, Admty; successive postings at home, in Africa, the Middle East, Ceylon and Hong Kong till 1953; promoted Executive Officer, 1945; Higher Executive Officer, 1949. Min. of Power, Asst Principal, 1954, Principal, 1957; seconded to HMOCS, 1957–62, Asst Sec., Govt of Northern Rhodesia; returned to MOP, 1962, Principal Private Sec. to Minister, 1965–66, Asst Sec., 1966, Under-Sec., Ministry of Technology, 1969–70, Cabinet Office, 1970–72, DTI, 1972–73; Dep. Sec., 1973. *Recreations:* gardening, music. *Address:* 1 Sondes Place Drive, Dorking, Surrey RH4 3ED. *T:* (01306) 884720. *Died 25 July 2005.*

VALENTIA, 15th Viscount *cr* 1622 (Ireland); **Richard John Dighton Annesley;** Bt 1620; Baron Mountnorris 1628; farmer in Zimbabwe, since 1957; *b* 15 Aug. 1929; *s* of 14th Viscount Valentia, MC, MRCS, LRCP, and Joan Elizabeth (*d* 1986), *d* of late John Joseph Curtis; *S* father, 1983; *m* 1957, Anita Phyllis, *o d* of William Arthur Joy, Bristol; two *s* one *d* (and one *s* decd). *Educ:* Marlborough; RMA Sandhurst; BA Univ. of S Africa. Commnd RA, 1950; retd, rank of Captain, 1957. Schoolmaster, Ruzawi Prep. Sch., Marondera, Zimbabwe, 1977–83. *Recreations:* sport, shooting, fishing, leisure riding. *Heir: s* Hon. Francis William Dighton Annesley [*b* 29 Dec. 1959; *m* 1982, Shaneen Hobbs; two *d*]. *Died 20 Aug. 2005.*

WAGNER, Gerrit Abram, KBE (Hon.) 1977 (CBE (Hon.) 1964); Kt, Order of Netherlands Lion, 1969; Grand Officer, Order of Oranje Nassau, 1983 (Commander 1977); Chairman, Supervisory Board, Royal Dutch Petroleum Co., 1977–87 (President, 1971–77); *b* 21 Oct. 1916; *m* 1946, M. van der Heul; one *s* three *d*. *Educ:* Leyden Univ. LLM 1939. After a period in a bank in Rotterdam and in Civil Service in Rotterdam and The Hague, joined Royal Dutch Shell Group, 1946; assignments in The Hague, Curaçao, Venezuela, London and Indonesia; apptd Man. Dir, Royal Dutch Petroleum Co. and Shell Petroleum Co. Ltd; Mem. Presidium of Bd of Directors of Shell Petroleum NV, 1964; Dir, Shell Canada Ltd, 1971–77; Chm., Cttee of Man. Dirs, Royal Dutch/Shell Group, 1972–77; Chm., Shell Oil USA, 1972–77. Former Chairman, Supervisory Board: De Nederlandsche Bank NV; Gist-Brocades NV; KLM; Smit Internat.; Vice-Chm., Supervisory Bd, Hoogovens Gp BV, Beverwijk; Member, International Advisory Committee: Chase Manhattan Bank, NY; Robert Bosch, Stuttgart. Hon. Dr Eindhoven, 1986; Hon. LLD Rochester, USA, 1987. Order of Francisco de Miranda, Grand Officer (Venezuela), 1965; Officier Légion d'Honneur (France), 1974. *Address:* 13 Teylingerhorstlaan 13, 2244 EJ Wassenaar, The Netherlands. *Died 8 Oct. 2003.*

WALKER, Sir James (Graham), Kt 1972; MBE 1963; Part Owner of Cumberland Santa Gertrudis Stud and Camden Park, Greenwoods and Wakefield sheep properties; *b* Bellingen, NSW, 7 May 1913; *s* of late Albert Edward Walker and Adelaide Mary, Sydney, NSW; *m* 1939, Mary Vivienne Maude Poole; two *s* three *d*. *Educ:* New England Grammar Sch., Glen Innes, NSW. Councillor, Longreach Shire Council, 1953– (Chm., 1957–91); Vice-Pres., Local Authorities of Qld, 1966, Sen. Vice-Chm., 1972–89. Dep. Chm., Longreach Pastoral Coll., since inception, 1966–78, Chm. 1978–89. Exec. Mem., Central Western Queensland Local Authorities' Assoc. and Queensland Local Authorities' Assoc., 1964–79. Chm., Central Western Electricity Bd, 1966–76; Dep. Chm., Capricornia Electricity Bd, 1968–76, Chm., 1976–85; Dep. Chm., Longreach Printing Co. Chm., Santa Gertrudis Assoc., Australia, 1976–77. Past Asst Grand Master, United Grand Lodge of Qld, 1970. Session Clerk, St Andrews Church, Longreach, 1948–78. Nat. Chm., Stockman's Hall of Fame and Out Back Heritage Centre, 1983–90. Fellow, Internat. Inst. of Community Service, 1975; Paul Harris Rotary Fellow, Longreach Rotary Club, 1985. Freeman, City of London, 1990. Hon. LLD Queensland Univ., 1985. *Recreations:* bowls, golf, surfing, painting. *Address:* Camden Park, Longreach, Queensland 4730,

Australia. *T:* (7) 46581331. *Clubs:* Queensland (Hon. Life Mem., 2002), Tattersall's (Brisbane); Longreach (Life Mem.), Longreach Rotary, Diggers (Longreach). *Died 9 July 2004.*

WARDLAW, Sir Henry (John), 21st Bt *cr* 1631, of Pitreavie; *b* 30 Nov. 1930; *s* of Sir Henry Wardlaw, 20th Bt, and Ellen (*d* 1977), *d* of John Francis Brady; *S* father, 1983, but his name does not appear on the Official Roll of the Baronetage; *m* 1962, Julie-Ann, *d* of late Edward Patrick Kirwan; five *s* two *d*. *Educ:* Melbourne Univ. (MB, BS). *Heir: s* (Henry) Justin Wardlaw [*b* 10 Aug. 1963; *m* 1988, Rachel Jane, *y d* of James Kennedy Pitney]. *Address:* Mandalay, 75–77 Two Bays Road, Mount Eliza, Vic 3930, Australia. *Died 8 Aug. 2005.*

WATSON, Henry, CBE 1969; QPM 1963; Chief Constable of Cheshire, 1963–74; *b* 16 Oct. 1910; *s* of John and Ann Watson, Preston, Lancs; *m* 1933, Nellie Greenhalgh; two *d*. *Educ:* Preston Victoria Junior Technical Coll. Admitted to Inst. of Chartered Accountants, 1934; joined Ashton-under-Lyne Borough Police, 1934; King's Lynn Borough Police, 1942; Norfolk County Constabulary, 1947; Asst Chief Constable, Cumberland and Westmorland, 1955, Chief Constable, 1959. CStJ 1973. *Recreation:* golf. *Died 22 Jan. 2004.*

WATT, His Honour Robert; QC (NI) 1964; County Court Judge, 1971–89; *b* 10 March 1923; *s* of John Watt, schoolmaster, Ballymena, Co. Antrim; *m* 1951, Edna Rea; one *d*. *Educ:* Ballymena Academy; Queen's Univ., Belfast (LLB). Called to Bar, Gray's Inn, 1946; called to Bar of Northern Ireland, 1946; Sen. Crown Prosecutor Counties Fermanagh and Tyrone. *Recreation:* sailing. *Address:* 12 Deramore Drive, Belfast BT9 5JQ. *Club:* Royal North of Ireland Yacht. *Deceased.*

WEBB, Sir Thomas (Langley), Kt 1975; *b* 25 April 1908; *s* of Robert Langley Webb and Alice Mary Webb; *m* 1942, Jeannette Alison Lang; one *s* one *d*. *Educ:* Melbourne Church of England Grammar Sch. Joined Huddart Parker Ltd, 1926 (Man. Dir, 1955–61). Served War, AIF, 1940–45. Dir, Commercial Bank of Aust., 1960–78 (Chm., 1970–78); Dir and Vice-Chm., McIlwraith McEacharn Ltd, 1961–92. Vice-Pres. and Hon. Treas., Royal Victorian Eye and Ear Hosp., 1963–82. *Recreations:* golf, tennis. *Address:* 18 Chastleton Avenue, Toorak, Vic 3142, Australia. *T:* (3) 98275259. *Clubs:* Australian, Melbourne, Royal Melbourne Golf, Royal South Yarra Tennis (all Melbourne). *Died 20 July 2005.*

WEE CHONG JIN, Hon.; Chief Justice of the Supreme Court, Singapore, 1963–90; *b* 28 Sept. 1917; *s* of late Wee Gim Puay and Lim Paik Yew; *m* 1955, Cecilia Mary Henderson; three *s* one *d*. *Educ:* Penang Free Sch.; St John's Coll., Cambridge. Called to Bar, Middle Temple, 1938; admitted Advocate and Solicitor of Straits Settlement, 1940; practised in Penang and Singapore, 1940–57; Puisne Judge, Singapore, 1957. Hon. DCL Oxon, 1987. *Recreation:* golf. *Address:* 80 Raffles Place #29–20, UOB Plaza 2, Singapore 048624. *Died 5 June 2005.*

WEE KIM WEE, Hon. GCB 1989; President of Singapore, 1985–93; *b* 4 Nov. 1915; *m* 1936, Koh Sok Hiong; one *s* six *d*. *Educ:* Pearl's Hill School; Raffles Instn. Joined Straits Times, 1930; United Press Assoc., 1941 and 1945–59; Straits Times, 1959–73 (Dep. Editor, Singapore); High Comr to Malaysia, 1973–80; Ambassador to Japan, 1980–84 and to Republic of Korea, 1981–84; Chm., Singapore Broadcasting Corp., 1984–85. Formerly Member: Rent Control Bd, Film Appeal Cttee; Land Acquisition Bd; Bd of Visiting Justices; Nat. Theatre Trust; former Chm., Singapore Anti-Tuberculosis Assoc.; former Pres., Singapore Badminton Assoc. and Vice-Pres., Badminton Assoc. of Malaya. JP 1966. Hon. DLitt Nat. Univ. of Singapore, 1994. Public Service Star, 1963;

Meritorious Service Medal, 1979. Order of Temasek, 1st cl. (Singapore), 1993; Most Esteemed Family Order Laila Utama (Brunei), 1990. *Publications:* Glimpses & Reflections, 2004. *Died 2 May 2005.*

WELLS, Thomas Umfrey, MA; Headmaster, Wanganui Collegiate School, New Zealand, 1960–80; *b* 6 Feb. 1927; *s* of Athol Umfrey and Gladys Colebrook Wells; *m* 1953, Valerie Esther Brewis; two *s* one *d*. *Educ:* King's College, Auckland, New Zealand; Auckland University (BA); (Orford Studentship to) King's College, Cambridge (BA 1951; MA 1954). Assistant Master, Clifton College, 1952–60 (Senior English Master, 1957–60). Pres., NZ Assoc. of Heads of Independent Secondary Schs, 1972–75. Member: Univs Entrance Bd, 1972–80; HMC; Tongariro Forest Park Promotion Cttee, 1984–87; Taumarunui and Dist Promotion and Develt Council, 1985–; Executive Member: CKC Visual Arts Trust, 1986– (Chm., 1986–91); Wanganui River Floats Coalition, 1987–; Taumarunui Community Arts Council, 1987–; Trustee: Avonlea, 1984–; Outdoor Pursuits Centre, Tawhiti-kuri, 1985–90; Taumarunui Museum Trust, 1987–. Synodsman, 1985–, Mem. Standing Cttee, 1989–, Waikato Dio.; Mem. of Vestry, Taumarunui Anglican Church, 1981–. Pres., Taumarunui Cricket Club Assoc., 1984–86, Patron, 1986–; Mem., Rotary Club of Wanganui, 1961–80 (Pres., 1979–80), of Taumarunui, 1980–95, of Te Awamuta, 1995–; Chm., Dist 993 Rotaract Cttee, 1983–85. *Recreations:* reading, theatre, cricket (NZU Blue, 1948–49 (Capt., 1949); Cambridge Blue, 1950), tennis, fishing; formerly Rugby football (Cambridge Blue, 1951; England Final Trial, 1951; Trial, 1954; Bristol, 1952–56; Glos, 1953–56). *Address:* c/o Windsor Court Rest Home, Sandes Street, Ohaupo, New Zealand. *Clubs:* MCC; Hawks (Cambridge). *Died 30 July 2001.*

WHITELEY, Samuel Lloyd; Deputy Chief Land Registrar, 1967–73; Legal Assistant to the Clerk to the Haberdashers' Company 1973–78, Freeman, 1978; *b* 30 April 1913; *s* of Rev. Charles Whiteley and Ann Letitia Whiteley; *m* 1939, Kathleen Jones (*d* 1988); two *d*. *Educ:* George Dixon Sch.; Birmingham Univ. LLB (Hons) 1933. Admitted Solicitor, 1935; HM Land Registry, 1936; seconded Official Solicitor's Dept, 1939; RAF, 1940–46; HM Land Registry, 1946–73. *Recreations:* sport, as a reminiscent spectator. *Address:* 8 Stonehaven Court, Knole Road, Bexhill, Sussex TN40 1LW. *T:* (01424) 213191. *Died 31 Dec. 2005.*

WIGGINS, Rt Rev. Maxwell Lester; Bishop of Victoria Nyanza, 1963–76; retired; *b* 5 Feb. 1915; *s* of Herbert Lester and Isobel Jane Wiggins; *m* 1941, Margaret Agnes Evans (decd); one *s* two *d*. *Educ:* Christchurch Boys' High Sch., NZ; Canterbury University College, NZ (BA). Asst Curate, St Mary's, Merivale, NZ, 1938; Vicar of Oxford, NZ, 1941; CMS Missionary, Diocese Central Tanganyika, 1945; Head Master, Alliance Secondary Sch., Dodoma, 1948; Provost, Cathedral of Holy Spirit, Dodoma, 1949; Principal, St Philip's Theological Coll., and Canon of Cathedral of Holy Spirit, Dodoma, 1954; Archdeacon of Lake Province, 1956; Asst Bishop of Central Tanganyika, 1959; Asst Bishop of Wellington, 1976–81; Pres., NZ CMS, 1986–96 (Gen. Sec., 1982–83). Sen. ChLJ, 1982–96. *Address:* 42 Otara Street, Christchurch 5, New Zealand. *Died 7 Aug. 2005.*

WILDE, Dr Christian; Joint Senior Partner, Freshfields Bruckhaus Deringer, 2000–04; *b* 21 Sept. 1939; *s* of Wolf Wilde and Inge Wilde (*née* Uibeleisen); *m* 1980, Gabriele Rocholl; two *s* one *d*. *Educ:* Univ. of Lausanne; Univ of Hamburg; Univ. of Göttingen (Dr Juris); Univ. of Calif, Berkeley (LLM). Associate, 1970, Partner, 1971–90, Stegemann Sieveking & Lutheroth; Partner, Bruckhaus Westrick Stegemann, 1991–2000. Non-exec. board mem. of several cos. *Recreations:* golf, reading. *Address:* c/o Freshfields Bruckhaus Deringer, Alsterarkaden 27, 20354 Hamburg, Germany. *Club:* Der Uebersee (Hamburg). *Died 9 May 2004.*

WILLIAMS, Sir Arthur (Dennis Pitt), Kt 1991; Chairman, Williams Holdings Ltd, since 1965; *b* 15 Oct. 1928; *s* of Arthur Henry Williams and Dora Ruth Williams; *m* 1st, 1951, Ngaire Garbett; three *s* two *d*; 2nd, 1989, Jeanne Brinkworth; one *s*. *Educ:* Salmerston; Margate College. Served RN, 1944–46. Apprentice carpenter, 1942–44 and 1946–47; carpenter, NZ, 1951–53; builder, 1953–, and property owner. Govt Appointee, Govt Property Services Ltd, 1991. Fellow: NZ Inst. of Builders; Aust. Inst. of Builders; NZ Inst. of Management. NZ Commemorative Medal, 1990. *Recreation:* horse breeding and racing. *Address:* Cranbrook, Cranbrook Grove, Waikanae, New Zealand. *T:* (business) (6) 3647739, *Fax:* (6) 3647605. *Club:* Wellesley (Wellington, NZ). *Died Nov. 2001.*

WILSON, Stanley John, CBE 1981; FCIS; Chairman, Burmah Oil (South Africa) (Pty) Ltd, 1982–87; Managing Director, 1975–82 and Chief Executive, 1980–82, The Burmah Oil Co. Ltd; *b* 23 Oct. 1921; *s* of Joseph Wilson and Jessie Cormack; *m* 1952, Molly Ann (*née* Clarkson); two *s*. *Educ:* King Edward VII Sch., Johannesburg; Witwatersrand Univ. CA (SA); ASAA, ACMA; FCIS 1945; CIMgt 1976; FInst Pet 1977. 1948–75: Chartered Accountant, Savory & Dickinson; Sec. and Sales Man., Rhodesian Timber Hldgs; Chm. and Chief Exec. for S Africa, Vacuum Oil Co.; Reg. Vice Pres. for S and E Asia, Mobil Petroleum; Pres., Mobil Sekiyu; Pres., subseq. Reg. Vice Pres. for Europe, Mobil Europe Inc.; Pres., Mobil East Inc., and Reg. Vice Pres. for Far East, S and SE Asia, Australia, Indian Sub-Continent; Reg. Pres. for Africa, etc. Freeman, City of London; Liveryman, Basketmakers' Co. FRSA. *Recreations:* golf, shooting, fishing. *Address:* The Jetty, PO Box 751, Plettenberg Bay, Cape Province, 6600, South Africa. *T:* (44) 5330547, *Fax:* (44) 5330556. *Clubs:* Royal Automobile; Royal & Ancient Golf; Plettenberg Bay Country (Cape Province); Kelvin Grove (Cape Town); Johannesburg Country (Johannesburg). *Died 13 Sept. 2005.*

WRIGHT, George Paul; Chief Superintendent, Royal Signals and Radar Establishment, Ministry of Defence, Baldock, 1976–80; *b* 27 April 1919; *s* of late George Maurice Wright, CBE, and of late Lois Dorothy Wright (*née* Norburn); *m* 1957, Jean Margaret Reid, *d* of Lt-Col Charles Alexander Reid Scott, DSO and Marjorie Reid Scott (*née* Mackintosh); one *s* one *d*. *Educ:* Bishops Stortford Coll.; Magdalen Coll., Oxford (BA 1948, MA 1951). FInstP. Admty Signal Estabt, 1939–45; Services Electronics Research Lab., 1945–57; Dept of Physical Research, Admty, 1957–63; Services Electronics Research Lab., 1963–76 (Dir, 1972–76). *Recreations:* music, sailing, gardening. *Address:* Tullom Grange, 11 Elwin Road, Tiptree, Essex CO5 0HL. *T:* (01621) 815239. *Clubs:* Civil Service; Blackwater Sailing (Maldon). *Died 22 Dec. 2005.*

A

ABBOTT, Sir Albert (Francis), Kt 1981; CBE 1974; Mayor, City of Mackay, Queensland, 1970–88; *b* Marvel Loch, WA, 10 Dec. 1913; *s* of late Albert Victor and Diana Abbott; *m* 1941, Gwendoline Joyce Maclean; two *s* four *d*. *Educ:* Mount Martin and Mackay State Schs, Qld. Served RAAF, 1941–45. Sugar cane farmer, 1950–; gave twenty years service to sugar industry organisations. Member: Picture, Theatre and Films Commn, 1975–90; Qld Local Govt Grants Commn, 1977–85. Returned Services League of Australia: Mem., 1946–; Pres., Mackay Sub-Br., 1960–65; Dist Pres., Mackay, 1965–74; Pres., Qld State, 1974–90; Hon. Life Pres., Qld State, 1991–; Hon. Life Vice Pres., Nat. Br., 1995–. President: N Qld Local Govt Assoc., 1975–84; Qld Local Govt Assoc., 1983–88; Aust. Local Govt Assoc., 1986–87; Lifeline Mackay, 1990–. Mem., Mackay Rotary Club. Governor, Utah Foundn, 1975–88. Hon. Dr Central Qld Univ., 1996. *Address:* 2 Tudor Court, Mackay, Qld 4740, Australia. *Clubs:* United Services (Brisbane); RSL Ex-Services, Golf, Trotting, Turf, Amateur Race, Diggers Race, Legacy (all in Mackay). *Died 10 Feb. 2006.*

ABBOTT, James Alan, PhD; Manager and Director of Research, Koninklijk/Shell Laboratorium, Amsterdam, Shell Research BV, 1981–88, retired; *b* 2 Dec. 1928; *s* of George Oswald and Eva Abbott; *m* 1954, Rita Marjorie Galloway, one *s* one *d*. *Educ:* Ilkeston Grammar School; University of Nottingham (BSc, PhD). Post-doctoral research, Univ. of Durham, 1952–53; served Royal Air Force, 1953–56 (Flt Lt RAF Technical Coll., Henlow). Shell companies, UK and Holland, 1956–88: Dir, Shell Research Ltd, Sittingbourne Research Centre, 1980–81. Officer, Order of Oranje-Nassau (The Netherlands), 1988. *Publications:* papers in Trans Faraday Soc., Proc. Royal Society. *Recreation:* bridge. *Died 24 May 2008.*

ABBOTT, Ronald William, CVO 1989; CBE 1979; FIA, ASA, FPMI; Consultant Partner, Bacon & Woodrow, Consulting Actuaries, 1982–94 (Senior Partner, 1972–81); *b* 18 Jan. 1917; *s* of late Edgar Abbott and Susan Mary Ann Abbott; *m* 1st, 1948, Hilda Mary Hampson (*d* 1972), *d* of late William George Clarke and Emily Jane Clarke; two *d*; 2nd, 1973, Barbara Constance, *d* of late Gilbert Hugh Clough and Harriet Clough. *Educ:* St Olave's Grammar Sch. FIA 1946; FPMI 1976. Actuarial Assistant: Atlas Assce Co., 1934–38; Friends Provident & Century Life Office, 1938–46; Sen. Actuary, Bacon & Woodrow, 1946, Partner 1948. Mem., Deptl Cttee on Property Bonds and Equity Linked Life Assce, 1971–73. Dep. Chm., 1973–82, Chm., 1982–87, Occupational Pensions Bd. Mem. Council: Inst. of Actuaries, 1966–74 (Hon. Treasurer, 1971–73); Indust. Soc., 1964–84 (Life Mem., 1984); Pensions Management Inst., 1977–81 (Vice-Pres., 1978–80). Master, Worshipful Co. of Ironmongers, 1986–87. FRSA. Finlaison Medal, Inst. of Actuaries, 1988. *Publications:* A Short History of the Association of Consulting Actuaries, 1991; contrib. to Jl of Inst. of Actuaries. *Recreation:* music. *Club:* Royal Automobile. *Died 19 Aug. 2006.*

ABEL, Kenneth Arthur, CBE 1984; Clerk and Chief Executive, Dorset County Council, 1967–91 (Clerk of the Peace, 1967–73); *b* 4 April 1926; *s* of late Arthur Abel, CBE and Frances Ethel Abel; *m* 1955, Sarah Matilda, *d* of late Capt. M. P. Poynor, TD and Norah Elizabeth Poynor; three *s*. *Educ:* Durham Sch.; Glasgow Univ.; Durham Univ. (LLB). Served RA, 1944–48. Admitted Solicitor, 1953; Assistant Solicitor: Warwicks CC, 1953–54; Leics CC, 1954–59; Sen. Asst Solicitor, Northants CC, 1959–63; Dep. Clerk and Dep. Clerk of the Peace, NR Yorks CC, 1963–67. Chm., Assoc. of County Chief Execs, 1982–83. Past Pres., Dorset County Golf Union. DL Dorset, 1977. *Recreations:* golf, gardening.

Address: Herne's Oak, Bradford Road, Sherborne, Dorset DT9 6BP. *T:* (01935) 813200. *Club:* Sherborne Golf (Sherborne) (Vice Pres.). *Died 13 Dec. 2010.*

ABERDEEN AND TEMAIR, June Marchioness of; (Beatrice Mary) June Gordon, CBE 1989 (MBE 1971); DL; Musical Director and Conductor, Haddo House Choral and Operatic Society (formerly Haddo House Choral Society), 1945–2005; *b* 29 Dec. 1913; *d* of Arthur Paul Boissier, MA, and Dorothy Christina Leslie Smith; *m* 1939, David George Ian Alexander Gordon (later 4th Marquess of Aberdeen and Temair, CBE, TD) (*d* 1974); two adopted *s* two adopted *d*. *Educ:* Southlands School, Harrow; Royal Coll. of Music. GRSM, ARCM. Teacher of Music, Bromley High School for Girls, 1936–39. Director of Haddo House Choral and Operatic Soc. and Arts Centre, 1945–2005. Chairman: Scottish Children's League, 1969–94; NE Scotland Music School, 1975–; Adv. Council, Scottish Opera, 1979–92; Chm. (local), Adv. Cttee, Aberdeen Internat. Festival of Music and the Performing Arts, 1980–96. Governor: Gordonstoun Sch., 1971–86; Royal Scottish Acad. of Music and Drama, 1979–82. FRCM 1967; FRSE 1983; FRSAMD 1985. DStJ 1977; GCStJ 1995. DL Aberdeenshire, 1971. Hon. LLD Aberdeen, 1968; Hon. DMus CNAA, 1991. *Publications:* contribs to Aberdeen Univ. Jl, RCM magazine. *Address:* Haddo House, Aberdeen AB41 7EQ. *T:* (01651) 851216. *Club:* New (Edinburgh). *Died 22 June 2009.*

ABSE, Leo; *b* 22 April 1917; *s* of Rudolph and Kate Abse; *m* 1st, 1955, Marjorie Davies (*d* 1996); one *s* one *d*; 2nd, 2000, Ania Czepulkowska. *Educ:* Howard Gardens High Sch.; LSE. Served RAF, 1941–46 (arrest for political activities in ME, 1944, precipitated parly debate). Solicitor; sen. partner, subseq. consultant in Cardiff law firm; first solicitor to be granted audience in High Court, 1986. Chm., Cardiff City Lab Party, 1951–53; Mem., Cardiff CC, 1953–58. Contested (Lab) Cardiff N, 1955. Fought a record 17 UK parly and local elections. MP (Lab): Pontypool, Nov. 1958–1983; Torfaen, 1983–87. Chm., Welsh Parly Party, 1976–87. Mem., Home Office Adv. Cttees on the Penal System, 1968, on adoption, 1972; first Chm., Select Cttee on Welsh Affairs, 1980; Mem., Select Cttee on Abortion, 1975–76; Sec., British-Taiwan Parly Gp, 1983–87. Led agitation for Suicide Act (ending criminality of attempted suicide), 1961; introd Infanticide Bills 1964 and 1969 to amend law relating to child murder; led final parly campaign for abolition of capital punishment, 1969; sponsor or co-sponsor of Private Mem.'s Acts relating to divorce, homosexuality, family planning, legitimacy, widows' damages, industrial injuries, congenital disabilities and relief from forfeiture; sponsored Children's Bill, 1973, later taken over by Govt to become Children's Act, 1975; sponsored Divorce Bill, 1983, later taken over by Govt to become Matrimonial and Family Proceedings Act, 1985; initiated first Commons debates on genetic engineering, Windscale, *in vitro* pregnancies. Led Labour anti-devolution campaign in Wales, 1979. Mem. Council, 1964–94, Vice Pres., 1995–, Centre for Crime and Justice Studies (formerly Inst. for Study and Treatment of Delinquency); Chm., Winnicott Clinic of Psychotherapy, 1988–91 (Trustee, 1980–2005); Pres., National Council for the Divorced and Separated, 1974–92; Vice-Pres., British Assoc. for Counselling, 1985–90; Chm., Parly Friends of WNO, 1985–87. Gov., Nat. Mus. of Wales, 1981–87; Member of Court: Univ. of Wales, 1981–87; UWIST. Regents' Lectr, Univ. of Calif, 1984. Received best dressed man award of Clothing Fedn, 1962. Order of Brilliant Star (China), 1988. *Publications:* Private Member: a psychoanalytically orientated study of

contemporary politics, 1973; (contrib.) In Vitro Fertilisation: past, present and future, 1986; Margaret, daughter of Beatrice: a psychobiography of Margaret Thatcher, 1989; Wotan, my enemy: can Britain live with the Germans?, 1994 (Wingate prize, Jewish Qly, 1994); The Man Behind the Smile: Tony Blair and the politics of perversion, 1996, new edn as Tony Blair: the man who lost his smile, 2003; Fellatio, Masochism, Politics and Love, 2000; The Bisexuality of Daniel Defoe: a psychoanalytic survey of the man and his works, 2006. *Recreations:* Italian wines, Cuban cigars, visits to European art galleries. *Address:* 54 Strand-on-the-Green, W4 3PD. *T:* (020) 8994 1166; Via Poggio di Mezzo, Nugola Vecchia, Livorno, Italy. *T:* (586) 977022. *Club:* Savile.
Died 19 Aug. 2008.

ACHESON, Sir (Ernest) Donald, KBE 1986; Chief Medical Officer, Departments of Health and of Social Security (formerly Department of Health and Social Security), Department of Education and Science and Home Office, 1983–91; *b* 17 Sept. 1926; *s* of Malcolm King Acheson, MC, MD, and Dorothy Josephine Rennoldson; *m* 1st, Barbara Mary Castle (marr. diss. 2002); one *s* four *d* (and one *d* decd); 2nd, 2002, Angela Judith Roberts; one *d*. *Educ:* Merchiston Castle Sch., Edinburgh; Brasenose Coll., Oxford (Theodore Williams Schol. in pathology, 1946; MA, DM; Hon. Fellow, 1989); Middlesex Hospital (Sen. Broderip Schol. in Med., Surg. and Pathol., 1950). FRCP 1967; FFPH (FFPHM 1972); FFOM 1985; FRCS 1988; FRCOG 1992. Acting Sqdn Leader, RAF Med. Br., 1953–55. Medical Practitioner, 1951; various clinical posts at Middlesex Hosp.; Radcliffe Trav. Fellow of University Coll., Oxford, 1957–59; Medical Tutor, Nuffield Dept of Medicine, Radcliffe Infirmary, Oxford, 1960; Dir, Oxford Record Linkage Study and Unit of Clin. Epidemiology, 1962; May Reader in Medicine, 1965; Fellow, Brasenose Coll., Oxford, 1968; Prof. of Clinical Epidemiology, Univ. of Southampton, and Hon. Consultant Physician, Royal South Hants Hosp., 1968–83; Foundation Dean, Faculty of Med., Southampton Univ., 1968–78; Dir, MRC Unit in Environmental Epidemiology, 1979–83. Member: Wessex Regional Hosp. Bd, 1968–74; Hampshire AHA (Teaching) 1974–78; Chm., SW Hants and Southampton DHA, 1981–83; Member: Adv. Cttee on Asbestos, Health and Safety Exec., 1978; Royal Commn on Environmental Pollution, 1979–83; UGC, 1982–83; GMC, 1984–91; MRC, 1984–91; Chairman: Slow Virus Group, DHSS, 1979–80; Primary Health Care Inner London Gp, DHSS, 1980–81; Enquiry into Public Health in England, 1988; Home Office Adv. Cttee on Health of Prisoners, 1992–94; Internat. Centre for Health and Society, UCL, 1996–2003; Ind. Inquiry into Inequalities in Health, DoH, 1997–98. UK Rep., Exec. Bd, WHO, 1988–90; Special Rep. of WHO in former Yugoslavia, 1992–93. Trustee, SCF, 1991–93. R. Samuel McLaughlin Vis. Prof., McMaster Univ., 1977; King's Fund Travelling Fellow, NZ Postgrad. Med. Fedn, 1979; Vis. Prof. of Internat. Health, Dept of Public Health and Policy, LSHTM, 1991–98. Lectures included: inaugural Adolf Streicher Meml, Stoke-on-Trent, 1978; Walter Hubert, British Assoc. for Cancer Res., 1981; Christie Gordon, Univ. of Birmingham, 1982; Edwin Chadwick Centennial, LSHTM, 1990; Harveian Orator, RCP, 1998. Examiner in Community Medicine: Univ. of Aberdeen, 1971–74; Univ. of Leicester, 1981–82; Examiner in Medicine, Univ. of Newcastle upon Tyne, 1975. Mem., Assoc. of Physicians of GB and Ire, 1965– (Pres. 1979); Pres., RIPH&H, 1999–2004. Founder FMedSci 1998. Hon. Fellow: LSHTM 1985; UCL, 1994. Hon. FRSocMed 1994. Hon. DM Southampton, 1984; Hon. DSc: Newcastle, 1984; Salford, 1991; Ulster, 1998; Hon. MD: QUB, 1987; Nottingham, 1989; Birmingham, 1991; Hon. LLD Aberdeen, 1988. Leon Bernard Foundn

Prize, WHO, 1994. *Publications:* Medical Record Linkage, 1967; Multiple Sclerosis, a reappraisal, 1966; Medicine, an outline for the intending student, 1970; One Doctor's Odyssey: the social lesion (memoir), 2007; scientific papers on epidemiology of cancer, multiple sclerosis and other chronic diseases, medical education and organisation and inequalities of medical care. *Recreations:* family, gardening, music. *Club:* Athenæum.
Died 10 Jan. 2010.

ACKERMANN, Georg K.; *see* Kahn-Ackermann.

ACKERS, Sir James George, Kt 1987; Chairman, West Midlands Regional Health Authority, 1982–93; *b* 20 Oct. 1935; *s* of James Ackers and Vera Harriet Ackers (*née* Edwards). *Educ:* Oundle Sch., Northants; LSE. BSc(Econ). Man. Dir, 1963, Chm., 1974–91, Ackers Jarrett Ltd; Chm., Ackers Jarrett Leasing Ltd, 1982–91; Vice Pres., Michael Doud Gill & Associates, Washington, DC, 1968–71. Pres., Walsall Chamber of Industry and Commerce, 1978; Association of British Chambers of Commerce, 1982–: Dep. Chm., 1982–84; Chm., 1984–86; Pres., 1986–90. Member: Cttee of Inquiry into Civil Service Pay, 1981–; Monopolies and Mergers Commn, 1981–90; Nat. Trng Task Force, 1989–91; NEDC, 1989–92. Chm., Fedn of Univ. Conservative Assocs, 1958; Vice-Chm., Bow Group, 1962–63. Pres., Jerome K. Jerome Soc., 1985–93. *Address:* 7 Gainsborough Drive, Mile Oak, Tamworth, Staffordshire B78 3PJ. *Died 31 March 2008.*

ACKNER, Baron *cr* 1986 (Life Peer), of Sutton in the county of West Sussex; **Desmond James Conrad Ackner,** Kt 1971; PC 1980; a Lord of Appeal in Ordinary, 1986–92; *b* 18 Sept. 1920; *s* of Dr Conrad and Rhoda Ackner; *m* 1946, Joan, *d* of late John Evans, JP, and *widow* of K. B. Spence; one *s* two *d*. *Educ:* Highgate Sch.; Clare Coll., Cambridge (MA; Hon. Fellow, 1983). Served in RA, 1941–42; Admty Naval Law Br., 1942–45. Called to Bar, Middle Temple, 1945; QC 1961; Recorder of Swindon, 1962–71; Judge of Courts of Appeal of Jersey and Guernsey, 1967–71; a Judge of the High Court of Justice, Queen's Bench Div., 1971–80; Judge of the Commercial Court, 1973–80; Presiding Judge, Western Circuit, 1976–79; a Lord Justice of Appeal, 1980–86. Mem. Gen. Council of Bar, 1957–61, 1963–70 (Hon. Treas., 1964–66; Vice-Chm., 1966–68; Chm., 1968–70); Bencher Middle Temple, 1965, Dep. Treasurer, 1983, Treasurer, 1984; Mem. Senate of the Four Inns of Court, 1966–70 (Vice-Pres., 1968–70); Pres., Senate of the Inns of Court and the Bar, 1980–82. Chm., Law Adv. Cttee, British Council, 1980–90 (Mem., 1991–); Mem., Lloyd's Arbitration Panel, 1992–. Pres., Arb. Appeal Tribunal, SFA, 1994–2002. Appeal Comr, PIA, 1994–2001; Dir, City Disputes Panel, 1994–98. Hon. Mem., Canadian Bar Assoc., 1973–. Pres., Soc. of Sussex Downsmen, 1993–96. Hon. Fellow, Soc. of Advanced Legal Studies, 1997. *Recreations:* reading, theatre. *Address:* House of Lords, SW1A 0PW. *T:* (020) 7219 6104; 4 Pump Court, Temple, EC4Y 7AN. *T:* (020) 7353 2656; 7 Rivermill, 151 Grosvenor Road, SW1V 3JN. *T:* (020) 7821 8068.
Died 21 March 2006.

ACKRILL, Prof. John Lloyd, FBA 1981; Professor of the History of Philosophy, Oxford University, 1966–89, then Emeritus; Fellow of Brasenose College, Oxford, 1953–89, then Emeritus; *b* 30 Dec. 1921; *s* of late Frederick William Ackrill and Jessie Anne Ackrill; *m* 1953, Margaret Walker Kerr; one *s* three *d*. *Educ:* Reading School; St John's Coll., Oxford (Scholar) (1940–41 and 1945–48; Hon. Fellow, 1996). War service (Royal Berks Regt and GS, Capt.), 1941–45. Assistant Lecturer in Logic, Glasgow Univ., 1948–49; Univ. Lectr in Ancient Philosophy, Oxford, 1951–52; Tutorial Fellow, Brasenose Coll., 1953–66. Gen. Ed., Clarendon Aristotle series, 1962–2000. Mem., Inst. for Adv. Study, Princeton, 1950–51, 1961–62; Fellow Coun. of Humanities, and Vis. Prof., Princeton Univ., 1955, 1964. *Publications:* Aristotle's *Categories* and *De*

Interpretatione (trans. with notes), 1963; Aristotle's Ethics, 1973; Aristotle the Philosopher, 1981; New Aristotle Reader, 1987; Essays on Plato and Aristotle, 1997; articles in philos. and class. jls. *Address:* 22 Charlbury Road, Oxford OX2 6UU. *T:* (01865) 556098.
Died 30 Nov. 2007.

ACLAND, Sir John (Dyke), 16th Bt *cr* 1644, of Columb John, Devon; *b* 13 May 1939; *s* of Sir Richard Thomas Dyke Acland, 15th Bt and Anne Stella (*née* Alford) (*d* 1992); *S* father, 1990; *m* 1st, 1961, Virginia (marr. diss. 2001), *yr d* of Roland Forge; two *s* one *d*; 2nd, 2001, Susan, *d* of Herbert Hooper. *Educ:* Clifton; Magdalene Coll., Cambridge; Univ. of West Indies (MSc). *Heir: s* Dominic Dyke Acland [*b* 19 Nov. 1962; *m* 1990, Sarah Anne, 3rd *d* of Ven. Kenneth Unwin; two *s* two *d* (of whom one *s* one *d* are twins)]. *Address:* 26A Cambridge Place, Cambridge CB2 1NS. *Died 25 Sept. 2009.*

ACLAND, Maj.-Gen. Sir John (Hugh Bevil), KCB 1980; CBE 1978; Vice Lord-Lieutenant of Devon, 1994–99; farmer; *b* 26 Nov. 1928; *s* of late Brig. Peter Acland, OBE, MC, TD and Bridget Susan Acland; *m* 1953, Myrtle Christian Euing, *d* of Brig. and Mrs Alastair Crawford, Auchentroig, Stirlingshire; one *s* one *d. Educ:* Eton Enlisted Scots Guards, 1946; commnd, 1948; served with 1st or 2nd Bn in Malaya, Cyprus, Egypt, Germany, Kenya, Zanzibar and NI, 1949–70; Equerry to HRH the Duke of Gloucester, 1957–59; Staff Coll., 1959; Bde Major, 4th Guards Armoured Bde, 1964–66; CO 2nd Bn Scots Guards, 1968–71; Col GS ASD, MoD, 1972–74; BGS, MoD, 1975; Comd Land Forces and Dep. Comd British Forces Cyprus, 1976–78; GOC South West Dist, 1978–81; Comd Monitoring Force, Southern Rhodesia, and Military Advr to the Governor, 1979–80; retired 1981. Dir of Liaison Res., Allied Vintners, 1982–93. Hon. Colonel: Exeter Univ. OTC, 1980–90; Royal Devon Yeomanry, 1983–92; Royal Wessex Yeomanry, 1989–92. Pres., Royal British Legion, Devon, 1982–90; Mem., Dartmoor National Park Authority, 1986. Chm., SW Regl Working Party on Alcohol, 1987–93. Mem. Steering Gp, Schools Health Educn Unit, Exeter Univ., 1986–92. Trustee, Exeter Cathedral Preservation Trust, 1984– (Chm., 1997–). Governor: Allhallows Sch., 1982–94; King's Sch., Ottery St Mary, 1994–99. Pres., Honiton and Dist Agricl Assoc., 1995–. DL Devon, 1984. *Publications:* articles in Country and other jls. *Recreations:* fishing, arboriculture, destroying vermin. *Address:* Sowton Farm, Buckerell, Honiton, Devon EX14 3EH. *Clubs:* Army and Navy, MCC, Blue Seal. *Died 17 Nov. 2006.*

ACTON, 4th Baron *cr* 1869, of Aldenham, Salop; **Richard Gerald Lyon-Dalberg-Acton;** Baron Acton of Bridgnorth (Life Peer) 2000; Bt 1644; Patrician of Naples, 1802; *b* 30 July 1941; *s* of 3rd Baron Acton, CMG, MBE, TD and Hon. Daphne, *o d* of 4th Baron Rayleigh, FRS and Lady Mary Hilda, 2nd *d* of 4th Earl of Leitrim; *S* father, 1989; *m* 1st, 1965, Hilary Juliet Sarah (*d* 1973), *d* of Dr Osmond Laurence Charles Cookson, Perth, WA; one *s*; 2nd, 1974, Judith (writer) (marr. diss. 1987), *d* of Hon. Sir (Reginald Stephen) Garfield Todd; 3rd, 1988, Patricia (Law Professor and writer), *o d* of late M. Morey Nassif and of Mrs Nassif, Iowa, USA. *Educ:* St George's Coll., Salisbury, Rhodesia; Trinity Coll., Oxford (BA History 1963, MA 1988). Mgt trainee, Amalgamated Packaging Industries Ltd, Britain, Rhodesia, USA and S Africa, 1963–66; Trainee Dir, 1967–70, Dir, 1970–74, Coutts & Co. Called to the Bar, Inner Temple, 1976; practising barrister, 1977–81; a Senior Law Officer, Min. of Justice, Legal and Parly Affairs, Zimbabwe, 1981–85. A cross-bencher, H of L, 1989–97; joined Lab. Party, 1997; Member: H of L Refreshment Cttee, 1998–99; H of L Constitution Cttee, 2001–05; Jt Cttee on Consolidation Bills, 2002–05, 2006–; H of L Select Cttee on Delegated Powers and Regulatory Reform, 2006–07. Patron: Jubilee Appeal, MIND, 1996–; The Mulberry Bush Sch., 1998–; APEX Trust, 2002–; Frank Longford Trust, 2002–; Hansard Soc., 2003–; Trustee, Old Creamery Th. Co., Iowa, 1995–. Hon. Pres., Assoc. of Amer. Study

Abroad Progs in the UK, 2006–. Throne/Aldrich Award, State Historical Soc. of Iowa, 1995. Hon. Citizen of Iowa, 2003. *Publications:* (contrib.) The Spectator Annual, 1993; (with Prof. P. Acton) To Go Free: a treasury of Iowa's legal heritage, 1995 (Benjamin F. Shambaugh award, 1996); A Brit Among the Hawkeyes, 1998; (contrib.) Outside In: African-American history in Iowa 1838–2000, 2001; (contrib.) The Biographical Dictionary of Iowa, 2008; contribs anthologies and periodicals. *Heir: s* Hon. John Charles Ferdinand Harold Lyon-Dalberg-Acton [*b* 19 Aug. 1966; *m* 1998, Lucinda, *d* of Brig. James Percival]. *Address:* 152 Whitehall Court, SW1A 2EL. *T:* (020) 7839 3077; 100 Red Oak Lane SE, Cedar Rapids, IA 52403, USA. *T:* (319) 3626181.
Died 10 Oct. 2010.

ADAM, Sir Christopher Eric Forbes, 3rd Bt *cr* 1917; *b* 12 Feb. 1920; *s* of Eric Graham Forbes Adam, CMG (*d* 1925) (2nd *s* of 1st Bt) and of Agatha Perrin, *d* of Reginald Walter Macan; *S* uncle, 1982; *m* 1957, Patricia Anne Wreford (*d* 2008), *y d* of late John Neville Wreford Brown; one adopted *d. Heir: cousin* Rev. (Stephen) Timothy Beilby Forbes Adam [*b* 19 Nov. 1923; *m* 1954, Penelope, *d* of George Campbell Munday, MC; four *d*]. *Address:* 46 Rawlings Street, SW3 2LS. *Died 17 Jan. 2009.*

ADAMS, John Crawford, OBE 1977; MD, MS, FRCS; orthopædic practice; Hon. Consulting Orthopædic Surgeon, St Mary's Hospital, London, 1979; Hon. Civil Consultant in Orthopædic Surgery, Royal Air Force, 1984 (Civil Consultant, 1964–84); *b* 25 Sept. 1913; *s* of Archibald Crawford Adams, W Hallam, Derbys; *m* 1940, Joan Bower Elphinstone (*d* 1981); *m* 1990, Marguerite Kyle (*d* 2010). *Educ:* MB, BS 1937; MRCS 1937; LRCP 1937; FRCS 1941; MD (London) 1943; MS (London) 1965. Formerly: Chief Asst, Orthopædic and Accident Dept, London Hosp.; Orthopædic Specialist, RAFVR; Resident Surgical Officer, Wingfield-Morris Orthopædic Hosp., Oxford; Consultant Orthopædic Surgeon: St Mary's Hosp., London and Paddington Green Children's Hosp., 1948–79; Brighton Gen. Hosp., 1948–58; St Vincent's Orthopædic Hosp., Pinner, 1952–65. FRSocMed 1948 (Hon. Mem., Sect. of Orthopædics, 1986); Hon. Fellow: British Orthopædic Assoc., 1994 (Hon. Sec., 1959–62; Vice-Pres., 1974–75; Robert Jones Gold Medal and Prize, 1961); Amer. Acad. of Orthopædic Surgeons, 1975. Mem., Council, Jl of Bone and Joint Surgery, 1974–84 (formerly Production Editor). *Publications:* (contrib.) Techniques in British Surgery, ed Maingot, 1950; Outline of Orthopædics, 1956, 14th edn 2007; Outline of Fractures, 1957, 11th edn 1999; Ischio-femoral Arthrodesis, 1966; Arthritis and Back Pain, 1972; Standard Orthopædic Operations, 1976, 4th edn 1992; Shakespeare's Physic, Lore and Love, 1989, new edn as Shakespeare's Physic, 2000; Francis, Forgiven Fraud, 1991; Associate Editor and contributor, Operative Surgery (ed Rob and Smith); contribs to Jl of Bone and Joint Surgery, etc. *Address:* The Old H H Inn, Cheriton, Alresford, Hampshire SO24 0PY. *Died 31 Oct. 2010.*

ADAMS, Rear-Adm. John Harold, CB 1967; LVO 1957; Senior Partner, John Adams Interviews, 1993–99; *b* Newcastle-on-Tyne, 19 Dec. 1918; *m* 1st, 1943, Mary Parker (marr. diss. 1961); one *s* decd; 2nd, 1961, Ione Eadie, MVO, JP (*d* 1998); two *s* two *d. Educ:* Glenalmond. Joined Navy, 1936; Home Fleet, 1937–39; Western Approaches, Channel and N Africa, 1939–42 (despatches); Staff Capt. (D), Liverpool, 1943–45; Staff Course, Greenwich, 1945; HMS Solebay, 1945–47; HMS Vernon, 1947–49; jssc 1949; comd HMS Creole, 1950; Staff Flag Officer Submarines, 1951–52; TAS, Warfare Div., Admty, 1953; Comdr, HM Yacht Britannia, 1954–57; Asst Dir, Underwater Weapons Matériel Dept, 1957–58; Capt. (SM) 3rd Submarine Sqdn, HMS Adamant, 1958–60; Captain Supt, Underwater Detection Estab., Portland, subseq. Admty Underwater Weapons Estab., 1960–62; idc 1963; comd HMS Albion, 1964–66; Asst Chief of Naval Staff (Policy),

1966–68; retd 1968. Lieut 1941; Lieut-Comdr 1949; Comdr 1951; Capt. 1957; Rear-Adm. 1966. Dir, Paper and Paper Products Industry Training Bd, 1968–71; Dir, Employers' Federation of Papermakers and Boardmakers, 1972–73; Dir Gen., British Paper and Board Industry Fedn, 1974–83. Dir, DUO (UK) Ltd, 1983–93. Chm. Governors, Cheam Sch., 1975–87. Paper Industry Gold Medal, 1984. *Recreations:* fishing, photography. *Address:* Yew Tree Cottage, Ibworth, Tadley, Hants RG26 5TJ. *Club:* Army and Navy. *Died 3 Nov. 2008.*

ADAMS, Richard Borlase, CBE 1983; Managing Director, Peninsular & Oriental Steam Navigation Co., 1979–84 (Director, 1970, Deputy Managing Director, 1974); *b* 9 Sept. 1921; *s* of James Elwin Cokayne Adams and Susan Mercer Porter; *m* 1951, Susan Elizabeth Lambert; two *s* one *d*. *Educ:* Winchester Coll.; Trinity Coll., Oxford, 1940. War service, Rifle Bde, 1940–46 (Major). Mackinnon Mackenzie Gp of Cos, Calcutta, New Delhi and Hongkong, 1947–63; Chm., Islay Kerr & Co. Ltd, Singapore, 1963–66; British India Steam Navigation Co. Ltd: Dir, 1966; Man. Dir, 1969; Chm., 1970. Dir, Clerical, Medical & General Life Assurance Soc., 1975–88. *Died 8 Nov. 2009.*

ADAMSON, Norman Joseph, CB 1981; QC (Scot.) 1979; Legal Secretary to the Lord Advocate and First Parliamentary Draftsman for Scotland, 1979–89, retired; Assistant Counsel to the Lord Chairman of Committees, House of Lords, 1989–95, retired; *b* 29 Sept. 1930; *o s* of Joseph Adamson, wine and spirit merchant, and Lily Thorrat, Glasgow; *m* 1961, Patricia Mary, *er d* of Walter Scott Murray Guthrie and Christine Gillies Greenfield, Edinburgh; four *d*. *Educ:* Hillhead High Sch., Glasgow; Glasgow Univ. (MA Hons Philosophy and Economics 1952; LLB 1955). Admitted to Faculty of Advocates, Scotland, 1957; called to English Bar, Gray's Inn, 1959. Army Legal Aid (Civil) (UK), 1956–57; practice at Scottish Bar, 1957–65; Partner, Joseph Adamson & Co., 1965–82; Standing Jun. Counsel, Bible Board, 1962; Standing Jun. Counsel, MoD (Army), 1963–65; Hon. Sheriff Substitute, 1963–65; Parly Draftsman and Legal Sec., Lord Advocate's Dept, London, 1965–89. Underwriting Mem. of Lloyd's, 1976–91. Jt Convener, Scottish YCs, 1953–55. Founder Chm., Laleham Soc. (Civic Trust), 1970–72. Pres., Woking and Dist Scottish Soc., 1980–81. Governor, Ashford (Middx) Secondary Schs, 1968–72. Contested (C) Glasgow (Maryhill), 1959 and 1964. TA, 1948–55. Elder of the Church of Scotland. *Publications:* (contrib.) Stair Memorial Encyclopedia of the Laws of Scotland, 1995; contribs to legal jls. *Recreations:* music, theatre. *Address:* Prospect House, 53 Lodge Hill Road, Lower Bourne, Farnham, Surrey GU10 3RD. *T:* (01252) 721988. *Club:* Civil Service. *Died 9 Dec. 2006.*

ADDISON, Kenneth George, OBE 1978; company director; Director, 1971–89, and Deputy Chief General Manager, 1976–84, Sun Alliance & London Insurance Group; *b* 1 Jan. 1923; *s* of Herbert George Addison and Ruby (*née* Leathers); *m* 1945, Maureen Newman; one *s* one *d*. *Educ:* Felixstowe Grammar Sch. LLB Hons London. Served RAF, 1942–46. Joined Alliance Assurance Co. Ltd, 1939; various subsequent appts; Asst Sec., Law Fire Insurance Office, 1960–64; Gen. Manager, Sun Alliance & London Insurance Group, 1971. Chm., Bourne Home Develts Ltd, 1989–93; Dir, Sabre Insurance Co. Ltd, 1990–96. Chairman: Fire Insurers' Res. & Testing Orgn, 1977–84; Management Cttee, Associated Insurers (British Electricity), 1977–84; Internat. Oil Insurers, 1979–82; Dir, Insurance Technical Bureau, 1977–84; Advr, Med. Defence Union, 1986–94 (Dir, 1991–94). Chm., Hearing Aid Council, 1971–78. Dir, Croydon Community Trust, 1990–94. FCIS; FCII (Pres., 1980); FCIArb (Pres., 1968–69). *Publications:* papers on insurance and allied subjects. *Recreations:* swimming, carpentry, gardening. *Died 23 Aug. 2010.*

ADELAIDE, Dean of; *see* Renfrey, Rt Rev. L. E. W.

AGNEW, Peter Graeme, MBE 1946; retired; Chairman, Bradbury Agnew & Co. Ltd (Proprietors of Punch), 1962–68; *b* 7 April 1914; *s* of late Alan Graeme Agnew; *m* 1937, Mary Diana (*née* Hervey) (*d* 2000); two *s* two *d*. *Educ:* Kingsmead, Seaford; Stowe School; Trinity College, Cambridge (BA). Student Printer, 1935–37; joined Bradbury Agnew & Co. Ltd, 1937. RAFVR 1937; served War of 1939–45; demobilised, 1945, as Wing Commander. *Recreations:* sailing, gardening. *Died 7 Oct. 2006.*

AGNEW-SOMERVILLE, Sir Quentin (Charles Somerville), 2nd Bt *cr* 1957, of Clendry, Co. Wigtown; insurance consultant; *b* 8 March 1929; *s* of Comdr Sir Peter Agnew, 1st Bt and Enid Frances (*d* 1982), *d* of late Henry Boan; assumed additional name of Somerville by Royal licence, 1950; *S* father, 1990; *m* 1963, Hon. April, *y d* of 15th Baron Strange; one *s* two *d*. *Educ:* RNC Dartmouth. *Heir:* *s* James Lockett Charles Agnew-Somerville, *b* 26 May 1970. *Died 13 Oct. 2010.*

AIRD, Captain Sir Alastair (Sturgis), GCVO 1997 (KCVO 1984; CVO 1977; LVO 1969); Comptroller, 1974–2002, and Private Secretary and Equerry, 1993–2002, to Queen Elizabeth the Queen Mother; an Extra Equerry to the Queen, since 2003; *b* 14 Jan. 1931; *s* of Col Malcolm Aird; *m* 1963, Fiona Violet Myddelton (CVO 2001); two *d*. *Educ:* Eton; RMA Sandhurst. Commnd 9th Queen's Royal Lancers, 1951; served in BAOR; Adjt 9th Lancers, 1956–59; retd from Army, 1964. Equerry to Queen Elizabeth the Queen Mother, 1960; Asst Private Sec. to the Queen Mother, 1964. Mem. Council, Feathers Assoc. of Youth Clubs, 1973–93; Trustee, RSAS Develt Trust, 1986–99. Hon. Bencher, Middle Temple, 1991. *Recreations:* shooting, fishing, golf. *Address:* The Paddock, Lovells Court, Marnhull, Sturminster Newton, Dorset DT10 1JJ. *Clubs:* Cavalry and Guards; Eton Ramblers; I Zingari. *Died 30 Sept. 2009.*

AITCHISON, Craigie (Ronald John), CBE 1999; RA 1988 (ARA 1978); painter; *b* 13 Jan. 1926; *yr s* of late Rt Hon. Lord Aitchison, PC, KC, LLD. *Educ:* Scotland; Slade Sch. of Fine Art. British Council Italian Govt Scholarship for painting, 1955; Edwin Austin Abbey Premier Scholarship, 1965; Lorne Scholarship, 1974–75. One-man Exhibitions: Beaux Arts Gall., 1959, 1960, 1964; Marlborough Fine Art (London) Ltd, 1968; Compass Gall., Glasgow, 1970; Basil Jacobs Gall., 1971; Rutland Gall., 1975; Knoedler Gall., 1977; Kettle's Yard Gall., Cambridge, 1979; Serpentine Gall. (major retrospective, 1953–81), 1981–82; Artis, Monte Carlo, Monaco, 1986; Albemarle Gall., 1987, 1989; Castlefield Gall., Manchester, 1990; Thomas Gibson Fine Art, London, 1993; Harewood House, Leeds (retrospective, 1954–94); Gall. of Modern Art, Glasgow (retrospective, 1956–96), 1996; Timothy Taylor Gall., Waddington Galls, 1998, 2001, 2004. Exhibited: Calouste Gulbenkian Internat. Exhibn, 1964; Il Tempo del imagine, 2nd Internat. Biennale, Bologna, 1967; Modern British Painters, Tokyo, Japan, 1969; 23rd Salon Actualité de l'Esprit, Paris, 1975; The Proper Study, British Council Lalit Kala Akademi, Delhi, 1984; Hard Won Image, Tate Gall., 1985; British Council Exhibn, Picturing People, Hong Kong and Zimbabwe, 1990; The Journey, Lincoln Cathedral, 1990; Nine Contemporary Painters, City of Bristol Mus. and Art Gall., 1990; British Council Exhibn, British Figurative Painting of 20th Century, Israel Mus., Jerusalem, 1992. Pictures in public collections: Tate Gall., Arts Council, Contemp. Art Soc., Scottish National Gall. of Modern Art, Glasgow Mus. and Art Gall., and Nat. Gall. of Melbourne, Australia; Truro Cathedral, Liverpool Cathedral and chapel of King's College, Cambridge. 1st Johnson Wax Prize, Royal Acad., 1982; Korn Ferry Internat. Award, Royal Acad., 1989 and 1991; 1st Jerwood Foundn Award, 1994; Nordstern Art Award, RA, 2000. *Address:* c/o Royal Academy of Arts, Burlington House, Piccadilly, W1V 0DS. *Died 21 Dec. 2009.*

AKEHURST, Gen. Sir John (Bryan), KCB 1984; CBE 1976; Deputy Supreme Allied Commander, Europe, 1987–90; b 12 Feb. 1930; s of late Geoffrey and Doris Akehurst; m 1955, Shirley Ann, er d of late Major W. G. Webb, MBE, and Ethel Webb; (one s one d decd). Educ: Cranbrook Sch.; RMA, Sandhurst. Commnd Northamptonshire Regt, 1949; Malay Regt (despatches), 1952–55; Adjt, 5th Northamptonshire Regt (TA), 1959–60; Staff Coll., Camberley, 1961; Brigade Major, 12 Infantry Bde Gp, 1962–64; Instructor, Staff Coll., Camberley, 1966–68; commanded 2nd Royal Anglian Regt, 1968–70; Directing Staff, IDC/RCDS, 1970–72; Comdt, Jun. Div., Staff Coll., 1972–74; Comdr, Dhofar Bde, Sultan of Oman's Armed Forces, 1974–76; Dep. Mil. Sec. (A), MoD (Army), 1976–79; GOC 4th Armoured Div., BAOR, 1979–81; Comdt, The Staff Coll., Camberley, 1982–83; Comdr, UK Field Army, and Inspector Gen., TA, 1984–87. Sen. Mil. Visitor to Saudi Arabia, 1985–87; Dep. Col, 1981–86, Col, 1986–91, Royal Anglian Regt. Comr, Commonwealth War Graves Commn, 1993–98. Chm., Council, TA&VRA, 1990–95; Mem. Council, RUSI, 1985–88; President: Reserve Forces Assoc., 1991–99; RBL Wilts, 2006–. Chm., 1982–84, Pres., 1984–90, Army Golf Assoc.; Vice Patron, Army Officers' Golf Soc., 1986– (Pres., 1983–86). Gov., Royal Star and Garter Home, 1990–91. Governor: Harrow Sch., 1982–97 (Chm. of Govs, 1991–97); John Lyon Sch., 1989–91; Princecroft Primary Sch., Warminster, 1990–2000 (Chm. of Govs, 1995–2000). Pres., Warminster Civic Trust, 1998–. Liveryman, Poulters' Co., 1997–. Order of Oman, 3rd Class (mil.), 1976. Publications: We Won a War, 1982; Generally Speaking, 1999. Recreations: reading, battlefield touring and guiding, trout fishing, travel. Address: Dresden Cottage, 46 Vicarage Street, Warminster, Wilts BA12 8JF. Clubs: Army and Navy; Woking Golf; Senior Golfers' Society (Pres., 2006–). Died 20 Feb. 2007.

ALCOCK, Prof. Leslie, OBE 1991; Professor of Archaeology, University of Glasgow, 1973–90, then Emeritus; b 24 April 1925; o s of Philip John Alcock and Mary Ethel (née Bagley); m 1950, Elizabeth A. Blair (decd); one s one d. Educ: Manchester Grammar Sch.; Brasenose Coll., Oxford. BA 1949, MA 1950. Supt of Exploration, Dept of Archaeology, Govt of Pakistan, 1950; Curator, Abbey House Museum, Leeds, 1952; Asst Lectr, etc, UC Cardiff, 1953; Prof. of Archaeology, UC Cardiff, 1973; Hon. Professorial Res. Fellow, Univ. of Glasgow, 1990. Member: Bd of Trustees, Nat. Mus. of Antiquities, Scotland, 1973–85; Ancient Monuments Bd, Scotland, 1974–90; Royal Commn on Ancient and Historical Monuments of Scotland, 1977–92; Royal Commn on Ancient and Historical Monuments in Wales, 1986–90. President: Cambrian Archaeological Assoc., 1982; Glasgow Archaeological Soc., 1984–85; Soc. of Antiquaries, Scotland, 1984–87. Lectures: Jarrow, 1988; Rhind, Soc. of Antiquaries, Scotland, 1988–89. FRHistS 1969. Hon. FSAScot, 1994. Publications: Dinas Powys, 1963; Arthur's Britain, 1971; Cadbury/Camelot, 1972; Economy, Society and Warfare, 1987; (co-ed) From the Baltic to the Black Sea, 1988; Cadbury Castle, Somerset, 1995; Kings and Warriors, Craftsmen and Priests in Northern Britain AD 550–850, 2002; articles and reviews in British and Amer. jls. Recreations: mountain and coastal scenery, music. Address: c/o 47 Upper Belmont Road, Bristol BS7 9DG. Died 7 June 2006.

ALDRIDGE, Trevor Martin; solicitor; President: Special Educational Needs and Disability Tribunal (formerly Special Educational Needs Tribunal), 1994–2003; Protection of Children Act Tribunal, 1999–2001; b 22 Dec. 1933; s of Dr Sidney and Isabel Aldridge; m 1966, Joanna, d of C. J. v. D. Edwards; one s one d. Educ: Frensham Heights School; Sorbonne; St John's College, Cambridge (MA). Partner in Bower Cotton & Bower, 1962–84; Law Comr, 1984–93. Chairman: Conveyancing Standing Cttee, 1989 (Mem., 1985–89); Commonhold Working Gp, reported 1987. Hon. Vis. Prof., City Univ., 1994–95. Pres., Frensham Heights School, 1996– (Chm. Govs, 1977–95). Hon. QC 1992;

Hon. Life Mem., Law Soc., 1995. General editor, Property Law Bulletin, 1980–84. Publications: Boundaries, Walls and Fences, 1962, 10th edn 2009; Finding Your Facts, 1963; Directory of Registers and Records, 1963. (consulting ed.) 5th edn 1993; Service Agreements, 1964, 4th edn 1982; Rent Control and Leasehold Enfranchisement, 1965, 11th edn as Aldridge's Residential Lettings, 1998; Betterment Levy, 1967; Letting Business Premises, 1971, 8th edn 2004; Your Home and the Law, 1975, 2nd edn 1979; (jtly) Managing Business Property, 1978; Criminal Law Act 1977, 1978; Guide to Enquiries of Local Authorities, 1978, 2nd edn 1982; Guide to Enquiries Before Contract, 1978; Guide to National Conditions of Sale, 1979, 2nd edn 1981; Leasehold Law, 1980; Housing Act, 1980, and as amended 1984, 2nd edn 1984; (ed) Powers of Attorney, 6th edn 1986 to 10th edn 2007; Guide to Law Society's Conditions of Sale, 1981, 2nd edn 1984; Questions of Law: Homes, 1982; Law of Flats, 1982, 3rd edn 1994; Practical Conveyancing Precedents, 1984; Practical Lease Precedents, 1987; Companion to Standard Conditions of Sale, 1990, 3rd edn 2003; Companion to Property Information Forms, 1990; First Registration, 1991; Companion to Enquiries of Local Authorities, 1991; Companion to the Law Society Business Lease, 1991; Implied Covenants for Title, 1995; Privity of Contract: Landlord and Tenant (Covenants) Act, 1995; Commonhold Law, 2002. Address: Birkitt Hill House, Offley, Hitchin, Herts SG5 3DB. T: (01462) 768261, e-mail: t.m.aldridge@btopenworld.com. Club: Oxford and Cambridge. Died 14 Sept. 2010.

ALEXANDER, Prof. Albert Geoffrey, FDSRCS; Professor of Conservative Dentistry, University of London, 1972–92, then Emeritus; b 22 Sept. 1932; s of William Francis Alexander and Muriel Katherine (née Boreham); m 1956, Dorothy Constance (née Johnson); one d. Educ: Bridlington Sch.; UCH Dental Sch., Univ. of London (BDS 1956; MDS 1968). LDSRCS 1955, FDSRCS 1961. Dental House Surgeon, Nat. Dental Hosp., 1955–56; Nat. Service, RADC, 1956–58; Clinical Asst, UCH Dental Dept, 1958; private dental practice, 1958–59; Lectr in Cons. Dentistry, 1959–62, Sen. Lectr in Cons. Dentistry and Periodontics, 1962–69, UCH Dental Sch.; Hon. Consultant, UCH Dental Hosp., 1967–92; Vice-Dean of Dental Studies, 1974–77, Dean, 1977–92, UCL Dental Sch., later UC and Middlesex Sch. of Dentistry; Vice-Dean, Faculty of Clinical Sciences, UCMSM, 1977–91; Prof. of Conservative Dentistry, Univ. of Hong Kong, 1992–94. Fellow, UCL, 1986; Member: Council, UCL, 1984–91; Senate, Univ. of London, 1987–91. Chm., Dental Educn Adv. Council, 1986–90; Member: GDC, 1986–92 (Treasurer, 1989–92); Bloomsbury HA, 1981–90. Fellow: Internat. Coll. of Dentists, 1975; Hong Kong Acad. of Medicine, 1993. Publications: (co-ed) The Prevention of Periodontal Disease, 1971; (jtly) Self-Assessment Manual, No 3, Clinical Dentistry, 1978; (co-ed) Companion to Dental Studies, Vol. 3, 1986, Vol. 2, 1988; scientific, technical and clinical articles on dentistry and dental research. Recreations: photography, blue and white Chinese ceramics. Died 2 June 2010.

ALEXANDER, Sir Charles G(undry), 2nd Bt cr 1945; MA, AIMarE; Chairman, Alexander Shipping Co. Ltd, 1959–87; b 5 May 1923; s of Sir Frank Alexander, 1st Bt, and Elsa Mary (d 1959), d of Sir Charles Collett, 1st Bt; S father, 1959; m 1st, 1944, Mary Neale, o c of S. R. Richardson; one s one d; 2nd, 1979, Eileen Ann Stewart. Educ: Bishop's Stortford College; St John's College, Cambridge. Served War as Lieut (E), RN, 1943–46. Chm., Governors Care Ltd, 1975–86; formerly Dep. Chm., Houlder Bros and Co. Ltd: Director: Furness-Houlder Insurance Ltd, until 1988; Furness-Houlder (Reinsurance Services) Ltd, until 1988; Inner London Region, National Westminster Bank Ltd, until 1987; Chm., Hull, Blyth & Co. Ltd, 1972–75. Chm., Bd of Governors, Bishop's Stortford College, until 1986. Mem. Court of Common Council, 1969; Alderman (Bridge Ward), 1970–76. Master, Merchant

Taylors' Co., 1981–82; Prime Warden, Shipwrights' Co., 1983–84. *Heir: s* Richard Alexander [*b* 1 Sept. 1947; *m* 1971, Lesley Jane Jordan (marr. diss.); two *s*]. *Address:* Newland House, 68 Newland, Sherborne, Dorset DT9 3AQ. *T:* (01935) 389758. *Club:* Royal Automobile.   *Died 31 Dec. 2009.*

ALEXANDER of Ballochmyle, Sir Claud Hagart-, 3rd Bt *cr* 1886, of Ballochmyle; JP; DL; Vice Lord-Lieutenant, Ayr and Arran, 1983–98; *b* 6 Jan. 1927; *s* of late Wilfred Archibald Alexander (2nd *s* of 2nd Bt) and Mary Prudence, *d* of Guy Acheson; *S* grandfather, 1945; assumed additional surname of Hagart, 1949; *m* 1959, Hilda Etain, 2nd *d* of Miles Malcolm Acheson, Ganges, BC, Canada; two *s* two *d*. *Educ:* Sherborne; Corpus Christi Coll., Cambridge (BA 1948). MInstMC 1980. Hon. Sheriff, S Strathclyde, Dumfries and Galloway, 1997–. DL Ayrshire, 1973; JP Cumnock and Doon Valley, 1983. *Heir: s* Claud Hagart-Alexander [*b* 5 Nov. 1963; *m* 1994, Elaine Susan, *d* of Vincent Park, Winnipeg; one *s*]. *Address:* Kingencleugh House, Mauchline, Ayrshire KA5 5JL. *T:* (01290) 550217. *Club:* New (Edinburgh).   *Died 23 Jan. 2006.*

ALEXANDER, Prof. (John) David, Hon. CBE 1998; DPhil; President Emeritus (formerly Trustees' Professor), Pomona College, since 1991 (President, 1969–91); *b* 18 Oct. 1932; *s* of John David Alexander, Sr and Mary Agnes McKinnon; *m* 1956, Catharine Coleman; one *s* two *d*. *Educ:* Southwestern at Memphis (BA); Louisville Presbyterian Theological Seminary; Oxford University (DPhil). Instructor to Associate Prof., San Francisco Theol. Seminary, 1957–64; Pres., Southwestern at Memphis, 1965–69. Trustee, Teachers Insurance and Annuity Assoc., NY, 1970–2002; Director: Great Western Financial Corp., Beverly Hills, 1973–97; KCET (Community Supported TV of S Calif.), 1979–89; Amer. Council on Educn, Washington DC, 1981–84; National Assoc. of Ind. Colls and Univs, 1984–88; British Inst., 1979–87; Member: Nat. Panel on Academic Tenure, 1971–72; Assoc. of Amer. Med. Colls Panel on Gen. Professional Preparation of Physicians, 1981–84; Bd of Overseers, Huntington Library, Art Collections and Botanical Gardens, 1991–. Amer. Sec., Rhodes Scholarship Trust, 1981–98. Ed., The American Oxonian, 1998–2000. Dir, Children's Hosp. of Los Angeles, 1993–99. Trustee: Woodrow Wilson Nat. Fellowship Foundn, 1978–98; Seaver Inst., 1992–; Wenner-Gren Foundn for Anthropological Res., NY, 1995–2007; Emeriti Consortium, Inc., 2005–. Vice-Pres., Soc. of Fellows, Phi Beta Kappa, 2000–; Dist. Friend, Oxford Univ., 2000; Pres., American Friends of Nat. Portrait Gall. (London) Foundn, 2004–. Fellow, Amer. Acad. of Arts and Scis, 2006. Hon. LLD: Univ. of S California, 1970; Occidental Coll., 1970; Centre Coll. of Kentucky, 1971; Pepperdine Univ., Calif, 1991; Albertson Coll. of Idaho, 1992; Pomona Coll., Calif, 1996; Hon. LHD Loyola Marymount Univ., 1983; Hon. LittD Rhodes Coll., Memphis, 1986. *Publications:* (contrib.) History of the Rhodes Trust, 2001; The Goddess Pomona: a harvest of digressions, 2007; articles in Biblical studies; articles and chapters on higher educn in USA. *Recreations:* music, book collecting. *Address:* 406 Taylor Drive, Claremont, CA 91711–4137, USA. *T:* (909) 6247848. *Clubs:* Athenæum; Century Association (NY); California (Los Angeles); Bohemian (San Francisco).   *Died 25 July 2010.*

ALEXANDER, Richard Thain; *b* 29 June 1934; *s* of Richard Rennie Alexander and Gladys Alexander; *m* 1st, 1966, Valerie Ann Winn (marr. diss. 1985); one *s* one *d*; 2nd, 1987, Pat Hanson. *Educ:* Dewsbury Grammar Sch., Yorks; University Coll. London (LLB Hons). Articled with Sir Francis Hill, Messrs Andrew & Co., Lincoln, 1957–60; Asst Solicitor, Messrs McKinnell, Ervin & Holmes, Scunthorpe, 1960–64; Sen. Partner, Messrs Jones, Alexander & Co., Retford, 1964–85, Consultant, 1986–90. MP (C) Newark, 1979–97; contested (C) same seat, 1997. Mem. (C) Newark and Sherwood DC, 2003–.

Recreation: golf. *Address:* 3 The Friary, Appletongate, Newark, Notts NG24 1JY. *Clubs:* Newark Conservative, Newark Town and District.   *Died 20 April 2008.*

ALEXANDER, (Walter) Ronald, CBE 1984; Chairman, Walter Alexander plc, 1979–90 (Managing Director, 1973–79); company director; *b* 6 April 1931; *s* of Walter Alexander and Katherine Mary Turnbull; *m* 1st, 1956, Rosemary Anne Sleigh (garden designer, Rosemary Alexander) (marr. diss. 1975); two *s* two *d*; 2nd, 1979, Mrs Lorna Elwes, *d* of Lydia Duchess of Bedford. *Educ:* Loretto Sch.; Clare Coll., Cambridge (MA Hons). Chm. and Man. Dir, Tayforth Ltd, 1961–71; Chm., Scottish Automobile Co. Ltd, 1971–73. Director: Scotcros plc, 1965–82 (Chm., 1972–82); Investors Capital Trust plc, 1967–99; Clydesdale Bank plc, 1971–96; RIT and Northern plc (formerly Great Northern Investment Trust plc), 1973–84; Dawson Internat. plc, 1979–96. Chm., Scottish Appeals Cttee, Police Dependants' Trust, 1974–81; Pres., Public Schs Golfing Soc., 1973–79; Chairman: PGA, 1982–85; Royal and Ancient Golf Club of St Andrews Trust, 1987–2003. Governor, Loretto Sch., 1961–89; Comr, Queen Victoria Sch., 1987–92. Hon. LLD St Andrews, 2001. Scottish Free Enterprise Award, 1977. *Recreation:* golf. *Address:* 54 Argyle Street, St Andrews, Fife KY16 9BU. *Clubs:* Royal and Ancient Golf (Captain, 1980–81); Hon. Company of Edinburgh Golfers; Prestwick Golf; Pine Valley Golf (USA).
                                     Died 19 Sept. 2006.

ALFONSÍN, Dr Raúl Ricardo; President of Argentina, 1983–89; *b* 12 March 1927; *s* of Serafín Raúl Alfonsín and Ana María Foulkes; *m* 1949, María Lorenza Barreneche; three *s* three *d*. *Educ:* Regional Normal School, Chascomús; Gen San Martín Mil. Acad.; Law Sch., Nat. Univ. of La Plata. Joined Radical Civic Union, 1945: Pres., 1983–91; Pres., Nat. Cttee, 1999–. Journalist, founder El Imparcial, Chascomús; Mem., Chascomús City Cttee, 1951, Mem. Council, 1954–55 (Pres., 1955 and 1959–61); Mem., Buenos Aires Provincial Legislature, 1952; Provincial Deputy, 1958–62; Deputy, Nat. Congress, 1963–66, 1973–76. Founder: Movimiento de Intransigencia y Renovación; Fundación Argentina para la Libre Información, 1992. Dr *hc*: New Mexico, New York, 1985; Bologna, Santiago de Compostela, Complutense de Madrid, 1988; Naples, 1990. Human Rights Prize (jtly), Council of Europe, 1986; numerous awards and foreign decorations. *Publications:* La Cuestión Argentina, 1980; Ahora, mi Propuesta Política, 1983; Que es el Radicalismo?, 1983; Alfonsín Responde, 1992; Democracia y Consenso, 1996. *Address:* Unión Cívica Radical, Alsina 1786, 1088 Buenos Aires, Argentina.   *Died 31 March 2009.*

ALLAIS, Prof. Maurice; Grand Officier de la Légion d'honneur, 2005 (Commandeur, 1989); Officier des Palmes académiques, 1949; Chevalier de l'économie nationale, 1962; Grand Croix de l'Ordre National du Mérite, 1998; French economist and engineer; *b* 31 May 1911; *s* of Maurice Allais and Louise (*née* Caubet); *m* 1960, Jacqueline Bouteloup (*d* 2003); one *d*. *Educ:* Lycée Lakanal à Sceaux; Lycée Louis-le-Grand; Ecole Polytechnique; Ecole Nationale Supérieure des Mines de Paris. Engineer, Dept of Mines and Quarries, Nantes, 1937–43; Dir, Bureau de Documentation Minière, 1943–48; Prof. of Economic Analysis, Ecole Nationale Supérieure des Mines de Paris, 1944–88; Dir, Centre for Economic Analysis, 1946–; Prof. of Economic Theory, Inst. of Statistics, Univ. of Paris, 1947–68; research in economics, 1948–; Dir of Res., Centre National de la Recherche Scientifique, 1954–80; Prof., Graduate Inst. of Internat. Studies, Geneva, 1967–70; Dir, Clément Juglar Centre of Monetary Analysis, Univ. of Paris, 1970–85. Fellow: Operations Res. Soc., 1958; Internat. Soc. of Econometrics, 1949. Mem. de l'Académie des Sciences Morales et Politiques, 1990; Hon. Mem., Amer. Econ. Assoc., 1976; Associate Foreign Member: US Nat. Acad. of Scis, 1989; Accademia Nazionale dei Lincei, Rome, 1991; l'Académie des Sciences de Russie, 1999. Dr *hc*: Univ. of Groningen, 1964; Univ. of Mons, 1992; Amer.

Univ. of Paris, 1992; Univ. of Lisbon, 1993; Ecole des Hautes Etudes Commerciales, 1993. Prizes from: L'Académie des Sciences, 1933; L'Académie des Sciences Morales et Politiques, 1954, 1959, 1983, 1984. Gravity Res. Foundn, 1959; also Lanchester Prize, Amer. Economic Assoc., 1958; Prix Galabert, 1959; Grand Prix André Arnoux, 1968; Gold Medal, Centre National de la Recherche Scientifique, 1978; Nobel Prize for Economics, 1988. *Publications* include: A la recherche d'une discipline économique, 1943, 2nd edn as Traité d'Economie Pure, 1952, 3rd edn 1994; Abondance ou misère, 1946; Economie et Intérêt, 1947, 2nd edn 1997; Les fondements comptables de la macroéconomique, 1954, 2nd edn 1992; Manifeste pour une société libre, 1959; L'Europe unie, route de la prosperité, 1960; The Role of Capital in Economic Development, 1963; Growth without Inflation, 1968; Les théories de l'équilibre économique général et de l'éfficacité maximale, 1971; Inequality and Civilization, 1973; L'impôt sur le capital et la réforme monétaire, 1977, 2nd edn 1988; La théorie générale des surplus, 1980, 2nd edn 1989; Frequency, Probability and Chance, 1982; Determination of Cardinal Utility, 1985; Les conditions monétaires d'une économie de marchés, 1987; Autoportraits, 1989; Pour l'indexation, 1990; Pour la réforme de la fiscalité, 1990; L'Europe face à son avenir, que faire, 1991; Erreurs et impasses de la construction européenne, 1992; Combats pour l'Europe, 1994; Cardinalism, 1994; L'Anisotropie de l'espace, 1997; La Crise Mondiale d'aujourd'hui, 1999; L'Union européenne: la mondialisation et le chômage, 1999; Des régularités significatives dans les observations interterométriques de Dayton C. Miller, 1997–2000; Fondements de la dynamique Monétaire, 2001; La Passion de la recherche, 2001; Un savant méconnu, 2002. *Address:* (office) 60 boulevard Saint Michel, 75006 Paris, France. *Died 9 Oct. 2010.*

ALLARDICE, His Honour William Arthur Llewellyn; DL; a Circuit Judge, 1972–96 (Midland and Oxford Circuit); *b* 18 Dec. 1924; *s* of late W. C. Allardice, MD, FRCSEd, JP, and Constance Winifred Allardice; *m* 1956, Jennifer Ann, *d* of late G. H. Jackson; one *s* one *d*. *Educ:* Stonyhurst Coll.; University Coll., Oxford (MA). Open Schol., Classics, 1942; joined Rifle Bde, 1943, commnd 1944; served with 52nd LI, Europe and Palestine, 1945; Oxford, 1946–48; called to Bar, Lincoln's Inn, 1950; practised Oxford Circuit, 1950–71. Chm., Trustees, William Salt Liby, 1990–96. DL Staffs, 1980. *Recreations:* local history, matters equestrian. *Address:* c/o Stafford Crown and County Courts, Stafford ST18 2QQ. *T:* (01785) 255217. *Died May 2006.*

ALLCHIN, Rev. Canon Arthur Macdonald, (Donald); Hon. Professor, University of Wales, Bangor, since 1992; *b* 20 April 1930; *s* of late Dr Frank Macdonald Allchin and Louise Maude Allchin. *Educ:* Westminster Sch.; Christ Church, Oxford (BLitt, MA); Cuddesdon Coll., Oxford. Curate, St Mary Abbots, Kensington, 1956–60; Librarian, Pusey House, Oxford, 1960–69; Warden, Community of Sisters of Love of God, Oxford, 1967–94; Res. Canon of Canterbury, 1973–87, Hon. Canon, 1988–. Programme Dir, St Theosevia Centre for Christian Spirituality, Oxford, 1987–96. Visiting Lecturer: General Theological Seminary, NY, 1967 and 1968; Catholic Theological Faculty, Lyons, 1980; Trinity Inst., NY, 1983; Vis. Prof., Nashotah House, Wisconsin, 1984, 1995. Editor, Sobornost, 1960–77; Jt Editor, Christian, 1975–80. Hon. DD: Bucharest Theol Inst., 1977; Nashotah House, 1985; Aarhus, 1992; Wales, 1993; Lambeth, 2006. *Publications:* The Silent Rebellion, 1958; The Spirit and the Word, 1963; (with J. Coulson) The Rediscovery of Newman, 1967; Ann Griffiths, 1976; The World is a Wedding, 1978; The Kingdom of Love and Knowledge, 1979; The Dynamic of Tradition, 1981; A Taste of Liberty, 1982; The Joy of All Creation, 1984, 2nd edn 1993; (with E. de Waal) Threshold of Light,

1986; Participation in God, 1988; The Heart of Compassion, 1989; Landscapes of Glory, 1989; Praise Above All, 1991; (ed with D. Jasper and contrib.) Heritage and Prophecy, 1993; God's Presence Makes the World, 1997; N. F. S. Grundtvig: an introduction to his life and work, 1997; Resurrection's Children, 1998; (with D. Morgan and P. Thomas) Sensuous Glory: the poetic vision of D. Gwenallt Jones, 2000; (ed with S. Bradley and contrib.) Grundtvig in International Perspective, 2000; Friendship in God: Evelyn Underhill and Sorella Maria, 2003; The Gift of Theology, 2005; contrib. Studia Liturgica, Irenikon, Theology, Eastern Churches Review, Worship, One in Christ, Planet, Logos, Collectanea Cisterciensia. *Recreations:* music, poetry, enjoying hill country. *Address:* 42 Hill Rise, Woodstock, Oxon OX20 1AB. *Died 23 Dec. 2010.*

ALLCHIN, Frank Raymond, PhD; FBA 1981; Fellow of Churchill College, since 1963, and Reader in Indian Studies, 1972–90, University of Cambridge; Reader Emeritus, since 1990; *b* 9 July 1923; *s* of late Frank MacDonald Allchin and Louise Maude Wright; *m* 1951, Bridget Gordon; one *s* one *d*. *Educ:* Westminster Sch.; Regent Street Polytechnic; Sch. of Oriental and African Studies, London Univ. (BA, PhD 1954); MA Cantab. Lectr in Indian Archaeology, SOAS, 1954–59; Univ. Lectr in Indian Studies, Cambridge, 1959–72. Jt Dir, Cambridge Univ. (British) Archaeol Mission to Pakistan, 1975–92. Chairman: Ancient India and Iran Trust, 1995– (Treas., 1978–86, 1989–2001); British Assoc. for Conservation of Cultural Heritage of Sri Lanka, 1996–2003 (Vice Chm., 1982–91; Acting Chm., 1990–96); Dir, British Anuradhapura Project, Sri Lanka, 1989–93. Consultant: UNESCO, 1969, 1972, 1975; UNDP, 1971. Hon. DLitt Deccan Coll., Pune, India, 2007. *Publications:* Piklihal Excavations, 1960; Utnur Excavations, 1961; Neolithic Cattle Keepers of South India, 1963; Kavitāvalī, 1964; The Petition to Rām, 1966; (with B. Allchin) Birth of Indian Civilization, 1968; (with N. Hammond) The Archaeology of Afghanistan, 1978; (with D. K. Chakrabarti) Sourcebook of Indian Archaeology, vol. 1, 1979, vol 2, 1997, vol 3, 2003; (with B. Allchin) The Rise of Civilization in India and Pakistan, 1982; (jtly) The Archaeology of Early Historic South Asia, 1995; (with B. Allchin) The Origins of a Civilisation, 1997; contribs to learned journals. *Recreations:* gardening, walking, reading, bat watching, writing memoirs (with B. Allchin). *Address:* 2 Shepreth Road, Barrington, Cambridge CB22 7SB. *T:* (01223) 870494. *Club:* India International Centre (New Delhi). *Died 4 June 2010.*

ALLDIS, John Trevor; conductor; *b* 10 Aug. 1929; *s* of W. J. and N. Alldis; *m* 1960, Ursula Margaret Mason; two *s*. *Educ:* Felsted School; King's Coll., Cambridge (MA). ARCO. Formed John Alldis Choir, 1962; Founder and Conductor, London Symphony Chorus, 1966–69; Conductor, London Philharmonic Choir, 1969–82; Joint Chief Conductor, Radio Denmark, 1971–77; Conductor, Groupe Vocal de France, 1979–83; Chorus Master, Hallé Choir, 1992–93. Choral Prof., Guildhall Sch. of Music, 1966–79 (FGSM 1976); Music Consultant, Israel Chamber Choir (Cameran Singers), 1989–91. Mem., Vaughan Williams Trust, 1976–2003. Fellow, Westminster Choir Coll., Princeton, NJ, 1978. Chevalier des Arts et des Lettres (France), 1984. *Address:* 3 Wool Road, Wimbledon, SW20 0HN. *T:* (020) 8946 4168. *Died 20 Dec. 2010.*

ALLEN OF ABBEYDALE, Baron *cr* 1976 (Life Peer), of the City of Sheffield; **Philip Allen,** GCB 1970 (KCB 1964; CB 1954); *b* 8 July 1912; *yr s* of late Arthur Allen and Louie Tipper, Sheffield; *m* 1938, Marjorie Brenda Coe (*d* 2002). *Educ:* King Edward VII Sch., Sheffield; Queens' Coll., Cambridge (Hon. Fellow 1974). Whewell

Schol. in Internat. Law, Cambridge Univ., 1934. Entered Home Office, 1934; Offices of War Cabinet, 1943–44; Commonwealth Fellowship in USA, 1948–49; Deputy Chm. of Prison Commn for England and Wales, 1950–52; Asst Under Sec. of State, Home Office, 1952–55; Deputy Sec., Min. of Housing and Local Govt, 1955–60; Deputy Under-Sec. of State, Home Office, 1960–62; Second Sec., HM Treasury, 1963–66; Permanent Under-Sec. of State, Home Office, 1966–72. Chairman: Occupational Pensions Bd, 1973–78; Nat. Council of Social Service, 1973–77; Gaming Bd for GB, 1977–85 (Mem., 1975); Mencap, 1982–88. Member Royal Commissions: on Standards of Conduct in Public Life, 1974–76; on Civil Liability and Compensation for Personal Injury, 1973–78; Member: Security Commn, 1973–91; tribunal of inquiry into Crown Agents, 1978–82. Chief Counting Officer, EEC Referendum, 1975. Chm. Council, RHBNC, London Univ., 1985–92 (Visitor, 1992–97). *Address:* Holly Lodge, Middle Hill, Englefield Green, Surrey TW20 0JP. *T:* (01784) 432291.
Died 27 Nov. 2007.

ALLEN, Colin Mervyn Gordon, CBE 1978; General Manager, Covent Garden Market Authority, 1967–89; *b* 17 April 1929; *s* of late Cecil G. Allen and Gwendoline L. Allen (*née* Hutchinson); *m* 1953, Patricia, *d* of late William and Doris Seddon; two *s* one *d*. *Educ:* King Edward's Sch., Bath. BA Open, 1985; MA London, 1986; MA London (Dist.), 1991. FCIPS (FInstPS 1967). Naval Store Dept, Admiralty, 1948–56; National Coal Board: London HQ, 1956–59; Area Stores Officer, NE Div., 1959–64; Covent Garden Market Authority: Planning Officer, 1964–66; Asst Gen. Man., 1967. President: Assoc. of Wholesale Markets within Internat. Union of Local Authorities, 1972–78; IPS, 1982–83. Chm., Vauxhall Cross Amenity Trust, 1982–83. *Publications:* Transplanting the Garden: the story of the relocation of Covent Garden Market, 1998; various papers on horticultural marketing and allied topics, supply and logistics matters, and ancient history and archaeology. *Recreation:* archaeology. *Address:* Grassington, 142 Gidley Way, Horspath, Oxford OX33 1TD. *T:* (01865) 872388. *Died 14 June 2010.*

ALLEN, Prof. Deryck Norman de Garrs; Professor of Applied Mathematics in the University of Sheffield, 1955–80, then Emeritus; Warden of Ranmoor House, 1968–82; *b* 22 April 1918; *s* of Leonard Lincoln Allen and Dorothy Allen (*née* Asplin). *Educ:* King Edward VII School, Sheffield; Christ Church, Oxford. Messrs Rolls Royce, 1940; Research Asst to Sir Richard Southwell, FRS, 1941; Lectr in Applied Mathematics at Imperial Coll., London, 1945; Visiting Prof. in Dept of Mechanical Engineering, Massachusetts Inst. of Technology, 1949; Reader in Applied Mathematics at Imperial Coll. in Univ. of London, 1950. Pro-Vice-Chancellor, Sheffield Univ., 1966–70; Chm., Jt Matriculation Bd, 1973–76. *Publications:* Relaxation Methods, 1954 (US); papers on Applied Maths and Engineering Maths in: Proc. Royal Soc.; Philosophical Trans. of Royal Soc.; Quarterly Jl of Mechanics and Applied Maths; Jl of Instn of Civil Engineers. *Recreation:* travel. *Address:* Broomcroft House Nursing Home, 416 Ecclesall Road, Sheffield S11 9PY.
Died 14 March 2010.

ALLEN, Donald George, CMG 1981; Deputy Parliamentary Commissioner for Administration (Ombudsman), 1982–90; *b* 26 June 1930; *s* of Sidney George Allen and Doris Elsie (*née* Abercombie); *m* 1955, Sheila Isobel Bebbington; two *s* (and one *s* decd). *Educ:* Southall Grammar School. Foreign Office, 1948; HM Forces, 1949–51; FO, 1951–54; The Hague, 1954–57; 2nd Sec. (Commercial), La Paz, 1957–60; FO, 1961–65: 1st Sec. 1962; Asst Private Sec. to Lord Privy Seal, 1961–63 and to Minister without Portfolio, 1963–64; 1st

Sec., Head of Chancery and Consul, Panama, 1966–69; FCO, 1969–72; Counsellor on secondment to NI Office, Belfast, 1972–74; Counsellor and Head of Chancery, UK Permanent Delegn to OECD, Paris, 1974–78; Inspector, 1978–80; Dir, Office of Parly Comr (Ombudsman), 1980–82, on secondment. Mem., Broadcasting Complaints Commn, 1990–97. *Recreations:* squash, tennis, golf. *Address:* 99 Parkland Grove, Ashford, Middx TW15 2JF. *T:* (01784) 255617. *Clubs:* Royal Automobile, MCC. *Died 12 March 2007.*

ALLEN, His Honour Francis Andrew; a Circuit Judge, 1979–2001; *b* 7 Dec. 1933; *s* of Andrew Eric Allen and Joan Elizabeth Allen; *m* 1st, 1961, Marjorie Pearce; one *s* three *d*; 2nd, 1994, Sheila Baggaley. *Educ:* Solihull School; Merton College, Oxford (MA). 2nd Lieut, Highland Light Infantry, 1957; called to the Bar, Gray's Inn, 1958. A Recorder of the Crown Court, 1978–79. Chm., Magisterial Cttee, Judicial Studies Bd, 1990–95. *Recreation:* walking. *Club:* Mountain Bothies Association (Scottish Highlands). *Died 17 March 2006.*

ALLEN, Frank Graham, CB 1984; Clerk of the Journals, House of Commons, 1975–84; *b* 13 June 1920; *s* of Percy and Gertrude Allen; *m* 1947, Barbara Caulton; one *d* (one *s* decd). *Educ:* Shrewsbury Sch. (Schol.); Keble Coll., Oxford (Exhibnr, BA). 7th Bn Worcs Regt, 1940–46, India, 1942–44; Allied Commn Austria, Vienna, 1945–46. Asst Clerk, House of Commons, 1946; Principal Clerk, 1973. Mem., House of Laity, Gen. Synod of C of E, 1970–80. Silver Jubilee Medal, 1977. *Address:* 3 Badger's Walk, Cedars Village, Chorleywood, Herts WD3 5GA. *T:* (01923) 350054. *Club:* Rhinefield Owners (Brockenhurst). *Died 12 Aug. 2007.*

ALLEN, Maj.-Gen. John Geoffrey Robyn, CB 1976; Senior Army Directing Staff, Royal College of Defence Studies, 1976–78; Lay Observer attached to Lord Chancellor's Department, 1979–85; *b* 19 Aug. 1923; *s* of R. A. Allen and Mrs Allen (*née* Youngman); *m* 1959, Ann Monica (*née* Morford); one *s* one *d*. Haileybury. Commissioned KRRC, 1942; trans. RTR, 1947; Bt Lt-Col, 1961; Lt-Col, CO 2 RTR, 1963; Mil. Asst (GSO1) to CGS, MoD, 1965; Brig., Comd 20 Armd Bde, 1967; IDC, 1970; Dir of Operational Requirements 3 (Army), MoD, 1971; Maj.-Gen., Dir-Gen., Fighting Vehicles and Engineer Equipment, MoD, 1973–74; Dir, RAC, 1974–76; retired 1979. Col Comdt, RTR, 1976–80; Hon. Colonel: Westminster Dragoons, 1982–87; Royal Yeomanry, 1982–87. Member: Adv. Cttee on Legal Aid, 1979–86; Booth Cttee on Procedure in Matrimonial Causes, 1982–85; Mgt Cttee, Friends of Chichester Hosps, 1987–2002 (Chm., 1991–97); Pres., 1997–2002); Appeal Tribunals, FIMBRA, 1989–98; Membership and Disciplinary Tribunal, PIA, 1994–98. *Address:* Meadowleys, Charlton, Chichester, W Sussex PO18 0HU. *T:* (01243) 811638. *Club:* Army and Navy. *Died 15 July 2010.*

ALLEN, Prof. Percival, FRS 1973; Professor of Geology, and Head of Geology Department, University of Reading, 1952–82, then Emeritus Professor; Director, Sedimentology Research Laboratory, 1965–82; *b* 15 March 1917; *s* of late Norman Williams Allen and Mildred Kathleen Hoad; British; *m* 1941, Frances Margaret Hepworth, BSc (*d* 2007); three *s* one *d*. *Educ:* Brede Council Sch.; Rye Grammar School; University of Reading. BSc 1939, PhD 1943, Hon. DSc, 1992, Reading; MA Cantab 1947. Univ. Demonstrator, 1942–45, Univ. Asst Lectr, 1945–46, Reading; University Demonstrator, 1946–47, Univ. Lectr, 1947–52, Cambridge; Dean of Science Faculty, Reading, 1963–66. Vis. Prof., Univ. of Kuwait, 1970. Served War of 1939–45. In Royal Air Force, 1941–42. Sedgwick Prize, Univ. of Cambridge, 1952; Daniel Pidgeon Fund, Geological Soc. of London, 1944; Leverhulme Fellowships Research Grant, 1948, 1949. Geological Soc. of London: Mem. Council, 1964–67; Lyell Medal, 1971; Pres., 1978–80; Royal Society: Mem. Council, 1977–79; a Vice-Pres., 1977–79; Chairman: Expeditions Cttee,

1974–; British Nat. Cttee for Geology, 1982–90; Sectional Cttee 5, 1983–88; Actg Chm., Earth Sciences Res. Priorities, 1987–89. Chm., Scottish Regional Cttee and Mem., Nat. and Eastern Reg. Cttees, UGC Earth Sciences Rev., 1987–90; Council Mem., NERC, 1971–74 and Royal Soc. Assessor, 1977–80; Chm., vis. group to Palaeont. Dept in British Mus. (Nat. Hist.), 1975, and Univ. of Strathclyde, 1982; External Appraiser (Geol. Depts): Meml Univ., Newfoundland, 1968; Jadavpur Univ., India, 1977; Univ. of Western Ontario, 1982; Univ. of London, 1982; Univ. of Malaya, 1983; Adv. Panel, UNDP Project on Nile Delta, 1972–; UNESCO/UNDP Geology Consultant, India, 1976–77. UK Editor, Sedimentology, 1961–67; Jt Editor, OUP Monographs in Geology and Geophysics series, 1980–87. Chm., Org. Cttees: VII Internat. Sedimentological Congress, 1967; first European Earth and Planetary Physics Colloquium, 1971; first Meeting European Geological Socs, 1975; UK Delegate to Internat. Union of Geol Sciences, Moscow, 1984; UK Corresp., IGCP Project 245, 1986–91. Sec.-Gen., Internat. Assoc. Sedimentologists, 1967–71; Pres., Reading Geol. Soc., 1976–78, 1987–88; Chm., British Inst. for Geological Conservation, 1987–91. Algerian Sahara Glacials Expedn, 1970; Sec., Philpots Quarry Ltd. Hon. Member: American Soc. of Economic Paleontologists and Mineralogists; Bulgarian Geological Soc.; Geologists' Assoc.; Internat. Assoc. of Sedimentologists; For. Fellow, Indian Nat. Sci. Acad., 1980. *Publications:* papers on Wealden (Lower Cretaceous) and Torridonian (Proterozoic) in various scientific journals. *Recreations:* chess, natural history, gardening, bicycling. *Address:* Postgraduate Research Institute for Sedimentology, University of Reading, Reading RG6 6AB. *T:* (0118) 931 6713.   *Died 3 April 2008.*

ALLERTON, Air Vice-Marshal Richard Christopher, CB 1989; DL; Director General of Supply, Royal Air Force, 1987–90; Chairman, Sharpe's of Aberdeen, 1995–98; *b* 7 Dec. 1935; *er s* of late Air Cdre Ord Denny Allerton, CB, CBE, and Kathleen Mary Allerton; *m* 1964, Marie Isobel Campbell Mackenzie, *er d* of Captain Sir Roderick Mackenzie, 11th Bt, CBE, DSC, RN, and Marie, Lady Mackenzie; two *s. Educ:* Stone House, Broadstairs; Stowe Sch. Commissioned RAF, 1954; served, 1955–78: RAF Hullavington, Oakington, Feltwell, Kinloss, RAF Unit HQ Coastal Command, Hereford, Little Rissington; Instructor, RAF Coll., Cranwell; Student, RAF Staff Coll., Bracknell; Staff, HQ RAF Germany; Chief Instructor, Supply and Secretarial Trng, RAF Coll., Cranwell; Student, Nat. Defence Coll., Latimer; MoD Harrogate; Dep. Dir, RAF Supply Policy, MoD, 1978–80; Station Comdr, RAF Stafford, 1980–82; RCDS 1983; Air Cdre, Supply and Movements, HQ Strike Comd, 1983–86. ADC to the Queen, 1980–82. Pres., RAF Cricket Assoc., 1987–89. Mem., St John Council for Cornwall, 1991–2000. DL Cornwall, 1995. *Recreations:* shooting, fishing, cricket. *Address:* c/o Lloyds TSB, 13 Broad Street, Launceston, Cornwall PL15 8AG. *Club:* Royal Air Force.   *Died 28 Oct. 2008.*

ALLSOP, Peter Henry Bruce, CBE 1984; Publishing Consultant, Publishers' Management Advisers, 1983–2004; *b* 22 Aug. 1924; *s* of late Herbert Henry Allsop and Elsie Hilpern (*née* Whittaker); *m* 1950, Patricia Elizabeth Kingwell Bown; two *s* one *d. Educ:* Haileybury; Caius Coll., Cambridge (MA). Called to Bar, Lincoln's Inn, 1948, Bencher, 1989. Temp. Asst Principal, Air Min., 1944–48; Barrister in practice, 1948–50; Sweet & Maxwell: Editor, 1950–59; Dir, 1960–64; Man. Dir, 1965–73; Chm., 1974–80; Dir, Associated Book Publishers, 1963, Asst Man. Dir, 1965–67, Man. Dir, 1968–76, Chm., 1976–88. Chm., Teleordering Ltd, 1978–91; Trustee and Vice-Chm., Yale University Press, 1984–99 (Dir, 1981–84); Director: J. Whitaker & Sons, 1987–98; Lloyd's of London Press, 1991–95. Mem. Council, Publishers Assoc., 1969–81 (Treasurer, 1973–75, 1979–81; Pres., 1975–77; Vice-Pres., 1977–78; Trustee, 1982–95); Member: Printing and Publishing Industry Trng Bd, 1977–79; Publishers' Adv. Cttee,

British Council, 1980–85; Chm., Management Cttee, Book House Training Centre, 1980–86. Chm., Social Security Appeal Tribunal, 1982–87 (Mem., 1979–82). Chm., Book Trade Benevolent Soc., 1986–92 (Trustee, 1976–85, 1994–98; Dir, 1985). Mem., St Albans City Council, 1955–58. Chm., DAC, Bath and Wells, 1985–94; Trustee, St Andrews Conservation Trust, Wells, 1987–99; Mem., Wells Cathedral Fabric Adv. Cttee, 1991–99. Chm. Council, King's Coll., Taunton, 1986–94 (Mem., 1983–86). Dir, Woodard Schools (Western Div.) Ltd, 1985–95. Editor, later Editor Emeritus: Current Law, 1952–90; Criminal Law Review, 1954–90. *Publications:* (ed) Bowstead's Law of Agency, 11th edn, 1951. *Recreations:* reading, theatre. *Club:* Garrick.   *Died 4 May 2010.*

ALSTON, Rt Rev. Mgr J(oseph) Leo; Parish Priest, Sacred Heart Church, Ainsdale, Southport, 1972–98; *b* 17 Dec. 1917; *s* of Benjamin Alston and Mary Elizabeth (*née* Moss). *Educ:* St Mary's School, Chorley; Upholland College, Wigan; English Coll., Rome; Christ's College, Cambridge. Priest, 1942; Licentiate in Theology, Gregorian Univ., Rome, 1942; BA (1st Cl. Hons Classics) Cantab 1945. Classics Master, Upholland Coll., Wigan, 1945–52, Headmaster, 1952–64; Rector, Venerable English Coll., Rome, 1964–71. Protonotary Apostolic, 1988. Mem., Cambridge Soc. *Recreation:* music. *Address:* St Marie's House, 27 Seabank Road, Southport, Merseyside PR9 0EJ. *T:* (01704) 501361.   *Died 27 Sept. 2006.*

ALTHAUS, Sir Nigel (Frederick), Kt 1989; Senior Broker to the Commissioners for the Reduction of the National Debt (Government Broker), 1982–89; *b* 28 Sept. 1929; *er s* of late Frederick Rudolph Althaus, CBE and Margaret Frances (*née* Twist); *m* 1958, Anne, *d* of P. G. Cardew; three *s* one *d. Educ:* Eton; Magdalen Coll., Oxford (Roberts Gawen Scholar; 2nd Cl. Lit. Hum. 1954). National Service, 60th Rifles, 1948–50. Joined Pember and Boyle (Stockbrokers), 1954; Partner, 1955–75, Sen. Partner, 1975–82; Sen. Partner, Mullens and Co., 1982–86. Mem., Stock Exchange, 1955–89; Chm., Stock Exchange Benevolent Fund, 1975–82. Treas., ICRF, 1991–2000. Master, Skinners' Co., 1977–78; Chm. Governors, Skinners' Co. Sch. for Boys, Tunbridge Wells, 1982–89. Chm., British Library of Tape Recordings for Hosp. Patients, 1975–97. Comr, Royal Hosp., Chelsea, 1988–94. Queen Victoria's Rifles (TA), 1950–60; Hon. Col, 39 Signal Regt (TA), 1982–88. *Publications:* (ed) British Government Securities in the Twentieth Century, 1976. *Recreations:* golf, shooting, music. *Address:* c/o Bank of England, Threadneedle Street, EC2R 8AH. *Clubs:* Boodle's, Beefsteak; Swinley Forest Golf (Ascot).   *Died 30 July 2007.*

ALTMAN, Lionel Phillips, CBE 1979; special adviser to parliamentary and public bodies and to private sector; Chairman: European Cleaning Services Group, 1991–94; Hydro-Lock Europe (formerly Hydro-Lock UK), 1992–96; Equity & General plc, 1978–91; Westminster Consultancy, since 1998; *b* 12 Sept. 1922; *s* of late Arnold Altman and Catherine Phillips; *m* Diana; one *s* two *d* by previous marriages. *Educ:* University Coll. and Business Sch., also in Paris. FIMI; FCIM; FMI; MCIPR. Director: Carmo Holdings Ltd, 1947–63; Sears Holdings Motor Gp, 1963–72; Sears Finance, 1965–71; C. & W. Walker Holdings Ltd, 1974–77; H. P. Information plc, 1985–91; Motor Agents Assoc. Ltd, 1986–89 (Mem., Nat. Council, 1965–; Pres., 1975–77); Chm., Pre-Divisional Investments Ltd, 1972–95 (Chief Exec., 1972–94). Chairman: Motor Industry Educnl Consultative Council Industry Working Party, producing Altman Report on recruitment and training, 1968; Retail Motor Industry Working Party on Single European Market, 1988–92. Vice-Pres., and Mem. Council, Inst. of Motor Industry, 1970–78. Chairman: Publicity Club of London, 1961–62; Industry Taxation Panel, 1977–86; United Technologists Estabt, 1980–; Dep. Chm., Technology Transfer Assoc., 1984–90; Member: Council, CBI, 1977–88; CBI

Industrial Policy Cttee, 1979–85; Dun & Bradstreet Industry Panel, 1982–86. Mem., Jt Consultative Cttee, London Ct of Internat. Arbitration, 1999–. Dep. Chm., Wallenberg Foundn, 1997–. Chairman: Automotive VIP Club, 1988–92; Barbican Assoc., 1995–98. Mem., Battle of Britain (London) Cttee, 2003–. Life Vice-Pres., Devon County Agricl Assoc., 1980. Gov., GSMD, 2000–. Trustee, Guildhall Sch. Trust, 2000–. Various TV and radio broadcasts. Mem., Court of Common Council, Corp. of London, 1996– (Member: Estabt Cttee, 2002–03; Policy and Resources Cttee, 2003–; Dep. Chm., Standards Cttee, 2001–04; Dep. Chm., 2001–03, Chm., 2003–, Libraries, Guildhall Art Gall. and Archives Cttee); Freeman: City of London, 1973; City of Glasgow, 1974; Liveryman and former Hon. Treas., Coachmakers' and Coach Harness Makers' Co.; Burgess Guild Brother, Cordwainers' Co. *Publications:* articles. *Address:* (office) 405 Gilbert House, Barbican, EC2Y 8BD. *T:* and *Fax:* (020) 7638 3023. *Died 6 Feb. 2009.*

ALTMAN, Robert Bernard; film director; *b* Kansas City, 20 Feb. 1925; *m* 3rd, Kathryn (*née* Reed); one *s* and one adopted *s*, and two *s* one *d* by previous marriages. *Educ:* Wentworth Mil. Acad. Served US Army, 1943–47. Industrial film maker, Calvin Co., Kansas City, 1950–57. Television writer, producer and director, 1957–65. *Films directed:* The Delinquents, 1957; (co-dir) The James Dean Story, 1957; Nightmare in Chicago, 1964; Countdown, 1968; That Cold Day in the Park, 1969; M★A★S★H★, 1970 (Grand Prix, Cannes, 1970); Brewster McCloud, 1971; McCabe and Mrs Miller, 1971; Images, 1972; The Long Goodbye, 1973; Thieves Like Us, 1974; Popeye, 1980; Come Back to the 5 & Dime Jimmy Dean, Jimmy Dean, 1982; OC & Stiggs, 1985; Fool for Love, 1986; Beyond Therapy, 1987; (jtly) Aria, 1987; Vincent & Theo, 1990; The Player, 1992 (Best Dir, Cannes Film Fest. 1992); Short Cuts, 1993; The Gingerbread Man, 1998; A Prairie Home Companion, 2006; *directed and produced:* California Split, 1974; Nashville, 1975; Buffalo Bill and the Indians, 1976; 3 Women, 1977; A Wedding, 1978; Quintet, 1979; A Perfect Couple, 1979; Health, 1980; Streamers, 1983; Secret Honor, 1984; Tanner '88, 1988 (series); Prêt à Porter, 1994; Kansas City, 1996; Jazz '34: remembrances of Kansas City swing, 1997; Cookie's Fortune, 1999; Dr T and the Women, 2000; Gosford Park, 2002; The Company, 2004; *produced:* Welcome to LA, 1977; The Late Show, 1977; Remember My Name, 1978; Rich Kids, 1979; Mrs Parker and the Vicious Circle, 1995; Afterglow, 1997; *also screenplay for:* The Delinquents; Images; 3 Women; (jointly): McCabe and Mrs Miller; Thieves Like Us; Buffalo Bill and the Indians; A Wedding; Quintet; A Perfect Couple; Health; Beyond Therapy; Short Cuts; Prêt à Porter; Kansas City; A Prairie Home Companion. *Play directed:* Resurrection Blues, Old Vic, 2006. *Address:* c/o Sandcastle 5 Productions, Inc., 545 W 45th Street, New York, NY 10036, USA. *Died 20 Nov. 2006.*

ALTON, Euan Beresford Seaton, MBE 1945; MC 1943; Under Secretary, Department of Health and Social Security, 1968–76; *b* 22 April 1919; *y s* of late William Lester St John Alton and Ellen Seaton Alton; *m* 1953, Diana Margaret Ede; one *s* one *d*. *Educ:* St Paul's Sch.; Magdalen Coll., Oxford (Exhibnr; MA). Served with Army, 1939–45; Major RA. Admin. Officer, Colonial Service and HM OCS, Gold Coast and Ghana, 1946–58; Admin. Officer, Class 1, 1957. Entered Civil Service as Asst Principal, Min. of Health, 1958; Principal, 1958; Asst Sec., 1961; Under Sec., 1968. *Recreations:* sailing, walking. *Address:* 19 Quay Courtyard, South Street, Manningtree, Essex CO11 1BA. *T:* (01206) 393419. *Club:* Stour Sailing (Manningtree). *Died 27 Oct. 2008.*

ALUN-JONES, Sir (John) Derek, Kt 1987; *b* 6 June 1933; *s* of Thomas Alun-Jones, LLB and Madge Beatrice Edwards; *m* 1960, Gillian Palmer; two *s* three *d*. *Educ:* Lancing College; St Edmund Hall, Oxford (MA Hons Jurisp.). Philips Electrical, 1957–59; H. C. Stephens, 1959–60; Expandite, 1960–71 (Man. Dir, 1966–71);

Man. Dir, Burmah Industrial Products, 1971–74; Man. Dir and Chief Exec., 1975–87, Chm., 1987–90, Ferranti, subseq. Ferranti Internat. Signal, then Ferranti Internat.; Director: Burmah Oil Trading, 1974–75; Royal Insurance Holdings plc (formerly Royal Insurance), 1981–96; Throgmorton Trust, 1978–84; SBAC, 1982–90; Reed International PLC, 1984–90; GKN plc, 1986–88; Consolidated Gold Fields PLC, 1988–89; Oyez Straker Gp, 1991–2003. Chm. of Govs, Lancing Coll., 1986–99. Fellow, Woodard Corp., 1986–2003. *Recreations:* fishing, golf, family. *Address:* The Willows, Effingham Common, Surrey KT24 5JE. *T:* (01372) 458158. *Clubs:* Effingham Golf, Swinley Forest Golf. *Died 19 Jan. 2008.*

AMBO, Rt Rev. George Somboba, KBE 1988 (OBE 1978); Archbishop of Papua New Guinea, 1983–89; Bishop of Popondota, 1977–89; Chairman, South Pacific Anglican Council, 1986–89; *b* Gona, Nov. 1925; *s* of late J. O. Ambo, Gona; *m* 1946, Marcella O., *d* of Karau; two *s* two *d*. *Educ:* St Aidan's College, Dogura; Newton Theological Coll., Dogura. Deacon, 1955; Priest, 1958. Curate of: Menapi, 1955–57; Dogura, 1957–58; Priest in charge of Boianai, Diocese of New Guinea, 1958–63; Missionary at Wamira, 1963–69; an Asst Bishop of Papua New Guinea, 1960 (first Papuan-born Anglican Bishop). *Publications:* St John's Gospel in Ewage. *Recreations:* reading, carpentry. *Address:* c/o Anglican Diocesan Office, PO Box 26, Popondetta, Papua New Guinea. *Died 6 July 2008.*

AMHERST OF HACKNEY, 4th Baron *cr* 1892; **William Hugh Amherst Cecil;** *b* 28 Dec. 1940; *s* of 3rd Baron Amherst of Hackney, CBE, and of Margaret Eirene Clifton Brown, *d* of late Brig.-Gen. Howard Clifton Brown; *S* father, 1980; *m* 1965, Elisabeth, *d* of Hugh Humphrey Merriman, DSO, MC, TD, DL; one *s* one *d*. *Educ:* Eton. Director: E. A. Gibson Shipbrokers Ltd, 1975–90; Seascope Sale and Purchase Ltd, 1994–97; Short Sea Europe plc, 1996–2002. Younger Brother, Trinity House, 1995. Member Council: New Forest Assoc., 1997–2000; RYA, 1999–2002. Patron: St John-at-Hackney; St John of Jerusalem, S Hackney. *Heir: s* Hon. Hugh William Amherst Cecil [*b* 17 July 1968; *m* 1996, Nicola Jane, *d* of Major Timothy Michels; one *s* two *d*]. *Address:* Hawthorn House, New Street, Lymington, Hampshire SO41 9BJ. *Clubs:* Royal Ocean Racing; Royal Yacht Squadron (Vice-Cdre, 1993–98, Cdre, 2001–05), Royal Cruising, Royal Lymington Yacht, Island Sailing. *Died 2 April 2009.*

AMOS, Air Comdt Barbara Mary D.; *see* Ducat-Amos.

ANDERSON, Rear-Adm. (Charles) Courtney, CB 1971; Flag Officer, Admiralty Interview Board, 1969–71; *b* 8 Nov. 1916; *s* of late Lt-Col Charles Anderson, Australian Light Horse, and Mrs Constance Powell-Anderson, OBE, JP; *m* 1940, Pamela Ruth Miles; three *s*. *Educ:* RNC, Dartmouth. Joined RN, 1930. Served War of 1939–45: in command of Motor Torpedo Boats, Destroyers and Frigates. Naval Intelligence, 1946–49 and 1955–57; Commanded HMS Contest, 1949–51; Comdr. 1952; BJSM, Washington, 1953–55; Capt., 1959; Naval Attaché, Bonn, 1962–65; Director, Naval Recruiting, 1966–68; ADC to Queen, 1968; Rear-Adm., 1969. Editor, The Board Bulletin, 1971–78. *Publications:* The Drum Beats Still, 1951; Seagulls in my Belfry, 1997; numerous articles and short stories. *Address:* 3 Lambourne Gardens, Breinton Lee, Hereford HR4 0TL. *Died 8 Dec. 2008.*

ANDERSON, Prof. Dennis, OBE 2008; CPhys, FInstP; CEng; Professor of Energy and Environmental Studies, Imperial College London, 1996–2005, then Emeritus; *b* 12 July 1937; *s* of Joseph and Alice Anderson; *m* 1980, Marsaleete Harman; two *d*. *Educ:* Imperial Coll. London (DIC 1960); Univ. of Manchester (MSc (Eng) 1963); LSE (MSc (Econs) 1967). CPhys 1964, FInstP 2003; CEng 1966, MIET 1966, MIMechE 1968. Apprentice, 1952–59; Reactor physicist and engr, CEGB, 1962–67; Economic Advr, CS, 1967–69; World Bank: Economist

and Energy and Ind. Advr, 1969–87 and 1991–96; Chief Economist, Royal Dutch Shell, 1987–89; Vis. Prof. of Econs, UCL, 1989–91. Advr, UN Global Envmt Facility, 1998–2004. Advr, H of C and H of L Select Cttees on Sci. and Technol., 2003–04. *Publications:* Electricity Economics: essays and case studies (with R. Turvey), 1977; Economics of Afforestation: a case study in Africa, 1989; numerous papers and reports for industry and govt and for academic jls. *Recreations:* walking, reading, dining with friends and family. *Club:* Reform.
Died 20 April 2008.

ANDERSON, Dr Ephraim Saul, CBE 1976; FRCP; FRS 1968; Director, Enteric Reference Laboratory, Public Health Laboratory Service, 1954–78; *b* 28 Oct. 1911; *e s* of Benjamin and Ada Anderson, Newcastle upon Tyne; *m* 1959, Carol Jean (*née* Thompson) (marr. diss.); three *s. Educ:* Rutherford Coll., and King's Coll. Med. Sch. (Univ. of Durham), Newcastle upon Tyne. MB, BS 1934; MD Durham, 1953; Dip.Bact. London, 1948; Founder Fellow, Royal Coll. of Pathologists, 1963. GP, 1935–39; RAMC, 1940–46; Pathologist, 1943–46; Registrar in Bacteriology, Postgrad. Med. Sch., 1946–47; Staff, Enteric Reference Lab., 1947–52, Dep. Dir, 1952–54. WHO Fellow, 1953; FIBiol 1973; FRCP 1975. Hon. Chm., Internat. Fedn for Enteric Phage Typing of Internat. Union of Microbiol. Socs, 1986– (Jt Chm., 1958–66; Chm., 1966–86); Dir, Internat. Ref. Lab. for Enteric Phage Typing of Internat. Fedn for Enteric Phage Typing, 1954–; Dir, Collab. Centre for Phage Typing and Resistance of Enterobacteria of WHO, 1960–; Mem., WHO Expert Adv. Panel for Enteric Diseases. Vis. Prof., Sch. of Biol Sciences, Brunel Univ., 1973–77; Royal Soc.–Israel Acad. Vis. Res. Prof., 1978–79. Lectures: Scientific Basis of Medicine, British Postgrad. Med. Fedn, 1966; Almroth Wright, Wright-Fleming Inst. of Microbiol., 1967; Holme, UCH, 1970; Cutter, Sch. of Public Health, Harvard, 1972; Marjory Stephenson Meml, Soc. for Gen. Microbiol., 1975. Hon. DSc Newcastle, 1975. *Publications:* contrib. to: The Bacteriophages (Mark Adams), 1959; The World Problem of Salmonellosis (Van Oye), 1964; Ciba Symposium: Bacterial Episomes and Plasmids, 1969; articles on bacteriophage typing and its genetic basis, microbial ecology, transferable drug resistance in bacteria, its evolution, and epidemiology, with special ref. to significance of bacterial plasmids. *Recreations:* music, photography.
Died 14 March 2006.

ANDERSON, Maj.-Gen. Sir John (Evelyn), KBE 1971 (CBE 1963); CEng, FIET; Associate and Director, Space and Maritime Applications Inc., 1988–93; *b* 28 June 1916; *e s* of Lt-Col John Gibson Anderson, Christchurch, NZ, and Margaret (*née* Scott), Edinburgh; *m* 1944, Jean Isobel, *d* of Charles Tait, farmer, Aberdeenshire; one *s* one *d. Educ:* King's Sch., Rochester; RMA, Woolwich. Commissioned in Royal Signals, 1936; Lt-Col 1956; Col 1960; Brig. 1964; Maj.-Gen. 1967; Signal Officer in Chief (Army), MoD, 1967–69; ACDS (signals), 1969–72. Col Comdt, Royal Corps of Signals, 1969–74. Hon. Col 71st (Yeomanry) Signal Regt TAVR, 1969–76; Hon. Col Women's Transport Corps (FANY), 1970–76. Dir Gen., NATO Integrated Communications System Management Agency, 1977–81; Exec. Dir, Europe Gp, AFCEA, 1981–88. Pres., Piscatorial Soc., 1981–87. CCMI. *Recreation:* fishing. *Address:* 23 Northfield Court, Aldeburgh, Suffolk IP15 5LU. *Club:* Flyfishers'.
Died 9 Sept. 2007.

ANDERSON, Prof. John Neil; (first) Professor of Dental Prosthetics, 1964–82 (then Emeritus), (first) Dean of Dentistry, 1972–76, 1980–82, University of Dundee; *b* 11 Feb. 1922; *s* of J. Anderson, Sheffield; *m* 1945, Mary G. Croll; one *s* one *d. Educ:* High Storrs Gram. Sch., Sheffield; Sheffield Univ. Asst Lectr, Sheffield Univ., 1945–46; Lectr, Durham Univ. 1946–48; Lectr, Birmingham Univ., 1948–52; Sen. Lectr, St Andrews Univ., 1952–64. External Examiner, Univs of Malaya, Baghdad, Newcastle upon Tyne, Bristol, Birmingham, Liverpool, RCSI. *Publications:* Applied Dental Materials,

1956; (with R. Storer) Immediate and Replacement Dentures, 1966, 3rd edn, 1981; contribs to leading dental jls. *Recreations:* music, gardening, carpentry. *Address:* Wyndham, Derwent Drive, Baslow, Bakewell, Derbyshire DE45 1RS.
Died 5 Sept. 2009.

ANDERSON, Brig. Hon. Dame Mary Mackenzie; *see* Pihl, Brig. Hon. Dame M. M.

ANDERSON, Mary Margaret, CBE 1996; FRCOG; Consultant Obstetrician and Gynaecologist, Lewisham Hospital, 1967–97; *b* 12 Feb. 1932; *d* of William Anderson and Lily Adams. *Educ:* Forres Acad.; Edinburgh Univ. (MB, ChB 1956). FRCOG 1974. Jun. hosp. posts in Scotland and England, including Hammersmith Hosp., and St Mary's Hosp., London (Sen. Registrar); Chm., Div. of Obst. and Gynaecol., Lewisham Hosp., 1984–87. Royal College of Obstetricians and Gynaecologists: Chm., Hosp. Recognition Cttee, 1987–89; Jun. Vice Pres., 1989–92. Chm., SE Thames RHA Specialist Sub Cttee, 1986–88; Member: Scientific Cttee, National Birthday Trust, 1990–; Council, Med. Defence Union, 1987–. *Publications:* Anatomy and Physiology of Obstetrics, 1979; Handbook of Obstetrics and Gynaecology, 1981; The Menopause, 1983; Pregnancy after Thirty, 1984; An A–Z of Gynaecology, 1986; Infertility, 1987; (contrib.) Ten Teachers in Obstetrics and Gynaecology, 1990. *Recreations:* reading, music, gardening. *Address:* Califer Croft, Rafford, Forres, Moray IV36 2RN.
Died 17 Feb. 2006.

ANDERSON, Vice Adm. Sir Neil (Dudley), KBE 1982 (CBE 1976); CB 1979; Chief of Defence Staff (NZ), 1980–83; *b* 5 April 1927; *s* of Eric Dudley Anderson and Margaret Evelyn (*née* Craig); *m* 1951, Barbara Lillias Romaine Wright; one *s* (and one *s* decd). *Educ:* Hastings High Sch.; BRNC. Joined RNZN, 1944; trng and sea service with RN, 1944–49; Korean War Service, 1950–51; qual. as navigation specialist; Navigator: HMS Vanguard, 1952–53; HMNZS Lachlan, 1954; HMS Saintes, 1958–59; Commanding Officer, HMNZS: Taranaki, 1961–62; Waikato, 1968–69; Philomel, 1969–70; Dep. Chief of Def. Staff, 1976–77; Chief of Naval Staff, 1977–80. Lieut 1949, Lt-Comdr 1957, Comdr 1960, Captain 1968, Cdre 1972, Rear Adm. 1977, Vice Adm. 1980. *Recreations:* croquet, fishing. *Address:* 2/248 Oriental Parade, Wellington 6001, New Zealand. *T:* and *Fax:* (4) 3858494. *Club:* Wellington (Wellington, NZ).
Died 5 June 2010.

ANDERSON, Robert (Woodruff); playwright; *b* NYC, 28 April 1917; *s* of James Hewston Anderson and Myra Esther (*née* Grigg); *m* 1st, 1940, Phyllis Stohl (*d* 1956); 2nd, 1959, Teresa Wright (marr. diss. 1978; she *d* 2005). *Educ:* Phillips Exeter Acad.; Harvard Univ. AB (*magna cum laude*) 1939, MA 1940. Served USNR, 1942–46 (Lt); won prize (sponsored by War Dept) for best play written by a serviceman overseas, Come Marching Home, 1945, subseq. prod., Univ. of Iowa and Blackfriars Guild, NY. Rockefeller Fellowship, 1946; taught playwrighting, American Theatre Wing Professional Trng Prog., 1946–50; organized and taught Playwright's Unit, Actors Studio, 1955; Writer in Residence, Univ. of N Carolina, 1969; Faculty: Salzburg Seminar in Amer. Studies, 1968; Univ. of Iowa Writers' Workshop, 1976. Member: Playwrights Co., 1953–60; Bd of Governors, American Playwrights Theatre, 1963–; Council, Dramatists Guild, 1954– (Pres., 1971–73); New Dramatists Cttee, 1949– (Pres., 1955–57); Vice-Pres., Authors' League of America; Chm., Harvard Bd of Overseers' Cttee to visit the Performing Arts, 1970–76. Wrote and adapted plays for TV and Radio, 1948–53. Elected to Theater Hall of Fame, 1980. Connecticut Commn on the Arts Award, 1992. *Plays:* Eden Rose, 1948; Love Revisited, 1952; Tea and Sympathy, 1953; All Summer Long, 1954; Silent Night, Lonely Night, 1959; The Days Between, 1965; You Know I Can't Hear You When the Water's Running (four short plays), 1967; I Never Sang For My Father, 1968; Solitaire/Double Solitaire, 1971; Free and Clear, 1983; The Kissing was Always the Best, 1987; The Last Act is a Solo, 1989; *screenplays:* Tea and Sympathy,

1956; Until They Sail, 1957; The Nun's Story, 1959; The Sand Pebbles, 1965; I Never Sang For My Father, 1970 (Writers Guild Award for Best Screenplay, 1971); The Patricia Neal Story, TV, 1981; Absolute Strangers, TV, 1991; The Last Act is a Solo, TV, 1991 (ACE Award). *Publications: novels:* After, 1973; Getting Up and Going Home, 1978; *anthology:* (jtly) Elements of Literature, 6 vols, 1988. *Recreations:* photography, tennis. *Club:* Harvard (New York City). *Died 9 Feb. 2009.*

ANDERSON, Rupert John; QC 2003; *b* 5 Aug. 1958; *s* of John David Bennett Anderson and Roberta Elizabeth Anderson. *Educ:* Cambridgeshire County High Sch.; Hills Road Sixth Form Coll., Cambridge; Pembroke Coll., Cambridge (MA). Called to the Bar, Inner Temple, 1981. Mem., Attorney-Gen.'s A panel of Counsel to Crown, 2000–03. *Publications:* (specialist ed) Copinger and Skone James on Copyright, 14th edn 1999; (contrib.) Weinberg and Blank on Takeovers and Mergers, 2000; (contrib.) PLC Competition Manual, 2002; contrib. to various jls. *Recreations:* classical history, baroque and choral music, dogs. *Address:* Prospect House, 92 North End, Bassingbourn, Royston, Herts SG8 5PD. *T:* (01763) 245932; *e-mail:* randerson@ monckton.com. *Died 30 July 2009.*

ANDRESKI, Prof. Stanislav Leonard; Professor of Sociology, University of Reading, 1964–84, then Emeritus; part-time Professor of Sociology, Polish University in London, 1969–99; *b* 18 May 1919; *m* 1977 Ruth Ash; two *s* two *d* from a former marriage. *Educ:* Secondary sch. in Poznan, 1928–37; Univ. of Poznan (Faculty of Economics and Jurisprudence), 1938–39; London Sch. of Economics, 1942–43. Military service in Polish Army (with exception of academic year 1942–43), 1937–38 and 1939–47 (commissioned, 1944). Lectr in Sociology, Rhodes Univ., SA, 1947–53; Sen. Research Fellow in Anthropology, Manchester Univ., 1954–56; Lectr in Economics, Acton Technical Coll., London, 1956–57; Lectr in Management Studies, Brunel Coll. of Technology, London, 1957–60; Prof. of Sociology, Sch. of Social Sciences, Santiago, Chile, 1960–61; Sen. Res. Fellow, Nigerian Inst. of Social and Economic Research, Ibadan, Nigeria, 1962–64; Hd, Dept of Sociology, Univ. of Reading, 1964–82. Vis. Prof. of Sociology and Anthropology, City Coll., City Univ. of New York, 1968–69; Vis. Prof. of Sociology, Simon Fraser Univ., Vancouver, 1976–77; pt-time Prof. of Social Scis, Duxx Sch. of Business, Monterey, Mexico, 1995–98; pt-time Prof., Wyższa Szkoła Języków Obcych i Ekonomii, Czestochowa, Poland, 1998–2002. *Publications:* Military Organization and Society (Internat. Library of Sociology and Social Reconstruction), 1954 (2nd aug. edn, 1968, USA, 1968, paperback, 1969); Class Structure and Social Development (with Jan Ostaszewski and others), (London), 1964 (in Polish); Elements of Comparative Sociology (The Nature of Human Society Series), 1964, Spanish edn 1972; The Uses of Comparative Sociology (American edn of the foregoing), 1965, paperback 1969; Parasitism and Subversion: the case of Latin America, 1966 (NY, 1967, rev. edn 1968, etc.; Buenos Aires (in Spanish with a postscript), 1968; paperback edn, London, 1970); The African Predicament: a study in pathology of modernisation, 1968 (USA, 1969); Social Sciences as Sorcery, 1972, Spanish edn 1973, German edn 1974, French edn 1975, Italian edn 1977, Japanese edn 1982, Polish edn 2002; Prospects of a Revolution in the USA, 1973; Max Weber's Insights and Errors, 1984, Polish rev. edn 1992, Chinese edn 2000; Syphilis, Puritanism and Witch-Hunts, 1989; Wars, Revolutions, Dictatorships, 1992; (with Alex Robinson) Is Marriage Doomed to Obsolescence?, 2004; Editor: Herbert Spencer, Principles of Sociology, 1968; Herbert Spencer, Structure, Function and Evolution, 1970; The Essential Comte, 1974; Reflections on Inequality, 1975; Max Weber on Capitalism, Bureaucracy and Religion, 1983; contribs to: A Dictionary of the Social Sciences (UNESCO); A Dictionary of Sociology (ed D. Mitchell); Brit. Jl of Sociology; Japanese Jl of Sociology; The Nature of Fascism (ed S. Woolf); Science Jl, Man, European Jl of

Sociology, Encounter, etc. *Recreation:* carpentry. *Address:* Farriers, Village Green, Upper Basildon, Berkshire RG8 8LS. *T:* (01491) 671318. *Died 26 Sept. 2007.*

ANDREWS, John Hayward, CMG 1988; Director, Logan Motorway Group (formerly Logan Toll Motorway Group), 1988–95; *b* 9 Nov. 1919; *s* of James Andrews and Florence Elizabeth Andrews; *m* 1947, June; one *s* one *d* (and one *s* decd). *Educ:* Univ. of Queensland (BEc). DipT&CP; DipCE. Served Royal Aust. Engineers, 1940–45. Local Govt City Engineer, Wagga Wagga and Tamworth, NSW, 1946–60; Deputy Commissioner, Main Roads Dept, Queensland, 1961–78; Administrator, Gold Coast City, 1978–79; private practice, 1979–81; Agent-Gen. for Qld, 1981–84; Chairman: Electoral Redistribution Commn for Qld, 1985–86; Sugar Bd (Qld), subseq. Qld Sugar Corp., 1986–92. Dir, White Industries Ltd, 1986–88. Freeman, City of London, 1981. *Recreations:* golf, painting, walking. *Club:* Twin Towns Services. *Died 3 Jan. 2006.*

ANDRUS, Francis Sedley, LVO 1982; Beaumont Herald of Arms Extraordinary, since 1982; *b* 26 Feb. 1915; *o s* of late Brig.-Gen. Thomas Alchin Andrus, CMG, JP, and Alice Loveday (*née* Parr); unmarried. *Educ:* Wellington Coll.; St Peter's Hall (later Coll.), Oxford (MA). Entered College of Arms as Member of Staff, 1938; Bluemantle Pursuivant of Arms, 1970–72; Lancaster Herald of Arms, 1972–82. Freeman, City of London, 1988. Lord of the Manor of Southfleet, Kent, 1952–. *Address:* 8 Oakwood Rise, Longfield, Kent DA3 7PA. *T:* (01474) 705424. *Died 9 Nov. 2009.*

ANGUS, Sir Michael (Richardson), Kt 1990; DL; Chairman, Whitbread PLC, 1992–2000 (Director, 1986–2000; Deputy Chairman, 1992); Deputy Chairman, The Boots Company PLC, 1998–2000 (Chairman, 1994–98); *b* 5 May 1930; *s* of William Richardson Angus and Doris Margaret Breach; *m* 1952, Eileen Isabel May Elliott; two *s* one *d*. *Educ:* Marling Sch., Stroud, Glos; Bristol Univ. (BSc Hons; Hon. Fellow, 1998). CCMI (CBIM 1979). Served RAF, 1951–54. Unilever, 1954–92: Marketing Dir, Thibaud Gibbs, Paris, 1962–65; Man. Dir, Res. Bureau, 1965–67; Sales Dir, Lever Brothers UK, 1967–70; Toilet Preparations Co-ordinator, 1970–76; Chemicals Co-ordinator, 1976–80; Regional Dir, N America, 1979–84; Chairman and Chief Executive Officer: Unilever United States, Inc., New York, 1980–84; Lever Brothers Co., New York, 1980–84; Chm., Unilever PLC, 1986–92 (Dir, 1970–92; Vice Chm., 1984–86); Vice Chm., Unilever NV, 1986–92 (Dir, 1970–92). Dir, Nat. Westminster Bank, 1991–2000 (a Dep. Chm., 1991–94); Chm., RAC Holdings Ltd, 1999; Jt Dep. Chm., 1989–93, Dep. Chm., 1993–2000, British Airways (Dir, 1988–2000); non-executive Director: Thorn EMI plc, 1988–93; Halcrow Gp Ltd, 2000–06. Jt Chm., Netherlands-British Chamber of Commerce, 1984–89; Internat. Counsellor, The Conference Board, 1984–96, Emeritus, 1996. Pres., CBI, 1992–94 (Dep. Pres., 1991–92, 1994–95). Vis. Fellow, Nuffield Coll., Oxford, 1986–92. Dir, Ditchley Foundn, 1994–. Trustee, Leverhulme Trust, 1984–2008 (Chm. Trustees, 1999–2008). Chairman of Governors: Ashridge Management Coll., 1991–2002 (Governor, 1974–2002; Pres., 2002–); RAC, Cirencester, 1992–2006 (Vice Pres., 2006–); Mem. Court of Govs, LSE, 1985–95. DL Gloucestershire, 1997. Hon. DSc: Bristol, 1990; Buckingham, 1994; Hon. LLD Nottingham, 1996. Holland Trade Award, 1990. Comdr, Order of Oranje-Nassau (Netherlands), 1992. *Recreations:* countryside, wine, mathematical puzzles. *Address:* Cerney House, North Cerney, Cirencester, Glos GL7 7BX. *Clubs:* Athenæum, Brooks's; University (New York). *Died 13 March 2010.*

ANSTEY, Edgar, MA, PhD; Deputy Chief Scientific Officer, Civil Service Department, and Head of Behavioural Sciences Research Division, 1969–77; *b* 5 March 1917; British; *s* of late Percy Lewis Anstey and Dr Vera Anstey; *m* 1939, Zoë Lilian Robertson (*d* 2000); one *s*. *Educ:* Winchester Coll.; King's Coll., Cambridge.

Assistant Principal, Dominions Office, 1938; Private Sec. to Duke of Devonshire, 1939. 2nd Lieut Dorset Regt, 1940; Major, War Office (DSP), 1941. Founder-Head of Civil Service Commission Research Unit, 1945; Principal, Home Office, 1951; Senior Principal Psychologist, Min. of Defence, 1958; Chief Psychologist, Civil Service Commn, 1964–69. Pres., N Cornwall Liberal Democrat Assoc., 1988–90 (N Cornwall Liberal Assoc., 1985–88). *Publications:* Interviewing for the Selection of Staff (with Dr E. O. Mercer), 1956; Staff Reporting and Staff Development, 1961; Committees - How they work and how to work them, 1962; Psychological Tests, 1966; The Techniques of Interviewing, 1968; (with Dr C. A. Fletcher and Dr J. Walker) Staff Appraisal and Development, 1976; An Introduction to Selection Interviewing, 1978; articles in Brit. Jl of Psychology, Occupational Psychology, etc. *Recreations:* fell-walking, surfing, bridge. *Address:* Sandrock, 3 Higher Tristram, Polzeath, Wadebridge, Cornwall PL27 6TF. *T:* (01208) 863324. *Club:* Royal Commonwealth Society. *Died 1 June 2009.*

ANSTRUTHER of that Ilk, Sir Ian Fife Campbell, 8th Bt *cr* 1694 (S), of Balcaskie, and 13th Bt *cr* 1700 (S), of Anstruther, and 10th Bt *cr* 1798 (GB), of Anstruther; Hereditary Carver; *b* 11 May 1922; *s* of Douglas Tollemache Anstruther, *g s* of 5th Bt, and Enid, *d* of Lord George Granville Campbell; *S* cousin, 2002; *m* 1st, 1951, Honor Blake (marr. diss. 1963); one *d*; 2nd, 1963, Susan Margaret Walker, *e d* of H. St J. B. Paten; two *s* three *d*. *Educ:* Eton; New Coll., Oxford. FSA 1975. Landowner and author. *Publications:* I Presume, 1956; The Knight and the Umbrella, 1963; The Scandal of the Andover Workhouse, 1973; Oscar Browning, 1983; Coventry Patmore's Angel, 1992; The Angel in the House, Books I and II, 1998; (with Patricia Aske) Dean Farrar and 'Eric', 2003; The Baronets' Champion, 2006. *Heir:* (to (S) Baronetcies): *s* Sebastian Paten Campbell Anstruther, *b* 13 Sept. 1962; (to (GB) Btcy): *s* Tobias Alexander Campbell Anstruther, *b* 16 Dec. 1968. *Died 29 July 2007.*

ANTONIONI, Michelangelo; film director; *b* Ferrara, Italy, 29 Sept. 1912; *s* of Ismaele and Elisabetta Roncagli; *m* 1st, 1942, Letizia Balboni (marr. diss.); 2nd, 1986, Enrica Fico. *Educ:* Univ. of Bologna (degree in Econs); Centro Sperimentale di Cinematografia, Rome. Formerly an asst dir, film critic to newspapers (Corriere padano, Italia libera), and script writer. Films directed include: documentaries, etc (incl. Gente del Po), 1943–50; subseq. full-length films: Cronaca di un Amore, 1950; one episode in Amore in Città, 1951; I Vinti, 1952; La Signora Senza Camelie, 1953; Le Amiche, 1955; Il Grido, 1957; L'Avventura, 1960; La Notte, 1961; L'Eclisse, 1962; Il Deserto Rosso, 1964 (Golden Lion, Venice Film Fest., 1964); one episode in I Tre Volti, 1965; Blow-Up, 1967 (Palme d'Or, Cannes Film Fest., 1967); Zabriskie Point, 1969; Chung Kuo-China, 1972; The Passenger, 1974; Il Mistero di Oberwald, 1979; Identificazione di una Donna, 1981; Beyond the Clouds, 1995; documentaries include: Kumbha Mela, 1989; Roma, 1989. Academy Award, 1995. Kt Grand Cross, Order of Merit (Italian Republic), 1992; Comdr, Order of Arts and Letters (France), 1992; Legion of Honour (France), 1996. *Publications:* Quel Bowling sul Tevere, 1983. *Recreations:* collecting blown glass, tennis, ping-pong. *Address:* Via Vincenzo Tiberio 18, 00191 Rome, Italy; (office) Via Fleming III, 00191 Rome, Italy. *Died 30 July 2007.*

APPEL, Karel Christian; Dutch artist (painter); *b* 25 April 1921; *s* of Jan Appel and Johanna Chevallier. *Educ:* Royal Academy of Art, Amsterdam. Began career as artist in 1940; founder mem., Cobra gp, 1948–51; joined Art Informel gp, Paris; work incl. stained glass windows and murals; with Min Tanaka conceived and designed ballet, 1987. One-man exhibitions in Europe, America and Asia, including: Kunstzaal van Lier, Amsterdam, 1951; Palais des Beaux-Arts, Brussels, 1953, 2004; Stedelijk Mus., Amsterdam, 1955, 1956, 1965; ICA, London, 1957; Palazzo dei Medici, Florence, 1985; Kunstforum Vienna, 2002; travelling exhibitions: museums in Calif, 1961;

museums in Canada and USA, 1972, 1973; museums in Brazil, Colombia, Mexico, 1978, 1981; 5 museums in Japan, 1989; Europe, 1990–92. UNESCO Prize, Venice Biennale, 1953; Lissone Prize, Italy, 1958; Acquisition Prize, São Paulo Biennale, Brazil, 1959; Graphique Internat. Prize, Ljubljana, Jugoslavia, 1959; Guggenheim National Prize, Holland, 1961; Guggenheim International Prize, 1961. *Publications:* Works on Paper, 1980; Street Art, 1985; Dupe of Being, 1989; Complete Sculptures 1936–1990, 1990; Karel Appel Sculpture: catalogue raisonné, 1994; Psychopathologisches Notizbuch, 1997; Der Machtwille der Planeten, 2000; *relevant publications:* Karel Appel, 1980; Karel Appel: the early years 1937–1957, 1988; Karel Appel, ein Farbgestus, 1998. *Died 3 May 2006.*

AQUINO, Maria Corazón Cojuangco, (Cory); President of the Philippines, 1986–92; *b* 25 Jan. 1933; *d* of late José and Demetria Cojuangco; *m* 1954, Benigno S. Aquino (*d* 1983); one *s* four *d*. *Educ:* St Scholastica's Coll. and Assumption Convent, Manila; Ravenhill Acad., Philadelphia; Notre Dame Sch., NY; Mount St Vincent Coll., NY (BA); Far Eastern Univ., Manila. Numerous honours, awards and hon. degrees from Philippine and overseas bodies. *Address:* 25 Times Street, Quezon City, Philippines. *Died 31 July 2009.*

ARBUTHNOT, Rev. Andrew Robert Coghill; Missioner, London Healing Mission, 1983–95; Director, Sun Alliance and London Insurance Ltd, 1970–91; *b* 14 Jan. 1926; *s* of Robert Wemyss Muir Arbuthnot and Mary Arbuthnot (*née* Coghill); *m* 1952, Audrey Dutton-Barker; one *s* one *d*. *Educ:* Eton; Southwark Ordination Course. Served 1944–47, Captain, Scots Guards, wounded. Dir, Arbuthnot Latham & Co. Ltd, 1953–82; Chm. and Chief Exec., Arbuthnot Latham Holdings, 1974–81; Chm., Arbuthnot Insurance Services, 1968–83. Contested (C) Houghton-le-Spring, 1959. Ordained Deacon, 1974; Priest, 1975. *Publications:* (with Audrey Arbuthnot) Love that Heals, 1986; Christian Prayer and Healing, 1989; All You Need is More and More of Jesus, 1993. *Recreations:* water colour painting, operas. *Address:* Greenacre, Bell Lane, Lower Broadheath, Worcs WR2 6RR. *T:* (01905) 641685. *Died 11 Dec. 2010.*

ARCHDALE, Sir Edward (Folmer), 3rd Bt *cr* 1928; DSC 1943; Captain, RN, retired; *b* 8 Sept. 1921; *s* of Vice-Adm. Sir Nicholas Edward Archdale, 2nd Bt, CBE, and Gerda (*d* 1969), 2nd *d* of late F. C. Sievers, Copenhagen; *S* father, 1955; *m* 1954, Elizabeth Ann Stewart (marr. diss. 1978), *d* of late Maj.-Gen. Wilfrid Boyd Fellowes Lukis, CBE; one *s* one *d* (and one *d* decd). *Educ:* Royal Naval Coll., Dartmouth. Joined Royal Navy, 1935; served War of 1939–45 (despatches, DSC). *Recreation:* civilization. *Heir:* *s* Nicholas Edward Archdale, *b* 2 Dec. 1965. *Died 31 July 2009.*

ARCHER, John Francis Ashweek; QC 1975; a Recorder of the Crown Court, 1974–97; *b* 9 July 1925; *s* of late George Eric Archer, FRCSE, and Frances Archer (*née* Ashweek); *m* 1960, Doris Mary Hennessey (*d* 1988); *m* 1995, Vivienne Frances Weatherhead (*née* Ecclestone). *Educ:* Winchester Coll., 1938–43; New Coll., Oxford, 1947–49 (BA 1949). Served War of 1939–45, 1944–47; Lieut RA, 1948. Called to Bar, Inner Temple, 1950, Bencher, 1984. Mem., Criminal Injuries Compensation Bd, 1987–2000. *Recreations:* motoring, bridge. *Address:* The Cottage, 68 High Street, Wicken, Cambs CB7 5XR. *Died 2 Nov. 2009.*

ARCHER, Prof. John Stuart, CBE 2002; PhD; FREng, FIChemE, FEI; FRSE; Principal and Vice-Chancellor, Heriot-Watt University, 1997–2006; *b* 15 June 1943; *s* of Stuart Leonard Archer and Joan (*née* Watkinson); *m* 1967, Lesley Oaksford; one *s* one *d*. *Educ:* County Grammar Sch., Chiswick; City Univ. (BSc Hons Ind. Chem.); Imperial Coll., London (DIC Advanced Chem. Engrg, PhD Combustion Engrg; FIC 1998). FInstE 1983; FInstPet 1984; FIMMM (FIMM 1986); FREng (FEng 1992); FRSE 1998. Sen. Res. Engr, Imperial Oil (Exxon), Canada, 1969–73; Sen. Petroleum Engr, British

Gas Corp., 1973–74; Manager, Reservoir Engrg, D&S Petroleum Consultants, 1974–77; Energy Resource Consultants Ltd: Founder Dir, 1977; Dir of Reservoir Studies, 1977–81; non-exec. Dir, 1982–90; Imperial College, London: Reader in Petroleum Engrg, 1980–86; Prof. of Petroleum Engrg, 1986–97; Hd, Petroleum Engrg, 1984–97; Hd, Dept of Mineral Resources Engrg, 1986–94; Dean, RSM, 1989–91; Pro Rector, then Dep. Rector, 1991–97. Vis. Prof., Univ. of Delft, 1990–93. Mem., EPSRC, 2000–06. Director: IMPEL Ltd, 1989–97; MTD Ltd, 1993–; non-exec. Chm., Scottish Enterprise, Edinburgh and Lothians (formerly Lothian Edinburgh Enterprise Ltd), 1998–2005. Convenor: Res. and Commercialisation Cttee, Cttee of Scottish Higher Educn Principals, 1999–2003; Univ. UK Res. Policy Strategy Gp, 2003–; Member, Scottish Executive, subseq. Scottish Government, committees: Nat. Clusters Liaison Gp, 1999–; Foresight Steering Cttee, Scotland, 1999–; Science Strategy Review Gp, 1999–; Taskforce on the Knowledge Economy, 2000–; Manufg Image Gp, 2000–. Mem., Soc. of Petroleum Engrs, 1973–; Dep. Pres., 2004, Pres., 2005–06, IChemE. Associate Editor: Jl Petroleum Sci. and Engrg, 1990–; Jls of Soc. Petroleum Engrs; Adv. Editor, Petroleum Engineering and Development Studies series, 1987–. FRSA 1990; FCGI 1996. Hon. DSc: City, 2002; Edinburgh, 2006. Distinguished Achievement Award, Soc. Petroleum Engrs, 1992. *Publications:* Petroleum Engineering: principles and practice, 1986; numerous papers in learned jls on petroleum reservoir engrg. *Recreations:* golf, gardening, theatre, music, the arts. *Address:* Heriot-Watt University, Edinburgh EH14 4AS. *T:* (0131) 449 5111. *Clubs:* Caledonian; New (Edinburgh). *Died 9 Dec. 2007.*

ARGENT, Eric William, FCA; FCIB; Director, Nationwide Anglia Building Society, 1987–88, retired (Joint General Manager, 1978–81, Director, 1978–87, Anglia Building Society); *b* 5 Sept. 1923; *s* of Eric George Argent and Florence Mary Argent; *m* 1949, Pauline Grant; two *d*. *Educ:* Chiswick Grammar Sch. FCA 1951. War Service, 1942–47. With City Chartered Accountants, 1940–42 and 1947–51; with London Banking House, Antony Gibbs & Sons Ltd, 1951–59; Hastings & Thanet Building Society, 1959–78: Sec. and Chief Accountant, 1962; Dep. Gen. Man., 1964; Gen. Man. and Sec., 1966; Dir and Gen. Man., 1976. *Recreations:* reading, gardening, travel. *Died 23 Nov. 2006.*

ARIS, John Bernard Benedict, TD 1967; with IMPACT Programme, 1990–99 (Director, 1990–95); *b* 6 June 1934; *s* of John (Jack) Woodbridge Aris and Joyce Mary (*née* Williams). *Educ:* Eton (King's Schol.); Magdalen Coll., Oxford (MA). FBCS; CITP. LEO Computers, 1958–63; English Electric Computers, 1963–69; ICL, 1969–75; Imperial Group, 1975–85 (Man., Gp Management Services, 1982–85); Dir, NCC, 1985–90. Non-exec. Dir, NCC, 1981–85; Chairman: FOCUS Private Sector Users Cttee (DTI), 1984–85; Alvey IT User Panel, 1985–88; Mem., IT 86 Cttee, 1986. Founder Freeman, Co. of Information Technologists, 1987 (Liveryman, 1992). FInstD; FRSA. *Publications:* (jtly) User Driven Innovation, 1996. *Recreations:* travel, music, art, gastronomy. *Died 6 Aug. 2010.*

ARMSTRONG, Anne Legendre, (Mrs Tobin Armstrong); Member, Board of Directors: General Motors, 1977–99; Halliburton Company, 1977–2000; Boise Cascade Corporation, 1978–2000; American Express, 1975–76 and 1981–2000; *b* New Orleans, Louisiana, 27 Dec. 1927; *d* of Armant Legendre and Olive Martindale; *m* 1950, Tobin Armstrong (*d* 2005); three *s* two *d*. *Educ:* Foxcroft Sch., Middleburg, Va; Vassar Coll., NY (BA). Deleg. Nat. Conventions, 1964, 1968, 1972, 1980, 1984; Mem. Republican Nat. Cttee, 1968–73 (Co-Chm., 1971–73); Counselor to the President, with Cabinet rank, 1973–74; Ambassador to the Court of St James's, 1976–77. Co-Chm., Reagan/Bush Campaign, 1980; Chm., President's Foreign Intelligence Adv. Bd, 1981–90. Center for Strategic and International Studies:

Chm., Bd of Trustees, 1987–99; Chm., Exec. Cttee, 1999–2006. Mem., Council on Foreign Relations, 1977–; Chm., E-SU of the US, 1977–80. Mem., Adv. Bd, Promontory Interfinancial Network LLC, 2003–07. Trustee: Southern Methodist Univ., 1977–86; Economic Club of NY, 1978–81 (Mem., 1982–); Amer. Associates of the Royal Acad. (Vice Chm., 1984–); Mem., Adv. Bd, Inst. Bioscis and Technology, 2003–. Citizen Regent, Smithsonian Instn, 1978–94, Emeritus, 1994–; Regent, Texas A & M Univ. System, 1997–2003. Kenedy County Comr, 2005–. Hon. Mem., City of London Br., Royal Soc. of St George, 1978; Mem. and Governor, Ditchley Foundn, 1977–87. Pres., Blair House Restoration Fund, 1985–91. Hon. LLD: Bristol, 1976; Washington and Lee, 1976; Williams Coll., 1977; St Mary's Univ., 1978; Tulane, 1978; Hon. LHD: Mt Vernon Coll., 1978; Ripon Coll., 1986; Hamilton Coll., 1990. Gold Medal, Nat. Inst. Social Scis, 1977. Josephine Meredith Langstaff Award, Nat. Soc. Daughters of British Empire in US, 1978; Republican Woman of the Year Award, 1979; Texan of the Year Award, 1981; Texas Women's Hall of Fame, 1986; Presidential Medal of Freedom, 1987; Golden Plate Award, Amer. Acad. of Achievement, 1989. Phi Beta Kappa. *Address:* Armstrong Ranch, Armstrong, TX 78338, USA. *Clubs:* Pilgrims (New York); Alfalfa (Washington). *Died 30 July 2008.*

ARMSTRONG, Robert George, CBE 1972; MC 1946; TD 1958; Deputy Director and Controller, Savings Bank, Department for National Savings, 1969–74; *b* 26 Oct. 1913; *s* of late George William Armstrong; *m* 1947, Clara Christine Hyde (*d* 2003); one *s* one *d*. *Educ:* Marylebone Grammar Sch.; University Coll. London. Post Office Engineering Dept, 1936–50. Served War of 1939–45, Royal Signals. Principal, PO Headquarters, 1950; Asst Sec., 1962; Dep. Dir of Savings, 1963; Dep. Dir and Controller, Post Office Savings Bank, 1964; Under-Sec., 1972. *Address:* c/o Avernish, Great North Road, Rockley, Retford, Notts DN22 0QR. *Died 1 April 2007.*

ARNDT, Ulrich Wolfgang, MA, PhD; FRS 1982; Member, Scientific Staff of Medical Research Council Laboratory of Molecular Biology, Cambridge, since 1962; *b* 23 April 1924; *o s* of E. J. and C. M. Arndt; *m* 1958, Valerie Howard (*d* 2004), *e d* of late Maj.-Gen. F. C. Hilton-Sergeant, CB, CBE, QHP; three *d*. *Educ:* Dulwich Coll.; King Edward VI High Sch., Birmingham; Emmanuel Coll., Cambridge (MA, PhD). Metallurgy Dept, Birmingham Univ., 1948–49; Davy-Faraday Laboratory of Royal Instn, 1950–63; Dewar Fellow of Royal Instn, 1957–61; Univ. of Wisconsin, Madison, 1956; Institut Laue-Langevin, Grenoble, 1972–73. *Publications:* (with B. T. M. Willis) Single Crystal Diffractometry, 1966; (with A. J. Wonacott) The Rotation Method in Crystallography, 1977; *posthumous publication:* Personal X-Ray Reflections (memoirs), 2006; papers in scientific jls. *Recreations:* walking, reading. *Address:* 28 Barrow Road, Cambridge CB2 2AS. *T:* (01223) 350660. *Died 24 March 2006.*

ARNELL, Richard Anthony Sayer; composer; conductor; poet; Principal Lecturer, Trinity College of Music, 1981–87 (Teacher of Composition, 1949–81); *b* 15 Sept. 1917; *s* of late Richard Sayer Arnell and Hélène Marie Scherf; *m* 1992, Joan Heycock; one *s* three *d* from former marriages. *Educ:* The Hall, Hampstead; University Coll. Sch., NW3; Royal Coll. of Music. Music Consultant, BBC North American Service, 1943–46; Lectr, Royal Ballet Sch., 1958–59. Editor, The Composer, 1961–64, 1991–93; Chairman: Composers' Guild of GB, 1965, 1974–75 (Vice-Pres., 1992–); Young Musicians' Symph. Orch. Soc., 1973–75. Vis. Lectr (Fulbright Exchange), Bowdoin Coll., Maine, 1967–68; Vis. Prof. Hofstra Univ., New York, 1968–70. Music Dir and Board Mem., London Internat. Film Sch., 1975–89 (Chm., Film Sch. Trust, 1981–87; Chm., Friends of LIFS, 1982–87, Vice-Pres., 1988–); Music Dir, Ram Filming Ltd, 1980–91; Director: Organic Sounds Ltd, 1982–87; A plus A Ltd, 1984–89. Chm., Friends of TCM Junior

Dept, 1986–87 (Vice-Pres., 1987–). Chairman: Tadcaster Civic Soc. Music and Arts Cttee, 1988–91; Saxmundham Music and Arts, 1992–95 (Pres., 1995–). Hon. FTCL. Composer of the Year, 1966 (Music Teachers Assoc. Award); Tadcaster Town Council Merit Award, 1990. *Compositions include:* 7 symphonies; 2 concertos for violin; concerto for harpsichord; 2 concertos for piano; string trio; 6 string quartets; 2 quintets; piano trio; piano works; songs; cantatas; organ works; music for string orchestra, wind ensembles, brass ensembles, song cycles; electronic music; *opera:* Love in Transit; Moonflowers; *music theatre:* Ça Va, 2004; *ballet scores:* Punch and the Child, for Ballet Soc., NY, 1947; Harlequin in April, for Arts Council, 1951; The Great Detective, 1953, The Angels, 1957, for Sadler's Wells Theatre Ballet; Giselle (Adam) re-orchestrated, for Ballet Rambert, 1965; *film scores:* The Land, 1941; The Third Secret, 1963; The Visit, 1964; The Man Outside, 1966; Topsail Schooner, 1966; Bequest for a Village, 1969; Second Best, 1972; Stained Glass, 1973; Wires Over the Border, 1974; Black Panther, 1977; Antagonist, 1980; Dilemma, 1981; Doctor in the Sky, 1983; Toulouse Lautrec, 1984; Light of the World, 1990; *other works:* Symphonic Portrait, Lord Byron, for Sir Thomas Beecham, 1953; Landscapes and Figures, for Sir Thomas Beecham, 1956, Petrified Princess, puppet operetta (libretto by Bryan Guinness), for BBC, 1959; Robert Flaherty, Impression for Radio Eireann, 1960; Musica Pacifica for Edward Benjamin, 1963; Festival Flourish, for Salvation Army, 1965; 2nd piano concerto, for RPO, 1967; Overture, Food of Love, for Portland Symph. Orch., 1968; My Ladye Greene Sleeves, for Hofstra Univ., 1968; Life Boat Voluntary, for RNLI, 1974; Call, for LPO, 1980; Ode to Beecham, for RPO, 1986; War God II, 1987; Con Amore, 1990; Xanadu, 1993; *mixed media:* Nocturne: Prague, 1968; I Think of all Soft Limbs, for Canadian Broadcasting Corp., 1971; Combat Zone, for Hofstra Univ., 1971; Astronaut One, 1973; Not Wanted on Voyage, 1990; 24 Hours in TR Scale, 1995; "B"—Queen Boudicca, 2004; Ode for Mandela, 2004. *Club:* Savage. *Died 10 April 2009.*

ARNOLD, Sir Malcolm (Henry), Kt 1993; CBE 1970; FRCM; composer; *b* 21 Oct. 1921; *s* of William and Annie Arnold, Northampton; *m* 1st, 1941, Sheila Nicholson, LRAM (marr. diss.); one *s* one *d*; 2nd, 1963, Isobel Gray (marr. diss.); one *s. Educ:* Royal Coll. of Music, London (Schol., 1938). FRCM 1983; FTCL 1992; FRNCM 1997. Principal Trumpet, London Philharmonic Orchestra, 1941–44; served in the Army, 1944–45; Principal Trumpet, London Philharmonic Orchestra, 1945–48; Mendelssohn Schol. (study in Italy), 1948; Coronation Ballet, Homage to the Queen, performed Royal Opera House, 1953. Awarded Oscar for music for film Bridge on the River Kwai, 1957; Ivor Novello Award for outstanding services to British Music, 1985; Wavendon Allmusic Composer of the Year, 1987; Ivor Novello Award for Inn of Sixth Happiness, 1958. Bard of the Cornish Gorsedd, 1969. Fellow, BASCA, 1991. Hon. RAM; Hon. Mem., Schubert Soc., 1988. Hon. DMus: Exeter, 1970; Durham, 1982; Leicester, 1984; Hon. Dr Arts and Humane Letters, Miami Univ., Ohio, 1990. Hon. Freeman, Borough of Northampton, 1989. Dist. Musicians Medal, ISM, 2004. *Publications: symphonies:* No 1, 1949; No 2, 1953; No 3, 1957; No 4, 1960; No 5, 1961; No 6, 1967; No 7, 1973; No 8, 1978; No 9, 1986; Symphony for Brass Instruments, 1979; *other works:* Beckus the Dandipratt, overture, 1943; Tam O'Shanter, overture, 1955; Peterloo, overture, 1967; eighteen concertos; six ballets: Homage to the Queen, Electra, Rinaldo Armida, Flowers of the Forest, Solitaire, Sweeney Todd; two one-act operas; two string quartets; two brass quintets; vocal, choral and chamber music. *Recreations:* reading, foreign travel. *Address:* Music Unites, 26 Springfields, Attleborough, Norfolk NR17 2PA. *T:* and *Fax:* (01953) 455420; *e-mail:* musicunites@btopenworld.com. *Club:* Savile. *Died 23 Sept. 2006.*

ARNOLD-BAKER, Charles, OBE 1966; Chairman, Longcross Press, since 1968; Consultant Lecturer, 1978, and Visiting Professor, 1985–94, City University; *b* 25 June 1918; *s* of Baron Albrecht v. Blumenthal and Alice Wilhelmine (*née* Hainsworth); adopted surname of mother's second husband, Percival Richard Arnold Baker, 1938; *m* 1943, Edith (*née* Woods); one *s* one *d. Educ:* Winchester Coll.; Magdalen Coll., Oxford. BA 1940. Called to Bar, Inner Temple, 1948. Army (Private to Captain), 1940–46. Admty Bar, 1948–52; Sec., Nat. Assoc. of Local Councils, 1953–78; Dep. Eastern Traffic Comr, 1978–90. Editor, Road Law, 1992–96. Mem., Royal Commn on Common Lands, 1955–58; Mem. European Cttee, Internat. Union of Local Authorities, 1960–78; a Deleg. to European Local Govt Assembly, Strasbourg, 1960–78. Occasional broadcaster, Radio 4, 1987–92. Gwylim Gibbons Award, Nuffield Coll., Oxford, 1959. King Haakon's Medal of Freedom (Norway), 1945. *Publications:* Norway (pamphlet), 1946; Everyman's Dictionary of Dates, 1954; Parish Administration, 1958; New Law and Practice of Parish Administration, 1966; The 5000 and the Power Tangle, 1967; The Local Government Act 1972, 1972; Local Council Administration, 1975, 6th edn 2001; The Local Government, Planning and Land Act 1980, 1981; Practical Law for Arts Administrators, 1983, 3rd edn 1992; The Five Thousand and the Living Constitution, 1986; The Companion to British History, 1996, 3rd edn 2009; For He is An Englishman: memoirs of a Prussian nobleman, 2007; Quacks and Quotes, 2008; many contribs to British and European local govt and legal jls. *Recreations:* travel, history, writing, music, cooking, journalism, wine, doing nothing. *Address:* Top Floor, 2 Mitre Court Buildings, Temple, EC4Y 7BX. *T:* (020) 7353 3490. *Club:* Union (Oxford). *Died 6 June 2009.*

ARNOTT, Prof. W(illiam) Geoffrey, PhD; FBA 1999; Professor of Greek Language and Literature, University of Leeds, 1968–91, then Emeritus; *b* 17 Sept. 1930; *s* of late Bertie Arnott and Edith May Arnott (*née* Smith); *m* 1955, Vera Hodson; three *d. Educ:* Bury Grammar Sch.; Pembroke Coll., Cambridge (Schol.; BA 1952; Porson Prize, 1952; MA 1956; PhD 1960). Asst Master, Bristol Grammar Sch., 1952–53; Carrington-Coe Res. Student, Univ. of Cambridge, 1953–54; Asst Lectr in Greek, Bedford Coll., London Univ., 1955–59; Asst Dir of Exams, Civil Service Commn, 1959–60; Asst Lectr in Classics, Univ. of Hull, 1960–61; Lectr in Classics, King's Coll., Univ. of Durham, 1960–63; Lectr in Classics, 1963–66, Sen. Lectr in Classics, 1966–67, Univ. of Newcastle upon Tyne. Vis. Mem., Inst. of Advanced Studies, Princeton, 1973; Vis. Schol., Univ. of British Columbia, 1982; Visiting Professor: Univ. of Wellington, 1982; Univ. of Alexandria, 1983; Univ. of Queensland, 1987; Univ. of Bologna, 1998; Vis. Fellow, Gonville and Caius Coll., Cambridge, 1987–88. Lectr, NADFAS, 1980–2004. Pres., Leeds Birdwatchers Club, 1981–84. Member: Classical Jls Bd, 1970–94; Bd of Mgt, Greece & Rome, 1981–89. Fellow, Italian Soc. for Study of Classical Antiquity, 1981. *Publications:* Menander's Dyskolos: a translation, 1960; Menander, Plautus, Terence, 1975; Menander, vol. I, 1979, vol. II, 1996, vol. III, 2000; Alexis: a commentary, 1996; Birds in the Ancient World from A–Z, 2007; papers and reviews in classical jls, etc. *Recreations:* birds and 19th century bird painting, crosswords, photography, travel. *Address:* 35 Arncliffe Road, Leeds LS16 5AP. *T:* (0113) 275 2751. *Died 1 Dec. 2010.*

ARTHUR, Prof. Geoffrey Herbert; Professor and Head of Department of Veterinary Surgery, University of Bristol, 1974–79, Professor Emeritus since 1980; *b* 6 March 1916; *s* of William Gwyn Arthur and Ethel Jessie Arthur; *m* 1948, Lorna Isabel Simpson; four *s* one *d. Educ:* Abersychan Secondary Sch.; Liverpool Univ. (BVSc 1939; MVSc 1945; DVSc 1957). MRCVS 1939, FRCVS 1957. Lectr in Veterinary Medicine, Liverpool Univ., 1941–48; Royal Veterinary College, University of London: Reader in Veterinary Surgery, 1949–51; Reader in Veterinary Surgery and Obstetrics, 1952–65; Prof. of Veterinary Obstetrics and Diseases of Reproduction, 1965–73. Regl Postgrad. Vet. Dean, W and SW England and S Wales, 1985–94. Examiner to Univs of Cambridge, Dublin, Edinburgh, Glasgow, Liverpool, London, Reading, Bristol and Ceylon. Visiting Professor: Univ. of Khartoum, 1964; Pahlavi Univ., 1976; Nairobi Univ., 1979; Clinical Prof., King Faisal Univ., Saudi Arabia, 1980–84. Chm., Soc. for Protection of Animals Abroad, 1992–94. *Publications:* Wright's Veterinary Obstetrics (including Diseases of Reproduction, 3rd edn), 1964, 5th edn, as Veterinary Reproduction and Obstetrics, 1982, 8th edn 2001; papers on medicine and reproduction in Veterinary Record, Veterinary Jl, Jl of Comparative Pathology, Jl Reprod. Fert., Equine Vet. Jl and Jl Small Animal Pract. (Editor). *Recreations:* observing natural phenomena and experimenting, North African and Middle Eastern travel. *Address:* Fallodene Farm, Stone Allerton, Axbridge, Som BS26 2NH. *Died 11 March 2007.*

ARTHUR, James Stanley, CMG 1977; HM Diplomatic Service, retired; British High Commissioner in Bridgetown, 1978–82, also British High Commissioner (non-resident) to Dominica, 1978–82, to St Lucia and St Vincent, 1979–82, to Grenada, 1980–82, to Antigua and Barbuda, 1981–82, and concurrently British Government Representative to West Indies Associated State of St Kitts-Nevis; *b* 3 Feb. 1923; *s* of Laurence and Catherine Arthur, Lerwick, Shetland; *m* 1950, Marion North; two *s* two *d*. *Educ:* Trinity Academy, Edinburgh; Liverpool Univ. (BSc). Scientific Civil Service, 1944–46; Asst Principal, Scottish Educn Dept, 1946; Min. of Educn/ Dept of Educn and Science, 1947–66: Private Sec. to Parly Sec., 1948–50; Principal Private Sec. to Minister, 1960–62; Counsellor, FO, 1966; Nairobi, 1967–70; Dep. High Comr, Malta, 1970–73; High Comr, Suva, 1974–78, and first High Comr (non-resident), Republic of Nauru, 1977–78. Mem. Court, Liverpool Univ., 1987–. *Recreations:* walking the dog, music. *Address:* Moreton House, Longborough, Moreton-in-Marsh, Glos GL56 0QQ. *T:* (01451) 830774. *Died 3 Sept. 2010.*

ARTHUR, Sir Stephen (John), 6th Bt *cr* 1841, of Upper Canada; *b* 1 July 1953; *s* of Hon. Sir Basil Malcolm Arthur, 5th Bt, MP, and of Elizabeth Rita, *d* of late Alan Mervyn Wells; S father, 1985; *m* 1978, Carolyn Margaret (marr. diss.), *d* of Burney Lawrence Daimond, Cairns, Queensland; one *s* two *d*. *Educ:* Timaru Boys' High School. *Heir: s* Benjamin Nathan Arthur, *b* 27 March 1979. *Died 15 May 2010.*

ASH, Rear-Adm. William Noel, CB 1977; LVO 1959; *b* 6 March 1921; *s* of late H. Arnold Ash, MRCS, LRCP; *m* 1951, Pamela, *d* of late Harry C. Davies, Hawkes Bay, NZ; one *s* one *d*. *Educ:* Merchant Taylors' School. Joined RN, 1938; HM Yacht Britannia, 1955–58; Captain 1965; Canadian NDC, 1965–66; Staff of SACLANT (NATO), 1966–69; Cabinet Office, 1969–71; comd HMS Ganges, 1971–73; Rear-Adm. 1974; Dir of Service Intelligence, 1974–77. Sec. Defence Press and Broadcasting Cttee, 1980–84. *Address:* c/o National Bank of New Zealand, PO Box 28074, Auckland, New Zealand. *Died 4 June 2008.*

ASHBEE, Paul; Archaeologist, University of East Anglia, 1969–83; *b* 23 June 1918; *s* of Lewis Ashbee and Hannah Mary Elizabeth Ashbee (*née* Brett); *m* 1952, Richmal Crompton Lamburn Disher (*d* 2005); one *s* one *d*. *Educ:* sch. in Maidstone, Kent; Univ. of London; Univ. of Leicester (MA; DLitt 1984). Post-grad. Dip. Prehistoric Archaeology, London. Royal W Kent Regt and REME, 1939–46; Control Commn for Germany, 1946–49; Univ. of London, Univ. of Bristol (Redland Coll.), 1949–54; Asst Master and Head of History, Forest Hill Sch., 1954–68. Excavation of prehistoric sites, mostly barrows both long and round for then Min. of Works, 1949–76, incl. Halangy Down, Isles of Scilly, 1964–76; Co-dir with R. L. S. Bruce-Mitford of BM excavations at Sutton-Hoo, 1964–69; Mem., Sutton Hoo Research Cttee, 1982–2002. Mem. Council and Meetings Sec., Prehistoric Soc., 1960–74; Sec. (Wareham Earthwork), British Assoc. Sub-Cttee for Archaeological Field Experiment, 1961–; one-time Sec., Neolithic and Bronze

Age Cttee, Council for British Archaeology; Mem. Royal Commn on Historical Monuments (England), 1975–85; Mem., Area Archaeological Adv. Cttee (DoE) for Norfolk and Suffolk, 1975–79. Pres., Cornwall Archæol Soc., 1976–80, Vice-Pres., 1980–84; Chm., Scole Cttee for E Anglian Archaeology, 1979–84. Patron, Kent Archaeol Soc., 2002–. FSA 1958; FRSAI 1987. *Publications:* The Bronze Age Round Barrow in Britain, 1960; The Earthen Long Barrow in Britain, 1970, 2nd edn 1984; Ancient Scilly, 1974; The Ancient British, 1978; chapter in Sutton Hoo, Vol. I, 1976; Wilsford Shaft, 1989; Halangy Down, Isles of Scilly, 2000; Kent in Prehistoric Times, 2005; numerous papers, articles and reviews in Archaeologia, Antiquaries Jl, Archaeological Jl, Proc. Prehistoric Soc., Antiquity, Cornish Archaeology, Arch. Cantiana, Proc. Dorset Arch. and Nat. Hist. Soc., Proc. Hants FC, Wilts Archaeol Magazine, Yorks Arch. Jl, etc. *Recreations:* East Anglia, historical architecture, bibliophilia. *Address:* The Old Rectory, Chedgrave, Norfolk NR14 6ND. *T:* (01508) 520595. *Club:* Norfolk (Norwich). *Died 19 Aug. 2009.*

ASHFORD, Ronald, CBE 1992; CEng, FIMechE, FRAeS; aviation and safety consultant; *b* 24 Aug. 1932; *s* of Russell Sutcliffe Ashford and Dorothy Ashford (*née* Shorland); *m* 1955, Françoise Louisa Gabrielle Génestal du Chaumeil; two *s*. *Educ:* St Edward's Sch., Oxford; De Havilland Aeronautical Tech. Sch. Flight Develt Engr, De Havilland Aircraft Co., 1953–56; Pilot Officer, RAF, 1956–58; Flight Develt Engr and Sen. Aerodynamicist, De Havilland/Hawker Siddeley Aviation, 1958–68; Design Surveyor, Air Registration Bd, 1968–72; Civil Aviation Authority: Surveyor and Head, Flight Dept, 1972–83; Dir-Gen., Airworthiness, 1983–88; Group Dir, Safety Regulation, and Board Mem., 1988–92; Sec. Gen., Eur. Jt Aviation Authorities, 1992–94. Wakefield Gold Medal, 1989, Hodgson Prize, 1991, RAeS; Dist. Service Award, Flight Safety Foundn, 1992; Award for Dist. Service, US Fed. Aviation Admin, 1992; Cumberbatch Trophy, GAPAN, 1992; James Clayton Prize, IMechE, 1995. *Publications:* papers in Jl RAeS. *Recreations:* walking, gardening. *Address:* Sheeplands, 17 Granville Road, Limpsfield, Oxted, Surrey RH8 0BX. *T:* (01883) 382917. *Club:* Royal Air Force. *Died 6 Oct. 2008.*

ASHLEY, Sir Bernard (Albert), Kt 1987; Founder, Laura Ashley Holdings plc, 1993 (Chairman, 1985–93; non-executive Director, 1991–98); Founder, designer and colourist, Elanbach, since 2000; *b* 11 Aug. 1926; *s* of Albert Ashley and Hilda Maud Ashley; *m* 1st, 1949, Laura Mountney (*d* 1985); two *s* two *d*; 2nd, 1990, Mme Regine Burnell. *Educ:* Whitgift Middle Sch., Croydon, Surrey. Army commission, 1944; Royal Fusiliers, 1944–46, seconded 1 Gurkha Rifles, 1944–45. Incorporated Ashley, Mountney Ltd, 1954; Chm., Ashley, Mountney Ltd, later Laura Ashley Ltd, 1954–93. Hon. DScEcon Wales, 1986. *Recreations:* sailing, flying. *Address:* Llangoed Hall, Llyswen, Brecon, Powys LD3 0YP. *Clubs:* Royal Thames Yacht (Southampton); Army Sailing Association. *Died 14 Feb. 2009.*

ASHMOLE, (Harold) David; Assistant Director and Head of Boys, Images of Dance, London Studio Centre, since 2002; Senior Principal Dancer, 1984–93, Guest Artist, since 1994, Australian Ballet; *b* 31 Oct. 1949; *s* of Richard Thomas Ashmole and Edith Ashmole; *m* Petal Miller. *Educ:* Sandye Place, Beds; Royal Ballet Sch.; Grad. Dip Visual and Performing Arts, Melbourne Univ. Solo Seal, Royal Acad. of Dancing; ARAD. Joined Royal Ballet Co., 1968; Soloist, 1972; Principal, 1975; transf. to Sadler's Wells Royal Ballet, 1976, Sen. Principal, 1978–84; Dir, Australian Ballet Foundn, 1995–99. Lectr in Classical Dance, Victorian Coll. of the Arts, Univ. of Melbourne, 1998–2001; Guest Teacher: London Studio Centre, 1999–2000, 2001; K Ballet UK, 2000; Singapore Dance Theatre, 2000; Birmingham Royal Ballet, 2001–; Winter Sch., Universal Ballet Acad., Korea, 2006. Appeared in: Dame Alicia Markova's Master Classes, BBC Television, 1980; Maina Gielgud's Steps, Notes and Squeaks, Aberdeen Internat.

Festival, 1981. Guest appearances with Scottish Ballet, 1981, with Bolshoi (for UNESCO Gala), 1986, with Sadler's Wells Royal Ballet at Royal Opera House, 1986 (season) and in Japan, Germany, S Africa and France. *Classical ballets include:* La Bayadère, Coppélia, Daphnis and Chloe, Giselle, Nutcracker, Raymonda, The Seasons, Sleeping Beauty, Swan Lake, La Sylphide; *other ballets include:* (choreography by Ashton): Cinderella, The Two Pigeons, La Fille Mal Gardée, Les Rendezvous, The Dream, Lament of the Waves, Symphonic Variations, Birthday Offering; (Balanchine): Apollo, Prodigal Son, Serenade, The Four Temperaments, Agon, Tchaikovsky Pas de Deux; (Béjart): Gaîté Parisienne, Webern Opus 5, Songs of a Wayfarer, Le Concours; (Bintley): Night Moves, Homage to Chopin, The Swan of Tuonela; (Cranko): Brouillards, Pineapple Poll, The Taming of the Shrew, Onegin; (Darrell): The Tales of Hoffmann; (de Valois): Checkmate, The Rake's Progress; (Fokine): Les Sylphides, Petrushka; (Hynd): Papillon; (Lander): Etudes; (Litar): Suite en Blanc, (MacMillan): Concerto, Elite Syncopations, Romeo and Juliet, Quartet, Song of the Earth, Symphony; (Massine): La Boutique Fantasque; (Miller-Ashmole): Snugglepot-and-Cuddlepie; (Nijinska): Les Biches; (Nureyev): Don Quixote; (Robbins): Dances at a Gathering, Requiem Canticles, In the Night, Concert; (Seymour): Intimate Letters, Rashomon; (Samsova): Paquita; (Tetley): Gemini, Laborintus, Orpheus; (van Manen): Grosse Fugue, 5 Tangos; (Wright): Summertide; (Prokovsky): The Three Musketeers; (Seregi): Spartacus. *Recreations:* Moorcroft pottery collection, gardening, fishing. *Address:* London Studio Centre, 42–50 York Way, N1 9AB.
Died 25 July 2009.

ASHTON OF HYDE, 3rd Baron *cr* 1911; **Thomas John Ashton**, TD; Director, Barclays Bank PLC and subsidiary companies, 1969–87; *b* 19 Nov. 1926; *s* of 2nd Baron Ashton of Hyde and Marjorie Nell (*d* 1993), *d* of late Hon. Marshall Jones Brooks; *S* father, 1983; *m* 1957, Pauline Trewlove, *er d* of late Lt-Col R. H. L. Brackenbury, OBE; two *s* two *d*. *Educ:* Eton; New Coll., Oxford (BA 1950, MA 1955). Sen. Exec. Local Dir, Barclays Bank, Manchester, 1968–81. Major retd, Royal Glos Hussars (TA). JP Oxon, 1965–68. *Heir: s* Hon. Thomas Henry Ashton [*b* 18 July 1958; *m* 1987, Emma, *d* of Colin Allinson; four *d*]. *Address:* Fir Farm, Upper Slaughter, Cheltenham GL54 2JR. *Club:* Boodle's.
Died 2 Aug. 2008.

ASHTON, Roy; a Recorder of the Crown Court, 1979–98; barrister-at-law; *b* 20 Oct. 1928; *s* of Charles and Lilian Ashton; *m* 1954, Brenda Alice Dales; one *s* one *d*. *Educ:* Boston Grammar Sch.; Nottingham Univ. (LLB Hons 1950). National Service, Directorate of Legal Services, RAF, 1951–53. Called to the Bar, Lincoln's Inn, 1954. Dep. Chairman, Agricultural Land Tribunal, 1978–. Mem., Bishops Stortford UDC, 1961–64. *Recreations:* bridge, reading, horse racing, film collecting. *Address:* c/o 22 Albion Place, Northampton NN1 1UD. *Club:* Northampton and County.
Died 30 April 2007.

ASHTOWN, 7th Baron *cr* 1800; **Nigel Clive Cosby Trench**, KCMG 1976 (CMG 1966); HM Diplomatic Service, retired; *b* 27 Oct. 1916; *s* of Clive Newcome Trench (*d* 1964), *g s* of 2nd Baron, and Kathleen (*d* 1979), 2nd *d* of Major Ivar MacIvor, CIE; *S* cousin, 1990; *m* 1st, 1939, Marcelle Catherine Clotterbooke Patyn (*d* 1994); one *s*; 2nd, 1997, Mary, Princess of Pless, *d* of late Lt Col and Mrs R. G. E. Minchin. *Educ:* Eton; Univ. of Cambridge. Served in KRRC, 1940–46 (despatches). Appointed a Member of the Foreign (subseq. Diplomatic) Service, 1946; Lisbon, 1946; First Secretary, 1948; returned Foreign Office, 1949; First Secretary (Commercial), Lima, 1952; transf. Foreign Office, 1955; Counsellor, Tokyo, 1961; Counsellor, Washington, 1963; Cabinet Office, 1967; HM Ambassador to Korea, 1969–71; CS Selection Board, 1971–73; Ambassador to Portugal, 1974–76. Mem., Police, Prison and Fire Service Selection Bds, 1977–86. Sungrye Medal, Order of

Diplomatic Service Merit (Korea), 1984. *Heir: s* Hon. Roderick Nigel Godolphin Trench [*b* 17 Nov. 1944; *m* 1st, 1967, Janet (*d* 1971), *d* of Harold Hamilton-Faulkner; one *s*; 2nd, 1973, Susan Barbara, *d* of L. F. Day, FRCS, DLO; one *d*]. *Died 6 March 2010.*

ASPELL, Col Gerald Laycock, TD (2 clasps); DL; FCA; Vice Lord-Lieutenant of Leicestershire, 1984–90; *b* 10 April 1915; *s* of Samuel Frederick Aspell and Agnes Maude (*née* Laycock); *m* 1939, Mary Leeson Carroll (*d* 1998), *d* of Rev. Ion Carroll, Cork; two *d* (one *s* decd). *Educ:* Uppingham Sch. FCA 1938. Commnd 2nd Lieut, 4th Bn Leicestershire Regt, TA, 1933; served War of 1939–45 in UK and Burma, RE, RA, RAF; commanded 579 Light Anti-Aircraft Regt, RA (TA), 1946–51. Partner, Coopers & Lybrand, 1952–78; mem. of various nat. and local cttees of Inst. of Chartered Accountants during that time. Dir, 1964–85, Chm., 1978–85, Leicester Building Soc.; Dep. Chm., Alliance and Leicester Building Soc., 1985; Local Dir, Eagle Star Insce Gp, 1949–84 (Chm., Midlands Bd, 1970–84). Chm., Leicester and Dist Local Employment Cttee, then Leics Dist Manpower Cttee, 1971–79. Mem., Leicester Diocesan Bd of Finance, 1952–77. Civil Defence Controller, then Sub-Regl Dir CD, Leics, Rutland and Northants, 1956–65. Member: Leics and Rutland TAA, then E Midlands TAVRA, 1947–80 (Chm., Leics Cttee, 1969–80). Hon. Colonel: Royal Anglian Regt (Leics), 1972–79; Leics and Northants ACF, 1979–84. Grand Treasurer, United Grand Lodge of England, 1974–75. Trustee, Uppingham Sch., 1964–87 (Chm., 1977–87). DL Leics, 1952. *Recreations:* cricket, tennis, squash, fishing, charitable involvements. *Address:* Laburnum House, Great Dalby, Melton Mowbray, Leics LE14 2HA. T: (01664) 411513. *Died 11 July 2006.*

ATKIN, Alec Field, CBE 1978; FREng; FRAeS; Managing Director, Marketing, Aircraft Group, British Aerospace, 1981–82; Director, AWA (Consultancy) Ltd, since 1983; *b* 26 April 1925; *s* of Alec and Grace Atkin; *m* 1948, Nora Helen Darby (marr. diss. 1982); one *s* one *d* (and one *s* decd); *m* 1982, Wendy Atkin (marr. diss. 1998); *m* 2006, Lynn Tonkinson. *Educ:* Riley High Sch.; Hull Technical Coll. (DipAe); Hull Univ. (BSc (Hons) Maths, ext. London). FIMechE 1945–2000; FRAeS 1952; FREng (FEng 1979). English Electric Co., Preston: Aerodynamicist, 1950; Dep. Chief Aerodyn., 1954; Head of Exper. Aerodyns, 1957; Asst Chief Engr, then Proj. Manager, 1959; Warton Div., British Aircraft Corporation Ltd: Special Dir, 1964; Dir, 1970; Asst Man. Dir, 1973–75; Dep. Man. Dir, 1975–76; Man. Dir, 1976–77; Man. Dir (Mil.), Aircraft Gp of British Aerospace, and Chm., Warton, Kingston-Brough and Manchester Divs, 1978–81. FRSA. Hon. DSc Hull, 1997. *Recreation:* sailing. *Address:* Les Fougères d'Icart, Icart Road, St Martin, Guernsey GY4 6JG. *Died 2 July 2009.*

ATKINSON, Arthur Kingsley Hall, CB 1985; Chief Executive, Intervention Board for Agricultural Produce, 1980–86; *b* 24 Dec. 1926; *er s* of Arthur Hall Atkinson and Florence (*née* Gerrans). *Educ:* Priory Sch., Shrewsbury; Emmanuel Coll., Cambridge (MA). RAF, 1948; MAFF: Asst Principal 1950; Private Sec. 1953; Principal 1956; Asst Sec. 1965; Under Sec., 1973; Cabinet Office, 1976–78; MAFF, 1978–80. *Recreations:* travel, music, gardening. *Died 15 Jan. 2009.*

ATKINSON, James Oswald, CMG 2004; HM Diplomatic Service, retired; Ambassador to Democratic Republic of Congo and (non-resident) to Republic of Congo, 2000–04; *b* 20 Oct. 1944; *s* of James Edward Atkinson and Helen (*née* Liuta); *m* 1980, Annemiek van Werkum; one *d*. *Educ:* Woolverstone Hall, Suffolk. Joined HM Diplomatic Service, 1966: Third Secretary: Nicosia, 1969–72; Gaborone, 1972–76; Second Sec., Damascus, 1976–79; FCO, 1980–84; First Secretary: Athens, 1984–88; Jakarta, 1988–90; FCO, 1990–93; Dep. High Comr, Kampala, 1993–97; Dep. Hd of Consular

Service, London, 1997–2000. *Recreations:* sailing, photography. *Address:* c/o Foreign and Commonwealth Office, King Charles Street, SW1A 2AH.
Died 20 July 2006.

ATTENBOROUGH, Philip John, CBE 1994; publisher; Deputy Chairman, Hodder Headline plc, 1993–96 (Chairman, Hodder & Stoughton Ltd and Hodder & Stoughton Holdings Ltd, 1975–93); *b* 3 June 1936; *er s* of late John Attenborough, CBE, and Barbara (*née* Sandle); *m* 1963, Rosemary, *y d* of late Dr (William) Brian Littler, CB, and Pearl Littler; one *s* one *d. Educ:* Rugby; Trinity Coll., Oxford. Christmas postman (parcels), 1952–54; Nat. Service, Sergeant 68th Regt RA, Oswestry, 1956; lumberjack, Blind River, Ont, 1957; joined Hodder & Stoughton, 1957: Export Manager, 1960; Dir, 1963–; Sales Dir, 1969. Chm., The Lancet Ltd, 1977–91; Dir, Book Tokens Ltd, 1985–96. Publishers Association: Mem. Council, 1976–92 (Treasurer, 1981–82; Vice-Pres., 1982–83, 1985–86; Pres., 1983–85); Leader, delegns of Brit. publishers to China, 1978, to Bangladesh, India and Pakistan, 1986, to India, 1990; Mem., Exec. Cttee, IPA, 1988–96 (Vice-Pres., 1992–96); Chairman: Book Develt Council, 1977–79; PA Freedom to Publish Cttee, 1987–92; Member: British Council Publishers Adv. Cttee, 1977–93 (Chm., 1989–93); British Library Adv. Council, 1986–89; UK Rep., Fédération des Editeurs Européens, 1986–93; Advr, UNESCO Publishing, 1992–95. Sponsor, Airey Neave Trust, 1979–2005. Governor: Judd Sch., Tonbridge, 1987–2004; Tonbridge Sch., 1998–2005. Chairman: Sir Thomas Smythe's Charity, 2000–; Lawrence Atwell's Charity, 2003–. Mem. Governing Body, SPCK, 1999–. Liveryman, Skinners' Co., 1970 (Mem. Court, 1995–; Master, 2000–01). *Recreations:* trout fishing, croquet (Jamaica Inn rules), dog and cat walking, watching cricket. *Address:* Coldhanger, Seal Chart, near Sevenoaks, Kent TN15 0EJ. *T:* (01732) 761516. *Clubs:* Garrick, MCC; Kent CC; Band of Brothers; Rye Golf; Piscatorial Society. *Died 4 April 2006.*

AUCHINCLOSS, Louis Stanton; author; Partner, Hawkins Delafield and Wood, NYC, 1957–86 (Associate, 1954–57); *b* NY, 27 Sept. 1917; *s* of J. H. Auchincloss and P. Stanton; *m* 1957, Adèle Lawrence (*d* 1991); three *s. Educ:* Groton Sch.; Yale Univ.; Univ. of Virginia (LLB). Lieut USNR; served, 1941–45. Admitted to NY Bar, 1941; Associate Sullivan and Cromwell, 1941–51. Mem. Exec. Cttee, Assoc. of Bar of NY City. Pres., Museum of City of NY, 1967; Trustee, Josiah Macy Jr Foundn. Mem., Nat. Inst. of Arts and Letters. *Publications:* The Indifferent Children, 1947; The Injustice Collectors, 1950; Sybil, 1952; A Law for the Lion, 1953; The Romantic Egoists, 1954; The Great World and Timothy Colt, 1956; Venus in Sparta, 1958; Pursuit of the Prodigal, 1959; The House of Five Talents, 1960; Reflections of a Jacobite, 1961; Portrait in Brownstone, 1962; Powers of Attorney, 1963; The Rector of Justin, 1964; Pioneers and Caretakers, 1966; The Embezzler, 1966; Tales of Manhattan, 1967; A World of Profit, 1969; Second Chance: tales to two generations, 1970; Edith Wharton, 1972; I Come as a Thief, 1972; Richelieu, 1972; The Partners, 1974; A Writer's Capital, 1974; Reading Henry James, 1975; The Winthrop Covenant, 1976; The Dark Lady, 1977; The Country Cousin, 1978; The House of the Prophet, 1980; The Cat and the King, 1981; Watch Fires, 1982; Honourable Men, 1986; Diary of a Yuppie, 1987; The Golden Calves, 1989; (ed) Hone and Strong Diaries of Old Manhattan, 1989; Fellow Passengers, 1990; J. P. Morgan, 1990; House of the Prophet, 1991; Lady of Situations, 1991; False Gods, 1992; Three Lives, 1993; Tales of Yesteryear, 1994; The Style's the Man, 1994; Collected Stories, 1994; The Education of Oscar Fairfax, 1995; The Man Behind the Book, 1996; La Gloire, 1996; The Atonement, 1997; The Anniversary, 1999; Her Infinite Variety, 2000; Woodrow Wilson, 2000; Theodore Roosevelt, 2002; Manhattan Monologues, 2002; East Side Story: a novel, 2004; The Scarlet Letters, 2004; The Headmaster's Dilemma, 2007;

Last of the Old Guard, 2008; pamphlets on American writers. *Address:* 1111 Park Avenue, New York, NY 10128–1234, USA. *Club:* Century Association (NY).
Died 26 Jan. 2010.

AUDLEY, Sir (George) Bernard, Kt 1985; Chairman: Caverswall Holdings, since 1990; Pergamon AGB plc, 1988–90; Founder, and Chairman, AGB Research PLC, 1973–88; *b* Stockton Brook, N Staffs, 24 April 1924; *s* of late Charles Bernard Audley and Millicent Claudia Audley; *m* 1950, Barbara, *d* of late Richard Arthur Heath; two *s* one *d. Educ:* Wolstanton Grammar Sch.; Corpus Christi Coll., Oxford (MA). Lieut, Kings Dragoon Guards, 1943–46. Asst Gen. Man., Hulton Press Ltd, 1949–57; Man. Dir, Television Audience Measurement Ltd, 1957–61; founded AGB Research, 1962. Chairman: Netherhall Trust, 1962–2002; Industry and Commerce Adv. Cttee, William and Mary Tercentenary Trust, 1985–89; Arts Access, 1986–98; Pres., EUROPANEL, 1966–70; Vice-Pres., Periodical Publishers Assoc., 1989– (Pres., 1985–89); Mem. Cttee, St Bride's World Wide Trust, 1991–2004. Vis. Prof. in Business and Management, Middlesex Univ. (formerly Poly.), 1989–2000. Governor, Hong Kong Coll., 1984–95. FRSA 1986. Freeman of City of London, 1978; Liveryman, Gold and Silver Wyre Drawers' Company, 1975–. *Recreations:* golf, reading, travel. *Address:* 56 River Court, SE1 9PE. *T:* (020) 7928 6576; Le Collet du Puits, Montauroux, 83440 Fayence, France. *T:* 494765287. *Clubs:* Cavalry and Guards, MCC; Rye Golf.
Died 4 Jan. 2008.

AULD, Margaret Gibson, RGN, RM, RMT; FRCN; MPhil; Chief Nursing Officer, Scottish Home and Health Department, 1977–88; *b* 11 July 1932; *d* of late Alexander John Sutton Auld and Eleanor Margaret Ingram. *Educ:* Glasgow; Cardiff High Sch. for Girls; Radcliffe Infirm., Oxford (SRN 1953); St David's Hosp., Cardiff; Queen's Park Hosp., Blackburn (SCM 1954). Midwife Teacher's Dip., 1962; Certif. of Nursing Admin, 1966, MPhil 1974, Edinburgh. Queen's Park Hosp., Blackburn, 1953–54; Staff Midwife, Cardiff Maternity Hosp., 1955, Sister, 1957; Sister, Queen Mary Hosp., Dunedin, NZ, 1959–60; Deptl Sister, Cardiff Maternity Hosp., 1960–66; Asst Matron, Simpson Meml Maternity Pavilion, Edinburgh, 1966–68, Matron, 1968–73; Actg Chief Reg. Nursing Officer, S-Eastern Reg. Hosp. Bd, Edinburgh, 1973; Chief Area Nursing Off., Borders Health Bd, 1973–76. Life Vice Pres., Royal Coll. of Midwives of UK, 1988. Chm., CRAG/SCOTMEG Review of Maternity Services in Scotland, 1992–96; Member: GNC (Scotland), 1973–76; Central Midwives Bd (Scotland), 1972–76; Cttee on Nursing (Briggs), 1970–72; Maternity Services Cttee, Integration of Maternity Work (Tennent Report), 1972–73; Human Fertilization and Embryol. Authy, 1990–93; Cttee on Ethics of Gene Therapy, 1990–93; Nuffield Council on Bioethics, 1991–94. Vice-Chm., Eildon Housing Assoc., 2001–08 (Mem., 1989–2008). Patron, Queen Margaret Univ. (formerly Queen Margaret Coll., subseq. Queen Margaret UC), Edinburgh, 1999– (Gov., 1989–2000; Chm. Bd of Govs, 1997–2000). FRCN 1981; CCMI (CBIM 1983). Hon. DSc CNAA, 1987. *Recreations:* reading, music, entertaining. *Address:* Staddlestones, Neidpath Road, Peebles EH45 8NN. *T:* (01721) 729594. *Died 10 Sept. 2010.*

AUSTIN, Prof. Colin François Lloyd, DPhil; FBA 1983; Fellow, Trinity Hall, Cambridge, 1965–2008, then Emeritus (Director of Studies in Classics, 1965–2005); Professor of Greek, University of Cambridge, 1998–2008; *b* Melbourne, Australia, 26 July 1941; *s* of Prof. Lloyd James Austin, FBA; *m* 1967, Mishtu Mazumdar, Calcutta, India; one *s* one *d. Educ:* Lycée Lakanal, Paris; Manchester Grammar Sch.; Jesus Coll., Cambridge (Scholar; MA 1965); Christ Church, Oxford (Sen. Scholar; MA, DPhil 1965); Freie Universität, West Berlin (Post-grad. Student). University of Cambridge: John Stewart of Rannoch Scholar in Greek and Latin, 1960; Battie Scholar, Henry Arthur Thomas Scholar and

Hallam Prize, 1961; Sir William Browne Medal for a Latin Epigram, 1961; Porson Prize, 1962; Prendergast Greek Student, 1962; Res. Fellow, Trinity Hall, 1965–69; Asst Univ. Lectr in Classics, 1969–73, Lectr, 1973–88; Reader in Greek Lang. and Lit., 1988–98; Leverhulme Res. Fellow, 1979 and 1981. Treas., Cambridge Philological Soc., 1971–. *Publications:* De nouveaux fragments de l'Erechthée d'Euripide, 1967; Nova Fragmenta Euripidea, 1968; (with Prof. R. Kasser) Papyrus Bodmer XXV et XXVI, 2 vols, 1969; Menandri Aspis et Samia, 2 vols, 1969–70; Comicorum Graecorum Fragmenta in papyris reperta, 1973; (with Prof. R. Kassel) Poetae Comici Graeci: vol. IV, Aristophon–Crobylus, 1983, vol. III 2, Aristophanes, Testimonia et Fragmenta, 1984, vol. V, Damoxenus–Magnes, 1986, vol. VII, Menecrates–Xenophon, 1989, vol. II, Agathenor–Aristonymus, 1991, vol. VIII, Adespota, 1995, vol. VI 2, Menander, Testimonia et Fragmenta apud scriptores servata, 1998, vol. I, Comoedia Dorica, Mimi, Phlyaces, 2001; (jtly) Posidippo di Pella Epigrammi, 2001; (with Prof. G. Bastianini) Posidippi Pellaei quae supersunt omnia, 2002; (with Prof. S. D. Olson) Aristophanes, Thesmophoriazusae, 2004; notes and reviews in classical periodicals. *Recreations:* cycling, philately, wine tasting. *Address:* 7 Park Terrace, Cambridge CB1 1JH. *T:* (01223) 362732; Trinity Hall, Cambridge CB2 1TJ. *Died 13 Aug. 2010.*

AUSTIN, Rt Rev. John Michael, OBE 2006; Bishop Suffragan of Aston, 1992–2005; *b* 4 March 1939; *s* of John Fenner Austin and Margaret Austin; *m* 1971, Rosemary Joan Elizabeth King; two *s* one *d. Educ:* Worksop Coll.; St Edmund Hall, Oxford (BA 1963); St Stephen's House, Oxford. Ordained deacon, 1964, priest, 1965; Assistant Curate: St John the Evangelist, E Dulwich, 1964–68; St James Cathedral, Chicago, 1968–69; St Christopher's, Pembroke Coll. Mission, 1969–76; Social Responsibility Advr, St Albans Dio., 1976–84; Dir, London Diocesan Bd for Social Responsibility, 1984–92. Prebendary, St Paul's Cathedral, 1982–87. Founding Chm., Church Action on Poverty, 1980–85; Mem., Follow-up Cttee for the Archbishop's Report, Faith in the City, 1986–92. Mem., Gen. Synod of C of E, 2000–05 (Chm., Inter-Faith Consultative Cttee, Bd for Mission, 1998–2005). Chairman: Newtown/S Aston City Challenge Bd, Birmingham, 1993–99; St Basil's Young Homeless Provision in Birmingham, 2000–05. Trustee, Church Urban Fund, 1999–. Hon. Dr UCE, 1996. *Recreations:* walking, cycling. *Address:* Bell House, The Row, Hartest, Bury St Edmunds, Suffolk IP29 4DL. *Died 17 Aug. 2007.*

AVENT, (John) Richard, FSA; Chief Inspector of Ancient Monuments and Historic Buildings, Cadw: Welsh Historic Monuments, since 1984; *b* 13 July 1948, *s* of Gp Capt. John Avent and Mary Day Avent (*née* Baird); *m* 1980, Sian Eluned Rees; two *s* one *d. Educ:* Reading Bluecoat Sch.; University Coll. Cardiff (BA 1970, MA 1974). FSA 1979. Asst Curator, Carmarthen Mus., 1971–73; Asst Inspector, 1973–76, Inspector, 1976–84, of Ancient Monuments, Wales. Mem. Council, Soc. of Antiquaries, 1989–92; Pres., Cambrian Archaeol Assoc., 2006–. *Publications:* Anglo-Saxon Garnet Inlaid Disc and Composite Brooches, 1975; Cestyll Tywysogion Gwynedd/Castles of the Princes of Gwynedd (bilingual), 1983; (ed jtly) Castles in Wales and the Marches, 1987; various guide books to Welsh castles; contribs to Brit. and foreign jls. *Recreations:* astronomy, gardening, visiting ruins. *Address:* Datchet House, Station Road, Raglan, Monmouthshire NP15 2EP. *Died 2 Aug. 2006.*

AVONSIDE, Lady; Janet Sutherland Shearer, OBE 1958; Scottish Governor, BBC, 1971–76; *b* 31 May 1917; *d* of William Murray, MB, ChB, and Janet Harley Watson; *m* 1954, Ian Hamilton Shearer, later Hon. Lord Avonside, PC (*d* 1996). *Educ:* St Columba's Sch., Kilmacolm; Erlenhaus, Baden Baden; Univ. of Edinburgh. LLB, Dip. of Social Science. Asst Labour Officer (Scot.), Min. of Supply, 1941–45; Sec. (Scot.),

King George's Fund for Sailors, 1945–53; Hon. Sec. (Scot.), Federal Union and United Europe, 1945–64; Scottish Delegate: Congress of Europe, 1947; Council of Europe, Strasburg, 1949. Contested (C), elections: Maryhill, Glasgow, 1950; Dundee East, 1951; Leith, 1955. Lectr in Social Studies, Dept of Educational Studies, Univ. of Edinburgh, 1962–70. Governor, Queen Margaret Coll., Edinburgh, 1986–89. *Recreation:* gardening. *Address:* 4A Dirleton Avenue, North Berwick, East Lothian EH39 4AY. *Clubs:* Caledonian (Associate Mem.); New (Edinburgh). *Died 15 Feb. 2008.*

AWDRY, Daniel (Edmund), TD; DL; *b* 10 Sept. 1924; *s* of late Col Edmund Portman Awdry, MC, TD, DL, Coters, Chippenham, Wilts, and Mrs Evelyn Daphne Alexandra Awdry, JP (formerly French); *m* 1950, Elizabeth Cattley (*d* 2007); three *d. Educ:* Winchester Coll. RAC, OCTU, Sandhurst, 1943–44 (Belt of Honour). Served with 10th Hussars as Lieut, Italy, 1944–45; ADC to GOC 56th London Div., Italy, 1945; Royal Wilts Yeo., 1947–62, Major and Sqdn Comdr, 1955–62. Qualified Solicitor, 1950. Mayor of Chippenham, 1958–59; Pres., Southern Boroughs Assoc., 1959–60. MP (C) Chippenham, Wilts, Nov. 1962–1979; PPS to Minister of State, Board of Trade, Jan.–Oct. 1964; PPS to Solicitor-Gen., 1973–74. Director: BET Omnibus Services, 1966–80; Sheepbridge Engineering, 1968–79; Rediffusion Ltd, 1973–85; Colonial Mutual Life Assurance Ltd, 1974–89. DL Wilts, 1979. *Recreation:* chess. *Address:* Old Manor, Beanacre, near Melksham, Wilts SN12 7PT. *T:* (01225) 702315. *Died 11 Oct. 2008.*

AXFORD, Sir (William) Ian, Kt 1996; PhD; FRS 1986; Director, Max Planck Institut für Aeronomie, Katlenburg-Lindau, Germany, 1974–82 and 1985–2001, then Emeritus; *b* 2 Jan. 1933; *s* of John Edgar Axford and May Victoria Axford; *m* 1955, Catherine Joy; two *s* two *d. Educ:* Univ. of Canterbury, NZ (MSc Hons, ME Dist.); Univ. of Manchester (PhD); Univ. of Cambridge. NZ Defence Science Corps, 1957–63; seconded to Defence Res. Bd, Ottawa, 1960–62; Associate Prof. of Astronomy, 1963–66, Prof. of Astronomy, 1966–67, Cornell Univ., Ithaca, NY; Prof. of Physics and Applied Physics, Univ. of Calif at San Diego, 1967–74; Vice-Chancellor, Victoria Univ. of Wellington, NZ, 1982–85. Pres., COSPAR, 1986–94; Vice-Pres., Scientific Cttee on Solar-Terrestrial Physics, 1986–90. Hon. Prof., Göttingen Univ., 1978; Regents Prof., Univ. of Calif., Riverside, 2003; Pei-Ling Chan Prof. of Physics, Univ. of Alabama, 2002–04; Adjunct Prof., Auckland Univ. of Technology, 2004–. Appleton Meml Lectr, URSI, 1969. Chm. Bd, NZ Foundn for Res., Sci. and Technol., 1992–95. Chm., Marsden Fund, 1994–98. Pres., European Geophysical Soc., 1990–92 (Hon. Mem., 1996); Vice Pres., Asia Oceania Geoscis Soc., 2004–05 (First Hon. Mem., 2006). Fellow, Amer. Geophysical Union, 1971; ARAS 1981; For. Associate, US Nat. Acad. of Scis, 1983; Member: Internat. Acad. of Astronautics, 1985; Academia Europaea, 1989. Hon. FRSNZ 1993. Hon. DSc: Canterbury, 1996; Victoria Univ. of Wellington, 1999. Space Science Award, AIAA, 1970; John Adam Fleming Medal, Amer. Geophysical Union, 1972; Tsiolkovsky Medal, Kosmonautical Fedn, USSR, 1987; Chapman Medal, RAS, 1994; NZ Sci. and Technol. Gold Medal, 1994; NZ Scientist of the Year, New Zealander of the Year, We Care Foundn, 1995. Freedom, City of Napier, NZ, 1999. *Publications:* In Soso's Web (with T. K. Breus), 2004; about 300 articles in scientific jls on aspects of space physics and astrophysics. *Address:* 2 Gladstone Road, Napier, New Zealand. *T:* (6) 8352188, *Fax:* (6) 8352176. *Died 13 March 2010.*

AYKROYD, Sir Michael David, 4th Bt *cr* 1920, of Lightcliffe, Yorks; *b* 14 June 1928; *s* of George Hammond Aykroyd, TD, and Margaret (*née* Aykroyd); *S* cousin, 2007; *m* 1952, Gillian, *o d* of Donald George Cowling, MBE; one *s* three *d. Educ:* USA. *Recreation:* shooting. *Heir:* *s* Henry Robert George Aykroyd [*b* 4 April 1954; *m* 1975, Lucy Merlin Brown; two *s* three *d* (incl. twin *d*)]. *Address:*

The Homestead, Killinghall, Harrogate, N Yorks HG3 2BQ. *T*: (01423) 506437; *e-mail*: michael.aykroyd@ ruralmail.net. *Died 21 March 2010.*

AYKROYD, Sir William Miles, 3rd Bt *cr* 1920; MC 1944; *b* 24 Aug. 1923; *s* of Sir Alfred Hammond Aykroyd, 2nd Bt, and Sylvia Ambler Aykroyd (*née* Walker) (*d* 1992), *widow* of Lieut-Col Foster Newton Thorne; S father, 1965. *Educ*: Charterhouse. Served in 5th Royal Inniskilling Dragoon Guards, Lieut, 1943–47. Dir, Hardy Amies Ltd, 1950–69. *Heir: cousin* Michael David Aykroyd [*b* 14 June 1928; *m* 1952, Oenone Gillian Diana, *o d* of Donald George Cowling, MBE; one *s* three *d*]. *Address*: Buckland Newton Place, Dorchester, Dorset DT2 7BX. *T*: (01300) 345259. *Club*: Boodle's. *Died 18 July 2007.*

AYLESFORD, 11th Earl of, *cr* 1714; **Charles Ian Finch-Knightley;** JP; Baron Guernsey, 1703; Lord-Lieutenant of West Midlands, 1974–93; *b* 2 Nov. 1918; *er s* of 10th Earl of Aylesford; S father, 1958; *m* 1946, Margaret Rosemary Tyer (*d* 1989); one *s* one *d* (and one *d* decd). *Educ*: Oundle. Lieut RSF, 1939; Captain Black Watch, 1947. Regional Dir, Birmingham and W Midlands Bd, Lloyds Bank, 1982–88. Mem., Water Space Amenity Commn, 1973–83. County Comr for Scouts, 1949–74, Patron 1974–. JP 1948, DL 1954, Vice-Lieutenant 1964–74, Warwicks. KStJ 1974. Hon. LLD Birmingham, 1989. *Recreation*: wild life and nature conservation. *Heir: s* Lord Guernsey, *b* 27 March 1947. *Address*: Packington Old Hall, Coventry, West Midlands CV7 7HG. *T*: (01676) 523273, (office) (01676) 523467. *Club*: Warwickshire CC (President, 1980–99). *Died 19 Feb. 2008.*

AYLING, Peter William, OBE 1989; BSc, CEng, FRINA; Secretary, Royal Institution of Naval Architects, 1967–89; *b* 25 Sept. 1925; *s* of late William Frank and Edith Louise Ayling; *m* 1949, Sheila Bargery; two *s* two *d*. *Educ*: Royal Dockyard Sch., Portsmouth; King's Coll., Univ. of Durham (BSc). Shipwright apprentice, HM Dockyard, Portsmouth, 1942–47; King's Coll., Univ. of Durham, 1947–50; Research and Principal Research Officer, British Ship Research Assoc., London, 1950–65; Principal Scientific Officer, Ship Div., Nat. Physical Laboratory, Feltham, 1965–67. *Publications*: papers on ship strength and vibration, Trans RINA, NECInst and IESS. *Recreations*: music, gardening, walking, motoring. *Address*: Oakmead, School Road, Camelsdale, Haslemere, Surrey GU27 3RN. *T*: (01428) 644474. *Died 8 July 2010.*

AYLMER, 13th Baron *cr* 1718; **Michael Anthony Aylmer;** Bt 1662; *b* 27 March 1923; *s* of Christopher Aylmer (*d* 1955) and Marjorie (*d* 1981), *d* of Percival Ellison Barber, surgeon, Sheffield; S cousin, 1982; *m* 1950, Countess Maddalena Sofia, *d* of late Count Arbeno Attems, Aiello del Friuli, Italy; one *s* one *d*. *Educ*: privately and Trinity Hall, Cambridge (Exhibnr, MA, LLM). Admitted a solicitor, 1948. Employed in Legal Dept of Equity & Law Life Assurance Society plc, 1951 until retirement, 1983. *Recreations*: reading, music. *Heir: s* Hon. (Anthony) Julian Aylmer [*b* 10 Dec. 1951; *m* 1990, Belinda Rosemary, *d* of Maj. Peter Parker; one *s* one *d*]. *Address*: Dovecot House, Jesse's Lane, Long Crendon, Bucks HP18 9AG. *T*: (01844) 208464. *Died 2 Aug. 2006.*

B

BABINGTON, His Honour Robert John, DSC 1943; QC (NI) 1965; appointed County Court Judge for Fermanagh and Tyrone, 1978; *b* 9 April 1920; *s* of David Louis James Babington and Alice Marie (*née* McClintock); *m* 1952, Elizabeth Bryanna Marguerite Alton (*d* 2000), *d* of Dr E. H. Alton, Provost of Trinity College, Dublin; two *s* one *d. Educ:* St Columba's Coll., Rathfarnham, Dublin; Trinity Coll., Dublin (BA). Called to the Bar, Inn of Court of NI, 1947. MP (U) North Down, Stormont, 1968–72. *Recreations:* golf, bird-watching. *Address:* c/o Royal Courts of Justice, Chichester Street, Belfast BT1 3JF. *Club:* Royal Belfast Golf.   *Died 17 Sept. 2010.*

BACKETT, Prof. (Edward) Maurice; Foundation Professor of Community Health, University of Nottingham, 1969–81, then Professor Emeritus; *b* 12 Jan. 1916; *o s* of late Frederick and Louisa Backett; *m* 1940, Shirley Paul-Thompson (*d* 2003); one *s* two *d. Educ:* University Coll., London; Westminster Hospital. Operational Research with RAF; Nuffield Fellow in Social Medicine; Research Worker, Medical Research Council; Lecturer, Queen's Univ., Belfast; Senior Lecturer, Guy's Hospital and London Sch. of Hygiene and Tropical Medicine; Prof. and Head of Dept of Public Health and Social Medicine, Univ. of Aberdeen, 1958–69. Hon. Member: Internat. Epidemiol Assoc., 1984; Soc. for Social Medicine, 1986. *Publications:* The Risk Approach to Health Care, 1984; papers in scientific journals. *Address:* Harvey Cottage, Fore Street, Totnes, Devon TQ9 5NJ. *T:* (01803) 865241; *e-mail:* c/o james.cowie@btinternet.com.   *Died 2 Dec. 2009.*

BACKHOUSE, Sir Jonathan Roger, 4th Bt *cr* 1901; formerly Managing Director, W. H. Freeman & Co. Ltd, Publishers; *b* 30 Dec. 1939; *s* of Major Sir John Edmund Backhouse, 3rd Bt, MC, and Jean Marie Frances, *d* of Lieut-Col G. R. V. Hume-Gore, MC, The Gordon Highlanders; *S* father, 1944; *m* 1997, Sarah Ann, *o d* of James Stott, Cromer, Norfolk; one *s* one *d. Educ:* Oxford. *Heir: s* Alfred James Stott Backhouse, *b* 7 April 2002.
       Died 15 Nov. 2007.

BADDILEY, Prof. Sir James, Kt 1977; PhD, DSc, ScD; FRS 1961; FRSE 1962; Professor of Chemical Microbiology, 1977–83, then Emeritus, and Director, Microbiological Chemistry Research Laboratory, 1975–83, University of Newcastle upon Tyne; SERC Senior Research Fellow, and Fellow of Pembroke College, University of Cambridge, 1981–85, then Emeritus; *b* 15 May 1918; *s* of late James Baddiley and Ivy Logan Cato; *m* 1944, Hazel Mary (*d* 2007), *yr d* of Wesley Wilfrid Townsend and Ann Rayner Townsend (*née* Kilner); one *s. Educ:* Manchester Grammar Sch.; Manchester University (BSc (1st Class Hons., Chem.) 1941, PhD 1944, DSc 1953; Sir Clement Royds Meml Schol., 1942, Beyer Fellow, 1943–44); MA 1981, ScD 1986, Cantab. Imperial Chemical Industries Fellow, Pembroke Coll., Cambridge, 1945–49; Swedish Medical Research Council Fellow, Wenner-Grens Institute for Cell Biology, Stockholm, 1947–49; Mem. of Staff, Dept of Biochemistry, Lister Institute of Preventive Medicine, London, 1949–55; Rockefeller Fellowship, Mass Gen. Hosp., Harvard Med. Sch., 1954; Prof. of Organic Chem., King's Coll., Univ. of Durham, 1954–77 (later Univ. of Newcastle upon Tyne); Head of Sch. of Chemistry, Newcastle upon Tyne Univ., 1968–78. Member: Council, Chemical Soc., 1962–65; Cttee, Biochemical Soc., 1964–67; Council, Soc. of Gen. Microbiol., 1973–75; Council, SERC (formerly SRC), 1979–81 (Mem., Enzyme Chem. and Technol Cttee, 1972–75; Biol Scis Cttee, 1976–79; Mem., Science Bd, 1979–81); Council, Royal Soc., 1977–79; Adv. Cttee, CIBA (later CIBA-GEIGY) Fellowships, 1966–88; Editorial Boards, Biochemical Preparations, 1960–70, Biochimica et Biophysica Acta, 1970–77, Cambridge Studies in Biotechnology, 1985–. Trustee, EPA Cephalosporin Fund, 1979–2004; Patron, Alzheimer's Res. Trust, 1993–. Karl Folkers Vis. Prof. in Biochem., Illinois Univ., 1962; Tilden Lectr, Chem. Soc., 1959; Special Vis. Lectr, Dept of Microbiology, Temple Univ., Pa, 1966; Leeuwenhoek Lectr, Royal Society, 1967; Pedler Lectr, Chem. Soc., 1978; Endowment Lectr, Bose Inst., Calcutta, 1980. Founder Mem., Interdisciplinary Cttee, Consejo Cultural Mundial. Hon. Mem., Amer. Soc. Biochem. and Molecular Biol. Hon. DSc Heriot Watt, 1979; Bath, 1986. Meldola Medal, RIC, 1947; Corday-Morgan Medal, Chem. Soc., 1952; Davy Medal, Royal Soc., 1974. Responsible for first chemical synthesis (structure definitive) of ADP and ATP; discovery of teichoic acids in bacterial cell walls and membranes. *Publications:* numerous contribs on chemistry and biochemistry of co-enzymes, bacterial cell walls and membranes in Journal of the Chemical Society, Nature, Biochemical Journal, etc; articles in various microbiological and biochemical reviews. *Recreations:* mountaineering, swimming, photography, music, fine arts. *Address:* 21 Grange Court, Pinehurst, Grange Road, Cambridge CB3 9BD; Department of Biochemistry, University of Cambridge, Tennis Court Road, Cambridge CB2 1QW. *T:* (01223) 333600.   *Died 19 Nov. 2008.*

BADEN, (Edwin) John, CA; Director, 1987–98, and Deputy Chairman, 1989–90 and 1996–98, Girobank plc; *b* 18 Aug. 1928; *s* of Percy Baden and Jacoba (*née* de Blank); *m* 1952, Christine Irene (*née* Grose) (*d* 2003); one *s* three *d* (and one *s* decd). *Educ:* Winchester Coll.; Corpus Christi Coll., Cambridge (MA Econ and Law). Audit Clerk, Deloitte Haskins & Sells, CA, 1951–54; Financial Dir/Co. Sec., H. Parrot & Co., Wine Importer, 1954–61; Dir of various subsids, C & A Modes, 1961–63; a Man. Dir, Samuel Montagu & Co. Ltd, 1963–78; Man. Dir Chief Exec., Italian International Bank Plc, 1978–89; Girobank: Chief Exec., 1989–91; Man. Dir, 1990–91; Chm., 1995–96. Dir, 1990–98, Dep. Chm., 1997–98, Alliance & Leicester Building Soc., then Alliance & Leicester PLC (Chm., Gp Credit Policy Cttee, 1998–2001). Member, Management Committee: Pan European Property Unit Trust, 1973–2001; N American Property Unit Trust, 1975–93 (Chm., 1980–93). Sec. Gen., Eurogiro (formerly European Post/Giro Dirs Gp), 1993–97 (Chm., 1990–92); Mem., EU Payment Systems Technical Develt Gp, 1990–97. Institute of Chartered Accountants of Scotland: Mem., Council, 1984–90; Mem., Res. Cttee, 1966–74, 1985–88, 1991–95. Trustee, Internat. Centre for Res. in Accounting, Univ. of Lancaster, 1975–96. Mem., Review Panel, Financial Reporting Council, 1990–95. Chm., Stammerham Amenity Assoc., 1998–2001; Dir, Rosebery Housing Assoc., 1999–2005. Liveryman, Co. of Information Technologists, 1992–. Cavaliere Ufficiale, Order of Merit, Italian Republic, 1986. *Publications:* (contrib.): Making Corporate Reports Valuable, 1988; Auditing into the 21st Century, 1993; Post Giro Banking in Europe, 1993; Internal Control and Financial Reporting, 1994; articles in professional magazines. *Recreations:* reading, sailing, shooting. *Address:* Lanaways Barn, Two Mile Ash, Horsham, W Sussex RH13 0LA. *T:* (01403) 733834, *Fax:* (01403) 732860.   *Died 13 May 2010.*

BADEN-POWELL, Lady; Patience Hélène Mary Baden-Powell, CBE 1986; DL; Vice President, The Girl Guides Association, 1990–2000; President, Commonwealth Youth Exchange Council, 1982–86; *b* 27 Oct. 1936; *d* of Mr and Mrs D. M. Batty, Zimbabwe; *m* 1963, 3rd Baron Baden-Powell. *Educ:* St Peter's Diocesan Sch., Bulawayo. Internat. Comr, 1975–79, Chief Comr, 1980–85, Girl Guides Assoc. Director: Laurentian

Financial Gp, 1981–94; Fieldguard Ltd, 1986–. President: Nat. Playbus Assoc., 1979–2004; Surrey Council for Voluntary Youth Services, 1986–; Woodlarks Camp Site for the Disabled, 2006– (Patron, 1978–2005); Patron: Surrey Antiques Fair, 1969–2003; E Africa Women's League UK, 2005–; Walton Firs Campsite and Activity Centre, 2006–. DL Surrey, 2004. *Address:* Weston Farmhouse, The Street, Albury, Surrey GU5 9AY. *T:* (01483) 205087. *Died 18 Dec. 2010.*

BAILEY, Sir Derrick Thomas Louis, 3rd Bt *cr* 1919; DFC; *b* 15 Aug. 1918; *s* of Sir Abe Bailey, 1st Bt, KCMG and Hon. Dame Mary Bailey (*née* Westenra) (DBE 1930), *o d* of 5th Baron Rossmore; *S* half-brother, 1946; *m* 1st, 1946, Katharine Nancy Stormonth Darling (marr. diss.; she *d* 1998); four *s* one *d*; 2nd, 1980, Mrs Jean Roscoe (marr. diss. 1990; she *d* 1996). *Educ:* Winchester. Capt., SAAF. Formerly engaged in farming, Hereford. Founded Aurigny Air Services, 1968. *Recreations:* all sports, all games. *Heir: s* John Richard Bailey [*b* 11 June 1947; *m* 1977, Jane, *o d* of John Pearson Gregory; two *s* one *d*]. *Address:* Bluestones, Alderney, CI GY99 9ZZ. *Club:* Rand (Johannesburg). *Died 19 June 2009.*

BAILEY, Air Vice-Marshal Dudley Graham, CB 1979; CBE 1970; RAF, 1943–80, retired; Deputy Managing Director, The Services Sound and Vision Corporation (formerly Services Kinema Corporation), 1980–93; Chairman, SSVC Pension Fund, 1993–99; *b* 12 Sept. 1924; *s* of P. J. Bailey and D. M. Bailey (*née* Taylor); *m* 1948, Dorothy Barbara Lovelace-Hunt; two *d*. *Educ:* Christ's Coll., Finchley; Teignmouth Grammar Sch. Pilot trng, Canada, 1943–45; Intell. Officer, Air HQ Italy, 1946–47 and HQ 23 Gp, 1948–49; Berlin Airlift, 1949; Flt Comdr No 50 and 61 Sqdns, Lincolns, 1950–52; exchange duties, USAF, B-36 aircraft, California, 1952–54; Canberra Sqdn: Flt Comdr, 1955; Sqdn Comdr, 1956; Air Min., 1956–58; Army Staff Coll., Camberley, 1959; OC No 57 (Victor) Sqdn, 1960–62; Air Warfare course, Manby, 1962; Wing Comdr Ops, HQ Air Forces Middle East, 1963–65; MoD Central Staffs, 1965–66; MoD (Air) Directorate of Air Staff Plans, 1966–68; OC RAF Wildenrath, 1968–70; Sen. Personnel Staff Officer, HQ Strike Comd, 1970–71; Royal Coll. of Defence Studies, 1972; Dir of Personnel (Air), RAF, 1972–74; SASO, RAF Germany, 1974–75; Dep. Comdr, RAF Germany, 1975–76; Dir Gen., Personal Services (RAF), MoD, 1976–80, retired. Chm., Central Council, 1990–99, Life Vice-Pres., 2000, RAFA. Gov., Piper's Corner Sch., Gt Kingshill, Bucks, 1991– (Chm., 2006–). *Address:* Firs Corner, Abbotswood, Speen, Bucks HP27 0SR. *T:* (01494) 488462. *Club:* Royal Air Force. *Died 1 Nov. 2006.*

BAILEY, Rt Rev. Jonathan Sansbury, KCVO 2005; Bishop of Derby, 1995–2005; Clerk of the Closet to the Queen, 1996–2005; Hon. Assistant Bishop, Diocese of Gloucester, since 2005; *b* 24 Feb. 1940; *s* of late Walter Eric and of Audrey Sansbury Bailey; *m* 1965, Rev. Susan Mary Bennett-Jones; three *s*. *Educ:* Quarry Bank High School, Liverpool; Trinity College, Cambridge (MA). Assistant Curate: Sutton, St Helens, Lancs, 1965–68; St Paul, Warrington, 1968–71; Warden, Marrick Priory, 1971–76; Vicar of Wetherby, Yorks, 1976–82; Archdeacon of Southend and Bishop's Officer for Industry and Commerce, dio. of Chelmsford, 1982–92; Suffragan Bishop of Dunwich, 1992–95. Chm., Churches Main Cttee, 2002–05. Entered H of L, 1999. DUniv Derby, 2006. *Recreations:* theatre, music, carpentry. *Address:* 28 Burleigh Way, Wickwar, Wotton-under-Edge, Glos GL12 8LR. *T:* (01454) 294112; *e-mail:* jonathan.s.bailey@gmail.com. *Died 9 Dec. 2008.*

BAILEY, Ronald William, CMG 1961; HM Diplomatic Service, retired; *b* 14 June 1917; *o s* of William Staveley Bailey and May Eveline (*née* Cudlipp), Southampton; *m* 1946, Joan Hassall (*d* 2001), *d* of late A. E. Gray, JP, Stoke-on-Trent; one *s* one *d*. *Educ:* King Edward VI Sch., Southampton; Trinity Hall, Cambridge (Wootton Isaacson Scholar in Spanish). Probationer Vice-Consul, Beirut, 1939–41; HM Vice-Consul,

Alexandria, 1941–45; Asst Oriental Sec., British Embassy, Cairo, 1945–48; 1st Sec., Foreign Office, 1948–49; British Legation, Beirut, 1949–52 (acted as Chargé d'Affaires, 1949, 1950 and 1951); British Embassy, Washington, 1952–55; Counsellor, Washington, 1955–57; Khartoum, 1957–60 (acted as Chargé d'Affaires in each of these years); Chargé d'Affaires, Taiz, 1960–62; Consul-Gen., Gothenburg, 1963–65; Minister, British Embassy, Baghdad, 1965–67; Ambassador to Bolivia, 1967–71; Ambassador to Morocco, 1971–75. Mem. Council, Anglo-Arab Assoc., 1978–85. Vice-Pres., 1975–87, Pres., 1987–89, Hon. Vice-Pres., 1989–2001, Soc. for Protection of Animals Abroad; Chm., Black Down Cttee, Nat. Trust, 1982–87; Founder, 1975, Hon. Pres., 1989–98, British-Moroccan Soc. *Publications:* (ed) Records of Oman 1867–1960 (12 vols), 1989–92. *Recreation:* music. *Address:* The Lodge, 22 Spicer Road, Exeter EX1 1SY. *T:* (01392) 494943. *Died 14 May 2010.*

BAILEY, Sir Stanley (Ernest), Kt 1986; CBE 1980; QPM 1975; DL; security consultant; *b* 30 Sept. 1926; *m* 1st, 1954, Marguerita Dorothea Whitbread (*d* 1997); 2nd, 1998, Maureen Shinwell. Joined Metropolitan Police, 1947; Asst Chief Constable, Staffs, 1966; Dir, Police Res., Home Office, 1970–72; Dep. Chief Constable, Staffs, 1973–75; Chief Constable, Northumbria, 1975–91; Regl Police Comdr, No 1 Home Defence Reg., 1981–91. Mem., IACP, 1970 (Chairman: Adv. Cttee on Internat. Policy, 1984–89; Europ. Sub-Cttee, 1984–89; Mem. Exec. Cttee, 1986–91; Life Mem., 1999); Rep., ICPO, 1986–88. Pres., ACPO, England, Wales & NI, 1985–86 (Vice-Pres., 1984–85; Immediate Past Pres., 1986–87; Chm., Crime Prevention Sub-cttee, 1986–91); Vice Pres., Police Mutual Assce Soc., 1986–94. Chairman: Cttee on Burglar Alarms, BSI, 1975–93; Cttee on Security Standards, BSI, 1976–93; Founder and Chm., 1st Internat. Police Exhibn and Conf., London, 1987; Founder and Jt Chm., Centre for Res. into Crime, Community and Policing, Univ. of Newcastle upon Tyne, 1989–92; Vice Chm., Crime Concern, 1989–93 (Mem., Adv. Bd, 1988–94); Member: Home Office Standing Conf. on Crime Prevention, 1977–91; Bd, Northumbria Coalition Against Crime, 1989–92; Chm. of cttees and working parties on crime prevention, intruder alarms, criminal intelligence, computer privacy, and physical stress in police work. Pres., Security Systems and Alarms Inspection Bd, 1995–. Observer, VIII UN Congress on Crime Prevention, Havana, 1990 (Organiser and Chm., First UN Meeting of Sen. Police Officials). Police Advr, AMA, 1987–91. President: Security Services Assoc., 1991–95; Ex Police in Commerce, 1998–2005 (Vice Pres., 1992–98). Presented papers etc in USA, Denmark, France, Hong Kong, NZ, Japan, Germany, Spain, Thailand, China, Holland, Portugal, Italy, Belgium and USSR on community crime prevention, measurement of effectiveness, and Private Security industry. Mem., NEI Associates, USA, 1984–. Trustee, Suzy Lamplugh Trust, 1991–93. Patron, Assoc. of Security Consultants, 1992–. Mem., Bd of Govs, Internat. Inst. of Security, 1990–99 (Hon. Fellow, 1991). Grad., Nat. Exec. Inst., FBI Washington, 1984. Freeman, City of London, 1988. CCMI (CBIM 1987). DL Tyne and Wear, 1986. ABIS—Ken Bolton Award for outstanding contribution to crime prevention, 1990. OStJ 1981. *Publications:* (jtly) Community Policing and Crime Prevention in America and England, 1993; articles in learned jls on policy issues. *Recreations:* gardening, travel. *Died 10 Aug. 2008.*

BAILLIE, Alastair Turner; HM Diplomatic Service, retired; Deputy High Commissioner in Calcutta, 1987–91; *b* 24 Dec. 1932; *s* of late Archibald Turner Baillie and Margaret Pinkerton Baillie; *m* 1st, 1965, Wilma Noreen Armstrong (marr. diss. 1974); one *s*; 2nd, 1977, Irena Maria Gregor; one step *s* one step *d*. *Educ:* Dame Allan's Sch., Newcastle upon Tyne; Christ's Coll., Cambridge (BA). National Service, commissioned Queen's Own Cameron Highlanders, 1951–53. HMOCS: North Borneo, subseq. Sabah, Malaysia,

1957–67; joined HM Diplomatic Service, 1967; FCO, 1967–73; Consul (Commercial), Karachi, 1973–77; First Sec. and Head of Chancery, Manila, 1977–80; Counsellor, Addis Ababa, 1980–81; Counsellor (Commercial), Caracas, 1981–83; Governor of Anguilla, 1983–87. *Recreations:* sport, reading, travelling. *Died 18 Nov. 2009.*

BAILLIE, Ian Fowler, CMG 1966; OBE 1962; Director, The Thistle Foundation, Edinburgh, 1970–81; *b* 16 Feb. 1921; *s* of late Very Rev. John Baillie, CH, DLitt, DD, LLD and Florence Jewel (*née* Fowler); *m* 1951, Sheila Barbour (*née* Mathewson); two *s* one *d*. *Educ:* Edinburgh Acad.; Corpus Christi Coll., Oxford (MA). War service, British and Indian Armies, 1941–46. HM Overseas Civil Service (formerly Colonial Service), 1946–66: Admin. Officer (District Comr), Gold Coast, 1946–54; Registrar of Co-operative Socs and Chief Marketing Officer, Aden, 1955; Protectorate Financial Sec., Aden, 1959; Dep. British Agent, Aden, 1962; Brit. Agent and Asst High Comr, Aden, 1963; Dir, Aden Airways 1959–66; Sen. Research Associate and Administrative Officer, Agricultural Adjustment Unit, Dept of Agricultural Economics, Univ. of Newcastle upon Tyne, 1966–69. *Publications:* (ed with S. J. Sheehy) Irish Agriculture in a Changing World, 1971. *Recreation:* angling. *Address:* Flat 4, 61 Grange Loan, Edinburgh EH9 2EG. *T:* (0131) 667 2647. *Died 29 Nov. 2008.*

BAIN, John Taylor, CBE 1975; Director of Education, Glasgow, 1968–75; Lay Observer (Solicitors Act) in Scotland, 1977–83; *b* 9 May 1912; *m* 1941, Anne Nicoll Dewar; one *s* two *d*. *Educ:* St Andrews Univ. (BSc, MA); Edinburgh Univ. (BEd). War Service, RAF (Technical Br.). Entered educational administration in 1947. JP Glasgow, 1971. *Died 2 March 2006.*

BAINBRIDGE, Dame Beryl, DBE 2000; FRSL; actress, writer; *b* 21 Nov. 1934; *d* of Richard Bainbridge and Winifred Baines; *m* 1954, Austin Davies (marr. diss.); one *s* one *d*; and one *d* by Alan Sharp. *Educ:* Merchant Taylors' Sch., Liverpool; Arts Educational Schools, Ltd, Tring. Weekly columnist, Evening Standard, 1987–93. FRSL 1978; Fellow, Hunterian Soc., 1997. Hon. LittD Liverpool, 1986. (Jtly) David Cohen Prize, Arts Council, 2003. *Plays:* Tiptoe Through the Tulips, 1976; The Warrior's Return, 1977; It's a Lovely Day Tomorrow, 1977; Journal of Bridget Hitler, 1981; Somewhere More Central (TV), 1981; Evensong (TV), 1986. *Publications:* A Weekend with Claud, 1967, rev. edn 1981; Another Part of the Wood, 1968, rev. edn 1979; Harriet Said..., 1972; The Dressmaker, 1973 (film, 1989); The Bottle Factory Outing, 1974 (Guardian Fiction Award); Sweet William, 1975 (film, 1980); A Quiet Life, 1976, repr. 1999; Injury Time, 1977 (Whitbread Award); Young Adolf, 1978; Winter Garden, 1980; English Journey, 1984 (TV series, 1984); Watson's Apology, 1984; Mum and Mr Armitage, 1985; Forever England, 1986 (TV series, 1986); Filthy Lucre, 1986; An Awfully Big Adventure, 1989 (staged, 1992; filmed, 1995); The Birthday Boys, 1991; Something Happened Yesterday (essays), 1993; Every Man for Himself, 1996 (Whitbread Award); Master Georgie, 1998 (James Tait Black Meml Prize, W. H. Smith Award); According to Queeney, 2001; Front Row, 2005. *Recreations:* painting, sleeping. *Address:* 42 Albert Street, NW1 7NU. *T:* (020) 7387 3113. *Died 2 July 2010.*

BAINS, Malcolm Arnold; JP, DL; Clerk of the Kent County Council and Clerk to the Lieutenancy of Kent, 1970–74; *b* 12 Sept. 1921; *s* of Herbert Bains, Newcastle-upon-Tyne; *m* 1st, 1942, Winifred Agnes Davies (marr. diss. 1961); three *s*; 2nd, 1968, Margaret Hunter. *Educ:* Hymers Coll.; Durham Univ. (LLB (Hons)); Solicitor. Commnd as Pilot in RAF, 1941–46. Solicitor with Taunton and Sunderland and with Notts and Hants County Councils, 1946–55; Dep. Clerk of Hants CC and Dep. Clerk of the Peace, 1955–60; Dep. Clerk of Kent CC, 1960–70; Chm., Working Group which advised Sec. of State for Envmt on future management of Local Authorities, 1971–73. Fellow, ANU and Advr to NSW Govt, 1977–78; Chm., Local Govt Review Bd of Victoria, 1978–79; Head of Norfolk Island Public Service, 1979–82. FRSA 1976. DL Kent 1976; JP Norfolk Is, 1980. *Publications:* The Bains Report, 1973; Management Reform in English Local Government, 1978; Local Government in NSW, 1980. *Recreations:* swimming, travel. *Address:* PO Box 244, Norfolk Island, via NSW 2899, Australia. *Died 17 Sept. 2006.*

BAIRD, Lt-Gen. Sir James (Parlane), KBE 1973; MD, FRCP, FRCPE; Medical Adviser, National Advice Centre for Postgraduate Education, 1977–84; *b* 12 May 1915; *s* of Rev. David Baird and Sara Kathleen Black; *m* 1948, Anne Patricia Anderson (*d* 2007); one *s* one *d*. *Educ:* Bathgate Academy; Univ. of Edinburgh; MD 1958. FRCPE 1952, FRCP 1959. Commissioned, RAMC, 1939; Lt-Col 1956; Prof. of Military Medicine, Royal Army Medical Coll., 1965; Cons. Physician, BAOR, 1967; Dir of Medicine and Consulting Physician to the Army, 1969–71; Comdt and Dir of Studies, Royal Army Med. Coll., 1971 73; Dir Gen , Army Medical Services, 1973–77. QHP 1969. QHA (Pakistan), 1982. *Publications:* Tropical Diseases Supplement to Principles and Practice of Medicine, 1968; (contrib.) The Oxford Companion to Medicine, 1986. *Recreation:* golf. *Died 26 May 2007.*

BAIRD, Susan, CBE 1991; JP; Vice Lord-Lieutenant, City of Glasgow, since 1996; Member (Lab), City of Glasgow Council (formerly Glasgow District Council, then Glasgow City Council), since 1974; *b* 26 May 1940; *d* of Archie and Susan Reilly; *m* 1957, George Baird; three *s* one *d*. *Educ:* St Mark's Secondary School, Glasgow. Mem. Labour Party, 1969; City of Glasgow Council (formerly Glasgow District Council, then Glasgow City Council): Bailie of the City, 1980–84; Convener, Manpower Cttee, 1980–84; Vice-Convener: Parks and Recreation Cttee, 1984–88; Strathclyde Fire and Rescue, 2006–. Lord Provost and Lord-Lieutenant of Glasgow, 1988–92. JP 1977, DL 1992, Glasgow. DUniv Glasgow, 1990. St Mungo Prize, St Mungo Trust, 1991. OStJ. *Recreations:* reading, walking. *Address:* 138 Downfield Street, Parkhead, Glasgow G32 8RZ. *T:* (0141) 778 7641. *Died 24 Jan. 2009.*

BAKER, Anthony Castelli, LVO 1980; MBE 1975; HM Diplomatic Service, retired; *b* 27 Dec. 1921; *s* of late Alfred Guy Baker and Luciana (*née* Castelli). *Educ:* Merchant Taylors' Sch., Northwood, Middx. Served War: munitions worker, 1940–41; volunteered for RAFVR and served in UK, ME and Italy, 1941–46 (Flt Lieut). Joined HM Diplomatic Service, 1946; served in Rome and Paris, 1946–50; Third Sec., Prague, 1951; Hamburg, 1953; Vice-Consul, Milan, 1954; Third, later Second Sec., Athens, 1959; Second Sec., Beirut, 1963; First Sec., Cairo, 1965; Naples, 1968; Turin, 1970; First Sec. Commercial, Calcutta, 1972; Consul, Montreal, 1975; First Sec. Commercial, Port of Spain, 1976; Consul, Genoa, 1979–81. Officer, Order of Merit (Italy), 1980. *Recreations:* watching cricket, travelling, jazz music. *Address:* Flat 16, Mourne House, 11 Maresfield Gardens, NW3 5SL. *Clubs:* Royal Air Force, MCC; Gloucestershire CC. *Died 8 Feb. 2008.*

BAKER, Arthur John, CBE 1981; Principal, Brockenhurst Tertiary College (formerly Brockenhurst Grammar School, then Brockenhurst Sixth Form College), 1969–88, retired; *b* 29 Nov. 1928; *s* of Arthur Reginald and Ruth Baker; *m* 1st, 1953, June Henrietta Dunham (*d* 1996); one *s* two *d*; 2nd, 1997, Maeve Mary Walker. *Educ:* Southampton Univ. (BSc; DipEd). Mathematics Master, Hampton Grammar Sch., 1952–55; Dep. Head, Sunbury Grammar Sch., 1955–61; Headmaster, Christchurch Grammar Sch., 1961–69. *Recreations:* walking, gardening, travel. *Address:* Honey Cottage, Crescent Drive, Barton-on-Sea, Hants BH25 7HS. *T:* (01425) 629049. *Died 3 March 2007.*

BAKER, Cecil John; Director, Alliance & Leicester Building Society (formerly Alliance Building Society), 1970–92 (Chairman, 1981–91); *b* 2 Sept. 1915; *s* of late

Frederick William Baker and Mildred Beatrice Palmer; *m* 1st, 1942, Kathleen Cecilia Henning (marr. diss. 1965); one *s*; 2nd, 1971, Joan Beatrice Barnes; one *d*. *Educ:* Whitgift Sch.; LSE (LLB 1939; BSc(Econ) 1949); Inst. of Actuaries. FIA 1948; ACII 1937. Sec., Insurance Inst. of London, 1945–49; Investment Manager, London Assurance, 1950–64; Investment Consultant, Hambros Bank Ltd, 1964–74; Chairman: Pension Fund Property Unit Trust, 1966–87; Charities Property Unit Trust, 1967–87; Agricl Property Unit Trust for Pension Funds and Charities, 1976–87; Victory Insurance Holdings Ltd, 1979–85; British American Property Unit Trust, 1982–87; United Real Property Trust plc, 1983–86 (Dir, 1982–86); Hunting Gate Group, 1980–90; Dir, Abbey Life Group plc, 1985–88. *Recreations:* golf, travel. *Address:* 3 Tennyson Court, 12 Dorset Square, NW1 6QB. *T:* (020) 7724 9716. *Died 15 April 2010.*

BAKER, Charles A.; *see* Arnold-Baker.

BAKER, Douglas Robert Pelham, FCA; Chairman: Portman Building Society, 1990–99; Hardy Oil and Gas plc, 1989–98; *b* 21 May 1929. With Touche Ross & Co., Chartered Accountants, 1945–47 and 1949–89 (Chm., 1984–88). Chm., Regency and W of England Building Soc. (merged with Portman Wessex Building Soc., 1990), 1988–90; Dir, Merrett Hldgs, 1988–94; Dep. Chm., London Internat. Gp, 1989–96. Royal Naval Service, 1947–49. Chm., Brighton HA, 1988–91. Treas., Univ. of Sussex, 1999–2002. *Address:* Hamsey Manor, Hamsey, E Sussex BN8 5TD. *Died 21 Jan. 2008.*

BAKER, Hon. Francis Edward N.; *see* Noel-Baker.

BAKER, His Honour Geoffrey; QC 1970; a Circuit Judge, 1978–95, a Deputy Circuit Judge, 1995–98; *b* 5 April 1925; *er s* of late Sidney and Cecilia Baker, Bradford; *m* 1948, Sheila (*née* Hill); two *s* one *d*. *Educ:* Bradford Grammar Sch.; Leeds Univ. (LLB (Hons)). Called to Bar, Inner Temple, 1947. Recorder: of Pontefract, 1967–71; of Sunderland, 1971; a Recorder of the Crown Court, 1972–78. Pres., Leeds and WR Medico-Legal Soc., 1984–85 (Mem. Cttee, 1980–94). Chm., Standing Cttee, Convocation of Leeds Univ., 1986–90 (Mem. 1980–); Member: Adv. Cttee on Law, Leeds Univ., 1983–; Court, Leeds Univ., 1984–88, 1996–98; Pres., Leeds Univ. Law Graduates' Assoc., 1981–2002. *Recreations:* gardening, painting, photography. *Address:* c/o Court Service, Symons House, Belgrave Street, Leeds LS2 8DD. *Died 31 July 2007.*

BAKER, Col James Henry, MBE 1999; Head of Conservation, Ministry of Defence, 1986–2003; *b* 15 Feb. 1938; *s* of late Lt-Col George Baker, TD, and Gwladys Joan Baker (*née* Russell), Dickhurst, Haslemere; *m* 1961, Lally Moss; one *s* one *d*. *Educ:* Harrow Sch. Commnd Irish Guards, 1957; served BAOR, Cyprus, Aden, Belize; ADC to Maj.-Gen. comdg Household Bde, 1965–67; CO, 1st Bn, Irish Guards, 1977–79; MA to QMG, 1979–81; Regtl Lt Col, Irish Guards, 1981–85. Standard Bearer, HM Body Guard of Hon. Corps of Gentlemen-at-Arms, 2003–08 (Harbinger, 2000–03). Commandeur, Order of Adolf-Nassau (Luxembourg), 1985. *Recreations:* fishing, shooting, archaeology. *Address:* Rovehurst, Chiddingfold, Surrey GU8 4SN. *T:* (01428) 644463. *Club:* MCC. *Died 16 Oct. 2009.*

BALCHIN, Prof. William George Victor, PhD; FKC; FRGS, FRMetS, FBCartS; Professor of Geography, University College of Swansea, University of Wales, 1954–78, then Professor Emeritus; *b* 20 June 1916; *s* of Victor Balchin and Ellen Winifred Gertrude Chapple; *m* 1939, Lily Kettlewood (*d* 1999); one *s* one *d* (and one *d* decd). *Educ:* Aldershot County High Sch. (State Scholar and County Major Scholar, 1934); St Catharine's Coll., Cambridge (1st Cl. Pt I Geographical Tripos, 1936; College Prize for Geography, 1936; BA 1937; MA 1941); King's Coll., London (PhD 1951; FKC 1984). FRGS 1937; FRMetS 1945; FBCartS 1996. Jun. Demonstrator in Geog., Univ. of Cambridge, 1937–39 (Geomorphologist on Spitsbergen Expedn, 1938);

Hydrographic Officer, Hydrographic Dept, Admiralty, 1939–45 (also part-time Lectr for Univ. of Bristol Regional Cttee on Educn and WEA Tutor and Lectr); Lectr in Geog., KCL, 1945–54 (Geomorphologist on US Sonora-Mohave Desert Expedn, 1952); University College of Swansea, University of Wales, Dept of Geog., 1954–78; Dean, Faculty of Pure and Applied Science, 1959–61; Vice-Principal, 1964–66 and 1970–73. Leverhulme Emeritus Fellow, 1982. Royal Geographical Society: Open Essay Prize, 1936; Gill Meml Award, 1954; Mem. Council, 1962–65, 1975–82, 1984–88; Chm., Educn Cttee, 1975–88; Vice-Pres., 1978–82; Chm., Ordnance Survey Cons. Cttee for Educn, 1983–92. Geographical Association: Hon. Annual Conf. Organiser, 1950–54; Mem. Council, 1950–81; Trustee, 1954–77; Pres., 1971; Hon. Mem., 1980. Pres., Section E (Geog.), BAAS, 1972. Member: Met. Res. Cttee, MoD, 1963–69; British Nat. Cttee for Cartography, 1961–71 and 1976–79, for Geography, 1964–70 and 1976–78; Council, British Geography, 1988–92. Treasurer, Second Land Utilisation Survey of Britain, 1961–; Chm., Land Decade Educnl Council, 1978–83. Mem., Nature Conservancy Cttee for Wales, 1959–68; Vice-Pres., Glam Co. Naturalists' Trust, 1961–80. Pres., Balchin Family Hist. Soc., 1993–. Member: Hydrology Cttee, ICE, 1962–76; Bradford Univ. Disaster Prevention and Limitation Unit, 1989–97. Member, Court of Governors: Nat. Mus. of Wales, 1966–74; Univ. of Wales Swansea (formerly UC of Swansea), 1980–; Mem. Council, St David's UC, 1968–80. *Publications:* (ed) Geography and Man (3 vols), 1947; (with A. W. Richards) Climatic and Weather Exercises, 1949; (with A. W. Richards) Practical and Experimental Geography, 1952; Cornwall (The Making of the English Landscape Series), 1954; (ed and contrib.) Geography: an outline for the intending student, 1970; (ed and contrib.) Swansea and its Region, 1971; (ed and contrib.) Living History of Britain, 1981; Concern for Geography, 1981; The Cornish Landscape, 1983; The Geographical Association: the first hundred years, 1993; (ed and contrib.) The Joint School Story, 1997; over 150 res. papers, articles and contribs on geomorphology, climatology, hydrology, econ. geography and cartography in learned jls. *Recreations:* travel, writing. *Address:* 10 Low Wood Rise, Ben Rhydding, Ilkley, West Yorks LS29 8AZ. *T:* (01943) 600768. *Clubs:* Royal Commonwealth Society (Life Fellow, 1978), Geographical. *Died 30 July 2007.*

BALCON, Dr Raphael, MD; FRCP, FACC; Consultant Cardiologist, Bart's and the London NHS Trust, retired; *b* 26 Aug. 1936; *s* of late Henry and Rhoda Balcon; *m* 1959, Elizabeth Ann Henry; one *d*. *Educ:* King's Coll., London; King's Coll. Hosp. Med. Sch. (MB, BS 1960, MD 1969). LRCP, MRCS 1960, MRCP 1965, FRCP 1977; FACC 1973. House Phys., Med. Unit, KCH, 1960; House Surg., KCH, Dulwich, 1960; House Phys., London Chest Hosp., 1961; Sen. House Officer, St Stephen's Hosp., 1962; Public Health Fellow in Cardiology, Wayne State Univ. Med. Sch., USA, 1963; British Heart Foundn Fellow, Dept of Cardiol., KCH, 1964, Med. Registrar 1965; Registrar, then Sen. Registrar, National Heart Hosp., 1966–70; Consultant Cardiologist, Nat. Heart and Chest Hosps, London Chest Hosp., subseq. Royal Brompton and Nat. Heart and Lung Hosps, Victoria Park, then Royal Hosps, later Bart's and the London, NHS Trust, 1970–2001; Dean, Cardiothoracic Inst., 1976–80. Hon. Treasurer, 1981–86, Pres., 1995–97, British Cardiac Soc. *Publications:* contrib. books on cardiological subjects; papers in BMJ, Lancet, Brit. Heart Jl, Amer. Jl of Cardiol., Circulation, Eur. Jl of Cardiol., Acta Medica Scandinavica. *Recreations:* ski-ing, mountain walking. *Died 15 Jan. 2008.*

BALDRY, Jack Thomas; Director, Purchasing and Supplies, Post Office, 1969–72; *b* 5 Oct. 1911; *s* of late John and Ellen Baldry; *m* 1936, Ruby Berenice (*née* Frost); three *d*. *Educ:* Framlingham Coll. Post Office: Asst Traffic Supt, 1930; Asst Surveyor, 1935; Asst Principal, 1940; Principal, 1947 (Private Sec. to PMG, 1950–53);

Asst Sec., 1953; Dep. Dir, External Telecommunications, 1960; Dir of Personnel, 1967. *Recreations:* farming, foreign travel, solving crossword puzzles, watching sport on TV. *Address:* 6 Tanyard Court, Bridge Street, Framlingham, Woodbridge IP13 9GA. *T:* (01728) 720129. *Died 15 March 2007.*

BALDWIN, John, OBE 1978; National Secretary, Amalgamated Engineering Union (formerly Amalgamated Union of Engineering Workers) Workers/Construction Section, 1976–88; *b* 16 Aug. 1923; *s* of Stephen John Baldwin and Elizabeth (*née* Hutchinson); *m* 1945, Grace May Florence (*née* Wilson) (*d* 2003); two *d. Educ:* Laindon High Road Sen. Sch., Essex. Boy service, RN, HMS Ganges, 1938; returned to civilian life, 1948; Steel Erector, CEU, 1950; played active part as Shop Steward and Site Convenor; elected full-time official, 1957; Asst Gen. Sec., AUEW/Construction Sect., 1969–76. Chm., Mechanical Handling Sector Working Party of NEDO; Member: Engrg Construction EDC, 1975; Construction Equipment and Mobile Cranes Sector Working Party of NEDO; National Jt Council for the Engrg Construction Industry. Mem., Labour Party, 1962–. *Recreation:* most sports. *Address:* Sanderstead, South Croydon, Surrey CR2 0AP. *Died 28 Nov. 2007.*

BALDWIN, Prof. John Evan, PhD; FRS 1991; Professor of Radioastronomy, 1989–99, then Emeritus, and Fellow of Queens' College, since 1989, University of Cambridge; Head of Mullard Radio Astronomy Observatory, Cavendish Laboratory, 1987–97; *b* 6 Dec. 1931; *s* of Evan Baldwin and Mary Wild; *m* 1969, Joyce Cox. *Educ:* Merchant Taylors', Crosby; Queens' Coll., Cambridge (MA; Clerk Maxwell Student, 1955–57; PhD 1956). FInstP 1997. Cambridge University: Research Fellow, later Fellow, Queens' Coll., 1956–74; Univ. Demonstrator in Physics, 1957–62; Asst Dir of Research, 1962–81; Reader, 1981–89. Guthrie Medal, Inst. of Physics, 1997; Hopkins Prize, Cambridge Philosophical Soc., 1997; Jackson Gwilt Medal, RAS, 2001. *Publications:* contribs to scientific jls. *Recreations:* gardening, mountain walking. *Address:* Cavendish Laboratory, 19 J. J. Thomson Avenue, Cambridge CB3 0HE. *T:* (01223) 337294. *Died 7 Dec. 2010.*

BALDWIN, Sir Peter (Robert), KCB 1977 (CB 1973); MA; Permanent Secretary, Department of Transport, 1976–82; *b* 10 Nov. 1922; *s* of Charles Baldwin and Katie Baldwin (*née* Field); *m* 1951, Margaret Helen Moar; two *s. Educ:* City of London Sch.; Corpus Christi Coll., Oxford (Hon. Fellow, 1980). Foreign Office, 1942–45; Gen. Register Office, 1948–54; HM Treasury, 1954–62; Cabinet Office, 1962–64; HM Treasury, 1964–76; Principal Private Sec. to Chancellor of Exchequer, July 1966–Jan. 1968; Under-Sec., HM Treasury, 1968–72; Dep. Sec., HM Treasury, 1972–76; Second Permanent Sec., DoE, 1976. Dir, Mitchell Cotts, 1983–87; Chairman: SE Thames RHA, 1983–91; Rural Village Develt Foundn, 1983–85 (Vice-Chm., 1985–90); Brent Dial-a-Ride, 1983–85; Westminster Dial-a-Ride, 1984–87; Community Transport, 1985–87; Disabled Persons Transport Adv. Cttee, 1986–93; President: ReadiBus, 1981–84; Disability Action Westminster, 1986–95 (Chm., 1983–86); Tripscope 1994–2006 (Chm., 1986–94); AFASIC, 1995–; Charities Aid Foundn, 1999–2003 (Mem. Bd, 1988–99; Vice Chm., 1993; Chm., 1994–99); Vice-President: RNID, 1983–91; Mobilise (formerly Disabled Drivers Motoring Club), 1985–; Hearing Dogs for Deaf People, 1986– (Chm., 1983–86); PHAB, 1988– (Vice-Chm., 1981, Chm., 1982–88; Vice-Pres., N Ireland, 1990–); RADAR, 1998– (Mem., 1983–96, Chm., 1992–96, Exec. Cttee); Right from the Start, 2007–08 (Trustee). Automobile Association: Vice-Pres., 1993–; Mem. Cttee, 1983–93, Vice-Chm. Cttee, 1990–93; AA Road Safety Research Foundation: Mem. Cttee, 1986–90; Chm., 1990–94; Mem., Chm's Res. Adv. Gp, 1994–2005. Member: Nat. Rly Mus. Cttee, 1983–87; Railway Heritage Trust Tech. Panel, 1984–; Bd, Public Finance Foundn, 1984–98;

Compact Wkg Gp, 1998–2002; Adv. Cttee, Air Ambulance Assoc., 2000–02; Chairman: Kent Air Ambulance Trust, 1992–94; Pets As Therapy, 1997–2006 (Trustee, 1990–2006; Pres., 2007–); Motorway Archive Trust, 2000–06; Help for All Trust, 2002–. Royal Society of Arts: FRSA; Mem., 1983–94, Chm., 1985–87, Council; Vice-Pres., 1987–94; Emeritus Vice-Pres., 1994–. Chm. Delegacy, KCH Med. and Dental Sch., 1991–98; Member: Bd, City Lit. Inst., 1990–95; Council, KCL, 1992–2003; Bd of Govs, UMDS of Guy's and St Thomas' Hosp., 1993–98. Chm., St Catherine's Home and Sch., Ventnor, 1961–78; Gov., Eltham Coll., 1984–85. Trustee, Flanders Club, 2002–04. Life Vice-Pres., CS Sports Council, 1982 (Vice-Chm., 1974–78; Chm., 1978–82). Freeman, City of London, 1992. MRSocMed 2008. FKC; FCILT; Hon. FIHT; CCMI; CompICE 2008. *Publications:* (ed with R. C. D. Baldwin) The Motorway Achievement: the British motorway system: visualisation, policy and administration, 2004; (ed with R. C. D. Baldwin and M. M. Chrimes) Visions of Reconstruction 1940–1948, 2005; (ed with R. C. D. Baldwin) The Motorway Achievement: the motorways of Southern and Eastern England, 2007. *Recreations:* painting, watching cricket. *Address:* 2 Stokes Cottages, Burwash Common, near Etchingham, E Sussex TN19 7LR. *T:* (01435) 883550. *Died 9 May 2010.*

BALFOUR, Comdr Colin James, RN; DL; Vice Lord-Lieutenant of Hampshire, 1996–99; *b* 12 June 1924; *s* of late Maj. Melville Balfour, MC, Wintershill Hall, Hants and Margaret, (Daisy), Mary Balfour (*née* Lascelles); *m* 1949, Prudence Elizabeth, JP, *d* of Adm. Sir Ragnar Colvin, KBE, CB; one *s* one *d. Educ:* Eton. Joined RN, 1942: served HMS Nelson, Mediterranean, 1943; D-Day and N Russia Convoys, 1944–45; HMS Cossack, Korean War, 1950–52; RNSC, 1955; 1st Lt, HM Yacht Britannia, 1956–57; Comdr 1957; Capt., HMS Finisterre, 1960–62; resigned 1965. Mem., Hants Local Valuation Panel, 1971–81 (Chm., 1977–81). Country Landowners' Association: Chm., 1980–81, Pres., 1987–94, Hants Br.; Chm., Legal and Parly Sub-cttee and Mem., Nat. Exec. Cttee, 1982–87; Chm., Charitable Trust, 1988–96. Pres., Hants Fedn of Young Farmers' Clubs, 1982. Liaison Officer (Hants), Duke of Edinburgh's Award Scheme, 1966–76. Governor: and Vice-Chm., Larkhills Special Sch., Winchester, 1975–80; Durley C of E Primary Sch., 1966–97 (Chm., 1980–96). High Sheriff 1972, DL 1973, Hants. Freeman, City of London, 1982; Liveryman, Farmers' Co., 1983–2005. *Recreations:* shooting, small woodland management. *Address:* Wintershill Farmhouse, Durley, Hants SO32 2AH. *Clubs:* Brooks's, Pratt's. *Died 13 Aug. 2009.*

BALFOUR, John Charles, OBE 1978; MC 1943; JP; Vice Lord-Lieutenant for Fife, 1988–96; Chairman, Fife Area Health Board, 1983–87 (Member, 1981–87); *b* 28 July 1919; *s* of late Brig. E. W. S. Balfour, CVO, DSO, OBE, MC, and Lady Ruth Balfour, CBE; *m* 1950, (Elizabeth) Jean Drew (CBE 1981); three *s. Educ:* Eton Coll.; Trinity Coll., Cambridge (BA). Served war, Royal Artillery, 1939–45 (Major), N Africa and Europe. Member, Royal Company of Archers, Queen's Body Guard for Scotland, 1949–. Member: Inter-departmental Cttee on Children and Young Persons, Scotland (Chm., Lord Kilbrandon), 1961–64; Scottish Council on Crime, 1972–75; Chairman: Children's Panel, Fife County, 1970–75; Fife Region 1975–77; Scottish Assoc. of Youth Clubs, 1968–79. JP 1957, DL 1958, Fife. *Address:* Kirkforthar House, Markinch, Glenrothes, Fife KY7 6LS. *T:* (01592) 752233, *Fax:* (01592) 610314. *Club:* New (Edinburgh). *Died 21 May 2009.*

BALFOUR, Richard Creighton, MBE 1945; *b* 3 Feb. 1916; *s* of Donald Creighton Balfour and Muriel Fonçeca; *m* 1943, Adela Rosemary Welch (*d* 2004); two *s. Educ:* St Edward's Sch., Oxford (Pres., Sch. Soc., 1985–86). FIB. Joined Bank of England, 1935; Agent, Leeds, 1961–65; Deputy Chief Cashier, 1965–70; Chief Accountant, 1970–75. Dir, Datasaab Ltd, 1975–81. Naval Service, Lt-Comdr RNVR, 1939–46. President: Royal National

Rose Soc., 1973 and 1974; World Fedn of Rose Socs, 1983–85 (Vice-Pres. for Europe, 1981–83; Chm., Classification Cttee, 1981–88); Chairman: 1976—The Year of the Rose; Internat. Rose Conf., Oxford, 1976; organiser and designer of the British Garden at Montreal Floralies, 1980. Master, Worshipful Co. of Gardeners, 1991–92; Freeman, City of London. DHM 1974. Gold Medal, World Fedn of Rose Socs, 1985; Australian Rose Award, 1989. *Publications:* articles in many horticultural magazines and photographs in many publications. *Recreations:* roses, gardening, photography, dancing, sea floating, collecting rocks and hat pins, travel, watching sport. *Address:* Albion House, Little Waltham, Chelmsford, Essex CM3 3LA. *T:* (01245) 360410.
Died 4 Feb. 2009.

BALFOUR-PAUL, (Hugh) Glencairn, CMG 1968; HM Diplomatic Service, retired; Director General, Middle East Association, 1978–79; Research Fellow, University of Exeter, since 1979; *b* 23 Sept. 1917; *s* of late Lt-Col J. W. Balfour Paul, DSO; *m* 1st, 1950, Margaret Clare Ogilvy (*d* 1971); one *s* three *d*; 2nd, 1974, Janet Alison Scott; one *s* one *d*. *Educ:* Sedbergh; Magdalen Coll., Oxford. Served War of 1939–45, Sudan Defence Force (seconded to A and SH, 1941–46). Sudan Political Service, Blue Nile and Darfur, 1946–54; joined Foreign Office, 1955; Santiago, 1957; Beirut, 1960; Counsellor, Dubai, 1964; Dep. Political Resident, Persian Gulf, 1966; Counsellor, FO, attached St Antony's Coll., Oxford, 1968; Ambassador to Iraq, 1969–71; Ambassador to Jordan, 1972–75; Ambassador to Tunisia, 1975–77. *Publications:* The End of Empire in the Middle East, 1991; (poems) A Kind of Kindness, 2000; Bagpipes in Babylon: a lifetime in the Arab world and beyond, 2006. *Recreations:* archaeology, poetry, pew ends. *Address:* Uppincott Barton, Shobrooke, Crediton, Devon EX17 1BE.
Died 2 July 2008.

BALGONIE, Lord; David Alexander Leslie Melville; DL; Director, Amerind Ltd (formerly Wood Conversion Ltd), since 1984; *b* 26 Jan. 1954; *s* and *heir* of 14th Earl of Leven and Melville; *m* 1981, Julia Clare, *yr d* of Col I. R. Critchley, Dornock Lodge, Crieff, Perthshire; one *s* one *d*. *Educ:* Eton. Lieut (acting Captain), Queen's Own Highlanders (GSM for N Ireland); RARO 1979–89. DL Nairn, 1998. *Heir: s* Hon. Alexander Ian Leslie Melville, *b* 29 Nov. 1984. *Address:* Glenferness House, Nairn IV12 5UP.
Died 14 Feb. 2007.

BALKWILL, Bryan Havell; conductor; Professor of Conducting, Indiana University, Bloomington, 1977–92; *b* 2 July 1922; *s* of Arthur William Balkwill and Dorothy Silver Balkwill (*née* Wright); *m* 1949, Susan Elizabeth Roberts (*d* 2006); one *s* one *d*. *Educ:* Merchant Taylors' Sch.; Royal Academy of Music (FRAM). Asst Conductor, New London Opera Co., 1947–48; Associate Conductor, Internat. Ballet, 1948–49; Musical Director and Principal Conductor, London Festival Ballet, 1950–52; Music staff and subseq. Associate Conductor, Glyndebourne Opera, 1950–58; Musical Dir, Arts Council 'Opera For All', 1953–63; Resident Conductor, Royal Opera House, Covent Garden, 1959–65; Musical Director: Welsh Nat. Opera Company, 1963–67; Sadler's Wells Opera, 1966–69; free-lance opera and concert conducting in N America, Europe and GB, 1970–. Guest Conductor: Royal Opera House, Covent Garden, English Nat. Opera, Glyndebourne, Wexford Festival, Aldeburgh, RPO, LPO, BBC. Life Mem. Royal Philharmonic Society. *Address:* 5 Reynolds Road, Beaconsfield, Bucks HP9 2NJ. *T:* (01494) 675265.
Died 25 Feb. 2007.

BALL, Arthur Beresford, OBE 1973; HM Diplomatic Service, retired; history teacher, 1989–91, language teacher, 1991–97, Gresham's School; *b* 15 Aug. 1923; *s* of Charles Henry and Lilian Ball; *m* 1961, June Stella Luckett; one *s* two *d*. *Educ:* Bede Collegiate Boys' Sch., Sunderland; Univ. of E Anglia (BA Hons 1987; MA 1989). Joined HM Diplomatic Service, 1949: Bahrain, 1949; Tripoli, 1950; Middle East Centre for Arab Studies, 1952; Ramullah, 1953; Damascus, 1954;

Foreign Office, 1957; Kuwait, 1959; HM Consul, New Orleans, 1963; Jedda, 1965; FO, 1967; São Paulo, 1969; Lisbon, 1972; Ankara, 1975; Consul-Gen., Perth, WA, 1978–80. *Recreations:* bookbinding, historical studies.
Died 23 Aug. 2008.

BALLARD, James Graham; novelist and short story writer; *b* 15 Nov. 1930; *s* of late James Ballard and Edna Ballard (*née* Johnstone); *m* 1954, Helen Mary Matthews (*d* 1964); one *s* two *d*. *Educ:* Leys School, Cambridge; King's College, Cambridge. *Publications:* The Drowned World, 1963; The 4-Dimensional Nightmare, 1963 (re-issued as The Voices of Time, 1985); The Terminal Beach, 1964; The Drought, 1965; The Crystal World, 1966; The Disaster Area, 1967; The Atrocity Exhibition, 1970; Crash, 1973 (filmed 1997); Vermilion Sands, 1973; Concrete Island, 1974; High Rise, 1975; Low-Flying Aircraft, 1976; The Unlimited Dream Company, 1979; Myths of the Near Future, 1982; Empire of the Sun, 1984 (filmed, 1988); The Venus Hunters, 1986; The Day of Creation, 1987; Running Wild, 1988; War Fever, 1990; The Kindness of Women, 1991; Rushing to Paradise, 1994; A User's Guide to the Millennium, 1996; Cocaine Nights, 1996; Super-Cannes, 2000; Millennium People, 2003; Kingdom Come, 2006; Miracles of Life: Shanghai to Shepperton (autobiog.), 2008. *Address:* 36 Old Charlton Road, Shepperton, Middlesex TW17 8AT. *T:* (01932) 225692.
Died 19 April 2009.

BALLINGER, Martin Stanley Andrew, FCILT; Chairman, Northgate plc, since 2005; *b* 19 Nov. 1943; *s* of Cyril Herbert Ballinger and Sylvia May Ballinger; *m* 1968, Diana Susan Edgoose; one *s* one *d*. *Educ:* Salesians, Chertsey; University College London. ACMA; FCILT (FCIT 1991). Accountant, 1972–82, Gen. Manager, 1982–87, National Bus Co.; Man. Dir, subseq. Chief Exec., Go-Ahead Gp plc, 1987–2004. Director: Samson Aviation Services Ltd, 1995–; Saint Cuthbert's Care, 2003–. *Recreations:* golf, private pilot. *Address:* Bolam Hall (East), Morpeth NE61 3UA. *T:* (01661) 881620. *Clubs:* Northern Counties (Newcastle upon Tyne); Newcastle upon Tyne Aero; Stocksfield Golf.
Died 27 Feb. 2007.

BALMFORTH, Ven. Anthony James; Archdeacon of Bristol, 1979–90, then Archdeacon Emeritus; *b* 3 Sept. 1926; *s* of Joseph Henry and Daisy Florence Balmforth; *m* 1952, Eileen Julia, *d* of James Raymond and Kitty Anne Evans; one *s* two *d*. *Educ:* Sebright School, Wolverley; Brasenose Coll., Oxford (BA 1950, MA 1951); Lincoln Theological Coll. Army service, 1944–48. Deacon 1952, priest 1953, dio. Southwell; Curate of Mansfield, 1952–55; Vicar of Skegby, Notts, 1955–61; Vicar of St John's, Kidderminster, Worcs, 1961–65; Rector of St Nicolas, King's Norton, Birmingham, 1965–79; Hon. Canon of Birmingham Cathedral, 1975–79; RD of King's Norton, 1973–79; Examining Chaplain to: Bishop of Birmingham, 1978–79; Bishop of Bristol, 1981–90. Hon. Canon of Bristol Cathedral, 1979–90. Mem., Gen. Synod of C of E, 1982–90. *Recreations:* cricket, gardening. *Address:* Slipper Cottage, Stag Hill, Yorkley, near Lydney, Glos GL15 4TB. *T:* (01594) 564016.
Died 20 Feb. 2009.

BAMBOROUGH, John Bernard; Principal of Linacre College, Oxford, 1962–88; Pro-Vice-Chancellor, Oxford University, 1966–88; *b* 3 Jan. 1921; *s* of John George Bamborough; *m* 1947, Anne (*d* 2007), *d* of Olav Indrehus, Indrehus, Norway; one *s* one *d*. *Educ:* Haberdashers' Aske's Hampstead Sch. (Scholar); New College, Oxford (Scholar). 1st Class, English Language and Literature, 1941; MA 1946. Service in RN, 1941–46 (in Coastal Forces as Lieut RNVR; afterwards as Educ. Officer with rank of Instructor Lieut, RN). Junior Lectr, New Coll., Oxford, 1946; Fellow and Tutor, Wadham Coll., Oxford, 1947–62 (Dean, 1947–54; Domestic Bursar, 1954–56; Sen. Tutor, 1957–61); Univ. Lectr in English, 1951–62; Mem. Hebdomadal Council, Oxford Univ., 1961–79. Hon. Fellow: New Coll., Oxford, 1967; Linacre Coll., Oxford, 1988; Wadham Coll., Oxford, 1988. Clerk of the Market, Oxford Univ., 1997–2002.

Editor, Review of English Studies, 1964–78. Cavaliere Ufficiale, Order of Merit (Italy), 1991. *Publications:* The Little World of Man, 1952; Ben Jonson, 1959; (ed) Pope's Life of Ward, 1961; Jonson's Volpone, 1963; The Alchemist, 1967; Ben Jonson, 1970; (ed) Burton's Anatomy of Melancholy, vols iv–vi, 1998–2000. *Address:* 18 Winchester Road, Oxford OX2 6NA. *T:* (01865) 559886.   *Died 13 Feb. 2009.*

BAMFIELD, Clifford, CB 1981; Under Secretary, Civil Service Department, 1974–80; *b* 21 March 1922; *s* of G. H. Bamfield. *Educ:* Wintringham Grammar Sch., Grimsby; Manchester Business Sch., 1966. Served War, RNVR, 1941–46. Customs and Excise: Exec. Officer, 1946; Private Sec. to Chm., 1959–61; Principal, 1961; Asst Sec., 1967; Under Sec., Comr and Dir of Estabs, 1973. Mem., 1982–91, Dep. Chm., 1989–91, CSAB; Civil Service Commn Panel of Selection Bd Chairmen, 1982–93. *Address:* 15 The Linkway, Sutton, Surrey SM2 5SE. *T:* (020) 8642 5377.   *Died 2 Nov. 2007.*

BANBURY, (Frederick Harold) Frith, MBE 2000; theatrical director, producer and actor; *b* 4 May 1912; *s* of Rear-Adm. Frederick Arthur Frith Banbury and Winifred (*née* Fink); unmarried. *Educ:* Stowe Sch.; Hertford Coll., Oxford; Royal Academy of Dramatic Art. First stage appearance in "If I Were You", Shaftesbury Theatre, 1933; for next 14 years appeared both in London and Provinces in every branch of theatre from Shakespeare to revue. Appearances included: Hamlet, New Theatre, 1934; Goodness How Sad, Vaudeville, 1938; (revue) New Faces, Comedy, 1939; Uncle Vanya, Westminster, 1943; Jacobowsky and the Colonel, Piccadilly, 1945; Caste, Duke of York's, 1947. During this time he also appeared in numerous films including The Life and Death of Colonel Blimp and The History of Mr Polly, and also on the television screen. From 1947 he devoted his time to production and direction, starting with Dark Summer at Lyric, Hammersmith (later transferred St Martin's), 1947; subseq. many, in both London and New York, including The Holly and the Ivy, Duchess, 1950; Waters of the Moon, Haymarket, 1951; The Deep Blue Sea, Duchess, 1951, and Morosco, New York, 1952; A Question of Fact, Piccadilly, 1953; Marching Song, St Martin's, 1954; Love's Labour's Lost, Old Vic, 1954; The Diary of Anne Frank, Phoenix, 1956; A Dead Secret, Piccadilly, 1957; Flowering Cherry, Haymarket, 1957, and Lyceum, New York, 1959; A Touch of the Sun, Saville, 1958; The Ring of Truth, Savoy, 1959; The Tiger and the Horse, Queen's, 1960; The Wings of the Dove, Lyric, 1963; The Right Honourable Gentleman, Billy Rose, New York, 1965; Howards End, New, 1967; Dear Octopus, Haymarket, 1967; Enter A Free Man, St Martin's, 1968; A Day In the Death of Joe Egg, Cameri Theatre, Tel Aviv, 1968; Le Valet, Théâtre de la Renaissance, Paris, 1968; On the Rocks, Dublin Theatre Festival, 1969; My Darling Daisy, Lyric, 1970; The Winslow Boy, New, 1970; Captain Brassbound's Conversion, Cambridge, 1971; Reunion in Vienna, Chichester Festival, 1971, Piccadilly, 1972; The Day After the Fair, Lyric, 1972, Shubert, Los Angeles, 1973; Glasstown, Westminster, 1973; Ardèle, Queen's, 1975; On Approval, Canada and SA, 1976, Vaudeville, 1977; directed in Australia, Kenya, USA, 1978–79; Motherdear, Ambassadors, 1980; Dear Liar, Mermaid, 1982; The Aspern Papers, Haymarket, 1984; The Corn is Green, Old Vic, 1985; The Admirable Crichton, Haymarket, 1988; Screamers, Arts, 1989; The Gin Game, Savoy, 1999; The Old Ladies (tour), 2003. *Recreation:* playing the piano.   *Died 14 May 2008.*

BANGHAM, Alec Douglas, MD; FRCP; FRS 1977; Research Worker, Agricultural Research Council, Institute of Animal Physiology, Babraham, 1952–82 and Head, Biophysics Unit, 1971–82; *b* 10 Nov. 1921; *s* of Dr Donald Hugh and Edith Bangham; *m* 1943, Rosalind Barbara Reiss; three *s* one *d. Educ:* Bryanston Sch.; UCL and UCH Med. Sch. (MD). FRCP 1997. Captain, RAMC, 1946–48. Lectr, Dept of Exper. Pathology, UCH, 1949–52; Principal Scientific Officer, 1952–63,

Senior Principal Scientific Officer (Merit Award), 1963–82, ARC, Babraham. Fellow, UCL, 1981–. *Publications:* contrib. Nature, Biochim. Biophys. Acta, and Methods in Membrane Biol. *Recreations:* horticulture, photographic arts, sailing. *Address:* 17 High Green, Great Shelford, Cambridge CB2 5EG. *T:* (01223) 843192; *e-mail:* alecbangham@wwr.co.uk; *web:* www.bangham.org.uk.   *Died 9 March 2010.*

BANISTER, Stephen Michael Alvin; Secretary, British and Foreign School Society, 1978–96; Founder Editor, Transport Reviews, since 1981; *b* 7 Oct. 1918; *s* of late Harry Banister and Idwen Banister (*née* Thomas); *m* 1944, Rachel Joan Rawlence; four *s. Educ:* Eton; King's Coll., Cambridge (MA). With Foreign Office, 1939–45; Home Guard (Major, 1944). Asst Principal, Min. of Civil Aviation, 1946; Principal, 1947; Private Sec. to six successive Ministers of Transport and Civil Aviation, 1950–56; Asst Sec., Min. of Transport and BoT, 1956–70; Under Sec., DoE, 1970–76, Dept of Transport, 1976–78. UK Shipping Delegate, UNCTAD, 1964; UK Dep., European Conf. of Ministers of Transport, 1976–78. Dir, Taylor and Francis, 1978–91. Mem., Nat. Insurance Tribunal, Kingston upon Thames, 1979–85. CMILT (MCIT 1994; MILT 1999). *Compositions:* (amateur) for singers, including Bluebeard. *Recreations:* countryside, walking, singing (formerly in opera, then in choirs); formerly cricket (Cambridge Crusader); played for CU *v* Australians, 1938. *Address:* Bramshaw, Lower Farm Road, Effingham, Surrey KT24 5JJ. *T:* (01372) 452778.   *Died 29 June 2006.*

BANKS, Tony; see Stratford, Baron.

BANNON, Yvonne Helen; see Carter, Y. H.

BANTOCK, John Leonard; Assistant Under Secretary of State, Home Office Police Department, 1980–84; *b* 21 Oct. 1927; *s* of Edward Bantock and Agnes Bantock; *m* 1947, Maureen McKinney; two *s. Educ:* Colfe's Sch., SE13; King George V Sch., Southport, Lancs; LSE, London Univ. (LLB 1951). Unilever Ltd, 1943–45; Army, 1945–48 (Staff Captain, UK, India and Cyprus); Colonial Office, 1951–52; Inland Revenue, 1952–69; Secretariat, Royal Commn on Constitution, 1969–73; Cabinet Office, 1973–76; Sec., Cttee of Privy Counsellors on Recruitment of Mercenaries, 1976; Asst Under Sec. of State, Home Office Radio Regulatory Dept, 1976–79 (Head, UK Delegn, World Admin. Radio Conf., 1979). *Club:* MCC.   *Died 18 July 2006.*

BANWELL, Derick Frank, CBE 1978; Member: Refugee Housing Association Ltd (formerly BCAR (Housing) Ltd), 1978–95 (Chairman, 1979–89); Refugee Housing Society Ltd (formerly BCAR (Homes) Ltd), 1978–95 (Chairman, 1979–86); *b* 19 July 1919; *s* of Frank Edward Banwell; *m* 1945, Rose Kathleen Worby; two *s* one *d. Educ:* Kent Coll., Canterbury. RA, 1939–46. Admitted as Solicitor, 1947; Asst Solicitor, Southend-on-Sea Co. Borough Coun., 1947–48; Sen. Asst Solicitor, Rochdale Co. Borough Coun., 1948–51; Chief Common Law Solicitor, City of Sheffield, 1951–56; Sen. Asst Solicitor, 1956–59, Asst Town Clerk, 1959–60, Southend-on-Sea Co. Borough Coun.; Dep. Town Clerk and Dep. Clerk of the Peace, Swansea Co. Borough Council, 1960–64; Gen. Manager, Runcorn Develt Corp., 1964–78. Sec., Church Bldgs Cttee, United Reformed Church, 1978–85. *Recreations:* history, music, model railways. *Address:* 57 Broad Street, Canterbury, Kent CT1 2LS.   *Died 8 Jan. 2006.*

BARBACK, Ronald Henry; Professor of Economics, University of Hull, 1965–76 (Dean, Faculty of Social Sciences and Law, 1966–69); *b* 31 Oct. 1919; *s* of late Harry Barback and Winifred Florence (*née* Norris); *m* 1950, Sylvia Chambers (*d* 2004); one *s* one *d. Educ:* Woodside Sch., Glasgow; UC, Nottingham (BScEcon); Queen's and Nuffield Colls, Oxford (MLitt). Asst Lectr in Econs, Univ. of Nottingham, 1946–48; Lectr in Econs, subseq. Sen. Lectr, Canberra University Coll., Australia, 1949–56; Univ. of Ibadan (formerly University

Coll., Ibadan): Prof. of Econs and Social Studies, 1956–63; Dean, Faculty of Arts, 1958–59; Dean, Faculty of Econs and Social Studies, 1959–63; Dir, Nigerian (formerly W African) Inst. of Social and Econ. Res., 1956–63; Sen. Res. Fellow, Econ. Res. Inst., Dublin, 1963–64; Prof. of Econs, TCD, 1964–65; Vis. Prof., Brunel Univ., 1984–86. Dep. Econ. Dir and Head, Econ. Res., CBI, 1977–81, Consultant, 1981–82. Nigeria: Mem., Ibadan Univ. Hosp. Bd of Management, 1958–63; Mem., Jt Econ. Planning Cttee, Fedn of Nigeria, 1959–61; Sole Arbitrator, Trade Disputes in Ports and Railways, 1958; Chm., Fed. Govt Cttee to advise on fostering a share market, 1959. UK Official Delegate, FAO meeting on investment in fisheries, 1970; Mem., FAO mission to Sri Lanka, 1975. Consultant, Div. of Fisheries, EC Directorate-Gen. of Agriculture, 1974; Specialist Advr, H of L Select Cttee on Eur. Communities, 1980–83; Commonwealth Scholarships Commn Adviser on Econs, 1971–76. Mem., Schools Council Social Sciences Cttee, 1971–80; Chm., Schs Council Econs and Business Studies Syllabus Steering Gp, 1975–77. Member: Hull and Dist Local Employment Cttee, 1966–73; N Humberside Dist Manpower Cttee, 1973–76; CNAA Business and Management Studies Bd, 1978–81, Economics Bd, 1982–86; Ct, Brunel Univ., 1979–83; Gov., Tunbridge Wells Girls' GS, 1996–98. Chm., Royal Tunbridge Wells Civic Soc., 1991–93 (Vice-Pres., 1994–96). Member: Editorial Bd, Bull. of Economic Research (formerly Yorks Bull. of Social and Economic Research), 1965–76 (Jt Editor, 1966–67); Editorial Adv. Bd, Applied Economics, 1969–80; Editor, Humberside Statistical Bull., nos 1–3, 1974, 1975, 1977. *Publications:* (contrib.) The Commonwealth in the World Today, ed J. Eppstein, 1956; (ed with Prof. Sir Douglas Copland) The Conflict of Expansion and Stability, 1957; (contrib.) The Commonwealth and Europe (EIU), 1960; The Pricing of Manufactures, 1964; (contrib.) Insurance Markets of the World, ed M. Grossmann 1964; (contrib.) Webster's New World Companion to English and American Literature, 1973; Forms of Co-operation in the British Fishing Industry, 1976; (with M. Breimer and A. F. Haug) Development of the East Coast Fisheries of Sri Lanka, 1976; The Firm and its Environment, 1984; contrib. New Internat. Encyc., FAO Fisheries Reports, and jls. *Recreations:* walking, music. *Died 26 April 2008.*

BARBOZA, Mario G.; *see* Gibson-Barboza.

BARCLAY, Sir Colville Herbert Sanford, 14th Bt *cr* 1668; painter; *b* 7 May 1913; *s* of late Rt Hon. Sir Colville Adrian de Rune Barclay, 3rd *s* of 11th Bt, and Sarita Enriqueta, *d* of late Herbert Ward; *S* uncle, 1930; *m* 1949, Rosamond Grant Renton Elliott; three *s. Educ:* Eton; Trinity Coll., Oxford. Third Sec., Diplomatic Service, 1937–41; enlisted in Navy, Nov. 1941; Sub-Lieut RNVR 1942; Lieut 1943; Lieut Commander 1945; demobilised, 1946. Exhibitor: Royal Academy, RBA, London Group, Bradford City and Brighton Art Galleries. Chm. Royal London Homoeopathic Hospital, 1970–74 (Vice-Chm., 1961–65; Chm., League of Friends, 1974–84). Plant-hunting expedns to Crete, Turkey, Cyprus, Réunion, Mauritius and Nepal, 1966–81. *Publications:* Crete: checklist of the vascular plants, 1986; articles in botanical jls. *Recreation:* gardening. *Heir: s* Robert Colraine Barclay [*b* 12 Feb. 1950; *m* 1980, Lucilia Saboia (marr. diss. 1986), *y d* of Carlos Saboia de Albuquerque, Rio de Janeiro; one *s* one *d*]. *Address:* 23 High Street, Broughton, near Stockbridge, Hants SO20 8AE. *Died 1 Sept. 2010.*

BARKER, Prof. David (Faubert), MA, DPhil, DSc; Professor of Zoology, University of Durham, 1962–87, then Professor Emeritus; *b* 18 Feb. 1922; *s* of Faubert and Doreen Barker; *m* 1st, 1945, Kathleen Mary Frances Pocock; three *s* two *d*; 2nd, 1978, Patricia Margaret Drake (Pat Barker, novelist, CBE 2000); one *s* one *d. Educ:* Bryanston Sch.; Magdalen Coll., Oxford. DSc 1972. Senior Demy of Magdalen Coll., 1946; Leverhulme

Research Scholar, Royal Coll. of Surgeons, 1946; Demonstrator in Zoology and Comparative Anatomy, Oxford, 1947; DPhil 1948; Rolleston Prizeman, 1948; Prof. of Zoology, Univ. of Hong Kong, 1950–62; led scientific expeditions to Tunisia, 1950, North Borneo, 1952; Dean of Faculty of Science, Hong Kong, 1959–60; Public Orator, Hong Kong, 1961; Sir Derman Christopherson Fellow, Durham Univ. Research Foundn, 1984–85. Emeritus Fellow, Leverhulme Trust, 1989–92. *Publications:* (Founder) Editor, Hong Kong Univ. Fisheries Journal, 1954–60; Editor, Symposium on Muscle Receptors, 1962; scientific papers, mostly on muscle innervation. *Address:* 10 The Avenue, Durham DH1 4ED. *T:* (0191) 384 0908. *Died 7 Jan. 2009.*

BARKER, Richard Philip; Headmaster, Sevenoaks School, 1981–96; *b* 17 July 1939; *s* of late Philip Watson Barker and Helen May Barker; *m* 1966, Imogen Margaret Harris; two *s* one *d. Educ:* Repton; Trinity Coll., Cambridge (MA 1962); Bristol Univ. (Cert. Ed. 1963). Head of Geography, Bedales Sch., 1963–65; Founder Dir, A level business studies project, 1966–73; Lectr, Inst. of Education, London Univ., 1973–74; Housemaster, Marlborough Coll., 1973–81. Resident Gov., British Sch., Colombo, Sri Lanka, 1996–97; Governor: Epsom Coll., 1996–2002; Chm. of Govs, Worth Sch., 1999–2002. Chm., Friends of Yehudi Menuhin Sch., 1996–2002. Mem., RSA. *Publications:* (ed) Understanding Business Series, 1976–98. *Recreations:* educational interests, beekeeping, croquet, fishing, repairing buildings, travelling. *Address:* Slyfield Farm House, Stoke D'Abernon, Cobham, Surrey KT11 3QE. *T:* (01932) 862634; *e-mail:* barker@slyfieldfh.freeserve.co.uk. *Died 5 Dec. 2009.*

BARKWORTH, Peter Wynn; actor, since 1948; director, since 1980; *b* 14 Jan. 1929; *s* of Walter Wynn Barkworth and Irene May Barkworth. *Educ:* Stockport Sch.; Royal Academy of Dramatic Art. Folkestone and Sheffield Repertory Cos, 1948–51. West End *plays* include: A Woman of No Importance, Savoy, 1953; Roar Like a Dove, Phoenix, 1957–60; The School for Scandal, Haymarket, 1962; Crown Matrimonial, Haymarket, 1972; Donkeys' Years, Globe, 1976; Can You Hear Me at the Back?, Piccadilly, 1979; A Coat of Varnish, Haymarket, 1982; Siegfried Sassoon, Apollo, 1987; Hidden Laughter, Vaudeville, 1990; The Winslow Boy, Globe, 1994; director: Night and Day, Leatherhead, 1980; Sisterly Feelings, nat. tour, 1982; The Eight O'Clock Muse, Riverside Studios, 1989; *television* serials: The Power Game, 1966; Manhunt, 1969; Telford's Change, 1979; Winston Churchill: The Wilderness Years, 1981; The Price, 1985; Late Starter, 1985; The Gospel According to St Matthew, 1986; *films:* Where Eagles Dare, 1968; Mr Smith, 1983; Escape from the Dark, 1983; Champions, 1984; Wilde, 1997. *Awards:* Best Actor, BAFTA, 1974 and 1977; RTS and BPG, 1977 (both 1977 awards for Professional Foul). *Publications:* About Acting, 1980; First Houses, 1983; More About Acting, 1984; The Complete About Acting, 1991; For All Occasions, 1997. *Recreations:* walking, gardening, music, looking at paintings. *Address:* 47 Flask Walk, NW3 1HH. *T:* (020) 7794 4591. *Club:* Academy of Film and Television Arts. *Died 21 Oct. 2006.*

BARLOW, Prof. Frank, CBE 1989; MA, DPhil; FBA 1970; FRSL 1971; FRHistS; Professor of History and Head of Department, University of Exeter, 1953–76, then Emeritus Professor; *b* 19 April 1911; *e s* of Percy Hawthorn and Margaret Julia Barlow; *m* 1936, Moira Stella Brigid Garvey; two *s. Educ:* Newcastle High Sch.; St John's Coll., Oxford (Open Schol., 1930; 1st Cl. Hons Sch. of Modern History, 1933; Bryce Student, 1933; BLitt 1934; Hon. Fellow, 2001); DPhil Oxon 1937. FRHistS 1957. Oxford Senior Student, 1934; Fereday Fellow, St John's Coll., Oxford, 1935–38; Asst Lecturer, University Coll., London, 1936–40; War service in the Army, 1941–46, commissioned into Intelligence Corps, demobilised as Major; Lecturer 1946, Reader 1949, Dep.

Vice-Chancellor, 1961–63, Public Orator, 1974–76, University of Exeter. Hon. DLitt Exon, 1981. *Publications:* The Letters of Arnulf of Lisieux, 1939; Durham Annals and Documents of the Thirteenth Century, 1945; Durham Jurisdictional Peculiars, 1950; The Feudal Kingdom of England, 1955; (ed and trans.) The Life of King Edward the Confessor, 1962; The English Church, 1000–1066, 1963; William I and the Norman Conquest, 1965; Edward the Confessor, 1970; (with Martin Biddle, Olof von Feilitzen and D. J. Keene) Winchester in the Early Middle Ages, 1976; The English Church 1066–1154, 1979; The Norman Conquest and Beyond (selected papers), 1983; William Rufus, 1983; Thomas Becket, 1986; Introduction to Devonshire Domesday Book, 1991; English Episcopal Acta, xi–xii (Exeter 1046–1257), 1996; (ed and trans.) Carmen de Hastingae Proelio, 1999; The Godwins, 2002. *Recreation:* gardening. *Address:* Middle Court Hall, Kenton, Exeter EX6 8NA. *T:* (01626) 890438. *Died 27 June 2009.*

BARLTROP, Roger Arnold Rowlandson, CMG 1987; CVO 1982; HM Diplomatic Service, retired; Ambassador to Fiji, 1988–89 (High Commissioner, 1982–88) and High Commissioner (non-resident) to Republic of Nauru and to Tuvalu, 1982–89; *b* 19 Jan. 1930; *s* of late Ernest William Barltrop, CMG, CBE, DSO, and Ethel Alice Lucy Barltrop (*née* Baker); *m* 1st, 1962, Penelope Pierrepont Dalton (marr. diss.); two *s* two *d*; 2nd, 1998, Bojana Komadina (*née* Jovanovic). *Educ:* Solihull Sch.; Leeds Grammar Sch.; Exeter Coll., Oxford (MA). Served RN, 1949–50, RNVR/RNR, 1950–64 (Lt-Comdr 1962). Asst Principal, CRO, 1954–56; Second Sec., New Delhi, 1956–57; Private Sec. to Parly Under-Sec. of State and Minister of State, CRO, 1957–60; First Sec., E Nigeria, 1960–62; Actg Dep. High Comr, W Nigeria, 1962; First Sec., Salisbury, Rhodesia, 1962–65; CRO, Commonwealth Office and FO, later FCO, 1965–69; First Sec. and Head of Chancery, Ankara, 1969–70; Dep. British Govt Rep., WI Associated States, 1971–73; Counsellor and Head of Chancery, Addis Ababa, 1973–77; Head of Commonwealth Coordination Dept, FCO, 1978–82. Mem., Commonwealth Observer Gp for elections in Bangladesh, Feb. 1991, and in St Kitts/Nevis, 1995; Mem., UK/OSCE Observer Gp for elections in Bosnia, 1996; Foreign Affairs Trng Advr, Solomon Is, 1994. Chm., Pacific Is Soc. of UK and Ireland, 1992–98. *Publications:* contribs to Round Table (Commonwealth jl of internat. affairs). *Recreations:* sailing, genealogy, opera. *Address:* 35 Highfield Drive, Hurstpierpoint, West Sussex BN6 9AU. *Club:* Royal Commonwealth Society. *Died 6 Dec. 2009.*

BARNA, Prof. Tibor, CBE 1974; Professor of Economics, University of Sussex, 1962–82, Professor Emeritus 1984; Member, Monopolies and Mergers Commission, 1963–78; *b* 19 April 1919; *m* 1944, Florence Marie Creaner Fox; two *d* (one *s* decd). *Educ:* London School of Economics. Lecturer, London School of Economics, 1944; Official Fellow, Nuffield College, Oxford, 1947; senior posts in UN Economic Commission for Europe, 1949; Assistant Director, National Institute of Economic and Social Research, London, 1955. *Publications:* Redistribution of Income through Public Finance in 1937, 1945; Investment and Growth Policies in British Industrial Firms, 1962; Agriculture towards the Year 2000, 1979; European Process Plant Industry, 1981; papers in Jl Royal Statistical Soc., Economic Jl, European Econ. Review. *Died 17 July 2009.*

BARNARD, Sir Joseph (Brian), Kt 1986; DL; Director, Northern Electric (formerly North Eastern Electricity Board), 1986–90; *b* 22 Jan. 1928; *s* of Joseph Ernest Barnard and Elizabeth Loudon (*née* Constantine); *m* 1959, Suzanne Hamilton Bray; three *s* (incl. twins). *Educ:* Bramcote School, Scarborough; Sedbergh School. Served Army, 1946–48, commissioned KRRC. Director: Joseph Constantine Steamship Line, 1952–66; Teesside Warehousing Co., 1966–97. Farms at East Harlsey. Chm., NE Electricity Cons. Council, 1986–90; Mem.,

Electricity Consumers' Council, 1986–90. Dir, Financial Consultancy Services Ltd, 2000–03. Vice-Chm., 1988–91, Chm., 1991–92, Nat. Union of Cons. and Unionist Assocs (Chm., Yorks Area, 1983–88); Chm., Cons. Assoc. for Cleveland and Yorks N Euro Constituency, 1993–94; Pres., Richmond Cons. Assoc., 2007–. Life Vice President: Yorkshire Conservative Clubs, 1994; Conservatives at Work, 1994. Chm. Governors, Ingleby Arncliffe C of E Primary School, 1979–91; Patron, St Oswald's, E Harlsey. JP Northallerton, 1973–94; Chm., Northallerton (formerly Allertonshire PSD), 1981–93; Mem., N Yorks Magistrates' Courts Cttee, 1981–93. DL N Yorks, 1988. *Recreations:* walking, shooting, gardening. *Address:* Harlsey Hall, Northallerton, N Yorks DL6 2BL. *T:* (01609) 882203. *Club:* Carlton. *Died 3 June 2010.*

BARNES, Alan Robert, CBE 1976; JP; Headmaster, Ruffwood School, Kirkby, Liverpool, 1959–87; Field Officer and Consultant, Secondary Heads Association, 1987–2000; *b* 9 Aug. 1927; *s* of Arthur Barnes and Ida Barnes; *m* 1951, Pearl Muriel Boughton (*d* 2008); (two *s* decd). *Educ:* Enfield Grammar Sch.; Queens' Coll., Cambridge (MA). National Service, RAEC. Wallington County Grammar Sch., 1951–55; Churchfields Sch., West Bromwich, 1955–59. Pres., Headmasters' Assoc., 1974, Treas., 1975–77; Chm., Jt Four Secondary Assocs, 1978; Treas., Secondary Heads Assoc., 1978–82; Vice-Chm., British Educn Management and Admin Soc., 1980–82, Chm. 1982–84. Schools Liaison Officer, Univ. of Essex, 1988–92. Chm., HMA Benevolent Fund, 1975–2005. Treasurer, HiPACT, 2000–04. JP Knowsley, Merseyside, 1967. *Publications:* (contrib.) Going Comprehensive (ed Halsall), 1970; (contrib.) Management and Headship in the Secondary School (ed Jennings), 1978; contrib. to: Education, BEMAS Jl, SHA publications. *Recreation:* bridge. *Address:* 2 Lark Valley Drive, Fornham St Martin, Bury St Edmunds, Suffolk IP28 6UF; *e-mail:* AlanBarnes@Larkvalley.fsnet.co.uk. *Died 20 Nov. 2008.*

BARNES, Clive Alexander, CBE 1975; Associate Editor and Chief Drama and Dance Critic, New York Post, since 1977; *b* London, 13 May 1927; *s* of Arthur Lionel Barnes and Freda Marguerite Garratt; *m* 1958, Patricia Winckley (marr. diss.); one *s* one *d*; *m* 2004, Valerie Taylor. *Educ:* King's Coll., London; St Catherine's Coll., Oxford. Served RAF, 1946–48. Admin. Officer, Town Planning Dept, LCC, 1952–61; concurrently freelance journalist; Chief Dance Critic, The Times, 1961–65; Exec. Editor, Dance and Dancers, Music and Musicians, and Plays and Players, 1961–65; a London Correspondent, New York Times, 1963–65, Dance Critic, 1965–77, Drama Critic (weekdays only), 1967–77; a NY correspondent, The Times, 1970–. Knight of the Order of Dannebrog (Denmark), 1972. *Publications:* Ballet in Britain since the War, 1953; (ed, with others) Ballet Here and Now, 1961; Frederick Ashton and his Ballets, 1961; Dance Scene, USA (commentary), 1967; (ed with J. Gassner) Best American Plays, 6th series, 1963–67, 1971, and 7th series, 1974; (ed) New York Times Directory of the Theatre, 1973; Nureyev, 1983; contribs to jls, inc. Punch, The New Statesman, The Spectator, The New Republic. *Recreations:* eating, drinking, walking, theatre-going. *Address:* c/o New York Post, 1211 6th Avenue, New York, NY 10036, USA. *Club:* Century (NY). *Died 19 Nov. 2008.*

BARNES, Rev. Cyril Arthur; Dean of Moray, Ross and Caithness, 1980–84; *b* 10 Jan. 1926; *s* of Reginald William and Mary Adeline Barnes; *m* 1951, Patricia Patience Allen. *Educ:* Penistone Grammar School; Edinburgh Theological Coll. (GOE 1950). King's Own Scottish Borderers and RAEC, 1944–47. Curate, St John's, Aberdeen, 1950–53; Rector, St John's, Forres, 1953–55; Priest-in-Charge, Wentbridge, Yorks, 1955–58; Vicar, St Bartholomew's, Ripponden with St John's, Rishworth, 1958–67, also St John's, Thorpe, 1966–67; Rector, Christ Church, Huntly with St Marnan's, Aberchirder, 1967–84, also Holy Trinity,

Keith, 1974–84; Canon of Inverness Cathedral, 1971–80; Synod Clerk, 1977–80. Editor: Huntly Express, 1985–91; Northern See, 1990–96; Newscan, 1991–93. *Recreations:* gardening, do-it-yourself. *Address:* Laurels Lodge Care Home, Station Road, Woodside, Aberdeen AB24 2UL.
Died 11 Jan. 2008.

BARNES, Geoffrey Thomas, CBE 1989; HM Overseas Civil Service, retired; *b* 18 Aug. 1932; *s* of late Thomas Arthur Barnes and Ethel Maud (*née* Walker); *m* 1962, Agnete Scot Madsen; three *s* one *d. Educ:* Dover College; St Catharine's College, Cambridge (MA). Nat. Service, 2nd Lieut QO Royal West Kent Regt; served Malaya, 1951–52; Lieut, Royal Warwickshire Regt, TA, 1952–55. Admin. Officer, HMOCS Sarawak, 1956–68; City and Guilds of London, 1968–70; HMOCS Hong Kong: Asst Defence Sec., 1970–72; Police Civil Sec., 1972–76; Asst Dir, Commerce and Industry Dept, 1976–77; Dep. Sec. for Security, 1977–81, for Health and Welfare, 1981–84; Comr, Ind. Commn Against Corruption, 1985–88; Sec. for Security, Hong Kong Govt, and Official Mem., Legislative Council, 1988–90. Consultant to FCO on anti-corruption measures in Jamaica, 1990, Peru, 1991, Venezuela, 1992 and Ecuador, 1993. Pres., ICAC Assoc., 1993–98. JP Hong Kong, 1980. *Publications:* Mostly Memories (autobiog.), 1996, rev. edn 1999; With the Dirty Half-Hundred in Malaya (autobiog.), 2001. *Recreations:* sailing, painting, golf, gardening. *Address:* Alloways, Cranleigh Road, Ewhurst, Surrey GU6 7RJ. *T:* (01483) 276490. *Clubs:* Royal Over-Seas League; Hong Kong (Hong Kong) (Life Mem.). *Died 11 Feb. 2010.*

BARNES, Prof. John Arundel, DSC 1944; FBA 1981; Professor of Sociology, University of Cambridge, 1969–82, then Emeritus; Fellow of Churchill College, Cambridge, since 1969; *b* Reading, 9 Sept. 1918; *s* of T. D. and M. G. Barnes, Bath; *m* 1942, Helen Frances, *d* of Charles Bastable; three *s* one *d. Educ:* Christ's Hosp.; St John's Coll., Cambridge; Sch. of African Studies, Univ. of Cape Town; Balliol Coll., Oxford. Fellow, St John's Coll., Cambridge, 1950–53; Simon Research Fellow, Manchester Univ., 1951–53; Reader in Anthropology, London Univ., 1954–56; Prof. of Anthropology, Sydney Univ., 1956–58; Prof. of Anthropology, Inst. of Advanced Studies, ANU, Canberra, 1958–69; Overseas Fellow, Churchill Coll., Cambridge, 1965–66. Australian National University: Vis. Fellow, 1978–79, 1985–92; Program Visitor, Sociology, Res. Sch. of Social Scis, 1992–98. *Publications:* Marriage in a Changing Society, 1951; Politics in a Changing Society, 1954; Inquest on the Murngin, 1967; Sociology in Cambridge, 1970; Three Styles in the Study of Kinship, 1971; Social Networks, 1972; The Ethics of Inquiry in Social Science, 1977; Who Should Know What?, 1979; Models and interpretations, 1990; A Pack of Lies, 1994. *Address:* Churchill College, Cambridge CB3 0DS.
Died 13 Sept. 2010.

BARNES, Sir Kenneth, KCB 1977 (CB 1970); Permanent Secretary, Department of Employment, 1976–82; *b* 26 Aug. 1922; *s* of Arthur and Doris Barnes, Accrington, Lancs; *m* 1948, Barbara Ainsworth (*d* 2001); one *s* two *d. Educ:* Accrington Grammar Sch.; Balliol Coll., Oxford. Lancs Fusiliers, 1942–45. Entered Ministry of Labour, 1948; Under-Sec., Cabinet Office, 1966–68; Dep. Sec., Dept of Employment, 1968–75. *Address:* South Sandhills, Sandy Lane, Betchworth, Surrey RH3 7AA. *T:* (01737) 842445. *Died 16 Sept. 2010.*

BARNES, Kenneth James, CBE 1969 (MBE 1964); Advisor (Finance), Directorate General for Development, Commission of the European Communities, 1982–87; *b* 8 May 1930; *s* of late Thomas Arthur Barnes and Ethel Maud Barnes; *m* 1st, 1953, Lesley Dawn Grummett Wright (*d* 1976); two *s* one *d;* 2nd, 1981, Anna Elisabeth Gustaf Maria Vanoorlé (marr. diss. 1988). *Educ:* Guildford and Hale Schs, Perth, WA; Dover Coll.; St Catharine's Coll., Cambridge (Crabtree exhibnr; MA); London Univ. Pilot Officer, RAF, 1949–50; Flying Officer, RAFVR, 1950–53.

Administrative Officer, HMOCS Eastern Nigeria, 1954–60; Asst Sec., Min. of Finance, Malawi, 1960–64, Sen. Asst Sec., 1965, Dep. Sec., 1966, Permanent Sec., 1967–71; Asst Sec., British Steel Corp., 1971–73; EEC: Principal Administrator, Directorate-Gen. for Develt, 1973–75; Head of Div. for Ind. Co-operation, Trade Promotion and Regional Co-operation, 1976–78; Hd of Div. for Caribbean, Indian and Pacific Oceans, 1979–80; Advr (Political), 1981–82; Advr (Finance), 1983–87. Chairman: Newbury Dist Liaison Group on Disablement, 1990–97; Internat. Cttee, RADAR, 1993–2001; Member: Council, Anti-Slavery Internat., 1991–98 (Jt Treas., 1992–97); Council, John Grooms Assoc. for Disabled, 1994–97. *Publications:* Polio and ME in Nigeria, Malawi, Belgium, England and Other Places, 1998; (contrib.) Palm Wine & Leopard's Whiskers, 1999; A Rough Passage: memories of Empire, vols I and II, 2006. *Recreations:* reading, esp. history, listening to music, mediaeval fortifications, strengthening European Community links, charities for the disabled. *Address:* 29 Bearwater, Charnham Street, Hungerford, Berks RG17 0NN. *T:* (01488) 684329, *Fax:* (01488) 681733; *e-mail:* kjbarnes@29bearwater.com. *Died 1 July 2010.*

BARNETT, Colin Michael; international business consultant, since 1990; Regional Secretary, North-West Regional Council of the Trades Union Congress, 1976–85; Divisional Officer, North-West Division of the National Union of Public Employees, 1971–84; *b* 27 Aug. 1929; *s* of Arthur Barnett and Kathleen Mary Barnett; *m* 1st, 1953, Margaret Barnett (marr. diss. 1980); one *s* one *d;* 2nd, 1982, Hilary Carolyn Hodge, PhD; one *s* one *d. Educ:* St Michael's Elem. Sch., Southfields; Wandsworth Grammar Sch.; London Sch. of Econs and Pol Science; WEA classes. Area Officer, NUPE, 1959, Asst Divl Officer 1961. Chm. Gp H, Duke of Edinburgh Conf. on Industry and Society, 1974. Secretary: NW Peace Council, 1979–; NW Cttee Against Racism, 1980–. Chm., MSC Area Bd, Gtr Manchester and Lancashire, 1978–83. Member: Merseyside District Manpower Bd, 1983–86; Industrial Tribunal, Manchester, 1974–99; Liverpool Social Security Appeal Tribunal, 1986–99. Dir, AT4 Community Prog. Agency, 1986–89. Debt and Industrial Advr, St Helens CAB, 1984–92; Marriage Guidance Counsellor, 1984–92. Organised: People's March for Jobs, 1981; (jtly) People's March for Jobs, 1983. British Representative: NW Russia Agency for Internat. Co-operation and Develt; St Petersburg British-Russia Soc.; Co-ordinator, UK projects for St Petersburg Health Dept. Employment Advr, This is Your Right, Granada TV, 1970–89. Governor: William Temple Foundn, 1980–87; Rainhill High Sch., 1994–2003; Settlebeck High Sch., 2004–06; Chm. Governors, Broadway Community High Sch., St Helens, 1999–2004. Chm. Trustees, Prescot and St Helens Victim Support Service. Chm., Sedbergh Book Town Cttee Ltd, 2004–08. *Recreations:* reading, promoting values of socialist ethics. *Address:* 17 Bainbridge Road, Sedbergh, Cumbria LA10 5AU. *T:* (01539) 620314. *Died 21 Dec. 2010.*

BARR, Danielle; Member, Broadcasting Standards Commission, 1994–99; *b* 7 Aug. 1940; *d* of Michael and Helen Brachfeld; *m* 1966, Marvin Stein; one *d,* and one step *s. Educ:* Tichon Hadash High Sch., Tel Aviv. Nat. Service, Israeli Army, 1958–60; Account Exec., Crane Advertising, 1961–64; Asst Advertising Manager, Goya, 1964–67; Brand Manager, 1967–76, Mktg Manager, 1976–80, Elida Gibbs; Dir, Geers Gross Advertising, 1980–84; Head of Advertising, Natwest Bank, 1984–87; Man. Dir, 1987–89, Chm., 1989–91, Publicis; Man. Dir, Third Age Mktg, 1993–95. Mem., Mktg Gp of GB, 1986–. *Recreations:* theatre, music, quilting. *Address:* 20 Jameson Street, W8 7SH. *T:* (020) 7221 2632. *Club:* Women's Advertising of London (Pres., 1985–86).
Died 23 Oct. 2009.

BARR, Prof. James, DD; FBA 1969; Professor of Hebrew Bible, Vanderbilt University, Nashville, Tennessee, 1989–98, Distinguished Professor, 1994–98, then Emeritus; *b* 20 March 1924; *s* of Rev. Prof. Allan Barr, DD; *m* 1950, Jane J. S. Hepburn, MA; two *s* one *d*. *Educ*: Daniel Stewart's Coll., Edinburgh; Edinburgh Univ. (MA 1948, BD 1951); MA 1976, BD, DD 1981, Oxon. Served War of 1939–45 as pilot in RNVR (Fleet Air Arm), 1942–45. Minister of Church of Scotland, Tiberias, Israel, 1951–53; Prof. of New Testament Lit. and Exegesis, Presbyterian Coll., Montreal, 1953–55; Prof. of Old Testament Lit. and Theology, Edinburgh Univ., 1955–61; Prof. of Old Testament Lit. and Theology, Princeton Theol Seminary, 1961–65; Prof. of Semitic Langs and Lits, Manchester Univ., 1965–76; Oriel Prof. of the Interpretation of Holy Scripture, and Fellow of Oriel Coll., Oxford Univ., 1976–78 (Hon Fellow, 1980); Regius Prof. of Hebrew, Oxford Univ., and Student of Christ Church, 1978–89, Prof. Emeritus, 1989. Visiting Professor: Hebrew Univ., Jerusalem, 1973; Chicago Univ., 1975, 1981; Strasbourg Univ., 1975–76; Brown Univ., Providence, RI, 1985, 1994; Univ. of Otago, NZ, 1986; Univ. of South Africa, 1986; Vanderbilt Univ., Nashville, Tenn, 1987–88; Heidelberg Univ., 1993; Chinese Univ. of Hong Kong, 2004; lectured: in Princeton Univ., 1962–63; in Union Theol Seminary, NY, 1963; in Pittsburgh Theol Seminary, 2000; in UCLA, 2002. Lectures: Currie, Austin Theol Seminary, Texas, 1964; Cadbury, Birmingham Univ., 1969; Faculty, Cardiff, 1969, 1986; Croall, Edinburgh Univ., 1970; Grinfield, on the Septuagint, Oxford Univ., 1974–78; Firth, Nottingham Univ., 1978; Sprunt, Richmond, Va, 1982; Sanderson, Ormond Coll., Melbourne, 1982; Schweich, British Acad., 1986; Cole, Vanderbilt, 1988; Sarum, Oxford, 1989; Read-Tuckwell, Bristol, 1990; Gifford, Edinburgh, 1991; Hensley Henson, Oxford, 1997; Alexander Robertson, Glasgow Univ., 1999; Guggenheim Meml Fellowship for study in biblical semantics, 1965. Mem., Inst. for Advanced Study, Princeton, NJ, 1985. Editor: Jl of Semitic Studies, 1965–76; Oxford Hebrew Dictionary, 1974–80. President: SOTS, 1973; British Assoc. for Jewish Studies, 1978. FRAS 1969; Fellow, Amer. Acad. of Arts and Scis, 1993. Corresp. Mem., Göttingen Acad. of Sciences, 1976; Member: Norwegian Acad. of Science and Letters, 1977; Royal Soc. of Scis, Uppsala, 1991; Amer. Philosophical Soc., 1993; Hon. Mem., Soc. of Biblical Lit. (USA), 1983. Hon. Fellow, SOAS, 1975. Hon. DD: Knox Coll., Toronto, 1964; Dubuque, 1974; St Andrews, 1974; Edinburgh, 1983; Victoria Univ., Toronto, 1988; Hon. DTheol: Univ. of South Africa, 1986; Protestant Theol Faculty, Paris, 1988; Oslo, 1991; Helsinki, 1997; Hon. MA Manchester, 1969. *Publications*: The Semantics of Biblical Language, 1961; Biblical Words for Time, 1962; Old and New in Interpretation, 1966; Comparative Philology and the Text of the Old Testament, 1968; The Bible in the Modern World, 1973; Fundamentalism, 1977; The Typology of Literalism, 1979; Explorations in Theology 7: The Scope and Authority of the Bible, 1980; Holy Scripture: Canon, Authority, Criticism, 1983; Escaping from Fundamentalism, 1984; The Variable Spellings of the Hebrew Bible, 1988; The Garden of Eden and the Hope of Immortality, 1992; Biblical Faith and Natural Theology, 1993; The Concept of Biblical Theology, 1999; History and Ideology in the Old Testament, 2000; articles in Semitic and biblical journals. *Recreation*: bird watching. *Address*: 890 East Harrison Avenue, #17, Pomona, CA 91767, USA. *Died 14 Oct. 2006.*

BARR, His Honour Reginald Alfred; a Circuit Judge (formerly Judge of County Courts), 1970–92; *b* 21 Nov. 1920; *s* of Alfred Charles Barr; *m* 1946, Elaine, 2nd *d* of James William Charles O'Bala Morris, Llanstephan, Carmarthenshire. *Educ*: Christ's Hospital; Trinity Coll., Oxford (MA). Served War, 1941–46, Middle East and Burma. Called to Bar, Middle Temple, 1954; Standing Counsel to Registrar of Restrictive Trading Agreements, 1962–70. Mem. Review Bd for Govt Contracts, 1969–70. *Address*: Aynhoe Park, Aynho, Banbury, Oxon OX17 3BQ. *Died 13 Sept. 2007.*

BARR, William Greig; DL; Rector, Exeter College, Oxford, 1972–82; *b* 10 June 1917; *s* of late William S. Barr, Glasgow; *m* 1st, 1954, Helen Georgopoulos (*d* 1988); two *s*; 2nd, 1991, Valerie Bowman (*née* Tatham). *Educ*: Sedbergh Sch.; Magdalen Coll., Oxford. Stanhope Prize, 1938; 1st cl., Hon. Sch. of Modern History, 1939. Served War, 1939–45: Lt-Col, Royal Devon Yeomanry. Exeter College, Oxford: Fellow, 1945–72; Sub-Rector, 1947–54; Sen. Tutor, 1960–66; Hon. Fellow, 1982; Oxford University: Lectr in Modern History, 1949–72; Jun. Proctor, 1951–52; Pro-Vice-Chancellor, 1980–82. Hon. Treas., Oxford Univ. Rugby Football Club, 1948–73. A Rhodes Trustee, 1975–87. Visiting Prof. of Hist., Univ. of South Carolina, 1968. DL Oxon 1974. *Address*: 24 Northmoor Road, Oxford OX2 6UR. *T*: (01865) 558253. *Died 23 April 2008.*

BARRACLOUGH, Air Chief Marshal Sir John, KCB 1970 (CB 1969); CBE 1961; DFC 1942; AFC 1941; FRAeS; Gentleman Usher to the Sword of State, 1980–88; Vice-Chairman, Commonwealth War Graves Commission, 1981–86 (Commissioner 1974–86); Director, Data-Track Fuel Services Ltd, since 1996; *b* 2 May 1918; *s* of late Horatio and Marguerite Maude Barraclough; *m* 1946, Maureen (*née* McCormack) (*d* 2001), *niece* of George Noble, Count Plunkett; one *d*. *Educ*: Cranbrook Sch. Mem., Artists' Rifles, 1935–38. Commissioned RAF, 1938. Air Vice-Marshal, 1964; Air Marshal, 1970; Air Chief Marshal, 1973. Served Near, Middle and Far East; commanded RAF Mogadishu, 1943; despatches 1945; first single-engined jet flight to S Africa, 1951. Examining Wing, Central Flying Sch., 1948–51; Staff of IDC, 1952–54; Station Commander, RAF Biggin Hill, 1954–56 and Middleton St George, 1956–58; GC Ops, FEAF, 1958–61; Dir of Public Relations, Air Ministry, 1961–64; AOC No 19 Group, and NATO Air Comdr, Central Sub-Area, Eastern Atlantic Comd, 1964–67; Harvard Business Sch., AMP, 1967; AOA, Bomber Command, 1967–68; AOA, Strike Comd, 1968–70; Vice-Chief of Defence Staff, 1970–72; Air Secretary, 1972–74; Comdt, Royal Coll. of Defence Studies, 1974–76, retired. Underwriting Mem. of Lloyd's, 1979–85. Hon. Air Cdre, No 3 (County of Devon) Maritime HQ Unit, RAuxAF, 1979–90; Hon. Inspector Gen., RAuxAF, 1984–89. Mem., RAF Training and Educn Adv. Bd, 1976–79; Vice Chairman: Air League Council, 1977–81; British Export Finance Adv. Council, 1982–89; Chm., Council, 1977–80, Vice-Pres., 1980–90, Vice-Patron, 1990–, RUSI; President: Air Public Relations Assoc., 1976–99 (Vice-Patron, 1999–); West Devon Area, St John Ambulance, 1977–85; Royal Crescent Soc., Bath, 1990–2003; Coastal Comd and Maritime Air Assoc., 1999–; Maritime Air Trust, 2003– (Chm., 1999–2003), Trustee and Chm., RAF Project Constant Endeavour, 2001–05); Special Advr, Air League, 1994–97; Vice President: Bomber Command Assoc., 2000–; Aircrew Assoc., 2001–; Artists' Rifles Assoc., 2006–. Editl Dir, 1978–81, Vice-Chm. of Editl Bd, 1981–86, NATO's Sixteen Nations. Freeman, City of London, 2001; Freeman, 1970, Liveryman, 2001, GAPAN. Air League Gold Medal, 1999. OStJ 1985. QCVSA 1951. *Publications*: (jtly) The Third World War, 1978; contrib. to The Third World War: The Untold Story, 1982; contribs to professional jls. *Recreations*: country pursuits, sailing (Irish Admiral's Cup Team, 1973), classic cars. *Address*: 28 The Royal Crescent, Bath BA1 2LT. *Clubs*: Boodle's, Royal Air Force; Bath and County; Royal Western Yacht. *Died 10 May 2008.*

BARRAN, Sir John (Napoleon Ruthven), 4th Bt *cr* 1895; Head of Information Technology, Central Office of Information, 1985–87; *b* 14 Feb. 1934; *s* of Sir John Leighton Barran, 3rd Bt, and Hon. Alison Mary (*d* 1973), 3rd *d* of 9th Baron Ruthven, CB, CMG, DSO; *S* father, 1974; *m* 1965, Jane Margaret, *d* of Sir Stanley Hooker, CBE, FRS; one *s* one *d*. *Educ*: Heatherdown Sch., Ascot; Winchester Coll.; University Coll., London (BA 1994). National Service, 1952–54, Lieut, 5th Roy. Inniskilling Dragoon Guards; served Canal Zone. Asst Account Executive: Dorland Advertising Ltd, 1956–58; Masius &

Fergusson Advertising Ltd, 1958–61; Account Executive, Ogilvy, Benson & Mather (New York) Inc., 1961–63; Overseas TV News Service, COI, 1964; First Sec. (Information), British High Commission, Ottawa, 1965–67; Central Office of Information: Home Documentary Film Section, 1967–72; Overseas TV and Film News Services, 1972–75; TV Commercials and Fillers Unit, 1975–78; Head of Viewdata Unit, 1978–85. Founded Video History to make documentaries, 1986. *Recreations:* entertaining, gardening, shooting. *Heir:* s John Ruthven Barran [*b* 10 Nov. 1971; *m* 2005, Helen Elizabeth Ward]. *Address:* 17 St Leonard's Terrace, SW3 4QG. *T:* (020) 7730 2801; The Hermitage, East Bergholt, Suffolk CO7 6RB; Middle Rigg Farm, Sawley, North Yorks HG4 3HA. *Died 25 March 2010.*

BARRATT-BOYES, Sir Brian (Gerald), KBE 1971 (CBE 1966); Surgeon-in-Charge, Cardio-Thoracic Surgical Unit, Greenlane Hospital, Auckland, 1964–88, then Hon. Consultant; Hon. Senior Cardio-Thoracic Surgeon, Mercy (formerly Mater Misericordiae) Hospital, Auckland, 1966–89; *b* 13 Jan. 1924; *s* of Gerald Cave Boyes and Edna Myrtle Boyes (*née* Barratt); *m* 1st, 1949, Norma Margaret Thompson (marr. diss. 1986); five *s*; 2nd, 1986, Sara Rose Monester. *Educ:* Wellington Coll.; Univ. of Otago. MB, ChB 1946; FRACS 1952; FACS 1960; ChM 1962. Lectr in Anatomy, Otago Univ. Med. Sch., 1947; House Surg. and Registrar, Wellington Hosp., 1948–50; Surgical Registrar and Pathology Registrar, Palmerston North Hosp., 1950–52; Fellow in Cardio-Thoracic Surgery, Mayo Clinic, USA, 1953–55; Nuffield Trav. Fellowship UK (Bristol Univ.), 1956; Sen. Cardio-Thoracic Surg., Greenlane Hosp., 1957. Hon. Prof. of Surgery, Auckland Univ., 1971; Sir Arthur Sims Commonwealth Travelling Prof., 1982. FRSNZ 1970. Hon. FACS 1977; Hon. FRCS 1985; Hon. Fellow, Royal Coll. of Surgeons of Thailand, 1987; Hon. FACC 1988; Hon. FRACP 1995. Hon. DSc, 1985. R. T. Hall Prize for Disting. Cardiac Surgery in Austr. and NZ, 1966; René Leriche Prize, Société Internationale de Chirurgie, 1987; Award for Excellence in Surgery, RACS, 1994; Dist. Alumni Award, Mayo Foundn, 2005. Depicted on special stamp issued by NZ Post (Famous New Zealanders series, science, medicine and education category), 1995. *Publications:* Heart Disease in Infancy: diagnosis and surgical treatment, 1973; (jtly) Cardiac Surgery, 1986, 3rd edn 2003; numerous in med. jls throughout the world. *Recreations:* farming, trout fishing, tennis. *Address:* 27 Beach Road, Milford, PO Box 31–408, Auckland 1330, New Zealand. *Club:* Northern (Auckland). *Died 8 March 2006.*

BARRE, Raymond; Chevalier de la Légion d'Honneur, Chevalier de l'Ordre National du Mérite agricole, Officier des Palmes Académiques; Grand Croix de l'Ordre National du Mérite, 1977; Député, Rhône, French National Assembly, 1978–2002; Mayor of Lyon, 1995–2001; *b* Saint-Denis, Réunion, 12 April 1924; *s* of René Barre and Charlotte Déramond; *m* 1954, Eve Hegedüs; two *s*. *Educ:* Lycée Leconte-de-Lisle, Saint-Denis-de-la-Réunion; Faculté de Droit, Paris; Institut d'Etudes Politiques, Paris. Professor at Faculté de Droit et des Sciences Economiques: Caen, 1950; Paris (Chair of Political Economy), 1963; Econs Res. Dir Foundation Nat. des Scis Politiques, 1958; Professor at Institut d'Etudes Politiques, Paris, 1961, 1982–94. Director of Cabinet of Mr J.-M. Jeanneney (Minister of Industry), 1959–62; Member: Cttee of Experts (Comité Lorain) studying financing of investments in France, 1963–64; Gen. Cttee on Economy and Financing of Fifth Plan, 1966; Vice-Chm., Commn of European Communities (responsible for Economic and Financial Affairs), 1967–72; Minister of Foreign Trade, Jan.–Aug. 1976; Prime Minister of France, 1976–81, and Minister of Economics and Finance, 1976–78; elected to National Assembly, from Rhône, 1978. Mem. Gen. Council, Banque de France, 1973; Chm. Cttee for studying Housing Financing Reform, 1975–76. *Publications:* Economie Politique, vol. 1, 1961, vol. 2, 1965; Une Politique pour l'Avenir, 1981; Refléxions pour Demain,

1984; Question de Confiance, 1987; Au Tournant du Siècle, 1988. *Address:* 4–6 avenue Emile-Acollas, 75007 Paris, France. *Died 25 Aug. 2007.*

BARRETT-LENNARD, Rev. Sir Hugh (Dacre), 6th Bt *cr* 1801; Priest, London Oratory; *b* 27 June 1917; *s* of Sir Fiennes Cecil Arthur Barrett-Lennard (*d* 1963) and Winifrede Mignon (*d* 1969), *d* of Alfred Berlyn; *S* cousin, 1977. *Educ:* Radley College, Berks; Pontifical Beda College, Rome. Teaching, 1936. Served War of 1939–45, NW Europe (despatches); enlisted London Scottish, Jan. 1940; commissioned 2nd Lt, Oct. 1940; Captain Essex Regt, 1945. Entered Brompton Oratory, 1946; ordained Priest in Rome, 1950. *Recreations:* on Isle of Eigg, Hebrides. *Heir: cousin* Peter John Barrett-Lennard, *b* 26 Sept. 1942. *Address:* The Oratory, Brompton Road, South Kensington, SW7 2RP. *Died 21 June 2007.*

BARRON, Brian Munro, MBE 2007; New York News Correspondent, BBC Television News and Current Affairs, since 2005; *b* 28 April 1940; *s* of Albert and Norah Barron; *m* 1974, Angela Lee, MA; one *d*. *Educ:* Bristol Grammar School. Junior Reporter, Western Daily Press, Bristol, 1956–60; Dep. Chief Sub-editor, Evening World, Bristol, 1960–61; Sub-editor, Daily Mirror, 1961–63; Dep. Chief Sub-editor, Evening Post, Bristol, 1963–65; Sub-editor, BBC External Services, London, 1965–67; Correspondent, BBC Radio: Aden, 1967–68; ME, Cairo, 1968–69; SE Asia, Singapore, 1969–71; Reporter, BBC TV News, 1971–73; Correspondent, BBC TV: Far East, Hong Kong, 1973–76; Africa, Nairobi, 1976–81; Ireland, 1981–83; Washington, 1983–86; Asia, 1986–94; New York, 1994–2000; Rome, 2000–04. Royal Television Society: Journalist of the Year, 1979–80; Internat. Reporting Award, 1985. *Recreations:* opera, cinema, running, tennis. *Address:* British Broadcasting Corporation, 450 West 33rd Street, New York, NY 10001, USA. *Clubs:* Oriental, Travellers. *Died 16 Sept. 2009.*

BARRON, Henry Denis; Judge of the Supreme Court, Ireland, 1997–2000; *b* 25 May 1928; *s* of Harrie and Lena Barron; *m* 1958, Rosalind Scheps (*d* 1997); two *s* two *d*. *Educ:* Castle Park Sch., Dalkey; Coll. of St Columba, Rathfarnham, Dublin; Trinity Coll., Dublin (BA, LLB); King's Inns, Dublin (BL). Called to the Irish Bar, 1951, Sen. Bar, 1970; called to the Bar, Middle Temple, 1953; Judge of the High Court, Ireland, 1982–97. Mem. (sole), Commn of Inquiry into bombings in Dublin, Monaghan, 1974, and Dundalk, 1975, 2000–05. Visitor, Univ. of Dublin, 1983–2003. *Recreations:* bridge, travel. *Club:* Kildare Street and University (Dublin). *Died 25 Feb. 2010.*

BARRON, Prof. John Penrose, MA, DPhil, FSA; Master of St Peter's College, Oxford, 1991–2003, Hon. Fellow, 2003; *b* 27 April 1934; *s* of George Barron and Minnie Leslie Marks; *m* 1962, Caroline Mary Hogarth (Prof. C. M. Barron, FSA); two *d*. *Educ:* Clifton Coll.; Balliol Coll., Oxford (Hon. Exhibnr). 1st Cl., Class. Hon. Mods, 1955; Lit. Hum., 1957; MA 1960, DPhil 1961: Thomas Whitcombe Greene Prize, 1955, and Scholar, 1957; Barclay Head Prize, 1959; Cromer Prize, British Academy, 1965. London University: Asst Lectr in Latin, Bedford Coll., 1959–61, and Lectr, 1961–64; Lectr in Archaeology, UCL, 1964–67; Reader in Archaeology and Numismatics, 1967–71; Prof. of Greek Lang. and Lit., 1971–91, and Head of Dept of Classics, 1972–84, KCL; Dean, Faculty of Arts, 1976–80; Dir, Inst. of Classical Studies, 1984–91; Dean, Insts for Advanced Study, 1989–91; Mem. Senate, 1977–81, 1987–91; Mem. Academic Council, 1977–81, 1985–89; Public Orator, 1978–81, 1986–88; Pro-Vice-Chancellor, 1987–89; Oxford University: Chairman: Conf. of Colls, 1993–95; Ashmolean Mus. Review, 1993–95; Admissions Cttee, 1997–2000. Mem., UFC, 1989–93. FKC 1988. Vis. Mem., Inst. for Advanced Study, Princeton, 1973. Blegen Distinguished Vis. Res. Prof., Vassar Coll., NY, 1981; T. B. L. Webster Vis. Prof., Stanford Univ., 1986; Visiting Professor: Aust. Archaeol Inst., Athens, 1994; KCL,

2003–; Dist. Sen. Fellow, Sch. of Advanced Study, London Univ., 2004–. Lectures: Eberhard L. Faber, Princeton, 1985; Woodward, Yale, 1985; Sotheby, Edinburgh, 1986; Dill, QUB, 1986; Batchelor, UEA, 1992; Dabis, Royal Holloway, 1996. Vice-Pres., Soc. for Promotion of Hellenic Studies, 1993– (Trustee, 1970–2000; Hon. Sec., 1981–90; Pres., 1990–93); Mem. Council, Soc. of Antiquaries, 2003–07 (Vice-Pres., 2004–07); MAE 1990. Trustee, Prince of Wales Inst. of Architecture, 1990–96. Jt Chm., Oxford & Cambridge Schs Exam. Bd, 1993–96. Chairman: Lambeth Palace Library Cttee, 1998–; Sir Ernest Cassel Educn Trust, 2005–. Governor: SOAS, 1989–99 (Vice-Pres., 1992–99); St Paul's Schools, London, 1991–2007; Clifton Coll., Bristol, 1996– (Pres., 1999–); Radley Coll., 1998–2003; Almoner, Christ's Hosp., 1975–80. *Publications:* Greek Sculpture, 1965 (new and rev. edn 1981); Silver Coins of Samos, 1966; articles in Classical Quarterly, Jl of Hellenic Studies, Bulletin of Inst. of Classical Studies, etc. *Recreations:* travel, gardens. *Address:* 9 Boundary Road, NW8 0HE. *Clubs:* Athenæum, Oxford and Cambridge.   *Died 16 Aug. 2008.*

BARROW, Captain Sir Richard John Uniacke, 6th Bt cr 1835; b 2 Aug. 1933; s of Sir Wilfrid John Wilson Croker Barrow, 5th Bt and (Gwladys) Patricia (née Uniacke); S father, 1960; m 1961, Alison Kate (marr. diss. 1974; she d 2009), yr d of late Capt. Russell Grenfell, RN, and of Mrs Lindsay-Young; one s two d. *Educ:* Abbey Sch., Ramsgate; Beaumont Coll., Old Windsor. Commnd 2nd Lieut Irish Guards, 1952; served: Germany, 1952–53; Egypt, 1953–56; Cyprus, 1958; Germany, 1959–60; retired, 1960; joined International Computers and Tabulators Ltd; resigned 1973. *Heir:* s Anthony John Grenfell Barrow [b 24 May 1962; m 1st, 1990, Rebecca Mary Long (marr. diss. 1996); 2nd, 2001, Elisa Isabel Marzo Pérez; one d; and one d]. *Address:* 2 Underwood House, Sycamore Gardens, W6 0AR.   *Died 16 Feb. 2009.*

BARROW, Simon William; JP; Headmaster, The Oratory School, 1992–2000; b 17 Jan. 1942; s of Alfred Francis Lendon Barrow and Ruth Mary Barrow; m 1977, Brenda Cora Mary Kelly; one s one d. *Educ:* Stonyhurst; Reading Univ. (BA Mod Hist). Asst Master, Caldicott Sch., Farnham Royal, 1963–69; The Oratory Sch., Woodcote, 1969–2000 (Housemaster, 1971; Dep. Head, 1982). Member: CAB, 2001–05; Young Offenders' Referral Panel, 2002–. Gov., Winterfold Hse Sch., 2002–. JP Reading 2002. *Recreations:* walking, gardening, giving others good advice. *Address:* 19 Treforgan, Hunters Chase, Caversham, Reading RG4 7XG.   *Died 8 Dec. 2006.*

BARRY, Prof. Brian Michael, FBA 1988; Lieber Professor of Political Philosophy, Columbia University, New York, 1998–2005, then Emeritus; b 7 Aug. 1936; s of James Frederick and Doris Rose Barry; m 1st, 1960, Joanna Hill Scroggs (marr. diss. 1988); one s; 2nd, 1991, Anni Parker. *Educ:* Taunton's Sch., Southampton; Queen's Coll., Oxford (MA; DPhil 1965). Lloyd-Muirhead Res. Fellow, Univ. of Birmingham, 1960–61; Rockefeller Fellow in Legal and Political Philosophy, and Fellow of Harvard College, 1961–62; Asst Lectr, Keele Univ., 1962–63; Lectr, Univ. of Southampton, 1963–65; Tutorial Fellow, University Coll., Oxford, 1965–66; Official Fellow, Nuffield Coll., Oxford, 1966–69 and 1972–75; Prof., Univ. of Essex, 1969–72 (Dean of Social Studies, 1971–72); Prof., Univ. of British Columbia, 1975–76; Fellow, Center for Advanced Study in the Behavioral Scis, 1976–77; Professor: Univ. of Chicago, 1977–82; California Inst. of Technology, 1982–86; European Univ. Inst., Florence, 1986–87; Prof. of Pol Sci., LSE, 1987–98, then Emeritus. Founding Editor, British Jl of Political Science, 1971–72; Editor, Ethics, 1979–82. *Publications:* Political Argument, 1965; Sociologists, Economists and Democracy, 1970; The Liberal Theory of Justice, 1973; (with Russell Hardin) Rational Man and Irrational Society?, 1982; Democracy, Power and Justice: collected essays, 1989, rev. edn 1991;

Theories of Justice, 1989; Justice as Impartiality, 1995; Culture and Equality, 2001; Why Social Justice Matters, 2005; articles in learned jls. *Recreations:* theatre, cooking.   *Died 10 March 2009.*

BARRY, His Honour James Edward; a Circuit Judge, 1994–2006; b 27 May 1938; s of James Douglas Barry and Margaret Elizabeth Barry (née Thornton); m 1963, Pauline Pratt; three s. *Educ:* Merchant Taylors' Sch., Crosby; Brasenose Coll., Oxford (schol.; MA Jurisp.). Called to the Bar, Inner Temple, 1963; in practice, NE Circuit, 1963–85; Stipendiary Magistrate for S Yorks, 1985–94; a Recorder, 1985–94. Part-time Chm., Industrial Tribunals, 1983–85. *Recreations:* reading, eating and drinking.   *Died 25 Oct. 2010.*

BART, André S.; *see* Schwarz-Bart.

BARTLETT, Prof. Neil, FRS 1973; Professor of Chemistry, University of California, Berkeley, 1969–93, then Professor Emeritus; Principal Investigator, Chemical Sciences Division, Lawrence Berkeley Laboratory, 1969–99; b Newcastle upon Tyne, 15 Sept. 1932; s of Norman Bartlett and Ann Willins Bartlett (née Vock), both of Newcastle upon Tyne; m 1957, Christina I., d of J. W. F. Cross, Guisborough, Yorks; three s one d. *Educ:* Heaton Grammar Sch., Newcastle upon Tyne; King's Coll., Univ. of Durham, Newcastle upon Tyne. BSc 1954, PhD 1958. Senior Chemistry Master, The Duke's Sch., Alnwick, Northumberland, 1957–58; Mem. Faculty (Dept of Chemistry), Univ. of British Columbia, 1958–66; Prof. of Chemistry, Princeton Univ., and Scientist, Bell Telephone Laboratories, Murray Hill, NJ, USA, 1966–69. Visiting Miller Prof., Univ. of Calif, Berkeley, 1967–68; Brotherton Vis. Prof., Univ. of Leeds, 1981; Erskine Fellow, Univ. of Canterbury, NZ, 1983; Vis. Fellow, All Souls, Oxford, 1984, etc. Foreign Associate: Nat. Acad. of Sciences, USA, 1979; Acad. des Scis, France, 1989; For. MAE, 1998; For. FRS(Can) 2001; Member: Deutsche Akademie der Naturforscher Leopoldina, 1969; Der Akademie der Wissenschaften in Göttingen, 1977; Amer. Chem. Soc., etc; Fellow: Amer. Acad. of Arts and Scis, 1977; Chem. Inst. of Canada. Hon. FRSC 2002. Sigma Xi. Hon. DSc: Waterloo, Canada, 1968; Colby Coll., Maine, USA, 1972; Newcastle, 1981; McMaster, 1992; UBC, 2006; Dr hc: Bordeaux, 1976; Ljubljana, 1989; Nantes, 1990; Hon. LLD Simon Fraser, 1993; Hon. Dr rer. nat. Freie Univ., Berlin, 1998. Corday-Morgan Medal and Prize of Chem. Soc., 1962; Res. Corp. Plaque and Prize, 1965; E. W. R. Steacie Prize, 1965; Robert A. Welch Award, 1976; Medal of Inst. Jožef Stefan, Ljubljana, 1980; W. H. Nichols Medal, NY Section, ACS, 1983; Prix Moissan, 1988; Amer. Chem. Soc. Award for Distinguished Service to Inorganic Chemistry, 1989, for Creative Work in Fluorine Chemistry, 1992; Pauling Medal, 1989; Bonner Chemicpreis, Bonn, 1992; Davy Medal, Royal Soc., 2002; Grand Prix de la Maison de la Chimie, Paris, 2004. *Publications:* The Chemistry of the Monatomic Gases, 1975; The Oxidation of Oxygen and Related Chemistry, 2001; scientific papers to: Jl of Chem. Soc., Inorganic Chem., etc; Mem. various editorial advisory bds in Gt Britain, France and USA. *Recreations:* water colour painting, walking in high country, gardening. *Address:* 6 Oak Drive, Orinda, CA 94563, USA; Chemistry Department, University of California, Berkeley, CA 94720, USA; e-mail: nbartlett@LBL.gov.   *Died 5 Aug. 2008.*

BARTOSIK, Rear-Adm. Josef Czeslaw, CB 1968; DSC 1943; b 20 July 1917; m 1st, 1943, Cynthia Pamela Bowman (marr. diss.); two s one d (and one s decd); 2nd, 1969, Jeannine Scott, MBE (née Bridgeman) (d 2007). Joined Polish Navy, 1935; served War 1939–45 as gunnery officer in destroyers in Norwegian campaign, E Mediterranean, Western Approaches, convoys to Malta, Murmansk and Atlantic, Normandy operation; transf. to RN, 1948; battleship trng, HMS Anson, 1948, HMS Vanguard, 1949; 1st Lieut HMS Loch Scavaig, 1950–51, Mediterranean Stn, Suez Canal guardship duties; commanded: HMS Comus, 1955–56, Far East Stn;

HMS Scarborough and 5th Frigate Sqn, 1960–61, Far East Stn; HMS Seahawk (RN Air Station Culdrose), 1962–63; HMS London, 1964–65, S Atlantic and Far East Stns; Rear-Adm. 1966; Asst Chief of Naval Staff (Ops), 1966–68; retired 1968. Co-ordinating Dir, European Jt Org., Australia Europe Container Service and Australia NZ Europe Container Service, 1969–81, retired 1981. *Address:* 33 Cheval Place, SW7 1EW.
Died 14 Jan. 2008.

BARTY-KING, Mark Baxter, MC 1958; Chairman, Wade & Doherty Literary Agency, since 2004; *b* 3 March 1938; *s* of George Ingram, (Tom), Barty-King and Barbara (*née* Baxter); *m* 1st, 1963, Margild Bolten (marr. diss. 1975); two *s*; 2nd, 1976, Marilyn Scott Barrett; two *s*. *Educ:* Winchester Coll. Nat. Service, 13th/18th Royal Hussars (QMO), Aden, Oman, Malaya, 1957–61 (Capt.). Abelard Schuman, NY, 1962–63; John Howell Books, San Francisco, 1964–65; Heinemann Gp, 1966–74 (Director: Peter Davies Ltd, 1969; William Heinemann Ltd, 1971); Granada Publishing: Editorial Dir, 1974–81; Man. Dir, Hardback Div., 1981–83; William Collins Ltd, 1983–84; Transworld Publishers Ltd, 1984–2004 (became part of Random House Group, 1998): Dep. Man. Dir, Publishing, 1992; Man. Dir and CEO, 1995–2000; Chm., 2001–03. Founder, Bantam Press, 1985. Chm. of Govs, St John's Sch., Northwood, 1997–2004. FRSA. Mem., Ct of Assts, Merchant Taylors' Co., 1992–. *Recreation:* countryside. *Address:* 46 Elms Road, SW4 9EX. *T:* (020) 7622 1544. *Clubs:* Groucho, Lansdowne.
Died 25 March 2006.

BARZEL, Dr Rainer Candidus; Member of the Bundestag, Federal Republic of Germany, 1957–87; *b* 20 June 1924; *s* of Dr Candidus Barzel, Senior Asst Master, and Maria Barzel; *m* 1948, Kriemhild Schumacher (*d* 1980); (one *d* decd); *m* 1982, Hilda Henselder (*d* 1995); *m* 1997, Ute Cremer. *Educ:* studied Jurisprudence and Political Economy, Univ. of Cologne (Referendar, Dr jur.). With Govt of North Rhine-Westphalia, 1949–56; Federal Minister in the Adenauer Govt, for all-German affairs, Dec. 1962–Oct. 1963; Chairman: Cttee on Economic Affairs, German Fed. Parlt, 1977–79; Cttee on Foreign Affairs, 1980–82; Fed. Minister for Inter-German Affairs, 1982–83; Pres. of Bundestag, 1983–84. Coordinator for German-French cooperation, Feb.-Dec. 1980, 1986–90. Chm., CDU, 1971–73 and Chm., CDU/CSU Group in German Federal Parlt, 1964–73. Pres., German-French Inst., 1980–83. *Publications:* (all publ. in Germany): Die geistigen Grundlagen der politischen Parteien, 1947; Die deutschen Parteien, 1952; Gesichtspunkte eines Deutschen, 1968; Es ist noch nicht zu spät, 1976; Auf dem Drahtseil, 1978; Das Formular, 1979; Unterwegs—Woher und wohin, 1982; Im Streit und umstritten, 1986; Geschichten aus der Politik, 1987; Ermland und Masuren—Zu Besuch, aber nicht als ein Fremder, 1988; Plädoyer für Deutschland, 1988; (ed) Sternstunden des Parlaments, 1989; So Nicht, 1993; Zwei ungehaltene Reden, 1996; Von Bonn nach Berlin, Deutschland verändert sich, 1997; Die Tür blieb offen, 1998; Ein gewagtes Leben, 2001; Fibel für Wahlkämpfer und Wähler beiderlei Geschlechts, 2002; Was war, wirkt nach—wohin geht's mit Deutschland, 2005.
Died 26 Aug. 2006.

BASING, 5th Baron *cr* 1887; **Neil Lutley Sclater-Booth;** *b* 16 Jan. 1939; *s* of 4th Baron Basing and Jeannette (*d* 1957), *d* of late Neil Bruce MacKelvie, New York; *S* father, 1983; *m* 1967, Patricia Ann, *d* of late George Bryan Whitfield, New Haven, Conn; two *s*. *Educ:* Eton; Harvard Univ. (BA). *Heir:* *s* Hon. Stuart Anthony Whitfield Sclater-Booth [*b* 18 Dec. 1969; *m* 1997, Kirsten Erica Oxboel; two *s* one *d*]. *Died 24 Nov. 2007.*

BASSET, Bryan Ronald, CBE 1988; Chairman, Royal Ordnance plc, 1985–87; *b* 29 Oct. 1932; *s* of late Ronald Lambart Basset and Lady Elizabeth Basset, DCVO; *m* 1960, Lady Carey Elizabeth Coke, *d* of 5th Earl of Leicester; three *s*. *Educ:* Eton; RMA Sandhurst. Captain, Scots Guards, 1952–57. Stockbroker, Toronto, Canada,

1957–59; Panmure Gordon & Co., Stockbrokers, 1959–72; Managing Director, Philip Hill Investment Trust, 1972–85. *Recreations:* shooting, fishing. *Address:* Farm House, Quarles, Wells-next-the-Sea, Norfolk NR23 1RY. *T:* (01328) 738105. *Club:* White's.
Died 8 Nov. 2010.

BASSETT, Douglas Anthony; Director, National Museum of Wales, 1977–86, then Senior Research Fellow; *b* 11 Aug. 1927; *s* of Hugh Bassett and Annie Jane Bassett; *m* 1955, Elizabeth Menna Roberts (marr. diss.); three *d*. *Educ:* Llanelli Boys' Grammar Sch.; University Coll. of Wales, Aberystwyth. Asst Lectr and Lectr, Dept of Geology, Glasgow Univ., 1952–59; Keeper, Dept of Geology, Nat. Museum of Wales, 1959–77. Member: Water Resources Bd, 1965–73 (Chm., Adv. Cttee for Wales, 1967–73); Nature Conservancy Council (and Chm., Adv. Cttee for Wales), 1973–85; Secretary of State for Wales' Celtic Sea Adv. Cttee, 1974–79; Ordnance Survey Rev. Cttee, 1978–79; Adv. Cttee for Wales, British Council, 1983–90; Founder Mem. and first Chm., Assoc. of Teachers of Geology, 1967–68; Chm., Royal Soc. Cttee on History of Geology, 1972–82. Dir, Nat. Welsh-American Foundn, 1980– (Vice-Pres., 1996–99). Prince of Wales' Cttee, 1977–86. Hon. Professorial Fellow, University Coll., Cardiff, 1977. Editor: Nature in Wales, 1982–87; Manual of Curatorship, Museums Assoc., 1983–. Aberconway Medal, Instn of Geologists, 1985; Silver Medal, Czechoslovakian Soc. for Internat. Relns, 1985; American Order of Ivorites Award, Nat. Welsh-American Foundn, 2007. Mem. White Order of Bards of GB, 1979; Officier de l'Ordre des Arts et des Lettres (received from Min. of Culture, Paris), 1983. *Publications:* Bibliography and Index of Geology and Allied Sciences for Wales and the Welsh Borders, 1897–1958, 1961; A Source-book of Geological, Geomorphological and Soil Maps for Wales and the Welsh Borders (1800–1966), 1967; Wales in Miniature, 1993; contribs to various geological, museum and historical jls and to biographical dictionaries. *Recreations:* bibliography, chronology. *Address:* 4 Romilly Road, Cardiff CF5 1FH. *Died 9 Nov. 2009.*

BASSETT, Nigel F.; *see* Fox Bassett.

BATE, Maj.-Gen. William, CB 1974; OBE 1963; DL; Secretary to the Council of TAVR Associations, 1975–86 (Deputy Secretary, 1973–75); *b* 6 June 1920; *s* of S. Bate, Warrington; *m* 1946, Veronica Mary Josephine (*née* Quinn); two *s* two *d*. Commnd. 1941; war service in Burma, 1941–46 (despatches three times); Senior Instructor, RASC Officers Sch., 1947–50; Co. Comd 7th and 11th Armoured Divs, 1951–53; psc 1954; DAA&QMG Q (Ops), WO, 1955–57; jssc 1957; Admin. Staff Coll., Henley, 1958; Directing Staff, Staff Coll., Camberley, 1958–60; AA&QMG, Ops and Plans, HQ BAOR, 1961–63; CO, 2 Div. Column, BAOR, 1963–65; Col GS, Staff Coll., Camberley, 1965–67; Brig. Q (Maint.), MoD, 1967–68; ADC to the Queen, 1969; idc 1969; Dir of Admin. Planning (Army), 1970; Dir of Movements (Army), MoD, 1971–73. Col Comdt, 1974–86, Rep. Col Comdt, RCT, 1975, 1977, 1982, 1986. Hon. Col, 163 Movement Control Regt, RCT(V), TAVR, 1974–79. President: RASC/RCT Benevolent Fund; Waggon Club. DL Surrey, 1980. *Recreations:* cricket, tennis. *Address:* Netherbury, 14 Belton Road, Camberley, Surrey GU15 2DE. *T:* (01276) 63529. *Clubs:* East India, Devonshire, Sports and Public Schools, MCC.
Died 13 Jan. 2008.

BATES, Sir Edward (Robert), 6th Bt *cr* 1880, of Bellefield, co. Lancaster; *b* 4 July 1946; *s* of Sir Geoffrey Bates, 5th Bt, MC and his 1st wife, Kitty Kendall Lane; *S* father, 2005. *Educ:* Aysgarth Sch.; Gordonstoun; Grenoble Univ. Edward Bates & Sons, merchant bankers, Liverpool, 1969; Spence Veitch, stockbrokers, London, 1970; Northcotes, stockbrokers, London, 1970–75. *Recreations:* tennis, shooting, bird watching. *Heir:* nephew James Geoffrey Bates, *b* 14 March 1985. *Address:* Gyrn Castle, Llanasa, Holywell, Flintshire CH8 9BG. *T:* (01492) 533663. *Died 25 March 2007.*

BATES, Sir Malcolm (Rowland), Kt 1998; Chairman: Premier Farnell plc, 1997–2005; HHG plc, 2003–05; *b* 23 Sept. 1934; *s* of late Rowland Bates and Ivy Bates (*née* Hope); *m* 1960, Lynda Margaret Price; three *d*. *Educ:* Portsmouth Grammar Sch.; Univ. of Warwick (MSc); Harvard Business Sch. FCIS 1963; FRAeS 1993; CCMI (CIMgt 1983). Flying Officer, RAF, 1956–58. Delta Group plc, 1959–68 (Man. Dir, Elkington & Co. plc, 1966–68); Adwest Gp plc, 1968–69; Industrial Reorgn Corp., 1969–70; Man. Dir, Spey Investments, 1970–72; Jt Man. Dir, Wm Brandt & Sons Ltd, 1972–75; General Electric Co. plc: Sen. Commercial Dir, 1976–80; Dir, 1980–97; Dep. Man. Dir, 1985–97. Special Advr to Paymaster General, HM Treasury, 1997–99. Chairman: AMP (UK) plc, 1996–2003; London Transport, 1999–2003. Non-executive Director: Enterprise Oil, 1991–95; Pearl Assurance, 1996–2005; London Life, 1996–2005; BICC plc, 1997–99; Wavetek, Wandel & Goltermann Inc. (formerly Wavetek Corp.) (USA), 1997–99; AMP Ltd (Australia), 1998–2003; Grass Valley Group (USA), 1999–2002; The New Theatre Royal Trustees (Portsmouth) Ltd, 1999–2001; NPI Ltd, 1999–2005. Advr, DLJ Phoenix Equity Partners II, 1997–2004. Chm., Engrg Deregulation Task Force, 1993–94; Member: Industrial Develt Adv. Bd, 1993–99; Private Finance Panel, 1993–96; IMRO, 1995–96; Finance Bd, RAeS, 1997–99. Chm., Business in the Arts, 1996–99; Mem. Council, ABSA, 1996–99; Advr, Nat. Musicians SO, 2001–04; Dir and Trustee, Oxford Philomusica Trust, 2006–08. Vice-Pres., London Playing Fields Soc., 2001– (Chm., Gen. Purposes Cttee, 1995–2001). Gov., Univ. of Westminster, 1995–2002 (Dep. Chm., 1999–2002). Freeman: City of London, 1985; Painter-Stainers' Co., 1985. Hon. FICPD, 1998. Hon. DLitt Westminster, 2002. *Recreations:* classical music, reading. *Address:* Mulberry Close, Croft Road, Goring-on-Thames, Oxon RG8 9ES. *T:* (01491) 872214. *Club:* Royal Air Force. *Died 30 May 2009.*

BATES, Paul Spencer; independent management consultant; *b* 1 Jan. 1940; *s* of Rev. John Spencer Bates and Margaret Annie Bates (*née* Harwood); *m* 1964, Freda Ann Spillard (marr. diss. 1998); two *s*; *m* 2004, Christine Dalby. *Educ:* St Edmund's Sch., Canterbury; Corpus Christi Coll., Cambridge (MA); Lincoln Theol Coll. Deacon 1965, priest 1966; Asst Curate, Hartcliffe, Bristol, 1965–69; Chaplain, Winchester Coll., 1970–80; Dir of Training, dio. of Winchester, 1980–90; Residentiary Canon, Westminster Abbey, 1990–94; Consultant, Alexander Corp., then Alexander, subseq. Sibson & Co., 1994–2000. *Publications:* contrib. SPCK Taleteller series. *Recreations:* watching cricket, piano playing, cooking. *Address:* 78 Claverton Street, SW1V 3AX. *T:* (020) 7592 0163; 15 Rue de l'Avenir, 1950 Brussels, Belgium. *T:* (2) /822256. *Died 29 May 2006.*

BATHO, (Walter) James (Scott), CBE 1998; Chairman: London and Quadrant Housing Trust, 1989–98; Crown Housing Association, 1996–2003; *b* 13 Nov. 1925; *er s* of Walter Scott Batho and Isabella Laidlaw Batho (*née* Common); *m* 1951, Barbara Kingsford; two *s* two *d*. *Educ:* Epsom County Grammar Sch.; Univ. of Edinburgh (MA Eng. Lit. and Lang.). Served War, RNVR, 1943–46. Air Min., 1950–53; WO, 1953–63 (Private Sec. to Perm. Under Sec. of State, 1956–57); MPBW, 1963–70; DoE, 1970–85, Under Sec., 1979–85 (Regl Dir and Chm., Regl Bd for Eastern Region, DoE and Dept of Transport, 1983–85). Chm., Noise Review Wkg Party, DoE, 1990. Pres., Ashtead Choral Soc., 1990–. *Recreations:* singing, reading, gardening. *Address:* Bushpeace, 16 Grays Lane, Ashtead, Surrey KT21 1BU. *T:* (01372) 273471. *Clubs:* Naval, MCC. *Died 17 Nov. 2009.*

BATLEY, John Geoffrey, OBE 1987; CEng; Consultant, Dan-Rail, Copenhagen, 1988–92; Transport Consultant, Carl Bro (UK), 1993–96; *b* 21 May 1930; *s* of John William and Doris Batley; *m* 1953, Cicely Anne Pindar; one *s* (one *d* decd). *Educ:* Keighley Grammar School. MICE. British Rail: trained and qualified as a chartered engineer in NE Region, 1947–53; Asst Divl Engr, Leeds,

1962; Management Services Officer, BR HQ, London, 1965; Dep. Principal, British Transport Staff Coll., Woking, 1970; Divl Manager, Leeds, 1976; Dep. Chief Secretary, BRB, London, 1982; Sec., BRB, 1984–87; Project Co-ordinator, World Bank/Tanzanian Railway Corp., 1988–92. *Recreations:* walking, golf, gardening. *Club:* Farmers. *Died 6 March 2010.*

BATTISCOMBE, (Esther) Georgina, BA; FRSL 1964; author; *b* 21 Nov. 1905; *d* of late George Harwood, MP, Master Cotton Spinner, Bolton, Lancs, and Ellen Hopkinson, *d* of Sir Alfred Hopkinson, KC, MP, first Vice-Chancellor of Manchester Univ.; *m* 1932, Lt-Col Christopher Francis Battiscombe, OBE, FSA (*d* 1964), Grenadier Guards; (one *d* decd). *Educ:* St Michael's Sch., Oxford; Lady Margaret Hall, Oxford. *Publications:* Charlotte Mary Yonge, 1943; Two on Safari, 1946; English Picnics, 1949; Mrs Gladstone, 1956; John Keble (James Tait Black Memorial Prize for best biography of year), 1963; Christina Rossetti, 1965; (ed, with M. Laski) A Chaplet for Charlotte Yonge, 1965; Queen Alexandra, 1969; Shaftesbury, 1974; Reluctant Pioneer: The Life of Elizabeth Wordsworth, 1978; Christina Rossetti: a divided life, 1981; The Spencers of Althorp, 1984; Winter Song, 1992. *Recreation:* looking at churches. *Address:* Thamesfield, Wargrave Road, Henley-on-Thames, Oxfordshire RG9 2LX. *T:* (01491) 575760. *Died 26 Feb. 2006.*

BAUMBERG, Prof. Simon, OBE 2005; DPhil; Professor of Bacterial Genetics, University of Leeds, 1996–2005, then Professor Emeritus; *b* 5 March 1940; *s* of Pincus and Esther Baumberg; *m* 1963, Ruth Elizabeth Geiger; three *s* (and one *s* decd). *Educ:* St Paul's Sch.; Merton Coll., Oxford (MA; DPhil 1964). University of Leeds: Lectr, 1966–76; Sen. Lectr, 1976–92; Reader, 1992–96. EMBO Long-Term Fellow, Univ. of Wisconsin-Madison, 1975–76. Ed., Jl Gen. Microbiol., 1986–91. Medical Research Council: Chairman: Molecular and Cellular Medicine Bd Grants Cttee B, and Mem., Molecular and Cellular Medicine Bd, 1993–97; Non-Clinical Trng Fellowships and Career Develt Awards Panel, 1997–99; Adv. Bd, 1997–2003. Stem Cell Bank User (Non-Clinical) Liaison Cttee, 2003–. Genetical Society: Sec., 1978–84; Vice-Pres., 1984–87 and 1996–99; Society for General Microbiology: Mem. Council, 1986–90; Convener, Physiol., Biochem. and Molecular Genetics Gp, 1992–97. *Publications:* (ed jtly) Microbial Products: new approaches, 1989; (ed jtly) Population Genetics of Bacteria, 1995; (ed jtly) Microbial Responses to Light and Time, 1998; (ed jtly) Transport of Molecules across Microbial Membranes, 1999; (ed) Prokaryotic Gene Expression, 1999; contrib. papers to scientific jls. *Recreations:* listening to classical music, playing the piano badly, hill walking, reading. *Address:* Institute of Integrative and Comparative Biology, L. C. Miall Building, University of Leeds, Leeds LS2 9JT. *T:* (0113) 343 3080. *Died 10 April 2007.*

BAVIN, Alfred Robert Walter, CB 1966; Deputy Secretary, Department of Health and Social Security, 1968–73 (Ministry of Health, 1966–68); *b* 4 April 1917; *s* of late Alfred and late Annie Bavin; *m* 1947, Helen Mansfield (*d* 1987); one *s* three *d*. *Educ:* Christ's Hosp.; Balliol Coll., Oxford. 1st cl. Hon. Mods 1937; 1st cl. Lit. Hum. 1939. Min. of Health, Asst Principal, 1939, Principal, 1946; Cabinet Office, 1948–50; Min. of Health, Principal Private Sec. to Minister, 1951; Asst Sec. 1952; Under-Sec. 1960. Nuffield Home Civil Service Travelling Fellowship, 1956. *Address:* Oakland Court Hotel, Admiralty Road, Felpham, Bognor Regis, West Sussex PO22 7DW. *Died 29 April 2006.*

BAXANDALL, Prof. Michael David Kighley, FBA 1982; Professor of the History of Art, University of California, Berkeley, 1987–96, then Emeritus; *b* 18 Aug. 1933; *o s* of late David Baxandall, CBE, and 1963, Katharina Simon; one *s* one *d*. *Educ:* Manchester Grammar Sch.; Downing Coll., Cambridge (MA); Univs of Pavia and Munich. Jun. Res. Fellow, Warburg Inst., 1959–61; Asst Keeper, Dept of Architecture and Sculpture, Victoria and

Albert Museum, 1961–65; Warburg Institute, University of London: Lectr in Renaissance Studies, 1965–73; Reader, 1973–81; Prof., History of the Classical Tradition, 1981–88. Slade Prof. of Fine Art, Univ. of Oxford, 1974–75; A. D. White Prof.-at-Large, Cornell Univ., 1982–88. *Publications:* Giotto and the Orators, 1971; Painting and Experience in Fifteenth-Century Italy, 1972; South German Sculpture 1480–1530 in the Victoria and Albert Museum, 1974; The Limewood Sculptors of Renaissance Germany, 1980; Patterns of Intention, 1985; (jtly) Tiepolo and the Pictorial Intelligence, 1994; Shadows and Enlightenment, 1995; Words for Pictures, 2003. *Died 12 Aug. 2008.*

BAXTER, Raymond Frederic, OBE 2003; FRSA; broadcaster and writer; *b* 25 Jan. 1922; *s* of Frederick Garfield Baxter and Rosina Baxter (*née* Rivers); *m* 1945, Sylvia Kathryn (*née* Johnson) (*d* 1996), Boston, Mass; one *s* one *d. Educ:* Ilford County High Sch. Joined RAF, 1940; flew Spitfires with 65, 93 and 602 Sqdns, in UK, Med. and Europe. Entered Forces Broadcasting in Cairo, still as serving officer, 1945; civilian deputy Dir, BFN Hamburg, 1947–49; subseq. short attachment BBC West Region and finally joined Outside Broadcast Dept, London; with BBC until 1966; Dir, Motoring Publicity, BMC, 1967–68. Member: Cttee of Management, RNLI, 1979–97 (Vice Pres., 1987–97; Life Vice Pres., 1997); Council, Air League, 1980–85. Hon. Freeman, City of London, 1978; Liveryman, GAPAN, 1983 (Award of Merit, 1995). Hon. Admiral, Assoc. of Dunkirk Little Ships, 1982–. Hon. CRAeS 1991. *Publications:* (with James Burke and Michael Latham) Tomorrow's World, Vol. 1, 1970, Vol. 2, 1971; Farnborough Commentary, 1980; (with Tony Dron) Tales of my Time, 2005; film commentaries, articles and reports on motoring and aviation subjects, etc. *Recreations:* motoring, boating. *Address:* The Green Cottage, Wargrave Road, Henley-on-Thames, Oxon RG9 3HX. *T:* (01491) 571081. *Clubs:* Royal Air Force, British Racing Drivers, etc. *Died 15 Sept. 2006.*

BAXTER, William Threipland; Professor of Accounting, London School of Economics, 1947–73, Hon. Fellow 1978; *b* 27 July 1906; *s* of W. M. Baxter and Margaret Threipland; *m* 1st, 1940, Marjorie Allanson (*d* 1971); one *s* one *d;* 2nd, 1973, Leena-Kaisa Laitakari-Kaila. *Educ:* George Watson's Coll.; Univ. of Edinburgh (BCom; Hon. Fellow, 1994). Chartered Accountant (Edinburgh), 1930; Commonwealth Fund Fellow, 1931, at Harvard Univ.; Lectr in Accounting, Univ. of Edinburgh, 1934; Prof. of Accounting, Univ. of Cape Town, 1937. Visiting Professor: Columbia, 1958–59; Baruch, 1978–79, 1982–83. Hon. DLitt: Kent at Canterbury, 1974; Heriot-Watt, 1976; Hon. DSc Buckingham, 1983; Hon. DSc(Econ) Hull. 1977. *Publications:* Income Tax for Professional Students. 1936; The House of Hancock, 1945; Depreciation, 1971; Accounting Values and Inflation, 1975; Collected Papers on Accounting, 1979; Inflation Accounting, 1984; Accounting Theory, 1996. *Address:* 1 The Ridgeway, NW11 8TD. *T:* (020) 8455 6810. *Died 8 June 2006.*

BAYLIS, Rear-Adm. Robert Goodwin, CB 1984; OBE 1963; Chief Executive, R. G. Baylis & Associates, since 1984; *b* 29 Nov. 1925; *s* of Harold Goodwin Baylis and Evelyn May (*née* Whitworth); *m* 1949, Joyce Rosemary Churchill (*d* 1995); two *s* one *d. Educ:* Highgate Sch.; Edinburgh Univ.; Loughborough Coll.; RN Engrg Coll.; Trinity Coll., Cambridge. MA Cantab. MRAeS. Joined Royal Navy, 1943; various appts at sea in Far East and Home Fleet and ashore in research and develt and trng establishments; Staff of C-in-C, S Atlantic and S America, 1958; British Navy Staff, Washington, and Special Projects (Polaris), 1964; Defence Fellow, Southampton Univ., 1969; Naval ADC to HM the Queen, 1978; Staff of Vice Chief of Defence Staff, 1979; President, Ordnance Board, 1981–84. Comdr 1961, Captain 1970, Rear-Adm. 1979. Dir, 1988–2000, Associate, 2000–, British Maritime Technol. Reliability

Consultants. Mem., Nuffield Theatre Bd, 1988– (Chm., 1989–93, 1995–97). Mem. (Emeritus), Australian Ordnance Council; Mem. Council, IEE, 1984–86. Vice-Patron, CP Centre, 2003–. *Recreations:* painting, playwriting. *Address:* Broadwaters, 4 Cliff Road, Hill Head, Fareham, Hants PO14 3JS. *Club:* Lansdowne. *Died 29 May 2009.*

BAYLISS, Sir Richard (Ian Samuel), KCVO 1978; MD, FRCP; FMedSci; Physician to the Queen, 1970–81, and Head of HM Medical Household, 1973–81; Consultant Physician, King Edward VII's Hospital for Officers, 1964–87; Vice-President, Private Patients Plan, 1989–98 (Director, 1979–89); *b* 2 Jan. 1917; *o s* of late Frederick William Bayliss, Tettenhall, and Muryel Anne Bayliss; *m* 1st, 1941, Margaret Joan Lawson (marr. diss. 1956); one *s* (one *d* decd); 2nd, 1957, Constance Ellen, *d* of Wilbur J. Frey, Connecticut; two *d;* 3rd, 1979, Marina de Borchgrave d'Altena, *widow* of Charles Rankin. *Educ:* Rugby; Clare Coll., Cambridge (Hon. Fellow, 1983); St Thomas' Hosp., London. MB, BChir Cambridge 1941; MRCS, LRCP 1941; MRCP 1942; MD Cambridge 1946; FRCP 1956. Casualty Officer, Ho.-Phys., Registrar, Resident Asst Phys., St Thomas' Hosp.; Off. i/c Med. Div., RAMC, India; Sen. Med. Registrar and Tutor, Hammersmith Hosp.; Rockefeller Fellow in Medicine, Columbia Univ., New York, 1950–51; Lectr in Medicine and Physician, Postgrad. Med. Sch. of London; Dean, Westminster Med. Sch., 1960–64; Physician to HM Household, 1964–70; Consulting Physician: Westminster Hosp., 1954–81; King Edward VII Hosp., Midhurst, 1973–82; Civilian Consultant in Medicine, RN, 1975–82. Asst Dir, RCP Res. Unit, 1982–88. Hon. Sec., Assoc. of Physicians, 1958–63, Cttee 1965–68, Pres., 1980–81; Pres., Section of Endocrinology, RSM, 1966–68; Examr in Medicine. Cambridge and Oxford Univs; Examr, MRCP. Chm., Med. Adv. Panel, ITC, 1980–. Member: Bd of Governors, Westminster Hosp., 1960–64, 1967–74; Council, Westminster Med. Sch., 1960–75; Soc. for Endocrinology (Council, 1956–60); Brit. Cardiac Soc., 1952; Council, RCP, 1968–71 (Second Vice-Pres., 1983–84); Bd of Advrs, Merck Inst. of Therapeutic Res., 1972–76. Med. Dir, Swiss Reinsurance Co. (UK), 1968–85; Dir, JS Pathology plc, 1984–90; Hon. Med. Adviser, Nuffield Nursing Home Trust, 1981–88; Consultant: Biotechnology Investments Ltd, 1984–99; Internat. Biotechnology Trust plc. Harveian Orator. RCP, 1983. Founder FMedSci 1998. Hon. FRCPath 1994. *Publications:* Thyroid Disease: the facts, 1982, 3rd edn 1998; Practical Procedures in Clinical Medicine, 3rd edn; various, in med. jls and textbooks, on endocrine, metabolic and cardiac diseases. *Recreations:* ski-ing, music. *Address:* Flat 7, 61 Onslow Square, SW7 3LS. *T:* (020) 7589 3087, *Fax:* (020) 7581 5937; *e-mail:* ricbayliss@ dial.pipex.com. *Club:* Garrick. *Died 21 April 2006.*

BAYNES, Pauline Diana, (Mrs F. O. Gasch); designer and book illustrator; *b* 9 Sept. 1922; *d* of Frederick William Wilberforce Baynes, CIE and Jessie Harriet Maud Cunningham; *m* 1961, Fritz Otto Gasch (*d* 1988). *Educ:* Beaufront Sch., Camberley; Farnham Sch. of Art; Slade Sch. of Art. MSIA 1951. Mem., Women's Internat. Art Club, 1938. Voluntary worker, Camouflage Develt and Trng Centre, RE, 1940–42; Hydrographic Dept, Admty, 1942–45. Designed world's largest crewel embroidery, Plymouth Congregational Church, Minneapolis, 1970. Kate Greenaway Medal, Library Assoc., 1968. *Publications: illustrated:* Farmer Giles of Ham. and subseq. books and posters by J. R. R. Tolkien, 1949; The Lion, the Witch and the Wardrobe, and subseq. Narnia books by C. S. Lewis, 1950; The Arabian Nights by Amabel Williams Ellis, 1957; The Puffin Book of Nursery Rhymes by Iona and Peter Opie, 1963; Recipes from an Old Farmhouse by Alison Uttley, 1966; Dictionary of Chivalry by Grant Uden, 1968; Snail and Caterpillar by Helen Piers, 1972; A Companion to World Mythology, 1979; The Enchanted Horse by Rosemary Harris, 1981; Frog and Shrew by Helen Piers, 1981; All Things Bright and Beautiful, 1986; The Story of Daniel by George MacBeth, 1986; Noah and the Ark, 1988; Bilbo's Last Song, 1990, new edn 2002; The Naming by Margaret Greaves, 1992; A book of Narnians: the Lion, the Witch and the others, by Peter Dickinson, 1994; I Believe, 2003; The Moses Basket, 2003; numerous other children's books, etc; *written and illustrated:* Victoria and the Golden Bird, 1948; How Dog Began, 1985; King Wenceslas, 1987; In the beginning, 1990. *Recreation:* going for walks with dogs. *Address:* Rock Barn Cottage, Dockenfield, Farnham, Surrey GU10 4HH. *T:* (01428) 713306. *Died 1 Aug. 2008.*

BAYÜLKEN, Ümit Halûk, Hon. GCVO 1967; President: Turkish Atlantic Treaty Association, since 1984; Turkish Parliamentarians' Union, 1992–97, then Hon. President; Atlantic Treaty Association, Paris, 1994–97, then Patron; *b* 7 July 1921; *s* of Staff Officer H. Hüsnü Bayülken and Mrs Melek Bayülken; *m* 1952, Mrs Valihe Salci; one *s* one *d. Educ:* Lycée de Haydarpasa, Istanbul; Faculty of Political Science (Diplomatic Sect.), Univ. of Ankara. Joined Min. of For. Affairs, 1944; 3rd Sec., 2nd Political Dept; served in Private Cabinet of Sec.-Gen.; mil. service as reserve Officer, 1945–47; Vice-Consul, Frankfurt-on-Main, 1947–49; 1st Sec., Bonn, 1950–51; Dir of Middle East Sect., Ankara, 1951–53; Mem. Turkish Delegn to UN 7th Gen. Assembly, 1952; Political Adviser, 1953–56, Counsellor, 1956–59, Turkish Perm. Mission to UN; rep. Turkey at London Jt Cttee on Cyprus, 1959–60; Dir-Gen., Policy Planning Gp, Min. of Foreign Affairs, 1960–63; Minister Plenipotentiary, 1963; Dep. Sec.-Gen. for Pol Affairs, 1963–64; Sec. with rank of Ambassador, 1964–66; Ambassador to London, 1966–69, to United Nations, 1969–71; Minister of Foreign Affairs, 1971–74; Secretary-General, Cento, 1975–77; Sec.-Gen., Presidency of Turkish Republic, 1977–80; Senator, 1980; Minister of Defence, 1980–83; MP, Antalya, 1983–87. Mem., Turkish Delegns to 8th–13th, 16th–20th Gen. Assemblies of UN; rep. Turkey at internat. confrs, 1953–66; Leader of Turkish Delegn: at meeting of For. Ministers, 2nd Afro-Asian Conf., Algiers, 1965; to Ministerial Councils of NATO, OECD, Cento and Regl Co-operation for Develt, 1971–74; Turkey and EEC Jt Assoc., 1971–74; to Cttee of Ministers, Council of Europe, 1972; at Conf. on European Security and Co-operation, 1973; Mem., Parly Assembly of European Council, 1984–87. Univ. of Ankara: Mem., Inst. of Internat. Relations; Lectr, Faculty of Pol Scis, 1963–66. Hon. Gov., Sch. of Oriental and African Studies, London; Hon. Mem., Mexican Acad. of Internat. Law. Isabel la Católica (Spain), 1964; Grand Cross of Merit (Germany), 1965; Sitara-i-Pakistan (Pakistan), 1970; Star, Order One (Jordan), 1972; Sirdar-i-Ali (Afghanistan), 1972. Tunisia, 1973; UAR, 1973; UN, 1975; Turkish Pres., 1980; Order of Madara Horseman (Bulgaria), 1997; Chevalier de la Légion d'Honneur (France), 2002. *Publications:* lectures, articles, studies and essays on subject of minorities, Cyprus, principles of foreign policy, internat. relations and disputes. *Recreations:* music, painting, reading. *Address:* Nergiz, Sokak no 15/20, Çankaya, Ankara 06680, Turkey. *Died 26 April 2007.*

BAZALGETTE, Rear-Adm. Derek Willoughby, CB 1976; *b* 22 July 1924; *yr s* of late H. L. Bazalgette; *m* 1st, 1947, Angela Hilda Vera (*d* 1991), *d* of late Sir Henry Hinchliffe, JP, DL; four *d*; 2nd, 1994, Ann, *widow* of Adm. Sir Peter Stanford, GCB, LVO. *Educ:* RNC Dartmouth. Served War of 1939–45; specialised in Gunnery, 1949; HMS Centaur, 1952–54; HMS Birmingham, 1956–58; SO 108th Minesweeping Sqdn and in comd HMS Houghton, 1958–59; HMS Centaur, 1963–65; Dep. Dir Naval Ops, 1965–67; comd HMS Aurora, 1967–68; idc 1969; Chief Staff Officer to Comdr British Forces Hong Kong, 1970–72; comd HMS Bulwark, 1972–74; Admiral President, RNC Greenwich, 1974–76; Comdr 1958; Captain 1965; Rear-Adm. 1974. ADC 1974. HQ Comr for Water Activities, Scout Assoc., 1976–87; Principal, Netley Waterside House, 1977–83; Ind. Inquiry Inspector, 1983–92. Lay Canon, Portsmouth Cathedral, 1984–2002; Mem., General Synod of C of E, 1985–90. Sen. Treas., Corp. of Sons of the Clergy,

1992–94. Chm., Portsmouth Housing Trust, 1989–95. Freeman, City of London, 1976; Liveryman, Shipwrights' Co., 1986–. FCMI (FBIM 1976). *Address:* Park House, Hambledon, Waterlooville, Hants PO7 4SB. *Died 22 July 2007.*

BEAL, Rt Rev. Robert George; Bishop of Wangaratta, 1985–94; *b* 17 Aug. 1929; *s* of Samuel and Phyllis Beal; *m* 1956, Valerie Francis Illich; two *s* four *d. Educ:* Sydney Grammar School; St Francis' College, Brisbane, Qld; Newcastle Univ., NSW (BA, ThL). Ordained, 1953; Priest, Asst Curate, St Francis', Nundah, Brisbane, 1953–55; Rector: South Townsville, 1955–59; Auchenflower, Brisbane, 1959–65; Dean of Wangaratta, 1965–72; Rector of Ipswich, Brisbane, and Residentiary Canon of St John's Cathedral, 1972–75; Dean of Newcastle, NSW, 1975–83; Archdeacon of Albury, 1983–85. *Recreation:* gardening. *Address:* 1 Pangari Place, New Lambton Gardens, Newcastle, NSW 2299, Australia. *Died 24 June 2009.*

BEALE, Anthony John; Solicitor and Legal Adviser, Welsh Office, 1980–91; Under Secretary (Legal), Welsh Office, 1983–91; *b* 16 March 1932; *o s* of late Edgar Beale and Victoria Beale; *m* 1969, Helen Margaret Owen-Jones; one *s* one *d. Educ:* Hitchin Grammar Sch.; King's Coll. London (LLB; AKC); BA Hons Open 1999. Solicitor of the Supreme Court, 1956. Legal Asst, 1960, Sen. Legal Asst, 1966, Min. of Housing and Local Govt and Min. of Health; Consultant, Council of Europe, 1973; Asst Solicitor, DoE 1974. ARPS. *Recreations:* photography, collecting old cheques. *Died 23 Nov. 2010.*

BEALE, Prof. Geoffrey Herbert, MBE 1947; PhD; FRS 1959; FRSE; Royal Society Research Professor, Edinburgh University, 1963–78; *b* 11 June 1913; *s* of Herbert Walter and Elsie Beale; *m* 1949, Betty Brydon McCallum (marr. diss. 1969); three *s. Educ:* Sutton County Sch.; Imperial Coll. of Science, London. Scientific Research Worker, John Innes Horticultural Institution, London, 1935–40. Served in HM Forces (1941–46). Research worker, Department of Genetics, Carnegie Institute, Cold Spring Harbor, New York, 1947; Rockefeller Fellow, Indiana Univ., 1947–48; Lecturer, Dept of Animal Genetics, 1948–59, Reader in Animal Genetics, 1959–63, Edinburgh Univ. Research Worker (part-time), Chulalongkorn Univ., Bangkok, 1976. FRSE 1966. Hon. DSc Chulalongkorn, 1996. *Publications:* The Genetics of Paramecium aurelia, 1954; (with Jonathan Knowles) Extranuclear Genetics, 1978; (with S. Thaithong) Malaria Parasites, 1992. *Died 16 Oct. 2009.*

BEALE, (Josiah Edward) Michael; Assistant Secretary, Department of Trade and Industry (formerly Board of Trade), 1968–85; *b* 29 Sept. 1928; *s* of late Mr and Mrs J. E. Beale, Upminster, Essex; *m* 1958, Jean Margaret McDonald; two *d* (and one *d* decd). *Educ:* Brentwood Sch.; Jesus Coll., Cambridge. Entered Civil Service, 1950; Principal, Min. of Transport, 1956–68; UK Shipping Advr, Singapore, 1968–71; Asst Sec., Monopolies and Mergers Commn, 1978–81. Hon. Officer, 1987–2002, Chm., 2002–04, Friends of Historic Essex. Churchwarden, Great Waltham, 1990–96. *Publications:* The Friends of Historic Essex: the first forty years, 1994; (contrib.) Essex, full of Profitable Things, 1996. *Address:* The Laurels, The Village, Great Waltham, Chelmsford, Essex CM3 1DE. *Died 8 June 2007.*

BEAN, Leonard, CMG 1964; MBE (mil.) 1945; MA; Secretary, Southern Gas Region, 1966–79; *b* 19 Sept. 1914; *s* of late Harry Bean, Bradford, Yorks, and late Agnes Sherwood Beattie, Worcester; *m* 1938, Nancy Winifred (*d* 1990), *d* of Robert John Neilson, Dunedin, NZ; one *d. Educ:* Canterbury Coll., NZ; Queens' Coll., Cambridge. Served War of 1939–45: Major, 2nd NZ Div. (despatches, MBE). Entered Colonial Service, N Rhodesia, 1945; Provincial Comr, 1959; Perm. Sec. (Native Affairs), 1961; acted as Minister for Native Affairs and Natural Resources in periods, 1961–64; Permanent

Secretary: to Prime Minister, 1964; also to President, 1964. Adviser to President, Zambia, 1964–66. *Recreations:* golf, gardening. *Clubs:* MCC; Bramshaw Golf.
Died 28 Sept. 2009.

BEARE, Robin Lyell Blin, MB, BS; FRCS; Hon. Consultant Plastic Surgeon: Queen Victoria Hospital, East Grinstead, since 1960; Brighton General Hospital and Brighton and Lewes Group of Hospitals, since 1960; Hon. Consulting Plastic Surgeon, St Mary's Hospital, London, since 1976 (Consultant Plastic Surgeon, 1959–76); *b* 31 July 1922; *s* of late Stanley Samuel Beare, OBE, FRCS, and late Cecil Mary Guise Beare (*née* Lyell); *m* 1947, Iris Bick; two *s* two *d. Educ:* Radley (scholar); Middlesex Hosp. Medical Sch. MB, BS (Hons) 1952 (dist. Surg.); FRCS 1955. Served with RAF Bomber Command (Aircrew) 1940–46. Formerly Ho. Surg., Casualty Officer, Asst Pathologist and Surgical Registrar, The Middlesex Hosp., 1952–56. Surg. Registrar, Plastic Surgery and Jaw Injuries Centre, Queen Victoria Hosp., East Grinstead, 1957–60. Examr in gen. surgery for FRCS, 1972–78. Fellow Assoc. of Surgeons of Gt Britain and Ireland; Fellow Royal Society Med.; Mem. Brit. Assoc. of Plastic Surgeons; Mem. of Bd of Trustees, McIndoe Memorial Research Unit, E Grinstead; Hon. Mem. Société Française de Chirurgie Plastique et Reconstructive. *Publications:* various on surgical problems in BMJ, Amer. Jl of Surgery, etc. *Recreations:* fishing, shooting. *Address:* Scraggs Farm, Cowden, Kent TN8 7EB. *T:* (01342) 850386.
Died 26 Nov. 2007.

BEARN, Prof. Alexander Gordon, MD; FRCP, FRCPEd, FACP; Executive Officer, American Philosophical Society, 1997–2002, then Emeritus; Professor of Medicine, Cornell University Medical College, 1966–79, then Professor Emeritus (Stanton Griffis Distinguished Medical Professor, 1977–79); Attending Physician, The New York Hospital, since 1966; *b* 29 March 1923; *s* of E. G. Bearn, CB, CBE; *m* 1952, Margaret, *d* of Clarence Slocum, Fanwood, NJ, USA; one *s* one *d. Educ:* Epsom Coll.; Guy's Hosp., London. Postgraduate Medical Sch. of London, 1949–51. Rockefeller Univ., 1951–66; Hon. Research Asst, University Coll. (Galton Laboratory), 1958–59; Prof. and Sen. Physician, Rockefeller Univ., 1964–66; Chm., Dept of Medicine, Cornell Univ. Med. Coll., 1966–77; Physician-in-Chief, NY Hosp., 1966–77; Sen. Vice Pres., Medical and Scientific Affairs, Merck Sharp and Dohme Internat., 1979–88. Woodrow Wilson Foundn Vis. Fellow, 1979–80; Dist. Vis. Fellow, 1996–97, Fellow Commoner, 1997–, Christ's Coll., Cambridge; Adjunct and Vis. Prof., Rockefeller Univ., 1966– (Hon. Physician, 1988–); Adjunct Prof., Univ. of Pennsylvania Sch. of Medicine, 1998–. Trustee: Rockefeller Univ., 1970–98; Howard Hughes Medical Inst., 1987–2005; Dir, Josiah Macy Jr Foundn, 1981–98. Mem. Editorial Bd, several scientific and med. jls. Lectures: Lowell, Harvard, 1958; Medical Research Soc., 1969; Lilly, RCP, 1973; Harvey, 1975; Lettsomian, Med. Soc., 1976. Macy Faculty Scholar Award, 1974–75. Alfred Benzon Prize, Denmark, 1979; Benjamin Franklin Medal, 2000; David Rockefeller Award, 2002. Member: Nat. Acad. Science; Amer. Philosophical Soc. (Exec. Officer, 1997–2002); Foreign Mem., Norwegian Acad. Science and Letters. Hon. MD Catholic Univ., Korea, 1968; Docteur *hc* Paris, 1975. *Publications:* Archibald Garrod and the individuality of man, 1993; Sir Clifford Allbutt, Scholar and Physician, 2007; Sir Francis Richard Fraser: a canny Scot shapes British medicine, 2008; articles on human genetics and liver disease, 1950–; (Co-Editor) Progress in Medical Genetics, annually, 1962–85; (Associate Editor) Cecil and Loeb: Textbook of Medicine. *Recreations:* biography, collecting snuff-mulls, aristology. *Address:* 241 South 6th Street, Philadelphia, PA 19106, USA. *T:* (215) 9252666; 31 Clarendon Street, Cambridge CB1 1JX. *Clubs:* Philadelphia (Pa); Knickerbocker, Century (NY); Hawks (Cambridge); Crail Golf (Scotland).
Died 15 May 2009.

BEASLEY, Prof. William Gerald, CBE 1980; PhD; FRHistS; FBA 1967; Professor of the History of the Far East, University of London, 1954–83, then Emeritus; Head of Japan Research Centre, School of Oriental and African Studies, 1978–83; *b* 22 Dec. 1919; *m* 1955, Hazel Polwin; one *s. Educ:* Magdalen Coll. Sch., Brackley; University Coll. London (BA). Served War, 1940–46, RNVR. Lectr, SOAS, Univ. of London, 1947–54. Mem., 1961–68, British Chm., 1964–68, Anglo-Japanese Mixed Cultural Commn. Vice-Pres., British Acad., 1974–75, Treasurer, 1975–79. Lectures: Raleigh, British Acad., 1969; Creighton, Univ. of London, 1984. Hon. Mem., Japan Acad., 1984. Hon. Fellow, SOAS, 1991. Hon. DLitt Hong Kong, 1978. Order of the Rising Sun (Third Class), Japan, 1983. *Publications:* Great Britain and the opening of Japan, 1951; Select Documents on Japanese foreign policy, 1853–1868, 1955; The Modern History of Japan, 1963; The Meiji Restoration, 1972; Japanese Imperialism 1894–1945, 1987; The Rise of Modern Japan, 1990; Japan Encounters the Barbarian: Japanese travellers in America and Europe, 1995; The Japanese Experience: a short history of Japan, 1999. *Address:* 172 Hampton Road, Twickenham TW2 5NJ.
Died 19 Nov. 2006.

BEAUMONT OF WHITLEY, Baron *cr* 1967 (Life Peer), of Child's Hill; **Rev. Timothy Wentworth Beaumont**, MA (Oxon); politician, priest and writer; *b* 22 Nov. 1928; *o s* of Major and Hon. Mrs M. W. Beaumont; *m* 1955, Mary Rose Wauchope; one *s* two *d* (and one *s* decd). *Educ:* Gordonstoun; Christ Church, Oxford; Westcott House, Cambridge. Asst Chaplain, St John's Cathedral, Hong Kong, 1955–57; Vicar, Christ Church Kowloon Tong, Hong Kong, 1957–59; Hon. Curate, St Stephen's Rochester Row, London, 1960–63; resigned orders, 1973; resumed orders, 1984; Vicar, St Philip and All Saints, with St Luke, Kew, 1986–91; licensed to officiate, Holy Spirit, Clapham, 1993–. Editor: Prism, 1960–63 and 1964; New Outlook, 1964, 1972–74; Chm., Studio Vista Books Ltd, 1963–68; Proprietor of New Christian, 1965–70. Food Columnist, Illustrated London News, 1976–80. Asst Dir (Public Affairs), Make Children Happy, 1977–78; Co-ordinator, The Green Alliance, 1978–80. Liberal Party Organisation: Jt Hon. Treas., 1962–63; Chm., Liberal Publications Dept, 1963–64; Head of Org., 1965–66; Chm., Liberal Party's Org. Cttee, 1966; Chm., Liberal Party, 1967–68; Pres., Liberal Party, 1969–70; Vice-Chm., Liberal Party Exec. and Dir, Policy Promotion, 1980–83; Mem., Lib Dem Policy Cttee, 1992–95. Liberal spokesman on education and the arts, H of L, 1968–86; Lib Dem spokesman on conservation and the countryside, H of L, 1993–98; Treas., All-Party Gp on St Helena and Dependencies, 1995–; Sec., All-Party Gp on Family Farms, 1998–; Vice-Chm., All-Party Gp on UK Overseas Territories, 1998–. Alternate Mem., Assemblies of Council of Europe and WEU, 1973–77, Leader of Liberal Delegn, 1977–78, Vice-Chm., Liberal Gp, 1977–78. Joined Green Party, 1999; spokesman on agriculture, 1999–. Pres., British Fedn of Film Socs, 1973–79. Chairman: Albany Trust, 1969–71; Inst. of Res. into Mental and Multiple Handicap, 1971–73; Exit, 1980–81. Mem., Exec. Cttee, British Council, 1974–78. Mem. Exec., Church Action on Poverty, 1983–86, 1991–94. *Publications:* (ed) Modern Religious Verse, 1965; ed and contrib., The Liberal Cookbook, 1972; (ed) New Christian Reader, 1974; (ed) The Selective Ego: the diaries of James Agate, 1976; Where shall I place my cross?, 1987; The End of the Yellowbrick Road, 1997. *Address:* 40 Elms Road, SW4 9EX. *T:* (020) 7498 8664; *e-mail:* beaumontt@parliament.uk.
Died 8 April 2008.

BEAUMONT, Sir Richard Ashton, KCMG 1965 (CMG 1955); OBE 1949; HM Diplomatic Service, retired; *b* 29 Dec. 1912; *s* of A. R. Beaumont, FRCS, Uppingham, and Evelyn Frances (*née* Rendle); *m* 1st, 1942, Alou (*d* 1985), *d* of M. Camran, Istanbul; one *d*; 2nd, 1989, Melanie Anns, *d* of Major H. Brummell. *Educ:* Repton; Oriel Coll., Oxford. Joined HM Consular

Service, 1936; posted Lebanon and Syria, 1936–41. Served War, 1941–44. Returned to Foreign Office, 1944; served in London, Iraq, Venezuela; Imperial Defence Coll., 1958; Head of Arabian Department, Foreign Office, 1959; Ambassador: to Morocco, 1961–65; to Iraq, 1965–67; Dep. Under-Sec. of State, FO, 1967–69; Ambassador to the Arab Republic of Egypt, 1969–72. Dir-Gen., Middle East Assoc., 1973–77; Chairman: Arab British Centre, 1976–77; Anglo-Arab Assoc., 1979–99; Arab-British Chamber of Commerce, 1980–96. Governor, SOAS, 1973–78. Trustee, Thomson Foundn, 1974–2000. *Address:* 82 Peterborough Road, SW6 3EB.
Died 23 Jan. 2009.

BEAUMONT-DARK, Sir Anthony (Michael), Kt 1992; investment adviser; *b* Birmingham, 11 Oct. 1932; *s* of Leonard Cecil Dark; *m* 1959, Sheelagh Irene, *d* of R. Cassey; one *s* one *d*. *Educ:* Birmingham Coll. of Arts and Crafts; Birmingham Univ. Mem., Birmingham Stock Exchange, 1958–; Consultant: Smith, Keen, Cutler, subseq. Smith Keen Murray, 1985–95 (Sen. Partner, 1959–85); Brewin Dolphin, 1995–2002; Dep. Chm., J. Saville Gordon plc, 1994–99 (Dir, 1989–99); Director: Wigham Poland (Midlands) Ltd, 1960–75; Nat. Exhibition Centre Ltd, 1971–73; Cope Allman Internat. Ltd, 1972–83; Birmid Qualcast PLC, 1983–89; Henderson (formerly TR) High Income Trust PLC, 1990– (Chm., 1994–2002); Birmingham Executive Airways, 1983– (Chm., 1983–86); ADR Net, 1993–94. Mem., Central Housing Adv. Cttee, DoE, 1970–76. Member: Birmingham City Council, 1956–67 (Alderman, 1967–74, Hon. Alderman, 1976); W Midlands CC, 1973–87 (Chm., Finance Cttee, 1977–83). Contested (C): Birmingham, Aston, 1959, 1964; Birmingham, Selly Oak, 1992. MP (C) Birmingham, Selly Oak, 1979–92. Mem., Treasury and Civil Service Select Cttee, 1979–92. Governor: Aston Univ., 1980–94; Birmingham Univ., 1984–92. Trustee, Birmingham Copec Housing Trust, 1975–80. FRSA 1993. *Address:* 124 Lady Byron Lane, Knowle, Solihull, West Midlands B93 9BA. *Died 2 April 2006.*

BECK, Prof. (John) Swanson, FRSE; Foundation Dean, International Medical College, Kuala Lumpur, 1993–97; Professor of Pathology, University of Dundee, 1971–93, then Professor Emeritus; *b* 22 Aug. 1928; *s* of late Dr John Beck and Mary (*née* Barbour); *m* 1960, Marion Tudhope Paterson; one *s* one *d*. *Educ:* Glasgow Acad.; Univ. of Glasgow (BSc, DSc, MB, ChB, MD). FRCPG, FRCPE, FRCPI, FRACP, FRCPath, FIBiol, CBiol, EurBiol. Lectr in Pathology, Univ. of Glasgow, 1958–63; Sen. Lectr in Pathology, Univ. of Aberdeen, 1963–71. Consultant Pathologist: N Eastern Regl Hosp. Bd, 1963–71; Eastern Regl Hosp. Bd, 1971–74; Tayside Health Bd, 1974–93. Vis. Prof. of Pharmacy, Univ. of Strathclyde, 1996–2003. Chairman: Breast Tumour Panel, MRC, 1979–90; Biomedical Res. Cttee, SHHD, 1983–93 (Mem. 1975–79). Member: Cell Biology and Disorders Bd, MRC, 1978–82; Health Services Res. Panel, MRC, 1981–82; Chief Scientist's Cttee, SHHD, 1983–93; Tayside Health Bd, 1983–91; Nat. Biol Standards Bd, 1988–93 (Chm., 1991–93, Mem., 1993–2001, Scientific Policy Adv. Cttee); Med. Adv. Bd, LEPRA, 1988–97. FRSE 1984 (Mem. Council, 1987–90, 1997–2003; Convenor, Grants Cttee, 1991–94; Meetings Sec., 1997–98; Prog. Convenor, 1998–2003). Distinguished Fellow, Internat. Med. Coll., 1998. DUniv Strathclyde, 1999. Bicentenary Medal, RSE, 2004. *Publications:* various papers in Jl of Pathology and other medical and scientific jls. *Recreations:* walking, gardening. *Address:* East Balloch Cottage, near Kirriemuir, Angus DD8 5EY. *T:* (01575) 574731, *Fax:* (01575) 575752; *e-mail:* jsbeck@clara.net. *Club:* New (Edinburgh). *Died 28 Jan. 2007.*

BECKE, Lt-Col William Hugh Adamson, CMG 1964; DSO 1945; *b* 24 Sept. 1916; *er s* of late Brig.-Gen. J. H. W. Becke, CMG, DSO, AFC, and Mrs A. P. Becke (*née* Adamson); *m* 1945, Mary Catherine, 3rd *d* of late Major G. M. Richmond, Kincairney, Murthly, Perthshire. *Educ:*

Charterhouse; RMC Sandhurst. Commissioned in The Sherwood Foresters, 1937. British Military Mission to Greece, 1949–52; Asst Military Adviser to the High Commissioner for the UK in Pakistan, 1957–59; Military Attaché, Djakarta, 1962–64; retd 1966. Private Sec. and Comptroller to Governor of Victoria, 1969–74; Personnel Officer, Gas and Fuel Corp. of Vic, 1974–82. *Address:* Melbourne, Australia. *Clubs:* Army and Navy; Melbourne. *Died 3 April 2009.*

BECKETT, Prof. Arnold Heyworth, OBE 1983; Professor of Pharmacy, Chelsea College (University of London), 1959–85, then Emeritus; *b* 12 Feb. 1920; *m* 1st, 1942, Miriam Eunice Webster; one *s* one *d*; 2nd, Susan Yvonne Harris; 3rd, 1991, Prof. Bozena W. Hadzija. *Educ:* Baines Grammar Sch., Poulton-le-Fylde; Sch. of Pharmacy and Birkbeck Coll., University of London. FRPharmS (FPS 1942); BSc 1947; PhD 1950; DSc London, 1959. Head, Dept of Pharmacy, Chelsea Coll. of Sci. and Technology, 1959–79. Chm., Med. Commn, Internat. Tennis Fedn, 1985–93; Mem., Med. Commn, Internat. Olympic Cttee, 1968–93; Mem., British Olympic Assoc. Med. Commn, until 1986; Chm., Bd of Pharmaceutical Sciences, Fédération Internat. Pharmaceutique, 1960–80; Mem. Council, Pharmaceutical, later Royal Pharmaceutical, Soc. of GB, 1965–90 (Pres., 1981–82). Jt Founder, Biovail Corp. Internat., 1978; Chairman: Bio-Dis, 1982–; Vitabiotics Ltd, 1994–. Vis. Prof. to Univs, USA and Canada. Examr in Pharmaceut. Chem., univs in UK, Nigeria, Ghana, Singapore. Internat. pharmaceutical and nutraceutical consultant. Pereira Medal, 1942; STAS Medal, Belg. Chem. Soc., 1962; Hanbury Meml Medal, 1974; Charter Gold Medal, 1977; Mem. of Olympic Order, Silver Medal, 1980. Hon. DSc: Heriot-Watt, 1976; Uppsala, 1977; Leuven, 1982. *Publications:* (co-author) Practical Pharmaceutical Chemistry, 1962; Part 1, 3rd edn, 1975, Part 2, 3rd edn, 1976; founder Co-editor, Jl of Medicinal Chemistry; research contribs to 450 jls. *Recreations:* travel, sport, photography. *Address:* 20 Braybrooke Gardens, Upper Norwood, SE19 2UN.
Died 25 Jan. 2010.

BECKWITH, Prof. Athelstan Laurence Johnson, AO 2004; FRS 1988; FAA; FRACI; Professor of Organic Chemistry, Research School of Chemistry, Australian National University, 1981–96, then Emeritus (Dean, 1989–91); *b* 20 Feb. 1930; *s* of Laurence Alfred Beckwith and Doris Grace Beckwith; *m* 1953, Phyllis Kaye Marshall, Perth, WA; one *s* two *d*. *Educ:* Perth Modern Sch.; Univ. of WA (BSc Hons); Oxford Univ. (DPhil 1956). FAA 1973; FRACI 1973. Lectr in Chemistry, Adelaide Univ., 1953; CSIRO Overseas Student, 1954; Res. Officer, CSIRO Melbourne, 1957; Adelaide University: Lectr in Organic Chemistry, 1958; Prof., 1965–81; Dean of Science, 1972–73. Temp. Lectr, Imperial Coll., London, 1962–63; Vis. Lectr, Univ. of York, 1968; Carnegie Fellow, 1968. Federal Pres., RACI, 1965 (Rennie Medal, 1960; H. G. Smith Meml Medal, 1981; Organic Chemistry Medal, 1992; Leighton Medal, 1997); Treas., Aust. Acad. of Sci., 1997–2001. *Publications:* numerous articles in Jl of Chem. Soc., Jl of Amer. Chem. Soc., etc. *Recreations:* golf, music, walking. *Address:* 3/9 Crisp Circuit, Bruce, ACT 2617, Australia. *T:* (2) 61253234, (2) 62530696. *Died 15 May 2010.*

BEDDINGTON, Charles Richard; Metropolitan Magistrate, 1963–80; *b* 22 Aug. 1911; *s* of late Charles Beddington, Inner Temple, and Stella (*née* de Goldschmidt); *m* 1939, Debbie, *d* of late Frederick Appleby Holt and Rae Vera Franz, *d* of Sir George Hutchinson; two *s* one *d*. *Educ:* Eton (scholar); Balliol Coll., Oxford. Barrister, Inner Temple, 1934. Joined TA, 1939; served RA, 1939–45, Major. Practised at the Bar in London and on SE Circuit. Mem. Mental Health Review Tribunal (SE Metropolitan Area), 1960–63. *Address:* 21 Mytten Close, Cuckfield, West Sussex RH17 5LN. *T:* (01444) 454063. *Died 6 May 2008.*

BEDFORD, Sybille, OBE 1981; CLit 1994; author; *b* 16 March 1911; *d* of Maximilian von Schoenebeck and Elizabeth Bernard; *m* 1935, Walter Bedford. *Educ:* privately, in Italy, England and France. Career in writing and literary journalism. Vice-Pres., PEN, 1979. FRSL. *Publications:* The Sudden View: a Mexican journey, 1953, repr. as A Visit to Don Otavio, 1960, 3rd edn 1982; The Best We Can Do (The Trial of Dr Adams), 1958, 2nd edn 1989; The Faces of Justice, 1961; Aldous Huxley, a Biography: Vol. I, The Apparent Stability, 1894–1939, 1973, 2nd edn 1987; Vol. II, The Turning Points, 1939–1963, 1974, 4th edn 2003; As It Was (essays), 1990; Pleasures and Landscape (essays), 2003; Quicksands (memoir), 2005; *fiction:* A Legacy, 1956, repr. 1992 (televised 1975); A Favourite of the Gods, 1962, 2nd edn 1993; A Compass Error, 1968, 2nd edn 1984; Jigsaw: an unsentimental education, 1989. *Recreations:* wine, reading, travel. *Address:* c/o Lutyens & Rubinstein, 231 Westbourne Park Road, W11 1EB. *Club:* PEN.
Died 17 Feb. 2006.

BEDSER, Sir Alec (Victor), Kt 1997; CBE 1982 (OBE 1964); Chairman, England Cricket Selection Committee, 1968–81 (Member, 1961–85); *b* 4 July 1918; twin *s* of late Arthur and Florence Beatrice Bedser. *Educ:* Monument Hill Secondary Sch., Woking. Served with RAF in UK, France (BEF), N Africa, Sicily, Italy, Austria, 1939–46. Joined Surrey County Cricket Club, as Professional, 1938; awarded Surrey CCC and England caps, 1946, 1st Test Match v India, created record by taking 22 wickets in first two Tests; toured Australia as Member of MCC team, 1946–47, 1950–51, 1954–55; toured S Africa with MCC, 1948–49; held record of most number of Test wickets (236), since beaten, 1953; took 100th wicket against Australia (first English bowler since 1914 to do this), 1953; Asst Man. to Duke of Norfolk on MCC tour to Australia, 1962–63; Manager: MCC team to Australia, 1974–75; England team tour of Australia and India, 1979–80; Mem., MCC Cttee, 1982–85. Pres., Surrey CCC, 1987–88. Founded own company (office equipment and supplies) with Eric Bedser, 1955. Freeman, City of London, 1968; Liveryman, Worshipful Co. of Environmental Cleaners, 1988. *Publications:* (with E. A. Bedser) Our Cricket Story, 1951; Bowling, 1952; (with E. A. Bedser) Following On, 1954; Cricket Choice, 1981; (with Alex Bannister) Twin Ambitions (autobiog.), 1986. *Recreations:* cricket, golf. *Clubs:* MCC (Hon. Life Mem., 1962; Hon. Life Vice Pres., 1999), East India, Devonshire, Sports and Public Schools (Hon. Life Mem.); Surrey County Cricket (Hon. Life Mem.); West Hill Golf (Hon. Life Mem.; Pres., 2006–). *Died 4 April 2010.*

BEESON, Prof. Paul Bruce, Hon. KBE 1973; FRCP; Professor of Medicine, University of Washington, 1974–82, then Emeritus; *b* 18 Oct. 1908; *s* of John Bradley Beeson, Livingston, Mont; *m* 1942, Barbara Neal, *d* of Ray C. Neal, Buffalo, NY; two *s* one *d*. *Educ:* Univ. of Washington, McGill Univ. Med. Sch. MD, CM, 1933. Intern, Hosp. of Univ. of Pa, 1933–35; Gen. practice of medicine, Wooster, Ohio, 1935–37; Asst Rockefeller Inst., 1937–39; Chief Med. Resident, Peter Bent Brigham Hosp., 1939–40; Instructor in Med., Havard Med. Sch., and Chief Phys., American Red Cross–Harvard Field Hosp. Unit, Salisbury, 1940–42; Asst and Assoc. Prof. of Med., Emory Med. Sch., 1942–46; Prof. of Med. Emory Med. Sch., 1946–52; Prof. of Med. and Chm. Dept of Med., Yale Univ., 1952–65; Nuffield Prof. of Clinical Med., Oxford Univ., and Fellow of Magdalen Coll., 1965–74, Hon. Fellow, 1975; Hon. Fellow RSM, 1976. Vis. Investigator, Wright-Fleming Inst., St Mary's Hosp., 1958–59. Pres., Assoc. Amer. Physicians, 1967; Master, Amer. Coll. of Physicians, 1975; Phillips Award, Amer. Coll. Physicians, 1975; Flexner Award, Assoc. Amer. Med. Colls, 1977. *Alumnus Summa Laude Dignatus,* Univ. of Washington, 1968; Hon. DSc: Emory Univ., 1968; McGill Univ., 1971; Yale Univ., 1975; Albany Med. Coll., 1975; Ohio Med. Coll., 1979. *Publications:* (ed jtly) The Oxford Companion to Medicine, 1986; edited: Cecil-Loeb Textbook of Medicine, 1959–82; Yale Journal Biology and Medicine, 1959–65; Journal

Amer. Geriatric Soc., 1981–84; numerous scientific publications relating to infectious disease, pathogenesis of fever, pyelonephritis and mechanism of eosinophilia. *Address:* 7 River Woods Drive, Exeter, NH 03833, USA.
Died 14 Aug. 2006.

BEETHAM, Roger Campbell, CMG 1993; LVO 1976; HM Diplomatic Service, retired; *b* 22 Nov. 1937; *s* of Henry Campbell and Mary Beetham; *m* 1st, 1965, Judith Rees (marr. diss. 1986); 2nd, 1986, Christine Marguerite Malerme. *Educ:* Peter Symonds Sch., Winchester; Brasenose Coll., Oxford (MA). Entered HM Diplomatic Service, 1960; FO, 1960–62; UK Delegation to Disarmament Conference, Geneva, 1962–65; Washington, 1965–68; News Dept, FCO, 1969–72; Head of Chancery, Helsinki, 1972–76; FCO, 1976; seconded to European Commission, Brussels, as Spokesman of the President, Rt Hon. Roy Jenkins, 1977–80; Counsellor (Econ. and Commercial), New Delhi, 1981–85; Head of Maritime, Aviation and Envmt Dept, FCO, 1985–90; Ambassador to Senegal and (non-resident) to Cape Verde, Guinea, Guinea-Bissau and Mali, 1990–93; UK Perm. Rep. (with personal rank of Ambassador) to Council of Europe, Strasbourg, 1993–97; European Manager, Surrey CC, 1998–2000. Trustee, Eur. Opera Centre, 2002– (Vice-Chm., 2005–). Order of the White Rose of Finland, 1976. *Publications:* (ed) The Euro Debate: persuading the people, 2001. *Recreations:* oenology, cooking, travel. *Club:* Cercle Royal Gaulois (Brussels). *Died 19 Sept. 2009.*

BÉJART, Maurice (Jean); choreographer; Director: Béjart Ballet Lausanne, 1987–92; Rudra Béjart Ballet School, since 1992; *b* 1 Jan. 1927; *s* of Gaston and Germaine Berger. *Educ:* Lycée de Marseilles. Début as ballet dancer with Marseilles Opéra, 1945; International Ballet, 1949–50; Royal Opera, Stockholm, 1951–52; co-founded Les Ballets de l'Etoile, later Ballet-Théâtre de Paris, 1954 (Dir, 1954–59); Director: Twentieth Century Ballet Co., 1959–87; Mudra Sch., 1972. Grand Prix National de la Musique, 1970; Prix Erasme de la danse, 1974. Chevalier des Arts et des Lettres; Commandeur de l'Ordre de Léopold (Belgium), 1982; Ordre du Soleil Levant (Japan), 1986; Grand Officier de l'Ordre de la Couronne (Belgium), 1988. Principal works include: La Belle au Boa, Symphonie pour un homme seul, 1955; Orphée, 1958; Le sacre du printemps, 1959; Boléro, 1961; The Tales of Hoffman, 1962; The Merry Widow, The Damnation of Faust, l'Oiseau de Feu, 1964; Romeo and Juliet, 1966; Messe pour le temps présent, 1967; Firebird, 1970; Song of a Wayfarer, Nijinsky: clown de Dieu, 1971; Le Marteau sans Maître, La Traviata, 1973; Ce que l'amour me dit, 1974; Notre Faust, 1975; Heliogabale, Pli selon Pli, 1976; Petrouchka, 1977; Gaîté Parisienne, Ce que la Mort me dit, 1978; Mephisto Waltzer, 1979; Casta Diva, Eros Thanatos, 1980; The Magic Flute, Les Chaises, Light, Les Uns et les Autres (film), Adagietto, 1981; Wien Wien nur du Allein, Thalassa Mare Nostrum, 1982; Salome, Messe pour le Temps Futur, Vie et mort d'une marionnette humaine, 1983; Dionysos, 1984; Le Concours, la Chauve Souris, 1985; Arepo, Malraux ou la Métamorphose des Dieux, 1986; Trois Etudes pour Alexandre, Souvenir de Léningrad, Après-midi d'un Faune, Fiche Signalétique, 1987; Patrice Chéreau…, Dibouk, Et Valse, Piaf, Paris-Tokyo, A force de partir…, 1988; 1789 et nous, Elégie pour elle, L…, aile, 1989; Ring um den Ring, Nijinsky Clown de dieu (theatrical version), Pyramides, Mozart Tangos, 1990; La Mort subite, La Tour, Paradoxe sur le comédien (film), Tod in Wien, Nijinski, 1991; Mr C, Episodes, A6-Roc, Le Mandarin merveilleux, La Crucifixion, Sissi, 1992; L'Art du pas de deux, AmoRoma, M(Mishima), Ballade de la rue Athina, 1993; King Lear–Prospero, Journal I, 1994; Ich stehe im Regen und warte, A propos de Shéhérazade, 1995; Le Presbytère n'a rien perdu de son charme ni le jardin de son éclat (Ballet for Life), IXe Symphonie, Juan Y Teresa, Barocco Bel Canto, 1997; Elton-Berg, 2000; Mère Teresa et les enfants du monde, 2003; L'Amour - La Danse; Zarathustra, 2005. *Publications:* Mathilde, ou le temps perdu (novel), 1963; La Reine Verte (play), 1963; L'autre chant de la danse, 1974; Un instant dans la vie d'autrui, 1979; La Mort Subite, 1991. *Address:* Ecole-Atelier Rudra Béjart, Chemin du Presbytère, Case Postale 25, 1000 Lausanne 22, Switzerland. *Died 22 Nov. 2007.*

BELCHER, John Rashleigh, FRCS; Consultant Thoracic Surgeon, NE Metropolitan Regional Hospital Board, 1950–82; Surgeon, London Chest Hospital, 1951–82; Thoracic Surgeon, Middlesex Hospital, 1955–82; *b* 11 Jan. 1917; *s* of late Dr Ormonde Rashleigh Belcher, Liverpool; *m* 1940, Jacqueline Mary, *d* of late C. P. Phillips; two *s* one *d. Educ:* Epsom Coll.; St Thomas' Hosp. MB BS 1939; FRCS 1942; MS 1945. Resident appointments at St Thomas' Hospital, 1939–46. RAF, 1940–46: Medical Service; general duties and surgical specialist; Squadron Leader. Resident and Asst posts at St Thomas', Brompton, London Chest, and Middlesex Hosps; followed by consultant appointments. Pres., Assoc. of Thoracic Surgeons, 1980; Member: Thoracic Soc.; Cardiac Soc.; Amer. Coll. of Chest Physicians. Mem. Bd of Governors: Hosps for Diseases of Chest and Heart, 1961–80. Toured: for British Council, Far East 1969, Cyprus and Greece 1973, Yugoslavia 1977; for FCO, Indonesia 1971, Bolivia 1975; personal lecture tours, Nepal and India 1969, Jamaica 1973, Mexico 1975. Hunterian Prof., RCS, 1979. Co-editor, Brit. Jl of Diseases of the Chest. *Publications:* Thoracic Surgical Management, 1953; chapters in standard text-books; papers in British and foreign medical journals. *Recreations:* photography, picture framing, opera. *Address:* 23 Hornton Court, Kensington High Street, W8 7RT. *T:* (020) 7937 7006. *Died 12 Jan. 2006.*

BELL, (Alexander) Scott, CBE 2000; Group Managing Director, Standard Life Assurance Co., 1988–2002; *b* 4 Dec. 1941; *s* of William Scott Bell and Irene Bell; *m* 1965, Veronica Jane (*née* Simpson); two *s* one *d. Educ:* Daniel Stewart's College, Edinburgh. FFA. Standard Life Assurance Co.: Asst Actuary for Canada, 1967; Dep. Actuary, 1972; South Region Manager, 1974; Asst Gen. Manager (Finance), 1979; Gen. Manager (Finance), 1985–88. Director: Bank of Scotland, 1988–96; Hammerson plc (formerly Hammerson Property and Develt Corp.), 1988–98; Prosperity SA, 1993–2002; Standard Life Healthcare, 1994–2002; Universities Superannuation Scheme Ltd, 1996–2005; Standard Life Bank, 1997–2002; Standard Life Investments, 1998–2002; Dunfermline Bldg Soc., 2002–; Chm., Associated Scottish Life Offices, 1994–96. Dir, ABI, 1999–2002. Hon. Canadian Consul in Scotland, 1994–2004. Hon. DLitt Heriot-Watt, 1997. *Recreations:* travel, golf, reading. *Clubs:* Hon. Co. of Edinburgh Golfers, Royal & Ancient Golf, Golf House (Elie), Bruntsfield Links Golfing Society. *Died 23 Aug. 2007.*

BELL, Arthur; *see* Bell, E. A.

BELL, Sir Brian (Ernest), KBE 1994 (OBE 1977); Chairman and Managing Director, Brian Bell & Co. Ltd, since 1956; *b* 3 July 1928; *s* of Ernest James Bell and Evelyn Ivy Alice Bell (*née* Zeller); *m* 1962, Jean Ann Clough (*d* 1992); one *s* one *d. Educ:* Chinchilla State Sch., Qld, Australia; Toowoomba Grammar Sch., Qld; Queensland Univ. (pharmaceutical chemist, 1949). Went to Papua New Guinea, 1954; Bulk Med. Store, Dept of Health, 1954–56; estabd first Appliance and Service Orgn, 1956. Mem., first Port Moresby CC, 1971–88 (Dep. Lord Mayor, 1973). Citizen of PNG, 1976. Hon. Consul for: Sweden, 1974–88 (Consul Gen., 1988–2005); Norway, 1984–88 (Consul Gen., 1988–2004). Chm., Port Moresby Gen. Hosp., 1994–. Mem., Salvation Army Adv. Bd, PNG, 1987– (Order of Dist. Auxiliary Service, 2006). Chm., Univ. of PNG Foundn, 1985–. Independence Medal (PNG), 1975; Silver Jubilee Medal, 1977; Tenth Anniversary Medal (PNG), 1985. CStJ 2004. Comdr, Royal Order of Polar Star (Sweden), 1990; Comdr, Royal Order of Merit (Norway), 2004 (Kt 1st Cl. 1992); Companion, Star of Melanesia (PNG), 2005. *Recreation:* interest in community affairs. *Address:* Brian Bell and Co. Ltd, PO Box 1228, Boroko, Papua New Guinea. *T:* 3255411; *e-mail:* bbadmin@brianbell.com.pg. *Club:* Papua (Port Moresby). *Died 25 July 2010.*

BELL, Prof. (Ernest) Arthur, CB 1988; PhD; FLS, CChem, FRSC; CBiol, FIBiol; Director, Royal Botanic Gardens, Kew, 1981–88; Visiting Professor, King's College London, since 1982; Adjunct Professor, University of Texas at Austin, since 1990; *b* 20 June 1926; *s* of Albert Bell and Rachel Enid (*née* Williams), Gosforth, Northumberland; *m* 1952, Jean Swinton Ogilvie; two *s* one *d. Educ:* Dame Allan's Sch., Newcastle upon Tyne; Univ. of Durham (King's Coll., Newcastle upon Tyne) BSc; Trinity Coll., Dublin (MA, PhD; Hon. Fellow, 1990). CChem, FRIC (later FRSC) 1961; FIBiol 1987. Res. Chemist, ICI, Billingham, 1946; Demonstr and holder of Sarah Purser Med. Res. Award, TCD, 1947; Asst to Prof. of Biochem., TCD, 1949; Lectr in Biochem., KCL, 1953; Reader in Biochem., Univ. of London, 1964–68; Prof. of Botany, Univ. of Texas, 1968–72; Prof. of Biology, London Univ., and Hd of Dept of Plant Scis, KCL, 1972–81; FKC 1982. Sen. Foreign Scientist Fellow, Nat. Sci. Foundn, USA, and Vis. Prof. of Biol., Univ. of Kansas, 1966; Visiting Professor: Univ. of Sierra Leone, 1977; Univ. of Reading, 1982–88; Cecil H. and Ida Green Vis. Prof., Univ. of British Columbia, 1987; Vis. Commonwealth Fellow, Australia, 1980; Emeritus Leverhulme Fellow, 1991–93. Scientific Dir, Texas Botanical Gardens Soc., 1988–. Consultant Dir, CAB-Internat. Mycological Inst. (formerly Commonwealth Mycol. Inst.), 1982–88; Member: Working Party on Naturally Occurring Toxicants in Food, 1983–94; Royal Mint Adv. Cttee, 1992–98. Hon. Botanical Adviser, Commonwealth War Graves Commn, 1983–89. President: Section K (Plant Biol.), BAAS, 1985–86; KCL Assoc., 1986–88; Vice Pres., Linnean Soc., 1983–85 (Mem. Council, 1980–85); Mem. Council, RHS, 1985–89; Hon. Mem., Phytochemical Soc. of Europe, 1985. *Publications:* contribs on plant biochem., chemotaxonomy, and chem. ecology to Phytochemistry, and Biochem. Jl. *Recreations:* walking, travel. *Address:* 3 Hillview, Wimbledon, SW20 0TA. *Club:* Athenæum. *Died 11 June 2006.*

BELL, Griffin Boyette; Attorney-General, USA, 1977–79; Senior Counsel, King & Spalding, Atlanta, since 2004; *b* Americus, Georgia, 31 Oct. 1918; *s* of A. C. Bell and Thelma Pilcher; *m* 1st, 1943, Mary Foy Powell (*d* 2000); one *s*; 2nd, 2001, Nancy Duckworth Kinnebrew. *Educ:* Southwestern Coll., Ga; Mercer Univ. (LLB *cum laude* 1948, LLD 1967). Served AUS, 1941–46, reaching rank of Major. Admitted to Georgia Bar, 1947; practice in Savannah and Rome, 1947–53. Partner in King & Spalding, Atlanta, 1953–59, 1976–77, 1979–2004, Managing Partner, 1959–61; United States Judge, 5th Circuit, 1961–76. Chairman: Atlanta Commn on Crime and Delinquency, 1965–66; CSCE, 1980. Mem., Vis. Cttee, Law Sch., Vanderbilt Univ.; Trustee, Mercer Univ.; Member: Amer. Law Inst.; Amer. Coll. of Trial Lawyers (Pres., 1985–86). *Address:* King & Spalding, 1180 Peachtree Street, Atlanta, GA 30309, USA. *Died 5 Jan. 2009.*

BELL, Peter Robert; Emeritus Professor of Botany, University of London; *b* 18 Feb. 1920; *s* of Andrew and Mabel Bell; *m* 1952, Elizabeth Harrison; two *s. Educ:* Simon Langton School, Canterbury; Christ's Coll., Cambridge (MA 1949). University College London: Asst Lecturer in Botany, 1946; Lectr in Botany, 1949; Reader in Botany, 1967; Prof. of Botany, 1967; Quain Prof. of Botany and Head of Dept of Botany and Microbiol., 1978–85; Dean of Science, 1979–82; Mem. Council, 1979–85. Visiting Professor: Univ. of California, Berkeley, 1966–67; Univ. of Delhi, India, 1970. British Council Distinguished Visitor, NZ, 1976; many other visits overseas, including exploration of Ecuadorian Andes. Vice-Pres., Linnean Soc., 1962–65; Mem. Biological Sciences Cttee, 1974–79 (Chm. Panel 1, 1977–79), SRC. *Publications:* Darwin's Biological Work, Some Aspects Reconsidered, 1959; (with C. F.

Woodcock) The Diversity of Green Plants, 1968, 3rd edn 1983; (trans., with D. E. Coombe) Strasburger's Textbook of Botany, 8th English edn, 1976; Green Plants: their origin and diversity, 1992, 2nd edn (with A. R. Hemsley) 2000; scientific papers on botanical topics, particularly reproductive cells of land plants, and on history of botany. *Recreation:* mountains. *Address:* 13 Granville Road, Barnet, Herts EN5 4DU. *T:* (020) 8449 9331. *Died 10 Jan. 2009.*

BELL, Scott; *see* Bell, Alexander Scott.

BELL DAVIES, Vice-Adm. Sir Lancelot (Richard), KBE 1977; *b* 18 Feb. 1926; *s* of late Vice-Adm. R. Bell Davies, VC, CB, DSO, AFC, and Mrs M. P. Bell Davies, Lee on Solent, Hants; *m* 1949, Emmeline Joan (*née* Molengraaff), Wassenaar, Holland; one *s* two *d*. *Educ:* Boxgrove Preparatory Sch., Guildford; RN Coll., Dartmouth. War of 1939–45: Midshipman, HMS Norfolk, 1943 (Scharnhorst sunk); joined Submarines, 1944. First Command, HMS Subtle, 1953; subseq. commands: HMS Explorer, 1955; Comdr, HMS Leander, 1962; Captain: HMS Forth, also SM7, 1967, and HMS Bulwark, 1972; Rear-Adm., 1973. Ministry of Defence Posts: (Comdr) Naval Staff, 1960; (Captain) Naval Asst to Controller, 1964; Director of Naval Warfare, 1969; Comdr, British Naval Staff, Washington, and UK Rep. to Saclant, 1973–75; Supreme Allied Commander Atlantic's Rep. in Europe, 1975–78; Comdt, Nato Defence Coll., Rome, 1978–81. Chm., Sea Cadet Council, 1983–92; President: HMS Norfolk Assoc., 1987–; Portsmouth Sea Cadets, 1992–2005; Square Rigger Club, 1997–2005. Pres., Southampton MND Assoc., 1998–2009; Vice Pres., Trincomalee Trust, 1999–2008. CCMI (FBIM 1977). *Recreations:* sailing, gardening. *Address:* Wessex Bungalow, Satchell Lane, Hamble, Hampshire SO31 4HS. *T:* (023) 8045 7415. *Clubs:* Naval and Military; Royal Yacht Squadron, Royal Naval Sailing Association. *Died 3 July 2010.*

BELLEW, 7th Baron *cr* 1848; **James Bryan Bellew;** Bt 1688; *b* 5 Jan. 1920; *s* of 6th Baron Bellew, MC, and Jeanie Ellen Agnes (*d* 1973), *d* of late James Ormsby Jameson; *S* father, 1981; *m* 1st, 1942, Mary Elizabeth (*d* 1978), *d* of Rev. Edward Eustace Hill; two *s* one *d*; 2nd, 1978, Gwendoline (*d* 2002), formerly wife of Major P. Hall and *d* of late Charles Redmond Clayton-Daubeny. Served War of 1939–45, Irish Guards (Captain). *Heir: s* Hon. Bryan Edward Bellew [*b* 19 March 1943; *m* 1968, Rosemary Sarah, *d* of Major Reginald Kilner Brasier Hitchcock; one *s* (and one *s* decd)]. *Address:* c/o Royal Bank of Scotland, 45 The Promenade, Cheltenham, Glos GL50 1PY. *Died 3 Aug. 2010.*

BELLOWS, James Gilbert; TV, newspaper, on-line executive; *b* 12 Nov. 1922; *s* of Lyman Hubbard Bellows and Dorothy Gilbert Bellows; *m* 1950, Marian Raines (decd); three *d*; *m* 1964, Maggie Savoy (decd); *m* 1971, Keven Ryan; one *d*. *Educ:* Kenyon Coll. (BA, LLB). Columbus (Ga) Ledger, 1947; News Editor Atlanta (Ga) Jl, 1950–57; Asst Editor, Detroit (Mich.) Free Press, 1957–58; Managing Editor Miami (Fla) News, 1958–61; Exec. Editor (News Ops), NY Herald Tribune, 1961–62; Editor, 1962–66; associate Editor, Los Angeles Times, 1966–75; Editor: Washington Star, 1975–78; Los Angeles Herald Examiner, 1979–82; Managing Editor, Entertainment Tonight (TV show), 1982–83; Exec. Editor, ABC-TV News, 1983–86; Dir of Editorial Develt, Prodigy, 1986–88; Managing Editor, USA Today on TV, 1988–89; Vice Pres. Editorial, MediaNews Gp, 1990–91; Los Angeles Bureau Chief, TV Guide, 1992–94; Exec. Editor, Excite Inc. Software, 1995–96; Chm., Editl Adv. Bd, Excite, 1997; Consultant, LA Daily News, 1998–99. Member: Kenyon Review Adv. Bd; Amer. Soc. of Newspaper Editors. *Publications:* The Last Editor: how I saved the New York Times, the Washington Post and the Los Angeles Times (memoir), 2002. *Address:* 555 South Barrington Avenue, Los Angeles, CA 90049–4344, USA. *Club:* Bel-Air Country (Los Angeles). *Died 6 March 2009.*

BENN, Anthony, OBE 1945; *b* 7 Oct. 1912; *s* of late Francis Hamilton Benn and Arta Clara Benn (*née* Boal); *m* 1943, Maureen Lillian Kathleen Benn (*née* Denbigh) (*d* 1992); two *s* four *d*. *Educ:* Harrow; Christ Church, Oxford (Scholar). Oxford Univ. Cricket XI, 1935. Price & Pierce Ltd, 1935 (Director, 1947, Chm., 1956–72). Joined Surrey and Sussex Yeomanry, 1936. Served War of 1939–45 (OBE): Staff Coll., 1942; Instructor, Middle East Staff Coll., 1943. Comdr, Order of the Lion of Finland, 1958. *Recreation:* travel. *Died 22 Sept. 2008.*

BENNETT, Corinne Marie Gillian, MBE 1988; FSA; historic buildings consultant, 1996–98; Cathedrals Architect at English Heritage, 1992–96; *b* 3 March 1935; *d* of Gilbert Wilson and Lucile (*née* Terroux); *m* 1979, Keith Charles Hugh Bennett. *Educ:* University Coll. London (BA Hons Arch. 1957; Inst. of Archaeology, London Univ. (Dip. Conservation of Historic Monuments 1964). ARIBA 1959. FSA 1996. Assistant Architect: Powell & Moya, 1958–61; Manning & Clamp, 1961–62; Architect, Ancient Monuments Br., MPBW, 1963–68; joined Purcell Miller Tritton, Associate, 1968, Partner, 1972–92. Consulting Surveyor, Archdeacons of Rochester Dio., 1969–84; Architect, Dean and Chapter of Winchester, 1974–89; Consultant Architect, Brighton BC (for Royal Pavilion), 1981–92. Mem., Cathedrals Fabric Commn for England, 1996–2006. DHS 1979, DCHS 1988, DGCHS 2000. *Recreations:* opera, walking, gardening. *Died 10 July 2010.*

BENNETT, John, MBE 1945; HM Senior Chief Inspector of Schools for Scotland, 1969–73; *b* 14 Nov. 1912; *m* 1940, Johanne R. McAlpine, MA; two *s* one *d*. *Educ:* Edinburgh Univ. MA (first class hons) 1934. Schoolmaster until 1951. Served War of 1939–45: Capt. REME, 79 Armd Div., 1940–46. HM Inspector of Schools, 1951. *Recreations:* mathematics, golf, bridge. *Died 19 July 2007.*

BENNETT, Patrick; QC 1969; a Recorder of the Crown Court, 1972–97; *b* 12 Jan. 1924; *s* of Michael Bennett; *m* 1951, Lyle Reta Pope; two *d*. *Educ:* Bablake Sch., Coventry; Magdalen Coll., Oxford. State Scholar, 1941. MA, BCL 1949. Served RNVR., 1943–46, Sub Lt. Called to Bar, Gray's Inn, 1949, Bencher 1976, Master of Students, 1980; Asst Recorder, Coventry, 1969–71; Dep. Chm., Lindsey QS, 1970–71. Mem., Mental Health Act Commn, 1984–86. Fellow: Internat. Soc. of Barristers, 1984; Nat. Inst. of Advocacy, 1980. Pres., Thomas More Soc., 1990–93. Associate Mem., Guild of Sommeliers of Northern France, 2007. *Publications:* Assessment of Damages in Personal Injury and Fatal Accidents, 1980; The Common Jury, 1986; Trial Techniques, 1986. *Recreations:* food, flying, spoiling two granddaughters. *Address:* (home) 22 Wynnstay Gardens, W8 6UR. *T:* (020) 7937 2110; 233 rue Nationale, Boulogne sur Mer, France. *T:* 321913339. *Club:* Spartan Flying (Denham). *Died 5 Dec. 2009.*

BENNETT, Richard Clement W.; *see* Wheeler-Bennett.

BENNEY, (Adrian) Gerald (Sallis), CBE 1995; RDI 1971; goldsmith and silversmith; Professor of Silversmithing and Jewellery, Royal College of Art, 1974–83; *b* 21 April 1930; *s* of late Ernest Alfred Benney and Aileen Mary Benney; *m* 1957, Janet Edwards; three *s* one *d*. *Educ:* Brighton Grammar Sch.; Brighton Coll. of Art (Nat. Dip. in Art); RCA (DesRCA). FSIAD 1975. Estabd 1st workshop, Whitfield Place, London, 1955; Consultant Designer, Viners Ltd, 1957–69; began designing and making Reading civic plate, 1963; discovered technique of texturing on silver, 1964; moved workshop to Bankside, London, 1969; began prodn of Beenham Enamels, 1970; retired as goldsmith, 1999. Held Royal Warrants of Appt to the Queen (designer and maker of 40th Anniversary Mace, for use at Commonwealth Ceremonies, 1992), the Duke of Edinburgh, Queen Elizabeth the Queen Mother and the Prince of Wales. Member: Govt's Craft Adv. Cttee,

1972–77; UK Atomic Energy Ceramics Centre Adv. Cttee, 1979–83; British Hallmarking Council, 1983–88. Metalwork Design Advisor to Indian Govt (UP State), 1977–78; Chm., Govt of India Hallmarking Survey, 1981; Export Advisor and Designer to Royal Selangor Pewter Co., Kuala Lumpur, 1986–. Consultant to Silver Trust, 1977– (commission of silver for loaning to No 10 Downing St and other govt estabs). Major exhibitions: Goldsmiths' Co., 1973, 2005 (retrospective); NY, 1994; Tel Aviv, 1995; major one man exhibn of oil paintings, Solomon Gall., 1988. Major commissions for: ICAEW; Christie's, UK; Schroders; ICI; Coventry Cathedral; St Paul's Cathedral; Westminster Abbey; All Saints', Princeton. Liveryman, Goldsmiths' Co., 1964. Hon. MA Leicester, 1963. Freeman, Borough of Reading, 1984. *Relevant publication*: Gerald Benney, Goldsmith, by Graham Hughes, 1998. *Recreations*: walking, oil painting, landscape gardening. *Address*: The Old Rectory, Chalderton, Salisbury, Wilts SP4 0DW. *T*: (01980) 629614, *Fax*: (01980) 629461; (show rooms) 73 Walton Street, Knightsbridge, SW3 2HT. *T*: (020) 7589 7002. *Club*: Groucho. *Died 26 June 2008.*

BENSON, (Harry) Peter (Neville), CBE 1982; MC 1945; FCA; Chairman, Davy Corporation PLC, 1982–85; *b* 10 Feb. 1917; *s* of Harry Leedham Benson and Iolanthe Benson; *m* 1948, Margaret Young Brackenridge; two *s* one *d*. *Educ*: Cheltenham Coll. FCA 1946. Served War, S Staffs Regt, 1939–45 (Major; MC). Moore Stephens, 1946–48; John Mowlem, 1948–51; Dir, 1951–54, Man. Dir, 1954–57, Waring & Gillow; Dir, APV Co., 1957–66; Man. Dir, 1966–77, Chm., 1977–82, APV Holdings. Director: Rolls Royce Motors, 1971–80; Vickers Ltd, 1980–82. *Recreation*: golf. *Address*: The Gate House, Little Chesters, Nursery Road, Walton-on-the-Hill, Tadworth, Surrey KT20 7TX. *T*: (01737) 813767. *Club*: Walton Heath Golf. *Died 23 July 2010.*

BENTSEN, Lloyd Millard, Jr; Chairman, New Holland, 1996–98; *b* 11 Feb. 1921; *s* of late Lloyd and of Edna Ruth Bentsen; *m* 1943, Beryl Ann Longino; two *s* one *d*. *Educ*: Univ. of Texas (LLB 1942). Served USAAF, 1942–45 (DFC; Air Medal). Admitted to Texas Bar, 1942; in private practice, 1945–48; Judge, Hidalgo County, Texas, 1946–48. Mem. of Congress, 1948–54; Mem. for Texas, US Senate, 1972–93; Sec. to US Treasury, 1993–94. Pres., Lincoln Consolidated, Houston, 1955–70. Democratic running mate to Michael Dukakis, US Presidential election, 1988. *Died 23 May 2006.*

BERESFORD-WEST, Michael Charles; QC 1975; a Recorder of the Crown Court, 1974–80; *b* 3 June 1928; *s* of late Arthur Charles, OBE, KPM and Ida Dagmar West; *m* 1st, 1956, Patricia Eileen Beresford (marr. diss.); two *s* one *d*; 2nd, 1986, Sheilagh Elizabeth Davies. *Educ*: St Peter's, Southbourne; Portsmouth Grammar Sch.; Brasenose Coll., Oxford (MA). Nat. Service, Intell. Corps, Middle East, SIME. Called to Bar, Lincoln's Inn, 1952, Inner Temple, 1980, Gray's Inn, 1980; Western Circuit, 1953–65; SE Circuit, 1965; a Chm., Independent Schools Tribunal and Tribunal (Children's Act 1948), 1974–80. *Recreations*: swimming, opera, music, golf, cruising. *Address*: 3/4 Farnham Hall, Farnham, Saxmundham, Suffolk IP17 1LB. *T*: and *Fax*: (01728) 602758. *Clubs*: Hampshire Hogs; Nomads; Aldeburgh Yacht, Bar Yacht; Aldeburgh Golf. *Died 25 Sept. 2006.*

BERGMAN, (Ernst) Ingmar; Swedish film and theatre producer; Director, Royal Dramatic Theatre, Stockholm; director of productions on television; *b* Uppsala, 14 July 1918; *s* of a Chaplain to the Royal Court at Stockholm; *m* 1971, Mrs Ingrid von Rosen (*d* 1995); three *s* three *d* (and one *s* decd) by previous marriages; one *d* with Liv Ullmann. *Educ*: Stockholm Univ. Producer, Royal Theatre, Stockholm, 1940–42; Producer and scriptwriter, Swedish Film Co., 1940–44; Theatre Director: Helsingborg, 1944–46; Gothenburg, 1946–49; Malmo, 1952–59. Produced: Hedda Gabler, Cambridge, 1970; Show, 1971; King Lear, 1985; Hamlet, 1986, Nat.

Theatre, 1987; Miss Julie, Nat. Th., 1987; Lady from the Sea, Oslo, A Doll's House, Theatre Royal Glasgow, 1990; Ghosts, Barbican, 2003. Films (British titles) produced include: Torment, 1943; Crisis, 1945; Port of Call, 1948; Summer Interlude, 1950; Waiting Women, 1952; Summer with Monika, 1952; Sawdust and Tinsel, 1953; A Lesson in Love, 1953; Journey into Autumn, 1954; Smiles of a Summer Night, 1955; The Seventh Seal, 1956–57; Wild Strawberries, 1957; So Close to Life, 1957; The Face, 1958; The Virgin Spring, 1960 (shown Edinburgh Fest., 1960); The Devil's Eye, 1961 (shown Edinburgh Fest., 1961); Through a Glass Darkly, 1961; Winter Light, 1962; The Silence, 1963; Now About all these Women, 1964 (first film in colour); Persona, 1967; Hour of the Wolf, 1968; Shame, 1968; The Rite, 1969; The Passion, 1970; The Fåro Document, 1970 (first documentary, shown Vienna Fest., 1980); The Touch, 1971; Cries and Whispers, 1972 (NY Film Critics Best Film Award, 1972); Scenes from a Marriage, 1974 (BBC TV Series, 1975; published, 1975; British première as play, Chichester, 1990); Face to Face, 1976 (BBC TV Series, 1979); The Serpent's Egg, 1977; Autumn Sonata, 1978; From the Life of the Marionettes, 1981; Fanny and Alexander, 1983 (published, 1989); Saraband, 2005; screenplays: The Best Intentions, 1991; Faithless, 2000. Gained several international awards and prizes for films; Goethe Prize, 1976; Great Gold Medal, Swedish Acad. of Letters, 1977. *Publications*: Four Stories, 1977; The Magic Lantern (autobiog.), 1988; Images: my life in film, 1994; Private Confessions, 1996. *Died 30 July 2007.*

BERGNE, (Alexander) Paul (A'Court), CBE 2002 (OBE 1985); HM Diplomatic Service, retired; author, broadcaster and consultant; *b* 9 Jan. 1937; *s* of Villiers A'Court Bergne and Diana Daphne Cuthbert (*née* Holman-Hunt); *m* 1963, Suzanne Hedwig Judith Wittich; one *s* one *d*. *Educ*: Winchester Coll.; Trinity Coll., Cambridge (BA); SOAS, London Univ. (MA). Krasicki Iran Expedn film cameraman, 1958–59; joined FO, 1959; served Vienna, 1961–63; Tehran, 1965–68; MECAS, 1970–72; Abu Dhabi, 1972–75; Cairo, 1975–77; Athens, 1980–84; Counsellor, Hong Kong, 1985–87; Cabinet Office, 1988–92; Ambassador to Uzbekistan, 1993–95, and to Tajikistan, 1994–95; Prin. Res. Officer, Res. and Analysis Dept, FCO, 1995–96. Director: Camco Trading Ltd, 1997–2000; London Information Network on Conflicts and State Building, 1999–2002. Specialist Advr, H of C Foreign Affairs Cttee, 1999–2000; Prime Minister's personal rep. for Afghan affairs, 2001. Member: Cttee for Central and Inner Asia, British Acad., 2002–; Council, Royal Soc. of Asian Affairs, 2003–; Council of Mgt, British Inst. of Persian Studies, 2003–. Sen. Associate Mem., St Antony's Coll., Oxford, 1997–. Writer/presenter, radio series: Reports from the Silk Road, 1997; Hidden London, 1999; Persian Studies in Britain, 2001. Mem. Editl Bd, Central Asian Survey, 1998–. *Publications*: The Birth of Tajikistan, 2007; articles on art, architecture and archaeology of the Middle East. *Recreations*: mountain walking, numismatics, archaeology. *Address*: PO Box 414, Bourton on the Water, Cheltenham GL54 2YY. *Died 5 April 2007.*

BERGQUIST, Prof. Dame Patricia (Rose), DBE 1994; DSc; FRSNZ; Professor of Zoology, University of Auckland, 1981–2000, then Emeritus; *b* 10 March 1933; *d* of William Smyth and Bertha Ellen Smyth (*née* Penny); *m* 1958, Peter Leonard Bergquist; one *d*. *Educ*: Devonport Primary Sch.; Takapuna Grammar; Univ. of Auckland (BSc 1954; MSc Hons 1957; PhD 1961; DSc 1979). University of Auckland: Lectr, then Sen. Lectr in Zool., 1958–69; Associate Prof., 1970–80; Head of Zool., 1986–92; Asst Vice-Chancellor Academic, 1989–96; Dep. Vice-Chancellor, 1993; Special Asst to Vice-Chancellor, 1997–2000. Research Fellow: Yale 1962 and 1968; Marseille, 1973; Natural Hist. Mus., London, 1978; Amer. Mus. of Natural Hist., 1990; Sen. Queen's Fellow in Marine Sci., Australia, 1984. FRSNZ 1981 (Hector Medal and Prize, 1989). *Publications*: Sponges, 1978; numerous papers and monographs in learned jls. *Recreations*: music, stamp collecting, swimming, wind-surfing. *Address:* Department of Anatomy, School of Medicine, University of Auckland, Private Bag 92019, Auckland, New Zealand. *T:* (9) 373599.   *Died 9 Sept. 2009.*

BERKSON, David Mayer; a Recorder of the Crown Court, 1978–99; an Assistant Judge Advocate General, 1988–99; Deputy Judge Advocate General, Germany, 1994–99; Magistrate of the Standing Civilian Courts, 1991–99; *b* 8 Sept. 1934; *s* of Louis Berkson and Regina Berkson (*née* Globe); *m* 1961, Pamela Anne (*née* Thwaite); one *d. Educ:* Birkenhead School. Called to the Bar, Gray's Inn, 1957. Dep. Judge Advocate, 1984–87. Legal Mem., Mental Health Review Tribunal for the Mersey Area, 1982–84. Part-time Special Adjudicator, Immigration Appeal Authority, 1998–2003.
Died 10 Dec. 2007.

BERNSTEIN OF CRAIGWEIL, Baron *cr* 2000 (Life Peer), of Craigweil, in the co. of West Sussex; **Alexander Bernstein;** Chairman, Granada Group plc, 1979–96 (Director, 1964–96); Director, Waddington Galleries, since 1966; *b* 15 March 1936; *s* of late Cecil Bernstein and of Myra Ella, *d* of Lesser and Rachel Lesser; *m* 1st, 1962, Vanessa Anne Mills (marr. diss. 1993; she *d* 2003); one *s* one *d;* 2nd, 1995, Angela Mary Serota (CBE 2008). *Educ:* Stowe Sch.; St John's Coll., Cambridge. Man. Dir, 1964–68, Chm., 1977–86, Granada TV Rental Ltd; Jt Man. Dir, Granada Television Ltd, 1971–75. Trustee: Civic Trust for the North-West, 1964–86; Granada Foundn, 1968–; Theatres Trust, 1996–2000; Trusthouse Charitable Foundn, 1996–; Chairman: Royal Exchange Theatre, 1983–94 (Dep. Chm., 1980–83); Old Vic Theatre Trust, 1998–2002. Mem., Nat. Theatre Develt Council, 1996–98. Member of Court: Univ. of Salford, 1976–87; Univ. of Manchester, 1983–98. Hon. DLitt Salford 1981; Hon. LLD Manchester, 1996. *Address:* c/o House of Lords, SW1A 0PW.   *Died 12 April 2010.*

BERRILL, Sir Kenneth (Ernest), GBE 1988; KCB 1971; Deputy Chairman, Universities' Superannuation Scheme, 1981–85 (Chairman Joint Negotiating Committee, 1990–2008); *b* 28 Aug. 1920; *m* 1st, 1941, Brenda West (marr. diss.); one *s;* 2nd, 1950, June Phillips (marr. diss.; she *d* 2003); one *s* one *d;* 3rd, 1977, Jane Marris. *Educ:* London Sch. of Economics; Trinity Coll., Cambridge. BSc(Econ) London; MA Cantab, 1949. Served War, 1939–45, REME. Economic Adviser to Turkey, Guyana, Cameroons, OECD, and World Bank. Univ. Lectr in Economics, Cambridge, 1949–69; Rockefeller Fellowship Stanford and Harvard Univs, 1951–52; Fellow and Bursar, St Catharine's Coll., Cambridge, 1949–62, Hon. Fellow, 1974; Prof., MIT, 1962; Fellow and First Bursar, King's Coll., Cambridge, 1962–69, Hon. Fellow, 1973; HM Treasury Special Adviser (Public Expenditure), 1967–69; Chm., UGC, 1969–73; Head of Govt Econ. Service and Chief Economic Advr, HM Treasury, 1973–74; Head of Central Policy Review Staff, Cabinet Office, 1974–80; Chm., Vickers da Costa Ltd and Vickers da Costa & Co. Hong Kong Ltd, 1981–85; Chm., SIB, 1985–88; Dep. Chm., 1982–87, Chm., 1987–90, Robert Horne Gp; Chm., Commonwealth Equities Fund, 1990–95; Chm., Moneda Chile Fund, 1995–2007. Mem., Stock Exchange, London, 1981–85. Member: Council for Scientific Policy, 1969–72; Adv. Bd for Research Councils, 1972–77; Adv. Council for Applied R&D, 1977–80; Brit. Nat. Commn for UNESCO, 1967–70; UN Cttee for Develt Planning, 1984–87; Inter-Univ. Council, 1969–73; UGC, Univ. of S Pacific, 1972–85; Council, Royal Economic Soc., 1972– (Vice Pres., 1986–); Adv. Bd, RCDS, 1974–80; Review Bd for Govt Contracts, 1981–85; Chm. Exec. Cttee, NIESR, 1988–96; (Nominated), Governing Council, Lloyd's, 1983–88. Dir, UK-Japan 2000 Gp, 1986–90. Advr, Nippon Credit Internat. Ltd, 1989–99; Dep. Chm., General Funds Investment Trust, 1982–85; Member: Baring Private Equity Partners Adv. Council, 1996–2000; Baring Eur. Private Equity Fund Adv. Council, 1999–; Director: Investing in Success

Investment Trust, 1965–67; Ionian Bank, 1969–73. Trustee: London Philharmonic, 1987–2006; Newnham Coll. Develt Trust, 1989–95; Nat. Extension Coll., 1990–2006 (Vice-Chm. Trustees, 1997–2006); Res. Inst. for Consumer Affairs, 1990–96. Pro-Chancellor, and Chm. Council, Open Univ., 1983–96; Governor: Admin. Staff Coll., Henley, 1969–84; ODI, 1969–73; Mem. Council, Salford Univ., 1981–84. McDonnell Scholar, World Inst. for Develt Economic Res., 1988, 1990. Mem., Cambridge City Council, 1963–67. CCMI (CBIM 1987). FRSA 1988; Hon. Fellow: LSE, 1970; Chelsea Coll., London, 1973; Hon. FKC 1989; Fellow, Open Univ., 1997. Hon. LLD: Cambridge, 1974; Bath, 1974; East Anglia, 1975; Leicester, 1975; DUniv Open, 1974; Hon. DTech Loughborough, 1974; Hon DSc Aston, 1974. Jephcott Lectr and Medallist, 1978; Stamp Meml Lectr, 1980. *Recreations:* gardening, sailing, music. *Address:* Salt Hill, Bridle Way, Grantchester, Cambs CB3 9NY. *T:* (01223) 840335, *Fax:* (01223) 845939. *Clubs:* Climbers (Hon. Mem.); Himalayan; Cambridge Alpine.
Died 30 April 2009.

BERRY, Anthony Arthur; Chairman, Berry Bros & Rudd Ltd, 1965–85; *b* 16 March 1915; *s* of Francis L. Berry and Amy Marie (*née* Freeman); *m* 1953, Sonia Alice, *d* of Sir Harold Graham-Hodgson, KCVO; one *s* one *d. Educ:* Charterhouse; Trinity Hall, Cambridge. Served War, RNVR, 1939–45, incl. 2¼ yrs in the Mediterranean. Joined the wine trade on leaving Cambridge, 1936; rejoined family firm of Berry Bros & Rudd on completion of war service; Dir, 1946–. Worshipful Co. of Vintners: Liveryman, 1946; Mem. Court, 1972–; Master, 1980–81. *Clubs:* Boodle's, MCC; Saintsbury; Royal Wimbledon Golf; Royal St George's Golf (Sandwich).   *Died 23 Feb. 2010.*

BERRY, Prof. Francis; Professor of English Language and Literature, Royal Holloway College, University of London, 1970–80, then Emeritus; *b* 23 March 1915; *s* of James Berry and Mary Augusta Jane Berry (*née* Ivens); *m* 1st, 1947, Nancy Melloney (*d* 1967), *d* of Cecil Newton Graham; one *s* one *d;* 2nd, 1970, Patricia (marr. diss. 1975), *d* of John Gordon Thomson; 3rd, 1979, Eileen, *d* of Eric Charles Lear. *Educ:* Hereford Cathedral Sch.; Dean Close Sch.; University Coll., Exeter (BA London (1st cl. hons); MA Exeter). Solicitor's articled clerk, 1931; University Coll., Exeter, 1937. War Service, 1939–46. University Coll., Exeter, 1946; successively Asst Lectr, Lectr, Sen. Lectr, Reader in English Literature, and Prof. of English Literature, Univ. of Sheffield, 1947–70. Visiting Lecturer: Carleton Coll., Minn, USA, 1951–52; UC of the West Indies, Jamaica, 1957; W. P. Ker Vis. Lectr, Glasgow, 1979; Lectr for British Council: in India, 1966–67; tour of univs in Japan, 1983, of univs of New Zealand, 1988; Vis. Fellow, ANU, Canberra, 1979; Vis. Prof. of English, Univ. of Malaŵi, 1980–81. Pres., SW of England Shakespeare Trust, 1985. FRSL 1968. Hon. Fellow, RHBNC, London Univ., 1987. *Publications:* Gospel of Fire, 1933; Snake in the Moon, 1936; The Iron Christ, 1938; Fall of a Tower, 1942; Murdock and Other Poems, 1947; The Galloping Centaur, 1952, 2nd edn 1970; Herbert Read, 1953, 2nd edn 1961; (ed) An Anthology of Medieval Poems, 1954; Poets' Grammar: time, tense and mood in poetry, 1958, 2nd edn, 1974; Morant Bay and other poems, 1961; Poetry and the Physical Voice, 1962; The Shakespeare Inset, 1965, 2nd edn 1971; Ghosts of Greenland, 1967; John Masefield: the Narrative Poet, 1968; (ed) Essays and Studies for the English Association, 1969; Thoughts on Poetic Time, 1972; I Tell of Greenland (novel), 1977; From the Red Fort: new and selected poems, 1984; Collected Poems, 1994; contributor: Review of English Studies; Essays in Criticism; Poetry Nat. Review; BBC Radio Three, ABC, etc. *Recreations:* following first-class cricket, chess, travel, gardening. *Address:* 4 Eastgate Street, Winchester, Hants SO23 8EB. *T:* (01962) 854439.
Died 10 Oct. 2006.

BERRY, Dr Robert Langley Page, CBE 1979; Chairman, 1968–78, Deputy Chairman, 1978–79, Alcoa of Great Britain Ltd; *b* 22 Nov. 1918; *s* of Wilfred Arthur and Mabel Grace Berry; *m* 1946, Eleanor Joyce (*née* Cramp); one *s* one *d*. *Educ*: Sir Thomas Rich's Sch., Gloucester; Birmingham Univ. (BSc (Hons), PhD). Served war, Royal Engrs, 1939–45. ICI Metals Div., 1951–66, Director, 1960–66; Man. Dir, Impalco, 1966–68. Non-Exec. Dir, Royal Mint, 1981–86. Dir, Nat. Anti-Waste Prog., 1976–80. President: Inst. of Metals, 1973; Aluminium Fedn, 1974. Chm., Friends of Fairford Church, 1985–97. *Publications*: several, in scientific jls. *Recreations*: fly-fishing, gardening. *Address*: Waterloo Cottage, Waterloo Lane, Fairford, Glos GL7 4BP. *T*: (01285) 712038. *Club*: Army and Navy. *Died 14 Dec. 2009.*

BERTHON, Vice-Adm. Sir Stephen (Ferrier), KCB 1980; *b* 24 Aug. 1922; *s* of late Rear-Adm. C. P. Berthon, CBE and Mrs C. P. Berthon (*née* Ferrier), *m* 1948, Elizabeth Leigh-Bennett; two *s* two *d*. *Educ*: Old Malthouse, Swanage; RNC Dartmouth. Served War of 1939–45 at sea, Mediterranean, Atlantic, Russia; spec. communications, 1945–46; Flag Lieut Singapore, 1946–48; submarines, 1949–51; East Indies Flagship, 1951–52; HMS Mercury, 1952–54; Staff of Flag Officer Aircraft Carriers, 1954–56; Fleet Communications Officer Mediterranean, 1957–59; jssc 1959; Comdr HMS Mercury, 1959–61; Jt Planning Staff, 1961–64; Naval Attaché, Australia, 1964–66; Dir of Defence Policy, MoD, 1968–71; Cdre HMS Drake, 1971–73; Flag Officer Medway and Port Adm. Chatham, 1974–76; Asst Chief of Naval Staff (Op. Req.), 1976–78; Dep. Chief of Defence Staff (Operational Requirements), 1978–81; retired 1981. Jt MFH, Avon Vale Hunt, 1981–84. *Recreations*: hunting, riding, gardening, walking, painting. *Club*: Army and Navy. *Died 30 Jan. 2007.*

BESAG, Prof. Julian E., FRS 2004; Professor of Statistics, University of Washington, Seattle, 1991–2007, then Emeritus; *b* 26 March 1945; one *s* one *d*. *Educ*: Univ. of Birmingham (BSc Hons Mathematical Stats 1968). Res. Asst, Univ. of Oxford, 1968–69; Lectr in Stats, Univ. of Liverpool, 1969–75; Reader in Stats, 1975–85, Prof. of Stats, 1985–89, Univ. of Durham; Prof. of Stats, Univ. of Newcastle upon Tyne, 1990–91. Visiting Professor: Princeton Univ., 1975; Univ. of Newcastle upon Tyne, 1987–88; Univ. of Washington, Seattle, 1989–90. *Recreation*: sailing. *Address*: Department of Statistics, Box 354322, University of Washington, Seattle, WA 98195, USA. *T*: (206) 5433871, *Fax*: (206) 6857419; *e-mail*: julian@stat.washington.edu. *Clubs*: Northwest Riggers Yacht, Washington Yacht. *Died 6 Aug. 2010.*

BESTERMAN, Edwin Melville Mack, MD; FRCP; FACC; Honorary Consultant Cardiologist: Department of Medicine, University of the West Indies (Mona Faculty, Jamaica), since 1985; St Mary's Hospital, London, since 1985; Paddington Green Children's Hospital, since 1985; Hon. Consultant Physician, Department of Medicine, Hammersmith Hospital, since 1981; *b* 4 May 1924; *s* of late Theodore Deodatus Nathaniel Besterman and Evelyn, *y* d of Arthur Mack, NY; *m* Audrey Heald (marr. diss.); one *s* (and one *s* decd); *m* 1955, Eleanor Mary Rymer Till (marr. diss.), *d* of T. Till, Caerleon; two *s*; *m* 1978, Perri Marjorie Burrowes, *d* of R. Burrowes, Kingston, Jamaica, WI. *Educ*: Stowe Sch.; Trinity Coll., Cambridge (BA 1943 (1st cl. hons Physiology); MA 1948; MB, BChir 1947; MD 1955 (Raymond Horton Smith Prize)); Guy's Hospital. MRCP 1949, FRCP 1967; FACC 1985. Out-patient Officer, Guy's Hosp., 1947; House Physician, Post-graduate Medical Sch., Hammersmith, 1948; Registrar, Special Unit for Juvenile Rheumatism, Canadian Red Cross Memorial Hosp., Taplow, Berks, 1949–52; First Asst (Lectr), Inst of Cardiology and Nat. Heart Hosp., 1953–56; Sen. Registrar, Middlesex Hosp., 1956–62; Consultant Cardiologist: St Mary's Hosp., London, 1962–85; Paddington Green Children's Hosp., 1972–85. Member: Brit. Cardiac Soc.; Caribbean Cardiac Soc.; Fellow, Amer. Coll. of Cardiology. Mem., Colony Photographic Club of Jamaica. *Publications*: (contrib.) Paul Wood, Diseases of the Heart and Circulation, 3rd edn, 1968; (contrib.) British Cardiology in the 20th Century, 2000; articles on phonocardiography, pulmonary hypertension, atherosclerosis, blood platelet function, lipid fractions and drug trials in angina and hypertension in Brit. Heart Jl, Brit. Med. Jl, Lancet, Circulation, Atherosclerosis Research, etc. *Recreations*: photography, gardening, dogs (Pres., German Shepherd Club, Jamaica). *Address*: PO Box 340, Stony Hill, Kingston 9, Jamaica, West Indies. *Died 3 Sept. 2007.*

BETHELL, 4th Baron *cr* 1922, of Romford; **Nicholas William Bethell**; Bt 1911; Member (C) London Region, European Parliament, 1999–2003; free-lance writer; *b* 19 July 1938; *s* of Hon. William Gladstone Bethell (*d* 1964) (3rd *s* of 1st Baron), and Ann Margaret Bethell (*d* 1996); *S* kinsman, 1967; *m* 1st, 1964, Cecilia Mary (marr. diss. 1971, she *d* 1977), *er d* of Prof. A. M. Honeyman; two *s*; 2nd, 1992, Bryony Lea Morgan, *e d* of Brian Griffiths; one *s*. *Educ*: Harrow; Pembroke Coll., Cambridge (PhD 1987). On editorial staff of Times Literary Supplement, 1962–64; a Script Editor in BBC Radio Drama, 1964–67. A Lord in Waiting (Govt Whip, House of Lords), June 1970–Jan. 1971. MEP (C), 1975–94 (London NW, 1979–94); contested (C) London NW, Eur. Parly elecns, 1994. President: Friends of Gibraltar's Heritage, 1992–2001; Friends of Cyprus, 2001– (Chm., 1981–2001). Pres., Uxbridge Conservative Assoc., 1995–99. Vice Pres., Brill CC, 1997–. Freeman, City of Gibraltar, 2004. Robert Schuman Award, 2003. Comdr, Order of Merit (Poland), 1991. *Publications*: Gomulka: his Poland and his Communism, 1969; The War Hitler Won, 1972; The Last Secret, 1974; Russia Besieged, 1977; The Palestine Triangle, 1979; The Great Betrayal, 1984; Spies and Other Secrets, 1994; *translations*: Six Plays, by Slawomir Mrozek, 1967; Elegy to John Donne, by Joseph Brodsky, 1967; Cancer Ward, by A. Solzhenitsyn, 1968; The Love Girl and the Innocent, by A. Solzhenitsyn, 1969; The Ascent of Mount Fuji, by Chingiz Aitmatov, 1975; dramatic works for radio and TV; occasional journalism. *Recreations*: poker, tennis. *Heir*: *s* Hon. James Nicholas Bethell [*b* 1 Oct. 1967. *Educ*: Harrow; Edinburgh Univ.]. *Address*: Manor Farm, Brill, Bucks HP18 9SL. *T*: (01844) 238446. *Clubs*: Garrick, Pratt's. *Died 8 Sept. 2007.*

BEVAN, Rear-Adm. Christopher Martin, CB 1978; Under Treasurer Gray's Inn, 1980–89; *b* London, 22 Jan. 1923; *s* of Humphrey C. Bevan and Mary F. Bevan (*née* Mackenzie); *m* 1948, Patricia C. Bedford; one *s* three *d*. *Educ*: Stowe Sch., Bucks; Victoria Univ., Wellington, NZ. Trooper in Canterbury Yeoman Cavalry (NZ Mounted Rifles), 1941; joined RN as Ord. Seaman, 1942; served remainder of 1939–45 war, Mediterranean and N Atlantic; commissioned 1943; Comdr 1958; Captain 1967; Supt Weapons and Radio, Dockyard Dept, MoD (Navy), 1967–70; Asst Dir, Weapons Equipment (Surface), later, Captain Surface Weapons Acceptance, Weapons Dept, MoD (Navy), 1970–73; Dir, Naval Officer Appts (Engrs), 1973–76; ADC to the Queen, 1976; Rear-Adm. 1976; Flag Officer Medway and Port Adm. Chatham, 1976–78. *Recreations*: photography, theatre, music, travel. *Address*: c/o Messrs C. Hoare and Co., 37 Fleet Street, EC4P 4DQ. *Club*: Boodle's. *Died 13 April 2008.*

BEVERIDGE, William Ian Beardmore, ScD, DVSc; Professor of Animal Pathology, Cambridge, 1947–75; Fellow of Jesus College, Cambridge, 1948–76, then Emeritus; *b* 23 April 1908; *s* of J. W. C. and Ada Beveridge; *m* 1935, Patricia, *d* of Rev. E. C. Thomson; one *s*. *Educ*: Cranbrook Sch., Sydney; St Paul's Coll., University of Sydney (DVSc); ScD Cantab 1974. Research bacteriologist, McMaster Animal Health Laboratory, Sydney, 1931–37; Commonwealth Fund Service Fellow at Rockefeller Inst. and at Washington, 1938–39; Walter and Eliza Hall Inst. for Medical Research, Melbourne, 1941–46; Visiting Worker, Pasteur

Inst., Paris, 1946–47; Vis. Prof., Ohio State Univ., 1953; Guest Lectr, Norwegian Veterinary Sch., 1955; first Wesley W. Spink Lectr on Comparative Medicine, Minnesota, 1971. Consultant: WHO, Geneva, 1964–79; Bureau of Animal Health, Canberra, 1979–84; Vis. Fellow, John Curtin Sch. of Med. Res., ANU, Canberra, 1979–84, Fellow, University House, 1980–85. Chm. Permanent Cttee of the World Veterinary Assoc., 1957–75. DVM (*hc*) Hanover, 1963; Hon. Associate RCVS, 1963; Life Fellow, Aust. Vet. Assoc., 1963; Hon. Member: British Veterinary Assoc., 1970; Amer. Vet. Med. Assoc., 1973; World Veterinary Congresses, 1975; Univ. House, Canberra, 1986; Hon. Foreign Mem., Académie Royale de Médicine de Belgique, 1970; Foundation Fellow, Aust. Coll. Vet. Scientists, 1971; Mem., German Acad. for Scientific Research, Leopoldina, 1974; Hon. Dip., Hungarian Microbiological Assoc., Budapest, 1976. Karl F. Meyer Goldheaded Cane Award, 1971; Gamgee Gold Medal, World Vet. Assoc., 1975; Medal of Honour, French Nat. Cttee of World Vet. Assoc., 1976. *Publications:* The Art of Scientific Investigation, 1950; Frontiers in Comparative Medicine, 1972; Influenza: the last great plague, 1977; Seeds of Discovery, 1980; Viral Diseases of Farm Livestock, 1981; Bacterial Diseases of Cattle, Sheep and Goats, 1983; Fighting Diseases: my varied scientific career, 1997; articles on infectious diseases of man and domestic animals and comparative medicine, in scientific jls. *Recreation:* bush-walking. *Address:* 5 Bellevue Road, Wentworth Falls, Blue Mountains, NSW 2782, Australia. *T:* (2) 47571606. *Died 14 Aug. 2006.*

BHUTTO, Benazir; Chairperson, Pakistan People's Party, since 1993; Prime Minister of Pakistan, 1988–90, and 1993–96; *b* 21 June 1953; *d* of late Zulfikar Ali Bhutto and of Begum Nusrat Bhutto; *m* 1987, Asif Ali Zardari; one *s* two *d. Educ:* Harvard Univ.; Lady Margaret Hall, Oxford (MPhil PPE; Dip. in Internat. Law and Diplomacy, 1977; Pres., Oxford Union Soc., 1977; Hon. Fellow, 1989). Co-Chair (with Begum Nusrat Bhutto), Pakistan People's Party, 1979–93; under house arrest, 1979–84; exile in London, 1984–86; returned to Pakistan, 1986; exile in Dubai, 1999–. Honorary Professor: Kyrghyz State Nat. Univ., Kyrghyzstan, 1995; Yassavi Kazakh Turkish Univ., Kazakhstan, 1995. Hon. Fellow, St Catherine's Coll., Oxford. Hon. FRCP. Hon. Dr Law Harvard; Hon. Dr Mendanao State Univ., 1995; Hon. Dr Econs Gakushuin Univ., Tokyo, 1996. *Publications:* Perspective on Pakistan Foreign Policy, 1978; Daughter of the East (autobiog.), 1988, 2nd edn 2007; *posthumous publication:* Reconciliation: Islam, Democracy and the West. *Recreations:* reading biographies, walking. *Address:* House No 8, Street 19, Sector F–8/2, Islamabad, Pakistan. *Club:* Oxford and Cambridge. *Died 27 Dec. 2007.*

BICKERTON, Frank Donald, CBE 1966; Director General, Central Office of Information, and Head of Government Information Service, 1971–74; *b* 22 June 1917; *s* of F. M. Bickerton and A. A. Hibbert; *m* 1945, Linda Russell; two *s. Educ:* Liverpool Collegiate Sch. Min. of Health, in Public Relations Div., 1935–40. Served War, RNVR, 1940–45. Min. of National Insurance (later Min. of Pensions and Nat. Insurance), 1946–61: initially Asst Press Officer and in charge of Information Div., 1952–61; Chief Information Officer, Min. of Transport, 1961–68; Controller (Home), COI, 1968–71. *Recreations:* walking, gardening. *Address:* 6 Diana Close, Granville Rise, Totland, Isle of Wight PO39 0EE. *Died 12 April 2008.*

BIDDULPH, Constance; see Holt, C.

BIDE, Sir Austin (Ernest), Kt 1980; Hon. President, Glaxo Holdings plc, 1985–95 (Chief Executive, 1973–80; Chairman, 1973–85); non-executive Chairman, BL plc, 1982–86 (Deputy Chairman, 1980–82; Director, 1977–86); *b* 11 Sept. 1915; *o s* of late Ernest Arthur Bide and Eliza Bide (*née* Young); *m* 1941, Irene (*née* Ward); three *d. Educ:* County Sch., Acton; Univ. of London. 1st cl. hons BSc Chemistry; FRSC, CChem. Govt Chemist's Dept, 1932–40; Research Chemist, Glaxo, 1940: i/c

Chemical Develt and Intellectual Property, 1944–54; Dep. Sec., 1954–59; Sec., 1959–65; Dir, 1963–71; Dep. Chm., 1971–73; Dir, J. Lyons & Co. Ltd, 1977–78. Member: Review Body, UGC, 1985–87; Working Party on Biotechnology (under auspices of ACARD/ABRD and Royal Soc.) (Report 1980); Adv. Cttee on Industry to the Vice-Chancellors and Principals of UK Univs, 1984–87; Chm., Information Technology 1986 Cttee, 1986. Member: Adv. Council, Inst. of Biotechnological Studies, 1985–89; Council, Inst. of Manpower Studies, 1985–91; Chairman: Visiting Cttee, Open Univ., 1982–89; Adam Smith Inst., 1986 (Mem., 1985). Chairman: QCA Ltd, 1985–89; Micro-test Res. Ltd, 1987–90; United Environmental Systems, 1988–90; CGEA (UK) Ltd, 1991–99; Comatech (UK) Ltd, 1992–99; Tyseley Waste Disposal, 1994–99; Onyx Environmental Group plc, 1998–99; Director: Oxford Consultancy Ltd, 1988–98 (Chm., 1994–98); Cie des Transports et Services Publiques, 1992–. Confederation of British Industry: Member: Council, 1974–85; President's Cttee, 1983–86; Chm., Res. and Technol. Cttee, 1977–86; Institute of Management (formerly British Institute of Management): CCMI (FBIM 1972); Mem. Council, 1976–88; Chm., Finance Cttee, 1976–79; Vice-Pres., 1992–; Dir, BIM Foundn, 1977–79. Medical Research Council: Mem., 1986–90; Chm., Investment Cttee, 1988–90; Chm., Pensions Trust, 1988–90; Mem., AIDS Cttee, 1987–90; Trustee, Nat. AIDS Trust (Chm., until 1991); Co-founder, and Chm., World Humanity Action Trust, 1992–98. Member: Editl Adv. Bd, Science in Parlt, 1994–98; Foundn for Sci. and Technol., 1994–. Chm. Court, Freight Transport Assoc., 1992–; Mem. Court, British Shippers Council, 1984–92 (Chm., 1989–92); Trustee, British Motor Industry Heritage Trust, 1983–86. Chm., Salisbury Cathedral Spire Appeal Cttee, 1987–92; Trustee, Salisbury Cathedral Spire Trust, 1987–; Mem., Confraternity of Benefactors, Salisbury Cathedral, 1992–. Chm. of Appeal, RCS, 1992– (Patron, 1996–). Mem. Council, Imperial Soc. of Knights Bachelor, 1980–97. FIEx 1987; FInstD 1989; Hon. FIChemE 1983; Hon. FIIM 1983 (Vice-Pres., 1983); Hon. Fellow: Inst. Biotechnological Studies 1985; St Catherine's Coll., Oxford, 1987. Hon. DSc: QUB, 1986; CNAA, 1990; DUniv OU, 1991. Gold Medal, BIM, 1983; Duncan Davies Medal, R&D Soc., 1990. *Publications:* papers in learned jls on organic chemical subjects. *Recreation:* fishing. *Club:* Hurlingham. *Died 11 May 2008.*

BIDSTRUP, (Patricia) Lesley, MD, FRCP, FRACP; Member, Medical Appeals Tribunal, 1970–88; private consulting concerned mainly with industrial medicine, since 1958; *b* 24 Oct. 1916; *d* of Clarence Leslie Bidstrup, Chemical Works Manager, South Australia, and Kathleen Helena Bidstrup (*née* O'Brien); *m* 1952, Ronald Frank Guymer, TD, MD, FRCP, FRCS, DPH, DIH; one step *s* one step *d. Educ:* Kadina High Sch. and Walford House, Adelaide, SA. MB, BS (Adel.) 1939; MD (Adel.) 1958; FRACP 1954; FRCP (Lond.) 1964. Resident Ho. Phys. and Registrar, Royal Adelaide Hosp., SA, 1939–41. Hon. Capt., AAMC, 1942–45. MO, UNRRA, Glyn-Hughes Hosp., Belsen, 1945–46. General practice: Acting Hon. Asst Phys., Royal Adelaide Hosp.; Tutor in Med., St Mark's Coll., Adelaide, and in Univ. of Adelaide Med. Sch.; Lectr in Med., Univ. of Adelaide Dental Faculty, 1942–45; Asst, Dept for Research in Industrial Medicine, MRC, 1947–58; Clinical Asst (Hon.), Chest Dept, St Thomas' Hosp., 1958–78. Member: Scientific Sub-Cttee on Poisonous Substances used in Agriculture and Food Storage, 1956–58; Industrial Injuries Adv. Council, 1970–83. Visiting Lectr, TUC Centenary Inst. of Occupational Health; Examiner for Diploma in Industrial Health: Conjoint Bd, 1965–71, 1980–82; Society of Apothecaries, 1970–76; External Examiner for Diploma in Industrial Health, Dundee, 1980–82. Fellow, Amer. Coll. of Occupational Medicine. William P. Yant Award, Amer. Industrial Hygiene Assoc., 1989. Mayoress, Royal Borough of Kingston-upon-Thames, 1959, 1960. *Publications:* The Toxicity of Mercury and

its Compounds, 1964; chapters in: Cancer Progress, 1960; The Prevention of Cancer, 1967; Clinical Aspects of Inhaled Particles, 1972; contribs to Brit. Jl Indust. Med., Lancet, BMJ, Proc. Royal Soc. Med., ILO Encyclopaedia on Industrial Diseases. *Recreations:* people, theatre, music. *Address:* 11 Sloane Terrace Mansions, Sloane Terrace, SW1X 9DG. *T:* (020) 7730 8720.
Died 14 Jan. 2010.

BIFFEN, Baron *cr* 1997 (Life Peer), of Tanat, in the co. of Shropshire; **William John Biffen;** PC 1979; DL; *b* 3 Nov. 1930; *s* of Victor W. Biffen; *m* 1979, Mrs Sarah Wood (*née* Drew); one step *s* one step *d. Educ:* Dr Morgan's Sch., Bridgwater; Jesus Coll., Cambridge (MA). Worked in Tube Investments Ltd, 1953–60; Economist Intelligence Unit, 1960–61. MP (C): Salop, Oswestry, Nov. 1961–1983; Shropshire N, 1983–97; Chief Sec. to the Treasury, 1979–81; Sec. of State for Trade, 1981–82; Lord Pres. of the Council, 1982–03; Leader of House of Commons, 1982–87 and Lord Privy Seal, 1983–87. Director: Glynwed International, 1987–2000; J. Bibby & Sons, 1988–97; Rockware Gp, 1988–91; Barlow International, 1998–2000. Trustee, The London Clinic, 1994–2002. DL Shropshire, 1993. *Publications:* Inside the House of Commons, 1989, Inside Westminster, 1996. *Address:* Tanat House, Llanyblodwel, Oswestry, Shropshire SY10 8NQ. *Died 14 Aug. 2007.*

BIGGS, Brig. Michael Worthington, CBE 1962 (OBE 1944); CEng, MICE; *b* 16 Sept. 1911; *s* of late Lt-Col Charles William Biggs, OBE, Cheltenham and late Winifred Jesse Bell Biggs (*née* Dickinson); *m* 1940, Katharine Mary, *d* of Sir Walter Harragin, CMG, QC, Colonial Legal Service, and Lady Harragin; two *d. Educ:* Cheltenham Coll.; RMA Woolwich; Pembroke Coll., Cambridge (MA 1966). MICE 1967. 2nd Lieut RE, 1931; served War of 1939–45, E Africa, Abyssinia (Bde Major), and Burma (GSO1 and CRE); Lt-Col 1942; Col 1954; Mil. Adviser to High Comr, Australia, 1954–57; Col GS, SME Chatham, 1957–60; Brig. 1960; Chief of Staff, E Africa Comd, 1960–62; Dir of Quartering (Army), MoD, 1963–66; retd, 1966. Group Building Exec., Forte's (Holdings) Ltd, 1966–67; Manager, Hatfield and Welwyn Garden City, Commn for New Towns, 1967–78. Member: Council, TCPA, 1978–86; Exec. Cttee, Hertfordshire Soc.; Chm., Herts Bldg Preservation Trust, 1978–86. Pres., KAR and EAF Officers' Dinner Club, 1972–97. Freeman, City of London, 1985. *Recreations:* tennis (incl. for Army), golf, gardening. *Address:* 1 Mildmay Court, Odiham, Hampshire RG29 1AX. *T:* (01256) 702715. *Club:* Army and Navy. *Died 15 April 2007.*

BINGHAM OF CORNHILL, Baron *cr* 1996 (Life Peer), of Boughrood in the County of Powys; **Thomas Henry Bingham,** KG 2005; Kt 1980; PC 1986; Senior Lord of Appeal in Ordinary, 2000–08; *b* 13 Oct. 1933; *o s* of late Dr T. H. Bingham and Dr C. Bingham, Reigate; *m* 1963, Elizabeth, *o d* of late Peter Loxley; two *s* one *d. Educ:* Sedbergh; Balliol Coll., Oxford (MA; Hon. Fellow, 1989). Royal Ulster Rifles, 1952–54 (2nd Lt); London Irish Rifles (TA) 1954–59. Univ. of Oxford: Gibbs Schol. in Mod. Hist., 1956; 1st cl. Hons, Mod. Hist., 1957. Eldon Law Schol., 1957; Arden Schol., Gray's Inn, 1959; Cert. of Honour, Bar Finals, 1959; called to Bar, Gray's Inn, 1959; Bencher, 1979. Standing Jun. Counsel to Dept of Employment, 1968–72; QC 1972; a Recorder of the Crown Court, 1975–80; Judge of the High Court of Justice, Queen's Bench Div., and Judge of the Commercial Court, 1980–86; a Lord Justice of Appeal, 1986–92; Master of the Rolls, 1992–96; Lord Chief Justice, 1996–2000. Leader, Investigation into the supply of petroleum and petroleum products to Rhodesia, 1977–78; Chm., King's Fund Working Parties into Statutory Registration of Osteopaths and Chiropractors, 1989–93; Inquiry into the Supervision of BCCI, 1991–92; Comr, Interception of Communications Act 1985, 1992–94. Chairman: Council of Legal Educn, 1982–86; Adv. Council, Centre for Commercial Law Studies, Queen Mary and Westfield Coll., London Univ.,

1989–92; Adv. Council on Public Records, 1992–96; Magna Carta Trust, 1992–96; Royal Commn on Historical Manuscripts, 1994–2003; Council of Mgt, British Inst. of Internat. and Comparative Law, 2001–. President: CIArb, 1991–95; British Records Assoc., 1992–96. Visitor: Balliol Coll., Oxford, 1986–; RPMS, 1989–96; UCL, 1992–96; Nuffield Coll., Oxford, 1992–96; London Business Sch., 1992–96; Templeton Coll., subseq. Green Templeton Coll., Oxford, 1996–; Darwin Coll., Cambridge, 1996; University Coll., Oxford, 2006–08; High Steward, Oxford Univ., 2001–08. Governor: Sedbergh, 1978–88; Atlantic Coll., 1984–89. Special Trustee, St Mary's Hosp., 1985–92 (Chm., 1988–92); Member: St Mary's Med. Sch. Delegacy, 1988–92; Council, KCL, 1989–93. Trustee, Pilgrim Trust, 1991–2006; Chm., Butler Trust, 2001–04. President: Seckford Foundn, 1994–; Hay Fest., 2000–. Fellow, Winchester, 1983–93; Presentation Fellow, KCL, 1992; Fellow, QMW, 1993; Hon. Fellow: Amer. Coll. of Trial Lawyers, 1994; Coll. of Estate Mgt, 1996; UCL, 1997; Acad. of Athens; Wolfson Coll., Oxford, 2008. Hon. FBA 2003. Hon. Bencher: Inn of Court of NI, 1993; Inner Temple, 1999; Middle Temple, 2002. Hon. LLD: Birmingham, 1993; Wales, London, 1998; Glamorgan, 1999; Dickinson Sch. of Law (Pennsylvania State Univ.), 2000; City, 2005, Roma Tre, 2008; Nottingham Trent, 2009; Hon. DCL Oxford, 1994; DU Essex, 1997. Onassis Internat. Prize in Law, Alexander S. Onassis Public Benefit Foundn and Inst. of France, 2009. *Publications:* Chitty on Contracts, (Asst Editor) 22nd edn, 1961; The Business of Judging, 2000; The Rule of Law, 2010. *Address:* House of Lords, SW1A 0PW.
Died 11 Sept. 2010.

BINGHAM, Dr Sheila Anne, (Mrs S. H. Rodwell), OBE 2009; Director, MRC Centre for Nutrition and Cancer, and Hon. Professor, University of Cambridge, since 2006; Head of Group, Dunn Human Nutrition Unit, MRC, since 1998; *b* 7 March 1947; *d* of Bernard Walter Harrison and Audrey Jean Harrison (*née* Wootton); *m* 1st, 1970, Roger Bingham (marr. diss. 1979); 2nd, 2000, Simon Hunter Rodwell. *Educ:* Loughborough High Sch.; King's Coll., London (BSc 1968; PhD 1983); MA Cantab 1996. Dietitian, University Coll. and St Phillip's Hosps, London, 1969–74; Dunn Human Nutrition Unit, 1976–: MRC Res Officer, 1976–88; MRC Scientific Staff, 1988–95; MRC Special Appt, 1995; Dep. Dir, 1998–2005. Associate Lectr, Faculty of Clinical Medicine, Univ. of Cambridge, 1992–. Vis. Prof., Univ. of Ulster, 1994–. Member: Cttee on Med. Aspects of Food Policy, 1991–2000; Scientific Adv. Cttee on Nutrition, 2000. FRSocMed 1993; FMedSci 2001. *Publications:* Dictionary of Nutrition, 1977; Everyman Companion to Food and Nutrition, 1987; numerous articles in learned jls. *Address:* High Hall, Norton Little Green, Bury St Edmunds, Suffolk IP31 3NN. *Died 16 June 2009.*

BINNING, Kenneth George Henry, CMG 1976; consultant, public policy and international regulation, since 1992; *b* 5 Jan. 1928; *o s* of late Henry and Hilda Binning; *m* 1953, Pamela Dorothy, *o d* of A. E. and D. G. Pronger; three *s* one *d. Educ:* Bristol Grammar Sch.; Balliol Coll., Oxford. Joined Home Civil Service, 1950; Nat. Service, 1950–52; HM Treasury, 1952–58; Private Sec. to Financial Sec., 1956–57; AEA, 1958–65; seconded to Min. of Technology, 1965; rejoined Civil Service, 1968; Dir-Gen. Concorde, 1972–76 and Under-Sec., DTI later Dept of Industry, 1972–83. Mem., BSC, 1980–83; Director of Government Relations: NEI Internat. subseq. NEI plc, 1983–90; Rolls Royce plc, 1991–93. Consultant on regulatory policy to govts of Hungary, Poland, Slovakia and Lithuania, 1993–2000. *Recreations:* music, appreciation of other people's gardens. *Address:* Flat 11, Oakbrook, 8 Court Downs Road, Beckenham, Kent BR3 6LR. *T:* (020) 8650 0273.
Died 15 Feb. 2009.

BIRCH, Prof. William; geographer; Director, Bristol Polytechnic, 1975–86; *b* 24 Nov. 1925; *s* of Frederick Arthur and Maude Olive Birch; *m* 1950, Mary Vine Stammers; one *s* one *d. Educ:* Ranelagh Sch.; Univ. of Reading. BA 1949, PhD 1957. Royal Navy, 1943–46, Sub-Lt RNVR. Lectr, Univ. of Bristol, 1950–60; Prof. of Geography, Grad. Sch. of Geog., Clark Univ., Worcester, Mass, USA, 1960–63; Prof., and Chm. of Dept of Geog., Univ. of Toronto, Canada, 1963–67; Prof., and Head of Dept of Geog., Univ. of Leeds, 1967–75. Visiting Professor: Inst. of Educn, London Univ., 1986–88; Univ. of Bristol, 1990–94. Pres., Inst. of British Geographers, 1976–77; Chm., Cttee of Directors of Polytechnics, 1982–84. Mem., ESRC, 1985–88. Hon. DLitt CNAA, 1989. *Publications:* The Isle of Man: a study in economic geography, 1964; The Challenge to Higher Education: reconciling responsibilities to scholarship and society, 1988; contribs on higher educn policy and on geography and planning, Trans Inst. Brit. Geographers, Geog. Jl, Economic Geog., Annals Assoc. Amer. Geographers, Jl Environmental Management, Studies in Higher Educn, etc. *Recreations:* yachting, travel, gardening, pottery. *Address:* 3 Rodney Place, Clifton, Bristol BS8 4HY. *T:* (0117) 973 9719. *Died 12 June 2009.*

BIRD, Ven. (Colin) Richard (Bateman); Minister Provincial, Third Order of the Society of St Francis (European Province), 2002–08; *b* 31 March 1933; *s* of Paul James Bird and Marjorie Bird (*née* Bateman); *m* 1963, Valerie Wroughton van der Bijl; two *d* one *s. Educ:* privately; County Technical Coll., Guildford; Selwyn Coll., Cambridge (MA); Cuddesdon Theol Coll. Curate: St Mark's Cathedral, George, S Africa, 1958–61; St Saviour's Claremont, Cape Town, 1961–64; Rector, Parish of Northern Suburbs, Pretoria, 1964–66; Rector, Tzaneen with Duiwelskloof and Phalaborwa, N Transvaal, 1966–70; Curate, Limpsfield, Surrey, 1970–75; Vicar of St Catherine, Hatcham, 1975–88; RD, Deptford, 1980–85; Hon. Canon of Southwark, 1982–88; Archdeacon of Lambeth, 1988–99; Priest-in-Charge, St Saviour's, Brixton Hill, 1989–94. *Recreations:* enjoying music and visual arts, enjoying my family, bird watching, baking bread. *Address:* 32 Bristol Road, Bury St Edmunds, Suffolk IP33 2DL. *T:* (01284) 723810; *e-mail:* dickbird@btopenworld.com. *Died 2 June 2010.*

BIRD, Peter Frederick, RIBA; FSA; Caroe & Partners Architects, since 1979 (Partner, since 1983); *b* 20 March 1947; *s* of W. J. and S. M. Bird; *m* 1971, Charlotte Maclagan; two *s. Educ:* Birmingham Sch. of Architecture; King Edward's Five Ways Sch., Birmingham; Univ. of Aston, Birmingham (BSc Hons; DipArch; SPAB Lethaby Schol. 1970). RIBA 1972; AABC 2000. Asst Architect, then Associate, Twist & Whitley, Cambridge, 1970–76; Conservation Architect, Bath CC, 1976–79. Cathedral Architect to St Davids, 1984–, Winchester, 1989–, Exeter, 1989– and Wells, 1994–. FSA 1994. *Publications:* (contrib.) Historic Floors: their care and conservation, ed J. Fawcett, 1998. *Recreations:* archaeology, history, engineering history, railways, canals. *Address:* Caroe & Partners, Penniless Porch, Market Place, Wells BA5 2RB. *T:* (01749) 677561; *e-mail:* wells@caroe.co.uk. *Died 10 Dec. 2010.*

BIRD, Ven. Richard; see Bird, Ven. C. R. B.

BIRDSALL, Doris, CBE 1985; Lord Mayor of Bradford Metropolitan District, 1975–76; *b* 20 July 1915; *d* of Fred and Violet Ratcliffe; *m* 1940, James Birdsall (decd); one *s* one *d. Educ:* Hanson Girls' Grammar School. Mem. Bradford City Council, 1958, Chm. of Educn Cttee, 1972–74; former Mem. Bradford Univ. Council. Hon. MA Bradford, 1975; DUniv Bradford, 1993; Hon. LHD Lesley Coll., Mass, 1976. *Address:* 4 Flower Mount, Station Road, Baildon, Bradford, West Yorks BD17 6SB. *Died 11 June 2008.*

BIRKS, His Honour Michael; a Circuit Judge, 1983–93; *b* 21 May 1920; *s* of late Falconer Moffat Birks, CBE, and Monica Katherine Lushington (*née* Mellor); *m* 1st, 1947, Ann Ethne (*d* 1999), *d* of Captain Henry Stafford Morgan; one *d*; 2nd, 1999, Anne Mary, *widow* of Lt-Col Richard Martin Power, RE. *Educ:* Oundle; Trinity Coll., Cambridge. Commissioned 22nd Dragoons, 1941; attached Indian Army, 1942, invalided out, 1943. Admitted Solicitor, 1946; Assistant Registrar: Chancery Div., High Court, 1953–60; Newcastle upon Tyne group of County Courts, 1960–61; Registrar: Birkenhead gp of County Courts, 1961–66; W London County Court, 1966–83; a Recorder of the Crown Court, 1979–83. Adv. Editor, Atkins Court Forms, 1966–91; Jt Editor, County Court Practice, 1976–83. Mem. County Court Rule Cttee, 1980–83. *Publications:* Gentlemen of the Law, 1960; Small Claims in the County Court, 1973; Enforcing Money Judgments in the County Court, 1980; The Young Hussar, 2007; contributed titles: County Courts and Interpleader (part), 4th edn Halsbury's Laws of England; Judgments and Orders (part), References and Inquiries (part), Service (part), and Transfer (part), County Courts Atkins Court Forms; contribs to legal jls. *Recreation:* painting. *Address:* Dreva, Rhinefield Road, Brockenhurst, Hants SO42 7SQ. *T:* (01590) 623353. *Died 11 Aug. 2008.*

BIRLEY, Anthony Addison, CB 1979; Clerk of Public Bills, House of Commons, 1973–82, retired; *b* 28 Nov. 1920; *s* of Charles Fair Birley and Eileen Mia Rouse; *m* 1951, Jane Mary Ruggles-Brise; two *d. Educ:* Winchester (exhibnr); Christ Church, Oxford (MA). Served War in RA (Ayrshire Yeomanry), 1940–45, in North Africa and Italian campaigns (wounded). Asst Clerk, House of Commons, 1948; Clerk of Standing Cttees, 1970. *Recreations:* gardening, walking, racing. *Club:* Army and Navy. *Died 21 June 2006.*

BIRTWISTLE, Maj.-Gen. Archibald Cull, CB 1983; CBE 1976 (OBE 1971); DL; Signal Officer in Chief (Army), 1980–83, retired; Master of Signals, 1990–97; *b* 19 Aug. 1927; *s* of Walter Edwin Birtwistle and Eila Louise Cull; *m* 1956, Sylvia Elleray; two *s* one *d. Educ:* Sir John Deane's Grammar School, Northwich; St John's Coll., Cambridge (MA Mech. Sciences). CEng, MIEE. Commissioned, Royal Signals, 1949; served: Korea (despatches, 1952); UK; BAOR; CCR Sigs 1 (Br) Corps, 1973–75; Dep. Comdt, RMCS, 1975–79; Chief Signal Officer, BAOR, 1979–80. Col Comdt, Royal Corps of Signals, 1983–89, and 1990–97; Hon. Colonel: Durham and South Tyne ACF, 1983–88; 34 (Northern) Signal Regt (Vol.), TA, 1988–90. Pres., British Korean Veterans Assoc., 1997–2006. DL N Yorks, 1991. *Recreations:* all sports, especially Rugby (former Chairman, Army Rugby Union), soccer and cricket; gardening. *Address:* c/o National Westminster Bank PLC, 97 High Street, Northallerton, North Yorks DL7 8PS. *Died 18 March 2009.*

BISHOP, George Robert, CBE 1993; DPhil; FRSE; CPhys, FInstP; Director General, Ispra Establishment, Joint Research Centre, European Commission, Ispra, Italy, 1983–92 (Director, 1982–83); *b* 16 Jan. 1927; *s* of George William Bishop and Lilian Elizabeth Garrod; *m* 1952, Adriana Giuseppina, *d* of Luigi Caberlotto and Giselda Mazzariol; two *s* one *d. Educ:* Christ Church, Oxford (MA, DPhil). ICI Research Fellow, Univ. of Oxford, 1951; Research Fellow, St Antony's Coll., Oxford, 1952; Chercheur, Ecole Normale Supérieure, Paris, 1954; Ingénieur-Physicien, Laboratoire de l'Accelerateur Linéaire, ENS, Orsay, 1958; Prof., Faculté des Sciences, Univ. de Paris, 1962; Kelvin Prof. of Natural Philosophy, Univ. of Glasgow, 1964–76; Dir, Dept of Natural and Physical Sciences, JRC, Ispra, 1974–82. Hon. DSc, Strathclyde, 1979. *Publications:* Handbuch der Physik, Band XLII, 1957; β and X-Ray Spectroscopy, 1960; Nuclear Structure and Electromagnetic Interactions, 1965; numerous papers in learned jls on nuclear and high energy physics. *Recreations:* literature, music, swimming, tennis, gardening, travel. *Address:* via Favretti 23/A, Mogliano Veneto, 31021 (TV), Italy. *T:* (41) 455813. *Died 11 Oct. 2008.*

BISHOP, Stanley Victor, MC 1944; Managing Director, British Printing Corporation, 1966–70; Director, Massey-Ferguson Europe Ltd, 1973–79; *b* 11 May 1916; *s* of George Stanley Bishop, MA; *m* 1946, Dorothy Primrose Dodds, Berwick-upon-Tweed; two *s* one *d. Educ:* Leeds. Articled to Beevers & Adgie, Leeds; CA 1937. Served War of 1939–45: enlisted London Scottish (TA), 1938; commissioned, West Yorkshire Regt, 1940; served overseas, 1940–45, Middle East, India and Burma (MC) (Hon. Major). Joined Albert E. Reed and Co. Ltd, 1946; Brush Group, 1951; Massey Ferguson Ltd, 1959–79; Perkins Diesel Engine Group, 1963. Chm. and Dir various cos, 1970–73 and 1979–92. Lectured to British Institute of Management, Institute of Chartered Accountants, Oxford Business Summer School, etc. *Publications:* Business Planning and Control, 1966. *Recreation:* pottering. *Died 3 March 2006.*

BISSON, Rt Hon. Sir Gordon (Ellis), Kt 1991; PC 1987; Judge of the Court of Appeal: New Zealand, 1986–91; Samoa, 1994–2004; Kiribati, 1999–2002; Chairman, New Zealand Banking Ombudsman Commission, 1992–97; *b* 23 Nov. 1918; *s* of Clarence Henry Bisson and Ada Ellis; *m* 1948, Myra Patricia Kemp; three *d. Educ:* Napier Boys' High Sch.; Victoria Coll., Wellington; Univ. of NZ. LLB. Served War of 1939–45, RN and RNZN, 1940–45 (mentioned in despatches); Lt Comdr RNZNVR. Partner, Bisson Moss Robertshawe & Co., Barristers and Solicitors, Napier, NZ, 1946–78; Crown Solicitor, Napier, 1961; Judge, Courts Martial Appeal Ct, 1976; Judge of Supreme Ct, 1978. Vice-Pres., NZ Law Soc., 1974–77; Chm., NZ Sect., Internat. Commn of Jurists, 1979–92. Chairman: Ind. Tribunal for Allocation of Meat Export Quotas, 1995–97; New Entrants Allocation Cttee, NZ Meat Bd, 1998–2005. Order of Samoa, 2005. *Publications:* (jtly) Criminal Law and Practice in New Zealand, 1961. *Recreations:* tennis, fly-fishing, golf. *Address:* 341/4 Fergusson Drive, Heretaunga, Wellington 5018, New Zealand. *Clubs:* Wellington, Royal Wellington Golf (Wellington, NZ). *Died 14 Nov. 2010.*

BLACK, Sir James (Whyte), Kt 1981; OM 2000; FRCP; FRS 1976; Professor of Analytical Pharmacology, King's College Hospital Medical School, University of London, 1984–93, then Emeritus; Chancellor, Dundee University, 1992–2006; *b* 14 June 1924; *m* 1st, 1944, Hilary Vaughan (*d* 1986); one *d*; 2nd, 1994, Prof. Rona McLeod MacKie, CBE. *Educ:* Beath High Sch., Cowdenbeath; Univ. of St Andrews (MB, ChB). Asst Lectr in Physiology, Univ. of St Andrews, 1946; Lectr in Physiology, Univ. of Malaya, 1947–50; Sen. Lectr, Univ. of Glasgow Vet. Sch., 1950–58; ICI Pharmaceuticals Ltd, 1958–64; Head of Biological Res. and Dep. Res. Dir, Smith, Kline & French, Welwyn Garden City, 1964–73; Prof. and Head of Dept of Pharmacology, University College, London, 1973–77; Dir of Therapeutic Research, Wellcome Res. Labs, 1978–84. Mem., British Pharmacological Soc., 1961–. Hon. FRSE 1986. Hon. Fellow, London Univ., 1990. Mullard Award, Royal Soc., 1978; (jtly) Nobel Prize for Physiology or Medicine, 1988. *Address:* James Black Centre, King's College School of Medicine, SE5 9NU. *Died 22 March 2010.*

BLACK, Prof. Robert Denis Collison, FBA 1974; Professor of Economics, and Head of Department of Economics, Queen's University Belfast, 1962–85, then Emeritus; *b* 11 June 1922; *s* of William Robert Black and Rose Anna Mary (*née* Reid), Dublin; *m* 1953, Frances Mary, *o d* of William F. and Mary Weatherup, Belfast; one *s* one *d. Educ:* Sandford Park Sch.; Trinity Coll., Dublin (Hon. Fellow, 1982). BA 1941, BComm 1941, PhD 1943, MA 1945. Dep. for Prof. of Pol Economy, Trinity Coll., Dublin, 1943–45; Asst Lectr in Economics, Queen's Univ., Belfast, 1945–46, Lectr, 1946–58, Sen. Lectr, 1958–61, Reader, 1961–62. Rockefeller Post-doctoral Fellow, Princeton Univ., 1950–51; Visiting Prof. of Economics, Yale Univ., 1964–65; Dean of Faculty of Economics and Social Sciences, QUB, 1967–70; Pro-Vice-Chancellor, 1971–75. President: Statistical & Social

Inquiry Soc. of Ireland, 1983–86; Section F, BAAS, 1984–85. Distinguished Fellow, History of Economics Soc., USA, 1987. MRIA 1974. Hon. DSc(Econ) QUB, 1988. *Publications:* Centenary History of the Statistical Society of Ireland, 1947; Economic Thought and the Irish Question 1817–1870, 1960; Catalogue of Economic Pamphlets 1750–1900, 1969; Papers and Correspondence of William Stanley Jevons, Vol. I, 1972, Vol. II, 1973, Vols III–VI, 1977, Vol. VII, 1981; Ideas in Economics, 1986; Economic Theory and Policy in Context, 1995; articles in Economic Jl, Economica, Oxford Econ. Papers, Econ. History Review, Oxford DNB, etc. *Recreations:* travel, music. *Address:* Queen's University, Belfast, Northern Ireland BT7 1NN. *T:* (028) 9024 5133. *Died 7 Dec. 2008.*

BLACK, Sheila (Psyche), OBE 1986; feature writer; Director, MAI plc (formerly Mills and Allen International), 1976–92; *b* 6 May 1920; *d* of Clement Johnston Black, CA, and Mildred Beryl Black; *m* 1st, 1939, Geoffrey Davien, sculptor (marr. diss. 1951); one *d* (one *s* decd); 2nd, 1951, L. A. Lee Howard, DFC (marr. diss. 1973; he *d* 1978). *Educ:* Dorset; Switzerland; RADA. Actress, until outbreak of War of 1939–45; Asst to production manager of an electrical engineering factory. Post-war, in advertising; then in journalism, from the mid-fifties; Woman's Editor, Financial Times, 1959–72; specialist feature writer, The Times, 1972–79; Chm., Interflex Data Systems (UK) Ltd, 1975–83. Features writer for The Director, Financial Weekly, Punch, Mediaworld, and many newspapers and magazines. Chairman: Nat. Gas Consumers' Council, 1981–86; Gas Consumers Council, 1986–88; Dir, Money Management Council, 1985–90; Member: Furniture Develt Council, 1967–70; Liquor Licensing Laws Special Cttee, 1971–72; (part-time) Price Commn, 1973–77; Nat. Consumer Council, 1981–91; Calcutt Cttee on Privacy and Related Matters, 1989–90. Dir, Countrywide Workshops Charitable Trust, 1982–88 and 1989–93. Mem. Council, Inst. of Directors, 1975–90. Freeman, City of London, 1985. *Publications:* The Black Book, 1976; Mirabelle: cuisine de qualité et tradition, 1979; The Reluctant Money Minder, 1980; various others. *Recreations:* gardening, grandchildren, football. *Address:* Flat 1, 11 Upper Grosvenor Road, Tunbridge Wells, Kent TN1 2DU. *Died Sept. 2007.*

BLACKER, Dr Carmen Elizabeth, OBE 2004; FBA 1989; FSA; Lecturer in Japanese, 1958–91, and Fellow of Clare Hall, 1965–91, then Fellow Emeritus, Cambridge University; Professor, Ueno Gakuen University, Tokyo, since 1996; *b* 13 July 1924; *d* of Carlos Paton Blacker, MC, GM, MA, MD, FRCP and Helen Maud Blacker (*née* Pilkington). *Educ:* Benenden School; School of Oriental Studies, London University; Somerville Coll., Oxford (Hon. Fellow, 1991) PhD London Univ., 1957. Visiting Professor: Columbia Univ., 1965; Princeton Univ., 1979; Ueno Gakuen Univ., Tokyo, 1991; Toronto Univ., 1992; Vis. Fellow, Kyoto Univ., 1986. Pres., Folklore Soc., 1982–84 (Hon. Mem., 1988). Minakata Kumagusu Prize, 1997. FSA 2004. Order of the Precious Crown (Japan), 1988. *Publications:* The Japanese Enlightenment: a study of the writing of Fukuzawa Yukichi, 1964; The Catalpa Bow: a study of Shamanistic practices in Japan, 1975, rev. edn 1986; Collected Papers, 2000; The Straw Sandal or The Scroll of the Hundred Crabs, 2008; articles in Monumenta Nipponica, Folklore, Trans of Asiatic Soc. of Japan, Asian Folklore Studies, etc. *Recreations:* walking, comparative mythology. *Address:* Willow House, Grantchester, Cambridge CB3 9NF. *T:* (01223) 840196. *Club:* University Women's. *Died 13 July 2009.*

BLACKLOCK, Sir Norman (James), KCVO 1993 (CVO 1989); OBE 1974; FRCS; Professor and Head of Department of Urological Surgery, Victoria University of Manchester, at Withington Hospital, 1978–91, then Professor Emeritus; an Extra Gentleman Usher to the Queen, since 1993; *b* 5 Feb. 1928; 2nd *s* of Prof. John and Ella Blacklock; *m* 1956, Marjorie Reid; one *s* one *d. Educ:*

McLaren High Sch., Perthshire; Glasgow Univ. (MB ChB 1950). FRCS 1957. Jun. appts, Royal Inf. and Western Inf., Glasgow, 1950–51; Nat. Service, RN, 1951–54, Surg. Lieut, HMSs Theseus and Warrior; Surg. Registrar and Lectr, Glasgow Royal Inf., 1954–56; Surg. Registrar, Ipswich and St Bart's Hosps, 1956–58; Royal Navy: Surg. Specialist, then Cons. in Gen. Surg., serving in naval hosps at Chatham, Devonport, Malta and Portsmouth, 1958–70; Cons. in Surg. and Urol., and Dir of Surg. Res., 1970–78; retd in rank of Surg. Capt., 1978; Dir, Lithotripter Centre, Withington Hosp., 1987–91. Med. Advr to HM Queen on overseas visits, 1976–93; Hon. Cons. in Urol., RN, 1978–93. Former Ext. Examnr in Surgery, Univs of Edinburgh, Newcastle upon Tyne and King Saud, Riyadh; Chm., Mil. Educn Cttee, Manchester Univ., 1986–91. Chm., Health Care Cttee, BSI, 1970–91 (mem. cttees concerned with safety of med. equipment etc). Member: Council, British Assoc. of Urolog. Surgs, 1975–78, 1987–91; Adv. Cttee in Urol., RCS, 1987–91. Gilbert Blane Medal, RCS and RCP, 1970; Errol Eldridge Prize, RN Med. Service, 1972. *Publications:* contributor to: Scientific Foundations of Urology, 1976, 3rd edn 1990; Urinary Infection, 1983; Textbook of Geriatric Medicine and Gerontology, 1985, 2nd edn 1991; Urinary Calculous Disease, 1979; Prostate Cancer, 1981; Western Diseases: their emergence and prevention, 1981; Recent Advances in Urology, 3rd edn 1981; Urolithiasis: clinical and basic research, 1982; Textbook of Genito-Urinary Surgery, 2 vols, 1985; Therapy of Prostatitis, 1986; Diagnostic Techniques in Urology, 1990; Tropical Urology and Renal Disease, 1992; many contribs to learned jls. *Recreations:* gardening, cookery, bread-making, pottering. *Address:* c/o Registrar, University of Manchester, Oxford Road, Manchester M13 9PT. *Died 7 Sept. 2006.*

BLACKWELL, Prof. Donald Eustace, MA, PhD; Savilian Professor of Astronomy, University of Oxford, 1960–88, then Emeritus; Fellow of New College, Oxford, 1960–88, then Emeritus; *b* 27 May 1921; *s* of John Blackwell and Ethel Bowe; *m* 1951, Nora Louise Carlton; two *s* two *d. Educ:* Merchant Taylors' Sch.; Sandy Lodge; Sidney Sussex Coll., Cambridge. Isaac Newton Student, University of Cambridge, 1947; Stokes Student, Pembroke Coll., Cambridge, 1948; Asst Director, Solar Physics Observatory, Cambridge, 1950–60. Various Astronomical Expeditions: Sudan, 1952; Fiji, 1955; Bolivia, 1958 and 1961; Canada, 1963; Manuae Island, 1965. Pres., RAS, 1973–75. *Publications:* papers in astronomical journals. *Died 3 Dec. 2010.*

BLACKWELL, John Charles, CBE 1988; education consultant, since 1995; farmer; *b* 4 Nov. 1935; *s* of Charles Arthur Blackwell and Louisa Amy Blackwell (née Sellers); *m* 1st, 1961, Julia Rose; one *s*; 2nd, 1978, Inger Beatrice Lewin; one step *s. Educ:* Glynn Grammar Sch., Ewell; Dudley Coll. of Educn (Cert. in Educn); Bristol Univ. (BA, MEd, PhD). Metropolitan Police Cadet, 1952–53; RAF, 1954–56; teacher, Dempsey Secondary Sch., London, 1958–60; British Council, 1966–95: Asst Rep., Tanzania, 1966–70; Educn Officer, Calcutta, 1971–72; Asst Educn Adviser, New Delhi, 1973–75; Head, Schools and Teacher Educn Unit, 1976–78; attached British Embassy, Washington, 1979; Dir, Educn Contracts Dept, 1980–83; Rep., Indonesia, 1983–89; Controller, later Dir, Sci. and Educn Div., 1989–92; Develt Advr, 1993–95. *Recreations:* boating, fishing, reading. *Address:* Agriomata, Paralia Vergas, Kalamata, Messinia 24100, Greece. *T:* and *Fax:* (2721) 097524. *Died 30 Jan. 2008.*

BLAIR, Claude, CVO 2005; OBE 1994; FSA 1956; Keeper, Department of Metalwork, Victoria and Albert Museum, 1972–82; *b* 30 Nov. 1922; *s* of William Henry Murray Blair and Lilian Wearing; *m* 1952, Joan Mary Greville Drinkwater (*d* 1996); one *s. Educ:* William Hulme's Grammar Sch., Manchester; Manchester Univ. (MA). Served War, Army (Captain RA), 1942–46.

Manchester Univ., 1946–51; Asst, Tower of London Armouries, 1951–56; Asst Keeper of Metalwork, V&A, 1956–66; Dep. Keeper, 1966–72. Hon. Editor, Jl of the Arms and Armour Soc., 1953–77. Consultant to Christie's, 1983–84; Member: Arch. Adv. Panel, Westminster Abbey, 1979–98; Council for the Care of Churches, 1991–96 (Mem. Exec. Cttee, 1983–91); Trustee, Churches Conservation Trust (formerly Redundant Churches Fund), 1982–97. Vice-Pres., Soc. of Antiquaries, 1990–93; Hon. Pres., Meyrick Soc., 1979–94; Hon. Vice-President: Soc. for Study of Church Monuments, 1984– (Hon. Pres., 1978–84); Monumental Brass Soc. Hon. Mem., Accademia di San Marciano, Turin, 2002. Hon. Liveryman, Cutlers' Co. Liveryman: Goldsmiths' Co.; Armourers and Brasiers' Co. Hon. LittD Manchester, 2004. Medal of Museo Militar, Barcelona, 1969; Medal of Arms and Armour Soc., 1986; Gold Medal, Soc. of Antiquaries, 1998. *Publications:* European Armour, 1958, 2nd edn 1972; European and American Arms, 1962; The Silvered Armour of Henry VIII, 1965; Pistols of the World, 1968; Three Presentation Swords in the Victoria and Albert Museum, 1972; The James A. de Rothschild Collection: Arms, Armour and Miscellaneous Metalwork, 1974; (gen. editor and contrib.) Pollard's History of Firearms, 1983; (ed) The History of Silver, 1987; (gen. editor and contrib.) The Crown Jewels, 1998; (with Marian Campbell) Marcy: oggetti d'arte della Galleria Parmeggiani di Reggio Emilia, 2008; numerous articles and reviews in Archaeological Jl, Jl of Arms and Armour Soc., Connoisseur, Waffen und Kostümkunde, etc. *Recreations:* travel, looking at churches, listening to music. *Address:* 90 Links Road, Ashtead, Surrey KT21 2HW. *T:* (01372) 275532. *Clubs:* Civil Service, Royal Over-Seas League. *Died 21 Feb. 2010.*

BLAIR, Sir Edward Thomas H.; *see* Hunter-Blair.

BLAKE, Sir (Thomas) Richard (Valentine), 17th Bt *cr* 1622, of Menlough; *b* 7 Jan. 1942; *s* of Sir Ulick Temple Blake, 16th Bt, and late Elizabeth Gordon (she *m* 1965, Vice-Adm. E. Longley-Cook, CB, CBE, DSO); *S* father, 1963; *m* 1st, 1976, Mrs Jacqueline Hankey; 2nd, 1982, Bertice Reading (marr. diss. 1986; she *d* 1991); 3rd, 1991, Wendy, *widow* of Anthony Ronald Roberts. *Educ:* Bradfield Coll., Berks. Member, Standing Council of Baronets. *Recreations:* classic cars, horses, gardening. *Heir:* kinsman Anthony Teilo Bruce Blake [*b* 5 May 1951; *m* 1988, Geraldine, *d* of Cecil Shnaps; one *s* two *d*]. *Address:* 46 chemin du Peylong Sud, route des Arcs, 83510 Lorgues, Var, France. *Clubs:* Cowdray Park Polo, Gordon-Keeble Owners, Rolls-Royce Enthusiasts, Goodwood Road Racing. *Died 29 May 2008.*

BLAKER, Baron *cr* 1994 (Life Peer), of Blackpool in the County of Lancashire, and of Lindfield in the County of West Sussex; **Peter Allan Renshaw Blaker,** KCMG 1983; PC 1983; MA; *b* Hong Kong, 4 Oct. 1922; *s* of late Cedric Blaker, CBE, MC and Louisa Douglas Blaker (née Chapple); *m* 1953, Jennifer, *d* of late Sir Pierson Dixon, GCMG, CB; one *s* two *d. Educ:* Shrewsbury; Trinity Coll., Toronto (BA, 1st class, Classics); New Coll., Oxford (MA). Served 1942–46: Argyll and Sutherland Highlanders of Canada (Capt., severely wounded). Admitted a Solicitor, 1948. New Coll., Oxford, 1949–52; 1st Class, Jurisprudence, Pass degree in PPE. Pres. Oxford Union. Called to Bar, Lincoln's Inn, 1952. Admitted to HM Foreign Service, 1953; Western Orgns, FO, 1953–55; HM Embassy, Phnom Penh, 1955–57 (Chargé d'Affaires, 1956); UK High Commn, Ottawa, 1957–60; Levant Dept, FO, 1960–62; Private Sec. to Minister of State for Foreign Affairs, 1962–64. Attended Cuba missile crisis, UN and Disarmament Conf., Geneva; UN Gen. Assembly, 1962 and 1963; signing of Nuclear Test Ban Treaty, Moscow, 1963. MP (C) Blackpool South, 1964–92; an Opposition Whip, 1966–67; PPS to Chancellor of Exchequer, 1970–72; Parliamentary Under-Secretary of State: (Army), MoD, 1972–74; FCO, 1974; Minister of State: FCO, 1979–81; for the Armed

Forces, MoD, 1981–83. Joint Secretary: Conservative Party Foreign Affairs Cttee, 1965–66; Trade Cttee, 1967–70; Exec. Cttee of 1922 Cttee, 1967–70; Vice-Chm., All-Party Tourism Cttee, 1974–79; Member: Select Cttee on Conduct of Members, 1976–77; Public Accounts Commn, 1987–92; Intelligence and Security Cttee, 1996–97; Chairman: Hong Kong Parly Gp, 1970–72, 1983–92; Cons. For. and Commonwealth Affairs Cttee, 1983–92 (Vice-Chm., 1974–79); Mem. Exec. Cttee, British-American Parly Gp, 1975–79; Hon. Sec., Franco-British Parly Relations Cttee, 1975–79. Chm., Bd, Royal Ordnance Factories, 1972–74; Chm. Governors, Welbeck Coll., 1972–74; Mem. Council: Chatham House, 1977–79, 1986–90; Council for Arms Control, 1983–99; Freedom Assoc., 1984–97; Vice-Chm., Peace Through NATO, 1983–93; Vice-Pres., 1983–92, Patron, 1993–, Cons. Foreign and Commonwealth Council; Mem. Council, Britain-Russia Centre (formerly GB-USSR Assoc.), 1974–79, and 1992–2000 (Vice-Chm., 1983 92); Governor, Atlantic Inst., 1978–79; Trustee, Inst. for Negotiation and Conciliation, 1984–92. Chm., Maclean Hunter Cablevision Ltd, 1989–94; farmer. *Publications:* Coping with the Soviet Union, 1977; Small is Dangerous: micro states in a macro world, 1984. *Recreations:* sailing, opera, shooting. *Address:* House of Lords, SW1A 0PW.
Died 5 July 2009.

BLAMIRE-BROWN, John; DL; County Clerk and Chief Executive, Staffordshire County Council, 1973–78; *b* 16 April 1915; *s* of Rev. F. J. Blamire Brown, MA; *m* 1945, Joyce Olivia Pearson; two *s. Educ:* Cheam Sch.; St Edmund's Sch., Canterbury. Solicitor 1937. Served War of 1939–45, Royal Marines (Captain). Asst Solicitor, Wednesbury, 1938, West Bromwich, 1946; Staffs CC, 1948; Deputy Clerk of County Council and of Peace, 1962; Clerk, Staffs CC, 1972; Clerk to Lieutenancy, 1972–78; Sec., Staffs Probation and After Care Cttee; Hon. Sec., W Mids Planning Authorities Conf., 1972–78. Dep. Chm., Manpower Services Commn Area Board, Staffs, Salop, W Midlands (North), 1978–83. Mem. Council, Beth Johnson Foundn, 1978–83; Governor, Newcastle-under-Lyme Endowed Schools, 1978–83; Chm., St Giles Hospice Ltd, 1979–84. Pres., Codsall Civic Soc., 1991–. DL Staffs, 1974. *Recreations:* local history, gardening, painting. *Address:* The Mount, Codsall Wood, Wolverhampton, West Midlands WV8 1QS. *T:* (01902) 842044. *Died 4 May 2008.*

BLANCH, Mrs Lesley, MBE 2001; FRSL; author; *b* 6 June 1904; *m* 2nd, 1945, Romain Kacew (Romain Gary) (marr. diss. 1962; he *d* 1980). *Educ:* by reading, and listening to conversation of elders and betters. FRSL 1969. *Publications:* The Wilder Shores of Love (biog.), 1954; Round the World in Eighty Dishes (cookery), 1956; The Game of Hearts (biog.), 1956; The Sabres of Paradise (biog.), 1960; Under a Lilac Bleeding Star (travels), 1963; The Nine Tiger Man (fict.), 1965; Journey into the Mind's Eye (autobiog.), 1968; Pavilions of the Heart (biog.), 1974; Pierre Loti: portrait of an escapist (biog.), 1983; From Wilder Shores: the tables of my travels (travel/autobiog.), 1989. *Recreations:* travel, opera, acquiring useless objects, animal welfare, gardening. *Died 7 May 2007.*

BLANCHARD, Francis; Commandeur de la Légion d'Honneur; Director-General, International Labour Office, 1974–89; *b* Paris, 21 July 1916; *m* 1940, Marie-Claire Boué; two *s. Educ:* Univ. of Paris. French Home Office; Internat. Organisation for Refugees, Geneva, 1947–51; Internat. Labour Office, Geneva, 1951–89: Asst Dir-Gen., 1956–68; Dep. Dir-Gen., 1968–74. Mem., French Econ. and Social Council, 1989–. Dr *hc* Brussels, Cairo and Manila. *Recreations:* ski-ing, hunting, riding. *Address:* Prébailly, 01170 Gex, France. *T:* 450415170. *Died 9 Dec. 2009.*

BLANCO WHITE, Thomas Anthony; QC 1969; *b* 19 Jan. 1915; *s* of late G. R. Blanco White, QC, and Amber Blanco White, OBE; *m* 1950, Anne Katherine Ironside-Smith; two *s* one *d. Educ:* Gresham's Sch.; Trinity Coll.,

Cambridge. Called to Bar, Lincoln's Inn, 1937, Bencher 1977, retired 1993. Served RAFVR, 1940–46. *Publications:* Patents for Inventions, 1950, 1955, 1962, 1974, 1983, etc. *Recreation:* photography. *Address:* 72 South Hill Park, NW3 2SN. *Died 12 Jan. 2006.*

BLANDFORD, Eric George, CBE 1967; Assistant Registrar of Criminal Appeals, Royal Courts of Justice, 1978–81; *b* 10 March 1916; *s* of George and Eva Blanche Blandford; *m* 1940, Marjorie Georgina Crane (decd); one *s. Educ:* Bristol Grammar Sch. Admitted Solicitor Supreme Court, England, 1939; LLB (London) 1939. War Service, 1939–46 (despatches): India, Burma, Malaya; rank on release Temp. Major RA. Solicitor in London, 1946–51; Asst Comr of Lands, Gold Coast, 1951; Dist Magistrate, Gold Coast, 1952; called to the Bar, Inner Temple, 1955; Chief Registrar, Supreme Court, Gold Coast, 1956; Registrar of High Court of Northern Rhodesia, 1958; Judge, Supreme Court of Aden, 1961–68; Dep. Asst Registrar of Criminal Appeals, 1968–78. Chm. Aden Municipality Inquiry Commn, 1962. *Publications:* Civil Procedure Rules of Court, Aden, 1967. *Recreation:* local history research. *Address:* Hays Park, Sedgehill, Shaftesbury, Dorset SP7 9JR. *Died 1 June 2006.*

BLEANEY, Prof. Brebis, CBE 1965; DPhil; FRS 1950; Warren Research Fellow, Royal Society, 1977–80, Leverhulme Emeritus Fellow, 1980–82; Fellow, 1957–77, Senior Research Fellow, 1977–82, Wadham College, Oxford, then Emeritus Fellow; Dr Lee's Professor of Experimental Philosophy, University of Oxford, 1957–77, then Emeritus Professor; *b* 6 June 1915; *m* 1949, Betty Isabelle Plumpton; one *s* one *d. Educ:* Westminster City Sch.; St John's Coll., Oxford (MA). Research Fellow, Harvard Univ. and Mass Institute of Technology, 1949. University Demonstrator and Lectr in Physics, Univ. of Oxford, 1945–57; Fellow and Lectr in Physics, 1947–57, Tutor, 1950–57, Hon. Fellow, 1968, St John's Coll., Oxford; Lectr in Physics at Balliol Coll., Oxford, 1947–50. Visiting Prof. in Physics in Columbia Univ., 1956–57; Harkins Lectr, Chicago Univ., 1957; Kelvin Lectr, Instn Electrical Engineers, 1962; Morris Loeb Lectr, Harvard Univ., 1981; Cherwell Simon Meml Lectr, Oxford Univ., 1981–82; John and Abigail Van Vleck Lectr, Univ. of Minnesota, 1985; Visiting Professor: Univ. of California, Berkeley, 1961; Univ. of Pittsburgh, 1962–63; Manitoba, 1968; La Plata, Argentina, 1971; Amer. Univ. in Cairo, 1978; Univ. of NSW, 1981. Mem. Council for Scientific and Industrial Res., 1960–62; Chm., British Radiofrequency Spectroscopy Gp, 1983–85. Fellow, Internat. Electron Paramagnetic Resonance Soc., 1995 (Gold Medallist, 1999); FRSSAf 1995. FRSA 1971. Corr. Mem. Acad. of Sciences, Inst. of France, 1974, Associé Etranger, 1978; For. Hon. Mem., Amer. Acad. of Arts and Scis, 1978; Hon. Prof., Kazan Univ., 1994. DSc *hc* Porto, Portugal, 1987. Charles Vernon Boys Prize, Physical Soc., 1952; Hughes Medal, Royal Society, 1962; ISMAR Prize, Internat. Soc. for Magnetic Resonance, 1983; Holweck Medal and Prize, Inst. of Physics and Société Française de Physique, 1984; Zavoisky Prize, Kazan, Physical-Technical Inst., 1992. *Publications:* (with B. I. Bleaney) Electricity and Magnetism, 1957, 3rd edn 1976, revd edn in 2 vols 1989; (with A. Abragam) Electron Paramagnetic Resonance, 1970, revd edn 1986; over 300 papers in Proceedings of the Royal Society and Proceedings of the Physical Society, etc. *Recreations:* music, travel. *Address:* Clarendon Laboratory, Parks Road, Oxford OX1 3PU. *Died 4 Nov. 2006.*

BLEASE, Baron *cr* 1978 (Life Peer), of Cromac in the City of Belfast; **William John Blease;** JP; *b* 28 May 1914; *e s* of late William and Sarah Blease; *m* 1939, Sarah Evelyn Caldwell (*d* 1995); three *s* one *d. Educ:* elementary and technical schs; Nat. Council of Labour Colls; WEA. Retail Provision Trade (apprentice), 1929; Retail Grocery Asst (Branch Manager), 1938–40; Clerk, Belfast Shipyard, 1940–45; Branch Manager, Co-operative Soc., Belfast, 1945–59; Divl Councillor, Union of Shop

Distributive Workers, 1948–59; NI Officer, 1959–75, Exec. Consultant, 1975–76, Irish Congress of Trade Unions; Divl Chm. and Nat. Exec. Mem., Nat. Council of Labour Colls, 1948–61; Exec. Mem., NI Labour Party, 1949–59 (Dep. Chm., 1957–58); Trustee, LPNI, 1986–90. Labour Party Spokesman in House of Lords, on N Ireland, 1979–82; Mem., British-Irish Inter-Parly Body, 1997–; Trade Union Side Sec., NI CS Industrial Jt Council, 1975–77. Member: NI Co-operative Develt Agency, 1987–92 (Patron, 1993–); NI Economic Council, 1964–75; Review Body on Local Govt, NI, 1970–71; Review Body on Ind. Relations, NI, 1970–73; Working Party on Discrimination in Employment, NI, 1972–73; NI Trng Res. Cttee, 1966–80; NI Regional Adv. Bd, BIM, 1971–80; NUU Vocational Guidance Council, 1974–83; Ind. Appeals Tribunals, 1974–76; Local Govt Appeals Tribunal, 1974–83; Irish Council of Churches Working Party, 1974–93; IBA, 1974–79; Standing Adv. Commn on Human Rights, NI, 1977–79; Police Complaints Bd, 1977–80; Conciliation Panel, Ind. Relations Agency, 1978–89; Security Appeal Bd, NI SC Commn, 1979–88; Chm., Community Service Order Cttee, 1979–80; Rapporteur, EEC Cross Border Communications Study on Londonderry/Donegal, 1978–80. President: NI Assoc., NACRO, 1982–85; NI Hospice, 1981–85 (Patron, 1986–); E Belfast Access Council for Disabled, 1982–88; NI Widows Assoc., 1985–89; Mem., Belfast Housing Aid, 1989–95. Trustee: Belfast Charitable Trust for Integrated Educn, 1984–88; TSB Foundn, NI, 1986–96. Hon. Mem., NI Cttee, Duke of Edinburgh's Award Scheme (Chm., NI Anniversary Appeal, 1981–82). Member: Bd of Govs, St Mae Nissis Coll., 1981–90; Mgt Bd, Rathgael Young People's Centre, 1989–93. Ford Foundn Travel Award, USA, 1959. Duke of Edinburgh's Sword, 1981. Hon. Res. Fellow, Univ. of Ulster, 1976–83; Jt Hon. Res. Fellow, TCD, 1976–79. Hon. FBIM 1981 (MBIM 1970). JP Belfast, 1976–. Hon. DLitt New Univ. of Ulster, 1972; Hon. LLD QUB, 1982. *Publications:* Encyclopaedia of Labour Law, vol. 1: The Trade Union Movement in Northern Ireland, 1983. *Recreations:* gardening, reading.
Died 16 May 2008.

BLEDISLOE, 3rd Viscount *cr* 1935; **Christopher Hiley Ludlow Bathurst;** QC 1978; *b* 24 June 1934; *s* of 2nd Viscount Bledisloe, QC, and Joan Isobel Krishaber (*d* 1999); *S* father, 1979; *m* 1962 (marr. diss. 1986); two *s* one *d. Educ:* Eton; Trinity Coll., Oxford. Called to the Bar, Gray's Inn, 1959; Bencher, 1986. Elected Mem., H of L, 1999. *Heir: s* Hon. Rupert Edward Ludlow Bathurst [*b* 13 March 1964; *m* 2001, Shera, *d* of Rohinton and Irma Sarosh; one *s* two *d*]. *Address:* Lydney Park, Glos GL15 6BT. *T:* (01594) 842566; Fountain Court, Temple, EC4Y 9DH. *T:* (020) 7583 3335.
Died 12 May 2009.

BLEEHEN, Prof. Norman Montague, CBE 1994; Cancer Research Campaign Professor of Clinical Oncology, 1975–95, then Emeritus, and Hon. Director of MRC Unit of Clinical Oncology and Radiotherapeutics, 1975–95, University of Cambridge (Director, Radiotherapeutics, and Oncology Centre, 1984–92); Fellow of St John's College, Cambridge, since 1976; *b* 24 Feb. 1930; *s* of Solomon and Lena Bleehen; *m* 1969, Tirza, *d* of Alex and Jenny Loeb. *Educ:* Manchester Grammar Sch.; Haberdashers' Aske's Sch.; Exeter Coll., Oxford (Francis Gotch medal, 1953); Middlesex Hosp. Med. School. BA 1951, BSc 1953, MA 1954, BM, BCh 1955, Oxon. MRCP 1957, FRCP 1973; FRCR 1964; DMRT 1962. MRC Res. Student, Biochem. Dept, Oxford, 1951; house appts: Middlesex Hosp., 1955–56; Hammersmith Hosp., 1957; Asst Med. Specialist Army, Hanover, 1957; Med. Specialist Army, Berlin, 1959 (Captain); Jun. Lectr in Medicine, Dept of Regius Prof. of Medicine, Oxford, 1959–60; Registrar and Sen. Registrar in Radiotherapy, Middlesex Hosp. Med. Sch., 1961–66; Lilly Res. Fellow, Stanford Univ., 1966–67; Locum Consultant, Middlesex Hosp., 1967–69; Prof. of Radiotherapy, Middlesex Hosp. Med. Sch., 1969–75. Consultant advr to CMO, DHSS, for radiation oncology,

1986–92. Cantor Lectr, RSA, 1979; Simon Lectr, RCR, 1986. Member: Jt MRC/CRC Cttee for jtly supported insts, 1971–74; Coordinating Cttee for Cancer Res., 1973–79, 1987–; Council, Imperial Cancer Res. Fund, 1973–76; Council, Brit. Inst. of Radiology, 1974–77; Sci. Cttee, Cancer Res. Campaign, 1976–90; MRC Cell Bd, 1980–84; UICC Fellowships Cttee, 1983–87; Council, European Organisation for Treatment of Cancer, 1983–88; Council, RCR, 1987–90; Vice-President: Bd of Dirs, Internat. Assoc. for Study of Lung Cancer, 1980–82, 1985–94; EEC Cancer Experts Cttee, 1987–96; Pres., Internat. Soc. of Radiation Oncology, 1985–89; Chairman: MRC Lung Cancer Wkg Party, 1973–89; MRC Brain Tumour Wkg Party, 1978–89; MRC Cancer Therapy Cttee, 1972–88; British Assoc. for Cancer Res., 1976–79; Soc. for Comparative Oncology, 1983–86. Hon. FACR 1984. Hon. Dr, Faculty of Pharmacy, Bologna, 1990. Roentgen Prize, British Inst. of Radiology, 1986. *Publications:* (ed jtly) Radiation Therapy Planning, 1983; (Scientific Editor) British Medical Bulletin 24/1, The Scientific Basis of Radiotherapy, 1973; various on medicine, biochemistry, cancer and radiotherapy. *Recreations:* gardening, television. *Address:* 21 Bentley Road, Cambridge CB2 2AW. *T:* (01223) 354320.
Died 1 Feb. 2008.

BLIN-STOYLE, Prof. Roger John, FRS 1976; Professor of Theoretical Physics, University of Sussex, 1962–90, then Emeritus; *b* 24 Dec. 1924; *s* of Cuthbert Basil St John Blin-Stoyle and Ada Mary (*née* Nash); *m* 1949, Audrey Elizabeth Balmford; one *s* one *d. Educ:* Alderman Newton's Boys' Sch., Leicester; Wadham Coll., Oxford (Scholar; MA, DPhil). FInstP; ARCM. Served Royal Signals, 1943–46 (Lieut). Pressed Steel Co. Res. Fellow, Oxford Univ., 1951–53; Lectr in Math. Physics, Birmingham Univ., 1953–54; Sen. Res. Officer in Theoret. Physics, Oxford Univ., 1952–62; Fellow and Lectr in Physics, Wadham Coll., Oxford, 1956–62, Hon. Fellow, 1987; Vis. Associate Prof. of Physics, MIT, 1959–60; Vis. Prof. of Physics, Univ. of Calif, La Jolla, 1960; Sussex University: Dean, Sch. of Math. and Phys. Sciences, 1962–68; Pro-Vice-Chancellor, 1965–67; Dep. Vice-Chancellor, 1970–72; Pro-Vice-Chancellor (Science), 1977–79. Chm., School Curriculum Develt Cttee, 1983–88. Member: Royal Greenwich Observatory Cttee, 1966–70; Nuclear Physics Bd, SRC, later SERC, 1967–70, 1982–84; Mem. Council, 1982–83, Chm. Educn Cttee, 1992–94, Royal Soc.; President: Inst. of Physics, 1990–92; Assoc. for Sci. Educn, 1993–94. Editor: Reports on Progress in Physics, 1977–82; Student Physics Series, 1983–87. Hon. DSc Sussex, 1990. Rutherford Medal and Prize, IPPS, 1976. Silver Jubilee Medal, 1977. *Publications:* Theories of Nuclear Moments, 1957; Fundamental Interactions and the Nucleus, 1973; Nuclear and Particle Physics, 1991; Eureka!, 1997; papers on nuclear and elementary particle physics in scientific jls. *Recreation:* making music.
Died 31 Jan. 2007.

BLOW, Sandra, RA 1978 (ARA 1971); *b* 14 Sept. 1925; *d* of Jack and Lily Blow. *Educ:* St Martin's School of Art; Royal Academy Sch.; Accademia di Belle Arti, Rome. Tutor, Painting School, Royal Coll. of Art, 1960–75. *Individual exhibitions:* Gimpel Fils, 1952, 1954, 1960, 1962; Saidenburg Gallery, NY, 1957; New Art Centre, London, 1966, 1968, 1971, 1973; Francis Graham-Dixon, 1991; Newlyn, 1995; New Millennium Gall., St Ives, 1997; Tate St Ives, 2001–02; *retrospective:* Royal Acad's Sackler Galls, 1994. Represented in group exhibitions in Britain (including British Painting 74, Hayward Gall.; Tate, St Ives, 1995, 1997), USA, Italy, Denmark, France, Ireland, UAE; first etching exhibited RA, 1996. Won British Section of Internat. Guggenheim Award, 1960; 2nd prize, John Moore's Liverpool Exhibition, 1961; Arts Council Purchase Award, 1965–66; Korn/Ferry Picture of the Year Award, 1998; *group exhibition:* Barbican, 2002. *Official purchases:* Peter Stuyvesant Foundation; Nuffield Foundation; Arts Council of Great Britain; Arts Council of N Ireland; Walker Art Gallery, Liverpool; Allbright Knox Art Gallery, Buffalo, NY; Museum of Modern Art, NY; Tate

Gallery; Chantry Bequest; Gulbenkian Foundation; Min. of Public Building and Works; Contemp. Art Society; Victoria and Albert Museum; Fitzwilliam Museum, Cambridge; City of Leeds Art Gall.; Graves Art Gall., Sheffield; Heathrow Airport (glass screen). *Address:* c/o Royal Academy of Arts, Piccadilly, W1V 0DS.
Died 22 Aug. 2006.

BLUNDEN, Sir Philip (Overington), 7th Bt *cr* 1766, of Castle Blunden, Kilkenny; artist and art restorer; *b* 27 Jan. 1922; *s* of Sir John Blunden, 5th Bt and Phyllis Dorothy (*d* 1967), *d* of Philip Crampton Creaghe; *S* brother, 1985; *m* 1945, Jeannette Francesca Alexandra (*d* 1999), *e d* of Captain D. Macdonald, RNR; two *s* one *d*. *Educ:* Repton. Served RN, 1941–46 (1939–45 Star, Atlantic Star, Defence Medal). Estate Manager, Castle Blunden, 1947–60; engaged in marketing of industrial protective coatings, 1962–83; in art and art restoration, 1976–. Solo exhibns bi-annually, Dublin, Celbridge and Galway. *Recreations:* fishing, field sports, reading. *Heir: s* Hubert Chisholm Blunden [*b* 9 Aug. 1948; *m* 1975, Eilish O'Brien; one *s* one *d*]. *Club:* Royal Dublin Society (Life Mem.). *Died 9 April 2007.*

BLYTH, 4th Baron *cr* 1907; **Anthony Audley Rupert Blyth;** Bt 1895; *b* 3 June 1931; *er s* of 3rd Baron Blyth and Edna Myrtle (*d* 1952), *d* of Ernest Lewis, Wellington, NZ; *S* father, 1977; *m* 1st, 1954, Elizabeth Dorothea (marr. diss. 1962), *d* of R. T. Sparrow, Vancouver, BC; two *d* (one *s* decd); 2nd, 1963, Oonagh Elizabeth Ann, *yr d* of late William Henry Conway, Dublin; one *s* one *d*. *Educ:* St Columba's College, Dublin. *Heir: s* Hon. James Audley Ian Blyth [*b* 13 Nov. 1970; *m* 2003, Elodie Bernadette Andrée Odette, *d* of Jean-Georges Cadet de Fontenay; one *s* one *d*]. *Address:* Blythwood Estate, Athenry, Co. Galway, Ireland. *Died 20 Jan. 2009.*

BOAG, Prof. John Wilson; Professor of Physics as Applied to Medicine, University of London, Institute of Cancer Research, 1965–76, then Emeritus; *b* Elgin, Scotland, 20 June 1911; *s* of John and Margaret A. Boag; *m* 1938, Isabel Petrie (*d* 2006); no *c*. *Educ:* Universities of Glasgow, Cambridge and Braunschweig. Engineer, British Thomson Houston Co., Rugby, 1936–41; Physicist, Medical Research Council, 1941–52; Visiting Scientist, National Bureau of Standards, Washington, 1953–54; Physicist, British Empire Cancer Campaign, Mount Vernon Hospital, 1954–64; Royal Society (Leverhulme) Visiting Prof. to Poland, 1964. President: Hosp. Physicists' Assoc., 1959; Assoc. for Radiation Res. (UK), 1972–74; Internat. Assoc. for Radiation Res., 1970–74; British Inst. of Radiology, 1975–76. L. H. Gray Medal, ICRU, 1973; Barclay Medal, BIR, 1975. *Publications:* (jtly) Kapitza in Cambridge and Moscow, 1990; papers on radiation dosimetry, statistics, radiation chemistry, radiodiagnosis. *Address:* 4/50 Gillsland Road, Edinburgh EH10 5BW. *Died 2 Jan. 2007.*

BOCK, Prof. Claus Victor, MA, DrPhil; Professor of German Language and Literature, Westfield College, University of London, 1969–84, then Emeritus; Hon. Research Fellow, Queen Mary, University of London (formerly Westfield College, later Queen Mary and Westfield College), since 1984, Fellow, 1993; *b* Hamburg, 7 May 1926; *o s* of Frederick Bock, merchant and manufacturer, and Margot (*née* Meyerhof). *Educ:* Quaker Sch., Eerde, Holland; Univs of Amsterdam, Manchester, Basl. DrPhil (insigni cum laude) Basle 1955. Asst Lectr in German, Univ. of Manchester, 1956–58; University of London: Lectr, Queen Mary Coll., 1958–69; Reader in German Lang. and Lit., 1964; Chm., Bd of Studies in Germanic Langs and Lit., 1970–73; Hon. Dir, Inst. of Germanic Studies, 1973–81 (Hon. Fellow, 1989); Dean, Fac. of Arts, 1980–84; Mem., Senate, 1981–83; Mem., Acad. Council, 1981–83; Mem., Central Research Fund (A), 1981–84. Mem. Council, English Goethe Soc., 1965–2006; Chm., Stichting Castrum Peregrini, 1984–98 (Mem., 1971–). Hon. Pres., Assoc. of Teachers of German, 1973–75. Mem., Maatschappij der Nederlandse Letteren, 1977. Mem. Editl Bd, Bithell Series of Dissertations, 1978–84. Officer,

Order of Merit (FRG), 1984. *Publications:* Deutsche erfahren Holland 1725–1925, 1956; Q. Kuhlmann als Dichter, 1957; ed (with Margot Ruben) K. Wolfskehl Ges. Werke, 1960; ed (with G. F. Senior) Goethe the Critic, 1960; Pente Pigadia und die Tagebücher des Clement Harris, 1962; ed (with L. Helbing) Fr. Gundolf Briefwechsel mit H. Steiner und E. R. Curtius, 1963; Wort-Konkordanz zur Dichtung Stefan Georges, 1964; ed (with L. Helbing) Fr. Gundolf Briefe Neue Folge, 1965; A Tower of Ivory?, 1970; (with L. Helbing and K. Kluncker) Stefan George: Dokumente seiner Wirkung, 1974; (ed) London German Studies, 1980; (with K. Kluncker) Wolfgang Cordan: Jahre der Freundschaft, 1982; Untergetaucht unter Freunden, 1985, 5th edn 2004; Besuch im Elfenbeinturm (selected essays), 1990; (ed) W. Frommel Templer und Rosenkreuz, 1991; (ed) W. Frommel Meditationen, 1994; (ed) W. Frommel Briefe an die Eltern 1920–1959, 1997; (ed) W. Frommel/R. v. Scheliha Briefwechsel, 2002; (ed) M. Claussner Gedichte, 2006; articles in English and foreign jls and collections. *Recreation:* foreign travel. *Address:* c/o Castrum Peregrini Presse, PB 645, 1000 AP Amsterdam, Netherlands. *T:* (20) 6230043. *Died 5 Jan. 2008.*

BOHR, Prof. Aage Niels, DSc, DrPhil; Danish physicist; Professor of Physics, University of Copenhagen, 1956–92; *b* Copenhagen, 19 June 1922; *s* of late Prof. Niels Bohr (Nobel Prize in Physics, 1922) and Margrethe Nørlund; *m* 1st, Marietta Bettina (*née* Soffer) (*d* 1978); two *s* one *d*, 2nd, 1981, Bente, *d* of late Chief Physician Johannes Meyer and Lone (*née* Rubow) and *widow* of Morten Scharff. *Educ:* Univ. of Copenhagen. Jun. Scientific Officer, Dept of Scientific and Industrial Research, London, 1943–45; Research Asst, Inst. for Theoretical Physics, Univ. of Copenhagen, 1946; Dir, Niels Bohr Inst. (formerly Inst. for Theoretical Physics), 1963–70. Bd Mem., Nordita, 1958–74, Dir, 1975–81. Member: Royal Danish Acad. of Science, 1955–; Royal Physiolog. Soc., Sweden, 1959–; Royal Norwegian Acad. of Sciences, 1962–; Acad. of Tech. Sciences, Copenhagen, 1963–; Amer. Phil. Soc., 1965–; Amer. Acad. of Arts and Sciences, 1965–; Nat. Acad. of Sciences, USA, 1971–; Royal Swedish Acad. of Sciences, 1974–; Yugoslavia Acad. of Sciences, 1976–; Pontificia Academia Scientiarum, 1978–; Norwegian Acad. of Sciences, 1979–; Polish Acad. of Sciences, 1980–; Finska Vetenskaps-Societeten, 1980–; Deutsche Akademie der Naturforscher Leopoldina, 1981–. Awards: Dannie Heineman Prize, 1960; Pius XI Medal, 1963; Atoms for Peace Award, 1969; H. C. Ørsted Medal, 1970; Rutherford Medal, 1972; John Price Wetherill Medal, 1974; (jointly) Nobel Prize in Physics, 1975; Ole Rømer Medal, 1976. Dr *hc:* Manchester, 1961; Oslo, 1969; Heidelberg, 1971; Trondheim, 1972; Uppsala, 1975. *Publications:* Rotational States of Atomic Nuclei, 1951; (with Ben R. Mottelson) Nuclear Structure, vol. I, 1969, vol. II 1975; (with Ben R. Mottelson and O. Ulfbeck) The Principle Behind Quantum Mechanics, 2004; contrib. learned jls. *Address:* Strandgade 34, 1st Floor, 1401 Copenhagen K, Denmark. *Died 8 Sept. 2009.*

BOLINGBROKE, 7th Viscount *cr* 1712, **AND ST JOHN,** 8th Viscount *cr* 1716; **Kenneth Oliver Musgrave St John;** Bt 1611; Baron St John of Lydiard Tregoze, 1712; Baron St John of Battersea, 1716; Founder, 1956, Chairman, 1958–75, Atlantic and Pacific Travel Ltd; *b* 22 March 1927; *s* of Geoffrey Robert St John, MC (*d* 1972) and Katherine Mary (*d* 1958), *d* of late A. S. J. Musgrave; *S* cousin, 1974; *m* 1st, 1953, Patricia Mary McKenna (marr. diss. 1972); one *s*; 2nd, 1972, Jainey Anne McRae (marr. diss. 1987); two *s*. *Educ:* Eton; Geneva Univ. Director: Shaw Savill Holidays Pty Ltd; Bolingbroke and Partners Ltd; Wata Investment Inc., Panama. Pres., Travel Agents Assoc. of NZ, 1965–67; Dir, World Assoc. of Travel Agencies, 1966–75; Chm., Aust. Council of Tour Wholesalers, 1972–75. Fellow, Aust. Inst. of Travel; Mem., NZ Inst. of Travel. *Recreations:* golf, cricket, tennis, history. *Heir: s* Hon. Henry Fitzroy St John, *b* 18 May 1957.
Died 5 July 2010.

BOLLAND, Sir Edwin, KCMG 1981 (CMG 1971); HM Diplomatic Service, retired; Ambassador to Yugoslavia, 1980–82; *b* 20 Oct. 1922; *m* 1948, Winifred Mellor; one *s* three *d* (and one *s* decd). *Educ:* Morley Grammar Sch.; University Coll., Oxford. Served in Armed Forces, 1942–45. Foreign Office, 1947; Head of Far Eastern Dept, FO, 1965–67; Counsellor, Washington, 1967–71; St Antony's Coll., Oxford, 1971–72; Ambassador to Bulgaria, 1973–76; Head of British delegn to Negotiations on MBFR, 1976–80. *Recreations:* walking, gardening. *Address:* 2A Dukes Meadow, Stapleford, Cambridge CB22 5BH. *T:* (01223) 847139.   *Died 5 Dec. 2008.*

BOLLERS, Hon. Sir Harold (Brodie Smith), Kt 1969; CCH 1982; Chairman, Elections Commission, 1982; Chief Justice of Guyana, 1966–80; *b* 5 Feb. 1915; *s* of late John Bollers; *m* 1st, 1951, Irene Mahadeo (*d* 1965); two *s* one *d*; 2nd, 1968, Eileen Hanoman; one *s*. *Educ:* Queen's Coll., Guyana; King's Coll., London; Middle Temple. Called to the Bar, Feb. 1938; Magistrate, Guyana, 1946, Senior Magistrate, 1959; Puisne Judge, Guyana, 1960. *Recreations:* reading, walking. *Address:* 252 South Road, Bourda, Georgetown, Guyana.   *Died 26 Dec. 2006.*

BOLTON, Roger William; General Secretary, Broadcasting, Entertainment, Cinematograph and Theatre Union, since 1993; *b* 7 Sept. 1947; *s* of William and Honara Bolton; *m* 1974, Elaine Lewis; one *d*. *Educ:* St Thomas More's Sch., London. Photographic Asst, Boots The Chemists, 1960–64; photographer: Belgrave Press Bureau, 1964–69; BBC TV News, 1969–79; Trade Union Official: Assoc. of Broadcasting Staff, 1979–84; Broadcasting Entertainment Trades Alliance, 1984–93. Mem., British Screen Adv. Council, 1994–. Gov., Nat. Film and TV Sch., 1994–. *Address:* (office) 373–377 Clapham Road, SW9 9BT. *T:* (020) 7346 0900.
Died 18 Nov. 2006.

BOND, Sir Kenneth (Raymond Boyden), Kt 1977; Vice-Chairman, The General Electric Company plc, 1985–90 (Financial Director, 1962–66; Deputy Managing Director, 1966–85), retired; *b* 1 Feb. 1920; *s* of late James Edwin and Gertrude Deplidge Bond; *m* 1958, Jennifer Margaret, *d* of late Sir Cecil and Lady Crabbe; two *s* three *d* (and one *s* decd). *Educ:* Selhurst Grammar School. Served TA, Europe and Middle East, 1939–46. FCA 1960 (Mem. 1949). Partner, Cooper & Cooper, Chartered Accountants, 1954–57; Dir, Radio & Allied Industries Ltd, 1957–62. Member: Industrial Develt Adv. Bd, 1972–77; Cttee to Review the Functioning of Financial Instns, 1977–80; Audit Commn, 1983–86; Civil Justice Rev. Adv. Cttee, 1985–88. *Address:* Woodstock, Wayside Gardens, Gerrards Cross, Bucks SL9 7NG. *T:* (01753) 883513.   *Died 13 May 2006.*

BONELLO DU PUIS, George, KOM 1995; LLD; High Commissioner for Malta in London, 1999–2005; *b* 24 Jan. 1928; *s* of Joseph Bonello and Josephine (*née* Du Puis); *m* 1957, Mary Iris sive Iris Gauci Maistre'; two *s* one *d*. *Educ:* St Catherine's High Sch., Malta; The Lyceum, Malta; Royal Univ. of Malta (LLD 1952). Law Practice, 1953–87 and 1995–98. MP, Malta, 1971–96; Minister of Finance, 1987–92; Minister for Econ. Services, 1992–95. Chm., Sliema Wanderers FC, 1961–87. *Recreations:* billiards and sports in general, football in particular. *Address:* The Park, Antonio Nani Street, Ta'Xbiex, Malta. *T:* 335415. *Clubs:* Royal Over-Seas League; Casino Maltese (Valletta, Malta).   *Died 19 Feb. 2010.*

BONHAM, Major Sir Antony Lionel Thomas, 4th Bt *cr* 1852; DL; late Royal Scots Greys; *b* 21 Oct. 1916; *o s* of Maj. Sir Eric H. Bonham, 3rd Bt, and Ethel (*d* 1962), *y d* of Col Leopold Seymour; *S* father, 1937; *m* 1944, Felicity (*d* 2003), *o d* of late Col. Frank L. Pardoe, DSO, Bartonbury, Cirencester; three *s*. *Educ:* Eton; RMC. Served Royal Scots Greys, 1937–49; retired with rank of Major, 1949. DL Glos 1983. *Heir:* *s* (George) Martin (Antony) Bonham [*b* 18 Feb. 1945; *m* 1979, Nenon Baillieu (marr. diss. 1992), *e d* of R. R. Wilson and Hon. Mrs Wilson, Durford Knoll, Upper Durford Wood,

Petersfield, Hants; one *s* three *d*]. *Address:* Greystones, The Croft, Fairford, Glos GL7 4BB. *T:* (01285) 712258.
Died 5 Oct. 2009.

BONHAM, Derek Charles, FCA, FCT; Chairman: Imperial Tobacco Group plc, 1996–2007; Cadbury Schweppes plc, 2000–03; *b* 12 July 1943; *m*; two *d*. *Educ:* Bedford Sch. Chartered Accountant, Whinney Murray; Management Accountant, Staflex Internat.; Hanson plc: Dep. Financial Controller, 1971; Finance Dir, 1981; Chief Exec., 1992–97; Dep. Chm., 1993–97; Chm., Energy Gp, 1997–98. Chairman: Marconi, 2001–02; Songbird Estates, 2004–05; non-executive Director: USI, 1995–96; Glaxo-Wellcome, 1995–2001; TXU Corp. (USA), 1998–2005. Member: Accounting Standards Cttee, 1987–90; Financial Accounting Standards Adv. Council, USA, 1990–93. Master, Feltmakers' Co., 2006–07. *Address:* 150 Brompton Road, SW3 1HX. *T:* (020) 7584 6798, *Fax:* (020) 7589 6485.
Died 3 Sept. 2007.

BONHAM-CARTER, Victor; Joint Secretary, Society of Authors, 1971–78, Consultant, 1978–82; Secretary, Royal Literary Fund, 1966–82; *b* 13 Dec. 1913; *s* of Gen. Sir Charles Bonham-Carter, GCB, CMG, DSO, and Gabrielle Madge Jeanette (*née* Fisher); *m* 1st, 1938, Audrey Edith Stogdon (marr. diss. 1979); two *s*; 2nd, 1979, Cynthia Claire Sanford. *Educ:* Winchester Coll.; Magdalene Coll., Cambridge (MA); Hamburg and Paris. Worked on The Countryman, 1936–37; Dir, School Prints Ltd, 1937–39, 1945–60; Army, R Berks Regt and Intell. Corps, 1939–45; farmed in W Somerset, 1947–59; historian of Dartington Hall Estate, Devon, 1951–66; on staff of Soc. of Authors, 1963–82. Active in Exmoor National Park affairs, 1955–; Pres., Exmoor Soc., 1975–; Partner, Exmoor Press, 1969–89. *Publications:* The English Village, 1952; (with W. B. Curry) Dartington Hall, 1958; Exploring Parish Churches, 1959; Farming the Land, 1959; In a Liberal Tradition, 1960; Soldier True, 1965; Surgeon in the Crimea, 1969; The Survival of the English Countryside, 1971; Authors by Profession, vol. 1 1978, vol. 2 1984; Exmoor Writers, 1987; The Essence of Exmoor, 1991; What Countryman, Sir?, 1996; many contribs to jls, radio, etc on country life and work; also on authorship matters, esp. Public Lending Right. *Recreations:* music, conversation. *Address:* The Mount, Milverton, Taunton TA4 1QZ.
Died 13 March 2007.

BONNEY, George Louis William, FRCS; Consulting Orthopædic Surgeon, St Mary's Hospital, London, since 1984; *b* 10 Jan. 1920; *s* of late Dr Ernest Bonney and Gertrude Mary Williams; *m* 1950, Margaret Morgan; two *d*. *Educ:* Eton (Scholar); St Mary's Hospital Medical Sch. (MB, BS; MS 1947). MRCS, LRCP 1943; FRCS 1945. Formerly: Surg.-Lieut RNVR; Res. Asst and Sen. Registrar, Royal Nat. Orthopædic Hosp.; Consultant Orthopædic Surgeon: Southend Group of Hospitals; St Mary's Hosp., London, 1954–84 (Sen. Consultant, 1979–84; Mem., Bd of Govs, Dist Mgt Team). Travelling Fellowship of BPMF, Univ. of London, 1950. Watson-Jones Lectr, RCS, 1976. Sen. FBOA; Hon. Fellow, Medical Defence Union; Mem., SICOT. Mem., Soc. of Authors. Associate Ed., Jl Bone and Joint Surgery. *Publications:* (jtly) Surgical Disorders of the Peripheral Nerves, 1998; The Battle of Jutland 1916, 2002, 2nd edn 2006; chapters in: Operative Surgery, 1957; Clinical Surgery, 1966; Clinical Orthopædics, 1983, 2nd edn 1995; Micro-reconstruction of Nerve Injuries, 1987; Current Therapy in Neurologic Disease, 1987; Medical Negligence, 1990, 3rd edn 2000; Clinical Neurology, 1991; Medical Negligence: cranium, spine and nervous system, 1999; papers in medical journals on visceral pain, circulatory mechanisms, nerve injuries and on various aspects of orthopædic surgery. *Recreations:* reading, writing, photography, music. *Address:* 6 Wooburn Grange, Grange Drive, Wooburn Green, Bucks HP10 0QU. *T:* (01628) 525598. *Club:* Leander.
Died 11 Feb. 2007.

BONYNGE, Dame Joan; *see* Sutherland, Dame Joan.

BOOLELL, Sir Satcam, GCSK 2006 (GOSK 1999); Kt 1977; High Commissioner for Mauritius in London, 1996–2001; *b* New Grove, Mauritius, 11 Sept. 1920; *s* of Sahadewoo Boolell and Cossilah Choony; *m* 1st, 1948, Inderjeet Kissoodaye (*d* 1986); two *s* one *d*; 2nd, 1987, Myrtha Poblete. *Educ:* primary and secondary schs in New Grove, Mare d'Albert, Rose Belle, and Port-Louis; LSE (LLB Hons 1951). Called to the Bar, Lincoln's Inn, 1952. Civil servant, Mauritius, 1944–48. Minister of Agric. and Natural Resources, 1959–82; Minister of Economic Planning, 1983–84; Dep. Prime Minister, Attorney General, Minister of Justice and Minister of External Affairs and Emigration, 1986–90. Mem. Central Exec., 1955–, Leader, 1985–90, Advr, 1990–, Mauritius Labour Party. Rep. Mauritius, internat. confs. Founder, English and French daily newspaper, The Nation. Hon. DCL Mauritius, 1986. GCSG 1999. Comdr, Légion d'Honneur (France), 1990. *Publications:* The Untold Stories, 1997; Reminiscences of Travels Abroad, 1998. *Recreations:* travel books, walking in the countryside. *Address:* 4bis Bancilhon Street, Port Louis, Mauritius. *T:* 2080079, *Fax:* 2089207.   *Died 23 March 2006.*

BOOTH, His Honour Alan Shore; QC 1975; a Circuit Judge, 1976–93; *b* Aug. 1922; 4th *s* of Parkin Stanley Booth and Ethel Mary Shore; *m* 1954, Mary Gwendoline Hilton; one *s* one *d*. *Educ:* Shrewsbury Sch.; Liverpool Univ. (LLB). Served War of 1939–45, RNVR, Fleet Air Arm, 1833 Sqdn (despatches 1944): Sub-Lt 1942; HMS Illustrious, Eastern and Pacific Fleets, 1943–45; Lieut 1944. Called to Bar, Gray's Inn, 1949. A Recorder of the Crown Court, 1972–76. Mem. Mgt Cttee, Hoylake Cottage Hosp., 1996–2004. Governor, Shrewsbury Sch., 1969–2003. Guide, Chester Cathedral, 1996–. Pres., Liverpool Ramblers AFC, 1992–94. *Recreation:* golf. *Address:* 18 Abbey Road, West Kirby, Wirral CH48 7EW. *T:* (0151) 625 5796. *Clubs:* Royal Liverpool Golf; Royal and Ancient (St Andrews).
                                                    Died 15 May 2006.

BOOTH, Rt Hon. Albert Edward; PC 1976; *b* 28 May 1928; *e s* of Albert Henry Booth and Janet Mathieson; *m* 1957, Joan Amis (*d* 2008); two *s* (and one *s* decd). *Educ:* St Thomas's Sch., Winchester; S Shields Marine Sch.; Rutherford Coll. of Technology. Engineering Draughtsman. Election Agent, 1951 and 1955. County Borough Councillor, 1962–65. Exec. Dir, S Yorks Passenger Transport Exec., 1983–87. MP (Lab) Barrow-in-Furness, 1966–83; Minister of State, Dept of Employment, 1974–76; Sec. of State for Employment, 1976–79; Opposition spokesman on transport, 1979–83. Chm., Select Cttee on Statutory Instruments, 1970–74. Treasurer, Labour Party, 1984. Contested (Lab): Tynemouth, 1964; Barrow and Furness, 1983; Warrington South, 1987. CompIMechE 1985. *T:* (020) 8650 5982.   *Died 6 Feb. 2010.*

BOOTH, Rev. Preb. William James, CVO 2007 (LVO 1999); Sub-Dean of Her Majesty's Chapels Royal, Deputy Clerk of the Closet, Sub-Almoner and Domestic Chaplain to The Queen, 1991–2007; Prebendary, St Paul's Cathedral, 2000–07; *b* 3 Feb. 1939; *s* of William James Booth and Elizabeth Ethel Booth. *Educ:* Ballymena Acad., Co. Antrim; TCD (MA). Curate, St Luke's Parish, Belfast, 1962–64; Chaplain, Cranleigh Sch., Surrey, 1965–74. Priest-in-Ordinary to The Queen, 1976–91; Priest-Vicar of Westminster Abbey, 1987–91. Chaplain, Westminster School, London, 1974–91 (Hon. Fellow 2006); Acting Chaplain, New Coll., Oxford, 2009. Organiser, PHAB annual residential courses at Westminster (and formerly at Cranleigh). *Recreations:* music, hi-fi, cooking. *Address:* 48 South Everard Street, King's Lynn, Norfolk PE30 5HJ.   *Died 2 June 2009.*

BORLAUG, Norman Ernest, PhD; Consultant, International Center for Maize and Wheat Improvement, since 1979; Distinguished Professor of International Agriculture, Texas A & M University, since 1984; *b* 25 March 1914; *s* of Henry O. and Clara Vaala Borlaug; *m* 1937, Margaret Gibson (*d* 2007); one *s* one *d*. *Educ:* Univ. of Minnesota (BS 1937; MS 1940; PhD 1942). US Forest

Service (USDA), 1935, 1937, 1938; Biologist, Dupont de Nemours & Co., 1942–44; Rockefeller Foundation: Plant Pathologist and Geneticist, Wheat Improvement, 1944–60; Associate Dir, Inter-American Food Crop Program, 1960–63; Dir of Wheat Res. and Production Program, International Center for Maize and Wheat Improvement (CIMMYT), 1964–79. Dir, Population Crisis Cttee, 1971–; Asesor Especial, Fundación para Estudios de la Población (Mexico), 1971; Member: Adv. Council, Renewable Natural Resources Foundn, 1973; Citizens' Commn on Science, Law and Food Supply, 1973–74; Council for Agricl Science and Tech., 1973–; Commn on Critical Choices for Americans 1973–74. Mem., Nat. Acad. of Scis (USA), 1968; Foreign Mem., Royal Soc., 1987. Outstanding Achievement Award, Univ. of Minnesota, 1959; Sitara-Imtiaz (Star of Distinction) (Pakistan), 1968, Hilal-I-Imtiaz 1978. Nobel Peace Prize, 1970. Holds numerous hon. doctorates in Science, both from USA and abroad; and more than 30 Service Awards by govts and organizations, including US Medal of Freedom, 1977, Congressional Gold Medal, 2007. *Publications:* more than 70 scientific and semi-popular articles. *Recreations:* hunting, fishing, baseball, wrestling, football, golf. *Address:* c/o International Center for Maize and Wheat Improvement (CIMMYT), Apartado Postal 6–641, 06600 Mexico DF, Mexico; Texas A & M University, Department of Crop Sciences, College Station, TX 77843–2474, USA.
                                                    Died 12 Sept. 2009.

BORRETT, Louis Albert Frank; a Chairman, Police Disciplinary Appeals, 1987–89; *b* 8 Aug. 1924; *e s* of late Albert B. Borrett and Louise Alfreda Eudoxie Forrestier; *m* 1946, Barbara Betty, *er d* of late Frederick Charles Bamsey and of Lily Gertrude Thompson. *Educ:* France and England; Folkestone Teachers' Trng Coll.; King's Coll., Univ. of London (LLB 1954). Served War, Army: volunteered, 1940; RASC, London Dist and South Eastern Comd; commnd Royal Sussex Regt, 1944; served India and Burma Border; Intell. Officer, 9th Royal Sussex, during invasion of Malaya, 1945; GSO III (Ops), ALFSEA, 1946 (Burma Star, Defence Medal, Victory Medal); demob., 1946 (Captain). Schoolmaster, 1947–53; called to the Bar, Gray's Inn, 1955; barrister, in practice on South-Eastern circuit, 1955–86; a Recorder, 1980–89. Asst Comr, Boundary Commn, 1964–67. *Recreations:* music, the French language. *Address:* Riders' Drift, 55 Judith Avenue, Knodishall, Saxmundham, Suffolk IP17 1UY.   *Died 29 Jan. 2007.*

BORWICK, 4th Baron *cr* 1922; **James Hugh Myles Borwick;** Bt *cr* 1916; MC 1944; Major, Highland Light Infantry, retired; *b* 12 Dec. 1917; *s* of 3rd Baron and Irene Phyllis, *d* of late Thomas Main Paterson, Littlebourne, Canterbury; S father, 1961; *m* 1954, Hyllarie Adalia Mary, *y d* of late Lt-Col William Hamilton Hall Johnston, DSO, MC, DL, Bryn-y-Groes, Bala, N Wales; four *d*. *Educ:* Eton; RMC, Sandhurst. Commissioned as 2nd Lieut, HLI, 1937; Capt. 1939; Major 1941; retired, 1947. *Recreations:* field sports, sailing. *Heir: nephew* Geoffrey Robert James Borwick [*b* 7 March 1955; *m* 1981, Victoria Lorne Peta (*née* Poore); three *s* one *d*]. *Club:* Royal Ocean Racing.   *Died 19 April 2007.*

BOSTOCK, James Edward, RE 1961 (ARE 1947); ARCA London; painter and engraver; *b* Hanley, Staffs, 11 June 1917; *s* of William George Bostock, pottery and glass-worker, and Amy (*née* Titley); *m* 1939, Gwladys Irene (*née* Griffiths); three *s*. *Educ:* Borden Grammar Sch., Sittingbourne; Medway Sch. of Art, Rochester; Royal College of Art. War Service as Sgt in Durham LI and Royal Corps of Signals. Full-time Teacher, 1946–78; Vice-Principal, West of England Coll. of Art, 1965–70; Academic Develt Officer, Bristol Polytechnic, 1970–78. Elected Mem. of Soc. of Wood Engravers, 1950. Mem. Council. Soc. of Staffs Artists, 1963. Mem., E Kent Art Soc., 1980. Exhibited water-colours, etchings, wood engravings and drawings at RA, NEAC, RBA, RE, RI and other group exhibitions and in travelling exhibitions to Poland, Czechoslovakia, South Africa, Far East, New

Zealand, USA, Sweden, Russia and Baltic States, and the provinces. One-man shows: Mignon Gall., Bath; Univ. of Bristol; Bristol Polytechnic; Margate Liby Gall.; Deal Liby Gall.; Broadstairs Liby Gall.; Folkestone Liby Gall.; Phillip Maslen Gall., Canterbury; Exeter Mus.; Hereford Mus.; Oxford Univ.; 20th Century Gall., SW6. Works bought by V & A Museum, British Museum, British Council, Hull, Swindon, Stoke-on-Trent and Bristol Education Cttees, Hunt Botanical Library, Pittsburgh, Hereford Mus., Medici Soc., and private collectors. Commissioned work for: ICI Ltd, British Museum (Nat. Hist.), Odhams Press, and other firms and public authorities. *Publications:* Roman Lettering for Students, 1959; wood engraved illustrations to Poems of Edward Thomas, 1988; articles in: Times, Guardian, Staffordshire Sentinel, Studio, Artist; reproductions in: Garrett, History of British Wood Engraving, 1978; Garrett, British Wood Engraving of the Twentieth Century, 1980. *Address:* White Lodge, 80 Lindenthorpe Road, Broadstairs, Kent CT10 1DB. *T:* (01843) 869782. *Died 26 May 2006.*

BOSTON, 10th Baron *cr* 1761; **Timothy George Frank Boteler Irby;** Bt 1704; *b* 27 March 1939; *s* of 9th Baron Boston, MBE, and Erica N. (*d* 1990), *d* of T. H. Hill; *S* father, 1978; *m* 1967, Rhonda Anne, *d* of R. A. Bate; two *s* one *d*. *Educ:* Clayesmore School, Dorset; Southampton Univ. (BSc Econ.). *Heir: s* Hon. George William Eustace Boteler Irby, BSc [*b* 1 Aug. 1971; *m* 1998, Nicola Sydney Mary, *d* of William Reid; two *s* two *d*]. *Address:* Cae'r Borth, Moelfre, Anglesey LL72 8NN. *T:* (01248) 410249. *Died 3 Feb. 2007.*

BOSTON, Richard; writer; *b* 29 Dec. 1938; *m* 1st, 1968, Anne (marr. diss. 1976); 2nd, 2004, Marie-Claude Chapuis. *Educ:* Stowe; Regent Street Polytechnic School of Art; King's Coll., Cambridge (MA). Taught English in Sicily, Sweden and Paris; acted in Jacques Tati's Playtime. Glenfiddich Special Award, 1976. Editorial staff of Peace News, TLS, New Society; columnist and feature writer, The Guardian, at intervals, 1972–2001. Editor: The Vole, 1977–80; Quarto, 1979–82. *Publications:* The Press We Deserve (ed), 1969; An Anatomy of Laughter, 1974; The Admirable Urquhart, 1975; Beer and Skittles, 1976; Baldness Be My Friend, 1977; The Little Green Book, 1979; C. O. Jones's Compendium of Practical Jokes, 1982; Osbert: a portrait of Osbert Lancaster, 1989; Boudu Saved from Drowning, 1994; Starkness at Noon, 1997. *Recreation:* shelling peas. *Address:* The Old School, Aldworth, Reading, Berks RG8 9TJ. *T:* (01635) 578587. *Died 22 Dec. 2006.*

BOSWORTH, (John) Michael (Worthington), CBE 1972; FCA; Deputy Chairman, British Railways Board, 1972–83 (Vice-Chairman, 1968–72); *b* 22 June 1921; *s* of Humphrey Worthington Bosworth and Vera Hope Bosworth; *m* 1955, Patricia Mary Edith Wheelock; one *s* one *d*. *Educ:* Bishop's Stortford Coll. Served Royal Artillery, 1939–46. Peat, Marwick, Mitchell & Co., 1949–68, Partner, 1960; Chairman: British Rail Engineering Ltd, 1969–71; British Rail Property Bd, 1971–72; British Rail Shipping and International Services Ltd, later Sealink UK Ltd, 1976–84; BR Hovercraft Ltd, 1976–81; British Transport Hotels, 1978–83; British Rail Investments Ltd, 1981–84; British Rail Trustee Co., 1984–86; Director: Hoverspeed (UK) Ltd, 1981–89; British Ferries, 1984–90. Vice Pres., Société Belgo-Anglaise des Ferry-Boats, 1979–87. Dir, Compass Hotels Ltd, 1988–99. *Recreations:* ski-ing, vintage cars. *Address:* 3 Ruscombe Close, Tunbridge Wells, Kent TN4 0SG. *Died 8 May 2007.*

BOTHA, Pieter Willem, DMS 1976; Star of South Africa, 1979; State President, Republic of South Africa, 1984–89; *b* 12 Jan. 1916; *s* of Pieter Willem and Hendriena Christina Botha; *m* 1st, 1943, Anna Elizabeth Rossouw (*d* 1997); two *s* three *d*; 2nd, 1998, Barbara Nola Robertson. *Educ:* Paul Roux; Bethlehem, Orange Free State; Univ. of Orange Free State, Bloemfontein. MP for George, 1948–84; Deputy Minister of the Interior, 1958; Minister of Community Development and of Coloured Affairs, 1961; Minister of Public Works,

1964; Minister of Defence, 1966–80; Prime Minister, and Minister of National Intelligence Service, 1978–84. Leader of the National Party in the Cape Province, 1966–86; Chief Leader of Nat. Party, 1978–89. Hon. Doctorate in: Military Science, Stellenbosch Univ., 1976; Philosophy, Orange Free State Univ., 1981; DAdmin *hc* Pretoria Univ., 1985. Grand Cross of Military Order of Christ, Portugal, 1967; Order of Propitious Clouds with Special Grand Cordon, Taiwan, 1980; Grand Collar, Order of Good Hope, Republic of S Africa, 1985. *Relevant publication:* Voice from the Wilderness, by Dr Daan Prinsloo, 1997. *Recreations:* horseriding, walking, reading, small game hunting. *Address:* Die Anker, Wilderness 6560, South Africa. *Died 31 Oct. 2006.*

BOUCHER, Prof. Robert Francis, CBE 2000; PhD; FREng, FIMechE, FASME; DL; Vice-Chancellor, University of Sheffield, 2001–07; Chairman, Museums Sheffield, since 2008; *b* 25 April 1940; *s* of Robert Boucher and Johanna (*née* Fox); *m* 1965, Rosemary Ellen Maskell; two *s* one *d* (and one *s* decd). *Educ:* St Ignatius Coll.; Borough Poly.; Nottingham Univ. (PhD 1966). FIMechE 1992; FREng (FEng 1994); FASME 1997. ICI Post-doctoral Fellow, Nottingham Univ., 1966; Queen's University, Belfast: Res. Fellow, 1966–68; Lectr, 1968–70; University of Sheffield: Lectr, 1970–76; Sen. Lectr, 1976–85; Prof. of Mech. Engrg, 1985–95; Pro-Vice-Chancellor, 1992–95; Principal and Vice-Chancellor, UMIST, 1995–2000. Chm., Engrg Profs' Council, 1993–95; Senator, Engrg Council, 1995–99; Member: Council, Royal Acad. of Engrg, 1996–99; Bd, British Council, 1996–2003 (Mem., 1996–2003, Chm., 1997–2003, CICHE); Council, ACU, 1997– (Treas., 2004–); User Panel, EPSRC, 1997–2001; Internat. Sector Gp, UUK (formerly CVCP), 1995–2006 (Chm., 1997–2006); Bd, UUK, 2002–; Bd, UCEA, 2004–; Chair, White Rose Univs Consortium, 2003–. Trustee, NPG, 2003–. Chairman: CSU Ltd, later Graduate Prospects, 1998–2004; Marketing Manchester, 1999–2000; Member: Bd of Patrons, Alliance Française de Manchester, 1997–2000; Bd, Yorkshire Forward, 2003–06. DL S Yorks, 2007. FCGI 2006. Hon. Mem., RNCM, 1999. Hon. DHL SUNY, 1998; Hon. DEng Sheffield, 2009. *Publications:* in engrg jls and confs incl. Proc. IMechE, Trans ASME, Trans IEEE, Inst. of Physics jls. *Recreations:* hill-walking, music, exercise. *Address:* Leader House, Surrey Street, Sheffield S1 2LH. *Club:* Athenæum. *Died 25 March 2009.*

BOULTER, Prof. Patrick Stewart, FRCSE, FRCS, FRCP; Consultant Surgeon Emeritus, Royal Surrey County Hospital and Regional Radiotherapy Centre, since 1991; President, Royal College of Surgeons of Edinburgh, 1991–94; *b* 28 May 1927; *s* of Frederick Charles Boulter, MC and Flora Victoria Boulter of Annan, Dumfriesshire; *m* 1946, Patricia Mary Eckersley Barlow, *d* of S. G. Barlow of Lowton, Lancs; two *d*. *Educ:* King's Coll. Sch.; Carlisle GS; Guy's Hosp. Med. Sch., Univ. of London (Sands Cox Schol. in Physiology, 1952; MB BS Hons and Gold Medal, 1955). FRCS 1958; FRCSE 1958; FRCPE 1993; FRCPSGlas 1993; FRCP 1997. Guy's Hospital and Medical School, University of London: House Surgeon, 1955–56; Res. Fellow, Dept of Surgery, 1956–57; Lectr in Anatomy, 1956–57; Sen. Surgical Registrar, 1959–62; Hon. Consultant Surgeon, 1963; Surgical Registrar, Middlesex Hosp., 1957–59; Consultant Surgeon, Royal Surrey County and St Luke's Hosps, Guildford, 1962–91; Vis. Surgeon, Cranleigh and Cobham Hosps, 1962–91; Surgical Dir, Jarvis Breast Screening Centre, DHSS, 1978–91. Sen. Mem., British Breast Gp (Mem., 1962–). Prof. Surrey Univ., 1986– (Hon. Reader, 1968–80); Vis. Prof., univs in USA, Australia, NZ, Pakistan and India; Wilson Wang Prof. in Surgery, Chinese Univ. of HK, 1993. Examnr, RCSGlas, and Univs of Edinburgh, London, Nottingham, Newcastle, Singapore and Malaya; Overseas Advr for sen. acad. appts in surgical specialities, Univ. of Malaya, 1993–; Ext. Advr for sen. surg. posts, King Saud Univ., Riyadh, 1993–; Advr, Anti-Cancer Council of Vic, Aust., 1992–. Mem. Clin. Adv. Gp,

Health Risk Resources Internat., 1995–; Trustee and Mem., Health and Welfare Cttee, Thalidomide Trust, 1995–; Overseas Mem., Australian and NZ Breast Cancer Study Gp, 1989–. Chm., Conf. of Colls and Faculties (Scotland), 1992–94; Mem., Senate of Surgery of UK and Ire., 1992–95; Fellow, Assoc. of Surgeons of GB and Ire., 1962 (Mem. Council, and Chm., Educn Adv. Cttee, 1986–90); Royal College of Surgeons: Handcock Prize, 1955; Surgical Tutor, 1964; Regl Advr, 1975; Penrose May teacher, 1985–; Royal College of Surgeons of Edinburgh: Examnr, 1979; Mem. Council, 1984–; Vice-Pres., 1989–91; Regent, 1995. Hon. FRACS 1985; Hon. FCS(SA) 1992; Hon. FCSSL 1992; Hon. FRCSI 1993; Hon. FCSHK 1993; Hon. FCEM (Hon. FFAEM 1997); Mem., Acad. of Medicine of Malaysia, 1993; Hon. Member: N Pacific Surgical Assoc., USA, 1991; Assoc. of Surgeons of India, 1993; Soc. of Surgeons of Nepal, 1994; Surgical Res. Soc., 1995; Fellow, Acad. of Medicine of Singapore, 1994. Internat. Master Surgeon, Internat. Coll. of Surgeons, 1994 DUniv Surrey, 1996. Hon. Citizen, State of Nebraska, USA, 1967. *Publications:* articles and book chapters on surgical subjects, esp. breast disease, surgical oncology and endocrine surgery. *Recreations:* mountaineering, ski-ing, fly-fishing. *Address:* Quarry Cottage, Salkeld Dykes, Penrith, Cumbria CA11 9LL. *T:* (01768) 898822. *Clubs:* Alpine, Caledonian; New (Edinburgh); Yorkshire Fly Fishers; Swiss Alpine (Pres., Assoc. of British Members, 1978–80). *Died 30 Nov. 2009.*

BOULTON, Sir William (Whytehead), 3rd Bt *cr* 1944; Kt 1975; CBE 1958, TD 1949; Secretary, Senate of the Inns of Court and the Bar, 1974–75; *b* 21 June 1912; *s* of Sir William Boulton, 1st Bt, and Rosalind Mary (*d* 1969), *d* of Sir John Davison Milburn, 1st Bt, of Guyzance, Northumberland; *S* brother, 1982; *m* 1944, Margaret Elizabeth, *o d* of late Brig. H. N. A. Hunter, DSO; one *s* two *d*. *Educ:* Eton (Captain of Oppidans, 1931); Trinity Coll., Cambridge. Called to Bar, Inner Temple, 1936; practised at the Bar, 1937–39. Secretary, General Council of the Bar, 1950–74. Gazetted 2nd Lieut TA (Essex Yeo.), 1934; retired with rank of Hon. Lieut-Col, 1949; served War of 1939 16; with 104th Regt RHA (Essex Yeo.) and 14th Regt RHA, in the Middle East, 1940–44; Staff Coll., Camberley, 1944. Control Commission for Germany (Legal Div.), 1945–50. *Publications:* A Guide to Conduct and Etiquette at the Bar of England and Wales, 1st edn 1953, 6th edn, 1975. *Heir: s* John Gibson Boulton, *b* 18 Dec. 1946. *Address:* The Quarters House, Alresford, near Colchester, Essex CO7 8AY. *T:* (01206) 822450. *Died 20 July 2010.*

BOURGEOIS, Louise; artist and sculptor; *b* Paris, 25 Dec. 1911; *m* 1938, Robert Goldwater (*d* 1973); three *s*. *Educ:* Sorbonne; Ecole du Louvre; Acad. des Beaux-Arts; Atelier Fernand Léger; Art Students League, NY. Emigrated to USA, 1938, naturalised 1953. Teaching posts include: Brooklyn Coll., 1963–68; Maryland Art Inst., Baltimore, 1984; NY Studio Sch.; Yale Univ. *Solo exhibitions* include: (paintings) Bertha Schaefer Gall., NY, 1945; Norlyst Gall., NY, 1947; Peridot Gall., NY, 1949, 1950, 1953; Allan Frumkin Gall., Chicago, 1953; Stable Gall., NY, 1964; Xavier Fourcade Gall., NY, 1978–80; (retrospective) MOMA, NY, 1982; Robert Miller Gall., NY, 1982, 1984, 1986, 1987–89, 1991; Serpentine Gall., London, 1985, 1998; Mus. Overholland, Amsterdam, 1988; (retrospective) Frankfurter Kunstverein, Frankfurt, 1989 (toured Europe, 1990); Galerie Lelong, Zurich, 1991; Hauser & Wirth, Zurich, 1996, 2000, 2002, 2008, London, 2005, 2007; (retrospective) Tate Modern, London, 2000, 2007 (travelled to Centre Georges Pompidou, Paris, Guggenheim Mus., NY, Mus. of Contemp. Art, LA and Hirshhorn Mus. and Sculpture Gdn (Washington); Rockefeller Center, NY, 2001; Guggenheim Mus., Bilbao, 2001; *group shows* include: Musée Rodin, Paris, 1965; Venice Biennale, 1993, 2007; *works in permanent collections* including: MOMA, Whitney Mus., Metropolitan Mus., New Mus. of Contemp. Art, Guggenheim Mus., NY; Musée Nat. d'Art Moderne,

Paris; Australian Nat. Gall., Canberra; MOMA, Vienna; Tate Modern, London; Uffizi Gall., Florence; *works* include: Personages, 1940s, The Blind Leading the Blind, 1947–49; Fillette, 1968; The Destruction of the Father, 1974; Cumul I, 1969; Cells, 1989–93; spider, Maman, 1999. Fellow, Amer. Acad. Arts and Scis, 1981. Gold Medal of Honor, Nat. Arts Club, NY, 1987; Grand Prix Nat. de Sculpture, Min. of Culture, France, 1991; Praemium Imperiale, Japan, 1999; Wolf Prize in Arts, Wolf Foundn, Israel, 2002. Officier, Order of Arts and Letters (France), 1984. *Address: c/o* Hauser & Wirth London, 196A Piccadilly, W1J 9DY. *Died 31 May 2010.*

BOURNE, Sir Clive (John), Kt 2004; Founder, Seabourne Shipping, 1962; Life President, Seabourne Group plc, since 1999; *b* 27 Sept. 1942; *s* of late Maurice Bourne and of Lily Bourne; *m* 1967, Joy Hilary Ingram; four *d*. *Educ:* William McEntee Sch., Walthamstow. Founded Prostate Cancer Charitable Trust, 1991, subseq. Prostate Cancer Res. Foundn, Founder Trustee, Mus. in Docklands, 1996–; Trustee, Transaid, 2000–. Sponsor, Mossbourne Community Acad., Hackney, 2002. JP Newham, 1990 (Chm., 1995). *Recreations:* bad tennis, UK's largest collection of inkwells, music. *Address:* 9 Lanark Square, Glengall Bridge, E14 9RE. *T:* (020) 7536 6360, *Fax:* (020) 7987 9889; *e mail:* cjbourneam@ supanet.com. *Died 10 Jan. 2007.*

BOVEY, Dr Leonard; Editor, Materials & Design, 1985–2000; Head of Technological Requirements Branch, Department of Industry, 1977–84; *b* 9 May 1924; *s* of late Alfred and Gladys Bovey; *m* 1944, Constance Hudson (*d* 1987); one *s* one *d*. *Educ:* Hele's Sch., Exeter; Emmanuel Coll., Cambridge (BA, PhD). FInstP; CPhys. Dunlop Rubber, 1943–46; Post-doctoral Fellow, Nat. Res. Council, Ottawa, 1950–52; AERE Harwell, 1952–65; Head W Mids Regional Office, Birmingham, Min. of Technology, 1966–70; Regional Dir, Yorks and Humberside, DTI, 1970–73; Counsellor (Scientific and Technological Affairs), High Commn, Ottawa, 1974–77. Foreign correspondent, Soc. for Advancement of Materials and Processes Engineering (USA) Jl, 1987–. Mem., London Diplomatic Sci, Club. *Publications:* Spectroscopy in the Metallurgical Industry, 1963; papers on spectroscopy in Jl Optical Soc. Amer., Spectrochimica Acta, Jl Phys. Soc. London. *Recreations:* repairing neglected household equipment, work, reading (particularly crime novels), walking, theatre, music. *Address:* 32 Radnor Walk, Chelsea, SW3 4BN. *T:* (020) 7352 4142. *Club:* Civil Service. *Died 4 Feb. 2009.*

BOWATER, Sir J(ohn) Vansittart, 4th Bt *cr* 1914; *b* 6 April 1918; *s* of Captain Victor Spencer Bowater (*d* 1967) (3rd *s* of 1st Bt) and Hilda Mary (*d* 1918), *d* of W. Henry Potter; *S* uncle, Sir Thomas Dudley Blennerhassett Bowater, 3rd Bt, 1972; *m* 1943, Joan Kathleen, (*d* 1982), *d* of late Wilfrid Scullard; one *s* one *d*. *Educ:* Branksome School, Godalming, Surrey. Served Royal Artillery, 1939–46. *Heir: s* Michael Patrick Bowater [*b* 18 July 1949; *m* 1968, Alison, *d* of Edward Wall; four *d*]. *Address:* 214 Runnymede Avenue, Bournemouth, Dorset BH11 9SP. *T:* (01202) 571782. *Died 24 April 2008.*

BOWEN, Maj.-Gen. Esmond John, CB 1982; Director, Army Dental Service, 1978–82; *b* 6 Dec. 1922; *s* of Major Leslie Arthur George Bowen, MC, and Edna Grace Bowen; *m* 1948, Elsie (*née* Midgley) (*d* 1996); two *s* two *d* (and one *d* decd). *Educ:* Clayesmore Sch.; Univ. of Birmingham. LDS Birmingham 1946. Commd Lieut, RADC, 1947; Captain 1948; Major 1955; Lt-Col 1962; Chief Instructor, Depot and Training Establishment RADC, 1966–69: CO Nos 2 and 3 Dental Groups, 1969–74; Asst Dir, Army Dental Service, 1974–76; Comdt, HQ and Training Centre, RADC, 1976–77; Brig. 1977; Dep. Dir, Dental Service, HQ BAOR, 1977–78. QHDS, 1977–82. Col Comdt, RADC, 1982–87. OStJ 1975. *Recreation:* muzzle loading shooting. *Address:* 72 Winchester Road, Andover, Hants SP10 2ER. *T:* (01264) 323252. *Club:* Lansdowne. *Died 7 April 2006.*

BOWETT, Sir Derek (William), Kt 1998; CBE 1983; QC 1978; LLD; FBA 1983; Whewell Professor of International Law, Cambridge University, 1981–91; Professorial Fellow of Queens' College, Cambridge, 1982–91 (Hon. Fellow, 1991); *b* 20 April 1927; *s* of Arnold William Bowett and Marion Wood; *m* 1953, Betty Northall; two *s* one *d*. *Educ*: William Hulme's Sch., Manchester; Downing Coll., Cambridge. MA, LLB, LLD (Cantab), PhD (Manchester). Called to the Bar, Middle Temple, 1953, Hon. Bencher, 1975. Lectr, Law Faculty, Manchester Univ. 1951–59; Legal Officer, United Nations, New York, 1957–59; Cambridge University: Lectr, Law Faculty, 1960–76, Reader, 1976–81; Fellow of Queens' Coll., 1960–69, President 1969–82. Gen. Counsel, UNRWA, Beirut, 1966–68. Member: Royal Commn on Environmental Pollution, 1973–77; Internat. Law Commn, 1991–96. Commander, Order of Dannebrog (Denmark), 1993; Grand Cross, Civil Order, Jose Cecilio del Valle (Honduras), 1993; White Cross (Slovakia), 2005. *Publications*: Self-defence in International Law, 1958; Law of International Institutions, 1964; United Nations Forces, 1964; Law of the Sea, 1967; Search for Peace, 1972; Legal Régime of Islands in International Law, 1978; The International Court of Justice: process, practice and procedure, 1997. *Recreation*: music. *Address*: 228 Hills Road, Cambridge CB2 2QE. *T*: (01223) 210688.   *Died 23 May 2009.*

BOWIE, Prof. Malcolm McNaughtan, DPhil; FBA 1993; FRSL; Master, Christ's College, Cambridge, 2002–06; Hon. Professor of French and Comparative Literature, University of Cambridge, since 2003; *b* 5 May 1943; *s* of George Alexander Bowie and Beatrice Georgina Betty (*née* Strowger); *m* 1979, Alison Mary Finch; one *s* one *d*. *Educ*: Woodbridge Sch.; Univ. of Edinburgh (MA 1965); Univ. of Sussex (DPhil 1970); MA Cantab 1969; MA Oxon 1992. FRSL 1999. Asst Lectr in French, UEA, 1967–69; University of Cambridge: Asst Lectr, 1969–72; Lectr, 1972–76; Fellow and Dir of Studies, Clare Coll., 1969–76, Tutor, 1971–76; University of London: Prof. of French Lang. and Lit., 1976–92; Hd, Dept of French, QMC, 1976–89; Founding Dir, Inst. of Romance Studies, 1989–92 (Hon. Sen. Res. Fellow, 1993); Marshal Foch Prof. of French Lit. and Fellow, All Souls Coll., 1992–2002, Dir, Eur. Humanities Res. Centre, 1998–2002, Oxford Univ. Vis. Prof., Univ. of California, Berkeley, 1983; Vis. Dist. Prof., Grad. Center, CUNY, 1989; Vis. Fellow, 1991, Associate Fellow, 2003–, Centre for Res. in Philosophy and Lit., Univ. of Warwick. Lectures: Andrew W. Mellon, Bucknell Univ., 1990; Cassal, London Univ., 1999. President: Assoc. of Univ. Profs of French, 1982–84; Soc. for French Studies, 1994–96; British Comparative Lit. Assoc., 1998–2004. Member: Exec. Cttee, Univs Council for Modern Langs, 1994–96; Council, British Academy, 1999–2002; Chm., Adv. Council, Inst. of Germanic and Romance Studies, Univ. of London, 2004–. Mem., Academia Europaea, 1989; Hon. Mem., Modern Language Assoc. of America, 2003. Gen. Editor, French Studies, 1980–87; Founding Gen. Editor, Cambridge Studies in French, 1980–95; Editor, Jl Inst. Romance Studies, 1992. Hon. DLit QMW, 1997. Truman Capote Award for Literary Criticism, 2001. Chevalier, 1987, Officier, 1996, de l'Ordre des Palmes Académiques (France). *Publications*: Henri Michaux: a study of his literary works, 1973; Mallarmé and the Art of Being Difficult, 1978; Freud, Proust and Lacan: theory as fiction, 1987; Lacan, 1991; Psychoanalysis and the Future of Theory, 1993; Proust Among the Stars, 1998; (jtly) A Short History of French Literature, 2003; contribs to learned jls and collective works. *Address*: c/o Master's Lodge, Christ's College, Cambridge CB2 3BU.   *Died 28 Jan. 2007.*

BOWIE, Stanley Hay Umphray, DSc; FRS 1975; FREng; FRSE, FIMMM, FMSA; Consultant Geologist; Assistant Director, Chief Geochemist, Institute of Geological Sciences, 1968–77; *b* 24 March 1917; *s* of Dr James Cameron and Mary Bowie; *m* 1948, Helen Elizabeth, *d* of Dr Roy Woodhouse and Florence

Elizabeth Pocock; two *s*. *Educ*: Grammar Sch. and Univ. of Aberdeen (BSc, DSc). Meteorological Office, 1942; commissioned RAF, 1943; HM Geological Survey of Gt Britain: Geologist, Sen. Geologist and Principal Geologist, 1946–55; Chief Geologist, Atomic Energy Div., 1955–67; Chief Consultant Geologist to UKAEA, 1955–77. Visiting Prof. of Applied Geology, Univ. of Strathclyde, 1968–85; Vis. Prof., Imperial Coll., London, 1985–92. Principal Investigator, Apollo 11 and 12 lunar samples, 1969–71; Chairman: Internat. Mineralogical Assoc., Commn on Ore Microscopy, 1970–78; Royal Soc. Sectl Cttee 5, 1977–79; Royal Soc. Working Party on Envtl Geochem. and Health, 1979–81; DoE Res. Adv. Gp, Radioactive Waste Management, 1984–85; Mem., Radioactive Waste Management Adv. Cttee. 1978–82. Vice-Pres., Shetland Sheep Soc. (formerly Gp), 1992– (Chm., 1989–91). Vice-Pres., Geological Soc., 1972–74; Mem. Council, Mineralogical Soc., 1954–57, 1962–65 (Chairman: Applied Mineralogy Gp, 1969–72; Geochem. Gp, 1972–75). FGS 1959; FMSA 1963; FRSE 1970; FIMM 1972 (Pres. 1976–77), Hon. FIMMM (Hon. FIMM 1987); FREng (FEng 1976). Silver Medal, RSA, 1959; Team Mem., Queen's Award for Technol Achievement, 1990 (for develt of Inductively Coupled Plasma Mass Spectrometer). New mineral (rhodium-iridium-platinum sulphide) named bowieite in honour of res. on identification of opaque minerals, 1984. *Publications*: (ed jtly) Uranium Prospecting Handbook, 1972; (ed jtly) Mineral Deposits of Europe, Vol. 1: North-West Europe, 1978; (with P. R. Simpson) The Bowie-Simpson System for the Microscopic Determination of Ore Minerals, 1980; (ed jtly) Environmental Geochemistry and Health, 1985; (with C. Bowie) Radon and Health—The Facts, 1991; Shetland's Native Farm Animals, 2005; contributions to: Nuclear Geology, 1954; Physical Methods in Determinative Mineralogy, 1967, 2nd edn 1977; Uranium Exploration Geology, 1970; Proceedings of the Apollo Lunar Science Conference, 1970; Proceedings of the Second Lunar Science Conference, 1971; Uranium Exploration Methods, 1973; Recognition and Evaluation of Uraniferous Areas, 1977; Theoretical and Practical Aspects of Uranium Geology, 1979; Nuclear Power Technology, 1983; Applied Environmental Geochemistry, 1983; numerous papers in scientific and technical jls on uranium geology and economics, mineralogy, geophysics and geochemistry, and articles on rare breeds of domesticated animals. *Recreations*: preservation of rare breeds, gardening, photography. *Address*: Tanyard Farm, Clapton, Crewkerne, Somerset TA18 8PS. *T*: (01460) 72093.   *Died 3 Sept. 2008.*

BOWLER, Geoffrey, FCIS; Chief General Manager, Sun Alliance & London Insurance Group, 1977–87; *b* 11 July 1924; *s* of James Henry Bowler and Hilda May Bowler. *Educ*: Sloane Sch., Chelsea. FCIS 1952. Dir, British Aviation Insurance Co., 1976–87 (Chm., 1977–83). Dep. Chm., British Insurance Assoc., 1977, Chm. 1979–80. *Address*: 13 Green Lane, Purley, Surrey CR8 3PP. *T*: (020) 8660 0756.   *Died 9 Oct. 2009.*

BOWLER, Ian John, CBE 1971 (OBE 1957); Chairman, International Management & Engineering Group Ltd, 1973 (Managing Director, 1964–68); *b* 1920; *s* of Major John Arthur Bowler; *m* 1963, Hamideh, *d* of Prince Yadollah Azodi, GCMG; two *d*, and one step *s* one step *d*. *Educ*: King's Sch., Worcester; privately; Oxford Univ. Director of Constructors, John Brown, 1961–64; Pres., Iranian Management & Engrg Gp, 1965. Director: IMEG (Offshore) Ltd, 1974–; MMC Gas, Kuala Lumpur. Mem., RNLI, 1983–. Sec., Azerbaijan Foundn, 1992. MInstPet. *Publications*: Predator Birds of Iran, 1973. *Recreations*: ornithology, yachting. *Clubs*: Royal Thames Yacht, Ocean Cruising; S.R.R. (La Rochelle, France).   *Died 10 May 2009.*

BOWRING, Air Vice-Marshal John Ivan Roy, CB 1977; CBE 1971; CEng, FRAeS; FCMI; management consultant, aircraft maintenance; Head of Technical Training and Maintenance, British Aerospace (formerly

British Aircraft Corporation), Riyadh, Saudi Arabia, 1978–88; *b* 28 March 1923; *s* of Hugh Passmore Bowring and Ethel Grace Bowring; *m* 1945, Irene Mary Rance; two *d*. *Educ*: Great Yarmouth Grammar Sch., Norfolk; Aircraft Apprentice, RAF Halton-Cosford, 1938–40; Leicester Tech. Coll. Commissioned, RAF, 1944; NW Europe, 1944–47; RAF, Horsham St Faith's, Engrg duties, 1947–48; RAF South Cerney, Pilot trng, 1949; Engr Officer: RAF Finningly, 1950–51; RAF Kai-Tak, 1951–53; Staff Officer, AHQ Hong Kong, ADC to Governor, Hong Kong, 1953–54; Sen. Engr Officer, RAF Coltishall, 1954–56; exchange duties with US Air Force, Research and Develt, Wright Patterson Air Force Base, Ohio, 1956–60; RAF Staff Coll., Bracknell, 1960; Air Min. Opl Requirements, 1961–64; OC Engrg Wing, RAF St Mawgan, 1964–67; Head of F111 Procurement Team, USA, 1967–68; OC RAF Aldergrove, NI, 1968–70; RCDS, 1971; Dir of Engrg Policy, MoD, 1972–73; AO Engrg, RAF Germany, 1973–74; SASO, RAF Support Comd, 1974–77; AO Maintenance, 1977. *Recreations*: sailing, golf. *Club*: Royal Air Force.
Died 2 Oct. 2010.

BOWSER of Argaty and the King's Lundies, David Stewart; a Forestry Commissioner, 1974–82; *b* 11 March 1926; *s* of late David Charles Bowser, CBE and Maysie Murray Bowser (*née* Henderson); *m* 1951, Judith Crabbe; one *s* four *d*. *Educ*: Harrow; Trinity Coll., Cambridge (BA Agric). Captain, Scots Guards, 1944–47. Member: Nat. Bd of Timber Growers Scotland Ltd (formerly Scottish Woodland Owners' Assoc.), 1960–82 (Chm. 1972–74); Regional Adv. Cttee, West Scotland Conservancy, Forestry Commn, 1964–74 (Chm. 1970–74). Chm., Scottish Council, British Deer Soc., 1989–94; Mem., Blackface Sheep Breeders' Assoc. (Vice-Pres., 1981–83; Pres., 1983–84); Pres., Highland Cattle Soc., 1970–72. Trustee, Scottish Forestry Trust, 1983–89. Mem. Perth CC, 1954–61. *Recreation*: fishing. *Address*: Auchlyne, Killin, Perthshire FK21 8RG. *Died 8 March 2010.*

BOYD, Dennis Galt, CBE 1988; Chief Conciliation Officer, Advisory, Conciliation and Arbitration Service, 1980–92; *b* 3 Feb. 1931; *s* of late Thomas Ayre Boyd and Minnie (*née* Galt); *m* 1953, Pamela Mary McLean; one *s* one *d*. *Educ*: South Shields High School for Boys. National Service, 1949–51; Executive Officer, Civil Service: Min. of Supply/Min. of Defence, 1951–66; Board of Trade, 1966–69; Personnel Officer, Forestry Commission, 1969–75; Director of Corporate Services Health and Safety Executive, Dept of Employment, 1975–79; Director of Conciliation (ACAS), 1979–80. Hon. FIPM 1985. *Recreation*: compulsory gardening. *Address*: Dunelm, Silchester Road, Little London, Tadley RG26 5EW. *Died 21 Feb. 2009.*

BOYD, Ian Robertson; HM Stipendiary Magistrate, West Yorkshire, 1982–89; a Recorder of the Crown Court, 1983–88; *b* 18 Oct. 1922; *s* of Arthur Robertson Boyd, Edinburgh, and Florence May Boyd (*née* Kinghorn), Leeds; *m* 1952, Joyce Mary Boyd (*née* Crabtree); one *s* one *d*. *Educ*: Roundhay Sch.; Leeds Univ. (LLB (Hons)). Served Army, 1942–47: Captain Green Howards; Royal Lincolnshire Regt in India, Burma, Malaya, Dutch East Indies. Leeds Univ., 1947; called to Bar, Middle Temple, 1952; practised North Eastern Circuit, 1952–72; HM Stipendiary Magistrate, sitting at Hull, 1972–82. Sometime Asst/Dep. Recorder of Doncaster, Newcastle, Hull and York. *Recreation*: gardener manqué. *Died 21 Jan. 2007.*

BOYD, James Edward, CA; Director and Financial Adviser, Denholm group of companies, 1968–96; *b* 14 Sept. 1928; *s* of Robert Edward Boyd and Elizabeth Reid Sinclair; *m* 1956, Judy Ann Christey Scott; two *s* two *d*. *Educ*: Kelvinside Academy; The Leys Sch., Cambridge. CA Scot. (dist.) 1951. Director: Lithgows (Hldgs), 1962–87; Ayrshire Metal Products plc, 1965–93 (Chm., 1991–93); Invergordon Distillers (Holdings) plc, 1966–88; GB Papers plc, 1977–87; Jebsens Drilling plc, 1978–85; Scottish Widows' Fund & Life Assurance Soc., 1981–93 (Dep. Chm., 1988–93); Shanks & McEwan

Gp Ltd, 1983–94; Scottish Exhibn Centre Ltd, 1983–89; British Linen Bank Ltd, 1983–94 (Gov., 1986–94); Bank of Scotland, 1984–94; Yarrow PLC, 1984–86 (Chm., 1985–86); Bank of Wales, 1986–88; Save and Prosper Gp Ltd, 1987–89; James River UK Hldgs Ltd, 1987–90; Chairman: London & Gartmore Investment Trust plc, 1978–91; English & Caledonian Investment plc, 1981–91. Partner, McClelland Ker & Co. CA (subseq. McClelland Moores & Co.), 1953–61; Finance Director: Lithgows Ltd, 1962–69; Scott Lithgow Ltd, 1970–78; Chm., Fairfield Shipbuilding & Engrg Co. Ltd, 1964–65; Man. Dir, Invergordon Distillers (Holdings) Ltd, 1966–67; Director: Nairn & Williamson (Holdings) Ltd, 1968–75; Carlton Industries plc, 1978–84. Dep. Chm., BAA plc (formerly British Airports Authority), 1985–94; Member: CAA (part-time), 1984–85; Clyde Port Authority, 1974–80; Working Party on Scope and Aims of Financial Accounts (the Corporate Report), 1971–75; Exec. Cttee, Accountants Jt Disciplinary Scheme, 1979–81; Mem. Council, Inst. of Chartered Accountants of Scotland, 1977–83 (Vice-Pres., 1980–82, Pres., 1982–83). Mem. Council, Glenalmond Coll., 1983–92. *Recreations*: tennis, golf, gardening, painting. *Address*: Dunard, Station Road, Rhu, Dunbartonshire, Scotland G84 8LW. *T*: (01436) 820441. *Died 25 March 2008.*

BOYER, John Leslie, OBE 1982; Chief Executive, Zoological Society of London, 1984–88; *b* 13 Nov. 1926; *s* of Albert and Gladys Boyer; *m* 1953, Joyce Enid Thomasson; one *s* two *d*. *Educ*: Nantwich; Acton Grammar Sch. Served Army, 1944–48: commnd into South Lancashire Regt, 1946, and attached to Baluch Regt, then Indian Army. Joined Hongkong and Shanghai Banking Corp., 1948: served Hong Kong, Burma, Japan, India, Malaysia, Singapore; General Manager, Hong Kong, 1973; Director, March 1977; Dep. Chm., Sept. 1977–81; Chm., Antony Gibbs Hldgs Ltd, 1981–83. *Recreations*: walking, swimming, bridge, reading. *Address*: 24 Fairacres, Roehampton Lane, SW15 5LX. *T*: (020) 8878 7345. *Clubs*: Oriental; Shek O (Hong Kong); Tanglin (Singapore). *Died 16 June 2006.*

BOYES, Sir Brian Gerald B.; *see* Barratt-Boyes.

BOYES, Roland; *b* 12 Feb. 1937; *m* 1962, Patricia James; two *s*. *Educ*: London Univ. (BSc Econ 1968); Bradford Univ. (MSc). Teacher, 1961–74; Asst Dir, Social Services Dept, Durham CC, 1975–79. Member (Lab) Durham, European Parliament, 1979–84. MP (Lab) Houghton and Washington, 1983–97; an opposition frontbench spokesman on: Parly environment team, 1985–88; Parly defence team, 1988–92; Member, Select Committee: on Envmt, 1992–94; on Nat. Heritage, 1994–97; Mem., Speaker's Panel of Chairmen, 1994–97. Founder Chm., All Party Photography Gp, 1987–97. Mem., GMB. Chm., Tribune Gp, 1985–86. Dir, Hartlepool United AFC, 1987–. Hon. degree, Sunderland, 1997. *Publications*: People in Parliament, 1990. *Address*: 12 Spire Hollin, Peterlee, Co. Durham SR8 1DA. *T*: (0191) 586 3917. *Died 16 June 2006.*

BOYLE, Leonard Butler, CBE 1977; Director and General Manager, Principality Building Society, Cardiff, 1956–78; *b* 13 Jan. 1913; *s* of Harold and Edith Boyle; *m* 1938, Alice Baldwin Yarborough (*d* 1989); two *s*. *Educ*: Roundhay Sch., Leeds. FCIB. Chief of Investment Dept, Leeds Permanent Building Soc., 1937; Asst Man., Isle of Thanet Bldg Soc., 1949; Jt Asst Gen. Man., Hastings and Thanet Bldg Soc., 1951, Sec. 1954. Building Societies Association: Mem. Council, 1956–78 (Chm. Gen. Purposes Cttee, 1958–60; Chm. Develt Cttee, 1967–71); Chm. of Council, 1973–75 (Dep. Chm. 1971–73; Vice-Pres., 1978); Vice-Pres., CIB (formerly CBSI), 1982–. *Recreations*: gardening, walking, golf. *Address*: Northwick Cottage, Marlpit Lane, Seaton, Devon EX12 2HH. *T*: (01297) 22194. *Died 3 Sept. 2006.*

BOYNE, (Donald Arthur) Colin (Aydon), CBE 1977; Director, 1974–85, Consultant, 1984–86, The Architectural Press; *b* 15 Feb. 1921; 2nd *s* of late Lytton Leonard Boyne and Millicent (*née* Nisbet); *m* 1947, Rosemary Pater; two *s* one *d*. *Educ:* Tonbridge Sch.; Architectural Assoc. School of Architecture, 1943–47. Indian Army, 8/13 FF Rifles, 1940–43. Editor, Architects' Jl, 1953–70; Chm., Editorial Bd, Architectural Review and Architects' Jl, 1971–84. Hon. FRIBA 1969. *Address:* Pound House, Southover, Wells, Somerset BA5 1UH. *T:* (01749) 674704. *Died 28 Sept. 2006.*

BOYNTON, Sir John (Keyworth), Kt 1979; MC 1944; LLB; MRTPI; DL; Chief Executive, Cheshire County Council, 1974–79; Solicitor; *b* 14 Feb. 1918; *s* of late Ernest Boynton, Hull; *m* 1st, 1947, Gabrielle Stanglmaier, Munich (*d* 1978); two *d*; 2nd, 1979, Edith Laane, The Hague. *Educ:* Dulwich Coll. Served War, 15th Scottish Reconnaissance Regt, 1940–46 (despatches, MC). Dep. Clerk, Berks CC, 1951–64; Clerk, Cheshire CC, 1964–74. Member: Planning Law Cttee of Law Soc., 1964–88; Economic Planning Council for NW, 1965; Exec. Council of Royal Inst. of Public Admin., 1970; Council of Industrial Soc., 1974–93; Council, PSI, 1978–83. Pres., RTPI, 1976. Election Commissioner, Southern Rhodesia, 1979–80. DL Cheshire, 1975. *Publications:* Compulsory Purchase and Compensation, 1964, 7th edn 1994; Job at the Top, 1986. *Recreation:* golf. *Address:* 40 High Sheldon, Sheldon Avenue, N6 4NJ. *T:* (020) 8348 5234. *Club:* Army and Navy. *Died 15 Jan. 2007.*

BOYSE, Prof. Edward Arthur, MD; FRS 1977; Distinguished Professor, University of Arizona, Tucson, 1989–94, then Emeritus Professor; Member, Sloan-Kettering Institute for Cancer Research, New York, 1967–89; Professor of Biology, Cornell University, 1969–89; *b* 11 Aug. 1923; *s* of late Arthur Boyse, FRCO, and Dorothy Vera Boyse (*née* Mellersh); *m* 1951, Jeanette (*née* Grimwood) (marr. diss. 1987); one *s* one *d* (and one *s* decd); *m* 1987, Judith Bard. *Educ:* St Bartholomew's Hosp. Med. Sch., Univ. of London (MB BS 1952; MD 1957). Aircrew, RAF, 1941–46, commnd 1943. Various hospital appts, 1952–57; research at Guy's Hosp., 1957–60; research appts at NY Univ. and Sloan-Kettering Inst., 1960–89. Amer. Cancer Soc. Res. Prof., 1977. Member: Amer. Acad. of Arts and Scis, 1977; Nat. Acad. of Scis, USA, 1979. Cancer Research Institute Award in Tumor Immunology, 1975; Isaac Adler Award, Rockefeller and Harvard Univs, 1976. *Publications:* papers relating genetics and immunology to development and cancer. *Address:* University of Arizona, 5340 N Post Trail, Tucson, AZ 85750, USA. *Died 14 July 2007.*

BRACEWELL, Hon. Dame Joyanne (Winifred), (Dame Joyanne Copeland), DBE 1990; a Judge of the High Court of Justice, Family Division, 1990–2006; *b* 5 July 1934; *d* of Jack and Lilian Bracewell; *m* 1963, Roy Copeland; one *s* one *d*. *Educ:* Manchester Univ. (LLB, LLM). Called to Bar, Gray's Inn, 1955; pupillage at the Bar, 1955–56; Mem., Northern Circuit, 1956–; a Recorder of the Crown Court, 1975–83; QC 1978; a Circuit Judge, 1983–90. Family Div. Liaison Judge for London, 1990–97. Chm., Children Act Adv. Cttee, 1993–97. Consulting Editor: Butterworth's Family Law Service, 1989–; Family Practice, 1993–. FRSA 1994. Hon. LLD Manchester, 1991. *Recreations:* antiques, cooking, reading, walking, wildlife conservation. *Died 9 Jan. 2007.*

BRADEN, Hugh Reginald, CMG 1980; DL; Mayor of Worthing, 1991–92; *b* 30 Jan. 1923; *s* of late Reginald Henry Braden and Mabel Braden (*née* Selby); *m* 1946, Phyllis Grace Barnes; one *d*. *Educ:* Worthing High School for Boys; Brighton College of Technology. Joined War Office, 1939; served War, Royal Navy, 1942–45; Far East Land Forces, 1946–50; British Army of the Rhine, 1953–56; War Office and Min. of Defence, 1956–66; jssc 1967; British Embassy, Washington, 1968–70; Min. of Defence, 1971–80 (Asst Under Sec. of State, 1978–80). Dir, A. B. Jay, 1981–90. Borough Councillor, Worthing,

1983–95; Chm., Worthing Cons. Assoc., 1992–95. DL W Sussex, 1993. *Address:* Field House, Honeysuckle Lane, High Salvington, Worthing, West Sussex BN13 3BT. *T:* (01903) 260203. *Died 22 April 2009.*

BRADLEY, Prof. Daniel Joseph, PhD; FRS 1976; FInstP; Professor of Optical Electronics, Trinity College Dublin, 1980–83, then Emeritus; Emeritus Professor of Optics, London University, 1980; *b* 18 Jan. 1928; *s* of late John Columba Bradley and Margaret Mary Bradley; *m* 1958, Winefride Marie Therese O'Connor; four *s* one *d*. *Educ:* St Columb's Coll., Derry; St Mary's Trng Coll., Belfast; Birkbeck and Royal Holloway Colls, London (BSc Maths, BSc Physics, PhD). Primary Sch. Teacher, Derry, 1947–53; Secondary Sch. Teacher, London area, 1953–57; Asst Lectr, Royal Holloway Coll., 1957–60; Lectr, Imperial Coll. of Science and Technol., 1960–64; Reader, Royal Holloway Coll., 1964–66; Prof. and Head of Dept of Pure and Applied Physics, QUB, 1966–73; Prof. of Optics, 1973–80, and Head of Physics Dept, 1976–80, Imperial Coll., London. Vis. Scientist, MIT, 1965; Consultant, Harvard Observatory, 1966. Lectures: Scott, Cambridge, 1977; Tolansky Meml, RSA, 1977. Chairman: Laser Facility Cttee, SRC, 1976–79; British Nat. Cttee for Physics, 1979–80; Quantum Electronics Commn, IUPAP, 1982–85; Member: Rutherford Lab. Estab. Cttee, SRC, 1977–79; Science Bd, SRC, 1977–80; Council, Royal Soc., 1979–80. Gov., Sch. of Cosmic Physics, DIAS, 1981–95. MRIA 1969; Fellow, Optical Soc. of America, 1975. Hon. DSc: NUU, 1983; QUB, 1986. Thomas Young Medal, Inst. of Physics, 1975; Royal Medal, Royal Soc., 1983; C. H. Townes Award, Optical Soc. of America, 1989; Cunningham Medal, RIA, 2001. *Publications:* papers on optics, lasers, spectroscopy, chronoscopy and astronomy in Proc. Roy. Soc., Phil. Mag., Phys. Rev., J. Opt. Soc. Amer., Proc. IEEE, Chem. Phys. Letts, Optics Communications. *Recreations:* television, walking, DIY. *Address:* Trinity College, Dublin 2, Ireland. *Died 7 Feb. 2010.*

BRADLEY, Michael John, CMG 1990; QC (Cayman Islands) 1983; Constitutional Adviser, Overseas Territories Department, Foreign and Commonwealth Office, 2001–09; Law Revision Commissioner for the Cayman Islands, 1994–2009; *b* 11 June 1933; *s* of late Joseph Bradley and Catherine Bradley (*née* Cleary); *m* 1965, Patricia Elizabeth Macauley, MBE; one *s*. *Educ:* St Malachy's Coll., Belfast; Queen's Univ., Belfast (LLB Hons). Solicitor, Law Soc. of NI, 1964; Attorney, Supreme Ct, Turks and Caicos Is, 1980; Barrister-at-law, Eastern Caribbean Supreme Ct, 1982. Solicitor, NI, 1964–67; State Counsel, Malawi, 1967–69; Volume Editor, Halsbury's Laws, 1970; Sen., later Chief, Parly Draftsman, Botswana, 1970–72; UN Legal Advr to Govt of Antigua, 1973–76; Reg. Legal Draftsman to Govts of E Caribbean, British Develt Div. in the Caribbean, FCO, 1976–82; Attorney General: British Virgin Is, 1977–78; Turks and Caicos Is, 1980; Montserrat, 1981; Cayman Is, 1982–87; Gov., Turks and Caicos Is, 1987–93. British Dependent Territories Law Reform and Law Revision Consultant, 1993. Pres., Cayman Is Gaelic FC, 2000–07; Chm., Cayman Is Celtic Supporters Club, 2004–. *Recreations:* reading, philately, travel, good wine. *Address:* 11 The Lays, Goose Street, Beckington, Somerset BA11 6RS. *T: and Fax:* (01373) 831059; PO Box 2394, George Town, Grand Cayman KY1–1105, Cayman Islands, West Indies. *T: and Fax:* 9455925; *e-mail:* m.bradley@mbzonline.net. *Clubs:* Civil Service, Royal Over-Seas League. *Died 2 March 2010.*

BRADLEY, Maj.-Gen. Peter Edward Moore, CB 1968; CBE 1964 (OBE 1955); DSO 1946; Trustee, Vindolanda Trust, 1982–85 (Secretary, 1975–82); *b* 12 Dec. 1914; *s* of late Col Edward de Winton Herbert Bradley, CBE, DSO, MC, DL; *m* 1st, 1944, Daphne Renshaw (marr. diss.); two *s*; 2nd, 1956, Margaret, *d* of late Norman Wardhaugh of Haydon Bridge, Northumberland; one *s*. *Educ:* Marlborough; Royal Military Academy, Woolwich. 2nd Lieut, Royal Signals, 1934. Served War of 1939–45; India, Middle East, Italy and North West Europe (DSO 6th Airborne Div.). Lieut-Col 1954; Col 1957; Brig. 1962; Maj.-Gen. 1965; Signal Officer in Chief (Army), Ministry of Defence, 1965–67; Chief of Staff to C-in-C Allied Forces Northern Europe, Oslo, 1968–70. Dunlop Ltd, 1970–75. Col Comdt, Royal Signals, 1967–82, Master of Signals, 1970–82; Col Gurkha Signals, 1967–74. CEng, FIET (FIEE, 1966). *Address:* c/o RHQ Royal Signals, Blandford Camp, Blandford Forum DT11 8RH. *Died 2 June 2010.*

BRADLEY, William Ewart; Special Commissioner of Income Tax, 1950–75; *b* 5 Sept. 1910; *s* of W. E. Bradley, Durham City; *m* 1949, Mary Campbell Tyre; one *s* (and one *s* decd). *Educ:* Johnston Sch., Durham; LSE, London Univ. Inland Revenue, 1929–50. *Address:* Abbeyfield House, 3 Kinburn Terrace, St Andrews, Fife KY16 9DU. *Died 5 March 2008.*

BRADSHAW, Prof. Anthony David, PhD; FRS 1982; Holbrook Gaskell Professor of Botany, University of Liverpool, 1968–88, then Emeritus; *b* 17 Jan. 1926; *m* Betty Margaret Bradshaw; three *d*. *Educ:* St Paul's Sch., Hammersmith; Jesus Coll., Cambridge (BA 1947; MA 1951); PhD Wales 1959. FIBiol 1971. Lectr, 1952–63, Sen. Lectr, 1963–64, Reader in Agricl Botany, 1964–68, UCNW, Bangor. Member: Nature Conservancy Council, 1969–78; Natural Environment Res. Council, 1969–74; Bd of Management, Sports Turf Res. Inst., 1976– (Vice Pres., 1982–). President: British Ecological Soc., 1981–83; Inst. Ecology and Envmtl Management, 1991–94; Merseyside Envmtl Trust, 1998–. Trustee, Nat. Museums and Galls on Merseyside, 1986–96 (Vice Chm., 1995–96). Mem. Bd, Groundwork Trust St Helens, 1981–2006. Hon. Fellow, Indian Nat. Acad. Sci., 1990. FLS 1982; FIEEM 1994 (MIEEM 1991). Hon. DSc: Lancaster, 1998; Hong Kong Baptist Univ., 2000. *Publications:* (ed jtly) Teaching Genetics, 1963; (with M. J. Chadwick) The Restoration of Land, 1980; (with others) Quarry Reclamation, 1982; (with others) Mine Wastes Reclamation, 1982; (with R. A. Dutton) Land Reclamation in Cities, 1982; (with Alison Burt) Transforming our Waste Land: the way forward, 1986; (ed jtly) Ecology and Design in Landscape, 1986; (ed jtly) The Treatment and Handling of Wastes, 1992; (with B. Hunt and T. J. Walmsley) Trees in the Urban Landscape, 1995; contribs to symposia and learned jls. *Recreations:* sailing, gardening, appreciating land. *Address:* 58 Knowsley Road, Liverpool L19 0PG. *Died 21 Aug. 2008.*

BRADSHAW, Sir Kenneth (Anthony), KCB 1986 (CB 1982); Clerk of the House of Commons, 1983–87; *b* 1 Sept. 1922; *s* of late Herbert and Gladys Bradshaw. *Educ:* Ampleforth Coll.; St Catharine's Coll., Cambridge (1st Cl. Hons History); MA 1947. War Service, 1942–45; served with Royal Ulster Rifles (2nd Bn), NW Europe. Temp. Asst Principal, Min. of Supply, Oct.-Dec. 1946; a Clerk in the House of Commons, 1947–87; seconded as Clerk of the Saskatchewan Legislature, 1966 session; Clerk of Overseas Office, 1972–76. Pres., Assoc. of Secs Gen. of Parlts, IPU, 1986–87 (Jt Sec., 1955–71; Vice-Pres., 1984–86). Administrator, 1988–97, Mem. Adv. Bd, 1997–2001, Compton Verney Opera Project. *Publications:* (with David Pring) Parliament and Congress, 1972, new edn 1982. *Died 31 Oct. 2007.*

BRAIN, Albert Edward Arnold; Regional Director (East Midlands), Department of the Environment, and Chairman of Regional Economic Planning Board, 1972–77; *b* 31 Dec. 1917; *s* of Walter Henry and Henrietta Mabel Brain; *m* 1947, Patricia Grace Gallop; two *s* one *d*. *Educ:* Rendcomb Coll., Cirencester; Loughborough College. BSc (Eng) London, external; DLC hons Loughborough; CEng, MICE, MIMunE. Royal Engineers, 1940–46; Bristol City Corp., 1946–48; Min. of Transport: Asst Engr, London, 1948–54; Civil Engr, Wales, 1954–63; Sen. Engr, HQ, 1963–67; Asst Chief Engr, HQ, 1967–69; Divl Road Engr, W Mids, then Regional Controller (Roads and Transportation), 1969–72. Pres., Old Rendcombian Soc., 1986–91.

Recreation: gardening. *Address:* Withyholt Lodge, Moorend Road, Charlton Kings, Cheltenham GL53 9BW. *T:* (01242) 576264. *Died 31 Dec. 2008.*

BRAITHWAITE, (Arthur) Bevan (Midgley), OBE 1993; FREng; Chief Executive, TWI, 1988–2004; *b* 27 July 1939; *s* of Frederick Arthur Bevan Braithwaite and Magnhild Katrina Braithwaite (*née* Dahl); *m* 1st, 1961, Rosemary Kerry Conrad Cooke (marr. diss. 2007); one *s* two *d*; 2nd, 2007, Vanda Jane Galer. *Educ:* Leighton Park Sch.; Jesus Coll., Cambridge (MA). FREng 1999. Joined British Welding Res. Assoc., subseq. The Welding Inst., then TWI, 1961; Dir of Develt, 1966–84; Man. Dir, 1984–88. Mem., Eastern Reg. IDB, 1994–98; Dir, Granta Park, 1997–2004. Mem, EPSRC, 1996–2001 (Chm., User Panel, 1996–2000). Pres., Internat. Inst. Welding, 1999–2002. Chairman: Bressingham Steam Mus., 2004–; Cambridge Mus. of Technology, 2004–07. *Publications:* contribs to various jls; several patents. *Recreations:* steam engines, house restoration. *Address:* De Freville Manor, High Green, Great Shelford, Cambs CB22 5EG. *Died 25 April 2008.*

BRAITHWAITE, His Honour Bernard Richard; a Circuit Judge (formerly County Court Judge), 1971–88; *b* 20 Aug. 1917; *s* of Bernard Leigh Braithwaite and Emily Dora Ballard Braithwaite (*née* Thomas); unmarried. *Educ:* Clifton; Peterhouse, Cambridge (BA (Hons) Law). Served War: 7th Bn Somerset LI, 1939–43; Parachute Regt, 1943–46; Captain, Temp. Major. Called to Bar, Inner Temple, 1946. *Recreations:* hunting, sailing. *Club:* Boodle's. *Died 4 Aug. 2008.*

BRAITHWAITE, Bevan; *see* Braithwaite, A. B. M.

BRAMALL, Margaret Elaine, OBE 1969; Vice-President, National Council for One Parent Families (formerly National Council for the Unmarried Mother and her Child) (Director, 1962–79); *b* 1 Oct. 1916; *d* of Raymond Taylor, MA and Nettie Kate Taylor, BA; *m* 1939, E. A. Bramall, later Sir Ashley Bramall (marr. diss.; he *d* 1999); two *s*. *Educ:* St Paul's Girls' Sch., Hammersmith; Somerville Coll., Oxford (BA 1939, MA 1942); LSE (Social Science Hon. Cert. 1950); Inst. of Almoners (Cert. 1951). Lectr, Applied Social Studies Course, Surrey Univ., 1979–89. Member: Probation Case Cttee; Management Cttee, Humming Bird Housing Assoc. Chm., Richmond on Thames Action for Southern Africa. JP Richmond, 1965. *Publications:* (contrib.) One Parent Families, ed Dulan Barber, 1975; contrib. social work jls. *Recreations:* gardening, family. *Died 11 Aug. 2007.*

BRAND, Alexander George, MBE 1945; *b* 23 March 1918; *s* of David Wilson Brand and Janet Ramsay Brand (*née* Paton); *m* 1947, Helen Constance Campbell (*d* 2004); one *s* one *d*. *Educ:* Ayr Academy; Univ. of Glasgow. MA 1940, LLB 1948. Admitted Solicitor, 1948. Served in Royal Air Force, 1940–46 (Flt Lt). Legal Asst: Dumbarton CC, 1948; in Office of Solicitor to the Secretary of State for Scotland, 1949; Sen. Legal Asst, 1955; Asst Solicitor, 1964; Dep. Solicitor, 1972–79. Sec. of Scottish Law Commn, 1965–72. Traffic Comr and Dep. Licensing Authy, Scotland, 1979–88. *Recreations:* sport on TV, theatre, music. *Died 14 April 2008.*

BRANDES, Lawrence Henry, CB 1982; Under Secretary and Head of Office of Arts and Libraries, 1978–82; *b* 16 Dec. 1924; *m* 1950, Dorothea Stanyon; one *s* one *d*. *Educ:* Beltane Sch.; London Sch. of Economics. Min. of Health, 1950; Principal Private Sec. to Minister, 1959; Nat. Bd for Prices and Incomes, 1966; Dept of Employment and Productivity, 1969; Under-Sec., DHSS, 1970; HM Treasury, 1975. Director: Dance Umbrella, 1984–94; London Internat. Festival of Theatre, 1985–92. Member: Dulwich Picture Gall. Mgt Cttee, 1984–94 (acting Chm., 1992; Chm., 1994); Museums and Galls Commn (Chm., Conservation Cttee), 1988–92. Chm., Textile Conservation Centre, 1993–98. Mem.

Delegacy, Goldsmiths' Coll., 1983–88. Trustee, SS Great Britain, 1987–98. *Address:* 4 Hogarth Hill, NW11 6AX.
Died 19 Sept. 2009.

BRANDON, Michael John Hamilton, FNAEA; Senior Partner, since 1992, and Deputy Chairman, since 2005, Jackson-Stops & Staff; *b* Derby, 27 June 1947; *s* of Reginald Brandon and Doris Cecily Brandon; *m* 1975, Rosalind Mary Attwood; one *s* one *d. Educ:* Shoreham Grammar Sch.; Chichester Coll. of Art and Technol. FNAEA 1985. Joined Jackson-Stops & Staff Consortium, 1967; Area Dir, Chichester, 1987. *Recreations:* sailing, walking, computing, classic cars, motor racing, horse-racing. *Address:* Jackson-Stops & Staff, 37 South Street, Chichester, W Sussex PO19 1EL. *T:* (01243) 786316, *Fax:* (01243) 533736; *e-mail:* michaelbrandon@jackson-stops.co.uk. *Club:* Goodwood Road Racing.
Died 7 Feb. 2009.

BRASH, Robert, CMG 1980; HM Diplomatic Service, retired; Ambassador to Indonesia, 1981–84; *b* 30 May 1924; *s* of Frank and Ida Brash; *m* 1954, Barbara Enid Clarke; three *s* one *d. Educ:* Trinity Coll., Cambridge (Exhbnr). War Service, 1943–46. Entered Foreign Service, 1949; Djakarta, 1951–55; FO, 1955–58; First Sec., 1956; Jerusalem, 1958–61; Bonn, 1961–64; Bucharest, 1964–66; FCO, 1966–70; Counsellor, 1968; Canadian Nat. Defence Coll., 1970–71; Counsellor and Consul-Gen., Saigon, 1971–73; Counsellor, Vienna, 1974–78; Consul-Gen., Düsseldorf, 1978–81. Chm., Guildford Rambling Club, 1986–91. *Recreations:* walking, gardening, stained glass, golf. *Address:* Pondside, 22 Appleton Road, Cumnor, Oxford OX2 9QH.
Died 22 Oct. 2007.

BRATBY, Jean Esme Oregon; *see* Cooke, J. E. O.

BRATT, Guy Maurice, CMG 1977; MBE 1945; HM Diplomatic Service, retired; Counsellor, Foreign and Commonwealth Office, 1977–80; *b* 4 April 1920; *s* of late Ernst Lars Gustaf Bratt and Alice Maud Mary Bratt (*née* Raper); *m* 1945, Françoise Nelly Roberte Girardet; two *s* one *d. Educ:* Merchant Taylors' Sch.; London Univ. (BA). Served Army, 1939–46 (MBE): Major, Royal Signals. Solicitor 1947. Asst Sec., Colonial Develt Corp.; joined HM Foreign (subseq. Diplomatic) Service, 1952; served FO, 1952–54; Berlin, 1954–56; Brussels, 1956–58; FO, 1958–62; Vienna, 1962–66; FCO, 1966–70; Geneva, 1970–72; FCO, 1972–74; Washington, 1974–77. Mem. various gps of Chiltern Soc. *Publications:* The Bisses of Valais: man-made watercourses in Switzerland, 1995; articles in railway and model railway jls. *Recreations:* music, railways, mountain walking. *Address:* 2 Orchehill Rise, Gerrards Cross, Bucks SL9 8PR. *T:* (01753) 883106. *Club:* Travellers. *Died 15 May 2006.*

BRAZAUSKAS, Dr Algirdas Mykolas; Prime Minister, Republic of Lithuania, 2001–06; *b* Rokishkis, Lithuania, 22 Sept. 1932; *s* of Kazimieras Brazauskas and Zofija Brazauskiene; *m* 1st, 1958, Julija Styraite-Brazauskiene (marr. diss.); two *d*; 2nd, Kristina Butrimine. *Educ:* Polytech. of Kaunas; Dr 1974. Construction work, Hydro-electric Power Stn, River Nemunas and other constructive orgns, 1956–65; Minister, Lithuanian SSR Bldg Materials Industry, 1965–67; Vice-Chm., Lithuanian SSR Planning Cttee, 1967–77; Dep., Supreme Council of Lithuanian SSR, 1969–90; Sec., 1977–88, First Sec., 1988–90, Central Cttee, Communist Party of Lithuania; Republic of Lithuania: Chm., Democratic Labour Party, 1990–93; Dep., Supreme Council and Parliament, 1990–93; Chm. Presidium, Supreme Council, 1990; Dep. Prime Minister, 1990–91; President, 1993–98; Chm., Social Democratic Party, 2001–. Hon. Dr: Vilnius Tech., Lithuania, 1994; Kiev, Ukraine, 1994. Royal Order of Seraphim (Sweden), 1995; Grand-Croix, Ordre de la Rose Blanche (Finland), 1995; Order of White Eagle (Poland), 1995; Order of Gen. San Martin (Argentina), 1996; Collar, Order of the Libertador (Venezuela), 1996; Gran Cordon de la Medallia de la Republica Oriental de Uruguay, 1996.

Publications: Lithuanian Divorce, 1992. *Recreations:* yachting, hunting. *Address:* Turniškiu 30, 2016 Vilnius, Lithuania. *T:* (2) 778787. *Died 26 June 2010.*

BREACH, Gerald Ernest John; Director, Project Group, Export Credits Guarantee Department, 1988–90; *b* 14 March 1932; *s* of Ernest Albert Breach and Jane Breach; *m* 1st, 1958, Joan Elizabeth Eckford; one *s* one *d*; 2nd, 1988, Sylvia Eileen Harding. *Educ:* Roan Sch., Greenwich. Nat. Service, Royal Signals, 1950–52. Joined: ECGD, 1952; ECGD Management Bd, 1988. *Recreations:* boating, rambling, bell-ringing (Mem., Guild of Church Bell-Ringers), archaeological excursions. *Address:* Clunbury, Shropshire. *Died 3 March 2008.*

BREITMEYER, Brig. Alan Norman; DL; Lieutenant, HM Body Guard, Honourable Corps of Gentlemen at Arms, 1993–94 (Member, 1976–94; Harbinger, 1992–93); *b* 14 March 1924; *s* of Cecil Breitmeyer and Clare Herbert-Smith; *m* 1st, 1952, Hon. June Jane Barrie (marr. diss. 1977); one *s* one *d*; 2nd, 1978, Susan Irwin (*née* Lipscomb). *Educ:* Winchester Coll.; RMA Sandhurst. Commissioned Grenadier Guards, 1943; served NW Europe, 1944–45 (despatches 1945); ADC to Field Marshal Montgomery, 1948–50 (despatches, Palestine, 1948); Staff College, 1954; commanded 2nd Bn Grenadier Guards, 1964–66; commanding Grenadier Guards, 1966–69; Brig., 1971; Dep. Comdr, NE Dist, 1972–74, retired 1974. County Councillor, Cambs, 1977–85. DL Cambs, 1978; High Sheriff Cambs, 1984. *Recreation:* shooting. *Address:* Elms Farm, Ashley, Newmarket, Suffolk CB8 9DU. *T:* (01638) 731843. *Clubs:* Boodle's, Pratt's. *Died 26 May 2006.*

BRENNAN, Edward A.; Director, Morgan Stanley Group Inc., 2004–06; *b* 16 Jan. 1934; *s* of Edward Brennan and Margaret (*née* Bourget); *m* 1955, Lois Lyon; three *s* three *d. Educ:* Marquette Univ., Wisconsin (BA). Joined Sears as salesman in Madison, Wisconsin, 1956; asst store manager, 1958, asst buyer, 1960, store manager, 1967 and other positions in diff. locations, to 1969; Asst Manager, NY group, 1969–72; Gen. Manager, Sears Western NY group, 1972–75; Admin. Asst to Vice-Pres., Sears Eastern Territory, 1975; Gen. Manager, Boston group, 1976; Exec. Vice Pres., Southern Territory, 1978; Pres., Sears, Roebuck, 1980; Chm. and Chief Exec., Sears Merchandise Group, 1981; Pres. and Chief Operating Officer, 1984, Chm. and CEO, 1986–95, Pres., 1989, Sears, Roebuck & Co.; Dir, AMR Corp., 1987– (Exec. Chm., 2003–04); Dir, Dean Witter, Discover & Co., subseq. Morgan Stanley Gp Inc., 1993–2003; dir of other cos. Member: President's Export Council; Business Roundtable; Conference Bd; business adv. council, Chicago Urban League; Civic Cttee, Commercial Club; Chm., Board of Governors, United Way of America; Member, Boards of Trustees: Savings and Profit Sharing Fund of Sears Employees; Univs of DePaul and Marquette; Chicago Museum of Science and Industry. *Address:* Morgan Stanley Group Inc., 1585 Broadway, New York, NY 10036, USA. *Died 27 Dec. 2007.*

BREWER, Prof. Derek Stanley, LittD; Master of Emmanuel College, Cambridge, 1977–90; Professor of English, University of Cambridge, 1983–90, then Emeritus Professor; *b* 13 July 1923; *s* of Stanley Leonard Brewer and Winifred Helen Forbes; *m* 1951, Lucie Elisabeth Hoole (*d* 2008); three *s* two *d. Educ:* elementary school; The Crypt Grammar Sch.; Magdalen Coll., Oxford (Matthew Arnold Essay Prize, 1948; BA, MA 1948); Birmingham Univ. (PhD 1956); LittD Cantab 1980. Commnd 2nd Lieut, Worcestershire Regt, 1942; Captain and Adjt, 1st Bn Royal Fusiliers, 1944–45. Asst Lectr and Lectr in English, Univ. of Birmingham, 1949–56; Prof. of English, Internat. Christian Univ., Tokyo, 1956–58; Lectr and Sen. Lectr, Univ. of Birmingham, 1958–64; Lectr in English, Univ. of Cambridge, 1965–76, Reader in Medieval English, 1976–83; Fellow of Emmanuel Coll., Cambridge, 1965–77, Life Fellow 1990. Founder, D. S. Brewer Ltd, for the publication of academic books, 1972; later part of Boydell and Brewer Ltd (Dir, 1979–96). Mem., Council

of the Senate, Cambridge, 1978–83; Chairman: Fitzwilliam Museum Enterprises Ltd, 1978–90; Univ. Library Synd., 1980–93; English Faculty Bd, Cambridge, 1984–86, 1989. Lectures: Sir Israel Gollancz Meml, British Academy, 1974; first William Matthews, Univ. of London, 1982; first Geoffrey Shepherd Meml, Univ. of Birmingham, 1983; Ballard Mathews, Univ. of Wales, Bangor, 1996. Sandars Reader, Univ. of Cambridge, 1991. First British Council Vis. Prof. of English to Japan, 1987; Vis. Prof., Japan Soc. for Promotion of Science, 1988; Cline Distinguished Vis. Prof., Univ. of Texas at Austin, 1992; Francqui Internat. Chair in Human Sciences, univs in Belgium, 1998. President: The English Assoc., 1982–83, 1987–90 (Hon. Fellow, 2001); Internat. Chaucer Soc., 1982–84; Chairman Trustees: Chaucer Heritage Trust, 1992–98; British Taiwan Cultural Inst., 1990–98; Trustee (Treas.), SOS Villages (UK), 1990–2002; Hon. Trustee, Osaka Univ. of Arts, 1987–. Hon. Mem., Japan Acad., 1981 (Commemorative Medal, 1997); Corresp. Fellow, Medieval Soc. of America, 1987. Hon. LLD: Keio Univ., Tokyo, 1982; Harvard Univ., 1984; Hon. DLitt: Birmingham, 1985; Williams Coll., USA, 1990; DUniv: York, 1985; Sorbonne, 1988; Univ. of Liège, 1990. Seatonian Prize, Univ. of Cambridge, 1969, 1972, 1983, 1986, 1988, 1993, 1999, (jtly) 1979, 1980, 1992, (prox. acc.) 1985, 1990. Editor, The Cambridge Review, 1981–86. Publications: Chaucer, 1953, 3rd edn 1973; Proteus, 1958 (Tokyo); (ed) The Parlement of Foulys, 1960; Chaucer in his Time, 1963; (ed and contrib.) Chaucer and Chaucerians, 1966; (ed) Malory's Morte Darthur: Parts Seven and Eight, 1968; (ed and contrib.) Writers and their Backgrounds: Chaucer, 1974; (ed) Chaucer: the Critical Heritage, 1978; Chaucer and his World, 1978; Symbolic Stories, 1980, 2nd edn 1988; (ed jtly) Aspects of Malory, 1981; English Gothic Literature, 1983; Tradition and Innovation in Chaucer, 1983; Chaucer: the Poet as Storyteller, 1984; Chaucer: an introduction, 1984; (ed) Beardsley's Le Morte Darthur, 1985; (with E. Frankl) Arthur's Britain: the land and the legend, 1985; (ed) Studies in Medieval English Romances, 1988; (ed) Medieval Comic Tales, 1996; (ed) A Critical Companion to the Gawain-poet, 1997; (ed) The Middle Ages after the Middle Ages, 1997; A New Introduction to Chaucer, 1998; Seatonian Exercises and Other Verses, 2000; Chaucer's World, 2000; numerous articles in learned jls, reviews, etc. Recreations: reading, travelling, publishing other people's books. Address: 240 Hills Road, Cambridge CB2 2QE; Emmanuel College, Cambridge CB2 3AP. T: (01223) 334200.
Died 23 Oct. 2008.

BRICE, Air Cdre Eric John, CBE 1971 (OBE 1957); CEng; AFRAeS; RAF retd; stockbroker; b 12 Feb. 1917; s of Courtenay Percy Please Brice and Lilie Alice Louise Brice (née Grey); m 1942, Janet Parks, Roundhay, Leeds, Yorks; two s one d. Educ: Loughborough Coll. (DLC). Joined RAF, 1939; served War, MEAF, 1943–46 (Sqdn Ldr). Air Ministry, 1946–50; Parachute Trng Sch., 1950–52; Wing Comdr, 1952; RAE, Farnborough, 1952–58; Comd, Parachute Trng Sch., 1958–60; RAF Coll., Cranwell, 1960–61; Gp Capt., 1961; RAF Halton, 1961–64; Comd, RAF Innsworth, Glos, 1964–66; Dir, Physical Educn, RAF, MoD, 1966–68; Air Cdre, 1968; Dep. AOA, RAF HQ, Maintenance Comd, 1968–71; April 1971, retd prematurely. MCMI. Hon. BSc Loughborough, 2009. Recreations: athletics (Combined Services and RAF athletic blues); Rugby football (RAF trialist and Blackheath Rugby Club); captained Loughborough Coll. in three sports. Address: Durns, Boldre, Lymington, Hampshire SO41 8NE. T: (01590) 672196. Club: Royal Lymington Yacht.
Died 12 March 2010.

BRICHTO, Rabbi Dr Sidney; Senior Vice-President, Union of Liberal and Progressive Synagogues, since 1992; b 21 July 1936; s of Solomon and Rivka Brichto; m 1st, 1959, Frances Goldstein (decd); one s one d; 2nd, 1971, Cathryn Goldhill; two s. Educ: New York Univ. (BA); Hebrew Union Coll., NY (MA, MHL, DD); University College London (Study Fellowship).

Associate Minister, Liberal Jewish Synagogue, 1961–64; Founder and Principal, Evening Inst. for Study of Judaism, 1962–65; Exec. Vice-Pres. and Dir, ULPS, 1964–89; Lectr, Oxford Centre for Postgrad. Hebrew Studies, 1991–96; Dir, Joseph Levy Charitable Foundn, 1989–99. Chairman: Conf. of Rabbis, ULPS, 1969–70, 1974–75; Council of Reform and Liberal Rabbis, 1974–76; Chief Rabbi's Consultative Cttee on Jewish-non-Jewish Relations, 1976–78. Vice-Pres., Nat. Assoc. of Bereavement Services, 1992–98. Founder and Chm., Adv. Cttee, Israel Diaspora Trust, 1982–; Mem. Exec. Council, Leo Baeck Coll., 1964–74; Dir, Inst. for Jewish Policy Res., 1996–99; Gov., Oxford Centre for Hebrew and Jewish Studies, 1994–2003. Publications: Funny...you don't look Jewish, 1995; (ed jtly) Two Cheers for Secularism, 1998; Ritual Slaughter, 2001; (ed jtly) He Kissed Him and They Wept, 2001; (ed and trans.) The People's Bible: Genesis, 2000; Samuel, 2000; Song of Songs, 2000; St Luke and the Apostles, 2000; The Conquest of Canaan, 2001; The Genius of Paul, 2001; Moses, Man of God and the Laws of Moses, 2003; Apocalypse, 2004; The New Testament, 2009; contribs to Service of the Heart (Liberal Jewish Prayer Book) and to national and Jewish jls. Recreations: pleasant lunches, reading, writing. T: (020) 8933 6216; e-mail: sidney@brichto.com Club: Athenæum.
Died 16 Jan. 2009.

BRICKWOOD, Sir Basil (Greame), 3rd Bt cr 1927; b 21 May 1923; s of Sir John Brickwood, 1st Bt and Isabella Janet Gibson (d 1967), d of James Gordon; S half-brother, 1974; m 1956, Shirley Anne Brown; two d. Educ: King Edward's Grammar Sch., Stratford-upon-Avon; Clifton. Served War, RAF, 1940–46. Heir: none. Club: Royal Air Force.
Died 16 May 2006 (ext).

BRIDGE OF HARWICH, Baron cr 1980 (Life Peer), of Harwich in the County of Essex; **Nigel Cyprian Bridge,** Kt 1968; PC 1975; a Lord of Appeal in Ordinary, 1980–92; b 26 Feb. 1917; s of late Comdr C. D. C. Bridge, RN; m 1944, Margaret Swinbank (d 2006); one s two d. Educ: Marlborough College; BScHons (Math. Scis) Open Univ. 2003. Army Service, 1940–46; commnd into KRRC, 1941. Called to the Bar, Inner Temple, 1947; Bencher, 1964, Reader, 1985, Treasurer, 1986; Junior Counsel to Treasury (Common Law), 1964–68; a Judge of High Court, Queen's Bench Div., 1968–75; Presiding Judge, Western Circuit, 1972–74; a Lord Justice of Appeal, 1975–80. Mem., Security Commn, 1977–85 (Chm. 1982–85); Chm., C of E Synodical Govt Review, 1993–97. Hon. Fellow, Amer. Coll. of Trial Lawyers, 1984. Hon. Fellow, Wolfson Coll., Cambridge, 1989. Address: House of Lords, SW1A 0PW.
Died 20 Nov. 2007.

BRIDGE, Very Rev. Antony Cyprian; Dean of Guildford, 1968–86; b 5 Sept. 1914; s of late Comdr C. D. C. Bridge, RN; m 1st, 1937, Brenda Lois Streatfeild (d 1995); one s two d; 2nd, 1996, Diana Joyce Readhead. Educ: Marlborough Coll; Lincoln Theol Coll. Scholarship to Royal Academy School of Art, 1932; professional painter thereafter. War of 1939–45: joined Army, Sept. 1939; commissioned Buffs, 1940; demobilised as Major, 1945. Ordained deacon, 1955, priest, 1956; Curate, Hythe Parish Church, 1955–58; Vicar of Christ Church, Lancaster Gate, London, 1958–68. Mem., Adv. Council, V&A Museum, 1976–79. FSA 1987. Publications: Images of God, 1960; Theodora: portrait in a Byzantine landscape, 1978; The Crusades, 1980; Suleiman The Magnificent, 1983; One Man's Advent, 1985; Richard the Lionheart, 1989. Recreations: bird-watching, reading. Address: 34 London Road, Deal, Kent CT14 9TE.
Died 23 April 2007.

BRIDGE, John, GC 1944; GM 1940 and Bar 1941; Director of Education for Sunderland Borough Council (formerly Sunderland County Borough Council), 1963–76, retired; b 5 Feb. 1915; s of late Joseph Edward Bridge, Culcheth, Warrington; m 1945, F. Jean Patterson (d 2006); three d. Educ: London Univ. (BSc Gen. Hons, 1936 and BSc Special Hons (Physics), 1937; Teacher's Dip., 1938). Schoolmaster: Lancs CC, Sept.–Dec. 1938;

Leighton Park, Reading, Jan.–Aug. 1939; Firth Park Grammar Sch., Sheffield, Sept. 1939–Aug. 1946 (interrupted by war service). Served War: RNVR June 1940–Feb. 1946, engaged on bomb and mine disposal; demobilised as Lt Comdr RNVR. *Recreations:* gardening, travel, photography. *Address:* 37 Park Avenue, Roker, Sunderland SR6 9NJ. *T:* (0191) 548 6356.
Died 14 Dec. 2006.

BRIDGES, Brian; Under Secretary in charge of Environmental and Food Safety, Department of Health, 1992–95; *b* 30 June 1937; 4th *s* of late William Ernest Bridges; *m* 1970, Jennifer Mary Rogers. *Educ:* Harrow Weald County Grammar Sch.; Univ. of Keele (BA 1961). Sec., Univ. of Keele Union, 1959–60. Joined Civil Service, 1961; Principal, 1967; Asst Sec. 1975; Under Sec., DHSS, 1985; Dir of Estabts and Personnel, DHSS, 1985–88; Under Sec. i/c of NHS dental, pharmaceutical and optical services and pharmaceutical industry, DoH, 1988–92. *Recreations:* long walks in the tow of dogs, a range of practical and intellectual pursuits including carpentry and local history. *Address:* Townsend House, Ullingswick, Herefordshire HR1 3JQ. *T:* (01432) 820312.
Died 6 June 2007.

BRIDGES, Sir Phillip (Rodney), Kt 1973; CMG 1967; *b* 9 July 1922; *e s* of late Captain Sir Ernest Bridges and Lady Bridges; *m* 1st, 1951, Rosemary Ann Streeten (marr. diss. 1961); two *s* one *d*; 2nd, 1962, Angela Mary, (Jill) (*née* Dearden), *widow* of James Huyton. *Educ:* Bedford School. Military Service (Capt., RA) with Royal W African Frontier Force in W Africa, India and Burma, 1941–47; Beds Yeo., 1947–54. Admitted Solicitor (England), 1951; Colonial Legal Service, 1954; Barrister and Solicitor, Supreme Court of The Gambia, 1954; Solicitor-General of The Gambia, 1963; QC (Gambia) 1964; Attorney-General of The Gambia, 1964–68; Chief Justice of The Gambia, 1968–83. *Address:* Weavers, Coney Weston, Bury St Edmunds, Suffolk IP31 1HG. *T:* (01359) 221316.
Died 26 Dec. 2007.

BRIDGEWATER, Allan, CBE 1998; LVO 2008; Chairman, Swiss Re GB plc (formerly Swiss Re Group UK), 1998–2007; *b* 26 Aug. 1936; *m* 1960, Janet Bridgewater; three *d*. *Educ:* Wyggeston Grammar Sch., Leicester. ACII, Chartered Insurer, FCIPD, CCMI. Norwich Union Insurance Group: Dir, 1985–97; Group Chief Exec., 1989–97. Director: Riggs Bank Europe, 1991–2005; Fox Pitt Kelton, 2000–04. Pres., Chartered Insurance Inst., 1989–90; Chm., Assoc. of British Insurers, 1993–95. Pres., Endeavour Training, 1997–2005 (Chm., 1987–97); Chm., C of E Pensions Bd, 1998–2008. Special Prof., Business Sch., Univ. of Nottingham, 1995–2006. Trustee: Duke of Edinburgh's Commonwealth Study Conf., 1993–2007 (Vice Chm.); Industry in Educn, 1993–97; Soc. for the Protection of Life from Fire, 1991–. Gov., Chartered Insurance Inst. College, 1985–2000. Vice Chm., Norwich Cathedral Trustees, 1998–. Chm. Trustees, Paul Golmick Fund, 2001–. FRSA 1989. Freeman, City of London, 1991; Liveryman, Insurers' Co., 1991– (Hon. Ct Asst). OStJ 1999. Insce Brokers Insce Personality of the Year, 1997; British Insce Achievement Award, 1998; Gold Medal, Chartered Insce Inst., 2005. *Died 5 Aug. 2010.*

BRIDGLAND, Milton Deane, AO 1987; FTSE; Chairman, ICI Australia Ltd, 1980–93; *b* 8 July 1922; *s* of late Frederick H. and Muriel E. Bridgland, Adelaide; *m* 1945, Christine L. Cowell; three *d*. *Educ:* St Peter's Coll., Adelaide; Adelaide Univ. (BSc). FRACI, FAIM. Joined ICI Australia Ltd, 1945; Technical Manager, Plastics Gp, 1955–62; Ops Dir, 1962–67; Man. Dir, 1967–71; Dulux Australia Ltd; Exec. Dir 1971, Man. Dir, 1978–84, ICI Australia Ltd. Chairman: Jennings Properties, later Centro Properties Ltd, 1985–92; ANZ Banking Group Ltd, 1989–92 (Dir, 1982–92; Dep. Chm., 1987–89); Director: Jennings Group (formerly Industries) Ltd, 1984–92; Freeport-McMoRan Australia Ltd, 1987–89. President: Aust. Chemical Industry Council, 1977; Aust. Industry Develt Assoc., 1982–83. Vice President: Aust. Business Roundtable, 1983; Business Council of Australia,

1983–84; Dir, Aust. Inst. of Petroleum, 1980–84; Mem., National Energy Adv. Cttee, 1977–80. Member, Board of Management: Univ. of Melbourne Grad. Sch. of Management, 1983–86; Crawford Fund for Internat. Agricl Res., 1989–94. Chm. Adv. Bd, Salvation Army, Southern Territory, 1986–90. Mem., Cook Soc. *Recreations:* the arts, gardening. *Address:* 1/42 Glen Street, Hawthorn, Vic 3122, Australia. *T:* (3) 98193939.
Died 26 July 2008.

BRIDLE, Rear-Adm. Gordon Walter, CB 1977; MBE 1952; *b* 14 May 1923; *s* of Percy Gordon Bridle and Dorothy Agnes Bridle; *m* 1944, Phyllis Audrey Page; three *s*. *Educ:* King Edward's Grammar Sch., Aston, Birmingham; Northern Grammar Sch., Portsmouth; Royal Dockyard Sch., Portsmouth (Whitworth Scholar); Imperial Coll., London (ACGI). CEng, FIET. jssc. Loan Service, Pakistan, 1950–52; served HM Ships: Implacable, St James, Gambia, Newfoundland, Devonshire; Proj. Manager, Sea Slug and Sea Dart, Mins of Aviation/Technol.; comd HMS Collingwood, 1969–71; Dir, Surface Weapons Projects, ASWE; Asst Controller of the Navy, 1974–77. *Address:* 25 Heatherwood, Midhurst, Sussex GU29 9LH. *T:* (01730) 812838.
Died 30 July 2009.

BRIEN, Alan; novelist and journalist; *b* 12 March 1925; *s* of Ernest Brien and Isabella Brien (*née* Patterson); *m* 1st, 1947, Pamela Mary Jones (*d* 1998); three *d*; 2nd, 1961, Nancy Newbold Ryan (*d* 1987); one *s* one *d*; 3rd, 1973, Jill Sheila Tweedie (*d* 1993); 4th, 1996, Jane Hill. *Educ:* Bede Grammar Sch., Sunderland; Jesus Coll., Oxford. BA (Eng Lit). Served war RAF (air-gunner), 1943–46. Associate Editor: Mini-Cinema, 1950–52; Courier, 1952–53; Film Critic and Columnist, Truth, 1953–54; TV Critic, Observer, 1954–55; Film Critic, 1954–56, columnist, 1956–58, Evening Standard; Drama Critic and Features Editor, Spectator, 1958–61; Columnist, Daily Mail, 1958–62; Columnist, Sunday Dispatch, 1962–63; Political Columnist, Sunday Pictorial, 1963–64; Drama Critic, Sunday Telegraph, 1961–67; Columnist: Spectator, 1963–65; New Statesman, 1966–72; Punch, 1972–84; Diarist, 1967–75, Film Critic, 1976–84, Sunday Times. Foreign correspondent: New York (for Evening Standard), 1956–58; Moscow (for Sunday Times), 1974; Saigon (for Sunday Times, Punch), 1972. Regular broadcaster on radio, 1952–, and television, 1955–. Hannen Swaffer (later IPC) Critic of Year, 1966, 1967. *Publications:* Domes of Fortune (essays), 1979; Lenin: the novel (novel), 1987. *Recreations:* procrastination, empyromancy. *Address:* The Cottage at 36A, Highgate High Street, N6 5JG. *T:* (020) 8348 4895.
Died 23 May 2008.

BRIERLEY, Ven. David James; Archdeacon of Sudbury, since 2006; *b* 12 Dec. 1953; *s* of Jack Brierley and Mary Brierley (*née* Connearn); *m* 1976, Gill Eatough; one *s* two *d*. *Educ:* Bristol Univ. (BA Hons Theol.); Oak Hill Theol Coll. (DPS). Ordained deacon, 1977, priest, 1978; Curate, Rochdale, 1977–80; Vicar: St Andrew, Eccles, 1980–85; Harwood, 1985–95; Vicar and RD, Walmsley, 1995–2002; Residentiary Canon, Bradford Cathedral, 2002–04; Diocesan Missioner, Bradford, 2004–06. Manchester Diocesan Ecumenical Officer, 1981–88; Chm., Decade of Evangelism Steering Cttee, 1999–2000. *Publications:* two working booklets. *Recreations:* walking (Labrador dog), biographies (Churchill), ornithology, 'soaps', the amber nectar, avid but now armchair Blackburn Rovers supporter. *Address:* Sudbury Lodge, Stanningfield Road, Great Whelnetham, Suffolk IP30 0TL. *T:* (01284) 386942; *e-mail:* archdeacon.david@stedmundsbury.anglican.org.
Died 1 Aug. 2009.

BRIGDEN, Wallace, MA, MD, FRCP; Consulting Physician: Royal London Hospital, and Cardiac Department, Royal London Hospital; National Heart Hospital; Consulting Cardiologist to the Royal Navy, then Emeritus; *b* 8 June 1916; *s* of Wallis Brigden and Louise Brigden (*née* Clarke); *m* 1st, 1942, Joan Mack (marr. diss. 1966); two *s* one *d*; 2nd, 1966, Everel Sankey;

one s, and one step s. *Educ:* Latymer School; University of Cambridge; King's College Hospital; Yale University. Senior Scholar, King's College, Cambridge; First Class Natural Sciences Tripos, Parts I and II, 1936, 1937; Henry Fund Fellowship, Yale University, USA, 1937–38; Burney Yeo Schol., King's College Hospital, 1938. RAMC, 1943–47, Med. Specialist and O/C Medical Division. Lecturer in Medicine, Post-Grad. Med. School of London; Physician, Hammersmith Hospital, 1948–49; Asst Physician, later Consultant Physician, London Hospital and Cardiac Dept of London Hosp., 1949–81; Asst Physician, later Consultant Physician, National Heart Hospital, 1949–81; Cons. Cardiologist, Special Unit for Juvenile Rheumatism, Taplow, 1955–59; Director Inst. of Cardiology, 1962–66. Cons. Physician to Munich Re-Insurance Co., 1974–90. Past Hon. Pres., Assurance Medical Society, 1987–89. St Cyres Lectr, 1956; R. T. Hall Lectr, Australia and New Zealand, 1961; Hugh Morgan Vis. Prof., Vanderbilt Univ., 1963. Late Assistant Editor, British Heart Journal Mem. British Cardiac Society and Assoc. of Physicians. *Publications:* Section on Cardio-vascular disease in Price's Textbook of Medicine; Myocardial Disease, Cecil-Loeb Textbook of Medicine; contributor to the Lancet, British Heart Jl, British Medical Jl. *Recreation:* painting. *Address:* Willow House, 38 Totteridge Common, N20 8NE. *T:* (020) 8959 6616.
Died 11 March 2008.

BRIGGS, (Peter) John; a Recorder of the Crown Court, 1978–97; *b* 15 May 1928; *s* of late Percy Briggs and Annie M. Folker; *m* 1956, Sheila Phyllis Walton; one *s* three *d*. *Educ:* King's Sch., Peterborough; Balliol Coll., Oxford. MA, BCL. Called to the Bar, Inner Temple, 1953. Legal Member: Mersey Mental Health Review Tribunal, 1969 (Dep. Chm., 1971, Chm., 1981–94); North-West Mental Health Review Tribunal, 1994–98; NW and W Midlands Mental Health Review Tribunal, 1998–2000. Pres., Merseyside Medico-Legal Soc., 1982–84. Chm., Merseyside Opera, 1996–99. *Recreations:* music, particularly amateur operatics. *Address:* 15 Dean's Lawn, Chesham Road, Berkhamsted, Herts HP4 3AZ. *T:* (01442) 871488.
Died 13 May 2010.

BRIGHTMAN, Baron *cr* 1982 (Life Peer), of Ibthorpe in the County of Hampshire; **John Anson Brightman,** Kt 1970; PC 1979; a Lord of Appeal in Ordinary, 1982–86; *b* 20 June 1911; 2nd *s* of William Henry Brightman, St Albans, Herts; *m* 1945, Roxane Ambatielo; one *s*. *Educ:* Marlborough College; St John's College, Cambridge (Hon. Fellow, 1982). Called to the Bar, Lincoln's Inn, 1932; Bencher 1966. QC 1961. Able Seaman, Merchant Navy, 1939–40; RNVR (Lieut-Commander), 1940–46; anti-sub. warfare base, Tobermory; N Atlantic and Mediterranean convoys; staff, SEAC; RNSC, 1944; Assistant Naval Attaché, Ankara, 1944. Attorney-General of the Duchy of Lancaster, 1969–70; Judge of the High Court of Justice, Chancery Div., 1970–79; a Lord Justice of Appeal, 1979–82; Judge, Nat. Industrial Relns Court, 1971–74. Chm., H of L and H of C Jt Cttee on Consolidation Bills, 1983–86; Chairman, House of Lords Select Committee: on Charities, 1983–84; on Abortion Law, 1987–88; on City of Bristol Develt, 1988; on Spitalfields Market, 1989; on British Waterways, 1991; on Property Law, 1994; on Private Internat. Law, 1994–95; on Family Homes and Domestic Violence, 1995; Member: Cttee on Parly procedures for tax simplification, 1996; Ecclesiastical Cttee, 1997–2004; H of L Working Gp on procedure, 1998; Jt Cttee on Tax Simplification Bills, 2001–04. Mem., General Council of the Bar, 1956–60, 1966–70. Mem. Adv. Cttee, Inst. of Advanced Legal Studies, 2000–03. Chm., Tancred's Charities, 1982–96. Hon. FRGS, 2001. *Recreations:* interested in High Arctic (Spitsbergen and Franz Josef Land), sailing, and legislative drafting in plain English. *Address:* House of Lords, SW1A 0PW. *T:* (020) 7219 2034.
Died 6 Feb. 2006.

BRINTON, Timothy Denis; self-employed broadcasting consultant, presentation tutor and communications adviser, retired 1999; *b* 24 Dec. 1929; *s* of late Dr Denis

Hubert Brinton; *m* 1st, 1954, Jane-Mari Coningham (marr. diss.); one *s* three *d*; 2nd, 1965, Jeanne Frances Wedge; two *d*. *Educ:* Summer Fields, Oxford; Eton Coll., Windsor; Geneva Univ.; Central Sch. of Speech and Drama. BBC staff, 1951–59; ITN, 1959–62; freelance, 1962–99. Mem., Kent CC, 1974–81. Chm., Dartford Gravesham HA, 1988–90. MP (C): Gravesend, 1979–83; Gravesham, 1983–87. Member: Court, 1979–95, Council, 1995–98, Univ. of London; Med. Sch. Council, St Mary's Hosp., Paddington, 1983–88; Gov., Wye Coll., London Univ., 1989–97. Mem., RTS. *Address:* 19 Grimston Gardens, Folkestone, Kent CT20 2PU. *T:* (01303) 226558.
Died 22 March 2009.

BRISE, Sir John Archibald R.; *see* Ruggles-Brise.

BRISTOW, Alan Edgar, OBE 1966; FRAeS; Managing Director, then Chairman, Bristow Helicopters Ltd, 1954–85; *b* 3 Sept. 1923; *m* 1st, 1945, Jean (decd); one *s* (one *d* decd); 2nd, Heather. *Educ:* Portsmouth Grammar School. Cadet, British India Steam Navigation Co., 1939–43; Pilot, Fleet Air Arm, 1943–46; Test Pilot, Westland Aircraft Ltd, 1946–49; Helicopair, Paris/Indo-China, 1949–51; Man. Dir, Air Whaling Ltd (Antarctic Whaling Expedns), 1951–54; Dir, British United Airways Ltd, 1960–70, Man. Dir 1967–70; Chairman: Briway Transit Systems Ltd, 1987–94; Alanta Ltd, 1996–. Invented water beds for cows and horses, 1995, patented 1997. Cierva Memorial Lectr, RAeS, 1967. FRAeS 1967. Croix de Guerre (France), 1950. *Publications:* papers to RAeS. *Recreations:* flying, shooting, sailing. *Address:* Meadowfield, Barhatch Road, Cranleigh, Surrey GU6 7DJ. *T:* (01483) 274674.
Died 26 April 2009.

BROADBENT, Dr Edward Granville, FRS 1977; FREng, FRAeS, FIMA; Visiting Professor and Senior Research Investigator, Imperial College of Science and Technology (Mathematics Department), London University, since 1983; *b* 27 June 1923; *s* of Joseph Charles Fletcher Broadbent and Lucetta (*née* Riley); *m* 1949, Elizabeth Barbara (*née* Puttick) (*d* 2001). *Educ:* Huddersfield Coll.; St Catharine's Coll., Cambridge (State Scholarship, 1941; Eng Scholar; MA, ScD). FRAeS 1959; FIMA 1965. Joined RAF (Structures Dept), 1943: worked on aero-elasticity (Wakefield Gold Medal, RAeS, 1960); transf. to Aerodynamics Dept, 1960; worked on various aspects of fluid mechanics and acoustics; DCSO (IM), RAE, 1969–83, retired. Gold Medal, RAeS, 1991. *Publications:* The Elementary Theory of Aero-elasticity, 1954. *Recreations:* bridge, chess, music, theatre. *Address:* 11 Three Stiles Road, Farnham, Surrey GU9 7DE. *T:* (01252) 714621.
Died 9 March 2008.

BROCK, Jonathan Simon; QC 1997; FCIArb; a Recorder, since 2000; *b* 13 July 1952; *s* of Rev. Preb. Patrick Laurence Brock, MBE and Patricia Addinsell Brock, RIBA; *m* 1st, 1977 (marr. diss. 1988)1 two *s* one *d*; 2nd, 1989, Lindsey Frances Oliver; two *s*. *Educ:* St Paul's Sch.; Corpus Christi Coll., Cambridge (MA 1975). FCIArb 1989. Called to the Bar, Lincoln's Inn, 1977, Bencher, 2007. An Asst Recorder, 1994–2000. Bar Council: Mem., 1992–98 and 2002–; Chairman: Commonwealth Internat. Relns Sub-cttee, 1993–98; European Cttee, 2006–; Co-Chm., Bar Policy and Res. Gp, 2005; Vice-Chm., Legal Services Cttee, 2005; Mem., Gen. Mgt Cttee, 2005–. Mem., Court of Appeal Users' Cttee, 1996–2002. Chm., London Common Law and Commercial Bar Assoc., 2002–03. Church Comr. 2002–. Trustee, Lambeth Palace Liby, 2004–. *Publications:* (ed) Woodfall on the Law of Landlord and Tenant. *Recreations:* cricket, football, ski-ing. *Address:* Falcon Chambers, Falcon Court, EC4Y 1AA. *Clubs:* Athenæum, MCC, Queen's; Snakepit Strollers (Chm.).
Died 10 July 2007.

BROCKBANK, Maj.-Gen. John Myles, (Robin), CBE 1972; MC 1943; Vice Lord-Lieutenant of Wiltshire, 1990–96; *b* 19 Sept. 1921; *s* of Col J. G. Brockbank, CBE, DSO, and Eireine Marguerite Robinson; *m* 1953, Gillian Findlay, *yr d* of Sir Edmund Findlay, 2nd Bt of Aberlour; three *s* one *d*.

Educ: Eton Coll.; Oxford Univ. Commissioned into 12 Royal Lancers, 1941. Served War, North Africa, Italy, 1941–45. Served Germany: 1955–58, 1964–68 and 1970–72; Cyprus, 1959; USA, 1961–64; Staff Coll., 1950; IDC 1969; CO, 9/12 Royal Lancers; Comdr, RAC, HQ 1 Corps; Chief of Staff, 1 Corps; Dir, RAC, 1972–74; Vice-Adjutant General, MoD, 1974–76, retd. Col, 9/12 Lancers, 1982–85. Dir, British Field Sports Soc., 1976–84. Chm., Wilts Trust for Nature Conservation, 1984–90. DL Wilts 1982. *Recreations:* field sports, gardening, bird watching. *Address:* 24 Harcourt Terrace, Salisbury, Wilts SP2 7SA.
Died 21 Aug. 2006.

BROCKMAN, Rev. John St Leger, CB 1988; Permanent Deacon, St Joseph's RC Church, Epsom, since 1988; Assistant Director for Permanent Diaconate, Diocese of Arundel and Brighton, 1996–2002; *b* 24 March 1928; *s* of late Prof. Ralph St Leger Brockman and Estelle Wilson; *m* 1954, Sheila Elizabeth Jordan; one *s* two *d* (and one *d* decd). *Educ:* Ampleforth; Gonville and Caius Coll., Cambridge. MA, LLB. Called to the Bar, Gray's Inn, 1952. Legal Asst, Min. of National Insurance, 1953; Sen. Legal Asst, Min. of Pensions and National Insurance, 1964; Asst Solicitor, DHSS, 1973; Under Sec. and Principal Asst Solicitor, DHSS, 1978; Solicitor to DHSS, to Registrar General and to OPCS, 1985–89. *Publications:* compiled and edited: The Law relating to Family Allowances and National Insurance, 1961; The Law relating to National Insurance (Industrial Injuries), 1961. *Address:* 304 The Greenway, Epsom, Surrey KT18 7JF. *T:* (01372) 812915. *Died 7 June 2009.*

BRODIE-HALL, Sir Laurence (Charles), Kt 1982; AO 1993; CMG 1976; Director, 1962–82, Consultant, 1975–82, Western Mining Corporation; Chairman, West Australian Foundation for the Museum of Science and Technology; *b* 10 June 1910; *m* 1st, 1940, Dorothy Jolly (decd); three *s* two *d*; 2nd, 1978, Jean Verschuer (AM 2001). *Educ:* Sch. of Mines, Kalgoorlie (Dip. Metallurgy 1947, DipME 1948). Served War, RAE. Geologist, Central Norseman Gold Corp., 1948–49; Tech. Asst to Man. Dir, Western Mining Corp., 1950–51; Gen. Supt, Gt Western Consolidated, 1951–58; Gen. Supt, 1958–68, Exec. Dir, WA, 1967–75, Western Mining Corp.; Chairman: Gold Mines of Kalgoorlie (Aust.) Ltd, 1974–82; Central Norseman Gold Corp. NL, 1974–82; Westintech Innovation Corp. Ltd, 1984–88; Director: Ansett WA (formerly Airlines WA), 1983–93; Coolgardie Gold NL, 1985–93; former Chm. or Dir of many subsidiaries, and Dir, Alcoa of Australia Ltd, 1971–83. Pres., WA Chamber of Mines, 1970–75 (Life Mem.); Past Pres., Australasian Inst. of Mining and Metallurgy (Institute Medal, 1977, Hon. Life Mem., 1987); Chairman: WA State Cttee, CSIRO, 1971–81; Bd of Management, WA Sch. of Mines, to 1991. Hon. DTech, WA Inst. Technology, 1978. *Address:* (office) 2 Cliff Street, West Perth, WA 6005, Australia. *Club:* Weld (Perth). *Died 1 Oct. 2006.*

BROOK, Leopold, BScEng, FICE, FIMechE; Director, Renishaw plc, since 1980; *b* 2 Jan. 1912; *s* of Albert and Kate Brook, Hampstead; *m* 1st, 1940, Susan (*d* 1970), *d* of David Rose, Hampstead; two *s*; 2nd, 1974, Mrs Elly Rhodes; two step *s* one step *d*. *Educ:* Central Foundation School, London; University College, London. L. G. Mouchel & Partners, Cons. Engineers, 1935–44; Simon Engineering Ltd, 1944–77 (Chief Exec., 1967–70; Chm., 1970–77); Chairman: Associated Nuclear Services Ltd, 1977–90; Brown & Sharpe Group (UK), 1979–88. Fellow, UCL, 1970–. CCMI; FRSA 1973. *Recreations:* music, theatre, walking. *Address:* 55 Kingston House North, Prince's Gate, SW7 1LW. *T:* (020) 7584 2041. *Clubs:* Athenæum, Hurlingham. *Died 16 March 2007.*

BROOKE, Arthur Caffin, CB 1972; Chairman, Arts Council of Northern Ireland, 1982–86 (Member, 1979–86); *b* 11 March 1919; *s* of late Rev. James M. Wilmot Brooke and Constance Brooke; *m* 1942, Margaret Florence Thompson; two *s*. *Educ:*

Abbotsholme Sch.; Peterhouse, Cambridge (MA). Served War, Royal Corps of Signals, 1939–46. Northern Ireland Civil Service, 1946–79; Ministry of Commerce, 1946–73: Asst Sec., Head of Industrial Development Div., 1955; Sen. Asst Sec., Industrial Development, 1963; Second Sec., 1968; Permanent Sec., 1969; Permanent Sec., Dept of Educn, 1973–79. *Address:* 4 Camden Court, Brecon, Powys LD3 7RP. *T:* (01874) 625617. *Died 19 March 2006.*

BROOKE-LITTLE, John Philip Brooke, CVO 1984 (MVO 1969); Norroy and Ulster King of Arms, and King of Arms, Registrar and Knight Attendant on the Most Illustrious Order of St Patrick, 1980–95; Librarian, 1974–94, and Treasurer, 1978–95, College of Arms; Clarenceux King of Arms, 1995–97; *b* 6 April 1927; *s* of late Raymond Brooke-Little, Unicorns House, Swalcliffe; *m* 1960, Mary Lee, *o c* of late John Raymond Pierce; three *s* one *d*. *Educ:* Clayesmore Sch; New Coll., Oxford (MA). Earl Marshal's staff, 1952–53; Gold Staff Officer, Coronation, 1953; Bluemantle Pursuivant of Arms, 1956–67; Richmond Herald, 1967–80; Registrar, Coll. of Arms, 1974–82. Dir, Heralds' Museum, 1991–97; Adviser on heraldry: Nat. Trust, 1983–; Shrievalty Assoc., 1983–. Founder of Heraldry Soc., 1947 (Chm., 1947–97; Pres., 1997–); Hon. Editor, The Coat of Arms, 1950–2004; Fellow, Soc. of Genealogists, 1969; Hon. Fellow, 1979, and Trustee, Inst. of Heraldic and Genealogical Studies. Chm., Harleian Soc., 1984–; Pres., English Language Literary Trust, 1985–96. Governor Emeritus, Clayesmore Sch. (Chm., 1971–83). Trustee, RAF Heraldic Trust, 1996. Freeman and Liveryman, Scriveners' Co. of London (Master, 1985–86). FSA 1961. KStJ 1975; Knight of Malta, 1955, Knight Grand Cross of Grace and Devotion, Order of Malta, 1974 (Chancellor, British Assoc., 1973–77); Comdr Cross of Merit of Order of Malta, 1964; Cruz Distinguida (1st cl.) de San Raimundo de Peñafort, 1955; Knight Grand Cross of Grace, Constantinian Order of St George, 1975. *Publications:* Royal London, 1953; Pictorial History of Oxford, 1954; Boutell's Heraldry, 1970, 1973, 1978 and 1983 (1963 and 1966 edns with C. W. Scott-Giles); Knights of the Middle Ages, 1966; Prince of Wales, 1969; Fox-Davies' Complete Guide to Heraldry, annotated edn, 1969; (with Don Pottinger and Anne Tauté) Kings and Queens of Great Britain, 1970; An Heraldic Alphabet, 1973, rev. edn 1997; (with Marie Angell) Beasts in Heraldry, 1974; The British Monarchy in Colour, 1976; Royal Arms, Beasts and Badges, 1977; Royal Ceremonies of State, 1979; genealogical and heraldic articles. *Recreations:* designing, humming. *Address:* Heyford House, Lower Heyford, Bicester, Oxon OX25 3NZ. *T:* (01869) 340337. *Club:* Chelsea Arts (Hon. Member). *Died 13 Feb. 2006.*

BROOKS, John Ashton, CBE 1989; FCIB; Director: Midland Bank plc, 1981–91; Hongkong and Shanghai Banking Corp., 1989–91; Thomas Cook Group Ltd, 1983–94 (Chairman, 1988–92); *b* 24 Oct. 1928; *s* of Victor Brooks and Annie (*née* Ashton); *m* 1959, Sheila (*née* Hulse); one *s* one *d*. *Educ:* Merchant Taylors' Sch., Northwood. Joined Midland Bank, 1949; Manager: 22 Victoria Street Br., 1970; Threadneedle Street Br., 1972; Gen. Man., Computer Operations, 1975; Dep. Gp Chief Exec., Midland Group, 1981–89. President: Chartered Inst. of Bankers, 1987–89; Assoc. of Banking Teachers, 1990–98. Trustee, Charities Aid Foundn, 1990–99; Dir and Chm., CafCash Ltd (formerly Charities Aid Foundn Money Management Ltd), 1993–99. *Recreations:* reading, walking. *Club:* Institute of Directors. *Died 3 Aug. 2010.*

BROTHERS, Air Cdre Peter Malam, CBE 1964; DSO 1944; DFC 1940, and Bar, 1943; Managing Director, Peter Brothers Consultants Ltd, 1973–86; *b* 30 Sept. 1917; *s* of late John Malam Brothers; *m* 1939, Annette (*d* 2005), *d* of late James Wilson; twod (and one *d* decd). *Educ:* N Manchester Sch. (Br. of Manchester Grammar). Joined RAF, 1936; Flt-Lieut 1939; RAF Biggin Hill, Battle of Britain, 1940; Sqdn-Ldr 1941; Wing Comdr

1942; Tangmere Fighter Wing Ldr, 1942–43; Staff HQ No. 10 Gp, 1943; Exeter Wing Ldr, 1944; US Comd and Gen. Staff Sch., 1944–45; Central Fighter Estab., 1945–46; Colonial Service, Kenya, 1947–49; RAF Bomber Sqdn, 1949–52; HQ No. 3 Gp, 1952–54; RAF Staff Coll., 1954; HQ Fighter Comd, 1955–57; Bomber Stn, 1957–59; Gp Capt., and Staff Officer, SHAPE, 1959–62; Dir of Ops (Overseas), 1962–65; Air Cdre, and AOC Mil. Air Traffic Ops, 1965–68; Dir of Public Relations (RAF), MoD (Air), 1968–73; retired 1973. Freeman, Guild Air Pilots and Air Navigators, 1966 (Liveryman, 1968; Warden, 1971; Master, 1974–75); Freeman, City of London, 1967. Editorial Adviser, Defence and Foreign Affairs publications, 1973–76. Chm., Battle of Britain Fighter Assoc., 2003– (Dep. Chm., 1993–2003); Patron, Spitfire Assoc., Australia, 1971–; Vice-President: Spitfire Soc., 1984–; Devon Emergency Volunteers, 1980–93 (Chm., 1981–93); Life Vice-Pres., Battle of Britain Meml Trust, 2003–; President: Hungerford Br., Aircrew Assoc., 2001–; Battle of Britain Histl Soc., 2003–. *Recreations:* golf, sailing, fishing, swimming, flying. *Address:* 11 Downs Close, Eastbury, W Berks RG17 7JW. *Clubs:* Royal Air Force; Deanwood Park Golf.   *Died 18 Dec. 2008.*

BROUGH, Edward; Chairman, Volker Stevin (UK) Ltd, 1980–82; *b* 28 May 1918; *s* of late Hugh and Jane Brough; *m* 1941, Peggy Jennings (decd); two *s. Educ:* Berwick Grammar School; Edinburgh University (MA). Joined Unilever Ltd, 1938. War service, KOSB, 1939–46 (Captain). Rejoined Unilever, 1946; Commercial Dir, 1951, Man. Dir, 1954, Lever's Cattle Foods Ltd; Chairman, Crosfields (CWG) Ltd, 1957; Lever Bros & Associates Ltd: Development Dir, 1960; Marketing Dir, 1962; Chm., 1965; Hd of Unilever's Marketing Div., 1968–71; Dir of Unilever Ltd and Unilever NV, 1968–74, and Chm. of UK Cttee, 1971–74. Chm., Adriaan Volker (UK) Ltd, 1974–80. Mem., NBPI, 1967–70. FCMI (FBIM 1967). *Recreations:* flyfishing, golf. *Address:* Flat 8, Ferndown Court, Frensham Road, Lower Bourne, Farnham, Surrey GU10 3PZ; St John's, Chagford, Devon TQ13 8HJ. *Club:* Farmers'.
Died 26 June 2006.

BROUGHSHANE, 3rd Baron *cr* 1945; **William Kensington Davison,** DSO 1945; DFC 1942; *b* 25 Nov. 1914; *yr s* of 1st Baron Broughshane and Beatrice Mary (*d* 1971), *d* of Sir Owen Roberts; *S* brother, 1995. *Educ:* Shrewsbury Sch.; Magdalen Coll., Oxford. Called to the Bar, Inner Temple, 1939. Served War, 1939–45 (Wing Commander, RAF). *Recreations:* music, opera, ballet, reading. *Heir:* none. *Address:* 3 Godfrey Street, SW3 3TA. *T:* (020) 7352 7826. *Club:* Garrick.
Died 24 March 2006 (ext).

BROUN, Sir William (Windsor), 13th Bt *cr* 1686 (NS), of Colstoun, Haddingtonshire; FCA; *b* 11 July 1917; *e s* of William Arthur Broun (*d* 1925) and Marie Victoria Broun (*d* 1964), *d* of William McIntyre; *S* cousin, 1995; *m* 1952, D'Hrie, *d* of late Frank R. King, Bingara, NSW; two *d. Educ:* North Sydney High Sch. FCA 1991. Vice Pres., Scottish Australian Heritage Council. Member: Royal Agricl Soc. of NSW; Royal Armoured Corps Assoc. *Recreations:* golf, bowls. *Heir: nephew* Wayne Hercules Broun [*b* 23 Jan. 1952; *m* 1st, 1976, Anna Maria Paolucci (marr. diss. 1998); one *s* one *d*; 2nd, 2001, Caroline Mary Lavender; one *d*]. *Address:* Tamarisk Gardens, 12/2–4 Reed Street, Cremorne, NSW 2090, Australia. *T:* (2) 99041020. *Clubs:* Royal Automobile of Australia (Sydney); Cromer Golf; Bombay Presidency Golf; Mosman Bowling.   *Died 17 March 2007.*

BROWALDH, Tore; Grand Cross, Order of Star of the North, 1974; Kt Comdr's Cross, Order of Vasa, 1963; Hon. Chairman, Svenska Handelsbanken, since 1988; Deputy Chairman, Nobel Foundation, 1966–88; *b* 23 Aug. 1917; *s* of Knut Ernfrid Browaldh and Ingrid Gezelius; *m* 1942, Gunnel Eva Ericson; three *s* one *d. Educ:* Stockholm Univ. (MA Politics, Economics and Law, 1941). Financial Attaché, Washington, 1943; Asst Sec., Royal Cttee of Post-War Econ. Planning, and

Admin. Sec., Industrial Inst. for Econ. and Social Res., 1944–45; Sec. to Bd of Management, Svenska Handelsbanken, 1946–49; Dir of Econ., Social, Cultural and Refugee Dept, Secretariat Gen., Council of Europe, Strasbourg, 1949–51; Exec. Vice Pres., Confedn of Swedish Employers, 1951–54; Chief Gen. Man., Svenska Handelsbanken, 1955–66, Chm., 1966–78, Vice-Chm., 1978–88. Chairman: Svenska Cellulosa AB, 1965–88; Sandrew theater and movie AB, 1963–; Swedish IBM, 1978–; Swedish Unilever AB, 1977–; Industrivärden, 1976–88; Deputy Chairman: Beijerinvest AB, 1975–82; AB Volvo, 1977–88; Director: Volvo Internat. Adv. Bd, 1980–88; IBM World Trade Corp., Europe/ME/Africa, New York, 1979–88; Unilever Adv. Bd, Rotterdam and London, 1976–88. Member: Swedish Govt's Econ. Planning Commn, 1962–73 and Res. Adv. Bd, 1966–70; Consultative Cttee, Internat. Fedn of Insts for Advanced Study, 1972–; UN Gp of Eminent Persons on Multinational Corporations, 1973–74. Member: Royal Swedish Acad. of Sciences; Hudson Inst., USA; Soc. of Scientists and Members of Parlt, Sweden; Royal Swedish Acad. of Engrg Sciences; Royal Acad. of Arts and Sciences, Uppsala; World Acad. of Art and Scis. Dr of Technol. *hc* Royal Inst. of Technol., 1967; Dr of Econs *hc* Gothenburg, 1980. St Erik's Medal, Sweden, 1961; Gold Medal for public service, Sweden, 1981. *Publications:* Management and Society, 1961; (autobiography): vol. I, The Pilgrimage of a Journeyman, 1976; vol. II, The Long Road, 1980; vol. III, Against the Wind, 1984. *Recreations:* jazz, piano, golf, chess. *Address:* (office) Svenska Handelsbanken, Kungsträdgårdsgatan 2, 10670 Stockholm, Sweden. *T:* (8) 229220; (home) Sturegatan 14, 11436 Stockholm, Sweden. *T:* (8) 6619643. *Club:* Sällskapet (Stockholm).   *Died 14 Feb. 2007.*

BROWN, Alan James; HM Diplomatic Service, retired, Deputy Commissioner-General, UN Relief and Works Agency for Palestine Refugees, 1977–84; *b* 28 Aug. 1921; *s* of W. Y. Brown and Mrs E. I. Brown; *m* 1966, Joy Aileen Key Stone (*née* McIntyre); one *s*, and two step *d. Educ:* Magdalene College, Cambridge (MA). Served with HM Forces, 1941–47; CRO 1948; 2nd Sec., Calcutta, 1948–50; CRO, 1951; Private Sec. to Parly Under-Secretary of State, 1951–52; 1st Secretary, Dacca, Karachi, 1952–55; CRO, 1955–57; Kuala Lumpur, 1957–62; CRO, 1962–63; Head of Information Policy Dept, 1963–64; Dep. High Comr, Nicosia, 1964; Head of Far East and Pacific Dept, CRO, 1964–66; Dep. High Comr, Malta, 1966–70; Dep High Comr, later Consul-Gen., Karachi, 1971–72; Ambassador to Togo and Benin, 1973–75; Head of Nationality and Treaty Dept, FCO, 1975–77. *Recreation:* sailing. *Address:* Oakwood, Treworthal Road, Perranarworthal, Truro TR3 7QB. *T:* (01872) 863027. *Club:* Oxford and Cambridge.
Died 10 Nov. 2006.

BROWN, A(rthur) I(vor) Parry, FRCA; Anæsthetist: London Hospital, 1936–73; London Chest Hospital, 1946–73; Harefield Hospital, 1940–73; Royal Masonic Hospital, 1950–73; *b* 23 July 1908; *s* of A. T. J. Brown; *m* Joyce Marion Bash. *Educ:* Tollington Sch., London; London Hospital. MRCS, LRCP, 1931; MB, BS London, 1933; DA, 1935; FFARCS, 1951. Member of the Board of the Faculty of Anæsthetists, RCS; Pres., Sect. of Anæsthetics, RSM, 1972–73; Fellow, Assoc. of Anæsthetists; Member, Thoracic Soc. *Publications:* chapter in Diseases of the Chest, 1952; contributions to: Thorax, Anæsthesia. *Address:* Long Thatch, Church Lane, Balsham, Cambridge CB1 6DS. *T:* (01223) 893012.
Died 15 Nov. 2007.

BROWN, Sir (Cyril) Maxwell Palmer, (Sir Max), KCB 1969 (CB 1965); CMG 1957; Permanent Secretary, Department of Trade, March–June 1974; *b* 30 June 1914; *s* of late Cyril Palmer Brown; *m* 1940, Margaret May Gillhespy (*d* 2006); three *s* one *d. Educ:* Wanganui College; Victoria University College, NZ; Clare College, Cambridge. Princ. Private Secretary to Pres. Board of Trade, 1946–49; Monopolies Commn, 1951–55; Counsellor (Commercial) Washington, 1955–57;

returned to Board of Trade; Second Permanent Sec., 1968–70; Sec. (Trade), DTI, 1970–74: Mem., 1975–81, Dep. Chm., 1976–81, Monopolies and Mergers Commn. Director: John Brown & Co., 1975–82; ERA Technology Ltd, 1974–86; RHP Gp plc (formerly Ransome Hoffmann Pollard Ltd), 1975–88. *Address:* 20 Cottenham Park Road, Wimbledon, SW20 0RZ. *T:* (020) 8946 7237. *Died 13 Aug. 2009.*

BROWN, David Colin, CMG 1995; HM Diplomatic Service, retired; Consultant, Home Estates Department, Foreign and Commonwealth Office, 1997 (Head, 1989–97); Project Director, Refurbishment of Foreign Office, Whitehall, 1989–97; *b* 10 Aug. 1939; *yr s* of Alan James Brown and Catherine Mary Brown; *m* 1960, Ann Jackson; two *s* one *d. Educ:* Lymm Grammar Sch. Joined CRO, 1960; Tech. Aid Administrator, Lagos, 1960–63; Admin. Officer, Kingston, Jamaica, 1964–66; Diplomatic Service Admin Office, 1966–68; Second Sec., FCO, 1968; Vice-Consul (Commercial), Johannesburg, 1969–73; seconded to Commn on Rhodesian Opinion, Bulawayo, 1971; News Dept, FCO, 1974–77; Dep. High Comr, Port Louis, 1977–81; Overseas Inspectorate, 1981–83; Asst Hd, W Indian and Atlantic Dept, FCO, 1983–86; Dep. Consul Gen., Milan, 1986–89; Counsellor, 1989. *Recreations:* walking, gardening, building conservation. *Died 27 Sept. 2010.*

BROWN, Sir Douglas (Denison), Kt 1983; Chairman, 1981–87 and Managing Director, 1954–87, James Corson & Co. Ltd; *b* 8 July 1917; *s* of Robert and Alice Mary Brown; *m* 1941, Marion Cruickshanks Emmerson (*d* 1992); one *s* one *d. Educ:* Bablake Sch., Coventry. Served Army, 1940–46: RE, 1940–41; commnd RA, 1941; India, ME, N Africa, Italy; mentioned in despatches; retd in rank of Major. Member: Exec. Cttee, Clothing Manufrs of GB, 1967–82; Cttee, Wooltac, 1988– (Vice Chm., 1982–92); Exec., BCIA, 1988–90 (Hon. Mem., Yorks Humberside BCIA, 1990); Chairman: Leeds and Northern Clothing Assoc., 1975–77; Clothing Initiative, 1988–90; Leeds Clothing and Textile Centre, 1993–97. Chairman: NW Leeds Cons. Assoc., 1961–74 (Pres. 1974); Yorks Area Cons. Assoc., 1978–83 (Treasurer, 1971–78); Mem., Nat. Exec. Cttee, Cons. and Unionist Assoc., 1971–90; Mem., Cons. Bd of Finance, 1971–78. Director: Computer Internat., 1993–94; Castleton Computers, 1995–2000. Mem., Gas Consumer Council, NE Area, 1981–86; Bd Mem., Yorkshire Water Authority, 1983–86. President: Water Aid Yorkshire, 1988; Leeds Gardeners' Fedn, 1991–94 and 1998. Vice-Chm., St Edmund's PCC, Roundhay, 1981–96. Chm., Bd of Governors, Jacob Kramer Coll. of Further Educn, 1978–92 (Gov., 1975–93); Chm. Govs, Leeds Coll. of Art and Design, 1993–2000 (Life Pres., 2001); Governor, Cross Green High Sch., 1989–96 (Chm., 1995–96). *Recreations:* gardening, Rugby, cricket, golf. *Address:* One Oak, 12 Elmete Grove, Leeds LS8 2JY. *T:* (0113) 273 5470. *Died 20 May 2007.*

BROWN, Prof. Gavin, AO 2006; PhD; FAA; FRSN; Inaugural Director, Royal Institution of Australia, since 2008; *b* Fife, Scotland, 27 Feb. 1942; *s* of F. B. D. and A. D. D. Brown; *m* 1st, 1966, Barbara Routh (*d* 2001); one *s* one *d*; 2nd, 2004, Diané Ranck. *Educ:* Univ. of St Andrews (MA); Univ. of Newcastle upon Tyne (PhD 1966). FAA 1981. Asst Lectr, then Lectr, and Sen. Lectr in Maths, Liverpool Univ., 1966–75; University of New South Wales: Prof. of Pure Maths, 1976–92, then Emeritus; Hd, Dept of Pure Maths, 1976–81, 1986–89; Hd, Sch. of Maths, 1981–85; Dean: Faculty of Sci., 1989–92; Bd of Studies in Sci. & Maths, 1990–92; Dep. Vice-Chancellor, 1992–93, Vice-Chancellor, 1994–96, Univ. of Adelaide; Vice-Chancellor and Principal, Univ. of Sydney, 1996–2008. Visiting Professor: Univ. of Paris, 1975; Univ. of York, 1979; Univ. of Cambridge, 1986; Tohoku Univ., 2008. FRSN 2010. Corresp. FRSE 2007. Hon. LLD: St Andrews, 1998; Dundee, 2004; Waseda, 2009; Hon. EdD Unitar, 2008; Hon. DSc:

Sydney, 2009; Edinburgh, 2010. *Publications:* numerous contribs to various maths jls. *Recreation:* racing. *Died 25 Dec. 2010.*

BROWN, Sir George (Noel), Kt 1991; legal consultant; Law Revision Commissioner, Belize, 1998–99; Chief Justice, Belize, 1990–98; *b* 13 June 1942; *s* of late Noel Todd Brown and Elma Priscilla Brown; *m* 1974, Magdalene Elizabeth Bucknor; two *d*, and one *s* one *d* from previous marriage. *Educ:* St Michael's Coll., Belize City; Carlton Univ., Ottawa (Cert. in Public Admin); Univ. of WI (LLB Hons); Norman Manley Law Sch., Council of Legal Educn, Univ. of WI (Legal Educn Cert.); Nairobi Law Sch., Kenya (Commonwealth Cert. in Legislative Drafting). Customs Examiner, Customs and Excise Dept, 1960–67; Clerk of Courts, Magistracy Dept, 1967–69; Admin. Asst, and Actg Trade Adminr, Min. of Trade and Ind., 1970–72; Actg Magistrate, Belize Judicial Dist and Itinerant countrywide, 1972–73; Crown Counsel, Attorney General's Ministry, 1978–81; Solicitor General, 1981–84; Puisne Judge, Supreme Court Justice, 1984–85 and 1986–90; Actg Chief Justice, 1985–86; Dep. Governor-Gen., Belize, 1985–94. Mem., Belize Adv. Council, 1985–2002. Chairman: Nat. Olympic Fairplay Commn, 2000–; Nat. Community Rehabilitation Cttee, 2002–. Pres., Sir George Noel Brown Foundn, 1998–; Chairman: Bd of Dirs, Tubal Trade and Vocational Sch., 2003–; Belize Maritime Trust, 2003–. Elder, Seventh Day Adventist Faith, 2000–04. *Publications:* Consumer Society and the Law, 1976; contribs to Caribbean Law Rev. *Recreations:* yachting, football (soccer), especially coaching and managing primary and secondary schools teams. *Address:* 6203 corner Park Avenue and Seashore Drive, Buttonwood Bay, Belize City, PO Box 236, Belize, Central America. *T:* (2) 233824. *Club:* Belize Yacht (Belize City). *Died 26 July 2007.*

BROWN, Harold James, AM 1980; BSc, ME; Hon. DSc; FIEAust; FIREE; management consultant, Adelaide, South Australia, 1976–85; Technical Director, Philips Industries Holdings Ltd, Sydney, 1961–76; *b* 10 July 1911; *s* of Allison James and Hilda Emmy Brown; *m* 1936, Hazel Merlyn Dahl Helm; two *s* two *d. Educ:* Fort Street Boys' High Sch.; Univ. of Sydney, NSW, Australia. BSc 1933; BE (Univ. Medal) 1935; ME (Univ. Medal) 1945; Hon. DSc 1976. Research Engineer, Amalgamated Wireless Australasia Ltd, 1935–37; Electrical Engineer, Hydro-electric Commission of Tasmania, 1937–39; Research Officer and Principal Research Officer, Council for Scientific and Industrial Research, 1939–45; Chief Communications Engineer, Australian Nat. Airways Pty Ltd, 1945–47; Prof. of Electrical Engineering, Dean of Faculty of Engineering and Asst Director, NSW Univ. of Technology, 1947–52; Controller R&D, Dept of Supply, Melbourne, 1952–54; Controller, Weapons Research Establishment, Department of Supply, Commonwealth Government of Australia, 1955–58; Technical Director, Rola Co. Pty Ltd, Melbourne, 1958–61. Silver Jubilee Medal, 1977. *Publications:* numerous technical articles in scientific journals. *Recreations:* gardening, bowling. *Address:* 20 Woodbridge, 6 Island Drive, West Lakes, SA 5021, Australia. *Died 3 Nov. 2006.*

BROWN, Henry Thomas C.; *see* Cadbury-Brown.

BROWN, Hugh Dunbar; *b* 18 May 1919; *s* of Neil Brown and Grace (*née* Hargrave); *m* 1947, Mary Glen Carmichael (*d* 2000); one *d. Educ:* Allan Glen's School and Whitehill Secondary School, Glasgow. Formerly Civil Servant, Ministry of Pensions and National Insurance. Member of Glasgow Corporation, 1954; Magistrate, Glasgow, 1961. MP (Lab) Provan Div. of Glasgow, 1964–87. Parly Under-Sec. of State, Scottish Office, 1974–79. *Recreation:* golf. *Address:* Allander Court, Flat 2, 86 Main Street, Milngavie, Glasgow G62 6JN. *Died 10 March 2008.*

BROWN, John B.; *see* Blamire-Brown.

BROWN, Prof. John Milton, PhD; FRS 2003; Professor of Chemistry, Oxford University, 1996–2008; Fellow, Exeter College, Oxford, since 1983; *b* 12 Sept. 1941; *s* of Arthur Godfrey Kilner Brown and Mary Denholm Brown; *m* 1964, Monika Bergstrom; two *s* one *d. Educ:* Cheltenham Coll.; Peterhouse, Cambridge (BA 1963; PhD 1966); MA Oxon. Lectr, 1970–82, Reader, 1982–83, Southampton Univ.; Lectr, Oxford Univ., 1983–96. *Publications:* Molecular Spectroscopy, 1998; Rotational Spectroscopy of Diatomic Molecules, 2003. *Recreations:* walking in mountains, bicycling, running. *Address:* Physical and Theoretical Chemistry Laboratory, South Parks Road, Oxford OX1 3QZ. *T:* (office) (01865) 275403, *Fax:* (01865) 275410; *e-mail:* jmb@physchem.ox.ac.uk. *Club:* Achilles. *Died 10 Sept. 2009.*

BROWN, June P.; *see* Paterson-Brown.

BROWN, Prof. L(ionel) Neville, OBE 1988; Professor of Comparative Law, University of Birmingham, 1966–90, Emeritus Professor, since 1990; Leverhulme Fellow, 1990–92; *b* 29 July 1923; *s* of Reginald P. N. Brown and Fanny Brown (*née* Carver); *m* 1957, Mary Patricia Vowles; three *s* one *d. Educ:* Wolverhampton Grammar Sch.; Pembroke Coll., Cambridge (Scholar; 1st Cl. Class. Tripos Pt I and Law Tripos Pt II; MA, LLM); Lyons Univ. (Dr en Droit). RAF, 1942–45; Cambridge, 1945–48; articled to Wolverhampton solicitor, 1948–50; Rotary Foundn Fellow, Lyons Univ., 1951–52; Lectr in Law, Sheffield Univ., 1953–55; Lectr in Comparative Law, Birmingham Univ., 1956, Sen. Lectr, 1957; Sen. Res. Fellow, Univ. of Michigan, 1960. Mem., Council on Tribunals, 1982–88; Chm., Birmingham Social Security Appeal Tribunal, 1990–96. Visiting Professor: Univ. of Tulane, New Orleans, 1968; Univ. of Nairobi, 1974; Laval, 1975, 1979, 1983, 1990; Limoges, 1986; Mauritius, 1988, 1989; Aix-en-Provence, 1991. Commonwealth Foundn Lectr (Caribbean), 1975–76. Pres., SPTL, 1984–85. Reader, C of E, Lichfield Dio., 1971–. Dr *hc* Limoges, 1989; Hon. LLD Laval, 1992. Commandeur, Ordre des Palmes Académiques (France), 2006 (Officier, 1987). *Publications:* (with F. H. Lawson and A. E. Anton) Amos and Walton's Introduction to French Law, 2nd edn 1963 and 3rd edn 1967; (with J. F. Garner) French Administrative Law, 1967, 5th edn (with J. S. Bell) 1998; (with F. G. Jacobs) Court of Justice of the European Communities, 1977, 5th edn (with T. Kennedy), 2000. *Recreations:* landscape gardening, country walking, music. *Address:* Willow Rise, 14 Waterdale, Compton Road West, Wolverhampton, West Midlands WV3 9DY. *T:* (01902) 426666. *Club:* Oxford and Cambridge. *Died 6 Nov. 2008.*

BROWN, Sir Max; *see* Brown, Sir C. M. P.

BROWN, Ronald, (Ron); *b* Edinburgh, 29 June 1940; *s* of James Brown (*né* Jänsch) and Margaret McLaren; *m* 1963, May Smart (*d* 1995); two *s. Educ:* Pennywell Primary Sch., Edinburgh; Ainslie Park High Sch., Edinburgh; Bristo Technical Inst., Edinburgh. National Service, Royal Signals. Five yrs engrg apprenticeship with Bruce Peebles and Co. Ltd, East Pilton, Edinburgh. Chm., Pilton Br., AUEW; President: AEU, Pilton, 1992–98; AEEU, Edinburgh, 1998–2000; formerly: Chm. Works Cttee, Edinburgh Dist of SSEB; Convenor of Shop Stewards, Parsons Peebles Ltd, Edinburgh. Formerly Councillor for Central Leith, Edinburgh Town Council; Regional Councillor for Royston/Granton, Lothian Reg. Council, 1974–79. MP (Lab) Edinburgh Leith, 1979–92; contested (Ind. Lab) Edinburgh Leith, 1992. Member: Lothian and Borders Fire Bd, 1974–79; Central Scotland Water Develt Bd, 1974–79. EC Mem. and Vice Chair, Edinburgh Trade Union Council, 1998–2000. Mem. Mgt Cttee, Leith CAB, 1998–2000. Columnist, Edinburgh Echo, 1998–2000. *Died 3 Aug. 2007.*

BROWN, Rowland Percival, OBE 1993; MA; JP; legal consultant, Secondary Heads Association, 1993–2002; Headmaster, Royal Grammar School, High Wycombe,

1975–93; *b* 8 Jan. 1933; *s* of late Percy and Gladys Mabel Brown; *m* 1959, Jessie Doig Connell; three *d. Educ:* Queen Mary's Sch., Basingstoke; Worcester Coll., Oxford (MA French and Russian, 1956). Called to the Bar, Inner Temple, 1966; ESU Walter Page Scholar, 1976. Intelligence Corps, 1951–53, Second Lieut. Hampton Sch., 1957–62; Head of Modern Langs, Tudor Grange Grammar Sch., Solihull, 1962–67; Head Master, King Edward VI Sch., Nuneaton, 1967–75. Legal Sec., Headmasters' Assoc. and SHA, 1975–85; Pres., SHA, 1985–86. Oxford Univ. Delegacy of Local Exams, 1986–96; Mem., RAF OASC Selection Bd, 1970–96. Educnl Advr, World Challenge Expedns, 1993–2001. Liveryman, Feltmakers' Co., 1991–. JP Bucks, 1978. *Publications:* Heads Legal Guide, 1984; The School Management Handbook, 1993; The Education Acts, 1998. *Recreations:* golf, walking, theatre, following sport. *Address:* Wildwood, Manor Road, Penn, Bucks HP10 8JA. *Club:* Phyllis Court (Henley). *Died 22 Sept. 2010.*

BROWN, Roy Dudley; Director, Association of West European Shipbuilders, 1977–83; *b* 5 Aug. 1916; *y s* of late Alexander and Jessie Brown; *m* 1941, Maria Margaret Barry McGhee (*d* 1996); one *s* one *d. Educ:* Robert Gordon's Coll., Aberdeen; Aberdeen Univ. (MA 1935, LLB 1937). In private law practice, Glasgow, 1937–38; joined Shipbldg Conf., London, 1938; War Service, RN; Jt Sec. on amalgamation of Shipbldg Conf., Shipbldg Employers Fedn, and Dry Dock Owners and Repairers Central Council into Shipbuilders and Repairers National Assoc., 1967; Dep. Dir, 1973, until dissolution of Assoc. on nationalization, 1977. Sec., Shipbldg Corp. Ltd, 1943–77. Freeman, Shipwrights' Co. *Recreations:* golf, wine, gardening. *Address:* St Vincent's Nursing Home, Wiltshire Lane, Eastcote, Pinner, Middlesex HA5 2NB. *Died 8 April 2008.*

BROWNE, Angelica Elizabeth; *see* Mitchell, A. E.

BROWNE, Air Cdre Charles Duncan Alfred, CB 1971; DFC 1944; RAF, retired; *b* 8 July 1922; *s* of late Alfred Browne and Catherine (*née* MacKinnon); *m* 1946, Una Félicité Leader (*d* 2001); (one *s* decd). War of 1939–45: served Western Desert, Italy, Corsica and S France in Hurricane and Spitfire Sqdns; post war service in Home, Flying Training, Bomber and Strike Commands; MoD; CO, RAF Brüggen, Germany, 1966–68; Comdt, Aeroplane and Armament Exp. Estab., 1968–71; Air Officer i/c Central Tactics and Trials Orgn, 1971–72. *Club:* Royal Air Force. *Died 24 March 2009.*

BROWNE, Mervyn Ernest, CBE 1976; ERD 1954; HM Diplomatic Service, retired 1976; *b* 3 June 1916; *s* of late Ernest Edmond Browne and of Florence Mary Browne; *m* 1st, 1942, Constance (*née* Jarvis) (*d* 1988); three *s*; 2nd, 1991, Cecily (*née* Baker) (*d* 2004). *Educ:* Stockport Sec. Sch.; St Luke's Coll., Exeter; University Coll., Exeter. BScEcon London; BA Exeter. RA, 1940–46; TA, 1947–53; AER, RASC, 1953–60. Distribution of industry res., BoT, 1948–56; HM Trade Comr Service: Trade Comr, Wellington, NZ, 1957–61 and Adelaide, 1961–64; Principal Trade Comr, Kingston, Jamaica, 1964–68; HM Diplomatic Service: Counsellor (Commercial), Canberra, 1968–70; Dir, Brit. Trade in S Africa, Johannesburg, 1970–73; Consul-Gen., 1974–76 and Chargé d'Affaires, 1974 and 1976, Brit. Embassy, Manila. *Recreations:* militaria, lepidoptery, squash rackets. *Address:* 32 Cydonia Court, Earlsdon Way, Highcliffe, Dorset BH23 5TD. *T:* (01425) 278529. *Died 16 Jan. 2006.*

BROWNE-EVANS, Hon. Dame Lois (Marie), DBE 1999; JP; Attorney-General of Bermuda, 1999–2003; *b* 1 June 1927; *d* of James T. Browne and Emmeline Browne (*née* Charles); *m* 1958, John Evans; one *s* two *d. Educ:* King's Coll., London (LLB). Called to the Bar: Middle Temple, June 1953; Bermuda, Dec. 1953; Jamaica, 1966; in practice at the Bar, own chambers, 1954–99. MP (Progressive Lab) Devonshire North,

Bermuda, 1963–2003; Leader of the Opposition, Bermuda, 1968–85; Shadow Minister of Legislative Affairs, 1985–98; Minister of Legislative Affairs, 1998–2003. Mem., Internat. Fedn of Women Lawyers. Hon. Rep. of Govt of Jamaica, Bermuda. *Recreations:* reading, travel. *Clubs:* Devonshire Recreation, Bermuda Business and Professional Women's (Bermuda).
Died 29 May 2007.

BROWNING, Rex Alan, CB 1984; Deputy Secretary, Overseas Development Administration, 1981–86; *b* 22 July 1930; *s* of Gilbert H. W. Browning and Gladys (*née* Smith); *m* 1961, Paula McKain; three *d*. *Educ:* Bristol Grammar Sch.; Merton Coll., Oxford (Postmaster) (MA). HM Inspector of Taxes, 1952; Asst Principal, Colonial Office, 1957; Private Sec. to Parly Under-Sec. for the Colonies, 1960; Principal, Dept of Techn. Co-operation, 1961; transf. ODM, 1964; seconded to Diplomatic Service as First Sec. (Aid), British High Commn, Singapore, 1969; Asst Sec., 1971; Counsellor, Overseas Develt, Washington, and Alternate UK Exec. Dir, IBRD, 1973–76; Under-Secretary: ODM, 1976–78; Dept of Trade, 1978–80; ODA, 1980–81. *Address:* 19 Lingdale Road, Prenton, Merseyside CH43 8TE.
Died 29 May 2009.

BROWNLEE, Prof. George; Professor of Pharmacology, King's College, University of London, 1958–78, then Emeritus; *b* 8 Sept. 1911; *s* of late George R. Brownlee and of Mary C. C. Gow, Edinburgh; *m* 1940, Margaret P. M. Cochrane (*d* 1970), 2nd *d* of Thomas W. P. Cochrane and Margaret P. M. S. Milne, Bo'ness, Scotland; three *s*; 2nd, 1977, Betty Jean Gaydon (marr. diss. 1981), *o d* of Stanley H. Clutterham and Margaret M. Fox, Sidney, Australia. *Educ:* Tynecastle Sch.; Heriot-Watt Coll., Edinburgh. BSc 1936, DSc 1950, Glasgow; PhD 1939, London. Rammell Schol., Biological Standardization Labs of Pharmaceutical Soc., London; subseq. Head of Chemotherapeutic Div., Wellcome Res. Labs, Beckenham; Reader in Pharmacology, King's Coll., Univ. of London, 1949. Editor, Jl of Pharmacy and Pharmacology, 1955–72. FKC, 1971. *Publications:* (with Prof. J. P. Quilliam) Experimental Pharmacology, 1952; papers on: chemotherapy of tuberculosis and leprosy; structure and pharmacology of the polymyxins; endocrinology; toxicity of drugs; neurohumoral transmitters in smooth muscle, etc., in: Brit. Jl Pharmacology; Jl Physiology; Biochem. Jl; Nature; Lancet; Annals NY Acad. of Science; Pharmacological Reviews, etc. *Recreations:* collecting books, making things. *Address:* 602 Gilbert House, Barbican, EC2Y 8BD. *T:* (020) 7638 9543. *Club:* Athenæum.
Died 19 May 2010.

BROWNLIE, Sir Ian, Kt 2009; CBE 1993; QC 1979; DCL; FBA 1979; International Law practitioner; Chichele Professor of Public International Law, then Emeritus, and Fellow of All Souls College, University of Oxford, 1980–99 (Distinguished Fellow, 2004); *b* 19 Sept. 1932; *s* of John Nason Brownlie and Amy Isabella (*née* Atherton); *m* 1st, 1957, Jocelyn Gale (marr. diss. 1975); one *s* two *d*; 2nd, 1978, Christine J. Apperley, LLM. *Educ:* Alsop High Sch., Liverpool; Hertford Coll., Oxford (Gibbs Scholar, 1952; BA 1953); King's Coll., Cambridge (Humanitarian Trust Student, 1955). DPhil Oxford, 1961; DCL Oxford, 1976. Called to the Bar, Gray's Inn, 1958, Bencher, 1987. Lectr, Nottingham Univ., 1957–63; Fellow and Tutor in Law, Wadham Coll., Oxford, 1963–76 and Lectr, Oxford Univ., 1964–76; Prof. of Internat. Law, LSE, Univ. of London, 1976–80. Reader in Public Internat. Law, Inns of Ct Sch. of Law, 1973–76; Dir of Studies, Internat. Law Assoc., 1982–91. Member: Panel of Conciliators and Panel of Arbitrators, ICSID (World Bank), 1988–98; Internat. Law Commn, UN, 1996– (Chm., 2007–08); Judge, 1995–, Pres., 1996–, Eur. Nuclear Energy Tribunal. Delegate, OUP, 1984–94. Lectr, Hague Acad. of Internat. Law, 1979, 1995. Editor, British Year Book of International Law, 1974–99. Mem., Inst. of Internat. Law, 1985– (Associate Mem., 1977; Third Vice-Pres.,

2001–). Hon. Member: Amer. Soc. of Internat. Law, 2004; Indian Soc. of Internat. Law. Japan Foundn Award, 1978. Comdr, Royal Norwegian OM, 1993. *Publications:* International Law and the Use of Force by States, 1963; Principles of Public International Law, 1966, 7th edn 2008 (Russian edn, ed G. I. Tunkin, 1977; Japanese edn, 1989; Portuguese edn, 1998; Chinese edn, 2003; Certif. of Merit, Amer. Soc. of Internat. Law, 1976); Basic Documents in International Law, 1967, 5th edn 2002; The Law Relating to Public Order, 1968; Basic Documents on Human Rights, 1971, 5th edn 2006; Basic Documents on African Affairs, 1971; African Boundaries, a legal and diplomatic encyclopaedia, 1979; State Responsibility, part 1, 1983; (ed jtly) Liber Amicorum for Lord Wilberforce, 1987. *Recreation:* travel. *Address:* Blackstone Chambers, Blackstone House, Temple, EC4Y 9BW. *T:* (020) 7583 1770.
Died 3 Jan. 2010.

BRUCE, Sir Hervey (James Hugh); see Bruce-Clifton, Sir H. J. H.

BRUCE-CLIFTON, Sir Hervey (James Hugh), 7th Bt *cr* 1804; hotelier, Oaklands Country Manor; *b* 3 Sept. 1952; *s* of Sir Hervey John William Bruce, 6th Bt, and Crista, (*d* 1984), *y d* of late Lt-Col Chandos De Paravicini, OBE; changed name to Bruce-Clifton on inheriting Clifton estate, 1996; *S* father, 1971; *m* 1st, 1979, Charlotte (marr. diss. 1991), *e d* of Jack Gore; one *s* one *d*; 2nd, 1992, Joanna (marr. diss. 2006), *y d* of Frank Pope; two *s*; 3rd, 2007, Caroline Mary, *d* of late Roger Naismith Tully. *Educ:* Eton; Officer Cadet School, Mons. Major, the Grenadier Guards, 1984–96. *Recreations:* bungee jumping, body surfing, riding, tapestry. *Heir: s* Hervey Hamish Peter Bruce, *b* 20 Nov. 1986. *Address:* PO Box 19, Van Reenen 3372, KwaZulu-Natal, South Africa. *Club:* Cavalry and Guards.
Died 9 Feb. 2010.

BRUCE-LOCKHART, Baron *cr* 2006 (Life Peer), of the Weald in the County of Kent; **Alexander, (Sandy), John Bruce-Lockhart,** Kt 2003; OBE 1995; Chairman, English Heritage, since 2007; *b* 4 May 1942; *s* of John McGregor Bruce-Lockhart, CB, CMG, OBE and Margaret Evelyn Bruce-Lockhart (*née* Hone); *m* 1966, Tess Pressland; two *s* one *d*. *Educ:* Dragon Sch., Oxford; Sedbergh Sch., Yorks; Royal Agricultural Coll., Cirencester. Farmer, Zimbabwe, 1963–65, Kent, 1966–. Kent County Council: Mem., 1989–; Leader, Cons. Gp, 1993–2005; Leader of Council, 1997–2005. Chairman: LGA, 2004–07 (Vice-Chm., 2002–04); Kent Thameside Delivery Bd, 2004–. Pres., Maidstone Cons. Assoc., 1993– (Chm., 1989–92). Trustee: Inst. of Social Justice, 2004–; Leeds Castle Foundn, 2006–; Nat. Horticultural Res. Inst., 2006–. Pres., Kent Handicapped Care Assoc., 2005–. Hon. DCL Kent, 2006; Hon. DBA Greenwich, 2006. *Publications:* (contrib.) Renewing One Nation, 2002. *Recreations:* family, walking, shooting. *Address:* House of Lords, SW1A 0PW. *Club:* Carlton.
Died 14 Aug. 2008.

BRUMFIT, Prof. Christopher John; Professor of Applied LInguistics, School of Humanities, University of Southampton, since 2003 (Professor of Education, 1984–2003); *b* 25 Oct. 1940; *s* of late John Raymond Brumfit and of Margaret May Brumfit (*née* Warner; she *m* 2nd, 1942, Frank Greenaway); *m* 1st, 1965, Elizabeth Ann Sandars (marr. diss.); one *s*; 2nd, 1986, Rosamond Frances Mitchell; one *s*. *Educ:* Glyn Grammar Sch., Epsom; Brasenose Coll., Oxford (BA English Lang. and Lit.); Univ. of Essex (MA Applied Linguistics); PhD London 1983; Makerere Coll., Univ. of East Africa (DipEd). Head of English, Tabora Govt Sch., Tanzania, 1964–68; Lectr in Educn, Univ. of Dar es Salaam, 1968–71; Lectr in English and Linguistics, City of Birmingham Coll. of Educn, 1972–74; Lectr in Educn with ref. to English for Speakers of Other Languages, Univ. of London Inst. of Educn, 1974–80; Reader in Educn, Univ. of London, 1980–84; Southampton University: Dir, Centre for Language in Educn, 1986–2003; Head, Sch. of Educn, 1986–90; Dean, Faculty of Educnl Studies, 1990–93 and 1996–99; Head, Res. and Grad. Sch. of Educn, 1997–2000; Head: Music, 2004; Modern Langs,

2004–05. Vis. Prof. of English, Univ. of Vienna, 2000–01. Chairman: BAAL, 1982–85; British Council English Teaching Adv. Cttee, 1991–98; British Assoc. of TESOL Qualifying Instns, 1991–94; Vice-Pres., Assoc. Internat. de Linguistique Appliquée, 1984–87; Member: Lang. Cttee, 1981–, Educn Cttee, 1992–, ESU; Lit. Adv. Cttee, British Council, 1989–97; Res. Cttee, Centre for Inf. on Lang. Teaching, 1991–; Bd, English 2000, 1996–98. Editor: ELT Documents, 1982–90; Review of English Language Teaching, 1990–96. Founding AcSS, 1999; Founding Fellow, British Inst. of English Lang. Teaching, 2000. *Publications*: (jtly) Teaching English as a Foreign Language, 1978; (with K. Johnson) The Communicative Approach to Language Teaching, 1979; Problems and Principles in English Teaching, 1980; English for International Communication, 1982; (with J. Roberts) An Introduction to Language and Language Teaching, 1983; (with M. Finocchiaro) The Functional-Notional Approach, 1983; Teaching Literature Overseas, 1983; Language Teaching Projects for the Third World, 1983; Communicative Methodology in Language Teaching, 1984; General English Syllabus Design, 1984; Language and Literature Teaching, 1985; (jtly) English as a Second Language in the UK, 1985; The Practice of Communicative Teaching, 1986; (with R. A. Carter) Literature and Language Teaching, 1986; Language in Teacher Education, 1988; (with R. Mitchell) Research in the Language Classroom, 1990; Literature on Language, 1991; Assessment in Literature Teaching, 1992; (with R. Bowers) Applied Linguistics and English Language Teaching, 1992; (with M. G. Benton) Teaching Literature, 1993; The Council of Europe and Language Teaching, 1995; (jtly) Language Education in the National Curriculum, 1995; Individual Freedom in Language Teaching, 2001; academic and professional papers. *Recreations*: Russian literature, academic cricket, opera, walking. *Address*: 4 The Finches, Southampton SO17 1UB. *T*: (023) 8055 7346. *Club*: Athenæum.
Died 18 March 2006.

BRUNTISFIELD, 2nd Baron *cr* 1942, of Boroughmuir; **John Robert Warrender**, OBE 1963; MC 1943; TD 1967; DL; Bt 1715; *b* 7 Feb. 1921; *s* of 1st Baron Bruntisfield, MC and Dorothy (*d* 1975), *y d* of Col R. H. Rawson, MP; *S* father, 1993; *m* 1st, 1948, (Anne) Moireen Campbell (*d* 1976), 2nd *d* of Sir Walter Campbell, KCIE; two *s* two *d*; 2nd, 1977, Mrs Shirley Crawley (*d* 1981), *o d* of E. J. L. Ross; 3rd, 1985, Mrs (Kathleen) Joanna Graham, JP, *o d* of David Chancellor. *Educ*: Eton; RMC, Sandhurst. Royal Scots Greys (2nd Dragoons), 1939–48; ADC to Governor of Madras, 1946–48; comd N Somerset Yeomanry/44th Royal Tank Regt, 1957–62; Dep. Brigadier RAC (TA), Southern and Eastern Commands, 1962–67. Mem., Queen's Body Guard for Scotland (Royal Co. of Archers) (Brigadier, 1973–85). DL Somerset 1965. *Recreations*: shooting, fishing. *Heir*: *s* Hon. Michael John Victor Warrender [*b* 9 Jan. 1949; *m* 1978, Baroness Walburga von Twickel; one *s*]. *Address*: 41 Park Road, Edinburgh EH6 4LA. *T*: (0131) 551 3701; 151 Skinnet, Melness, by Lairg, Sutherland IV27 4YP. *Clubs*: Puffin's, New (Edinburgh).
Died 14 July 2007.

BRUNTON, Sir (Edward Francis) Lauder, 3rd Bt *cr* 1908; physician; *b* 10 Nov. 1916; *s* of Sir Stopford Brunton, 2nd Bt, and Elizabeth, *o d* of late Professor J. Bonsall Porter; *S* father, 1943; *m* 1946, Marjorie, *o d* of David Sclater Lewis, MSc, MD, CM, FRCP (C); one *s* one *d*. *Educ*: Trinity College School, Port Hope; Bryanston School; McGill Univ. BSc 1940; MD, CM 1942. Served as Captain, RCAMC. Hon. attending Physician, Royal Victoria Hosp., Montreal. Fellow: American Coll. of Physicians; Internat. Soc. of Hematology; Life Mem., Montreal Mus. of Fine Arts; Life Governor, Art Gall. of Nova Scotia. *Heir*: *s* James Lauder Brunton, MD, FRCP(C) [*b* 24 Sept. 1947; *m* 1st,1967, Susan (marr. diss. 1983), *o d* of Charles Hons; one *s* one *d*; 2nd, 1984, Beverly Anne Freedman; one *s*]. *Address*: PO Box 140, Guysborough, Nova Scotia B0H 1N0, Canada.
Died 1 Jan. 2007.

BRUS, Prof. Wlodzimierz, PhD; Professor of Modern Russian and East European Studies, University of Oxford, 1985–88, then Emeritus Professor; Professorial Fellow, Wolfson College, 1985–88, then Emeritus Fellow; Senior Research Fellow, St Antony's College, Oxford, 1989–91; *b* 23 Aug. 1921; *s* of Abram Zylberberg and Helena (*née* Askanas); changed surname to Brus, 1944; *m* 1st, 1940, Helena Wolińska; 2nd, 1945, Irena Stergień; two *d*; 3rd, 1956, Helena Wolińska; one *s*. *Educ*: Saratov, USSR (MA Economic Planning); Warsaw, Poland (PhD Pol. Econ.). Polish Army, 1944–46. Junior Editor, Nowe Drogi (theoretical journal of Polish Workers' (later United Workers') Party), 1946–49; Asst (later Associate) Prof. of Political Economy, Central Sch. of Planning & Statistics, Warsaw, 1949–54; Hd of Dept of Political Economy, Inst. of Social Sciences attached to Central Cttee, Polish United Workers' Party, 1950–56; Prof. of Political Econ., Univ. of Warsaw, 1954–68; Dir, Research Bureau, Polish Planning Commn, 1956–58; Vice-Chm., Econ. Adv. Council of Poland, 1957–63; research worker, Inst. of Housing, Warsaw, 1968–72; Vis. Sen. Res. Fellow, Univ. of Glasgow, 1972–73; Sen. Res. Fellow, St Antony's Coll., Oxford, 1973–76; Univ. Lectr and Fellow, Wolfson Coll., Oxford, 1976–85. Visiting Professor (or Senior Fellow): Rome, 1971; Catholic Univ. of Louvain, 1973; Columbia, 1982; Johns Hopkins Bologna Centre, 1983; Siena, 1991. Consultant to World Bank, 1980–82, 1984. Officers' Cross, Order of Polonia Restituta, Poland, 1954; Polish and Soviet war medals, 1944, 1945. *Publications*: The Law of Value and Economic Incentives, 1956 (trans Hungarian, 1957); General Problems of Functioning of the Socialist Economy, 1961 (published in 10 langs); Economics and Politics of Socialism, 1973 (published in 6 langs); Socialist Ownership and Political Systems, 1975 (published in 8 langs); Economic History of Eastern Europe, 1983 (published in 6 langs); (with K. Laski) From Marx to the Market: socialism in search of an economic system, 1989; contribs to Soviet Studies, Jl of Comparative Economics, Cambridge Jl of Economics. *Recreations*: walking, swimming. *Address*: 21 Bardwell Court, Bardwell Road, Oxford OX2 6SX. *T*: (01865) 553790.
Died 31 Aug. 2007.

BRYANT, Richard Charles, CB 1960; Under-Secretary, Board of Trade, 1955–68; *b* 20 Aug. 1908; *s* of Charles James and Constance Byron Bryant, The Bounds, Hernhill, Faversham, Kent; *m* 1938, Elisabeth Ellington (*d* 1994), *d* of Dr. A. E. Stansfeld, FRCP; two *s* two *d*. *Educ*: Rugby; Oriel College, Oxford. Entered Board of Trade, 1932; Ministry of Supply, 1939–44. *Address*: Marsh Farm House, Brancaster, Norfolk PE31 8AE. *T*: (01485) 210206. *Club*: Travellers.
Died 22 May 2008.

BRYCE, Most Rev. Jabez Leslie; Bishop in Polynesia, since 1975; Archbishop and Co-Presiding Bishop, Anglican Church in Aotearoa, New Zealand and Polynesia, since 2006; *b* 25 Jan. 1935. *Educ*: St John's College, Auckland, NZ (LTh); St Andrew's Seminary, Manila, Philippines (BTh). Deacon 1960, priest 1962, Polynesia; Curate of Suva, 1960–63; Priest-in-charge: Tonga, 1964; St Peter's Chinese Congregation, Manila, 1965–67; Archdeacon of Suva, 1967–69; Deputy Vicar-General, Holy Trinity Cathedral, Suva, 1967–72; Lectr, St John Baptist Theological Coll., Suva, 1967–69; Vicar of Viti Levu W, 1969–75; Archdeacon in Polynesia, 1969–75; Vicar-General of Polynesia, 1972–75. Chm., Pacific Conf. of Churches, 1976–86; Sec., S Pacific Anglican Council, 1970– (Chm., 1995–); Pres., WCC for Oceania, 1998–. *Recreations*: tennis, golf. *Address*: Bishop's House, PO Box 35, Suva, Fiji Islands. *T*: (office) 304716, (home) 302553, *Fax*: 302687.
Died 11 Feb. 2010.

BUCCLEUCH, 9th Duke of, *cr* 1663, **AND QUEENSBERRY**, 11th Duke of, *cr* 1684; **Walter Francis John Montagu Douglas Scott**, KT 1978; VRD; JP; Baron Scott of Buccleuch, 1606; Earl of Buccleuch, Baron Scott of Whitchester and Eskdaill, 1619; Earl of Doncaster and Baron Tynedale (Eng.), 1662; Earl of Dalkeith, 1663; Marquis of Dumfriesshire, Earl of Drumlanrig and Sanquhar, Viscount of Nith,

Torthorwold, and Ross, Baron Douglas, 1684; Hon. Captain RNR; President of the Council, the Queen's Body Guard for Scotland, Royal Company of Archers, 1996–2001; Lord-Lieutenant of Roxburgh, 1974–98, of Ettrick and Lauderdale, 1975–98; Chancellor, Order of the Thistle, since 1992; *b* 28 Sept. 1923; *o s* of 8th Duke of Buccleuch, KT, GCVO, PC, and Vreda Esther Mary (*d* 1993), *er d* of late Major W. F. Lascelles and Lady Sybil Lascelles, *d* of 10th Duke of St Albans; *S* father, 1973; *m* 1953, Jane, *d* of John McNeill, QC, Appin, Argyll; three *s* one *d*. *Educ*: Eton; Christ Church, Oxford. Served War of 1939–45, RNVR. MP (C) Edinburgh North, 1960–73; PPS to the Sec. of State for Scotland, 1962–64. Chairman: Buccleuch Heritage Trust, 1985–; Living Landscape Trust, 1986–; Assoc. of Lord Lieutenants, 1990–98; President: Royal Highland & Agricultural Soc. of Scotland, 1969; St Andrew's Ambulance Assoc.; Royal Scottish Agricultural Benevolent Inst.; Scottish Nat. Inst. for War Blinded; Royal Blind Asylum & School; RADAR; Galloway Cattle Soc.; East of England Agricultural Soc., 1976; Commonwealth Forestry Assoc., 1979–99; Royal Scottish Forestry Soc., 1994–96; Vice-Pres., Children First; Hon. President: Moredun Foundn for Animal Welfare; Scottish Agricultural Organisation Soc. FRAgS 1995. DL, Selkirk 1955, Roxburgh 1962, Dumfries 1974; JP Roxburgh 1975. Countryside Award, Countryside Commn and CLA, 1983; Bledisloe Gold Medal, RASE, 1992. *Recreations*: country pursuits, painting, classical music, tormenting a French horn, works of art study, overseas travel. *Heir*: *s* Earl of Dalkeith, KBE, *b* 14 Feb. 1954. *Address*: Bowhill, Selkirk TD7 5ET. *T*: (01750) 720732. *Died 4 Sept. 2007.*

BUCHANAN, Rev. Canon Eric; Vicar of St Mary's, Higham Ferrers, 1990–97; Chaplain to the Queen, 1992–2002; *b* 2 Feb. 1932; *s* of Oswald Stanley Buchanan and Dorothy Aletta Buchanan (*née* Parkinson); *m* 1st, 1961, Julie Anne Taylor (*d* 1977); one *s* two *d*; 2nd, 1977, Julie Annette Howard (*née* Chamberlain); one step *s* two step *d*. *Educ*: Rotherham Grammar Sch.; Leeds Univ. (BA Hons Phil.); Coll. of the Resurrection, Mirfield. Ordained deacon, 1956, priest, 1957; Asst Curate, St Mark's, Coventry, 1956–59; Asst Chaplain, Univ. of London, 1959–64; Vicar: St Luke's, Duston, Northants, 1964–79; All Hallows, Wellingborough, 1979–90. Rural Dean of Wootton, 1974–79; Non-residentiary Canon of Peterborough Cathedral, 1977–97, Canon Emeritus, 1997–. Chm., House of Clergy, Peterborough Diocesan Synod, 1978–91. *Recreations*: listening to classical music and jazz, gardening, theatre, detective fiction. *Address*: 8 College Street, Higham Ferrers, Northants NN10 8DZ. *T*: (01933) 411232. *Died 4 March 2006.*

BUCHANAN-DUNLOP, Richard; QC 1966; *b* 19 April 1919; *s* of late Canon W. R. Buchanan-Dunlop and Mrs R. E. Buchanan-Dunlop (*née* Mead); *m* 1948, Helen Murray Dunlop (*d* 2006); three *d*. *Educ*: Marlborough College; Magdalene College, Cambridge. Served in Royal Corps of Signals, 1939–46 (Hon. Major). BA (Hons) Law, Cambridge, 1949; Harmsworth Scholar, 1950. Called to the Bar, 1951. *Publications*: Skiathos and other Poems, 1984; Old Olive Men, 1986; Hie Paeeon: songs from the Greek Isles, 1989; The Painted Veil, 2003. *Recreations*: painting, writing. *Address*: Skiathos, Greece. *Died 19 Sept. 2010.*

BUCHANAN-JARDINE, Sir Andrew Rupert John; *see* Jardine.

BUCHWALD, Arthur, (Art); American journalist, author, lecturer and columnist; *b* Mount Vernon, New York, 20 Oct. 1925; *s* of Joseph Buchwald and Helen (*née* Kleinberger); *m* 1952, Ann McGarry (marr. diss.), Warren, Pa; one adopted *s* two adopted *d*. *Educ*: University of Southern California. Sergeant, US Marine Corps, 1942–45. Columnist, New York Herald Tribune: in Paris, 1949–62; in Washington, 1962–. Syndicated columnist whose articles appear in 550 newspapers throughout the world. Mem., AAAL, 1986–. Pulitzer Prize for outstanding commentary, 1982. *Publications*: (mostly published later in England) Paris After Dark,

1950; Art Buchwald's Paris, 1954; The Brave Coward, 1957; I Chose Caviar, 1957; More Caviar, 1958; A Gift from the Boys, 1958; Don't Forget to Write, 1960; Art Buchwald's Secret List to Paris, 1961; How Much is That in Dollars?, 1961; Is it Safe to Drink the Water?, 1962; I Chose Capitol Punishment, 1963; . . . and Then I told the President, 1965; Son of the Great Society, 1966; Have I Ever Lied to You?, 1968; The Establishment is Alive and Well in Washington, 1969; Sheep on the Runway (Play), 1970; Oh, to be a Swinger, 1970; Getting High in Government Circles, 1971; I Never Danced at the White House, 1973; I Am not a Crook, 1974; Bollo Caper, 1974; Irving's Delight, 1975; Washington is Leaking, 1976; Down the Seine and up the Potomac, 1977; The Buchwald Stops Here, 1978; Laid Back in Washington, 1981; While Reagan Slept, 1984; You Can Fool All of the People All the Time, 1985; I Think I Don't Remember, 1987; Whose Rose Garden is it Anyway?, 1989; Lighten Up, George, 1991; Leaving Home: a memoir, 1994; I'll Always Have Paris, 1996. *Recreations*: tennis, chess, marathon running. *Died 17 Jan. 2007.*

BUCKLAND, Maj.-Gen. Ronald John Denys Eden, CB 1974; MBE 1956; DL; Chief Executive, Adur District Council, 1975–85; *b* 27 July 1920; *s* of Geoffrey Ronald Aubert Buckland, CB and Lelgarde Edith Eleanor (*née* Eden); *m* 1968, Judith Margaret Coxhead, MBE, DL; two *d*. *Educ*: Winchester; New College, Oxford (MA). Commissioned into Coldstream Gds, Dec. 1940. Served War of 1939–45: NW Europe, with 4th Coldstream Gds, 1944–45 (wounded twice). GSO3, Gds Div., BAOR, 1946; Adjt, 1st Bn Coldstream Gds, Palestine and Libya, 1948; DAA&QMG, 2nd Guards Bde and 18th Inf. Bde, Malaya, 1950–52 (Dispatches); DAAG, 3rd Div., Egypt, 1954; jssc 1956; Bde Major, 1st Gds Bde, Cyprus, 1958; Bt Lt-Col 1959; Bde Major, 51st Inf. Bde, 1960; commanded 1st Bn, Coldstream Gds, 1961, British Guiana, 1962; GSO1, 4th Div., BAOR, 1963; Brig. 1966; Comdr, 133 Inf. Bde (TA), 1966; ACOS, Joint Exercises Div., HQ AFCENT, Holland, 1967; idc 1968; DA&QMG, 1st British Corps, BAOR, 1969; Maj.-Gen. 1969; Chief of Staff, HQ Strategic Command, 1970; Maj.-Gen. i/c Admin, UKLF, 1972–75. DL W Sussex, 1986. *Recreations*: travel, watching cricket, bricklaying. *Clubs*: MCC; Leander; Sussex. *Died 22 Jan. 2008.*

BUCKLEY, Eric Joseph, MA; FIP3; Printer to the University of Oxford, 1978–83; Emeritus Fellow of Linacre College, Oxford, 1983 (Fellow, 1979–83); *b* 26 June 1920; *s* of Joseph William Buckley and Lillian Elizabeth Major (*née* Drake); *m* 1st, 1945, Joan Alice Kirby (*d* 1973); one *s* one *d*; 2nd, 1978, Harriett (*d* 1995), *d* of Judge and Mrs Robert Williams Hawkins, Caruthersville, Mo, USA. *Educ*: St Bartholomew's, Dover. MA Oxon 1979 (by special resolution; Linacre College). Served War, RAOC and REME, ME and UK, 1939–45. Apprentice, Amalgamated Press, London, 1935; Dir, Pergamon Press Ltd, 1956–74; joined Oxford Univ. Press as Dir, UK Publishing Services, 1974. Liveryman, Stationers and Newspaper Makers Co., 1981; Freeman, City of London, 1980. FIP3 (FIOP 1981). *Recreations*: reading, theatre, cats. *Address*: Clover Cottage, Hazler Road, Church Stretton, Shropshire SY6 7AF. *T*: (01694) 723536. *Died 19 May 2010.*

BUCKLEY, Peter Neville; Chairman, Caledonia Investments plc, since 1994 (Deputy Chairman, 1987–94; Chief Executive, 1987–2002); President, Royal Horticultural Society, since 2006; *b* 23 Sept. 1942; *s* of Maj. Edward Richard Buckley and Ina Heather (*née* Cayzer); *m* 1967, Mary Barabel Stewart; two *d*. *Educ*: Eton; Manchester Business Sch. (DipBA). Served articles with McClelland Moores & Co. (later Ernst & Young); qualified as Chartered Accountant, 1966; joined Brit. & Commonwealth Shipping Co., later Brit. & Commonwealth Hldgs PLC, 1968; Exec. Dir, 1974–88. Chairman: English & Scottish Investors, 1988–2002; Sterling Inds, 1988–2005; Bristow Helicopter Gp, 1991–2004; Bristow Aviation Hldgs, 1996–; Cayzer Trust Co., 1996–; non-executive Director: RHS

Enterprises, 1993–2006; Kerzner Internat. Ltd (formerly Sun Internat. Hotels), 1994–2006; Close Brothers Gp, 1995–2007; Offshore Logistics, subseq. Bristow Gp, Inc., 1996–. *Recreations:* gardening, golf, shooting. *Address:* Caledonia Investments plc, Cayzer House, 30 Buckingham Gate, SW1E 6NN. *T:* (020) 7802 8080.
Died 2 Dec. 2008.

BUCKMASTER, 3rd Viscount *cr* 1933, of Cheddington; **Martin Stanley Buckmaster,** OBE 1979; Baron 1915; HM Diplomatic Service, retired; *b* 11 April 1921; *s* of 2nd Viscount Buckmaster and Joan, Viscountess Buckmaster (*d* 1976), *d* of Dr Garry Simpson; *S* father, 1974. *Educ:* Stowe. Joined TA, 1939; served Royal Sussex Regt (Captain) in UK and Middle East, 1940–46. Foreign Office, 1946; Middle East Centre for Arab Studies, Lebanon, 1950–51; qualified in Arabic (Higher Standard); served in Trucial States, Sharjah (1951–53) and Abu Dhabi (Political Officer, 1955–58) and subsequently in Libya, Bahrain, FO, Uganda, Lebanon and Saudi Arabia, 1958–73; First Sec., FCO, 1973–77; Head of Chancery and Chargé d'Affaires, Yemen Arab Republic, 1977–81. Deputy Chairman: Council for the Advancement of Arab-British Studies; Christian Broadcasting Council. FRGS 1954. *Recreations:* walking, music, railways; Arab and African studies. *Heir: nephew* Adrian Charles Buckmaster [*b* 2 Feb. 1949; *m* 1975, Dr Elizabeth Mary Mark; one *s* two *d*]. *Address:* 90 Cornwall Gardens, SW7 4AX. *Club:* Travellers. *Died 8 June 2007.*

BUDDEN, Julian Medforth, OBE 1991; FBA 1987; *b* 9 April 1924; *s* of Prof. Lionel Bailey Budden and Dora Magdalene (*née* Fraser). *Educ:* Stowe Sch.; Queen's Coll., Oxford (MA); Royal Coll. of Music; Trinity Coll. of Music (BMus 1955). Joined BBC Music Dept, 1951, as clerk; Music Producer, 1956–70; Chief Producer, Opera (Radio), 1970–76; External Services Music Organiser, 1976–83. *Publications:* The Operas of Verdi, vol. I 1973, vol. II 1978, vol. III 1981; Verdi, 1985; Puccini, 2002; contribs to various musicological periodicals. *Address:* (March, April, July–Sept.) 94 Station Road, N3 2SG. *T:* (020) 8349 2954; (Oct.–Feb., May, June) Via Aretina 166, 50069 Sieci, Pontassieve (F1), Italy. *T:* (55) 8328775.
Died 28 Feb. 2007.

BULL, Dr John Prince, CBE 1973; Director of MRC Industrial Injuries and Burns Unit, 1952–82; *b* 4 Jan. 1917; *s* of Robert James Bull and Ida Mary Bull; *m* 1939, Irmgard Bross; four *d*. *Educ:* Burton-on-Trent Grammar Sch.; Cambridge Univ.; Guy's Hospital. MA, MD, BCh Cantab; MRCS, FRCP. Casualty Res. Officer, Min. of Home Security, 1941; RAMC, 1942–46; Mem. Research Staff 1947, Asst Dir 1948, MRC Unit, Birmingham Accident Hosp. Member: MRC, 1971–75; Med. Commn on Accident Prevention, 1975– (Chm., Transport Cttee, 1981–94); Chairman: Regional Res. Cttee, West Midlands RHA, 1966–82; Inst. of Accident Surgery, 1980–2003. Mem., Med. Res. Soc. FRSocMed. *Publications:* contrib. scientific and med. jls. *Recreation:* bricolage. *Address:* 9 Queensdale Place, W11 4SQ. *T:* (020) 7603 0073. *Died 7 Aug. 2008.*

BULLARD, Sir Julian (Leonard), GCMG 1987 (KCMG 1982 CMG 1975); HM Diplomatic Service, retired; Fellow of All Souls College, Oxford, 1950–57 and since 1988; *b* 8 March 1928; *s* of late Sir Reader Bullard, KCB, KCMG, CIE, and Miriam, *d* of A. L. Smith, Master of Balliol Coll., Oxford; *m* 1954, Margaret Stephens; two *s* two *d*. *Educ:* Rugby; Magdalen Coll., Oxford. Army, 1950–52; HM Diplomatic Service, 1953–88: served at: FO, 1953–54; Vienna, 1954–56; Amman, 1956–59; FO, 1960–63; Bonn, 1963–66; Moscow, 1966–68; Dubai, 1968–70; Head of E European and Soviet Dept, FCO, 1971–75; Minister, Bonn, 1975–79; Dep. Under-Sec. of State, 1979–84 and Dep. to Perm. Under Sec. of State and Political Dir, 1982–84, FCO; Ambassador, Bonn, 1984–88. Birmingham University: Mem. Council, 1988–97; Chm. Council and Pro-Chancellor, 1989–94; Hon. LLD 1994. *Publications:* (ed with Margaret Bullard)

Inside Stalin's Russia: the diaries of Reader Bullard 1930–34, 2000. *Address:* 18 Northmoor Road, Oxford OX2 6UR. *T:* (01865) 512981. *Died 25 May 2006.*

BULLEN, Air Vice-Marshal Reginald, CB 1975; GM 1945; MA; Senior Bursar and Fellow, Gonville and Caius College, Cambridge, 1976–87, Life Fellow and Property Developments Consultant, since 1988; *b* 19 Oct. 1920; *s* of Henry Arthur Bullen and Alice May Bullen; *m* 1952, Christiane (*née* Phillips); one *s* one *d*. *Educ:* Grocers' Company School. 39 Sqdn RAF, 458 Sqdn RAAF, 1942–44; Air Min., 1945–50; RAF Coll. Cranwell, 1952–54; psa 1955; Exchange USAF, Washington, DC, 1956–58; RAF Staff Coll., Bracknell, 1959–61; Admin. Staff Coll., Henley, 1962; PSO to Chief of Air Staff, 1962–64; NATO Defence Coll., Paris, 1965; Adjutant General, HQ Allied Forces Central Europe, 1965–68; Dir of Personnel, MoD, 1968–69; idc 1970; Dep. AO i/c Admin, HQ Maintenance Comd, 1971; AOA Training Comd, 1972–75. Chm., Huntingdon DHA, 1981–92. MA Cantab, 1975. FCMI (FBIM 1979; MBIM 1971). *Publications:* various articles. *Address:* Gonville and Caius College, Cambridge CB2 1TA. *Club:* Royal Air Force.
Died 27 Jan. 2008.

BULLERS, Ronald Alfred, CBE 1988; QFSM 1974; FIFireE; consultant fire prevention engineer; Chief Executive Officer, London Fire and Civil Defence Authority, 1986–87; *b* 17 March 1931; *m* 1954, Mary M. Bullers. *Educ:* Queen Mary's Grammar Sch., Walsall. Deputy Asst Chief Officer, Lancashire Fire Brigade, 1971; Dep. Chief Officer, Greater Manchester Fire Brigade, 1974, Chief Officer, 1977; Chief Officer, London Fire Bde, 1981–86. Adviser: Nat. Jt Council for Local Authority Fire Brigades, 1977; Assoc. of Metropolitan Authorities, 1977. FCMI. OStJ. *Recreations:* gardening, travel. *Address:* 31 Pavillion Close, Aldridge, Walsall WS9 8LS. *Died 9 Feb. 2010.*

BULLOUGH, Prof. William Sydney, PhD, DSc Leeds; Professor of Zoology, Birkbeck College, University of London, 1952–81, then Emeritus; *b* 6 April 1914; *o s* of Rev. Frederick Sydney Bullough and Letitia Anne Cooper, both of Leeds; *m* 1942, Dr Helena F. Gibbs (*d* 1975), Wellington, NZ; one *s* one *d*. *Educ:* William Hulme's Grammar Sch., Manchester; Grammar Sch., Leeds; Univ. of Leeds. Lecturer in Zoology, Univ. of Leeds, 1937–44; McGill Univ., Montreal, 1944–46; Sorby Fellow of Royal Society of London, 1946–51; Research Fellow of British Empire Cancer Campaign, 1951–52; Hon. Fellow: Soc. for Investigative Dermatology (US); AAAS, 1981. Vice-Pres., Zoological Soc., 1983–84. *Publications:* Practical Invertebrate Anatomy, 1950; Vertebrate Sexual Cycles, 1951; (for children) Introducing Animals, 1953; Introducing Animals-with-Backbones, 1954; Introducing Man, 1958; The Evolution of Differentiation, 1967; The Dynamic Body Tissues, 1983; scientific papers on vertebrate reproductive cycles, hormones, and chalones published in a variety of journals. *Recreation:* gardening. *Address:* 75 Hillfield Court, Belsize Avenue, NW3 4BG. *T:* (020) 7435 4558. *Died 27 Dec. 2010.*

BUNCH, Sir Austin (Wyeth), Kt 1983; CBE 1978 (MBE 1974); Vice-Patron, British Limbless Ex-Servicemen's Association, 1992 (National President, 1983–92); *b* 20 March 1918; *s* of Horace William and Winifred Ada Bunch; *m* 1944, Joan Mary Peryer (*d* 2005); four *d*. *Educ:* Christ's Hospital. FCA; FIET. Deloitte, Plender, Griffiths, 1935–48; Southern Electricity Board, 1949–76: Area Man., Newbury, 1962; Area Man., Portsmouth, 1966; Dep. Chm., 1967; Chm., 1974; Dep. Chm., Electricity Council, 1976–81, Chm., 1981–83; Chm., British Electricity Internat. Ltd, 1977–83; retd. Chm., Queen Mary's Roehampton Hosp. Trust, 1983–89. *Recreation:* sports for the disabled. *Address:* 35 Draycott Road, Chiseldon, Swindon SN4 0LT. *Died 30 June 2008.*

BUNN, Douglas Henry David; Chairman: All England Jumping Course, Hickstead; White Horse Caravan Co. Ltd; *b* 1 March 1928; *s* of late George Henry Charles Bunn and Alice Ann Bunn; *m* 1st, 1952, Rosemary Pares Wilson; three *d*; 2nd, 1960, Susan Dennis-Smith; two *s* one *d*; 3rd, 1979, Lorna Kirk (*d* 1995); one *s* two *d*. *Educ:* Chichester High Sch.; Trinity Coll., Cambridge (MA). Called to Bar, Lincoln's Inn; practised at Bar, 1953–59; founded Hickstead, 1960; British Show Jumping Team, 1957–68; Pres., BSJA, 2001–05 (Chm., 1969, 1993–96; Vice-Chm., 1969–93; Vice-Pres., 1996–2001); Mem. British Equestrian Fedn; founded White Horse Caravan Co. Ltd, 1958; Chm., Southern Aero Club, 1968–72. Jt Master, 1976–2000, Vice-Chm., 2000–, Mid Surrey Drag Hounds. *Recreations:* horses, flying, books, wine. *Address:* Hickstead Place, Sussex RH17 5NU. *T:* (01273) 834666, *T:* (office) (01273) 834315, *Fax:* (01273) 834452. *Clubs:* Saints and Sinners (Chm., 1989–90), Annabel's, Sussex.
Died 16 June 2009.

BURBIDGE, Prof. Geoffrey Ronald, FRS 1968; Professor of Physics, University of California, San Diego, since 1988; *b* 24 Sept. 1925; *s* of Leslie and Eveline Burbidge, Chipping Norton, Oxon; *m* 1948, Margaret Peachey (Dr (Eleanor) Margaret Burbidge, FRS); one *d*. *Educ:* Chipping Norton Grammar Sch.; Bristol University; Univ. Coll., London. BSc (Special Hons Physics) Bristol, 1946; PhD London, 1951. Asst Lectr, UCL, 1950–51; Agassiz Fellow, Harvard Univ., 1951–52; Research Fellow, Univ. of Chicago, 1952–53; Research Fellow, Cavendish Lab., Cambridge, 1953–55; Carnegie Fellow, Mount Wilson and Palomar Observatories, Caltech, 1955–57; Asst Prof., Dept of Astronomy, Univ. of Chicago, 1957–58; Associate Prof., 1958–62; University of California, San Diego: Associate Prof., 1963–64; Prof., 1964–78; Emeritus Prof., 1984–88; Dir, Kitt Peak Nat. Observatory, Arizona, 1978–84. Phillips Vis. Prof., Harvard Univ., 1968. Elected Fellow: UCL, 1970; Amer. Acad. of Arts and Scis, 1970. Pres., Astronomical Soc. of the Pacific, 1974–76 (Catherine Wolfe Bruce Medal, 1999); Trustee, Assoc. Universities Inc., 1973–82. Gold Medal, RAS, 2005. Editor, Annual Review Astronomy and Astrophysics, 1973–2004; Scientific Ed., Astrophysical Jl, 1996–2002. *Publications:* (with Margaret Burbidge) Quasi-Stellar Objects, 1967; (with Sir Fred Hoyle and J. V. Narlikar) A Different Approach to Cosmology, 2000; (with J. V. Narlikar) Facts and Speculations in Cosmology, 2008; scientific papers in Astrophysical Jl, Nature, Rev. Mod. Phys, Handbuch der Physik, etc. *Address:* Department of Physics and Center for Astrophysics and Space Sciences, 0424 University of California, San Diego, La Jolla, CA 92093, USA. *T:* (858) 5346626.
Died 26 Jan. 2010.

BURCH, Rear Adm. Jonathan Alexander, CBE 1991; CEng; Chief Executive (formerly Executive Secretary), Royal Academy of Engineering, 2000–03; *b* 18 June 1949; *s* of late Lt Comdr Walter H. Burch and of Mary Angela Burch; *m* 1976, Ursula Georgette Victoria Maria Villiers Bear (*née* Villiers) (*d* 2008); one step *s*. *Educ:* Chorister Sch., Durham; Durham Sch.; BRNC, Dartmouth; RNEC Manadon (BSc). CEng 1972. HM Submarines, 1972–84; Australian Staff Coll., 1984; Assistant Director: Dockyard Privatisation, 1985–88; Commitments (Middle East), 1989–92; Superintendent Ships, Devonport, 1992–94; rcds 1995; Naval Base Comdr, Devonport (Cdre), 1996–98; DG Aircraft (Navy), 1998–2000 and Chief Naval Engr Officer, 1999. FCMI (FIMgt 1989); FIMarEST (FIMarE 2000). President: Devonport Field Gun, 1996–98; RN Volleyball, 1998–2000. *Recreations:* travel, walking, history, music.
Died 4 Nov. 2009.

BURCHAM, Prof. William Ernest, CBE 1980; FRS 1957; Emeritus Professor of Physics, Birmingham University, since 1981; *b* 1 Aug. 1913; *er s* of Ernest Barnard and Edith Ellen Burcham; *m* 1st, 1942, Isabella Mary (*d* 1981), *d* of George Richard Todd and of Alice Louisa Todd; one *d* (and one *d* decd); 2nd, 1985, Patricia Newton, *er d* of Frank Harold Newton Marson and

Miriam Eliza Marson. *Educ:* City of Norwich Sch.; Trinity Hall, Cambridge. Stokes Student, Pembroke Coll., Cambridge, 1937; Scientific Officer, Ministry of Aircraft Production, 1940, and Directorate of Atomic Energy, 1944; Fellow of Selwyn Coll., Cambridge, 1944; Univ. Demonstrator in Physics, Cambridge, 1945; Univ. Lecturer in Physics, Cambridge, 1946; Oliver Lodge Prof. of Physics, Univ. of Birmingham, 1951–80. Member: SRC, 1974–78; Council, Royal Soc., 1977–79. Hon. Life Fellow, Coventry Polytechnic, 1984. *Publications:* Nuclear Physics: an Introduction, 1963; Elements of Nuclear Physics, 1979; (with M. Jobes) Nuclear and Particle Physics, 1995; papers in Nuclear Physics A, Phys. Letters B, Phys. Rev. Letters. *Address:* 95 Witherford Way, Birmingham B29 4AN. *T:* (0121) 472 1226.
Died 5 Nov. 2008.

BURGESS, Geoffrey Harold Orchard; Chief Scientist (Agriculture and Horticulture), Ministry of Agriculture, Fisheries and Food, 1982–86; *b* 28 March 1926; *s* of late Harold Frank and Eva M. F. Burgess, Reading; *m* 1952, Barbara Vernon, *y d* of late Rev. Gilbert Vernon Yonge; two *s*. *Educ:* Reading Sch.; Univ. of Reading; UC Hull. BSc Reading, 1951 (Colin Morley Prizewinner 1950); PhD London, 1955. Special research appt, Univ. of Hull, 1951; Sen. Scientific Officer, DSIR, Humber Lab., Hull, 1954; PSO, Torry Res. Stn, Aberdeen, 1960; Officer i/c, Humber Lab., Hull, 1962; Director, Torry Res. Station, 1969–79; Head of Biology Div., Agricl Science Service, and Officer i/c Slough Lab., MAFF, 1979–82. Hon. Res. Lectr in Fish Technology, Univ. of Aberdeen, 1969–79; Buckland Lectr, 1964; Hon. Lectr in Fish Technology, Univ. of Leeds, 1966–69; Mem. Adv. Cttee on Food Science, Univ. of Leeds, 1970–86; Mem., Panel of Fish Technology Experts, FAO, 1962–79. *Publications:* Developments in the Handling and Processing of Fish, 1965; (with Lovern, Waterman and Cutting) Fish Handling and Processing, 1965; The Curious World of Frank Buckland, 1967; scientific and technical papers, reviews, reports etc concerning handling, processing, transport and preservation for food, of fish, from catching to consumption.
Died 11 Sept. 2009.

BURGON, Geoffrey; composer; *b* 15 July 1941; *s* of Alan Wybert Burgon and Ada Vera Isom; *m* 1st, 1963, Janice Elizabeth Garwood (marr. diss.); one *s* one *d*; 2nd, 1992, Jacqueline Krofchak; one *s*. *Educ:* Pewley Sch., Guildford; Guildhall School of Music and Drama; studied composition with Peter Wishart, trumpet with Bernard Brown. Freelance trumpeter, 1964–71: Royal Opera House (stage band), Philomusica, London Mozart Players, Northern Sinfonia, Jacques and Capriol Orchestras, also session work, theatres and jazz bands. Full time composer and conductor, 1971–; work in almost every musical genre, particularly orchestral, choral, and music for dance, film & TV; commissions from many Festivals, incl. Bath, Edinburgh, Cheltenham, Southern Cathedrals, Three Choirs, and Camden; also many works for Dance, incl. Ballet Rambert and London Contemporary Dance Theatre; work performed internationally. *Major works:* Gending; Alleluia Nativitas; The World Again; Acquainted with Night; Think on Dreadful Domesday; Canciones del Alma; Requiem; Revelations; Title Divine; Short Mass; The Golden Eternity; The Fire of Heaven, Dos Coros; A Hymn to the Creatures; The Golden Fish; The Calm; Running Figures; Goldbergs Dream; Songs, Lamentations and Praises; Mass; The Trials of Prometheus; Hymn to Venus; Five Sonnets of John Donne; Four Guitars; Six Studies for Solo Cello; Worldes Blisse; Trumpet Concerto: the Turning World; First Was the World; City Adventures; Merciless Beauty; The Wanderer; Piano Concerto; A Different Dawn; Magic Words, Heavenly Things; Three Mysteries; Cello Concerto; Viola Concerto; Minterne Dances; On the Street; *opera:* Hard Times; *film scores:* Life of Brian; Dogs of War; Turtle Diary; Robin Hood; Labyrinth; *television scores:* Tinker, Tailor, Soldier, Spy; Brideshead Revisited; Bleak House; Happy Valley; Chronicles of Narnia; Children of the North; Martin Chuzzlewit; Silent Witness; Cider with Rosie; Longitude (BAFTA award); The Forsyte Saga (BAFTA award); Island at War; Love Lies Bleeding. Prince Pierre of Monaco Award, 1969; Ivor Novello Award, 1979, 1981; Gold Disc for Brideshead record, 1986. *Recreations:* playing jazz, cricket, Bristol motor cars, sleeping. *Address:* c/o Chester Music, 14–15 Berners Street, W1T 3LJ. *T:* (020) 7434 0066; *e-mail:* promotion@musicsales.co.uk. *Died 21 Sept. 2010.*

BURLISON, Baron *cr* 1997 (Life Peer), of Rowlands Gill in the co. of Tyne and Wear; **Thomas Henry Burlison;** DL; *b* 23 May 1936; *s* of Robert Burlison and Georgina (*née* Doige); *m* 1981, Valerie Stephenson; two *s* one *d.* *Educ:* Edmondsley, Co. Durham. Panel beater, 1951–57; professional footballer, 1953–65; RAF, 1959–61; General and Municipal Workers' Union, then General, Municipal, Boilermakers and Allied Trades Union, later GMB: Regl Officer, 1965–78; Regl Sec., 1978–91; Dep. Gen. Sec., 1991–96. Treas., Labour Party, 1992–96. A Lord in Waiting, (Govt Whip), 1999–2001 Member: WEU, 2005; Council of Europe, 2005. Bd of Govs, Northumbria Univ., 2003. DL Tyne and Wear, 1997. *Recreation:* gardening. *Address:* House of Lords, SW1A 0PW. *Died 20 May 2008.*

BURN, Michael Clive, MC 1945; writer; *b* 11 Dec. 1912; *s* of late Sir Clive Burn and Phyllis Stoneham; *m* 1947, Mary Booker (*née* Walter) (*d* 1974); no *c.* *Educ:* Winchester; New Coll., Oxford (open scholar); Hons Degree in Soc. Scis, Oxford, 1945, with distinction in all subjects (awarded whilst POW at Colditz). Journalist, The Times, 1936–39; Lieut 1st Bn Queens Westminsters, KRRC, 1939–40; Officer in Independent Companies, Norwegian Campaign, 1940, subseq. Captain No. 2 Commando; taken prisoner in raid on St Nazaire, 1942; prisoner in Germany, 1942–45. Foreign Correspondent for The Times in Vienna, Jugoslavia and Hungary, 1946–49. Mem., Welsh Acad., 2006. Keats Poetry First Prize, 1973. Légion d'Honneur, 5th class (France), 2006. *Plays:* The Modern Everyman (prod. Birmingham Rep., 1947); Beyond the Storm (Midlands Arts Co., and Vienna, 1947); The Night of the Ball (prod. New Theatre, 1956). *Publications: novels:* Yes, Farewell, 1946, repr. 1975; Childhood at Oriol, 1951; The Midnight Diary, 1952; The Trouble with Jake, 1967; *sociological:* Mr Lyward's Answer, 1956; The Debatable Land, 1970; *poems:* Poems to Mary, 1953; The Flying Castle, 1954; Out On A Limb, 1973; Open Day and Night, 1978; *play:* The Modern Everyman, 1948; *non-fiction:* Mary and Richard, 1988; Turned Towards the Sun (autobiog.), 2003; Poems as Accompaniment to a Life, 2006. *Address:* Beudy Gwyn, Minffordd, Gwynedd, N Wales LL48 6EN. *Died 3 Sept. 2010.*

BURNETT, Sir John (Harrison), Kt 1987; *b* 21 Jan. 1922; *s* of Rev. T. Harrison Burnett, Paisley; *m* 1945, E. Margaret, *er d* of Rev. Dr E. W. Bishop; two *s.* *Educ:* Kingswood Sch., Bath; Merton Coll., Oxford (BA, MA 1947; DPhil 1953; Christopher Welch Scholar, 1947; Hon. Fellow, 1997). FRSE 1957; FIBiol 1969. Served 1942–46 as Lieut RNVR (despatches). Lecturer, Lincoln Coll., 1948–49; Fellow (by Exam.) Magdalen Coll., 1949–53; Univ. Lecturer and Demonstrator, Oxford, 1949–53; Lecturer, Liverpool Univ., 1954–55; Prof. of Botany: Univ. of St Andrews, 1955–60; King's Coll., Newcastle, Univ. of Durham, 1961–63, Univ. of Newcastle, 1963–68; Dean of Faculty of Science, St Andrews, 1958–60, Newcastle, 1966–68; Public Orator, Newcastle, 1966–68; Regius Prof. of Botany, Univ. of Glasgow, 1968–70; Oxford University: Sibthorpian Prof. of Rural Economy and Fellow, St John's Coll., 1970–79; Member: Gen. Bd of Faculties, 1972–77 (Vice-Chm, 1974–76); Hebdomodal Council, 1974–79; Prin. and Vice-Chancellor, Univ. of Edinburgh, 1979–87. Exec. Sec., World Council for the Biosphere, 1987–93; Chm. and Founder, Internat. Orgn for Plant Inf., 1991–96. Lectures: Delgarno, Univ. of Manitoba, 1979–80; Bewley Meml, 1982; Peacock Meml, Dundee Univ., 1982; St Leonard's, Univ. of St Andrews, 1988. Chairman: Scottish Horticultural Research Inst., 1959–74;

Co-ordinating Commn for Biol Recording, 1989–2003; Nat. Biodiversity Network Trust, 2000–05; Member: Nature Conservancy Scottish Cttee, 1961–66, English Cttee, 1966–69; Nature Conservancy Council, 1987–89 (Dep. Chm. and Acting Chm., 1988–89; Mem. Scottish Cttee, 1980–87); Nuffield Foundn Biol. Project, 1962–68 (Chm., 1965–68); British Mycological Soc. (Pres., 1982–83); Trustee, The New Phytologist, 1962–85, Advr, 1985–99; Member: Academic Adv. Council, Univs of St Andrews and Dundee, 1964–66; Council, Univ. of Buckingham, 1989–96. Member: Newcastle Reg. Hosp. Bd, 1964–68; Kingswood Assoc. (Pres., 1989). Hon. Consultant: Nat. Grid Co., 1990–99; Heritage Lottery Fund, 1995–99. Hon. Res. Prof., Open Univ., 1996–99. Hon. Fellow: RCSE, 1983; Green Coll., Oxford, 1988. Hon. DSc: Buckingham, 1981; Pennsylvania, 1983; Hon LLD: Dundee, 1982; Strathclyde, 1983; Glasgow, 1987; Dr *hc* Edinburgh, 1988. Commendatore, Order of Merit (Italy), 1990. *Publications:* Vegetation of Scotland, ed and contrib., 1964; Fundamentals of Mycology, 1968, 3rd edn 1994; Mycogenetics, 1975; Fungal Walls and Hyphal Growth, ed and contrib., 1979; Edinburgh University Portraits II, 1986; Speciation and Evolution in Fungi, 1989; (ed jtly and contrib.) The Maintenance of the Biosphere, 1989; (ed jtly and contrib.) Surviving with the Biosphere, 1994; Biological Recording in the UK: present practice and future development, 1996; Fungal Populations and Species, 2003; papers in various books and scientific journals. *Recreations:* walking, writing, gardens. *Address:* 13 Field House Drive, Oxford OX2 7NT. *Clubs:* Athenæum, Royal Over-Seas League. *Died 22 July 2007.*

BURNETT-STUART, Joseph; Chairman, Robert Fleming Holdings Ltd, 1981–90 (Director, 1963–90); *b* 11 April 1930; *s* of late George Eustace Burnett-Stuart, CBE and Etheldreda Cecily (*née* Edge); *m* 1954, Mary Hermione, *d* of late John A. M. Stewart of Ardvorlich, TD; three *s* one *d.* *Educ:* Eton Coll.; Trinity Coll., Cambridge (BA). Bankers Trust Co., 1953–62. A Church Commissioner, 1984–94. *Recreations:* gardening, shooting, fishing. *Club:* New (Edinburgh). *Died 21 May 2010.*

BURNLEY, Christopher John; Burnley and Evans, Chartered Accountants, Halesowen, 1989–2003; *b* 1 May 1936; *s* of John Fox Burnley and Helena Burnley; *m* 1960, Carol Joan Quirk; two *d.* *Educ:* King William's College, Isle of Man. Chartered Accountant. Articled Clerk, 1953–59; Military service, 1959–62; Computer Systems Analyst, IBM, 1962–66; Management Consultant, Peat Marwick, 1966–67; Systems Planning Manager, Castrol, 1967–68; Sen. Planner, IBM, 1969–72; Financial Dir, Foseco FS, 1972–74; Group Treasurer, Foseco Minsep, 1974–75; Financial Dir, BAA, 1975–86; Finance Dir, Dan Air Engrg, 1987–88. *Recreation:* railway enthusiast. *Address:* Thirlmere, 173 Worcester Road, West Hagley, West Midlands DY9 0PB. *T:* (01562) 883592. *Died 30 Dec. 2006.*

BURNS, Michael; Chairman, South Yorkshire County Association, since 1986; *b* 21 Dec. 1917; *s* of Hugh Burns and Jane Ellin Burns; *m* 1939, Vera Williams (*d* 1984); two *d.* *Educ:* Thorne Grammar Sch. Served War, 1940–46: 1939–45 Star, France and Germany Star, War Medal, Defence Medal. Miner, Hatfield Main Colliery, 1934–40 and 1946–66; Thorpe Marsh Power Stn, 1966–70; Sch. Caretaker, Hatfield Travis Sch., 1970–81 (due to wife's illness); retd 1981. Mem., Nat. Cttee, NUPE, 1979–81; Chm., Health and Safety Local Govt Nat. Cttee, NUPE, 1979–81. Member: S Yorks CC, 1973–86 (Chm., 1982–83); Hatfield Town Council, 1995–2007 (Dep. Mayor, 1995–96, 2005–06; Dep. Ldr, 1995; Mayor, 1996–97, 2006–07; Ldr, 2000–07). Mem., Doncaster MBC Robin Hood Doncaster/Sheffield Airport Consultative Cttee, 2005–06. Chairman: Hatfield and Dunscroft Lab Party, 1965–86 (Vice Chm., 1997–); Goole CLP, 1977–83; Doncaster CVS, 1984–92 (Mem., 1977); Thorne No 2 Sub-Div., Police Community Liaison Forum, 1987–; Founder Chm., Doncaster Victim

Support Scheme, 1984–95 (Life Pres., 1995); Exec. Mem., Doncaster Intermediate Treatment Orgn, 1990–99; Member: S Yorks Valuation Panel, 1974–89; S Yorks Charity Information Service, 1983–90; Nat. Exec., CVSNA, 1985–87; Doncaster FPC, 1985–86; Doncaster Jt Consultative Cttee, 1985–89; Yorks Local Council Assoc., 1995. Trustee: S Yorks Foundn Charity, 1986–90; Hatfield Church Bldg Trust, 1997–2004; Chm., Friends of S Yorks Training Trust, 1986–2003 (Vice-Pres., 2003–). Pres., Hatfield Br., Arthritic Care, 1980–86. Governor, Hatfield High Sch., 1974–88; Chairman: Hatfield Ash Hill Sch. Bd of Governors, 1974–88 and 1989–92 (Vice-Chm., 1988–89); Govs, Hatfield Sheepdip Lane Sch., 1974–2003; Hatfield Chase Sch. (ESNS), 1983–2003. Hatfield Spiral Youth Club Cttee, 1974–99; Hatfield/Thorne Moors Forum, 1996–2000. Church Warden, Christ Church, Dunscroft, 1964–79. *Recreations:* DIY, oil painting, politics. *Address:* 1 Grange Avenue, Hatfield, Doncaster, South Yorks DN7 6RH. *T:* (01302) 844146. *Died 7 Nov. 2009.*

BURRELL, Sir (John) Raymond, 9th Bt *cr* 1774; *b* 20 Feb. 1934; *s* of Sir Walter Raymond Burrell, 8th Bt, CBE, TD, and Hon. Anne Judith (OBE) (*d* 1987), *o d* of 3rd Baron Denman, PC, GCMG, KCVO; *S* father, 1985; *m* 1st, 1959, Rowena Frances (marr. diss. 1971), *d* of late M. H. Pearce; one *s*; 2nd, 1971, Margot Lucy, *d* of F. E. Thatcher, Sydney, NSW; one *s* one *d. Educ:* Eton; Royal Agricultural Coll., Cirencester. *Heir: s* Charles Raymond Burrell [*b* 27 Aug. 1962; *m* 1993, Isabella Elizabeth Nancy, adopted *d* of M. L. Tree; one *s* one *d*]. *Address:* Rosemont, 14 Rosemont Avenue, Woollahra, Sydney, NSW 2025, Australia. *Club:* Boodle's. *Died 29 May 2008.*

BURRIDGE, Alan; Certification Officer for Trade Unions and Employers' Associations, 1981–85; *b* 15 Feb. 1921; *m* 1961, Joan Edith Neale; one *s. Educ:* William Ellis Sch.; Bristol Univ. (BA 1st Cl. Hons 1950). Served War, Army, 1939–46. Northern Assurance Co., 1936–39; Bristol Univ., 1947–50; Swinton Coll., 1950–53; London Municipal Soc., 1953–56; General Electric Co., 1956–67; Dept of Employment, 1967–81. *Address:* 1 Castle Hill Avenue, Berkhamsted, Herts HP4 1HJ. *T:* (01442) 865276. *Died 26 July 2006.*

BURROW, Prof. John Wyon, FBA 1986; FRHistS 1971; Professor of European Thought, and Fellow of Balliol College, University of Oxford, 1995–2000, Emeritus Fellow, since 2001; *b* 4 June 1935; *s* of Charles and Alice Burrow; *m* 1958, Diane Dunnington; one *s* one *d. Educ:* Exeter School; Christ's College, Cambridge (MA, PhD). Research Fellow, Christ's College, Cambridge, 1959–62; Fellow, Downing Coll., Cambridge, 1962–65; Lectr, Sch. of European Studies, Univ. of East Anglia, 1965–69; Reader in History, 1969–82, Prof. of Intellectual History, 1982–95, Univ. of Sussex. Vis. Prof., Univ. of California, Berkeley, 1981 and 1989; Visiting Fellow: History of Ideas Unit, ANU, 1983; All Souls Coll., Oxford, 1994–95; Res. Prof. of Intellectual Hist., Univ. of Sussex, 2000–03. Carlyle Lectr, Oxford, 1985; Christian Gauss Seminars, Princeton Univ., 1988. Editor in Chief, History of European Ideas, 1996–2005. Hon. Dr Scienze Politiche, Bologna, 1988. *Publications:* Evolution and Society, 1966; A Liberal Descent, 1981 (Wolfson History Prize, 1981); (with S. Collini and D. Winch) That Noble Science of Politics, 1983; Gibbon, 1985; Whigs and Liberals, 1988; The Crisis of Reason, 2000; A History of Histories, 2007. *Recreation:* cooking. *Address:* Balliol College, Oxford OX1 3BJ; 22 Bridge Street, Witney, Oxon OX28 1HY. *T:* (01993) 700306. *Died 3 Nov. 2009.*

BURROWES, Edmund Spencer Stanley, CMG 1959; Financial Secretary, Barbados, 1951–66; *b* 16 Dec. 1906; *m* 1st, 1934, Mildred B. Jackson (decd); one *s* three *d*; 2nd, 1965, Gwen Searson. *Educ:* Queen's Coll., British Guiana. British Guiana Colonial Secretariat, 1924; Inspector of Labour, 1940; Deputy Commissioner, 1945; Labour Commissioner, Barbados, 1947. *Publications:* Occupational Terms on Sugar Estates in British Guiana,

1945. *Recreation:* wild life watching. *Address:* 18B Butler's Way, Great Yeldham, Halstead, Essex CO9 4QN. *Died 12 Nov. 2006.*

BURROWS, (Lionel) John, CBE 1974; Chief Inspector of Schools, Department of Education and Science, 1966–73; Educational Adviser, Methodist Residential Schools, 1974–84; *b* 9 March 1912; *s* of H. L. Burrows, HM Inspector of Schools, and Mrs C. J. Burrows; *m* 1939, Enid Patricia Carter; one *s* one *d. Educ:* King Edward VI Sch., Southampton; Gonville and Caius Coll., Cambridge. BA Cantab (1st cl. hons Mod. Langs Tripos) 1933. West Buckland Sch., Devon, Tiffin Sch., Kingston-upon-Thames and primary schools in London and Surrey, 1934–41; HM Forces (RASC and Intell. Corps), 1941–46; Commendation from US Army Chief of Staff, 1945; HM Inspector of Schools, 1946; Divisional Inspector, Metropolitan Div., 1960. Vice-Pres., Nat. Assoc. for Gifted Children, 1975–88. *Publications:* The Middle School: high road or dead end?, 1978. *Recreations:* natural history, fell-walking. *Address:* 34 Groby Road, Ratby, Leicester LE6 0LJ. *Club:* English-Speaking Union. *Died 28 Aug. 2008.*

BURSTALL, Dr Clare, FBPsS; Director, National Foundation for Educational Research in England and Wales, 1983–93 (Deputy Director, 1972–83); *b* 3 Sept. 1931; *d* of Alfred and Lily Wells; *m* 1955, Michael Lyle Burstall (marr. diss. 1977); one *s* one *d. Educ:* King's Coll. and Birkbeck Coll., Univ. of London (BA Hons French, BA Hons Psychology, PhD Psychology); La Sorbonne, Paris. FBPsS 1975. Project Leader of team evaluating teaching of French in British primary schs, NFER, 1964–72. Charter Fellow, Coll. of Preceptors, 1988; FRSA 1990; Mem., Soc. of Authors, 2000; Hon. Mem., CGLI, 1987. Hon. DSc Hull, 1988; Hon. DEd De Montford, 1993. *Publications:* French from Eight: a national experiment, 1968; French in the Primary School: attitudes and achievement, 1970; Primary French in the Balance, 1974; French from Age Eight or Eleven?, 1975; translated with Vladimir Kisselnikov: Zhitinsky, The Staircase, and Cheops and Nefertiti, 2000; Red Star Under the Baltic, by Viktor Korzh, 2004; Leningrad Under Siege: firsthand accounts of the ordeal, by A. Adamovich and D. Granin, 2006; jl articles on various aspects of educnl research (eg, second language learning, large-scale assessment of achievement, class size, and management of educnl res.). *Recreations:* sailing, art collection, music, needlework. *Address:* Taskalinrinne 4, 49400 Hamina, Finland. *T:* and *Fax:* (5) 388668; *e-mail:* clare.burstall@pp.inet.fi. *Died 31 May 2006.*

BURTON, Sir George (Vernon Kennedy), Kt 1977; CBE 1972 (MBE (mil.) 1945); DL; Chairman, Fisons plc, 1973–84 (Chief Executive, 1966–76, Senior Vice-Chairman, 1966–71, Deputy Chairman, 1971–72); *b* 21 April 1916; *s* of late George Ethelbert Earnshaw Burton and Francesca (*née* Holden-White); *g s* of Sir Bunnell Burton, Ipswich; *m* 1st, 1945, Sarah Katherine Tcherniavsky (marr. diss.); two *s*; 2nd, 1975, Priscilla Margaret Gore (MBE 1996), *d* of late Cecil H. King. *Educ:* Charterhouse; Germany. Served RA, 1939–45, N Africa, Sicily, Italy, Austria. Director: Barclays Bank Internat. plc, 1976–82; Thomas Tilling, 1976–83; Rolls-Royce Ltd, 1976–84. Member: Export Council for Europe, 1965–71 (Dep. Chm., 1967–71); Council, CBI, 1970–84 (Chm., CBI Overseas Cttee, 1975–81); BOTB, 1972–73 (BOTB European Trade Cttee, 1972–81; British Overseas Trade Adv. Council, 1975–79); Investment Insce Adv. Cttee, ECGD, 1971–76; Council on Internat. Develt of ODM, 1977–79; Council, BIM, 1968–70 (FBIM); NEDC, 1975–79; Whitford Cttee to Consider Law on Copyright and Designs, 1974–77; Ipswich County Borough Council, 1947–51; Ipswich Gp HMC; Assoc. for Business Sponsorship of the Arts, 1978–84; Governing Body, British National Cttee of Internat. Chamber of Commerce, 1979–86; Governor, Sutton's Hosp. in Charterhouse, 1979–92; Chm., Ipswich Conservative Assoc., 1982–84. FRSA 1978. DL Suffolk, 1980. Commander: Order of Ouissam Alaouite,

Morocco, 1968; Order of Léopold II, Belgium, 1974. *Recreation:* music. *Address:* Aldham Mill, Hadleigh, Suffolk IP7 6LE. *Died 19 Nov. 2009.*

BURTON, Prof. Kenneth, FRS 1974; Professor of Biochemistry, 1966–88, then Emeritus, and Dean of Faculty of Science, 1983–86, University of Newcastle upon Tyne; *b* 26 June 1926; *s* of Arthur and Gladys Burton; *m* 1955, Hilda Marsden; one *s* one *d. Educ:* High Pavement Sch., Nottingham; Wath-upon-Dearne Grammar Sch.; King's Coll., Cambridge (MA, PhD). Asst Lectr in Biochem., Univ. of Sheffield, 1949, Lectr, 1952; Res. Associate, Univ. of Chicago, 1952–54; MRC Unit for Research in Cell Metabolism, Oxford, 1954–66. Vis. Lectr in Medicine, Harvard, 1964; William Evans Vis. Prof., Univ. of Otago, 1977–78. *Publications:* scientific articles, especially on nucleic acids. *Recreation:* music. *Address:* Byways, The Broadway, Alfriston, Polegate, East Sussex BN26 5XH. *Died 22 Nov. 2010.*

BUSH, Maj.-Gen. Peter John, OBE 1968; Controller, Army Benevolent Fund, 1980–87; *b* 31 May 1924; *s* of Clement Charles Victor Bush and Kathleen Mabel Peirce; *m* 1948, Jean Mary Hamilton (decd); two *s* one *d. Educ:* Maidenhead County Sch. Commnd Somerset LI, 1944; comd LI Volunteers, 1966; GSO 1 HQ 14 Div./Malaya Dist, 1968; Comdr 3 Inf. Bde, 1971 (mentioned in despatches, 1973); Asst Comdt RMA Sandhurst, 1974; Chief of Staff and Head of UK Delegn to Live Oak, SHAPE, 1977–79, retd. Col, The Light Infantry, 1977–82. *Recreations:* natural history, walking, reading. *Address:* Thorndean, Boyndon Road, Maidenhead, Berks SL6 4EU. *Died 12 June 2009.*

BUSHE, Frederick Joseph William, OBE 1994; RSA 1986 (ARSA 1977); Founder, 1979, and Director, 1979–96, Scottish Sculpture Workshop; *b* 1 March 1931; *s* of Frederick M. C. Bushe and Kathleen Welch; *m* 1st, 1956, Rosemary R. Beattie; three *s* one *d*; 2nd, 1984, Fiona M. S. Marr; one *d. Educ:* Our Lady's High Sch., Motherwell; Glasgow Sch. of Art (DA). Temp. Captain RAEC, 1954–58. Art teacher, Midlothian, 1958–60; Berwickshire, 1960–62; Lectr in Art Educn, Notre Dame, Liverpool, 1962–69, Aberdeen Coll. of Educn, 1969–79. Curator, Scandex, 15th anniv. touring exhibn of Scottish sculpture, 1994–95. Governor, Edinburgh Coll. of Art, 1983–88. Invited Artist: Formaviva Internat. Symposium of Sculptors, Yugoslavia, 1988; Terra Internat. Symposium, Kikinda, Yugoslavia, 1990. Work in numerous public collections; one man exhibitions: Edinburgh, 1962, 1971, 1982; Liverpool, 1966; Glasgow, 1974; Manchester, 1975; Stirling, 1978; group exhibns. *Recreations:* listening to music, cooking. *Address:* Rose Cottage, Lumsden, Huntly, Aberdeenshire AB54 4JJ. *T:* (01464) 861394; Muirhead Private Nursing Home, Muir of Fowlis, by Alford, Aberdeenshire AB33 8NU. *Died 18 May 2009.*

BUSHNELL, Alexander Lynn, CBE 1962; County Clerk and Treasurer, Perth County Council, 1946–75; *b* 13 Aug. 1911; *s* of William and Margaret Bushnell; *m* 1939, Janet Braithwaite Porteous (*d* 2005); two *d. Educ:* Dalziel High Sch., Motherwell; Glasgow University. Dep. County Clerk and Treas., Inverness CC, 1939; County Clerk and Treas., Kirkcudbright CC, 1944. *Recreation:* golf. *Died 7 March 2009.*

BUTCHER, John Patrick; Partner, J. & A. Butcher Associates, since 1996; *b* 13 Feb. 1946; *s* of Russell Patrick Butcher and Kathleen (*née* Read); *m* 1970, Anne Lowe; one *s* two *d. Educ:* Huntingdon Grammar Sch.; Birmingham Univ. (BSocSc). Marketing exec. and Product Manager, computer industry, 1968–79. Mem., Birmingham City Council, 1972–78 (Vice-Chm., Educn Cttee). Chm., Texas Instruments Ltd, 1990–98. MP (C) Coventry SW, 1979–97; Parly Under Sec. of State, DoI, 1982–83, DTI, 1983–88, DES, 1988–89. Co-Chm., All-Party Manufacturing Industry Gp. Chm., Inst. of Dirs, 1997–2001. FIET (CompIEE). Bicentenary Medal, RSA,

1986. *Recreations:* the Lake District, fell-walking, pre-Conquest history, remote places, occasional journalism. *Died 25 Dec. 2006.*

BUTLER, Rt Hon. Sir Adam (Courtauld), Kt 1986; PC 1984; Vice Lord-Lieutenant, Warwickshire, 1998–2005; Director, H. P. Bulmer Holdings plc, 1988–97; *b* 11 Oct. 1931; *s* of late Baron Butler of Saffron Walden, KG, CH, PC and Sydney, *o c* of late Samuel Courtauld; *m* 1955, Felicity Molesworth-St Aubyn; two *s* one *d. Educ:* Eton; Pembroke College, Cambridge. National Service, 2nd Lieut KRRC, 1949–51. Cambridge (BA History/Economics), 1951–54. ADC to Governor-General of Canada, 1954–55; Courtaulds Ltd, 1955–73; Director: Aristoc Ltd, 1966–73; Kayser Bondor Ltd, 1971–73; Capital and Counties Property Co., 1973–79; Dep. Chm., CMW Gp, 1989–93. MP (C) Bosworth, 1970–87. PPS to: Minister of State for Foreign Affairs, 1971–72; Minister of Agriculture, Fisheries and Food, 1972–74; PPS to Leader of the Opposition, 1975–79; an Asst Govt Whip, 1974; an Opposition Whip, 1974–75; Minister of State: DoI, 1979–81; NI Office, 1981–84; Defence Procurement, 1984–85. Chm., British Hallmarking Council, 1998–2004. Mem. NFU. Mem. Court of Assistants, Goldsmiths' Co., 1987– (Prime Warden, 1999–2000). Chairman: Samuel Courtauld Trustees, 1989–2005; Airey Neave Trust, 1989–99. Mem. Council, RSA, 1986–90. Pres., BHS, 1990–92. DL Warwicks, 1993. *Recreations:* field sports, music, pictures. *Address:* The Old Rectory, Lighthorne, Warwick CV35 0AR. *T:* (01926) 651214. *Died 9 Jan. 2008.*

BUTLER, Anthony John; Director, Oxford University Careers Service, 1996–2006; Professorial Fellow, New College, Oxford, 1996–2006, then Emeritus Fellow; *b* 30 Jan. 1945; *s* of Martin Edward and Freda Alice Butler; *m* 1967, Margaret Ann, *d* of George and Margaret Randon; one *s* one *d. Educ:* Maidstone Grammar Sch.; University Coll., Oxford (Exhibnr, Mod. Hist.; MA); Inst. of Criminology and Trinity Hall, Cambridge (Dip. Crim.); Cambridge-Columbia Fellow, Columbia Law Sch., NY. FCIPD. Joined Home Office as Asst Principal, 1969; Police and Criminal Depts, 1969–72; Private Sec. to Minister of State, Home Office, 1972–74; Principal, Gen. Dept, Sex Discrimination and Race Relations Legislation Units and Broadcasting Dept, 1974–79; Private Sec. to Sec. of State for the Home Dept, 1979–80; Asst Sec., Broadcasting, Finance and Prisons Depts, 1980–88; Asst Under-Sec. of State, seconded to DoE, 1988 as Dir, Inner Cities; Principal Finance Officer, Home Office, 1990; Dir of Personnel and Finance, then of Personnel, later of Services, HM Prison Service, 1990–96. Ind. Assessor, DCMS, 2000–07. Dir, 2000–06, Chm., 2005–06, CVs.ac.uk Ltd. Treas., 2002–04, Pres., 2004–06, Assoc. of Grad. Careers Adv. Services. Trustee, University Coll. Oxford Old Members' Trust, 1988–94 (Chm. Trustees, 1991–94). Foundn Gov., St Gregory the Great Sch., Oxford, 2007–. *Publications:* (ed with M. Dane) AGCAS: reflections on change 1967–2007, 2007. *Recreations:* lead guitarist (The Muskrats, 1960–62, 2007–), virtual walking, under-gardening. *Died 13 Nov. 2010.*

BUTLER, His Honour Gerald Norman; QC 1975; a Circuit Judge, 1982–97; Senior Judge at Southwark Crown Court, 1984–97; *b* 15 Sept. 1930; *s* of Joshua Butler and Esther Butler (*née* Lampel); *m* 1959, Stella, *d* of Harris and Leah Isaacs; two *d* (one *s* decd). *Educ:* Ilford County High Sch.; London Sch. of Economics; Magdalen Coll., Oxford. LLB London 1952, BCL Oxon 1954. 2nd Lieut, RASC, 1956–57. Called to Bar, Middle Temple, 1955; a Recorder of the Crown Court, 1977–82. Inquiry and Reports into: English RFU, 1997; Central Casework at CPS, 1999; prosecution of Regina *v* Doran and others, 2000; Treasury Counsel instructed by CPS, 2000. Non-exec. Chm., Mark Butler Associates Ltd. *Recreations:* Rugby, opera, Japanese pottery, walking. *Address:* 1 Essex Court, Temple, EC4Y 9AR. *Clubs:* Garrick, MCC. *Died 28 Feb. 2010.*

BUTLER, Maj.-Gen. Hew Dacres George, CB 1975; DL; *b* 12 March 1922; *s* of late Maj.-Gen. Stephen Seymour Butler, CB, CMG, DSO; *m* 1954, Joanna, *d* of late G. M. Puckridge, CMG, ED; two *s* one *d*. *Educ*: Winchester. Commnd Rifle Bde, 1941; Western Desert, 1942–43; wounded POW, 1943–45; psc 1951; BM 7th Armd Bde, 1951–53; Kenya, 1954–55; Instructor, Staff Coll., 1957–60; CO 1 RB, 1962–64; Cyprus (despatches, 1965); comd 24 Inf. Bde, Aden, 1966–67; idc 1969; ACOS G3 Northag, 1970–72; GOC Near East Land Forces, 1972–74. Chief of Staff (Contingencies Planning), SHAPE, 1975–76; retired 1977. Sec., Beit Trust, 1978–93. DL 1980, High Sheriff 1983, Hants. *Recreations*: shooting, racing, horticulture. *Address*: Bury Lodge, Hambledon, Hants PO7 4QL. *Clubs*: Army and Navy, MCC. *Died 10 July 2007.*

BUTLER, Keith Stephenson, CMG 1977; HM Diplomatic Service, retired; Appeal Director for various charities, since 1978; *b* 3 Sept. 1917; *s* of late Raymond R. Butler and Gertrude Stephenson; *m* 1st, 1952, Geraldine Marjorie Clark (*d* 1979); 2nd, 1979, Mrs Priscilla Wittels; no *c*. *Educ*: King Edward's Sch., Birmingham; Liverpool Coll.; St Peter's Coll., Oxford (MA). HM Forces, 1939–47 (despatches): served, RA, in Egypt, Greece and Crete; POW, Germany, 1941–45. Foreign Correspondent for Sunday Times and Kemsley Newspapers, 1947–50. Joined HM Foreign Service, 1950; served: First Sec., Ankara and Caracas; Canadian Nat. Defence Coll.; Paris; Montreal. HM Consul-General: Seville, 1968; Bordeaux, 1969; Naples, 1974–77. *Publications*: contrib. historical and political reviews. *Recreation*: historical research. *Address*: Sheilings, 10 Station Road, Kintbury, near Newbury, Berks RG17 9UP. *T*: (01488) 658350. *Died 16 Oct. 2008.*

BUTLER, Prof. Michael Gregory, PhD, LittD; Professor of Modern German Literature, University of Birmingham, 1986–2003, then Emeritus; *b* 1 Nov. 1935; *s* of Maurice Gregory Butler and Winifred May Butler (*née* Barker); *m* 1960, Jean Mary Griffith; one *s* one *d*. *Educ*: High Pavement Sch., Nottingham; Fitzwilliam Coll., Cambridge (BA, MA; LittD 1999); Trinity Coll., Oxford (DipEd 1958); CNAA (PhD 1974). Assistant Master: King's Sch., Worcester, 1958–61; Reuchlin Gymnasium, Pforzheim, FRG, 1961–62; Hd of German, Ipswich Sch., 1962–70; University of Birmingham: Lectr, 1970–80; Sen. Lectr, 1980–86; Head: Dept of German Studies, 1984–2001; Sch. of Mod. Langs, 1988–93; Professorial Fellow, Inst. for German Studies, 1997–; Public Orator, 1997–2005; Fellow, Inst. for Advanced Res. in Arts and Social Scis, 2003–. Vis. Fellow, Humanities Res. Centre, ANU, 1979. Vice-Pres., 1994–96, Pres., 1996–99, Conf. of Univ. Teachers of German in GB and Ireland. Gov., Abbey High Sch., Redditch, 1971–87. Editor, Samphire, New Poetry, 1968–81; Jt Gen. Editor, New Perspectives in German Studies, 2000–. Taras Schevchenko Meml Prize, 1961. Knight's Cross, Order of Merit (FRG), 1998. *Publications*: The Novels of Max Frisch, 1975; (ed) Englische Lyrik der Gegenwart, 1981; The Plays of Max Frisch, 1985; Frisch: Andorra, 1985, 2nd edn 1994; (ed) Rejection and Emancipation: writing in German-speaking Switzerland 1945–1991, 1991; (ed) The Narrative Fiction of Heinrich Böll: social conscience and literary achievement, 1995; (ed) The Challenge of German Culture, 2000; (ed) The Making of Modern Switzerland 1848–1998, 2000; Marks of Honour: public ovations 1997–2005, 2007; contrib. many articles and essays to edited bks and learned jls; regular contrib. TLS. *Recreation*: avoiding retirement. *Address*: 45 Westfields, Catshill, Bromsgrove B61 9HJ. *T*: (01527) 874189; Department of German Studies, University of Birmingham, Edgbaston, Birmingham B15 2TT. *T*: (0121) 414 6174. *Died 25 Nov. 2007.*

BUTLER, Prof. Neville Roy, MD; FRCP; FRCOG; Director, International Centre for Child Studies, since 1983; Professor of Child Health, Bristol University, 1965–85, Emeritus Professor, since 1985; Visiting Fellow, Centre for Longitudinal Studies, London University, since 1998; *b* Harrow, 6 July 1920; *o s* of late Dr C. J. Butler, MRCS, and Ida Margaret Butler; *m* 1954, Jean Ogilvie (marr. diss.; she *d* 1998), *d* of late John McCormack; two *d*. *Educ*: Epsom Coll.; Charing Cross Hosp. Med. Sch. (MB BS 1942; MD 1949). MRCP 1946, FRCP 1965; DCH 1949; FRCOG 1979. Served RAMC, 1942–44, temp. Captain. First Assistant to Paediatric Unit, UCH, 1950; Med. Registrar and Pathologist, Hosp. for Sick Children, Gt Ormond St, 1953; Consultant Paediatrician, Oxford and Wessex RHB, 1957–63; Dir, Perinatal Mortality Survey, Nat. Birthday Trust Fund, 1958; Consultant Physician, Hosp. for Sick Children, Gt Ormond St and Sen. Lectr, Inst. of Child Health, London Univ., 1963–65; Hon. Cons. Paediatrician, Bristol & Weston Teaching Dist and Southmead Dist, 1965–85. Co-Dir, Nat. Child Develt Study (1958 cohort), 1965–75; Dir, Child Health and Educn Study (1970 cohort), and Youthscan UK, 1975–89. Harding Meml Lect., RIBA, 1983. Member: BPA, 1958–; Neonatal Soc., 1961–; Cuban Paediatric Soc., 1973–; Hungarian Paediatric Soc., 1979–. Hon. FRCPCH 1996. *Publications*: jointly: Perinatal Mortality, 1963; 11,000 Seven Year Olds, 1966; Perinatal Problems, 1969; From Birth to Seven, 1972; ABO Haemolytic Diseases of the Newborn, 1972; The Social Life of Britain's Five Year Olds, 1984; Ethnic Minority Children, 1985; The Health of Britain's Five Year Olds, 1986; papers in scientific and med. jls. *Address*: International Centre for Child Studies, 86 Cumberland Road, Bristol BS1 6UG. *T*: (0117) 925 0835, *Fax*: (0117) 909 3739; *e-mail*: NRButler@childstudies.org; Centre for Longitudinal Studies, Institute of Education, University of London, 20 Bedford Way, WC1H 0AL; *e-mail*: NRButler@ aol.com. *Club*: Savage. *Died 22 Feb. 2007.*

BUTTER, Major Sir David (Henry), KCVO 1991; MC 1941; JP; landowner and farmer; company director; HM Lord-Lieutenant of Perth and Kinross, 1975–95; *b* 18 March 1920; *s* of late Col Charles Butter, OBE, DL, JP, Pitlochry, and Agnes Marguerite (Madge), *d* of late William Clark, Newark, NJ, USA; *m* 1946, Myra Alice (CVO 1992), *d* of Hon. Maj.-Gen. Sir Harold Wernher, 3rd Bt, GCVO, TD; one *s* four *d*. *Educ*: Eton; Oxford. Served War of 1939–45: 2nd Lieut Scots Guards, 1940, Western Desert and North Africa, Sicily (Staff), 1941–43; Italy (ADC to GOC 8th Army, Gen. Sir Oliver Leese, 1944); Temp. Major, 1946; retd Army, 1948. Captain, Queen's Body Guard for Scotland (Royal Company of Archers); Pres., Highland T&AVR, 1979–84. County Councillor, Perth, 1955–74; DL Perthshire, 1956, Vice-Lieutenant of Perth, 1960–71; HM Lieutenant of County of Perth, 1971–75, and County of Kinross, 1974–75. *Recreations*: shooting, golf, ski-ing, travel. *Address*: Cluniemore, Pitlochry, Scotland PH16 5NE. *T*: (01796) 472006; 64 Rutland Gate, SW7 1PJ. *T*: (020) 7589 6731. *Clubs*: Turf; Royal and Ancient (St Andrews). *Died 29 May 2010.*

BUTTER, John Henry, CMG 1962; MBE 1946; Financial Director to Government of Abu Dhabi, 1970–83; *b* 20 April 1916; *s* of late Captain A. E. Butter, CMG, and Helen Ciceley Butter (*née* Kerr, later Baird); *m* 1950, Joyce Platt; three *s*. *Educ*: Charterhouse; Christ Church, Oxford. Indian Civil Service, 1939–47; Pakistan Admin. Service, 1947–50 (served in Punjab, except for period 1942–46 when was Asst to Political Agent, Imphal, Manipur State). HM Overseas Civil Service, Kenya, 1950–65 (Perm. Sec. to the Treasury, 1959–65); Financial Adviser, Kenya Treasury, 1965–69. *Publications*: Uncivil Servant, 1989. *Recreations*: golf, bridge. *Address*: Whitehill, Gordon, Berwickshire TD3 6LQ. *Club*: East India. *Died 28 Oct. 2008.*

BUTTERFIELD, Charles Harris; QC (Singapore) 1952; HMOCS, retired; *b* 28 June 1911; 2nd *s* of William Arthur Butterfield, OBE, and Rebecca Butterfield; *m* 1st, 1938, Monica, *d* of Austin Harrison, London; one *d*; 2nd, by special permission of the Holy See, Ellen, *d* of Ernest John Bennett, Singapore and *widow* of J. E. King, Kuala

Lumpur, Singapore and Hooe. *Educ:* Downside; Trinity Coll., Cambridge. Barrister-at-law, Middle Temple, 1934. Entered Colonial Legal Service, 1938; Crown Counsel, Straits Settlements, 1938. Served Singapore RA (Volunteer) and RA, 1941–46; POW, 1942–45. Solicitor-General, Singapore, 1948–55, Attorney-General, 1955–57; Legal Adviser's Dept CRO and FCO, 1959–69; DoE and Sec. of State's Panel of Inspectors (Planning), 1969–74. *Recreations:* beagling, walking.
Died 15 April 2008.

BUTTON, Henry George; author; *b* 11 Aug. 1913; *e s* of late Rev. Frank S. and Bertha B. Button; *m* 1938, Edith Margaret Heslop (*d* 1972); two *d. Educ:* Manchester Grammar Sch.; Christ's Coll., Cambridge (Scholar). Mod. and Medieval Langs Tripos, Part II, 1st Class (with dist.) 1934; MLitt 1977; Tiarks German Scholar (research at Univ. of Bonn), 1934–35; Sen. Studentship of Goldsmiths' Company, 1935–36. Entered Civil Service, 1937; Board of Trade, 1937–57 (served in Min. of Production, 1942; Counsellor, UK Delegn to OEEC, Paris, 1952–55; on staff of Monopolies Commn, 1955–56); transf. Min. of Agriculture, Fisheries and Food, 1957; Under-Sec., Min. of Agriculture, Fisheries and Food, 1960–73 (Principal Finance Officer, 1965–73). Res. Student, 1974–76, Fellow-Commoner, 1982–, Christ's Coll., Cambridge. Mem. Agricultural Research Council, 1960–62. Leader of various UK Delegns to FAO in Rome. BBC Brain of Britain for 1962; rep. Great Britain in radio quiz in Johannesburg, 1966; Bob Dyer's TV show, Sydney, 1967. *Publications:* The Guinness Book of the Business World (with A. Lampert), 1976; contribs to various jls both learned and unlearned, and to newspapers. *Recreations:* reading, writing, studying old businesses (hon. review ed., Business Archives Council, 1966–75; Hon. Sec., Tercentenarians' Club, 1970–2001), showing visitors round the colleges. *Address:* 7 Amhurst Court, Grange Road, Cambridge CB3 9BH. *T:* (01223) 355698. *Club:* Civil Service.   *Died 11 March 2008.*

BUXTON OF ALSA, Baron *cr* 1978 (Life Peer), of Stiffkey in the County of Norfolk; **Aubrey Leland Oakes Buxton,** KCVO 1996; MC 1943; DL; Director, Anglia Television, since 1958 (Chairman, 1986–88); *b* 15 July 1918; *s* of Leland Wilberforce Buxton and Mary, *d* of Rev. Thomas Henry Oakes; *m* 1st, 1946, Pamela Mary (*d* 1983), *d* of Sir Henry Birkin, 3rd Bt; two *s* four *d*; 2nd, 1988, Mrs Kathleen Peterson, Maine, USA. *Educ:* Ampleforth; Trinity Coll., Cambridge. Served 1939–45, RA; combined ops in Arakan, 1942–45 (despatches, 1944). Extra Equerry to Duke of Edinburgh. A Trustee of the British Museum (Natural History), 1971–73. Member: Countryside Commn, 1968–72; Royal Commission on Environmental Pollution, 1970–74; Nature Conservancy Council, 1988–92; British Vice Pres., World Wildlife Fund; Trustee, Wildfowl Trust; Treasurer, London Zoological Soc., 1978–83; Former Pres., Royal Television Soc.; Chairman: Independent Television Cos Assoc., 1972–75; UPITN Inc., USA, 1981–83; ITN, 1981–86. Wildlife Film Producer, Anglia TV. Golden Awards, Internat. TV Festival, 1963 and 1968; Silver Medal, Zoological Society of London, 1967; Silver Medal, Royal TV Society, 1968; Queen's Award to Industry, 1974; Gold Medal, Royal TV Soc., 1977. High Sheriff of Essex 1972; DL Essex, 1975–85. *Publications:* (with Sir Philip Christison) The Birds of Arakan, 1946; The King in his Country, 1955. *Recreations:* travel, natural history, painting, sport. *Address:* Old Hall Farm, Stiffkey, Norfolk NR23 1QJ. *Club:* White's.   *Died 1 Sept. 2009.*

BUXTON, Prof. John Noel, FBCS; CEng; Chairman, Room Underwriting Systems Ltd, 1993–97; Professor of Information Technology, King's College, London, 1984–94; *b* 25 Dec. 1933; *s* of John William Buxton and Laura Frances Buxton; *m* 1958, Moira Jean O'Brien; two *s* two *d. Educ:* Bradford Grammar Sch.; Trinity Coll., Cambridge (BA 1955, MA 1959). FBCS 1968. Flight Trials Engr, De Havilland Propellers, 1955–59; Ops Res. Scientist, British Iron and Steel Res. Assoc., 1959–60; Applied Science Rep., IBM UK, 1960–62; Lectr, Inst. of Computer Science, Univ. of London, 1962–66; Chief Software Consultant, CEIR (later Scicon Ltd) 1966–68; Prof. of Computer Science, Univ. of Warwick, 1968–84. UNDP Proj. Manager, Internat. Computing Educn Centre, Budapest, 1975–77; Vis. Scholar, Harvard Univ., 1979–80; Dir of Systems Engrg, DTI, 1989–91 (on secondment). Hon. Vice-Pres. (Engrg), BCS, 1997–2000. *Publications:* (ed) Simulation Programming Languages, 1968; (ed jtly) Software Engineering Concepts and Techniques (Procs of NATO Confs 1968 and 1969), 1976; (jtly) The Craft of Software Engineering, 1987; three computer programming languages; papers in professional jls. *Recreations:* mountaineering, music, ancient houses, genealogy, local history. *Address:* The Guildhall, Church Street, Eye, Suffolk IP23 7BD.
Died 3 Nov. 2009.

BUXTON, Paul William Jex; Northern Ireland Office, 1974–85 (Under Secretary, 1981–85); *b* 20 Sept. 1925; *s* of of late Denis Buxton and Emily Buxton (*née* Hollins); *m* 1st, 1950, Katharine Hull (marr. diss. 1971, she *d* 1977); two *s* one *d*; 2nd, 1971, Hon. Margaret Evelyn Aston, DPhil, FBA, *d* of 1st Baron Bridges, KG, GCB, GCVO, MC, PC, FRS; one *d* (and one *d* decd). *Educ:* Rugby Sch.; Balliol Coll., Oxford (MA). Coldstream Guards, 1944–47. HM Foreign, later Diplomatic, Service, 1950–71; served Delhi, UN, Guatemala and Washington, latterly as Counsellor. Investment banking, 1972–74; on staff of Monopolies and Mergers Commn, 1985–91. Treasurer: Anti-Slavery International (formerly Anti-Slavery Soc.), 1986–2002; Howard League for Penal Reform, 1991–97 (Mem. Council, 1985–99); Hon. Treas., Prisoners' Advice Service, 1991–96. *Recreation:* forestry. *Address:* Castle House, Chipping Ongar, Essex CM5 9JT. *T:* (01277) 362642. *Club:* Brooks's.   *Died 5 Jan. 2009.*

BUXTON, Raymond Naylor, OBE 1975; BEM 1957; QPM 1971; *b* 16 Sept. 1915; *s* of late Tom Bird Buxton and Ethel Buxton, Rushall, Walsall; *m* 1939, Agatha (*d* 2001), *d* of late Enoch and Elizabeth Price, Essington, Wolverhampton; three *s. Educ:* King Edward VI Grammar Sch., Stafford. Constable to Chief Supt in Staffordshire Co. Police. Served War, RAF, Navigator, 1943–45 (FO). Police Coll. Staff, 1958–61; Asst Chief Constable, then Dep. Chief Constable of Herts, 1963–69; Chief Constable, 1969–77; HM Inspector of Constabulary, 1977–79.   *Died 25 Jan. 2006.*

BUYERS, Thomas Bartlett, OBE 1975; HM Chief Inspector of Prisons for Scotland, 1985–89; *b* 21 March 1926; *s* of Charles Stuart Buyers and Bessie Heywood Buyers; *m* 1951, Agnes Lodge Alexander; three *d. Educ:* Glasgow Acad., Glasgow; Glasgow Univ. (BSc); BA Open Univ. 1998. MIChemE. Res. Chemist, Shell, 1947–50; professional and management posts, BP Chemicals, Grangemouth and Baglan Bay, 1951–73; Dir, Scottish Petroleum Office, 1973–74; Dir of Engrg, Offshore Supplies Office, Dept of Energy, 1974–75; BP Rep./Commissioning Man., Sullom Voe Terminal, Shetland, 1975–80; Special Projects Man., BP Chemicals, London, 1980–84. *Recreations:* gardening, hill walking, voluntary work.   *Died 20 Dec. 2010.*

BYRNE, John Keyes; *see* Leonard, Hugh.

C

CACHELIN, Commissioner Francy; International Evangelist, The Salvation Army, 1987–89, retired; *b* 4 Aug. 1923; *s* of Maurice Cachelin and France Hauswirth; *m* 1951, Geneviève Irène Catherine Booth; two *s* two *d*. *Educ:* Lausanne School of Arts. Commissioned Salvation Army Officer, 1944; served in Switzerland as Corps Officer; Editor, The War Cry, in Belgium, 1951; responsible for youth work, France, 1957; Field Secretary, Switzerland, 1966; Chief Secretary, France, 1975, British Territory, 1977; Territorial Commander, Germany, 1979; British Comr, 1984. Federal Cross of Merit (FRG), 1984. *Recreation:* biblical languages. *Died 16 Aug. 2007.*

CADBURY, Peter (Egbert); Chairman, Preston Publications Ltd, since 1985; *b* Great Yarmouth, Norfolk, 6 Feb. 1918; *s* of late Sir Egbert Cadbury, DSC, DFC; *m* 1st, 1947, Eugenie Benedicta (marr. diss. 1968), *d* of late Major Ewen Bruce, DSO, MC and of Mrs Bruce; one *s* one *d*; 2nd, 1970, Mrs Jennifer Mary Victoria Morgan-Jones (marr. diss. 1976; she *m* 3rd, Robin D'Abo, and *d* 2003), *d* of Major Michael Hammond Maude, Ramsden, Oxon; one *s*; 3rd, 1976, Mrs Jane Mead; two *s*. *Educ:* Leighton Park Sch.; Trinity Coll., Cambridge (BA, MA 1939). Called to Bar, Inner Temple, 1946; practised at Bar, 1946–54. Served Fleet Air Arm, 1940, until released to Ministry of Aircraft Production, 1942, as Prodn, Research and Experimental Test Pilot. Contested (L) Stroud (Glos), 1945. Member, London Travel Cttee, 1958–60; Chm. and Man. Dir, Keith Prowse Group, 1954–71; Chairman: Alfred Hays Ltd, 1955–71; Ashton & Mitchell Ltd and Ashton & Mitchell Travel Co. Ltd, 1959–71; Air Westward Ltd, 1977–79; Air West Ltd, 1977–79; Educational Video Index Ltd, 1981–83; Westward Travel Ltd, 1982–84; Testworth Ltd, 1996–; Exec. Chm., Westward Television Ltd, 1960–80; Chm., Preston Estates, 1973–90; Director: Independent Television News Ltd, 1972–79; Willett Investments Ltd, 1955–. Chm., George Cadbury Trust, 1979–; Trustee: Help the Aged, 1986–; Mus. of Army Flying, 1986–; Winchester Cathedral Trust, 1986–. Freeman of City of London, 1948. *Recreations:* theatre, racing, flying, golf, tennis, sailing. *Address:* Upton Grey Lodge, Upton Grey, near Basingstoke, Hants RG25 2RE. *T:* (01256) 862374, *Fax:* (01256) 862988. *Clubs:* Royal Thames Yacht, Buck's, XL (Forty), MCC (Hon. Life Mem.), Lord's Taverners; Hawks (Cambridge); Island Sailing, Royal Motor Yacht, RAF Yacht. *Died 17 April 2006.*

CADBURY-BROWN, Henry Thomas, OBE 1967; TD; RA 1975 (ARA 1971); FRIBA; Professor of Architecture, Royal Academy, 1975–88; architect, in partnership with John F. Metcalfe and Elizabeth R. Cadbury-Brown, 1962–84; *b* 20 May 1913; *s* of Henry William Cadbury-Brown and Marion Ethel Sewell; *m* 1953, Elizabeth Romeyn (*d* 2002), *d* of Prof. A. Elwyn, Croton on Hudson, NY. *Educ:* Westminster Sch.; AA Sch. of Architecture (Hons Diploma). Architect in private practice after winning competition for British Railways Branch Offices, 1937. Work includes pavilions for "The Origins of the People", main concourse and fountain display at Festival of Britain; schools, housing, display and interiors. Architect for new civic centre at Gravesend and halls for residence for Birmingham Univ. and, with Sir Hugh Casson and Prof. Robert Goodden, for new premises for Royal College of Art; awarded London Architecture Bronze Medal, 1963; lecture halls for Univ. of Essex; for RBK & C: Tavistock Cres. housing; World's End redevelt (in gp partnership Eric Lyons, Cadbury-Brown, Metcalfe & Cunningham); interior alterations in Burlington House for RA. Taught at Architectural Association Sch., 1946–49; Tutor at Royal Coll. of Art, 1952–61. Invited as Visiting Critic to Sch. of Architecture, Harvard Univ., 1956. Retrospective exhibn, Elegant Variation, RA, 2006–07. Member: RIBA Council, 1951–53; MARS (Modern Architectural Research) group. Pres. Architectural Assoc., 1959–60. TA and military service, 1931–45; Major RA (TD). Hon. Fellow: RCA; Kent Inst. of Art and Design, 1992. DU Essex, 1989. *Recreations:* numerous, including work. *Address:* 3 Church Walk, Aldeburgh, Suffolk IP15 5DU. *T:* (01728) 452591. *Died 9 July 2009.*

CADELL, Patrick Moubray, CBE 2001; FSAScot; Keeper of the Records of Scotland, 1991–2000; *b* 17 March 1941; *s* of late Col Henry Moubray Cadell of Grange, OBE and Christina Rose Nimmo or Cadell; *m* 1st, 1968, Sarah Margaret Florence King (*d* 1996); two *s* one *d*; 2nd, 2001, Rachel Watson. *Educ:* Merchiston Castle Sch.; Trinity Coll., Cambridge (BA 1962); Toulouse Univ. FSAScot 1985. British Museum: guide lectr, Dept of Admin, 1964–66; Asst Keeper, Dept of Manuscripts, 1966–68; National Library of Scotland: Asst Keeper, Dept of Manuscripts, 1968–83; Keeper, Dept of Manuscripts, 1983–90. Bailie, Abbey Court of Holyrood, 1995–. Officier de l'Ordre des Arts et des Lettres (France), 2002. *Publications:* The Iron Mills at Cramond, 1973; (contrib.) The Water of Leith, 1984; The Abbey Court and High Constables of Holyrood, 1985; (contrib.) A Sense of Place: studies in Scottish Local history, 1988; (contrib.) For the Encouragement of Learning: Scotland's National Library 1689–1989, 1989; The Third Statistical Account of Scotland, Vol. for West Lothian, 1992; contribs on historical subjects to books and jls. *Recreations:* walking, the French language. *Address:* 5 Morham Park, Edinburgh EH10 5GF. *T:* (0131) 447 0635. *Died 11 June 2010.*

CADMAN, Surg. Rear-Adm. (D) (Albert) Edward, CB 1977; Director of Naval Dental Services, 1974–77; *b* 14 Oct. 1918; *m* 1st, 1946, Margaret Henrietta Tomkins-Russell (*d* 1974); one *s* one *d*; 2nd, 1975, Mary Croil Macdonald (*d* 1987), Superintendent, WRNS; 3rd, 1988, Irene Davies (*née* Lowther). *Educ:* Dover Grammar Sch.; Guy's Hosp. Dental Sch. LDS RCS 1941. Surg. Lieut (D) RNVR, 1942; transf. to RN, 1947; served as Asst to Dir, Naval Dental Services, 1967–70; Comd Dental Surgeon on staff of Flag Officer, Naval Air Comd, 1970–74. QHDS 1974–77. *Address:* 28 Newton Lane, Romsey, Hampshire SO51 8GX. *T:* (01794) 522870. *Died 24 April 2010.*

CADOGAN, Peter William; lecturer, writer and campaigner; Chairman, London Alliance for Local Democracy, since 1998; *b* 26 Jan. 1921; *s* of Archibald Douglas Cadogan and Audrey Cadogan (*née* Wannop); *m* 1949, Joyce (marr. diss. 1969), *d* of William Stones, MP; one *d*. *Educ:* Tynemouth Sch., Tynemouth; Univ. of Newcastle, 1946–51 (BA (Hons) History, DipEd; Joseph Cowen Meml Prize, 1951). Served War, Air Sea Rescue Service, RAF, 1941–46. Teaching, Kettering and Cambridge, 1951–65; Tutor in Adult Educn, Birkbeck Coll. and WEA, 1981–93. Committed to the Far Left, 1945–60; broke with Marxism, 1960. Founding Secretary, East Anglian Committee of 100: exploring theory and practice of non-violent direct action, 1961; Sec., Internat. Sub-Cttee of Cttee of 100, 1962; Sec. (full-time), National Cttee of 100, 1965–68. Mem., Nat. Council of CND, mid-sixties; Founding Sec., Save Biafra Campaign, 1968–70; Gen. Sec., South Place Ethical Soc., 1970–81; Co-Founder: Turning Point, 1975; Peace Anonymous, Action '84 and Summit '84, 1983–84; broke with Protest, 1987; Co-Chm., Anglo-Afghan Circle, 1987–92; Sec., NI Project, Gandhi Foundn, 1988–2001. Founder Mem., New Consensus/New Dialogue, 1990; Co-founder: Values and Vision, 1991; John Macmurray Fellowship, 1991; Kilburn 2000, 1995. Chm., Blake Soc. of St James', 1988–94 (Vice-Pres., 1994). *Publications:* Extra-

Parliamentary Democracy, 1968; Direct Democracy, 1974, rev. 1975; Early Radical Newcastle, 1975; Six Ballads for the Seventies, 1976; The People Power Papers, 2004; Historical Idealism, 2006; many articles in learned jls, periodicals and elsewhere. *Recreations:* reading, gardening, social invention. *Address:* 3 Hinchinbrook House, Greville Road, NW6 5UP. *T:* (020) 7328 3709; *e-mail:* petercadogan@aol.com. *Died 18 Nov. 2007.*

CAFFERTY, Michael Angelo; HM Diplomatic Service; Consul-General, Melbourne, Australia, 1983–87; *b* 3 March 1927; *m* 1950, Eileen E. Geer; two *s* three *d. Educ:* Univ. of London. BoT, 1951; Asst Trade Comr, Johannesburg, 1955, Pretoria, 1957; seconded to FO. Buenos Aires, 1958; Trade Comr, Singapore, 1964; FCO, 1968; Consul (Commercial), Milan, 1974; First Sec. and Head of Chancery, Rome (Holy See), 1977; Ambassador and Consul-Gen., Santo Domingo, 1979–83. *Address:* 12 Brackendale Way, Earley, Reading RG6 1DZ. *Died 10 May 2010.*

CAHN, Prof. Robert Wolfgang, PhD, ScD; FRS 1991; FIMMM; FInstP; Distinguished Research Fellow (formerly Senior Associate), Department of Materials Science and Metallurgy, Cambridge University, since 1986; *b* 9 , Sept. 1924; *s* of Martin and Else Cahn; *m* 1947, Patricia Lois Hanson; two *s* two *d. Educ:* Trinity Coll., Cambridge (BA 1945; PhD 1950; ScD 1963). FIMMM (FIM 1962); FInstP 1959. SO, later SSO, Harwell, 1947–51; Lectr, Sen. Lectr, then Reader, Physical Metallurgy Dept, Birmingham Univ., 1951–62; Professor of Materials Technol., UCNW, 1962–64; Prof. of Materials Sci., Sussex Univ., 1965–81, then Prof. Emeritus (Dean of Engrg, 1973–78); Prof. of Physical Metallurgy, Université de Paris–Sud, 1981–83; Vis. Res. Fellow, General Electric Corporate Res., NY, 1985; Fairchild Distinguished Scholar, CIT, 1985–86. Commonwealth Vis. Prof., Monash Univ., Melbourne, 1976; Visiting Professor: Univ. of Surrey, 1986–92; Univ. Autónoma de Barcelona, 1993. David Turnbull Lectr, Materials Res. Soc., USA, 2002. Editor, several scientific jls and book series. Mem., Soc. of Scholars, Johns Hopkins Univ., 2005; Foreign Member: Göttingen Acad. Arts and Scis, 1987; Chinese Acad. of Sci., 1996; Foreign Corresp. Mem., Real Academia de Ciencias Exactas, Fisicas y Naturales, Madrid, 1995; Foreign Fellow, Indian Nat. Sci. Acad., 1997; Fellow: Amer. Soc. for Materials Internat., 1997; Minerals, Metals and Materials Soc., USA, 2000; Hon. Member: Indian Inst. of Metals, 1972; Materials Res. Soc. of India, 1991. FRSA. Ste Claire Deville Medal, Société Française de Métallurgie, 1978; A. A. Griffith Medal, Materials Science Club, 1983; Heyn Medal, Deutsche Ges. für Materialkunde, 1996; Luigi Losana Gold Medal, Assoc. Italiana di Metallurgia, 2001; Gold Medal, Acta Materialia Inc., 2002. *Publications:* (ed) Physical Metallurgy, 1965, 4th edn 1996; (ed) Processing of Metals and Alloys, 1991; Artifice and Artefacts—100 Essays in Materials Science, 1992; (contrib.) Twentieth Century Physics, ed B. R. Pippard *et al,* 1995; The Coming of Materials Science, 2001; The Art of Belonging: a memoir, 2005; contrib. scientific jls incl. Nature and Acta Metallurgica. *Recreations:* composing English prose, literature, looking at and collecting pictures, mountains and alpine flowers, music. *Address:* Department of Materials Science and Metallurgy, Pembroke Street, Cambridge CB2 3QZ. *T:* and *Fax:* (01223) 334381; 6 Storey's Way, Cambridge CB3 0DT. *T:* (01223) 360143; *e-mail:* robert.pat.cahn@btinternet.com. *Died 9 April 2007.*

CAIN, Sir (Henry) Edney (Conrad), Kt 1986; OBE 1975 (MBE 1965); Order of Distinguished Service (Belize) 2006; FCCA; CA (Belize); first Governor, Central Bank of Belize, 1982–83, reappointed 1991; *b* 2 Dec. 1924; *s* of Henry Edney Conrad Cain I and Rhoda Cain (*née* Stamp); *m* 1951, Leonie (*née* Locke); two *d. Educ:* St George's Coll., Belize; St Michael's Coll., Belize; Balham and Tooting Coll. of Commerce, London. FCCA 1977 (ACCA 1961); CA Belize 1984.

Belize Government Service, 1940–: Examr of Accts, Audit Dept, 1954; Auditor, Audit Dept, 1959; Asst Accountant Gen., 1961; Accountant Gen., 1963; Man. Dir, Monetary Authority of Belize, 1976; Ambassador to USA, 1983; High Comr to Canada (resident in Washington, DC), 1984; Financial Sec., Ministry of Finance, Belize, 1985–87; High Comr to UK, 1987–90. Director: Belize Bank Ltd (Chm., 1995–2004); Carlisle Hldgs Ltd (formerly Belize Holdings Inc., then BHI Corp.), 1992–. *Publications:* When the Angel says 'Write' (verse), 1948, 2001. *Recreations:* music, reading, current affairs. *Address:* PO Box 238, 3 Amethyst Street, Orchid Gardens, Belmopan, Belize. *T:* (8) 222492. *Died 17 Jan. 2008.*

CAIRNS, Air Vice-Marshal Geoffrey Crerar, CBE 1970; AFC 1960; FRAeS 1979; Chief of Staff No 18 Group, Strike Command, 1978–80; *b* 21 May 1926; *s* of late Dr J. W. Cairns, MD, MCh, DPH and Marion Cairns; *m* 1948, Carol (*d* 1985), *d* of H. I. F. Evernden, MBE; four *d. Educ:* Loretto School, Musselburgh; Cambridge Univ. Joined RAF, 1944; served: Sqdns 43 and 93, Italy; Sqdn 73, Malta, 1946–49; Sqdn 72, UK, 1949–51; Adjutant, Hong Kong Auxiliary Air Force; test pilot A&AEE, Boscombe Down, 1957–60; Jt Planning Staff, MoD, 1961; Chief Instructor, Helicopters, CFS, RAF Ternhill, 1963; JSSC 1966; Supt Flying A&AEE 1968; Dir, Defence Operational Requirements Staffs, MoD, 1970; Commandant, Boscombe Down, 1972–74; ACAS (Op. Requirements), MoD, 1974–76; Comdr, Southern Maritime Air Region, 1976–78. Dir, Trago Aircraft Ltd, 1982–87. Consultant: Marconi Avionics, 1980–81; FLS Aerospace (Lovaux) Ltd, 1992–94. *Recreations:* golf, railways. *Club:* Royal Air Force. *Died 6 Feb. 2009.*

CALDERWOOD, Sir Robert, Kt 1990; Chairman, Greater Glasgow Health Board, 1993–97; Chief Executive, Strathclyde Regional Council, 1980–92; Director, GEC (Scotland) Ltd, 1991–99; *b* 1 March 1932; *s* of Robert Calderwood and Jessie Reid (*née* Marshall); *m* 1958, Meryl Anne (*née* Fleming); three *s* one *d. Educ:* William Hulme's Sch., Manchester; Manchester Univ. (LLB (Hons)). Admitted solicitor, 1956; Town Clerk: Salford, 1966–69; Bolton, 1969–73; Manchester, 1973–79. Dir, Glasgow Garden Fest. 1988 Ltd, 1985–88; Chm., Strathclyde Buses, 1989–93. Member: Parole Bd for England and Wales, 1971–73; Soc. of Local Authority Chief Execs, 1974–92 (Pres., 1989–90); Scottish Consultative Cttee, Commn for Racial Equality, 1981–88; Employers Panel, Industrial Tribunals in Scotland, 1992–98; Local and Central Govt Relations Res. Cttee, Joseph Rowntree Foundn, 1992–97. Director: European Summer Special Olympic Games 1990 (Strathclyde) Ltd, 1989–90; Scottish Opera, 1991–96 (Dep. Chm., 1992–96); Quality Scotland Foundn, 1991–92. Mem. Council, Industrial Soc., 1983–92. Gov., Glasgow Caledonian Univ., 1994–96. Chm., Clyde Heritage Trust, 1997–98. Hon. Mem., Incorporation of Coopers, Trades House of Glasgow. 1994–; Hon. Patron, Scottish Overseas Aid, 1993–98. Hon. FIWEM 1992. *Recreations:* theatre, watching Rugby. *Address:* 6 Mosspark Avenue, Milngavie, Glasgow G62 8NL. *Died 28 May 2006.*

CALLANDER, Maj. (John) Henry; landowner and farmer; Vice Lord-Lieutenant, Midlothian, since 1996; *b* 9 May 1948; *s* of late Maj. John David Callander, MC and Mary Callander (*née* Crompton-Roberts); *m* 1987, Jacqueline Hulda (*née* Crocker); two *s* one *d. Educ:* Eton Coll. Royal Scots Greys; Royal Scots Dragoon Guards; retd 1991. Trustee: Baird Trust; Housing and Loan Fund, C of S; Crichton Collegiate Church Trust. DL Midlothian. *Recreation:* field sports. *Address:* Prestonhall, Pathhead, Midlothian EH37 5UG. *T:* (01875) 320949. *Died 4 Nov. 2010.*

CALLOW, His Honour Henry William, CBE 1994; HM Second Deemster, Isle of Man, 1988–93; *b* 16 May 1926; 2nd *s* of Frederick Henry Callow and Elizabeth Callow (*née* Cowley); *m* 1952, Mary Elaine Corlett. *Educ:*

Douglas High Sch.; King William's Coll., IOM. Served Army, 1945–48. Advocate, Manx Bar, 1950; High Bailiff and Coroner of Inquests, IOM, 1969–88; Chairman: IOM Criminal Injuries Compensation Tribunal, 1988–93; IOM Licensing Appeal Court, 1988–93. Police Complaints Comr, IOM, 1994–2003. Chairman of Trustees: Noble's Hosp., IOM, 1987–98; Ellan Vannin Home, 1988–97; Trustee, Grest Home, 1995–. Pres., Ramsey Male Choir, 1997–; Chm., IOM Church Music Assoc., 1997–2000. Hon. Freeman, Douglas, 2001. *Recreations:* music, walking. *Club:* Laxey Sailing (Laxey).
Died 14 April 2006.

CALNAN, Prof. James Stanislaus, FRCP; FRCS; Professor of Plastic and Reconstructive Surgery, University of London, at the Royal Postgraduate Medical School and Hammersmith Hospital, 1970–81, then Emeritus; *b* 12 March 1916; *e s* of James and Gertrude Calnan, Eastbourne, Sussex; *m* 1949, Joan (formerly County Councillor for Great Berkhamsted and Dacorum District Councillor, and Town Councillor, Berkhamsted), *e d* of George Frederick and Irene Maud Williams, Roath Park, Cardiff; one *d. Educ:* Stonyhurst Coll.; Univ. of London at London Hosp. Med. Sch. LDS RCS 1941; MRCS, LRCP 1943; DA 1944; DTM&H 1948; MRCP (London and Edinburgh) 1948; FRCS 1949; FRCP 1971. Served War of 1939–45, F/Lt RAF, UK, France, India. RMO, Hosp. for Tropical Diseases, 1948; Sen. Lectr, Nuffield Dept of Plastic Surgery, Oxford, 1954; Hammersmith Hospital and Royal Postgraduate Med. Sch.: Lectr in Surgery, 1960; Reader, 1965; Professor, 1970. Hunterian Prof. RCS, 1959. Vis. Prof. in Plastic Surgery, Univ. of Pennsylvania, 1959. Member: BMA, 1941–82; British Assoc. of Plastic Surgeons, 1949–71; Sen. Mem., Surgical Research Soc., 1962–82. Fellow, Royal Soc. of Medicine, 1943; FCST 1966. Mem., Soc. of Authors, 1985–90. Clemson Award for Bioengineering, 1980. *Publications:* Speaking at Medical Meetings, 1972, 2nd edn 1981; Writing Medical Papers, 1973; How to Speak and Write: a practical guide for nurses, 1975; One Way to do Research, 1976; Talking with Patients, 1983; Coping with Research: the complete guide for beginners, 1984; The Hammersmith 1935–1985: the first 50 years of the Royal Postgraduate Medical School, 1985; Principles of Surgical Research, 1989; contribs to medical and scientific jls and chapters in books, on cleft palate, wound healing, lymphatic diseases, venous thrombosis, research methods and organisation. *Recreations:* gardening, carpentry, reading and writing. *Address:* 4 Park House, Park Street, Berkhamsted, Herts HP4 1HY. *T:* (01442) 862320. *Died 23 Feb. 2010.*

CALVOCORESSI, Peter (John Ambrose); author; *b* 17 Nov. 1912; *s* of Pandia Calvocoressi and Irene (Ralli); *m* 1st, 1938, Barbara Dorothy Eden (*d* 2005), *d* of 6th Baron Henley; two *s*; 2nd, 2006, Margaret Rachel, *d* of Hon. Ernest Scott, KCMG, MVO and Lady Scott. *Educ:* Eton (King's Scholar); Balliol Coll., Oxford. Called to Bar, 1935. RAF Intelligence, 1940–45; Wing Comdr. Trial of Major War Criminals, Nuremberg, 1945–46. Contested (L) Nuneaton, 1945. Staff of Royal Institute of International Affairs, 1949–54 (Mem. Council, 1955–70); Dir of Chatto & Windus Ltd and The Hogarth Press Ltd, 1954–65; Editorial Dir, 1972–76, Publisher and Chief Exec., 1973–76, Penguin Books. Chm., Open Univ. Educnl Enterprises Ltd, 1979–88. Reader (part time) in International Relations, Univ. of Sussex, 1965–71; Member: Council, Inst. for Strategic Studies, 1961–71; Council, Inst. of Race Relations, 1970–71; UN Sub-Commn on the Prevention of Discrimination and Protection of Minorities, 1962–71; Chm., The Africa Bureau, 1963–71; Mem., Internat. Exec., Amnesty International, 1969–71; Chm., The London Library, 1970–73; Dep. Chm., N Metropolitan Conciliation Cttee, 1967–71. DUniv Open, 1990. *Publications:* Nuremberg: The Facts, the Law and the Consequences, 1947; Surveys of International Affairs, vol. 1, 1947–48, 1950; vol. 2, 1949–50, 1951; vol. 3, 1951, 1952; vol. 4, 1952, 1953; vol. 5, 1953, 1954; (with Guy Wint) Middle East Crisis,

1957; South Africa and World Opinion, 1961; World Order and New States, 1962; World Politics since 1945, 1968, 9th edn, 2009; (with Guy Wint) Total War, 1972, 2nd rev. edn (with John Pritchard) 1989; The British Experience 1945–75, 1978; Top Secret Ultra, 1980; Independent Africa and the World, 1985; A Time for Peace, 1987; Who's Who in the Bible, 1987; Resilient Europe 1870–2000, 1991; Threading My Way (memoirs), 1994; Fall Out: World War II and the shaping of Europe, 1997. *Address:* Old Mill Lane Farmhouse, Marnhull, Dorset DT10 1JY; Flat U, 12–18 Bloomsbury Street, WC1B 3GA. *Club:* Garrick.
Died 5 Feb. 2010.

CAMERON, Roy James, CB 1982; PhD; Australian Statistician, 1977–85; *b* 11 March 1923; *s* of Kenneth Cameron and Amy Jean (*née* Davidson); *m* 1951, Dorothy Olive Lober; two *s* one *d. Educ:* Univ. of Adelaide (BEc 1st Cl. Hons, MEc); PhD Harvard. Lecturer in Economics, Canberra UC, 1949–51; Economist, World Bank, 1954–56; Australian Treasury official, 1956–73; Australian Ambassador to OECD, Paris, 1973–77. Chairman: ACT Taxi Fares Adv. Cttee, 1987–89; Cttee of Inquiry into Distribution of Federal Roads Grants, 1985–86. Associate Comr, Industries Assistance Commn, 1989–90. Mem. Council, Canberra Coll. of Advanced Educn, 1986–89. *Recreation:* lawn bowls.
Died 3 Oct. 2006.

CAMPBELL, Sir Alan (Hugh), GCMG 1979 (KCMG 1976; CMG 1964); HM Diplomatic Service, retired; *b* 1 July 1919; *y s* of late Hugh Campbell and Ethel Campbell (*née* Warren); *m* 1947, Margaret Taylor (*d* 1999); three *d. Educ:* Sherborne Sch.; Caius Coll., Cambridge. Served in Devonshire Regt, 1940–46. 3rd Sec., HM Foreign (later Diplomatic) Service, 1946; appointed to Lord Killearn's Special Mission to Singapore, 1946; served in Rome, 1952, Peking, 1955; UK Mission to UN, New York, 1961; Head of Western Dept, Foreign Office, 1965; Counsellor, Paris, 1967; Ambassador to Ethiopia, 1969–72; Asst Under-Sec. of State, FCO, 1972–74; Dep. Under-Sec. of State, FCO, 1974–76; Ambassador to Italy, 1976–79; Foreign Affairs adviser to Rolls Royce Ltd, 1979–81. Director: National Westminster Bank, 1979–89; Mercantile and General Reinsurance Co., 1979–89; H. Clarkson (Hldgs), 1979–89; Agricola (UK) Ltd, 1987–92. Chairman: Soc. of Pension Consultants, 1982–87; British-Italian Soc., 1983–90; British Sch. at Rome, 1987–94 (Mem. Council, 1982–94); Mem. Council, London Philharmonic Orchestra, 1982–90. Governor, Sherborne Sch., 1973–87 (Chm. of Governors, 1982–87). *Publications:* Colleagues and Friends (autobiog.), 1988; articles in Internat. Affairs, contrib. to Oxford DNB. *Recreation:* painting in watercolour. *Address:* 45 Carlisle Mansions, Carlisle Place, SW1P 1HY. *Clubs:* Brooks's, Beefsteak. *Died 7 Oct. 2007.*

CAMPBELL, Alexander Buchanan, RSA 2005 (ARSA 1973); FRIBA, PPRIAS; architect; Senior Partner, A. Buchanan Campbell and Partners, Glasgow, 1949–90; *b* 14 June 1914; *s* of Hugh Campbell and Elizabeth Flett; *m* 1939, Sheila Neville Smith; one *s* one *d. Educ:* Royal Technical Coll., Glasgow; Glasgow School of Art; Univ. of Strathclyde (BArch). Assistant: Prof. T. Harold Hughes, 1937; G. Grey Wornum, 1938; City Architect, Glasgow, 1939; served War, Royal Engineers, 1940–46; Inspector, Inspectorate of Elect. and Mech. Equipment, 1947; Chief Technical Officer, Scottish Building Centre, 1948, Dep. Dir, 1949. Principal works include: Dollan Swimming Baths and Key Youth Centre, East Kilbride; Whittingehame Court, Ascot; Flats, Great Western Road, Glasgow; St Christopher's Church, Glasgow; Priesthill Church, Glasgow; St James Primary Sch., Renfrew; Callendar Park Coll. and Craigie College of Education at Falkirk and Ayr (Civic Trust Awards); High Rise Flats, Drumchapel. President: Glasgow Inst. of Architects, 1974–76; Royal Incorporation of Architects in Scotland, 1977–79. *Recreations:* music, art, golf. *Address:* 19 Lochan Avenue, Kirn, Dunoon, Argyll PA23 8HT. *T:* (01369) 703674. *Club:* Glasgow Art (President, 1972–74). *Died 13 May 2007.*

CAMPBELL, David Arthur; Chief Executive, British Vita Plc, 2001–05; non-executive Director: Fenner plc, since 2005; Zotefoams plc, since 2007; *b* 5 March 1950; *s* of Arthur and Anne Campbell; *m* 1974, Sylvia; two *d.* *Educ:* BA Hons Business Studies. British Vita Plc, 1974–2005: Dir, 1999–2005; Man. Dir, 2000–01. Mem. Bd, Stahl BV, 2007–. FCIPD; CCMI. *Address:* c/o Fenner plc, Hesslewood Country Office Park, Ferriby Road, Hessle, E Yorks HU13 0PW. *Died 29 Nov. 2010.*

CAMPBELL, Ian; JP; *b* 26 April 1926; *s* of William Campbell and Helen Crockett; *m* 1950, Mary Millar; two *s* three *d. Educ:* Dumbarton Academy; Royal Technical Coll., Glasgow (later Strathclyde Univ.). Formerly CEng, MIMechE. Engineer with South of Scotland Electricity Board for 17 years. Councillor, Dumbarton, 1958–70; Provost of Dumbarton, 1962–70. MP (Lab): Dunbartonshire W, 1970–83; Dumbarton, 1983–87. PPS to Sec. of State for Scotland, 1976–79. Member: Dumbarton Dist Enterprise Trust, 1987–98; Strathclyde Region Local Valuation Panel, 1988–2000. *Address:* The Shanacles, Gartocharn, Alexandria, Dunbartonshire G83 8NB. *T:* (01389) 752286. *Died 9 Sept. 2007.*

CAMPBELL, Ian Dugald, FRCPE, FFPH; Treasurer, Royal College of Physicians of Edinburgh, 1981–85; *b* Dornie, Kintail, 22 Feb. 1916; *s* of John Campbell and Margaret Campbell; *m* 1943, Joan Carnegie Osborn; one *s* two *d. Educ:* Dingwall Acad.; Edinburgh Univ. (MB, ChB 1939). FRCPE 1973, FFPH (FFCM 1974). Served War, 1941–46: UK, BAOR, MEF, RAMC; final appt OC Field Amb. (Lt-Col). Med. Supt, St Luke's Hosp., Bradford, 1946–49; Asst SMO, Leeds Reg. Hosp. Bd, 1949–57; Dep. Sen. Admin. MO, S-Eastern Reg. Hosp. Bd, Scotland, 1957–72, Sen. Admin. MO, 1972–73; Chief Admin. MO, Lothian Health Bd, 1973–80. QHP 1977–80. WHO assignments, SE Asia, 1969, 1971, 1975. *Publications:* various medical. *Recreations:* fishing, shooting, golf. *Address:* 5 Succoth Park, Edinburgh EH12 6BX. *T:* (0131) 539 5965. *Clubs:* New (Edinburgh); Hon. Company of Edinburgh Golfers (Muirfield); Royal Burgess Golfing Society (Barnton, Edinburgh). *Died 26 Sept. 2008.*

CAMPBELL, James Hugh; Consultant, Bird Semple Fyfe Ireland, WS, Glasgow, Edinburgh and London, 1991–93; *b* 13 Nov. 1926; *s* of William Campbell and Agnes Wightman Campbell; *m* 1953, Iris Burnside (*née* Hercus); two *s* one *d. Educ:* Univ. of Glasgow, 1944–45 and 1948–50 (BL). Service in RAF, Japan, 1946–48. Solicitor; Partner, Bird Son & Semple, 1952–73, Sen. Partner, 1965–73; Sen. Partner, Bird Semple & Crawford Herron, subseq. Bird Semple Fyfe Ireland, 1973–91. President: Glasgow Juridical Soc., 1951–52; Law Soc. of Scotland, 1991–92 (Mem. Council, 1986–95; Vice-Pres., 1990–91). Hon. Mem., Royal Faculty of Procurators, Glasgow, 1997. Deacon, Incorp. of Wrights, Glasgow, 1980–81. *Recreations:* music, reading, golf. *Address:* 2 Lincuan Avenue, Giffnock, Glasgow G46 6QN. *T:* (0141) 638 2630. *Clubs:* Western, Glasgow Art (Glasgow); East Renfrewshire Golf. *Died 24 May 2006.*

CAMPBELL, Ken; actor, director and writer; *b* 10 Dec. 1941; *s* of late Colin Campbell and Elsie (*née* Handley); *m* 1977, Prunella Gee; one *d. Educ:* RADA. Founder and Dir, Science Fiction Th. of Liverpool, 1976; Artistic Dir, Everyman Th., Liverpool, 1980; Prof. of Ventriloquism, RADA, 1999–. Director: War with the Newts, Riverside, 1981; Carmilla, Almeida, 1982; Waiting for Godot, Young Vic, 1982; The Complete Berk, Edinburgh Fest., 1985; Outbreak of God in Area 9, Young Vic, 1987; Beauty and the Beast, Battersea Arts Centre, 1993; The Warp, Albany, 1998; writer: *plays for television* include: Unfair Exchanges, 1985; The Blackheath Poisonings, 1992; *film:* The Madness

Museum, 1988 (also dir); actor: *television* includes: In Sickness and In Health; Brookside; *theatre:* Art, Wyndhams, 2000; one man shows (also writer): The Recollections of a Furtive Nudist, Pigspurt and Jamais Vu (trilogy), RNT, 1993 (Evening Standard Best Comedy Award); Mystery Bruises, Almeida, 1994; Theatre Stories, Royal Court, 1996; Violin Time, 1996, Pidgin Macbeth, 1998, RNT; History of Comedy, Part 1: Ventriloquism, RNT, 2000 (also toured in UK, Europe, Canada and USA). *Publications:* plays: You See the Thing is This, 1972; Old King Cole, 1975; Skungpoomery, 1980; Jack Sheppard; The Clown Plays; The Bald Trilogy; Violin Time. *Recreations:* dog agility, ventriloquism. *Address:* 40 Baldwins Hill, Loughton, Essex IG10 1SF. *T:* (020) 8508 8599. *Died 31 Aug. 2008.*

CAMPBELL, Ross, OC 2006; DSC 1944; President, InterCon Consultants Ltd, Ottawa, since 1996 (Senior Partner, 1983–96); *b* 4 Nov. 1918; *s* of late William Marshall Campbell and of Helen Isabel Harris; *m* 1945, Penelope Grantham-Hill; two *s. Educ:* Univ. of Toronto Schs; Trin. Coll., Univ. of Toronto. BA, Faculty of Law, 1940. Served RCN, 1940–45. Joined Dept of Ext. Affairs, Canada, 1945; Third Sec., Oslo, 1946–47; Second Sec., Copenhagen, 1947–50; European Div., Ottawa, 1950–52; First Sec., Ankara, 1952–56; Head of Middle East Div., Ottawa, 1957–59; Special Asst to Sec. of State for Ext. Aff., 1959–62; Asst Under-Sec. of State for Ext. Aff., 1962–64; Adviser to Canadian Delegns to: UN Gen. Assemblies, 1958–63; North Atlantic Coun., 1959–64; Ambassador to Yugoslavia, 1964–67, concurrently accredited Ambassador to Algeria, 1965–67; Ambassador and Perm. Rep. to NATO, 1967–73 (Paris May 1967, Brussels Oct. 1967); Ambassador to Japan, 1973–75, and concurrently to Republic of Korea, 1973. Chm., Atomic Energy of Canada Ltd, 1976–79; President: Atomic Energy of Canada International, 1979–80; Canus Technical Services Corp., Ottawa, 1981–83; Dir, Adopac Ltd, 1992–. *Recreation:* gardening. *Address:* Rivermead House, 890 Aylmer Road, Gatineau, QC J9H 5T8, Canada; (office) Suite 1300, 100 Queen Street, Ottawa, ON K1P 1J9, Canada. *Club:* Rideau (Ottawa). *Died 15 Aug. 2007.*

CANE, Prof. Violet Rosina; Professor of Mathematical Statistics, University of Manchester, 1971–81, then Emeritus; *b* 31 Jan. 1916; *d* of Tubal George Cane and Annie Louisa Lansdell. *Educ:* Newnham Coll., Cambridge (MA, Dipl. in Math. Stats). BoT, 1940; Univ. of Aberdeen, 1941; FO, 1942; Min. of Town and Country Planning, 1946; Statistician to MRC Applied Psychol. Unit, 1948; Queen Mary Coll., London, 1955; Fellow, Newnham Coll., Cambridge, 1957; Lectr, Univ. of Cambridge, 1960. Mem., UGC, 1974–79. Mem., Cambridge CC, 1965–72, 1982–90 (Hon. Councillor, 1990). Hon. MSc Manchester, 1974. *Publications:* (contrib.) Current Problems in Animal Behaviour, 1961; (contrib.) Perspectives in Probability and Statistics, 1975; papers in Jl of Royal Stat. Soc., Animal Behaviour, and psychol jls. *Recreation:* supporting old houses. *Died 27 June 2008.*

CANNON, John Francis Michael; Keeper of Botany, Natural History Museum (formerly British Museum (Natural History)), 1978–90; *b* 22 April 1930; *s* of Francis Leslie Cannon and Aileen Flora Cannon; *m* 1954, Margaret Joy (*née* Herbert); two *s* one *d. Educ:* Whitgift Sch., South Croydon, Surrey; King's Coll., Newcastle upon Tyne, Univ. of Durham (BSc 1st Cl. Hons Botany). Dept of Botany, British Museum (Nat. History), 1952, Dep. Keeper 1972. President: Botanical Soc. of the British Isles, 1983–85; Ray Soc., 1986–88. *Publications:* papers in scientific periodicals and similar pubns. *Recreations:* travel, music, gardening. *Died 31 March 2008.*

CANT, Rev. Harry William Macphail; Minister of St Magnus Cathedral, Kirkwall, Orkney, 1968–90; Chaplain to the Queen in Scotland, 1972–91, and Extra Chaplain, since 1991; *b* 3 April 1921; *s* of late J. M. Cant and late Margaret Cant; *m* 1951, Margaret Elizabeth Loudon; one *s* two *d*. *Educ*: Edinburgh Acad.; Edinburgh Univ. (MA, BD); Union Theological Seminary, NY (STM). Lieut, KOSB, 1941–43; Captain, King's African Rifles, 1944–46; TA Chaplain, 7th Argyll and Sutherland Highlanders, 1953–61. Asst Minister, Old Parish Church, Aberdeen, 1950–51; Minister of Fallin Parish Church, Stirling, 1951–56; Scottish Sec., Student Christian Movt, 1956–59; Minister of St Thomas' Parish Church, 1960–68. *Publications*: Preaching in a Scottish Parish Church: St Magnus and Other Sermons, 1970; Springs of Renewal in Congregational Life, 1980; (ed jtly) Light in the North, 1989; Pilgrimage of a Pupil, Preacher and Pastor: the mystery and the miracle of the Church, 1999. *Recreations*: angling, golf. *Address*: Quoylobs, Holm, Orkney KW17 2RY. *Died 13 Feb. 2007.*

CAPEY, Montague Martin; Under Secretary and Director of Establishments and Organisation, Department for Education (formerly Department of Education and Science), 1988–93; *b* 16 July 1933; *s* of Ernest Paton Capey and Lettice Isabel Capey; *m* 1960, Diana Mary Barnes; one *s* one *d*. *Educ*: The Leys Sch., Cambridge; Clare Coll., Cambridge (MA); Didsbury Coll., Bristol; Univ. of Bristol (BA). Methodist Minister, 1958–71. Principal 1971–76, Asst Sec. 1976–88, DES. *Recreations*: gardening, music, enjoying Cornwall. *Address*: Bramble Cottage, West Kitty, St Agnes, Cornwall TR5 0SU. *Died 25 Feb. 2006.*

CAPLAN, Hon. Lord; Philip Isaac Caplan; a Senator of the College of Justice in Scotland, 1989–2000; *b* 24 Feb. 1929; *s* of Hyman and Rosalena Caplan; *m* 1st, 1953, Elaine Marcia Caplan; two *s* one *d*; 2nd, 1974, Joyce Ethel Stone; one *d*. *Educ*: Eastwood Sch., Renfrewshire; Glasgow Univ. (MA, LLB). Solicitor, 1952–56; called to Bar, 1957; Standing Junior Counsel to Accountant of Court, 1964–70; QC (Scot.) 1970; Sheriff of Lothian and Borders, 1979–83; Sheriff-Principal of North Strathclyde, 1983–89. Member: Sheriff Court Rules Council, 1984–89; Adv. Council on Messengers-at-Arms and Sheriff Officers, 1987–89. Chairman: Plant Varieties and Seeds Tribunal, Scotland, 1977–79; Scottish Assoc. for Study of Offending (formerly Delinquency), 1985–89 (Hon. Vice-Pres., 1990–); Family Mediation Scotland (formerly Scottish Assoc. of Family Conciliation Services), 1989–94 (Hon. Pres., 1994–; Hon. Life Patron, 2006); Bd of Trustees, CommunicAbility (formerly James Powell UK Trust), 1992–. FRPS 1988; AFIAP 1985. Hon. LLD Glasgow, 1996. *Recreations*: photography, reading, music. *Club*: New (Edinburgh). *Died 7 Nov. 2008.*

CARDEN, Derrick Charles, CMG 1974; HM Diplomatic Service, retired; Ambassador, Sudan, 1977–79; *b* 30 Oct. 1921; *s* of Canon Henry Craven Carden and Olive (*née* Gorton); *heir pres.* to Sir John Craven Carden, 7th Bt; *m* 1952, Elizabeth Anne Russell; two *s* two *d*. *Educ*: Marlborough; Christ Church, Oxford. Sudan Political Service, 1942–54. Entered HM Diplomatic Service, 1954; Foreign Office, 1954–55; Political Agent, Doha, 1955–58; 1st Sec., Libya, 1958–62; Foreign Office, 1962–65; Head of Chancery, Cairo, 1965; Consul-General, Muscat, 1965–69; Dir, ME Centre of Arab Studies, 1969–73; Ambassador, Yemen Arab Republic, 1973–76. Governor, IDS, Sussex Univ., 1981–87. Mem. Bd, CARE Britain, 1988–90. JP Fareham, 1980–91. *Recreation*: pleasures of the countryside. *Address*: Apartment 47, The King's House, Peninsula Square, Winchester SO23 8GJ. *Club*: Vincent's (Oxford). *Died 26 April 2006.*

CARDEN, Sir John Craven, 7th Bt *cr* 1787; *b* 11 March 1926; *s* of Capt. Sir John V. Carden, 6th Bt and Dorothy Mary, *d* of Charles Luckraft McKinnon; *S* father, 1935; *m* 1947, Isabel Georgette (*d* 2007), *y d* of late Robert de Hart; one *d*. *Educ*: Eton. *Heir*: *cousin* John Craven Carden [*b* 17 Nov. 1953; *m* 1983, Celia Howitt; one *s*]. *Address*: Chalet Abaco, Green Road, St Clement, Jersey, CI JE2 6QA. *Club*: White's. *Died 4 April 2008.*

CARDIFF, Jack, OBE 2000; film director and cameraman; *b* 18 Sept. 1914; *s* of John Joseph and Florence Cardiff; *m* 1940, Julia Lily Mickleboro; three *s*; *m* 1997, Angela Gray; one *s* and one adopted *s* one adopted *d*. *Educ*: various schools, incl. Medburn Sch., Herts. Started as child actor, 1918; switched to cameras, 1928. World travelogues, 1937–39. Photographed, MOI Crown Film Unit: Western Approaches, 1942; best known films as cinematographer include: A Matter of Life and Death, 1946; Black Narcissus (Acad. Award; Golden Globe Award), 1947; The Red Shoes, 1948; Scott of the Antarctic, 1948; Under Capricorn, 1949; Pandora and the Flying Dutchman, 1951; African Queen, 1951; The Barefoot Contessa, 1954; War and Peace (British Acad. of Cinematographers Award), 1956. Started as Director, 1958. *Films include: directed:* Sons and Lovers (New York Critics Award for best film direction, Golden Globe Award, outstanding directorial award, Directors Guild of America), 1960; My Geisha, 1962; The Lion, 1962; The Long Ships, 1964; Young Cassidy, 1965; The Liquidator, 1965; The Mercenaries, 1968; Girl on a Motorcycle, 1968; The Mutation, 1974; *photographed:* Ride a Wild Pony, 1975; The Prince and the Pauper, 1977; Death on the Nile, 1978; Behind the Iron Mask, 1979; Avalanche Express, 1979; The Awakening, 1980; The Dogs of War, 1980; Ghost Story, 1981; The Wicked Lady, 1983; Scandalous, 1984; The Far Pavilions (TV), 1984; The Last Days of Pompeii (TV), 1984; Conan the Destroyer, 1984; Rambo: First Blood II, 1985; Cat's Eye, 1985; Million Dollar Mystery, 1987; Call from Space, 1989; Magic Balloon, 1990; *directed and photographed:* music documentaries, Delius, Vivaldi's Four Seasons. *Exhibitions:* Jack Cardiff: portraits from a Hollywood master, Regan Gall., Cardiff, 2003; Icons, RCA, 2004; Hallion Club, Edinburgh, 2004. FRPS 1945; Fellow, BFI, 2003. Hon. Member: Assoc. Française de Cameramen, 1971; BAFTA, 1995. Hon. Dr of Art: Rome, 1953; RCA, 2000; Hon. DLitt Bradford, 1996; Hon. PhD APU, 2001. Coup Ce Soir (France), 1951; Film Achievement Award, Look Magazine; Internat. Award for Outstanding Achievement, 1944, Hollywood Internat. Life Achievement Award, 1995, Amer. Soc. of Cinematographers; Contribn to Art of Photography award, British Acad. of Cinematographers, 1996; London Film Critics Life Achievement Award, 1997; Lumière Award, RPS, 1999; Academy Award for Lifetime Achievement, 2001; BAFTA Special Award, 2001; first Alexander Korda Award, 2004; Lifetime Achievement Award, Heritage Foundn, 2006. *Publications:* Magic Hour (autobiog.), 1996. *Recreations:* tennis, cricket, painting. *Clubs:* MCC, Groucho, Arts. *Died 22 April 2009.*

CAREY, Group Captain Alban Majendie, CBE 1943; owner/farmer Church Farm, Great Witchingham, since 1973; *b* 18 April 1906; *m* 1st, 1934, Enid Morten Bond (*d* 1991); one *s*; 2nd, 2000, Barbara Roberts. *Educ:* Bloxham. Commissioned RAF 1929; served in night bombers, flying boats and as flying boat and landplane instructor; Pilots Cert. no 5283 for Public Transport; Navigator's Licence no 175, 1936; Sen. Op. Trng Officer, Coastal Command, 1939–42; Station Commander: Pembroke Dock, 1942–43; Gibraltar, 1943–45; Haverfordwest, 1945; St Eval, 1945–46. Chairman: Shaw & Sons Ltd, 1946–79; Jordan & Sons Ltd, 1953–68; Hadden Best Ltd, 1957–72; Shaw & Blake Ltd, 1960–68; H. T. Woodrow & Co., 1961–68; Chirit Investment Co., 1970–; Leutromedia Computers Internat., 1971–; Maden Park Property Investment Co., 1975–; East Coast Plastics, 1984–2002; Viking Opticals, 1986–; Dep. Chm., Tridant Group Printers plc 1972–78; Senior Partner: Carey Farm Syndicate, 1972–; Park Farm Syndicate, Snettisham, 1988–. Pres., Nat. Assoc. of Engravers and Die Stampers, 1954; Pres., Central London Br., British Fedn of Printing Industries, 1963; Chm., Nat. Assoc. of Law Stationers, 1963–68; Pres., Egham and Thorpe, Royal Agr. Assoc., 1961, 1962; Chm., Egham and Dist Abbeyfield Assoc., 1970–82. Trustee: Pensthorpe Waterfowl Trust, 1986–; Thursford Collection of Steam Engines, 1990–. *Recreations:* shooting, fishing, yachting. *Address:* Church Farm, Great

Witchingham, Norfolk NR9 5PQ. *T*: (01603) 872511. *Clubs*: Royal Air Force; Royal Air Force Yacht.
Died 11 March 2008.

CARMICHAEL, Catherine McIntosh, (Kay); social worker; *b* 22 Nov. 1925; *d* of John D. and Mary Rankin; *m* 1948, Neil George Carmichael (later Baron Carmichael of Kelvingrove) (marr. diss.; he *d* 2001); one *d*; *m* 1987, David Vernon Donnison. *Educ*: Glasgow and Edinburgh. Social worker, 1955–57; psychiatric social work, 1957–60; Dep. Dir, Scottish Probation Training Course, 1960–62; Lectr, 1962, Sen. Lectr, 1974–80, Dept of Social Administration and Social Work, Univ. of Glasgow. Mem., 1969–75, Dep. Chm., 1975–80, Supplementary Benefits Commn. Mem., Gareloch Horticulturalists; lifelong peace protester. *Publications*: Ceremony of Innocence, 1991; For Crying Out Loud, 1993; Sin and Forgiveness, 2003. *Recreation*: Alexander technique. *Address*: 23 Bank Street, Glasgow G12 8JQ. *T*: (0141) 334 5817. *Died 26 Dec. 2009.*

CARMICHAEL, Ian (Gillett), OBE 2003; actor; *b* 18 June 1920; *s* of Arthur Denholm Carmichael, Cottingham, E Yorks, and Kate Gillett, Hessle, E Yorks; *m* 1st, 1943, Jean Pyman Maclean (*d* 1983), Sleights, N Yorks; two *d*; 2nd, 1992, Kathryn Ann Fenton, (Kate Fenton, novelist). *Educ*: Scarborough Coll.; Bromsgrove Sch. Studied at RADA, 1938–39. Served War of 1939–45 (despatches). First professional appearance as a Robot in "RUR", by Karel and Josef Capek, The People's Palace, Stepney, 1939; *stage appearances* include: The Lyric Revue, Globe, 1951; The Globe Revue, Globe, 1952; High Spirits, Hippodrome, 1953; Going to Town, St Martin's, 1954; Simon and Laura, Apollo, 1954; The Tunnel of Love, Her Majesty's, 1958; The Gazebo, Savoy, 1960; Critic's Choice, Vaudeville, 1961; Devil May Care, Strand, 1963; Boeing-Boeing, Cort Theatre, New York, 1965; Say Who You Are, Her Majesty's, 1965; Getting Married, Strand, 1968; I Do! I Do!, Lyric, 1968; Birds on the Wing, O'Keefe Centre, Toronto, 1969; Darling I'm Home, S African tour, 1972; Out on a Limb, Vaudeville, 1976; Overheard, Theatre Royal, Haymarket, 1981; Pride and Prejudice, Theatre Royal, York and nat. tour, 1987; The Circle, nat. tour, 1990; The School for Scandal, Chichester, 1995. *Films* include: (from 1955) Simon and Laura; Private's Progress; Brothers in Law; Lucky Jim; Happy is the Bride; The Big Money; Left, Right and Centre; I'm All Right Jack; School for Scoundrels; Light Up The Sky; Double Bunk; The Amorous Prawn; Hide and Seek; Heavens Above!; Smashing Time; The Magnificent Seven Deadly Sins; From Beyond the Grave; The Lady Vanishes. *TV series* include: The World of Wooster; Bachelor Father; Lord Peter Wimsey; All For Love; Obituaries; Strathblair; Wives and Daughters, 1999; The Royal, 2002–. Hon. DLitt Hull, 1987. *Publications*: Will the Real Ian Carmichael... (autobiog.), 1979. *Recreations*: cricket, gardening, photography and reading. *Address*: c/o Diamond Management, 31 Percy Street, W1T 2DD. *Club*: MCC. *Died 5 Feb. 2010.*

CARMICHAEL, Kay; see Carmichael, C. M.

CARNEGY OF LOUR, Baroness *cr* 1982 (Life Peer), of Lour in the District of Angus; **Elizabeth Patricia Carnegy of Lour**; formerly a farmer; *b* 28 April 1925; *e d* of late Lt Col U. E. C. Carnegy, DSO, MC, DL, JP, 12th of Lour, and Violet Carnegy, MBE. *Educ*: Downham Sch., Essex. Served Cavendish Lab., Cambridge, 1943–46. With Girl Guides Association, 1947–89: County Comr, Angus, 1956–63; Trng Adviser, Scotland, 1958–62; Trng Adviser, Commonwealth HQ, 1963–65; Pres. for Angus, 1971–79, for Scotland, 1979–89. Co-opted to Educn Cttee, Angus CC, 1967–75; Tayside Regional Council: Councillor, 1974–82; Convener: Recreation and Tourism Cttee, 1974–76; Educn Cttee, 1977–81. Chairman: Working Party on Prof. Trng for Community Education in Scotland, 1975–77; Scottish Council for Community Educn, 1981–88 (Mem., 1978–88); Tayside Cttee on Med. Res. Ethics, 1990–93. Member: MSC,

1979–82 (Chm., Cttee for Scotland, 1981–83); Council for Tertiary Educn in Scotland, 1979–84; Scottish Economic Council, 1981–93; Council, Open Univ., 1984–96; Admin. Council, Royal Jubilee Trusts, 1985–88; Court, St Andrews Univ., 1991–96. House of Lords: Mem., Scrutiny Cttees on European Community, 1983–97; Mem., Select Cttee on Delegated Powers and Regulatory Reform, 2002–05. Trustee, Nat. Museums of Scotland, 1987–91. Hon. Sheriff, 1969–84; DL Angus, 1988–2001. Hon. LLD: Dundee, 1991; St Andrews, 1997; DUniv Open, 1998. *Address*: Lour, by Forfar, Angus DD8 2LR. *T*: (01307) 820237; 33 Tufton Court, Tufton Street, SW1P 3QH. *Clubs*: Lansdowne; New (Edinburgh). *Died 9 Nov. 2010.*

CARNOCK, 4th Baron *cr* 1916, of Carnock; **David Henry Arthur Nicolson;** Bt (NS) of that Ilk and Lasswade 1629, of Carnock 1637; Chief of Clan Nicolson; solicitor; *b* 10 July 1920; *s* of 3rd Baron Carnock, DSO, and Hon. Katharine (*d* 1968), *e d* of 1st Baron Roborough; *S* father, 1982. *Educ*: Winchester; Balliol Coll., Oxford (MA). Admitted Solicitor, 1949; Partner, Clifford-Turner, 1953–86. Served War of 1939–45, Royal Devon Yeomanry and on staff, Major. *Recreations*: shooting, fishing, gardening. *Heir*: *cousin* Adam Nicolson [*b* 12 Sept. 1957; *m* 1st, 1982, Olivia Mary Rokeby Fane (marr. diss. 1992); three *s*; 2nd, 1993, Sarah Clare Raven; two *d*]. *Address*: 90 Whitehall Court, SW1A 2EL; Ermewood House, Harford, Ivybridge, S Devon PL21 0JE. *Clubs*: Travellers, Beefsteak.
Died 26 Dec. 2008.

CARPENTER, Harry Leonard, OBE 1991; sports commentator, BBC, 1949–94; *b* 17 Oct. 1925; *s* of Harry and Adelaide May Carpenter; *m* 1950, Phyllis Barbara Matthews; one *s*. *Educ*: Ashburton School, Shirley; Selhurst Grammar School, Croydon. Greyhound Express, 1941; RN, 1943–46; Greyhound Owner, 1946–48; Speedway Gazette, 1948–50; Sporting Record, 1950–54; Daily Mail, 1954–62; BBC TV, full-time 1962–94. Sports Personality of the Year, TV and Radio Industries, 1989; Internat. Award, Amer. Sportscasters' Assoc., 1989. *Publications*: Masters of Boxing, 1964; Illustrated History of Boxing, 1975; The Hardest Game, 1981; Where's Harry? My Story, 1992. *Recreations*: golf, chess, classical music. *Address*: Sommerfield Holdings plc, 35 Old Queen Street, SW1H 9JD. *Died 20 March 2010.*

CARPENTER, Maj.-Gen. (Victor Harry) John, CB 1975; MBE 1945; FCILT; Senior Traffic Commissioner, Western Traffic Area and Licensing Authority, 1990–91; *b* 21 June 1921; *s* of Harry and Amelia Carpenter; *m* 1946, Theresa McCulloch (*d* 2007); one *s* one *d*. *Educ*: Army schools; Apprentice Artificer RA; RMC Sandhurst. Joined the Army, Royal Artillery, 1936; commissioned into Royal Army Service Corps as 2nd Lieut, 1939. Served War of 1939–45 (Dunkirk evacuation, Western Desert, D-Day landings, Sicily and Normandy). Post-war appts included service in Palestine, Korea, Aden, and Singapore; also commanded a company at Sandhurst. Staff College, 1951; JSSC, 1960; served WO, BAOR, FARELF, 1962–71; Transport Officer-in-Chief (Army), MoD, 1971–73; Dir of Movements (Army), MoD, 1973–75; Chm., Traffic Comrs, NE Traffic Area (formerly Yorks Traffic Area), 1975–85; Traffic Comr, W Traffic Area, 1985–90. Col Comdt, 1975–87, Representative Col Comdt, 1976, 1978 and 1985, RCT. Nat. Pres., 1940 Dunkirk Veterans Assoc., 1991–2000; President: Artificers Royal Artillery Assoc., 1974–2001; RASC/RCT Assoc., 1977–87; Somerset Br., Normandy Veterans Assoc., 1994–2006. Chm., Yorkshire Section, CIT, 1980–81; Pres., Taunton Gp, IAM, 1990–2008. Hon. FIRTE 1987. Commander, Order of Leopold II (Belgium), 1992. *Recreation*: gardening. *Club*: Royal Over-Seas League. *Died 8 July 2009.*

CARR, Christopher; QC 1983; barrister; *b* 30 Nov. 1944; *s* of Edwin Wilfred Carr and Kathleen Carr; *m*; one *s* two *d*. *Educ*: Skegness Grammar Sch.; London Sch. of Economics; Clare Coll., Cambridge. Called to the Bar, Lincoln's Inn, 1968, Bencher, 1991. Lectr in Law, LSE,

1968–69 and 1972–73; Asst Prof. of Law, Univ. of British Columbia, 1969–72; Associate Prof. of Law, Univ. of Toronto, 1973–75; part-time Lectr, QMC, London, 1975–78; in practice at the Bar, 1975–. *Publications:* articles and notes in English and Canadian law jls. *Recreations:* mathematics, philosophy, history. *Address:* 1 Essex Court, Temple, EC4Y 9AR. *Club:* Athenæum.
Died 2 March 2007.

CARR, Dr Eric Francis, FRCP, FRCPsych; Lord Chancellor's Medical Visitor, 1979–89; Member: Mental Health Act Commission, since 1983; Parole Board, since 1988; *b* 23 Sept. 1919; *s* of Edward Francis Carr and Maude Mary Almond; *m* 1954, Janet Gilfillan (marr. diss. 1980); two *s* one *d*. *Educ:* Mill Hill Sch.; Emmanuel Coll., Cambridge (MA, MB BChir). FRCP 1971, FRCPsych 1972; DPM. Captain, RAMC, 1944–46. Consultant Psychiatrist: St Ebba's Hosp., 1954–60; Netherne Hosp., 1960–67; Epsom and West Park Hosps, 1967–76; Hon. Consultant Psychiatrist, KCH, 1960–76; SPMO, DHSS, 1976–79. *Recreations:* reading, listening to music, studying foreign languages (Spanish and French). *Address:* 116 Holly Lane East, Banstead, Surrey SM7 2BE. *T:* (01737) 353675.
Died 27 Dec. 2006.

CARR, Ian Henry Randell; freelance trumpeter, composer, author and broadcaster, since 1960; Associate Professor, Guildhall School of Music and Drama, since 1982; *b* 21 April 1933; *s* of late Thomas Randell Carr and Phyllis Harriet Carr; *m* 1963, Margaret Blackburn Bell (*d* 1967); one *d*; 2nd, 1972, Sandra Louise Major (marr. diss. 1993). *Educ:* Barnard Castle Sch.; King's Coll., Newcastle upon Tyne (BA Hons English Lang. and Lit. 1955). Nat. Service, 2nd Lieut, Royal Northumberland Fusiliers, 1956–58. Member: Emcee Five Quintet, 1960–62; Don Rendell/Ian Carr Quintet, 1963–69; Ian Carr's Nucleus, 1969–88 (toured world-wide); Founder Mem., United Jazz and Rock Ensemble, 1975–. Documentary, The Miles Davis Story, Channel 4 (Internat. Emmy Arts Documentary Award), 2001. Mem., Royal Soc. of Musicians of GB, 1982. Calabria Award for outstanding contrib. in the field of jazz (Italy), 1982. *Compositions:* Solar Plexus, 1970; Labyrinth, 1973; Will's Birthday Suite, 1974 (for Globe Theatre Trust); Out of the Long Dark, 1978; Old Heartland, 1988; Sounds and Sweet Airs, for trumpet and Cathedral organ, 1992; many broadcasts for BBC Radio 3. *Publications:* Music Outside, 1973; Miles Davis: a critical biography, 1982, 3rd edn 1998 (as Miles Davis: the definitive biography); (jtly) Jazz: the essential companion, 1987; Keith Jarrett: the man and his music, 1991; (jtly) The Rough Guide to Jazz, 1995; contrib. BBC Music mag. *Recreations:* music, the visual arts, world literature, travel. *Club:* Ronnie Scott's.
Died 25 Feb. 2009.

CARR-GOMM, Richard Culling, OBE 1985; founder, Abbeyfield Society; *b* 2 Jan. 1922; *s* of Mark Culling Carr-Gomm and Amicia Dorothy (*née* Heming); *m* 1957, Susan (*d* 2007), *d* of Ralph and Dorothy Gibbs; two *s* three *d*. *Educ:* Stowe School. Served War: commnd Coldstream Guards, 1941; served 6th Guards Tank Bde, NW Europe (twice wounded, mentioned in despatches); Palestine, 1945; ME; resigned commn, 1955. Founded: Abbeyfield Soc., 1956; Carr-Gomm Soc., 1965; Morpeth Soc. (charity socs), 1972. Templeton UK Project Award, 1984; Beacon Lifetime Achievement Award, 2004; Pride of Britain Award, 2005. Croix de Guerre (Silver Star), France, 1944. KStJ. *Publications:* Push on the Door (autobiog.), 1979, 2nd edn as All Things Considered, 2004; Loneliness—the wider scene, 1987. *Recreations:* golf, backgammon, painting. *Address:* 9 The Batch, Batheaston, Somerset BA1 7DR. *T:* (01225) 858434.
Died 27 Oct. 2008.

CARSON, Robert Andrew Glendinning, FBA 1980; Keeper, Department of Coins and Medals, British Museum, 1978–83; *b* 7 April 1918; *s* of Andrew and Mary Dempster Carson; *m* 1949, Meta Fransisca De Vries; one *s* one *d*. *Educ:* Kirkcudbright Acad.; Univ. of Glasgow (MA (1st Cl. Hons Classics) 1940; Foulis Schol. 1940). FSA 1965. Served War, RA, 1940–46,

NW Europe; 2nd Lieut 1941, Captain 1945. Asst Keeper, 1947, Dep. Keeper, 1965, Dept of Coins and Medals, British Museum. Pres., Internat. Numismatic Commn, 1979–86. Editor, Numismatic Chronicle, 1966–73; Mem., Adv. Cttee on Historic Wreck Sites, 1973–80; Pres., Royal Numismatic Soc., 1974–79 (Medallist, 1972; Hon. Fellow, 1980); Patron, Australian Numismatic Soc., 1984–. Hon. Vis. Fellow, Univ. of Tasmania, 1990. Hon. Assoc., Powerhouse Mus., Sydney, 1986. Hon. Member: Romanian Numismatic Soc., 1977; British Numismatic Soc., 1979; Corresponding Member: Amer. Numismatic Soc., 1967; Austrian Numismatic Soc., 1971; Foreign Mem., Finnish Soc. of Science and Letters, 1986. Hon. DLitt Glasgow, 1983. Medallist: Soc. française de Numismatique, 1970; Luxembourg Museum, 1971; Amer. Numismatic Soc., 1978. Silver Jubilee Medal, 1977. *Publications:* (with H. Mattingly and C. H. V. Sutherland) Roman Imperial Coinage, 1951–; ed, Essays in Roman Coinage presented to Harold Mattingly, 1956; (with P. V. Hill and J. P. C. Kent) Late Roman Bronze Coinage, 1960; Coins, ancient, mediæval and modern, 1962, 2nd edn 1972; Catalogue of Roman Imperial Coins in the British Museum, vol. VI, 1962; ed, Mints, Dies and Currency, 1971; Principal Coins of the Romans, vol. I, 1978, vol. II, 1980, vol. III, 1981; ed, Essays presented to Humphrey Sutherland, 1978; History of the Royal Numismatic Society, 1986; Coins of the Roman Empire, 1990; articles in Numismatic Chron., Rev. Numismatique, etc. *Address:* 7 Ontario Avenue, Roseville, NSW 2069, Australia.
Died 24 March 2006.

CARTER, Baron *cr* 1987 (Life Peer), of Devizes in the County of Wiltshire; **Denis Victor Carter;** PC 1997; agricultural consultant and farmer, since 1957; *b* 17 Jan. 1932; *s* of Albert William and Annie Julia Carter; *m* 1957, Teresa Mary Greengoe; (one *s* one *d* decd). *Educ:* Xaverian Coll., Brighton; East Sussex Inst. of Agriculture; Essex Inst. of Agriculture (NDA, Queen's Prize); Worcester Coll., Oxford (BLitt). Nat. Service, Canal Zone, GHQ MELF, 1950–52. Audit clerk, 1949–50 and 1952–53; farmworker, 1953–54; student of agriculture, 1954–57. Founded AKC Ltd, Agricultural Accounting and Management, 1957; commenced farming, Oxfordshire, Hants and Wilts, 1975. Sen. Research Fellowship in Agricultural Marketing, MAFF, 1970–72. Opposition frontbench spokesman on agric. and rural affairs, 1987–97, also on social security, 1988–90, and health, 1989–92; Dep. Chief Opposition Whip, H of L, 1990–92; Captain, Hon. Corps of Gentlemen at Arms (Govt Chief Whip in H of L), 1997–2002. Contested (Lab) Basingstoke, 1970. Exec. Prod., LINK, 1988–97. Chairman: UK Co-operative Council, 1993–97; BBC Rural Affairs and Agricl Adv. Cttee, 1987–90; Vice-Chairman: English Farming and Food Partnership, 2002–; British Assoc. for Biofuels and Oils, 2002–; President: British Inst. of Agricl Consultants, 1992–97; Guild of Agricl Journalists, 1994–96; Inst. of Agricl Mgt, 1996–97 and 2002–; Forestry and Timber Assoc., 2002–; Royal Assoc. of British Dairy Farmers, 2003–. Trustee: Rural Housing Trust, 1992–97; John Arlott Meml Trust, 1993–97. Vice-Pres., Shaw Trust, 1991–97. DUniv Essex, 1998. *Recreations:* walking, reading, supporting Southampton Football Club. *Clubs:* Farmers' (Chm., 1982; Trustee, 1986–97; Vice-Pres., 1997–); Turners (Stockbridge); Grasshoppers (Amesbury).
Died 18 Dec. 2006.

CARTER, Eric Stephen, CBE 1986; Convener, Standing Conference on Countryside Sports, 1988–2005; *b* 23 June 1923; *s* of Albert Harry Carter, MBE and Doris Margaret (*née* Mann); *m* 1948, Audrey Windsor; one *s*. *Educ:* Grammar Sch., Lydney; Reading Univ. (BSc (Agric) 1945). Techn. Officer, Gloucester AEC, 1945–46; Asst District Officer, Gloucester NAAS, 1946–49, Dist Officer, 1949–57; Sen. Dist Officer, Lindsey (Lincs) NAAS, 1957–63, County Agric. Officer, 1963–69; Yorks and Lancs Region: Dep. Regional Dir, NAAS, 1969–71; Regional Agric. Officer, ADAS,

1971–73; Regional Officer, (ADAS), 1973–74; Chief Regional Officer, MAFF, 1974–75; Dep. Dir-Gen., Agricl Develt and Advisory Service, 1975–81; Adviser, Farming and Wildlife Adv. Gp, 1981–88. Pres., Lincs Agricl Soc., 1998–99; Member: Nuffield Farming Scholarships Trust Selection Cttee, 1981–92 (Hon. Nuffield Farming Scholar, 1992); Adv. Cttee, Welsh Plant Breeding Station, 1987–89; Governing Body, AFRC Inst. for Grassland and Envmtl Res., 1989–91. FIBiol 1974, CBiol 1974 (Vice-Pres., 1993–96); FRAgS 1985; Hon. FRASE 1988 (Hon. Vice-Pres., 1997–). FRSA 1998. Editor, Jl of Royal Agricl Soc. of England, 1985–94. *Publications:* (with M. H. R. Soper) Modern Farming and the Countryside, 1985, 2nd edn (with M. H. R. Soper) as Farming and the Countryside, 1991; (with J. M. Stansfield) British Farming: changing policies and production systems, 1994; contrib. agric. and techn. jls. *Recreations:* travel, reading, music, countryside. *Address:* 15 Farrs Lane, East Hyde, Luton, Beds LU2 9PY. *T:* (01582) 760501. *Club:* Farmers'.
Died 20 Dec. 2006.

CARTER, Prof. Yvonne Helen, (Mrs M. J. Bannon), CBE 2009 (OBE 2000); DL; MD; FRCGP; Dean, Warwick Medical School, since 2004, and Pro-Vice-Chancellor (Regional Engagement), since 2007, University of Warwick; *b* 16 April 1959; *d* of Percival Anthony Daniel Carter and Ellen Carter (*née* Bore); *m* 1988, Dr Michael Joseph Bannon; one *s*. *Educ:* Notre Dame High Sch., Liverpool; St Mary's Hosp. Med. Sch., Univ. of London (BSc, MB BS, MD 1994; DRCOG, DCH). FRCGP 1994. S Sefton Vocational Trng Scheme, Liverpool, 1984–87; General Practitioner: Liverpool, 1987–90; Newcastle-under-Lyme, 1990–93; Sen. Lectr, Dept of General Practice, Univ. of Birmingham, 1992–96; GP Tutor, Queen Elizabeth Postgrad. Med. Centre, Birmingham, 1994–96; Prof., and Hd of Dept of Gen. Practice and Primary Care, St Bartholomew's and Royal London Sch. of Medicine and Dentistry, QMW, subseq. Bart's and The London, Queen Mary's Sch. of Medicine and Dentistry, Univ. of London, 1996–2003 (Hon. Fellow, Queen Mary, Univ. of London, 2004–); Vice-Dean, Leicester Warwick Med. Schs, 2003–06. Hon. Res. Fellow, Keele Univ., 1990–92. Chm. of Res., RCGP, 1996–2000. DL W Midlands, 2008. Founder FMedSci 1998. *Publications:* (ed with C. Thomas) Research Methods in Primary Care, 1996; (ed jtly) Handbook of Palliative Care, 1998, 2nd edn 2005; (ed jtly) Handbook of Sexual Health in Primary Care, 1998, 2nd edn 2006; (ed jtly) Research Opportunities in Primary Care, 1999; papers in med. jls on injury prevention (accidents to children and older people; child protection and aggression and violence in general practice and primary care). *Recreations:* reading, theatre, interior design. *Address:* Warwick Medical School, University of Warwick, Coventry CV4 7AL. *T:* (024) 7657 3080. *Club:* Royal Society of Medicine. *Died 20 Oct. 2009.*

CARTLAND, Sir George (Barrington), Kt 1963; CMG 1956; Vice-Chancellor of the University of Tasmania, 1968–77; Chairman, Australian National Accreditation Authority for Translators and Interpreters, 1977–83; *b* 22 Sept. 1912; *s* of William Arthur and Margaret Cartland, West Didsbury; *m* 1937, Dorothy Rayton (*d* 1993); one *s* (and one *s* decd). *Educ:* Manchester Central High Sch.; Manchester Univ. (BA Hons Hist.); Hertford Coll., Oxford. Entered Colonial Service, Gold Coast, 1935; served Colonial Office, 1944–49; Head of African Studies Br. and Founding Ed. Jl of Afr. Adminis., 1945–49; Sec. London Afr. Conf., 1948; Admin. Sec., Uganda, 1949; Sec. for Social Services and Local Govt, Uganda, 1952; Min. for Social Services, Uganda, 1955; Min. of Education and Labour, Uganda, 1958; Chief Sec., Uganda, 1960; Deputy Gov. of Uganda, 1961–62 (Acting Gov., various occasions, 1952–62); Registrar of Univ. of Birmingham, 1963–67. Part-time Mem., West Midlands Gas Bd, 1964–67. Member: Exec. Cttee, Inter Univ. Council for Higher Educn Overseas (UK), 1963–67; Commonwealth Scholarship Commn (UK), 1964–67. Dep. Chm., Australian Vice-Chancellors' Cttee, 1975

and 1977. Chairman: Adv. Cttee on National Park in SW Tasmania, 1976–78; Tasmanian Council of Australian Trade Union Trng Authority, 1979. Appointed to review: Library and Archives Legislation of Tasmania, 1978; Tasmanian Govt Admin, 1979. Mem., Australian Nat. Cttee of Hoover Awards for Marketing, 1968–82. Chm., St John Council, Uganda, 1958–59; Pres., St John Council, Tasmania, 1969–78. Member Council: Makerere Coll., 1952–60; Royal Tech. Coll., Nairobi, 1952–60; UC of Rhodesia, 1963–67; Univ. of S Pacific, 1972–76. FACE 1970. Hon. LLD Univ. of Tasmania, 1978. KStJ 1972; awarded Belgian Congo medal, 1960. *Publications:* (jtly) The Irish Cartlands and Cartland Genealogy, 1978. *Recreation:* fly fishing. *Address:* 5 Aotea Road, Sandy Bay, Hobart, Tasmania 7005, Australia. *Clubs:* Athenæum; Tasmanian, Royal Tasmanian Yacht (Hobart). *Died 31 July 2008.*

CARTWRIGHT, Harry, CBE 1979 (MBE 1946); MA, CEng, MIMechE, MIET; Director, Atomic Energy Establishment, Winfrith, 1973 83; *b* 16 Sept. 1919; *s* of Edwin Harry Cartwright and Agnes Alice Cartwright (*née* Gillibrand); *m* 1950, Catharine Margaret Carson Bradbury (*d* 2007); two *s*. *Educ:* William Hulme's Grammar Sch., Manchester; St John's Coll., Cambridge (Schol.). 1st cl. Mechanical Sciences Tripos, 1940. Served War, RAF, 1940 46: Flt Lt, service on ground radar in Europe, India and Burma. Decca Navigator Co., 1946–47; English Electric Co., 1947–49; joined Dept of Atomic Energy, Risley, as a Design and Project Engr, 1949; Chief Engr, 1955; Dir in charge of UKAEA consultancy services on nuclear reactors, 1960–64; Dir, Water Reactors, 1964–70, and as such responsible for design and construction of Winfrith 100 MW(e) SGHWR prototype power station; Dir, Fast Reactor Systems, 1970–73. Pres., British Nuclear Energy Soc., 1979–82; Pres., European Nuclear Soc., 1983–85 (Vice-Pres., 1980–83). Chm. of Trustees, Corfe Castle Charities, 1991–98. Chm. of Govs, Purbeck Sch., 1985–88. *Publications:* various techn. papers. *Recreations:* walking, gardening. *Address:* Tabbit's Hill House, Corfe Castle, Wareham, Dorset BH20 5HZ. *T:* (01929) 480582. *Club:* Oxford and Cambridge. *Died 6 June 2009.*

CARTWRIGHT, Rt Rev. Richard Fox; Assistant Bishop, Diocese of Exeter, since 1988; *b* 10 Nov. 1913; *s* of late Rev. George Frederick Cartwright, Vicar of Plumstead, and Constance Margaret Cartwright (*née* Clark); *m* 1947, Rosemary Magdalen (*d* 2003), *d* of Francis Evelyn Bray, Woodham Grange, Surrey; one *s* three *d*. *Educ:* The King's School, Canterbury; Pembroke Coll., Cambridge (BA 1935, MA 1939); Cuddesdon Theological Coll. Deacon, 1936; Priest, 1937; Curate, St Anselm, Kennington Cross, 1936–40; Priest-in-Charge, Lower Kingswood, 1940–45; Vicar, St Andrew, Surbiton, 1945–52; Proctor in Convocation, 1950–52; Vicar of St Mary Redcliffe, Bristol (with Temple from 1956 and St John Bedminster from 1965), 1952–72; Hon. Canon of Bristol, 1960–72; Suffragan Bishop of Plymouth, 1972–81; Asst Bishop, dio. of Truro, 1982–91. Sub-Chaplain, Order of St John, 1957–; Director: Ecclesiastical Insurance Office Ltd, 1964–85; Allchurches Trust Ltd, 1985–91. Chm. Governors, Kelly Coll., 1973–88. Hon. DD Univ. of the South, Tennessee, 1969. *Recreations:* fly-fishing, gardening, water-colour painting. *Address:* Cadogan Court, Barley Lane, Exeter, Devon EX4 1TA. *Club:* Army and Navy. *Died 10 April 2009.*

CARVER, James, CB 1978; CEng, FIMMM; consulting mining engineer; *b* 29 Feb. 1916; *s* of late William and Ellen Carver; *m* 1944, Elsie Sharrock; one *s* two *d* (incl. twin *s* and *d*). *Educ:* Wigan Mining and Technical Coll. Certificated Mine Manager. Asst Mine Manager, Nos 5, 6 and 7 mines, Garswood Hall, Lancs, 1941–43; HM Jun. Inspector Mines and Quarries, W Midlands Coalfields, 1943; Dist Inspector, Mines and Quarries, N Staffordshire, 1951; Senior District Inspector: M&Q, London Headquarters, 1957; M&Q, Doncaster Dist (in charge), 1962; Principal Inspector, M&Q, London Headquarters, 1967; Dep. Chief, M&Q, 1973; Chief Inspector, M&Q, 1975–77; Member, Health and Safety Exec., 1976–77. *Publications:* author or co-author, papers in Trans IMinE; several papers to internat. mining confs. *Address:* 196 Forest Road, Tunbridge Wells, Kent TN2 5JB. *T:* (01892) 526748. *Died 25 March 2007.*

CASE, Humphrey John; Keeper, Department of Antiquities, Ashmolean Museum, 1973–82; *b* 26 May 1918; *s* of George Reginald Case and Margaret Helen (*née* Duckett); *m* 1st, 1942, Margaret Adelia (*née* Eaton); 2nd, 1949, Jean Alison (*née* Orr); two *s*; 3rd, 1979, Jocelyn (*née* Herickx). *Educ:* Charterhouse; St John's Coll., Cambridge (MA); Inst. of Archaeology, London Univ. Served War, 1939–46. Ashmolean Museum: Asst Keeper, 1949–57; Sen. Asst Keeper, 1957–69; Dep. Keeper, Dept of Antiquities, 1969–73. Vice-Pres., Prehistoric Soc., 1969–73; directed excavations in England, Ireland and France. FSA 1954. *Publications:* in learned jls (British and foreign): principally on neolithic in Western Europe, prehistoric metallurgy and regional archaeology. *Recreations:* drawing, reading, music, gardening. *Address:* Pitt's Cottage, 187 Thame Road, Warborough, Wallingford, Oxon OX10 7DH. *Died 13 June 2009.*

CASS, Edward Geoffrey, CB 1974; OBE 1951; Alternate Governor, Reserve Bank of Rhodesia, 1978–79; *b* 10 Sept. 1916; *s* of Edward Charles and Florence Mary Cass; *m* 1941, Ruth Mary Powley; four *d.* *Educ:* St Olave's; University Coll., London (Scholar); BSc (Econ.) London (1st Cl.) 1937; The Queen's Coll., Oxford (Scholar); George Webb Medley Scholarship, 1938; BA Oxon (1st Cl. PPE) 1939, MA 1987. Lecturer in Economics, New Coll., Oxford, 1939. From 1940 served in Min. of Supply, Treasury, Air Ministry, MoD; Private Sec. to the Prime Minister, 1949–52; Chief Statistician, Min. of Supply, 1952; Private Sec. to Min. of Supply, 1954; Imperial Defence Coll., 1958; Asst Under-Sec. of State (Programmes and Budget), MoD, 1965–72; Dep. Under-Sec. of State (Finance and Budget), MoD, 1972–76. Mem., Review Bd for Govt Contracts, 1977–84; Chm., Verbatim Reporting Study Gp, 1977–79. *Address:* 60 Rotherwick Road, NW11 7DB. *T:* (020) 8455 1664. *Died 30 May 2006.*

CASTILLO, Rudolph Innocent, MBE 1976; Secretary, National Advisory Commission on Belize-Guatemala Relations, 2000–03; Director, Secretariat of Relations with Guatemala, 2003; *b* 28 Dec. 1927; *s* of late Justo S. and Marcelina Castillo; *m* 1947, Gwen Frances Powery; three *s* four *d.* *Educ:* St John's Coll., Belize. Training assignments with BBC and COI, London. Lectr in Maths, Spanish and Hist., St John's Coll., 1946–52; Radio Belize: Announcer, 1952–53; Sen. Announcer, 1953–55; Asst Prog. Organizer, 1955–59; Govt Information Services: Information Officer, 1959–62; Chief Information Officer, 1962–74; Permanent Secretary: Agriculture, 1974–76; Education, 1976–79; Sec. to Cabinet, 1980–83; Chief of Protocol, 1981–83 and 2002; first High Comr for Belize in London, and first Belize Ambassador to France, Fed. Republic of Germany, Holy See, EEC and Unesco, 1983–85; retired from public service, 1985; first resident High Comr for Belize in Canada, 1990–93; Rep. to ICAO, 1991–93; business consultant, 1994–2000. Pres., Our Lady of Guadalupe Co-Cathedral Parish Council, Belmopan, 2002. ITV Commercial Productions (voicing commentary). Citation Award, Audubon Soc., 1994. Order of Belize, 2006. *Publications:* The Rt Hon. George Price, PC: man of the people, 2002; Holy Redeemer Credit Union (HRCU): 60 years of growth, 2004. *Recreations:* photography, theatre, watercolour painting. *Address:* 29 Mahogany Street, Belmopan, Belize, Central America. *T:* (8) 220412; *e-mail:* ceeush@yahoo.com. *Died 19 March 2010.*

CASTLEMAN, Christopher Norman Anthony; Advisory Director, Standard Chartered Bank, since 2001; Senior Adviser, UBS Investment Bank (formerly UBS Warburg), since 2001; *b* 23 June 1941; *s* of late S. Phillips and Mrs Joan S. R. Pyper; *m* 1st, 1965, Sarah Victoria (*née* Stockdale) (*d* 1979); one *s* one *d*; 2nd, 1980, Caroline Clare (*née* Westcott) (marr. diss. 1990); two *d*; 3rd, 1990, Suzy M. Diamond (*née* Twycross); one *s* one *d.* *Educ:* Harrow; Clare Coll., Cambridge (MA Law). Joined M. Samuel & Co. Ltd, 1963; General Manager, Hill Samuel Australia Ltd, 1970–72; Director, Hill Samuel & Co. Ltd, 1972; Man. Dir., Hill Samuel Group (SA) Ltd and Hill Samuel (SA) Ltd, 1978–80; Chief Executive: Hill Samuel Gp Plc, 1980–87; Blue Arrow PLC, 1987–88; Exec. Dir, Standard Chartered Bank, 1991–2001. Director: Macquarie Bank Ltd, 1985–92; Consolidated Gold Fields plc, 1988–89; Christopher Castleman & Co., 1988–89; Chairman: Nat. Investment Hldgs, 1988–90; Johnson Fry PLC (formerly LIT Holdings), 1991–95 (Chief Exec., 1989–91); ABP Holdings, 1991–94. *Recreations:* sport, travel. *Address:* Standard Chartered Bank, 4th Floor, 22 Billiter Street, EC3M 2RY. *T:* (020) 7280 7008, *Fax:* (020) 7280 7522. *Died 26 April 2006.*

CATER, Sir Jack, KBE 1979 (CBE 1973; MBE 1956); JP; Consultant, Hong Kong Nuclear Investment Co., since 1990 (Managing Director, 1987–89); Director, Guangdong Nuclear Power Joint Venture Co. Ltd, 1986–89 (First Deputy General Manager, 1985–86); *b* 21 Feb. 1922; *yr s* of Alfred Francis Cater and Pamela Elizabeth Dukes; *m* 1950, Peggy Gwenda Richards; one *s* two *d.* *Educ:* Sir George Monoux Grammar Sch., Walthamstow. Served War of 1939–45, Sqdn Ldr, RAFVR; British Military Administration, Hong Kong, 1945; joined Colonial Administrative Service, 1946, appointed Hong Kong; attended 2nd Devonshire Course, Oxford (The Queen's Coll.), 1949–50; various appts, incl. Registrar of Co-operative Societies and Director of Marketing, Dir of Agriculture and Fisheries, Dep. Economic Sec.; IDC 1966; Defence Sec./Special Asst to Governor/Dep. Colonial Sec. (Special Duties), 1967; Executive Dir, HK Trade Development Council, 1968–70; Director, Commerce and Industry, 1970–72; Secretary for Information, 1972; for Home Affairs and Information, 1973; Founding Commissioner, Independent Commn Against Corruption, 1974–78; Chief Secretary, Hong Kong, 1978–81; actg Governor and Dep. Governor on several occasions; MEC and MLC, variously 1970–81; Hong Kong Comr in London, 1982–84; Adviser to Consultative Cttee for the Basic Law, Hong Kong, 1986–90. Chairman: HG (Asia) Ltd, 1992–95 (Director: Hoare Govett (Asia), 1990–92; HG (Asia), later ABN AMRO HG (Asia), subseq. ABN AMRO, 1995–2001); Oriental Develt Co. Ltd, 1992–2001; Director: Hong Kong Cable Communications Ltd, 1990–92; The Scottish Asian Development Co. Ltd, 1990–2000; Hong Kong Inst. of Biotechnol./Syntex Ltd, 1991–95; Television Broadcasts Ltd, 1992–2001; Television Entertainment (Holdings) Ltd, 1992–96; Springfield Bank and Trust, 1994–99; Consultant: Philips & Co., China and Hong Kong, 1990–92; Internat. Bechtel Inc., 1990–97; DAO Heng Bank Ltd, 1996–2001. Pres., Agency for Volunteer Service, Hong Kong, 1982–99; Member: Internat. Bd of Dirs, United World Colls, UK, 1981–92; Court, Univ. of Hong Kong, 1982–2000; Bd of Govs, Hong Kong Baptist Univ., 1991–99; Dir, Li Po Chun United World Coll. of Hong Kong, 1991–2001. Hon. DSSc Univ. of Hong Kong, 1982; Hon. LLD Bath, 1995. *Address:* Bryanston, Clos du Petit Bois, Rue Cauchez, St Martins, Guernsey GY4 6NX. *Club:* Hong Kong. *Died 14 April 2006.*

CATFORD, Sir (John) Robin, KCVO 1993; CBE 1990; Secretary for Appointments to the Prime Minister and Ecclesiastical Secretary to the Lord Chancellor, 1982–93; *b* 11 Jan. 1923; *er s* of late Adrian Leslie Catford and Ethel Augusta (*née* Rolfe); *m* 1948, Daphne Georgina (*d* 2005), *o d* of late Col J. F. Darby, CBE, TD; three *s* one *d.* *Educ:* Hampton Grammar Sch.; Univ. of St Andrews (BSc); St John's Coll., Cambridge (DipAgric). Sudan Civil Service: Dept of Agriculture and Forests: Kordofan Province, 1946; Equatoria Province, 1948; Blue Nile Province (secondment to White Nile Schemes Bd), 1952–55; various posts in industry and commerce, mainly in UK,

1955–66; Home Civil Service: Principal, MAFF, 1966; Sec. to Cttee of Inquiry on Contract Farming, 1971; Asst Sec., 1972; Under-Sec. (Agricultural Resources Policy and Horticulture), 1979; transferred to PM's Office, 1982. Member: Economic Development Cttee for Hotels and Catering, 1972–76; EDC for Agriculture, 1979–82. Mem. Chichester Dio. Synod, 1979–84 and 1988–90. Crafts Advr, Radcliffe Trust, 1993–. *Recreations:* sailing, theatre, travel, arts, avoiding gardening. *Address:* Priory Cottage, Priory Road, Chichester, West Sussex PO19 1NS. *T:* (01243) 783197. *Club:* Oxford and Cambridge.
Died 27 May 2008.

CATLIN, His Honour Brian Ernest Frederick; a Circuit Judge, 1995–2004; *b* 7 Feb. 1937; *s* of Ernest William Catlin and Winifred May Catlin (*née* White); *m* 1962, Patricia Ann Wheeldon; two *s* one *d. Educ:* Welwyn Garden City Grammar Sch. Served RN, 1955–57. Clerk, Bower Cotton & Bower, 1953–60; Clerk, Kidd Rapinet, 1960–67; admitted solicitor, 1967; Partner, Kidd Rapinet, 1969–84; Dist Judge, 1984–95; a Recorder, 1991–95. *Recreations:* golf, grandchildren, gardening, steeplechasing. *Club:* Mapledurham Golf.
Died 11 Aug. 2006.

CATO, Brian Hudson; Full-time Chairman of Industrial Tribunals, 1975–92, Regional Chairman, Newcastle upon Tyne, 1989–92; *b* 6 June 1928; *s* of Thomas and Edith Willis Cato; *m* 1963, Barbara Edith Myles; one *s. Educ:* LEA elem. and grammar schs; Trinity Coll., Oxford; RAF Padgate. MA Oxon, LLB London. RAF, 1952–54 Called to Bar, Gray's Inn, 1952; in practice NE Circuit, 1954–75; a Recorder of the Crown Court, 1974–75. Special Lectr (part-time) in Law of Town and Country Planning, King's Coll., later Univ. of Newcastle, 1956–75; Hon. Examnr, Inst. of Landscape Architects, 1960–75. Pres., N of England Medico-legal Soc., 1973–74. Corresp. Sec., Berwickshire Naturalists Club, 1992–96. Freeman of City of Newcastle upon Tyne by patrimony; Founder Mem. Scriveners' Co., Newcastle upon Tyne (Clerk, 1992–2006); Freeman, City of London, 1985. Hon. ALI. *Recreations:* bibliomania, antiquarian studies, family life. *Address:* 2 Croft Place, Newton-by-the-Sea, Alnwick, Northumberland NE66 3DL. *T:* (01665) 576334. *Died 19 Aug. 2010.*

CAWSON, Prof. Roderick Anthony, MD; FDS, RCS and RCPS Glasgow; FRCPath; Professor (Hon. Consultant) and Head of Department of Oral Medicine and Pathology, United Medical and Dental Schools, Guy's Hospital, 1966–86, then Emeritus; *b* 23 April 1921; *s* of Capt. Leopold Donald Cawson and Ivy Clunies-Ross; *m* 1949, Diana Hall, SRN; no *c. Educ:* King's College Sch. Wimbledon; King's College Hosp. Med. Sch. MD (London); MB, BS, BDS (Hons) (London); FDS, RCS; FDS, RCPS Glasgow; MRCPath, LMSSA. Served RAF, 1944–48; Nuffield Foundn Fellow, 1953–55; Dept of Pathology, King's Coll. Hosp., Sen. Lectr in Oral Pathology, King's Coll. Hosp. Med. Sch., 1955–62; Sen. Lectr in Oral Pathology, Guy's Hosp. Med. Sch., 1962–66. Examinerships: Pathology (BDS) London, 1965–69; Univ. of Wales, 1969–71; Dental Surgery (BDS), Glasgow, 1966–70; BChD Leeds, 1966–70; Newcastle, 1967–71; FDS, RCPS Glasgow, 1967–86; BDS Lagos, 1975–78; RCPath, 1984–87. Chairman: Dental Formulary Sub-cttee (BMA); Dental and Surgical Materials Cttee, Medicines Division, 1976–80; recently First Chm., Univ. Teachers' Gp (BDA). *Publications:* Essentials of Dental Surgery and Pathology 1962, 5th edn 1991, 6th edn as Oral Pathology and Oral Medicine (with E. W. Odell), 1998; Medicine for Dental Students (with R. H. Cutforth), 1960; (with R. G. Spector) Clinical Pharmacology in Dentistry, 1975, 5th edn 1989; Aids to Oral Pathology and Diagnosis, 1981; (with C. Scully) Medical Problems in Dentistry, 1982, 4th edn 1998; (with A. W. McCracken and P. B. Marcus) Pathology: the mechanisms of disease, 1982, 2nd edn 1989; (with A. W. McCracken) Clinical and Oral Microbiology, 1982; (with J. W. Eveson) Oral Pathology and Diagnosis, 1987, 2nd edn as Oral Disease: clinico-

pathological correlations, 1993; (jtly) Lucas's Pathology of Tumours of the Oral Tissues, 5th edn 1998; *festschrift:* Horizons in Oral Medicine and Pathology, 2003; numerous papers, etc, in med. and dental jls. *Recreations:* reading, music, gardening (reluctantly). *Address:* 40 Court Lane, Dulwich, SE21 7DR. *T:* (020) 8693 5781.
Died 25 April 2007.

CHADWICK, Rt Rev. Graham Charles; Principal, then Director, Institute for Christian Spirituality, Sarum College, Salisbury, 1995–98; *b* 3 Jan. 1923; *s* of William Henry and Sarah Ann Chadwick; *m* 1955, Jeanne Suzanne Tyrrell; one *s. Educ:* Swansea Grammar School; SOAS; Keble Coll., Oxford (MA); St Michael's Coll., Llandaff. RNVR, 1942–46. Deacon 1950, priest 1951; Curate, Oystermouth, Dio. Swansea and Brecon, 1950–53; Diocese of Lesotho, 1953–63; Chaplain, University Coll., Swansea, 1963–68; Senior Bursar, Queen's Coll., Birmingham, 1968–69; Diocesan Missioner, Lesotho, and Warden of Diocesan Training Centre, 1970–76; Bishop of Kimberley and Kuruman, 1976–82; Chaplain, St Asaph Cathedral, and Advr on Spirituality, Dio. of St Asaph, 1983–90; Asst Bishop of Liverpool, 1990–95. *Address:* 66 Hulse Road, Salisbury SP1 3LY. *T:* (01722) 505801; *e-mail:* Gcchadwick@aol.com. *Died 28 Oct. 2007.*

CHADWICK, Prof. Henry, KBE 1989; DD; FBA 1960; MRIA; Master of Peterhouse, Cambridge, 1987–93 (Hon. Fellow, 1993); Regius Professor Emeritus of Divinity, University of Cambridge, 1983 (Regius Professor, 1979–83); *b* 23 June 1920; 3rd *s* of late John Chadwick, Barrister, Bromley, Kent, and Edith (*née* Horrocks); *m* 1945, Margaret Elizabeth, *d* of late W. Pemell Brownrigg; three *d. Educ:* Eton (King's Scholar); Magdalene Coll., Cambridge (Music Schol.). John Stewart of Rannoch Scholar, 1939. MusB. Asst Master, Wellington Coll., 1945; University of Cambridge: Fellow of Queens' Coll., 1946–58; Hon. Fellow, 1958; Junior Proctor, 1948–49. Regius Professor of Divinity and Canon of Christ Church, Oxford, 1959–69; Dean of Christ Church, Oxford, 1969–79 (Hon. Student, 1979); Pro-Vice-Chancellor, Oxford Univ., 1974–75; Delegate, OUP, 1960–79; Fellow, Magdalene Coll., Cambridge, 1979–87 (Hon. Fellow 1962). Fellow, Eton, 1976–79; Hon. Fellow: St Anne's Coll., Oxford, 1979; Trinity Coll., Cambridge, 1987. Gifford Lectr, St Andrews Univ., 1962–64; Birkbeck Lectr, Cambridge, 1965; Burns Lectr, Otago, 1971; Sarum Lectr, Oxford, 1982–83. Editor, Journal of Theological Studies, 1954–85. Member, Anglican-Roman Catholic International Commn, 1969–81 and 1983–90. Mem., Amer. Philosophical Soc.; For. Hon. Mem., Amer. Acad. Arts and Sciences; Correspondant de l'Académie des Inscriptions et des Belles Lettres, Institut de France; Member Société des Bollandistes, Brussels; Bavarian Acad., Munich; Corresponding Member: Göttingen Acad. of Scis; Rhineland Acad. of Scis; Erfurt Acad. Hon. DD, Glasgow, Yale, Harvard, Surrey, Manchester, Jena and Lateran (Augustinianum); Hon. Teol Dr, Uppsala; D Humane Letters, Chicago. Humboldt Prize, 1983; Lucas Prize, Tübingen, 1991. Order pour le mérite (Germany), 1993. *Publications:* Origen, Contra Celsum, 1953, 3rd edn 1980, repr. 2004; Alexandrian Christianity (with J. E. L. Oulton), 1954; Lessing's Theological Writings, 1956; The Sentences of Sextus, 1959, repr. 2004; Early Christian Thought and the Classical Tradition, 1966; The Early Church (Pelican), 1967, 2nd edn 1993; The Treatise on the Apostolic Tradition of St Hippolytus of Rome, ed G. Dix (rev. edn), 1968; Priscillian of Avila, 1976; Boethius, 1981; History and Thought of the Early Church, 1982; Augustine, 1986; (ed) Atlas of the Christian Church, 1987; Augustine's Confessions, 1991; Heresy and Orthodoxy in the Early Church, 1991; Tradition and Exploration, 1994; The Church in Ancient Society: from Galilee to Gregory the Great, 2001; East and West: the making of a rift in the Church, 2003; Studies on Ancient Christianity, 2006; (contrib.) Oxford History of the Classical World, 1986; (contrib.) Oxford Illustrated History of Christianity, 1990; (contrib.) Cambridge

Ancient History, vol. XIII, 1997. *Recreation:* music. *Address:* 46 St John Street, Oxford OX1 2LH. *T:* (01865) 512814. *Died 17 June 2008.*

CHAMBERLAIN, Prof. Owen, AB, PhD; Professor of Physics, University of California, 1958–89, then Emeritus; *b* San Francisco, 10 July 1920; *s* of W. Edward Chamberlain and Genevieve Lucinda Owen; *m* 1st, 1943, Babette Copper (marr. diss. 1978; she *d* 1988); one *s* three *d*; 2nd, 1980, June Greenfield Steingart (*d* 1991); 3rd, 1998, Senta Pugh (*née* Gaiser). *Educ:* Philadelphia; Dartmouth Coll., Hanover, NH (AB). Atomic research for Manhattan District, 1942, transferred to Los Alamos, 1943; worked in Argonne National Laboratory, Chicago, 1947–48, and studied at University of Chicago (PhD); Instructor in Physics, University of California, 1948; Asst Professor, 1950; Associate Professor, 1954. Guggenheim Fellowship, 1957; Loeb Lecturer in Physics, Harvard Univ., 1959. Fellow: American Phys. Soc.; Amer. Acad. of Arts and Scis; Mem., Nat. Acad. of Sciences, 1960; Berkeley Fellow, 1992. Nobel Prize (joint) for Physics, 1959; Berkeley Citation, 1989. *Publications:* papers in Physical Review, Physical Review Letters, Nature, Nuovo Cimento. *Address:* Department of Physics, University of California, Berkeley, CA 94720, USA. *Died 28 Feb. 2006.*

CHAMBERS, Dr Douglas Robert; HM Coroner, City of London, 1994–2002; *b* 2 Nov. 1929; *s* of Douglas Henry Chambers and Elizabeth Paterson; *m* 1955, Barbara June Rowe; one *s* two *d*. *Educ:* Shene Grammar Sch.; King's College, London (MB BS; AKC 1953); LLB London Univ. (ext.) 1960; MA Univ. of Wales, 1989. FIBiol 1992. Called to the Bar, Lincoln's Inn, 1965. RAF Med. Br., 1955–58; Med. Advr, Parke Davis, 1959–61, Nicholas Laboratories, 1961–63, Pharmacia, 1964–65; Med. Dir, Hoechst Pharmaceuticals, 1965–70; Dep. Coroner, West London, 1969–70; HM Coroner, Inner North London, 1970–94. Hon. Sen. Clin. Lectr in med. law, UCL, 1978–96; Hon. Sen. Lectr, medical law, Royal Free Hosp., 1978–2002. Chairman: Richmond Div., BMA, 1969–70; Animal Research and Welfare Panel, Biological Council, 1986–92; Animal Welfare in Res. and Educn Cttee, Inst. of Biology, 1992–95; Pres., Library (sci. research) section, RSocMed, 1979–80; Pres., British sect., Anglo-German Med. Soc., 1980–84; Pres., Coroners' Soc., 1985–86. Hon. Mem., British Micro-circulation Soc., 1986 (Hon. Treas., 1968–86). Dist Comr, Richmond & Barnes Dist Scouts, 1976–85 (Silver Acorn 1984). Pres., Kensington Rowing Club, 1973–78. Baron C. ver Heyden de Lancey Prize for services to law and medicine, RSocMed, 1990. *Publications:* (jtly) Coroners' Inquiries, 1985; (consultant ed.) Jervis on Coroners, (with Dr J. Burton) 11th edn 1993, (with Dr J. Burton and M. J. C. Burgess) 12th edn 2002; papers on medico-legal subjects. *Recreation:* local history of coroners and of scouting. *Address:* 4 Ormond Avenue, Richmond, Surrey TW10 6TN. *T:* (020) 8940 7745. *Club:* Auriol-Kensington Rowing. *Died 1 Jan. 2009.*

CHAN, Baron *cr* 2001 (Life Peer), of Oxton in the County of Merseyside; **Michael Chew Koon Chan,** MBE 1991; MD; FRCP, FRACP, FRCPCH; part-time Advisor on Ethnic Health, Regional Public Health Directorate, Government Office of the North West, since 2000; Consultant on Cultural Awareness and Communication, Merseyside Police, since 1999; Visiting Professor in Ethnic Health, University of Liverpool, since 1996; *b* 6 March 1940; *s* of James Chieu Kim Chan and Rosie Chan; *m* 1965, Irene Wei-Len Chee; one *s* one *d*. *Educ:* Raffles Instn, Singapore; Guy's Hosp. Med. Sch. London Univ. (MB BS); MD Singapore 1969. FRCP 1986; FRACP 1975; FRCPCH 1996; MFPHM 1996. Lectr, Dept of Paediatrics, 1970–73, Sen. Lectr and Consultant Paediatrician, 1973–76, Univ. of Singapore; BPA Heinz Res. Fellow, Inst. of Child Health, Univ. of London and Gt Ormond St Hosp. for Sick Children, 1974–75; Sen. Lectr and Consultant Paediatrician, Liverpool Sch. of Tropical Medicine, 1976–94; Dir, NHS Ethnic Health Unit, 1994–97. Advr on Ethnic Health,

Commn for Health Improvement, 2001–02; Chairman: Acupuncture Regulatory Wkg Gp, DoH, 2002–03; Malaria Consortium, 2003–; Patient's Choice Nat. Trustee, DoH, 2002–03. Non-executive Director: Wirral and W Cheshire Community NHS Trust, 1999–2002; Birkenhead and Wallasey Primary Care Trust, 2002–. Mem., PCC, 2002–. Church Elder, Liverpool Chinese Gospel Church. *Publications:* (ed jtly) Diseases of Children in the Subtropics and Tropics, 1991; (contrib.) Roberton, Textbook of Neonatology, 1986, 3rd edn 1999; (contrib.) The Future of Multi Ethnic Britain: the Parekh Report, 2000; contrib. learned jls. *Recreations:* overseas travel, Chinese cooking, community involvement, preaching, gardening. *Address:* 1 Rathmore Drive, Oxton, Wirral CH43 2HD. *T:* (0151) 653 6956; House of Lords, SW1A 0PW. *T:* (020) 7219 8726. *Died 21 Jan. 2006.*

CHANCE, Sqdn Ldr Dudley Raymond, FRGS; a Recorder of the Crown Court, 1980–86; *b* 9 July 1916; *s* of Captain Arthur Chance, Sherwood Foresters, and Byzie Chance; *m* 1958, Jessie Maidstone, widow, *d* of John and Alice Dewing. *Educ:* Nottingham High Sch.; London Univ. (BA Oriental Religions and Philosophies, LLB 1969); BA Hons Internat. Politics and For. Policy, Open Univ., 1980. Called to Bar, Middle Temple, 1955; Dep. Circuit Judge, 1973–80. Commissioned in Royal Air Force, 1936; served Egypt, Transjordan, 1936–37; Bomber Comd (4 Gp), 1938; served in Bomber Comd Nos 97 and 77 Sqdns; took part in first raids on Norway; crashed off Trondheim; picked up later from sea by HMS Basilisk, later sunk at Dunkirk; Air Ministry, Whitehall, 1941–42, later in 2 Group, Norfolk, 21 Sqdn; also served in SEAC, Bengal/Burma. Sqdn Ldr, RAFO, until March 1961; gazetted to retain rank of Sqdn Ldr from that date. Member: panel of Chairmen of Medical Appeal Tribunals (DHSS), 1978–88; panel of Independent Inspectors for motorway and trunk road inquiries for DoE, 1978–83. Contested (C) Norwich North, 1959. FRGS 1979. *Recreations:* violin, painting. *Address:* Lamb Buildings, Temple, EC4Y 7AS; Fenners Chambers, 4 Madingley Road, Cambridge CB3 0EE. *Club:* Goldfish (RAF aircrew rescued from sea). *Died 2 Aug. 2009.*

CHANDLER, Tony John; Hon. Research Fellow, University College London, since 1989; Visiting Professor, King's College, London, since 1989; *b* 7 Nov. 1928; *s* of Harold William and Florence Ellen Chandler; *m* 1954, Margaret Joyce Weston (decd); one *s* one *d*. *Educ:* King's Coll., London. MSc. PhD, AKC, MA. Lectr, Birkbeck Coll., Univ. of London, 1952–56; University Coll. London: Lectr, 1956–65; Reader in Geography, 1965–69; Prof. of Geography, 1969–73; Prof. of Geography, Manchester Univ., 1973–77; Master of Birkbeck Coll., Univ. of London, 1977–79. Sec., Royal Meteorological Soc., 1969–73, Vice-Pres., 1973–75. Member: Council, NERC; Health and Safety Commn; Cttee of Experts on Major Hazards; Royal Soc. Study Gp on Pollution in the Atmosphere, 1974–77; Clean Air Council; Royal Commn on Environmental Pollution, 1973–77; Standing Commn on Energy and the Environment 1978. *Publications:* The Climate of London, 1965; Modern Meteorology and Climatology, 1972, 2nd edn 1981; contribs to: Geographical Jl, Geography, Weather, Meteorological Magazine, Bulletin of Amer. Meteorological Soc., etc. *Recreations:* horology, music, reading, travel. *Address:* 15 Durrell Close, Langney, Eastbourne, East Sussex BN23 7AN. *Died 17 July 2008.*

CHANDRACHUD, Hon. Yeshwant Vishnu; Chief Justice of India, 1978–85; *b* Poona (Maharashtra), 12 July 1920; *s* of Vishnu Balkrishna Chandrachud and Indira; *m* Prabha; one *s* one *d*. *Educ:* Bombay Univ. (BA, LLB). Advocate of Bombay High Court, 1943, civil and criminal work; part-time Prof. of Law, Government Law Coll., Bombay, 1949–52; Asst Govt Pleader, 1952; Govt Pleader, 1958; Judge, Bombay High Court, 1961–72; one-man Pay Commn for Bombay Municipal Corporation officers, later Arbitrator in dispute between Electricity Supply and Transport Undertaking and its employees' union; one-man Commn to inquire into circumstances leading to death of Deen Dayal Upadhyaya; Judge, Supreme Court of India, 1972–78. President: Internat. Law Assoc. (India Branch), 1978; Indian Law Inst., 1978–85. *Address:* (official) 7–B Samata, General Bhosale Marg, Mumbai 400021, India. *T:* (22) 2042474. *Died 14 July 2008.*

CHAPLAIS, Pierre Théophile Victorien Marie, FBA 1973; Reader in Diplomatic in the University of Oxford, 1957–87, then Reader Emeritus; Professorial Fellow, Wadham College, Oxford, 1964–87, then Emeritus Fellow; *b* Châteaubriant, Loire-Atlantique, France, 8 July 1920; *s* of late Théophile Chaplais and Victorine Chaplais (*née* Roussel); *m* 1948, (Mary) Doreen Middlemast (*d* 2000); two *s. Educ:* Collège St-Sauveur, Redon, Ille-et-Vilaine; Univ. of Rennes, Ille-et-Vilaine (Licence en Droit, Licence ès-Lettres); Univ. of London (PhD). Editor, Public Record Office, London, 1948–55; Lectr in Diplomatic, Univ. of Oxford, 1955–57; Literary Dir, Royal Hist. Soc., 1958–64 (Hon. Vice-Pres., 2004–). Corresp. Fellow, Mediaeval Acad. of America, 1979. Médaille de la Résistance, 1946. *Publications:* Some Documents regarding . . . The Treaty of Brétigny, 1952; The War of St Sardos, 1954; Treaty Rolls, vol. I, 1955; (with T. A. M. Bishop) Facsimiles of English Royal Writs to AD 1100 presented to V. H. Galbraith, 1957; Diplomatic Documents, vol. I, 1964; English Royal Documents, King John-Henry VI, 1971; English Medieval Diplomatic Practice, Part II, 1975, Part I, 1982; Essays in Medieval Diplomacy and Administration, 1981; Piers Gaveston, Edward II's Adoptive Brother, 1994; English Diplomatic Practice in the Middle Ages, vol. I, 2003; articles in Bulletin of Inst. of Historical Research, English Hist. Review, Jl of Soc. of Archivists, etc. *Recreations:* gardening, fishing. *Address:* Lew Lodge, Mount Owen Road, Lew, Bampton, Oxfordshire OX18 2BE. *T:* (01993) 850613. *Died 26 Nov. 2006.*

CHAPMAN, Baroness *cr* 2004 (Life Peer), of Leeds in the County of West Yorkshire; **Nicola Jane Chapman;** Chair, Leeds Centre for Integrated Living, since 2004 (Member, since 1993); *b* 3 Aug. 1961; *d* of Peter Leslie Chapman and late Marlene Chapman. *Educ:* John Jamieson Sch. for Physically Disabled Children; Park Lane Coll. of Further Educn, Leeds; Trinity and All Saints Coll., Leeds. Volunteer Tutor, Apex Trust, 1985–86; Leeds City Council: Finance Clerk, 1986–89; IT Tutor, 1989–92; IT Tutor, E Leeds Women's Workshops, 1992–93. Member: Cttee, Habinteg Housing Assoc., 1993–; Leeds Utd Disabled Orgn, 1994–2004 (Chm., 1997–). *Recreations:* Leeds Utd FC, reading. *Address:* House of Lords, SW1A 0PW; *e-mail:* chapmann@ parliament.uk. *Died 3 Sept. 2009.*

CHAPMAN, His Honour Cyril Donald; QC 1965; a Circuit Judge, 1972–86; *b* 17 Sept. 1920; *s* of Cyril Henry Chapman and Frances Elizabeth Chapman (*née* Braithwaite); *m* 1st, 1950, Audrey Margaret Fraser (*née* Gough) (marr. diss. 1959); one *s*; 2nd, 1960, Muriel Falconer Bristow; one *s. Educ:* Roundhay Sch., Leeds; Brasenose Coll., Oxford (MA). Served RNVR, 1939–45. Called to Bar, 1947; Harmsworth Scholar, 1947; North Eastern Circuit, 1947; Recorder of Huddersfield, 1965–69, of Bradford, 1969–71. Contested (C) East Leeds 1955, Goole 1964, Brighouse and Spenborough, 1966. *Address:* Hill Top, Collingham, Wetherby, W Yorks LS22 5BB. *T:* (01937) 572813. *Died 10 Nov. 2008.*

CHAPMAN, Honor Mary Ruth, CBE 1997; FRICS; Executive Chairman, Future London, 2004–08; *b* 29 July 1942; *d* of Alan Harry Woodland and Frances Evelyn (*née* Ball); *m* 1966, David Edwin Harold Chapman (marr. diss. 1997). *Educ:* Coll. of Estate Mgt, London Univ. (BSc Estate Mgt 1963); University Coll. London (MPhil Town Planning 1966). MRTPI 1971; FRICS 1979. Surveyor, Valuation Dept, LCC, 1963–64; with Nathaniel Lichfield & Partners (Econ. and Planning Consultants), 1966–76 (Partner, 1971–76); freelance Consultant, 1976–79; Sloan Fellow, London Business Sch., 1977; Chm., Research, then Internat. Partner, Jones Lang Wootton, 1979–2000;

Consultant, Jones Lang LaSalle, 2000–03; Chief Exec. (on secondment half-time), London First Centre, 1993–95 (Dir, 1993–99). Dir, Legal and General plc, 1993–2001. Vice-Chm., 2000–03, Chm., 2003–04, London Develt Agency; Board Member: English Estates, 1984–92; Cardiff Bay Urban Develt Corp., 1987–94; a Crown Estate Comr, 1997–2004. Gov. and Mem., Exec. Cttee, Centre for Economic Policy Res., 1988–96. Chm., Burlington Gardens Client Cttee, Royal Academy, 2001–07. FRSA 1992. *Recreations:* dairy farming, watching people do things well. *Club:* University Women's. *Died 22 Aug. 2009.*

CHAPMAN, Prof. Norman Bellamy, MA, PhD; CChem, FRSC; G. F. Grant Professor of Chemistry, Hull University, 1956–82, then Emeritus; Pro-Vice-Chancellor, 1973–76; *b* 19 April 1916; *s* of Frederick Taylor Chapman and Bertha Chapman; *m* 1949, Fonda Maureen Bungey; one *s* one *d. Educ:* Barnsley Holgate Grammar Sch.; Magdalene Coll., Cambridge (Entrance Scholar). 1st Cl. Parts I and II Nat. Sciences Tripos, 1937 and 1938; BA 1938, MA 1942, PhD 1941. Bye-Fellow, Magdalene Coll., 1939–42; Univ. Demonstrator in Chemistry, Cambridge, 1945; Southampton Univ.: Lectr, 1947; Senior Lectr, 1949; Reader in Chemistry, 1955. R. T. French Visiting Prof., Univ. of Rochester, NY, 1962–63; R. J. Reynolds Vis. Prof., Duke Univ., N Carolina, 1971; Cooch Behar Prof., Calcutta, 1982. Universities Central Council on Admissions: Dep. Chm., 1979–83; Chm., Technical Cttee, 1974–79; Chm., Statistics Cttee, 1983–89. Hon. DSc Hull, 1984. *Publications:* (ed with J. Shorter) Advances in Free Energy Relationships, 1972; (ed) Organic Chemistry, Series One, vol. 2: Aliphatic Compounds (MTP Internat. Review of Science), 1973, Series Two, vol. 2, 1976; (ed with J. Shorter) Correlation Analysis in Chemistry: recent advances, 1978; contribs to Jl Chem. Soc., Analyst, Jl Medicinal Chem., Tetrahedron, Jl Organic Chemistry, Chemistry and Industry. *Recreations:* music, gardening, cricket, Rugby football. *Address:* 5 The Lawns, Molescroft, Beverley, E Yorks HU17 7LS. *Died 6 March 2008.*

CHARKHAM, Jonathan Philip, CBE 2002; director of companies; Adviser to the Governors, Bank of England, 1988–93 (Chief Adviser, 1985–88); *b* 17 Oct. 1930; *s* of late Louis Charkham and Phoebe Beatrice Barquet (*née* Miller); *m* Moira Elizabeth Frances, *d* of late Barnett A. Salmon and Molly Salmon; twin *s* one *d. Educ:* St Paul's Sch.; Jesus Coll., Cambridge (BA 1952). Called to Bar, Inner Temple, 1953. Morris Charkham Ltd, 1953–63 (Man. Dir, 1957–63); Div. Dir, Rest Assured Ltd, 1963–68. Civil Service Department: Principal, Management Services, later Pay, 1969–73; Asst Sec., 1973–78, Personnel Management, 1973–75; Dir, Public Appts Unit, 1975–82; Under Sec., 1978, Management and Organisation, 1980–82; on secondment from Bank of England as Dir, PRO NED, 1982–85. Director: Great Universal Stores, 1993–2001; CrestaCare, 1993–99; CLM, 1993–99; Leopold Joseph Hldgs, 1994–2002; PRS Ltd, 1996–97; Rostrum plc, 2001–; London Bd, Mizuho Internat. plc, 2002–; Consultant: Pensions and Investment Research Consultants, 1994–2000; Hermes Focus Asset Mgt Ltd, 2005; Mem., London Adv. Bd, Industrial Bank of Japan, 1997–2000. Member: Council, Royal Inst. of Public Admin., 1981–82; Industry and Finance Cttee, NEDC, 1988–90; Steering Cttee, Corporate Takeovers Inquiry, 1990–91; Instnl Investors Project Adv. Bd, Columbia Univ. of NY Center for Law and Econ. Studies, 1989–93; City Transportation Task Force, 1990–92; Cttee on Financial Aspects of Corporate Governance, 1991–93; US subcouncil on Corporate Governance and Financial Mkts, 1992–94; CII Working Party on Financing Transport Infrastructure, 1992–93; Steering Cttee on Corporate Governance in NHS, 1993–94; Adv. Bd, Centre of Bd Leadership (USA), 1997; Fabian Soc. Commn on Taxation and Citizenship, 1998–2000; Global Corp. Governance Forum, World Bank, 1999–; Lay Mem., Jt Disciplinary Scheme of Accounting Profession,

1993–2006. Vis. Prof., Sir John Cass Business Sch., City of London (formerly City Univ. Business Sch.), 1997–. Mem., Duke of Edinburgh's 7th Commonwealth Study Conf., 1990–92; Chm., Knightsbridge Assoc., 1998–2004 (Mem. Cttee, 1989–2004). Chm., CU Labour Club, 1952. Master, Worshipful Co. of Upholders, 1979–80, 1980–81; Sheriff, City of London, 1994–95; Mem., Court of Common Council, 1997–2003 (Chief Commoner, 2002–03). CCMI. Hon. DSc City, 2003. *Publications:* Keeping Good Company: a survey of corporate governance in five countries, 1994, 2nd edn, as Keeping Better Company, 2005; Conversations with a Silent Friend, 1998; (with Anne Simpson) Fair Shares, 1999; booklets and pamphlets on non-executive directors, boards and shareholders. *Recreations:* music, playing golf, antique furniture, wine. *Address:* The Yellow House, 22 Montpelier Place, SW7 1HL. *T:* (020) 7589 9879, *Fax:* (020) 7581 8520. *Clubs:* Athenæum, MCC. *Died 30 May 2006.*

CHARLES, Jack; Director of Establishments, Greater London Council, 1972–77; *b* 18 Jan. 1923; *o s* of late Frederick Walter Charles and Alice Mary Charles; *m* 1959, Jean (*d* 1991), *d* of late F. H. Braund, London; one *s* one *d. Educ:* County High Sch., Ilford. Air Min., 1939–42; RAF, 1942–46; Min. of Supply, 1947–59 (Private Sec. to Minister of Supply, 1952–54); War Office, 1959–60; UKAEA, 1960–68 (Authority Personnel Officer, 1965–68); Dep. Dir of Estabs, GLC, 1968–72. *Recreations:* gardening, walking. *Address:* Kings Warren, Enborne Row, Wash Water, Newbury, Berks RG20 0LY. *T:* (01635) 30161. *Died 19 Jan. 2006.*

CHARLTON, Graham; see Charlton, T. A. G.

CHARLTON, Prof. Kenneth; Emeritus Professor of History of Education, King's College, University of London, since 1983; *b* 11 July 1925; 2nd *s* of late George and Lottie Charlton; *m* 1953, Maud Tulloch Brown, *d* of late P. R. Brown, MBE and M. B. Brown; one *s* one *d. Educ:* City Grammar Sch., Chester; Univ. of Glasgow. MA 1949, MEd 1953, Glasgow. RNVR, 1943–46. History Master, Dalziel High Sch., Motherwell, and Uddingston Grammar Sch., 1950–54; Lectr in Educn, UC N Staffs, 1954–64; Sen. Lectr in Educn, Keele Univ., 1964–66; Prof. of History and Philosophy of Educn, Birmingham Univ., 1966–72; Prof. of History of Educn and Head of Dept of Educn, King's Coll., Univ. of London, 1972–83. *Publications:* Recent Historical Fiction for Children, 1960, 2nd edn 1969; Education in Renaissance England, 1965; Women, Religion and Education in Early Modern England, 1999; (contrib.) Cambridge History of Early Modern English Literature 1530–1675, 2002; (contrib.) A Companion to Early Modern Women's Writing, 2002; contrib. Oxford DNB; contribs to Educnl Rev., Brit. Jl Educnl Psych., Year Bk of Educn, Jl Hist. of Ideas, Brit. Jl Educnl Studies, Internat. Rev. of Educn, Trans Hist. Soc. Lancs and Cheshire, Irish Hist. Studies, Northern Hist., Hist. of Educn, Hist. of Educn Quarterly. *Recreations:* gardening, listening to music. *Address:* 128 Ridge Langley, Sanderstead, Croydon CR2 0AS. *Died 4 Nov. 2008.*

CHARLTON, (Thomas Alfred) Graham, CB 1970; Secretary, Trade Marks, Patents and Designs Federation, 1973–84; *b* 29 Aug. 1913; 3rd *s* of late Frederick William and Marian Charlton; *m* 1940, Margaret Ethel, *yr d* of A. E. Furst; three *d. Educ:* Rugby School; Corpus Christi Coll., Cambridge. Asst Principal, War Office, 1936; Asst Private Secretary to Secretary of State for War, 1937–39; Principal, 1939; Cabinet Office, 1947–49; Asst Secretary, 1949; International Staff, NATO, 1950–52; War Office, later MoD, 1952–73; Asst Under-Sec. of State, 1960–73. Coronation Medal, 1953. *Recreation:* gardening. *Address:* Room 14, Bradbury House, Windsor End, Beaconsfield, Bucks HP9 2JW. *Died 12 Dec. 2006.*

CHARPAK, Georges; Physicist, Organisation européenne pour la recherche nucléaire (CERN), 1959–91; *b* Poland, 8 March 1924; *s* of Anne Szapiro and Maurice Charpak; *m* 1953, Dominique Vidal; two *s* one *d. Educ:* Ecole des Mines de Paris; Collège de France, Paris (PhD Physics 1954). Went to France at age 7; served in French Resistance; imprisoned for 1 year in Dachau. Centre national de la recherche scientifique (CNRS), 1948; CERN, Geneva, 1959; in 1968 invented multiwire proportional chamber (linked to computers) for detecting particles in atom smashers. Mem., Acad. des Sciences, France, 1985; Foreign Associate of Nat. Acad. of Sciences, USA, 1986. Nobel Prize for Physics, 1992. *Publications:* (jtly) Megawatts and Megatons: a turning point in the nuclear age?, 2001; (jtly) Debunked, 2004; many papers. *Recreations:* ski-ing, travel, music. *Address:* CERN, 1211 Geneva 23, Switzerland. *T:* (22) 7672144, *Fax:* (22) 7677555. *Died 29 Sept. 2010.*

CHATFIELD, 2nd Baron *cr* 1937, of Ditchling; **Ernle David Lewis Chatfield;** *b* 2 Jan. 1917; *s* of 1st Baron Chatfield, PC, GCB, OM, KCMG, CVO (Admiral of the Fleet Lord Chatfield), and Lillian Emma St John Matthews (*d* 1977); *S* father, 1967; *m* 1969, (Felicia Mary) Elizabeth, *d* of late Dr John Roderick Bulman, Hereford. *Educ:* RNC Dartmouth; Trinity Coll., Cambridge. ADC to Governor-General of Canada, 1940–44. *Heir:* none. *Address:* 535 Island Road, Victoria, BC V8S 2T7, Canada. *Died 30 Sept. 2007 (ext).*

CHERRY, Alan Herbert, CBE 2003 (MBE 1984); DL; FRICS; Founder Director, 1971, and Chairman, since 1981, Countryside Properties plc; *b* 4 Aug. 1933; *s* of William Alfred Cherry and Helen Grace (*née* Parrish); *m* 1976, Fay Angela Robbins; two *s. Educ:* Mayfield Sch. Founder Partner, Bairstow Eves, 1958–81; Dep. Chm., Workspace Gp plc, 1987–2004. Non-exec. Dir, MEPC Ltd, 2006–. Member: Inquiry into British Housing, 1985–87; Urban Task Force, 1998–99. Dir, E of England Investment Agency, 1997–2002; Mem. Bd, E of England Develt Agency, 1999–2002; Chm., E of England, CBI, 2001–03. Nat. Pres., Home Builders' Fedn, 1988. Chm. Govs, Anglia Poly. Univ., 1988–2002. Hon. MRTPI 1991. DL Essex, 2002. Hon. Freeman, Brentwood, 2008. *Recreations:* ski-ing, walking, swimming. *Address:* (office) Countryside House, The Drive, Brentwood, Essex CM13 3AT. *T:* (01277) 260000. *Died 23 Jan. 2010.*

CHESHAM, 6th Baron, *cr* 1858; **Nicholas Charles Cavendish;** *b* 7 Nov. 1941; *s* of 5th Baron Chesham, TD, PC and Mary Edmunds, *d* of late David G. Marshall; *S* father, 1989; *m* 1st, 1965, Susan Donne Beauchamp (marr. diss. 1969); 2nd, 1973, Suzanne Adrienne, *d* of late Alan Gray Byrne; two *s. Educ:* Eton. Chartered Accountant. Capt. of the Yeoman of the Guard (Dep. Govt Chief Whip in H of L), 1995–97. *Recreations:* tennis, ski-ing, shooting. *Heir: s* Hon. Charles Gray Compton Cavendish [*b* 11 Nov. 1974; *m* 2002, Sarah Elizabeth, *d* of Bruce Dawson; one *s* one *d*]. *Address:* The Old Post House, Church Street, Ropley, Alresford, Hants SO24 0DR. *Clubs:* Pratt's; Australian (Sydney); Royal Sydney Golf. *Died 27 Aug. 2009.*

CHESTERTON, Sir Oliver (Sidney), Kt 1969; MC 1943; Consultant, Chestertons, Chartered Surveyors, London, since 1980 (Partner, 1936, Senior Partner, 1945–80); *b* 28 Jan. 1913; *s* of Frank and Nora Chesterton; *m* 1944, Violet Ethel Jameson (*d* 2004); two *s* one *d. Educ:* Rugby Sch. Served War of 1939–45, Irish Guards. Director: Woolwich Equitable Building Soc., 1962–86 (Chm., 1976–83); Property Growth Assurance, 1972–85; London Life Assoc., 1975–84; Estates Property Investment Co., 1979–88. Vice-Chm., Council of Royal Free Med. Sch., 1964–77; Crown Estate Comr, 1969–82. Past Pres., Royal Instn of Chartered Surveyors, Hon. Sec., 1972–79; Pres., Commonwealth Assoc. Surveying and Land Economy, 1969–77; first Master, Chartered Surveyors' Co., 1977–78. Governor, Rugby Sch., 1972–88. *Recreations:* golf, fishing, National Hunt racing. *Address:* Hookfield House, Abinger Common, Dorking, Surrey RH5 6JF. *Club:* New Zealand Golf. *Died 14 Oct. 2007.*

CHETWOOD, Sir Clifford (Jack), Kt 1987; FCIOB, FRSH; *b* 2 Nov. 1928; *s* of Stanley Jack Chetwood and Doris May Palmer; *m* 1953, Pamela Phyllis Sherlock; one *s* three *d*. George Wimpey & Co. Ltd, later George Wimpey PLC: Director, 1969; Chm., Bd of Management, 1975–79; a Gp Man. Dir, 1978–82; Chief Exec., 1982–90; Chm., 1984–92; Chairman: Wimpey Construction UK, 1979–83; Wimpey Homes Holdings, 1981–83; Broadgate Properties, 1994–96 (Dir, 1993–94). Pres., Building Employers' Confedn, 1989–92; Chm., Construction ITB, 1990–96. Mem. Council, Imperial Soc. of Knights Bachelor, 1988–95; Trustee: V&A Museum, 1985–97; London Zoological Soc. Develt Trust, 1986–90; Chm. of Trustees, Develt Trust, ICE, 1988–96; Pres., Bldg Industry Youth Trust, 1990–95; Vice-President: C&G, 1992–97; Tennis and Rackets Assoc., 1992–. Master, Guild of Freemen, City of London, 1993–94. FRSA; Hon. FICE 1990; Hon. FCGI 1991. Prince Philip Medal, CGLI, 1987. Man of the Year, Architects and Surveyors Inst., 1989. *Recreations:* Real tennis (Pres., Royal Court Club, 1991–96), lawn tennis. *Address:* The Old Dairy, 9 The Courtyard, Cobham Park, Downside Bridge Road, Cobham, Surrey KT11 3LX. *Died 9 Feb. 2007.*

CHEW, (Victor) Kenneth, TD 1958; Research Fellow of the Science Museum, London, 1977–95; *b* 19 Jan. 1915; *yr s* of Frederick and Edith Chew. *Educ:* Christ's Hospital; Christ Church, Oxford (Scholar). 1st class, Final Honours School of Natural Science (Physics), 1936; BA (Oxon) 1936, MA 1964. Asst Master, King's Sch., Rochester, 1936–38; Winchester Coll., 1938–40. Served War: Royal Signals, 1940–46. Asst Master, Shrewsbury Sch., 1946–48 and 1949–58; Lecturer in Education, Bristol Univ., 1948–49. Entered Science Museum as Asst Keeper, 1958; Deputy Keeper and Sec. to Advisory Council, 1967; Keeper, Dept of Physics, 1970–78. *Publications:* official publications of Science Museum. *Recreations:* hill walking, photography. *Address:* 701 Gilbert House, Barbican, EC2Y 8BD. *Died 7 May 2008.*

CHEYNE, Major Sir Joseph (Lister Watson), 3rd Bt *cr* 1908; OBE 1976; Curator, Keats Shelley Memorial House, Rome, 1976–90; *b* 10 Oct. 1914; *e s* of Sir Joseph Lister Cheyne, 2nd Bt, MC, and Nelita Manfield (*d* 1977), *d* of Andrew Pringle, Borgue; *S* father, 1957; *m* 1st, 1938, Mary Mort (marr. diss. 1955; she *d* 1959), *d* of late Vice-Adm. J. D. Allen, CB; one *s* one *d*; 2nd, 1955, Cicely, *d* of late T. Metcalfe, Padiham, Lancs; two *s* one *d*. *Educ:* Stowe Sch.; Corpus Christi Coll., Cambridge. Major, The Queen's Westminsters (KRRC), 1943; served Africa, 1943–44 (African Star); Italian Campaign. 2nd Sec. (Inf.), British Embassy, Rome, 1968, 1st Sec., 1971, 1st Sec. (Inf.), 1973–76. *Heir: s* Patrick John Lister Cheyne [*b* 2 July 1941; *m* 1968, Helen Louise Trevor, *yr d* of Louis Smith, Southsea; one *s* three *d*] *Address:* The Haa, Gloup, Cullivoe, Yell, Shetland ZE2 9DD. *Club:* Circolo della Caccia (Rome). *Died 16 Feb. 2007.*

CHICHESTER, Sir (Edward) John, 11th Bt *cr* 1641; *b* 14 April 1916; *s* of Comdr Sir Edward George Chichester, 10th Bt, RN, and Phyllis Dorothy, *d* of late Henry F. Compton, Minstead Manor, Hants; *S* father, 1940; *m* 1950, Hon. Mrs Anne Rachel Pearl Moore-Gwyn, JP, *widow* of Capt. Howel Moore-Gwyn, Welsh Guards, and *d* of 2nd Baron Montagu of Beaulieu and late Hon. Mrs Edward Pleydell-Bouverie; two *s* two *d* (and one *d* decd). *Educ:* Radley; RMC Sandhurst. Commissioned RSF, 1936; served throughout War of 1939–45; formerly Capt., Royal Scots Fusiliers and Lieut RNVR. A King's Foreign Service Messenger, 1947–50. Employed by ICI Ltd, 1950–60. Patron of one living. *Heir: s* James Henry Edward Chichester [*b* 15 Oct. 1951; *m* 1990, Anne, *d* of late Major J. W. Chandos-Pole; two *s*]. *Address:* Battramsley Lodge, Boldre, Lymington, Hants SO41 8PT. *Club:* Naval. *Died 14 May 2007.*

CHILD, Christopher Thomas; National President, Bakers' Union, 1968–77; former Consultant to Baking Industry, Industrial Relations Officer and Training Officer, Baking Industry and Health Food Products,

1970–85; *b* 8 Jan. 1920; *s* of late Thomas William and Penelope Child; *m* 1943, Lilian Delaney; two *s* one *d*. *Educ:* Robert Ferguson Sch., Carlisle; Birmingham Coll. of Food and Domestic Science. Apprenticed baker, 1936; gained London City and Guilds final certificates in Breadmaking, Flour Confectionery and Bakery Science, 1951, and became Examiner in these subjects for CGLI. Full-time trade union official in Birmingham, 1958. Member: Birmingham Trades Council Exec., 1958–68; Adv. Council, Midland Regional TUC, 1959–68; Disablement Adv. Cttee, Birmingham, 1959–68. Former Chairman: Nat. Council Baking Education; Nat. Joint Apprenticeship Council for Baking. Mem., Industrial Training Bd, Food, Drink and Tobacco, 1968–78; former Vice-Pres., EEC Food Group and Mem., EEC Cttees on Food Products, Vocational Training, and Food Legislation; former Sec., Jt Bakers' Unions of England, Scotland and Ireland. Mem., TEC C4 programme Cttee, Hotel, Food, Catering and Institutional Management. *Recreations:* fishing, gardening, climbing in English Lake District. *Address:* Moss Cottages, 14 Hodwell, Ashwell, Baldock, Herts SG7 5QG. *T:* (01462) 743454. *Died 12 May 2008.*

CHILTON, Brig. Sir Frederick Oliver, Kt 1969; CBE 1963 (OBE 1957); DSO 1941 and bar 1944; Chairman, Repatriation Commission, Australia, 1958–70; *b* 23 July 1905. *Educ:* Univ. of Sydney (BA, LLB). Solicitor, NSW, 1929. Late AIF; served War of 1939–45, Libya, Greece, New Guinea and Borneo (despatches, DSO and bar); Controller of Joint Intelligence, 1946–48; Asst Sec., Dept of Defence, Australia, 1948–50; Dep. Sec., 1950–58. *Address:* Box 129, Avalon PO, NSW 2107, Australia. *Clubs:* Melbourne, Union, Naval and Military (Melbourne). *Died 1 Oct. 2007.*

CHIONA, Most Rev. James; Archbishop of Blantyre, (RC), 1967–2001; *b* 12 Sept. 1924. *Educ:* Nankhunda Minor Seminary, Malaŵi; Kachebere Major Seminary, Malaŵi. Priest, 1954; Asst Parish Priest, 1954–57; Prof., Nankhunda Minor Seminary, 1957–60; study of Pastoral Sociology, Rome, 1961–62; Asst Parish Priest, 1962–65; Auxiliary Bishop of Blantyre and Titular Bishop of Bacanaria, 1965; Vicar Capitular of Archdiocese of Blantyre, 1967. *Recreation:* music. *Address:* c/o Archdiocese of Blantyre, PO Box 385, Blantyre, Malaŵi. *Died 18 Aug. 2008.*

CHIPP, David Allan; Editor in Chief, Press Association, 1969–86; *b* 6 June 1927; *s* of late Thomas Ford Chipp and Isabel Mary Ballinger; unmarried. *Educ:* Geelong Grammar Sch., Australia; King's Coll., Cambridge (MA). Served with Middlesex Regt, 1944–47; Cambridge, 1947–50. Joined Reuters as Sports Reporter, 1950; Correspondent for Reuters: in SE Asia, 1953–55; in Peking, 1956–58; various managerial positions in Reuters, 1960–68; Editor of Reuters, 1968. Asst News Dir, The Observer, 1985–93; Director: Reuter Foundn, 1986–90; TV-am News Co., 1986–92; Lloyds of London Press, 1990–93; Teletext UK, 1992–2005; Talk Radio UK, 1994–95; Chm., News World, 1994–96. Mem., Press Complaints Commn, 1991–93. *Recreations:* reading, opera. *Address:* 2 Wilton Court, 59/60 Eccleston Square, SW1V 1PH. *T:* (020) 7834 5579. *Clubs:* Garrick, Beefsteak; Leander (Henley-on-Thames); Hawks (Cambridge). *Died 9 Sept. 2008.*

CHITTY, (Margaret) Beryl, (Mrs Henry Fowler), CMG 1977; HM Diplomatic Service, retired; *b* 2 Dec. 1917; *d* of Wilfrid and Eleanor Holdgate; *m* 1st, 1949, Keith Chitty, FRCS (*d* 1958); 2nd, 1989, Henry Fowler, CD (*d* 2007), Kingston, Jamaica. *Educ:* Belvedere Sch. (GPDST), Liverpool; St Hugh's Coll., Oxford (BA, MA; Hon. Fellow, 1982). Dominions Office, 1940; Private Sec. to Parly Under-Sec. of State, 1943–45; Principal, 1945; CRO, 1947–52; First Sec., Commonwealth Office, 1958; Jt Sec., First Commonwealth Educn Conf., 1959; UK Mission to UN, New York, 1968–70; FCO, 1970–71; Dep. (and Acting) British High Comr in Jamaica, 1971–75; Head of Commonwealth Co-ord. Dept, FCO, 1975–77. Appeal Sec., St Hugh's Coll.,

Oxford, 1978–81; Appeal Dir, St Peter's Coll., Oxford, 1982–88. Non-Press Mem., Press Council, 1978–80. Mem., Governing Body, Queen Elizabeth House, Oxford, 1977–80. *Address:* 79 Bainton Road, Oxford OX2 7AG. *T:* (01865) 553384.   *Died 22 Aug. 2009.*

CHOLMONDELEY CLARKE, Marshal Butler; Master of the Supreme Court of Judicature (Chancery Division), 1973–92; *b* 14 July 1919; *s* of Major Cecil Cholmondeley Clarke and Fanny Ethel Carter; *m* 1947, Joan Roberta Stephens (*d* 2004); two *s. Educ:* Aldenham. Admitted a solicitor, 1943; Partner, Burton Yeates & Hart, Solicitors, London, WC2, 1946–72. Pres., City of Westminster Law Soc., 1971–72; Mem. Council, Law Soc., 1966–72; Chm., Family Law Cttee, 1970–72; Chm., Legal Aid Cttee, 1972; Chancery Procedure Cttee, 1968–72. *Publications:* The Supreme Court Practice (Chancery ed.), 1985, 1991, 1993. *Recreations:* reading, genealogy. *Address:* 44 Pelham Court, 145 Fulham Road, SW3 6SH. *Club:* Turf.   *Died 21 Nov. 2007.*

CHRISTIE, Ann Philippa; *see* Pearce, A. P.

CHRISTIE, Sir William, Kt 1975; MBE 1970; JP; Lord Mayor of Belfast, 1972–75; a Company Director; *b* 1 June 1913; *s* of Richard and Ellen Christie, Belfast; *m* 1935, Selina Pattison (*d* 2000); one *s* two *d* (and one *s* decd). *Educ:* Ward Sch., Bangor, Northern Ireland. Belfast City Councillor, 1961; High Sheriff of Belfast, 1964–65; Deputy Lord Mayor, 1969; Alderman, 1973–77. JP Belfast, 1951; DL Belfast, 1977. Freeman, City of London, 1975. Salvation Army Order of Distinguished Auxiliary Service, 1973. *Recreations:* travel, walking, boating, gardening.   *Died 10 Aug. 2008.*

CHRISTIE, William James; Sheriff of Tayside, Central and Fife at Kirkaldy, 1979–97; *b* 1 Nov. 1932; *s* of William David Christie and Mrs Anne Christie; *m* 1957, Maeve Patricia Gallacher; three *s. Educ:* Holy Cross Acad., Edinburgh; Edinburgh Univ. (LLB). Nat. Service, 1954–56; commnd Royal Scots. Private Practice, 1956–79. Mem. Council, Law Soc. of Scotland, 1975–79; President: Soc. of Procurators of Midlothian, 1977–79; Soc. of Solicitors in the Supreme Court, 1979. *Recreations:* music, reading, shooting. *Address:* Woodville Court, 63/6 Canaan Lane, Edinburgh EH10 4SG.
           Died 8 Aug. 2010.

CHRISTOPHER, Colin Alfred; National Secretary, Construction, Furniture, Timber and Allied Section, GMB, 1993–96; *b* 6 Nov. 1932; *s* of Alfred and Ivy Christopher; *m* 1952, Mary (*née* Wells); one *s* one *d. Educ:* Woodland Secondary Modern Sch., Gillingham, Kent. Apprentice upholsterer, furniture industry, 1947–52. Nat. Service, RAOC, 1952–54. Furniture, Timber and Allied Trades Union: Dist Organiser for Kent/Sussex/ Hampshire area, 1968; Nat. Trade Organiser for Soft Furnishing and Bedding Sect., 1978; Gen. Sec., 1986–93. Mem. Bd, FIRA, 1986–; Mem., Exec. Cttee, IFBWW, 1989–. Active Mem., British Labour Party, at Constituency and Nat. Level, 1960–. *Recreations:* gardening, reading, classical music, ballet.
           Died 1 Aug. 2007.

CHRISTOPHERSON, Harald Fairbairn, CMG 1978; Commissioner of Customs and Excise, 1970–80; *b* 12 Jan. 1920; *s* of late Captain Harald and Mrs Laura Christopherson; *m* 1947, Joyce Winifred Emmett (*d* 1979); one *s* two *d. Educ:* Heaton Grammar Sch., Newcastle upon Tyne; King's Coll., Univ. of Durham (BSc and DipEd). Served in RA, 1941–46, Captain 1945. Teacher and lecturer in mathematics, 1947–48. Entered administrative class, Home CS, Customs and Excise, 1948; seconded to Trade and Tariffs Commn, W Indies, 1956–58; Asst Sec., 1959; seconded to Treasury, 1965–66; Under Sec., 1969. Senior Clerk, Committee Office: House of Commons, 1980–85; House of Lords, 1985–86. Mem. Cttee for Southern Region, Nat. Trust, 1986–94. *Recreations:* music, museums and galleries,

books, travel. *Address:* 57a York Road, Sutton, Surrey SM2 6HN. *T:* (020) 8642 2444. *Club:* Reform (Chm., 1998–99).   *Died 21 May 2010.*

CHURCH, James Anthony, (Tony); Dean, National Theatre Conservatory, Denver, USA, 1989–96, then Emeritus; *b* 11 May 1930; *s* of Ronald Frederic and Margaret Fanny Church; *m* 1st, 1958, Margaret Ann Blakeney (marr. diss. 2003); one *s* two *d*; 2nd, 2003, Mary Gladstone. *Educ:* Hurstpierpoint Coll.; Clare Coll., Cambridge. MA 1954. First perf. as professional, Arts Theatre, London, 1953; frequent television, radio, regional theatre perfs; founder mem., RSC, 1960, and Associate Artist, 1960–; roles there include: Henry IV; Polonius (twice); King Lear; John of Gaunt; Friar Laurence; Ulysses; Pandarus; York in Richard II; Trelawney in Maydays; Horsham in Waste; Director of Nuclear Plant in Sarcophagus; Wizard in Wizard of Oz, 1987; Cymbeline, Gonzalo and Antigonus in the late Shakespeares, NT, 1988. Extensive tours of USA, 1974–: King Lear, 1982; Falstaff (Santa Cruz), 1984; Prospero, Shylock (Colorado), 1987; Denver Center Theatre Company: Scrooge, 1990; Malvolio, 1991; Uncertainty, 1992; The Quick Change Room, King Lear, 1995; Sir in The Dresser, 1995; Valley Song, Taking Leave, Travels with my Aunt, Prospero, 1998; First Player and Gravedigger in Hamlet, 2003; Tubal and the Duke, Merchant of Venice, 2004; Give 'em a Bit of Mystery (solo devised performance), 1999, 2000. Recorded 26 Shakespeare roles, 1956–66. Founder dir, Northcott Theatre, Exeter, 1967–71; Dir of Drama, GSMD, 1982–88; Drama Advr, Hong Kong Govt, 1982–85. Member: Arts Council, 1982–85 (Chm., Drama Panel, 1982–85); British Council Drama Cttee, 1985–88. Hon. MA Exeter, 1971; Hon. DHL Denver, 1998. *Recreations:* listening to music, narrowboats, travel. *Address:* c/o The Post Office, Hydra 18040, Greece. *T:* (Greece) (22980) 53652.   *Died 25 March 2008.*

CHURCHILL, Winston Spencer; author; journalist; parliamentarian; *b* 10 Oct. 1940; *s* of late Hon. Randolph Frederick Edward Spencer Churchill, MBE and Hon. Mrs Averell Harriman, US Ambassador to France, 1993–97; *m* 1st, 1964, Mary Caroline, (Minnie) (marr. diss. 1997), *d* of Sir Gerard d'Erlanger, CBE; two *s* two *d*; 2nd, 1997, Luce Engelen. *Educ:* Eton; Christ Church, Oxford (MA). War correspondent in Yemen, Congo and Angola, 1963; Correspondent: Borneo and Vietnam, 1966; Middle East, 1967; Chicago, Czechoslovakia, 1968; Nigeria, Biafra and Middle East, for The Times, 1969–70; Special Correspondent: China, for The Observer, 1972; Portugal, for The Daily Telegraph, 1975. Presenter, This Time of Day, BBC Radio, 1964–65. Lecture tours of the US and Canada, 1965–2005. Contested Gorton Div. of Manchester, Nov. 1967. MP (C) Stretford, 1970–83, Davyhulme, Manchester, 1983–97. PPS to Minister of Housing and Construction, 1970–72, to Minister of State, FCO, 1972–73; Sec., Cons. Foreign and Commonwealth Affairs Cttee, 1973–76; Conservative Party front-bench spokesman on Defence, 1976–78. Member: Select Cttee on Defence, 1983–97; Select Cttee on H of C (Services), 1985–86. Vice-Chm., Cons. Defence Cttee, 1979–83; Cons. Party Co-ordinator for Defence and Multilateral Disarmament, 1982–84; Mem. Exec., 1922 Cttee, 1979–85, Treas., 1987–88. Sponsored Motor Vehicles (Passenger Insce) Act 1972, Crown Proceedings (Armed Forces) Act 1987. Pres., Trafford Park Indust. Council, 1971–97. Member, Council: Consumers' Assoc., 1990–93; British Kidney Patients Assoc., 1990–2004. Founder President: Friends of Airborne Forces, 1996–2004; War Memls Trust (formerly Friends of War Memls), 1997–; UK National Defence Assoc., 2007–; Chairman: Nat. Benevolent Fund for the Aged, 1994– (Trustee, 1974–); Winston Churchill Meml Trust, 2002–09 (Trustee, 1965–); Trustee, Sandy Gall's Afghanistan Appeal, 1995–2009. Governor, English-Speaking Union, 1975–80; Vice-Pres., British Technion Soc., 1976–. Hon. Fellow, Churchill Coll., Cambridge, 1969. Hon. FSE 1989. Hon. LLD Westminster Coll.,

Fulton, Mo, USA, 1972; Hon. DSc Technion, Israel, 1997. *Publications:* First Journey, 1964; Six Day War, 1967; Defending the West, 1981; Memories and Adventures, 1989; His Father's Son, 1996; The Great Republic, 1999; (ed) Never Give In!: the best of Winston Churchill's speeches, 2003. *Recreations:* tennis, sailing, ski-ing, golf, trekking in the Himalayas. *Clubs:* White's, Buck's, Press; Air Squadron; St Moritz Tobogganing; Queenwood Golf (Everglades, USA).
Died 2 March 2010.

CITRINE, 3rd Baron *cr* 1946, of Wembley; **Dr Ronald Eric Citrine,** MRCS, LRCP; *b* 19 May 1919; *yr s* of 1st Baron Citrine, GBE, PC and Doris Helen (*d* 1973), *d* of Edgar Slade; *S* brother, 1997 but does not use the title; *m* 1945, Mary (*d* 1995), *d* of Reginald Williams. *Heir:* none. *Address:* 1 Rosella Place, Maunu, Whangarei, New Zealand. *T:* (9) 4380872.   *Died 5 Aug. 2006 (ext).*

CLANCY, Michael John; HM Diplomatic Service; Governor and Commander-in-Chief, St Helena and Dependencies, 2004–07; *b* 31 March 1949; *s* of William John Clancy and Chrissie Melinda Clancy (*née* Clarke); *m* 1994, Claire Elizabeth Coates; one *s* one *d. Educ:* Lewis Sch., Pengam; Trinity Coll., Cambridge (BA Econs Tripos 1970). Trainee and Private Sec. to Sec. of State, Welsh Office, 1972–81; Principal, Hong Kong Govt, 1981–86; Hd, Personnel Mgt, Welsh Office, 1986–90; Sen. Consultant, Hay Mgt Consultants, 1990–92; Dir for Wales, Dept of Employment, 1992–95; Housing, Welsh Office, 1995–97; Chief Sec., St Helena Govt, 1997–2000; Hd of Investment, Nat. Assembly for Wales, 2001–04. *Recreations:* horse-riding, sailing, hill-walking, cycling. *Address:* c/o Foreign and Commonwealth Office, SW1A 2AH. *Club:* St Helena Yacht.   *Died 23 Feb. 2010.*

CLANWILLIAM, 7th Earl of, *cr* 1776 (Ire.); **John Herbert Meade;** Bt 1703; Viscount Clanwilliam, Baron Gillford 1766; Baron Clanwilliam (UK) 1828; *b* 27 Sept. 1919; 2nd *s* of Adm. Hon. Sir Herbert Meade Fetherstonhaugh, GCVO, CB, DSO (*d* 1964) (3rd *s* of 4th Earl) and Margaret Ishbel Frances (*d* 1977), *d* of Rt. Rev. Hon. Edward Carr Glyn, DD; *S* cousin, 1989; *m* 1956, Maxine (*d* 2004), *o d* of late J. A. Hayden-Scott; one *s* two *d. Educ:* RNC Dartmouth. *Heir: s* Lord Gillford, *b* 28 Dec. 1960. *Address:* Blundells House, Tisbury, Wilts SP3 6JP. *Club:* Turf.
Died 24 Dec. 2009.

CLARE, Prof. Anthony Ward, MD; FRCPsych; FRCPI; Adjunct Professor of Psychiatry, Trinity College, Dublin, since 2001 (Clinical Professor of Psychiatry, 1989–2000); Consultant Psychiatrist: St Patrick's Hospital, Dublin, since 1989 (Medical Director, 1989–2000); St Edmundsbury Hospital, Lucan, since 2000; *b* 24 Dec. 1942; *s* of late Bernard Joseph Clare and Mary Agnes (*née* Dunne); *m* 1966, Jane Carmel Hogan; three *s* four *d. Educ:* Gonzaga Coll., Dublin; University Coll., Dublin. MB, BCh, BAO 1966, MD 1982; MPhil 1972; FRCPsych 1985 (MRCPsych 1973), FRCPI 1983 (MRCPI 1971). Auditor, Literary and Historical Soc., 1963–64. Internship, St Joseph's Hosp., Syracuse, New York, 1967; psychiatric training, St Patrick's Hosp., Dublin, 1967–69; Psychiatric Registrar, Maudsley Hosp., London, 1970–72, Sen. Registrar, 1973–75; research worker, General Practice Research Unit, Inst. of Psychiatry, 1976–79, Sen. Lectr, 1980–82; Prof. and Head of Dept of Psychol Medicine, St Bartholomew's Hosp. Med. Coll., 1983–88. Radio series: In the Psychiatrist's Chair, 1982–2001; All in the Mind, 1988–98; Men in Crisis, 2000; TV series: Motives, 1983; The Enemy Within, 1995. Hon. FRCP 1998. *Publications:* Psychiatry in Dissent, 1976, 2nd edn 1980; (ed with P. Williams) Psychosocial Disorders in General Practice, 1979; (with S. Thompson) Let's Talk About Me, 1981; (ed with R. Corney) Social Work and Primary Health Care, 1982; (ed with M. Lader) Psychiatry and General Practice, 1982; In the Psychiatrist's Chair, 1984, 1992, 1995, 1998; Lovelaw, 1986; (with S. Milligan) Depression and How To Survive It, 1993; On Men: masculinity in crisis, 2000. *Recreations:* literature, cinema,

travel. *Address:* St Patrick's Hospital, PO Box No 136, James's Street, Dublin 8, Ireland. *T:* 6798055; St Edmundsbury Hospital, Lucan, Co. Dublin, Ireland.
Died 28 Oct. 2007.

CLARENDON, 7th Earl of, *cr* 1776; **George Frederick Laurence Hyde Villiers;** Baron Hyde 1756; Managing Director, 1962–93, and Chairman, 1985–93, Seccombe Marshall and Campion plc; *b* 2 Feb. 1933; *o s* of Lord Hyde (*d* 1935) and Hon. Marion Féodorovna Louise Glyn, Lady Hyde (*d* 1970), *er d* of 4th Baron Wolverton; *S* grandfather, 1955; *m* 1974, Jane Diana, DL, *d* of late E. W. Dawson; one *s* one *d.* Page of Honour to King George VI, 1948–49; Lieut RHG, 1951–53. Mem. Ct of Assts, Fishmongers' Co., 1988– (Prime Warden, 1999–2000). *Heir: s* Lord Hyde, *b* 12 Feb. 1976. *Address:* Holywell House, Swanmore, Hants SO32 2QE. *T:* (01489) 896090.   *Died 4 July 2009.*

CLARFELT, Jack Gerald; Chairman, Heathcourt Properties Ltd, since 1987; *b* 7 Feb. 1914; *s* of Barnett Clarfelt and Rene (*née* Frankel); *m* 1948, Baba Fredman; one *s* one *d. Educ:* Grocers' Co. Sch.; Sorbonne. Qualified as Solicitor, 1937; Man. Dir, Home Killed Meat Assoc., 1940–43 and 1945–54; Queen's Royal Surreys, 1943–45; Man. Dir, Fatstock Marketing Corp., 1954–60; Chm., Smithfield & Zwanenberg Gp Ltd, 1960–75; Exec. Dep. Chm., 1975–79, Dir, 1979–83, FMC Ltd. Dir, S. and W. Berisford Ltd, 1973–75; Chm., Linhay Frizzell Insurance Brokers Ltd, 1984–88. Farming, Hampshire. Master, Worshipful Co. of Butchers, 1978. *Recreations:* golf, swimming. *Address:* 76 Hamilton Terrace, NW8 9UL. *T:* (020) 7289 7143. *Club:* Farmers'.   *Died 9 May 2009.*

CLARK, Charles David Lawson; Adviser, Freedom to Publish, Publishers' Association, 2000–02; Legal Adviser: Publishers' Association, 1984–99; Copyright Licensing Agency, 1988–99 (Chairman, 1985–88); General Counsel, International Publishers Copyright Council, 1990–99; Copyright Representative, Federation of European Publishers, 1990–99; *b* 12 June 1933; *s* of Alec Fulton Charles Clark, CB, and of Mary Clark; *m* 1960, Fiona McKenzie Mill; one *s* three *d. Educ:* Edinburgh Acad.; Jesus Coll., Oxford (Exhibnr; MA). Called to the Bar, Inner Temple, 1960. Second Lieut 4th Regt RHA. Editor: Sweet and Maxwell, 1957–60; Penguin Books, 1960–66; Managing Director: Penguin Educn, 1966–72; Allen Lane the Penguin Press, 1967–69; Dir, LWT (Holdings) Ltd, 1982–84. Chairman: Bookrest, 1975–78; Book Marketing Council, 1979–81; Hutchinson Publishing Group, 1972–80 (Man. Dir, 1972); Chief Exec., Hutchinson Ltd, 1980–84. Member: Book Trade Working Party, 1970–72; Brit. Copyright Council, 1976–79 and 1984–99 (Treas. 1987–93); Legal Adv. Bd, EC, 1990–99; Council of Management, Common Law Inst. of Intellectual Property, 1990–94; Council of Management, MIND, the Nat. Assoc. of Mental Health, 1970–79 (Chm. MIND, 1976–79, Vice-Pres., 1980–). *Publications:* (ed) Publishing Agreements, 1980, 5th edn 1997; The Answer to the Machine is in the Machine, and other collected writings, 2005. *Recreations:* music, reading. *Address:* 19 Kennington Palace Court, Sancroft Street, SE11 5UL. *T:* (020) 7582 9971. *Club:* Groucho.
Died 6 Oct. 2006.

CLARK, Michael William, CBE 1977; DL; Deputy Chairman and Deputy Chief Executive, Plessey Co. plc, 1970–87; *b* 7 May 1927; *yr s* of late Sir Allen Clark and late Jocelyn Anina Maria Louise Clark (*née* Emerson Culverhouse); *m* 1st, 1955, Shirley (*née* MacPhadyen) (*d* 1974); two *s* one *d* (and one *d* decd); 2nd, 1985, Virginia, Marchioness Camden. *Educ:* Harrow. 1st Foot Guards, Subaltern, 1945–48. Plessey Co. plc, 1950–87: founded and built Electronics Div., 1951; Main Bd Dir, 1953; Dir, Corporate Planning, 1965, Man. Dir, Telecommunications Gp, 1967; Chief. Exec., Defence Electronics, 1970–87. Member: Electronics EDC, 1975–80; Council, Inst. of Dirs; Nat. Electronics Council; Ct of Univ. of Essex. President: Essex Br., SSAFA, 1988–99; Essex Br., Grenadier Guards Assoc., 1988–99. FIET (CompIEE, 1964); CompIERE, 1965.

FCMI (FBIM 1974). DL Essex, 1988, High Sheriff, 1991–92. *Recreations:* fishing, shooting, forestry. *Address:* Braxted Park, Witham, Essex CM8 3EN. *Clubs:* Boodle's, Pratt's.   *Died 27 July 2010.*

CLARK, His Honour Paul Nicholas Rowntree; a Circuit Judge, 1985–2003; *b* 17 Aug. 1940; *s* of late Henry Rowntree Clark and Gwendoline Victoria Clark; *m* 1st, 1967, Diana Barbara Bishop (marr. diss.); two *s* one *d*; 2nd, 1997, Her Honour Judge Jacqueline Davies. *Educ:* Bristol Grammar Sch.; New Coll., Oxford (Open Schol.; MA (Lit. Hum.)). Called to the Bar, Middle Temple, 1966 (Harmsworth Schol.), Bencher 1982, Reader 2005; in practice on Midland and Oxford (formerly Oxford) Circuit, 1966–85; a Recorder, 1981–85. Pres., Council of HM Circuit Judges, 1998. Chm., Disciplinary Court, Oxford Univ., 2002–04. Chm., Friends of the Ashmolean Mus., 1996–2005. Pres., Old Bristolians' Soc., 1999–2000. *Address:* 2 Harcourt Buildings, Temple, EC4Y 9DB. *T:* (020) 7353 6961. *Club:* Garrick.
                                            Died 6 Oct. 2008.

CLARKE, Prof. Alan Maxwell, CMG 1995; FRACS; Executive Director, New Zealand Spinal Trust, since 1995; *b* 12 Dec. 1932; *s* of John Maxwell Clarke and Daisy Martha Clarke; *m* 1956, Jane Malloch; three *s* one *d*. *Educ:* King's Coll., Auckland; Otago Univ., Dunedin (MB ChB 1956; ChM 1969). FRACS 1961. Otago University: Sen. Lectr in Surgery, 1964–69; Prof. of Surgery, 1970–85; Dean, Christchurch Sch. of Medicine, 1986–93; Dir, Spinal Injuries Unit, Burwood Hosp., Christchurch, 1993–99. James IV Traveller in Surgery, 1970; Nuffield Travelling Fellow, 1963–64. Amer. Cancer Soc. Award, 1968 and 1976. *Publications:* Understanding Cancer, 1982; Cancer Consensus Manual, 1984; numerous papers in learned jls. *Recreations:* art, reading, flying light aeroplanes. *Address:* New Zealand Spinal Trust, Burwood Hospital, Private Bag 4708, Christchurch, New Zealand. *T:* (3) 3839487; *e-mail:* alanc@burwood.org.nz.   *Died 21 Jan. 2007.*

CLARKE, Allen; see Clarke, C. A. A.

CLARKE, Sir Arthur (Charles), Kt 1998; CBE 1989; *b* 16 Dec. 1917; *s* of Charles Wright Clarke and Nora Mary Willis; *m* 1953, Marilyn Mayfield (marr. diss. 1964). *Educ:* Huish's Grammar Sch., Taunton; King's Coll., London (BSc; FKC 1977). FRAS. HM Exchequer and Audit Dept, 1936–41. Served RAF, 1941–46. Instn of Electrical Engineers, 1949–50. Techn. Officer on first GCA radar, 1943; originated communications satellites, 1945. Chm., British Interplanetary Soc., 1946–47, 1950–53. Asst Ed., Science Abstracts, 1949–50. From 1954 engaged on underwater exploration on Gt Barrier Reef of Australia and coast of Sri Lanka (formerly Ceylon). Extensive lecturing, radio and TV in UK and US. Chancellor, Moratuwa Univ., Sri Lanka, 1979–2002; Vikram Sarabhai Prof., Physical Research Lab., Ahmedabad, 1980; Marconi Internat. Fellowship, 1982; Hon. Fellow, AIAA, 1976 (Aero-space Communications Award, 1974). Hon. DSc: Beaver Coll., Pa, 1971; Univ. of Moratuwa, Sri Lanka, 1979; Hon. DLitt: Bath, 1988; Liverpool, 1995; Baptist Univ., Hong Kong, 1996. Freeman of Minehead, 1992. Unesco, Kalinga Prize, 1961; Acad. of Astronautics, 1961; World Acad. of Art and Science, 1962; Stuart Ballantine Medal, Franklin Inst., 1963; Westinghouse-AAAS Science Writing Award, 1969; Nebula Award, Science Fiction Writers of America, 1972, 1974, 1979; John Campbell Award, 1974; Hugo Award, World Science Fiction Convention, 1974, 1980; Vidya Jyothi Medal (Presidential Science Award), 1986; Grand Master, SF Writers of America, 1986; Charles Lindbergh Award, 1987; Lord Perry Award, 1992; von Karman Award, Internat. Acad. of Astronautics, 1996. *Publications: non-fiction:* Interplanetary Flight, 1950; The Exploration of Space, 1951; The Young Traveller in Space, 1954 (publ. in USA as Going into Space); The Coast of Coral, 1956; The Making of a Moon, 1957; The Reefs of Taprobane, 1957; Voice Across the Sea, 1958; The Challenge of the Spaceship, 1960; The Challenge of the Sea, 1960; Profiles of the Future, 1962; Voices from the Sky, 1965; (with

Mike Wilson): Boy Beneath the Sea, 1958; The First Five Fathoms, 1960; Indian Ocean Adventure, 1961; The Treasure of the Great Reef, 1964; Indian Ocean Treasure, 1964; (with R. A. Smith) The Exploration of the Moon, 1954; (with Editors of Life) Man and Space, 1964; (ed) The Coming of the Space Age, 1967; The Promise of Space, 1968; (with the astronauts) First on the Moon, 1970; Report on Planet Three, 1972; (with Chesley Bonestell) Beyond Jupiter, 1973; The View from Serendip, 1977; (with Simon Welfare and John Fairley) Arthur C. Clarke's Mysterious World, 1980 (also TV series); (with Simon Welfare and John Fairley) Arthur C. Clarke's World of Strange Powers, 1984 (also TV series); Ascent to Orbit, 1984; 1984: Spring, 1984; (with Peter Hyams) The Odyssey File, 1985; (with editors of OMNI) Arthur C. Clarke's July 20, 2019, 1986; (with Simon Welfare and John Fairley) Arthur C. Clarke's Chronicles of the Strange and Mysterious, 1987; Astounding Days, 1988; How the World was One, 1992; (with Simon Welfare and John Fairley) Arthur C. Clarke's A–Z of Mysteries, 1993; By Space Possessed, 1993; The Snows of Olympus, 1994; Greetings, Carbon-based Bipeds!, 1999; *fiction:* Prelude to Space, 1951; The Sands of Mars, 1951; Islands in the Sky, 1952; Against the Fall of Night, 1953; Childhood's End, 1953; Expedition to Earth, 1953; Earthlight, 1955; Reach for Tomorrow, 1956; The City and the Stars, 1956; Tales from the White Hart, 1957; The Deep Range, 1957; The Other Side of the Sky, 1958; A Fall of Moondust, 1961; Tales of Ten Worlds, 1962; Dolphin Island, 1963; Glide Path, 1963; (with Stanley Kubrick) novel and screenplay, 2001: A Space Odyssey, 1968; The Lost Worlds of 2001, 1972; The Wind from the Sun, 1972; Rendezvous with Rama, 1973; Imperial Earth, 1975; The Fountains of Paradise, 1979; 2010: Space Odyssey II, 1982 (filmed 1984); The Songs of Distant Earth, 1986; 2061: Odyssey III, 1988; (with Gentry Lee) Cradle, 1988; Rama II, 1989; The Ghost from the Grand Banks, 1990; The Garden of Rama, 1991; (with Gregory Benford) Beyond the Fall of Night, 1991; The Hammer of God, 1993; (with Gentry Lee) Rama Revealed, 1993; (with Mike McQuay) Richter 10, 1996; 3001: The Final Odyssey, 1997; (with Michael Kube-McDowell) The Trigger, 1999; (with Stephen Baxter) The Light of Other Days, 2000; (with Stephen Baxter) Time's Eye, 2004; (with Stephen Baxter) Sunstorm, 2005; *posthumous publication:* (with Stephen Baxter) Firstborn, 2008; *anthologies:* Across the Sea of Stars, 1959; From the Ocean, From the Stars, 1962; Prelude to Mars, 1965; The Nine Billion Names of God, 1967; Of Time and Stars, 1972; The Best of Arthur C. Clarke, 1973; The Sentinel, 1983; A Meeting with Medusa, 1988; Tales from Planet Earth, 1990; More than One Universe, 1991; The Collected Short Stories, 2001; papers in Electronic Engineering, Wireless World, Wireless Engineer, Aeroplane, Jl of British Interplanetary Soc., Astronautics, etc. *Recreations:* diving, table-tennis. *Address:* 25 Barnes Place, Colombo 7, Sri Lanka. *T:* (11) 2699757, (11) 2694255, *Fax:* (11) 2698730; c/o David Higham Associates, 5 Lower John Street, Golden Square, W1R 3PE. *Clubs:* British Sub-Aqua; Colombo Swimming, Otters.   *Died 19 March 2008.*

CLARKE, Sir Chris(topher James), Kt 2005; OBE 2000; business and communications consultant; Chairman, South Gloucestershire Primary Care Trust, since 2006; Managing Director, Word on the Street Ltd, since 2006; *b* 24 March 1941; *s* of Thomas Edward Clarke and Theresa Margaret Clarke (*née* Kiernan); *m* 1st, 1964, Sheila Ann Ridgway (marr. diss. 1995); one *s* one *d*; 2nd, 2006, Elizabeth Boait. *Educ:* Westcliff-on-Sea Grammar Sch.; City of London Coll. Commercial apprentice, 1959–62, mkt res. exec., 1962–65, Rank Orgn; retail merchandise and mktg manager, G. J. Keddie & Sons, 1965–71; retail consultant, then sen. consultant, then gen. manager, C. & J. Clark Ltd, 1971–90; business journalist, then business consultant, later implementation manager: self-employed, 1990–2005; with Improvement and Develt Agency, 2005–. Mem. Council, Arts Council England SW, 2005–. Member (Lib Dem): Richmondshire (N Yorks) DC, 1983–84; Somerset CC,

1985–2005 (Leader, 1993–2001); Mendip DC, 1991–95 (Leader, 1992–93); founder Chm., SW Regl Assembly, 1998–2000. Lib Dem Dep. Leader, 1999–2001, Lib Dem Leader and Dep. Chm., 2001–05, LGA. Member: Inst. Business Counsellors, 1992–; Inst. Journalists, 1991–. FRSA 2006. *Recreations:* cycling, swimming, reading, music, arts. *Address:* Old School House, Tibberton, Glos GL19 3AQ. *T:* (01452) 790369; *e-mail:* chrisclarke001@tesco.net. *Died 15 Dec. 2009.*

CLARKE, (Cyril Alfred) Allen, MA, DLitt; Headmaster, Holland Park Secondary School, 1957–71; *b* 21 Aug. 1910; *s* of late Frederick John Clarke; *m* 1934, Edna Gertrude Francis (*d* 1971); two *s* (and one *s* decd). *Educ:* Langley Sch., Norwich; Culham Coll. of Educn, Oxon; Birkbeck Coll., Univ. of London; King's Coll., Univ. of London. DLitt Knightsbridge Univ., Copenhagen, 1993. Entered London Teaching Service, 1933; Royal Artillery, 1940–46; Staff Officer (Major) in Educn Br. of Mil. Govt of Germany, 1945–46; Asst Master, Haberdashers' Aske's Hatcham Boys' Sch., 1946–51; Headmaster: Isledon Sec Sch., 1951–55; Battersea Co. Sec. Sch., 1955–57. Hon. Gov., Langley Sch., 1994–. *Recreations:* photography, writing, reading, archaeology. *Died 12 July 2007.*

CLARKE, Sir Ellis (Emmanuel Innocent), TC 1969; GCMG 1972 (CMG 1960); Kt 1963 (but did not use the title within Republic of Trinidad and Tobago); President of Trinidad and Tobago, 1976–86 (Governor General and C-in-C, 1973–76); *b* 28 Dec. 1917; *o c* of late Cecil Clarke and Elma Clarke; *m* 1952, Eyrmyntrude (*née* Hagley) (*d* 2002); one *s* one *d*. *Educ:* St Mary's Coll., Trinidad (Jerningham Gold Medal, 1936, and other prizes); London Univ. (LLB 1940). Called to the Bar, Gray's Inn, 1940. Private practice at Bar of Trinidad and Tobago, 1941–54; Solicitor-Gen., Oct. 1954, Dep. Colonial Sec., Dec. 1956; Attorney-Gen., 1957–62; Actg Governor, 1960; Chief Justice designate, 1961; Trinidad and Tobago Perm. Rep. to UN, 1962–66; Ambassador: to United States, 1962–73; to Mexico, 1966–73; Rep. on Council of OAS, 1967–73. Chm. of Bd, British West Indian Airways, 1968–72. KStJ 1973. *Address:* (office) 116 Frederick Street, Port of Spain, Trinidad, West Indies. *T:* 6272150. *Clubs:* Queen's Park Cricket (Port of Spain); Trinidad Turf, Arima Race (Trinidad); Tobago Golf (President, 1969–75). *Died 30 Dec. 2010.*

CLARKE, Frederick, BSc; FBCS; Director: DS Information Systems, since 1991; DS Group Holdings Ltd; *b* 8 Dec. 1928; *s* of George and Edna Clarke; *m* 1955, Doris Thompson (marr. diss. 1987); two *d*; *m* 1988, Dorothy Sugrue. *Educ:* King James I Grammar Sch., Bishop Auckland; King's Coll., Durham Univ. (BSc 1951). FBCS 1972. Served RAF, 1951–54. Schoolmaster, 1954–57; IBM, 1957–82 (final appts, Gen. Manager and Dir); Chm., Royal Ordnance plc (formerly Royal Ordnance Factories), 1982–85. Chm., Lingfield Park Racecourse, 1988–90; Dir, Leisure Investments, 1985–90. Freeman, City of London, 1987. *Recreations:* golf, cricket, racing, reading. *Address:* Arran, Bute Avenue, Petersham, Richmond, Surrey TW10 7AX. *Died 14 May 2007.*

CLARKE, James Samuel, MC 1943 and Bar 1944; Under-Secretary and Principal Assistant Solicitor, Inland Revenue, 1970–81, retired; Managing Director, Bishop and Clarke Ltd, 1981–96; *b* 19 Jan. 1921; *s* of James Henry and Deborah Florence Clarke; *m* 1949, Ilse Cohen; two *d*. *Educ:* Reigate Grammar Sch.; St Catharine's Coll., Cambridge (MA). Army Service, 1941–45: Royal Irish Fusiliers; served 1st Bn N Africa and Italy; Major 1943. Called to Bar, Middle Temple, 1946. Entered Legal Service (Inland Rev.), 1953; Sen. Legal Asst, 1958; Asst Solicitor, 1965. *Recreation:* gardening. *Address:* Dormers, The Downs, Givons Grove, Leatherhead, Surrey KT22 8LH. *T:* (01372) 378254. *Clubs:* National Liberal, Royal Automobile. *Died 2 March 2006.*

CLARKE, Marshal Butler C.; *see* Cholmondeley Clarke.

CLARKE, Prof. Martin Lowther; *b* 2 Oct. 1909; *s* of late Rev. William Kemp Lowther Clarke; *m* 1942, Emilie de Rontenay Moon (*d* 1991), *d* of late Dr R. O. Moon; two *s*. *Educ:* Haileybury Coll.; King's Coll., Cambridge. Asst, Dept of Humanity, Edinburgh Univ., 1933–34; Fellow of King's Coll., Cambridge, 1934–40; Asst Lecturer in Greek and Latin, University Coll., London, 1935–37. Foreign Office, 1940–45. Lecturer, 1946–47, and Reader, 1947–48, in Greek and Latin, University Coll., London; Prof. of Latin, University Coll. of North Wales, 1948–74, Vice-Principal, 1963–65, 1967–74. *Publications:* Richard Porson, 1937; Greek Studies in England, 1700 to 1830, 1945; Rhetoric at Rome, 1953; The Roman Mind, 1956; Classical Education in Britain, 1500–1900, 1959; George Grote, 1962; Bangor Cathedral, 1969; Higher Education in the Ancient World, 1971; Paley, 1974; The Noblest Roman, 1981. *Address:* 61 Ilges Lane, Cholsey, Wallingford OX10 9PA. *T:* (01491) 651389. *Died 29 May 2010.*

CLARKE, Nicholas Campbell, (Nick); Presenter, World at One, BBC Radio Four, since 1994; *b* 9 June 1948; *s* of John Campbell Clarke and Ruth Wilda (*née* McNeile); *m* 1st, 1973, Sue Armstrong (marr. diss. 1990); two *s* one *d* (incl. twin *s* and *d*); 2nd, 1991, Barbara Want; twin *s*. *Educ:* Bradfield Coll., Berks; Fitzwilliam Coll., Cambridge (BA Hons). Yorkshire Evening Post, 1970–72; Reporter and Industrial Corresp., BBC North-West, 1973–79; Reporter, Money Prog., BBC, 1980–85; Political Corresp. and Presenter, Newsnight, BBC, 1986–89; Presenter, World This Weekend, Radio 4, 1989–94. Chm., Round Britain Quiz, Radio 4, 1997–. Pres., Fitzwilliam Soc., 2001–02. Best Individual Contributor to Radio, Voice of the Listener and Viewer, 1999; Radio Broadcaster of the Year, RPG, 2000. *Publications:* Alistair Cooke: The Biography, 1999; The Shadow of a Nation, 2003. *Recreations:* cricket, cooking, wine, worrying. *Address:* c/o BBC News Centre, Wood Lane, W12 7RJ. *T:* (020) 8624 9730. *Club:* Groucho. *Died 23 Nov. 2006.*

CLARKE, Prof. Patricia Hannah, DSc; FRS 1976; Emeritus Professor, University of London, since 1984; *b* 29 July 1919; *d* of David Samuel Green and Daisy Lilian Amy Willoughby; *m* 1940, Michael Clarke (decd); two *s*. *Educ:* Howells Sch., Llandaff; Girton Coll., Cambridge (BA). DSc London. Armament Res. Dept, 1940–44; Wellcome Res. Labs, 1944–47; National Collection of Type Cultures, 1951–53; University College London: Lectr, Dept of Biochemistry, 1953; Reader in Microbial Biochemistry, 1966; Prof. of Microbial Biochemistry, 1974–84; Hon. Fellow, 1995. Leverhulme Emer. Fellow, 1984–87; Hon. Professorial Fellow, UWIST, Univ. of Wales, 1984–90; Kan Tong-Po Prof., Chinese Univ. of Hong Kong, 1986. Chm., Inst. for Biotechnological Studies, 1986–87. Hon. Gen. Sec., Soc. for General Microbiology, 1965–70 (Hon. Mem., 1996); Mem., CNAA, 1973–79. Gov., Cirencester Deer Park Comprehensive Sch., 1988–99. Lectures: Royal Soc. Leeuwenhoek, 1979; Marjory Stephenson, Soc. for Gen. Microbiology, 1981; A. J. Kluyver, Netherlands Soc. for Microbiology, 1981. A Vice-Pres., Royal Soc., 1981–82. Hon. DSc: Kent, 1984; CNAA, 1990. *Publications:* Genetics and Biochemistry of Pseudomonas (ed with M. H. Richmond), 1975; papers on genetics, biochemistry and enzyme evolution in Jl of Gen. Microbiol. and other jls. *Recreations:* walking, gardening, travelling. *Died 28 Jan. 2010.*

CLARKE, Major Sir Peter Cecil, KCVO 1992 (CVO 1969; LVO 1964); Chief Clerk, Duchy of Lancaster, 1969–92; Extra Equerry to HRH Princess Alexandra, the Hon. Lady Ogilvy; *b* 9 Aug. 1927; *s* of late Captain E. D. Clarke, CBE, MC, Binstead, Isle of Wight; *m* 1950, Rosemary Virginia Margaret Harmsworth, *d* of late T. C. Durham, Appomattox, Virginia, USA; one *s* two *d*. *Educ:* Eton; RMA, Sandhurst. 3rd The King's Own Hussars and 14th/20th King's Hussars, 1945–64; Adjt 3rd The King's Own Hussars, GSO2 2 Inf. Div., psc 1959. Seconded as

Asst Private Secretary to HRH Princess Marina, Duchess of Kent, 1961–64; Comptroller, 1964–68; Comptroller to HRH Princess Alexandra, 1964–69. Mem. Court of Assts, Corp. of Sons of the Clergy, 1987–98. JP Hants, 1971–81. *Recreations:* golf, fishing. *Address:* 6 Gordon Place, W8 4JD. *T:* (020) 7937 0356. *Club:* Cavalry and Guards. *Died 6 June 2006.*

CLARKE, Peter James, CBE 1993; Secretary of the Forestry Commission, 1976–94; *b* 16 Jan. 1934; *s* of Stanley Ernest Clarke and Elsie May (*née* Scales); *m* 1966, Roberta Anne, *y d* of Robert and Ada Browne; one *s* one *d. Educ:* Enfield Grammar Sch.; St John's Coll., Cambridge (MA). Exec. Officer, WO, 1952–62 (univ., 1957–60), Higher Exec. Officer, 1962; Sen. Exec. Officer, Forestry Commn, 1967; Principal 1972; Principal, Dept of Energy, 1975. *Recreations:* gardening, walking, travel. *Address:* 5 Murrayfield Gardens, Edinburgh EH12 6DG. *T:* (0131) 337 3145. *Died 15 Aug. 2010.*

CLARKE HALL, Denis; architect; President, Architectural Association, 1958–59; Chairman, Architects Registration Council of the UK, 1963–64; *b* 4 July 1910; *s* of Sir William Clarke Hall and Edna (*née* Waugh); *m* 1936, Mary Garfitt; one *s* two *d. Educ:* Bedales. AA Dip. Own practice, 1937–71. *Address:* Moorhouse, Iping, Midhurst, W Sussex GU29 0PJ. *Died 31 July 2006.*

CLAY, His Honour John Lionel, TD 1961; a Circuit Judge, 1977–88; *b* 31 Jan. 1918; *s* of Lionel Pilleau Clay and Mary Winifred Muriel Clay; *m* 1952, Elizabeth, *d* of Rev. Canon Maurice Ponsonby, MC and Lady Phyllis Ponsonby, OBE, *d* of 1st Earl Buxton, GCMG, PC; one *s* three *d. Educ:* Harrow Sch.; Corpus Christi Coll., Oxford (MA). Served War of 1939–45 (despatches) in 1st Bn Rifle Bde, N Africa (8th Army), Italy, 1941–44; Instr, Infantry Heavy Weapons Sch., 1944–45; 1st Bn Rifle Bde, Germany, 1945–46. London Rifle Bde Rangers (TA); Major (2nd i/c Bn) and 23 SAS (TA), 1948–60. Called to the Bar, Middle Temple, 1947; a Recorder of the Crown Court, 1975–77. Chm., Horserace Betting Levy Appeal Tribunal for England and Wales, 1974–77. Freeman of City of London, 1980; Liveryman, Gardeners' Co., 1980. *Recreation:* gardening. *Address:* Tamarisk, 3 The Hooks, Henfield, West Sussex BN5 9UY. *Died 29 March 2008.*

CLAY, Prof. Dame Marie (Mildred), DBE 1987; FRSNZ; Professor of Education, University of Auckland, New Zealand, 1975–91, then Emeritus, and Head of Department of Education, 1975–78 and 1986–88; *b* 3 Jan. 1926; *d* of Donald Leolin Irwin and Mildred Blanche Irwin (*née* Godier); *m* 1951, Warwick Victor Clay; one *s* one *d. Educ:* Wellington East Girls' College; Wellington Teachers' College; Univ. of New Zealand (MA Hons, DipEd); Univ. of Minnesota; Univ of Auckland (PhD). Teacher Training, 1943–45; Teacher of Retarded Children, 1945; Sen. Scholar in Educn, Univ. of New Zealand, 1946; Asst Psychologist, 1948–50; Fulbright Scholar, Univ. of Minnesota, 1950–51; Teacher, 1953–54; Psychologist, 1955–59; University of Auckland: Univ. Lectr, 1960–67; Sen. Lectr, 1968–72; Associate Prof., 1973–74. Distinguished Vis. Prof., Ohio State Univ., 1984–85; Vis. Fellow, Wolfson Coll., Oxford, 1987–88; George A. Miller Vis. Prof., Univ. of Illinois, 1991; Sen. Fulbright Fellow, Ohio State Univ., 1991; Vis. Prof., Univ. of London, 1991–93; President's Scholar, Texas Woman's Univ., 1994. Pres., Internat. Reading Assoc., 1992–93. FNZPsS 1978; FRSNZ 1994; Hon. FNZEl 1976. Hon. LHD Lesley Coll., Mass., 1994; Hon. DHL: Ohio State Univ., 1998; Texas Woman's Univ., 2003; Hon. DLitt London, 2002; Hon. EdD Purdue, 2002. David H. Russell Award, Nat. Council of Teachers of English, USA, 1979; Internat. Citation of Merit, 1978, William S. Gray Citation of Merit, 1995, Internat. Reading Assoc.; Mackie Medal, ANZAAS, 1983; McKenzie Foundn Award, NZ Assoc. for Res. in Educn, 1993; (jtly) Dana Foundn Award for Educn, 1993; New Zealander of the Year, We Care Foundn, 1994. *Publications:* What Did I

Write, 1975; Reading: the patterning of complex behaviour, 1972, 2nd edn 1979; The Early Detection of Reading Difficulties, 1972, 3rd edn 1985; Children of Parents Who Separate, 1978; (jtly) Reading Begins at Home, 1979; Observing Young Readers, 1982; Round About Twelve, 1983; (jtly) Record of Oral Language, 1983; Writing Begins at Home, 1987; Quadruplets and Higher Multiple Births, 1989; Becoming Literate: the Construction of Inner Control, 1991; An Observation Survey, 1993, 2nd edn 2002; Reading Recovery: guidelines for teachers in training, 1993; (jtly) Instrumento de Observation de los Logros de la Lecto-escritura Inicial, 1994; By Different Paths to Common Outcomes, 1998; Change Over Time in Children's Literacy Development, 2001; Le Sondage d'Observation en Lecture-écriture, 2003; Literacy Lessons Designed for Individuals, 2005. *Died 13 April 2007.*

CLEARY, Jon Stephen; novelist; *b* 22 Nov. 1917; *s* of Matthew Cleary and Ida (*née* Brown); *m* 1946, Constantine Lucas (*d* 2003); one *d* (and one *d* decd). *Educ:* Marist Brothers' Sch., Randwick, NSW. Variety of jobs, 1932–40; served with AIF, 1940–45; freelance writer, 1945–48; journalist with Australian News and Information Bureau: London, 1948–49; New York, 1949–51; subseq. full-time writer. Jt winner, Nat. Radio Play Contest, ABC, 1945; second prize, Sydney Morning Herald Novel Comp., 1946; Australian Lit. Soc. Gold Medal, 1950; regional winner, NY Herald Tribune World Short Story Contest, 1950; First Lifetime Award, Aust. Crime Writers' Soc., 1998. *Publications:* These Small Glories (short stories), 1946; You Can't See Round Corners, 1947 (2nd Prize, Novel Contest, Sydney Morning Herald); The Long Shadow, 1949; Just Let Me Be, 1950 (Crouch Gold Medal for best Australian novel); The Sundowners, 1952; The Climate of Courage, 1953; Justin Bayard, 1955; The Green Helmet, 1957; Back of Sunset, 1959; North from Thursday, 1960; The Country of Marriage, 1962; Forests of the Night, 1963; A Flight of Chariots, 1964; The Fall of an Eagle, 1964; The Pulse of Danger, 1966; The High Commissioner, 1967; The Long Pursuit, 1967; Season of Doubt, 1968; Remember Jack Hoxie, 1969; Helga's Web, 1970; Mask of the Andes, 1971; Man's Estate, 1972; Ransom, 1973; Peter's Pence (Edgar Award for best crime novel; Mystery Writers of America, Best Crime Novel), 1974; The Safe House, 1975; A Sound of Lightning, 1976; High Road to China, 1977; Vortex, 1977; The Beaufort Sisters, 1979; A Very Private War, 1980; The Golden Sabre, 1981; The Faraway Drums, 1981; Spearfield's Daughter, 1982; The Phoenix Tree, 1984; The City of Fading Light, 1985; Dragons at the Party, 1987; Now and Then, Amen, 1988; Babylon South, 1989; Murder Song, 1990; Pride's Harvest, 1991; Dark Summer, 1992; Bleak Spring, 1993; Autumn Maze, 1994; Winter Chill, 1995; Endpeace, 1996; A Different Turf, 1997; Five Ring Circus, 1998; Dilemma, 1999; Bear Pit, 2000; Yesterday's Shadow, 2001; The Easy Sin, 2002; Degrees of Connection, 2003; Miss Amber Regrets, 2004; Morning's Gone, 2006; Four-Cornered Circle, 2007. *Recreation:* reading. *Address:* c/o HarperCollins, 77–85 Fulham Palace Road, W6 8JB. *Died 19 July 2010.*

CLEASBY, Very Rev. (Thomas Wood) Ingram; Dean of Chester, 1978–86, Dean Emeritus, since 1986; *b* 27 March 1920; *s* of T. W. Cleasby, Oakdene, Sedbergh, Yorks, and Jessie Brown Cleasby; *m* 1st, 1956, Olga Elizabeth Vibert Douglas (*d* 1967); one *s* one *d* (and one *d* decd); 2nd, 1970, Monica, *e d* of Rt Rev. O. S. Tomkins; one *d. Educ:* Sedbergh Sch., Yorks; Magdalen Coll., Oxford; Cuddesdon Coll., Oxford. BA, MA (Hons Mod. History) 1947. Commissioned, 1st Bn Border Regt, 1940; served 1st Airborne Div., 1941–45, Actg Major. Ordained, Dio. Wakefield, 1949 (Huddersfield Parish Church). Domestic Chaplain to Archbishop of York, 1952–56; Anglican Chaplain to Univ. of Nottingham, 1956–63; Archdeacon of Chesterfield, 1963–78; Vicar of St Mary and All Saints, Chesterfield, 1963–70; Rector of Morton, Derby, 1970–78. *Recreations:* fell-walking, bird-

watching, gardening, fishing, local history. *Address:* Low Barth, Dent, Cumbria LA10 5SZ. *T:* (01539) 625476.
Died 9 Feb. 2009.

CLEMENT, John Handel, CB 1980; *b* 24 Nov. 1920; *s* of late William and Mary Hannah Clement; *m* 1946, Anita Jones; one *d* (and one *d* decd). *Educ:* Pontardawe Grammar Sch. RAF, 1940–46, Flt Lt (despatches). Welsh Board of Health: Clerical Officer, 1938; Exec. Officer, 1946; Higher Exec. Officer, 1948; Sen. Exec. Officer, 1956; Principal, Welsh Office, Min. of Housing and Local Govt, 1960, Asst Sec., 1966; Private Sec. to Sec. of State for Wales, 1966; Under-Sec., 1971–81, Dir of Industry Dept, 1976–81, Welsh Office. Sec., Council for Wales, 1955–59; Chm., Welsh Planning Bd, 1971–76. Member: Wales Tourist Bd, 1982–88; Midland Bank Adv. Council for Wales, 1985–94. Hon. MA Wales, 1982. *Recreations:* Welsh Rugby, fishing. *Died 24 May 2007.*

CLEMENTS, Julia; *see* Seton, Lady, (Julia).

CLEMENTS, Richard Harry; author and journalist; Director, Citizens Income Trust, 1993–96; *b* 11 Oct. 1928; *s* of Harry and Sonia Clements; *m* 1952, Bridget Mary MacDonald; two *s*. *Educ:* King Alfred Sch., Hampstead; Western High Sch., Washington, DC; Regent Street Polytechnic. Middlesex Independent, 1949; Leicester Mercury, 1951; Editor, Socialist Advance (Labour Party Youth paper), 1953; industrial staff, Daily Herald, 1954; joined Tribune, 1956, Editor, 1961–82; Political Adviser to the Leader of the Opposition, Rt Hon. Michael Foot, 1982–83; Exec. Officer to Leader of the Opposition, Rt Hon. Neil Kinnock, 1983–87. *Publications:* Glory without Power: a study of trade unions, 1959. *Recreation:* woodwork. *Address:* 68 Strafford Road, High Barnet, Herts EN5 4TR.
Died 23 Nov. 2006.

CLEMINSON, Sir James (Arnold Stacey), KBE 1990; Kt 1982; MC 1945; DL; Deputy Chairman, J. H. Fenner plc, 1993–97 (Director, 1989–97); *b* 31 Aug. 1921; *s* of Arnold Russel Cleminson and Florence Stacey; *m* 1950, Helen Juliet Measor; one *s* two *d*. *Educ:* Rugby Sch. Served War, 1940–46, mainly in Parachute Regt. Reckitt & Colman, 1946–86: Chief Exec., 1973–80; Chm., 1977–86; Chairman: Jeyes Hygiene, 1986–89; Riggs A P Bank, 1987–91 (Dir, 1985–2002); Director: Norwich Union, 1979–92 (Vice-Chm., 1981–92); United Biscuits, 1982–89; Eastern Counties Newspaper Gp, 1987–93; Riggs Nat. Bank of Washington, 1991–93; Member: Council, CBI, 1978–86 (Dep. Pres., 1983; Pres., 1984–86); London Cttee, Toronto Dominion Bank, 1982–90; NEDC, 1984–86. Jt Chm., Netherlands British Chamber of Commerce Council, 1978–84; Chairman: Food and Drink Industries Council, 1983–84; Nurses' Independent Pay Review Body, 1986–90; BOTB, 1986–90. President: Endeavour Trng, 1984–98; Arnhem Veterans Club, 2008–; Trustee, Airborne Forces Security Fund, 1972–2006. Chm., Theatre Royal Norwich Trust, 1991–98. Pro-Chancellor, Hull Univ., 1985–94. Hon. LLD Hull, 1985. DL Norfolk, 1983. *Recreations:* field sports, golf. *Address:* 18 Earsham Street, Bungay, Norfolk NR35 1AG. *Club:* Norfolk (Norwich). *Died 14 Sept. 2010.*

CLEVELAND, (James) Harlan; President, World Academy of Art and Science, 1991–2000, then President Emeritus; Professor, 1980–88 and Dean, 1980–87, Hubert H. Humphrey Institute of Public Affairs, University of Minnesota, then Professor Emeritus; *b* 19 Jan. 1918; *s* of Stanley Matthews Cleveland and Marian Phelps (*née* Van Buren); *m* 1941, Lois W. Burton; one *s* two *d*. *Educ:* Phillips Acad., Andover, Mass; Princeton Univ.; Oxford Univ. (Rhodes Scholar). Farm Security Admin, Dept of Agric., 1940–42; Bd of Econ. Warfare (subseq. Foreign Econ. Admin), 1942–44; Exec. Dir Econ. Sect., 1944–45, Actg Vice-Pres., 1945–46, Allied Control Commn, Rome; Mem. US Delegn, UNRRA Council, London, 1945; Dept Chief of Mission, UNRRA Italian Mission, Rome, 1946–47; Dir,

UNRRA China Office, Shanghai, 1947–48; Dir, China Program, Econ. Coop. Admin, Washington, 1948–49; Dept Asst Adminstr, 1949–51; Asst Dir for Europe, Mutual Security Agency, 1952–53; Exec. Editor, The Reporter, NYC, 1953–56, Publisher, 1955–56; Dean, Maxwell Sch. of Citizenship and Pub. Affairs, Syracuse Univ., 1956–61; Asst Sec. for Internat. Orgn Affairs, State Dept, 1961–65; US Ambassador to NATO, 1965–69; Pres., Univ. of Hawaii, 1969–74; Dir, Program in Internat. Affairs, Aspen Inst. for Humanistic Studies, 1974–80. Distinguished Vis. Tom Slick Prof. of World Peace, Univ. of Texas at Austin, 1979. Delegate, Democratic National Convention, 1960. Chairman: Weather Modification Adv. Bd, US Dept of Commerce, 1977–78; Nat. Retiree Volunteer Coalition, 1989–92; Volunteers in Technical Assistance, 1994–96. Holds hon. degrees. Woodrow Wilson Award, Princeton Univ., 1968; Prix de Talloires, Groupe de Talloires, 1981; Elmer Staats Lifetime Public Service Award, Amer. Soc. for Public Admin, 2003. US Medal of Freedom, 1946; foreign orders. *Publications:* Next Step in Asia (jtly), 1949; (ed jtly) The Art of Overseasmanship, 1957, (jtly) The Overseas Americans, 1960; (ed) The Promise of World Tensions, 1961; (ed jtly) The Ethic of Power, 1962; (ed jtly) Ethics and Bigness, 1962; The Obligations of Power, 1966; NATO: the Transatlantic Bargain, 1970; The Future Executive, 1972; China Diary, 1976; The Third Try at World Order, 1977; (jtly) Humangrowth: an essay on growth, values and the quality of life, 1978; (ed) Energy Futures of Developing Countries, 1980; (ed jtly) Bioresources for Development, 1980; (ed) The Management of Sustainable Growth, 1981; The Knowledge Executive, 1985; The Global Commons, 1990; Birth of a New World, 1993; Leadership and the Information Revolution, 1997; Nobody in Charge, 2002. *Address:* 46891 Grissom Street, Sterling, VA 20165, USA. *T:* and *Fax:* (703) 4500428. *Club:* Century (NY).
Died 30 May 2008.

CLEWS, Michael Arthur; Master of the Supreme Court Taxing Office, 1970–87; *b* Caudebec, France, 16 Sept. 1919; *s* of late Roland Trevor Clews and late Marjorie (*née* Baily); *m* 1947, Kathleen Edith, *d* of Adam Hollingworth, OBE, JP; one *s* two *d*. *Educ:* Epworth Coll., Rhyl; Clare Coll., Cambridge (MA). Served in Indian Army (Major, RA and V Force), 1940–46. Solicitor, 1953; Partner, W. H. House & Son, and Knocker & Foskett, Sevenoaks, 1957–70. Mem., Lord Chancellor's Adv. Cttee on Legal Aid, 1977–84. *Address:* Hameau de Coriolan 9, 83120 Plan de la Tour, Var, France. *Died 18 May 2010.*

CLINTON, (Robert) Alan; Director, 1986–95, Managing Director, 1987–95, Picton House Group of Companies, property development cos; *b* 12 July 1931; *s* of John and Leah Clinton; *m* 1956, Valerie Joy Falconer. *Educ:* George Dixon Grammar Sch., Edgbaston, Birmingham; Manchester Business Sch. On leaving school, joined the Post Office, 1948; Member, North Western Postal Board, 1970; Asst Director (Personnel), London, 1975; Asst Director (Operations), London, 1976; Director of Eastern Postal Region, Colchester, 1978; Director of Postal Operations, London, 1979; Member Post Office Board, 1981–85: for Mails Network and Develt, 1981; for Mails Ops and Estates, 1982; for Corporate Services, 1984–85; Man. Dir, Counter Services, 1984–85. Mem. Mgt Cttee, Royal Assoc. in Aid of Deaf People, 1994–97. Pres., Clacton and NE Essex Arts and Literary Soc., 1992–97; Mem. Cttee, St Osyth Historical Soc., 1995–2006. Chm., St Osyth Almshouse Charity, 1995–; Consultant, Hampton Discretionary Trust, 1997–2002. FCILT (FCIT 1982). Mem., Worshipful Company of Carmen, 1981; Freeman of City of London, 1979. *Recreations:* music, walking, cooking. *Address:* Summer Cottage, The Quay, St Osyth, Clacton-on-Sea, Essex CO16 8EZ. *T:* (01255) 820368; *e-mail:* alanclinton@uwclub.net. *Club:* City of London. *Died 14 Jan. 2009.*

CLOKIE, Hilary Ann; *see* Nicolle, H. A.

CLOSE, Roy Edwin, CBE 1973; Director General, British Institute of Management, 1976–85; *b* 11 March 1920; *s* of Bruce Edwin and Minnie Louise Close; *m* 1947, Olive Joan Forty (*d* 2009); two *s. Educ:* Trinity County Sch., N London; MSc Aston 1973. Served Army, 1939–46; RASC; Para Regt; SAS, 1943–46 (Captain). Editorial Staff, The Times; Asst Editor, The Times Review of Industry, 1949–56; Executive, Booker McConnell GP; Dir, Bookers Sugar Estates, 1957–65; Directing Staff, Admin. Staff Coll., Henley, 1965; Industrial Adviser, NEDO, 1966–69; Industrial Dir, NEDO, 1969–73; Chm., Univ. of Aston Management Centre, and Dean of Faculty of Management, 1973–76; Proprietor, Management Adv. Services, 1986–92. Director: Davies and Perfect, 1985–87; Flextech plc, 1985–87; Kepner Tregoe Ltd, 1986–89; Broad Street Group, 1986–91 (Chm., 1986–88); Equity Development Ltd, 1996–2000 (Chm., 1996–99); Equity I (formerly Equity Develt) Ltd, 2000–06. Chm., Open Univ. Mgt Educn Sector Bd, Open Business Sch., 1984–87; Mem., Open Univ. Business Sch. Industrial and Professional Adv. Cttee, 1988–93 (Chm., 1988–90). Chm., Conservation Foundn, 1987–98 (Dir, 1986–98). Mem. Council, Farm-Africa, 1987–92. CCMI (FBIM 1979); FIIM (FIWM 1979); FRSA 1980. DUniv Open, 1987. *Publications:* The Cruellest of Tests (novel), 2005; In Action with the SAS: a soldier's odyssey from Dunkirk to Berlin (war memoirs), 2005; various articles on industrial, economic subjects. *Recreations:* swimming, walking, reading, listening to music. *Address:* Cathedral Cottage, Church Lane, North Elmham, Dereham, Norfolk NR20 5JU. *Clubs:* Reform, Special Forces.
Died 18 April 2010.

CLOTHIER, Sir Cecil (Montacute), KCB 1982; QC 1965; Chairman, Council on Tribunals, 1989–92; *b* 28 Aug. 1919; *s* of Hugh Montacute Clothier, Liverpool; *m* 1st, 1943, Mary Elizabeth (*d* 1984), *o d* of late Ernest Glover Bush; one *s* two *d*; 2nd, 1992, Diana Stevenson (*née* Durrant). *Educ:* Stonyhurst Coll.; Lincoln Coll., Oxford (BCL, MA; Hon. Fellow 1984). Served 1939–46, 51 (Highland) Div.; British Army Staff, Washington, DC; Hon. Lt-Col Royal Signals. Called to Bar, Inner Temple, 1950, Bencher, 1973. Recorder of Blackpool, later of the Crown Court, 1965–78; Judge of Appeal, IoM, 1972–78. A Legal Assessor to Gen. Medical and Gen. Dental Councils, 1972–78; Mem., Royal Commn on NHS, 1976–78; Parly Comr for Admin, and Health Service Comr for England, Wales and Scotland, 1979–84; Chm., Police Complaints Authority, 1985–89; Mem., Sen. (formerly Top) Salaries Rev. Body, 1989–95; Vice-Pres., Interception of Communications Tribunal, 1986–96; Chairman: Cttee on Ethics of Gene Therapy, 1990–92; Inquiry into Deaths in Devonport Hosp., 1972; Allitt Inquiry, 1993–94; Review Body on Police Services in Jersey, 1996–97; Review Panel on Machinery of Govt in Jersey, 1999–2001. Mem., Adv. Council, British Library, 1993–98. Chm., Harefield Res. Foundn, 2001–03. Hon. Life Pres., Magdi Yacoub Inst., 2005. John Snow Meml Lectr (Assoc. of Anaesthetists of GB and Ireland/Amer. Assoc. of Anaesthesiologists), 1981. Hon. Mem., Assoc. of Anaesthetists of GB and Ireland, 1987; Hon. FRPharmS 1990; Hon. FRCP 1998. Rock Carling Fellow, Nuffield Provincial Hosps Trust, 1987. Hon. LLD Hull, 1982. *Address:* 1 Temple Gardens, Temple, EC4Y 9BB. *Died 8 May 2010.*

CLUCAS, Sir Kenneth (Henry), KCB 1976 (CB 1969); Permanent Secretary, Department of Trade, 1979–82; Chairman, Nuffield Foundation Committee of Inquiry into Pharmacy, 1983–86; *b* 18 Nov. 1921; *o s* of late Rev. J. H. Clucas and Ethel Clucas (*née* Sim); *m* 1960, Barbara (*d* 1993), *e d* of late Rear-Adm. R. P. Hunter, USN, Washington; two *d. Educ:* Kingswood Sch.; Emmanuel Coll., Cambridge. Royal Signals, 1941–46 (despatches). Joined Min. of Labour as Asst Principal, 1948; 2nd Sec. (Labour), British Embassy, Cairo, 1950; Principal, HM Treasury, 1952; Min. of Labour, 1954; Private Sec. to Minister, 1960–62; Asst Sec., 1962; Under-Sec., 1966–68; Sec., Nat. Bd for Prices and Incomes, 1968–71; First Civil Service Comr, and Dep. Sec., CSD, 1971–73; Dep. Sec., DTI, 1974; Permanent Sec., Dept of Prices and Consumer Protection, 1974–79. Member: Council on Tribunals, 1983–89; Adv. Panel, Freedom of Information Campaign, 1984–; RIPA Wkg Gp on Politics and the Civil Service, 1985–86; Chairman: Cttee of Inquiry into Advertising Controls, 1986–87; Monitoring Cttee, ABI Code of Practice, 1989–93; FIMBRA, 1993–98 (Mem. Council, 1986–); Dep. Chm., CIBA Foundn Media Resource Steering Cttee, 1984–93; Chm., Lloyd's Wkg Pty on Consumer Guarantees, 1985; Lloyd's Members Ombudsman, 1988–94. Chm., Nat. Assoc. of Citizens' Advice Bureaux, 1984–89 (Vice Chm., 1983–84; Chm. Surrey and W Sussex Area Cttee, 1982–84); Mem. Management Cttee, Godalming CAB, 1982–85; Vice Pres., and Chm. of Trustees, Friends of CAB, 1991–95. FRSA. Hon. FRPharmS, 1989. *Recreations:* walking, theatre, opera, composing and solving puzzles. *Address:* Cariad, Knoll Road, Godalming, Surrey GU7 2EL. *T:* (01483) 416430. *Died 27 Aug. 2010.*

CLUTTERBUCK, Vice-Adm. Sir David Granville, KBE 1968; CB 1965; *b* Gloucester, 25 Jan. 1913; *m* 1937, Rose Mere Vaile, Auckland, NZ; two *d*. Joined RN, 1929. Served War of 1939–45 (despatches twice): navigating officer of cruisers HMS Ajax, 1940–42, HMS Newfoundland, 1942–46 (present Japanese surrender at Tokyo). Subsequently commanded destroyers Sluys and Cadiz, 1952–53; Naval Attaché at British Embassy, Bonn; Capt. (D) of Third Training Squadron in HMS Zest, Londonderry, 1956–58; commanded cruiser HMS Blake, 1960–62; Chief of Staff to C-in-C Home Fleet and C-in-C Allied Forces Eastern Atlantic, 1963–66; Rear-Adm., 1963; Vice-Adm. 1966; Dep. Supreme Allied Comdr. Atlantic, 1966–68. *Died 13 Dec. 2008.*

CLUTTON, Rafe Henry, CBE 1992; FRICS; Partner, Cluttons, Chartered Surveyors, London, 1955–92 (Senior Partner, 1982–92); *b* 13 June 1929; *s* of late Robin John Clutton and Rosalie Muriel (*née* Birch); *m* 1954, Jill Olwyn Evans; four *s* one *d. Educ:* Tonbridge Sch., Kent. FRICS 1959. Director: Legal & General Group PLC (formerly Legal & General Assurance Soc. Ltd), 1972–93; Rodamco (UK) BV (formerly Haslemere Estates), 1990–96. Member: Royal National Theatre Bd, 1976–93; Salvation Army London Adv. Bd, 1971–93; Royal Commn for Exhibn of 1851, 1988–99. Governor, Royal Foundn of Grey Coat Hosp., 1967–2002 (Chm., 1981–2001). *Publications:* Take One Surveyor (autobiog.), 2004. *Recreations:* grandchildren, books, admiring the view. *Address:* Providence Cottage, Church Road, Barcombe, East Sussex BN8 5TP. *T:* (01273) 400763. *Club:* Royal Thames Yacht. *Died 8 Oct. 2010.*

CLWYD, 3rd Baron *cr* 1919; **John Anthony Roberts;** Bt 1908; *b* 2 Jan. 1935; *s* of 2nd Baron Clwyd and Joan de Bois (*d* 1985); *d* of late Charles R. Murray; *S* father, 1987; *m* 1969, Geraldine, *yr d* of Charles Eugene Cannons, Sanderstead; three *s. Educ:* Harrow; Trinity College, Cambridge. Called to the Bar, Gray's Inn, 1970. *Heir: s* Hon. John Murray Roberts, *b* 27 Aug. 1971. *Address:* 24 Salisbury Avenue, Cheam, Sutton, Surrey SM1 2DJ. *Died 10 Oct. 2006.*

CLYDE, Baron *cr* 1996 (Life Peer), of Briglands in Perthshire and Kinross; **James John Clyde;** PC 1996; a Lord of Appeal in Ordinary, 1996–2001; *b* 29 Jan. 1932; *s* of Rt Hon. Lord Clyde; *m* 1963, Ann Clunie Hoblyn; two *s. Educ:* Edinburgh Academy; Corpus Christi Coll., Oxford (BA; Hon. Fellow, 1996); Edinburgh Univ. (LLB). Called to Scottish Bar, 1959; QC (Scot.) 1971; Advocate-Depute, 1973–74. Chancellor to Bishop of Argyll and the Isles, 1972–85; a Judge of the Courts of Appeal of Jersey and Guernsey, 1979–85; a Senator of the College of Justice in Scotland, 1985–96; Justice Oversight Comr, NI, 2003–06. Chairman: Med. Appeal Tribunal, 1974–85; Cttee of Investigation for Scotland on Agricl Mktg, 1984–85; Scottish Valuation Adv. Council, 1987–96 (Mem., 1972–96); Faculty of Advocates' Disciplinary Tribunal, 2004–07; Orkney Children

Inquiry, 1991–92; Children in Scotland, 2003–06. Mem., UK Delegn to CCBE, 1978–84 (Leader, 1981–84). Assessor to Chancellor, 1989–97, Vice-Chm., 1993–96, Court of Edinburgh Univ.; Chm., Europa Inst., Edinburgh Univ., 1990–97; Pres., Scottish Univs Law Inst., 1991–98. Dir, Edinburgh Acad., 1979–88; Trustee: St Mary's Music Sch., 1976–92; Nat. Library of Scotland, 1977–93; Chm. of Govs, St George's Sch. for Girls, 1989–97; Gov., Napier Polytechnic, 1989–93. Chm. Special Trustees, St Mary's Hosp., Paddington, 1997–99; Pres., Dumfries Burns Club, 1996–97. Vice-Pres., Royal Blind Asylum and Sch., 1987–; Pres., SSAFA, Edinburgh & Lothians Br., 2007–. Hon. Pres., Scottish Young Lawyers' Assoc., 1988–97. Hon. Bencher, Middle Temple, 1996. DUniv Heriot-Watt, 1991; Dr *hc* Edinburgh, 1997; Hon. DLitt Napier, 1995. *Publications:* (ed jtly) Armour on Valuation, 3rd edn, 1961, 5th edn, 1985; (jtly) Judicial Review, 2000. *Recreations:* music, gardening. *Address:* House of Lords, SW1A 0PW. *Club:* New (Edinburgh). *Died 6 March 2009.*

COADY, Aubrey William Burleton, CMG 1959; Chairman, Electricity Commission of NSW, 1959–75 (Member, 1950–75); *b* Singleton, NSW, 15 June 1915; *s* of W. A. Coady, Belmont; *m* 1964, Phyllis K., *d* of late G. W. Mathews. *Educ:* Newcastle High Sch.; Sydney Univ. (BA, BEc). Under-Sec. and Comptroller of Accounts, NSW Treasury, 1955–59. *Died Sept. 2006.*

COATES, David Randall, CB 2000; consulting economist; Chairman, North West Economic Forecasting Panel, since 2003; *b* 22 March 1942; *m* Julia Hagedorn (*d* 1995); one *s* one *d*. *Educ:* Leeds Grammar Sch.; Queen's Coll., Oxford; LSE. Res. Assistant, Univ. of Manchester and Manchester Business Sch., 1966–68; Economic Advr, Min. of Technology and DTI, 1968–74; Sen. Economic Advr, Dept of Trade and DTI, 1974–82; Department of Trade and Industry: Asst Sec., 1982–89; Grade 3, 1989; Chief Economic Advr, and Hd of Econs Profession, 1990–2002. *Recreations:* family, gardening, travel, music. *Address:* e-mail: david.r.coates@ btopenworld.com. *Died 10 Oct. 2008.*

COATES, John Francis, OBE 1955; Deputy Director, Ship Design, Ministry of Defence, 1977–79; *b* 30 March 1922; *s* of Joseph Edward Coates and Ada Maria Coates; *m* 1954, Jane Waymouth (*d* 2008); two *s*. *Educ:* Clifton Coll.; Queen's Coll., Oxford (MA 1946). Entered RCNC, 1943; RCDS, 1971; Supt, Naval Construction Res. Estabt, Dunfermline, 1974. Dir, The Trireme Trust, 1985–. Hon. DSc Bath, 1989. *Publications:* (with J. S. Morrison): The Athenian Trireme, 1986, 2nd edn (with N. B. Rankov) 2000; The Age of the Galley, 1995; Greek and Roman Oared Warships, 1996; papers on naval architecture of ancient ships. *Recreation:* nautical research. *Address:* Sabinal, Lucklands Road, Bath BA1 4AU. *T:* (01225) 423696. *Died 10 July 2010.*

COATES, Kenneth Sidney; Special Professor in Continuing Education, University of Nottingham, 1990–2004 (Reader, 1980–89); *b* 16 Sept. 1930; *s* of Eric Arthur Coates and Mary Coates; *m* 1969, Tamara Tura; three *s* three *d* (and one *d* decd). *Educ:* Nottingham Univ. (Mature State Scholar, 1956; BA 1st Cl. Hons Sociology, 1959). Coal miner, Notts Coalfield, 1948–56; student, 1956–60; Asst Tutor, Tutor, and Sen. Tutor in Adult Educn, Univ. of Nottingham, 1960–80. MEP (Lab 1989–98, Ind. Lab 1998–99), Nottingham, 1989–94, Notts N and Chesterfield, 1994–99. Chm., Human Rights Subcttee, 1989–94, Rapporteur, Temp. Cttee on Employment, 1994–95, EP. Member: Bertrand Russell Peace Foundn, 1965–; Inst. of Workers' Control, 1968–; Jt Sec., European Nuclear Disarmament Liaison Cttee, 1981–89. Ed., The Spokesman, 1970–. *Publications:* (with A. J. Topham) Industrial Democracy in Great Britain, 1967, 3rd edn 1976; (with R. L. Silburn) Poverty, the Forgotten Englishmen, 1970, 4th edn 1983; (with A. J. Topham) The New Unionism, 1972, 2nd edn 1974; (with A. J. Topham) Trade Unions in Britain, 1980, 3rd edn 1988; Heresies, 1982; The Most Dangerous Decade, 1984; (with A. J. Topham) Trade Unions and Politics,

1986; Think Globally, Act Locally, 1988; (with A. J. Topham) The Making of the Transport and General Workers' Union, 1991; Clause IV: common ownership and the Labour Party, 1995; The Right to Work, 1995; (with S. Holland) Full Employment for Europe, 1995; (jtly) Dear Commissioner, 1996; (with M. Barratt Brown) The Blair Revelation, 1996; Community Under Attack, 1998; Worker's Control, 2003; Empire No More!, 2004. *Recreations:* walking, reading. *Address:* Russell House, Bulwell Lane, Nottingham NG6 0BT. *T:* (0115) 978 4504. *Died 27 June 2010.*

COATS, Sir William David, Kt 1985; DL; Chairman, Coats Patons PLC, 1981–86 (Deputy Chairman, 1979–81); Deputy Chairman, Clydesdale Bank, 1985–93 (Director, since 1962); *b* 25 July 1924; *s* of Thomas Heywood Coats and Olivia Violet Pitman; *m* 1950, Hon. Elizabeth Lilian Graham MacAndrew; two *s* one *d*. *Educ:* Eton Coll. Entered service of J. & P. Coats Ltd, later Coats Patons PLC, 1948: Director: The Central Agency Ltd (subsid. co.), 1953–55; Coats Patons PLC, 1960–86; Murray Caledonian Trust Co. Ltd, 1961–81; Weir Group Ltd, 1970–83; Murray Investment Trusts, 1986–92. Mem., S of Scotland Electricity Bd, 1972–81. Hon. LLD Strathclyde, 1977. DL Ayr and Arran, 1986. *Recreation:* golf. *Club:* Western (Glasgow). *Died 1 May 2009.*

COBHAM, 11th Viscount *cr* 1718; **John William Leonard Lyttelton;** Bt 1618; Baron Cobham 1718; Lord Lyttelton, Baron of Frankley 1756 (renewed 1794); Baron Westcote (Ire.) 1776; DL; *b* 5 June 1943; *e s* of 10th Viscount Cobham, KG, PC, GCMG, GCVO, TD, and Elizabeth Alison Viscountess Cobham (*d* 1986), *d* of J. R. Makeig-Jones, CBE; *S* father, 1977; *m* 1974, Penelope Ann (Penelope, Viscountess Cobham) (marr. diss. 1995); *m* 1997, Dr Lisa Clayton. *Educ:* Eton; Christ's College, New Zealand; Royal Agricultural College, Cirencester. DL West Midlands, 2000. *Recreations:* golf, cricket. *Heir:* *b* Hon. Christopher Charles Lyttelton [*b* 23 Oct. 1947; *m* 1973, Tessa Mary, *d* of late Col A. G. J. Readman, DSO; one *s* one *d*]. *Address:* Hagley Hall, Hagley, Worcs DY9 9LG. *T:* (01562) 885823. *Club:* MCC. *Died 13 July 2006.*

COBHAM, Sir Michael (John), Kt 1995; CBE 1981; FRAeS; Life President, Cobham plc (formerly Flight Refuelling (Holdings) Ltd, subseq. FR Group plc), (Chief Executive, 1969–92; Chairman, 1969–95); *b* 22 Feb. 1927; *s* of Sir Alan John Cobham, KBE, AFC, and Lady (Gladys) Cobham; *m* 1st, 1954, June Oakes (marr. diss. 1972); 2nd, 1973, Nadine Felicity, *e d* of William Abbott, Wimborne, Dorset; one *d*. *Educ:* Malvern; Trinity Coll., Cambridge (BA 1949, MA 1965). Served RN, 1945–47. Called to the Bar, Inner Temple, 1952; practised, 1952–55. Flight Refuelling Ltd: Dir, 1952; Man. Dir, 1964–77. Pres., 1976–77, Treasurer, 1980–84, SBAC; Mem. Council, Inst. of Dirs, 1976–97. Life Vice-Pres., Air League, 1992 (Chm., 1990–92); Trustee, Fleet Air Arm Museum, 1987–2006. Hon. DEng Bournemouth, 1994; DUniv Southampton, 2001. *Recreations:* ski-ing, sailing. *Address:* The Manor House, Martin, near Fordingbridge, Hants SP6 3LN. *Clubs:* Naval and Military; Royal Thames Yacht; Royal Southern Yacht (Hamble). *Died 13 April 2006.*

COCHRANE, Christopher Duncan; QC 1988; *b* 29 Aug. 1938; *s* of Harold Hubert and Joan Cochrane; *m* 1st, 1960, Caroline Beatrice Carey; two *d*; 2nd, 1970, Patricia Joan Godley; 3rd, 1984, Doreen Ann Suffolk; one step *d*. *Educ:* Ampleforth Coll.; Magdalen Coll., Oxford (Schol.; MA). Called to the Bar, Middle Temple, 1965; a Recorder, 1985. *Recreations:* travel, theatre, spectator sport, dining out. *Address:* 2–3 Gray's Inn Square, Gray's Inn, WC1R 5JH. *T:* (020) 7242 4986. *Died 23 May 2008.*

COCKAYNE, Prof. David John Hugh, DPhil; FRS 1999; Professor of the Physical Examination of Materials, University of Oxford, 2000–09; Fellow, Linacre College, Oxford, 2000–09, then Emeritus; *b* 19 March 1942; *s* of John Henry Cockayne and Ivy Cockayne; *m* 1967, Jean

Mary Kerr; one *s* two *d*. *Educ*: Geelong C of E Grammar Sch., Australia; Trinity Coll., Univ. of Melbourne (BSc 1964; MSc 1966); Magdalen Coll., Oxford (DPhil 1970). Res. Lectr and Jun. Res. Fellow, Christ Church, and Res. Fellow, Dept of Materials, Univ. of Oxford, 1969–74; Dir, Electron Microscope Unit, 1974–2000, Prof. of Physics, 1992–2000, Hon. Prof., 2001–, Univ. of Sydney; Dir, Aust. Key Centre for Microscopy and Microanalysis, 1996–2000. Visiting Research Scientist: Atomic Energy of Canada, 1970; Univ. of Calif at Berkeley, 1979; Royal Soc. Anglo-Australasian Vis. Fellow, Univ. of Oxford, 1982; Hon. Professor: Univ. of Sci. and Tech., Beijing, 2005–; Lanzhou Univ. of Tech., 2006–07; Vis. Prof., Univ. of Paris, 1993. General Secretary: Cttee, Asia Pacific Socs, Electron Microscopy, 1984–96; Internat. Fedn of Socs for Electron Microscopy, 1995–2002 (Pres., 2003–06); Chm., Nat. Cttee, Electron Microscopy, Australian Acad. of Sci., 1986–94. FAIP; FInstP 1999. Massey Medal and Prize, Inst. of Physics and Australian Inst. of Physics, 2008. *Publications*: over 200 scientific articles. *Recreation*: walking. *Address*: Department of Materials, University of Oxford, Parks Road, Oxford OX1 3PH. *Died 22 Dec. 2010.*

COCKE, Dr Thomas Hugh, FSA; Chief Executive, National Association of Decorative and Fine Arts Societies, 2001–06; *b* 19 Feb. 1949; *s* of late J. W. G. Cocke, TD, MA and E. J. Cocke (*née* Ferguson); *m* 1973, Carolyn Marina Clark, *d* of K. W. Clark (MBE 2000); one *s* one *d*. *Educ*: Marlborough Coll.; Pembroke Coll., Cambridge (MA); Courtauld Inst. (MA, PhD 1982). Lectr, History of Art Dept, Univ. of Manchester, 1973–76; Investigator, RCHM for England, 1976–90; Mem., Faculty of Architecture and History of Art, Univ. of Cambridge, 1985–2000; Fellow, Darwin College, Cambridge, 1987–2001; Sec., Council for the Care of Churches, 1990–2001. Mem., Westminster Abbey Fabric Commn, 2000–; Vice-Chm., St Edmundsbury Cathedral Fabric Adv. Council, 2001–; Chairman: Mausolea and Monuments Trust, 2005–; Bury St Edmunds Art Gallery, 2006–. FSA 1983 (Mem. Council, 2001–). Extra Mem. Court, Skinners' Co., 1988–91. *Publications*: Churches of South East Wiltshire, 1987; (with P. Kidson) Salisbury Cathedral: perspectives on the architectural history, 1993; Nine Hundred Years: the restorations of Westminster Abbey, 1995; (ed) The Churchyards Handbook, 4th edn, 2001; contribs to British and European learned jls and exhibn catalogues. *Recreations*: gardening, topography, Italian travel. *Address*: Landguard House, Stonham Aspal, Stowmarket, Suffolk IP14 6AQ. *Died 23 April 2008.*

COCKFIELD, Baron *cr* 1978 (Life Peer), of Dover in the County of Kent; **Francis Arthur Cockfield,** Kt 1973; PC 1982; a Vice-President, Commission of the European Communities, 1985–88; *b* 28 Sept. 1916; 2nd *s* of late Lieut C. F. Cockfield (killed on the Somme in Aug. 1916) and Louisa (*née* James); *m* 1st, 1943, Ruth Francis Simonis (marr. diss.); one *s* one *d*; 2nd, 1970, Aileen Monica Mudie (*d* 1992), choreographer. *Educ*: Dover Grammar Sch.; London Sch. of Economics (LLB, BSc (Econ.)). Called to Bar, Inner Temple, 1942. Home Civil Service, Inland Revenue, 1938; Asst Sec. to Board of Inland Revenue, 1945; Commissioner of Inland Revenue, 1951–52; Dir of Statistics and Intelligence to Board of Inland Revenue, 1945–52; Boots Pure Drug Co. Ltd: Finance Dir, 1953–61; Man. Dir, and Chm. Exec. Management Cttee, 1961–67. Chm., Price Commn, 1973–77. Minister of State, HM Treasury, 1979–82; Sec. of State for Trade and Pres., BoT, 1982–83; Chancellor of the Duchy of Lancaster, 1983–84. Mem., NEDC, 1962–64, 1982–83; Advr on Taxation Policy to Chancellor of Exchequer, 1970–73. Mem., Court of Governors, Univ. of Nottingham, 1963–67. Pres., Royal Statistical Soc., 1968–69. Hon. Fellow, LSE, 1972. Hon. LLD: Fordham Univ., NY, 1989; Sheffield, 1990; Sussex, 2002; DUniv Surrey, 1989. Grand Cross, Order of Leopold II, Belgium, 1990.

Publications: The European Union: creating the single market, 1994. *Address*: House of Lords, SW1A 0PW. *Died 8 Jan. 2007.*

CODRINGTON, John Ernest Fleetwood, CMG 1968; *b* 19 June 1919; *s* of late Stewart Codrington; *m* 1951, Margaret, *d* of late Sir Herbert Hall Hall, KCMG; three *d*. *Educ*: Haileybury; Trinity Coll., Cambridge. Served RNVR, 1940–42: HMS Enchantress, HMS Vanity; Royal Marines, 1942–46: 42 (RM) Commando; Colonial Administrative Service, 1946: Gold Coast (later Ghana), 1947–58; Nyasaland, 1958–64; Financial Sec., Bahamas, 1964–70; Bahamas Comr in London, 1970–73, acting High Comr, 1973–74; Financial Sec., Bermuda, 1974–77. Consultant, FCO, 1991–94. *Recreation*: sailing. *Address*: 2 Bryn Road, St Davids, Pembs SA62 6SG. *Club*: Army and Navy. *Died 7 July 2010.*

CODRINGTON, Sir William (Alexander), 8th Bt *cr* 1721; FNI; Director, World-Wide Shipping Agency Ltd, 1994–97; Port Captain, Hong Kong, for Worldwide Shipping Agency, 1979–97; *b* 5 July 1934; *e s* of Sir William Richard Codrington, 7th Bt, and Joan Kathleen Birelli, *e d* of Percy E. Nicholas, London, NW; *S* father, 1961. *Educ*: St Andrew Coll., *S* Africa; *S* African Naval Coll., General Botha. FNI 1976. Joined Merchant Navy, 1952; joined Union Castle Mail Steamship Co., 1960; Master Mariner's Certificate of Competency, 1961. Joined Worldwide Shipping 1976. Chm., HK Br., Nautical Inst., 1994–97. Mem., Hon. Co. of Master Mariners. *Recreations*: model engineering, sailing. *Heir*: *b* Giles Peter Codrington [*b* 28 Oct. 1943; *m* 1989, Shirley Linda Duke; two *s* one *d*]. *Address*: 206 Westcliffe Apartments, 1 South Wharf Road, W2 1JB. *Club*: Naval. *Died 1 Dec. 2006.*

COHEN, Prof. Gerald Allan, FBA 1985; Chichele Professor of Social and Political Theory, Oxford University, 1985–2008, then Professor Emeritus; Fellow of All Souls College, Oxford, 1985–2008; *b* 14 April 1941; *s* of Morrie Cohen and Bella Lipkin; *m* 1st, 1965, Margaret Florence Pearce (marr. diss. 1996); one *s* two *d*; 2nd, 1999, Michèle Jacottet. *Educ*: Morris Winchevsky Jewish School, Montreal; Strathcona Academy, Montreal; Outremont High School, Montreal; McGill University (BA 1961); New College, Oxford (BPhil 1963). Lectr in Philosophy, University College London, 1963, Reader, 1978–84. Vis. Asst Prof. of Political Science, McGill Univ., 1965; Vis. Associate Prof. of Philosophy, Princeton Univ., 1975; Vis. Prof., McGill Univ., 2000–. *Publications*: Karl Marx's Theory of History: a defence, 1978, expanded edn 2000; History, Labour and Freedom: themes from Marx, 1988; Self-ownership, Freedom and Equality, 1995; If You're An Egalitarian, How Come You're So Rich?, 2000; Rescuing Justice and Equality, 2009; Why Not Socialism, 2009; articles in anthologies, philosophical and social-scientific jls. *Recreations*: Guardian crosswords, the visual arts, patience, travel. *Address*: All Souls College, Oxford OX1 4AL. *T*: (01865) 279379. *Died 5 Aug. 2009.*

COHEN, Laurence Jonathan, FBA 1973; Fellow and Praelector in Philosophy, 1957–90, Senior Tutor, 1985–90, Queen's College, Oxford, then Emeritus Fellow; British Academy Reader in Humanities, Oxford University, 1982–84; *b* 7 May 1923; *s* of Israel and Theresa Cohen; *m* 1953, Gillian Mary Slee; three *s* one *d*. *Educ*: St Paul's Sch., London; Balliol Coll., Oxford (MA 1947; DLitt 1982). Served War: Naval Intell. in UK and SEAC, 1942–45, and Lieut (Sp.) RNVR. Asst in Logic and Metaphysics, Edinburgh Univ., 1947–50; Lectr in Philosophy, St Andrews Univ. at Dundee, 1950–57; Commonwealth Fund Fellow in Logic at Princeton and Harvard Univs, 1952–53. Vis. Lectr, Hebrew Univ. of Jerusalem, 1952; Visiting Professor: Columbia Univ., 1967; Yale Univ., 1972; Northwestern Univ. Law Sch., 1988; Hon. Prof., Northwest Univ., Xian, China, 1987. Vis. Fellow, ANU, 1980. British Acad. Philosophical Lectr, 1975; Fry Lectr, Bristol Univ., 1976; Austin Lectr, UK Assoc. for Legal and Social Philos., 1982. Sec., Internat. Union of History and Philosophy of Science

(Div. of Logic, Methodology and Philosophy of Science), 1975–83, Pres., 1987–91; Pres., British Soc. for Philosophy of Science, 1977–79; Chairman: British Nat. Cttee for Logic, Methodology and Philosophy of Science, 1987–91; Section K (Phil.), British Acad., 1994–96; Sec.-Gen., ICSU, 1993–96; Member: Comité Directeur, Fédn Internat. des Socs de Philosophie, 1983–91; Nat. Cttee for Philosophy, 1993–. Governor: Bartholomew Sch., Eynsham, 1989–93; Wood Green Sch., Witney, 1990–93. General Editor, Clarendon Library of Logic and Philosophy, 1973–. *Publications*: The Principles of World Citizenship, 1954; The Diversity of Meaning, 1962; The Implications of Induction, 1970; The Probable and the Provable, 1977; (ed jtly) Applications of Inductive Logic, 1980; (ed jtly) Logic, Methodology and Philosophy of Science, 1982; The Dialogue of Reason, 1986; An Introduction to the Philosophy of Induction and Probability, 1989; An Essay on Belief and Acceptance, 1992; Knowledge and Language, 2002; articles in academic jls. *Recreations*: gardening; work for Campaign to Protect Rural England. *Address*: Queen's College, Oxford OX1 4AW. *Died 26 Sept. 2006.*

COHEN, Hon. Leonard Harold Lionel, OBE 1995; barrister-at-law; *b* 1 Jan. 1922; *s* of Rt Hon. Lord Cohen, PC (Life Peer), and Adelaide, Lady Cohen (*née* Spielmann); *m* 1949, Eleanor Lucy Quixano Henriques; two *s* one *d*. *Educ*: Eton Coll.; New Coll., Oxford (MA). War Service, Rifle Bde (wounded), Captain, 1941–45. Called to Bar, Lincoln's Inn, 1948, Bencher, 1989; practised at Chancery Bar, 1949–61. Chm., Secure Retirement PLC, 1987–92; Dir, M. Samuel & Co. Ltd (subseq. Hill Samuel & Co. Ltd), 1961–76. Dir-Gen., Accepting Houses Cttee, 1976–82; Chairman: United Services Trustee, 1976–82; Council, Royal Free Hosp. Med. Sch., 1982–92; Community Trust for Berkshire, 1988–93; Pres., Jewish Colonization Assoc., 1976–92. Master of the Skinners' Co., 1971–72. Hon. Col, 39th (City of London) Signal Regt (V), 1973–78. High Sheriff of Berks, 1987–88. *Recreation*: reading. *Address*: Dovecote House, Swallowfield Park, Reading RG7 1TG. *T*: (0118) 988 4775. *Club*: White's. *Died 25 Dec. 2007.*

COHN, Prof. Norman, DLitt; FBA 1978; FRHistS; Astor-Wolfson Professor of History, University of Sussex, 1973–80, then Professor Emeritus; *b* London, 12 Jan. 1915; *yr s* of August Cohn and Daisy (*née* Reimer); *m* 1st, 1941, Vera Broido (*d* 2004); one *s*; 2nd, 2004, Marina Voikhanskaya. *Educ*: Gresham's Sch.; Christ Church, Oxford (Scholar; 1st Class Hons, Sch. of Medieval and Mod. Languages, 1936; MA); DLitt Glasgow, 1957. Served War of 1939–45, Queen's Royal Regt and Intell. Corps. Lectr in French, Glasgow Univ., 1946–51; Professor of French: Magee UC (then associated with TCD), 1951–60; King's Coll., Durham Univ., 1960–63; changed career to become Dir, Columbus Centre, Sussex Univ. and Gen. Editor, Columbus Centre's Studies in the Dynamics of Persecution and Extermination, 1966–73. Professorial Fellow, Sussex Univ., 1966–73; advr on comparative study of genocide, Concordia Univ., Montreal, 1982–85; advr, Montreal Inst. for Genocide Studies, 1985–; Vis. Prof., KCL, 1986–89. Hugh Le May Fellow, Rhodes Univ., 1950; Fellow, Center for Advanced Study in the Behavioral Sciences, Stanford, Calif, 1966; Vis. Fellow, Center for Humanities, Wesleyan Univ., Conn, 1971; Fellow, Netherlands Inst. for Advanced Study, 1975–76; Canadian SSHRC Vis. Fellow, 1982, Canadian Commonwealth Vis. Fellow, 1983. Hon. LLD Concordia Univ., 1985. *Publications*: Gold Khan and other Siberian legends, 1946; The Pursuit of the Millennium: revolutionary millenarians and mystical anarchists of the middle ages, 1957, 4th edn 1993 (trans. German, French, Spanish, Portuguese, Italian, Norwegian, Greek, Polish, Hebrew, Dutch and Japanese); Warrant for Genocide: the myth of the Jewish world-conspiracy and the Protocols of the Elders of Zion, 1967, 3rd edn 1996 (Anisfield-Wolf Award in Race Relations, 1967) (trans. German, French, Spanish, Portuguese, Italian, Russian, Serbian, Hebrew and Japanese); Europe's Inner Demons: the demonization of

Christians in medieval Christendom, 1975, 3rd edn 1993 (trans. French, Spanish, Portuguese, Hungarian, Romanian, Norwegian and Japanese); Cosmos, Chaos and the World to Come: the ancient roots of apocalyptic faith, 1993 (trans. German, Spanish, Portuguese, French, Polish and Japanese), 2nd edn 2001; Noah's Flood: the Genesis story in western thought, 1996 (trans. Japanese); contributor to various symposia, learned jls, and reviews. *Recreations*: walking, looking at pictures, butterfly-watching. *Address*: 20 Garden Walk, Cambridge CB4 3EN. *T*: (01223) 367747. *Club*: Athenæum. *Died 31 July 2007.*

COHN, Prof. Paul Moritz, FRS 1980; Emeritus Professor of Mathematics, University of London, and Hon. Research Fellow in Mathematics, University College London, since 1989; *b* Hamburg, 8 Jan. 1924; *o c* of late James Cohn and late Julia Cohn (*née* Cohen); *m* 1958, Deirdre Sonia Sharon; two *d*. *Educ*: Trinity Coll., Cambridge. BA 1948, MA, PhD 1951. Chargé de Recherches, Univ. de Nancy, 1951–52; Lectr, Manchester Univ., 1952–62; Reader, London Univ., at Queen Mary Coll., 1962–67; Prof. of Maths, London Univ. at Bedford Coll., 1967–84, at UCL, 1984–86; Astor Prof. of Maths, UCL, 1986–89. Visiting Professor: Yale Univ., 1961–62; Univ. of California (Berkeley), 1962; Univ. of Chicago, 1964; State Univ. of New York (Stony Brook), 1967; Rutgers Univ., 1967–68; Univ. of Paris, 1969; Tulane Univ., 1971; Indian Inst. of Technology, Delhi, 1971; Univ. of Alberta, 1972, 1986; Carleton Univ., Ottawa, 1973; Technion, Haifa, 1975; Iowa State Univ., 1978; Univ. of Bielefeld, 1979; Bar Ilan Univ., Ramat Gan, 1987; Univ. of Hamburg, 1992. Member: Mathematics Cttee, SRC, 1977–80; Council, Royal Soc., 1985–87; IMU Rep., Royal Soc. Internat. Relns Cttee, 1990–93; London Mathematical Society: Sec., 1965–67; Mem. Council, 1968–71, 1972–75, 1979–84; Pres., 1982–84; Editor, London Math. Soc. Monographs, 1968–77, 1980–93. Lester R. Ford Award (Mathematical Assoc. of America), 1972; Senior Berwick Prize, London Mathematical Soc., 1974. *Publications*: Lie Groups, 1957; Linear Equations, 1958; Solid Geometry, 1961; Universal Algebra, 1965, 2nd edn 1981 (trans foreign langs); Free Rings and their Relations, 1971, 2nd edn 1985; Algebra, vol. I, 1974, 2nd edn 1982, vol. II, 1977, 2nd edn 1989, vol. III, 1990; Skew Field Constructions, 1977; Algebraic Numbers and Algebraic Functions, 1991; Elements of Linear Algebra, 1994; Skew Fields, vol. 57 of Encyclopedia of Mathematics and its Applications, 1995; An Introduction to Ring Theory, 2000; Classic Algebra, 2000; Basic Algebra, 2002; Further Algebra and Applications, 2003; Free Ideal Rings and Localization in General Rings, 2006; contribs to Encyclopedia Britannica, Oxford DNB; papers on algebra in various mathematical periodicals. *Recreations*: linguistics, etymology. *Address*: Department of Mathematics, University College London, Gower Street, WC1E 6BT. *T*: (020) 7679 4459. *Died 20 April 2006.*

COLDSTREAM, Prof. John Nicolas, FSA; FBA 1977; Yates Professor of Classical Art and Archaeology, 1983–92, then Emeritus, Hon. Fellow, 1993, University College London; *b* 30 March 1927; *s* of Sir John Coldstream and Phyllis Mary Hambly; *m* 1970, Imogen Nicola Carr. *Educ*: Eton; King's College, Cambridge (Class. Tripos, BA 1951, MA 1956). FSA 1964. Nat. Service, Buffs and HLI (Egypt and Palestine), 1945–48. Asst Master, Shrewsbury Sch., 1952–56; Temp. Asst Keeper, Dept of Greek and Roman Antiquities, BM, 1956–57; Macmillan Student, British Sch. at Athens, 1957–60; Bedford College, London: Lectr, 1960–66; Reader, 1966–75; Prof. of Aegean Archaeology, 1975–83. Geddes-Harrower Vis. Prof. of Classical Archaeology, Univ. of Aberdeen, 1983; Vis. Prof., Australian Archaeol Inst., Athens, 1989; T. B. L. Webster Meml Vis. Prof., Stanford Univ., Calif, 1990; Vis. Prof., Univ. of Athens, 1992. Mem., 1966–, Chm., 1987–91, Managing Cttee, British Sch. at Athens. Chm., Nat. Organizing Cttee, XI Internat. Congress of Classical

Archaeol., London, 1978. Member: European Acad. of Scis and Arts, Salzburg, 1991; Deutsches Archäologisches Inst., 1978; Corresponding Member: Nordrhein-Westfälische (formerly Rheinisch-Westfälische) Akademie der Wissenschaften, 1984; Acad. of Athens, 1993; Hon. Mem., Archaeol Inst. of America, 1994. Hon. Fellow, Archaiologikē Hetaireia Athenōn, 1987. Sir F. Kenyon Medal for Classical Studies, British Acad., 2003. Editor, Annual of the British School at Athens, 1968–73. *Publications:* Greek Geometric Pottery, 1968, 2nd edn 2008; (with G. L. Huxley) Kythera: Excavations and Studies, 1972; Knossos: The Sanctuary of Demeter, 1973; Geometric Greece, 1977, 2nd edn, 2003; (with H. W. Catling) Knossos, the North Cemetery: early Greek tombs, 4 vols, 1996; (jtly) Knossos, Pottery Handbook II: Greek and Roman, 2001; articles in British and foreign classical and archaeological journals. *Recreations:* music, travel. *Address:* 180 Ebury Street, SW1W 8UP. *Died 21 March 2008.*

COLEMAN, Bernard, CMG 1986; HM Diplomatic Service, retired; Ambassador to Paraguay, 1984–86; *b* 3 Sept. 1928; *s* of William Coleman and Ettie Coleman; *m* 1st, 1950, Sonia Dinah Walters (*d* 1995); two *d*; 2nd, 1996, Georgina Edith Dorndorf; three step *d*. *Educ:* Alsop High Sch., Liverpool. HM Forces (RAEC), 1946–48. Entered Foreign (later Diplomatic) Service, 1950; FO, 1950–53; Lima, 1953–56; Detroit, 1956–59; Second Secretary (Information): Montevideo, 1959–62; Caracas, 1962–64; First Sec. (Inf.), Caracas, 1964–66; FCO, 1967–69; First Sec. (Inf.), Ottawa, 1969–73; FCO, 1973–74; seconded to DTI, 1974–75; Consul-Gen., Bilbao, 1976–78; First Sec. (Commercial), Dublin, 1979–80; High Commissioner, Tonga, 1980–83. *Recreations:* golf, bowls, bridge, reading, walking, travel. *Died 28 Jan. 2009.*

COLEMAN, Ronald Frederick, CB 1991; DSc; CChem, FRSC; consultant in technology management, since 1992; Chief Engineer and Scientist, Department of Trade and Industry, 1987–92; *b* 10 Nov. 1931; *s* of late Frederick George Coleman and Dorothy Alice Coleman (*née* Smith); *m* 1954, Maureen Mary Salt; one *s* one *d*. *Educ:* King Edward VI Sch., Birmingham; College of Technology, Birmingham (BSc, DSc). Chance Brothers Glassworks, Smethwick, 1949–54; UKAEA: Aldermaston, 1954–71; Harwell, 1972; Laboratory of the Government Chemist, 1973–77; National Physical Laboratory, 1977–81; Government Chemist, 1981–87. Dir, Beard Dove Ltd, 1994–95. Visiting Professor: Kingston Polytechnic, 1981–91; Royal Holloway and Bedford New Coll., 1985–92. Pres., British Acad. of Forensic Sciences, 1982–83. Member: SERC, 1987–92; AFRC, 1987–92. Pres., BioIndustry Assoc., 1992–96. Chm., Bd of Govs, Kingston Univ. (formerly Polytechnic), 1991–95. DUniv Surrey, 1987; Hon. DSc: Poly. of Central London, 1989; Cranfield Inst. of Technology, 1992. *Publications:* various papers on analytical chemistry, nuclear chemistry and forensic science. *Recreations:* music, golf, gardening. *Address:* Lime Cottage, Thames Street, Sonning on Thames, Berks RG4 6UR. *T:* (0118) 969 9837. *Died 30 Dec. 2006.*

COLGRAIN, 3rd Baron *cr* 1946, of Everlands; **David Colin Campbell;** *b* 24 April 1920; *s* of 2nd Baron Colgrain, MC, and of Margaret Emily (*d* 1989), *d* of late P. W. Carver; *S* father, 1973; *m* 1st, 1945, Veronica Margaret (marr. diss. 1964), *d* of late Lt-Col William Leckie Webster, RAMC; one *s* one *d*; 2nd, 1973, Mrs Sheila M. Hudson. *Educ:* Eton; Trinity Coll., Cambridge. Served War of 1939–45, 9th Lancers. Manager, Grindlays Bank Ltd, India and Pakistan, 1945–49; joined Antony Gibbs and Sons Ltd, 1949, Director, 1954–83, retired. *Heir: s* Hon. Alastair Colin Leckie Campbell [*b* 16 Sept. 1951; *m* 1979, Annabel Rose, *yr d* of Hon. Robin Warrender; two *s*]. *Address:* Bushes Farm, Weald, Sevenoaks, Kent TN14 6ND. *Died 7 Feb. 2008.*

COLLARD, Douglas Reginald, OBE 1976; HM Diplomatic Service, retired; *b* 7 April 1916; *s* of late Hebert Carthew Collard and late Mary Ann (*née* Pugh); *m*

1947, Eleni Alkmini Kiortsi (marr. diss. 1969); two *s* three *d*. *Educ:* Wallasey Grammar Sch.; privately. Army Service, 1940–46 (despatches); UNRRA, Greece, 1946–47; Asst Commercial Adviser, British Econ. Mission to Greece, 1947; Consul, Patras, Greece, 1947–52; Beirut, 1952–54; Khartoum, 1954–56; Copenhagen, 1958–61; Tripoli, 1961–65; Lahore, 1965–67; Montevideo, 1969–71; Algiers, 1971–73; Consul-Gen., Bilbao, 1973–76. Director: Anglo-Arab Assoc., 1976–90; Arab British Centre, 1981–90. *Recreations:* reading, meditation, good company. *Address:* Henry Nihill House, 94 Priory Field Drive, Edgware, Middlesex HA8 9PU. *Died 22 Oct. 2007.*

COLLIER-WRIGHT, John Hurrell, CBE 1966; Member, British Transport Docks Board, 1974–77; *b* 1 April 1915; *s* of John Robert Collier Collier-Wright and Phyllis Hurrell Walters; *m* 1940, Pauline Beatrice Platts (*d* 2003); three *s* (and one *s* decd). *Educ:* Bradfield Coll.; Queen's Coll., Oxford (MA). FCIT. Traffic Apprentice, LNER, 1936–39. Served War of 1939–45, RE, France, Iraq and Iran (Lt-Col; US Legion of Merit). East African Railways and Harbours, 1946–64; Chief Commercial Supt; joined British Transport Docks Bd, 1964; Chief Commercial Man., 1964–70; Asst Man. Dir, 1970–72; Dep. Man. Dir, 1972–77; Dir, British Transport Advertising, 1966–81. *Address:* 62 Marygate, York YO3 7BH. *Club:* Nairobi (Kenya). *Died 29 Oct. 2006.*

COLLIN, Maj.-Gen. Geoffrey de Egglesfield, CB 1975; MC 1944; DL; *b* 18 July 1921; *s* of late Peter Charles de Egglesfield Collin and Catherine Mary Collin; *m* 1949, Angela Stella (*née* Young); one *s* three *d*. *Educ:* Wellington Coll., Berks. Served War of 1939–45: commissioned as 2nd Lt, RA, 1941; in India and Burma, 1942–45. Qualified as Army Pilot, 1946; attended Staff Coll., Camberley, 1951; Instructor at RMA, Sandhurst, 1954–56; served Kenya, 1956–58; JSSC, 1958; Instructor at Staff Coll., Camberley, 1960–62; comd 50 Missile Regt, RA, 1962–64; GSO 1 Sch. of Artillery, 1965; CRA, 4th Div., 1966–67; attended Imperial Defence College, London, 1968; Comdt, Royal School of Artillery, 1969–71; Maj.-Gen. RA, HQ BAOR, 1971–73; GOC North East District, York, 1973–76; retired 1976. Col Comdt, RA, 1976–83 (Rep. Col Comdt, 1982). Chairman: CS Selection Bd, 1981–91 (Mem., 1978); Retired Officer Selection Bd, 1979–2001. Hon. Dir, Great Yorks Show, 1976–87; Pres., Yorks Agricl Soc., 1988–89. Guide, Ripon Cathedral, 1981–. DL N Yorks, 1977. *Recreations:* fishing, ornithology, music, keeping gun dog and garden under control. *Address:* c/o Lloyds TSB, 8 Cambridge Crescent, Harrogate HG1 1PQ. *Club:* Army and Navy. *Died 14 Feb. 2009.*

COLLINGS, Very Rev. Neil; Dean of St Edmundsbury, 2006–09, then Dean Emeritus; *b* 26 Aug. 1946; *s* of James Philip Sanford Collings and Edith Lilian Collings (*née* Neill). *Educ:* Torquay Grammar Sch.; King's Coll. London (BD, AKC); St Augustine's Coll., Canterbury. Ordained deacon, 1970, priest 1971; Curate, 1970–72; Team Vicar, 1972–74; Littleham cum Exmouth; Chaplain, Westminster Abbey, 1974–79; Dir of Ordinands and Post-ordination Trng, Dio. Hereford, and Preb., Hereford Cathedral, 1979–86; Chaplain to the Bishop of Hereford, 1982–86; Rector: St Nicholas, Hereford, 1979–86; St Nicholas, Harpenden, 1986–99; Hon. Canon, St Alban's Cathedral, 1996–99; Canon Residentiary and Treas., Exeter Cathedral, 1999–2006. Chaplain, Devon and Cornwall Constabulary, 1999–2006. *Publications:* Young Person's Guide to Westminster Abbey, 1979. *Recreations:* swimming, cats, Queen Victoria, 'The Archers', travel. *Club:* National. *Died 26 June 2010.*

COLLINGWOOD, John Gildas, FREng, FIChemE; Director: Unilever Ltd, 1965–77; Unilever NV, 1965–77; Head of Research Division of Unilever Ltd, 1961–77; *b* 15 June 1917; *s* of Stanley Ernest Collingwood and Kathleen Muriel (*née* Smalley); *m* 1942, Pauline Winifred Jones (*d* 1998); one *s* one *d*. *Educ:*

Wycliffe Coll., Stonehouse, Glos; University Coll. London (BSc; Fellow, 1970). English Charcoal, 1940–41; British Ropeway Engrg Co., 1941–44; De Havilland Engines, 1944–46; Olympia Oil and Cake Mills Ltd, 1946–49; British Oil and Cake Mills Ltd, 1949–51; Mem., UK Milling Group of Unilever Ltd, 1951–60; Dir, Advita Ltd, 1951–60; Dir, British Oil & Cake Mills Ltd, 1955–60. Mem. Research Cttee, 1963–68, Mem. Council, 1964–67, IChemE. Member: Council, Univ. of Aston, 1971–83 (Chm., Academic Advisory Cttee, 1964–71); Research Cttee, CBI, 1970–71; Council for Scientific Policy, 1971–72; Exec. Cttee, British Nutrition Foundn, 1978–82 (Council, 1970–85); Food Standards Cttee, 1972–80; Royal Commn on Environmental Pollution, 1973–79; Standing Commn on Energy and the Environment, 1978–81. A Gen. Sec., BAAS, 1978–83, 1986–88. Vice Pres., Nat. Children's Home, 1989– (Chm., F and GP Cttee, 1983–89); Pres., Wycliffe Coll., Stonehouse, Glos, 1997–2006 (Mem. Council, 1967–2006; Chm., 1985–89; Vice-Pres., 1989–97). Hon. DSc Aston, 1966. *Recreations:* sailing, music. *Address:* 54 Downs Road, Coulsdon, Surrey CR5 1AA. *T:* (01737) 554817. *Club:* Athenæum. *Died 24 July 2010.*

COLLINS, Basil Eugene Sinclair, CBE 1983; Chairman, Nabisco Group, 1984–89; *b* 21 Dec. 1923; *s* of Albert Collins and Pauline Alicia (*née* Wright); *m* 1942, Doris Slott (*d* 2004); two *d*. *Educ:* Great Yarmouth Grammar School. Sales Manager, L. Rose & Co. Ltd, 1945; Export Dir, Schweppes (Overseas) Ltd, 1958; Group Admin. Dir, Schweppes Ltd, 1964, Chm. of Overseas Gp 1968; Chm. of Overseas Gp, Cadbury Schweppes Ltd, 1969, Dep. Man. Dir 1972, Man. Dir 1974, Dep. Chm. and Group Chief Exec., Cadbury Schweppes plc, 1980–83; Director: Thomas Cook Gp, 1980–85; British Airways Bd, 1982–88; Royal Mint, 1984–88. Royal College of Nursing: Chm., Finance and General Purposes Cttee, 1970–86; Hon. Treasurer, 1970–86; Vice-Pres., 1972, Life Vice-Pres., 1986. Fellow Inst. of Dirs, 1974, Council Mem., 1982–89; Managing Trustee, Inst. of Economic Affairs, 1987–91; Mem. Council, UEA, 1987–94. FZS 1975; CCMI (FBIM 1976); Fellow, Amer. Chamber of Commerce, 1979, Dir, 1984–89. FRSA 1984. Hon. Fellow, UEA, 1995. *Recreations:* music, languages, travel, English countryside. *Died 15 Aug. 2009.*

COLLINS, Prof. Philip Arthur William; Professor of English, University of Leicester, 1964–82, then Emeritus; *b* 28 May 1923; *er s* of Arthur Henry and Winifred Nellie Collins; *m* 1st, 1952, Mildred Lowe (marr. diss. 1963); 2nd, 1965, Joyce Dickins; two *s* one *d*. *Educ:* Brentwood Sch.; Emmanuel Coll., Cambridge (Sen. Schol.; MA 1948). Served War (RAOC and Royal Norfolk Regt), 1942–45. Leicester: Staff Tutor in Adult Educn, 1947; Warden, Vaughan Coll., 1954; Leicester University: Sen. Lectr in English, 1962–64; Head, English Dept, 1971–76, 1981–82; Public Orator, 1975–78, 1980–82. Visiting Prof.: Univ. of California, Berkeley, 1967; Columbia, 1969; Victoria Univ., NZ, 1974. Sec., Leicester Theatre Trust Ltd, 1963–87; Member: Drama Panel, Arts Council of GB, 1970–75; National Theatre Bd, 1976–82; British American Drama Acad. Bd, 1983–97; Pres., Dickens Fellowship, 1983–85; Chm. Trustees, Dickens House Museum, 1984–92; Chm., Tennyson Soc., 1984–97. Many overseas lecture-tours; performances, talks and scripts for radio and television. *Publications:* James Boswell, 1956; (ed) English Christmas, 1956; Dickens and Crime, 1962; Dickens and Education, 1963; The Canker and the Rose (Shakespeare Quater-centenary celebration) perf. Mermaid Theatre, London, 1964; The Impress of the Moving Age, 1965; Thomas Cooper the Chartist, 1969; A Dickens Bibliography, 1970; Dickens's Bleak House, 1971; (ed) Dickens, the Critical Heritage, 1971; (ed) A Christmas Carol: the public reading version, 1971; Reading Aloud: a Victorian Métier, 1972; (ed) Dickens's Public Readings, 1975; Dickens's David Copperfield, 1977; (ed) Dickens: Interviews and Recollections, 1981; (ed) Thackeray: Interviews and Recollections, 1983; Trollope's London, 1983; (ed) Dickens: Sikes and Nancy

and other Readings, 1983; Tennyson, Poet of Lincolnshire, 1984; (co-ed) The Annotated Dickens, 1986; contrib. to: Encyclopaedia Britannica, Listener, TLS, sundry learned journals. *Recreations:* theatre, music. *Address:* 26 Knighton Drive, Leicester LE2 3HB. *T:* (0116) 270 6026. *Died 6 May 2007.*

COLLINS, Terence Bernard; Chairman, 1984–87, Vice Chairman, 1976–84, Group Managing Director, 1975–86, Berger Jenson Nicholson; *b* 3 March 1927; *s* of George Bernard Collins and Helen Theresa Collins; *m* 1956, Barbara (*née* Lowday); two *s* two *d*. *Educ:* Marist Coll., Hull; Univ. of St Andrews (MA Hons). Trainee, Ideal Standard, 1951–52; Blundell Spence: Area Manager, 1953–55; Regl Manager, 1955–57; UK Sales Manager, 1957–59; Berger Jenson Nicholson: Sales Manager, 1959–62; Man. Dir, Caribbean, 1962–69; Overseas Regl Exec., 1969–70; Gp Dir UK, 1970–74. Chairman: Cranfield Conf. Services Ltd, 1987–93; Cranfield Ventures Ltd, 1990–93; CIT Hldgs Ltd, 1991–92 (Dir, 1989–93); Interact Design and Print Ltd (formerly Interact Ltd), 1994–2001; Director: A. G. Stanley Hldgs, 1977–87; Hoechst UK, 1979–87; Hoechst Australia Investments, 1980–87; Mayborn Gp PLC, 1986–91; Phoenix Develts Ltd, 1987–94, 1995–2001 (Chm., 2000–01); Aldehurst Consultants Ltd, 1987–94; Cranfield Precision Engineering Ltd, 1990–95; Chm., Management Bd, Kingline Consultants Ltd, 1989–90. Mem., Duke of Edinburgh's Award Internat. Panel, 1978–86; Trustee, Atlas Econ. Foundn UK, 1986–93. Cranfield University (formerly Institute of Technology): Mem. Court, 1977–98; Mem. Council, 1981–93; Treasurer, 1991–92; Chm., Finance Cttee, 1991–92; University of Buckingham: Vice-Chm. Council, 1987–95; Chm., F and GP Cttee, 1987–94. DUniv Buckingham, 1994. *Recreations:* music, gardening. *Address:* Woodbridge, Suffolk. *Died 19 Feb. 2009.*

COLQUHOUN OF LUSS, Captain Sir Ivar (Iain), 8th Bt *cr* 1786; JP; DL; Hon. Sheriff (formerly Hon. Sheriff Substitute); Chief of the Clan; Grenadier Guards; *b* 4 Jan. 1916; *s* of Sir Iain Colquhoun, 7th Bt, and Geraldine Bryde (Dinah) (*d* 1974), *d* of late F. J. Tennant; *S* father, 1948; *m* 1943, Kathleen (*d* 2007), 2nd *d* of late W. A. Duncan and of Mrs Duncan, 53 Cadogan Square, SW1; one *s* one *d* (and one *s* decd). *Educ:* Eton. JP 1951, DL 1952, Dunbartonshire. *Heir:* *s* Malcolm Rory Colquhoun, Younger of Luss [*b* 20 Dec. 1947; *m* 1st, 1978, Susan Timmerman (marr. diss.); one *s*; 2nd, 1989, Katharine, *e d* of A. C. Mears; one *s* one *d*]. *Address:* Camstraddan, Luss, Argyllshire G83 8NX. *Clubs:* White's, Royal Ocean Racing. *Died 31 Jan. 2008.*

COLVILLE OF CULROSS, 4th Viscount *cr* 1902; **John Mark Alexander Colville;** QC; 14th Baron (Scot.) *cr* 1604; 4th Baron (UK) *cr* 1885; a Circuit Judge, 1993–99; *b* 19 July 1933; *e s* of 3rd Viscount and Kathleen Myrtle (*d* 1986), OBE 1961, *e d* of late Brig.-Gen. H. R. Gale, CMG, RE, Bardsey, Saanichton, Vancouver Island; *S* father, 1945; *m* 1st, 1958, Mary Elizabeth Webb-Bowen (marr. diss. 1973); four *s*; 2nd, 1974, Margaret Birgitta, Viscountess Davidson, LLB, JP, Barrister, *o d* of Maj.-Gen. C. H. Norton, CB, CBE, DSO; one *s*. *Educ:* Rugby (Scholar); New Coll., Oxford (Scholar) (MA; Hon. Fellow, 1997). Lieut Grenadier Guards Reserve. Barrister-at-law, Lincoln's Inn, 1960 (Buchanan prizeman), Bencher, 1986; QC 1978; a Recorder, 1990–93. Minister of State, Home Office, 1972–74; elected Mem., H of L, 1999. Dir, Securities and Futures Authy (formerly Securities Assoc.), 1987–93. Chm., Norwich Information and Technology Centre, 1983–85; Director: Rediffusion Television Ltd, 1961–68; British Electric Traction Co. Ltd, 1968–72, 1974–84 (Dep. Chm., 1980–81); Mem., CBI Council, 1982–84. Chairman: Mental Health Act Commn, 1983–88; Alcohol Educn and Res. Council, 1984–90; Parole Bd, 1988–92; UK rep., UN Human Rights Commn, 1980–83; Mem., UN Working Gp on Disappeared Persons, 1980–84 (Chm., 1981–84); Special Rapporteur on Human Rights in Guatemala, 1983–86; Mem., UN

Human Rights Cttee, 1995–2000; Asst Surveillance Comr, 2001–. Reports on Prevention of Terrorism Act and NI Emergency Powers Act, for HM Govt, 1986–93. Mem. Council, Univ. of E Anglia, 1968–72. Mem., Royal Company of Archers (Queen's Body Guard for Scotland). Governor, BUPA, 1990–93. Hon. DCL UEA, 1998. *Heir: s* Master of Colville, *b* 5 Sept. 1959. *Address:* House of Lords, SW1A 0PW. *Died 8 April 2010.*

COLVIN, Sir Howard (Montagu), Kt 1995; CVO 1983; CBE 1964; MA; FBA 1963; FRHistS; FSA, 1980; Fellow of St John's College, Oxford, 1948–87, then Emeritus (Tutor in History, 1948–78; Librarian, 1950–84); Reader in Architectural History, Oxford University, 1965–87; *b* 15 Oct. 1919; *s* of late Montagu Colvin; *m* 1943, Christina Edgeworth (*d* 2003), *d* of late H. E. Butler, Prof. of Latin at University Coll. London; two *s. Educ:* Trent Coll.; University Coll., London (Fellow, 1974). Served in RAF, 1940–46 (despatches). Asst Lecturer, Dept of History, University Coll., London, 1946–48. Member: Royal Fine Art Commn, 1962–72; Royal Commn on Historical Monuments, England, 1963–76; Historic Buildings Council for England, 1970–84; Royal Commn on Ancient and Historical Monuments of Scotland, 1977–89; Royal Commn on Historical Manuscripts, 1981–88; Reviewing Cttee on the Export of Works of Art, 1982–83; Historic Buildings and Monuments Commn, 1984–85; Historic Buildings Adv. Cttee, 1984–2000. Pres., Soc. of Architectural Historians of GB, 1979–81. Hon. FRIBA; Hon. FSA (Scot.) 1986. DUniv York, 1978. Wolfson Literary Award, 1978. *Publications:* The White Canons in England, 1951; A Biographical Dictionary of English Architects 1660–1840, 1954, 2nd edn as A Biographical Dictionary of British Architects 1600–1840, 1978, 4th edn 2007; (General Editor and part author) The History of the King's Works, 6 Vols, 1963–82; A History of Deddington, 1963; Catalogue of Architectural Drawings in Worcester College Library, 1964; Architectural Drawings in the Library of Elton Hall (with Maurice Craig), 1964; (ed with John Harris) The Country Seat, 1970; Building Accounts of King Henry III, 1971; (introduction) The Queen Anne Churches, 1980; (ed with John Newman) Roger North, Of Architecture, 1981; Unbuilt Oxford, 1983; Calke Abbey, Derbyshire, 1985; The Canterbury Quadrangle, St John's College, Oxford, 1988; (with J. S. G. Simmons) All Souls: an Oxford college and its buildings, 1989; Architecture and the After-Life, 1991; (ed with Susan Foister) Anthonis van den Wyngaerde, The Panorama of London, 1996; Essays in English Architectural History, 1999; articles on mediæval and architectural history in Archaeological Journal, Architectural Review, etc. *Recreation:* gardening. *Address:* 50 Plantation Road, Oxford OX2 6JE. *T:* (01865) 557460. *Died 27 Dec. 2007.*

COMPTON, Rt Hon. Sir John (George Melvin), KCMG 1997; OCC 2002; PC 1983; Prime Minister and Minister of Finance and Physical Development, St Lucia, since 2006; *b* 29 April 1926; *m* 1968, Janice, *d* of Sir Frederick Joseph Clarke; five *c. Educ:* London School of Economics. Called to the Bar, Gray's Inn; practice in St Lucia, 1951. Indep. Mem., Legislative Council, 1954; joined Labour Party, 1954; Dep. Leader, 1957–61; resigned, and formed Nat. Labour Movement, 1961 (later United Workers' Party; Leader, 1964–96 and 2005–); Chief Minister of St Lucia, 1964–67, Premier, 1967–79, Prime Minister, Feb.-July 1979 and 1982–96; Minister for Finance, Planning and Develt, 1982–96; Sen. Minister, St Lucia, 1996–97. *Address:* Prime Minister's Office, 5th Floor, Greaham Louisy Administrative Building, Waterfront, Castries, St Lucia. *Died 7 Sept. 2007.*

COMPTON, Robert Edward John; DL; Chairman: Time-Life International Ltd, 1979–90 (Chief Executive Officer, 1985–88); Time SARL, 1985–90; *b* 11 July 1922; *yr s* of late Major Edward Robert Francis Compton, JP, DL, and Sylvia Farquharson; *m* 1951, Ursula Jane Kenyon-Slaney; two *s. Educ:* Eton; Magdalen Coll.,

Oxford, 1940–41. Served War, Coldstream Guards, 1941–46 (wounded); Mil. Asst to British Ambassador, Vienna, 1946. Studied fruit growing and horticulture (Diploma), 1946–48; with W. S. Crawford Ltd, Advertising Agency, 1951–54; joined Time International, 1954; advertising sales, 1954–58, UK Advertising Dir, 1958–62; also Dir, Time-Life Internat. Ltd, 1958–79. Pres., Highline Finances Services, SA, and Dir, Highline Leasing Ltd, 1985–94; Bd Dir, Extel Corp., Chicago, 1973–80; Dir, Transtel Communications Ltd, Slough, 1974–83. Vice-Chm., Yorks. Nat. Trust, 1970–85. President: Nat. Council for the Conservation of Plants and Gardens, 1994– (Chm., 1988–94); N of England Horticultural Soc., 1984–86; Northern Horticultural Soc., 1986–96; Yorks Agricl Soc., 1995–96; Vice Pres., RHS, 1996. High Sheriff, 1978–79, DL 1981, N Yorks. VMH 1994. *Recreations:* gardening, music. *Address:* The Manor House, Marton Le Moor, Ripon, N Yorks HG4 5AT. *T:* (01423) 323315; Newby Hall Estate Office, Ripon, Yorkshire HG4 5AE. *T:* (01423) 322583. *Club:* White's. *Died 14 Nov. 2009.*

CONNELL-SMITH, Prof. Gordon Edward, PhD; FRHistS; Professor of Contemporary History, University of Hull, 1973–85; *b* 23 Nov. 1917; 2nd *s* of George Frederick Smith and Margaret Smith (*née* Woolerton); surname changed to Connell-Smith by deed-poll, 1942; *m* 1954, Wendy Ann (*d* 1987), *o d* of John Bertram and Kathleen Tomlinson; one *s* one *d. Educ:* Richmond County Sch., Surrey; University Coll. of SW of England, Exeter (BA); Birkbeck Coll., London (PhD). FRHistS 1959. Served War, RA and Staff, 1940–46 (Staff Major). Julian Corbett Prize, Inst. of Historical Res., 1949; University of Hull: Staff Tutor/Lectr in Adult Educn and History Depts, 1952–63; Sen. Lectr, 1963–69; Reader in Contemp. Internat. History, 1969–73. Mem., Cttee of Management, Univ. of London Inst. of Latin Amer. Studies, 1973–85. Chm., Latin American Newsletters, Ltd, London, 1969–72. *Publications:* Forerunners of Drake, 1954; Pattern of the Post-War World, 1957; The Inter-American System, 1966 (Spanish edn 1971); (co-author) The Relevance of History, 1972; The United States and Latin America, 1974 (Spanish edn 1977); The Future of History, 1975; Latin American Relations with the World 1826–1976, 1976; contrib. to Bull. Inst. of Historical Res., Contemp. Rev., Econ. History Rev., Eng. Historical Rev., History, Internat. Affairs, Jl of Latin Amer. Studies, World Today, etc. *Recreations:* travel, sport. *Address:* 7 Braids Walk, Kirk Ella, Hull HU10 7PA. *T:* (01482) 652624. *Died 8 July 2009.*

CONROY, Harry; author, financial journalist; Proprietor, Conroy Associates, public relations consultants, since 1992; Editor, Scottish Catholic Observer, 2000–07 (Managing Editor, 2001–05); *b* Scotland, 6 April 1943; *s* of Michael Conroy and Sarah (*née* Mullan); *m* 1965, Margaret Craig (*née* Campbell); twin *s* one *d.* Trainee Lab. Technician, Southern Gen. Hosp., 1961–62; Night Messenger (copy boy), 1962–63; Jun. Features Sub-Editor, 1963–64; Scottish Daily Express; Daily Record: Reporter, 1964–66 and 1967–69; Financial Correspondent, 1969–85; Reporter, Scottish Daily Mail, 1966–67. Campaign Dir, Scottish Constitutional Convention, 1990–92. Mem., ASTMS, 1961–62. National Union of Journalists: Mem., 1963– (Hon. Mem., 2000); Mem., Nat. Exec. Council, 1976–85; Vice-Pres., 1980–81; Pres., 1981–82; Gen. Sec., 1985–90. Bureau Mem., Internat. Fedn of Journalists, 1986–90; Founding Mem., Inst. of Employment Rights, 1989. Associate Mem., GMBATU, 1984–85. Trustee, Share Charity, 1993–; Dir, Consumer Credit Counselling (Glasgow) Ltd, 1996–99; Mem. UK Bd, Affinity Trust (formerly TACT), 2008– (Chm., TACT Scotland, 2008–09). *Publications:* (with Jimmy Allison) Guilty By Suspicion, 1995; (with Allan Stewart) The Long March of the Market Men, 1996; Off The Record: a life in journalism, 1997; (ed) The People Say Yes: the making of Scotland's Parliament, 1997; (ed) They Rose Again, 2003; Callaghan, 2006. *Recreations:* stamp and post-card collecting, supporting Glasgow

Celtic FC. *Address:* 44 Redwood Crescent, Cambuslang, Glasgow G72 7FZ. *T:* (0141) 641 9071; *e-mail:* harry@conroy.co.uk.   *Died 24 April 2010.*

CONSTANTINOU, Sir Georgkios, (Sir George), Kt 1997; OBE 1992; Chairman, Constantinou Group of Companies; *b* 11 May 1930; *s* of Costas Savva Constantinou and Eleni Lazarou; *m* 1955, Maria (separated); two *s* two *d*; Cecelia; three *s* three *d*. *Educ:* in Cyprus. Established companies which form Constantinou Group: Papuan Welders, 1954; Papuan Transport Contractors/Roadmakers, 1955; Rouna Quarries Pty Ltd, 1960; Hebou Constructions (PNG) Pty Ltd, 1973; Airways Hotel & Apartments Pty Ltd, 1986; Yodda Resources Pty Ltd, 1996; Kidu Kidu Pty Ltd, 1996. Hon. Consul of Cyprus in PNG, 1986–. *Recreations:* fishing, walking. *Address:* PO Box 120, Port Moresby, Papua New Guinea. *T:* 3253077. *Clubs:* Royal Papua Yacht (Port Moresby); Queensland Turf.   *Died 16 Dec. 2008.*

CONWAY, Sari Elizabeth; restaurateur, since 2001, *b* 3 March 1951; *d* of late Gordon and of Gladys Mary Wright; *m* 1973, Vincent Conway; three *s*. *Educ:* Leeds Polytechnic (Teaching Cert.); Leeds Univ. (Advanced Diploma in Guidance and Counselling; Postgrad. Cert. in Educn of Maladjusted Children); Nottingham Univ. (MPhil); Warwick Univ. (MEd); Leeds Business Sch. (MBA 2000). Teacher of Home Econs, Leeds LEA, 1973–75; Head of Home Economics, Nat. Children's Home, Leeds, 1975–77; Sen. Mistress, Disruptive Unit, and Head of Girls' Studies, Calderdale, 1977–79; part-time Adult Educn Tutor/Organiser, Youth Worker, and Lectr in Further Educn, Derbys, 1979–82; Educn Advr, Leics CC, 1982–88; Asst Dir of Community and Continuing Educn, South Tyneside MBC, 1988–91; Dir of Educn, City of Bradford MBC, 1991–95; Interim Chief Exec., London Borough of Lambeth, 1994–95; Chief Exec., Eastbourne BC, 1995–2001. Freeman, City of London. *Publications:* Educational Perceptions of Unemployed Adolescents in an LEA, 1984; Women Senior Officers in the Statutory Youth Service, 1992. *Recreations:* travel, dressmaking, theatre, voluntary youth work. *Address:* The Fish Shop, The Mint, Rye, E Sussex TN31 7EN. *T:* (01797) 223268.   *Died 24 July 2006.*

CONYNGHAM, 7th Marquess *cr* 1816; **Frederick William Henry Francis Conyngham;** Baron Conyngham, 1781; Viscount Conyngham, 1789; Earl Conyngham, Viscount Mount Charles, 1797; Earl of Mount Charles, Viscount Slane, 1816; Baron Minster (UK), 1821; late Captain Irish Guards; *b* 13 March 1924; *e s* of 6th Marquess Conyngham and Antoinette Winifred (*d* 1966), *er d* of late J. W. H. Thompson; *S* father, 1974; *m* 1st, 1950, Eileen Wren (marr. diss. 1970), *o d* of Capt. C. W. Newsam, Ashfield, Beauparc, Co. Meath; three *s*; 2nd, 1971, Mrs Elizabeth Anne Rudd; 3rd, 1980, Mrs D. G. A. Walker (*d* 1986); 4th, 1987, Annabelle Agnew. *Educ:* Eton. *Heir: s* Earl of Mount Charles, *b* 23 May 1951. *Address:* Myrtle Hill, Andreas Road, Ramsey, Isle of Man IM8 3UA. *T:* (01624) 815532. *Club:* Royal St George Yacht.   *Died 3 March 2009.*

COOK, Beryl Frances, OBE 1996; painter; *b* 10 Sept. 1926; *d* of Adrian Lansley and Ella Farmer-Francis; *m* 1948, John Victor Cook; one *s*. *Educ:* Kendrick Girls' Sch., Reading, Berks. *Exhibitions:* Plymouth Arts Centre, 1975, 1995; Whitechapel Art Gallery, London, 1976; The Craft of Art, Walker Art Gallery, 1979; Musée de Cahors, 1981; Chelmsford Museum, 1982; Portal Gall., 1985, 1991, 2000, 2001; travelling, Plymouth, Stoke-on-Trent, Preston, Nottingham and Edinburgh, 1988–89; Drumcroon Arts Centre, Wigan, 1993; travelling, Blackpool, Durham, Stockton-on-Tees, Hartlepool, 1998; Durham, 2003; Stoke-on-Trent, 2004; Portal Gallery, London, 2006; Baltic Centre, Gateshead, 2007. *Publications:* The Works, 1978; Private View, 1980; Seven Years and a Day (illustrations), 1980; One Man Show, 1981; Bertie and the Big Red Ball (illustrations), 1982; My Granny (illustrations), 1983, repr. 2003; Beryl Cook's New York, 1985; Beryl Cook's London, 1988; Mr Norris

Changes Trains (illustrations), 1990; Bouncers, 1991; The Loved One (illustrations), 1993; Happy Days, 1995; The Prime of Miss Jean Brodie (illustrations), 1998; Cruising, 2000; The Bumper Edition, 2000. *Recreation:* reading.   *Died 28 May 2008.*

COOK, Rear-Adm. James William Dunbar, CB 1975; DL; Vice President, Surrey Branch of Soldiers', Sailors', and Airmen's Families Association; *b* 12 Dec. 1921; *s* of James Alexander Cook, Pluscarden, Morayshire; *m* 1st, 1949, Edith May Williams (*d* 1997); one *s* two *d*; 2nd, 2000, Elizabeth Provan (*née* Gooding). *Educ:* Bedford Sch.; HMS Worcester. CO, HM Ships Venus, Dido and Norfolk; Sen. British Naval Officer, S Africa, 1967–69 (as Cdre); Dir, RN War College, 1969–71; Asst Chief of Naval Staff (Ops), 1973–75; retired from RN, 1975. Comdr 1957; Captain 1963; Rear-Adm. 1973; jssc 1958; sowc 1970. Pres., Age Concern (Haslemere), 1990–. DL Surrey, 1989. *Recreations:* golf, gardening. *Address:* Springways Cottage, Farnham Lane, Haslemere, Surrey GU27 1EY. *T:* (01428) 643615. *Club:* Army and Navy.   *Died 26 Jan. 2007.*

COOKE OF ISLANDREAGH, Baron *cr* 1992 (Life Peer), of Islandreagh in the County of Antrim; **Victor Alexander Cooke,** OBE 1981; DL; CEng, FIMechE; Chairman: Henry R. Ayton Ltd, Belfast, 1970–89; Springvale EPS (formerly Polyproducts) Ltd, 1964–2000, *b* 18 Oct. 1920; *s* of Norman Victor Cooke and Alice Harman Cooke (*née* Peavey); *m* 1951, Alison Sheila Casement; two *s* one *d*. *Educ:* Marlborough Coll., Wilts; Trinity Coll., Cambridge (MA). Engineer Officer, Royal Navy, 1940–46 (Lieut (E) RN). Henry R. Ayton Ltd, Belfast, 1946–89; Chairman: Belfast Savings Bank, 1963; Harland & Wolff Ltd, 1980–81 (Dir, 1970–87); Dir, NI Airports, 1970–85. Member: Senate, Parliament of N Ireland, 1960–68; N Ireland Economic Council, 1974–78; Commissioner, Belfast Harbour, 1968–79; Commissioner of Irish Lights, 1983–95 (Chm. of Comrs, 1990–92). DL Co. Antrim, 1970. *Recreations:* sailing, shooting. *Club:* Naval.   *Died 13 Nov. 2007.*

COOKE OF THORNDON, Baron *cr* 1996 (Life Peer), of Wellington in New Zealand and of Cambridge in the County of Cambridgeshire; **Robin Brunskill Cooke,** ONZ 2002; KBE 1986; Kt 1977; PC 1977; PhD; President, Court of Appeal of New Zealand, 1986–96 (Judge, 1976–86); *b* 9 May 1926; *s* of Hon. Philip Brunskill Cooke, MC (Judge of Supreme Court), and Valmai Digby Gore; *m* 1952, (Phyllis) Annette Miller; three *s*. *Educ:* Wanganui Collegiate Sch.; Victoria University Coll., Wellington (LLM); Clare Coll., Cambridge; Gonville and Caius Coll., Cambridge (MA, PhD). Trav. Scholarship in Law, NZ, 1950; Res. Fellow, Gonville and Caius Coll., Cambridge, 1952–56 (Yorke Prize), 1954), Hon. Fellow, 1982. Called to the Bar, Inner Temple, 1954, Hon. Bencher 1985; practised at NZ Bar, 1955–72; QC 1964; Judge of Supreme Court, 1972–76; Pres., Court of Appeal of Samoa (formerly Western Samoa), 1982 and 1994–, of Cook Is, 1981 and 1982, of Kiribati, 1999; Judge of Supreme Court of Fiji, 1995–2001; a Lord of Appeal, UK, 1996–2001; arbitrator, London, 2002–; Non-Perm. Judge, Hong Kong Court of Final Appeal, 1997–. Chm., Commn of Inquiry into Housing, 1970–71; Commn Mem., Internat. Commn of Jurists, 1993–; Mem., London Court of Arbitration, 2003–. Life Mem., Lawasia. Special Status Mem., Amer. Law Inst., 1993–. Vis. Fellow, All Souls Coll., Oxford, 1990; Hon. Fellow, Legal Res. Foundn, NZ, 1993; Distinguished Fellow, Victoria Univ. of Wellington, 1996–. Lectures include: Sultan Azlan Shah Law, Malaysia, 1990; Peter Allan Meml, Hong Kong, 1994; Hamlyn (4), UK, 1996. Hon. LLD: Victoria Univ. of Wellington, 1989; Cambridge Univ., 1990; Hon. DCL Oxford, 1991. *Publications:* (ed) Portrait of a Profession (Centennial Book of NZ Law Society), 1969; (Editor in Chief) The Laws of New Zealand, 1990–; Turning Points of the Common Law (Hamlyn Lectures), 1997; articles in law reviews and papers at internat. law confs. *Recreations:*

theatre, The Times crossword, watching cricket (Patron, Wellington Cricket Assoc., 1995–). *Address:* 4 Homewood Crescent, Karori, Wellington, New Zealand. *T:* (4) 4768059; House of Lords, SW1A 0PW; Brick Court Chambers, 7–8 Essex Street, WC2R 3LD; *e-mail:* densem@attglobal.net. *Clubs:* Oxford and Cambridge; Wellington, Wellington Golf (NZ).
Died 30 Aug. 2006.

COOKE, Prof. Brian Ernest Dudley; Professor Emeritus, University of Wales, 1983; Professor of Oral Medicine and Oral Pathology, University of Wales, Dean of Welsh National School of Medicine Dental School and Consultant Dental Surgeon to University Hospital of Wales, 1962–82; *b* 12 Jan. 1920; *e s* of Charles Ernest Cooke and Margaret Beatrice Wood; *m* 1948, Marion Neill Orkney Hope; one *s* one *d. Educ:* Merchant Taylors' Sch.; London Univ. LDSRCS 1942; LRCP, MRCS 1949; FDSRCS 1952; MDSU London 1959; MRCPath 1965, FRCPath 1974. Served RNVR (Dental Br.), 1943–46. Nuffield Dental Fellow, 1950–52; Trav. Nuffield Fellow, Australia, 1964. Lectr 1952–57, Reader in Dental Med. 1958–62, Guy's Hosp. Dental School. Rep. Univ. of Wales on Gen. Dental Council, 1964–82; Mem. Bd of Faculty of Dental Surgery, RCS England, 1964–72 (Vice-Dean 1971–72); Chm., Dental Educn Adv. Council, GB, 1975–78 (Mem. 1962–82); Sec.-Gen., Assoc. for Dental Educn in Europe, 1982–84. Adviser in Dental Surgery to Welsh Hosp. Bd, 1962–74; Civilian Consultant in Dental Surgery to RN, 1967–83. Hon. Adviser, Editorial Bd, British Jl of Dermatology, 1967–76. Mem., S Glamorgan AHA, 1974–76. Mem. Bd of Governors: United Cardiff Hosps, 1965–71; HMC (Cardiff) Univ. Hosp. of Wales, 1971–74. Vice-Provost, Welsh Nat. Sch. of Medicine, 1974–76. Examr in Dental Surgery and Oral Pathology, Liverpool, Manchester and London Univs; Examr for Primary Fellowship in Dental Surgery, RCS, 1967–73. Hon. Mem., Pierre Fauchard Acad., 1967. Charles Tomes Lectr, RCS, 1963; Guest Lectr, Students' Vis. Lectrs Trust Fund, Witwatersrand Univ., 1967; Vis. Prof., Univ. of Sydney Dental Sch., 1986–87. Pres., Section of Odontology, RSocMed, 1975 (Hon. Mem., 1990); Founder Pres., British Soc. for Oral Medicine, 1981. Hon. Coll. Fellow, Univ. of Wales Coll. of Medicine, 1990. Cartwright Prize and Medal, RCS, 1955; Chesterfield Prize and Medal, St John's Hosp. for Diseases of Skin, 1955. *Publications:* (jtly) Oral Histopathology, 1959, 2nd edn 1970; scientific contribs to medical and dental jls. *Recreation:* various. *Address:* 22 Rocky Park, Pembroke SA71 4NY.
Died 28 Sept. 2007.

COOKE, Gilbert Andrew, FCA; Chairman and Chief Executive, C. T. Bowring & Co. Ltd, 1982–88; Director, Marsh & McLennan Companies Inc., 1980–88; *b* 7 March 1923; *s* of Gilbert N. Cooke and Laurie Cooke; *m* 1949, Katherine Margaret Mary McGovern; one *s* one *d. Educ:* Bournemouth Sch. FCA 1950. Sen. Clerk, chartered accountants, 1950–54; Bowmaker Ltd: Chief Accountant, 1955; Dir, 1968; Man. Dir, 1968; Dep. Chm. and Chief Exec., 1972; C. T. Bowring & Co. Ltd: Dir, 1969; Gp Man. Dir, 1976–82. Chm., Bowring UK, 1984–88. Chm., Finance Houses Assoc., 1972–74. *Recreations:* music, reading. *Address:* Kilmarth, 66 Onslow Road, Burwood Park, Walton-on-Thames, Surrey KT12 5AY. *T:* (01932) 240451. *Died 17 Sept. 2009.*

COOKE, Jean Esme Oregon, RA 1972 (ARA 1965); (professional name Jean E. Cooke); Lecturer in Painting, Royal College of Art, 1964–74; *b* 18 Feb. 1927; *d* of Arthur Oregon Cooke, grocer, and of Dorothy Emily Cooke (née Cranefield); *m* 1953, John Randall Bratby, RA (marr. diss. 1977; he *d* 1992); three *s* one *d. Educ:* Blackheath High Sch.; Central Sch. of Arts and Crafts, Camberwell; City and Guilds; Goldsmiths' Coll. Sch. of Art; Royal Coll. of Art (Royal Schol.). NDD in Sculpture, 1949. Pottery Workshop, 1950–53; Tutor, Summer Sch., Swiss Alps, 1992–94. Member: Council, Royal Acad., 1983–85, 1992–94 (Sen. Hanger, 1993, 1994) and 2001–02; Academic Bd, Blackheath Sch. of

Art, 1986–88; Governor: Central Sch. of Art and Design, 1984–86; Tertiary Educn Bd, Greenwich, 1984–86. Life Pres., Friends of Woodlands Art Gall., Blackheath, 1990. Purchase of self-portrait, 1969, and portrait of John Bratby (called Lilly, Lilly on the Brow), 1972, by Chantrey Bequest; portraits: Dr Egon Wellesz and Dr Walter Oakshott for Lincoln Coll., Oxford; Mrs Bennett, Principal, for St Hilda's Coll., Oxford, 1976; Peter Carlisle, 1985–86; Clare Chalmers and Jane Lee, 1987–88; John Petty, 1989. Started Homage to Birling Gap (large painting), 1985. Television film: Portrait of John Bratby, BBC, 1978. *One-man shows include:* Establishment Club, 1963; Leicester Gall., 1964; Bear Lane Gall., Oxford, 1965; Arun Art Centre, Arundel; Ashgate Gall., Farnham; Moyan Gall., Manchester; Bladon Gall., Hampshire, 1966; Lane Gall., Bradford, 1967; Gallery 66, Blackheath, 1967; Motley Gall., Lewisham, 1968; Phoenix, Suffolk, 1970; New Grafton Gall., 1971; Ansdell Gall., 1974; Woodlands Gall., Blackheath, 1976 and 1991; J. K. Taylor Gall., Cambridge, 1976; Garden Gall., Greenwich, 1983; Alpine Gall., 1986; Friends Room, RA, 1990; Bardolf Hall, Sussex, 1990, in aid of Birling Gap Safety Boat; Blackheath Concert Halls, 1990; Linton Court Gall., Settle, 1991; In the Looking Glass, touring, 1996–97; Piano Nobile Gall., London, 2007; open studio for: Greenwich Festival, 1977–94; Blackheath High Sch. Art Fund, 1979; Bakehouse Gall., Blackheath, 1980; open studio in aid of: Royal Acad. Trust, 1982; Birling Gap Safety Boat, 1989. *Works exhibited:* annually, RA, 1956–; Furneaux Gall., 1968; Upper Grosvenor Gall., 1968; Ashgate Gall., 1973; Agnews, 1974; Gall. 10, Richmond Hill, 1974; Leonie Jonleigh Gall., 1976; Dulwich Coll. Picture Gall., 1976; British Painting 1952–77, Royal Acad., 1977; Business Art Galleries, 1978; New Ashgate Gall., 1979; Tate Gall., 1979; Grosvenor Street Gall., 1979, 1980; Norwich Gall., 1979, 1980; Imp. Coll. Gall., 1980; Patrick Seale Gall., Belgravia, 1981; WEA, 1987; Foss Gall. Gp, 1987, 1988, 1990; RCA, 1988; Hurlingham Gall., 1990; Patterson Gall., 1990, 1991, 1992, 1993, 1994; King Street Gall., 1992; Thompson's Gall., 1992; Sacker Galls, RA, 1993; Boston Coll., Lincoln, 1997; Woodlands Gall., 1997; Grimsby Art Centre, 1997; Highgate Fine Arts, 1997; Blackfriars Art Centre, 1997; A. T. Kearney, 1998; Visual Wit, RA, 2002; John Madejski Fine Rooms, RA, 2007. *Works in collections include:* Govt Art Collections Fund (HM the Queen); Nat. Gall. (Sir Brinsley Ford); Usher Gall. (self portrait); Tate (self portrait, 1969). *Publications:* Contemporary British Artists; The Artist, 1980; The Artist's Garden, 1989; *relevant publications:* Frances Borzello, Seeing Ourselves: women's self-portraits, 1998; Philip Vann, Face to Face: British self portraits in the twentieth century, 2004. *Recreations:* ungardening, talking, shouting, walking along the beach.
Died 6 Aug. 2008.

COOKE, (Patrick) Joseph (Dominic), FCMC; Vice-Chairman, Daily Telegraph, 1994–96 (Managing Director, 1987–94); *b* Galway, 9 Aug. 1931; *s* of Patrick Cooke and Mary (née Naughton); *m* 1960, Margaret Mary Brown; two *s* four *d. Educ:* St Joseph's Coll.; University Coll., Galway (BE). CEng, MICE, MIMechE; FCMC (FIMC 1968); AIIRA. United Steel Cos, 1952–54; Workington Iron & Steel Co., 1954–61; Urwick, Orr and Partners Ltd, 1961–73: Sen. Partner, 1967; Principal Partner, 1970; founded Cooke Management Consultants Ltd, 1973; non-exec. Dir, EMAP plc, 1984–96; Consultant, Daily Telegraph, 1985–87; non-executive Director: IFRA, 1990–94 (Senator, 1994–); Hollinger, 1992–94. Sandford Smith Award, Inst. Management Consultants, 1967. *Recreations:* golf, gardening. *Address:* Apartment 305, Bâtiment les Terrasses, Parc Saint Roman, 7 Avenue Saint Roman, MC 98000, Monaco. *Club:* Monte-Carlo (Pres., 2003–04). *Died 1 Jan. 2009.*

COOKSON, Lt-Col Michael John Blencowe, OBE 1986; TD 1969; Vice Lord-Lieutenant of Northumberland, 1987–2002; land owner, agriculturist; *b* 13 Oct. 1927; *s* of late Col John Charles Blencowe

Cookson, DSO, TD, DL; *m* 1957, Rosemary Elizabeth, *d* of David Aubrey Haggie; one *s* three *d*. *Educ*: Eton; Cirencester Agricl Coll., 1951–52. Served with: E African Forces, Kenya, 1947–48; Northumberland Hussars (TA), 1952–69; Queen's Own Yeomanry, 1969–72; Chm., Northumberland Hussars (TA) Regtl Assoc., 1977–87. Hon. Col, Northumberland Hussars Sqn QOY, 1988–92. Chm., Co. Cttee, Northumberland Assoc. Boys' Clubs, 1974–86 (Mem., 1964–73). Chm., Northumberland Queen's Silver Jubilee Appeal, 1978. High Sheriff, 1976, DL 1983, Northumberland. *Recreations:* hunting (Joint Master: Haydon Foxhounds, 1955–57; Morpeth Foxhounds, 1960–64, 1971–95), gardening. *Address:* Needless Hall, Northside, Meldon, Morpeth, Northumberland NE61 3SR. *T:* (01670) 772661. *Club:* Northern Counties (Newcastle upon Tyne).
Died 3 Jan. 2007.

COOKSON, Prof. Richard Clive, MA, PhD; FRS 1968; FRSC; Research Professor of Chemistry in the University of Southampton, 1983–85, then Emeritus Professor (Professor of Chemistry, 1957–83); *b* 27 Aug. 1922; *s* of late Clive Cookson; *m* 1948, Ellen Fawaz (*d* 2002); two *s*. *Educ:* Harrow Sch.; Trinity Coll., Cambridge. BA 1944; MA, PhD Cantab 1947. Research Fellow, Harvard Univ., 1948; Research Div. of Glaxo Laboratories Ltd, 1949–51; Lectr, Birkbeck Coll., London Univ., 1951–57. *Publications:* papers, mainly in Jl Chem. Soc. *Address:* Northfield House, Coombe Bissett, Salisbury, Wilts SP5 4JZ. *Died 17 Dec. 2008.*

COOMBE, His Honour Michael Ambrose Rew; a Circuit Judge, 1985–2003, at Central Criminal Court, 1986–2003; *b* 17 June 1930; *s* of late John Rew Coombe and Phyllis Mary Coombe; *m* 1961, Elizabeth Anne Hull (*d* 1998); two *s* one *d* (and one *s* decd). *Educ:* Berkhamsted; New Coll., Oxford. MA (Eng. Lang. and Lit.). Called to Bar, Middle Temple, 1957 (Harmsworth Scholar); Bencher, 1984; Autumn Reader, 2001. 2nd Prosecuting Counsel to the Inland Revenue at Central Criminal Court and 5 Courts of London Sessions, 1971; 2nd Counsel to the Crown at Inner London Sessions, Sept. 1971; 1st Counsel to the Crown at Inner London Crown Court, 1974; 4th Junior Treasury Counsel at Central Criminal Court, 1974, 2nd Jun. Treasury Counsel, 1975, 1st Jun. Treasury Counsel, 1977; Recorder of the Crown Court, 1976–85; Sen. Prosecuting Counsel to the Crown, CCC, 1978–85. Freeman, City of London, 1986; Liveryman: Stationers' Co.; Fruiterers' Co. *Recreations:* theatre, antiquity, art and architecture, printing. *Club:* Garrick. *Died 20 Oct. 2007.*

COOMBS, Prof. Robert Royston Amos, (Robin), ScD; FRCPath 1969; FRS 1965; Quick Professor in Immunology, University of Cambridge, 1966–88, then Emeritus; Fellow of Corpus Christi College, since 1962; *b* 9 Jan. 1921; *s* of Charles Royston Amos and Edris Owen Amos (formerly Coombs); *m* 1952, Anne Marion Blomfield; one *s* one *d*. *Educ:* Diocesan Coll., Cape Town; Edinburgh Univ. (BSc, MRCVS 1943); PhD 1947, ScD 1966, Cantab. University of Cambridge: Stringer Fellow, King's Coll., 1947–56; Asst Director of Research, Dept of Pathology, 1948; Reader in Immunology, 1963–66. Foreign Hon. Mem., Royal Belgium Acad. of Medicine, 1991. Hon. FRCP 1973; Hon. Fellow, Amer. Coll. of Allergists, 1979; Hon. FRSocMed 1992; Hon. Member: Amer. Assoc. of Immunologists, 1973–; British Blood Transfusion Soc., 1984–; British Soc. for Immunology, 1988–; British Soc. Allergy and Clin. Immunology, 1988–; Pathol. Soc. of GB and Ire., 1990–; British Soc. Haematology, 1993–. Hon. MD Linköping Univ. 1973; Hon. dr med. vet. Copenhagen, 1979; Hon. DSc. Guelph, 1981; Edinburgh, 1984. Landsteiner Award, Amer. Assoc. of Blood Banks, 1961; Gairdner Foundn Award, 1965; Henry Steele Gold Medal, RCVS, 1966; James Calvert Spence Medal, British Paediatric Assoc., 1967; Philip Levine Medal, Amer. Soc. Clin. Pathol., 1969; Oliver Meml Award, 1979; Clemens von Pirquet Medal,

Austrian Soc. of Allergy and Immunology, 1988; British Soc. Haematology Medal, 1993. *Publications:* (with Anne M. Coombs and D. G. Ingram) Serology of Conglutination and its relation to disease, 1960; (ed with P. G. H. Gell) Clinical Aspects of Immunology, 1963, 3rd edn (also with P. J. Lachmann), 1975; (with W. E. Parish and A. F. Walls) Sudden Infant Death Syndrome: could a healthy infant succumb to inhalation-anaphylaxis during sleep leading to cot death?, 2000; numerous scientific papers on immunology. *Recreation:* retreat to the country. *Address:* 6 Selwyn Gardens, Cambridge CB3 9AX. *T:* (01223) 352681. *Died 25 Jan. 2006.*

COOPER, Sir Richard (Powell), 5th Bt *cr* 1905, of Shenstone Court, Co. Stafford; *b* 13 April 1934; *s* of Sir Francis Ashmole Cooper, 4th Bt and of Dorothy Frances Hendrika, *d* of late Emile Deen; *S* father, 1987; *m* 1957, Angela Marjorie (*d* 2004), *e d* of Eric Wilson, Norton-on-Tees; one *s* two *d*. *Educ:* Marlborough. Chm., Rare Breeds Survival Trust, 1978–80, 1990–92. Chm., Royal Smithfield Club, 2000–02. *Recreation:* foxhunting. *Heir: s* Richard Adrian Cooper, *b* 21 Aug. 1960. *Address:* Lower Farm, Chedington, Beaminster, Dorset DT8 3JA. *T:* (01935) 891463. *Club:* Carlton. *Died 5 March 2006.*

COOPER, Sidney Pool; Head of Public Services, British Museum, 1973–76; *b* 29 March 1919; *s* of late Sidney Charles Henry Cooper and Emily Lilian Baptie; *m* 1940, Denise Marjorie Peverett (*d* 2003); two *s* one *d*. *Educ:* Finchley County Sch.; Northern Polytechnic (BSc); University Coll. London (MSc). Laboratory of the Government Chemist, 1947; Asst Keeper, National Reference Library of Science and Invention, British Museum, 1963; Dep. Keeper, NRLSI, 1969. *Address:* 11 Bridgewater Hill, Northchurch, Berkhamsted, Herts HP4 1LW. *T:* (01442) 864145. *Died 28 Nov. 2009.*

COORAY, His Honour (Bulathsinhalage) Anura (Siri); a Circuit Judge, 1991–97; *b* 20 Jan. 1936; *s* of (Bulathsinhalage) Vincent Cooray, accountant, and Dolly Perera Manchanayake, Etul Kotte, Sri Lanka; *m* 1957, Manel Therese, *d* of late George Perera, planter, and late Myrtle Perera, Kandy, Sri Lanka; two *s* three *d*. *Educ:* Christian Coll., Kotte, Sri Lanka; London Univ. Called to the Bar, Lincoln's Inn, 1968. Served RAF, Cranwell and Locking, 1952–55 (RAF Boxing Assoc. Sigrist Trophy, 1953–54); served Royal Ceylon Air Force, 1955–60. Practised in Common Law Chambers at Middle Temple; later, Dep. Head of Chambers at No 1 Gray's Inn Sq.; Mem., South Eastern Circuit; Prosecuting Counsel for DPP and Met. Police Solicitors, 1969–82; a Metropolitan Stipendiary Magistrate, 1982–91; a Recorder, 1989–91. Mem., Cttee of Magistrates, 1989. *Recreations:* wine making (and tasting too!), gardening. *Address:* 1 Gray's Inn Square, WC1R 5AA; Kingsland, Etul Kotte, Kotte, Sri Lanka. *Died 30 April 2009.*

COPELAND, Dame Joyanne Winifred; *see* Bracewell, Hon. Dame J. W.

COPELAND, Rev. Canon Charles McAlester; Provost of St John's Cathedral, Oban, 1959–79, and Dean of Diocese of Argyll and The Isles, 1977–79; *b* 5 April 1910; *s* of Canon Alexander Copland and of Violet Williamina Somerville McAlester; *m* 1946, Gwendoline Lorimer Williamson (*d* 2001); two *d*. *Educ:* Forfar Academy; Denstone Coll.; Corpus Christi Coll., Cambridge (MA); Cuddesdon College. Reserve of Officers, 1933–38. Curate, Peterborough Parish Church, 1934–38; Mission Priest, Chanda, CP, India, 1938–53 (Head of Mission, 1942–53); Canon of Nagpur, 1952; Rector, St Mary's, Arbroath, 1953–59; Canon of Dundee, 1953; Hon. Canon of Oban, 1979. *Publications:* Chanda: history of a mission, 1988; India: past glimpses of country life, 2007. *Recreations:* formerly Rugby football, athletics; rifle shooting (shot for Cambridge, for Scotland 1932–84). *Address:* 3 West Hill Road, Kirriemuir, Angus DD8 4PR. *T:* (01575) 575415. *Died 12 Dec. 2009.*

COPP, Darrell John Barkwell, OBE 1981; General Secretary, Institute of Biology, 1951–82; *b* 25 April 1922; *s* of J. J. H. Copp and L. A. Hoad; *m* 1944, Margaret Henderson; two *s* one *d*. *Educ:* Taunton's Sch., Southampton; Southampton Univ. (BSc). Scientific Officer, Admty Signals Estabt, 1942–45; Asst Sec., British Assoc. for Advancement of Science, 1947–51. Sec., Council for Nature, 1958–63; originator and co-ordinator of first National Nature Week, 1963. Hon. Treas., Parly and Scientific Cttee, 1980–83; Sec., European Community Biologists' Assoc., 1975–85. Trustee, Rye Art Gall., 1985–90. Hon. MTech Bradford, 1975; Hon. FIBiol 1984. *Publications:* reports and reviews in scientific jls. *Recreations:* walking, renovating farm buildings. *Address:* Underhill Farmhouse, Wittersham, Tenterden, Kent TN30 7EU. *T:* (01797) 270633.
Died 4 April 2010.

CORBETT, Hon. Michael McGregor; Chief Justice of South Africa, 1989–96; *b* 14 Sept. 1923; *s* of Alan Frederick Corbett and Johanna Sibella McGregor; *m* 1949, Margaret Murray Corbett (*née* Luscombe); two *s* two *d*. *Educ:* Rondebosch Boys' High Sch.; Univ. of Cape Town (BA, LLB); Trinity Hall, Cambridge (Elsie Ballot Scholarship, 1946; Law Tripos 1st cl. 1947; LLB 1st cl. 1948; Hon Fellow, 1992). Enlisted S African Tank Corps, 1942, commissioned 1943; active service, Egypt and Italy with Royal Natal Carbineers, 1943–44. Admitted Advocate, Cape Bar, 1948; QC 1961; Judge, Cape Provincial Div., Supreme Court, 1963; Judge of Appeal, 1974. Hon. Bencher, Lincoln's Inn, 1991; Hon. Mem., Amer. Bar Assoc., 1997. Hon. LLD: Cape Town, 1982; Orange Free State, 1990; Rhodes, 1990; Pretoria, 1993; Witwatersrand, 1994; Stellenbosch, 1996. President of Convocation Medal, Univ. of Cape Town, 1998. Order for Meritorious Service (S Africa), 1996. *Publications:* (jtly) The Quantum of Damages in Bodily and Fatal Injury Cases, 1960, 3rd edn 1985; (jtly) The Law of Succession in South Africa, 1980, 2nd edn 2001. *Recreations:* tennis, walking. *Address:* 18 Ladies Mile Extension, Constantia, Cape 7800, South Africa. *Clubs:* City and Civil Service (Cape Town); Kelvin Grove (Newlands, Cape).
Died 16 Sept. 2007.

CORBIN, Maurice Haig Alleyne; Justice of Appeal, Supreme Court, Trinidad and Tobago, 1972–81; *b* 26 May 1916; *s* of L. A. Corbin; *m* 1943, Helen Jocelyn Child (decd); one *s* two *d*; *m* 1968, Jean Barcant (decd). *Educ:* Harrison Coll., Barbados; Queen's Royal Coll., Trinidad. Solicitor, 1941; appointed Magistrate, Trinidad, 1945; called to the Bar, Middle Temple, 1949; Crown Counsel, 1953; Registrar, Supreme Court, 1954; Puisne Judge, Supreme Court, 1957–72. *Address:* 77 Brook Road, Goodwood Park, Pt Cumana, Trinidad. *Club:* Queen's Park Cricket (Port of Spain, Trinidad).
Died 27 Oct. 2007.

CORBY, Sir (Frederick) Brian, Kt 1989; FIA; Chairman, Prudential Corporation plc, 1990–95; *b* 10 May 1929; *s* of Charles Walter and Millicent Corby; *m* 1952, Elizabeth Mairi McInnes; one *s* two *d*. *Educ:* Kimbolton Sch.; St John's Coll., Cambridge (MA). Joined Prudential Assce Co. Ltd, 1952; Dep. Gen. Manager, 1974; Gen. Manager, 1976–79; Gp Gen. Manager, Prudential Corp. Ltd, 1979–82; Dir, 1981–89; Chief Gen. Manager, 1982–85; Chm., 1985–89; Prudential Assce Co. Ltd; Chief Exec., Prudential Corp., 1982–90. Dir, 1982–90, Chm., 1985–90, Mercantile & General Reinsce Co. Chm., South Bank Bd, 1990–98; a Dir, Bank of England, 1985–93; Member Board of Governors: NASD Inc., 2001–07; FINRA Inc., 2007–. Vice-President, Inst. of Actuaries, 1979–82; Chm., Assoc. of British Insurers, 1985–87; President: CBI, 1990–92; NIESR, 1994–2003. Chancellor, Univ. of Hertfordshire, 1992–96. Hon. DSc: City, 1989; Hertfordshire, 1996; Hon. DLitt CNAA, 1991. *Publications:* contribs to Jl of Inst. of Actuaries. *Recreations:* reading, golf.
Died 23 April 2009.

COREN, Alan; writer and broadcaster; *b* 27 June 1938; *s* of Samuel and Martha Coren; *m* 1963, Anne Kasriel; one *s* one *d*. *Educ:* East Barnet Grammar Sch.; Wadham Coll., Oxford (Open scholar; MA); Yale; Univ. of California, Berkeley. Asst Editor, Punch, 1963–66, Literary Editor 1966–69, Dep. Editor 1969–77, Editor, 1978–87; Editor, The Listener, 1988–89. TV Critic, The Times, 1971–78; Columnist: Daily Mail, 1972–76; Mail on Sunday, 1984–92; The Times, 1988–; Sunday Express, 1992–96; contributor to: Sunday Times, Atlantic Monthly, TLS, Spectator, Observer, Tatler, London Review of Books. *TV series:* The Losers, 1978; Call My Bluff, 1996–; *radio series:* The News Quiz, 1975–; Freedom Pass, 2003–. Commonwealth Fellowship, 1961–63. Rector, St Andrews Univ., 1973–76. Hon. DLitt Nottingham, 1993. *Publications:* The Dog It Was That Died, 1965; All Except the Bastard, 1969; The Sanity Inspector, 1974; The Bulletins of Idi Amin, 1974; Golfing For Cats, 1975; The Further Bulletins of Idi Amin, 1975; The Lady From Stalingrad Mansions, 1977; The Peanut Papers, 1977; The Rhinestone as Big as the Ritz, 1979; Tissues for Men, 1980; The Best of Alan Coren, 1980; The Cricklewood Diet, 1982; Present Laughter, 1982; (ed) The Penguin Book of Modern Humour, 1983; Bumf, 1984; Something For The Weekend, 1986; Bin Ends, 1987; Seems Like Old Times, 1989; More Like Old Times, 1990; A Year in Cricklewood, 1991; Toujours Cricklewood?, 1993; Sunday Best, 1993; (ed) Animal Passions, 1994; A Bit on the Side, 1995; The Alan Coren Omnibus, 1996; The Cricklewood Dome, 1998; The Cricklewood Tapestry, 2000; Waiting for Jeffrey, 2002; (ed) The Pick of Punch (annual), 1979–87; (ed) The Punch Book of Short Stories, Bk 1, 1979, Bk 2, 1980, Bk 3, 1981; The Arthur Books (for children), 1976–83. *Recreations:* bridge, riding, broadcasting. *Address:* Robson Books, Chrysalis Books Group, The Chrysalis Building, Bramley Road, W10 6SP.
Died 18 Oct. 2007.

CORNBERG, Catherine, (Mrs Sol Cornberg); *see* Gaskin, C.

CORNISH, Jack Bertram; HM Civil Service; Under-Secretary, Department of Health and Social Security, 1976–78; *b* 26 June 1918; *s* of Bertram George John Cornish and Nora Jarmy; *m* 1946, Mary Milton (decd); three *d*. *Educ:* Price's Grammar Sch., Fareham; Cotham Grammar Sch., Bristol. Admiralty, 1937–61: London, Bath, Plymouth, Singapore; DHSS, 1961–78. Supply Ships in Singapore and Newfoundland, 1941 and 1942. *Recreations:* music, painting, gardening.
Died 24 Dec. 2007.

CORNWALLIS, 3rd Baron *cr* 1927, of Linton, Kent; **Fiennes Neil Wykeham Cornwallis,** OBE 1963; DL; *b* 29 June 1921; *s* of 2nd Baron Cornwallis, KCVO, KBE, MC, and Cecily Etha Mary (*d* 1943), *d* of Sir James Walker, 3rd Bt; *S* father, 1982; *m* 1st, 1942, Judith Lacy Scott (marr. diss. 1948); one *s* (one *d* decd); 2nd, 1951, Agnes Jean Russell Landale (*d* 2001); one *s* three *d*; 3rd, 2002, Stephanie Coleman (*d* 2009). *Educ:* Eton. Served War, Coldstream Guards, 1940–44. Pres., British Agricultural Contractors Assoc., 1952–54; Pres., Nat. Assoc. of Agricultural Contractors, 1957–63 and 1986–98; Vice-Pres., Fedn of Agricl Co-operatives, 1984–86; Chm., Smaller Firms Council, CBI, 1978–81. Representative, Horticultural Co-operatives in the EEC, 1974–87. Chm., English Apples & Pears Ltd, 1990–94; Dir, Town & Country Building Soc. (formerly Planet, then Magnet & Planet, Bldg Soc.) 1967–92 (Chm., 1973–75; Dep. Chm., 1975–77; Chm., 1978–81 and 1991–92). Dep. Chm. and Exec. Gov., Cobham Hall Sch., 1969–72; Mem., Bd of Trustees, Chevening Estate, 1979–98. Fellow, Inst. of Horticulture, 1986; FRPSL 1998. Pro Grand Master, United Grand Lodge of England, 1982–91. DL Kent, 1976. *Recreations:* fishing, philately. *Heir:* *s* Hon. (Fiennes Wykeham) Jeremy Cornwallis [*b* 25 May 1946; *m* 1969, Sara Gray de Neufville, *d* of Lt-Col Nigel Stockwell, Benenden, Kent;

one *s* two *d*]. *Address:* Old Parsonage Cottage, Goudhurst, Cranbrook, Kent TN17 1AN. *T:* (01580) 211226. *Clubs:* Brooks's, Flyfishers'.   *Died 6 March 2010.*

COROB, Sidney, CBE 1993; Chairman: Corob Consolidated Ltd, 1984–2004; Corob Holdings Ltd, 1959–2004; *b* 2 May 1928; *s* of Wolf and Rachel Corob; *m* 1949, Elizabeth Springer; three *d*. *Educ:* Tree of Life Coll. Chief Exec., W. Corob & Son, 1951–59; Chairman: Corob Construction Co. Ltd, 1952–2001; Western & Northern Investments Ltd, 1964–68; Corob Intercity Ltd, 1968–77; Mayfair & City Properties plc, 1984–87. Lloyds Underwriter, 1978–85. Chairman: British Technion Soc., 1984–2000 (Hon. Pres., 2000–); Internat. Centre for Enhancement of Learning Potential, 1991–. Director: Eur. Jewish Publication Soc., 1995–; Jewish Assoc. for Business Ethics, 1994–. Vice President: CCJ, 1995– (Vice-Chm., 1978–95); British ORT, 1996–; Central Council for Jewish Social Services, 1989–99; Westmount Housing Assoc., 1974–. Life Pres., The HOPE Charity, 1998–. Hon. DSc Technion, Israel Inst. of Engrg and Technology, 1986. *Recreations:* foreign travel, hiking, Bible studies, opera, reading. *Address:* 62 Grosvenor Street, W1K 3JF. *T:* (020) 7499 4301.
                                    Died 27 Feb. 2009.

CORY, (Charles) Raymond, CBE 1982; Chairman: John Cory & Sons Ltd, 1965–91 (Director 1948–91); Milford Haven Port Authority (formerly Conservancy Board), 1982–94; *b* 20 Oct. 1922; *s* of Charles and Ethel Cory; *m* 1st, 1946, Vivienne Mary Roberts (*d* 1988), Kelowna, BC, Canada; three *d*; 2nd, 1989, Betty (*d* 2000), *widow* of Lt-Col Roy Horley. *Educ:* Harrow; Christ Church, Oxford. Served RNVR, Ord. Seaman to Lieut, 1942–46; Russian and N Atlantic convoys and Normandy landings (C-in-C's Commendation June 1944). Vice-Chm., A. B. Electronics Products Group PLC, 1979–92. Dir and Mem. Executive, Baltic and Internat. Maritime Conf., Copenhagen, 1957–67; Mem., Lloyd's Register of Shipping, 1963–67. Chairman: Barry Pilotage Authority, 1963–74 (Mem. 1953); Port Talbot Pilotage Authority, 1970–74; SE Wales Pilotage Authority, 1974–80; Welsh Council Mission to Seamen, 1984–95; Vice-Chm., BTDB, 1969–79 (Mem., 1966–79); Chm., S Wales Local Bd, 1966); Pres., Cardiff Chamber of Commerce, 1959–60. Chm., S Glamorgan HA, 1974–84. Church in Wales: Member: Governing Body, 1957–60; Rep. Body, 1960–97 (Dep. Chm., 1985–95; Treasurer, 1988–); Finance Cttee, 1960–88 (Vice-Chm. 1971, Chm. 1975–88); Dep. Chm., Finance and Resources Cttee, 1988–95. RNLI: Chm. Cardiff Br., 1950–73; Mem. Cttee of Management, 1954–97; Vice-Pres. 1969–97, Life Vice-Pres., 1997; Dep. Chm., 1985–93; Mem., Exec. Cttee, 1970–93. Chm., Council, Univ. of Wales Coll. of Medicine, 1988–97 (Mem., 1984–97). *Publications:* A Century of Family Shipowning, 1954. *Recreations:* formerly ski-ing, sailing and gardening. *Address:* The Coach House, Llanblethian, Cowbridge, Vale of Glamorgan CF71 7JF. *T:* (01446) 772251. *Club:* Cardiff and County.   *Died 16 Feb. 2007.*

COSSHAM, Christopher Hugh, CB 1989; Senior Assistant Director of Public Prosecutions (Northern Ireland), 1973–89; *b* 12 April 1929; *s* of Lorimer and Gwendolin Cossham; *m* 1958, Joanna Howard Smith; one *s* one *d*. *Educ:* Monkton Combe Sch.; Bristol Univ.; BA Open Univ. Called to Bar, Gray's Inn, 1958. Board of Trade, 1958–62; Director of Public Prosecutions Dept, 1962–73. Dep. Metropolitan Stipendiary Magistrate, 1978–86. Mem., Wkg Party on handling of complaints against police, 1974. *Recreations:* cycling, listening to music, writing humorous verse. *Address:* Valhalla, 1 The Grange, High Street, Portishead, Bristol BS20 6QL. *T:* (01275) 845237. *Clubs:* Civil Service, Northern Law.
                                    Died 21 Dec. 2008.

COSTELLO, Gordon John; Chief Accountant of the Bank of England, 1975–78; *b* 29 March 1921; *s* of late Ernest James Costello and Hilda May Costello; *m* 1946, Joan Lilian Moore; two *s* one *d*. *Educ:* Varndean Sch. Served War, 1939–45 (RA). Bank of England, 1946;

worked in various Departments; Asst Chief Accountant, 1964; Asst Sec., 1965; Dep. Sec., 1968; Dep. Chief Cashier, 1970. *Recreations:* music, travel, walking, tennis. *Address:* 26 Peacock Lane, Brighton, Sussex BN1 6WA. *T:* (01273) 552344.   *Died 27 June 2007.*

COTTERELL, Geoffrey; author; *b* 24 Nov. 1919; *yr s* of late Graham Cotterell and Millicent (*née* Crews). *Educ:* Bishop's Stortford College. Served War of 1939–45, Royal Artillery, 1940–46. *Publications:* Then a Soldier, 1944; This is the Way, 1947; Randle in Springtime, 1949; Strait and Narrow, 1950; Westward the Sun, 1952 (repr. 1973); The Strange Enchantment, 1956 (repr. 1973); Tea at Shadow Creek, 1958; Tiara Tahiti, 1960 (filmed 1962, screenplay with Ivan Foxwell); Go, said the bird, 1966; Bowers of Innocence, 1970; Amsterdam, the life of a city, 1972. *Recreation:* golf. *Address:* 2 Fulbourne House, Blackwater Road, Eastbourne, Sussex BN20 7DN. *Clubs:* Royal Automobile; Cooden Beach Golf.   *Died 6 Dec. 2010.*

COTTON, Sir Bill; *see* Cotton, Sir W. F.

COTTON, Christopher P.; *see* Powell-Cotton.

COTTON, Hon. Sir Robert (Carrington), KCMG 1978; AO 1993; FCPA; Chairman of Directors, Kleinwort Benson Australian Income Fund Inc., since 1986; *b* 29 Nov. 1915; *s* of H. L. Carrington Cotton; *m* 1937, Eve Elizabeth Macdougall; one *s* two *d*. *Educ:* St Peter's Coll., Adelaide, SA. FCPA 1977. State President of Liberal Party (NSW), 1956–59; Federal Vice-Pres., 1960–61; elected to Senate, 1965; Minister for Civil Aviation, 1969–72; Shadow Minister for Manufacturing Industry (in Opposition), 1972–75; Minister for Industry and Commerce, 1975–77; Australian Consul-Gen. in NY, 1978–81; Ambassador to USA, 1982–85. Chm. (acting), Alders International Pty Ltd, Australia, 1987. Sen. Advr, Hill & Knowlton Inc., 1988–93. Mem. Bd, Reserve Bank of Australia, 1982–83; Dir, Thomson-CSF Pacific Holdings Pty Ltd, 1996–. Chairman: Australian Nat. Gall. Foundn, 1991–94; Australian Photonics Co-operative Res. Centre, 1992–. Hon. DSc Sydney, 1995. *Recreations:* swimming, writing, photography. *Address:* Apartment 11, Southern Cross Gardens, 2 Spruson Street, Neutral Bay, NSW 2089, Australia. *T:* (2) 99545066. *Clubs:* The Brook, Pilgrims (NY); Australian (Sydney); Commonwealth (Canberra).   *Died 25 Dec. 2006.*

COTTON, Sir William Frederick, (Sir Bill Cotton), Kt 2001; CBE 1989 (OBE 1976); Chairman, Meridian Broadcasting, 1996–2001 (Deputy Chairman, 1992–96); Director, Alba plc, 1988–2006; *b* 23 April 1928; *s* of late William Edward (Billy) Cotton and Mabel Hope; *m* 1st, 1950, Bernadine Maud (*née* Sinclair) (*d* 1964); three *d*; 2nd, 1965, Ann Corfield (*née* Bucknall) (marr. diss. 1989); 3rd, 1990, Kathryn Mary (*née* Ralphs). *Educ:* Ardingly College. Jt Man. Dir, Michael Reine Music Co., 1952–56; BBC-TV: Producer, Light Entertainment Dept, 1956–62; Asst Head of Light Entertainment, 1962–67; Head of Variety, 1967–70; Head of Light Entertainment Gp, 1970–77; Controller, BBC 1, 1977–81; Dep. Man. Dir, 1981–82; Dir of Programmes, Television, and Dir of Develt, BBC, 1982; Chm., BBC Enterprises, 1982–86 and 1987–88 (Vice Chm., 1986–87); Man. Dir, Television, BBC, 1984–88. Chm., Noel Gay TV, 1988–97; Director: Noel Gay Orgn, 1988–97; Billy Marsh Associates, 1998–. Vice-Pres., Marie Curie Cancer Care (formerly Marie Curie Foundn), 1990–. FRTS 1983 (Vice-Pres., 1984–92; Pres., 1992–95); Fellow, BAFTA, 1998. Hon. DA Bournemouth Univ., 2001. *Publications:* Double Bill: 80 years of entertainment (autobiog.), 2000. *Recreations:* golf, theatre. *Address:* Summer Hill, The Glebe, Studland, Swanage, Dorset BH19 3AS. *Clubs:* Garrick, Hurlingham; Royal & Ancient Golf (St Andrews); Royal Motor Yacht.   *Died 11 Aug. 2008.*

COTTRELL, Bryce Arthur Murray; Chairman, JWM Partners (UK) Ltd, 1999–2005; *b* 16 Sept. 1931; *s* of late Brig. A. F. B. Cottrell, DSO, OBE and Mrs M. B.

Cottrell (née Nicoll); m 1955, Jeane Dolores Monk; two s two d. Educ: Charterhouse; Corpus Christi Coll., Oxford (MA). Joined Phillips & Drew, 1955; Partner, 1963; Sen. Partner, 1983; Chm., 1985–88. Dir, Long Term Capital Portfolio (GP) Ltd, 1994–99. Fellow and Funding Dir, Corpus Christi Coll., Oxford, 1990–92. Recreations: sport, railways. Address: Portreeves House, East Street, Tonbridge TN9 1HP. T: (01732) 773277.
Died 20 Jan. 2006.

COUPLAND, Prof. Rex Ernest; Professor of Human Morphology, 1967–89, and Dean of Medicine, 1981–87, University of Nottingham; Hon. Consultant, Trent Regional Hospital Board, 1970–89; b 30 Jan. 1924; s of late Ernest Coupland, company dir and Doris Coupland; m 1947, (Lucy) Eileen Sargent; one s one d. Educ: Mirfield Grammar Sch.; University of Leeds. MB, ChB with honours, 1947; MD with distinction, 1952; PhD 1954; DSc 1970. House appointments, Leeds General Infirmary, 1947; Demonstrator and Lecturer in Anatomy, University of Leeds, 1948, 1950–58; Asst Prof. of Anatomy, University of Minnesota, USA, 1955–56; Prof. of Anatomy, Queen's Coll., Dundee, University of St Andrews, 1958–67. Medical Officer, RAF, 1948–50. FRSE 1960. Member: Biological Research Board of MRC, 1964–70; Med. Adv. Bd, Crippling Diseases Foundn, 1971–75; CMO's Academic Forum, 1984–89; Chm., MRC Non-Ionizing Radiations Cttee, 1970–89; Derbyshire AHA, 1978–81; Trent RHA, 1981–88; Chm., Nottingham Div., BMA, 1978–79; GMC, 1982–88; Med. sub-cttee, UGC, 1984–89. President: Anat. Soc. GB and Ireland, 1976–78; British Assoc. of Clinical Anat., 1977–82. Wood Jones Medal for contrib. to clinical anatomy, RCS, 1984. Publications: The Natural History of the Chromaffin Cell, 1965; (ed jtly) Chromaffin, Enterochromaffin and Related Cells, 1976; (ed jtly) Peripheral Neuroendocrine Interaction, 1978; papers in jls of anatomy, physiology, endocrinology, pathology and pharmacology on endocrine and nervous systems and in jls of radiology on NMR imaging; chapters on: Anatomy of the Human Kidney, in Renal Disease (ed Black), 1962, 1968, 1973; The Chromaffin System, in Catecholamines (ed Blaschko and Muscholl), 1973; The Blood Supply of the Adrenal Gland, in Handbook of Physiology, 1974; The Adrenal Medulla, in The Cell in Medical Science (ed Beck and Lloyd), 1976; Endocrine System, in Textbook of Human Anatomy (ed W. J. Hamilton), 1976; contribs to: Hormones and Evolution, Vol. I, ed Barrington, 1979; Biogenic Amines in Development, ed Parvez and Parvez, 1980; Hormones in Human Tissues, Vol. I, ed Fotherby and Pal, 1981; Asst Editor, Gray's Anatomy (ed Davies), 1967. Recreations: shooting, gardening, watercolour painting. Address: Foxhollow, Quaker Lane, Farnsfield, Newark, Notts NG22 8EE. T: (01623) 882028. Died 22 June 2008.

COURT, Hon. Sir Charles (Walter Michael), AK 1982; KCMG 1979; Kt 1972; OBE 1946; MLA (Liberal Party) for Nedlands, 1953–82; Premier of Western Australia, 1974–82; also Treasurer, and Minister co-ordinating Economic and Regional Development, 1974–82; b Crawley, Sussex, 29 Sept. 1911; s of late W. J. Court, Perth; m 1st, 1936, Rita M. (d 1992), d of L. R. Steffanoni; five s; 2nd, 1997, Judith Butt. Educ: Leederville and Rosalie State Schs; Perth Boys' Sch. Chartered Accountant, 1933; Foundn Partner, Hendry, Rae & Court, 1938–70. Served AIF, 1940–46, Lt-Col. State Registrar, Inst. Chartered Accountants in Aust. (WA Br.), 1946–52, Mem. State Council, 1952–55. Dep. Leader, 1957–59, 1971–72, and Leader, 1972–74, of Opposition, WA; Minister, Western Australia: for Industrial Development and the NW, 1959–71; for Railways, 1959–67; for Transport, 1965–66. Chairman: Adv. Cttee under WA Prices Control Act, 1948–52; Taiwan Trade Assoc., 1984–87; President: WA Band Assoc., 1954–59; Order of Australia Assoc., 1987–89 (Hon. Life Mem., 1994). Warden, WA State War Meml, 1991–92. Chm. Adv. Council, Asia Res. Council, Murdoch Univ. Patron: WA Div., PGA; WA Youth Orch.; WA Opera Co. Hon. Colonel: WA Univ. Regt,

1969–75; SAS Regt, 1976–80. Paul Harris Fellow, 1982, Sapphire Pin, 1991, Rotary. FCA; FCIS; FASA. Hon. FAIM 1980. Freeman: City of Nedlands, 1982; Shire of West Kimberley, WA, 1983. Hon. LLD Univ. of WA. 1969; Hon. DTech WA Inst. of Technol., 1982; Hon. Dr Murdoch Univ., 1995; Hon. DLitt Edith Cowan Univ., 1999. Manufacturers' Export Council Award, 1969; James Kirby Award, Inst. of Production Engrs, 1971; Australian Chartered Accountant of the Year, 1983. Life Member: Musicians Union, 1953; ASA, 1979; Returned Services League, 1981; Inst. of Chartered Accountants in Australia, 1982; Gold Star Medal and Life Mem., Strategic Studies Assoc., Va, 2005. Order of the Sacred Treasure, 1st cl. (Japan), 1983; Kt Comdr, Order of Merit (Italian Republic), 1991; Order of Brilliant Star with Grand Cordon (Taiwan), 1991. Publications: many professional papers on accountancy, and papers on economic and resource development. Recreation: music and other cultural and sporting interests. Address: Unit 83, 4 Albert Street, Claremont, WA 6010, Australia. Clubs: Weld, Western Australian (Hon. Life Mem.), Commercial Travellers Association (Perth); Nedlands Rotary, Lions.
Died 22 Dec. 2007.

COUSINS, Brian Harry, CBE 1981; Principal Establishment and Finance Officer, Lord Chancellor's Department, 1989–93; b 18 July 1933; s of late William and Ethel Margaret Cousins; m 1957, Margaret (née Spark); two s. Educ: Devonport High School. Served RAF, pilot, 1952–54. Joined Ministry of Defence, 1954; Private Sec. to Permanent Secretary, 1962–65; Private Sec. Parliamentary Secretary, 1971–72; ndc 1972; Civil Sec., British Forces Germany, 1973–76; Asst Under Sec. of State, MoD, 1981–85, 1986–89; Chm., CSSB, 1985–86. Recreations: golf, local affairs, music, gardening. Address: c/o HSBC, Ewell, Surrey. Club: Royal Automobile. Died 19 Aug. 2007.

COUVE DE MURVILLE, Most Rev. Maurice Noël Léon; Archbishop of Birmingham, (RC), 1982–99; b 27 June 1929; s of Noël Couve de Murville and Marie, d of Sir Louis Souchon. Educ: Downside School; Trinity Coll., Cambridge (MA); STL (Institut Catholique, Paris); MPhil (Sch. of Oriental and African Studies, Univ. of London). Priest, 1957; Curate, St Anselm's, Dartford, 1957–60; Priest-in-Charge, St Francis, Moulsecoomb, 1961–64; Catholic Chaplain: Univ. of Sussex, 1961–77; Univ. of Cambridge, 1977–82. Principal Chaplain, British Assoc., Order of Malta, 1987–91, 2000–05. DUniv Open, 1994; Hon. DD Birmingham, 1996. Grand Cross Conventual Chaplain, SMO Malta, 1982. Publications: (with Philip Jenkins) Catholic Cambridge, 1983; John Milner 1752–1826, 1986; Karl Leisner, 1988; Pierre Toussaint, 1995; Junípero Serra, 2000; (trans.) J. P. Charbonnier, History of Christians in China, 2007. Recreations: gardening, local history. Address: 53 North Parade, Horsham, W Sussex RH12 2DE. Clubs: Athenæum, Lansdowne. Died 3 Nov. 2007.

COWDREY, Rev. (Herbert Edward) John, FBA 1991; Emeritus Fellow, St Edmund Hall, Oxford, since 1994 (Senior Research Fellow in Modern History, 1987–94); b 29 Nov. 1926; s of Herbert and Winifred Cowdrey; m 1959, Judith Watson Davis (d 2004); one s two d. Educ: Queen Mary's Sch., Basingstoke; Trinity Coll., Oxford (BA Modern Hist. and Theology, 1951; MA); St Stephen's House, Oxford (Hon. Fellow, 2005); DD Oxon 2000. Nat. service, RN, 1945–47. Deacon, 1952; priest, 1953; Tutor and Chaplain, St Stephen's House, Oxford, 1952–56; Fellow and Tutor in Modern History, St Edmund Hall, Oxford, 1956–87. Leverhulme Emeritus Fellow, 1996–98. Publications: The Cluniacs and the Gregorian Reform, 1970; The Epistolae vagantes of Pope Gregory VII, 1972; Two Studies in Cluniac History, 1978; The Age of Abbot Desiderius, 1983; Popes, Monks and Crusaders, 1984; Pope Gregory VII, 1998; The Crusades and Latin Monasticism, 1999; Popes and Church Reform in the 11th Century, 2000; The Register of Pope Gregory VII, 2002; Lanfranc: scholar, monk and

archbishop, 2003; articles and reviews in learned jls. *Recreation:* listening to music. *Address:* 19 Church Lane, Old Marston, Oxford OX3 0NZ. *T:* (01865) 794486.
Died 4 Dec. 2009.

COWGILL, Bryan; television producer; Consultant, Sports' Masters International, since 2002; *b* 27 May 1927; *m* 1966, Jennifer E. Baker; two *s. Educ:* Clitheroe Grammar School. Marine, subseq. Lieut, 3rd Royal Marine Commando Bde, SE Asia, 1943–47. Copy boy, then reporter, then feature writer with Lancashire Evening Post and Preston Guardian Group, 1942–50; edited local newspaper, Clitheroe, 1950–55; joined BBC TV as Outside Broadcasts prodn asst, 1955; produced Sportsview and Grandstand, 1957–63; Head of BBC Sport, 1963; founder, Match of the Day, 1964, Sportsnight, 1968; coined phrase 'action replay' for slow motion video, first introd. in BBC World Cup coverage, 1966; Head of TV Outside Broadcasts Group, 1972; Controller, BBC1, 1974–77; Dir, News and Current Affairs, BBC, 1977; Man. Dir, Thames Television, 1977–85; Man. Dir, Championship Television, 1989–90. Chairman: Euston Films, 1977–85; Cosgrove Hall Productions, 1977–85; Thames Television Internat., 1982–85; WTN (formerly UPITN), 1983–85; Thames Cable and Satellite Services, 1984–85. BAFTA Awards: Olympic Games, Rome, 1960; BBC coverage of World Cup, 1966; Olympic Games, Mexico City, 1968; Judges' Special Award, RTS Sports Awards, 2007. FRTS 1984. *Publications:* Mr Action Replay, 2006. *Recreations:* reading, theatre, cinema, music, watching television sport. *Address:* 38 Saxon Close, Stratford-upon-Avon, Warwicks CV37 7DX.
Died 14 July 2008.

COWPERTHWAITE, David Jarvis; Under-Secretary, Scottish Home and Health Department, 1974–81, retired; *b* 14 Sept. 1921; *s* of J. J. Cowperthwaite and Mrs J. W. B. Cowperthwaite (*née* Jarvis); *m* 1944, Patricia Stockdale (*d* 1993); two *d. Educ:* Edinburgh Academy; Exeter Coll., Oxford (MA). Nigerian Admin. Service, 1942–48; joined Home Civil Service (Scottish Home Dept), 1948. *Address:* 69 Northumberland Street, Edinburgh EH3 6JG. *T:* (0131) 557 0215.
Died 20 Oct. 2006.

COWPERTHWAITE, Sir John James, KBE 1968 (OBE 1960); CMG 1964; International Adviser to Jardine Fleming & Co. Ltd, Hong Kong, 1972–81; Financial Secretary, Hong Kong, 1961–71; *b* 25 April 1915; *s* of late John James Cowperthwaite and Jessie Wemyss Barron Jarvis Cowperthwaite; *m* 1941, Sheila Mary, *d* of Alexander Thomson, Aberdeen; (one *s* decd). *Educ:* Merchiston Castle Sch.; St Andrews Univ; Christ's Coll., Cambridge. Entered Colonial Administrative Service, Hong Kong, 1941; seconded to Sierra Leone, 1942–45. *Address:* 25 South Street, St Andrews, Fife KY16 9QS. *T:* (01334) 474759. *Clubs:* Hong Kong Jockey, Hong Kong Golf; Royal and Ancient.
Died 21 Jan. 2006.

COWTAN, Maj.-Gen. Frank Willoughby John, CBE 1970 (MBE 1947); MC 1942 and Bar, 1945; *b* 10 Feb. 1920; *s* of late Air Vice-Marshal F. C. Cowtan, CB, CBE, KHS and Mrs N. A. Cowtan (*née* Kennedy); *m* 1949, Rose Isabel Cope; one *s* one *d. Educ:* Wellington Coll.; RMA Woolwich. 2nd Lieut Royal Engineers, 1939; served War of 1939–45, BEF, N Africa, Italy, NW Europe (Captain); Palestine, Kenya, Middle East, 1945–50 (Major); psc 1951; Middle East, UK, BAOR, 1952–58; Liaison Officer to US Corps of Engrs, USA, 1958–60 (Bt Lt-Col); CO 131 Parachute Engr Regt, 1960–62; CO Victory Coll., RMA Sandhurst, 1962–65 (Lt-Col); Comd 11 Engr Bde, BAOR, 1965–67 (Brig.); ndc (Canada) 1967–68; Dir of Quartering (Army), 1968–70; Maj.-Gen. 1969; Dep. QMG, 1970–71; Comdt, RMCS, 1971–75. Hon. Col, 131 Ind. Commando Sqn, RE, 1975–80; Col Comdt RE, 1977–82. Dep. Dir, CLA Game Fair, 1978–86. *Recreations:* travel, languages, crosswords, support of field sports, particularly wildfowling. *Address:* Rectory Cottage, Coleshill, Swindon SN6 7PR.
Died 1 Jan. 2010.

COX, Prof. (Charles) Brian, CBE 1990; John Edward Taylor Professor of English Literature, University of Manchester, 1976–93, then Emeritus; *b* 5 Sept. 1928; *s* of late Hedley E. Cox and Rose Thompson; *m* 1954, Jean Willmer; one *s* two *d. Educ:* Wintringham Sec. Sch.; Pembroke Coll., Cambridge (MA, MLitt). Lectr, Univ. of Hull, 1954–66; Manchester University: Prof. of English Lit., 1966–76; Dean, Faculty of Arts, 1984–86; Pro-Vice-Chancellor, 1987–91. Vis. Associate Prof., Univ. of Calif, Berkeley, 1964–65; Brown Fellow, Univ. of the South, Sewanee, Tennessee, 1980; Lord Northcliffe Lectr, UCL, 1991; Visiting Professor: KCL, 1994–96; Sheffield Hallam Univ., 1994–98. Pres., Nat. Council for Educnl Standards, 1984–89 (Chm., 1979–84); Mem., Kingman Cttee, 1987–88; Chm., Nat. Curriculum English Working Gp, 1988–89. Chairman: NW Arts Bd, 1994–2000; Arvon Foundn, 1994–97; Mem., Arts Council of England, 1996–98. Co-editor: Critical Qly, 1959–; Black Papers on Education, 1969–77. FRSL 1993. Hon. Fellow, Westminster Coll., Oxford, 1994. Hon. DLitt De Montfort, 1999. *Publications:* The Free Spirit, 1963; (ed with A. E. Dyson) Modern Poetry, 1963; (ed with A. E. Dyson) Practical Criticism of Poetry, 1965; Joseph Conrad: the modern imagination, 1974; Every Common Sight (poems), 1981; Two-Headed Monster (poems), 1985; Cox on Cox: an English curriculum for the 1990s, 1991; The Great Betrayal (autobiog.), 1992; Collected Poems, 1993, The Battle for the English Curriculum, 1995; (ed) African Writers, 1996; (ed) Literacy is not Enough, 1998; Emeritus (poems), 2001; My Lightieth Year to Heaven (poems), 2007. *Recreations:* Manchester United, walking. *Address:* 20 Park Gates Drive, Cheadle Hulme, Stockport SK8 7DF. *T:* (0161) 485 2162. *Club:* Lansdowne.
Died 24 April 2008.

COX, Dennis George; Under-Secretary (Industrial Relations), Department of Employment, 1971–74; a Deputy Chairman, Central Arbitration Committee, 1977–84; *b* 23 Feb. 1914; *s* of George and Amelia Cox; *m* 1938, Victoria Barraclough (*d* 2000); one *s* (and one *s* decd). *Educ:* University College Sch.; Queens' Coll., Cambridge. Royal Navy, 1942–45; served with Netherlands and Norwegian navies, Lieut RNVR. Entered Min. of Labour, 1936; Asst Sec. 1966; Regional Controller, SW Region. *Recreations:* gardening, fishing. *Address:* 105 Court Road, Lewes, East Sussex BN7 2RZ. *T:* (01273) 472818.
Died 31 Oct. 2007.

COX, Sir Geoffrey (Sandford), CNZM 2000; Kt 1966; CBE 1959 (MBE (mil.) 1945); *b* 7 April 1910; *s* of Sandford Cox, Wellington, NZ, and Mary Cox (*née* MacGregor); *m* 1935, Cecily Barbara Talbot Turner (*d* 1993); two *s* two *d* (twins). *Educ:* Southland High Sch., New Zealand; Otago Univ., New Zealand (MA): Rhodes Scholar, 1932–35; Oriel Coll., Oxford (BA). Reporter, Foreign and War Corresp, News Chronicle, 1935–37, Daily Express, 1937–40. Enlisted New Zealand Army, 1940; commissioned, Dec. 1940; served in 2 New Zealand Div., Greece, Crete, Libya, Italy; Major, Chief Intelligence Officer, Gen. Freyberg's staff (despatches twice). First Sec. and Chargé d'Affaires, NZ Legation, Washington, 1943; NZ Rep., first UNRRA Conf., 1943; Political Corresp., News Chronicle, 1945; Asst Editor, News Chronicle 1954. Regular Contributor, BBC radio and TV, 1945–56; Editor and Chief Exec., Independent Television News, 1956–68; founded News at Ten, 1967; Dep. Chm., Yorkshire Television, 1968–71; Chm., Tyne Tees Television, 1971–74; Chm., LBC Radio, 1978–81; independent Dir, The Observer, 1981–89. FRTS (Silver Medal, 1963; Gold Medal, 1978); Fellow, British Kinematograph and TV Soc. TV Producers' Guild Award Winner, 1962. Hon. DLitt Otago, 1999. *Publications:* Defence of Madrid, 1937; The Red Army Moves, 1941; The Road to Trieste, 1946; The Race for Trieste, 1977; See It Happen, 1983; A Tale of Two Battles, 1987; Countdown to War, 1988; Pioneering Television News, 1995; Eyewitness, 1999. *Recreations:* fishing, tracing Roman roads. *Club:* Garrick.
Died 2 April 2008.

COX, Vice-Adm. Sir John (Michael Holland), KCB 1982; Director, Sound Alive, 1988–97; Flag Officer Naval Air Command, 1982–83; *b* Peking, China, 27 Oct. 1928; *s* of late Thomas Cox, MBE, and of Daisy Anne Cox; *m* 1962, Anne Garden Farquharson Seth-Smith; one *s* one *d*. *Educ*: Hilton Coll., Natal, SA. Joined BRNC, 1946; ADC to C-in-C Allied Forces, N Europe, 1952–53; ADC to Governor of Victoria, 1955; commanded HM Ships: Dilston, 1957 (despatches); Stubbington, 1958; sc Camberley, 1960; Cadet Trng Officer, BRNC Dartmouth, 1962; CSO, London Div., RNR, 1963; commanded HMS: Surprise, 1964; Naiad, 1965; Comdr, Sea Trng, Staff of Flag Officer Sea Trng, 1967; Naval Attaché, Bonn, 1969; comd HMS Norfolk, 1972; Dir, Naval Ops and Trade, 1973–75; Comdr, Standing Naval Force Atlantic, 1976–77; COS to C-in-C, Naval Home Command, 1977–79; Flag Officer Third Flotilla and Comdr Anti-Submarine Group Two, 1979–82. Dir, Spastics Soc., 1984–88. *Recreation*: gardening. *Club*: Lansdowne. *Died 3 Oct. 2006.*

COX, Norman Ernest, CMG 1973; MA; HM Diplomatic Service, retired; *b* 28 Aug. 1921; *s* of late Ernest William Cox and late Daisy Beatrice (*née* Edmonds); *m* 1945, Mary Margarita (*née* Cruz); one *d* (one *s* decd). *Educ*: Lycée Français de Madrid; King's Coll., London (BA (Hons) 1956); Inst. of Latin Amer. Studies, London Univ. (MA 1973). Tax Officer, Inland Revenue, 1938–41; Army, Intell. Corps, 1941–45: Gibraltar, 1942–45; Attaché, Madrid, 1945–47; FO, 1947–50; 2nd Sec., Sofia, 1950–52; 2nd Sec., Montevideo, 1952–54; FO, 1954–57; Dep. Regional Information Officer for SE Asia, Singapore, 1957–60; FO, 1960–62: Laos Conf., Geneva, 1961; Sec. to UK Conf. Delegn to ECSC, Luxemburg, 1962–63; 1st Sec. (Commercial), Madrid, 1963–66; Counsellor (Information), Mexico, Regional Information Officer for Central American Republics, PRO to Duke of Edinburgh for 1968 Olympics, 1966–68; Counsellor (Commercial), Moscow, 1969–72; Diplomatic Service Inspector, 1973–74; Ambassador to: Ecuador, 1974–77; Mexico, 1977–81. Res. student, LSE, 1981–84. Vice-Pres., British Mexican Soc., 1985– (Chm., 1982–84). Hon. Mem. Bd, Anglo-Mexican Cultural Inst., Mexico, 1996. Order of Aztec Eagle (Mexico), 1994. *Publications*: (jtly) Politics in Mexico, 1985. *Recreations*: archaeology, history, genealogy, linguistics, comparative religion. *Died 6 April 2008.*

COX, Oliver Jasper, CBE 1982; RIBA; Principal, Oliver Cox, Consultant Architect, since 2007 (Partner, Jean & Oliver Cox, 1989–2007); *b* 20 April 1920; *s* of William Edward and Elsie Gertrude Cox; *m* 1953, Jean (*d* 2007); one *s* two *d*. *Educ*: Mill Hill Sch.; Architectural Association School of Architecture (AADip Hons). DistTP. Architects Dept, Herts CC, New Schools Division, 1948–49; Architects Dept, LCC Housing Division, 1950–59; Dep. Chief Architect, and Leader, Research and Development Gp, Min. of Housing and Local Govt, 1960–64; Partner, Shankland/Cox Partnership, 1965–85. *Publications*: Upgrading and Renewing the Historic City of Port Royal, Jamaica, 1985; (jtly) Lauderdale Revealed, 1993; The Naval Hospitals of Port Royal, Jamaica, 1996; Oracabessa: the town, the people and the waterfront development, 1997; (jtly) Lauderdale Reborn, 2003. *Recreations*: painting, drawing and screen printing. *Address*: 22 Grove Terrace, NW5 1PL. *T*: (020) 7485 6929. *Died 24 April 2010.*

COX, His Honour Roger Charles; a Circuit Judge, 1988–2004; *b* 18 April 1941; *s* of late Reginald William Cox and Hilda Cox; *m* 1970, Patricia Anne Edwards. *Educ*: Cheltenham Grammar Sch.; Birmingham Univ. (LLB, LLM). Called to the Bar, Gray's Inn, 1965. Asst Lectr, Faculty of Law, Bristol Univ., 1964–66; Lord Justice Holker Sen. Schol., Gray's Inn, 1966; a Recorder, 1986. *Publications*: (contrib.) Guidelines for the

Assessment of Damages in Personal Injury Cases. *Recreations*: travel, music, theatre, reading, Freemasonry. *Died 6 April 2009.*

CRABB, Most Rev. Frederick Hugh Wright; DD; *b* Luppitt, Devon, 24 April 1915; *s* of William Samuel and Florence Mary Crabb; *m* 1946, (Alice) Margery Coombs; two *s* two *d*. *Educ*: Luppitt Parochial Sch.; Univ. of London (St John's Hall, Highbury, London); BD Lond. (1st Cl. Hons); ALCD (1st Cl. Hons). Ordained deacon 1939, priest 1940; Asst Curate, St James', West Teignmouth, Devon, 1939–41; Asst Priest, St Andrew's, Plymouth, 1941–42; Missionary at Akot, S Sudan, 1942–44; Principal, Bishop Gwynne Divinity Sch., S Sudan, 1944–51; Vice Principal, London Coll. of Divinity, 1951–57; Principal, Coll. of Emmanuel and St Chad, Saskatoon, Sask., 1957–67; Associate Priest, Christ Church, Calgary, Alberta, 1967–69; Rector, St Stephen's Church, Calgary, 1969–75; Bishop of Athabasca, 1975–83; Metropolitan of Rupert's Land, 1977–82; Hon. Asst, St Cyprian, Calgary, and Dir, Anglican Sch. of Lay Ministry, 1983–87. Hon. Chaplain, Calgary Div., Royal Canadian Mounted Police Veterans' Assoc., 1985–2004 (Hon. Life Mem. 1998). Mem. Governing Council, Athabasca Univ., 1982–85. Hon. DD: Wycliffe Coll., Toronto, 1960; St Andrew's Coll., Saskatoon, 1967; Coll. of Emmanuel and St Chad, Saskatoon, 1979. *Publications*: (jtly) Rupert's Land: A Cultural Tapestry, 1988. *Recreations*: gardening, mountain hiking. *Address*: Statesman Life Centre, Suite 324, 6700 Hunterview Drive NW, Calgary, AB T2K 6K4, Canada. *Died 24 Feb. 2007.*

CRABTREE, Prof. Lewis Frederick, PhD; FRAeS, FAIAA; Sir George White Professor of Aeronautical Engineering, University of Bristol, 1973–85, then Emeritus; *b* 16 Nov. 1924; *m* 1955, Averil Joan Escott; one *s* one *d*. *Educ*: Grange High Sch., Bradford; Univ. of Leeds; Imperial Coll. of Science and Technology; Cornell Univ., USA. BSc (Mech. Eng) Leeds, 1945; DIC (Aeronautics), 1947; PhD (Aero Eng), Cornell, 1952. Air Engr Officer, RNVR, 1945–46. Grad. apprentice, Saunders-Roe Ltd, E Cowes, IoW, 1947–50; ECA Fellowship, Grad. Sch. of Aero. Engrg, Cornell Univ., 1950–52; Aerodynamics Dept, RAE, Farnborough, 1953–73; Head of: Hypersonics and High temperature Gasdynamics Div., 1961–66; Low Speed Aerodynamics Div., 1966–70; Propulsion Aerodynamics and Noise Div., 1970–73. Visiting Prof., Cornell Univ., 1957. First Chm., Aerospace Technol. Bd, DSAC, 1980–83. Chairman: Brecknock Wildlife Trust, 1988–91; Welsh Wildlife Trusts Ltd, 1994–95. Lectures to RAeS: Lanchester Meml, 1977; Handley Page, 1979; Barnwell, 1981. Pres., RAeS, 1978–79 (Usborne Meml Prize, 1955). *Publications*: Elements of Hypersonic Aerodynamics, 1965; contributor to: Incompressible Aerodynamics, 1960; Laminar Boundary Layers, 1963; Engineering Structures, 1983; articles chiefly in Jl RAeS, Aeron. Quart., Jl Aeron. Sci., Jahrbuch der WGLR, and Reports and Memos of ARC. *Address*: Carlton House, 25 High Street, Crickhowell, Powys NP8 1BE. *T*: (01873) 810507. *Died 8 May 2006.*

CRABTREE, Simon; see Wharton, M. B.

CRACROFT-ELEY, Bridget Katharine, CVO 2008; Lord-Lieutenant of Lincolnshire, 1995–2008; *b* 29 Oct. 1933; *d* of Weston Cracroft-Amcotts and Rhona (*née* Clifton-Brown); *m* 1959, Robert Peel Charles Cracroft-Eley (*d* 1996); one *s* one *d*. *Educ*: Lincoln Girls' High Sch.; Crofton Grange Sch., Buntingford, Herts. Voluntary and charity work, including: WRVS, 1974–94; Lincs Old Churches Trust, 1980–; Girl Guides, 1984–; RNIB Looking Glass Appeal, 1990–91. Parish Councillor, Hackthorn and Cold Hanworth, 1980–. Governor: Hackthorn C of E Primary Sch., 1988–2006; King's Sch., Grantham, 1995–. High Sheriff, Lincs, 1989–90. Hon. Col, Lincs ACF, 2001–06. DStJ 1996. Hon. LLD: De Montfort, 1999; Lincoln, 2003. *Recreations*: upholstery,

gardening, the arts. *Address:* The Little House, Hackthorn, Lincoln LN2 3PQ. *T:* (01673) 860212.
Died 29 Aug. 2008.

CRADDOCK, (William) Aleck, LVO 1981; Director, Harrods Ltd, 1964–88 (Managing Director, 1980–84, Chairman, 1981–86, Deputy Chairman, 1987–88); Director, Cartier Ltd, 1986–97; *b* Nov. 1924; *m* 1947, Olive May Brown; one *s* one *d. Educ:* City of London School. Joined Druce and Craddock, Craddock and Tomkins Ltd (family firm), Meat and Provision Merchants, Marylebone, London, 1946; joined Harrods Ltd as Asst to Food Manager, 1954; Member of the Board, 1964; Director and General Manager, 1970; Asst Managing Director, 1975; a Director of House of Fraser, 1980–91. Vice Chm., Drapers' Cottage Homes, 1987–94 (Pres., Appeal, 1985–86); Pres., Twenty Club, 1988. Liveryman, Worshipful Company of Cooks, 1972 (Mem., Court of Assts, 1993–96). Cavaliere Ufficiale (Fourth Cl.), Order Al Merito Della Repubblica Italiana, 1980. *Recreation:* watercolour painting. *Address:* 17 Tretawn Park, Mill Hill, NW7 4PS. *Club:* Guards' Polo (Life Mem.). *Died 6 Oct. 2008.*

CRADDOCK, Rt Hon. Sir Percy, GCMG 1983 (KCMG 1980; CMG 1968); PC 1993; the Prime Minister's Foreign Policy Adviser, 1984–92; *b* 26 Oct. 1923; *m* 1953, Birthe Marie Dyrlund. *Educ:* St John's Coll., Cambridge (MA, LLM; Hon. Fellow, 1982). Pres., Cambridge Union, 1950. Called to the Bar, Middle Temple, 1953. Served Foreign Office, 1954–57; First Sec., Kuala Lumpur, 1957–61, Hong Kong, 1961, Peking, 1962; Foreign Office, 1963–66; Counsellor and Head of Chancery, Peking, 1966–68; Chargé d'Affaires, Peking, 1968–69; Head of Planning Staff, FCO, 1969–71; Under-Sec., Cabinet Office, 1971–75; Ambassador to German Democratic Republic, 1976–78; Leader, UK Delegn to Comprehensive Test Ban Discussions at Geneva, 1977–78; Ambassador to People's Republic of China, 1978–83; Leader of UK team in negotiations over Hong Kong, 1982–83; Dep. Under Sec. of State, FCO, supervising Hong Kong negotiations, 1984; Chm., Jt Intelligence Cttee, 1985–92. *Publications:* Experiences of China, 1994; In Pursuit of British Interests, 1997; Know Your Enemy, 2002. *Club:* Reform. *Died 22 Jan. 2010.*

CRAIG, Douglas, OBE 1965; freelance opera producer, adjudicator and lecturer; *b* 26 May 1916; *m* 1955, Dorothy Dixon; two *d. Educ:* Latymer Upper Sch.; St Catharine's Coll., Cambridge (MA). FRCM, FRSA. Winchester Prize, Cambridge, 1938. Intell. Corps, 1940–46, Major 1944. Baritone, Sadler's Wells Opera and elsewhere, 1946–; Artistic Dir, Opera for All, 1949–65; Stage Dir, Glyndebourne, 1952–55; Asst Gen. Man., Glyndebourne, 1955–59; Producer, Royal Coll. of Music, 1958–; Freelance Opera Producer, 1959–; Dep Dir, London Opera Centre, 1965–66; Administrator, Welsh Nat. Opera, 1966–70; Dir, Sadler's Wells Theatre, 1970–78; Dir, Opera and Drama Sch., RCM, 1976–80. Master Teacher in Residence, Adelaide Coll. of the Arts, 1981; taught in Adelaide, Canberra, Melbourne, Sydney and Hong Kong, 1984 (specialist tour award from British Council); prodns for S Australia Coll. of Advanced Educn and for NSW State Conservatorium of Music, master classes and lectures, Australia, 1985; Nat. Adjudicator, Australian Singing Competition, 1985. President: Council of Friends of Sadler's Wells, 1982–95; Sussex Opera and Ballet Soc., 1997–. Mem. Exec. and Editor, Music Jl of ISM, 1979–84. *Publications:* (ed) Delius: Koanga (opera), 1975. *Recreation:* travel. *Address:* 43 Park Road, Radlett, Herts WD7 8EG. *T:* (01923) 857240. *Club:* Garrick. *Died 26 July 2009.*

CRAIG, Rev. Maxwell Davidson; General Secretary, Action of Churches Together in Scotland, 1990–98; Chaplain to the Queen in Scotland, 1986–2001, then an Extra Chaplain; *b* 25 Dec. 1931; *s* of Dr William Craig and Alice M. Craig (*née* Semple); *m* 1957, Janet Margaret Macgregor; one *s* three *d. Educ:* Oriel Coll., Oxford (MA (Hons) Lit.Hum.); Edinburgh Univ. (BD); Princeton

Theol Seminary, NJ (ThM). 2nd Lieut, 1st Bn Argyll and Sutherland Highlanders, 1954–56. Asst Principal, Ministry of Labour, 1957–61. Ordained minister, Grahamston Parish Church, Falkirk, 1966; Minister: Wellington Church, Glasgow, 1973–89; St Columba's Parish Church, Aberdeen, 1989–90; St Andrew's Ch, Jerusalem, 1999–2000. Convener of the Church and Nation Cttee, Church of Scotland, 1984–88. Chairman: Falkirk Children's Panel, 1970–72; Hillhead Housing Assoc., 1977–89; Scottish Churches Housing Agency, subseq. Action, 2000–06. *Publications:* Stella: the story of Stella J. Reekie, 1984; For God's Sake Unity, 1998. *Recreations:* hill-walking, choral singing. *Address:* 3 Queens Road, Stirling FK8 2QY. *T:* (01786) 472319. *Died 26 Sept. 2009.*

CRAIG, Norman; Assistant Under-Secretary of State, Ministry of Defence, 1972–79; *b* 15 May 1920; *s* of George Craig, OBE; *m* 1st, 1946, Judith Margaret Newling (marr. diss. 1957); one *s*; 2nd, 1960, Jane Hudson; two *s* one *d. Educ:* Penarth County Sch.; Cardiff Univ. Army Service, Royal Sussex Regt, 1940–47. Board of Trade, 1948; Min. of Supply (later Aviation), 1953; Private Sec. to Minister, 1959–60; Min. of Technology, 1964; Sec. to Cttee of Inquiry into Aircraft Industry, 1964–65; course at IDC, 1968; MoD, 1971. Lord Chancellor's Department: official, 1979–85; consultant, 1986–87; lay observer, 1990. *Publications:* The Broken Plume, 1982. *Address:* 51 Hayes Lane, Beckenham, Kent BR3 6RE. *T:* (020) 8650 7916. *Died 22 Dec. 2009.*

CRAIGEN, Desmond Seaward; Director: Prudential Corporation plc, 1982–89; Pioneer Concrete (Holdings) Ltd, 1982–89; *b* 31 July 1916; *s* of late John Craigen and Ann Amelia Craigen (*née* Brebner); *m* 1961, Elena Ines (*née* Oldham Florez) (*d* 1995); one *s* one *d. Educ:* Holloway Sch.; King's Coll., London (BA Hons). Prudential Assurance Co. Ltd, 1934–81; India, 1950–57; attached O&M Div., Treasury, 1957–58; Dep. General Manager, 1968–69; General Manager, 1969–78; Chief General Manager, 1979–81; Chm., Vanbrugh Life Assurance Co. Ltd, 1982–87. Served War of 1939–45: 53rd Reconnaissance Regt RAC (Major; despatches). *Recreations:* music, reading. *Address:* Tregolls Manor, Tregolls Road, Truro TR1 1XQ. *Died 9 Jan. 2009.*

CRAMPHORN, Colin Ralph, CBE 2006; QPM 2004; DL; Chief Constable, West Yorkshire Police, since 2002; *b* 1 April 1956; *s* of Ralph Howard Cramphorn and Iris Cramphorn (*née* Tucker); *m* 1988, Lynne Wendy Atkinson; two *s. Educ:* King's Coll., London (LLB 1984, AKC); Univ. of Salford (MSc 1997). Apptd Constable, Surrey Constabulary, 1975; Supt, Gtr Manchester Police, 1990; Asst Chief Constable, W Mercia Constabulary, 1995–98; rcds 1997; Dep. Chief Constable, RUC GC, subseq. Police Service of NI, 1998–2002. Member: Centre for Crime and Justice Studies, 1984–; Inst. of Business Ethics, 2001–. Mem. Council, W and S Yorks, St John Ambulance, 2002–. DL W Yorks, 2006. FRSA 1998; MInstD 2004; FCMI 2004. Hon. LLD Bradford, 2005. *Publications:* articles on police-related topics in Police Res. & Mgt, Criminal Justice Matters and Seaford House Papers. *Recreations:* running, fell walking, music. *Address:* West Yorkshire Police HQ, PO Box 9, Laburnum Road, Wakefield WF1 3QP. *T:* (01924) 292002, *Fax:* (01924) 292490; *e-mail:* JH12@westyorkshire.pnn.police.uk. *Club:* Royal Over-Seas League. *Died 30 Nov. 2006.*

CRAMPTON SMITH, Alex; *see* Smith, A. C.

CRANMER, Philip; Secretary, Associated Board of the Royal Schools of Music, 1974–83; *b* 1 April 1918; *s* of Arthur Cranmer and Lilian Phillips; *m* 1939, Ruth Loasby (*d* 2000); one *s* three *d. Educ:* Wellington; Christ Church, Oxford (BMus, MA). Asst Music Master, Wellington Coll. 1938–40; served RA, 1940–46; Major, Education Officer, Guards Div., 1946; Dir of Music, King Edward's Sch., Birmingham, 1946; Staff Accompanist, Midland Region, BBC, 1948; Lectr in Music, Birmingham Univ., 1950; Hamilton Harty Prof. of Music, Queen's Univ.,

Belfast, 1954–70; Prof. of Music, Univ. of Manchester, 1970–74. Pres., Incorporated Soc. of Musicians, 1971; Chm., Musicians' Benevolent Fund, 1980–87. FRCO 1947; FRNCM 1974; FRCM 1976. Hon. RAM 1967. Hon. DMus QUB, 1985. Chevalier de l'Ordre de Léopold II, 1947; Croix de Guerre Belge, 1947. *Publications:* The Technique of Accompaniment, 1970; Sight-reading for Young Pianists, 1979; How to Follow a Score, 1982; Two Sonatinas for piano duet, 1981 and 1985. *Died 1 July 2006.*

CRANSTON, Prof. William Ian; Professor of Medicine, United Medical and Dental Schools of Guy's and St Thomas' Hospitals (formerly St Thomas's Hospital Medical School), 1964–93, then Emeritus; *b* 11 Sept. 1928; *s* of Thomas and Margaret Cranston; *m* Pamela Isabel Pearson (*d* 2000); four *s. Educ:* High Sch. for Boys, Glasgow; Aberdeen Grammar Sch.; Boys' High Sch., Oswestry; University of Aberdeen (MB, ChB (Hons), 1949; MD 1957); MA Oxon 1962. MRCP 1952, FRCP 1965. Royal Infirmary, Aberdeen: House Physician, 1949–50; Medical Registrar, 1952–53; Asst in Medical Unit, St Mary's Hospital, Paddington, 1953–56; 1st Asst in Dept of Regius Prof. of Med., Radcliffe Infirmary, Oxford, 1961–64. Mem., Med. Res. Soc. *Recreation:* reading. *Address:* 31 Kiln Road, Fareham, Hants PO16 7UQ. *Died 22 Feb. 2007.*

CRAWFORD, Maj.-Gen. (Ian) Patrick, GM 1964; FFCM, FFOM; Commandant and Postgraduate Dean, Royal Army Medical College, Millbank, 1989–93; *b* 11 Oct. 1933; *s* of Donald Patrick and Florence Ireland Crawford; *m* 1956, Juliet Treharne James; two *s* one *d. Educ:* Chatham House, Ramsgate; St Thomas' Hosp., London. MRCS, LRCP; FFCM 1982; FFOM 1987; DPH, DIH, DTM&H. House Surgeon, Casualty and Orthopaedics and House Physician, Royal Sussex County Hosp., 1959–60; Nat. Service, RAMC, 1960–63; on active service, Borneo, 1962–64; commnd 1963; Regimental MO, 20 Regt RA and 1st/7th Gurkha Rifles, Malaya and Borneo, 1963–68; Staff Officer: Army Health Home Counties Dist, 1968; HQ Singapore Dist, 1968–70; Instructor, Sch. of Army Health, 1970–71; MoD, 1971–72; Exchange Officer, Australia, 1972–75; MoD, 1975–78; HQ 1 BR Corps, 1978–81; Parkes Prof. of Preventive Medicine, Royal Army Med. Coll., 1981–84; Defence Med. Services Directorate, 1984–86; Comdr, Saudi Arabian Nat. Guard Med. Team, 1986–88; Defence Med. Services Directorate, 1988–89. QHP 1991–93. Specialist in Preventive Medicine, Singapore, Australia, PNG, BAOR, Saudi Arabia and UK; Consultant Advr, Saudi Arabia Nat. Guard, Jeddah, 1986–88. Chm. Court of Govs, 1997–, and Mem. Bd, 1994–, LSHTM. Mem. Council, Shipwrecked Fishermen and Mariners' Royal Benevolent Soc., 1994–; Trustee, Florence Nightingale Mus., 1993–. Hon. Lectr, Dept of Occupational Med., Queensland Univ., 1973–75. FRSocMed 1981. OStJ 1992. *Publications:* papers and pubns on military preventive medicine. *Recreations:* golf, computing, travel, bridge. *Address:* Mill Cottage, Mill Lane, Cocking, near Midhurst, W Sussex GU29 0HJ. *T:* (01730) 817982. *Died 21 Feb. 2009.*

CRAWFORD ADAMS, John; *see* Adams.

CRAWLEY, John Cecil, CBE 1972 (MBE 1944); Chairman of Trustees of Visnews, 1976–86; *b* 29 June 1909; *s* of John and Kathleen Crawley; *m* 1933, Constance Mary Griffiths (*d* 1998); two *d. Educ:* William Ellis Sch. War Service, Army, 1939–45. Journalism: Reynolds, 1927; Central News Agency, 1928; National Press Agency, 1929; Press Secretaries, 1933; BBC: Sub-Editor, 1945; Foreign Correspondent, New York, 1959–63; Foreign News Editor, 1963–67; Editor of News and Current Affairs, 1967–71; Chief Asst to Dir-Gen., BBC, 1971–75. *Recreations:* walking, bird-watching. *Address:* 157 Clarence Gate Gardens, NW1 6AP. *T:* (020) 7723 6876. *Died 22 Feb. 2006.*

CRAXTON, John Leith, RA 1993; artist; *b* 3 Oct. 1922; *s* of late Harold Craxton, OBE, LRAM and Essie Craxton. *Educ:* various private schs incl. Betteshanger, Kent; Westminster and Central Schs of Art; Goldsmiths' Coll. (with Lucian Freud). First solo exhibn, Leicester Galls, 1944; with Lucian Freud, worked in Scilly Is, then Greece, 1945–47, and held joint exhibn, London Gall., 1947; designed sets and costumes for Daphnis and Chloë, Royal Ballet, 1951, Apollo, 1966; Cotteral Meml Tapestry for Stirling Univ., 1971–74. Principal solo exhibitions include: St George's Gall., London, 1945; Galerie Gasser, Zürich, 1946; British Council, Athens, 1946, 1949, 1985; Mayor Gall., London, 1950; Leicester Galls, London, 1951, 1954, 1956, 1961, 1966; Crane Gall., Manchester, 1955; Whitechapel Art Gall., 1967; Hamet Gall., London, 1971; Christopher Hull Gall., London, 1982, 1985, 1987, 1993; Chrysostomos Gall., Hania, 1985; Pallant House Gall., Chichester, 1998. Work in public collections includes: Tate Gall.; V&A; BM; Gall. of Modern Art, Edinburgh; Nat. Mus. of Wales; Arts Council; British Council; Govt Picture Collection; Nat. Gall., Melbourne; Metropolitan Mus., NY; work in many private collections. HM Consular Correspondent, Hania, Crete, 1992–. *Relevant publication:* Illustrated Monograph 1941–1948, by Geoffrey Grigson, 1948. *Recreations:* music, museums, motorbikes, archaeology, seafood, cooking. *Address:* Moschon 1, Hania, Crete, Greece; c/o Royal Academy of Arts, Burlington House, Piccadilly, W1V 0DJ. *Died 17 Nov. 2009.*

CREAN, Hon. Francis Daniel, (Hon. Frank); *b* Hamilton, Vic, 28 Feb. 1916; *s* of J. Crean; *m* 1946, Mary Isobel (AM 2006), *d* of late A. E. Findlay; three *s. Educ:* Hamilton High Sch.; Melbourne High Sch.; Melbourne Univ. BA Hons; BCom. DPA; FCPA. Income Tax Assessor, 1934–45. MLA: for Albert Park, Vic, 1945–47; for Prahran, 1949–51; MHR for Melbourne Ports, 1951–77; Mem. Exec., Federal Parly Labour Party, 1956–72, Dep. Leader, 1975–76; Mem., Jt Parly Cttee on Public Accounts, 1952–55; Treasurer, Commonwealth of Australia, 1972–74; Minister for Overseas Trade, 1974–75, also Deputy Prime Minister, 1975. Chm., Council of Adult Educn, 1947–74. Pres., Vict. Br., Aust. Inst. Internat. Affairs, 1983–86; Chairman: Vict. Br., Freedom from Hunger Campaign, 1979; South-Central Migrant Resource Centre, 1980–. *Publications:* (with W. J. Byrt) Government and Politics in Australia, 1972, 2nd edn 1982. *Address:* 31/27 Queens Road, Melbourne, Vic 3004, Australia. *Died 2 Dec. 2008.*

CREASY, Leonard Richard, CB 1972; OBE 1961; CEng, FICE, FIStructE; civil engineer in private practice with son, 1974–2000; *b* 20 Dec. 1912; *s* of William and Ellen Creasy; *m* 1937, Irene Howard (*d* 1989); one *s* one *d. Educ:* Wimbledon Technical Coll.; BSc(Eng) London. Served War, RE, E Africa, 1944–46. Service in Industry, 1928–34; HM Office of Works, Asst Engr, 1935; Min. of Works, Suptg Engr, 1959; Ministry of Public Buildings and Works: Dir, Civil Engrg, 1966; Dir, Central Services, 1968; Dir of Civil Engrg Develt, DoE, 1970–73. Concerned with Inquiries into disasters at Aberfan, Ronan Point and Brent, and with design of Radio and Radar Towers, London Heathrow and Birmingham; Plant House, Royal Botanical Gardens, Edinburgh; Wind Tunnels, Bedford RAE; and other structures. Pres., IStructE, 1973 (Bronze Medal and Certif. of Merit of the Instn); Bronze Medal, Reinforced Concrete Assoc.; Manby and Telford Premiums, Instn Civil Engrs. *Publications:* Pre-stressed Concrete Cylindrical Tanks, 1961; James Forrest Lecture, 1968; many other papers on civil and structural engrg projects and engrg economics. *Recreations:* music, opera, languages. *Address:* Riding High, Miller's Farm, Church Road, Hilgay, Downham Market, Norfolk PE38 0JL. *T:* (01366) 385040. *Died 13 Feb. 2007.*

CRESPIN, Régine; Commandeur de la Légion d'Honneur, 1994 (Chevalier, 1969; Officier, 1981); Grand Croix de l'Ordre National du Mérite, 2005

(Chevalier, 1965; Commandeur, 1990; Grand Officier, 1997); Commandeur des Arts et des Lettres, 1974; soprano singer; Professor of Singing, Conservatoire National Supérieur de Musique de Paris, 1976–92; *b* Marseille, 23 Feb. 1927; *d* of Henri Crespin and Marguerite (*née* Meirone); *m* 1962, Lou Bruder (marr. diss.), French novelist, critic, poet, translator. *Educ:* Nîmes; Conservatoire National, Paris (Baccalauréat). Worked at the Opera, Paris, 1951–, in all the famous opera houses of Europe and all over the world, giving concerts, recitals, etc.; *Operas include:* Otello, Tosca, Il Trovatore, Le Nozze di Figaro, Ballo in Maschera, Der Rosenkavalier, Tannhäuser, Lohengrin, Die Walküre, Parsifal, Les Troyens, Dialogues of the Carmelites, Tales of Hoffmann, Iphigenie auf Tauris, Carmen, Le Medium. *Publications:* La vie et l'amour d'une femme (autobiog.), 1982; A la scène, à la ville, 1997 (English edn, On stage, off stage, 1997). *Recreations:* sea, sun, sleep, books, theatre, and my dog! *Address:* 3 Avenue Frochot, 75009 Paris, France.   *Died 5 July 2007.*

CREWE, Albert Victor, PhD; Professor, Department of Physics and the Enrico Fermi Institute, 1963–96, then Emeritus (Assistant Professor, 1956–59; Associate Professor, 1959–63; William E. Wrather Distinguished Service Professor, 1977–97), Dean of Physical Sciences Division, 1971–81, University of Chicago; *b* 18 Feb. 1927; US citizen, 1961; *m* 1949, Doreen Patricia Blunsdon; one *s* three *d. Educ:* Univ. of Liverpool (BS, PhD). Asst Lectr, 1950–52, Lectr, 1952–55, Univ. of Liverpool; Div. Dir, Particle Accelerator Division, Argonne National Laboratory, 1958–61; Dir, Argonne National Laboratory, 1961–67. Mem. Bd of Dirs, R. R. Donnelley & Sons, Co., 1974–93; Pres., Orchid One Corp., 1987–90. Member: Nat. Acad. of Sciences; Amer. Acad. of Arts and Sciences. Artist Mem., Palette and Chisel Acad., Chicago. Hon. FRMS 1984. Named Outstanding New Citizen by Citizenship Council of Chicago, 1962; received Immigrant's Service League's Annual Award for Outstanding Achievement in the Field of Science, 1962; Illinois Sesquicentennial Award, 1968; Industrial Research Award, 1970; Distinguished Service Award, Electron Microscope Soc. of America, 1976; Albert A. Michelson Award, Franklin Inst., 1977; Ernst Abbe Award, NY Microscope Soc., 1979; Duddell Medal, Inst. of Physics, 1980. *Publications:* Research USA (with J. J. Katz), 1964; contribs to: Proc. Royal Soc.; Proc. Phys. Soc.; Physical Review; Science; Physics Today; Jl of Applied Physics; Reviews of Scientific Instruments; Optik; Ultramicroscopy, etc. *Address:* 8 Summit Drive, Dune Acres, IN 46304, USA. *T:* (219) 7875018. *Clubs:* Quadrangle, Wayfarers' (Chicago).   *Died 18 Nov. 2009.*

CRICHTON, Maj.-Gen. Edward Maitland-Makgill-, OBE 1948 (MBE 1945); GOC 51st Highland Division, 1966–68; *b* 23 Nov. 1916; *s* of late Lt-Col D. E. Maitland-Makgill-Crichton, Queen's Own Cameron Highlanders and Phyllis (*née* Cuthbert); *m* 1951, Sheila Margaret Hibbins (*d* 2004), Bexhill-on-Sea; two *s* (and one *s* decd). *Educ:* Bedford Sch.; RMC Sandhurst. 2nd Lieut Queen's Own Cameron Highlanders, 1937; Adjt 5th Bn Cameron Highlanders, 1939; served with 5th Cameron Highlanders and 51 (Highland) Div., N Africa, Sicily, Normandy, NW Europe, 1940–45; GSO 1, HQ British Commonwealth Occupation Force, Japan, 1946–47; Mobilisation Br., WO 1948–50; 1st Bn Cameron Highlanders, Tripoli and Canal Zone, 1950–52; Jt Services Staff Coll., 1953; GSO 1, 3rd Inf. Div. (UK Strategic Reserve), Canal Zone, Egypt, UK and Suez, 1953–57; with 1st Bn Cameron Highlanders, Aden, 1957; comd 1st Liverpool Scottish, 1958–61; Comdr 152 (Highland) Inf. Bde, 1962–64; Dep. Dir Army Staff Duties, MoD, 1965–66. *Recreations:* shooting, golf, gardening, fishing. *Address:* c/o Coldon, Port of Menteith, Stirling FK8 3RD.   *Died 22 Dec. 2009.*

CRICHTON, (John) Michael, MD; author; film director; *b* Chicago, 23 Oct. 1942; *m* 2005, Sherri Alexander; one *d* by a previous marriage. *Educ:* Harvard Univ. (AB *summa cum laude* 1964); Harvard Med. Sch. (MD 1969). Henry Russell Shaw Travelling Fellow, 1964–65; Vis. Lectr in Anthropology, Univ. of Cambridge, 1965; Post-doctoral Fellow, Salk Inst. for Biol Scis, La Jolla, Calif, 1969–70. Vis. Writer, MIT, 1988. *Television:* creator and Co-Exec. Producer, ER, 1994–; *films:* writer/director: Westworld, 1973; Coma, 1977; The Great Train Robbery, 1978; Looker, 1981; Runaway, 1984; director: Pursuit, 1972; Physical Evidence, 1989; writer: Rising Sun, 1993; Jurassic Park, 1993; producer: Disclosure, 1995; Twister, 1996; Sphere, 1998. Member: Authors' Guild; Writers' Guild Amer.; Dirs' Guild Amer.; Producers' Guild; PEN Amer. *Publications: novels:* The Andromeda Strain, 1969; The Terminal Man, 1972; The Great Train Robbery, 1975; Eaters of the Dead, 1976; Congo, 1980; Sphere, 1987; Jurassic Park, 1990; Rising Sun, 1992; Disclosure, 1993; The Lost World, 1995; Airframe, 1996; Timeline, 1999; Prey, 2002; State of Fear, 2004; Next, 2006; (as John Lange): Odds On, 1966; Scratch One, 1967; Easy Go, 1968; The Venom Business, 1969; Zero Cool, 1969; Grave Descend, 1970; Drug of Choice, 1970; Binary, 1972; Pirate Latitudes, 2009 (published posthumously); (as Jeffery Hudson) A Case of Need, 1968; (as Michael Douglas) (with D. Crichton) Dealing, 1971; *non-fiction:* Five Patients, 1970; Jasper Johns, 1977; Electronic Life, 1983; Travels (autobiog.), 1988; *screenplays:* Westworld, 1975; (with A.-M. Martin) Twister, 1996. *Address:* 2118 Wilshire Boulevard #433, Santa Monica, CA 90403, USA; c/o Jenkins Financial Services, 433 N Camden Drive #770, Beverly Hills, CA 90210, USA.   *Died 4 Nov. 2008.*

CRICK, Sir Bernard, Kt 2002; BSc (Econ.), PhD (London); writer; Emeritus Professor, University of London; *b* 16 Dec. 1929; *s* of Harry Edgar and Florence Clara Crick; *m* (marr. diss.); two *s. Educ:* Whitgift Sch.; University Coll., London. Research student, LSE, 1950–52; Teaching Fellow, Harvard, 1952–54; Asst Prof., McGill, 1954–55; Vis. Fellow, Berkeley, 1955–56; Asst Lectr, later Lectr, later Sen. Lectr, LSE, 1957–65; Prof. of Political Theory and Institutions, Sheffield Univ., 1965–71; Prof. of Politics, Birkbeck Coll., Univ. of London, 1971–84. Vis. Prof., Univ. of Glasgow, 2006–07. Joint Editor, Political Quarterly, 1966–80; Chm., Political Qly Publishing Co., 1980–93; Literary Ed., Political Qly, 1993–2000. Joint Sec., Study of Parlt Gp, 1964–68; Jt Chm., British S African Conf., 1991–95. Chairman: Cttee on Teaching Citizenship in English Schs, 1997–98; Living in the UK (adv. gp), 2003–04; Adv. Bd for Naturalisation and Integration, 2004–05. Adviser on Citizenship to: DfEE, 1998–2001; Home Office, 2002–04. Hon. President: Politics Assoc., 1970–76; Assoc. for Citizenship Teaching, 2001–; Vice Pres., Political Studies Assoc., 1995–; Hon. Mem., Hansard Soc., 1993 (Mem. Council, 1962–93). Vis. Fellow, Woodrow Wilson Centre, 1995–96; Hon. Fellow in Politics, Univ. of Edinburgh, 1986–. Hon. Fellow: Birkbeck Coll., 1999; UCL, 2001. Senate of Australia Lectr, 2008. Hon. DSc QUB, 1986; Hon. DLitt: Sheffield, 1990; E London Poly., 1990; Kingston, 1996; Glasgow, 2006. *Publications:* The American Science of Politics, 1958; In Defence of Politics, 1962, 5th edn 2000 (trans. German, Japanese, Spanish, Italian); The Reform of Parliament, 1964, 2nd edn 1968; (ed) Essays on Reform, 1967; (ed with W. A. Robson) Protest and Discontent, 1970; (ed) Machiavelli: The Discourses, 1971; Political Theory and Practice, 1972; (ed with W. A. Robson) Taxation Policy, 1973; Basic Forms of Government, 1973; Crime, Rape and Gin, 1975; (ed with Alex Porter) Political Education and Political Literacy, 1978; George Orwell: a Life, 1980, 3rd edn 1992; (ed) Unemployment, 1981; (ed) Clarendon edn, Orwell's Nineteen Eighty-Four, 1984; (ed with Audrey Coppard) Orwell Observed, 1984; Socialism, 1987; Essays on Politics and Literature, 1989; Political Thoughts and Polemics, 1990; (ed) National Identities, 1991; (with David Millar) To Make the Parliament of Scotland a Model for Democracy, 1995; Essays on Citizenship, 2000; Crossing Borders, 2001; (ed) Citizens: towards a citizenship culture, 2001; Democracy, 2002. *Recreations:* polemicising, talking, theatre, city-walking. *Address:* 8A Bellevue Terrace, Edinburgh EH7 4DT. *T:* (0131) 557 2517. *Club:* Savile.   *Died 19 Dec. 2008.*

CRICK, R(onald) Pitts, FRCS, FRCOphth; Ophthalmic Surgeon, King's College Hospital, 1950–82 (Hon. Consultant, 1982–87); Recognised Teacher in the Faculty of Medicine, University of London, 1960–87; Lecturer in Opthalmology, King's College Hospital Medical School, 1950–1982, Emeritus Lecturer, 1982–87; *b* 5 Feb. 1917; *yr s* of Owen J. Pitts Crick and Margaret Daw, Minehead, Som; *m* 1941, Jocelyn Mary Grenfell Robins, *yr d* of Leonard A. C. Robins and Geraldine Grenfell, Hendon; four *s* one *d*. *Educ:* Latymer Upper Sch., London; King's Coll. and (Science Schol.) King's Coll. Hosp. Med. Sch., Univ. of London. MRCS, LRCP 1939; DOMS 1946; FRCS 1950; FRCOphth 1988 (Hon. FRCOphth 2008). Surgeon, MN, 1939–40; Surg. Lieut, RNVR, 1940–46. Ophthalmic Registrar, King's Coll. Hosp., 1946–48; Surgical First Asst, Royal Eye Hosp., 1947–50; Ophth. Surg., Epsom County Hosp., 1948–49; Ophth. Registrar, Belgrave Hosp. for Children, 1948–50; Ophth. Surg., Sevenoaks Hosp., 1948–50; Sen. Ophthalmic Surg., Royal Eye Hosp., 1950–69; Ophthalmic Surg., Belgrave Hosp. for Children, 1950–66. Vis. Res. Fellow, Univ. of Sussex, 1976–98. Chm., Ophthalmic Post-Grad. Trng, SE Thames RHA, 1972–82. Examr to RCS for Diploma in Ophthalmology, 1961–68. Hon. Ophth. Surg., Royal London Soc. for the Blind, 1954–57. FRSocMed, Vice-Pres. Ophthalmological Section, 1964, and Mem. Council Ophthalmolog. Section, 1953–54 and 1956–58. Member: Oxford Ophthalmol Congress; Southern Ophthalmol Soc. (Vice-Pres., 1969; Pres., 1970); Founder and Chm. Internat. Glaucoma Assoc., 1974–2000 (Pres., 2000–05); Charter Member: Internat. Glaucoma Congress, USA, 1977; Internat. Assoc. of Ocular Surgeons, 1981. Alim Meml Lectr, Ophthalmol Soc. of Bangladesh, Dhaka, 1991. Sir Stewart Duke-Elder Glaucoma Award, Internat. Glaucoma Congress, 1985; Lederle Medal for Ophthalmology, Amer. Soc. of Contemp. Ophthalmol., 1985. *Publications:* All About Glaucoma, 1981; A Textbook of Clinical Ophthalmology, 1986, 3rd edn (with Peng T. Khaw) 2003; Cardiovascular Affections, Arteriosclerosis and Hypertension (Section in Systemic Ophthalmology, ed A. Sorsby), 1950 and 1958; Computerised Monitoring of Glaucoma (Section in Glaucoma, ed J. G. Bellows), 1979; Diagnosis of Primary Open Angle Glaucoma (in Glaucoma, ed J. E. Cairns), 1986; medical and ophthalmic contribs to Brit. Jl Ophthalmology, BMJ, Lancet, Eye, Ophthalmic and Physiol Optics, etc. *Recreations:* motoring, sailing, economics. *Address:* International Glaucoma Association, Woodcote House, 15 Highpoint Business Village, Henwood, Ashford, Kent TN24 8DH. *T:* (01233) 648160, *Fax:* (01233) 648179; *e-mail:* r_crick@sky.com; 10 Golden Gates, Sandbanks, Poole, Dorset BH13 7QN. *T:* (01202) 707560, *Fax:* (01202) 701560. *Clubs:* Royal Automobile; Royal Motor Yacht.
                    Died 10 June 2009.

CRISP, Prof. Arthur Hamilton, MD, DSc; FRCP, FRCPE, FRCPsych; Professor of Psychiatry, University of London at St George's Hospital Medical School, 1967–95, then Professor Emeritus of Psychological Medicine; *b* 17 June 1930; *s* of John and Elizabeth Crisp; *m* 1958, Irene Clare (*née* Reid); three *s*. *Educ:* Watford Grammar Sch.; Univ. of London (MD; DSc). FRCPsych 1971 (Hon. FRCPsych 1996); FRCPE 1972; FRCP 1973. Previously Lectr, then Sen. Lectr in Psych., Middlesex Hosp. Med. Sch., London; Hd, Dept of Psychiatry, later Dept of Mental Health Scis, St George's Hosp. Med. Sch., 1967–95; Dean, Faculty of Medicine, Univ. of London, 1976–80. Chairman: Educn Cttee, GMC, 1982–88; Adv. Cttee on Med. Educn, EEC, 1983–85. Chm., Changing Minds Campaign, RCPsych, 1998–2003. *Publications:* (jtly) Sleep, Nutrition and Mood, 1976; Anorexia Nervosa: Let Me Be, 1980; (jtly) Anorexia Nervosa and the Wish to Change, 1990; (jtly)

Anorexia Nervosa: guidelines for assessment and treatment in primary and secondary care, 1994; (jtly) Every Family in the Land, 2000; approx. 350 articles in learned jls. *Recreations:* golf, study of the River Wandle and of poetic insights into relationship between sleep and depression. *Clubs:* Athenæum; Royal Wimbledon Golf, Thorpeness Golf and Country.   *Died 13 Oct. 2006.*

CROAN, Thomas Malcolm; Sheriff of North Strathclyde, 1983–2004; *b* 7 Aug. 1932; *s* of John Croan and Amelia Sydney; *m* 1959, Joan Kilpatrick Law; one *s* three *d*. *Educ:* St Joseph's Coll., Dumfries; Edinburgh University. MA 1953; LLB 1955. Admitted to Faculty of Advocates, 1956; Standing Junior Counsel, to Scottish Develt Dept, 1964–65 and (for highways work) 1967–69; Advocate Depute, 1965–66; Sheriff of Grampian, Highland and Islands (formerly Aberdeen, Kincardine and Banff), 1969–83. *Recreations:* sailing, reading. *Address:* Overdale, 113 Bentinck Drive, Troon KA10 6JB.
                    Died 8 June 2008.

CROCKER, His Honour Peter Vernon; a Circuit Judge, 1974–91; *b* 29 June 1926; *s* of Walter Angus Crocker and Fanny Victoria Crocker (*née* Dempster); *m* 1950, Nancy Kathleen Sargent (*d* 2005). *Educ:* Oundle; Corpus Christi Coll., Cambridge (BA). Called to Bar, Inner Temple, 1949. *Recreations:* gardening, tennis, swimming, horseracing.   *Died 13 Feb. 2006.*

CROCKETT, Rt Rev. (Phillip) Anthony; Bishop of Bangor, since 2004; *b* 23 Aug. 1945; *s* of Arthur and Mary Crockett; *m* 1999, Caroline (*née* Owen); one *s* two *d* by a previous marriage. *Educ:* Pontypridd Boys' Grammar Sch.; King's Coll. London (BA (Classics) 1967; BD, AKC 1970); St Michael's Coll., Llandaff; UCW Cardiff (DPS; MA 1991). Ordained deacon, 1971, priest, 1972; Curate: Aberdare, 1971–74; Whitchurch, 1974–78; Vicar, Llanafan y Trawsgoed, Llanfihangel y Creuddyn, Llanwnnws and Ysbyty Ystwyth, 1978–86; Rector of Dowlais, 1986–91; Sec., Bd of Ministry, Church in Wales, 1991–99; Archdeacon of Carmarthen, and Vicar of Cynwyl Elfed, Cwmduad and Newchurch, 1999–2004. Winston Churchill Fellow, 1983. *Recreations:* walking, fly-fishing and fly-tying, cooking, reading. *Address:* Ty'r Esgob, Bangor, Gwynedd LL57 2SS. *T:* (01248) 362895, *Fax:* (01248) 354866; *e-mail:* bishop.bangor@churchinwales.org.uk.
                    Died 30 June 2008.

CROFT, His Honour David Legh; QC 1982; a Circuit Judge, 1987–2004; *b* 14 Aug. 1937; *s* of late Alan Croft and Doreen Mary Berry (*née* Mitchell); *m* 1963, Susan Mary (*née* Bagnall); two *s*. *Educ:* Haileybury and ISC; Nottingham Univ. (LLB). Called to the Bar, Middle Temple, 1960; called to the Hong Kong Bar, 1984; a Recorder, 1985–87. *Recreation:* resting. *Club:* The Castle (Rochester).   *Died 21 Jan. 2009.*

CROFT, Stanley Edward, TD 1951; life insurance consultant; formerly HM Diplomatic Service; *b* 18 Oct. 1917; *s* of Edward John Croft and Alice Lucy Croft; *m* 1950, Joan Mary Kaye; four *s* two *d*. *Educ:* Portsmouth Grammar School. TA, 1939; served War of 1939–45, RA, Middle East, Aden, Italy, Germany. Min. of Labour, 1935; Admty, 1937–39 and 1946–47; transf. to Diplomatic Service, 1947; Vice-Consul, Barcelona, 1950; 2nd Sec., Lahore, 1951; Washington, 1955; Madrid, 1956; 1st Sec., FO, 1960; Consul, Geneva, 1961; FO and CRO, 1965–70; Consul-Gen., Madrid, 1970; Counsellor and Consul-Gen., Luanda, 1974–77. Sen. Associate, Abbey Life Assurance Co., 1977–90. *Recreations:* swimming, tennis, camping, fishing, carpentry.
                    Died 15 June 2007.

CROFTON, 7th Baron *cr* 1797 (Ire.); **Guy Patrick Gilbert Crofton;** Bt 1758; Lieutenant Colonel, 9/12 Royal Lancers (Prince of Wales's), retired; *b* 17 June 1951; *s* of 5th Baron Crofton and of Ann Pamela, *d* of late Gp Capt. Charles Herbert Tighe, OBE, DFC; *S* brother, 1989; *m* 1985, Gillian, *o d* of late Harry Godfrey Mitchell Bass, CMG; twin *s*. *Educ:* Theresianistische Akademie,

Vienna; Midhurst GS. Commissioned 9/12 Royal Lancers, 1971; Defence Attaché, Berne, 1995–98; Staff Officer, DERA, 1999–2002; Defence Attaché, Luanda, 2003–06; retired 2006. *Recreations:* shooting, ski-ing. *Heir: er* twin *s* Hon. Edward Harry Piers Crofton, *b* 23 Jan. 1988. *Address:* Hamilton House, High Street, Bruton, Som BA10 0AH. *Club:* Cavalry and Guards.
Died 25 Nov. 2007.

CROFTON, Sir John (Wenman), Kt 1977; Professor of Respiratory Diseases and Tuberculosis, University of Edinburgh, 1952–77; *b* 27 March 1912; *s* of Dr W. M. Crofton; *m* 1945, Eileen Chris Mercer, MBE 1984; two *s* three *d*. *Educ:* Tonbridge; Sidney Sussex Coll., Cambridge (BA 1933; MB BChir 1937; MD 1947); St Thomas's Hosp. FRCP 1951; FRCPE 1957. War of 1939–45, RAMC; France, Middle East, Germany. Lecturer in Medicine, Postgraduate Medical Sch. of London, 1947–51, Senior Lecturer, 1951; Part-time Tuberculosis Unit, Medical Research Council, Brompton Hosp., 1947–50; Dean of Faculty of Medicine, 1963–66, and Vice-Principal, 1969–70, Univ. of Edinburgh. Vice-Pres., 1972–73, Pres., 1973–76, RCPE. Hon. Mem., Acads of Medicine of Argentina, Catalonia and Singapore. Hon. FRCPI 1975; Hon. FRACP 1976; Hon. FACP 1976; Hon. FFCM 1978; Hon. FRCPE 1987; Hon. FRSE 1997; Hon. FRSocMed 2003. Dr *hc* Bordeaux, 1997; Hon. DSc London, 2001. Weber-Parkes Prize, RCP, 1966; City of Edinburgh Medal for Sci. and Soc., 1995; Galen Medal, Soc. of Apothecaries, 2001; Union Medal, Internat. Union against Tuberculosis and Lung Disease, 2005; Edwin Chadwick Medal, LSHTM, 2008. *Publications:* (jtly) Respiratory Diseases, 1969, 3rd edn 1981; (jtly) Clinical Tuberculosis, 1992, 3rd edn 2009; Housing and Health in Scotland, 1993; (co-ed) Tobacco and Health, 1996; (jtly) Tobacco or Health: a global threat, 2001; contributor to BMJ, Lancet, Thorax, etc. *Recreations:* reading science and history, mountains. *Address:* 13 Spylaw Bank Road, Edinburgh EH13 0JW. *T:* (0131) 441 3730.
Died 3 Nov. 2009.

CROLL, Prof. Elisabeth Joan, CMG 2007; PhD; Professor of Chinese Anthropology, since 1995, and Vice Principal (External Relations), since 2002, School of Oriental and African Studies, University of London; *b* 21 Sept. 1944; *d* of Colston Robert Sprackett and Kathleen Joan Sprackett; *m* 1966, Prof. James George Arthur Croll (marr. diss. 1997); one *s* one *d*. *Educ:* Univ. of Canterbury, NZ (BA 1965, MA Hons 1967); Sch. of Oriental and African Studies, London (MA 1971; PhD 1977). Fellow, Contemporary China Inst., SOAS, London, 1973–77; res. consultant, Internat. Labour Office, UN, Geneva, 1977; Visiting Fellow: Inst. of Develt Studies, Univ. of Sussex, 1978; Dept of E Asian Studies, Princeton Univ., 1979; res. consultant, Res. Inst. for Social Develt, UN, Geneva, 1979–81; Mem., Fac. of Soc. Studies, Univ. of Oxford, 1981; Leverhulme Fellow, Queen Elizabeth House, Oxford, 1981–83; Vis. Fellow, Inst. of Soc. Studies, The Hague, 1984; Fellow, Wolfson Coll., Oxford, 1984–86; School of Oriental and African Studies, University of London: Res. Fellow, Dept of Anthropology, 1987–90; Lectr, 1990–91, Sen. Lectr, 1991–92, in Anthropology of China; Reader in Chinese Anthropology, 1992–95; Chm., Centre of Chinese Studies, 1992–96; Hd, Dept of Develt Studies, 1996–99. Member: Bd, GB-China Centre, 1999– (Vice-Chm., 2004–); Prime Minister's China Task Force, 2005–. United Nations University Council: UK Mem., 1998–; Vice Chm., Envmt and Sustainable Develt, 2000; Chm., 2002–04. AcSS 2004. *Publications:* Feminism and Socialism in China, 1978; Women and Rural Development: the case of the People's Republic of China, 1979; The Politics of Marriage in Contemporary China, 1980; The Family Rice Bowl: food and the domestic economy in China, 1982; Chinese Women since Mao, 1984; Women and Rural Development in China, 1986; Food Supply in China and the Nutritional Status of Children, 1986; Wise Daughters from Foreign Lands: six European women writers in China, 1989; From Heaven to Earth:

images and experiences of development in China, 1994; Changing Identities of Chinese Women: rhetoric, experience and self-perception, 1995; Endangered Daughters: discrimination and development in Asia, 2000; China's New Consumers: social development and domestic demand, 2006; articles in learned jls and reports commnd by UK public bodies and internat. develt agencies. *Recreations:* swimming, travelling, embroidery, reading, music. *Address:* School of Oriental and African Studies, University of London, Thornhaugh Street, Russell Square, WC1H 0XG. *T:* (020) 7898 4486, *Fax:* (020) 7898 4019; *e-mail:* ec2@soas.ac.uk.
Died 3 Oct. 2007.

CROMPTON, His Honour Ian William; a Circuit Judge, 1994–2004; *b* 28 June 1936; *s* of Thomas and Hilda Crompton; *m* 1962, Audrey (*née* Hopewell); two *s*. *Educ:* Manchester Grammar School; Victoria University of Manchester (LLB). Asst Solicitor, County Magistrates' Court, Strangeways, Manchester, 1961–62; Asst Solicitor, O'Collier, Littler & Kilberg, 1962–65, Partner, 1965–72; Clerk to the Justices: County Magistrates' Court, Strangeways, 1972–74; Eccles Magistrates' Court, 1974–83; Stipendiary Magistrate for S Yorks, 1983–94; a Recorder, 1989–94. *Recreations:* ballroom and Latin American dancing, golf. *Club:* Davyhulme Park Golf (Urmston).
Died 6 Nov. 2006.

CROOK, Prof. John Anthony, MA; Professor of Ancient History, University of Cambridge, 1979–84, then Emeritus; Fellow of St John's College, Cambridge, since 1951; *b* 5 Nov. 1921; *s* of Herbert Crook and Hilda Naomi (*née* Flower). *Educ:* St Mary's C of E Sch., Balham; Dulwich Coll.; St John's Coll., Cambridge 1939–41 and 1945–47 (John Stewart of Rannoch Scholar); BA 1947, Craven Student, 1947; Research Student of Balliol Coll., Oxford, 1947–48; MA (Cantab) 1949. Served War, Private and Corporal, 9th Royal Fusiliers, 1941–43 (PoW Stalag VIIIB, 1943–45); Sgt, RAEC, 1945. Univ. Asst Lectr in Classics, Reading Univ., 1948, Lectr, 1949–51; St John's Coll., Cambridge: Tutor, 1956–64; President, 1971–75; Univ. Asst Lectr in Classics, Cambridge Univ., 1953, Lectr, 1955–71, Reader in Roman History and Law, 1971–79, and Brereton Reader, 1974–79. FBA 1970–80. Dr jur *hc* Freiburg, 1995. *Publications:* Consilium Principis, 1955; Law and Life of Rome, 1967; Legal Advocacy in the Roman World, 1995; (contrib.) The Cambridge Ancient History, 2nd edn, vol. IX, 1994, vol. X, 1996. *Address:* St John's College, Cambridge CB2 1TP. *T:* (01223) 338621.
Died 7 Sept. 2007.

CROOME, (John) Lewis, CMG 1957; *b* 10 June 1907; *s* of John and Caroline Croome; *m* 1st, 1931, Honoria Renée Minturn (*née* Scott; as Honor Croome, Editorial Staff of The Economist) (*d* 1960); four *s* one *d* (and one *s* decd); 2nd, 1961, Pamela Siola (*d* 2003), *o d* of Lt-Col Tyrrel Hawker, Hurstbourne Priors, Hants; one *s*. *Educ:* Henry Thornton Sch., Clapham; London Sch. of Economics. Imperial Economic Cttee, 1931–39; Ministry of Food, 1939–48; Deputy (later Head), British Food Mission, Ottawa, 1942–46; HM Treasury (Central Economic Planning Staff), 1948–51; Min. of Food, 1951–54; UK Delegation to OEEC, Paris, 1954–57; Ministry of Agriculture, Fisheries and Food, 1957–58; Chief Overseas Relations Officer, UKAEA, 1958–72, retired. *Recreations:* reading, cooking. *Address:* 8 The Holdens, Bosham, West Sussex PO18 8LN. *T:* (01243) 572292.
Died 7 March 2008.

CROSS, Hannah Margaret, (Mrs E. G. Wright); barrister-at-law; *b* 25 April 1908; *o d* of late F. J. K. Cross and Eleanor Mary Cross (*née* Phillimore); *m* 1936, Edmund Gordon Wright, Barrister-at-Law (*d* 1971); one *s* one *d*. *Educ:* Downe House Sch.; St Hilda's Coll., Oxford. BA 1929. Called to Bar, Lincoln's Inn, 1931; first woman Mem. of Gen. Council of Bar, 1938–45. Civil Defence, 1939–45. *Address:* The Quay House, Sidlesham, near Chichester, West Sussex PO20 7LX. *T:* (01243) 641258.
Died 19 Jan. 2008.

CROSSLAND, Prof. Ronald Arthur, FSA 1982; Professor of Greek, University of Sheffield, 1958–82, then Emeritus (Dean, Faculty of Arts, 1973–75); *b* 31 Aug. 1920; *s* of late Ralph Crossland, BSc, and Ethel Crossland (*née* Scattergood). *Educ:* Stanley Road Elementary Sch., Nottingham; Nottingham High Sch.; King's Coll., Cambridge. Major Scholar in Classics, King's Coll., Cambridge, 1939–41 and 1945–46. National Service in Royal Artillery, 1941–45. Henry Fellow, Berkeley Coll., Yale Univ., 1946–47; Instructor in Classics, Yale Univ., 1947–48; Senior Student of Treasury Cttee for Studentships in Foreign Languages and Cultures (for research in Hittite Philology and Linguistics), 1948–51; Hon. Lectr in Ancient History, University of Birmingham, 1950–51; Lecturer in Ancient History, King's Coll., University of Durham, Newcastle upon Tyne, 1951–58. Harris Fellow of King's Coll., Cambridge, 1952–56. Vis. Prof., Univ. Texas, 1962; Collitz Vis. Prof., Univ. Michigan, 1967; Vis. Fellow: Victoria Univ. of Wellington, NZ, 1979; German Democratic Republic Acad. of Scis, 1981. Pres., South Shields Archaeological and Historical Soc., 1976–77. *Publications:* Bronze Age Migrations in the Aegean (with A. Birchall), 1973; Teaching Classical Studies, 1976; chapters on: Immigrants from the North, in Cambridge Ancient History, rev. edn, 1967; Linguistic Problems of the Balkan Area, in Cambridge Ancient History, rev. edn, 1982; Early Greek Migrations, in Civilization of the Ancient Mediterranean (ed M. Grant), 1987; articles in Trans Philological Soc., Archivum Linguisticum, Studia Balcanica, Past and Present, Antiquity. *Recreations:* music, travel, pastime with good company. *Address:* 59 Sherlock Close, Cambridge CB3 0HP. *T:* (01223) 358085, *T:* (enquiries) (0114) 222 2555. *Died 29 Jan. 2006.*

CROSSLEY, Geoffrey Allan, CMG 1974; HM Diplomatic Service, retired; Director, External Relations, Continuing Education, European Institute of Business Administration, INSEAD, Fontainebleau, 1980–84; *b* 11 Nov. 1920; *s* of Thomas Crossley and Winifred Mary Crossley (*née* Ellis); *m* 1945, Aline Louise Farcy; two *s* one *d. Educ:* Penistone; abroad; Gonville and Caius Coll., Cambridge (Scholar). Served War of 1939–45: Min. of Supply, 1941; Foreign Office, 1942; in Algeria and France. Foreign (later Diplomatic) Service, 1945–80: Second Sec., Paris, 1945–48; FO, 1948–49; Alternate UK Deleg. on UN Balkans Commn, Greece, 1949–52; Dep. Regional Inf. Officer with Commissioner-Gen. for SE Asia, Singapore, 1952–55; FO, 1955–57; Consulate-Gen., Frankfurt, for Saar Transition from France to Germany, 1957–59; Political Office, NE Command, Cyprus (later in charge), 1959–61; Head of Chancery, Berne, 1961–65; on secondment to Min. of Overseas Development, as Head of W and N African Dept, 1965–67; Dep. High Comr, Lusaka, 1967–69; Counsellor, Oslo, 1969–73; Ambassador to Colombia, 1973–77; Envoy to the Holy See, 1978–80. Founder Mem., Cambridge Soc. Mem., French Inst. of Internat. Relations. *Recreation:* various. *Address:* La Houlette, Le Pin, 24520 Saint Germain et Mons, Dordogne, France. *Died 13 June 2009.*

CROSTHWAIT, Timothy Leland, CMG 1964; MBE 1944; HM Diplomatic Service, retired; *b* 5 Aug. 1915; *s* of Lt-Col L. G. Crosthwait, Survey of India; *m* 1959, Anne Marjorie, *d* of Col T. M. M. Penney. *Educ:* Wellington Coll.; Peterhouse, Cambridge (MA). Appointed to Indian Civil Service, 1937; Asst Private Sec. to Viceroy, 1942–44; Air Min., 1948–55; Commonwealth Relations Office, 1955; British Deputy High Commissioner in Ceylon, 1957–61; Asst Sec., CRO, 1961–63; British High Commissioner, Zanzibar, 1963–64; British Deputy High Commissioner, Malta, 1965–66; British High Commissioner, Guyana, 1966–67; Ambassador, Malagasy Republic, 1970–75. *Address:* 39 Eaton Terrace, SW1W 8TP. *T:* (020) 7730 9553. *Club:* Oxford and Cambridge. *Died 9 Nov. 2006.*

CROW, (Hilary) Stephen, CB 1995; FRTPI, FRICS; FRGS; Chief Planning Inspector and Chief Executive, Planning Inspectorate, executive agency in Department of the Environment and Welsh Office, 1992–94; Hon. Professor of Planning Practice and Policy, Cardiff School of City and Regional Planning, Cardiff University (formerly University of Wales College of Cardiff), since 1995; *b* 2 Sept. 1934; *s* of late Aubrey Everard Crow and Ivy Marion (*née* Warltier); *m* 1958, Margaret Anderson; two *s* one *d. Educ:* Leek High Sch.; William Ellis Sch.; St Catharine's Coll., Cambridge (MA). FRGS 1963; FRTPI 1986; FRICS 1992. Planning Asst, various grades, with Lancashire CC and Southport CBC, 1957–72; Divl Planning Officer, 1972–74, Prin. Asst County Planning Officer, 1974–76, Herts CC; joined Planning Inspectorate, 1976: Prin. Inspector for Wales, 1982–85; Asst Chief Inspector, 1985–88; Dep. Chief Inspector, then Chief Inspector, 1988–94. Chm., public examn of draft regl planning guidance for SE England, 1999. Chm., Casino Adv. Panel, 2005–07. C of E Lay Reader, 1979–. *Recreations:* music, reading, garden. *Address:* The Pines, Lyncombe Vale Road, Bath BA2 4LS; *e-mail:* stephen.crow@btopenworld.com. *Died 5 Dec. 2007.*

CROWDY, Maj.-Gen. Joseph Porter, CB 1984; Commandant and Postgraduate Dean, Royal Army Medical College, 1981–84, retired; Hon. Consultant on nutrition to Army, 1985–88; *b* 19 Nov. 1923; *s* of late Lt-Col Charles R. Crowdy and Kate Crowdy (*née* Porter); *m* 1948, Beryl Elisabeth Sapsford (*d* 1997); four *d. Educ:* Gresham's Sch.; Edinburgh Univ. MB, ChB 1947, DTM&H 1956, DPH 1957, DIH 1957; FFPH (FFCM 1974); MFOM 1981; FRSPH (FRIPHH 1982). House Surgeon, Norfolk and Norwich Hosp., 1947–48; joined RAMC, 1949; North Africa, 1952–55; Singapore, 1960–62; Head of Applied Physiology, Army Personnel Res. Estabt, 1963–73; Prof. of Army Health, Royal Army Med. Coll., 1973–76; SMO, Land Forces Cyprus, 1976–78; Dir, Army Preventive Medicine, 1978–81. Col Comdt, RAMC, 1985–88. QHP 1981–84. Editor, RAMC Jl, 1978–83. *Publications:* articles in medical jls, on smoking and health, nutrition, physical fitness and obesity. *Recreations:* antique furniture restoration, family genealogy, embroidery. *Address:* Pepperdon Mine, Lustleigh, Newton Abbot, Devon TQ13 9SN. *T:* and *Fax:* (01647) 277419; *e-mail:* crowdy@btinternet.com. *Died 28 June 2009.*

CROWE, William James, Jr, DDSM; DSM; Ambassador of the United States of America to the Court of St James's, 1994–97; Professor, US Naval Academy, since 1999; *b* Kentucky, 2 Jan. 1925; *s* of William James Crowe and Eula (*née* Russell); *m* 1954, Shirley Mary Grenell; two *s* one *d. Educ:* US Naval Acad. (BS 1946); Stanford Univ. (MA 1956); Princeton (PhD 1965). Commnd Ensign, USN, 1946; Comdr, ME Force, Bahrain, 1976–77; Dep. Chief of Naval Ops, Navy Dept, Washington, 1977–80; C-in-C Allied Forces, S Europe, 1980–83; C-in-C Pacific, 1983–85; Chm., Jt Chiefs of Staff, 1985–89; retd 1989 in rank of Adm. Prof. of Geopolitics, Oklahoma Univ., 1989–94. Chm., Foreign Intelligence Adv. Bd, Washington, 1993–94. Director of several public cos. Numerous US and foreign decorations incl. Navy, Air Force, Army and Coastguard DSMs and Medal of Freedom. *Publications:* (jtly) The Line of Fire, 1993; Reducing Nuclear Danger: the road away from the brink, 1993; articles on military and foreign policy. *Died 18 Oct. 2007.*

CROWFOOT, Maj.-Gen. Anthony Bernard, CB 1991; CBE 1982 (MBE 1974); General Officer Commanding North West District, 1989–91, retired; *b* 12 Aug. 1936; *s* of Thomas Bernard Crowfoot and Gladys Dorothy Crowfoot; *m* 1960, Bridget Sarah Bunting; three *s* one *d. Educ:* King Edward VII Sch., Norfolk; Royal Military Academy, Sandhurst, psc. Commissioned 1956; 1 E Yorks 1PWO: BAOR, UK, Aden, Gibraltar, 1956–60; Instructor, School of Infantry, 1960–62; 1PWO: BAOR, UK, Aden, 1962–66; Army Staff Coll. 1967; Brigade Major, HQ 5 Inf. Bde, 1968–69; Coy

Comd 1PWO, Cyprus, 1970–71; DAAG, MoD, 1971–73; CO 1PWO: UK, BAOR, N Ireland, 1973–76; Instructor, Army Staff College, 1976–77; Col GS, MoD, 1977–80; Comd 39 Inf. Bde, N Ireland, 1980–82; Student, US Army War Coll., 1982–83; Dep. Comdr/COS, HQ British Forces Hong Kong, 1983–86; Dir Gen. Army Manning and Recruiting, MoD, 1986–89. Col, PWO Regt of York, 1986–96. *Died 13 Sept. 2008.*

CROWTHER, Eric (John Ronald), OBE 1977; Metropolitan Magistrate, 1968–89; a Recorder of the Crown Court, 1983–96; *b* 4 Aug. 1924; *s* of Stephen Charles Crowther, company secretary, and Olive Beatrix Crowther (*née* Selby); *m* 1959, Elke Auguste Ottilie Winkelmann; one *s* one *d. Educ:* University College Sch., Hampstead. Royal Navy, 1943–47 (Medit. Area of Ops). Awarded Tancred Studentship in Common Law, 1948; Called to Bar, Lincoln's Inn, 1951; winner of Inns of Court Contest in Advocacy, 1951; Lectr and Student Counsellor, British Council, 1951–81; Lecturer: on Elocution and Advocacy for Council of Legal Educn, 1955–91 (Dir of Studies, Post-Final Gps, 1975–77); on Evidence to RN, 1968–89. Joined Inner Temple *ad eundem*, 1960. Practised at Criminal Bar, 1951–68. Sen. Resident Magistrate, Montserrat, 1996. Chairman: Inner London Magistrates' Assoc. Trng Sub-Cttee, 1981–89; Prisoners' Wives Service, 1982–85. Mem. Council, British Council, 1985– (lectures world-wide); Mem., Bd of Academic Studies, St Catherine's, Cumberland Lodge, 1977–82; Director of Studies: Cromwell Sch. of English, 1973–91; Oxford Study Centre, 1992–94. Trustee: Professional and Academic Regional Visits Organisation, 1977–89; Fair Trials Abroad, 1997–2000; Outside Chance, 2000–. Vice-Patron, Missing Persons' Helpline, 1994–. Mem. Cttee, RADA, 1979–84. Hon. Officer, Internat. Students' Hse, 1981–. Volunteer dog walker, Battersea Dogs' Home, 1999–. Freeman, City of London, 2004. Editor, Commonwealth Judicial Jl, 1973–77. *Publications:* Advocacy for the Advocate, 1984; Last in the List, 1988; Look What's on the Bench!, 1992; Russian Roulette, 1997. *Recreations:* travel, transport, the theatre, debating, student welfare, Scottish dancing. *Club:* International Students' House. *Died 6 Feb. 2006.*

CROZIER, Julian Smyth, CB 1995; business consultant; Chief Executive, Training and Employment Agency, Northern Ireland, 1990–95; *b* 19 Sept. 1935; *m* 1961, Rose Mary Maurna; two *s* one *d. Educ:* Campbell Coll., Belfast; Queens' Coll., Cambridge (BA). HMOCS, N Rhodesia, 1958–64; N Ireland Civil Service, 1965–95: served in Dept of Agriculture, Office of Comr for Complaints (Ombudsman), Depts of Health and Social Services, Finance and Personnel, Economic Develt. Dep. Chm., Probation Bd for NI, 1998–2003. Dir, Springvale Learning. Member: Council, Young Enterprise NI; Ulster Community Investment Trust. Chm., S Down Br., Alliance Party, 2000– (Mem. Party Exec., 2002–). Dir, Action Mental Health. *Recreations:* farming, country pursuits, golf, fishing, sailing, reading. *Clubs:* Royal Commonwealth Society; Royal Co. Down Golf. *Died 14 Sept. 2006.*

CRUFT, John Herbert; Music Director, Arts Council of Great Britain, 1965–79; *b* 4 Jan. 1914; *er s* of late Eugene and Winifred Cruft; *m* 1938, Mary Margaret Miriam (*d* 2003), *e d* of late Rev. Pat and Miriam McCormick; two *s. Educ:* Westminster Abbey Choir Sch.; Westminster Sch.; Royal College of Music (K. F. Boult Conducting Scholar). Oboist in BBC Television, London Philharmonic and Suisse Romande Orchestras, 1936–40. Served with Royal Corps of Signals, 1940–46. London Symphony Orchestra: Oboist, 1946–49; Sec., 1949–59. British Council: Dir of Music Dept, 1959–61; Dir of Drama and Music Dept, 1961–65. Member: Council, RCM, 1983–90, Life Gov., 1990; Council for Dance Educn and Trng, 1990–92; a Dir, National Jazz Centre, 1982–87. Trustee: Loan Fund for Musical Instruments, 1979–2005; Electro-Acoustic Music Trust, 1980–88; Governor: London Festival Ballet Trust Ltd, 1980–84; Contemporary Dance Trust Ltd, 1982–88. Hon. Treas., Royal Soc. of Musicians, 1976–87. FRCM, Hon. RAM.

Publications: The Royal College of Music: a Centenary Record 1883–1983 (with H. C. Colles), 1982. *Address:* 11 Broadhinton Road, Clapham, SW4 0LU. *T:* (020) 7720 2330. *Died 17 May 2008.*

CRUICKSHANK, Prof. Durward William John, PhD, ScD; FRS 1979; CChem, FRSC; Professor of Chemistry (Theoretical Chemistry), University of Manchester Institute of Science and Technology, 1967–83, then Emeritus; *b* 7 March 1924; *s* of William Durward Cruickshank, MB, ChB, and Margaret Ombler Meek, MA, MRCS, LRCP; *m* 1953, Marjorie Alice Travis (*d* 1983), MA, PhD; one *s* one *d. Educ:* St Lawrence Coll., Ramsgate; Loughborough Coll. (DLC 1944; BScEng 1st Cl. Hons London, 1944); St John's Coll., Cambridge (Wrangler, Math Tripos, 1949; Dist. Pt III Math. Tripos, 1950; BA 1949, MA 1954, ScD 1961; PhD Leeds, 1952. CChem, FRIC 1971. Engrg Asst, SOE and Admiralty (Naval Opl Res.), 1944–46; Leeds University: Res. Asst, Chemistry Dept, 1946–47; Lectr, 1950–57; Reader in Math. Chemistry, 1957–62; Fellow, St John's Coll., Cambridge, 1953–56; Joseph Black Prof. of Chem. (Theor. Chem.), Glasgow Univ., 1962–67; Dep. Principal, UMIST, 1971–72. Hon. Vis. Prof. of Physics, York Univ., 1985–88; Bragg Lectr, British Crystallographic Assoc., 1997. Treasurer, 1966–72, and Gen. Sec., 1970–72, Internat. Union of Crystallography. Companion of UMIST, 1992. Hon. DSc Glasgow, 2004. 1977 Chemical Soc. Award for Struct. Chem., 1978; (first) Dorothy Hodgkin Prize, British Crystallographic Assoc., 1991. *Publications:* (ed jtly) P. P. Ewald and his Dynamical Theory of X-ray Diffraction, 1992; (ed jtly) Time-resolved Macromolecular Crystallography, 1992; scientific papers on crystallography, molecular structure determination and theoretical chemistry in Acta Cryst., Proc. Royal Soc., and Jl Chem. Soc. *Recreations:* golf, genealogy. *Address:* 105 Moss Lane, Alderley Edge, Cheshire SK9 7HW. *T:* (01625) 582656. *Died 13 July 2007.*

CRUICKSHANK, Prof. Eric Kennedy, OBE 1961; MD; FRCP, FRCPGlas; Dean of Postgraduate Medicine, University of Glasgow, 1972–80; *b* 29 Dec. 1914; *s* of John Cruickshank, CBE, and Jessie (*née* Allan); *m* 1st, 1951, Ann Burch; two *s* two *d*; 2nd, 1969, Josephine Williams. *Educ:* Aberdeen Grammar Sch.; Univ. of Aberdeen (MB, ChB Hons, 1937; MD Hons and gold medal, 1948). Fellow, Harvard and Massachusetts Gen. Hosp., USA, 1938–39; Lectr, then Sen. Lectr, Dept of Medicine, Univ. of Aberdeen, 1939–50; Hon. Consultant in Medicine, NHS, 1948–50; First Dean, Medical Faculty, and Prof. of Medicine, Univ. of West Indies, Kingston, Jamaica, 1950–72. Served War of 1939–45: Captain RAMC, Medical Specialist, Changi Prisoner of War Camp, Singapore (despatches twice). WHO Consultant in Medical Educn, 1959–, Nutrition, 1955–; Member: GMC, 1972–80; Inter-Univ. Council, 1972–84; Greater Glasgow Health Bd, 1972–80. Hon. FACP 1969. *Publications:* on nutrition, neurology, medical educn. *Recreations:* gardening, ornithology. *Address:* Parsonage House, Oare, Wilts SN8 4JA. *Died 8 Aug. 2007.*

CUCKNEY, Baron *cr* 1995 (Life Peer), of Millbank in the City of Westminster; **John Graham Cuckney,** Kt 1978; *b* 12 July 1925; *s* of Air Vice-Marshal E. J. Cuckney, CB, CBE, DSC and Bar, and Lilian (*née* Williams); *m* 2nd, 1960, Muriel (*d* 2004), *d* of late Walter Scott Boyd; 3rd, 2007, (Priscilla) Jane Newell (*née* Watts), OBE. *Educ:* Shrewsbury; St Andrews Univ. (MA). War Service, Royal Northumberland Fusiliers, King's African Rifles, followed by attachment to War Office (Civil Asst, Gen. Staff), until 1957; subseq. appts with various industrial and financial cos including: Chairman: Brooke Bond Gp, 1981–84 (Dir, 1979–84); Thomas Cook Gp, 1978–87; John Brown, 1983–86 (Dir, 1981–86; Dep. Chm., 1982–83); Westland Gp, 1985–89; Royal Insce Hldgs plc, 1985–94 (Dir, 1979–89; Dep. Chm., 1983–85); Investors in Industry Gp, subseq. 3i Gp, 1987–92 (Dir, 1986–92); Orion Publishing Gp Ltd, 1994–97; Dep. Chm., TI Gp,

1985–90; Vice Chm., Glaxo, 1993–95 (Dir, 1990–95); Director: Lazard Brothers, 1964–70 and 1988–90; Midland Bank, 1978–88; Brixton Estate, 1985–96. Public appointments include: Chm., Mersey Docks and Harbour Board, 1970–72; Chief Executive (Second Perm. Sec.), Property Services Agency, DoE, 1972–74; Chm., International Military Services Ltd (an MoD company), 1974–85; Sen. Crown Agent and Chm. of Crown Agents, for Oversea Governments and Administrations, 1974–78. Advr to Sec. of State for Social Security on Maxwell pensions affair, and Founder Chm., Maxwell Pensioners' Trust, 1992–95. Independent Mem., Railway Policy Review Cttee, 1966–67; special Mem., Hops Marketing Bd, 1971–72; Chairman: EDC for Building, 1976–80; Port of London Authority, 1977–79; Internat. Maritime Bureau, Internat. Chamber of Commerce, 1981–85; NEDC Working Party on European Public Purchasing, 1990–92; Member: Docklands Joint Cttee, 1977–79; Council, British Exec. Service Overseas, 1981–84; Council, Foundn for Science and Technology, 1987–90; Dir, SBAC, 1986–89. Vice Pres., Liverpool Sch. of Tropical Med., 1985–93. Governor, Centre for Internat. Briefing, Farnham Castle, 1974–84; Chm., Understanding Industry Trust, 1988–91; Controller, ROH Develt Land Trust, 1993–96; Trustee, RAF Mus., 1987–99. Freeman, City of London, 1987. Elder Brother of Trinity House, 1980. Hon. DSc Bath, 1991; Hon. LLD St Andrews, 1993. *Address:* House of Lords, SW1A 0PW. *T:* (020) 7219 3000. *Club:* Athenæum.
Died 30 Oct. 2008.

CUENOD, Hugues; Swiss tenor; *b* 26 June 1902; *s* of Frank Cuenod and Gabrielle de Meuron; civil union 2007, Alfred Augustin. *Educ:* Swiss schools and colleges; Conservatoire Basel; Vienna; with Mme Singer-Burian. First concert, Paris, 1928; gave many performances of classical and light music, incl. musical comedy, in Europe and USA; numerous concerts with Clara Haskil and Nadia Boulanger; taught at Conservatoire de Genève, 1940–46; after returning to Paris, concentrated on sacred and classical music; sang in all major opera houses, incl. Glyndebourne (début 1954) and NY Metropolitan (début 1987); latterly specialised in French songs; many master classes; teacher of vocal interpretation of French songs. 33 recordings, of Couperin, Fauré, Debussy, Schubert, Bach, etc, many re-issued on CD; Grand Prix du Disque, 1980, for Socrate, by Erik Satie. Hon. Citizen of Boston, 1972. Händel and Haydn Soc. Medal, Boston, 1972; Fidelio Medal, Geneva, 1987. Commandeur de l'Ordre des Arts et des Lettres (France), 1976. *Relevant publications:* Hugues Cuenod: un diable de musicien, by Jerôme Spycket, 1978; Hugues Cuenod d'une voix légère: entretiens avec François Hudry, 1995. *Address:* 21 Place du Marché, 1800 Vevey, Switzerland; Château de Lully sur Morges, Vaud, Switzerland. *Died 3 Dec. 2010.*

CUEVAS-CANCINO, Francisco, Hon. GCVO 1985; Founder and Professor, Instituto de Educación Superior Simón Bolívar, Xalapa, Veracruz, since 1997; Mexican Ambassador Emeritus; *b* 7 May 1921; *s* of José Luis Cuevas and Sofía Cancino; *m* 1946, Ana Hilditch; two *s* one *d; m* Cristina Flores de Cuevas. *Educ:* Free School of Law, Mexico (lawyer, 1943); McGill Univ., Montreal (MCL 1946). Entered Mexican Foreign Service, as Vice-Consul, 1946, reaching rank of Ambassador by own merit; Permanent Representative to UN, 1965–70; Mexican Rep. to UNESCO, 1971–75, and Mem. Exec. Council during first four years; Perm. Rep. to UN, 1978–79; Ambassador: to Brazil, 1979–80; to Belgium, 1980–83; to UK and to Republic of Ireland, 1983–85; to Austria, 1986–90; Perm. Mexican Rep. to UNIDO and IAEA, 1986. Chm., Group of 77, Vienna, 1988. Order of the Liberator, 1970, Order Andrés Bello, 1971, (Venezuela); Medal of Mexican For. Service (25 years), 1972; Order Cruzeiro do Sul (Brazil), 1980; Great Cross of Order of the Crown (Belgium), 1983. *Publications:* La nullité des actes juridiques, 1947; La doctrina de Suárez en el derecho natural (award, Madrid), 1952; Roosevelt y la buena vecindad, 1955; Del Congreso de Panamá a la

Conferencia de Caracas, 1955, re-ed 1979; Tratado sobre la organización internacional, 1962; (ed) Porvenir de México by Luis G. Cuevas, 1961; (ed) Pacto de Familia (vol. forms part of Hist. Archives of Mexican Diplomatic Service, 2nd series), 1963; (ed) Foro Internacional, 1961–62; Cuentos de la Síndone, 1995; Las máscaras americanas del heroísmo, 1997; Homenaje a Agatha Christie, 2000; El asesinato del Gran Mariscal de Ayacucho, 2001; Las Memorias de Hugo Grocio, 2004; Grotius' *De Iure Belli* (modern version in Spanish), 2005; Manual de Derecho Internacional Privado Mexicano, 2007; contrib. to book of essays in homage to Hans Morgenthau, 1978; several works and articles on Bolivarian theatre, and on Simón Bolívar (The Liberator), incl.: Visión Surrealista del Libertador, (Bogotá) 1980; Homenaje a Bolívar en el Sesquicentenario de su Muerte, (Bogotá) 1980. *Address:* Instituto de Educación Superior Simón Bolivar, Revolución 279, Xalapa Centro, 91000 Veracruz, Mexico. *Died 18 Feb. 2008.*

CULLEN, Terence Lindsay Graham; QC 1978; *b* 29 Oct. 1930; *s* of late Eric Graham Cullen and Jean Morrison Hunter (*née* Bennett); *m* 1958, Muriel Elisabeth Rolfe; three *s. Educ:* RNC, Dartmouth. RN, 1948–55; Prestige Group Ltd, 1955–61. Called to the Bar: Lincoln's Inn, 1961 (Bencher, 1986); Singapore, 1978; Malaysia, 1980; Hong Kong, 1986; Bermuda, 1990; retired, 1998. *Recreation:* the Turf. *Address:* The Old School House, 1 Clare Lane, East Malling, Kent ME19 6BN.
Died 3 June 2010.

CULLINGFORD, Eric Coome Maynard, CMG 1963; *b* 15 March 1910; *s* of Francis James and Lilian Mabel Cullingford; *m* 1938, Friedel Fuchs (*d* 2003); one *s* one *d* (and one *s* decd). *Educ:* City of London Sch.; St Catharine's Coll., Cambridge (Exhibitioner). Entered Ministry of Labour as Third Class Officer, 1932; Principal, 1942. Served with Manpower Div. of CCG, 1946–50. Asst Sec., Min. of Labour, 1954. Labour Attaché, Bonn, 1961–65, 1968–72. Regional Controller, Eastern and Southern Region, Dept of Employment and Productivity, 1966–68; retired 1973. *Publications:* Trade Unions in West Germany, 1976; Pirates of Shearwater Island, 1983. *Address:* The Chace Rest Home, Chase Road, Upper Welland, Worcs WR14 4JY.
Died 4 April 2009.

CUMMINS, Frank; Examinations Liaison Officer, Sandwell Local Education Authority, 1987–89; Headmaster, Thomas Telford High School, Sandwell, West Midlands, 1973–87; *b* 20 Jan. 1924; *s* of Archibald Ernest and Ruth Elizabeth Cummins; *m* 1st, 1943, Joyce Swale (marr. diss.); three *s;* 2nd, 1973, Brenda Valerie Swift. *Educ:* Whitgift Middle Sch., Croydon; London School of Economics and Institute of Education, London Univ. Served Royal Signals, 1943–46. Assistant Teacher, Shireland Boys' Sch., Smethwick, 1949; Dep. Headmaster, 1956, Headmaster, 1961, Sandwell Boys' Sch., Smethwick. W Midlands Examinations Board: Chm., Exams Cttee, 1983–86 (Vice-Chm., 1980–83); Vice-Chm., Council, 1986–89; Chm., Bd, 1989–92; Mem. Jt Management Cttee, 1985–94, Governing Council, 1993–94, Midland Examining Gp for GCSE (Chm. Appeals Cttee, 1991–94). Chairman, Community Relations Councils: Warley, 1969, Sandwell, 1974; part-time Commissioner for Racial Equality, 1977–82; Chm., Schools Council Steering Group on Educn in a Multi-Cultural Soc., 1981–83. *Recreations:* cooking, caravanning, diabetes research, animal welfare. *Address:* 21 Green Street, Smethwick, Warley, West Midlands B67 7EB. *T:* (0121) 558 8484. *Died 9 Jan. 2007.*

CUNDY, Rt Rev. Ian Patrick Martyn; Bishop of Peterborough, since 1996; Assistant Bishop, Diocese of Ely, since 2004; *b* 23 April 1945; *s* of late Henry Martyn Cundy and Kathleen Ethel Cundy; *m* 1969, Josephine Katherine Boyd; two *s* one *d. Educ:* Monkton Combe Sch.; Trinity Coll., Cambridge (BA 1967; MA 1971); Tyndale Hall, Bristol. Ordained: deacon, 1969; priest, 1970; Asst Curate, Christ Church, New Malden, 1969–73; Tutor and Lectr in Church History, Oak Hill

Coll., London, 1973–77; Team Rector, Mortlake with East Sheen, 1978–83; Warden, Cranmer Hall, St John's Coll., Durham, 1983–92; Suffragan Bishop of Lewes, 1992–96. Church Comr, 2004–. Chm., Council for Christian Unity, 1998–2008. Pres., St John's Coll., Durham, 1999–2008. Trustee, Uppingham and Oakham Schs, 1996–. *Publications:* Ephesians—2 Thessalonians, 1981. *Recreations:* walking, music, photography, vintage cars. *Address:* Bishop's Lodging, The Palace, Peterborough, Cambs PE1 1YA. *T:* (01733) 562492, *Fax:* (01733) 890077.   *Died 7 May 2009.*

CUNNINGHAM, Merce; Artistic Director, Merce Cunningham Dance Company, since 1953; *b* 16 April 1919; *s* of Clifford D. Cunningham. *Educ:* Cornish Coll., Seattle, Washington. Martha Graham Dance Co., 1939–45; 1st solo concert, NY, 1944; choreographed: The Seasons, for Ballet Society (later NY City Ballet), 1947; Un Jour ou deux, for Ballet of Paris Opéra, 1973; more than 200 works for own company; other works revived for NY City Ballet, American Ballet Theatre, Rambert Dance Co. (formerly Ballet Rambert), Théâtre du Silence, France, Ohio Ballet, Boston Ballet, Pacific Northwest Ballet, Zürich Ballet, Netherlands Ballet, Ballet de Lyon. Hon. Mem., Amer. Acad. and Inst. of Arts and Letters, 1984. DLitt Univ. of Illinois, 1972; Hon. DHL Minnesota, 2004. Samuel H. Scripps American Dance Festival Award for lifetime contribs to dance, 1982; Award of Honor for Arts and Culture, NY, 1983; MacArthur Award, 1985; Kennedy Center Honors, 1985; Laurence Olivier Award, 1985; Meadows Award for excellence in the arts, Meadows Sch. of Arts, Southern Methodist Univ., Dallas, 1987; Nat. Medal of Arts, USA, 1990; Digital Dance Premier Award, 1990; Golden Lion, Venice Biennale, 1995; Premio Internazionale, Gino Tani, 1999; Dorothy and Lillian Gish Prize, 2000; Nijinsky Special Prize, Monaco, 2000; Praemium Imperiale, Tokyo, 2005. Comdr, Order of Arts and Letters, France, 1982; Officier de la Légion d'Honneur, 2004 (Chevalier, 1989). *Publications:* Changes: notes on choreography (ed Frances Starr), 1968; Le Danseur et la danse: entretiens avec Jacqueline Lesschaeve, 1980, English edn The Dancer and the Dance, 1985; Other Animals: drawings and journals, 2002; articles in 7 Arts, trans/formation, TriQuarterly. *Address:* 55 Bethune Street, New York, NY 10014, USA. *T:* (212) 2558240.   *Died 26 July 2009.*

CURE, Kenneth Graham, OBE 1984; Executive Councilman, Amalgamated Engineering Union, 1979–89, retired; Member, Labour Party National Executive, 1981–89; *b* 22 Feb. 1924; *s* of Herbert and Doris Edith Cure; *m* 1949, Kathleen (*née* Taylor) (decd); two *s* one *d*. *Educ:* King Edward VI Grammar School, Birmingham. Apprentice, BSA; trained as Universal Miller and draughtsman; served War of 1939–45, RN (Atlantic convoys and combined ops). Joined AEU, 1952; Founder Sec., Castle Vale Birmingham Branch, 1970; held numerous offices in Branch and District; former Mem., W Midlands Regional Labour Party Exec.; former Chm., Disputes Cttee, Lab. Party NEC; former Mem., Gen. Purposes Cttee, TUC. Former Director: Co-operative Press Ltd; Prince's Trust Educn and Training. Member: Panel, Central Arbitration Cttee; ACAS. Chair, East Birmingham Coll. Corp. (formerly Govs), 1973–98; Chm., Birmingham Metropolitan Inst. of Technology, 1992–96; Governor, Fircroft Coll., 1981–94. Hon. Chancellor, City Coll., Birmingham, 1998–. FRSA. Hon. MSc CNAA, 1986. *Recreation:* reading.   *Died 29 April 2007.*

CURIE, Eve, (Mrs Henry R. Labouisse); writer and journalist; *b* Paris, 6 Dec. 1904; *d* of late Marie and Pierre Curie; *m* 1954, Henry Richardson Labouisse (*d* 1987). *Educ:* Sévigné College; Bachelor of Science and Bachelor of Philosophy. Accompanied her mother in her tour of the US 1921; devoted several years to the study of the piano and gave her first concert in 1925 in Paris; later she took up musical criticism and under a pseudonym acted for several years as musical critic of the

weekly journal Candide; after the death of her mother in 1934 she collected and classified all the papers, manuscripts, and personal documents left by Mme Curie and went to Poland in 1935 to obtain material as to Mme Curie's youth; wrote Mme Curie's biography; went to America again in 1939 and several times afterwards on lecture tours; was a co-ordinator of the women's war activities at the Ministry of Information in Paris at the beginning of the war; after the French capitulation went to live in London for six months, then to America for her third lecture tour; Vichy Govt deprived her of French citizenship in April 1941; in 1942, travelled, as a war correspondent to the battlefronts of Libya, Russia, Burma, China; enlisted in the Fighting French corps, Volontaires Françaises, 1943, as a private; received basic training in England; 2nd Lieut 1943; 1st Lieut 1944. Co-publisher of Paris-Presse, an evening paper in Paris, 1944–49. Special Adviser to the Sec. Gen. of NATO, Paris, Aug. 1952–Nov. 1954. *Publications:* Madame Curie (in US), 1937 (trans. into 32 langs), Journey Among Warriors, 1943. *Recreation:* swimming. *Address:* 1 Sutton Place South, New York, NY 10022, USA.   *Died 22 Oct. 2007.*

CURRAN, Prof. Robert Crowe, MD; Leith Professor of Pathology, Birmingham University, 1966–86, then Emeritus; Hon. Consultant Pathologist, Birmingham Central Health District, 1966–86; *b* 28 July 1921; *s* of John Curran and Sarah Crowe, Netherton, Wishaw, Lanarkshire; *m* 1947, Margaret Marion Park; one *s* one *d*. *Educ:* Glasgow Univ. MB, ChB 1943, MD 1956; FRCPath 1967; FRCP 1969. RAMC, 1945–47. Lectr in Pathology, Glasgow Univ., 1950–55. Sen. Lectr and Cons. Pathologist, Sheffield Univ., 1955–58; Prof. of Pathology, St Thomas's Hospital Medical Sch., 1958–66. Registrar, Royal Coll. of Pathologists, 1968–73; Vice-Pres., 1977–80, Pres., 1981–84; Mem., GMC, 1979–86; Hon. Sec., Conf. of Med. Royal Colls and their Faculties in UK, 1982–86. Hon. FFPath, RCPI, 1983. *Publications:* Colour Atlas of Histopathology, 1966, 4th edn 2000; The Pathological Basis of Medicine, 1972; Gross Pathology—a Colour Atlas, 1974; Tumours: Structure and Diagnosis, 1991; scientific papers on lymphoid tissue, disorders of connective tissue, neoplasia. *Recreations:* golf, music. *Address:* 34A Carpenter Road, Edgbaston, Birmingham B15 2JH.   *Died 5 Sept. 2006.*

CURRY, Dr Alan Stewart; Controller, Forensic Science Service, Home Office, 1976–82; *b* 31 Oct. 1925; *s* of late Richard C. Curry and of Margaret Curry; *m* 1973, J. Venise Hewitt; one *s* by previous marriage. *Educ:* Arnold Sch., Blackpool; Trinity Coll., Cambridge (Scholar; MA; PhD 1952). CChem, FRSC, FRCPath. Served War of 1939–45 with RAF. Joined Home Office Forensic Science Service, 1952; served in NE Region, 1952–64; Dir, Nottingham Forensic Sci. Lab., 1964–66; Dir, Home Office Central Research Estabt, Aldermaston, 1966–76. Pres., Internat. Assoc. of Forensic Toxicologists, 1969–75; UN Consultant in Narcotics, 1972–91; Hon. Consultant in Forensic Toxicology to RAF, 1973–91; Consultant in Toxicology to British Airways, 1982–91. Fellow, Indian Acad. of Forensic Scis; Mem., Amer. Acad. of Forensic Scis (Lucas Gold Medal, 2002); Hon. Mem., Belg. Pharmaceutical Soc. Hon. DSc Ghent, 1985. Stas Gold Medal, Gesellschaft für Toxicologische und Forensische Chemie, 1983. *Publications:* Poison Detection in Human Organs, 1962, 4th edn 1988; (ed) Methods in Forensic Science, vols 3 and 4, 1964–65; Advances in Forensic and Clinical Toxicology, 1973; (ed) Analytical Methods in Human Toxicology, Part 1 1985, Part 2 1986; (ed with wife) The Biochemistry of Women: Clinical Concepts; Methods for Clinical Investigation, 1974; over 100 papers in med. and sci. and police jls. *Recreations:* sailing, amateur radio. *T:* (0118) 958 1481. *Club:* Athenæum.   *Died 20 Aug. 2007.*

CURRY, (Thomas) Peter (Ellison); QC 1966, 1973; *b* 22 July 1921; *s* of Maj. F. R. P. Curry; *m* 1950, Pamela Joyce, *d* of late Group Capt. A. J. Holmes, AFC, JP; two *s* two *d*. *Educ:* Tonbridge; Oriel Coll., Oxford (BA 1948;

MA 1951). Served War of 1939–45; enlisted 1939; commnd, 1941; 17th Indian Div., India and Burma, 1941–45. War Office, 1946. Called to Bar, Middle Temple, 1953, Bencher, 1979. QC 1966. Solicitor, 1968; partner in Freshfields, Solicitors, 1968–70; returned to Bar; re-appointed QC 1973. Pres., Aircraft and Shipbuilding Industries Arbitration Tribunal, 1978–80. Chm., Chancery Bar Assoc., 1980–85; Dep. Chm., Barristers' Benevolent Assoc., 1989–91 (Hon. Treas., 1964–71, 1984–89). Rep. Army and Sussex at Squash Racquets (described as fastest mover in squash, 1947); triple blue, squash, cross country and athletics, Oxford (twice cross country winner; unbeaten, cross country, 1946–48); World Student Games (5000 m), 1947; British Steeplechase champion 1948, Olympic Games, 1948. Served on AAA Cttee of Inquiry, 1967. Holder of French certificate as capitaine-mécanicien for mechanically propelled boats. *Publications:* (ed jtly) Palmer's Company Law, 1959; (ed jtly) Crew on Meetings, 1966, 1975. *Recreations:* gardening, the Turf. *Address:* Hurlands, Dunsfold, Surrey GU8 4NT. *T:* (01483) 200356.
Died 25 Jan. 2010.

CUSHING, David Henry, DPhil; FRS 1977; Deputy Director, Fisheries Research, England and Wales, 1974–80; *b* 14 March 1920; *s* of W. E. W. Cushing and Isobel (*née* Batchelder); *m* 1943, Diana R. C. Antona-Traversi; one *d*. *Educ:* Duke's Sch., Alnwick; Newcastle upon Tyne Royal Grammar Sch.; Balliol Coll., Oxford (MA, DPhil). RA, 1940–45; 1st Bn, Royal Fusiliers, 1945–46. Fisheries Lab., 1946–80. Rosenstiel Gold Medal for Oceanographic Science, Rosenstiel Inst. for Marine and Atmospheric Scis, Miami, 1980; Albert Medal for Oceanography, Institut Océanographique, Paris, 1984; Award for Excellence, Amer. Fisheries Soc., 1986; Ecology Inst. Prize, 1993. *Publications:* The Arctic Cod, 1966; Fisheries Biology, 1968 (USA); Detection of Fish, 1973; Fisheries Resources and their Management, 1974; Marine Ecology and Fisheries, 1975; Science and the Fisheries, 1977; Climate and Fisheries, 1982; The Provident Sea, 1988; Population Production and Regulation in the Sea, 1995; Towards the Science of Recruitment, 1996. *Address:* 198 Yarmouth Road, Lowestoft, Suffolk NR32 4AB. *T:* (01502) 565569.
Died 14 March 2008.

CUTHBERTSON, Ian Jardine; Senior Partner, Corporate Recovery, Dundas & Wilson, since 1997; *b* 8 May 1951; *s* of James and Catherine Cuthbertson; *m* 1974, Sally Jane Whittick; one *s* two *d*. *Educ:* Jordanhill Coll. Sch.; Univ. of Glasgow (LLB). Admitted solicitor, 1974; NP 1975; licensed as Insolvency Practitioner, 1986; Partner: Boyds, 1978–79; and Jt Founder, Dorman Jeffrey, 1979; Dundas & Wilson, 1997– (following merger with Dorman Jeffrey). Founding Mem., Internat. Insolvency Inst., 2005. FInstD 1988; FIPA 1990; Fellow, Assoc. of Business Recovery Professionals, 1990; Fellow, Inst. of Contemp. Scotland, 2003. *Recreations:* sport (Rugby, football), reading, art. *Address:* Dundas & Wilson, 191 West George Street, Glasgow G2 2LD. *T:* (0141) 222 2200, *Fax:* (0141) 222 2201; *e-mail:* ian.cuthbertson@dundas-wilson.com.
Died 28 Oct. 2009.

CUTLER, Hon. Sir Charles (Benjamin), KBE 1973; ED 1960; Director, 1976–88, Chairman, 1978–88, Sun Alliance (Australia); *b* Forbes, NSW, 20 April 1918; *s* of George Hamilton Cutler and Elizabeth Cutler; *m* 1943, Dorothy Pascoe (OBE 1976); three *s* one *d*. *Educ:* rural and high schs, Orange, NSW. Government of New South Wales: MLA for Orange, NSW; 1947; Leader of Country Party (NSW), 1959; Dep. Premier and Minister for Educn, 1965; Dep. Premier, 1972–76, Minister for Local Govt, 1972–76, and Minister for Tourism, 1975–76. Chm., United World Colls (Aust.) Trust,

1977. Hon. DLitt Newcastle Univ., NSW, 1968. *Recreation:* golf. *Address:* 52 Kite Street, Orange, NSW 2800, Australia. *T:* (2) 63626418. *Clubs:* Royal Automobile, Imperial Service, Union (Sydney); Orange Golf.
Died 23 Sept. 2006.

CUTLER, Ivor; humorist, poet, illustrator, playwright, singer and composer, since 1957; *b* 15 Jan. 1923; *s* of Jack and Polly Cutler; marr. diss.; two *s*. *Educ:* Shawlands Academy; Jordanhill Coll., Glasgow. Teacher: Summerhill Sch., Suffolk; ILEA, 1954–80. *Radio and television:* Monday Night at Home, Radio 4, 1959–63; John Peel, Radio 1, 1969–; 14 radio plays, Radio 3, 1979–88; Prince Ivor (opera), Radio 3, 1983; King Cutler I to VI (with Phyllis King), Radio 3, 1990–; Magical Mystery Tour, TV, 1967; Ivor Cutler has 15, 1990, Cutler the Lax, 1991, Radio 4 (radio archive selections); A Stuggy Pren (series), Radio 3, 1994; A Jelly Mountain (series), Radio 3, 1996; A Wet Handle (series), Radio 3, 1997; *stage:* Establishment Club (cabaret), 1961–62; An Evening of British Rubbish, Comedy Th., 1963. Cartoonist, Private Eye and Observer, 1962–63. Pye Radio Award for humour, 1980. *Recordings:* Ivor Cutler of Y'hup, 1959; Get Away from the Wall, 1961; Who Tore Your Trousers?, 1961; Ludo, 1967, reissued 1997; Dandruff, 1974; Velvet Donkey, 1975; Jammy Smears, 1976; Life in a Scotch Sitting Room, vol. 2, 1978, reissued 1987 and 1995; Privilege, 1983; Women of the World (single), 1983; Prince Ivor, 1986; Gruts, 1986; A Wet Handle, 1997; A Flat Man, 1998; Cute, (H)ey?, 1999. Poetry cartoons, Scotland on Sunday mag., 1992–93. *Publications:* stories: Cockadoodledon't, 1967; (illustr. Martin Honeysett): Gruts, 1961, repr. 1986; Life in a Scotch Sitting Room, vol. 2, 1984, 2nd edn 1998; Fremsley, 1987; Glasgow Dreamer, 1990, 2nd edn 1998; *children's books:* (illustr. Helen Oxenbury): Meal One, 1971; Balooky Klujypop, 1974; The Animal House, 1977; (illustr. Alfreda Benge): Herbert the Chicken, 1984; Herbert the Elephant, 1984; (illustr. M. Honeysett) One and a Quarter, 1987; (illustr. Patrick Benson) Herbert: Five Stories, 1988; (illustr. Jill Barton) Grape Zoo, 1990; (illustr. Claudio Muñoz) Doris the Hen, 1992; (illustr. Claudio Muñoz) The New Dress, 1995; *poetry:* Many Flies Have Feathers, 1973; A Flat Man, 1977; Private Habits, 1981; Large et Puffy, 1984; Fresh Carpet, 1986; A Nice Wee Present from Scotland, 1988; (illustr. M. Honeysett) Fly Sandwich and other Menu, 1992; Is that your flap, Jack?, 1992; (photogr. Katrina Lithgow) A Stuggy Pren, 1994; A Wet Handle, 1997; A Flat Man, 1998; South American Bookworms, 1999; Under the Spigot, 2002; *philosophy:* (illustr. Martin Honeysett) Befriend a Bacterium, 1992. *Recreation:* 2000 catalyst and hypocrite. *Address:* c/o BBC, Broadcasting House, W1A 1AA.
Died 3 March 2006.

CUTTER, Prof. Elizabeth Graham, PhD, DSc; FRSE; FLS; George Harrison Professor of Botany, University of Manchester, 1979–89, then Emeritus; *b* 9 Aug. 1929; *d* of Roy Carnegie Cutter and Alexandra (*née* Graham). *Educ:* Rothesay House Sch., Edinburgh; Univ. of St Andrews (BSc, DSc); Univ. of Manchester (PhD). Asst Lecturer in Botany, 1955–57, Lectr in Botany, 1957–64, Univ. of Manchester; Associate Professor of Botany, 1964–68, Professor of Botany, 1968–72, Univ. of California, Davis; Sen. Lectr in Cryptogamic Botany, 1972–74, Reader in Cryptogamic Botany, 1974–79, Univ. of Manchester. ARPS 1998. *Publications:* Trends in Plant Morphogenesis (principal editor), 1966; Plant Anatomy: Experiment and Interpretation, pt 1, Cells and Tissues, 1969, 2nd edn 1978; pt 2, Organs, 1971. *Recreations:* photography, fishing. *Address:* Barnyard Butts, Bakers Road, Gattonside, Melrose, Roxburghshire TD6 9NA. *T:* (01896) 822139.
Died 23 Oct. 2010.

D

da CUNHA, His Honour John Wilfrid; JP; a Circuit Judge (formerly Judge of County Courts), 1970–92; *b* 6 Sept. 1922; 2nd *s* of Frank C. da Cunha, MD, DPH, and Lucy (*née* Finnerty); *m* 1953, Janet, MB, ChB, *d* of Louis Savatard, (Hon.) MSc, LSA, and Judith Savatard, MB, BS; one *s* four *d*. *Educ*: Stonyhurst Coll., Lancs; St John's Coll., Cambridge. MA Cantab 1954. Served 1942–47: 23rd Hussars (RAC); wounded Normandy, 1944; Judge Advocate Gen. (War Crimes); Hon. Major. Called to Bar, Middle Temple, 1948; Northern Circuit. Chm., Local Appeal Tribunal, Min. of Social Security (Wigan), 1964–69. Asst Recorder, Oldham County Borough QS, 1966–70; Chm., Industrial Tribunals, 1966–70; Dep. Chm., Lancs County QS, 1968–71. Comr, NI (Emergency Provisions) Act, 1973; Member: Appeals Tribunal; Parole Bd, 1976–78; Criminal Injuries Compensation Bd, 1992–97. Pres., Bristol Medico-Legal Soc., 1989–91. Governor, Mount Carmel Sch., Alderley Edge, 1962–78. JP Lancs, 1968. *Recreations*: gardening, pottering. *Died 12 May 2006.*

D'AETH, Prof. (Hugh) Richard (Xenophon), PhD; President, Hughes Hall, Cambridge, 1978–84; *b* 3 June 1912; *e s* of Walter D'Aeth and Marion Turnbull; *m* 1943, Pamela Straker; two *d*. *Educ*: Bedford Sch.; Emmanuel Coll., Cambridge (Scholar; 1st Cl. Hons Nat. Sci., PhD); Harvard Univ. (Commonwealth Fellow; AM). Served War, RAF, 1941–46 (Wing Comdr). Master, Gresham's Sch., 1938–40; HM Inspector of Schs, 1946–52; Prof. of Education: University Coll. of West Indies, 1952–58; Univ. of Exeter, 1958–77. Mem., Internat. Assoc. for Advancement of Educnl Res. (Pres., Warsaw, 1969); sometime mem. cttees of Schools Council, BBC, Schs Broadcasting Council, RCN and NSPCC. *Publications*: Education and Development in the Third World, 1975; articles in jls. *Address*: Barton House, Rydon Acres, Stoke Gabriel, Totnes, Devon TQ9 6QJ.
Died 19 Feb. 2008.

DAHRENDORF, Baron *cr* 1993 (Life Peer), of Clare Market in the City of Westminster; **Ralf Dahrendorf,** KBE 1982; DPhil, DrPhil; FBA 1977; Warden of St Antony's College, Oxford, 1987–97; *b* Hamburg, 1 May 1929; adopted British nationality, 1988; *s* of Gustav Dahrendorf and Lina Dahrendorf (*née* Witt); *m* 1st, 1954, Vera Banister; three *d*; 2nd, 1980, Ellen de Kadt; 3rd, Christiane. *Educ*: several schools, including Heinrich-Hertz Oberschule, Hamburg; studies in philosophy and classical philology, Hamburg, 1947–52; DrPhil 1952; postgrad. studies at London Sch. of Economics, 1952–54; Leverhulme Research Schol., 1953–54; PhD 1956. Habilitation, and University Lecturer, Saarbrücken, 1957; Fellow at Center for Advanced Study in the Behavioral Sciences, Palo Alto, USA, 1957–58; Prof. of Sociology, Hamburg, 1958–60; Vis. Prof. Columbia Univ., 1960; Prof. of Sociology, Tübingen, 1960–66; Vice-Chm., Founding Cttee of Univ. of Konstanz, 1964–66; Prof. of Sociology, Konstanz, 1966–69; Parly Sec. of State, Foreign Office, W Germany, 1969–70; Mem., EEC, Brussels, 1970–74; Dir, 1974–84, Governor, 1986–, LSE; Prof. of Social Sci., Konstanz Univ., 1984–87. Chm., Delegated Powers Select Cttee, H of L, 2002–06. Member: Hansard Soc. Commn on Electoral Reform, 1975–76; Royal Commn on Legal Services, 1976–79; Cttee to Review Functioning of Financial Instns, 1977–80. Trustee, Ford Foundn, 1976–88. Chm. Bd, Friedrich Naumann Stiftung, 1982–88; non-executive Director: Glaxo Holdings PLC, 1984–92; Bankges. Berlin (UK) plc, 1996–2001. Vis. Prof. at several Eur. and N American univs. Reith Lecturer, 1974; Jephcott Lectr, RSocMed, 1983. Hon. Fellow: LSE; Imperial Coll. Hon. MRIA 1974; Fellow, St Antony's Coll., Oxford, 1976. Foreign Hon. Member: Amer. Acad. of Arts and Sciences, 1975–; Nat. Acad. of Sciences, USA, 1977; Amer. Philosophical Soc., 1977; FRSA 1977; Hon. FRCS 1982. 26 hon. degrees from univs in 12 countries. Journal Fund Award for Learned Publication, 1966; Agnelli Prize, Giovanni Agnelli Foundation, 1992; Heuss Prize, Theodor-Heuss Stiftung, 1997. Grand Croix de l'Ordre du Mérite du Sénégal, 1971; Grosses Bundesverdienstkreuz mit Stern und Schulterband (Federal Republic of Germany), 1974; Grand Croix de l'Ordre du Mérite du Luxembourg, 1974; Grosses goldenes Ehrenzeichen am Bande für Verdienste um die Republik Österreich (Austria), 1975; Grand Croix de l'Ordre de Léopold II (Belgium), 1975; Comdr's Cross, Order of Civil Merit (Spain), 1990. *Publications include*: Marx in Perspective, 1953; Industrie- und Betriebssoziologie, 1956; Soziale Klassen und Klassenkonflikt, 1957 (Class and Class Conflict, 1959); Homo Sociologicus, 1959; Die angewandte Aufklärung, 1963; Gesellschaft und Demokratie in Deutschland, 1965 (Society and Democracy in Germany, 1966); Pfade aus Utopia, 1967 (Uscire dall'Utopia, 1971); Essays in the Theory of Society, 1968; Konflikt und Freiheit, 1972; Plädoyer für die Europäische Union, 1973; The New Liberty, 1975; Life Chances, 1979; On Britain, 1982; Die Chancen der Krise, 1983; Reisen nach innen und aussen, 1984; Law and Order, 1985; The Modern Social Conflict, 1988; Reflections on the Revolution in Europe, 1990; LSE: a history of the London School of Economics and Political Science 1895–1995, 1995; After 1989, 1997; Liberal und unabhängig: Gerd Bucerius und seine Zeit, 2000; Universities after Communism, 2000; Über Grenzen, 2002; Auf der Suche nach einer neuen Ordnung, 2003; Der Wiederbeginn der Geschichte, 2004; Versuchungen der Unfreiheit, 2006. *Address*: House of Lords, SW1A 0PW. *Clubs*: PEN, Reform, Garrick.
Died 17 June 2009.

DAKIN, Dorothy Danvers, OBE 1982; JP; Assistant Chaplain, HM Prison and Remand Centre, Pucklechurch, 1984–87; *b* 22 Oct. 1919; *d* of Edwin Lionel Dakin, chartered civil engr and Mary Danvers Dakin (*née* Walker), artist. *Educ*: Sherborne Sch. for Girls; Newnham Coll., Cambridge. MA Geography. 2nd Officer WRNS (Educn), 1943–50; Housemistress, Wycombe Abbey Sch., 1950–60; Headmistress, The Red Maids' School, Bristol, 1961–81; Chm., ISIS Assoc., 1982–84. President: West of England Br., Assoc. of Headmistresses, 1969–71; Assoc. of Headmistresses of Girls' Boarding Schs, 1971–73; Girls' Schs Assoc. (Independent), 1973–75; Chm. Council, ISIS, 1975–81. Licensed Reader, C of E, 1982–86. FRSA 1988. JP Bristol, 1974. *Recreations*: fencing, painting, embroidery. *Address*: 41 Park Grove, Henleaze, Bristol BS9 4LF. *Died 22 May 2009.*

DALITZ, Prof. Richard Henry, FRS 1960; Royal Society Research Professor, Oxford University, 1963–90, then Professor Emeritus, and Fellow of All Souls College, 1964–90, then Emeritus Fellow; *b* 28 Feb. 1925; *s* of Frederick W. and Hazel B. Dalitz, Melbourne, Australia; *m* 1946, Valda (*née* Suiter), Melbourne, Australia; one *s* three *d*. *Educ*: Scotch Coll., Melbourne; Ormond Coll., Univ. of Melbourne; Trinity Coll., Univ. of Cambridge, PhD Cantab, 1950. Lecturer in Mathematical Physics, Univ. of Birmingham, 1949–55; research appointments in various Univs, USA, 1953–55; Reader in Mathematical Physics, Univ. of Birmingham, 1955–56; Prof. of Physics, Univ. of Chicago, 1956–66. Mem. Council, Royal Soc. 1979–81. Corresp. Mem., Australian Acad. of Science, 1978; Foreign Member: Polish Acad. of Sci., 1980; Nat. Acad. of India, 1990; For. Assoc., US Nat. Acad. Scis, 1991. Maxwell Medal and Prize, Institute of Physics and the Physical Soc., 1966; Bakerian Lectr and Jaffe Prize, 1969, Hughes Medal, 1975, Royal Medal, 1982, Royal

Soc.; J. Robert Oppenheimer Meml Prize, Univ. of Miami, 1980; Harrie Massey Prize, Inst. of Physics and Aust. Inst. of Physics, 1990. *Publications*: Strange Particles and Strong Interactions, 1962; Nuclear Interactions of the Hyperons, 1965; (ed jtly) High Energy Physics, 1965; (jtly) Nuclear Energy Today and Tomorrow, 1971; (jtly) Paul A. M. Dirac 1902–1984, 1986; (jtly) A Breadth of Physics, 1988; (ed) Collected Works of P. A. M. Dirac 1924–48, 1995; (jtly) Selected Scientific Papers of Sir Rudolf Peierls, 1997; (ed jtly) The Foundations of Newtonian Scholarship, 2000; numerous papers on theoretical physics in various British and American scientific jls. *Recreations*: travelling, biographical research, study of the Sorbian (Wendish) people, especially their language and emigration. *Address*: Rudolf Peierls Centre for Theoretical Physics, 1 Keble Road, Oxford OX1 3NP. *T*: (01865) 273966; All Souls College, Oxford.
Died 13 Jan. 2006.

DALRYMPLE-HAY, Sir John (Hugh), 7th Bt *cr* 1798, of Park Place, Wigtownshire; *b* 16 Dec. 1929; 2nd *s* of Lt-Col Brian George Rowland Dalrymple-Hay (*d* 1943) and Beatrice (*d* 1935), *d* of A. W. Inglis; *S* brother 2005; *m* 1962, Jennifer, *d* of Brig. Robert Johnston, OBE; one *s*. *Educ*: Blundell's Sch., Tiverton; RMA Sandhurst. Commnd RSF, 1950; served with KOSB, Korea (despatches, 1952) and Malaya; retired in rank of Captain, 1957. Industrial Relations Manager, Shell Co. (Fedn of Malaya) Ltd, 1960–62; various appointments with: Distillers Co. (CO_2) Ltd; Messer Gresheim. *Recreations*: sailing, ski-ing, golf (mainly golf now). *Heir*: *s* Malcolm John Robert Dalrymple-Hay, FRCS [*b* 1 April 1966; *m* 1998, Vanessa Long; three *d*]. *Died 20 Jan. 2009.*

DALRYMPLE-WHITE, Sir Henry Arthur Dalrymple, 2nd Bt *cr* 1926; DFC 1941 and Bar 1942; *b* 5 Nov. 1917; *o s* of Lt-Col Sir Godfrey Dalrymple Dalrymple-White, 1st Bt, and late Hon. Catherine Mary Cary, *d* of 12th Viscount Falkland; *S* father, 1954; *m* 1948, Mary (marr. diss. 1956), *o d* of Capt. Robert H. C. Thomas; one *s*. *Educ*: Eton; Magdalene Coll., Cambridge; London Univ. Served War of 1939–45. Formerly Wing Commander RAFVR. *Heir*: *s* Jan Hew Dalrymple-White [*b* 26 Nov. 1950; *m* 1st, 1979, Elizabeth (marr. diss.); 2nd, 1984, Angela Stevenson (marr. diss.); one *s*; 3rd, 1990, Betty Smith]. *Address*: Fairseat Foundation, PO Box 670, Village Market, Nairobi, Kenya. *Died 30 June 2006.*

DALTON, Sir Alan (Nugent Goring), Kt 1977; CBE 1969; DL; Chairman: British Railways (Western) Board, 1978–92; Devon and Cornwall Development Company, 1988–91; *b* 26 Nov. 1923; *s* of Harold Goring Dalton and Phyllis Marguerite (*née* Ash). *Educ*: Shendish Prep. Sch., King's Langley; King Edward VI Sch., Southampton. Man. Dir, English Clays, Lovering Pochin & Co. Ltd, 1961–84; Dep. Chm., 1968–84, Chm., 1984–89, English China Clays PLC. Member: Sun Alliance & London Assurance Group Bd, 1976–89; Western (formerly SW) Adv. Bd, Nat. Westminster Bank PLC, 1977–91; Director, Westland plc (formerly Westland Aircraft), 1980–85. DL Cornwall, 1982. *Recreations*: sailing, painting, reading. *Died 15 Sept. 2006.*

DALTON, Sir Howard, Kt 2007; FRS 1993; Professor, Department of Biological Sciences, Warwick University, since 1983; Chief Scientific Adviser, Department for Environment, Food and Rural Affairs, 2002–07; *b* 8 Feb. 1944; *s* of Leslie Alfred and Florence Dalton; *m* 1971, Kira Rozdestvensky; one *s* one *d*, and two step *s*. *Educ*: Queen Elizabeth Coll., London Univ. (BSc); Univ. of Sussex (DPhil). Univs of London, 1962–65, and Sussex, 1965–68; Postdoctoral Fellow: Purdue Univ., Indiana, 1968–70; Sussex Univ., 1970–73; posts at Warwick Univ., 1973–. Member: NERC, 2002–; BBSRC, 2002–. President: Soc. for Gen. Microbiology, 1997–2000; Marine Biol Assoc., 2007–. Leeuwenhoek Lectr, Royal Soc., 2000. *Publications*: contribs to learned scientific jls. *Recreations*: Real tennis, Japanese gardening. *Address*: Groves Mill, Shakers Lane, Long Itchington, Warwickshire CV47 9QB. *T*: (01926) 632746. *Club*: Leamington Tennis Court. *Died 12 Jan. 2008.*

DALY, His Eminence Cardinal Cahal Brendan; Archbishop Emeritus of Armagh, (RC) and Primate Emeritus of All Ireland; *b* 1 Oct. 1917. *Educ*: St Malachy's Coll., Belfast; Queen's Univ., Belfast (BA Hons, Classics, MA); St Patrick's Coll., Maynooth (LTh 1942, DTh 1944; DD); Institut Catholique, Paris (LPh 1953); DHL Sacred Heart Univ., Conn, USA. Ordained priest, 1941. Classics Master, St Malachy's Coll., Belfast, 1945–46; Lecturer in Scholastic Philosophy, 1946–63; Reader, 1963–67, Queen's Univ., Belfast; consecrated Bishop, 1967; Bishop of Ardagh and Clonmacnois, 1967–82; Bishop of Down and Connor, 1982–90; Archbishop of Armagh and Primate of All Ireland, 1990–96. Cardinal, 1991. Hon. DD: QUB: Exeter; Hon. DLitt TCD; Hon. LLD: NUI; Notre Dame, Indiana; St John's, NY; Sacred Heart, Fairfield, Conn. *Publications*: Morals, Law and Life, 1962; Natural Law Morality Today, 1965; Violence in Ireland and Christian Conscience, 1973; Theologians and the Magisterium, 1977; Peace the Work of Justice, 1979; The Price of Peace, 1991; Tertullian: the Puritan and his influence, 1993; Morals and Law, 1993; Northern Ireland—Peace—Now is the Time, 1994; Love begins at Home, 1995; Moral Philosophy in Britain from Bradley to Wittgenstein, 1996; Steps on my Pilgrim Journey, 1998; The Minding of Planet Earth, 2000; chapters in: Prospect for Metaphysics, 1961; Intellect and Hope, 1968; New Essays in Religious Language, 1969; Understanding the Eucharist, 1969. *Address*: Ard Mhacha, 23 Rosetta Avenue, Belfast BT7 3HG.
Died 31 Dec. 2009.

DALY, Lawrence; General Secretary, National Union of Mineworkers, 1968–84; *b* 20 Oct. 1924; *s* of James Daly and late Janet Taylor; *m* 1948, Renée M. Baxter; four *s* one *d*. *Educ*: primary and secondary schools. Glencraig Colliery (underground), 1939; Workmen's Safety Inspector, there, 1954–64. Part-time NUM lodge official, Glencraig, 1946; Chm., Scottish NUM Youth Committee, 1949; elected to Scottish Area NUM Exec. Cttee, 1962; Gen. Sec., Scottish NUM, 1964; National Exec., NUM, 1965. Mem., TUC General Council, 1971–81. TUC Gold Badge, 1981. *Publications*: (pamphlets): A Young Miner Sees Russia, 1946; The Miners and the Nation, 1968. *Recreations*: literature, politics, folk-song. *Died 23 May 2009.*

DALZIEL, Geoffrey Albert; British Commissioner, Leader of Salvation Army activities in Great Britain, 1974–80; *b* 10 Dec. 1912; *s* of Alexander William and Olive Mary Dalziel; *m* 1939, Ruth Edith Fairbank (*d* 1990); two *s* (one *d* decd). *Educ*: Harrow Elementary Sch. Commissioned Salvation Army Officer, 1934; Corps Officer in Gt Britain, to 1946; on Internat. Trng Coll. Staff, 1946–51; Divisional Youth Sec., 1951–59; Trng Coll. Principal, Melbourne, Aust., 1959–64; Chief Side Officer, Internat. Trng Coll., London, 1964–66; Chief Secretary: Sydney, Aust., 1966–68; Toronto, Canada, 1968–70; Territorial Comdr, Kenya, Uganda and Tanzania, E Africa, 1970–74. *Recreations*: walking, gardening, reading. *Died 2007.*

DALZIEL, Malcolm Stuart, CBE 1984; international funding consultant, 1991–2003; *b* 18 Sept. 1936; *s* of late Robert Henderson Dalziel and Susan Aileen (*née* Robertson); *m* 1961, Elizabeth Anne Harvey; one *s* two *d*. *Educ*: Banbury Grammar Sch.; St Catherine's Coll., Oxford (BA 1960, MA 1965). National Service, 2nd Lieut Northamptonshire Regt, 1955–57. The British Council, 1960–87: student, SOAS, 1960; Asst Educn Officer, Lahore, Pakistan, 1961–63; Regional Dir, Penang, Malaya, 1963–67; Regional Rep., Lahore, 1967–70; Rep., Sudan, 1970–74; Dir, Management Services Dept, and Dep. Controller, Estabs Div., 1975–79; Rep., Egypt, and Counsellor (Cultural), British Embassy, Cairo, 1979–83; Controller, Higher Educn Div., British Council and Sec., IUPC, 1983–87; Associate Consultant, 1988–96, Dir, 1990–96, Consultants in Economic Regeneration in Europe Services; Associate Consultant, Eur. Econ. Develt Services, 1996–2001.

Affiliate, Internat., Develt Centre, Queen Elizabeth House, Oxford Univ., 1988–. Dep. Chm., Council for Educn in the Commonwealth, 1990–2000 (Mem. Exec. Cttee, 1986–2003); Mem. Court, Univ. of Essex, 1986–88. Mem., Methodology Soc., 2004–. Vice-Pres., 1990–2007, Sen. Mem., 2007–, Northants CCC. *Recreations:* theatre, ballet, walking, Rugby. *Address:* 62 Victoria Road, Oxford OX2 7QD. *T:* (01865) 558969. *Club:* Oxford and Cambridge.   *Died 26 June 2009.*

DANIELL, Ralph Allen, CBE 1965 (OBE 1958); HM Diplomatic Service, retired; *b* 26 Jan. 1915; 2nd *s* of late Reginald Allen Daniell; *m* 1943, Diana Lesley (*née* Tyndale) (*d* 2004); one *s* three *d. Educ:* Lancing Coll.; University Coll., Oxford. Appointed to Board of Trade, 1937. Joined HM Forces, 1942; served with Royal Tank Regt in North Africa and Italian campaigns, 1943–45. Appointed to HM Foreign Service as First Sec., 1946; Mexico City, 1946; Rome, 1949; Foreign Office, 1951; Helsinki, 1953; Counsellor, 1958; Washington, 1958; New York, 1959; Cairo, 1962; Wellington, 1967; Consul-Gen., Chicago, 1972–74. *Address:* St Ives House, Ashley Heath, Ringwood, Hants BH24 2ED. *Died 12 Nov. 2007.*

DANIELS, Harold Albert; *b* 8 June 1915; *s* of Albert Pollikett Daniels and Eleanor Sarah Maud Daniels (*née* Flahey); *m* 1946, Frances Victoria Jerdan; one *s* decd. *Educ:* Mercers' Sch., Christ's Coll., Cambridge. BA 1937; Wren Prize 1938; MA 1940. Asst Principal, Post Office, 1938; Admiralty, 1942; Post Office, 1945; Principal, 1946; Asst Sec., 1950; Under-Sec., 1961; Min. of Posts and Telecommunications, 1969; Asst Under Sec. of State, Home Office, 1974–76. *Address:* Lyle Court Cottage, Bradbourne Road, Sevenoaks, Kent TN13 3PZ. *T:* (01732) 454039.   *Died 6 Feb. 2009.*

DANKWORTH, Sir John (Philip William), Kt 2006; CBE 1974; FRAM 1973; musician; *b* 20 Sept. 1927; British; *m* 1958, Clementine Dinah Laine (Dame Cleo Laine); one *s* one *d. Educ:* Monoux Grammar Sch. Studied Royal Academy of Music, 1944–46. ARAM 1969. Closely involved with post-war development of British jazz, 1947–60; formed large jazz orchestra, 1953; with Cleo Laine founded Stables Theatre, Wavendon, 1969. Pops Music Dir, LSO, 1985–90; Principal Guest Pops Conductor, San Francisco Orch., 1987–89. *Compositions* for combined jazz and symphonic musicians including: Improvisations (with Matyas Seiber), 1959; Escapade (commissioned by Northern Sinfonia Orch.), 1967; Tom Sawyer's Saturday, for narrator and orchestra (commissioned by Farnham Festival), 1967; String Quartet, 1971; Piano Concerto (commissioned by Westminster Festival), 1972; Grace Abounding (for RPO), 1980; The Diamond and the Goose (for City of Birmingham Choir and Orch.), 1981; Reconciliation (commnd for Silver Jubilee of Coventry Cathedral), 1987; Woolwich Clarinet Concerto (for Emma Johnson), 1995; Mariposas (for Peter Fisher), for violin and piano, 1996, rescored for violin and string orch., 2001; Double Vision (for BBC Big Band, world première, BBC Proms), 1997; Objective 2000 (for combined orchs of Harpur Trust Schs), 2000; many important *film scores,* 1964–, including: Saturday Night and Sunday Morning, Darling, The Servant, Morgan, Accident, Gangster No 1; other works include: Palabras, 1970; dialogue and songs for Colette, Comedy, 1980. Numerous record albums, incl. Echoes of Harlem, Misty, Symphonic Fusions. Variety Club of GB Show Business Personality Award (with Cleo Laine), 1977. Hon. Fellow, Leeds Coll. of Music, 1999. Hon. MA Open Univ., 1975; Hon. DMus: Berklee Sch. of Music, 1982; York, 1993. Distinguished Artists Award, Internat. Soc. for the Performance Arts, 1999; (with Cleo Laine) Bob Harrington Lifetime Achievement Award, Back Stage, 2001; Lifetime Achievement Award, BBC Radio Jazz Awards, 2002. *Publications:* Sax from the Start, 1996; Jazz in Revolution (autobiog.), 1998. *Recreations:* driving, household maintenance. *Address:* The Old Rectory, Wavendon, Milton Keynes MK17 8LT. *Fax:* (01908) 584414.   *Died 6 Feb. 2010.*

DANN, Most Rev. Robert William; *b* 28 Sept. 1914; *s* of James and Ruth Dann; *m* 1949, Yvonne (*née* Newnham); one *s* two *d. Educ:* Trinity Coll., Univ. of Melbourne. BA Hons Melbourne 1946. Deacon, 1945; Priest, 1946. Dir of Youth and Religious Education, Dio. Melbourne, 1946; Incumbent: St Matthew's, Cheltenham, 1951; St George's, Malvern, 1956; St John's, Footscray, 1961; Archdeacon of Essendon, 1961; Dir of Evangelism and Extension, Dio. Melbourne, 1963; Bishop Coadjutor, Dio. Melbourne, 1969–77; Archbishop of Melbourne and Metropolitan of Province of Victoria, 1977–83. *Address:* 101 Cameron Close, 155 Warrigal Road, Burood, Vic 3125, Australia. *Died 11 April 2008.*

DARBY, Sir Peter (Howard), Kt 1985; CBE 1973; QFSM 1970; HM Chief Inspector of Fire Services, 1981–86; *b* 8 July 1924; *s* of William Cyril Darby and Beatrice Colin; *m* 1948, Ellen Josephine Glynn; one *s* one *d. Educ:* City of Birmingham Coll. of Advanced Technology. Fire Brigades: Dep. Ch. Officer, Suffolk and Ipswich FB, 1963; Chief Officer, Nottingham FB, 1966; Chief Officer, Lancashire FB, 1967; County Fire Officer, Greater Manchester FB, 1974; Regional Fire Comdr (No 10) NW Region, 1974–76; Regional Fire Adviser (No 5) Greater London Region, 1977; Chief Officer of the London Fire Brigade, 1977–80. Pres., Chief and Asst Chief Fire Officers' Assoc., 1975–76; Mem. Adv. Council, Central Fire Brigades, 1977; Principal Adviser to Sec. of State on Fire Service matters, 1981–86; Chm., Fire Services Central Examinations Bd, 1985. Chm., Certifire Ltd, 1987–. Foundation Gov., St James's Catholic High (formerly Secondary Modern) Sch., Barnet, 1985– (Chm. Governors, 1987–). Freeman, City of London; Liveryman, Worshipful Co. of Basketmakers. CStJ 1983. *Recreations:* tell-walking, golf, fishing, sailing. *Address:* Darby, York House, 7 Twatling Road, Barnt Green, Birmingham B45 8HX. *Clubs:* City Livery, KSC. *Died 21 May 2008.*

DARCY DE KNAYTH, Baroness (18th in line), *cr* 1332; **Davina Marcia Ingrams,** DBE 1996; *b* 10 July 1938; *née* Herbert; *d* of late Squadron Leader Viscount Clive (*d* on active service, 1943) (17th Baron Darcy de Knayth, and *s* of 4th Earl of Powis), and Vida (*d* 2003), *o d* of late Captain James Harold Cuthbert, DSO, Scots Guards (she *m* 2nd, 1945, Brig. Derek Schreiber, MVO (*d* 1972)); *S* to father's Barony, 1943; *m* 1960, Rupert George Ingrams (*d* 1964), *s* of late Leonard Ingrams and Mrs Ingrams; one *s* two *d.* Elected Mem., H of L, 1999. *Heir: s* Hon. Caspar David Ingrams [*b* 5 Jan. 1962; *m* 1996, Catherine, *er d* of Bryan Baker and of Mrs Bryan Barnes; three *s*]. *Address:* Camley Corner, Stubbings, Maidenhead, Berks SL6 6QW.   *Died 24 Feb. 2008.*

D'ARCY HART, Philip Montagu; *see* Hart.

DARK, Sir Anthony Michael B.; *see* Beaumont-Dark.

DARKE, Marjorie Sheila; writer, since 1962; *b* 25 Jan. 1929; *d* of Christopher Darke and Sarah Ann (*née* Palin); *m* 1952, M. K. Twiselton; two *s* one *d. Educ:* Worcester Grammar Sch. for Girls; Leicester Coll. of Art and Technol.; Central Sch. of Art, London. Worked in textile studio of John Lewis Partnership, 1950–54. *Publications:* Ride the Iron Horse, 1973; The Star Trap, 1974; A Question of Courage, 1975; The First of Midnight, 1977; A Long Way to Go, 1978; Comeback, 1981; Tom Post's Private Eye, 1982; Messages and Other Shivery Tales, 1984; A Rose from Blighty, 1990; *for young children:* Mike's Bike, 1974; What Can I Do, 1975; Kipper's Turn, 1976; The Big Brass Band, 1976; My Uncle Charlie, 1977; Carnival Day, 1979; Kipper Skips, 1979; Imp, 1985; The Rainbow Sandwich, 1989; Night Windows, 1990; Emma's Monster, 1992; Just Bear and Friends, 1996. *Recreations:* reading, music, sewing, country walks. *Address:* c/o Rogers, Coleridge & White Ltd, Literary Agency, 20 Powis Mews, W11 1JN. *Clubs:* Society of Authors; International PEN.   *Died 21 July 2009.*

DARWIN, Kenneth; Deputy Secretary, Department of Finance (Northern Ireland), 1977–81; *b* 24 Sept. 1921; *s* of late Robert Lawrence and Elizabeth Darwin (*née* Swain), Ripon, Yorks; unmarried. *Educ:* Elementary Sch.; Ripon Grammar Sch.; University Coll., Durham; Oflag VIIB (1943–45). BA 1947, MA 1948. Served 2nd Bn Lancs Fus., N Africa, (Captain) POW, 1942–46; TA Captain (Intelligence Corps), 1949–54. Asst Keeper, Public Record Office (NI), 1948; Dep. Keeper of Records of N Ireland, 1955–70; Vis. Lectr in Archives, UC Dublin, 1967–71; Fellow Commoner, Churchill Coll., Cambridge, 1970; Asst Sec., Min. of Commerce (NI), 1970–74; Sen. Asst Sec., Dept of Finance (NI) and Dept of Civil Service (NI), 1974–77. Dir, Fountain Publishing, Belfast, 1995–. Member: Irish MSS Commn, Dublin, 1955–70; Adv. Bd for New History of Ireland, Royal Irish Acad., 1968–; Trustee: Ulster Historical Foundn, 1956–87; Ulster Museum, 1982–88 (Vice-Chm., 1984–86); Lyric Th., Belfast, 1966–69. Mem., Bangor Drama Club. Ed., Familia: Ulster Genealogical Rev., 1985–93. *Publications:* (ed jtly) Passion and Prejudice: Nationalist-Unionist conflict in Ulster in the 1930s and the founding of the Irish Association, 1993; articles on archives, history and genealogy, in jls and Nat. Trust guides. *Recreations:* travel, piano playing, walking, gardening. *Address:* 18 Seymour Road, Bangor, Co. Down BT19 1BL. *T:* (028) 9146 0718. *Clubs:* Royal Commonwealth Society; Royal British Legion (Bangor, Co. Down). *Died 20 Aug. 2009.*

DATTA, Dr Naomi, FRS 1985; Professor Emeritus, London University; *b* 17 Sept. 1922; *d* of Alexander and Ellen Henrietta Goddard; *m* 1943, S. P. Datta; two *d* (one *s* decd). *Educ:* St Mary's Sch., Wantage; University Coll. London; W London Hosp. Med Sch. MB BS (external); MD London. Junior medical posts, 1946–47; Bacteriologist in PHLS, 1947–57; Lectr, later Prof. of Microbiol Genetics, RPMS, London Univ., 1957–84; retired 1984. *Publications:* papers on the genetics and epidemiology of antibiotic resistance in bacteria. *Recreations:* gardening, cooking, travelling. *Address:* 9 Duke's Avenue, W4 2AA. *T:* (020) 8995 7562. *Died 30 Nov. 2008.*

DAUSSET, Prof. Jean Baptiste Gabriel Joachim; Grand Croix de la Légion d'Honneur; Professeur de Médecine Expérimentale au Collège de France, 1977–87; *b* 19 Oct. 1916; *s* of Henri Dausset and Elizabeth Brullard; *m* 1962, Rose Mayoral; one *s* one *d. Educ:* Lycée Michelet, Paris; Faculty of Medicine, University of Paris. Associate Professor, 1958–68, Professor of Immunohaematology, 1968–77, University of Paris. Institut Nationale de la Santé et de la Recherche Médicale: Director of Research Unit on Immunogenetics of Human Transplantation, 1968–84; Centre National de la Recherche Scientifique: Co-Director, Oncology and Immunohaematology Laboratory, 1968–84. Gairdner Foundn Prize, 1977; Koch Foundn Prize, 1978; Wolf Foundn Prize, 1978; Nobel Prize for Physiology or Medicine, 1980. *Publications:* Immuno-hématologie biologique et clinique, 1956; (with F. T. Rapaport) Human Transplantation, 1968; (with G. Snell and S. Nathanson) Histocompatibility, 1976; (with M. Fougereau) Immunology 1980, 1980; (with M. Pla) HLA, 1985; Clin d'oeil à la vie (autobiog.), 1998. *Recreation:* plastic art. *Address:* 44 rue des Ecoles, 75005 Paris, France. *Died 6 June 2009.*

DAVEY, Geoffrey Wallace; a Recorder of the Crown Court, 1974–97; *b* 16 Oct. 1924; *s* of late Hector F. T. Davey and Alice M. Davey; *m* 1st, 1950, Barbara Jean Fairbairn (marr. diss. 1963); one *s* one *d*; 2nd, 1964, Joyce Irving Steel (*d* 1995); one step *s*; 3rd, 1995, June Mary Wheldon; two step *s. Educ:* Queen Elizabeth Grammar Sch., Faversham; Wadham Coll., Oxford (MA). Called to Bar, Lincoln's Inn, 1954; admitted Ghana Bar, 1957; resumed practice NE Circuit, 1970; retired, 1998. Chm., Med. Appeal Tribunal, 1982–96; Dep. Chm., Agricl Land Tribunal, 1982–96. FCIArb 1993 (ACIArb 1992). *Recreations:* cooking, carpentry, local government.

Address: 22 Mill Hill Lane, Northallerton, N Yorkshire DL6 1DN. *T:* (01609) 780418; Fountain Chambers, Cleveland Business Centre, 1 Watson Street, Middlesbrough TS1 2RQ. *T:* (01642) 804040. *Died 18 May 2007.*

DAVEY, Keith Alfred Thomas, CB 1973; Solicitor and Legal Adviser, Department of the Environment, 1970–82; *b* 1920; *s* of W. D. F. Davey; *m* 1949, Kathleen Elsie, *d* of Rev. F. J. Brabyn; one *s* one *d. Educ:* Cambridge and County High Sch.; Fitzwilliam House, Cambridge (MA). Served War of 1939–45, Middle East (Captain). Called to the Baz, Middle Temple, 1947. Principal Asst Solicitor, DHSS, 1968–70. *Recreations:* looking at churches, reading history, keeping cats and dogs. *Address:* 172 Duxford Road, Whittlesford, Cambridge CB22 4NJ. *Club:* Athenæum. *Died 8 Nov. 2007.*

DAVEY, Roy Charles; Headmaster, King's School, Bruton, 1957–72; *b* 25 June 1915; *s* of William Arthur Davey and Georgina (*née* Allison); *m* 1940, Kathleen Joyce Sumner (*d* 2002); two *d. Educ:* Christ's Hospital; Brasenose Coll., Oxford (Open Scholar). Asst Master, Weymouth Coll., 1937–40. War Service, Royal Artillery, 1940–46. Senior Master, 1946–49, Warden, 1949–57, The Village Coll., Impington. FRSA. *Recreations:* poetry, botany, gardening, games. *Clubs:* East India, Devonshire, Sports and Public Schools. *Died 2 Jan. 2007.*

DAVID, Baroness *cr* 1978 (Life Peer), of Romsey in the City of Cambridge; **Nora Ratcliff David;** JP; *b* 23 Sept. 1913; *d* of George Blockley Blakesley, JP, and Annie Edith Blakesley; *m* 1935, Richard William David, CBE (*d* 1993); two *s* two *d. Educ:* Ashby-de-la-Zouch Girls' Grammar School; St Felix, Southwold; Newnham Coll., Cambridge (MA; Hon. Fellow 1986). Mem. Bd, Peterborough Develt Corp., 1976–78. A Baroness-in-Waiting (Government Whip), 1978–79; Opposition Whip, 1979–82; Dep. Chief Opposition Whip, 1982–87; opposition spokesman on education, 1987–97. Member: Cambridge City Council, 1964–67, 1968–74; Cambs County Council, 1974–78. Fellow, Anglia Ruskin Univ. (formerly Anglia Poly. Higher Educn Coll.), 1989. JP Cambridge City, 1965. *Recreations:* theatre, travel. *Address:* Windmill Court, St Minver, Cornwall PL27 6RD. *T:* (01208) 863293; House of Lords, SW1A 0PW. *T:* (020) 7219 3159. *Died 29 Nov. 2009.*

DAVIDSON, Hon. Lord; Charles Kemp Davidson, FRSE 1985; a Senator of the College of Justice in Scotland, 1983–96; Chairman, Scottish Law Commission, 1988–96; *b* Edinburgh, 13 April 1929; *s* of Rev. Donald Davidson, DD, Edinburgh; *m* 1960, Mary (OBE 1994), *d* of Charles Mactaggart, Campbeltown, Argyll; one *s* two *d. Educ:* Fettes Coll., Edinburgh; Brasenose Coll., Oxford; Edinburgh Univ. Admitted to Faculty of Advocates, 1956; QC (Scot.) 1969; Vice-Dean, 1977–79; Dean, 1979–83; Keeper, Advocates' Library, 1972–76. Procurator to Gen. Assembly of Church of Scotland, 1972–83. Dep. Chm., Boundary Commn for Scotland, 1985–96. *Address:* 22 Dublin Street, Edinburgh EH1 3PP. *T:* (0131) 556 2168. *Died 18 June 2009.*

DAVIDSON, Basil Risbridger, MC 1945; author and historian; *b* 9 Nov. 1914; *s* of Thomas and Jessie Davidson; *m* 1943, Marion Ruth Young; three *s*. Served War of 1939–45 (despatches twice, MC, US Bronze Star, Jugoslav Zasluge za Narod); British Army, 1940–45 (Balkans, N Africa, Italy); Temp. Lt-Col demobilised as Hon. Major. Editorial staff of The Economist, 1938–39; The Star (diplomatic correspondent, 1939); The Times (Paris correspondent, 1945–47; chief foreign leader-writer, 1947–49); New Statesman (special correspondent, 1950–54); Daily Herald (special correspondent, 1954–57); Daily Mirror (leader-writer, 1959–62). Vis. Prof., Univ. of Ghana, 1964; Vis. Prof., 1965, Regents' Lectr, 1971, Univ. of California; Montagu Burton Vis. Prof. of Internat. Relations, Edinburgh Univ., 1972; Sen. Simon Res. Fellow, Univ. of Manchester, 1975–76; Hon. Res. Fellow, Univ. of Birmingham, 1978–; Agnelli Vis.

Prof., Univ. of Turin, 1990. A Vice-Pres., Anti-Apartheid Movement, 1969–85. Author/presenter, Africa (8-part TV documentary series), 1984. Associate Mem., Acad. des Scis d'Outre-Mer, Paris, 1973. Freeman of City of Genoa, 1945. Hon. Fellow, SOAS, London Univ., 1998. DLitt *hc*: Ibadan, 1975; Dar es Salaam, 1985; Edinburgh, 1981; Western Cape, S Africa, 1997; Bristol, 1999; DUniv Open, 1980. Haile Selassie African Research Award, 1970. Medalha Amílcar Cabral (Republic of Guinea-Bissau), 1976; Grand Officer, Order of Prince Henry the Navigator (Portugal), 2002; First Degree, Order Amílcar Cabral (Republic of Cape Verde), 2003. *Publications: novels*: Highway Forty, 1949; Golden Horn, 1952; The Rapids, 1955; Lindy, 1958; The Andrassy Affair, 1966; *non-fiction*: Partisan Picture, 1946; Germany: From Potsdam to Partition, 1950; Report on Southern Africa, 1952; Daybreak in China, 1953; (ed) The New West Africa, 1953; The African Awakening, 1955; Turkestan Alive, 1957; Old Africa Rediscovered, 1959; Black Mother, 1961, rev. edn 1980; The African Past, 1964; Which Way Africa?, 1964; The Growth of African Civilisation: West Africa AD 1000–1800, 1965; Africa: History of a Continent, 1966; A History of East and Central Africa to the late 19th Century, 1967; Africa in History: Themes and Outlines, 1968; The Liberation of Guiné, 1969; The Africans, An Entry to Cultural History, 1969; Discovering our African Heritage, 1971; In the Eye of the Storm: Angola's People, 1972; Black Star, 1974; Can Africa Survive?, 1975; Discovering Africa's Past, 1978 (Children's Rights Workshop Award, 1978); Africa in Modern History, 1978; Crossroads in Africa, 1980; Special Operations Europe, 1980; The People's Cause, 1980; No Fist is Big Enough, 1981; Modern Africa, 1982, 3rd edn 1994; The Story of Africa, 1984; The Fortunate Isles, 1989; African Civilisation Revisited, 1991; The Black Man's Burden: Africa and the curse of the nation-state, 1992; The Search for Africa (essays), 1994; West Africa before the Colonial Era: a history to 1850, 1998. *Died 9 July 2010.*

DAVIDSON, Charles Kemp; *see* Davidson, Hon. Lord.

DAVIDSON, Ivor Macaulay; Chairman, D. O. Sanbiet Ltd, since 1980; *b* 27 Jan. 1924; *s* of late James Macaulay and Violet Alice Davidson; *m* 1st, 1948, Winifred Lowes (*d* 2002); four *s* one *d*; 2nd, 2004, Maureen Dingley Edwards (*née* Sambrook). *Educ:* Bellahouston Sch.; Univ. of Glasgow. Royal Aircraft Establishment, 1943; Power Jets (R&D) Ltd, 1944; attached RAF, 1945; National Gas Turbine Establishment, 1946: Dep. Dir, 1964; Dir, 1970–74; Dir-Gen. Engines, Procurement Exec., MoD, 1974–79. *Publications:* numerous, scientific and technical. *Recreations:* music, gardening. *Died 22 Jan. 2008.*

DAVIDSON, Keith; *see* Davidson, W. K.

DAVIDSON, Sir Robert (James), Kt 1989; Chairman, Devonport Management Ltd, 1994–96; Director, BICC plc, 1991–96; *b* 21 July 1928; *m* 1953, Barbara Elsie Eagles; one *s* two *d* (and one *s* decd). *Educ:* Royal Tech Coll., Glasgow (DRC 1949); Imperial Coll., London (DIC 1953). FREng (FEng 1984); FIMechE. Joined English Electric Co. as grad. apprentice, 1949; Develt Engr, 1951–52; Design Engr, Hydro Electric Project, 1953–55; Project Manager, Priest Rapids Hydro-Electric Power Stn, USA, 1956–61; Manufg Manager, then Gen. Manager, Netherton Works, 1962–69; English Electric taken over by GEC, 1969; Manager, Outside Construction Dept, 1969–72; Manufg Dir, 1972–74; Man. Dir, 1974–88, GEC Turbine Generators Ltd; Dir, GEC plc, 1985–91; Man. Dir, GEC Power Systems Ltd, 1988–89; Vice-Chm. and Chief Exec. Officer, GEC Alsthom NV, 1989–91; Chm. and Man. Dir, GEC ALSTHOM Ltd, 1989–91; Dir, GEC ALSTHOM SA, 1989–91; Chairman: NNC, 1988–91; Balfour Beatty Ltd, 1991–94. Mem., British Coal Corp., 1993. Hon. DSc Strathclyde, 1991. *Recreations:* walking, gardening, listening to music. *Died 1 Aug. 2007.*

DAVIDSON, Dr (William) Keith, CBE 1982; FRCGP; JP; Chairman, Scottish Health Service Planning Council, 1984–90; *b* 20 Nov. 1926; *s* of James Fisher Keith Davidson and Martha Anderson Davidson (*née* Milloy); *m* 1952, Dr Mary Waddell Aitken Davidson (*née* Jamieson); one *s* one *d*. *Educ:* Coatbridge Secondary Sch.; Glasgow Univ. DPA 1967; FRCGP 1980. MO 1st Bn Royal Scots Fusiliers, 1950; 2nd Command (Major) 14 Field Ambulance, 1950–51; MO i/c Holland, 1952. Gen. Medical Practitioner, 1953–90. Chairman: Glasgow Local Medical Cttee, 1971–75; Glasgow Area Medical Cttee, 1975–79; Scottish Gen. Medical Services Cttee, 1972–75; Dep. Chm., Gen. Medical Services Cttee (UK), 1975–79; Member: Scottish Medical Practices Cttee, 1968–80; Scottish Council on Crime, 1972–75; GMC, 1983–94; Scottish Health Service Policy Bd, 1985–88; Greater Glasgow Health Bd, 1989–93. British Medical Association: Mem. Council, 1972–81; Fellow, 1975; Chm., Scottish Council, 1978–81; Vice-Pres., 1983–. Hon. Pres., Glasgow Eastern Med. Soc., 1984–85; Pres., Scottish Midland and Western Med. Soc., 1985–86; FRSocMed 1986. Chm., Chryston High Sch. Bd, 1995–98 (Vice-Chm., 1990–95). Mem., Bonnetmaker Craft. Elder, Church of Scotland, 1956–; Session Clerk: Ruchazie Parish Church, 1961–71; Stepps Parish Church, 1983–98. JP Glasgow, 1962. SBStJ 1976. *Recreation:* gardening. *Address:* Dunvegan, 2 Hornshill Farm Road, Stepps, Glasgow G33 6DE. *T:* (0141) 779 2103. *Died 21 May 2007.*

DAVIES, Sir (Alfred William) Michael, Kt 1973; a Judge of the High Court of Justice, 1973–91, Acting High Court Judge, 1991–97, Queen's Bench Division; *b* 29 July 1921; *er s* of Alfred Edward Davies, Stourbridge; *m* 1947, Margaret (*d* 2003), *y d* of Robert Ernest Jackson, Sheffield; one *s* three *d*. *Educ:* King Edward's Sch., Birmingham; University of Birmingham (LLB). Called to Bar, Lincoln's Inn, 1948, Bencher 1972, Treasurer 1991; QC 1964; Dep. Chm. Northants QS, 1962–71; Recorder of: Grantham, 1963–65; Derby, 1965–71; Crown Court, 1972–73; Leader of Midland Circuit, 1968–71; Jt Leader of Midland and Oxford Circuit, 1971–73; Barrister, NSW, 1996. Chm. Mental Health Review Tribunal, for Birmingham Area, 1965–71; Comr of Assize (Birmingham), 1970; Chancellor, Dio. of Derby, 1971–73; Mem., Gen. Council of the Bar, 1968–72. Chm., Hospital Complaints Procedure Cttee, 1971–73. Conducted Visitor's Inquiry, UC, Swansea, 1992–93. Founding Chm., Expert Witness Inst., 1996–98. Over 100 TV and radio broadcasts, 1991–. Pres., Holdsworth Club, Univ. of Birmingham, 2003–04. *Publications:* articles and stories. *Recreations:* golf, the theatre. *Address:* Elliot House, Wolverley, Kidderminster, Worcs DY11 5XE. *T:* (01562) 851111. *Club:* Garrick. *Died 5 Sept. 2006.*

DAVIES, (Angie) Michael; Chairman: National Express Group, 1992–2004; Simon Group (formerly Simon Engineering), 1993–2003; Corporate Services Group, 1999–2002; *b* 23 June 1934; *s* of Angelo Henry and Clarice Mildred Davies; *m* 1962, Jane Priscilla, *d* of Oliver Martin and Kathleen White; one *d* (one *s* decd). *Educ:* Shrewsbury; Queens' College, Cambridge. Director: Ross Group, 1964–82; Fenchurch Insurance Holdings, 1969–76; Brown Brothers Corp., 1976–81; Imperial Group, 1972–82; Chairman: Imperial Foods, 1979–82; Tozer Kemsley & Millbourn (Holdings) plc, 1982–86; Bredero Properties, 1986–94; John Perkins Meats, then Perkins Foods, 1987–2001; Worth Investment Trust, 1987–95; Wiltshier, 1988–95; Calor Group, 1989–97 (Dir, 1987–97); Shearings Gp plc, 1997–2000; Deputy Chairman: TI Gp, 1990–93 (Dir, 1984–93); AerFi (formerly GPA) Gp plc, 1993–2000; Director: Littlewoods Organisation, 1982–88; Avdel (formerly Newman Industries), 1983–95; British Airways, 1983–2002; TV-am, 1983–89; Broadwell Land, 1984–90; James Wilkes, 1987–88; Blue Arrow, later

Manpower, 1987–92; Worcester Gp, 1991–92; Falcon Agencies, 1994–99. *Address:* Little Woolpit, Ewhurst, Cranleigh, Surrey GU6 7NP. *T:* (01483) 277344.
Died 3 April 2007.

DAVIES, Dr Arthur Gordon; Managing Director, Medical & Electrical Instrumentation Co. Ltd, 1965–90; *b* 6 Nov. 1917; *s* of Louis Bernard Davies and Elizabeth Davies; *m* 1945, Joan (*née* Thompson) (*d* 2003); two *d. Educ:* Westminster Hosp. (MB, BS 1943). LRCP, MRCS 1943. Called to the Bar, Lincoln's Inn, 1955. Served War, RAMC (Captain). Coroner to the Royal Household, 1959–83; Coroner, Inner South London, 1959–87. *Recreations:* chess, bridge, photography, electronics.
Died 19 Jan. 2008.

DAVIES, Caleb William, CMG 1962; FFPH; MRCS; LRCP; DPH; Regional Specialist in Community Medicine, 1974–82 (Acting Regional Medical Officer, 1977–78, 1979–80), South Western Regional Health Authority; *b* 27 Aug. 1916; *s* of Caleb Davies, KIH, MB, ChB, and Emily (*née* Platt); *m* 1939, Joan Heath (*d* 2003); three *s* one *d. Educ:* Kingswood Sch., Bath; University Coll. and University Coll. Hosp. Med. Sch., London; Edinburgh Univ.; London Sch. of Hygiene and Tropical Med. Kenya: MO, 1941; MOH, Mombasa, 1946; Tanganyika: Sen. MO, 1950; Asst Dir of Med. Services, 1952; Uganda: Dep. Dir of Medical Services, 1958; Permanent Sec. and Chief Medical Officer, Ministry of Health, 1960; retired 1963; South-Western Regional Hosp. Bd: Asst SMO, 1963–66; Principal Asst SMO, 1966–74. *Recreations:* swimming, photography. *Address:* St Joseph's Care Home, Gay Bowers Road, Danbury, Essex CM3 4JQ. *Died 1 Nov. 2007.*

DAVIES, Air Vice-Marshal David Brian Arthur Llewellyn, FRCGP; Principal Medical Officer, Headquarters RAF Support Command, 1989–91; *b* 4 Feb. 1932; *s* of Graham and Iris Davies; *m* 1958, Jean Mary Goate; two *s. Educ:* University Coll. London (BSc); University Coll. Hosp. (MB BS). DAvMed. Sen. MO, various RAF units, incl. Brize Norton, Scampton, Gütersloh and HQ AFCENT, 1958–80; Dep. Dir, Medical Personnel, MoD, 1980–82; OC RAF Hosp., Wegberg, 1982–85; Comdt, Central Med. Estabt, 1985–87; Dep. PMO, Strike Command, 1987–88. Consultant in Public Health Medicine, 1986–; Consultant Advr to DGMS (RAF), 1990–91. QHP, 1989–91. *Recreations:* travel, music, theatre, gardening. *Address:* c/o Royal Bank of Scotland, 127–128 High Holborn, WC1V 2PQ. *Club:* Royal Air Force.
Died 1 June 2006.

DAVIES, David Levric, CB 1982; OBE 1962; Under Secretary (Legal), Treasury Solicitor's Office, 1977–82; *b* 11 May 1925; *s* of Benjamin and Elizabeth Davies; *m* 1955, Beryl Justine Hammond. *Educ:* Llanrwst Grammar Sch.; University Coll. of Wales, Aberystwyth (LLB Hons). Called to the Bar, Middle Temple, 1949. Served War, 1943–46: Sub-Lt RNVR. Crown Counsel, Aden, 1950–55; Tanganyika: Asst to Law Officers, 1956–58; Parly Draftsman, 1958–61; Solicitor-Gen., 1961–64; Home Civil Service, 1964–82: seconded to Jamaica as Sen. Parly Draftsman, 1965–69, and to Seychelles as Attorney-Gen., 1970–72; Sen. Legal Asst, Treasury Solicitor's Office, 1972–73; Asst Treasury Solicitor, 1973–77. *Recreations:* gardening, loafing, reading. *Address:* Greystones, Breach Lane, Shaftesbury, Dorset SP7 8LF. *T:* (01747) 851224. *Died 7 Feb. 2008.*

DAVIES, Rt Rev. Howell Haydn; Bishop of Karamoja, Uganda, 1981–87; Vicar of St Jude's Parish, Wolverhampton, 1987–93; *b* 18 Sept. 1927; *s* of Ivor Thomas Davies and Sarah Gladys Davies (*née* Thomas); *m* 1958, Jean Wylam (*née* King); three *s* three *d. Educ:* Birmingham; DipArch (Birm.) 1954; ARIBA 1955. Corporal Clerk (Gen. Duties) RAF, Mediterranean and Middle East, 1945–48. Assistant Architect, 1952–56. Deacon 1959, priest 1960; Curate, St Peter's Parish, Hereford, 1959–61; Missionary of Bible Churchmen's Missionary Soc., Kenya, 1961–79, Uganda, 1981–87;

Archdeacon of Maseno North, 1971–74; Provost of Nairobi, 1974–79; Vicar of Woking, 1979–81. Buildings designed and completed in Kenya: Church Trng Centre, Kapsabet; Teachers' Coll. Chapel, Mosoriot; St Andrew's Parish Centre, Kapenguria; Cathedral Church of the Good Shepherd, Nakuru; three-storey admin block, bookshop and staff housing for Maseno N Dio., Kakamega; various church and mission staff housing in Kenya and Uganda. *Recreations:* walking, reading, d-i-y, building design. *Address:* 2 Cherry Tree Close, Cherry Tree Road, Sheffield S11 9AF. *Died 30 Nov. 2009.*

DAVIES, Humphrey; *see* Davies, M. W. H.

DAVIES, Ian Leonard, CB 1983; CEng, FIEE; Director, Admiralty Underwater Weapons Establishment, 1975–84; *b* 2 June 1924; *s* of late H. Leonard Davies and Mrs J. D. Davies; *m* 1951, Hilary Dawson, *d* of late Rear-Adm. Sir Oswald Henry Dawson, KBE; two *s* two *d. Educ:* Barry County Sch.; St John's Coll., Cambridge (Schol. and Prizeman; Mechanical Scis Tripos, 1944, and Mathematical Tripos Pt 2 (Wrangler), 1949; MA). Telecommunications Research Estabt, 1944; Blind Landing Experimental Unit, 1946. TRE (later the Royal Radar Establishment), 1949–69; Imperial Defence Coll., 1970; Asst Chief Scientific Adviser (Projects), MoD, 1971–72; Dep. Controller Electronics, 1973, Dep. Controller Air Systems (D), 1973–75, MoD(PE). Tech. Advr, Monopolies and Mergers Commn, 1986. Mem. Council, IEE, 1974–77 (Chm., Electronics Div. Bd, 1975–76). *Publications:* papers on information theory, radar, and lasers. *Recreations:* music, walking. *Address:* 37 Bowleaze Coveway, Preston, Weymouth, Dorset DT3 6PL. *T:* (01305) 832206. *Club:* Athenæum.
Died 4 June 2006.

DAVIES, John Richard; QC 2003; *b* 18 Sept. 1958; *s* of late Geoffrey William and Jean Dawson Davies; partner, Barbara Kelly; one *d. Educ:* Eastbourne Coll.; Downing Coll., Cambridge (BA 1980, MA 1984). Called to the Bar, 1981; in practice as commercial, company and employment barrister, 1981–. *Recreations:* Burgundy (both red and white), Bordeaux, golf and almost all matters sporting. *Address:* Littleton Chambers, 3 King's Bench Walk North, Temple, EC4Y 7HR. *T:* (020) 7797 8600, *Fax:* (020) 7797 8699. *Died 30 Sept. 2009.*

DAVIES, His Honour Joseph Marie; QC 1962; a Circuit Judge (formerly Judge of County Courts), 1971–91; *b* 13 Jan. 1916; *s* of Joseph and Mary Davies, St Helen's; *m* 1948, Eileen Mary (*née* Dromgoole); two *s* two *d. Educ:* Stonyhurst Coll.; Liverpool Univ. Called to Bar, Gray's Inn, Nov. 1938; practice in Liverpool; Recorder of Birmingham, 1970–71; Cumberland Co. Quarter Sessions: Dep. Chm., 1956–63, 1970–71; Chm., 1963–70. Served War of 1939–45; The King's Regt, Nov. 1939–Dec. 1941; RIASC and Staff Allied Land Forces, SE Asia, 1942–46. *Address:* 4 Elm Grove, Eccleston Park, Prescot, Lancs L34 2RX. *T:* (0151) 426 5415. *Died 21 Sept. 2006.*

DAVIES, Sir Lancelot Richard B.; *see* Bell Davies.

DAVIES, Michael; *see* Davies, A. M.

DAVIES, Sir Michael; *see* Davies, Sir A. W. M.

DAVIES, Prof. (Morgan Wynn) Humphrey, MBE 2002; DSc; CEng, FIET; FCGI; Professor of Electrical Engineering, Queen Mary College, University of London, 1956–79, then Emeritus (Fellow of the College, 1984); *b* 26 Dec. 1911; *s* of late Richard Humphrey Davies, CB; *m* 1944, Gwendolen Enid (decd), *d* of late Rev. Canon Douglas Edward Morton, Camborne, Cornwall; one *s. Educ:* Westminster Sch.; University College of N Wales, Bangor (BSc 1931); Charlottenburg Technische Hochschule, Berlin; Commonwealth Fellow, MIT, 1938–39 (MSc 1940). Grad. Apprentice with Metropolitan-Vickers, 1933; Lectr in Electrical Engineering, Univ. of Wales, 1935–42; Educn Officer to Instn of Electrical Engineers, 1944–47; Lectr, 1947, and Univ. Reader, 1952, in Electrical Engineering, Imperial

Coll., London, 1947–56; Dean of Engrg, Univ. of London, 1976–79. Member: Council, IEE, 1948–51, 1958–61 (Chm., Science and Gen. Div. 1964–65). Council, City & Guilds of London Inst., 1952–62; Engineering Adv. Cttee, BBC, 1965–71; Computer Bd for Univs and Res. Councils, 1968–71; Chm. Bd, Univ. of London Computer Centre, 1968–79; University of Wales, Bangor (formerly UCNW, Bangor): Mem. Council, 1976–2005 (Chm., F and GP Cttee, 1981–2005); Chm., and Trustee, Develt Trust, 1984–2000; Sec., Bangor Univ. Foundn, 2000–05; Adv. Cttee, Alumni Bangor, 2005–. Gov., Howell's Sch., Denbigh, 1987–96; Chm., Educn Cttee, 1991–96. Freeman, City of London, 1996; Liveryman, Drapers' Co., 2007– (Freeman, 1995). Hon. LLM London, 1977; Hon. DSc Wales, 1985. *Publications:* Power System Analysis (with J. R. Mortlock), 1952; papers in Proc. of Instn of Electrical Engineers. *Recreation:* travel. *Address:* Church Bank, Beaumaris, Anglesey LL58 8AB. *Club:* Athenæum.   *Died 24 June 2007.*

DAVIES, Richard Llewellyn; QC 1994; *b* 7 April 1948; *s* of Richard Henry Davies and Margaret Davies; *m* 1979, Elizabeth Ann Johnston; one *s* one *d. Educ:* St Julian's High Sch., Newport, Gwent; Univ. of Liverpool (LLB Hons). Called to the Bar, Inner Temple, 1973, Bencher, 2002. *Recreations:* music, wine, reading, cycling. *Address:* 39 Essex Street, WC2R 3AT.   *Died 11 Nov. 2008.*

DAVIES, Robert, CMG 2000; Chief Executive Officer, The Prince of Wales International Business Leaders Forum, since 1990; *b* 21 April 1951; *s* of Bob Davies and late Betty Davies; *m* 1993, Noriko Suzuki (marr. diss. 2001). *Educ:* Brierly Hill GS; Univ. of Durham (BA Hons 1972); LSE (post-grad. res., 1975–79). Manager, various charities and regl arts initiatives, 1971–74; NCVO, 1974–80; Dir and Jt Founder, Nat. Energy Action, 1979–83; Chm. and Founder, Rainbow Educational TV Productions, 1982–90; Dir of Develt, 1983–86, Dep. Chief Exec., 1986–90, BITC; Founder and Exec. Dir, Digital Partnership, 2000–; Dir, Digital Partnership (S Africa), 2002–05. Chairman: Marylebone & Soho CHC, 1979–80; Kensington & Chelsea and Westminster FHSA, 1984–96; Coll. of Health, 1989–94; Vice Chm., Westminster Assoc. for Mental Health, 1980–86; Jt Chair, Kensington & Chelsea and Westminster NHS Health Commning Jt Authy, 1994–96. Member: Crown Agents Foundn, 1997–; Performance and Innovation Unit Trade Adv. Gp, Cabinet Office, 1999–2000; External Mem., Comprehensive Spending Review, DFID, 1997–98; Bd Mem., UK Know-How Fund, DFID, 1998–99. Founder and Council Mem., Urban Villages Forum, 1992–2001; Bd Mem., British Hungarian Small Business Foundn, 2001–05; Member: Gov. Council, El Foro de la Empresa y Responsabilidad Social en las Américas, 2002–; Internat. Bd, Global Rainwater Harvesting Collective, 2003–; Bd, Dubai Ethics Resource Centre, 2005–. Chm., Internat Business Leaders Forum N America Inc., 2006–. Trustee: Sch. for the Performing Arts Trust, 1985–2000; New Acad. of Business, 1998–2005; Central Sch. of Ballet, 2001–06; Stars Foundn, 2001–06; Jordan River Foundn (UK), 2005–; Advisor: Abu Dhabi Higher Colls of Technol., 2000–04; Pure Resonance Ltd, 2006–; Mem., Internat. Adv. Bd, Academia Engelberg, 2002–; Adv. Bd, Global Inst. for Tomorrow, 2005–. Comr, St Petersburg Action Commn, Centre for Internat. Strategic Studies, 1994–96; Dir, Pushkin Cultural Trust, 1995–; Mem. Adv. Bd, Russia Partnership, 2003–. Patron, Youth Business China, 2003–. *Publications:* (contrib.) Making Globalisation Good, 2003. *Recreations:* ski-ing, opera, urban life, technology. *Address:* International Business Leaders Forum, 15–16 Cornwall Terrace, Regent's Park, NW1 4QP. *T:* (020) 7467 3666, *Fax:* (020) 7467 3610; *e-mail:* robert.davies@iblf.org.   *Died 18 Aug. 2007.*

DAVIES-SCOURFIELD, Brig. Edward Grismond Beaumont, CBE 1966 (MBE 1951); MC 1945; DL; General Secretary, National Association of Boys Clubs, 1973–82; *b* 2 Aug. 1918; 4th *s* of H. G. Davies-Scourfield and Helen (*née* Newton); *m* 1945, Diana Lilias (*née*

Davidson); one *s* one *d. Educ:* Winchester Coll.; RMC Sandhurst. Commnd into KRRC, 1938; served War of 1939–45 (despatches 1945); psc; commanded: 1st Bn The Rifle Bde, 1960–62; Green Jackets Bde, 1962–64; British Jt Services Trng Team (Ghana), 1964–66; British Troops Cyprus and Dhekelia Area, 1966–69; Salisbury Plain Area, 1970–73; retd 1973. DL Hants, 1984. *Publications:* In presence of my foes: travels and travails of a POW, 1991. *Recreation:* country pursuits. *Address:* c/o Lloyds TSB Bank plc, Cox's and King's Branch, PO Box 1190, 7 Pall Mall, SW1Y 5NA. *Clubs:* Army and Navy, Mounted Infantry.   *Died 20 Nov. 2006.*

DAVIS, Brig. John Anthony; Chairman, Commonwealth Society for the Deaf (Sound Seekers), since 2006 (Chief Executive, 1994–2003); Director, 2003–06; Trustee, since 2003); *b* 2 Dec. 1936; *s* of late Horace Albert Davis and Jean Isobel Davis (*née* Marshall); *m* 1960, Deirdre Telford; two *d. Educ:* Hurstpierpoint Coll.; RMA, Sandhurst. FCIS 1979. Commnd York and Lancaster Regt, 1958; served BAOR, Cyprus, Swaziland, Aden, Kenya; Green Howards, 1968, tranf. RAPC, 1970; HQ 1 Armd Div., 1966–68; DAA&QMG, HQ Dhekelia Area, 1972–74; Staff Paymaster, HQ 2 Armd Div., 1978–80; Chief Instructor, RAPC Trng Centre, 1980–83; Comd Finance HQ 1 (BR) Corps, 1983–86; Regtl Paymaster, Regtl Pay Office, Glasgow, 1986–88; Dep. Paymaster-in-Chief, 1988–89; Comd Finance HQ BAOR, 1989–92. Dep. Controller, SSAFA, 1992–94. *Recreations:* photography, travel. *Address:* Pear Tree Cottage, 31 Basingbourne Road, Fleet, Hants GU52 6TG.   *Died 27 Nov. 2008.*

DAVIS, John Michael N.; *see* Newsom-Davis.

DAVIS, Michael McFarland; Director for Wales, Property Services Agency, Department of the Environment, 1972–77; *b* 1 Feb. 1919; 2nd *s* of Harold McFarland and Gladys Mary Davis; *m* 1942, Aline Seton Butler; three *d. Educ:* Haberdashers' Aske's, Hampstead. Entered Air Ministry, 1936. Served War, RAF, 1940–45 (PoW, 1942–45). Private Sec. to Chiefs and Vice-Chiefs of Air Staff, 1945–49, and to Under-Secretary of State for Air, 1952–54; Harvard Univ. Internat. Seminar, 1956; Student, IDC, 1965; Command Sec., FEAF, 1966–69; on loan to Cabinet Office (Central Unit on Environmental Pollution), 1970; transf. to Dept of Environment, 1971. Delegate to UN Conf. on Human Environment, Stockholm, 1972. *Recreations:* music, bonsai, wine. *Address:* Avalon, 1 Foxborough Road, Radley OX14 3AB. *T:* (01235) 535541.   *Died 11 Nov. 2007.*

DAVIS, Raymond, Jr, PhD; Adjunct Professor of Astronomy, University of Pennsylvania, since 1984; *b* Washington, DC, 14 Oct. 1914; *s* of Raymond Davis and Ida Rogers (*née* Younger); *m* 1948, Anna Marsh Torrey; three *s* two *d. Educ:* Univ. of Maryland (BS, MS Chemistry); Yale Univ. (PhD Chemistry). Monsanto Chemical Co., 1945–48; Sen. Scientist, Brookhaven Nat. Lab., 1948–84. Honorary DSc: Pennsylvania, 1990; Laurentian, 1997; Chicago, 2000. Comstock Prize, US Nat. Acad. of Scis, 1978; Searle Prize, Amer. Chem. Soc., 1978; Bonner Prize, 1988, Panofsky Prize, 1992, APS; Tinsley Prize, 1995, Hale Prize, 1996, AAS; Pontecorvo Prize, Jt Inst. for Nuclear Res., Dubna Russia, 1999; Wolf Prize, Wolf Foundn, Israel, 2000; US Nat. Medal of Sci., 2001; (jtly) Nobel Prize for Physics, 2002; Benjamin Franklin Medal, Franklin Inst., Philadelphia, 2003; Enrico Fermi Award, US Dept of Energy, 2003. *Publications:* (ed) Solar Neutrinos: the first 30 years, 1994; articles on neutrinos in several encyclopaedias; contribs on solar neutrinos and lunar sci. to Physical Rev., Jl of Geophys. Res., Science, Phys. Rev. Letters, Procs Apollo 11 Lunar Sci. Conf., Nature, Astrophys. Jl, Nuclear Physics, etc. *Address:* 28 Bergen Lane, Blue Point, NY 11715, USA. *T:* (631) 363 6521.   *Died 31 May 2006.*

DAVIS, Hon. Sir Thomas (Robert Alexander Harries), KBE 1981; MD; Pa Tu Te Rangi Ariki 1979; Prime Minister, Cook Islands, 1978–87; *b* 11 June 1917; *s* of Sidney Thomes Davis and Mary Anne Harries; *m* 1940,

Myra Lydia Henderson; one *s* (and two *s* decd); *m* 1979, Pa Tepaeru Ariki (decd); *m* 2000, Carla Frances Cassata; one *d*. *Educ*: King's Coll., Auckland, NZ; Otago Univ. Med. Sch. (MB, ChB 1945); Sch. of Tropical Medicine, Sydney Univ., Australia (DTM&H 1950); Harvard Sch. of Public Health (Master of Public Health 1952). FRSTM&H 1949. MO and Surg. Specialist, Cook Islands Med. Service, 1945–48; Chief MO, Cook Is Med. Service, 1948–52; Res. Staff, Dept of Nutrition, Harvard Sch. of Public Health, 1952–55; Chief, Dept of Environmental Medicine, Arctic Aero-medical Lab., Fairbanks, Alaska, 1955–56; Res. Physician and Dir, Div. of Environmtl Med., Army Medical Res. Lab., Fort Knox, Ky, 1956–61; Dir of Res., US Army Res. Inst. of Environmtl Med., Natick, 1961–63; Res. Exec., Arthur D. Little, Inc., 1963–71. Involved in biol aspects of space prog., first for Army, later for NASA, 1957–71. Formed Democratic Party, Cook Islands, 1971; private med. practice, Cook Islands, 1974–78 and 1987–. Mem., RSocMed, 1960; twice Pres., Med. and Dental Assoc., Cook Islands. Chancellor, S Seas Univ., 2000–. President: Liby and Mus. Soc., 1991–92; Cook Islands Voyaging Soc., 1992–; Cook Islands Yachting Fedn, 1995–; Pacific Islands Voyaging Soc. (Internat.), 1995–. Designed, built and sailed Polynesian voyaging canoes, Takitumu, 1991–92, Te Au o Tonga, 1994–98, Aotearoa, 2001. Cook Islander Man of the Year, 1996; Pacific Islander of the Century, Achiever's Magazine, 2000. Silver Jubilee Medal, 1977; Order of Merit, Fed. Republic of Germany, 1978; Papua New Guinea Independence Medal, 1985. *Publications*: Doctor to the Islands, 1954; Makutu, 1956; Island Boy, 1992; Vaka, 1992; over 150 scientific and other pubns. *Recreations*: deep sea fishing, yacht racing, agriculture/planting, amateur radio. *Address*: PO Box 116, Avarua, Rarotonga, Cook Islands; *e-mail*: sirthomasdavis@paradise.net.nz. *Clubs*: Harvard (Boston, Mass); Wellington (NZ); Avatiu Sports (patron), Ivans (Pres. 1990), Rarotonga Yacht (patron); Avatiu Cricket (patron).   *Died 23 July 2007.*

DAVIS-RICE, Peter; Director of Nursing and Personnel, North Western Regional Health Authority, 1990–94; *b* 1 Feb. 1930; *s* of Alfred Davis-Rice and Doris Eva (*née* Bates); *m* 1967, Judith Anne Chatterton; one *s* two *d*; *m* 1993, Joan Margaret Walton. *Educ*: Riley High Sch., Hull; Royal Coll. of Nursing, Edinburgh; Harefield Hosp., Middx; City Hosp., York. SRN; British Tuberculosis Assoc. Cert.; MCMI; NAdmin(Hosp)Cert. Staff Nurse, Charge Nurse, St Luke's Hosp., Huddersfield, 1954–57; Theatre Supt, Hull Royal Infirmary, 1957–62; Asst Matron (Theatres), Walton Hosp., Liverpool, 1962–66; Matron, Billinge Hosp., Wigan, 1966–69; Chief Nursing Officer, Oldham and District HMC, 1969–73; Regl Nursing Officer, 1973–90, Asst Gen. Manager (Personnel Services), 1985–90, N Western RHA. Caseworker, High Peak Div., SSAFA, Forces Help, 1996–. Mem. Mgt Cttee, Tameside CAB, 2001–. *Publications*: contrib. Nursing Times. *Recreations*: walking, music. *Address*: 17 Storthbank, Simmondley, Glossop, Derbys SK13 6UX. *T*: (01457) 856224.   *Died 28 April 2006.*

DAWS, Dame Joyce (Margaretta), DBE 1975; FRCS, FRACS; Surgeon, Queen Victoria Memorial Hospital, Melbourne, Victoria, Australia, 1958–85; Thoracic Surgeon, Prince Henry's Hospital, Melbourne, 1975, retired; President, Victorian Branch Council, Australian Medical Association, 1976; *b* 21 July 1925; *d* of Frederick William Daws and Daisy Ethel Daws. *Educ*: Royal School for Naval and Marine Officers' Daughters, St Margaret's, Middx; St Paul's Girls' Sch., Hammersmith; Royal Free Hosp., London. MB, BS (London) 1949; FRCS 1952, FRACS. Ho. Surg., Royal Free Hosp.; SHMO, Manchester Royal Infirmary; Hon. Surg., Queen Victoria Meml Hosp., Melb., 1958; Asst Thoracic Surg., Prince Henry's Hosp., Melb., 1967–75. Pres., Bd of Management, After-Care Hosp., Melbourne, 1980–85; Chairman: Victorian Nursing Council, 1983–89; Academic and Professional Panel, Victoria, for Churchill Fellowship Awards, 1984; Jt Adv. Cttee on Pets in

Society, 1984; Internat. Protea Assoc., 1987–96. Hon. Sec., Victorian Br., AMA, 1974. *Recreations*: opera, ballet, theatre, desert travel, protea grower. *Address*: Hilltop Aged Care, 10 Hotham Street, Preston, Vic 3072, Australia. *Clubs*: Lyceum, Soroptimist International (Melbourne).   *Died 13 June 2007.*

DAWSON, Hon. Lord; Thomas Cordner Dawson; a Senator of the College of Justice in Scotland, since 1995; *b* 14 Nov. 1948; *s* of Thomas Dawson and Flora Chisholm (*née* Dunwoodie); *m* 1975, Jennifer Richmond Crombie; two *s*. *Educ*: Royal High Sch. of Edinburgh; Edinburgh Univ. (LLB Hons). Advocate, 1973; QC (Scot.) 1986. Lectr, Univ. of Dundee, 1971–74; Advocate Depute, 1983–87; Solicitor-Gen. for Scotland, 1992–95. Member: Supreme Court Legal Aid Cttee, 1980–83; Criminal Injuries Compensation Bd, 1988–92. *Recreations*: golf, cricket, reading, crosswords. *Address*: 19 Craiglea Drive, Edinburgh EH10 5PB. *T*: (0131) 447 4427. *Club*: Royal Northern and University (Aberdeen).   *Died 1 June 2007.*

DAWSON, Sir (Hugh) Michael (Trevor), 4th Bt *cr* 1920, of Edgewarebury; *b* 28 March 1956; *s* of Sir (Hugh Halliday) Trevor Dawson, 3rd Bt; *S* father, 1983. *Heir*: *b* Nicholas Antony Trevor Dawson, *b* 17 Aug. 1957.   *Died 26 Nov. 2007.*

DAWSON, James Gordon, CBE 1981; FREng, FIMechE, FSAE; Consultant; *b* 3 Feb. 1916; *s* of James Dawson and Helen Mitchell (*née* Tawse); *m* 1941, Doris Irene (*née* Rowe) (*d* 1982); one *s* one *d*. *Educ*: Aberdeen Grammar Sch.; Aberdeen Univ. (BScEng Hons Mech. Eng, BScEng Hons Elect. Eng). Develt Test Engr, Rolls Royce Ltd, Derby, 1942; Chief Engr, Shell Research Ltd, 1946; Technical Dir, Perkins Engines Ltd, 1955; Dir, Dowty Group Ltd, 1966; Man. Dir, Zenith Carburetter Co. Ltd, 1969, Chm., 1977–81. Pres., IMechE, 1979–80; FIMechE 1957; Hon. FIMechE 1986. *Publications*: technical papers publd in UK and abroad. *Recreation*: golf. *Address*: Mildmay House, Apethorpe, Peterborough PE8 5DP. *T*: (01780) 470348.   *Died 30 Jan. 2007.*

DAWSON, Sir Michael; *see* Dawson, Sir H. M. T.

DAWSON, Thomas Cordner; *see* Dawson, Hon. Lord.

DAY, Lucienne, OBE 2004; RDI 1962; in freelance practice, since 1948; Consultant, with Robin Day, to John Lewis Partnership, 1962–87; *b* 1917; *d* of Felix Conradi and Dulcie Lilian Duncan-Smith; *m* 1942, Robin Day, OBE, RDI; one *d*. *Educ*: Convent Notre Dame de Sion, Worthing; Croydon School of Art; Royal Coll. of Art. ARCA 1940; FSIAD 1955. Teacher, Beckenham Sch. of Art, 1942–47; began designing full-time, dress fabrics and later furnishing fabrics, carpets, wallpapers, table-linen, 1947 for Edinburgh Weavers, Heal's Fabrics, Cavendish Textiles, Tomkinsons, Wilton Royal, Thos Somerset etc, and firms in Scandinavia, USA and Germany; also china decoration for Rosenthal China, Selb, Bavaria, 1956–68; work for Barbican Art Centre, 1979; latterly designing and making silk wall-hangings (silk mosaics). Retrospective exhibitions: Whitworth Art Gall., Manchester, and RCA, 1993; Aberdeen, 1994: Barbican, 2001; Mackintosh Gall., Glasgow, 2003. Work in permanent collections: V&A; Whitworth Art Gall. Museum; Trondheim Museum, Norway; Cranbrook Museum, Michigan, USA; Art Inst. of Chicago; Röhsska Mus., Gothenberg, Sweden; Musée des Arts Décoratifs, Montreal. Member: Rosenthal Studio-line Jury, 1960–68; Cttee, Duke of Edinburgh's Prize for Elegant Design, 1960–63; Council, RCA, 1962–67; RSA Design Bursaries Juries; Cttee, Sir Misha Black Awards, 1980–2007. Master, Faculty of Royal Designers for Industry, 1987–89. Hon. FRIBA 1997. Sen. Fellow, RCA, 1999. Hon. DDes: Southampton, 1995; Buckingham, 2003. First Award, Amer. Inst. of Decorators, 1950; Gold Medal, 9th Triennale di Milano, 1951; Gran Premio, 10th Triennale di Milano, 1954: Design Council Awards, 1957, 1960, 1968; Silver Medal, Weavers' Co., 2005. *Relevant publication*: Robin and

Lucienne Day: pioneers of contemporary design, by Lesley Jackson, 2001. *Recreation:* gardening. *Address:* 21 West Street, Chichester, W Sussex PO19 1QW. *T:* (01243) 781429.   *Died 30 Jan. 2010.*

DAY, Robin, OBE 1983; RDI 1959; FCSD (FSIAD 1948); design consultant and freelance designer; *b* 25 May 1915; *s* of Arthur Day and Mary Shersby; *m* 1942, Lucienne Conradi (Lucienne Day, OBE, RDI) (*d* 2010); one *d. Educ:* Royal Coll. of Art (ARCA). National scholarship to RCA, 1935–39; teacher and lectr for several yrs; Design Consultant: Hille International, 1948–; John Lewis Partnership, 1962–87. Commissions include: seating for many major concert halls, theatres, stadia, etc.; interior design of Super VC10 and other aircraft. Mem., juries for many national and internat. indust. design competitions. Sen. Fellow, RCA, 1991; Hon. FRIBA; Hon. Fellow, Kent Inst. of Art & Design, 1998. Hon. DDes Buckingham Chilterns UC, 2003. Many awards for design work, including: 6 Design Centre awards; Gold Medal, Triennale di Milano, 1951, and Silver Medal, 1954; Designs Medal, SIAD, 1957. *Relevant publication:* Robin and Lucienne Day: pioneers of contemporary design, by Lesley Jackson, 2001. *Recreations:* mountaineering, ski touring, hill-walking. *Address:* 21 West Street, Chichester, W Sussex PO19 1QW. *T:* (01243)   781429.   *Clubs:*   Alpine,   Alpine   Ski.
                                    Died 9 Nov. 2010.

DEAN OF HARPTREE, Baron *cr* 1993 (Life Peer), of Wedmore in the County of Somerset; **Arthur Paul Dean,** Kt 1985; PC 1991; company director; *b* 14 Sept. 1924; *s* of Arthur Percival Dean and Jessie Margaret Dean (*née* Gaunt); *m* 1st, 1957, Doris Ellen Webb (*d* 1979); 2nd, 1980, Peggy Parker (*d* 2002). *Educ:* Ellesmere Coll., Shropshire; Exeter Coll., Oxford (MA, BLitt). Former President Oxford Univ. Conservative Assoc. and Oxford Carlton Club. Served War of 1939–45, Capt. Welsh Guards; ADC to Comdr 1 Corps BAOR. Farmer, 1950–56. Resident Tutor, Swinton Conservative Coll., 1957; Conservative Research Dept, 1957–64, Assistant Director from 1962. MP (C) Somerset North, 1964–83, Woodspring, Avon, 1983–92. A Front Bench Spokesman on Health and Social Security, 1969–70; Parly Under-Sec. of State, DHSS, 1970–74; Dep. Chm. of Ways and Means and Dep. Speaker, 1982–92. Member: Exec. Cttee, CPA, UK Branch, 1975–92; House of Commons Services Select Cttee, 1979–82; House of Commons Chairman's Panel, 1979–82; Chm., Conservative Health and Social Security Cttee, 1979–82. A Dep. Speaker, H of L, 1995–. Mem., Exec. Cttee, Assoc. of Conservative Peers, 1995–. Formerly, Member Governing Body of Church in Wales. *Publications:* contributions to political pamphlets. *Recreation:* fishing. *Address:* Archer's Wyck, Knightcott, Banwell, Weston-super-Mare, Avon BS24 6HS. *Club:* Oxford and Cambridge.   *Died 1 April 2009.*

DEAN, His Honour Joseph (Jolyon); a Circuit Judge, South Eastern Circuit, 1975–87; *b* 26 April 1921; *s* of late Basil Dean, CBE; *m* 1962, Hon. Jenefer Mills, *yr d* of 5th Baron Hillingdon, MC, TD; one *s* two *d. Educ:* Elstree Sch.; Harrow Sch.; Merton Coll., Oxford (MA Classics and Law). 51st (Highland) Div., RA, 1942–45. Called to the Bar, Middle Temple, 1947; Bencher 1972. Member (C): Westminster City Council, 1961–65; Ashford BC, 1991–95. Chm., E Ashford Rural Trust, 1988–91. *Publications:* Hatred, Ridicule or Contempt, 1953 (paperback edns 1955 and 1964). *Address:* The Hall, West Brabourne,   Ashford,   Kent   TN25   5LZ.
                                    Died 11 Jan. 2010.

DEAN, Katharine Mary Hope, (Mrs Robert Dean); *see* Mortimer, K. M. H.

DEANE, Prof. (Samuel) Basil; Professor of Music, University of Birmingham, 1987–92, then Emeritus; *b* 27 May 1928; *s* of Rev. Canon Richard A. Deane and Lorna Deane; *m* 1955, Norma Greig (*d* 1991); two *s. Educ:* Armagh Royal School; The Queen's Univ., Belfast (BA, BMus); PhD Glasgow. FRNCM 1978. Lecturer in Music, Glasgow Univ., 1953–59; Senior Lectr, Melbourne Univ., 1959–65; Lectr, Nottingham Univ., 1966–68; Prof., Sheffield Univ., 1968–74; Prof., Manchester Univ., 1975–80; Music Dir, Arts Council, 1980–83; Dir, Hongkong Acad. for Performing Arts, 1983–87. Member of Arts Council, 1977–79 (Chairman, Music Advisory Panel, 1977–79); Chairman of Music Board, Council for Nat. Academic Awards, 1978–80. *Publications:* Albert Roussel, 1962; Cherubini, 1965; Hoddinott, 1979; contribs to periodicals. *Address:* 21 Lough Shore Road, Portaferry, Co. Down, N Ireland BT22 1PD.   *Died 23 Sept. 2006.*

DEARING, Baron *cr* 1998 (Life Peer), of Kingston upon Hull in the co. of the East Riding of Yorkshire; **Ronald Ernest Dearing,** Kt 1984; CB 1979; *b* 27 July 1930; *s* of late E. H. A. Dearing and of M. T. Dearing (*née* Hoyle), *m* 1954, Margaret Patricia Riley; two *d. Educ:* Doncaster Grammar Sch.; Hull Univ. (BScEcon); London Business Sch. (Sloan Fellow). Min. of Labour and Nat. Service, 1946–49; Min. of Power, 1949–62; HM Treasury, 1962–64; Min. of Power, Min. of Technology, DTI, 1965–72; Regional Dir, N Region, DTI, 1972–74, and Under-Sec., DTI later Dept of Industry, 1972–76; Dep. Sec. on nationalised industry matters, Dept of Industry, 1976–80; Dep. Chm., 1980–81, Chm., 1981–87, Post Office Corp.; Chairman: Co. Durham Develt Co., 1987–90; Northern Develt Co., 1990–94; Camelot Gp, 1993–95. Director (non-executive): Whitbread Co. plc, 1987–90; Prudential plc, 1987–91; IMI plc, 1988–95; British Coal, 1988–91; Erisson Ltd, 1988–93; English Estates, 1988–90; SDX Business Systems, 1996–99. Chairman: NICG, 1983–84; Accounting Standards Review Cttee, CCAB, 1987–88; Financial Reporting Council, 1990–93. Mem. Council, Industrial Soc., 1985–99. CCMI (CBIM 1981; Mem. Council, 1985–88; Vice-Chm., 1986; Gold Medal, 1994). Chairman: CNAA, 1987–88; PCFC, 1988–93; UFC, 1991–93; HEFCE, 1992–93; SCAA, 1993–96; Nat. Cttee of Inquiry into Higher Educn, 1996–97; Cttee of Inquiry into Church Schs, 2000–01; Report on Languages in Schs, 2007. McKechnie Lectr, Liverpool Univ., 1995. Mem. Governing Council, London Business Sch., 1985–89, Fellow, 1988; Member: Council, Durham Univ., 1988–91; Governing Body, Univ. of Melbourne, 1997–2000; Chm., London Educn Business Partnership, 1989–92; Chm. Trustees, Higher Educn Policy Inst., 2002–04. Pres., Council of Church Colls Assoc., 2000–03. Chm., Northern Sinfonia Appeals Cttee, 1993–94. Pres., Inst. of Direct Mkting, 1994–97. Chancellor, Nottingham Univ., 1993–2001. Patron: Sascha Lasserson Meml Trust, 1995; Music in Allendale, 1995; Univ. for Industry, 2000– (Chm., 1999–2000); Guildford Community Family Trust, 2001–; Trident Trust, 2005–. Trustee, TRAC, 1995–97. Freeman, City of London, 1982. Hon. FREng (Hon. FEng 1992); Hon. FTCL 1993; Hon. Fellow, Inst. of Educn, 1995. Hon. Fellow, Sunderland Poly., 1991. Hon. DSc Hull, 1986; Hon. DTech: CNAA, 1991; Staffordshire, 1995; Hon. DCL: Durham, 1992; Northumbria, 1993; Hon. LLD Nottingham, 1993; Dr *hc* Humberside, 1993; DUniv Open, 1995; Hon. DLitt: Brighton, 1998; Exeter, 1998; Melbourne, 2000; Gloucestershire, 2002. *Recreations:* car boot sales, DIY, gardening. *Address:* House of Lords, SW1A 2PW.   *Died 19 Feb. 2009.*

DEARNALEY, Dr Geoffrey, FRS 1993; President, Cambritec Consulting, since 1999; Vice-President, Materials and Structures Division, Southwest Research Institute, 1994–99; *b* 22 June 1930; *s* of Eric and Dora Dearnaley; *m* 1957, Jean Rosalind Beer; two *s. Educ:* Univ. of Cambridge (MA 1955; PhD 1956). Research Fellow, Pembroke Coll., Cambridge, 1955–58; joined AERE, Harwell, Nuclear Physics Division, 1958: Individual Merit Promotion, 1975; Chief Scientist, Surface Technologies, 1991–93; joined Southwest Res. Inst., Texas, 1993, Inst. Scientist, 1993–94. Vis. Prof. in Physics, Sussex Univ., 1972–. *Publications:* Semiconductor Counters for Nuclear Radiations, 1963; Ion Implantation, 1973; numerous articles on interaction of energetic ion beams with materials. *Recreations:* travel, walking, the life and work of William Blake. *Died 5 May 2009.*

DeBAKEY, Dr Michael Ellis, MD, MS; Chancellor, Baylor College of Medicine, 1979–96, then Emeritus (Director, DeBakey Heart Center, since 1985; Distinguished Service Professor, since 1968, and Olga Keith Wiess Professor of Surgery, since 1981, Michael E. DeBakey Department of Surgery; Professor and Chairman, Department of Surgery, 1948–93, President, 1969–79, Chief Executive Officer, and Vice-President for Medical Affairs, 1968–69); Surgeon-in-Chief, Ben Taub General Hospital, Houston, Texas, 1963–93; Senior Attending Surgeon, Methodist Hospital, Houston; Director, National Heart and Blood Vessel Research and Demonstration Center, 1976–84; President, DeBakey Medical Foundation, since 1961; Consultant in Surgery to various Hospitals etc., in Texas, and to Walter Reed Army Hospital, Washington, DC; *b* 7 Sept. 1908; *s* of Shaker Morris and Raheeja Zorba DeBakey; *m* 1st, 1936, Diana Cooper (*d* 1972); two *s* (and two *s* decd); 2nd, 1975, Katrin Fehlhaber; one *d*. *Educ:* Tulane Univ., New Orleans, La, USA (BS 1930; MD 1932; MS 1935; Hon LLD 1965; Alumni Assoc. Distinguished Alumnus of Year, 1974; Sesquicentennial Medal for Most Distinguished Alumni, 1997; Lifetime Achievement of Outstanding Alumnus award, 2000). Residency in New Orleans, Strasbourg, and Heidelberg, 1933–36; Instructor, Dept of Surgery, Tulane Univ., 1937–40; Asst Prof. of Surgery, 1940–46; Associate Prof. of Surgery, 1946–48. Colonel Army of US (Reserve). In Office of Surgeon-General, 1942–46, latterly Director Surgical Consultant Div. (US Army Legion of Merit, 1945). Chairman, President's Commission on Heart Disease, Cancer and Stroke, 1964 (Report to the President published in 2 vols, 1964, 1965); US Chm., Task Force for Mechanical Circulatory Assistance, Jt US-USSR Cttee, 1974; Dir, Cardiovascular Res. and Trng Center, Methodist Hosp. (Houston), 1964–75; Adv. Council, Nat. Heart, Lung, Blood Inst., 1982–86; Mem., VTEL Med. Adv. Panel, 1996; served on governmental and university cttees, etc., concerned with public health, research and medical education; Mem., Bd of Dirs, Albert and Mary Lasker Foundn, 2005. Member, Advisory Editorial Boards, including: Ann. Surg., 1970–; Coeur, 1969–; Biomaterials, Med. Devices & Artificial Organs (formerly Biomedical Materials and Artificial Organs), 1971–; Founding Editor, Jl of Vascular Surgery, 1984–88. Member and Hon. Member of medical societies, including: Inst. of Medicine, Nat. Acad. of Sciences; American Assoc. for Thoracic Surgery (Pres. 1959); International Cardiovascular Society (Pres. 1957–59); BMA (Hon. Foreign Corresp. Member 1966); Royal Society Med., London; Acad. of Medical Sciences, USSR; US-China Physicians Friendship Assoc., 1974; Assoc. Internat. Vasc. Surgeons (Pres., 1983, 1990); Southern Surgical Assoc. (Pres., 1990); Assoc. Française de Chirurgie, 1991; Acad. of Athens, 1992; Royal Coll. of Physicians and Surgeons of USA (Hon. Dist. Fellow, 1992); Amer. Inst. Med. and Biol Engrg (Founding Fellow, 1993); Soc. for Biomaterials (Fellow, Biomaterials Sci. and Engrg, 1994). Received numerous awards from American and foreign medical institutions, and over 50 honorary doctorates; Hektoen Gold Medal, Amer. Med. Assoc., 1954, 1970; Albert Lasker Award for Clin. Res., 1963; Presidential Medal of Freedom with Distinction, 1969; Meritorious Civilian Service Medal, Sec. of Defense, 1970; USSR Acad. of Science 50th Anniversary Jubilee Medal, 1973; Nat. Medal of Science, 1987; Markowitz Award, Acad. of Surgical Res., 1988; Special Recognition Award, Assoc. of Amer. Med. Colls., 1988; Crile Award, Internat. Platform Assoc., 1988; Thomas Alva Edison Foundn Award, 1988; Scripps Clinic and Res. Foundn Inaugural Award, 1989; Centennial Award, 1980, and first Michael DeBakey Medal, 1989, ASME; Jacobs Award, Amer. Task Force for Lebanon, 1991; Gibbon Award, Amer. Soc. for Extracorporeal Tech., 1993; Maxwell Finland Award, Nat. Foundn for Infectious Diseases, 1992; Ellis Island Medal of Honor,

1993; Lifetime Achievement Award, Amer. Heart Assoc., Texas Chapter, 1994; Boris Petrovsky Internat. Surgeons Award and first Gold Medal, Russian Mil. Med. Acad., 1997; Global Peace and Tolerance Lifetime Achievement Award, Children Uniting Nations, 1999; Jonathan Rhoads Medal, Amer. Philosophical Soc., 2000; Bicentennial Living Legend Award, Liby of Congress, 2000; NASA Invention of the Year Award, 2001; Methodist DeBakey Heart Center, 2001; Mendel Medal Award, Villanova Univ., 2001; Lindbergh-Carrel Prize, 2002; Foundn for Biomed. Res. Michael E. DeBakey Journalism Award, 2002; Golden Hippocrates Internat. Prize for Excellency in Medicine, 2003; Olaf Acrel Medallion, Swedish Surgical Soc., 2003; Lomonosov Gold Medal, Russian Acad. of Scis, 2004; US House of Reps Cert. of Congressional Recognition, 2004; David E. Rogers Award, Assoc. of Amer. Med. Colls and Robert Wood Johnson Foundn, 2004; Outstanding Surgical Patient Safety Award, Amer. Coll. of Scis, 2005; Torch of Hope Award, Cancer League of Houston, 2005; Lifetime Achievement Award, New Cardiovascular Horizons, 2006; Physician of the Century Award, Nat. Amer. Lebanese Med. Assoc., 2006; Michael E. DeBakey Life Science Award, BioHouston, 2006. Merit Order of the Republic, 1st class (Egypt), 1980; The Independence of Jordan Medal, 1st class, 1980; Commander Cross of Merit, Sovereign Order of the Knights of the Hospital of St John (Denmark), 1980; Commander's Cross, Order of Merit (Germany), 1992; Order of Independence 1st cl. medal (UAE), 1992; Nat. Order of Vasco Nuñez de Balboa (Panama), 1995. *Publications:* The Blood Bank and the Technique and Therapeutics of Transfusions, 1942; (jtly) Battle Casualties, 1952; (jtly) Cold Injury, Ground Type, 1958; (jtly) Buerger's Disease: a follow-up study of World War II army cases, 1963; (jtly) A Surgeon's Visit to China, 1974; (jtly) The Living Heart, 1977; (jtly) The Living Heart Diet, 1984; (jtly) The Living Heart Brand Name Shopper's Guide, 1992; (jtly) The Living Heart Guide to Eating Out, 1993; (jtly) The New Living Heart Diet, 1996; (jtly) The New Living Heart, 1997; contributions to standard textbooks of medicine and surgery, and many symposia; Editor, Year Book of General Surgery, etc; over 1,600 articles in medical journals. *Recreations:* literature, music, gardening. *Address:* Baylor College of Medicine, One Baylor Plaza, Houston, TX 77030, USA. *T:* (713) 7903185. *Clubs:* Cosmos, The Jonathan (Reagan Dist. American Award, 2006), University, Federal City (Washington); River Oaks Country, Criterion, Doctor's, Heritage, Houston, Petroleum, Plaza, University, University Faculty, Warwick (Houston, Texas). *Died 11 July 2008.*

DEEDES, Baron *cr* 1986 (Life Peer), of Aldington in the County of Kent; **William Francis Deedes,** KBE 1999; MC 1944; PC 1962; DL; Editor, The Daily Telegraph, 1974–86; *b* 1 June 1913; *s* of (Herbert) William Deedes; *m* 1942, Evelyn Hilary Branfoot (*d* 2004); one *s* three *d* (and one *s* decd). *Educ:* Harrow. Journalist with Morning Post, 1931–37; war correspondent on Abyssinia, 1935. Served war of 1939–45, Queen's Westminsters (12 KRRC). MP (C) Ashford Div. of Kent, 1950–Sept. 1974; Parliamentary Sec., Ministry of Housing and Local Government, Oct. 1954–Dec. 1955; Parliamentary Under-Sec., Home Dept., 1955–57; Minister without Portfolio, 1962–64. DL, Kent, 1962. Hon. DCL Kent, 1988. *Publications:* Dear Bill: W. F. Deedes Reports (autobiog.), 1997; At War with Waugh: the real story of 'Scoop', 2003; Brief Lives, 2004; Words and Deedes: selected journalism 1931–2006, 2006. *Address:* New Hayters, Aldington, Kent TN25 7DT. *T:* (01233) 720269. *Club:* Carlton. *Died 17 Aug. 2007.*

DEER, Prof. William Alexander, MSc Manchester, PhD Cantab; FRS 1962; FGS; Emeritus Professor of Mineralogy and Petrology, Cambridge University; Master of Trinity Hall, Cambridge, 1966–75 (Hon. Fellow, 1978); *b* 26 Oct. 1910; *s* of William Deer; *m* 1939, Margaret Marjorie (*d* 1971), *d* of William Kidd; two *s* one *d*; *m* 1973, Rita Tagg. *Educ:* Manchester Central High Sch.; Manchester Univ.; St John's Coll., Cambridge.

Graduate Research Scholar, 1932, Beyer Fellow, 1933, Manchester Univ.; Strathcona Studentship, St John's Coll., Cambridge, 1934; Petrologist on British East Greenland Expedition, 1935–36; 1851 Exhibition Senior Studentship, 1938; Fellow, St John's Coll., Cambridge, 1939; served War of 1939–45, RE, 1940–45. Murchison Fund Geological Soc. of London, 1945 (Murchison Medal, 1974); Junior Bursar, St John's Coll., 1946; Leader NE Baffin Land Expedition, 1948; Bruce Medal, Royal Society of Edinburgh, 1948; Tutor, St John's Coll., 1949; Prof. of Geology, Manchester Univ., 1950–61; Fellow of St John's Coll., Cambridge, 1961–66, Hon. Fellow, 1969; Prof. of Mineralogy and Petrology, 1961–78, Vice-Chancellor, 1971–73, Cambridge Univ. Percival Lecturer, Univ. of Manchester, 1953; Joint Leader East Greenland Geological Expedition, 1953; Leader British East Greenland Expedition, 1966. Trustee, British Museum (Natural History), 1967–75. President: Mineralogical Soc., 1967–70; Geological Soc., 1970–72; Member: NERC, 1968–71; Marshall Aid Commemoration Commn, 1973–79. Hon. DSc Aberdeen, 1983. Publications: (jtly) Rock-forming Minerals, 5 vols, 1962–63, 2nd edn 1978– (vol. IIA 1978, vol. IA 1982, vol. IB 1986, vol. IIB 1997, Introduction 1992); Introduction to Rock-forming Minerals, 1966, 2nd edn 1992; papers in Petrology and Mineralogy. Address: 12 Barrington House, Southacre Drive, Cambridge CB2 2TY. Died 8 Feb. 2009.

DE FREYNE, 7th Baron cr 1851; Feudal Baron of Coolavin; **Francis Arthur John French;** Knight of Malta; b 3 Sept. 1927; s of 6th Baron and Victoria (d 1974), d of Sir J. Arnott, 2nd Bt; S father 1935; m 1st, 1954, Shirley Ann Pobjoy (marr. diss. 1978); two s one d; 2nd, 1978, Sheelin Deirdre, widow of William Walker Stevenson and y d of late Lt-Col H. K. O'Kelly, DSO. Educ: Ladycross, Glenstal. Heir: s Hon. Fulke Charles Arthur John French [b 21 April 1957; m 1986, Julia Mary, o d of Dr James H. Wellard; two s]. Address: The Old School, Sutton Courtenay, Oxon OX14 4AW. Died 24 Nov. 2009.

de GENNES, Prof. Pierre-Gilles, PhD; Professor of Condensed Matter Physics, Collège de France, 1971–2004; b 24 Oct. 1932; s of Robert de Gennes and Yvonne de Gennes (née Morin-Pons). Educ: Ecole Normale Supérieure, Paris. Prof., Univ. Orsay, 1961–71; Dir, Ecole de Physique et Chimie, Paris, 1976–2002. Foreign Mem., Royal Soc., 1984. Nobel Prize in Physics, 1991. Publications: Superconductivity of Metals and Alloys, 1966; The Physics of Liquid Crystals, 1974; Scaling Concepts in Polymer Physics, 1979; Les objets fragiles, 1994; Gouttes, Bulles, Perles et Ondes, 2002. Recreation: sketching. Address: Biophysique Institut Curie, 11 rue P. Curie, Paris 75005, France. T: 142346797. Died 18 May 2007.

de GREY, Flavia, (Lady de Grey), (Flavia Irwin), RA 1996; RWEA; painter; b 15 Dec. 1916; d of Clinton and Everilda Irwin; m 1942, Sir Roger de Grey, KCVO, PPRA (d 1995); two s one d. Educ: Hawnes Sch., Ampthill; Chelsea Sch. of Art. Teacher, 1960–97: Bexley Girls' Sch.; Sheppey Comprehensive Sch.; Medway Coll. of Art; City and Guilds of London Art Sch. (Head of Decorative Arts). Exhibitions include: London Gp, 1938; Andsell Gall. (solo); Shad Thames, 1994; Curwen and Phoenix Galls, 1996; Friends' Room, RA (solo), 2001. Pictures in various public and private collections, incl. Carlisle City Art Gall. and Walker Art Gall. Recreations: swimming, walking. Address: Camer Street, Meopham, Kent DA13 0XR. Died 1 Aug. 2009.

DEHQANI-TAFTI, Rt Rev. Hassan Barnaba; Hon. Assistant Bishop of Winchester, 1990–2006 (Assistant Bishop, 1982–90); b 14 May 1920; s of Muhammad Dehqani-Tafti and Sakineh; m 1952, Margaret Isabel Thompson; three d (one s decd). Educ: Stuart Memorial Coll., Isfahan; Iran; Tehran Univ.; Ridley Hall, Cambridge. Iran Imperial Army, 1943–45; layman in Diocese of Iran, 1945–47; theological coll., 1947–49; Deacon, Isfahan, 1949; Priest, Shiraz, 1950; Pastor: St

Luke's Church, Isfahan, 1950–60; St Paul's Church, Tehran, 1960–61; Bishop in Iran, 1961–90, Vicar-Gen., 1990–91; Pres.-Bishop, Episcopal Church in Jerusalem and Middle East, 1976–86; Episcopal Canon, St George's Cathedral, Jerusalem, 1976–90; Commissary to Bishop in Iran, 1991–2000. Hon. DD Virginia Theol Seminary, USA, 1981. Publications: many books in Persian; in English: Design of my World, 1959; The Hard Awakening, 1981; Christ and Christianity in Persian Poetry, 1986; The Unfolding Design of My World: a pilgrim in exile, 2000; Norman Sharp's Persian Designs, 2001. Recreations: Persian poetry, painting in water colours, walking. Died 29 April 2008.

DELACOURT-SMITH OF ALTERYN, Baroness cr 1974 (Life Peer), of Alteryn, Gwent; **Margaret Rosalind Delacourt-Smith;** b 5 April 1916; d of Frederick James Hando and Alice Hando (née Stanton); m 1st, 1939, Charles George Percy Smith (subsequently Baron Delacourt-Smith (Life Peer), PC) (d 1972); one s two d; 2nd, 1978, Professor Charles Blackton (d 2007). Educ: Newport High School for Girls; St Anne's College, Oxford (MA). Died 8 June 2010.

DELAFONS, John, CB 1982; Visiting Professor, Department of Land Management and Development, University of Reading, 1993–2001; b 14 Sept. 1930; m 1957, Sheila Egerton; four d. Educ: Ardingly; St Peter's College, Oxford (1st cl. Hons English). Asst Principal, Min. of Housing and Local Govt, 1953; Harkness Fellowship, Harvard, 1959–60; Principal, 1959–66; Principal Private Sec. to Minister, 1965–66; Department of the Environment: Assistant Sec., 1966–72; Under Sec., 1972–77; Under Sec., Cabinet Office, 1977–79; Dep. Sec., DoE, 1979–90, retd. Leverhulme and Nuffield Fellowship, 1989–90; Res. Associate, Inst. of Urban and Regl Develt, Univ. of California, 1990, Associate, Dept of Land Economy, Univ. of Cambridge, 1990–93. Chm., 1981–83, Vice Pres., 1985–92, RIPA; Mem. Council, 1992–95, 1997–99, Vice-Pres., 2000–, TCPA. Publications: Land-Use Controls in the United States, 1962, revd edn 1969; Development Impact Fees, 1990; Aesthetic Control, 1991; Politics and Preservation, 1997. Recreations: woodturning, travel. Address: 34 Castlebar Road, W5 2DD. Died 10 June 2007.

DELL, Ven. Robert Sydney; Archdeacon of Derby, 1973–92, then Archdeacon Emeritus; Canon Residentiary of Derby Cathedral, 1981–92, then Canon Emeritus; b 20 May 1922; s of Sydney Edward Dell and Lilian Constance Palmer; m 1953, Doreen Molly Layton; one s one d. Educ: Harrow County Sch.; Emmanuel Coll., Cambridge (MA); Ridley Hall. Curate of: Islington, 1948; Holy Trinity, Cambridge, 1950; Asst Chaplain, Wrekin Coll., 1953; Vicar of Mildenhall, Suffolk, 1955; Vice-Principal of Ridley Hall, Cambridge, 1957; Vicar of Chesterton, Cambridge, 1966 (Dir, Cambridge Samaritans, 1966–69). Mem., Archbishops' Commn on Intercommunion, 1965–67; Proctor in Convocation and Mem. Gen. Synod of C of E, 1970–85. Vis. Fellow, St George's House, Windsor Castle, 1981. Hon. Fellow, Univ. of Derby, 1994. Publications: Atlas of Christian History, 1960; Honest Thinker—John Rawlinson 1884–1960: theologian, bishop, ecumenist, 1998; contributor to: Charles Simeon, 1759–1836: essays written in commemoration of his bi-centenary, 1959; Jl of Ecclesiastical History. Recreations: reading, writing poetry, travelling. Address: Pinehurst Lodge, 35 Grange Road, Cambridge CB3 9AU. T: (01223) 365466. Died 19 Jan. 2008.

DEMPSTER, Nigel Richard Patton; Editorial Executive, Mail Newspapers Plc (formerly Associated Newspapers), 1973–2003; Editor: Mail Diary, 1973–2003; Mail on Sunday Diary, 1986–2003; b 1 Nov. 1941; s of Eric R. P. Dempster and Angela Grace Dempster (née Stephens); m 1st, 1971, Emma de Bendern (marr. diss. 1974), d of Count John de Bendern and late Lady Patricia Douglas, d of 11th Marquess of Queensberry; 2nd, 1977, Lady Camilla Godolphin Osborne (marr. diss. 2004), o c of 11th Duke of Leeds and late Audrey (who *m* 1955, Sir David Lawrence, 3rd Bt); one *d*. *Educ*: Sherborne. Broker, Lloyd's of London, 1958–59; Stock Exchange, 1959–60; PR account exec., Earl of Kimberley Associates, 1960–63; journalist, Daily Express, 1963–71; columnist, Daily Mail, 1971–2004. London correspondent, Status magazine, USA, 1965–66; contributor to Queen magazine, 1966–70; columnist ('Grovel'), Private Eye magazine, 1969–85. Broadcaster with ABC (USA) and CBC (Canada), 1976–, and with TV-am, 1983–92; resident panellist, Headliners, Thames TV, 1987–89. FGS. *Publications*: HRH The Princess Margaret—A Life Unfulfilled (biog.), 1981; Heiress: the story of Christina Onassis, 1989; Nigel Dempster's Address Book, 1990; (with Peter Evans) Behind Palace Doors, 1993; Dempster's People, 1998. *Recreations*: photography, squash, running marathons, bicycling. *Clubs*: Royal Automobile; Chappaquiddick Beach (Mass, USA). *Died 12 July 2007.*

DENISON, John Law, CBE 1960 (MBE (mil.) 1945); FRCM; Hon. RAM; Hon. GSM; Director, South Bank Concert Halls (formerly General Manager, Royal Festival Hall), 1965–76; Chairman, Arts Educational Schools, 1977–91; *b* 21 Jan. 1911; *s* of late Rev. H. B. W. and Alice Dorothy Denison; *m* 1st, 1936, Annie Claudia Russell Brown, comedienne as Anna Russell (marr. diss. 1946; she *d* 2006); 2nd, 1947, Evelyn Mary Donald (*née* Moir) (*d* 1958), *d* of John and Mary Scott Moir, Edinburgh; one *d*; 3rd, 1960, Audrey Grace Burnaby (*née* Bowles) (*d* 1970); 4th, 1972, Françoise Charlotte Henriette Mitchell (*née* Garrigues) (*d* 1985). *Educ*: St George's Sch., Windsor; Brighton Coll.; Royal Coll. of Music. Played horn in BBC Symphony, London Philharmonic, City of Birmingham, and other orchestras, 1934–39. Served War of 1939–45; gazetted Somerset Light Inf., 1940; DAA and QMG 214 Inf. Bde and various staff appts, 1941–45 (despatches). Asst Dir, Music Dept, British Council, 1946–48; Music Dir, Arts Council of Great Britain, 1948–65. Chairman: Cultural Programme, London Celebrations Cttee, Queen's Silver Jubilee, 1976–78; Royal Concert Cttee, St Cecilia Fest., 1976–88; Hon. Treasurer, Royal Philharmonic Soc., 1977–89 (Hon. Mem., 1989); Member: Council, RCM, 1975–90; Council, Musicians Benevolent Fund, 1992– (Exec. Cttee, 1984–92); Trustee, Prince Consort Foundn, 1990–96. FRSA. Comdr, Order of Lion (Finland), 1976; Chevalier de l'Ordre des Arts et des Lettres (France), 1988. *Publications*: articles for various musical publications. *Address*: 9 Hays Park, near Shaftesbury, Dorset SP7 9JR. *Clubs*: Garrick, Army and Navy. *Died 31 Dec. 2006.*

DENMAN, Sir (George) Roy, KCB 1977 (CB 1972); CMG 1968; Ambassador and Head of European Communities Delegation in Washington, 1982–89; *b* 13 June 1924; *s* of Albert Edward and Gertrude Ann Denman; *m* 1966, Moya Lade; one *s* one *d*. *Educ*: Harrow Grammar Sch.; St John's Coll., Cambridge. War Service 1943–46; Major, Royal Signals. Joined BoT, 1948; Asst Private Sec. to successive Presidents, 1950–52; 1st Sec., British Embassy, Bonn, 1957–60; UK Delegn, Geneva, 1960–61; Counsellor, Geneva, 1965–67; Under-Sec., 1967–70, BoT; Deputy Secretary: DTI, 1970–74; Dept of Trade, 1974–75; Second Permanent Sec., Cabinet Office, 1975–77; Dir-Gen. for External Affairs, EEC Commn, 1977–82. Business Fellow, John F. Kennedy Sch. of Govt, Harvard, 1989–90. Mem. negotiating delegn with European Communities, 1970–72. Mem., British Overseas Trade Bd, 1972–75. *Publications*: Missed Chances: Britain and Europe in the twentieth century, 1996; The Mandarin's Tale (autobiog.), 2002; Britannia and the Hun, 2005. *Address*: c/o Coutts & Co., 2 Lower Sloane Street, SW1W 8BJ. *Club*: Oxford and Cambridge. *Died 4 April 2006.*

DENNY, Rev. Norwyn Ephraim; Methodist minister; President of the Methodist Conference, 1982–83; *b* 23 Oct. 1924; *s* of Percy Edward James Denny and Dorothy Ann Denny (*née* Stringer); *m* 1950, Ellen Amelia Shaw; three *d*. *Educ*: City of Norwich School; Wesley College,

Bristol. BD (Hons), London Univ. Ordained Methodist Minister, 1951; Methodist Minister in Jamaica, 1950–54; Minister in Peterborough, 1955–61; Member of Notting Hill Group (Ecumenical) Ministry, 1961–75; Chm., Liverpool Dist Methodist Church, 1975–86; Supt, Lowestoft and E Suffolk Methodist Circuit, 1986–91. Mem., Fellowship of Reconciliation. *Publications*: (with D. Mason and G. Ainger) News from Notting Hill, 1967; Caring, 1976; Worship, 1995; Words on the Way, 2005. *Recreations*: gardening, astronomy, association football, World Development movement. *Address*: 5 Red Hill, Lodge Park, Redditch, Worcs B98 7JE. *T*: (01527) 522426. *Died 9 Sept. 2010.*

DENT, Maj.-Gen. Jonathan Hugh Baillie, CB 1984; OBE 1974; Director General, Fighting Vehicles and Engineer Equipment, Ministry of Defence, 1981–85; *b* 19 July 1930; *s* of Joseph Alan Guthrie Dent and Hilda Ina Dent; *m* 1957, Anne Veronica Inglis; one *s* three *d*. *Educ*: Winchester College. Commissioned, Queen's Bays, 1949; regtl and instructional employment in BAOR, UK, Jordan, Libya, 1949–61; Adjt 1958; Adjt Shropshire Yeomanry, 1959–60; Staff trng, RMCS, 1962–63; Staff Coll. Camberley, 1964; Sqdn Comd, Queen's Dragoon Guards, N Ireland and Borneo, 1965–66; MoD (Operational Requirements), 1967–69; Second in Comd, Queen's Dragoon Guards, 1970; Ministry of Defence: MGO Secretariat, 1971–74; Project Manager Chieftain, 1974–76; RCDS 1977; Defence R&D Attaché, British Embassy, Washington, 1978–80. *Recreations*: fishing, bird watching, walking, shooting, classical music. *Died 23 Feb. 2007.*

DENTON, Sir Eric (James), Kt 1987; CBE 1974; FRS 1964; ScD; Director, Laboratory of Marine Biological Association, Plymouth, 1974–87; Member, Royal Commission on Environmental Pollution, 1973–76; *b* 30 Sept. 1923; *s* of George Denton and Mary Anne (*née* Ogden); *m* 1946, Nancy Emily, *d* of Charles and Emily Jane Wright; two *s* one *d*. *Educ*: Doncaster Grammar Sch.; St John's Coll., Cambridge. Biophysics Research Unit, University Coll. London, 1946–48; Lectr in Physiology, Univ. of Aberdeen, 1948–56; Physiologist, Marine Biological Assoc. Lab., Plymouth, 1956–74; Royal Soc. Res. Professor, Univ. of Bristol, 1964–74, Hon. Professor, 1975. Fellow, University Coll. London, 1965. Hon. Sec., Physiological Soc., 1963–69. Hon. DSc: Exeter, 1976; Göteborg, 1978. Royal Medal, Royal Soc., 1987; Frink Medal, Zool Soc. of London, 1987; Internat. Prize for Biology, Japan Soc. for the Promotion of Science, 1989. *Publications*: scientific papers in Jl of Marine Biological Assoc., etc. *Recreation*: gardening. *Address*: Fairfield House, St Germans, Saltash, Cornwall PL12 5LS. *T*: (01503) 230204. *Died 2 Jan. 2007.*

de PALACIO del VALLE LERSUNDI, Loyola; a Vice President and Commissioner for Energy and Transport, European Commission, 1999–2004; *b* Madrid, 16 Sept. 1950; *d* of Luis de Palacio and Luisa del Valle-Lersundi. *Educ*: Univ. Complutense de Madrid (Law degree). First Pres., Nuevas Generaciones de Alianza Popular, 1977–78. Parliament of Spain: Member for Segovia and Dep. Pres., Popular Party, 1986–99; Minister for Agric., Fisheries and Food, 1996–99. Chm., Foreign Policy Council, Popular Party, 2005–. Chm., High Level Gp on Pan-Eur. Mediterranean Transport Network, Eur. Commn, 2004; Eur. Co-ordinator, Priority Transport Project, Lyon-Turin, 2005–. Guest Prof., European Univ. Inst., San Domenico di Fiesole, 2005–. Dr *hc* Maritime Economy and Transport, Genoa. *Address*: c/o Popular Party, Genova 13, 28004 Madrid, Spain. *T*: (91) 5577346. *Died 13 Dec. 2006.*

DERAMORE, 6th Baron *cr* 1885; **Richard Arthur de Yarburgh-Bateson;** Bt 1818; Chartered Architect, retired; *b* 9 April 1911; *s* of 4th Baron Deramore and of Muriel Katherine (*née* Duncombe); *S* brother, 1964; *m* 1948, Janet Mary, *d* of John Ware, BA Cantab, MD Edin., Askham-in-Furness, Lancs; one *d*. *Educ*: Harrow; St John's Coll., Cambridge (MA 1936). AA Diploma, 1935; ARIBA 1936. Associate, A. W. Kenyon, FRIBA,

1936–39. Served as Navigator, RAFVR, 1940–45: 14 Sqdn, RAF, 1942–44 and 1945. County Architect's Dept, Herts, 1949–52; in private practice, London, Buckinghamshire and Yorkshire, 1952–81. Member: Council, Queen Mary Sch., Duncombe Park, Helmsley, 1977–85; Management Cttee, Purey Cust Nursing Home, York, 1976–84; Governor: Heslington Sch., York, 1965–88; Tudor Hall Sch., Banbury, 1966–75. Fellow, Woodard Schs (Northern Div.) Ltd, 1978–84. *Publications:* (jtly) Winged Promises, 1996; freelance articles and short stories. *Recreation:* water-colour painting. *Heir:* none. *Address:* Heslington House, Aislaby, Pickering, North Yorks YO18 8PE. *Clubs:* Royal Air Force, Royal Automobile. *Died 20 Aug. 2006 (ext).*

DERHAM, Sir Peter (John), AC 2001; Kt 1980; FAIM; FPIA; FInstD; Chairman: Circadian Technologies Ltd (formerly Circadian Pharmaceuticals Ltd), 1984–2006; See Australia (formerly Partnership Australia Domestic Ltd), 1999–2005; Red Hill Wines plc, 2001–05; *b* 21 Aug. 1925; *s* of John and Mary Derham; *m* 1950, Averil C. Wigan; two *s* one *d*. *Educ:* Melbourne Church of England Grammar School; Univ. of Melbourne (BSc 1958); Harvard Univ. (Advanced Management Programme, 1965). Served RAAF and RAN, 1944–46. Joined Moulded Products (Australasia) Ltd (later Nylex Corp.), 1943; Dir, 1953–82, Sales Dir, 1960, Gen. Manager, 1967, Man. Dir, 1972–80. Chairman: Internat. Pacific Corp. Ltd, later Rothschild Australia Ltd, 1981–85; Australia New Zealand Foundn, 1978–83; Australian Canned Fruits Corp., 1981–89; Robert Bryce & Co. Ltd, 1982–91; Davy McKee Pacific Pty, 1984–90; Leasing Corp. Ltd, 1987–93; Multistack, 1993–99; Greenchip Develt Capital Ltd, 1993–99; Greenchip Investments Ltd, 1997–99; Vos Industries Ltd, 1997–2001; Bays and Peninsulas, 1999–2000; Deputy Chairman: Prime Computer of Australia Ltd, 1986–92; Australian Mutual Provident Society State Board of Advice, 1990–91 (Dir, Victoria Br. Bd, 1974–90); Director: Lucas Industries Aust., 1981–84; Station 3XY Pty, 1980–87; Radio 3XY Pty, 1980–87; Perpetual Trustees Victoria Ltd, 1992–93; Perpetual Trustees Australia Ltd, 1993–97; Advance Australia Foundn, 1983–96; Jt Chm., Advance Australia America Cup Challenge Ltd, 1981–83; Councillor Enterprise Australia, 1975–82 (Dep. Chm., 1975–78). Chairman: Nat. Training Council, 1971–80; Adv. Bd, CSIRO, 1981–86; Australian Tourist Commn, 1981–85; Member: Manufg Industries Adv. Council, 1971–74; Victorian Econ. Develt Corp., 1981–82. Federal Pres., Inst. of Directors in Australia, 1980–82 (Mem., 1975–89, Chm., 1975–82, Victorian Council; Life Mem., 1986); Councillor: Yooralla Soc. of Victoria, 1972–79 (Chm. Workshops Cttee, 1972–81); Aust. Industries Develt Assoc., 1975–80; State Councillor, Industrial Design Council, 1967–73, Federal Councillor, 1970–73; Mem. Council, Inst. of Public Affairs, 1971–; Life Mem., Plastics Inst. of Australia Inc. (Victorian Pres., 1964–66; Nat. Pres., 1971–72); Mem. Board of Advisors, Inst. of Cultural Affairs, 1971–81. Victorian State Treas., Liberal Party of Australia, 1981–83. Member: Rotary Club of Melbourne (Mem., Bd of Dirs, 1974–75, 1975–76); Victorian State Cttee, Child Accident Prevention Foundn of Australia; Appeal Cttee, Royal Victorian Eye and Ear Hosp.; Bd of Management, Alfred Hosp., 1980–93 (Pres., 1990–92), Amalgamated Alfred, Caulfield and Royal Southern Meml Hosp., 1987–93; Alfred Foundn Bd, 1993–; St John Ambulance, 1988– (Chm., State Council, 1991–96; Pres., Victoria, 1996–99); Chm., Caulfield Hosp. Cttee, 1984–87 (Dir, 1981–87; Vice Pres., 1989). President: Alcohol and Drug Foundn (formerly Victorian Foundn on Alcoholism and Drug Dependence), 1986–91 (Appeal Chm., 1981–86); Victorian Soc. for Prevention of Child Abuse and Neglect, 1987–96; Dep Chm., Australian Assoc. for Support of Educn, 1983–87; Mem., Melbourne C of E Grammar Sch. Council, 1974–75, 1977–80; Pres., Old Melburnians, 1974–75; Governor, Ian Clunies Ross Meml Foundn, 1981–99; Chairman: Trade & Industry Cttee, Victoria's 150th Anniv. Celebration; Police Toy Fund for Underprivileged

Children; Pres., Somers Area, Boy Scout Assoc. of Australia, 1985–90; Vict. Trustee, Australian Koala Foundn Inc., 1986–92; Trustee, H & L Hecht Trust, 1990–; Life Governor, Assoc. for the Blind. Rotary Paul Harris Fellowship, 1997. CStJ 1995. *Recreations:* golf, sailing, tennis, gardening, viticulture. *Address:* 2a Ashley Grove, Malvern, Vic 3144, Australia. *T:* (3) 98220770; *e-mail:* pjderham@bigpond.com. *Clubs:* Australian, Melbourne (Melbourne); Royal Melbourne Golf, Flinders Golf. *Died 24 Sept. 2008.*

de ROHAN, Maurice John, AO 2006; OBE 1992; Agent General for South Australia, since 1998; *b* 13 May 1936; *s* of late Louis Maurice Virgil de Rohan and Joann Stewart de Rohan (*née* Roger); *m* 1958, Margaret Jennifer Roads; one *s* one *d* (and one *d* decd). *Educ:* Univ. of Adelaide; South Australian Inst. of Technology (BTech Civil Engrg 1958). FIEAust 1971. Partner, Kinnaird Hill de Rohan & Young, 1959–73; Man. Dir, Kinhill Engrs Pty Ltd, Adelaide, 1973–76; Dep. Chm. and Man. Dir, Llewelyn-Davies International, London, 1976–78; Chairman: Tibbalds Monro Ltd, 1978–96; Transcon Ltd, 1979–94; Davis Brody & Associates, NY, 1988–95; Facilities Management Pty Ltd, 1988–95. Dir, Australian Business in Europe, London, 1976–2002 (Pres., 1982–83; Hon. Life Mem., 1983). Dir, Gracechurch Bellyard Ltd, 1997–2000. Mem. Council, 1996–, Chm., Exec. Cttee, 1998–2000, Maritime Trust, Chm., Cutty Sark Trust, 2000–; Pres., Regent's Canal Boatowners' Assoc., 1990–. Mem., Supervisory Bd, Menzies Centre for Australian Studies, 2002–. Freeman, City of London, 1998; Liveryman, Engineers' Co., 2000–. Founding Chm., Herald Families Assoc., 1987–97; Chairman: Herald Charitable Trust, 1990–; Founding Chairman: Disaster action, 1991–; Australia Day Foundn, UK, 2003–; Cook Soc., 2003 (Mem. Cttee, 1997–2000, 2002–04). Mem., S Australian Cricket Assoc. Hon. Dr SA, 2003. Centenary Medal, Australia, 2003. *Recreations:* narrow boating, following cricket, theatre. *Address:* 114 Clifton Hill, St John's Wood, NW8 0JS. *T:* (020) 7887 5124. *Clubs:* East India, MCC (Mem. Cttee, Exec. Bd, 2000–; Chm., Estates Cttee, 1999–), Middlesex CC; Adelaide (Adelaide). *Died 5 Oct. 2006.*

DERRICK, Patricia, (Mrs Donald Derrick); *see* Lamburn, P.

de TRAFFORD, Sir Dermot Humphrey, 6th Bt *cr* 1841; VRD 1963; Director, 1977–90, Chairman, 1982–90, Low & Bonar plc (Deputy Chairman, 1980–82); Chairman: GHP Group Ltd, 1965–77 (Managing Director, 1961); Calor Gas Holding, 1974–88; *b* 19 Jan. 1925; *s* of Sir Rudolph de Trafford, 5th Bt, OBE and June Lady Audley (*née* Chaplin), MBE (*d* 1977); *S* father, 1983; *m* 1st, 1946, Patricia Mary Beeley (marr. diss. 1973); three *s* five *d* (and one *d* decd); 2nd, 1973, Mrs Xandra Caradini Walter (*d* 2002). *Educ:* Harrow Sch.; Christ Church, Oxford (MA). Trained as Management Consultant, Orr & Boss and Partners Ltd, 1949–52; Director: Monks Investment Trust; Imperial Continental Gas Assoc., 1963–87 (Dep. Chm., 1972–87); Petrofina SA, 1971–87. Chm. Council, Inst. of Dirs, 1990–93. *Recreations:* theatre, travel. *Heir:* *s* John Humphrey de Trafford [*b* 12 Sept. 1950; *m* 1975, Anne, *d* of J. Faure de Pebeyre; one *s* one *d*]. *Address:* 1 Roper's Orchard, Danvers Street, SW3 5AX. *Clubs:* White's, Royal Ocean Racing; Island Sailing. *Died 22 Jan. 2010.*

de VERE, Anthony Charles Mayle, CMG 1986; HM Diplomatic Service, retired; Foreign and Commonwealth Office, 1986–93; *b* 23 Jan. 1930; *m* 1st, 1959, Geraldine Gertrude Bolton (*d* 1980); 2nd, 1986, Rosemary Edith Austin. *Educ:* St John's College, Cambridge. Served Army, Malaya, 1950–52; joined Colonial Service (later HMOCS), 1953, Provincial Admin, Tanganyika; Kibondo, 1953–56; in charge Kondoa-Irangi Develt Scheme, 1957–59; Res. Magistrate, Singida, 1959; Dist Comr, Tunduru, 1960–61, Kigoma, 1961–62; Head of local govt, Western Region, 1962–63, retired 1963; joined FO, later FCO, 1963; First Sec., Lusaka, 1967–70, NY, 1972–74; Counsellor, Washington, 1982–86.

Recreations: riding, most things rural, sculpture, music, books. *Address:* Haddiscoe Hall, Norfolk NR14 6PE.
Died 17 Sept. 2008.

de VIRION, Tadeusz, Cross of Valour, Cross of the Home Army, Warsaw Uprising Cross, 1944; practising lawyer in penal law; Polish Ambassador to the Court of St James's, 1990–93; *b* 28 March 1926; *s* of Jerzy de Virion (killed in Auschwitz, 1941); *m* 1985, Jayanti Kazra; two *d*. *Educ:* Univ. of Warsaw (LLM). Barrister, 1950–, specialising in criminal law; Judge of Tribunal of State, elected by Polish Parlt, 1989, 1990, 1993–. Cross of Knights of Malta, 1980; Golden Insignia of Barrister's Merit, 1988; Comdr's Cross, Order of Polonia Restituta; Grand Officier, Order of Pro Merito Melitensi. *Recreations:* Jayanti, books. *Address:* ul. Zakopiańska 17, 03 934 Warsaw, Poland. *T:* (2) 6178880. *Clubs:* Polish Hearth, Travellers, Special Forces; Polish Business Centre (Warsaw). *Died 25 Oct. 2010.*

DEVLIN, Rt Rev. Mgr Bernard Patrick, CMG 1996; Bishop of Gibraltar, (RC), 1985–98, then Emeritus; *b* Youghal, Co. Cork, 10 March 1921. *Educ:* Mount Melleray Cistercian Coll.; Holy Cross Seminary, Dublin; Nat. Univ. of Ireland (BA 1942); Pontifical Beda Coll. Ordained, 1945; Curate, Cathedral of St Mary the Crowned, Gibraltar, 1946–60; Parish Priest, St Theresa's Church, Gibraltar, 1961–85; Vicar General, 1976–85. Freeman, City of Gibraltar, 1999. *Recreations:* golf, painting. *Address:* c/o Cathedral of St Mary the Crowned, 215 Main Street, Gibraltar. *T:* 76688.
Died 15 Dec. 2010.

DEVONS, Prof. Samuel, FRS 1955; Professor of Physics, Columbia University, New York, 1960–85, then Emeritus, and Special Research Scientist (Chairman, Dept of Physics, 1963–67); Director, History of Physics Laboratory, Barnard College, Columbia University, 1970–85; *b* 30 Sept. 1914; *s* of Rev. David I. Devons and E. Edleston; *m* 1938, Celia Ruth Toubkin; four *d*. *Educ:* Trinity Coll., Cambridge (BA 1935; MA, PhD 1939). Exhibition of 1851 Senior Student, 1939. Scientific Officer, Senior Scientific Officer, Air Ministry, MAP, and Ministry of Supply, 1939–45. Lecturer in Physics, Cambridge Univ., Fellow and Dir of Studies, Trinity Coll., Cambridge, 1946–49; Prof. of Physics, Imperial Coll. of Science, London, 1950–55; Langworthy Prof. of Physics and Dir of Physical Laboratories, Univ. of Manchester, 1955–60. Royal Soc. Leverhulme Vis. Prof., Andhra Univ., India, 1967–68; Balfour Vis. Prof., History of Science, Weizmann Inst., Rehovot, Israel, 1973; Racah Vis. Prof. of Physics, Hebrew Univ., Jerusalem, 1973–74. Rutherford Meml Lectr, Royal Soc., Australia, 1989. Fellow, NY Acad. of Scis, 2001. Rutherford Medal and Prize, Inst. of Physics, 1970. *Publications:* Excited States of Nuclei, 1949; (ed) Biology and Physical Sciences, 1969; (ed) High Energy Physics and Nuclear Structure, 1970; contributions to Proc. Royal Society, Proc. Phys. Soc., etc. *Recreations:* plastic arts, survival. *Address:* Nevis Laboratory, Columbia University, PO Box 137, Irvington-on-Hudson, NY 10533, USA. *T:* (914) 5912860, *Fax:* (914) 5917080. *Died 6 Dec. 2006.*

de WAAL, Rt Rev. Hugo Ferdinand; an Hon. Assistant Bishop, diocese in Europe, since 2002; *b* 16 March 1935; *s* of Bernard Hendrik and Albertine Felice de Waal; *m* 1960, Brigit Elizabeth Townsend Massingberd-Mundy; one *s* three *d*. *Educ:* Tonbridge School; Pembroke Coll., Cambridge (MA); Münster Univ., Germany; Ridley Hall, Cambridge. Ordained deacon 1960, priest 1961; Curate, St Martin's-in-the Bull Ring, Birmingham, 1960–64; Chaplain, Pembroke Coll., Cambridge, 1964–68; Rector of Dry Drayton, Cambs, 1964–73, with Bar Hill Ecumenical Area, 1967–73; Vicar of St John's, Blackpool Parish Church, 1974–78; Principal, Ridley Hall Theol Coll., Cambridge, 1978–91; Bp Suffragan of Thetford, 1992–2000. Hon. Canon, Ely Cathedral, 1986–91. *Recreations:* music, fly-fishing. *Address:* Folly House, The Folly, Haughley, Stowmarket, Ipswich IP14 3NS. *T:* (01449) 774915. *Died 6 Jan. 2007.*

DEWAR, His Honour Thomas; a Circuit Judge (formerly Judge of the County Court), 1962–84; Joint President, Council of Circuit Judges, 1980 (Vice-President, 1979); *b* 5 Jan. 1909; *s* of James Stewart Dewar and Katherine Rose Dewar; *m* 1950, Katherine Muriel Johnson; one *s* decd. *Educ:* Penarth Intermediate School; Cardiff Technical Coll.; Sch. of Pharmacy, University of London; Birkbeck Coll., University of London. Pharmaceutical Chemist, 1931; BPharm 1931, PhD 1934, BSc (Botany, 1st cl. hons) 1936, London. Called to Bar, Middle Temple, 1939; Blackstone Pupillage Prize, 1939. Admin. staff of Pharmaceutical Soc., 1936–40; Sec., Middx Pharmaceutical Cttee, 1940–41; Asst Dir, Min. of Supply, 1943; Sec., Wellcome Foundation, 1943–45. Mem. of Western Circuit, 1945–62; Judge of the County Court (circuit 59, Cornwall and Plymouth), 1962–65, (circuit 38, Edmonton, etc), 1965–66 (circuit 41, Clerkenwell), 1966–71; Circuit Judge, SE circuit, 1972–84. Presided over inquiry into X-ray accident at Plymouth Hosp., 1962. Mem. Executive Council, Internat. Law Assoc., 1974–89. Governor, Birkbeck Coll., 1944–46 and 1971–82 (Fellow, 1981). *Publications:* Textbook of Forensic Pharmacy, 1946 and four subsequent editions; scientific papers in Quarterly Jl of Pharmacy and Pharmacology. *Recreations:* horticulture, travel. *Address:* 1 Garden Court, Temple, EC4Y 9BJ. *T:* (020) 7353 3326. *Club:* Royal Over-Seas League.
Died 31 Dec. 2007.

DEWHURST, Prof. Sir (Christopher) John, Kt 1977; FRCOG, FRCSE; Professor of Obstetrics and Gynaecology, University of London, at Queen Charlotte's Hospital for Women, 1967–85, then Professor Emeritus; *b* 2 July 1920; *s* of John and Agnes Dewhurst; *m* 1952, Hazel Mary Atkin; two *s* one *d*. *Educ:* St Joseph's Coll., Dumfries; Manchester Univ. (MB, ChB). Surg. Lieut, RNVR, 1943–46. Sen. Registrar, St Mary's Hosp., Manchester, 1948–51; Lectr, Sen. Lectr and Reader, Sheffield Univ., 1951–67. Pres., RCOG, 1975–78. Hon. FACOG 1976; Hon. FRCSI 1977; Hon. FCOG (SA) 1978; Hon. FRACOG 1985. Hon. DSc Sheffield, 1977; Hon. MD Uruguay, 1980. *Publications:* A Student's Guide to Obstetrics and Gynaecology, 1960, 2nd edn 1965; The Gynaecological Disorders of Infants and Children, 1963; (jtly) The Intersexual Disorders, 1969; (ed) Integrated Obstetrics and Gynaecology for Postgraduates, 1972, 3rd edn 1981; (jtly) A General Practice of Obstetrics and Gynaecology, 1977, 2nd edn 1984; Practical Paediatric and Adolescent Gynaecology, 1980; Royal Confinements, 1980; Female Puberty and its Abnormalities, 1984. *Recreations:* cricket, gardening, music. *Address:* 21 Jack's Lane, Harefield, Middlesex UB9 6HE. *T:* (01895) 825403. *Died 1 Dec. 2006.*

DEYERMOND, Prof. Alan David, DLitt; FSA; FBA 1988; Professor of Spanish, Queen Mary and Westfield College, London (formerly Westfield College), 1969–97, then Research Professor; *b* 24 Feb. 1932; *s* of late Henry Deyermond and Margaret Deyermond (*née* Lawson); *m* 1957, Ann Marie Bracken; one *d*. *Educ:* Quarry Bank High Sch., Liverpool; Victoria Coll., Jersey; Pembroke Coll., Oxford (MA; BLitt 1957; DLitt 1985). FSA 1987. Westfield, subseq. Queen Mary and Westfield, College, London: Asst Lectr, 1955; Lectr, 1958; Reader, 1966; Senior Tutor, 1967–72; Dir, Medieval Hispanic Res. Seminar, 1967–97; Dean, Faculty of Arts, 1972–74, 1981–84; Head of Dept of Spanish, 1983–89; Vice-Principal, 1986–89; Dir of Grad. Studies, Sch. of Modern Langs, 1995–97; Hon. Fellow, 2000. Visiting Professor, Universities of: Wisconsin, 1972; California LA, 1977; Princeton, 1978–81; Victoria, 1983; N Arizona, 1986; Johns Hopkins, 1987; Nacional Autónoma de México, 1992; A Coruña, 1996; California Irvine, 1998–99; Consejo Superior de Investigaciones Científicas, Madrid, 2002–; Scholar in Residence, Indiana Univ., 1998. Lectures: Sir Henry Thomas, Univ. of Birmingham, 1985; Taylorian, Univ. of Oxford, 1999; Ramsden and Gybbon-Monypenny, Univ. of Manchester, 2003. Chm. Trustees, Kentish's Educnl Foundn, 1992–98. President: London Medieval Soc., 1970–74; Internat. Courtly

Literature Soc., 1977–83, Hon. Life Pres., 1983; Asociación Internacional de Hispanistas, 1992–95 (Vice-Pres., 1983–89; Hon. Life Pres., 1995). Corresponding Fellow: Medieval Acad. of America; Real Acad. de Buenas Letras de Barcelona; Mem., Hispanic Soc. of America; Hon. Fellow: Asociación Hispánica de Literatura Medieval, 1985; Sociedad de Estudios Medievales y Renacentistas, 2006. Hon. LHD Georgetown, 1995; Dr hc Valencia, 2005. Premio Internacional Elio Antonio de Nebrija, 1994. Gen. Ed., Papers of Medieval Hispanic Res. Seminar, 1995–. *Publications:* The Petrarchan Sources of La Celestina, 1961, 2nd edn 1975; Epic Poetry and the Clergy, 1969; A Literary History of Spain: The Middle Ages, 1971; Apollonius of Tyre, 1973; Lazarillo de Tormes: a critical guide, 1975; Historia y crítica de la literatura española: Edad Media, 1980, supplement, 1991; El Cantar de Mio Cid y la épica medieval española, 1987; Tradiciones y puntos de vista en la ficción sentimental, 1993; La literatura perdida de la Edad Media castellana: catálogo y estudio, vol. 1, 1995; Point of View in the Ballad, 1996; The Libro de Buen Amor in England, 2004; The Department of Hispanic Studies: a biographical dictionary, 2005; Poesía de cancionero del siglo xv, 2007; (ed) A Century of Medieval Studies, 2007; contribs to Hispanic Res. Jl etc. *Recreations:* psephology, vegetarian cookery. *Address:* 20 Lancaster Road, St Albans, Herts AL1 4ET. *T:* (01727) 855383; *e-mail:* alandeyermond@waitrose.com.   *Died 19 Sept. 2009.*

DHRANGADHARA, Maharaja Sriraj of Halvad-, His Highness Jhaladhip Maharana Sriraj Meghrajji III, KCIE 1947; 45th Ruler (dynastic salute of 13 guns) and Head of Jhalla-Makhvan Clan; *b* 3 March 1923; *s* of HH Ghanashyamsinhji Bava, GCIE, KCSI; *S* father 1942, assumed powers 1943 on termination of political minority; *m* 1943, Princess Brijrajkunvarba of Jodhpur; three *s. Educ:* Dhrangadhara Rajmahal Shala (Palace Sch.) which was moved to UK to become Millfield Sch., Som., 1935; Heath Mount Sch.; Haileybury Coll.; St Joseph's Acad., Dehra Dun; Sivaji Military Sch., Poona; later, Christ Church, Oxford, 1952–58 (Mem. High Table and Sen. Common Room); Philosophy course; Ruskin Sch. of Drawing; Associate Vice Pres., Amateur Fencing Assoc. of GB; Postgrad. Diploma in Social Anthropology (with distinction), 1955; research in Hindu sacraments, 1956–58; BLitt (Oxon). FRAS, FRAI; Associate, RHistS. As Darbar-in-Council proclaimed fundamental rights; estab. public adv. body; accepted attachment of Lakhtar, Sayla, Chuda and Muli States and the transfer of British suzerainty over them to the Dhrangadhara Darbar, 1943, and laws enacted: local self-govt, removal of untouchability, compulsory free primary educn, women's property rights, Hindu widows' remarriage, child marriage restraint, labour laws. Mem., Standing Cttee, Chamber of Princes, 1945–47; proposed Confedn of Saurashtra, 1945, and carried it in States-General meeting (as Chm.), 1946; received in private audience by King George VI and witnessed final reading of India Independence Bill, H of C, 1947; reserving sovereignty acceded to India, 1947; instituted Dhrangadhara Coronation Medal, 1942 and Accession to India Medal, 1947; under Covenant ceded admin and army to United State of Saurashtra, 1948; nominated to India's Constituent Assembly, instead became Uparajpramukh, Actg Rajpramukh and C-in-C of State Forces of United State of Saurashtra, 1948–52; First Pres., State Bank of Saurashtra; proclaimed India's constitution for United State of Saurashtra, 1949; resigned to attend Oxford Univ., 1952. Elected Mem. for Jhalavad (Gujarat), Lok Sabha, 1967–70 (introd. Referendum Bill to counter Bill empowering Parlt to abridge fundamental rights; led resistance to Govt's derecognition of all Rulers); Intendant General, Consultation of Rulers of Indian States in Concord for India, 1967. Life Member: Indian Council of World Affairs and Inst. of Const. and Parly Studies; Indian Parly Gp and CPA, 1967; Linguistic Soc. of India; Internat. Phonetic Assoc. and Simplified Spelling Soc., London; WWF; Wildlife Preservation Soc. of India; Cricket Club of India; India Internat. Centre.

Perm. Pres., Srirajman (Educ.) Foundn; Founder President: Sriraj Jhaleśvar Rajkarma Śakti Asthâ, 1990; Jhâlâmâ Unnati Asthâ, 1990. Pres., Rajkumar Coll., Rajkot, 1966–2000. Patron, Bhandarkar Oriental Res. Inst. *Heir: s* Maharajkumar Shri Sodhsalji, *b* 22 March 1944. *Address:* Ajitnivas Palace, Dhrangadhara, Jhalavad, Gujarat 363310, India.   *Died 1 Aug. 2010.*

DIAMOND, His Honour Anthony Edward John; QC 1974; a Circuit Judge, 1990–98; international and maritime arbitrator; *b* 4 Sept. 1929; *s* of late Arthur Sigismund Diamond, former Master of the Supreme Court, and of Gladys Elkah Diamond (*née* Mocatta); *m* 1965, Joan Margaret Gee; two *d. Educ:* Rugby; Corpus Christi Coll., Cambridge (MA). Served RA, 1947–49. Called to the Bar, Gray's Inn, 1953 (Bencher, 1985); practised at Bar as a specialist in commercial law, 1958–90; Head of Chambers at 4 Essex Court, EC4, 1984–90; Dep. High Court Judge, 1982–90; a Recorder, 1985–90; Judge i/c of Central London County Court Business List, 1994–98. Chm., Banking Act Appeals, 1980; Mem., indep. review body under colliery review procedure, 1985. *Publications:* papers on maritime law and arbitration. *Recreation:* the visual arts. *Club:* Athenæum.
Died 6 July 2006.

DIAMOND, Prof. Aubrey Lionel; Professor of Law, University of Notre Dame, 1987–99 and Co-Director, London Law Centre, 1987–99; Emeritus Professor of Law, University of London; solicitor; *b* 28 Dec. 1923; *s* of Alfred and Millie Diamond, London; *m* 1955, Dr Eva M. Bobasch; one *s* one *d. Educ:* elementary schs; Central Foundation Sch., London; London Sch. of Economics (LLB, LLM; Hon. Fellow, 1984). Clerical Officer, LCC, 1941–48. Served RAF, 1943–47. Admitted a solicitor, 1951. Sen. Lectr, Law Society's Sch. of Law, 1955–57; Asst Lectr, Lectr and Reader, Law Dept, LSE, 1957–66; Prof. of Law, Queen Mary Coll., Univ. of London, 1966–71; Law Comr, 1971–76; Prof. of Law and Dir, Inst. of Advanced Legal Studies, Univ. of London, 1976–86, then Emeritus; Hon. Fellow, QMW, 1989 (Fellow, QMC, 1984). Partner in Lawford & Co., Solicitors, 1959–71 (consultant, 1986–99). Part-time Chm. of Industrial Tribunals, 1984–90; Dep. Chm., Data Protection Tribunal, 1985–96; Consultant, DTI, 1986–88. Member: Central London Valuation Court, 1956–73; Consumer Advisory Council, BSI, 1961–63; Council, Consumers' Assoc., 1963–71 (Vice-Pres., 1981–84); Consumer Council, 1963–66, 1967–71; Cttee on the Age of Majority, 1965–67; Council, Law Society, 1976–92. Chairman: Social Sciences and the Law Cttee, SSRC, 1977–80; Hamlyn Trust, 1977–88; Advertising Adv. Cttee, IBA, 1980–88. President: Nat. Fedn of Consumer Groups, 1977–81 (Chm., 1963–67); British Insurance Law Assoc., 1988–90; Vice-Pres., Inst. of Trading Standards Administration, 1975–. Visiting Professor: University Coll. Dar es Salaam, Univ. of E Africa, 1966–67; Law Sch., Stanford Univ., 1971; Melbourne Univ., 1977; Univ. of Virginia, 1982; Tulane Univ., 1984; Vis. teacher, LSE, 1984–93. Hon. QC 1992. Hon. MRCP 1990. Hon. DCL City, 1992. *Publications:* The Consumer, Society and the Law (with Gordon Borrie, later Lord Borrie), 1963, 4th edn, 1981; Introduction to Hire-Purchase Law, 1967, 2nd edn, 1971; (ed) Instalment Credit, 1970; (co-ed) Sutton and Shannon on Contracts, 7th edn, 1970; Commercial and Consumer Credit: an introduction, 1982; A Review of Security Interests in Property, 1989; articles and notes in legal and medical jls and symposia.
Died 6 July 2006.

DIBDIN, Michael; author; *b* 21 March 1947; *s* of Frederick John Dibdin and Peigi (*née* Taylor); *m* 1st, 1971, Benita Mitbrodt (marr. diss. 1986); one *d;* 2nd, 1987, Sybil Sheringham (marr. diss. 1995); one *d;* 3rd, 1997, Kathrine Beck. *Educ:* Univ of Sussex (BA English Lit.); Univ. of Alberta (MA). Gold Dagger, CWA, 1988; Grand Prix de Littérature Policière (France), 1994. *Publications:* The Last Sherlock Holmes Story, 1978; A Rich Full Death, 1986; Ratking, 1988; The Tryst, 1989;

Vendetta, 1990; Dirty Tricks, 1991; Cabal, 1992; The Dying of the Light, 1993; (ed) The Picador Book of Crime Writing, 1993; Dead Lagoon, 1994; Dark Spectre, 1995; Così Fan Tutti, 1996; A Long Finish, 1998; Blood Rain, 1999; Thanksgiving, 2000; And Then You Die, 2002; Medusa, 2003; Back to Bologna, 2005; *posthumous publication:* End Games, 2007. *Recreations:* music, travel. *Address:* c/o Pat Kavanagh, Peters Fraser & Dunlop, Drury House, 34–43 Russell Street, WC2B 5HA. *T:* (020) 7344 1000. *Club:* Groucho. *Died 30 March 2007.*

DICK, Gavin Colquhoun; Vice-Chairman, Mobile Radio Training Trust, 1990–2002; *b* 6 Sept. 1928; *s* of late John Dick and Catherine MacAuslan Henderson; *m* 1953, Elizabeth Frances, *e d* of late Jonathan Hutchinson; two *d. Educ:* Hamilton Academy; Glasgow Univ. (MA 1950); Balliol Coll., Oxford (Snell Exhibnr, 1949, MA 1957); SOAS (Cert. in Turkish, 1986). National Service, 3rd RTR (Lieut), 1952–54. Asst Principal, BoT, 1954, Principal, 1958; UK Trade Comr, Wellington, NZ, 1961–64; Asst Sec., 1967; Jt Sec., Review Cttee on Overseas Representation, 1968–69; Under-Sec., 1975–84, Dept of Industry, 1981–84. Consultant: Office of Telecommunications, 1984–87; DTI Radiocommunications Div., 1987–89. Bd Mem., English Industrial Estates Corp., 1982–84. Governor, Coll. of Air Training (Hamble), 1975–80. *Recreation:* words. *Address:* Fell Cottage, Bayley's Hill, Sevenoaks, Kent TN14 6HS. *T:* (01732) 453704. *Club:* Oxford and Cambridge. *Died 24 May 2007.*

DICK, Air Vice-Marshal Ronald, CB 1988; writer and lecturer in aviation and military history; Head of British Defence Staff, Washington, and Defence Attaché, 1984–88, retired; *b* Newcastle upon Tyne, 18 Oct. 1931; *s* of Arthur John Craig Dick and Lilian Dick; *m* 1955, Pauline Lomax; one *s* one *d. Educ:* Beckenham and Penge County Grammar Sch.; RAF Coll., Cranwell. Commnd 1952; served, 1953–69: No 64 Fighter Sqdn; Flying Instr, No 5 FTS; Central Flying Sch. Examg Wing and Type Sqdn; Flt Comdr, 3615th Pilot Trng Sqdn, USAF, and No IX Bomber Sqdn; Trng (Operational) 2a (RAF), MoD; RAF Staff Coll., Bracknell; Ops B2 (RAF), MoD; Jt Services Staff Coll.; OC No IX Bomber Sqdn, RAF Akrotiri, 1970–72; Staff, RCDS, 1972–74; PSO to Dep. SACEUR, SHAPE, 1974–77; OC RAF Honington, 1978–80; Air Attaché, Washington, DC, 1980–83; Dir of Organization and Estabts, 1983–84, of Organization and Quartering, 1984, RAF. Internat. Fellow, Nat. Air and Space Mus., Smithsonian Instn, 1988–91; Vis. Prof. in Air Power History, USAF Air Univ., Ala, 1992–94. Mem., Bd of Trustees, Amer. Airpower Heritage Foundn, 1987–94. Consulting Editor, Air & Space Smithsonian Magazine, 1990–. FRAeS 1987. Wright Jubilee Aerobatic Trophy Winner, 1956. *Publications:* (jtly) The Means of Victory, 1992; (jtly) Classic RAF Battles, 1995; Lancaster, 1996; American Eagles: a history of the United States Air Force, 1997; Messerschmitt Bf109, 1997; Spitfire, 1997; Reach and Power: the heritage of the United States Air Force, 1997; Hurricane, 2000; The Aviation Century, 5 vols, 2003; articles for Air and Space Smithsonian, Air Power History, Flight, and other aviation jls and magazines. *Recreations:* wildlife conservation, bird watching, private flying, military history, opera. *Address:* 6 Shadwell Court, Fredericksburg, VA 22406, USA. *Club:* Royal Air Force. *Died 25 March 2008.*

DICKENSON, Joseph Frank, PhD, CEng, FIMechE; Director, North Staffordshire Polytechnic, 1969–86; *b* 26 Nov. 1924; *s* of late Frank Brand Dickenson and Maud Dickenson (*née* Beharrell); *m* 1948, Sheila May Kingston; two *s* one *d. Educ:* College of Technology, Hull. BSc (1st Cl. Hons) Engrg, PhD (both London). Engrg apprenticeship and Jun. Engr's posts, 1939–52; Lectr and Sen. Lectr, Hull Coll. of Technology, 1952–59; Head of Dept of Mechanical Engrg and later Vice-Principal, Lanchester Coll. of Technology, 1960–64; Principal, Leeds Coll. of Technology, 1964–69. *Recreations:* motor

cars, computers. *Address:* 6 Burlington Court, Burlington Place, Eastbourne BN21 4AU. *T:* (01323) 725039. *Died 30 March 2010.*

DICKINSON, Basil Philip Harriman; Under Secretary, Department of the Environment (formerly Ministry of Transport), 1959–74; *b* 10 Sept. 1916; *yr s* of F. H. and I. F. Dickinson; *m* 1941, Beryl Farrow; three *s* one *d. Educ:* Cheltenham Coll.; Oriel Coll., Oxford. *Address:* c/o Child & Co., 1 Fleet Street, EC4Y 1BD. *Died 19 Jan. 2006.*

DICKINSON, Sir Harold (Herbert), Kt 1975; *b* 27 Feb. 1917; *s* of late William James Dickinson and Barwon Venus Clarke; *m* 1946, Elsie May Smith; two *d. Educ:* Singleton Public Sch.; Tamworth High Sch.; Univ. of Sydney (LLB, 1st Cl. Hons). Barrister-at-Law. Served War, 2nd AIF HQ 22 Inf. Bde, 1940–45 (despatches); Japanese POW (Sgt). Dept of Lands, NSW, 1933–40; NSW Public Service Bd, 1946–60: Sec. and Sen. Inspector, 1949–60; Chief Exec. Officer, Prince Henry Hosp., 1960–63; NSW Public Service Bd: Mem., 1963–70; Dep. Chm., 1970–71; Chm., 1971–79. Formerly: Chm., AFT Property Co.; Director: Development Finance Corp.; Australian Fixed Trusts Ltd. Hon. Mem., NSW Univs Bd, 1967–71; Hon. Dir, Prince Henry, Prince of Wales, Eastern Suburbs Teaching Hosps, 1965–75, Chm. of Dirs, 1975–82; Governor, NSW Coll. of Law, 1972–77. *Publications:* contribs to administration jls. *Recreation:* sailing. *Address:* 15/8–10 Diaram Street, Hunters Hill, NSW 2110, Australia. *Club:* Probus (Sydney). *Died 11 July 2008.*

DICKINSON, William Michael, MBE 1960; Managing Director, Africa Research Ltd, 1966–90; *b* 13 Jan. 1930; *s* of late Comdr W. H. Dickinson, RN, and Ruth Sandeman Betts; *m* 1971, Enid Joy Bowers (*d* 1997); one *s* two *d. Educ:* St Edward's Sch., Oxford. Army Service, 1948–51; 2/Lieut, Oxford and Bucks LI, Sept. 1948; seconded Somaliland Scouts; Lieut 1950; Colonial Service Devonshire Course, 1951–52; Somaliland Protectorate: Admin. Officer, 1952; Dist Officer, 1953–54; Asst Sec. (Political), 1955–56; seconded to British Liaison Orgn, Ethiopia, as Sen. Asst Liaison Officer, 1957–59; Brit. Liaison Officer in charge, 1959; transf. N Rhodesia as Dist Officer, 1960; Dist Comr, 1961; seconded to FO as HM Consul-Gen., Hargeisa, 1961–63; Principal, External Affairs Section, Office of Prime Minister, N Rhodesia, during 1964; Sen. Principal, Min. of Foreign Affairs, Govt of Zambia, 1964–65. *Address:* Lian, Dark Lane, Camelford, Cornwall PL32 9UQ. *T:* (01840) 213492. *Died 16 Feb. 2006.*

DICKSON, Prof. Gordon Ross; Professor of Agriculture, University of Newcastle upon Tyne, 1973–97; Chairman, North England Regional Advisory Committee, Forestry Commission, 1987–97; *b* 12 Feb. 1932; *s* of T. W. Dickson, Tynemouth; *m* 1st, 1956, Dorothy Stobbs (*d* 1989); two *s* one *d*; 2nd, 1991, Violet Adams. *Educ:* Tynemouth High Sch.; Durham Univ. BSc (Agric) 1st cl. hons 1953, PhD (Agric) 1958, Dunelm. Tutorial Research Student, Univ. Sch. of Agric., King's Coll., Newcastle upon Tyne, 1953–56; Asst Farm Dir, Council of King's Coll., Nafferton, Stocksfield-on-Tyne, 1956–58; Farms Director for the Duke of Norfolk, 1958–71; Principal, Royal Agric. Coll., Cirencester, 1971–73. Chm., Agricl Wages Bd for England and Wales, 1981–84; Dep. Chm., Home-Grown Cereals Authy, 1982–94. FRAgS; FIAgrM 1992. *Address:* The West Wing, Bolam Hall, Morpeth, Northumberland NE61 3UA. *Died 6 Oct. 2008.*

DICKSON MABON, Rt Hon. Jesse; *see* Mabon.

DIGBY, Very Rev. Richard Shuttleworth W.; *see* Wingfield Digby.

DIGGORY, Elizabeth Mary; High Mistress, St Paul's Girls' School, 1998–2006; *b* 22 Dec. 1945; *d* of Clarence Howard Diggory and Beatrice Mary Diggory. *Educ:* Shrewsbury High Sch. for Girls; Westfield Coll., Univ. of London (BA Hons Hist.); Hughes Hall, Univ. of

Cambridge (PGCE). King Edward VI High School for Girls, Birmingham: Asst Teacher, 1968–73; Hd of History Dept, 1973–82; Head Mistress: St Albans High Sch. for Girls, 1983–94; Manchester High Sch. for Girls, 1994–98. Pres., GSA, 1991–92; Mem., Gen. Teaching Council, 2000–02; Vice-Chm., ISC, 2006–. Trustee, HSBC Educn Trust, 2004–. FRSA 1993. *Recreations:* theatre, the arts in general, travel, walking. *Died 18 March 2007.*

DILNOT, Mary, (Mrs Thomas Ruffle), OBE 1982; Director, IPC Women's Magazines Group, 1976–81; Editor, Woman's Weekly, 1971–81; *b* 23 Jan. 1921; 2nd *d* of George Dilnot, author, and Ethel Dilnot; *m* 1974, Thomas Ruffle. *Educ:* St Mary's Coll., Hampton. Joined Woman's Weekly, 1939. *Recreations:* home interests, reading, travel. *Address:* Emberbrook Care Centre, Raphael Drive, Thames Ditton KT7 0EB. *Died 5 Nov. 2010.*

DINGLE, Prof. Robert Balson, PhD; FRSE; Professor of Theoretical Physics, University of St Andrews, 1960–87, then Emeritus; *b* 26 March 1926; *s* of late Edward Douglas Dingle and Nora Gertrude Balson; *m* 1958, Helen Glenronnie Munro; two *d. Educ:* Bournemouth Secondary Sch.; Cambridge University. PhD 1951. Fellow of St John's Coll., Cambridge, 1948–52; Theoretician to Royal Society Mond Lab., 1949–52; Chief Asst in Theoretical Physics, Technical Univ. of Delft, Holland, 1952–53; Fellow, Nat. Research Council, Ottawa, 1953–54; Reader in Theoretical Physics, Univ. of WA, 1954–60. *Publications:* Asymptotic Expansions: their derivation and interpretation, 1973; contribs to learned journals. *Recreations:* music, local history. *Address:* 6 Lawhead Road East, St Andrews, Fife, Scotland KY16 9ND. *T:* (01334) 474287. *Died 2 March 2010.*

DIXON, Bernard Tunbridge; legal consultant; *b* 14 July 1928; *s* of Archibald Tunbridge Dixon and Dorothy Dixon (*née* Cardinal); *m* 1962, Jessie Netta Watson Hastie; one *s* three *d. Educ:* Owen's Sch.; University Coll. London (LLB). Admitted Solicitor, 1952 (Edmund Thomas Child Prize); Partner in Dixon & Co., Solicitors, 1952–59; Legal Asst/Sen. Legal Asst with Treasury Solicitor, 1959–67; Sen. Legal Asst with Land Commission, 1967–70; Sen. Legal Asst with Charity Comrs, 1970–74; Dep. Charity Comr, 1975–81; Charity Comr, 1981–84. *Recreations:* photography, exploring Lancashire. *Address:* c/o Maxwell Hodge, 9C Altway, Old Roan, Aintree, Liverpool L10 3JA. *Died 16 Sept. 2008.*

DIXON-LEWIS, Prof. Graham, DPhil; FRS 1995; Professor of Combustion Science, University of Leeds, 1978–87, then Emeritus; *b* Newport, Gwent, 1 July 1922; *s* of Daniel Watson Dixon-Lewis and Eleanor Jane Dixon-Lewis; *m* 1950, Patricia Mary Best; one *s* two *d. Educ:* Newport High Sch.; Jesus Coll., Oxford (MA; DPhil 1948). Research Chemist, Courtaulds, 1946–49; Sen. Scientific Officer, Gas Res. Bd, Beckenham, 1949–53; University of Leeds: Gas Council Sen. Res. Fellow, 1953–70; Reader, 1970–78. Vis. Prof., Applied Physics Lab., Johns Hopkins Univ., 1965; Vis. Scientist, Sandia Nat. Labs, Calif, 1987. Alfred Egerton Gold Medal 1990, Silver Medal 1990, Combustion Inst.; Award for Combustion and Hydrocarbon Oxidation Chemistry, RSC, 1993; Dionizy Smoleński Medal, Thermodynamics and Combustion Cttee, Polish Acad. of Scis, 1995. *Publications:* numerous scientific papers on combustion topics, chemically reacting flows, and molecular transport processes. *Recreations:* walking, gardening. *Address:* 16 West Park Grove, Leeds LS8 2HQ. *T:* (0113) 266 2269. *Died 5 Aug. 2010.*

DOBBS, (William) Bernard (Joseph); HM Diplomatic Service, retired; Ambassador to Laos (Lao People's Democratic Republic), 1982–85; *b* 3 Sept. 1925; *s* of late William Evelyn Joseph Dobbs and Maud Clifford Dobbs (*née* Bernard); *m* 1952, Brigid Mary Bilitch; one *s* one *d. Educ:* Shrewsbury Sch.; Trinity Coll., Dublin (BA

Hons Mod. History 1951; MA 1977). Served Rifle Bde/7th Gurkha Rifles, 1943–47 (Captain). Forbes Forbes Campbell and Co. Ltd, 1952–56; Examiner, Patent Office, 1957–61; British Trade Commission, 1961–65: Lagos, 1961–64; Freetown, 1964–66; HM Diplomatic Service: Freetown, London, Rangoon, Milan, Kinshasa, Vientiane, 1965–85. *Recreations:* reading, walking, writing. *Club:* Royal Automobile. *Died 19 April 2007.*

DOBRYNIN, Anatoly Fedorovich; Hero of Socialist Labour; Order of Lenin (five awards); Order of Red Banner of Labour; Secretary, Central Committee, Communist Party of the Soviet Union, 1986–91; Deputy, Supreme Soviet of the USSR, 1986–91; *b* 16 Nov. 1919; *m* Irina Nikolaevna Dobrynina; one *d. Educ:* Moscow Inst. of Aviation, 1942; Higher Sch. of Diplomacy, 1946 (doctorate in History). Asst to Dean of Faculty, Moscow Inst. of Aviation, engr-designer, 1942–44; Official, Min. of For. Affairs, 1946–52; Counsellor, Counsellor-Minister, Embassy to USA, 1952–54; Asst to Minister for For. Affairs, 1955–57; Dep. Sec. Gen., UN, 1957 60; Chief, Dept of Amer. Countries, Min. of For. Affairs, 1960–62; Amb. to USA, 1962–86. Mem., CPSU Central Cttee, 1971–91 (Candidate Mem., 1966–71); Chief, Internat. Dept, CPSU Central Cttee, 1986–91. *Publications:* In Confidence: Moscow's Ambassador to six Cold War presidents, 1995. *Died 6 April 2010.*

DOBSON, Sir Patrick John H.; *see* Howard-Dobson.

DODDS-PARKER, Sir (Arthur) Douglas, Kt 1973; company director since 1946; *b* 5 July 1909; *o s* of A. P. Dodds-Parker, FRCS, Oxford; *m* 1946, Aileen, *d* of late Norman B. Coster and late Mrs Alvin Dodd, Grand Detour, Ill., USA; one *s. Educ:* Winchester; Magdalen Coll., Oxford (BA in Modern History, 1930; MA 1934). Entered Sudan Political Service, 1930; Kordofan Province, 1931–34; Asst Private Sec. to Governor-General, Khartoum, 1934–35; Blue Nile Province, 1935–38; Public Security Dept, Khartoum, 1938–39; resigned 1938; joined Grenadier Guards, 1939; employed on special duties, March 1940; served in London, Cairo, East African campaign, North Africa, Italy and France, 1940–45; Mission Comdr, SOE, Western and Central Mediterranean, 1943–44; Col, 1944 (despatches, French Legion of Honour, Croix de Guerre). MP (C): Banbury Div. of Oxon, 1945–Sept. 1959; Cheltenham, 1964–Sept. 1974; Jt Parly Under-Sec. of State for Foreign Affairs, Nov. 1953–Oct. 1954, Dec. 1955–Jan. 1957; Parly Under-Sec. for Commonwealth Relations, Oct. 1954–Dec. 1955. Chairman: British Empire Producers Organisation; Joint East and Central Africa Board, 1947–50; Conservative Commonwealth Council, 1960–64; Cons. Parly Foreign and Commonwealth Cttee, 1970–73; Europe Atlantic Gp, 1976–79; Delegate to Council of Europe, North Atlantic and W European Assemblies, 1965–72; led Parly Delegn to China, 1972, Mem., British Parly Delegn to European Parlt, Strasbourg, 1973–75. Mem., Adv. Bd, 1947–99, Vice-Pres., 1999–, FANY (Princess Royal's Volunteer Corps). Freeman, City of London, 1983. *Publications:* Setting Europe Ablaze, 1983; Political Eunuch, 1986. *Address:* 9 North Court, Great Peter Street, SW1P 3LL. *Clubs:* Special Forces (Pres., 1977–81); Vincent's (Oxford); Leander. *Died 13 Sept. 2006.*

DOLE, John Anthony; Controller and Chief Executive of HM Stationery Office, and the Queen's Printer of Acts of Parliament, 1987–89, retired; *b* 14 Oct. 1929; *s* of Thomas Stephen Dole and Winifred Muriel (*née* Henderson); *m* 1952, Patricia Ivy Clements; two *s. Educ:* Bideford Grammar Sch.; Berkhamsted Sch. Air Ministry: Exec. Officer, 1950; Higher Exec. Officer, 1959; Principal, 1964; Ministry of Transport: Principal, 1965; Asst Sec. (Roads Programme), 1968; Administrator of Sports Council, 1972–75; Under Sec., Freight Directorate, 1976–78; Dir, Senior Staff Management, Depts of the Environment and Transport, 1978–82; Controller of Supplies, PSA, DoE, 1982–84; Controller of the Crown Suppliers, 1984–86. *Publications:* plays: Cat on the Fiddle, 1964; Shock Tactics, 1966; Lucky for Some, 1968; Once in a Blue Moon, 1972; Top Gear, 1976; *verse:* Odd Bodikins, 1992. *Recreations:* writing, philately. *Died 19 March 2008.*

DONEGALL, 7th Marquess of, *cr* 1791; **Dermot Richard Claud Chichester,** LVO 1986; Viscount Chichester and Baron of Belfast, 1625; Earl of Donegall, 1647; Earl of Belfast, 1791; Baron Fisherwick (GB), 1790; Baron Templemore, 1831; Hereditary Lord High Admiral of Lough Neagh; late 7th Queen's Own Hussars; Standard Bearer, Honourable Corps of Gentlemen at Arms, 1984–86 (one of HM Bodyguard, since 1966); *b* 18 April 1916; 2nd *s* of 4th Baron Templemore, KCVO, DSO, PC, and Hon. Clare Meriel Wingfield (*d* 1969), 2nd *d* of 7th Viscount Powerscourt, PC Ireland; *S* father to Barony of Templemore, 1953, and cousin to Marquessate of Donegall, 1975; *m* 1946, Lady Josceline Gabrielle Legge (*d* 1995), *y d* of 7th Earl of Dartmouth, GCVO, TD; one *s* two *d. Educ:* Harrow; RMC, Sandhurst. 2nd Lieut 7th Hussars, 1936; Lieut 1939; served War of 1939–45 in Middle East and Italy (prisoner); Major, 1944; retired, 1949. *Recreations:* hunting, shooting, fishing. *Heir: s* Earl of Belfast, *b* 9 May 1952. *Address:* Dunbrody Park, Arthurstown, Co. Wexford, Eire. *T:* (51) 389104. *Clubs:* Cavalry and Guards; Kildare Street and University (Dublin). *Died 19 April 2007.*

DONKIN, Dr Robin Arthur, FBA 1985; Reader in Historical Geography, 1990–96, then Emeritus, and Fellow of Jesus College, 1972–96, then Emeritus, University of Cambridge; *b* Morpeth, 28 Oct. 1928; *s* of Arthur Donkin and Elizabeth Jane Kirkup; *m* 1970, Jennifer Gay Kennedy; one *d. Educ:* Univ. of Durham (BA 1950; PhD 1953); MA Cantab 1971; LittD Cantab 1993. Lieut, Royal Artillery, 1953–55 (Egypt). King George VI Meml Fellow, Univ. of California, Berkeley, 1955–56; Asst Lectr, Dept of Geography, Univ. of Edinburgh, 1956–58; Lectr, Dept of Geography, Univ. of Birmingham, 1958–70; Lectr in the Geography of Latin America, Univ. of Cambridge, 1971–90; Tutor, Jesus Coll., Cambridge, 1975–96. Leverhulme Research Fellow, 1966; Vis. Associate Prof. of Geography, Univ. of Toronto, 1969. Carl O. Sauer Meml Lectr, Univ. of Calif, Berkeley, 1995. Field work in Middle and S America, NW Africa, India, China, Turkestan. *Publications:* The Cistercian Order in Europe: a bibliography of printed sources, 1969; Spanish Red: cochineal and the Opuntia cactus, 1977; The Cistercians: studies in the geography of medieval England and Wales, 1978; Agricultural Terracing in the Aboriginal New World, 1979; Manna: an historical geography, 1980; The Peccary, 1985; The Muscovy Duck, 1986; Meleagrides: an historical and ethnogeographical study of the Guinea fowl, 1991; Beyond Price: pearls and pearl-fishing, origins to the Age of Discoveries, 1998; Dragon's Brain Perfume: an historical geography of camphor, 1999; Between East and West: the Moluccas and the traffic in spices up to the arrival of Europeans, 2003; articles in geographical, historical and anthropological jls. *Address:* Jesus College, Cambridge CB5 8BL; 13 Roman Hill, Barton, Cambridge. *T:* (01223) 262572. *Died 1 Feb. 2006.*

DONNE, Hon. Sir Gaven (John), KBE 1979; Chief Justice: of Nauru, 1985–2000; of Tuvalu, 1986–2001; Member, Kiribati Court of Appeal, 1987–92; *b* 8 May 1914; *s* of Jack Alfred Donne and Mary Elizabeth Donne; *m* 1946, Isabel Fenwick (*d* 2005), *d* of John Edwin Hall; two *s* two *d. Educ:* Palmerston North Boys' High Sch.; Hastings High Sch.; Victoria Univ., Wellington; Auckland Univ. (LLB New Zealand). Called to the Bar and admitted solicitor, 1938. Military Service, 2nd NZEF, Middle East and Italy, 1941–45. Stipendiary Magistrate, NZ, 1958–75; Puisne Judge, Supreme Court of Western Samoa, 1970–71; Chief Justice, Western Samoa, 1972–75, Mem. Court of Appeal of Western Samoa, 1975–82; Judge, High Court of Niue, 1973; Chief Justice of the Cook Islands, 1975–82, and of Niue, 1974–82; Queen's Rep. in the Cook Islands, 1982–84. Hon. Counsellor, Internat.

Assoc. of Youth Magistrates, 1974–. Member: Takapuna Bor. Council, 1957–58; Auckland Town Planning Authority, 1958; Bd of Governors, Westlake High Sch., 1957–58. Grand Cross 2nd Cl., Order of Merit of Fed. Republic of Germany, 1978. *Recreation:* walking. *Address:* Otaramarae, Rotorua, New Zealand. *Club:* University (Auckland). *Died 28 March 2010.*

DONNISON, Kay; *see* Carmichael, C. M.

DONOVAN, Charles Edward; Board Member, 1981–92, and Senior Managing Director, Corporate Activities, 1991–92, British Gas plc; *b* 28 Jan. 1934; *s* of Charles and Sarah Donovan; *m* 1963, Robina Evelyn (*née* Anderson); three *s. Educ:* Camphill Sch., Paisley; Royal Technical Coll., Glasgow. FIPM 1990; CIGEM (CIGasE 1985). Personnel Officer: HQ, BEA, 1962; London and SE, Richard Costain Ltd, Constr. and Civil Engrs, 1963; Sen. Personnel Officer, Engrg, W Midlands Gas Bd, 1966; Southern Gas, 1970–77: Personnel Manager, 1973; Personnel Dir, 1975; British Gas: Dir, Indust. Relations, 1977–81; Man. Dir, Personnel, 1981–91, also Group Services, 1989–91. Dir, Inst. of Citizenship Studies, 1992–97. CCMI (CBIM 1991); FRSA 1992. *Recreations:* model sailing, music. *Address:* 65 Moss Lane, Pinner, Middx HA5 3AZ. *Died 25 Nov. 2007.*

DOOGE, Prof. James Clement Ignatius; Professor of Civil Engineering, University College, Dublin, 1970–84, then Professor Emeritus; research consultant; Consultant: United Nations specialised agencies; European Commission; President, Royal Irish Academy, 1987–90; *b* 30 July 1922; *s* of Denis Patrick Dooge and Veronica Catherine Carroll; *m* 1946, Veronica O'Doherty; two *s* three *d. Educ:* Christian Brothers' Sch., Dun Laoghaire; University Coll., Dublin (BE, BSc 1942, ME 1952); Univ. of Iowa (MSc 1956). FICE; FASCE. Jun. Civil Engr, Irish Office of Public Works, 1943–46; Design Engr, Electricity Supply Bd, Ireland, 1946–58; Prof. of Civil Engrg, UC Cork, 1958–70. Irish Senate: Mem., 1965–77 and 1981–87; Chm., 1973–77; Leader, 1983–87; Minister for Foreign Affairs, Ireland, 1981–82. President: ICEI, 1968–69 (Hon. FICEI; Kettle Premium and Plaque, 1948, 1985; Mullins Medal, 1951, 1962); Internat. Assoc. for Hydrologic Scis, 1975–79; Member: Exec. Bureau, Internat. Union for Geodesy and Geophysics, 1979–87; Gen. Cttee, ICSU, 1980–86, 1988–2002 (Sec. Gen., 1980–82; Pres., 1993–96). Fellow, Amer. Geophysical Union (Horton Award, 1959; Bowie Medal, 1986); Hon. Mem., Eur. Geophysical Soc., 1993 (John Dalton Medal, 1998). Foreign Member: Polish Acad. of Scis, 1985; Russian Acad. of Scis, 1994; Spanish Acad. of Sci., 1998; Royal Acad. of Engrg, 2000. Hon. DAgrSc Wageningen, 1978; Hon. DTech. Lund, 1980; Hon. DSc: Birmingham, 1986; Heriot-Watt, 2000; NUI, 2000; Univ. Complutense, Madrid, 2001; Hon. ScD Dublin, 1988; Hon. Dr Technical Univ. of Cracow, 2000. Internat. Prize for Hydrology, 1983; Internat. Prize for Meteorology, 1999; Prince Philip Gold Medal, Royal Acad. of Engrg, 2005. *Address:* 2 Belgrave Road, Monkstown, Co. Dublin, Ireland. *Died 20 Aug. 2010.*

DORWARD, William, OBE 1977; Commissioner for Hong Kong Economic Affairs, United States, 1983–87, retired; *b* 25 Sept. 1929; *s* of Alexander and Jessie Dorward; *m* 1960, Rosemary Ann Smith; one *s. Educ:* Morgan Academy, Dundee. Colonial Office, 1951–53; Commerce and Industry Dept, Hong Kong Govt, 1954–74; Counsellor (Hong Kong Affairs) UK Mission, Geneva, 1974–76; Hong Kong Government: Dep. Dir of Commerce and Industry, 1974–77; Comr of Industry and Customs, 1977–79; Dir of Trade, Industry and Customs, 1979–82; Sec. for Trade and Industry, 1982–83; MLC, 1979–83. Mem., GATT Dispute Settlement Panel, 1991–96. *Address:* Waulkmill House, Skirling, by Biggar ML12 6HB. *Clubs:* Carlton, Royal Over-Seas League; Hong Kong. *Died 18 Oct. 2006.*

DOUGAL, James Joseph; writer and broadcaster, public affairs consultant and media trainer; Director, Dougal Media, since 2006; *b* 19 March 1945; *s* of Samuel and Christine Dougal; *m* 1970, Deirdre O'Neill; one *s* three *d*. *Educ:* St Mary's Christian Brothers Grammar Sch., Belfast; St Gabriel's Seminary, Enniskillen. NI Pol and News Ed., RTE, 1977–90; NI Pol Ed., BBC, 1990–97; Hd of NI Repn, 1997–2002, Hd of Repn in UK, 2002–04, EC. Presenter, BBC Radio, 2004–; maker of documentaries for Ulster TV. DUniv QUB, 2003. *Recreations:* walking, driving, going to the gym.   *Died 15 Oct. 2010.*

DOUGAN, (Alexander) Derek; company director and marketing consultant; *b* 20 Jan. 1938; *s* of John and Josephine Dougan; *m* 1963, Jutta Maria; two *s*. *Educ:* Mersey Street primary sch., Belfast; Belfast Technical High School. Professional footballer with: Distillery, NI, 1953–57; Portsmouth, 1957–59; Blackburn Rovers, 1959–61; Aston Villa, 1961–63; Peterborough, 1963–65; Leicester, 1965–67; Wolverhampton Wanderers, 1967–75. Represented N Ireland at all levels, from schoolboy to full international, more than 50 times. Chm., PFA, 1970–78. Chief Exec., Kettering Town FC, 1975–77; Chm. and Chief Exec., Wolverhampton Wanderers' FC, 1982–85. Sports Presenter, Yorkshire Television. Mem. Council, Co-Operation North, 1987–. *Publications:* Attack! (autobiog.), 1969; The Sash He Never Wore (autobiog.), 1972, rev. edn, The Sash He Never Wore: 25 years on, 1997; The Footballer (novel), 1974; On the Spot (football as a profession), 1974; Doog (autobiog.), 1980; How Not to Run Football, 1981; (with Patrick Murphy) Matches of the Day 1958–83, 1984. *Recreations:* watching football, playing squash. *Address:* 25 Campbell Park Avenue, Belfast, N Ireland BT4 3FL.   *Died 24 June 2007.*

DOUGHTY, Sir (Graham) Martin, Kt 2001; Chair, Natural England, since 2006; *b* 11 Oct. 1949; *s* of late Harold Doughty and Eva Mary (*née* Swift); *m* 1st, 1974, Eleanor Lamont (*d* 1988); two *d*; 2nd, 1996, Gillian Gostick. *Educ:* New Mills Grammar Sch.; Imperial Coll., London (BSc Eng, MSc). Res. Chem. Engr, Booth (Internat.), 1971–72; Lectr, 1973–90, Sen. Lectr, 1990–95, Sheffield Poly., later Sheffield Hallam Univ. Mem. (Lab), Derbys CC, 1981–2005 (Chairman: Highways and Transport, 1983–86; Planning and Countryside, 1986–92; Council Leader, 1992–2001). Chair, English Nature, 2001–06. Board Member: E Midlands Develt Agency, 1998–2001; Countryside Agency, 1999–2005. Mem., Peak Dist Nat. Park Authy, 1987–2005 (Chm., 1993–2002, Vice-Chm., 2002–04); Chm., Assoc. of Nat. Park Authorities, 1997–2001; Mem., Rural Affairs Forum for England, 2002–04. Non-executive Director: Entrust, 1996–2003; Derbys Ambulance Services NHS Trust, 1996–98. Vice-Pres., Arkwright Soc., 2003–. Nat. Forest Ambassador, 2004–. Patron, Inst. of Ecology and Envmtl Mgt, 2002–. DUniv: Sheffield Hallam, 2002; Derby, 2006; Hon. DSc Cranfield, 2005. *Publications:* The Park under the Town, 2001. *Recreations:* hill-walking, gardening, cooking fish well, natural history. *Address:* Natural England, 1 East Parade, Sheffield S1 2ET; *e-mail:* martin.doughty@naturalengland.org.uk. *Club:* Royal Commonwealth Society.   *Died 4 March 2009.*

DOUGLAS, Anthony Jude; Director, Gravitas Communications, since 2001; *b* 14 Dec. 1944; *s* of Arthur Sidney Douglas and Margaret Mary Douglas; *m* 1968, Jacqueline English; two *d*. *Educ:* Cardinal Vaughan Grammar Sch., London; Southampton Univ. (BA Hons English). Head of Client Services, Lintas Advertising, 1967–81; Jt Chm. and Chief Exec., DMB&B Advertising, 1981–95; Chief Exec., COI, 1996–98; Chm., FCB Europe, 1998–99. Dir, Effective TV, 2003–. *Recreations:* cooking, walking, reading, anthropology. *Address:* 20 Malbrook Road, Putney, SW15 6UE. *T:* (020) 8788 3209.   *Died 12 Oct. 2010.*

DOUGLAS, Gavin Stuart, RD 1970; QC (Scot.) 1971; *b* 12 June 1932; *y s* of late Gilbert Georgeson Douglas and Rosena Campbell Douglas. *Educ:* South Morningside Sch.; George Heriot's Sch.; Edinburgh Univ. MA 1953, LLB 1955. Qual. as Solicitor, 1955; nat. service with RN, 1955–57. Admitted to Faculty of Advocates, 1958; Sub-editor (part-time), The Scotsman, 1957–61; Mem. Lord Advocate's Dept in London (as Parly Draftsman), 1961–64; returned to practice at Scots Bar, 1964; Junior Counsel to BoT, 1965–71; Counsel to Scottish Law Commn, 1965–96; Hon. Sheriff in various sheriffdoms, 1965–71; a Chm. of Industrial Tribunals, 1966–78; Counsel to Sec. of State for Scotland under Private Legislation Procedure (Scotland) Act 1936, 1969–75, Sen. Counsel under that Act, 1975–2002; Temporary Sheriff, 1990–99. Mem., Lothian Health Bd, 1981–85. Pres., Temporary Sheriffs' Assoc., 1998–99. Mem. Bd, Leith Nautical Coll., 1981–84. Editor, Session Cases, 7 vols, 1976–82. *Recreations:* golf, ski-ing. *Clubs:* Royal Scots (Edinburgh); Rolls-Royce Enthusiasts'; Hon. Company of Edinburgh Golfers (Muirfield).   *Died 6 March 2008.*

DOUGLAS, James Murray, CBE 1985; Director-General, Country Landowners' Association, 1970–90; *b* 26 Sept. 1925; *s* of Herbert and Amy Douglas, Brechin; *m* 1950, Julie Kemmner; one *s* one *d*. *Educ:* Morrison's Acad., Crieff; Aberdeen Univ.; Balliol Coll., Oxford. Entered Civil Service, 1950; Treasury, 1960–63; Asst Sec., Min. of Housing and Local Govt, 1964; Sec. to Royal Commn on Local Govt, 1966–69. Dir, Booker Countryside, 1990–93. Vice-Pres., Confedn of European Agriculture, 1971–88 (Chm., Environment Cttee, 1988–90); Mem., Econ. Develt Cttee for Agriculture, 1972–90; Sec., European Landowning Orgns Gp, 1972–87. Mem., Council, CBI, 1986–89. *Publications:* various articles on local govt planning, agriculture and landowning. *Address:* 1 Oldfield Close, Bickley, Kent BR1 2LL. *T:* (020) 8467 3213. *Club:* Oxford and Cambridge.   *Died 3 Aug. 2006.*

DOUGLAS, Margaret Elizabeth, (Mrs T. Lancaster), OBE 1994; Supervisor of Parliamentary Broadcasting, 1993–99; *b* 22 Aug. 1934; *d* of Thomas Mincher Douglas and Dorothy Jones; *m* 2000, Terence Lancaster (decd). *Educ:* Parliament Hill Grammar Sch., London. Joined BBC as sec., 1951; subseq. researcher, dir and producer in Current Affairs television, working on Panorama, Gallery, 24 Hours and on special progs with Lord Avon and Lord Stockton; Editor, Party Conf. coverage, 1972–83; Chief Asst to Dir-Gen., 1983–87; Chief Political Advr, BBC, 1987–93. *Recreation:* watching politics and football. *Address:* Flat 49, The Anchor Brewhouse, 50 Shad Thames, SE1 2LY.   *Died 20 Aug. 2008.*

DOUGLAS, Dame (Margaret) Mary, DBE 2007 (CBE 1992); FBA 1989; Avalon Foundation Professor in the Humanities, Northwestern University, 1981–85, then Professor Emeritus; *b* 25 March 1921; *d* of late Gilbert Charles Tew and Phyllis Twomey, *m* 1951, James A. T Douglas, OBE (*d* 2004); two *s* one *d*. *Educ:* Sacred Heart Convent, Roehampton; St Anne's Coll., Oxford (MA, BSc, DPhil; Hon. Fellow, 1992). Returned to Oxford, 1946, to train as anthropologist; fieldwork in Belgian Congo, 1949–50, 1953 and 1987; Lectr in Anthropology, Univ. of Oxford, 1950; Univ. of London, 1951–78, Prof. of Social Anthropology, UCL, 1970–78. Res. Scholar, Russell Sage Foundn, NY, 1977–81; Vis. Prof., Princeton Univ., 1986–88. Gifford Lectr, Univ. of Edinburgh, 1989. MAE 1988. Foreign Mem., Royal Swedish Acad. of Letters. Hon. Res. Fellow, UCL, 1994. Hon. Dr of Philosophy, Univ. of Uppsala, 1986; Hon. LLD Univ. of Notre Dame, 1988; Hon. DLitt: East Anglia, Jewish Theol Seminary of America, 1992; Warwick, 1993; Exeter, 1995; Oxon, 2003; DU Essex, 1992; Hon. DPhil Oslo, 1997; Hon. DHL Pennsylvania, 1999; DUniv Surrey, 1999; Hon DSc: London, Brunel, 2001. *Publications:* The Lele of the Kasai, 1963; Purity and Danger, 1966; Natural Symbols, 1970; Implicit Meanings, 1975; (with Baron Isherwood) The World of Goods: towards an anthropology of consumption, 1979; Evans-Pritchard, 1980; (with Aaron Wildavsky) Risk and Culture, 1982; In the Active

Voice, 1982; Risk Acceptability, 1986; How Institutions Think, 1986; Risk and Blame, 1992; In the Wilderness, 1993; Thought Styles, 1996; (with Steven Ney) Missing Persons, 1998; Leviticus as Literature, 1999; Jacob's Tears, 2004; Thinking in Circles, 2007. *Address:* 84 Bedford Court Mansions, Bedford Avenue, WC1B 3HE. *Died 16 May 2007.*

DOUGLAS, Prof. Thomas Alexander; Professor of Veterinary Biochemistry and Head of Department of Veterinary Biochemistry (Clinical), University of Glasgow, 1977–90; *b* 9 Aug. 1926; *s* of Alexander and Mary Douglas; *m* 1957, Rachel Ishbel McDonald; two *s*. *Educ:* Battlefield Public Sch.; High Sch. of Glasgow; Glasgow Vet. Coll., Univ. of Glasgow (BSc; Animal Health Schol., 1950–54; PhD). MRCVS. General Veterinary Practice: Ulverston, 1948–49; Lanark, 1949–50; University of Glasgow: Faculty of Sci., 1950–54; Asst Lectr, Biochemistry, 1954–57; Lectr 1957–71, Sen. Lectr 1971–77, in Vet. Biochem., Vet. Sch.; Dean of Faculty of Vet. Medicine, 1982–85. Mem. Council, RCVS, 1982–85. Mem., UGC, 1986–89 (Chm., Agriculture and Veterinary Studies Sub-Cttee, 1986–89). *Publications:* sci. articles in vet. and biochem. jls. *Recreations:* golf, hill walking. *Address:* 77 South Mains Road, Milngavie, Glasgow G62 6DE. *T:* (0141) 956 2751. *Died 7 Jan. 2009.*

DOUGLAS-SCOTT, Douglas Andrew Montagu; *see* Scott.

DOVER, Sir Kenneth James, Kt 1977; DLitt; FRSE 1975; FBA 1966; Chancellor, University of St Andrews, 1981–2005; *b* 11 March 1920; *o s* of Percy H. J. Dover, London, civil servant; *m* 1947, Audrey Ruth Latimer (*d* 2009); one *s* one *d*. *Educ:* St Paul's Sch. (Scholar); Balliol Coll., Oxford (Domus Scholar); Gaisford Prize, 1939; 1st in Classical Hon. Mods., 1940; Ireland Scholar, 1946; Cromer Prize (British Academy), 1946; 1st in Lit. Hum., Derby Scholar, Amy Mary Preston Read Scholar, 1947; Harmsworth Sen. Scholar, Merton Coll., 1947 (Hon. Fellow, 1980); DLitt Oxon 1974. Served War of 1939–45: Army (RA), 1940–45; Western Desert, 1941–43, Italy, 1943–45 (despatches). Fellow and Tutor, Balliol Coll., 1948–55 (Hon. Fellow, 1977); Prof. of Greek, 1955–76, Dean of Fac. of Arts, 1960–63, 1973–75, Univ. of St Andrews; Pres., Corpus Christi Coll., Oxford, 1976–86 (Hon. Fellow, 1986); Prof. of Classics (Winter Quarter), Stanford Univ., 1988–92. Vis. Lectr, Harvard, 1960; Sather Prof. of Classical Literature, Univ. of California, 1967; Prof.-at-large, Cornell Univ., 1984–89. President: Soc. for Promotion of Hellenic Studies, 1971–74; Classical Assoc., 1975; Jt Assoc. of Classical Teachers, 1985. Pres., British Acad., 1978–81. For. Hon. Mem., Amer. Acad. of Arts and Sciences, 1979; For. Mem., Royal Netherlands Acad. of Arts and Sciences, 1979. Hon. LLD: Birmingham, 1979; St Andrews, 1981; Hon. DLitt: Bristol, 1980; London, 1980; St Andrews, 1981; Durham, 1984; Hon. LittD Liverpool, 1983; Hon. DHL Oglethorpe, 1984. Kenyon Medal, British Acad., 1993. *Publications:* Greek Word Order, 1960; Commentaries on Thucydides, Books VI and VII, 1965; (ed) Aristophanes' Clouds, 1968; Lysias and the Corpus Lysiacum, 1968; (with A. W. Gomme and A. Andrewes) Historical Commentary on Thucydides, vol. IV, 1970, vol. V, 1981; (ed) Theocritus, select poems, 1971; Aristophanic Comedy, 1972; Greek Popular Morality in the Time of Plato and Aristotle, 1974; Greek Homosexuality, 1978; (ed) Plato, Symposium, 1980; (ed and co-author) Ancient Greek Literature, 1980; The Greeks, 1980 (contrib., The Greeks, BBC TV series, 1980); Greek and the Greeks, 1987; The Greeks and their Legacy, 1989; (ed) Perceptions of the Ancient Greeks, 1992; (ed) Aristophanes, Frogs, 1993; Marginal Comment (memoirs), 1994; The Evolution of Greek Prose Style, 1997; articles in learned journals; Co-editor, Classical Quarterly, 1962–68. *Recreations:* historical linguistics, gardening. *Address:* 49 Hepburn Gardens, St Andrews, Fife KY16 9LS. *Died 7 March 2010.*

DOWDESWELL, Lt-Col (John) Windsor, MC 1943; TD 1947; Chairman, Gateshead Health Authority, 1984–93; Vice Lord-Lieutenant of Tyne and Wear, 1987–93; *b* 11 June 1920; *s* of Thomas Reginald Dowdeswell and Nancy Olivia Pitt Dowdeswell; *m* 1948, Phyllis Audrey Horsfield; one *d* (one *s* decd). *Educ:* Malvern Coll. Commnd RA (TA), 1938; served War, RA 50 (N) Division: France, 1940; Western Desert, 1941–43; Sicily, 1943; NW Europe, 1944–46; Lt-Col Comdg 272 (N) Field Regt, RA (TA), 1963–66; Hon. Col, 101 (N) Field Regt, RA (TA), 1981–86. Emerson Walker Ltd, 1946–68 (Man. Dir, 1961–68); Clarke Chapman Ltd, 1968–77; NEI plc, 1977–83. JP Gateshead, 1955–90 (Chm., 1979–86); DL Tyne and Wear, 1976. *Address:* 40 Oakfield Road, Gosforth, Newcastle upon Tyne NE3 4HS. *T:* (0191) 285 2196. *Club:* Northern Counties (Newcastle upon Tyne). *Died 24 Jan. 2007.*

DOWLING, Rt Rev. Owen Douglas; Bishop of Canberra and Goulburn, 1983–92; *b* 11 Oct. 1934; *s* of Cecil Gair Mackenzie Dowling and Winifred Hunter; *m* 1st, 1958, Beverly Anne Johnston (*d* 1985); two *s* one *d*; 2nd, 1993, Gloria Helen Goodwin. *Educ:* Melbourne High School; Trinity Coll., Melbourne Univ. (BA, DipEd, ThL). Victorian Education Dept, Secondary Teacher, 1956–60; ordained to ministry of Anglican Church, 1960; Asst Curate, Sunshine/Deer Park, Dio. Melbourne, 1960–62; Vicar of St. Philip's, W Heidelberg, 1962–65; Precentor and Organist, St Saviour's Cathedral, Goulburn, 1965–67; Rector of South Wagga Wagga, 1968–72; Rector of St John's, Canberra, 1972–81; Archdeacon of Canberra, 1974–81; Asst Bishop, Dio. Canberra and Goulburn, 1981–83; Rector: St James's, New Town, Hobart, 1993–96; Christ Church, Longford, Tas, 1996–99. Comr, Australian Heritage Commn, 1993–95. *Recreation:* pipe organ and piano playing. *Address:* 1/12 Key Street, Campbell, ACT 2612, Australia. *Club:* Southern Cross (Canberra). *Died 7 May 2008.*

DOWN, Antony Turnbull L.; *see* Langdon-Down.

DOWNES, Sir Edward (Thomas), Kt 1991; CBE 1986; Associate Music Director and Principal Conductor, Royal Opera House, Covent Garden, since 1991; *b* 17 June 1924; *m* 1955, Joan (*d* 10 July 2009); one *s* one *d*. FRCM. Royal Opera House, Covent Garden, 1952–69; Music Dir, Australian Opera, 1972–76; Prin. Conductor, BBC Northern Symphony Orch., subseq. BBC Philharmonic Orch., 1980–91, then Conductor Emeritus. *Address:* c/o Royal Opera House, Covent Garden, WC2E 7QA. *Died 10 July 2009.*

DOWNES, George Robert, CB 1967; Director of Studies, Royal Institute of Public Administration, 1972–94; *b* 25 May 1911; *o s* of late Philip George Downes; *m* 1947, Edna Katherine Millar; two *d*. *Educ:* King Edward's Grammar School, Birmingham; Grocers', London. Entered GPO, 1928; Assistant Surveyor, 1937; Asst Principal, 1939. Served War of 1939–45: RNVR, in destroyers, 1942–45. Principal, GPO, 1946; Principal Private Sec. to: Lord President of the Council, 1948–50; Lord Privy Seal, 1951; Assistant Secretary, 1951; Imperial Defence College, 1952; Deputy Regional Director, GPO London, 1955; Dir, London Postal Region, 1960–65; Dir of Postal Services, 1965–67; Dir, Operations and Overseas, PO, 1967–71. *Recreations:* music, gardening. *Address:* Orchard Cottage, Frithsden, Berkhamsted, Herts HP4 1NW. *Died 7 Jan. 2008.*

DOWNEY, Air Vice-Marshal John Chegwyn Thomas, CB 1975; DFC 1945, AFC; Deputy Controller of Aircraft (C), Ministry of Defence, 1974–75; *b* 26 Nov. 1920; *s* of Thomas Cecil Downey and Mary Evelyn Downey; *m* Diana, (*née* White); one *s* two *d*. *Educ:* Whitgift Sch. Entered RAF 1939; served War of 1939–45 in Coastal Command (DFC 1945 for his part in anti-U-boat ops). Captained Lincoln Aries III on global flight of 29,000 miles, during which London-Khartoum record was broken. RAE Farnborough

1956–58; commanded Bomber Comd Develt Unit 1959–60; head of NE Defence Secretariat, Cyprus, 1960–62; Comd RAF Farnborough, 1962–64; a Dir. Op. Requirements (RAF) MoD, 1965–67; IDC, 1968: Comdt, RAF Coll. of Air Warfare, Manby, Jan./Oct. 1969; Comdr Southern Maritime Air Region, 1969–71; Senior RAF Mem., RCDS, 1972–74. *Publications:* Management in the Armed Forces: an anatomy of the military profession, 1977; (contrib.) Yearbook of World Affairs, 1983. *Recreations:* sailing, ski-ing. *Address:* c/o Lloyds TSB, 7 Pall Mall, SW1Y 5NA. *Club:* Royal Air Force. *Died 14 Feb. 2010.*

DOWNEY, William George, CB 1967; *b* 3 Jan. 1912; *s* of late William Percy Downey; *m* 1936, Iris (*d* 2000), *e d* of late Ernest Frederick Pickering; three *d*. *Educ:* Southend Grammar Sch. ACWA 1935, ACA 1937, FCA 1960. Ministry of Aircraft Production, 1940; Ministry of Supply, 1946 (Director of Finance and Administration, Royal Ordnance Factories, 1952–57); Ministry of Aviation, 1959; Under-Secretary, 1961; Chm., Steering Gp, Develt Cost Estimation, 1964–66; Min. of Technology, 1967, Min. of Aviation Supply, 1970; DTI, 1971; Management Consultant to Procurement Exec., MoD, 1972–74; Under Sec., NI Office, 1974–75; Dir, Harland and Wolff, 1975–81; Consultant to CAA, 1976–79, to Dept of Energy, 1980. *Address:* Cornhill Cross, Cheadle Road, Leek, Staffs ST13 5RE. *T:* (01538) 383761 *Died 23 June 2007.*

DOWNING, Dr Anthony Leighton, FREng; Consultant, Binnie & Partners, Consulting Engineers, 1986–96 (Partner, 1974–86); *b* 27 March 1926; *s* of Sydney Arthur Downing and Frances Dorothy Downing; *m* 1952, Kathleen Margaret Frost; one *d*. *Educ:* Arnold Sch., Blackpool; Cambridge and London Universities. BA Cantab. 1946; BSc Special Degree 2 (1) Hons. London, 1950; DSc London 1967. Joined Water Pollution Research Lab., 1946; seconded to Fisheries Research Lab., Lowestoft, 1947–48; granted transfer to Govt Chemist's Lab., 1948; returned to WPRL as Scientific Officer, 1950; subsequently worked mainly in field of biochemical engrg; Dir, Water Pollution Res. Lab., 1966–73. Vis. Prof., Imperial Coll. of Science and Technology, 1978–82. FIChemE 1975; FIWPC 1965 (Pres., 1979); FIBiol 1965; Hon. FIPHE 1965; FIWES 1975; Hon. FCIWEM 1987; FREng (FEng 1991). Freeman, City of London, 1988. Member: Probus Club, Stevenage, 1995– (Chm., 2002); CGA, 2000–. *Publications:* Water on the Brain (memoirs), 2005; 120 papers in scientific and technical journals. *Recreations:* golf, snooker, gardening. *Address:* 2 Tewin Close, Tewin Wood, Welwyn, Herts AL6 0HF. *T:* (01438) 798474. *Club:* Knebworth Golf. *Died 1 Jan. 2009.*

DOWSON, Graham Randall; Partner, Graham Dowson and Associates, since 1975; Chairman, Dowson Shurman (formerly Dowson-Salisbury) Associates Ltd, since 1987; *b* 13 Jan. 1923; *o s* of late Cyril James Dowson and late Dorothy Celia (*née* Foster); *m* 1954, Fay Weston (marr. diss. 1974); two *d*; *m* 1975, Denise Shurman. *Educ:* Alleyn Court Sch.; City of London Sch.; Ecole Alpina, Switzerland. Served War of 1939–45 (1939–43 and Africa Stars, Atlantic, Defence and Russian Arctic Medals, etc); RAF, 1941–46 (Pilot, Sqdn-Ldr). US Steel Corporation (Columbia Steel), Los Angeles, 1946–49; Sales Senior Commentator, Mid South Network (MBS), radio, US, 1949–52; Dir, Rank Organization Ltd, 1960–75, Chief Exec., 1974–75; Chairman: Erskine House Investments, 1975–83; Moolaya Investments, 1975–78; Pincus Vidler Arthur Fitzgerald Ltd, 1979–83; Marinex Petroleum, 1981–83; Nash Industries, 1988–90; Premier Speakers, 1987–91; Chm. and Chief Exec., Teltech Ltd, 1984–87; Deputy Chairman: Nimslo European Hldgs, 1978–87; Nimslo International Ltd, 1981–87; Nimslo Ltd, 1978–87 (Dir, 1978); Paravision (UK) Ltd, 1988–91; Director: A. C. Nielsen Co., Oxford, 1953–58; Carron Co. (Holdings) Ltd, 1976–84; Carron Investments Ltd, 1976–84; RCO Holdings PLC (formerly Barrowmill Ltd), 1979–94; Nimslo Corp., 1978–87; Filmbond plc,

1985–88; Fairhaven Internat. Ltd, 1988–95; Grovewood Securities, 1990–91. Chm., European League for Econ. Co-operation (British Section), 1974–87 (Pres., 1987–); Vice Pres., NPFA, 1972–; Chm., Migraine Trust. 1985–88; Patron, Internat. Centre for Child Studies. Liveryman, Distillers' Co.; Mem., Court of Common Council, City of London, 1992–95. FInstD 1957; CCMI (CBIM 1969); FInstM 1971. Officier de l'Ordre des Coteaux de Champagne, 1998. *Recreations:* sailing, shooting. *Address:* 193 Cromwell Tower, Barbican, EC2Y 8DD. *Clubs:* Carlton, Royal Air Force, Saints and Sinners, Thirty; Royal London Yacht (Ex-Commodore). *Died 10 June 2006.*

DRAYCOTT, Gerald Arthur; a Recorder of the Crown Court, 1972–86; *b* 25 Oct. 1911; *s* of Arthur Henry Seely Draycott and Maud Mary Draycott; *m* 1939, Phyllis Moyra Evans (decd); two *s* one *d*. *Educ:* King Edward's Sch., Stratford-on-Avon. FCII. Called to Bar, Middle Temple, 1938. Served in RAF, 1939–46 (Sqdn Ldr; despatches). Practised at Bar, SE Circuit, 1946–90; Dep. Recorder, Bury St Edmunds and Great Yarmouth, 1966–72. Chairman: Eastern Rent Assessment Panel, 1965–77; Nat. Insurance Tribunal, Norwich, 1970–84; E Anglia Med. Appeal Tribunal, 1978–84. *Address:* Nethergate House, Saxlingham Nethergate, Norwich NR15 1PB. *T:* (01508) 498306. *Died 15 March 2008.*

DRAYSON, Robert Quested, DSC 1943; MA; Headmaster of Stowe, 1964–79; *b* 5 June 1919; *s* of late Frederick Louis Drayson and late Elsie Mabel Drayson; *m* 1943, Rachel, 2nd *d* of Stephen Spencer Jenkyns; one *s* two *d*. *Educ:* St Lawrence Coll., Ramsgate; Downing Coll., Cambridge, 1938–39, 1946–47 (History Tripos, BA 1947; MA 1950). Served RNVR, 1939–46; Lieut in command HM Motor Torpedo Boats. Asst Master and Housemaster, St Lawrence Coll., 1947–50; Asst Master, Felsted Sch., 1950–55; Headmaster, Reed's Sch., Cobham, 1955–63. Resident Lay Chaplain to Bishop of Norwich, 1979–84; Lay Reader, 1979. Member: HMC Cttee, 1973–75 (Chm., Midland Div., 1974–75); Council, McAlpine Educnl Endowments Ltd, 1979–97; Allied Schools Council, 1980–94; Gen. Council, S Amer. Missionary Soc., 1980–96 (Chm. Selection Cttee, 1980–95); Scholarship Cttee, Ind. Schs Travel Assoc., 1982–2003; Martyrs' Meml and C of E Trust, 1983–94. Treas., Swifts Sports Trust, 1988–2004. Chm. of Govs, Riddlesworth Hall, 1980–84; Governor: Parkside, 1958–63; Beachborough, 1965–79; Bilton Grange, 1966–79; Beechwood Park, 1967–79; Monkton Combe, 1976–85; Felixstowe Coll., 1981–84; Vice President: Reed's Sch., 1991–; St Lawrence Coll., 1993– (Gov., 1977–93). Chm., E Sussex Coastal Forces Veterans Assoc., 2000–; Organiser, Sandhurst WRVS Social Car Service, 1988–2008 (Queen's Long Service Medal). IRSA 1968. *Recreations:* formerly hockey (Cambridge Blue, 1946, 1947; Kent XI (Captain), 1947–56; England Final Trial, 1950); now walking, reading. *Address:* Three Gables, Linkhill, Sandhurst, Cranbrook, Kent TN18 5PQ. *T:* (01580) 850447. *Clubs:* Hawks (Cambridge); Acrostics; Rye Golf; Band of Brothers. *Died 15 Oct. 2008.*

DREW, Peter Robert Lionel, OBE 1979; Hon. Director, World Trade Centers Association, New York, since 1992; Chairman, Taylor Woodrow Group of Companies, 1989–92; *b* 4 Sept. 1927; *s* of Sydney Herbert Drew and Edith Mary Drew (*née* Ball); *m* 1st, 1952, June Durham; one *s* one *d*; 2nd, 1966, Monica Margaret Mary Allman (marr. diss. 1993); (one *d* decd); 3rd, 1993, Wendy Ferris. *Educ:* Kingston College (Dip. Eng., later Architecture); Hendon Coll. (Dip. BIM 1959). Helicopter research, Don Juan de la Cierva enterprise, 1949; archit. studies and practice, London, 1951; started housing co., Lytham St Anne's, for Sir Lindsay Parkinson & Co., 1954; Willetts and Bernard Sunley Investment Trust, 1962–90; Taylor Woodrow Property Co., 1965, Dir, 1979–92; Founder Chm., St Katharine by the Tower Ltd (pioneer, London Docks redevelt), 1970–92; founded

World Trade Centre, London, 1973. Chm. and Vice-Pres., internat. WTCA movement, 1974–89; Pres., London World Trade Centre Assoc., 1985–89. Dir, Develt Bd, 1990–2000, Gov., 1992–2000, Museum of London; Trustee, Jubilee Walkway Trust, 1977–. Gov., Sadler's Wells, 1990–95. CCMI (CBIM 1990); FRSA. Church Warden, All Hallows by the Tower, 1972–94. Founder, Worshipful Co. of World Traders, 2000– (first Master; Guild of World Traders, 1982; Co. of World Traders, 1993); Liveryman, Painter-Stainers' Co., 1984–; Freeman, Co. of Watermen and Lightermen, 1975. *Publications:* Buy Your Own Home!, 1957; papers on world trade and urban renewal. *Recreations:* painting, sailing, public speaking. *Address:* 18 Westgate Street, Bury St Edmunds, Suffolk IP33 1QG. *T:* (01284) 725990.
Died 4 June 2007.

DRIVER, Sir Eric (William), Kt 1979; Chairman: Mersey Regional Health Authority, 1973–82; National Staff Committee, (Works), 1979–82; *b* 19 Jan. 1911; *s* of William Weale Driver and Sarah Ann Driver; *m* 1st, 1938, Winifred Bane; two *d*; 2nd, 1972, Sheila Mary Johnson. *Educ:* Strand Sch., London; King's Coll., London Univ. (BSc). FICE. Civil Engr with ICI Ltd, 1938–73, retd as Chief Civil Engr Mond Div. *Recreations:* walking, gardening, travel, bridge, chess. *Address:* Conker Tree Cottage, South Bank, Great Budworth, Cheshire CW9 6HG. *Clubs:* Budworth Sailing; Northwich Probus.
Died 4 June 2010.

DRNOVŠEK, Dr Janez; President of Slovenia, 2002–07 (Prime Minister, 1992–2002); *b* Celje, 17 May 1950. *Educ:* Univ. of Ljubljana (Master (Econs) 1981); Maribor Univ. (PhD (Econs) 1986). Economist, IGM Zagorje, 1973–75; Hd, Dept of Economy, GIP Beton Zagorje, 1975–77, 1978–82; Chief Exec., Trbovlje Br., Ljubljanska Bank, 1982–84; advr on econ. affairs, Yugoslavian Embassy, Egypt; Slovenian Rep., Collective Presidency, 1989–91, Hd of Presidency, 1989–90, former Yugoslavia; Chm., Summit of Non-Aligned, Belgrade, 1989; principal negotiator between Slovene leadership, leaders of former Yugoslavia and Yugoslav People's Army during independence negotiations, 1991; Founder, Liberal Democracy of Slovenia party, 1991 (Pres., 1992–2002). Hon. DJur Boston, 1994; Dr *hc* Illinois Wesleyan, 1999. Le prix de la Méditerranée, Crans Montana Forum, Malta, 1995; Public Leadership Award, Univ. of Minnesota, 1997; Fund for American Studies award, American Inst. of Political and Econ. Systems, Prague, 1998; Diálogo Europeo award, Spain, 1998; Ramón Trias Fargas award, Foundn Liberty and Democracy, Barcelona, 2003. Golden Order of Freedom, Slovenia, 1992; Royal Order of the Seraphin (Sweden), 2004. *Publications:* Moja resnica, 1996 (Escape from Hell); Meine Wahrheit, 1998; El laberinto de los Balcanes, 1999; numerous articles on credit control, monetary policy and internat. financial relns. *Address:* c/o Office of the President, Erjavčeva 17, 1000 Ljubljana, Slovenia.
Died 23 Feb. 2008.

DRONFIELD, Ronald; Chief Insurance Officer for National Insurance, Department of Health and Social Security, 1976–84, retired; *b* 21 Dec. 1924; *m* 1966, Marie Renie (*née* Price) (*d* 2007). *Educ:* King Edward VII Sch., Sheffield; Oriel Coll., Oxford. RN, 1943–46. Entered Min. of National Insurance, 1949; Principal Private Sec. to Minister of Pensions and Nat. Insurance, 1964–66; Cabinet Office, 1970–71. *Recreations:* reading, biography. *Address:* 8 Beechrow, Ham Common, Richmond, Surrey TW10 5HE. *Died 17 Dec. 2007.*

DRUMMOND, Sir John (Richard Gray), Kt 1995; CBE 1990; writer and broadcaster; *b* 25 Nov. 1934; *s* of late Captain A. R. G. Drummond and Esther (*née* Pickering), Perth, WA. *Educ:* Canford; Trinity Coll., Cambridge (MA History). RNVR, 1953–55. BBC Radio and Television, 1958–78, latterly as Asst Head, Music and Arts; programmes produced incl.: Tortelier Master Classes, 1964; Leeds Piano Comp., 1966 (1st Prize, Prague Fest., 1967); Diaghilev, 1967; Kathleen Ferrier, 1968; Music Now, 1969; Spirit of the Age, 1975;

The Lively Arts, 1976–78; Dir, Edinburgh Internat. Fest., 1978–83; Controller of Music, 1985–92, and of Radio 3, 1987–92, BBC; Dir, BBC Prom. Concerts, 1986–95. Dir, European Arts Fest., 1992. Pres., Kensington Soc., 1985–2001; Vice Pres., British Arts Festivals Assoc., 1993–2004 (Vice-Chm., 1981–83); Chm., Nat. Dance Co-ordinating Cttee, 1986–94; Mem. various adv. councils and cttees concerning music, theatre and dance; Governor, Royal Ballet, 1986–2000; Mem., Theatres Trust, 1989–2001 (Chm., 1998–2001). FRCM 1995; Hon. GSM 1988; Hon. RAM 1994; Hon. FRNCM 1994; Hon. FTCL 1994. FRSA. DUniv UCE, 1997; Hon. DMus Keele, 1998; Hon. DArts De Montfort, 1998. Chevalier, Légion d'Honneur (France), 1996. *Publications:* (with Joan Bakewell) A Fine and Private Place, 1977; (with N. Thompson) The Turn of Dance?, 1984; Speaking of Diaghilev, 1997; Tainted by Experience (autobiog.), 2000. *Recreations:* conversation, looking at architecture, browsing in bookshops. *Address:* 3 Caburn Court, Station Street, Lewes, E Sussex BN7 2DA. *T:* (01273) 470975. *Club:* New (Edinburgh).
Died 6 Sept. 2006.

DRUON, Maurice Samuel Roger Charles, Hon. KBE 1999 (Hon. CBE 1988); Grand Croix de la Légion d'Honneur; Commandeur des Arts et Lettres; author; Member of the French Academy since 1966 (Permanent Secretary, 1986–2000); Member: French Parliament (Paris), 1978–81; Assembly of Council of Europe, 1978–81; European Parliament, 1979–80; Franco-British Council, since 1972; *b* Paris, 23 April 1918; *s* of René Druon de Reyniac and Léonilla Jenny Samuel-Cros; *m* 1968, Madeleine Marignac. *Educ:* Lycée Michelet and Ecole des Sciences Politiques, Paris. Ecole de Cavalerie de Saumur, aspirant, 1940; joined Free French Forces, London, 1942; Attaché Commissariat à l'Intérieur et Direction de l'Information, 1943; War Correspondent, 1944–45; Lieut de réserve de cavalerie. Journalist, 1946–47; Minister for Cultural Affairs, France, 1973–74. Member: Acad. of Morocco, 1980; Athènes' Acad., 1981; Acad. Bresilienne de Lettres, 1995; Acad. Roumaine, 1996; Acad. Sciences Russie, 2006; Pres., Franco-Italian Assoc., 1985–91. Dr *hc*: York Univ., Ontario, 1987; Boston Univ.; Tirana Univ. Prix de Monaco, 1966. Commandeur du Phénix de Grèce; Grand Officer de l'Ordre de l'Honneur de Grèce; Grand Officier du Mérite de l'Ordre de Malte; Commandeur de l'Ordre de la République de Tunisie; Grand Officier du Lion du Sénégal; Grand Croix du Mérite de la République Italienne; Grand Croix de l'Aigle Aztèque du Mexique; Grand Officier Ouissam Alaouite (Morocco); Commandeur de Saint-Charles de Monaco; Grand Officier, Cruseiro del Sul (Brazil); Grand Officier, Ordre du Cèdre (Lebanon); Comdr, Ordre de Léopold (Belgium); Grand Officier, Ordre de Mai (Argentina); Grand Officier, Etoile (Romania); Commandeur du Mérite Culturel (Monaco); Grand Croix, Ordre du Christ (Portugal), 1994. *Publications:* Lettres d'un Européen, 1944; La Dernière Brigade (The Last Detachment), 1946 (publ. in England 1957); Les Grandes Familles (Prix Goncourt, 1948), La Chute des Corps, Rendez-Vous aux Enfers, 1948–51 (trilogy publ. in England under title The Curtain falls, 1959); La Volupté d'Etre (Film of Memory), 1954 (publ. in England 1955); Les Rois Maudits (The Accursed Kings), 1955–60 (six vols: The Iron King, The Strangled Queen, The Poisoned Crown, The Royal Succession, The She-Wolf of France, The Lily and the Lion, publ. in England 1956–61); Tistou les pouces verts (Tistou of the green fingers), 1957 (publ. in England 1958); Alexandre le Grand (Alexander the God), 1958 (publ. in Eng. 1960); Des Seigneurs de la Plaine- (The Black Prince and other stories), 1962 (publ. in Eng. 1962); Les Mémoires de Zeus I (The Memoirs of Zeus), 1963 (in Eng. 1964); Bernard Buffet, 1964; Paris, de César à Saint Louis (The History of Paris from Caesar to St Louis), 1964 (in Eng. 1969); Le Pouvoir, 1965; Le Bonheur des Uns, 1967; Les Mémoires de Zeus II (The Memoirs of Zeus II), 1967; L'Avenir en désarroi, 1968; Vézelay, colline éternelle, 1968; Nouvelles lettres d'un Européen, 1970; Une Eglise qui se trompe de siècle, 1972; La Parole et le Pouvoir, 1974; Oeuvres complètes, 25 vols, 1973–79; Quand un roi perd la France (Les Rois Maudits 7), 1977; Attention la France!, 1981; Réformer la Démocratie, 1982; Lettre aux Français sur leur langue et leur âme, 1994; Circonstances, 1997; Circonstances politiques, 1998 (Prix Saint Simon, 1998); Circonstances politiques II, 1999; La France aux ordres d'un cadavre, 2000 (Prix Agrippa d'Aubigné); Ordonnances pour un Etat malade, 2002; Le Franc-parler, 2003; L'Aurore vient du fond du ciel (mémoires), vol. 1, 2006; *plays:* Mégarée, 1942; Un Voyageur, 1953; La Contessa, 1962; *song:* Le Chant des Partisans (with Joseph Kessel and Anna Marly), 1943 (London). *Recreations:* riding, travel. *Address:* 81 rue de Lille, 75007 Paris, France; Abbaye de Faise, 33570 Les Artigues de Lussac, Lussac, France. *Clubs:* Savile, Garrick; Travellers (Paris).   *Died 14 April 2009.*

DU BOULAY, Prof. (Francis) Robin (Houssemayne), FBA 1980; Emeritus Professor of Mediæval History in the University of London, 1982; *b* 19 Dec. 1920; *er s* of late Philip Houssemayne Du Boulay and Mercy Tyrrell (*née* Friend); *m* 1st, 1948, Cecilia Burnell Matthews (*d* 2000); two *s* one *d*; 2nd, 2004, Margaret Mary Darby. *Educ:* Christ's Hospital; Phillip's Academy, Andover, Mass., USA; Balliol Coll., Oxford. Williams Exhibitioner at Balliol Coll., 1939; Friends' Ambulance Unit and subsequently Royal Artillery, 1940–45; MA 1947; Asst Lecturer at Bedford Coll., 1947, Lecturer, 1949; Reader in Mediæval History, in University of London, 1955, Prof., 1960–82. Hon. Sec., RHistS, 1961–65. Mem. Court, Univ. of Hull, 1992 95. *Publications:* The Register of Archbishop Bourgchier, 2 vols, 1953–55; Medieval Bexley, 1961, 2nd edn 1994; Documents Illustrative of Medieval Kentish Society, 1964; The Lordship of Canterbury, 1966; An Age of Ambition, 1970; (ed jtly) The Reign of Richard II, 1972; Germany in the later Middle Ages, 1983; Legion, and other poems, 1983; The England of Piers Plowman, 1991; various essays and papers on late medieval subjects, English and German, in specialist journals and general symposia. *Address:* 11 Munts Meadow, Weston, Herts SG4 7AE.   *Died 2 Jan. 2008.*

DUCAT-AMOS, Air Comdt Barbara Mary, CB 1974; RRC 1971; Director of Royal Air Force Nursing Services and Matron-in-Chief, Princess Mary's Royal Air Force Nursing Service, 1972–78; Nursing Sister, Medical Department, Cable and Wireless plc, 1978–85; *b* 9 Feb. 1921; *d* of late Captain G. W. Ducat-Amos, Master Mariner, and Mrs M. Ducat-Amos. *Educ:* The Abbey Sch., Reading; St Thomas's Hosp., London (The Nightingale Trng Sch.). SRN 1943; CMB Pt 1 1948. PMRAFNS, 1944–47: served in RAF Hosps, UK and Aden; further training; nursing in S Africa and SW Africa, 1948–52; rejoined PMRAFNS, 1952: served in RAF Hosps as General Ward and Theatre Sister, UK, Germany, Cyprus, Aden and Changi (Singapore); Matron 1967; Sen. Matron 1968; Principal Matron 1970. QHNS 1972–78. Vice-Pres., Girls' Venture Corps Air Cadets, 1991– (Nat. Chm., 1982–91). CStJ 1975. *Recreations:* music, theatre, travel. *Club:* Royal Air Force.   *Died 7 Jan. 2008.*

DUCK, Hywel Ivor, CMG 1998; Hon. Director-General, Council of the European Union, since 1998; Director of Fisheries, Secretariat General, Council of Ministers of European Communities, 1987–98; *b* 12 June 1933; *s* of Dr Ernest Frank Duck and Minnie Isabel Duck (*née* Peake); *m* 1st, 1963, Theodora Mary Fitzgerald Mugnaini (*née* Creighton) (marr. diss. 1975); four step *d*; 2nd, 1980, Dr Barbara Elisabeth Huwe (*d* 1994); one *s* one *d*; 3rd, 2002, Patricia Anne-Louise de Graeve. *Educ:* King's School, Canterbury; Trinity College, Cambridge (MA); Diplôme d'Etudes Supérieures Européennes, Nancy. ARCO 2002. Called to the Bar, Gray's Inn, 1956. Foreign Office, 1956; served Warsaw, FO, Cairo, Khartoum, Damascus; Second later First Sec., Bonn, 1964; DSAO, later FCO, 1968; Consul (Commercial), Zürich and Dep. Dir, British Export Promotion in Switzerland, 1970–73;

Head of Div., Secretariat Gen., Council of Ministers, EC, 1973–75; Dir of Ops and Translation, 1975–84; Dir, Directorate-Gen. for Agriculture and Fisheries, 1984–87. *Recreation:* classical music. *Club:* Oxford and Cambridge.   *Died 30 Oct. 2009.*

DUDLEY, Prof. Norman Alfred, CBE 1977; FREng; Lucas Professor of Engineering Production, University of Birmingham, 1959–80, Emeritus Professor, 1981; *b* 29 Feb. 1916; *s* of Alfred Dudley; *m* 1940, Hilda Florence, *d* of John Miles; one *s* two *d*. *Educ:* Kings Norton Grammar Sch.; Birmingham Coll. of Technology; BSc London; PhD Birmingham. Nat. Service, 1943–46 (Medal). Industrial training and appts: H. W. Ward & Co. Ltd, 1932–39; Imperial Typewriter Co. Ltd, 1940–45; Technical Coll. Lectr, 1945–52; Sen. Lectr, Wolverhampton and Staffs, 1948–52; University of Birmingham: Lectr in Enrg Prodn, 1952; Reader, 1956; Hd, Dept of Engrg Prodn and Dir, Lucas Inst. of Engrg Prodn, 1955–80; Chm., Manufacturing Processes Div., Birmingham Univ. Inst. for Advanced Studies in Engineering Sciences, 1965 68. Director: Birmingham Productivity Services Ltd; West Midlands Low Cost Automation Centre. Member: SRC Manufacturing Technol. Cttee; SRC and DoI Teaching Company Cttee, 1977–80. Chm., Cttee of Hds of Univ. Depts of Production Studies, 1970–80. Governor: Dudley and Staffs Tech. Coll., and Walsall and Staffs Tech. Coll., 1955–60; Letchworth Coll. of Technol., 1964–66. Member: Council, West Midlands Productivity Assoc.; Council, Internat. Univ. Contact for Management Education, 1957; UK Delegn to UNCSAT Geneva, 1963; W Midlands Economic Planning Council, 1970–78; British Council Mission to Bulgaria, 1971; Adv Panel on Economic Develt, West Midlands Metropolitan CC, 1976–77; Council, Nat. Materials Handling Centre. Institution of Production Engineers: Mem. Council, 1959–61; Chm., Res. Cttee, 1965–66; J. D. Scaife Silver Medal, 1958; Viscount Nuffield Meml Lectr, 1969. Pres., Midlands Operational Research Soc., 1966–80. Mem., Ergonomics Res. Soc.; Emeritus Mem., Internat. Inst. of Production Engrg Research. FREng (FEng 1981); Fellow, World Acad. of Productivity Sci., 2000; FCMI; Hon. FIMgE; Hon. FIEE. Hon. Member: Japanese Industrial Management Assoc.; Internat. Foundn of Prodn Research. Hon. DTech Loughborough, 1981. Editor, International Journal of Production Research, 1961–80. Norman Dudley Lect. inaugurated at 11th Internat. Conf. on Prodn Res., China, 1991; Norman Dudley award estab. by Internat. Jl of Production Res., 1996. Granted armorial bearings, 1994. *Publications:* Work Measurement; Some Research Studies, 1968; (co-ed) Production and Industrial Systems, 1978; The Bulstrodes alias Bolstridges of Bedworth, 1991; The Dudleys of Northwich Hundred, 1994; various papers on Engineering Production. *Address:* 37 Abbots Close, Knowle, Solihull, W Midlands B93 9PP. *T:* (01564) 775976.   *Died 9 Feb. 2006.*

DUKE, Neville Frederick, DSO 1943; OBE 1953; DFC and two Bars, 1942, 1943, 1944; AFC 1948; Managing Director, Duke Aviation; Technical Adviser and Consultant Test Pilot; *b* 11 Jan. 1922; *s* of Frederick and Jane Duke, Tonbridge, Kent; *m* 1947, Gwendoline Dorothy Fellows. *Educ:* Convent of St Mary, and Judd Sch., Tonbridge, Kent. Joined Royal Air Force (cadet), 1940, training period, 1940; 92 Fighter Sqdn, Biggin Hill, 1941; Desert Air Force: 112 Fighter Sqdn, Western Desert, 1941–42, 92 Fighter Sqdn, Western Desert, 1943, Chief Flying Instructor, 73 Operational Training Unit, Egypt, 1943–44, Commanding 145 Sqdn Italy (Fighter), 1944, 28 enemy aircraft destroyed. Hawker Aircraft Ltd test flying, 1945; Empire Test Pilots Sch., 1946; RAF high speed flight, 1946 (world speed record); test flying Aeroplane and Armament Experimental Estab., Boscombe Down, 1947–48; resigned from RAF as Sqdn Leader, 1948; test flying Hawker Aircraft Ltd, 1948; Commanding 615 (County of Surrey) Sqdn, Royal Auxiliary Air Force, Biggin Hill, 1950; Chief Test Pilot, Hawker Aircraft Ltd, 1951–56 (Asst Chief, 1948–51).

FRSA 1970; FRAeS 1993 (ARAeS 1948). Member: RAF Escaping Soc.; United Service & Royal Aero Club (Associate); FAA Officers Assoc.; Hon. Mem., FAA Sqdn. Hon. Fellow, Soc. of Experimental Test Pilots, 1991. Hon. Pres., Tangmere Mil. Aviation Mus., 1988. World records: London-Rome, 1948; London-Karachi, 1949; London-Cairo, 1950; World Speed Record, Sept. 1953; Closed Circuit World Speed Record, 1953. Gold Medal Royal Danish Aero Club, 1953; Gold Medal, Royal Aero Club, 1954; two De la Vaux Medals, FAI, 1954; Segrave Trophy, 1954; Queen's Commendation, 1955; Jeffrey Quill Medal, Air League, 2002; Award of Honour, GAPAN, 2003. MC (Czech) 1946. *Publications:* Sound Barrier, 1953; Test Pilot, 1953; Book of Flying, 1954; Book of Flight, 1958; The Crowded Sky (anthology), 1959; The War Diaries of Neville Duke, 1995. *Recreations:* sporting flying, yachting. *Clubs:* Royal Air Force; Royal Cruising, Royal Naval Sailing, Royal Lymington Yacht. *Died 7 April 2007.*

DUKES, Justin Paul; Chairman, ECIC Management (formerly European Communications Industries Consortium), since 1990; *b* 19 Sept. 1941; *s* of late John Alexander Dukes and Agnes Dukes; *m* 1990, Jane Macallister; one *s* one *d*, and two *s* one *d* by a previous marriage. *Educ:* King's Coll., Univ. of Durham. Dir, Financial Times Ltd, 1975–81; Chm., Financial Times (Europe) Ltd, 1978–81; Man. Dir, Channel Four TV Co., 1981–88; Chief-Exec., Galileo Co., 1988–89. Chm., Risk Avert, 2005–; Dir, Herald Investment Trust plc, 1994–2005. Pres., Inst. of Information Scientists, 1982–83; Mem. Council, Foundn for Management Educn, 1979–90. Mem., British Screen Adv. Council, 1986–88. Trustee, Internat. Inst. of Communications, 1986–91. FRTS 1986; FRSA 1986; CCMI (CBIM 1988). Chevalier, Ordre des Arts et des Lettres (France), 1988. *Recreations:* changing institutions, walking. *Died 1 Oct. 2008.*

DUNBAR, Ian Malcolm, CB 1993; Director of Inmate Administration, Prison Service, Home Office, 1990–94; *b* 6 Jan. 1934; *s* of Thomas Dunbar and Rose (*née* Hook); *m* 1966, Sally Ann Hendrickson; two *s* one *d*. *Educ:* Buckhurst Hill County High Sch.; Keele Univ.; Reed Coll., Portland, USA; LSE. Joined Prison Service, 1959; Leyhill Prison, 1960; Prison Service Coll., 1965; Dep. Gov., Long Lartin, 1970; Gov., Usk Borstal and Detention Centre, 1972; Prison Dept 4 Div., Home Office, 1974; Governor: Feltham Borstal, 1978; Wakefield Prison, 1979; Wormwood Scrubs, 1983; seconded to HM Inspectorate of Prisons, 1985; Regl Dir, SW Reg., Prison Service, 1985. NI Sentence Review Comr, 1998– (NI Transitional Life Sentence Review Comr, 2001–02). *Publications:* A Sense of Direction, 1985; (with A. Langdon) Tough Justice: sentencing and penal policies in the 1990s, 1998. *Recreations:* bee-keeping, gardening, photography, walking, reading. *Died 21 May 2010.*

DUNCAN, David Francis; HM Diplomatic Service, retired; *b* 22 Feb. 1923; *s* of late Brig. William Edmonstone Duncan, CVO, DSO, MC, and Magdalene Emily Duncan (*née* Renny-Tailyour). *Educ:* Eton; Trinity Coll., Cambridge. Served War, RA, 1941–46 (despatches). Entered Foreign (later Diplomatic) Service, 1949; Foreign Office, 1949–52; Bogotá, 1952–54; UK Delegn to ECSC, Luxembourg, 1954–55; FO, 1955–58; Baghdad, 1958; Ankara, 1958–60; FO, 1960–62; Quito, 1962–65; Phnom Penh, 1965 (as Chargé d'Affaires); FO (later Foreign and Commonwealth Office), 1965–70; Islamabad, 1970–71; Counsellor, UK Delegn to Geneva Disarm. Conf., 1971–74; Ambassador to Nicaragua, 1974–76; retired 1976. *Recreations:* walking, photography, travel. *Address:* 133 Rivermead Court, Ranelagh Gardens, SW6 3SE. *T:* (020) 7736 1576. *Died 31 Aug. 2007.*

DUNCAN, George Alexander; Fellow Emeritus of Trinity College, Dublin, since 1967; *b* 15 May 1902; *s* of Alexander Duncan and Elizabeth Linn; *m* 1932, Eileen Stone, MSc (*d* 1997), *d* of William Henry Stone and Sarah Copeland; one *d*. *Educ:* Ballymena Academy; Campbell

Coll., Belfast; Trinity Coll., Dublin; University of North Carolina. BA, LLB 1923, MA 1926; Research Fellow on the Laura Spelman Rockefeller Memorial Foundation. 1924–25; Prof. of Political Economy in the University of Dublin, 1934–67; Registrar of TCD, 1951–52, and Bursar, 1952–57; Pro-Chancellor, Univ. of Dublin, 1965–72. Leverhulme Res. Fellow, 1950; Vis. Fellow, Princeton Univ., 1963–64. Mem. of IFS Commissions of Inquiry into Banking, Currency and Credit, 1934–38; Agriculture, 1939; Emigration and Population, 1948. Planning Officer (temp.) in Ministry of Production, London, 1943–45; Economic Adviser to British Nat. Cttee of Internat. Chambers of Commerce, 1941–47. Past Vice-Pres., Royal Dublin Society; Life Mem., Mont Pelerin Soc.; Founder Mem., Edmund Burke Inst., Dublin, 1993. Formerly Member: Irish National Productivity Cttee; Council Irish Management Inst.; Exec. Bd, Dublin Economic Research Inst.; Internat. Inst. of Statistics; Bd of Visitors, Nat. Mus. of Ireland. *Publications:* numerous papers in the economic periodicals. *Recreations:* travel, walking. *Address:* 7 Braemor Park, Churchtown, Dublin 14, Ireland. *T:* (1) 4922442. *Died 14 Jan. 2006.*

DUNCAN, John Spenser Ritchie, CMG 1967; MBE 1953; HM Diplomatic Service, retired; High Commissioner in the Bahamas, 1978–81; *b* 26 July 1921; *s* of late Rev. J. H. Duncan, DD and H. P. Duncan (*née* Ritchie); *m* 1950, Sheila Conacher (*d* 2000), MB, ChB, DObstRCOG; one *d*. *Educ:* George Watson's Boys' Coll.; Glasgow Acad.; Dundee High Sch.; Edinburgh Univ. Entered Sudan Political Service, 1941. Served in HM Forces, 1941–43. Private Sec. to Governor-Gen. of the Sudan, 1954; Dep. Adviser to Governor-Gen. on Constitutional and External Affairs, 1955; appointed to Foreign (subseq. Diplomatic) Service, 1956; seconded to Joint Services Staff Coll., 1957; Political Agent, Doha, 1958; Dep. Dir-Gen., British Information Services, New York, 1959–63; Consul-Gen., Muscat, 1963–65; Head of Personnel Dept, Diplomatic Service, 1966–68; Minister, British High Commn, Canberra, 1969–71; High Comr, Zambia, 1971–74; Ambassador to Morocco, 1975–78. *Publications:* The Sudan: A Record of Achievement, 1952; The Sudan's Path to Independence, 1957. *Address:* St Luke's Hospital, Latimer Road, Oxford OX3 7PF. *Died 12 Sept. 2006.*

DUNLOP, Rear-Adm. Colin Charles Harrison, CB 1972; CBE 1963; *b* 4 March 1918; *s* of late Engr Rear-Adm. S. H. Dunlop, CB; *m* 1st, 1941, Moyra Patricia O'Brien Gorges (*d* 1991); two *s* (and one *s* decd); 2nd, 1995, Comdt Elizabeth Craig-McFeely, CB. *Educ:* Marlborough Coll. Joined RN, 1935; served War of 1939–45 at sea in HM Ships Kent, Valiant, Diadem and Orion; subseq. HMS Sheffield, 1957–59; Sec. to 1st Sea Lord, 1960–63; comd HMS Pembroke, 1964–66; Programme Evaluation Gp, MoD, 1966–68; Director, Defence Policy (A), MoD, 1968–69; Comdr, British Navy Staff, Washington, 1969–71; Chief Naval Supply and Secretariat Officer, 1970–74; Flag Officer, Medway, and Port Adm., Chatham, 1971–74, retd 1974. Director General: Cable TV Assoc., 1974–83; Nat. TV Rental Assoc., 1974–83. DL Kent 1976. *Recreations:* cricket, country pursuits. *Address:* 1 The Gatehouse, Elliscombe Park, Holton, Wincanton, Som BA9 8EA. *T:* (01963) 31534. *Clubs:* Army and Navy; MCC, I Zingari, Free Foresters, RN Cricket, Band of Brothers. *Died 8 March 2009.*

DUNN, Air Marshal Sir Eric (Clive), KBE 1983; CB 1981; BEM 1951; *b* 27 Nov. 1927; *s* of late W. E. and K. M. Dunn; *m* 1951, Margaret Gray; three *d*. *Educ:* Bridlington Sch. CEng, FRAeS. RAF aircraft apprentice, 1944–47; commnd Engr Br., 1954; Staff Coll., 1964; Jt Services Staff Coll., 1967; Sen. Engrg Officer, RAF Boulmer, 1968; MoD, 1969–70; Comd Electrical Engr, NEAF, 1971–72; Dir of Engrg Policy (RAF), 1973–75; RCDS, 1976; AO Wales, and Stn Comdr RAF St Athan, 1977; Air Officer Maintenance. RAF Support Comd, 1977–81; Air Officer Engineering,

HQ Strike Comd, 1981–83; Chief Engr, RAF, 1983–86. Dir, Hellermann Deutsch, 1986–90; Engrg Consultant, Dowty Gp, 1986–90. *Club:* Royal Air Force. *Died 16 July 2008.*

DUNN, Rt Rev. Kevin John, JCD; Bishop (RC) of Hexham and Newcastle, since 2004; *b* 9 July 1950; *s* of Stephen and Kathline Dunn. *Educ:* Oscott Coll., Birmingham; Pontifical Univ. of St Thomas, Rome (JCD 1992). Ordained priest, 1976; Chaplain to Caribbean Community, Birmingham, 1980–89; Parish Priest: Our Lady's, Stoke-on-Trent, 1989–90; St Austin's, Stafford, 1993–2002; Episcopal Vicar for Religious, Birmingham Archdio., Wolverhampton, Walsall, Black Country, and Worcs, 2002–04. *Recreations:* walking, golf, reading. *Address:* Bishop's House, 800 West Road, Newcastle upon Tyne NE5 2BJ. *T:* (0191) 228 0003; *e-mail:* bishop@rcdhn.org.uk. *Died 1 March 2008.*

DUNNILL, Prof. Peter, OBE 1999; DSc, PhD, FREng, FIChemE; Professor of Biochemical Engineering, University College London, since 1984; Chairman, The Advanced Centre for Biochemical Engineering, since 2001 (Director, 1991–2001); *b* 20 May 1938; *s* of Eric and Marjorie Dunnill; *m* 1962, Patricia Mary Lievesley; one *s*. *Educ:* University College London (BSc; DSc 1978; Fellow, 1991). Royal Instn MRC staff, 1963–64; Lectr, 1964–79, Reader, 1979–84, UCL. Member: Internat. Cttee on Econ. and Applied Microbiol., 1974–82; Scientific and Technical Cttee, Central Lab. of Nat. Blood Transfusion Service, 1978–82; Biotechnol. Directorate Management Cttee, SERC, 1982–88, 1993–94; Biotechnol. Adv. Gp to Heads of Res. Councils, 1987–90; Biotechnol. Jt Adv. Bd, 1989–92; BBSRC, 1994–96; Steering Gp, BioSci. Innovation and Growth Team, DTI and DoII, 2002–03. FREng (FEng 1985). Donald Medal, IChemE, 1995; Heatley Medal, Biochem. Soc., 1997. *Publications: c* 200 pubns in learned jls. *Recreation:* music. *Address:* The Advanced Centre for Biochemical Engineering, University College London, Torrington Place, WC1E 7JE. *T:* (020) 7679 7031. *Died 10 Aug. 2009.*

DUNNING, Prof. John Harry, OBE 2008; PhD; Emeritus Professor of International Business, University of Reading, since 1992; State of New Jersey Professor of International Business, Rutgers University, US, 1989–2002; *b* 26 June 1927; *m* 1st, 1948, Ida Teresa Bellamy (marr. diss. 1975); one *s*; 2nd, 1975, Christine Mary Brown. *Educ:* Lower Sch. of John Lyon, Harrow; University Coll. London (BSc (Econ); PhD). Sub-Lieut, RNVR, 1945–48. Research Asst, University Coll. London, 1951–52; Lectr and Sen. Lectr, Univ. of Southampton, 1952–64; University of Reading: Prof. of Economics, 1964–74; Hd of Dept of Economics, 1964–87; Esmée Fairbairn Prof. of Internat. Investment and Business Studies, 1975–87; ICI Res. Prof. of Internat. Business, 1988–92. Visiting Professor: Univ. of Western Ontario, Canada, 1968–69; Univ. of California (Berkeley), 1968, 1987; Boston Univ., USA, 1976; Stockholm Sch. of Economics, 1978; HEC, Univ. of Montreal, Canada, 1980; Walker-Ames Prof., Univ. of Washington, Seattle, 1981; Seth Boyden Distinguished Prof., Rutgers Univ., 1987; Hon. Prof., Univ. of Internat. Business and Econs, Beijing, 1995. Consultant to UN, 1974–; OECD, 1975–; and EC, 1985–. Member: SE Economic Planning Council, 1966–68; Chemicals EDC, 1968–77; UN Study Gp on Multinational Corps, 1973–74. Chm., Economists Advisory Gp Ltd, 1975–2001. Pres., Internat. Trade Assoc., 1994. Fellow, Acad. of Internat. Business (Pres., 1987–88). Hon. Dr: Uppsala, 1975; Universidad Autónoma de Madrid, 1990; Antwerp, 1997; Chinese Culture Univ., Taiwan, 2007; Lund, 2007; Reading, 2008. *Publications:* American Investment in British Manufacturing Industry, 1958, 2nd edn 1998; (with C. J. Thomas) British Industry, 1963; Economic Planning and Town Expansion, 1963; Studies in International Investment, 1970; (ed) The Multinational Enterprise, 1971; (with E. V. Morgan) An Economic Study of the City of London, 1971; (ed) International

Investment, 1972; (ed) Economic Analysis and the Multinational Enterprise, 1974; US Industry in Britain, 1976; (with T. Houston) UK Industry Abroad, 1976; International Production and the Multinational Enterprise, 1981; (ed with J. Black) International Capital Movements, 1982; (with J. Stopford) Multinationals: Company Performance and Global Trends, 1983; (with R. D. Pearce) The World's Largest Industrial Companies 1962–83, 1985; (ed) Multinational Enterprises, Economic Structure and International Competitiveness, 1985; Japanese Participation in British Industry, 1986; (with J. Cantwell) World Directory of Statistics on International Direct Investment and Production, 1987; Explaining International Production, 1988; Multinationals, Technology and Competitiveness, 1988; (ed with A. Webster) Structural Change in the World Economy, 1990; Multinational Enterprises and the Global Economy, 1993, new and rev. edn (with S. Lundan) 2008; The Globalization of Business, 1993; (ed with R. Narula) Foreign Direct Investment and Governments, 1996; (ed with K. Hamdani) The New Globalism and Developing Countries, 1997; Alliance Capitalism and Global Business, 1997; (ed) Governments, Globalisation and International Business, 1997; (ed) Globalization, Trade and Foreign Direct Investment, 1998; (ed) Regions, Globalisation and the Knowledge Based Economy, 2000; Global Capitalism at Bay, 2001; Theories and Paradigms of International Business Activity, 2002; Global Capitalism FDI and Competitiveness, 2002; (ed) Making Globalisation Good, 2003; (with R. Narula) Multinationals and Industrial Competitiveness: a new agenda, 2004; (ed with P. Gugler) Foreign Direct Investment, Location and Competitiveness, 2008; Seasons of a Scholar, 2008; numerous articles in learned and professional jls. *Address:* School of Business, University of Reading, Whiteknights Park, Reading, Berks RG6 2AA; *e-mail:* jill.mturner@virgin.net. *Club:* Athenæum. *Died 29 Jan. 2009.*

DUNSTER, (Herbert) John, CB 1979; consultant in radiation protection; *b* 27 July 1922; *s* of Herbert and Olive Grace Dunster; *m* 1945, Rosemary Elizabeth, *d* of P. J. Gallagher; one *s* three *d*. *Educ:* University Coll. Sch.; Imperial College of Science and Technology (ARCS, BSc). FSRP 1988. Scientist, UK Atomic Energy Authority, 1946–71; Asst Dir, Nat. Radiological Protection Bd, 1971–76; Dep. Dir Gen., HSE, 1976–82; Dir, NRPB, 1982–87. Member: Internat. Commn on Radiological Protection, 1977–97 (Emer. Mem., 1997); Sci. and Tech. Cttee, Euratom, 1982–93; Sci. Adv. Cttee, IAEA, 1982–87. *Publications:* numerous papers in technical jls. *Recreation:* music. *Address:* 15A Wood Street, Wallingford, Oxon OX10 0AY. *T:* (01491) 825244; *e-mail:* hjohn.dunster@virgin.net. *Died 23 April 2006.*

DUNWOODY, Gwyneth (Patricia); MP (Lab) Crewe and Nantwich, since 1983 (Crewe, Feb. 1974–1983); *b* 12 Dec. 1930; *d* of late Morgan Phillips and Baroness Phillips; *m* 1954, Dr John Elliott Orr Dunwoody, CBE (marr. diss. 1975; he *d* 2006); two *s* one *d*. MP (Lab) Exeter, 1966–70; Parly Sec. to BoT, 1967–70; Mem., European Parlt, 1975–79; Front Bench Spokesman on Foreign Affairs, 1980, on Health Service, 1980–83, on Transport, 1984–85; Parly Campaign Co-ordinator, 1983–84; Chm., Select Cttee on Transport, 1997–. Member: Labour Party NEC, 1981–88; Chairmen's Panel, 1992–2001. Life Pres., Labour Friends of Israel, 1995– (Chm., 1988–93; Pres., 1993–95); Vice-Pres., Socialist Internat. Women, 1986–92. Dir, Film Production Assoc. of GB, 1970–74. *Address:* c/o House of Commons, SW1A 0AA. *Died 17 April 2008.*

DUNWOODY, Dr John (Elliott Orr), CBE 1986; general practitioner; Vice-Chairman, Merton, Sutton and Wandsworth Local Medical Committee, since 1996; *b* 3 June 1929; *s* of Dr W. O. and late Mrs F. J. Dunwoody; *m* 1st, 1954, Gwyneth Patricia Phillips (marr. diss. 1975); two *s* one *d*; 2nd, 1979, Evelyn Louise (*née* Borner). *Educ:* St Paul's Sch.; King's Coll., London Univ.; Westminster Hosp. Med. Sch. MB, BS London; MRCS, LRCP 1954.

House Surgeon, Westminster (Gordon) Hosp., 1954; House Physician, Royal Berks Hosp., 1954–55; Sen. House Physician, Newton Abbot Hosp., 1955–56; Family Doctor and Medical Officer, Totnes District Hosp., 1956–66; MO, Staff Health Service, St George's Hosp., 1976–77. MP (Lab) Falmouth and Camborne, 1966–70; Parly Under-Sec., Dept of Health and Social Security, 1969–70. Vice-Chm., 1974–77, Chm., 1977–82, Kensington, Chelsea and Westminster AHA (T); Chm., Bloomsbury DHA, 1982–90. Member: Exec. Cttee, British Council, 1967–69; Council, Westminster Med. Sch., 1974–82; (co-opted) Social Services Cttee, Westminster City Council, 1975–78; Nat. Exec. Council, FPA, 1979–87 (Dep. Chm., 1980, Chm., 1981–87). Council Mem., UCL, 1982–90. Hon. Dir, Action on Smoking and Health, 1971–73. Governor, Pimlico Sch., 1972–75. *Publications:* (jtly) A Birth Control Plan for Britain, 1972. *Recreations:* travel, cooking. *Address:* 9 Cautley Avenue, SW4 9HX. *T:* (020) 8673 7471.
Died 26 Jan. 2006.

DUPREE, Sir Peter, 5th Bt *cr* 1921; *b* 20 Feb. 1924; *s* of Sir Victor Dupree, 4th Bt and of Margaret Cross; *S* father, 1976, but his name does not appear on the Official Roll of the Baronetage; *m* 1947, Joan (*d* 2000), *d* of late Captain James Desborough Hunt. *Heir: cousin* Thomas William James David Dupree, *b* 5 Feb. 1930.
Died 12 Sept. 2006.

DURIE, Thomas Peter, OBE 2003 (MBE 1958); GM 1951; Chairman, United Bristol Healthcare NHS Trust, 1991–94; *b* 1 Jan. 1926; *s* of Col Thomas Edwin Durie, DSO, MC, late RA and Madeleine Louise Durie; *m* 1st, 1952, Pamela Mary Bowlby (*d* 1982); one *s* one *d*; 2nd, 1983, Constance Christina Mary Linton. *Educ:* Fettes Coll.; Queen's Univ., Belfast. Commissioned RA 1945, served with RHA and Airborne Forces, India, Palestine, Cyprus, BAOR; Lt Col Directing Staff, Staff Coll., Camberley; retired 1964; Courage Ltd, 1964–86 (Main Bd Dir and Group Asst Man. Dir, 1974); Chm., Bristol & Weston DHA, 1986–90. University of Bristol: Mem. Court and Council, 1982–2001; Chm., Buildings Cttee, 1992–96; Pro-Chancellor, 1994–2004. Master, Soc. of Merchant Venturers, 1988–89. DL Avon, 1992–96, Somerset, 1996–2002. Hon. LLD Bristol, 2002. *Recreations:* gardening, music, ski-ing, tennis. *Address:* 2 Bells Walk, Wrington, Somerset BS40 5PU. *Club:* Army and Navy.
Died 2 March 2010.

DUTTON, James Macfarlane; HM Diplomatic Service, retired; *b* 3 June 1922; *s* of late H. St J. Dutton and Mrs E. B. Dutton; *m* 1958, Jean Mary McAvoy; one *s*. *Educ:* Winchester Coll.; Balliol Coll., Oxford. Dominions Office, 1944–46; Private Sec. to Permanent Under Sec., 1945; Dublin, 1946–48; CRO, 1948–50; Asst Private Sec. to Sec. of State, 1948; 2nd Sec., New Delhi, 1950–53; CRO, 1953–55; 1st Sec., Dacca and Karachi, 1955–58, Canberra, 1958–62; Head of Constitutional and Protocol Dept, CRO, 1963–65; Canadian Nat. Defence Coll., 1965–66; Dep. High Comr and Counsellor

(Commercial), Colombo, 1966–70; Head of Rhodesia Econ. Dept, FCO, 1970–72; attached CSD, 1972–73; seconded to: British Electrical & Allied Manufacturers Assoc. (Dir, Overseas Affairs), 1973–74; Wilton Park and European Discussion Centre, 1974–75; Consul-Gen., Gothenburg, 1975–78. *Recreations:* golf, trout-fishing. *Address:* Cockerhurst, Tyrrells Wood, Leatherhead, Surrey KT22 8QH.
Died 20 June 2006.

DUTTON, Reginald David Ley; *b* 20 Aug. 1916; *m* 1951, Pamela Jean (*née* Harrison); two *s* one *d*. *Educ:* Magdalen Coll. Sch., Oxford. Joined OUP; subseq. joined leading British advertising agency, London Press Exchange (later Lopex plc), 1937. During War of 1939–45 served in Royal Navy. Returned to agency after his service; there, he worked on many of major accounts; Dir, 1954; Man. Dir and Chief Exec., 1964–71; Chm., 1971–76; retired 1976. Pres. Inst. Practitioners in Advertising, 1969–71; Chm., Jt Ind. Council for TV Advertising Research, 1973–75; Mem. Council, BIM, 1970–74; FIPA 1960. Councillor, Canterbury CC, 1976–77. *Recreations:* fishing, amateur radio. *Address:* Butts Fold, Stalham Road, Hoveton, Norwich NR12 8DU. *T:* (01603) 783145.
Died 2 Nov. 2006.

DYNEVOR, 9th Baron *cr* 1780; **Richard Charles Uryan Rhys;** *b* 19 June 1935; *s* of 8th Baron Dynevor, CBE, MC; *S* father, 1962; *m* 1959, Lucy (marr. diss. 1978), *d* of Sir John Rothenstein, CBE; one *s* three *d*. *Educ:* Eton; Magdalene Coll., Cambridge. Patron of the arts: theatre producer; founded Dynevor Fest., Newton House, 1966; publisher, Black Raven Press. *Heir: s* Hon. Hugo Griffith Uryan Rhys, *b* 19 Nov. 1966.
Died 12 Nov. 2008.

DYSON, Prof. Roger Franklin, PhD; Honorary Professor, since 1989, and Director of Clinical Management Unit Centre for Health Planning and Management, 1989–2001, Keele University; *b* 30 Jan. 1940; *s* of John Franklin Dyson and Edith Mary Jobson; *m* 1st, 1964, Anne Greaves (marr. diss. 1994); one *s* one *d*; 2nd, 1995, Ann Frances Naylor, *d* of late Alfred Worsfold and Mabel (*née* Burt). *Educ:* Counthill Grammar Sch., Oldham; Keele Univ. (BA Hons 1st cl. Hist. and Econs, 1962); Leeds Univ. (PhD 1971). Asst Lectr, 1963, Lectr, 1966, Adult Educn Dept, Leeds Univ.; Dep. Dir and Sen. Lectr in Ind. Relations, Adult Educn Dept, 1974, Prof. and Dir of Adult and Continuing Educn, 1976–89, Keele Univ. Consultant Advr on Ind. Relations to Sec. of State, DHSS, 1979–81. Chm., N Staffs HA, 1982–86. Mem. (C) Essex CC, 2001– (Chm., Health Overview and Scrutiny Cttee, 2003–05; Dep. Cabinet Mem. for Adult Social Care, 2005–). Mem., RSocMed. Hon. MRCP 1997. Editor, Health Manpower Management (formerly Health Services Manpower Review), 1975–91. Gold Medal, RCAnaes, 2000. *Publications:* (ed jtly) Management for Hospital Doctors, 1994; contribs to BMJ. *Recreations:* gardening, gastronomy. *Address:* 4 Huskards, Fryerning, Ingatestone, Essex CM4 0HR. *T:* (01277) 354841. *Club:* Carlton.
Died 26 May 2006.

E

EAMES, Eric James, MBE 2010; JP; Lord Mayor of Birmingham, 1974–75, Deputy Lord Mayor, 1975–76; *b* Highley, Shropshire, 13 April 1917; *s* of George Eames; *m* (marr. diss.); one *s*. *Educ:* Highley Sch., Highley, Shropshire. Member (Lab): Birmingham City Council, 1949–92; W Midlands CC, 1974–77. Mem., Governing Board, Internat. Center for Information Co-operation and Relationship among World's Major Cities. Dir, Assoc. for Neighbourhood Democracy (formerly Councils), 1992–. Governor, Harper Adams Agricl Coll., 1953–90. JP Birmingham, 1972. *Recreations:* gardening, do-it-yourself enthusiast. *Died 10 April 2010.*

EARLE, Ion, TD 1946; Assistant to the Directors, Clive Discount Co., 1973–81, retired; *b* 12 April 1916; *s* of late Stephen Earle and of E. Beatrice Earle (*née* Blair White); *m* 1946, Elizabeth Stevens, US citizen; one *s* one *d*. *Educ:* Stowe Sch.; University Coll., Oxford; Université de Grenoble. Federation of British Industries, Birmingham, 1938–51, London, 1952–60; Chief Executive, Export Council for Europe, 1960–64; Dep. Dir-Gen., BNEC, 1965–71 (Dir, 1964–65); Head of Personnel, Kleinwort Benson Ltd, 1972. Royal Artillery, TA, 1939–46 (Major). *Recreations:* golf, gardening. *Address:* Apartment 23, Strand Court, Harsfold Road, Rustington, West Sussex BN16 2NT. *T:* (01903) 773350. *Died 1 March 2006.*

EARNSHAW, (Thomas) Roy, CBE 1978 (OBE 1971); Director and General Manager of Division, TBA Industrial Products Ltd, Rochdale, 1966–76; *b* 27 Feb. 1917; *s* of Godfrey Earnshaw and Edith Annie (*née* Perry); *m* 1953, Edith Rushworth; two *d*. *Educ:* Marlborough Coll., Liverpool. MICS. Served War, Army, 1940–46: Major Lancs Fusiliers. Shipbroking, Liverpool, 1933–39; appts with subsid. cos of Turner & Newall Ltd: Turner Brothers Asbestos Co. Ltd, Rochdale (mainly Export Sales Manager), 1939–40 and 1946–53; Dir, AM&FM Ltd, Bombay, 1954–59; Export Dir, Ferodo Ltd, Chapel-en-le-Frith, 1959–66. British Overseas Trade Board: Mem. Adv. Council, 1975–82; Export Year Advr, 1976–77; Export United Advr, 1978–83. Director: Actair Holdings Ltd, 1979–83; Actair Internat. Ltd, 1979–83; Unico Finance Ltd, 1979–81. Formerly: Pres., Rochdale Chamber of Commerce; Chm., NW Region Chambers of Commerce; UK Delegate to European Chambers of Commerce. London Economic Adviser to Merseyside CC, 1980–82. Vis. Fellow, Henley Management Coll. (formerly ASC), 1981–90. Chm, Henley Crime Prevention Panel, 1992–94; Mem., Bd of Managers, Henley YMCA, 1989–91; Sec., Henley Wildlife Gp, 1994–99. *Publications:* Glad Hearts in Export Year, 1991. *Recreations:* gardening, oil painting, hill walking, cycling. *Died 19 Dec. 2008.*

EASON, Anthony Gordon, CBE 1995; JP; Executive Director, Hong Kong Experts Consultancy Co. Ltd, 1997–98; *b* 30 May 1938; *s* of Aubrey Eason and Helen Eason (*née* Hajj); *m* 1962, Teresa Wong; two *d*. *Educ:* Chatham House Grammar Sch., Ramsgate; RMA, Sandhurst. Served RA, 1959–62. Hong Kong Civil Service: Exec. Officer, 1962–68; Admin. Service, 1968–89; Dir, Buildings and Lands, 1989–92; Sec. for Planning, Envmt and Lands, 1992–95. Mem., HK Housing Soc., 1989–. JP Hong Kong, 1996. *Recreations:* reading, walking, writing. *Died 28 Dec. 2009.*

EASON, Henry, CBE 1967; JP; a Vice-President of the Institute of Bankers, 1969–75, and Consultant with special reference to overseas relationships, 1971–74 (Secretary-General, 1959–71); *b* 12 April 1910; *s* of late H. Eason and F. J. Eason; *m* 1939 (at Hexham Abbey), Isobel (*d* 1992), *d* of late Wm and Dorothy Stevenson; one *s* one *d* (and one

d decd). *Educ:* Yarm (Schol.); King's Coll., University of Durham (BCom with distinction). Barrister-at-law, Gray's Inn. Served Lloyds Bank until 1939; Asst Sec., Institute of Bankers, 1939. Served War of 1939–45 and until 1946, with Royal Air Force (Wing Commander, despatches twice). Asst Dir, Military Gov. (Banking), NW Europe, 1944–46; UN Adviser (Banking) to Pakistan Govt, 1952; Dep. Sec., Institute of Bankers, 1956. Director: Internat. Banking Summer Sch., Christ Church, Oxford, 1961, 1964, 1970; Cambridge Banking Seminar, Christ's Coll., Cambridge, 1968 and 1969. Gen. Comr of Income Tax, Bromley, 1973–76. Mem., British National Cttee., Internat. Chamber of Commerce, 1959–74. JP Bromley, 1967. Governor, City of London Coll., 1958–69. Editor, Jl Inst. of Bankers, 1959–71. Hon. Fellow, Inst. of Bankers, 1971. *Publications:* contributions to professional journals. *Recreations:* golf, walking, gardening, world travel. *Address:* 12 Redgate Drive, Hayes Common, Bromley BR2 7BT. *T:* (020) 8462 1900. *Club:* Gresham. *Died 30 Jan. 2007.*

EASTCOTT, Harry Hubert Grayson, (Felix), MS; FRCS; FRCOG; Consulting Surgeon, St Mary's Hospital; Consultant in Surgery and Vascular Surgery to the Royal Navy, 1957–82, then Emeritus; *b* 17 Oct. 1917; *s* of Harry George and Gladys Eastcott; *m* 1941, Doreen Joy (*d* 2007), *e d* of Brenchley Ernest and Muriel Mittell, four *d*. *Educ:* Latymer Sch.; St Mary's Hosp. Medical School and Middlesex Hospital Medical Sch., University of London; Harvard Med. Sch. War of 1939–45, Junior surgical appts and service as Surgeon Lieut, RNVR up till 1946. Surg. Lieut Comdr RNVR, London Div., until 1957. MRCS; LRCP; MB, BS (Hons), 1941; FRCS 1946; MS (London), 1951. Sen. Registrar, 1950 as Hon. Cons. to St Mary's and Asst Dir Surgical Unit; Research Fellow in Surgery, Harvard Med. Sch., and Peter Bent Brigham Hosp., Boston, Mass, 1949–50; recognised teacher, 1953, and Examr, 1959, in surgery, University of London; Cons. Surgeon, St Mary's Hosp. and Lectr in Surgery, St Mary's Hosp. Med. Sch., 1955–82; Surgeon, Royal Masonic Hosp., 1964–80; Cons. Surgeon, King Edward VII Hosp. for Officers, 1965–87; Hon. Surg., RADA, 1959–; External Examr in Surgery: Queen's Univ., Belfast, 1964–67; Cambridge Univ., 1968–84; Univ. of Lagos, Nigeria, 1970–71. Editorial Sec., British Jl of Surgery, 1972–78. Royal College of Surgeons: Hunterian Prof., 1953; Mem. Court of Examrs, 1964–70; Mem. Council, 1971–83; Bradshaw Lectr, 1980; Vice-Pres., 1981–83; Cecil Joll Prize, 1984; RCS Visitor to RCOG Council, 1972–80; Mem. Court of Patrons, 1997–. FRSocMed (Hon. Sec., Section of Surgery, 1963–65, Vice-President, 1966, Pres., 1977; Pres., United Services Section, 1981–83, Hon. Mem., 1992). Fellow Medical Soc. of London (Hon. Sec., 1962–64, Vice-Pres. 1964, Pres., 1976, Fothergill Gold Medal, 1974, Trustee 1988). Pres., Assoc. of Surgeons of GB and Ireland, 1982–83. Mem., Soc. Apothecaries, 1967 (Galen Medal, 1993). Hon. FACS, 1977; Hon. FRACS, 1978; Hon. Fellow: Amer. Surgical Assoc., 1981; Amer. Heart Assoc.; Stroke Council, 1981; Hon. Member: Purkinje Med. Soc., Czechoslovakia, 1984; Internat. Union of Angiology, 1995; Eur. Soc. for Vascular Surgery, 1995. Leriche Prize, Internat. Surg. Soc., 2001. *Publications:* Arterial Surgery, 1969, 3rd edn 1992; A Colour Atlas of Operations on the Internal Carotid Artery, 1984; various articles on gen. and arterial surgery, Lancet, Brit. Jl of Surg., etc.; contrib. chap. of peripheral vascular disease, Med. Annual, 1961–80; various chaps in textbooks on these subjects. *Recreations:* music, travel, and a lifelong interest in aeronautics. *Address:* 16 White Cross Road, Haddenham, Bucks HP17 8BA. *T:* (01844) 290629. *Club:* Garrick. *Died 25 Oct. 2009.*

EASTON, Sir Robert (William Simpson), Kt 1990; CBE 1980; CEng, FIMarEST, FRINA; Chairman: Yarrow Shipbuilders Ltd, 1979–94; GEC Scotland, 1989–99; *b* 30 Oct. 1922; *s* of James Easton and Helen Agnes (*née* Simpson); *m* 1948, Jean, *d* of H. K. Fraser and Jean (*née* Murray); one *s* one *d. Educ:* Royal Technical Coll., Glasgow. Fairfield Shipbuilding Co., 1939–51; Manager, Yarrow & Co. Ltd, 1951–65; Yarrow Shipbuilders Ltd: Director, 1965; Dep. Managing Director, 1970; Managing Director, 1977–91; Main Board Director, Yarrow & Co. Ltd, 1970–77. Vice Pres., Clyde Shipbuilders, 1972–79; Chm., Clyde Port Authy, 1983–93. Chm., GEC Naval Systems, 1991–94; Director: Genships (Canada), 1979–80; Supermarine Consortium Ltd, 1986–90; W of Scotland Water Authy, 1995–97; Caledonian MacBrayne Ltd, 1997–2000. Chancellor, Paisley Univ., 1993–2003. President: Inst. of Welding, 1991–93; Inst. of Engineers and Shipbuilders, Scotland, 1997–99; Member: Council, RINA, 1983–91 (Hon. Vice Pres., 1991–); Worshipful Company of Shipwrights, 1982–96; Merchants House of Glasgow, 1989–; Incorporation of Hammermen, 1989–. Hon. FIMechE 2000. *Recreations:* walking, golf, gardening. *Address:* Springfield, Stuckenduff, Shandon, Argyll & Bute G84 8NW. *T:* (01436) 820677. *Clubs:* Caledonian; Ross Priory Golf (Strathclyde). *Died 10 Oct. 2008.*

ECCLES, Jack Fleming, CBE 1980; trade union official; *b* 9 Feb. 1922; *s* of Tom and Dora Eccles; *m* 1952, Milba Hartley Williamson; one *s* one *d. Educ:* Chorlton High Sch.; Univ. of Manchester. BA (Com). Gen. and Municipal Workers Union: District Organiser, 1948–60; Nat. Industrial Officer, 1960–66; Regional Sec. (Lancs), 1966–86. Trades Union Congress: Gen. Council, 1973–86; Chm., 1984–85; Pres., 1985. Non-Executive Director: Remploy Ltd, 1976–90; English Industrial Estates, 1976–92; Plastics Processing ITB, 1982–88 (Chm.); British Steel plc (formerly BSC), 1986–91. *Address:* Terange, 11 Sutton Road, Alderley Edge, Cheshire SK9 7RB. *T:* (01625) 583684. *Died 13 Jan. 2010.*

ECCLESTON, Harry Norman, OBE 1979; PPRE (RE 1961; ARE 1948); RWS 1975 (ARWS 1964); RWA 1991; Artist Designer at the Bank of England Printing Works, 1958–83 (appointed first full-time bank-note designer, 1967); *b* 21 Jan. 1923; *s* of Harry Norman Eccleston and Kate Pritchard, Coseley, Staffs; *m* 1948, Betty Doreen Gripton (*d* 1995); two *d. Educ:* Sch. of Art, Bilston; Coll. of Art, Birmingham; Royal College of Art. ATD 1947; ARCA (1st Class) 1950. Studied painting until 1942. Served in Royal Navy, 1942–46; Temp. Commn, RNVR, 1943. Engraving Sch., Royal College of Art, 1947–51; engraving, teaching, free-lance graphic design, 1951–58. Pres., Royal Soc. of Painter-Etchers and Engravers, 1975–89. Hon. RBSA 1989; Hon. NEAC, 1995. Hon. PhD (DA) Wolverhampton, 2003. *Recreation:* reading. *Address:* 110 Priory Road, Harold Hill, Romford, Essex RM3 9AL. *T:* (01708) 340275. *Club:* Arts. *Died 30 April 2010.*

ECEVIT, Bülent; Prime Minister of Turkey, 1974, 1977, 1978–79, and 1999–2002; Chairman, Democratic Left Party, 1989–2004; *b* Istanbul, 28 May 1925; *s* of late Prof. Fahri Ecevit and Nazli Ecevit; *m* 1946, Rahşan Aral. *Educ:* Robert Coll., Istanbul (BA Lit. 1944); Univ. of Ankara; SOAS, Univ. of London; Harvard Univ. (Rockefeller Foundn Fellow, 1957–58). Press and Publicity Dept, Turkish Govt, 1944–46; Press Attaché's Office, Turkish Embassy, London, 1946–50; joined Ulus (Republican People's Party newspaper) as art critic and translator, 1950; held posts of Foreign News Ed., Man. Dir, then Pol Ed.; pol columnist, 1956–61. Served Turkish army, 1951–52 (attained rank of Lt). MP (Republican People's Party), Turkey, 1957–60, 1961–80; Mem., Constituent Assembly, 1960–61;

Minister of Labour, 1961–65; Sec.-Gen., 1966–71, Chm., 1972–80, Republican People's Party; Dep. Prime Minister, 1997–98. Imprisoned by mil. regime, 1980 and 1981–82. *Publications:* Left of Centre, 1966; The System Must Change, 1968; Atatürk and Revolution, 1970; Conversations, 1974; Democratic Left, 1974; Foreign Policy, 1975; Workers and Peasants Together, 1976; Poems, 1976 (trans. German, Russian, Serbian, Danish and Romanian); translations into Turkish: Gitanjali (R. Tagore), 1941; Straybirds (R. Tagore), 1943; Cocktail Party (T. S. Eliot), 1963. *Address:* Or-an, Şehri 69/5, Ankara, Turkey. *Died 5 Nov. 2006.*

ECHLIN, Sir Norman David Fenton, 10th Bt *cr* 1721; Captain 14/1st Punjab Regiment, Indian Army; *b* 1 Dec. 1925; *s* of Sir John Frederick Echlin, 9th Bt, and Ellen Patricia (*d* 1971), *d* of David Jones, JP, Dublin; *S* father, 1932; *m* 1953, Mary Christine, *d* of John Arthur, Oswestry, Salop. *Educ:* Masonic Boys' School, Dublin. *Heir:* none. *Address:* Nartopa, 36 Marina Avenue, Appley, Ryde, IoW PO33 1NJ. *Died 11 April 2007 (dormant)*

ECKERSLEY, Sir Donald (Payze), Kt 1981; OBE 1977; farmer, since 1946; Inaugural President, National Farmers' Federation of Australia, 1979–81; *b* 1 Nov. 1922; *s* of Walter Roland Eckersley and Ada Gladys Moss; *m* 1949, Marjorie Rae Clarke; one *s* two *d. Educ:* Muresk Agricl Coll. (Muresk Diploma in Agriculture). Aircrew, RAAF, 1940–45. Pres., Milk Producers' Assoc., 1947–50; Farmers' Union of WA: Executive, 1962–67; Pres., Milk Sect., 1965–70; Vice-Pres., 1969–72; Gen. Pres., 1972–75; Pres., Australian Farmers' Fedn, 1975–79; Austr. Rep., Internat. Fedn of Agric., 1979–81. Pres., Harvey Shire Council, 1970–79; Director: Chamberlain John Deere, 1980–; Br. Bd. Australian Mutual Provident Soc., 1983–. Chairman: Leschenault Inlet Management Authority, 1977–80; Artificial Breeding Bd of WA, 1981–; SW Develt Authority, 1989–96; Bd, Muresk Inst. of Agric., 1984–88; Member: WA Waterways Commn, 1977–80; Nat. Energy Adv. Cttee, 1979–; Comr, WA State Housing Commn, 1982–. Mem., Senate, Univ. of WA, 1981–86. Mem., Harvey Rotary Club. JP WA, 1982–86. Hon. DTech Curtin, 1989. WA Citizen of Year award, 1976; Man of Year, Austr. Agriculture, 1979. *Publications:* (contrib.) Farm Focus: the '80s, 1981. *Recreations:* golf, fishing. *Address:* 323 Korijekop Avenue, WA 6220, Australia. *T:* (8) 97291472. *Clubs:* Weld (Perth); Harvey Golf. *Died 12 April 2009.*

EDE, Jeffery Raymond, CB 1978; Keeper of Public Records, 1970–78; *b* 10 March 1918; *e s* of late Richard Arthur Ede; *m* 1944, Mercy (*d* 2001), *d* of Arthur Radford Sholl; one *s* one *d. Educ:* Plymouth Coll.; King's Coll., Cambridge (MA). Served War of 1939–45, Intell. Corps (despatches); GSO2 HQ 8 Corps District, BAOR, 1945–46. Asst Keeper, Public Record Office, 1947–59; Principal Asst Keeper, 1959–66; Dep. Keeper, 1966–69. Lectr in Archive Admin., Sch. of Librarianship and Archives, University Coll., London, 1956–61; Unesco expert in Tanzania, 1963–64. Chm., British Acad. Cttee on Oriental Documents, 1972–78; Vice Pres., Internat. Council on Archives, 1976–78. Pres., Soc. of Archivists, 1974–77. FRHistS 1969. Hon. Mem., L'Institut Grand-Ducal de Luxembourg, 1977. Freeman: Goldsmiths' Company, 1979; City of London, 1979. *Publications:* Guide to the Contents of the Public Record Office, Vol. II (major contributor), 1963; articles in archival and other professional jls. *Recreation:* countryside. *Address:* Vaughan Lee House, Orchard Vale, Ilminster, Som TA19 0EX. *Died 6 Dec. 2006.*

EDEY, Prof. Harold Cecil, FCA; Professor of Accounting, London School of Economics, University of London, 1962–80, then Emeritus; *b* 23 Feb. 1913; *s* of Cecil Edey and Elsie (*née* Walmsley); *m* 1944, Dilys Mary Pakeman Jones (*d* 2000); one *s* one *d. Educ:* Croydon High Sch. for Boys; LSE (BCom; Hon. Fellow, 1986). Chartered Accountant, 1935. Commnd in RNVR, 1940–46. London School of Economics: Lectr in Accounting and Finance, 1949–55; Reader in

Accounting, 1955–62; Pro-Dir, 1967–70. Mem., UK Adv. Council on Educn for Mgt, 1961–65; Mem., Academic Planning Bd for London Grad. Sch. of Business Studies, 1961–71, and Governor, 1965–71; Chm., Arts and Social Studies Cttee, CNAA, 1965–71, and Mem. Council, 1965–73; Chm., Bd of Studies in Econs, 1966–71, Mem. Senate, 1975–80, University of London; Mem. Council, ICAEW, 1969–80. Freeman, City of London, 1986; Hon. Freeman, 1981, Hon. Liveryman, 1986, Co. of Chartered Accountants in England and Wales. Hon. Professor, UCW, Aberystwyth, 1980–95; Patron, Univ. of Buckingham, 1984–. Hon. LLD CNAA, 1972. Bard of the Cornish Gorsedd, 1933. Silver Jubilee Medal, 1977, Centenary Award, 1987, ICAEW; Lifetime Achievement Award, British Accounting Assoc., 2004. *Publications:* (with A. T. Peacock) National Income and Social Accounting, 1954; Business Budgets and Accounts, 1959; Introduction to Accounting, 1963; (with B. S. Yamey and H. Thomson) Accounting in England and Scotland 1543–1800, 1963; (with B. V. Carsberg) Modern Financial Management, 1969; (with B. S. Yamey) Debits, Credits, Finance and Profits, 1974; (with L. H. Leigh) The Companies Act 1981, 1981; Accounting Queries, 1982; articles in various jls.
Died 12 March 2007.

EDKINS, George Joseph, (John), FCA; Chief Executive, Cystic Fibrosis Trust, 1991–96; *b* 18 June 1930; *s* of late George Henry John Edkins and Olympia Edkins (*née* Izzillo); *m* 1954, Audrey Joan Paul; one *s* (and one *s* one *d* decd). *Educ:* Mitcham GS; Oxted GS. FCA 1960. Naval Fighter Intelligence, RAF, 1948–50. Shell Internat. Petroleum, 1950–55; Chartered Accountant: Frazer Whiting, 1955–60; Pike-Russell & Co., 1960–70; Sen. Partner, Russell Limebeer, 1978–88; Sen. Partner, Fraser Russell, 1988–90. Exec. Mem. and Treas., Internat. Cystic Fibrosis Assoc., 1991–98; Council Mem., AMRC, 1991–96. Chm., Inst. of Meat, 1999–2004. Liveryman, Co. of Butchers, 1974– (Master, 2005–06). FInstM; FRSA 2006. *Recreations:* charity work, sports (Rugby and cricket). *Address:* Birchwood Cottage, Mizen Way, Cobham, Surrey KT11 2RG. *T:* (01932) 863017. *Clubs:* MCC, City of London, Royal Automobile.
Died 24 April 2007.

EDMONDS, Robert Humphrey Gordon, CMG 1969; MBE 1944; writer; HM Diplomatic Service, retired; *b* 5 Oct. 1920; *s* of late Air Vice-Marshal C. H. K. Edmonds, CBE, DSO; *m* 1st, 1951, Georgina Combe (marr. diss. 1975); three *s* (and one *s* decd); 2nd, 1976, Mrs Enid Balint (*d* 1994), *widow* of Dr Michael Balint; 3rd, 1998, Mrs Gillian Pawley. *Educ:* Ampleforth; Brasenose Coll., Oxford. Pres., Oxford Union, 1940. Served Army, 1940–46; attached to Political Div., Allied Commn for Austria, 1945–46. Entered Foreign Service, Dec. 1946; served Cairo, 1947; FO, 1949; Rome, 1953; Warsaw, 1957; FO, 1959; Caracas, 1962; FO, CO and FCO, 1966–69; Minister, Moscow, 1969–71; High Comr, Nicosia, 1971–72; Asst Under Sec. of State, FCO, 1974–77, retd 1978. Vis. Fellow, Glasgow Univ., 1973–74; Fellow, Woodrow Wilson Internat. Centre for Scholars, Washington, 1977; Leverhulme Res. Fellow, 1989–91; Hon. Fellow, Glasgow Inst. of Soviet and E European Studies, 1988–91. Adviser, Kleinwort Benson, 1978–83, consultant, 1984–86. Mem. Council, RIIA, 1986–92. *Publications:* Soviet Foreign Policy: the paradox of superpower, 1975; Soviet Foreign Policy: the Brezhnev years, 1983; Setting the Mould: the United States and Britain 1945–1950, 1986; The Big Three, 1990; (contrib.) Churchill, ed Blake and Louis, 1992; Pushkin: the man and his age, 1994; articles and review articles in International Affairs, TLS and Survival. *Club:* Turf.
Died 12 April 2009.

EDMONDSON, His Honour Anthony Arnold; a Circuit Judge (formerly County Court Judge and Commissioner, Liverpool and Manchester Crown Courts), 1971–91; *b* 6 July 1920; *s* of late Arnold Edmondson; *m* 1947, Dorothy Amelia Wilson; three *s* one *d*. *Educ:* Liverpool Univ. (LLB Hons); Lincoln Coll.,

Oxford (BCL Hons). Served RA (Adjutant), 1940–44; RAF (Pilot), 1944–46; thereafter RA (TA) and TARO. Called to the Bar, Gray's Inn, 1947; William Shaw Schol. 1948; practised on Northern Circuit, 1948–71; Chairman, Liverpool Dock Labour Bd Appeal Tribunal, 1955–66; Mem. Court of Liverpool Univ., 1960–. Dep. Chm., Lancashire QS, 1970–71; Pres., S Cumbria Magistrates' Assoc., 1977–87; JP Lancs, 1970. *Recreations:* walking, fishing. *Address:* County Sessions House, Preston, Lancs PR1 2PD.   *Died 18 Aug. 2007.*

EDMONDSON, Leonard Firby; Executive Council Member, Amalgamated Union of Engineering Workers, 1966–77; *b* 16 Dec. 1912; *s* of Arthur William Edmondson and Elizabeth Edmondson; unmarried. *Educ:* Gateshead Central Sch. Served apprenticeship as engr, Liner Concrete Machinery Co. Ltd, Newcastle upon Tyne, 1929–34; worked in a number of engrg, ship-bldg and ship-repairing firms; shop steward and convener of shop stewards in several firms. AUEW: Mem., Tyne Dist Cttee, 1943–53; Tyne Dist Sec., 1953–66; CSEU: Mem., Exec. Council, 1966–78; Pres., 1976–77; Mem., Gen. Council of TUC, 1970–78. Member: Shipbldg Industry Trng Bd, 1966–79; Council, ACAS, 1976–78; Royal Commn on Legal Services, 1976–79; Council on Tribunals, 1978–84; Cttee of Inquiry into Prison Services, 1978–79. Mem., Birtley Canine Soc. *Recreation:* exhibiting Shetland sheep dogs. *Address:* 6 Kenwood Gardens, Low Fell, Gateshead, Tyne and Wear NE9 6PN. *T:* (0191) 487 9167. *Clubs:* Northern Counties Shetland Sheep Dog; Manors Social (Newcastle-upon-Tyne).   *Died 20 Nov. 2006.*

EDWARDS, Arthur Frank George; Vice-Chairman, Thames Water Authority, 1973–83; *b* 27 March 1920; *o s* of Arthur Edwards and Mabel (Elsie) Edwards; *m* 1946, Joyce May Simmons; one *s* one *d*. *Educ:* West Ham Grammar Sch.; Garnett Coll., London; West Ham Coll. of Technology; City of London Polytechnic (MSc 1990); King's College London (MPhil 2000). CEng, FIChemE; Hon. FIWM. Various posts with Ever Ready (GB) Ltd, 1936–50; Prodn Man., J. Burns & Co. Ltd, 1950–53; various lectrg posts, 1954–65; Organiser for science and techn. subjects, London Boroughs of Barking and Redbridge, 1965–83. Member: West Ham Co. Borough Council, 1946–65; Newham Council, 1964–86 (Mayor, 1967–68); GLC, 1964–86 (Dep. Chm., 1970–71; Chm., Public Services Cttee, 1973–77). Chm. of Governors, NE London Polytechnic, 1972–87. Hon. Alderman, London Borough of Newham, 2004. Hon. Prof., Moscow Univ. of Humanities, 1996. Mem., Fabian Soc. *Recreations:* reading, Association football (watching West Ham United). *Address:* 18 Wanstead Park Avenue, E12 5EN. *T:* (020) 8530 6436. *Clubs:* West Ham Supporters'; Aldersbrook Bowls.   *Died 27 Nov. 2008.*

EDWARDS, Frederick Edward, LVO 1992; RD 1968 and Clasp, 1977; CEnv; voluntary worker; Director of Social Work, Strathclyde Region, 1976–93; *b* 9 April 1931; *s* of Reginal Thomas Edwards and Jessie Howard Simpson; *m* 1st, 1957, Edith Jocelyn Price (marr. diss. 1990); two *s* one *d*; 2nd, 1990, Mary Olds (*née* Ellis). *Educ:* St Edward's Coll., Liverpool; Univ. of Glasgow (Dip. Applied Soc. Studies 1965). BA 1973, MA 2003, Open Univ. CEnv 2005. Merchant Navy Deck Officer, 1948–58; Perm. Commn, RNR, 1953, Lt-Comdr 1963; sailed Barque Mayflower to USA, 1957. Morgan Refractories, 1958–60; Probation Service, Liverpool, 1960–69; Dir of Social Work: Moray and Nairn, 1969–74; Grampian, 1974–76. Vis. Prof., Dept of Social Policy (formerly Social Admin.) and Social Work, Univ. of Glasgow, 1988–93. Member: Scottish Marriage Guidance Council, 1970– (Chm., 1980–83); Scottish Council on Crime, 1972–75; Adv. Council on Social Work, 1976–81; Bd, Scottish Envmt Protection Agency, 1999–2006. Chairman: Scottish Sen. Alliance Volunteering for the Envmt, 1989–2005; Carnegie Third Age Prog. Cttee, 1993–96; Capability Scotland, 1997–2005; President: Volunteer Develt Scotland, 1994–2000; Disability Scotland, 1995–99; Scottish

Environment LINK, 2004–07. Trustee, New Lanark Trust, 1993–2008. FCMI; MIEEM 2004. MUniv Open, 1988; DUniv Paisley, 1993. *Recreations:* walking, natural history, reading. *Address:* Gardenfield, Ninemileburn, Midlothian EH26 9LT.   *Died 18 Oct. 2008.*

EDWARDS, Prof. John Hilton, FRCP; FRS 1979; Professor of Genetics, and Fellow of Keble College, University of Oxford, 1979–95, then Emeritus; *b* 26 March 1928; *s* of late Harold Clifford Edwards, CBE, FRCS, FRCOG; *m* 1953, Felicity Clare, *d* of Dr C. H. C. Toussaint; two *s* two *d*. *Educ:* Univ. of Cambridge (MB, BChir). FRCP 1972. Ship's Surgeon, Falkland Islands Dependency Survey, 1952–53; Mem., MRC Unit on Population Genetics, Oxford, 1958–60; Geneticist, Children's Hosp. of Philadelphia, 1960–61; Lectr, Sen. Lectr, and Reader, Birmingham Univ., 1961–67; Hon. Consultant Paediatrician, Birmingham Regional Bd, 1967; Vis. Prof. of Pediatrics, Cornell Univ., and Sen. Investigator, New York Blood Center, 1967–68; Consultant, Human Genetics, Univ. of Iceland, 1967–; Prof. of Human Genetics, Birmingham Univ., 1969–79. *Publications:* Human Genetics, 1978; scientific papers. *Recreations:* gliding, ski-ing. *Address:* 78 Old Road, Headington, Oxford OX3 7LP; *e-mail:* jheox@ntlworld.com.   *Club:* Athenæum.   *Died 11 Oct. 2007.*

EDWARDS, (John) Michael, CBE 1986; QC 1981; *b* 16 Oct. 1925; *s* of Dr James Thomas Edwards and Constance Amy Edwards, *yr d* of Sir John McFadyean; *m* 1st, 1952, Morna Joyce Piper (marr. diss.); one *s* one *d*; 2nd, 1964, Rosemary Ann Moore (MBE 2004); two *s*. *Educ:* Andover Grammar Sch. (schol.); University Coll., Oxford (BCL, MA). Called to the Bar, Middle Temple, 1949, Bencher, 1993; barrister-at-law, 1950–55 and 1993–2001; Asst Parly Counsel, HM Treasury, 1955–60; Dep. Legal Advr and Dir of subsid. cos trading in E Europe, Courtaulds Ltd, 1960–67; British Steel Corporation: Dir, Legal Services, 1967–71; Man. Dir, BSC (Internat.) Ltd, 1968–81; Chm. and Man. Dir, BSC (Overseas Services) Ltd, 1973–81; Provost, City of London Polytechnic, 1981–88. Dir, 1982–90, and Man. Dir, 1988–89, Bell Group Internat. Ltd; Dir, Bell Resources Ltd (Australia), 1983–88. Member: Overseas Projects Bd, 1973–81; E European Trade Council, 1973–81; Educn Assets Bd, 1988–98. Deputy Chairman: Disciplinary Appeal Cttee, Assoc. of Certified Accountants, 1990–95 (Chm., 1987–90); Independent Appeals Authy for Sch. Exams, 1991–99. Member: Gen. Council of Bar, 1971–79, 1980–83; Senate of Inns of Court and Bar, 1974–79, 1980–83; Gen. Cttee, Bar Assoc. for Commerce, Finance and Industry, 1967–92 (Vice-Pres., 1980–82, 1992–; Chm., 1972–74); Acad. Council, Inst. of Internat. Business Law and Practice, ICC, Paris, 1982–88. FCIArb 1984, Chartered Arbitrator, 1999 (Chm., London Br., CIArb, 2000–01). Chairman: Eastman Dental Hosp., 1983–96 (Gov., 1981–83); Management Cttee, Eastman Dental Inst. (formerly Inst. of Dental Surgery), Univ. of London, 1984–96; Mem., Governing Body, BPMF, 1988–96. UCL Hosps Foundn Fellow, 1999. Mem., Council, Regional Opera Trust, (Kent Opera), 1981–88 (Chm., 1983–86). Chm., Sussex Adv. Bd, Salvation Army, 2001–05; Council Mem., Chichester Diocesan Assoc. for Family Support Work, 2002–06. CCMI (CBIM 1985; Mem. Council, BIM, 1978–81). FDS, Eastman Dental Inst., 2004. Freeman, City of London, 1979; Mem. Court, Ironmongers' Co., 1982– (Master, 1994–95). *Recreations:* family (numerous), other people. *Club:* Garrick.   *Died 9 Feb. 2007.*

EDWARDS, Owen; Director, Sianel 4 Cymru (Welsh Fourth Channel Authority), 1981–89; *b* 26 Dec. 1933; *s* of Sir Ifan ab Owen Edwards and Eirys Mary Edwards; *m* 1st, 1958, Shân Emlyn (marr. diss. 1994); two *d*; 2nd, 1994, Rosemary Allen. *Educ:* Ysgol Gymraeg, Aberystwyth; Leighton Park, Reading; Lincoln Coll., Oxford (MA). Cataloguer, Nat. Library of Wales, 1958–60; BBC Wales: Compère, TV Programme Heddiw, 1961–66; Programme Organiser, 1967–70;

Head of Programmes, 1970–74; Controller, 1974–81. Chairman: Assoc. for Film and TV in Celtic Countries, later Celtic Film and TV Assoc., 1983–85, 1989–91; Royal Nat. Eisteddfod of Wales, 1986–89 (Vice-Chm., 1985–86). Hon. LLD Wales, 1989. Gold Medal, RTS, 1989; BAFTA Cymru Special Award, 1995. *Address:* 2 Riversdale, Llandaff, Cardiff CF5 2QL. *T:* (029) 2055 5392.   *Died 31 Aug. 2010.*

EDWARDS, His Honour Quentin Tytler; QC 1975; a Circuit Judge, 1982–97; *b* 16 Jan. 1925; *s* of Herbert Jackson Edwards and Juliet Hester Edwards; *m* 1948, Barbara Marian Guthrie (*d* 2006); two *s* one *d*. *Educ:* Bradfield Coll.; Council of Legal Educn. Royal Navy, 1943–46. Called to Bar, Middle Temple, 1948; Bencher, 1972. A Recorder of the Crown Court, 1974–82; Chancellor: Dio. of Blackburn, 1977–90; Dio. of Chichester, 1978–99. Licensed Reader, Dio. of London, 1967–2003; Chm., Ecclesiastical Law Soc., 1990–96; Member: Legal Adv. Commn of General Synod of Church of England, 1973–2001; Dioceses Commn, 1978–96. Pres., Highgate Literary and Scientific Instn, 1988–93. Hon. MA (Archbp of Canterbury), 1961. *Publications:* (with Peter Dow) Public Rights of Way and Access to the Countryside, 1951; (with K. Macmorran, et al) Ecclesiastical Law, 3rd edn, Halsbury's Laws of England, 1955; What is Unlawful?, 1959; (with J. N. D. Anderson, et al) Putting Asunder, 1966. *Recreations:* open air, architecture.   *Club:* Athenæum.   *Died 19 Dec. 2010.*

EDWARDS, Prof. Richard Humphrey Tudor, FRCP; Professor of Research and Development for Health and Social Care, University of Wales College of Medicine, Cardiff, and Director of Research and Development for Health and Social Care in Wales, 1996–99, then Emeritus Professor; *b* 28 Jan. 1939; *s* of Hywel Islwyn Edwards and Menna Tudor Edwards (*née* Davies); *m* 1964, Eleri Wyn Roberts; one *d* (one *s* decd). *Educ:* Llangollen Grammar Sch.; Middlesex Hosp. Med. Sch., London (BSc, PhD, MB, BS). Ho. appts, Middlesex, National Heart and Hammersmith Hosps, 1964–65; Res. Fellow, Asst Lectr, then Lectr (Wellcome Sen. Res. Fellow in Clin. Science), Hon. Cons. Physician (Respiratory Med.), Royal Postgrad. Med. Sch., Hammersmith Hosp., 1966–76; Wellcome Swedish Res. Fellow, Karolinska Inst., Stockholm, 1970; Prof. of Human Metabolism, UCH Med. Sch., 1976–84; Hd of Dept of Medicine, UCL, 1982–84; University of Liverpool: Prof. and Head of Dept of Medicine, 1984–96; Dir, Magnetic Resonance Res. Centre, 1987–96; Dir., Muscle Res. Centre, 1986–96. Hon. Consultant Physician: Royal Liverpool Univ. Hosp., 1984–96; Robert Jones and Agnes Hunt Orthopaedic Hosp., Oswestry, 1979–96. *Publications:* Clinical Exercise Testing, 1975; sci. papers on human muscle in health and disease and on various fields of medicine in Jl of Physiology, Clinical Sci., Clinical Physiol., Muscle and Nerve, etc. *Recreations:* Wales—planting trees, mountain walking, gardening, music. *Address:* Berthlwyd, Nantgwynant, Caernarfon, Gwynedd LL55 4NL. *T:* (01766) 890364.   *Died 5 Dec. 2009.*

EDWARDS, Prof. Ronald Walter, CBE 1992; DSc; FIBiol, FIFM; Professor and Head of Department of Applied Biology, University of Wales Institute of Science and Technology, 1968–90, then Emeritus; *b* 7 June 1930; *s* of Walter and Violet Edwards. *Educ:* Solihull Sch., Warwicks; Univ. of Birmingham (BSc, DSc). FIBiol 1965; FIWEM (FIWPC 1981). Biologist, Freshwater Biol Assoc., 1953–58; Sen., Principal, and Sen. Principal Scientific Officer, Water Pollution Res. Lab., 1958–68. Chairman: Nat. Parks Rev. Panel, 1989–91; Sea Empress Envmtl Evaluation Cttee, 1996–98; Dep. Chm., Welsh Water Authority, 1983–89 (Mem., 1974–89); Member: NRA, 1988–94; NERC, 1970–73 and 1982–85; Nat. Cttee, European Year of the Environment, 1987–88; Envmt Agency, 1995–97; Council, RSPB, 1988–92; Brecon Beacons Nat. Park Cttee, 1993–95; Vice Pres., Council for Nat. Parks, 1993–; Pres., Envmtl Educn

Council for Wales, 1997–2001; County Pres., CPRW, 1999–2006. Trustee, WWF-UK, 1999–2001. *Publications:* (co-ed) Ecology and the Industrial Society, 1968; (co-ed) Conservation and Productivity of Natural Waters, 1975; (with Dr M. Brooker) The Ecology of the River Wye, 1982; Acid Waters in Wales, 1990; (co-ed) The Sea Empress Oil Spill, 1998; about 100 papers in learned jls. *Recreations:* music, collecting Staffordshire pottery. *Address:* Rhydowen, Llandysul, Ceredigion.
Died 11 July 2007.

EDWARDS, William (Henry); *b* 6 Jan. 1938; *s* of Owen Henry Edwards and S. Edwards; *m* 1961, Ann Eleri Rogers; one *s* three *d. Educ:* Sir Thomas Jones' Comprehensive Sch.; Liverpool Univ. (LLB). Solicitor. MP (Lab) Merioneth, 1966–Feb. 1974; contested (Lab) Merioneth, Oct. 1974; Prospective Parly Cand. (Lab), Anglesey, 1981–83. Mem., Historic Building Council for Wales, 1971–76. Editor, Solicitors Diary. *Recreations:* golf, Association football (from the terraces).
Died 16 Aug. 2007.

EGAN, Patrick Valentine Martin; Chairman, Fisons plc, 1992–94; *b* 17 July 1930; *s* of Eric and Sandy Egan; *m* 1953, Tessa Coleman; three *d. Educ:* Worth Prep. Sch., Crawley; Downside Sch., Bath. Signals Instructor, RA, 1948–50; joined Unilever, 1951; appts UK and abroad; joined main board, 1978; retired from Unilever, 1992; joined board of Fisons plc, 1985. Chairman: English Hops Ltd, 1993–; Botanix Ltd (formerly English Hop Products Ltd), 1993–. Mem. Council, Lloyd's of London, 1989–92. Exec. Trustee, E Malling Trust for Horticl Res., 1996–. *Recreations:* fishing, gardening.
Died 5 Feb. 2006.

EGERTON, Maj.-Gen. (Sir) David Boswell, (16th Bt *cr* 1617); CB 1968; OBE 1956; MC 1940; *b* 24 July 1914; *s* of Vice-Admiral W. de M. Egerton, DSO, and Anita Adolphine (*née* David); *S* cousin, Sir John Grey Egerton, 15th Bt, 2008, but did not use the title; *m* 1946, Margaret Gillian, ARCM (*d* 2004), *d* of Canon C. C. Inge; one *s* two *d. Educ:* Stowe; RMA Woolwich. Commissioned Royal Artillery, Aug. 1934; served in India, 1935–39; ops in Waziristan, 1937; France and Belgium, 1940 (MC); Egypt 1942, Italy 1944 (wounded; lost left leg). Technical Staff course, RMCS, 1946; BJSM, Washington, DC, 1950–52; Asst Chief Engineer in charge of ammunition development, Royal Armament R&D Estabt, 1955–58; idc 1959; Army Mem., Defence Research Policy Staff, 1959–62; Comdt, Trials Estabt Guided Weapons, RA, 1962–63; Army Mem., Air Defence Working Party, 1963–64; Dir-Gen. of Artillery, Army Dept, 1964–67; Vice-Pres., Ordnance Board, 1967–69; President, 1969–70; retired 1970. Col Comdt, RA, 1970–74. Gen. Sec., Assoc. of Recognised Eng. Lang. Schs, 1971–79. *Recreations:* enjoying my family's progress, reading, keeping going! Heir: *s* William de Malpas Egerton [*b* 27 April 1949; *m* 1971, Ruth, *d* of late Rev. George Watson; two *s*]. *Address:* Bosworth Retirement Home, Preston, Dorset DT3 6HR. *Died 17 Nov. 2010.*

EGERTON, Sir Philip John Caledon G.; *see* Grey Egerton.

EGERTON, Sir Stephen (Loftus), KCMG 1988 (CMG 1978); HM Diplomatic Service, retired; *b* 21 July 1932; *o s* of late William le Belward Egerton, ICS, and Angela Doreen Loftus Bland; *m* 1958, Caroline (OBE 2003), *er d* of late Major and Mrs E. T. E. Cary-Elwes ; one *s* one *d. Educ:* Summer Fields; Eton; Trinity Coll., Cambridge (BA 1956, MA 1960). 2nd Lieut, 60th Rifles (KRRC), 1952–53. Entered Foreign Service, 1956; Middle East Centre for Arab Studies, Lebanon, 1956–57; Political Officer and Court Registrar, Kuwait, 1958–61; Private Sec. to 8th Marquess of Lansdowne, Jt Parly Under-Sec. of State, FO, 1961–62; Northern Dept, FO, 1962–63; Oriental Sec. and later also Head of Chancery, Baghdad, 1963–67; First Sec., UK Mission to the UN, New York, 1967–70; Asst Head of Arabian and Near Eastern Depts, FCO, 1970–72; Counsellor and Head of Chancery, Tripoli, 1972–73; Head of Energy Dept, FCO, 1973–77;

Consul-Gen., Rio de Janeiro, 1977–80; Ambassador to Iraq, 1980–82; Asst Under-Sec. of State, FCO, 1982–85; Ambassador: to Saudi Arabia, 1986–89; to Italy, 1989–92; (non-resident) to Republic of Albania, May–July 1992. Consultant, Enterprise Oil plc, 1992–2002. Dir, 1994–99, Trustee, 1999–, St Andrew's Trust, Lambeth Palace. Mem., Internat. Links Gp, Norwich Cathedral, 2000–. Pres., Soc. for Libyan Studies, 1994–98; Vice-Pres., British Sch. of Archaeology in Iraq, 1994–; Vice-Chm., Council, Keats-Shelley Meml Assoc., 1995–. Order of King Feisal bin Abdul Aziz, 1st class, 1987; Grand Cross of the Italian Republic, 1990. *Recreations:* topiary, argument. *Address:* (mid-week) 32 Poplar Grove, W6 7RE. *T:* (020) 7602 7876. *Clubs:* Brooks's, Greenjackets.
Died 7 Sept. 2006.

ELEY, Bridget Katharine C.; *see* Cracroft-Eley.

ELIOT, Lord; Jago Nicholas Aldo Eliot; *b* 24 March 1966; *s* and *heir* of 10th Earl of St Germans; *m* 2002, Bianca, *d* of Mrs Joseph Ciambriello, Plymouth; one *s* two *d* (twins). *Educ:* Univ. of Plymouth (BSc (Hons) Medialab Arts). Heir: *s* Hon. Albert Charger Eliot, *b* 2 Nov. 2004. *Club:* Colony Room.
Died 15 April 2006.

ELLEN, Patricia Mae Hayward; *see* Lavers, P. M.

ELLES, Baroness *cr* 1972 (Life Peer), of the City of Westminster; **Diana Louie Elles;** *b* 19 July 1921; *d* of Col Stewart Francis Newcombe, DSO and Elisabeth Chaki; *m* 1945, Neil Patrick Moncrieff Elles (*d* 2008); one *s* one *d. Educ:* private Schs, England, France and Italy; London University (BA Hons). Served WAAF, 1941–45. Barrister-at-law. Care Cttee worker in S London, 1956–72. UK Deleg to UN Gen. Assembly, 1972; Mem., UN Sub-Commn on Prevention of Discrimination and Protection of Minorities, 1973–75; UN special rapporteur on Human Rights, 1973–75; Mem., British delegn to European Parlt, 1973–75. Mem., Cripps Cttee on legal discrimination against women; Chm., Sub-cttee of Women's Nat. Adv. Cttee (Conservative Party) on one-parent families (report publ. as Unhappy Families); Internat. Chm., European Union of Women, 1973–79; Chm., Cons. Party Internat. Office, 1973–78; Opposition front bench spokesman on foreign and Eur. affairs, H of L, 1975–79; Mem., H of L Eur. Communities Select Cttee, 1989–94 (Chm., Law and Institutions Sub-Cttee, 1992); Mem., 1996 IGC Sub-Cttee, 1995. European Parliament: MEP (C) Thames Valley, 1979–89; EDG spokesman on NI, 1980–87; Vice-Pres., 1982–87; Chm., Legal Affairs Cttee, 1987–89. Vice-Pres., UK Assoc. of European Lawyers, 1985. Of Counsel, Van Bael and Bellis, Brussels, 1989–2002. Mem. Council, Caldecott Community, 1990–97; Mem. Res. Council, Eur. Univ. Inst., Florence, 1986–95; Trustee: Cumberland Lodge, 1982–96; Industry and Parlt Trust, 1905–96; Chm। Bd of Govs, British Inst., Florence, 1996 (Gov., 1986–96, Vice Chm., Bd of Govs, 1994–96, Life Gov., 1997); Gov., Reading Univ., 1986–96. Hon. Bencher, Lincoln's Inn, 1993. *Publications:* The Housewife and the Common Market (pamphlet), 1971; Fair Share for the Fair Sex, (pamphlet), 1972; Human Rights of Aliens, 1980; articles, etc. *Address:* 26 Sheffield Terrace, W8 7NA. *Died 17 Oct. 2009.*

ELLES, Neil Patrick Moncrieff; Chairman, Value Added Tax Appeals Tribunal, 1972–92; *b* 8 July 1919; *s* of Edmund Hardie Elles, OBE and Ina Katharine Hilda Skene; *m* 1945, Diana Louie Newcombe (later Baroness Elles); one *s* one *d. Educ:* Eton; Christ Church, Oxford (MA). War Service, RAF, 1939–45. Called to the Bar, Inner Temple, 1947; Sec., Inns of Court Conservative and Unionist Taxation Cttee, 1957–71; Mem., Special Study Gp, Commn on Law of Competition, Brussels, 1962–67. *Publications:* The Law of Restrictive Trade Practices and Monopolies (with Lord Wilberforce and Alan Campbell), 1966; Community Law through the Cases, 1973. *Recreations:* fishing, listening to music, the cultivation of vines. *Address:* 75 Ashley Gardens, SW1P

1HG. *T:* (020) 7828 0175; Villa Fontana, Ponte del Giglio, Lucca, Italy. *Clubs:* Flyfishers', MCC.
Died 29 June 2008.

ELLIOT, Prof. Harry, CBE 1976; FRS 1973; Emeritus Professor of Physics, University of London; Professor of Physics at Imperial College, London, 1960–80 (Assistant Director of Physics Department, 1963–71); *b* 28 June 1920; *s* of Thomas Elliot and Hannah Elizabeth (*née* Littleton), Weary Hall, Cumberland; *m* 1943, Betty Leyman (*d* 2007); one *s* one *d. Educ:* Nelson Sch., Wigton; Manchester Univ. MSc, PhD. Served War, Signals Branch, RAF, incl. liaison duties with USAAF and USN, 1941–46. Manchester University: Asst Lectr in Physics, 1948–49; Lectr in Physics, 1949–54; Imperial College, London: Lectr in Physics, 1954–56; Sen. Lectr in Physics, 1956–57; Reader in Physics, 1957–60; Sen. Res. Fellow, 1982–87. Member: Science Research Council, 1971–77 (Chm., Astronomy, Space and Radio Bd, 1974–77); Council, Royal Soc., 1978–79; Science Adv. Cttee, ESA, 1979–80 (Chm., 1980–81). Hon. Prof., Universidad Mayor de San Andres, 1957; Hon. ARCS, 1965. Fellow, World Acad. of Arts and Scis, 1978. Holweck Prize and Medal, Inst. of Physics and Société Française de Physique, 1976. *Publications:* papers on cosmic rays, solar physics and magnetospheric physics in scientific jls; contrib. scientific reviews and magazine articles. *Recreation:* painting. *Address:* Rosan, Broadwater Down, Tunbridge Wells, Kent TN2 5PE.
Died 5 July 2009.

ELLIOTT, Hon. Lord; Walter Archibald Elliott, MC 1943; Chairman, Scottish Land Court, 1978–92; President, Lands Tribunal for Scotland, 1971–92; *b* 6 Sept. 1922; 2nd *s* of late Prof. T. R. Elliott, CBE, DSO, FRS, Broughton Place, Broughton, Peeblesshire; *m* 1954, Susan Isobel Mackenzie Ross, Kaimend, North Berwick; two *s. Educ:* Eton; Trinity Coll., Cambridge; Edinburgh Univ. Active service in Italy and North West Europe with 2nd Bn Scots Guards, 1943–45 (MC); demobilised, Staff Capt., 1947. Barrister-at-law, Inner Temple, 1950; Advocate at Scottish Bar, 1950; QC (Scotland) 1963. Chm., Med. Appeal Tribunals, 1971–78. Ensign, Royal Company of Archers (Queen's Body Guard for Scotland). *Publications:* Us and Them: a study of group consciousness, 1986; Esprit de Corps, 1996. *Recreations:* gardening, travelling. *Address:* Morton House, Fairmilehead, Edinburgh EH10 7AW. *T:* (0131) 445 2548. *Club:* New (Edinburgh). *Died 9 Aug. 2008.*

ELLIOTT, Prof. James Philip, PhD; FRS 1980; Professor of Theoretical Physics, University of Sussex, 1969–94, then Professor Emeritus; *b* 27 July 1929; *s* of James Elliott and Dora Kate Smith; *m* 1955, Mavis Rosetta Avery; one *s* two *d. Educ:* University College, Southampton; London External degrees: BSc 1949, PhD 1952. FInstP. Senior Scientific Officer, AERE Harwell, 1951–58; Vis. Associate Prof., Univ. of Rochester, USA, 1958–59; Lecturer in Mathematics, Univ. of Southampton, 1959–62; Reader in Theoretical Physics, Univ. of Sussex, 1962–69. Rutherford Medal, Inst. of Physics, 1994; Lise Meitner Prize, Eur. Physical Soc., 2002. *Publications:* Symmetry in Physics, 1979; contribs include: The Nuclear Shell Model, Handbuch der Physik, vol 39, 1957; many papers, mostly published in Proc. Roy. Soc. and Nuclear Phys. *Recreations:* gardening, sport and music. *Address:* 36 Montacute Road, Lewes, Sussex BN7 1EP. *T:* (01273) 474783. *Died 21 Oct. 2008.*

ELLIOTT, Katharine Barbara; Deputy Director General, Regions, Department of Trade and Industry, 2003–05; *b* 18 Dec. 1950; *d* of Geoffrey Gordon Lawrance and Margaret Sydney Lawrance (*née* Salkeld); *m* 1973, Timothy Stanley Elliott, QC; one *s* one *d. Educ:* Norwich High Sch GPDST; St Hugh's Coll., Oxford (BA Hons PPE). Joined DTI as admin. trainee, 1973; Private Sec. to Minister of State for Prices and Consumer Protection, 1976–78; Principal, 1978; Asst Sec., 1989; Head, European Staffing Unit, Cabinet Office, 1989–93; Director: Contracting Out, Companies House, 1994–96; Sen. Staff Mgt, DTI, 1997–2002; Chief Exec., Central

Arbitration Cttee, 2002–03. *Recreations:* theatre, cinema, walking. *Address:* c/o Keating Chambers, 15 Essex Street, WC2R 3AA. *Died 17 May 2008.*

ELLIOTT, Dr Michael, CBE 1982; FRS 1979; Lawes Trust Senior Fellow, Rothamsted Experimental Station, since 1989; *b* 30 Sept. 1924; *s* of Thomas William Elliott and Isobel Constance (*née* Burnell); *m* 1950, Margaret Olwen James; two *d. Educ:* Skinners' Co. Sch., Tunbridge Wells, Kent; The Univ., Southampton (BSc, PhD); King's Coll., Univ. of London (DSc; FKC 1984). FRSC. Postgrad. res., University Coll., Southampton, 1945–46, and King's Coll., Univ. of London, 1946–48; Rothamsted Experimental Station: Organic Chemist, Dept of Insecticides and Fungicides, 1948–85; SPSO 1971–79; DCSO 1979–83 (Hd of Dept of Insecticides and Fungicides, 1979–83, and Dep. Dir, 1980–83); Hon. Scientist and Consultant, Chemistry of Insecticides, 1983–85. Vis. Res. Scientist, Div. of Entomology, Univ. of Calif at Berkeley, 1969, 1974 and 1986–88; Vis. Prof., Imperial Coll. of Sci. and Tech., 1978–. For. Associate, US Nat. Acad. of Scis, 1996. Hon. DSc Southampton, 1985. Burdick and Jackson Internat. Award for Res. in Pesticide Chemistry, 1975; Holroyd Medal and Lectureship, Soc. of Chem. Ind., 1977; John Jeyes Medal and Lectureship, Chem. Soc., 1978; Mullard Medal, Royal Soc., 1981; Grande Médaille de la Société Française de Phytiatrie et de Phytopharmacie, 1983; Fine Chemicals and Medicinals Gp Award, RSC, 1984; British Crop Protection Council Award, 1986; Wolf Foundn Prize in Agriculture, 1989; Prix de la Fondation de la Chimie, Paris, 1989; Envmt Medal, SCI, 1993. *Publications:* Synthetic Pyrethroids, 1977; papers on chemistry of insecticides and relation of chemical structure with biological activity; chapters in books on insecticides. *Recreations:* photography, designing insecticides. *Address:* 45 Larkfield, Ewhurst, Cranleigh, Surrey GU6 7QU. *T:* (01483) 277506.
Died 17 Oct. 2007.

ELLIOTT, Sir Randal (Forbes), KBE 1977 (OBE 1976); President, New Zealand Medical Association, 1976; *b* 12 Oct. 1922; *s* of Sir James Elliott and Lady (Ann) Elliott (*née* Forbes), MBE; *m* 1949, Pauline June Young; one *s* six *d. Educ:* Wanganui Collegiate Sch.; Otago Univ. MB, ChB (NZ), 1947; DO, 1953; FRCS, FRACS. Group Captain, RNZAF. Ophthalmic Surgeon, Wellington Hospital, 1953–88. Chm. Council, NZ Med. Assoc. GCStJ 1987 (KStJ 1978). *Publications:* various papers in medical jls. *Recreations:* sailing, ski-ing, mountaineering. *Address:* Highwic Apt 4, 32 Hobson Street, Thorndon, Wellington 6011, New Zealand. *T:* (4) 4731080. *Club:* Wellington (NZ) (Life Mem.). *Died 20 July 2010.*

ELLIOTT, Walter Archibald; *see* Elliott, Hon. Lord.

ELLIS, Prof. Hadyn Douglas, CBE 2004; PhD, DSc; CPsych, FBPsS; Professor of Psychology, since 1988, and Deputy Vice-Chancellor, 2001–04 and since 2006, Cardiff University; *b* 25 Oct. 1945; *s* of A. Douglas Ellis and Myrtle M. Ellis (*née* Oliver); *m* 1966, Diane Margaret Newton; three *s. Educ:* St Julian's High Sch., Newport, Mon; Reading Univ. (BA 1967; PhD 1971); Aberdeen Univ. (DSc 1988). CPsych 1986; FBPsS 1986. Lectr, 1970–79, Sen. Lectr, 1979–86, Aberdeen Univ.; Prof. of Applied Psychol., UWIST, 1986–88; Cardiff University: Head, Dept of Psychology, 1989–2001; Dean, Grad. Studies, 1995–; Pro Vice-Chancellor (Res.), 1995–99 and 2000–01; Provost, Coll. of Humanities and Scis, 2004–06. Member: Bd, QAA, 1997–2000; Council, ESRC, 2000–04 (Chm., Trng Bd). *Publications:* (jtly) Perceiving and Remembering Faces, 1981; (jtly) Identification Evidence, 1982; (jtly) Aspects of Face Processing, 1986; (with A. Young) Handbook of Face Processing, 1989; (with N. Macrae) Validation in Psychology, 2001; contrib. articles to psychol., psychiatry and neurol. jls. *Recreation:* bricolage. *Address:* Llwynarthen House, Castleton, Cardiff CF3 2UN. *T:* (01633) 680213.
Died 2 Nov. 2006.

ELLIS, (Robert) Thomas; *b* 15 March 1924; *s* of Robert and Edith Ann Ellis; *m* 1949, Nona Harcourt Williams (*d* 2009); three *s* one *d. Educ:* Universities of Wales and Nottingham. Works Chemist, ICI, 1944–47; Coal Miner, 1947–55; Mining Engineer, 1955–70; Manager, Bersham Colliery, N Wales, 1957–70. MP Wrexham, 1970–83 (Lab, 1970–81; SDP, 1981–83). Contested: Clwyd South West (SDP) 1983, (SDP/Alliance) 1987; Pontypridd (SLD) Feb. 1989. Mem., European Parlt, 1975–79. *Publications:* Mines and Men, 1971; Dan Loriau Maelor, 2003; After the Dust Has Settled, 2004; R. S. Thomas a'i gerddi, 2008. *Recreations:* golf, reading, music. *Address:* 3 Old Vicarage, Ruabon, Wrexham LL14 6LG. *T:* (01978) 821128. *Died 14 April 2010.*

ELRINGTON, Prof. Christopher Robin, FSA, FRHistS; Editor, Victoria History of the Counties of England, 1977–94; Professor of History, Institute of Historical Research, University of London, 1992–94, then Professor Emeritus; *b* 20 Jan. 1930; *s* of late Brig. Maxwell Elrington, DSO, OBE, and Beryl Joan (*née* Ommanney); *m* 1951, Jean Margaret (*née* Buchanan), RIBA; one *s* one *d. Educ:* Wellington Coll., Berks; University Coll., Oxford (MA); Bedford Coll., London (MA). FSA 1964; FRHistS 1969. Asst to Editor, Victoria County History, 1954; Editor for Glos, 1960; Dep. Editor, 1968. British Acad. Overseas Vis. Fellow, Folger Shakespeare Library, Washington DC, 1976. Mem., Adv. Bd for Redundant Churches, 1982–96. Pres., 1984–85, Hon. Gen. Ed., Glos Record Series, 1995–, Bristol and Glos Archaeol Soc.; Hon. Gen. Editor, 1962–72, Pres., 1983–, Wilts Record Soc. *Publications:* Divers Letters of Roger de Martival, Bishop of Salisbury, 2 vols, 1963, 1972; Wiltshire Feet of Fines, Edward III, 1974; articles in Victoria County History and in learned jls. *Address:* 34 Lloyd Baker Street, WC1X 9AB. *T:* (020) 7837 4971. *Died 3 Aug. 2009.*

ELSDEN, Sidney Reuben, PhD (Cambridge); Professor of Biology, University of East Anglia, 1965–85; *b* 13 April 1915; *er s* of late Reuben Charles Elsden, Cambridge; *m* 1st, 1942, Frances Scott Wilson (*d* 1943); 2nd, 1948, Erica Barbara Scott, *er d* of late Grahame Scott Gardiner, Wisbech, Cambs; twin *s. Educ:* Cambridge and County High Sch. for Boys; Fitzwilliam House, Cambridge (Exhibn, Goldsmiths' Co.; BA 1936). Lecturer, Biochemistry, University of Edinburgh, 1937–42; Mem. Scientific Staff of ARC Unit for Animal Physiology, 1943–48; Sen. Lectr in Microbiology, 1948–59, West Riding Prof. of Microbiology, 1959–65, Sheffield Univ.; Hon. Dir, ARC Unit for Microbiology, Univ. of Sheffield, 1952–65; Dir, ARC Food Research Inst., 1965–77. Visiting Prof. of Microbiology, Univ. of Illinois, Urbana, Ill, USA, 1956. Pres., Soc. for General Microbiology, 1969–72, Hon. Mem. 1977. Hon. DSc Sheffield, 1985. *Publications:* contribs to scientific jls on metabolism of micro-organisms. *Recreations:* gardening, angling. *Address:* Oakwood House, Old Watton Road, Colney, Norwich NR4 7TP. *Died 29 April 2006.*

ELSMORE, Sir Lloyd, Kt 1982; OBE 1977; JP; Mayor of Manukau City, 1968–84; *b* 16 Jan. 1913; *s* of George and Minnie Elsmore; *m* 1935, Marie Kirk (decd); two *s* two *d. Educ:* Greymouth High Sch. Commenced grocery business on own account, 1933; President: Grocers' Assoc., 1949, 1950, 1952, Life Member, 1954; NZ Grocers' Federation, 1955, Life Member, 1959. Mem., Auckland Harbour Bd, 1971–83. Local Body involvement, 1953–; Mayor of Ellerslie Borough Council, 1956–62. *Recreations:* boating, fishing, gardening. *Address:* 47 Park Avenue, Pakuranga Park, Pakuranga, Manukau City, New Zealand. *Club:* Rotary (Pakuranga). *Died 12 Nov. 2007.*

ELSOM, Cecil Harry, CBE 1976; Consultant, EPR Partnership (formerly Elsom Pack & Roberts, Architects), since 1980 (Senior Partner, 1947–80); *b* 17 Jan. 1912; *s* of Julius Israelson and Leah Lazarus; name changed by deed poll to Elsom, 1930; *m* 1940, Gwyneth Mary Buxton Hopkin (*d* 1997); two *s. Educ:* Upton Cross Elem. Sch.; West Ham Polytechnic; Northern Polytechnic

Architectural School. FRIBA. Started practice by winning competition for town hall, Welwyn Garden City, 1933; partner in Lyons Israel & Elsom, 1936; won two more competitions, Town Hall, Consett, Co. Durham and Health Clinic in Bilston, Staffs. Served with Ordnance Corps, RE, 1940–46, ending war as Captain. Began new practice, as Sen. Partner, Elsom Pack & Roberts, 1947. Works include housing, schools and old people's homes for GLC, Lambeth BC and Westminster CC; office buildings and flats for Church Commissioners, Crown Estate Commissioners, BSC, LWT (Eternit Prize for offices, Victoria St, 1977); stores in Wolverhampton, Guildford and London for Army & Navy Stores; town centres in Slough, Chesterfield, Derby and Tamworth (three Civic Trust Awards, four Commendations). Adviser to DoE on Lyceum Club, Liverpool; Assessor for Civic Trust Awards, 1980. Pres., Nightingale House Old People's Home, 1973–93. Liveryman, Clockmakers' Co., 1979. FSA 1979. *Recreation:* horology. *Address:* Nightingale House, 105 Nightingale Lane, SW12 8NB. *Died 3 April 2006.*

ELTON, (Peter) John, MC 1944; *b* 14 March 1924; 2nd *s* of Sydney George Elton; *m* 1948, Patricia Ann Stephens; two *d. Educ:* Eastbourne Coll.; Clare Coll., Cambridge (BA Hons Econs and Law 1947). Served Indian Army, 14th Punjab Regt, 1942–45 (twice wounded). Alcan Aluminium (UK) Ltd, subseq. British Alcan Aluminium: Dir, 1962–99; Man. Dir, 1967–74; Exec. Chm. 1974–76, non-Exec. Chm., 1976–78; Chm., Alcan Booth Industries Ltd, 1968–76; Director: Alcan Aluminium Ltd, 1972–77; Hill Samuel Group, 1976–87; Consolidated Goldfields, 1977–88; Spillers, 1978–80; TVS Entertainment, 1988–90. *Recreations:* sailing, gardening. *Address:* Tober Lodge, Ruette Rabey, St Martins, Guernsey GY4 6DU. *T:* (01481) 238555, *Fax:* (01481) 237473. *Died 21 May 2008.*

ELY, 8th Marquess of, *cr* 1801; **Charles John Tottenham;** Bt 1780; Baron Loftus, 1785; Viscount Loftus, 1789; Earl of Ely, 1794; Baron Loftus (UK), 1801; Headmaster, Boulden House, Trinity College School, Port Hope, Ontario, 1941–81; *b* 30 May 1913; *s* of G. L. Tottenham, BA (Oxon) and Cécile Elizabeth, *d* of J. S. Burra, Bockhanger, Kennington, Kent; *g s* of C. R. W. Tottenham, MA (Oxon), Woodstock, Newtown Mount Kennedy, Co. Wicklow, and Plâs Berwyn, Llangollen, N Wales; *S* cousin, 1969; *m* 1st, 1938, Katherine Elizabeth (*d* 1975), *d* of Col W. H. Craig, Kingston, Ont; three *s* one *d*; 2nd, 1978, Elspeth Ann (*d* 1996), *o d* of late P. T. Hay, Highgate. *Educ:* Collège de Genève, Internat. Sch., Geneva; Queen's Univ., Kingston, Ont (BA). Career as Schoolmaster. *Recreation:* gardening. *Heir: e s* Viscount Loftus, *b* 2 Feb. 1943. *Address:* Trinity College School, Port Hope, ON L1A 3W2, Canada. *T:* (905) 8855209. *Died 1 Feb. 2006.*

EMANUEL, Aaron, CMG 1957; Consultant to OECD, 1972–81; *b* 11 Feb. 1912; *s* of Jack Emanuel and Jane (*née* Schaverien); *m* 1936, Ursula Pagel; two *s* one *d. Educ:* Henry Thornton Sch., Clapham; London Sch. of Economics (BSc Econ.). Economist at International Institute of Agriculture, Rome, 1935–38; Board of Trade, 1938; Ministry of Food, 1940; Colonial Office, 1943; Ministry of Health, 1961; Dept. of Economic Affairs, 1965; Under Secretary: Min. of Housing and Local Govt, 1969; Dept of the Environment, 1970–72. Chm., West Midlands Econ. Planning Bd, 1968–72; Vis. Sen. Lectr, Univ. of Aston in Birmingham, 1972–75. *Publications:* Issues of Regional Policies, 1973. *Died 13 March 2008.*

EMANUEL, Richard Wolff, DM; FRCP; Physician to Department of Cardiology, Middlesex Hospital, 1963–87; Lecturer in Cardiology, Middlesex Hospital Medical School, 1963–87; Physician to National Heart Hospital, 1963–90; Lecturer to National Heart and Lung Institute (formerly Institute of Cardiology), 1963–90; *b* 13 Jan. 1923; *s* of Prof. and Mrs J. G. Emanuel, Birmingham; *m* 1950, Lavinia Hoffmann; three *s. Educ:* Bradfield Coll.; Oriel Coll., Oxford (MA, DM); Middlesex Hospital.

House aAppts at Middx Hospital, 1948 and 1950; Captain RAMC, 1948–50; Med. Registrar, Middx Hosp., 1951–52; Sen. Med. Registrar, Middx Hosp., 1953–55; Sen. Med. Registrar, Nat. Heart Hosp., 1956–58; Fellow in Med., Vanderbilt Univ., 1956–57; Sen. Med. Registrar, Dept of Cardiology, Brompton Hosp., 1958–61; Asst Dir, Inst. of Cardiology and Hon. Asst Physician to Nat. Heart Hosp., 1961–63. Advr in Cardiovascular Disease to Sudan Govt, 1969–; Civil Consultant in Cardiology, RAF, 1979–89. Vis. Lecturer: Univ. of Med. Sciences and Chulalongkorn Univ., Thailand; Univ. of the Philippines; Univ. of Singapore; Univ. of Malaya; Khartoum Univ.; St Cyre's Lectr, London, 1968; Ricardo Molina Lectr, Philippines, 1969. Addressed numerous Heart Socs in SE Asia. Member: British Cardiac Soc., 1955– (Asst Sec., 1966–68; Sec., 1968–70; Mem. Council, 1981–85); Council, British Heart Foundn, 1967–73, 1979–92 (Chm., Cardiac Care Cttee, 1987–92); Cardiol Cttee, RCP, 1967–85 (Sec., 1972–79; Chm., 1979–85); Brit. Acad. of Forensic Sciences (Med.); Assoc. of Physicians of GB and Ireland; Chest, Heart and Stroke Assoc., 1978–91. FACC; Hon. Fellow, Philippine Coll. of Cardiology; Hon. Mem., Heart Assoc. of Thailand. Gov., National Heart and Chest Hosps Bd, 1972–75; Mem. Exec. Cttee, Gordon Meml Coll. Trust Fund, 1987–2006 (Trustee, 1999–2006). Mem., Editl Cttee, British Heart Journal, 1964–72. Grand Comdr of Most Distinguished Order of Crown of Pahang, 1990. *Publications:* various articles on diseases of the heart in British and American jls. *Recreations:* XVIIIth century glass, fishing. *Address:* 6 Lansdowne Walk, W11 3LN. *T:* (020) 7727 6688. *Club:* Oriental. *Died 12 April 2007.*

EMERY, Eleanor Jean, CMG 1975; HM Diplomatic Service, retired; *b* 23 Dec. 1918; *d* of Robert Paton Emery and Nellie Nicol (*née* Wilson). *Educ:* Western Canada High Sch., Calgary, Alberta; Glasgow Univ. (MA Hons in History, 1941). Dominions Office, 1941–45; Asst Private Sec. to Sec. of State, 1942–45; British High Commn, Ottawa, 1945–48; CRO, 1948–52; Principal Private Sec. to Sec. of State, 1950–52; First Sec., British High Commn, New Delhi, 1952–55; CRO, 1955–58; First Sec., British High Commn, Pretoria/Cape Town, 1958–62; Head of South Asia Dept, CRO, 1962–64; Counsellor, British High Commn, Ottawa, 1964–68; Head of Pacific Dependent Territories Dept, FCO, 1969–73; High Comr, Botswana, 1973–77. Chm., UK Botswana Soc., 1984–88, Vice-Chm., 1981–84 and 1988–92. Governor, Commonwealth Inst., 1980–85. *Address:* c/o Zachariah, Kelvinbrae, Wisborough Lane, Storrington, W Sussex RH20 4ND. *Club:* Royal Commonwealth Society. *Died 22 June 2007.*

EMERY, George Edward, CB 1980; Director General of Defence Accounts, Ministry of Defence, 1973–80, retired; *b* 2 March 1920; *s* of late Frederick and Florence Emery; *m* 1946, Margaret (*née* Rice); two *d. Educ:* Bemrose Sch., Derby. Admiralty, 1938; Min. of Fuel and Power, 1946; Min. of Supply, 1951; Min. of Aviation, 1959; Min. of Technology, 1967; Principal Exec. Officer, 1967; Asst Sec., Min. of Aviation Supply, 1970; Ministry of Defence: Asst Sec., 1971; Exec. Dir, 1973; Under-Sec., 1973. *Address:* 3 The Orchard, Freshford, Bath BA2 7WX. *Died 26 Jan. 2009.*

EMMERSON, Rt Rev. Ralph; an Assistant Bishop, Diocese of Ripon and Leeds (formerly Diocese of Ripon), since 1986; *b* 7 June 1913; *s* of Thomas and Alys Mary Emmerson; *m* 1st, 1942, Ann Hawthorn Bygate (*d* 1982); no *c*; 2nd, 2000, Elizabeth Anne Firth. *Educ:* Leeds Grammar Sch.; King's Coll., London (BD, AKC); Westcott House, Cambridge. Leeds Educn Authority Youth Employment Dept, 1930–35; Curate, St George's, Leeds, 1938–41; Priest-in-Charge, Seacroft Estate, 1941–48; Rector of Methley and Vicar of Mickletown, 1949–56; Vicar of Headingley, 1956–66; Hon. Canon of Ripon Cath., 1964; Residentiary Canon and Canon Missioner for Dio. Ripon, 1966–72; Bishop Suffragan of

Knaresborough, 1972–79; Asst Bishop, Dio. Wakefield, 1980–86. *Address:* Flat 1, 15 High Saint Agnesgate, Ripon HG4 1QR. *T:* (01765) 601626. *Died 31 Dec. 2007.*

ENGLEFIELD, Dermot John Tryal; Librarian, House of Commons, 1991–93; *b* 27 Aug. 1927; *o s* of Major Henry Wotton Englefield and Blanchfield Bernardine Englefield (*née* O'Halloran); *m* 1962, Dora, *o d* of Josip and Maca Grahovac, Karlovac, Croatia; one *s* one *d. Educ:* Mount St Mary's Coll.; Trinity Coll. Dublin (MA); Sarah Purser Scholarship (Hist. of Art) 1951. MCLIP (ALA 1966). Served RAF, 1946–48. St Marylebone Ref. Liby, 1952–54; House of Commons Liby, 1954–93; Asst Librarian (Parly Div.), 1967; Dep. Librarian, 1976. H of C corresp. to European Centre of Parly Res. and Documentation, 1977–93; Consultant to: Council of Europe, 1970; European Parlt, 1973; proposed Scottish Assembly, 1978; NI Assembly, 1982; Hong Kong Legislative Council, 1988; Romanian Parlt, 1993; Slovakian Parlt, 1993; Eur. Parlt, 1993–94; Swaziland, 1994, 1995; Malaŵi, 1994; Kenya, 1996; Zimbabwe, 1996; Ghana, 1996; Slovakia, 1996–97; Palestine, 1997, 1998–2000; Croatia, 1998. Member: Parly Libraries Sect., IFLA (Sec., 1981–85; Chm., 1985–89); Study of Parlt Gp (1970– (Chm., 1987–90). Dir of Studies, RIPA Internat., 1994–99. Gov., Dulwich Coll., 1985–99. Editor for Industry and Parlt Trust, 1984–. Silver Jubilee Medal, 1977. *Publications:* The Printed Records of the Parliament of Ireland 1613–1800, 1978; Parliament and Information, 1981; Whitehall and Westminster, 1985; The Study of Parliament Group, 1985; (jtly) Facts About the British Prime Ministers, 1995; *edited:* (with G. Drewry) Information Sources in Politics and Political Science, 1984; Commons Select Committees, 1984; Today's Civil Service, 1985; Legislative Libraries and Developing Countries, 1986; Local Government and Business, 1987; Parliamentary Libraries and Information Services, 1990; Workings of Westminster, 1991; Getting the Message Across: the media, business and government, 1992; Guidelines for Legislative Libraries, 1993; chapters in books and contribs to jls. *Recreations:* travel, theatre. *Address:* 19 Woodhall Drive, Dulwich, SE21 7HJ. *T: and Fax:* (020) 8693 1471. *Clubs:* Arts, Authors'. *Died 9 July 2007.*

ERICKSON, Prof. Charlotte Joanne; Paul Mellon Professor of American History, University of Cambridge, 1983–90, then Professor Emeritus; Life Fellow of Corpus Christi College, Cambridge, since 1990 (Fellow, 1982–90); *b* 22 Oct. 1923; *d* of Knut Eric Erickson and Lael A. R. Johnson; *m* 1952, G. L. Watt (marr. diss. 1992); two *s. Educ:* Augustana Coll., Rock Island, Ill (BA 1945); Cornell Univ., Ithaca, NY (MA 1947; PhD 1951). Instructor in History, Vassar Coll., Poughkeepsie, NY, 1950–52; Research Fellow, NIESR, 1952–55; Lillian Gilmore Fellow, Cornell Univ., April–Sept. 1954; Asst Lectr, 1955, Lectr, 1958, Sen. Lectr, 1966, Reader, 1975, Prof., 1979–82, in Economic History, London School of Economics. Guggenheim Fellow, Washington, DC, 1966–67; Sherman Fairchild Distinguished Scholar, Calif Inst. of Technology, 1976–77; MacArthur Fellow, John D. and Dorothy MacArthur Foundn, Chicago, 1990–95. Hon. DHumLet Augustana College, 1977. *Publications:* British Industrialists, Steel and Hosiery 1850–1950, 1958; American Industry and the European Immigrant 1860–1885, 1969; Invisible Immigrants, The Adaptation of English and Scottish Immigrants in Nineteenth Century America, 1972; Emigration from Europe 1815–1914, 1976; Leaving England: essays on British emigration in the Ninteenth Century, 1994; articles in professional jls and collective works. *Recreations:* music, gardening. *Address:* Corpus Christi College, Cambridge CB2 1RH; 8 High Street, Chesterton, Cambridge CB4 1NG. *Died 9 July 2008.*

ERNSTING, Air Vice-Marshal John, CB 1992; OBE 1959; PhD; FRCP, FFOM, FRAeS; Hon. Civil Consultant in Aviation Medicine to RAF, since 1993; *b* 21 April 1928; *s* of late Reginald James Ernsting and Phyllis May Josephine Ernsting (*née* Allington); *m* 1st,

1952, Patricia Mary Woolford (*d* 1969); one *s* one *d* (and one *s* decd); 2nd, 1970, Joyce Marion Heppell. *Educ:* Chislehurst and Sidcup County Grammar Sch. for Boys; Guy's Hosp. Med. Sch. (BSc 1949; MB BS 1952; PhD 1964). MFOM 1981, FFOM 1993; MRCP 1985. Guy's Hosp., 1952–53; Guy's-Maudsley Neurosurgical Unit, 1953–54; RAF Medical Branch, 1954; Lectr in Physiology, Guy's Hosp. Med. Sch., 1961–85; RAF Consultant in Aviation Physiology, 1964; RAF Consultant Adviser in Aviation Medicine, 1971–89; Dep. Dir and Dir of Research, 1976–88, Comdt, 1988–92, RAF Inst. of Aviation Medicine; Dean of Air Force Medicine, 1990–91; Sen. Consultant (RAF) 1991–93, retd. QHS, 1989–93. Visiting Professor: KCL, 1987–; Imperial Coll., London, 1993–96. *Publications:* (ed) Aviation Medicine, 1978, 3rd edn 1999; papers and chapters in books on aviation physiology and aviation medicine. *Recreations:* music, reading, travel. *Address:* White Gables, 2A Greenways, Fleet, Hants GU52 7UG. *T:* (01252) 621788. *Club:* Royal Air Force.
Died 2 June 2009.

ERSKINE, Sir (Thomas) David, 5th Bt *cr* 1821; JP; Vice Lord-Lieutenant, Fife Region, 1981–87; Convener, Fife County Council, 1970–73; *b* 31 July 1912; *o* surv. *s* of Sir Thomas Wilfred Hargreaves John Erskine, 4th Bt, and late Magdalen Janet, *d* of Sir Ralph Anstruther, 6th Bt of Balcaskie; *S* father, 1944; *m* 1947, Ann, *er d* of late Lt-Col Neil Fraser-Tytler, DSO, MC, and late Christian Helen Fraser-Tytler, CBE; two *s* (one *d* decd). *Educ:* Eton; Magdalene Coll., Cambridge. Employed by Butterfield & Swire, London and China, in 1934 and served with them in China, 1935–41. Joined HM Forces in India and commissioned into Indian Corps of Engineers. Served with them in Mid-East, India and Malaya, being demobilised in 1945 with rank of Major. JP Fife, 1951; DL Fife, 1955–81. *Heir:* *s* Thomas Peter Neil Erskine [*b* 28 March 1950; *m* 1972, Catherine, *d* of Col G. H. K. Hewlett; two *s* two *d*]. *Address:* West Newhall House, Kingsbarns, Fife KY16 8QD. *T:* (01333) 450228. *Club:* New (Edinburgh).
Died 21 March 2007.

ERVINE, David Walter; Member (PU) Belfast East, Northern Ireland Assembly, since 1998; *b* 21 July 1953; *s* of Walter and Elizabeth Ervine; *m* 1972, Jeanette Cunningham; two *s*. *Educ:* Orangefield Boys' Sec. Sch. Mem. (PU), Belfast CC, 1997–. Averell Harriman Peace Award, 1998; J. F. Kennedy Courage in Democracy Award, 1998. *Recreations:* restaurants, spectator sports. *Address:* Northern Ireland Assembly, Parliament Buildings, Belfast BT4 3XX. *Club:* Raven (Belfast).
Died 8 Jan. 2007.

ESER, Prof. Dr Günter Otto; Director General, International Air Transport Association, Montreal/ Geneva, 1985–92; *b* 10 Sept. 1927; *s* of Ernst Eser and Martha Siering; *m* 1976, Florida Huisman, two *s*. *Educ:* Bonn Univ.; Federal Acad. of Finance, Siegburg; Harvard (Management Programme). Auditor, Fed. German Min. of Finance, 1953–55; Lufthansa German Airlines, 1955–84: Head, Persian subsidiary, Teheran; Head, Munich Dist Office for Southern Germany; Sales Dir, Germany; Gen. Man., N and Central America; Mem., Chief Exec. Bd. Member: Adv. Bd, Europäische Reiseversicherung, 1978–; Adv. Bd, Amer. Univ., 1982–. Vis. Prof., Pace Univ., NY, 1978. Bundesverdienstkreuz 1st Class (FRG), 1985; Commendatore Officiale (Italy), 1967. *Recreations:* trekking, ocean-fishing, literature, music. *Address:* La Bellangère, ch. de Sodome, 1271 Givrins, Vaud, Switzerland.
Died 22 Oct. 2007.

ESPLIN, Air Vice-Marshal Ian (George), CB 1963; OBE 1946; DFC 1943; retired (voluntarily) 1965; *b* 26 Feb. 1914; *s* of late Donald Thomas Esplin and Emily Freame Esplin; *m* 1944, Patricia Kaleen Barlow (*d* 2002); one *s* one *d*. *Educ:* Shore Sch.; Sydney Univ. (BEc 1936); Oxford Univ. (MA 1939). Rowing Blue, 1934 and 1935. NSW Rhodes Schol., 1937. Entered RAF from Oxford, 1939. Served War of 1939–45, as Pilot in Night-Fighters; destroyed three enemy aircraft at night; also served at CFS and in HQ, SEAC; Air Min. (Policy),

1945; Comd RAF Desford, 1947; Dep. Senior Personnel Staff Officer, HQ Reserve Comd, 1948; Directing Staff, RAF Staff Coll., 1950–51; Comd first Jet All Weather Wing, Germany (No 148), 1952–54; Air War Coll. Course, 1954; Dep. Dir of Operational Requirements, Air Min., 1955–58; Comd RAF Wartling, 1958–60; Dir of Operational Reqts, 1960–62; Comdr, RAF Staff and Air Attaché, Washington, DC, 1963–65; Dean, Air Attaché Corps, 1964–65. *Recreations:* golf, swimming. *Address:* 141 The Villas, 15 Hale Road, Mosman, NSW 2088, Australia. *Clubs:* Vincent's (Oxford); Leander (Henley-on-Thames); Elanora Country (Sydney).
Died 15 April 2008.

ESSEX, Francis; author, producer and composer; *b* 24 March 1929; *s* of Harold and Beatrice Essex-Lopresti; *m* 1956, Jeanne Shires; (one *s* decd) one step *s*. *Educ:* Cotton Coll., N Staffs. Light Entertainment Producer, BBC Television, 1954–60; Sen. Prod., ATV Network Ltd, 1960–65; Controller of Progs, Scottish Television, 1965–69; ATV Network Ltd: Prodn Controller, 1969–76; Mem., Bd of Dirs, 1974; Dir of Production, 1976–81. Chm., Children's Network Cttee, ITV, 1976–81. Chm., Conservatives Abroad, Javea, 1990–92. Wrote and presented, The Bells of St Martins, St Martin's Theatre, 1953; devised and directed, Six of One, Adelphi, 1964; author, Jolson, Victoria Palace, 1995; *television film scripts include:* Shillingbury Tales, Gentle Flame, Silent Scream; Cuffy series; *scores:* Luke's Kingdom; Seas Must Live; The Lightning Tree; Maddie With Love, etc; writer of plays and songs. Fellow, Royal Television Soc., 1974. British Acad. Light Entertainment Award, 1964; Leonard Brett Award, 1964, 1981; Olivier Award for Best Musical, 1996. *Publications:* Shillingbury Tales, 1983; Skerrymor Bay, 1984. *Recreations:* tennis, gardening. *Address:* Punta Vista, Buzon No 1, Aldea de las Cuevas, 19, 03759 Benidoleig, Prov. de Alicante, Spain.
Died 5 March 2009.

ETHERINGTON-SMITH, (Raymond) Gordon (Antony), CMG 1962; HM Diplomatic Service, retired; *b* 1 Feb. 1914; *o s* of late T. B. Etherington-Smith and Henriette de Pitner; *m* 1950, Mary Elizabeth Besly (*d* 1989); one *s* two *d* (and one *d* decd). *Educ:* Downside; Magdalen Coll., Oxford; Sch. of Oriental and African Studies, London Univ. Entered FO, 1936; served at: Berlin, 1939; Copenhagen, 1939–40; Washington, 1940–42; Chungking, 1943–45; Kashgar, 1945–46; Moscow, 1947; Foreign Office, 1947–52; Holy See, 1952–54; Counsellor, Saigon, 1954–57; The Hague, 1958–61; Office of UK Commissioner-Gen. for South-East Asia, Singapore, 1961–63; Ambassador to Vietnam, 1963–66; Minister, and Dep. Commandant, Berlin, 1966–70; Ambassador to Sudan, 1970–74. *Publications:* Maximilian's Lieutenant, 1993. *Recreation:* physical and mental exercise. *Address:* The Coach House, 25A West Street, Wilton, Salisbury, Wilts SP2 0DI. *T:* (01722) 743429. *Club:* Oriental.
Died 14 April 2007.

ETTEDGUI, Joseph; fashion designer and retailer; Joint Founder, and Chairman until 2005, Joseph Ltd; *b* 22 Feb. 1936; Casablanca; *m* Isabelle; one *d*, and two *s* by a previous marriage. Came to London, 1960; with brother opened hairdressing salon and clothes shop, King's Road, Chelsea; opened over 20 Joseph shops, incl. outlets in London, Manchester, Leeds, and in USA, France and Germany. Contemporary Collection Award, British Fashion Awards, 2000.
Died 18 March 2010.

EUSTON, Earl of; James Oliver Charles FitzRoy, MA, FCA; *b* 13 Dec. 1947; *s* and *heir* of 11th Duke of Grafton, KG; *m* 1972, Lady Clare Kerr, MA, *d* of 12th Marquess of Lothian, KCVO; one *s* four *d*. *Educ:* Eton; Magdalene Coll., Cambridge (MA). Dir, Smith St Aubyn & Co. (Holdings) plc, 1980–86; Executive Director: Enskilda Securities, 1982–87; Jamestown Investments, 1987–91; Finance Director: Central Capital Hldgs, 1988–91; Capel-Cure Myers Capital Management, 1988–97. *Heir:* *s* Viscount Ipswich, *b* 6 April 1978. *Address:* The Racing Stables, Euston, Thetford, Norfolk IP24 2QT. *Club:* Turf (Chm.).
Died 1 Oct. 2009.

EVANS, Prof. Anthony Glyn, PhD; FRS 2001; FREng; Alcoa Chair and Professor of Materials and Mechanical Engineering, University of California, Santa Barbara, since 2001; *b* 4 Dec. 1942; *s* of William Glyn Evans and Annie May Evans; *m* 1967, Trisha Cross; three *d. Educ:* Imperial Coll., London (BSc 1964; PhD 1967). Member, Technical Staff; AERE, 1967–71; Nat. Bureau of Standards, 1971–74; Gp Leader, Rockwell Internat. Sci. Center, 1974–78; Prof., Dept of Materials Sci. and Mineral Engrg, Univ. of Calif, Berkeley, 1978–85; Alcoa Prof. and Chair, Materials Dept, UCSB, 1985–94; Gordon McKay Prof. of Materials Engrg, Div. of Applied Scis, Harvard Univ., 1994–98; Gordon Wu Prof. of Mechanical and Aerospace Engrg, and Dir, Princeton Materials Inst., Princeton Univ., 1998–2001. FREng 2006. Member: NAE, 1995; Amer. Acad. Arts and Scis, 2000; NAS, 2005. *Publications:* Metal Foams: a design guide, 2000; contribs to numerous scientific pubns in fields of materials and mechanical engrg. *Address:* Department of Materials, University of California, Santa Barbara, CA 93106–5050, USA. *T:* (805) 8937839, *Fax:* (805) 8938486; *e-mail:* agevans@engineering.ucsb.edu.
Died 9 Sept. 2009.

EVANS, David John; Chairman, Broadreach Group (formerly Broadreach Services) Ltd, 1990–2002; *b* 23 April 1935; *s* of Violet Edith Evans and Arthur Thomas Evans; *m* 1956, Janice Hazel (*née* Masters); two *s* one *d. Educ:* Raglan Road School; Tottenham Tech. College. Professional cricketer (Glos and Warwicks) and footballer (Aston Villa); founded Exclusive Office Cleaning Ltd, 1960; Chm. and Man. Dir, Brengreen (Holdings), first co. with contract for refuse collection and street cleansing services (Southend-on-Sea Borough Council), 1960–86 (Brengreen (Holdings) acquired by BET plc, 1986). MP (C) Welwyn, Hatfield, 1987–97; contested (C) same seat, 1997. Parliamentary Private Secretary: to Minister of State for Industry, DTI, 1990–91; to Minister for Corporate Affairs, DTI, 1991–92; to Minister of State for Local Govt and Inner Cities, DoE, 1992–93; to Sec. of State for Wales, 1993. Member: Select Cttee on Deregulation, 1995–97; Exec., 1922 Cttee, 1993–97; Cons. Party Bd of Treasurers, 1996–97. Chm., Luton Town Football and Athletic Co. Ltd, 1984–89 (Dir, 1977–90); Mem. Council, Lord's Taverners, 1978–96 (Chm., 1982–84; Chm., Finance Cttee, 1992–96). *Address:* Little Radley, Mackerye End, Harpenden, Herts AL5 5DS. *T:* (01582) 460302. *Clubs:* MCC, Lord's Taverners.
Died 21 Oct. 2008.

EVANS, David Milne; Cabinet Office, 1977–81; *b* 8 Aug. 1917; *s* of Walter Herbert Evans, MSc and Florence Mary Evans (*née* Milne); *m* 1946, Gwynneth May (*née* Griffiths), BA. *Educ:* Charterhouse (Scholar); Gonville and Caius Coll., Cambridge (Schol.; Wrangler, Math. Tripos). Administrative Class, Home Civil Service (War Office), 1939. Served in Army (Major, RA), 1940–45. Asst Sec., 1954; Imp. Def. Coll., 1954; Asst Under-Sec. of State, MoD, 1967–77 (Under-Sec., CS Dept, 1972). Coronation Medal, 1953; Silver Jubilee Medal, 1977. *Address:* 1 Church Rise, Walston Road, Wenvoe, Cardiff, South Glamorgan CF5 6DE. *T:* (029) 2059 7129.
Died 7 Aug. 2006.

EVANS, Eben, OBE 1976; Controller, Books Division, British Council, 1976–80; *b* 1 Nov. 1920; *s* of John Evans and Mary Evans; *m* 1946, Joan Margaret Howells; two *s* two *d. Educ:* Llandovery Grammar Sch.; University Coll. of Wales, Aberystwyth (BA 1948). Served War, 1941–46 (Army, Captain). Appointed to British Council, 1948; Cardiff, 1948–55; Thailand, 1955–59; Gambia, 1959–62; Ghana, 1962–64; Personnel Dept, London, 1964–68; Representative: Algeria, 1968–73; Yugoslavia, 1973–76. *Recreations:* walking, music.
Died 5 June 2009.

EVANS, Edward Stanley Price, FRTPI; City Planning Officer, Liverpool, 1974–84, retired; *b* 13 April 1925; *s* of late Bernard James Reuben Evans and of Nellie Evans; *m* 1948, Eva Magdalena Emma Fry; one *s* (and one *s* decd). *Educ:* Wolverhampton Grammar Sch.; Nottingham Coll. of Art and Crafts (DipTP). FRTPI 1966 (MTPI 1954).

Chief Town Planning Officer, Norwich, 1957; City Planning Officer, Nottingham, 1966–74. Member: DoE Environmental Bd, 1977–79; DoE Panel of Local Plan Inspectors, 1985–94. *Recreations:* travel, gardening, bridge (social).
Died 26 July 2006.

EVANS, Prof. (Henry) John, CBE 1997; PhD; FRCPE, FRCSE; FIBiol; FRSE; Director, Medical Research Council Human Genetics (formerly Clinical and Population Cytogenetics) Unit, Edinburgh, 1969–94; *b* 24 Dec. 1930; *s* of David Evans and Gwladys Evans (*née* Jones); *m* 1st, 1957, Gwenda Rosalind (*née* Thomas) (*d* 1974); 2nd, 1976, Roslyn Rose (*née* Angell); four *s. Educ:* Llanelli Boys Grammar Sch.; UCW, Aberystwyth (BSc, PhD 1955). FRSE 1969; FIBiol 1982; FRCPE 1988; FRCSE 1992. Res. Scientist, MRC Radiobiology Unit, Harwell, 1955–65, Head of Cell Biology Section, 1962–65; Vis. Fellow, Brookhaven Nat. Laboratory, Brookhaven, NY, USA, 1960–61; Prof. of Genetics, Univ. of Aberdeen, 1965–69. Chm., Assoc. Radiation Research, 1970–72; Mem., MRC Biological Res. Bd, 1968–72; Council Mem., MRC, 1978–82. Member: Cttee on Biological Effects of Ionizing Radiation, US Nat. Acad. Sci., 1972; Genetic Manipulation Adv. Gp, 1976–80; DHSS Cttee, Mutagenicity of Foods and Chemicals, 1978–96; Nat. Radiology Protection Bd, 1982–94; Lister Scientific Adv. Council, 1982–90; Sci. Council, Internat. Agency for Research on Cancer, 1982–86 (Chm., 1985–86); Scientific Cttee, CRC, 1983–95 (Chm., 1990–95); Vice Counsellor, 1995–); Chief Scientist Cttee, SHHD, 1983–87; Council, Imperial Cancer Res. Fund, 1985–90; Cttee on Med. Aspects of Radiation in the Environment, DHSS, 1985–94; Scientific Rev. Cttee, Alberta Heritage Foundn for Med. Res., 1986–98; Internat. Commn for Protection of Envmt from Mutagens and Chemicals, 1986–91; Radiation Waste Management Adv. Cttee, DoE, 1988–92; Human Genome Orgn, 1990–95; Hong Kong Cancer Inst., 1994–. Member, Board of Governors: Beatson Inst. Cancer Res., 1985–99 (Chm., 1991–99); Lister Inst. of Preventive Medicine, 1988–2003; Inveresk Res. Foundn, 1988–89; Caledonian Res. Foundn, 1989–2004 (Chm., 1999–2004); Inst. Cancer Res., 1990–94. Hon. Prof., Univ. of Edinburgh; Vis. Prof., Kyoto Univ., Japan, 1981; Boerhaave Prof., Univ. of Leiden, 1994–95. Hon. Fellow: UK Clinical Cytogenetics Soc., 1984; UK Environmental Mutagen Soc., 1984; Russian Med. Genetics Soc., 1992. Hon. DSc Edinburgh, 1996. Lectures include: Douglas Lea Meml, 1979; Railford Robinson, Adelaide, 1981; Honeyman-Gillespie, 1984; Woodhull, Royal Instn, 1992. Lilly Prize, 1985, Ballantyne Prize, 1990, RCPE; Frank Rose Meml Prize, CRC, 1993; Frits Sobels Award, Eur. Envmtl Mutagen Soc., 1995. *Publications:* papers on radiation cytology, mutagenesis, chromosome structure and human cytogenetics in various internat. jls; editor of various books and jls in the field of genetics and radiobiology. *Recreations:* golf, music, fishing. *Address:* 45 Lauder Road, Edinburgh EH9 1UE. *T:* (0131) 667 2437. *Club:* New (Edinburgh).
Died 1 July 2007.

EVANS, Maj.-Gen. John Alan Maurice, CB 1989; Vice-Chairman, AEI Cables, 1993–96 (Managing Director, 1992–93); *b* 13 Feb. 1936; *s* of John Arthur Mortimer Evans and Margaret (*née* Lewis); *m* 1958, Shirley Anne May; one *s* one *d. Educ:* Grammar schs in Wales and England; RMA Sandhurst; Trinity Coll., Cambridge (MA). Various Staff and RE appointments; CO, 22 Engr Regt, 1976–78; Comd, Berlin Inf. Bde, 1980–82; RCDS, 1983; Comdt, RMCS, Shrivenham, 1985–87; Sen. Army Mem., RCDS, 1988–90. Col Comdt, RE, 1991–96. With GEC Wire and Cables Gp. 1990. Pres., Inst. of Royal Engineers, 1990–93. *Recreations:* music, reluctant DIY, travel. *Address:* East Mead, Homington Road, Coombe Bissett, Salisbury SP5 4ND.
Died 7 May 2009.

EVANS, Rt Rev. Kenneth Dawson; Assistant Bishop of Guildford, 1986–90; *b* 7 Nov. 1915; *s* of late Dr Edward Victor Evans, OBE; *m* 1939, Margaret (*d* 2001), *d* of J. J.

Burton; one s. *Educ:* Dulwich Coll.; Clare Coll., Cambridge. Ordained, 1938; Curate of: St Mary, Northampton, 1938–41; All Saints', Northampton, 1941–45; Rector of Ockley, 1945–49; Vicar of Dorking, 1949–63; Archdeacon of Dorking and Canon Residentiary of Guildford Cathedral, 1963–68; Bishop Suffragan of Dorking, 1968–85. Hon. Canon of Guildford, 1955–63 and 1979–85. Mem., Bishop's Finance Commn, 1957. *Address:* 3 New Inn Lane, Burpham, Guildford, Surrey GU4 7HN. *T:* (01483) 567978. *Died 29 June 2007.*

EVANS, Hon. Dame Lois (Marie) B.; *see* Browne-Evans.

EVANS, Prof. Trevor, FRS 1988; Personal Professor, University of Reading, 1968–92, Emeritus Professor, 1992; *b* 26 April 1927; *s* of late Henry and Margaret Evans; *m* Patricia Margaret Booth (*née* Johnson); two *s*, and two step *s*. *Educ:* Bridgend Grammar Sch.; Univ. of Bristol (BSc, PhD, DSc). FInstP. Physicist: British Nylon Spinners, 1955–56; Tube Investments Res. Lab., 1956–58; Physics Department, University of Reading, 1958–92: Res. Physicist, 1958–61; successively, Lectr, Reader, Personal Prof., 1961–92; Hd of Dept, 1984–88; Warden of Wantage Hall, Reading Univ., 1971–84. For. Associate, RSSAf 1995. *Publications:* papers in Proc. Royal Soc. and Phil. Mag., almost entirely concerning synthetic and natural diamond. *Recreation:* gardening. *Address:* Aston, Tutts Clump, Reading, Berks RG7 6JZ. *T:* (0118) 974 4498. *Died 10 Oct. 2010.*

EVANS, Sir (William) Vincent (John), GCMG 1976 (KCMG 1970; CMG 1959); MBE 1945; QC 1973; Barrister-at-Law; a Judge of the European Court of Human Rights, 1980–91; *b* 20 Oct. 1915; *s* of Charles Herbert Evans and Elizabeth (*née* Jenkins); *m* 1947, Joan Mary Symons; one *s* two *d*. *Educ:* Merchant Taylors' Sch., Northwood; Wadham Coll., Oxford (1st Class Hons, Jurisprudence, 1937; BCL 1938; MA 1941; Hon. Fellow, 1981). Elected Cassel Scholar, Lincoln's Inn, 1937; called to Bar, Lincoln's Inn, 1939 (Hon. Bencher, 1983). Served in HM Forces, 1939–46. Legal Adviser (Lt-Col) to British Military Administration, Cyrenaica, 1945–46; Asst Legal Adviser, Foreign Office, 1947–54; Legal Counsellor, UK Permanent Mission to the United Nations, NY, 1954–59; Legal Counsellor, FO, 1959–60; Dep. Legal Adviser, FO, 1960–68; Legal Adviser, FCO, 1968–75, retired. Chm., Bryant Symons & Co. Ltd, 1964–85. Chm., European Cttee on Legal Cooperation, Council of Europe, 1969–71; UK Rep. Council of Europe Steering Cttee on Human Rights, 1976–80 (Chm., 1979–80); Mem., Human Rights Cttee set up under Internat. Covenant on Civil and Political Rights, 1977–84 (Vice-Chm., 1979–80); Mem., Permanent Court of Arbitration, 1987–97. Vice-Pres., British Inst. of Human Rights, 1992–2004; Member: Adv. Bd, Centre for Internat. Human Rights Law, Univ. of Essex, 1983–94; Council of Management, British Inst. of Internat. and Comparative Law, 1969–2005; Diplomatic Service Appeals Bd, 1976–86; Sch. Cttee, Merchant Taylors' Co., 1985–93. Pres., Old Merchant Taylors' Soc., 1984–85; Vice-Pres., Hon. Soc. of Cymmrodorion, 1987–. DUniv Essex, 1986. *Recreation:* gardening. *Address:* (home) 4 Bedford Road, Moor Park, Northwood, Middx HA6 2BB. *T:* (01923) 824085. *Club:* Athenæum. *Died 18 May 2007.*

EVERARD, Sir Robin (Charles), 4th Bt *cr* 1911; *b* 5 Oct. 1939; *s* of Sir Nugent Henry Everard, 3rd Bt and Frances Audrey (*d* 1975), *d* of J. C. Jesson; *S* father, 1984; *m* 1963, Ariel Ingrid, *d* of late Col Peter Cleasby-Thompson, MBE, MC; one *s* two *d*. *Educ:* Sandroyd School; Harrow; RMA Sandhurst. Short service commn, Duke of Wellington's Regt, 1958–61. Money Broker; Jt Managing Director, P. Murray-Jones, 1962–76; Consultant, 1976–91. *Heir: s* Henry Peter Charles Everard [*b* 6 Aug. 1970; *m* 2003, Nicola Anne de Poher Wilkinson, *d* of late Geoffrey de la Poer Wilkinson; one *s* one *d*]. *Address:* Church Farm, Shelton, Long Stratton, Norwich NR15 2SB. *Died 31 Aug. 2010.*

EVERARD, William Fielding; His Honour Judge Everard; a Circuit Judge, Midland Circuit, since 2004; *b* 25 April 1949; *s* of Richard and Mary Everard; *m* 1980, Christine Bell. *Educ:* Repton; QUB (LLB 1972). Called to the Bar, Middle Temple, 1973; Hd of Chambers, KCH Barristers, Nottingham, 1996–2004; Asst Recorder, 1996–2000, Recorder, 2000–04. *Recreations:* flyfishing, shooting. *Address:* Leicester Crown Court, 90 Wellington Street, Leicester LE1 6HG. *Clubs:* Gentlemen of Leicestershire Cricket; Leicester Hockey. *Died 1 Feb. 2009.*

EVERETT, Katharine Winn; Director of Change, BBC, since 2004; *b* 3 July 1952; *d* of Comdr Peter Everett, OBE, RN retd, and Penelope Everett (*née* Stapleton); *m* 1988, Horacio Queiro; one *s* one *d*. *Educ:* Lady Margaret Hall, Oxford (MA Eng. Lang. and Lit.). BBC Television: wardrobe asst, 1975–76; res. trainee, 1977–78; Producer, BBC Science, 1982–93; Finance Manager, BBC One, 1994–97; Hd of Programming, BBC Choice, 1997–99; Controller: Interactive TV, 1999–2001; BBC New Media, 2001–03. Vice-Chm., Relate Richmond, Kingston, Hounslow, 2006–. Mem., RTS, 2001. *Recreations:* walking, singing. *Address:* Media Centre, BBC White City, W12 7TQ. *Died 3 Feb. 2009.*

EVERITT, Prof. Alan Milner, PhD; FRHistS; FBA 1989; Hatton Professor and Head of Department of English Local History, University of Leicester, 1968–82, then Professor Emeritus (Associate Professor, 1982–84); *b* 17 Aug. 1926; *s* of Robert Arthur Everitt and Grace Beryl Everitt (*née* Milner). *Educ:* Sevenoaks Sch.; Univ. of St Andrews (MA 1951); Inst. of Historical Res., London Univ. (Carnegie Scholar; PhD 1957). FRHistS 1969. Editorial Assistant, ACU, 1951–54; Department of English Local History, University of Leicester: Res. Assistant, 1957–59; Res. Fellow in Urban Hist., 1960–65; Lectr in Eng. Local Hist., 1965–68. Lectures: Gregynog, Univ. of Wales, 1976; Helen Sutermeister, UEA, 1982; James Ford Special, Univ. of Oxford, 1983; W. G. Hoskins, Univ. of Leicester, 1999. *Publications:* The County Committee of Kent in the Civil War, 1957; Suffolk and the Great Rebellion 1640–1660, 1960; The Community of Kent and the Great Rebellion 1640–60, 1966, 3rd edn 1986; Change in the Provinces: the seventeenth century, 1969; The Pattern of Rural Dissent: the nineteenth century, 1972; Perspectives in English Urban History, 1973; (with Margery Tranter) English Local History at Leicester 1948–1978, 1981; Landscape and Community in England, 1985; Continuity and Colonization: the evolution of Kentish settlement, 1986; (with John Chartres) Agricultural Markets and Trade 1500–1750, 1990; contribs to: The Agrarian History of England and Wales; Past and Present, Trans of RHistS, Agricl Hist. Rev., Urban History Yearbook, Jl of Histl Geog., Jl of Transport Hist., Archaeologia Cantiana, Local Historian, TLS, Nomina, Rural England, Landscapes, and other learned publications. *Recreation:* topographical research. *Address:* Fieldedge, Poultney Lane, Kimcote, Lutterworth, Leics LE17 5RX. *Died 8 Dec. 2008.*

EVISON, Dame (Helen June) Patricia, DBE 1993 (OBE 1980); freelance actress on stage, film, radio and television in New Zealand and Australia; *b* 2 June 1924; *d* of Rev. Ernest Oswald Blamires and Annie (*née* Anderson); *m* 1948, Roger Douglas Evison; two *s* one *d*. *Educ:* Solway Coll., Masterton; Victoria Univ. (BA 1943); Auckland Teachers' Training Coll. (postgrad. course 1944); Auckland Univ. (DipEd 1944); LTCL (speech) 1942. Directors course, Old Vic Theatre Centre, 1947–48 (first NZ bursary); Assistant to Michel Saint-Denis, Young Vic Theatre Co., 1947–48; freelance director, Wellington, 1949–52; tutor for NZ Opera and NZ Ballet Schs, 1953–79. *Theatre includes:* Happy Days, 1964, 1974; Father's Day, 1966; The Killing of Sister George, 1968; An Evening with Katherine Mansfield (one-woman show), 1972; Awatea, 1974; Home, 1976; Juno and the Paycock, 1977; Hot Water, 1983; Last Days in Woolloomooloo, 1983; Ring Round the Moon, 1990;

Steel Magnolias, 1991; Lettice and Lovage, 1993; The Cripple of Inishmaan, 1999; *films*: Tim, 1979 (Best Supporting Actress, Aust. Film Inst., 1979); The Earthling, 1981; Starstruck, 1982; Bad Blood, 1982; The Silent One, 1983; The Clinic, 1983; What the Moon Saw, 1988; Moonrise, 1992; *television*: All Earth to Love, 1963; Pukemanu, 1971 (Cummings award for Best NZ Actress, 1972); Pig in a Poke, 1974 (Logie award for best individual acting perf., 1974); They Don't Clap Losers, 1974; Close to Home (series), 1975–82; The Emigrants, 1977; A Town Like Alice, 1982; Flying Doctors (series), 1984–87. Charter Member: Wellington Zonta Club; Zonta Club for Port Nicholson. *Publications*: Happy Days in Muckle Flugga (autobiog.), 1998. *Recreations*: music, watching cricket and soccer, reading, swimming, travel. *Address*: 11 Beerehaven Road, Seatoun Heights, Wellington 6022, New Zealand. *T*: (4) 3888766.
Died 30 May 2010.

EWING OF KIRKFORD, Baron *cr* 1992 (Life Peer), of Cowdenbeath in the District of Dunfermline; **Harry Ewing;** DL; Chairman, Fife Healthcare NHS Trust, 1996–98; *b* 20 Jan. 1931; *s* of Mr and Mrs William Ewing; *m* 1954, Margaret Greenhill; one *s* one *d*. *Educ*: Foulford Primary Sch., Cowdenbeath; Beath High Sch., Cowdenbeath. Contested (Lab) East Fife, 1970; MP (Lab) Stirling and Falkirk, Sept. 1971–Feb. 1974, Stirling, Falkirk and Grangemouth, Feb. 1974–83, Falkirk East, 1983–92. Parly Under-Sec. of State, Scottish Office, with special responsibility for devolution, 1974–79. Chm., Ewing Inquiry into availability of housing for wheelchair and other disabled, 1993 (report, 1994). Jt Chm., Scottish Const. Convention, 1990–96. Mem. Educn Cttee, Church of Scotland, 1999–. Nat. Hon. Pres., Girls' Brigade, Scotland, 1993–; Nat. Hon. Mem., UCW; Hon. President: Bowhill Peoples Burns' Club, 1980–; E Fife Male Voice Choir, 1998–; Patron: Scotland Patients Assoc.; Scottish Fisheries Mus. DL Fife, 1995. DUniv Stirling, 1998. Paul Harris Fellow, Rotary Internat., 1999. *Recreation*: gardening. *Address*: Gowanbank, 45 Glenlyon Road, Leven, Fife KY8 4AA. *T*: (01333) 426123.
Died 9 June 2007.

EWING, Margaret Anne; Member (SNP) Moray, Scottish Parliament, since 1999; *b* 1 Sept. 1945; *d* of John and Peggie McAdam; *m* 1968, Donald Straiton Bain; *m* 1983, Fergus Stewart Ewing. *Educ*: Univ. of Glasgow (MA 1967); Strathclyde Univ. (BA Hons 1973). Asst Teacher, Our Lady's High, Cumbernauld, 1968–70; St Modan's High, Stirling: Special Asst Teacher, 1970–73; Principal Teacher, Remedial Educn, 1973–74. MP (SNP): East Dunbartonshire, Oct. 1974–1979; Moray, 1987–2001. Contested (SNP) Strathkelvin and Bearsden, 1983. Sen. Vice-Chm., SNP, 1984–87; Leader, SNP

Parly Gp, 1987–99. Convener, SNP Gp, Scottish Parlt, 1999–2003. *Recreations*: the arts in general, folk music in particular. *Address*: Burns Cottage, Tulloch's Brae, Lossiemouth, Morayshire IV31 6QY. *T*: (01343) 812222.
Died 21 March 2006.

EXTON, Clive Jack; scriptwriter and playwright; *b* 11 April 1930; *s* of late J. E. M. Brooks and Marie Brooks (*née* Rolfe); *m* 1951, Patricia Fletcher Ferguson (marr. diss. 1957); two *d*; *m* 1957, Margaret Josephine Reid; one *s* two *d*. *Educ*: Christ's Hospital. *TV plays*: No Fixed Abode, 1959; The Silk Purse; Where I Live; Some Talk of Alexander; Hold My Hand, Soldier; I'll Have You to Remember; The Big Eat; The Trial of Doctor Fancy; Land of my Dreams; The Close Prisoner; The Bone Yard; Conceptions of Murder (series); Are You Ready for the Music?; The Rainbirds; Killers (series); Stigma; Henry Intervenes; (with Tom Stoppard) The Boundary; The Crezz (series); Dick Barton—Special Agent (series); Wolf to the Slaughter, A Guilty Thing Surprised, Shake Hands for Ever (dramatizations of novels by Ruth Rendell); Jeeves and Wooster (Writers' Guild Award, 1992); Something's Got to Give; Rosemary and Thyme; The Man Who Could Write Miracles; many scripts and script consultant for Agatha Christie's Poirot. *Stage plays*: Have You Any Dirty Washing, Mother Dear?; Twixt; Murder is Easy; Dressing Down; Barking in Essex; Nedi and Bumps. *Films*: Night Must Fall; Isadora; Entertaining Mr Sloane; Ten Rillington Place; Running Scared; Doomwatch; The House in Nightmare Park; The Awakening. *Publications*: No Fixed Abode (in Six Granada Plays, anthol.), 1960; Have You Any Dirty Washing, Mother Dear? (in Plays of the Year, vol. 37), 1970. *Recreation*: panification. *Address*: c/o Rochelle Stevens & Co., 2 Terret's Place, N1 1QZ. *T*: (020) 7359 3900. *Club*: Groucho.
Died 16 Aug. 2007.

EYRE, Hon. Dean Jack; New Zealand High Commissioner to Canada, 1968–73 and 1976–80; *b* Westport, NZ, 1914; *m*; two *s* one *d*. *Educ*: Hamilton High Sch.; Auckland University Coll. Served War of 1939–45, Lieut in RNVR. Electrical importer and manufacturer. Government of New Zealand: MP (Nat) North Shore, 1949–66; Minister of Customs, Industries and Commerce, 1954–57; Minister of Social Security and Tourist and Health Resorts, 1956–57; Minister of Housing, State Advances and Defence, 1957; Minister in Charge of Police, 1960–63; Minister of Defence, 1960–66; Minister i/c Tourism, 1961–66. *Recreations*: yachting, fishing. *Address*: 550 Wilbrod Street, Ottawa, ON K1N 9M3, Canada. *Clubs*: Royal New Zealand Yacht Squadron, Northern (Auckland); Royal Ottawa Golf.
Died 19 May 2007.

F

FABER, Sir Richard (Stanley), KCVO 1980; CMG 1977; FRSL; HM Diplomatic Service, retired; Ambassador to Algeria, 1977–81; *b* 6 Dec. 1924; *er s* of late Sir Geoffrey Faber and Enid, *d* of Sir Henry Erle Richards, KCSI, KC; unmarried. *Educ:* Westminster Sch.; Christ Church, Oxford (1st cl. Lit. Hum.; MA). RNVR, 1943–46. Pres., Oxford Union Soc., 1949. Joined HM Foreign (subseq. Diplomatic) Service, 1950; service in FO and in Baghdad, Paris, Abidjan, Washington; Head of Rhodesia Political Dept, FCO, 1967–69; Counsellor: The Hague, 1969–73; Cairo, 1973–75; Asst Under Sec. of State, FCO, 1975–77. Hon. Treas., RSL, 1986–91. *Publications:* Beaconsfield and Bolingbroke, 1961; The Vision and the Need: Late Victorian Imperialist Aims, 1966; Proper Stations: Class in Victorian Fiction, 1971; French and English, 1975; The Brave Courtier (biog. of Sir William Temple), 1983; High Road to England, 1985; Young England, 1987; A Brother's Murder, 1992; A Chain of Cities (autobiog.), 2000. *Address:* Flat 1, 170 High Street, Lewes BN7 1YE. *Club:* Travellers.
Died 18 Oct. 2007.

FACK, Robbert; Commander, Order of Orange-Nassau, 1979; Chevalier, Order of Netherlands Lion, 1971; Netherlands diplomat; Ambassador of the Netherlands to the Court of St James's, 1976–82; also, concurrently, Ambassador to Iceland, 1976–82; *b* 1 Jan. 1917; *m* 1943, Patricia H. Hawkins; four *s. Educ:* Univ. of Amsterdam. Military service, 1937–45. Min. of Foreign Affairs, The Hague, 1945–46; New York (UN), 1946–48; Min. of Foreign Affairs, 1948–50; Rome, 1950–54; Canberra, 1954–58; Bonn, 1958–63; Min. of Foreign Affairs, 1963–68; Ambassador-at-large, 1968–70; Perm. Rep. to UN, New York, 1970–74. Holder of various foreign decorations. *Publications:* Gedane Zaken (Finished Business), (reminiscences), 1984. *Address:* Widden Hill House, Horton, near Chipping Sodbury, S Glos BS37 6QU. *Club:* Dutch. *Died 17 June 2010.*

FAIR, (James) Stuart, CBE 1997; WS; Chairman, Dundee Incubator Ltd, 1997–2003; Consultant, Thorntons, WS, Dundee, 1991–97; *b* 30 Sept. 1930; *s* of James Stuart Fair and Margaret Fair (*née* McCallum); *m* 1957, Anne Lesley Cameron (*d* 2003); two *s* one *d. Educ:* Perth Acad.; St Andrews Univ. (MA); Edinburgh Univ. (LLB); MSc in Criminal Justice, Napier Univ., 2000. Admitted solicitor, 1956; Sen. Partner, Thorntons, WS, 1984–91; Hon. Sheriff, Dundee, 1978–; Temp. Sheriff, 1988–98. Clerk to General Comrs of Income Tax, Dundee Div., 1975–96. Chairman: Dundee Port Authy, 1992–96; Dundee Teaching Hosps NHS Trust, 1993–96. Pres., Dundee & Tayside Chamber of Commerce and Industry, 1980–81; Dep. Chm., Tayside Cttee on Medical Research Ethics, 1990–95. Dean, Faculty of Procurators and Solicitors in Dundee, 1977–79. Chm. Court, Univ. of Dundee, 1988–93; Trustee, Sir James Caird's Travelling Scholarships Trust, 1988– (Administrator and Sec., 1993–96). Mem., Develt Adv. Bd, Nat. Museums of Scotland, 1999–2002. Trustee, Dundee Heritage Trust, 2000–03. Hon. LLD Dundee, 1994. *Address:* Apt 8, 33 Murrayfield Road, Edinburgh EH12 6EP. *T:* (0131) 346 2716. *Club:* New (Edinburgh). *Died 16 Nov. 2006.*

FAIRHALL, Hon. Sir Allen, KBE 1970; MHR (L) Paterson, NSW, 1949–69; *b* 24 Nov. 1909; *s* of Charles Edward and Maude Fairhall; *m* 1936, Monica Clelland, *d* of James and Ellen Ballantyne; one *s. Educ:* East Maitland Primary and High Sch.; Newcastle Tech. Inst. Founded commercial broadcasting stn 2KO, 1931; Supervising Engr, Radio and Signals Supplies Div., Min. of Munitions, 1942–45; Pres., Austr. Fedn of Commercial Broadcasting Stns, 1942–43. Mem. Australian Delegn to UN Gen. Assembly, 1954; Government of New South Wales: Minister for Interior and Works, 1956–58; Minister for Supply, 1961–66; Minister for Defence, 1966–69. Mem. Newcastle CC, 1941. FRSA 1970. Hon. DSc Newcastle, NSW, 1968. *Recreations:* amateur radio, deep sea fishing. *Address:* Apt 4, The Breakwater, 304 Wharf Road, Newcastle, NSW 2300, Australia. *T:* (2) 49291510. *Club:* Newcastle (Newcastle). *Died 4 Nov. 2006.*

FAIRTLOUGH, Gerard Howard, CBE 1989; Chief Executive, Celltech Ltd, 1980–90; *b* 5 Sept. 1930; *s* of late Maj.-Gen. Eric V. H. Fairtlough, DSO, MC, and Λ. Zoë Fairtlough (*née* Barker); *m* 1954, Elizabeth A. Betambeau; two *s* two *d. Educ:* Cambridge Univ. (BA Biochemistry, Pt II). Royal/Dutch Shell Group, 1953–78; Managing Director, Shell Chemicals UK Ltd, 1973–78; Divisional Director, NED, 1978–80. Director: Cantab Pharmaceuticals plc, 1990–2001; Xenova Gp plc, 2001–03; Chairman: Coverdale Orgn, 1974–93; Therexsys Ltd, 1992–96; Landmark Inf. Gp Ltd, 1994–97; Triarchy Press Ltd. Mem., SERC, 1989–94. Hon. DSc: City, 1987; CNAA, 1990. *Publications:* Creative Compartments, 1994; The Power of the Tale, 2002; New York Changed My Life, 2004; The Three Ways of Getting Things Done, 2005. *Recreations:* walking, yoga, theatre. *Died 15 Dec. 2007.*

FAKLEY, Dennis Charles, OBE 1973; Ministry of Defence, 1963–84; *b* 20 Nov. 1924; *s* of Charles Frederick and Ethel May Fakley; *m* 1976, Louise Grace Swindell. *Educ:* Chatham House Grammar Sch., Ramsgate; Queen Mary Coll., Univ. of London (BSc Special Physics). Royal Naval Scientific Service, 1944–63. *Recreations:* reading, cricket. *Address:* 14 Coval Gardens, SW14 7DG. *T:* (020) 8876 6856. *Died 3 April 2009.*

FALCONER, Hon. Sir Douglas (William), Kt 1981; MBE 1946; a Judge of the High Court of Justice, Chancery Division, 1981–89; *b* 20 Sept. 1914; *s* of late William Falconer, S Shields; *m* 1st, 1941, Joan Beryl Argent (*d* 1989), *d* of late A. S. Bishop, Hagley, Worcs; one *s* one *d*; 2nd, 1997, Constance M. F. Drew. *Educ:* South Shields; King's Coll., Durham Univ.; BSc (Hons) Physics, 1935. Served War of 1939–45 (Hon. Major): commissioned E Yorks Regt, 1939. Called to Bar, Middle Temple, 1950, Bencher 1973; QC 1967. Apptd to exercise appellate jurisdiction of BoT, later DoT, under Trade Marks Act, 1970–81; Member: Departmental Cttee to review British trade mark law and practice, 1972–73; Standing Adv. Cttee on Patents, 1975–79; Standing Adv. Cttee on Trade Marks, 1975–79; Senate of Four Inns of Court, 1973–74; Senate of Four Inns of Court and the Bar, 1974–77; Chm., Patent Bar Assoc., 1971–80. *Publications:* (Jt Editor) Terrell on the Law of Patents, 11th edn, 1965, 12th edn, 1971. *Recreations:* music, theatre. *Address:* 1 Sandbourne Court, West Overcliff Drive, Bournemouth, Dorset BH4 8AB. *T:* (01202) 760302. *Died 18 Dec. 2007.*

FALLAIZE, Prof. Elizabeth Anne, PhD; Professor of French, 2002–08, and Pro-Vice-Chancellor, 2005–08, University of Oxford; Fellow, St John's College, Oxford, since 1990; *b* 3 June 1950; *d* of John and Jill Fallaize; *m* Michael Driscoll (marr. diss. 1996); one *s* one *d*; *m* 1998, Prof. Alan Grafen. *Educ:* Univ. of Exeter (BA, MA; PhD). Lectr in French, Univ. of Birmingham, 1977–90; Lectr, Univ. of Oxford, 1990–2002. Trustee, Rhodes Trust, 2006–. Co-Ed., French Studies, 1996–2004. Commandeur des palmes académiques (France), 2009 (Officier, 2002). *Publications:* The Novels of Simone de Beauvoir, 1990; French Women's Writing: recent fiction, 1993; Simone de Beauvoir: a critical reader, 1998; French Fiction in the Mitterand Years, 2000; The Oxford Book of French Short Stories, 2002. *Address:* St John's College, Oxford OX1 3JP; *e-mail:* elizabeth.fallaize@sjc.ox.ac.uk. *Died 6 Dec. 2009.*

FANNER, His Honour Peter Duncan; a Circuit Judge, 1986–95; *b* 27 May 1926; *s* of late Robert William Hodges Fanner, solicitor, and Doris Kitty Fanner; *m* 1949, Sheila Eveline England; one *s* one *d*. *Educ:* Pangbourne Coll. Admitted Solicitor of the Supreme Court, 1951 (holder Justices' Clerks' Society's prize). Served War of 1939–45, Pilot in Fleet Air Arm, Lieut (A) RNVR, 1944–47. Asst Clerk to Bromley Justices, 1947–51; Dep. Clerk to Gore Justices, 1951–56; Clerk to Bath Justices, 1956–72; Metropolitan Stipendiary Magistrate, 1972–86; a Dep. Circuit Judge, 1974–80; a Recorder, 1980–86. Mem. Council of Justices' Clerks' Society, 1966–72; Assessor Mem. of Departmental Cttee on Liquor Licensing, 1971–72. Chairman: Bath Round Table, 1963–64; Claverton Parish Council, 1998–2005. *Publications:* Stone's Justices' Manual; contrib. to Justice of the Peace, The Magisterial Officer, The Lawyer's Remembrancer. *Recreations:* travel, railways. *Address:* c/o The Law Courts, Small Street, Bristol BS1 1DA. *T:* (0117) 976 3030. *Died 28 Dec. 2009.*

FANTHORPE, Ursula Askham, CBE 2001; freelance writer, since 1989; *b* 22 July 1929; *d* of late His Honour Judge Richard Fanthorpe and Winifrid Elsie Askham (*née* Redmore); partner, Dr Rosemarie V. Bailey. *Educ:* St Catherine's Sch., Bramley; St Anne's Coll., Oxford (MA; Hon. Fellow 2003); Inst. of Educn, London (DipEd); Univ. of Swansea (Dip. Sch. Counselling). Cheltenham Ladies' College: Asst English Mistress, 1954–62; Hd of English, 1962–70; temp. clerical work, Bristol, 1973–74; clerk/receptionist, Burden Neurological Hosp., Bristol, 1974–89. Arts Council Writer-in-Residence, St Martin's Coll., Lancaster, 1983–85; Northern Arts Fellow, Durham and Newcastle Univs, 1987. FRSL 1988. Hawthornden Fellowship, 1987, 1997, 2002. Member: Poetry Soc.; Soc. of Authors (Travelling Fellowship, 1983); International PEN. Hon. Fellow, Sarum Coll., 2004. Hon. DLitt: UWE, 1995; Bath, 2006; Hon. PhD Gloucester, 2000. Queen's Gold Medal for Poetry, 2003. *Publications:* Side Effects, 1978; Standing To, 1982; Voices Off, 1984; Selected Poems, 1986; A Watching Brief, 1987; Neck-Verse, 1992; Safe as Houses, 1995; Consequences, 2000; Christmas Poems, 2002; Queueing for the Sun, 2003; Collected Poems, 2005; Homing In, 2006; From Me to You, 2007. *Recreations:* mediaeval parish churches, inland waterways. *Address:* Culverhay House, Wotton under Edge, Gloucestershire GL12 7LS. *T:* and *Fax:* (01453) 843105; *e-mail:* fanthorpe.bailey@ googlemail.com. *Died 28 April 2009.*

FARLEY, Prof. Martyn Graham, CEng, FRAeS, FIMechE, FIET; engineering and management consultant, 1976–95; Emeritus Professor, Royal Military College of Science, Shrivenham and Cranfield Institute of Technology, since 1986; *b* 27 Oct. 1924; *s* of Herbert Booth Farley and Hilda Gertrude (*née* Hendey); *m* 1948, Freda Laugharne; two *s* one *d*. *Educ:* Merchant Venturers Tech. Coll., Bristol; Bristol Aeroplane Co. Tech. Coll. CEng, FRAeS 1968; FIMechE 1969; FIET (FIProdE 1975); FIIM 1988. Engine Div., Bristol Aeroplane Co.: Design Apprentice, 1939–45; Engine Design, 1945–46; Develt Engr, 1946–51; Bristol Aero Engines Ltd: Sen. Designer, Gas Turbine Office, 1951–55; Asst Chief Develt Engr, 1955–59; Bristol Siddeley Engines: Asst Chief Mech. Engr, 1959–62; Chief Develt Engr, Small Engines Div., 1962–65; Chief Engr, 1965–67; Small Engines Div., Rolls-Royce: Chief Engr, 1967–68; Gen. Works Manager, 1968–72; Manufg and Prodn Dir, 1972–74; HQ Exec. to Vice-Chm. of Rolls-Royce (1971) Ltd, 1974–75; Prof. and Head of Dept of Management Sciences, RMCS, 1975–84; Vice-Chm., Sch. of Management and Maths, RMCS Faculty of Cranfield Inst. of Technology, 1984–86. Dir, World Tech Ventures, 1984–86; Chairman: RECSAM Components Ltd, 1986–89; Harwell Computer Power Ltd, 1991–93. Vis. Res. Prof., Luton Univ., 1992–98. Royal Aeronautical Society: Mem. Council, 1972–92; Vice Pres., 1980–83; Pres., 1983–84; Dir, Aeronautical Trusts, 1975–88; Hon. Treasurer, 1984–88. Vice Pres., Instn of Indust. Engrs, 1981–92; Pres., IProdE, 1984–85

(Mem. Council, 1973–; Chm. Council, 1978–80; Vice-Pres., 1982–83); Chm., British Management Data Foundn Ltd, 1978–92; Founder Chm., Alliance of Manufg and Management Orgns, 1981; Member: EEF Manufg Trng Cttee, 1975–91; Guggenheim Medal Bd of Award, 1983; Adv. Council, RN Engrg Coll., Manadon, 1988–95; Court, Brunel Univ., 1977–80, Loughborough Univ., 1977–83, Cranfield Inst. of Technol., 1977–, Bath Univ., 1983–, Luton Univ., 1995–98. External Examiner: RAF Cranwell, RNEC and RMCS, 1979–; RNEC and Plymouth Univ., 1988–95. Mem., Sen. Awards Cttee. 1979–99, Fellows Cttee, 1992–, and Hon. Mem. Council, 1985–99, City and Guilds of London Inst.; Hon. CGIA 1981 (Pres., CGIA Assoc., 1984–98, Hon. Life Pres., 1998); Hon. FCGI 1990; Designer and Project Co-ordinator, EITB Manufg Fellowships, 1977–91. CCMI (CBIM 1980). Hon. FIIPE 1979; Hon. Member: Amer. Inst. of Indust. Managers, 1979; Australian Inst. of Indust. Engrs, 1981; Amer. Soc. of Manufg Engrs, 1985 (elected Charter Fellow, 1986). Freeman, City of London, 1981; Mem., Co. of Coachmakers and Coach Harness Makers. Hon. DSc RNEC and Plymouth Univ., 1994. Internat. Archimedes Award, Amer. Soc. of Prof. Engrs, 1979; First Shuttle Contributions Medal, 1981; Educn Gold Medal Award, ASME, 1983; Amer. Instn Advanced Engr Medal, 1984; NASA/Rocketdyne Tech. Award, 1984; Internat. Engr of Year Award, LA Council of Engrs and Scientists, 1984; California State Engrg Commendation, 1985; NASA Contribs Award, 1985; W. B. Johnson Award, ASME, 1988. *Publications:* articles and technical pubns; procs of conferences. *Address:* Willow End, Vicarage Lane, Shrivenham, Swindon, Wilts SN6 8DT. *T:* (01793) 782319. *Clubs:* Athenæum, Advanced Class; Shrivenham (Shrivenham); Ariel Rowing (Bristol). *Died 3 Nov. 2007.*

FARNCOMBE, Charles Frederick, CBE 1977; FRAM; Musical Director: Handel Opera Society, 1955–85; Malcolm Sargent Festival Choir, 1985–2006; *b* 29 July 1919; *o s* of Harold and Eleanor Farncombe, both of London; *m* 1963, Sally Mae (*née* Felps) (*d* 2003), Riverside, Calif, USA; one *d*. *Educ:* London Univ., 1936–40 (Archibald Dawnay Scholarship in Civil Engrg, 1936; BSc Hons (Eng) 1940); Royal Sch. of Church Music, 1947–48; Royal Academy of Music, 1948–51 (RAM, Mann Prize). Civil Engr to John Mowlem & Co. 1940–42. Served War, 1942–47, as Captain in REME, in 21st Army Gp. Freelance Conductor: formed Handel Opera Soc. 1955; Musical Dir, 1968–79, Chief Conductor, 1970–79, Royal Court Theatre, Drottningholm, Sweden; Chief Guest Conductor, 1979–85, Chief Conductor, annual Handel Fest., 1985–95, Badisches Staatstheater, Karlsruhe, 1979–; Guest Conductor, Komische Oper Berlin, 1994–. Dir, Treadam Barn Trust, 1994–. AMICE 1945 (resigned later); FRAM 1963 (ARAM 1962); Hon. Fellow, Royal Swedish Acad. of Music, 1972. Hon DMus: Columbus Univ., Ohio, USA, 1959; Yankton Univ., S Dakota, 1959; City Univ., 1988. Gold Medal of the Friends of Drottningholm, 1971; Gold Medal, Karlsruhe Handel Fest. Cttee, 1992. Kt Comdr, Order of North Star, Sweden, 1982. *Recreations:* cajoling singers, swimming, farm on Offa's Dyke. *Address:* 32 Trinity Court, 170A Gloucester Terrace, W2 6HS. *Died 30 June 2006.*

FARQUHARSON of Whitehouse, Captain Colin Andrew; JP; FRICS; chartered surveyor and land agent; Lord Lieutenant of Aberdeenshire, 1987–98 (Vice Lord-Lieutenant, 1983–87); *b* 9 Aug. 1923; *s* of late Norman Farquharson of Whitehouse; *m* 1st, 1948, Jean Sybil Mary (*d* 1985), *d* of late Brig.-Gen. J. G. H. Hamilton, Skene, DSO, JP, DL; two *d* (and one *d* decd); 2nd, 1987, Clodagh, *widow* of Ian Houldsworth, Dallas Lodge, Moray, and *d* of Sir Kenneth Murray, Geanies, Ross-shire; three step *s* two step *d*. *Educ:* Rugby. FLAS 1956, FRICS 1970. Served Grenadier Guards, 1942–48: ADC to Field Marshal Sir Harold Alexander (later (1st) Earl Alexander of Tunis), 1945. Member, Queen's Body Guard for Scotland (Royal Company of Archers), 1964–. Chartered surveyor and land agent in private practice in

Aberdeenshire, 1953–; Director, MacRobert Farms (Douneside) Ltd, 1971–87. Member, Bd of Management for Royal Cornhill Hosps, 1962–74; Chm., Gordon Local Health Council, 1975–81; Mem., Grampian Health Bd, 1981–89. DL 1966, JP 1969, Aberdeenshire. *Recreations:* shooting, fishing. *Address:* Whitehouse, Alford, Aberdeenshire AB33 8DP. *Clubs:* MCC; Royal Northern and University (Aberdeen).   *Died 13 March 2010.*

FARR, Dennis Larry Ashwell, CBE 1991; FMA; Director, Courtauld Institute Galleries, 1980–93; *b* 3 April 1929; *s* of late Arthur William Farr and Helen Eva Farr (*née* Ashwell); *m* 1959, Diana Pullein-Thompson (writer), *d* of Captain H. J. Pullein-Thompson, MC, and Joanna (*née* Cannan); one *s* one *d. Educ:* Luton Grammar Sch.; Courtauld Inst. of Art, London Univ. (BA, MA). Asst Witt Librarian, Courtauld Inst. of Art, 1952–54; Asst Keeper, Tate Gallery, 1954–64; Curator, Paul Mellon Collection, Washington, 1965–66; Sen. Lectr in Fine Art, and Dep. Keeper, University Art Collections, Univ. of Glasgow, 1967–69; Dir, City Museums and Art Gallery, Birmingham, 1969–80. Fred Cook Meml Lecture, RSA, 1974. Hon. Art Adviser, Calouste Gulbenkian Foundn, 1969–73; Member: British Council Fine Arts Adv. Cttee, 1971–80; Wright Cttee on Provincial Museums and Galls, 1971–73; Museums Assoc. Council, 1971–74 (Vice-Pres., 1978–79, 1980–81; Pres., 1979–80; Hon Councillor, 1991–93); Art Panel, Arts Council, 1972–77; ICOM (UK) Exec. Bd, 1976–85; Cttee, Victorian Soc., 1980–95; Exec. Cttee, Assoc. of Art Historians, 1981–87 (Chm. of Assoc., 1983–86); History of Art and Design Bd, CNAA, 1981–87; Comité Internat. d'Histoire de l'Art, 1983–94 (Hon Mem., 1994); Registration Cttee, Museums and Galls Commn, 1993–99. Trustee: Birmingham Mus. and Art Gall. Appeal Fund, 1980– (Chm. Trustees, 1978–00), Nat. Heritage, 2005–; Mount Pleasant, 1980– (Chm. Trustees, 2006–); Secretary: Home House Soc. Trustees, 1986–90; Samuel Courtauld Trust, 1990–93. Guest Curator, Francis Bacon: a retrospective, USA tour, 1999. JP Birmingham, 1977–80. Hon. Sec., CS Riding Club, 1958–60. FRSA 1970; FMA 1972. Hon. DLitt Birmingham, 1981. Gen. Editor, Clarendon Studies in the History of Art, 1985–2001. *Publications:* William Etty, 1958; (with M. Chamot and M. Butlin) Catalogue of the Modern British School Collection, Tate Gallery, 1964; British Sculpture since 1945, 1965; New Painting in Glasgow, 1968; Pittura Inglese 1660–1840, 1975; English Art 1870–1940, 1978, 2nd edn 1984; (contrib.) British Sculpture in the Twentieth Century, 1981; (with W. Bradford) The Courtauld Collection (catalogue for exhibns in Tokyo and Canberra), 1984; (with W. Bradford) The Northern Landscape (catalogue for exhibn in New York), 1986; (contrib.) In Honor of Paul Mellon, Collector and Benefactor, 1986; (jtly) Impressionist and Post-Impressionist Masterpieces: the Courtauld Collection, 1987; (ed and contrib.) 100 Masterpieces from the Courtauld Collections: Bernardo Daddi to Ben Nicholson, 1987; (jtly) The Oxford Dictionary of Art, 1988; (with Eva Chadwick) Lynn Chadwick: Sculptor, a complete catalogue 1947–88, 1990, 3rd edn 2006; (ed and contrib.) Thomas Gambier Parry as Artist and Collector, 1993; (ed and contrib.) Francis Bacon: a retrospective, 1999; Lynn Chadwick: Tate Britain exhibition, 2003; articles in: Apollo, Burlington Magazine, DNB, Oxford DNB, TLS, etc. *Recreations:* riding, reading, music, foreign travel. *Address:* Orchard Hill, Swan Barn Road, Haslemere, Surrey GU27 2HY. *T:* (01428) 641880. *Club:* Athenæum.   *Died 6 Dec. 2006.*

FARR, Air Vice-Marshal Peter Gerald Desmond, CB 1968; OBE 1952; DFC 1942; Director, Brain Research Trust, 1973–83; *b* 26 Sept. 1917; *s* of late Gerald Farr and Mrs Farr (*née* Miers); *m* 1949, Rosemarie (*d* 1983), *d* of late R. S. Haward; two *s* one *d. Educ:* Tonbridge Sch. Commnd in RAF, 1937; served War of 1939–45, Middle East, India and Burma; OC, No 358 Sqdn, 1944–45; OC, RAF Pegu, 1945–46; OC, 120 Sqdn, 1950–51; Dep. Dir, Jt Anti-Submarine Sch., 1952–54; OC, RAF Idris, 1954–55; Directing Staff, Jt Services Staff Coll., 1959;

SASO, Malta, 1960–63; OC, RAF Kinloss, 1963–64; Air Officer Administration: RAF Germany, 1964–68; Strike Comd, 1969–72. *Recreations:* golf, music. *Address:* c/o Lloyds TSB, Great Missenden, Bucks HP16 0AT. *Club:* Royal Air Force.   *Died 21 Oct. 2009.*

FARRAR-HOCKLEY, Gen. Sir Anthony Heritage, GBE 1982 (MBE 1957); KCB 1977; DSO 1953 and bar 1964; MC 1944; author (military history), defence consultant and lecturer; Commander-in-Chief Allied Forces Northern Europe, 1979–82; ADC General to the Queen, 1981–83; retired 1983; *b* 8 April 1924; *s* of late Arthur Farrar-Hockley and Agnes Beatrice (*née* Griffin); *m* 1945, Margaret Bernadette Wells (*d* 1981); two *s* (and one *s* decd); *m* 1983, Linda Wood. *Educ:* Exeter Sch. War of 1939–45 (despatches, MC): enlisted under-age in ranks of The Gloucestershire Regt and served until Nov. 1942: commissioned into newly forming 1st Airborne Div., campaigning in Greece, Italy, S France, to 1945 (despatches 1943). Palestine, 1945–46; Korea, 1950–53 (despatches 1954); Cyprus and Port Said, 1956; Jordan, 1958; College Chief Instructor, RMA Sandhurst, 1959–61; commanded parachute bn in Persian Gulf and Radfan campaign, 1962–65; Col GS to Dir of Borneo Ops, 1965–66; Comdr, 16 Parachute Bde, 1966–68; Defence Fellowship, Exeter Coll., Oxford, 1968–70 (BLitt); DPR (Army), 1970; Comdr, Land Forces, N Ireland, 1970–71; GOC 4th Armoured Div., 1971–73; Dir, Combat Development (Army), 1974–77; GOC SE District, 1977–79. Colonel Commandant: Prince of Wales's Div., 1974–80; Parachute Regt, 1977–83; Col, The Gloucestershire Regt, 1978–84. President: UK–Korea Forum, 1991–99; Army Records Soc., 2002–. *Publications:* The Edge of the Sword, 1954; (cd) The Commander, 1957; The Somme, 1964; Death of an Army, 1968; Airborne Carpet, 1969; War in the Desert, 1969; General Student, 1973; Goughie: the Life of General Sir Hubert Gough, GCB, GCMG, KCVO, 1975; Opening Rounds, 1988; The British Part in the Korean War, vol. I: A Distant Obligation, 1990, vol. II: An Honourable Discharge, 1995; Army in the Air, 1994; contributor: (and associate ed.) The D-Day Encyclopaedia, 1994; Oxford Illustrated History of the British Army, 1994; Oxford Companion to the Second World War, 1995; DNB; Oxford DNB. *Recreations:* cricket, sailing, walking. *Address:* c/o National Westminster Bank, 30 Wellington Street, Aldershot, Hants GU11 1EB.   *Died 11 March 2006.*

FARTHING, (Richard) Bruce (Crosby); Chairman, 1999–2000, President, since 2001, Maritime London; *b* 9 Feb. 1926; *s* of late Col Herbert Hadfield Farthing and late Marjorie Cora (*née* Fisher); *m* 1st, 1959, Anne Brenda Williams (marr. diss. 1986), LLB, barrister, *d* of late Thomas Williams, solicitor; one *s* one *d*; 2nd, 1986, Moira Roupell, *o d* of late Lt-Col R. A. Curties and late Ida Curties. *Educ:* Alleyn's Sch. (Dulwich and Rossall); St Catharine's Coll., Cambridge (MA). Commissioned RA and RHA, 1944–48. Called to Bar, Inner Temple, 1954; Govt Legal Service, 1954–59; joined Chamber of Shipping of UK, 1959; Asst Gen. Manager, 1966; Sec., Cttee of European Shipowners and Cttee of European Nat. Shipowners' Assocs, 1967–74; Sec.-Gen., Council of European and Japanese Nat. Shipowners' Assocs (CENSA), 1974–76; Dir, 1976–80, Dep. Dir-Gen., 1980–83, Gen. Council of British Shipping. Rapporteur, Sea Transport Commn, ICC, 1976–96; Consultant Dir, Internat. Assoc. of Dry Cargo Shipowners, 1984–99. Freeman, City of London, 1979; Liveryman, Shipwrights' Co., 1982–; Mem. Court of Common Council (Aldgate Ward), 1981–. Pres., Aldgate Ward Club, 1985 (Vice-Pres., 1984). Governor: City of London Sch., 1983–99 (Dep. Chm., 1988–89, 1993–94, Chm., 1990–93); SOAS, 1985–2000; GSMD, 2001–; Mem. Council, City Univ., 1994–98. Mem. Court, Hon. Irish Soc., 1992–94. Trustee, Nautical Museums Trust, 1983–2001. Mem., British Cttee, Registro Italiano Navale, 1997–2003. Chm., King of Norway Reception Cttee, 1988. FCMI. Commander, Royal Norwegian Order of Merit, 1988. *Publications:* ed, Vol. 20, Aspinalls Maritime Law Cases,

1961; International Shipping, 1987, 3rd edn 1997. *Recreations:* sailing, music, writing. *Address:* 44 St George's Drive, SW1V 4BT. *Clubs:* MCC, Royal Ocean Racing.
Died 21 April 2007.

FASHAM, Dr Michael John Robert, FRS 2000; Hon. Professor, Southampton Oceanography Centre, University of Southampton, since 2002; *b* 29 May 1942; *s* of Ronald Henry Alfred Fasham and Hazel Grace Fasham (*née* Day); *m* 1967, Jocelyn Mary Hart; one *s*. *Educ:* Kilburn Grammar Sch.; Birmingham Univ. (BSc; PhD 1968). Sen. Geophysicist, Wimpey Labs, 1967–68; SSO, Nat. Inst. Oceanography, 1968–73; PSO, Inst. Oceanographic Scis, 1973–93; SPSO, Southampton Oceanography Centre, 1993–2002. Chm. Scientific Cttee, Jt Global Ocean Flux Study, 1998–2000. Silver Medal, Challenger Soc., 2002. *Publications:* (ed) Flows of Energy and Materials in Marine Ecosystems: theory and practice, 1984; (ed jtly) Towards a Model of Ocean Biogeochemical Processes, 1993; contrib. papers to oceanographic jls. *Recreations:* genealogy, British history, gardening. *Address:* White Cottage, Hill Road, Grayshott, Hindhead, Surrey GU26 6HL. *T:* (01428) 606119.
Died 7 June 2008.

FATEH, Abul Fazal Muhammad Abul; Hon. Representative of Royal Commonwealth Society in Bangladesh, 1985–94; *b* 16 May 1924; *s* of Abdul Gafur and Zohra Khatun; *m* 1956, Mahfuza Banu; two *s*. *Educ:* Dhaka, Bangladesh. MA (English Lit.); special course, LSE, 1949–50. Carnegie Fellow in Internat. Peace, 1962–63. Entered Pakistan Foreign Service, 1949; 3rd Secretary: Paris, 1951–53; Calcutta, 1953–56; 2nd Sec., Washington, DC, 1956–60; Dir, Min. of Foreign Affairs, Karachi, 1961–65; 1st Sec., Prague, 1965–66; Counsellor, New Delhi, 1966–67; Dep. High Comr for Pakistan, Calcutta, 1968–70; Ambassador of Pakistan, Baghdad, 1970–71; Adviser to Actg President of Bangladesh, Aug. 1971–Jan. 1972; Foreign Sec., Bangladesh, Oct. 1971–Jan. 1972; Ambassador of Bangladesh to France and Spain, 1972–75; Permanent Deleg. to UNESCO, 1972–76; High Comr for Bangladesh in London, 1976–77; Ambassador, Algeria, 1977–82. Leader, Bangladesh Delegation: Commonwealth Youth Ministers' Conf., Lusaka, 1973; Meeting of UN Council on Namibia, Algiers, 1980; Ministerial Meeting of Non-aligned Countries Co-ordination Bureau on Namibia, Algiers, 1981. Chm., Commonwealth Human Ecology Council Symposium, 1977. Mem., Poetry Soc., 1994–99. *Address:* 3 Hertford Lodge, 15 East End Road, Finchley Church End, N3 3NJ. *Died 4 Dec. 2010.*

FAY, His Honour Edgar Stewart; QC 1956; a Circuit Judge (formerly an Official Referee of the Supreme Court of Judicature), 1971–80; *b* 8 Oct. 1908; *s* of late Sir Sam Fay; *m* 1st, 1930, Kathleen Margaret (*d* 1970), *e d* of late C. H. Buell, Montreal, PQ, and Brockville, Ont; two *s* (and one *s* decd); 2nd, Jenny Julie Henriette (*d* 1990), *yr d* of late Dr Willem Roosegaarde Bisschop, Lincoln's Inn; one *s*; 3rd, Eugenia Bishop, *yr d* of late Piero Biganzoli, Milan. *Educ:* Courtenay Lodge Sch.; McGill Univ.; Pembroke Coll., Cambridge (MA). FCIArb 1981–2008. Called to Bar, Inner Temple, 1932; Master of the Bench, 1962. Recorder: of Andover, 1954–61; of Bournemouth, 1961–64; of Plymouth, 1964–71; Dep. Chm., Hants QS, 1960–71. Member: Bar Council, 1955–59, 1966–70; Senate of Four Inns of Court, 1970–72. Chm., Inquiry into Crown Agents, 1975–77. *Publications:* Why Piccadilly?, 1935; Londoner's New York, 1936; Discoveries in the Statute Book, 1937; The Life of Mr Justice Swift, 1939; Official Referees' Business, 1983. *Address:* 95 Highgate West Hill, N6 6NR. *T:* (020) 8348 5780. *Died 14 Nov. 2009.*

FEARN, Sir (Patrick) Robin, KCMG 1991 (CMG 1983); HM Diplomatic Service, retired; Associate Director, Centre for Political and Diplomatic Studies, Oxford, since 2000; *b* 5 Sept. 1934; *s* of late Albert Cyprian Fearn and Hilary (*née* Harrison); *m* 1961, Sorrel Mary Lynne Thomas; three *s* one *d*. *Educ:* Ratcliffe Coll.; University Coll., Oxford (MA Hons, Mod.

Langs). Nat. Service, Intelligence Corps, 1952–54. Overseas marketing, Dunlop Rubber Co. Ltd, 1957–61; entered Foreign Service, 1961; FO, 1961–62; Third, later Second Sec., Caracas, 1962–64; Havana, 1965; First Sec., Budapest, 1966–68; FCO, 1969–72; Head of Chancery, Vientiane, 1972–75; Asst Head of Science and Technol. Dept, FCO, 1975–76; Counsellor, Head of Chancery and Consul Gen., Islamabad, 1977–79; Head of S America Dept, FCO, 1979–82; Head of Falkland Islands Dept, FCO, 1982; RCDS, 1983; Ambassador to Cuba, 1984–86; Asst Under-Sec. of State (Americas), FCO, 1986–89; Ambassador to Spain, 1989–94. Dir, Foreign Service Prog., Oxford Univ., and Vis. Fellow, UC, Oxford, 1995–99. Trustee, Imperial War Mus., 2001–. Chm., Anglo-Spanish Soc., 1999–2002. Mem. Council, Univ. of Bath, 2000–03; Chm. Council, King's Coll., Madrid, 2003–. *Recreations:* tennis, music, reading, family life. *Address:* c/o Barclays Bank, 9 Portman Square, W1A 3AL. *Club:* Oxford and Cambridge. *Died 26 Aug. 2006.*

FEATHERSTONE, Hugh Robert, CBE 1984 (OBE 1974); FCIS; Director-General, Freight Transport Association, 1969–84; *b* 31 March 1926; *s* of Alexander Brown Featherstone and Doris Olive Martin; *m* 1948, Beryl Joan Sly; one *s* one *d*. *Educ:* Minchenden Sch., Southgate, London. FCIS 1956. Served War, RNVR, 1943–46 (Sub-Lt). Assistant Secretary: Nat. Assoc. of Funeral Dirs, 1946–48; Brit. Rubber Develt Bd, 1948–58; Asst Sec. 1958–60, Sec. 1960–68, Traders Road Transport Assoc. *Publications:* contrib. to jls concerned with transport and admin. *Recreations:* golf, gardening, languages, travel, bridge, cookery. *Died 24 July 2009.*

FEDIDA, Sam, OBE 1980; independent consultant, information systems, retired; inventor of Prestel, viewdata system (first public electronic information service); *b* 4 May 1918; *m* 1942, Joan Iris Druce (decd); three *s* (one *d* decd). Served Royal Air Force, Radar Officer, 1940–46. Became Asst Dir of Research, The English Electric Company; started research for the Post Office, 1970; Prestel first in use 1979, as public service; MacRobert Award, Council of Engineering Instns, 1979; Prestel sold in Europe, USA, Far East. *Died 10 Aug. 2007.*

FEE, John Fitzgerald; Member (SDLP) Newry & Armagh, Northern Ireland Assembly, 1998–2003; *b* 7 Dec. 1963; *s* of Patrick and Deirdre Fee; *m* 1995, Collette Byrne. *Educ:* St Patrick's Primary Sch., Crossmaglen; St Colman's Coll., Newry; Queen's Univ., Belfast. Member: Rural Develt Council for NI, 1990–94; European Cttee of the Regions, 1998. Mem. (SDLP) Newry and Mourne DC, 1989. Editor, Creggan Historical Jl, 1986–87. *Recreations:* traditional Irish music, local history, golf, reading. *Address:* Aras Ceíli, Crossmaglen, Co. Armagh, N Ireland BT35 9BF. *T:* (028) 3086 8824. *Died 11 Nov. 2007.*

FEILDEN, Sir Bernard (Melchior), Kt 1985; CBE 1976 (OBE 1969); FRIBA 1968 (ARIBA 1949); Consultant, Feilden and Mawson, Chartered Architects (Partner, 1956–77); Member, Cathedrals Advisory Commission for England, 1981–90; *b* 11 Sept. 1919; *s* of Robert Humphrey Feilden, MC, and Olive Feilden (*née* Binyon); *m* 1st, 1949, Ruth Mildred Bainbridge (*d* 1994); two *s* two *d*; 2nd, 1995, Christina Matilda Beatrice Murdoch. *Educ:* Bedford Sch. Exhibr, Bartlett Sch. of Architecture, 1938 (Hon. Fellow, UCL, 1985). Served War of 1939–45: Bengal Sappers and Miners. AA Diploma (Hons), 1949; Bratt Colbran Schol., 1949. Architect, Norwich Cathedral, 1963–77; Surveyor to the Fabric: York Minster, 1965–77; St Paul's Cathedral, 1969–77; Consultant Architect, UEA, 1969–77. Dir, Internat. Centre for the Preservation and Restoration of Cultural Property, Rome, 1977–81. Hoffman Wood Prof. of Architecture, Leeds Univ., 1973–74. Member: Ancient Monuments Bd (England), 1964–77; Council, RIBA, 1972–77; Cathedrals Fabric Commn, 1990–95; Cathedrals Fabric Cttees, Bury St Edmunds and Ely, 1990–2006. President: Ecclesiastical Architects' and

Surveyors' Assoc., 1975–77; Guild of Surveyors, 1976–77. FSA 1969; FRSA 1973; Hon. FAIA 1987. Corresp. Mem., Architectes en Chef, France. DUniv York, 1973; Hon. DLitt: Gothenburg, 1988; East Anglia, 1989. Aga Khan Award for Architecture, 1986. Order of St William of York, 1976. *Publications:* The Wonder of York Minster, 1976; Introduction to Conservation, 1979; Conservation of Historic Buildings, 1982, 3rd edn 2003; Between Two Earthquakes, 1987; Guidelines for Conservation (India), 1989; Guidelines for Management of World Cultural Heritage Sites, 1993; articles in Architectural Review, Chartered Surveyor, AA Quarterly. *Recreations:* painting, fishing. *Address:* The Old Barn, Hall Farm Place, Bawburgh, Norwich NR9 3LW. *T:* (01603) 747472. *Club:* Norfolk (Norwich).
Died 14 Nov. 2008.

FEILDEN, Sir Henry (Wemyss), 6th Bt *cr* 1846; *b* 1 Dec. 1916; *s* of Col Wemyss Gawne Cunningham Feilden, CMG (*d* 1943) (3rd *s* of 3rd Bt) and Winifred Mary Christian (*d* 1980), *d* of Rev. William Cosens, DD; *S* cousin, Sir William Morton Buller Feilden, 5th Bt, 1976; *m* 1943, Ethel May (*d* 2010), 2nd *d* of John Atkinson, Annfield Plain, Co. Durham; one *s* two *d*. *Educ:* Canford Sch.; King's Coll., London. Served War, RE, 1940–46. Clerical Civil Service, 1960–79. *Recreations:* watching cricket, reading. *Heir: s* Henry Rudyard Feilden, BVetSc, MRCVS [*b* 26 Sept. 1951; *m* 1st, 1982, Anne Shepperd (marr. diss. 1996); one *s*; 2nd, 1998, Geraldine, *d* of Major G. R. Kendall; one *s* one *d*]. *Address:* Little Dene, Heathfield Road, Burwash, Etchingham, East Sussex TN19 7HN. *T:* (01435) 882205. *Club:* MCC. *Died 12 Dec. 2010.*

FELLGETT, Prof. Peter Berners, PhD; FRS 1986; Professor of Cybernetics, University of Reading, 1965–87, then Emeritus; *b* 11 April 1922; *s* of Frank Ernest Fellgett and Rose, (Rowena), (*née* Wagstaffe); *m* 1947, Janet Mary (*d* 1998), *o d* of late Prof. G. E. Briggs, FRS, and Mrs Nora Briggs; one *s* two *d*. *Educ:* The Leys Sch., Cambridge; Univ. of Cambridge (BA 1943, MA 1947, PhD 1952). Isaac Newton Student, Cambridge Observatories, 1950–51; Lick Observatory, Calif, 1951–52; Cambridge Observatories, 1952–59; Royal Observatory, Edinburgh, 1959–65. *Publications:* approx. 75 pubns in learned jls and 32 gen. articles. *Recreations:* making musical instruments, high quality audio, gardening, fun-running, not being interrupted and not being hurried. *Address:* Little Brighter Farm, St Kew Highway, Bodmin, Cornwall PL30 3DU.
Died 15 Nov. 2008.

FELLNER, Christine; Social Security and Child Support Commissioner, since 1999; *b* 1 April 1946; *d* of Gustav Michael Fellner and Gwyneth Mary Fellner (*née* Hughes). *Educ:* Chiswick Co. Grammar Sch.; St Anne's Coll., Oxford (BA Jurisp., BCL). Lectr in Law, Southampton Univ., 1969–72; solicitor, 1974–81; called to the Bar, Middle Temple, 1981; in practice as barrister, 1981–95; occasional lectr, QMW and City Univ. Business Sch., 1984–92; Chm. (part-time), Social Security, Medical and Disability Appeal Tribunals, 1986–95; Chm., Independent Tribunal Service, 1995–99. *Publications:* The Future of Legal Protection for Industrial Design, 1985; Industrial Design Law, 1995; contribs to periodicals on intellectual property. *Address:* Commissioners' Office, Third Floor, Procession House, 55 Ludgate Hill, EC4M 7JW. *Died 1 April 2007.*

FENN, Prof. John Bennett, PhD; Professor of Analytical Chemistry, Virginia Commonwealth University, since 1993; *b* 15 June 1917; *s* of late Herbert Bennett Fenn and Jeanette Clyde Fenn (*née* Dingman); *m* 1st, 1939, Margaret Elizabeth Wilson (*d* 1992); one *s* two *d*; 2nd, Frederica Mullen; two step *d*. *Educ:* Berea Coll. (AB 1937); Yale Univ. (PhD 1940). Research Chemist: Monsanto Chemical Co., 1940–43; Sharples Chemicals Inc., 1943–45; Vice-Pres., Experiment Inc., 1945–52; Dir, Project SQUID, 1952–62, Prof. of Mech. Engrg, 1959–63, Prof. of Aerospace Scis, 1963–66, Princeton Univ.; Prof. of Applied Sci. and Chemistry, 1967–80,

Prof. of Engrg, 1980–87, Yale Univ., then Emeritus. Pres., Relay Develt Corp., 1975–. (Jtly) Nobel Prize in Chemistry, 2002. *Address:* Department of Chemistry, Virginia Commonwealth University, 1001 W Main Street, PO Box 842006, Richmond, VA 23284–2006, USA. *Died 12 Dec. 2010.*

FENNER, Prof. Frank John, AC 1989; CMG 1976; MBE 1944; FRS 1958; FAA; University Fellow, 1980–82, Visiting Fellow, 1983–2007, John Curtin School of Medical Research, Australian National University; *b* 21 Dec. 1914; *s* of Charles and Emma L. Fenner; *m* 1944, Ellen Margaret Bobbie Roberts (*d* 1995); one *d* (and one *d* decd). *Educ:* Thebarton Technical High Sch.; Adelaide High Sch.; Univ. of Adelaide (MB, BS 1938; MD 1942); DTM Sydney 1940. FAA 1954. Served as Medical Officer, Hospital Pathologist, and Malariologist, AIF, 1940–46; Francis Haley Research Fellow, Walter and Eliza Hall Inst. for Medical Research, Melbourne, 1946–48; Rockefeller Foundation Travelling Fellow, 1948–49; Prof. of Microbiology, 1949–67, Dir, John Curtin Sch. of Med. Research, 1967 73, Prof. of Environmental Studies and Dir, Centre for Resource and Environmental Studies, 1973–79, ANU; Overseas Fellow, Churchill Coll., Cambridge, 1961–62. Fogarty Schol., Nat. Insts of Health, USA, 1973–74, 1982–83. Chm., Global Commn for Certification of Smallpox Eradication, WHO, 1978–80. For. Associate, Nat. Acad. of Scis, USA, 1977. Harvey Lecture, Harvey Soc. of New York, 1957; Royal Society: Leeuwenhoek Lecture, 1961, Florey Lecture, 1983; Copley Medal, 1995; Australian Acad. of Science: Matthew Flinders Lecture, 1967; Burnet Lecture, 1985. Emeritus Mem., Amer. Soc. Virol., 1991. Fellow, World Acad. of Art and Sci., 1986. Hon. FRACP 1959; Hon. FRCP 1967; Hon. Fellow, University House, 2002. Hon. MD Monash, 1966; Dr *hc* Liège, 1992; Hon. DSc: Oxford Brookes Univ., 1995; ANU, 1996; DUniv Adelaide, 2007. David Syme Prize, Univ. of Melbourne, 1949; Mueller Medal, Australian and New Zealand Assoc. for the Advancement of Science, 1964; Britannica Australia Award for Medicine, 1967; ANZAC Peace Award, 1980; ANZAAS Medal, 1980; Stuart Mudd Award, Internat. Union of Microbiol Socs, 1986; Japan Prize (Preventive Medicine), Sci. & Technol. Foundn of Japan, 1988; Albert Einstein World Award for Science, 2000; Clunies Ross Nat. Sci. and Technol. Lifetime Contribution Award, 2002; Prime Minister's Prize for Science, 2002; Australian of the Year, 2003, Sen. Australian of the Year, 2006, ACT. *Publications:* The Production of Antibodies (with F. M. Burnet), 1949; Myxomatosis (with F. N. Ratcliffe), 1965; The Biology of Animal Viruses, 1968, 2nd edn 1974; Medical Virology (with D. O. White), 1970, 4th edn 1994; Classification and Nomenclature of Viruses, 1976; (with A. L. G. Rees) The Australian Academy of Science: the First Twenty-five Years, 1980; (jtly) Veterinary Virology, 1987, 2nd edn 1993; (jtly) Smallpox and its Eradication, 1988; (with Z. Jezek) Human Monkeypox, 1988; (with A. Gibbs) Portraits of Viruses: a history of virology, 1988; (jtly) The Orthopoxviruses, 1989; History of Microbiology in Australia, 1990; The Australian Academy of Science: the first forty years, 1995; (with B. Fantini) The Biological Control of Vertebrate Pests, 1999; (with D. R. Curtis) History of the John Curtin School of Medical Research 1948–1998, 2001; The Australian Academy of Science: the first fifty years, 2005; Nature, Nurture and Chance: the lives of Frank and Charles Fenner, 2006; numerous scientific papers, dealing with virology, epidemiology, bacteriology, environmental problems and history of science. *Recreation:* gardening. *Address:* 8 Monaro Crescent, Red Hill, Canberra, ACT 2603, Australia. *T:* (2) 62959176.
Died 22 Nov. 2010.

FENNESSY, Sir Edward, Kt 1975; CBE 1957 (OBE 1944); BSc; FIET, FRIN; Managing Director, Telecommunications, 1969–77, and Deputy Chairman, 1975–77, Post Office Corporation; *b* 17 Jan. 1912; *m* 1st, 1937, Marion Banks (*d* 1983); one *s* one *d*; 2nd, 1984, Leonora Patricia Birkett, *widow* of Trevor Birkett. *Educ:*

Queen Mary Coll., London (Hon. Fellow, QMW, 1998). Telecommunications Research, Standard Telephones and Cables, 1934–38; Radar Research, Air Min. Research Station, Bawdsey Manor, 1938. War of 1939–45: commissioned RAFVR, 1940; Group Captain, 1945; staff No 60 Group, RAF, 1940–45; resp. for planning and construction radar systems for defence of UK, and Bomber Ops. Joined Bd of The Decca Navigator Co., 1946; Managing Director: Decca Radar Ltd, 1950–65; The Plessey Electronics Group, 1965–69. Chairman: British Telecommunications Research Ltd, 1966–69; Electronic Engineering Assoc., 1967–68. Chairman: IMA Microwave Products Ltd, 1979–83; LKB Biochrom, 1978–87; British Medical Data Systems, 1981–91; Dep. Chm., LKB Instruments, 1978–87. Pres., Royal Institute of Navigation, 1975–78. DUniv Surrey, 1971. *Address:* Northbrook, Littleford Lane, Shamley Green, Surrey GU5 0RH. *T:* (01483) 892444.
Died 21 Nov. 2009.

FENTON, Rev. Canon John Charles; Canon of Christ Church, Oxford, 1978–91, Hon. Canon, 1991–92, then Hon. Canon Emeritus and Emeritus Student; *b* 5 June 1921; *s* of Cornelius O'Connor Fenton and Agnes Claudina Fenton; *m* 1st, 1945, Mary Hamilton Ingoldby (*d* 1960); two *s* two *d*; 2nd, 1963, Linda Brandham; two *s* one *d*. *Educ:* St Edward's Sch., Oxford; Queen's Coll., Oxford (BA 1943, MA 1947, BD 1953); Lincoln Theol Coll. Deacon 1944, priest 1945. Asst Curate, All Saints, Hindley, Wigan, 1944–47; Chaplain, Lincoln Theol Coll., 1947–51, Sub-Warden, 1951–54; Vicar of Wentworth, Yorks, 1954–58; Principal: Lichfield Theol Coll., 1958–65; St Chad's Coll., Durham, 1965–78. DD Lambeth, 2001. *Publications:* Preaching the Cross, 1958; The Passion according to John, 1961; Crucified with Christ, 1961; Saint Matthew (Pelican Commentaries), 1963; Saint John (New Clarendon Bible), 1970; What was Jesus' Message?, 1971; (with M. Hare Duke) Good News, 1976; Finding the Way through John, 1988; Sunday Readings, 1991; Affirmations, 1993; Finding the Way through Mark, 1995; The Matthew Passion, 1996; Galatians, 1996, with 1 & 2 Thessalonians, 1999 (People's Bible Commentary); More About Mark, 2001; contrib. Theol., Jl of Theol Studies, and Church Times. *Address:* 8 Rowland Close, Wolvercote, Oxford OX2 8PW. *T:* (01865) 554099.
Died 27 Dec. 2008.

FERGUSON, John McIntyre, CBE 1976; FREng; FIET; FIMechE; engineering consultant, 1973, retired 1986; *b* 16 May 1915; *s* of Frank Ferguson and Lilian (*née* Bowen); *m* 1941, Margaret Frances Tayler; three *s*. *Educ:* Armstrong Coll., Durham Univ. BScEng (1st Cl. Hons). English Electric Co., Stafford: Research, 1936; Chief Engr, 1953; Dir Engrg, Heavy Electric Products, 1965; Dir of Engrg, GEC Power Engrg Co., 1969. Member: Metrication Bd, 1969–76; Science Res. Council, 1972–76; UGC, 1977–82. President: IEE, 1977–78; IEETE, 1979–81. FREng (FEng 1978). Hon. FIEEIE. Hon. DSc Birmingham, 1983. *Recreations:* golf, sailing. *Address:* 11 Appledore Close, Baswich, Stafford ST17 0EW. *T:* (01785) 664700.
Died 27 Jan. 2008.

FERGUSON, Richard; QC 1986; QC (NI) 1973; SC (Ireland) 1983; *b* 22 Aug. 1935; *o* *s* of late Wesley Ferguson and Edith Ferguson (*née* Hewitt); *m* 1st, Janet Irvine Magowan (marr. diss.); three *s* one *d*; 2nd, Roma Felicity Whelan; one *s*. *Educ:* Rainey Sch., Magherafelt; Methodist Coll., Belfast; Trinity Coll., Dublin (BA); Queen's Univ. of Belfast (LLB). Called to NI Bar, 1956, to Bar of England and Wales, Gray's Inn, 1972 (Bencher, 1994). Chairman: NI Mental Health Review Tribunal, 1973–84; Criminal Bar Assoc. of England and Wales, 1993–95. MP (OU) S Antrim, Nov. 1968–1970. Mem., Irish Sports Council, 1978–81. FRGS 1980. *Recreation:* watching the Arsenal. *Address:* Carmelite Chambers, 9 Carmelite Street, EC4Y 0DR. *T:* (020) 7936 6300. *Club:* Garrick.
Died 26 July 2009.

FEROZE, Sir Rustam Moolan, Kt 1983; MD; FRCS, FRCOG; (first) President, European Association of Obstetrics and Gynaecology, 1985–88, then Hon.

President; Consulting Obstetrician, Queen Charlotte's Maternity Hospital; Consulting Surgeon, Chelsea Hospital for Women; *b* 4 Aug. 1920; *s* of Dr J. Moolan-Feroze; *m* 1947, Margaret Dowsett; three *s* (one *d* decd). *Educ:* Sutton Valence Sch.; King's Coll. and King's Coll. Hospital, London. MRCS, LRCP 1943; MB, BS 1946; MRCOG 1948; MD (Obst. & Dis. Wom.) London 1952; FRCS 1952; FRCOG 1962; Hon. FRCSI 1984; Hon. FRACOG 1985; Hon. FACOG 1986. Surg.-Lt, RNVR, 1943–46. King's Coll. Hosp., 1946; RMO, Samaritan Hosp. for Women, 1948; Sen. Registrar: Hosp. for Women, Soho Sq., and Middlesex Hosp., 1950–53; Chelsea Hosp. for Women, and Queen Charlotte's Maternity Hosp., 1953–54; Consultant Obstetrician and Gynaecologist, King's Coll. Hosp., 1952–85. Dean, Inst. of Obstetrics and Gynaecology, Univ. of London, 1954–67; Dir, Postgrad. Studies, RCOG, 1975–80; Pres., RCOG, 1981–84; Chm., Conf. of Royal Colls and Faculties, 1982–84. McIlrath Guest Prof., Royal Prince Alfred Hosp., Sydney, 1970. Lectures: Soc. of Obstetrics and Gynaecology of Canada, Winnipeg, 1978; Bartholomew Mosse, Dublin, 1982; Shirodkar Meml, Bombay, 1982; Charter Day, National Maternity Hosp., Dublin, 1984. Past Examiner: RCOG; Univs of London, Cambridge, Birmingham and Singapore. *Publications:* contributor: Integrated Obstetrics and Gynaecology for Postgraduates, 1981; Gynaecological Oncology, 1981, rev. edn 1992; Bonney's Gynaecological Surgery, 1986; contribs to med. jls. *Recreations:* Bonsai, music. *Address:* 9 Arbor Close, Beckenham, Kent BR3 6TW. *Club:* Royal Automobile.
Died 8 Feb. 2010.

FESSEY, Mereth Cecil, CB 1977; Director, Business Statistics Office, 1969–77, retired; *b* Windsor, Berks, 19 May 1917; *s* of late Morton Fessey and Ethel Fessey (*née* Blake), Bristol; *m* 1945, Grace Lilian (*d* 2004), *d* of late William Bray, Earlsfield, London; one *s* two *d*. *Educ:* Westminster City Sch.; LSE, Univ. of London. London Transport, 1934; Army, 1940; Min. of Transport, 1947; Board of Trade, 1948; Statistician, 1956; Chief Statistician, 1965. Statistical Adviser to Syrian and Mexican Govts, 1979; Consultant, Statistical Office, Eur. Communities, 1990–95. Chm. of Council, Inst. of Statisticians, 1970–73; Vice Pres. and Mem., Council, Royal Statistical Soc., 1974–78; Chm., Cttee of Librarians and Statisticians, LA/Royal Stat. Soc., 1978–97. Hon. FCLIP (Hon. FLA 1984). *Publications:* articles and papers in: Economic Trends; Statistical News; Jl of Royal Statistical Soc.; The Statistician; Annales de Sciences Economiques Appliquées, Louvain; etc. *Recreations:* chess, walking. *Address:* Undy House, Undy, Caldicot, Monmouthshire NP26 3BX. *T:* (01633) 880478.
Died 20 April 2006.

FETHERSTON-DILKE, Capt. Charles Beaumont, RN retired; Vice Lord-Lieutenant, Warwickshire, 1990–96; *b* 4 April 1921; *s* of late Dr Beaumont Albany Fetherston-Dilke, MBE and Phoebe Stella (*née* Bedford); *m* 1943, Pauline Stanley-Williams; one *s* one *d*. *Educ:* RNC, Dartmouth. Entered RN, 1935; served throughout War of 1939–45 and Korean War, 1952–54 (underwater warfare specialist); Comdr 1955; Danish Naval Staff, 1955–58; Directing Staff, RN Tactical Sch., 1958–60; staff of C-in-C S Atlantic and S America Station, 1960–61; Captain 1961; Naval Dep. to UK Nat. Mil. Rep., SHAPE, 1962–64; comd HMS St Vincent, 1964–66; Defence Policy Staff, MOD, 1966–68; retired 1968. Warwickshire: JP 1969–91; CC, 1970–81 (Chm., 1978–80); Chm., CLA, 1984–87; High Sheriff 1974; DL 1974. SBStJ 1986 (Mem. Council, 1977–92). Seigneur de Vangalême, Jersey. *Publications:* A Short History of Maxstoke Castle, 1985. *Recreation:* country pursuits. *Address:* Keeper's Cottage, Maxstoke, Coleshill, Warwicks B46 2QA. *T:* (01675) 465100.
Died 2 April 2007.

FEVERSHAM, 6th Baron *cr* 1826; **Charles Antony Peter Duncombe;** free-lance journalist; *b* 3 Jan. 1945; *s* of late Col Antony John Duncombe-Anderson and G. G. V. McNalty; *S* (to barony of) kinsman, 3rd Earl of

Feversham (the earldom having become extinct), 1963; *m* 1st, 1966, Shannon (*d* 1976), *d* of Sir Thomas Foy, CSI, CIE; two *s* one *d*; 2nd, 1979, Pauline, *d* of John Aldridge, Newark, Notts; one *s*. *Educ*: Eton; Middle Temple. Chairman: Standing Conf. of Regional Arts Assocs, 1969–76; Trustees, Yorkshire Sculpture Park, 1981–2004; President: Yorkshire Arts Assoc., 1987–91 (Chm., 1969–80); Soc. of Yorkshiremen in London, 1974; The Arvon Foundn, 1976–86; Yorks and Cleveland Local Councils Assoc., 1977–99; Nat. Assoc. of Local Councils, 1986–99. Governor, Leeds Polytechnic, 1969–76. *Publications*: A Wolf in Tooth (novel), 1967; Great Yachts, 1970. *Heir*: *s* Hon. Jasper Orlando Slingsby Duncombe, *b* 14 March 1968. *Address*: Duncombe Park, Helmsley, York YO62 5EB.   *Died 29 March 2009.*

FICKLING, Benjamin William, CBE 1973; FRCS, FDS RCS; Honorary Consultant Dental Surgeon, since 1974, formerly Dental Surgeon: St George's Hospital, SW1, 1936–74; Royal Dental Hospital of London, 1935–74; Mount Vernon Centre for Plastic and Jaw Surgery (formerly Hill End), 1941–74; *b* 14 July 1909; *s* of Robert Marshall Fickling, LDS RCS, and Florence (*née* Newson); *m* 1943, Shirley Dona, *er d* of Albert Latimer Walker, FRCS; two *s* one *d*. *Educ*: Framlingham; St George's Hosp. Royal Dental Hospital. William Brown Senior Exhibition, St George's Hosp., 1929; LDS RCS, 1932; MRCS, LRCP, 1934; FRCS 1938; FDS RCS 1947; MGDSRCS 1979; Dip. in Gen. Dental Practice, RCS, 1992; FFGDP (UK) 2002. Lectures: Charles Tomes, RCS, 1956; Everett Magnus, Melbourne, 1971; Webb-Johnson, RCS, 1978. Examiner (Chm.), Membership in Gen. Dental Surgery, 1979–83; formerly Examiner: in Dental Surgery, RCS; Univ. of London and Univ. of Edinburgh Dean of Faculty of Dental Surgery, 1968–71, and Mem. Council, Royal College of Surgeons, 1968–71 (Vice-Dean, 1965; Colyer Gold Medal, 1979); Fellow Royal Society of Medicine (Pres. Odontological Section, 1964–65); Pres., British Assoc. of Oral Surgeons, 1967–68; Mem. GDC, 1971–74. Director: Med. Sickness Annuity and Life Assurance Soc. Ltd, 1967–86; Permanent Insurance Co. Ltd, 1974–86; Medical Sickness Finance Corp. Ltd, 1977–86. Civilian Dental Consultant to RN, 1954–76. *Publications*: (joint) Injuries of the Jaws and Face, 1940; (joint) Chapter on Faciomaxillary Injuries and Deformities in British Surgical Practice, 1951. *Address*: 29 Maxwell Road, Northwood, Middx HA6 2YG. *T*: (01923) 822035. *Club*: Ski Club of Great Britain.   *Died 27 Jan. 2007.*

FIELDING, Sir Colin (Cunningham), Kt 1986; CB 1981; *b* 23 Dec. 1926; *s* of Richard Cunningham and Sadie Fielding; *m* 1953, Gillian Aerona (*née* Thomas) (*d* 2005); one *d*. *Educ*: Heaton Grammar Sch., Newcastle upon Tyne; Durham Univ. BSc Hons Physics. British Scientific Instruments Research Assoc., 1948–49; RRE Malvern, 1949–65; Asst Dir of Electronics R&D, Min. of Technology, 1965–68; Head of Electronics Dept, RRE Malvern, 1968–73; RCDS, 1973–74; Dir of Scientific and Technical Intelligence, MoD, 1975–77; Dir, Admiralty Surface Weapons Estabt, 1977–78; Dep. Controller, R&D Estabts and Res. A, and Chief Scientist (RN), MoD, 1978–80; Dep. Chief of Defence Procurement (Nuclear), and Dir, AWRE, MoD, 1980–82; Controller of R&D Estabts, Res. and Nuclear Progs, MoD, 1982–86. Dir, Cray Research (UK), 1988. *Publications*: papers in Proc. IEE, Proc. IERE, Nature. *Recreations*: yachting, tennis, music, golf.   *Died 6 Oct. 2010.*

FIELDS, Terence; *b* 8 March 1937; *s* of late Frank Fields; *m* 1962, Maureen Mongan; two *s* two *d*. Served RAMC, 1955–57. Fireman, Merseyside County Fire Bde, 1957–83. Former Vice-Chm., Bootle Constit. Lab. Party; former Mem., NW Regl Exec. Cttee, Lab. Party. MP Liverpool, Broad Green, 1983–92 (Lab, 1983–91, Ind, 1991–92); contested (Soc. Lab) Liverpool, Broad Green, 1992. *Address*: 20 John Hunter Way, Bootle, Merseyside L30 5RJ.   *Died 28 June 2008.*

FIFOOT, Paul Ronald Ninnes, CMG 1978; HM Diplomatic Service, retired; *b* 1 April 1928; *o s* of late Ronald Fifoot, Cardiff; *m* 1952, Erica, *er d* of late Richard Alford, DMD; no *c*. *Educ*: Monkton House Sch., Cardiff; Queens' Coll., Cambridge. BA 1948, MA 1952. Military Service, 1948–50. Called to Bar, Gray's Inn, 1953; Crown Counsel, Tanganyika, 1953; Asst to the Law Officers, 1960; Legal Draftsman (later Chief Parliamentary Draftsman), 1961; retd from Tanzania Govt Service, 1966; Asst Legal Adviser, Commonwealth Office, 1966; Legislative Counsel, Province of British Columbia, 1967; Asst Legal Adviser, Commonwealth (later Foreign and Commonwealth) Office, 1968; Legal Counsellor, 1971; Agent of the UK Govt in cases before the European Commn and Court of Human Rights, 1971–76; Counsellor (Legal Advr), UK Mission to UN, NY, 1976–79; Legal Counsellor, FCO, 1979–84; Dep. Leader, UK Delegation to 3rd UN Conference on the Law of the Sea, 1981–82; Leader, UK Delegation to Preparatory Commn for Internat. Sea Bed Authority, 1983–84; Dep. Legal Advr, FCO, 1984–88. Special Legal Advr/Consultant, FCO, 1988, 1990, and 1992–2001; consultant and constitutional advr to various overseas govts, 1988–2001; consultant, Council on Tribunals, 1988–89. *Publications*: articles and reviews in journals, etc. *Address*: Zebrato, Lynwood Avenue, Epsom, Surrey KT17 4LQ.   *Died 22 Feb. 2008.*

FIGGIS, His Honour Arthur Lenox; a Circuit Judge (formerly Judge of County Courts), 1971–92; *b* 12 Sept. 1918; *s* of late Frank Fernesley Figgis and Frances Annie Figgis; *m* 1953, Alison, *d* of late Sidney Bocher Ganthony and Doris Ganthony; two *s* three *d*. *Educ*: Tonbridge; Peterhouse, Cambridge (MA). Served War, 1939–46, Royal Artillery. Barrister-at-Law, Inner Temple, 1947. *Recreations*: rifle shooting half blue, 1939, and shot for Ireland (Elcho Shield), 1935–39; walking. *Address*: The Forge, Shamley Green, Guildford, Surrey GU5 0UB. *T*: (01483) 898360.   *Died 28 May 2006.*

FIGURES, Sir Colin (Frederick), KCMG 1983 (CMG 1978); OBE 1969; HM Diplomatic Service, retired; Deputy Secretary, Cabinet Office, 1985–89; *b* 1 July 1925; *s* of Frederick and Muriel Figures; *m* 1956, Pamela Ann Timmis; one *s* two *d*. *Educ*: King Edward's Sch., Birmingham; Pembroke Coll., Cambridge (MA). Served Worcestershire Regt, 1943–48. Joined Foreign Office, 1951; attached Control Commn, Germany, 1953–56; Amman, 1956–58; FCO, 1958–59; Warsaw, 1959–62; FCO, 1962–66; Vienna, 1966–69; FCO, 1969–85 (Dep. Sec.). *Recreations*: watching sport, gardening, beachcombing. *Address*: c/o HSBC, 130 New Street, Birmingham B2 4JU. *Club*: Old Edwardians (Birmingham).   *Died 8 Dec. 2006.*

FILBY, Ven. William Charles Leonard; Archdeacon of Horsham, 1983–2002, then Emeritus; *b* 21 Jan. 1933; *s* of William Richard and Dorothy Filby; *m* 1958, Marion Erica, *d* of Prof. Terence Wilmot Hutchison, FBA; four *s* one *d*. *Educ*: Ashford County Grammar School; London Univ. (BA); Oak Hill Theological Coll. Curate, All Souls, Eastbourne, 1959–62; Curate-in-charge, Holy Trinity, Knaphill, 1962–65; Vicar, Holy Trinity, Richmond-upon-Thames, 1965–71; Vicar, Bishop Hannington Memorial Church, Hove, 1971–79; Rector of Broadwater, 1979–83; RD of Worthing, 1980–83; Hon. Canon of Chichester Cathedral, 1981–83. Proctor in Convocation, 1975–90. Chm., Redcliffe Missionary Trng Coll., Chiswick, 1970–91; Mem., Keswick Convention Council, 1973–93; Pres., Chichester Diocesan Evangelical Union, 1978–84; Chairman: Diocesan Stewardship Cttee, 1983–89; Sussex Churches Broadcasting Cttee, 1984–96; Diocesan Cttee for Mission and Renewal, 1989–93; Diocesan Industrial Mission Adv. Panel, 1989–2002; Diocesan Gp, Archbishops' Commn on Rural Areas, 1998–2002. Bishops Advr for Hosp. Chaplains, 1986–98. Governor: St Mary's Hall, Brighton, 1984–2002; UC, Chichester (formerly W Sussex Inst. of Higher Educn), 1985–2002. *Recreations*: sport, music.

Address: Kymber Cottage, Hale Hill, West Burton, Pulborough, W Sussex RH20 1HE. *T:* (01798) 831269.
Died 31 Dec. 2009.

FINESTEIN, His Honour Israel, MA; QC 1970; a Circuit Judge, 1972–87; *b* 29 April 1921; *y c* of late Jeremiah Finestein, Hull; *m* 1946, Marion Phyllis (*d* 2004), *er d* of Simon Oster, Hendon, Middx. *Educ:* Kingston High School, Hull; Trinity Coll., Cambridge (Major Scholar and Prizeman; MA 1946). Called to the Bar, Lincoln's Inn, 1953. Sometime Pres., Mental Health Review Tribunal. President: Jewish Hist. Soc. of England, 1973–75, 1994–95; Bd of Deps of British Jews, 1991–94; sometime Chm., London Jewish Mus. Pres., Norwood Child Care, 1983–90. Hon. LLD Hull. *Publications:* Short History of the Jews of England, 1956; Jewish Society in Victorian England, 1993; Anglo-Jewry in Changing Times 1840–1914, 1999; Scenes and Personalities in Anglo-Jewry 1800–2000, 2002; Studies and Profiles in Anglo-Jewish History from Picciotto to Bermant, 2008. *Recreation:* reading history. *Address:* 18 Buttermere Court, Boundary Road, NW8 6NR.
Died 12 Oct. 2009.

FINGLETON, David Melvin; Metropolitan Stipendiary Magistrate, 1980–95; *b* 2 Sept. 1941; *s* of Laurence Fingleton and Norma Phillips (*née* Spiro); *m* 1975, Clare, *yr d* of late Ian Colvin. *Educ:* Aldwickbury Sch., Harpenden; Stowe Sch.; University Coll., Oxford (Exhibnr; BA Hons Modern History, MA). Called to Bar, Middle Temple, 1965; South Eastern Circuit. Member: Bd, Trinity Coll. of Music, 1986–98; Trinity Coll. of Music Corp., 1986–2005; Trustee, Samuel Butler's Educnl Foundn, 1968–. Music Correspondent, Contemporary Review, 1969–92; Opera and Ballet Critic, Tatler and Bystander, 1970–78; Stage Design Corresp., Arts Review, 1976–95; Associate Editor, Music and Musicians, 1977–80; Music Critic: Evening News, 1979–80; Daily Express, 1982–98; Restaurant Critic, Spectator, 1996–99; Opera Critic, Sunday Express, 2001–. *Publications:* Kiri, 1982; articles in Contemp. Rev., Tatler and Bystander, Music and Musicians, Arts Rev., Evening News, Daily Express, Sunday Express, Spectator. *Recreations:* listening to and writing about music, gastronomy. *Address:* 36 Devonshire Mews West, W1G 6QQ. *Clubs:* Garrick, MCC. *Died 18 Feb. 2006.*

FINLAY, Ian Hamilton, CBE 2002; artist and writer; *b* 28 Oct. 1925; *s* of James Hamilton Finlay and Annie Whitelaw Finlay; *m* 1st, Marion; 2nd, Sue; one *s* one *d.* Served Army, 1944–47. Hon. Prof., Univ. of Dundee, 1999. *Solo exhibitions* include: Inter Artes et Naturam, Musée d'Art Moderne, Paris, 1987; Ideologische Ausserungen, Frankfurt, 1991; Philadelphia Mus. of Art, 1991; Wildwachsende Blumen, Munich, 1993; Works: Pure and Political, Hamburg, 1995; Variations on Several Themes, Joan Miró Foundn, Barcelona, 1999; Maritime Works, Tate St Ives, 2002; Idylls and Interventions, London, 2002; Sentences, Royal Botanic Garden, Edinburgh, 2005; began landscaped garden at Little Sparta, 1966; perm. installations in gardens and parks, incl. garden of Max Planck Inst., Stuttgart, 1975; Kröller-Müller Sculpture Gdn, Otterlo, 1982; campus of UCSD, 1991; Serpentine Gall., London, 1999; Wallraff-Richartz Mus., Cologne, 2000; St George's Ch, Bristol, 2002; Nat. Mus. of Scotland, Edinburgh, 2003. Hon. Prof., Univ. of Dundee, 1999. Hon. DLitt: Aberdeen, 1987; Heriot-Watt, 1993; Glasgow, 2002. Scottish Horticl Medal, Royal Caledonian Horticl Soc., 2002; Creative Scotland Award, Scottish Arts Council, 2003. *Publications:* books include: A Wartime Garden, 1990; Poet of the Woodland, 1991; Works in Europe 1972–1995, 1995; The Dancers Inherit the Party, and the Glasgow Beasts, 1996; Little Sparta, 1998; Modern Antiquities, 2000; Souvenirs, 2000. *Recreation:* model building. *Address:* Stonypath, Little Sparta, Dunsyre, Lanark ML11 8NG. *T:* (01899) 810500. *Died 27 March 2006.*

FISCHER, Prof. Ernst Otto; Emeritus Professor of Inorganic Chemistry, Munich Technical University; *b* Munich, 10 Nov. 1918; *s* of Prof. Karl T. Fischer and Valentine (*née* Danzer); unmarried. *Educ:* Tech. Univ., Munich. Dip. Chem., 1949; Dr rer. nat., 1952, Habilitation 1954. Associate Prof. of Inorganic Chem., Univ. of Munich, 1957, Prof. 1959, Prof. and Dir, Inorganic Chem. Inst., Tech. Univ., Munich, 1964. Member: Bavarian Acad. of Sciences; Akad. deutscher Naturforscher Leopoldina, 1969; Austrian Acad. of Scis, 1976; Accad. dei Lincei, Italy, 1976; Göttingen Akad. der Wissenschaften, 1977; Rheinisch-Westfälische Akad. der Wissenschaften, 1987; Soc. of German Chemists, etc; Centennial For. Fellow, Amer. Chem. Soc., 1976. Hon. Dr rer. nat.: Munich, 1972; Erlangen, 1977; Veszprem, 1983; Hon. DSc Strathclyde, 1975. Received many prizes and awards including the Nobel Prize for Chemistry, 1973 (jointly with Prof. Geoffrey Wilkinson) for pioneering work, performed independently, on the chem. of organometallic "sandwich compounds". *Publications:* (with H. Werner) Metall-pi-Komplexe mit di- und oligoolefinischen Liganden, 1963 (trans. as Metal pi-Complexes Vol. 1, Complexes with di- and oligo-olefinic Ligands, 1966–); numerous contribs to learned jls on organometallic chem., etc. *Recreations:* art, history, travel. *Address:* 16 Sohnckestrasse, 81479 München, Germany.
Died 23 July 2007.

FISH, John, OBE 1996; Under-Secretary, Head of Establishment General Services Division, Department of Industry, 1974–80; *b* 16 July 1920; *m* 1948, Frances; two *s. Educ:* Lincoln School. BA Open Univ., 1989. Entered Customs and Excise, 1937; Exchequer and Audit Dept, 1939; War service, Pilot in RAF, 1940–46; Exchequer and Audit Dept, 1946; BoT, 1949; Principal, 1950; Min. of Materials, 1951; Volta River Preparatory Commn, Accra, 1953; BoT, 1956; Asst Sec., 1960; Min. of Health, 1962; BoT, 1965; DTI, 1970; Under-Sec., 1973; Dept of Industry, 1974. Civil Service Retirement Fellowship: Mem. Cttee of Mgt, 1985–95; Trustee, 1998–2001; formerly Sec., Vice Chm., Chm. and Pres., Warwicks Br. *Address:* Galanos House, Banbury Road, Southam, Warwicks CV47 2BL. *Club:* Civil Service.
Died 14 March 2009.

FISHER, Arthur J.; *see* Jeddere-Fisher.

FISHER, Sir George Read, Kt 1967; CMG 1961; Mining Engineer; President, MIM Holdings Ltd, 1970–75; *b* 23 March 1903; *s* of George Alexander Fisher and Ellen Harriett Fisher; *m* 1st, 1927, Eileen Elaine Triggs (*d* 1966); one *s* three *d*; 2nd, 1973, Marie C. Gilbey. *Educ:* Prince Alfred Coll., Adelaide; Adelaide Univ. (BE). Formerly Gen. Manager of Operations for Zinc Corporation Ltd, Broken Hill, NSW; Chm., Mount Isa Mines Ltd, 1953–70. *Recreations:* shooting, bowling. *Clubs:* Queensland, Brisbane (Brisbane).
Died 13 July 2007.

FISHER, Maurice, RCNC; General Manager, HM Dockyard, Rosyth, 1979–83; retired; *b* 8 Feb. 1924; *s* of William Ernest Fisher and Lily Edith (*née* Hatch); *m* 1955, Stella Leslie Sumsion; one *d. Educ:* St Luke's Sch., Portsmouth; Royal Dockyard Sch., Portsmouth; Royal Naval Coll., Greenwich. Constructor-in-Charge, HM Dockyard, Simonstown, 1956–60; Staff of Director of Naval Construction, 1960–63; Staff of C-in-C Western Fleet, 1963–65; Dep. Supt, Admiralty Experiment Works, Haslar, 1965–68; Dep. Prodn Manager, HM Dockyard, Devonport, 1968–72; Personnel Manager, HM Dockyard, Portsmouth, 1972–74; Planning Manager, 1974–77, Prodn Manager, 1977–79, HM Dockyard, Devonport. *Recreation:* game fishing. *Address:* 9 Roman Row, Bank Street, Bishops Waltham, Hants SO32 1RW. *Died 27 Dec. 2008.*

FISHLOCK, David Jocelyn, OBE 1983; Editor, R&D Efficiency, since 1991 (Publisher, 1992–2002); *b* 9 Aug. 1932; *s* of William Charles Fishlock and Dorothy Mary Turner; *m* 1959, Mary Millicent Cosgrove; one *s. Educ:* City of Bath Boys' Sch. (now Beechen Cliff Sch.); Bristol Coll. of Technol. FIBiol 1988; FEI (Comp. Inst. of Energy, 1987). National Service, REME, 1955–58. Westinghouse Brake & Signal Co. Ltd, 1948–55;

McGraw-Hill, 1959–62; New Scientist, 1962–67; Science Editor, Financial Times, 1967–91. Columnist: Nuclear Europe Worldscan, 1981–2002; Business in East Anglia, 1997–; Erotic Review, 1998–; Chemistry World (formerly Chemistry in Britain), RSC, 2000–. Glaxo Travelling Fellow, 1978; Associate Fellow, Centre for Res. in Innovation & Competitiveness, 1998–2001. Member: R&D Soc., 1994–; Scientific Instrument Soc., 1994–. Hon. DLitt Salford, 1982; Hon. DSc Bath, 1993. Chemical Writer of the Year Award, BASF, 1982; Worthington Pump Award, 1982; British Press Award, 1986. Silver Jubilee Medal, 1977. *Publications:* The New Materials, 1967; Man Modified, 1969; The Business of Science, 1975; The Business of Biotechnology, 1982; (with Elizabeth Antébi) Biotechnology: strategies for life, 1986. *Recreations:* writing, reading, collecting old medical/pharmaceutical equipment. *Address:* Traveller's Joy, Copse Lane, Jordans, Bucks HP9 2TA. *T:* (01494) 873242. *Club:* Athenæum. *Died 18 Sept. 2009.*

FISON, Sir (Richard) Guy, 4th Bt *cr* 1905; DSC 1944; *b* 9 Jan. 1917; *er s* of Sir William Guy Fison, 3rd Bt; *S* father, 1964; *m* 1952, Elyn Hartmann (*d* 1987); one *s* one *d*. *Educ:* Eton; New Coll., Oxford. Served RNVR, 1939–45. Entered Wine Trade, 1948; Master of Wine, 1954; Dir, Saccone & Speed Ltd, 1952–82; Chairman: Saccone & Speed Internat., 1979–82; Percy Fox & Co. Ltd, 1982–83; Wine Develt Bd, 1982–83; Fine Vintage Wines Plc, 1985–95; Pres., Wine and Spirit Assoc., 1977–78. Hon. Freeman, 1976, Renter Warden, 1981–82, Upper Warden, 1982–83, Master, 1983–84, Vintners' Co. *Heir: s* Charles William Fison, *b* 6 Feb. 1954. *Died 1 Oct. 2008.*

FITCH, Douglas Bernard Stocker, FRICS; FAAV; MRAC; Director, Land and Water Service, Agricultural Development and Advisory Service, Ministry of Agriculture, Fisheries and Food, 1980–87; *b* 16 April 1927; *s* of William Kenneth Fitch and Hilda Barrington; *m* 1952, Joyce Vera Griffiths (*d* 2002); three *s*. *Educ:* St Albans Sch.; Royal Agricl Coll. (Dip. 1951). FRICS 1977. Served Army, RE, 1944–48. Joined Land Service, MAFF, 1951; Divl Surveyor, Guildford, 1971; Regional Surveyor, SE Reg., 1979. Mem., European Faculty of Land Use and Develt, 1985–2002 (Prof., Rural Planning and Natural Resource Mgt, 1985–97). Royal Institution of Chartered Surveyors: Mem., Agric. Divl Council, 1980–87; Mem., Gen. Council, 1980–86. Internat. Fedn. of Surveyors deleg., 1988–91, and Chm., Standing Conf. on Marine Resource Management, 1985–89. Chm. Adv. Cttee, Centre for Rural Studies, 1990–96; Mem., Bd of Governors, Royal Agricl Coll., 1981–2001. *Recreation:* golf. *Clubs:* Farmers', Civil Service. *Died 9 July 2006.*

FITZALAN-HOWARD, Maj.-Gen. Lord Michael, GCVO 1981 (KCVO 1971; MVO 1952); CB 1968; CBE 1962; MC 1944; DL; Extra Equerry to the Queen, since 1999; Her Majesty's Marshal of the Diplomatic Corps, 1972–81; *b* 22 Oct. 1916; 2nd *s* of 3rd Baron Howard of Glossop, MBE, and Baroness Beaumont (11th in line), OBE; *b* of 17th Duke of Norfolk, KG, GCVO, CB, CBE, MC; granted title and precedence of a Duke's son, 1975; *m* 1st, 1946, Jean (*d* 1947), *d* of Sir Hew Hamilton-Dalrymple, 9th Bt; one *d*; 2nd, 1950, Margaret (*d* 1995), *d* of Capt. W. P. Meade-Newman; four *s* one *d*; 3rd, 1997, Victoria Winifred Baring, *widow* of Sir Mark Baring, KCVO. *Educ:* Ampleforth Coll.; Trinity Coll., Cambridge. Joined Scots Guards, 1938. Served in: North West Europe, 1944–45; Palestine, 1945–46; Malaya, 1948–49; Egypt, 1952–53; Germany, 1956–57 and 1961–66; Commander Allied Command Europe Mobile Forces (Land), 1964–66; Chief of Staff, Southern Command, 1967–68; GOC London Dist, and Maj.-Gen. comdg The Household Division, 1968–71. Colonel: The Lancs Regt (Prince of Wales's Volunteers), 1966–70; The Queen's Lancashire Regiment, 1970–78; Colonel of The Life Guards, 1979–99; Gold Stick to the Queen, 1979–99; Joint Hon. Col, Cambridge Univ. OTC, 1968–71. Chm. Council, TAVR Assocs, 1973–81, Pres., 1981–84; Patron, Council, TA&VRA, 1984–; Hon.

Recorder, British Commonwealth Ex-Service League, 1991–2001. DL Wilts, 1974. Freeman, City of London, 1985. *Address:* Fovant House, Church Lane, Fovant, Salisbury, Wilts SP3 5LA. *T:* (01722) 714617. *Clubs:* Buck's, Pratt's. *Died 2 Nov. 2007.*

FITZPATRICK, James Bernard, CBE 1983; JP; DL; Immigration Appeal Adjudicator, 1990–2002; Member, Criminal Injuries Compensation Appeals Panel, since 2000; *b* 21 April 1930; *s* of late B. A. Fitzpatrick and Mrs J. E. Fitzpatrick; *m* 1965, Rosemary, *d* of late Captain E. B. Clark, RD and bar, RNR and Mrs K. E. Clark, Claughton; one *s* one *d*. *Educ:* Bootle Grammar Sch.; London Univ. (LLB). Admitted Solicitor, 1962; FCIT 1973. Joined Mersey Docks and Harbour Bd, 1951: various management posts from 1965; Personnel and Industrial Relns Dir, 1971, on formation of Mersey Docks and Harbour Co.; Jt Man. Dir, 1974; Dep. Chief Exec., 1975; Man. Dir and Chief Exec., 1977; Chm., 1984–87. Director: Plan Invest Group plc, 1984–91; Teesside Hldgs, 1992–95; Mem., 1979–89, Chm., 1988–89, Merseyside Enterprise Forum. Chairman: Nat. Assoc. of Port Employers, 1979–82 (Vice-Chm., 1973–79); Employers' Assoc. of Port of Liverpool, 1974–83; Member: Liverpool Dock Labour Bd, 1974–76 (Chm., 1976); Exec. Council, British Ports Assoc., 1976–87 (Dep. Chm., 1985–87); Nat. Dock Labour Bd, 1978–84. Chairman: Liverpool HA, 1986–91; Royal Liverpool Univ. Hosp. NHS Trust, 1991–95; Royal Liverpool and Broadgreen Univ. Hosps NHS Trust, 1995–96. Chm., The Appeals Service, 1992–2000. Mem. Council, Industrial Soc., 1989–92. Liverpool University: Mem. Council, 1988–89, 1991–98; Chm., Inst. of Irish Studies, 1990–98. Chm., Denbighshire Br., CPRW, 2004–. JP Liverpool 1977; DL Merseyside, 1985. CCMI; FRSA Hon. Fellow, Liverpool John Moores Univ. (formerly Liverpool Polytechnic), 1988. *Recreations:* fell walking, gardening, music, reading. *Address:* Waen Ffynnon, Pentre Coch, Ruthin, Denbighshire LL15 2YF. *T:* (01824) 703425. *Clubs:* Oriental, Pilgrims. *Died 3 Feb. 2006.*

FLACK, Bertram Anthony, CMG 1979; HM Diplomatic Service, retired; *b* 3 Feb. 1924; *y s* of Dr F. H. Flack and Alice Cockshut, Nelson, Lancs; *m* 1948, Jean W. Mellor (decd); two *s* two *d*. *Educ:* Epsom Coll.; Liverpool Univ. (LLB Hons). Enlisted Gren. Gds, 1942; commissioned E Lancashire Regt, 1943; served in NW Europe (Captain). Joined Foreign Service, 1948; served Karachi, 1948–50; Alexandria, 1950–52; Stockholm, 1955–58; Accra, 1958–61; Johannesburg, 1964–67; Dep. High Comr, E Pakistan, 1967–68; Inspector, Diplomatic Service, 1968–70; Head of Communications Dept, FCO, 1971–73; Commercial Counsellor, Stockholm, 1973–75; Canadian Nat. Defence Coll., 1975–76; Dep. High Comr, Ottawa, 1976–79; High Comr, Repub. of Uganda, 1979–80. *Recreations:* cricket, golf. *Address:* Abbotswood House Nursing Home, Crossag Road, Ballasalla, Isle of Man IM9 3DZ. *Died 16 Feb. 2009.*

FLAGG, Rt Rev. John William Hawkins; General Secretary, South American Missionary Society, 1986–93; *b* 16 April 1929; *s* of Wilfred John and Emily Flagg; *m* 1954, Marjorie Lund (*d* 1999); one *s* four *d* and one adopted *s*. *Educ:* All Nations Christian Coll.; Clifton Theological Coll. Agricultural missionary, Chile, 1951; Chaplain and Missionary Superintendent, St Andrew's, Asunción, Paraguay, 1959–64; Archdeacon, N Argentine, 1964–69; Diocesan Bishop of Paraguay and N Argentine, 1969–73; Asst Bishop for Chile, Peru and Bolivia, 1973–77; Bishop, Diocese of Peru, 1977; Asst Bishop, Diocese of Liverpool, 1978–86; Vicar, St Cyprian's with Christ Church, Edge Hill, 1978–85; Priest-in-Charge of Christ Church, Waterloo, 1985–86; Hon. Assistant Bishop: of Rochester, 1986–92; of Southwell, 1992–97. Member of Anglican Consultative Council, 1974–79; Presiding Bishop of Anglican Council of South America (CASA), 1974–77. Diocesan Advr in rural ministry, and stewardship, 1993–96, and overseas relns, 1994–96, Southwell. *Publications:* From Ploughshare to Crook, 2000. *Died 1 Oct. 2008.*

FLANAGAN, Barry, OBE 1991; RA 1991 (ARA 1987); sculptor; *b* 11 Jan. 1941; *m* Sue Lewis (marr. diss. 1997; she *d* 2002); two *d*; one *s* one *d* with Renate Widmann; partner, Jessica Sturgess. *Educ:* Birmingham Coll. of Arts and Crafts; St Martin's Sch. of Art. Teacher, St Martin's Sch. of Art and Central Sch. of Art and Design, 1967–71. One-man exhibitions include: Rowan Gall., 1966, 1968, 1970–74; Fischbach Gall., NY, 1969; Galleria del Leone, Venice, 1971; Mus. of Modern Art, NY, Mus. of Modern Art, Oxford, 1974; Hogarth Galls, Sydney, 1975; Centro de Arte y Communicación, Buenos Aires, 1976; (retrospective) Van Abbemuseum, Eindhoven, Arnolfini Gall., Bristol, Serpentine Gall. (tour), 1977–79; Galerie Durand-Dessert, Paris, 1980, 1982, 1988, 1992, 1996; Waddington Galls, 1980–81, 1983, 1985, 1990, 1994, 1998, 2001, 2004; Inst. of Contemporary Arts (prints and drawings), 1981–82; British Pavilion, XL Venice Biennale, and tour, 1982–83; Centre Georges Pompidou, Paris, 1983; Pace Gall., NY, 1983, 1990, 1994; Fuji Television Gall., Tokyo, 1985, 1991; Tate Gall., 1986; Laing Art Gall., Newcastle upon Tyne, Mus. of Contemporary Art, Belgrade, City Gall., Zagreb, Mus. of Modern Art, Ljubljana (tour), 1987–88; (retrospective) Madrid and Nantes, 1993–94; RHA Gallagher Gall., Dublin, 1995; Park Ave., NY, Grant Park, Chicago, 1995–96; Galerie Xavier Hufkens, Brussels, 1999; Tate, Liverpool, 2000; Kunsthalle Recklinghausen, Germany, Musée d'Art Moderne et d'Art Contemporaine, Nice (tour), 2002; Irish Mus. of Modern Art, Dublin, 2006. Work includes: outdoor sculpture for Sint Pietersplein, Ghent, 1980; Camdonian sculpture, Lincoln's Inn Fields, 1980; bronze sculptures: Baby Elephant and Hare on Bell, Equitable Life Tower West, NY, 1984; Nine Foot Hare, Victoria Plaza, London, 1984; The Boxing Ones, Capability Green, Luton Hoo Estate, Beds, 1986; Kouros Horse, Stockley Park, Uxbridge, 1987; The Cricketer, 1989, Jesus Coll., Cambridge; two bronze Leaping Hare sculptures for Kawakyo Co., Osaka, 1990. Choreographed two pieces for dance gp, Strider, 1972. Judge, Bath Sculpture Competition, 1985. *Address:* c/o Waddington Galleries, 11 Cork Street, W1S 3LT. *Died 31 Aug. 2009.*

FLANNERY, Martin Henry; *b* 2 March 1918; *m* 1949, Blanche Howson; one *s* two *d*. *Educ:* Sheffield Grammar Sch.; Sheffield Teachers' Trng College. Served with Royal Scots, 1940–46. Teacher, 1946–74, Head Teacher, 1969–74. MP (Lab) Hillsborough, Sheffield, Feb. 1974–1992. Chairman: Tribune Group, 1980–81; PLP's NI Cttee, 1983–92; PLP Consultant MP for NUT, 1974–92. *Recreations:* music, rambling. *Address:* 530 Manchester Road, Sheffield S10 5PQ. *Died 16 Oct. 2006.*

FLEET, Stephen George, PhD; FInstP; Master, Downing College, Cambridge, 2001–03; Registrary, University of Cambridge, 1983–97, then Emeritus; *b* 28 Sept. 1936; *er s* of late George Fleet and Elsie Fleet, Lewes, Sussex; *m* 2002, Alice, *d* of late William and Eithne Boyle and *widow* of Michael Percival. *Educ:* Brentwood Sch.; Lewes County Grammar Sch.; St John's Coll., Cambridge (Scholar; MA; PhD 1962). FInstP 1972. Res. Physicist, Mullard Res. Labs, Surrey, 1961–62; University of Cambridge: Demonstr in Mineralogy, 1962–67; Lectr in Mineralogy, 1967–83; Fellow: Fitzwilliam House, 1963–66; Fitzwilliam Coll., 1966–73 (Jun. Bursar, 1967–73; Dir of Studies in Physical Sciences, 1971–74; Hon. Fellow, 1997); Downing Coll., 1974–2000 (Bursar, 1974–83; Pres., 1983–85; Vice-Master, 1985–88, 1991–94 and 1997–2000; Hon. Fellow, 2003); Mem., Univ. Council of Senate, 1975–82; Mem., Financial Bd, 1979–83; Chm., Bd of Exams, 1974–83; Chm., Bursars' Cttee, 1980–83; Dep. Vice-Chancellor, 2001–03; President: Fitzwilliam Soc., 1977, 1999; Downing Assoc., 1991.

Member: Finance Cttee, Internat. Union of Crystallography, 1987–; Jt Negotiating Cttee, Universities Superannuation Scheme, 1992–2005. Treasurer: Cambridge Commonwealth Trust, 1983–; Cambridge Overseas Trust, 1988–; Cambridge Housing Soc., 1999–; Gates Cambridge Trust, 2000–; Chairman of Trustees: Foundn of Edward Storey, 1984–88, 1999–; Strangeways Res. Lab., 1997–; Trustee, Mineralogical Soc. of GB, 1977–87; Mem., Cttee of Management, Charities Property Unit Trust, 1983–88. FRSA 1995. *Publications:* res. pubns in scientific jls. *Recreations:* books, music, history of Sussex. *Address:* 20 Champneys Walk, Cambridge CB3 9AW. *T:* (01223) 461142. *Clubs:* Athenæum, Royal Over-Seas League. *Died 18 May 2006.*

FLEMING, Thomas Kelman, (Tom), CVO 1998; OBE 1980; *b* 29 June 1927; *s* of late Rev. Peter Fleming and Kate Ulla Fleming (*née* Barker). *Educ:* Daniel Stewart's Coll., Edinburgh. Actor, writer, producer and broadcaster; toured India with Edith Evans, 1945; RN, 1945–47; co-founder and Dir, Edinburgh Gateway Co., 1953–65; RSC, 1962–64, toured Europe, USA, USSR; founder and Dir, Royal Lyceum Theatre Co., 1965–66; Dir, Scottish Mil. Tattoo, Washington, 1976; Governor, Scottish Theatre Trust, 1980–82; Dir, Scottish Theatre Co., 1982–87; numerous Edinburgh Festival performances and productions. Member: Drama Adv. Panel, British Council, 1983–89; Lamp of Lothian Collegiate Trust, 1970–95; Scottish Internat. Educn Trust, 1996–2007. Pres., Edinburgh Sir Walter Scott Club, 2000. Leader, Corporate Ministry, Canonmills Baptist Ch, 1989–2007. Hon. Mem., Royal Scottish Pipers' Soc.; Hon. Life Mem., Saltire Soc. Hon. FRSAMD 1986; DDra 2003. DUniv Heriot-Watt, 1984; Hon. DLitt Queen Margaret UC, 1999. *Films* include: King Lear; Mary Queen of Scots; Meetings with Remarkable Men; *television:* title rôles include, 1952–: Redgauntlet; Rob Roy; Jesus of Nazareth; Henry IV; Weir of Hermiston; Reith; over 2000 broadcasts, 1944–; *television and radio:* BBC commentator, royal events, incl. Queen's Coronation, 1953, Silver Jubilee, 1977, and Queen's Birthday Parades, 1970–94; Cenotaph service, 1961, 1965–99; D Day, VE Day and VJ Day commems, 1994, 1995; Edinburgh Military Tattoo, 1966–2008; also funeral services of HRH Duke of Windsor, King Frederick IX of Denmark, HRH Duke of Gloucester, Cardinal Heenan, Viscount Montgomery of Alamein, Pope John Paul I, Earl Mountbatten of Burma, President Tito, Princess Grace of Monaco, King Olav V of Norway, Diana, Princess of Wales and Queen Elizabeth, the Queen Mother. Proposed Immortal Memory of Robert Burns, Kremlin, 1991. Andrew Fletcher of Saltoun Award for services to Scotland, 2000. *Publications:* It's My Belief, 1953; So That Was Spring (poems), 1954; Miracle at Midnight (play), 1954; Voices out of the Air, 1981; (contrib.) BBC Book of Memories, 1991; (contrib.) A Scottish Childhood, 1998. *Recreations:* noticing, remembering and wondering. *Address:* c/o United Agents, 12–26 Lexington Street, W1F 0LE. *Clubs:* Royal Commonwealth Society; Scottish Arts (Hon. Mem.) (Edinburgh). *Died 18 April 2010.*

FLETCHER, Alan Gerard, RDI 1972; designer; freelance practice, since 1993; *b* Nairobi, Kenya, 27 Sept. 1931; *s* of Bernard Fletcher and Dorothy Murphy; *m* 1956, Paola Biagi; one *d*. *Educ:* Christ's Hosp. Sch.; Central Sch. of Arts and Crafts; Royal Coll. of Art (ARCA); Sch. of Architecture and Design, Yale Univ. (Master of Fine Arts). FCSD (FSIAD 1964). Designer, Fortune Magazine, New York, 1958–59; freelance practice, London, 1959–62; Partner: Fletcher Forbes Gill, 1962–65; Crosby Fletcher Forbes, 1965–72; Founding Partner, Pentagram Design, 1972–92. Pres., Designers and Art Dirs Assoc., 1973; Internat. Pres., Alliance Graphique Internat., 1982–85. Sen. Fellow, RCA, 1989. Hon. Fellow, London Inst., 2000. Hon. DDes Kingston, 2003. Designers and Art Dirs Assoc. Gold Award for Design, 1974, and President's Award for Outstanding Contribn to Design, 1977; One Show Gold Award for

Design, New York, 1974; Design Medal, SIAD, 1983; Prince Philip Prize for Designer of the Year, 1993; Hall of Fame, Amer. Art Directors, 1994. *Publications:* (jtly) Graphic Design: a visual comparison, 1963; (also illus.) Was Ich Sah, 1967; (jtly) A Sign Systems Manual, 1970; (jtly) Identity Kits, 1971; (jtly) Living by Design, 1978; (jtly) Ideas on Design, 1987; (jtly) Pentagram, The Compendium, 1993; Beware Wet Paint, 1995; The Art of Looking Sideways, 2001; *posthumous publication:* Picturing and Poeting, 2006. *Address:* 12 Pembridge Mews, W11 3EQ. *T:* (020) 7229 7095, *Fax:* (020) 7229 8120. *Died 21 Sept. 2006.*

FLETCHER, Sir James Muir Cameron, Kt 1980; ONZ 1997; FCA; Managing Director, 1942–79, Chairman, 1972–80, Fletcher Holdings Ltd; *b* Dunedin, NZ, 25 Dec. 1914; *s* of Sir James Fletcher; *m* 1942, Margery Vaughan, *d* of H. H. Gunthorp; three *s. Educ:* Waitaki Boys' High School; Auckland Grammar School. South British Insurance Co., 1931–37; then Fletcher Construction Co. and Fletcher Holdings; Pres. and Dir, Fletcher Challenge Ltd, 1981–90. *Address:* Fletcher Challenge Ltd, Private Bag 92114, Auckland, New Zealand; 119 St Stephens Avenue, Parnell, Auckland, New Zealand. *Died 29 Aug. 2007.*

FLETCHER, Comdt Marjorie Helen (Kelsey), CBE 1988; Director, Women's Royal Naval Service, 1986–88; *b* 21 Sept. 1932; *d* of late Norman Farler Fletcher and Marie Amelie Fletcher (*née* Adams). *Educ:* Avondale High Sch.; Sutton Coldfield High Sch. for Girls. Solicitor's Clerk, 1948–53; joined WRNS as Telegraphist, 1953; progressively, 3rd Officer to Chief Officer, 1956–76; Supt, 1981; served in Secretarial, Careers Advisor, Intelligence and Staff appts; ndc 1979; Directing Staff, RN Staff Coll., 1980–81; psc 1981; Internat. Mil. Staff, NATO HQ, 1981–84; Asst Dir, Dir Naval Staff Duties, 1984–85. ADC to the Queen, 1986–88. *Publications:* The WRNS, 1989. *Recreations:* reading, needlework. *Died 11 Oct. 2008.*

FLEW, Prof. Antony Garrard Newton; Emeritus Professor, University of Reading, since 1983; *b* 11 Feb. 1923; *o s* of Rev. Dr R. N. Flew; *m* 1952, Annis Ruth Harty; two *d. Educ:* St Faith's Sch., Cambridge; Kingswood Sch., Bath; Sch. of Oriental and African Studies, London; St John's Coll., Oxford (John Locke Schol., MA); DLitt Keele, 1974. Lecturer: Christ Church, Oxford, 1949–50; Univ. of Aberdeen, 1950–54; Professor of Philosophy: Univ. of Keele, 1954–71; Univ. of Calgary, 1972–73; Univ. of Reading, 1973–82; (part-time) York Univ., Toronto, 1983–85; Distinguished Res. Fellow (part-time), Social Philosophy and Policy Center, Bowling Green State Univ., Ohio, 1986–91. Many temp. vis. appts. Gavin David Young Lectr, Adelaide, 1963; Gifford Lectr, St Andrews, 1986. A Vice-Pres., Rationalist Press Assoc., 1973–88; Chm., Voluntary Euthanasia Soc., 1976–79. Fellow, Acad. of Humanism, 1983–. Phillip E. Johnson Award for Liberty and Truth, Biola Univ., 2006. *Publications:* A New Approach to Psychical Research, 1953; Hume's Philosophy of Belief, 1961; God and Philosophy, 1966; Evolutionary Ethics, 1967; An Introduction to Western Philosophy, 1971; Crime or Disease?, 1973; Thinking About Thinking, 1975; The Presumption of Atheism, 1976; Sociology, Equality and Education, 1976; A Rational Animal, 1978; Philosophy: an introduction, 1979; The Politics of Procrustes, 1981; Darwinian Evolution, 1984; Thinking About Social Thinking, 1985; Hume, Philosopher of Moral Science, 1986; (with G. Vesey) Agency and Necessity, 1987; The Logic of Mortality, 1987; Power to the Parents, 1987; Equality in Liberty and Justice, 1989; Atheistic Humanism, 1993; Shephard's Warning: setting schools back on course, 1994; Philosophical Essays of Antony Flew, 1998; How to Think Straight, 1998; Social Life and Moral Judgement, 2003; (with R. A. Varghese) There is No A God: how the world's most notorious atheist changed his mind, 2007; articles in philosophical and other jls.

Recreations: walking, climbing, house maintenance. *Address:* 26 Alexandra Road, Reading, Berks RG1 5PD. *T:* (0118) 926 1848. *Died 8 April 2010.*

FLOISSAC, Rt Hon. Sir Vincent (Frederick), Kt 1992; CMG 1985; OBE 1973; PC 1992; Chief Justice and President of the Court of Appeal, Eastern Caribbean Supreme Court, 1991–96; *b* 31 July 1928; *m* 1954, Marilyn (*née* Bristol); twin *d. Educ:* St Mary's Coll., St Lucia; UCL (LLM 1953). Called to the Bar, Gray's Inn, 1952 (Hon. Bencher, 1992); in practice, St Lucia, 1953–91; QC (St Lucia) 1969; Mem., Seychelles Ct of Appeal, 1988–91. Nominated Mem. and Dep. Speaker, St Lucia House of Assembly, 1969–75; first Pres., Senate of St Lucia, 1979; Acting Governor Gen., St Lucia, 1987–88. Member: Judicial Cttee, Privy Council, 1992–; Regl Judicial and Legal Services Commn, 2003–08; Chm., Judicial Services Commn for Turks and Caicos Is, 2007–09. Chm., St Lucia Central Water Authority, 1965–72; Dir, St Lucia Co-op Bank Ltd, 1960–91. *Recreations:* football, table tennis, tennis. *Address:* c/o Floissac Fleming & Associates, PO Box 722, Castries, St Lucia, West Indies. *Died 25 Sept. 2010.*

FLOWERS, Baron *cr* 1979 (Life Peer), of Queen's Gate in the City of Westminster; **Brian Hilton Flowers,** Kt 1969; FRS 1961; Chancellor, Manchester University, 1994–2001; Chairman, Nuffield Foundation, 1987–98 (a Managing Trustee, 1982–98); *b* 13 Sept. 1924; *o s* of late Rev. Harold J. Flowers, Swansea; *m* 1951, Mary Frances, *er d* of late Sir Leonard Behrens, CBE; two step *s. Educ:* Bishop Gore Grammar Sch., Swansea; Gonville and Caius Coll. (Exhibitioner), Cambridge (MA); Hon. Fellow, 1974; University of Birmingham (DSc). Anglo-Canadian Atomic Energy Project, 1944–46; Research in nuclear physics and atomic energy at Atomic Energy Research Establishment, Harwell, 1946–50; Dept of Mathematical Physics, University of Birmingham, 1950–52; Head of Theoretical Physics Div., AERE, Harwell, 1952–58; Prof. of Theoretical Physics, 1958–61, Langworthy Prof. of Physics, 1961–72, Univ. of Manchester; on leave of absence as Chm., SRC, 1967–73; Rector of Imperial Coll. of Sci. and Technol., 1973–85; Vice-Chancellor, Univ. of London, 1985–90. Chairman: Royal Commn on Environmental Pollution, 1973–76; Standing Commn on Energy and the Environment, 1978–81; Univ. of London Working Party on future of med. and dent. teaching resources, 1979–80; Cttee of Vice-Chancellors and Principals, 1983–85; Select Cttee on Science and Technology, H of L, 1989–93 (Mem., 1980–93, 1994–98, 1999–2002). Mem., AEA, 1970–80. President: Inst. of Physics, 1972–74; European Science Foundn, 1974–80; Nat. Soc. for Clean Air, 1977–79; Parly and Scientific Cttee, 1993–97. Chm., Computer Bd for Univs and Research Councils, 1966–70. Member: Council, RPMS, 1990–97 (Vice Chm., 1991–97); Bd of Management, LSHTM, 1992–95 (Chm., 1994–95). Gov., Middx Univ., 1992–2001. Founding Mem. and Mem. Exec. Council, Academia Europaea, 1988. Founder Mem., SDP, 1981. FInstP 1961; Hon. FInstP 1996; Hon. FCGI, 1975; Hon. MRIA (Science Section), 1976; Hon. FIET (Hon. FIEE, 1975); Hon. FRCP 1992; Sen. Fellow, RCA, 1983; Hon. Fellow: UMIST, 1985; Royal Holloway, London Univ., 1996; Univ. of Wales, Swansea, 1996; Corresp. Mem., Swiss Acad. of Engrg Sciences, 1986. MA Oxon, 1956; Hon. DSc: Sussex, 1968; Wales, 1972; Manchester, 1973; Leicester, 1973; Liverpool, 1974; Bristol, 1982; Oxford, 1985; NUI, 1990; Reading, 1996; London, 1996; Hon. DEng Nova Scotia, 1983; Hon. ScD Dublin, 1984; Hon. LLD: Dundee, 1985; Glasgow, 1987; Manchester, 1995; DU Middlesex, 2001. Rutherford Medal and Prize, 1968, Glazebrook Medal and Prize, 1987, IPPS; Chalmers Medal, Chalmers Univ. of Technol., Sweden, 1980. Officier de la Légion d'Honneur, 1981 (Chevalier, 1975). *Publications:* (with E. Mendoza) Properties of Matter, 1970; An Introduction to Numerical Methods in C++, 1995; contribs to scientific periodicals on structure of the atomic nucleus, nuclear reactions, science policy, energy and the environment. *Recreations:* music, walking, computing, gardening. *Address:* 53 Athenaeum Road, N20 9AL. *T:* (020) 8446 5993. *Died 25 June 2010.*

FLOYD, Keith; cook, broadcaster; *b* 28 Dec. 1943; *s* of late Sydney Albert Floyd and of Winnifred Margaret Floyd; *m* 1995, Theresa Mary (*née* Smith) (marr. diss. 2008); one *s* one *d* by prev. marriages. *Educ:* Wellington Sch. Commnd, 3rd RTR 1963; journalist, 1961–; broadcaster, 1986– (19 TV series). *Publications:* Floyd's Food, 1981; Floyd on Fish, 1985; Floyd on Fire, 1986; Floyd on France, 1987; Floyd on Britain and Ireland, 1988; Floyd in the Soup, 1988; A Feast of Floyd, 1989; Floyd's American Pie, 1989; Floyd on Oz, 1991; Floyd on Spain, 1992; Floyd on Hangovers, 1992; Far Flung Floyd, 1993; Floyd on Italy, 1994; The Best of Floyd, 1995; Floyd on Africa, 1996; Floyd's Barbies, 1997; Floyd's Fjord Fiesta, 1998; Floyd Uncorked, 1998; Floyd Around the Med, 1999; Out of the Frying Pan (autobiog.), 2000; Floyd's India, 2001; Flash Floyd, 2002; Floyd's Great Curries, 2004; Floyd's China, 2005; Splash and a Dash, 2006; Floyd's Thailand, 2006. *Posthumous publication:* Stirred but not Shaken (autobiog.), 2009. *Recreations:* Rugby, fishing, drinking, gardening. *Address:* c/o Stan Green Management, PO Box 4, Dartmouth, Devon TQ6 0YD. *T:* (01803) 770046, *Fax:* (01803) 770075. *Died 14 Sept. 2009.*

FLYNN, Desmond James; Inspector General and Chief Executive, Insolvency Service, Department for Business, Enterprise and Regulatory Reform (formerly Department of Trade and Industry), 2001–07; *b* 21 March 1949; *s* of James Joseph Flynn and Kathleen Eithne Flynn (*née* Fagan); *m* 1975, Kumari Ramdewar; one *s* one *d*. *Educ:* Univ. of E Anglia (BA Hons 1974). Trainee examr, Official Receiver, London, 1968–71; Examr, Official Receiver, Birmingham, 1976–80; Asst Official Receiver, Birmingham and London, 1980–86; Principal, Internat. Trade Policy Div., DTI, 1986–88; Principal Inspector of Official Receivers, 1988–89; Dep. Inspector Gen., Insolvency Service, DTI, 1989–2001. *Publications:* (contrib.) Insolvency Law: theory and practice, ed H. Rajak, 1993. *Recreations:* reading, golf. *Club:* Letchworth Golf. *Died 22 March 2008.*

FOGDEN, Michael Ernest George, CB 1994; Chairman, Accountancy Investigation and Disciplinary Board, 2004–08; *b* 30 May 1936; *s* of late George Charles Arthur and of Margaret May Fogden; *m* 1957, Rose Ann Diamond; three *s* one *d*. *Educ:* High Sch. for Boys, Worthing. Nat. Service, RAF, 1956–58. Ministry of Pensions and National Insurance, later Department of Health and Social Security: Clerical Officer, 1958–59; Exec. Officer, 1959–67; Private Sec. to Parly Sec., 1967–68; Asst Private Sec. to Sec. of State for Social Services, 1968–70; Principal, 1970–76; Asst Sec., 1976–83; Under Sec., 1983–84; Under Sec., Dept of Employment, then DFEE, 1984–96 (Chief Exec. Employment Service, 1987–96). Chm., Nat. Blood Authy, 1998–2005. Dep. Chm., Civil Service Appeal Bd, 1999–2006. Chm., First Div. Assoc. of Civil Servants, 1980–83. Chairman: London Council, RIPA, 1989–93; Public Management Forum (formerly London Inst. of Public Admin), 1994–98; Exec. Cttee, Public Mgt and Policy Assoc., 1998–2003; Investigation and Disciplinary Bd, Accountancy Foundn, 2001–03. FRSA. *Recreations:* gardening, talking, music. *Address:* 59 Mayfield Avenue, Orpington, Kent BR6 0AH. *T:* (01689) 77395. *Club:* Royal Commonwealth Society. *Died 10 Oct. 2009.*

FOGG, Alan Hampson, MBE 1994; Chairman, Royal Philanthropic Society, 1982–90; former Director, PA International; *b* 19 Sept. 1921; *o s* of John Fogg, Dulwich; *m* 1948, Mary Marsh; two *s* one *d*. *Educ:* Repton; Exeter Coll., Oxford (MA, BSc). Served with RN, 1944–47. *Publications:* (with Barnes, Stephens and Titman) Company Organisation: theory and practice, 1970; various papers on management subjects. *Recreations:* travel, gardening, youth charities. *Address:* 124 Nutfield Road, Merstham, Redhill, Surrey RH1 3HG. *T:* (01737) 642023. *Died 23 Feb. 2010.*

FOGGON, George, CMG 1961; OBE 1949 (MBE 1945); Director, London Office, International Labour Organisation, 1976–82, retired; *b* 13 Sept. 1913; *s* of late Thomas and Margaret Foggon; *m* 1st, 1938, Agnes McIntosh (*d* 1968); one *s*; 2nd, 1969, Audrey Blanch (*d* 2002). Joined Min. of Labour, 1930. Served War of 1939–45 (MBE), Wing-Comdr, RAFVR, 1941–46. Seconded to FO, 1946; on staff of Mil. Gov., Berlin, 1946–49; Principal, CO, 1949; Asst Sec., W African Inter-Territorial Secretariat, Gold Coast (later Ghana), 1951–53; Comr of Labour, Nigeria, 1954–58; Labour Adviser: to Sec. of State for Colonies, 1958–61; to Sec. for Techn. Co-op., 1962–64; to Min. of Overseas Development, 1965–66; Overseas Labour Advr, FO later FCO, 1966–76, retd. *Recreations:* history, photography. *Address:* 3 Castle Hill House, Wylam, Northumberland NE41 8JG. *T:* (01661) 852257. *Clubs:* Athenæum, Oriental. *Died 18 Feb. 2006.*

FOOT, Sir Geoffrey (James), Kt 1984; Chairman and Commissioner, Hydro Electric Commission of Tasmania, 1987–89 (Associate Commissioner, 1984–87); *b* 20 July 1915; *s* of James P. Foot and Susan J. Foot; *m* 1940, Mollie W. Snooks; two *s* one *d*. *Educ:* Launceston High Sch. AASA; ACIS. MLC, Tasmania, 1961–72 (Leader for Govt, 1969–72). Chairman: Tasmania Permanent Bldg Soc., 1982–85; Launceston Gas Co., 1982–84; Gas Corp. of Tasmania, 1984–87. Mem., Lilydale Commn—Local Govt, 1983–85. Mem. Council, Univ. of Tasmania, 1970–85. Freeman, City of Launceston, 1990. Hon. LLD Tasmania, 1988. *Recreations:* reading, music. *Address:* Manor Complex, Guy Street, Kings Meadows, Tas 7250, Australia. *T:* (03) 63431143. *Died 4 May 2009.*

FOOT, Rt Hon. Michael (Mackintosh); PC 1974; *b* 23 July 1913; *s* of late Rt Hon. Isaac Foot, PC; *m* 1949, Jill Craigie (*d* 1999). *Educ:* Forres Sch., Swanage; Leighton Park Sch., Reading; Wadham Coll., Oxford (Exhibitioner). Pres. Oxford Union, 1933; contested (Lab) Mon, 1935; MP (Lab): Devonport Div. of Plymouth, 1945–55; Ebbw Vale, Nov. 1960–1983; Blaenau Gwent, 1983–92; Sec. of State for Employment, 1974–76; Lord President of the Council and Leader of the House of Commons, 1976–79; Leader of the Opposition, 1980–83. Mem., Labour Party Nat. Exec. Cttee, 1971–83; Deputy Leader of the Labour Party, 1976–80; Leader of the Labour Party 1980–83. Asst Editor, Tribune, 1937–38; Acting Editor, Evening Standard, 1942; Man. Dir, Tribune, 1945–74, Editor, 1948–52, 1955–60; political columnist on the Daily Herald, 1944–64; former Book Critic, Evening Standard. Hon. Fellow, Wadham Coll., Oxford, 1969. *Publications:* Guilty Men (with Frank Owen and Peter Howard), 1940; Armistice 1918–39, 1940; Trial of Mussolini, 1943; Brendan and Beverley, 1944; Still at Large, 1950; Full Speed Ahead, 1950; Guilty Men (with Mervyn Jones), 1957; The Pen and the Sword, 1957; Parliament in Danger, 1959; Aneurin Bevan: Vol. I, 1897–1945, 1962; Vol. II, 1945–60, 1973; Debts of Honour, 1980; Another Heart and Other Pulses, 1984; Loyalists and Loners, 1986; The Politics of Paradise, 1988; H. L. G.: the history of Mr Wells, 1995; Dr Strangelove, I Presume, 1999; The Uncollected Michael Foot, 2003. *Recreations:* Plymouth Argyle supporter, chess, reading, walking. *Address:* c/o Tribune, 9 Arkwright Road, NW3 6AN. *Died 3 March 2010.*

FOOT, Prof. Philippa Ruth, FBA 1976; Griffin Professor, University of California at Los Angeles, 1988–91, then Emeritus (Professor of Philosophy, 1974–91); *b* 3 Oct. 1920; *d* of William Sydney Bence Bosanquet, DSO, and Esther Cleveland Bosanquet, *d* of Grover Cleveland, Pres. of USA; *m* 1945, Michael Richard Daniell Foot, CBE, TD (marr. diss. 1960); no *c*. *Educ:* St George's Sch., Ascot; privately; Somerville Coll., Oxford (BA 1942, MA 1946). Somerville College, Oxford: Lectr in philosophy, 1947; Fellow and Tutor, 1950–69; Vice-Principal, 1967–69; Sen. Res. Fellow, 1970–88; Hon. Fellow, 1988. Formerly Vis. Prof., Cornell Univ., MIT, Univ. of California at Berkeley,

Princeton Univ., City Univ. of NY; Fellow, Center for Advanced Studies in Behavioral Scis, Stanford, 1981–82. Pres., Pacific Div., Amer. Philos. Assoc., 1982–83. Fellow, Amer. Acad. of Arts and Scis, 1983. Hon. Dr Sofia, 2000. *Publications:* Theories of Ethics (ed), 1967; Virtues and Vices, 1978; Natural Goodness, 2001; Moral Dilemmas, 2002; articles in Mind, Aristotelian Soc. Proc., Philos. Rev., New York Rev., Philosophy and Public Affairs. *Address:* 15 Walton Street, Oxford OX1 2HG. *T:* (01865) 557130. *Died 3 Oct. 2010.*

FOOTE, Prof. Peter Godfrey; Emeritus Professor of Scandinavian Studies, University of London; *b* 26 May 1924; 4th *s* of late T. Foote and Ellen Foote, Swanage, Dorset; *m* 1951, Eleanor Jessie McCaig (*d* 2006), *d* of late J. M. McCaig and Margaret H. McCaig; one *s* two *d*. *Educ:* Grammar Sch., Swanage; University Coll., Exeter; Univ. of Oslo; University Coll., London. BA London 1948; MA London 1951; Fil. dr *hc* Uppsala, 1972; dr phil. *hc* Univ. of Iceland, 1987. Served with RNVR, 1943–46. University College London. Asst Lectr, Lectr and Reader in Old Scandinavian, 1950–63; Prof. of Scandinavian Studies, 1963–83; Fellow, 1989. Jt Sec., Viking Soc., 1956–83 (Pres., 1974–76; 1990–92; Hon. Life Mem., 1983). Member: Royal Gustav Adolfs Academy, Uppsala, 1967; Kungliga Humanistiska Vetenskapssamfundet, Uppsala, 1968; Vísindafélag Islands, 1969; Vetenskapssocieteten, Lund, 1973; Kungliga Vetenskapssamhället, Göteborg; Det kongelige Norske Videnskabers Selskab, 1977; Societas Scientiarum Fennica, 1979; Det norske Videnskapsakademi, 1986; Hon. Member: Islenska Bókmenntafélag, 1965; Thjóðvinafélag Íslenska í Vesturheimi, 1975; Félag íslenzkra fræða, 1995; Corresp. Mem., Kungliga Vitterhets Hist. och Antikvitets Akad., Stockholm, 1971. Crabtree Orator, 1968. Commander with star, Icelandic Order of the Falcon, 1984 (Comdr, 1973); Knight, Order of Dannebrog (Denmark); Comdr, Royal Order of North Star (Sweden), 1977; Comdr, Royal Order of Merit (Norway), 1993. *Publications:* Gunnlaugs saga ormstungu, 1957; Pseudo-Turpin Chronicle in Iceland, 1959; Laing's Heimskringla, 1961; Lives of Saints: Icelandic manuscripts in facsimile IV, 1962, and XIX, 1990; (with G. Johnston) The Saga of Gisli, 1963; (with D. M. Wilson) The Viking Achievement, 1970, 2nd edn 1980; (jt trans. and ed) Laws of Early Iceland, vol. I, 1980, vol. II, 2000; Aurvandilstá (selected papers), 1984; (ed) Olaus Magnus: a description of the Northern Peoples, vol. I, 1996, vols II and III, 1998; (ed) Jóns saga Hólabyskups ens helga, 2003; Kreddur (more selected papers), 2004; papers in Saga-Book, Arv, Studia Islandica, Islenzk Tunga, etc. *Recreations:* bell-ringing, walking. *Address:* 18 Talbot Road, N6 4QR. *T:* (020) 8340 1860. *Died 29 Sept. 2009.*

FOOTS, Sir James (William), Kt 1975; AO 1992; mining engineer; Chairman: MIM Holdings Ltd, 1970–83 (Director, 1956–87); Westpac Banking Corporation, 1987–89 (Director, 1971–89); *b* 12 July 1916; *m* 1939, Thora H. Thomas; one *s* two *d*. *Educ:* Melbourne Univ. (BME). President: Austr. Inst. Mining and Metallurgy, 1974; Austr. Mining Industry Council, 1974 and 1975; 13th Congress, Council of Mining and Metallurgical Instns, 1986. Fellow, Australian Acad. of Technol Scis. University of Queensland: Mem. Senate, 1970–92; Chancellor, 1985–92. Hon. DEng Univ. of Qld, 1982. *Address:* c/o 53 Royston Street, Brookfield, Qld 4069, Australia. *Died 21 Aug. 2010.*

FORBES, Donald James, MA; Headmaster, Merchiston Castle School, 1969–81; *b* 6 Feb. 1921; *s* of Andrew Forbes; *m* 1945, Patricia Muriel Yeo; two *s* one *d*. *Educ:* Oundle; Clare Coll., Cambridge (Mod. Lang. Tripos). Capt. Scots Guards, 1941–46; 1st Bn Scots Guards, 1942–46, N Africa, Italy. Asst Master, Dulwich Coll., 1946–55; Master i/c cricket, 1951–55; Headmaster, Dauntsey's Sch., 1956–69. Diploma in Spanish, Univ. of Santander, 1954; Lectr in Spanish, West Norwood Tech. Coll., 1954–55. *Recreations:* cricket, Rugby football, tennis, Rugby fives, curling, golf; history, literature;

instrumental and choral music. *Address:* 33 Coates Gardens, Edinburgh EH12 5LG. *Club:* Hawks (Cambridge). *Died 23 Feb. 2006.*

FORBES, Major Sir Hamish (Stewart), 7th Bt *cr* 1823, of Newe; MBE (mil.) 1945; MC 1945; Welsh Guards, retired; *b* 15 Feb. 1916; *s* of Lt-Col James Stewart Forbes (*d* 1957) (*g s* of 3rd Bt) and Feridah Frances Forbes (*d* 1953), *d* of Hugh Lewis Taylor; *S* cousin, 1984; *m* 1st, 1945, Jacynthe Elizabeth Mary, *d* of late Eric Gordon Underwood; one *s* three *d*; 2nd, 1981, Mary Christine, MBE, *d* of late Ernest William Rigby. *Educ:* Eton College; Lawrenceville, USA; SOAS. Served Welsh Guards, France, Germany, Turkey, 1939–58. Calmic Chemicals, Gillette, and Shell-Mex BP, 1959–64. Gen. Sec., Church Lads' Bde, 1964–73; Mem., Church Lads' and Church Girls' Bde Incorporated Soc., 1978–92; Vice-Pres., Church Lads' and Church Girls' Bde Assoc., 2000– (Pres., 1974–2000). Patron, Lonach Highland and Friendly Soc., 1984–. KStJ 1984 (Sec., Order of St John, 1973–83) *Recreations:* shooting, sculpture. *Heir:* s James Thomas Stewart Forbes [*b* 28 May 1957; *m* 1986, Kerry Lynne, *o d* of Rev. Lee Toms; two *d*]. *Address:* Newe, Strathdon, Aberdeenshire AB36 8TY. *T:* (019756) 51431. *Clubs:* Turf, Chelsea Arts, Pilgrims. *Died 3 Sept. 2007.*

FORD, Rt Rev. Douglas Albert; Bishop of Saskatoon, 1970–81; *b* 16 July 1917; *s* of Thomas George Ford and Elizabeth Eleanor (Taylor), both English; *m* 1944, Doris Ada (Elborne); two *s* one *d*. *Educ:* primary and secondary schs, Vancouver; Univ. of British Columbia (BA); Anglican Theological Coll. of BC (LTh); General Synod (BD). Deacon, 1941; Priest, 1942; Curate, St Mary's, Kerrisdale, 1941–42; St George's, Vancouver, 1942–44; Vicar of Strathmore, 1944–49; Rector of: Okotoks, 1949–52; Vermilion, 1952–55; St Michael and All Angels, Calgary, 1955–62; St Augustine, Lethbridge, 1962–66; Dean and Rector, St John's Cath., Saskatoon, 1966–70; Asst Bishop of Calgary, 1981–87; Incumbent of All Saints', Cochrane, dio. Calgary, 1981–85. Hon. DD: Coll. of Emmanuel and St Chad, Saskatoon, 1970; Anglican Theological Coll. of BC, Vancouver, 1971. *Address:* 126 Hawkstone Manor NW, Calgary, AB T3G 3X2, Canada. *Died 23 Jan. 2007.*

FORD, Sir Edward (William Spencer), GCVO 1998 (KCVO 1957; MVO 1949); KCB 1967 (CB 1952); ERD 1987; DL; Secretary and Registrar of the Order of Merit, 1975–2003; Secretary to the Pilgrim Trust, 1967–75; *b* 24 July 1910; 4th (twin) *s* of late Very Rev. Lionel G. B. J. Ford, Headmaster of Repton and Harrow and Dean of York, and of Mary Catherine, *d* of Rt Rev. E. S. Talbot, Bishop of Winchester and Hon. Mrs Talbot; *m* 1949, Virginia (*d* 1995), *er d* of 1st and last Baron Brand, CMG, and *widow* of John Metcalfe Polk, NY; two *s*. *Educ:* Eton (King's Schol.); New Coll., Oxford (Open Scholar; 1st Class Hon. Mods; 2nd Class Lit. Hum. (Greats); MA; Hon. Fellow, 1982). Law Student (Harmsworth Scholar), Middle Temple, 1934–35; Tutor to King Farouk of Egypt, 1936–37; called to Bar, Middle Temple, 1937 and practised 1937–39; 2nd Lieut (Supplementary Reserve of Officers) Grenadier Guards, 1936; Lieut 1939; served in France and Belgium, 1939–40 (despatches), and in Tunisia and Italy, 1943–44 (despatches), Brigade Major 10th Infantry and 24th Guards Brigades; Instructor at Staff Coll., Haifa, 1944–45; psc†. Asst Private Secretary to King George VI, 1946–52, and to the Queen, 1952–67; Extra Equerry to the Queen, 1955. Dir, London Life Assoc., 1970–83. Mem., Central Appeals Adv. Cttee, BBC and IBA, 1969–72, 1976–78; Mem., Council, St Christopher's Hospice, Sydenham, 1980–90 (Pres., 1990–2000); Chairman: UK/USA Bicentennial Fellowships Cttee, 1975–80; St John Council for Northamptonshire, 1976–82; Grants Cttee, Historic Churches Preservation Fund, 1977–90. Trustee: York Glaziers' Trust, 1977–2002; Butler Trust, 1986–90; Hon. Treas., Children's Country Holidays Fund, 1958–73; Vice-Pres., 1973–; Governor, The Ditchley

Foundn, 1966–89. FRSA. Mem. Ct of Assts, Goldsmiths' Co., 1970– (Prime Warden, 1979). High Sheriff, 1970, DL 1972, Northants. OStJ 1976. *Address:* Canal House, 23 Blomfield Road, W9 1AD. *T:* (020) 7286 0028. *Clubs:* White's, Beefsteak, Pratt's, MCC.
Died 19 Nov. 2006.

FORD, Air Marshal Sir Geoffrey (Harold), KBE 1979; CB 1974; FREng; Secretary, The Institute of Metals, 1985–88; *b* 6 Aug. 1923; *s* of late Harold Alfred Ford, Lewes, Sussex; *m* 1951, Valerie, *d* of late Douglas Hart Finn, Salisbury; two *s*. *Educ:* Lewes County Grammar Sch.; Bristol Univ. (BSc). Served War of 1939–45: commissioned, 1942; 60 Gp, 1943; Italy and Middle East, 1944–46. 90 (Signals) Gp, 1946–49; Bomber Development, 1954–57; Air Ministry, 1958–61; RAF Technical Coll., 1961–62; Min. of Aviation, 1963–64; Chief Signals Officer, RAF Germany, 1965–68; MoD, 1968–72; RCDS, 1972; AO Engineering, Strike Command, 1973–76; Dir-Gen. Engineering and Supply Management, RAF, 1976–78; Chief Engr (RAF), 1978–81. Dir, The Metals Soc., 1981–84. FIET (Council, IEE, 1977–82); FREng (FEng 1987). *Address:* c/o Barclays Bank, Lewes, East Sussex BN7 2JP. *Club:* Royal Air Force. *Died 1 April 2007.*

FORD, Gerald Rudolph; President of the United States of America, Aug. 1974–Jan. 1977; lawyer; company director; *b* Omaha, Nebraska, 14 July 1913; (adopted) *s* of Gerald R. Ford and Dorothy Gardner; *m* 1948, Elizabeth (*née* Bloomer); three *s* one *d*. *Educ:* South High Sch., Grand Rapids; Univ. of Michigan (BA); Law Sch., Yale Univ. (LLB). Served War: US Navy (Carriers), 1942–46. Partner in law firm of Ford and Buchen, 1941–42; Member, law firm of Butterfield, Keeney and Amberg, 1947–49; subseq. with Amberg, Law and Buchen. Member US House of Representatives for Michigan 5th District, 1948–73; Member: Appropriations Cttee, 1951; Dept of Defense Sub-Cttee, etc; House Minority Leader, Republican Party, 1965–73; Vice President of the United States, Dec. 1973–Aug. 1974. Attended Interparly Union meetings in Europe; Mem. US-Canadian Interparly Gp. Advr to Bd, American Express Co.; Hon. Mem. Bd, Citigroup Inc. Several hon. degrees. Delta Kappa Epsilon, Phi Delta Phi. Holds Amer. Pol. Sci. Assoc.'s Distinguished Congressional Service Award, 1961; Congressional Gold Medal, 1999; Presidential Medal of Freedom, 1999. *Publications:* (with John R. Stiles) Portrait of an Assassin, 1965; A Time to Heal, 1979; Humor and the Presidency, 1987. *Recreations:* outdoor sports (formerly football), skiing, tennis, golf. *Address:* PO Box 927, Rancho Mirage, CA 92270, USA. *Died 26 Dec. 2006.*

FORD, Prof. Sir Hugh, Kt 1975; FRS 1967; FREng; Professor of Mechanical Engineering, 1969–80, Professor Emeritus, since 1980, Pro-Rector, 1978–80, University of London (Imperial College of Science and Technology); Chairman, Sir Hugh Ford & Associates Ltd, since 1982; *b* 16 July 1913; *s* of Arthur and Constance Ford; *m* 1st, 1942, Wynyard (*d* 1991), *d* of Major F. B. Scholfield; two *d*; 2nd, 1993, Mrs Thelma Jensen. *Educ:* Northampton Sch.; City and Guilds Coll., Univ. of London. DSc (Eng); PhD. Practical trng at GWR Locomotive Works, 1931–36; researches into heat transfer, 1936–39; R&D Engrg, Imperial Chemical Industries, Northwich, 1939–42; Chief Engr, Technical Dept, British Iron and Steel Fedn, 1942–45, then Head of Mechanical Working Div., British Iron and Steel Research Assoc., 1945–47; Exec. Dir, Paterson Engrg Ltd, 1947–48; Reader in Applied Mechanics, Univ. of London (Imp. Coll. of Science and Technology), 1948–51, Prof., 1951–69; Head of Dept of Mech. Engineering, 1965–78. Mem. Bd of Governors, Imperial Coll., 1982–89. Technical Dir, Davy-Ashmore Group, 1968–71; Director: Ford & Dain Research Ltd, 1972–93; Alfred Herbert Ltd, 1972–79; Air Liquide UK Ltd, 1979–95; Ricardo Consulting Engrs Ltd, 1980–88; Chm., Adv. Bd, Prudential Portfolio Managers, 1985–88; Mem., Adv. Bd, Brown and Root (UK), 1983–92. John

Player Lectr, 1973, Hugh Ford Management Lectr, 1988, IMechE. First Pres., Inst. of Metals, 1985–87 (merger of Inst. of Metallurgists and Metals Soc.); President: Section 6, British Assoc., 1975–76; Welding Inst., 1983–85; Founder Fellow, Fellowship (later Royal Acad.) of Engineering, 1976 (Vice-Pres., 1981–83, Mem. Council, 1986–92); Member: Council, IMechE (Vice-Pres., 1972, 1975, Sen. Vice-Pres., 1976, Pres., 1977–78); SRC, 1968–72 (Chm. Engineering Bd); Council, Royal Soc., 1973–74; ARC, 1976–81. FICE; Whitworth Schol.; FCGI; FIC 1982; Sen. Fellow, RCA, 1987. Foreign Mem., Finnish Acad. of Technology, 1979. Hon. MASME, 1980; Hon. FIMechE 1984; Hon. FIChemE 1987. Hon. DSc: Salford, 1976; QUB, 1977; Aston, 1978; Bath, 1978; Sheffield, 1984; Sussex, 1990. Thomas Hawksley Gold Medallist, IMechE, 1948, for researches into rolling of metals; Robertson Medal, Inst. of Metals, 1954; James Alfred Ewing Gold Medal, ICE, 1982; James Watt Internat. Gold Medal, 1985. *Publications:* Advanced Mechanics of Materials, 1963; papers to Royal Soc., IMechE, Iron and Steel Inst., Inst. of Metals, foreign societies, etc. *Recreations:* gardening, music, model engineering. *Address:* 18 Shrewsbury House, Cheyne Walk, SW3 5LN; Shamley Cottage, Stroud Lane, Shamley Green, Surrey GU5 0ST. *Club:* Athenæum.
Died 28 May 2010.

FORD, James Allan, CB 1978; MC 1946; *b* 10 June 1920; 2nd *s* of Douglas Ford and Margaret Duncan (*née* Allan); *m* 1948, Isobel Dunnett; one *s* one *d*. *Educ:* Royal High School, Edinburgh; University of Edinburgh. Served 1940–46, Capt. Royal Scots. Entered Civil Service, 1938; Asst Sec., Dept of Agriculture and Fisheries for Scotland, 1958; Registrar Gen. for Scotland, 1966–69; Principal Establishment Officer, Scottish Office, 1969–79. A Trustee, Nat. Library of Scotland, 1981–91. *Publications:* The Brave White Flag, 1961; Season of Escape, 1963; A Statue for a Public Place, 1965; A Judge of Men, 1968; The Mouth of Truth, 1972. *Address:* 6 Hillpark Court, Edinburgh EH4 7BE. *T:* (0131) 336 5398. *Club:* Royal Scots (Edinburgh).
Died 30 March 2009.

FORD, (John) Peter, CBE 1969; Chairman and Managing Director, International Joint Ventures Ltd, 1974–2003; *b* 20 Feb. 1912; *s* of Ernest and Muriel Ford; *m* 1939, Phoebe Seys, *d* of Herbert McGregor Wood, FRIBA; one *s* two *d*. *Educ:* Wrekin Coll.; Gonville and Caius Coll., Cambridge (BA (Hons Nat. Sci. Tripos) 1934; MA 1937). Cambridge Univ. Air Sqdn, 1932–35 (Pilot's A Licence, 1933–). Air Ministry (subsequently FO, RAFVR), 1939–40; Coventry Gauge and Tool Co. Ltd (Asst to Chm.), 1941–45; Gen. Man., Brit. Engineers Small Tools and Equipment Co. Ltd, and Gen. Man. Scientific Exports (GB) Ltd, 1945–48; Man. Dir, Brush Export Ltd, Associated British Oil Engines (Export) Ltd and National Oil Engines (Export) Ltd, and Dir of other associated cos of The Brush Group, 1949–55; Dir, Associated British Engineering Ltd and subsidiaries, 1957–58; Man. Dir, Coventry Climax International Ltd, 1958–63; Director: Plessey Overseas Ltd, 1963–70; Bryant & May (Latin America) Ltd, 1970–73; Chm., Metra Martech Ltd, 1988–2000. Chm. Institute of Export, 1954–56, 1965–67; President: Soc. of Commercial Accountants, 1970–74 (Vice-Pres., 1956–70); Inst. of Company Accountants, 1974–75; Member: Council, London Chamber of Commerce, 1951–72 (Dep. Chm., 1970–72; Vice-Pres., 1972–2003); London Ct of Arbitration, 1970–73; FBI, Overseas Trade Policy Cttee, 1952–63; Council, British Internal Combustion Engine Manufacturers Assoc., 1953–55; BNEC Cttee for Exports to Latin America, 1964–71 (Chm. 1968–71); NEDO Cttee for Movement of Exports, 1972–75; British Overseas Trade Adv. Council, 1975–82. Chm., British Shippers' Council, 1972–75 (Dep. Chm., 1971–72). Chm., British Mexican Soc., 1973–77; Vice-Pres., Hispanic and Luso Brazilian Council, 1980–. Freeman of City of London, 1945; Mem. Ct of Assistants, Ironmongers' Co. (Master, 1981); Governor: Wrekin Coll., 1953–57; Oversea Service

Coll., 1966–86. CEng, CIMechE, CIMarE, MIEE. Order of Rio Branco (Brazil), 1977. *Publications:* contributor to technical press and broadcaster on international trade subjects. *Recreation:* Athletics (Cambridge Univ. and Internat. Teams, 1932–35; held various county championships, 1932–37; Hon. Treas., 1947–58, Vice-Pres., 1990–, Achilles Club; Pres., London Athletic Club, 1964–66). *Clubs:* Oxford and Cambridge, MCC; Hawks (Cambridge); Royal Wimbledon Golf. *Died 7 March 2007.*

FORDER, Ven. Charles Robert; Archdeacon Emeritus, Diocese of York, since 1974; *b* 6 Jan. 1907; *s* of late Henry Forder, Worstead, Norfolk; *m* 1933, Myra (decd), *d* of late Harry Peat, Leeds; no *c. Educ:* Paston Sch., North Walsham; Christ's Coll., Cambridge (Exhibnr and Prizeman, 1926; 1st Cl. Math. Trip. Part I, 1926, BA (Sen. Opt. Part II) 1928, MA 1932); Ridley Hall, Cambridge. Curate: St Peter's, Hunslet Moor, 1930–33; Burley, 1933–34; Vicar: Holy Trinity, Wibsey, 1934–40; St Clement's, Bradford, 1940–47; Organising Sec., Bradford Church Forward Movement Appeal, 1945–47; Vicar of Drypool, 1947–55; Rector of Routh and Vicar of Wawne, 1955–57; Canon, and Prebendary of Fenton, York Minster, 1957–76; Rector of Sutton-on-Derwent, 1957–63; Rector of Holy Trinity, Micklegate, York, 1963–66; Archdeacon of York, 1957–72. Chaplain to HM Prison, Hull, 1950–53; Proctor in Convocation, 1954–72; Organising Sec., Diocesan Appeal, 1955–76; Church Comr, 1958–73. *Publications:* A History of the Paston Grammar School, 1934, 2nd edn 1975; The Parish Priest at Work, 1947; Synods in Action, 1970; Churchwardens in Church and Parish, 1976; contrib. to Encyclopædia Britannica. *Recreation:* reading and writing. *Address:* Dulverton Hall, Esplanade, Scarborough YO11 2AR. *T:* (01723) 340112. *Died 10 Oct. 2008*

FORMAN, Roy; Managing Director and Chief Executive, Private Patients Plan Ltd, 1985–94; *b* 28 Dec. 1931; *s* of Leslie and Ena Forman; *m* 1954, Mary (née Nelson); three *s* one *d. Educ:* Nunthorpe Grammar Sch., York; Nottingham Univ. (BA Hons). RAF, 1953–56. Business economist, 1956–61; electricity supply industry, 1961–80: Chief Commercial Officer, S Wales Elec. Bd, 1972–76; Commercial Adviser, Electricity Council, 1976–80; Private Patients Plan Ltd: Gen. Manager, Marketing and Sales, 1980–81; Marketing Dir, 1981–85; Man. Dir, Age Concern Enterprises Ltd, 1995–96; Director: General Healthcare Group PLC, 1994; Reliastar Reinsurance Group (UK) Ltd, 1997. FRSA 1992. *Recreations:* music, walking, reading. *Died 15 June 2009.*

FORRESTER, John Stuart; *b* 17 June 1924; *s* of Harry and Nellie Forrester; *m* 1945, Gertrude H. Weaver. *Educ:* Eastwood Council Sch.; City Sch. of Commerce, Stoke-on-Trent; Alsager Teachers' Training Coll. Teacher, 1946–66. MP (Lab) Stoke-on-Trent, N, 1966–87. Sec., Constituency Labour Party, 1961–84. Mem., Speaker's Panel of Chairmen, 1982–87; Member: NUT, 1949–87; APEX, 1942–43, 1946–49, 1984–. Councillor, Stoke-on-Trent, 1970–2000. Freedom of Stoke-on-Trent, 1992. *Address:* 13 Cadeby Grove, Milton, Stoke-on-Trent ST2 7BY. *Died 22 Nov. 2007.*

FORRESTER, Maj.-Gen. Michael, CB 1969; CBE 1963 (OBE 1960); DSO 1943 and Bar, 1944; MC 1939 and Bar, 1941; retired 1970; *b* 31 Aug. 1917; 2nd *s* of late James Forrester, formerly of Kirklinton, Cumbria and Elsie (née Mathwin), Chilworth, Hants; *m* 1947, Pauline Margaret Clara (marr. diss. 1960), *d* of late James Fisher, Crossmichael; two *s. Educ:* Haileybury. 2nd Lieut, SRO, Queen's Royal Regt, 1936, Regular Commn, 1938; served in Palestine (Arab Rebellion), 1938–39; served War of 1939–45 in Palestine, Egypt, Greece, Crete, Western Desert, Syria, N Africa, Italy and France; Intell. Officer, GHQ Cairo, 1940; GSO3 (Ops) British Military Mission, Greece, 1940–41; GSO3 (Ops), HQ Western Desert Force and HQ 13 Corps, 1941–42; Staff Coll., Haifa, 1942; Bde Major, 132 Inf. Bde, 1942 (despatches); GSO2 (Ops), HQ 13 Corps and HQ 18 Army Gp, 1943;

Comdr, 1st/6th Bn, Queen's Royal Regt, 1943–44; wounded, Normandy; GSO1 (Ops), HQ 13 Corps, 1945–46; Mil. Asst to Supreme Allied Comdr Mediterranean, 1947; Mil. Asst to Comdr Brit. Army Staff and Army Mem., Brit. Jt Services Mission, Washington, DC, 1947–50; Co. Comdr, 2nd Bn Parachute Regt, Cyprus and Canal Zone, 1951–52; Dirg Staff, Staff Coll., Camberley, 1953–55; GSO1 (Ops), GHQ East Africa, 1955–57; transf. to Parachute Regt, 1957; Comdr, 3rd Bn Parachute Regt, 1957–60 (incl. Jordan, 1958); Col, Military Operations (4), War Office, 1960–61; Comdr, 16 Parachute Bde Gp, 1961–63; Imp. Def. Coll., 1964; GOC 4th Div., BAOR, 1965–67; Dir of Infantry, MoD, 1967–70. Col Comdt, The Queen's Division, 1968–70. Lay Co-Chm., Alton Deanery Synod, 1984–88; Mem., Winchester Diocesan Synod, 1988–91. Vice-Pres., UK Crete Veterans' Assoc., 1993–2001; Pres., UK Crete Veterans' and Friends' Soc., 2001–. Hon. Citizen, Canea, Crete, 1966. *Address:* Hammonds, West Worldham, near Alton, Hants GU34 3BH. *T:* (01420) 84470. *Died 15 Oct. 2006.*

FORRESTER, Prof. Peter Garnett, CBE 1981; Professor Emeritus, Cranfield Institute of Technology; *b* 7 June 1917; *s* of Arthur Forrester and Emma (née Garnett); *m* 1942, Marjorie Hewitt (*d* 2000), Berks; two *d. Educ:* Manchester Grammar Sch.; Manchester Univ. (BSc, MSc). Metallurgist, Thomas Bolton & Son Ltd, 1938–40; Research Officer, later Chief Metallurgist, Tin Research Inst., 1940–48; Chief Metallurgist and Research Man., Glacier Metal Co. Ltd, 1948–63; Dep. Principal, Glacier Inst. of Management, 1963–64; Consultant, John Tyzack & Partners, 1964–66; Prof. of Industrial Management, Coll. of Aeronautics, Cranfield, 1966; Dir, Cranfield Sch. of Management, 1967–82, Dean of Faculty, 1972; Pro-Vice-Chancellor, Cranfield Inst. of Technol., 1976–82; Chm., Conf. of Univ Management Schs, 1976–77. Chm., Rye and Winchelsea Centre, Nat. Trust, 1991–93. Mem., Bd of Trustees, European Foundation for Management Develt, 1976–82. CCMI. Hon. DSc Cranfield Inst. of Technol., 1983. Burnham Medal, BIM, 1979. *Publications:* The British MBA, 1986; papers and reports on management educn; numerous scientific and technological papers on metallurgy, bearing materials, tribology. *Recreations:* sailing, walking. *Address:* Strawberry Hole Cottage, Ewhurst Lane, Northiam, near Rye, Sussex TN31 6HJ. *T:* (01797) 252255. *Died 23 March 2008.*

FORSTER, Neil Milward; Chairman: Air UK Ltd, 1982–90; Air UK Group Ltd, 1990–97; *b* 29 May 1927; *s* of Norman Milward Forster and Olive Christina Forster (née Cockrell); *m* 1954, Barbara Elizabeth Smith; one *s* two *d. Educ:* Hurstpierpoint Coll., Sussex; Pembroke Coll., Cambridge (BA Law and Economics). Fellow, Inst. of Transport. Joined Clan Line Steamers, 1952; Chm., Calcutta Liners Conf., 1962–66; Director: Clan Line, 1967; Group and Associated cos, British & Commonwealth Shipping Co., 1974–78; British and Commonwealth Hldgs plc, 1974–88 (Gp Man. Dir, 1982–86); S African Marine Corp., 1977–99; KLM UK, 1997–99. Chairman: Europe/SA Shipping Confs. 1977–87; UK S Africa Trade Assoc., 1985–87. Rep. England and GB at hockey, 1951–58. *Recreations:* golf, gardening. *Address:* The Orchard, Upper Slaughter, Cheltenham, Glos GL54 2JB. *T:* (01451) 822025. *Clubs:* Oriental, MCC. *Died 8 Nov. 2006.*

FORSYTE, Charles; see Philo, G. C. G.

FORSYTHE, Air Cdre James Roy, (Paddy), CBE 1966; DFC; Director of Development, 1976–81, Joint Chief Executive, 1981–86, Look Ahead Housing Association Ltd; *b* 10 July 1920; *s* of W. R. and A. M. Forsythe; *m* 1st, 1946, Barbara Mary Churchman (*d* 1983); two *s* two *d;* 2nd, 1989, Mrs W. P. Newbery. *Educ:* Methodist Coll., Belfast; Queen's Univ., Belfast. Bomber Comd, 1944–45; OC, Aberdeen Univ. Air Sqdn, 1952–54; psa 1955; Principal Staff Officer to Dir-Gen. Orgn (RAF), 1956–58; OC, 16 Sqdn, 1958–60; Directing Staff, Coll. of Air Warfare, Manby, 1960–62;

Head of RAF Aid Mission to India, 1963; Stn Comdr, RAF Acklington, 1963–65; Dep. Dir Air Staff Policy, MoD, 1965–68; Dir Public Relations, Far East, 1968–70; Dir Recruiting, RAF, 1971–73; Dir, Public Relations, RAF, 1973–75. Chm., RAF RU, 1972, 1973, 1974; Chm., Combined Services RU, 1974; Vice-Pres., 1979, Chm., 1988–90, Pres., 1990–92, London Irish RFC. Chm., League of Friends, Royal Brompton Hosp., 1992–98. MCIPR. *Recreations:* Rugby, golf. *Address:* 104 Earls Court Road, W8 6EG. *T:* (020) 7937 5291. *Club:* Royal Air Force. *Died 28 Aug. 2009.*

FORT, Dame Maeve (Geraldine), DCMG 1998 (CMG 1990); DCVO 1999; HM Diplomatic Service, retired; High Commissioner, South Africa, 1996–2000; *b* 19 Nov. 1940; *d* of late F. L. and R. E. Fort. *Educ:* Trinity College, Dublin (MA); Sorbonne, Paris. Joined Foreign Service, 1963; UKMIS, NY, 1964; CRO, 1965; seconded to SEATO, Bangkok, 1966; Bonn, 1968; Lagos, 1971; Second, later First Sec., FCO, 1973; UKMIS, NY, 1978; Counsellor, FCO, 1982; RCDS, 1983; Counsellor, Hd of Chancery and Consul-Gen., Santiago, 1984–86; Head of W African Dept, FCO, 1986–89, and Ambassador (non-resident) to Chad, 1987–89; Ambassador to: Mozambique, 1989–92; Lebanese Republic, 1992–96. Trustee: Beit Trust, 2000–; BRCS, 2001–07. *Address:* 5 Simon Close, Portobello Road, W11 3DJ. *Died 18 Sept. 2008.*

FORTE, Baron *cr* 1982 (Life Peer), of Ripley in the county of Surrey; **Charles Forte,** Kt 1970; President, Forte (formerly Trusthouse Forte) PLC, 1992–96 (Chairman, 1982–92, Executive Chairman, 1978–81; Deputy Chairman, 1970–78, and Chief Executive, 1971–78); *b* 26 Nov. 1908; *m* 1943, Irene Mary Chierico; one *s* five *d.* *Educ:* Alloa Academy; Dumfries Coll.; Mamiani, Rome. Fellow and Mem. Exec. Cttee, Catering Inst., 1949; Member: Small Consultative Advisory Cttee to Min. of Food, 1946; London Tourist Board. Hon. Consul Gen. for Republic of San Marino. FCMI (FBIM 1971); FRSA. Grand Officier, Ordine al Merito della Repubblica Italiana; Cavaliere di Gran Croce della Repubblica Italiana; Cavaliere del Lavoro (Italy). *Publications:* Forte (autobiog.), 1986; articles for catering trade papers. *Recreations:* golf, fishing, shooting, fencing, music. *Address:* c/o House of Lords, SW1A 0PW. *Clubs:* Carlton, Caledonian. *Died 28 Feb. 2007.*

FORTESCUE, Trevor Victor Norman, (Tim), CBE 1984; Secretary-General, Food and Drink Industries Council, 1973–83; *b* 28 Aug. 1916; *s* of Frank Fortescue; *m* 1st, 1939, Margery Stratford (marr. diss. 1975), *d* of Dr G. H. Hunt; one *s* one *d* (and one *s* decd); 2nd, 1975, Anthea Maureen, *d* of Robert M. Higgins. *Educ:* Uppingham Sch.; King's Coll., Cambridge. BA 1938; MA 1945. Colonial Administrative Service, Hong Kong, 1939–47 and Kenya, 1949–51 (interned by Japanese, 1941–45); FAO, UN, Washington, DC, 1947–49 and Rome, 1951–54; Chief Marketing Officer, Milk Marketing Bd of England and Wales, 1954–59; Manager, Nestlé Gp of Cos, Vevey, Switz., 1959–63 and London, 1963–66. MP (C) Liverpool, Garston, 1966–Feb. 1974; an Asst Govt Whip, 1970–71; a Lord Comr of HM Treasury, 1971–73. Chairman: Conference Associates Ltd, 1978–87; Standing Cttee, Confedn of Food and Drink Industries of European Community (CIAA), 1982–84; Pres., British Food Manufg Industries Res. Assoc., 1984–92; Member: Meat Promotion Rev. Body, 1984; Council, British Industrial Biol. Res. Assoc., 1980–83. Develt Manager (with A. M. Fortescue), Winchester Cathedral, 1989–90; Dir, Winchester Cathedral Enterprises Ltd, 1990–2000. Trustee, Uppingham Sch., 1957–63; Patron and Trustee, The Quest Community, Birmingham, 1971–85. *Publications:* Lovelines, 1987; Lovelines from Winchester, 1996. *Recreation:* marriage to Anthea. *Address:* 4 Compton Road, Winchester, Hants SO23 9SL. *T:* (01962) 854693. *Died 29 Sept. 2008.*

FORTH, Rt Hon. Eric; PC 1997; MP (C) Bromley and Chislehurst, since 1997 (Mid Worcestershire, 1983–97); *b* 9 Sept. 1944; *s* of late William and Aileen Forth; *m* 1st, 1967, Linda St Clair (marr. diss. 1994); two *d*; 2nd, 1994, Mrs Carroll Goff; one step *s. Educ:* Jordanhill Coll. Sch., Glasgow; Glasgow Univ. (MA Hons Politics and Econs). Chm., Young Conservatives', Constituency CPC, 1970–73; Member: Glasgow Univ. Cons. Club, 1962–66; Brentwood UDC, 1968–72. Contested (C) Barking, Feb. and Oct. 1974. Member (C), North Birmingham, European Parlt, 1979–84; Chm., Backbench Cttee, European Democ. Gp, European Parlt, 1979–84. PPS to Minister of State, DES, 1986–87; Parly Under Sec. of State: DTI, 1988–90; Dept of Employment, 1990–92; DFE, 1992–94; Minister of State, DFE, later DFEE, 1994–97; Shadow Leader of H of C, 2001–03. Member: H of C Commn, 2000–03; Chairmen's Panel, 2004–; Select Committee: on Employment, 1986; on Standards and Privileges, 1999–2001; on Procedure, 1999–2001; on Statutory Instruments, 2004–; Chm., Jt Cttee on Statutory Instruments, 2005–; Admin Cttee, 2005–; Finance and Services Cttee, 2005–. Chm., Cons. Backbench European Affairs Cttee, 1987–88 (Vice-Chm., 1983–86). Chm., Cons. Way Forward, 1997–2001. *Publications:* Regional Policy—A Fringe Benefit?, 1983. *Recreations:* cinema, reading, biographies, travel. *Address:* House of Commons, SW1A 0AA. *Club:* Bromley Conservative. *Died 17 May 2006.*

FOSSETT, Steve; adventurer; *b* California, 22 April 1944; *m* 1968, Peggy Viehland. *Educ:* Stanford Univ. (BA 1966); Washington Univ. (MBA 1968). Cert. Public Accountant, State of Illinois, 1972. Pres., Larkspur Securities Inc., 1980–. Record holder: *ballooning:* first solo flight across Pacific (Seoul, S Korea, to Mendham, Saskatchewan), 1995; Roziere balloon altitude flight (8 US records), 1996; first solo balloon flight round the world and absolute round the world speed record (Northam, Western Australia, to Queensland, Australia), 19 June–4 July 2002, fastest speed by manned balloon, 322.25 kmh (200.24 mph), 1 July 2002, and 24 hr balloon distance record, 5,128.65 km (3,186.80 statute miles), 30 June–1 July 2002; *sailing:* Round Ireland, 1993; Pacific Ocean singlehanded (Yokohama to San Francisco), 1996; Newport to Bermuda singlehanded, 1999; Newport to Bermuda, 2000; Transatlantic (NY to England), 2001; Isle of Wight, 2001; Fastnet course, 2002; Round Britain and Ireland, 2002; Round the World, 2004; *gliding:* world speed records, with Terry Delore: 500 km triangle, 2002; 1000 km out-and-return, 2002; *airplane flying:* US transcontinental records: East to West, non-military jet, 2000; West to East, non-military jet, 2003; turboprop, unlimited, 2003; round the world records, medium airplane H-class, eastbound and westbound, 2000; trans-Atlantic flight in replica of 1st World War Vickers Vimy biplane, 2005; other world records include: fastest world record by non-supersonic airplane, 1,194.17 kmh (742.02 mph), Perth-Hobart, 2000; 5000 km speed record, H-class, 2000; fastest solo flight around the globe without stopping or refuelling, 2005; other activities include: swimming, English Channel, 1985; mountain climbing: climbed highest peak on six continents; Everest expeditions, 1987, 1992; dogsled racing, Iditarod, 1992; auto racing, Le Mans, 1993, 1996; Ironman Triathlon, 1996; cross country ski-ing: Aspen to Eagle record, 2000; completed all 14 races in World Loppet League. Member: World Scout Cttee, World Scout Orgn; Nat. Exec. Bd, Boy Scouts of America; President's Council, Experimental Aircraft Assoc; Trustee, Youth Foundn. FRGS. Many awards incl. Diplôme de Montgolfier, 1996, Prix de la Vaulx, 1995, 1997, 1998, 2002, Fédération Aéronautique Internat.; Rolex Yachtsman of 2001, US Sailing Assoc., 2002; Explorers Medal, Explorers Club, 2003; Médaille de l'Aéronautique (France), 2003; Grand Médaille de l'Aéro Club de France, 2002; Gold Medal, Royal Aero Club of UK, 2002. *Clubs:* Adventurers (Hon. Mem.) (Chicago); Explorers (New York) (Fellow); Aéro Club (France) (Hon. Mem.);

National Yacht, Ireland (Dun Laoghaire) (Hon. Mem.), Newport Harbor Yacht (Hon. Mem.), Royal Temple Yacht (Ramsgate) (Hon. Mem.). *Died Sept. 2007.*

FOSTER, Sir John (Gregory), 3rd Bt *cr* 1930; Consultant Physician, George, Cape Province, until 2001; *b* 26 Feb. 1927; *s* of Sir Thomas Saxby Gregory Foster, 2nd Bt, and Beryl, *d* of late Dr Alfred Ireland; *S* father, 1957; *m* 1956, Jean Millicent Watts; one *s* three *d*. *Educ:* Michaelhouse Coll., Natal. South African Artillery, 1944–46; Witwatersrand Univ., 1946–51; MB, BCh 1951; Postgraduate course, MRCPE 1955; Medical Registrar, 1955–56; Medical Officer, Cape Town, 1957. DIH London, 1962; FRCPE 1981. *Recreation:* outdoor sport. *Heir: s* Saxby Gregory Foster [*b* 3 Sept. 1957; *m* 1989, Rowen Audrey, *d* of R. A. Ford; two *s*]. *Address:* 7 Caledon Street, PO Box 1325, George 6530, Cape Province, South Africa. *T:* (44) 8743333, *Fax:* (44) 8732507. *Club:* Johannesburg Country (S Africa).
Died 24 Nov. 2006.

FOSTER, (John) Peter, OBE 1990; Surveyor of the Fabric of Westminster Abbey, 1973–88, then Emeritus; *b* 2 May 1919; *s* of Francis Edward Foster and Evelyn Marjorie, *e d* of Sir Charles Stewart Forbes, 5th Bt of Newe; *m* 1944, Margaret Elizabeth Skipper; one *s* one *d*. *Educ:* Eton; Trinity Hall, Cambridge. BA 1940, MA 1946; ARIBA 1949. Commnd RE 1941; served Norfolk Div.; joined Guards Armd Div. 1943, served France and Germany; Captain SO,RE(2) 30 Corps 1945; discharged 1946. Marshall Sisson, Architect: Asst 1948, later Partner; Sole Principal 1971; Surveyor of Royal Academy of Arts, 1965–80. Partner with John Peters of Vine Press, Hemingford Grey, 1957–63. Member: Churches Cttee for Historic Building Council for England, 1977–84; Adv. Bd for Redundant Churches, 1979–91; Exec. Cttee, Georgian Gp, 1983–91; Fabric Cttee, Canterbury Cathedral, 1987–91 (Chm., 1990); Council, Ancient Monuments Soc., 1988–; Fabric Cttee, Ely Cathedral, 1990–2008. Chm., Cathedral Architects Assoc., 1987–90; President: Cambridge Antiquarian Soc., 1968–70; Assoc. for Studies in Conservation of Historic Buildings, 2001. Art Workers' Guild: Mem., 1971; Master, 1980; Trustee, 1985–2002. Pres., Surveyors Club, 1980. Governor, Suttons Hosp., Charterhouse, 1982–2000. FSA 1973; FRSA 1994. CStJ 1987. *Publications:* Holiday Painter: watercolours 1935–1998, 2000. *Recreations:* painting, books, travel. *Address:* Harcourt, Hemingford Grey, Huntingdon, Cambs PE28 9BJ. *T:* (01480) 462200. *Club:* Athenæum. *Died 6 March 2010.*

FOSTER, Maj.-Gen. Peter Beaufoy, MC 1944; Major-General Royal Artillery, British Army of the Rhine, 1973–76; retired June 1976; *b* 1 Sept. 1921; *s* of F. K. Foster, OBE, JP, Allt Dinas, Cheltenham; *m* 1947, Margaret Geraldine, *d* of W. F. Henn, sometime Chief Constable of Glos; two *s* one *d* (and one *s* decd). *Educ:* Uppingham School. Commnd RA, 1941; psc 1950; jssc 1958; OC Para. Light Battery, 1958–60; DAMS MS5, WO, 1960–63; Mil. Assistant to C-in-C BAOR, 1963–64; CO 34 Light Air Defence Regt RA, 1964–66; GSO1, ASD5, MoD, 1966–68; BRA Northern Comd, 1968–71; Comdt Royal Sch. of Artillery, 1971–73. Col Comdt, RA, 1977–82; Regimental Comptroller, RA, 1985–86. Vice President: RA Assoc., 1986–; RHA Assoc., 1994–. Chapter Clerk, Salisbury Cathedral, 1978–85. *Recreations:* shooting, gardening, beagling, walking, reading. *Address:* The Lodge, Wallop House, Nether Wallop, Stockbridge, Hants SO20 2HE.
Died 7 June 2007.

FOULIS, Sir Iain (Primrose Liston), 13th Bt *cr* 1634, of Colinton; Bt 1661, of Ravelston, but for the attainder; Language Tutor, Madrid, 1966–83; *b* 9 Aug. 1937; *s* of Lieut-Colonel James Alistair Liston-Foulis, Royal Artillery (killed on active service, 1942), and Mrs Kathleen de la Hogue Moran (*d* 1991), 2nd *d* of Lt-Col John Moran, Indian Army and Countess Olga de la Hogue, *yr d* of Marquis de la Hogue, Mauritius; *S* cousin, Sir Archibald Charles Liston Foulis, 12th Bt, 1961. *Educ:* Hodder; St Mary's Hall; Stonyhurst Coll.; Cannington

Farm Inst., Somerset (Dip. Agr.); Madrid (Dip. in Spanish). National Service, 1957–59; Argyll and Sutherland Highlanders, Cyprus, 1958 (Gen. Service Medal). Landowner, 1961–. Language Teacher, Estremadura and Madrid, 1959–61; Trainee, Bank of London and South America, 1962; Trainee, Bank of London and Montreal (in Nassau, 1963, Guatemala City, 1963–64; Managua, Nicaragua, 1964–65); Toronto (Sales), 1965–66. Mem., Standing Council of Baronets, 1988–. Life Mem., Nat. Trust for Scotland. Member: Spanish Soc. of the Friends of Castles; Friends of the St James Way. Cert. from Archbishop of Santiago de Compostela for pilgrimage on foot, Somport to Santiago, Jubilee Year, 1971. *Recreations:* swimming, walking, mountaineering, travelling, foreign languages and customs, reading, Spanish medieval history (especially Muslim Spain), car racing and rallies, country pursuits, hunting. *Address:* Apartado de Correos 7, San Agustin de Guadalix, 28750 Madrid, Spain. *T:* and *Fax:* (91) 8418978; Calle Universidad 28, Escalera 2, 5-D Jaca, Huesca, Spain. *Died 5 Feb. 2006 (ext).*

FOUYAS, Metropolitan Methodios, of Pisidia; Metropolitan of Pisidia, since 1988; Archbishop of Thyateira and Great Britain, 1979–88; Greek Orthodox Archbishop of Great Britain, 1979–88; *b* 14 Sept. 1925. *Educ:* BD (Athens), 1952; PhD (Manchester), 1962. Vicar of Greek Church in Munich, 1951–54; Secretary-General, Greek Patriarchate of Alexandria, 1954–56; Vicar of Greek Church in Manchester, 1960–66; Secretary, Holy Synod of Church of Greece, 1967–78; Archbishop of Aksum (Ethiopia), 1968–79. Estabd Foundn for Hellenism in GB, 1982. Founder, Harmony of Otherness, 2000. Member, Academy of Religious Sciences, Brussels, 1974–. Dist. Lectr, Univ. of Berkeley, 1992. Hon. DD: Edinburgh, 1970; Gr. Th. Sch. of Holy Cross, Boston, 1984. Grand Cordon, Order of Phoenix (Greece); of Sellassie (Ethiopia). Editor: Ekklesiastikos Pharos (Prize of Academy of Athens), 11 Volumes; Ecclesia and Theologia, vols I-XII, 1980–93; Texts and Studies: a review of the Foundn for Hellenism in GB, Vols I–X, 1982–91; Founder-Editor, Abba Salama Review of Ethio-Hellenic Studies, 10 Volumes. *Publications:* History of the Church in Corinth, 1968, 2nd edn 1997; Orthodoxy, Roman Catholicism and Anglicanism, 1972, 2nd edn 1984, 3rd edn in Greek 1996; Letters of Meletius Pegas, Pope and Patriarch of Alexandria 1590–1601, 1976, 2nd edn 1998; The Person of Jesus Christ in the Decisions of the Ecumenical Councils, 1976, 2nd edn in Greek 1997; Christianity and Judaism in Ethiopia, Nubia and Meroe, 1st Vol., 1979, 2nd Vol., 1982; Theological and Historical Studies, Vols 1–18, 1979–2003; Greeks and Latins, 1990, 2nd edn 1994; Hellenism, the Pedestal of Christianity, 1992; Contemporary History of the Church of Alexandria, 1993; Hellenism, the Pedestal of Islam, 1994, 2nd edn 1995; Hellenism and Judaism, 1995; The Hellenistic Jewish Tradition, 1996; Hellenic Problems, 1997; Hellenism, the Pedestal of European Civilisation, 1999; The World Wise Spreading of the Hellenic Civilization, 2001; contrib. to many other books and treatises. *Recreation:* gardening. *Address:* 9 Riga Feraiou Street, Khalandri, 15232 Athens, Greece. *T:* (210) 6824793.
Died 7 July 2006.

FOWDEN, Sir Leslie, Kt 1982; FRS 1964; Director of Arable Crops Research, Agricultural and Food Research Council, 1986–88; *b* Rochdale, Lancs, 13 Oct. 1925; *s* of Herbert and Amy D. Fowden; *m* 1949, Margaret Oakes (decd); one *s* one *d*. *Educ:* University Coll., London. PhD Univ. of London, 1948. Scientific Staff of Human Nutrition Research Unit of the MRC, 1947–50; Lecturer in Plant Chemistry, University Coll. London, 1950–55, Reader, 1956–64; Prof. of Plant Chemistry, 1964–73; Dean of Faculty of Science, UCL, 1970–73; Dir, Rothamsted Exptl Station, 1973–86. Rockefeller Fellow at Cornell Univ., 1955; Visiting Prof. at Univ. of California, 1963; Royal Society Visiting Prof., Univ. of Hong Kong, 1967. Consultant Dir, Commonwealth Bureau of Soils, 1973–88. Chm., Agric. and Vet. Adv.

Cttee, British Council, 1987–95; Member: Advisory Board, Tropical Product Inst., 1966–70; Council, Royal Society, 1970–72; Radioactive Waste Management Adv. Cttee, 1983–91. Royal Botanic Gardens, Kew: Mem., Scientific Adv. Panel, 1977–83; Trustee, 1983–93; Trustee, Bentham-Moxon Trust, 1994–. Foreign Member: Deutsche Akademie der Naturforscher Leopoldina, 1971; Lenin All-Union Acad. of Agricultural Sciences of USSR, 1978–92; Acad. of Agricl Scis of GDR, 1986–91; Russian Acad. of Agricl Scis, 1992–; Corresponding Mem., Amer. Soc. Plant Physiologists, 1981; Hon. Mem., Phytochemical Soc. of Europe, 1985. Hon. DSc Westminster, 1993. *Publications:* contribs to scientific journals on topics in plant biochemistry.
Died 16 Dec. 2008.

FOWELLS, Joseph Dunthorne Briggs, CMG 1975; DSC 1940; Deputy Director General, British Council, 1976–77; *b* 17 Feb. 1916; *s* of late Joseph Fowells and Maud Dunthorne, Middlesbrough; *m* 1st, 1940, Edith Agnes McKerracher (marr. diss. 1966); two *s* one *d*; 2nd, 1969, Thelma Howes (*d* 1974). *Educ:* Sedbergh Sch.; Clare Coll., Cambridge (MA). School teaching, 1938; service with Royal Navy (Lt-Comdr), 1939–46; Blackie & Son Ltd, Educnl Publishers, 1946; British Council, 1947: Argentina, 1954; Representative Sierra Leone, 1956; Scotland, 1957; Dir Latin America and Africa (Foreign) Dept, 1958; Controller Overseas B Division (foreign countries excluding Europe), 1966; Controller Planning, 1968; Controller European Div., 1970; Asst Dir Gen. (Functional), 1972; Asst Dir Gen. (Regional), 1973–76. *Recreations:* golf, sailing. *Address:* The Manor, Edward Gardens, Old Bedhampton, Havant, Hants PO9 3JJ. *T:* (023) 9249 8317. *Died 6 Aug. 2010.*

FOWLER, Beryl, (Mrs Henry Fowler); *see* Chitty, M. B.

FOWLER, Derek, CBE 1979; Deputy Chairman, Capita Group, 1990–2000; Chairman: Kier Group Pension Scheme, 1992–97; Railways (formerly BR) Pension Trustee Co., 1986–96; *b* 26 Feb. 1929; *s* of late George Edward Fowler and Kathleen Fowler; *m* 1st, 1953, Ruth Fox (*d* 1996); one *d*; 2nd, 1998, Nina Krzyzagorska. *Educ:* Grantham, Lincs. Financial appointments with: Grantham Borough Council, 1944–50; Spalding UDC, 1950–52; Nairobi City Council, 1952–62; Southend-on-Sea CBC, 1962–64. British Railways Board: Internal Audit Manager, 1964–67, and Management Acct, 1967–69, W Region; Sen. Finance Officer, 1969–71; Corporate Budgets Manager, 1971–73; Controller of Corporate Finance, 1973–75; Finance Mem., 1975–78; a Vice-Chm., 1981–90; Dep. Chm., 1990. Dir, Kier Gp, 1992–97. Mem., UK Accounting Standards Cttee, 1982–84. Vice-Chm., Papworth Hosp. NHS Trust, 1996–97 (Dir, 1995–97). Freeman, City of London, 1981; Liveryman, Co. of Loriners, 1981. JDipMA.
Died 7 Jan. 2006.

FOWLER, Ian, OBE 1993; Principal Chief Clerk and Clerk to the Committee of Magistrates for the Inner London area, 1979–94; *b* 20 Sept. 1932; *s* of Major Norman William Frederick Fowler, OBE, QPM, and late Alice May (*née* Wakelin); *m* 1961, Gillian Cecily Allchin, JP; two *s* one *d*. *Educ:* Maidstone Grammar Sch.; Skinners Sch., Tunbridge Wells; King's Sch., Canterbury; St Edmund Hall, Oxford (MA). National Service, commnd 2nd Bn The Green Howards, 1951–53. Called to Bar, Gray's Inn, 1957; entered Inner London Magistrates Courts Service, 1959. Dep. Traffic Comr, Eastern Traffic Area, 1987–99. Councillor: Herne Bay UDC and Canterbury CC, 1961–83 (Mayor, 1976–77). Mem. Court, Univ. of Kent at Canterbury, 1976–. *Recreation:* reading. *Address:* 6 Dence Park, Herne Bay, Kent CT6 6BG. *Died 13 April 2006.*

FOX, Rt Hon. Sir Michael John, Kt 1975; PC 1981; a Lord Justice of Appeal, 1981–92; *b* 8 Oct. 1921; *s* of late Michael Fox; *m* 1954, Hazel Mary Stuart, (Lady Fox, CMG); three *s* one *d*. *Educ:* Drayton Manor Sch., Hanwell; Magdalen Coll., Oxford (BCL, MA).

Admiralty, 1942–45. Called to the Bar, Lincoln's Inn, 1949, Bencher, 1975; QC 1968. Judge of the High Court of Justice, Chancery Div., 1975–81.
Died 9 April 2007.

FOX, Ruth W.; *see* Winston-Fox.

FOX, Prof. Wallace, CMG 1973; MD, FRCP, FFPH; Professor of Community Therapeutics, Cardiothoracic Institute, Brompton Hospital, 1979–86, then Emeritus; Director, Medical Research Council Tuberculosis and Chest Diseases Unit, Brompton Hospital, 1965–86; Hon. Consultant Physician, Brompton Hospital, 1969–86; WHO Consultant, since 1961; *b* 7 Nov. 1920; *s* of Samuel and Esther Fox; *m* 1956, Gaye Judith Akker; three *s*. *Educ:* Cotham Grammar Sch., Bristol; Guy's Hosp. MB, BS (London) 1943; MRCS, LRCP, 1943; MRCP 1950; MD (Dist.) (London) 1951; FRCP 1962; FFPH (FFCM 1976). Ho. Phys., Guy's USA Hosp., 1945–46; Resident Phys., Preston Hall Sanatorium, 1946–50; Registrar, Guy's Hosp., 1950–51; Asst Chest Physician, Hammersmith Chest Clinic, 1951–52; Mem. Scientific Staff of MRC Tuberculosis and Chest Diseases Unit, 1952–56, 1961–65; seconded to WHO, to establish and direct Tuberculosis Chemotherapy Centre, Madras, 1956–61; Dir, WHO Collaborating Centre for Tuberculosis Chemotherapy and its Application, 1976–87. Lectures: Marc Daniels, RCP, 1962; First John Barnwell Meml, US Veterans Admin, 1968; Philip Ellman, RSocMed, 1976; Martyrs Meml, Bangladesh Med. Assoc., 1977; first Quezon Meml, Philippine Coll. of Chest Physicians, 1977; Morriston Davies Meml, BTA, 1981; Mitchell, RCP, 1982; E. Merck Oration, Indian Chest Soc., 1983; A. J. S. McFadzean, Univ. of Hong Kong, 1986; Ranbaxy-Robert Koch Oration, Tuberculosis Assoc. of India, 1989. Waring Vis. Prof. in Medicine, Univ. of Colorado and Stanford Univ., 1974. Mem. Tropical Med. Research Bd, 1968–72; Mem., several MRC Cttees; Member: WHO Expert Adv. Panel on Tuberculosis, 1965–91; BCG Vaccination Sub-Cttee, Min. of Health, 1968–; Mem. Council, Chest, Heart & Stroke Assoc., 1974–90; International Union Against Tuberculosis: Mem., later Chm., Cttee of Therapy, 1964–71; Associate Mem., Scientific Cttees, 1973; Mem., Exec. Cttee, 1973–85 (Chm., 1973–77). Chm., Acid Fast Club, 1971–72. Editor, Advances in Tuberculosis Research. Life Mem., BMA, 1994; Elected Corresp. Mem., Amer. Thoracic Soc., 1962; Mem., Mexican Acad. of Medicine, 1976; Hon. Life Mem., Canadian Thoracic Soc., 1976; Corresp. Mem., Argentine Nat. Acad. of Medicine, 1977; Corresp. For. Member: Argentine Soc. of Phthisiol. and Thoracic Pathol., 1977; Coll. of Univ. Med. Phthisiologists of Argentine, 1978; Hon. Member: Argentine Med. Assoc., 1977; Singapore Thoracic Soc., 1978. Sir Robert Philip Medal, Chest and Heart Assoc., 1969; Weber Parkes Prize, RCP, 1973; Carlo Forlanini Gold Medal, Fedn Ital. contra la Tuberculosi e le Malattie Polmonari Sociali, 1976; Hon. Medal, Czech. Med. Soc., 1980; Robert Koch Centenary Medal, Internat. Union against Tuberculosis, 1982; Presidential Citation Award, Amer. Coll. of Chest Physicians, 1982; Presidential Commendation, Amer. Thoracic Soc., 1989. *Publications:* Reports on tuberculosis services in Hong Kong to Hong Kong Government: Heaf/Fox, 1962; Scadding/Fox, 1975; Fox/Kilpatrick, 1990; contribs to med. jls: on methodology of controlled clinical trials, on epidemiology and on chemotherapy, particularly in tuberculosis, and carcinoma of the bronchus. *Address:* 28 Mount Ararat Road, Richmond, Surrey TW10 6PG. *Club:* Athenæum. *Died 22 Jan. 2010.*

FOX BASSETT, Nigel; Commissioner, Building Societies Commission, 1993–2001; Member Council: London First, since 1998; London Chamber of Commerce and Industry, 1993–99; *b* 1 Nov. 1929; *s* of Thomas Fox Bassett and Catherine Adriana Wiffen; *m* 1961, Patricia Anne Lambourne; one *s* one *d*. *Educ:* Taunton Sch.; Trinity Coll., Cambridge (MA Hons History and Law). Articled, Coward Chance, 1953;

admitted Solicitor, 1956; Partner, Coward Chance, later Clifford Chance, 1960–93 (Sen. Partner, 1990–93). Dir, London First, later London First Centre, 1993–98. Member: Council, British Inst. of Internat. and Comparative Law, 1977–2005 (Chm., Exec. Cttee, 1986–96; Hon. Mem., 2004; Mem. Adv. Bd, 2005–); Council, British Gp, Internat. Assoc. for Protection of Indust. Property, 1984–89; Council, British Branch, Internat. Law Assoc., 1971–86 (Chm., Cttee on Internat. Securities Regulation, 1989–93); Business Section, Internat. Bar Assoc., 1969–93; European Gp, Law Soc., 1969–93; Cttee, Amer. Bar Assoc., 1979–93; Deleg., Banking and Finance Mission to Poland, 1989. Liveryman, City of London Solicitors' Co. Pres. Council, Taunton Sch., 1994–97 (Mem. Council, 1985–97; Hon. Life Vice-Pres., 2005). Mem., charitable, sports, opera concerns. *Publications:* (contrib.) Branches and Subsidiaries in the European Common Market, 1976; (contrib.) Business Law in Europe, 1982, 2nd edn 1990; articles in law professional jls. *Recreations:* shooting, painting, cricket, art, opera. *Address:* 10 Upper Bank Street, E14 5JJ. *T:* (020) 7006 1000. *Clubs:* Garrick, Pilgrims, MCC; Seaview Yacht. *Died 26 Oct. 2008.*

FRAENKEL, Peter Maurice, FREng, FICE, FIStructE, FIHT; Founder and Senior Partner, Peter Fraenkel & Partners, since 1972 (Chairman, 1995–2006); Director, Peter Fraenkel BMT Ltd, 1990–95 (Chairman, 1990–93); Chairman, Peter Fraenkel Maritime Ltd, 1995–2007; *b* 5 July 1915; *s* of Ernest Fraenkel and Luise (*née* Tessmann); *m* 1946, Hilda Muriel, *d* of William Norman; two *d*. *Educ:* Battersea Polytechnic; Imperial Coll., London. BScEng. FICE 1954, FIStructE 1954; FREng (FEng 1984); FIHT 1992. Asst Engr with London firm of contractors, engaged on design and construction of marine and industrial structures, 1937–40; served in Army, 1941–42; Works Services Br., War Dept, 1942–45; Rendel, Palmer & Tritton, Cons. Engineers: Civil Engr, 1945; Sen. Engr, 1953; Partner, 1961–72. Dir, British Maritime Technology, 1990–96. Was responsible for, or closely associated with, technical and management aspects of many feasibility and planning studies, and planning, design and supervision of construction of large civil engrg projects, incl. ports, docks, offshore terminals, inland waterways, highways, power stations and tunnels in Gt Britain, Middle East, India, Far East and Australia, including: new Oil port at Sullom Voe, Shetland; new Naval Dockyard, Bangkok; Shatin to Tai Po coastal Trunk Road, Hong Kong; comprehensive study for DoE, of maintenance and operational needs of canals controlled by Brit. Waterways Bd (Fraenkel Report), and new port at Limassol, Cyprus. James Watt Medal, 1963, Telford Gold Medal, 1971, ICE. *Publications:* (jtly) papers to Instn of Civil Engrs: Special Features of the Civil Engineering Works at Aberthaw Power Station, 1962; Planning and Design of Port Talbot Harbour, 1970. *Address:* Little Paddock, Rockfield Road, Oxted, Surrey RH8 0EL. *T:* (01883) 712927. *Club:* Athenæum. *Died 18 Nov. 2009.*

FRANCIS, Dick, (Richard Stanley), CBE 2000 (OBE 1984); FRSL; author; *b* 31 Oct. 1920; *s* of George Vincent Francis and Catherine Mary Francis; *m* 1947, Mary Margaret Brenchley (*d* 2000); two *s*. *Educ:* Maidenhead County Boys' School. Pilot, RAF, 1940–45 (Flying Officer). Amateur National Hunt jockey, 1946–48, Professional, 1948–57; Champion Jockey, season 1953–54. Racing Correspondent, Sunday Express, 1957–73. Mem., CWA. FRSL 1998. Hon. LHD Tufts, 1991. Edgar Allan Poe Grand Master Award, 1996. *Publications:* Sport of Queens (autobiog.). 1957, 3rd updated edn, 1982; Dead Cert, 1962; Nerve, 1964; For Kicks, 1965; Odds Against, 1965; Flying Finish, 1966; Blood Sport, 1967; Forfeit, 1968 (Edgar Allan Poe Award, 1970); Enquiry, 1969; Rat Race, 1970; Bonecrack, 1971; Smoke Screen, 1972; Slay-Ride, 1973; Knock Down, 1974; High Stakes, 1975; In the Frame, 1976; Risk, 1977; Trial Run, 1978; Whip Hand, 1979 (Golden Dagger Award, Crime Writers' Assoc.,

1980; Edgar Allan Poe Award, 1980); Reflex, 1980; Twice Shy, 1981; Banker, 1982; The Danger, 1983; Proof, 1984; Break In, 1985; Lester, the official biography. 1986; Bolt, 1986; Hot Money, 1987; The Edge, 1988; Straight, 1989; Longshot, 1990; Comeback, 1991; (ed jtly) Great Racing Stories, 1989; Driving Force, 1992; Decider, 1993; Wild Horses, 1994; Come to Grief, 1995 (Edgar Allan Poe Award, 1996); To the Hilt, 1996; 10lb Penalty, 1997; Field of Thirteen, 1998; Second Wind, 1999; Shattered, 2000; Under Orders, 2006; (with Felix Francis) Dead Heat, 2007; (with Felix Francis) Silks, 2008; (with Felix Francis) Even Money, 2009. *Recreations:* boating, travel. *Address:* c/o Johnson and Alcock Ltd, 45/47 Clerkenwell Green, EC1R 0HT. *Club:* Garrick. *Died 14 Feb. 2010.*

FRANCIS, Norman; *see* Francis, W. N.

FRANCIS, Richard Stanley; *see* Francis, Dick.

FRANCIS, His Honour (William) Norman; a Circuit Judge (formerly Judge of County Courts), 1969–93; *b* 19 March 1921; *s* of Llewellyn Francis; *m* 1951, Anthea Constance (*née* Kerry); one *s* one *d*. *Educ:* Bradfield; Lincoln Coll., Oxford (BCL, MA). Served War of 1939–45, RA. Called to Bar, Gray's Inn, 1946. Dep. Chm., Brecknock QS, 1962–71. Member: Criminal Law Revision Cttee, 1977–; Policy Adv. Cttee on Sexual Offences, 1977–85; County Court Rule Cttee, 1983–88 (Chm., 1987–88). Pres., Council of HM Circuit Judges, 1987. Chancellor, Dio. of Llandaff, 1979–99. Fellow, Woodard Corp. (Western Div.), 1985–91. *Address:* 2 The Woodlands, Lisvane, near Cardiff CF14 0SW. *T:* (029) 2075 3070. *Died 6 Jan. 2009.*

FRANKEL, William, CBE 1970; Editor, Jewish Chronicle, 1958–77; *b* 3 Feb. 1917; *s* of Isaac and Anna Frankel, London; *m* 1st, 1939, Gertrude Freda Reed (marr. diss.); one *s* (one *d* decd); 2nd, 1973, Mrs Claire Neuman. *Educ:* elementary and secondary schs in London; London Univ. (LLB Hons). Called to Bar, Middle Temple, 1944; practised on South-Eastern circuit, 1944–55. General Manager, Jewish Chronicle, 1955–58. Special Adviser to The Times, 1977–81. Chm., Jewish Chronicle Ltd, 1991–94 (Dir, 1959–95). Pres., Mental Health Review Appeal Tribunal, 1978–89; Chm., Social Security Appeal Tribunal, 1979–89. Vis. Prof., Jewish Theological Seminary of America, 1968–69. Pres., New Israel Fund, 1997–. Vice-Pres., Inst. for Jewish Policy Res. (formerly Inst. of Jewish Affairs), 1993–; Emeritus Gov., Oxford Centre for Hebrew Studies; Mem. Bd of Govs, Cambridge Centre for Modern Hebrew Studies. Hon. Fellow, Girton Coll., Cambridge. JP Co. of London, 1963–69. *Publications:* (ed) Friday Nights, 1973; Israel Observed, 1980; (ed) Survey of Jewish Affairs (annual), 1982–92; Tea with Einstein and Other Memories, 2006. *Address:* 30 Montagu Square, W1H 2LQ. *T:* (020) 7935 1202. *Clubs:* Savile, MCC. *Died 18 April 2008.*

FRANKS, Sir Arthur Temple, (Sir Dick Franks), KCMG 1979 (CMG 1967); HM Diplomatic Service, retired; *b* 13 July 1920; *s* of late Arthur Franks, Hove; *m* 1945, Rachel Marianne (*d* 2004), *d* of late Rev. A. E. S. Ward, DD; one *s* two *d*. *Educ:* Rugby; Queen's Coll., Oxford. HM Forces, 1940–46 (despatches). Entered Foreign Service, 1949; British Middle East Office, 1952; Tehran, 1953; Bonn, 1962; FCO, 1966–81. *Address:* Roefield, Alde Lane, Aldeburgh, Suffolk IP15 5DZ. *Clubs:* Travellers; Aldeburgh Golf. *Died 12 Oct. 2008.*

FRANKS, His Honour Desmond Gerald Fergus; a Circuit Judge, 1972–93; *b* 24 Jan. 1928; *s* of F. Franks, MC, late Lancs Fus., and E. R. Franks; *m* 1952, Margaret Leigh (*née* Daniel); one *d*. *Educ:* Cathedral Choir Sch., Canterbury; Manchester Grammar Sch.; University Coll., London (LLB). Called to Bar, Middle Temple, 1952; Northern Circuit; Asst Recorder, Salford, 1966; Deputy Recorder, Salford, 1971; a Recorder of the Crown

Court, 1972. Pres., SW Pennine Br., Magistrates' Assoc., 1977–93. Chm., Selcare (Gtr Manchester) Trust, 1978–84. *Recreations:* gardening, music, photography.
Died 28 Aug. 2009.

FRANKS, Sir Dick; *see* Franks, Sir A. T.

FRASER, Sir Campbell; *see* Fraser, Sir J. C.

FRASER, Donald Hamilton, RA 1985 (ARA 1975); artist; Member, Royal Fine Art Commission, 1986–99; *b* 30 July 1929; *s* of Donald Fraser and Dorothy Christiana (*née* Lang); *m* 1954, Judith Wentworth-Sheilds; one *d*. *Educ:* Maidenhead Grammar Sch.; St Martin's Sch. of Art, London; Paris (French Govt Scholarship). Tutor, Royal Coll. of Art, 1958–83, Fellow 1970, Hon. FRCA 1984. Held 70 one-man exhibitions in Britain, Europe, N America and Japan. Work in public collections includes: Museum of Fine Arts, Boston; Albright-Knox Gall., Buffalo; Carnegie Inst., Pittsburgh; City Art Museum, St Louis; Wadsworth Athenaeum, Hartford, Conn; Hirshhorn Museum, Washington, DC; Yale Univ. Art Museum; Palm Springs Desert Museum; Nat. Gall. of Canada, Ottawa; Nat. Gall. of Vic, Melbourne; many corporate collections and British provincial galleries; Arts Council, DoE, etc. Designed Commonwealth Day issue of postage stamps, 1983. Vice-Pres. Artists Gen. Benevolent Inst., 1981– (Chm., 1981–87); Vice-Pres., Royal Over-Seas League, 1986–. Trustee: British Instn Fund, 1982–93; Royal Acad., 1993–99 (Hon. Curator, 1992–99). *Publications:* Gauguin's 'Vision after the Sermon', 1969; Dancers, 1989. *Address:* Bramham Cottage, Remenham Lane, Henley-on-Thames, Oxon RG9 2LR. *T:* (01491) 574253. *Club:* Leander (Henley).
Died 2 Sept. 2009.

FRASER, George MacDonald, OBE 1999; author and journalist; *b* 2 April 1925; *s* of late William Fraser, MB, ChB and Anne Struth Donaldson; *m* 1949, Kathleen Margarette, *d* of late George Hetherington, Carlisle; two *s* one *d*. *Educ:* Carlisle Grammar Sch.; Glasgow Academy. Served in British Army, 1943–47: Infantryman XIVth Army, Lieut Gordon Highlanders. Newspaperman in England, Canada and Scotland from 1947; Dep. Editor, Glasgow Herald, 1964–69. FRSL 1998. *Publications:* Flashman, 1969; Royal Flash, 1970; The General Danced at Dawn, 1970; The Steel Bonnets, 1971; Flash for Freedom!, 1971; Flashman at the Charge, 1973; McAuslan in the Rough, 1974; Flashman in the Great Game, 1975; Flashman's Lady, 1977; Mr American, 1980; Flashman and the Redskins, 1982; The Pyrates, 1983; Flashman and the Dragon, 1985; The Sheikh and the Dustbin, 1988; The Hollywood History of the World, 1988; Flashman and the Mountain of Light, 1990; Quartered Safe Out Here, 1992; The Candlemass Road, 1993; Flashman and the Angel of the Lord, 1994; Black Ajax, 1997; Flashman and the Tiger, 1999; The Light's on at Signpost, 2002; Flashman on the March, 2005; The Reavers, 2007; *film screenplays:* The Three Musketeers, 1974; The Four Musketeers, 1975; Royal Flash, 1975; The Prince and the Pauper, 1977; Octopussy, 1983; Red Sonja, 1985; Casanova, 1987; The Return of the Musketeers, 1989. *Recreations:* snooker, talking to wife, history, singing. *Address:* Baldrine, Isle of Man.
Died 2 Jan. 2008.

FRASER, Lt-Comdr Ian Edward, VC 1945; DSC 1943; RD and Bar 1948; JP; Chairman, since 1947, Managing Director, 1947–65 and since 1983, Universal Divers Ltd; *b* 18 Dec. 1920; *s* of S. Fraser, Bourne End, Bucks; *m* 1943, Melba Estelle Hughes; four *s* one *d* (and one *d* decd). *Educ:* Royal Grammar Sch., High Wycombe; HMS Conway. Merchant Navy, 1937–39; Royal Navy, 1939–47; Lt-Comdr, RNR, 1951–65. Jt Man. Dir, North Sea Diving Services Ltd, 1965–76; Dir, Star Offshore Services Ltd, 1977–82. Younger Brother of Trinity House, 1980. JP Wallasey, 1957. Hon. Freeman, Metropolitan Bor. of Wirral, 1993. Officer, American Legion of Merit. *Publications:* Frogman VC, 1957. *Address:* Sigyn, 1 Lyndhurst Road, Wallasey, Wirral CH45 6XA.

T: (0151) 639 3355. *Clubs:* Hoylake Sailing (life mem.); New Brighton Rugby (life mem.); Leasowe Golf (life mem.; Captain, 1975). *Died 1 Sept. 2008.*

FRASER, Sir (James) Campbell, Kt 1978; FRSE 1978; Chairman: Scottish Television plc, 1975–91; Director: Arlen PLC, 1991–95 (Chairman, 1993–95); Barkers Communications Scotland Ltd, 1992–95 (Chairman, 1994–95); *b* 2 May 1923; *s* of Alexander Ross Fraser and Annie McGregor Fraser; *m* 1950, Maria Harvey (*née* McLaren), JP, SRN (*d* 1995); two *d*. *Educ:* Glasgow Univ.; McMaster Univ.; Dundee Sch. of Economics (BCom). Served RAF, 1941–45. Raw Cotton Commn, Liverpool, 1950–52; Economist Intelligence Unit, 1952–57; Dunlop Rubber Co. Ltd, 1957–83: Public Relations Officer, 1958; Group Marketing Controller, 1962; Man. Dir, Dunlop New Zealand Ltd, 1967; Exec. Dir, 1969; Jt Man. Dir, 1971; Man. Dir, 1972; Chm., Dunlop Holdings, 1978–83; Chm. and Man. Dir, Dunlop Ltd, 1977–83; Chm., Dunlop Internat. AG, 1978–83. Director: British Petroleum, 1978–92 (Mem., Scottish Adv. Bd, 1990–97); BAT Industries, 1980–93; FFI, 1980–82; Charterhouse J. Rothschild, 1982–84; Bridgewater Paper Co., 1984–99; Alexander Proudfoot PLC, 1987–95; Tandem Inc., 1993–96; Chairman: Green Park Health Care, 1985–89; Tandem Computers Ltd, 1985–97; Internat. Adv. Bd, Wells Fargo, 1990–95; Pauline Hyde & Assocs, 1991–93; Riversoft Ltd, 1997–99. Pres., CBI, 1982–84 (Dep. Pres., 1981–82). Founder Mem., Past Chm., and Pres., 1972–84, Soc. of Business Economists; Mem. Exec. Cttee, SMMT, 1973–82. Trustee, The Economist, 1978–2006. Vis. Professor: Strathclyde Univ., 1980–85; Stirling Univ., 1980–88. Chm., Strathclyde Univ. Business Sch., 1976–81; Mem. Court, St Andrews Univ., 1987–90. CCMI (CBIM 1971); FPRI 1978. Hon. LLD Strathclyde, 1979; DUniv Stirling, 1979; Hon. DCL Bishop's Univ., Canada, 1990. *Publications:* many articles and broadcasts. *Recreations:* reading, theatre, cinema, gardening, walking. *Club:* Caledonian.
Died 27 April 2007.

FRASER, Peter Marshall, MC 1944; MA; FBA 1960; Fellow of All Souls College, Oxford, 1954–85, then Emeritus, and Acting Warden, 1985–87 (Sub-Warden, 1980–82); Lecturer in Hellenistic History, 1948–64, Reader 1964–85; *b* 6 April 1918; *y s* of late Archibald Fraser; *m* 1st, 1940, Catharine, *d* of late Prebendary Heaton-Renshaw (marr. diss.); one *s* three *d*; 2nd, 1955, Ruth Elsbeth, *d* of late F. Renfer, Bern, Switzerland; two *s*; 3rd, 1973, Barbara Ann Stewart, *d* of late L. E. C. Norbury, FRCS. *Educ:* City of London Sch.; Brasenose Coll., Oxford (Hon. Fellow 1977). Seaforth Highlanders, 1941–45; Military Mission to Greece, 1943–45. Sen. Scholar, Christ Church, Oxford, 1946–47; Junior Proctor, Oxford Univ., 1960–61; Domestic Bursar, All Souls Coll., 1962–65. Dir, British Sch. at Athens, 1968–71. Vis. Prof. of Classical Studies, Indiana Univ., 1973–74. Chm., Managing Cttee, Soc. of Afghan Studies, 1972–82; Vice Pres., Soc. for S Asian Studies, 1985–90. Ordinary Mem., German Archaeol. Soc., 1979; Corresp. Fellow, Archaeolog. Soc. of Athens, 1971 (Hon. Vice-Pres., 1999). Gen. Editor and Chm., British Acad. Cttee, Lexicon of Greek Personal Names, 1973–95. For. Mem., Acad. of Athens, 2003. Hon. Dr. phil Trier, 1984; Hon. DLitt La Trobe, 1996; Hon. DPhil Athens, 2002. *Publications:* (with G. E. Bean) The Rhodian Peraea and Islands, 1954; (with T. Rönne) Boeotian and West Greek Tombstones, 1957; Rostovtzeff, Social and Economic History of the Roman Empire, 2nd edn, revised, 1957; Samothrace, The Inscriptions, (Vol. ii, Excavations of Samothrace), 1960; E. Löfstedt, Roman Literary Portraits, trans. from the Swedish (Romare), 1958; The Wares of Autolycus; Selected Literary Essays of Alice Meynell (ed), 1965; E. Kjellberg and G. Säflund, Greek and Roman Art, trans. from the Swedish (Grekisk och romersk konst), 1968; Ptolemaic Alexandria, 1972; Rhodian Funerary Monuments, 1977; A. J. Butler, Arab Conquest of Egypt, 2nd edn, revised, 1978; (ed with E. Matthews) A Lexicon

of Greek Personal Names, vol. 1, 1987, vol. 3A, 1997, vol. 3B, 2000, vol. 4, 2005; (ed) Memorial Addresses of All Souls College, 1989; Cities of Alexander, 1996. *Address:* All Souls College, Oxford OX1 4AL.
Died 15 Sept. 2007.

FREDE, Prof. Michael, PhD; FBA 1994; Professor of the History of Philosophy, and Fellow of Keble College, Oxford University, 1991–2005; *b* Berlin, 31 May 1940; *m* 1st, Dorothea von Nicolai (marr. diss.); one *s* one *d*; 2nd, Gabriele Thiede (marr. diss.); twin *d*; partner, Katerina Ierodiakonou. *Educ:* Univ. of Göttingen (PhD 1966). Philosophy Res. Assistant, Univ. of Göttingen, 1966–71; Loeb Fellow, Harvard Univ., 1971; University of California at Berkeley: Vis. Lectr, 1968–69; Asst, then Associate, Professor of Philosophy, 1971–74; Prof. of Philosophy, 1974–76; Princeton University: Prof. of Philosophy, 1976–89; Stewart Prof. of Philosophy, 1989–91. *Publications:* Essays in Ancient Philosophy, 1987; (ed jtly) Rationality in Greek Thought, 1996; (ed jtly) Pagan Monotheism in Antiquity, 1999; contrib. to learned jls. *Died 11 Aug. 2007.*

FREE, Prof. John Brand, CMG 1995; ScD, DSc; Hon. Professor, School of Pure and Applied Biology, University of Wales, Cardiff (formerly University College, Cardiff), 1984–98; *b* 21 Aug. 1927; *s* of Frederick Charles Free and Gladys Ellen Free; *m* 1953, Nancy Wilson Speirs; two *s* one *d*. *Educ:* Cambridge and County High Sch.; Jesus Coll., Cambridge (BA 1950, MA 1955, ScD 1982); PhD 1954, DSc 1967, London. FIBiol 1970. Served Army, 1945–48, Suffolk Regiment: commnd RPC; seconded to High Commnd Territory Corps in ME: Rothamsted Experimental Station: ARC Scholar, 1951–54; on staff, 1954–87; SPSO 1983. NRCC Fellow, Apiculture Dept, Univ. of Guelph, Ontario, 1958–59; Nuffield/NRCC lecture tour of Canadian univs and res. centres, 1967; Leverhulme Emeritus Fellow, 1987, 1988. Visited several tropical countries for ODA and British Council to initiate and advise on bee-keeping and crop pollination projects, 1972–. Vice-Chm., Internat. Bee Res. Assoc., 1975–83 (Hon. Vice-Pres., 1993); President: Central Assoc. of Beekeepers, 1977–83; Apimondia Standing Commn on Pollination, 1985–89 (Hon. Mem. Apimondia, 1989); Chm., British Section, Internat. Union for Study of Social Insects, 1979–82 (Hon. Mem., 1988). Hon. Fellow, British Beekeepers' Assoc., 1990. *Publications:* Bumblebees (with C. G. Butler), 1959; Insect Pollination of Crops, 1970, 2nd edn 1993; The Social Organisation of Honeybees, 1977; Bees and Mankind, 1982; (ed) Honeybee Biology, 1982; Pheromones of Social Bees, 1987; (ed) Keeping Bees, 1992; *children's books:* Honeybees, 1978; Insects We Need, 1980; (with R. Dutton) Arab Village, 1980; Life Under Stones, 1981; contrib. res. papers and rev. papers to scientific jls on: social orgn of bees and their behaviour within the colony and in the field; improving honey prodn and bee pollination of agricl crops; use of pheromones (natural and synthetic) that control bee activities; insect pests of oil seed rape. *Recreations:* photography (produced many educational slide series and film-strips—mostly on insects and tropical agriculture), ancient civilisations, painting, walking. *Address:* 37 Plainwood Close, Summersdale, Chichester, West Sussex PO19 5YB. *T:* (01243) 533822. *Died 31 Dec. 2006.*

FREEMAN, George Vincent; Under-Secretary (Legal), Treasury Solicitor's Department, 1973–76, retired; *b* 30 April 1911; *s* of Harold Vincent Freeman and Alice Freeman; *m* 1945, Margaret Nightingale (*d* 2008); one *d*. *Educ:* Denstone Coll., Rocester. Admitted Solicitor, 1934; in private practice Birmingham until 1940. Served RN, 1940–46, Lieut RNVR. Legal Asst, Treasury Solicitor's Dept, 1946; Sen. Legal Asst 1950; Asst Treasury Solicitor 1964. *Recreation:* gardening. *Address:* 8 Shelley Close, Ashley Heath, Ringwood, Hants BH24 2JA. *Clubs:* Civil Service; Conservative (Ringwood). *Died 7 March 2006.*

FREEMAN, Paul, DSc (London), ARCS, FRES; Keeper of Entomology, British Museum (Natural History), 1968–81; *b* 26 May 1916; *s* of Samuel Mellor Freeman and Kate Burgis; *m* 1942, Audrey Margaret Long; one *d* (and one *d* decd). *Educ:* Brentwood Sch., Essex; Imperial Coll., London. Demonstrator in Entomology, Imperial Coll., 1938. Captain, RA and Army Operational Research Group, 1940–45. Lecturer in Entomology, Imperial Coll., 1945–47. Asst Keeper, Dept of Entomology, British Museum (Nat. Hist.), 1947–64, Dep. Keeper, 1964–68. Royal Entomological Soc. of London: Vice-Pres., 1956, 1957; Hon. Sec., 1958–62; Hon. Fellow, 1984. Sec., XIIth Internat. Congress of Entomology, London, 1964. *Publications:* Diptera of Patagonia and South Chile, Pt III-Mycetophilidae, 1951; Simuliidae of the Ethiopian Region (with Botha de Meillon), 1953; numerous papers in learned jls, on taxonomy of Hemiptera and Diptera. *Recreations:* gardening, natural history. *Address:* Briardene, 75 Towncourt Crescent, Petts Wood, Orpington, Kent BR5 1PH. *T:* (01689) 827296. *Died 31 July 2010.*

FREESON, Rt Hon. Reginald; PC 1976; Director, Reg Freeson & Associates, urban renewal consultants, since 1987; freelance writer and speaker; *b* 24 Feb. 1926; *m* 1st, 1971, Anne Levy (marr. diss. 1983); one *s* one *d*; 2nd, 1993, Charlotte Nolte. *Educ:* Jewish Orphanage, West Norwood. Served in Army, 1944–47. Middle East magazines and newspapers, 1946–48. Joined: Labour Party on return to United Kingdom, 1948; IVS, 1956; UN Assoc. Internat. Service, 1958; Co-operative Party, 1958; Fabian Society, 1960; Poale Zion-Labour Zionists, 1964 (incorporated into Jewish Labour Movt, 2004) and Labour Finance and Industry Gp, 1990–2001. Journalist, 1948–64: magazines, newspaper agencies and television; John Bull, Today, News Review, Everybody's Weekly, Tribune, News Chronicle, Daily Mirror. Asst Press Officer with Min. of Works, British Railways Board. Some short story writing, research and ghosting of books and pamphlets. Editor: Searchlight, against fascism and racism, 1964–67; Jewish Vanguard, Jewish Labour Movt (formerly Labour-Zionist) qly, 1987–. Radio and television: housing, urban planning, race relations and foreign affairs. Elected Willesden Borough Council, 1952; Alderman, 1955; Leader of Council, 1958–65; Chm. of new London Borough of Brent, 1964–65 (Alderman, 1964–68); Mem. (Lab), Brent LBC, 2002–. MP (Lab): Willesden E, 1964–74; Brent E, Feb. 1974–1987. PPS to Minister of Transport, 1964–67; Parly Secretary: Min. of Power, 1967–69; Min. of Housing and Local Govt, 1969–70; Labour front-bench spokesman: on housing and urban affairs, 1970–74; on social security, 1979–81; Minister for Housing and Construction and Urban Affairs, DoE, 1974–79; responsible for New Towns, planning, land and local govt, 1976–79; Mem., Select Cttee on the Environment, 1981–84 (Chm., 1982–83). Member: Council of Europe Parly Assembly, 1984–87; Western Eur. Assembly, 1984–87. Dir, Labour Friends of Israel, 1992–93. Dir, JBG Housing Soc., 1981–83; Mem. Exec., Housing Centre Trust, 1987–98; Exec. Mem., Nat. Housing and Planning Council, 1998–2002; Room@RTPI 2002. Mem., Internat. Voluntary Service and UNA International Service. Sponsor, three Willesden housing co-operatives, 1958–60. Member: CPA; London Labour Mayors' Assoc. Founder-Chairman: Willesden (then Brent) Coun. of Social Service, 1960–62; Willesden Social Action, 1961–63; Willesden Internat. Friendship Council (then Brent Community Relns Council), 1959–63 (Vice-Pres., 1967); Chairman: Warsaw Memorial Cttee, 1964–71; Poale Zion, 1984–87; Vice-Pres., Campaign for Democracy in Ulster; Founder-Sponsor, Internat. Centre for Peace in ME; Mem., Jewish Welfare Bd, 1971–74 (Mem. Exec., 1973–74); Mem., Labour Campaign for Electoral Reform, 1983–. Mem., TCPA; Life Member: YHA, 1957; Nat. Trust, 1987. Pres., Norwood (Jewish Orphanage) Old Scholars' Assoc. Writer and speaker on urban and envmtl regeneration, housing, construction industry and planning. *Publications:* policy papers, pamphlets, reports and articles for Borrie Commn on

Social Justice, Lab. Party Commn on Envmt, Labour Finance and Industry Gp, Fabian Rev., Rowntree Foundn, Housing Rev., Roof, Housing and Planning Rev., Axis, Tribune, Commonweal. *Recreations:* gardening, tree planting, music, theatre, reading, country walking, community environmental action. *Address:* 1 Christchurch Court, 171 Willesden Lane, NW6 7XF.
Died 9 Oct. 2006.

FREETH, Denzil Kingson, MBE 1997; *b* 10 July 1924; *s* of late Walter Kingson and Vera Freeth. *Educ:* Highfield Sch., Liphook, Hants; Sherborne Sch. (Scholar); Trinity Hall, Cambridge (Scholar). Served War, 1943–46: RAF (Flying Officer). Pres. Union Soc., Cambridge, 1949; Chm. Cambridge Univ. Conservative Assoc. 1949; debating tour of America, 1949, also debated in Ireland; Mem. Exec. Cttee Nat. Union, 1955. MP (C) Basingstoke Division of Hants, 1955–64. PPS to Minister of State, Bd of Trade, 1956, to Pres. of the Bd of Trade, 1957–59, to Minister of Educn, 1959–60; Parly Sec. for Science, 1961–63. Mem. Parliamentary Cttee of Trustee Savings Bank Assoc., 1956–61. Mem. Select Cttee on Procedure, 1958–59. Employed by and Partner in stockbroking firms, 1950–61 and 1964–89; Mem. of Stock Exchange, 1959–61, 1965–91. Chm. Finance Cttee, London Diocesan Fund, 1986–94. Churchwarden, All Saints' Church, Margaret St, W1, 1977–96. *Recreations:* good food, wine and conversation. *Address:* 3 Brasenose House, 35 Kensington High Street, W8 5BA. *T:* (020) 7937 8685. *Clubs:* Carlton; Pitt (Cambridge).
Died 26 April 2010.

FRETWELL, Elizabeth Drina, OBE 1977; professional adjudicator and vocal coach, retired 1998; operatic and dramatic soprano; *b* Melbourne, Australia, 13 Aug. 1920; *m* 1958, Robert Simmons (decd); one *s* one *d*. *Educ:* privately. Joined National Theatre, Melbourne, 1950; came to Britain, 1955; joined Sadler's Wells, 1956; Australia, Elizabethan Opera Co., 1963; tour of W Germany, 1963; USA, Canada and Covent Garden, 1964; tour of Europe, 1965; guest soprano with Cape Town and Durban Opera Cos, South Africa, 1970; Australian Opera, 1970–87. Rôles include Violetta in La Traviata, Leonora in Fidelio, Ariadne in Ariadne auf Naxos, Senta in The Flying Dutchman, Minnie in The Girl of the Golden West, Leonora in Il Trovatore, Aida, Ellen Orford in Peter Grimes, Leonora in Forza del Destino, Alice Ford in Falstaff, Amelia in Masked Ball, Georgetta in Il Tabarro, opening season of Sydney Opera Hse, 1973. Has sung in BBC Promenade Concerts and on TV. Mem., Music Bd, Opera Foundn Australia, 1982. *Recreation:* rose-growing. *Died 5 June 2006.*

FREUD, Sir Clement (Raphael), Kt 1987; writer, broadcaster, caterer; *b* 24 April 1924; *s* of late Ernst and Lucie Freud; *m* 1950, June Beatrice, (Jill), 2nd *d* of H. W. Flewett, MA; three *s* two *d*. Apprenticed, Dorchester Hotel, London. Served War, Royal Ulster Rifles; Liaison Officer, Nuremberg war crimes trials, 1946. Trained, Martinez Hotel, Cannes. Proprietor, Royal Court Theatre Club, 1952–62. Sports writer, Observer, 1956–64; Cookery Editor: Time and Tide, 1961–63; Observer Magazine, 1964–68; Daily Telegraph Magazine, 1968–. Sports Columnist, Sun, 1964–69; Columnist: Sunday Telegraph, 1963–65; News of the World, 1965; Financial Times, 1964–; Daily Express, 1973–75; Saga magazine, 1987–2002; Radio Times, 1992–; Independent, 1997–; Times Diarist, 1988–98, Columnist, 1992–96. Consultant: Intercity, 1990–97; Rail Gourmet, 1998–; Compass Gp, 1999–. Contested (L) Cambridgeshire NE, 1987. MP (L): Isle of Ely, July 1973–1983; Cambridgeshire NE, 1983–87. Liberal spokesman on education, the arts and broadcasting; sponsor, Official Information Bill. Chm., Standing Cttee, Liberal Party, 1982–86. Rector: Univ. of Dundee, 1974–80; St Andrews Univ., 2002–06. Pres., Down's Syndrome (formerly Down's Children) Assoc., 1988–90. £5,000 class winner, Daily Mail London–NY air race, 1969; line honours, Cape Town-Rio yacht race, 1971. Award winning petfood commercial: San Francisco, Tokyo, Berlin, 1967. BBC (sound) Just a Minute, 1968–. MUniv Open, 1989; Hon. LLD St Andrews, 2005. *Publications:* Grimble, 1968; Grimble at Christmas, 1973; Freud on Food, 1978; Clicking Vicky, 1980; The Book of Hangovers, 1981; Below the Belt, 1983; No-one Else has Complained, 1988; The Gourmet's Tour of Great Britain and Ireland, 1989; Freud Ego (autobiog.), 2001; contributor to, New Yorker, etc (formerly to Punch). *Recreations:* racing, backgammon, pétanque. *Address:* 14 York House, Upper Montagu Street, W1H 1FR. *T:* (020) 7724 5432; Westons, Walberswick, Suffolk IP18 6UH; Casa de Colina, Praia da Luz, Algarve. *Clubs:* MCC, Lord's Taverners', Groucho. *Died 15 April 2009.*

FRIEDMAN, Prof. Milton, PhD; Economist, USA; Senior Research Fellow, Hoover Institution, Stanford University, since 1976; Professor Emeritus of Economics, University of Chicago, since 1982 (Professor of Economics, 1948–82); Member of Research Staff, National Bureau of Economic Research, 1948–81; Economic Columnist, Newsweek, 1966–84; *b* Brooklyn, New York, 31 July 1912; *s* of Jeno Saul and Sarah E. Friedman; *m* 1938, Rose Director; one *s* one *d*. *Educ:* Rutgers (AB), Chicago (AM), and Columbia (PhD) Univs. Associate Economist, Natural Resources Cttee, Washington, 1935–37; Nat. Bureau of Economic Research, New York, 1937–45 (on leave 1940–45). During 1941–45: Principal Economist, Tax Research Div., US Treasury Dept, 1941–43; Associate Dir., Statistical Research Gp, Div. of War Research, Columbia Univ., 1943–45. Fulbright Lecturer, Cambridge Univ., 1953–54; Vis. Prof., Econs, Columbia Univ., 1964–65, etc. Member: President's Commn on an All-Volunteer Armed Force, 1969–70; Commn on White House Fellows, 1971–73. Mem. Bd of Editors, Econometrica, 1957–65; Pres., Amer. Economic Assoc., 1967; Pres., Mont Pelerin Soc., 1970–72. John Bates Clark Medal, Amer. Econ. Assoc., 1951; Member various societies, etc., incl. Royal Economic Soc. (GB). Fellowships and awards, in USA. Holds several hon. doctorates. Nobel Memorial Prize for Economics, 1976; Nat. Medal of Sci., USA, 1988. Grand Cordon, Sacred Treasure (Japan), 1986; US Presidential Medal of Freedom, 1988. *Publications:* Income from Independent Professional Practice (with Simon Kuznets), 1946; Sampling Inspection (with others), 1948; Essays in Positive Economics, 1953; (ed) Studies in the Quantity Theory of Money, 1956; A Theory of the Consumption Function, 1957; A Program for Monetary Stability, 1960; Capitalism and Freedom, 1962; Price Theory: a Provisional Text, 1962; A Monetary History of the United States 1867–1960 (with Anna J. Schwartz), 1963; Inflation: Causes and Consequences, 1963; The Balance of Payments: Free versus Flexible Exchange Rates (with Robert V. Roosa), 1967; Dollars and Deficits, 1968; Optimum Quantity of Money and Other Essays, 1969; Monetary vs Fiscal Policy (with Walter W. Heller), 1969; Monetary Statistics of the United States (with Anna J. Schwartz), 1970; A Theoretical Framework for Monetary Analysis, 1971; Social Security: Universal or Selective? (with Wilbur J. Cohen), 1972; An Economist's Protest, 1972; Money and Economic Development, 1973; There's No Such Thing as a Free Lunch, 1975; Price Theory, 1976; Free to Choose (with Rose Friedman), 1980; Monetary Trends in the United States and the United Kingdom (with Anna J. Schwartz), 1982; Bright Promises, Dismal Performance, 1983; (with Rose Friedman) Tyranny of the Status Quo, 1984; Monetarist Economics, 1991; Money Mischief, 1992; (with Thomas S. Szasz) Friedman and Szasz on Liberty and Drugs, 1992; (with Rose Friedman) Two Lucky People: memoirs, 1998. *Recreations:* tennis, carpentry. *Address:* Hoover Institution, Stanford, CA 94305–6010, USA. *Club:* Quadrangle (Chicago). *Died 16 Nov. 2006.*

FRINDALL, William Howard, (Bill), MBE 2004; freelance cricket statistician, broadcaster, writer, and editor, since 1965; *b* 3 March 1939; *s* of late Arthur Howard Frindall and Evelyn Violet Frindall (*née*

McNeill); *m* 1st, 1960, Maureen Doris Wesson (marr. diss. 1970); two *s* one *d*; 2nd, 1970, Jacqueline Rose Seager (marr. diss. 1980); 3rd, 1992, Deborah Margaret Brown; one *d*. *Educ*: Reigate Grammar Sch.; Kingston upon Thames Sch. of Art. Asst Prodn Manager, Lutterworth Press, 1958; Royal Air Force, 1958–65, commnd Secretarial Br., 1964. BBC cricket statistician, 1966–; Editor, Playfair Cricket Annual, 1986–; Cricket Corresp., Mail on Sunday, 1987–89; cricket statistician, The Times, 1994–; cricket archivist to Sir Paul and Lady Getty, 1996–. President: British Blind Sport, 1984–2004; BBC Cricket Club, 1998–. Patron: German Assoc. of Cricket Umpires and Scorers, 2005–; German Cricket Bd, 2006–. Hon. DTech Staffordshire, 1998. Statistician of the Year, Assoc. of Cricket Statisticians and Historians, 1996. *Publications*: The Wisden Book of Test Cricket, 1979, 5th edn 2000; The Wisden Book of Cricket Records, 1981, 4th edn 1998; The Guinness Book of Cricket Fact and Feats, 1983, 4th edn 1996; England Test Cricketers, 1989; Ten Tests for England, 1989; Gooch's Golden Summer, 1991; A Tale of Two Captains, 1992; Playfair Cricket World Cup Guide, 1996; Limited-Overs International Cricket: the complete record, 1997; NatWest Playfair Cricket World Cup, 1999; Bearders - My Life in Cricket, 2006. *Recreations*: cricket, sketching, painting, photography, philately, elementary gardening (under supervision from my wife). *Address*: Urchfont, Wiltshire. *Clubs*: MCC, Lord's Taverners; Cricket Writers'; Forty; Master's. *Died 30 Jan. 2009.*

FRITH, Anthony Ian Donald; Chairman, South West Region, British Gas, 1973–90; *b* 11 March 1929; *s* of Ernest and Elizabeth Frith; *m* 1952, Joyce Marcelle Boyce; one *s* one *d*. *Educ*: various grammar schs and tech. colls. CEng. Various appts in North Thames Gas Bd and Gas Light & Coke Co., 1945–65; Sales Man. 1965–67, Dep. Commercial Man. 1967–68, North Thames Gas Bd; Marketing Man., Domestic and Commercial Gas, Gas Council, 1968–72; Sales Dir, British Gas Corp., 1972–73. Board Member: Bristol Water Hldgs plc, 1989–99; Bath Dist HA, 1990–94; non-exec. Dir, Wilts and Bath Health Commn, 1992–94. *Publications*: various techn. and prof. in Gas Engineering and other jls. *Recreations*: fishing, golf. *Address*: Greenacres, Hayeswood Road, Timsbury, Bath BA2 0HH. *Died 29 Feb. 2008.*

FRODSHAM, Anthony Freer, CBE 1978; company director and management consultant, retired; Director-General, Engineering Employers' Federation, 1975–82; *b* Peking, China, 8 Sept. 1919; *er s* of late George William Frodsham and Constance Violet Frodsham (*née* Neild); *m* 1953, Patricia Myfanwy, *o c* of late Cmdr A. H. Wynne-Edwards, DSC, RN; two *s*. *Educ*: Ecole Lacordaire, Paris; Faraday House Engineering Coll., London. DFH, CEng, FIMechE, CCMI. Served War, 1940–46: Engineer Officer, RN, Asst Fleet Engr Officer on staff of C-in C Mediterranean, 1944–46 (despatches, 1945). P-E Consulting Group Ltd, 1947–73: Man. Dir and Gp Chief Exec., 1963–72; Group Specialist Adviser, United Dominions Trust Ltd, 1973–74. Director: TACE Ltd, 1973–76; Arthur Young Management Services, 1973–79; F. Pratt Engrg Corp. Ltd, 1982–85; Greyfriars Ltd, 1984–88 (Dep. Chm., 1986–88). Chairman: Management Consultants Assoc., 1968–70; Machine Tools EDC, 1973–79; Independent Chm., Internat. Compressed Air and Allied Machinery Cttee, 1976–96; Chairman: European Business Foundn Adv. Cttee, 1982–2001; Council, European Business Sch., 1986–91 (Mem., 1983–91); Vice-Chm., British Export Finance Adv. Council, 1982–87; President: Inst. of Management Consultants, 1967–68; Inst. of Linguists, 1986–89; Member: CBI Grand Council, 1975–82; CBI President's Cttee, 1979–82; Engineering Industry Training Bd, 1975–79; W European Metal Working Employers' Assoc., 1975–82; Manadon Adv. Council, RNEC, 1988–94; Enterprise Counsellor, DTI, 1988–91. A General Commissioner of Tax, 1975–94. Conducted MoD Study into Provision of Engineer Officers for Armed Services, 1983. Hon. FCIL (Hon. FIL 1986). Hon. DBA RNEC, 1991. *Publications*: contrib. to

technical jls; lectures and broadcasts on management subjects. *Address*: 36 Fairacres, Roehampton Lane, SW15 5LX. *T*: (020) 8878 9551. *Club*: Royal Automobile. *Died 3 Nov. 2007.*

FROGGATT, Sir Leslie (Trevor), Kt 1981; Chairman, Ashton Mining Ltd, 1981–94; *b* 8 April 1920; *s* of Leslie and Mary Helena Froggatt (*née* Brassey); *m* 1945, Jessie Elizabeth Grant; three *s*. *Educ*: Birkenhead Park Sch., Cheshire. Joined Asiatic Petroleum Co. Ltd, 1937; Shell Singapore, Shell Thailand, Shell Malaya, 1947–54; Shell Egypt, 1955–56; Dir of Finance, Gen. Manager, Kalimantan, Borneo, and Dep. Chief Rep., PT Shell Indonesia, 1958–62; Shell International Petroleum Co. Ltd: Area Co-ordinator, S Asia and Australia, 1962–63; assignment in various Shell cos in Europe, 1964–66; Shell Oil Co., Atlanta, 1967–69; Chm. and Chief Exec. Officer, Shell Gp in Australia, 1969–80; non-exec. Dir, Shell Australia Ltd, 1981–87. Chairman: Pacific Dunlop, 1986–90 (Vice-Chm., 1981; Dir, 1978–90); BRL Hardy, 1992–95; Director: Australian Industry Develt Corp., 1978–90; Australian Inst. of Petroleum Ltd, 1976–80, 1982–84 (Chm., 1977–79); Moonee Valley Racing Club Nominees Pty Ltd, 1977–92; Tandem Australia, 1989–98 (Chm., 1992–98). Member: Australian Nat. Airlines Commn (Australian Airlines), 1981–87 (Vice-Chm., 1984–87); Internat. Bd of Advice, ANZ Banking Gp, 1986–91; Internat. Adv. Council, Tandem Computers Inc., USA, 1988–98; Bd, CARE Australia, 1989– (Vice Chm., 1995–2002). Chm., Co-op. Res. Centre for Cochlear Implant. *Recreations*: reading, music, racing, golf. *Address*: 3 Teringa Place, Toorak, Vic 3142, Australia. *T*: (3) 9827 2362. *Clubs*: Melbourne, Australian, Victoria Racing, Victoria Amateur Turf, Moonee Valley Racing, Commonwealth Golf (Melbourne). *Died 21 Oct. 2010.*

FROOD, Alan Campbell, CBE 1988; Managing Director, Crown Agents for Oversea Governments and Administrations, 1978–88; Crown Agent, 1980–88; *b* 15 May 1926; *s* of James Campbell Frood, MC and Margaret Helena Frood; *m* 1960, Patricia Ann Cotterell; two *s* two *d*. *Educ*: Cranleigh Sch.; Peterhouse, Cambridge. Royal Navy, 1944–47 (Sub-Lt RNVR). Bank of England, 1949; Colonial Admin. Service, 1952; Bankers Trust Co., 1962; Dir, Bankers Trust Internat. Ltd, 1967; Gen. Man., Banking Dept, Crown Agents, 1975; Dir of Financial Services, Crown Agents, 1976–78. Trustee, Queen's Nursing Inst., 1986–2000 (Hon. Treas., 1973–94). *Recreations*: sailing, gardening. *Address*: 2 Dolforgan Court, Louisa Terrace, Exmouth, Devon EX8 2AQ. *T*: (01395) 267744. *Died 5 Nov. 2007.*

FROST, Albert Edward, CBE 1983; Director, Marks & Spencer Ltd, 1976–87; Chairman: Remploy, 1983–87; Trustees, Remploy Pension Fund, 1989–98; *b* 7 March 1914; *s* of Charles Albert Frost and Minnie Frost; *m* 1942, Eugénie Maud Barlow (*d* 2008). *Educ*: Oulton Sch., Liverpool; London Univ. Called to the Bar, Middle Temple (1st Cl. Hons). HM Inspector of Taxes, Inland Revenue, 1937; Imperial Chemical Industries Ltd: Dep. Head, Taxation Dept, 1949; Dep. Treasurer, 1957; Treasurer, 1960; Finance Dir, 1968; retd 1976. Director: British Airways Corp., 1976–80; BL Ltd, 1977–80; S. G. Warburg & Co., 1976–83; British Steel, 1980–83 (Chm., Audit and Salaries Cttees); Guinness Peat Gp, 1983–84; Chairman: Guinness Mahon Hldgs Ltd, 1983–84; Guinness Mahon & Co., 1983–84; Billingsgate City Securities, 1989–90. Mem. Council, St Thomas's Med. Sch., London, 1974– (Chm., Finance Cttee, 1978–85); Governor, United Med. Schs of Guy's and St Thomas's Hosps, 1982–98 (Dep. Chm. of Govs, 1989–97; Chm., Finance and Investment Cttees, 1982–85; Hon. Fellow, 1994). Member: Council and Finance Cttee, Morley Coll., London, 1975–85; Exec. Cttee for Develt Appeal, Royal Opera House, Covent Garden, 1975–87; Arts Council of GB, 1982–84; Vice Pres., ABSA, 1992– (Mem. Council, 1976–93; Jt Dep. Chm., 1985–92); Chairman: Robert Mayer Trust for Youth and Music, 1981–90 (Dir, 1977–90); Jury, and of Org. Cttee, City of

London Carl Flesch Internat. Violin Competition, 1984–92. Trustee and Treas., Loan Fund for Mus. Instruments, 1980–2006; Dir, City Arts Trust, 1982–93. FRSA. *Publications:* (contrib.) Simon's Income Tax, 1952; (contrib.) Gunns Australian Income Tax Law and Practice, 1960; articles on financial matters affecting industry and on arts sponsorship. *Recreations:* violinist (chamber music); swimming (silver medallist, Royal Life Saving Assoc.); athletics (county colours, track and cross country); walking; arts generally. *Club:* Royal Automobile. *Died 13 Aug. 2010.*

FRY, Ronald Ernest, FSS; Director of Economics and Statistics, Departments of the Environment and Transport, 1975–80, retired; *b* 21 May 1925; *s* of Ernest Fry and Lilian (*née* Eveling); *m* 1954, Jeanne Ivy Dawson; one *s* one *d*. *Educ:* Wilson's Grammar Sch., Camberwell; Birkbeck Coll., Univ. of London (BSc (Special)). MIS. Telecommunications Technician, Royal Signals, 1944–47; Scientific Asst, CEGB (London Region), 1948–52; Statistician: Glacier Metal Co., London, 1952–54; CEGB HQ, London, 1954–64; Gen. Register Office, 1965–66; Asst Dir of Research and Intelligence, GLC, 1966–69; Chief Statistician: (Social Statistics) Cabinet Office, 1969–74; (Manpower Statistics) Dept of Employment, 1974–75. *Publications:* various technical pubns in statistical and other professional jls. *Recreations:* photography, reading, motoring. *Address:* 39 Claremont Road, Hadley Wood, Barnet, Herts EN4 0HR. *T:* (020) 8440 1393. *Died 13 Sept. 2006.*

FULFORD, Robert John; Keeper, Department of Printed Books, British Library (formerly British Museum), 1967–85; *b* 16 Aug. 1923; *s* of John Fulford, Southampton; *m* 1950, Alison Margaret Rees (*d* 1996); one *s* one *d*. *Educ:* King Edward VI Sch., Southampton; King's Coll., Cambridge; Charles Univ., Prague. Asst Keeper, Dept of Printed Books, British Museum, 1945–65; Dep. Keeper, 1965–67 (Head of Slavonic Div., 1961–67); Keeper, 1967–85. *Address:* 7 Tulip Tree Close, Tonbridge, Kent TN9 2SH. *T:* (01732) 350356; Maumont, 24390 Hautefort, France. *T:* (5) 53505007. *Died 3 April 2008.*

FULLER, Hon. Sir John (Bryan Munro), Kt 1974; President: Arthritis Foundation of Australia, 1980–91 (Emeritus Vice-President, since 1991); Barnardo's Australia, 1985–95 (Member, Management Committee, 1980–85); *b* 22 Sept. 1917; *s* of late Bryan Fuller, QC; *m* 1940, Eileen, *d* of O. S. Webb; one *s* one *d*. *Educ:* Knox Grammar Sch., Wahroonga. Chm., Australian Country Party (NSW), 1959–64; MLC, NSW, 1961–78; Minister for Decentralisation and Development, 1965–73; NSW Minister for Planning and Environment, 1973–76; Vice-Pres. of Exec. Council and Leader of Govt in Legis. Council, 1968–76; Leader of Opposition, 1976–78; Leader, NSW Govt trade missions to various parts of the world. Pres., Assoc. of Former Mems of NSW Parlt, 1988–92. Australian Institute of Export: Federal Pres., 1986–91; Mem., Federal Council, 1985–92; Pres., NSW, 1985; Fellow, 1969; Hon. Life Fellow, 1991. Vice-Pres., Graziers Assoc. of NSW, 1965; Member: Council, Univ. of NSW, 1967–78; Cttee, United World Colls Trust, NSW, 1978–88; Bd, Foundn for Res. and Treatment Alcohol and Drug Dependence, 1980–85; Council, Nat. Heart Foundn, NSW, 1980–. Chm., Rushcutters Bay Maritime Reserve Trust, 1993–96. Nat. Patron, Australian Monarchist League, 1997–. *Recreations:* tennis, bowls. *Address:* 54/8 Fullerton Street, Woollahra, NSW 2025, Australia. *Clubs:* Australian (Sydney); Royal Sydney Golf, Australian Jockey. *Died 31 Jan. 2009.*

FURCHGOTT, Prof. Robert Francis, PhD; Emeritus Professor of Pharmacology, State University of New York Health Science Center, Brooklyn, since 1990; *b* Charleston, SC, 4 June 1916; *m* 1st, 1941, Lenore Mandelbaum (*d* 1983); three *d*; 2nd, Margaret Gallagher Roth (*d* 2004). *Educ:* Univ. of N Carolina (BS 1937); Northwestern Univ. (PhD Biochem. 1940). Medical College, Cornell University: Res. Fellow in Medicine,

1940–43; Res. Associate, 1943–47; Instructor in Physiol., 1943–48; Asst Prof. of Med. Biochem., 1947–49; Asst Prof., then Associate Prof. of Pharmacol., Med. Sch., Washington Univ., 1949–56; SUNY Health Science Center, Brooklyn: Chm., Dept of Pharmacol., 1956–83; Prof., 1956–88; Univ. Dist. Prof., 1988–90. Visiting Professor: Univ. of Geneva, 1962–63; Univ. of Calif., San Diego, 1971–72; Med. Univ., SC, 1980; UCLA, 1980; Adjunct Prof. of Pharmacol., Sch. Medicine, Univ. of Miami, 1989–2001; Vis. Dist. Prof., Med. Univ., SC, 2002–. Member: ACS, 1937; AAAS, 1940; Amer. Soc. Biochem., 1948; Amer. Soc. Pharmacol. and Exptl Therapeutics, 1952 (Pres., 1971–72; Goodman and Gilman Award, 1984); NAS, 1991; Harvey Soc. Hon. degrees from Univs of Lund, N Carolina, Ghent, Ohio State, Autonomous Univ. of Madrid, Mt Sinai Med. Sch., Med. Univ. of S Carolina, Med. Coll. of Ohio, Northwestern Univ., UCL and Charles Univ., Prague. Awards include: Res. Achievement Award, Amer. Heart Assoc., 1990; Bristol-Myers Squibb Award for Achievement in Cardiovascular Res., 1991; Medal, NY Acad. Medicine, 1992; Wellcome Gold Medal, Brit. Pharmacol. Soc., 1995; Gregory Pincus Award for Res., 1996; Lasker Award for Med. Res., 1996; Nobel Prize for Physiology or Medicine, 1998. *Address:* One Garden Way, Apt 252, Charleston, SC 29412, USA. *Died 19 May 2009.*

FURMSTON, Bentley Edwin, FRICS; Director of Overseas Surveys, Ordnance Survey, 1984–89; *b* 7 Oct. 1931; *s* of Rev. Edward Bentley Furmston and Mary Furmston (*née* Bennett); *m* 1957, Margaret (*née* Jackson); two *s* one *d*. *Educ:* The Nelson Sch., Wigton, Cumbria; Victoria Univ., Manchester (BSc Mathematics). Entered Civil Service as Surveyor, Directorate of Overseas Surveys, 1953, with service in Gambia, Swaziland, Basutoland, N Rhodesia; Sen. Surveyor, N Rhodesia, 1960; Sen. Computer, DOS, 1963; seconded to Govt of Malawi as Dep. Commissioner of Surveys, 1965; Principal Survey Officer, DOS, 1968; Overseas Supervisor, Sch. of Military Survey; Regional Survey Officer, W Africa; Asst Director (Survey), 1971; Asst Dir (Cartography), Ordnance Survey, 1973; Dep. Dir, Field Survey, Ordnance Survey, 1974; Dep. Dir (Survey), DOS, 1977; Dir, Overseas Surveys and Survey Advr, Min. of Overseas Develt, 1980. *Publications:* contribs to technical jls. *Recreations:* reading, gardening, hill walking. *Address:* The Orchards, Carter's Clay Road, Newtown, Romsey, Hants SO51 0GL. *Died 7 Oct. 2007.*

FURNELL, Very Rev. Raymond; Dean of York, 1994–2003; *b* 18 May 1935; *s* of Albert George Edward and Hetty Violet Jane Furnell; *m* 1967, Sherril Witcomb; one *s* three *d*. *Educ:* Hinchley Wood School, Surrey; Brasted Place Theological Coll.; Lincoln Theol Coll. Thomas Meadows & Co. Ltd, 1951; RAF, 1953; Lummus Co. Ltd, 1955; Geo. Wimpey & Co. Ltd, 1960; Brasted Place, 1961; Lincoln Theol Coll., 1963; Curate, St Luke's, Cannock, 1965; Vicar, St James the Great, Clayton, 1969; Rector, Hanley Team Ministry and RD, Stoke North, 1975–81; Provost, St Edmundsbury, 1981–94. Mem., Gen. Synod of C of E, 1988–2003; Chairman: Assoc. of English Cathedrals, 1994–2000; Council for the Care of Churches, 1999–2003. Chm. Bd, Theatre Royal, York, 1996–2003. Chm., W Suffolk, Cruse, 2003–. DUniv York, 2000. KStJ 2004 (Dean, Priory of England and the Is, 2004–). *Recreations:* music, drama. *Address:* 9 Well Street, Bury St Edmunds, Suffolk IP33 7EQ. *T:* (01284) 706335; *e-mail:* r.furnell@ tiscali.co.uk. *Club:* Carlton. *Died 10 July 2006.*

FURNER, Air Vice-Marshal (Derek) Jack, CBE 1973 (OBE 1963); DFC 1943; AFC 1954; *b* 14 Nov. 1921; *s* of Vivian J. Furner; *m* 1948, Patricia Donnelly; three *s*. *Educ:* Westcliff High Sch., Essex. Joined RAF, 1941; commnd as navigator, 1942; Bomber Comd (2 tours), 1942–44; Transport Comd, Far East, 1945–47; Navigation Instructor, 1948–50; trials flying, Boscombe Down, 1951–53 and Wright-Patterson, Ohio, 1953–56; Air Min., 1957; OC Ops Wing, RAF Waddington, 1958–60;

Planning Staff, HQ Bomber Comd, 1961–63 and SHAPE, Paris, 1964–65; Dep. Dir Manning, MoD (Air), 1966–67; OC RAF Scampton, 1968; AOC Central Reconnaissance Estab., 1969–70; Sec., Internat. Mil. Staff, NATO, Brussels, 1970–73; Asst Air Secretary, 1973–75. Gen. Manager, 1976–81, Dir, 1977–81, Harlequin Wallcoverings. FCIPD (FIPM 1975); FCMI (FBIM 1975). Mem., Mensa, 1989. *Recreations:* music, literature, computing. *Address:* 6 Sutherland Court Gardens, Overstrand Road, Cromer, Norfolk NR27 0DA. *T:* and *Fax:* (01263) 510255. *Club:* Royal Air Force. *Died 1 Jan. 2007.*

FURNER, Air Vice-Marshal Jack; *see* Furner, Air Vice-Marshal D. J.

FURSDON, Maj.-Gen. Francis William Edward, CB 1980; MBE 1958; defence correspondent; *b* 10 May 1925; *s* of late G. E. S. Fursdon and Mrs Fursdon; *m* 1950, Joan Rosemary (*née* Worssam); one *s* one *d*. *Educ:* Westminster Sch., MLitt Aberdeen, 1978; DLitt Leiden, 1979. AMIMechE. Enlisted RE, 1942; RE Course, Birmingham Univ., 1943; in ranks until commnd, 1945; 1945–67: Royal W Afr. Frontier Force, India, Burma and Gold Coast; Student RMCS; staff and regtl duty, UK, Singapore, Canal Zone and Cyprus; Staff Coll.; DAA&QMG 19 Inf Bde, UK (MBE for Gallantry, 1958)

and Port Said; GSO2 RE Sch. of Inf.; JSSC; OC 34 Indep. Fd Sqdn, E Africa and Kuwait; Instr, Staff Coll., Camberley; Borneo; 2 i/c 38 Engr Regt; Admin. Staff Coll., Henley; CO 25 Engr Regt, BAOR, 1967–69; AA&QMG HQ Land Forces, Gulf, 1970–71; Dep. Comd and COS Land Forces, Gulf, 1971; Col Q (Qtg) HQ BAOR, 1972–73; Dir of Def. Policy (Europe and NATO), MoD, 1974; Dir of Def. Policy (Europe and NATO), MoD, 1974–77; Dir, Military Assistance Office, MoD, 1977–80; Mil. Adv. to Governor of Rhodesia, and later Senior British Officer, Zimbabwe, 1980, retired 1980. Dir of Ceremonies, Order of St John, 1980–94. Defence and Military Correspondent, The Daily Telegraph, 1980–86; Correspondent, Army Qly & Defence Jl, 1985–2000; RN Correspondent, Navy Internat., 1991–94; Contributing Editor Europe, Asia-Pacific Defence Reporter, 1989–94; UK Armed Forces Correspondent, Salut (S Africa), 1995–2000; Special Corresp., S Africa Soldier, 2001–. Freeman, City of London, 1987. FCMI; MCIJ. KStJ 1980. *Publications:* Grains of Sand, 1971; There are no Frontiers, 1973; The European Defence Community. A History, 1980; Falklands Aftermath: picking up the pieces, 1988. *Recreations:* photography (IAC Internat. Award, 1967), gardening, travel. *Club:* Special Forces. *Died 3 Jan. 2007.*

G

GADSBY, (Gordon) Neville, CB 1972; *b* 29 Jan. 1914; *s* of William George and Margaret Sarah Gadsby; *m* 1938, Jeanne (*née* Harris) (*d* 2004); two *s* one *d. Educ:* King Edward VI Sch., Stratford-upon-Avon; University of Birmingham (BSc 1935, DipEd 1937, Cadbury Prizeman 1937). FRSC, CChem. Princ. Lectr, RMCS, 1946–51; Supt, Army Operational Research Gp, 1951–55; Dep. Sci. Adviser to Army Coun., 1955–59; idc 1960; Dir of Army Operational Science and Research, 1961; Dir, Army Operational Res. Estab., 1961–64; Dir of Biol. and Chem. Defence, MoD, 1965–67; Dep. Chief Scientist (Army), MoD, 1967–68; Dir, Chemical Defence Estabt, Porton, Wilts, 1968–72; Minister, Defence R&D, British Embassy, Washington, 1972–75, retired. *Publications:* Lubrication, 1949; An Introduction to Plastics, 1950. *Recreations:* oil painting, photography. *Died 29 Dec. 2007.*

GADSDEN, Sir Peter (Drury Haggerston), GBE 1979; Hon. AC 1988; FREng; Lord Mayor of London for 1979–80; *b* Canada, 28 June 1929; *er s* of late Basil Claude Gadsden, ACT, ThL, and Mabel Florence Gadsden (*née* Drury); *m* 1955, Belinda Ann, *e d* of late Captain Sir (Hugh) Carnaby de Marie Haggerston, 11th Bt; four *d. Educ:* Rockport, Northern Ireland; The Elms, Colwall; Wrekin Coll., Wellington; Jesus Coll., Cambridge (MA; Hon. Fellow, 1988). 2nd Lieut King's Shropshire LI, attached Oxf. and Bucks LI and Durham LI, Germany, 1948–49. Man. Dir, London subsid. of Australian Mineral Sands Producer, 1964–70; Marketing Economist (Mineral Sands) to UN Industrial Development Organisation, 1969; pt-time Mem., Crown Agents for Oversea Govts and Admins, 1981–87. Director: City of London (Arizona) Corp., 1970–88 (Chm., 1985–88); Wm Jacks plc, 1984–2006; W. Canning plc, 1989–99 (Dep. Chm., 1990–99); PPP Healthcare Gp (formerly Private Patients Plan Ltd), 1981–96 (Chm., 1984–96; Pres., 1996–98); Albox Australia Pty Ltd, 2002–; Chairman: PPP Healthcare Medical Trust, 1996–99; PPP Healthcare Foundn, 1996–2005; Anglo Pacific Minerals Ltd, 2005–. Chm. City of London Br., Inst. of Dirs, 1995–99 (Pres. Emeritus, 2004–). Dir, Clothworkers' Foundn, 1978–2006; Hon. Mem. London Metal Exchange. President: Nat. Assoc. of Charcoal Manufacturers, 1970–86; City of London Rifle & Pistol Club (formerly Embankment Rifle Club), 1975–87; Leukaemia Res. Fund, City of London Br., 1975–86; Metropolitan Soc. for the Blind, 1979–2004 (Mem. Council, 1972–82); Publicity Club of London, 1983–2001; Council, London World Trade Centre Assoc., 1980–92; St John Ambulance (Eastern Area), 1981–86 (Mem. Council, Shropshire Br.); British-Australasian Heritage Soc., 1986–; Australian-NZ Chamber of Commerce, 1997–2006. Sheriff, City of London, 1970–71; Common Councilman (Cripplegate Within and Without), 1969–71; Alderman, City of London (Ward of Farringdon Without), 1971–99, Sen. Alderman, 1996–99; HM Lieutenant, City of London, 1979–99; Founder Master, Engineers' Co., 1983–85 (Hon. Liveryman, 2004); Liveryman, Clothworkers' Co. (Master 1989–90); Hon. Liveryman: Plaisterers' Co., 1975–; Marketors Co., 1978–; Fruiterers' Co., 1999–; Freeman, Shrewsbury Drapers' Co., 1998– (Patron, Shrewsbury Drapers Hall Preservation Trust, 1998–); Hon. Freeman, Actuaries' Co., 1981–; Master, Cripplegate Ward Club, 1982–83; Member: Guild of Freemen, 1963– (Master 1984–85; Hon. Asst, 1995); Company of World Traders (formerly Guild of World Traders in London), 1985– (Master, 1987–88); Royal Soc. of St George (City of London Br.), 1970–; Council, City Univ., 1985–86 (Chancellor, 1979–80); Council, Britain Australia Soc., 1978–92 (Chm., 1989–92; Vice Pres., 1992–); Bermuda Soc., 1987– (Founder Chm., 1987–89). Chairman: Britain Australia Bicentennial Cttee, 1984–88;

UK Europe, Order of Australia Assoc., 1991–93; Cook Soc., 1999. Hon. Freeman, Borough of Islwyn, S Wales, 1983. Vice-President: Sir Robert Menzies Meml Trust; League of Friends, Robert Jones and Agnes Hunt, Orthopaedic Hosp., 1980–; Nuffield Nursing Homes Trust, subseq. Nuffield Hosps, 1984–; Commonwealth Trust, 1984–95; Shropshire Soc. in London, 1986–89; Blackwood Little Theatre, 1986–. Fellowship of Engrg Distinction Lectr, 1980; Wm Menelaus Meml Lectr, SW Inst. of Engrs, 1983; paper to MANTECH Symposium, 1983; Royal Instn Lectr, 1991. Trustee: St Bartholomew's and St Mark's Hosps, 1981–88; Britain-Australia Bicentennial Trust, 1986–; Britain-Australia Bicentennial Schooner Trust, 1986–92; Britain-Australia Soc. Educnl Trust, 1990–; Edward King Hse, Lincoln, 1988–2000; Battle of Britain Meml Trust, 1990–93; Nat. History Mus. Devel Trust, 1992–98; Shropshire Regt Museum, 2000– (Chm., Appeal, 1991–99); Ludlow Mus. Devel Trust, 2000–; Chm., London Bridge Mus. Trust, 2000–; President: Ironbridge Gorge Museum Develt Trust, 1981–; Upper Severn Navigation Trust Ltd, 1992–; Shropshire Horticultural Soc., 1992–93; Patron, Telford and Wrekin Community Trust, 1998– (Chm., Community Chest 2000, 1999–); Gov., Hereford Cathedral Perpetual Trust, 2001–. Life Pres., Freemen of City of London in Islwyn, 1995. Member: Management Council, Shakespeare Theatre Trust, 1979–86; Royal Commn for the 1851 Exhibn, 1986–99; Chm. and Mem. Council, 1984–88, Vice-Pres., 1988–89, Royal Commonwealth Soc.; Patron: Museum of Empire and Commonwealth Trust, 1986–; Guild of Rahere, 1986–; Royal Soc. Project Science, 1996–; Shropshire and Mid Wales Hospice, 1998– (Vice Pres., 1989–98). Vice-Pres., Royal Nat. Coll. for the Blind, 2001–. Governor: Hon. Irish Soc., 1984–87; The Elms, Colwall, 1993–2004; Wrekin Coll., 1997–99. JP, City of London, 1971–99 (Inner London Area of Greater London, 1969–71). Hon. FCIM; FIMMM (FIMM 1979); CEng 1979, FREng (FEng 1980); Hon. Mem., Instn of Royal Engrs, 1986; Hon. FRSH 1992; Hon. FRCA 1994. Hon. DSc 1979. Hon. Mem. Court, HAC, 1971–99; Hon. Col 5th (Shropshire and Hereford) Bn LI (Vol.), 1988–93 (Hon. Mem. of Mess). KStJ 1980 (OStJ 1977). Christ Church-Midnite Award, Perth, WA, 1997. Officier de l'Etoile Equatoriale de la République Gabonaise, 1970. *Publications:* articles in: InstMM Transactions, 1971; RSM Jl, 1979; Textile Institute and Industry, 1980; articles on titanium, zirconium, and hafnium in Mining Jl Annual Reviews, 1969–86. *Recreations:* walking, photography, fishing. *Address:* Cheriton, Middleton Scriven, Bridgnorth, Shropshire WV16 6AG. *T:* (01746) 789650. *Clubs:* Boodle's, City Livery (Mem. Council), United Wards, Farringdon Ward (Patron, 1971–99), City of London (Hon.), City of London Pickwick (Pres., 1999–), Light Infantry (Hon.); Bligny (Shrewsbury) (Pres., 2006–); Royal London Yacht (Hon.). *Died 4 Dec. 2006.*

GAINSBOROUGH, 5th Earl of, (2nd) *cr* 1841; **Anthony Gerard Edward Noel;** JP; Bt 1781; Baron Barham, 1805; Viscount Campden, Baron Noel, 1841; *b* 24 Oct. 1923; *s* of 4th Earl and Alice Mary (*d* 1970), *e d* of Edward Eyre, Gloucester House, Park Lane, W1; *S* father, 1927; *m* 1947, Mary, *er d* of late Hon. J. J. Stourton, TD and Mrs Kathleen Stourton; four *s* three *d. Educ:* Georgetown, Garrett Park, Maryland, USA. Chairman: Oakham RDC, 1952–67; Executive Council RDC's Association of England and Wales, 1963 (Vice-Chairman 1962, Pres., 1965); Pres., Assoc. of District Councils, 1974–80; Vice-Chm. Rutland CC, 1958–70, Chm., 1970–73; Chm., Rutland Dist Council, 1973–76. Chm., Bd of Management, Hosp. of St John and St Elizabeth, NW8, 1970–80 (Pres., 1995–). Chm., Hosp. Mgt Trust, 1985–2002. Mem. Court of Assistants, Worshipful Co. of

Gardeners of London, 1960 (Upper Warden, 1966; Master, 1967). Hon. FICE (Hon. FIMunE 1969). JP Rutland, 1957, Leics, 1974. Knight of Malta, 1948; Bailiff Grand Cross Order of Malta, 1958; Pres. Br. Assoc., SMO, Malta, 1968–74. KStJ 1970. *Recreations:* shooting, sailing. *Heir: s* Viscount Campden, *b* 16 Jan. 1950. *Address:* Horn House, Exton Park, Oakham, Rutland LE15 7QU. *T:* (office) (01780) 460772. *Clubs:* Brooks's, Pratt's; Bembridge Sailing. *Died 29 Dec. 2009.*

GAINSBOROUGH, George Fotheringham, CBE 1973; PhD, FIET; Barrister-at-law; Secretary, Institution of Electrical Engineers, 1962–80; *b* 28 May 1915; *o s* of late Rev. William Anthony Gainsborough and of Alice Edith (*née* Fennell); *m* 1937, Gwendoline (*d* 1976), *e d* of John and Anne Berry; two *s. Educ:* Christ's Hospital; King's Coll., London; Gray's Inn. Scientific Staff, Nat. Physical Laboratory, 1938–46; Radio Physicist, British Commonwealth Scientific Office, Washington, DC, USA, 1944–45; Administrative Civil Service (Ministries of Supply and Aviation), 1946–62. Imperial Defence College, 1960. Hon. Sec., Commonwealth Engineering Conf., 1962–69; Hon. Sec.-General, World Fedn of Engineering Organizations, 1968–76. *Publications:* papers in Proc. Instn of Electrical Engineers. *Address:* c/o 3 Methley Street, SE11 4AL. *Club:* Athenæum. *Died 3 Oct. 2008.*

GAIUS, Rev. Sir Saimon, KBE 1988 (OBE 1975); *b* 6 Aug. 1920; *s* of Peni Tovarur and Miriam Ia Pea; *m* 1941, Margaret Ia Kubak; four *s* one *d* (and two *s* one *d* decd). *Educ:* Mission Sch., East New Britain; theological training, PNG and Sydney, Aust. Ordained 1960; worked as United Church Minister; Principal, Pastors' Training Coll., 1967–68; Bishop of New Guinea Island Region, 1968–77; retired as Minister of Religion, 1983. SIIStJ 1976. *Recreation:* reading. *Address:* United Church, PO Box 90, Rabaul, East New Britain, Papua New Guinea. *Died 14 July 2006.*

GAJDUSEK, Daniel Carleton, MD; Director of Program for Study of Child Growth and Development and Disease Patterns in Primitive Cultures, and Laboratory of Slow Latent and Temperate Virus Infections, National Institute of Neurological Disorders (formerly of Neurological and Communicative Disorders and Stroke), National Institutes of Health, Bethesda, Md, 1958–97; Chief, Central Nervous System Studies Laboratory, NINDS, 1970–97; *b* Yonkers, NY, 9 Sept. 1923; *s* of Karol Gajdusek and Ottilia Dobroczki; sixty-seven adopted *s* and *d* (all from New Guinea and Micronesia). *Educ:* Marine Biological Lab., Woods Hole, Mass; Univ. of Rochester (BS *summa cum laude*); Harvard Medical Sch. (MD); California Inst. of Technology (Post-Doctoral Fellow). Residencies: Babies Hosp., NY, 1946–47; Children's Hosp., Cincinatti, Ohio, 1947–48; Children's Hosp., Boston, Mass, 1949–51; Sen. Fellow, Nat. Research Council, Calif Inst. of Tech., 1948–49; Children's Hosp., Boston, Mass, 1949–51; Research Fellow, Harvard Univ. and Sen. Fellow, Nat. Foundn for Infantile Paralysis, 1949–52; Walter Reed Army Medical Center, 1952–53; Institut Pasteur, Tehran, Iran and Univ. of Maryland, 1954–55; Vis. Investigator, Nat. Foundn for Infantile Paralysis and Walter and Eliza Hall Inst., Australia, 1955–57. Adjunct Prof., Inst. of Human Virology, Baltimore, 1996–97; Guest Scientist, CNRS, Institut Alfred Fessard, Gif-sur-Yvette, France, 1998–; Visiting Professor: Human Retrovirus Lab., Univ. of Amsterdam, 1998–; Univ. of Tromsø, 1998–. Member: Nat..Acad. of Sciences, 1974; Amer. Philos. Soc., 1978; Amer. Acad. of Arts and Scis, 1978; Amer. Acad. of Neurol.; Infectious Dis. Soc. of America; Amer. Pediatric Soc.; Amer. Epidemiological Soc.; Amer. Soc. for Virology; Deutsche Akademie der Naturforscher Leopoldina, 1982; Czechoslovak, Portuguese, Australian, Russian, Sakha and Korean Acads of Science; Mexican Nat. Acad. of Medicine; Nat. Acad. of Medicine, Colombia; Royal Acad. of Medicine of Belgium. Mem., Scientific Council, Fondn pour l'Etude du Système Nerveux, Geneva, 1983–96. Discovered slow virus infections of man; studied child growth and develt and disease patterns in primitive and isolated populations, virus encephalitides, hemorrhagic fevers, hantavirus and human retrovirus infections, chronic degenerative brain diseases, cerebral amyloidoses, and aging, spontaneous generation of infectious agents by nucleating induction of infectious conformation of host precursor proteins, molecular casting. E. Meade Johnson Award, Amer. Acad. Pediatrics, 1963; DHEW Superior Service Award, 1970; DHEW Distinguished Service Award, 1975; Lucien Dautrebande Prize, Belgium, 1976; shared with Dr Baruch Blumberg Nobel Prize in Physiology or Medicine, for discoveries concerning new mechanisms for the origin and dissemination of infectious diseases, 1976; George Cotzias Meml Prize, Amer. Acad. of Neurol., 1978; Huxley Medal, RAI, 1988; Gold Medal, Slovak Acad. of Scis, 1996; Premio Gargano, Inst. di Cultura, Manfredouia, 2000; Qi Liu Friendship Prize, Shandong, 2000. Hon. Curator, Melanesian Ethnography, Peabody Mus., Salem, Mass; Hon. Pres., World Hantavirus Soc., 1994–; Hon. Advr, Shandong Acad. Scis, 2000–. Hon. Prot., many med. colls and univs in China, incl. Beijing, 1987, Ningxia Med. Coll., 2001, Youjiang Med. Coll. for Nationalities, Baise, 2003, and Sichuan, 2006. Hon. DSc: Univ. of Rochester, 1977; Med. Coll. of Ohio, 1977; Washington and Jefferson Coll., 1980; Harvard Med. Sch. (Bicentennial), 1982; Hahnemann Univ., 1983; Univ. of Medicine and Dentistry of NJ, 1987; Hon. LHD: Hamilton Coll., 1977; Univ. of Hawaii, 1986; Comenius Univ., Bratislava, 1996; Docteur *hc*: Univ. of Marseille, 1977; Univ. of Lisbon, 1991; Univ. of Ust-Kamenogorsk, 1995; Univ. of Kharkov, 1995; Univ. of Las Palmas, 1996; Hon. LLD Aberdeen, 1980; Laurea *hc* Univ. of Milan, 1992. *Publications:* Acute Infectious Hemorrhagic Fevers and Mycotoxicoses in the USSR, 1953; (ed with C. J. Gibbs, Jr and M. P. Alpers) Slow, Latent and Temperate Virus Infections, 1965; Journals 1937–2005, 75 vols, 1958–2005; Smadel-Gajdusek Correspondence 1955–1958; (ed with J. Farquhar) Kuru, 1981; Viliuisk Encephalitis, 1996; over 1000 papers in major jls of medicine, microbiology, immunology, pediatrics, neurology, developmental biology, psychosexual development, neurobiology, genetics, evolution, anthropology and linguistics. *Died 11 Dec. 2008.*

GALBRAITH, James Hunter, CB 1985; Under Secretary, Department of Employment Industrial Relations Division, 1975–85; *b* 16 July 1925; *o s* of late Prof. V. H. Galbraith, FBA, and Dr Georgina Rosalie Galbraith (*née* Cole-Baker); *m* 1954, Isobel Gibson Graham; two *s. Educ:* Dragon Sch.; Edinburgh Academy; Balliol Coll., Oxford. 1st Cl. Litt Hum. Fleet Air Arm (pilot), 1944–46. Entered Ministry of Labour, 1950; Private Sec. to Permanent Sec., 1953–55; Jun. Civilian Instructor, IDC, 1958–61; Private Sec. to Minister of Labour, 1962–64; Chm. Central Youth Employment Exec., 1964–67; Sen. Simon Research Fellow, Manchester Univ., 1967–68; Asst Under-Sec. of State, Dept of Employment and Productivity (Research and Planning Div.), 1968–71; Dir, Office of Manpower Economics, 1971–73; Under-Sec., Manpower Gen. Div., Dept of Employment, 1973–74; Sec., Manpower Services Commn, 1974–75. Mem., Employment Appeal Tribunal, 1986–96. Chm., Bd of Govs. Volunteer Centre UK, 1989–93. *Recreations:* Rugby (Oxford Blue), golf, fishing. *Address:* The Orangery, Alde House, Aldeburgh, Suffolk IP15 5EE. *T:* (01728) 452594. *Died 23 Jan. 2009.*

GALBRAITH, Prof. John Kenneth; Paul M. Warburg Professor of Economics, Harvard University, 1949–75, then Emeritus Professor; *b* Ontario, Canada, 15 Oct. 1908; *s* of William Archibald and Catherine Galbraith; *m* 1937, Catherine M. Atwater; three *s* (and one *s* decd). *Educ:* Univ. of Guelph; California Univ. BS, MS, PhD. Tutor, Harvard Univ., 1934–39; Social Science Research Fellow, Cambridge Univ., 1937; Asst Prof. of Economics, Princeton Univ., 1939; Asst Administrator, Office of Price Administration, 1941; Deputy

Administrator, 1942–43; Dir, State Dept Office of Economic Security Policy, 1945; Mem. Bd of Editors, *Fortune* Magazine, 1943–48. United States Ambassador to India, 1961–63 (on leave from Professorship). Reith Lecturer, 1966; Vis. Fellow, Trinity Coll., Cambridge, 1970–71 (Hon. Fellow, 1987). TV series, *The Age of Uncertainty*, 1977. Chm., Americans for Democratic Action, 1967–69; President: Amer. Econ. Assoc., 1972; Amer. Acad. of Arts and Letters, 1984 (Mem., 1982–). Hon. LLD: Bard, 1958; Miami Univ., 1959; Univ. of Toronto, 1961; Brandeis Univ., 1963; Univ. of Mass, 1963; Univ. of Saskatchewan, 1965; Rhode Island Coll., 1966; Boston Coll., 1967; Hobart and William Smith Colls, 1967; Univ. of Paris, 1975; and others. President's Certificate of Merit; Medal of Freedom, 2000. *Publications*: American Capitalism, the Concept of Countervailing Power, 1952; The Great Crash, 1929, 1955, new edn 1979; The Affluent Society, 1958, 4th edn, 1985; Journey to Poland and Yugoslavia, 1958; The Liberal Hour, 1960; Made to Last, 1964; The New Industrial State, 1967, rev. edn, 1978; Indian Painting, 1968; Ambassador's Journal, 1969; Economics, Peace and Laughter, 1971; A China Passage, 1973; Economics and the Public Purpose, 1974; Money: whence it came, where it went, 1975; The Age of Uncertainty, 1977; Almost Everyone's Guide to Economics, 1978; Annals of an Abiding Liberal, 1979; The Nature of Mass Poverty, 1979; A Life in Our Times, 1981; The Anatomy of Power, 1983; China Passage, 1983; A View from the Stands, 1987; A History of Economics, 1987; (with S. Menshikov) Capitalism, Communism and Coexistence, 1989; A Tenured Professor (novel), 1990; A Short History of Financial Euphoria, 1990; The Culture of Contentment, 1992; A Journey through Economic Time, 1994; The Good Society: the humane agenda, 1996; Letters to Kennedy, ed James Goodman, 1998; Name-Dropping: from FDR on, 1999; The Economics of Innocent Fraud, 2004; contribs to learned jls. *Address*: 206 Littauer Center, Harvard University, Cambridge, MA 02138, USA; 30 Francis Avenue, Cambridge, MA 02138, USA. *Clubs*: Century (NY); Federal City (Washington). *Died 29 April 2006*.

GALE, (Gwendoline) Fay, AO 1989; PhD; FASSA; President: Association of Asian Social Science Research Councils, 2001–03; Academy of the Social Sciences in Australia, 1998–2000; *b* 13 June 1932; *d* of Rev. George Jasper Gilding and Kathleen Gertrude Gilding; *m* 1957, Milton Gale (marr. diss.) one *s* one *d*. *Educ*: Adelaide Univ. (BA 1952, Hons I 1954; PhD 1962). University of Adelaide: Lectr, 1966–71; Sen. Lectr, 1972–74; Reader, 1975–77; Prof., 1978–89; Pro-Vice-Chancellor, 1988–89; Vice-Chancellor, Univ. of WA, 1990–97. Pres., Australian Vice-Chancellors' Cttee, 1996–97. Comr, Australian Heritage Commn, 1989–95. Mem. Nat. Cttee, UNESCO, 1999–2005. Elin Wagner Fellow, 1971; Catherine Helen Spence Fellow, 1972. FASSA 1978. Hon. Life Fellow, Inst. of Australian Geographers, 1994 (Pres., 1989). DUniv Adelaide, 1994; Hon. DLitt WA, 1998. British Council Award, 1972; John Lewis Gold Medal, RGS, SA, 2000; Griffith Taylor Medal, Inst. of Aust. Geographers, 2001. *Publications*: Race Relations in Australia: the Aboriginal situation, 1975; Urban Aborigines, 1972; Poverty among Aboriginal families in Adelaide, 1975; Adelaide Aborigines, a case study of urban life 1966–81, 1982; We are bosses ourselves: the status and role of Aboriginal women today, 1983; Tourists and the National Estate: procedures to protect Australia's heritage, 1987; Aboriginal youth and the criminal justice system: the injustice of justice, 1990; Changing Australia, 1991; Inventing Places: studies in cultural geography, 1992; Juvenile Justice: debating the issues, 1993; Tourism and the Protection of Aboriginal Cultural Sites, 1994; (ed) Cultural Geographics, 1999; (ed) Youth in Transition: the challenges of generational change in Asia, 2005. *Recreations*: bush walking, music, theatre. *Address*: c/o Vice Chancellory, University of Adelaide, North Terrace, Adelaide, SA 5005, Australia. *Died 3 May 2008*.

GALE, Michael Denis, PhD; FRS 1996; John Innes Professor, University of East Anglia, 2000–03, then Professorial Fellow, School of Biological Sciences; Associate Research Director, John Innes Centre, Norwich, 1994–98, 1999–2003, then John Innes Foundation Emeritus Fellow (Research Director, 1999); *b* 25 Aug. 1943; *s* of Sydney Ralph Gale and Helen Mary (*née* Johnson); *m* 1979, Susan Heathcote Rosbotham; two *d*. *Educ*: W Buckland Sch., Barnstaple; Birmingham Univ. (BSc Hons); UCW, Aberystwyth (PhD). Plant Breeding Institute, subseq. AFRC Institute of Plant Science Research, Cambridge: Researcher, 1968–86; Head, Cereals Res. Dept, and Individual Merit SPSO, Cambridge Lab., 1986–92; Head of Cambridge Lab., Norwich, 1992–94. Mem., Consultative Gp on Internat. Agricultural Res., Science Council, 2004–. Farrer Meml Bicentennial Fellow, NSW Dept of Agric., 1989; Hon. Res. Prof., Inst. of Crop Germplasm Resources, Acad. Sinica, 1992. Advr, Inst. of Genetics, Beijing, 1992; Chm., Internat. Adv. Bd, Chinese Acad. of Agricl Sci., 2007–. Foreign Fellow, Chinese Acad. of Engrg, 1999. Hon. DSc Birmingham, 2005; Hon. Dr, Norwegian Univ. of Life Scis, Ås, Norway, 2005. Res. Medal, RASE, 1994; Rank Prize for Nutrition, 1997; Darwin Medal, Royal Soc., 1998. *Publications*: 300 scientific papers and articles on plant genetics and cytogenetics, esp. dwarfism, quality and genome res. in wheat. *Recreations*: golf, poker (Dropsy Champion, Llangollen, 2002, 2004). *Address*: John Innes Centre, Norwich Research Park, Colney, Norwich NR4 7UH. *T*: (01603) 450000. *Club*: Royal Norwich Golf. *Died 18 July 2009*.

GALL, Thomas Mitchell; Hon. Mr Justice Gall; Judge of the Court of the First Instance of the High Court (formerly Judge of the High Court), Hong Kong, since 1991; *b* 20 Nov. 1942; *s* of John Berry Gall and Helen Lucy (*née* Mitchell); *m* 1966, Barbara Smart; one *s* one *d*. *Educ*: Univ. of Adelaide (LLB). Admitted barrister and solicitor, 1966; Colin D. Rowe & Co., Barristers and Solicitors, 1966–73; Hong Kong: Crown Counsel, 1973–76; Sen. Crown Counsel, 1976–78; Asst Principal Crown Counsel, 1978–81; Dist Judge, 1981–91. Hon. Sec., Council Early Childhood Educn; Chm., Childsafe Action Gp, 1992–. Vice-Chm., Criminol Soc., Hong Kong, 1992–. Gov., Winchester Internat. Sch., Hong Kong, 1989–. *Address*: High Court Building, 38 Queensway, Hong Kong. *Died 20 Jan. 2006*.

GALLINER, Peter; Director, International Press Institute, Zürich/London, 1975–93, then Emeritus; Chairman: Peter Galliner Associates, since 1970; International Encounters, since 1995; *b* 19 Sept. 1920; *s* of Dr Moritz and Hedwig Galliner; *m* 1st, 1948, Edith Marguerite Goldschmidt (decd); one *d*; 2nd, 1990, Helga Stenschke. *Educ*: Berlin and London. Reuters, 1942–47; Foreign Manager, Financial Times, 1947–60; Chm. and Man. Dir, Ullstein Publishing Co., Berlin, 1960–64; Vice-Chm. and Man. Dir, British Printing Corporation Publishing Gp, 1965–70; international publishing consultant, 1965–67 and 1970–. Press Freedom Award, Turkey, 1995; Europäischer Media and Communications Award, Germany, 1998. Order of Merit. 1st cl., 1961, and Comdr's Cross, 1990 (GFR); Ecomienda, Orden de Isabel la Católica (Spain), 1982. *Recreations*: reading, music. *Address*: Bregenzer Strasse 3, 10707 Berlin, Germany. *T*: (30) 8871166; 8001 Zürich, Untere Zäune 9, Switzerland. *T*: (1) 2518664. *Club*: Reform. *Died 19 Dec. 2006*.

GALLOWAY, Rev. Prof. Allan Douglas; Professor of Divinity, University of Glasgow, 1968–82, then Emeritus Professor; Principal of Trinity College, Glasgow, 1972–82; *b* 30 July 1920; *s* of late William Galloway and Mary Wallace Galloway (*née* Junor); *m* 1948, Sara Louise Phillipp; two *s*. *Educ*: Stirling High Sch.; Univ. of Glasgow; Christ's Coll., Cambridge; Union Theol Seminary, New York. MA, BD, STM, PhD. Ordained, Asst Minister, Clune Park Parish, Port Glasgow, 1948–50; Minister of Auchterhouse, 1950–54; Prof. of Religious Studies, Univ. of Ibadan, Nigeria, 1954–60; Sen. Lectr,

1960–66, Reader in Divinity, 1966–68, Univ. of Glasgow. Hensley Henson Lectr in Theology, Oxford Univ., 1978; Cunningham Lectr, Edinburgh, 1979; Gifford Lectr, Glasgow, 1984. FRSE 1985. *Publications:* The Cosmic Christ, 1951; Basic Readings in Theology, 1964; Faith in a Changing Culture, 1966; Wolfhart Pannenberg, 1973; History of Christian Theology, Vol. 1, Pt III, 1986. *Recreation:* sailing. *Address:* 5 Straid Bheag, Clynder, Helensburgh, Dunbartonshire G84 0QX.
Died 4 Feb. 2006.

GALLWEY, Sir Philip Frankland P.; *see* Payne-Gallwey.

GALPIN, His Honour Brian John Francis; a Circuit Judge, 1978–93; an Official Referee, Western Circuit, 1986–93; *b* 21 March 1921; *s* of late Christopher John Galpin, DSO and Gladys Elizabeth Galpin (*née* Souhami); *m* 1st, 1947, Ailsa McConnel (*d* 1959); one *d* decd; 2nd, 1961, Nancy Cecilia Nichols; two adopted *s. Educ:* Merchant Taylors' Sch., Hertford Coll., Oxford (MA 1947). FCIArb. RAF Officer, 1941–45. Editor, Isis, 1946. Called to the Bar, 1948; a Recorder of the Crown Court, 1972–78. Councillor, Metropolitan Borough of Fulham, 1950–59. Chm., Galpin Soc. for Study of Musical Instruments, 1954–72, Vice-Pres., 1974–; Pres., Madrigal Soc., 1989–91; Mem. Bach Choir, 1947–93 (Mem. Cttee, 1954–61). Trustee, Horniman Mus., 1990–2002 (Vice-Chm., 1990–96). Pres., Old Merchant Taylors' Soc., 1988 and 1991; Vice-Pres., Hertford Soc., 2004–. *Publications:* A Manual of International Law, 1950; Maxwell's Interpretation of Statutes, 10th edn 1953 and 11th edn 1962; Every Man's Own Lawyer, 69th edn 1962, 70th edn 1971, 71st edn 1981; contrib. Halsbury's Laws of England, 3rd and 4th edns, Encycl. of Forms and Precedents, Galpin Soc. Jl. *Recreations:* cricket (retired), music, chess. *Address:* St Bruno House, Charters Road, Sunningdale, Berks SL5 9QB. *Clubs:* Travellers, Pratt's.
Died 24 May 2006.

GAMMELL, John Frederick, MC 1943; Headmaster, Repton Sch., 1968–78; *b* 31 Dec. 1921; 2nd *s* of Lieut-Gen. Sir James A. H. Gammell, KCB, DSO, MC; *m* 1947, Margaret Anne, *d* of Ralph Juckes, Fiddiston Manor, Tewkesbury; two *s* one *d. Educ:* Winchester Coll.; Trinity Coll., Cambridge (MA 1953). Asst Master, Horris Hill, Newbury, 1940–41. War Service with KRRC, 1941–44; wounded, 1943; invalided out, 1944. Trinity Coll., Cambridge, 1946–47 (BA); Asst Master, Winchester Coll., 1944–45 and 1947–68; Exchange with Sen. Classics Master, Geelong Grammar Sch., Australia, 1949–50; Housemaster of Turner's, Winchester Coll., 1958–68; Asst Sec., Cambridge Univ. Careers Service, 1978 83. *Recreation:* friends. *Address:* 11 Church Lane, Seaton, Oakham LE15 9HR. *T:* (01572) 747835.
Died 4 July 2007.

GANDY, Christopher Thomas; HM Diplomatic Service, retired; *b* 21 April 1917; *s* of late Dr Thomas H. Gandy and Mrs Ida Gandy (authoress of A Wiltshire Childhood, Around the Little Steeple, etc); unmarried. *Educ:* Marlborough; King's Coll., Cambridge. On active service with Army and RAF, 1939–45. Entered Foreign Office, Nov. 1945; Tehran, 1948–51; Cairo, 1951–52; FO, 1952–54; Lisbon, 1954–56; Libya, 1956–59; FO, 1960–62; apptd HM Minister to The Yemen, 1962, subsequently Counsellor, Kuwait; Minister (Commercial) Rio de Janeiro, 1966–68. Sen. Common Room Mem., St Antony's Coll., Oxford, 1973–. *Publications:* articles in Asian Affairs, Middle East International, The New Middle East, The Annual Register of World Events, Art International, Arts of Asia, Jl of Royal Asiatic Soc., British Jl of Middle Eastern Studies, and Financial Times. *Recreations:* music, gardening. *Address:* c/o G. M Gandy, 21 Nightingale Avenue, Cambridge CB1 8SG. *Club:* Travellers.
Died 9 Dec. 2009.

GANZ, Prof. Peter Felix; Professor of German, University of Oxford, 1972–85, then Emeritus; *b* 3 Nov. 1920; *s* of Dr Hermann and Dr Charlotte Ganz; *m* 1st, 1949, Rosemary (*née* Allen) (*d* 1986); two *s* two *d*; 2nd,

1987, Prof. Nicolette Mout, Univ. of Leiden. *Educ:* Realgymnasium, Mainz; King's Coll., London (MA 1950; PhD 1954); MA Oxon 1960. Army service, 1940–45. Asst Lectr, Royal Holloway Coll., London Univ., 1948–49; Lectr, Westfield Coll., London Univ., 1949–60; Reader in German, 1960–72; Fellow of Hertford Coll., Oxford Univ., 1963–72 (Hon. Fellow, 1977); Fellow of St Edmund Hall, 1972–85, then Emeritus Fellow; Resident Fellow, Herzog August Bibliothek, Wolfenbüttel, W Germany, 1985–88. Vis. Professor: Erlangen-Nürnberg Univ., 1964–65 and 1971 (Hon. Dr 1993); Munich Univ., 1970 and 1974. Comdr, Order of Merit, Germany, 1973. Jt Editor: Beiträge zur Geschichte der deutschen Sprache und Literatur, 1976–90; Oxford German Studies, 1978–90. *Publications:* Der Einfluss des Englischen auf den deutschen Wortschatz 1740–1815, 1957; Geistliche Dichtung des 12. Jahrhunderts, 1960; Graf Rudolf, 1964; (with F. Norman and W. Schwarz) Dukus Horant, 1964; (with W. Schröder) Probleme mittelalterlicher Überlieferung und Textkritik, 1967; Jacob Grimm's Conception of German Studies, 1973; Gottfried von Strassburgs 'Tristan', 1978; Jacob Burckhardt, Über das Studium der Geschichte, 1981; articles on German medieval literature and language in jls. *Recreations:* music, walking, travel. *Address:* Oranje Nassaulaan 27, 2361 LB Warmond, Netherlands.
Died 17 Aug. 2006.

GARDAM, David Hill; QC 1968; *b* 14 Aug. 1922; *s* of late Harry H. Gardam, Hove, Sussex; *m* 1954, Jane Mary Pearson (OBE 2009); two *s* one *d. Educ:* Oundle Sch.; Christ Church, Oxford. MA 1948. War Service, RNVR, 1941–46 (Temp. Lieut). Called to the Bar, Inner Temple, 1949; Bencher 1977. *Recreations:* painting, etching, printing. *Address:* 1 Atkin Building, Gray's Inn, WC1R 5BQ. *T:* (020) 7404 0102; Haven House, Sandwich, Kent CT13 9ES.
Died 15 Jan. 2010.

GARDEN, Baron *cr* 2004, of Hampstead in the London Borough of Camden; **Timothy Garden,** KCB 1994 (CB 1992); Liberal Democrat spokesman on defence, House of Lords, since 2004; Visiting Professor, Centre for Defence Studies, King's College London, since 2000; *b* 23 April 1944; *s* of Joseph Garden and Winifred M. Garden (*née* Mayes); *m* 1965, Susan Elizabeth, *d* of Henry George Button, author; two *d. Educ:* King's Sch., Worcester; St Catherine's Coll., Oxford (MA 1967; Hon. Fellow, 1994); Magdalene Coll., Cambridge (MPhil 1982). FRAeS 1994. Joined RAF 1963; Pilot, 3 Sqn, 1967–71; Flying Instructor, 1972–75; Army Staff Coll., 1976; PSO to Air Mem. for Personnel, 1977–79; OC 50 Sqn, 1979–81; Dir Defence Studies RAF, 1982–85; Station Comdr RAF Odiham, 1985–87; Asst Dir, Defence Programmes, 1987–88; Dir Air Force Staff Duties, 1988–90; ACAS, 1991–92; ACDS (Programmes), 1992–94; Air Marshal; Comdt, RCDS, 1994–95; retired 1996. Dir, RIIA, 1997–98. Dist. Citizen Fellow, 2001, Wells Prof., 2004, Indiana Univ. Member, House of Lords Select Committee: on Delegated Powers and Regulatory Reform, 2004–06; on Regulators, 2006–; Convenor, All Party Parly Gp on Global Security and Nonproliferation, 2005–. Liberal Democratic Party: foreign and security policy advr, 2000–04; Member: Exec. Cttee, European Gp, 2002–04; Fed. Policy Cttee, 2003–05; Federal Exec., 2004–06. Ed., SourceUK.net, 1998–2001. Member of Advisory Board: NATO Defense Coll., Rome, 1996–2001; Internat. Studies Centre, Cambridge Univ., 1996–; Centre for Strategic Studies, Univ. of Hull, 1996–; Academic Study Gp on Israel and ME, 1996–2006; Königswinter Conf., 1997–; Oxford Res. Gp, 2001–; SaferWorld, 2001–; Crisis Action, 2005–; Member: DERA Analysis Bd, 1997–2000; Commn on Globalisation, 2002–04. Mem. Develt Council, St Catherine's Coll., Oxford, 1992–2006; Gov., King's Sch., Worcester, 1986–94. Dir, Asia Pacific Technol. Network, 1997–2000. Trustee, World Humanity Action Trust, 1996–2000. Chm., Rippon Gp, 2000–06. Member: RUSI, 1981– (Mem. Council, 1984–87, 2005–; FRUSI 1996); IISS, 1982–; RIIA, 1994– (Associate Fellow, 2000–); Council, RAeS,

1999–2002; Pugwash Conf., 1999–. Fellow, World Economic Forum, 1997–99. President: CCF, 2000–03; Trading Standards Inst., 2005–. President: British Gp, Liberal Internat., 2004–07; Camden Lib Dems, 2005–. Hon. Vice President: RAF Rowing Assoc., 1996 (Pres., 1992–95); St Catherine's Coll. Rowing Soc., 2003–; Hon. Pres., London and SE Reg. ATC, 1997–; President: Adastral Burns Club, 1999–; RAF Oxford and Cambridge Soc., 2005– (Chm., 1998–2005). Liveryman, GAPAN, 1997–. FCGI 2003. Chevalier, Légion d'Honneur (France), 2003. *Publications:* Can Deterrence Last?, 1984; The Technology Trap: science and the military, 1989; contribs to books and jls on internat. relations. *Recreations:* writing, bridge, photography, computing, grandchildren. *Address:* House of Lords, SW1A 0PW. *T:* (020) 7219 2747; *e-mail:* tgarden@ mac.com. *Clubs:* Beefsteak, Royal Air Force.
Died 9 Aug. 2007.

GARDNER, Rear-Adm. Herbert, CB 1976; Chartered Engineer; *b* 23 Oct. 1921; *s* of Herbert and Constance Gladys Gardner; *m* 1946, Catherine Mary Roe, Perth, WA. *Educ:* Taunton Sch.; Weymouth Coll. War of 1939–45; joined Dartmouth, 1940; RN Engineering Coll., Keyham, 1940; HMS Nigeria, Cumberland, Adamant, and 4th Submarine Sqdn, 1944; HM S/M Totem, 1945. Dept of Engr-in-Chief, 1947; HM S/M Telemachus, 1949; Admty Develt Establishment, Barrow-in-Furness, 1952; HMS Eagle, 1954; Comdr, 1956; HMS Caledonia, 1956; HMS Blackpool, 1958; Asst to Manager Engrg Dept, Rosyth Dockyard, 1960; HMS Maidstone, 1963; Capt., 1963; Dep. Manager, Engrg Dept, Devonport Dockyard, 1964; Chief Engr and Production Manager, Singapore Dockyard, 1967; Chief Staff Officer (Technical) to Comdr Far East Fleet, 1968; course at Imperial Defence Coll., 1970; Chief of Staff to C-in-C Naval Home Comd, 1971–73; Vice Pres., Ordnance Bd, 1974–76, Pres., 1976–77. *Recreations:* sailing, golf. *Address:* 41 Mayfair Street, Mount Claremont, Perth, WA 6010, Australia. *Club:* Royal Freshwater Bay Yacht (Perth). *Died 21 March 2006.*

GARFITT, His Honour Alan; a Circuit Judge, 1977–92, and Judge, Cambridge County Court and Wisbech County Court, 1978–92; *b* 20 Dec. 1920; *s* of Rush and Florence Garfitt; *m* 1st, 1941, Muriel Ada Jaggers; one *s* one *d*; 2nd, 1973, Ivie Maud Hudson; 3rd, 1978, Rosemary Lazell; one *s* one *d*. *Educ:* King Edward VII Grammar Sch., King's Lynn; Metropolitan Coll. and Inns of Court Sch. of Law. Served War of 1939–45, RAF, 1941–46. LLB London 1947; called to the Bar, Lincoln's Inn, 1948. Hon. Fellow, Faculty of Law, Cambridge, 1978. *Publications:* Law of Contracts in a Nutshell, 4 edns 1949–56; The Book for Police, 5 vols, 1958; jt ed, Roscoe's Criminal Evidence, Practice and Procedure, 16th edn, 1952; contribs to Jl of Planning Law, Solicitors' Jl and other legal pubns. *Recreations:* farming, gardening, DIY activities, horse riding and, as a member since 1961 and President 1978–93 of the Association of British Riding Schools (Fellow, 1989), the provision of good teaching and riding facilities for non-horse owners, dinghy sailing, boat building. *Address:* Leap House, Barcham Road, Soham, Ely, Cambs CB7 5TU.
Died 18 Dec. 2008.

GARLICK, Kenneth John; Keeper of Western Art, Ashmolean Museum, Oxford, 1968–84; Professorial Fellow of Balliol College, Oxford, 1968–84, then Emeritus; *b* 1 Oct. 1916; *s* of late D. E. Garlick and Annie Hallifax. *Educ:* Elmhurst Sch., Street; Balliol Coll., Oxford; Courtauld Inst. of Art, London. MA Oxon, PhD Birmingham; FMA. RAF Signals, 1939–46. Lectr, Bath Academy of Art, 1946–48; Asst Keeper, Dept of Art, City of Birmingham Museum and Art Gallery, 1948–50; Lectr (Sen. Lectr 1960), Barber Inst. of Fine Arts, Univ. of Birmingham, 1951–68. Governor, Royal Shakespeare Theatre, 1978–95. FRSA. Hon. DLitt Birmingham, 1996. *Publications:* Sir Thomas Lawrence, 1954; Walpole Society Vol. XXXIX (Lawrence Catalogue Raisonné), 1964; Walpole Society Vol. XLV

(Catalogue of Pictures at Althorp), 1976; (ed with Angus Macintyre) The Diary of Joseph Farington, Vols I–II, 1978, III–VI, 1979; Sir Thomas Lawrence, 1989; Portraits in the Bodleian Library Catalogue, 2004; numerous articles and reviews. *Recreations:* travel, music. *Address:* The Cotswold Home, Bradwell Village, Burford OX18 4XA. *Died 22 July 2009.*

GARNETT, Thomas Ronald, OAM 1996; MA; Head Master, Geelong Church of England Grammar School, Australia, 1961–73; *b* 1 Jan. 1915; *s* of E. N. Garnett; *m* 1946, Penelope, *d* of Philip Frere; three *s* two *d*. *Educ:* Charterhouse (Scholar); Magdalene Coll., Cambridge (Scholar; BA 1936, MA 1946). Assistant Master: Westminster School, 1936–38; Charterhouse, 1938–52; Master of Marlborough College, 1952–61. Served War of 1939–45, RAF, India and Burma, 1941–46, Squadron Leader (despatches). Cricket for Somerset, 1939. *Publications:* Stumbling on Melons, 1984; (ed) A Gardener's Potpourri, 1986; Man of Roses: Alister Clark of Glenara, 1990; The Evolution of a Gardener, 1993; A Gardener's Guide to the Climatic Zones of Australia, 1997; From the Country, 2001; Bits and Pieces: articles from The Age, vols 1–8, 2003–05. *Recreations:* gardening, ornithology. *Address:* 7 McGrath Street, Castlemaine, Vic 3450, Australia. *Died 22 Sept. 2006.*

GARRETT, Anthony David, CBE 1993; Deputy Master and Comptroller, Royal Mint, 1988–92; *b* 26 Aug. 1928; *s* of Sir William Garrett, MBE and Lady Garrett; *m* 1952, Monica Blanche Harris; three *s* one *d*. *Educ:* Ellesmere College; Clare College, Cambridge (MA). National Service, Subaltern IVth QO Hussars, 1946–48. Procter & Gamble Co., 1953–82 (Vice-Pres., 1975–82); Bd Mem., 1983–87, and Man. Dir of Parcels, 1986–87, Post Office. Dir, Nat. Provident Instn, 1988–94. FRSA 1991. *Recreations:* golf, bridge, chess, walking. *Address:* 2 Harlequin Place, Harlequin Lane, Crowborough, East Sussex TN6 1HZ. *T:* (01892) 663648. *Died 19 Feb. 2006.*

GARRETT, John Laurence; *b* 8 Sept. 1931; *s* of Laurence and Rosina Garrett; *m* 1959, Wendy Ady; two *d*. *Educ:* Selwyn Avenue Primary Sch., London; Sir George Monoux Sch., London; University Coll., Oxford (MA, BLitt); Grad. Business Sch. of Univ. of California at Los Angeles (King George VI Fellow). Labour Officer, chemical industry, 1958–59; Head of Market Research, motor industry, 1959–63; Management Consultant, Dir of Public Services, 1963–74, and Associate Dir, 1983–87, Inbucon Ltd. Consultant to Fulton Cttee on CS, 1966–68. Hon. Lectr in Govt, UEA, 1998–. Mem. (Lab), Norfolk CC, 1997–2001 (spokesman on planning and transportation, 1997–98). MP (Lab) Norwich South, Feb. 1974–1983, and 1987–97; contested (Lab) same seat, 1983. PPS to Minister for Civil Service, 1974, to Minister for Social Security, 1977–79; Opposition Treasury spokesman, 1979–80; spokesman: on industry, 1980–83; on energy, 1987–88; on industry, 1988–89; on civil service, 1993–94; Campaigns Co-ordinator, Southern and Eastern England, 1989–92. LRPS. *Publications:* Visual Economics, 1966; (with S. D. Walker) Management by Objectives in the Civil Service, 1969; The Management of Government, 1972; Administrative Reform, 1973; Policies Towards People, 1973 (Sir Frederic Hooper Award); Managing the Civil Service, 1980; Westminster, 1992; articles and papers on industry, management and govt. *Recreations:* theatre, dabbling, arguing. *Address:* 217 College Road, Norwich NR2 3JD.
Died 11 Sept. 2007.

GARRIOCH, Sir (William) Henry, Kt 1978; Chief Justice, Mauritius, 1977–78, retired; *b* 4 May 1916; *s* of Alfred Garrioch and Jeanne Marie Madeleine Colin; *m* 1964, Jeanne Louise Marie-Thérèse Desvaux de Marigny. *Educ:* Royal Coll., Mauritius. Called to the Bar, Gray's Inn, 1952. Civil Service (clerical), Mauritius, 1936–48; law student, London, 1949–52; Dist Magistrate, Mauritius, 1955; Crown Counsel, 1958; Sen. Crown Counsel, 1960; Solicitor-Gen., 1964; Dir of

Public Prosecutions, 1966; Puisne Judge, 1967; Sen. Puisne Judge, 1970; Actg Governor-Gen., 1977–78. KCSG 1996. *Recreations:* reading, chess. *Address:* Lees Street, Curepipe, Mauritius. *T:* 6752708.
Died 18 Feb. 2008.

GARROD, Lt-Gen. Sir (John) Martin (Carruthers), KCB 1988; CMG 1999; OBE 1980; DL; UN Regional Administrator of Mitrovica, Kosovo, 1999; *b* 29 May 1935; *s* of Rev. William Francis Garrod and Isobel Agnes (*née* Carruthers); *m* 1963, Gillian Mary, *d* of late Lt-Col R. G. Parks-Smith, RM; two *d. Educ:* Sherborne School. Joined Royal Marines, 1953; served Malta, Cyprus, DS Officers' Training Wing, RM School of Music, Malaya, Borneo, 1955–66; Staff Coll., Camberley, 1967; HQ 17 Div., Malaya, 1968–69; HQ Farelf, Singapore, 1970–71; 40 Commando RM (Co. Comdr, Plymouth and N Ireland), 1972–73 (despatches); GSO2 Plans, Dept of CGRM, 1973–76; GSO1, HQ Commando Forces RM, 1976–78; CO 40 Commando RM, 1978–79 (OBE operational, NI); Col Ops/Plans, Dept of CGRM, 1980–82; Comdr 3 Commando Bde RM, 1983–84; ADC to the Queen, 1983–84; COS to Comdt Gen. RM, 1984–87; Comdt Gen., RM, 1987–90. Mem., EC Monitor Mission in Bosnia, 1993–94; COS to EU Adminr, Mostar, 1994–96; EU Special Envoy, Mostar, 1996; Head, 1997–98, a Dep. High Rep., 1998, Regl Office of High Representative resp. for Southern Bosnia and Hercegovina. Dep. Dir, Maastricht Referendum Campaign, 1993. Freeman, City of London, 1990. DL Kent, 1992. *Recreation:* portrait photography. *Address:* c/o Lloyds TSB, 2 High Street, Deal, Kent CT14 7AD. *Club:* East India. *Died 17 April 2009.*

GARSON, Cdre Robin William, CBE 1975; RN retd; Director of Leisure Services, London Borough of Hillingdon, 1975–86; *b* 13 Nov. 1921; *s* of late Peter Garson and Ada Frances (*née* Newton); *m* 1946, Joy Ligertwood Taylor (*née* Hickman); one *s* one *d. Educ:* School of Oriental and African Studies. Japanese Interpreter. Entered Royal Navy, 1937; served War of 1939–45, HM Ships: Resolution, Nigeria, Cyclops, and HM Submarines: Seawolf, H.33, Spark; subsequent principal appointments: In Command HM Submarines: Universal, Uther, Seraph, Saga, Sanguine, Springer, Thule, Astute, 1945–54; Chief Staff Officer Intelligence, Far East, 1966–68; Sen. Polaris UK Rep., Washington, 1969–71; Captain 1st Submarine Sqdn, 1971–73; Commodore, HMS Drake, 1973–75; ADC to the Queen, 1974. Adviser to AMA on Arts and Recreation, 1976–86; Adviser to Sports Council, 1985–86; Mem., Library Adv. Council (England), 1977–83. Patron, RN Submarine Mus., 1990–. *Recreations:* golf, ski-ing, tennis. *Address:* Gateways, Hamilton Road West, Old Hunstanton, Norfolk PE36 6JB. *Clubs:* Army and Navy, Royal Navy of 1765 and 1785; Hunstanton Golf.
Died 26 Jan. 2006.

GARTON, George Alan, PhD, DSc; FRSE 1966; FRS 1978; Hon. Professorial Fellow, Rowett Research Institute, Bucksburn, Aberdeen, since 1992; Hon. Research Fellow, University of Aberdeen, since 1987; *b* 4 June 1922; *o s* of late William Edgar Garton, DCM, and Frances Mary Elizabeth Garton (*née* Atkinson), Scarborough, N Yorks; *m* 1951, Gladys Frances Davison, BSc; two *d. Educ:* Scarborough High Sch.; Univ. of Liverpool (BSc: (War Service) 1944, (Hons Biochem.) 1946; PhD 1949, DSc 1959). Experimental Asst, Chemical Inspection Dept, Min. of Supply, 1942–45; Johnston Research and Teaching Fellow, Dept of Biochem., Univ. of Liverpool, 1949–50; Rowett Research Inst., Bucksburn, Aberdeen: Biochemist, 1950; Dep. Dir, 1968–83; Head of Lipid Biochem. Dept, 1963–83; Hon. Res. Associate, 1983–92; Hon. Res. Associate, Univ. of Aberdeen, 1966–86. Sen. Foreign Fellow of Nat. Science Foundn (USA), and Vis. Prof. of Biochem., Univ. of N Carolina, 1967. Chm., British Nat. Cttee for Nutritional and Food Sciences, 1982–87; Pres., Internat. Confs on Biochem. Lipids, 1982–89. Scientific Gov., British Nutrition Foundn, 1982–2003, Gov.

Emeritus, 2004–; a Dir, The Mother and Child Foundn, 1995–2000. MStJ 1986. *Publications:* papers, mostly on aspects of lipid biochemistry, in scientific jls.
Died 13 May 2010.

GARVEY, Thomas, (Tom); Deputy Director General (Environment, Nuclear Safety and Civil Protection), European Commission, 1992–98; *b* 27 May 1936; *s* of Thomas and Brigid Garvey; *m* 1961, Ellen Devine; two *s* two *d. Educ:* University Coll., Dublin (MA Econ). Fellow, Management Inst. Ireland. Various marketing and internal trade appts, 1958–69; Chief Exec., Irish Export Bd, 1969–76; EEC Delegate, Nigeria, 1977–80; Chief Exec., An Post (Irish Postal Service), 1980–84; Dir, Internal Market and Ind. Affairs, EEC, 1984–89; Dir, DG1 (External Relns), EC, 1990–92. Mem. Gen. Assembly and Life Fellow, Regl Envmt Centre, Budapest, 1996; Chm., Regl Envmt Centre, Moldova, 1999. Visiting Lecturer: Univ. of Pittsburgh, 1998; Univ. of Cape Town; Internat. Univ., Venice. Life FRSA 1990. *Publications:* (jtly) Where to Now?: ideas on the future of the EU, 2005; various, in industrial, trade and academic jls. *Recreations:* golf, music. *Died 11 April 2008.*

GARY, Lesley; *see* Blanch, L.

GASCH, Pauline Diana, (Mrs F. O. Gasch); *see* Baynes, P. D.

GASCOIGNE, Stanley, CMG 1976; OBE 1972; Secretary to the Cabinet, Bermuda, 1972–76; Member, Senate, 1976–85 (Vice-President, 1980–85); *b* 11 Dec. 1914; *s* of George William Gascoigne and Hilda Elizabeth Gascoigne; *m* 1st, 1941, Sybil Wellspring Outerbridge (*d* 1980); 2nd, 1980, Sandra Alison Lee, two *s. Educ:* Mt Allison Univ., Canada (BA 1937): London Univ., England (DipEd 1938); Boston Univ., USA (MEd 1951). Teacher, 1939–51; Inspector of Schools, 1951–59; Director, Marine and Ports Authority, 1959–69; Permanent Sec., Education, 1969–72. Exec. Dir, Inst. of Chartered Accountants of Bermuda, 1976–89. *Recreation:* ornithology. *Address:* #17 Panorama, 153 South Road, Paget, DV 04, Bermuda. *T:* 2367053; *e-mail:* gascoigne@northrock.bm. *Club:* Royal Hamilton Amateur Dinghy (Bermuda). *Died 20 April 2006.*

GASH, Prof. Norman, CBE 1989; FBA 1963; FRSL 1973; FRSE 1977; FRHistS; Professor of History, St Salvator's College, University of St Andrews, 1955–80, then Emeritus; *b* 16 Jan. 1912; *s* of Frederick and Kate Gash; *m* 1st, 1935, Ivy Dorothy Whitehorn (*d* 1995); two *d*; 2nd, 1997, Mrs Ruth Frances Jackson. *Educ:* Reading Sch.; St John's Coll., Oxford (Hon. Fellow 1987). Scholar, St John's Coll.; 1st cl. Hons Mod. Hist., 1933; BLitt, 1934; MA 1938. FRHistS 1953. Temp. Lectr in Modern European History, Edinburgh, 1935–36; Asst Lectr in Modern History, University Coll., London, 1936–40. Served War, 1940–46: Intelligence Corps; Capt. 1942; Major (Gen. Staff), 1945. Lectr in Modern British and American History, St Salvator's Coll., University of St Andrews, 1946–53; Prof. of Modern History, University of Leeds, 1953–55; Vice-Principal, 1967–71, Dean of Faculty of Arts, 1978–80, St Andrews Univ. Hinkley Prof. of English History, Johns Hopkins Univ., 1962; Ford's Lectr in English History, Oxford Univ., 1963–64; Sir John Neale Lectr in English Hist., UCL, 1981; Wellington Lectr, Southampton Univ., 1992. Vice-Pres., Hist. Assoc. of Scotland, 1963–64. Hon. DLitt: Strathclyde, 1984; St Andrews, 1985; Southampton, 1988. *Publications:* Politics in the Age of Peel, 1953; Mr Secretary Peel, 1961; The Age of Peel, 1968; Reaction and Reconstruction in English Politics, 1832–1852, 1966; Sir Robert Peel, 1972; Peel, 1976; (jtly) The Conservatives: a history from their origins to 1965, 1978; Aristocracy and People: England 1815–1865, 1979; Lord Liverpool, 1984; Pillars of Government, 1986; (ed) Wellington: studies in the military and political career of the first Duke of Wellington, 1990; Robert Surtees and Early Victorian Society, 1993; (ed) W. B. Ferrand "The Working Man's Friend" 1809–1889, by John Ward, 2002; articles and reviews in Eng. Hist. Review, Trans.

Royal Historical Society, and other learned jls. *Recreations:* gardening, swimming. *Address:* Old Gatehouse, Portway, Langport, Som TA10 0NQ. *T:* (01458) 250334.
Died 1 May 2009.

GASKIN, Catherine; author; *b* Co. Louth, Eire, 2 April 1929; *m* 1955, Sol Cornberg (*d* 1999). *Educ:* Holy Cross Coll., Sydney, Australia; Conservatorium of Music, Sydney. Brought up in Australia; lived in London, 1948–55, New York, 1955–65, Virgin Islands, 1965–67, Ireland, 1967–81, Isle of Man, 1981–2000. *Publications:* This Other Eden, 1946; With Every Year, 1947; Dust In Sunlight, 1950; All Else Is Folly, 1951; Daughter of the House, 1952; Sara Dane, 1955; Blake's Reach, 1958; Corporation Wife, 1960; I Know My Love, 1962; The Tilsit Inheritance, 1963; The File on Devlin, 1965; Edge of Glass, 1967; Fiona, 1970; A Falcon for a Queen, 1972; The Property of a Gentleman, 1974; The Lynmara Legacy, 1975; The Summer of the Spanish Woman, 1977; Family Affairs, 1980; Promises, 1982; The Ambassador's Women, 1985; The Charmed Circle, 1988. *Recreations:* music, reading. *Address:* Villa 139, The Manors, 15 Hale Road, Mosman, NSW 2088, Australia.
Died 6 Sept. 2009.

GATHERCOLE, Ven. John Robert; Archdeacon of Dudley, 1987–2001; *b* 23 April 1937; *s* of Robert Gathercole and Winifred Mary Gathercole (*née* Price); *m* 1963, Joan Claire (*née* London); one *s* one *d*. *Educ:* Judd School, Tonbridge; Fitzwilliam Coll., Cambridge (BA 1959, MA 1963); Ridley Hall, Cambridge. Deacon 1962, priest 1963; Curate: St Nicholas, Durham, 1962–66; St Bartholomew, Croxdale, 1966–70; Social and Industrial Adviser to Bishop of Durham, 1967–70; Industrial Chaplain, Redditch, dio. Worcester, 1970–87; RD of Bromsgrove, 1978–85; Team Leader, and Sen. Chaplain, Worcs Industrial Mission, 1985–91; RD of Droitwich, 2007–08. Member: General Synod of C of E, 1995–2001; Council for the Care of Churches, 1998–2001. *Publications:* The Riley Imp: histories and profiles, 2008. *Recreations:* vintage sports cars, music. *Address:* Wisteria Cottage, Main Road, Ombersley, Worcs WR9 0EL. *T:* (01905) 676128.
Died 8 Oct. 2010.

GAY, Geoffrey Charles Lytton; Consultant, Knight, Frank & Rutley, 1975–85 (Senior Partner, 1969–75); World President, International Real Estate Federation (FIABCI), 1973–75; a General Commissioner for Inland Revenue, 1953–89; *b* 14 March 1914; *s* of late Charles Gay and Ida, *d* of Sir Henry A. Lytton (famous Savoyard); *m* 1947, Dorothy Ann, *d* of Major Eric Rickman; one *s* two *d*. *Educ:* mainly by parents and grandparents; St Paul's School. FRICS. Joined Knight, Frank & Rutley, 1929. Served War of 1939–45: Durham LI, BEF, 1940; psc; Lt-Col; Chief of Staff, Sind District, India, 1943. Mem. Westminster City Council, 1962–71. Governor: Benenden Sch., 1971–86; Clayesmore Sch. Council; Mem. Council of St John, London, 1971–84; Liveryman, Broderers' Co. Licentiate, RPS, 1983; FRSA 1983. Chevalier de l'Ordre de l'Economie Nationale, 1960. OStJ 1961; KStJ 1979. *Recreations:* photography, fishing, music, theatre, planning for the future. *Address:* Amesbury Abbey, Amesbury, Wilts SP4 7EX. *T:* and *Fax:* (01980) 524153; *e-mail:* poohbah@dial.pipex.com. *Clubs:* Carlton, MCC, Flyfishers'. *Died 19 Aug. 2007.*

GEDDES, His Honour Andrew Campbell; a Circuit Judge, 1994–2009; Designated Civil Judge, Worcester (formerly Coventry) Group of Courts, 1998–2009; *b* 10 June 1943; *s* of Hon. Alexander Campbell Geddes, OBE, MC, TD and Hon. Margaret Kathleen Geddes (*née* Addis); *m* 1st, 1974, Jacqueline Tan Bunzl; two *s*; 2nd, 1985, Bridget Bowring; one *s* one *d*. *Educ:* Stowe; Christ Church, Oxford (MA). Founder, Building Products Index, 1965. Called to the Bar, Inner Temple, 1972; a Recorder, 1990; authorised to sit as High Court Judge, 1995. Mem., Interviewing Panel, Judicial Appts Commn, 2008–. *Publications:* Product and Service Liability in the EEC, 1992; Public Procurement, 1993; Protection of Individual Rights under EC Law, 1995; Public and Utility Procurement, 1996; contribs to learned jls. *Recreations:* music, walking, reading, writing, gardening.
Died 27 June 2009.

GELLING, Margaret Joy, OBE 1995; PhD; FBA 1998; FSA; President, English Place-Name Society, 1986–98; *b* 29 Nov. 1924; *d* of Lucy and William Albert Midgley; *m* 1952, Peter Stanley Gelling (*d* 1983). *Educ:* Chislehurst Grammar Sch.; St Hilda's Coll., Oxford (BA 1945; MA 1951; Hon. Fellow, 1993); University Coll. London (PhD 1957). FSA 1986. Temp. Civil Servant, 1945–46; Res. Asst, English Place-Name Soc., 1946–53. Hon. Reader, Univ. of Birmingham, 1981–. Vice-Pres., Internat. Council for Onomastic Scis, 1993–99. Hon. DLitt: Nottingham, 2002; Leicester, 2003. *Publications:* English Place-Name Society volumes: Oxfordshire, part 1, 1953, part 2, 1954; Berkshire, part 1, 1973, part 2, 1974, part 3, 1976; Shropshire, part 1, 1990, part 2, 1995, part 3, 2001, part 4, 2004, part 5, 2006; (jtly) The Names of Towns and Cities in Britain, 1970; Signposts to the Past, 1978, 3rd edn 1997; The Early Charters of the Thames Valley, 1979; Place-Names in the Landscape, 1984; The West Midlands in the Early Middle Ages, 1992; (jtly) The Landscape of Place-Names, 2000; papers in Medieval Archaeology, Anglo-Saxon England, etc. *Recreation:* gardening. *Address:* 31 Pereira Road, Harborne, Birmingham B17 9JG. *T:* (0121) 427 6469.
Died 24 April 2009.

GENDERS, Rt Rev. Roger Alban Marson, (Bishop Anselm), CR; *b* 15 Aug. 1919; *yr s* of John Boulton Genders and Florence Alice (*née* Thomas). *Educ:* King Edward VI School, Birmingham; Brasenose College, Oxford (Sen. Scholar 1938, BA Lit. Hum. 1946, MA 1946). Served War, Lieut RNVR, 1940–46. Joined Community of the Resurrection, Mirfield, 1948; professed, 1952; ordained, 1952; Tutor, College of the Resurrection, 1952–55; Vice-Principal 1955, and Principal 1957–65, Codrington Coll., Barbados; Exam. Chaplain to Bishop of Barbados, 1957–65; Treasurer of St Augustine's Mission, Rhodesia, 1966–75; Archdeacon of Manicaland, 1970–75; Asst Bursar, Community of the Resurrection, Mirfield, 1975–77; Bishop of Bermuda, 1977–82; Assistant Bishop of Wakefield, 1983–89. *Publications:* contribs to Theology. *Address:* Community of the Resurrection, House of the Resurrection, Mirfield, W Yorks WF14 0BN. *Died 19 June 2008.*

GEORGE, Baron *cr* 2004 (Life Peer), of St Tudy in the County of Cornwall; **Edward Alan John George,** GBE 2000; PC 1999; DL; Governor, Bank of England, 1993–2003; *b* 11 Sept. 1938; *s* of Alan George and Olive Elizabeth George; *m* 1962, Clarice Vanessa Williams; one *s* two *d*. *Educ:* Dulwich Coll.; Emmanuel Coll., Cambridge (BAecon 2nd Cl. (i); MA). Joined Bank of England, 1962; worked initially on East European affairs; seconded to Bank for International Settlements, 1966–69, and to International Monetary Fund as Asst to Chairman of Deputies of Committee of Twenty on Internat. Monetary Reform, 1972–74; Adviser on internat. monetary questions, 1974–77; Dep. Chief Cashier, 1977–80; Asst Dir (Gilt Edged Div.), 1980–82; Exec. Dir, 1982–90; Dep. Gov., 1990–93. DL Cornwall, 2006. Hon. DSc: (Econ) Hull, 1993; City, 1995; Cranfield, 1997; UMIST, 1998; Buckingham, 2000; Hon. DLitt: Loughborough, 1994; Sheffield, 1999; Hon. DPhil London Guildhall, 1996; Hon. LLD: Exeter, 1997; Bristol, 1999; Herts, 1999; Cantab, 2000; DUniv London Metropolitan, 2002. *Recreations:* family, sailing, bridge.
Died 18 April 2009.

GEORGE, Rear Adm. Anthony Sanderson, CB 1983; CEng, FIIM; Port Manager, Portsmouth, since 1987; *b* 8 Nov. 1928; *s* of Sandys Parker George and Winifred Marie George; *m* 1953, Mary Veronica Frances Bell; two *d*. *Educ:* Royal Naval Coll., Dartmouth; Royal Naval Engrg Coll., Manadon. MIMechE 1957; FIIM 1979. Sea-going appts, 1950–62; warship design, Ship Dept of MoD, 1962–64; RN Staff Coll., 1965; British High Commn, Canberra, 1966–67; MEO, HMS Hampshire, 1968–69; Staff of Flag Officer Sea Trng, 1970–71; Dep.

Prodn Manager, HM Dockyard, Portsmouth, 1972–75; RCDS, 1976; CSO (Trng) to C-in-C Naval Home Comd, 1977–78; Prodn Manager, HM Dockyard, Portsmouth, 1979–81; Dir, Dockyard Prodn and Support, 1981–82; Chief Exec., Royal Dockyards, 1983–86. Chief Exec., World Energy Business, 1986. Comdr 1965, Captain 1972, Rear Adm. 1981. FCMI (FBIM 1977). *Recreations:* sailing, swimming, walking, painting. *Address:* c/o National Westminster Bank, 5 East Street, Chichester, West Sussex PO19 1HH. *Died 28 June 2007.*

GEORGE, Llewellyn Norman Havard; a Recorder of the Crown Court, 1980–91; Consultant, V. J. G. Johns & Son, Solicitors, since 1991 (Partner, 1950–91, Senior Partner, 1972–91); *b* 13 Nov. 1925; *s* of Benjamin William George, DSO, RNR, and Annie Jane George; *m* 1950, Mary Patricia Morgan (*née* Davies); one *d*. *Educ:* Cardiff High Sch.; Fishguard Grammar Sch. HM Coroner, 1965–80; Recorder, Wales and Chester Circuit, 1980. President: West Wales Law Society, 1973–74; Pembrokeshire Law Society, 1981–83; Chairman: (No 5) South Wales Law Society Legal Aid Cttee, 1979; Agricl Land Tribunal (Wales), 1985–90 (Dep. Chm., 1983–85). Mem., Farrand Cttee, 1984–85. *Recreations:* golf, reading, chess. *Address:* Fourwinds, 3 Pantycelyn, Penyraber, Fishguard, Pembs SA65 9EH. *T:* (01348) 872040. *Clubs:* Pembrokeshire County; Newport (Pembs) Golf (Life Pres., 1988). *Died 24 March 2006.*

GEORGE, Peter John, OBE 1974; HM Diplomatic Service, retired; Counsellor and Consul General, British Embassy, Manila, 1976–79; Chargé d'Affaires *ai*, 1978; *b* 12 Dec. 1919; *s* of late Cecil John George and Mabel George; *m* 1946, Andrée Louise Pernon (*d* 2003); one *d*. *Educ:* Sutton Grammar Sch., Plymouth. Served War, 1939–46: Captain. Home Civil Service, 1936; HM Diplomatic Service, 1966; First Secretary, Commercial: Colombo, 1967–70; Seoul, 1971–73 (Chargé d'Affaires *ai*, 1971 and 1972); Prague, 1973–76. *Recreations:* reading, golf, swimming. *Address:* St Just, Walton Park, Walton-on-Thames, Surrey KT12 3EU. *Died 20 Feb. 2008.*

GERTYCH, Prof. Zbigniew; Professor, Botanical Garden, Polish Academy of Sciences, Warsaw, since 1990; *b* 26 Oct. 1922; *s* of Tadeusz Gertych and Maria Gertych (*née* Marecka); *m* 1st, 1945, Roza (*née* Skrochowska) (decd); one *s* two *d*; 2nd, 1970, Zofia (*née* Dobrzanska). *Educ:* Uniw. Jagiellonski, Krakow. MA eng 1946, DAgric 1950. Joined Army as volunteer and participated in September campaign, 1939; during Nazi occupation took part in clandestine activities, was detained in camps and Gestapo prisons; after escape served Home Army (AK) to 1945 (wounded in partisan combat). Polish Academy of Sciences (PAN), 1946–83: Head of Pomology Dept, Dendrology Research Centre, Kórnik, 1947–53; Dir Exp. Fruit Growing Research Centre, Brzeźna, 1953–64; Dir, Research Centre, Agric. and Forestry Econ. Science, 1964–78; Vice-Dir and Dir, Vegetable Growing Inst., Skierniewice, 1964–82; Vice-Sec. and Sec., Agric. and Forestry Scis Dept, 1964–87; First Dep. Gen. Sec., 1981–83; Mem., PAN, 1976; Mem., Presidium of PAN, 1978–86; Asst Prof., 1963, Associate Prof., 1969, Prof., 1979, Jagiellonian Univ., Cracow and Polish Acad. of Scis. MP, Nowy Sacz, 1957–89; Dep. Speaker, Sejm, 1982–85 (Chm., Budget Commn, Social and Economic Council and Main Cttee, Nat. Action for School Assistance); Dep. Chm., Council of Ministers, 1985–87; Ambassador of Poland to the Court of St James's and to Republic of Ireland, 1987–90. Pres., Homo et Planta Foundn, 1991–; Mem., Supreme Council and Exec. Cttee, Internat. Soc. of Hort. Scis. Hon. Dr, Acad. of Agric. Scis, Berlin, 1974; DAgr *hc* Szczecin Univ., 1989. Cross of Valour, 1944; Comdr's Cross, Order of Polonia Restituta, 1984; other Polish decorations; numerous foreign honours and awards. *Publications:* contribs to sci. jls. *Recreations:* music, art, travels. *Address:* Botanical Garden, Polish Academy of Sciences, vl. Prawdziwka 2, POB 84, 02–973 Warsaw 34, Poland. *Club:* Rotary. *Died 4 July 2008.*

GESTETNER, David; President, Gestetner Holdings PLC, 1987–95; *b* 1 June 1937; *s* of late Sigmund Gestetner and Henny Gestetner, OBE; *m* 1st, 1961, Alice Floretta Sebag-Montefiore (*d* 2000); one *s* three *d*; 2nd, 2006, Mrs Angela Howard. *Educ:* Midhurst Grammar Sch.; Bryanston Sch.; University Coll., Oxford (MA). Gestetner Holdings: Dir, 1967–2005; Jt Chm., 1972–86; Man. Dir, 1982–86; Jt Pres., 1986–87. Director: Alphameric PLC, 1994–2000; Nipson Digital Printing Systems PLC, 2004–. *Recreations:* sailing, book collecting. *Clubs:* Reform, MCC. *Died 3 April 2010.*

GHURBURRUN, Sir Rabindrah, Kt 1981; Vice-President, Republic of Mauritius, 1992–97; *b* 27 Sept. 1929; *s* of Mrs Sookmeen Ghurburrun; *m* 1959; one *s* one *d*. *Educ:* Keble Coll., Oxford. Called to the Bar, Middle Temple; QC Mauritius, 1991; practised as Lawyer, 1959–68; High Comr for Mauritius in India, 1968–76; MLA 1976; Minister of Justice, 1976; Minister of Economic Planning and Development, 1977–82. Member: Central Board; Bar Council (Chm., 1991–92). Former President: Mauritius Arya Sabha; Mauritius Sugar Cane Planters' Assoc.; Hindu Educn Authority; Nat. Congress of Young Socialists. Patron, Commonwealth ESU in Mauritius. Grand Order of the Star and Key, Mauritius, 1993. *Address:* 18 Dr Lesur Street, Cascadelle, Beau Bassin, Mauritius. *T:* 4546421. *Died 21 April 2008.*

GIBB, Walter Frame, DSO 1945; DFC 1943; Chairman, 1980–84, and Managing Director, 1978–84, British Aerospace, Australia, Ltd; retired; *b* 26 March 1919; British; *m* 1944, Pauline Sylvia Reed; three *d*. *Educ:* Clifton Coll. Apprentice, Bristol Aero Engines, 1937. RAF, 1940–46. Test Pilot, Bristol Aircraft Ltd, 1946; Asst Chief Test Pilot, 1953; Chief Test Pilot, Bristol Aeroplane Co. Ltd, 1956–60; Product Support Manager, BAC Filton, 1960–78. World Altitude Height Record 63,668 feet in Olympus-Canberra, 1953, and second record 65,890 ft in same machine, 1955. MRAeS. JP Bristol, 1974. *Recreation:* sailing. *Address:* Merlin Haven Lodge, Wotton-under-Edge, Glos GL12 7BA. *Club:* Royal Air Force. *Died 4 Oct. 2006.*

GIBBERD, Dr Frederick Brian, MD; FRCP, FRCPE; Consultant Neurologist, Chelsea and Westminster Hospital, 1965–96, then Hon. Consultant Neurologist; *b* 7 July 1931; *s* of late George Frederick Gibberd, CBE and Margaret Erica (*née* Taffs); *m* 1960, Margaret Clare Sidey; four *d*. *Educ:* Aldenham Sch. (Schol.); Gonville and Caius Coll., Cambridge (Schol.); BA 1954; MA, MB BChir 1957; MD 1974); Westminster Med. Sch. (Schol.). FRCP 1972; FRCPE 1993. Nat. Service, commnd RA, 1949–51. Jun. doctor posts at Westminster, Addenbrookes, Brompton, Nat. Queen Square and Royal London Hosps, 1957–65; Consultant Neurologist, Queen Mary's Hosp., Roehampton, 1965–96. Mem., GMC, 1992–96; Neurologist, The Lister Hosp., 1996–2004. Chm., Westminster Hosp. Med. Cttee, 1983–86; Mem., Riverside Dist HA, 1987–90. Royal College of Physicians: Censor, 1991–92; Council Mem., 1970–72 and 1990–96; Royal Society of Medicine: Pres., Clinical Section, 1972–74; Hon. Librarian, 1975–79. President: Harveian Soc., 1995; Hunterian Soc., 2003–04. Society of Apothecaries: Liveryman, 1968; Master, 1996–97. Hon. FFOM 1995. *Publications:* (contrib.) Medical Negligence, 1994; MRCP (UK) Examination Book, 1995; articles and papers on epilepsy, Parkinson's Disease, Refsum's Disease, and neurological diseases. *Recreations:* gardening, travelling, history. *Address:* Chelsea and Westminster Hospital, 369 Fulham Road, SW10 9NH. *T:* (020) 8746 8134; 2 Ferrings, Dulwich, SE21 7LU. *T:* (020) 8693 8106. *Died 20 Feb. 2006.*

GIBBS, Rt Rev. John; Bishop of Coventry, 1976–85; *b* 15 March 1917; *s* of late A. E. Gibbs, Bournemouth; *m* 1943, G. Marion (*d* 2005), *d* of late W. J. Bishop, Poole, Dorset; one *s* one *d*. *Educ:* Univ. of Bristol; Western Coll., Bristol; Lincoln Theological Coll. BA (Bristol); BD (London). In the ministry of the Congregational Church,

1943–49. Student Christian Movement: Inter-Collegiate Sec., 1949–51; Study Sec. and Editor of Student Movement, 1951–55. Curate of St Luke's, Brislington, Bristol, 1955–57; Chaplain and Head of Divinity Dept, Coll. of St Matthias, Bristol, 1957–64, Vice-Principal, 1962–64; Principal, Keswick Hall Coll. of Education, Norwich, 1964–73; Examining Chaplain to Bishop of Norwich, Hon. Canon of Norwich Cathedral, 1968–73; Bishop Suffragan of Bradwell, Dio. Chelmsford, 1973–76. Hon. Asst to Bps of Gloucester and Bristol, 1985–. Member, Durham Commn on Religious Education, 1967–70; Chairman: C of E Children's Council, 1968–71; C of E Bd of Educn Publications Cttee, 1971–79, Education and Community Cttee, 1974–76; Assoc. of Voluntary Colls, 1985–87; Further and Higher Educn Cttee, General Synod Bd of Educn, 1986–91; BCC Wkg Parties: Chm., The Child in the Church, 1973–76; Chm., Understanding Christian Nurture, 1979–81; Anglican Chm., Anglican-Lutheran European Reg. Commn, 1980–82. Founder, Myton Hamlet Hospice, Warwick (Chm., 1982–85); Chm., Cotswold Care Hospice, 1986–96. Introduced into H of L, 1982. *Recreations:* music, bird watching. *Address:* Farthingloe, Southfield, Minchinhampton, Stroud, Glos GL6 9DY. *Died 20 Dec. 2007.*

GIBSON, Prof. Frank William Ernest, AM 2004; FRS 1976; FAA; Emeritus Professor of Biochemistry, Australian National University, since 1989 (Visiting Fellow, 1989); *b* 22 July 1923; *s* of John William and Alice Ruby Gibson; *m* 1st, 1949, Margaret Isabel Nancy (marr. diss. 1979); two *d*; 2nd, 1980, Robin Margaret; one *s*. *Educ:* Queensland Univ.; Melbourne Univ. (BSc, DSc); DPhil Oxon. Research Asst, Melbourne and Queensland Univs, 1938–47; Sen. Demonstrator, Melbourne Univ., 1948–49; ANU Scholar, Oxford, 1950–52. Melbourne University: Sen. Lectr, 1953–58; Reader in Chem. Microbiology, 1959–65; Prof. of Chem. Microbiology, 1965–66; Australian National University: Prof. of Biochem., 1967–88; Hd of Biochem. Dept, 1967–76, Chm., Div. of Biochemical Scis, 1988, John Curtin Sch. of Medical Res.; Howard Florey Prof. of Medical Res., and Dir, John Curtin Sch. of Med. Res., 1977–79. Newton-Abraham Vis. Prof. and Fellow of Lincoln Coll., Oxford Univ., 1982–83. David Syme Research Prize, Univ. of Melb., 1963. FAA 1971. *Publications:* scientific papers on the biochemistry of bacteria, particularly the biosynthesis of aromatic compounds, energy metabolism. *Recreations:* tennis, ski-ing. *Address:* 7 Waller Crescent, Campbell, ACT 2612, Australia. *Died 11 July 2008.*

GIBSON, John Sibbald; historian; Under Secretary, Scottish Office, 1973–83, retired; *b* 1 May 1923; *s* of John McDonald Frame Gibson and Marion Watson Sibbald; *m* 1948, Moira Helen Gillespie; one *s* one *d*. *Educ:* Paisley Grammar Sch.; Glasgow Univ. Army, 1942–46, Lieut in No 1 Commando from 1943; Far East. Joined Admin. Grade Home Civil Service, 1947; Asst Principal, Scottish Home Dept, 1947–50; Private Sec. to Parly Under-Sec., 1950–51; Private Sec. to Perm. Under-Sec. of State, Scottish Office, 1952; Principal, Scottish Home Dept, 1953; Asst Sec., Dept of Agriculture and Fisheries for Scotland, 1962; Under Secretary: Scottish Office, 1973; Dept of Agriculture and Fisheries for Scotland, 1979. Mem., Agricl Res. Council, 1979–83. Organiser, Scottish Office Centenary Exhibn, 1985. *Publications:* Ships of the '45: the rescue of the Young Pretender, 1967; Deacon Brodie: Father to Jekyll and Hyde, 1977; The Thistle and the Crown, 1985; Playing the Scottish Card: the Franco-Jacobite invasion of 1708, 1988; (contrib.) The '45: to keep an image whole, 1988; (jtly) The Jacobite Threat: a source book, 1990; (jtly) Summer Hunting a Prince, 1992; Lochiel of the '45, 1994; Edinburgh in the '45, 1995; The Gentle Lochiel, 1998. *Recreation:* historical research. *Died 15 May 2008.*

GIBSON, Robin Warwick, OBE 2001; art historian and writer; Chief Curator, National Portrait Gallery, 1994–2001; *b* 3 May 1944; *s* of Walter Edward Gibson and Freda Mary Yates (*née* Partridge). *Educ:* Royal

Masonic Sch., Bushey; Magdalene Coll., Cambridge (BA 1966). Asst Keeper, City Art Gall., Manchester, 1967–68; National Portrait Gallery: Asst Keeper, 1968–83; Curator, Twentieth Century Collection, 1983–94. Member of Committee: NT Foundn for Art, 1991–2000; Fry Art Gall., Saffron Walden, 2008–. *Publications:* The McDonald Collection, 1970; (jtly) British Portrait Painters, 1971; Flower Painting, 1976; The Clarendon Collection, 1977; 20th Century Portraits, 1978; Glyn Philpot, 1984; John Bellany: new portraits, 1986; (jtly) Madame Yevonde, 1990; John Bratby Portraits, 1991; The Portrait Now, 1993; (jtly) The Sitwells, 1994; (jtly) Glenys Barton, 1997; The Face in the Corner, 1998; (jtly) Painting the Century, 2000; contrib. to Oxford DNB; various catalogue essays; articles and reviews for Burlington Mag., Museums Jl, The Independent, Folio, Modern Painters. *Recreations:* composing music, village organist, plants, my dog, paintings other than portraiture. *Address:* Maple Cottage, 1 The Bull Ring, Thaxted, Essex CM6 2PL; *e-mail:* robline@btinternet.com. *Died 9 Aug. 2010.*

GIBSON-BARBOZA, Mario, Hon. GCMG 1968; Brazilian Ambassador to the Court of St James's, 1982–86; *b* Olinda, Pernambuco, 13 March 1918; *s* of Oscar Bartholomeu Alves Barboza and Evangelina Gibson Barboza; *m* 1975, Julia Blacker Baldassarri Gibson-Barboza. *Educ:* Law School of Recife, Pernambuco (graduated in Law, 1937); Superior War College, 1951. Entered Brazilian Foreign Service, 1940; served: Houston, Washington and Brussels, 1943–54; Minister-Counsellor: Buenos Aires, 1956–59; Brazilian Mission to United Nations, New York, 1959–60; Ambassador: to Vienna, 1962–66; to Asunción, 1967–68; Secretary General for Foreign Affairs, 1968–69; Ambassador to Washington, 1969; Minister of State for External Relations, 1969–74; Ambassador: to Athens, 1974–77; to Rome, 1977–82. Several Grand Crosses of Orders of Brazil and other countries. *Recreations:* riding, reading, theatre. *Clubs:* Athenæum, Travellers, White's; Jockey Clube Brasileiro (Rio de Janeiro). *Died 26 Nov. 2007.*

GIDDINGS, Air Marshal Sir (Kenneth Charles) Michael, KCB 1975; OBE 1953; DFC 1945; AFC 1950 and Bar 1955; *b* 27 Aug. 1920; *s* of Charles Giddings and Grace Giddings (*née* Gregory); *m* 1946, Elizabeth McConnell; two *s* two *d*. *Educ:* Ealing Grammar Sch. Conscripted, RAF, 1940; Comd, 129 Sqdn, 1944; Empire Test Pilots Sch., 1946; Test pilot, RAE, 1947–50; HQ Fighter Command, 1950–52; RAF Staff Coll., 1953; OC, Flying Wing, Waterbeach, 1954–56; CFE, 1956–58; OC, 57 Sqdn, 1958–60; Group Captain Ops, Bomber Command, 1960–62; Supt of Flying, A&AEE, 1962–64; Dir Aircraft Projects, MoD, 1964–66; AOC, Central Reconnaissance Estabt, 1967–68; ACAS (Operational Requirements), 1968–71; Chief of Staff No 18 (M) Group, Strike Command, RAF, 1971–73; Dep. Chief of Defence Staff, Op. Requirements, 1973–76. Dir, Nat. Counties Building Soc., 1982–85. Ind. Panel Inspector, DoE, 1979–91. *Recreations:* golf, gardening, music. *Address:* 16 Grasmere Court, Wordsworth Road, Worthing, W Sussex BN11 3JE. *T:* (01903) 205731. *Died 5 April 2009.*

GIFFARD, Adam Edward; *b* 3 June 1934; *o s* of 3rd Earl of Halsbury, FRS; *S* father as 4th Earl, 2000, but did not use the title; *m* 1976, Joanna Elizabeth, *d* of late Frederick Harry Cole; two *d*. *Educ:* Jesus Coll., Cambridge (MA 1961); BSc Open Univ. 1995. *Died 31 Dec. 2010 (ext).*

GILBERT, Prof. Alan David, AO 2008; DPhil; first President and Vice-Chancellor, University of Manchester, 2004–10; *b* 11 Sept. 1944; *s* of Garnet E. Gilbert and Violet Gilbert (*née* Elsey); *m* 1967, Ingrid Sara Griffiths; two *d*. *Educ:* ANU (BA Hons 1965; MA 1967); Oxford Univ. (DPhil History 1973). Lectr, Univ. of Papua New Guinea, 1967–69; University of New South Wales: Lectr, 1973–77; Sen. Lectr, 1977–79; Associate Prof., 1979–81; Prof. of History, 1981–88; Pro-Vice-

Chancellor, 1988–91; Vice-Chancellor: Univ. of Tasmania, 1991–95; Univ. of Melbourne, 1996–2004. Member: Australian Higher Educn Council, 1991–95; Council for Sci. and Technol., 2007–; UK Commn for Employment and Skills, 2007–. FASSA 1990. Hon. degrees: Tasmania; McGill; Melbourne; Edinburgh, 2004. *Publications:* Religion and Society in Industrial England, 1976; The Making of Post-Christian Britain, 1980; (with R. Currie and L. Horsley) Churches and Churchgoers, 1977; (Gen. Editor) Australians: a historical library, 11 Vols, 1987. *Recreation:* golf. *Address:* c/o Office of the President and Vice-Chancellor, University of Manchester, Oxford Road, Manchester M13 9PL.
Died 27 July 2010.

GILBERT, Michael Francis, CBE 1980; TD 1950; crime writer; *b* 17 July 1912; *s* of Bernard Samuel Gilbert and Berwyn Minna Cuthbert; *m* 1947, Roberta Mary, *d* of Col R. M. W. Marsden; two *s* five *d. Educ:* Blundell's Sch.; London University. LLB 1937. Served War of 1939–45, Hon. Artillery Co., 12th Regt RHA, N Africa and Italy (despatches 1943). Joined Trower Still & Keeling, 1947 (Partner, 1952–83). Legal Adviser to Govt of Bahrain, 1960. Member: Arts Council Cttee on Public Lending Right, 1968; Royal Literary Fund, 1969; Council of Soc. of Authors, 1975; (Founder) Crime Writers' Assoc. (Diamond Dagger, 1994); Mystery Writers of America, Grand Master, 1987. FRSL 1999. *Publications: novels:* Close Quarters, 1947; They Never Looked Inside, 1948; The Doors Open, 1949; Smallbone Deceased, 1950; Death has Deep Roots, 1951; Death in Captivity, 1952; Fear to Tread, 1953; Sky High, 1955; Be Shot for Sixpence, 1956; The Tichborne Claimant, 1957; Blood and Judgement, 1958; After the Fine Weather, 1963; The Crack in the Tea Cup, 1965; The Dust and the Heat, 1967; The Etruscan Net, 1969; The Body of a Girl, 1972; The Ninety Second Tiger, 1973; Flash Point, 1974; The Night of the Twelfth, 1976; The Empty House, 1978; Death of a Favourite Girl, 1980; The Final Throw, 1983; The Black Seraphim, 1983; The Long Journey Home, 1985; Trouble, 1987; Paint Gold and Blood, 1989; The Queen against Karl Mullen, 1991; Roller Coaster, 1993; Ring of Terror, 1995; Into Battle, 1997; Over and Out, 1998; *short stories:* Game Without Rules, 1967; Stay of Execution, 1971; Petrella at Q, 1977; Mr Calder and Mr Behrens, 1982; Young Petrella, 1988; Anything for a Quiet Life, 1990; *plays:* A Clean Kill; The Bargain; Windfall; The Shot in Question; *edited:* Crime in Good Company, 1959; The Oxford Book of Legal Anecdotes, 1986; The Fraudsters, 1988; Prep School, 1991; has also written radio and TV scripts. *Recreations:* walking, contract bridge. *Address:* The Old Rectory, Luddesdown, Gravesend, Kent DA13 0XE. *T:* (01474) 814272. *Died 8 Feb. 2006.*

GILBERT, Patrick Nigel Geoffrey; General Secretary of the Society for Promoting Christian Knowledge, 1971–92; *b* 12 May 1934; adopted *s* of late Geoffrey Gilbert and Evelyn (*née* Miller), Devon. *Educ:* Cranleigh Sch.; Merton Coll., Oxford. Lectr, S Berks Coll. of Further Educn, 1959–62; PA to Sir Edward Hulton, 1962–64; OUP, 1964–69; Linguaphone Group (Westinghouse), 1969–71 (Man. Dir in Group, 1970). World Assoc. for Christian Communication: Trustee, 1975–87; European Vice-Chm., 1975–82; representative to EEC, 1975–82, to Conf. of Eur. Churches, 1976–82, to Council of Europe, 1976–82, and to Central Cttee, 1979–84. Member: Bd for Mission and Unity of Gen. Synod, 1971–78 (Mem. Exec., 1971–76); Archbishops' Cttee on RC Relations, 1971–81; Church Inf. Cttee, 1978–81; Church Publishing Cttee, 1980–84; Council, Conf. of British Missionary Socs, 1971–78; Council, Christians Abroad, 1974–79; Exec., Anglican Centre, Rome, 1981–91 (Vice Chm. of Friends, 1984–91); British National Cttee, UNESCO World Book Congress, 1982. Greater London Arts Association: Mem. Exec., 1968–78; Hon. Life Mem., 1978; Chm., 1980–84 (Dep. Chm., 1979–80); Initiator, 1972 Festivals of London. Art Workers' Guild: Hon. Brother, 1971; Chm. Trustees and Hon. Treas., 1976–86 (Trustee, 1975).

Chairman: Gp Eight Opera, 1962–72; Standing Conf. of London Arts Councils, 1975–78; Embroiderers' Guild, 1977–78 (Hon. Treas., 1974–77); Concord Multicultural Arts Trust, 1980–89; Harold Buxton Trust, 1983–92; Nikaean Club, 1984–92; Vice-President: Camden Arts Council, 1974–89 (Chm., 1970–74); Nat. Assoc. of Local Arts Councils, 1980–89 (Founder Chm., 1976–80); Mem., Arts Adv. Cttee, CRE, 1979; Steward, Artists' Gen. Benevolent Instn, 1971–93. Rep. of Archbishop of Canterbury to Inter-Church Travel, 1987–92; Consultant, Saga Travel, 1994–98. Trustee: Overseas Bishoprics Fund, 1971–92; All Saints Trust, 1978–92 (Chairman: F and GP and Investment Cttees); Schulze Trust, 1980–83 (Chm.); Dancers' Resettlement Fund, 1982–90 (Chm., Finance Cttee); Richards Trust, 1971–92; ACC Res. Fund, 1982–84; Vis. Trustee, Seabury Press, NY, 1978–80; Chm., Dancers' Resettlement Trust, 1987–90. Member, Executive: GBGSA, 1981–84, 1988–89; Assoc. of Vol. Colls, 1979–87; Member, Governing Body: SPCK India, 1971–92; SPCK Australia, 1977–92; SPCK (USA), 1984–92; SPCK NZ, 1989–92; Partners for World Mission, 1979–92; Governor: Contemp. Dance Trust, 1981–90; All Saints Coll., Tottenham, 1971–78; St Martin's Sch. for Girls, 1971–92 (Vice Chm., 1978–91); Rep. to Tertiary Educn Council, 1983–89); Ellesmere Coll., 1977–87 (Mem ISCO Exec., 1984–86); St Michael's Sch., Petworth, 1978–88 (rcp. to GBGSA); Roehampton Inst., 1978–92 (rep. to Assoc. of Vol. Colls, 1978–88; Chm., Audit Cttee, 1989–92); Pusey House, 1985–92; Patron, Pusey House Appeal, 1984–88; Fellow, Corp. of SS Mary and Nicholas (Woodard Schs), 1972–92 (Mem. Exec., 1981–92; Chm., S Div. Res. Cttee, 1972–84; Trustee, Endowment Fund, Dir, Corp. Trustee Co.). Member Development Cttee: SPAB, 1985–87; London Symphony Chorus, 1985–87; Nat. Sch. of Osteopathy, 1986–90; Bd Mem., Nat. Youth Dance Co., 1988–92; Mem. Council, Publishers Assoc., 1990–92. Cttee, London Europe Soc., 1985–93; Mem. Court, City Univ., 1986–92. Dir, Surrey Building Soc., 1988–93. Dep. Chm. and Chm., Exec. Cttee, Athenæum Club, 1985–89. Hon. Member: Assoc. for Develt in the Arts; Georgia Salzburger Soc., USA, 1986. JP Inner London, 1971–75. Freeman, City of London, 1966; Liveryman, Worshipful Co. of Woolmen (Master, 1985–86; Rep. to City and Guilds, 1986–92); Parish Clerk, All Hallows, Bread Street, 1981–93; Mem., Guild of Freemen (Court, 1991–93); Hon. Citizen, Savannah, Georgia, 1986. FRSA 1978; FCMI (FBIM 1982); FInstD 1982. Hon. DLitt Columbia Pacific, 1982. Order of St Vladimir, 1977. *Publications:* articles in various jls. *Recreations:* mountain walking, reading, travel, enjoying the Arts, golf. *Address:* 3 The Mount Square, NW3 6SU. *T:* (020) 7794 8893; PO Box 118, Udon Thani 41000, Thailand. *T:* (42) 347338. *Died 16 Aug. 2009.*

GILBERT, Stuart William, CB 1983; Vice-President, Upkeep (Trust for training and education in building maintenance), since 2003 (Trustee, 1988–2002; Chairman, 1993–96); *b* 2 Aug. 1926; *s* of Rodney Stuart Gilbert and Ella Edith (*née* Esgate); *m* 1955, Marjorie Laws Vallance (*d* 2004); one *s* one *d. Educ:* Maidstone Grammar Sch.; Emmanuel Coll., Cambridge (Open Exhibnr and State Scholar; MA). Served RAF, 1944–47. Asst Principal, Min. of Health, 1949; Asst Private Secretary: to Minister of Housing and Local Govt, 1952; to Parly Sec., 1954; Principal, 1955; Sec., Parker Morris Cttee on Housing Standards, 1958–61, Rapporteur to ECE Housing Cttee, 1959–61; Reporter to ILO Conf. on Workers' Housing, 1960; Asst Sec., Local Govt Finance Div., 1964; Under-Sec., DoE, 1970–80 (for New Towns, 1970, Business Rents, 1973, Construction Industries, 1974, Housing, 1974, Planning Land Use, 1977); Dep. Dir, 1980–81, Dir (Dep. Sec.), 1981–86, Dept for Nat. Savings. *Recreations:* computing, music, painting, woodwork. *Address:* Flat 8, Darwin Manor, Jeavons Lane, Great Cambourne, Cambridge CB23 5JH. *T:* (0954) 718192. *Died 23 Nov. 2007.*

GILL, Air Vice-Marshal Bill; *see* Gill, Air Vice-Marshal L. W. G.

GILL, Air Vice-Marshal Harry, CB 1979; OBE 1968; Director-General of Supply, Royal Air Force, 1976–79; *b* 30 Oct. 1922; *s* of John William Gill and Lucy Gill, Newark, Notts; *m* 1951, Diana Patricia, *d* of Colin Wood, Glossop; one *d. Educ:* Barnby Road Sch.; Newark Technical Coll. Entered RAF, 1941; pilot trng, 1942; commnd 1943; flying duties, 1943–49; transf. to Equipment Br., 1949; Officer Commanding: Supply Sqdns, RAF Spitalgate and RAF North Coates, 1949–52; HQ Staff No 93 Maintenance Unit Explosives and Fuels Supply Ops, 1952–55; Explosives and Fuels Sch., 1955–58; Staff Officer Logistics Div., HQ Allied Forces Northern Europe, 1958–61; Head of Provision Br., Air Min., 1961–64; Chief Equipment Officer, No 25 Maintenance Unit, RAF Hartlebury, 1964–66; Equipment Staff Officer, HQ Air Forces Middle East, 1966–67; Dep. Dir Supply Systems, MoD Air, 1968–70; RCDS, 1971; Comdt, RAF Supply Control Centre, 1972–73; Dir, Supply Management, MoD Air, 1973–76. Internat. rifle and pistol shot; Silver Medallist, King's Prize, Bisley, 1951. *Recreations:* shooting, fishing, tennis, cricket, gardening. *Address:* c/o Lloyds TSB, 37 Castlegate, Newark, Notts NG24 1BD. *Club:* Royal Air Force. *Died 20 Jan. 2008.*

GILL, Maj.-Gen. Ian Gordon, CB 1972; OBE 1959 (MBE 1949); MC 1940, Bar 1945; idc, psc; Colonel, 4/7 Royal Dragoon Guards, 1973–78; *b* Rochester, 9 Nov. 1919; *s* of late Brig. Gordon Harry Gill, CMG, DSO and Mrs Doris Gill, Rochester, Kent; *m* 1963, Elizabeth Vivian Rohr, MD, MRCP (*d* 1990), *o d* of late A. F. Rohr; no *c. Educ:* Edinburgh House, Hants; Repton School. Commnd from SRO into 4th/7th Roy. Dragoon Guards, 1938; served with Regt in: BEF, France, 1939–40; BLA, NW Europe, 1944–45 (despatches, 1945); Palestine, 1946–48; Tripolitania, 1951–52; Instructor, Armoured Sch., 1948–50; Staff Coll., Camberley, 1952; Bde Maj., HQ Inf. Bde, 1953–55; comdg 4th/7th RDG, 1957–59; Asst Mil. Sec., HQ, BAOR, 1959–61; Coll. Comdt RMA Sandhurst, 1961–62; Imp. Def. Coll., 1963; Comdr, 7th Armoured Bde, 1964–66; Dep. Mil. Sec. 1, MoD (Army), 1966–68; Head, British Defence Liaison Staff, Dept of Defence, Canberra, 1968–70; Asst Chief of Gen. Staff (Op. Requirements), 1970–72, retired. Hon. Liveryman, Coachmakers' Co., 1974. *Recreations:* equitation, ski-ing, cricket, squash rackets. *Address:* Park House Nursing Home, 27 Park Crescent, Peterborough PE1 4DX. *Clubs:* Cavalry and Guards, MCC. *Died 23 Nov. 2006.*

GILL, Kenneth; General Secretary, Manufacturing, Science, Finance, 1989–92 (Joint General Secretary, 1988–89); Chairman, Morning Star, 1984–95; *b* 30 Aug. 1927; *s* of Ernest Frank Gill and Mary Ethel Gill; *m* 1st, 1953, Jacqueline Manley (marr. diss. 1964); 2nd, 1967, S. Tess Paterson (marr. diss. 1990); two *s* one *d*; 3rd, 1997, Norma Bramley. *Educ:* Chippenham Secondary School. Engrg apprentice, 1943–48; Draughtsman Designer, Project Engr, Sales Engr in various cos, 1948–62; District Organiser, Liverpool and Ireland TASS, 1962–68; Editor, TASS Union Jl, 1968–72; Dep. Gen. Sec., 1972–74; Gen. Sec. AUEW (TASS), 1974–86, TASS—the Manufacturing Union, 1986–88. Pres., CSEU, 1988–89. Mem., Gen. Council, TUC, 1974–92 (Chm., 1985–86); Pres. of TUC, 1985–86. Mem., Commn for Racial Equality, 1981–87. Hon. Pres., Cuba Solidarity Campaign, 2008– (Chm., 1992–2008). *Recreations:* sketching, political caricaturing. *Address:* c/o Cuba Solidarity Campaign, Unite, Woodberry, 218 Green Lanes, N4 2HB. *T:* (020) 8800 0155. *Died 23 May 2009.*

GILL, Air Vice-Marshal Leonard William George, (Bill), DSO 1945; Consultant in personnel planning, since 1973; Director, Merton Associates, since 1979 (Chairman, 1984–94); Consultant, Randle Cooke & Associates, since 1994; Senior Consultant, MSL (formerly Austin Knight Ltd), since 1997; Managing Director,

Windsor Personnel Consultants, since 1999; *b* 31 March 1918; *s* of L. W. Gill, Hornchurch, Essex and Marguerite Gill; *m* 1st, 1943, Joan Favill Appleyard (marr. diss.); two *s* two *d*; 2nd, Mrs Constance Mary Cull. *Educ:* University Coll. Sch., London. Joined RAF, 1937; served in Far East until 1942; then UK as night fighter pilot; comd No 68 Sqdn for last 6 months of war; subseq. served in various appts incl. comd of Nos 85 and 87 night fighter Sqdns and tour on directing staff at RAF Staff Coll.; Stn Comdr No 1 Flying Trng Sch., Linton-on-Ouse, 1957–60; Dir of Overseas Ops, 1960–62; Nat. Def. Coll. of Canada, 1962–63; Dir of Organisation (Estabs), 1963–66; SASO, RAF Germany, 1966–68; Dir-Gen., Manning (RAF), MoD, 1968–73, retired. Manpower and Planning Advr, P&O Steam Navigation Co., 1973–79. Vice-Pres., RAF Assoc., 1973– (Pres. E Area, 1974–81; Vice-Chm., Central Council, 1984–88); Pres., Mosquito Aircrew Assoc., 2003–. Chm., River Thames Soc., 1994–2000. FIPD; FCMI. Order of King George of Bohemia (Czech and Slovak Republic), 1991. *Recreations:* shooting, cricket, boats, amateur woodwork. *Address:* Flat 15, 35 Cranley Gardens, Kensington, SW7 3BD. *T:* (020) 7370 2716. *Clubs:* Royal Air Force; Phyllis Court (Henley). *Died 13 July 2007.*

GILL, His Honour Stanley Sanderson; a Circuit Judge, 1972–87; *b* Wakefield, 3 Dec. 1923; *s* of Sanderson Henry Briggs Gill, OBE and Dorothy Margaret Gill (*née* Bennett); *m* 1954, Margaret Mary Patricia Grady; two *d* (one *s* decd). *Educ:* Queen Elizabeth Grammar Sch., Wakefield; Magdalene Coll., Cambridge (MA). Served in RAF, 1942–46: 514 and 7 (Pathfinder) Sqdns, Flt Lt 1945. Called to the Bar, Middle Temple, 1950; Asst Recorder of Bradford, 1966; Dep. Chm., WR Yorks QS, 1968; County Court Judge, 1971. Mem., County Court Rule Cttee, 1980–84. Chm., Rent Assessment Cttee, 1966–71. *Recreations:* walking, reading, music, history, painting. *Address:* 19 Hereford Court, Hereford Road, Harrogate HG1 2PX. *Died 20 Dec. 2010.*

GILLESPIE, Prof. John Spence; Head of Department of Pharmacology, Glasgow University, 1968–92; *b* 5 Sept. 1926; *s* of Matthew Forsyth Gillespie and Myrtle Murie Spence; *m* 1956, Jemima Simpson Ross; four *s* one *d. Educ:* Dumbarton Academy; Glasgow Univ. MB ChB (Commendation), PhD. FRCP; FRSE. Hosp. Residency (Surgery), 1949–50; Nat. Service as RMO, 1950–52; hosp. appts, 1952–53; McCunn Res. Schol. in Physiology, Glasgow Univ., 1953–55; Faulds Fellow then Sharpey Schol. in Physiology Dept, University Coll. London, 1955–57; Glasgow University: Lectr in Physiol., 1957–59; Sophie Fricke Res. Fellow, Royal Soc., in Rockefeller Inst., 1959–60; Sen. Lectr in Physiol., 1961–63; Henry Head Res. Fellow, Royal Soc., 1963–68; Vice-Principal, 1983–87, 1988–91. *Publications:* articles in Jls of Physiol. and Pharmacol. *Recreations:* gardening, painting. *Address:* 5 Boclair Road, Bearsden, Glasgow G61 2AE. *T:* (0141) 943 1395. *Died 8 Nov. 2009.*

GILLETT, Sir Robin (Danvers Penrose), 2nd Bt *cr* 1959; GBE 1976; RD 1965; Underwriting Member of Lloyd's; Lord Mayor of London for 1976–77; *b* 9 Nov. 1925; *o s* of Sir (Sydney) Harold Gillett, 1st Bt, MC, and Audrey Isabel Penrose Wardlaw (*d* 1962); *S* father, 1976; *m* 1950, Elizabeth Marion Grace (*d* 1997), *e d* of late John Findlay, JP, Busby, Lanarks; two *s*; *m* 2000, Alwyne Winifred Cox (separated), JP, *widow* of His Honour Albert Edward Cox. *Educ:* Nautical Coll., Pangbourne. Served Canadian Pacific Steamships, 1943–60; Master Mariner 1951; Staff Comdr 1957; Hon. Comdr RNR 1971. Elder Brother of Trinity House; Fellow and Founder Mem., Nautical Inst. City of London (Ward of Bassishaw): Common Councilman 1965–69; Alderman 1969–96; Sheriff 1973; one of HM Lieuts for City of London, 1975; Chm. Civil Defence Cttee, 1967–68; Pres., City of London Civil Defence Instructors Assoc., 1967–78; Vice-Pres., City of London Centre, St John Ambulance Assoc.; Pres., Nat. Waterways Transport Assoc., 1979–83; Dep. Commonwealth Pres., Royal Life

Saving Soc., 1981–96; Chm. Council, Maritime Volunteer Service, 1998–2000, Gov., 2000–. Vice-Chm., PLA, 1979–84. Master, Hon. Co. of Master Mariners, 1979–80. Trustee, Nat. Maritime Mus., 1982–92. Chm. of Governors, Pangbourne Coll., 1978–92. Chancellor, City Univ., 1976–77. FIAM (Pres., 1980–84; Gold Medal, 1982); FRCM 1991. Hon. DSc City, 1976. Gentleman Usher of the Purple Rod, Order of the British Empire, 1985–2000. KStJ 1977 (OStJ 1974). Gold Medal, Administrative Management Soc., USA, 1983. Officer, Order of Leopard, Zaire, 1973; Comdr, Order of Dannebrog, 1974; Order of Johan Sedia Mahkota (Malaysia), 1974; Grand Cross of Municipal Merit (Lima), 1977. *Publications:* A Fish out of Water (autobiog.), 2001; Dogwatch Doggerel, 2004. *Recreation:* sailing. *Heir:* s Nicholas Danvers Penrose Gillett, BSc, ARCS [b 24 Sept. 1955; m 1987, Haylie (marr. diss. 1998), er d of Dennis Brooks]. *Clubs:* City Livery, City Livery Yacht (Admiral), Guildhall, Royal Yacht Squadron, Royal London Yacht (Cdre, 1984–85), St Katharine's Yacht (Admiral).
Died 21 April 2009.

GILLINGHAM, (Francis) John, CBE 1982 (MBE mil. 1944); FRSE 1970; Professor of Neurological Surgery, University of Edinburgh, 1963–80, then Emeritus; at Royal Infirmary of Edinburgh and Western General Hospital, Edinburgh, 1963–80; Consultant Neuro-Surgeon to the Army in Scotland, 1966–80; b 15 March 1916; s of John H. Gillingham, Upwey, Dorset; m 1945, Irene, (Judy), Jude; three s (and one s decd). *Educ:* Hardye's Sch., Dorset; St Bartholomew's Hosp. Medical Coll., London. Matthews Duncan Gold Medal, 1939, MRCS, LRCP Oct. 1939; MB BS (London) Nov. 1939; FRCS 1947; FRCSE 1955; FRCPE 1967. Prof. of Surgical Neurol., King Saud Univ. Saudi Arabia, 1983–85, then Emeritus. Advr in Neuro-Surgery, MoD, Kingdom of Saudi Arabia, 1980–83. Hon. Consultant in Neurosurgery, St Bartholomew's Hosp., London, 1981–. Hunterian Prof., RCS, 1957; Morison Lectr, RCP of Edinburgh, 1960; Colles Lectr, College of Surgeons of Ireland, 1962; Elsberg Lectr, College of Physicians and Surgeons, NY, 1967; Penfield Lectr, Middle East Med. Assembly, 1970; Syme Derby Lectr, Univ. of Hong Kong, 1982; Adlington Syme Oration, RACS, 1983. Hon. Mem., Soc. de Neurochirurgie de Langue Française, 1964; Hon. Mem., Soc. of Neurol. Surgeons (USA), 1965; Hon. Mem., Royal Academy of Medicine of Valencia, 1967; Hon. and Corresp. Mem. of a number of foreign neuro-surgical societies; Hon. Pres., World Fedn of Neurosurgical Socs. President: Medico-Chirurgical Soc. of Edinburgh, 1965–67; European Soc. of Stereostatic and Functional Neurosurgery, 1972–76; RCSE, 1979–82 (Vice-Pres., 1974–77; Mem., Court of Regents, 1990–2001). FRSA 1991. Hon. FRACS 1980; Hon. FCS Sri Lanka 1980; Hon. FRCSI 1981; Hon. FRCSGlas 1982. Hon. MD Thessaloniki, 1973. Jim Clark Foundn Award, 1979; Medal of City of Gdansk, Poland, 1980; Medal, Soc. of British Neurological Surgeons, 2008. *Publications:* Clinical Surgery: Neurological Surgery, 1969; Parkinson's Disease, 1969; Head Injuries, 1971; papers on surgical management of cerebral vascular disease, head and spinal injuries, Parkinsonism and the dyskinesias, epilepsy and other neurosurgical subjects. *Recreations:* sailing, travel, gardening (cactus). *Address:* 6 Prebendal Court, Station Road, Shipton-under-Wychwood, Chipping Norton, Oxon OX7 6BB. *Club:* Nautico (Javea, Alicante).
Died 3 Jan. 2010.

GILMOUR OF CRAIGMILLAR, Baron cr 1992 (Life Peer), of Craigmillar in the District of the City of Edinburgh; **Ian Hedworth John Little Gilmour;** PC 1973; Bt 1926; b 8 July 1926; er s of Lt-Col Sir John Little Gilmour, 2nd Bt, and Hon. Victoria Laura, OBE, TD (d 1991), d of late Viscount Chelsea (e s of 5th Earl Cadogan); S father, 1977; m 1951, Lady Caroline Margaret Montagu-Douglas-Scott, yr d of 8th Duke of Buccleuch and Queensberry, KT, GCVO, PC; four s one d. *Educ:* Eton; Balliol Coll., Oxford (Hon. Fellow, 1999). Served with Grenadier Guards, 1944–47; 2nd Lieut 1945.

Called to the Bar, Inner Temple, 1952. Editor, The Spectator, 1954–59. MP (C) Norfolk Central, Nov. 1962–1974, Chesham and Amersham, 1974–92. Parly Under-Sec. of State, MoD, 1970–71; Minister of State: for Defence Procurement, MoD, 1971–72; for Defence, 1972–74; Sec. of State for Defence, 1974; Lord Privy Seal, 1979–81. Chm., Cons. Res. Dept, 1974–75. President: Med. Aid for Palestinians, 1993–96; Foundn of Al-Quds Med. Sch., 1996–; HACAN Clearskies, 1999–2005. Chm., Byron Soc., 2003–06; Pres., Isleworth Soc., 1993–. DU Essex, 1995. *Publications:* The Body Politic, 1969; Inside Right: a study of Conservatism, 1977; Britain Can Work, 1983; Riot, Risings and Revolution: governance and violence in 18th Century England, 1992; Dancing with Dogma: Britain under Thatcherism, 1992; (jtly) Whatever Happened to the Tories: a history of the Conservative Party since 1945, 1997; The Making of the Poets: the early lives of Byron and Shelley, 2002. *Heir:* (to baronetcy): s Hon. David Robert Gilmour [b 14 Nov. 1952; m 1975, Sarah Anne, d of M. H. G. Bradstock; one s three d]. *Address:* The Ferry House, Old Isleworth, Middx TW7 6BD. T. (020) 8560 6769. *Clubs:* Pratt's, White's.
Died 21 Sept. 2007.

GILMOUR, Alexander Clement, CVO 1990; Chairman, On Bourse Ltd, since 2001; b 23 Aug. 1931; s of Sir John Little Gilmour, 2nd Bt, and Lady Mary Gilmour; m 1st, 1954, Barbara M. L. Constance Berry (marr. diss. 1983); two s one d; 2nd, 1983, Susan Lady Chetwode. *Educ:* Eton. National Service, commn in Black Watch, 1950–52. With Joseph Sebag & Co. (subseq. Carr, Sebag), 1954–82; Director: Safeguard Industrial Investments, 1974–84; Tide (UK) Ltd, 1986–87; Exec. Dir, Equity Finance Trust Ltd, 1984–86. Dir, SW London, subseq. Thames, Community Foundn, 1995–2000. Consultant, Grieveson Grant, 1982. Chm., Nat. Playing Fields Assoc., 1976–88 (Past-Chm. Appeals Cttee, 10 yrs). Dir, Tate Gallery Foundn, 1986–88. Governor, LSE, 1969 (Hon. Fellow, 2002). *Recreations:* tennis, fishing, gardening. *Address:* c/o Drummonds Branch, Royal Bank of Scotland, 49 Charing Cross, SW1A 2DX. *Club:* Queen's.
Died 5 Jan. 2009.

GILMOUR, Col Sir John (Edward), 3rd Bt cr 1897; DSO 1945; TD; JP; Lord-Lieutenant of Fife, 1980–87 (Vice Lord-Lieutenant, 1979–80); Lord High Commissioner, General Assembly of the Church of Scotland, 1982 and 1983; b 24 Oct. 1912; o s of Col Rt Hon. Sir John Gilmour, 2nd Bt, GCVO, DSO, MP, and Mary Louise (d 1919), e d of late E. T. Lambert, Telham Court, Battle, Sussex; S father, 1940; m 1941, Ursula Mabyn (d 2004), yr d of late F. O. Wills; two s. *Educ:* Eton; Trinity Hall, Cambridge. Served War of 1939–45 (DSO). Bt Col 1950; Captain, Royal Company of Archers (Queen's Body Guard for Scotland); Hon. Col, The Highland Yeomanry, RAC, T&AVR, 1971–75. MP (C) East Fife, 1961–79. Chm., Cons. and Unionist Party in Scotland, 1965–67. DL Fife, 1953. *Heir:* s John Gilmour [b 15 July 1944; m 1967, Valerie, yr d of late G. W. Russell, and of Mrs William Wilson; two s two d]. *Address:* Montrave, Leven, Fife KY8 5NZ. *T:* (01333) 426159. *Club:* Royal & Ancient Golf (St Andrews).
Died 1 June 2007.

GINGELL, Air Chief Marshal Sir John, GBE 1984 (CBE 1973; MBE 1962); KCB 1978; KCVO 1992; Gentleman Usher of the Black Rod, Serjeant-at-Arms, House of Lords, and Secretary to the Lord Great Chamberlain, 1985–92; b 3 Feb. 1925; e s of late E. J. Gingell; m 1949, Prudence, d of late Brig. R. F. Johnson; two s one d. *Educ:* St Boniface Coll., Plymouth. Entered RAF, 1943; Fleet Air Arm, 1945–46 as Sub-Lt (A) RNVR; returned to RAF, 1951; served with Nos 58 and 542 Sqdns; CFS 1954; psc 1959; jssc 1965; comd No 27 Sqdn, 1963–65; Staff of Chief of Defence Staff, 1966; Dep. Dir Defence Ops Staff (Central Staff), 1966–67; Mil. Asst to Chm. NATO Mil. Cttee, Brussels, 1968–70; AOA, RAF Germany, 1971–72; AOC 23 Group, RAF Trng Comd, 1973–75; Asst Chief of Defence Staff (Policy), 1975–78; Air

Member for Personnel, 1978–80; AOC-in-C, RAF Support Comd, 1980–81; Dep. C-in-C, Allied Forces Central Europe, 1981–84. Mem., Commonwealth War Graves Commn, 1986–91. Hon. Bencher, Inner Temple, 1990. *Recreations:* gardening, walking, music. *Club:* Royal Air Force.   *Died 10 Dec. 2009.*

GINZBURG, Prof. Vitaly Lazarevich, PhD, DSc; Professor, P. N. Lebedev Physical Institute, Russian Academy of Sciences; *b* 4 Oct. 1916; *s* of late Lazar Efimovich Ginzburg and Augusta Veniaminovna Vildauer-Ginzburg; *m* 1st, 1937, Olga Zamsha (marr. diss. 1946); one *d*; 2nd, 1946, Nina Ivanovna Ermakova. *Educ:* Moscow State Univ. (PhD 1940; DSc 1942). P. N. Lebedev Physical Inst., USSR, subseq. Russian, Acad. of Scis, 1940–: Hd, I. E. Tamm Theory Dept, 1971–88. Visiting Professor: Gorky State Univ., 1945–68; Moscow Inst. for Physics and Technol., 1968–. (Jtly) Nobel Prize for Physics, 2003. *Publications include:* Propagation of Electromagnetic Waves in Plasma, 1961; (jtly) Spatial Dispersion in Crystal Optics and the Theory of Exitons, 1966; (jtly) The Origin of Cosmic Rays, 1964; Theoretical Physics and Astrophysics, 1979; (jtly) High-Temperature Superconductivity, 1982; Waynflete Lectures on Physics, 1983; Physics and Astrophysics: a selection of key problems, 1985; (jtly) Astrophysics of Cosmic Rays, 1990; (jtly) Transition Radiation and Transition Scattering, 1990; (jtly) Superconductivity, 1994; The Physics of a Lifetime, 2001; articles in learned jls. *Address:* I. E. Tamm Theory Department, P. N. Lebedev Physical Institute, Russian Academy of Sciences, 53 Leninsky prospect, Moscow 119991, Russia.
Died 8 Nov. 2009.

GIOLITTI, Dr Antonio; Member, Commission of the European Communities, 1977–85; Senator, Italian Parliament, 1987–92; *b* 12 Feb. 1915; *s* of Giuseppe and Maria Giolitti; *m* 1939, Elena d'Amico; one *s* two *d*. *Educ:* Rome Univ. (Dr Law); Oxford; München. Dep., Italian Parlt, 1946–76; Minister of Budget and Economic Planning, 1964, 1970–72, 1973–74. Member: Italian Communist Party, 1943–57; Italian Socialist Party, 1958–83; Exec., Italian Socialist Party, 1958–83; Sinistra Indipendente, 1987–92. *Publications:* Riforme e rivoluzione, 1957; Il comunismo in Europa, 1960; Un socialismo possibile, 1967; Lettere a Marta, 1992. *Recreations:* music, walking. *Address:* Piazza Cairoli 6, 00186 Rome, Italy.   *Died 8 Feb. 2010.*

GIRDWOOD, Prof. Ronald Haxton, CBE 1984; MD, PhD, FRCP, FRCPE, FRCPI; FRCPath; FRSE 1978; Professor of Therapeutics and Clinical Pharmacology, University of Edinburgh, 1962–82, then Emeritus; President, Royal College of Physicians of Edinburgh, 1982–85; *b* 19 March 1917; *s* of late Thomas Girdwood and Elizabeth Stewart Girdwood (*née* Haxton); *m* 1945, Mary Elizabeth, *d* of late Reginald Williams, Calstock, Cornwall; one *s* one *d*. *Educ:* Daniel Stewart's Coll., Edinburgh; University of Edinburgh (MB, ChB (Hons) 1939); Ettles Schol., Leslie Gold Medallist, Royal Victoria Hosp.; Tuberculosis Trust Gold Medallist, Wightman, Beaney and Keith Memorial Prize Winner, 1939; MD (Gold Medal for thesis), 1954. Pres. Edinburgh Univ. Church of Scotland Soc., 1938–39. Served RAMC, 1942–46 (mentioned in Orders); Nutrition Research Officer and Officer i/c Med. Div. in India and Burma. Lectr in Medicine, University of Edinburgh, 1946; Rockefeller Research Fellow, University of Michigan, 1948–49; Cons. Phys., Chalmers Hosp., Edinburgh, 1950–51; Sen. Lectr in Med., 1951–58; Vis. Lectr, Dept of Pharmacology, Yale Univ., 1956; Reader in Med., 1958, Dean of Faculty of Medicine, 1975–79, Edinburgh Univ.; Consultant Physician, Royal Infirmary of Edinburgh, 1951–82. Sometime External Examiner for Universities of London, Sheffield, St Andrews, Dundee, Dublin, Glasgow and Hong Kong, and for Med. Colls in Singapore, Dhaka and Karachi. Chm., SE Scotland Blood Transfusion Assoc., 1970–95; Mem. Council, RCPE, 1966–70, 1978–80, Vice-Pres., 1981–82, Pres. 1982–85; Member: South-Eastern Reg. Hosp. Board (Scotland),

1965–69; Board of Management, Royal Infirmary, Edinburgh, 1958–64; Cttee on Safety of Medicines, 1972–83; Exec., Medico-Pharmaceutical Forum, 1972–74 (Vice-Chm., 1983–85; Chm., 1985–87); Chairman: Scottish Group of Hæmophilia Soc., 1954–60; Non-Professorial Medical Teachers and Research Workers Gp Cttee (Scot.) of BMA, 1956–62; Scottish Gp of Nutrition Soc., 1961–62; Consultative Council, Edinburgh Medical Gp, 1977–82; Scottish Nat. Blood Transfusion Assoc., 1980–95; Pres. Brit. Soc. for Hæmatology, 1963–64; Member: Coun. Brit. Soc. of Gastroenterology, 1964–68; Council of Nutrition Soc., 1957–60 and 1961–64; Pres., Univ. of Edinburgh Graduates' Assoc., 1991–93 (Vice-Pres., 1989–91). British Council visitor to W African Hosps, 1963, to Middle East, 1977, to India, 1980; Visiting Prof. and WHO Consultant, India, 1965, Pakistan, 1985. Gov., St Columba's Hospice, 1985–97. Former Chm., Bd of Management, Scottish Med. Jl and Mem., Editl Bds, Blood, and British Jl of Haematology; Mem. Editl Bd, Brit. Jl of Nutrition, 1960–65. Mem., Greenbank Ch, Edinburgh, 2002–. Awarded Freedom of the township of Sirajgunj, Bangladesh, 1984. Hon. FACP 1983; Hon. FRACP 1985. Cullen Prize, 1970, Lilly Lectr, 1979, RCPE; Suniti Panja gold medal, Calcutta Sch. Trop. Med., 1980; Oliver Meml Award (for services to blood transfusion), 1991. *Publications:* about 350, particularly in relation to nutrition, hæmatology, gastroenterology and medical history; (contrib.) Davidson's Principles and Practice of Medicine, all edns 1952–81; (ed with A. N. Smith) Malabsorption, 1969; (ed with S. Alstead) Textbook of Medical Treatment, 12th edn 1971 to 14th edn 1978, (ed with J. Petrie) 15th edn, 1987 (trans. Spanish, 1992); (ed) Blood Disorders due to Drugs and Other Agents, 1973; (ed) Clinical Pharmacology, 23rd edn 1976 to 25th edn 1984; Travels with a Stethoscope, 1991. *Recreations:* photography, writing.
Died 25 April 2006.

GIVEN, Edward Ferguson, CMG 1968; CVO 1979; HM Diplomatic Service, retired; *b* 13 April 1919; *s* of James K. Given, West Kilbride, Ayrshire; *m* 1st, 1946, Philida Naomi Bullwinkle; one *s*; 2nd, 1954, Kathleen Margaret Helena Kelly. *Educ:* Sutton County Sch.; University Coll., London. Served RA, 1939–46. Entered HM Foreign Service, 1946; served at Paris, Rangoon, Bahrain, Bordeaux, Office of Political Adviser to C-in-C Far East, Singapore, Moscow, Beirut; Ambassador: United Republic of Cameroon and Republic of Equatorial Guinea, 1972–75; Bahrain, 1975–79, retired, 1979. Dir-Gen., Middle East Assoc., 1979–83. *Address:* 16 Monmouth Court, Church Lane, Lymington, Hants SO41 3RB.   *Died 5 Feb. 2006.*

GLANVILLE, Alec William; Assistant Under-Secretary of State, Home Office, 1975–81; *b* 20 Jan. 1921; *y s* of Frank Foster and Alice Glanville; *m* 1941, Lilian Kathleen Hetherton; one *s* one *d*. *Educ:* Portsmouth Northern Secondary Sch.; Portsmouth Municipal Coll. War service, RAMC, 1939–46. Exchequer and Audit Dept, 1939–47; General, Criminal, Police and Probation and After-care Depts, Home Office, 1947–81 (seconded to Cabinet Office, 1956–58); Private Sec. to Permanent Under Sec. of State, 1949–50; Principal Private Sec. to Sec. of State, 1960–63; Sec., Interdepartmental Cttee on Mentally Abnormal Offenders, 1972–75.   *Died 22 Sept. 2008.*

GLANVILLE-JONES, Thomas; *see* Jones.

GLASBY, (Alfred) Ian; HM Diplomatic Service, retired; *b* 18 Sept. 1931; *s* of Frederick William Glasby and Harriet Maria Glasby; *m* 1970, Herma Fletcher; one *d*. *Educ:* Doncaster Grammar Sch.; London School of Economics and Political Science (BSc). Served HM Forces, 1950–52. Home Office, 1952–68; Second Sec., CO, 1968–71; Second, later First Sec. (Commercial and Energy), Washington, 1971–76; Dep. High Comr, Hd of Chancery and Consul, Kampala, 1976; Hd, British Interests Sect., French Embassy, Kampala, 1976–77; First Sec., Hd of Chancery and

Consul, Yaoundé, 1977–81, concurrently non-resident Chargé d'Affaires, Central Afr. Empire, Gabon, and Equatorial Guinea; Asst Hd, Consular Dept, FCO, 1981–84; Dep. Consul Gen., Sydney, 1984–88; Ambassador to People's Republic of the Congo, 1988–90. Director: Trust Co. of Australia (UK) Ltd, 1990–2004; Truco (Australia) Europe Ltd, 1990–2004. Hon. Chevalier, Ordre de Mérite (République Populaire du Congo). *Recreations:* Rugby, cricket, gardening. *Address:* Longridge, 3 Love Lane, Shaftesbury, Dorset SP7 8BG. *T:* (01747) 850389; 5 rue du Collet, Spéracèdes, near Grasse 06530, France. *T:* 493605311. *Clubs:* Royal Commonwealth Society, Lansdowne; Australasian Pioneers, NSW Rugby (Sydney). *Died 17 May 2009.*

GLASS, Norman Jeffrey, CB 2000; Chief Executive, National Centre for Social Research, since 2001; *b* 31 May 1946; *s* of Philip Harris Glass and Anne (*née* Stein); *m* 1974, Marie-Anne Verger; one *s* one *d. Educ:* Trinity Coll., Dublin (BA); Univ. of Amsterdam (Post Grad. Dip). Shell Mex and BP, 1969–70; Economic Models Ltd, 1970–72; Lectr, Univ. of Newcastle upon Tyne, 1972–74; Res. Scholar, Internat. Inst. for Applied Systems Analysis, Vienna, 1974–75; Economic Adviser: DHSS, 1975–77; HM Treasury, 1977–79; Exchequer and Audit Dept, 1979–81; Sen. Econ. Advr, DHSS, 1981–86; Asst Sec., DoH, 1986–89; Dir, Analytical Services, DSS, 1989–92; Chief Economist, DoE, 1992–95; Dep. Dir (Micro-econs), HM Treasury, 1995–2001. Chm., Economic Policy Cttee, EU, 1999–2001 (Vice-Chm., 1997–99). Non-exec. Dir, Govt Offices for the Regions Bd, 2002–04. Board Member: Countryside Agency, 2003–06; Skillforce, 2004–06; Commn for Rural Communities, 2006–. Chairman: High/Scope UK, 2001–06; Capacity, 2004–06. *Publications:* articles on social policy. *Recreations:* music, languages, gardening. *Address:* National Centre for Social Research, 35 Northampton Square, EC1V 0AX. *Died 13 June 2009.*

GLAZE, Michael John Carlisle, (James), CMG 1988; HM Diplomatic Service, retired; Deputy Secretary-General, Order of St John of Jerusalem, 1994–2001; *b* 15 Jan. 1935; *s* of late Derek Glaze and Shirley Gardner (formerly Glaze, *née* Ramsay); *m* 1965, Rosemary Duff; two step *d. Educ:* Repton; St Catharine's Coll., Cambridge (open Exhibitioner, BA 1958); Worcester Coll., Oxford. Colonial Service, Basutoland, 1959–65; HMOCS, Dep. Permanent Sec., Finance, Lesotho, 1966–70; Dept of Trade (ECGD), 1971–73; FCO, 1973–75; Abu Dhabi, 1975–78; Rabat, 1978–80; Consul-Gen., Bordeaux, 1980–84; Ambassador: Republic of Cameroon, 1984–87; Angola, 1987–90; Ethiopia, 1990–94. OStJ 2000. *Recreations:* golf, grand opera, the garden *Died 6 Feb. 2007.*

GLAZEBROOK, (Reginald) Mark; writer, curator, painter and lecturer on art; *b* 25 June 1936; *s* of late Reginald Field Glazebrook; *m* 1st, 1965, Elizabeth Lea Claridge (marr. diss. 1969); one *d*; 2nd, 1974, Wanda Barbara O'Neill (*née* Osińska) (marr. diss. 2000); one *d*; 3rd, 2004, Cherry Moorsom (*née* Long Price). *Educ:* Eton; Pembroke Coll., Cambridge (MA); Slade School of Fine Art. Worked at Arts Council, 1961–64; Lectr at Maidstone Coll. of Art, 1965–67; Art Critic, London Magazine, 1967–68; Dir, Whitechapel Art Gall., 1969–71; Head of Modern English Paintings and Drawings, P. and D. Colnaghi & Co. Ltd, 1973–75; Gallery Director and Art History Lectr, San José State Univ., 1977–79; Dir, Albemarle Gall. Ltd, London, 1986–93. One-man exhibn, Mayor Gall., London, 2000. FRSA 1971. *Publications:* (comp.) Artists and Architecture of Bedford Park 1875–1900 (catalogue), 1967; (comp.) David Hockney: paintings, prints and drawings 1960–1970 (catalogue), 1970; Edward Wadsworth 1889–1949: paintings, prints and drawings (catalogue), 1974; (introduction) John Armstrong 1893–1973 (catalogue), 1975; (introduction) John Tunnard (catalogue), 1976; Sean Scully (catalogue),

1997; articles in: London Magazine, Modern Painters, Royal Acad. Magazine, Spectator. *Recreations:* cooking, cinema, swimming. *Address:* Flat 1, 28 Draycott Place, SW3 2SB. *Clubs:* Beefsteak, Chelsea Arts, Lansdowne. *Died 3 Nov. 2009.*

GLENCONNER, 3rd Baron *cr* 1911; **Colin Christopher Paget Tennant;** Bt 1885; Governing Director, Tennants Estate Ltd, 1967–91; Chairman, Mustique Co. Ltd, 1969–87; *b* 1 Dec. 1926; *s* of 2nd Baron Glenconner and Pamela Winefred (*d* 1989), 2nd *d* of Sir Richard Paget, 2nd Bt; *S* father, 1983; *m* 1956, Lady Anne Coke, LVO, *e d* of 5th Earl of Leicester, MVO; one *s* twin *d* (and two *s* decd). *Educ:* Eton; New College, Oxford. Director, C. Tennant Sons & Co. Ltd, 1953; Deputy Chairman, 1960–67, resigned 1967. Goodwill Ambassador for St Lucia, 2006. *Heir: g s* Cody Charles Edward Tennant, *b* 2 Feb. 1994. *Address:* Beau Estate, PO Box 250, Soufrière, St Lucia, West Indies. *T:* and *Fax:* 4595057; *e-mail:* beauestate@candw.lc. *Died 27 Aug. 2010.*

GLENCROSS, David, CBE 1994; Chairman, Disasters Emergency Committee, 1999–2005 (Member, 1997–2005); *b* 3 March 1936; *s* of John William Glencross and Elsie May Glencross; *m* 1965, Elizabeth Louise, *d* of John and Edith Richardson; one *d. Educ:* Salford Grammar School; Trinity College, Cambridge. BBC: general trainee, 1958; talks producer, Midlands, 1959; TV Midlands at Six, 1962; Staff Training section, 1964; Senior Producer, External Services, 1966; Asst Head of Programmes, N Region, 1968; Senior Programme Officer, ITA, 1970; Head of Programme Services, IBA, 1976; Dep. Dir, 1977, Dir, 1983–90, Television, IBA; Chief Exec., ITC, 1991–96; Chm., British Screen Adv Council, 1996–97. Trustee: Sandford St Martin Trust, 1998–2007; One World Broadcasting Trust, 2000–06; Help the Aged, 2005–; Elizabeth R Fund, 2006–. FRTS 1981. Hon. MA Salford, 1993. *Publications:* (contrib.) Yearbook of Media and Entertainment Law, 1996; articles on broadcasting in newspapers and jls. *Recreations:* music, reading, listening to radio, walking. *Address:* c/o Help the Aged, 207–221 Pentonville Road, N1 9UZ. *Club:* Garrick. *Died 6 Aug. 2007.*

GLENDEVON, 2nd Baron *cr* 1964, of Midhope, Co. Linlithgow; **Julian John Somerset Hope;** opera producer; *b* 6 March 1950; *er s* of 1st Baron Glendevon and Elizabeth Mary (*d* 1998), *d* of (William) Somerset Maugham, CH; *S* father, 1996. *Educ:* Eton; Christ Church, Oxford. Resident Prod., WNO, 1973–75; Assoc. Prod., Glyndebourne Festival, 1974–81; other prodns for San Francisco Opera, Wexford and Edinburgh Festivals. *Heir: b* Hon. Jonathan Charles Hope, *b* 23 April 1952. *Died 29 Sept. 2009.*

GLENDYNE, 3rd Baron *cr* 1922; **Robert Nivison;** Bt 1914; Chairman, Glenfriars Holdings Ltd, 1977–93; *b* 27 Oct. 1926; *o s* of 2nd Baron Glendyne and Ivy May Rose, *S* father, 1967; *m* 1953, Elizabeth, *y d* of late Sir Cecil Armitage, CBE; one *s* two *d. Educ:* Harrow. Grenadier Guards, 1944–47. Partner, 1947–67, Sen. Partner, 1967–86, R. Nivison & Co., stockbrokers. *Heir: s* Hon. John Nivison, *b* 18 Aug. 1960. *Address:* Craigeassie, by Forfar, Angus DD8 3SE. *Died 27 June 2008.*

GLOSSOP, Peter; Principal Baritone, Royal Opera House, Covent Garden, until 1967, then Guest Artist; *b* 6 July 1928; *s* of Cyril and Violet Elizabeth Glossop; *m* 1st, 1955, Joyce Elizabeth Blackham (marr. diss. 1977); no *c*; 2nd, 1977, Michèle Yvonne Amos (marr. diss. 1986); two *d. Educ:* High Storrs Grammar Sch., Sheffield. Began singing professionally in chorus of Sadler's Wells Opera, 1952, previously a bank clerk; promoted to principal after one season; Covent Garden Opera, 1962–67. Début in Italy, 1964; La Scala, Milan, début, Rigoletto, 1965. Sang Otello and Rigoletto with Metropolitan Opera Company at Newport USA Festival, Aug. 1967; Rigoletto and Nabucco with Mexican National Opera Company, Sept. 1967. Guest Artist (Falstaff, Rigoletto, Tosca) with American National Opera Company, Oct. 1967. Sang in opera houses of Bologna, Parma Catania, Vienna,

1967–68, Berlin and Buenos Aires. Recording artist. Hon. DMus, Sheffield, 1970. Winner of 1st Prize and Gold Medal in First International Competition for Young Opera Singers, Sofia, Bulgaria, 1961; Gold Medal for finest performance (in Macbeth) of 1968–69 season, Barcelona; Amici di Verdi Gold Medal, 1995. *Films:* Pagliacci, Otello. *Publications:* The Story of a Yorkshire Baritone (autobiog.), 2004. *Recreations:* New Orleans jazz music, golf. *Address:* End Cottage, Hawkchurch, Axminster, Devon EX13 5TY.   *Died 7 Sept. 2008.*

GLOVER, Maj.-Gen. Peter James, CB 1966; OBE 1948; *b* 16 Jan. 1913; *s* of late G. H. Glover, CBE, Sheephatch House, Tilford, Surrey, and Mrs G. H. Glover; *m* 1946, Wendy Archer; one *s* two *d*. *Educ:* Uppingham; Cambridge (MA). 2nd Lieut RA, 1934; served War of 1939–45, BEF France and Far East; Lieut-Col 1956; Brig. 1961; Comdt, Sch. of Artillery, Larkhill, 1960–62; Maj.-Gen. 1962; GOC 49 Infantry Division TA and North Midland District, 1962–63; Head of British Defence Supplies Liaison Staff, Delhi, 1963–66; Director, Royal Artillery, 1966–69, retd. Col Comdt, RA, 1970–78. *Address:* Garden Cottage, Wallop House, Nether Wallop, Stockbridge, Hants SO20 8HE.
Died 17 March 2009.

GLOVER, Trevor David; consultant, book and music publishing, since 2001; *b* 19 April 1940; *s* of Frederick Percy and Eileen Frances Glover; *m* 1967, Carol Mary Roberts (*d* 2005); one *s* one *d*. *Educ:* Tiffin Sch., Kingston-upon-Thames; Univ. of Hull (BA Hons English Lang. and Lit.). Newspaper reporter, BC, Canada, 1963; began publishing career as college rep. with McGraw-Hill, Sydney, 1964; Coll. Sales Manager, 1966, later Gen. Manager, Professional and Reference Book Div., McGraw-Hill, UK; joined Penguin UK, 1970; UK Sales Manager, later UK Sales and Marketing Dir; Viking Penguin, NY, 1975–76; Man. Dir, 1976–87, Chm., 1987–95, Penguin Australia; UK Man. Dir, Penguin Gp, 1987–95; Man. Dir, Boosey & Hawkes Music Publishers Ltd, 1996–2001. Pres., Australian Book Publishers Assoc., 1983–85 and 1986–87; Pres., Publishers Assoc., 1997–98; Chm., Booktrust, 2002–05. Sec.-Gen., Rachmaninoff Foundn, 2001–; Adv. Bd Mem., Making Music, 2002–06. Mem. Council, Friends of BL, 2002–06. *Recreation:* choral singing. *Club:* Groucho.   *Died 12 Sept. 2007.*

GODBER, Sir George (Edward), GCB 1971 (KCB 1962; CB 1958); Chief Medical Officer, Department of Health and Social Security, Department of Education and Science, and Home Office, 1960–73; *b* 4 Aug. 1908; *s* of late I. Godber, Willington Manor, Bedford; *m* 1935, Norma Hathorne Rainey (*d* 1999); two *s* one *d* (and two *s* two *d* decd). *Educ:* Bedford Sch.; New Coll., Oxford (Hon. Fellow, 1973); London Hospital; London Sch. of Hygiene. BA 1930, BM 1933, DM 1939, Oxon; MRCP 1935, FRCP 1947; DPH London 1936. Medical Officer, Min. of Health, 1939; Dep. Chief Medical Officer, Min. of Health, 1950–60. Chm., Health Educn Council, 1977–78 (Mem., 1976–78). QHP, 1953–56. Scholar in Residence, NIH Bethesda, 1975. Vice-Pres., RCN, 1973. Fellow: American Hospital Assoc., and American Public Health Assoc., 1961; British Orthopaedic Assoc.; Mem. Dietetic Assoc., 1961; Hon. Member: Faculty of Radiologists, 1958; British Pædiatric Assoc.; Royal Pharmaceut. Soc., 1973. FRCOG *ad eundem* 1966; FRCPsych 1973; FFCM 1974. Hon. FRCS 1973; Hon. FRCGP 1973; Hon. FRSocMed 1973. Hon. LLD: Manchester, 1964; Hull, 1970; Nottingham, 1973; Hon. DCL: Newcastle 1972; Oxford 1973; Hon. DSc Bath, 1979. Hon. Fellow, London Sch. of Hygiene and Tropical Medicine, 1976. Bisset Hawkins Medal, RCP, 1965; 150th Anniversary Medal, Swedish Med. Soc. 1966; Leon Bernard Foundn Medal, 1972; Ciba Foundn Gold Medal, 1970; Therapeutics Gold Medal, Soc. of Apothecaries, 1973. Lectures: Thomas and Edith Dixon Belfast, 1962; Bartholomew, Rotunda, Dublin, 1963; Woolmer, Bio-Engineering Soc., 1964; Monkton Copeman, Soc. of Apothecaries, 1968; Michael M. Davis,

Chicago, 1969; Harold Diehl, Amer. Public Health Assoc., 1969; Rhys Williams, 1969; W. M. Fletcher Shaw, RCOG, 1970; Henry Floyd, Inst. of Orthopaedics, 1970; First Elizabeth Casson Meml, Assoc. of Occ. Therapists, 1973; Cavendish, W London Med.-Chir. Soc., 1973; Heath Clark, London Univ., 1973; Rock Carling, Nuffield Provincial Hosps Trust, 1975; Thom Bequest, RCSE, 1975; Maurice Bloch, Glasgow, 1975; Ira Hiscock, Yale, 1975; John Sullivan, St Louis, 1975; Fordham, Sheffield, 1976; Lloyd Hughes, Liverpool, 1977; Gale Meml, SW England Faculty RCGP, 1978; Gordon, Birmingham, 1979; Samson Gamgee, Birm. Med. Inst., 1979; W. H. Duncan, Liverpool, 1984; W. Pickles, RCGP, 1985; Green Coll., Oxford, 1988. *Publications:* (with Sir L. Parsons and Clayton Fryers) Survey of Hospitals in the Sheffield Region, 1944; The Health Service: past, present and future (Heath Clark Lectures), 1974; Change in Medicine (Rock Carling monograph), 1975; British National Health Service: Conversations, 1977; papers in Lancet, BMJ, Public Health. *Recreation:* gardening.   *Died 7 Feb. 2009.*

GODFREY, Gerald Michael, CBE 2001; chartered arbitrator; a Justice of Appeal, 1993–2000, and Vice-President, 2000, Court of Appeal of the High Court (formerly Supreme Court) of Hong Kong; *b* 30 July 1933; *s* of late Sidney Godfrey and Esther (*née* Lewin); *m* 1960, Anne Sheila, *er d* of late David Goldstein; three *s* two *d*. *Educ:* Lower Sch. of John Lyon, Harrow; King's Coll., London Univ. LLB 1952, LLM 1954. FCIArb 1990. Called to the Bar: Lincoln's Inn, 1954 (Bencher 1978); Bahamas, 1972; Hong Kong, 1974; Kenya, 1978; Singapore, 1978; Malaysia, 1979; Brunei, 1979. National Service as 2nd Lt, RASC, 1955; Temp. Captain, 1956. In practice at the Chancery Bar, 1957–86; QC 1971; a Judge of the High Court, Hong Kong, 1986–93. Chm., Justice Cttee on Parental Rights and Duties and Custody Suits (Report, 1975); DoT Inspector into Affairs of Saint Piran Ltd (Report, 1981). Member: Senate of Inns of Court and the Bar, 1974–77, 1981–84 (Chm., Law Reform Cttee, 1981–83); Council of Justice, 1976–81. Vis. Lectr. Harvard and Tufts Univs, 2001; Legal Assessor, GMC, 2002–07. *Publications:* Editor, Business Law Review. 1958. *Address:* 11 Stone Buildings, Lincoln's Inn, WC2A 3TG; The Garden Flat, 76 Hamilton Terrace, NW8 9UL. *Clubs:* Athenæum, MCC.   *Died 29 Oct. 2007.*

GODLEY, Prof. Hon. Wynne Alexander Hugh; Professor of Applied Economics, University of Cambridge, 1980–93, then Emeritus (Director, 1970–85, Acting Director, 1985–87, Department of Applied Economics); Fellow of King's College, Cambridge, 1970–98, then Emeritus; *b* 2 Sept. 1926; *yr s* of Hugh John, 2nd Baron Kilbracken, CB, KC and Elizabeth Helen Monteith, *d* of Vereker Monteith Hamilton; *m* 1955, Kathleen Eleonora, *d* of Sir Jacob Epstein, KBE; one *d*. *Educ:* Rugby; New Coll., Oxford; Conservatoire de Musique, Paris. Professional oboist, 1950. Joined Economic Section, HM Treasury, 1956; Dep. Dir, Economic Sect., HM Treasury, 1967–70. Dir, Investing in Success Equities Ltd, 1970–85. Official Advr, Select Cttee on Public Expenditure, 1971–73; an Economic Consultant, HM Treasury, 1975; Mem., Panel of Indep. Forecasters, 1992–95. Visiting Professor: Aalborg Univ., 1987–88; Roskilde Univ., 1995; Distinguished Scholar, Jerome Levy Econs Inst., Annandale-on-Hudson, NY, 1991–92, 1993–95, 1996–2001; Vis. Sen. Res. Fellow, Cambridge Endowment for Res. and Finance, Univ. of Cambridge, 2001–04. Dir, Royal Opera House, Covent Garden, 1976–87. Excellence in Journalism Prize, Amer. Psychoanalytic Assoc., 2003. *Publications:* (with T. F. Cripps) Local Government Finance and its Reform, 1976; The Planning of Telecommunications in the United Kingdom, 1978; (with K. J. Coutts and W. D. Nordhaus) Pricing in the Trade Cycle, 1978; (with T. F. Cripps) Macroeconomics, 1983; (with M. Lavoie) Monetary Economics, 2007; articles, in National Institute Review, Economic Jl, London and Cambridge Economic Bulletin, Cambridge Economic Policy Review, Economica, Jl of Policy Modelling, Manchester

School, Jl of Post Keynesian Econs, Banco Nazionale del Lavoro, Nationalokonomisk Tidsskrift, Political Qly, New Statesman and Society, Observer, Guardian, London Review of Books, Financial Times, Challenge, Cambridge Jl of Econs, Jl of Post Keynesian Econs. *Address:* Jasmine House, The Green, Cavendish, Suffolk CO10 8BB. *T:* (01787) 281166.
Died 13 May 2010.

GOGUEN, Prof. Joseph Amadee, PhD; Professor of Computer Science and Director, Meaning and Computation Laboratory (formerly Program in Advanced Manufacturing), University of California at San Diego, 1996–2006; *b* 28 June 1941; *s* of Joseph Amadee Goguen and Helen Stratton; *m* 1st, 1961, Nancy Hammer; one *s* one *d*; 2nd, 1981, Kathleen Morrow; one *d*; 3rd, Ryoko Amadee Goguen. *Educ:* Harvard Univ. (BA); Univ. of California at Berkeley (MA, PhD). Asst Prof., Cttee on Inf. Sciences, Univ. of Chicago, 1968–73; Academic Staff, Naropa Inst., Boulder Colo, 1974–78; Prof., Computer Sci. Dept, UCLA, 1973–79; Man. Dir, Structural Semantics, Palo Alto, 1978–88; Sen. Staff Scientist, SRI Internat., Menlo Park, Calif, 1979–88; Sen. Mem., Center for Study of Language and Inf., Stanford Univ., 1984–88; Prof. of Computing Sci., Oxford Univ., 1988–96. IBM Postdoctoral Fellowship, T. J. Watson Res. Center, 1971; Sen. Vis. Fellow, Univ. of Edinburgh, 1976, 1977, 1983. Fellow, Japan Soc. for Promotion of Sci., 1999. Exceptional Achievement Award, SRI Internat., 1984. *Publications:* (ed) Theory and Practice of Software Technology, 1983; (ed jtly) Requirements Engineering: social and technical issues, 1994; (jtly) Algebraic Semantics of Imperative Programs, 1996; Software Engineering with OBJ, 2000; over 220 articles in professional jls. *Address:* Department of Computer Science and Engineering, University of California at San Diego, 9500 Gilman Drive, La Jolla, CA 92093–0114, USA.
Died 3 July 2006.

GOHEEN, Robert Francis; educator; President Emeritus, and Senior Fellow, Public and International Affairs, since 1981, Princeton University; *b* Venguria, India, 15 Aug. 1919; *s* of Dr Robert H. H. Goheen and Anne Ewing; *m* 1941, Margaret M. Skelly; two *s* four *d*. *Educ:* Princeton Univ. AB 1940; PhD 1948. Princeton University: Instructor, Dept of Classics, 1948–50; Asst Prof., 1950–57; Prof., 1957–72; President, 1957–72. Chm., Council on Foundns, 1972–77; US Ambassador to India, 1977–80; Dir, Mellon Fellowships in Humanities, 1982–92. Sen. Fellow in Classics, Amer. Academy in Rome, 1952–53; Dir Nat. Woodrow Wilson Fellowship Program, 1953–56. Member: Adv. Council, Centre for Advanced Study of India, Univ. of Pennsylvania; American Philosophical Soc.; American Academy of Arts and Sciences; Phi Beta Kappa; Trustee: Nat. Humanities Center; Bharatiya Vidya Bhavan (USA). Former Mem. Internat. Adv. Bd, Chemical Bank; former Member of Board: Amer. Univ. in Beirut; Carnegie Foundn for Advancement of Teaching; Carnegie Endowment for Internat. Peace; United Bd of Christian Higher Educn in Asia; Rockefeller Foundn; Asia Soc.; Amer. Acad. in Rome; Inst. of Internat. Educn; Equitable Life; Thomson Newspapers Inc.; Dreyfus Third Century Fund; Midlantic Nat. Bank; Reza Shah Kabir Univ., Iran; Univ. Service Cttee, Hong Kong. Hon. degrees: Harvard, Rutgers, Yale, Temple, Brown, Columbia, New York, Madras, Pennsylvania, Hamilton, Middlebury, Saint Mary's (Calif), State of New York, Denver, Notre Dame, N Carolina, Hofstra, Nebraska, Dropsie, Princeton; Tusculum Coll.; Trinity Coll., USA; Coll. of Wooster; Jewish Theological Seminary of America; Ripon Coll.; Rider Coll. *Publications:* The Imagery of Sophocles' Antigone, 1951; The Human Nature of a University, 1969; articles. *Recreations:* books, golf. *Address:* 1 Orchard Circle, Princeton, NJ 08540, USA. *T:* (609) 9242751. *Clubs:* Princeton; Century Association (New York); Cosmos (Washington); Nassau, Pretty Brook (Princeton); Gymkhana, Delhi Golf (Delhi).
Died 31 March 2008.

GOLDBERG, Prof. Sir Abraham, Kt 1983; Regius Professor of the Practice of Medicine, University of Glasgow, 1978–89, then Emeritus (Regius Professor of Materia Medica, 1970–78); Consultant Physician, Western Infirmary, Glasgow, since 1959; Hon. Professorial Research Fellow in Modern History, University of Glasgow, 1996–99 (Hon. Senior Research Fellow, 1990–96); *b* 7 Dec. 1923; *s* of late Julius Goldberg and Rachel Goldberg (*née* Varinofsky); *m* 1957, Clarice Cussin; two *s* one *d*. *Educ:* George Heriot's Sch., Edinburgh; Edinburgh University (MB, ChB 1946, MD (Gold Medal for thesis) 1956); DSc Glasgow 1966. FRCPGlas 1964; FRCPE 1965; FRCP 1967; FFPM 1989; FRSE 1971. Nat. Service, RAMC, 1947–49. Nuffield Research Fellow, UCH Med. Sch., London, 1952–54; Eli Lilly Trav. Fellow in Medicine (MRC) in Dept of Medicine, Univ. of Utah, 1954–56; Lectr in Medicine 1956, Titular Prof. 1967, Univ. of Glasgow. Mem., Grants Cttee, Clinical Res. Bd, MRC, 1971–77; Chm., Grants Cttee I, Clinical Res. Bd, MRC, 1973–77. Mem., Chief Scientist Cttee, SHHD, 1977–83; Chm., Biomed. Res. Cttee, SHHD Chief Scientist Orgn, 1977–83; Chm., Cttee on Safety of Medicines, 1980–86. Mem., Editorial Bd, Jt Formulary Cttee, British Nat. Formulary, 1972–78. Foundn Pres., Faculty of Pharmaceutical Medicine, RCP, 1989–91. Editor, Scottish Medical Jl, 1962–63. Lectures: Sydney Watson Smith, RCPE, 1964; Henry Cohen, Hebrew Univ., Jerusalem, 1973; Fitzpatrick, RCP, 1988; Archibald Goodall Meml, RCPSG, 1989. Watson Prize, RCPGlas, 1959; Alexander Fleck Award, Univ. of Glasgow, 1967. Lord Provost's Award for Public Service, City of Glasgow, 1988. *Publications:* (jtly) Diseases of Porphyrin Metabolism, 1962; (ed jtly) Recent Advances in Haematology, 1971; (jtly) Disorders of Porphyrin Metabolism, 1987; (ed jtly) Pharmaceutical Medicine and the Law, 1991; papers on clinical and investigative medicine. *Recreations:* walking, swimming, writing. *Address:* 16 Birnam Crescent, Bearsden, Glasgow G61 2AU.
Died 1 Sept. 2007.

GOLDING, Prof. Raymund Marshall, AO 1994; FNZIC; FRACI; FInstP; FTSE; FRAS; Vice-Chancellor, James Cook University of North Queensland, 1986–96, then Emeritus Professor; *b* 17 June 1935; *s* of Austin E. Golding and Marion H. R. Golding; *m* 1962, Ingeborg Carl; two *d*. *Educ:* Auckland Univ., NZ (BSc 1957, MSc 1958); Cambridge Univ. (PhD 1963). FNZIC 1966; FInstP 1969; FRACI 1974; FTSE 1995; FRAS 2004. Res. and Sen. Res. Scientist, DSIR, NZ, 1957–68; University of New South Wales: Prof. of Theoretical and Physical Chemistry, 1968–86, then Emeritus Prof.; Mem., Bd of Sen. Sch. Studies, 1975–86; Pro-Vice-Chancellor, 1978–86. Dir, St George Hosp., 1982–86. Chm., Aust. Marine Sci. Consortium, 1984–2002; Dep. Chm., Consultative Gp on Marine Industries Sci. and Technol., 1990–94. Dir, PACON Internat., 1990–2002 (Hon. Chm., Australian Chapter, 1990–2002; Fellow, 2002); Chm., Nat. Unit for Multidisciplinary Studies of Spinal Pain, Townsville Gen. Hosp., 1996–2002; Member: Educn Cttee, NSW Chiropractic Registration Bd, 1983–2002; Chiropractors and Osteopaths Bd of Qld, 1991–2002. Mem. Council, PNG Univ. of Technol., 1986–93. Chm., Aust. Fest. of Chamber Music Pty, 1990–96; Director: Tropic Line Res. Theatre Ltd, 1992–94; Townsville Enterprise Ltd, 1990–96; Aust. Tourism Res. Inst., 1990–97. Mem., Crown-of-Thorns Res. Cttee, 1986–96. Trustee, WWF (Australia), 1988–94. FRSA 1977. Hon. Fellow, Korean Chem. Soc., 1985. Hon. DSc Univ. of NSW, 1986. *Publications:* Applied Wave Mechanics, 1969; The Goldings of Oakington, 1992; Quantum Mechanics in Chemical Physics—an exploration, 2008; contribs to books on chem. and med. subjects; numerous research papers and articles. *Recreations:* music, photography, astronomy, family history. *Address:* 5 Tolson Road, Mooloolah, Qld 4553, Australia. *T:* and *Fax:* (7) 54947689.
Died 21 Nov. 2009.

GOLDMAN, Sir Samuel, KCB 1969 (CB 1964); *b* 10 March 1912; *y s* of late Philip and Sarah Goldman; *m* 1st, 1933, Pearl Marre (*d* 1941); one *s*; 2nd, 1943, Patricia Rosemary Hodges (*d* 1990). *Educ:* Davenant Foundation Sch.; Raine's Sch.; London Sch. of Economics (London Univ. Inter-Collegiate Scholar; BSc (Econ.), First Class Hons in Econs and Gladstone Meml Prize, 1931; MSc (Econ.), 1933; Hutchinson Silver Medallist; Hon. Fellow). Moody's Economist Services, 1934–38; Joseph Sebag & Co., 1938–39; Bank of England, 1940–47. Entered Civil Service, 1947, as Statistician in Central Statistical Office; transferred to Treasury, Sept. 1947; Chief Statistician, 1948; Asst Sec., 1952; Under-Sec., 1960–62; Third Sec., 1962–68; Second Perm. Sec., 1968–72. UK Alternate Exec. Dir, International Bank, 1961–62. Exec. Dir, 1972–74; Man. Dir, 1974–76, Orion Bank Ltd. Chm., Henry Ansbacher Holdings Ltd and Henry Ansbacher Ltd, 1976–82. Chm., Covent Garden Market Authority, 1976–81. *Publications:* Public Expenditure Management and Control, 1973. *Recreations:* music, gardening. *Address:* 3 Little Tangley, Wonersh, Guildford, Surrey GU5 0PW. *T:* (01483) 568913.
Died 28 July 2007.

GOLDSMITH, Edward René David; Founder, The Ecologist, 1969 (Editor, 1970–89, and 1997–98); *b* 8 Nov. 1928; *s* of late Frank B. H. Goldsmith, OBE, TD, MP (C) for Stowmarket, Suffolk, 1910–18, and Marcelle (*née* Mouiller; *m* 1st, 1953, Gillian Marion Pretty; one *s* two *d*; 2nd, 1981, Katherine Victoria James; two *s*. *Educ:* Magdalen Coll., Oxford (MA Hons). Adjunct Associate Prof., Univ. of Michigan, 1975; Vis. Prof., Sangamon State Univ., 1984. Contested (Ecology Party): Eye, Feb. 1974; Cornwall and Plymouth, European parly election, 1979. Hon. Right Livelihood Award, Stockholm, 1991; Internat. Forum on Globalization, First Annual Edward Goldsmith Lifetime Achievement Award, 2007. Chevalier, Légion d'Honneur, 1991. *Publications:* (ed) Can Britain Survive?, 1971; (with R. Prescott-Allen) A Blueprint for Survival, 1972; The Stable Society, 1977; (ed with J. M. Brunetti) La Médecine à la Question, 1981; (with N. Hildyard) The Social and Environmental Effects of Large Dams, vol. I, 1984, (ed) vol. II, 1986, (ed) vol. III, 1992; (ed with N. Hildyard) Green Britain or Industrial Wasteland?, 1986; (ed with N. Hildyard) The Earth Report, 1988; The Great U-Turn, 1988; (with N. Hildyard and others) 5,000 Days to Save the Planet, 1990; The Way: an ecological world view, 1992; (ed with J. Mander) The Case against the Global Economy and for a Turn Towards the Local, 1996, UK edn as The Case against the Global Economy and for a Turn Towards Localisation, 2000. *Address:* 9 Montague Road, Richmond, Surrey TW10 6QW. *Clubs:* Brooks's; Travellers (Paris). *Died 21 Aug. 2009.*

GOLDSMITH, John Stuart, CB 1984; Director General Defence Accounts, Ministry of Defence, 1980–84; *b* 2 Nov. 1924; *o s* of R. W. and S. E. Goldsmith; *m* 1948, Brenda; two *s* one *d*. *Educ:* Whitgift Middle Sch.; St Catharine's Coll., Cambridge. Royal Signals, 1943–47 (Captain). War Office, 1948; Principal, 1952; Treasury, 1961–64; Asst Sec., MoD, 1964; RCDS 1971; Asst Under-Sec. of State, MoD, 1973; Chm. Civil Service Selection Bd, 1973. *Recreations:* gardening, jazz, travel. *Address:* 16 Church Lane, Rode, Frome BA11 6PN. *T:* (01373) 830681. *Died 19 July 2007.*

GOMM, Richard Culling C.; *see* Carr-Gomm.

GOOBEY, Alastair R.; *see* Ross Goobey.

GOOCH, Major Sir Timothy (Robert Sherlock), 13th Bt *cr* 1746, of Benacre Hall, Suffolk; MBE 1970; DL; company director; landowner; *b* 7 Dec. 1934; *y s* of Col Sir Robert Gooch, 11th Bt, KCVO, DSO and Katharine Clerveaux, *d* of Maj. Gen. Sir Edward Chaytor, KCMG, KCVO, CB; *S* brother, 1999; *m* 1963, Susan Barbara Christie, *o d* of Maj. Gen. K. C. Cooper, CB, DSO, OBE; two *d*. *Educ:* Eton; RMA Sandhurst. Commissioned, The Life Guards, 1955; served in Egypt, Aden, Oman, Germany, Malaya, Hong Kong and Northern Ireland; retd 1972. Mem., HM Body Guard, Hon. Corps of Gentlemen-at-Arms, 1986–2003, Standard Bearer, 2000–03. DL Suffolk, 1999. *Recreations:* shooting, reading, walking. *Heir: cousin* Arthur Brian Sherlock Gooch [*b* 1 June 1937; *m* 1963, Sarah Diana Rowena Perceval Scott; two *d*]. *Address:* The Cedars, Covehithe, Wrentham, Beccles, Suffolk NR34 7JW. *T:* (01502) 675266. *Clubs:* White's, Cavalry and Guards.
Died 9 April 2008.

GOODALL, Rt Rev. Maurice John, MBE 1974; Bishop of Christchurch, 1984–90; *b* 31 March 1928; *s* of John and Alice Maud Goodall; *m* 1st, 1953, Nathalie Ruth Cummack (decd); two *s* four *d*; 2nd, 1981, Beverley Doreen Moore. *Educ:* Christchurch Technical Coll.; College House, Univ. of NZ (BA 1950); Univ. of Canterbury (LTh 1964); Dip. Social Work (Distinction) 1977; CQSW 1982. Asst Curate, St Albans, Dio. of Christchurch, 1951–54; Vicar of: Waikari, 1954–59; Shirley, 1959–67; Hon. Asst, Christchurch, St John's 1967–69; Chaplain, Kingslea Girls' Training Centre, 1967–69; City Missioner (dio. Christchurch), 1969–76; Nuffield Bursary, 1973; Dir, Community Mental Health Team, 1976–82; Dean of Christchurch Cathedral, 1982–84. *Publications:* (with Colin Clark) Worship for Today, 1967; (contrib.) Christian Responsibility in Society (ed Yule), 1977; contribs to journals. *Recreations:* walking, reading, NZ history. *Address:* Flat 1, 50 Crofton Road, Harewood, Christchurch 5, New Zealand.
Died 27 Oct. 2010.

GOODALL, Ralph William; Chairman, Volex Group, 1992–2002 (Director, 1988–2002); Vice Lord-Lieutenant of Lancashire, 1999–2002; *b* 15 Oct. 1931; *s* of James Goodall and Evelyn (*née* Hamer); *m* 1959, Marjory Audrey Ellen Flint; three *s* one *d*. *Educ:* Haileybury Coll.; Leeds Univ. (BSc Textile Inds); Pembroke Coll., Cambridge (MA Econs). CText 1967; ATI 1967; CompTI 1983. Flying Officer/Engr, RAF, 1954–56. Joined Scapa Dryers Ltd as Mgt Trainee, 1956; Scapa Group plc: Asst Gp Man. Dir, 1969–76; Gp Man. Dir and Chief Exec., 1976–86; Chm., 1986–93; Dir and Chm., Carbo (formerly Hopkinsons Gp) plc, 1992–2002; Dir, Manweb plc, 1993–95 (Chm., 1994–95); Chm., Inveresk PLC, 1994–2001. Mem., Econ. Situation Cttee, CBI, 1983–92; Chm., Textile and other Manufrs Cttee and Consumer Technol. Res. Cttee, DTI, 1987–92. Pres., Textile Inst., 1985–87. Fishing trawler owner, 1968–96. Mem., Chancellor of Duchy of Lancaster's Adv. Cttee on appt of JPs, 1990–95. Gov., Queen Elizabeth's Grammar Sch., Blackburn, 1979–2007 (Chm., 1993–98); Council Mem., UMIST, 1992–2001 (Dep. Chm., 1997–99); Dep. Pro Chancellor, Lancaster Univ., 1997–2002. Pres., Royal Lancs Agricl Soc., 1997–98. FRSA 1983. Freeman, City of London, 1986; Liveryman, Feltmakers' Co., 1986–. DL 1988, High Sheriff, 1995–96, Lancs. Hon. DEng Leeds Univ., 1990. *Recreations:* shooting, golf, walking, music. *Address:* The Old Vicarage, Hoghton, near Preston, Lancs PR5 0SJ. *Clubs:* Farmers', Oxford and Cambridge; District & Union, Pleasington Golf (Blackburn). *Died 16 March 2008.*

GOODCHILD, David Hicks, CMG 1992; CBE 1973; Partner of Clifford Chance (formerly Clifford-Turner), Solicitors, 1962–91 (resident in Paris); *b* 3 Sept. 1926; *s* of Harold Hicks Goodchild and Agnes Joyce Wharton Goodchild (*née* Mowbray); *m* 1954, Nicole Marie Jeanne (*née* Delamotte); one *s* one *d*. *Educ:* Felsted School. Lieut., Royal Artillery, 1944–48; articled clerk, Longmores, Hertford; qual. Solicitor, 1952; Mem., Paris Bar, 1992–2002. HAC, 1952–56. Chairman: Hertford British Hosp. Corp., 1976–2001; Victoria Home, 1982–2006. Hon. Pres., Franco-British Chamber of Commerce and Industry (formerly British Chamber of Commerce in France), 1982–2004 (Pres., British Chamber of Commerce in France, 1970–72). *Recreations:* golf, cricket. *Address:* 53 Avenue Montaigne, 75008 Paris, France. *T:* 42254927. *Clubs:* MCC, HAC, Sloane. *Died 27 Aug. 2009.*

GOODFELLOW, Rosalind Erica; JP; Moderator of the General Assembly of the United Reformed Church, 1982–83; *b* 3 April 1927; *d* of late Rev. William Griffith-Jones and Kathleen (*née* Speakman); *m* 1949, Keith Frank Goodfellow, QC (*d* 1977); two *s* one *d*. *Educ:* Milton Mount Coll. (later Wentworth Coll.); Royal Holloway Coll., London Univ. (BA Hons). Member: BCC Div. of Community Affairs Bd, 1980–83; Churches' Council for Covenanting, 1981–82; Chm., World Church and Mission Dept, URC, 1983; Moderator, Churches' Council for Inter-faith Relations, CCBI, 1994–99. Chairman: Surrey and W Sussex CAB, 1985; Age Concern Surrey, 1990–93. Mem. Council, Brunel Univ., 1995–2000. JP Surrey (Esher and Walton PSD), 1960. *Address.* 2 Judge Walk, Claygate, Surrey KT10 0RP. *T:* (01372) 467656. *Died 25 Aug. 2008.*

GOODHEW, Sir Victor (Henry), Kt 1982; *b* 30 Nov. 1919; *s* of late Rudolph Goodhew, Mannings Heath, Sussex; *m* 1st, 1940, Sylvia Johnson (marr. diss.); one *s* (one *d* decd); 2nd, 1951, Suzanne Gordon-Burge (marr. diss. 1972); 3rd, 1972, Eva Rittinghausen (marr. diss. 1981). *Educ:* King's Coll. Sch. Served War of 1939–45: RAF, 1939–46; comd Airborne Radar Unit, attached 6th Airborne Div.; Sqdn Ldr 1945. Member: Westminster City Council, 1953–59; LCC, 1958–61. Contested (C) Paddington North, 1955; MP (C) St Albans Div., Herts, Oct. 1959–83. PPS to Mr C. I. Orr-Ewing, OBE, MP (when Civil Lord of the Admiralty), May 1962–63; PPS to Hon. Thomas Galbraith, MP (Jt Parly Sec., Min. of Transport), 1963–64; Asst Govt Whip, June–Oct. 1970; a Lord Comr, HM Treasury, 1970–73. Member: Speaker's Panel of Chairmen, 1975–83; Select Cttee, House of Commons Services, 1978–83; House of Commons Commn, 1979–83; Jt Sec. 1922 Cttee, 1979–83; Vice-Chm., Cons. Defence Cttee, 1974–83. Chm., Bd of Management, Inst. of Sports Medicine, 1982– (Mem., 1967–70, 1973–82). *Recreations:* swimming, reading. *Clubs:* United and Cecil, 1900; Constitutional (Windsor). *Died 11 Oct. 2006.*

GOODISON, Sir Alan (Clowes), KCMG 1985 (CMG 1975); CVO 1980; HM Diplomatic Service, retired; *b* 20 Nov. 1926; *o s* of late Harold and Winifred Goodison (*née* Ludlam); *m* 1956, Anne Rosemary Fitton (*d* 1994); one *s* two *d*. *Educ:* Colfe's Grammar Sch.; Trinity Coll., Cambridge (Scholar, Mod. and Medieval Langs Tripos, 1st cl.; MA 1951); DipTh London 1995; MA (Theol) London 1997. Army, Lieut, 1947–49. Foreign Office, Third Sec., 1949; Middle East Centre for Arab Studies, 1950; served in Cairo, Tripoli, Khartoum, Lisbon, Amman, and Bonn, with spells in Foreign Office, 1950–68; Counsellor, Kuwait, 1969–71; Head of Trg Dept and Dir, Diplomatic Service Lang. Centre, FCO, 1971–72; Head of S European Dept, FCO, 1973–76; Minister, Rome, 1976–80; Asst Under Sec. of State, FCO, 1980–83; Ambassador, Dublin, 1983–86. Dir, Wates Foundn, 1988–92. Chm., Charities Evaluation Services, 1993–97; Trustee, Hampstead Wells and Campden Trust, 1993–2006. Pres., Beckenham Chorale, 1972–73. Licensed Reader of Anglican Church, 1959–62, 1966–82, 1988–; a Bishops' Selector for ABM (formerly ACCM), 1989–96; Moderator of Reader Training, Edmonton Episcopal Area, 1990–92. Mem. Council: Jerusalem and the East Mission, 1964–65; Anglican Centre, Rome, 1977–80. Grande Ufficiale dell'Ordine al Merito della Repubblica Italiana (Hon.), 1980. *Publications:* articles on devotional subjects and trans. for Encyclopaedia of Islam. *Recreations:* theology, music, theatre, reading. *Address:* 12 Gardnor Mansions, Church Row, NW3 6UR. *Died 30 June 2006.*

GOODRIDGE, Rt Rev. Sehon Sylvester; Bishop of the Windward Islands, 1994–2002; *b* Barbados, 9 Oct. 1937; *s* of late Simeon Goodridge and Vernese (*née* Burrows); *m* 1966, Janet Rosalind Thomas; one *s* two *d*. *Educ:* Harrison Coll., Barbados; Codrington Coll., Barbados; King's Coll. London (BD 1966, AKC 1991). Asst Master, Grenada Boys' Sec. Sch., 1957–58. Deacon 1963, priest 1964, Windward Is; Curate, Holy Trinity, St Lucia,

1964–66; Anglican Chaplain, Univ. of W Indies and part-time Teacher, Kingston Coll., 1967–69; Anglican Tutor, United Theol Coll. of W Indies, Mona, Jamaica, 1969–71; Principal, Codrington Coll., Barbados, 1971–82; Warden/Student Counsellor, Univ. of W Indies, Cave Hill Campus, Barbados, 1983–89; Mem., Synod Council, Dio. Barbados, 1973–87; Hon. Canon, Dio. Barbados, 1976–; Principal, Simon of Cyrene Theol Inst., 1989–94. Chaplain to the Queen, 1993–94. Univ. Preacher, Univ. of St Andrews, 1997. Member: Inter-Anglican Theol and Doctrinal Commn, 1981–85; Bd of Govs, Coll. of Ascension, Birmingham, 1989–94; Standing Cttee on Theol Educn, CCBI, 1989–94; Bd for Social Responsibility, Gen. Synod, C of E, 1990–94; Council of Southwark Ordination Course, 1990–94; Partnership Adv. Gp, USPG, 1990–94; URC Trng Cttee, 1991–94; Initial Ministerial Educn Cttee, ABM, 1991–94; Gov. Body, SPCK, 1991–94; Bd, William Temple Foundn, 1992–94. Chm. Adv. Cttee, Sch. of Continuing Studies, Univ. of W Indies, St Vincent and the Grenadines, 1998–. Exam. Chaplain to Bishop of Southwark, 1990–94. Vis. Prof., Gen. Theol Seminary, NY, 1986. Hon. DD: Huron Coll., Univ. of W Ont, 1977; Gen. Theol Seminary, NY, 1995. Mem. of Privy Council, Barbados, 1986–91. *Publications:* St Mary's: 1827–1977, 1977; Facing the Challenge of Emancipation, 1981; A Companion to Liberation Theology, 1984; (ed jtly) Facing the Challenge of Racism, 1994, (contrib.) Window on Salvation, 1994; (contrib.) The Terrible Alternative, 1998; *monographs:* Politics and the Caribbean Church, 1971; The Church Amidst Politics and Revolution, 1977; The Abortion Question, 1977; articles in Bull. F Caribbean Affairs, The Bajan, Caribbean Contact, Christian Action Jl, The Month, Crucible. *Recreations:* reading, cricket, gardening. *Address:* c/o Bishop's Court, Montrose, PO Box 502, St Vincent, WI. *Died 28 Dec. 2007.*

GOODWIN, Leonard George, CMG 1977; FRCP; FRS 1976; Director, Nuffield Laboratories of Comparative Medicine, Institute of Zoology, The Zoological Society of London, 1964–80; Director of Science, Zoological Society of London, 1966–80; Consultant, Wellcome Trust, since 1984; *b* 11 July 1915; *s* of Harry George and Lois Goodwin; *m* 1940, Marie Evelyn Coates (*d* 2004); no *c*. *Educ:* William Ellis Sch., London; University Coll. London (Fellow, 1981); School of Pharmacy, London; University Coll. Hospital. BPharm 1935, BSc 1937, MB BS 1950 (London). MRCP 1966, FRCP 1972. Demonstrator, Sch. of Pharmacy, London, 1935–39; Head of Wellcome Labs of Tropical Medicine, 1958–63 (Protozoologist, 1939–63). Jt Hon. Sec., Royal Soc. of Tropical Medicine and Hygiene, 1968–74, Pres., 1979–81. Chairman: Trypanosomiasis Panel, ODM, 1974–77; Filariasis Steering Cttee, WHO Special Programme, 1978–82. Hon. Dir, Wellcome Museum for Med. Sci., 1984–85. Hon. FRPharmS (Hon. FPS 1977) Hon. DSc Brunel, 1986. Soc. of Apothecaries Gold Medal, 1975; Harrison Meml Medal, 1978; Schofield Medal, Guelph Univ., 1979; Silver Medal, Zoological Soc., 1980; Manson Medal, RSTM&H, 1992. Chm. Editorial Bd, Parasitology, 1980–. *Publications:* (pt author) Biological Standardization, 1950; (contrib.) Biochemistry and Physiology of Protozoa, 1955; (jointly) A New Tropical Hygiene, 1960, 2nd edn 1972; (contrib.) Recent Advances in Pharmacology, 1962; many contribs to scientific jls, mainly on pharmacology and chemotherapy of tropical diseases, especially malaria, trypanosomiasis and helminth infections. *Recreations:* dabbling in arts and crafts especially pottery (slipware), gardening and passive participation in music and opera. *Address:* Shepperlands Farm, Park Lane, Finchampstead, Berks RG40 4QF. *T:* (0118) 973 2153. *Died 25 Nov. 2008.*

GOODWIN, Prof. Trevor Walworth, CBE 1975; FRS 1968; Johnston Professor of Biochemistry, University of Liverpool, 1966–83; *b* 22 June 1916; British; *m* 1944, Kathleen Sarah Hill (decd); three *d*. *Educ:* Birkenhead Inst.; Univ. of Liverpool. Lectr 1944, Sen. Lectr 1949, in Biochemistry, University of Liverpool; Prof. of

Biochemistry and Agricultural Biochemistry, UCW, Aberystwyth, 1959. NSF Sen. Foreign Scientist, Univ. of Calif at Davis, 1964. Chairman: British Photobiol. Gp, 1964–66; Phytochemical Soc., 1968–70; MRC Biol Grants Cttee B, 1969–73; Cttee, Biochem. Soc., 1971–74 (Mem., 1953–57, 1962–64); Brit. Nat. Cttee for Biochem., 1976–82; Royal Soc. Internat. Exchange Cttee (Panel A), 1986–89, 1994–; Member: Council, Royal Society, 1972, 1974, 1985; UGC, 1974–81; SRC Science Bd, 1975–78; ARC Grants Bd, 1975–82; Wirral Educn Cttee, 1974–84; Lawes Agricl Trust Cttee, 1977–91; Exec. Cttee, FEBS, 1975–83 (Chm., Publication Cttee, 1975–83); Vice-Pres., Comité Internat. de Photobiologie, 1967–69. Mem. Court, UCW, Aberystwyth, 1965–; Rep. of Lord Pres. of Council on Court, Univ. of N Wales, Bangor, 1983–; Royal Soc. Rep., Court, Univ. of Liverpool, 1985–92. Governor: Birkenhead Inst., 1976–79; Wirral County Grammar Sch. for Girls, 1980–94 (Chm., 1990–94). Morton Lectr, Biochem. Soc., 1983. Corresp. Mem., Amer. Soc. Plant Physiologists, 1982; Hon. Member: Phytochemical Soc. of Europe, 1983; Biochem. Soc., 1985. Diplôme d'honneur, FEBS, 1984. Ciba Medallist, Biochemical Soc., 1970; Prix Roussel, Société Roussel Uclaf, 1982. Editor, Protoplasma, 1968–80; Mem., Editl Bd, Phytochemistry, 1966–96. *Publications:* Comparative Biochemistry of Carotenoids, 1952 (trans. Russian, 1956), 2nd edn, vol. 1 1980, vol. 2 1983; Recent Advances in Biochemistry, 1960; Biosynthesis of Vitamins, 1964 (trans. Japanese, 1966); (ed) Chemistry and Biochemistry of Plant Pigments, 1965, 3rd edn 1988; (with E. I. Mercer) Introduction to Plant Biochemistry, 1972, 2nd edn 1982 (trans. Russian, 1986); History of the Biochemical Society, 1987; (Subject Editor) Oxford Dictionary of Biochemistry and Molecular Biology, 1997; numerous articles in Biochem. Jl, Phytochemistry, etc. *Recreation:* gardening. *Address:* Monzar, 9 Woodlands Close, Parkgate, Neston CH64 6RU. *T:* (0151) 336 4494; *e-mail:* goodwinbiochemistry@bushinternet.com.
Died 7 Oct. 2008.

GORDON, Sir Charles (Addison Somerville Snowden), KCB 1981 (CB 1970); Clerk of the House of Commons, 1979–83; *b* 25 July 1918; *s* of C. G. S. Gordon, TD, Liverpool, and Mrs E. A. Gordon, Emberton and Wimbledon; *m* 1943, Janet Margaret, (Jane), Beattie (*d* 1995); one *s* (one *d* decd); partner, Pamela Fernant. *Educ:* Winchester; Balliol Coll., Oxford. Served in Fleet Air Arm throughout War of 1939–45. Apptd Asst Clerk in House of Commons, 1946; Senior Clerk, 1947; Fourth Clerk at the Table, 1962; Principal Clerk of the Table Office, 1967; Second Clerk Assistant, 1974; Clerk Asst, 1976. Sec., Soc. of Clerks-at-the-Table in Commonwealth Parliaments, and co-Editor of its journal, The Table, 1952–62. *Publications:* Parliament as an Export (jointly), 1966; Editor, Erskine May's Parliamentary Practice, 20th edn, 1983 (Asst Editor, 19th edn); contribs to: The Table; The Parliamentarian. *Recreation:* dolce far niente. *Address:* 279 Lonsdale Road, Barnes, SW13 9QB. *T:* (020) 8748 6735. *Died 1 March 2009.*

GORDON, Nadia, (Mrs Charles Gordon); *see* Nerina, N.

GORDON, Sir Sidney (Samuel), Kt 1972; CBE 1968 (OBE 1965); GBM 1999; CA; JP; Director, Sir Elly Kadoorie & Sons, Ltd; *b* 20 Aug. 1917; *s* of late P. S. Gordon and late Angusina Gordon; *m* 1950, Olive W. F. Eldon (*d* 1992), *d* of late T. A. Eldon and Hannah Eldon; two *d*. *Educ:* Hyndland Sch., Glasgow; Glasgow Univ. Sen. Partner, Lowe Bingham & Matthews, Chartered Accountants, Hong Kong, 1956–70. MLC, 1962–66, MEC, Hong Kong, 1965–80. Chairman: Univ. and Polytechnic Grants Cttee, 1974–76; Standing Commn on Civil Service Salaries and Conditions of Service, 1988–2000. JP Hong Kong, 1961. Hon. LLD The Chinese University of Hong Kong, 1970. *Recreation:* racing. *Address:* 7 Headland Road, Hong Kong. *T:* 28122577. *Clubs:* Oriental; Hong Kong, Hong

Kong Jockey (Hon. Steward), Hong Kong Golf (Hon. Life Mem.; formerly, Pres. and Captain), Hong Kong Country, Hong Kong Cricket, etc.
Died 11 April 2007.

GORDON JONES, Air Marshal Sir Edward, KCB 1967 (CB 1960); CBE 1956 (OBE 1945); DSO 1941; DFC 1941; idc; jssc; qs; Air Officer Commanding-in-Chief, Near East Air Force, and Administrator, Sovereign Base Areas, 1966–69; Commander, British Forces Near East, 1967–69; retired 1969; *b* 31 Aug. 1914; *s* of late Lt-Col Dr Albert Jones, DSO, MC, MD, DPH; *m* 1938, Margery Thurston Hatfield, BSc (*d* 2002); two *s*. Served War of 1939–45 (despatches, DFC, DSO, OBE, Greek DFC). ACOS (Intelligence), Allied Air Forces Central Europe, 1960–61; Air Officer Commanding RAF Germany, 1961–63; Senior RAF Directing Staff, Imperial Defence Coll., 1963–65; AOC, RAF, Malta, and Dep. C-in-C (Air), Allied Forces, Mediterranean, 1965–66. Comdr, Order of Orange Nassau. *Recreations:* sport (Rugby for Lancashire and RAF), music. *Address:* 20 Marlborough Court, Grange Road, Cambridge CB3 9BQ. *T:* (01223) 363029. *Club:* Royal Air Force. *Died 20 Feb. 2007.*

GORE, (Francis) St John (Corbet), CBE 1986; FSA; *b* 8 April 1921; *s* of late Francis Gore and Kirsteen Corbet-Singleton; *m* 1st, 1951, Priscilla (marr. diss. 1975), *d* of Cecil Harmsworth King; one *s* one *d*; 2nd, 1981, Lady Mary Strachey (*d* 2000), *d* of 3rd Earl of Selborne, PC, CH; 3rd, 2009, Mary Barrow. *Educ:* Wellington; Courtauld Inst. of Art. Served War, 1940–45, Captain, Royal Northumberland Fusiliers. Employed Sotheby's, 1950–55; National Trust: Adviser on pictures, 1956–86, Hon. Advr, 1986–; Historic Buildings Sec., 1973–81. Mem., Exec. Cttee, Nat. Art Collections Fund, 1964–97; Trustee: Wallace Collection, 1975–89; National Gall., 1986–94. *Publications:* Catalogue, Worcester Art Museum, Mass (British Pictures), 1974; various exhibn catalogues, incl. RA; contribs to Apollo, Country Life, etc. *Recreation:* sight-seeing. *Address:* Flat 5, 42 Sutherland Street, SW1V 4JZ. *Clubs:* Brooks's, Beefsteak. *Died 23 April 2010.*

GORE, Frederick John Pym, CBE 1987; RA 1972 (ARA 1964); painter; Head of Painting Department, St Martin's School of Art, WC2, 1951–79, and Vice-Principal, 1961–79; *b* 8 Nov. 1913; *s* of Spencer Frederick Gore and Mary Johanna Kerr; *m* Constance; one *s* two *d*. *Educ:* Lancing Coll.; Trinity Coll., Oxford; studied art at Ruskin, Westminster and Slade Schs. Taught at: Westminster Sch. of Art, 1937; Chelsea and Epsom, 1947; St Martin's, 1946–79. Chm., RA exhibitions cttee, 1976–87. Trustee, Imperial War Mus., 1967–84 (Chm., Artistic Records Cttee, 1972–86). *One-man exhibitions:* Gall. Borghèse, Paris, 1938; Redfern Gall., 1937, 1949, 1950, 1953, 1956, 1962; Mayor Gall., 1958, 1960; Juster Gall., NY, 1963; RA (retrospective), 1989. *Paintings in public collections include:* Contemporary Art Soc., Leicester County Council, GLC, Southampton, Plymouth, Rutherston Collection and New Brunswick. Served War of 1939–45: Mx Regt and RA (SO Camouflage). *Publications:* Abstract Art, 1956; Painting, Some Basic Principles, 1965; Piero della Francesca's 'The Baptism', 1969. *Recreation:* Russian folk dancing. *Address:* Flat 3, 35 Elm Park Gardens, SW10 9QF. *T:* (020) 7352 4940. *Died 31 Aug. 2009.*

GORE, Sir Nigel (Hugh St George), 14th Bt *cr* 1621 (Ire.), of Magherabegg, Co. Donegal; grazier and farmer, since 1945; *b* 23 Dec. 1922; *yr s* of St George Richard Gore (*d* 1952, *great nephew* of Sir St George Ralph Gore, 9th Bt), and Loo Loo Ruth (*d* 1961), *d* of E. P. Amesbury; *S* nephew, 1993; *m* 1952, Beth Allison (*d* 1976), *d* of R. W. Hooper; one *d*. *Educ:* Church of England Grammar Sch., Brisbane; Gatton Agricl Coll. Served Army, 1940–45. *Heir: cousin* Hugh Frederick Corbet Gore [*b* 31 Dec. 1934; *m* 1963, Jennifer Mary Copp; one *s* two *d*]. *Clubs:* Toowoomba Range Probus, Returned Soldiers League (Toowoomba). *Died 23 Sept. 2008.*

GORE, St John; see Gore, F. St J. C.

GORELL, 4th Baron cr 1909; **Timothy John Radcliffe Barnes;** b 2 Aug. 1927; e s of 3rd Baron Gorell and Elizabeth, d of Alexander Nelson Radcliffe; S father, 1963; m 1954, Joan Marion, y d of late John Edmund Collins, MC, Sway, Hants; two adopted d. Educ: Groton Sch., USA; Eton Coll.; New Coll., Oxford. Lieut, Rifle Brigade, 1946–48. Barrister, Inner Temple, 1951. Sen. Executive, Royal Dutch/Shell Group, 1959–84. Heir: nephew John Picton Gorell Barnes [b 29 July 1959; m 1989, Rosanne; one s one d]. Address: 4 Roehampton Gate, SW15 5JS. T: (020) 8876 5522.
Died 25 Sept. 2007.

GORHAM, Col Sir Richard (Masters), Kt 1995; CBE 1978; DFC 1945; JP; Chairman: The Supermart Ltd, since 1954; Gorham's Ltd, 1964–98, then Chairman Emeritus; b 3 Oct. 1917; s of late Arthur John Gorham and Muriel Irene Gorham; m 1948, Barbara McIntire; three s two d. Educ: Saltus Grammar Sch., Bermuda; Ridley Coll., St Catherines, Canada; Shaw Business Sch., Toronto. Served in Bermuda Volunteer Engineers, 1938, Bermuda Militia Artillery, 1942; RA, 1942; Pilot, Army Air Comd, Artillery Spotter, Captain RA, in UK, N Africa, Italy (DFC), Austria, Yugoslavia. Mem., Pembroke Vestry, 1958–64; Chm., Pembroke W Constituency, 1964; Mem., Central Cttee, United Bermuda Party, 1964; Chm., Finance Cttee, UBP, 1965–75; MLC, 1968–76; First Parly Sec. and First Parly Sec. for Finance, Bermuda, 1968–77. Dir, Bank of Bermuda, 1966–90. Financial Advisor: New Testament Church of God, 1974–; Girl Guide Assoc. of Bermuda and UK, 1989–; business consultant to service orgns, Salvation Army and numerous other charitable bodies; Founder and Chairman: Summerhave Home for Physically Handicapped, 1974–; Volunteer Independent Pension and Community Services Fund, 1976–; funded eponymous Room: Mus. of Army Flying, Middle Wallop, Hants, 1986; Bermuda Military Heritage Exhibit, Comr's House, Bermuda, in honour of Bermuda's war veterans, 2002. Mem., HAC, 1992–; Hon. Col RA, 1996–. Coronation Medal. Recreations: military history; formerly ocean racing, Rugby, table tennis. Address: Westmorland, 9 Fairylands Road, Pembroke West HM 06, Bermuda. T: (441) 2955321. Clubs: Royal Air Force; Royal Bermuda Yacht, Coral Beach, Mid-Ocean (Bermuda); Metropolitan (NYC); Fishers Island, Hay Harbor (NY). Died 8 July 2006.

GORST, Sir John (Michael), Kt 1994; b 28 June 1928; s of late Derek Charles Gorst and Tatiana (née Kolotinsky); m 1954, Noël Harington Walker; five s. Educ: Ardingly Coll.; Corpus Christi Coll., Cambridge (MA). Advertising and Public Relations Manager, Pye Ltd, 1953–63; Trade Union and Public Affairs Consultant, John Gorst & Associates, 1964–95. Public relations adviser to: British Lion Films, 1964–65; Fedn of British Film Makers, 1964–67; Film Production Assoc. of GB, 1967–68; BALPA, 1967–69; Guy's Hosp., 1968–74. Founder: Telephone Users' Assoc., 1964–80 (Sec. 1964–70); Local Radio Assoc. 1964 (Sec., 1964–71). Contested (C) Chester-le-Street, 1964; Bodmin, 1966; MP (C) Hendon North, 1970–97; contested (C) Hendon, 1997. Sec., Cons. Consumer Protection Cttee, 1973–74; Member: Employment Select Cttee, 1979–87; Nat. Heritage Select Cttee, 1992–97; Vice-Chm., All Party War Crimes Cttee, 1987–97; Chairman: Cons. Media Cttee, 1987–90; British Mexican Gp, 1992–97. Recreations: woodwork, chess. Address: Holway Mill Barn, Sandford Orcas, Sherborne, Dorset DT9 4RZ. T: (01963) 220395; e-mail: sirjohng@hotmail.com.
Died 31 July 2010.

GOSLING, Col Richard Bennett, OBE 1957; TD 1947; DL; b 4 Oct. 1914; 2nd s of late T. S. Gosling, Dynes Hall, Halstead; m 1st, 1950, Marie Terese Ronayne (d 1976), Castle Redmond, Co. Cork; one adopted s one adopted d (one s decd); 2nd, 1978, Sybilla Burgers van Oyen, widow of Bernard Burgers, 't Kasteel, Nijmegen. Educ: Eton; Magdalene Coll., Cambridge (MA). CEng.

Served with Essex Yeomanry, RHA, 1939–45; CO, 1953–56; Dep. CRA, East Anglian Dist, 1956–58. Dir-Gen., British Agricl Export Council, 1971–73. Chairman: Constructors, 1965–68; Hearne & Co., 1971–82. Director: P-E International, 1956–76; Doulton & Co., 1962–72; Revertex Chemicals, 1974–81; Press Mouldings, 1977–92. DL 1954, High Sheriff 1982, Essex. DU Essex, 1993. French Croix de Guerre, 1944. Recreation: country pursuits. Address: Canterburys Lodge, Margaretting, Essex CM4 0EE. T: (01277) 353073.
Died 7 May 2007.

GOTTLIEB, Bernard, CB 1970; Under-Secretary, Ministry of Posts and Telecommunications, 1969–73; b 1913; s of late James Gottlieb and Pauline (née Littau); m 1955, Sybil N. Epstein; one s one d. Educ: Haberdashers' Hampstead Sch.; Queen Mary Coll., London Univ. BSc First Class Maths, 1932. Entered Civil Service as an Executive Officer in Customs and Excise, 1932. Air Ministry, 1938; Asst Private Sec., 1941, and Private Sec., 1944, to Permanent Under-Sec. of State (late Sir Arthur Street), Control Office for Germany and Austria, 1945; Asst Sec., 1946. Seconded to National Coal Board, 1946; Min. of Power, 1950; Under-Sec., 1961, Dir of Establishments, 1965–69. Secretariat, Pay Board, 1973–74, Royal Commn for Distribution of Income and Wealth, 1974–78; research with Incomes Data Services, 1978–90. Gwilym Gibbon Research Fellow, Nuffield Coll., Oxford, 1952–53. Club: Reform.
Died 21 Feb. 2010.

GOUDIE, Rev. John Carrick, CBE 1972; Assistant Minister at St John's United Reformed Church, Northwood, 1985–88; b 25 Dec. 1919; s of late Rev. John Goudie, MA and Mrs Janet Goudie, step s of late Mrs Evelyn Goudie; unmarried. Educ: Glasgow Academy; Glasgow Univ. (MA); Trinity Coll., Glasgow. Served in RN: Hostilities Only Ordinary Seaman and later Lieut RNVR, 1941–45; returned to Trinity Coll., Glasgow to complete studies for the Ministry, 1945; Asst Minister at Crown Court Church of Scotland, London and ordained, 1947–50; Minister, The Union Church, Greenock, 1950–53; entered RN as Chaplain, 1953; Principal Chaplain, Church of Scotland and Free Churches (Naval), 1970–73; on staff of St Columba's Church of Scotland, Pont Street, 1973–77; Minister of Christ Church URC, Wallington, 1977–80; on staff of Royal Scottish Corp., London, 1980–84. QHC 1970–73. Recreations: tennis, the theatre. Address: 309 Howard House, Dolphin Square, SW1V 3PF. T: (020) 7798 8537. Club: Army and Navy.
Died 20 Sept. 2010.

GOULD, Prof. Frank William; Vice-Chancellor, University of East London, 1992–2001; b 12 Aug. 1937; s of Frank Gould and Bridget (née Tyler); m 1963, Lesley Hall; one s two d. Educ: University Coll. London (BA Hons); Univ. of NSW (MA). Nat. Service, Russian linguist, RAF, 1956–58. Tutor in Econs, Univ. of NSW, 1964–66; Econs Journalist, Beaverbrook Newspapers, 1966–67; Lectr in Econs, Kingston Poly., 1967–73; Principal Lectr in Econs and Dean of Faculty, Poly. of Central London, 1973–85; Asst Dir, Leeds Poly., 1985–88; Pro-Rector, NE London Poly., 1988–92. Vice-Chm., Bd of Dirs, Open Learning Foundn, 1994–96; Chairman: Open Learning Foundn Enterprises, 1989–95; UEL Business Services (formerly E London Trng and Consultancy Co.), 1994–2001; NE London Workforce Develt Bd (formerly Confedn), NHS, 2002–06; Member: Bd, London East TEC, 1993–96; Bd, E London Business Assoc., 1997–2001; Adv. Council, Economic and Regl Analysis, 1997–2001. Dir, London Docklands Business Sch., 1994–2001; non-exec. Dir, Newham Healthcare NHS Trust, 2001–. Member, Board of Trustees: Toynbee Housing Assoc., 2001–03; The Place2Be, 2001– (Dep. Chm., 2005–). FRGS 1996. Publications: contribs to books and scientific jls in econs, pol sci. and social policy on govt and the economy and develt of public expenditure. Recreation: horse-riding and horse-driving. Club: Reform. Died 3 June 2008.

GOULDING, Sir Marrack (Irvine), KCMG 1997 (CMG 1983); Warden of St Antony's College, Oxford, 1997–2006; *b* 2 Sept. 1936; *s* of Sir Irvine Goulding; *m* 1st, 1961, Susan Rhoda D'Albiac (marr. diss. 1996), *d* of Air Marshal Sir John D'Albiac, KCVO, KBE, CB, DSO, and of Lady D'Albiac; two *s* one *d*; 2nd, 1996, Catherine Pawlow (marr. diss. 2004), *d* of Alexandre Pawlow and Alla Sobkevitch de Vicens. *Educ:* St Paul's Sch.; Magdalen Coll., Oxford (1st cl. hons Lit. Hum. 1959). Joined HM Foreign (later Diplomatic) Service, 1959; MECAS, 1959–61; Kuwait, 1961–64; Foreign Office, 1964–68; Tripoli (Libya), 1968–70; Cairo, 1970–72; Private Sec., Minister of State for Foreign and Commonwealth Affairs, 1972–75; seconded to Cabinet Office (CPRS), 1975–77; Counsellor, Lisbon, 1977–79; Counsellor and Head of Chancery, UK Mission to UN, NY, 1979–83; Ambassador to Angola, and concurrently to São Tomé e Principe, 1983–85; United Nations, New York: Under Sec.-Gen., Special Political Affairs, later Peace-Keeping Ops, 1986–93; Under Sec.-Gen., Political Affairs, 1993–97. *Publications:* Peacemonger, 2002. *Recreations:* travel, birdwatching. *Address:* 11 St Gabriel's Manor, 25 Cormont Road, SE5 9RH. *T:* (020) 7820 0284. *Club:* Oxford and Cambridge. *Died 9 July 2010.*

GOVAN, Sir Lawrence (Herbert), Kt 1984; President, Lichfield (NZ) Ltd, 1991–98 (Director, 1949–79; Deputy Chairman, 1979–91); *b* 13 Oct. 1919; *s* of Herbert Cyril Charles Govan and Janet Armour Govan (*née* Edmiston); *m* 1946, Clara Hiscock (*d* 1998); one *s* three *d. Educ:* Christchurch Boys' High School. Started in garment industry with Lichfield (NZ) Ltd, 1935, Managing Director, 1950. Pres., NZ Textile and Garment Fedn, 1961–63, Life Mem., 1979. Patron, Canterbury Med. Res. Foundn, 2001– (Pres., 1987–2001). *Recreations:* golf, swimming, horticulture. *Address:* Villa 3, Merivale Retirement Village, 60 Browns Road, Merivale, Christchurch, New Zealand. *T:* (3) 3551012. *Club:* Rotary (Christchurch) (Pres. 1963–64). *Died 6 Nov. 2007.*

GOW, Neil; QC (Scot.) 1970; Sheriff of South Strathclyde, at Ayr, 1976–2005; *b* 24 April 1932; *s* of Donald Gow, oil merchant, Glasgow; *m* 1959, Joanna, *d* of Comdr S. D. Sutherland, Edinburgh; one *s. Educ:* Merchiston Castle Sch., Edinburgh; Glasgow and Edinburgh Univs. MA, LLB. Formerly Captain, Intelligence Corps (BAOR). Carnegie Scholar in History of Scots Law, 1956. Advocate, 1957–76. Standing Counsel to Min. of Social Security (Scot.), 1964–70. Contested (C): Kirkcaldy Burghs, Gen. Elections of 1964 and 1966; Edinburgh East, 1970; Mem. Regional Council, Scottish Conservative Assoc. An Hon. Sheriff of Lanarkshire, 1971. Pres., Auchinleck Boswell Soc. Jt editor, Crime and Prejudice, Channel 4, 1993; writer, Tests of Evidence, Radio Scotland, 1995 (Gold Medal, NY Radio City Awards, 1998). FSA (Scot.). *Publications:* A History of Scottish Statutes, 1959; Jt Editor, An Outline of Estate Duty in Scotland, 1970; A History of Belmont House School, 1979; numerous articles and broadcasts on legal topics and Scottish affairs. *Recreations:* golf, shooting, classic cars. *Address:* Old Auchenfail Hall, by Mauchline, Ayrshire KA5 5TA. *T:* (01290) 550822. *Clubs:* Western (Glasgow); Prestwick Golf. *Died 16 Dec. 2007.*

GOWING, Prof. Noel Frank Collett; Emeritus Professor of Pathology, University of London; Consultant Pathologist and Director of the Department of Histopathology, The Royal Marsden Hospital, SW3, 1957–82; Professor of Tumour Pathology (formerly Senior Lecturer), Institute of Cancer Research: The Royal Cancer Hospital, 1971–82; *b* 3 Jan. 1917; *s* of Edward Charles Gowing and Annie Elizabeth Gowing; *m* 1942, Rela Griffel; one *d. Educ:* Ardingly Coll., Sussex; London Univ. MRCS, LRCP 1941; MB BS, London, 1947; MD London, 1948. Served RAMC (Capt.), 1942–46, 52nd (Lowland) Div. Lectr in Pathology, St George's Hosp. Med. Sch., 1947–52; Sen. Lectr in Pathology and Hon. Cons. Pathologist, St George's Hosp., 1952–57. Vis. Pathologist, St Vincent's Hosp.,

Worcester, Mass and Vis. Prof. of Pathology, Univ. of Mass, 1979. Sometime Examiner in Pathology to: Univ. of London; RCPath; Univ. of Newcastle upon Tyne; Univ. of Malta; Nat. Univ. of Malaysia. Lectures: Kettle Meml, RCPath, 1968; Whittick Meml, Saskatchewan Cancer Soc., 1974; Symeonidis Meml, Thessaloniki Cancer Inst., Greece, 1977. Pres., Assoc. of Clinical Pathologists, 1982–83. FRCPath (Founder Fellow, Coll. of Pathologists, 1964). *Publications:* A Colour Atlas of Tumour Histopathology, 1980; articles on pathology in medical journals. *Recreations:* gardening, astronomy. *Died 17 Sept. 2007.*

GRAHAM, Sir (Albert) Cecil, Kt 2008; FRCP. FRCPCH; Consultant Paediatrician, Queen Elizabeth Hospital, St Michael, Barbados, 1964–95, then Emeritus; Consultant Paediatrician, Children's Development Centre, St Michael, Barbados, 1981–95, then Emeritus; *b* Bridgetown, Barbados, 22 Jan. 1928; *s* of George Washington Graham and Cecil Graham; *m* 1975, Margaret Letitia McCurdy; one *s* three *d* by a previous marriage. *Educ:* Harrison Coll.; McGill Univ.; Guy's Hosp., London (MB BS 1954; DCH 1955). MRCP 1962, FRCP 1974; FRCPCH 1985, Hon. FRCPCH 2002. Commonwealth Scholar, 1961–62, House Officer, Neonatal Unit, 1962, Hammersmith Hosp. Founder Mem., Parent Educn for the Develt of Barbados, 1972–; Advr, Caribbean Assoc. for Mental Retardation and Develtd Disabilities. Mem., Imperial Soc. of Knights Batchelor. Gold Cross of Merit (Barbados), 1982. *Recreations:* music, gardening. *Address:* Cap Rock, 39 Prior Park, 7th Avenue, St James, BB23006, Barbados. *T:* 4246444, *Fax:* 4217287; *e-mail:* m.b@caribsurf.com. *Club:* Rotary (Barbados). *Died 28 Aug. 2009.*

GRAHAM, Colin, OBE 2002; stage director, designer, lighting designer, and author; Artistic Director, Opera Theatre of St Louis, since 1984 (Associate Artistic Director, 1979–84); *b* 22 Sept. 1931; *s* of Frederick Eaton Graham-Bonnalie and Alexandra Diana Vivian Findlay. *Educ:* Northaw Prep. Sch.; Stowe Sch.; RADA (Dip.). Dir of Productions, English Opera Gp, 1963–74; Associate Dir of Prodns, Sadler's Wells Opera/ENO, 1967–75; Dir of Prodns, 1977–84, then Associate Artist, ENO; Artistic Director: Aldeburgh Fest., 1969–89; English Music Theatre, 1975–79. Principal productions for: English Music Theatre; Royal Opera, Covent Garden; Scottish Opera; New Opera Co.; Glyndebourne Opera; BBC TV; Brussels National Opera; St Louis Opera Theatre; Santa Fe Opera; Metropolitan Opera, New York; NYC Opera; San Franscisco Opera; Chicago Lyric Opera; Washington Opera, etc; dir. world premières: of all Benjamin Britten's operas since 1954; of other contemp. composers. Theatre productions for: Old Vic Co.; Bristol Old Vic; Royal Shakespeare Co. Ordained minister, New Covenant Church, St Louis, Mo, 1987. Hon. DA: Webster Univ., 1985; Univ. of Missouri, 1992. Arts and Education Council Award, 1993. Orpheus award (Germany) for best opera production, 1973 (War and Peace, ENO); Opera America award for production, 1988 (Albert Herring, Banff Fest. Opera). *Publications:* A Penny for a Song (libretto for Richard Rodney Bennett), 1969; The Golden Vanity (libretto for opera by Britten), 1970; King Arthur (libretto for new version of Purcell opera), 1971; The Postman Always Rings Twice (libretto for opera by Stephen Paulus), 1981; Jōruri (libretto for opera by Minoru Miki), 1985; The Woodlanders (libretto for opera by Stephen Paulus), 1984; Anna Karenina (libretto for opera by David Carlson); production scores for Britten's: Curlew River, 1969; The Burning Fiery Furnace, 1971; The Prodigal Son, 1973; contrib. Opera. *Recreations:* The Bible, motor cycles, movies, weight training. *Address:* PO Box 191910, Saint Louis, MO 63119, USA. *Died 6 April 2007.*

GRAHAM, Euan Douglas, CB 1985; Principal Clerk of Private Bills, House of Lords, 1961–84; *b* 29 July 1924; *yr s* of Brig. Lord (Douglas) Malise Graham, CB, DSO, MC, RA; *m* 1st, 1954, Pauline Pitt-Rivers (*née* Tennant)

(marr. diss. 1972); one adopted s; 2nd, 1972, Caroline (marr. diss.), d of late K. W. B. Middleton and Ruth, Lady Kinross; two d. Educ: Eton; Christ Church, Oxford (MA). Served RAF, 1943–47. Joined Parliament Office, House of Lords, 1950; Clerk, Judicial Office, 1950–60; Principal Clerk of Private Bills, Examiner of Petitions for Private Bills, Taxing Officer, 1960–85. Recreations: deer stalking, mountain bicycling. Club: Beefsteak. Died 14 Dec. 2007.

GRAHAM, Sir Norman (William), Kt 1971; CB 1961; FRSE; Secretary, Scottish Education Department, 1964–73; b 11 Oct. 1913; s of William and Margaret Graham; m 1949, Catherine Mary Strathie; two s one d. Educ: High Sch. of Glasgow; Glasgow Univ. Dept of Health for Scotland, 1936; Private Sec. to Permanent Under-Sec. of State, 1939–40; Ministry of Aircraft Production, 1940; Principal Private Sec. to Minister, 1944–45; Asst Sec., Dept of Health for Scotland, 1945; Under-Sec., Scottish Home and Health Dept, 1956–63. Hon. DLitt Heriot-Watt, 1971; DUniv Stirling, 1974. Recreation: gardening. Address: 42 Charteris Road, Longniddry, East Lothian EH32 0NT. T: (01875) 852130. Club: New (Edinburgh). Died 25 Feb. 2010.

GRAHAM, Sir Peter (Alfred), Kt 1987; OBE 1969; FCIB; Chairman, Crown Agents for Oversea Governments and Administrations, 1983–90; b 25 May 1922; s of Alfred Graham and Margaret (née Winder); m 1953, Luned Mary (née Kenealy Jones); two s two d. Educ: St Joseph's Coll., Beulah Hill. FCIB (FIB 1975). Served War, RNVR: Pilot, FAA. Joined The Chartered Bank of India, Australia and China, 1947; 24 yrs overseas banking career, incl. appts in Japan, India and Hong Kong; i/c The Chartered Bank, Hong Kong, 1962–70; Chm. (1st), Hong Kong Export Credit Insurance Corp., 1965–70; General Manager, 1970, Dep. Man. Dir, 1975, Gp Man. Dir, 1977–83, Sen. Dep. Chm., 1983–87, Chm., 1987–88, Standard Chartered Bank, London. Director: Standard Chartered Finance Ltd, Sydney (formerly Mutual Acceptance Corp.), 1974–87; First Bank Nigeria, Lagos, 1976–87; Union Bank Inc., Los Angeles, 1979–88; Singapore Land Ltd, 1988–89; Employment Conditions Abroad Ltd, 1988–94; Dolphin Hldgs Ltd, Bermuda, 1995–99; Chairman: Standard Chartered Merchant Bank Ltd, 1977–83; Mocatta Commercial Ltd, 1983–87; Mocatta & Goldsmid Ltd, 1983–87; Equatorial Bank, 1989–93; Deputy Chairman: Chartered Trust plc, 1983–85; Governing Body, ICC UK, 1985–92; Mem., Bd of Banking Supervision, 1986–87; Pres., Inst. of Bankers, 1981–83. City University: Chm., Adv. Cttee, 1981–86, Council, 1986–92, Business Sch.; Chm., Council, 1986–92; Mem., Court, 1997–2000. Formerly Chm., Exchange Banks' Assoc., Hong Kong; Mem., Govt cttees connected with trade and industry, Hong Kong. CCMI (CDIM 1981); FRSA 1983. Freeman, City of London, 1982. Hon. DSc City Univ., 1985. Recreations: golf, tennis. Clubs: Naval, Royal Automobile, Oriental; Hong Kong (Hong Kong); Rye Golf. Died 10 June 2009.

GRANGER, Sir Clive (William John), Kt 2005; PhD; Research Professor, Department of Economics, University of California, San Diego, 1974–2003; b 4 Sept. 1934; s of Edward John Granger and Evelyn Agnes Granger; m 1960, Patricia Anne Loveland; one s one d. Educ: Univ. of Nottingham (BA 1st cl. (Maths); PhD (Stats) 1959). Lectr, then Reader, then Prof., Dept of Maths and Econs, Univ. of Nottingham, 1956–74. Hon. DSc: Nottingham, 1992; Carlos III, Madrid, 1996; Stockholm Sch. of Econs, 1998; Loughborough, 2002; Aarhus, 2003. Nobel Prize in Econs, 2003. Publications: Spectral Analysis of Economic Time Series, 1964, trans. French 1969; (jtly) Predictability of Stock Market Prices, 1970; (jtly) Speculation, Hedging and Forecasts of Commodity Prices, 1970, trans. Japanese 1976; (jtly) Forecasting Economic Time Series, 1977, 2nd edn 1986; (jtly) Introduction to Bilinear Time Series Models, 1978; Forecasting in Business and Economics, 1980, 2nd edn

1989, trans. Chinese 1993, Japanese, 1994; Modeling Economics Series: readings in econometric methodology, 1990; (ed jtly) Long Run Economic Relationships: readings in cointegration, 1991; (jtly) Modeling Nonlinear Dynamic Relationships, 1993; Empirical Modeling in Economics: specification and evaluation, 1999; (jtly) The Dynamics of Deforestation and Economic Growth in the Brazilian Amazon, 2003; Festschrift: Cointegration, Causality, and Forecasting, ed. Robert F. Engle and Halbert White, 1999; Essays in Econometrics: collected papers of Clive W. J. Granger, ed E. Ghysels et al, 2 vols, 2001; numerous contribs to jls. Recreations: body surfing in summer, walking all the year round, reading, art appreciation. Address: Department of Economics, University of California, San Diego, La Jolla, CA 92093–0508, USA. T: (858) 5343856, Fax: (858) 5347040; e-mail: cgranger@ucsd.edu. Died 27 May 2009.

GRANT, His Honour (Hubert) Brian; a Circuit Judge of Sussex and Kent (formerly Judge of County Courts), 1965–82; b Berlin, 5 Aug. 1917; m 1946, Jeanette Mary Carroll; one s three d. Educ: Trinity Coll., Cambridge (Sen. Schol.). 1st cl. hons, Law Tripos, 1939; MA. War service, 1940–44: Commandos, 1942–44. Called to the Bar, Gray's Inn, 1945 (Lord Justice Holker Senior Scholar). Mem., Law Reform Cttee, 1970–73. Vice-Chm., Nat. Marriage Guidance Council, 1970–72; Founder Pres., Parenthood, 1979. Publications: Marriage, Separation and Divorce, 1946; Family Law, 1970; Conciliation and Divorce, 1981; The Quiet Ear, 1987; The Deaf Advance, 1990; Not Guilty, 1994. Address: 33 Arthur Street, Penrith CA11 7TU. Club: Penrith Golf. Died 22 March 2008.

GRAY OF CONTIN, Baron cr 1983 (Life Peer), of Contin in the District of Ross and Cromarty; **James, (Hamish), Hector Northey Gray**; PC 1982; Lord-Lieutenant, Inverness, 1996–2002; President, British-Romanian Chamber of Commerce, 1999–2002; b 28 June 1927; s of late J. Northey Gray, Inverness, and Mrs E. M. Gray; m 1953, Judith Waite Brydon, BSc, Helenburgh; two s one d. Educ: Inverness Royal Academy. Served in Queen's Own Cameron Hldrs, 1945–48. A director of private and family companies, 1950–70; parly and business consultant, 1986–2000. MP (C) Ross and Cromarty, 1970–83; an Asst Govt Whip, 1971–73; a Lord Comr, HM Treasury, 1973–74; an Opposition Whip, 1974–Feb. 1975; Opposition spokesman on Energy, 1975–79; Minister of State: Dept of Energy, 1979–83; Scottish Office, 1983–86; Govt spokesman on Energy, H of L, 1983–86. Contested (C) Ross, Cromarty and Skye, 1983. Member, Inverness Town Council, 1965–70. DL, 1989–94, Vice Lord-Lieut. 1994–96, Lochaber, Inverness, Badenoch and Strathspey. Recreations: golf, cricket, walking, family life. Address: Achneim House, Flichity, Inverness-shire IV2 6XD. Died 14 March 2006.

GRAY, Cecil; see Gray, T. C.

GRAY, (Clemency Anne) Rose, MBE 2010; chef and owner, The River Cafe London, since 1987; b 28 Jan. 1939; d of Clement Nelson Swann and Elizabeth Anne Lawrence; m 1961, Michael Selby Gray (marr. diss.); one s two d; m 2004, David Robin MacIlwaine; one s. Educ: Guildford Sch. of Art (BA Fine Art). Teacher of fine art, London, 1960–63; designer and manufacturer of paper lights and furniture, 1963–68; importer of French stoves and cookers, 1969–80; chef, Nell's Nightclub, NY, 1985–86. Founder, Cooks in Schs, 2005. Publications: with Ruth Rogers: River Cafe Cook Book, 1995; River Cafe Cook Book Two, 1997; The Italian Kitchen, 1998; River Cafe Cook Book Green, 2000; River Cafe Cook Book Easy, 2003; River Cafe Two Easy, 2005; River Cafe Pocket Books, 2006; River Cafe Classic Italian Cookbook, 2009. Recreations: gardening, wine, travelling, eating. T: (020) 7386 4250, Fax: (020) 7386 4201; e-mail: info@rivercafe.co.uk. Died 28 Feb. 2010.

GRAY, Dr Denis Everett, CBE 1983 (MBE 1972); JP; Resident Staff Tutor, since 1957, and Senior Lecturer, 1967–84, Department of Extramural Studies, University of Birmingham; *b* 25 June 1926; *s* of Charles Norman Gray and Kathleen Alexandra (*née* Roberts); *m* 1949, Barbara Joyce, *d* of Edgar Kesterton. *Educ:* Bablake Sch., Coventry; Univ. of Birmingham (BA); Univ. of London; Univ. of Manchester (PhD). Tutor-organiser, WEA, S Staffs, 1953–57. Chairman: Jt Negotiating Cttees for Justices' Clerks and Justices' Clerks' Assts, 1978–86; Central Council of Magistrates' Courts Cttees, 1980–86 (Dep. Chm., 1978–80); Member: Magistrates' Courts Rule Cttee, 1982–86; Lord Chancellor's Adv. Cttee on Trng of Magistrates, 1974–84. JP Solihull, 1962; Dep. Chm., 1968–71 and 1978–82, Chm., 1971–75, Solihull Magistrates; Chm., Licensing Cttee, 1972–76. *Publications:* Spencer Perceval: the evangelical Prime Minister, 1963. *Recreations:* travel, church architecture, reading. *Address:* 11 Brueton Avenue, Solihull, West Midlands B91 3EN. *T:* (0121) 705 2935.
Died 19 April 2008.

GRAY, John Malcolm, CBE 1996; Chairman, Hongkong and Shanghai Banking Corporation Ltd, 1993–96; *b* 28 July 1934; *s* of Samuel Gray and Christina (*née* Mackay-Sim); *m* 1st, 1966, Nicole de Fournier (marr. diss. 1979); two *d*; 2nd, 1984, Ursula Siong Koon; one *d*. *Educ:* Strathallan Sch., Scotland. With Hongkong and Shanghai Banking Corp. Ltd, 1952–96; Dep. Chm., Harvey Nichols Gp, 1996–2002. Dir, World Maritime Ltd, Bermuda, 1984–2004. Chm., Hong Kong Port Develt Bd, 1990–96. MEC, Hong Kong, 1993–95; Mem., Governor's Business Council, Hong Kong, 1993–96. *Recreations:* reading, golf. *Clubs:* Hong Kong (Hong Kong); Penang (Malaysia).
Died 19 Nov. 2009.

GRAY, Margaret Caroline, MA Cantab; Headmistress, Godolphin and Latymer School, 1963–73; *b* 25 June 1913; *d* of Rev. A. Herbert Gray, DD, and Mrs Gray (Mary C. Dods, *d* of Principal Marcus Dods of New Coll., Edinburgh). *Educ:* St Mary's Hall, Brighton; Newnham Coll., Cambridge. Post graduate fellowship to Smith Coll., Mass, USA, 1935–36. Asst History mistress, Westcliff High Sch. for Girls, 1937–38; Head of History Dept, Mary Datchelor Girls' Sch., Camberwell, 1939–52; Headmistress, Skinners' Company's Sch., Stamford Hill, 1952–63. Chm., Nat. Advisory Centre on Careers for Women, 1970–91. Governor: Francis Holland Schs, 1974–99; Hampton Sch., 1976–88; West Heath Sch., Sevenoaks, 1974–89; Unicorn Sch., Kew, 1974–89; Chm. of Trustees, Godolphin and Latymer Bursary Fund, 1976–. Hon. Sec., IndependentAge (formerly RUKBA), Kingston-upon-Thames, 1973–. Elder, St John's Wood URC, 1960–. *Recreations:* gardening, motoring, walking. *Address:* 1 Ennerdale Road, Kew, Richmond TW9 3PG. *T:* (020) 8940 4439.
Died 5 July 2010.

GRAY, Monique Sylvaine, (Mrs P. F. Gray); *see* Viner, M. S.

GRAY, Robert, CBE 1988; JP; building consultant and clerk of works; Vice Lord-Lieutenant, City of Glasgow, 1992–96; *b* 3 March 1928; *s* of John Gray and Mary (*née* McManus); *m* 1955, Mary (*née* McCartney); one *d*. *Educ:* St Mungo's Acad., Glasgow. LIOB 1970. Lecturer: Glasgow Coll. of Building, 1964–65; Anniesland Coll., 1965–70; Sen. Lectr, Cardonald Coll., 1970–84. Mem. (Lab) City of Glasgow (formerly Glasgow Dist, then Glasgow City) Council, 1974; Lord Provost and Lord-Lieutenant of Glasgow, 1984–88. Deacon, Incorporation of Wrights of Glasgow, 1996. DL City of Glasgow, 1988. OStJ. Fellow, Glasgow Coll. of Technol., 1987. Hon. LLD Strathclyde, 1987. *Recreations:* walking, reading, music. *Address:* 106 Churchill Drive, Glasgow G11 7EZ. *T:* (0141) 357 3328. *Club:* Art (Glasgow).
Died 10 Sept. 2008.

GRAY, Rose; *see* Gray, C. A. R.

GRAY, Simon James Holliday, CBE 2005; writer; *b* 21 Oct. 1936; *s* of Dr James Davidson Gray and Barbara Cecelia Mary Holliday; *m* 1965, Beryl Mary Kevern (marr. diss. 1997); one *s* one *d*; *m* 1997, Victoria Katherine Rothschild. *Educ:* Westminster; Dalhousie Univ.; Trinity Coll., Cambridge (MA). Trinity Coll., Cambridge: Sen. Schol., Research Student and Harper-Wood Trav. Student, 1960; Supervisor in English, 1960–63; Sen. Instructor in English, Univ. of British Columbia, 1963–64; Lectr in English, QMC, London Univ., 1965–85 (Hon. Fellow, 1985). Co-dir, The Common Pursuit, Promenade Theatre, NY, 1986, and dir, Phoenix Theatre, 1988. Screenplay: A Month in the Country, 1987. *Publications: novels:* Colmain, 1963; Simple People, 1965; Little Portia, 1967, repr. 1986; (as Hamish Reade) A Comeback for Stark, 1968; Breaking Hearts, 1997; *plays:* Wise Child, 1968; Sleeping Dog, 1968; Dutch Uncle, 1969; The Idiot, 1971; Spoiled, 1971; Butley, 1971; Otherwise Engaged, 1975 (voted Best Play, 1976–77, by NY Drama Critics Circle); Plaintiffs and Defendants, 1975; Two Sundays, 1975; Dog Days, 1976; Molly, 1977; The Rear Column, 1978; Close of Play, 1979; Stage Struck, 1979; Quartermaine's Terms, 1981 (televised 1987); adap. Tartuffe (for Washington, DC; unpublished), 1982; The Common Pursuit, 1984 (televised 1992); Plays One, 1986; Melon, 1987; The Holy Terror, Tartuffe, 1990; Hidden Laughter, 1990; Cell Mates, 1995; Simply Disconnected, 1996; Life Support, 1997; Just the Three of Us, 1997; The Late Middle Classes, 1999; Japes, 2001; The Old Masters, 2004; *television plays:* After Pilkington, 1987; Old Flames, 1990; They Never Slept, 1991; Running Late, 1992; Unnatural Pursuits, 1993; Femme Fatale, 1993; *radio plays:* The Rector's Daughter, 1992; Suffer the Little Children, 1993; With a Nod and a Bow, 1993; Little Nell, 2006; *non-fiction:* An Unnatural Pursuit and Other Pieces, 1985; How's That for Telling 'Em, Fat Lady?, 1988; Fat Chance, 1995; Enter a Fox: further adventures of a paranoid, 2001; The Smoking Diaries (memoirs), 2004; The Year of the Jouncer, 2006; The Last Cigarette, 2008. *Recreations:* watching cricket and soccer, tennis, swimming. *Address:* c/o Judy Daish Associates, 2 St Charles Place, W10 6EG.
Died 6 Aug. 2008.

GRAY, Prof. (Thomas) Cecil, CBE 1976; KCSG 1982; MD; FRCP, FRCS, FRCA; Professor of Anæsthesia, The University of Liverpool, 1959–76, then Emeritus; Dean of Postgraduate Medical Studies, 1966–70, of Faculty of Medicine, 1970–76; *b* 11 March 1913; *s* of Thomas and Ethel Gray; *m* 1st, 1937, Marjorie Kathleen (*née* Hely) (*d* 1978); one *s* one *d*; 2nd, 1979, Pamela Mary (*née* Corning); one *s*. *Educ:* Ampleforth Coll.; University of Liverpool (MB ChB 1937; MD 1947). FRCA (FFARCS 1948); FRCS 1968; FRCP 1972. General Practice, 1937–42; Hon. Cons. Anæsthetist to various hospitals, 1941–47. Active Service, RAMC, 1942–44 (Captain; invalided out). Demonstrator in Anæsthesia, University of Liverpool, 1942, 1944–46; Reader in Anæsthesia and Hd of Dept of Anæsthesia, University of Liverpool, 1947–59; Hon. Cons Anæsthetist: United Liverpool Hosps, Royal Infirmary Branch; Liverpool Thoracic Surgical Centre, Broadgreen Hosp. Ed., British Jl of Anæsthesia, 1948–64. Mem. Bd, Faculty of Anæsthetists, RCS, 1948–69 (Vice-Dean, 1952–54; Dean, 1964–67); Member Council: RCS, 1964–67; Assoc. of Anæsthetists of GB and Ire., 1948–76 (Hon. Treas. 1950–55; Pres. 1956–59; Hon. Mem., 1977–); ASME, 1972–76; FRSocMed (Mem. Council, 1958–61; Pres. Anæsthetic Section, 1955–56; Mem. Council, Sect. of Med. Educn, 1969–72; Hon. Fellow, 1979); Chm., BMA Anæsthetic Group, 1957–62; Mem., Liverpool Regional Hosp. Board, 1968–74 (Chm., Anæsthetic Adv. Cttee, 1948–70; Chm., Med. Adv. Council, 1970–74); Mem., Merseyside RHA, 1974–77; Mem., Bd of Governors, United Liverpool Hosp., 1969–74; Pres., Liverpool Medical Inst., 1974; Mem. Clinical Res. Bd, MRC, 1965–69; Mem. Exec., Univ. Hosps Assoc., 1975–77; Pres., 1962–64, Vice-Pres., 1964–65, Life Vice-Pres., 1973, Liverpool Soc. of Anæsthetists. Hon. Civilian Consultant in Anæsthetics to the Army at Home,

1960–78 (Guthrie Medal 1977), Emeritus Consultant to the Army, 1979–. Mem., delegn of anæsthetists to USSR, 1964. Member Council, Order of St John for Merseyside, 1974–82; St John Rep., Bd of Mgt, Royal Liverpool Hosp., 1974–82; Asst Dir-Gen., St John Ambulance, 1977–82; Vice-Pres., 1954–61 and 1983–88, Mem., 1961–83, Treas., 1976–81, Med. Defence Union; Foundn Mem. and first Chm., Bd of Governors, Linacre Centre for Study of Ethics of Health Care, 1973–83. Examiner in FFARCS, 1953–70; FFARCSI 1967–70: Dip. Vet. Anæsth. Part II, RCVS, 1968–70, 1972–75. Hon. Member: Sheffield and East Midlands Soc. of Anæsthetists; Yorks Soc. of Anæsthetists; SW Regl Soc. of Anæsthetists; Austrian Soc. of Anæsthetists; Soc. Belge d'Anesthesie et de Reanimation; Argentinian and Brazilian Socs of Anesthesiologists; Australian and Malaysian Socs of Anæsthetists; Assoc. of Veterinary Anæsthetists; W African Assoc. of Surgeons; Hon. Corresp. Mem., Sociedade das Ciencias Medical di Lisboa. Lectures: Clover (and Medal), RCS, 1954; Med. Soc. of London, 1946; Simpson-Smith Meml, W London Sch. of Med., 1956; Sir James Young Simpson Meml (and gold medal), RCSE, 1957; Jenny Hartmann Meml, Univ. of Basle, 1958; Eastman, Univ. of Rochester, NY, 1958; Torsten Gordh, Swedish Soc. of Anaesthetists, 1978; Kirkpatrick (and silver medal), Faculty of Anaesthetists, RCSI, 1981; John Gilhes, Scottish Soc. of Anaesthetists, 1982; Mitchiner Meml, RAMC, 1983; Florence Elliott, Royal Victoria Hosp., Belfast, 1984. Sims Commonwealth Travelling Prof., 1961. JP City of Liverpool, 1966 (retd list). Freeman, City of London, 1984; Liveryman, Soc. of Apothecaries, 1956. OStJ 1979. Hon. FFARCSI 1962; Hon. FANZCA 1992. Medallist, Univ. of Liège, 1947; Henry Hill Hickman Medal, RSocMed, 1972; Guthrie Medal, RAMC, 1977; Hon. Gold Medal, RCS, 1978; Ralph M. Waters medal and award, Illinois Soc. of Anesthesiologists, 1978; John Snow Silver Medal, 1982, Magill Gold Medal, 2003, Assoc. of Anaesthetists of GB & Ire. Papal Gold Medal, 1982. *Publications:* Modern Trends in Anæsthesia (ed jtly), 1958, 3rd edn 1967; (ed jtly) General Anæsthesia, 1959, 4th edn 1980; (ed with G. J. Rees) Paediatric Anæsthesia, 1981; Dr Richard Formby, Founder of the Liverpool Medical School, 2003; many contribs to gen. med. press and specialist jls. *Recreations:* music, reading, writing. *Address:* 6 Ravenmeols Lane, Formby, Liverpool L37 4DF.
Died 5 Jan. 2008.

GREATHEAD, Dr David John; Director, International Institute of Biological Control, 1985–91; Hon. Principal Research Fellow, Centre for Population Biology, Imperial College of Science, Technology and Medicine at Silwood Park; *b* 12 Dec. 1931; *s* of Harold Merriman Greathead and Kathleen May (*née* Collett); *m* 1958, Annette Helen Blankley; one *s* two *d*. *Educ:* Merchant Taylors' Sch., Middx; Imperial Coll., London Univ. (BSc, PhD, DSc). ARCS; CBiol; FIBiol. Anti-Locust Res. Centre, 1953–59; research on desert locust in Ethiopia, Somalia, Kenya, Aden Protectorates, Desert Locust Survey, 1959–61; Commonwealth (later Internat.) Institute of Biological Control: set up and managed East African Station in Uganda, res. on crop pests and weeds, 1962–73; based in UK, 1973–91; Asst Dir, 1976–85. *Publications:* A Review of Biological Control in the Ethiopian Region, 1971; A Review of Biological Control in Western and Southern Europe, 1976; (with J. K. Waage) Insect Parasitoids, 1986; (with N. L. Evenhuis) World Catalog of Bee Flies, 1999; numerous publications in learned jls. *Recreations:* natural history, walking, travelling. *Address:* Centre for Population Biology, Imperial College at Silwood Park, Ascot, Berks SL5 7PY. *T:* (020) 7594 2475; 6 The Walled Garden, Wargrave, Reading, Berks RG10 8L. *Died 13 Oct. 2006.*

GREAVES, Graham Charles; aviation consultant, since 2005; *b* 5 July 1945; *s* of Joseph Clarence Greaves and Jane Isabella Greaves; *m* 1975, Pamela Ann Ellson; two *d*. *Educ:* Loughborough Univ. (BSc Hons Transport Mgt and Planning). FCILT (FCIT 1995; FILT 2000). Civil Engr, City of Birmingham, 1964–71; Professional and Technol. Officer, Civil Engr, W Midlands Regl Office, Depts of Transport and the Envmt, 1971–79; various mgt posts, HQ London, Heathrow and Gatwick, BAA, 1979–85; Ops Manager, Manchester Airport, 1985–87; Ops Dir/Man. Dir, Cardiff Airport, 1987–95; Mgt Cons., BAe and independent, 1995–98; Dir Gen. and Chief Exec., CIT, 1998–99; independent aviation consultant, 2000–02; Airport Develt Dir, Newquay Cornwall Internat. Airport, 2002–04; Man. Dir, Gloucestershire Airport Ltd, 2004. Visiting Lecturer: in aviation studies, Loughborough Univ., 1995–2009, IATA, 2008–09; Cranfield Univ., 2009; in business mgt in transport studies, UWE, 2001–06. MCMI (MIMgt 1984). *Publications:* ACI Marketing Handbook, 1995. *Recreations:* British history, military and civil aviation, photography, cricket. *Address:* Grove House, Lyonshall, Herefordshire HR5 3JP. *Died 22 Aug. 2010.*

GREAVES, John Western, CMG 1998; Vice President, Canning House, since 2005 (Chairman, 2001–05); Chairman, Lattitude Global Volunteering (formerly GAP Activity Projects), since 2007, *b* 6 Sept. 1939, *s* of Sir Western Greaves, KBE and Marjorie Nahir (*née* Wright); *m* 1965, Margaret Anne Berg; one *s* three *d*. *Educ:* Uppingham Sch.; Leeds Univ. (BSc Hons Chem. Engrg). Business Manager: ICI Argentina, Buenos Aires, 1965–73; ICI Europa, Brussels, 1973–79; ICI Plastics, 1979–81; Corporate Planning, ICI, 1981 85; Regl Exec., Latin America, Zeneca, 1992–97; Business Dir, Zeneca Agrochemicals, 1997–2000. Chairman: Latin American Crop Protection Assoc., 1993–96; Latin American Trade Adv. Gp, 1995–98. Dir, Bd, Inst. of Latin American Studies, London Univ., 1996–99. *Recreations:* family, home, travel, reading, sailing, ten grandchildren. *Address:* Bramshott Thatch, Rectory Lane, Bramshott, Hants GU30 7QZ, T; (01428) 722243; Las Terrazas, Portals, Mallorca. *Clubs:* Liphook Golf; Tortugas Country (Buenos Aires), Santa Ponsa Yacht (Mallorca).
Died 3 May 2010.

GREEN, Arthur Edward Chase, MBE (mil.) 1955; TD (and Bar) 1950; DL; FRICS; Chartered Surveyor; Chief Estates Surveyor, Legal and General Assurance Society, 1946–71 (Surveyor, 1934–46); *b* 5 Nov. 1911; *s* of Harry Catling and Sarah Jane Green, Winchmore Hill, London; *m* 1941, Margaret Grace (*d* 1991), *yr d* of John Lancelot and Winifred Churchill, Wallington, Surrey; one *s* one *d* (and one *d* decd). *Educ:* Merchant Taylors' Sch.; Coll. of Estate Management. HAC, 1932–: King's Prize, 1938; commnd, 1939; Adjt 11 (HAC) Regt RHA, 1941–42; Western Desert, ME; PoW 1942; on release, Germany, 1945, commanded unit collecting evidence of atrocities against POWs, Brunswick area; despatches, Germany, 1945; attended Brunswick/Hanover War Crimes Trials, 1946; Territorial Efficiency Medal and bar; Court of Assistants, HAC, 1946–76, Treasurer, 1966–69, Vice-Pres., 1970 72; Metropolitan Special Constabulary, HAC Div., 1937–39 and 1946–74 (Long Service Medal and bar; Champion Shot, Met. Special Constab., 1958); Hon. Mem., Transvaal Horse Artillery. Property Advr, J. H. Schroder Wagg & Co., 1972–82; Advr, Schroder Property Fund for Pension Funds and Charities, 1972–82; Dir, Schroder Properties Ltd, 1974–82; Member: Cttee of Management, Pension Fund Property Unit Trust, 1972–82; Transcontinental Property Unit Trust, 1974–82; Advr on Policy, Post Office Staff Superannuation Fund, 1973–77, Dir, Mereacre Ltd, and Mereacre Farms Ltd (PO Staff Superann. Fund), 1977–83; Director: Franey & Co. Ltd, and subsids, 1965–76; Percy Bilton (Industrial Development) Ltd, 1972–76. Member: Chancellor of the Exchequer's Property Adv. Panel, 1975–80; Govt Cttee of Inquiry into Agriculture in GB, 1977–79 (Northfield Cttee). Chm., Elecrent Properties Ltd (Electronic Rentals Gp), 1974–83; Director: Lock Estate Ltd, 1974–82; Marlborough Property Hldgs plc, 1978–86; Studley Farms Ltd, 1980–82. Mem., TA&VR Assocs for City of London, 1970–77, and for Greater London, 1970–81. Pres., Camden and Islington Corps, 1974–75, City of London Bde (formerly City of London and Hackney Corps), 1975–, St John Ambulance.

Governor: Bridewell Royal Hosp. (King Edward's Sch., Witley), 1962–88; City of London Sch., 1976–81; Queenswood Sch., 1966–78; Corp. of Sons of the Clergy, 1986– (Mem. Court of Assistants, 1964–86). Brunswick Youth Club Trust (formerly Brunswick Boys' Club Trust): Founder-Trustee, 1945–78, elected while POW, Oflag 79, Germany; Vice-Pres., 1978–2003; Pres., 2003–. City of London Court of Common Council (Bread Street Ward), 1971–81. Freedom of the City of London, 1939; Liveryman: Merchant Taylors' Co., 1946; Gunmakers' Co., 1954. DL Greater London, 1967 (Representative DL for London Borough of Islington, 1967–81). CStJ 1988. *Recreation:* various. *Address:* The Old Rectory, Ewhurst, Cranleigh, Surrey GU6 7PX. *T:* (01483) 267195. *Clubs:* HAC, Guildhall, Bread Street Ward, Cordwainer Ward.   *Died 21 March 2006.*

GREEN, Arthur Jackson; Under Secretary, Department of Education for Northern Ireland, 1983–87, retired; *b* 12 Nov. 1928; *s* of F. Harvey Green and Sylvia Green (*née* Marsh), MB; *m* 1957, Rosemary Bradley, MA; two *s*. *Educ:* Friends Sch., Lisburn, Co. Antrim; Leighton Park Sch., Reading; Lincoln Coll., Oxford (BA Mod. Hist.); Haverford Coll., Philadelphia (MA Philosophy). Asst Principal, NICS, 1952; Secretary: Cameron Commn, 1969; Scarman Tribunal, 1969–72; Asst Sec., NI Dept of Finance, 1972–78; Under Sec., NI Office, 1978–79; Dir, NI Court Service (Lord Chancellor's Dept), 1979–82; Fellow, Center for Internat. Affairs, Harvard Univ., 1982–83. English teacher, Poland, 1993–2000. Mem. Bd, British Council, 1992–97. *Publications:* articles on Anglo-Irish topics; contribs to Oxford DNB. *Address:* 36 St Patrick's Road, Saul, Downpatrick, N Ireland BT30 7JQ. *T:* (028) 4461 4360. *Club:* Reform.   *Died 16 Nov. 2006.*

GREEN, Father Benedict; *see* Green, Rev. H. C.

GREEN, Charles Frederick; Director, 1982–89, and Deputy Group Chief Executive, 1986–89, National Westminster Bank; *b* 20 Oct. 1930; *m* 1956, Rev. Pauline (*née* Jackson); two *s* one *d*. *Educ:* Harrow County School. FCIB (FIB 1971). Nat. Service, RAF, 1949–51 (Flying Officer). Joined National Provincial Bank, 1946, Secretary, 1967–70; Head of Planning, National Westminster Bank, 1970; Manager, Lombard Street, 1972; Managing Dir, Centre-file, 1974; General Manager: Business Develt Div., 1977; Financial Control Div., 1982. Chairman: CBI/ICC Multinational Affairs Panel, 1982–87; Overseas Cttee, CBI, 1987–89; Dir, Business in the Community, 1981–91 (Vice-Chm., 1985–89); Mem. Council, PSI, 1984–98 (Treas., 1984–93). Mem., General Synod, 1980–90; Vice-Chm., C of E Bd for Social Responsibility, 1983–91; Chm., Industrial and Econ. Affairs Cttee, 1986–93; Mem., Central Stewardship Cttee, Central Bd of Finance, 1991–99 (Chm., 1993–99); Trustee, Church Urban Fund, 1987–89. Chm., Co. of Glos Community Foundn, 1991–2000 (Trustee, 1990–2005; Vice Pres., 2005–); Vice-Chm., Dio. of Gloucester Bd of Finance, 1991–2000; Mem., Council for Charitable Support, 1989–93; Chm., Glenfall House Trust, 1996–2002; Trustee: Small Business Res. Trust, 1986–96; Monteverdi Choir, 1986–2001; Charities Aid Foundn, 1989–98; Church Housing Trust, 1992–2005. Governor: Westonbirt Sch., 1990–2003; Monkton Combe Sch., 1990–96; Mem. Council, Cheltenham & Gloucester Coll. of Higher Educn, subseq. Univ. of Gloucestershire, 1993–2002 (Vice-Chm. Council, 1994–2002; Fellow, 1990). FCMI (FBIM 1982); FRSA 1994. Hon. FLCM 1988. Freeman, City of London, 1990. *Recreations:* opera, concert music, drama. *Address:* The Old House, Parks Farm, Old Sodbury, Bristol BS37 6PX. *Clubs:* Athenæum, Langbourn Ward.   *Died 22 May 2010.*

GREEN, Prof. Dennis Howard, FBA 1992; Schröder Professor of German, University of Cambridge, 1979–89; Fellow of Trinity College, Cambridge, since 1949; *b* 26 June 1922; *s* of Herbert Maurice Green and Agnes Edith Green (*née* Fleming); *m* 1st, 1947, Dorothy Warren (marr. diss. 1972; she *d* 2006); one *d*; 2nd, 1972, Margaret Parry

(*d* 1997); 3rd, 2001, Sarah Redpath. *Educ:* Latymer Upper Sch., London; Trinity Coll., Cambridge; Univ. of Basle. Univ. of Cambridge, 1940–41 and 1945–47; Univ. of Basle (Dr Phil.), 1947–49; Military service (RAC), 1941–45; Univ. Lectr in German, St Andrews, 1949–50; Research Fellowship, Trinity Coll., Cambridge (first year held *in absentia*), 1949–52; Univ. Lectr in German, Cambridge, 1950–66; Teaching Fellowship, Trinity Coll., Cambridge, 1952–66; Head of Dept of Other Languages, 1956–79, and Prof. of Modern Languages, Cambridge, 1966–79; Visiting Professor: Cornell Univ., 1965–66; Auckland Univ., 1966; Yale Univ., 1969; ANU, Canberra, 1971; UCLA, 1975; Univ. of Pennsylvania, 1975; Univ. of WA, 1976; Univ. of Freiburg, 1990; Vis. Fellow, Humanities Res. Centre, Canberra, 1978. Fellow, Netherlands Inst. for Advanced Study, Wassenaar, 1998. Pres., MHRA, 1997. *Publications:* The Carolingian Lord, 1965; The Millstätter Exodus: a crusading epic, 1966; (with Dr L. P. Johnson) Approaches to Wolfram von Eschenbach, 1978; Irony in the Medieval Romance, 1979; The Art of Recognition in Wolfram's Parzival, 1982; Medieval Listening and Reading, 1994; Language and History in the early Germanic World, 1998; The Beginnings of Medieval Romance: fact and fiction 1150–1220, 2002; Women Readers in the Middle Ages, 2007; reviews and articles in learned journals. *Recreation:* walking and foreign travel. *Address:* Trinity College, Cambridge CB2 1TQ. *T:* (01223) 339517.   *Died 5 Dec. 2008.*

GREEN, Geoffrey Hugh, CB 1977; Deputy Under-Secretary of State (Policy), Procurement Executive, Ministry of Defence, 1975–80; *b* 24 Sept. 1920; *o s* of late Duncan M. Green and Kate Green, Bristol; *m* 1948, Ruth Hazel Mercy; two *d*. *Educ:* Bristol Grammar Sch.; Worcester Coll., Oxford (Exhibnr), 1939–41, 1945–47 (MA). Served with Royal Artillery (Ayrshire Yeomanry): N Africa and Italy, 1942–45 (Captain). Entered Min. of Defence, Oct. 1947; Principal, 1949; Asst Sec., 1960; Asst Under-Sec. of State, 1969; Dep. Under-Sec. of State, 1974. *Recreations:* reading, music. *Address:* 47 Kent Avenue, Ealing, W13 8BE.   *Died 10 May 2007.*

GREEN, Rev. Humphrey Christian, (Father Benedict Green, CR); Principal, College of the Resurrection, Mirfield, 1975–84; *b* 9 Jan. 1924; *s* of late Rev. Canon Frederick Wastie Green and Marjorie Susan Beltt Green (*née* Gosling). *Educ:* Dragon Sch., Oxford; Eton (King's Scholar); Merton Coll., Oxford (Postmaster; BA 1949, MA 1952). Served War, RNVR, 1943–46. Deacon 1951, priest 1952; Asst Curate of Northolt, 1951–56; Lectr in Theology, King's Coll., London, 1956–60; professed in Community of the Resurrection (taking additional name of Benedict), 1962; Vice-Principal, Coll. of the Resurrection, 1965–75; Associate Lectr in Dept of Theology and Religious Studies, Univ. of Leeds, 1967–87. Mem., SNTS, 1989–. *Publications:* The Gospel according to Matthew (New Clarendon Bible), 1975; Lay Presidency at the Eucharist, 1994; Matthew: poet of the Beatitudes, 2001; *contributor:* Towards a Church Architecture (ed P. Hammond), 1962; The Anglican Synthesis (ed W. R. F. Browning), 1964; Synoptic Studies (ed C. M. Tuckett), 1984; The Making of Orthodoxy (ed R. Williams), 1989; The Synoptic Gospels: source criticism and the new literary criticism (ed C. Focant), 1993; contrib. Oxford DNB, theological jls. *Recreations:* walking, music, synoptic criticism. *Address:* House of the Resurrection, Mirfield, W Yorks WF14 0BN. *T:* (01924) 483328, *Fax:* (01924) 490489.   *Died 3 Sept. 2007.*

GREEN, Sir Kenneth, Kt 1988; MA; Vice-Chancellor (formerly Director), Manchester Metropolitan University (formerly Manchester Polytechnic), 1981–97; *b* 7 March 1934; *s* of James William and Elsie May Green; *m* 1961, Glenda (*née* Williams); one *d*. *Educ:* Helsby Grammar Sch.; Univ. of Wales, Bangor (BA 1st Cl. Hons); Univ. of London (MA). 2nd Lieut, S Wales Borderers, 1955–57. Management Trainee, Dunlop Rubber Co., 1957–58; Teacher, Liverpool, 1958–60; Lecturer: Widnes

Technical Coll., 1961–62; Stockport College of Technology, 1962–64; Sen. Lectr, Bolton College of Education, 1964–68; Head of Educn, City of Birmingham College of Education, 1968–72; Dean of Faculty, Manchester Polytechnic, 1973–81. Vice-Chm., Manchester TEC, 1989–93 (Mem. Bd, 1989–93); Member: Council, CNAA, 1985–93; UFC, 1989–93. Non-exec. Dir, Halton PCT, 2002–06. Chm., Council of Mgt, Rathbone Soc., 1993–95; Jt Chm., Rathbone Community Industry Ltd, 1995–97. Member, Governing Body: The Heath Comprehensive Sch., Runcorn, 1988–92; Victoria Rd Co. Primary Sch., Runcorn, 1990– (Chm., 1993–2003). Chm., Halton Duke of Edinburgh Award Cttee, 1998–. CCMI (CIMgt 1996). Hon. Mem., Manchester Literary & Philosophical Soc.; Hon. MRNCM; Hon. Fellow, Bolton Inst. of Higher Educn, 1997. Hon. LLD Manchester, 1992; Hon. DLitt: Salford, 1997; Manchester Metropolitan, 1998. *Recreations:* Rugby football, beer tasting. *Address:* 40 Royden Avenue, Runcorn, Cheshire WA7 4SP. *T:* (01928) 575201.   *Died 28 July 2010.*

GREEN, Rt Rev. Mark, MC 1945; an Assistant Bishop, Diocese of Chichester, 1982–2006; *b* 28 March 1917; *s* of late Rev. Ernest William Green, OBE, and Miranda Mary Green; unmarried. *Educ:* Rossall Sch.; Lincoln Coll., Oxford (MA). Curate, St Catharine's, Gloucester, 1940; Royal Army Chaplains' Dept, 1943–46 (despatches, 1945); Dir of Service Ordination Candidates, 1947–48; Vicar of St John, Newland, Hull, 1948–53; Short Service Commn, Royal Army Chaplains' Dept, 1953–56; Vicar of South Bank, Teesside, 1956–58; Rector of Cottingham, Yorks, 1958–64; Vicar of Bishopthorpe and Acaster Malbis, York, 1964–72; Hon. Chaplain to Archbp of York, 1964–72; Rural Dean of Ainsty, 1964–68; Canon and Prebendary of York Minster, 1963–72; Bishop Suffragan of Aston, 1972–82; Hon. Assistant: Christ Church, St Leonards-on-Sea, 1982–94; St Mary, Eastbourne, 1994–2006. Chm. of Governing Body, Aston Training Scheme, 1977–83; Provost, Woodard Schs Southern Div., 1982–89. Hon. DSc Aston, 1989. *Publications:* Diary of Doubt and Faith, 1974. *Address:* The College of St Barnabas, Blackberry Lane, Lingfield RH7 6NJ. *T:* (01342) 872824.   *Died 2 Aug. 2009.*

GREEN, Robert James; Member (Lib Dem), Reading Borough Council, 1995–2008; Mayor of Reading, 2000–01; *b* 27 Jan. 1937; *er s* of Ronald Percy Green and Doris Rose (*née* Warman); *m* 1960, Jill Marianne Small; one *d* (one *s* decd). *Educ:* Kent College, Canterbury. Executive Officer, Board of Trade, 1957; Asst Principal, 1963, Principal, 1967, Min. of Housing and Local Govt; Secretary, Water Resources Board, 1972–74; Asst Secretary: Dept of the Environment, 1974; Dept of Transport, 1980, Under Sec., 1982; Regl Dir, Northern Reg., 1982–83, and Yorks and Humberside Reg., 1982–86; Dir of Rural Affairs, DoE, 1988–91; Dir, Local Govt, 1991–92; Prin. Estabt and Finance Officer, Office of the Rail Regulator, 1993–94. Non-exec. Dir, Butterley Bricks Ltd, 1988–90. Mem. (Lib Dem), Berks CC, 1995–98. Hon. Freeman, Bor. of Reading, 2008. *Recreations:* theatre, including amateur dramatics. *Address:* Runge's Cottage, 11 St Andrews Road, Caversham, Reading RG4 7PH.   *Died 7 Dec. 2009.*

GREEN, Maj.-Gen. Robert Leslie Stuart; *b* 1 July 1925; *s* of Leslie Stuart Green and Eliza Dorothea Andrew; *m* 1952, Nancy Isobel Collier; two *d*. *Educ:* Chorlton Sch. 2nd Bn Black Watch, India, 1944–46; 6 Airborne Div., Palestine, 1946; 2 Parachute Bde, UK and Germany, 1946–47; 1st Bn HLI, UK, ME and Cyprus, 1947–56; ptsc 1959; jssc 1962; 1st Bn Royal Highland Fusiliers, UK, Aden, Germany and Gibraltar, 1959–69, Comd 1967–69; staff appt 1970; Military Dir of Studies, RMCS, 1970–72; Sen. Military Officer, Royal Armament Res. and Develt Estabt, 1973–75; Vice-Pres., Ordnance Bd, 1976–78, Pres., March–June 1978. Col, The Royal Highland Fusiliers, 1979–91. Hon. Vice Pres., CARE, 1995– (Exec. Gov., 1980–90;

Chm., 1991–95). Freeman, City of London, 1983. FCMI. *Recreations:* fishing, music. *Address:* Royal Bank of Scotland, 43 Curzon Street, Mayfair, W1Y 7RF.   *Died 8 April 2009.*

GREEN, Terence Arthur; Director and Deputy Group Chief Executive, National Westminster Bank, 1987–89; *b* 19 May 1934; *m* 1957, Leeta (*née* Beales); two *s* one *d*. *Educ:* South East Essex County Technical College; Harvard Business School (AMP 1980). ACIB. Joined Westminster Bank, 1950; Dep. Gen. Manager, Internat. Banking Div., Nat. Westminster Bank, 1982; Gen. Manager, Business Development Div., 1985. *Recreations:* golf, cricket, fishing.   *Died 19 Jan. 2008.*

GREEN, Thomas Charles, CB 1971; Chief Charity Commissioner, 1966–75; *b* 13 Oct. 1915; *s* of late Charles Harold Green and Hilda Emma Green (*née* Thomas); *m* 1945, Beryl Eva Barber, *widow* of Lieut N. Barber; one *d* (and one step *d*). *Educ:* Eltham Coll.; Oriel Coll., Oxford. Entered Home Office, 1938. Served with RAF, 1940–45. Asst Secretary: Home Office, 1950–64; Charity Commn, 1964–65. UK representative on UN Commn on Narcotic Drugs, 1957–64. Nuffield Travelling Fellowship, 1959–60. *Recreations:* gardening, photography. *Address:* Coombe Bungalow, Coombe Lane, Compton Bishop, Somerset BS26 2HE.   *Died 20 Oct. 2007.*

GREENFIELD, Dr Peter Rex; Senior Principal Medical Officer, Department of Health (formerly of Health and Social Security), 1983–91; *b* 1 Dec. 1931; *s* of late Rex Youhill Greenfield and Elsie Mary Greenfield (*née* Douthwaite); *m* 1954, Faith Stella, *d* of George and Stella Gigg; eight *s* two *d*. *Educ:* Cheltenham College, Pembroke College, Cambridge (BA 1954; MB BChir 1957, MA 1985); St George's Hosp. Med. Sch., London. DObst RCOG 1960. 2nd Lieut, R Signals, 1950–51; House appts, St George's Hosp., 1958; Gen. Med. Pract., Robertsbridge, Sussex, 1959–69; MO, Vinehall Sch., Robertsbridge, 1964–69; MO, Battle Hosp., 1964–69; joined DHSS, 1969; Chief Med. Advr (Social Security), 1983–86. Mem., Jt Formulary Cttee, British Nat. Formulary, 1978–82; Chm., Informal Working Gp on Effective Prescribing, 1981–82. Divl Surgeon, St John Ambulance Bde, 1965–89. Medical Mem., The Appeals Service, 1996–2001. Chm. of Trustees, Chaseley Home for Disabled Ex-Servicemen, Eastbourne, 1995–2001 (Trustee, 1983–2003). QHP 1987–90. Hon. Mem., BPA, 1991–96; Hon. FRCPCH 1996. Mem., Salehurst PCC, 1995–2010. *Publications:* contribs to med. jls on geriatric day care, hypothermia and DHSS Regional Med. Service. *Recreations:* swimming, walking, music, pinball. *Address:* Lorne House, Bellhurst Road, Robertsbridge, East Sussex TN32 5DW. *T:* (01580) 880209.   *Died 30 Dec. 2010.*

GREENING, Rear-Adm. Sir Paul (Woollven), GCVO 1992 (KCVO 1985); Master of HM's Household, 1986–92; an Extra Equerry to the Queen, since 1983; *b* 4 June 1928; *s* of late Captain Charles W. Greening, DSO, DSC, RN, and Mrs Molly K. Greening (*née* Flowers); *m* 1951, Monica (*d* 2008), *d* of late Mr and Mrs W. E. West, East Farndon, Market Harborough; one *s* one *d*. *Educ:* Mowden Sch., Brighton; Nautical Coll., Pangbourne. Entered RN, 1946; Midshipman, HMS Theseus, 1947–48; Sub-Lt and Lieut, HM Ships Zodiac, Neptune, Rifleman, Asheldham (CO), and Gamecock, 1950–58; Lt-Comdr, HM Ships Messina (CO), Loch Killisport, Urchin, and Collingwood, 1958–63; Comdr 1963; CO HMS Lewiston, and SO 2nd Minesweeping Sqdn, 1963–64; jssc 1964; Naval Plans, MoD (Navy), 1965–67; CO HMS Jaguar, 1967–68; Fleet Plans Officer, Far East Fleet, 1969–70; Captain 1969; CO HMS Aurora, 1970–71; Captain Naval Drafting, 1971–74; Sen. Officers War Course, 1974; Dir of Officers Appts (Seamen), MoD (Navy), 1974–76; Captain BRNC Dartmouth, 1976–78; Naval Secretary, 1978–80; Flag Officer, Royal Yachts, 1981–85; retired 1985. ADC to the Queen, 1978. Mem. Council, Mission to Seafarers (formerly Missions to Seamen), 1994–2007. Younger

Brother of Trinity House, 1984–. Vice Pres., Assoc. of Royal Yachtsmen, 1999–. *Recreations:* golf, gardening, following cricket. *Clubs:* Army and Navy; Corhampton Golf. *Died 5 Nov. 2008.*

GREENOUGH, Beverly, (Mrs P. B. Greenough); *see* Sills, B.

GREENWOOD, Allen Harold Claude, CBE 1974; FRAeS; JP; Deputy Chairman, British Aerospace, 1977–83 (Member, Organizing Committee, 1976–77); Chairman, British Aircraft Corporation, 1976 (Deputy Chairman, 1972–75); *b* 4 June 1917; *s* of Lt-Col Thomas Claude Greenwood and Hilda Letitia Greenwood (*née* Knight). *Educ:* Cheltenham Coll.; Coll. of Aeronautical Engineering. Pilot's Licence, 1939. Joined Vickers-Armstrongs Ltd, 1940; served RNVR (Fleet Air Arm), 1942–52 (Lt-Cmdr); rejoined Vickers-Armstrongs Ltd, 1946, Dir, 1960; British Aircraft Corp., 1962, Dep. Man. Dir, 1969; Director: British Aircraft Corp. (Holdings), 1972; BAe Australia Ltd, 1977–83; Chm., BAe Inc., 1977–80. Director: SEPECAT SA, 1964; Europlane Ltd, 1974–83; Chairman: Panavia GmbH, 1969–72; Remploy Ltd, 1976–79 (Vice-Chm., 1973). Pres., Assoc. Européenne des Constructeurs de Material Aerospatial, 1974–76; Pres., 1970–72, Dep. Pres., 1981–82, SBAC; Vice-Pres., Engineering Employers' Fedn, 1982–83; Mem., National Def. Industry Council, 1970–72. Pres., Cheltenham Coll. Council, 1980–85; Member: Council, Cranfield Inst. of Technology, 1970–79; Council, CBI, 1970–77; Assoc. of Governing Bodies of Public Schools, 1982–85; Council, St John's Sch., Leatherhead, 1970–85 (Chm., 1979–85). FRAeS 1965. JP Surrey 1962, Hampshire, 1975. Freeman, City of London. Liveryman, Company of Coachmakers, Guild of Air Pilots. General Comr for Income Tax, 1970–74. *Address:* Belmoir Lodge, Milford Road, Lymington, Hants SO41 8DJ. *T:* (01590) 671515. *Clubs:* White's, Royal Automobile; Royal Lymington Yacht. *Died 21 May 2009.*

GREENWOOD, David Ernest; Research Director, Centre for European Security Studies, Groningen, since 1997; *b* 6 Feb. 1937; *s* of Ernest Greenwood and Doris (*née* Cowsill); *m* 1st, 1960, Helen Ramshaw (marr. diss.); two *s*; 2nd, 1986, Margaret McRobb (*née* Cruickshank). *Educ:* Manchester Grammar Sch.; Liverpool Univ. (BA, MA). Educn Officer, RAF, 1959–66; Economic Advr, MoD, 1966–67; University of Aberdeen: Lectr 1967, Sen. Lectr 1970, Reader 1975, in Higher Defence Studies; Dir, Centre for Defence Studies, 1976–97. Vis. Fellow, IISS, 1974–75; Visiting Professor: Nat. Defense Acad., Yokosuka, 1981–82; Univ. of Nat. and World Econ., Sofia, 1994–; Czech Mil. Acad., Brno, 1996–; Olin Prof., USAF Acad., Colorado Springs, 1991–92. Member: FCO Adv. Panel on Arms Control and Disarmament, 1974–; Honeywell Adv. Council, 1981–85; ACOST Study Gp on Defence R&D, 1987–88. *Publications:* Budgeting for Defence, 1972; (jtly) British Security Policy and the Atlantic Alliance: prospects for the 1990s, 1987; The European Defence Market, 1991; Resource Allocation and Resources Management in Defence, 1996; (jtly) Towards Shared Security: seven-nation perspectives, 2001; (jtly) Organising National Defences for NATO Membership, 2001; numerous monographs, res. reports, contribs to symposia, jl and newspaper articles. *Recreations:* cooking, golf, racing. *Address:* 7 Westhill Grange, Westhill AB32 6QJ. *T:* (01224) 741508; 31a Lutkenieuwstraat, 9712 AW Groningen, Netherlands. *T:* (50) 3132520. *Club:* Royal Air Force. *Died 11 May 2009.*

GREENWOOD, Duncan Joseph, CBE 1993; PhD, DSc; FRS 1985; CChem, FRSC, FIHort; Head of Soils and Crop Nutrition, 1966–92, Associate Fellow, Warwick University, since 2004, Warwick Horticulture Research International (formerly National Vegetable Research Station, later AFRC Institute of Horticultural Research, then Horticulture Research International), Wellesbourne, Warwick (Emeritus Fellow, 1992–2004); *b* 16 Oct. 1932; *s* of Herbert James Greenwood and Alison Fairgrieve Greenwood. *Educ:* Hutton Grammar

Sch., near Preston; Liverpool Univ. (BSc 1954); Aberdeen Univ. (PhD 1957; DSc 1972). CChem, FRSC 1977; FIHort 1986. Res. Fellow, Aberdeen Univ., 1957–59; Res. Leader, National Vegetable Res. Station, 1959–66. Vis. Prof. of Plant Scis, Leeds Univ., 1985–93; Hon. Prof. of Agricl Chem., Birmingham Univ., 1986–93. Chm., Agriculture Gp, Soc. of Chemical Industry, 1975–77; President: Internat. Cttee of Plant Nutrition, 1978–82; British Soc. of Soil Science, 1990–92. Lectures: Blackman, Univ. of Oxford, 1982; Distinguished Scholars, QUB, 1982; Hannaford, Univ. of Adelaide, 1985; Shell, Univ. of Kent, 1988; Amos, Wye Coll., 1989. Hon. Lifetime Mem., Assoc. of Applied Biologists, 2004. Sir Gilbert Morgan Medal, Soc. of Chemical Industry, 1962; Res. Medal, RASE, 1979; inaugural Grower of the Year Award for Lifetime Achievement, 2000; President's Medal, Inst. of Horticulture, 2004. *Publications:* over 180 scientific papers on soil science, crop nutrition and fertilizers. *Address:* 23 Shelley Road, Stratford-upon-Avon, Warwicks CV37 7JR. *T:* (01789) 204735. *Died 13 Feb. 2010.*

GREENWOOD, Ronald, CBE 1981; Manager, England Association Football Team, 1977–82, retired; *b* 11 Nov. 1921; *s* of Sam and Margaret Greenwood; *m* Lucy Joan Greenwood; one *s* one *d.* *Educ:* Alperton School. Apprenticed signwriter, 1937; joined Chelsea FC, 1940; served RAF, 1940–45; Bradford Park Avenue FC, 1945 (Captain); Brentford FC, 1949 (over 300 matches); rejoined Chelsea FC, 1952 (League Champions, 1954–55); Fulham FC, Feb. 1955; coached Oxford Univ. team, 3 years, Walthamstow Avenue FC, 2 years; Manager, Eastbourne United FC and England Youth team; Asst Manager, Arsenal FC, 1958; Team Manager, England Under-23, 1958–61; Manager and Coach, later Gen. Manager, West Ham United FC, 1961–77 (FA Cup, 1964 and 1975; European Cup Winners' Cup, 1965); a FIFA technical adviser, World Cup series, 1966 and 1970. *Publications:* Yours Sincerely, 1984. *Died 9 Feb. 2006.*

GREETHAM, (George) Colin; Headmaster, Bishop's Stortford College, 1971–84; *b* 22 April 1929; *s* of late George Cecil Greetham and of Gertrude Greetham (*née* Heavyside); *m* 1963, Rosemary (*née* Gardner); two *s* one *d.* *Educ:* York Minster Song Sch.; St Peter's Sch., York; (Choral Scholar) King's Coll., Cambridge. BA (Hons) History Tripos Cantab, Class II, Div. I, 1952; Cert. of Educn (Cantab), 1953. *Recreations:* music, choral training, horticulture, bowls. *Address:* 2 Millbuie Street, Elgin, Morayshire IV30 6GE. *Died 5 May 2010.*

GREGORY, Clifford; Chief Scientific Officer, Department of Health and Social Security, 1979–84, retired; *b* 16 Dec. 1924; *s* of Norman and Grace Gregory; *m* 1948, Wyn Aveyard; one *d* (one *s* decd). *Educ:* Royal Coll. of Science, London Univ. (2nd Cl. Hons Physics; ARCS). Served War, RN, 1943–46. Lectr, Middx Hosp. Med. Sch., 1949; Sen. Physicist, Mount Vernon Hosp., 1954; Dep. Reg. Physicist, Sheffield, 1960; Sen. Principal Scientific Officer, Min. of Health, 1966; Dep. Chief Scientific Officer, DHSS, 1972. *Publications:* scientific papers in med. and scientific jls. *Recreations:* outdoor pursuits, natural history. *Address:* 22 Lansdown Road, Gloucester GL1 3JD. *Died 25 Feb. 2006.*

GREGORY, (John) Peter; JP; CEng, FIMechE; Director, ASL Ltd, 1986–91; *b* 5 June 1925; *s* of Mr and Mrs P. Gregory; *m* 1949, Lilian Mary (*née* Jarvis); one *s* one *d.* *Educ:* Ernest Bailey Sch., Matlock; Trinity Hall, Cambridge (Scholar, MA). CEng, FIMechE 1970. Served War, RAF Pilot, 1943–47. Joined Cadbury Bros Ltd, 1949, Dir 1962; Vice Chm., Cadbury Ltd, 1969–70, Dir, Cadbury Schweppes, 1971–82 (Chm., Overseas Gp and Internat. Tech. Dir, 1973–80); Director: National Vulcan Engrg Insce Group Ltd, 1970–79; Amalgamated Power Engrg Ltd, 1973–81; Chm., Data Recording Instruments Ltd, 1982–84. Gen. Comr of Income Tax, 1978–82. Chm. Trustees, Middlemore Homes, 1970–82. Liveryman, Needlemakers' Co. JP Birmingham, 1979. *Recreations:* music, bridge, country pursuits, sailing.

Address: 5 Place Stables, Place Road, Fowey, Cornwall PL23 1DR. *Clubs:* Carlton; Royal Fowey Yacht.
Died 4 Feb. 2009.

GREGORY, Leslie Howard James; former National Officer of EETPU; *b* 18 Jan. 1915; *s* of J. F. and R. E. Gregory; *m* 1949, D. M. Reynolds; one *s* one *d*. *Educ:* Junior Section, Ealing College (formerly Acton Coll.) and state schools. Mem. Exec. Council, ETU, 1938–54; full-time Nat. Officer, 1954–79, retired. Member: CSEU Nat. Sub-Cttees, for Shipbuilding, 1966–79, for Railway Workshops, 1968–78; Craft Training Cttees of Shipbuilding ITB, 1965–77, and Engineering ITB, 1965–68; EDC for Elec. Engrg, 1967–74; EDC for Shipbuilding, 1974–76; Org. Cttee, British Shipbuilders, 1976–77; Bd, British Shipbuilders (part-time), 1977–80.
Died 26 March 2007.

GREGORY, Peter; *see* Gregory, J. P.

GREGORY, Prof. Richard Langton, CBE 1989; DSc; FRS 1992; FRSE 1969; Professor of Neuropsychology and Director of Brain and Perception Laboratory, University of Bristol, 1970–88, then Professor Emeritus and Senior Research Fellow; *b* 24 July 1923; *s* of C. C. L. Gregory, astronomer, and Patricia (*née* Gibson); *m* 1st, 1953, Margaret Hope Pattison Muir (marr. diss. 1966); one *s* one *d*; 2nd, 1967, Freja Mary Balchin (marr. diss. 1976). *Educ:* King Alfred Sch., Hampstead; Downing Coll., Cambridge, 1947–50 (Hon. Fellow, 1999); DSc Bristol, 1983. Served in RAF (Signals), 1941–46; Research, MRC Applied Psychology Research Unit, Cambridge, 1950–53; Univ. Demonstrator, then Lecturer, Dept of Psychology, Cambridge, 1953–67; Fellow, Corpus Christi Coll., Cambridge, 1962–67 (Hon. Fellow, 1997); Professor of Bionics, Dept of Machine Intelligence and Perception, Univ. of Edinburgh, 1967–70 (Chm. of Dept, 1968–70). Founder and Chm. Trustees, 1983–91, Pres., 1991–99, The Exploratory Hands-on Science Centre. President: Section J, British Assoc. for Advancement of Science, 1975, Section X, 1986, and Section Q, 1989 and 1990; Experimental Psychol. Soc., 1981–82. Member: Royal Soc. Cttee for Public Understanding of Sci., 1986–92; BBC Sci. Consultative Gp, 1988–93. Royal Institution: Manager, 1971–74; Mem. Council and Vice-Pres., 1991–94; Christmas Lectr, 1967–68. Medawar Lectr, Royal Soc., 2001. Hon. FInstP 1999; Hon. Fellow, BAASc 2006. DUniv: Open, 1990; Stirling, 1990; Hon. LLD Bristol, 1993; Hon. DSc: E Anglia, 1996; Exeter, 1996; York, 1998; UMIST, 1998; Keele, 1999; Edinburgh, 2000; Wolverhampton 2004. Craik Prize for Physiological Psychology, St John's Coll., Cambridge, 1958; CIBA Foundn Research Prize, 1959; Waverley Gold Medal, 1960; Capire Internat. Prize, Internat. Cttee for Promotion of Advanced Educnl Res., Italy; Primo Rovis Prize, Trieste Internat. Foundn for Scientific Progress and Freedom, Italy; Michael Faraday Medal, Royal Soc., 1993; Lord Crook Medal, Spectacle Makers' Co., 1996; Hughlings Jackson Medal, RSocMed, 2000. Founder Editor, Perception, 1972. *Publications:* Recovery from Early Blindness (with Jean Wallace), 1963; Eye and Brain, 1966, 5th edn 1998; The Intelligent Eye, 1970; Concepts and Mechanisms of Perception, 1974; (ed jtly) Illusion in Nature and Art, 1973; Mind in Science, 1981; Odd Perceptions (essays), 1986; (ed) Oxford Companion to the Mind, 1987, 2nd edn 2004; Evolution of the Eye and Visual System, vol. 2 of Vision and Visual Dysfunction, 1991; Even Odder Perceptions (essays), 1994; The Artful Eye, 1995; Mirrors in Mind, 1996; Seeing Through Illusions, 2009; articles in various scientific jls and patents for optical and recording instruments and a hearing aid; radio and television appearances. *Recreation:* punning and pondering. *Address:* 23 Royal York Crescent, Clifton, Bristol BS8 4JX. *Clubs:* Athenæum, Chelsea Arts.
Died 17 May 2010.

GREGORY, Ronald, CBE 1980; QPM 1971; DL; Chief Constable of West Yorkshire Metropolitan Police, 1974–83; *b* 23 Oct. 1921; *s* of Charles Henry Gregory and Mary Gregory; *m* 1942, Grace Miller Ellison; two *s*. *Educ:*
Harris College. Joined Police Service, Preston, 1941. RAFVR, 1942–44; RNVR(A), 1944–46. Dep. Chief Constable, Blackpool, 1962–65; Chief Constable, Plymouth, 1965–68; Dep. Chief Constable, Devon and Cornwall, 1968–69; Chief Constable, West Yorkshire Constabulary, 1969–74. DL West Yorks, 1977. *Recreations:* golf, sailing, ski-ing. *Died 9 April 2010.*

GREGSON, Baron *cr* 1975 (Life Peer), of Stockport in Greater Manchester; **John Gregson,** AMCT, CIMgt; DL; non-Executive Director, Fairey Group plc (formerly Fairey Holdings Ltd), 1989–94; with British Steel plc (formerly British Steel Corporation), 1976–94; *b* 29 Jan. 1924. Joined Stockport Base Subsidiary, 1939; Fairey R&D team working on science of nuclear power, 1946; appointed to Board, 1966. Non-executive Dir, Innvotec Ltd (formerly Electra Corporate Ventures Ltd), 1989–99; non-exec. Dir, OSC Process Engineering Ltd, 1995. Mem., NRA, 1992–95. Member: H of L Select Cttee on Sci. & Technol., 1980–99; H of L Select Cttee on Sustainable Develt, 1994–96; President: Parly and Scientific Cttee, 1986–89; Finance and Industry Gp of Labour Party. Vice Pres., Assoc. of Metropolitan Authorities, 1984. President: Defence Manufacturers Assoc., 1984–2000; Envmtl Industries Commn, 1994–96. Chairman: Waste Mgt Industry Trng and Adv. Bd, 1985–2000; Onyx Envmtl Trust, 1997–2003. Chm. Adv. Council, RMCS Shrivenham, 1985–99; Member Court: UMIST, 1976–99; Univ. of Manchester, 1995–97. Hon. Fellow, Manchester Polytechnic, 1983; Hon. FIProdE 1982; Hon. FREng (Hon. FEng 1986); Hon. FICE 1987; Hon. FIET. DUniv Open, 1986; Hon. DSc: Aston, 1987; Cranfield; Hon. DTech Brunel, 1989; Hon. DSc RMCS, 1990. DL Greater Manchester, 1979. *Recreation:* gardening. *Address:* 12 Rosemont Road, Richmond-upon-Thames, Surrey TW10 6QL. *T:* and *Fax:* (020) 8948 2244; The Spinney, Cragg Vale, Mytholmroyd, Hebden Bridge, West Yorks HX7 5SR; 407 Hawkins House, Dolphin Square, SW1V 3XL.
Died 12 Aug. 2009.

GRESHAM, Prof. (Geoffrey) Austin, TD 1966; FRCPath, FRCPE; Professor of Morbid Anatomy and Histopathology, Cambridge, 1973–92; Fellow, 1964–92, then Emeritus, and President, 1976–79, Jesus College, Cambridge; Home Office Pathologist, 1968–92; *b* 1 Nov. 1924; *s* of Thomas Michael and Harriet Anne Gresham; *m* 1950, Gweneth Margery Leigh; three *s* two *d*. *Educ:* Grove Park Sch., Wrexham; Gonville and Caius Coll., Cambridge (Tancred Student and Schol.; Schuldham Plate; MA; ScD; Hon. Fellow, 2001); King's Coll. Hosp., London (Burney Yeo Schol., Todd and Jelf Medallist; MB BChir, MD). FRCPath 1973; FRCPE 1994. Served RAMC, 1950–52, Lt-Col RAMC V, 1961. Cambridge University: Demonstrator and Lectr in Pathology, 1953–62; Univ. Morbid Anatomist, 1962–73; Sec., Faculty Bd of Medicine, 1956–61; Chm., MD Cttee, 1991–2003; Dep. to Regius Prof. of Physic, 1991–2003; Dep. to Vice Chancellor, 1993–95. Consultant Mem., Cambridge Dist Management Team, 1974–84; Chairman: Cambridge Dist Medical Cttee, 1974–84; Medical Staff Leave Cttee, 1974–84; Cambridge Dist Ethical Cttee, 1974–84; Member: European Atherosclerosis Soc., 1959–; British Atherosclerosis Discussion Gp, 1965–. Roy Cameron Meml Lectr, RCPath, 1983. Mem. Bd of Governors, United Cambridge Hosps, 1972–74. Hon. Fellow, British Assoc. of Forensic Medicine, 1996. Scientific Medal, Univ. of Tokyo, 1985. *Publications:* Introduction to Comparative Pathology, 1962; Biological Aspects of Occlusive Vascular Disease, 1964; Colour Atlas of General Pathology, 1971, 2nd edn 1993; Primate Atherosclerosis, 1976; Colour Atlas of Forensic Pathology, 1977; Post Mortem Procedures, 1979; Reversing Atherosclerosis, 1980; Arterial Pollution, 1981; Wounds and Wounding, 1987; contrib. chapters, and papers in many jls, about pathology. *Recreations:* gardening, playing organ, wine, silver, talking. *Address:* 18 Rutherford Road, Cambridge CB2 8HH. *T:* (01223) 841326. *Died 24 July 2009.*

GREY EGERTON, Sir (Philip) John (Caledon), 15th Bt *cr* 1617; *b* 19 Oct. 1920; *er s* of Sir Philip Grey Egerton, 14th Bt; *S* father, 1962; *m* 1st, 1952, Margaret Voase (*d* 1971) (who *m* 1941, Sqdn Ldr Robert A. Ullman, *d* 1943), *er d* of late Rowland Rank; 2nd, 1986, Frances Mary (who *m* 1941 Sqdn Ldr William Dudley Williams, DFC, *d* 1976), *y d* of late Col R. M. Rainey-Robinson. *Educ:* Eton. Served Welsh Guards, 1939–45. *Recreation:* fishing. *Heir: cousin* Maj.-Gen. David Boswell Egerton [*b* 24 July 1914; *m* 1946, Margaret Gillian (*d* 2004), *d* of Canon C. C. Inge; one *s* two *d*]. *Address:* Meadow House, West Stafford, Dorchester, Dorset DT2 8AQ.
Died 19 Feb. 2008.

GRIBBON, Maj.-Gen. Nigel St George, OBE 1960; Assistant Chief of Staff, (Intelligence), Supreme Headquarters Allied Powers Europe, 1970–72; *b* 6 Feb. 1917; *s* of late Brig. W. H. Gribbon, CMG, CBE; *m* 1943, Rowan Mary MacLiesh; two *s* one *d*. *Educ:* Rugby Sch.; RMC Sandhurst. King's Own Royal Regt, 1937–42; Aldershot, 1937; Madras, 1938–39; Karachi, 1940; active service, Iraq, 1941–42 (Habbaniya-Felujah, 1942) (wounded); GSO3 10th Indian Div., 1942; Staff Coll. Quetta, 1943; G2 HQ 55 Inf. Div., 1944; Army Airborne Transport Develt Centre, 1945; Parachute Course, 1945; Bde Major, 1st Parachute Bde, 1946; served Palestine, 1946, Trieste, 1947–48, GSO2 Jt Intelligence Cttee (Far E), 1948–50; RAF Staff Coll., 1947; DAAG WO, 1953–55; HK, 1954–55; OC 5 King's Own, 1958–60; AMS WO, 1960–62; Comdr 161 Bde, 1963–65; Canadian Nat. Defence Coll., 1965–66; DMC MoD, 1966–67; Dep. Chm., South Arabian Action Gp, MoD/FCO, 1966–68; BGS (I) BAOR and ACOS Northern Army Gp, 1967–69. Man. Dir, Partnerplan Public Affairs Ltd, 1973–75; BAC Delegate, Congrès Atlantique, Paris, 1975; Man. Dir, Sallingbury Ltd, 1977–85 (Chm., 1975–77 and 1984–85); Sallingbury Casey Ltd, 1986–87; Dir, Gatewood Engineers Ltd, 1976–83; non-exec. Dir, Chancellor Insurance Co. Ltd, 1986–92; Operational Planning Consultant, Venice-Simplon Orient Express, 1980–84. Chm., 1982–97, Vice-Pres., 1997–2001, UK Falkland Is Trust. Canada-UK Chamber of Commerce: Mem. Council, 1979–99; Chm., Trade Cttee, 1980; Pres., 1981; Chm., Jt Cttee, Canada-UK and Canadian Chambers of Commerce, 1982–91. Hd of Secretariat, European Channel Tunnel Gp and Public Affairs Cttee, 1980–85; Chairman: Forces Financial Services, 1983–85; SHAPE Assoc. (UK Chapter), 1984–; Member: Eur. Atlantic Gp, 1974–87; Council, British Atlantic Cttee, 1975–93 (Mem. Exec. Cttee, 1983–88); Council, Mouvement Européen Français (Londres), 1979–87; Council, Wyndham Place Trust, 1979–82; Cttee, Amer. European Atlantic Cttee, 1985–92; Adv. Cttee, Shackleton Meml Fund, 1995–97; Mil. Mem., Canadian War Meml Foundn, 1988–94. Vice-Pres., King's Own Affairs, 1974–88; Founder and Hon. Vice-Pres., Lancaster Mil. Heritage Group, 2000–04. Associate, Armed Forces Art Soc., 2005–. Member: Woodland Trust; Exec. Council, Rugbeian Soc. Commentator, BBC Radio 4, 1979–80; lectr on public affairs; organiser of chamber music concerts, 1991–. Freeman, City of London; Freeman, Worshipful Co. of Shipwrights, 2008 (Liveryman, 1982–88). *Recreation:* watercolour sketching. *Address:* Danny House, Hurstpierpoint, W Sussex BN6 9BB. *Clubs:* Army and Navy (Mem., Gen. and Finance Cttees, 1989–92), Little Ship (Rear Commodore Training, 1978–80; Hon. Life Mem.).
Died 9 Jan. 2009.

GRIERSON, Sir Michael (John Bewes), 12th Bt *cr* 1685 (NS), of Lag, Dumfriesshire; *b* 24 July 1921; *s* of Lt-Col Alexander George William Grierson, RM retd (*d* 1951) (2nd *s* of 9th Bt) and Violet Ethel (*d* 1980), *d* of Lt-Col Arthur Edward Bewes, CMG; *S* cousin, 1987; *m* 1971, Valerie Anne, *d* of late Russell Wright, Gidea Park, Essex; one *d*. *Educ:* Warden House School, Deal; St Edmund's School, Canterbury. Served War, RAF, 1941–46; subsequent career in civil engineering and local government; retired, 1986. *Recreations:* gardening,

motoring, plane spotting, woodwork, photography. *Heir:* none. *Address:* 40c Palace Road, Streatham Hill, SW2 3NJ.
Died 24 March 2008 (ext).

GRIERSON, Prof. Philip, LittD; FBA 1958; FSA; Fellow, since 1935, Librarian, 1944–69, and President, 1966–76, Gonville and Caius College, Cambridge; Professor of Numismatics, University of Cambridge, 1971–78, then Emeritus; Professor of Numismatics and the History of Coinage, University of Brussels, 1948–81; Hon. Keeper of the Coins, Fitzwilliam Museum, Cambridge, since 1949; *b* 15 Nov. 1910; *s* of Philip Henry Grierson and Roberta Ellen Jane Pope. *Educ:* Marlborough Coll.; Gonville and Caius Coll., Cambridge (MA 1936, LittD 1971). University Lectr in History, Cambridge, 1945–59; Reader in Medieval Numismatics, Cambridge, 1959–71. Literary Dir of Royal Historical Society, 1945–55; Ford's Lectr in History, University of Oxford, 1956–57. Advr in Byzantine Numismatics to the Dumbarton Oaks Library and Collections, Harvard Univ., at Washington, USA, 1955–98. Pres. Royal Numismatic Society, 1961–66. Corresp. Fellow, Mediaeval Acad. of America, 1972; Corresp. Mem., Koninklijke Vlaamse Acad., 1955; Assoc. Mem., Acad. Royale de Belgique, 1968. Hon. LittD: Ghent, 1958; Leeds, 1978; Hon. LLD Cambridge, 1993. *Publications:* Les Annales de Saint-Pierre de Gand, 1937; Books on Soviet Russia, 1917–42, 1943; Sylloge of Coins of the British Isles, Vol. I (Fitzwilliam Museum: Early British and Anglo-Saxon Coins), 1958; Bibliographie numismatique, 1966, 2nd edn 1979; English Linear Measures: a study in origins, 1973; (with A. R. Bellinger) Catalogue of the Byzantine Coins in the Dumbarton Oaks Collection and in the Whittemore Collection, vols 1, 2, 3, 5, 1966–99; Numismatics, 1975; Monnaies du Moyen Age, 1976; The Origins of Money, 1977; Les monnaies, 1977; Dark Age Numismatics, 1979; Later Medieval Numismatics, 1979; Byzantine Coins, 1982; Medieval European Coinage, vol. 1 (with M. Blackburn) The Early Middle Ages, 1986, vol. 14 (with L. Travaini) Italy III, 1998; The Coins of Medieval Europe, 1991; Tarì, Follari e Denari, 1991; (with M. Mays) Catalogue of Late Roman Coins in the Dumbarton Oaks Collection and in the Whittemore Collection, 1992; Scritti storici e numismatici, 2001; trans. F. L. Ganshof, Feudalism, 1952; editor: C. W. Previté-Orton, The Shorter Cambridge Medieval History, 1952; H. E. Ives, The Venetian Gold Ducat and its Imitations, 1954; Studies in Italian History presented to Miss E. M. Jamison, 1956; (with U. Westermark) O. Mørkholm, Early Hellenistic Coins, 1991; Studies in Numismatic Method, presented to Philip Grierson (Festschrift), 1983. *Recreation:* science fiction. *Address:* Gonville and Caius College, Cambridge CB2 1TA. *T:* (01223) 332450.
Died 15 Jan. 2006.

GRIEW, Prof. Stephen, PhD; Emeritus Professor and Senior Scholar, Atkinson College, York University, Toronto, since 1993; *b* 13 Sept. 1928; *e s* of late Harry and Sylvia Griew, London, England; *m* 1st, 1955, Jane le Geyt Johnson (marr. diss.); one *s* two *d* (and one *s* decd); 2nd, 1977, Eva Margareta Ursula, *d* of late Dr and Fru Johannes Ramberg, Stockholm, Sweden; one *d* and one step *s*. *Educ:* Univ. of London (BSc, Dip Psych); Univ. of Bristol (PhD). Vocational Officer, Min. of Labour, 1951–55; Univ. of Bristol: Research Worker, 1955–59; Lectr, 1959–63; Kenneth Craik Research Award, St John's Coll., Cambridge, 1960; Prof. of Psychology: Univ. of Otago, Dunedin, NZ, 1964–68 (Dean, Faculty of Science, 1967–68); Univ. of Dundee, 1968–72; Vice-Chancellor, Murdoch Univ., Perth, WA, 1972–77; Chm., Dept of Behavioural Science, Faculty of Medicine, Univ. of Toronto, 1977–80; Pres., 1980–85, University Prof., 1986–87, Athabasca Univ.; Dean, 1987–90, Prof. of Admin. Studies, 1990–93, Atkinson Coll., York Univ., Toronto; Pres., Senior Univ., Toronto, 1990–95; Adjunct Prof. of Psychol., 1993–, Dir, Inst. for Behavioural Res. in Health, 1996–97, Curtin Univ. of Technol., Perth, WA; Adjunct Prof. of Gerontol., St Thomas Univ., Fredericton, 2001–08 (Vis. Prof., 1998–99). Consultant, OECD, Paris, 1963–64;

Expert, ILO, Geneva, 1966–67; Mem., Social Commn of Rehabilitation Internat., 1967–75; Consultant, Dept of Employment, 1970–72; Vis. Prof., Univ. of Western Ont., London, Canada, 1970 and 1971; Vis. Fellow, Wolfson Coll., Cambridge, 1985–86; Vis. Professorial Fellow, Curtin Univ. of Technol., Perth, 1993. Vice-Pres., Australian Council on the Ageing, 1975–76. FBPsS 1960; Fellow, Gerontological Soc. (USA), 1969. *Publications:* Beyond Permissiveness, 1992; handbooks and monographs on ageing and vocational rehabilitation, and articles in Jl of Gerontology and various psychological jls. *Recreations:* music, travel, writing. *Address:* c/o Department of Gerontology, St Thomas University, Fredericton, NB E3B 5G3, Canada.
Died 2 Oct. 2010.

GRIFFIN, Major Sir (Arthur) John (Stewart), KCVO 1990 (CVO 1974; MVO 1967); Press Secretary to HM Queen Elizabeth the Queen Mother, 1956–91; *b* 20 Feb. 1924; s of Arthur Wilfrid Michael Stewart Griffin and Florence May Griffin; *m* 1962, Henrietta Montagu Douglas Scott (*d* 2008); two *s. Educ:* Harrow School. Regular Army Officer, The Queen's Bays, later The Queen's Dragoon Guards, 1942–58. *Recreations:* cricket, fishing, shooting. *Address:* Barton's Cottage, Bushy Park, Teddington, Middx TW11 0EA. *Club:* MCC.
Died 1 April 2009.

GRIFFITH, (Edward) Michael (Wynne), CBE 1986; Vice Lord-Lieutenant for the County of Clwyd, 1986–2008; *b* 29 Aug. 1933; *e s* of Major H. W. Griffith, MBE; *m* Jill Grange, *d* of Major D. P. G. Moseley, Dorfold Cottage, Nantwich; one *s* (and two *s* decd). *Educ:* Eton; Royal Agricultural College. Regional Dir, National Westminster Bank Ltd, 1974–92; Mem. Welsh Bd, Nationwide Anglia Bldg Soc., 1986–89. High Sheriff of Denbighshire, 1969. Chairman: Clwyd HA, 1980–90; National Trust Cttee for Wales, 1984–91 (Mem., National Trust Exec. and Council, 1989–2000); Countryside Council for Wales, 1991–2000; Glan Clwyd Hosp. Trust, 1993–2001; Denbighshire and Conway Hosp. Trust, 1993–2001; Council, Univ. of Wales Coll. of Medicine, 1997–2004; Univ of Wales Audit Cttee, 2002–; Higher Educn Wales Chairs, 2002–04; Dir, Land Authority Wales, 1989–90. Member: Countryside Commn Cttee for Wales, 1972–78; Min. of Agriculture Regional Panel, 1972–77; ARC, 1973–82; UFC (Wales), 1989–92; HEFCW, 1992–95; British Library Bd, 1992–95. Pres., CPRW, 2003–06. Mem. Council, Cardiff Univ., 2004–. FRSA 1993; FLS 1995. DL Clwyd, 1985. *Address:* Greenfield, Trefnant, Clwyd LL16 5UE. *T:* (01745) 730633. *Club:* Boodle's.
Died 27 June 2009.

GRIFFITH, Prof. John Aneurin Grey, LLB London, LLM London; Hon. LLD Edinburgh 1982, York, Toronto, 1982, Manchester 1987; FBA 1977; Barrister-at-law; Chancellor of Manchester University, 1986–93; Emeritus Professor of Public Law, University of London; *b* 14 Oct. 1918; *s* of Rev. B. Grey Griffith and Bertha Griffith; *m* 1941, Barbara Eirene Garnet, *d* of W. Garnet Williams; two *s* one *d. Educ:* Taunton Sch.; LSE. British and Indian armies, 1940–46. Lectr in Law, UCW, Aberystwyth, 1946–48; Lectr in Law and Reader, LSE, 1948–59, Prof. of English Law, 1959–70, Prof. of Public Law, 1970–84. Vis. Professor of Law: Univ. of California at Berkeley, 1966; York Univ., 1985. Mem., Marlow UDC, 1950–55, and Bucks CC, 1955–61. Editor, Public Law, 1956–81. *Publications:* (with H. Street) A Casebook of Administrative Law, 1964; Central Departments and Local Authorities, 1966; (with H. Street) Principles of Administrative Law, 5th edn, 1973; Parliamentary Scrutiny of Government Bills, 1974; (with T. C. Hartley) Government and Law, 1975, 2nd edn 1981; (ed) From Policy to Administration, 1976; The Politics of the Judiciary, 1977, 5th edn 1997; Public Rights and Private Interests, 1981; (with M. T. Ryle) Parliament, 1989; Judicial Politics, since 1920: a chronicle, 1993; articles in English, Commonwealth and American jls of law, public

administration and politics. *Recreations:* drinking beer, writing bad verse. *Address:* 2 The Close, Spinfield Lane, Marlow, Bucks SL7 2LA. *Died 8 May 2010.*

GRIFFITH, Kenneth; actor, writer and documentary film-maker; formed own film company, Breakaway Productions Ltd, 1982; *b* 12 Oct. 1921; *g s* of Ernest and Emily Griffith; three marriages dissolved; three *s* two *d. Educ:* council and grammar schs, Tenby, Pembrokeshire, SW Wales. Became a professional actor at Festival Theatre, Cambridge, 1937; films and television; served War, RAF; post war, associated with Tyrone Guthrie at Old Vic; unknown number of films, partic. for Boulting brothers; unknown number of television plays; rarely theatre; made first documentary film at invitation of David Attenborough and Huw Wheldon, 1964; best documentaries include: Life of Cecil Rhodes; Hang Up Your Brightest Colours (life of Michael Collins; suppressed by Lew Grade at behest of IBA for twenty years, until broadcast in 1993); The Public's Right to Know; The Sun's Bright Child (life of Edmund Kean); Black as Hell, Thick as Grass (the 24th Regt in Zulu War); The Most Valuable Englishman Ever (life of Thomas Paine for BBC TV); Clive of India (Channel 4); The Light (life of David Ben Gurion for Channel 4); But I Have Promises to Keep (life of Jawaharlal Nehru for Indian Govt), 1987; The Girl Who Didn't Run (on Zola Budd for BBC TV), 1989; Roger Casement, the Heart of Darkness (for BBC TV), 1992; The Untouchable (life of Dr Ambedkar for BBC TV), 1996; The Legend of George Rex (Channel 4), 1997; Against Empire (to commemorate 2nd Anglo-Boer War, for BBC), 1999; *relevant film:* The Tenby Poisoner (film biography, BBC TV), 1993. *Publications:* Thank God we kept the Flag Flying, 1974; (with Timothy O'Grady) Curious Journey, 1981 (based on unshown TV documentary); The Discovery of Nehru, 1989; The Fool's Pardon (autobiog.), 1994. *Recreations:* talking; collecting British Empire military history (envelopes, post-cards), also ephemera connected with southern Africa. *Address:* 110 Englefield Road, Islington, N1 3LQ. *T:* (020) 7226 9013.
Died 25 June 2006.

GRIFFITH, Michael; see Griffith, E. M. W.

GRIFFITHS, David Howard, OBE 1982; Chairman, Eastern Region, British Gas Corporation, 1981–87; *b* 30 Oct. 1922; *s* of David Griffiths and Margaret (*née* Jones); *m* 1949, Dilys Watford John; two *d. Educ:* Monmouth Sch.; Sidney Sussex Coll., Cambridge (Exhibnr; BA 1941, MA 1946, LLB 1946). Admitted Solicitor of the Supreme Court, 1948. Asst Solicitor, Newport Corp., 1948; Wales Gas Board: Solicitor, 1949; Management Develt Officer, 1965; Dir of Develt, 1967; Wales Gas: Dir of Conversion, 1970; Sec., 1973; Dep. Chm., Eastern Gas, 1977. Vice Pres., Contemporary Arts Soc., Wales, 1977. *Recreations:* reading, golf, music. *Address:* 12 Fallows Green, Harpenden, Herts AL5 4HD.
Died 14 Dec. 2006.

GRILLET, Alain R.; see Robbe-Grillet.

GRIMA, Andrew Peter; Jeweller by appointment to HM the Queen; Managing Director, Andrew Grima Ltd, since 1966; *b* 31 May 1921; *s* of late John Grima and Leopolda Farnese; *m* 1st, 1947, Helène Marianne Haller (marr. diss. 1977); one *s* two *d*; 2nd, 1977, Joanne Jill, (Jojo), Maughan-Brown, *d* of late Captain Nigel Maughan-Brown, MC and of Mrs Graham Rawdon; one *d. Educ:* St Joseph's Coll., Beulah Hill; Nottingham Univ. Served War of 1939–45, REME, India and Burma, 1942–46 (despatches, 1945); commanded div. workshop. Director and jewellery designer. Exhibitions worldwide, designed and made prestige watch collection for Omega, "About Time", 1971; 40 year retrospective exhibn, Goldsmiths' Hall, 1991. Opened shops in Jermyn Street, 1966; Sydney and New York, 1970; Zürich, 1971; Tokyo, 1973; Lugano, 1987; Gstaad, 1992. Duke of Edinburgh Prize for Elegant Design, 1966; Queen's Award to Industry, 1966; 12 Diamond Internat. New York Awards, 1963–67. Freeman, City of London, 1964; Liveryman, Worshipful

Co. of Goldsmiths, 1968. *Publications:* contribs to: International Diamond Annual, S Africa, 1970; 6 Meister Juweliere unserer Zeit, 1971; By Royal Command, 1999; Artists and Authors at War, 1999; *relevant publications:* Grima 1951–1991, by Johann Willsberger, 1991; Grima: a jeweller's world, 2003. *Recreations:* paintings, sculpture, food and wine. *Address:* Vieux Gstaad, 3780 Gstaad, Switzerland; Albany, Piccadilly, W1J 0AZ.
Died 26 Dec. 2007.

GRIMSHAW, Maj.-Gen. Ewing Henry Wrigley, CB 1965; CBE 1957 (OBE 1954); DSO 1945; *b* 30 June 1911; *s* of Col E. W. Grimshaw; *m* 1943, Hilda Florence Agnes Allison (*d* 1993); one *s* one *d* (and one *s* decd). *Educ:* Brighton Coll. Joined Indian Army, 1931. Served War of 1939–45, Western Desert and Burma (despatches twice, DSO), Java; Brig. 1944 (youngest on active service). Transferred to Royal Inniskilling Fusiliers, 1947; active service in Malaya, 1948 and 1950, Kenya, 1954, Suez, 1956 and Cyprus, 1958; GOC 44th Div. (TA) and Home Counties Dist, 1962–65. Col, The Royal Inniskilling Fusiliers, 1966–68; Dep. Col, The Royal Irish Rangers, 1968–73. Dep. Chief Constable, Dover Castle, 1962–65.
Died 1 Nov. 2007.

GRINDROD, Most Rev. John Basil Rowland, KBE 1983; Archbishop of Brisbane and Metropolitan of Queensland, 1980–89; Primate of Australia, 1982–89; *b* 14 Dec. 1919; *s* of Edward Basil and Dorothy Gladys Grindrod; *m* 1949, Ailsa W. (*d* 1981), *d* of G. Newman; two *d*; *m* 1983, Mrs Dell Cornish, *d* of S. J. Caswell. *Educ:* Repton School; Queen's College, Oxford (BA 1949; MA 1954); Lincoln Theological College. Deacon, 1951, priest, 1952, Manchester; Curate: St Michael's, Hulme, 1951–54; Bundaberg, Qld, 1954–56; Rector: All Souls, Ancoats, Manchester, 1956–60; Emerald, Qld, 1960–61; St Barnabas, N Rockhampton, Qld, 1961–65; Archdeacon of Rockhampton, Qld, 1960–65; Vicar, Christ Church, S Yarra, Vic, 1965–66; Bishop of Riverina, NSW, 1966–71; Bishop of Rockhampton, 1971–80. Hon. ThD 1985. *Address:* Unit 7152, 101 Lindfield Road, Helensvale, Qld 4212, Australia.
Died 4 Jan. 2009.

GRINSTEAD, Sir Stanley (Gordon), Kt 1986; FCA; Chairman and Director, Harmony Leisure Group, 1989–92; *b* 17 June 1924; *s* of Ephraim Grinstead and Lucy Grinstead (*née* Taylor); *m* 1955, Joyce Preston; two *d*. *Educ:* Strodes, Egham. Served Royal Navy, 1943–46 (Pilot, FAA). Franklin, Wild & Co., Chartered Accountants, 1946–56; Hotel York Ltd, 1957; Grand Metropolitan Ltd, 1957–62; Union Properties (London) Ltd, 1958–66; Grand Metropolitan Ltd, 1964–87: Dep. Chm. and Group Man. Dir, 1980–82; Gp Chief Exec., 1982–86; Chm., 1982–87; Chm., Reed Internat., 1988–89 (Dir, 1981–90). Trustee, FAA Museum. Vice-Pres., CGLI, 1986–90. CCMI. Master, Brewers' Co., 1983–84. *Recreations:* gardening, cricket, racing, breeding of thoroughbred horses. *Clubs:* Army and Navy, MCC; Surrey County Cricket (Hon. Treas., 1987–94).
Died 13 July 2009.

GRIST, Prof. Norman Roy, FRCPE; Professor of Infectious Diseases, University of Glasgow, 1965–83, then Emeritus; *b* 9 March 1918; *s* of Walter Reginald Grist and Florence Goodwin Grist (*née* Nadin); *m* 1943, Mary Stewart McAlister. *Educ:* Shawlands Acad., Glasgow; University of Glasgow (BSc 1939; MB ChB (Commendation), 1942). MRCPE 1950, FRCPE 1958; Founder Mem., 1963, FRCPath 1967; MRCPGlas 1980, FRCPGlas 1983. Ho. Phys. Gartloch Hosp., 1942–43; RAMC, GDO 223 Fd Amb. and RMO 2/KSLI, 1943–46; Ho. Surg. Victoria Inf., Glasgow, 1946–47; Res. Phys., Ruchill Hosp., Glasgow, 1947–48; Research Asst, Glasgow Univ. Dept of Infectious Diseases, 1948–52; Lectr in Virus Disease, Glasgow Univ., 1952–62, and Regional Adviser in Virology to Scottish Western Reg. Hosp. Bd, 1960–74; Reader in Viral Epidemiology, Glasgow Univ., 1962–65. Mem., Expert Adv. Panel on Virus Diseases to WHO, 1967–2001. Pres., Glasgow Natural History Soc., 1993–96. Hon.

Mem., Assoc. of Clin. Pathology, 1989. Bronze Medal, Helsinki Univ., 1973; Orden Civil de Sanidad, cat. Encomienda, Spain, 1974. *Publications:* Diagnostic Methods in Clinical Virology, 1966, 3rd edn, 1979; (with D. Reid and I. W. Pinkerton) Infections in Current Medical Practice, 1986; (with D. O. Ho-Yen, E. Walker and G. R. Williams) Diseases of Infection, 1987, 2nd edn 1993; numerous contribs to British and international med. jls. *Recreations:* gardener's mate, natural history. *Address:* Red Cross House, Erskine Home, Bishopton, Renfrewshire PA7 5PU.
Died 7 June 2010.

GROBLER, Richard Victor, CBE 1996; Deputy Secretary of Commissions, Lord Chancellor's Department, 1984–96; *b* Umtali, S Rhodesia, 27 May 1936; *m* 1961, Julienne Nora de la Cour (*née* Sheath); one *s* three *d*. *Educ:* Bishop's, Capetown; Univ. of Cape Town (BA). Called to the Bar, Gray's Inn, 1961; joined staff of Clerk of the Court, Central Criminal Court, 1961; Dep. Clerk of the Court, 1970; Dep. Courts Administrator, 1972; Courts Administrator, Inner London Crown Court, 1974; Sec., Lord Chancellor's Adv. Cttee on Justices of the Peace for Inner London and Jt Hon. Sec., Inner London Br. of Magistrates' Assoc., 1974–77; Courts Administrator, Central Criminal Court, and Co-ordinator, Crown Courts Taxations, SE Circuit, 1977–79; Dep. Circuit Administrator, S Eastern Circuit, 1979–83. Dir, Housing Solutions Ltd, 2000–. Gov., Furze Platt Sen. Sch., 1997–. Liveryman, Worshipful Company of Gold and Silver Wyre Drawers. *Recreations:* gardening, swimming, golf. *Address:* Meadowsweet, 5 Pinkneys Drive, Maidenhead, Berks SL6 5DS. *T:* (01628) 624280.
Died 21 July 2008.

GROUÈS, Henri Antoine, (Abbé Pierre); Grand Officier de la Légion d'Honneur, 2001 (Officier, 1980); French priest; Founder of the Companions of Emmaüs; *b* Lyon, 5 Aug. 1912; 5th *c* of Antoine Grouès, Soyeux. *Educ:* Collège des Jésuites, Lyon. Entered Capuchin Monastery, 1930; studied at Capuchin seminary, Crest, Drôme, and Faculté de Théologie, Lyon. Secular priest, St Joseph Basilica, Grenoble. Served war of 1939–45 (Officier de la Légion d'Honneur, Croix de Guerre, Médaille de la Résistance); Alsatian and Alpine fronts; Vicar of the Cathedral, Grenoble; assumed name of Abbé Pierre and joined resistance movement, 1942; Chaplain of French Navy at Casablanca, 1944; of whole Free French Navy, 1945. Elected (Indep.) to 1st Constituent Assembly of 4th French Republic, 1945; elected as candidate of Mouvement Républicain Populaire to 2nd Constituent Assembly; re-elected 1946; contested (Indep.), 1951. Président de l'Exécutif du Mouvement Universel pour une Confédération Mondiale, 1949. Founded the Companions of Emmaüs, a movement to provide a roof for the "sanslogis" of Paris, 1949. *Publications* include: 23 Mois de Vie Clandestine; L'Abbé Pierre vous Parle; Vers l'Homme; Feuilles Eparses; Emmaüs ou Venger l'homme; Dieu merci; Dieu et les hommes; Testament...; Fraternité; Mémoire d'un croyant. *Address:* 183 bis rue Vaillant Couturier BP91, 94143 Alfortville Cedex, Val de Marne, France. *T:* (1) 48932950.
Died 22 Jan. 2007.

GROVE, Sir Edmund (Frank), KCVO 1982 (CVO 1974; LVO 1963; MVO 1953); Chief Accountant of the Privy Purse, 1967–82, and Serjeant-at-Arms, 1975–82; *b* 20 July 1920; *s* of Edmund Grove and Sarah Caroline (*née* Hunt); *m* 1945, Grete Elisabet (*d* 2007), *d* of Martinus Skou, Denmark; two *d*. Served War, RASC, ME, 1940–46 (C-in-C's Commendation). Entered the Household of King George VI, 1946 and of Queen Elizabeth II, 1952. Chevalier: Order of the Dannebrog, Denmark, 1974; Légion d'Honneur, France, 1976; Officer, Order of the Polar Star, Sweden, 1975. *Recreation:* gardening. *Address:* Chapel Cottage, West Newton, King's Lynn, Norfolk PE31 6AU.
Died 28 June 2010.

GROVES, John Dudley, CB 1981; OBE 1964; Director-General, Central Office of Information, 1979–82; Head of Profession for Government Information Officer Group, 1981–82; *b* 12 Aug. 1922; *y* s of late Walter Groves; *m* 1943, Pamela Joy Holliday (*d* 2007); one *s* two *d*. *Educ:* St Paul's Sch. Reporter, Richmond Herald, 1940–41; Queen's Royal Regt, 1941–42; commnd in 43rd Reconnaissance Regt, 1942; served in NW Europe, 1944–45 (despatches); Observer Officer, Berlin, 1945; Press Association (Press Gallery), 1947–51; Times (Press Gallery and Lobby), 1951–58; Head of Press Sect., Treasury, 1958–62; Dep. Public Relations Adviser to Prime Minister, 1962–64 (Actg Adviser, 1964); Chief Information Officer, DEA, 1964–68; Chief of Public Relations, MoD, 1968–77; Dir of Information, DHSS, 1977–78. Mem., Working Party on Censorship, 1983. *Publications:* (with R. Gill) Club Route, 1945. *Recreations:* walking, painting. *Address:* Mortimers, Manningford Bohune, Pewsey, Wilts SN9 5PG. *Died 26 Dec. 2007.*

GRUENBERG, Prof. Karl Walter; Professor of Pure Mathematics in the University of London, at Queen Mary and Westfield (formerly Queen Mary) College, 1967–93, then Emeritus; *b* 3 June 1928; *s* of late Paul Gruenberg and Anna Gruenberg; *m* 1st, Katherine; one *s* one *d*; 2nd, 1973, Margaret Semple. *Educ:* Shaftesbury Grammar Sch.; Kilburn Grammar Sch.; Cambridge Univ. BA 1950, PhD 1954. Asst Lectr, Queen Mary Coll., 1953–55; Commonwealth Fund Fellowship, 1955–57 (at Harvard Univ., 1955–56; at Inst. for Advanced Study, Princeton, 1956–57). Queen Mary College: Lectr, 1957–61; Reader, 1961–67. Visiting Professor: Univ. of Michigan, 1961–62, 1978; Cornell Univ., 1966–67; Univ. of Illinois, 1972; Australian Nat. Univ., 1979 and 1987. Mem., Maths Cttee, SERC, 1983–86. *Publications:* Cohomological Topics in Group Theory, 1970; Relation Modules of Finite Groups, 1976; Linear Geometry (jtly with A. J. Weir), 2nd edn 1977; Una Introduzione all' Algebra Omologica, 2002; articles on algebra in various learned jls. *Address:* School of Mathematical Sciences, Queen Mary and Westfield College (University of London), Mile End Road, E1 4NS. *T:* (020) 7882 5472. *Died 10 Oct. 2007.*

GRUFFYDD JONES, Daniel; *see* Jones.

GRUGEON, Sir John (Drury), Kt 1980; DL; Chairman, Kent Police Authority, 1992–98; *b* 20 Sept. 1928; *s* of Drury Grugeon and Sophie (*née* Pratt); *m* 1st, 1955, Mary Patricia (*née* Rickards) (marr. diss. 1986); one *s* one *d*; 2nd, 1989, Pauline Lois (*d* 2006), *widow* of Dr Roland Phillips. *Educ:* Epsom Grammar Sch.; RMA Sandhurst. Commissioned, The Buffs, Dec. 1948; served 1st Bn in Middle and Far East and Germany; Regimental Adjt, 1953–55; Adjt 5th Bn, 1956–58; left Army, 1960. Joined Save and Prosper Group, 1960. Kent County Council: Mem., 1967–2001; Leader, 1973–82; Vice-Chm., 1987–89; Chm., 1989–91, 1997–99; Chairman: Superannuation Fund, 1982–87; Fire and Public Protection Cttee, 1984–87. Chm., Policy Cttee, Assoc. of County Councils, 1978–81 (Chm., Finance Cttee, 1976–79); Vice Chm., Assoc. of Police Authorities, 1997–98 (Chm., Finance Gp, 1997–98). Dir, Internat. Garden Fest. '84, Liverpool, 1982–83. Chm., Tunbridge Wells HA, 1984–92. Member: SE Economic Planning Council, 1971–74; Medway Ports Authority, 1977–93; Dep. Chm., Medway (Chatham) Dock Co., 1983–92. Jt Vice-Chm., Cons. Nat. Adv. Cttee for Local Govt, 1975–82. Chm., Brett Envmt Trust, 2001–07. Liveryman, Ironmongers' Co., 1977–. DL Kent, 1986. Hon. Fellow, Canterbury Christ Church UC, 2002. *Recreations:* cricket, shooting, local govt. *Address:* 3 Eastgate Road, Tenterden, Kent TN30 7AH. *T:* (01580) 763494. *Clubs:* Carlton, MCC; Kent CC. *Died 22 Nov. 2009.*

GUERITZ, Rear-Adm. Edward Findlay, CB 1971; OBE 1957; DSC 1942, and Bar, 1944; *b* 8 Sept. 1919; *s* of Elton and Valentine Gueritz; *m* 1947, Pamela Amanda Bernhardina Britton, *d* of Commander L. H. Jeans, and *widow* of Lt-Comdr E. M. Britton, RN; one *s* one *d*. *Educ:* Cheltenham Coll. Entered Navy, 1937; Midshipman, 1938; served War of 1939–45 (wounded; DSC and Bar): HMS Jersey, 5th Flotilla, 1940–41; Combined Ops

(Indian Ocean, Normandy), 1941–44; HMS Saumarez (Corfu Channel incident), 1946; HMS Troubridge, 1947; Army Staff Coll., Camberley, 1948; Staff of C-in-C S Atlantic and Junior Naval Liaison Officer to UK High Comr, S Africa, 1954–56; Near East Operations, 1956 (OBE); Staff of FO Sea Training, 1957–58; Dep. Dir, RN Staff Coll., 1959–61; Naval Staff, Admty, 1961–63; idc 1964; Captain of Fleet, Far East Fleet, 1965–66; Dir of Defence Plans (Navy), 1967; Dir, Jt Warfare Staff, MoD, 1968; Admiral-President, Royal Naval Coll., 1968–70 (concurrently first Pres., RN Staff Coll.); Comdt, Jt Warfare Estabt, 1970–72. Lt-Comdr 1949; Comdr 1953; Captain 1959; Rear-Adm. 1969; retd 1973. Dep. Dir and Editor, 1976–79, Dir and Editor-in-Chief, 1979–81, RUSI. Specialist Adviser, House of Commons Select Cttee on Defence, 1975–95. Chief Hon. Steward, Westminster Abbey, 1975–85. President: Soc. for Nautical Res., 1974–90 (Hon. Vice Pres., 1990); J and K Class Destroyer Assoc., 1990–99; Vice-Pres., RN Commando Assoc., 1993–2004; Vice Chairman: Council for Christian Approaches to Defence and Disarmament, 1974–80; Victoria League, 1985–88; Marine Soc., 1988–93 (Vice Pres., 1991); Member Council: Fairbridge-Drake Soc., 1981–90; British Atlantic Cttee, 1977–89; HOST (Hosting for Overseas Students Trust), 1987–90 (founding Governor). Mem., Bd of War Studies, Univ. of London, 1969–85. *Publications:* (jtly) The Third World War, 1978; (ed jtly) Ten Years of Terrorism, 1979; (ed jtly) Will the Wells Run Dry, 1979; (ed jtly) Nuclear Attack: Civil Defence, 1982; editor, RUSI Brassey's Defence Year Book, 1977–78, 1978–79, 1980, 1981. *Recreations:* history, gardening. *Address:* Hemyngsby, 56 The Close, Salisbury, Wilts SP1 2EL. *Club:* Army and Navy. *Died 21 Dec. 2008.*

GUINNESS, James Edward Alexander Rundell, CBE 1986; Director, Guinness Peat Group, 1973–87 (Joint Chairman, 1973–77; Deputy Chairman, 1977–84); Deputy Chairman, Provident Mutual Life Assurance Association, 1983–89; *b* 23 Sept. 1924; *s* of Sir Arthur Guinness, KCMG and Frances Patience Guinness, MBE (*née* Wright); *m* 1953, Pauline Mander; one *s* four *d*. *Educ:* Eton; Oxford. Served in RNVR, 1943–46. Joined family banking firm of Guinness Mahon & Co., 1946, Partner 1953; Chm., Guinness Mahon Hldgs Ltd, 1968–72. Chm., Public Works Loan Bd, 1979–90 (Comr, 1960–90). *Recreations:* shooting, fishing. *Address:* Coldpiece Farm, Hound Green, Hook, Hants RG27 8LQ. *T:* (01734) 326292. *Clubs:* Brooks's, Pratt's; Royal Yacht Squadron (Cowes). *Died 26 March 2006.*

GUISE, Sir John (Grant), 7th Bt *cr* 1783; Jockey Club Official, 1968; *b* 15 Dec. 1927; *s* of Sir Anselm William Edward Guise, 6th Bt and Nina Margaret Sophie (*d* 1991), *d* of Sir James Augustus Grant, 1st Bt; S father. 1970; *m* 1992, Sally, *d* of late Cdre H. G. C. Stevens, RN. *Educ:* Winchester; RMA Sandhurst. Regular officer, 3rd The King's Own Hussars, 1948–61. *Recreations:* hunting, shooting. Heir: *b* Christopher James Guise [*b* 10 July 1930; *m* 1969, Mrs Carole Hoskins Benson, *e d* of Jack Master; one *s* one *d*]. *Address:* Elmore Court, Gloucester GL2 3NT. *T:* (01452) 720293. *Died 15 May 2007.*

GUN-MUNRO, Sir Sydney Douglas, GCMG 1979; Kt 1977; MBE 1957; FRCS; Governor-General of St Vincent and the Grenadines, 1979–85, retired (Governor, 1977–79); *b* 29 Nov. 1916; *s* of Barclay Justin Gun-Munro and Marie Josephine Gun-Munro; *m* 1943, Joan Estelle Benjamin; two *s* one *d*. *Educ:* Grenada Boys' Secondary Sch.; King's Coll. Hosp., London (MB BS Hons 1943); Moorfields Hosp., London (DO 1952). MRCS, LRCP 1943; FRCS 1985. House Surg., EMS Hosp., Horton, 1943; MO, Lewisham Hosp., 1943–46; Dist MO, Grenada, 1946–49; Surg., Gen. Hosp., St Vincent, 1949–71; Dist MO, Bequia, St Vincent, 1972–76. *Recreations:* tennis, boating. *Address:* PO Box 51, Bequia, St Vincent and the Grenadines, West Indies. *T:* 83261. *Died 1 March 2007.*

GUNN, Marion Ballantyne; Head of Fire Service and Emergency Planning Division, Scottish Executive Justice Department (formerly Scottish Office Home and Health, then Home, Department), 1992–2001; *b* 31 Oct. 1947; *d* of Dr Allan Christie Tait and Jean Ballantyne Hay; *m* 1985, Donald Hugh Gunn (*d* 2007); one step *s. Educ:* Jordanhill College School; Dumfries Academy; Univ. of Edinburgh (MA Hons 1969); Open Univ. (BA 1975). Management trainee, Lewis's, Bristol, 1969–70; joined Scottish Office, 1970; posts in Scottish Educn Dept and Scottish Develt Dept, 1970–90; Asst Sec., 1984; Head of Roads Policy and Programme Div., 1987; Head of Water Policy Div., 1990. Research Fellow, Univ. of Glasgow, 1983–84. *Recreations:* gardening, badminton. *Address:* 32 Warriston Avenue, Edinburgh EH3 5NB. *T:* (0131) 552 4476. *Died 17 July 2009.*

GUNNELL, (William) John; *b* 1 Oct. 1933; *s* of late William Henry and Norah Gunnell; *m* 1955, Jean Louise (*d* 2007), *d* of late Frank and Harriet Louise Lacey; three *s* one *d. Educ:* King Edward's Sch., Birmingham; Univ. of Leeds (BSc Hons). Hospital porter, St Bartholomew's, London, 1955–57; Teacher, Leeds Modern Sch., 1959–62; Head of Science, United Nations International Sch., New York, 1962–70; Lectr, Centre for Studies in Science and Mathematics Education, Univ. of Leeds, 1970–88. Chm., Crown Point Foods, 1988–90. County Councillor for Hunslet, 1977–86; Leader of Opposition, 1979–81, Leader, 1981–86, W Yorks MCC; Mem. for Hunslet, Leeds MDC, 1986–92 (Chm., Social Services Cttee, 1990–92). MP (Lab) Leeds South and Morley, 1992–97, Morley and Rothwell, 1997–2001. Member, Select Committee: on Broadcasting, 1992–97; on Public Service, 1995–97; on Health, 1997–2001. Chm., Educn and Employment Deptl Cttee, 1997–99. Chairman: Yorkshire Enterprise Ltd (formerly W Yorks Enterprise Bd), 1982–90 and 1994–96 (Vice-Chm., 1990–94); Yorkshire Fund Management Ltd, 1989–97 (non-exec. Dir, 1989–2003). Chairman: Yorks and Humberside Develt Assoc., 1981–93 (Hon. Pres., 1993–97); Leeds/Bradford Airport jt cttee, 1981–83; N of England Regional Consortium, 1984–92 (Hon. Pres., 1992–97); Member: Audit Commn, 1983–90; Leeds Develt Corp., 1988–92; Leeds Eastern AHA, later Leeds Health Care, 1990–92. Advr to Conseil des Régions d'Europe, subseq. Assembly of Regions of Europe, 1986–2001 (Mem. Bureau, 1985–86). Hon. Pres., RETI, 1985–87. Spokesman for MCCs in their campaign against abolition, 1983–85. Mem., Fabian Soc., 1972–. Director: Opera North, 1982–2001; Leeds Theatre Trust, 1986–93. Hon. Alderman, City of Leeds, 2001. *Publications:* Selected Experiments in Advanced Level Chemistry, 1975, and other texts (all with E. W. Jenkins); (contrib.) Local Economic Policy, 1990. *Recreations:* music, opera, watching cricket and soccer. *Clubs:* Warwickshire CC; Yorkshire CC. *Died 28 Jan. 2008.*

GUTHRIE, Robert Isles Loftus, (Robin); Director of Social and Economic Affairs, Council of Europe, 1992–98; *b* 27 June 1937; *s* of late Prof. W. K. C. Guthrie, FBA and of Adele Marion Ogilvy, MA; *m* 1963, Sarah Julia Weltman; two *s* one *d. Educ:* Clifton Coll.; Trinity Coll., Cambridge (MA); Liverpool Univ. (CertEd); LSE (MScEcon). Head of Cambridge House (Univ. settlement in S London), 1962–69; teacher, ILEA, 1964–66; Social Develt Officer, Peterborough Develt Corp., 1969–75; Asst Dir, Social Work Service, DHSS, 1975–79; Dir, Joseph Rowntree Meml Trust, 1979–88; Chief Charity Comr for England and Wales, 1988–92. Mem., expedns in Anatolia, British Inst. of Archaeol. at Ankara, 1958–62. Member: Arts Council of GB, 1979–81 and 1987–88 (Regional Cttee, 1976–81); Council, Policy Studies Institute, 1979–88; Council, York Univ., 1982–94; UK Cttee, Eur. Cultural Foundn, 2004–; Council, Leeds Univ., 2004–05; Chairman: Yorkshire Arts Assoc., 1984–88; Council of Regional Arts Assocs, 1985–88; Jessie's Fund, 1998–; Yorkshire Regl Arts Bd, 2000–02; Rodolfus Choir, 2001– (Trustee, 1998–); York Mus and Gall. Trust, 2002–; York St John Coll., 2003–08; Trustee: York Early Music Foundn, 1995–2003

(Chm., 1995–2001); Thalidomide Trust, 1999–. FRSA. Hon. DLitt Bradford, 1991. *Publications:* (ed) Outlook, 1963; (ed) Outlook Two, 1965; The Good European's Dilemma, 2000; various articles, speeches and lectures. *Recreations:* music, mountains, travel, sheep. *Address:* Braeside House, Acomb Road, York YO24 4EZ. *Died 12 April 2009.*

GUTTERIDGE, Prof. William Frank, MBE (mil.) 1946; Director, Research Institute for the Study of Conflict and Terrorism, 1994–2001; *b* 21 Sept. 1919; *s* of Frank Leonard Gutteridge and Nora Conwy (*née* Tighe); *m* 1944, Margaret McCallum Parker; three *d. Educ:* Stamford Sch., Lincs; Hertford Coll., Oxford (MA Mod. Hist., DipEd). Served War, 1939–46: commnd Manchester Regt; India/Burma, 1942/45: Staff Officer, 33 Indian Corps, finally DAAG 2nd British Div. Sen. Lectr in Commonwealth Hist. and Govt, RMA Sandhurst, 1949–63; Nuffield Foundn/Home CS Travelling Fellow studying rôle of Armed Forces in Commonwealth Africa, 1960–61; Hd, Langs and Mod. Studies Dept, Lanchester Poly., Coventry, 1963–71; Aston University: Dir, Complementary Studies, 1971–80; Prof. of Internat. Studies, 1976–82; Hd, Pol and Econ. Studies Dept, 1980–82; Prof. Emeritus, 1982; Editl Cons., Inst. for Study of Conflict, 1982–89; Exec. and Editl Dir, Res. Inst. for Study of Conflict and Terrorism, 1989–94. Sec., Brit. Pugwash Gp for Sci. and World Affairs, 1965–86. Chm., CNAA Cttee for Arts and Social Studies, 1978–84. *Publications:* Armed Forces in New States, 1962; Military Institutions and Power in New States, 1965; The Military in African Politics, 1969; Military Regimes in Africa, 1975; The New Terrorism, 1986; South Africa from Apartheid to National Unity 1981–94, 1995; South Africa's Defence and Security Forces into the 21st Century, 1996; (with J. E. Spence) Violence in Southern Africa, 1997; Latin America and the Caribbean: prospects for democracy, 1997; South Africa: potential of Mbeki's presidency, 1999. *Recreations:* research, writing. *Died 22 May 2008.*

GUY, Geoffrey Colin, CMG 1964; CVO 1966; OBE 1962 (MBE 1957); Governor and Commander in Chief, St Helena and its Dependencies, 1976–81, retired; first elected Speaker of the Legislative Council, St Helena, 1989; *b* 4 Nov. 1921; *s* of late E. Guy, 14 Woodland Park Road, Headingley, Leeds, and of Constance Reed Guy (*née* Taylor); *m* 1946, Joan Elfreda Smith; one *s. Educ:* Chatham House Sch., Ramsgate; Brasenose Coll., Oxford. Served RAF, 1941–46: reconnaissance pilot Spitfires and Hurricanes, Middle East and Burma, 1943–45; Special Force 136, 1945 (Flight Lieut). Asst Ed., Courtaulds Works Mag., 1948; management staff, Scribbans-Kemp Ltd, 1948–51; Colonial Administrative Service, Sierra Leone: Cadet, 1951; Asst Sec. Chief Comr Protectorate, 1953–54; District Comr, Tonkolili Dist, 1955; Administrator, Turks and Caicos Islands, and Chm. and Man. Dir, Turks Island Salt Co., 1958–65; Administrator, Dominica, 1965–67, Governor, March–Nov. 1967; Asst Sec., Soil Assoc., 1968; Sec., Forces Help Soc. and Lord Roberts' Workshops, 1970–73; Administrator, Ascension Island, 1973–76. *Recreations:* reading, walking, swimming. *Clubs:* Royal Air Force, Victory Services. *Died 1 Dec. 2006.*

GUYATT, Richard Gerald Talbot, CBE 1969; Rector, Royal College of Art, 1978–81 (Pro-Rector, 1974–78); Professor of Graphic Arts, 1948–78); *b* 8 May 1914; *s* of Thomas Guyatt, sometime HM Consul, Vigo, Spain and Cecil Guyatt; *m* 1941, Elizabeth Mary Corsellis (*d* 2005); one step *d. Educ:* Charterhouse. Freelance designer: posters for Shell-Mex and BP, 1935. War Service: Regional Camouflage Officer for Scotland, Min. of Home Security. Dir and Chief Designer, Cockade Ltd, 1946–48; Co-designer of Lion and Unicorn Pavilion, Festival of Britain, 1951; Consultant Designer to: Josiah Wedgwood & Sons, 1952–55, 1967–70; Central Electricity Generating Bd, 1964–68; British Sugar Bureau, 1965–68; W. H. Smith, 1970–87. Vis. Prof., Yale Univ., 1955 and 1962. Ceramic Designs for Min. of

Works (for British Embassies), King's Coll. Cambridge, Goldsmiths' Co. and Wedgwood commem. mugs for Coronation, 1953, Investiture, 1969, Royal Silver Wedding, 1973, Millennium, 2000, Golden Jubilee, 2002 and 50th Anniv. of Coronation, 2003. Designed: silver medal for Royal Mint, Mint Dirs Conf., 1972; 700th Anniv. of Parlt stamp, 1965; Postal Order forms, 1964 for Post Office; Silver Jubilee stamps, 1977; commem. crown piece for 80th birthday of HM Queen Elizabeth The Queen Mother, 1980. Member: Stamp Adv. Cttee, 1963–74; Internat. Jury, Warsaw Poster Biennale, 1968; Bank of England Design Adv. Cttee, 1968–75; Adv. Council, Victoria and Albert Mus., 1978–81. Chm., Guyatt/Jenkins Design Group. Governor, Imperial Coll. of Sci. and Technol., 1979–81. FSIA; Hon. ARCA. Misha Black Meml Medal, for distinguished services to design educn, SIAD, 2000. *Address:* Forge Cottage, Ham, Marlborough, Wilts SN8 3RB. *T:* (01488) 668270.
Died 17 Oct. 2007.

GWYNN, Edward Harold, CB 1961; Deputy Under-Secretary of State, Ministry of Defence, 1966–72; retired 1972; *b* 23 Aug. 1912; *y s* of late Dr E. J. Gwynn, Provost of Trinity Coll., Dublin, and Olive Ponsonby; *m* 1937, Dorothy (*d* 2002), *d* of late Geoffrey S. Phillpotts, Foxrock, Co. Dublin; one *s* two *d* (and two *d* decd). *Educ:* Sedbergh School; Trinity Coll., Dublin. Entered Home Office, 1936; Assistant Secretary, 1947; Assistant Under-Secretary of State, 1956; Principal Finance Officer (Under-Secretary), Ministry of Agriculture, 1961–62; Deputy Under-Secretary of State, Home Office, 1963–66. *Recreations:* gardening, the countryside. *Address:* The Chestnuts, Minchinhampton, Glos GL6 9AR. *T:* (01453) 832863.
Died 3 Feb. 2007.

GWYNN-JONES, Sir Peter (Llewellyn), KCVO 2010 (CVO 1998; LVO 1994); Garter Principal King of Arms, 1995–2010; Genealogist, Order of the Bath, Order of St Michael and St George, and Order of St John, 1995–2010; *b* 12 March 1940; *s* of late Major Jack Llewellyn Gwynn-Jones, Cape Town, and Mary Muriel Daphne, *d* of Col Arthur Patrick Bird Harrison, and step *s* of late Lt-Col Gavin David Young, Long Burton, Dorset. *Educ:* Wellington Coll.; Trinity Coll., Cambridge (MA). Assistant to Garter King of Arms, 1970; Bluemantle Pursuivant of Arms, 1973; Secretary, Harleian Society, 1981–94; Lancaster Herald of Arms, 1982–95. Inspector of Regtl Colours, 1995–2010, of RAF Badges, 1996–2010. Freeman and Liveryman: Painter Stainers' Co., 1997; Scriveners' Co., 1997. Hon. Citizen, State of Tennessee, 1991. FSA 1997. KStJ 1995. *Publications:* Heraldry, 1993; The Art of Heraldry, 1998; The Coati Sable: the story of a herald, 2010. *Recreations:* tropical forests, wildlife conservation, fishing. *Address:* 79 Harcourt Terrace, SW10 9JP. *T:* (020) 7373 5859.
Died 21 Aug. 2010.

H

HAAN, Christopher Francis, LLB; Director: Firecrest Hambro Ltd, since 2002; Firecrest Capital Ltd, merchant bankers, since 2002. Admitted solicitor, 1968. Partner: Herbert & Gowers, 1969–71; Linklaters & Paines, 1974–81; S. J. Berwin & Co., 1982–92 (Sen. Partner, 1988–92); Coudert Brothers, 1992–94; Partner, 1995–2001, Consultant, 2001–03, Hammonds (formerly Hammond Suddards), solicitors. Chm. Bd, Local Investment Fund, 1994–; Dir, Dartington Hall Trust, 2000–. *Address:* Firecrest Hambro Ltd, 4 Park Place, SW1A 1LP. *T:* (020) 7898 9020, *Fax:* (020) 7898 9263; *e-mail:* c.haan@firecresthambro.com.
Died 10 March 2007.

HACKNEY, Arthur, RWS 1957 (VPRWS 1974–77); RE 1960 (Hon. RE 1982); ARCA 1949; artist; Principal Lecturer (formerly Deputy Head), Fine Art Department, West Surrey College of Art and Design (Farnham Centre) (formerly Farnham School of Art), 1979–85; *b* 13 March 1925; *s* of late J. T. Hackney; *m* 1955, Mary Baker, ARCA; two *d*. *Educ:* Burslem Sch. of Art; Royal Coll. of Art, London. Served in Royal Navy, Western Approaches, 1942–46. Travelling scholarship, Royal College of Art, 1949; part-time Painting Instructor, Farnham Sch. of Art, 1950, Lecturer, 1962; Head of Dept: Graphic, 1963–68; Printmaking, 1968–79. Work represented in Public Collections, including Bradford City Art Gallery, Victoria and Albert Museum, Guildhall Art Gall., Ashmolean Museum, Wellington Art Gallery (NZ), Nottingham Art Gallery, Keighley Art Gallery (Yorks), Wakefield City Art Gallery, Graves Art Gallery, Sheffield, Preston Art Gallery, City of Stoke-on-Trent Art Gall., Kent Educn Cttee, Staffordshire Educn Cttee, RCA. Mem., Fine Art Bd, CNAA, 1975–78. Work reproduced in 20th Century Painters and Sculptors, by Francis Spalding, 1990. *Address:* Woodhatches, Spoil Lane, Tongham, Farnham, Surrey GU10 1BP. *T:* (01252) 323919. *Club:* Chelsea Arts.
Died 12 May 2010.

HADFIELD, (Geoffrey) John, CBE 1980; TD 1963; FRCS; Surgeon, Stoke Mandeville Hospital, 1960–88, retired; Hon. Tutor in Surgery, University College Hospital Medical School, 1968–88; *b* 19 April 1923; *s* of late Prof. Geoffrey Hadfield, MD, and Eileen D'Arcy Irvine; *m* 1960, Beryl, *d* of late Hubert Sleigh, Manchester; three *d*. *Educ:* Merchant Taylors' Sch.; St Bartholomew's Hosp., London Univ. (MB BS 1947; MS 1954). MRCS, LRCP 1946; FRCS 1948. Ho. Officer Appts, Demonstr of Anatomy, Registrar and Sen. Lectr in Surgery, St Bart's Hosp.; Fellow in Surgery, Memorial Hosp., New York; served RAMC, Far East, 1948–50; TAVR, 1950–73; Lt-Col, RAMC, Hon. Col 219 Gen. Hosp., TAVR. Royal College of Surgeons of England: Arris and Gale Lectr, 1954; Hunterian Prof., 1959; Erasmus Wilson Demonstr, 1969; Arnott Demonstr, 1972; Stamford Cade Meml Lectr, 1978; Mem., Council, 1971–83, Vice-Pres., 1982–83; Mem., Court of Examiners, Final FRCS, 1972–78 (Chm., 1977–78); Mem., Ct of Examiners, Primary FRCS, 1982–85. Examiner in Surgery for Univs of Liverpool, Bristol and Leeds, and Vis. Examiner to univs in Middle and Far East. Fellow, 1955, Sen. Fellow, 1988, Assoc. of Surgs of GB and Ireland; Senior Member: British Assoc. of Urol Surgs (Mem. Council, 1979–82); British Assoc. of Surg. Oncology (Mem., Nat. Cttee, 1972–75); British Assoc. of Clin. Anatomists (Mem. Council, 1976–80). Hon. FCPS (Pak) (Liaison Officer), 1991. SPk 2000. *Publications:* (with M. Hobsley) Current Surgical Practice, vol. 1, 1976, vol. 2, 1978, vol. 3, 1981, vol. 4, 1986, vol. 5, 1990; (with M. Hobsley and B. C. Morson) Pathology in Surgical Practice, 1985; (jtly) Imaging in Surgical Practice, 1989; articles in jls and chapters in books on diseases of the breast, cancer, urology, trauma, varicose veins and med. educn.

Recreations: ocean racing and cruising, travel, walking, golf. *Address:* Milverton House, 6 St John's Close, Bishopsteignton, near Teignmouth, Devon TQ14 9RT. *T:* (01626) 779537. *Clubs:* Army and Navy; Teign Corinthian Yacht.
Died 26 Dec. 2006.

HADFIELD, James Irvine Havelock, FRCS, FRCSE; Anatomy Supervisor, Jesus College, and Demonstrator, Department of Anatomy, University of Cambridge, since 1995; Consultant Surgeon (Urologist), Bedford General Hospital, 1965–95; *b* 12 July 1930; *s* of Prof. G. Hadfield and S. V. E. Hadfield (*née* Irvine); *m* 1957, Ann Pickernell Milner; one *s* two *d*. *Educ:* Radley College; Brasenose College, Oxford (MA, BM, BCh 1955, MCh Pt I 1960); St Thomas's Hosp. Med. Sch. FRCS 1960, FRCSE 1960; FICS 1990. House Surgeon, St Thomas' Hosp., 1955; Lectr in Anatomy, St Thomas's Hosp. Med. Sch., 1956–57; RSO, Leicester Royal Inf., 1960–62; Surgical Tutor, Oxford Univ., 1962–66; Med. Dir, Bedford Hosp. NHS Trust, 1990–95. Arris and Gale Lectr, RCS, 1967; Examnr in Surgery, Univ. of Cambridge, 1976–82; Examnr in MRCS, LRCP, 1974–80; Examnr, FRCSE, 1989–95. *Publications:* Topics in Core Clinical Anatomy, 1999; articles in surgical jls on Metabolic Response to Trauma, Urology, and Surgical Anatomy of the Veins of the Legs. *Recreations:* watching rowing, shooting, unwilling gardener, trying to catch unwilling salmon in South West Wales. *Address:* Baker's Barn, Stagsden West End, near Bedford MK43 8SZ. *T:* (01234) 824514. *Clubs:* Vincent's (Oxford); Leander, London Rowing.
Died 17 May 2006.

HADFIELD, John; *see* Hadfield, G. J.

HAGGERSTON GADSDEN, Sir Peter Drury; *see* Gadsden.

HAIG, 2nd Earl *cr* 1919; **George Alexander Eugene Douglas Haig,** OBE 1966; RSA 2006 (ARSA 1988); Viscount Dawick, *cr* 1919; Baron Haig and 30th Laird of Bemersyde; painter; Member, Queen's Body Guard for Scotland; *b* 15 March 1918; *o s* of 1st Earl and Hon. Dorothy Vivian (*d* 1939) (author of A Scottish Tour, 1935), *d* of 3rd Lord Vivian; *S* father, 1928; *m* 1st, 1956, Adrienne Thérèse, *d* of Derrick Morley; one *s* two *d*; 2nd, 1981, Donna Geroloma Lopez y Royo di Taurisano. *Educ:* Stowe; Christ Church, Oxford. MA Oxon. 2nd Lieut Royal Scots Greys, 1938; retired on account of disability, 1951, rank of Captain; Hon. Major on disbandment of HG 1958. Studied painting Camberwell School of Art; paintings in collections of Arts Council and Scottish Nat. Gallery of Modern Art. War of 1939–45 (prisoner). Member: Royal Fine Art Commission for Scotland, 1958–61; Council and Executive Cttee, Earl Haig Fund, Scotland, 1950–65 and 1966– (Pres., 1980–86); Scottish Arts Council, 1969–75; President, Scottish Craft Centre, 1950–75. Member Council, Commonwealth Ex-Services League, 1960–96; President: Officers' Association (Scottish Branch), 1987–95 (Chm., 1977–87); Nat. Ex-Prisoner of War Assoc., 1998–2005; Vice-President: Friends of St George's Meml Church, Ypres, 1955–; Scottish National Institution for War Blinded; Royal Blind Asylum and School; President Border Area British Legion, 1955–61; Chairman SE Scotland Disablement Advisory Cttee, 1960–73; Vice-Chairman, British Legion, Scotland, 1960, Chairman, 1962–65, Pres., 1980–86; Chm., Bd of Trustees, Scottish National War Memorial, 1983–95 (Trustee, 1961–95); Trustee, National Gallery of Scotland, 1962–72; Chairman: Berwickshire Civic Soc., 1971–73; Friends of DeMarco Gall., 1968–71. Berwickshire: DL 1953; Vice-Lieutenant, 1967–70; DL Ettrick and Lauderdale (and Roxburghshire), 1977–93. KStJ 1977. FRSA 1951. *Publications:* My Father's Son (autobiog.), 2000. *Heir:* *s* Viscount Dawick, *b* 30 June

1961. *Address:* Bemersyde, Melrose, Scotland TD6 9DP. *T:* (01835) 822762. *Clubs:* Cavalry and Guards; New (Edinburgh). *Died 10 July 2009.*

HAIG, General Alexander Meigs, Jr; Chairman and President, Worldwide Associates, Inc., since 1984; Secretary of State, USA, 1981–82; *b* 2 Dec. 1924; *m* 1950, Patricia Fox; two *s* one *d. Educ:* schs in Pennsylvania; Univ. of Notre Dame; US Mil. Acad., West Point (BS); Univs of Columbia and Georgetown (MA); Ground Gen. Sch., Fort Riley; Armor Sch., Fort Knox; Naval and Army War Colls. 2nd Lieut 1947; Far East and Korea, 1948–51; Europe, 1956–59; Vietnam, 1966–67; CO 3rd Regt, subseq. Dep. Comdt, West Point, 1967–69; Sen. Mil. Adviser to Asst to Pres. for Nat. Security Affairs, 1969–70; Dep. Asst to Pres. for Nat. Security Affairs, 1970–73; Vice-Chief of Staff, US Army, Jan.–July 1973, retd; Chief of White House Staff, 1973–74 when recalled to active duty; Supreme Allied Commander Europe, 1974–79, and Commander-in-Chief, US European Command, 1974–79. President and Chief Operating Officer, United Technologies, 1979–81. Sen. Fellow, Hudson Inst. for Policy Research, 1982–84. Strategic Advr, SaVi Media Gp, 2005–; Director: MGM Mirage Inc.; Metro-Goldwyn-Mayer Inc.; Interneuron Pharmaceuticals, Inc.; SDC International, Inc.; CompuServe Interactive Services Inc. Member: Presidential Cttee on Strategic Forces, 1983–; Presidential Commn on Chemical Warfare Review, 1985; Bd of Special Advisers, President's Commn on Physical Fitness and Sports, 1984. Host of own weekly television progs, World Business Review, then 21st Century Business. Hon. LLD: Niagara; Utah; hon. degrees: Syracuse, Fairfield, Hillsdale Coll., 1981. Awarded numerous US medals, badges and decorations; also Vietnamese orders and Cross of Gallantry; Medal of King Abd el-Aziz (Saudi Arabia). *Publications:* Caveat: realism, Reagan and foreign policy, 1984; Inner Circles, 1992. *Recreations:* tennis, golf. *Address:* e-mail: ahaig@aol.com. *Died 20 Feb. 2010.*

HAJNAL, John, FBA 1966; Professor of Statistics, London School of Economics, 1975–86 (Reader, 1966–75); *b* 26 Nov. 1924; *s* of late Kálmán and Eva Hajnal-Kónyi; *m* 1950, Nina Lande; one *s* three *d. Educ:* University Coll. Sch., London; Balliol Coll., Oxford. Employed by: Royal Commission on Population, 1944–48; UN, New York, 1948–51; Office of Population Research, Princeton Univ., 1951–53; Manchester Univ., 1953–57; London Sch. of Economics, 1957–86. Vis. Fellow Commoner, Trinity Coll., Cambridge, 1974–75; Vis. Prof., Rockefeller Univ., NY, 1981. Mem. Internat. Statistical Institute. *Publications:* The Student Trap, 1972; papers on demography, statistics, mathematics, etc. *Address:* 95 Hodford Road, NW11 8EH. *T:* (020) 8455 7044. *Died 30 Nov. 2008.*

HALL, Alfred Charles, CBE 1977 (OBE 1966); HM Diplomatic Service, retired; *b* 2 Aug. 1917; *s* of Alfred Hall and Florence Mary Hall; *m* 1945, Clara Georgievna Strunina, Moscow; five *s* one *d. Educ:* Oratory Sch.; Open Univ. (BA); Univ. of Kent (MA 1995). Served War, RA and Intell. Corps, 1939–43. LCC, 1934–39 and 1946–49; FO, with service in Saudi Arabia, Algeria, Egypt, Iran and USSR, 1943–46; FCO (formerly CRO and CO), with service in Pakistan, India, Nigeria, Canada and Australia, 1949–75; Dep. High Comr in Southern India, 1975–77. Grants Officer, SCF, 1979–82. *Publications:* papers on foreign and Commonwealth relations. *Recreations:* music, politics. *Address:* 10A Castle Avenue, Dover CT16 1EZ. *Club:* Royal Commonwealth Society. *Died 4 Jan. 2006.*

HALL, Prof. (Alfred) Rupert, LittD; FBA 1978; Professor of the History of Science and Technology, Imperial College of Science and Technology, University of London, 1963–80; *b* 26 July 1920; *s* of Alfred Dawson Hall and Margaret Ritchie; *m* 1st, 1942, Annie Shore Hughes (marr. diss.); two *d*; 2nd, 1959, Marie Boas, (Dr Marie Boas Hall, FBA). *Educ:* Alderman Newton's Boy's Sch., Leicester; Christ's Coll., Cambridge (scholar). LittD Cantab 1975. Served in Royal Corps of Signals, 1940–45.

1st cl. Historical Tripos Part II, 1946; Allen Scholar, 1948; Fellow, Christ's Coll., 1949–59, Steward, 1955–59; Curator, Whipple Science Mus., Cambridge and University Lectr, 1950–59. Medical Research Historian, University of Calif, Los Angeles, 1959–60, Prof. of Philosophy, 1960–61; Prof. of History and Logic of Science, Indiana Univ., 1961–63. Royal Society Lectures: Wilkins, 1973; Leeuwenhoek, 1988. FRHistS. Pres., British Soc. for History of Science, 1966–68; Pres., Internat. Acad. of the History of Science, 1977–81; Wellcome Trust: Chm., Adv. Panel on History of Medicine, 1974–80; Co-ordinator, History of Medicine, 1981–85. Co-editor, A History of Technology, 1951–58. Corresp. Mem., Soc. for the History of Technology, 1970. Hon. Laureate, Univ. of Bologna, 1999. Silver Medal, RSA, 1974; (jtly) Sarton Medal, History of Science Soc., 1981. *Publications:* Ballistics in the Seventeenth Century, 1952; The Scientific Revolution, 1954; From Galileo to Newton, 1963; The Cambridge Philosophical Society: a history 1819–1969, 1969; Philosophers at War, 1980; Short History of the Imperial College, 1982; The Revolution in Science 1500–1750, 1983; Henry More: Magic, Religion and Experiment, 1990; with Marie Boas Hall: Unpublished Scientific Papers of Isaac Newton, 1962; Correspondence of Henry Oldenburg, 1965–86; (with Laura Tilling) Correspondence of Isaac Newton, vols 5–7, 1974–77; (ed with Norman Smith) History of Technology, 1976–83; (with B. A. Bembridge) Physic and Philanthropy: a history of the Wellcome Trust, 1986; Isaac Newton: Adventurer in Thought, 1992; Newton, his Friends and his Foes, 1993; All was Light, 1993; Essays on the History of Science and Technology, 1994; Isaac Newton: Eighteenth Century perspectives, 1998; contributor to Isis, Annals of Science, etc. *Address:* 14 Ball Lane, Tackley, Oxford OX5 3AG. *T:* (01869) 331257. *Died 5 Feb. 2009.*

HALL, Denis C.; *see* Clarke Hall.

HALL, Denis Whitfield, CMG 1962; Provincial Commissioner, Coast Province, Kenya, 1959–63; *b* 26 Aug. 1913; *s* of late H. R. Hall, Haslemere, Surrey; *m* 1940, Barbara Carman; two *s. Educ:* Dover College; Wadham Coll., Oxford. Dist Officer, Kenya, 1936; Personal Asst to Chief Native Comr, 1948; Senior Dist Comr, 1955–59. Dep. Chm., Sussex Church Campaign, 1964–73. *Recreations:* sailing, tennis, walking, motoring. *Address:* Martins, Priory Close, Boxgrove, West Sussex PO18 0EA. *Clubs:* Oxford Union; Oxford University Yacht. *Died 20 Feb. 2006.*

HALL, Prof. James Snowdon, CBE 1976; Professor of Agriculture, Glasgow University, and Principal, West of Scotland Agricultural College, 1966–80; *b* 28 Jan. 1919; *s* of Thomas Blackburn Hall and Mary Milburn Hall; *m* 1942, Mary Smith; one *s* one *d. Educ:* Univ. of Durham (BSc Hons). FRAgS, FIBiol. Asst Technical Adviser, Northumberland War Agric. Exec. Commn, 1941–44; Lectr in Agriculture, Univ. of Newcastle upon Tyne, 1944–54; Principal, Cumbria Coll. of Agriculture and Forestry, 1954–66. *Died 18 Nov. 2008.*

HALL, Prof. Laurance David, PhD; FRS(Can.) 1982; CChem, FRSC, FCIC; (first) Herchel Smith Professor of Medicinal Chemistry, University of Cambridge, 1984–2005, and Fellow, Emmanuel College, since 1987; *b* 18 March 1938; *s* of Daniel William Hall and Elsie Ivy Hall; *m* 1962, Winifred Margaret (*née* Golding); twin *s* two *d. Educ:* Leyton County High Sch.; Bristol Univ. (BSc 1959; PhD 1962); MA Cantab 1990. FCIC 1973; FRSC 1985. Post-doctoral Fellow, Ottawa Univ., 1962–63; Dept of Chemistry, Univ. of British Columbia: Instr II, 1963–64; Asst Prof., 1964–69; Associate Prof., 1969–73; Prof., 1973–84. Alfred P. Sloan Foundn Res. Fellow, 1971–73; Canada Council Killam Res. Fellow, 1982–84. Lederle Prof., RSM, 1984; Vis. Professor: Univ. of NSW, 1967; Univ. of Cape Town, 1974; Northwestern Univ., Evanston, Ill, 1982. Lectures include: Van Cleave, Univ. of Saskatchewan, Regina, 1983; Cecil Green, Galveston

Univ., Texas, 1983; Brotherton, Leeds Univ., 1985; Philip Morris, Richmond Univ., Va, 1985; Scott, Cambridge Univ., 1986; Larmor, Cambridge Philosophical Soc., 1986; C. B. Purves, McGill Univ., 1987; Eduard Faber Med. Physics, Univ. of Chicago, 1990; Friday Evening Discourse, Royal Instn, London, 1991, 1997; Merck Frosst, Montreal, 1994; public, 1995, Henderson Trust, 1996, RSChem; Horizon, Cleveland Clinic Foundn, Ohio, 1995; Harry Hallam Meml, Swansea, 1998. Fellow, Cambridge Philosophical Soc. Hon. DSc Bristol, 2000. Jacob Bielly Faculty Res. Prize, Univ. of BC, 1974; Tate and Lyle Award for Carbohydrate Chemistry, Chemical Soc., 1974; Merck, Sharpe and Dohme Lecture Award, Chemical Inst. of Canada, 1975; Corday Morgan Medal and Prize, Chemical Soc., 1976; Barringer Award, Spectroscopy Soc. of Canada, 1981; Interdisciplinary Award, RSC, 1988; Chemical Analysis and Instrumentation Award, RSC, 1990. *Publications:* over 530 research pubns. *Recreations:* music, travel, research. *Address:* Emmanuel College, St Andrew's Street, Cambridge CB2 3AP; *e-mail:* ldh11@cam.ac.uk. *Died 28 Aug. 2009.*

HALL, Sir Laurence Charles B.; see Brodie-Hall.

HALL, Dr Marie Boas, FBA 1994; Reader in History of Science and Technology, University of London, 1964–80, Reader Emeritus, since 1980; *b* 18 Oct. 1919; *d* of Ralph Philip Boas and Louise (*née* Schutz); *m* 1959, Prof. (Alfred) Rupert Hall, FBA (*d* 2009). *Educ:* Radcliffe Coll. (AB 1940; MA 1942); Cornell Univ. (PhD 1949). Assistant Professor of History: Univ. of Mass, 1949–52; Brandeis Univ., 1952–57; Associate Prof., UCLA, 1957–61; Prof. of Hist. and Logic of Sci., Indiana Univ., 1961–63; Sen. Lectr, Imperial Coll., Univ. of London, 1963–64. Guggenheim Fellow, 1955–56. Mem., Liby Cttee, Royal Soc., 1983–93. Fellow, Amer. Acad. of Arts and Scis, 1955–63. Mem., Académie internat. d'histoire des sciences, 1960; Sec., Hist. of Science Soc., 1953–57. Pfizer Award, 1959, (jtly) Sarton Medal, 1981, Hist. of Science Soc. *Publications:* The Establishment of the Mechanical Philosophy, 1952, 2nd edn 1981; Robert Boyle and Seventeenth Century Chemistry, 1958; The Scientific Renaissance 1450–1630, 1962, repr. 1994; Robert Boyle on Natural Philosophy, 1965; All Scientists Now: the Royal Society in the Nineteenth Century, 1984; Promoting Experimental Learning: experiment and the Royal Society 1660–1727, 1991; The Library and Archives of the Royal Society, 1992; Henry Oldenburg: shaping the Royal Society, 2002; with A. R. Hall: Unpublished Scientific Papers of Isaac Newton, 1962; A Brief History of Science, 1962, 2nd edn 1988; The Correspondence of Henry Oldenburg, 13 vols, 1965–86; contribs to major history of science jls. *Address:* 14 Ball Lane, Tackley, via Kidlington, Oxon OX5 3AG. *T:* (01869) 331257. *Died 23 Feb. 2009.*

HALL WILLIAMS, Richard; see Williams.

HALLIDAY, Prof. Fred, FBA 2002; ICREA Research Professor, Institut Barcelona d'Estudis Internacionals, since 2008; *b* 22 Feb. 1946; *s* of Arthur Halliday and Rita (*née* Finigan); *m* 1979, Prof. Maxine Molyneux; one *s*. *Educ:* Ampleforth Coll.; Univ. of Oxford (BA 1st Cl.); School of Oriental and African Studies (MSc); London School of Economics (PhD 1985). London School of Economics and Political Science: Dept of Internat. Relations, 1983–2008; Prof. of Internat. Relations, 1985–2008; Montague Burton Prof. of Internat. Relations, 2005–08. Visiting Professor: Fundación CIDOB, 2004–05; Institut Barcelona d'Estudis Internacionals, 2005–08; Internat. Advr, Barcelona Centre for Contemporary Culture, 2005–. Fellow, Transnational Inst., Amsterdam and Washington, 1973–85. Mem., Adv. Council, The Foreign Policy Centre, 1999–2004; Gov., LSE, 1994–98. AcSS 1999–2006. Contributing Ed., Middle East Reports, 1978–; Mem. Editl Bd, New Left Rev., 1969–83; columnist: Opendemocracy, 2004–; La Vanguardia, 2004–. *Publications:* Arabia without Sultans, 1974; Iran: dictatorship and development, 1978; (with Maxine Molyneux) The Ethiopian Revolution, 1981; Threat from the East?, 1982; The Making of the Second Cold War, 1983, 2nd edn 1986; Cold War, Third World, 1989; Revolution and Foreign Policy: the case of South Yemen 1967–1987, 1990; Arabs in Exile: the Yemen communities in Britain, 1992; Rethinking International Relations, 1994; Islam and the Myth of Confrontation, 1996; Revolution and World Politics: the rise and fall of the sixth great power, 1999; Nation and Religion in the Middle East, 2000; The World at 2000, 2000; Two Hours That Shook the World, 2001; The Middle East in International Relations, 2005; 100 Myths About the Middle East, 2005. *Recreations:* translation, travel, lunch, photography. *Address:* Institut Barcelona d'Estudis Internacionals, Elisabets 10, 08006 Barcelona, Spain; *e-mail:* fhalliday@ibei.org. *Died 26 April 2010.*

HALLIDAY, Vice-Adm. Sir Roy (William), KBE 1980; DSC 1944; Director General of Intelligence, Ministry of Defence, 1981–84; *b* 27 June 1923; *m* 1945, Dorothy Joan Meech. *Educ:* William Ellis Sch.; University College Sch. Joined Royal Navy, 1941; served in Fleet Air Arm (fighter pilot) in World War II, in HMS Chaser, HMSs Victorious and Illustrious; test pilot, Boscombe Down, 1947–48; Comdg Officer 813 Sqdn (Wyverns, HMS Eagle), 1954; Army Staff Coll., Camberley; Comdr, 1958; Exec. Officer Coastal Forces Base (HMS Diligence), 1959; Sen. Officer 104th Minesweeping Sqdn, Far East Flt, in comd (HMS Houghton), 1961–62; Naval Asst to Chief of Naval Information, 1962–64; comdr (Air) HMS Albion, 1964–66; Captain, 1966; Dep. Dir Naval Air Warfare, 1966–70; HMS Euryalus in comd and as Captain D3 Far East Fleet and D6 Western Fleet, 1970–71; Commodore, 1971; Cdre Amphibious Warfare, 1971–73; Cdre Intelligence, Defence Intelligence Staff, 1973–75; Comdr British Navy Staff, Washington, Naval Attaché, and UK Nat. Liaison Rep. to SACLANT, 1975–78; Dep. Chief of Defence Staff (Intelligence), 1978–81. ADC to the Queen, 1975. *Recreations:* gardening, walking. *Address:* Willow Cottage, Bank, Lyndhurst, Hants SO43 7FD. *Club:* Naval. *Died 23 Nov. 2007.*

HALLIDAY, S. F. P.; see Halliday, F.

HALSBURY, 4th Earl of; see Giffard, A. E.

HALSEY, Rt Rev. (Henry) David; Bishop of Carlisle, 1972–89; *b* 27 Jan. 1919; *s* of George Halsey, MBE and Gladys W. Halsey, DSc; *m* 1947, Rachel Margaret Neil Smith; four *d*. *Educ:* King's Coll. Sch., Wimbledon; King's Coll., London (BA); Wells Theol College. Curate, Petersfield, 1942–45; Chaplain, RNVR, 1946–47; Curate, St Andrew, Plymouth, 1947–50; Vicar of: Netheravon, 1950–53; St Stephen, Chatham, 1953–62; Bromley, and Chaplain, Bromley Hosp., 1962–68; Rural Dean of Bromley, 1965–66; Archdeacon of Bromley, 1966–68; Bishop Suffragan of Tonbridge, 1968–72. Entered House of Lords, 1976. *Recreations:* cricket, sailing, reading, gardening, walking. *Address:* Bramblecross, Gully Road, Seaview, Isle of Wight PO34 5BY. *Died 16 May 2009.*

HALWARD, Robin Paul, CB 2005; Deputy Director General, Immigration and Nationality Directorate, Home Office, 2002–04; *b* 10 June 1951; *s* of Raymond Silburn Halward and Joan Margaret Halward (*née* Whittles); *m* 1974, Valerie Jean Taylor; one *s* one *d*. *Educ:* Royal Grammar Sch., Guildford; Trinity Coll., Cambridge (MA). Housemaster, Gaynes Hall Borstal, 1973–77; Assistant Gov., Gartree Prison, 1977–80; Tutor, Prison Service Coll., Wakefield, 1980–84; Dep. Gov., Manchester Prison, 1984–88; Asst Dir, Prison Service N Reg., 1988–90; Governor: Leeds Prison, 1990–92; Manchester Prison, 1992–95; Prison Service Area Manager, Mersey and Manchester, 1996–97; Sec., Metropolitan Police Cttee, 1997–98; Dir Gen., NI Prison Service, 1998–2002. Non-exec. Dir, Bury NHS PCT, 2004–06; Mem. Bd, Partners of Prisoners and Families Support Gp, 2006–07. *Recreations:* city life in Manchester, badminton, hill-walking. *Died 10 April 2007.*

HAMBLEN, Derek Ivens Archibald, CB 1978; OBE 1956; *b* 28 Oct. 1917; *s* of late Leonard Tom Hamblen and Ruth Mary Hamblen, *d* of Sir William Frederick Alphonse Archibald; *m* 1950, Pauline Alison (*d* 2002), *d* of late Gen. Sir William Morgan, GCB, DSO, MC; one *s* one *d*. *Educ:* St Lawrence Coll., Ramsgate; St John's Coll., Oxford (Casberd Exhibn); Portuguese Essay Prize, 1938; BA Hons (Mod. Langs) 1940, MA 1949. Served War, 1940–46: 1st Army, N Africa, 1942–43; Major, GS, AFHQ, N Africa and Italy, and Adv. Mission to British Mil. HQ, Greece, 1944–45; GSO1, Allied Commn for Austria, 1945–46; Lt-Col, 1946. War Office, later Ministry of Defence, 1946–77: seconded HQ British Troops, Egypt, 1946–47; Asst Sec., Office of UK High Commn in Australia, 1951–55; seconded Foreign Office, 1957–60; Asst Sec., 1964–68; a Special Advr to NATO and SHAPE, 1968–74; Under Sec., 1974–77, retired. Mem. Bd of Governors, St Lawrence Coll., 1977–91 (Vice-Pres., 1991–2004). FRSA 1987. Medal of Merit, 1st cl. (Czechoslovakia), 1946. *Recreations:* cricket, hockey (represented Oxford *v* Cambridge, 1940), golf, music, reading. *Address:* c/o Lloyds TSB, East Grinstead, West Sussex RH19 1AH. *Clubs:* MCC; Vincent's (Oxford).
Died 7 Jan. 2009.

HAMBLING, Sir (Herbert) Hugh, 3rd Bt *cr* 1924; *b* 3 Aug. 1919; *s* of Sir (Herbert) Guy (Musgrave) Hambling, 2nd Bt; *S* father, 1966; *m* 1st, 1950, Anne Page Oswald (*d* 1990), Spokane, Washington, USA; one *s*; 2nd, 1991, Helen (*d* 2004), *widow* of David Gavin. *Educ:* Wixenford Preparatory Sch.; Eton Coll. British Airways Ltd, 1937–39. RAF Training and Atlantic Ferry Command, 1939–46. British Overseas Airways: Montreal, 1948; Seattle, 1950; Manager, Sir Guy Hambling & Son, 1956; BOAC Representative, Douglas, Los Angeles, and Boeing Co., Seattle, 1957–75; Royal Brunei Airlines Rep., Boeing Co., Seattle, 1975–96. *Heir: s* (Herbert) Peter Hugh Hambling [*b* 6 Sept. 1953; *m* 1st, 1982, Jan Elizabeth Frederick (marr. diss. 1989); 2nd, 1991, Lorayn Louise, *d* of late Frank Koson; three *s*]. *Address:* 1219 Evergreen Point Road, Medina, WA 98039, USA. *T:* (425) 4540905, *Fax:* (425) 4542048; Rookery Park, Yoxford, Suffolk IP17 3HQ. *T:* (01728) 668310.
Died 6 May 2010.

HAMBRO, Richard Alexander; Chairman, J. O. Hambro Investment Management Ltd, since 1986; *b* 1 Oct. 1946; 2nd *s* of late Jocelyn Olaf Hambro, MC; *m* 1st, 1973, Hon. Charlotte Soames (marr. diss. 1982); one *d*; 2nd, 1984, Juliet Mary Elizabeth Grana (*née* Harvey) (marr. diss. 1992); 3rd, 1993, Mary James (*née* Briggs). *Educ:* Eton; Univ. of Munich. Joined Hambros Bank, 1966, Director, 1979; Pres., Hambro America Inc., 1977–82; Chairman: I. Hennig & Co., 1987–; The Money Portal plc, 2003 ; Wilton's (St James's), 2003– (Dir, 1968–); Smith's Hldgs Ltd, 2003–; Newmarket Racecourses Trust, 2004–; Franco's, 2005–. Chm., SA Business Initiative, 1995–. Dep. Pres., Macmillan Cancer Support (formerly Cancer Relief Macmillan Fund, then Macmillan Cancer Relief), 2001– (Chm., 1991–2001); Pres., Bowel Cancer UK (formerly Colon Cancer Concern), 2004– (Chm., 1995–2004); Chairman: Jt British Cancer Charities, 1995–; Develt Bd, Inst. of Cancer Res., 2003–. Trustee, Burdett Trust for Nursing, 2005–. Trustee, London Clinic, 2000–. *Recreations:* golf, horse racing. *Address:* Waverton House, Sezincote, Moreton-in-Marsh, Glos GL56 9TB. *T:* (01386) 700700. *Clubs:* White's, Jockey; The Brook (New York) (Gov.).
Died 25 April 2009.

HAMBURGER, Michael Peter Leopold, OBE 1992; *b* Berlin, 22 March 1924; *e s* of late Prof. Richard Hamburger and Mrs L. Hamburger (*née* Hamburg); *m* 1951, Anne Ellen File; one *s* two *d*. *Educ:* Westminster Sch.; Christ Church, Oxford (MA). Army Service, 1943–47; freelance writer, 1948–52; Asst Lectr in German, UCL, 1952–55; Lectr, then Reader in German, Univ. of Reading, 1955–64. Florence Purington Lectr,

Mount Holyoke Coll., Mass, 1966–67; Vis. Prof., SUNY, at Buffalo, 1969, at Stony Brook, 1971; Vis. Fellow, Center for Humanities, Wesleyan Univ., Conn, 1970; Vis. Prof., Univ. of S Carolina, 1973; Regent's Lectr, Univ. of California, San Diego, 1973; Vis. Prof., Boston Univ., 1975–77; part-time Prof., Univ. of Essex, 1978. Bollingen Foundn Fellow, 1959–61, 1965–66. FRSL 1972–86. Corresp. Mem., Deutsche Akademie für Sprache und Dichtung, Darmstadt, 1973. Hon. LittD UEA, 1988; Hon. Dr Phil Technische Univ., Berlin, 1995. Cholmondeley Award for Poetry, 2000; Hölderlin Prize, Tübingen, 1991; Petrarc Prize, Modena, 1992; Horst Bienek Prize, Munich, 2001; translation prizes: Deutsche Akademie für Sprache und Dichtung, Darmstadt, 1964; Arts, Inter Nationes, Bonn, 1976; Medal, Inst. of Linguists, 1977; Schlegel-Tieck, London, 1978, 1981; Wilhelm-Heinse (medallion), Mainz, 1978; Goethe Medal, 1986; Austrian State Prize for Literary Translation, 1988. *Publications: poetry:* Flowering Cactus, 1950; Poems 1950–1951, 1952; The Dual Site, 1958; Weather and Season, 1963; Feeding the Chickadees, 1968; Penguin Modern Poets (with A. Brownjohn and C. Tomlinson), 1969; Travelling, 1969; Travelling, I–V, 1973; Ownerless Earth, 1973; Travelling VI, 1975; Real Estate, 1977; Moralities, 1977; Variations, 1981; Collected Poems, 1984; Trees, 1988; Selected Poems, 1988; Roots in the Air, 1991; Collected Poems 1941–1994, 1995; Late, 1997; Intersections, 2000; From a Diary of Non-Events, 2002; Wild and Wounded, 2004; Circling the Square, 2007; *translations:* Poems of Hölderlin, 1943, rev. edn as Hölderlin: Poems, 1952; C. Baudelaire, Twenty Prose Poems, 1946, repr. 1968 and 1988; L. van Beethoven, Letters, Journals and Conversations, 1951, repr. 1967 and 1984; J. C. F. Hölderlin, Selected Verse, 1961, repr. 1986; G. Trakl, Decline, 1952; A. Goes, The Burnt Offering, 1956; (with others) H. von Hofmannsthal, Poems and Verse Plays, 1961; B. Brecht, Tales from the Calendar, 1961; (with C. Middleton) Modern German Poetry 1910–1960, 1962; (jtly) H. von Hofmannsthal, Selected Plays and Libretti, 1964; G. Büchner, Lenz, 1966; H. M. Enzensberger, Poems, 1966; (with C. Middleton) G. Grass, Selected Poems, 1966; J. C. F. Hölderlin, Poems and Fragments, 1967 (Arts Council trans. prize, 1969), rev. edn 2004; (with J. Rothenberg and the author) H. M. Enzensberger, The Poems of Hans Magnus Enzensberger, 1968; H. M. Enzensberger, Poems For People Who Don't Read Poems, 1968; (with C. Middleton) G. Grass, The Poems of Günter Grass, 1969; P. Bichsel, And Really Frau Blum Would Very Much Like To Meet The Milkman, 1968; G. Eich, Journeys, 1968; N. Sachs, Selected Poems, 1968; Peter Bichsel, Stories for Children, 1971; Paul Celan, Poems, 1972, new enlarged edn, as Poems of Paul Celan, 1988 (European Translation Prize, 1990), 3rd edn 2007; (ed) East German Poetry, 1972; Peter Huchel, Selected Poems, 1974; German Poetry 1910–1975, 1977; Helmut Heissenbüttel, Texts, 1977; Franco Fortini, Poems, 1978; An Unofficial Rilke, 1981; Peter Huchel, The Garden of Theophrastus, 1983, 2nd edn 2004; Goethe, Poems and Epigrams, 1983, 3rd edn 2006; Günter Eich, Pigeons and Moles, 1991; H. M. Enzensberger, Selected Poems, 1994; G. Grass, Novemberland, 1996; Goethe, Roman Elegies and other Poems and Epigrams, 1996; H. M. Enzensberger, Kiosk (poetry), 1997; Ernst Jandl, Thingsure (poetry), 1997; Friedrich Hölderlin, Selected Poems and Fragments, 1998; G. Grass, Selected Poems 1956 to 1993, 1999; W. G. Sebald, After Nature, 2002; W. G. Sebald, Unrecounted, 2004; *prose:* Testimonies, selected shorter prose 1950–1987, 1989; Michael Hamburger in Conversation with Peter Dale (interview), 1998; *criticism:* Reason and Energy, 1957; From Prophecy to Exorcism, 1965; The Truth of Poetry, 1970, new edn 1996; Hugo von Hofmannsthal, 1973; Art as Second Nature, 1975; A Proliferation of Prophets, 1983; After the Second Flood: essays in modern German Literature, 1986; *memoirs:* A Mug's Game, 1973, rev.

edn as String of Beginnings, 1991. *Recreations:* gardening, walking. *Address:* c/o Johnson & Alcock Ltd, Clerkenwell House, 45/47 Clerkenwell Green, EC1R 0HT. *Died 7 June 2007.*

HAMILTON, 15th Duke of, *cr* 1643, Scotland, **AND BRANDON,** 12th Duke of, *cr* 1711, Great Britain; **Angus Alan Douglas Douglas-Hamilton;** Marquess of Douglas 1633; Lord Abernethy and Jedburgh Forest 1633; Marquess of Clydesdale 1643; Earl of Angus; Earl of Arran, Lanark and Cambridge; Lord Aven and Innerdale 1643; Lord Machanshire and Polmont; Baron Dutton (GB) 1711; Premier Peer of Scotland; Hereditary Keeper of Palace of Holyroodhouse; *b* 13 Sept. 1938; *e s* of 14th Duke of Hamilton and Brandon, PC, KT, GCVO, AFC, and Lady Elizabeth Percy, OBE, DL, *er d* of 8th Duke of Northumberland, KG; *S* father, 1973; *m* 1st, 1972, Sarah Jane (marr. diss. 1987; she *d* 1994), *d* of Sir Walter Scott, 4th Bt; two *s* two *d*; 2nd, 1988, Jillian Hulton (*née* Robertson) (marr. diss. 1995); 3rd, 1998, Kay Carmichael, *d* of Norman Dutch. *Educ:* Eton; Balliol Coll., Oxford (BA (Engrg) 1960; MA 1982). CEng, MIMechE; FBIS. Flt Lieut RAF; invalided, 1967. Flying Instructor, 1965; Sen. Commercial Pilot, 1968; Test Pilot, Scottish Aviation, 1970–72; Authorised Display Pilot, 1998. Mem. Council, Cancer Res. UK (formerly CRC), 1978–. Mem., Queen's Body Guard for Scotland, 1975–. Mem., Royal Scottish Pipers Soc., 1977; Mem., Piobaireachd Soc., 1979; Patron, British Airways Pipe Band, 1977–. Hon. Air Cdre, No 2 (City of Edinburgh) Maritime HQ Unit, RAuxAF, 1982–93. KStJ 1974 (Prior, Order of St John in Scotland, 1975–82). *Publications:* Maria R, 1991. *Heir: s* Marquess of Douglas and Clydesdale, *b* 31 March 1978. *Address:* Lennoxlove, Haddington, E Lothian EH41 4NZ. *T:* (01620) 823720. *Club:* Royal Air Force. *Died 5 June 2010.*

HAMILTON OF DALZELL, 4th Baron *cr* 1886; **James Leslie Hamilton;** DL; *b* 11 Feb. 1938; *s* of 3rd Baron Hamilton of Dalzell, GCVO, MC and Rosemary Olive (*d* 1993), *d* of Maj. Hon. Sir John Coke, KCVO; *S* father, 1990; *m* 1967, Corinna, *yr d* of Sir Pierson Dixon, GCMG, CB; four *s* (incl. twins). *Educ:* Eton. Served Coldstream Guards, 1956–58. Mem., Stock Exchange, 1967–80. Dir, Rowton Hotels plc, 1978–84; Chairman: Queen Elizabeth's Foundn for the Disabled, 1989–; Surrey Springboard Trust, 1996–; Nat. Council for Conservation of Plants and Gardens, 1997–; Trustee, Henry Smith's Charity, 1990–. Pres., Ludlow Cons. Assoc., 1996–99. Mem. Council, Freedom Assoc., 2000–. Freeman, City of London; Liveryman, Drapers' Co., 1977–. DL Surrey, 1993. *Heir: s* Hon. Gavin Goulburn Hamilton [*b* 8 Oct. 1968; *m* 1997, Harriet, *yr d* of Thomas Roskill; twin *d*]. *Address:* Stockton House, Stockton, Norton Shifnal, Salop TF11 9EF; Betchworth House, Betchworth, Surrey RH3 7AE. *Died 28 Sept. 2006.*

HAMILTON, Sir Edward (Sydney), 7th and 5th Bt, *cr* 1776 and 1819; *b* 14 April 1925; *s* of Sir (Thomas) Sydney (Percival) Hamilton, 6th and 4th Bt, and Bertha Muriel, *d* of James Russell King, Singleton Park, Kendal; *S* father, 1966. *Educ:* Canford Sch. Served Royal Engineers, 1943–47; 1st Royal Sussex Home Guard, 1953–56. *Recreations:* Spiritual matters, music. *Heir:* none. *Address:* The Cottage, Fordwater Road, East Lavant, Chichester, West Sussex PO18 0AL. *T:* (01243) 527414. *Died 21 Dec. 2008 (ext).*

HAMILTON, Myer Alan Barry K.; *see* King-Hamilton.

HAMILTON FRASER, Donald; *see* Fraser.

HAMMOND, Eric Albert Barratt, OBE 1977; General Secretary, Electrical, Electronic, Telecommunication and Plumbing Union, 1984–92; *b* 17 July 1929; *s* of Arthur Edgar Hammond and Gertrude May Hammond; *m* 1953, Brenda Mary Edgeler; two *s*. *Educ:* Corner Brook Public Sch. Shop Steward, 1953–63; Branch Sec., 1958–63; Exec. Councillor, 1963–84, EETPU. Borough and Urban District Councillor, 1958–63. Mem., TUC Gen. Council, 1983–88. Member: Electronics EDC, 1967–92;

Industrial Development Adv. Bd, 1977–87; Adv. Council on Energy Conservation, 1974–77; (part-time) Monopolies and Mergers Commn, 1978–84; Engrg Council, 1984–90; ACARD, 1985–87; NEDC, 1989–92; Lord Chancellor's Adv. Cttee on Legal Educn and Conduct, 1991–98; Employment Appeal Tribunal, 1992–2000; Chm., Electronic Components and Technology Sector Gp (formerly Electronic Components Sector Working Party), 1975–92. Mem. Bd, Kent Thame-side, Groundwork, 1991–95. Life Pres., Support Kent Schs, 2009– (Chm., 1998). Gov., Gravesend Grammar Sch. for Boys, 1987– (Vice-Chm., 1989–94, Chm., 1994–2006). *Publications:* Maverick: the life of a union rebel, 1992. *Recreations:* gardening, photography. *Address:* 9 Dene Holm Road, Northfleet, Kent DA11 8LF. *Club:* Gravesend Rugby. *Died 30 May 2009.*

HAMPDEN, 6th Viscount *cr* 1884; **Anthony David Brand;** DL; land agent; *b* 7 May 1937; *s* of 5th Viscount Hampden and Imogen Alice Rhys, *d* of 7th Baron Dynevor; *S* father, 1975; *m* 1969, Cara Fiona (marr. diss. 1988), *e d* of Claud Proby; two *s* one *d*; *m* 1993, Mrs Sally Snow, *d* of Sir Charles Hambro, KBE, MC. *Educ:* Eton. Lazard Brothers, merchant bankers, 1956–69; Hoare Govett, stockbrokers, 1970–82; Estate Manager, Glynde Estates, 1984–2002. Chairman: Sussex Br., CLA, 1985–87 (Pres., 2003–); SE Reg., HHA, 2001–05; Governing Body, Emanuel Sch., 1985–2004 (Gov., 1965–2005). DL E Sussex, 1986. *Publications:* Henry and Eliza, 1980; A Glimpse of Glynde, 1997. *Heir: s* Hon. Francis Anthony Brand [*b* 17 Sept. 1970; *m* 2004, Dr Caroline Pryor, *d* of His Honour Robert Charles Pryor, QC]. *Address:* Glynde Place, Glynde, Lewes, Sussex BN8 6SX. *Club:* White's. *Died 4 Jan. 2008.*

HAMYLTON JONES, Keith, CMG 1979; HM Diplomatic Service, retired; HM Ambassador, to Costa Rica, 1974–79, to Honduras, 1975–78, and to Nicaragua, 1976–79; *b* 12 Oct. 1924; *m* 1953, Eira Morgan; one *d*. *Educ:* St Paul's Sch.; Balliol Coll., Oxford (Domus Scholar in Classics, 1943); BA 1948; MA 1950. Welsh Guards, 1943; Italy, 1944 (Lieut); S France, 1946 (Staff Captain). HM Foreign Service, 1949; 3rd Sec., Warsaw, 1950; 2nd Sec., Lisbon, 1953; 1st Sec., Manila, 1957; Head of Chancery and HM Consul, Montevideo, 1962; Head of Chancery, Rangoon, 1967; Asst Head of SE Asia Dept, FCO, 1968; Consul-General, Lubumbashi, 1970–72; Counsellor, FCO, 1973–74. Operation Raleigh: Chm. for Devon and Cornwall, 1983–85; led internat. expedn to Costa Rica, Feb–May 1985. Chairman: Anglo-Costa Rican Soc., 1983–88; Anglo-Central American Soc., 1988–91. *Publications:* (as Peter Myllent) The Ideal World, 1972. *Recreations:* reading, writing, walking. *Died 23 Nov. 2007.*

HANCOCK, Maj.-Gen. Michael Stephen, CB 1972; MBE 1953; Planning Inspector, Department of the Environment, 1972–87; *b* 19 July 1917; *s* of late Rev. W. H. M. Hancock and Mrs C. C. Hancock (*née* Sherbrooke); *m* 1st, 1941, Constance Geraldine Margaret Ovens (*d* 1999), *y d* of late Brig.-Gen. R. M. Ovens, CMG; one *s* one *d*; 2nd, 2001, Margaret Alicia Griffin, *d* of Lt-Col F. E Walter, DSO and *widow* of Maj. J. R. Griffin. *Educ:* Marlborough Coll.; RMA Woolwich. Commnd into Royal Signals, 1937; Comdr, Corps Royal Signals, 1st British Corps, 1963–66; Sec., Mil. Cttee, NATO, 1967–68; Chief of Staff, FARELF, 1968–70; VQMG, MoD, 1970–72, retired. Col Comdt, Royal Signals, 1970–77. Chm., CCF Assoc., 1972–82, Vice Pres., 1982–96; Chm., NE Surrey Dist Scouts, 1979–82, Pres., 1982–2001. CEng; FIEE. *Publications:* Lucky Signaller, 1998. *Recreation:* chess. *Died 17 Feb. 2006.*

HAND, Rt Rev. Geoffrey David, KBE 1984 (CBE 1975); *b* 11 May 1918; *s* of Rev. W. T. Hand. *Educ:* Oriel College, Oxford (BA 1941, MA 1946); Cuddesdon Theological Coll. Deacon 1942, priest 1943; Curate of Heckmondwike, 1942–46; Missioner, Diocese of New Guinea, 1946–50; Priest in charge: Sefoa, 1947–48; Sangara, 1948–50; Archdeacon, North New Guinea,

1950–65; Bishop Coadjutor of New Guinea, 1950–63; Bishop of New Guinea (later Papua New Guinea), 1963–77; Archbishop of Papua New Guinea, 1977–83; Bishop of Port Moresby, 1977–83; Priest-in-charge, East with West Rudham, Houghton next Harpley, Syderstone, Tatterford and Tattersett, dio. Norwich, 1983–85. *Address:* PO Box 28, N Waigani, NCD, Papua New Guinea. *T:* 3260317. *Died 6 April 2006.*

HANDLEY, Vernon George, CBE 2004; FRCM; Principal Guest Conductor, Royal Liverpool Philharmonic Orchestra, 1989–95, then Conductor Emeritus; Associate Conductor, Royal Philharmonic Orchestra, since 1994 (Guest Conductor, 1961–94); *b* 11 Nov. 1930; 2nd *s* of Vernon Douglas Handley and Claudia Lilian Handley, Enfield; *m* 1st, 1954, Barbara (marr. diss.), *e d* of Kilner Newman Black and Joan Elfriede Black, Stoke Gabriel, Devon; one *s* one *d* (and one *s* decd); 2nd, 1977, Victoria (marr. diss.), *d* of Vaughan and Nona Parry-Jones, Guildford, Surrey; one *s* one *d*; 3rd, 1987, Catherine, *e d* of Kenneth and Joan Newby, Harrogate, Yorks; one *s. Educ:* Enfield Sch.; Balliol Coll., Oxford (BA; Hon. Fellow, 1999); Guildhall Sch. of Music. Conductor: Oxford Univ. Musical Club and Union, 1953–54; OUDS, 1953–54; Tonbridge Philharmonic Soc., 1958–61; Hatfield Sch. of Music and Drama, 1959–61; Proteus Choir, 1962–81; Musical Dir and Conductor, Guildford Corp., and Conductor, Guildford Philharmonic Orch. and Choir, 1962–83, Conductor Emeritus, Guildford Philharmonic Orch., 1984; Prof. at RCM for Orchestra and Conducting, 1966–72, for Choral Class, 1969–72. Principal Conductor: Ulster Orch., 1985–89 (Conductor Laureate, 2003); Malmö SO, 1985–88; Chief Conductor, W Australian SO, 1993–96. Guest Conductor from 1961: Bournemouth Symph. Orch.; Birmingham Symph. Orch.; BBC Welsh Orch.; BBC Northern Symph. Orch.; Ulster Orch.; Scottish Nat. Orch.; Philharmonia Orch.; Strasbourg Philharmonic Orch., 1982–; Helsinki Philharmonic, 1984–; Amsterdam Philharmonic, 1985; Guest Conductor, 1961–83, Principal Guest Conductor, 1983–85, BBC Scottish Symphony Orch.; Guest Conductor, 1961–83, Associate Conductor, 1983–86, London Philharmonic Orch.; Chief Guest Conductor, Melbourne SO, 1992–95; conducted London Symphony Orch. in internat. series, London, 1971; toured: Germany, 1966, 1980; S Africa, 1974; Holland, 1980; Sweden, 1980, 1981; Germany, Sweden, Holland and France, 1982–83; Australia, 1986; Japan, 1988; Australia, 1989; Artistic Dir, Norwich and Norfolk Triennial Fest., 1985. Regular broadcaster and made many recordings. Vice-President: Delius Soc., 1983–; Elgar Soc., 1984–; Fellow Goldsmiths Coll. 1987; Hon. Mem., Royal Philharmonic Soc., 1989. Hon. RCM, 1970; FRCM 1972; FRWCMD (FWCMD 2002). Arnold Bax Meml Medal for Conducting, 1962; Conductor of the Year, British Composers' Guild, 1974; Hi-Fi News Audio Award, 1982; BPI Classical Award, 1986, 1988; Gramophone Record of the Year, 1986, 1989; Classic CD Magazine Record of the Year (Contemporary), 1995; Lifetime Achievement Award, Classical BRIT Awards, 2007. DUniv Surrey, 1980; Hon. DMus Liverpool, 1993. *Recreations:* bird photography, old-fashioned roses. *Died 10 Sept. 2008.*

HANHAM, Sir Michael (William), 12th Bt *cr* 1667; DFC 1945; RAFVR; *b* 31 Oct. 1922; *s* of Patrick John Hanham (*d* 1965) and Dulcie (*d* 1979), *yr d* of William George Daffarn and *widow* of Lynn Hartley; *S* kinsman, Sir Henry Phelips Hanham, 11th Bt, 1973; *m* 1954, Margaret Jane (*d* 2007), *d* of W/Cdr Harold Thomas, RAF retd, and Joy (*née* MacGeorge); one *s* one *d. Educ:* Winchester. Joined RAF 1942, as Aircrew Cadet; served No 8 (Pathfinder) Gp, Bomber Command, 1944–45; FO 1945. At end of war, retrained as Flying Control Officer; served UK and India, 1945–46; demobilised, 1946. Joined BOAC, 1947, Traffic Branch; qualified as Flight Operations Officer, 1954; served in Africa until 1961; resigned, 1961. Settled at Trillinghurst Farmhouse, Kent and started garden and cottage furniture making business,

1963; moved to Wimborne, 1974; later engaged with upkeep of family house and estate. Governor, Wimborne Minster, 1977–. *Recreations:* conservation (Vice-Chm. Weald of Kent Preservation Soc., 1972–74, 1976–2000); Mem. Cttee, Wimborne Civic Soc., 1977–2007); preservation of steam railways, painting. *Heir: s* William John Edward Hanham [*b* 4 Sept. 1957; *m* 1st, 1982, Elizabeth Anne Keyworth (marr. diss. 1988), *yr d* of Paul Keyworth, Farnham and Mrs Keith Thomas, Petersfield; 2nd, 1996, Jennifer (marr. diss. 2005), *o d* of Harold Henry Sebag-Montefiore]. *Club:* Royal Air Force. *Died 30 May 2009.*

HANKINS, Prof. Harold Charles Arthur, CBE 1996; PhD; FREng, FIET; Principal, 1984–95, Vice-Chancellor, 1994–95, University of Manchester Institute of Science and Technology; *b* 18 Oct. 1930; *s* of Harold Arthur Hankins and Hilda Hankins; *m* 1955, Kathleen Higginbottom; three *s* one *d. Educ:* Crewe Grammar Sch.; Univ. of Manchester Inst. of Science and Technol. (BSc Tech, 1st Cl. Hons Elec. Engrg, 1955; PhD 1971). CEng, FREng (FEng 1993); FIET (FIEE 1975); AMCT 1952. Engrg Apprentice, British Rail, 1947–52; Electronic Engr, subseq. Asst Chief Engr, Metropolitan Vickers Electrical Co. Ltd, 1955–68; Univ. of Manchester Inst. of Science and Technology: Lectr in Elec. Engrg, 1968–71; Sen. Lectr in Elec. Engrg, 1971–74; Prof. of Communication Engrg, and Dir of Med. Engrg Unit, 1974–84; Vice Principal, 1979–81; Dep. Principal, 1981–82; Actg Principal, 1982–84. Non-executive Director: THORN EMI Lighting Ltd, 1979–85; Bodycote International, 1992–97; Dir, Inward, 1992–95; Mem. Bd, Trafford Park Develt Corp., 1996–98; Chairman: Trafford Park Manufacturing Inst., 1997–2002 (Hon. Pres., 2002–); Elliott Absorbant Products, 1999–. Instn of Electrical Engineers: Mem., NW Centre Cttee, 1969–77, Chm. 1977–78; Chm., M2 Exec. Cttee, 1979–82; Mem., Management and Design Div. Bd, 1980–82. Chm., Chemical Engrg, Instrumentation, Systems Engrg Bd, CNAA, 1975–81; Member: Cttee for Science and Technol., CNAA, 1975–81; Cttee of Vice-Chancellors and Principals, 1984–95; Parly Scientific Cttee, 1985–95; Engrg Council, 1993–95; Bd of Govs, Manchester Polytechnic, 1989–2001 (Hon. Fellow, 1984); Bd of Govs, South Cheshire Coll., 1990–96; Pres., Cheadle Hulme Sch., 1996–; Chm., Mil. Educn Cttee, Gtr Manchester Univs, 2002–07. Hon. DSc Manchester, 1995; DUniv Open, 1996; Hon. DEng UMIST, 1996. Reginald Mitchell Gold Medal, Assoc. of Engrs, 1990. *Publications:* 75 papers in learned jls; 10 patents for research into computer visual display systems. *Recreations:* military history, hill walking, music, choral work. *Address:* Rosebank, Kidd Road, Glossop, Derbyshire SK13 7PN. *T:* (01457) 853895. *Died 2 May 2009.*

HANMER, Sir John (Wyndham Edward), 8th Bt *cr* 1774; JP; DL; *b* 27 Sept. 1928; *s* of Sir (Griffin Wyndham) Edward Hanmer, 7th Bt, and Aileen Mary (*d* 1967), *er d* of Captain J. E. Rogerson; *S* father, 1977; *m* 1954, Audrey Melissa, *d* of Major A. C. J. Congreve; two *s. Educ:* Eton. Captain (retired), The Royal Dragoons. Director: Chester Race Co., 1978–2004; Ludlow Race Club, 1980–2004; Bangor-on-Dee Races, 1980–2003. Lord of the Manor, Bettisfield, Co. of Wrexham. JP Flintshire, 1971; High Sheriff of Clwyd, 1977; DL Clwyd, 1978. *Recreations:* horseracing, shooting. *Heir: s* (Wyndham Richard) Guy Hanmer [*b* 27 Nov. 1955; *m* 1986, Elizabeth A., *yr d* of Neil Taylor; two *s* one *d*]. *Address:* The Mere House, Hanmer, Whitchurch, Shropshire SY13 3DG. *T:* (01948) 830383. *Club:* Army and Navy. *Died 29 Dec. 2008.*

HANN, Air Vice-Marshal Derek William; Director-General RAF Personal Services, Ministry of Defence, 1987–89; *b* 22 Aug. 1935; *s* of Claude and Ernestine Hann; *m* 1st, 1958, Jill Symonds (marr. diss. 1987); one *s* one *d*; 2nd, 1987, Sylvia Jean Holder. *Educ:* Dauntsey's Sch., Devizes. Joined RAF, 1954; served in Fighter (65 Sqdn) and Coastal (201 and 203 Sqdns) Commands and at HQ Far East Air Force, 1956–68; MoD, 1969–72 and

1975–77; Comd No 42 Sqdn, RAF St Mawgan, 1972–74; Comd RAF St Mawgan, 1977–79; RCDS 1980; Dir of Operational Requirements 2, MoD, 1981–84; C of S, HQ No 18 Gp, 1984–87. *Recreations:* theatre, music, horology, campanology. *Address: e-mail:* hannderek@yahoo.co.uk. *Died 14 Sept. 2010.*

HANNAM, Michael Patrick Vivian, CBE 1980; HM Diplomatic Service, retired; Consul General, Jerusalem, 1976–80; *b* 13 Feb. 1920; *s* of Rev. Wilfrid L. Hannam, BD, and Dorothy (*née* Parker); *m* 1947, Sybil Huggins (*d* 2005); one *s* one *d*. *Educ:* Westminster Sch. LMS Railway, 1937–40. Served in Army, 1940–46 (Major, RE). LMS Railway, 1946–50; Malayan Railway, 1950–60. FO, 1960–62; First Sec., British Embassy, Cairo, 1962–65; Principal British Trade Comr, Hong Kong, 1965–69 (and Consul, Macao, 1968–69); Counsellor, Tripoli, 1969–72; Counsellor (Economic and Commercial), Nairobi, 1972–73, Dep. High Commissioner, Nairobi, 1973–76. Mem. Exec. Cttee, Palestine Exploration Fund, 1982–92 (Keeper of Written Archive, 1989–92). Chm. Governors, Rose Hill Sch., Tunbridge Wells, 1980–85; Chm. Council, British Sch. of Archaeology in Jerusalem, 1983–90. *Recreations:* music, research into 19th century Jerusalem, translating Homer. *Address:* Little Oaklands, Langton Green, Kent TN3 0HP. *T:* (01892) 862163. *Died 17 Aug. 2007.*

HANNIGAN, James Edgar, CB 1981; Deputy Secretary, Department of Transport, 1980–88; *b* 12 March 1928; *s* of late James Henry and Kathleen Hannigan; *m* 1955, Shirley Jean Bell (*d* 2001); two *d*. *Educ:* Eastbourne Grammar Sch.; Sidney Sussex Coll., Cambridge (BA). Civil Service, 1951; Asst Sec., Housing Div., Min. of Housing and Local Govt, 1966–70; Asst Sec., Local Govt Div., DoE, 1970–72. Under Sec. 1972; Regional Dir for West Midlands, DoE, 1972–75; Chm., West Midlands Economic Planning Bd, 1972–75; Dir of Housing 'B', DoE, 1975–78; Dep. Sec., 1978; NI Office, 1978–80. Mem., Internat. Exec. Cttee, PIARC, 1985–90. Trustee, Clapham Junction Disaster Fund, 1989–90. *Died 22 Oct. 2008.*

HANRAHAN, Brian; Diplomatic Editor, BBC Television, since 1997; *b* 22 March 1949; *s* of Thomas Hanrahan and Kathleen McInerney; *m* 1986, Honor Wilson; one *d*. *Educ:* Essex University (BA). BBC, 1971–: Far East correspondent, 1983–85; Moscow correspondent, 1986–89; Diplomatic correspondent, 1989–97. DU Essex, 1990. *Publications:* (with Robert Fox) I Counted Them All Out and I Counted Them All Back, 1982. *Address:* c/o World Affairs Unit, BBC TV Centre, Wood Lane, W12 7RJ. *Died 20 Dec. 2010.*

HANROTT, Francis George Vivian, CBE 1981; Chief Officer, Technician Education Council, 1973–82; *b* 1 July 1921; *s* of late Howard Granville Hanrott and Phyllis Sarah Hanrott; *m* 1953, Eileen Winifred Appleton (*d* 2009); three *d*. *Educ:* Westminster Sch.; King's Coll., Univ. of London (BA Hons). Served War, RN (Air Br.), 1940–45; Lieut (A) RNVR. Asst Master, St Marylebone Grammar Sch., 1948–50; Lectr, E Berks Coll. of Further Educn, 1950–53; Asst Educn Officer, Wilts, 1953–56; Staff Manager, GEC Applied Electronics Labs, 1956–59; Asst Educn Officer, Herts, 1959–66; Registrar and Sec., CNAA, 1966–73. Hon. MA Open Univ., 1977. *Address:* Coombe Down House, Salcombe Road, Malborough, Kingsbridge, Devon TQ7 3BX. *T:* (01548) 842721. *Died 28 March 2010.*

HARBOTTLE, Rev. Anthony Hall Harrison, LVO 1979; Priest-in-charge of East Dean with Friston and Jevington, 1995–96 (Rector, 1981–95); Chaplain to the Queen, 1968–95; *b* 3 Sept. 1925; *y s* of Alfred Charles Harbottle, ARIBA, and Ellen Muriel, *o d* of William Popham Harrison; *m* 1955, Gillian Mary, *o d* of Hugh Goodenough; three *s* one *d*. *Educ:* Sherborne Sch.; Christ's Coll., Cambridge (MA). Wycliffe Hall, Oxford. Served War in Royal Marines, 1944–46. Deacon 1952, priest 1953; Asst Curacies: Boxley, 1952–54; St Peter-in-Thanet, 1954–60; Rector of Sandhurst with Newenden,

1960–68; Chaplain of the Royal Chapel, Windsor Great Park, 1968–81. Founder Mem., Kent Trust for Nature Conservation, 1954; Mem., Green Alliance, 1984. County Chaplain, Royal British Legion (Sussex), 1982–2002. Special Life Mem., British Entomol and Natural Hist. Soc., 1998. FRES 1971. *Publications:* contribs to entomological jls, on lepidoptera. *Recreations:* butterflies and moths, nature conservancy, entomology, ornithology, philately, coins, Treasury and bank notes, painting, cooking, lobstering. *Address:* 44 Summerdown Road, Eastbourne BN20 8DQ. *Died 2 Dec. 2009.*

HARDAKER, Rev. Canon Ian Alexander; Clergy Appointments Adviser, 1985–98; Chaplain to the Queen, 1994–2002; *b* 14 May 1932; *s* of Joseph Alexander Hardaker and Edna Mary (*née* Theede); *m* 1963, Susan Mary Wade Bottom; two *s* two *d*. *Educ:* Kingston Grammar Sch.; Royal Military Acad., Sandhurst; King's Coll., London (BD, AKC). Commnd East Surrey Regt, 1952. Curate, Beckenham Parish Ch, 1960–65; Vicar of Eynsford and Rector of Lullingstone, 1965–70; Vicar of St Stephen's, Chatham, 1970–85; Rural Dean of Rochester, 1978–85. St Augustine's Medal, 1998. *Recreations:* walking, photography, family, gardening. *Address:* The Old Post Office, Huish Champflower, Wiveliscombe, Taunton, Somerset TA4 2EY. *Died 7 Nov. 2010.*

HARDIE, Michael John, OBE 1989; HM Diplomatic Service, retired; *b* 14 July 1938; *s* of John Thomas Hardie and Annie Smethurst; *m* 1st, 1967, Patricia Louisa Hulme (marr. diss. 1986); two *s* one *d*; 2nd, 1990, Jean Fish; one step *s* one step *d*. *Educ:* St Ambrose Coll., Hale Barns, Cheshire; De La Salle Coll., Salford. HM Forces (Intelligence Corps), 1957–59; FO 1959; served Bahrain, Elisabethville, Bathurst, Sofia, Vienna, Munich and Cape Town, to 1979; First Secretary, 1979; BMG Berlin, 1979–81; Malta, 1981–83; FCO, 1983–86; Lagos, 1986–89; Counsellor, 1988; New Delhi, 1990–93; High Comr, Gambia, 1994–95. *Recreations:* golf, music. *Address:* 4 Came Court, Woodhall Spa, Lincs LN10 6DA. *Died 29 May 2008.*

HARDING, Wilfrid Gerald, CBE 1978; FRCP, FFCM, DPH; Area Medical Officer, Camden and Islington Area Health Authority (Teaching), 1974–79; Hon. Consultant in Community Medicine, University College Hospital, London, 1971–79; *b* 17 March 1915; *s* of late Dr *hc* Ludwig Ernst Emil Hoffmann and Marie Minna Eugenie (*née* Weisbach); *m* 1st, 1938, Britta Charlotta Haraldsdotter, Malmberg (marr. diss. 1970); three *s*; 2nd, 1973, Hilary Maxwell. *Educ:* Französisches Gymnasium, Berlin; Süddeutsches Landerziehungsheim, Schondorf, Bavaria; Woodbrooke Coll., Selly Oak, Birmingham; University Coll. London; University Coll. Hosp. Med. Sch. MRCS, LRCP 1941; DPH London 1949; MRCP 1968; FFCM 1972; Hon. FFCM 1986; FRCP 1972. Interned twice, in 1939 and 1940. Ho. Phys. and Ho. Surg., UCH, 1941–42; Asst MOH, City of Oxford, 1942–43; RAMC, 1943–47, Field Units in NW Europe, 1 Corps Staff and Mil. Govt, Lt-Col (Hygiene Specialist). In charge of health services, Ruhr Dist of Germany. CCG, 1947–48; LSHTM, 1948–49; career posts in London public health service, 1949–64; MOH, London Bor. of Camden, and Principal Sch. MO, ILEA, 1965–74. Hon. Lectr, Dept of Sociol., Bedford Coll., London Univ., 1969–77; Civil Consultant in Community Medicine to RAF, 1974–78. Chm. of Council, Soc. of MOH, 1966–71 (Pres. 1971–72); Chm., Prov. Bd of FCM, Royal Colls of Physicians of UK, 1971–72 (Vice-Pres., 1972–75, Pres., 1975–78). Member: Central Health Services Council and Standing Med. Adv. Cttee, 1966–71 and 1975–78; Standing Mental Health Adv. Cttee, 1966–71; Bd of Studies in Preventive Med. and Public Health, Univ. of London, 1963–79; Council, UCH Med. Sch., 1965–78; Bd of Management, LSHTM, 1968–82; Council for Educn and Trng of Health Visitors, 1965–77; Council, ASH, 1970–73 and 1978–82; Public Health Laboratory Service Bd, 1972–83. Armed Services Med. Adv. Bd, 1975–78; GMC, 1979–84; Vice-Chm.,

Dartford and Gravesham CHC, 1984–89. Chm., DHSS Working Gp on Primary Health Team, 1978–80 (reported 1981). Hon. Advr, Office of Health Econs. Councillor, Sevenoaks DC, 1979–99 (Vice-Chm., 1996–97; Chm., 1997–98); Chm., Farningham Parish Council, 1983–89. Chm., Farningham Woods Nature Reserve, 1983–2001. Broadcasts on public health and community medicine. *Publications:* papers on public health and community med. in medical books and jls; Parkes Centenary Meml Lecture (Community, Health and Service), 1976. *Recreations:* watching river birds, music, wine. *Address:* Bridge Cottage, High Street, Farningham, Dartford DA4 0DW. *T:* (01322) 862733. *Club:* Athenæum.   *Died 5 March 2010.*

HARDWICK, Christopher, MD, FRCP; Physician Emeritus, Guy's Hospital, since 1976; *b* 13 Jan. 1911; *s* of Thomas Mold Hardwick and Harriet Taylor; *m* 1938, Joan Dorothy Plummer; two *s. Educ:* Berkhamsted Sch.; Trinity Hall, Cambridge; Middlesex Hospital. MRCS, LRCP 1935; MA (Cambridge) 1937; MD (Cambridge) 1940; FRCP 1947. House Physician, House Surgeon and Med. Registrar, Middlesex Hosp., 1935 and 1938–41; House physician and Registrar, Hosp. for Sick Children, Gt Ormond Street, 1936–38. Wing Comdr, Medical Specialist, RAF Med. Service, 1941–46. Physician, Guy's Hosp., 1946–76. Hon. Vis. Phys., Johns Hopkins Hosp., Baltimore, 1954. Mem. Council, RCP, 1965–68; Mem. Board of Governors, Guy's Hospital, 1967–74. Chm., British Diabetic Assoc., 1974–80. *Publications:* contribs to medical literature. *Recreations:* gardening, reading. *Address:* Nower House, Coldharbour Lane, Dorking, Surrey RH4 3BL.   *Died 16 Aug. 2008.*

HARDWICK, Donald, CBE 1980; PhD; Director, Johnson & Firth Brown plc, 1973–89 (Chairman, Steel Division, 1975–85); *b* 1926; *m* 1950, Dorothy Mary Hardwick; two *s. Educ:* Tadcaster Grammar Sch.; Sheffield Univ. (BMet 1st Cl. Hons 1947, Mappin Medal; PhD 1954). FIMMM. After appointments with English Electric Co., BISRA, and BSA Gp Research Centre, became first C. H. Desch Res. Fellow, Sheffield Univ. Joined Brown Firth Res. Laboratories, 1959; Man. Dir, Firth Brown Ltd, 1974–78; Mem. Bd, Johnson & Firth Brown, on amalgamation with Richard Johnson & Nephew, 1973. Director: Mitchell Somers Gp, 1974–89; Eagle Trust plc, 1987–89. Pres., BISPA, 1977–79. *Recreations:* fell walking, gardening. *Address:* 43 Dore Road, Dore, Sheffield S17 3NA.   *Died 19 Aug. 2006.*

HARDY, Rev. Prof. Daniel Wayne; Director, Center of Theological Inquiry, Princeton, New Jersey, 1990–95; *b* 9 Nov. 1930; *s* of John Alexander Hardy and Barbara Wyndham Harrison; *m* 1958, Kate Perrin Enyart; two *s* two *d. Educ:* Phillips Exeter Acad., Exeter, NH; Haverford Coll., Haverford, Penn (BA); Gen. Theological Seminary, NY (STB, STM); St John's Coll., Univ. of Oxford. Deacon 1955, priest 1956; Asst Minister, Christ Ch, Greenwich, Conn, 1955–59; Vicar, St Barnabas Ch, Greenwich, 1956–59; Instr, Rosemary Hall, Greenwich, 1957–59; Fellow and Tutor, Gen. Theol Seminary, NY, 1959–61; Lectr in Modern Theol Thought, 1965–76, Sen. Lectr, 1976–86, Univ. of Birmingham; Van Mildert Prof. of Divinity, Univ. of Durham, and Residentiary Canon, Durham Cathedral, 1986–90 (Hon. Fellow, Durham Univ., 1991). Hon. Mem. and Advr, Centre for Advanced Religious and Theol Studies, Cambridge Univ., 1996–; Chm., Governing Council, Cambridge Theol Fedn, 2003–. Moderator, Gen. Ministerial Exam., C of E, 1983–89. Pres., Soc. for the Study of Theology, 1987–88. Editor, Cambridge Studies in Christian Doctrine, 1991–. *Publications:* (with D. F. Ford) Jubilate: theology in praise, 1984; (with D. F. Ford) Praising and Knowing God, 1985; Education for the Church's Ministry, 1986; God's Ways with the World, 1996; Finding the Church, 2001; *contributor to:* Schleiermacher and Barth: beyond the impasse, 1987; Keeping the Faith, 1987; The Modern Theologians, 1989, 3rd edn 2006; (and ed jtly) On Being

the Church, 1989; (and ed jtly) The Weight of Glory: essays in honour of Peter Baelz, 1991; Christ and Context, 1993; Worship and Ethics: Lutherans and Anglicans in dialogue, 1996; Essentials of Christian Community: essays in honour of Daniel W. Hardy, 1996; The Doctrine of Creation, 1997; The Common Good: dialogue between religions, 1997; Spirituality and Theology, 1998; Science Meets Faith: theology and science in conversation, 1998; Where Shall Wisdom Be Found?, 1999; Seeing Beyond the Word: visual arts and the Calvinist tradition, 1999; Christian Missions and the Enlightenment, 2001; Textual Reasonings: Jewish philosophy and text study after modernity, 2002; Holiness Past and Present, 2003; Reading Texts, Seeking Wisdom, 2003; articles in Theology, Expository Times, Anglican Theol Rev., Internat. Jl for Study of the Christian Church, etc; *festschrift:* Essentials of Christian Community: essays in honour of Daniel W. Hardy, 1996. *Recreations:* swimming, ski-ing, music, photography. *Address:* 101 Millington Lane, Newnham, Cambridge CB3 9HA.   *Died 15 Nov. 2007.*

HARDYMAN, Norman Trenchard, CB 1984; Secretary, Universities Funding Council, 1988–90 (University Grants Committee, 1982–89); *b* 5 Jan. 1930; *s* of late Rev. Arnold Victor Hardyman and Laura Hardyman; *m* 1961, Carol Rebecca Turner; one *s* one *d. Educ:* Clifton Coll.; Christ Church, Oxford. Asst Principal, Min. of Educn, 1955; Principal 1960; Private Sec. to Sec. of State for Educn and Science, 1966–68; Asst Sec. 1968–75, Under-Sec., 1975–79, DES; Under-Sec., DHSS, 1979–81. Mem., UGC for Univ. of S Pacific, 1990–2001 Treasurer, Univ. of Exeter, 1991–2001. Hon. LLD Exeter, 2002. *Recreations:* walking, gardening, reading, photography. *Address:* 3 Hill View Road, Hanbury Park, Worcester WR2 4PN. *T:* (01905) 339368.   *Died 24 Dec. 2008.*

HARE, Rt Rev. (Thomas) Richard; Suffragan Bishop of Pontefract, 1971–92; *b* 29 Aug. 1922; *m* 1963, Sara (*d* 1999), *d* of Lt-Col J. E. Spedding, OBE; one *s* two *d. Educ:* Marlborough; Trinity Coll., Oxford; Westcott House, Cambridge. RAF, 1942–45. Curate of Haltwhistle, 1950–52; Domestic Chaplain to Bishop of Manchester, 1952–59; Canon Residentiary of Carlisle Cathedral, 1959–65; Archdeacon of Westmorland and Furness, 1965–71; Vicar of St George with St Luke, Barrow-in-Furness, 1965–69; Vicar of Winster, 1969–71. *Address:* Wood Cottage, Mirehouse, Keswick, Cumbria CA12 4QE. *T:* (017687) 72996.   *Died 18 July 2010.*

HARFORD, Sir (John) Timothy, 3rd Bt *cr* 1934;; Vice-Chairman, 1985–87, Deputy Chairman, 1987–93, Chairman, 1993–99, Wesleyan and General, then Wesleyan Assurance Society; *b* 6 July 1932; *s* of Sir George Arthur Harford, 2nd Bt and Anstice Marion (*d* 1993), *d* of Sir Alfred Tritton, 2nd Bt, *S* father, 1967; *m* 1962, Carolyn Jane Mullens; two *s* one *d. Educ:* Harrow Sch.; Worcester Coll., Oxford (BA); Harvard Business Sch. Philip Hill Higginson Erlangers Ltd, 1960–63; Director: Birmingham Industrial Trust Ltd, 1963–67; Singer & Friedlander Ltd, 1970–88 (Local Dir, 1967–69); Dep. Chm., Wolseley-Hughes Gp, then Wolseley Gp, 1983–97; Chm., 1990–94, Dep. Chm., 1994–97, Kwik Save Gp; Dep. Chm., Wagon Industrial Holdings, 1991–98. *Recreations:* wine and food, travel. *Heir:* *s* Mark John Harford [*b* 6 Aug. 1964; *m* 1999, Louise, *d* of Robert Langford; three *d*]. *Address:* South House, South Littleton, Evesham, Worcs WR11 8TJ. *T:* (01386) 830478. *Club:* Boodle's.   *Died 22 Aug. 2010.*

HARGROVES, Brig. Sir (Robert) Louis, Kt 1987; CBE 1965; DL; *b* 10 Dec. 1917; *s* of William Robert and Mabel Mary Hargroves (*née* Lalonde); *m* 1940, Eileen Elizabeth Anderson; four *d. Educ:* St John's College, Southsea. Commissioned South Staffordshire Regt, 1938; served War of 1939–45, India, Sicily, Italy; CO 1 Staffords, 1959–61; GSO1, RMA Sandhurst, 1962–63; Brig. 1964; comd Aden Bde, 1964–66; MoD, 1966–69; N Command, 1969–72; retired, 1972. Col. Staffordshire

Regt, 1971–77. DL Staffs 1974. *Address:* Nazareth House, London Road, Charlton Kings, Cheltenham GL52 6YJ. *T:* (01242) 516905. *Died 22 Feb. 2008.*

HARINGTON, Gen. Sir Charles (Henry Pepys), GCB 1969 (KCB 1964; CB 1961); CBE 1957 (OBE 1953); DSO 1944; MC 1940; ADC (General) to the Queen, 1969–71; *b* 5 May 1910; *s* of Lt-Col H. H. Harington and Dorothy Pepys; *m* 1942, Victoire Marion Williams-Freeman (*d* 2000); one *s* two *d. Educ:* Malvern; Sandhurst. Commissioned into 22nd (Cheshire) Regt, 1930. Served War of 1939–45: France and Belgium (incl. Dunkirk), 2nd Bn Cheshire Regt, 1939–40; CO, 1st Bn Manchester Regt and GSO1, 53 (Welch) Div., NW Europe, 1944–45. DS Staff Coll., 1946; GSO1 Mil. Mission Greece, 1948; CO 1st Bn The Parachute Regt, 1949; Mil. Asst to CIGS, 1951; SHAPE, 1953; Comdr 49 Inf. Bde in Kenya, 1955; idc 1957; Comdt Sch. of Infantry, 1958; GOC 3rd Div., 1959; Comdt, Staff Coll., Camberley, 1961; C-in-C Unified Command Middle East, 1963; DCGS, 1966; Chief of Personnel and Logistics, to the three Services, 1968–71, retired; Col The Cheshire Regt, 1962–68. Col Comdt, Small Arms Sch. Corps, 1964–70; Col Comdt, The Prince of Wales Div., 1968–71. President: Combined Cadet Force Assoc., 1971–80; Milocarian (Tri-Service) Athletic Club, 1966–99. Chm. Governors, Royal Star and Garter Home, 1972–80. Commissioner: Royal Hosp., Chelsea, 1970–79; Duke of York's Royal Military Sch., 1971–89. Vice-President: Royal Star and Garter Home, 1980–; Dogs' Home, Battersea, 1993–. Knight Officer with swords, Order of Orange Nassau (Netherlands), 1945. *Clubs:* Army and Navy, Hurlingham (Chm., 1970–77; Pres., 1979–2000). *Died 13 Feb. 2007.*

HARINGTON, Kenneth Douglas Evelyn Herbert; Metropolitan Magistrate, 1967–84; *b* 30 Sept. 1911; *yr s* of late His Honour Edward Harington; *m* 1st, 1939, Lady Cecilia Bowes-Lyon (*d* 1947), *er d* of 15th Earl of Strathmore; 2nd, 1950, Maureen Helen McCalmont (*d* 1992), *d* of Brig.-Gen. Sir Robert McCalmont, KCVO, CBE, DSO; two *s. Educ:* Stowe. War of 1939–45: Served NW Europe (Major, Coldstream Guards). Hon. Attaché, British Legation, Stockholm, 1930–32; Barrister, Inner Temple, 1952; Acting Deputy Chm., Inner London and NE London Quarter Sessions, 1966–67. *Recreations:* shooting, fishing. *Address:* Baker's Cottage, Great Rissington, Cheltenham, Glos GL54 2LP. *T:* (01451) 820858. *Died 13 Jan. 2007.*

HARKNESS, Rear-Adm. James Percy Knowles, CB 1971; Director-General, Naval Manpower, 1970, retired 1972; *b* 28 Nov. 1916; *s* of Captain P. Y. Harkness, West Yorkshire Regt, and Gladys Dundas Harkness (*née* Knowles); *m* 1949, Joan, *d* of late Vice-Adm. N. A. Sulivan, CVO; two *d. Educ:* RN Coll., Dartmouth. Entered RN, 1930; Comdr, 1951; Captain, 1961; Asst Dir of Plans, 1962; Cdre Naval Drafting, 1966. *Died 7 June 2009.*

HARLAND, Bryce; see Harland, W. B.

HARLAND, Rt Rev. Ian; an Hon. Assistant Bishop: Diocese in Europe, since 2000; Diocese of Bradford, since 2002; *b* 19 Dec. 1932; *s* of late Canon Samuel James Harland and of Brenda Gwendolyn Harland; *m* 1967, Susan Hinman; one *s* three *d. Educ:* Dragon School, Oxford; Haileybury; Peterhouse, Cambridge (MA); Wycliffe Hall, Oxford. Teaching at Sunningdale School, 1956–58; Curate, Melton Mowbray, 1960–63; Vicar, Oughtibridge, Sheffield, 1963–72; Member, Wortley RDC, 1969–73; Vicar, St Cuthbert, Fir Vale, Sheffield, 1972–75; Priest-in-charge, All Saints, Brightside, 1973–75; RD of Ecclesfield, 1973–75; Vicar of Rotherham, 1975–79; RD of Rotherham, 1976–79; Archdeacon of Doncaster, 1979–85; Bishop Suffragan of Lancaster, 1985–89; Bishop of Carlisle, 1989–2000. Proctor in Convocation, 1975–85. Hon. Treas., The Middle Way, 1998–2000. Pres., Abbotsholme Sch., 1999–2002. Entered H of L, 1996. *Recreations:* politics,

sport. *Address:* White House, 11 South Street, Gargrave, Skipton BD23 3RT. *T:* (01756) 748623. *Died 27 Dec. 2008.*

HARLAND, (William) Bryce, QSO 1992; Director, New Zealand Institute of International Affairs, 1997–2001; High Commissioner for New Zealand in the United Kingdom, 1985–91; *b* 11 Dec. 1931; *s* of Edward Dugard Harland and Annie McDonald Harland (*née* Gordon); *m* 1st, 1957, Rosemary Anne Gordon (marr. diss. 1977); two *s* (and one *s* decd); 2nd, 1979, (Margaret) Anne Blackburn; one *s. Educ:* Victoria Univ., Wellington, NZ (MA Hons); Fletcher School of Law and Diplomacy, Boston, Mass, USA (AM). Joined NZ Dept of External Affairs, 1953; diplomatic postings: Singapore, 1956; Bangkok, 1957; NY, 1959; Wellington, 1962; Washington, 1965; Wellington, 1969; first NZ Ambassador to China, 1973–75; Ministry of Foreign Affairs, Wellington: Head of African and European Divs, 1976–77; Asst Sec., 1977–82; Perm. Rep. of NZ to the UN, NY, 1982–85 (Chm., Economic and Financial Cttee, Gen. Assembly, 1984). Vis. Fellow, All Souls Coll., Oxford, 1991. Hon. Freeman, City of London, 1987. KStJ 1985. *Publications:* On Our Own: New Zealand in the emerging tripolar world, 1992; Asia—What Next?, 1992; Collision Course: America and East Asia in the past and the future, 1996; sundry articles. *Recreations:* reading history, walking. *Address:* 9 Tinakori Road, Wellington, New Zealand. *Clubs:* Royal Over-Seas League (Vice Pres.); Wellington. *Died 1 Feb. 2006.*

HARMAN, Very Rev. Desmond; see Harman, Very Rev. R. D.

HARMAN, Gen. Sir Jack (Wentworth), GCB 1978 (KCB 1974); OBE 1962; MC 1943; Deputy Supreme Allied Commander, Europe, 1978–81; *b* 20 July 1920; *s* of late Lt-Gen. Sir Wentworth Harman, KCB, DSO, and late Dorothy Harman; *m* 1st, 1947, Gwladys May Murphy (*d* 1996), *d* of Sir Idwal Lloyd and *widow* of Lt-Col R. J. Murphy; one *d,* and two step *d;* 2nd, 2001, Sheila Florence Perkins (*née* Gurdon), *widow* of Maj. Christopher Perkins, Hampshire Regt. *Educ:* Wellington Coll.; RMC Sandhurst. Commissioned into The Queen's Bays, 1940, Bt Lt-Col, 1958; Commanding Officer, 1st The Queen's Dragoon Guards, 1960–62; commanded 11 Infantry Bde, 1965–66; attended IDC, 1967; BGS, HQ Army Strategic Command, 1968–69; GOC, 1st Div., 1970–72; Commandant, RMA Sandhurst, 1972–73; GOC 1 (British) Corps, 1974–76; Adjutant-General, 1976–78. ADC Gen. to the Queen, 1977–80. Col, 1st The Queen's Dragoon Guards, 1975–80; Col Comdt, RAC, 1977–80. Dir, Wilsons Hogg Robinson (formerly Wilsons (Insurance Brokers)), 1982–88. Vice-Chairman: Nat. Army Museum, 1980–87; AA, 1984–90 (Mem. Cttee, 1981–85). *Address:* Sandhills House, Dinton, near Salisbury, Wilts SP3 5ER. *T:* (01722) 716288. *Club:* Cavalry and Guards. *Died 28 Dec. 2009.*

HARMAN, Very Rev. (Robert) Desmond; Dean of Christ Church Cathedral, Dublin, since 2004; *b* 20 June 1941; *s* of Herbert and Hannah Harman; *m* 1971, Susan Lalor; one *s* two *d. Educ:* Sligo Grammar Sch.; TCD (BA 1965, MA 1971). Ordained deacon 1967, priest 1968; Curate Asst, Taney Parish, Dublin, 1967–73; Rector: Santry and Glasnevin, 1973–86; Sandford and Milltown, 1986–2004; Canon of Christ Church Cathedral, Dublin, 1991–2004. Hon. Sec., C of I Bishops' Appeal, 1971–99; Clerical Hon. Sec., Gen. Synod, 1999–. Ed., Church Review, 1981–2000. *Recreations:* gardening, dog walking, music. *Address:* The Deanery, St Werburgh's Street, Dublin 8, Ireland. *T:* (home) (1) 4781797, (office) (1) 6778099, *Fax:* (home) (1) 4753442, (office) (1) 6798991; *e-mail:* dean@ dublin.anglican.org. *Died 18 Dec. 2007.*

HARNDEN, Arthur Baker, CB 1969; TD; CEng, FIET; FIMgt; Chairman, Appeals Tribunals, Supplementary Benefits Commission, 1970–82; *b* 6 Jan. 1909; *s* of Cecil Henry Harnden and Susan (*née* Baker); *m* 1st, 1935, Maisie Elizabeth Annie (*d* 1970), *d* of A. H. Winterburn,

LRIBA; one *s*; 2nd, 1971, Jean Kathleen (*d* 2000), *d* of H. F. Wheeler and *widow* of Eric J. Dedman; one step *s*. *Educ:* various state schools; Northampton Inst. (BSc London Univ. 1937). Exec. Engr, GPO, 1933; Royal Corps of Signals, 1939–45; Lt-Col GSO1, WO, 1942; DCSO Antwerp, 1944, Hamburg 1945. Dir, London Telecommunications Region, GPO, 1962; Senior Dir, Operations, PO (Telecommunications), 1967–69. Principal, Comrie House Sch., Finchley, 1971–72. *Recreation:* painting and potting.   *Died 23 Feb. 2008.*

HARPER, James Norman; barrister; a Recorder of the Crown Court, 1980–84; *b* 30 Dec. 1932; *s* of late His Honour Judge Norman Harper and Iris Irene Harper; *m* 1956, Blanka Miroslava Eva Sigmund (*d* 1999); one *s* one *d*. *Educ:* Marlborough Coll.; Magdalen Coll., Oxford (BA Hons). Called to the Bar, Gray's Inn, 1957; Attorney Gen. of NE Circuit, 1992–96. Pres., Northumberland County Hockey Assoc., 1982–2002. *Recreations:* cricket, hockey, painting. *Address:* (chambers) 33 Broad Chare, Newcastle upon Tyne NE1 3DQ. *T:* (0191) 232 0541. *Club:* MCC.   *Died 1 June 2010.*

HARPER, Prof. John Lander, CBE 1989; DPhil; FRS 1978; Emeritus Professor of Botany, University of Wales, since 1982: Head, Unit of Plant Population Biology, School of Plant Biology, Bangor, 1982–90; *b* 27 May 1925; *s* of John Hindley Harper and Harriett Mary (*née* Archer); *m* 1954, Borguy Lerø; one *s* two *d*. *Educ:* Lawrence Sheriff Sch., Rugby; Magdalen Coll., Oxford (BA, MA, DPhil). Demonstr, Dept of Agriculture, Univ. of Oxford, 1951, Lectr 1953; Rockefeller Foundn Fellow, Univ. of Calif, 1960–61; Prof. of Agricultural Botany, 1960, Prof. of Botany, 1977–82 and Head of Sch. of Plant Biology, 1967–82, University Coll. of North Wales, Bangor. Vis. Prof., Univ. of Exeter, 1999–. Member: NERC, 1971–81; AFRC, 1980–90; Jt Nature Conservation Cttee, 1991–94. Trustee, Natural Hist. Mus., 1993–97. For. Assoc., US Nat. Acad. of Sciences, 1984. Hon. DSc Sussex, 1984; Dr (*hc*) Univ. Nacional Autónoma de México, 1997. *Publications:* Biology of Weeds, 1960; Population Biology of Plants, 1977; (with M. Begon and C. Townsend) Ecology: organisms, populations and communities, 1985, 4th edn 2006; Fundamentals of Ecology, 2000, 3rd edn 2008; papers in Jl of Ecol., New Phytologist, Annals of Applied Biol., Evolution, and Proc. Royal Soc. (Editor, Series B, 1993–98). *Recreation:* gardening. *Address:* The Lodge, Chapel Road, Brampford Speke, Exeter EX5 5HG. *T:* (01392) 841929. *Club:* Farmers'.   *Died 22 March 2009.*

HARPER, John Mansfield; Managing Director, Seaford Head Advisers, 1995–2005; *b* 17 July 1930; *s* of late T. J Harper and May (*née* Charlton); *m* 1956, Berenice Honorine, *d* of Harold Haydon; one *s* one *d*. *Educ:* Merchant Taylors' Sch.; St John's Coll., Oxford. 2nd Lieut Royal Corps of Signals, 1948–49. Asst Principal, Post Office, 1953; Private Sec. to Dir-Gen., 1956–58; Principal, 1958–66; Asst Sec., Reorganization Dept, 1966–69; Dir, North-Eastern Telecommunications Region, 1969–71; Dir, Purchasing and Supply, 1972–75; Sen. Dir, Planning and Provisioning, 1975–77; Asst Man. Dir, Telecommunications, 1978–79; Dep. Man. Dir, British Telecommunications (Post Office), 1979–81; Dir, and Man. Dir Inland Div., BT, 1981–83, retired. Sen. Partner, Lullington Gp, 1993–96. Advr to Bd, NEC (UK) Ltd, 1985–92; Advr, BICC Ltd, 1994–96; Specialist Advr, Parly Select Cttee on Trade and Industry, 1994 and 1997, on Welsh Affairs, 2002–03. Vis. Fellow, Sci. Policy Res. Unit, Univ. of Sussex, 1992–93. Chm., Infrastructure Policy Gp, Electronic Engrg Assoc., 1989–90. Vice-Chm., Polegate and E Dean Lib Dems, 2001–05. Chm., E Dean Histl Gp, 2005–06. FIET. *Publications:* Telecommunications and Computing: the uncompleted revolution, 1986; Telecommunications Policy and Management, 1989; The Third Way: telecommunications and the environment, 1990; A 21st Century Structure for UK Telecoms, 1991; Monopoly and Competition in British

Telecommunications, 1997. *Recreations:* music, gardening, amateur radio. *Address:* 4 Friston Downs, Friston, Eastbourne, E Sussex BN20 0ET.   *Died 3 March 2008.*

HARRER, Prof. Heinrich; author and explorer; awarded title of Professor by President of Austrian Republic, 1964; *b* Hüttenberg, 6 July 1912; *m* 1st, 1938, Charlotte Wegener (marr. diss.); one *s*; 2nd, 1953, Margaretha Truxa (marr. diss. 1958); 3rd, 1962, Katharina Haarhaus. *Educ:* University of Graz, Austria (graduated in Geography, 1938). First ascent, Eiger North Wall, 1938; Himalayan Expedition, 1939; interned in India, 1939–44; Tibet, 1944–51; Himalayan Expedition, 1951: expeditions: to the Andes, 1953; to Alaska, 1954; to Ruwenzori (Mountains of the Moon), Africa, 1957; to West New Guinea, 1961–62; to Nepal, 1965; to Xingu Red Indians in Mato Grosso, Brazil; to Bush Negroes of Surinam (Surinam Expedn with King Leopold of Belgium), 1966; to the Sudan, 1970; to North Borneo (Sabah) (with King Leopold of Belgium), 1971; N-S crossing of Borneo, 1972; Valley of Flowers (Alaknanda), 1974; Andaman Islands, 1975; Zangkar-Ladakh, 1976. Inauguration of Heinrich Harrer Mus., Hüttenberg, 1992; inauguration of Lingkor (Tibetan pilgrim path), Hüttenberg, 1995. Mem., Austrian Acad. of Scis, 1995. Hon. Mem., Humboldt Soc. for Sci., Art and Educn. 35 short films on expeditions. Prize for best documentary book, Donanland, 1982; Golden medal, Humboldt Soc., 1985; Medal, Explorers' Club, NY, 1991; Internat. Prize for Literature, Italy, 1998. Hon. Citizen, Hüttenberg, 1983; Orders from Germany, Austria, Carinthia, Styria, 70th birthday, 1982; highest orders from Carinthia, Styria, 80th birthday, 1992. Austrian National Amateur Golf Champion, 1958; Austrian National Seniors Golf Champion, 1970. Hon. Pres, Austrian Golf Association, 1964 (Pres., 1949–64). *Publications:* Seven Years in Tibet, 1953 (Great Britain, and numerous other countries; filmed, 1997); Meine Tibet-Bilder, 1953 (Germany); The White Spider, History of the North Face of the Eiger, 1958; Tibet is My Country: biography of Thubten Jigme Norbu, *e b* of Dalai Lama, 1960 (Eng.); I Come from the Stone Age, 1964 (London); The Last 500, 1975; The Last Caravan, 1976; Return to Tibet, 1984; Meine Forschungsreisen, 1986; Das Buch vom Eiger, 1988; Borneo, 1988; Bhutan, 1989; Lost Lhasa, 1992. *Address:* Barbarasiedlung 15, 9376 Knappenberg, Austria. *Clubs:* Alpine (Hon. Mem.); Explorers' (New York) (Hon. Mem.); Royal and Ancient (St Andrews); PEN (Liechtenstein).   *Died 7 Jan. 2006.*

HARRINGTON, 11th Earl of, *cr* 1742; **William Henry Leicester Stanhope;** Viscount Stanhope of Mahon and Baron Stanhope of Elvaston, Co. Derby, 1717; Baron Harrington, 1729; Viscount Petersham, 1742; late Captain 15th/19th Hussars; *b* 24 Aug. 1922; *o s* of 10th Earl and Margaret Trelawney (Susan) (*d* 1952), *d* of Major H. H. D. Seaton; *S* father, 1929; *m* 1st, 1942, Eileen (from whom he obtained a divorce, 1946; she *d* 1999), *o d* of late Sir John Grey, Enville Hall, Stourbridge; one *s* one *d* (and one *d* decd); 2nd, 1947, Anne Theodora (from whom he obtained a divorce, 1962), *o d* of late Major Richard Arenbourg Blennerhassett Chute; one *s* two *d*; 3rd, 1964, Priscilla Margaret, *d* of Hon. A. E. Cubitt and Mrs Ronald Dawnay; one *s* one *d*. *Educ:* Eton; RMC Sandhurst. Served War of 1939–45, demobilised 1946. Owner of about 700 acres. Became Irish Citizen, 1965. *Heir:* *s* Viscount Petersham, *b* 20 July 1945. *Address:* The Glen, Ballingarry, Co. Limerick, Eire.   *Died 12 April 2009.*

HARRIS OF HIGH CROSS, Baron *cr* 1979 (Life Peer), of Tottenham in Greater London; **Ralph Harris;** Founder President, Institute of Economic Affairs, since 1990 (General Director, 1957–87, Chairman, 1987–89); *b* 10 Dec. 1924; *m* 1949, Jose Pauline Jeffery; one *d* (two *s* decd). *Educ:* Tottenham Grammar Sch.; Queens' Coll., Cambridge (Exhibnr, Foundn Schol.; 1st cl. Hons Econs; MA). Lectr in Political Economy, St Andrews Univ., 1949–56; Leader-writer, Glasgow Herald, 1956.

Dir (Ind. Nat.), Times Newspapers Hldgs Ltd, 1988–2001. Contested: (LU) Kirkcaldy, 1951; (C) Edinburgh Central, 1955. Trustee: Wincott Foundn; Ross McWhirter Foundn.; Inst. for Study of Civil Soc., 2000–05. Chairman: Bruges Gp, 1989–91; FOREST, 1989–2004; Jt Chm., Internat. Centre for Res. into Economic Transformation, Moscow, 1990–95. Mem. Council, Univ. of Buckingham, 1980–95. Chm., Birling Gap Cliff Protection Assoc., 1997–2003. Free Enterprise Award, 1976. Hon. DSc Buckingham, 1984. *Publications:* Politics without Prejudice, a biography of R. A. Butler, 1956; Hire Purchase in a Free Society, 1958, 3rd edn 1961; (with Arthur Seldon) Advertising in a Free Society, 1959; Advertising in Action, 1962; Advertising and the Public, 1962; (with A. P. Herbert) Libraries: Free for All?, 1962; Choice in Welfare, 1963; Essays in Rebirth of Britain, 1964; Choice in Welfare, 1965; Right Turn, 1970; Choice in Welfare, 1970; Down with the Poor, 1971; (with Brendan Sewill) British Economic Policy 1970–74, 1975; Crisis '75, 1975; Catch '76, 1976; Freedom of Choice: consumers or conscripts, 1976; (with Arthur Seldon) Pricing or Taxing, 1976; Not from Benevolence, 1977; (ed with Arthur Seldon) The Coming Confrontation, 1978; (with Arthur Seldon) Over-ruled on Welfare, 1979; End of Government, 1980; Challenge of a Radical Reactionary, 1981; No, Minister!, 1985; What Price Democracy?, 1985; The Enemies of Progress, 1986; Morality and Markets, 1986; (with Arthur Seldon) Welfare Without the State, 1987; Beyond the Welfare State, 1988; Murder a Cigarette, 1998; Smoking Out the Truth, 2005; (contrib.) Towards a Liberal Utopia, 2005; columnist in Truth, Statist, etc. *Recreations:* reading, writing, talking, swimming. *Address:* 5 Cattley Close, Wood Street, Barnet, Herts EN5 4SN. *Clubs:* Political Economy, Mont Pelerin Society.
Died 19 Oct. 2006.

HARRIS, Rt Rev. Augustine; Bishop (RC) of Middlesbrough, 1978–92, then Bishop Emeritus; *b* 27 Oct. 1917; *s* of Augustine Harris and Louisa Beatrice (*née* Rycroft). *Educ:* St Francis Xavier's Coll., Liverpool; Upholland Coll., Lancs. Ordained, 1942; Curate at: St Oswald's, Liverpool, 1942–43; St Elizabeth's, Litherland, Lancs, 1943–52; Prison Chaplain, HM Prison, Liverpool, 1952–65; Sen. RC Priest, Prison Dept, 1957–66; English Rep. to Internat. Council of Sen. Prison Chaplains (RC), 1957–66; Titular Bishop of Socia and Auxiliary Bishop of Liverpool, 1965–78. Mem. Vatican Delegn to UN Quinquennial Congress on Crime, London, 1960 and Stockholm, 1965; Liaison between English and Welsh Hierarchy (RC) and Home Office, 1966–92; Episcopal Moderator to Fédération Internationale des Associations Médicales Catholiques, 1967–76; Episcopal Pres., Commn for Social Welfare (England and Wales), 1972–83; Chm., Dept for Social Responsibility, Bishops Conf. of Eng. and Wales, 1984–92. Mem., Central Religious Advisory Council to BBC and IBA, 1974–78. *Publications:* articles for criminological works. *Address:* Ince Blundell Hall, Ince Blundell, Liverpool L38 6JL.
Died 30 Aug. 2007.

HARRIS, Basil Vivian, CEng, MIET; Chief Engineer, Communications Division, Foreign and Commonwealth Office, 1979–81; *b* 11 July 1921; *s* of late Henry William and Sarah May Harris; *m* 1943, Myra Winifred Mildred Newport (*d* 1997). *Educ:* Watford Grammar School. GPO Engineering Dept (Research), 1939; served RAF, 1943–46; GPO Engineering Dept (Radio Branch), 1946; Diplomatic Wireless Service, FCO, 1963; Dep. Chief Engineer, Communications Division, FCO, 1971. *Publications:* contribs to technical jls on communications. *Recreations:* golf, photography, travel. *Address:* 13 Decoy Drive, Eastbourne, Sussex BN22 0AB. *T:* (01323) 505819. *Club:* Royal Eastbourne Golf.
Died 16 March 2010.

HARRIS, David; Director, Commission of the European Communities, Directorate for Social and Demographic Statistics, 1973–87; *b* 28 Dec. 1922; *s* of David and Margaret Jane Harris; *m* 1946, Mildred Alice Watson;

two *d. Educ:* Bootle Grammar Sch.; LSE (BScEcon). FSS. Statistician, BoT, 1960; Statistician 1966 and Chief Statistician 1968, HM Treasury; Chief Statistician, Central Statistical Office, Cabinet Office, 1969. *Recreations:* swimming, economics. *Address:* 64 Rue de Rodenbourg, 6950 Olingen, Luxembourg.
Died 2006.

HARRIS, Sir Jack Wolfred Ashford, 2nd Bt *cr* 1932; Chairman, Bing Harris & Co. Ltd, Wellington, NZ, 1935–78 (Director until 1982); *b* 23 July 1906; *er s* of Rt Hon. Sir Percy Harris, 1st Bt, PC, and Frieda Bloxam (*d* 1962); *S* father, 1952; *m* 1933, Patricia (*d* 2002), *o d* of A. P. Penman, Wahroonga, Sydney, NSW; two *s* one *d. Educ:* Shrewsbury Sch.; Trinity Hall, Cambridge. BA (Cantab) History; then one year's study in Europe. Joined family business in New Zealand, 1929, and became director shortly afterwards. Past Pres. Wellington Chamber of Commerce. Served during War of 1939–45, for three years in NZ Home Forces. *Publications:* Memoirs of a Century (autobiog.), 2007. *Recreations:* gardening, fishing, swimming. *Heir: s* Christopher John Ashford Harris [*b* 26 Aug. 1934; *m* 1957, Anna, *d* of F. de Malmanche, Auckland, NZ; one *s* two *d*]. *Address:* Parkwood, Warbler Grove, Belvedere Road, Waikanae, Wellington, New Zealand. *Clubs:* Union (Sydney); Wellington (Wellington, NZ).
Died 26 Aug. 2009.

HARRIS, Dr John Edwin, MBE 1981; FRS 1988; FREng; nuclear scientist; *b* 2 June 1932; *s* of late John Frederick Harris and Emily Margaret (*née* Prosser); *m* 1956, Ann Foote; two *s* two *d. Educ:* Larkfield Grammar Sch., Chepstow; Dept of Metallurgy, Univ. of Birmingham (BSc 1953, PhD 1956, DSc 1973). FIMMM (FIM 1974); FREng (FEng 1987); FInstP 1992. Joined Associated Electrical Industries, 1956; CEGB, 1959–89; seconded to Sheffield Univ., 1959–61; Berkeley Nuclear Labs, 1961–89, Sect. Head, 1966–89; Univ. Liaison Manager, Nuclear Electric plc, 1989–90. Visiting Professor: Nuclear Engrg, Manchester Univ., 1991–; Corrosion Sci., UMIST, 1992–2004; Materials and Manufacture, Univ. of Plymouth (formerly Plymouth Poly.), 1992–; Visiting Lecturer: Bristol Univ., 1992–; Oxford Univ., 1992–. Member: Bd, British Nuclear Energy Soc., 1974–88; Watt Cttee Wkg Party on Atmospheric Attack on Inorganic Materials, 1987; Hon. Advisor on materials: repairs to St Paul's Cathedral, 1979; restoration of Albert Meml, 1988; roofing of BM, 1999. Mem., Home Office Wkg Party on Adjudications in HM Prisons, 1974; Chm., Leyhill Prison Bd of Visitors, 1973–74. Mem., Assoc. of British Science Writers. Vice Chm., British Pugwash, 2002–. Public Lectr, Tate Gall., 1984; Molecule Club Lectr, 1985 and 1987; Friday Evening Discourse, Royal Instn, 1998. Member, Editorial Board: Material Science and Technology, 1985–; Euro Materials, 1994–; Ed., Interdisciplinary Sci. Reviews, 1996–2002, subseq. Ed. Emeritus. FRSA 1989. Internat. Metallographic Soc. Award, 1976; Esso Gold Medal, Royal Soc., 1979; Interdisciplinary Award, RSC, 1987; Andrew Bryan Award, IMMM, 2006. *Publications:* (ed) Physical Metallurgy of Reactor Fuel Elements, 1975; Vacancies '76, 1977; (jtly) Metals and the Royal Society, 1999; scientific papers on nuclear metallurgy, deformation and corrosion; articles in New Scientist and The Guardian. *Recreations:* writing popular science articles, studying decay of buildings. *Address:* Church Farm House, 28 Hopton Road, Upper Cam, Dursley, Glos GL11 5PB. *T:* (01453) 543165; *e-mail:* j.harris106@btinternet.com. *Club:* Cam Bowling (non-playing member).
Died 3 Feb. 2009.

HARRIS, John Robert, FRIBA; architect; Founder, John R. Harris Architects, London, 1949 (also Founder of associated firms in Brunei, Qatar, Dubai, France, Hong Kong); *b* 5 June 1919; *s* of late Major Alfred Harris, CBE, DSO and Rosa Alfreda Alderson; *m* 1950, Gillian, *d* of Col C. W. D. Rowe, CB, MBE, TD, DL, JP; one *s* one *d. Educ:* Harrow Sch.; Architectural Assoc. Sch. of Architecture (AA Dipl. Hons). Membre de l'Ordre des Architectes Français, 1978. Served War, TA and Active Service, 1939–45 (TEM 1945); Lieut RE, Hong Kong, 1940–41; POW of Japanese, 1941–45; Mem., British Army Aid Gp, China, Hong Kong Resistance, 1943–45. Projects won in internat. competition: State Hosp., Qatar, 1953; New Dubai Hosp., 1976; Corniche and Traffic Intersection, Dubai, 1978; HQ for Min. of Social Affairs and Labour, Oman, 1979; Tuen Mun Hosp., Hong Kong, 1981 (internat. assessment); Ruler's Office, Dubai, 1985. Architects and planners for: Zhuhai New Town, Economic Zone, People's Republic of China, 1984; Deira Sea Corniche masterplan, Dubai, 1993. Major works in UK include: hospitals: Royal Northern, London, 1973; Ealing, 1976; RAF Upper Heyford, 1982; RAF Bentwaters, 1982; Stoke Mandeville, 1983; Wellesley House and St Peter's Court School, 1975; apartments, Hyde Park, 1983; dept stores in Barnstaple, Basildon, Cwmbran, Eltham, Harlow, Hammersmith, Sutton Coldfield and Worthing; refurbishment, Natural Hist. Mus., 1982–89; redevelt, Dorchester Hotel, 1989; develt, Gloucester Road Station site; redevelt and extension, Sheraton Grand Hotel, Edinburgh, 1993; Royal residence adjoining Windsor Park, 1998. Major works overseas include: National Bank of Dubai HQ Bldg, 1968; Sulaibikhat Hosp., Kuwait, 1968; Grindlay's Bank, Muscat, 1969; Rashid Hosp., Dubai, 1973; dept stores in Antwerp, Brussels, Lille, Paris and Strasbourg, 1973–83; shopping centres, Oman, 1978 and 1984; Internat. Trade Centre (40 storeys), Dubai, 1979; British Embassy, Chancery Offices and Ambassador's Residence, Abu Dhabi, 1982; University Teaching Hosp., Maiduguri, Nigeria, 1982; Caritas Hosp., Hong Kong, 1983; Women's Hosp., Doha, 1984; Shell Recreation Centre, Brunei, 1984; Wafi Shopping Mall, Dubai, 1991–; British Bank of ME HQ, Dubai, 1993; 3,000 seat Conf. Centre, Doha, 1997; Equine Hosp., Dubai, 1997; design, Harrow Internat Sch., Bangkok, 1997; Internat. Hotel Develt, Armenia, 1998; Palace Develt, Bahrain, 1998. FRSA 1982. Cert., Internat. Hosp. Fedn, 1993; Structural Steel Design Award, London Docklands, 1993. Silver Jubilee Medal, 1977. *Publications:* (jtly) John R. Harris Architects, 1984; (with O. Lindsay) The Battle for Hong Kong 1941–1945: hostage to fortune, 2004; contrib. to books and architectural and technical jls. *Recreations:* architecture, sailing, travel. *Address:* 24 Devonshire Place, W1G 6BX. *T:* (020) 7935 9353. *Clubs:* Special Forces, Royal Thames Yacht.   *Died 15 Feb. 2008.*

HARRIS, Lyndon Goodwin, RI 1958; RSW 1952; RWA 1947; artist in oil, water-colour, stained glass, and etching; *b* 25 July 1928; *s* of late S. E. Harris, ACIS and Mary Elsie Harris. *Educ:* Halesowen Grammar Sch. Studied Art at: Birmingham Coll. of Art; Slade Sch. of Fine Art, 1946–50; University of London Inst. of Education, 1950–51; Courtauld Inst.; Central Sch. of Art and Crafts, London. Leverhulme Schol., Pilkington Schol., Slade Schol., and Slade Anatomy Prizeman; Dip. Fine Art (London) 1949; Courtauld Certificate, 1950; ATD 1951. *Works exhibited:* Paris Salon (Gold Medal, Oil Painting; Honourable Mention, Etching); RA (first exhibited at age of 13), RSA, RI, RSW, NEAC, RBA, RGI, RWA, and principal provincial galleries. *Works in permanent collections:* Govt Art Collection; University Coll., London; Birmingham and Midland Inst.; City of Worcester; (stained glass) Overend Methodist Mission Church, Halesowen. *Recreation:* music (organ and pianoforte).   *Died 4 June 2006.*

HARRIS, Philip; Principal, Monopolies and Mergers Commission, 1977–85; *b* Manchester, 15 Dec. 1915; *er s* of S. D. Harris and Sarah Chazan; *m* 1939, Sarah Henriques Valentine (*d* 1996); three *d*. *Educ:* Manchester Grammar Sch.; Trinity Hall, Cambridge (Open Scholarship, BA 1st Cl (with dist.), Historical Tripos, MA 1970). Asst Principal, Board of Trade, 1938–40. Served War, 1940–45; Anti-Aircraft Command and Western Europe; 2nd Lieut RA, 1941; Lieut, 2/8th Lancs Fusiliers, 1944; Capt., 6th Royal Welch Fusiliers, 1945. Principal, Board of Trade, 1946; Asst Sec., Board of Trade, 1948–64; Asst Registrar, Office of the Registrar of Restrictive Trading Agreements, 1964–66, Principal Asst Registrar, 1966–73; Principal Asst Registrar, Fair Trading Div. I, DTI, 1973; Dir, Restrictive Trade Practices Div., Office of Fair Trading, 1973–76. Nuffield Travelling Fellowship, 1956–57 (study of Indian Industrial Development). UK Mem., EEC Adv. Cttee on Cartels and Monopolies, 1973–76; Mem., Labour Finance and Industry Gp, 1990–. Leader, UK Delgn to Internat. Cotton Advisory Cttee, 1960, 1963. Lectr, Univ. of the Third Age, London, 1995–2000. *Publications:* various articles on monopolies and restrictive trade practices policy and current developments in UK competition law and administration. *Recreation:* history. *Address:* c/o 14 Greatdown Road, W7 1JS.   *Died 2 June 2008.*

HARRIS, Richard Reader; *b* 4 June 1913; *s* of Richard Reader Harris; *m* 1st, 1940, Pamela Rosemary Merrick Stephens (marr. diss. 1963); three *d*; 2nd, Una; (one *s* decd). *Educ:* St Lawrence Coll., Ramsgate. Called to the Bar, 1941. Fire Service, 1939–45. MP (C) Heston and Isleworth, 1950–70. *Recreations:* squash, tennis.   *Died 7 July 2009.*

HARRIS, Rosina Mary; Consultant, Taylor Joynson Garrett, 1989–95; Partner, Joynson-Hicks, Solicitors, 1954–89 (Senior Partner, 1977–86); *b* 30 May 1921; *d* of late Alfred Harris, CBE, DSO, and Rosa Alfreda Harris. *Educ:* St Swithun's Sch., Winchester; Oxford Univ. (BA 1946, MA; BCL 1947). Joined American Ambulance of GB, 1940. Member, Whitford Committee (a Cttee set up under the Chairmanship of Hon. Mr Justice Whitford to enquire into and report as to copyright law), 1973. Silver Jubilee Medal, 1977. *Recreations:* theatre, riding. *Address:* 16 Upper Wimpole Street, W1G 6LT.   *Died 28 Sept. 2010.*

HARRISON, Claude William, RP 1961; artist; portrait painter and painter of conversation pieces, imaginative landscapes and murals, etc; *b* Leyland, Lancs, 31 March 1922; *s* of Harold Harrison and Florence Mildred Ireton; *m* 1947, Audrey Johnson (*d* 2005); one *s*. *Educ:* Hutton Grammar Sch., Lancs. Served in RAF, 1942–46. Royal Coll. of Art, 1947–49; Studio in Ambleside, 1949–52. Exhibited from 1950 at: RA; RSA; Royal Society Portrait Painters; New English Art Club, etc. Hon. RP 1990. *Publications:* The Portrait Painter's handbook, 1968. *Recreation:* painting. *Address:* 1 Rue Palmaro, 06500 Menton, France. *T:* (4) 93419721.   *Died 13 Sept. 2009.*

HARRISON, Sir Ernest (Thomas), Kt 1981; OBE 1972; FCA; Chairman, Racal Electronics Plc, 1966–2000 (Chief Executive, 1966–92); Director, Camelot Group plc, 1993–2000; *b* 11 May 1926; *s* of late Ernest Horace Harrison and Gertrude Rebecca Gibbons Harrison; *m* 1st (marr. diss. 1959); twin *s*; 2nd, 1960, Phyllis Brenda Knight, (Janie); one *s* two *d*. *Educ:* Trinity Grammar Sch., Wood Green, London. Qualified as Chartered Accountant, 1950; served Articles with Harker Holloway & Co.; joined Racal Electronics as Secretary and Chief Accountant, when company commenced manufacturing, 1951; Director, 1958, Dep. Man. Dir, 1961. Chairman: Racal Telecom, then Vodafone Gp, Plc, 1988–98; Chubb Security, 1992–97. Active in National Savings movement, 1964–76, for which services awarded OBE. Chm., Royal Free Cancer Research (formerly Ronald Raven Chair in Clinical Oncology, subseq. Ronald Raven Cancer Research) Trust, 1991–2006. Mem., Jockey Club, 1990–. Mem., RSA. Liveryman, Scriveners' Co. CompIERE 1975; CCMI (CBIM 1976); FIET (CompIEE 1978). Sch. Fellowship, Royal Free Hosp. Sch. of Medicine, 1995. Hon. FCGI 1990; Hon. FREng (Hon. FEng 1997); Hon. Fellow, UCL, 2006. Hon. DSc: Cranfield, 1981; City, 1982; DUniv: Surrey, 1981; Edinburgh, 1983. Businessman of the Year, 1981; Founding Society's Centenary Award, ICA, 1990; Mountbatten Medal, Nat. Electronic Council, 1992. *Recreations:* horse racing (owner), gardening, wild life, sport, espec. soccer.   *Died 16 Feb. 2009.*

HARRISON, Maj.-Gen. Ian Stewart, CB 1970; Captain of Deal Castle, since 1980; *b* 25 May 1919; *s* of Leslie George Harrison and Evelyn Simpson Christie; *m* 1942, Winifred Raikes Stavert (*d* 2005); one *s* one *d*. *Educ:* St Albans Sch. Commissioned, Royal Marines, 1937; service at sea, in Norway, Middle East, Sicily, BAOR, 1939–45; Staff Coll., Camberley (student), 1948; HQ 3rd Commando Bde, 1949–51 (despatches); Staff of Comdt-Gen., RM, 1951–52; Staff Coll., Camberley (Directing Staff), 1953–55; Commandant, RM Signal Sch., 1956–58; Joint Services Staff Coll. (Student), 1958; CO 40 Commando, RM, 1959–61; Dir, Royal Marines Reserves, 1962; Staff of Comdt-Gen., RM, 1963–64; Joint Warfare Estabt, 1965–67; British Defence Staff, Washington, DC, 1967–68; Chief of Staff to Comdt-Gen., RM, 1968–70, retired. ADC to HM the Queen, 1967–68. Representative Col Comdt, Royal Marines, 1981–82. Dir-Gen., British Food Export Council, 1970–77; Dir, British Consultants Bureau, 1977–87. Chm., Chichester Festivities, 1979–89. Governor, E. Hayes Dashwood Foundn, 1977–99. *Recreations:* sailing, Real tennis, golf. *Address:* Manor Cottage, Runcton, Chichester, W Sussex PO20 1PU. *T:* (01243) 785480. *Clubs:* Army and Navy; Royal Yacht Squadron, Royal Naval Sailing Association, Royal Marines Sailing (Commodore, 1968–70). *Died 2 April 2008.*

HARRISON, Surgeon Vice-Adm. Sir John (Albert Bews), KBE 1982; FRCP, FRCR; Medical Director General (Naval), 1980–83; *b* 20 May 1921; *s* of late Albert William Harrison and Lilian Eda Bews, Dover, Kent; *m* 1943, Jane (*née* Harris) (*d* 1988); two *s*. *Educ:* Queens' Coll., Cambridge; St Bartholomew's Hosp. Surg. Lt RNVR, transf. RN, 1947; served, 1947–83: RM Infirmary, Deal, 1948; HMS Sparrow, Amer. WI stn, 1949; RN Hosp., Plymouth, 1951; HMS Ganges, 1952; Admiralty Med. Bd and St Bartholomew's Hosp., 1953; RN Hosps, Hong Kong, 1955, Chatham, 1958, Haslar, 1959; St Bart's and Middlesex Hosps, 1961; RN Hosps Malta, 1962, Haslar, 1964–75; Adviser in Radiol., 1967–79; Dep. Med. Dir Gen. and Dir Med. Personnel and Logistics, 1975–77; Dean of Naval Medicine and Surgeon Rear-Adm., Inst. of Naval Medicine, 1977–80. Mem., Council for Med. Postgrad. Educn of Eng. and Wales, 1977–79. Pres., Section of Radiology, RSM, 1984–85. Fellow: RSM; MedSocLond (Pres. 1985–86). CStJ 1983. QHP 1976–83. *Publications:* Hyperbaric Osteonecrosis et al, 1975; articles in med. press on sarcoidosis, tomography, middle ear disease, and dysbaric osteonecrosis. *Recreations:* fishing, cricket, countryman. *Address:* c/o Alexandra Cottage, Swanmore, Hampshire SO32 2PB. *Club:* MCC. *Died 7 March 2010.*

HARRISON, Kenneth Cecil, OBE 1980 (MBE mil. 1946); FCLIP; City Librarian, Westminster, 1961–80, retired; Consultant Librarian, Ranfurly Library Service, 1983–90; *b* 29 April 1915; *s* of Thomas and Annie Harrison; *m* 1941, Doris Taylor (*d* 2005); two *s*. *Educ:* Grammar Sch., Hyde. Asst, Hyde Public Library, 1931–37; Branch Librarian, Coulsdon and Purley Public Libraries, 1937–39; Borough Librarian: Hyde, 1939–47; Hove (also Curator), 1947–50; Eastbourne, 1950–58; Hendon, 1958–61. HM Forces, 1940–46; commnd RMC Sandhurst, 1942; served with E Yorks Regt in Middle East, Sicily and NW Europe (wounded, 1944; Major 1944–46). President: Library Assoc., 1973; Commonwealth Library Assoc., 1972–75 (Exec. Sec., 1980–83); Vice-President: Internat. Assoc. Metropolitan Libraries; Westminster Arts Council (Hon. Sec. 1965–80). Member: IFLA Public Libraries Cttee, 1969–81; Central Music Library Council, 1961–80; Library Assoc. Council, 1953–79; MCC Arts and Library Cttee, 1973–89; Westminster Abbey Liby Cttee, 1973–80; Chm. Jt Organising Cttee for Nat. Library Week, 1964–69. British Council: Cultural Exchange Scholar to Romania, 1971; Mem., Library Adv. Panel, 1974–80; Consultant to Sri Lanka, 1974, to India, 1981. UNESCO Consultant to the Seychelles and Mauritius, 1977–78; Commonwealth Relations Trust Consultant to Ghana, Sierra Leone and The Gambia, 1979; Library

Consultant, Bermuda, 1983. President: Rotary Club of Eastbourne, 1957–58; Past Rotarians Club of Eastbourne, 2000–01; Sec., Assoc. of Past Rotarians, 1996–99. Commonwealth Foundn Scholar, E and Central Africa, 1975. C. C. Williamson Meml Lectr, Nashville, Tenn, 1969. Governor, Westminster College, 1962–80. Editor, The Library World, 1961–71. Knight, First Class, Order of the Lion (Finland), 1976. *Publications:* First Steps in Librarianship, 1950, 5th edn 1980; Libraries in Scandinavia, 1961, 2nd edn 1969; The Library and the Community, 1963, 3rd edn 1977; Public Libraries Today, 1963; Facts at your Fingertips, 1964, 2nd edn 1966; British Public Library Buildings (with S. G. Berriman), 1966; Libraries in Britain, 1968; Public Relations for Librarians, 1973, 2nd edn 1982; International Librarianship, 1989; A Librarian's Odyssey, 2000; *edited:* Prospects for British Librarianship, 1976; Public Library Policy, 1981; Public Library Buildings 1975–83, 1987; Library Buildings 1984–89, 1990; contribs to many British and foreign jls and encyclopædias. *Recreations:* reading, writing, travel, wine, cricket, crosswords. *Address:* 5 Tavistock, Devonshire Place, Eastbourne, E Sussex BN21 4AG. *T:* (01323) 726747; *e-mail:* kcharrison88@hotmail.com. *Clubs:* Royal Commonwealth Society, MCC. *Died 19 Feb. 2006.*

HARROWBY, 7th Earl of, *cr* 1809; **Dudley Danvers Granville Coutts Ryder,** TD; Baron Harrowby, 1776; Viscount Sandon, 1809; *b* 20 Dec. 1922; *er s* of 6th Earl of Harrowby and Lady Helena Blanche Coventry (*d* 1974), *e d* of late Viscount Deerhurst; *S* father, 1987; *m* 1st, 1949, Jeanette Rosalthé (*d* 1997), *yr d* of late Captain Peter Johnston-Saint; one *s* one *d*; 2nd, 2003, Janet Mary Pierette, *y d* of late Alan Edward Stott, JP, DL. *Educ:* Eton. Lt-Col RA; OC 254 (City of London) Field Regt, RA (TA), 56 Armoured Div., 1962–64. Served War of 1939–45: 59 Inf. Div., in NW Europe (wounded); 5 Para. Bde, India and Java (political offr), 1941–45. Man. Dir, 1949–89, Dep. Chm., 1970–89, Coutts & Co.; Director: Dinorwic Slate Quarries Co., 1951–69; United Kingdom Provident Institution, 1955–86 (Dep. Chm., 1956–64); National Provincial Bank, 1964–69; National Westminster Bank Plc, 1968–87 (Dep. Chm., 1971–87); Olympia Group, 1968–73 (Chm., 1971–73); Sheepbridge Engrg Ltd, 1977–79; Saudi Internat. Bank, 1980–82, 1985–87; Powell Duffryn Trustees Ltd, 1981–86; Orion Pacific Ltd, 1980–81; Orion Pension Trustee Co. Ltd, 1980–81; Chairman: International Westminster Bank Plc, 1977–87; Powell Duffryn Gp, 1981–86 (Dir, 1976–86); National Westminster Unit Trust Managers, 1979–83; Orion Bank Ltd, 1979–81; Bentley Engineering Co. Ltd, 1983–86; NatWest Investment Bank, 1986–87; Dowty Group, 1986–91 (Dir, 1986–91); The Private Bank & Trust Co., 1989–92; Private Financial Hldgs, 1992–94. Chm., Nat. Biol Standards Bd, 1973–88. Mem. Kensington Borough Council, 1950–65 (Chm., Gen. Purposes Cttee, 1957–59), Kensington and Chelsea BC, 1965–71 (Chm., Finance Cttee, 1968–71); Mem. Exec. Cttee, London area Cons. Assoc., 1949–50; Hon. Treasurer, S Kensington Cons. Assoc., 1953–56; Pres., Wolverhampton SW Cons. Assoc., 1959–68. Pres., Historical and Civic Soc. Hon. Treasurer: Family Welfare Assoc., 1951–65; Central Council for the Care of Cripples, 1953–60. General Commissioner for Income Tax, 1954–71; Member: Lord Chancellor's Adv. Investment Cttees, for Court of Protection, 1965–77, for Public Trustee, 1974–77; Inst. Internat. d'Etudes Bancaires, 1977–87; Trilateral Commn, 1980–94. Manager, Fulham and Kensington Hosp. Group, 1953–56; Member: Cttee of Management, Inst. of Psychiatry, 1953–73 (Chm. 1965–73); Board of Governors, Bethlem Royal and Maudsley (Postgraduate Teaching) Hosps, 1955–73 (Chm. 1965–73); Dep. Chm., London Postgraduate Cttee, Teaching Hosps Assoc., 1968–69; Trustee, Psychiatry Research Trust, 1982–99; Mem. Bd of Govs, Univ. of Keele, 1965–68. Pres., Staffordshire Soc., 1957–59 (Hon. Treas., 1947–51). Dep. Pres., Staffs Army Cadet League. Mem., Ct of Assts, Goldsmiths' Co., 1972–77. Governor, Atlantic Inst. for

Internat. Affairs, 1983–88. Hon. FRCPsych. Hon. DSc Keele, 1996. *Heir: s* Viscount Sandon, *b* 18 March 1951. *Address:* Apt 20, Albert Bridge House, 127 Albert Bridge Road, SW11 4PL. *T:* (020) 7223 7535; Sandon Hall, Stafford ST18 0BZ. *T:* (01889) 508338; Burnt Norton, Chipping Campden, Glos GL55 6PR. *T:* (01386) 841488.   *Died 9 Oct. 2007.*

HART, Alan Edward; Chief Executive, Equal Opportunities Commission, 1985–89; *b* 28 July 1935; *m* 1961, Ann Derbyshire; one *s* one *d*. *Educ:* Varndean County Grammar Sch., Brighton; Lincoln Coll., Univ. of Oxford (MA). Solicitor. Dep. Town Clerk, City of Salford, 1970–73; Dir of Admin, 1973–75, Chief Exec., 1975–85, Wigan MBC.   *Died 26 June 2006.*

HART, Alexander Hendry; QC (Canada) 1969; Agent General for British Columbia in the United Kingdom and Europe, 1981–87; *b* Regina, Sask, 17 July 1916; *s* of Alexander Hart and Mary (*née* Davidson); *m* 1948, Janet MacMillan Mackay; three *s* one *d*. *Educ:* Dalhousie Law School (LLB). Served War, Royal Canadian Artillery, 1939–45; retired with rank of Major. Read law with McInnis, Mcquarrie and Cooper; called to Bar of Nova Scotia, 1947. Vice-Pres., Marketing, 1967–71; Sen. Vice-Pres., Canadian Nat. Rlwys, 1971–81. Dep. Internat. Pres., Pacific Basin Economic Council, 1980–81; Pres., Canada-UK Chamber of Commerce, 1983; Past Pres., Vancouver Board of Trade; Past Chm., Western Transportation Adv. Council; Past Mem., University Council of British Columbia; Past Pres., Canada Japan Soc. of Vancouver. *Recreation:* golf. *Address:* 1515 Dorcas Point Road, Nanoose Bay, BC V9P 9B4, Canada. *Clubs:* Royal & Ancient Golf (St Andrews); Vancouver, Men's Canadian, Shaughnessy Golf and Country (Vancouver). *Died 4 Feb. 2009.*

HART, His Honour Donald; QC 1978; a Circuit Judge, 1989–98; President, Mental Health Review Tribunals (restricted patients), 1983–2000; *b* 6 Jan. 1933; *s* of Frank and Frances Hart; *m* 1st, 1958, Glenys Thomas (marr. diss. 1990); two *s* two *d*; 2nd, 1990, Joan Turton. *Educ:* Altrincham Grammar Sch.; Magdalen Coll., Oxford. MA. Macaskie Scholar, Arden and Atkin Prize, Lee Essay Prize (Gray's Inn), 1956. Called to the Bar, Gray's Inn, 1956; Northern Circuit, 1956; a Recorder, 1978–89; Designated Family Judge for Liverpool, 1992–98. *Recreations:* garden, opera, cuisine. *Address:* 217 Knutsford Road, Grappenhall, Cheshire WA4 2TX. *T:* (01925) 604228.   *Died 24 April 2007.*

HART, Hon. Sir Michael (Christopher Campbell), Kt 1998; **Hon. Mr Justice Hart;** a Judge of the High Court of Justice, Chancery Division, since 1998; *b* 7 May 1948; *s* of Raymond David Campbell Hart and Penelope Mary Hart (*née* Ellis); *m* 1st, 1972, Melanie Jane Sandiford (marr. diss. 1996); two *d*; 2nd, 1996, Sara Jane Hargreaves; one *s*. *Educ:* Winchester Coll.; Magdalen Coll., Oxford (MA, BCL). Called to the Bar, Gray's Inn, 1970, Bencher, 1995 (Master of Moots, 2000–04); QC 1987; QC (NI) 1994. Chancery Supervising Judge for Midland, Western, and Wales and Chester Circuits, 2004–. Fellow, All Souls College, Oxford, 1970–77, 1979–86, 1993–95, 2001–. *Address:* c/o Royal Courts of Justice, Strand, WC2A 2LL.   *Died 20 Feb. 2007.*

HART, P(hilip) M(ontagu) D'Arcy, CBE 1956; MA, MD (Cambridge); FRCP; Medical Research Council grant holder, National Institute for Medical Research, 1965–93, then Visiting Scientist (Director, Tuberculosis Research Unit, Medical Research Council, 1948–65); *b* 25 June 1900; *s* of late Henry D'Arcy Hart and Hon. Ethel Montagu; *m* 1941, Ruth, *d* of late Herbert Meyer and Grete Meyer-Larsen; one *s*. *Educ:* Clifton Coll.; Gonville and Caius Coll., Cambridge; University Coll. Hospital. Dorothy Temple Cross Fellowship to USA, 1934–35; Consultant Physician, UCH, 1934–37; Mem. Scientific Staff, MRC, 1937–48. Mem. Expert Cttee on Tuberculosis, WHO, 1947–64. Hon. FMedSci 1999. Goldsmith Entrance Exhibnr, Filliter Exhibnr, Magrath Scholarship, Tuke Medals, UCH Medical Sch., 1922–25;

Horton Smith MD Prize, Cambridge, 1930; Royal College of Physicians: Milroy Lecture, 1937; Mitchell Lecture, 1946; Weber-Parkes Prize, 1951; Marc Daniels Lecture, 1967; Stewart Prize, BMA, 1964; British Thoracic Soc. Medal, 1996. *Publications:* scientific papers on respiratory disease, epidemiology and cell biology. *Address:* 37 Belsize Court, NW3 5QN. *T:* (020) 7435 4048. *Club:* Athenæum.   *Died 30 July 2006.*

HARTOG, Harold Samuel Arnold; Knight, Order of the Netherlands Lion; KBE (Hon.) 1970; Advisory Director, Unilever NV, 1971–75 (Chairman, 1966–71); *b* Nijmegen, Holland, 21 Dec. 1910; *m* 1963, Ingeborg Luise Krahn. *Educ:* Wiedemann Coll., Geneva. Joined Unilever, 1931. After service with Dutch forces during War of 1939–45 he joined management of Unilever interests in France, and subseq. took charge of Unilever cos in the Netherlands; elected to Bds of Unilever, 1948; Mem. Rotterdam Group Management and responsible for Unilever activities in Germany, Austria and Belgium, 1952–60; subseq. Mem. Cttee for Unilever's overseas interests, in London; became, there, one of the two world co-ordinators of Unilever's foods interests, 1962. Hon. Dr CPhil Tel Aviv, 2001. *Recreations:* history of art, collecting Chinese pottery and porcelain. *Clubs:* Dutch; Ubersee (Hamburg); Golf (Falkenstein). *Died 23 Sept. 2007.*

HARVEY OF TASBURGH, 2nd Baron *cr* 1954, of Tasburgh, Norfolk, **Peter Charles Oliver Harvey,** FCA; Bt 1868; *b* 28 Jan. 1921; *er s* of 1st Baron Harvey of Tasburgh, GCMG, GCVO, CB, and Maud Annora (*d* 1970), *d* of late Arthur Watkin Williams-Wynn; *S* father, 1968; *m* 1957, Penelope Anne (*d* 1995), *d* of Lt-Col Sir William Makins, 3rd Bt; two *d*. *Educ:* Eton; Trinity College, Cambridge. Served 1941–46 with Royal Artillery, Tunisia, Italy. Bank of England, 1948–56; Binder Hamlyn & Co., 1956–61; Lloyds Bank International Ltd (formerly Bank of London and South America), 1961–75; English Transcontinental Ltd, 1975–78; Brown, Shipley & Co., 1978–81. *Recreations:* sailing, music. *Heir: nephew* Charles John Giuseppe Harvey, *b* 4 Feb. 1951. *Address:* Crownick Woods, Restronguet, Mylor, Falmouth, Cornwall TR11 5ST. *Clubs:* Brooks's; Royal Cornwall Yacht. *Died 18 April 2010.*

HARVEY, Alan Frederick Ronald, OBE 1970; HM Diplomatic Service, retired; *b* 15 Dec. 1919; *s* of Edward Frederick and Alice Sophia Harvey; *m* 1946, Joan Barbara (*née* Tuckey); one *s*. *Educ:* Tottenham Grammar Sch. Air Ministry, 1936–40 (Civil Service appt). Served War, RAF, 1940–46. Air Min., 1946–49; Foreign Office, 1949–52 (on transfer to Diplomatic Service); HM Vice-Consul, Turin, 1953–55; Second Sec.: Rome, 1956; Tokyo, 1957–59; HM Consul (Information): Chicago, 1959–62; FO, 1963–65; First Sec. (Commercial): Belgrade, 1965–67; Tokyo, 1967–72; Commercial Counsellor: Milan, 1973–74; Rome, 1975–76; Consul-General in Perth, 1976–78. *Recreations:* gardening, golf. *Address:* Tresibbett, Altarnun, near Launceston, Cornwall PL15 7RF. *Clubs:* Royal Commonwealth Society, Civil Service.   *Died 17 Nov. 2006.*

HARVEY, Prof. David Robert, FRCP, FRCPCH; Professor of Paediatrics and Neonatal Medicine, Imperial College Faculty of Medicine (formerly Royal Postgraduate Medical School) at Hammersmith Hospital, 1995–2002, then Emeritus; Consultant Paediatrician, Queen Charlotte's and Chelsea (formerly Queen Charlotte's Maternity) Hospital, 1970–2002; *b* 7 Dec. 1936; *s* of Cyril Francis Harvey and Margarita Harvey (*née* Cardew Smith); partner 1970, Teck Ong (*d* 2004). *Educ:* Dulwich Coll.; Guy's Hosp. Med. Sch. (MB BS 1960). MRCP 1963, FRCP 1976; FRCPCH 1997. House Officer: Guy's Hosp., 1960–61; Central Middx Hosp., 1961–62; Amer. Hosp., Paris, 1963; Neonatal House Officer, 1964, Neate Res. Fellow, 1964–65, Hammersmith Hosp.; House Officer, Hosp. for Sick Children, Gt Ormond St, 1966; Paediatric Registrar, Hammersmith and Hillingdon Hosps, 1966–68; Nuffield

Res. Fellow, Oxford, 1968–69; Paediatric Sen. Registrar, Hammersmith Hosp., 1969–70; Consultant Paediatrician: St Charles' Hosp., London, 1970–87; St Mary's Hosp., London, 1987–92; Sen. Lectr, RPMS, 1992–95. Hon. Secretary: Neonatal Soc., 1975–79; BPA, 1979–84. Handcock Prize, RCS, 1960. *Publications:* (ed jtly) Biology of Play, 1977; (jtly) The Sick Newborn Baby, 1981; (ed jtly) Child Health, 1985; (ed) New Parents, 1988; (ed jtly) The Baby under 1000 grams, 1989; (ed jtly) The Stress of Multiple Births, 1991; (jtly) Colour Guide: Neonatology, 1991; (ed jtly) Community Child Health and Paediatrics, 1995; contrib. to professional jls. *Recreations:* listening to opera, learning Chinese.
Died 10 April 2010.

HARVEY, John Edgar, CBE 1994; Director, Burmah Oil Trading Ltd and subsidiary companies in Burmah Oil Group, 1974–80; *b* 24 April 1920; *s* of John Watt Harvey and Charlotte Elizabeth Harvey; *m* 1945, Mary Joyce Lane, BA, JP (*d* 2007); one *s. Educ:* Xaverian Coll., Bruges, Belgium; Lyme Regis Grammar Sch. Radio Officer, in the Merchant Navy, 1939–45. Contested (C): St Pancras North, 1950; Walthamstow East, 1951; Mem. Nat. Exec. Cttee., Conservative Party, 1950–55; Chm., Woodford Conservative Assoc., 1954–56. MP (C) Walthamstow East, 1955–66. Founder Chm., Cttee of Greater London Cons. MPs, 1963–66. Mem., Speaker's Conf. on Electoral Reform, 1965–66. Regular broadcaster on parly affairs, BBC French Service, 1957–63. Pres., Wanstead & Woodford Conservative Assoc., 1986–93. A Founding Mem., Internat. Churchill Socs' Churchill Center, Washington, 1996. Mem., NSPCC Central Executive Cttee, 1963–68. Governor, Forest Sch., 1966–78. Verderer of Epping Forest, 1970–98; Reeve of Forest, Parish of Loughton, 1998–. Freeman, State of Texas, 1957. Freeman, City of London, 1966; Past Master, Guild of Freemen of City of London; Liveryman, Basketmakers' Co. *Recreation:* various in moderation. *Address:* 43 Traps Hill, Loughton, Essex IG10 1TB. *T:* (020) 8508 8753. *Club:* City of London.
Died 13 Jan. 2008.

HARVEY-JONES, Sir John (Henry), Kt 1985; MBE 1952; Chairman: Parallax Enterprises, 1987–96; Imperial Chemical Industries PLC, 1982–87; business executive; *b* London, 16 April 1924; *s* of Mervyn Harvey-Jones, OBE, and Eileen Harvey-Jones; *m* 1947, Mary Evelyn Bignell; one *d. Educ:* Tormore Sch., Deal, Kent; RNC Dartmouth, Devon. Served RN, 1937–56: specialised in submarines; qual. as Russian interpreter, 1946, and subseq. as German interpreter; appts in Naval Intell. (MBE); resigned, 1956, Lt-Comdr. Joined ICI as Work Study Officer, Wilton, 1956; commercial appts at Wilton and Heavy Organic Chemicals Div. until apptd Techno-Commercial Dir, 1967; Dep. Chm., HOC Div., 1968; Chm., ICI Petrochemicals Div., 1970–73; Main Bd, ICI, 1973, Dep. Chm., 1978–82. Chairman: Phillips-Imperial Petroleum, 1973–75; Burns Anderson, 1987–90 (non-exec. Dir, 1987–91); The Economist, 1989–94 (Dir, 1987–94); Trendroute Ltd, 1988–91; Didacticus Video Productions Ltd, 1989–97; Deputy Chairman: GPA Ltd, 1989–93 (Dir, 1987–93); Director: ICI Americas Inc., 1975–76; Fiber Industries Inc., 1975–78; Carrington Viyella Ltd, 1981–82 (non-exec. Dir, 1974–79); Grand Metropolitan PLC, 1983–94 (Dep. Chm., 1987–91); non-exec. Dir, Reed International PLC, 1975–84. Vice Pres., Indust. Participation Assoc., 1983–; Hon. Vice-Pres., Inst. of Marketing, 1982–89. Member: Welsh Develt Internat., 1989–93; Foundn Bd, Internat. Management Inst., Geneva, 1984–87; Internat. Council, Eur. Inst. of Business Admin, 1984–87; Adv. Council, Prince's Youth Business Trust, 1986–97; Soc. of Chem. Industry, 1978–; Hon. Consultant, RUSI, 1987–. Chancellor, Bradford Univ., 1986–91; Chm. Council, St James's and the Abbey Sch., Malvern, 1987–93; Vice-President: Hearing & Speech Trust, 1985–; Heaton Woods Trust, 1986–; Book Trust Appeal Fund, 1987–; Fellow, Smallpeice Trust, 1988–; Trustee: Conf. Bd, 1984–86; Multiple Sclerosis Res. Charitable Trust, 1999–; Hon. Trust Mem., Andrea Adams Trust, 2000–.

Chm. Council, Wildfowl Trust, 1987–94. Hon. President: Univ. of Bradford MBA Alumni Assoc., 1989; Friends of Brecon Jazz, 1989–. Patron: MSC Nat. Trng Awards, 1987; Steer Orgn, 1988–; Nat. Canine Defence League, 1990–; Kingwood Trust, 1996–; Royal Nat. Submarine Mus. Centennial Appeal, 1999–; Modem, 2000–; Amor Foundn for Street Children in El Salvador, 2000–; Soc. of Turnaround Professionals, 2000–06; Professional Contractors' Gp, 2000–06; Vice-Patron, British Polio Fellowship, 1988–; Corporate Patron, Primrose Earth Awareness Trust, 2001–; supporter, Campaign for Adventure (Risk and Enterprise in Society), 2001–. Gov., E-SU, 1987–91. Chm. Judges, Teaching Awards, 1999–2000. Hon. FRSC 1985; Hon. FIChemE 1985; Hon. Mem. CGLI, 1988; Hon. FCIPS 2001; FRSA 1979 (Vice-Pres., 1988–92). Sen. Ind. Fellow, Leicester Polytechnic, 1990; Hon. Fellow, Polytechnic of Wales. Hon. LLD: Manchester, 1985; Liverpool, 1986; London, 1987; Cambridge, 1987; DUniv Surrey, 1985; Hon. DSc: Bradford, 1986; Leicester, 1986; Keele, 1989; Exeter, 1989; Hon. DCL Newcastle, 1988; Hon. DBA Internat. Management Centre, 1990; Hon. DTech Loughborough, 1991. Gold Medal, BIM, 1985; Centenary Medal, SCI, 1986; J. O. Hambro British Businessman of the Year, 1986; Award of Excellence in Communication, Internat. Assoc. of Business Communicators, 1987; Radar Man of the Year, 1987; CGIA in Technol. (*hc*), 1987. Comdr's Cross, Order of Merit, Germany. Television: Troubleshooter (series), 1990; Troubleshooter Specials—Eastern Europe, 1991; Troubleshooter 2, 1992; Troubleshooter Returns, 1995; Troubleshooter: Back in Business, 2000. *Publications:* Making it Happen: reflections on leadership, 1987; Troubleshooter, 1990; Getting it Together, 1991; Troubleshooter 2, 1992; Managing to Survive, 1993; All Together Now, 1994; Troubleshooter Returns, 1995. *Recreations:* ocean sailing, swimming, the countryside, cooking, contemporary literature. *Address:* c/o PO Box 18, Ross-on-Wye, Herefordshire HR9 7PH. *T:* (01989) 567171, *Fax:* (01989) 567173. *Clubs:* Garrick, Groucho.
Died 9 Jan. 2008.

HASELDEN, Prof. Geoffrey Gordon; Brotherton Professor of Chemical Engineering, University of Leeds, 1960–86, then Emeritus; *b* 4 Aug. 1924; *s* of George A. Haselden and Rose E. (*née* Pleasants); *m* 1945, Eileen Doris Francis; three *d. Educ:* Sir Walter St John's Sch.; Imperial Coll. of Science and Technology (BScChemEng 1944; PhD (Eng) Chem Eng, 1947; DScEng, 1962; DIC). CEng; FIMechE; FIChemE; FInstR; FCGI. Mem. Gas Research Bd, 1946–48; Lectr in Low Temperature Technology, Chemical Engrg Dept, 1948–57, Senior Lectr in Chemical Engrg, 1957–60, Imperial Coll. Chm., British Cryogenics Council, 1967–71. President: Commn A3, Internat. Inst. of Refrigeration, 1971–79; Inst. of Refrigeration, 1981–84; Vice-Pres., IChemE, 1984–85. Gen. Editor, Internat. Jl of Refrigeration, 1978–88. *Publications:* Cryogenic Fundamentals, 1971; research papers in Trans Inst. Chem. Eng., etc. *Recreation:* Methodist lay preacher.
Died 1 Feb. 2007.

HASHIMOTO, Ryutaro; MHR (LDP) Okayama, District 2, 1963–96, District 4, 1996–2005; Prime Minister of Japan, 1996–98; *b* 29 July 1937; *s* of Ryogo Hashimoto and Masa Hashimoto; *m* 1966, Kumiko Nakamura; two *s* three *d. Educ:* Dept of Law, Keio Univ. (BSc). Vice-Minister of Health and Welfare, 1970–71; Dir, Social Affairs Div., 1972–74, Dep. Chm., 1974–76, Policy Res. Council, LDP; Chm., Standing Cttee on Social and Labor Affairs, House of Reps, 1976–78; Minister of Health and Welfare, 1978–79; Policy Research Council, Liberal Democratic Party: Chairman, Research Commission on: Public Admin and Finances, 1980–86; Fundamental Policies for Medical Care, 1984–86; Minister of Transport, 1986–87; Actg Sec.-Gen., 1987–89, Sec.-Gen., 1989, LDP; Minister of Finance, 1989–91; Liberal Democratic Party: Chairman: Res. Commn on Fundamental Policies for Envmtl Issues, 1993; Policy Res. Council, 1993–94; Pres., 1995–98; Minister of Internat. Trade and Industry, 1994–96; Dep.

Prime Minister, 1995–96; Minister for Admin Reform, 2000–01. Grand-Croix: Ordre de la Couronne (Belgium), 1996; Ordre National de Mérite (France), 1996; Das Grosskreuz (Germany), 1997. *Publications:* Vision of Japan, 1993. *Recreations:* mountain climbing, photography, Kendo (Japanese fencing). *Died 1 July 2006.*

HASKINS, Sam, (Samuel Joseph); photographic designer; *b* 11 Nov. 1926; *s* of Benjamin G. Haskins and Anna E. Oelofse; *m* 1952, Alida Elzabé van Heerden; two *s*. *Educ:* Helpmekaar Sch.; Witwatersrand Technical Coll.; Bolt Court Sch. of Photography. Freelance work: Johannesburg, 1953–68; London, 1968–. One-man Exhibitions: Johannesburg, 1953, 1960; Tokyo, 1970, 1973, 1976, 1981, 1985, 1987–88, 1990, 1992, 1993, 1996, 1999; London, 1972, 1976, 1978, 1980, 1987, 1999; Paris, 1973; Amsterdam, 1974; NY, 1981; San Francisco, 1982; Toronto, 1982; Bologna, 1982; Auckland, 1991; Sydney, 1991; Hong Kong, 1991; Taipei, 1991; Singapore, 1991; Osaka, 1990, 1992, 1993, 1997, 2000; Prague, 1993; Palermo, 1993; Glasgow, 1997; Berlin, 2000; Australian Nat. Portrait Gall., Canberra, 2006. *Publications:* Five Girls, 1962; Cowboy Kate and other stories, 1964 (Prix Nadar, France, 1964), rev. repr. 2006; November Girl, 1966; African Image, 1967 (Silver Award, Internat. Art Book Contest, 1969); Haskins Posters, 1972 (Gold Medal, New York Art Directors Club, 1974); Photo-Graphics, 1980 (Kodak Book Award); Cowboy Kate—Director's Cut, 2006; portfolios in most major internat. photographic magazines. *Recreations:* sculpting, books, music. *Address:* e-mail: sam@haskins.com; *web:* www.haskinsblog.com. *Died 26 Nov. 2009.*

HASLAM, Rear Adm. Sir David William, KBE 1984 (OBE 1964); CB 1979; President, Directing Committee, International Hydrographic Bureau, Monaco, 1987–92; *b* 26 June 1923; *s* of Gerald Haigh Haslam and Gladys Haslam (*née* Finley). *Educ:* Ashe Prep. Sch., Etwall; Bromsgrove Sch., Worcs. FRGS, FRIN, FRICS. Special Entry Cadet, RN, 1941; HMS Birmingham, HMAS Quickmatch, HMS Resolution (in Indian Ocean), 1942–43; specialised in hydrographic surveying, 1944; HMS White Bear (surveying in Burma and Malaya), 1944–46; comd Survey Motor Launch 325, 1947; RAN, 1947–49; HMS Scott, 1949–51; HMS Dalrymple, 1951–53; i/c RN Survey Trng Unit, Chatham, 1953–56; HMS Vidal, 1956–57; comd, HMS Dalrymple, 1958; comd, HMS Dampier, 1958–60; Admty, 1960–62; comd, HMS Owen, 1962–64; Exec. Officer, RN Barracks, Chatham, 1964–65; Hydrographer, RAN, 1965–67; comd, HMS Hecla, 1968–70; Asst Hydrographer, MoD, 1970–72; comd, HMS Hydra, 1972–73; Asst Dir (Naval) to Hydrographer, 1974–75; sowc 1975, Hydrographer of the Navy, 1975–85. Acting Conservator, River Mersey, 1985–87; Advr on Port Appts, Dept of Transport, 1986–87. Underwriting Mem., Lloyd's, 1986–93. Pres., Hydrographic Soc., 1977–79. Vice-Pres., Bromsgrove Sch., 1997– (Gov., 1977–97). President: English Schs Basketball Assoc., 1973–96; Derbyshire CCC, 1991–92. Liveryman, Chartered Surveyors' Co., 1983–. FRSA. *Address:* 146 Worcester Road, Bromsgrove, Worcs B61 7AS. *T:* (01527) 574068. *Died 4 Aug. 2009.*

HASLAM, (William) Geoffrey, OBE 1985; DFC 1944; Director, Prudential Corporation PLC, 1980–87 (Deputy Chairman, 1980–84); *b* 11 Oct. 1914; *yr s* of late William John Haslam and Hilda Irene Haslam; *m* 1941, Valda Patricia Adamson (decd); two *s* one *d*. *Educ:* New Coll. and Ashville Coll., Harrogate. War Service with RAF, No 25 Sqdn (night fighters), 1940–46. Joined Prudential Assurance Co. Ltd, 1933: Dep. Gen. Manager, 1963; Gen. Manager, 1969; Chief Gen. Manager, 1974–78; Chief Exec., 1979; Dep. Chm., 1980–84. Chairman: Industrial Life Offices Assoc., 1972–74; British Insurance Assoc., 1977–78. Chm., St Teresa's Hospital, Wimbledon, 1983–87; Vice Pres., NABC, 1983–2003.

Recreation: golf. *Address:* 6 Ashbourne Road, W5 3ED. *T:* (020) 8997 8164. *Clubs:* Royal Air Force, MCC. *Died 20 May 2007.*

HASSETT, Gen. Sir Francis (George), AC 1975; KBE 1976 (CBE 1966; OBE 1945); CB 1970; DSO 1951; LVO 1954; Chief of the Defence Force Staff, 1975–77, retired; *b* 11 April 1918; *s* of John Francis Hassett, Sydney, Australia; *m* 1946, Margaret Hallie Roberts, *d* of Dr Edwin Spencer Roberts, Toowoomba, Qld; one *s* two *d* (and one *s* decd). *Educ:* RMC Duntroon, Australia. Graduated RMC, 1938. Served War of 1939–45, Middle East and South West Pacific Area (Lt-Col; wounded; despatches twice); CO 3 Bn Royal Australian Regt, Korea, 1951–52; Marshal for ACT Royal Tour, 1954; Comd 28 Commonwealth Bde, 1961–62; idc, 1963; DCGS, 1964–65; Head of Aust. Jt Services Staff, Australia House, 1966–67; GOC Northern Comd, Australia, 1968–70; Chm., Army Rev. Cttee, 1969–70; Vice Chief of Gen. Staff, Australia, 1971–73; CGS, Australia, 1973–75. Extra Gentleman Usher to the Queen, 1966–68. *Recreations:* gardening, writing. *Address:* 42 Mugga Way, Red Hill, Canberra, ACT 2603, Australia. *Club:* Commonwealth. *Died 11 June 2008.*

HASTINGS, 22nd Baron *cr* 1290; **Edward Delaval Henry Astley;** Bt 1660; *b* 14 April 1912; *s* of 21st Baron and Lady Marguerite Nevill (*d* 1975), *d* of 3rd Marquess of Abergavenny; *S* father, 1956; *m* 1954, Catherine Rosaline Ratcliffe Coats, 2nd *d* of late Capt. H. V. Hinton; two *s* one *d*. *Educ:* Eton and abroad. Supplementary Reserve, Coldstream Guards, 1934; served War of 1939–45, Major 1945; farming in Southern Rhodesia, 1951–57. Mem. of Parliamentary delegation to the West Indies, 1958; a Lord in Waiting, 1961–62; Jt Parly Sec., Min. of Housing and Local Govt, 1962–64. Chairman: British-Italian Soc., 1957–62 (Pres., 1972–95); Italian People's Flood Appeal, 1966–67; Governor: Brit. Inst. of Florence, 1959–97; Royal Ballet, 1971–93; Chairman: Royal Ballet Benevolent Fund, 1966–84; Dance Teachers Benevolent Fund, 1982–99; President: British Epilepsy Assoc., 1965–93; Epilepsy Res. Foundn, 1996– (Chm., 1990–96); Joint Epilepsy Council, 1997–. Grand Officer, Order of Merit (Italy), 1968. *Recreations:* riding, ballet, foreign travel. *Heir: s* Hon. Delaval Thomas Harold Astley [*b* 25 April 1960; *m* 1987, Veronica, *er d* of Richard Smart; one *s* one *d*]. *Address:* Seaton Delaval Hall, Whitley Bay, Northumberland NE26 4QR. *T:* (0191) 237 0786. *Clubs:* Brooks's, Army and Navy; Northern Counties (Newcastle); Norfolk (Norwich). *Died 25 April 2007.*

HASWELL, (Anthony) James (Darley), OBE 1985; Insurance Ombudsman, 1981–89; Chairman, Appeals Tribunals, Financial Intermediaries, Managers and Brokers Regulatory Association, 1989; *b* 4 Aug. 1922; *s* of Brig. Chetwynd Henry Haswell, CIE, and Dorothy Edith (*née* Berry); *m* 1957, Angela Mary (*née* Murphy) (*d* 2004); three *s* one *d*. *Educ:* Winchester Coll.; St John's Coll., Cambridge (MA). Solicitor of the Supreme Court. Admitted Solicitor, 1949; RAC Legal Dept, 1949; private practice, London and Cornwall, 1950–51; commnd, Army Legal Services Staff List (Captain), 1952; Temp. Major 1956; Lt-Col 1967; retired from Army Legal Corps, 1981. Dep. Chm., Money Mgt Council, 1994–99. Freeman, City of London, 1987; Liveryman, Insurers' Co., 1987. *Publications:* Insurance Ombudsman Bureau annual reports for years 1981–88; miscellaneous articles in industry jls. *Recreations:* writing, chamber music, theatre, drawing, woodwork, London Phoenix (formerly Insurance) Orchestra (formerly Chm. and playing member). *Address:* 31 Chipstead Street, SW6 3SR. *T:* (020) 7736 1163. *Died 9 Oct. 2008.*

HATCH, Sir David (Edwin), Kt 2004; CBE 1994; JP; Chairman: Parole Board of England and Wales, 2000–04; Services Sound and Vision Corporation, since 2000 (Vice-Chairman, 1991–99; Board Member, 1981–90); *b* 7 May 1939; *s* of Rev. Raymond Harold Hatch and Winifred Edith May (*née* Brookes); *m* 1964, Ann Elizabeth Martin (*d* 1997); two *s* one *d*; *m* 1999, Mary

Clancy. *Educ:* St John's Sch., Leatherhead; Queens' Coll., Cambridge (MA, DipEd). Actor, Cambridge Circus, 1963; BBC: I'm Sorry I'll Read That Again, 1964; originator and producer, Weekending, I'm Sorry I Haven't a Clue, Just a Minute, 1964–74; Network Editor Radio, Manchester, 1974; Head of Light Entertainment Radio, 1978; Controller: Radio Two, 1980–83; Radio 4, 1983–86; Dir of Programmes, Radio, 1986–87; Man. Dir, Network Radio BBC (formerly BBC Radio), 1987–93; Vice-Chm., BBC Enterprises, 1987–93; Advr to Dir-Gen., BBC, 1993–95. Chm., NCC, 1996–2000. Dir, The Listener, 1988–90. Vice-Chm., EBU Radio Prog. Cttee, 1987–94; Pres., TRIC, 1990. Mem., Leggatt Review of Tribunals, 2000. Governor, St John's Sch., Leatherhead, 2001–. CCMI; FRSA. JP Aylesbury, 1993. *Recreations:* laughing, family. *Address:* Stone Cottage, High Street, Chalfont St Giles, Bucks HP8 4QA. *Clubs:* Garrick, Lord's Taverners. *Died 13 June 2007.*

HATFULL, Alan Frederick; Counsellor (Labour), Bonn, 1981–87; *b* 12 June 1927; *s* of Frederick George Hatfull and Florence May Hatfull (*née* Dickinson); *m* 1951, Terttu Kaarina Wahlroos (*d* 2003); one *s* one *d. Educ:* St Olave's and St Saviour's Grammar School; London School of Economics (BSc (Econ) 1951). Assistant Principal, Min. of Labour, 1951, Principal 1957, Assistant Sec., 1965; Director, Commn on Industrial Relations, 1970–73; Counsellor (Labour), Paris, 1977–81. *Address:* 75 Darwin Court, Gloucester Avenue, NW1 7BQ. *Died 27 Oct. 2006.*

HATTO, Prof. Arthur Thomas, MA; FBA 1991; Head of the Department of German, Queen Mary College, University of London, 1938–77; *b* 11 Feb. 1910; *s* of Thomas Hatto, LLB and Alice Walters; *m* 1935, Margot Feibelmann (*d* 2000); one *d. Educ:* Dulwich Coll.; King's Coll., London (Fellow, 1971); University Coll. London. BA (London) 1931; MA (with Distinction), 1934. Lektor für Englisch, University of Berne, 1932–34; Asst Lectr in German, KCL, 1934–38; Queen Mary Coll., University of London, 1938 (Head of Dept of German). Temp. Sen. Asst, Foreign Office, 1939–45; part-time Lectr in German, University Coll., London, 1944–45; returned to Queen Mary Coll., 1945; Reader in German Language and Literature, 1946, Prof. of German Language and Literature, 1953, University of London. Governor: SOAS, Univ. of London, 1960 (Foundn Day Lecture, 1970; Hon. Fellow, 1981); QMC, Univ. of London, 1968–70 (Hon. Fellow, QMW, 1992). Chairman: London Seminar on Epic; Cttee 'A' (Theol. and Arts), Central Research Fund, Univ. of London, 1969. Fellow: Royal Anthropological Institute; Royal Asiatic Society (lecture: Plot and character in Kirghiz epic poetry of the mid 19th cent., 1976); Leverhulme Emeritus Fellow (heroic poetry in Central Asia and Siberia), 1977–. Lectr, Rheinisch-Westfälische Akad. der Wissenschaften, Düsseldorf, 1990. Corresp. Mem., Finno-Ugrian Soc., 1978; Associate Mem., Seminar für Sprach- und Kulturwissenschaft Zentralasiens, Univ. of Bonn, 1984. *Publications:* (with R. J. Taylor) The Songs of Neidhart von Reuental, 1958; Gottfried von Strassburg, Tristan (trans. entire for first time) with Tristran of Thomas (newly trans.) with an Introduction, 1960; The Nibelungenlied: a new translation, with Introduction and Notes, 1964; editor of Eos, an enquiry by fifty scholars into the theme of the alba in world literature, 1965; (ed for first time with translation and commentary) The Memorial Feast for Kökötöy-khan: a Kirghiz epic poem, 1977; Essays on Medieval German and Other Poetry, 1980; Parzival, Wolfram von Eschenbach, a new translation, 1980; gen. editor, Traditions of Heroic and Epic Poetry, vol. I 1980, vol. II 1989; (re-ed with trans. and commentary) The Manas of Wilhelm Radloff, 1990; The Mohave Epic of Inyo-kutavêre, 1999; articles in learned periodicals. *Recreation:* reading. *Died 6 Jan. 2010.*

HAUGHEY, Charles James; Taoiseach (Prime Minister of Ireland), 1979–81, March–Dec. 1982 and 1987–92; *b* 16 Sept. 1925; *s* of Seán Haughey and late Sarah Ann (*née*

McWilliams); *m* 1951, Maureen Lemass; three *s* one *d. Educ:* Scoil Mhuire, Marino, Dublin; St Joseph's Christian Brothers' Sch., Fairview, Dublin; University College Dublin (BCom); King's Inns, Dublin. Called to Irish Bar, 1949. Member, Dublin Corporation, 1953–55; Member (FF) Dail Eireann for a Dublin constituency, 1957–92 (Dublin NE, 1957–77, then Dublin Artane, later Dublin N Central); Parly Sec. to Minister for Justice, 1960–61; Minister: for Justice, 1961–64; for Agriculture, 1964–66; for Finance, 1966–70; Chairman, Jt Cttee on the Secondary Legislation of the European Communities, 1973–77; Minister for Health and Social Welfare, 1977–79; Leader of the Opposition, 1982–87. President: Fianna Fail Party, 1979–92; European Council, Jan.–June 1990. Hon. Fellow, RHA. Hon. doctorates: Dublin City Univ.; UC Dublin; Univ. of Clermont-Ferrand; Univ. of Notre Dame, USA. *Recreations:* music, art, sailing, riding, swimming. *Address:* Abbeville, Kinsaley, Co. Dublin, Ireland. *T:* (1) 8450111. *Clubs:* Ward Union Hunt (Dublin); Howth Yacht; Royal Cork Yacht. *Died 13 June 2006.*

HAUSER, Frank Ivor, CBE 1968; free-lance director; *b* 1 Aug. 1922; *s* of late Abraham and of Sarah Hauser; unmarried. *Educ:* Cardiff High Sch.; Christ Church, Oxford. Oxford, 1941–42; RA, 1942–45; Oxford, 1946–48. BBC Drama Producer, 1948–51; Director: Salisbury Arts Theatre, 1952–53; Midland Theatre Co., 1945–55. Formed Meadow Players Ltd, which re-opened the Oxford Playhouse, 1956, Dir of Productions, 1956–73; took Oxford Playhouse Co. on tour of India, Pakistan and Ceylon, 1959–60. Produced at Sadler's Wells Opera: La Traviata, 1961; Iolanthe, 1962; Orfeo, 1965; produced: at Oxford Playhouse: Antony and Cleopatra, 1965; Phèdre, 1966; The Promise, 1966; The Silent Woman, 1968; Pippa Passes, 1968; Uncle Vanya, 1969; Curtain Up, 1969; The Merchant of Venice, 1973; also: Il Matrimonio Segreto, Glyndebourne, 1965; A Heritage and its History, Phoenix, 1965; The Promise, Fortune, 1967; Volpone, Garrick, 1967; The Magic Flute, Sadler's Wells, 1967; Kean, Globe, 1971; The Wolf, Apollo, 1973; Cinderella, Casino, 1974; On Approval, Haymarket, 1975; All for Love, Old Vic, 1977; The Importance of Being Earnest, Old Vic, 1980; Captain Brassbound's Conversion, Haymarket, 1982; An Enemy of the People, NY, 1985; Thursday's Ladies, Apollo, 1987; Candida, Arts, 1988; Getting Married, Chichester, 1993; Hobson's Choice, Chichester, 1995. *Recreation:* piano. *Died 14 Oct. 2007.*

HAVARD, John David Jayne, CBE 1989; MD; Secretary, British Medical Association, 1980–89; Chairman, Commonwealth Medical Trust, 2001–05 (Hon. Secretary, Commonwealth Medical Association, 1986–2001); *b* 5 May 1924; *s* of late Dr Arthur William Havard and Ursula Jayne Vernon Humphrey; *m* 1st, 1950, Margaret Lucy Lumsden Collis (marr. diss. 1982); two *s* one *d*; 2nd, 1982, Audrey Anne Boutwood, FRCOG (*d* 2009), *d* of Rear Adm. L. A. Boutwood, CB, OBE. *Educ:* Malvern Coll.; Jesus Coll., Cambridge (MA, MD, LLM); Middlesex Hosp. Med. Sch. FRCP 1994. Called to the Bar, Middle Temple, 1953. Professorial Med. Unit, Middlesex Hosp., 1950; National Service, RAF, 1950–52; general practice, Lowestoft, 1952–58 (Sec., E Suffolk LMC, 1956–58). British Medical Assoc.: Asst Sec., 1958–64; Under-Sec., 1964–76; Dep. Sec., 1976–79. Short-term Cons., Council of Europe, 1964–67, OECD 1964–69, WHO 1967–89, on Road Accident Prevention. Dep. Chm., Staff Side, Gen. Whitley Council for the Health Services, 1975–89; Sec., Managerial, Professional and Staffs Liaison Gp, 1978–89; Member: various Govt Working Parties on Coroners' Rules, Visual Standards for Driving, Licensing of Professional Drivers, etc. Chm., Internat. Driver Behaviour Res. Assoc., 1971–94. Pres., British Acad. of Forensic Scis, 1984–85. Mem., GMC, 1989–94 (Mem., Professional Conduct and Standards Cttee, 1989–94). Lectr, Green Coll., Oxford, 1989. Governor, Malvern Coll., 1984. Hon. FRCGP 1997. Gold Medal, Inter-Scandinavian Union for Non-Alcoholic Traffic, 1962;

Stevens Lectr and Gold Medallist, 1989; Widmark Award, Internat. Cttee on Alcohol, Drugs and Traffic Safety, 1989; BMA Gold Medal for Dist. Merit, 1990. Pres., CUAC, 1945–46; Captain United Hosps AC, 1946–47; London Univ. Record for 100 yards, 1947. Member, Editorial Board: Blutalkohol, 1968–90; Forensic Science Rev. 1989–. *Publications:* Detection of Secret Homicide (Cambridge Studies in Criminology), 1960; Research on Effects of Alcohol and Drugs on Driving Behaviour (OECD), 1968; chapters in textbooks on legal medicine, research advances on alcohol and drugs, etc; many articles in med., legal and sci. periodical lit.; several WHO reports. *Recreations:* history, English countryside. *Address:* 1 Wilton Square, N1 3DL. *T:* (020) 7359 2802, *Fax:* (020) 7354 9690. *Clubs:* Oxford and Cambridge; Achilles. *Died 23 May 2010.*

HAWKE, 11th Baron *cr* 1776, of Towton; **Edward George Hawke,** TD; FRICS; *b* 25 Jan. 1950; *s* of 10th Baron and of his 2nd wife, Georgette Margaret, *d* of George S. Davidson; *S* father, 1992; *m* 1993, Bronwen, *d* of William James, MRCVS; one *s* one *d. Educ:* Eton. 2nd Lt, 1st Bn Coldstream Guards, 1970–73; Territorial Army, Queen's Own Yeomanry, 1973–93 (Major). Hon. Col, Cheshire Yeomanry, 1998–2005. Dir, Lambert Smith Hampton (Manchester). Chm., Edward Mayes Trust. Governor, Terra Nova Sch. *Heir: s* Hon. William Martin Theodore Hawke, *b* 23 June 1995. *Died 2 Dec. 2009.*

HAWKEN, Lewis Dudley, CB 1983; a Deputy Chairman of the Board of Customs and Excise, 1980–87, *b* 23 Aug. 1931; *s* of late Richard and Doris May Evelyn Hawken; *m* 1954, Bridget Mary Gamble (*d* 1989); two *s* one *d. Educ:* Harrow County Sch. for Boys; Lincoln Coll., Oxford (MA). Comr of Customs and Excise, 1975. *Recreation:* collecting wood engravings. *Address:* 21 Sherleys Court, Wood Lane, Ruislip, Middx HA4 6DH. *T:* (01895) 632405. *Clubs:* Oxford and Cambridge, MCC. *Died 9 April 2010.*

HAWKES, David, MA, DPhil; Research Fellow, All Souls College, Oxford, 1973–83, then Emeritus; *b* 6 July 1923; *s* of Ewart Hawkes and Dorothy May Hawkes (*née* Davis); *m* 1950, Sylvia Jean Perkins; one *s* three *d. Educ:* Bancroft's Sch. Open Scholarship in Classics, Christ Church, Oxford, 1941; Chinese Hons Sch., Oxford, 1945–47; Research Student, National Peking Univ., 1948–51. Formerly University Lecturer in Chinese, Oxford; Prof. of Chinese, Oxford Univ., 1959–71. *Publications:* Ch'u Tz'ŭ, Songs of the South, 1959, rev. edn as The Songs of the South: an Ancient Chinese Anthology of Poems by Qu Yuan and Other Poets, 1985; A Little Primer of Tu Fu, 1967, repr. 1987; The Story of the Stone, vol. 1, 1973, vol. 2, 1977, vol. 3, 1980; Classical, Modern and Humane: essays in Chinese Literature (ed J. Minford and Siu-kit Wong), 1989, Liu Yi and the Dragon Princess: a thirteenth-century Zaju play by Shang Zhongxian, 2003; Letters from a Godless Grandfather, 2004. *Died 31 July 2009.*

HAWKES, Prof. John Gregory, OBE 1994; Mason Professor of Botany and Head of Plant Biology Department, University of Birmingham, 1967–82, then Emeritus; *b* 27 June 1915; *s* of C. W. and G. M. Hawkes; *m* 1941, Ellen Barbara Leather (*d* 2005); two *s* two *d. Educ:* Univ. of Cambridge. BA, MA, PhD, ScD. Botanist, Potato Res. Station of Commonwealth Agricultural Bureaux, 1939–48, 1951–52; Dir of Potato Research Project, Min. of Ag., Colombia, S America, 1948–51; Birmingham University: Lectr and Sen. Lectr in Taxonomic Botany, 1952–61; Prof. of Taxonomic Botany (Personal Chair), 1961–67. Pres., Linnean Soc. of London, 1991–94. Linnean Soc. Gold Medal, 1984. *Publications:* (with J. P. Hjerting) The Potatoes of Argentina, Brazil, Paraguay and Uruguay, 1969; (with D. A. Cadbury and R. C. Readett) A Computer-Mapped Flora, 1971; (with O. H. Frankel) Crop Genetic Resources for Today and Tomorrow, 1975; Conservation and Agriculture, 1978; (with R. N. Lester and A. D. Skelding) The Biology and Taxonomy of the

Solanaceae, 1979; The Diversity of Crop Plants, 1983; (with J. P. Hjerting) The Potatoes of Bolivia, 1989; The Potato: evolution, biodiversity and genetic resources, 1990; (with J. M. M. Engels and M. Worede) Plant Genetic Resources of Ethiopia, 1991; Genetic Conservation of World Crop Plants, 1991; (jtly) Solanaceae III - taxonomy, chemistry, evolution, 1991; (jtly) Plant Genetic Conservation: the *in situ* approach, 1996; (jtly) The *Ex Situ* Conservation of Plant Genetic Resources, 2000; contribs to various botanical and plant breeding jls. *Recreations:* walking, gardening, travel, art, archaeology. *Address:* 16 Erleigh Road, Reading RG1 5LH. *Died 6 Sept. 2007.*

HAWKINS, Prof. Eric William, CBE 1973; Director, Language Teaching Centre, University of York, 1965–79, then Professor Emeritus; *b* 8 Jan. 1915; *s* of James Edward Hawkins and Agnes Thompson (*née* Clarie); *m* 1938, Ellen Marie Thygesen, Copenhagen; one *s* one *d. Educ:* Liverpool Inst. High Sch.; Trinity Hall, Cambridge (Open Exhibn). MA, CertEd, FCIL. War Service, 1st Bn The Loyal Regt, 1940–46 (despatches 1945); wounded N Africa, 1943; Major 1945. Asst Master, Liverpool Coll., 1946–49; Headmaster: Oldershaw Grammar Sch., Wallasey, 1949–53; Calday Grange Grammar Sch., Ches, 1953–65. Member: Central Adv. Council for Educn (England) (Plowden Cttee), 1963–66; Rampton Cttee (educn of ethnic minorities), 1979–81. Hon. Prof., University Coll. of Wales, Aberystwyth, 1979–89. Comenius Fellow, Centre for Inf. on Lang. Teaching, 2000. Hon. DLitt Southampton, 1997. Gold Medal, Inst. Linguists, 1971. Comdr, Ordre des Palmes Académiques (France), 1986. *Publications:* (ed) Modern Languages in the Grammar School, 1961; (ed) New Patterns in Sixth Form Modern Language Studies, 1970; A Time for Growing, 1971; Le français pour tout le monde, vols 1–5, 1974–79; Modern Languages in the Curriculum, 1981; Awareness of Language: an introduction, 1984; (ed) Intensive Language Teaching and Learning, 1988; (ed) 30 Years of Language Teaching, 1996; Listening to Lorca, 1999. *Recreation:* walking. *Died 31 Oct. 2010.*

HAWLEY, Sir Donald (Frederick), KCMG 1978 (CMG 1970); MBE 1955; HM Diplomatic Service, retired; British High Commissioner in Malaysia, 1977–81; Barrister-at-law; consultant in Middle Eastern and South East Asian affairs; *b* 22 May 1921; *s* of late Mr and Mrs F. G. Hawley, Little Gaddesden, Herts; *m* 1964, Ruth Morwenna Graham Howes, DL, *d* of late Rev. P. G. Howes and of Mrs Howes, Charmouth, Dorset; one *s* three *d. Educ:* Radley; New Coll., Oxford (MA). Served in HM Forces, 1941. Sudan Political Service, 1944; joined Sudan Judiciary, 1947. Called to Bar, Inner Temple, 1951. Chief Registrar, Sudan Judiciary, and Registrar-Gen. of Marriages, 1951; resigned from Sudan Service, 1955; joined HM Foreign Service, 1955; FO, 1956: Political Agent, Trucial States, in Dubai, 1958; Head of Chancery, British Embassy, Cairo, 1962; Counsellor and Head of Chancery, British High Commission, Lagos, 1965; Vis. Fellow, Dept of Geography, Durham Univ., 1967; Counsellor (Commercial), Baghdad, 1968; HM Consul-General, Muscat, 1971; HM Ambassador to Oman, 1971–75; Asst Under Sec. of State, FCO, 1975–77. Mem., London Adv. Cttee, Hongkong and Shanghai Banking Corp.; Chairman: Ewbank Preece Gp, 1982–86, Special Advr, 1986–; Centre for British Teachers, 1987–91. Pres. Council, Reading Univ., 1987–94 (Mem., Court, 1994–); Vice-Pres., Anglo-Omani Soc., 1981–; Chairman: British Malaysian Soc., 1983–95 (Vice Pres., 1993–); Sudan Pensioners Assoc., 1992–; Royal Soc. for Asian Affairs, 1994–2002 (Vice Pres., 2002–); Sir William Luce Meml Fund, 1995–; Mem. Council, RGS, 1985–87. Gov., ESU, 1989–95. Pres., Sudan Defence Force Dinner Club. Hon. DLitt Reading, 1994; Hon. DCL Durham, 1997. *Publications:* Handbook for Registrars of Marriage and Ministers of Religion, 1963 (Sudan Govt pubn); Courtesies in the Trucial States, 1965; The Trucial States, 1971; Oman and its

Renaissance, 1977, 3rd edn 2005; Courtesies in the Gulf Area, 1978; Manners and Correct Form in the Middle East, 1984, 2nd edn 1996; Sandtracks in the Sudan, 1995; (ed) Sudan Canterbury Tales, 1999; Desert Wind and Tropic Storm (autobiog.), 2000; (ed) Khartoum Perspectives 1940s, 2001; The Emirates: witness to a metamorphosis, 2007. *Recreations:* tennis, travel, gardening. *Address:* Cheverell Place, Little Cheverell, near Devizes, Wilts SN10 4JJ. *T:* (01380) 813322. *Clubs:* Travellers, Beefsteak. *Died 31 Jan. 2008.*

HAWORTH, Rev. Betsy Ellen; Non-Stipendiary Minister, St Paul, Astley Bridge, Bolton, Diocese of Manchester, 1989–99; *b* 23 July 1924; *d* of Ambrose and Annie Kenyon; *m* 1953, Rev. Fred Haworth (*d* 1981); one *s* two *d*. *Educ:* William Temple Coll. (C of E), Hawarden (IDC). Licensed as lay worker, dio. Manchester, 1952, dio. Blackburn, 1965; elected Mem., Church Assembly, 1965–70, Gen. Synod, 1970–75, 1975–80, 1980–85, Ex-officio Mem., 1985–88. Advr for Women's Ministry, dio. Manchester, 1971–81. Third Church Estates Comr, 1981–88. Deaconess 1980; ordained Deacon, 1989. Examining Chaplain to Bishop of Manchester, 1981–94. *Address:* 14 Sharples Hall Fold, Sharples, Bolton, Lancs BL1 7EH. *Died 17 July 2007.*

HAWTHORNE, James Burns, CBE 1982; management consultant; Partner, James Hawthorne Associates, since 1993 (Director, 1987–92); *b* 27 March 1930; *s* of Thomas Hawthorne and Florence Hawthorne (*née* Burns); *m* 1958, Patricia King (*d* 2002); one *s* two *d*. *Educ:* Methodist Coll.; Queen's Univ., Belfast (BA); Stranmillis Coll. of Educn. Master at Sullivan Upper Sch., Holywood, 1951–60; joined Educn Dept, BBC, 1960; Schools Producer in charge, N Ireland, 1967; Chief Asst, N Ireland, 1969–70; seconded to Hong Kong Govt, as Controller Television, 1970; Dir of Broadcasting, Hong Kong, 1972–77 (resigned from BBC staff, 1976, ie seconded status ended; rejoined BBC, Jan. 1978); Controller, BBC NI, 1978–87. Member: NI Council for Educn Develt, 1980–85; Fair Employment Agency, 1988–89; Accreditation Panel, Hong Kong Acad. for the Performing Arts, 1988. Chairman: Ulster History Circle, 1987–89; NI Health Promotion Agency (formerly Unit), 1988–97; Cultural Traditions Gp, 1989–90; NI Community Relations Council, 1990–96; Prison Arts Foundn, 1997–. Comr, Commn for Racial Equality, NI, 1997–2000. Vis. Prof., Media Studies, Univ. of Ulster, 1993–99. Chm., Lecale Histl Soc., 2000–. JP Hong Kong, 1972–77. Queen's Univ. New Ireland Soc. award for community relations work, 1967; Winston Churchill Fellowship, 1968; FRTS 1988 (Cyril Bennett Award, 1986). Hon. LLD QUB, 1988. *Publications:* (ed) Two Centuries of Irish History, 1966, repr. 1967, 1969, rev. edn 1974; Reporting Violence: lessons from Northern Ireland, 1981. *Recreations:* angling, music, local history. *Address:* The Long Mill, Lissara, 67 Kilmore Road, Crossgar, N Ireland BT30 9HJ. *Club:* BBC. *Died 7 Sept. 2006.*

HAXBY, Donald Leslie, CBE 1988; principal of veterinary practice, Southwell, 1979–93; *b* 4 Aug. 1928; *s* of Leslie Norman Haxby and Ruth Blount; *m* 1953, Barbara Mary Smith (marr. diss. 1986); one *s* two *d*. *Educ:* Queen Elizabeth Grammar Sch., Barnet; Royal Veterinary Coll., London. MRCVS 1953. Army Service, Queen's Royal Regt, RAEC, Sudan Defence Force, 1946–48 (Warrant Officer I). Practice in Leics and Shropshire, 1953–55; research, Boots Pure Drug Co., 1955–57 (clinical pathologist); vet. practice, Southwell, 1957–93. Man. Dir, Don Haxby Associates, 1993–96. Lecturer: Animal Husbandry, Nottingham Coll. of Agriculture, 1969–93; Poultry Production and Public Health, London and Glasgow Univs, 1978–93; External Examiner: Vet. Medicine, Glasgow Univ., 1980–85; Animal Husbandry, Bristol Univ., 1987–93. Official Vet. Surgeon, Newark DC, 1979–85; Consultant to: W. & J. B. Eastwood, 1972–78; Hillsdown Holdings, 1982–90; Smith Kline Beecham Animal Health, 1982–89;

Cyanamid GB, 1982–85; Duphar-Philips Solvay, 1982–93; I. M. C. & Cambridge-Naremco Products, USA, 1985–90. Mem., Parly and Sci. Cttee, H of C, 1979–86; Sci. Advr to Agric. Select Cttee, H of C, 1989–93. Mem. Council, 1983–84, Hon. Lectr, 1984–91, Royal Vet. Coll.; President: E Midlands Vet. Assoc. (and Treasurer), 1973–75; BVA, 1977–78 (Mem. Council, 1958–); RCVS, 1983–84 (Mem. Council, 1971–99); Mem., Animal Health and Tech. Cttee, British Poultry Fedn, 1974–90; Chm., World Vet. Poultry Assoc., 1985–89. Mem., Farm Animal Welfare Council, 1981–92; Trustee and Treasurer, Gordon Meml Trust, 1982–93; Governor, Houghton Poultry Res. Station, 1983–90. Hon. FRCVS 2003. *Recreations:* work, reading, gardening. *Address:* Candant House, Main Street, Upton, Newark, Notts NG23 5ST. *T:* and *Fax:* (01636) 812020. *Clubs:* Farmers', Savile. *Died 21 Aug. 2006.*

HAY, Sir David (Osborne), Kt 1979; CBE 1962; DSO 1945; retired public servant; *b* 29 Nov. 1916; 2nd *s* of late H. A. Hay, Barwon Heads, Victoria; *m* 1944, Alison Marion Parker Adams (*d* 2002); two *s*. *Educ:* Geelong Grammar Sch.; Brasenose Coll., Oxford; Melbourne Univ. Joined Commonwealth Public Service, 1939. Australian Imperial Force, 1940–46: Major, 2nd Sixth Infantry Bn; served in Western Desert, Greece, New Guinea. Rejoined External Affairs Dept, 1947; Imp. Def. Coll., 1954; Minister (later Ambassador) to Thailand, 1955–57; High Comr in Canada, 1961–64; Ambassador to UN, New York, 1964–65; First Asst Secretary, External Affairs, 1966; Administrator of Papua and New Guinea, 1967–70; Sec., Dept of External Territories, Canberra, 1970–73; Defence Force Ombudsman, 1974–76; Sec., Dept of Aboriginal Affairs, 1977–79. *Publications:* The Delivery of Services financed by the Department of Aboriginal Affairs, 1976; Nothing Over Us: the story of the 2nd Sixth Australian Infantry Battalion, 1985; The Life and Times of William Hay of Boomanoomana 1816–1908, 1990. *Address:* Boomanoomana Homestead, via Mulwala, NSW 2647, Australia. *Clubs:* Australian, Melbourne (Melbourne). *Died 18 May 2009.*

HAY, Sir Hamish (Grenfell), Kt 1982; JP; Mayor of Christchurch, New Zealand, 1974–89; Director: Canterbury Development Corporation, 1983–96; Christchurch International Airport Ltd, 1988–96; *b* 8 Dec. 1927; twin *s* of Sir James Lawrence Hay, OBE, and Lady (Davidina) Hay; *m* 1955, Judith Leicester Gill (QSO 1987; CNZM 1998); one *s* four *d*. *Educ:* St Andrew's Coll., Christchurch; Univ. of Canterbury, NZ (BCom). FCA(NZ). Councillor: Christchurch City Council, 1959–74; Canterbury Regl Council, 1995–2003 (Dep. Chm., 1998–2001). Member: Victory Park Bd, 1974–89; Lyttelton Harbour Bd, 1983–89. Chairman: Christchurch Town Hall Board of Management, 1962–92; Canterbury Museum Trust Bd, 1981–84; Canterbury United Council, 1983–86; Museum of New Zealand, Wellington, 1992–98 (Chm., 1992–94). President: Christchurch Aged People's Welfare Council, 1974–89; Christchurch Civic Music Council, 1974–89; Christchurch Symphony Orchestra, 1982–88; Chm., Christchurch Arts Festival, 1965–74; past Mem., Queen Elizabeth II Arts Council. Chm., New Zealand Soc. of Accountants (Canterbury Br.), 1958; Dep. Man. Dir, Haywrights Ltd, 1962–74. Mem. Council, Univ. of Canterbury, 1974–89 (Mem., Foundn Patrons Gp); Chm. of Governors, McLean Inst., 1974–89; Governor, St Andrew's Coll., 1986–92. Vice-Pres., Municipal Assoc. of NZ, 1974–88. Trustee, Canterbury Savings Bank, 1962–88 (Pres., 1974–75); Dir, Trust Bank Canterbury Ltd, 1988–95. Mem., Charles Upham Trust, 1986– (Dep. Chm., 1990–); Trustee: J. L. Hay Charitable Trust, 1959–; Trust Bank Canterbury Community Trust, 1988–96; Christchurch City Mission Foundn, 1999–. Paul Harris Fellow, Rotary Internat., 1997; Emeritus Fellow, Nat. Bd, NZ Inst. of Management. JP New Zealand, 1990. Silver Jubilee Medal, 1977; Commemoration Medal, NZ, 1990; Order of the Rising Sun (with Gold Rays), Japan,

1990. *Publications:* Hay Days (autobiog.), 1989. *Recreations:* gardening, listening to good music. *Address:* PO Box 36224, Merivale, Christchurch 8005, New Zealand. *T:* (3) 3047102; 95 Rue Balguerie, Akaroa, New Zealand. *Club:* Christchurch Rotary (New Zealand). *Died 7 Sept. 2008.*

HAY, Sir James Brian D.; *see* Dalrymple-Hay.

HAY, Sir John Hugh D.; *see* Dalrymple-Hay.

HAYDAR, Dr Loutof Allah; Syrian Ambassador to the People's Republic of China, 1990–99; *b* 22 March 1940; *s* of Haydar and Mary; *m* 1968, Hayat Hassan; one *s* three *d*. *Educ:* Damascus Univ. (BA English Literature 1964); Moscow State Univ. (PhD 1976). Joined Foreign Office, 1965; served at Syrian Embassy: London, 1965–67; Bonn, 1967–68; Moscow, 1970–75; served with Syrian Delegation to UN, New York, 1978–82; Syrian Ambassador to UK, 1982–86. *Publications:* The Ancient History of Palestine and the Middle East (PhD Thesis), 1976; The Grand Spring: a collection of literary short stories, 1997; The Hut and the Mermaid, 2003. *Died 15 Nov. 2008.*

HAYHOE, Prof. Frank George James, MD, FRCP, FRCPath; Leukaemia Research Fund Professor of Haematological Medicine, University of Cambridge, 1968–88; Fellow, Darwin College, Cambridge, since 1964, Vice-Master, 1964–74; *b* 25 Oct. 1920; *s* of late Frank Stanley and Catherine Hayhoe; *m* 1945, Jacqueline Marie Marguerite (*née* Dierkx); two *s*. *Educ:* Selhurst Grammar Sch.; Trinity Hall, Cambridge; St Thomas's Hospital Medical Sch. BA Cantab 1942; MRCS, LRCP 1944; MB, BChir Cantab 1945; MRCP 1949; MA Cantab 1949; MD Cantab 1951; FRCP 1965; FRCPath 1971. Captain RAMC, 1945–47. Registrar, St Thomas' Hosp., 1947–49. Elmore Research Student, Cambridge Univ., 1949–51; Royal Soc. Exchange Res. Schol., USSR, 1962–63; Lectr in Medicine, Cambridge Univ., 1951–68; Mem. Council of Senate, 1967–71. Member: Bd of Governors, United Cambridge Hospitals, 1971–74; Cambs AHA, 1974–75; GMC, 1982–88. Lectures: Langdon Brown, RCP, 1971; Cudlip Meml, Ann Arbor, 1967; vis. lectr at med. schs in N and S America, Europe, Middle East, Africa, India. Hon. MD: L'Aquila, 1992; Montpellier, 1993. G. F. Götz Foundn Prize, Zürich Univ., 1974; Suniti Rana Panja Gold Medal, Calcutta Sch. of Trop. Med., 1979. *Publications:* (ed) Lectures in Haematology, 1960; Leukaemia: Research and Clinical Practice, 1960; (jtly) Cytology and Cytochemistry of Acute Leukaemia, 1964; (ed) Current Research in Leukaemia, 1965; (with R. J. Flemans) An Atlas of Haematological Cytology, 1969, 3rd edn 1992; (with J. C. Cawley) Ultrastructure of Haemic Cells, 1973; (jtly) Leukaemia, Lymphomas and Allied Disorders, 1976; (jtly) Hairy Cell Leukaemia, 1980; (with D. Quaglino) Haematological Cytochemistry, 1980, 3rd edn 1994; (ed with D. Quaglino) The Cytobiology of Leukaemias and Lymphomas, 1985; (with D. Quaglino) Haematological Oncology, 1992; contribs to med. and scientific jls, on haematological topics, especially leukaemia. *Address:* 20 Queen Edith's Way, Cambridge CB1 7PN. *T:* (01223) 248381. *Died 28 Nov. 2009.*

HAYWARD, Ven. (John) Derek (Risdon), OBE 2000; Vicar of Isleworth, 1964–94; General Secretary, Diocese of London, 1975–93; Archdeacon of Middlesex, 1974–75, then Archdeacon Emeritus; *b* 13 Dec. 1923; *s* of late Eric Hayward and of Barbara Olive Hayward; *m* 1965, Teresa Jane Kaye; one *d* (one *s* decd). *Educ:* Stowe; Trinity Coll., Cambridge (BA 1956, MA 1964). Served War of 1939–45, Lieut 27th Lancers, Middle East and Italy, 1943–45 (twice wounded). Man. Dir, Hayward Waldie & Co., Calcutta (and associated cos), 1946–53. Trinity Coll., Cambridge, 1953–56, Westcott House, Cambridge, 1956–57. Asst Curate, St Mary's Bramall Lane, Sheffield, 1957–58; Vicar, St Silas, Sheffield, 1959–63. Mem., General Synod, 1975–90. Chm., SCM Press, 1992–98 (Dir, 1985–99); Trustee: Church Urban Fund, 1987–94; Bath Preservation Trust, 1996–2007;

Herschel Mus., Bath, 1997– (Chm., 1997–2007). Chm. Council, St Luke's Hosp. for the Clergy, 1991–2001. Bronze Star (US) 1945. *Recreations:* walking, playing with my computer. *Address:* Garden Flat, 29a Great Pulteney Street, Bath BA2 4BU. *T:* (01225) 336305; *e-mail:* derekhayward@tantraweb.co.uk.
Died 26 April 2010.

HAYWARD ELLEN, Patricia Mae; *see* Lavers, P. M.

HAYWOOD, Sir Harold, KCVO 1988; OBE 1974; DL; Chairman, BBC/ITC Central Appeals Advisory Committee, 1989–93; Chairman, YMCA, 1989–93; *b* 30 Sept. 1923; *s* of Harold Haywood and Lilian (*née* Barrett); *m* 1944, Amy (*née* Richardson); three *s*. *Educ:* Guild Central Sch., Burton-on-Trent; Westhill Coll. of Educn, Selly Oak, Birmingham (Certificate of Educn, 1948). Organiser, St John's Clubland, Sheffield, 1948–51; Tutor, Westhill Coll. of Educn, 1951–53; Regional Organiser, Methodist Youth Dept, 1954–55; Dir of Education and Trng, 1955–66, Dir of Youth Work, 1966–74, NAYC; Gen. Sec., Educnl Interchange Council, 1974–77; Dir, Royal Jubilee and Prince's Trusts, 1977–88. Chm., Assoc. of Charitable Foundns, 1989–92; Trustee, Charities Aid Foundn, 1988–98 (Chm., Grants Council, 1989–97); Patron, Kids Internat. UK, 1994–; Vice-President: Commonwealth Youth Exchange Council, 1988–; Derbys Community Foundn, 1998–; Patron, Multi-Faith Campaign, Univ. of Derby, 2001– (Chm., 1999–2001); Pres, RBL, Oakwood, Derbys, 2000. DL Greater London, 1983. FRSA. *Recreations:* the garden, books. *Club:* Civil Service. *Died 23 May 2010.*

HAZELL, Bertie, CBE 1962 (MBE 1946); Chairman, Special Programme Board, North Yorkshire, Manpower Services Commission, 1978–83; *b* 18 April 1907; *s* of John and Elizabeth Hazell; *m* 1936, Dora A. Barham; one *d*. *Educ:* various elementary schs in Norfolk. Agricultural worker, 1921; apptd Sec. and Agent to E Norfolk Divisional Labour Party, Sept. 1933; District Organiser, Nat. Union of Agricl Workers, 1937–64, Pres., 1966–78; Mem. W Riding of Yorks, War Agricultural Executive Cttee, 1939 (Chm. several of its Cttees, throughout war period). Contested (Lab) Barkston Ash Parliamentary Division, 1945 and 1950 Gen. Elections; MP (Lab) North Norfolk, 1964–70. Chairman: E and W Ridings Regional Bd for Industry, 1954–64; N Yorks AHA, 1974–82; York DHA, 1981–84; Vice-Chm., Agricultural, Horticultural and Forestry Trng Bd, 1972–74; Member: E Riding Co. Agricultural Exec. Cttee, 1964–64; Agricultural Wages Board, 1946–78; Leeds Regional Hosp. Board, 1948–74 (Chm. Works and Buildings Cttee); Potato Marketing Bd, 1970–79. Magistrate, City of York, 1950–; Chairman: York and District Employment Cttee, 1963–74; N Yorks District Manpower Cttee, 1975–80; Vice-Chm., Leeds Regional Hosp. Bd, 1967–74. Mem. Council, Univ. of E Anglia. MUniv York, 1984. *Recreation:* gardening. *Died 11 Jan. 2009.*

HÁZI, Dr Vencel; Hungarian Diplomatic Service, retired; *b* 3 Sept. 1925; *m* 1952, Judit Zell; one *d*. *Educ:* Technical Univ. and Univ. of Economics, Budapest. Entered Diplomatic Service, 1950; served in Min. of Foreign Affairs, Budapest, 1950; Press Attaché, Hungarian Legation, London, 1951–53; Counsellor, Legation, Stockholm, 1957–58; Ambassador: to Iraq, and to Afghanistan, 1958–61; to Greece, and to Cyprus, 1962–64; Head of Western Dept, Min. of Foreign Affairs, Budapest, 1964–68; Dep. Foreign Minister, Budapest, 1968–70; Ambassador to UK, 1970–76; Dep. Foreign Minister, Budapest, 1976–83; Ambassador to USA, 1983–89. Golden Grade of Order of Merit for Labour, 1962, and of Medal of Merit of Hungarian People's Republic, 1953; Grand Cordon of Order of Omayoun, 1st Class, Iran. *Recreations:* reading, music, swimming, chess. *Address:* 1025 Budapest, II Kulpa utca 8, Hungary. *Club:* Opera Fans (Budapest). *Died 21 Jan. 2007.*

HAZLEWOOD, Air Vice-Marshal Frederick Samuel, CB 1970; CBE 1967 (OBE 1960); AFC 1951 (Bar to AFC, 1954); retired; *b* 13 May 1921; *s* of Samuel Henry

Hazlewood and Lilian Hazlewood; *m* 1943, Isabelle Mary (*née* Hunt); one *s*. *Educ*: Kimbolton Sch. Served War of 1939–45: joined RAF, 1939; ops with Bomber Command, 1941; MEAF and UK Coastal Command, 1940–45. Lancaster Units, 1948–53; Comdg Officer, No 90 Valiant Sqdn, 1958–61; HQ, Bomber Comd, 1961–63; HQ, RAF, Germany, 1963–64; OC RAF Lyneham, 1965–67; HQ, RAF, Germany, 1968–69; AOC and Commandant, Central Flying School, 1970–72; AOC 38 Gp, RAF, 1972–74; Comdt, Jt Warfare Estab., 1974–76. *Recreations*: golf, tennis, rough shooting. *Clubs*: Royal Air Force; Bath and County.
Died 12 July 2007.

HEAD, Alan Kenneth, AO 1992; PhD, DSc; FAA 1971; FRS 1988; Hon. Research Fellow, Commonwealth Scientific and Industrial Research Organization, Australia, since 1990 (Chief Research Scientist, 1969–90); *b* 10 Aug. 1925; *s* of Rowland Henry John Head and Elsie May (*née* Burrell); *m* 1951, Gwenneth Nancy Barlow. *Educ*: Ballarat Grammar Sch.; Scotch Coll.; Univ. of Melbourne (BA, BSc, DSc); Univ. of Bristol (PhD). Research Scientist: CSIR Div. of Aeronautics, 1947–50; Aeronautical Res. Labs, 1953–57; CSIRO Division: of Tribophysics, 1957–81; of Chemical Physics, 1981–86; of Materials Science, 1987. Visiting Professor: Brown Univ., 1961–62; Univ. of Florida, 1971; Christensen Fellow, 1986, Vis. Fellow, 1990–, St Catherine's Coll., Oxford. *Publications*: Computed Electron Micrographs and Defect Identification, 1973, Chinese edn 1979; numerous contribs to sci. jls. *Address*: 10 Ellesmore Court, Kew, Vic 3101, Australia. *T*: (office) (3) 95452861, *T*: (home) (3) 98530673, *Fax*: (office) (3) 95441128.
Died 9 Jan. 2010.

HEAF, Peter Julius Denison, OBE 2002; MD; FRCP; Chairman, Medical Sickness Annuity and Life Insurance Society Ltd, 1988–93; *b* 1922; *s* of late Prof. F. R. G. Heaf, CMG; *m* 1947, Rosemary Cartledge; two *s* two *d*. *Educ*: Stamford Sch., Lincs; University Coll., London, Fellow 1973. MB, BS 1946; MD London 1952; MRCP 1954; FRCP 1965. House Physician and Surg., also RMO, University Coll. Hosp., and Capt. RAMC, 1947–49; Research Asst, Brompton Hosp., 1953–54; Sen. Registrar, St Thomas' Hosp., 1955–58; Consultant Physician, UCH, 1958–86, retired. Hon. Med. Cons to RBL, 1980–2002. *Publications*: papers on chest disease and pulmonary physiology, in Lancet, etc. *Recreations*: painting, gardening. *Address*: Ferrybrook House, Chalmore Gardens, Wallingford, Oxon OX10 9EP. *T*: (01491) 839176.
Died 11 June 2009.

HEALEY, Lady; Edna May Healey; writer; *b* 14 June 1918; *d* of Rose and Edward Edmunds; *m* 1945, Denis Winston Healey (later Baron Healey, CH, MBE, PC); one *s* two *d*. *Educ*: Bell's Grammar School, Coleford, Glos; St Hugh's College, Oxford (BA, Dip Ed; Hon. Fellow, 2003). Taught English and History: Keighley Girls' Grammar School, 1940–44; Bromley Girls' High Sch., 1944–47; freelance lecturer, England and America; television writer and presenter; radio writer and broadcaster. *Publications*: Lady Unknown: life of Angela Burdett-Coutts, 1978; Wives of Fame, 1986; Coutts & Co. 1692–1992: the portrait of a private bank, 1992; The Queen's House: a history of Buckingham Palace, 1997; Emma Darwin, 2001; Part of the Pattern (memoir), 2006. *Recreations*: gardening, listening to music.
Died 21 July 2010.

HEANLEY, Charles Laurence, TD 1950; FRCS; Consulting Surgeon; *b* 28 Feb. 1907; *e s* of Dr C. M. Heanley; *m* 1935; three *s*. *Educ*: Epsom Coll.; Downing Coll., Cambridge (Exhib., Schol.); London Hosp. BA Cambridge (Nat. Sci. Tripos) 1929, MA 1934; MRCS, LRCP 1932; MB, BCh Cambridge 1934; FRCS 1933; MRCP 1935. London Hosp., 1929; Surg. First Asst, 1936. Served War of 1939–45; France, Surgical Specialist, 17th Gen. Hosp., 1939–40; Surgeon Specialist, RAMC Park Prewitt Plastic Unit, 1941–42; India, OC No 3 British Maxillo-Facial Surgical Unit and

Lieut-Col OC Surgical Div., 1942–45; Surg. in charge of Dept of Plastic Surg., London Hosp. (later Royal London Hosp.), 1946–64. Cons. Surg. Worthing Hosp., Bethnal Green Hosp., and Plastic Unit Queen Victoria Hosp., East Grinstead, 1945; Plastic Surg. London Hosp.; Hon. Cons. Plastic Surg. Royal National and Golden Square Hosps, 1969. Hon. Mem., Joseph Nazeno Plastic Soc., 1994. *Publications*: varied medical articles. *Recreations*: swimming, archæology. *Address*: Flat 1, 60 Cromwell Road, Hove BN3 3ES. *T*: (01273) 728974.
Died 9 Feb. 2008.

HEAP, Dr John Arnfield, CMG 1991; Director, 1992–97, Executive Director, 1998, Scott Polar Research Institute, Cambridge University; *b* 5 Feb. 1932; *s* of late David and Ann Heap; *m* 1960, Margaret Grace Gillespie, 3rd *d* of Captain Sir Stewart Dykes Spicer, 3rd Bt, RN; one *s* two *d*. *Educ*: Leighton Park Sch.; Edinburgh Univ. (MA 1955); Clare Coll., Cambridge (PhD 1962). Falkland Islands Dependencies Survey, 1955–62; Res. Fellow, Dept of Geology, 1962–63, Great Lakes Res. Div., 1963–64, Univ. of Michigan; Polar Regions Section, FCO, 1964–92: Head of Section, 1975–92; Adminr, British Antarctic Territory, 1989–92. Mem., UK Delegns to Antarctic Treaty Consultative Meetings, 1966–92; UK Comr, Commn for Conservation of Antarctic Marine Living Resources, 1982–92. Treas., Internat. Glaciological Soc., 1980–; Chairman: UK Antarctic Heritage Trust, 1996–; Trans-Antarctic Assoc., 1998–. Mem. (Lib Dem), S Cambs DC, 1999–. Editor, Handbook of the Antarctic Treaty System, 1977–94. *Publications*: Sea Ice in the Antarctic, 1963. *Address*: The New House, 27 High Street, Harston, Cambridge CB2 5PX. *T*: (01223) 870288; Acharonich, Ulva Ferry, Isle of Mull PA73 6LY. *T*: (01688) 500219.
Died 8 March 2006.

HEARD, Peter Graham, CB 1987; FRICS; IRRV; Deputy Chief Valuer, Valuation Office, Board of Inland Revenue, 1983–89; *b* 22 Dec. 1929; *s* of late Sidney Horwood Heard and Doris Winifred Heard, MBE; *m* 1953, Ethne Jean Thomas; two *d*. *Educ*: Exmouth Grammar School. Articled to W. W. Needham, 1946; joined Valuation Office, 1950; served in Exeter, Kidderminster, Dudley, Leeds; District Valuer, Croydon, 1971; Superintending Valuer, Chief Valuer's Office, 1973; Asst Sec., Bd of Inland Revenue, 1975; Superintending Valuer, Midlands, 1977; Asst Chief Valuer, 1978. *Recreations*: cricket, golf, countryside, walking the dog, theatre. *Address*: Romany Cottage, High Street, Lindfield, Sussex RH16 2HR. *T*: (01444) 482095. *Clubs*: MCC, Civil Service; Piltdown Golf; E Devon Golf.
Died 28 April 2009.

HEARST, Stephen, CBE 1980; FRSA; independent television producer and consultant, since 1986; *b* Vienna, Austria, 6 Oct. 1919; *m* 1948, Lisbeth Edith Neumann; one *s* one *d*. *Educ*: Vienna Univ.; Reading Univ. (Dip. Hort.); Brasenose Coll., Oxford (MA). Free lance writer, 1949–52; joined BBC as producer trainee, 1952; Documentary television: script writer, 1953–55; writer producer, 1955–65; Exec. Producer, Arts Programmes Television, 1965–67; Head of Arts Features, Television, 1967–71; Controller, Radio 3, 1972–78; Controller, Future Policy Gp, 1978–82; Special Adviser to Dir-Gen., BBC, 1982–86. Vis. Fellow, Inst. for Advanced Studies, Edinburgh Univ., 1988. FRSA 1980. *Publications*: Two Thousand Million Poor, 1965; Artistic Heritage and its Treatment by Television, 1982; (contrib.) The Third Age of Broadcasting (ed Wenham), 1982; (contrib.) Television and the Public Interest (ed Jay G. Blumler), 1991; (contrib.) Literacy is not enough (ed Brian Cox), 1998. *Recreations*: gardening, swimming, reading, listening to music. *Address*: c/o British Academy of Film and Television Arts, 195 Piccadilly, W1V 9LG.
Died 27 March 2010.

HEATH, John Moore, CMG 1976; HM Diplomatic Service, retired; *b* 9 May 1922; *s* of late Philip George and Olga Heath; *m* 1952, Patricia Mary Bibby; one *s* one *d*. *Educ*: Shrewsbury Sch.; Merton Coll., Oxford (MA).

Served War of 1939–45, France, Belgium and Germany: commnd Inns of Court Regt, 1942; Capt. GSO3 11th Armoured Div., 1944–45 (despatches). Merton Coll., 1940–42, 1946–47. Entered Foreign Service, 1950; 2nd Sec., Comr-Gen.'s Office, Singapore, 1950–52; 1st Sec. (Commercial), Jedda, 1952–56; 1st Sec., FO, 1956–58; Nat. Def. Coll., Kingston, Ont., 1958–59; Head of Chancery and HM Consul, Brit. Embassy, Mexico City, 1959–62; Head of Chancery, Brit. Embassy, Kabul, Afghanistan, 1963–65; Counsellor and Head of Establishment and Organisation Dept, FCO (formerly DSAO), 1966–69; Counsellor (Commercial), Brit. Embassy, Bonn, 1969–74; Overseas Trade Advr, Assoc. of British Chambers of Commerce, on secondment, 1974; Consul-Gen., Chicago, 1975–79; Ambassador to Chile, 1980–82. Dir Gen., Canning House (Hispanic and Luso-Brazilian Council), 1982–87. Chm., Anglo-Chilean Soc., 1987–89. FRPSL 1999. Orden al Merito por Servicios Distinguidos, Peru, 1984; Orden al Merito, Gran Oficial, Chile, 1991. *Publications:* The British Postal Agencies in Mexico 1825–1876, 1969; The Heath family engravers 1779–1878, 3 vols, 1993–98; Mexican Maritime Mail from Colonial Times to the Twentieth Century, 1997; Mexico - The 1868 Issue, 2004. *Recreation:* book collecting. *Address:* 6 Cavendish Crescent, Bath, N Somerset BA1 2UG. *Club:* Naval and Military.   *Died 13 Sept. 2009.*

HEATH, Air Vice-Marshal Michael Christopher, CBE 1998; FRAeS; Special Adviser to Commander, US Central Command, 2005–07; *b* 21 Dec. 1950; *s* of late Stanley Frank Heath and Mary Bridget Heath; *m* 1978, Margaret Bolton; one *s* one *d. Educ:* St John's Coll., Southsea. Commnd, 1969; qualified navigator, 1971; Electronic Warfare Instructor, RN, 1974; Staff Navigation Instructor, 1978; qwi 1979; OC 20 Sqn (Tornado), 1991–92; Station Comdr, RAF Benson, 1996–97; rcds, 1998; Dir, Targetting and Inf. Ops, 1999–2003; Sen. British Mil. Advr to US Central Comd, 2003–05. FRAeS 2000. *Recreations:* gliding, golf, walking. *Address:* c/o Lloyds Bank TSB, Cox's & King's Branch, 7 Pall Mall, SW1Y 5NA. *Club:* Royal Air Force.
                    Died 17 Nov. 2007.

HEATH-STUBBS, John (Francis Alexander), OBE 1989; poet; Lecturer in English Literature, College of St Mark and St John, Chelsea, 1963–73; *b* 9 July 1918; *s* of Francis Heath Stubbs and Edith Louise Sara (*née* Marr). *Educ:* Bembridge School; Worcester Coll. for the Blind, and privately; Queen's Coll., Oxford. English Master, Hall Sch., Hampstead, 1944–45; Editorial Asst, Hutchinson's, 1945–46; Gregory Fellow in Poetry, Leeds Univ., 1952–55; Vis. Prof. of English: University of Alexandria, 1955–58; University of Michigan, 1960–61. Pres., Poetry Soc., 1993–. FRSL 1953. Queen's Gold Medal for Poetry, 1973; Oscar Williams/Jean Durwood Award, 1977; Cholmondeley Award, 1989; Commonwealth Poetry Prize, 1989; Howard Sargeant Award, 1989. *Publications: verse:* Wounded Thammuz, 1942; Beauty and the Beast, 1943; The Divided Ways, 1946; The Swarming of the Bees, 1950; A Charm against the Toothache, 1954; The Triumph of the Muse, 1958; The Blue Fly in his Head, 1962; Selected Poems, 1965; Satires and Epigrams, 1968; Artorius, 1973; A Parliament of Birds, 1975; The Watchman's Flute, 1978; Mouse, the Bird and the Sausage, 1978; Birds Reconvened, 1980; Buzz Buzz, 1981; Naming the Beasts, 1982; The Immolation of Aleph, 1985; Cats' Parnassus, 1987; Time Pieces, 1988; Collected Poems, 1988; A Partridge in a Pear Tree, 1988; A Ninefold of Charms, 1989; Selected Poems, 1990; The Parson's Cat, 1992; Sweetapple Earth, 1993; Chimeras, 1994; Galileo's Salad, 1996; The Torriano Sequences, 1997; The Sound of Light, 1999; *drama:* Helen in Egypt, 1958; *criticism:* The Darkling Plain, 1950; Charles Williams, 1955; The Pastoral, 1969; The Ode, 1969; The Verse Satire, 1969; Literary Essays, 1998; *translations:* (with Peter Avery) Hafiz of Shiraz, 1952; (with Iris Origo) Leopardi, Selected Prose and Poetry, 1966; (with Carol A. Whiteside) The Poems of Anyte, 1974; (with Peter Avery) The Rubaiyat of Omar

Khayyam, 1979; The Eight Poems of Sulpicia, 2000; *edited:* Selected Poems of Jonathan Swift, 1948; Selected Poems of P. B. Shelley, 1948; Selected Poems of Tennyson, 1948; Selected Poems of Alexander Pope, 1964; (with David Wright) The Forsaken Garden, 1950; Images of Tomorrow, 1953; (with David Wright) Faber Book of Twentieth Century Verse, 1953; (with Martin Green) Homage to George Barker on his Sixtieth Birthday, 1973; Selected Poems of Thomas Gray, 1983; (with Phillips Salman) Poems of Science, 1984; David Gray, In the Shadows, 1991; *autobiography:* Hindsights, 1993. *Recreation:* taxonomy. *Address:* 22 Artesian Road, W2 5AR. *T:* (020) 7229 6367.   *Died 26 Dec. 2006.*

HEATHCOTE, Sir Michael Perryman, 11th Bt *cr* 1733; *b* 7 Aug. 1927; *s* of Sir Leonard Vyvyan Heathcote, 10th Bt, and Joyce Kathleen Heathcote (*d* 1967); *S* father, 1963; *m* 1956, Victoria Wilford, *e d* of Comdr J. E. R. Wilford, RN, retd; two *s* one *d. Educ:* Winchester Coll.; Clare Coll., Cambridge. Started farming in England, 1951, in Scotland, 1961. In remainder to Earldom of Macclesfield. *Recreations:* fishing, shooting, farming. *Heir:* *s* Timothy Gilbert Heathcote, *b* 25 May 1957. *Address:* Warborne Farm, Boldre, Lymington, Hants SO41 5QD. *T:* (01590) 673478.   *Died 13 April 2007.*

HEDDY, Brian Huleatt; HM Diplomatic Service, retired; Regional Co-ordinator and Resettlement Officer, British Refugee Council, 1979–82; *b* 8 June 1916; *o s* of late Dr William Reginald Huleatt Heddy, Barrister-at-Law, and Ruby Norton-Taylor; *m* 1st, 1940, Barbara Ellen Williams (*d* 1965); two *s* one *d*; 2nd, 1966, Ruth Mackarness (*née* Hogan) (*d* 1967); one step *s* two step *d*; 3rd, 1969, Horatia Clare Kennedy. *Educ:* St Paul's Sch.; Pembroke Coll., Oxford. Commissioned in 75th (Highland) Field Regt, Royal Artillery, Nov. 1939; served in France 1940; WA, 1943; War Office and France, 1944–45. Mem. of Gray's Inn. Entered Foreign Service, 1945; appointed to Brussels, 1946; Denver, 1948; Foreign Office, 1952; Tel Aviv, 1953; UK Delegation to ECSC, Luxembourg, 1955; Foreign Office, 1959; promoted Counsellor, 1963; Consul-Gen. at Lourenço Marques, 1963–65; Head of Nationality and Consular Dept, Commonwealth Office, 1966–67; Head of Migration and Visa Dept, FCO, 1968–71; Consul-Gen. in Durban, 1971–76. *Recreations:* travel, reading. *Address:* Abbots Litten Cottage, Long Street, Sherborne, Dorset DT9 3BU. *T:* (01935) 813335. *Clubs:* East India, Devonshire, Sports and Public Schools, MCC.
                    Died 23 Jan. 2007.

HEDGECOE, Prof. John, Dr RCA; FCSD; Professor of Photography, Royal College of Art, London, 1975–94, then Emeritus; Pro Rector, 1981–93, Acting Rector, 1983–84; *b* 24 March 1937; *s* of William Hedgecoe and Kathleen Don; *m* 1st, 1960, Julia Mardon (marr. diss. 1995); two *s* one *d*; 2nd, 2001, Jennifer M Ogilvie Hogg, *d* of Col D. O. Hogg, OBE, MC, TD, JP, DL. *Educ:* Gulval Village Sch., Cornwall; Guildford Sch. of Art. Staff Photographer, Queen Magazine, 1957–72; Freelance: Sunday Times and Observer, 1960–70; most internat. magazines, 1958–; Portrait, HM the Queen, for British and Australian postage stamps, 1966; photographed The Arts Multi-Projection, British Exhibn, Expo Japan Show, 1970. Royal College of Art: started Photography Sch., 1965: Head of Dept and Reader in Photography, 1965–74; Fellow, 1973; awarded Chair of Photography, 1975; started Audio/Visual Dept, 1980; Chm., Student Fund Awards, 1981–93; started Holography Unit, 1982; Managing Trustee, 1983; Sen. Fellow, 1992. Vis. Prof., Norwegian Nat. Television Sch., Oslo, 1985. Associate Ed., Country Illustrated, 2006–. Chm., Abacus Ltd (furniture stores), 1962–66; Managing Director: Lion & Unicorn Press Ltd, 1986–94; Mobius Books Internat. Ltd, 1986–92; Director: John Hedgecoe Ltd, 1965–95; Perennial Pictures Ltd, 1980, 1991. Mem. Photographic Bd, CNAA, 1976–78; Gov., W Surrey Coll. of Art (and Mem. Acad. Adv. Bd), 1975–; Acad. Gov., Richmond Coll., London; Trustee, The Minories Victor Batte-Lay Trust, 1985–88. Consultant,

English Heritage, 1995–98 (Head of External Pubns). Illustrated numerous books, 1958–; contributed to numerous radio broadcasts. Television: Tonight, Aust. TV, 1967; Folio, Anglia, 1980; 8 progs on Photography, Channel Four, 1983, repeated 1984; Winners, Channel Four, 1984; Light and Form, US Cable TV, 1985. Exhibitions: London, Sydney, Toronto, Edinburgh, Venice, Prague; one-man exhibitions: RCA, 2000; Nat. Portrait Gall., 2000; Sainsbury Centre for Visual Arts, UEA, 2000; Westcliffe Gall., Sheringham, 2000, 2002; Waterside Gall., Norfolk, 2000; Guild House Gall., Guildford, 2001; Christchurch Mansion Wolsey Art Gall., Ipswich, 2001; Royal Cornwall Mus., 2003; Poetry-next-the-Sea, Wells, Norfolk, 2003; Gables Yard, Norwich, 2003; Wells, 2004; St Paul's Sch., London, 2005; Beijing, Nanjing and Shanghai, China (rep. GB), 2005; Reflections, Horning, Norwich, 2008; Fifty Years of Modern British Art, Robert Sandelson Gall., London, 2008; permanent exhibn, Grove Clinic, Norfolk & Norwich Univ. Hosp.; collections: V&A Museum; Art Gall. of Ontario; Nat. Portrait Gall., London; Citibank, London; Henry Moore Foundn; Museum of Modern Art, NY; Leeds City Art Gall.; Ministry of Culture, Morocco. FRSA. Hon. FIIPC. Laureate and Medal for contribution to photography, Govt of Czechoslovakia, 1989; Lente de Plata Photography, Govt of Mexico, 2002. *Publications:* Henry Moore, 1968 (prize best art book, world-wide, 1969); (jtly) Kevin Crossley-Holland book of Norfolk Poems, 1970; Sculptures of Picasso, 1970; (jtly) Photography, Material and Methods, 1971–74 edns; Henry Moore, Energy in Space, 1973; The Book of Photography, 1976, new edn 2007; Handbook of Photographic Techniques, 1977, 3rd edn 1992; The Art of Colour Photography, 1978, new edn 2007 (Kodak Photobuchpreis Stuttgart 1979; Grand Prix Technique de la Photographie, Musée Français de la Photographie, Paris 1980); Possessions, 1978; The Pocket Book of Photography, 1979; Introductory Photography Course, 1979; Master Classes in Photography: Children and Child Portraiture, 1980; (illus.) Poems of Thomas Hardy, 1981; (illus.) Poems of Robert Burns, 1981; The Book of Advanced Photography, 1982; What a Picture!, 1983; The Photographer's Work Book, 1983, new edn 1997; Aesthetics of Nude Photography, 1984; The Workbook of Photo Techniques, 1984, 2nd edn 1997; The Workbook of Darkroom Techniques, 1984, 2nd edn 1997; Pocket Book of Travel and Holiday Photography, 1986; Henry Moore: his ideas, inspirations and life as an artist, 1986, new edn 1999; The Three Dimensional Pop-up Photography Book, 1986; (with A. L. Rowse) Shakespeare's Land, 1986; Photographer's Manual of Creative Ideas, 1986, new edn 1999; (with A. L. Rowse) Rowse's Cornwall, 1987; Practical Portrait Photography, 1987, 2nd edn 2000; Practical Book of Landscape Photography, 1988, 2nd edn 2000; Hedgecoe on Video, 1988; Hedgecoe on Photography, 1988; Complete Photography Guide, 1990; Video Photographer's Handbook, 1992; Zillij, 1992; John Hedgecoe's Complete Guide to Video, 1992; (jtly) The Art of Moroccan Ceramics, 1993; John Hedgecoe's Basic Photography, 1993; The New Book of Photography, 1994, 3rd edn 2004; Black and White Photography, 1994; Camcorder Basics, 1995; John Hedgecoe—a Complete Introductory Guide to Video, 1995; Breakfast with Dolly (novel), 1996; Figure and Form, 1996; John Hedgecoe's New Introductory Photography Course, 1996; The Spirit of the Garden, 1997; England's World Heritage, 1997; A Monumental Vision: the sculpture of Henry Moore, 1998; The Art of Colour Photography, 1998; Photography Sourcebook of Creative Ideas, 1998; John Hedgecoe's 35mm Photography, 1999; Portraits by John Hedgecoe, 2000; Photographing your Children, 2000; How to Take Great Photographs, 2001; (with Marie Pacheco) Dark Night of the Soul, 2001; Photographing Babies, 2002; How to Take Great Vacation Photography, 2003; New Manual of Photography, 2003 (trans. 37 lang), 2nd edn 2005 (German and Russian rev. edns); The Art of Digital Photography, 2006. *Recreations:* sculpture, building,

gardening. *Address:* c/o Dorling Kindersley, Penguin Books, 80 Strand, WC2R 0RL. *Clubs:* Arts; Norfolk (Norwich).   *Died 3 June 2010.*

HEDGELAND, Air Vice-Marshal Philip Michael Sweatman, CB 1978; OBE 1957 (MBE 1948); CEng, FIET; *b* 24 Nov. 1922; *s* of Philip and Margaret Hedgeland, Maidstone, Kent; *m* 1946, Jean Riddle Brinkworth (*d* 2006), *d* of Leonard and Anne Brinkworth, Darlington, Co. Durham; two *s*. *Educ:* Maidstone Grammar Sch.; City and Guilds Coll., Imperial Coll. of Science and Technology, London. BSc(Eng), ACGI (Siemens Medallist). Served War: commnd into Technical Br., RAF, 1942; despatches, 1943; Radar Officer, Pathfinder Force and at TRE, Malvern. Radar Develt Officer, Central Bomber Estabt, 1945–48; Radio Introd. Unit Project Officer for V-Bomber Navigation and Bombing System, 1952–57; Wing Comdr Radio (Air) at HQ Bomber Comd, 1957–60; jssc 1960; Air Ministry Technical Planning, 1961–62; aws 1963; Dir of Signals (Far East), Singapore, 1963–65; commanded RAF Stanbridge (Central Communications Centre), 1966–67; SASO, HQ Signals Comd/90 Gp, 1968–69; IDC, 1970; MoD Procurement Exec., Project Dir for Airborne Radar, 1971–74; Vice-Pres., Ordnance Bd, 1975–77, Pres., 1977–78. FCGI 1977. Pres., Pathfinder Assoc., 1985–87. *Address:* 34 Castle Court, Hadlow Road, Tonbridge, Kent TN9 1QU. *T:* (01732) 350196. *Club:* Royal Air Force.   *Died 25 Dec. 2009.*

HEDLEY, Ronald Henderson, CB 1986; DSc, PhD; FIBiol; Director, British Museum (Natural History), 1976–88; *b* 2 Nov. 1928; *s* of Henry Armstrong Hedley and Margaret Hopper; *m* 1957, Valmai Mary Griffith, New Zealand; one *s*. *Educ:* Durham Johnston Sch.; King's Coll., Univ. of Durham. Commissioned in Royal Regt of Artillery, 1953–55. Sen. Scientific Officer, British Museum (Natural History), 1955–61; New Zealand Nat. Research Fellow, 1960–61; Principal Scientific Officer, 1961–64; Dep. Keeper of Zoology, 1964–71; Dep. Dir, 1971–76. Vis. Lectr in Microbiology, Univ. of Surrey, 1968–75. Mem. Council, Fresh Water Biological Assoc., 1972–76; Trustee, Percy Sladen Meml Fund, 1972–77; Pres., British Section, Soc. of Protozoology, 1975–78; Member Council: Marine Biol Assoc., 1976–79, 1981–92; Zoological Soc., London, 1981–85 (Hon. Sec., 1977–80; Vice-Pres., 1980–85); Mem., Internat. Trust for Zoological Nomenclature, 1977–90. Member: Council, Royal Albert Hall, 1982–88; National Trust, 1985–88. *Publications:* (ed with C. G. Adams) Foraminifera, vols 1–3, 1974, 1976, 1978; (with C. G. Ogden) Atlas of Testate Amoebae, 1980; technical papers, mainly on biology, cytology and systematics of protozoa, 1956–. *Recreations:* horology, horticulture, humour. *Club:* Civil Service.   *Died 11 July 2006.*

HEDLEY-MILLER, Dame Mary (Elizabeth), DCVO 1989; CB 1983; Ceremonial Officer, Cabinet Office, 1983–88; *b* 5 Sept. 1923; *d* of late J. W. Ashe; *m* 1950, Roger Latham Hedley-Miller (*d* 2004); one *s* two *d*. *Educ:* Queen's Sch., Chester; St Hugh's Coll., Oxford (MA). Joined HM Treasury, 1945; served in UK Treasury Delegn, Washington DC, 1947–49; Under-Sec., HM Treasury, 1973–83. Alternate Dir, Monetary Cttee, EEC, and Alternate Exec. Dir, European Investment Bank, 1977–83. *Recreations:* family, including family music; reading. *Address:* 48 Elms Road, SW4 9EX. *T:* (020) 7627 8834. *Club:* Oxford and Cambridge.   *Died 20 March 2010.*

HEISBOURG, Georges; Ambassador of Luxembourg, retired; *b* 19 April 1918; *s* of Nicolas Heisbourg and Berthe (*née* Ernsterhoff); *m* 1945, Hélène Pinet; two *s* one *d*. *Educ:* Athénée, Luxembourg; Univs of Grenoble, Innsbruck and Paris. Head of Govt Press and Information Office, Luxembourg, 1944–45; Attaché 1945–48, Sec. 1948–51, of Legation, London; Head of Internat. Organisations Section, Dir of Political Affairs, Min. of For. Affairs, Luxembourg, 1951–58; Luxembourg Ambassador to USA, Canada and Mexico, 1958–64; Perm. Rep. to UN, 1958–61; Luxembourg Ambassador:

to Netherlands, 1964–67; to France, 1967–70; Perm. Rep. to OECD, 1967–70; Sec. Gen., WEU, 1971–74; Ambassador to USSR, Finland, Poland and Outer Mongolia, 1974–77; Perm. Rep. to Council of Europe, 1978–79; Ambassador to Fed. Rep. of Germany and to Denmark, 1979–83. Médaille de l'Ordre de la Résistance, Grand Officer, Nat. Order of Crown of Oak, 1980 (Chevalier, 1958), Comdr, Order of Adolphe de Nassau, 1963, and Grand Officer, Order of Merit, 1976, Luxembourg; also holds decorations from Austria, Belgium, France, Germany, Italy, Mexico, and the Netherlands. *Publications:* Le Gouvernement Luxembourgeois en exil 1940, Vol. I, 1986, Vol. II, 1987, Vol. III, 1989, Vol. IV, 1991. *Recreation:* swimming. *Address:* 9A Boulevard Joseph II, 1840 Luxembourg.
Died 28 April 2008.

HENAO, Rev. Sir Ravu, Kt 1982; OBE 1975; Executive Secretary, Bible Society of Papua New Guinea, 1980–87; *b* 27 March 1927; *s* of Boga Henao and Gaba Asi; *m* 1944, Lahui Peri; four *s* five *d. Educ:* Port Moresby (completed standard 5); Lawes Theol Coll., Fife Bay, Milne Bay Province. Primary sch. teacher, various schs in Central Dist, 1944–66 (pastor as well as teacher, 1946); Chm. (full-time), Papua Ekalesia (national church related to London Missionary Soc.), 1967; Bishop of United Church for Papua Mainland Region, 1968–80. Hon. DTech PNG Univ. of Technology, 1987. *Publications:* (with Raymond Perry) Let's Discuss These Things, 1966; (with Alan Dunstan) Paul's Letter to the Galatians, 1974. *Recreations:* fishing, hunting, gardening. *Address:* c/o PO Box 1224, Port Moresby, Papua New Guinea. *T:* 217893.
Died 18 Oct. 2007.

HENDER, John Derrik, CBE 1986; DL; public sector consultant; Chief Executive, West Midlands Metropolitan County Council, 1973–86; *b* 15 Nov. 1926; *s* of late Jessie Peter and Jennie Hender; *m* 1949, Kathleen Nora Brown; one *d. Educ:* Great Yarmouth Grammar School. IPFA, FCA. Deputy Borough Treasurer: Newcastle-under-Lyme, 1957–61; Wolverhampton County Borough, 1961–64; City Treas. 1965–69, Chief Exec. and Town Clerk 1969–73, Coventry County Borough. FCMI. DL West Midlands, 1975. *Publications:* numerous articles relating to various aspects of local govt and related matters. *Recreation:* gardening. *Address:* 11 Osborne Court, Lime Tree Road, Norwich NR2 2NN.
Died 31 Aug. 2009.

HENDERSON, Rt Rev. Charles Joseph; Auxiliary Bishop in Southwark, (RC), 1972–2001, then Emeritus; Titular Bishop of Tricala, since 1972; *b* 14 April 1924; *s* of Charles Stuart Henderson and Hanora Henderson (*née* Walsh). *Educ:* Mount Sion Sch., Waterford; St John's Seminary, Waterford Priest, 1948; Curate, St Stephen's, Welling, Kent, 1948–55; English Martyrs, Streatham, SW16, 1955–58; Chancellor, RC Diocese of Southwark, 1958–70; Vicar General, RC Diocese of Arundel and Brighton, 1965–66; Episcopal Vicar for Religious, Southwark, 1968–73; Vicar General, RC Archdiocese of Southwark, 1969–2003; Parish Priest, St Mary's, Blackheath, 1969–82; Canon of Cathedral Chapter, 1972; Provost of Cathedral Chapter, 1973–2001; Area Bp with responsibility for SE Pastoral area of Metropolitan RC See of Southwark, 1980–2001. Member: Ecumenical Commn for England and Wales, 1976–92; Nat. Catholic Commn for Racial Justice, 1978–81; English Anglican/RC Cttee, 1982–, Co. Chm. 1983–92; Methodist/RC Nat. Ecumenical Cttee, 1983 and Co. Chm. 1984–92; Chairman: RC Cttee for Dialogue with Other Faiths, 1984–2001; RC Nat. Cttee for Catholic-Jewish Relations, 1992–2001; RC Consultant-Observer, BCC, 1982–86; Exec. Cttee, inter-faith network for UK, 1987–2002; Member: Pontifical Council for Inter-religious Dialogue, 1990–2000; Exec. Cttee, CCJ, 1992–2003; Greenwich Univ. Assembly, 1993–. Papal Chamberlain, 1960; Prelate of Papal Household, 1965. Freeman, City of Waterford, 1973. Kt Comdr with Star of Equestrian Order of Holy Sepulchre, Jerusalem, 1973 (Prior, Southwark Sect., 1994–); Silver Palm of Jerusalem,

1998; Gold Medallion Award, Internat. CCJ, 2001. *Recreation:* special interest in sport. *Address:* Park House, 6A Cresswell Park, Blackheath, SE3 9RD. *T:* (020) 8318 1094.
Died 10 April 2006.

HENDERSON, Dr Derek Scott, FRSSAf; Principal and Vice-Chancellor, Rhodes University, Grahamstown, South Africa, 1975–96; *b* 28 Oct. 1929; *s* of late Ian Scott and Kathleen Elizabeth Henderson (*née* White); *m* 1958, Thelma Muriel, *d* of W. E. B. Mullins; two *d. Educ:* St John's Coll., Johannesburg; Rhodes University Coll. (BSc); Oxford Univ. (MA); Cambridge Univ. (MA); Harvard Univ. (PhD). FRSSAf 1995. Exec. Trainee, Anglo American Corp. of S Africa, 1953–56; Engr, Advanced Systems Develt, IBM Corp., Poughkeepsie, NY, 1960–62; Univ. of the Witwatersrand: Dir of Computer Centre, 1964–69; Prof. of Computer Science, 1967–75; Dean of Science Faculty, 1974–75. Chm., J. L. B. Smith Inst. of Ichthyology, 1976–96; Mem. Council, CSIR, 1982–87; Mem., Scientific Adv. Council, 1988–93; Mem. Bd, SABC, 1990–93; Vice-Chm., Leather Res. Inst., 1976–96; Mem. Council, Grahamstown (formerly 1820) Foundn (Vice-Chm., 1976–89; Exec. Dir, 1999–2002); Pres., SA Council of Automation and Computation, 1974. Chairman: Hillbrow Br., Progressive Party, 1964–65; Johannesburg Br., Kolbe Assoc. of Catholic Graduates, 1964; Mem. Council, St Andrew's Coll., 1986–2003; Trustee, SA Foundn, 1976–96; Patron, All Saints Coll., Bisho, 1986–96. Dir, Sabinet, 1983–88. Fellow, Computer Soc. of SA, 1974. Hon. LLD Rhodes, 1997. *Recreation:* golf. *Address:* 1 Ross Street, Grahamstown, 6139, S Africa. *T:* (46) 6223908. *Club:* Port Elizabeth (Port Elizabeth, S Africa).
Died 7 Aug. 2009.

HENDERSON, Douglas Mackay, CBE 1985; FRSE 1966; FLS; HM Botanist in Scotland, since 1987; *b* 30 Aug. 1927; *s* of Captain Frank Henderson and Adine C. Mackay; *m* 1952, Julia Margaret Brown; one *s* two *d. Educ:* Blairgowrie High Sch.; Edinburgh Univ. (BSc). Scientific Officer, Dept of Agriculture and Fisheries for Scotland, 1948–51. Royal Botanic Garden, Edinburgh, 1951–87, Regius Keeper, 1970–87; Adminr, Inverewe, Nat. Trust for Scotland, 1987–92. Hon. Prof., Edinburgh Univ., 1983–. Sec., Internat. Assoc. of Botanical Gardens, 1969–81. Curator of Library and Museum, Royal Soc. of Edinburgh, 1978–87. Mem. Council, Nat. Trust for Scotland, 1992–2002; Sec., Highland Cttee, Help the Aged, 1995–. VMH, 1985. *Publications:* British Rust Fungi (with M. Wilson), 1966; (with J. H. Dickson) A Naturalist in the Highlands: the life and travels of James Robertson in Scotland 1767–1771, 1993; A Checklist of the Rust Fungi of the British Isles, 2000; many papers on taxonomy of cryptogams. *Recreations:* music, hill walking, painting. *Address:* Isle View Care Home, Aultbea, W Ross IV22 2HU. *T:* 07756 025604; 38E Cramond Vale, Edinburgh EH4 6RB. *T:* (0131) 312 8432.
Died 10 Nov. 2007.

HENDERSON, Dr James Ewart, CVO 1988; DSc; President, Mastiff Electronic Systems Ltd, 1995–2002 (Managing Director, 1982–90; Chairman, 1985–95); *b* 29 May 1923; *s* of late Rev. James Ewart Henderson, MA, BD and Agnes Mary (*née* Crawford); *m* 1st, 1949, Alice Joan Hewlitt (*d* 1999); one *d;* 2nd, 1966, Nancy Maude Dominy; two *s. Educ:* private sch.; Glasgow Univ. (MA); Edinburgh Univ. Operational research on air rockets and guns, MAP, 1943–44; hon. commn in RAFVR, 1944–46; operational assessment of air attacks in Belgium, Holland and Germany, 2TAF, 1944–45; exper. research on fighter and bomber capability, and on the use of radar and radio aids: RAF APC Germany, 1945–46, Fighter Comd, 1946–49 and CFE, 1949–52; research on weapons effects and capability: Air Min., 1952–54, AWRE 1955, Air Min., 1955–58; Asst Scientific Adviser (Ops), Air Min., 1958–63; Dep. Chief Scientist (RAF), MoD, 1963–69; Chief Scientist (RAF) and Mem., Air Force Bd, 1969–73. Aviation Consultant, Hawker Siddeley Aviation Ltd, 1973–77; Financial Consultant, Charles

Stapleton & Co. Ltd, 1973–78; freelance Operational Res. and Management Consultant, 1975–78; Scientific Advr, BAe, 1978–82; Director: Lewis Security Systems Ltd, 1976–77; Mastiff Security Systems Ltd, 1977–82; Pres. and Chief Exec., Mastiff Systems US Inc., 1982–88; Chm., TIB Netherlands, 1982–86. Life Vice-Pres., Air League, 1994 (Mem. Council, 1979–80; Chm., 1981–87; Pres., 1987–94); Chm., Air League Educational Trust, 1983–87. FInstD 1978. *Publications:* technical papers on operational capability of aircraft and weapons; UK manual on Blast Effects of Nuclear Weapons. *Recreations:* sailing, golf, opera, photography. *Club:* Moor Park Golf.
Died 6 May 2006.

HENDERSON, Sir (John) Nicholas, GCMG 1977 (KCMG 1972; CMG 1965); KCVO 1991; HM Diplomatic Service, retired; re-appointed, Ambassador to Washington, 1979–82; author and company director; *b* 1 April 1919; *s* of Prof. Sir Hubert Henderson; *m* 1951, Mary Xenia Barber (*née* Cawadias) (OBE 1988) (*d* 2004); one *d. Educ:* Stowe Sch.; Hertford Coll., Oxford (Hon. Fellow 1975). Mem. HM Diplomatic Service. Served Minister of State's Office, Cairo, 1942–43; Asst Private Sec. to the Foreign Sec., 1944–47; HM Embassy, Washington, 1947–49; Athens, 1949–50; Permanent Under Secretary's Dept, FO, 1950–53; HM Embassy, Vienna, 1953–56; Santiago, 1956–59; Northern Dept, FO, 1959–62; Permanent Under Secretary's Dept, 1962–63; Head of Northern Dept, Foreign Office, 1963; Private Sec. to the Sec. of State for Foreign Affairs, 1963–65; Minister in Madrid, 1965–69; Ambassador to Poland, 1969–72, to Federal Republic of Germany, 1972–75, to France, 1975–79. Lord Warden of the Stannaries, Keeper of the Privy Seal of the Duke of Cornwall, and Mem. of Prince's Council, 1985–90. Mem., BBC General Adv. Council, 1983–87; Chm., Channel Tunnel Gp, 1985–86; Director: Foreign & Colonial Investment Trust, 1982–88; M&G Reinsurance, 1982–90; Hambros, 1983–89; Tarmac, 1983–89; F&C Eurotrust, 1984–; Eurotunnel, 1986–88; Supervisory Bd, Fuel-Tech NV, 1987–; Sotheby's, 1989–. Trustee, Nat. Gallery, 1985–89. Pres., Hertford Soc., 1984–89. Romanes Lectr, 1986. Hon. DCL Oxford, 1987. *Publications:* Prince Eugen of Savoy (biography), 1964; The Birth of Nato, 1982; The Private Office, 1984; Channels and Tunnels, 1987; Mandarin: the diaries of Nicholas Henderson, 1994; Old Friends and Modern Instances (memoirs), 2000; The Private Office Revisited, 2001; various stories and articles in Penguin New Writing, Horizon, Apollo, Country Life, The Economist and History Today. *Recreation:* gardening. *Address:* 6 Fairholt Street, SW7 1EG. *T:* (020) 7589 4291. *Clubs:* Brooks's, Pratt's. *Died 16 March 2009.*

HENDERSON, Leslie Edwin, CBE 1982; Director of Contracts, Property Services Agency, 1978–82; *b* 16 Dec. 1922; *s* of Thomas Edwin and Mabel Mary Henderson; *m* 1946, Marjorie (*née* Austin); two *s. Educ:* Ealing County Sch., London. Entered Civil Service (BoT) as Clerical Officer, 1939; Min. of Shipping, 1939; served in RAF, 1941–46; Min. of War Transport, 1946; subsequently in: Min. of Transport and Civil Aviation, MoT, DoE; Head of Contracts, Highways, Dept of Transport, 1968–78. *Recreations:* gardening, do-it-yourself. *Address:* Greenacres, The Rookery, Scotter, Lincs DN21 3FB. *T:* (01724) 763850. *Died 3 Oct. 2008.*

HENDERSON, Sir Nicholas; *see* Henderson, Sir J. N.

HENDRICKSE, Prof. Ralph George, MD; FRCP, FRCPE; Professor of Tropical Paediatrics and International Child Health, 1988–91, then Professor Emeritus, Head of Department of Tropical Paediatrics, 1974–91, and Dean, 1988–91, Liverpool School of Tropical Medicine; *b* 5 Nov. 1926; *s* of William George Hendrickse and Johana Theresa Hendrickse (*née* Dennis); *m* 1948, Begum Johanara Abdurahman; one *s* four *d. Educ:* Livingstone High Sch.; Univ. of Cape Town (MD). FMCPaed (Hon. Foundn Fellow). Res. MO, McCord Zulu Hosp., Durban, 1949–54, incl. secondment to Willis F. Pierce Meml Hosp., S Rhodesia, as MO i/c,

1951; postgrad. studies, Glasgow and Edinburgh, 1955; Sen. Registrar, UCH, Ibadan, Nigeria, 1955–57; Sen. Lectr, Univ. of Ibadan, 1957–62, and Hon. Consultant Paediatrician, UCH, 1957–69; Prof. and Head of Paediatrics, Univ. of Ibadan, 1962–69; Dir, Inst. of Child Health, 1964–69; Sen. Lectr, 1969–74, Prof. of Tropical Paediatrics, 1974–87, Liverpool Univ. Sch. of Trop. Med. Mem., Standing Panel of Experts in Public Health Medicine, Univ. of London, 1990–. Hon. Vis. Prof., Santo Tomas Univ., Philippines. Hon. Founder FRCPCH 1996; Hon. Member: BPA, 1995; Philippines Paed. Soc. Founder and Editor-in-Chief, Annals of Tropical Paediatrics, 1981–2004. Hon. DSc (Med.) Cape Town, 1998. Frederick Murgatroyd Prize, RCP, 1970. *Publications:* Paediatrics in the Tropics: current review, 1981; (ed and contrib.) Paediatrics in the Tropics, 1991; papers in learned jls. *Recreations:* photography, sketching, theatre, swimming, travel. *Address:* Beresford House, 25 Riverbank Road, Heswall, Wirral, Merseyside CH60 4SQ. *T:* (0151) 342 5510. *Died 6 May 2010.*

HENHAM, His Honour John Alfred; a Circuit Judge, 1983–95; *b* 8 Sept. 1924; *s* of Alfred and Daisy Henham; *m* 1946, Suzanne Jeanne Octavie Ghislaine Pinchart (*d* 1972); two *s. Educ:* County Tech. Coll., Kent. Served RAF, 1942–45. Asst to Justices' Clerks, 1940–60; admitted Solicitor, 1959; Clerk to Justices: Wednesbury Gp, 1960–61; Arundel and Worthing Divs, 1961–75; Stipendiary Magistrate for S Yorks, 1975–82; a Recorder of the Crown Court, 1979–82. *Publications:* Magistrates' Summary Jurisdiction: guide to sentencing powers, 1971, 3rd edn 1974. *Died 29 Aug. 2008.*

HENN, Charles Herbert; Assistant Under Secretary of State, Ministry of Defence, 1979–88; *b* 11 July 1931; *s* of Herbert George Henn and Ellen Anne Henn; *m* 1955, Ann Turner; one *s* one *d. Educ:* King's Coll. Sch., Wimbledon; Queen's Coll., Oxford (BA). National Service, REME, 1952–54 (2/Lieut). Scientific Officer, WO, 1954; Sen. Scientific Officer, 1957; Principal, 1964; Private Sec. to Minister of State for Defence, 1969; Asst Sec., 1972. *Recreations:* walking, running, listening to music. *Died 24 Dec. 2009.*

HENRY, Rt Hon. Sir Denis (Robert Maurice), Kt 1986; PC 1993; a Lord Justice of Appeal, 1993–2002; *b* 19 April 1931; *o s* of late Brig. Maurice Henry and Mary Catherine (*née* Irving); *m* 1963, Linda Gabriel Arthur; one *s* one *d* (and one *d* decd). *Educ:* Shrewsbury; Balliol Coll., Oxford (MA). 2nd Lieut, KORR, 1950–51. Called to the Bar, Inner Temple, 1955, Bencher, 1985; QC 1977; a Recorder, 1979–86; a Judge of the High Court, QBD, 1986–93. Chm., Judicial Studies Bd, 1994–99. Part-time Tutor, New Coll., Oxford, 1985–90. Mem., Civil Justice Council, 1998–99. *Recreation:* golf. *Address:* c/o Royal Courts of Justice, Strand, WC2A 2LL. *Died 6 March 2010.*

HENRY, Hon. Sir Trevor (Ernest), Kt 1970; Judge, Fiji Court of Appeal, 1974–85; *b* 9 May 1902; *s* of John Henry and Edith Anna (*née* Eaton); *m* 1930, Audrey Kate Sheriff; one *s* one *d. Educ:* Rotorua District High Sch.; Univ. of New Zealand, Auckland (LLB 1925, LLM Hons 1926). Solicitor of Supreme Court of NZ, 1923, Barrister, 1925. Judge of the Supreme Court of NZ, 1955–77. *Recreation:* fishing. *Address:* 10 Gerard Way, Meadowbank, Auckland, New Zealand. *Club:* Northern (Auckland). *Died 20 June 2007.*

HEPBURN, Prof. Ronald William; Professor of Moral Philosophy, University of Edinburgh, 1975–96 (Professor of Philosophy, 1964–75), then Professor Emeritus; *b* 16 March 1927; *s* of late W. G. Hepburn, Aberdeen; *m* 1953, Agnes Forbes Anderson; two *s* one *d. Educ:* Aberdeen Grammar Sch.; University of Aberdeen. MA 1951, PhD 1955 (Aberdeen). National service in Army, 1944–48. Asst, 1952–55, Lecturer, 1955–60, Dept of Moral Philosophy, University of Aberdeen; Visiting Associate Prof., New York University, 1959–60; Prof. of Philosophy, University of Nottingham, 1960–64. Stanton Lecturer in the Philosophy of Religion, Cambridge,

1965–68. *Publications:* (jtly) Metaphysical Beliefs, 1957; Christianity and Paradox, 1958; Wonder and Other Essays: eight studies in aesthetics and neighbouring fields, 1984; The Reach of the Aesthetic: collected essays, 2001; contrib. to books and learned journals; broadcasts. *Address:* 8 Albert Terrace, Edinburgh EH10 5EA.
Died 23 Dec. 2008.

HERBERT, Frederick William; Emeritus Fellow in Industrial Relations, International Management Centre, Buckingham, 1985–92; Chairman, NALGO Insurance Association Ltd, 1981–93; *b* London, 18 Dec. 1922; *s* of late William Herbert and Alice Herbert; *m* 1948, Nina Oesterman; two *d*. *Educ:* Ealing Boys' Grammar Sch. Served RAFVR, 1942–46. Local Govt Finance, Middx CC, 1939–65; Greater London Council: Local Govt Finance, 1965–72; Personnel Management, Estabt Officer, 1972–77; Asst Dir of Personnel, 1977–80; Head of Industrial Relations, 1980–82; Controller of Personnel, 1982–84. Parly Correspondent, Eurotunnel (UK), 1986–87. FRSA 1986. *Recreations:* cricket, music (classical and jazz), theatre, Antient Society of Cogers (debating). *Address:* 20 Priory Hill, Wembley, Middx HA0 2QF. *T:* (020) 8904 8634. *Clubs:* Royal Over-Seas League, MCC.
Died 26 Oct. 2010.

HERBERT, Sir Walter William, (Sir Wally), Kt 2000; Polar explorer; *b* 24 Oct. 1934; *s* of Captain W. W. J. Herbert and Helen (*née* Manton); *m* 1969, Marie, *d* of Prof. C. A. McGaughey; one *d* (and one *d* decd). Trained as surveyor in RE; Egypt, 1953–54, demob. 1955; travelled in Middle East, 1955; Surveyor with Falkland Is Dependencies Survey; Hope Bay, Antarctica, 1955–58; travelled in S America, 1958–59; Mem. expedn to Lapland and Spitzbergen, 1960; travelled in Greenland, 1960; Surveyor, NZ Antarctic Expedn, 1960–62; leader Southern Party; mapped 26,000 sq. miles of Queen Maud Range and descended Amundsen's route to Pole on 50th anniv.; led expedn to NW Greenland, 1966–67; dog-sledged 1,400 miles Greenland to Canada in trng for trans-Arctic crossing; led British Trans-Arctic Expedn, 1968–69, which made 3,800 mile first surface crossing of Arctic Ocean from Alaska via North Pole to Spitzbergen; led Ultima Thule expedn (filming Eskimos, Thule District), 1971–73; led expedn to Lapland, 1975; led expedn to Greenland, 1978–82 (attempting first circumnavigation by dog sledge and skin boat); led filming expedn to NW Greenland, Ellesmere Island and North Pole, 1987. One-man exhibitions: QE-2, 1994; Explorers Club, NY, 1994; Jamestown Coll., NY, 1994; Australian Geographic Soc., 1994; Travellers' Club, London, 1997; Atlas Gallery, 1999. Hon. Mem., British Schools Exploring Soc.; Jt Hon. Pres., World Expeditionary Assoc. FRGS. Hon. Fellow, New World Acad., 1993. Polar Medal 1962, and clasp 1969; Livingstone Gold Medal, RSGS, 1969, Founder's Gold Medal, RGS, 1970; City of Paris Medal, 1983; French Geog. Soc. Medal, 1983; Explorers' Medal, Explorers' Club, 1985; Finn Ronne Award, 1985. *Publications:* A World of Men, 1968; Across the Top of the World, 1969; (contrib.) World Atlas of Mountaineering, 1969; The Last Great Journey on Earth, 1971; Polar Deserts, 1971; Eskimos, 1976 (Jugendbuchpreis, 1977); North Pole, 1978; (contrib.) Expeditions the Expert's Way, 1977; (contrib.) Bell House Book, 1978; Hunters of the Polar North, 1982; The Noose of Laurels, 1989; The Third Pole, 2003. *Recreation:* painting. *Address:* Catlodge, Laggan, Inverness-shire PH20 1AH. *T:* and *Fax:* (01528) 544396. *Club:* Explorers (NY).
Died 12 June 2007.

HERBISON, Dame Jean (Marjory), DBE 1985; CMG 1976; Associate Director, Christchurch Polytechnic, New Zealand, 1975–84, retired; *b* 29 April 1923; *d* of William Herbison and Sarah Jane Herbison (*née* McKendry). *Educ:* Univ. of Canterbury (BA); Auckland Teachers' Coll. (Dip Teaching); Univ. of Northern Iowa (MA); Inst. of Education, Univ. of London. AIE 1974. Teaching, Avonside Girls' High School, Christchurch, 1952–59; Dean, 1960–68, Vice-Principal, 1968–74, Christchurch Teachers' Coll.; Assoc. Dir, Christchurch Polytechnic,

1975–84; Mem. Council, 1970–84, Chancellor, 1979–84, Univ. of Canterbury. Chairperson, NZ Council for Educnl Research, 1986–88 (Mem., 1977–88); Member: UGC, 1985–90; Ministerial Cttee of Inquiry into Curriculum, Assessment and Qualifications in the Senior Secondary Sch., 1985–87; Commonwealth Council for Educnl Admin, 1970– (Vice-Pres., 1982–86); NZ Vice-Chancellors' Cttee, Univ. Review Panel, 1987. Fellow: Commonwealth Council for Educnl Admin., 1986; NZ Educnl Admin. Soc., 1990; Hon. Fellow: NZ Educnl Inst.; NZ Inst. of Management. Hon. DLitt Canterbury, 1987. Queen's Silver Jubilee Medal, 1977. *Recreations:* gardening, walking, reading. *Address:* 2/172 Soleares Avenue, Christchurch 8008, New Zealand. *T:* (3) 3849086.
Died 20 May 2007.

HERITAGE, John Langdon, CB 1991; Director, Chesham Building Society, 1989–2001 (Chairman, 1992–97); *b* 31 Dec. 1931; *s* of Frank and Elizabeth Heritage; *m* 1956, Elizabeth Faulkner, *d* of Charles and Ethel Robertson; two *s* one *d*. *Educ:* Berkhamsted Sch., Exeter Coll., Oxford (MA). Called to the Bar, Middle Temple, 1956. National Service, Royal Hampshire Regt and Royal W African Frontier Force. Legal Asst, Treasury Solicitor's Office, 1957, Sen. Legal Asst 1964; Asst Solicitor, Lord Chancellor's Dept, 1973; Sec., Royal Commn on Legal Services, 1976 79; Under Sec., 1983; Circuit Administrator, South Eastern Circuit, 1983–88; Hd of Judicial Appts, Lord Chancellor's Dept, 1989–92. *Publications:* articles in legal jls. *Recreation:* amateur physiotherapy. *Address:* Hurdle House, 1 Chestnut Lane, Amersham, Bucks HP6 6EN. *Club:* Oxford and Cambridge.
Died 22 Jan. 2009.

HERITAGE, Robert Charles, CBE 1980; RDI 1963; DesRCA, FCSD; Professor, School of Furniture Design, Royal College of Art, 1974–85; *b* 2 Nov. 1927; *m* Dorothy (*d* 2005); two *s* one *d*. *Educ:* Royal College of Art, RCA, 1950. Freelance designer, 1961. *Recreations:* tennis, fishing. *Address:* 12 Jay Mews, Kensington Gore, SW7 2EP.
Died 23 Nov. 2008.

HERLIE, Eileen; actress; *b* Glasgow, 8 March 1920; *d* of Patrick Herlihy (Irish) and Isobel Cowden (Scottish); *m* 1st, 1942, Philip Barrett (marr. diss.); 2nd, 1951, Witold Kuncewicz (marr. diss.). *Educ:* Shawlands Academy, Glasgow. First stage appearance, Lyric, Glasgow, 1938; first London appearance, as Mrs de Winter in Rebecca, Ambassadors', 1942; varied repertoire with own company, 1942–44; Old Vic Co., Playhouse, Liverpool, 1944–45, including: Lady Sneerwell in The School for Scandal, Doll Common in The Alchemist; Lyric, Hammersmith, 1945–46, including: Andromache in The Trojan Women, Alcestis in Thracian Horses, Queen in The Eagle Has Two Heads; title rôle in Medea, Globe, 1948; Paula in The Second Mrs Tanqueray, Haymarket, 1950; Mrs Marwood in The Way of the World, Belvidera in Venice Preserv'd, Lyric, Hammersmith, 1953; Irene in A Sense of Guilt, King's, Glasgow, 1953; Mrs Molloy in The Matchmaker, Haymarket, 1954, transf. NY, 1955; Emilia Marty in The Makropoulos Secret, NY, 1957; Paulina in The Winter's Tale, Beatrice in Much Ado About Nothing, Stratford, Ont, 1958; Ruth Gray in Epitaph for George Dillon, NY, 1958; Lily in Take Me Along (musical), NY, 1959; Elizabeth Hawkes-Bullock in All American (musical), NY, 1962; Stella in Photo Finish, NY, 1963; Queen Gertrude in Hamlet, NY, 1964; Lady Fitzbuttress in Halfway up the Tree, NY, 1967; Martha in Who's Afraid of Virginia Woolf?, Chicago, 1971; Countess Matilda Spina in Emperor Henry IV, 1973; Queen Mary in Crown Matrimonial, NY, 1973. *Films:* Hungry Hill, 1947; Hamlet, 1948; Angel with the Trumpet, 1949; Gilbert and Sullivan, 1952; Isn't Life Wonderful?, 1952; She Didn't Say No!, 1958; Freud, 1962; The Seagull, 1968. *Television:* Myrtle Fargate in All My Children, ABC TV, 1976–. *Recreations:* riding, reading, music. *Address:* Apt 13P, 405 East 54th Street, New York, NY 10022, USA.
Died 8 Oct. 2008.

HERMON, Sir John (Charles), Kt 1982; OBE 1975; QPM 1988; Chief Constable, Royal Ulster Constabulary, 1980–89; *b* 23 Nov. 1928; *s* of late William Rowan Hermon and Agnes Hermon; *m* 1954, Jean Webb (*d* 1986); one *s* one *d*; *m* 1988, Sylvia Paisley (later Sylvia Hermon, MP); two *s*. *Educ:* Larne Grammar Sch. Accountancy training and business, 1946–50; joined RUC, 1950; Head Constable, 1963–66; Dep. Chief Constable, 1976–79. Pres., Internat. Professional Security Assoc., 1993–96. CStJ 1984. *Publications:* Holding the Line: an autobiography, 1997.   *Died 6 Nov. 2008.*

HERON, Robert, CVO 1988; MA; Director, Duke of Edinburgh's Award Scheme, 1978–87; *b* 12 Oct. 1927; *s* of James Riddick Heron and Sophie Leathem; *m* 1953, Patricia Mary Pennell; two *s* one *d*. *Educ:* King Edward's Sch., Birmingham; St Catharine's Coll., Cambridge. Housemaster: Strathallan, Perthshire, 1952–59; Christ Coll., Brecon, 1959–62; Headmaster, King James I Sch., IOW, 1962–66. Head of Educational Broadcasting, ATV Network Ltd, 1966–69, responsible for production of TV programme series in the scis, langs, soc. documentary, leisure interests, music, drama; Deleg., EBU study gps on educnl broadcasting, 1967–69; Programme Dir, The Electronic Video Recording Partnership (CBS Inc. USA/ ICI/Ciba-Geigy UK), 1970–77; Managing Dir, EVR Ltd, 1974–77, and of EVR Enterprises Ltd, 1975–77. Freeman, City of London, 1981. Formerly 6/7th Bn, The Black Watch (RHR) TA. *Recreations:* travel, sport. *Clubs:* Rugby; Hawks (Cambridge); Achilles.
Died 21 Nov. 2009.

HERRING, Cyril Alfred; management consultant; Senior Partner, Cyril Herring & Associates, since 1978; Chairman and Managing Director, Southern Airways Ltd, since 1978; *b* Dulwich, 17 Jan. 1915; *s* of Alfred James Herring and Minnie Herring (*née* Padfield); *m* 1939, Helen (*née* Warnes); three *s*. *Educ:* Alleyn's Sch.; London School of Economics (BSc(Econ)). FCMA; JDipMA; IPFA; FCILT. Chief Accountant, Straight Corporation Ltd, 1936–46; joined BEA, 1946; Chief Accountant, 1951–57; Personnel Director, 1957–65; Financial Director, 1965–71; Executive Board Member, 1971–74; Mem., British Airways Bd, 1972–78; Chief Executive, British Airways Regional Div., 1972–74; Finance Dir, 1975–78; Chm. and Man. Dir, British Air Services Ltd, 1969–76; Chairman: Northeast Airlines Ltd, 1969–76; Cambrian Airways Ltd, 1973–76; London Rail Adv. Cttee, 1976–80; CIPFA Public Corporations Finance Group, 1976–78. Member Council: Chartered Inst. of Transport, 1971–74; Inst. of Cost and Management Accountants, 1967–77 (Vice-Pres., 1971–73, Pres., 1973–74); CBI, 1975–78 (Mem. Financial Policy Cttee, 1975–78, Finance and General Purposes Cttee, 1977–78). Freeman, City of London; Liveryman, GAPAN. *Recreations:* flying, motoring, boating. *Address:* Cuddenbeake, St Germans, Cornwall PL12 5LY. *Club:* Reform.   *Died 25 Dec. 2009.*

HERSCHELL, 3rd Baron *cr* 1886; **Rognvald Richard Farrer Herschell;** late Captain Coldstream Guards; *b* 13 Sept. 1923; *o s* of 2nd Baron and Vera (*d* 1961), *d* of Sir Arthur Nicolson, 10th Bt, of that Ilk and Lasswade; *S* father, 1929; *m* 1948, Lady Heather, *d* of 8th Earl of Dartmouth, CVO, DSO; one *d*. *Educ:* Eton. Page of Honour to the King, 1935–40. Served World War II, 1942–45. *Heir:* none. *Address:* Westfield House, Ardington, Wantage, Oxon OX12 8PN. *T:* (01235) 833224.   *Died 26 Oct. 2008 (ext).*

HESTER, Rev. Canon John Frear; Canon Residentiary and Precentor of Chichester Cathedral, 1985–97, Canon Emeritus 1997; Chaplain to the Queen, 1984–97; *b* 21 Jan. 1927; *s* of William and Frances Mary Hester; *m* 1959, Elizabeth Margaret (*d* 2004), *d* of Sir Eric Riches, MC, MS, FRCS; three *s*. *Educ:* West Hartlepool Grammar School; St Edmund Hall, Oxford (MA); Cuddesdon Coll., Oxford. Captain RAEC, 1949–50. Personal Asst to Bishop of Gibraltar, 1950; Deacon, 1952; Priest, 1953; Assistant Curate: St George's, Southall, 1952–55; Holy Redeemer, Clerkenwell, 1955–58; Sec., Actors' Church

Union, 1958–63; Chaplain, Soc. of the Sisters of Bethany, Lloyd Sq., 1959–62; Dep. Minor Canon of St Paul's Cathedral, 1962–75; Rector of Soho, 1963–75; Priest-in-charge of St Paul's, Covent Garden, 1969–75; Senior Chaplain, Actors' Church Union, 1970–75; Chaplain to Lord Mayor of Westminster, 1970–71; in residence at St George's Coll. and the Ecumenical Inst., Tantur, Jerusalem, 1973; Chm., Covent Garden Conservation Area Adv. Cttee, 1971–75; Vicar of Brighton, 1975–85; Canon and Prebendary of Chichester Cathedral, 1976–85; RD of Brighton, 1976–85; Commissary of the Bishop of Nakuru, 1991–2000. Chm., Chichester Diocesan Overseas Council, 1985–94. Editor, Christian Drama, 1957–59. Lectr and preacher, US, 1961–; Leader of Pilgrimages to the Holy Land, Turkey, etc, 1962–. Mem., Worshipful Co. of Parish Clerks, 1970–86; Mem., Oving Parish Council, 1999–2003. Chaplain, Brighton and Hove Albion FC, 1979–97; Vice-Pres., Actors' Church Union, 2000– (Southern Area Chaplain, 1992–2000); Vice-Pres., 1979– and Hon. Chaplain, 1975–79 and 1988–, Royal Theatrical Fund (formerly Royal Gen. Theatrical Fund Assoc.). Chm. of Trustees, Chichester Centre of Arts, 1989–98; Chm., Chichester Arts Liaison Gp, 1990–95; Trustee, Chichester Fest. Theatre, 1990–2003 (Hon. Patron, 2003–); Pres., Forum Soc., 1985–2000; Vice-Pres., Sussex Guild (formerly Guild of Sussex Craftsmen), 1991–; Governor: Lavant House Sch., 1993–95; Lavant House Rosemead, 1995–2004 (Chm. Govs, 1995–99). Hon. Life Mem., British Actors' Equity Assoc. Chichester Civic Award, 1996. *Publications:* Soho Is My Parish, 1970. *Recreations:* sitting down; pulling legs; watching soccer and other drama; Middle Eastern studies. *Address:* The Hovel, Oving, Chichester PO20 2DE. *T:* (01243) 782071; *e-mail:* thehovel@bigfoot.com.   *Died 9 Feb. 2008.*

HESTON, Charlton; actor (films, stage and television), USA; *b* Evanston, Ill, 4 Oct. 1924; *né* John Charles Carter; *s* of Russell Whitford Carter and Lilla Carter (*née* Charlton, later Heston); *m* 1944, Lydia Marie Clarke (actress), Two Rivers, Wisconsin; one *s* one *d*. *Educ:* New Trier High Sch., Ill; Sch. of Speech, Northwestern Univ., 1941–43. Served War of 1939–45, with 11th Army Air Forces in the Aleutians. Co-Dir (with wife), also both acting, Thomas Wolfe Memorial Theatre, Asheville, NC (plays: the State of the Union, The Glass Menagerie, etc). In Antony and Cleopatra, Martin Beck Theatre, New York, 1947; also acting on Broadway, 1949 and 1950, etc; London stage début (also dir.), The Caine Mutiny Court Martial, Queen's, 1985 (filmed, 1988); A Man for All Seasons, Savoy, 1987, tour 1988; (with wife) Love Letters, UK tour, 1997. *Films:* (1950–) include: Dark City, Ruby Gentry, The Greatest Show on Earth, Arrowhead, Bad For Each Other, The Savage, Pony Express, The President's Lady, Secret of the Incas, The Naked Jungle, The Far Horizons, The Private War of Major Benson, The Ten Commandments (Moses), The Big Country, Ben Hur (Acad. Award for best actor, 1959), The Wreck of the Mary Deare, El Cid, 55 Days at Peking, The Greatest Story Ever Told, Major Dundee, The Agony and the Ecstacy, Khartoum, Will Penny, Planet of the Apes, Soylent Green, The Three Musketeers, Earthquake, Airport 1975, The Four Musketeers, The Last Hard Men, Battle of Midway, Two-Minute Warning, Gray Lady Down, Crossed Swords, The Mountain Men, The Awakening, Mother Lode, Music Box, Treasure Island, Solar Crisis, True Lies, Alaska, Hamlet, Any Given Sunday. TV appearances, esp. in Shakespeare. Mem., Screen Actors' Guild (Pres., 1966–69); Mem., Nat. Council on the Arts, 1967–; Chm., Amer. Film Inst., 1961–; Chm., Center Theatre Group, LA, 1963; Chm. on the Arts for Presidential Task Force on the Arts and Humanities, 1981–. Hon. Dr: Jacksonville Univ., Fla; Abilene Christian Univ., Texas. Jean Hersholt Humanitarian Award, Acad. Awards, 1977. *Publications:* (ed Hollis Alpert) The Actor's Life: Journals 1956–1976, 1979; Beijing Diary, 1990; In the Arena (autobiog.), 1995. *Club:* All England Lawn Tennis.
Died 5 April 2008.

HETHERINGTON, Sir Thomas Chalmers, (Tony), KCB 1979; CBE 1970; TD; QC 1978; Director of Public Prosecutions, 1977–87; Head of the Crown Prosecution Service, 1986–87; *b* 18 Sept. 1926; *er s* of William and Alice Hetherington; *m* 1953, June Margaret Ann Catliff; four *d*. *Educ*: Rugby Sch.; Christ Church, Oxford. Served in Royal Artillery, Middle East, 1945–48; Territorial Army, 1948–67. Called to Bar, Inner Temple, 1952; Bencher, 1978. Legal Dept, Min. of Pensions and Nat. Insce, 1953; Law Officers' Dept, 1962, Legal Sec., 1966–75; Dep. Treasury Solicitor, 1975–77. Jt Head, War Crimes Inquiry, 1988–89. Trustee, Maxwell Pension Trust, 1995–97. Pres., Old Rugbeians Soc., 1988–90. *Publications*: Prosecution and the Public Interest, 1989. *Address*: Rosemount, Mount Pleasant Road, Lingfield, Surrey RH7 6BH. *T*: (01342) 833923.   *Died 28 March 2007.*

HEWARD, Edmund Rawlings, CB 1984; Chief Master of the Supreme Court (Chancery Division), 1980–85 (Master, 1959–79); *b* 19 Aug. 1912; *s* of late Rev. Thomas Brown Heward and Kathleen Amy Rachel Rawlings; *m* 1945, Constance Mary Sandiford (*d* 2004), *d* of late George Bertram Crossley, OBE. *Educ*: Repton; Trinity Coll., Cambridge (BA 1933; LLB 1934; LLM 1960). Admitted a solicitor, 1937. Enlisted Royal Artillery as a Gunner, 1940; released as Major, DAAG, 1946. Partner in Rose, Johnson and Hicks, 9 Suffolk St, SW1, 1946. *Publications*: Guide to Chancery Practice, 1962, 5th edn 1979; Matthew Hale, 1972; (ed) Part 2, Tristram and Coote's Probate Practice, 24th edn, 1973, 26th edn 1983; (ed) Judgments and Orders in Halsbury's Laws of England, 4th edn; Lord Mansfield, 1979; Chancery Practice, 1983, 2nd edn 1990; Chancery Orders, 1986; Lord Denning—A Biography, 1990, 2nd edn 1997; Masters in Ordinary, 1991; The Great and the Good—a life of Lord Radcliffe, 1995; A Victorian Law Reformer—a life of Lord Selborne, 1998; Lives of the Judges: Jessel, Cairns, Bowen and Bramwell, 2001. *Club*: Travellers.   *Died 11 Dec. 2006.*

HEWITT, His Honour Harold; a Circuit Judge, 1980–90; *b* 14 March 1917; *s* of George Trueman Hewitt and Bertha Lilian Hewitt; *m* 1946, Doris Mary Smith (*d* 2001); two *s*. *Educ*: King James I Grammar Sch., Bishop Auckland. Admitted solicitor (Hons), 1938; HM Coroner, S Durham, 1948–80; a Recorder of the Crown Court, 1974–80. Chairman (part-time): Industrial Tribunal, 1975–80; Milk and Dairies Tribunal, Northern Region, 1975–80. Member Council, Law Society, 1976–80. Pres., NE Region, YMCA, 1981–2001. *Recreations*: music, French literature. *Address*: 5 Primlea Court, Aydon Road, Corbridge, Northumberland NE45 5ES. *T*: (01434) 632860. *Club*: Carlton.   *Died 19 June 2007.*

HEWITT, Peter McGregor, OBE 1967; Regional Director, East Midlands, Departments of the Environment and Transport, 1984–89; *b* 6 Oct. 1929; *e s* of late Douglas McGregor Hewitt and Audrey Vera Hewitt; *m* 1962, Joyce Marie Gavin; three *d*. *Educ*: De Aston Sch., Market Rasen, Lincs; Keble Coll., Oxford (MA). National Service (Army), 1947–49. HM Overseas Civil Service, 1952–64: served in Malaya and N Borneo; HM Diplomatic Service, 1964–71: served in FO, Shanghai and Canberra; Home Civil Service: Principal, 1971–77; Asst Sec., 1977–83; Grade 4, 1984. *Recreations*: cricket, music, gardening. *Address*: 14 Dovedale Road, West Bridgford, Nottingham NG2 6JA. *Club*: Royal Commonwealth Society.   *Died 17 Nov. 2010.*

HEY, Air Vice-Marshal Ernest, CB 1967; CBE 1963 (OBE 1954); CEng; Air Member for Technical Services, Department of Air, Canberra, 1960–72, retired; *b* Plymouth, Devon, 29 Nov. 1912; *s* of Ernest Hey, Terrigal, NSW; *m* 1936, Lorna, *d* of Sqdn Ldr A. Bennett, Melbourne; one *s* one *d*. *Educ*: Sydney Technical High Sch.; Sydney University. RAAF cadet, 1934; served War of 1939–45; Dir Technical Services, 1947–54; AOC

Maintenance Comd, 1956–57; Imp. Defence Coll., 1957; Liaison Air Materiel Comd, USAF, 1958–59.   *Died 31 May 2006.*

HEYWOOD-LONSDALE, Lt-Col Robert Henry, MBE 1952; MC 1945; Vice Lord-Lieutenant for Oxfordshire, 1989–96; *b* 18 Dec. 1919; *s* of Col John Pemberton Heywood-Lonsdale, DSO, OBE, TD and Hon. Helen Annesley; *m* 1952, Hon. Jean Helen Rollo, *d* of 12th Lord Rollo; one *s* three *d*. *Educ*: Eton. Grenadier Guards, 1938–56; Royal Wilts Yeo., 1961–67. Farmer. Co. Comr for Scouts, Oxfordshire, 1981–86. High Sheriff, Wilts, 1975; DL Wilts, 1972, Oxon, 1983. *Recreation*: country pursuits. *Address*: Mount Farm, Churchill, Oxon OX7 6NP. *T*: (01608) 658316. *Club*: Boodle's.   *Died 24 Dec. 2009.*

HEZLET, Vice-Adm. Sir Arthur Richard, KBE 1964; CB 1961; DSO 1944 (Bar 1945); DSC 1941; *b* 7 April 1914; *s* of late Maj.-Gen. R. K. Hezlet, CB, CBE, DSO; *m* 1948, Anne Joan Patricia, *e d* of late G. W. N. Clark, Carnabane, Upperlands, Co. Derry; two adopted *d*. *Educ*: RN College, Dartmouth. Comd HM Submarines: H44, Ursula, Trident, Thrasher and Trenchant, 1941–45; comd HMS Scorpion, 1949–50; Chief Staff Officer to Flag Officer (Submarines), 1953–54; Capt. (D), 6th Destroyer Squadron 1955–56; Dir, RN Staff Coll., Greenwich, 1956–57; comd HMS Newfoundland, 1958–59; Rear-Adm. 1959; Flag Officer (Submarines), 1959–61; Flag Officer, Scotland, 1961–62; Vice-Adm. 1962; Flag Officer, Scotland and Northern Ireland, 1963–64; retired 1964. Legion of Merit (Degree of Commander) (US), 1945. *Publications*: The Submarine and Sea Power, 1967; Aircraft and Sea Power, 1970; The 'B' Specials, 1972; Electron and Sea Power, 1975; The Trenchant at War, 2001; British and Allied Submarine Operations in World War II, 2002. *Address*: Bovagh House, Mullaghinch Road, Aghadowey, Co. Londonderry, N Ireland BT51 4AU. *T*: (028) 7086 8206. *Clubs*: Army and Navy, Royal Ocean Racing.   *Died 7 Nov. 2007.*

HIBBERT, Christopher, MC 1945; author; *b* 5 March 1924; *s* of late Canon H. V. Hibbert; *m* 1948, Susan Piggford; two *s* one *d*. *Educ*: Radley; Oriel Coll., Oxford (MA). Served in Italy, 1944–45; Capt., London Irish Rifles. Partner in firm of land agents, auctioneers and surveyors, 1948–59. Fellow, Chartered Auctioneers' and Estate Agents' Inst., 1948–59. Pres., Johnson Soc., 1980. FRSL, FRGS. Hon. DLitt Leicester, 1996. Heinemann Award for Literature, 1962; McColvin Medal, LA, 1989. *Publications*: The Road to Tyburn, 1957; King Mob, 1958; Wolfe at Quebec, 1959; The Destruction of Lord Raglan, 1961; Corunna, 1961; Benito Mussolini, 1962; The Battle of Arnhem, 1962; The Roots of Evil, 1963; The Court at Windsor, 1964; Agincourt, 1964; (ed) The Wheatley Diary, 1964; Garibaldi and His Enemies, 1965; The Making of Charles Dickens, 1967; (ed) Waterloo: Napoleon's Last Campaign, 1967; (ed) An American in Regency England: The Journal of Louis Simond, 1968; Charles I, 1968; The Grand Tour, 1969; London: Biography of a City, 1969; The Search for King Arthur, 1970; (ed) The Recollections of Rifleman Harris, 1970; Anzio: the bid for Rome, 1970; The Dragon Wakes: China and the West, 1793–1911, 1970; The Personal History of Samuel Johnson, 1971; (ed) Twilight of Princes, 1971; George IV, Prince of Wales, 1762–1811, 1972; George IV, Regent and King, 1812–1830, 1973; The Rise and Fall of the House of Medici, 1974; (ed) A Soldier of the Seventy-First, 1975; Edward VII: a portrait, 1976; The Great Mutiny: India 1857, 1978; Disraeli and His World, 1978; The Court of St James's, 1979; (ed) Boswell's Life of Johnson, 1979; The French Revolution, 1981; (ed) Greville's England, 1981; Africa Explored: Europeans in the Dark Continent, 1769–1889, 1982; (ed with Ben Weinreb) The London Encyclopaedia, 1983; Queen Victoria in Her Letters and Journals, 1984; Rome, Biography of a City, 1985; Cities and Civilizations, 1986; The English: A Social History 1066–1945, 1987; A Guide to Royal London, 1987; The Grand Tour, 1987;

London's Churches, 1988; (ed) The Encyclopaedia of Oxford, 1988; Venice: biography of a city, 1988; Redcoats and Rebels: the war for America 1770–1781, 1990; The Virgin Queen: the personal history of Elizabeth I, 1990; (ed) Captain Gronow: his reminiscences of Regency and Victorian Life 1810–60, 1991; The Story of England, 1992; Cavaliers and Roundheads: the English at war 1642–1649, 1993; Florence: biography of a city, 1993; Nelson: a personal history, 1994; No Ordinary Place: Radley College and the public school system, 1997; Wellington: a personal history, 1997; George III: a personal history, 1998; Queen Victoria: a personal history, 2000; The Marlboroughs: John and Sarah Churchill 1650–1744, 2001; Napoleon: his wives and women, 2002; Disraeli: a personal history, 2004. *Recreations:* gardening, travel, cooking, crosswords. *Address:* 6 Albion Place, West Street, Henley-on-Thames, Oxon RG9 2DT. *Club:* Army and Navy.   *Died 21 Dec. 2008.*

HICKLING, Rev. Canon Colin John Anderson; Canon Theologian, Leicester Cathedral, 1982–96, Canon Emeritus, since 1998; Hon. Lecturer in Biblical Studies, University of Sheffield, since 1986; *b* 10 July 1931; *s* of late Charles Frederick Hickling, CMG, ScD, and Marjorie Ellerington, *d* of Henry Blamey. *Educ:* Taunton Sch.; Epsom Coll.; King's Coll., Cambridge (BA 1953, MA 1957); Chichester Theol Coll. Deacon 1957, priest 1958; Asst Curate, St Luke's, Pallion, Sunderland, 1957–61; Asst Tutor, Chichester Theol Coll., 1961–65; Asst Priest Vicar, Chichester Cath., 1964–65; Asst Lectr in New Testament Studies, King's Coll., Univ. of London, 1965–68, Lectr, 1968–84; Dep. Minor Canon, St Paul's Cath., 1969–78; Hon. Asst Priest, St John's, E Dulwich, 1970–84; Dep. Priest in Ordinary to the Queen, 1971–74; Priest in Ordinary to the Queen, 1974–84; Subwarden of King's Coll. Hall, 1969–78; Warden of King's Coll. Hostel, 1978–81; Tutor in Biblical Studies, Queen's Coll., Birmingham, 1984–85; E. W. Benson Fellow, Lincoln Theol Coll., 1985–86; Vicar of All Saints, Arksey, Sheffield, 1986–98; Hon. Asst Priest, St Mary's, Sprotbrough, 1999–2004. Mem., Liturgical Commn, 1981–86. Boyle Lectr, 1973–76; Select Preacher: Univ. of Cambridge, 1979; Univ. of Oxford, 1983. *Publications:* contributed to: Church without Walls, 1968; Catholic Anglicans Today, 1968; Bible Bibliography 1967–73, 1974; (also ed jtly) What About the New Testament?, 1975; St Paul: Teacher and Traveller, 1975; L'Evangile de Jean, 1977; Les Actes des Apôtres, 1979; The Ministry of the Word, 1979; This is the Word of the Lord, 1980; Studia Biblica 1978, Vol. III, 1980; Logia: the sayings of Jesus, 1982; Studia Evangelica, Vol. VII, 1982; A Dictionary of Biblical Interpretation, 1990; The Bible in Three Dimensions, 1990; Memorial Volume for J. Anastasiou, 1992; Resurrection, 1994; The Corinthian Correspondence, 1996; reviews and articles. *Recreation:* music. *Address:* The College of St Barnabas, Blackberry Lane, Lingfield, Surrey RH7 6NJ. *T:* (01342) 871649.   *Died 19 Nov. 2007.*

HICKLING, Reginald Hugh, CMG 1968; QC (Gibraltar) 1970; PhD; *b* 2 Aug. 1920; *er s* of late Frederick Hugh Hickling and Elsie May Hickling, Malvern, Worcs; *m* 1945, Beryl Iris (*née* Dennett); two *s* one *d* (and one *s* decd). *Educ:* Buxton Coll.; Nottingham Univ.; PhD London. RNVR, 1941–46. Dep. Solicitor, Evening Standard, London, 1946–50; Asst Attorney-Gen., Sarawak, 1950–55; Legal Adviser, Johore, 1956; Legal Draftsman, Malaya, 1957; Parly Draftsman, Malaya, 1959; Comr of Law Revision, Malaya, 1961; Commonwealth Office, 1964; Legal Adviser to High Comr, Aden and Protectorate of S Arabia, 1964–67; Maritime Law Adviser: Thailand, 1968–69; Malaysia, 1969; Sri Lanka, 1970; Yemen Arab Republic, 1984, 1986; Attorney-General, Gibraltar, 1970–72. Lectr in SE Asian Law, SOAS, 1976–78, 1981–82; Visiting Professor, Faculty of Law: Univ. of Singapore, 1974–76 and 1978–80; Univ. of Malaya, 1983–84, 1986–88; Nat. Univ. of Malaysia, 1988–94; Adjunct Professor of Law: Charles Darwin Univ. (formerly Northern Territory

Univ.), 1995–; Universiti Kebangsaan Malaysia, 2004–06. Advr on consumer law, Fiji, 1990, 1992, on legislative drafting, Fiji, 1996, 1998. Hon. JMN (Malaya), 1960. *Publications:* The Furious Evangelist, 1950; The English Flotilla, 1954 (US as Falconer's Voyage, 1956); Sarawak and Its Government, 1955; Festival of Hungry Ghosts, 1957; (ed) Malayan Constitutional Documents, 1958; An Introduction to the Federal Constitution, 1960; Lieutenant Okino, 1968; A Prince of Borneo, 1985; The Ghost of Orchard Road and other stories, 1985; Malaysian Law, 1987, 2nd edn 2001; Essays in Malaysian Law, 1991; Essays in Singapore Law, 1992; So Lucky and Other Stories, 1992; The Dog Satyricon, 1994; Finding Hobbes, 1994; (with Min Aun Wu) Conflict of Laws in Malaysia, 1995; Malaysian Public Law, 1997, 2nd edn 2003; The Lotus-eaters, 1997; Ikhlas in England, 2000; Memoir of a Wayward Lawyer, 2000; Waltzing Mice, 2003. *Recreation:* not watching TV. *Address:* 40 St Peter's Road, Malvern, Worcs WR14 1QS. *T:* (01684) 573477.   *Died 11 Feb. 2007.*

HICKOX, Richard Sidney, CBE 2002; FRCO(CHM); conductor; Music Director: City of London Sinfonia, since 1971; City of London Sinfonia (formerly Richard Hickox) Singers, since 1971; London Symphony Chorus, since 1976; Opera Australia, since 2005; Associate Conductor, London Symphony Orchestra, since 1985; *b* Stokenchurch, Bucks, 5 March 1948; *m* 1976, Frances Ina Sheldon-Williams (marr. diss.); one *s*; *m* 1995, Pamela Helen Stephen; one *s* one *d*. *Educ:* in organ, piano and composition, Royal Acad. of Music (LRAM); Queens' Coll., Cambridge (Organ Scholar; MA; Hon. Fellow, 1996). Début as professional conductor, St John's Smith Square, 1971; Organist and Master of the Music, St Margaret's, Westminster, 1972–82; Prom début, 1973; Principal Conductor, BBC Nat. Orch. of Wales, 2000–06, subseq. Conductor Emeritus. Artistic Director: Wooburn Fest., 1967–89; St Endellion Fest., 1974–; Christ Church Spitalfields Fest., 1978–94; Truro Fest., 1981–; Chester Summer Fest., 1989–; Northern Sinfonia, 1982–90 (Conductor Emeritus, 1996–); City of London Fest., 1994; Music Dir, Bradford Festival Choral Soc., 1978–98; Principal Guest Conductor: Dutch Radio Orch., 1980–84; Associate Conductor, San Diego Symphony Orch., 1983–84; also regularly conducts Philharmonia, RPO, Bournemouth Symphony Orch. and Sinfonietta, Royal Liverpool Phil. Orch., BBC Symphony, Concert, Scottish and Welsh Orchs, BBC Singers, Hallé Orch.; San Francisco Symphony Orch.; Detroit Symphony Orch.; Houston Symphony Orch.; National Symphony Orch., Washington; Rotterdam Philharmonic; Oslo Philharmonic; Turku Philharmonia; Salzburg Mozarteum; Suisse Romande; Stockholm Philharmonic. Conducted: ENO, 1979, 1996, 2000; Opera North, 1982, 1986, 1995; Scottish Opera, 1985, 1987; Royal Opera, 1985, 1999, 2001; appeared at many music festivals incl. Proms, Flanders, Bath and Cheltenham. Co-founder, Opera Stage, 1985. Many recordings of choral and orchestral music. *Address:* c/o Intermusica Artists' Management, 16 Duncan Terrace, N1 8BZ.   *Died 23 Nov. 2008.*

HICKS, Maj.-Gen. (William) Michael (Ellis), CB 1982; OBE 1967; Secretary, Royal College of Defence Studies, 1983–93; *b* 2 June 1928; *s* of late George Capt William Charles Hicks, AFC, and Nellie Kilbourne (*née* Kay); *m* 1950, Jean Hilary Duncan; three *s*. *Educ:* Eton Coll.; RMA Sandhurst. Commnd 2 Lieut Coldstream Guards, 1948; served, 1948–67: regtl service, UK, Tripoli and Canal Zone; Instr. Sch. of Inf. (Captain); Staff Coll. (Major); GSO2 (Ops) HQ 4 Div.; regtl service, BAOR, UK and Kenya; JSSC; GSO (DS) Staff Coll.; GSO1 MO1, MoD, 1967–70 (Lt-Col); CO 1st Bn Coldstream Guards, 1970–72; RCDS, 1973 (Col); comd 4th Guards Armoured Bde, 1974–76 (Brig.); BGS Trng HQ UKLF, 1977–79; BGS (Author) attached to DMO, MoD, 1979; GOC NW Dist, 1980–83, retd. *Recreation:* gardening. *Address:* c/o Lloyds TSB, Cox's & King's, PO Box 1190, 7 Pall Mall, SW1Y 5NA.   *Died 27 Dec. 2008.*

HIGGINBOTTOM, Donald Noble; HM Diplomatic Service, retired; Counsellor, Foreign and Commonwealth Office, 1976–79; *b* 19 Dec. 1925; *s* of late Harold Higginbottom and Dorothy (*née* Needham); *m* 1950, Sarah Godwin. *Educ:* Calday Grange Grammar Sch., Cheshire; King's Coll., Cambridge (1st Cl. Hons Hist.); Yale Univ., USA (MA Hist.). Lectr in Humanities, Univ. of Chicago, 1951. Entered Foreign Office, 1953; Buenos Aires, 1955; Peking, 1958; Saigon, 1960; Phnom Penh, 1962; Singapore, 1964; Bangkok, 1971; Buenos Aires, 1974. *Recreations:* electronic clocks, power boating. *Address:* Apartado 54, 12580 Benicarló, Castellón, Spain. *Club:* Yacht Club Olivos (Buenos Aires). *Died 11 Jan. 2006.*

HIGGINS, Prof. Peter Matthew, OBE 1987; Bernard Sunley Professor and Chairman of Department of General Practice, United Medical Schools of Guy's and St Thomas' Hospitals (formerly Guy's Hospital Medical School), University of London, 1974–88, then Emeritus Professor; *b* 18 June 1923; *s* of Peter Joseph Higgins and Margaret Higgins; *m* 1952, Jean Margaret Lindsay Currie; three *s* one *d. Educ:* St Ignatius' Coll., London; UCH, London. MB, BS; FRCP, FRCGP. House Phys., Medical Unit, UCH, 1947; RAMC, 1948–49; House Phys , UCH, St Pancras, 1950; Resident MO, UCH, 1951–52; Asst Med. Registrar, UCH, 1953. Gen. Practice, Rugeley, Staffs, 1954–66, and Castle Vale, Birmingham, 1966–68; Sen. Lectr, Guy's Hosp. Med. Sch., 1968–74. Regl Advr in General Practice, SE Thames, 1970–88; Vice-Chm., SE Thames RHA, 1976–92; Chm., Kent FHSA, 1990–92. Mem., Attendance Allowance Bd, 1971–74; Chairman: Inquiry into A&E Dept, KCH, 1992; Review of Arrangements for Emergency Admissions, Ealing Hosp., 1994. Mem., National Council, 1985–95; Nat. Exec. Cttee, 1991–95, Family Service Units. Vice Chm. Governors, Linacre Centre for the Study of Medical Ethics, 1983–86; Mem. Court, Kent Univ., 1984–98. Hon. DSc Greenwich, 1998. *Publications:* articles in Lancet, BMJ, Jl RCGP, Epidemiology and Infection, British Jl of Psychiatry. *Address:* Wallings, Heathfield Lane, Chislehurst, Kent BR7 6AH. *T:* (020) 8467 2756. *Died 10 June 2010.*

HIGGINS, Rear-Adm. William Alleyne, CB 1985; CBE 1980; *b* 18 May 1928; *s* of Comdr H. G. Higgins, DSO, RN, and Mrs L. A. Higgins; *m* 1963, Wiltraud Hiebaum; two *s* one *d. Educ:* Wellington College. Joined Royal Navy, 1945; Commander 1965; Captain 1973; Commodore, HMS Drake, 1980–82; Flag Officer Medway and Port Adm. Chatham, 1982–83; Dir. Gen. Naval Personal Services, 1983–86; Chief Naval Supply and Secretariat Officer, 1986–92. Sec., Defence, Press and Broadcasting Cttee, 1986–92. *Recreations:* ski-ing, mountaineering, Austin Sevening. *Club:* Royal Naval and Royal Marines Mountaineering. *Died 20 Jan. 2007.*

HIGGS, Sir Derek (Alan), Kt 2004; FCA; Chairman: Partnerships UK plc, 2000–07; Alliance & Leicester plc, since 2005; *b* 3 April 1944; *s* of Alan Edward Higgs and Freda Gwendoline Higgs (*née* Hope); *m* 1970, Julia Mary Arguile; two *s* one *d. Educ:* Solihull Sch.; Univ. of Bristol (BA 1965). FCA 1978. Chartered Accountant, Price Waterhouse & Co., 1965–69; Corp. Finance Exec., Baring Brothers & Co., Ltd, 1969–72; S. G. Warburg & Co. Ltd: Corp. Finance Exec., 1972–86; Head of Corp. Finance, 1986–94; Chm., 1994–96; Chm., Prudential Portfolio Managers Ltd, 1996–2000. Chairman: Bramdean Asset Mgt LLP, 2004–; Gleacher Shacklock LLP, 2008–; Director: S. G. Warburg Gp plc, 1987–96; Prudential Corp. plc, 1996–2000; Jones Lang LaSalle Inc., 1999–; London Regl Transport, 1999–2003; Egg plc, 2000–05; The British Land Co. PLC, 2000–06 (Dep. Chm., 2001–06); Allied Irish Banks plc, 2000–05. Sen. Advr in the UK, UBS Warburg, subseq. UBS Investment Bank, 2001–05. Dep. Chm., BITC, 1999–2006; Chm., Business in the Envmt, 1999–2004. Member: Adv. Cttee on Business and the Envmt, 1993–99; Financial Reporting Council, 1996–2004; Adv. Council, Envmtl Change Inst., 2000–05; FTSE4Good Adv. Cttee,

2001–03; Dep. Chm., Fund Managers Assoc., 1998–2000. Hd, Inquiry into Role and Effectiveness of Non-executive Directors, 2002–03. Dir, Coventry City Football Club (Hldgs) Ltd, 1996–2008. Dep. Chm., City Arts Trust, 1995–2001 (Dir, 1995–2001). Mem. Council, 1994–97, Pro-Chancellor, 2002–, Univ. of Bristol. Trustee: Alan Edward Higgs Charity, 1979–; Textile Conservation Centre Foundn, 1979–; Architecture Foundn, 1998–2002; Scott Trust, 2008–. CCMI; FRSA 1992. Hon. LLD Bristol, 2005. *Address:* 2C Melbury Road, W14 8LP. *T:* (020) 7603 7874. *Club:* Royal Thames Yacht. *Died 28 April 2008.*

HIGHAM, Rear-Adm. Philip Roger Canning, CB 1972; Keeper, HMS Belfast, Imperial War Museum, 1978–83 (Director, HMS Belfast Trust, 1973–78); *b* 9 June 1920; *s* of Edward Higham, Stoke Bishop, Bristol; *m* 1942, Pamela Bracton Edwards (*d* 2001), *er d* of Gerald Edwards, Southport, Lancs; two *s. Educ:* RNC Dartmouth. Cadet, 1937; Midshipman, 1938; Sub-Lt 1940; Lieut 1942; qual. Gunnery Officer, 1944; Second Gunnery Off., HMS Vanguard, Royal Tour of S Africa, 1947; psc 1948; Exper. Dept, HMS Excellent, 1951–52; Comdr, Devonport Gunnery Sch., 1953; Trials Comdr, RAE Aberporth, 1954–55; jssc 1956; Exper. Comdr, HMS Excellent, 1957–59; Admty (DTWP), 1960–61; Naval Attaché, Middle East, 1962–64; idc 1965; Dep. Chief Polaris Exec., 1966–68; Cdre i/c Hong Kong, 1968–70; Asst Chief of Naval Staff (Op. Requirements), 1970–72; retired list 1973. Trustee, Portsmouth Naval Base Property Trust, 1985–92. *Address:* 1 John King Shipyard, King Street, Emsworth, Hants PO10 7AY. *T:* (01243) 372195. *Died 22 June 2006.*

HIGMAN, Prof. Graham, DPhil; FRS 1958; Waynflete Professor of Pure Mathematics, Oxford University, and Fellow of Magdalen College, Oxford, 1960–84, then Professor Emeritus; *b* 19 Jan. 1917; 2nd *s* of Rev. Joseph Higman; *m* 1941, Ivah May Treleaven (*d* 1981); five *s* one *d. Educ:* Sutton Secondary Sch., Plymouth; Balliol Coll., Oxford (MA; Hon. Fellow 1984). Meteorological Office, 1940–46; Lecturer, University of Manchester, 1946–55; Reader in Mathematics at Oxford Univ., 1955–60; Senior Research Fellow, Balliol Coll., Oxford, 1958–60. George A. Miller Vis. Prof., Univ. of Illinois, 1984–86. Hon. DSc: Exeter, 1979; NUI, 1992. De Morgan Medal, London Mathematical Soc., 1974; Sylvester Medal, Royal Soc., 1979. *Publications:* papers in Proc. London Math. Soc., and other technical jls. *Died 8 April 2008.*

HILL, George Raymond, FCA, FCIT, FIH; Director, Ashford International Hotel PLC, 1987–99; *b* 25 Sept. 1925; *s* of George Mark and Jill Hill; *m* 1948, Sophie (*née* Gilbert); two *d. Educ:* St Dunstan's Coll., London. Royal Marines, 1943–46 (Lieut). Distillers Co. Ltd (Industrial Group), 1952–66; BP Chemicals Ltd, 1967–69; British Transport Hotels Ltd: Chief Exec., 1970–76; Chm., 1974–76; Dir, Bass PLC, 1976–84 (Mem. Exec. Cttee); Chm., Bass UK Ltd, 1978–80; Chairman: Howard Machinery PLC (later H. M. Holdings PLC), 1984–85; Sims Catering Butchers plc, 1985–87; Director: Prince of Wales Hotels PLC, 1985–86; Chester Internat. Hotel, 1987–92; Regal Hotel Gp, 1989–92 (non-exec. Chm.). Member Boards: British Railways (Scottish), and British Rail Hovercraft Ltd, 1972–76; British Tourist Auth., 1981–89 (Chm., Marketing Cttee, 1985–89); Chairman: Liquor Licensing Working Party, 1985–; Channel Tunnel Nat. Tourism Working Pty, 1986–89. Member: Hotel and Catering Industry Trng Bd, 1973–80; Civil Service Final Selection Bd, 1973–80; Cttee of Inquiry on Motorway Service Areas, 1978; BHRCA (Bd Chm., 1979–80; Nat. Council Chm., 1985–86; Fellow, BHA); Pres., Licensed Victuallers Schs, 1982–83. Mem., HAC. FRSA 1980. *Publications:* Figuring For Fun: a ladder of opportunity, 1999. *Recreations:* music, theatre, works of art, country life. *Address:* 23 Sheffield Terrace, W8 7NQ. *Died 22 March 2008.*

HILL, Rt Rev. Henry Gordon; Co-Chairman, Anglican-Orthodox Joint Doctrinal Commission, 1980–90; *b* 14 Dec. 1921; *s* of Henry Knox Hill and

Kathleen Elizabeth (*née* Cunningham); unmarried. *Educ:* Queen's Univ., Kingston, Ont. (BA 1945); Trinity Coll., Toronto (LTh 1948); St John's Coll., Cambridge (MA 1952). Deacon, Dio. Ont., 1948; Priest (Bp of Ely for Ontario), 1949; Curate, Belleville, Ont., 1950; Rector of Adolphustown, Ont., 1951; Chaplain, St John's Coll., Cambridge, Eng., 1952; Curate, Wisbech, Cambs, 1955; Rector, St Thomas, Reddendale, Ont., 1957; Asst Prof., Canterbury Coll., Assumption Univ., Windsor, 1962–68 (Vice-Principal, 1965–68); Associate Prof. of History, Univ. of Windsor, Ont., 1968–74; Bishop of Ontario, 1975–81; Asst Bishop of Montreal, 1981–83. Warden, Sisters of St John the Divine, 1978–88; Vice-Pres., Fellowship of St Alban and St Sergius, 1980. Episcopal Consultant for the Eastern and Oriental Orthodox Churches, Lambeth Conf., 1988; formerly on staff of Primate of Canada, episcopal liaison with non-Chalcedonian orthodox church; estabd Scholarship of St Basil the Great, 1995 (for student exchanges between Anglican Ch of Canada, Oriental Orthodox Chs and Ch of the East). Hon. DD: Trinity Coll., Toronto, 1976; Montreal Dio. Theol Coll., 1976; Hon. LLD Univ. of Windsor, 1976; Hon. Dr, Theological Inst., Bucharest, 1977. KLJ 1980. Patriarchal Cross of Romanian Orthodox Church, 1969. *Publications:* Contemplation and Ecumenism (Monastic Studies No 15), 1984; Light Out of the East: chapters on the life and worship of the ancient orthodox churches, 1988; Engolpion, HH Ignatius Zakka Ivas, Syrian Orthodox Patriarch of Damascus, 1988; (ed and contrib.) Light from the East, 1988; (contrib.) Dictionary of the Ecumenical Movement, 1991; articles in Cdn Jl of Theology, Sobornost, Jl Fellowship of St Alban and St Sergius. *Recreations:* walking, reading. *Address:* St John's Convent, 233 Cummer Avenue, ON M2M 2E8, Canada.   *Died 21 Dec. 2006.*

HILL, Ian Macdonald, MS, FRCS; Consulting Cardiothoracic Surgeon, St Bartholomew's Hospital, since 1984 (Consultant Cardio-thoracic Surgeon, 1950–84); Hon. Consultant Thoracic Surgeon, SE Thames Regional Health Authority, since 1984 (Consultant Thoracic Surgeon, 1950–84); *b* 8 June 1919; British; *m* 1944, Agnes Mary Paice; three *s* one *d*. *Educ:* Stationers' Company Sch.; St Bartholomew's Hosp. Medical Coll. Undergrad. schols and medals, 1937–41; MB, BS (Hons) London, 1942; MRCS, LRCP 1942; FRCS 1944; MS London 1945. Demonstrator of Anatomy, St Bartholomew's, 1943; Surgical Chief Asst, St Bart's Hosp., 1944; RAF Medical Branch, 1946; Wing Comdr i/c Surg. Div. No 1 RAF Gen. Hosp., 1947; Senior Registrar, Thoracic Surg. Unit, Guy's Hosp., 1948; Surgical Chief Asst, Brompton Hosp. and Inst. of Diseases of the Chest, 1950. Sub-Dean, St Bart's Hosp. Med. Coll., 1964–73. FRSocMed. Member: Soc. of Apothecaries; Soc. of Thoracic Surgeons; Thoracic and Cardiac Socs. Governor, St Bartholomew's Hosp. Med. Coll., 1985–97. Freeman of City of London. *Publications:* articles in professional jls, mainly relating to lung and cardiac surgery, 1942–61. *Recreations:* old cars, furniture, keyboard instruments; gardening and house care. *Address:* Bracken Wood, Church Lane, Fernham, Faringdon, Oxon SN7 7PB. *T:* (01367) 820475.
                                        Died 22 Sept. 2007.

HILL, Brig. James; see Hill, Brig. S. J. L.

HILL, John Edward Bernard; farming in Suffolk since 1946; *b* 13 Nov. 1912; *o s* of late Capt. Robert William Hill, Cambs Regt, and Marjorie Jane Lloyd-Jones, *d* of Edward Scott-Miller; *m* 1944, Edith Luard (*d* 1995), *widow* of Comdr R. A. E. Luard, RNVR, and 5th *d* of late John Maxwell, Cove, Dunbartonshire; one adopted *d*. *Educ:* Charterhouse; Merton Coll., Oxford (MA). Various journeys; Middle East, Far East, India, USA, 1935–37; Far East, 1956–57; USA, 1958. Called to Bar, Inner Temple (Certificate of Honour), 1938. RA (TA), 1939; Air Observation Post Pilot, 1942; War Office, 1942; 651 (Air OP) RAF, Tunisia, 1942; wounded, 1943; invalided out, 1945. MP (C) South Norfolk, Jan. 1955–Feb. 1974; Mem. Parliamentary delegns: W

Germany and Berlin, 1959; Ghana, 1965; IPU Conf., Teheran, 1966; CPA Conf., Uganda, 1967; Bulgaria, 1970; Council of Europe and WEU, 1970–72; Mem., European Parlt, 1973–74; Chm., Cons. Educn Cttee, 1971–73; Member: Select Cttee on Agriculture, 1967–69; Select Cttee on Procedure, 1970–71; Asst Govt Whip, 1959–60; a Lord Comr of the Treasury, 1960–64. Mem. East Suffolk and Norfolk River Board, 1952–62. Mem. Exec. Cttee, CLA, 1957–59, 1977–82. Member: Governing Body, Charterhouse Sch., 1958–90; Langley Sch., Norfolk, 1962–77; Governing Body, Sutton's Hosp., Charterhouse, 1966–97; GBA Cttee, 1966–79, 1980–83; Council, Univ. of East Anglia, 1975–82. *Publications:* Better Late Than Never? an illustrated diary of 1935, 2002; Indian Spring: a diary of a visit to Bengal in 1937, 2005. *Recreations:* Association football, cricket, concerts, picture galleries. *Clubs:* Garrick, Farmers'.
                                        Died 6 Dec. 2007.

HILL, Sir John McGregor, Kt 1969; BSc, PhD; FRS 1981; FREng, FInstP, FInstE; Chairman: Rea Brothers Group, 1987–95; British Nuclear Fuels PLC, 1971–83; Amersham International PLC, 1975–88; Aurora Holdings PLC, 1984–88; *b* 21 Feb. 1921; *s* of late John Campbell Hill and Margaret Elizabeth Park; *m* 1947, Nora Eileen Hellett; two *s* one *d*. *Educ:* King's Coll., London; St John's Coll., Cambridge. Flt Lieut, RAF, 1941. Cavendish Laboratory, Cambridge, 1946; Lecturer, London Univ., 1948. Joined UKAEA, 1950, Mem. for Production, 1964–67, Chm., 1967–81. Member: Advisory Council on Technology, 1968–70; Nuclear Power Adv. Bd, 1973–81; Energy Commn, 1977–79. Pres., British Nuclear Forum, 1984–92. FREng (FEng 1982). Hon. FIChemE 1977; Hon. FIET (Hon. FIEE 1981); Foreign Associate, US Nat. Acad. of Engineering, 1976. Hon. DSc Bradford, 1981. Melchett Medal, Inst. of Energy, 1974; Sylvanus Thompson Medal, Inst. of Radiology, 1978. *Recreation:* golf. *Address:* Dominic House, Sudbrook Lane, Richmond, Surrey TW10 7AT. *T:* (020) 8940 7221. *Club:* East India.   *Died 14 Jan. 2008.*

HILL, Brig. (Stanley) James (Ledger), DSO 1942, and Bars, 1944, 1945; MC 1940; Vice-Chairman, Powell Duffryn Ltd, 1970–76 (Director, 1961–76); Chairman, Pauls & Whites Ltd, 1973–76 (Director, since 1970); Director: Lloyds Bank, 1972–79; Lloyds Bank UK Management Committee Ltd, 1979–81; *b* 14 March 1911; *s* of late Maj.-Gen. Walter Pitts Hendy Hill, CB, CMG, DSO, West Amesbury House, Wilts; *m* 1st, 1937, Denys, *d* of late E. Hubert Gunter-Jones, MC, JP, Gloucester House, Ledbury; one *d*; 2nd, 1986, Joan Patricia Haywood. *Educ:* Marlborough; RMC Sandhurst (Sword of Honour). 2nd Bn, Royal Fusiliers, 1931–35; 2nd Bn, RF, BEF, 1939; DAAG, GHQ, BEF, 1940; comd 1st Bn, Parachute Regt, N Africa landing, 1942; comd 3rd Parachute Bde, 1943–45; took part in Normandy and Rhine crossing (wounded thrice); comdr 4th Parachute Bde (TA), 1947–48. Apptd to Bd of Associated Coal & Wharf Cos Ltd, 1948; Pres., Powell Duffryn Group of Cos in Canada, 1952–58. Legion of Honour (France), 1942 (Grand Officier, 2000); Silver Star (USA), 1945; King Haakon VII Liberty Cross (Norway), 1945. *Recreation:* birdwatching. *Address:* Hidden House, Guilden Road, Chichester PO19 7LA. *T:* (01243) 789083. *Clubs:* Army and Navy; Island Sailing (IoW).
                                        Died 16 March 2006.

HILL-SMITH, His Honour Derek Edward, VRD 1958; FCIArb; a Circuit Judge, 1972–87, a Deputy Circuit Judge, 1987–96; *b* 21 Oct. 1922; *s* of Charles Hill-Smith and Ivy (*née* Downs); *m* 1950, Marjorie Joanna, *d* of His Honour Montague Berryman, QC; one *s* one *d*. *Educ:* Sherborne; Trinity Coll., Oxford (MA). RNVR, 1942–46; Lt-Comdr RNR. Trinity Coll., Oxford, 1941–42 and 1946–47 (MA, Classics and Modern Greats); BEA, 1947–48; business, 1948–50; teaching, 1950–54; called to Bar, Inner Temple, 1954; Dep. Chm., Kent QS, 1970; Recorder, 1972. Chm., Mental Health Review Tribunals, 1987–95. FCIArb 1994 (ACIArb 1993). *Publications:* contrib. Law Guardian. *Recreations:* the theatre, food and wine, collecting and restoring Old Masters and New Mistresses, the study of mediaeval church frescoes in Cyprus and Asia Minor. *Address:* c/o National Westminster Bank, North Street, Bishop's Stortford, Herts. *Club:* Garrick.   *Died 21 Oct. 2006.*

HILLARY, Sir Edmund (Percival), KG 1995; ONZ 1987; KBE 1953; author; lecturer; mountaineer; *b* 20 July 1919; *s* of Percival Augustus Hillary and Gertrude Hillary (*née* Clark); *m* 1st, 1953, Louise Mary Rose (*d* 1975), *d* of J. H. Rose; one *s* one *d* (and one *d* decd); 2nd, 1989, June Mulgrew, *widow* of Peter Mulgrew. *Educ:* Auckland Grammar Sch., Auckland, New Zealand. Apiarist, 1936–43. RNZAF, navigator on Catalina flying boats in Pacific Area, 1944–45. Apiarist (in partnership with brother W. F. Hillary), 1951–70. NZ High Comr to India, Nepal and Bangladesh, 1985–88. Himalayan Expeditions: NZ Gawhal Expedition, 1951; British Everest Reconnaissance, 1951; British Cho Oyu Expedition, 1952; Everest Expedition, 1953; with Sherpa Tenzing reached summit of Mount Everest, May 1953 (KBE). Leader of NZ Alpine Club Expedition to Barun Valley, East of Everest, 1954. Appointed, 1955, leader of New Zealand Transantarctic Expedition; completed overland journey to South Pole, Jan. 1958. Expeditions in Everest region, 1960–61, 1963, 1964, 1965, 1981; led expedition to Antarctic for geological and mountaineering purposes incl. first ascent of Mt Herschel, 1967; expedition to E Nepal (explored Himalayan rivers with two jet boats; first ascent of 180 miles of Sun Kosi river from Indian border to Katmandu), 1968; jet boat expedition up the Ganges, 1977. Built first hosp. for Sherpas in Everest area, with public subscription and NZ doctor, 1966; latterly Everest region had 25 schools, 2 hosps, 12 med. clinics, bridges, difficult access paths, fresh water pipelines; also re-afforestation prog. in Sagarmatha (Everest) Nat. Park. Internat. Dir, WWF; UNICEF Special Rep., Children of the Himalayas, 1991–. Consultant to Sears Roebuck & Co., Chicago, on camping and outdoor equipment. Hon. LLD: Univ. of Victoria, BC, Canada, 1969; Victoria Univ., Wellington, NZ, 1970. Hubbard Medal (US), 1954; Star of Nepal 1st Class; US Gold Cullum Geographical Medal, 1954; Founder's Gold Medal, Royal Geographical Society, 1958; Polar Medal, 1958. *Publications:* High Adventure, 1955; East of Everest, 1956 (with George Lowe); The Crossing of Antarctica, 1958 (with Sir Vivian Fuchs); No Latitude for Error, 1961; High in the Thin Cold Air, 1963 (with Desmond Doig); School House in the Clouds, 1965; Nothing Venture, Nothing Win (autobiog.), 1975; From the Ocean to the Sky: jet boating up the Ganges, 1979; (with Peter Hillary) Two Generations, 1983; Sagarmatha; View From the Summit (autobiog.), 1999. *Recreations:* mountaineering, ski-ing, camping. *Address:* 278A Remuera Road, Auckland 5, New Zealand. *Clubs:* New Zealand Alpine (Hon. Mem.; Pres. 1965–67); Explorers (New York) (Hon. Pres); Hon. Mem. of many other NZ and US clubs.   *Died 11 Jan. 2008.*

HILLERY, Dr Patrick John; Uachtarán na hÉireann (President of Ireland), 1976–90; *b* Miltown Malbay, Co. Clare, 2 May 1923; *s* of Dr Michael Joseph Hillery and Ellen (*née* McMahon); *m* 1955, Dr Mary Beatrice Finnegan; one *s* (one *d* decd). *Educ:* Miltown Malbay National Sch.; Rockwell Coll.; University Coll., Dublin. BSc; MB BCh, BAO, DPH. Mem. Health Council, 1955–57; MO, Miltown Malbay, 1957–59; Coroner for West Clare, 1958–59; TD (Mem. Dáil Eireann), Clare, 1951–73; Minister: for Educn, 1959–65; for Industry and Commerce, 1965–66; for Labour, 1966–69; of Foreign Affairs, 1969–72 (negotiated Ireland's accession to European Communities); Comr for Social Affairs and a Vice-Pres., Commn of the European Communities, 1973–76. MRIA 1963; Life Fellow, Irish Management Inst., 1981. Hon. FRCSI 1977; Hon. FFDRCSI 1977; Hon. FRCPI 1978; Hon. FRCGP 1982; Hon. FFCM RCSI, 1986; Hon. Fellow: Pharmaceutical Soc. of Ireland, 1984; All-India Inst. of Medical Sciences, 1978. Hon. LLD: NUI, 1962; Univ. of Dublin, 1977; Univ. of Melbourne, 1985; Hon. DPh Pontifical Univ. of

Maynooth, 1988. Robert Schuman Gold Medal (France), 1986. Grand Cross and Grand Cordon, Order of Merit (Italy), 1986; Grand Cross of the Netherlands Lion, 1986; Grand Cross of the Legion of Honour (France), 1988; Collar of the Pian Order (Vatican State), 1989. *Address:* Grasmere, Greenfield Road, Sutton, Dublin 13, Ireland.
Died 12 April 2008.

HILLS, David Henry, CBE 1993; Director-General of Intelligence, Ministry of Defence, 1988–93; *b* 9 July 1933; *s* of Henry Stanford Hills and Marjorie Vera Lily Hills; *m* 1957, Jean Helen Nichols; one *s* two *d*. *Educ:* Varndean Sch., Brighton; Univ. of Nottingham (BA Econs). Served Army Intell. Corps, 1954–56. Entered MoD, 1956; other appointments include: NBPI, 1967–70; National Indust. Relations Court, 1971–73; Dir of Marketing, Defence Sales Orgn, MoD, 1979–82; Dir of Economic and Logistic Intell., MoD, 1982–88. *Recreations:* gardening, music.   *Died 3 Dec. 2009.*

HILTON, Rear-Adm. John Millard Thomas, FIMechE, FIET; consulting engineer; *b* 24 Dec. 1934; *s* of late Edward Thomas Hilton and Margaret Norah Attrill (*née* Millard); *m* 1st, 1958, Patricia Anne Kirby (marr. diss. 1979); one *s* one *d*; 2nd, 1985, Cynthia Mary Caroline Seddon-Brown (*née* Hargreave); one step *d*. *Educ:* Wyggeston Grammar Sch. for Boys, Leicester; County High Sch., Clacton; RNC Dartmouth; RNEC Manadon; RNC Greenwich; City Univ. (MSc 1968); Imperial Coll. of Science and Technology (DIC 1973). Joined RN 1951; various sea and shore appts, 1951–80; Dep. Chief Naval Signal Officer, MoD, London, 1980–83; Project Dir, ARE Portsdown, 1984–87; Vice-Pres. (Navy), Ordnance Bd, 1987–88, Pres., Ordnance Bd, 1988–90. Dir, Christian Engineers in Develt, 1997– (Chm., 2000–03). Non-exec. Dir, mi2g, 2004–. Hon. Sen. Vis. Fellow, Sch. of Engrg, City Univ., 1993–96. Hon. DSc City, 2000. ADC to the Queen, 1985–88. Master, 2000–01, Hon. Treas., 2001–05, Scientific Instrument Makers' Co. *Publications:* professional papers. *Recreations:* personal computing, photography, Christian discipleship, family life. *Address:* 29 Grenehurst Way, The Village, Petersfield, Hants GU31 4AZ.
Died 14 July 2009.

HILTON, Prof. Peter John, MA, DPhil Oxon, PhD Cantab; Distinguished Professor of Mathematics, State University of New York at Binghamton, 1982–93, Emeritus since 1993; *b* 7 April 1923; *s* of late Dr Mortimer Hilton and Mrs Elizabeth Hilton; *m* 1949, Margaret (*née* Mostyn); two *s*. *Educ:* St Paul's Sch.; Queen's Coll., Oxford. Asst Lectr, Manchester Univ., 1948–51, Lectr, 1951–52; Lectr, Cambridge Univ., 1952–55; Senior Lecturer, Manchester Univ., 1956–58; Mason Prof. of Pure Mathematics, University of Birmingham, 1958–62; Prof. of Mathematics, Cornell Univ., 1962–71, Univ. of Washington, 1971–73; Beaumont Univ. Prof., Case Western Reserve Univ., 1972–82. Distinguished Prof. of Maths, Univ. of Central Florida, 1994–. Visiting Professor: Cornell Univ., USA, 1958–59; Eidgenössische Techn. Hochschule, Zürich, 1966–67, 1981–82, 1988–89; Courant Inst., NY Univ., 1967–68; Univ. Aut. de Barcelona, 1989; Erskine Fellow, Univ. of Canterbury, NZ, 2001, 2002. Mahler Lectr, Australian Math. Soc., 1997. Mathematician-in-residence, Battelle Research Center, Seattle, 1970–82. Chairman: US Commn on Mathematical Instruction, 1971–74; NRC Cttee on Applied Maths Trng, 1977–; First Vice-Pres., Math. Assoc. of Amer., 1978–80. Corresp. Mem., Brazilian Acad. of Scis, 1979; Hon. Mem. Belgian Mathematical Soc., 1955. Hon. DHum N Michigan, 1977; Hon. DSc: Meml Univ. of Newfoundland, 1983; Univ. Aut. de Barcelona, 1989. Silver Medal, Univ. of Helsinki, 1975; Centenary Medal, John Carroll Univ., 1985. *Publications:* Introduction to Homotopy Theory, 1953; Differential Calculus, 1958; Homology Theory (with S. Wylie), 1960; Partial Derivatives, 1960; Homotopy Theory and Duality, 1965; (with H. B. Griffiths) Classical Mathematics, 1970; General Cohomology Theory and K- Theory, 1971;

(with U. Stammbach) Course in Homological Algebra, 1971, 2nd edn 1996; (with Y.-C. Wu) Course in Modern Algebra, 1974; (with G. Mislin and J. Roitberg) Localization of Nilpotent Groups and Spaces, 1975; (with J. Pedersen) Fear No More, 1983; Nilpotente Gruppen und Nilpotente Räume, 1984; (with J. Pedersen) Build Your Own Polyhedra, 1987; (ed) Miscellanea Mathematica, 1991; (with D. Holton and J. Pedersen) Mathematical Reflections, 1996; Mathematical Vistas, 2002; numerous research articles on algebraic topology, homological algebra and category theory in British and foreign mathematical journals. *Recreations:* travel, sport, reading, theatre, chess, bridge, broadcasting. *Address:* Department of Mathematical Sciences, State University of New York, Binghamton, NY 13902–6000, USA.
Died 6 Nov. 2010.

HIME, Martin, CBE 1987; HM Diplomatic Service, retired; *b* 18 Feb. 1928; *s* of Percy Joseph Hime and Esther Greta (*née* Howe); *m* 1st, 1960, Henrietta Fehling (marr. diss.); one *s* three *d*; 2nd, 1971, Janina Christine Majcher (*d* 2002); one *d*. *Educ:* King's Coll. Sch., Wimbledon; Trinity Hall, Cambridge (MA; Lawn Tennis blue). Served RA, 1946–48. Called to the Bar, Inner Temple, 1951; Marks and Spencer Ltd, 1952–58; joined HM Diplomatic Service, 1960; served in Tokyo, Kobe, Frankfurt and Buenos Aires, 1960–69; 2nd Sec., FCO, 1970–72; Consul, Johannesburg, 1972–74; 1st Sec. (Econ.), Pretoria, 1974–76; Asst Head, S Pacific Dept, FCO, 1976–79; Dep. High Comr in Bangladesh, 1979–82; Consul-General: Cleveland, Ohio, 1982–85; Houston, Texas, 1985–88; Personnel Assessor, FCO, 1988–93. Administrator, NHS Network, 1996–98. Mem. (C) Wandsworth BC, 2002–06. Gov., Granard Sch., Putney, 1995–2006. *Recreations:* golf, lawn tennis, books, table games. *Address:* Field House, 248 Dover House Road, Roehampton, SW15 5DA. *Clubs:* All England Lawn Tennis; Hawks (Cambridge); Royal Wimbledon Golf.
Died 7 Aug. 2010.

HINDSON, William Stanley, CMG 1962; FIMechE; engineering and metallurgical consultant, 1974–94; *b* 11 Jan. 1920; *s* of late W. A. L. Hindson, Darlington; *m* 1944, Mary Sturdy (*d* 1961); one *s* one *d*; *m* 1965, Catherine Leikine, Paris, France; one *s*. *Educ:* Darlington Grammar Sch.; Coatham Sch., Redcar; BScEng. MIMMM. With Dorman Long (Steel) Ltd, Middlesbrough, 1937–55; Metallurgical Equipment Export Co. Ltd and Indian Steelworks Construction Co. Ltd, 1956–62; Wellman Engineering Corp. Ltd, 1963–69; Cementation Co. Ltd, 1970–71; Humphreys & Glasgow, 1971–74. *Recreations:* chess, philately. *Address:* 36 Eresby House, Rutland Gate, SW7 1BG. *T:* (020) 7589 3194.
Died 8 Dec. 2006.

HINTON, Prof. Denys James, FRIBA; Chairman, Redditch New Town Development Corporation, 1978–85; *b* 12 April 1921; *s* of James and Nell Hinton; *m* 1971, Lynette Payne (*née* Pattinson); one *d*. *Educ:* Reading Sch.; Architectural Assoc. (MSc; AADip.). FRIBA. Asst, Wells Coates, 1950–52; Birmingham Sch. of Architecture: Lectr, 1952–57; Sen. Lectr, 1957–64; Dir, 1964–72; Prof. of Architecture, Univ. of Aston, 1966–81, then Emeritus. Sen. Partner, Hinton Brown Langstone, Architects, Warwick, 1960–86. Chairman: Architects Registration Council of UK, 1983–86; Fabric Adv. Cttee, St Philip's Cathedral, Birmingham, 1992–93; Pres., EC Architects' Directive Adv. Cttee, 1992–93; Vice-Pres. (formerly Vice-Chm.), Exec. Cttee, Internat. New Towns Assoc., 1980–85. *Publications:* Performance Characteristics of the Athenian Bouleterion, RIBA Athens Bursary, 1962; Great Interiors: High Victorian Period, 1967; contrib. RIBA and Architects Jl, papers on architectural education, Inst. Bulletin (worship and religious architecture), Univ. of Birmingham. *Recreations:* travel, moving house, water colours. *Address:* 7 Hill View Road, S Witham, Lincs NG33 5QW. *T:* (01572) 767572.
Died 10 Feb. 2010.

HOARE, Sir Timothy Edward Charles, 8th Bt *cr* 1784; OBE 1996; Director: Career Plan Ltd, since 1970; New Metals and Chemicals Ltd, 1968–2005; *b* 11 Nov. 1934; *s* of Sir Edward O'Bryen Hoare, 7th Bt and Nina Mary (*d* 1995), *d* of late Charles Nugent Hope-Wallace, MBE; *S* father, 1969; *m* 1969, Felicity Anne, *o d* of late Peter Boddington; one *s* twin *d*. *Educ:* Radley College; Worcester College, Oxford (MA Modern Hist.); Birkbeck Coll., London (MA Manpower Studies). FLS 1980; FZS 1982. Dir, World Vision of Britain, 1983–95. Mem., Church Assembly, 1960–70; General Synod of Church of England: Mem., 1970–2000; Mem., Standing Cttee, 1981–98; Chairman: Law of Marriage Gp, 1984–88 (report, An Honourable Estate); Clergy Conditions of Service Steering Gp, 1991–98. Member: Chadwick Commn on Church and State, 1964–70; ACCM, 1971–86; Crown Appointments Commn, 1987–92. Treas., dio. of London, 1994–2005. Deleg., WCC, Canberra, 1991. Trustee, Intercontinental Church Soc., 1975–98. Mem. Council, St John's Coll., Durham Univ., 1995–2000; Gov., Canford Sch., 1965–2003. *Publications:* (contrib.) Hope for the Church of England, 1986; (contrib.) New Dictionary of Christian Ethics and Pastoral Theology, 1995; (contrib.) Our National Life: a Christian perspective on the state of the nation, 1998. *Recreations:* the work of God in nature, and of man in art. *Heir: s* Charles James Hoare [*b* 15 March 1971; *m* 2000, Hon. Eleanor Filumena Flower, *o d* of 11th Viscount Ashbrook; one *s* one *d*]. *Address:* 10 Belitha Villas, N1 1PD. *Clubs:* National, MCC.
Died 18 Jan. 2008.

HOBDEN, Reginald Herbert, DFC 1944; HM Diplomatic Service, retired; *b* 9 Nov. 1919; *s* of William Richard and Ada Emily Hobden; *m* 1945, Gwendoline Ilma Vowles (*d* 2004); two *s* one *d*. *Educ:* Sir William Borlase's Sch., Marlow. Apptd Colonial Office, Dec. 1936. Served War of 1939–45 (despatches, DFC). Returned to Colonial Office, 1946; seconded to Dept of Technical Co-operation, 1961; First Sec., UK Commn, Malta, 1962–64; HM Diplomatic Service, Nov. 1964: CRO until April 1968; Head of British Interests Section, Canadian High Commn, Dar es Salaam, April 1968; British Acting High Comr, Dar es Salaam, July–Oct. 1968, and Counsellor, Dar es Salaam, Oct. 1968–69; Counsellor (Economic and Commercial), Islamabad, 1970–75; Inst. of Develt Studies, Sussex Univ., 1975; High Comr, Lesotho, 1976–78. Clerk in Clerk's Dept, House of Commons, 1978–84. *Recreations:* chess, bridge.
Died 12 Aug. 2008.

HOBSON, David Constable, CBE 1991; Chartered Accountant; Partner, Coopers & Lybrand, 1953–84, Senior Partner, 1975–83; *b* 1 Nov. 1922; *s* of late Charles Kenneth and Eileen Isabel Hobson; *m* 1961, Elizabeth Anne Drury; one *s* one *d*. *Educ:* Marlborough Coll.; Christ's Coll., Cambridge (Scholar). MA. ACA 1950; FCA 1958. Served War, REME, 1942–47 (Captain). Joined Cooper Brothers & Co. (later Coopers & Lybrand), 1947; Mem., Exec. Cttee, Coopers & Lybrand (International), 1973–83. Chairman: Cambrian & General Securities, 1986–89; Fleming High Income Investment Trust, 1991–93 (Dir, 1989–93); Dir, The Laird Gp, 1985–98. Inspector (for Dept of Trade), London & County Securities Group Ltd, 1974; Advr, Prime Minister's Policy Unit, 1983–86. Member: Accounting Standards Cttee, 1970–82; City Capital Markets Cttee, 1980–84; Nat. Biological Standards Bd, 1983–88; Building Socs Commn, 1986–92; Board Mem. (repr. UK and Ireland), Internat. Accounting Standards Cttee, 1980–85. Hon. Treasurer, Lister Inst., 1986–98. Member of Council: Marlborough Coll., 1967–92 (Chm., 1987–92); Francis Holland Schools, 1975–95. *Address:* Magnolia, Chiswick Mall, W4 2PR. *T:* (020) 8994 7511. *Club:* Reform.
Died 13 April 2009.

HOCKING, Philip Norman; *b* 27 Oct. 1925; *s* of late Fred Hocking, FIOB; *m* 1950, Joan Mable (marr. diss. 1970), *d* of Horace Ernest Jackson, CBE, Birmingham; three *d*. *Educ:* King Henry VIII Sch., Coventry; Birmingham Sch. of Architecture. Formerly Dir of building and devclt cos. Mem. Coventry City Council, 1955–60. Prominent Mem., Young Cons. Movement. MP (C) Coventry South, 1959–64; PPS to Minister of State, FO, 1963–64. Contested Coventry S, 1964 and 1966. Chm., Conservative Back Benchers' Housing and Local Govt Cttee, 1962–64. Life Mem., Shropshire Sheep Breeders' Soc.; show judge of sheep. *Recreations:* gardening, field sports, hunting with foot hound packs (Chm., Leadon Vale Basset Hounds, 1992–99), observing nature, researching early history of the USA. *Address:* 2A Homepiece Cottages, Snowshill, Broadway, Worcs WR12 7JX. *Died 17 Aug. 2008.*

HOCKLEY, Gen. Sir Anthony Heritage F.; *see* Farrar-Hockley.

HODDER, Prof. Bramwell William, PhD; Professor of Geography, School of Oriental and African Studies, University of London, 1970–83, then Emeritus; *b* 25 Nov. 1923; *s* of George Albert Hodder and Emily Griggs, Eastbourne; *m* 1971, Elizabeth Scruton; two step *d*; three *s* two *d* by previous marriages. *Educ:* Oldershaw, Wallasey; Oriel Coll., Oxford (MA, BLitt); PhD London. Served War, 1942–47, commissioned in Infantry (Cameronians), Lieut. Lecturer, Univ. of Malaya, Singapore, 1952–56; Lectr, then Sen. Lectr, Univ. of Ibadan, Nigeria, 1956–63; Lectr, Univ of Glasgow, 1963–64; Lectr, then Reader, Queen Mary Coll., Univ. of London, 1964–70. Chm., Commonwealth Geog. Bureau, 1968–72; Hon. Dir, 1981–82, Mem. Exec. Council, 1981–84, Internat. African Inst. Joint Hon. Pres., World Expeditionary Assoc., 1972–. *Publications:* Man in Malaya, 1959; Economic Development in the Tropics, 1968, 3rd edn 1980; (jtly) Markets in West Africa, 1969; (jtly) Africa in Transition, 1967; (jtly) Economic Geography, 1974; Africa Today, 1979; articles in various learned jls. *Recreation:* music. *Address:* 4 Ascham Road, Cambridge CB4 2BD. *T:* (01223) 301086. *Died 12 Sept. 2006.*

HODDER-WILLIAMS, Paul, OBE 1945; TD; publisher; *b* 29 Jan. 1910; *s* of late Very Rev. (Frank) Garfield Hodder Williams, OBE, sometime Dean of Manchester, and (Sarah) Myfanwy (*née* Nicholson); *m* 1936, Felicity (*d* 1986), 2nd *d* of late Rt Rev. Claude Martin Blagden, DD, sometime Bishop of Peterborough; two *s* two *d*. *Educ:* Rugby; Gonville and Caius Coll., Cambridge (MA). Joined Hodder & Stoughton Ltd, 1931; Dir, 1936, Chm., 1961–75, Consultant, 1975–93. Served with HAC (Major, 1942), 99th (London Welsh) HAA Regt RA (Lt-Col Comdg, 1942–45). *Address:* Bradbury House, Windsor End, Beaconsfield, Bucks HP9 2JW. *T:* (01494) 672609. *Died 17 June 2007.*

HODDINOTT, Prof. Alun, CBE 1983; DMus; FRNCM; Professor of Music, University College, Cardiff, 1967–87, then Emeritus (Fellow, 1983); *b* 11 Aug. 1929; *s* of Thomas Ivor Hoddinott and Gertrude Jones; *m* 1953, Beti Rhiannon Huws; one *s*. *Educ:* University Coll. of S Wales and Mon. Lecturer: Cardiff Coll. of Music and Drama, 1951–59; University Coll. of S Wales and Mon, 1959–65; Reader, University of Wales, 1965–67. Member: BBC Music Central Adv. Cttee, 1971–78; Welsh Arts Council, 1968–74; Member Council: Welsh Nat. Opera, 1972–75; Composers' Guild of GB, 1972–; Nat. Youth Orchestra, 1972–. Chm., Welsh Music Archive, 1977–78, 1983–87. Artistic Dir, 1967–89, Pres., 1990–, Cardiff Music Festival. Governor: Welsh Nat. Theatre, 1968–74; St John's Coll., Cardiff, 1991–. FRNCM 1981; Fellow: Welsh Coll. of Music and Drama, 1991; Swansea Inst., 2006. Hon. RAM. Hon. DMus Sheffield, 1993; DUniv Wales, 2007. Walford Davies Prize, 1954; Arnold Bax Medal, 1957; John Edwards Meml Award, 1967; Hopkins Medal, St David's Soc., NY, 1980; Glyndwr Medal, 1997; Cymry for the World Award, 2004. *Publications: opera:* The Beach of Falesá, 1974; The Magician, 1975; What the Old Man does is always right, 1975; The Rajah's Diamond, 1979; The Trumpet Major, 1981; Tower, 1999; *choral:* Rebecca, 1961; oratorio, Job, 1962; Medieval Songs, 1962; Danegeld, 1964; Four Welsh Songs, 1964; Cantata:

Dives and Lazarus, 1965; An Apple Tree and a Pig, 1968; Ballad, Black Bart, 1968; Out of the Deep, 1972; The Tree of Life, 1971; Four Welsh Songs, 1971; The Silver Swimmer, 1973; Sinfonia Fidei, 1977; Dulcia Iuventutis, 1978; Voyagers, 1978; Hymnus ante Somnum, 1979; Te Deum, 1982; Charge of the Light Brigade, 1983; In Parasceve Domini, 1983; King of Glory, 1984; Bells of Paradise, 1984; Jubilate, 1985; Lady and Unicorn, 1985; In Gravescentem Aetatem, 1985; Ballad of Green Broom, 1985; Christ is Risen, 1986; Sing a New Song, 1986; Flower Songs, 1986; In Praise of Music, 1986; The Legend of St Julian, 1987; Lines from Marlowe's Dr Faustus, 1988; Emynau Pantycelyn, 1990; Advent Carols, 1990; Vespers Canticle, 1992; Gloria, 1992; Three Motets, 1993; Missa Sancti David, 1994; Three Hymns for mixed choir and organ, 1994; Shakespeare Songs for unaccompanied voices, 1994; The Poetry of Earth, 1995; Missa Camargue, 1996; Magnificat and Nunc Dimittis, 1996; *vocal:* Roman Dream, 1968; Ancestor Worship, 1972; Ynys Mon, 1975; A Contemplation upon Flowers, 1976; Six Welsh Songs, 1982; The Silver Hound, 1986; Songs of Exile (tenor and orch.), 1989; The Silver Swimmer (soprano and ensemble), 1994; Five Poems of Becquer (baritone and piano), 1994; One Must Always Have Love: songs for high voice and piano, 1994; Tymhorau: four poems of Gwyn Thomas (baritone and piano), 1995; The Poetry of Earth (baritone and harp), 1997; Grongar Hill (baritone and ensemble), 1998; To the Poet (Pushkin songs, for baritone and piano), 1999; La Serenissima Cycle for baritone and piano, 2000; Promontory of Dreams (baritone, horn and strings), 2004; Seven Folk Songs (baritone and harp), 2005; Images of Venice (soprano, baritone and orchestra), 2005–06; Towy Landscape (soprano, baritone and piano duet), 2006; Blake Songs (voice and violin), 2007; *orchestral:* Symphonies: no 1 1955, no 2 1962, no 3 1968, no 4 1969, no 5 1975, no 6 1984, no 7, for organ and orch., 1989, no 8, for brass and percussion, 1992, no 9, A Vision of Eternity, 1993, no 10 1999; Nocturne, 1952; Welsh Dances I, 1958, II 1969; Folk Song Suite, 1962; Variations, 1963; Night Music, 1966; Sinfonietta I, 1968, II, 1969, III, 1970, IV, 1971; Fioriture, 1968; Investiture Dances, 1969; Divertimento, 1969; the sun, the great luminary of the universe, 1970; the hawk is set free, 1972; Welsh Airs and Dances for Symphonic Band, 1975; Landscapes, 1975; French Suite, 1977; Passaggio, 1977; Nightpiece, 1977; Lanterne des Morts, 1981; Five Studies, 1983; Four Scenes, 1983; Quodlibet, 1984; Hommage à Chopin, 1985; Welsh Dances–3rd Suite, 1985; Scena, 1986; Fanfare with Variants; Concerto for Orchestra; Star Children, 1989; Celebration Dances, 1999; Badger in the Bag, 2004; Celebration Fanfare for strings, trumpets and organ for Royal Wedding, 2005; Taliesin, 2007; *concertos:* Clarinet I, 1951, II, 1987; Oboe, 1954; Harp, 1958; Viola, 1958; Piano I, 1950, II, 1960, III, 1966; Violin, 1961; Organ, 1967; Horn, 1969; Nocturnes and Cadenzas (cello), 1969; Ritornelli (trombone), 1974; The Heaventree of Stars, for violin and orchestra, 1980; Doubles (oboe); Scenes and Interludes (trumpet), 1985; Violin, Cello, Piano (Triple Concerto); Divisions (horn); Noctis Equi (cello and orch.), 1989; MISTRAL: concerto for violin and orch., 1995; Shining Pyramid (trumpet and orch.), 1995; Dragon Fire (timpani and percussion), 1998; concerto for percussion and brass, 2000; concerto for euphonium and orch., 2001; Lizard, concerto for orch., 2002; concerto for trombone and orch., 2004; Concerto Grosso for brass, 2004; *chamber:* Septet, 1956; Sextet, 1960; Variations for Septet, 1962; Wind Quartet, 1963; String Quartet, 1965, no 2 1984, no 3 1988, no 4 1996, no 5 2001; Nocturnes and Cadenzas for Clarinet, Violin and Cello, 1968; Divertimento for 8 instruments, 1968; Piano Trio, 1970, no 2 1985, no 3 1996; Piano Quintet, 1972; Scena for String Quartet, 1979; Ritornelli for Brass Quintet, 1979; Ritornelli for four double basses, 1981; Masks for oboe, bassoon, piano, 1985; Divertimenti for flute, bassoon, double-bass and percussion, 1985; Sonata for Four Clarinets; chorales, variants and fanfares, 1992; Wind Quintet, 1993; six Bagatelles for string quartet, 1994; Bagatelles for wind quintet, 1999; Doubles, quintet for oboe, piano and string trio, 2000; Bagatelles for 11 instruments, 2001; Dream Wanderer: trio for horn, violin and piano, 2001; Bagatelles for four trombones, 2004; Music for string quartet, 2006; *instrumental:* sonatas for: piano, 1959, 1962, 1965, 1966, 1968, 1972, 1984, 1986, 1989 (two), 1993, 1994, 2000; harp, 1964; clarinet and piano, 1967, 1996; violin and piano, 1969, 1970, 1971, 1976, 1992, 1997; cello and piano, 1970, 1977, 1996; horn and piano, 1971; organ, 1979; two pianos, 1986; flute and piano, 1991; oboe and harp, 1995; euphonium and piano, 2003; piano duet, 2004; sonatinas for: clavichord, 1963; 2 pianos, 1978; guitar, 1978; Suite for Harp, 1967; Fantasy for Harp, 1970; Italian Suite for Recorder and Guitar, 1977; Nocturnes and Cadenzas for Solo Cello, 1983; Bagatelles for Oboe and Harp, 1983; Passacaglia and Fugue for Organ, 1986; Little Suite (trumpet and piano), 1988; Sonata Notturna for Harp, 1990; Tempi: sonata for harp, 1997; Island of Dragons Variants for cello, 1998; Lizard: variants for recorder. *Died 12 March 2008.*

HODGE, Hon. Sir Henry (Egar Garfield), Kt 2004; OBE 1993; **Hon. Mr Justice Hodge;** a Judge of the High Court of Justice, Queen's Bench Division, since 2004; President, Asylum and Immigration Tribunal, since 2005; *b* 12 Jan. 1944; *s* of late Raymond Garfield Hodge and Ruth (*née* Egar); *m* 1st, 1971, Miranda Tufnell (marr. diss. 1975); 2nd, 1978, Margaret Eve Hodge (later Rt Hon. Margaret Hodge, MBE, MP); two *d*, and one step *s* one step *d. Educ:* Chigwell Sch., Essex; Balliol Coll., Oxford (BA Law 1965). Admitted solicitor, 1970; Legal Sec., Justice, 1971; Solicitor and Dep. Dir, CPAG, 1972–77; Sen. Partner, Hodge Jones & Allen, Solicitors, 1977–99; Asst Recorder, 1993–97; a Recorder, 1997–99; a Circuit Judge, 1999–2004; Chief Immigration Adjudicator, 2001–04. Mem. (Lab), Islington Borough Council, 1974–78 (Vice-Chm., Housing Cttee, 1976–78). Member: Lord Chancellor's Legal Adv. Cttee, 1977–83; Matrimonial Causes Rules Cttee, 1986–90. Law Society: Mem. Council, 1984–96 (Legal Aid Specialist); Chm., Courts and Legal Services Cttee, 1987–90; Chairman: Race Relns Cttee, 1992–94; Equal Opportunities Cttee, 1994–95. Dep. Chm., Legal Aid Bd, 1996–99; Member: Supplementary Benefits Commn, 1978–80; Social Security Adv. Cttee, 1980–92; Civil Justice Council, 1998–2000. Chairman: NCCL, 1974–75; Nat. CAB Trng Cttee, 1982–84; Camden CAB, 1983–88. Vice-Chm., Soc. of Labour Lawyers, 1992–99; Dep. Vice-Pres., Law Soc. of England and Wales, 1994–95. Contested (Lab) Croydon S, Feb. 1974. Mem. Council, Richmond Fellowship, 2001–05. Gov., Coll. of Law, 1991–2005. Gov., Middx Univ., 1996–2002. *Publications:* Legal Rights, 1974; numerous articles on legal aid and legal rights. *Recreations:* Arsenal supporter, motor-cycling, golf, gardening. *Address:* Royal Courts of Justice, Strand, WC2A 2LL. *Died 18 June 2009.*

HODGES, Air Chief Marshal Sir Lewis (Macdonald), KCB 1968 (CB 1963); CBE 1958; DSO 1944 and Bar 1945; DFC 1942 and Bar 1943; DL; *b* 1 March 1918; *s* of late Arthur Macdonald Hodges and Gladys Mildred Hodges; *m* 1950, Elisabeth Mary, *e d* of late G. H. Blackett, MC; two *s. Educ:* St Paul's Sch.; RAF Coll., Cranwell. Bomber Command, 1938–44; SE Asia (India, Burma, Ceylon), 1944–45; Palestine, 1945–47; Air Ministry and Min. of Defence, 1948–52; Bomber Command, 1952–59; Asst Comdt, RAF Coll., Cranwell, 1959–61; AO i/c Admin., Middle East Comd, Aden, 1961–63; Imperial Def. Coll., 1963; SHAPE, 1964–65; Ministry of Defence, Asst Chief of Air Staff (Ops), 1965–68; AOC-in-C, RAF Air Support Comd, 1968–70; Air Mem. for Personnel, MoD, 1970–73; Dep. C-in-C, Allied Forces Central Europe, 1973–76, retired. Air ADC to the Queen, 1973–76. Dir, Pilkington Bros Ltd (Optical Div.), 1979–83; Governor, BUPA Med. Foundn Ltd, 1973–85; Chm. of Governors, Duke of Kent School, 1979–86; Chm., RAF Benevolent Fund Educn Cttee, 1979–86; Pres., RAF Escaping Soc., 1979–2000; Pres., Royal Air Forces Assoc., 1981–84. DL Kent, 1992.

Grand Officier, Légion d'Honneur (France), 1988 (Commandeur, 1950); Croix de Guerre (France), 1944. *Recreations:* gardening, shooting, bee-keeping. *Address:* c/o Lloyds TSB, High Street, Tonbridge, Kent. *Clubs:* Royal Air Force (Vice Patron, 1993–), Special Forces. *Died 4 Jan. 2007.*

HODGKINSON, Air Chief Marshal Sir (William) Derek, KCB 1971 (CB 1969); CBE 1960; DFC 1941; AFC 1942; *b* 27 Dec. 1917; *s* of late Ernest Nicholls Hodgkinson; *m* 1939, (Nancy) Heather Goodwin; one *s* one *d. Educ:* Repton. Joined RAF 1936; served war of 1939–45, POW Germany, 1942–45; OC 210 and 240 (GR) Sqns; DS Aust. Jt Anti-Sub. Sch. and JSSC, 1946–58; Gp Captain, 1958; OC RAF St Mawgan, 1958–61; Staff of CDS, and ADC to the Queen, 1961–63; Air Cdre, 1963; IDC, 1964; Comdt RAF Staff Coll., Andover, 1965; Air Vice-Marshal, 1966; ACAS, Operational Requirements, 1966–68; SASO, RAF Training Command, 1969; Air Marshal, 1972; AOC-in-C, Near East Air Force, Commander British Forces Near East, and Administrator, Sovereign Base Areas, Cyprus, 1970–73; Air Secretary, 1973–76; Air Chief Marshal, 1974; retired 1976. Report on RAF Officer Career Structure, 1969. Pres., Regular Forces Employment Assoc., 1982–86 (Vice-Chm., 1977–80; Chm., 1980–82). *Recreations:* fishing, cricket. *Clubs:* Royal Air Force, MCC. *Died 29 Jan. 2010.*

HODGSON, Ven. (John) Derek; Archdeacon of Durham, 1993–97, then Emeritus, and Canon Residentiary of Durham Cathedral, 1983–97, then Emeritus; *b* 15 Nov. 1931; *s* of Frederick and Hilda Hodgson; *m* 1956, Greta Wilson; two *s* one *d. Educ:* King James School, Bishop Auckland; St John's Coll., Durham (BA Hons History); Cranmer Hall, Durham (Dip. Theology). Short service commission, DLI, 1954–57. Deacon 1959, priest 1960; Curate: Stranton, Hartlepool, 1959–62; St Andrew's, Roker, 1962–64; Vicar: Stillington, 1964–66; Consett, 1966–75; Rector of Gateshead, 1975–83; RD of Gateshead, 1976–83; Hon. Canon of Durham, 1978–83; Archdeacon of Auckland, 1983–93. Chm. of Govs, Durham Sch.; 1997–2001; Vice-Provost, Northern Div., Woodard Schs Corp., 1999–2001. *Recreations:* walking, music, theatre, sport. *Address:* 45 Woodside, Barnard Castle, Co. Durham DL12 8DZ. *T:* (01833) 690557. *Died 22 Nov. 2007.*

HODGSON, William Donald John; General Manager, Independent Television News, 1960–82 (Director, 1972–86); *b* 25 March 1923; *s* of James Samuel Hodgson and Caroline Maud Albrecht; *m* 1946, Betty Joyce Brown (*d* 2004); two *s* six *d. Educ:* Beckenham Grammar School. Served Beds and Herts Regt, 1940–42; pilot, RAF and Fleet Air Arm, 1942–46. Documentary and feature film editor (with Jean Renoir on The River, Calcutta). 1946–50; Organiser, Festival of Britain Youth Programme, 1950–51; Asst Sec., Central Bureau for Educational Visits and Exchanges, 1951–54; Asst Gen. Man., Press Assoc., 1954–60; Dir of Develt, ITN, 1982–86. Dir, UPITN Corp., 1967–73. Executive Producer: Battle for the Falklands, 1982; Theft of a Thoroughbred, 1983; Victory in Europe, 1985; writer and producer, Welcome to the Caley (Royal Caledonian Schs), 1987. *Recreations:* grandchildcare, private flying, club cricket. *Address:* 38 Lakeside, Wickham Road, Beckenham, Kent BR3 6LX. *T:* (020) 8650 8959. *Died 14 Feb. 2008.*

HOFFENBERG, Sir Raymond, (Bill), KBE 1984; President, Wolfson College, Oxford, 1985–93; Professor of Medical Ethics, University of Queensland, 1993–95; *b* 6 March 1923; *er s* of Benjamin and Dora Hoffenberg; *m* 1949, Margaret Rosenberg (*d* 2005); two *s*; *m* 2006, Madeleine Douglas. *Educ:* Univ. of Cape Town (MB, ChB 1948; MD, PhD). FRCP 1971. Wartime Service with S African Armed Forces, N Africa and Italy. Sen. Lectr, Dept of Medicine, Univ. of Cape Town, 1955–67; banned by S African Govt, 1967; emigrated to UK, 1968. Sen. Scientist, MRC (UK), 1968–72; William Withering

Prof. of Medicine, Univ. of Birmingham, 1972–85. Mem. MRC, 1978–82. Royal College of Physicians: Pres., 1983–89; Harveian Orator, 1991. *Publications:* Clinical Freedom, 1987 (Rock Carling Fellowship. Nuffield Provincial Hospitals Trust); papers on endocrinology and metabolism. *Address:* 304/57A Newstead Terrace, Newstead, Qld 4006, Australia. *Died 22 April 2007.*

HOFFMAN, Rev. Canon Stanley Harold, MA; Chaplain in Ordinary to the Queen, 1976–87; Hon. Canon of Rochester Cathedral, 1965–80, then Emeritus; *b* 17 Aug. 1917; *s* of Charles and Ellen Hoffman, Denham, Bucks; *m* 1943, Mary Mifanwy Patricia (*d* 1991), *d* of late Rev. Canon Creed Meredith, Chaplain to the Queen, and Mrs R. Creed Meredith, Windsor; one *s* one *d. Educ:* The Royal Grammar Sch., High Wycombe, Bucks; St Edmund Hall, Oxford (BA 1939, MA 1943); Lincoln Theol Coll., 1940–41. Deacon, 1941; Priest, 1942; Curate: Windsor Parish Ch., 1941–44; All Saints, Weston, Bath, 1944–47; Chertsey (in charge of All SS), 1947–50; Vicar of Shottermill, Haslemere, Sy, 1951–64; Diocesan Director of Education, Rochester, 1965–80; Warden of Readers, 1974–80. Proctor in Convocation, Church Assembly, 1969–70; Exam. Chaplain to Bp of Rochester, 1973–80. Member: Kent Educn Cttee, 1965–80; Bromley Educn Cttee, 1967–80; Kent Council of Religious Educn, 1965–80; Archbps' Commn on Christian Initiation, 1970. Vice-Chm., Christ Church Coll., Canterbury, 1973–80. Hon. MA Kent, 1982. *Publications:* Morning Shows the Day: the making of a priest (autobiog.), 1995; part author: A Handbook of Thematic Material, 1968; Christians in Kent, 1972; Teaching the Parables, 1974; contrib. various pubns on Preaching and Religious Educn; numerous Dio. study papers. *Recreations:* music, walking. *Address:* Flat 3, Ramsay Hall, Byron Road, Worthing, W Sussex BN11 3HN. *T:* (01903) 217332. *Died 27 Dec. 2008.*

HOGARTH, James, CB 1973; Under-Secretary, Scottish Home and Health Department, 1963–74, retired; *b* 14 Aug. 1914; *s* of George Hogarth; *m* 1940, Katherine Mary Cameron; two *s* one *d. Educ:* George Watson's, Edinburgh; Edinburgh Univ.; Sorbonne, Paris. Joined Dept of Health for Scotland as Asst Principal, 1938; Principal, 1944; Asst Sec., 1948; Under-Sec., 1963. *Publications:* Payment of the General Practitioner, 1963; translations from French, German, Russian, etc. *Recreation:* travel. *Address:* 3 Oswald Road, Edinburgh EH9 2HE. *T:* (0131) 667 3878. *Died 22 Aug. 2006.*

HOGG OF CUMBERNAULD, Baron *cr* 1997 (Life Peer), of Cumbernauld in North Lanarkshire; **Norman Hogg;** a Deputy Speaker, House of Lords, 2002–05; Lord High Commissioner, General Assembly, Church of Scotland, 1998 and 1999; *b* 12 March 1938; *s* of late Norman Hogg, CBE, LLD, DL, JP, and Mary Wilson; *m* 1964, Elizabeth McCall Christie. *Educ:* Causewayend Sch., Aberdeen; Ruthrieston Secondary Sch., Aberdeen. Local Government Officer, Aberdeen Town Council, 1953–67; District Officer, National and Local Govt Officers Assoc., 1967–79. MP (Lab) Dunbartonshire East, 1979–83, Cumbernauld and Kilsyth, 1983–97. Mem., Select Cttee on Scottish Affairs, 1979–82; Scottish Labour Whip, 1982–83; Chm., Scottish Parly Lab Gp, 1981–82; Dep. Chief Opposition Whip, 1983–87; Scottish Affairs spokesman, 1987–88; Member: Chairman's Panel, 1988–97; Public Accounts Cttee, 1991–92. Mem., H of L Select Cttee on Delegated Powers and Regulatory Reform, 1999–2002. Chm., Bus Appeals Body, 2000–. Hon. Pres., YMCA Scotland, 1998–2005; Hon. Vice Pres., CCJ, 1997–. Patron, Scottish Centre for Children with Motor Impairments, 1998–. Hon. LLD Aberdeen, 1999. *Recreation:* music. *Address:* House of Lords, SW1A 0PW. *Died 8 Oct. 2008.*

HOGG, Rear-Adm. Peter Beauchamp, CB 1980; Head of British Defence Liaison Staff and Defence Adviser, Canberra, 1977–80, retired; *b* 9 Nov. 1924; *s* of Beauchamp and Sybil Hogg; *m* 1951, Gabriel Argentine Alington (*d* 2004); two *s* two *d. Educ:* Connaught House,

Weymouth; Bradfield Coll., Berks; Royal Naval Engineering Coll., Keyham. Lieut, HMS Sirius, 1947–49; Advanced Engrg Course, RNC Greenwich, 1949–51; HMS Swiftsure and HMS Pincher, 1951–53; Lt Comdr. Loan Service with Royal Canadian Navy, 1953–56; Staff of RN Engrg Coll., Manadon, 1956–58; Comdr (Trng Comdr), HMS Sultan, 1959–62; Marine Engr Officer, HMS Hampshire, 1962–64; JSSC, Latimer, 1964; Ship Dept, Bath, 1965–67; Captain, Ship Dept, Bath, 1968–69; CO, HMS Tyne, 1970–71; RCDS, 1972; CO, HMS Caledonia, 1973–74; Dir of Naval Recruiting, 1974–76. Sec., Sixth Centenary Appeal, and Bursar i/c building works, Winchester Coll., 1980–88. Chairman: Hereford Cathedral Fabric Adv. Cttee, 1991–; Herefordshire Historic Churches Trust, 1995–2003. *Address:* c/o National Westminster Bank, 14 Old Town Street, Plymouth PL1 1DG. *Died 10 March 2007.*

HOGG, Prof. Richard Milne, FBA 1994; FRSE; Smith Professor of English Language and Medieval Literature, University of Manchester, since 1980; *b* 20 May 1944; *s* of Charles Milne Hogg and Norenne Hogg (*née* Young); *m* 1969, Margaret Kathleen White; two *s. Educ:* Royal High Sch., Edinburgh; Univ. of Edinburgh (MA, Dip. Gen. Linguistics, PhD). FRSE 2004. Lecturer in English Language: Univ. van Amsterdam, 1969–73; Univ. of Lancaster, 1973–80. Leverhulme Major Res. Fellow, 2000–02. Gen. Editor, Cambridge History of the English Language, 6 vols, 1992–2001; Jt Editor, English Language and Linguistics, 1997–. *Publications:* English Quantifier Systems, 1977; Metrical Phonology, 1986; A Grammar of Old English, 1992; (ed jtly) A History of the English Language, 2006; contribs to learned jls. *Recreation:* Altrincham Football Club. *Address:* Department of Linguistics and English Language, University of Manchester, Oxford Road, Manchester M13 9PL. *T:* (0161) 275 3164; *e-mail:* r.m.hogg@manchester.ac.uk. *Died 6 Sept. 2007.*

HOLBOROW, Eric John, MD, FRCP, FRCPath; Emeritus Professor of Immunopathology and Honorary Consultant Immunologist, London Hospital Medical College, E1, retired 1983; *b* 30 March 1918; *s* of Albert Edward Ratcliffe Holborow and Marian Crutchley; *m* 1943, Cicely Mary Foister; two *s* one *d. Educ:* Epsom Coll.; Clare Coll., Cambridge; St Bart's Hosp. MA, MD (Cantab). Served War of 1939–45, Major, RAMC. Consultant Bacteriologist, Canadian Hosp., Taplow, 1953; Mem. Scientific Staff, MRC Rheumatism Unit, Taplow, 1957; Director, 1975; Head, MRC Group, Bone and Joint Res. Unit, London Hosp. Med. Coll., 1976–83. Visiting Prof., Royal Free Hosp. Med. Sch., 1975. Bradshaw Lectr, RCP, 1982. Chm., Smith Kline Foundn, 1987–89 (Trustee, 1977–89). Editor, Jl Immunol. Methods, 1971–85. *Publications:* Autoimmunity and Disease (with L. E. Glynn), 1965; An ABC of Modern Immunology, 1968, 2nd edn 1973; (with W. G. Reeves) Immunology in Medicine, 1977, 2nd edn 1983; (with A. Maroudas) Studies in Joint Disease, vol. 1, 1981, vol. 2, 1983; Fingest: stony ground (local history), 1999; books and papers on immunology. *Recreations:* glebe terriers, ecclesiastical records. *Died 3 Feb. 2009.*

HOLBROOKE, Richard Charles; Counselor, Council on Foreign Relations, since 2001; United States Representative to the United Nations, 1999–2001; *b* 2 April 1941; *s* of Dan Holbrooke and Trudi (*née* Moos); *m* 1st, 1964, Larrine Sullivan (marr. diss.); two *s*; 2nd, 1977, Blythe Babyak (marr. diss.); 3rd, 1995, Kati Marton. *Educ:* Brown Univ. (BA). Foreign Service Officer in Vietnam and related posts, 1962–66; White House Vietnam staff. 1966–67; Special Asst to Under Secs of State Nicholas Katzenbach and Elliot Richardson, and Mem., US Delegn to Paris peace talks on Vietnam, 1967–69; Dir. Peace Corps, Morocco, 1970–72; Man. Dir, Foreign Policy mag., 1972–76; Consultant, President's Commn on Orgn of Govt for Conduct of Foreign Policy, 1974–75; Contrib. Ed., Newsweek, 1974–75; Co-ordinator, Nat. Security Affairs, Carter-Mondale

Campaign, 1976; Asst Sec. of State for E Asian and Pacific Affairs, 1977–81; Vice-Pres., Public Strategies, 1981–85; Man. Dir, Lehman Bros, 1985–93; Ambassador to Germany, 1993–94; Asst Sec. of State for Eur. and Canadian Affairs, 1994–96; Vice-Chm., Credit Suisse First Boston Corp., 1996–99; Advr, Baltic Sea Council, 1996–97; Special Presidential Envoy for Cyprus, to Yugoslavia, 1997–98. Numerous hon. degrees, including: Maryland, and Heidelberg, 1994; Georgetown, 1996; Amer. Univ. of Paris, 1996; Central Euro-Atlantic Bucaresti, Romania, 1996; Tufts, 1997; Brown, 1997; Amer. Univ. in Athens, 1998; Lawrence, 1998; Dayton, 1998. Dist. Public Service Award, Dept of Defense, 1994 and 1996; Excellence in Diplomacy Award, Amer. Acad. of Diplomacy, 1996; Gold Medal for Dist. Service to Humanity, Nat. Inst. of Social Scis, 1996; Citation of Honor, USAF Assoc., 1996; Nahum Goldmann Award, World Jewish Congress, 1996; America's First Freedom Award, 1996; Sec. of State's Dist. Service Award, 1996; Manfred Woerner Award, FRG, 1997; Humanitarian of Year Award, American Jewish Congress, 1998; Nat. Diplomatic Award, Foreign Policy Assoc., 1998; Community Service Award, Mt Sinai Med. Center, 1999. *Publications:* (jtly) Counsel to the President, 1991; To End a War, 1998; contrib. various articles and essays. *Recreations:* tennis, ski-ing. *Address:* c/o Council on Foreign Relations, The Harold Pratt House, 58 East 68th Street, New York, NY 10065, USA. *T:* (212) 4349400.
Died 13 Dec. 2010.

HOLCROFT, Sir Peter (George Culcheth), 3rd Bt *cr* 1921; JP; *b* 29 April 1931; *s* of Sir Reginald Culcheth Holcroft, 2nd Bt, TD, and Mary Frances (*d* 1963), *yr d* of late William Swire, CBE; *S* father, 1978; *m* 1956, Rosemary Rachel (marr. diss. 1987), *yr d* of late G. N. Deas; three *s* one *d*. *Educ:* Eton. High Sheriff of Shropshire, 1969; JP 1976. *Recreation:* the countryside. *Heir: s* Charles Anthony Culcheth Holcroft [*b* 22 Oct. 1959; *m* 1986, Mrs Elizabeth Carter, *y d* of John Raper, Powys; one *s* one *d*]. *Address:* Appartado de Correos 223, 07210 Algaida, Mallorca, Spain. *Died 26 Oct. 2009.*

HOLDSWORTH, Sir (George) Trevor, Kt 1982; CVO 1997; Chairman, GKN plc, 1980–88; *b* 29 May 1927; *s* of late William Albert Holdsworth and Winifred Holdsworth (*née* Bottomley); *m* 1st, 1951, Patricia June Ridler (*d* 1993); three *s*; 2nd, 1995, Jenny Watson. *Educ:* Hanson Grammar Sch., Bradford; Keighley Grammar Sch. FCA 1950. Rawlinson Greaves & Mitchell, Bradford, 1944–51; Bowater Paper Corp., 1952–63 (financial and admin. appts; Dir and Controller of UK paper-making subsids); joined Guest, Keen & Nettlefolds (later GKN plc), 1963; Dep. Chief Accountant, 1963–64; Gp Chief Accountant, 1965–67; General Man. Dir, GKN Screws & Fasteners Ltd, 1968–70; Dir, 1970–88; Gp Controller, 1970–72; Gp Exec. Vice Chm., Corporate Controls and Services, 1973–74; Dep. Chm., 1974–77; Man. Dir and Dep. Chm., 1977–80. Chairman: Allied Colloids Gp, 1983–96; British Satellite Broadcasting, 1987–90; National Power, 1990–95; Beauford, 1991–99; Lambert Howarth Gp, 1993–98; Industrial Finance Gp, 1997–2002; Director: Equity Capital for Industry, 1976–84; THORN EMI, 1977–87; Midland Bank plc, 1979–88; Prudential Corp., 1986–96 (Jt Dep. Chm., 1988–92); Owens-Corning Fiberglas Corp., 1994–98. Member: AMF Inc. Eur. Adv. Council, 1982–85; European Adv. Bd, Owens Corning Fiberglas Inc., 1990–93; Adv. Bd, LEK, 1992–99. Confederation of British Industry: Mem. Council, 1974–90; Mem., Econ. and Financial Policy Cttee, 1978–80; Mem., Steering Gp on Unemployment, 1982; Mem., Special Programmes Unit, 1982; Chm., Tax Reform Working Party, 1984–86; Dep. Pres., 1987–88; Pres., 1988–90. Chairman: Review Body on Doctors' and Dentists' Remuneration, 1990–93; Adv. Council, Foundn for Manufacturing and Industry, 1993–99; Inst. for Manufacturing, 1999–2000; Dep. Chm., Financial Reporting Council, 1990–93; Mem., Business in the Community, 1984–92; British Institute of Management: Mem. Council, 1974–84; Vice-Chm., 1978; Mem., Bd

of Fellows, 1979; Chm., 1980–82; a Vice-Pres., 1982–; Gold Medal, 1987. Vice Pres., Engineering Employers' Fedn, 1980–88; Jt Dep. Chm., Adv. Bd, Inst. of Occupational Health, 1980; Duke of Edinburgh's Award: Mem., Internat. Panel, 1980 (Chm., 1987); Internat. Trustee, 1987–94; UK Trustee, 1988–96; Member: Exec. Cttee, SMMT, 1980–83; Engineering Industries Council, 1980–88 (Chm., 1985); Court of British Shippers' Council, 1981–89; British-North American Cttee, 1981–85; Council, RIIA, 1983–88; Internat. Council of INSEAD, 1985–92; Eur. Adv. Cttee, New York Stock Exchange, 1985–97. Chm., Wigmore Hall Trust, 1992–99; Member: Council, Royal Opera House Trust (Trustee, 1981–84); Council, Winston Churchill Meml Trust, 1985–96. Hon. Pres., Council of Mechanical and Metal Trade Assocs, 1987. Dir, UK-Japan 2000 Gp, 1987. Trustee: Anglo-German Foundn for the Study of Industrial Society, 1980–92; Brighton Fest. Trust, 1980–90 (Chm. 1982–87); Philharmonia Trust, 1982–93; Thrombosis Res. Trust, 1989–98. Governor, Ashridge Management Coll., 1978; Chancellor, Bradford Univ., 1992–97. Vice-Pres., Ironbridge Gorge Museum Develt Trust, 1981–. Internat. Counsellor, Conference Bd, 1984. CIEx 1987. FRSA 1988. Freeman, City of London, 1977; Liveryman, Worshipful Co. of Chartered Accountants in England and Wales, 1978. Hon. DTech Loughborough, 1981; Hon. DSc: Aston, 1982; Sussex, 1988; Hon. DEng: Bradford, 1983; Birmingham, 1992; Hon. DBA Internat. Management Centre, Buckingham, 1986. Chartered Accountants Founding Socs' Centenary Award, 1983; Hon. CGIA 1989. *Recreations:* music, theatre. *Club:* Athenæum. *Died 28 Sept. 2010.*

HOLLAND, David Cuthbert Lyall, CB 1975; Librarian of the House of Commons, 1967–76; *b* 23 March 1915; *yr s* of Michael Holland, MC, and Marion Holland (*née* Broadwood); *m* 1949, Rosemary Griffiths, *y d* of David Ll. Griffiths, OBE; two *s* one *d*. *Educ:* Eton; Trinity Coll., Cambridge (MA). War service, Army, 1939–46; PoW. Appointed House of Commons Library, 1946. Chm., Study of Parlt Gp, 1973–74. *Publications:* book reviews, etc. *Recreation:* book collecting. *Address:* The Barn, Milton Street, Polegate, East Sussex BN26 5RP. *T:* (01323) 870379. *Club:* Athenæum.
Died 21 Sept. 2007.

HOLLAND, (Robert) Einion, FIA; Chairman: Pearl Assurance PLC, 1983–89; Pearl Group PLC, 1985–89 (Director, since 1985); *b* 23 April 1927; *s* of late Robert Ellis Holland and Bene Holland; *m* 1955, Eryl Haf Roberts (*d* 1988); one *s* two *d*; *m* 2008, Maifrona Davies. *Educ:* University Coll. of N Wales, Bangor (BSc). FIA 1957. Joined Pearl Assurance Co. Ltd, 1953: Dir, 1973; Chief Gen. Manager, 1977–83; Chm., Industrial Life Offices Assoc., 1976–78; Director: Aviation & General Insurance Co. Ltd, 1972–89 (Chm. 1976–78, 1984–85); British Rail Property Board, 1987–90; Community Reinsurance Corp. Ltd, 1973–89 (Chm., 1973–76); Crawley Warren Group, 1987–99; Pearl American Corp., 1972–84; Scottish Legal Life Assurance Soc. Ltd, 1995–97. Member: Welsh Develt Agency, 1976–86; CS Pay Research Unit Bd, 1980–81; Council, Univ. of Wales, 1990–95. *Recreation:* golf and Welsh literature. *Address:* 55 Corkscrew Hill, West Wickham, Kent BR4 9BA. *T:* (020) 8777 1861. *Died 23 June 2009.*

HOLLEY, Rear Adm. Ronald Victor, CB 1987; FRAeS; Independent Inspector, Lord Chancellor's Panel, 1992–2001; *b* 13 July 1931; *s* of late Mr and Mrs V. E. Holley; *m* 1954, Sister Dorothy Brierley, QARNNS; two *s* twin *d*. *Educ:* Rondebosch, S Africa; Portsmouth GS; RNEC Manadon; RAFC Henlow (post graduate); Dip. Music Open Univ. 2003. MIMechE, MIET; FRAeS 1988. Served HM Ships Implacable, Finisterre, Euryalus, Victorious, Eagle (899 Sqdn); NATO Defence Coll., Rome, 1968; Naval Plans, 1969–71; Aircraft Dept, 1971–73; Air Engr Officer, HMS Seahawk, 1973–75; Naval Asst to Controller of the Navy, 1975–77; RCDS, 1978; Seaman Officer Develt Study, 1979; Dir, Helicopter Projects, Procurement Exec., 1979–82;

RNEC in command, 1982–84; Sen. Naval Mem., Directing Staff, RCDS, 1984–85; Dir Gen. Aircraft (Navy), 1985–87. Tech. Dir, Shell Aircraft, 1987–92. Sec., European Helicopter Operators Cttee, 1988–91. President: RN Volunteer Bands, 1983–87; RN Amateur Fencing Assoc., 1986–87 (Chm., 1983–86). Member: Parly Gp for Engrg Develt, 1993–2007; Parly Mull of Kintyre Gp, 2003–. Henson and Stringfellow Lectr, RAeS, 1987. *Publications:* contribs to Naval Jls, and Seaford House Papers, 1978. *Recreation:* the Philharmonia Orchestra. *Died 13 Aug. 2010.*

HOLLIDAY, Leslie John, FCIOB; Chairman and Chief Executive, John Laing plc, 1982–85 (Director, 1978–85); Chairman, John Laing Construction Ltd, 1980–85 (Director, 1966–85); *b* 9 Jan. 1921; *s* of John and Elsie Holliday; *m* 1943, Kathleen Joan Marjorie Stacey; two *s. Educ:* St John's, Whitby. FCIOB 1969. Denaby & Cadby Colliery, 1937–40; served Merchant Navy, 1940–45; joined John Laing & Son Ltd, 1947, Dir 1977; Chairman: Laing Homes Ltd, 1978–81; Super Homes Ltd, 1979–81; Laing Management Contracting Ltd, 1980–81; John Laing Internat. Ltd, 1981–82; Director: Declan Kelly Holdings, 1985–89; RM Douglas Holdings, 1986–89; Admiral Homes Ltd, 1989–96; Redrow Gp, 1989–92. Mem., EDC for Bldg, 1979–82. CCMI (CBIM 1982). Freeman, City of London, 1984; Liveryman, Plaisterers' Co., 1984–. *Recreations:* yachting, golf. *Address:* 6 Priestland Gardens, Castle Village, Berkhamsted, Herts HP4 2GT. *Club:* Berkhamsted Golf. *Died 7 Jan. 2006.*

HOLLINGS, Sir (Alfred) Kenneth, Kt 1971; MC 1944; Judge of the High Court of Justice, Family Division (formerly Probate, Divorce and Admiralty Division), 1971–93; *b* 12 June 1918; *s* of Alfred Holdsworth Hollings and Rachel Elizabeth Hollings; *m* 1949, Harriet Evelyn Isabella, *d* of W. J. C. Fishbourne, OBE, Brussels; one *s* one *d. Educ:* Leys Sch., Cambridge; Clare Coll., Cambridge. Law Qualifying and Law Tripos, Cambridge, 1936–39; MA. Served RA (Shropshire Yeomanry), 1939–46. Called to Bar, Middle Temple, 1947 (Harmsworth Schol.); Master of the Bench, 1971. Practised Northern Circuit; QC 1966; Recorder of Bolton, 1968; Judge of County Courts, Circuit 5 (E Lancs), 1968–71; Presiding Judge, Northern Circuit, 1975–78. *Clubs:* Hurlingham; Tennis and Racquets (Manchester). *Died 27 Dec. 2008.*

HOLME OF CHELTENHAM, Baron *cr* 1990 (Life Peer), of Cheltenham in the County of Gloucestershire; **Richard Gordon Holme,** CBE 1983; PC 2000; Chairman, Globescan Research, since 2003; *b* 27 May 1936; *s* of J. R. Holme and E. M. Holme (*née* Eggleton); *m* 1958, Kathleen Mary Powell; two *s* two *d. Educ:* Royal Masonic Sch.; St John's Coll., Oxford (Hon. Fellow, 1999); Harvard Business Sch. (PMD). Commnd 10th Gurkha Rifles, Malaya, 1954–56. Vice-Chm., Liberal Party Exec., 1966–67; Pres., Liberal Party, 1980–81; contested: East Grinstead (L) 1964 and by-election, 1965; Braintree (L) Oct. 1974; Cheltenham (L) 1983, (L/ Alliance) 1987. Lib Dem spokesman on NI, H of L, 1992–99; Chm., Select Cttee on the Constitution, H of L, 2004–. Chm., Lib Dem Gen. Elect. Campaign, 1997. Dir, Campaign for Electoral Reform, 1976–85; Sec., Parly Democracy Trust, 1977–; Chm., Constitutional Reform Centre, 1985–94; Hon. Treasurer, Green Alliance, 1978–90. Chairman: DPR Publishing (formerly Dod's Publishing and Research), 1988–98; Black Box Publishing, 1988–95; Hollis Directories, 1989–98; Brasseys Ltd, 1996–98; Dep. Chm., ITC, 1999; Director: Political Quarterly, 1988–2004; RTZ-CRA, later Rio Tinto plc, 1995–98. Chm., Broadcasting Standards Commn, 1999–2000. Visiting Professor: in Business Administration, Middlesex Polytechnic, 1990–94; Thunderbird Sch. of Internat. Mgt, Phoenix, Arizona, 2002–. Associate Mem., Nuffield Coll., 1985–89; Exec. Mem., Campaign for Oxford, 1990–. Chairman: Hansard Soc. for Parly Govt, 2001–; Royal African Soc., 2004–; LEAD Internat., 2004–. Chairman: English Coll.

Foundn, Prague, 1991–2008; Adv. Bd, British American Proj., 2000–; Mem. Council, ODI, 1998–. Trustee: Citizenship Foundn, 1994–2001; Saïd Business Sch., Oxford, 2005–. Chancellor, Univ. of Greenwich, 1998–. *Publications:* No Dole for the Young, 1975; A Democracy Which Works, 1978; The People's Kingdom, 1987; (ed jtly) 1688–1988, Time for a New Constitution, 1988. *Address:* House of Lords, SW1A 0PW. *Clubs:* Brooks's, Reform, Royal Automobile. *Died 4 May 2008.*

HOLMER, Paul Cecil Henry, CMG 1973; HM Diplomatic Service, retired; Ambassador to Romania, 1979–83; *b* 19 Oct. 1923; *s* of late Bernard Cecil and Mimi Claudine Holmer; *m* 1946, Irene Nora, *e d* of late Orlando Lenox Beater, DFC; two *s* two *d. Educ:* King's Sch., Canterbury; Balliol Coll., Oxford. Served in RA, 1942–46. Entered Civil Service, 1947; Colonial Office, 1947–49; transferred to HM Foreign Service, 1949; FO, 1949–51; Singapore, 1951–55; FO, 1955–56; served on Civil Service Selection Bd, 1956; FO, 1956–58; Moscow, 1958–59; Berlin, 1960–64; FO, 1964–66; Counsellor, 1966; Dep. High Comr, Singapore, 1966–69; Head of Security Dept, FCO, 1969–72; Ambassador, Ivory Coast, Upper Volta and Niger, 1972–75; Minister and UK Dep. Perm. Rep. to NATO, 1976–79. Dir, African Develt Fund, 1973–75. *Died 22 May 2006.*

HOLMES, Prof. George Arthur, PhD; FBA 1985; Chichele Professor of Medieval History, University of Oxford, and Fellow of All Souls College, 1989–94; *b* 22 April 1927; *s* of late John Holmes and Margaret Holmes, Aberystwyth; *m* 1953, Evelyn Anne, *d* of late Dr John Klein and Audrey (*née* McFarlane); one *s* two *d* (and one *s* decd). *Educ:* Ardwyn County Sch., Aberystwyth; UC, Aberystwyth; St John's Coll., Cambridge (MA, PhD). Fellow, St John's Coll., Cambridge, 1951–54; Tutor, St Catherine's Society, Oxford, 1954–62; Fellow and Tutor, St Catherine's Coll., Oxford, 1962–89 (Vice-Master, 1969–71; Emeritus Fellow, 1990). Mem., Inst. for Advanced Study, Princeton, 1967–68. Vis. Prof., Harvard Univ. Centre for Italian Renaissance Studies, Florence, 1995–. Chm. Bd, Warburg Inst., London Univ., 1993–95. Chm., Victoria County Hist. Cttee, Inst. of Hist. Res., 1979–89. Jt Ed., English Historical Review, 1974–81; Delegate, Oxford Univ. Press, 1982–91. FRHistS 1956. Ellen MacArthur Prize for Economic Hist., Cambridge Univ., 1957; Serena Medal for Italian Studies, British Acad., 1993. *Publications:* The Estates of the Higher Nobility in Fourteenth-Century England, 1957; The Later Middle Ages, 1962; The Florentine Enlightenment 1400–1450, 1969; Europe: hierarchy and revolt 1320–1450, 1975; The Good Parliament, 1975; Dante, 1980; Florence, Rome and the Origins of the Renaissance, 1986; (ed) The Oxford Illustrated History of Medieval Europe, 1988; The First Age of the Western City 1300–1500, 1990; (ed) Art and Politics in Renaissance Italy, 1993; Renaissance, 1996; (ed) The Oxford Illustrated History of Italy, 1997; articles in learned jls. *Recreations:* walking in the country, looking at pictures. *Address:* Highmoor House, Bampton, Oxon OX18 2HY. *T:* (01993) 850408. *Died 29 Jan. 2009.*

HOLMES, Prof. William; Professor of Agriculture, Wye College, University of London, 1955–87, Professor Emeritus, since 1985, Fellow, 1993; *b* Kilbarchan, Renfrewshire, 16 Aug. 1922; *s* of William John Holmes, Bank Manager; *m* 1949, Jean Ishbel Campbell, BSc (*d* 2002); two *d. Educ:* John Neilson Sch., Paisley; Glasgow Univ.; West of Scotland Agricultural Coll. BSc (Agric), NDD, 1942; NDA (Hons), 1943; PhD Glasgow, 1947; DSc London, 1966. FIBiol 1974. Asst Executive Officer, S Ayrshire AEC, 1943–44; Hannah Dairy Research Inst.: Asst in Animal Husbandry, 1944–47; Head of Dept of Dairy and Grassland Husbandry, 1947–55. Member: Cttee on Milk Composition in the UK, 1958–60; technical cttees of ARC, JCO MAFF, MMB and MLC, 1960–90. Governor, Grassland Research Inst., 1960–75; President: British Grassland Soc., 1968–69 (1st recipient, British Grassland Soc. Award, 1979); British Soc. of

Animal Production, 1969–70. Chm., E Kent VSO, 1998–2005. Pres., Wye Gardeners' Soc., 1988–2000. Correspondent Étranger, Acad. d'Agric. de France, 1984. Ed., Jl Wye Coll. Agricola Club, 1987–97. Scout Wood Badge, Gilwell, 1948. *Publications:* (ed) Grass, its production and utilization, 1980, 2nd edn 1989; (ed) Grassland Beef Production, 1984; (jtly) The Blean: the woodlands of a cathedral city, 2002, 2nd edn 2005; papers in technical agricl jls incl. Jl of Agricl Sci. *Recreations:* grandchildren, woodland ecology, gardening, beekeeping, travel. *Address:* Amage, Wye, Kent TN25 5DF. *T:* (01233) 812372.   *Died 28 Jan. 2006.*

HOLMES SELLORS, Sir Patrick John; *see* Sellors.

HOLT, Constance, CBE 1975; Area Nursing Officer, Manchester Area Health Authority (Teaching), 1973–77; *b* 5 Jan. 1924; *d* of Ernest Biddulph and of Ada Biddulph (*née* Robley); *m* 1975, Robert Lord Holt, OBE, FRCS (decd). *Educ:* Whalley Range High Sch. for Girls, Manchester; Manchester Royal Infirmary (SRN); Queen Charlotte's Hosp., London; St Mary's Hosp., Manchester (SCM); Royal Coll. of Nursing, London Univ. (Sister Tutor Dipl.); Univ. of Washington (Florence Nightingale Schol., Fulbright Award). Nursing Officer, Min. of Health, 1959–65; Chief Nursing Officer: United Oxford Hosps, 1965–69; United Manchester Hosps, 1969–73. Pres., Assoc. of Nurse Administrators (formerly Assoc. of Hosp. Matrons), 1972–. Reader licensed by Bishop of Sodor and Man. Hon. Lectr, Dept of Nursing, Univ. of Manchester, 1972. Hon. MA Manchester, 1980. *Publications:* articles in British and internat. nursing press. *Recreations:* reading, gardening, music. *Address:* 3c Princess Towers, The Promenade, Port Erin, Isle of Man IM9 6LH. *T:* (01624) 833509.   *Died 2 March 2009.*

HOLT, Prof. John Riley, FRS 1964; Professor of Experimental Physics, University of Liverpool, 1966–83, then Emeritus; *b* 15 Feb. 1918; *er s* of Frederick Holt and Annie (*née* Riley); *m* 1949, Joan Silvester Thomas (*d* 2001); two *s*. *Educ:* Runcorn Secondary Sch.; University of Liverpool; PhD 1941. British Atomic Energy Project, Liverpool and Cambridge, 1940–45; University of Liverpool: Lectr, 1945–53; Sen. Lectr, 1953–56; Reader, 1956–66. *Publications:* papers in scientific journals on nuclear physics and particle physics. *Recreation:* gardening. *Address:* Rydalmere, Stanley Avenue, Higher Bebington, Wirral CH63 5QE. *T:* (0151) 608 2041.
Died 6 Jan. 2009.

HOLT, Prof. Peter Malcolm, FBA 1975; FSA; Professor of History of the Near and Middle East, School of Oriental and African Studies, University of London, 1975–82, then Professor Emeritus; *b* 28 Nov. 1918; *s* of Rev. Peter Holt and Elizabeth Holt; *m* 1953, Nancy Bury (*née* Mawle) (decd); one *s* one *d*. *Educ:* Lord Williams's Grammar Sch., Thame; University Coll., Oxford (Schol.; MA, DLitt). Sudan Civil Service: Min. of Education, 1941–53; Govt Archivist, 1954–55; School of Oriental and African Studies, London, 1955–82, Prof. of Arab History, 1964–75. FRHistS 1973; FSA 1980. Hon. Fellow, SOAS, 1985. Gold Medal of Science, Letters and Arts, Repub. of Sudan, 1980. *Publications:* The Mahdist State in the Sudan, 1958, 2nd edn 1970; A Modern History of the Sudan, 1961, 4th edn (with M. W. Daly) as A History of the Sudan from the Coming of Islam to the Present Day, 1988, 5th edn 2000; (co-ed with Bernard Lewis) Historians of the Middle East, 1962; Egypt and the Fertile Crescent, 1966; (ed) Political and Social Change in Modern Egypt, 1968; (co-ed with Ann K. S. Lambton and Bernard Lewis) The Cambridge History of Islam, 1970; Studies in the History of the Near East, 1973; (ed) The Eastern Mediterranean Lands in the period of the Crusades, 1977; The Memoirs of a Syrian Prince, 1983; The Age of the Crusades, 1986; trans. P. Thorau, The Lion of Egypt, 1992; Early Mamluk Diplomacy, 1995; The Sudan of the three Niles, 1999; trans. C. Cahen, The Formation of Turkey, 2001; The Crusader States and their Neighbours, 2004; articles in: Encyclopaedia of Islam, Bulletin of SOAS, Sudan Notes and Records, Der Islam, English Historical Rev., etc. *Address:* Dryden

Spinney, Bletchington Road, Kirtlington, Kidlington, Oxon OX5 3HF. *T:* (01869) 350477. *Club:* Oxford and Cambridge.   *Died 2 Nov. 2006.*

HOLTON, Michael; Assistant Secretary, Ministry of Defence, 1976–87, retired as Secretary of Air Staff Secretariat; *b* 30 Sept. 1927; 3rd *s* of late George Arnold Holton and Ethel (*née* Fountain); *m* 1st, 1951, Daphne Bache (marr. diss. 1987); one *s* two *d*; 2nd, 1987, Joan Catherine Thurman (*née* Hickman), (OBE 1994), Huddersfield. *Educ:* Finchley County Grammar Sch.; London Sch. of Economics. RAFVR, 1946–48; Min. of Food, 1948–54; Air Ministry, 1955–61; MoD, 1961–68; Secretary: Countryside Commn for Scotland, 1968–70; Carnegie UK Trust, 1971–75. Sec., European Conservation Year Cttee for Scotland, 1970; Mem. Council, 1976–93, Hon. Sec., 1988–93, RSNC; Member: YHA, 1946–; Bd, Cairngorm Chairlift Co., 1973–95; Museums Assoc., 1976–95. Hon. Secretary: RAF Mountaineering Assoc., 1952–54 (Hon. Mem., 1964–); British Mountaineering Council, 1954–59 (Hon. Mem., 1997–); RAF Mountain Rescue Assoc., 1993–95 (Hon. Mem., 1996–). *Publications:* Training Handbook for RAF Mountain Rescue Teams, 1953, 7th edn 2006. *Address:* 4 Ludlow Way, Hampstead Garden Suburb, N2 0LA. *T:* (020) 8444 8582. *Clubs:* Athenæum, Alpine; Himalayan.   *Died 24 March 2006.*

HOLZACH, Dr Robert; Hon. Chairman, Union Bank of Switzerland, 1988–96; *b* 28 Sept. 1922. *Educ:* Univ. of Zürich (Dr of Law). Union Bank of Switzerland: trainee, Geneva, London, 1951–52; Vice-Pres., 1956; Senior Vice-Pres., Head of Commercial Div., Head Office, 1962; Mem., Exec. Board, 1966; Exec. Vice-Pres., 1968; President, 1976; Chm. of Board, 1980–88. *Publications:* Herausforderungen, 1988. *Address:* Erbstrasse 7, 8700 Küsnacht, Switzerland.   *Died 24 March 2009.*

HOMAN, Rear-Adm. Thomas Buckhurst, CB 1978; *b* 9 April 1921; *s* of late Arthur Buckhurst Homan and Gertrude Homan, West Malling, Kent; *m* 1945, Christine Oliver; one *d*. *Educ:* Maidstone Grammar Sch. RN Cadet, 1939; served War of 1939–45 at sea; Comdr 1958; Sec., British Defence Staff, Washington, 1961; Captain 1965; Defence Intell. Staff, 1965; Sec. to Comdr Far East Fleet, 1967; idc 1970; Dir Naval Officer Appts (S), 1971; Captain HMS Pembroke, 1973; Rear-Adm. 1974; Dir Gen., Naval Personal Services, 1974–78. Sub-Treasurer, Inner Temple, 1978–85.   *Died 1 March 2008.*

HOME, Prof. George, BL; FCIBS; Professor of International Banking, Heriot-Watt University, Edinburgh, 1978–85, then Professor Emeritus; *b* 13 April 1920; *s* of George Home and Leah Home; *m* 1946, Muriel Margaret Birleson; two *s* one *d*. *Educ:* Fort Augustus Village Sch.; Trinity Academy, Edinburgh; George Heriot's Sch., Edinburgh; Edinburgh Univ. (BL 1952). Joined Royal Bank of Scotland, 1936; served RAF, 1940–46; Dep. Man. Dir, Royal Bank of Scotland Ltd, 1973–80; Dep. Gp Man. Dir, Royal Bank of Scotland Gp Ltd, 1976–80; Director: Williams & Glyn's Bank Ltd, 1975–80; The Wagon Finance Corp. plc, 1980–85. Vice-Pres., Inst. of Bankers in Scotland, 1977–80. Chm., George Heriot's Trust, 1989–96. FCMI. *Recreations:* fishing, gardening, reading, travel. *Address:* Bickley, 12 Barnton Park View, Edinburgh EH4 6HJ. *T:* (0131) 312 7648.   *Died 23 Sept. 2009.*

HONE, Robert Monro, MA; Headmaster, Exeter School, 1966–79; *b* 2 March 1923; *s* of late Rt Rev. Campbell R. Hone; *m* 1958, Helen Isobel, *d* of late Col H. M. Cadell of Grange, OBE; three *d*. *Educ:* Winchester Coll. (Scholar); New Coll., Oxford (Scholar). Rifle Brigade, 1942–45. Asst Master, Clifton Coll., 1948–65 (Housemaster, 1958–65). *Address:* 3 The Orchard, Throwleigh, Okehampton, Devon EX20 2HT.
Died 10 March 2006.

HONEYCOMBE, Sir Robert (William Kerr), Kt 1990; FRS 1981; FREng; Goldsmiths' Professor of Metallurgy, University of Cambridge, 1966–84, then Emeritus; *b* 2

May 1921; *s* of William and Rachel Honeycombe (*née* Kerr); *m* 1947, June Collins (decd); two *d*. *Educ*: Geelong Coll.; Univ. of Melbourne. Research Student, Department of Metallurgy, University of Melbourne, 1941–42; Research Officer, Commonwealth Scientific and Industrial Research Organization, Australia, 1942–47; ICI Research Fellow, Cavendish Laboratory, Cambridge, 1948–49; Royal Society Armourers and Brasiers' Research Fellow, Cavendish Laboratory, Cambridge, 1949–51; Senior Lecturer in Physical Metallurgy, University of Sheffield, 1951–55; Professor, 1955–66. Fellow of Trinity Hall, Cambridge, 1966–73, Hon. Fellow, 1975; Pres. 1973–80, Fellow, 1980–88, Emeritus Fellow, 1988, Clare Hall, Cambridge. Pres., Instn of Metallurgists, 1977; Pres., Metals Soc., 1980–81; Vice-Pres., Royal Institution, 1977–78; Treas., 1986–92, a Vice Pres., 1986–92, Royal Soc. Visiting Professor: University of Melbourne, 1962; Stanford Univ., 1965; Monash Univ., 1974; Hatfield Meml Lectr, Sheffield Univ., 1979. FREng (FEng 1980). Hon. Member: Iron and Steel Inst. of Japan, 1979; Soc. Française de Métallurgie, 1981; Japan Inst. of Metals, 1983 (Gold Medallist, 1983); Indian Inst. of Metals, 1984. Mem. Ct of Assts, Goldsmiths' Co., 1977– (Prime Warden, 1986–87). Hon. DAppSc Melbourne, 1974; Hon. DMet Sheffield, 1983; Dr *hc* Montanistischen Wissenschaften Leoben, 1990. Rosenhain Medal of Inst. of Metals, 1959; Sir George Beilby Gold Medal, 1963; Ste-Claire-Deville Medal, 1971; Inst. of Metals Lectr and Mehl Medallist, AIMF, 1976; Sorby Award, Internat. Metallographic Soc., 1986. *Publications*: The Plastic Deformation of Metals, 1968, 2nd edn 1984; Steels—Microstructure and Properties, 1981, 2nd cdn (with H. K. D. H. Bhadeshia) 1995; papers in Proc. Royal Soc., Metal Science, etc. *Recreations*: gardening, photography, walking. *Address*: Barrabool, 46 Main Street, Hardwick, Cambridge CB3 7QS. *T*: (01954) 210501. *Died 14 Sept. 2007*.

HOOD, Rear-Adm. John, CBE 1981; CEng, FIMechE; Director General Aircraft (Naval), 1978–81; *b* 23 March 1924; *s* of Charles Arthur Hood, architect, and Nellie Ormiston Brown Lamont; *m* 1948, Julia Mary Trevaskis (*d* 1993); three *s*. *Educ*: Plymouth Coll.; RN Engineering Coll., Keyham. Entered Royal Navy, 1945; RNEC, 1945–48; served in Illustrious, 1948; RN Air Stations, Abbotsinch, Anthorn, RAF West Raynham (NAFDU), 1948–51; HQ Min. of Supply, 1951–53; Air Engineer Officer, 1834 Sqdn, 1953–55, Aeroplane and Armament Experimental Estabt, 1955–57; Staff of Dir Aircraft Maintenance and Repair, 1957–59; AEO, HMS Albion, 1959–61; Sen. Air Engr, RNEC, Manadon, 1961–62; Development Project Officer, Sea Vixen 2, Min. of Aviation, 1962–65; AEO, RNAS, Lossiemouth, 1965–67; Staff of Dir of Officer Appointments (E), 1967–69; Defence and Naval Attaché, Argentina and Uruguay, 1970–72; Sen. Officers War Course, 1973; Asst Dir, Naval Manpower Requirements (Ships), 1974–75; Head of Aircraft Dept (Naval), 1975–78. Comdr 1962, Captain 1969, Rear-Adm. 1979. *Recreations*: sailing, gardening. *Club*: RN Sailing Association. *Died 20 March 2006*.

HOOD, Prof. Neil, CBE 2000; FRSE; Professor of Business Policy, University of Strathclyde, 1979–2003, then Emeritus; *b* 10 Aug. 1943; *s* of Andrew Hood and Elizabeth Taylor Carruthers; *m* 1966, Anna Watson Clark; one *s* one *d*. *Educ*: Wishaw High Sch.; Univ. of Glasgow (MA, MLitt). FRSE 1987. Res. Fellow, Scottish Coll. of Textiles, 1966–68; Lectr, later Sen. Lectr, Paisley Coll. of Technol., 1968–78; Economic Advr, Scottish Economic Planning Dept, 1979; University of Strathclyde: Associate Dean, 1982–85, Dean, 1985–87, Strathclyde Business Sch.; Co-Dir, 1983–87, Dir, 1992–2001, Strathclyde Internat. Business Unit; Dep. Principal (Develt), then Special Advr to Principal, 1991–94. Dir, Locate In Scotland, 1987–89, and Dir, Employment and Special Initiatives, 1989–90, Scottish Develt Agency (on secondment). Vis. Prof. of Internat. Business, Univ. of Texas, Dallas, 1981; Vis. Prof., Stockholm Sch. of Economics, 1983–89. Trade Adviser,

UNCTAD-GATT, 1980–85; Economic Consultant to Sec. of State for Scotland, 1980–87; Consultant to: Internat. Finance Corp., World Bank, 1982–84, 1991–; UN Centre on Transnational Corporations, 1982–84. Mem., Irvine Develt Corp., 1985–87. Non-executive Director: Euroscot Meat Exports Ltd, 1983–86; Scottish Develt Finance Ltd, 1984–90, 1993–96; Lanarkshire Industrial Field Executive Ltd, 1984–86; Prestwick Holdings PLC, 1986–87; Lamberton (Hldgs) Ltd, 1989–92; GA (Hldgs) Ltd, 1990–92; Shanks & McEwan Gp PLC, 1990–94; First Charlotte Assets Trust plc, 1990–92; Charlotte Marketing Services Ltd, 1991–94; Kwik-Fit plc, 1991–2001; I & S UK Smaller Cos Trust plc, 1992–98; The Malcolm Group (formerly Grampian Hldgs plc), 1993–2005; I & S Trustlink Ltd, 1994–97; Chm., John Dickie Gp Ltd, 1995–2000; Dep. Chm., British Polythene Industries plc, 1998–2005. Investment Advr, Castleforth Fund Managers Ltd, 1984–88; Corporate Advr, Scottish Power plc, 1990–; Chairman: Scottish Adv. Council, FI Gp, subseq. Xansa plc, 1992–97 (non exec. Dir, 1997–2005); Scottish Equity Partners Ltd, 2000–; STL Ltd, 2001–; Clyde Waterfront Strategic Partnership Bd, 2004–; Dep. Chm., Scottish Enterprise, 2001–04; Mem., Scottish Business Forum, 1998–2000. Member: various boards, CNAA, 1971–83; Industry and Employment Cttee, ESRC, 1985–87. Pres., European Internat. Business Assoc., 1986. Fellow, European Inst. of Advanced Studies in Management, Brussels, 1985–87. Hon. DBA Strathclyde, 2003. *Publications*: (with S. Young): Chrysler UK: Corporation in transition, 1977; Economics of Multinational Enterprise, 1979; European Development Strategies of US-owned Manufacturing Companies Located in Scotland, 1980; Multinationals in Retreat: the Scottish experience, 1982, Multinational Investment Strategies in the British Isles, 1983; (ed) Industrial Policy and the Scottish Economy, 1984; (with P. Draper, I. Smith and W. Stewart) Scottish Financial Sector, 1987; (ed with J. E. Vahlne) Strategies in Global Competition, 1987; (with S. Young and J. Hamill) Foreign Multinationals and the British Economy, Impact and Policy, 1988; (ed with S. Shaw) Marketing in Evolution, 1996; (ed with R. Kilis and J. E. Vahlne) Transition in the Baltic States, 1997; (ed with J. Birkinshaw) Multinational Corporate Evolution and Subsidiary Development, 1998; (ed with S. Young) The Globalisation of Multinational Enterprise and Economic Development, 1999; (ed jtly) Scotland in the Global Economy, 2002; Whose Life is it Anyway?, 2002; God's Payroll: whose work is it anyway?, 2003; The Multinational Subsidiary: management, economic development and public policy, 2003; God's Wealth: whose money is it anyway?, 2004; Learning at the Crossroads: a traveller's guide to Christian life, 2005; articles on internat. business, marketing, economic development and business policy, in various jls. *Recreations*: reading, writing, swimming, golf, gardening. *Address*: 95 Mote Hill, Hamilton ML3 6EA. *T*: (01698) 424870. *Died 2 Feb. 2006*.

HOOD, Samuel Harold; Director, Defence Operational Analysis Establishment, Ministry of Defence, 1985–86; *b* 21 Aug. 1926; *s* of Samuel N. and Annie Hood; *m* 1959, Frances Eileen Todd; two *s* four *d*. *Educ*: Larne Grammar Sch., Co. Antrim; Queen's Univ., Belfast (BA Hons Maths). Joined Civil Service, staff of Scientific Advr, Air Min., 1948; Staff of Operational Res. Br., Bomber Comd, 1950; Scientific Officer, BCDU, RAF Wittering, 1954; Operational Res. Br., Bomber Comd, 1959; Staff of Chief Scientist (RAF), 1964; joined DOAE, 1965; Supt, Air Div., DOAE, 1969; Dir, Defence Sci. Divs 1 and 7, MoD, 1974; Head, Systems Assessment Dept, RAE, 1981. *Recreations*: walking, gardening, bird watching. *Address*: 29 St James Avenue, Richmond 7020, Nelson, New Zealand. *Died 30 Sept. 2008*.

HOOK, Sister Patricia Mary, DCNZM 2001; RSM; Sister of Mercy; *b* 4 Aug. 1921; *d* of Stanley M. and Mary Hook. *Educ*: Dominican Coll., South Is, NZ; Mercy Hosp. Sch. of Nursing, Auckland (Registered Nurse 1947); Wellington (DipNAdmin 1957); Gonzaga Univ.,

Washington (MA Spiritual Studies 1982). Served War of 1939–45, RNZAF: Section Officer (WAAF) RDF (Filter) Units Central and Northern Gps; discharged 1944. Entered St Mary's Convent, Sisters of Mercy, Auckland, 1948, professed as Sister Mary de Montfort, 1951; Mercy Hospital, Auckland: Registered Nurse, 1947–58; Midwife, 1958–64; Principal Nurse, Hosp. Admin, 1964–79; founder, and Director, Retreat and Spiritual Direction Centre (run by Sisters of Mercy), Epsom, Auckland, 1982–2000. Mem., Nat. Adv. Cttee to Minister of Health, NZ Health Planning, 1975–78. *Recreations:* reading, gardening, tramping. *Address:* St Mary's Convent, PO Box 47025, Ponsonby, Auckland, New Zealand. *T:* (3) 3786795, *Fax:* (3) 3602306.
Died 12 Jan. 2010.

HOOKER, Ronald George, CBE 1985; FREng; Chairman: Management & Business Services Ltd, since 1972; London Ventures Ltd, since 1991; company directorships; *b* 6 Aug. 1921; *m* 1954, Eve Pigott; one *s* one *d*. *Educ:* Wimbledon Technical Coll.; London Univ. (external). Hon. FIET (FIProdE 1980); FREng (FEng 1984). CIMgt (CBIM 1972). Apprentice, Philips Electrical Ltd, 1937–41, Develt Engr, 1945–48; FBI, 1948–50; Dir and Gen. Man., Brush Electrical Engineering Co. Ltd, 1950–60; Man. Dir, K & L Steelfounders & Engineers Ltd, 1960–65; Man. Dir, Associated Fire Alarms Ltd, 1965–68; Chm. and Man. Dir, Crane Fruehauf Trailers Ltd, 1968–71; Dir of Manufacture, Rolls Royce (1971) Ltd, 1971–73; Chm. and Man. Dir, John M. Henderson (Holdings) Ltd, 1973–75; Chairman: Thomas Storey Ltd, 1984–96; EAC Ltd, 1993–2006. Dir, Computing Devices Hldgs Ltd, 1986–92. Pres., Engrg Employers' Fedn, 1986–88 (Mem. Management Bd, 1977–); Mem., Engrg Council, 1982–86. Past Pres., IProdE, 1974–75 (Hon. Life MIProdE 1980); CCMI; FRSA. Freeman, City of London. *Publications:* papers on management and prodn engrg to BIM, ICMA, IProdE and IMechE. *Recreations:* gardening, reading, music. *Address:* Loxborough House, Bledlow Ridge, near High Wycombe, Bucks HP14 4AA. *T:* (01494) 481486. *Clubs:* Athenæum, Lansdowne.
Died 13 June 2010.

HOOLAHAN, Anthony Terence; QC 1973; a Recorder of the Crown Court, 1976–97; a Social Security Commissioner, 1986–97; a Child Support Commissioner, 1993–98; *b* 26 July 1925; *s* of late Gerald and Val Hoolahan; *m* 1949, Dorothy Veronica Connochie; one *s* one *d* (and one *d* decd). *Educ:* Dorset House, Littlehampton, Sussex; Framlingham Coll., Suffolk; Lincoln Coll., Oxford (MA). Served War, RNVR, 1943–46. Oxford Univ., 1946–48. Called to Bar, Inner Temple, 1949, Bencher, 1980; called to the Bar of Northern Ireland, 1980, QC (Northern Ireland) 1980. Chairman: Richmond Soc., 1976–80; Trustees, Richmond Museum, 1988–95. Gov., St Elizabeth's Sch., Richmond, 1990–99. *Publications:* Guide to Defamation Practice (with Colin Duncan, QC), 2nd edn, 1958; contrib. to Halsbury's Laws of England, Atkin's Court Forms. *Recreation:* swimming. *Address:* Fair Lawn, Ormond Avenue, Richmond, Surrey TW10 6TN.
Died 11 March 2006.

HOPE, Sir John (Carl Alexander), 18th Bt *cr* 1628 (NS), of Craighall; *b* 10 June 1939; *s* of Sir Archibald Philip Hope, 17th Bt, OBE, DFC, AE and of Ruth, *y d* of Carl Davis; *S* father, 1987; *m* 1968, Merle Pringle, *d* of late Robert Douglas, Holbrook, Ipswich; one *s* one *d*. *Educ:* Eton. *Heir:* *s* Alexander Archibald Douglas Hope [*b* 16 March 1969; *m* 2002, Emmeline Grace, *d* of Simon H. Barrow; two *s*]. *Address:* 29 Nicholas Court, Corney Reach Way, W4 2TS.
Died 30 Oct. 2007.

HOPKIN, Sir Bryan; see Hopkin, Sir W. A. B.

HOPKIN, His Honour John Raymond, DL; a Circuit Judge, 1979–2002; a Chairman, Mental Health Review Tribunals, 2001–05; *b* 23 June 1935; *s* of George Raymond Buxton Hopkin and Muriel Hopkin; *m* 1965, Susan Mary Limb; one *s* one *d*. *Educ:* King's Sch.,

Worcester. Called to Bar, Middle Temple, 1958; in practice at the Bar, 1959–79. A Recorder of the Crown Court, 1978–79. A Chm. of Disciplinary Tribunals, Council of Inns of Court, 1987–90. Mem. Bd, Law Sch., Nottingham Trent Univ., 1998–2004; Chm. of Governors, Nottingham High Sch. for Girls, 1992–2006. Mem., Cathedral Council, Southwell Minster, 2005–. DL Notts, 1996. *Recreations:* fell walking and climbing, gardening, golf, the theatre. *Club:* Nottingham and Notts Services.
Died 22 July 2010.

HOPKIN, Sir (William Aylsham) Bryan, Kt 1971; CBE 1961; Hon. Professorial Fellow, Swansea University (formerly University College, Swansea), since 1988; *b* 7 Dec. 1914; *s* of late William Hopkin and Lilian Hopkin (*née* Cottelle); *m* 1938, Renée Ricour (*d* 2002); two *s*. *Educ:* Barry (Glam.) County Sch.; St John's Coll., Cambridge (Hon. Fellow, 1982); Manchester Univ. Ministry of Health, 1938–41; Prime Minister's Statistical Branch, 1941–45; Royal Commn on Population, 1945–48; Econ. Sect., Cabinet Office, 1948–50; Central Statistical Office, 1950–52; Dir, Nat. Inst. of Econ. and Soc. Research, 1952–57; Sec., Council on Prices, Productivity, and Incomes, 1957–58; Dep. Dir, Econ. Sect., HM Treasury, 1958–65; Econ. Planning Unit, Mauritius, 1965; Min. of Overseas Develt, 1966–67; Dir-Gen. of Economic Planning, ODM, 1967–69; Dir-Gen., DEA, 1969; Dep. Chief Econ. Adviser, HM Treasury, 1970–72; Prof. of Econs, UC Cardiff, 1972–82 (on leave of absence, Head of Govt Economic Service and Chief Economic Advr, HM Treasury, 1974–77). Mem., Commonwealth Develt Corp., 1972–74. Chm., Manpower Services Cttee for Wales, 1978–79. *Address:* Bedford Charterhouse, Kimbolton Road, Bedford MK40 2PU. *T:* (01234) 267757.
Died 10 Oct. 2009.

HOPWOOD, Prof. Anthony George; American Standard Companies Professor of Operations Management, University of Oxford, and Student of Christ Church, Oxford, 1997–2009; *b* 18 May 1944; *s* of late George and Violet Hopwood; *m* 1967, Caryl Davies; two *s*. *Educ:* Hanley High School; LSE (BSc Econ); Univ. of Chicago (MBA, PhD). Fulbright Fellow, Univ. of Chicago, 1965–70; Lectr in Management Accounting, Manchester Business Sch., 1970–73; Senior Staff, Admin. Staff Coll., Henley, 1973–76; Professorial Fellow, Oxford Centre for Management Studies, 1976–78; ICA Prof. of Accounting and Financial Reporting, London Business Sch., 1978–85; Arthur Young, subseq. Ernst and Young, Prof. of Internat. Accounting and Financial Management, LSE, 1985–95; Oxford University: Prof. of Management Studies, and Fellow, Templeton Coll., 1995–97; School of Management Studies, later Saïd Business School: Dep. Dir, 1995–98; Dir, then Peter Moores Dean, 1999–2006; Visitor, Ashmolean Mus., 2000–03. Vis. Prof. of Management, European Inst. for Advanced Studies in Management, Brussels, 1972– (Pres., 1995–2003; Hon. Fellow, 2003); Associate Fellow, Industrial Relations Research Unit, Univ. of Warwick, 1978–80; Dist. Internat. Vis. Lectr, 1981, Presidential Schol., 2006, Amer. Accounting Assoc. (Lifetime Achievement Award, 2002, 2008); Distinguished Vis. Prof. of Accounting, Pennsylvania State Univ., 1983–88. Foreign Mem., Swedish Royal Soc. of Scis, 2003. Mem., Management and Industrial Relations Cttee, SSRC, 1975–79; Chm., Management Awards Panel, SSRC, 1976–79; Pres., European Accounting Assoc., 1977–79 and 1987–88 (Academic Leadership Award, 2005); Member: Council, Tavistock Inst. of Human Relations, 1981–91; Research Bd, ICA, 1982–98; Dir, Greater London Enterprise Bd, 1985–87. Accounting Advr, EC, 1989–90; Accounting Cons., OECD, 1990–91. Chm., Prince's Foundn for the Built Envmt, 2006–; Mem. Exec. Bd, Prince's Accounting for Sustainability Proj., 2008– (Sen. Advr, 2006–07). Editor-in-Chief, Accounting, Organizations and Society, 1976–. Hon. DEcon: Turku Sch. of Econs, Finland, 1989; Gothenburg, 1992; Hon. DSc Lincolnshire and Humberside, 1999; Hon. Dr Mercaturae. Copenhagen Business Sch., 2000; DUniv Siena, 2003. Dist. Academic Award, BAA, 1998.

Publications: An Accounting System and Managerial Behaviour, 1973; Accounting and Human Behaviour, 1973; (with M. Bromwich) Essays in British Accounting Research, 1981; (with M. Bromwich and J. Shaw) Auditing Research, 1982; (with M. Bromwich) Accounting Standard Setting, 1983; (with H. Schreuder) European Contributions to Accounting Research, 1984; (with C. Tomkins) Issues in Public Sector Accounting, 1984; (with M. Bromwich) Research and Current Issues in Management Accounting, 1986; Accounting from the Outside: the collected papers of Anthony G. Hopwood, 1988; International Pressures for Accounting Change, 1989; (with M. Page and S. Turley) Understanding Accounting in a Changing Environment, 1990; (with M. Bromwich) Accounting and the Law, 1992; (with P. Miller) Accounting as Social and Institutional Practice, 1994; (with C. Leuz and D. Pfaff) The Economics and Politics of Accounting, 2004; (with C. Chapman and M. Shields) Handbook of Management Accounting Research, vols 1 and 2, 2007, vol. 3, 2009; articles in learned and professional jls. *Address:* Saïd Business School, University of Oxford, Park End Street, Oxford OX1 1HP. *T:* (01865) 288800.   *Died 8 May 2010.*

HORDEN, Prof. John Robert Backhouse, FSA, FSAScot, FRSL; Emeritus Professor of Bibliographical Studies, University of Stirling, since 1988; Editor, Dictionary of Scottish Biography; *o s* of late Henry Robert Horden and Ethel Edith Horden (*née* Backhouse), Warwicks; *m* 1948, Aileen Mary (*d* 1984), *o d* of late Lt Col and Mrs W. J. Douglas, Warwicks and S Wales; one *s*. *Educ:* Oxford, Cambridge, Heidelberg, Sorbonne, Lincoln's Inn. Revived and ed The *Isis*, 1945–46. Previously: Tutor and Lectr in English Literature, Christ Church, Oxford; Director, Inst. of Bibliography and Textual Criticism, Univ. of Leeds; Dir, Centre for Bibliographical Studies, Univ. of Stirling. Vis. professorial appts, Univs of Pennsylvania State, Saskatchewan, Erlangen-Nürnberg, Texas at Austin, Münster; Cecil Oldman Meml Lectr in Bibliography and Textual Criticism, 1971. Hon. Life Mem., Modern Humanities Res. Assoc., 1976. DHL (*hc*) Indiana State Univ., 1974. Marc Fitch Prize for Bibliography, 1979. Devised new academic discipline of Publishing Studies and designed first British degree course at Univ. of Leeds, 1972 (MA); initiated first British degree in Public Relations (MSc), Univ. of Stirling, 1987. *Publications:* Francis Quarles: a bibliography of his works to 1800, 1953; (ed) Francis Quarles' Hosanna and Threnodes, 1960, 3rd edn 1965; John Quarles (1625–1665): an analytical bibliography, 1960; Arthur Warwick's Spare Minutes (1634): an analytical bibliography, 1965; (ed) Annual Bibliography of English Language and Literature, 1967–75; (ed) English and Continental Emblem Books (22 vols), 1968–76; Art of the Drama, 1969; (ed) George Wither's A Collection of Emblemes, 1973; Everyday Life in Seventeenth-century England, 1974; (contrib.) New Cambridge Bibliography of English Literature, 1974; Techniques of Bibliography, 1977; (ed) Dictionary of Concealed Authorship, vol. 1, 1980 (1st vol. of rev. Halkett and Laing); (initiator and first editor) Index of English Literary Manuscripts (11 vols), 1980–97; John Freeth: political ballad writer and innkeeper, 1988, 2nd edn 1993; (ed) Bibliographia, 1992; (ed jtly) Francis Quarles' Emblemes and Hieroglyphikes, 1993; numerous contribs to learned jls. *Recreations:* golf (represented England, Warwicks, Oxford, and Cambridge); music, painting. *Address:* 57 Churchill Drive, Bridge of Allan, Stirlingshire FK9 4TJ. *T:* (01786) 833925. *Clubs:* Athenæum; Vincent's (Oxford); Hawks' (Cambridge).   *Died 21 June 2007.*

HORLOCK, Henry Wimburn Sudell; Underwriting Member of Lloyd's, 1957–2004; Director, Stepping Stone School, 1962–87; *b* 19 July 1915; *s* of Rev. Henry Darrell Sudell Horlock, DD, and Mary Haliburton Laurie; *m* 1960, Jeannetta Robin, *d* of F. W. Tanner, JP. *Educ:* Pembroke Coll., Oxford (MA). Army, 1939–42. Civil Service, 1942–60. Court of Common Council, City of London, 1969–2001 (Chm., West Ham Park Cttee, 1979–82; Chm., Police Cttee, 1987–90); Deputy, Ward

of Farringdon Within, 1978–99; Sheriff, City of London, 1972–73; Chm., City of London Sheriffs' Soc., 1985–2003; Liveryman: Saddlers Co., 1937–, Master, 1976–77; Plaisterers' Co. (Hon.), 1975–; Fletchers' Co., 1977–; Gardeners' Co., 1980–; Member: Parish Clerks' Co., 1966–, Master, 1981–82; Guild of Freemen, 1972–, Master, 1986–87; Farringdon Ward Club, 1970–, Pres., 1978–79; United Wards Club, 1972–, Pres., 1980–81; City Livery Club, 1969–, Pres., 1981–82; City of London Br., Royal Society of St George, 1972–, Chm., 1989–90. Commander: Order of Merit, Federal Republic of Germany, 1972; National Order of the Aztec Eagle of Mexico, 1973; Order of Wissam Alouite, Morocco, 1987. *Recreations:* Freemasonry, gardening, travel. *Address:* Copse Hill House, Lower Slaughter, Glos GL54 2HZ. *T:* (01451) 820276. *Clubs:* Athenæum, Guildhall, City Livery.   *Died 26 Aug. 2009.*

HORNBY, Prof. James Angus; Professor of Law in the University of Bristol, 1961–85, then Emeritus; *b* 15 Aug. 1922; twin *s* of James Hornby and Evelyn Gladys (*née* Grant). *Educ:* Bolton County Grammar Sch.; Christ's Coll., Cambridge (BA 1944, LLB 1945, MA 1948). Called to Bar, Lincoln's Inn, 1947. Lecturer, Manchester Univ., 1947–61. *Publications:* An Introduction to Company Law, 1957, 5th edn 1975; contribs to legal journals. *Recreations:* listening to music, reading, walking. *Address:* Flat 9, St Monica Court, Cote Lane, Westbury-on-Trym, Bristol BS9 3TL.   *Died 4 Oct. 2009.*

HORNBY, Richard Phipps, MA; Chairman, Halifax Building Society, 1983–90 (Director, 1976; Vice-Chairman, 1981–83); *b* 20 June 1922; *e s* of late Rt Rev. Hugh Leycester Hornby, MC; *m* 1951, Stella Hichens; two *s* one *d* (and one *s* decd). *Educ:* Winchester Coll.; Trinity Coll., Oxford (Scholar). Served in King's Royal Rifle Corps, 1941–45. 2nd Cl. Hons in Modern History, Oxford, 1948 (Soccer Blue). History Master, Eton Coll., 1948–50; with Unilever, 1951–52; with J. Walter Thompson Co., 1952–63, 1964–81 (Dir, 1974–81); Director: McCorquodale plc, 1982–86; Cadbury Schweppes plc, 1982–93. Contested (C) West Walthamstow: May 1955 (gen. election) and March 1956 (by-election); MP (C) Tonbridge, Kent, June 1956–Feb. 1974. PPS to Rt Hon. Duncan Sandys, MP, 1959–63; Parly Under-Sec. of State, CRO and CO, Oct. 1963–Oct. 1964. Member: BBC Gen. Adv. Council, 1969–74; Cttee of Inquiry into Intrusions into Privacy, 1970–72; British Council Exec. Cttee, 1971–74. *Recreations:* shooting, fishing, walking. *Address:* Ebble Thatch, Bowerchalke, near Salisbury, Wilts SP5 5BW.   *Died 22 Sept. 2007.*

HORNBY, Sir Simon (Michael), Kt 1988; Director, 1974–94, Chairman, 1982–94, W. H. Smith Group (formerly W. H. Smith & Son (Holdings) plc); Director: Pearson plc (formerly S. Pearson & Son Ltd), 1978–97; Lloyds TSB Group (formerly Lloyds Bank), 1988–99; Lloyds Abbey Life PLC, 1991–97 (Chairman, 1992–97); *b* 29 Dec. 1934; *s* of late Michael Hornby and Nicolette Joan, *d* of Hon. Cyril Ward, MVO; *m* 1968, Sheran Cazalet. *Educ:* Eton; New Coll., Oxford; Harvard Business Sch. 2nd Lieut, Grenadier Guards, 1953–55. Entered W. H. Smith & Son, 1958, Dir, 1965; Gp Chief Exec., W. H. Smith & Son (Holdings), 1978–82. Mem. Exec. Cttee, 1966–93, Property Cttee, 1979–86, Council 1976–2001, National Trust; Mem. Adv. Council, Victoria and Albert Museum, 1971–75; Council, RSA, 1985–90; Trustee, British Museum, 1984–85; Chairman: Design Council, 1986–92; Assoc. for Business Sponsorship of the Arts, 1988–97; Nat. Literacy Trust, 1993–2001 (Pres., 2001–); President: Book Trust, 1990–96 (Dep. Chm., 1976–78, Chm., 1978–80, NBL); Newsvendors' Benevolent Instn, 1989–94; RHS, 1994–2001 (Mem. Council, 1992–2001); Chelsea Soc., 1994–2000. DUniv Stirling, 1992; Hon. DLitt: Hull, 1994; Reading, 1996. *Recreations:* gardening, cooking. *Address:* The Ham, Wantage, Oxon OX12 9JA. *T:* (01235) 770222.   *Died 17 July 2010.*

HORNE, Frederic Thomas; Chief Taxing Master of the Supreme Court, 1983–88 (Master, 1967–83); *b* 21 March 1917; *y s* of Lionel Edward Horne, JP, Moreton-in-Marsh, Glos; *m* 1944, Madeline Hatton; two *s* two *d*. *Educ:* Chipping Campden Grammar Sch. Admitted a Solicitor (Hons), 1938. Served with RAFVR in General Duties Branch (Pilot), 1939–56. Partner in Iliffe Sweet & Co., 1956–67. Mem., Lord Chancellor's Adv. Cttee on Legal Aid, 1983–91; Chm., Working Party on the Simplification of Taxation, 1980–83 (Horne Report, 1983). Pres., Assoc. of Law Costs Draftsmen, 1991–97. *Publications:* Cordery's Law Relating to Solicitors, 7th edn (jtly) 1981, 8th edn 1987; (contrib.) Atkins Encyclopaedia of Court Forms, 2nd edn, 1983; (ed jtly) The Supreme Court Practice, 1985 and 1988 edns; (contrib.) Private International Litigation, 1987. *Recreations:* cricket, music, archaeology. *Address:* Dunstall, Quickley Lane, Chorleywood, Herts WD3 5AF. *Club:* MCC. *Died 24 Jan. 2010.*

HORSBRUGH, Ian Robert; Principal, Guildhall School of Music & Drama, 1988–2002; *b* 16 Sept. 1941; *s* of Walter and Sheila Horsbrugh; *m* 1965, Caroline Everett; two *s* two *d*. *Educ:* St Paul's Sch.; Guildhall Sch. of Music and Drama (AGSM); Royal Coll. of Music (ARCM). FGSM 1988; FRCM 1988; FRSAMD 1993; FRNCM 1993. Head of Music: St Mary's Sch., Hendon, 1969–72; Villiers High Sch., Southall, 1972–79; Dep. Warden, ILEA Music Centre, 1979–84; Vice-Dir, Royal Coll. of Music, 1985–88. Mem., Music Panel and Chm., New Music Sub-Cttee, Arts Council, 1981–87; Member: Music Adv. Cttee, British Council, 1987–97; Steering Cttee, Nat. Studio for Electronic Music, 1986–89; Bd, City Arts Trust, 1989–2002; Management Bd, London Internat. String Quartet Competition, 1989–2002; Council, NYO, 1989–2002; Arts and Entertainment Training Council, 1990–94; Bd, Bath Fests Trust, 1997–2004; Bd, English Touring Opera, 1998–; Dep. Chm., London Arts Bd, 1991–99. Vice-Pres., Nat. Assoc. of Youth Orchestras, 1989–2002; Pres., Assoc. of European Conservatoires, 1996–2004 (Hon. Pres. 2004–). Trustee, Parkhouse Award, 1990– (Chm., 1990–92). Treasurer, 1977–79, Chm., 1979–84, New Macnaghten Concerts. Hon. RAM 1993; FRSA. Hon. DMus: City, 1995; New England Conservatory, Boston, Mass. *Publications:* Leoš Janáček: the field that prospered, 1981. *Recreations:* watching Rugby football and cricket, reading, walking, cycling. *Address:* 10 Dorchester Mews, Twickenham, Middx TW1 2LE. *Club:* MCC. *Died 22 July 2006.*

HORSFIELD, Maj.-Gen. David Ralph, OBE 1962; FIET; *b* 17 Dec. 1916; *s* of late Major Ralph B. and Morah Horsfield (*née* Baynes); *m* 1948, Sheelah Patricia Royal Eagan; two *s* two *d*. *Educ:* Oundle Sch.; RMA Woolwich; Clare Coll., Cambridge Univ. (MA). Commnd in Royal Signals, 1936; British troops, Egypt, 1939–41; comd Burma Corps Signals, 1942; Instr, Staff Coll., Quetta, 1944–45; comd 2 Indian Airborne Signals, 1946–47; Instr, RMA Sandhurst, 1950–53 (Company Comdr to HM King Hussein of Jordan); comd 2 Signal Regt, 1956–59; Principal Army Staff Officer, MoD, Malaya, 1959–61; Dir of Telecommunications (Army), 1966–68; ADC to the Queen, 1968–69; Deputy Communications and Electronics, Supreme HQ Allied Powers, Europe, 1968–69; Maj.-Gen. 1969; Chief Signal Officer, BAOR, 1969–72; Col Comdt, Royal Signals, 1972–78. Pres., Indian Signals Assoc. of GB, 1978–; Vice Pres., Nat. Ski Fedn, 1978–81. *Recreations:* ski-ing (British Ski Champion, 1949), the visual arts. *Address:* Preybrook Farm, Preywater Road, Wookey, Wells BA5 1LE. *T:* (01749) 673241. *Club:* Ski Club of Great Britain. *Died 7 Dec. 2008.*

HORSFORD, Maj.-Gen. Derek Gordon Thomond, CBE 1962 (MBE 1953); DSO 1944 and Bar 1945; *b* 7 Feb. 1917; *s* of late Captain H. T. Horsford, The Gloucestershire Regt, and Mrs V. E. Horsford; *m* 1st, 1948, Sheila Louise Russell Crawford (*d* 1995); one *s*, and one step *s* two step *d*; 2nd, 1996, Gillian Patricia Moorhouse, *d* of K. O'B. Horsford; two step *s*. *Educ:* Clifton Coll.; RMC, Sandhurst. Commissioned into 8th Gurkha Rifles, 1937; NW Frontier, 1939–41; despatches 1943 and 1945; comd 4/1 Gurkha Rifles, Burma, 1944–45; transf. to RA, 1948; Instructor Staff Coll., 1950–52; transf. to King's Regt, 1950, Korea, 1952–53; GSO1, 2nd Infantry Div., 1955–56; comd 1st Bn, The King's Regt, 1957–59; AAG, AG2, War Office, 1959–60; Comdr 24th Infantry Brigade Group, Dec. 1960–Dec. 1962, Kenya and Kuwait; Imperial Defence Coll., 1963; Brig., Gen. Staff, HQ, BAOR, 1964–66. Maj.-Gen. 1966; GOC 50 (Northumbrian) Div./Dist, 1966–67; GOC Yorks Dist, 1967–68; GOC 17 Div./Malaya District, 1969–70; Maj.-Gen., Brigade of Gurkhas, 1969–71; Dep. Comdr Land Forces, Hong Kong, 1970–71, retired. Col, The King's Regt, 1965–70; Col, The Gurkha Transport Regt, 1973–78. Sec., Council, League of Remembrance (Pres., 2004). *Recreations:* travel, reading, all sport. *Died 5 Oct. 2007.*

HOSKYNS, Sir Benedict (Leigh), 16th Bt, *cr* 1676; *b* 27 May 1928; *s* of Rev. Sir Edwyn Clement Hoskyns, 13th Bt, MC, DD and Mary Trym (*d* 1994), *d* of Edwin Budden, Macclesfield; *S* brother 1956; *m* 1953, Ann Wilkinson; two *s* two *d*. *Educ:* Haileybury; Corpus Christi Coll., Cambridge; London Hospital. BA Cantab 1949; MB, BChir Cantab 1952. House Officer at the London Hospital, 1953. RAMC, 1953–56. House Officer at Royal Surrey County Hospital and General Lying-In Hospital, York Road, SE1, 1957–58; DObstRCOG 1958; in general practice, 1958–93. *Heir:* *s* Edwyn Wren Hoskyns [*b* 4 Feb. 1956; *m* 1981, Jane, *d* of John Sellars; one *s* one *d*. *Educ:* Nottingham Univ. Medical School (BM, BS). MRCP, FRCPCH. Cons. Paediatrician, Leicester Gen. Hosp, 1993–]. *Address:* Russell House, Wherry Corner, High Street, Manningtree, Essex CO11 1AP. *T:* (01206) 396432. *Died 2 June 2010.*

HOUGH, George Hubert, CBE 1965; PhD; FRAeS; Founder Director, British Aerospace, 1977; *b* 21 Oct. 1921; *m* Hazel Ayrton (*née* Russel); one *s* two *d*. *Educ:* Winsford Grammar Sch.; King's Coll., London (BSc (Hons Physics), PhD). Admiralty Signals Estabt, 1940–46; Standard Telecommunication Laboratories (ITT), 1946–51 (as external student at London Univ. prepared thesis on gaseous discharge tubes); de Havilland Propellers Ltd: early mem. Firestreak team in charge of develt of guidance systems and proximity fusing, 1951–59; Chief Engr (Guided Weapons), 1959; Chief Executive (Engrg), 1961; Dir, de Havilland Aircraft Co., 1962; Hawker Siddeley Dynamics Ltd: Technical Dir, 1963; Dep. Managing Dir, 1968; Man. Dir, 1977; Dep. Chief Exec., Dynamics Group, British Aerospace, 1977. Chairman and Chief Executive: British Smelter Constructions Ltd, 1978–80; Magnetic Components Ltd, 1986–89; Fernau Hldgs Ltd, 1989–94; Fernau Avionics Ltd, 1989–94; Chairman: Forthstar Ltd, 1980–99; Abasec Ltd, 1988–92; Director: Sheepbridge Engrg Ltd, 1977–79; Scientific Finance Ltd, 1979–84; Programmed Neuro Cybernetics (UK) Ltd, 1979–85; Landis & Gyr Ltd, 1980–85; Leigh Instruments Ltd (Canada), 1987–88. *Publications:* (with Dr P. Morris) The Anatomy of Major Projects, 1987. *Recreation:* golf. *Address:* Trelyon, Rock, near Wadebridge, Cornwall PL27 6LB. *T:* (01208) 863454. *Died 26 July 2006.*

HOUSSEMAYNE du BOULAY, (Edward Philip) George, CBE 1985; FRCR, FRCP; Professor of Neuroradiology, University of London at Institute of Neurology, 1975–84, then Emeritus; Hon. Research Fellow, Zoological Society of London (Head, X-Ray Department, Nuffield Laboratories, Institute of Zoology, 1965–86); Director, Radiological Research Trust, since 1985; *b* 28 Jan. 1922; *yr s* of Philip Houssemayne du Boulay and Mercy Tyrrell (*née* Friend); *m* 1944, Vivien M. Glasson (marr. diss.); four *s* (and two *s* decd); *m* 1968, Pamela Mary Verity; two *d*. *Educ:* Christ's Hospital; King's Coll., London; Charing Cross Hosp. (Entrance Schol. 1940; MB, BS, DMRD). Served RAF (Medical),

1946–48; Army Emergency Reserve, 1952–57. House appts, Charing Cross Hosp. and Derby City Hosp., 1945–46; Registrar (Radiology), Middlesex Hosp., 1948–49; Sen. Registrar (Radiology): St Bartholomew's Hosp., 1949–54; St George's Hosp., 1951–52; Consultant Radiologist: Nat. Hosp. for Nervous Diseases, Maida Vale, 1954–68; Bartholomew's Hosp., 1954–71; Nat. Hosp. for Nervous Diseases, Queen Square, 1968–75 (Head, Lysholm Radiol Dept, 1975–84). Editor, Neuroradiology, 1974–91. Pres., Brit. Inst. of Radiology, 1976–77, Appeal Co-ordinator 1976–84; Hon. Member: Société Française de Neuroradiologie; Amer. Soc. of Neuroradiology; Swedish Soc. of Neuroradiology; German Soc. Neuroradiology. Trustee, Nat. Hosp. Develt Foundn. Glyn Evans Meml Lectr, RCR, 1970; Ernestine Henry Lectr, RCP, 1976. Hon. FACR. Hon. DSc Leicester Polytechnic, 1992. Barclay Medal, BIR, 1968. *Publications:* Principles of X-Ray Diagnosis of the Skull, 1965, 2nd edn 1979; (jtly) 4th edn of A Text Book of X-Ray Diagnosis by British Authors: Neuroradiology Vol. 1, 5th edn 1984; (jtly) The Cranial Arteries of Mammals, 1973; (jtly) An Atlas of Normal Vertebral Angiograms, 1976; works in specialist jls. *Recreation:* gardening. *Address:* Old Manor House, Brington, Huntingdon, Cambs PE28 5AF. *T:* (01832) 710353.
Died 25 March 2009.

HOVING, Thomas Pearsall Field; President, Hoving Associates, Inc., since 1977; Editor-in Chief, Connoisseur, 1982–91; *b* 15 Jan. 1931; *s* of late Walter Hoving and Mary Osgood (*née* Field); *m* 1953, Nancy Melissa Bell; one *d*. *Educ:* Princeton Univ. BA Highest Hons, 1953; Nat. Council of the Humanities Fellowship, 1955; Kienbusch and Haring Fellowship, 1957; MFA 1958; PhD 1959. Dept of Medieval Art and The Cloisters, Metropolitan Museum of Art: Curatorial Asst, 1959; Asst Curator, 1960; Associate Curator, 1963; Curator, 1965; Commissioner of Parks, New York City, 1966; Administrator of Recreation and Cultural Affairs, New York City, 1967; Dir, Metropolitan Museum of Art, 1967–77. Distinguished Citizen's Award, Citizen's Budget Cttee, 1967. Hon. Mem. AIA, 1967. Hon. LLD, Pratt Inst., 1967; Dr *hc* Princeton; New York Univ. Middlebury and Woodrow Wilson Awards, Princeton. *Publications:* The Sources of the Ada Group Ivories (PhD thesis), 1959; Guide to The Cloisters, 1962; The Chase and The Capture, 1976; Two Worlds of Andrew Wyeth, 1977; Tutankhamun, the Untold Story, 1978; King of the Confessors, 1981; Masterpiece (novel), 1986; Discovery (novel), 1989; Making the Mummies Dance: inside the Metropolitan Museum of Art, 1993; (introd.) Andrew Wyeth: autobiography, 1995; False Impressions: the hunt for big time art fakes, 1996; Greatest Works of Art of Western Civilization, 1997; Art for Dummies, 1999; The Art of Dan Namingha, 2000; Master Pieces: the curator's game, 2005; articles in Apollo magazine and Metropolitan Museum of Art Bulletin. *Recreations:* sailing, ski-ing, bicycling, flying. *Address:* (office) Hoving Associates, 150 East 73rd Street, New York, NY 10021, USA.
Died 10 Dec. 2009.

HOWARD, Anthony Michell, CBE 1997; journalist and broadcaster; Obituaries Editor, 1993–99, weekly columnist, 1999–2005, The Times; *b* 12 Feb. 1934; *s* of late Canon Guy Howard and Janet Rymer Howard; *m* 1965, Carol Anne Gaynor. *Educ:* Westminster Sch.; Christ Church, Oxford (Hon. Student, 2003). Chm., Oxford Univ. Labour Club, 1954; Pres., Oxford Union, 1955. Called to Bar, Inner Temple, 1956. Nat. Service, 2nd Lieut, Royal Fusiliers, 1956–58; Political Corresp., Reynolds News, 1958–59; Editorial Staff, Manchester Guardian, 1959–61 (Harkness Fellowship in USA, 1960); Political Corresp., New Statesman, 1961–64; Whitehall Corresp., Sunday Times, 1965; Washington Corresp., Observer, 1966–69 and Political Columnist, 1971–72; Asst Editor, 1970–72, Editor, 1972–78, New Statesman; Editor, The Listener, 1979–81; Dep. Editor, The Observer, 1981–88; Presenter: Face the Press, Channel Four, 1982–85; The Editors, Sky News TV, 1989–90; Reporter, BBC TV News and Current Affairs (Panorama

and Newsnight), 1989–92; Chief political book reviewer, Sunday Times, 1990–2004. Hon. LLD Nottingham, 2001; Hon. DLitt Leicester, 2003. Gerald Barry Award, What the Papers Say, 1999. *Publications:* (contrib.) The Baldwin Age, 1960; (contrib.) Age of Austerity, 1963; (with Richard West) The Making of the Prime Minister, 1965; (ed) The Crossman Diaries: selections from the Diaries of a Cabinet Minister, 1979; Rab: the life of R. A. Butler, 1987; Crossman: the pursuit of power, 1990; (contrib.) Secrets of the Press, 1999; Basil Hume: the Monk Cardinal, 2005. *Address:* 11 Campden House Court, 42 Gloucester Walk, W8 4HU. *T:* (020) 7937 7313. *Clubs:* Garrick, Beefsteak.
Died 19 Dec. 2010.

HOWARD, Rev. Canon Donald; Provost, St Andrew's Cathedral, Aberdeen, 1978–91, retired; *b* 21 Jan. 1927; *s* of William Howard and Alexandra Eadie (*née* Buchanan); unmarried. *Educ:* Hull Coll. of Technology; London Univ. (BD, AKC). AFRAeS 1954–58. Design Engineer, Blackburn Aircraft, 1948–52; Hunting Percival Aircraft, 1952–54; English Electric Co., 1954–55. Assistant Minister, Emmanuel Church, Saltburn by-the-Sea Yorks, 1959–62; Rector and Mission Director, Dio. Kimberley and Kuruman, S Africa, 1962–65; Rector of St John the Evangelist, East London, S Africa, 1965–72; Rector of Holy Trinity Episcopal Church, Haddington, Scotland, 1972–78. Honorary Canon: Christ Church Cathedral, Hartford, Conn, USA, 1978–91; St Andrew's Cathedral, Aberdeen, 1991. *Address:* 42 Waterside, Bondgate, Ripon, North Yorkshire HG4 1RA. *T:* (01765) 692144.
Died 30 Jan. 2007.

HOWARD, James Boag, CB 1972; Assistant Under-Secretary of State, Home Office, 1963–75; *b* 10 Jan. 1915; *yr s* of William and Jean Howard, Greenock; *m* 1943, Dorothy Jean Crawshaw (*d* 2000); two *d*. *Educ:* Greenock High Sch.; Glasgow Univ. (MA, BSc; 1st cl. Hons Mathematics and Natural Philosophy). Asst Principal, Home Office, 1937; Private Sec. to Permanent Sec., Ministry of Home Security, 1940–41; Principal, 1941; Asst Sec., 1948. *Address:* 12 Windhill, Bishop's Stortford, Herts CM23 2NG. *T:* (01279) 651728.
Died 22 May 2010.

HOWARD, Air Vice-Marshal Peter, CB 1989; OBE 1957; FRCP, FRAeS; Commandant, RAF Institute of Aviation Medicine, 1975–88; The Senior Consultant, RAF, 1987–88; *b* 15 Dec. 1925; *s* of late Edward Charles Howard and Doris Mary Howard (*née* Cure); *m* 1950, Norma Lockhart Fletcher; one *s* one *d*. *Educ:* Farnborough Grammar Sch.; St Thomas's Hosp. Med. Sch. (MB BS 1949, PhD 1964). FRCP 1977; FFOM 1981; FRAeS 1973. House Physician, 1950, Registrar, 1951. St Thomas' Hosp.; RAF Medical Branch, 1951–88; RAF Consultant in Aviation Physiology, 1964; RAF Consultant Adviser in Occupational Medicine, 1983–85; Dean of Air Force Medicine, 1985–87. QHP 1982–88. Chm., Defence Med. Services Postgraduate Council, 1986–87; Registrar, Faculty of Occupational Medicine, RCP, 1986–91. *Publications:* papers and chapters in books on aviation physiology, medicine, occupational medicine. *Recreations:* fly fishing, computing. *Address:* 135 Aldershot Road, Church Crookham, Fleet, Hants GU52 8JU. *T:* (01252) 617309. *Club:* Royal Air Force.
Died 21 Oct. 2007.

HOWARD, Peter Milner; freelance journalist; Editor, Jane's Defence Industry, 2001–05; *b* 27 June 1937; *s* of Thomas Roland Howard and Margaret A. Howard (*née* Potter); *m* 1965, Janet Crownshaw; one *s* one *d*. *Educ:* St Thomas C of E Sch., Heaton Chapel; Dialstone Lane Mod. Sec., Stockport; Woodseats Co., Sheffield; Sheffield Coll. of Commerce and Tech. (NCTJ Prof. Cert. 1960); Univ. of Chichester (BA Hons History 2006). Copy boy, reporter, sports reporter and sub-editor, The Star, Sheffield, 1952–58; Nat. Service, Army, 1958–60; The Star, Sheffield: sports reporter and sub-editor, 1960–73; Sports Editor, 1973–75; Inf. Officer, MoD, 1975–83; Sen. Inf. Officer and Editor, Soldier Mag., 1983–85; Jane's Defence Weekly: Features Editor, 1985–87; Man. Editor, 1987–89; Editor,

1989–95; Man. Editor, Military and Tri-Service Gp, 1995–98, Editor, Jane's Navy Internat., 1998–2001, Jane's Inf. Gp. *Publications:* Secret Operations: underwater raid on the Tirpitz, 2006. *Recreations:* military history, military music, golf, walking. *Address:* Mildmay Cottage, Hawkley Road, West Liss, Hants GU33 6JL. *T:* (01730) 893307. *Died 17 Feb. 2007.*

HOWARD-DOBSON, Gen. Sir Patrick John, GCB 1979 (KCB 1974; CB 1973); *b* 12 Aug. 1921; *s* of late Canon Howard Dobson, MA; *m* 1946, Barbara Mary Mills (*d* 2004); two *s* one *d*. *Educ:* King's Coll. Choir Sch., Cambridge; Framlingham College. Joined 7th Queen's Own Hussars, Egypt, Dec. 1941; served in: Burma, 1942; Middle East, 1943; Italy, 1944–45; Germany, 1946; psc 1950; jssc 1958; comd The Queen's Own Hussars, 1963–65 and 20 Armoured Bde, 1965–67; idc 1968; Chief of Staff, Far East Comd, 1969–71; Comdt, Staff Coll., Camberley, 1972–74; Military Secretary, 1974–76; Quartermaster General, 1977–79; Vice-Chief of Defence Staff (Personnel and Logistics), 1979–81; ADC Gen. to the Queen, 1978–81. Col Comdt, ACC, 1976–82. Nat. Pres., Royal British Legion, 1981–87. Virtuti Militari (Poland), 1945; Silver Star (US), 1945. *Recreations:* sailing, golf. *Address:* 1 Drury Park, Snape, Saxmundham, Suffolk IP17 1TA. *Clubs:* Royal Cruising; Senior Golfers' Society. *Died 8 Nov. 2009.*

HOWE, Josephine Mary O'C.; *see* O'Connor Howe.

HOWELL, Air Vice-Marshal (Evelyn Michael) Thomas, CBE 1961; CEng, FRAeS; *b* 11 Sept. 1913; *s* of Sir Evelyn Berkeley Howell, KCIE, CSI; *m* 1st, 1937, Helen Joan, *o d* of late Brig. W. M. Hayes, CBE, FRICS (marr. diss. 1972); one *s* three *d*; 2nd, 1972, Rosemary, *e d* of late I. A. Cram, CEng, MICE; one *s* one *d*. *Educ:* Downside Sch.; RAF Coll., Cranwell. Commissioned, 1934; Dir of Air Armament Research and Devt, Min. of Aviation, 1960–62; Comdt, RAF Techn. Coll., 1963–65; SASO, HQ Technical Training Command RAF, 1966–67; retired, 1967. Gen. Manager, Van Dusen Aircraft Supplies, Oxford, Minneapolis, St Louis, Helsingborg, 1967–79. Mem. Livery of Clothworkers' Co., 1938. *Recreations:* swimming, conservation, boating. *Address:* 6 Summerhill, Kendal, Cumbria LA9 4JU. *Club:* Royal Air Force. *Died 5 May 2008.*

HOWELL, Paul Frederic; farmer; Director: ESU Group plc, since 2004; ESU Bio-Africa, since 2006; *b* 17 Jan. 1951; *s* of Sir Ralph Howell; *m* Angela; one *s*, and two *s* by a previous marriage. *Educ:* Gresham's Sch., Holt, Norfolk; St Edmund Hall, Oxford (MA Agric. and Econ.). Conservative Research Dept, 1973–75. MEP (C) Norfolk, 1979–94; contested (C) Eur. Parly elecns, 1994. Mem., Agricl, Foreign Affairs and Fisheries Cttees, European Parlt, 1979–94; spokesman for EDG: on youth culture, educn, information and sport, 1984–86; on agriculture, 1989–92; on fisheries, 1989–94; Mem. and EDG spokesman, Regl Cttee, 1992–94; Member, European Parliament's delegation: to Central America, 1987–94; to Soviet Union, 1989–91; to CIS, 1991–94; to Russia, Ukraine, Georgia, Armenia and Azerbaijan, 1993–94; Vice-Chm., Eur. Parlt/Comecon Delegn, 1984; Pres., Council of Centre for Eur. Educn, 1985–87. Chm., Riceman Insurance Investments plc, 1995–99; Special Ops Manager, WRG plc, 2000. Mem. Council, and Trustee, RSPB, 1992–95; Trustee, Nuffield Russia Trust, 1991–. *Recreation:* all sports. *Address:* The White House Farm, Bradenham Road, Scarning, East Dereham, Norfolk NR19 2LA. *Died 20 Sept. 2008.*

HOWELL, Sir Ralph (Frederic), Kt 1993; *b* 25 May 1923; *m* 1950, Margaret (*née* Bone) (*d* 2005); two *s* one *d*. *Educ:* Diss Grammar Sch., Norfolk. Navigator/Bomb-aimer, RAF, 1941–46; farmer, 1946–. MP (C) N Norfolk, 1970–97. Mem., European Parlt, 1974–79. Member: Treasury and Civil Service Select Cttee, 1981–87; Select Cttee on Employment, 1994–97. Vice-Chm., Cons. Parly Finance Cttee, 1979–84; Chairman: Cons. Parly Employment Cttee, 1984–87; Cons. Parly Agriculture Cttee, 1988; Mem. Exec., 1922 Cttee,

1984–90; Mem., Council of Europe and WEU, 1987–97. *Publications:* Why Work, 1976, 2nd edn 1981; Why Not Work, 1991; Putting Britain Back to Work, 1995. *T:* (01362) 687247. *Clubs:* Farmers'; Norfolk (Norwich). *Died 14 Feb. 2008.*

HUCKER, Michael; His Honour Judge Hucker; a Circuit Judge, since 1994; *b* 25 Oct. 1937; *o s* of Ernest George Hucker, CBE and Mary Louise Hucker (*née* Jowett); *m* 1961, Hazel Zoë Drake, JP; one *s* one *d* (and one *s* decd). *Educ:* St Dunstan's Coll.; LSE. Regular Commission, RE, 1957; served BAOR, Cameroons, Malaysia, NI, MoD; attached Army Legal Services, 1974–76; retired 1976. Called to the Bar, Lincoln's Inn, 1974, Gibraltar, 1988; in practice, London and SE Circuit, 1977–94, Head of Chambers, 1978–91; Counsel for Army and Air Force Boards in CMAC and House of Lords, 1979–94; Recorder, 1992–94. Chm., Lord Chancellor's Adv. Cttee for SW London, 1996–2000. Freeman, City of London, 1978. *Address:* The Crown Court, 6–8 Penrhyn Road, Kingston-upon-Thames KT1 2BB. *T:* (020) 8240 2500. *Died 28 May 2006.*

HUDSON, Prof. George, FRCP, FRCPath; Professor of Experimental Haematology, University of Sheffield, 1975–89, then Emeritus; *b* 10 Aug. 1924; *s* of George Hudson, blacksmith, and Edith Hannah (*née* Bennett); *m* 1955, Mary Patricia Hibbert (decd); one *d*. *Educ:* Edenfield C of E Sch.; Bury Grammar Sch.; Manchester Univ. (MSc, MB, ChB); MD, DSc Bristol. House Officer, Manchester Royal Inf., 1949–50; Demonstr in Anatomy, Univ. of Bristol, 1950–51; RAMC, 1951–53; University of Bristol: Lectr, later Reader, in Anatomy, 1953–68; Preclinical Dean, 1963–68; Vis. Prof., Univ. of Minnesota (Fulbright Award), 1959–60; Sheffield University: Admin. Dean, 1968–83; Hon. Clinical Lectr in Haematology, 1968–75; Head, Dept of Haematology, 1981–89; Postgrad. Dean, 1984–91. Hon. Cons. Haematologist, United Sheffield Hosps, 1969–89. Chm., Conf. of Deans of Provincial Med. Schs, 1980–82; Member: Sheffield RHB, 1970–74; Sheffield HA, 1974–84; DHSS Working Party on NHS Adv. and Representative Machinery, 1980–81; Council for Postgraduate Med. Educn for England and Wales, 1980–83. Hon. LLD Sheffield, 1993. *Publications:* papers in medical and scientific jls on haematological subjects. *Recreations:* lay reader since 1953, history of medicine, cavies, garden. *Address:* Box Cottage, Hill Bottom, Whitchurch Hill RG8 7PU. *T:* (0118) 984 2671. *Died 26 Oct. 2006.*

HUDSON, Ian Francis, CB 1976; Deputy Secretary, Department of Employment, 1976–80; *b* 29 May 1925; *s* of Francis Reginald Hudson and Dorothy Mary Hudson (*née* Crabbe); *m* 1952, Gisela Elisabeth Grettka; one *s* one *d*. *Educ:* City of London Sch.; New Coll., Oxford. Royal Navy, 1943–47. Customs and Excise, 1947–53; Min. of Labour, 1953–56, 1959–61, 1963–64; Treasury, 1957–58; Dept of Labour, Australia, 1961–63; Asst Sec., 1963; DEA, 1964–68; Under-Sec., 1967; Dept of Employment, 1968–73; Dep. Sec. 1973; Sec., Pay Board, 1973–74; Sec., Royal Commn on Distribution of Income and Wealth, 1974–76. *Died 8 Oct. 2006.*

HUDSON, Prof. John Pilkington, CBE 1975 (MBE (mil.) 1943); GM 1944 and Bar 1945; BSc, MSc, PhD; NDH; FIBiol; Emeritus Professor; former Director, Long Ashton Research Station, and Professor of Horticultural Science, University of Bristol, 1967–75; *b* 24 July 1910; *o s* of W. A. Hudson and Bertha (*née* Pilkington); *m* 1936, Mary Gretta (*d* 1989), *d* of late W. N. and Mary Heath, Westfields, Market Bosworth, Leics; one *s* (and one *s* decd). *Educ:* New Mills Grammar Sch.; Midland Agricultural Coll.; University Coll., Nottingham. Hort. Adviser, E Sussex CC, 1935–39. Served War, 1939–45, Royal Engineers Bomb Disposal (Major). Horticulturist, Dept of Agric., Wellington, NZ, 1945–48; Lecturer in Horticulture, University of Nottingham Sch. of Agric., 1948–50; Head of Dept of Horticulture, University of Nottingham, 1950–67 (as Prof. of Horticulture, 1958–67, Dean, Faculty of Agriculture and Horticulture, 1965–67);

seconded part-time to Univ. of Khartoum, Sudan, to found Dept of Horticulture, 1961–63. Associate of Honour, Royal New Zealand Institute of Horticulture, 1948. Chm., Jt Advisory Cttee on Agricultural Education (HMSO report published, 1973); former Mem., RHS Exam. Bd; PP and Hon. Mem., Hort. Educn Assoc. Hon. Fellow: RASE, 1977; Inst. of Hort., 1985. VMH, 1976. Editor, Experimental Agriculture, 1965–82; Past Mem. Editorial Bds, Jl Hort. Sci., SPAN. *Publications:* (ed) Control of the Plant Environment, 1957; numerous technical instructions on dealing with unexploded bomb fuses, where unambiguity was a matter of life and death; many contribs on effects of environment on plant growth and productivity to scientific jls. *Recreations:* choral singing, gardening, walking, talking with my friends. *Address:* The Spinney, Ladywell, Wrington, Bristol BS40 5LT.   *Died 6 Dec. 2007.*

HUDSON, Thomas Charles, CBE 1975; Chairman, ICL Ltd, 1972–80; Chartered Accountant (Canadian); *b* Sidcup, Kent, 23 Jan. 1915; British parents; *m* 1st, 1944, Lois Alma Hudson (marr. diss. 1973); one *s* one *d* (and one *s* decd); 2nd, 1986, Susan Gillian van Kan (marr. diss. 2004). *Educ:* Middleton High Sch., Nova Scotia. With Nightingale, Hayman & Co., Chartered Accountants, 1935–40. Served War, Royal Canadian Navy, Lieut, 1940–45. IBM Canada, as Sales Rep., 1946–51 (transf. to IBM, UK, as Sales Manager, 1951, and Managing Dir, 1954–65). Plessey Company: Financial Dir, 1967; Dir, 1969–76; Dir, ICL, 1968. Councillor for Enfield, GLC, 1970–73. *Recreations:* tennis, ski-ing, gardening. *Address:* Hele Farm, North Bovey, Devon TQ13 8RW. *T:* (01647) 440249. *Club:* Carlton.   *Died 19 Oct. 2009.*

HUGGINS, Sir Alan (Armstrong), Kt 1980; Vice-President, Court of Appeal, Hong Kong, 1980–87; *b* 15 May 1921; *yr s* of late William Armstrong Huggins and Dare (*née* Copping); *m* 1st, 1950, Catherine Davidson (marr. diss.), *d* of late David Dick; two *s* one *d*; 2nd, 1985, Elizabeth Low (*d* 2007), *d* of late Christopher William Lumley Dodd, MRCS, LRCP. *Educ:* Radley Coll.; Sidney Sussex Coll., Cambridge (MA). TARO (Special List), 1940–48 (Actg Major); Admiralty, 1941–46. Called to Bar, Lincoln's Inn, 1947. Legal Associate Mem., TPI, 1949–70. Resident Magistrate, Uganda, 1951–53; Stipendiary Magistrate, Hong Kong, 1953–58; District Judge, Hong Kong, 1958–65. Chm., Justice (Hong Kong Br.), 1965–68; Judicial Comr, State of Brunei, 1966–2000 (Pres., Court of Appeal, 2000–02); Judge of Supreme Court, Hong Kong, 1965–76; Justice of Appeal, Hong Kong, 1976–80; Justice of Appeal: Gibraltar, 1988–96; St Helena, 1988–97; British Antarctica, 1988–2002 (Pres., 2000–02); Falkland Is, 1988–2002 (Pres., 1991–2002); Bermuda, 1989–2000; British Indian Ocean Territory, 1991–2002 (Pres.); Mem., Ct of Final Appeal, HKSAR, China, 1997–2003. Hon. Lectr, Hong Kong Univ., 1979–87. Chm., Adv. Cttee on Legal Educn, 1972–87. Diocesan Reader, Dio. of Hong Kong and Macao, 1954–87; Reader, Dio. of Exeter, 1988–. Past Pres., YMCAs of Hong Kong. Hon. Life Governor, Brit. and For. Bible Soc; Hon. Life Mem., Amer. Bible Soc. Liveryman, Leathersellers' Company, 1942–91. *Recreations:* forestry, boating, archery, amateur theatre, tapestry. *Address:* Widdicombe Lodge, Widdicombe, Kingsbridge, Devon TQ7 2EF. *T:* (01548) 580727. *Club:* Royal Over-Seas League.   *Died 10 Dec. 2009.*

HUGHES, Edmwnd Goronwy M.; *see* Moelwyn-Hughes.

HUGHES, Howard, OBE 2009; World Managing Partner, Price Waterhouse, 1992–98; *b* 4 March 1938; *s* of Charles William Hughes and Ethel May Hughes (*née* Howard); *m* 1st, 1964, Joy Margaret Pilmore-Bedford (*d* 1984); two *s* one *d*; 2nd, 1988, Christine Margaret Miles; one *s*. *Educ:* Rydal School. FCA. Articled Bryce Hanmer & Co., Liverpool, 1955; joined Price Waterhouse, London, 1960: Partner, 1970; Dir, London Office, 1982; Managing Partner, UK, 1985–91; Member: World Bd, 1988–98; World Mgt Cttee, 1990–98. Auditor, Duchy of Cornwall, 1983–98. Mem., Agricl Wages Bd, 1990–99.

Chairman: Royal London Soc. for the Blind, 2000–05 (Vice Pres., 2007–); British Heart Foundn, 2006–08 (Trustee, 1998–). Chairman: Govs, Dorton House Sch., 1998–2001; Utd Westminster Schs, 2002– (Trustee, 2000–); Governor: Westminster City Sch., 1998–; Emanuel Sch., 2002–; Sutton Valance Sch., 2002–. Liveryman, Chartered Accts' Co., 1991–. *Recreations:* golf, music. *Address:* Witham, Woodland Rise, Seal, Sevenoaks, Kent TN15 0HZ. *T:* (01732) 761161, *Fax:* (01732) 763553. *Clubs:* Carlton, MCC; Wildernesse Golf (Sevenoaks).   *Died 4 Feb. 2009.*

HUGHES, Sir Jack (William), Kt 1980; chartered surveyor; Chairman, Bracknell Development Corporation, 1971–82; Consultant, Jones, Lang, Wootton, 1976–99 (a Senior Partner, 1949–76); *b* 26 Sept. 1916; 2nd *s* of George William Hughes and Isabel Hughes, Maidstone, Kent; *m* 1st, 1939, Marie-Theresa (Slade School scholar) (*d* 1987), *d* of Graham Parmley and Jessie Thompson; 2nd, 1994, Helena, *d* of Franciszek and Katrzyna Kanik. *Educ:* Maidstone Grammar Sch.; Univ. of London (BSc (Est. Man.)), DA Hons Open 1991. FRICS; FRIPH. Served with Special Duties Br., RAF, 1940–46; demobilised Squadron Leader. Chm., Property Adv. Gp, DoE, 1978–82; Director: South Bank Estates and subsid. cos, 1960–2002; URPT, 1961–86; MEPC, 1971–86; Housing Corporation (1974) Ltd, 1974–77; BR Property Bd, 1976–86; BR Investment Co., 1981–84; Property and Reversionary Investments, 1982–87; TR Property Investment Trust and subsid. cos, 1982–91; Brighton Marina Co. (Rep., Brighton Corp.), 1974–86; Undercliff Hldgs Ltd, 1986–93; Brighton Square Develts, 2002–03; Mem. Cttee, Mercantile Credit Gp Property Div.; Mem. Cttee of Management, Charities Property Unit Trust, 1967–74; first Chm., South Hill Park Arts Centre Trust, Bracknell, 1972–79; Member: Adv. Gp to DoE on Commercial Property Develt, 1974–78; DoE Working Party on Housing Tenure, 1976–77. Founder Mem., Continuing Professional Develt Foundn (Mem. Adv. Bd, 1980–). A Vice-Pres., Pestalozzi Children's Village Trust, 1994–. Trustee, New Towns Pension Fund, 1975–82. Freeman, City of London, 1959–; Liveryman, Painter Stainers Guild, 1960–. FICPD 1998; FRSA. *Publications:* (jtly) Town and Country Planning Act 1949 (RICS); (Chm. of RICS Cttee) The Land Problem: a fresh approach; (co-ed) Glossary of Property Terms, 1990; techn. articles on property investment, develt and finance. *Recreations:* golf, travel, reading. *Address:* Challoners, The Green, Rottingdean, Brighton, Sussex BN2 7DD. *Club:* Royal Air Force.
                                                   Died 28 Feb. 2006.

HUGHES, John; *b* 29 May 1925; *m* Josephine Brown; two *s*. *Educ:* Durham. Served with Fleet Air Arm, 1943–45. Apprentice joiner; then miner and mechanic; worked for GEC, and Unipart (TGWU convener). Mem., Coventry City Council, 1974–82; Chm., Coventry NE Lab Party, 1978–81. MP (Lab) Coventry North East, 1987–92; contested (Ind. Lab) Coventry North East, 1992. *Address:* 15 Stafford Close, Bulkington, Bedworth, Nuneaton, Warwicks CV12 9QX.   *Died 14 Aug. 2009.*

HUGHES, Very Rev. John Chester; Vicar of Bringhurst with Great Easton and Drayton, 1978–87; *b* 20 Feb. 1924; *m* 1950, Sybil Lewis McClelland; three *s* two *d* (and one *s* decd). *Educ:* Dulwich Coll.; St John's Coll., Durham (BA 1948; DipTh 1950; MA 1951). Curate of Westcliff-on-Sea, Essex, 1950–53; Succentor of Chelmsford Cathedral, 1953–55; Vicar of St Barnabas, Leicester, 1955–61; Vicar of Croxton Kerrial with Branston-by-Belvoir, 1961–63; Provost of Leicester, 1963–78. ChStJ 1974. *Publications:* The Story of Launde Abbey, 1998. *Address:* 29 High Street, Hallaton, Market Harborough, Leics LE16 8UD. *T:* (01858) 555622.   *Died 16 Oct. 2008.*

HUGHES, John Richard Poulton; DL; County Clerk and Chief Executive, Staffordshire County Council, and Clerk to the Lieutenancy, 1978–83; *b* 21 Oct. 1920; *s* of Rev. John Evan Hughes and Mary Grace Hughes; *m* 1943, Mary Margaret, *e d* of Thomas Francis Thomas; one *s*. *Educ:* Bromsgrove Sch.; LLB Hons London; DPA;

LMRTPI. Solicitor. Served War, RN and RNVR, 1940–46; discharged with rank of Lieut, RNVR. Articled in private practice, 1937–40; Asst Solicitor: West Bromwich County Borough Council, 1947–48; Surrey CC, 1948–50; Staffs County Council: Sen. Asst Solicitor, subseq. Chief Asst Solicitor, and Dep. Clerk, 1950–74; Dir of Admin, 1974–78; Sec., Staffs Probation and After Care Cttee, 1978–83. Sec., Staffs Historic Bldgs Trust, 1983–89; Trustee and Advr, Soc. for the Prevention of Solvent Abuse, 1984– (Vice-Pres., 1989). DL Staffs, 1979. *Recreations:* forestry, antiques restoration, sailing, fishing. *Address:* Plas Isa Cottage, Llanbedr Dyffryn Clwyd, near Ruthin, Clwyd LL15 1UP. *Died 26 May 2006.*

HUGHES, Kevin Michael; *b* 15 Dec. 1952; *s* of Leonard and Annie Hughes; *m* 1972, Lynda Saunders; one *s* one *d. Educ:* local state schs; Sheffield Univ. (3 yrs day release). Coal miner, 1970–90. Branch delegate, 1981–90, Mem., Yorks Area Exec. Cttee, 1983–86, NUM. Councillor, Doncaster MBC, 1986–92 (Chm., Social Services, 1987–92). MP (Lab) Doncaster N, 1992–2005. An Asst Govt Whip, 1997–2001. *Recreations:* golf, walking, listening to opera. *Clubs:* Doncaster Trade Union and Labour; Skellow Grange Workingmen's. *Died 16 July 2006.*

HUGHES, Sir Trevor Denby L.; *see* Lloyd-Hughes.

HUGHES-MORGAN, His Honour Maj.-Gen. Sir David (John), 3rd Bt *cr* 1925; CB 1983; CBE 1973 (MBE 1959); a Circuit Judge, 1986–98; *b* 11 Oct. 1925; *s* of Sir John Hughes-Morgan, 2nd Bt and Lucie Margaret (*d* 1987), *d* of late Thomas Parry Jones-Parry; *S* father, 1969; *m* 1959, Isabel Jean (*d* 1994), *d* of J. M. Lindsay; three *s. Educ:* RNC, Dartmouth. Royal Navy, 1943–46. Admitted solicitor, 1950. Commissioned, Army Legal Services, 1955; Brig., Legal Staff, HQ UKLF, 1976–78; Dir, Army Legal Services, BAOR, 1978–80, MoD, 1980–84; a Recorder, 1983–86. *Heir: s* Ian Parry David Hughes-Morgan [*b* 22 Feb. 1960; *m* 1992, Julia, *er d* of R. J. S. Ward; three *d*]. *Address:* Chorleywood Lodge, Rickmansworth Road, Chorleywood, Herts WD3 5BY. *Died 15 July 2006.*

HUME, Sir Alan (Blyth), Kt 1973; CB 1963; *b* 5 Jan. 1913; *s* of late W. Alan Hume; *m* 1943, Marion Morton Garrett; one *s* one *d. Educ:* George Heriot's Sch.; Edinburgh Univ. Entered Scottish Office, 1936; Under-Sec., Scottish Home Department, 1957–59; Asst Under-Sec. of State, Scottish Office, 1959–62; Under-Sec., Min. of Public Bldg and Works, 1963–64; Secretary, Scottish Develt Dept, 1965–73. Chairman: Ancient Monuments Bd, Scotland, 1973–81; Edinburgh New Town Conservation Cttee, 1975–90. *Recreations:* golf, fishing. *Address:* 5/4 Oswald Road, Edinburgh EH9 2HE. *T:* (0131) 667 2440. *Clubs:* English-Speaking Union; New (Edinburgh). *Died 21 Feb. 2006.*

HUNNISETT, Dr Roy Frank, FSA, FRHistS; on staff of Public Record Office, 1953–88; *b* 26 Feb. 1928; *s* of Frank Hunnisett and Alice (*née* Budden); *m* 1st, 1954, Edith Margaret Evans (marr. diss. 1989); 2nd, 1989, Janet Heather Stevenson. *Educ:* Bexhill Grammar Sch.; New Coll., Oxford (1st Cl. Hons Mod. Hist., 1952; Amy Mary Preston Read Scholar, 1952–53; MA, DPhil 1956). FRHistS 1961; FSA 1975. Lectr, New Coll., Oxford, 1957–63. Royal Historical Society: Alexander Prize, 1957; Mem. Council, 1974–77; Vice-Pres., 1979–82; Selden Society: Mem. Council, 1975–84, 1987–; Vice-Pres., 1984–87; Treasurer, Pipe Roll Soc., 1973–87; Literary Dir, Sussex Record Soc., 2003–09 (Mem. Council, 1992–2003). *Publications:* Calendar of Inquisitions Miscellaneous: (ed jtly) vol. IV, 1957 and vol. V, 1962; (ed) vol. VI, 1963 and vol. VII, 1968; The Medieval Coroners' Rolls, 1960; The Medieval Coroner, 1961; (ed) Bedfordshire Coroners' Rolls, 1961; (ed) Calendar of Nottinghamshire Coroners' Inquests 1485–1558, 1969; (contrib.) The Study of Medieval Records: essays in honour of Kathleen Major, 1971; Indexing for Editors, 1972; Editing Records for Publication, 1977; (ed jtly and contrib.) Medieval Legal

Records edited in memory of C. A. F. Meekings, 1978; (ed) Wiltshire Coroners' Bills 1752–1796, 1981; (ed) Sussex Coroners' Inquests 1485–1558, 1985; (ed) Sussex Coroners' Inquests 1558–1603, 1996, and 1603–1688, 1998; (ed) East Sussex Coroners' Records 1688–1838, 2005; articles and revs in historical and legal jls. *Recreations:* Sussex, music, cricket. *Address:* 23 Byron Gardens, Sutton, Surrey SM1 3QG. *T:* (020) 8661 2618. *Died 7 Dec. 2009.*

HUNT OF TANWORTH, Baron *cr* 1980 (Life Peer), of Stratford-upon-Avon in the county of Warwickshire; **John Joseph Benedict Hunt,** GCB 1977 (KCB 1973; CB 1968); Secretary of the Cabinet, 1973–79; Chairman, Prudential Corporation, 1985–90; *b* 23 Oct. 1919; *er s* of Major Arthur L. Hunt and Daphne Hunt; *m* 1st, 1941, Hon. Magdalen Mary Lister Robinson (*d* 1971), *yr d* of 1st Baron Robinson; two *s* (and one *d* decd); 2nd, 1973, Madeleine Frances (*d* 2007), *d* of Sir William Hume, CMG, FRCP, and *widow* of Sir John Charles, KCB, FRCP; one step *s* one step *d. Educ:* Downside; Magdalene College, Cambridge (Hon. Fellow, 1977). Served Royal Naval Volunteer Reserve, 1940–46, Lieut; Convoy escort, Western Approaches and in Far East. Home Civil Service, Admin. Class, 1946; Dominions Office, 1946; Priv. Sec. to Parly Under-Sec., 1947; 2nd Sec., Office of UK High Comr in Ceylon, 1948–50; Principal, 1949; Directing Staff, IDC, 1951–52; 1st Sec., Office of UK High Comr in Canada, 1953–56; Private Secretary to Sec. of Cabinet and Perm. Sec. to Treasury and Head of Civil Service, 1956–58; Assistant Secretary: CRO, 1958; Cabinet Office, 1960; HM Treasury, 1962–67, (Under-Sec., 1965); Dep. Sec., 1968 and First Civil Service Comr, Civil Service Dept, 1968–71; Third Sec., Treasury, 1971–72; Second Permanent Sec., Cabinet Office, 1972–73. Dir, 1980–92, Dep. Chm., 1982–85, Prudential Corp.; Dep. Chm., Prudential Assurance Co. Ltd, 1982–85; Chairman: Banque Nat. de Paris plc, 1980–97; BNP UK Hldgs, 1991–97; Dir, IBM (UK) Ltd, 1980–90; Adv. Dir, Unilever plc, 1980–90. Chairman: Sub-Cttee A, H of L European Communities Select Cttee, 1992–95; H of L Select Cttee on Relations between Central and Local Govt, 1995–96. Chm., Disasters Emergency Cttee, 1981–89. Chm., Inquiry into Cable Expansion and Broadcasting Policy, 1982. Chm., European Policy Forum, 1992–98. Chm., Ditchley Foundn, 1983–91. Dir, The Tablet Publishing Co. Ltd, 1984–99 (Chm., 1984–96). Pres., Local Govt Assoc., 1997–2001. Hon. DCL Northumbria, 2003. Officier, Légion d'Honneur (France), 1987; Kt Comdr, Order of Pius IX (Holy See), 1997. *Recreation:* gardening. *Address:* 8 Wool Road, Wimbledon, SW20 0HW. *T:* (020) 8947 7640. *Died 17 July 2008.*

HUNT, Hon. Sir (Patrick) James, Kt 2000; **Hon. Mr Justice Hunt;** a Judge of the High Court, Queen's Bench Division, since 2000; *b* 26 Jan. 1943; *s* of Thomas Ronald Clifford Hunt and Doreen Gwyneth Katarina Hunt; *m* 1969, Susan Jennifer Goodhead, JP; one *s* three *d. Educ:* Ashby de la Zouch Boys' Grammar Sch.; Keble Coll., Oxford (MA Mod. History). Called to the Bar, Gray's Inn, 1968 (Bencher, 1994; Master of Educn, 2002–); in practice on Midland and Oxford Circuit, from London chambers; Leader, Midland and Oxford Circuit, 1996–99 (Dep. Leader, 1992–96); a Recorder, 1982–2000; QC 1987; a Dep. High Court Judge, 1994–2000. Mem., Gen. Council of the Bar, 1989–91, 1996–99. Legal Assessor to Disciplinary Cttee, RCVS, 1990–2000; Chm., Code of Practice Appeal Bd, Assoc. of British Pharmaceutical Industry, 1999–2000. *Recreations:* singing, gardening, stonework, writing doggerel. *Address:* Royal Courts of Justice, Strand, WC2A 2LL. *Club:* Royal Automobile. *Died 8 Nov. 2006.*

HUNTER, Hon. Lord; John Oswald Mair Hunter, VRD; a Senator of the College of Justice in Scotland, 1961–86; *b* 21 Feb. 1913; *s* of John Mair Hunter, QC (Scot.) and Jessie Donald Frew; *m* 1st, 1939, Doris Mary Simpson (*d* 1988); one *s* one *d*; 2nd, 1989, Mrs Angela Marion McLean. *Educ:* Edinburgh Acad.; Rugby; New

Coll., Oxford (BA 1934, MA 1961); Edinburgh Univ. (LLB 1936, LLD 1975). Entered RNVR, 1933; served War 1939–45 (despatches); Lt-Comdr RNVR; retired list 1949. Called to Bar, Inner Temple, 1937; admitted to Faculty of Advocates, 1937; QC (Scot.) 1951. Advocate Depute (Home), 1954–57; Sheriff of Ayr and Bute, 1957–61. Chairman: Deptl Cttee on Scottish Salmon and Trout Fisheries, 1962–65; Lands Valuation Appeal Court, 1966–71; Scottish Law Commn, 1971–81; Scottish Council on Crime, 1972–75; Dep. Chm., Boundary Commn for Scotland, 1971–76. Pres., Scottish Univs Law Inst., 1972–77; Member: Scottish Records Adv. Council, 1966–81; Statute Law Cttee, 1971–81; Chm., later Hon. Pres., Cttee, RNLI (Dunbar), 1969–80 and 1981–2001; Hon. Pres., Scottish Assoc. for Study of Delinquency, 1971–88.   *Died 20 March 2006.*

HUNTER, Brig. Ian Murray, CVO 1954; AM 1994; MBE 1943; ED 1996; FAIM; FAICD; FIMMM; Chairman, I. M. & R. Holdings Pty Ltd, since 1972; *b* Sydney, Aust, 10 July 1917; *s* of late Dr James Hunter, Stranraer, Scotland; *m* 1947, Rosemary Jane Batchelor; two *s* two *d. Educ:* Cranbrook Sch., Sydney; RMC, Duntroon. Lieut Aust. Staff Corps, and AIF, 1939; 2/1 MG Bn, 1939–40; T/Capt. 1940; Staff Capt., 25 Inf. Bde, 1940–41; Middle East Staff Coll., Haifa, 1941; DAQMG (1), HQ 6 Div., 1941–42; T/Major 1942; AQMG, NT Force (MBE), 1942–43; Staff Sch. (Aust.), 1943; psc 1943; Gen. Staff 3 Corps and Advanced HQ Allied Land Forces, 1943–44; Lieut-Col 1945; Instructor, Staff Sch., 1945; AQMG, and Col BCOF, 1946–47; AQMG, AHQ and JCOSA, 1947; AA&QMG, HQ, 3 Div., 1948–50; Royal Visit, 1949; Exec. Commonwealth Jubilee Celebrations, 1950–51; CO 2 Recruit Trg Bn, 1952; CO 4 RAR, 1953; Executive and Commonwealth Marshal, Royal Visit, 1952, and 1954; Command and Gen. Staff Coll., Fort Leavenworth, USA, 1954–55; fsc (US) 1955; Military Mission, Washington, 1955–56; Officer i/c Admin, N Comd, 1956–59; Comd 11 Inf. Bde, 1959–60; Command 2nd RQR, 1960–62; Chief of Staff 1st Div., 1963; Commandant, Australian Staff Coll., 1963–65; Comdr, Papua New Guinea Comd, 1966–69; DQMG, Army HQ, 1969. Chm., 1970–2005, Man. Dir, 1981–2005, Allied Rubber Products (Qld). Ind. Mem., Presbyterian Church Property Commn, 1974–84. Chm., Australian Red Cross Soc. (Qld), 1990–94. FAIM 1964; FAICD 1990; FIMMM (FIM 1993); Fellow, Australian Plastic and Rubber Inst., 1994. *Recreations:* golf, squash, swimming, riding. *Address:* Garthland, 5 Sword Street, Ascot, Brisbane, Qld 4007, Australia; Finchley, Hargreaves Street, Blackheath, NSW 2785, Australia. *Clubs:* Australian (Sydney); Queensland (Brisbane); Royal Sydney Golf.   *Died 5 Nov. 2006.*

HUNTER, His Honour John; a Circuit Judge, 1980–93; *b* 12 April 1921; *s* of Charles and Mary Hunter; *m* 1956, Margaret Cynthia Webb; one *s* two *d. Educ:* Fitzwilliam House, Cambridge (MA). Called to the Bar, Lincoln's Inn, 1952. Served War, Army, 1939–46. Industry, 1952–62; practised at the Bar, 1962–80. *Recreations:* sailing, gardening. *Address:* 230 Compass House, Smugglers Way, SW18 1DQ. *Club:* London Rowing.   *Died 15 Nov. 2009.*

HUNTER, John Murray, CB 1980; MC 1943; *b* 10 Nov. 1920; *s* of Rev. Dr John Hunter and Frances Hunter (*née* Martin); *m* 1948, Margaret (*d* 1997), *d* of late Stanley Cursiter, CBE, RSW, RSA, and Phyllis Eda (*née* Hourston); two *s* three *d. Educ:* Fettes Coll.; Clare Coll., Cambridge. Served Army, 1941–45: Captain, The Rifle Bde. Served in Diplomatic Service at Canberra, Bogotá, Baghdad, Prague, Buenos Aires and in FCO (Head of Consular Dept, 1966, and of Latin America Dept, 1971–73); idc 1961, sowc 1965, jssc (Senior Directing Staff), 1967–69. Sec., 1973–75, Comr for Admin and Finance, 1976–81, Forestry Commn. Vice-Chm., 1981–83, Chm., 1983–86, Edinburgh West End Community Council. Scottish Tourist Guide, 1983–97. *Recreations:* music, reading; formerly Rugby football

(Cambridge 1946, Scotland 1947), curling. *Address:* 14–37 Maxwell Street, Edinburgh EH10 5HU.   *Died 31 March 2006.*

HUNTER, John Oswald Mair; *see* Hunter, Hon. Lord.

HUNTER, Muir Vane Skerrett; QC 1965; MA Oxon; Barrister-at-Law; *b* 19 Aug. 1913; *s* of late H. S. Hunter, Home Civil Service, and Bluebell M. Hunter, novelist; *m* 1st, 1939, Dorothea Eason, JP (*d* 1986), *e d* of late P. E. Verstone; one *d*; 2nd, 1986, Gillian Victoria Joyce Petrie, MA, *d* of late Dr Alexander Petrie, CBE, MD, FRCS, FRCP. *Educ:* Westminster Sch.; Christ Church, Oxford (Scholar). Voluntary war relief work, Spain, 1937. Called to the Bar, Gray's Inn, 1938 (*ad eundem* Inner Temple, 1965); Holker Senior Scholar; Bencher, Gray's Inn, 1975. Served 1940–46: Royal Armoured Corps (Hon. Lt-Col); GS Intelligence, GHQ (India); GSO 1 attd War and Legislative Depts, Mil. Judge of Anti-Corruption Tribunals, Govt of India, 1943–45; returned to the Bar, 1946; standing counsel (bankruptcy) to Bd of Trade, 1949–65; Dep. Chm., Advisory Cttee on Service Candidates, HO, 1960–95; Member: EEC Bankruptcy Adv. Cttee, Dept of Trade, 1973–76; Insolvency Law Review Cttee, Dept of Trade, 1977–82; Advr, Law Reform Commn, Kenya Govt, 1991–96; Consultant on law reform, Govt of The Gambia/USAID, 1992. Visiting Professor of Insolvency Law: Bournemouth Univ., 1997– ; Kingston Univ., 2007–. Presenter, Back–Handers (Poulson bankruptcy case), BBC4 documentary, 2006. Founder-Chairman, N Kensington Neighbourhood Law Centre, 1969–71; Mem., Exec. Cttee, British-Polish Legal Assoc., 1991–97; Hon. Mem. of Council, Justice. Amnesty/ICJ International Observer: Burundi, 1962; Rhodesia, 1969; Turkey, 1972. Gov., Royal Shakespeare Theatre, 1964–83, then Hon. Life Gov.; Mem. Council, Royal Shakespeare Theatre Trust, 1978–97; Pres., East Street Poets, Blandford, 1995–97; Sec., Kick Start Poets, Salisbury, 2000–02. Chairman: Gdansk Hospice Fund, 1989–92; Polish Hospices Fund, 1992–2002. Hon. Legal Advr, Nairobi Hospice, Kenya, 1989–92. Hon. Life Mem., Commercial Law League of America, 1985. Mem. Editl Board, Insolvency Law & Practice, 1985–95; Editl Consultant, Sweet & Maxwell Ltd, 1999–2004. (With Gillian Petrie Hunter) Aid and Co-operation Medals, Polish Govt, 1996. Hon. LLD Bournemouth, 2000. *Publications:* Senior Editor, Williams on Bankruptcy, 1958–78, Williams and Muir Hunter on Bankruptcy, 1979–84, Muir Hunter on Personal Insolvency, 1987–; Emergent Africa and the Rule of Law, 1963; Jt Editor: Halsbury's Laws, 4th edn, Vol. 3; Atkins' Forms, Vol. 7; Editor, Kerr, The Law and Practice as to Receivers and Administrators, 17th edn, 1988, 18th edn as Kerr & Hunter, The Law and Practice on Receivers and Administrators, 2004, First Supplement, 2006; Part Editor, Butterworth's Civil Court Precedents (formerly County Court Precedents and Pleadings), 1984–; Going Bust?: how to resist and survive bankruptcy and winding-up, 2007; (contrib.) Tears in the Fence (poetry), 1994; The Grain of My Life (poetry), 1997; contrib. Jl of Business Law, Commercial Law League Jl (US). *Recreations:* writing poetry, theatre, travel, music. *Address:* (chambers) 3–4 South Square, Gray's Inn, WC1R 5HP. *T:* (020) 7696 9900, *Fax:* (020) 7696 9911; Hunterston, Donhead St Andrew, Shaftesbury, Dorset SP7 9EB. *T:* (01747) 828779; *e-mail:* mvshunterqc@aol.com. *Clubs:* Hurlingham; Oxford Union.   *Died 18 Oct. 2008.*

HUNTER, Philip Brown, TD; Chairman, John Holt & Co. (Liverpool) Ltd, 1967–71; *b* 30 May 1909; *s* of Charles Edward Hunter and Marion (*née* Harper); *m* 1937, Joyce Mary Holt (*d* 2005); two *s* two *d. Educ:* Birkenhead Sch.; London University. Practised as Solicitor, 1933–80. Chm., Guardian Royal Exchange Assurance (Sierra Leone) Ltd, 1972–79; Director: Cammell Laird & Co. Ltd, 1949–70 (Chm. 1966–70); John Holt & Co. (Liverpool) Ltd, 1951–71 (Exec. Dir, 1960); Guardian Royal Exchange, 1969–79; Guardian Assurance Co. Ltd, 1967–69; Royal Exchange (Nigeria) Ltd, 1972–79; Lion of Africa Insurance Co. Ltd, 1972–79;

Enterprise Insurance Co. Ltd, Ghana, 1972–79. *Address:* Bryn Hyfryd, Lixwm, Holywell, Flintshire CH8 8LT. *T:* (01352) 780054. *Died 28 June 2007.*

HUNTER, William Hill, CBE 1971; JP; DL; CA; Partner, McLay, McAlister & McGibbon, Chartered Accountants, 1946–91; *b* 5 Nov. 1916; *s* of Robert Dalglish Hunter and Mrs Margaret Walker Hill or Hunter; *m* 1947, Kathleen, *d* of William Alfred Cole; one *s* (and one *s* decd). *Educ:* Cumnock Academy. Chartered Accountant, 1940. Served War: enlisted as private, RASC, 1940; commissioned RA, 1941; Staff Capt., Middle East, 1944–46. Director: Abbey National Building Soc. Scottish Adv. Bd, 1966–86; City of Glasgow Friendly Soc., 1966–88 (Pres., 1980–88); J. & G. Grant Glenfarclas Distillery, 1966–92. President: W Renfrewshire Conservative and Unionist Assoc., 1972–99; Scottish Young Unionist Assoc., 1958–60; Scottish Unionist Assoc., 1964–65. Contested (U) South Ayrshire, 1959 and 1964. Chairman: Salvation Army Adv. Bd in W Scotland, 1982–93 (Vice-Chm., 1972–82; Hon. Life Mem., 2001); Salvation Army Housing Assoc. (Scotland) Ltd, 1986–91; Salvation Army hostel named after him, Glasgow, 1991. Hon. Financial Advr and Mem. Council, Erskine Hosp., 1972; Hon. Treasurer, Quarrier's Homes, 1979–94 (Acting Chm., 1989–92). Deacon Convener, Trades House of Glasgow, 1986–87. Hon. Vice-Pres., Royal Scottish Agricl Benevolent Inst., 1993–2008; Hon. Pres., Friends of Glasgow Botanic Gardens, 1994–2004. Session Clerk, Kilmacolm Old Kirk, 1967–72. JP 1970, DL 1987, Renfrewshire. Mem., Order of Distinguished Auxiliary Service, Salvation Army, 1981. *Recreations:* gardening, swimming. *Address:* 8 Woodrow Court, Port Glasgow Road, Kilmacolm, Renfrewshire PA13 4QA. *T:* (01505) 872444. *Died 1 Sept. 2010.*

HUNTER-BLAIR, Sir Edward (Thomas), 8th Bt *cr* 1786, of Dunskey; landowner and forester since 1964; *b* 15 Dec. 1920; *s* of Sir James Hunter Blair, 7th Bt and Jean Galloway (*d* 1953), *d* of T. W. McIntyre, Sorn Castle, Ayrshire; *S* father, 1985; *m* 1st, 1956, Norma (*d* 1972), *d* of late W. S. Harris; one adopted *s* one adopted *d*; 2nd, 2003, Jonet, *e d* of David Reid. *Educ:* Balliol Coll., Oxford (BA); Univ. of Paris (Diploma, French Lang. and Lit.). Temp. Civil Servant, 1941–43; journalist (Asst Foreign Editor), 1944–49; in business in Yorkshire, manager and director of own company, 1950–63. Mem. Council, Wyndham Trust, 1992–96. Mem., Kirkcudbright CC, 1970–71. Mem. Cttee, Scottish Assoc. for Public Transport, 1993–. Former Pres., Dumfries and Galloway Mountaineering Club. 1939–45 Star, Gen. Service Medal, 1946. *Publications:* Scotland Sings, and A Story of Me, 1981; A Future Time (With an Earlier Life), 1984; A Mission in Life, 1987; Nearing the Year 2000, 1990; Our Troubled Future, 1993; Problems of Today, 2002; articles on learned and other subjects. *Recreations:* gardening, hill-walking. *Heir: cousin* Patrick David Hunter Blair [*b* 12 May 1958; *m* 1984, Margaret O'Neill; three *s* (incl. twins) two *d*]. *Address:* Parton House, Castle Douglas, Scotland DG7 3NB. *T:* (01644) 470234. *Clubs:* Royal Over-Seas League; Western Meeting (Ayr). *Died 21 Oct. 2006.*

HUNTER SMART, (William) Norman, CA; Senior Partner, Hays Allan, Chartered Accountants, 1983–86; *b* 25 May 1921; *s* of William Hunter Smart, CA, and Margaret Thorburn Inglis; *m* 1st, 1948, Bridget Beryl Andreae (*d* 1974); three *s* (and one *s* decd); 2nd, 1977, Sheila Smith Stewart (*née* Speirs) (*d* 2000). *Educ:* George Watson's Coll., Edinburgh. Served War, 1939–45; commnd 1st Lothians & Border Horse, 1941; Warwickshire Yeomanry, 1942; Adjt-Captain, 1945; mentioned in despatches. Qualif. as CA 1948; Hays Allan, Chartered Accountants, 1950–86 (Partner, 1950–83). Chairman: Charterhouse Develt Capital Fund Ltd, 1987–96; C. J. Sims Ltd, 1990–99. Chm., Assoc. of Scottish Chartered Accountants in London, 1972–73; Institute of Chartered Accountants of Scotland: Council Mem., 1970–75; Vice-Pres., 1976–78; Pres., 1978–79.

Member: Gaming Bd for GB, 1985–90; Scottish Legal Aid Bd, 1986–89. *Address:* Greenhouse Cottage, Lilliesleaf, Melrose, Roxburghshire TD6 9EP. *Club:* Caledonian. *Died 1 Jan. 2010.*

HURRELL, Sir Anthony (Gerald), KCVO 1986; CMG 1984; HM Diplomatic Service, retired; *b* 18 Feb. 1927; *s* of late William Hurrell and Florence Hurrell; *m* 1951, Jean Wyatt; two *d*. *Educ:* Norwich Sch.; St Catharine's Coll., Cambridge. RAEC, 1948–50; Min. of Labour, 1950–53; Min. of Educn, 1953–64; joined Min. of Overseas Develt, 1964; Fellow, Center for International Affairs, Harvard, 1969–70; Head of SE Asia Develt Div., Bangkok, 1972–74; Under Secretary: Internat. Div., ODM, 1974–75; Central Policy Rev. Staff, Cabinet Office, 1976; Duchy of Lancaster, 1977; Asia and Oceans Div., ODA, 1978–83; Ambassador to Nepal, 1983–86. Pres., St Catharine's Soc., 1993–94. *Recreations:* bird-ringing, bird-watching, digging ponds, music. *Address:* Lapwings, Dunwich, Saxmundham, Suffolk IP17 3DR. *Died 19 April 2009.*

HURRELL, Air Vice-Marshal Frederick Charles, CB 1986; OBE 1968; Director General, Royal Air Force Medical Services and Deputy Surgeon General (Operations), 1986–87; retired 1988; *b* 24 April 1928; *s* of Alexander John Hurrell and Maria Del Carmen Hurrell (*née* De Biedma); *m* 1950, Jay Jarvis; five *d*. *Educ:* Royal Masonic School, Bushey; St Mary's Hosp., Paddington (MB BS 1952). MRCS, LRCP 1952; DAvMed 1970; MFOM 1981, FFOM 1987. Joined RAF 1953; served UK, Australia, Singapore and USA; Dep. Dir, Aviation Medicine, RAF, 1974–77; British Defence Staff, Washington DC, 1977–80; CO Princess Alexandra Hosp., RAF Wroughton, 1980–82; Dir, Health and Research, RAF, 1982–84; PMO Strike Command, 1984–86. Dir of Appeals, RAF Benevolent Fund, 1988–95. Vice Pres., Royal Internat. Air Tattoo, 1997–2003. QHP 1984–88. FRAeS 1987. CStJ 1986. Chadwick Gold Medal, 1970. *Recreations:* painting, photography. *Address:* Hale House, 4 Upper Hale Road, Farnham, Surrey GU9 0NJ. *T:* (01252) 714190. *Club:* Royal Air Force. *Died 3 Oct. 2008.*

HUSSEY OF NORTH BRADLEY, Baron *cr* 1996 (Life Peer), of North Bradley in the county of Wiltshire; **Marmaduke James Hussey**; Chairman, Board of Governors, BBC, 1986–96; Chairman, Royal Marsden Hospital, 1985–98; *b* 29 Aug. 1923; *s* of late E. R. J. Hussey, CMG and Mrs Christine Hussey; *m* 1959, Lady Susan Katharine Waldegrave (Lady Susan Hussey, DCVO), 5th *d* of 12th Earl Waldegrave, KG, GCVO; one *s* one *d*. *Educ:* Rugby Sch.; Trinity Coll., Oxford (Scholar, MA; Hon. Fellow 1989). Served War of 1939–45, Grenadier Guards, Italy. Joined Associated Newspapers, 1949, Dir 1964; Man. Dir, Harmsworth Publications, 1967–70; Thomson Organisation Exec. Bd, 1971–82; Chief Exec., Times Newspapers Ltd, 1971–82; Jt Chm., Great Western Radio, 1985–86; Dir, William Collins plc, 1985–89. Chairman: Ruffer Investment Management Ltd, 1995–2002; Cadweb, 1996–2003; Director: Colonial Mutual Gp, 1985–97; Dialog Corp., 1996–2000. Mem. Bd, British Council, 1983–96. Mem., Select Cttee on EC, H of L, 1997–. Member: Govt Working Party on Artificial Limb and Appliance Centres in England, 1984–86; Management Cttee and Educn Cttee, King Edward's Hosp. Fund for London, 1987–99; Chm., King's Fund London Commn, 1991–92, 1995. President: Royal Bath and West of England Soc., 1990–91; Somerset, RBL, 1999– (Patron, 1999–). Trustee: Rhodes Trust, 1972–91; Royal Acad. Trust, 1988–96. *Publications:* Chance Governs All (autobiog.), 2001. *Address:* Flat 15, 47 Courtfield Road, SW7 4DB. *T:* (020) 7370 1414. *Club:* Brooks's. *Died 27 Dec. 2006.*

HUSSEY, Prof. Joan Mervyn, MA, BLitt, PhD; FSA, FRHistS; Professor of History in the University of London, at Royal Holloway College, 1950–74, then Emeritus; *b* 5 June 1907. *Educ:* privately; Trowbridge High Sch.; Lycée Victor Duruy, Versailles; St Hugh's

Coll., Oxford. Research Student, Westfield Coll., London, 1932–34; Internat. Travelling Fellow (FUW), 1934–35; Pfeiffer Research Fellow, Girton, 1934–37; Gamble Prize, 1935. Asst Lectr in Hist., Univ. of Manchester, 1937–43; Lectr in Hist., 1943–47, Reader in Hist., 1947–50, at Bedford Coll., Univ. of London. Visiting Prof. at Amer. Univ. of Beirut, 1966. Leverhulme Foundn Emeritus Res. Fellow, 1974. Pres., Brit. Nat. Cttee for Byzantine Studies, 1961–71; Hon. Vice-Pres., Internat. Cttee for Byzantine Studies, 1976. Governor, Girton Coll., Cambridge, 1935–37; Member Council: St Hugh's Coll., Oxford, 1940–46; Royal Holloway Coll., 1966–86. Hon. Fellow, St Hugh's Coll., Oxford, 1968; Hon. Res. Associate, RHBNC, 1986. Hon. Fellow, Instituto Siciliano di Studi Bizantini, 1975. *Publications:* Church and Learning in the Byzantine Empire 867–1185, 1937 (repr. 1961); The Byzantine World, 1957, 3rd edn 1966; Cambridge Medieval History IV, Pts I and II: ed and contributor, 1966–67; The Finlay Papers, 1973; The Orthodox Church in the Byzantine Empire, 1986, rev. edn 1990; (ed) Journals and Correspondence of George Finlay, 2 vols, 1995; reviews and articles in Byzantinische Zeitschrift, Byzantinoslavica, Trans Roy. Hist. Soc., Jl of Theological Studies, Jahrbuch der Österreichischen Byzantinistik, Enc. Britannica, Chambers's Enc., New Catholic Enc., Oxford DNB, etc. *Address:* 16 Clarence Drive, Englefield Green, Egham, Surrey TW20 0NL. *Died 20 Feb. 2006.*

HUTCHINSON, Patricia Margaret, CMG 1981; CBE 1982; HM Diplomatic Service, retired; *b* 18 June 1926; *d* of late Francis Hutchinson and Margaret Peat. *Educ:* abroad; St Paul's Girls' Sch.; Somerville Coll., Oxford (PPE, MA, Hon Fellow, 1980). ECE, Geneva, 1947; Bd of Trade, 1947–48; HM Diplomatic Service, 1948: 3rd Sec., Bucharest, 1950–52; Foreign Office, 1952–55; 2nd (later 1st) Sec., Berne, 1955–58; 1st Sec. (Commercial), Washington, 1958–61; FO, 1961–64; 1st Sec., Lima, 1964–67 (acted as Chargé d'Affaires); Dep. UK Permanent Rep. to Council of Europe, 1967–69; Counsellor: Stockholm, 1969–72; UK Delegn to OECD, 1973–75; Consul-Gen., Geneva, 1975–80; Ambassador to Uruguay, 1980–83; Consul-Gen., Barcelona, 1983–86. Pres., Somerville ASM, 1988–91. *Recreations:* music, reading. *Address:* 12A Ashley Gardens, SW1P 1HL. *Club:* Oxford and Cambridge. *Died 11 Dec. 2008.*

HUTCHISON, Prof. Terence Wilmot, FBA 1992; Professor of Economics, University of Birmingham, 1956–78, then Emeritus Professor; Dean of the Faculty of Commerce and Social Science, 1959–61; *b* 13 Aug. 1912; *m* 1st, 1935, Loretta Hack (*d* 1981); one *s* two *d*; 2nd, 1983, Christine Donaldson (*d* 2003). *Educ:* Tonbridge Sch.; Peterhouse, Cambridge. Lector, Univ. of Bonn, 1935–38; Prof., Teachers' Training Coll., Bagdad, 1938–41. Served Indian Army, in intelligence, in Middle East and India, 1941–46; attached to Govt of India, 1945–46. Lecturer, University Coll., Hull, 1946–47;

Lecturer, 1947–51 and Reader, 1951–56, London Sch. of Economics. Visiting Professor: Columbia Univ., 1954–55; Univ. of Saarbrücken, 1962, 1980; Yale Univ., 1963–64; Dalhousie Univ., 1970; Keio Univ., Tokyo, 1973; Univ. of WA, 1975; Univ. of California, Davis, 1978; Visiting Fellow: Univ. of Virginia, 1960; Aust. Nat. Univ., Canberra, 1967. Mem. Council, Royal Economic Soc., 1967–72. *Publications:* The Significance and Basic Postulates of Economic Theory, 1938 (2nd edn 1960); A Review of Economic Doctrines 1870–1929, 1953; Positive Economics and Policy Objectives, 1964; Economics and Economic Policy 1946–66, 1968; Knowledge and Ignorance in Economics, 1977; Keynes *v* the Keynesians, 1977; Revolutions and Progress in Economic Knowledge, 1978; The Politics and Philosophy of Economics, 1981; Before Adam Smith, 1988; Changing Aims in Economics, 1992; The Uses and Abuses of Economics, 1994; The Methodology of Economics and the Formalist Revolution, 2000; articles, reviews in jls. *Address:* 13 Watersmeet, Chesil Street, Winchester, Hants SO23 0HU. *T:* (01798) 831269. *Died 5 Oct. 2007.*

HUTTON, (Hubert) Robin, OBE 1993; Director-General, British Merchant Banking and Securities Houses Association, 1988–92; *b* 22 April 1933; *e s* of late Kenneth Douglas and of Dorothy Hutton; *m* 1st, 1956, Valerie Riseborough (marr. diss. 1967); one *s* one *d*; 2nd, 1969, Deborah Berkeley; two step *d*. *Educ:* Merchant Taylors' Sch.; Peterhouse, Cambridge (Scholar; MA 1960). Royal Tank Regt, 1952–53 (commnd). Economic Adviser to Finance Corp. for Industry Ltd, 1956–62; economic journalist and consultant; Dir, Hambros Bank Ltd, 1966–70; Special Adviser: to HM Govt, 1970–72; to Min. of Posts and Telecommunications, 1972–73. Chm., Cttee of Inquiry into Public Trustee Office, 1971; Dir of Banking, Insurance and Financial Instns in EEC, Brussels, 1973–78; Exec. Dir, S. G. Warburg & Co. Ltd, 1978–82; Chm., Soc. des Banques S. G. Warburg et Leu SA, Luxembourg, 1979–82; Director-General: Accepting Houses Cttee, 1982–87; Issuing Houses Assoc., 1983–88. Director: Ariel Exchange Ltd, 1982–86; Associated Book Publishers PLC, 1982–87; Northern Rock plc (formerly Northern Rock Building Soc.), 1986–2001; Rock Asset Management Ltd, Rock Asset Management (Unit Trust) Ltd, 1988–93; Singer & Friedlander Hldgs Ltd, 1993–2001; Chairman: LondonClear Ltd, 1987–89; Homes Intown plc, 1989–94. Dir, IMRO, 1986–2000; Lay Mem., Disciplinary Cttee, ICAEW, 1988–98; Member: Exec. Cttee, BBA, 1982–92 (Chm., Securities Cttee, 1987–91); Council of Foreign Bondholders, 1983–89; Adv. Cttee, European Business Inst., 1983–94; Chm., Nat. Adv. Cttee on Telecommunications for England, 1985–93. FRSA 1990. *Recreations:* cricket, skiing, gardening, travel. *Address:* Church Farm, Athelington, Suffolk IP21 5EJ. *T:* (01728) 628361. *Club:* MCC. *Died 25 Jan. 2008.*

I

IEVERS, Frank George Eyre, CMG 1964; Postmaster-General, East Africa, 1962–65, retired; *b* 8 May 1910; *s* of Eyre Francis and Catherine Ievers; *m* 1936, Phyllis Robinson; two *s*. *Educ*: Dover Coll. Asst Traffic Supt, Post Office, 1933; Traffic Supt, East Africa, 1946; Telecommunications Controller, 1951; Regional Dir, 1959. *Recreations*: golf, photography. *Address*: 20 Heron Close, Worcester WR2 4BW. *T*: (01905) 427121. *Clubs*: Nairobi (Kenya); Sudan (Khartoum).
Died 14 Oct. 2006.

ILCHESTER, 9th Earl of, *cr* 1756; **Maurice Vivian de Touffreville Fox-Strangways;** Baron Ilchester of Ilchester, Somerset, and Baron Strangways of Woodsford Strangways, Dorset, 1741; Baron Ilchester and Stavordale of Redlynch, Somerset, 1747; Group Captain, Royal Air Force, retired; Vice-Chairman, County Border News Ltd and Bromley News Ltd, since 1995 (Managing Director, 1984–95); *b* 1 April 1920; *s* of 8th Earl of Ilchester and Laure Georgine Emilie (*d* 1970), *d* of late Evanghelos Georgios Mazaraki, sometime Treasurer of Suez Canal Company; *S* father, 1970; *m* 1941, Diana Mary Elizabeth (Pres., WAAF Assoc.), *e d* of late George Frederick Simpson, Cassington, Oxfordshire. *Educ*: Kingsbridge Sch. CEng; MRAeS; FINucE (Pres., 1982–84). Served RAF, 1936–76 (Gp Captain). Vice Chm., Biggin Hill Airport Consultative Cttee, 1976–95. Dir, 1982–90, Vice Chm., 1985–86, Nottingham Building Soc. Mem., H of L Select Cttee on Science and Technology, 1984–89. President: Soc. of Engineers, 1974 (Hon. FSE 1989); Biggin Hill Br., 1973–2003, SE Area, 1978–2003, RAFA; Darent River Preservation Soc., 1993–2003; Grant Maintained Schools Foundn, 1991–99; Cannock Sch., 1992–95 (Chm. Govs, 1978–92); Kent and Downs Reg. Newspaper Soc., 1994–95; Westerham Br., RBL, 1996–2003. President: 285 Sqn, ATC, 1973–2000; 2427 Sqn, ATC, 1977–. FCMI. Hon. FCP 1994. *Recreations*: outdoor activities, enjoyment of the arts. *Heir: nephew* Robin Maurice Fox-Strangways [*b* 2 Sept. 1942; *m* 1969, Margaret Elizabeth, *d* of late Geoffrey Miles; one *s* one *d*]. *Address*: Farley Mill, Westerham, Kent TN16 1UB. *T*: (01959) 562314. *Club*: Royal Air Force.
Died 2 July 2006.

ILLINGWORTH, David Gordon, CVO 1987 (LVO 1980); MD, FRCPE; Surgeon Apothecary to HM Household at Holyrood Palace, Edinburgh, 1970–86; *b* 22 Dec. 1921; *yr s* of Sir Gordon Illingworth; *m* 1946, Lesley Beagrie, Peterhead; two *s* one *d*. *Educ*: George Watson's Coll.; Edinburgh University. MB, ChB Edinburgh, 1943; MRCPE 1949; MD (with commendation) 1963; FRCPE 1965; FRCGP 1970. Nuffield Foundn Travelling Fellow, 1966. RN Medical Service, 1944–46 (2nd Escort Gp); medical appts, Edinburgh Northern Hosps Group, 1946–82. Dep. CMO, Scottish Life Assurance Co., 1973–92. Hon. Sen. Lectr in Rehabilitation Studies, Dept of Orthopaedic Surgery, Edinburgh Univ., 1977–82; Lectr in Gen. Practice Teaching Unit, Edinburgh Univ., 1965–82. Member: Cancer Planning Group, Scottish Health Service Planning Council, 1976–81; Tenovus, Edinburgh, 1978–92; ASH, Royal Colleges Jt Cttee, 1978–82; Specialty Sub-Cttee on Gen. Practice, 1980–82; Nat. Med. Cons. Cttee, 1980–82. AFOM, RCP, 1980. Mem., Harveian Soc. Life Governor, Imperial Cancer Res. Fund, 1978. *Publications*: Practice (jtly), 1978; (contrib.) By Royal Command, ed H. Buckton, 1997; The Bridge With Broken Arches (autobiog.), 2003; contribs to BMJ, Jl of Clinical Pathology, Gut, Lancet, Medicine. *Recreations*: golf, gardening. *Address*: 19 Napier Road, Edinburgh EH10 5AZ. *T*: (0131) 229 8102. *Clubs*: University (Edinburgh); Bruntsfield Links Golfing Soc.
Died 12 Sept. 2009.

INGHAM, Prof. Kenneth, OBE 1961; MC 1946; Professor of History, 1967–84, Part-time Professor of History, 1984–86, then Emeritus Professor, and Head of History Department, 1970–84, University of Bristol; *b* 9 Aug. 1921; *s* of Gladson and Frances Lily Ingham; *m* 1949, Elizabeth Mary Southall (*d* 2009); one *s* one *d*. *Educ*: Bingley Grammar Sch.; Keble Coll., Oxford (Exhibitioner). Served with West Yorks Regt, 1941–46 (despatches, 1945). Frere Exhibitioner in Indian Studies, University of Oxford, 1947; DPhil 1950. Lecturer in Modern History, Makerere Coll., Uganda, 1950–56, Prof., 1956–62; Dir of Studies, RMA, Sandhurst, 1962–67. MLC, Uganda, 1954–61. *Publications*: Reformers in India, 1956; The Making of Modern Uganda, 1958; A History of East Africa, 1962; The Kingdom of Toro in Uganda, 1975; Jan Christian Smuts: the conscience of a South African, 1986; Politics in Modern Africa, 1990; Obote: a political biography, 1994; contrib. to Encyclopædia Britannica, Britannica Book of the Year. *Address*: The Woodlands, 94 West Town Lane, Bristol BS4 5DZ.
Died 13 Sept. 2010.

INGLEBY, 2nd Viscount *cr* 1955, of Snilesworth; **Martin Raymond Peake;** landowner; Director, Hargreaves Group Ltd, 1960–80; *b* 31 May 1926; *s* of 1st Viscount Ingleby, and Joan, Viscountess Ingleby (*d* 1979); *S* father, 1966; *m* 1st, 1952, Susan (*d* 1996), *d* of late Henderson Russell Landale; four *d* (one *s* decd); 2nd, 2003, Dobrila, *d* of late Radomir Radović. *Educ*: Eton; Trinity Coll., Oxford (MA). Called to the Bar, Inner Temple, 1956. Sec., Hargreaves Group Ltd, 1958–61. Administrative Staff Coll., 1961. CC Yorks (North Riding), 1964–67. Mem., N Yorks Moors Nat. Park Planning Cttee, 1968–78. *Heir: none. Address*: Shepherd Hill House, Shepherd Hill, Swainby, Northallerton, North Yorks DL6 3DL.
Died 14 Oct. 2008 (ext).

INGLEFIELD-WATSON, Lt-Col Sir John (Forbes), 5th Bt *cr* 1895, of Earnock, Co. Lanarks; *b* 16 May 1926; *s* of Sir Derrick William Inglefield Watson, Bt, TD (who changed family surname to Inglefield-Watson by Deed Poll, 1945) and Margrett Georgina (*née* Robertson-Aikman, later Savill) (*d* 1995); *S* father, 1987. *Educ*: Eton College. Enlisted RE, 1944; short course, Trinity Coll., Cambridge, 1944–45; commnd RE, 1946; served in Iraq, Egypt, Kenya, Libya, Cyprus, Germany, N Ireland; psc 1958; Major 1959; Lt-Col 1969; retired 1981. Association Football Referee: Class I, 1954; Chm. Army FA Referees Cttee, 1974–78; FA Staff Referee Instructor, 1978–. Mem. Council, Kent County FA, 1975–81; Hon. Vice-Pres., Army FA, 1982–92. MCMI. *Recreations*: Association football refereeing, philately. *Heir: cousin* Simon Conran Hamilton Watson [*b* 11 Aug. 1939; *m* 1971, Madeleine Stiles (*d* 1998), *e d* of late Wagner Mahlon Dickerson]. *Address*: The Ross, Hamilton, Lanarkshire ML3 7UF. *T*: (01698) 283734.
Died 7 Feb. 2007.

INGOLD, Cecil Terence, CMG 1970; DSc 1940; Professor of Botany in University of London, Birkbeck College, 1944–72; Vice-Master, Birkbeck College, 1965–70, Fellow, 1973; *b* 3 July 1905; *s* of late E. G. Ingold; *m* 1933, Leonora Mary Kemp; one *s* three *d*. *Educ*: Bangor (Co. Down) Grammar Sch.; Queen's Univ., Belfast. (BSc 1925). Asst in Botany, QUB, 1929; Lectr in Botany, University of Reading, 1930–37; Lecturer-in-charge of Dept of Botany, University Coll., Leicester, 1937–44; Dean of Faculty of Science, London Univ., 1956–60. Dep. Vice-Chancellor, London Univ., 1966–68, Chm. Academic Council, 1969–72. Chm., University Entrance and School Examinations Council, 1958–64; Vice-Chm., Inter-Univ. Council for Higher Educn Overseas, 1969–74. Chm., Council Freshwater Biol. Assoc., 1965–74; Pres., Internat. Mycological Congress, 1971. Hooker Lectr, Linnean Soc., 1974. Hon.

FLS 2000 (FLS 1934). Hon. DLitt Ibadan, 1969; Hon. DSc Exeter, 1972; Hon. DCL Kent, 1978. Linnean Medal (Botany), 1983; de Bary Medal (Mycology), Internat. Mycological Assoc., 1996; Millennium Gold Medal, 15th Internat. Botanical Congress, 1999. *Publications:* Spore Discharge in Land Plants, 1939; Dispersal in Fungi, 1953; The Biology of Fungi, 1961; Spore Liberation, 1965; Fungal Spores: their liberation and dispersal, 1971. *Address:* The Old Vicarage, 26 Cottage Road, Wooler, Northumberland NE71 6AD. *Died 31 May 2010.*

INGRAM, Prof. Vernon Martin, FRS 1970; John and Dorothy Wilson Professor of Biology, Massachusetts Institute of Technology, since 1988; *b* Breslau, 19 May 1924; *s* of Kurt and Johanna Immerwahr; *m* 1st, 1950, Margaret Young (marr. diss.); one *s* one *d*; 2nd, 1984, Elizabeth Hendee. *Educ:* Birkbeck Coll., Univ. of London. PhD Organic Chemistry, 1949; DSc Biochemistry, 1961. Analytical and Res. Chemist, Thos Morson & Son, Mddx, 1941–45; Lecture Demonstrator in Chem., Birkbeck Coll., 1945–47; Asst Lectr in Chem., Birkbeck Coll., 1947–50; Rockefeller Foundn Fellow, Rockefeller Inst., NY, 1950–51; Coxe Fellow, Yale, 1951–52; Mem. Sci. Staff, MRC Unit for Molecular Biology, Cavendish Lab., Cambridge, 1952–58; Assoc. Prof. 1958–61, Prof. of Biochemistry, 1961–, MIT; Lectr (part-time) in Medicine, Columbia, 1961–73; Guggenheim Fellow, UCL, 1967–68. Jesup Lectr, Columbia, 1962; Harvey Soc. Lectr, 1965. Mem., Amer. Acad. of Arts and Sciences, 1964. Fellow, Amer. Assoc. for Advancement of Science, 1987. William Allen Award, Amer. Soc. for Human Genetics, 1967. *Publications:* Haemoglobin and Its Abnormalities, 1961; The Hemoglobins in Genetics and Evolution, 1963; The Biosynthesis of Macromolecules, 1965, new edn, 1971; articles on human genetics, nucleic acids, differentiation and molecular biology of aging and developmental neurobiology, Alzheimer's Disease, in Nature, Jl Mol. Biol., Jl Cell Biol., Develt Biol., Jl Biol Chem., Brain Research, etc. *Recreations:* music; photographer of abstract images. *Address:* Massachusetts Institute of Technology, Massachusetts Avenue, Cambridge, MA 02139, USA. *T:* (617) 2533706. *Died 17 Aug. 2006.*

INNES of Coxton, Sir David (Charles Kenneth Gordon), 12th Bt *cr* 1686 (NS); consultant in electronics for petro-chemical and power generation fields; *b* 17 April 1940; *s* of Sir Charles Innes of Coxton, 11th Bt and Margaret Colquhoun Lockhart (*d* 1992), *d* of F. C. L. Robertson; *S* father, 1990; *m* 1969, Majorie Alison, *d* of E. W. Parker; one *s* one *d*. *Educ:* Haileybury Coll.; City & Guilds Coll. of Imperial Coll., London Univ. BSc(Eng); ACGI. Technical Dir, Peak Technologies, 1974–78; Man. Dir, Peak Combustion Controls, 1978–81. *Recreations:* electronics, aeronautics, astronomy. *Heir: s* Alastair Charles Deverell Innes, *b* 17 Sept 1970. *Address:* 28 Wadham Close, Shepperton, Middlesex TW17 9HT. *T:* (01932) 228273. *Died 21 Aug. 2010.*

INNES, Lt-Col William Alexander Disney; DL; Vice Lord-Lieutenant of Banffshire, 1971–86; *b* 19 April 1910; 2nd *s* of late Captain James William Guy Innes, CBE, DL, JP, RN, of Maryculter, Kincardineshire; *m* 1st, 1939, Mary Alison (*d* 1997), *d* of late Francis Burnett-Stuart, Howe Green, Hertford; two *s*; 2nd, 2001, Patricia Joan (*née* Callender), *widow* of George Gordon. *Educ:* Marlborough Coll., RMC, Sandhurst. Gordon Highlanders: 2nd Lieut, 1930; Captain 1938; Temp. Major 1941; Major, 1946; Temp. Lt-Col, 1951; retd, 1952. Served War of 1939–45: Far East (PoW Malaya and Siam, 1942–45). Chm., Banffshire T&AFA, 1959. DL 1959–87, JP 1964–86, Banffshire. *Recreation:* gardening. *Address:* Heath Cottage, Aberlour, Banffshire AB38 9QD. *T:* (01340) 871266. *Died 20 March 2008.*

IRVINE, His Honour James Eccles Malise; a Circuit Judge, 1972–96 (Leicester County and Crown Courts, 1972–82; Oxford and Northampton Combined Courts Centres, 1982–96); *b* 10 July 1925; *y s* of late Brig.-Gen. A. E. Irvine, CB, CMG, DSO, Wotton-under-Edge; *m*

1954, Anne, *e d* of late Col G. Egerton-Warburton, DSO, TD, JP, DL, Grafton Hall, Malpas; one *s* one *d*. *Educ:* Stowe Sch. (Scholar); Merton Coll., Oxford (Postmaster; MA Oxon 1953). Served Grenadier Guards, 1943–46 (France and Germany Star); Hon. Captain Grenadier Guards, 1946. Called to Bar, Inner Temple, 1949 (Poland Prizeman in Criminal Law, 1949); practised Oxford Circuit, 1949–71; Prosecuting Counsel for Inland Revenue on Oxford Circuit, 1965–71; Dep. Chm., Glos QS, 1967–71. Lay Judge of Court of Arches of Canterbury and Chancery Court of York, 1981–2000. Pres. Oxon Br., Grenadier Guards Assoc., 1990–. Pres., Heyford and Dist. Br., RBL, 1999–. *Publications:* Parties and Pleasures: the Diaries of Helen Graham 1823–26, 1957. *Address:* 2 Harcourt Buildings, Temple, EC4Y 9DB. *Died 29 Dec. 2007.*

IRWIN, Maj.-Gen. Brian St George, CB 1975; Director General, Ordnance Survey, 1969–77; *b* 16 Sept. 1917; *s* of late Lt-Col Alfred Percy Bulteel Irwin, DSO, andEileen Irwin (*née* Holberton); *m* 1939, Audrey Lilla (*d* 1994), *d* of late Lt-Col H. D. Steen, IMS; two *s*; *m* 2005, Pamela Mary, *widow* of Major D. T. Arnott, RE. *Educ:* Rugby Sch.; RMA Woolwich; Trinity Hall, Cambridge (MA). Commnd in RE, 1937; war service in Western Desert, 1941–43 (despatches); Sicily and Italy, 1943–44 (despatches); Greece, 1944–45; subseq. in Cyprus, 1956–59 (despatches) and 1961–63; Dir of Military Survey, MoD, 1965–69. Col Comdt, RE, 1977–82. FRICS (Council 1969–70, 1972–76); FRGS (Council 1966–70; Vice-Pres., 1974–77). *Recreation:* genealogy. *Address:* 16 Northerwood House, Swan Green, Lyndhurst, Hants SO43 7DT. *T:* (023) 8028 3499. *Club:* Army and Navy. *Died 6 March 2006.*

IRWIN, Flavia; *see* de Grey, F.

ISHAM, Sir Ian (Vere Gyles), 13th Bt *cr* 1627; *b* 17 July 1923; *s* of Lt-Col Vere Arthur Richard Isham, MC (*d* 1968) and Edith Irene (*d* 1973), *d* of Harry Brown; *S* cousin, Sir Gyles Isham, 12th Bt, 1976. Served War of 1939–45, Captain RAC. *Heir: b* Norman Murray Crawford Isham, OBE [*b* 28 Jan. 1930; *m* 1956, Joan, *d* of late Leonard James Genet; two *s* one *d*]. *Address:* 50 Willow Court, Ackender Road, Alton, Hants GU34 1JW. *Died 20 Oct. 2009.*

ISLES, Maj.-Gen. Donald Edward, CB 1978; OBE 1968; DL; *b* 19 July 1924; *s* of Harold and Kathleen Isles; *m* 1948, Sheila Mary Stephens (formerly Thorpe); three *s* one *d*. *Educ:* Roundhay; Leeds Univ.; RMCS. jssc 1961. Italian campaign, Palestine, Egypt, Sudan, Syria, with 1st Bn, Duke of Wellington's Regt, 1944–47; Asst Mil. Attaché, Paris, 1963–65; CO, 1DWR, BAOR and UN Forces in Cyprus, 1965–67; AMS, MoD, 1968; Col GS, MoD, 1968–71; Dir of Munitions, Brit. Defence Staff Washington, 1972–75; Dir-Gen. Weapons (Army), 1975–78, retired. Dep. Man. Dir, British Manufacture & Res. Co., 1979–89. Col, The Duke of Wellington's Regt, 1975–82; Col Comdt, The King's Div., 1975–79; Vice-Chm., Yorks and Humberside TA&VRA, 1984–87. Hon. Colonel: 3rd Bn, Yorkshire Volunteers, 1977–83; Leeds Univ. OTC, 1985–90. Mem., Court, Leeds Univ., 1987–95. Pres., Lincs and S Humberside RBL, 1990–96; Patron, Lincs RBL, 1996–2004. DL Lincs, 1990. *Recreation:* shooting. *Club:* Army and Navy. *Died 12 Nov. 2008.*

ISMAY, Walter Nicholas; Managing Director, Worcester Parsons Ltd, 1975–82; *b* 20 June 1921; *s* of late John Ismay, Maryport, Cumberland. *Educ:* Taunton's Sch., Southampton; King's Coll., University of London (BSc). Royal Aircraft Establishment, 1939–40; Ministry of Supply, 1940–43; served Army (Capt., General List), 1943–46; Imperial Chemical Industries, Metals Division, 1948–58 (Technical Dir, 1957–58); Dir, Yorkshire Imperial Metals, 1958–67; Dep. Chm. Yorkshire Imperial Plastics, 1966–67; Dep. Chm. and Man. Dir, Milton Keynes Devilt Corp., 1967–71; McKechnie Britain Ltd, 1972–75. FIMechE. *Recreation:* sailing. *Address:* 8–9 The

Close, Saffron Meadow, New Street, Stratford-upon-Avon, Warwickshire CV37 6GD. *Club:* Royal Lymington Yacht. *Died 25 Aug. 2006.*

ISRAEL, Rev. Dr Martin Spencer, FRCPath; Priest-in-Charge, Holy Trinity with All Saints Church, South Kensington, 1983–97; *b* 30 April 1927; *s* of Elie Benjamin Israel, ophthalmic surgeon, and Minnie Israel. *Educ:* Parktown Boys' High Sch., Johannesburg; Univ. of the Witwatersrand (MB ChB). MRCP 1952, FRCPath 1972. Ho. Phys., Hammersmith Hosp., 1952; Registrar in Pathology, Royal Hosp., Wolverhampton, 1953–55; service in RAMC, 1955–57; Lectr and Sen. Lectr in Pathology, 1958–82, Hon. Sen. Lectr 1982–, RCS. Ordained priest in C of E, 1975. President: Guild of Health, 1983–90; Churches' Fellowship for Psychical and Spiritual Studies, 1983–98. *Publications: medical:* General Pathology (with J. B. Walter), 1963, 6th edn 1987; *spiritual matters:* Summons to Life, 1974; Precarious Living, 1976; Smouldering Fire, 1978; The Pain that Heals, 1981; Living Alone, 1982; The Spirit of Counsel, 1983; Healing as Sacrament, 1984; The Discipline of Love, 1985; Coming in Glory, 1986; Gethsemane, 1987; The Pearl of Great Price, 1988; The Dark Face of Reality, 1989; The Quest for Wholeness, 1989; Creation, 1989; Night Thoughts, 1990; A Light on the Path, 1990; Life Eternal, 1993; Dark Victory, 1994; Angels—Messengers of Grace, 1995; Exorcism: the removal of evil influences, 1997; Doubt: the way of growth, 1997; Happiness That Lasts, 1999; Learning to Love, 2001; (with Neil Broadbent) The Devout Life, 2001. *Recreations:* music, conversation. *Address:* 21 Soudan Road, SW11 4HH. *T:* (020) 7622 5756. *Died 23 Oct. 2007.*

IVES, Prof. Kenneth James, CBE 1996; FREng; FICE; Chadwick Professor of Civil Engineering, University College London, 1984–92; *b* 29 Nov. 1926; *s* of Walter Ives and Grace Ives (*née* Curson); *m* 1952, Brenda Grace Tilley; one *s* one *d*. *Educ:* William Ellis Grammar School, London; University College London (BSc Eng, PhD, DSc Eng; Fellow, 1996). FREng (FEng 1986); FICE 1983. Junior Engineer, Metropolitan Water Board, London, 1948–55; Lectr, Reader, Prof., University Coll. London, 1955–92. Research Fellow, Harvard Univ., 1958–59; Visiting Professor: Univ. of North Carolina, 1964; Delft Technical Univ., 1977; Consultant Expert Adviser, WHO, 1966–92. Mem., Badenoch Cttee on Cryptosporidium in Water Supplies, 1989–95. For. Associate, NAE, US, 2003. Gans Medal, Soc. for Water Treatment, 1966; Gold Medal, Filtration Soc. Internat., 1983; Jenkins Medal, IAWPRC, 1990; Freese Award, ASCE, 1994. *Publications:* Scientific Basis of Filtration, 1975; Scientific Basis of Flocculation, 1978; Scientific Basis of Flotation, 1984; contribs to sci. and eng. jls on water purification. *Recreation:* ballroom dancing. *Address:* Department of Civil and Environmental Engineering, University College London, Gower Street, WC1E 6BT. *Died 8 Sept. 2009.*

IVORY, Thomas Peter Gerard; QC 1998; *b* 29 Sept. 1956; *s* of late Patrick Ivory and of Rosaleen Ivory; *m* 1985, Deborah Mary Stinson. *Educ:* St Patrick's Coll., Knock, Belfast; St Catharine's Coll., Cambridge (BA 1977; MA). Called to the Bar, Lincoln's Inn, 1978. Fellow, St Catharine's Coll., Cambridge, 1983–90. *Recreation:* golf. *Address:* 1 Essex Court, Temple, EC4Y 9AR. *T:* (020) 7583 2000. *Died 2 Nov. 2008.*

J

JACK, Prof. Ian Robert James, FBA 1986; Professor of English Literature, University of Cambridge, 1976–89, Emeritus 1989; Fellow of Pembroke College, Cambridge, 1961–89, Emeritus 1989; *b* 5 Dec. 1923; *s* of John McGregor Bruce Jack, WS, and Helena Colburn Buchanan; *m* 1st, 1948, Jane Henderson MacDonald (marr. diss.); two *s* one *d*; 2nd, 1972, Margaret Elizabeth Crone; one *s*. *Educ:* George Watson's Coll. (John Welsh Classical Schol., 1942); Univ. of Edinburgh (James Boswell Fellow, 1946; MA 1947); Merton Coll., Oxford (DPhil 1950; Hon. Fellow, 1998); LittD Cantab 1973. Brasenose College, Oxford: Lectr in Eng. Lit., 1950–55; Sen. Res. Fellow, 1955–61; Cambridge University: Lectr in English, 1961–73; Reader in English Poetry, 1973–76; Librarian, Pembroke Coll., 1965–75. Visiting Professor: Alexandria, 1960; Chicago (Carpenter Prof.), 1968–69; California at Berkeley, 1968–69; British Columbia, 1975; Virginia, 1980–81; Tsuda Coll., Tokyo, 1981; New York Univ. (Berg Prof.), 1989; de Carle Lectr, Univ. of Otago, NZ, 1964; Warton Lectr in English Poetry, British Acad., 1967; Guest Speaker, Nichol Smith Seminar, ANU, 1976; Guest Speaker, 50th anniversary meeting of English Literary Soc. of Japan, 1978; Leverhulme Emeritus Fellow, 1990, 1991; numerous lecture-tours for British Council and other bodies. President: Charles Lamb Soc., 1970–80; Browning Soc., 1980–83; Johnson Soc., Lichfield, 1986–87; Vice-Pres., Brontë Soc., 1973–. General Editor: Brontë novels (Clarendon edn), 7 vols, 1969–92; The Poetical Works of Browning, 1983–95. *Publications:* Augustan Satire, 1952; English Literature 1815–1832 (Vol. X, Oxf. Hist. of Eng. Lit.), 1963; Keats and the Mirror of Art, 1967; Browning's Major Poetry, 1973; The Poet and his Audience, 1984; *edited:* Sterne: A Sentimental Journey, etc, 1968; Browning: Poetical Works 1833–1864, 1970; (with Hilda Marsden) Emily Brontë: Wuthering Heights, 1976; The Poetical Works of Browning: co-edited: (with M. Smith) Vol. 1 (Pauline, Paracelsus), 1983; (with M. Smith) Vol. 2 (Sordello), 1984; (with R. Fowler) Vol. 3 (Bells and Pomegranates, i–vi), 1988; (with R. Fowler and M. Smith) Vol. 4 (Bells and Pomegranates, vii–viii, Christmas-Eve and Easter-Day), 1991; (with R. Inglesfield) Vol. 5 (Men and Women), 1995; contrib. TLS, RES, etc. *Recreations:* collecting books, travelling hopefully, thinking about words. *Address:* Highfield House, High Street, Fen Ditton, Cambridgeshire CB5 8ST. *T:* (01223) 292697; Pembroke College, Cambridge CB2 1RF.   *Died 3 Sept. 2008.*

JACKSON, Albert Leslie Samuel; JP; Chairman, Birmingham Technology Ltd (Aston Science Park), 1984–2005; *b* 20 Jan. 1918; *s* of Bert Jackson and Olive Powell; *m* Gladys Burley; one *s* one *d*. *Educ:* Handsworth New Road Council Sch. War service, Radio Mechanic, RAF. Mem., Birmingham CC, 1952–86; Lord Mayor, 1975–76, Dep. Lord Mayor, 1978–79, Birmingham. Dir and Cttee Chm., NEC, 1984–87; Dir, National Exhibition Centre (Developments) PLC, 1997–2006. JP 1968. Hon. DSc Aston, 1999. *Recreations:* chess, sailing. *Address:* Dickies Meadow, Dock Lane, Bredon, near Tewkesbury GL20 7LG. *T:* (01684) 772541.
            Died 25 May 2010.

JACKSON, Yvonne Brenda, OBE 1985; DL; Chairman, West Yorkshire Metropolitan County Council, 1980–81; *b* 23 July 1920; *d* of Charles and Margaret Wilson; *m* 1946, Edward Grosvenor Jackson (decd); twin *s* (one *d* decd). *Educ:* Edgbaston C of E Coll., Birmingham; Manchester Teachers' Trng Coll. (Dip. Domestic Science and qualified teacher). School Meals Organizer, West Bromwich, Staffs, 1942–45. Mem., W Riding CC, 1967–73 (local govt reorganisation); Mem. W Yorks CC, 1973–86; Chm., Fire and Public Protection Cttee, 1977–80; Deputy Leader and Shadow Chairman: Fire

Cttee, 1981–86; Trading Standards Cttee, 1981–86; Police Cttee, 1982–86. Chm., Yorks Electricity Consultative Council, 1982–90; Mem., Yorks RHA, 1982–87. Mem. Exec. Cttee, Nat. Union of Cons. Assocs. 1981–88 (Dep. Chm., Yorks Area Finance and Gen. Purposes Cttee, 1982–88; Divl Pres., Elmet, 1985–93). Mem. Council and Court, Leeds Univ. DL W Yorks, 1983, High Sheriff, 1986–87. *Recreations:* badminton, fishing; former County hockey and tennis player; former motor rally driver (competed in nat. and internat. events incl. Monte Carlo, Alpine and Tulip rallies).
            Died 28 March 2010.

JACOB, David Oliver L.; *see* Lloyd Jacob.

JACOBI, Sir James (Edward), Kt 1989; OBE 1978; Medical Practitioner (private practice), since 1960; *b* 26 Aug. 1925; *s* of Edward William Jacobi and Doris Stella Jacobi; *m* 1946, Joy; one *s* two *d*; *m* 1974, Nora Maria; two *s*. *Educ:* Maryborough State High School; Univ. of Queensland (MB, BS, PhC). Clerk, Public Service, 1941; RAAF, 1943–46; served navigator-wireless operator, Beaufighter Sqdn, SW Pacific. Apprentice pharmaceutical chemist, 1946–50; pharm. chem., 1950–54, and Univ. student, 1954–60; Resident MO, Brisbane, 1961; MO, Dept of Health, Papua New Guinea, 1962–63; GP Port Moresby, 1963–. *Recreations:* Past President, PNG Rugby Football League. *Address:* Jacobi Medical Centre, Box 1551, Boroko, Papua New Guinea. *T:* 3255355. *Clubs:* United Services (Brisbane); City Tattersalls, NSW Leagues (Sydney); Brisbane Polo; Papua (Port Moresby).
            Died 21 June 2009.

JACOBS, Rabbi Dr Louis, CBE 1990; Rabbi, New London Synagogue, since 1964; Visiting Professor, University of Lancaster, since 1987; *b* 17 July 1920; *s* of Harry and Lena Jacobs; *m* 1944, Sophie Lisagorska (*d* 2005); two *s* one *d*. *Educ:* Manchester Central High Sch.; Manchester Talmudical Coll.; BA Hons, PhD, London. Rabbinical Ordination; Rabbi, Central Synagogue, Manchester, 1948–54; New West End Synagogue, 1954–60; Tutor, Jews' Coll., London, 1959–62; Dir, Society Study of Jewish Theology, 1962–64. Vis. Prof., Harvard Divinity Sch., 1985–86. Hon. Fellow: UCL, 1988; Leo Baeck Coll., 1988. Hon. DHL: Spertus Coll., Chicago, 1987; Hebrew Union Coll., Cincinnati, 1989; Jewish Theol. Seminary, NY, 1989; Hon. DLitt Lancaster, 1991. Hon. Citizen: Texas, 1961; New Orleans, 1963. *Publications:* Jewish Prayer, 1955; We Have Reason to Believe, 1957, 5th edn 2004; Guide to Rosh Hashanah, 1959; Guide to Yom Kippur, 1959; Jewish Values, 1960; (trans.) The Palm Tree of Deborah, 1960; Studies in Talmudic Logic, 1961; (trans.) Tract on Ecstasy, 1963; Principles of Jewish Faith, 1964; Seeker of Unity, 1966; Faith, 1968; Jewish Law, 1968; Jewish Ethics, Philosophy and Mysticism, 1969; Jewish Thought Today, 1970; What Does Judaism Say About . . .?, 1973; A Jewish Theology, 1973; Theology in the Responsa, 1975; Hasidic Thought, 1976; Hasidic Prayer, 1977; Jewish Mystical Testimonies, 1977; TEKYU: the unsolved problem in the Babylonian Talmud, 1981; The Talmudic Argument, 1985; A Tree of Life, 1985, 2nd edn 2000; Holy Living, 1990; Helping with Inquiries (autobiog.), 1989; God, Torah, Israel, 1990; Structure and Form of the Babylonian Talmud, 1991; Religion and the Individual, 1991; The Jewish Religion: a companion, 1995; Concise Companion to the Jewish Religion, 1999; Beyond Reasonable Doubt, 1999; Ask the Rabbi, 1999; Jewish Preaching, 2004; Their Heads in Heaven, 2004; Judaism and Theology, 2005; Rabbinic Thought, 2005; contribs to learned jls, collections and festschriften. *Recreations:* reading thrillers, watching television, hill walking. *Address:* 27 Clifton Hill, St John's Wood, NW8 0QE. *T:* (020) 7624 1299.
            Died 1 July 2006.

JAFFRÉ, Philippe Serge Yves, Chevalier de la Légion d'Honneur; Ordres du Mérite et du Mérite Agricole; Executive Vice President, Alstom, since 2005; *b* 2 March 1945; *s* of Yves-Frédéric Jaffré and Janine Jaffré (*née* Alliot); *m* 1974, Elisabeth Coulon; one *s* two *d. Educ:* Faculté de Law, Paris; Inst. d'études politiques, Paris (diploma); Ecole Nat. d'Administration (Bachelor of Law). Inspecteur des Finances, 1974; Dept of the Treasury, 1977–88; Gen. Sec., Comité Interministeriel pour l'Aménagement des Structures Industrielles, 1978; Tech. Advr to Minister of Economy, 1979; Dep. Dir, Dept of Govt Holdings, 1984; Head of Dept for Monetary and Financial affairs, 1986–88; Dir, Banque Stern, 1988; Chief Exec. Officer, Crédit Agricole, 1988–93; Chm. and Chief Exec. Officer, Elf Aquitaine, 1993–99; Chm., Europatweb, 2000–02; Chief Financial Officer, Alstom, 2002–05. *Publications:* La Monnaie et la politique Monétaire, 1990; Pour ou Contre les Stocks-options, 2002. *Recreation:* golf. *Address:* 26 Avenue Hamoir, 1180 Uccle, Belgium. *Died 5 Sept. 2007.*

JAGAN, Janet, OE 1993; President, Republic of Guyana, 1997–99; *b* Chicago, 20 Oct. 1920; *d* of Charles and Kathryn Roberts; *m* 1943, Dr Cheddi Jagan (*d* 1997), former President of Guyana; one *s* one *d. Educ:* Univ. of Detroit; Wayne Univ.; Michigan State Coll. Founder Mem., 1946, Political Affairs Cttee, which became People's Progressive Party, Guyana, in 1950: Exec. Mem., 1950–; Gen. Sec., 1950–70; Editor, Thunder (party jl), 1950–57, 2005–; Internat. Affairs Sec., 1970–80. First woman elected to Georgetown CC, 1950; MP Guyana, 1953, 1957–61, 1963–64, 1976–97; Dep. Speaker, House of Assembly, 1953; imprisoned for six months, Sept. 1954–Feb. 1955; Minister of Labour, Health and Housing, 1957–61, of Home Affairs, 1963–64; Prime Minister of Guyana, May–Dec. 1997. Mem., Elections Commn, 1967–68. Pres., Union of Guyanese Journalists, 1970–90. Mem., Council of Women World Leaders, 1999–. Trustee, Cheddi Jagan Res. Centre, 2000–. Editor, Mirror newspaper, 1973–97. Gandhi Gold Medal for Democracy, Peace and Women's Rights, UNESCO, 1997. Order of the Liberator (Venezuela), 1998. *Publications:* History of the PPP, 1960; Army Intervention in 1973 Elections, 1973; *for children:* When Grandpa Cheddi was a Boy, 1993; Patricia the Baby Manatee and other stories, 1995; Children's Stories of Guyana's Freedom Struggles, 1995; Anastasia the Anteater and other stories, 1997; The Dog Who Loved Flowers, 2000; The Alligator Ferry Service and other stories from Guyana, 2001; (ed) Anthology of Children's Stories by Guyanese Writers, 2002. *Recreation:* swimming. *Address:* 65 Plantation Bel Air, Georgetown, Guyana; HQ of People's Progressive Party, 41 Robb Street, Georgetown, Guyana. *T:* 72095. *Died 28 March 2009.*

JAMES, Anne Eleanor S.; *see* Scott-James.

JAMES, Anthony Trafford, CBE 1979; PhD; FRS 1983; Member of Executive Committee of Unilever Research Colworth Laboratory, also Head of Division of Biosciences, 1972–85; *b* Cardiff, Wales, 6 March 1922; *s* of J. M. and I. James; *m* 1st, 1945, O. I. A. Clayton (*d* 1980); two *s* one *d*; 2nd, 1983, L. J. Beare; one *s. Educ:* University College Sch.; Northern Polytechnic; University Coll. London (BSc, PhD; Fellow 1975); Harvard Business Sch. (AMP). President: Union Soc., UCL, 1944–45; Jt Student Representative Council, Univs of Wales and London, 1944–45; NUS, 1944–46. MRC Junior Fellowship at Bedford Coll., Univ. of London (with Prof. E. E. Turner, subject: Antimalarials), 1945–47; Jun. Mem. staff, Lister Inst. for Preventive Med., London (with Dr R. L. M. Synge, Nobel Laureate, subject: Structure of Gramicidin S), 1947–50; Mem. scientific staff, Nat. Inst. for Med. Res., London (special appt awarded, 1961), 1950–62 (with Dr A. J. P. Martin, FRS, Nobel Laureate, 1950–56); Unilever Research Lab., Sharnbrook: Div. Manager and Head of Biosynthesis Unit, 1962–67; Head of Div. of Plant Products and Biochemistry, 1967–69; Gp Manager, Biosciences Gp,

1969–72. Industrial Prof. of Chemistry, Loughborough Univ. of Technology, 1966–71. Non-exec. Dir, Wellcome Foundn, 1985–92. Member: SRC, 1973–77; Food Sci. and Technol. Bd, MAFF, 1975–80; Manpower Cttee, SERC, 1981–84; ABRC, 1983–; Council, Royal Soc., 1988–90; Chairman: Food Composition, Quality and Safety Cttee, MAFF, 1975–80; Biotechnol. Management Cttee, SERC, 1981–85. Hon. Dr Dijon, 1981; Hon. DSc Cranfield Inst. of Technology, 1985. Various awards incl. some from abroad. *Publications:* (ed with L. J. Morris) New Biochemical Separations, 1964; (with M. I. Gurr) Lipid Biochemistry—an introduction, 1972. *Recreations:* glass engraving, antique collecting, gardening. *Address:* 9 High Street, Harrold, Beds MK43 7DQ. *Died 7 Dec. 2006.*

JAMES, Basil; Special Commissioner, 1963–82, Presiding Special Commissioner, 1982–83; *b* 25 May 1918; *s* of late John Elwyn James, MA (Oxon.), Cardiff, and Mary Janet (*née* Lewis), Gwaelodygarth, Glam; *m* 1943, Moira Houlding Rayner, MA (Cantab.), *d* of late Capt. Benjamin Harold Rayner, North Staffs Regt, and Elizabeth (*née* Houlding), Preston, Lancs; one *s* twin *d. Educ:* Llandovery Coll.; Canton High Sch., Cardiff; Christ's Coll., Cambridge (Exhibnr). Tancred Law Student, Lincoln's Inn, 1936; Squire Law Scholar, Cambridge, 1936. BA 1939; MA 1942. Called to Bar, Lincoln's Inn, 1940. Continuous sea service as RNVR officer in small ships on anti-submarine and convoy duties in Atlantic, Arctic and Mediterranean, 1940–45. King George V Coronation Scholar, Lincoln's Inn, 1946. Practised at Chancery Bar, 1946–63. Admitted to Federal Supreme Court of Nigeria, 1962. *Publications:* contrib. to Atkin's Court Forms and Halsbury's Laws of England. *Recreations:* music, gardening. *Died 12 May 2009.*

JAMES, Rt Rev. Colin Clement Walter; Bishop of Winchester, 1985–95; *b* 20 Sept. 1926; *yr s* of late Canon Charles Clement Hancock James and Gwenyth Mary James; *m* 1962, Margaret Joan, (Sally), Henshaw (*d* 2001); one *s* two *d. Educ:* Aldenham School; King's College, Cambridge (MA, Hons History); Cuddesdon Theological College. Assistant Curate, Stepney Parish Church, 1952–55; Chaplain, Stowe School, 1955–59; BBC Religious Broadcasting Dept, 1959–67; Religious Broadcasting Organizer, BBC South and West, 1960–67; Vicar of St Peter with St Swithin, Bournemouth, 1967–73; Bishop Suffragan of Basingstoke, 1973–77; Canon Residentiary of Winchester Cathedral, 1973–77; Bishop of Wakefield, 1977–85. Member of General Synod, 1970–95; Chairman: Church Information Cttee, 1976–79; C of E's Liturgical Commn, 1986–93. Chm., BBC and IBA Central Religious Adv. Cttee, 1979–84. President: Woodard Corp., 1978–93; RADIUS, 1980–93. Chm., USPG, 1985–88. Hon. DLitt Southampton, 1996. *Recreations:* theatre, travelling. *Address:* 3 Back Street, Winchester SO23 9SB. *T:* (01962) 868874. *Died 10 Dec. 2009.*

JAMES, Dr (David) Geraint, FRCP; Consultant Ophthalmic Physician, St Thomas' Hospital, London, since 1973; Teacher, University of London, since 1979; *b* 2 Jan. 1922; *s* of David James and Sarah (*née* Davies); *m* 1951, Sheila Sherlock, (Dame Sheila Sherlock, DBE, FRS; *d* 2001); two *d. Educ:* Jesus Coll., Cambridge (MA 1945); Middx Hosp. Med. Sch., London (MD 1953); Columbia Univ., NYC. FRCP 1964. Consultant Physician, Royal Northern Hosp., 1959–86 (Dean, 1968–86). Adjunct Prof. of Medicine, Univ. of Miami, Fla, 1973–, and Prof. of Epidemiology, 1981–; Adjunct Prof., Royal Free Hosp. Med. Sch., 1987–; Consulting Phys. to RN, 1972–86; Hon. Consultant Phys., US Veterans' Admin, 1978–; Hon. Consulting Phys., Sydney Hosp., Australia, 1969–79. President: Internat. Cttee on Sarcoidosis, 1987–99 (World Exec. Sec., 1980–86); Italian Congress on Sarcoidosis, 1983; World Assoc. of Sarcoidosis, 1987–; Vice-Pres., Fellowship of Postgrad. Medicine; Past President: Med. Soc. of London (Hon. Fellow); Harveian Soc.; Osler Club (Hon. Fellow); Pres., London Glamorgan Soc., 1989–99; Vice-Pres.,

Cymmrodorion Soc., 2004–. Lectures: Tudor Edwards, RCP and RCS, 1983; George Wise Meml, New York City, 1983. Foreign Corresponding Mem., French Nat. Acad. of Medicine, 1987; Hon. Corresp. Mem., Thoracic Socs of Italy, France, Dominican Republic and Portugal; Hon. FACP 1990; Hon. FRCOphth, 1994. Editor, Internat. Rev. of Sarcoidosis, 1984–95. Freeman, City of London, 1961. Hon. LLD Wales, 1982. Chesterfield Medal, Inst. of Dermatology, London, 1957; Gold Medal, Barraquer Inst. of Ophthalmology, 1958; Carlo Forlanini Gold Medal, Italian Thoracic Soc., 1983. Gold Medal, Milan, 1987. Kt of Order of Christopher Columbus (Dominican Republic), 1987. *Publications*: Diagnosis and Treatment of Infections, 1957; Sarcoidosis, 1970; Circulation of the Blood, 1978; Atlas of Respiratory Diseases, 1981, 2nd edn 1992; Sarcoidosis and other Granulomatous Disorders, 1985; Textbook on Sarcoidosis and other Granulomatous Disorders, 1994; The Granulomatous Disorders, 1999. *Recreations*: history of medicine, international Welshness, Rugby football. *Address*: 41 York Terrace East, NW1 4PT. *T*: (020) 7486 4560. *Club*: Athenæum.　　　　　*Died 20 Oct. 2010.*

JAMES, (Edwin) Kenneth (George); Chairman, Photon plc, 1986–89; Chief Scientific Officer, Civil Service Department, 1970–76; *b* 27 Dec. 1916; *s* of late Edwin and Jessie Marion James; *m* 1941, Dorothy Margaret Pratt (*d* 1998); (one *d* decd). *Educ*: Latymer Upper Sch.; Northern Polytechnic. BSc London; FRSC; FOR. Joined War Office, 1938; Chem. Defence Exper. Stn, 1942; Aust. Field Exper. Stn, 1944–46; Operational Research Gp, US Army, Md, 1950–54; Dir, Biol and Chem. Defence, WO, 1961; Army (later Defence) Op. Res. Estab., Byfleet, 1965; HM Treasury (later Civil Service Dept), 1968. Chm., PAG Ltd, 1984–87 (Dir, 1977–84). Chm., Maths Cttee, SRC, 1974–77. Mem., Soc. of Authors. Silver Medal, Op. Res. Soc., 1979; CompOR 2007. *Publications*: Strew on her Roses, Roses (memoir), 2000; Escoffier: the King of Chefs, 2002; A to Z of What to Cook, 2003; A to Z of Puddings, 2004; Sage in May (novel), 2004; Biography of a Century, 2005; A to Z of Starters and Light Lunches, 2006; They Made Us What We Are, 2007. *Recreation*: writing. *Address*: 5 Watersmeet Road, Harnham, Salisbury, Wilts SP2 8JH. *T*: (01722) 334099. *Club*: Athenæum.
　　　　　　　　　　　　　　　　Died 30 Dec. 2010.

JAMES, Evan Maitland; *b* 14 Jan. 1911; *er s* of late A. G. James, CBE, and late Helen James (*née* Maitland); *m* 1st, 1939, Joan Goodnow (*d* 1989), *d* of late Hon. J. V. A. MacMurray, State Dept, Washington, DC; one *s* one *d* (and one *d* decd); 2nd, 1992, Miriam Beatriz Porter, *d* of late George and Elizabeth Wansbrough. *Educ*: Durnford; Eton (Oppidan Scholar); Trinity Coll., Oxford (MA). Served War of 1939–45: War Reserve Police (Metropolitan), 1939; BBC Overseas (Propaganda Research) Dept, 1940–41; Ordinary Seaman/Lieut, RNVR, 1941–46. Clerk of the Merchant Taylors' Company, 1947–62; Steward of Christ Church, Oxford, 1962–78. *Address*: Upwood Park, Besselsleigh, Abingdon, Oxon OX13 5QE. *T*: (01865) 390535. *Club*: Travellers.
　　　　　　　　　　　　　　　　Died 5 Dec. 2008.

JAMES, Geraint; see James, D. G.

JAMES, Kenneth; see James, E. K. G.

JAMES, Lionel Frederic Edward, CBE 1977 (MBE (mil.) 1944); Comptroller, Forces Help Society and Lord Roberts Workshops, 1970–82; *b* 22 Feb. 1912; *s* of late Frederic James, Westmount, Exeter; *m* 1st, 1933, Harriet French-Harley (decd); one *s* one *d*; 2nd, 1992, Aurea Maidment. *Educ*: Royal Grammar Sch., Worcester. Investment Co., 1933–39. Served War with Royal Engineers, 1939–46: BEF; Planning Staff, Sicilian Invasion; N Africa, Sicily, Greece and Italy (Major). Dep. Dir, Overseas Service, Forces Help Soc., 1946, Dir, 1948; Asst Sec. of Society, 1953, Company Sec., 1963. *Recreation*: vetting and restoration of art and antiques.
　　　　　　　　　　　　　　　　Died 27 Feb. 2006.

JAMES, Richard Austin, CB 1980; MC 1945; Receiver for Metropolitan Police District, 1977–80; *b* 26 May 1920; *s* of late Thomas Morris James, Headmaster of Sutton Valence Sch., and Hilda Joan James; *m* 1948, Joan Boorer; two *s* one *d*. *Educ*: Clifton Coll.; Emmanuel Coll., Cambridge. British American Tobacco Co., 1938; Royal Engrs, 1939–41; Queen's Own Royal W Kent Regt, 1941–46; Home Office, 1948; Private Sec. to Chancellor of Duchy of Lancaster, 1960; Asst Sec., 1961; Dep. Receiver for Metropolitan Police District, 1970–73; Asst Under-Sec. of State, Police Dept, Home Office, 1974–76; Dep. Under-Sec. of State, 1980. Vice-Pres., Distressed Gentlefolk's Aid Assoc., 1992–96 (Gen. Sec., 1981–82; Mem., Council of Mgt, 1982–88); Mem., Cttee of Management, Sussex Housing Assoc. for the Aged, 1985–88. Pres., Brunswick Boys Club Trust, Fulham, 1990–95. Freeman, City of London, 1961. *Recreation*: cricket. *Address*: 5 Gadge Close, Thame, Oxfordshire OX9 2BD. *T*: (01844) 261776. *Clubs*: Athenæum, MCC.　　　　　　　　*Died 10 Sept. 2008.*

JAMES, Thomas Garnet Henry, CBE 1984; FBA 1976; Keeper of Egyptian Antiquities, British Museum, 1974–88; *b* 8 May 1923; *s* of late Thomas Garnet James and Edith (*née* Griffiths); *m* 1956, Diana Margaret (*d* 2002), *y d* of late H. L. Vavasseur-Durell; one *s*. *Educ*: Neath Grammar Sch.; Exeter Coll., Oxford (2nd Cl. Lit. Hum. 1947; 1st Cl. Oriental Studies 1950, MA 1948; Hon. Fellow, 1998). Served War of 1939–45, RA; NW Europe; 2nd Lieut 1943; Captain 1945. Asst Keeper, Dept of Egyptian and Assyrian Antiquities, 1951; Dep. Keeper (Egyptian Antiquities), 1974. Laycock Student of Egyptology, Worcester Coll., Oxford, 1954–60; Wilbour Fellow, Brooklyn Museum, 1964; Visiting Professor: Collège de France, 1983; Memphis State Univ., 1990. Vice Pres., Egypt Exploration Soc., 1990– (Chm., 1983–89); Mem., German Archæological Inst., 1974. Chm. Cttee, Freud Mus., 1986–2003. Foreign Corresp., l'Institut de France, 2000. Editor: Jl of Egyptian Archæology, 1960–70; Egyptological pubns of Egypt Exploration Soc., 1960–89. *Publications*: The Mastaba of Khentika called Ikhekhi, 1953; Hieroglyphic Texts in the British Museum I, 1961; The Hekanakhte Papers and other Early Middle Kingdom Documents, 1962; (with R. A. Caminos) Gebel es-Silsilah I, 1963; Egyptian Sculptures, 1966; Myths and Legends of Ancient Egypt, 1969; Hieroglyphic Texts in the British Museum, 9, 1970; Archæology of Ancient Egypt, 1972; Corpus of Hieroglyphic Inscriptions in the Brooklyn Museum, I, 1974; (ed) An Introduction to Ancient Egypt, 1979; (ed) Excavating in Egypt, 1982; (with W. V. Davies) Egyptian Sculpture, 1983; Pharaoh's People, 1984; Egyptian Painting, 1985; Ancient Egypt: the land and its legacy, 1988; Howard Carter, the Path to Tutankhamun, 1992; Egypt: the living past, 1992; A Short History of Ancient Egypt, 1996; Egypt Revealed, 1997; Tutankhamun: the eternal splendours of the boy Pharaoh, 2000; Ramesses II, 2002; The British Museum Concise Introduction: Ancient Egypt, 2005; contributed to: W. B. Emery: Great Tombs of the First Dynasty II, 1954; T. J. Dunbabin: Perachora II, 1962; Cambridge Ancient History, 3rd edn, Vol. II, i, 1973, Vol III, ii, 1991; Encyclop. Britannica, 15th edn, 1974; (ed English trans.) H. Kees: Ancient Egypt, 1961; articles in Jl Egyptian Arch., etc; reviews in learned jls. *Recreations*: music, cooking. *Address*: 113 Willifield Way, NW11 6YE. *T*: (020) 8455 9221. *Club*: Oxford and Cambridge.　　　　　*Died 16 Dec. 2009.*

JAMES, Prof. Walter, CBE 1977; Dean and Director of Studies, Faculty of Educational Studies, 1969–77, Professor of Educational Studies, 1969–84, Open University; *b* 8 Dec. 1924; *s* of late George Herbert James and Mary Kathleen (*née* Crutch); *m* 1948, Joyce Dorothy Woollaston; two *s*. *Educ*: Royal Grammar Sch., Worcester; St Luke's Coll., Exeter; Univ. of Nottingham. BA 1955. School teacher, 1948–52; Univ. of Nottingham: Resident Tutor, Dept of Extra-Mural Studies, 1958–65; Lectr in Adult Educn, Dept of Adult Educn, 1965–69. Consultant on Adult Educn and Community Develt to Govt of Seychelles and ODA of

FCO, 1973; Adviser: to Office of Educn, WCC, 1974–76; on Social Planning, to State of Bahrain, 1975; Council of Europe: UK Rep., Working Party on Develt of Adult Education, 1973–81; UK Rep. and Project Adviser, Adult Educn for Community Develt, 1982–87, Adult Educn for Social Change, 1988–93. Chairman: Nat. Council for Voluntary Youth Services, 1970–76; Review of Training of part-time Youth and Community Workers, 1975–77; Religious Adv. Bd, Scout Assoc., 1977–82; Inservice Training and Educn Panel for Youth and Community Service, 1978–82; Council for Educn and Trng in Youth and Community Work, 1982–85; Nat. Adv. Council for the Youth Service, 1985–88; Council for Local Non-Stipendiary Ministerial Training, dio. of Southwark, 1992–95; Eastbourne, Seaford and Wealden CHC, 1998–2002; non-exec. Dir, Eastbourne Downs Primary Care Trust, 2002–06. Member: DES Cttee on Youth and Community Work in 70s, 1967–69; ILO Working Party on Use of Radio and TV for Workers' Educn, 1968; Gen. Synod, C of E, 1970–75; Exec. Cttee, Nat. Council of Social Service, 1970–75; Univs' Council for Educn of Teachers, 1970–84; Univs Council for Adult Educn, 1971–76; BBC Further Educn Adv. Council, 1971–75; Exec. Cttee and Council, Nat. Inst. of Adult Educn, 1971–77; Library Adv. Council for England, 1974–76; Adv. Council, HM Queen's Silver Jubilee Appeal, 1976–78; Bd of Educn, Gen. Synod of C of E, 1991–2001; Bd of Govs, S Eastern Museums Service, 1997–2001; SE Arts Bd, 1998. Trustee: Young Volunteer Force Foundn, 1972–77; Trident Educnl Trust, 1972–86; Community Projects Foundn, 1977–90; Community Develt Foundn, 1990–96; President: Inst. of Playleadership, 1972–74; Fair Play for Children, 1979–82; London and SE Regl Youth Work Unit, 1992–94. Councillor (Lib Dem), Eastbourne BC, 1994–98. *Publications:* (with F. J. Bayliss) The Standard of Living, 1964; (ed) Virginia Woolf, Selections from her essays, 1966; (contrib.) Encyclopaedia of Education, 1968; (contrib.) Teaching Techniques in Adult Education, 1971; (contrib.) Mass Media and Adult Education, 1971; (with H. Janne and P. Dominice) The Development of Adult Education, 1980; (with others) The 14 Pilot Experiments, Vols 1–3, 1984; Some Conclusions from the Co-operation of 14 Development Projects, 1985; Handbook on Co-operative Monitoring, 1986; The Uses of Media for Community Development, 1988; (contrib.) Tomorrow is Another Country: education in a postmodern world, 1996; (contrib.) Called to New Life, 1999. *Recreation:* living. *Address:* 25 Kepplestone, Staveley Road, Eastbourne BN20 7JZ. *T:* (01323) 417029. *Died 25 Dec. 2010.*

JAMESON, John, CBE 1998; QFSM 1995; Firemaster, Strathclyde Fire Brigade, 1991–2000; *b* 12 April 1946; *s* of John Jameson and Catherine Clark Jameson; *m* 1970, Helen Mulvey; one *s* one *d. Educ:* St Aloysius and St Patrick's High Sch., Coatbridge. AIFireE 1995. Lanarkshire Fire Brigade, 1965–70; Glasgow Fire Service, 1970–75; Strathclyde Fire Brigade, 1975–2000: Asst Firemaster, 1987–88; Dep. Firemaster, 1988–91. Churchill Fellowship, 1983. CCMI (FBIM 1991). Fire Brigade Long Service and Good Conduct Medal, 1985; Strathclyde Regl Medal for Bravery, 1987. *Recreations:* historic buildings, cooking. *Address:* Iona, 56 Dunellan Road, Douglas Mains Estate, Milngavie, Glasgow G62 7RE. *Died 11 Dec. 2006.*

JAMIESON, Kenneth Douglas, CMG 1968; HM Diplomatic Service, retired; *b* 9 Jan. 1921; *s* of Rt Hon. Lord Jamieson, PC, KC, Senator of College of Justice in Scotland and Violet Rhodes; *m* 1946, Pamela Hall; two *s* one *d. Educ:* Rugby; Balliol Coll., Oxford. War Service: 5th Regt RHA, 1941–45; HQ, RA 7th Armoured Div., 1945–46. Joined Foreign Service, 1946; served in: Washington, 1948; FO, 1952; Lima, 1954; Brussels, 1959; FO, 1961; Caracas, 1963; Dir of Commercial Training, DSAO, 1968; Head of Export Promotion Dept, FCO, 1968–70; Minister and UK Dep. Permanent

Representative, UN, NY, 1970–74; Ambassador to Peru, 1974–77; Sen. Directing Staff, RCDS, 1977–80. *Address:* Mill Hill House, Bucks Green, Rudgwick, W Sussex RH12 3HZ. *Died 14 Feb. 2006.*

JANES, Maj.-Gen. Mervyn, CB 1973; MBE 1944; *b* 1 Oct. 1920; *o s* of W. G. Janes; *m* 1946, Elizabeth Kathleen McIntyre; two *d. Educ:* Sir Walter St John's Sch., London. Commnd 1942; served with Essex Yeo. (104 Regt RHA), 1942–46, Middle East and Italy; psc 1951; served with 3 RHA, 1952–53; 2 Div., BMRA, 1954–55; Chief Instructor, New Coll., RMAS, 1956–57; Batt. Comd, 3 RHA, 1958–60; Asst Army Instructor (GSO1), Imperial Defence Coll., 1961–62; comd 1st Regt RHA, 1963–65; Comdr, RA, in BAOR, 1965–67; DMS2 (MoD(A)), 1967–70; GOC 5th Division, 1970–71; Dir, Royal Artillery, 1971–73. Col Comdt, RA, 1973–81. *Recreations:* music, ornithology. *Address:* Lucy's Cottage, North Street, Theale, Reading, Berks RG7 5EX. *Club:* Army and Navy. *Died 7 Dec. 2008.*

JARDINE of Applegirth, Sir Alexander Maule, (Sir Alec), 12th Bt *cr* 1672 (NS); 23rd Chief of the Clan Jardine; farmer; *b* 24 Aug. 1947; *s* of Col Sir William Edward Jardine of Applegirth, 11th Bt, OBE, TD, JP, DL, and Ann Graham, *yr d* of late Lt-Col Claud Archibald Scott Maitland, DSO; *S* father, 1986; *m* 1982, Mary Beatrice, *d* of late Hon. John Michael Inigo Cross and of Mrs Anne Parker-Jervis, *d* of late Maj. Thomas Prain Douglas Murray, MBE, TD, JP, DL; three *s* two *d. Educ:* Gordonstoun; Scottish Agricl Coll., Aberdeen (DipFBOM 1988). Member of Queen's Body Guard for Scotland, Royal Co. of Archers. *Heir: s* William Murray Jardine, *yr* of Applegirth, *b* 4 July 1984. *Address:* Ash House, Thwaites, Millom, Cumbria LA18 5HY. *Died 6 April 2008.*

JARDINE, Sir (Andrew) Rupert (John) Buchanan-, 4th Bt *cr* 1885; MC 1944; DL; landowner and farmer; *b* 2 Feb. 1923; *s* of Sir John William Buchanan-Jardine, 3rd Bt and Jean Barbara (*d* 1989), *d* of late Lord Ernest Hamilton; *S* father, 1969; *m* 1950, Jane Fiona (marr. diss. 1975), 2nd *d* of Sir Charles Edmonstone, 6th Bt; one *s* one *d. Educ:* Harrow; Royal Agricultural College. Joined Royal Horse Guards, 1941; served in France, Holland and Germany; Major 1948; retired, 1949. Joint-Master, Dumfriesshire Foxhounds, 1950–2001. JP Dumfriesshire, 1957; DL Dumfriesshire, 1978. Bronze Lion of the Netherlands, 1945. *Recreation:* country pursuits. *Heir: s* John Christopher Rupert Buchanan-Jardine [*b* 20 March 1952; *m* 1975, Pandora Lavinia, *d* of Peter Murray Lee; one *s* five *d*]. *Address:* Dixons, Lockerbie, Dumfriesshire DG11 2PR. *T:* (01576) 202508. *Club:* MCC. *Died 24 Aug. 2010.*

JARRE, Maurice Alexis; French composer; *b* 13 Sept. 1924; *s* of André Jarre and Gabrielle Jarre (*née* Boullu); *m* 1984, Khong Fui Fong; two *s* one *d* by previous marriages. *Educ:* Lycée Ampère, Lyons; Univ. of Lyons; Univ. of Paris, Sorbonne; Conservatoire Nat. Supérieur de Musique. Musician, Radiodiffusion Française, 1946–50; Dir of Music, Théâtre Nat. Populaire, 1950–63. Work includes symphonic music, music for theatre and ballet; film scores include: Hôtel des Invalides, 1952; Sur le pont d'Avignon, 1956; Sundays and Cybele, 1962; The Longest Day, 1962; Lawrence of Arabia, 1962 (Acad. Award for best original score); Dr Zhivago, 1965 (Acad. Award for best original score); Gambit, 1966; The Fixer, 1968; Ryan's Daughter, 1970; El Condor, 1970; The Life and Times of Judge Roy Bean, 1972; The Man Who Would Be King, 1975; Jesus of Nazareth, 1977; Shogun, 1980; Firefox, 1982; The Year of Living Dangerously, 1983; A Passage To India, 1985 (Acad. Award for best original score); Mad Max 3, 1985; Witness, 1985; The Mosquito Coast, 1986; Tai-Pan, 1987; Fatal Attraction, 1987; Gorillas in the Mist, 1989; Dead Poets Society, 1989; Ghost, 1990; A Walk in the Clouds, 1995; La Jour et la Nuit, 1997; Sunshine, 1999; I Dreamed of Africa, 2000. Hon. Citizen: Lyon; Lille; Officier, Légion d'honneur (France); Commandeur des Arts et des Lettres (France); Comdr, Ordre Nat. du Mérite (France). *Address:* c/o Sacem, 225 avenue Charles de Gaulle, 92521 Neuilly-sur-Seine, France. *Died 29 March 2009.*

JARVIS, Patrick William, CB 1985; CEng, FIET, FIMarEST; RCNC; Deputy Controller (Warships), Ministry of Defence (Procurement Executive), and Head of Royal Corps of Naval Constructors, 1983–86; *b* 27 Aug. 1926; *s* of Frederick Arthur and Marjorie Winifred Jarvis; *m* 1951, Amy (*née* Ryley); two *s. Educ:* Royal Naval Coll., Greenwich; Royal Naval Engrg Coll., Keyham, Devonport. BScEng. Trade apprentice, HM Dockyard, Chatham, 1942–46; Design Engineer, Admiralty, Bath, 1946–62; Warship Electrical Supt, Belfast, 1962–63; Suptg Engr, MoD(N), Bath, 1963–72; Ship Department, MoD (PE), Bath: Asst Dir and Dep. Dir, 1972–78; Under Sec., 1978; Dir of Naval Ship Production, 1979–81; Dir of Ship Design and Engrg, and Dep. Head of Royal Corps of Naval Constructors, 1981–83; Dep. Sec., 1983. *Address:* Ranworth, Bathampton Lane, Bath BA2 6ST. *Died 9 Nov. 2009.*

JAUNCEY OF TULLICHETTLE, Baron *cr* 1988 (Life Peer), of Comrie in the District of Perth and Kinross; **Charles Eliot Jauncey;** PC 1988; a Lord of Appeal in Ordinary, 1988–96; *b* 8 May 1925; *s* of late Captain John Henry Jauncey, DSO, RN, Tullichettle, Comrie, and Muriel Charlie, *d* of late Adm. Sir Charles Dundas of Dundas, KCMG; *m* 1st, 1948, Jean (marr. diss. 1969), *d* of Adm. Sir Angus Cunninghame Graham of Gartmore, KBE, CB; two *s* one *d*; 2nd, 1973, Elizabeth (marr. diss. 1977), *widow* of Major John Ballingal, MC; 3rd, 1977, Camilla, *d* of late Lt-Col Charles Cathcart of Pitcairlie, DSO; one *d. Educ:* Radley; Christ Church, Oxford (BA 1947; Hon. Student, 1990); Glasgow Univ. (LLB 1949). Served in War, 1943–46, Sub-Lt RNVR. Advocate, Scottish Bar, 1949; Standing Junior Counsel to Admiralty, 1954; QC (Scotland) 1963; Kintyre Pursuivant of Arms, 1955–71; Sheriff Principal of Fife and Kinross, 1971–74; Judge of the Courts of Appeal of Jersey and Guernsey, 1972–79; a Senator of College of Justice, Scotland, 1979–88. Hon. Sheriff-Substitute of Perthshire, 1962. Mem. of Royal Co. of Archers (Queen's Body Guard for Scotland), 1951. Mem., Historic Buildings Council for Scotland, 1971–92. *Recreations:* fishing, bicycling, genealogy. *Address:* Tullichettle, Comrie, Perthshire PH6 2HU. *T:* (01764) 670349; House of Lords, SW1A 0PW. *Died 18 July 2007.*

JAY, Prof. Barrie Samuel, MD, FRCS; FRCOphth; Professor of Clinical Ophthalmology, University of London, 1985–92, then Emeritus; Consulting Surgeon, Moorfields Eye Hospital, since 1992 (Consultant Surgeon, 1969–92); Hon. Secretary: Academy of Medical Royal Colleges, 1994–99; Specialist Training Authority, Medical Royal Colleges, 1996–99; *b* 7 May 1929; *er s* of late Dr M. B. Jay and Julia Sterling; *m* 1954, Marcelle Ruby Byre; two *s. Educ:* Perse Sch., Cambridge; Gonville and Caius Coll., Cambridge (MA, MD); University Coll. Hosp., London. FRCS 1962; FCOphth 1988 (Hon. FRCOphth 1994). House Surgeon and Sen. Resident Officer, Moorfields Eye Hosp., 1959–62; Sen. Registrar, Ophthalmic Dept, London Hosp., 1962–65; Institute of Ophthalmology, University of London: Shepherd Res. Scholar, 1963–64; Mem., Cttee of Management, 1972–77, 1979–91; Clinical Sub-Dean, 1973–77; Dean, 1980–85; Ophthalmic Surgeon, The London Hosp., 1965–79. Consultant Advr in Ophthalmol., DHSS, 1982–88. Examiner: Dip. in Ophthal., 1970–75; British Orthoptic Council, 1970–78; Ophthalmic Nursing Bd, 1971–87; Mem. Ct of Examrs, RCS, 1975–80. Brit. Rep., Monospecialist Section of Ophthal., Eur. Union of Med. Specialists, 1973–85. Mem. Council: Section of Ophthal., RSM, 1965–77 (Editorial Rep., 1966–77); Faculty of Ophthalmologists, 1970–88 (Asst Hon. Sec., 1976–78; Hon. Sec., 1978–86; Pres., 1986–88); RCS (co-opted Mem. for Ophthalmology), 1983–88; Coll. of Ophthalmologists, 1988–92 (Vice-Pres., 1988–92); Nat.

Ophthalmic Treatment Bd Assoc., 1971–75; Internat. Pediatric Ophthal. Soc., 1975–92; Ophthal. Soc. UK, 1985–88; Member: Ophthal. Nursing Bd, 1974–88; Orthoptists Bd, Council for Professions Supplementary to Medicine, 1977–92 (Vice Chm., 1982–88); Specialist Adv. Cttee in Ophthalmology, 1979–88 (Chm., 1982–88); Standing Med. Adv. Cttee, DHSS, 1980–84; Transplant Adv. Panel, DHSS, 1983–88. Trustee: Fight for Sight, 1973–94; Wolfson Foundn, 1986–92; Wolfson Family Charitable Trust, 1992–. Fellow, Eugenics Soc.; FRPSL (Hon. Sec., 1992–98; Vice-Pres., 1996–98; Pres., 1998–2000; Tilleard Medal, 2002; Roll of Distinguished Philatelists, 2005); Hon. FRCPCH 1996; Hon. Member: British Paediatric Assoc., 1995; Canadian Ophthalmol Soc. Mem., Ct of Assts, Soc. of Apothecaries (Master, 1995–96; Hon. Treas., 1999–2004); Liveryman: Co. of Barbers; Co. of Spectacle Makers. Mem., Bd of Governors, Moorfields Eye Hosp., 1971–90. Mem. Editorial Board: Ophthalmic Literature, 1962–91 (Asst Editor, 1977–78; Editor, 1978–85); British Jl of Ophthalmology, 1965–90; Jl of Medical Genetics, 1971–76; Metabolic Ophthalmology, 1975–78; Survey of Ophthalmology, 1976–2004; Ophthalmic Paediatrics and Genetics, 1981–94; Editor, Postal History, 1994–2005. Lifetime Achievement Award, Eur. Paediatric Ophthalmol Soc., 2004. *Publications:* contrib. on ophthalmology and genetics to med. jls. *Recreations:* postal history, gardening. *Address:* 10 Beltane Drive, SW19 5JR. *T:* (020) 8947 1771. *Died 10 March 2007.*

JEAFFRESON, David Gregory, CBE 1981; Deputy Chairman, Big Island Holdings (formerly Big Island Contracting) (HK) Ltd, since 1992; *b* 23 Nov. 1931; *s* of late Bryan Leslie Jeaffreson, MD, FRCS, MRCOG and Margaret Jeaffreson; *m* 1959, Elisabeth Marie Jausions; two *s* two *d* (and one *d* decd). *Educ:* Bootham Sch., York; Clare Coll., Cambridge (MA). 2nd Lieut, RA, 1950. Dist Officer, Tanganyika, 1955–58; Asst Man., Henricot Steel Foundry, 1959–60; Admin. Officer, Hong Kong Govt, 1961; Dep. Financial Sec., 1972–76; Sec. for Economic Services, 1976–82; Sec. for Security, 1982–88; Comr, Independent Commn Against Corruption, 1988–92. *Recreations:* history, music, sailing, walking. *Address:* A2 Cherry Court, 12 Consort Rise, Hong Kong. *T:* 28188025. *Club:* Royal Hong Kong Yacht. *Died 30 Oct. 2008.*

JEANNE-CLAUDE; artist, as Christo and Jeanne-Claude; Jeanne-Claude de Guillebon, *b* Casablanca, 13 June 1935; *m* Christo Javacheff; one *s*. Emigrated to USA 1964. Completed works include: Wrapped Objects, 1958; Stacked Oil Barrels and Dockside Packages, Cologne Harbour, 1961; Iron Curtain Wall of Oil Barrels, blocking Rue Visconti, Paris, 1962; Store Fronts, NYC, 1964; Wrapped Kunsthalle, Berne, and Wrapped Fountain and Wrapped Medieval Tower, Spoleto, Italy, 1968; 5,600 Cubicmeter Package, Documenta 4, Kassel, 1968; Wrapped Floor and Stairway, Mus. of Contemporary Art, Chicago, 1969; Wrapped Coast, Little Bay, Sydney, Australia, 1969; Wrapped Monuments, Milan, 1970; Wrapped Floors and Covered Windows and Wrapped Walk Way, Krefeld, Germany, 1971; Valley Curtain, Grand Hogback, Rifle, Colo, 1970–72; The Wall, Wrapped Roman Wall, Via V. Veneto and Villa Borghese, Rome, 1974; Ocean Front, Newport, RI, 1974; Running Fence, Sonoma and Marin Counties, Calif, 1972–76; Wrapped Walk Ways, Kansas City, Mo, 1977–78; Surrounded Islands, Biscayne Bay, Miami, Fla, 1980–83; The Pont Neuf Wrapped, Paris, 1975–85; The Umbrellas, Japan-USA, 1984–91; Wrapped Floors and Stairways and Covered Windows, Mus. Würth, Künzelsau, Germany, 1995; Wrapped Reichstag, Berlin, 1971–95; Wrapped Trees, Switzerland, 1997–98; The Gates, Central Pk, NYC, 2005. *Fax:* (212) 9662891; *web:* www.christojeanneclaude.net. *Died 18 Nov. 2009.*

JEDDERE-FISHER, Arthur; Solicitor, Customs and Excise, 1982–85; *b* 15 July 1924; *s* of late Major Harry and Sarah Jeddere-Fisher; *m* 1947, Marcia Vincent, *d* of Kenneth Clarence Smith; two *s* one *d* (and one *s* decd). *Educ:* Harrow Sch.; Christ Church, Oxford (MA). Served War of 1939–45, Air Engineer, Royal Navy, 1942–46 (despatches). Called to Bar, Inner Temple, 1949; Magistrate, Senior Magistrate and Chairman Land Tribunal, Fiji, 1953–69; joined Solicitor's Office, HM Customs and Excise, 1970, Solicitor, 1979–82. *Recreations:* the collection and use of historic machinery, cricket, bird photography. *Address:* Apsley Cottage, Kingston Blount, Chinnor OX39 4SJ. *T:* (01844) 351300. *Clubs:* MCC, Vintage Sports Car.
Died 26 Feb. 2007.

JEFFRIES, Lionel Charles; actor since 1949, screen writer since 1959, and film director since 1970; *b* 10 June 1926; *s* of Bernard Jeffries and Elsie Jackson; *m* 1951, Eileen Mary Walsh; one *s* two *d*. *Educ:* Queen Elizabeth's Grammar Sch., Wimborne, Dorset; Royal Academy of Dramatic Art (Dip., Kendal Award, 1947). War of 1939–45: commissioned, Oxf. and Bucks LI, 1945; served in Burma (Burma Star, 1945); Captain, Royal West African Frontier Force. Stage: (West End) plays: Carrington VC; The Enchanted; Blood Wedding; Brouhaha; Hello Dolly, Prince of Wales, 1984; See How They Run, Two Into One, Rookery Nook, Shaftesbury, 1985–86; Pygmalion, Broadway, 1987; The Wild Duck, Phoenix, 1990; *films* include: Bhowani Junction, Lust for Life, The Baby and The Battleship, 1956; Colditz Story, Doctor at Large, 1957; Law and Disorder, 1958; The Nun's Story, 1959; Idle on Parade; Two Way Stretch, The Trials of Oscar Wilde, 1960; Fanny, 1961; The Notorious Landlady (Hollywood), The Wrong Arm of the Law, 1962; The First Men in the Moon, 1964; The Truth about Spring, 1965; Arrivederci Baby, The Spy with a Cold Nose, 1966; Camelot (Hollywood), 1967; Chitty, Chitty, Bang Bang, 1968; Baxter, 1973 (also dir; Golden Bear Award for Best Film, Europe); The Prisoner of Zenda, 1979; Eyewitness, 1981; Ménage à Trois; Chorus of Disapproval, 1989; Danny Champion of the World; Ending Up; First and Last. Wrote and directed: The Railway Children, 1970 (St Christopher Gold Medal, Hollywood, for Best Film); The Amazing Mr Blunden, 1972 (Gold Medal for Best Screen Play, Internat. Sci. Fiction and Fantasy Film Fest., Paris, 1974); Wombling Free, 1977; co-wrote and directed: The Water Babies, 1979; *television:* Cream in my Coffee, 1980; Shillingbury Tales, 1981; Father Charlie; Tom, Dick, and Harriet, 1983; Rich Tea and Sympathy, 1991; Look at it This Way, 1993. *Recreations:* painting, writing scripts, articles and a book. *Address:* c/o Liz Hobbs, MBE Management Ltd, 65 London Road, Newark, Notts NG24 1RZ.
Died 19 Feb. 2010.

JEGER, Baroness *cr* 1979 (Life Peer), of St Pancras in Greater London; **Lena May Jeger;** *b* 19 Nov. 1915; *e d* of Charles and Alice Chivers, Yorkley, Glos; *m* 1948, Dr Santo Wayburn Jeger (*d* 1953); no *c. Educ:* Southgate County Sch., Middx; Birkbeck Coll., London University (BA; Hon. Fellow, 1994). Civil Service: Customs and Excise, Ministry of Information, Foreign Office, 1936–49; British Embassy Moscow, 1947; Manchester Guardian, later The Guardian, London Staff, 1951–54, 1961–79. Mem. St Pancras Borough Council, 1945–59; Mem. LCC for Holborn and St Pancras South, 1952–55. Mem., Nat. Exec. Cttee, Labour Party, 1968–80 (Vice-Chm., 1978–79; Chm., 1980). MP (Lab) Holborn and St Pancras South, Nov. 1953–1959 and 1964–74, Camden, Holborn and St Pancras South, 1974–79. Mem., Chairmen's Panel, House of Commons, 1971–79. Chm., Govt Working Party on Sewage Disposal, 1969–70. Member, Consultative Assembly: Council of Europe, 1969–71; WEU, 1969–71; UK delegate, Status of Women Commn, UN, 1967. Medal of Merit (1st grade): Czech Republic, 2003; Slovak Republic, 2003.
Died 26 Feb. 2007.

JEJEEBHOY, Sir Jamsetjee, 7th Bt *cr* 1857; *b* 19 April 1913; *s* of Rustamjee J. C. Jamsetjee (*d* 1947), and Soonabai Rustomjee Byramjee Jeejeebhoy (*d* 1968); *S* cousin, Sir Jamsetjee Jejeebhoy, 6th Bt, 1968, and assumed name of Jamsetjee Jejeebhoy in lieu of Maneckjee Rustamjee Jamsetjee; *m* 1943, Shirin J. H. Cama; one *s* one *d. Educ:* St Xavier's Coll., Bombay (BA). Chairman: Sir Jamsetjee Jejeebhoy Charity Funds; Sir J. J. Parsee Benevolent Instn; H. B. Wadia Fire Temple Charity Fund; Iran League; Rustomjee Jamsetjee Jejeebhoy Gujarat Schools' Fund; Bombay Panjrapole; Framjee Cowasjee Inst.; Fasli Atash-Kadeh Trust; Chairman Emeritus: M. F. Cama Athornan Instn; M. M. Cama Educn Fund; Trustee: Byramjee Jeejeebhoy Parsee Charitable Instn; A. H. Wadia Charity Trust; Parsi Surat Charity Fund; Cowasji Behramji Divecha Charity Trust; Ashburner Fire Temple Trust; Vatcha Fire Temple and Charity Trust; Zoroastrian Bldg Fund; Mem., Exec. Cttee, B. D. Petit Parsee Gen. Hosp.; Dir, Beaulieu Investment Pvte Ltd, 1975–. Hon. Freeman and Liveryman, Clockmakers' Co., 1995. *Heir:* s Rustom Jejeebhoy [*b* 16 Nov. 1957; *m* 1984, Delara, *d* of Jal N. Bhaisa; one *s*]. *Address:* (residence) Beaulieu, 95 Worli Sea Face, Mumbai 400025, India. *T:* 24930955; (office) Kalpataru Heritage, 127 Mahatma Gandhi Road, Fort, Mumbai 400001. *T:* 22673843. *Clubs:* Willingdon Sports, Royal Western India Turf, Ripon, Malabar Hill (Mumbai).
Died 10 Aug. 2006.

JELLICOE, 2nd Earl *cr* 1925; **George Patrick John Rushworth Jellicoe,** KBE 1986; DSO 1942; MC 1944; PC 1963; FRS 1990; Viscount Brocas of Southampton, 1925; Viscount Jellicoe of Scapa, 1918; Baron Jellicoe of Southampton (Life Peer), 1999; President, Crete Veterans Association, since 1990; *b* 4 April 1918; *o s* of Admiral of the Fleet 1st Earl Jellicoe and late Florence Gwendoline, *d* of Sir Charles Cayzer, 1st Bt; godson of King George V; *S* father, 1935; *m* 1st, 1944, Patricia Christine (marr. diss., 1966), *o d* of Jeremiah O'Kane, Vancouver, Canada; two *s* two *d*; 2nd, 1966, Philippa, *o d* of late Philip Dunne; one *s* two *d. Educ:* Winchester; Trinity Coll., Cambridge (Exhibnr). Hon. Page to King George VI; served War of 1939–45, Coldstream Guards, No 8 Commando, 1 SAS Regt, SBS Regt (despatches three times), DSO, MC, Légion d'Honneur, Croix de Guerre, Greek War Cross). Entered HM Foreign Service, 1947; served as 1st Sec. in Washington, Brussels, Baghdad (Deputy Sec. General Baghdad Pact). Lord-in-Waiting, Jan.-June 1961; Jt Parly. Sec., Min. of Housing and Local Govt, 1961–62; Minister of State, Home Office, 1962–63; First Lord of the Admiralty, 1963–64; Minister of Defence for the RN, April-Oct. 1964; Dep. Leader of the Opposition, H of L, 1967–70; Lord Privy Seal and Minister in Charge, Civil Service Dept, 1970–73; Leader of the House of Lords, 1970–73. Chairman: British Adv. Cttee on Oil Pollution of the Sea, 1968–70; 3rd Internat. Conf. on Oil Pollution of the Sea, 1968. Chm., MRC, 1982–90. Chairman: Tate & Lyle, 1978–83 (Dir, 1974–93); Davy Corp., 1985–90; Booker Tate, 1988–91; Director: Sotheby's, 1973–85; Smiths Industries, 1973–86; Morgan Crucible, 1973–87; S. G. Warburg, 1973–88; Chm., European Capital Ltd, 1991–95. Chm., BOTB, 1983–86; President: London Chamber of Commerce and Industry, 1979–82; E European Trade Council, 1990–95 (Chm., 1986–90); Chm., 1978–86, Patron, 1986–, Anglo-Hellenic League; Chm., Greece Fund, 1988–94. A Governor, Centre for Environmental Studies, 1967–70; President: Nat. Fedn of Housing Socs, 1965–70; Parly and Scientific Cttee, 1980–83; Review of Prevention of Terrorism Act, 1983. President: BHF, 1990–95; RGS, 1993–97; SAS Regtl Assoc., 1996–2000. Chm. of Council, KCL, 1977–84; Chancellor, Southampton Univ., 1984–95. FKC 1979. Hon. LLD: Southampton, 1985; London; Long Island Univ., 1987. Grand Comdr, Order of Honour (Greece), 1992. *Recreations:* travel, opera. *Heir:* s Viscount Brocas, *b* 29 Aug. 1950. *Address:* Tidcombe Manor, Tidcombe, near Marlborough, Wilts SN8 3SL. *T:* (01264) 731225, *Fax:* (01264) 731418; Flat 5, 97 Onslow Square, SW7 3LT. *T:* (020) 7584 1551. *Clubs:* Brooks's, Special Forces.
Died 22 Feb. 2007.

JENKINS, Alan Roberts; editorial consultant; *b* 8 June 1926; *s* of Leslie Roberts Jenkins and Marjorie Kate Cawston; *m* 1st, 1949, Kathleen Mary Baker (*d* 1969); four *s*; 2nd, 1971, Helen Mary Speed; one *s*. *Educ:* Aylesbury Grammar Sch. Commnd Royal Berks Regt, 1945; Captain, W African Liaison Service, GHQ India; Staff Captain Public Relations, Royal W African Frontier Force, Lagos; DADPR W Africa Comd (Major). Reporter, Reading Mercury and Berkshire Chronicle, 1948; Sub-editor, Daily Herald; Daily Mail: Sub-editor; Night Editor, 1962–69; Northern Editor, 1969–71; Asst Editor, Evening Standard, 1971; Dep. Editor, Sunday People, 1971–72; Asst Editor, Sunday Mirror, 1972–77; Editor, Glasgow Herald, 1978–80; Editorial exec., The Times, 1981–89; Gp Consultant, The New Straits Times, Malaysia, 1989–92. *Address:* Old Rose Cottage, Kirkton of Balmerino, Fife DD6 8SA. *Died 24 June 2007.*

JENKINS, Surg. Vice Adm. Ian Lawrence, CB 2006; CVO 2000; FRCS; Constable and Governor of Windsor Castle, since 2008; *b* 12 Sept. 1944; *s* of Gordon Eaton Jenkins, MBE and Edith Jenkins (*née* Rouse); *m* 1968, Elizabeth Philippa Anne Lane; one *s* one *d*. *Educ:* Howardian Grammar Sch.; Welsh Nat. Sch. of Medicine (MB BCh 1968). FRCS 1973. Joined RN, 1975; HMS Ark Royal, 1975; RN Hosp. Haslar, 1976, 1979; Newcastle Gen. Hosp., 1977–79; OC 1 RN Surg. Support Team (3rd Cdo Bde), 1976–79; RN Hosp. Gibraltar, 1979–82; Consultant Urological Surg., 1982–90, MO i/c, 1990–96, RN Hosp. Haslar; Prof. of Naval Surgery, RN and RCS, 1988–90; Defence Postgrad. Med. Dean and Comdt, Royal Defence Med. Coll., 1996–99; Med. Dir Gen. (Naval), MoD, 1999–2002; Surgeon Gen. to the Armed Forces, 2002–06. QHS 1994–2006. Chm., Portsmouth Cathedral Council, 2001–. Gov., Sutton's Hosp. In Charterhouse, 2006–. Mem. Council, White Ensign Assoc.; Chm., Seafarers UK, 2007–. Patron, COFEPOW, 2005–. CStJ 2000. *Publications:* contribs to med. jls on various urological subjects. *Recreations:* swimming, game fishing, music, painting in watercolour, travel. *Address:* Windsor Castle, Windsor, Berks SL4 1NJ. *Club:* Naval. *Died 19 Feb. 2009.*

JENKINS, John George, CBE 1971; farmer; *b* 26 Aug. 1919; *s* of George John Jenkins, OBE, FRCS and Alice Maud Jenkins, MBE; *m* 1948, Chloe Evelyn (*née* Kenward); one *s* three *d*. *Educ:* Winchester; Edinburgh University. Farmed in Scotland, 1939–62; farmed in England (Cambs), 1957–. Pres., NFU of Scotland, 1960–61; Chm., Agricultural Marketing Development Exec. Cttee, 1967–73. Chm., United Oilseeds Ltd, 1984–87; Director: Childerley Estates Ltd, 1957–; Agricultural Mortgage Corporation Ltd, 1968–90. Compère, Anglia Television programme Farming Diary, 1963–80. *Publications:* contrib. Proc. Royal Soc., RSA Jl, etc. *Recreations:* bridge, music. *Address:* Childerley Hall, Dry Drayton, Cambridge CB3 8BB. *T:* (01954) 210271. *Club:* Farmers'. *Died 19 July 2007.*

JENKINS, John Owen, MBE 1978; FCSP; Chartered Physiotherapist; Senior Lecturer, St Mary's Hospital School of Physiotherapy, W2, 1975–88 (Lecturer, 1959); *b* 4 Nov. 1922; *s* of late J. O. Jenkins, JP, and M. E. Jenkins, Great House, Dilwyn, Hereford; *m* 1953, Catherine MacFarlane Baird, MCSP; three *d*. *Educ:* Worcester College for the Blind; NIB School of Physiotherapy, London. TMMG, TET, FCSP 1990. Chartered Society of Physiotherapy: Mem. Council, 1952–81; Chm., Finance and Gen. Purposes Cttee, 1955–79; Member: Education Cttee, 1953–71; Executive Cttee, 1955–79; Trustee, Members' Benevolent Fund, 1956–96. CSP Examiner, 1954–88; Pres., Orgn of Chartered Physiotherapists in Private Practice, 1980–86. Physiotherapy Representative: Min. of Health Working Party on Statutory Registration, 1954; Council for Professions Supplementary to Medicine, 1961–76; Chm., Physiotherapists' Board, 1962–76. Director, LAMPS, 1969–96, Chm., 1980–87; Pres., 1988–96; Trustee, Moira Pakenham-Walsh

Foundn, 1978–96. Churchwarden, St James the Great, N20, 1974–81. *Publications:* contribs to Physiotherapy and Rehabilitation. *Recreation:* freemasonry (Pres., Southgate Masonic Centre, 1997). *Address:* The New House, 34A Ravensdale Avenue, N12 9HT. *T:* (020) 8445 6072. *Died 19 April 2008.*

JENKINS, (Margaret) Elizabeth (Heald), OBE 1981; writer; *b* 31 Oct. 1905; *d* of James Heald Jenkins and Theodora Caldicott Jenkins (*née* Ingram). *Educ:* St Christopher School, Letchworth; Newnham College, Cambridge. *Publications:* The Winters, 1931; Lady Caroline Lamb, a Biography, 1932; Harriet (awarded the Femina Vie Heureuse Prize), 1934; The Phoenix' Nest, 1936; Jane Austen, a Biography, 1938; Robert and Helen, 1944; Young Enthusiasts, 1946; Henry Fielding (The English Novelists Series), 1947; Six Criminal Women, 1949; The Tortoise and the Hare, 1954; Ten Fascinating Women, 1955; Elizabeth the Great (biography), 1958; Elizabeth and Leicester, 1961; Brightness, 1963; Honey, 1968; Dr Gully, 1972; The Mystery of King Arthur, 1975; The Princes in the Tower, 1978; The Shadow and the Light, 1983; A Silent Joy, 1992; The View from Downshire Hill (memoir, ed by Sir Michael Jenkins), 2004. *Died 5 Sept. 2010.*

JENKYNS, Henry Leigh; Under-Secretary, Department of the Environment, 1969–75; *b* 20 Jan. 1917; *y s* of H. H. Jenkyns, Indian Civil Service; *m* 1947, Rosalind Mary Home (decd); two *s* one *d*. *Educ:* Eton, Balliol Coll., Oxford. War Service in Royal Signals; Lt-Col, East Africa Command, 1944. Treasury, 1945–66; Private Sec. to Chancellor, 1951–53. Treasury Representative in Australia and New Zealand, 1953–56; UK Delegation to OECD, Paris, 1961–63; Asst Under-Sec. of State, DEA, 1966–69; Chm., SE Economic Planning Bd, 1968–71. Mem., Southwark Diocesan Adv. Cttee for Care of Churches, 1977–78. Mem., Exmoor Study Team, 1977. *Recreations:* music, garden, sailing, mending things. *Died 28 Sept. 2007.*

JENNETT, Frederick Stuart, CBE 1985; consultant architect and town planner in own firm, since 1990; *b* 22 April 1924; *s* of Horace Frederick Jennett and Jenny Sophia Jennett; *m* 1948, Nada Eusebia Phillips; two *d*. *Educ:* Whitchurch Grammar School; Welsh School of Architecture, UWIST (Dip. in Architecture (dist.)). FRIBA, MRTPI, FRSA. T. Alwyn Lloyd & Gordon, Architects, Cardiff, 1949; Cwmbran Develt Corp., 1951; Louis de Soissons Peacock Hodges & Robinson, Welwyn Garden City, 1955; S. Colwyn Foukes & Partners, Colwyn Bay, 1956; Associate, 1962, Partner, 1964, Sir Percy Thomas & Son, Bristol; Chm. and Sen. Partner, Percy Thomas Partnership, 1971–89; Consultant: Studio BAAD, architects, Hebden Bridge, 1990–93; Mouchel Mgt Ltd, W Byfleet, 1990–92; NHS Estates, Leeds, 1991–92; Carnell Green Nightingale, architects, 1993; garden design with Nada Jennett, Weston Park, Shropshire, 1990–. Experience ranged over new town neighbourhood planning, public housing and private houses; ecclesiastical, university and hospital projects in the UK and overseas, and refurbishment of historic/listed buildings. *Publications:* papers on hospital planning and fast track construction. *Recreations:* water colour painting, calligraphy, hill walking, running. *Address:* Portland Lodge, Lower Almondsbury, Bristol BS32 4EJ. *T:* (01454) 615175. *Club:* Royal Over-Seas League. *Died 30 Jan. 2006.*

JENNETT, Prof. (William) Bryan, CBE 1992; FRCS; Professor of Neurosurgery, University of Glasgow, 1968–91, then Emeritus (Dean of the Faculty of Medicine, 1981–86); *b* 1 March 1926; *s* of Robert William Jennett and Jessie Pate Loudon; *m* 1950, Sheila Mary Pope; three *s* one *d*. *Educ:* Univ. of Liverpool (MB ChB 1949, MD 1960). House Physician to Lord Cohen of Birkenhead, 1949; Ho. Surg. to Sir Hugh Cairns, 1950; Surgical Specialist, RAMC, 1951–53; Registrar in Neurosurgery, Oxford and Cardiff, 1954–56; Lectr in Neurosurgery, Univ. of Manchester, 1957–62; Rockefeller Travelling Fellow, Univ. of California, LA,

1958–59; Cons. Neurosurgeon, Glasgow, 1963–68. Member: MRC, 1979–83; GMC, 1984–91; Chief Scientists' Cttee, 1983–; Inst. of Med. Ethics, 1986–. Mem. Ct, Univ. of Glasgow, 1988–91. Rock Carling Fellow, London, 1983. Hon. DSc St Andrews, 1993. *Publications:* Epilepsy after Blunt Head Injury, 1962, 2nd edn 1975; Introduction to Neurosurgery, 1964, 5th edn 1994; (with G. Teasdale) Management of Head Injuries, 1981; High Technology Medicine: benefits and burdens, 1984, 2nd edn 1986; The Vegetative State: medical facts, ethical and legal dilemmas, 2002; many papers in Lancet, BMJ and elsewhere. *Recreations:* cruising under sail, writing. *Address:* 3/3 Lauderdale Mansions, 47 Novar Drive, Glasgow G12 9UB. *T:* (0141) 334 5148; *e-mail:* bryan.jennett@ntlworld.com. *Club:* Royal Society of Medicine. *Died 26 Jan. 2008.*

JENNINGS, Anthony Francis; QC 2001; a Recorder, since 2002; *b* 11 May 1960; *s* of late Robert Jennings and Margaret (Irene) Jennings (*née* Conlon); *m* 1993, Louise McKeon; one *s* one *d. Educ:* St Patrick's Coll., Belfast; Univ. of Warwick (LLB Hons); Inns of Court Sch. of Law. Called to the Bar, Gray's Inn, 1983, Inns of Court, NI, 1987; barrister specialising in crime and human rights. *Publications:* (contributing ed.) Archbold, Criminal Pleading: evidence and practice, annually 1995–2004; (ed) Justice Under Fire: the abuse of Civil Liberties in Northern Ireland, 1988; (contrib.) Criminal Justice, Police Powers and Human Rights, 2001; (contrib.) Human Rights and Criminal Justice; contrib. to Judicial Studies Bd specimen directions. *Recreations:* Italy, Irish literature, Liverpool FC. *Address:* Matrix Chambers, Griffin Building, Gray's Inn, WC1R 5LN. *T:* (020) 7404 3447. *Club:* Liverpool Supporters. *Died 21 Jan. 2008.*

JENNINGS, Very Rev. Kenneth Neal; Dean of Gloucester, 1983–96, then Emeritus; *b* 8 Nov. 1930; *s* of Reginald Tinsley and Edith Dora Jennings; *m* 1972, Wendy Margaret Stallworthy; one *s* one *d. Educ:* Hertford Grammar School; Corpus Christi College, Cambridge (MA); Cuddesdon College, Oxford. Asst Curate, Holy Trinity, Ramsgate, 1956–59; Lecturer 1959–61, Vice-Principal 1961–66, Bishop's College, Calcutta; Vice-Principal, Cuddesdon Theological Coll., 1967–73; Vicar of Hitchin, 1973–76; Team Rector of Hitchin, 1977–82. *Recreations:* music, exploring the countryside. *Address:* The School House, Keasden, Clapham, Lancaster LA2 8EY. *T:* (01524) 251455. *Died 14 Dec. 2007.*

JEWELL, David John, MA, MSc; Master of Haileybury and Imperial Service College, 1987–96; *b* 24 March 1934; *s* of late Wing Comdr John Jewell, OBE, FRAeS, and Rachel Jewell, Porthleven, Cornwall; *m* 1958, Katharine Frida Heller; one *s* three *d. Educ:* Blundell's Sch., Tiverton; St John's Coll., Oxford (Hons Sch. of Natural Sci. (Chem.), BA 1957, MA 1961; BSc Physical Scis, 1959, MSc 1981). National Service with RAF, 1952–54. Head of Science Dept, Eastbourne Coll., 1958–62; Winchester Coll., 1962–67; Dep. Head, Lawrence Weston Comprehensive Sch., Bristol, 1967–70; Head Master, Bristol Cathedral Sch., 1970–78; Headmaster, Repton Sch., 1979–87. Vis. Prof., Rollins Coll., Florida, 1987. Chairman: HMC, 1990 (Chairman: Direct Grant Sub-Cttee, 1977–78; Professional Develt Cttee, 1987–89); Choir Schools' Assoc., 1976–77. Vice-Chm. of Govs, Truro Sch., 1994– (Gov., 1990–); Chm. of Govs, Blundell's Sch., 1996–2000 (Gov., 1994–2000). Mem. Council, Engrg and Marine Trng Authy, 1996–99. FRSA 1981. *Publications:* papers and articles in various scientific and educnl jls. *Recreations:* music, cricket, theology, Cornwall. *Address:* Merghwidden, Loe Bar Road, Porthleven, Cornwall TR13 9EL. *T:* (01326) 561737. *Clubs:* East India, Devonshire, Sports and Public Schools, MCC, Lord's Taverners; Bristol Savages. *Died 21 May 2006.*

JOBLING, Captain James Hobson, RN; Metropolitan Stipendiary Magistrate, 1973–87; *b* 29 Sept. 1921; *s* of late Captain and Mrs J. S. Jobling, North Shields, Northumberland; *m* 1946, Cynthia (*d* 2004), *o d* of late F.

E. V. Lean, Beacon Park, Plymouth; one *s* one *d. Educ:* Tynemouth High Sch.; London Univ. (LLB Hons, 1971). Entered Royal Navy, 1940; HMS Furious, 1941; HMS Victorious, 1941–45; awarded Gedge Medal and Prize, 1946; called to Bar, Inner Temple, 1955; Comdr, 1960; JSSC course, 1961–62; Dir, Nat. Liaison, SACLANT HQ, USA, 1962–65; Chief Naval Judge Advocate, in rank of Captain, 1969–72; retd, 1973. Planning Inspector, DoE, 1973; a Dep. Circuit Judge, 1976–82. *Recreations:* gardening, walking. *Died 21 Sept. 2009.*

JOGEE, Dr Moussa, OBE 2002 (MBE 1996); Joint Deputy Chairman, Commission for Racial Equality, 1999–2002 (Commissioner, 1994–2002); *b* 11 Nov. 1930; *s* of Ebrahim Moosa and Aysha Ebrahim; *m* 1948, Fatma Seedat; one *s* two *d* (and one *d* decd); partner, Elizabeth Hall; two *s. Educ:* India; South Africa; Newbattle Abbey Coll., Edinburgh. Activist in South Africa against apartheid; Founder and Editor, Lalkar jl, South Africa; exiled to Britain, 1965; caterer and restaurateur, Edinburgh, 1973–. Exec. Editor, Inter-Arts jl, 1986–91. FRSA 1996. JP Edinburgh, 1985. Hon. DLitt Edinburgh, 1996. Hind Ratan, India, 1989. *Recreations:* cricket, cooking, poetry (Urdu). *Died 17 June 2006.*

JOHNSON, Charles Ernest; JP; Councillor (Lab), Salford, 1986–2002; *b* 2 Jan. 1918; adopted *s* of Henry and Mary Johnson; *m* 1942, Betty, *d* of William Nelson Hesford, farmer; one *s. Educ:* elementary school. Commenced work as apprentice coppersmith, 1932; called up to Royal Navy, 1940, demobilised, 1946. Councillor and Alderman, Eccles Town Council, 1952–73; Mayor, 1964–65; Chm. of various cttees, incl. Housing, for 14 years, and of Local Employment Cttee, for ten years; Councillor, Greater Manchester County Council, 1974–86 (Chairman, 1982–83). Mem., Police Authy, Gtr Manchester, 1986–88. Mem., Assoc. of Municipal Councils, 1958–. JP Eccles, 1965. 1939–45 Medal, Atlantic Medal, Africa Star, Victory Medal; Imperial Service Medal, 1978. *Recreations:* gardening, watching football, swimming. *Address:* 17 Dartford Avenue, Winton, Eccles, Manchester M30 8NF. *T:* (0161) 789 4229. *Died July 2007.*

JOHNSON, Prof. Francis Rea; Professor of Anatomy, London Hospital Medical College, 1968–86, then Emeritus (Pre-clinical Sub-Dean, 1979–86); *b* 8 July 1921; *s* of Marcus Jervis Johnson and Elizabeth Johnson; *m* 1951, Ena Patricia Laverty; one *s* one *d. Educ:* Omagh Academy, N Ire.; Queen's Univ., Belfast. MB, BCh, BAO 1945, MD 1949. House appts, Belfast City Hosp., 1946; Demonstrator in Anatomy and Physiology, QUB, 1947–50; Lectr in Anatomy, Sheffield Univ., 1950–57; Reader in Anatomy, London Hosp. Med. Coll., 1957–64; Prof. of Histology, London Hosp. Med. Coll., 1964–68. *Publications:* papers on histochemistry and ultrastructure of tissues and organs in various jls. *Recreations:* motoring, camping, gardening. *Address:* 1 Lakeholme Gardens, Oswestry, Shropshire SY11 1RJ. *Died 6 July 2007.*

JOHNSON, Frank Robert; Parliamentary Sketch Writer and Columnist, The Daily Telegraph, since 2000; *b* 20 Jan. 1943; *s* of late Ernest Johnson, pastry cook and confectioner, and Doreen (*née* Skinner); *m* 1998, Virginia, widow of Hon. Simon Fraser, Master of Lovat; two step *s* two step *d. Educ:* Chartesey Secondary Sch., Shoreditch; Shoreditch Secondary Sch. Messenger Boy, Sunday Express, 1959–60; Reporter on local and regional newspapers, Walthamstow, Barrow-in-Furness, Nottingham and LIverpool, 1960–69; Political Staff, Sun, 1969–72; Parly Sketch Writer and Leader Writer, Daily Telegraph, 1972–79; Columnist, Now! Magazine, 1979–81; The Times: Parly Sketch Writer, 1981–83; Paris Diarist, 1984; Bonn Corresp., 1985–86; Parly Sketch Writer, 1986–87; Associate Editor, 1987–88; The Sunday Telegraph: Associate Editor, 1988–93; Dep. Editor (Comment), 1993–94; Dep. Editor, 1994–95; Editor, The Spectator, 1995–99, Columnist, 1999–.

Chm., Literary Panel, Royal Philharmonic Soc. Awards, 2000–03. Parly Sketch Writer of the Year Award, Granada, What The Papers Say, 1977; Columnist of the Year, British Press Awards, 1981. *Publications:* Out of Order, 1982; Frank Johnson's Election Year, 1983. *Recreations:* opera, ballet. *Address:* c/o The Daily Telegraph, 1 Canada Square, Canary Wharf, E14 5DT. *Clubs:* Garrick, Beefsteak. *Died 15 Dec. 2006.*

JOHNSON, Air Vice-Marshal Frank Sidney Roland, CB 1973; OBE 1963; *b* 4 Aug. 1917; *s* of Major Harry Johnson, IA, and Georgina Marklew; *m* 1943, Evelyn Hunt; two *s. Educ:* Trinity County Secondary Sch., Wood Green. Enlisted, 1935; served in UK and India; commnd, 1943; Germany (Berlin Airlift), 1948; Western Union Defence Organisation, 1955–57; Directing Staff, RAF Staff Coll., 1958–60; comd 113 MU, RAF Nicosia, 1960–63; Chief Instructor Equipment and Secretarial Wing, RAF Coll. Cranwell, 1963–64; Dep. Dir MoD, 1965–66; idc 1967; Chief Supply Officer, Fighter and Strike Comds, 1968–70; Dir-Gen. of Supply, RAF, 1971–73; Supply Manager, BAC, Saudi Arabia, 1974–76; Base Manager, BAC RSAF, Khamis Mushayt, Saudi Arabia, 1976–77, Dhahran, 1978–82. CCMI. *Recreations:* golf, squash, hockey, cricket. *Club:* Royal Air Force. *Died 10 May 2009.*

JOHNSON, Nevil; Nuffield Reader in the Comparative Study of Institutions, University of Oxford, and Professorial Fellow, Nuffield College, 1969–96, then Emeritus Fellow; *b* 6 Feb. 1929; *s* of G. E. Johnson and Doris Johnson, MBE, Darlington; *m* 1957, Ulla van Aubel; two *s. Educ:* Queen Elizabeth Grammar Sch., Darlington; University Coll., Oxford (BA PPE 1952, MA 1962). Army service, 1947–49. Admin. Cl. of Home Civil Service: Min. of Supply, 1952–57; Min. of Housing and Local Govt, 1957–62; Lectr in Politics, Univ. of Nottingham, 1962–66; Sen. Lectr in Politics, Univ. of Warwick, 1966–69. Chm. Board, Faculty of Social Studies, Oxford, 1976–78. Visiting Professor: Ruhr Univ. of Bochum, 1968–69; Univ. of Munich, 1980. Mem., ESRC (formerly SSRC), 1981–87 (Chm., Govt and Law Cttee, 1982–86). Civil Service Comr (pt-time), 1982–85. Mem. Exec. Council, RIPA, 1965–87; Chm., Study of Parlt Gp, 1984–87. Hon. Editor, Public Administration, 1967–81. *Publications:* Parliament and Administration: The Estimates Committee 1945–65, 1967; Government in the Federal Republic of Germany, 1973; In Search of the Constitution, 1977 (trans. German, 1977); (with A. Cochrane) Economic Policy-Making by Local Authorities in Britain and Western Germany, 1981; State and Government in the Federal Republic of Germany, 1983; The Limits of Political Science, 1989 (trans. Spanish, 1991); Reshaping the British Constitution, 2004; articles in Public Admin, Political Studies, Parly Affairs, Govt and Opposition, Ztschr. für Politik, Die Verwaltung, and Der Staat. *Recreation:* gardening. *Address:* 2 Race Farm Lane, Kingston Bagpuize, Oxon OX13 5AU. *T:* (01865) 820777. *Died 30 April 2006.*

JOHNSON, Stanley, CBE 1970; FCA; FCIT; Managing Director, British Transport Docks Board, 1967–75; *b* 10 Nov. 1912; *s* of late Robert and Janet Mary Johnson; *m* 1st, 1940, Sheila McLean Bald (*d* 1994); two *s* two *d;* 2nd, 1998, Ellen Elaine Sholten; three step *s* one step *d. Educ:* King George V Sch., Southport. Served as Lieut (S) RINVR, 1942–45. Joined Singapore Harbour Board, 1939; Asst Gen. Man. 1952; Chm. and Gen. Man. 1958–59; Chief Docks Man., Hull Docks, 1962; Asst Gen. Man. 1963, Mem. and Dep. Dir 1966, British Transport Docks Board. Chm. Major Ports Cttee, Dock and Harbour Authorities Assoc., 1971–72. Mem., Exec. Council, British Ports Assoc., 1973–75; Vice-Pres., Internat. Assoc. of Ports and Harbours, 1975–77. Vice-Pres., CIT, 1973–75. *Recreations:* walking, reading, travel. *Address:* 2425 20th Street, Apt 113, Vero Beach, FL 32960, USA. *Died 23 Dec. 2007.*

JOHNSON, Sir Vassel (Godfrey), Kt 1994; CBE 1979 (OBE 1970); JP; Director: Fidelity Bank (Cayman) Ltd (formerly British American Bank), 1983–2005, then Director Emeritus; Monetary Authority, Cayman Islands, 1997–2000; *b* 18 Jan. 1922; *s* of late Charles McKintha Johnson and of Theresa Virginia Johnson (*née* McDoom); *m* 1952, Rita Joanna Hinds; two *s* four *d* (and one *s* decd). *Educ:* Govt Secondary Sch., Grand Cayman; Bennett Coll., England; Wolsey Hall; Sussex Univ. Entered Cayman Is CS, 1942; transferred to Cayman Co. of Jamaica Home Guard, 1942–45; Clerical Officer, Dept of Treasury, Customs and PO, 1945–55; Asst to Dep. Treas., 1955–59; Clerk of Courts, 1959–60; Public Recorder, 1962–76; Treas. and Collector of Taxes, 1965–82; Hd of Exchange Control, 1966–80; Inspector of Banks and Trust Cos, 1966–73; Chm., Cayman Is Currency Bd, 1971–82; Mem., Exec. Council, resp. for Finance and Develt, 1972–82; Actg Gov., Cayman Is, 1977; Chm., Govt Vehicles Funding Scheme, 1977–82; retd from CS, 1983. Chm., Public Service Commn, 1983–84; MLA, George Town, 1984–88; Mem., Exec. Council, resp. for Develt and Nat. Resources, 1984–80. Cayman Airways Ltd: Founding Dir, 1968; Chm., 1971–77 and 1984–85; Chm., Cayman Is Corp. (Airport), 1969–77; Trustee, Swiss Bank & Trust Corp., 1983–97; Man. Dir, Montpelier Properties (Cayman) Ltd, 1983–97. JP Cayman Is, 1977. Chm., Bd of Govs, Cayman Prep. Sch., 1982–84 and 1993–95. Silver Jubilee Medal, 1977. *Publications:* Cayman Islands Economic and Financial Review 1904–1981, 1982; As I See It: how Cayman became a leading financial centre (autobiog.), 2001. *Recreations:* bridge, church work (Senior Elder, United Church). *Address:* PO Box 78G, Grand Cayman, Cayman Islands. *T:* 9499217, *Fax:* 9459326. *Died 12 Nov. 2008.*

JOHNSON, Prof. William, DSc, MA; FRS 1982; FREng, FIMechE; Professor of Mechanics, Engineering Department, Cambridge University, 1975–82, then Professor Emeritus; Professorial Fellow, Fitzwilliam College, Cambridge, 1975–82; *b* 20 April 1922; *er s* of James Johnson and Elizabeth Johnson (*née* Riley); *m* 1946, Heather Marie (*née* Thornber) (*d* 2004); three *s* two *d. Educ:* Manchester Central High Sch.; Manchester Coll. of Science and Technology (BScTech 1943; DSc 1960); BSc Maths, London (ext.) 1949; UCL (Hist. and Phil. of Sci. MSc course, 1950; Fellow, 1982); MA Cantab. CEng, FREng (FEng 1983). Commnd REME, UK, Italy and Austria, 1943–47. Asst Principal, Administrative Grade, Home Civil Service, 1948–50; Lecturer, Northampton Polytechnic, London, 1950–51; Lectr in Engineering, Sheffield Univ., 1952–56; Senior Lectr in Mechanical Engineering, Manchester Univ., 1956–60; Prof. of Mechanical Engrg, 1960–75, Dir of Medical Engrg, 1973–75, UMIST. Visiting Professor: McMaster Univ., Canada, 1969; Springer Prof., Univ. of Calif, Berkeley, 1980; Singapore, 1982; Allied Irish Banks Prof., Univ. of Belfast, 1983; UMIST, 1983–94; Industrial Engrg Dept. Purdue Univ., Indiana, 1984 and 1985; Taiwan, 1985; United Technologies Dist. Prof. of Engrg, Purdue Univ., 1988 and 1989. Hon. Sec., Yorks Br. of IMechE, 1953–56, and Chm., NW Br., 1974–75; Vis. for DoI to Prodn Engrg Res. Assoc. and Machine Tool Res. Assoc., 1973–75; President: Manchester and Salford Med. Engrg Club, 1971–72; Manchester Assoc. of Engrs, 1972–73; Manchester Technol. Assoc., 1983–84. Founder, and Editor-in-Chief: Internat. Jl Mech. Sciences, 1960–87; Internat. Jl Impact Engineering, 1983–87; Chm., Internat. Jl Mech. Engrg Educn, 1960–84. For. Fellow, Nat. Acad. of Athens, 1982; For. Mem., Russian Acad. of Scis, Ural Br., 1993; Hon. Mem., Indian Nat. Acad. Engrg, 1999. Hon. DTech Bradford, 1976; Hon. DEng: Sheffield, 1986; UMIST, 1995. Premium Award, Jl RAeS, 1956; T. Constantine Medal, Manchester Assoc. of Engrs, 1962; Bernard Hall Prize (jt), IMechE, 1965–66 and 1966–67; James Clayton Fund Prize (jt), IMechE, 1972 and 1978; Safety in Mech. Engrg Prize, (jt) 1980, 1991; Silver Medal, Inst. of Sheet Metal Engrg, 1987; James Clayton Prize, IMechE, 1987; W. Johnson Gold Medal for Lifetime Achievement in Materials Processing

Technology, Dublin, 1995; Engr-Historian Award, ASME, 2000; Sustainability Award, RAEng, 2007. *Publications:* Plasticity for Mechanical Engineers (with P. B. Mellor), 1962; Mechanics of Metal Extrusion (with H. Kudo), 1962; Plane Strain Slip Line Fields (with R. Sowerby and J. B. Haddow), 1970; Impact Strength of Materials, 1972; Engineering Plasticity (with P. B. Mellor), 1973; Lectures in Engineering Plasticity (with A. G. Mamalis), 1978; Crashworthiness of Vehicles (with A. G. Mamalis), 1978; Plane-Strain Slip-Line Fields for Metal-Deformation Processes (with R. Sowerby and R. Venter), 1982; Collected Works on B. Robins and G. Hutton, 2001; Record and Services, Satisfactory (memoir), 2003; papers in mechanics of metal forming, impact engineering, mechanics of sports and games, solids, medical and bioengineering, and history of engineering mechanics. *Address:* c/o 39 Whinfell Court, Sheffield S11 9QA. *Died 13 June 2010.*

JOHNSON SMITH, Rt Hon. Sir Geoffrey, Kt 1982; PC 1996; DL; *b* 16 April 1924; *s* of late J. Johnson Smith; *m* 1951, Jeanne Pomeroy, MD; two *s* one *d. Educ:* Charterhouse; Lincoln Coll., Oxford. Served War of 1939–45: Royal Artillery, 1942–47; Capt. RA, 1946. BA Hons, Politics, Philosophy and Economics, Oxford, 1949. Mem., Oxford Union Soc. Debating Team, USA, 1949. Information Officer, British Information Services, San Francisco, 1950–52; Mem. Production Staff, Current Affairs Unit, BBC TV, 1953–54; London County Councillor, 1955–58; Interviewer, Reporter, BBC TV, 1955–59. MP (C): Holborn and St Pancras South, 1959–64; East Grinstead, Feb. 1965–1983; Wealden, 1983–2001. PPS, Board of Trade and Min. of Pensions, 1960–63; Opposition Whip, 1965; Parly Under-Sec. of State for Defence for the Army, MoD, 1971–72; Parly Sec., CSD, 1972–74. Chm., Cons. Back-bench Defence Cttee, 1988–93 (Vice-Chm., 1980–88); Chm., Select Cttee on Members' Interests, 1980–95; Vice-Chm., 1922 Cttee, 1988–2001 (Mem. Exec., 1979–2001). A Vice-Chm., Conservative Party, 1965–71. Chm., Churchill Chapter, Primrose League, 1977–2004. Member: IBA Gen. Adv. Council, 1975–80; N Atlantic Assembly, 1980–2001 (Chm., Military Cttee, 1985–89; Leader, UK Delegn to Assembly, 1987–97; Treas., 1996–2001). Governor, BFI, 1980–88. Trustee, Handicapped Anglers, 1985–; Chm., Salmon and Trout Trust, 1987–2003. Pres., High Weald Area of Outstanding Natural Beauty, 2000. Freeman, City of London, 1980. DL East Sussex, 1986. *Club:* Travellers. *Died 12 Aug. 2010.*

JOHNSTON, Rt Hon. Lord; Alan Charles Macpherson Johnston; PC 2005; a Senator of the College of Justice in Scotland, since 1994; *b* 13 Jan. 1942; *s* of Hon. Lord Dunpark, TD; *m* 1966, Anthea Jean Blackburn; three *s. Educ:* Edinburgh Academy; Loretto School; Jesus Coll., Cambridge (BA Hons); Edinburgh Univ. (LLB). Called to the Bar, 1967; QC (Scot.) 1980. Standing Junior, Scottish Home and Health Dept, 1974–79; Advocate Depute, 1979–82; Treasurer, 1977–89, Dean, 1989–94, Faculty of Advocates. Chairman: Industrial Tribunal, 1982–85; Med. Appeal Tribunal, 1985–89. DUniv Heriot-Watt, 2001. *Publications:* (asst editor) Gloag and Henderson, Introduction to Scots Law, 7th edn 1968. *Recreations:* shooting, fishing, golf, walking. *Address:* 3 Circus Gardens, Edinburgh EH3 6TN. *Clubs:* University Pitt (Cambridge); New (Edinburgh). *Died 14 June 2008.*

JOHNSTON, Very Rev. Frederick Mervyn Kieran; Dean of Cork, 1967–71, retired; *b* 22 Oct. 1911; *s* of Robert Mills Johnston and Florence Harriet O'Hanlon; *m* 1938, Catherine Alice Ruth FitzSimons; two *s. Educ:* Grammar Sch., Galway; Bishop Foy Sch., Waterford; Trinity Coll., Dublin. BA 1933. Deacon, 1934; Priest, 1936; Curate, Castlecomer, 1934–36; Curate, St Luke, Cork, 1936–38; Incumbent of Kilmeen, 1938–40; Drimoleague, 1940–45; Blackrock, Cork, 1945–58;

Bandon, 1958–67; Rector of St Fin Barre's Cathedral and Dean of Cork, 1967; Examng Chaplain to Bishop of Cork, 1960–78. *Address:* 24 Lapps Court, Hartlands Avenue, Cork, Republic of Ireland. *Died 2006.*

JOHNSTON, Maj.-Gen. James Frederick Junor, CB 1993; CBE 1984; Chairman, Westminster Gardens Ltd, 1991–2003; *b* 5 Aug. 1939; *s* of late William Johnston and Margaret Macrae Ward Johnston (*née* Junor). *Educ:* George Watson's College; Welbeck College; RMA Sandhurst. BSc; CEng, Eur Ing, FIMechE; psc, rcds. Commissioned REME, 1959; Comd 7 Field Workshop, 1974–76; Directing Staff, Staff Coll., 1976–79; Comd Maint., 3 Armd Div., 1979–81; Dep. Chief of Staff, 4 Armd Div., 1981–84; Asst Chief of Staff, HQ BAOR, 1986–89; Dir Manning (Army), 1989; Dir Gen., Army Manning and Recruiting, MoD, 1990–93, retd. Col Comdt, REME, 1994–2000. Chairman: Crown Housing Trust, 1993–94; Broomleigh Housing Assoc., 1996–97; Brooke Hospital for Animals, 1998–2000. Trustee of several charities. FInstD; FCMI. *Recreations:* travel, photography, postal history, genealogy, animal welfare. *Address:* c/o Royal Bank of Scotland, Lawrie House, Victoria Road, Farnborough, Hants GU14 7NR. *Clubs:* Army and Navy; Fadeaways. *Died 20 April 2006.*

JOHNSTON, Lt-Col Sir John (Frederick Dame), GCVO 1987 (KCVO 1981; CVO 1977; MVO 1971); MC 1945; Comptroller, Lord Chamberlain's Office, 1981–87 (Assistant Comptroller, 1964–81); *b* 24 Aug. 1922; *m* 1949, Hon. Elizabeth Hardinge (*d* 1995), JP Windsor 1971, *d* of 2nd Baron Hardinge of Penshurst, GCB, GCVO, MC, PC and Lady Hardinge of Penshurst; one *s* one *d. Educ:* Ampleforth. Served in Grenadier Guards, 1941–64. Extra Equerry to the Queen, 1965–. Pres., King George V Fund for Actors and Actresses. *Publications:* The Lord Chamberlain's Blue Pencil, 1990. *Address:* Studio Cottage, The Great Park, Windsor, Berks SL4 2HP. *T:* (01784) 431627; Stone Hill, Newport, Pembrokeshire SA42 0QD. *T:* (01239) 820978. *Club:* Swinley Forest Golf. *Died 10 Sept. 2006.*

JOHNSTON, Thomas Lothian; DL; Principal and Vice-Chancellor of Heriot-Watt University, 1981–88; President, Royal Society of Edinburgh, 1993–96; *b* 9 March 1927; *s* of late T. B. Johnston and Janet Johnston; *m* 1956, Joan, *d* of late E. C. Fahmy, surgeon; two *s* three *d. Educ:* Hawick High Sch.; Univ. of Edinburgh (MA 1951, PhD 1955); Univ. of Stockholm. FRSE 1979; FEIS 1989. Served RNVR, 1944–47 (Sub-Lt). Asst Lectr in Pol Economy, Univ. of Edinburgh, 1953–55, Lectr 1955–65; Res. Fellow, Queen's Univ., Canada, 1965; Prof. and Hd of Dept of Econs, Heriot-Watt Univ., 1966–76. Visiting Professor: Univ. of Illinois, 1962–63; Internat. Inst. for Labour Studies, Geneva, 1973; Western Australia Inst. of Technol., 1979. Sec., Scottish Econ. Soc., 1958–65 (Pres., 1978–81); Member: Scottish Milk Marketing Bd, 1967–72; Nat. Industrial Relations Court, 1971–74; Scottish Cttee on Licensing Laws, 1971–73; Scottish Telecommunications Bd, 1977–84; Scottish Economic Council, 1977–91; Council for Tertiary Educn in Scotland, 1979–83; Chm., Manpower Services Cttee for Scotland, 1977–80; Economic Consultant to Sec. of State for Scotland, 1977–81. Trustee, Nat. Galls of Scotland, 1989–95. Director: First Charlotte Assets Trust, 1981–92; Universities Superannuation Scheme, 1985–88; Scottish Life Assurance, 1989–97; Hodgson Martin Ltd, 1989–97. A Dir, Edinburgh Sci. Festival, 1989–91. Chairman: Scottish Cttee, Industry Year 1986; Scottish Cttee, Industry Matters, 1987–89; Scottish Cttee, RSA, 1991–95; Univ. Authorities Pay Panel, 1985–88. Chairman: Enquiry into staff representation, London Clearing Banks, 1978–79; Water Workers' Enquiry, 1983; Mem., Review Cttee for NZ Univs, 1987; Arbitrator; Overseas Corresp., Nat. Acad. of Arbitrators, USA. FRSA 1981; CCMI (CBIM 1983); FIPD (FIPM 1986). For. Mem., Swedish Royal Acad. of Engrg Scis, 1985. DL Edinburgh, 1987. Dr *hc* Edinburgh, 1986; Hon. DEd CNAA, 1989; Hon. LLD Glasgow, 1989; DUniv Heriot-Watt, 1989; Hon. DLitt Napier, 1997. Comdr,

Royal Swedish Order of the Polar Star, 1985. *Publications:* Collective Bargaining in Sweden, 1962; (ed and trans.) Economic Expansion and Structural Change, 1963; (jtly) The Structure and Growth of the Scottish Economy, 1971; Introduction to Industrial Relations, 1981; numerous translations from Swedish; articles in learned jls. *Recreations:* gardening, walking. *Address:* 14 Mansionhouse Road, Edinburgh EH9 1TZ. *T:* (0131) 667 1439.   *Died 25 March 2009.*

JOLLIFFE, Christopher, CBE 1971; Chairman, Abbeyfield Richmond Society, 1980–87; Director, Science Division, Science Research Council, 1969–72 (Director for University Science and Technology, 1965–69); *b* 14 March 1912; *s* of William Edwin Jolliffe and Annie Etheldreda Thompson; *m* 1936, Miriam Mabel Ash. *Educ:* Gresham's Sch., Holt; University Coll., London. Asst Master, Stowe Sch., 1935–37; Dept of Scientific and Industrial Research, 1937–65. Vice-Chm., Council for Science and Society, 1978–82; Dir, Leverhulme Trust Fund, 1976–77. *Address:* Abbeyfield, Victoria House, 4 Ennerdale Road, Kew, Richmond, Surrey TW9 3PG. *T:* (020) 8940 4265.
                                              Died 1 March 2006.

JOLLY, Air Cdre Robert Malcolm, CBE 1969; retired; *b* 4 Aug. 1920; *s* of Robert Imrie Jolly and Ethel Thompson Jolly; *m* 1946, Josette Jacqueline (*née* Baindeky); no *c. Educ:* Skerry's Coll., Newcastle upon Tyne. Commnd in RAF, 1943; served in: Malta, 1941–45; Bilbeis, Egypt, 1945; Shaibah, Iraq, 1945–46; Malta, 1946–49; Air Cdre 1971; Dir of Personal Services, MoD, 1970–72; Dir of Automatic Data Processing (RAF), 1973–75, retd. Man. Dir, Leonard Griffiths & Associates, 1975–77; Vice-Pres., MWS Consultants Inc., 1978–80; Gen. Man., Diebold Europe SA and Dir, Diebold Research Program Europe, 1983–84. Hon. Archivist, St Paul's Anglican Pro-Cathedral, Malta GC, 1992–. *Address:* Villa Grey Golf, 26 Triq Galata, High Ridge, St Andrews STJ 03, Malta GC. *T:* 370282. *Club:* Royal Air Force.   *Died 18 July 2008.*

JONES, Rt Rev. Alwyn Rice; Archbishop of Wales, 1991–99; Bishop of St Asaph, 1982–99; *b* 25 March 1934; *s* of John Griffith and Annie Jones, Capel Curig, Caernarvonshire; *m* 1968, Meriel Anne Thomas; one *d. Educ:* Llanrwst Grammar School, Denbighshire; St David's Coll., Lampeter (BA Hons Welsh 1955); Fitzwilliam House, Cambridge (BA 1957 Theology Tripos, MA 1961); St Michael's Coll., Llandaff. Deacon 1958, priest 1959, Bangor Cathedral; Asst Curate, Llanfairisgaer, 1958–62; Secretary for SCM in N Wales Colleges and SCM in schools, 1962–65; Director of Education, Diocese of Bangor, 1965–75; Chaplain, St Winifred's School, Llanfairfechan, 1965–67; Diocesan Warden of Ordinands, 1970–75; Vicar of Porthmadog, dio. Bangor, 1975–79; Exam. Chaplain to Archbishop of Wales, 1970–79; Hon. Canon, Bangor Cathedral, 1974–78, Preb. of Llanfair, 1978–79; Dean of Brecon Cathedral, 1979–82. Mem., IBA Panel of Religious Advisers and Welsh Cttee, IBA, 1972–76; Asst Tutor in Religious Education, UCNW, Bangor, 1973–76. Pres., CCBI, 1997–2000. Fellow, Trinity Coll., Carmarthen, 1993. *Recreations:* music, walking. *Address:* 7 Llwyn Onn, Bishop's Walk, St Asaph, Denbighshire LL17 0SQ.
                                              Died 12 Aug. 2007.

JONES, Beti, CBE 1980; *b* 23 Jan. 1919; *d* of Isaac Jones and Elizabeth (*née* Rowlands). *Educ:* Rhondda County Sch. for Girls; Univ. of Wales (BA (Hons) History, Teaching Diploma). Grammar Sch. teaching, 1941–43; S Wales Organiser, Nat. Assoc. of Girls' Clubs, 1943–47; Youth Officer, Educn Branch, Control Commission, Germany, 1947–49; Children's Officer, Glamorgan CC, 1949–68; Chief Adviser on Social Work, Scottish Office, 1968–80. Fellow, University Coll., Cardiff, 1982 (Hon. Fellow, Dept of Social Administration, 1970). *Address:* 5 Belgrave Crescent, Edinburgh EH4 3AQ. *T:* (0131) 332 2696.   *Died 14 Sept. 2006.*

JONES, Gen. Sir (Charles) Edward (Webb), KCB 1989; CVO 2001; CBE 1985; Gentleman Usher of the Black Rod and Serjeant-at-Arms, House of Lords, and Secretary to the Lord Great Chamberlain, 1995–2001; *b* 25 Sept. 1936; *s* of Gen. Sir Charles Phibbs Jones, GCB, CBE, MC and of Ouida Margaret Wallace; *m* 1965, Suzanne Vere Pige Leschallas; two *s* one *d. Educ:* Portora Royal School, Enniskillen. Commissioned Oxford and Bucks LI, 1956; 1st Bn Royal Green Jackets, 1958; served BAOR, 1968–70; served NI, 1971–72 (despatches 1972); Directing Staff, Staff Coll., 1972; CO 1st Bn RGJ, 1974–76; Comdr 6th Armd Brigade, 1981–83; Comdr, British Mil. Adv. and Training Team, Zimbabwe, 1983–85; Dir Gen., TA and Organisation, 1985–87; Comdr, 3rd Armoured Div., 1987–88; QMG, MoD, 1988–91; UK Mil. Rep. to NATO, 1992–95. Colonel Commandant: RAEC, 1986–92; RGJ, 1988–95; Dep. Col Comdt, AGC, 1992–93. Comr, Royal Hosp. Chelsea, 1995–2001; Governor: Wellington Coll., 1997–; Eagle House Sch., 1999–. Vice-Patron, St Dunstan, 1998–; Pres., Craft Club, 2001–. *Recreations:* golf, fishing. *Address:* River House, Rushall, Pewsey, Wilts SN9 6EN. *T:* (01980) 630397. *Club:* Army and Navy.   *Died 14 May 2007.*

JONES, Daniel Gruffydd; Registrar and Secretary, University of Wales, Aberystwyth, 1990–99; *b* 7 Dec. 1933; *o s* of late Ifor Ceredig Jones and Gwendolen Eluned Jones; *m* 1969, Maureen Anne Woodhall; three *d. Educ:* Ardwyn Grammar Sch., Aberystwyth; University Coll. of N Wales, Bangor (BA). RAEC, 1957–59 (BAOR). Asst Principal, Min. of Housing and Local Govt, 1960; Private Sec. to Parly Sec., 1962–63; Principal, 1963; Private Sec. to Sec. of Cabinet, 1967–69; Asst Sec., 1969; Sec., Water Resources Bd, 1969–73; DoE, 1973; Sec., Prime Minister's Cttee on Local Govt Rules of Conduct, 1973–74; Under Sec., 1975; Prin. Finance Officer, Welsh Office, 1975–79; Director: Local Govt Directorate, DoE, 1980–82; Central Directorate of Envmtl Protection, DoE, 1982–86; Regl Dir, SE Reg., DoE and Dept of Transport, 1986–90. Mem., Royal Commn on the Ancient and Historical Monuments of Wales, 1991–2001. Chm., Hafod Adv. Cttee, Forest Enterprise, 1992–97. FRSA 1985. High Sheriff of Dyfed, 2000–01. *Address:* 40 Marchwood Gate, Marchwood, Chichester, W Sussex PO19 5HA. *T:* (01243) 531205.
                                              Died 23 Jan. 2007.

JONES, David Hugh; Hon. Associate Director, Royal Shakespeare Company, since 1966; Masterclass Film Professor, Columbia University, since 2004; *b* 19 Feb. 1934; *s* of John David Jones and Gwendolen Agnes Langworthy (*née* Ricketts); *m* 1964, Sheila Allen (marr. diss.); two *s. Educ:* Taunton Sch.; Christ's Coll., Cambridge (MA 1st Cl. Hons English). 2nd Lieut RA, 1954–56. Production team of Monitor, BBC TV's 1st arts magazine, 1958–62, Editor, 1962–64; joined RSC, 1964; Aldwych Co. Dir, 1968–72; Artistic Dir, RSC (Aldwych), 1973–77; Producer, Play of the Month, BBC TV, 1977–78; Artistic Dir, Brooklyn Acad. of Music Theatre Co., 1979–81; Adjunct Prof. of Drama, Yale Univ., 1981. Productions for RSC incl. plays by Arden, Brecht, Gorky, Granville Barker, Günter Grass, Graham Greene, Mercer, O'Casey, Shakespeare, and Chekhov; dir. prodns for Chichester and Stratford, Ontario, Festival Theatres; other productions include: Old Times, Theatre Royal, Haymarket, and Los Angeles (LA Dramalogue Award for direction), 1985; No Man's Land, NY, 1994; The Hothouse, Chichester Fest., 1995; Taking Sides, NY, 1996; The Caretaker, NY, 2003; Triptych, NY, 2004; The Controversy of Valladolid, NY, 2005; On the Razzle, 2005, Sweet Bird of Youth, 2006, The Autumn Garden, 2007, Williamstown Fest.; The Last Confession, Chichester Fest. and Theatre Royal, Haymarket, 2007. Dir, films for BBC TV, including: biography of poet, John Clare, 1969; adaptations of Hardy and Chekhov short stories, 1972 and 1973; Pinter's screenplay, Langrishe, Go Down, 1978; Merry Wives of Windsor, Pericles, 1982–83; The Devil's Disciple, 1987; Look Back in Anger, 1989 (ACE Award); directed for American TV:

The Christmas Wife, 1988; Sensibility and Sense, 1990; The End of a Sentence, 1991; Fire in the Dark, 1991; And Then There Was One, 1994; Is There Life Out There?, 1994; Sophie and the Moonhanger, 1995; The Irvine Fertility Scandal, 1996; Time to Say Goodbye?, 1997; An Unexpected Life, 1998; A Christmas Carol, 1999; Custody of the Heart, 2000. Feature films directed: Pinter's Betrayal, 1982; 84 Charing Cross Road (royal film performance), 1987 (Christopher and Scriptor Awards, 1988); Jacknife, 1989; Kafka's The Trial, 1993; The Confession, 1998. Obie Awards, NY, for direction of RSC Summerfolk, 1975, for innovative programming at BAM Theatre Co., 1980. *Publications:* (with Richard Nelson) Making Plays, 1995. *Recreations:* restaurants, reading modern poetry, exploring mountains and islands. *Address:* 250 West 27th Street (# 6B), New York, NY 10001–5924, USA.   *Died 19 Sept. 2008.*

JONES, David Lewis, CBE 2005; FSA; Librarian, House of Lords, 1991–2006; *b* 4 Jan. 1945; *s* of late Gwilym Morgan Jones and of Joyce Jones (*née* Davies). *Educ:* Aberaeron County Sch.; Jesus Coll., Oxford (MA); Coll. of Librarianship, Wales. FSA 1998. Asst Librarian, Inst. of Histl Res., 1970–72; University of Wales, Aberystwyth: Asst Librarian, 1972–75; Law Librarian, 1975–77; Dep. Librarian, H of L, 1977–91. Hon. Sec., Honourable Soc. of Cymmrodorion, 1994–96. Trustee, Cross Inn, Llanon, Sch. and School-House, 1975–. Gorsedd y Beirdd (Aelod er Anrhydedd), 1996. Freeman, City of London, 1993; Liveryman, Stationers' and Newspapermakers' Co., 1994. FRHistS 2003; FRSA 2006. *Publications:* Books in English on the Soviet Union 1917–73, 1975; Paraguay: a bibliography, 1979; Debates and proceedings of the British Parliaments: a guide to printed sources, 1986; (ed jtly) Peers, politics and power: the House of Lords 1603–1911, 1986; A parliamentary history of the Glorious Revolution, 1988; Eirene: a tribute, 2001. *Address:* 10 Heathfield Court, Heathfield Terrace, W4 4LP. *T:* (020) 8995 6029. *Club:* Beefsteak.   *Died 15 Oct. 2010.*

JONES, Sir Derek A.; *see* Alun-Jones.

JONES, Derek John Claremont, CMG 1979; Senior Fellow, Trade Policy Research Centre, 1986–90; *b* 2 July 1927; *er s* of Albert Claremont Jones and Ethel Lilian Jones (*née* Hazell); *m* 1st, 1951, Jean Cynthia Withams; one *s* two *d*; 2nd, 1970, Kay Cecile Thewlis; one *s*. *Educ:* Colston Sch., Bristol; Bristol Univ.; London Sch. of Economics and Political Science. Economic Asst, Economic Section, Cabinet Office, 1950–53; Second Sec., UK Delegn to OEEC/NATO, Paris, 1953–55; Asst Principal, Colonial Office, 1955–57; Principal, Colonial Office, 1957–66; First Secretary, Commonwealth Office, 1966–67; Counsellor (Hong Kong Affairs), UK Mission, Geneva, 1967–71; Government of Hong Kong: Dep. Economic Sec., 1971–73; Sec. for Economic Services, 1973–76; Sec. for the Environment, 1976–81; Sec. for Transport, 1981–82; Minister for Hong Kong Relns with EC and Member States, 1982–86. *Recreations:* reading, travel, conversation. *Address:* Cliff House, Trevaunance Cove, St Agnes, Cornwall TR5 0RZ. *T:* (01872) 552334. *Clubs:* Hong Kong, Hong Kong Jockey.   *Died 4 Oct. 2008.*

JONES, Gen. Sir Edward; *see* Jones, Gen. Sir C. E. W.

JONES, Air Marshal Sir Edward G.; *see* Gordon Jones.

JONES, Prof. Emrys, PhD; FBA 2003; FRGS; Professor of Geography, University of London, at London School of Economics, 1961–84, then Emeritus; *b* Aberdare, 17 Aug. 1920; *s* of Samuel Garfield and Anne Jones; *m* 1948, Iona Vivien, *d* of R. H. Hughes; one *d* (and one *d* decd). *Educ:* Grammar Sch. for Boys, Aberdare; University Coll. of Wales, Aberystwyth (BSc (1st Class Hons in Geography and Anthropology), 1941; MSc1945; PhD 1947). Fellow of the University of Wales, 1946–47; Asst Lectr, University Coll., London, 1947–50; Fellow, Rockefeller Foundation, 1948–49; Lectr, Queen's Univ., Belfast, 1950–58; Sen. Lectr, 1958; Reader, LSE, 1959–61. O'Donnel Lectr, Univ. of Wales, 1977.

Chairman: Regional Studies Assoc., 1967–69; Council, Hon. Soc. of Cymmrodorion, 1984–89 (Mem., 1977–; Pres., 1989–2002); Mem. Council, RGS, 1973–77 (Vice-Pres., 1978–81). Mem. Council, University Coll. of Wales, Aberystwyth, 1978–85. Consultant on urbanisation and planning. Hon. Mem., Gorsedd y Beirdd, 2005. Hon. Fellow, UCW, 1991. Hon. DSc Belfast, 1978; DUniv Open, 1990. Victoria Medal, RGS, 1977; Medal, Hon. Soc. of Cymmrodorion, 2001. *Publications:* Hon. Editor, Belfast in its Regional Setting, 1952; (jointly) Welsh Rural Communities, 1960; A Social Geography of Belfast, 1961; Human Geography, 1964; Towns and Cities, 1966; Atlas of London, 1968; (ed jtly) Man and his Habitat, 1971; (contrib.) The Future of Planning, 1973; (with E. van Zandt) The City, 1974; Readings in Social Geography, 1975; (with J. Eyles) Introduction to Social Geography, 1977; (Chief Editor) The World and its Peoples, 1979; Metropolis: the world's great cities, 1990; The Welsh in London 1500–2000, 2001; articles in geographical, sociological and planning jls. *Recreations:* books, music. *Address:* 51 Lower King's Road, Berkhamsted, Herts HP4 2AA. *T:* (01442) 875422. *Club:* Athenæum.   *Died 30 Aug. 2006.*

JONES, Fiona Elizabeth Ann; *b* 27 Feb. 1957; *d* of Fred Hamilton; *m* 1982, Christopher Jones; two *s*. *Educ:* Mary Help of Christians Convent, Liverpool; Wirral Coll. of Art; Preston Coll. Journalist. Contested (Lab) Gainsborough and Horncastle, 1992; MP (Lab) Newark, 1997–2001; contested (Lab) same seat, 2001.   *Died 28 Jan. 2007.*

JONES, Gwyn Owain, CBE 1978; DSc Oxon; PhD Sheffield; Director, National Museum of Wales, 1968–77; *b* 29 March 1917; *s* of Dr Abel John Jones, OBE, HMI, and Rhoda May Jones, Cardiff and Porthcawl; *m* 1st, 1944, Sheila Heywood (marr. diss.); two *d*; 2nd, 1973, Elizabeth Assunta Blandino, studio potter. *Educ:* Monmouth Sch.; Port Talbot Secondary Sch.; Jesus Coll., Oxford (Meyricke Schol.; MA). Glass Delegacy Research Fellow of University of Sheffield, later mem. of academic staff, 1939–41; Mem. UK Government's Atomic Energy project, 1942–46; Nuffield Foundation Research Fellow at Clarendon Laboratory, Oxford, 1946–49; Reader in Experimental Physics in University of London, at Queen Mary Coll., 1949–53; Prof. of Physics in Univ. of London, and Head of Dept of Physics at Queen Mary Coll., 1953–68; Hon. Fellow of Queen Mary and Westfield (formerly Queen Mary) Coll. Visiting Prof. Univ. of Sussex, 1964. Member: Court and Council, UWIST, 1968–74; Court, University Coll., Swansea, 1981–84; Hon. Professorial Fellow, University Coll., Cardiff, 1969–79. Yr Academi Gymreig (English Language Section) 1971 (Chm., 1978–81); Gorsedd y Beirdd (Aelod er Anrhydedd) 1974. Governor, Commonwealth Institute, 1974–77. FMA 1976. *Publications:* Glass, 1956; (in collab.) Atoms and the Universe, 1956; papers on solid-state, glass, low-temperature physics; *novels:* The Catalyst, 1960; Personal File, 1962; Now, 1965; A Close Family, 1998; *story sequence:* The Conjuring Show, 1981. *Address:* 12 Squitchey Lane, Summertown, Oxford OX2 7LB. *T:* (01865) 510363.   *Died 3 July 2006.*

JONES, James Larkin, (Jack), CH 1978; MBE 1950; FCILT (FCIT 1970); General Secretary, Transport and General Workers' Union, 1969–78; Member, TUC General Council, 1968–78; Chairman, TUC International, Transport and Nationalised Industries Committees, 1972–78; Deputy Chairman, National Ports Council, 1967–79; *b* 29 March 1913; *m* 1938, Evelyn Mary Taylor (*d* 1998); two *s*. *Educ:* elementary sch., Liverpool. Worked in engineering and docks industries, 1927–39. Liverpool City Councillor, 1936–39; served in Spanish Civil War; wounded Ebro battle, Aug. 1938; Coventry District Sec., Transport and General Workers' Union, also District Sec., Confedn of Shipbuilding and Engineering Unions, 1939–55; Midlands Regional Sec., Transport and General Workers' Union, 1955–63, Executive Officer, 1963–69. Mem., Midland Regional

Bd for Industry, 1942–46, 1954–63; Chm., Midlands TUC Advisory Cttee, 1948–63. Coventry City Magistrate, 1950–63; Executive Chm., Birmingham Productivity Cttee, 1957–63; Member: Labour Party Nat. Exec. Cttee, 1964–67; Nat. Cttee for Commonwealth Immigrants, 1965–69; NEDC, 1969–78; Council, Advisory, Conciliation and Arbitration Service, 1974–78; British Overseas Trade Board, 1974–79; Cttee of Inquiry into Industrial Democracy, 1976–77 (Chm., Labour Party Wkg Party on Industrial Democracy, 1967); Bd, Crown Agents, 1978–80; Royal Commn on Criminal Procedure, 1978–80; Jt Chm. (with Lord Aldington), Special Cttee on the Ports, 1972. Pres., EFTA Trade Union Council, 1972–73; Founder Mem., European TUC, 1973 Vice-President: ITF, 1974–79; Anti-Apartheid Movement, 1976–; Age Concern, England, 1978–; European Fed of Retired and Elderly Persons, 1991–; Pres., Retired Members Assocs, TGWU, 1979–; Life President: Nat Pensioners' Convention, 2000; Internat. Bde Meml Trust, 2002–. Chm., Trustees, Nat. Museum of Labour History, 1988–2003. Vis. Fellow, Nuffield Coll., Oxford, 1970–78; Associate Fellow, LSE, 1978–82. Dimbleby Lecture, BBC, 1977. Hon. Fellow: Liverpool Poly. (later Liverpool John Moores Univ.), 1988; Central Lancs Univ., 1993. Hon. DLitt: Warwick, 1978; Coventry, 1996; DUniv Open, 2000. Freeman, City of London, 1979. Award of Merit, City of Coventry, 1978. *Publications:* (contrib.) The Incompatibles, 1967; (contrib.) Industry's Democratic Revolution, 1974; (with Max Morris) A-Z of Trade Unionism and Industrial Relations, 1982; Union Man (autobiog.), 1986, 2nd edn 2008. *Recreation:* walking. *Address:* 74 Ruskin Park House, Champion Hill, SE5 8TH. *T:* (020) 7274 7067. *Died 21 April 2009.*

JONES, Jennifer, (Mrs Norton Simon); film actress (US); *b* Tulsa, Okla, 2 March 1919; *née* Phylis Isley; *d* of Philip R. Isley and Flora Mae (*née* Suber); *m* 1st, 1939, Robert Walker (marr. diss. 1945); one *s* (and one *s* decd); 2nd, 1949, David O. Selznick (*d* 1965); (one *d* decd); 3rd, 1971, Norton Simon (*d* 1993). *Educ:* schools in Okla and Tex; Northwestern Univ., Evanston, Illinois; American Academy of Dramatic Arts, New York City. Films include: Dick Tracy's G-Men, 1939; The New Frontier, 1939; The Song of Bernadette, 1943; Since You Went Away, 1944; Love Letters, 1945; The American Creed, 1946; Cluny Brown, 1946; Duel in the Sun, 1946; Portrait of Jenny, 1948; Madame Bovary, 1949; We Were Strangers, 1949; The Wild Heart, 1950; Ruby Gentry, 1952; Carrie, 1952; Indiscretion of an American Wife, 1953; Beat the Devil, 1954; Good Morning, Miss Dove, 1955; Love is a Many-Splendoured Thing, 1955; The Man in the Gray Flannel Suit, 1956; The Barretts of Wimpole Street, 1957; A Farewell to Arms, 1957; Tender is the Night, 1962; The Idol, 1966; Angel, Down We Go, 1969; The Towering Inferno, 1974. Awards include: American Academy of Motion Pictures, Arts and Sciences Award, 1943 (for Song of Bernadette); 4 other Academy nominations, etc. Pres., Norton Simon Mus., Pasadena, 1989. Medal for Korean War Work. *Died 17 Dec. 2009.*

JONES, Sir John Henry H.; see Harvey-Jones.

JONES, Air Vice-Marshal John Maurice, CB 1986; *b* 27 Jan. 1931; *s* of E. Morris Jones and Gladys Jones (*née* Foulkes); *m* 1962, Joan (*née* McCallum); one *s* one *d*. *Educ:* Liverpool Institute High Sch.; Univ. of Liverpool (BDS). LDSRCS, FDSRCS 1987. Hospital appt, Liverpool Dental Hosp., 1954; RAF Dental Branch: appts UK and abroad, incl. Christmas Island, Malta, Cyprus and Fontainebleau, 1955–73; Dep. Dir of RAF Dental Services, 1973; OC RAF Inst. of Dental Health and Training, 1976; Principal Dental Officer: HQ RAF Germany, 1979; HQ RAF Support Command, 1982; Dir, RAF Dental Services, 1983–88, and Dir, Defence Dental Services, MoD, 1985–88; QHDS, 1983–87. Sec., Ski Club of GB, 1988–91. Pres., RAF Squash Rackets Assoc., 1986–88. OBStJ 1978. *Recreations:* golf, fishing,

ski-ing. *Address:* Wyckenhurst, St Michael's Close, Halton Village, Wendover, Bucks HP22 5NW. *T:* (01296) 624184. *Clubs:* Royal Air Force, Kandahar. *Died 2 Feb. 2010.*

JONES, Sir John P.; see Prichard-Jones.

JONES, Karen Ida Boalth S.; see Spärck Jones.

JONES, Keith H.; see Hamylton Jones.

JONES, Mervyn; author; *b* 27 Feb. 1922; *s* of Ernest Jones and Katharine (*née* Jokl); *m* 1948, Jeanne Urquhart; one *s* two *d*. *Educ:* Abbotsholme School; New York University. Assistant Editor: Tribune, 1955–59; New Statesman, 1966–68; Drama Critic, Tribune, 1959–67. *Publications:* No Time to be Young, 1952; The New Town, 1953; The Last Barricade, 1953; Helen Blake, 1955; On the Last Day, 1958; Potbank, 1961; Big Two, 1962; A Set of Wives, 1965; Two Ears of Corn, 1965; John and Mary, 1966; A Survivor, 1968; Joseph, 1970; Mr Armitage Isn't Back Yet, 1971; Life on the Dole, 1972; Holding On, 1973; The Revolving Door, 1973; Strangers, 1974; Lord Richard's Passion, 1974; The Pursuit of Happiness, 1975; Scenes from Bourgeois Life, 1976; Nobody's Fault, 1977; Today The Struggle, 1978; The Beautiful Words, 1979; A Short Time to Live, 1980; Two Women and their Man, 1982; Joanna's Luck, 1985; Coming Home, 1986; Chances, 1987; That Year in Paris, 1988; A Radical Life, 1991; Michael Foot, 1994; The Amazing Victorian, 1999. *Address:* c/o 51 Upper Lewes Road, Brighton, E Sussex BN2 3HH. *Died 23 Feb. 2010.*

JONES, Rt Rev. Noël Debroy, CB 1986; an Hon. Assistant Bishop, diocese of York, since 2003, *b* 25 Dec. 1932; *s* of Brinley and Gwendoline Jones; *m* 1969, Joyce Barbara Leelavathy Arulanandam; one *s* one *d*. *Educ:* Haberdashers' West Monmouth Sch.; St David's Coll., Lampeter (BA); Wells Theol Coll. Dio. of Monmouth, 1955–59; Vicar of Kano, N Nigeria, 1960–62; Chaplain, RN, 1962; GSM Brunei 1962, Borneo 1963; RM Commando Course prior to service in Aden with 42 Cdo, 1967; GSM S Arabia, 1967; Mid Service Clergy Course at St George's House, Windsor Castle, 1974; Staff Chaplain, MoD, 1974–77; Chaplain of the Fleet and Archdeacon for the Royal Navy, 1984–89; Bishop of Sodor and Man, 1989–2003. QHC 1983–89. OStJ 1995. *Recreations:* squash, swimming, music, family; formerly Rugby. *Club:* Army and Navy. *Died 28 Aug. 2009.*

JONES, Norman Arthur W.; see Ward-Jones.

JONES, Brig. Percival de Courcy, OBE 1953; Chief Secretary, The Royal Life Saving Society, 1965–75; *b* 9 Oct. 1913; *s* of P. de C. Jones, Barnsley; *m* 1st, 1947, Anne Hollins (marr. diss., 1951); one *s*; 2nd, 1962, Elaine Garnett. *Educ:* Oundle; RMC, Sandhurst. Commissioned KSLI 1933; Staff Coll., 1942; comd 1st Northamptons, Burma, 1945; Staff Coll. Instructor, 1949–50; AA & QMG, 11th Armoured Div., 1951–53; comd 1st KSLI, 1953–55; AQMG, War Office, 1955–58; NATO Defence Coll., 1958–59; Bde Comdr, 1959–62. Mem., Aylesbury Vale DC, 1976–79. Commonwealth Chief Sec., RLSS, 1965–75. Silver Medallion, Fedn Internat. de Sauvetage, 1976. *Recreation:* gardening. *Address:* Fairfield House, Ford, Shrewsbury, Shropshire SY5 9LG. *Died 9 Dec. 2010.*

JONES, Peter Ferry, MA, MChir, FRCS, FRCSE; Surgeon to the Queen in Scotland, 1977–85; Honorary Consulting Surgeon, Aberdeen Royal Infirmary and Royal Aberdeen Children's Hospital, Aberdeen (Consultant Surgeon, 1958–85); Clinical Professor of Surgery, University of Aberdeen, 1983–85, then Emeritus; *b* 29 Feb. 1920; *s* of Ernest and Winifred Jones; *m* 1950, Margaret Thomson; two *s* two *d*. *Educ:* Emmanuel Coll., Cambridge (MA); St Bartholomew's Hosp. Med. Sch., London (MB, MChir). FRCS 1948; FRCSE 1964. Served War, RAMC, 1944–46, Captain. House Surgeon, St Bartholomew's Hosp., 1943; Surg. Registrar, N Middlesex Hosp., 1948–51; Surg. Tutor, St Bartholomew's Hosp., 1951–53; Sen. Surg. Registrar,

Central Middlesex Hosp. and the Middlesex Hosp., London, 1953–57; Reader in Surg. Paediatrics, Univ. of Aberdeen, 1965–83. *Publications:* Abdominal Access and Exposure (with H. A. F. Dudley), 1965; Emergency Abdominal Surgery in Infancy, Childhood and Adult Life, 1974, 2nd edn 1987, 3rd edn (jtly) 1998; (jtly) Integrated Clinical Science: Gastroenterology, 1984; A Colour Atlas of Colo-Rectal Surgery, 1985; A Surgical Revolution: surgery in Scotland 1837–1901, 2007; papers on paediatric and gen. surgery in Brit. Jl of Surg., BMJ, Lancet, etc. *Recreations:* gardening, surgical history. *Address:* 7 Park Road, Cults, Aberdeen AB15 9HR. *T:* (01224) 867702. *Died 17 Oct. 2009.*

JONES, Peter George Edward Fitzgerald, CB 1985; Director, Atomic Weapons Research Establishment, 1982–87; Consultant to the Ministry of Defence, 1987–2006; *b* 7 June 1925; *s* of John Christopher Jones and Isobel (*née* Howell); *m* 1st; one *s* (and one *s* decd); 2nd, Jacqueline Angela (*née* Gilbert); two *s* one *d*. *Educ:* various schs; Dulwich Coll.; London Univ. (BSc (Special) Physics 1st Cl. Hons 1951). FInstP. Served RAF, flying duties, 1943–47. GEC Res. Labs, 1951–54; AWRE and Pacific Test Site, 1955–63; Asst Dir of Res., London Communications Security, 1963; Atomic Weapons Research Establishment: Supt, Electronics Res., 1964; Head, Electronics Div., 1966; Head, Special Projects, 1971; Chief, Warhead Develt, 1974; Principal Dep. Dir, 1980. *Recreation:* motoring. *Address:* Yew Tree Cottage, Upper Llanover, Abergavenny, Gwent NP7 9ER. *T:* (01873) 880779. *Died 26 Sept. 2010.*

JONES, Sir Peter Llewellyn G.; *see* Gwynn-Jones.

JONES, Philip James, DPhil; FBA 1984; FRHistS; Fellow and Tutor, Modern History, 1963–89, Librarian, 1965–89, then Emeritus Fellow, Brasenose College, Oxford; *b* 19 Nov. 1921; *s* of John David Jones and Caroline Susan Jones (*née* Davies); *m* 1954, Carla Susini (*d* 2004); one *s* one *d*. *Educ:* St Dunstan's College; Wadham College, Oxford (1st class Hons Mod. Hist. 1945, MA, DPhil). Senior Demy, Magdalen College, Oxford, 1945–49; Amy Mary Preston Road Scholar, 1946; Bryce Research Student, 1947; Asst in History, Glasgow Univ., 1949–50; Leeds University: Lectr in Med. Hist., 1950–61; Reader in Med. Hist., 1961–63; Eileen Power Meml Student, 1956–57. Corresp. Mem., Deputazione Toscana di Storia Patria, 1975–. Serena Medal for Italian Studies, British Acad., 1988. *Publications:* The Malatesta of Rimini, 1974; Economia e Societa nell'Italia medievale, 1980; contribs to: Cambridge Economic History, Vol. 1, 2nd edn, 1966; Storia d'Italia, vol. 2, 1974; Storia d'Italia, Annali, Vol. 1, 1978; The Italian City-State: from commune to signoria, 1997; articles and reviews in hist. jls. *Address:* 167 Woodstock Road, Oxford OX2 7NA. *T:* (01865) 557953. *Died 26 March 2006.*

JONES, Raymond Edgar; HM Diplomatic Service, retired; *b* 6 June 1919; *s* of Edgar George Jones, Portsmouth; *m* 1942, Joan Mildred Clark; one *s* two *d*. *Educ:* Portsmouth Northern Grammar Sch. Entered Admiralty service as Clerical Officer, 1936; joined RAF, 1941; commissioned, 1943; returned to Admty as Exec. Officer, 1946; transf. to Foreign Service, 1948; Singapore, 1949; Second Sec., Rome, 1950; Bahrain, 1952; Rio de Janeiro, 1955; Consul, Philadelphia, 1958; FO, 1961; First Sec., Copenhagen, 1963; Consul, Milan, 1965; Toronto (Dir of British Week), 1966; Dep. High Comr, Adelaide, 1967–71; FCO, 1971–76; Consul-Gen., Genoa, 1976–79. *Recreations:* music, gardening. *Died 20 Sept. 2006.*

JONES, Robert Brannock; Chairman, Redrow plc, since 2000 (Director, since 1997); Director, Freeport (formerly Freeport Leisure) plc, since 1998; *b* 26 Sept. 1950; *s* of late Ray Elwin Jones and of Iris Pamela Jones; *m* 1989, Jennifer Anne, *d* of late Lewis Emmanuel Sandercock and Iris Delphia Sandercock, Braunton, Devon. *Educ:* Merchant Taylors' Sch.; Univ. of St Andrews (MA Hons Modern History). Marketing Develt Exec., Tay Textiles Ltd, Dundee, 1974–76; Head of Res., NHBC, 1976–78;

Housing Policy Adviser, Conservative Central Office, 1978–79; Parly Adviser, Fedn of Civil Engrg Contractors, 1979–83. Member: St Andrews Burgh Council, 1972–75; Fife CC, 1973–75; Chiltern DC, 1979–83. Vice-Pres., Assoc. of Dist Councils, 1983–94. MP (C) Hertfordshire West, 1983–97; contested (C) Hemel Hempstead, 1997. Parly Under-Sec. of State, DoE, 1994–95; Minister of State (Minister for Construction, Planning and Energy Efficiency), DoE, 1995–97. Chairman: Environment Select Cttee, 1992–94 (Mem., 1983–94); Cons. Party Orgn Cttee, 1986–94. Vice-Pres., Wildlife Hosp. Trust, 1985–. Freeman, City of London; Liveryman, Merchant Taylors' Co. *Publications:* New Approaches to Housing, 1976; Watchdog: guide to the role of the district auditor, 1978; Ratepayers' Defence Manual, 1980; Town and Country Chaos: critique of the planning system, 1982. *Recreations:* music, gardening, food and wine. *Died 16 April 2007.*

JONES, Robert Hefin, CVO 1969; PhD; Under Secretary, Welsh Office, 1980–92; *b* 30 June 1932; *s* of late Owen Henry and Elizabeth Jones, Blaenau Ffestiniog. *Educ:* Ysgol Sir Ffestiniog; University Coll. of Wales, Aberystwyth (BSc); University of London (PhD). Asst Master, Whitgift Sch., 1957–63; HM Inspector of Schools (Wales), 1963; seconded to Welsh Office as Sec., Prince of Wales Investiture Cttee, and Personal Asst to the Earl Marshal, 1967; Welsh Office: Principal, 1969; Asst Sec. 1972; Hd, Educn Dept, 1980–92. Member: HEFCW, 1992–95; Council on Tribunals, 1993–99. Dir, WNO, 1992–94; Mem., Welsh Cttee, Live Music Now, 1992–2002. *Recreations:* music, reading, cooking. *Address:* 34 The Grange, Llandaff, Cardiff CF5 2LH. *T:* (029) 2056 4573. *Died 7 Dec. 2006.*

JONES, Robin Francis McN.; *see* McNab Jones.

JONES, Terence Leavesley; Under-Secretary, Department of the Environment, 1974–84; *b* 24 May 1926; *s* of late Reginald Arthur Jones and Grace Jones; *m* 1966, Barbara Hall (*d* 2001); one *s*. *Educ:* Nottingham High Sch.; Jesus Coll., Cambridge (MA). RNVR, 1944–46 (Sub-Lt). Asst Inspector of Ancient Monuments, Min. of Works, 1949; Principal, 1957; Sec., Historic Buildings Council for England, 1961–67; Asst Sec., 1967; on loan to Housing Corp., 1979–81. *Recreations:* music, archæology. *Address:* Meadow View, Woodlands Road, Mildenhall, Marlborough, Wilts SN8 2LP. *T:* (01672) 512481. *Died 9 April 2007.*

JONES, Thomas Glanville; barrister; a Recorder of the Crown Court, 1972–99; *b* 10 May 1931; *s* of late Evan James and Margaret Olive Jones; Welsh; *m* 1964, Valma Shirley Jones; three *s*. *Educ:* St Clement Dane's Grammar Sch.; University Coll., London (LLB). Called to Bar, 1956. Hd of Angel Chambers, 1972–. Chm., Jt Professional Cttees of Swansea Local Bar and Swansea Law Soc. and W Wales Law Soc., 1976–; Founder Mem. and Exec. Cttee Mem., Wales Medico-Legal Soc., 1990; Founder Mem. and Trustee, Swansea Legal Charitable Foundn, 1994. Exec. Mem., Swansea Festival of Music and the Arts, 1967; Pres., Guild for Promotion of Welsh Music, 1996– (Chm., 1970); Mem., Grand Theatre Trust, 1988–. *Recreations:* Welsh culture, Rugby, reading, music, poetry, gardening. *Address:* Gelligron, 12 Eastcliff, Southgate, Swansea SA3 2AS. *T:* (01792) 233118. *Club:* Ffynone (Swansea). *Died 16 Sept. 2008.*

JOYCE, William R., Jr; lawyer, since 1951; Director and Secretary-Treasurer, Battle of Britain Museum Foundation (USA), since 1976; President, Canterbury Institute Trust (USA), since 1989; Director and President, Hanaya Financial Corporation, Tokyo and Washington, since 1996; *b* 18 May 1921; *s* of William R. Joyce and Winifred Lowery; *m* 1956, Mary-Hoyt Sherman; one *s* two *d*. *Educ:* Loyola Univ. (BA); New York and Harvard Law Schs. JD. Lawyer, in private practice, New York City and Washington, DC; member of firm, Vance Joyce & Carbaugh, 1977–; Consul General *ad hon.*, Republic of Bolivia (Washington, DC), 1963–. Pres., Consular Corps of Washington, DC, 1982–. Mem., Bd of Dirs, Council on Egyptian-American Relns, 2000–. Lectr, Inter-American Defense Coll., Washington, 1970; Founder Mem., US Naval War Coll., Newport, RI, 1973. FRGS. Academician, Catholic Acad. of Scis, USA, 1999. Kt 1973, Kt Comdr (pro Merito Melitensi), Order of Malta, 1977; Kt, Equestrian Order of Holy Sepulchre, Jerusalem, 1976, KCHS 1999; Kt Comdr of Grace, Order of Constantine and S George (Borbon-Two Sicilies), Naples, 1977; Order of Condor of the Andes, Bolivia, 1978; Order of Simon Bolivar the Liberator, Bolivia, 1988. *Recreations:* sailing, golf. *Address:* (residence) 3700 Blackthorn Court, Chevy Chase, MD 20815–4942, USA. *T:* (301) 6573292. *Clubs:* The Brook, India House (New York City); Metropolitan, Chevy Chase (Washington); Cooperstown Country (New York); Royal Malta Yacht (Malta).   *Died 17 April 2007.*

JUDA, Annely, CBE 1998; Director, Annely Juda Fine Art, since 1967; *b* 23 Sept. 1914; *m* 1939, Paul Juda (marr. diss. 1955); one *s* two *d. Educ:* von Meysenburg Sch., Kassel; Reimann Art Sch., London. Founded: Molton Gall., 1960; Hamilton Gall., 1963; Annely Juda Fine Art, 1967. *Publications:* specialised catalogues. *Recreation:* skiing. *Club:* Teatro.   *Died 13 Aug. 2006.*

JUDD, Nadine; *see* Nerina, Nadia.

K

KAHN-ACKERMANN, Georg; Secretary General, Council of Europe, 1974–79; *b* 4 Jan. 1918; *m* 1945, Rosmarie Müller-Diefenbach; one *s* three *d*. *Educ:* in Germany and Switzerland. Served in Armed Forces, 1939–45. Press Reporter and Editor from 1946; Commentator with Radio Bavaria and wrote for newspaper, Abendzeitung, 1950. Author of several books, a publisher's reader, and mem. Exec. Cttee of Bavarian Assoc. of Journalists. Dir, VG WORT, Munich, 1972–74; Vice-Chm., Bd of Deutschlandfunk (Cologne). Mem., Social Democratic Party (SDP), from 1946, and of the German Federal Parliament, 1953–57, 1962–69 and 1970–74. Previous appts include: Vice-Pres., Western European Union Assembly, 1967–70; Chm., Political Commn of Western European Union, 1971–74; Vice-Pres., Consultative Assembly of Council of Europe until elected Secretary General in 1974. Mem. Council, Deutsche Welthunger hilfe; Pres., VG WORT. *Recreation:* ski-ing. *Address:* Sterzenweg 3, 82541 Ammerland, Bayern, Germany.   *Died 6 Sept. 2008.*

KAISER, Philip Mayer; political and economic consultant; *b* 12 July 1913; *s* of Morris Kaiser and Temma Kaiser (*née* Sloven); *m* 1939, Hannah Greeley; three *s*. *Educ:* University of Wisconsin; Balliol Coll., Oxford (Rhodes Scholar). Economist, Bd of Governors, Fed. Reserve System, 1939–42; Chief, Project Ops Staff, also Chief, Planning Staff, Bd Economic Warfare and Foreign Econ. Admin., 1942–46; Expert on Internat. Organization Affairs, US State Dept., 1946; Exec. Asst to Asst Sec. of Labor in charge of internat. labor affairs, US Dept of Labor, 1947–49; Asst Sec. of Labor for Internat. Labor Affairs, 1949–53; mem., US Govt Bd of Foreign Service, Dept of State, 1948–53; US Govt mem., Governing Body of ILO, 1948–53; Chief, US delegn to ILO Confs, 1949–53; Special Asst to Governor of New York, 1954–58; Prof. of Internat. Relations and Dir, Program for Overseas Labor and Industrial Relations, Sch. of Internat. Service, American Univ., 1958–61; US Ambassador, Republic of Senegal and Islamic Republic of Mauritania, 1961–64; Minister, Amer. Embassy, London, 1964–69; Chm., Encyclopaedia Britannica International Ltd, 1969–75; Dir, Guinness Mahon Holdings Ltd, 1975–77; US Ambassador to Hungary, 1977–80, to Austria, 1980–81. Member: US Govt Interdepartmental Cttee on Marshall Plan, 1947–48; Interdepartmental Cttee on Greek-Turkish aid and Point 4 Technical Assistance progs, 1947–49. Sen. Consultant, SRI International, 1981–97. Professorial Lectr, Johns Hopkins Sch. of Adv. Internat. Studies, 1983–84; Woodrow Wilson Vis. Fellow, Hartford Univ. of W Hartford, Connecticut, 1983. Board Member: Soros Hungarian Foundn; Amer. Ditchley Foundn; Council of Amer. Ambassadors; Amer. Acad. of Diplomacy; Inst. for Diplomatic Studies; Partners for Democratic Change; Member: Council on Foreign Relations; Washington Inst. of Foreign Affairs; IISS. *Publications:* Journeying Far and Wide: a political and diplomatic memoir, 1993. *Recreations:* tennis, swimming, music. *Address:* 2101 Connecticut Avenue NW, Washington, DC 20008, USA.   *Died 24 May 2007.*

KAMBA, Prof. Walter Joseph; Herbert Chitepo/ UNESCO Professor of Human Rights and Democracy, University of Zimbabwe, 2000; Distinguished Professor, Institute of Peace, Leadership and Governance, Africa University, Zimbabwe, since 2005; Founding Dean, and UNESCO Professor of Human Rights, Democracy and Law, Faculty of Law, University of Namibia, 1994–2000, then Emeritus Professor of Law; *b* 6 Sept. 1931; *s* of Joseph Mafara and Hilda Kamba; *m* 1960, Angeline Saziso Dube; two *s* (and one *s* decd). *Educ:* University of Cape Town (BA, LLB); Yale Law School (LLM). Attorney of the High Court of Rhodesia (later Zimbabwe), 1963–66; Research Fellow, Institute of Advanced Legal Studies, London Univ., 1967–68; Lecturer, then Sen. Lectr, in Comparative Law and Jurisprudence, 1969–80, Dean of the Faculty of Law, 1977–80, Univ. of Dundee; Prof. of Law, 1980–91, Vice-Prin., 1980–81, Vice-Chancellor, 1981–91, Univ. of Zimbabwe; Inaug. Dist. Knight Prof. of Law and Educn, Univ. of Manitoba, 1992; Inaug. UNESCO Africa Prof., Utrecht Univ., 1992–96. Chm., Kingstons (booksellers and distributors) (Zimbabwe), 1984–. Chm., Bd of Governors, Zimbabwe Broadcasting Corp., 1987 (Vice-Chm., 1980–87); Member: Public Service Professional Qualifications Panel, Harare, 1981–83; Council, ACU, 1981–83 (Member: Working Party on future policy, 1981; Budget Review Cttee, 1982–83); Commonwealth Standing Cttee on student mobility, 1981–88; Exec. Bd, Assoc. of African Univs, 1984 (Chm., Finance and Admin Cttee, 1985); Nat. Commn, Law and Popn Studies Project, Zimbabwe, 1986–; Chairman: Assoc. of Eastern and Southern African Univs, 1984–87; Bd, UNITWIN, 1992–; Vice-President: Internat. Assoc. of Univs, 1985–90; ACP-EEC Foundn for Cultural Co-op., Brussels, 1986–88; Mem., Zimbabwe Nat. Commn for UNESCO, 1987–. Mem., Univ. of Swaziland Commn on Planning, 1986. Legal Adviser, ZANU (Patriotic Front), until 1980; Chm., Electoral Supervisory Commn, 1984–94; Mem., S African Ind. Electoral Commn, 1994; Co-Chm., Malawi Nat. Constitutional Conf., 1995; Mem. Adv. Bd, Global Governance Review, 1994–. Trustee: Zimbabwe Mass Media Trust, 1981–; Conservation Trust of Zimbabwe, 1981–87; Legal Resources Foundn, Zimbabwe, 1984–90; African-American Inst., NY, 1985–; Zimbabwe Cambridge Trust, 1987–; Centre for Higher Educn Transformation, S Africa, 1995–; Internat. Trustee, Press Trust of Malawi, 1996–; Member: Bd of Trustees, Michael Gelfand Med. Res. Foundn, Zimbabwe, 1986–; Internat. Bd, United World Colls, 1985–87; Mem. Council: Univ. for Peace, Costa Rica, 1981–86; Univ. of Zambia, 1981–86; United Nations Univ., Tokyo, 1983–89 (Chm., Council, 1985–86; Mem., Cttee on Institutional and Programmatic Develt); Univ. of Lesotho, 1987–; Mem., Internat. Adv. Cttee, Synergos Inst., NY, 1987–; Patron, Commonwealth Legal Educn Assoc., 1986–; Governor, Ranche House Coll., Harare, 1980–; Member Board of Governors: Zimbabwe Inst. of Development Studies, 1981– (Chm. Bd, 1986–); Internat. Devclt Res. Centre, Canada, 1986–; Commonwealth of Learning, 1988– (Vice-Chm., 1989–); Member: St John's Ambulance Council for Republic of Zimbabwe, 1982–87; Ind. Internat. Commn on Health Res. for Develt, 1987–; Bd, Internat. Cttee for Study of Educnl Exchange, 1988–; Exec. Cttee, Internat. Devclt Res. Centre, Canada, 1989–. Hon. LLD: Dundee, 1982; Natal, 1995; Zimbabwe, 1998; Hon. DHL Rhode Is, 1991; Hon. DLett Charles Sturt, 1995. 50th anniv. Distinguished Service Award, Lesotho, 1995; Ten Years of Democracy Award, Ind. Electoral Commn, SA, 2004. Officier dans l'Ordre des Palmes Académiques (France). *Publications:* articles in Internat. and Comparative Law Quarterly, Juridical Review. *Recreation:* tennis. *Address:* Faculty of Law, University of Zimbabwe, PO Box MP 167, Mount Pleasant, Harare, Zimbabwe. *T:* (4) 333570, *Fax:* (4) 333563; *e-mail:* wkamba@yahoo.com.   *Died 18 May 2007.*

KANE, Prof. George, FBA 1968; Professor of English Language and Medieval Literature, 1965–76 and Head of English Department, 1968–76, King's College, London, Professor Emeritus, University of London, since 1976; *b* 4 July 1916; *o s* of George Michael and Clara Kane; *m* 1946, Katherine Bridget, *o d* of Lt-Col R. V. Montgomery, MC; one *d* (one *s* decd). *Educ:* St Peter's Coll.; British Columbia University; Toronto Univ.; University Coll.,

London. BA (University of BC), 1936; Research Fellow, University of Toronto, 1936–37; MA (Toronto), 1937; Research Fellow, Northwestern Univ., 1937–38; IODE Schol., for BC, 1938–39. Served War of 1939–45: Artists' Rifles, 1939–40; Rifle Bde, 1940–46 (despatches). PhD (London), 1946; Asst Lecturer in English, University Coll., London, 1946, Lecturer, 1948, Reader in English, 1953, Fellow, 1971; Prof. of English Language and Literature and Head of English Dept, Royal Holloway College, London Univ., 1955–65; William Rand Kenan Jr Prof. of English in Univ. of N Carolina at Chapel Hill, 1976–87, Chm. of Div. of Humanities, 1980–83, Prof. Emeritus, 1987–. Fellow, KCL, 1976. Vis. Prof., Medieval Acad. of America, 1970, 1982, Corresp. Fellow, 1975, Fellow, 1978; Fellow: Amer. Acad. of Arts and Scis, 1977–91 (resigned); Nat. Humanities Center, 1987–88; Sen. Fellow, Southeastern Inst. of Medieval and Renaissance Studies, 1978. Member: Council, Early English Text Soc., 1969–88; Governing Body, SOAS, 1970–76; Council, British Acad., 1974–76; Governing Body, Univ. of N Carolina Press, 1979–84. Sir Israel Gollancz Memorial Prize, British Acad., 1963, 1999; Haskins Medallist, Med. Acad. of Amer., 1978. Lectures: Chambers Meml, UCL, 1965; Accademia Nazionale dei Lincei, Rome, 1976; John Coffin Meml, Univ. of London, 1979; M. W. Bloomfield Meml, Harvard, 1989; Tucker-Cruse Meml, Bristol Univ., 1991; Public Orator, Univ. of London, 1962–66; Annual Chaucer Lectr, New Chaucer Soc., 1980. Gen. editor of London Edn of Piers Plowman. *Publications:* Middle English Literature, 1951; (ed) Piers Plowman, the A Version, 1960, the B Version, 1975, the C Version, 1997; Piers Plowman: The Evidence for Authorship, 1965; Geoffrey Chaucer, 1984; Chaucer and Langland, 1989; (ed) Chaucer, The Legend of Good Women, 1995; Piers Plowman Glossary, 2005; articles and reviews. *Recreation:* fishing. *Clubs:* Athenæum, Flyfishers'. *Died 27 Dec. 2008.*

KANE, Col John Mark, CMG 2002; OBE 1994; Defence Attaché, Harare, since 2005; *b* 8 Aug. 1954; *s* of Dr John Edward Kane and Margaret Mary Kane; *m* 1976, Moira Clark Chalmers; one *d. Educ:* Thames Valley Grammar Sch.; RMA, Sandhurst; RMCS; Army Staff Coll., Camberley. Commnd RCT, 1974; regtl duty, Germany, UK, NI, Cyprus; Army Staff Course, 1985–86; OC 6 Sqdn RCT, Germany and Ireland, 1989–90; Defence Intelligence Staff, 1991–94; CO 1 Gen. Support Regt RLC, Germany and Bosnia, 1994–97; Liaison Officer, US Army Combined Arms Centre, 1998–2000; Mem., NATO Special Negotiating Teams, Serbia and Macedonia, 2001; Chief, Current Intelligence and Warning Br., HQ NATO, 2000–03; Exec. Dir, Kofi Annan Internat. Peacekeeping Trng Centre, Accra, Ghana, 2003–05. *Recreations:* golf, ski-ing, running. *Address:* British Embassy, 7th Floor, Corner House, Cnr Samora Machel Avenue/Leopold Takawira Street, PO Box 4490, Harare, Zimbabwe; *e-mail:* johnandmoira@hotmail.com. *Died 8 Sept. 2008.*

KAPI, Hon. Sir Mari, KCMG 2008; Kt 1988; CBE 1983; Chief Justice of Papua New Guinea, 2003–08 (Deputy Chief Justice, 1982–2003); a Justice of the Court of Appeal: Solomon Islands, 1982; Fiji, 1992; *b* 12 Dec. 1950; *s* of Kapi 'Ila and Mea Numa; *m* 1973, Tegana Kapi; three *s* three *d. Educ:* Univ. of Papua New Guinea (LLB); SOAS, Univ. of London (LLM). Admitted to practice in PNG and Australia, 1974. Dep. Public Solicitor, 1976; Associate Public Solicitor, 1977; Public Solicitor, 1978; a Judge of Nat. and Supreme Courts of PNG, 1979. Cross of Solomon Islands, 1994. *Recreations:* tennis, touch Rugby. *Address:* PO Box 7018, Boroko, Papua New Guinea. *T:* 3259273. *Died 25 March 2009.*

KAPLICKY, Jan; Founder and Partner, Future Systems, since 1979; *b* Prague, 18 April 1937; *s* of Josef Kaplicky and Jirina Kaplicka (*née* Florova); *m* 1991, Amanda Levete (marr. diss. 2006); one *s; m* 2007, Eliska Fuchsova; one *d. Educ:* Coll. of Applied Arts and Architecture, Prague (DipArch 1962). Architect: private practice, Prague, 1964–68; Denys Lasdun & Partners, 1969–71; Piano &

Rogers, 1971–73; Spencer & Webster, 1974–75 (Associate); Foster & Partners, 1977–83. *Projects* include: Space Station Wardroom Table (NASA Cert. of Recognition, 1989); MOMI Tent, 1991 (British Construction Industry Award, 1992); Stonehenge Visitor Centre (AJ/Bovis Royal Acad. Award), 1993; Hauer-King House, London, 1994 (Aluminium Imagination Award, Civic Trust, 1996); West India Quay Bridge, Canary Wharf, 1995 (Millennium Product Award, Civic Trust, and RIBA Award, 1998); Wild at Heart flower shop (RIBA Award), 1998; Comme des Garçons, NY and Tokyo, 1999; NatWest Media Centre, Lord's Cricket Ground (Millennium Product Award, and Aluminium Imagination Award, Civic Trust; Stirling Prize, RIBA), 1999; Marni shops, London, Milan, Tokyo, Paris, NY, 1999; Selfridges, Birmingham, 2003; Czech Nat. Liby, 2007. *Exhibitions* include: RIBA, 1982, 1991; Arch. Assoc., London, 1987; Storefront, NY, 1992; New Urban Environments, Tokyo, 1998; ICA, 1998, 2005; Nat. Gall., Prague, 1999; The Cube, Manchester, 1999; FS Originals, Faggionato Fine Arts, 2001. Broadcasts on TV and radio. *Publications:* For Inspiration Only, 1996; More for Inspiration Only, 1999; Confessions, 2002; Czech Inspiration, 2005; *relevant publications:* Future Systems, 1987; Future Systems: the story of tomorrow, 1993; Future Systems, ed M. Field, 1999; Unique Building, 2001; Sketches, 2005; Future Systems, by Deyan Sudjic, 2006; exhibn catalogues; articles in jls throughout the world. *Recreation:* history of modern architecture. *Address:* Future Systems, 20 Victoria Gardens, W11 3PE. *T:* (020) 7243 7670. *Club:* Architecture. *Died 14 Jan. 2009.*

KARMEL, Prof. Peter Henry, AC 1976; CBE 1967; Chairman, National Institute of the Arts, Australian National University, 1992–2003; Professor Emeritus, University of Adelaide, 1965; *b* 9 May 1922; *s* of Simeon Karmel; *m* 1946, Lena Garrett; one *s* five *d. Educ:* Caulfield Grammar Sch.; Univ. of Melbourne (BA); Trinity Coll., Cambridge (PhD). Research Officer, Commonwealth Bureau of Census and Statistics, 1943–45; Lectr in Econs, Univ. of Melbourne, 1946; Rouse Ball Res. Student, Trinity Coll., Cambridge, 1947–48; Sen. Lectr in Econs, Univ. of Melbourne, 1949; Prof. of Econs, Univ. of Adelaide, 1950–62; Principal-designate, Univ. of Adelaide at Bedford Park (subseq. Flinders Univ. of SA), 1961–66; Vice-Chancellor, Flinders Univ. of SA, 1966–71; Chancellor, Univ. of Papua and New Guinea, 1969–70 (Chm., Interim Council, 1965–69); Chairman: Univs Commn, 1971–77; Commonwealth Tertiary Educn Commn, 1977–82; Vice-Chancellor, ANU, 1982–87. Chairman: Aust. Inst. of Health, 1987–92; Nat. Council on AIDS, 1988–92. Mem. Council, Univ. of Adelaide, 1955–69; Vis. Prof. of Econs, Queen's Univ., Belfast, 1957–58; Mem. Commonwealth Cttee: on Future of Tertiary Educn, 1961–65; of Economic Enquiry, 1963–65; Mem., Australian Council for Educn Research, 1968– (Pres., 1979–99); Chairman: Cttee of Enquiry into Educn in SA, 1969–70; Interim Cttee for Aust. Schools Commn, 1972–73; Cttee of Enquiry on Med. Schs, 1972–73; Cttee of Enquiry on Open Univ., 1973–74; Australia Council, 1974–77; Cttee on Post-Secondary Educn in Tasmania, 1975–76; Quality of Educn Review Cttee, 1984–85; Member: Commonwealth Govt Cttee to Review Efficiency and Effectiveness in Higher Educn, 1985–86; Adv. Cttee of Cities Commn, 1972–74; CSIRO Adv. Council, 1979–82; Australian Stats Adv. Council, 1988–97. Leader, OECD Review of US Educn Policy, 1978–79 and NZ Educn Policy, 1982. Chm., Canberra Inst. of the Arts, 1988–91. Mem. Council, Chinese Univ. of Hong Kong, 1990–94. FASSA 1952 (Pres., 1987–90); FACE 1969. Hon. LLD: Univ. of Papua and New Guinea, 1970; Univ. of Melbourne, 1975; Univ. of Queensland, 1985; ANU, 1996; Hon. LittD Flinders Univ. of SA, 1971; Hon. DLit Murdoch Univ., 1975; Hon. DLitt Macquarie, 1992; DU Newcastle, NSW, 1978. Mackie Medal, 1975; Aust. Coll. of Educn Medal, 1981. *Publications:* Applied Statistics for Economists, 1957, 1962 (1970 edn with M. Polasek, 4th edn 1977),

Portuguese edn, 1972; (with M. Brunt) Structure of the Australian Economy, 1962, repr. 1963, 1966; (with G. C. Harcourt and R. H. Wallace) Economic Activity, 1967 (Italian edn 1969); articles in Economic Record, Population Studies, Jl Royal Statistical Assoc., Australian Jl of Education, and other learned jls. *Address:* 4/127 Hopetoun Circuit, Canberra, ACT 2600, Australia.
Died 30 Dec. 2008.

KATZIR, Prof. Ephraim (Katchalski), PhD; Institute Professor, Weizmann Institute of Science, since 1978; President, State of Israel, 1973–78; *b* Kiev, Ukraine, 16 May 1916; *s* of Yehuda and Tsila Katchalski; *m* 1938, Nina Gotlieb (*d* 1986); one *s* (two *d* decd). *Educ:* Rehavia High Sch., Jerusalem; Hebrew Univ., Jerusalem (chemistry, botany, zool., bacteriol.; MSc *summa cum laude* 1937; PhD 1941). Settled in Israel with parents, 1922; involved in Labour youth movement; Inf. Comdr, Jewish Self-Defence Forces (Hagana). Asst, Dept of Theoretical and Macromolecular Chem., Hebrew Univ., 1941–45; Res. Fellow, Polytechnic Inst., and Columbia Univ., NY, 1946–48; Actg Head, Dept of Biophys., Weizmann Inst. of Science, Rehovot, Israel, 1949–51, Head 1951–73 (mem. founding faculty of Inst.); Chief Scientist, Israel Def. Min., 1966–68; Head, Dept of Biotechnology, Tel Aviv Univ., 1980–88. Vis. Prof. of Biophys., Hebrew Univ., 1953–61; Guest Scientist, Harvard Univ., 1957–59; Vis. Prof., Rockefeller Univ., NY, and Univ. of Mich, Ann Arbor, 1961–65; Sen. Foreign Scientist Fellowship, UCLA, 1964; Battelle Seattle Res. Center, Washington, 1971; Regents Prof., Univ. of Calif., San Diego, 1979; First Herman F. Mark Chair in Polymer Sci., Poly. Inst., NY, 1979. President: World ORT Union, 1986–90; Cobiotech, 1989–95. Member: Biochem. Soc. of Israel; Israel Acad. of Sciences and Humanities; Israel Chem. Soc.; Council, Internat. Union of Biochem.; AAAS; Assoc. of Harvard Chemists; Leopoldina Acad. of Science, Germany; World Acad. of Art and Science; New York Acad. of Science (Life Mem.). Centennial Foreign Fellow, Amer. Chem. Soc.; For. Associate, Nat. Acad. of Sciences of USA. For. Member: The Royal Soc.; Amer. Philosoph. Soc.; Acad. des Scis, France, 1989. Hon. Fellow, Scientific Acad. of Argentina, 1986; Hon. Member: Amer. Acad. of Arts and Sciences; Amer. Soc. of Biol Chemists; Harvey Soc.; Romanian Acad. of Scis, 1991; Hon. MRI 1989. Hon. PhD: Hebrew Univ., 1973; Poly. Inst. of NY, 1975; Brandeis Univ., Univ. of Mich, and Hebrew Union Coll., 1975; Weizmann Inst. of Science, 1976; Northwestern Univ., Evanston, 1978; Harvard, 1978; McGill, 1980; ETH Zurich, 1980; Thomas Jefferson, 1981; Oxford, 1981; Miami, 1983; Technion, Israel Inst. of Technology, 1983; Univ. of Buenos Aires, 1986. Tchernikhovski Prize, 1948; Weizmann Prize, 1950; Israel Prize in Nat. Sciences, 1959; Rothschild Prize in Nat. Sciences, 1961; Linderstrøm Lang Gold Medal, 1969; Hans Krebs Medal, 1972; Alpha Omega Achievement Medal, 1979; Underwood Prescott Award, MIT, 1982; first Japan Prize, Science and Technol. Foundn of Japan, 1985; Internat. Enzyme Engineering Award, 1987. Hon. Founding Editor, Biopolymers, 1986– (Mem., Editorial Bd, 1963–86). Comdr, Legion of Honour (France), 1990. *Address:* Weizmann Institute of Science, Rehovot 76100, Israel. *Died 30 May 2009.*

KAUSIMAE, Sir David, KBE 1995 (OBE 1974); Founder and Deputy Chairman, Pacific Asia Evangelical Association, since 1976; *b* Solomon Is, 12 Oct. 1931; *s* of Joe Poraiwai and Patricia Hagar Keraapu; *m* 1951, Bethezel Kalifera; three *s* three *d*. No formal educn. MLC, Solomon Is, 1965–67; Member: Exec. Council, 1966; Forestry Rev. Cttee, 1968–69; Select Cttee on Tourist Bill, 1969–70; Governing Council, 1970–74; Chm., Natural Resources, Commerce and Industry, 1970–74; MLA, 1974–77; Minister of Foreign Trade, Commerce and Industry, 1974–75; Mem., Constitutional Cttee, 1975–76; Dep. Speaker, Nat. Parlt, 1976–77; Chairman: Special Cttee on Provincial Govt, 1977–79; Electoral Rev. Cttee, 1995; Mem., Police Force Rev. Cttee, 1989–90. Founder Mem., People's Alliance Party, 1976 (Pres., 1976). Chairman: Ports Authy, 1981–84 and

1989–91; Tourist Authy, 1991. Pres., S Pacific Ports Assoc., 1982–83. Chairman: 'Are'Are Maasina Develt Co. Ltd, 1970–80; Solomon Wholesale Union Ltd, 1972–73; Maasina Enterprises Ltd, 1973–74; Solomon Is Investment Ltd, 1973–75; Property Develt Co. Ltd, 1985–94; Sasape Mariner Ltd, 1985–86; Solomon Taiyo Ltd, 1986–87; Burns Philp Toyota (SI) Ltd, 1993–; Director: Concrete Industry Ltd, 1980–82; Central Bank of Solomon Is, 1990–92; Island Hotels Ltd, 1994–; King Solomon Hotel Ltd, 1994–; Gizo Hotel Ltd, 1994–. Chm., Praise the Lord Corp. Ltd, 1995–. Mem. Exec. Council, South Seas Evangelical Ch, 1972–73. Life Mem., CPA, 1966. *Address:* PO Box 335, Honiara, Solomon Islands; Maasina Hill, via Kiu Postal Agency, West 'Are'Are, Malaita Province, Solomon Islands. *T:* 22959. *Clubs:* Honiara Golf; Lions (Guadalcanal).
Died 14 Sept. 2007.

KAWHARU, Prof. Sir (Ian) Hugh, ONZ 2002; Kt 1989; FRSNZ 1994; Professor, Maori Studies, and Head of Department of Anthropology, 1985–93, Professor Emeritus, and Director, James Henare Maori Research Centre, 1993–95, University of Auckland; *b* 18 Feb. 1927; *s* of Wiremu and Janet Paora Kawharu; *m* 1st, 1957, Nina; three *d*; 2nd, 1970, Freda; two *d*. *Educ:* Univ. of New Zealand (BSc); Emmanuel Coll., Cambridge (MA); DPhil Oxon (Hon. Fellow, Exeter Coll., Oxford, 1993). Dept of Maori Affairs, housing, welfare and trust admin, variously, 1953–65; Lectr, Dept of Anthropology, Univ. of Auckland, 1965–70; Prof. (personal chair), Social Anthropology and Maori Studies, Massey Univ., 1970–84. Consultant: FAO, 1961–63; NZ Govt, 1968–; Unesco, 1974–76; NZ Council for Educnl Res., 1976–89; NZ Maori Council, 1981–. Chm., Ngati Whatua Tribal Trusts, 1978–; Member: NZ Nat. Commn for Unesco, 1969–73; Royal Commn on the Courts, 1976–78; Waitangi Tribunal, 1986–94; Bd of Maori Affairs, 1987–90; Trust Bd, Auckland War Meml Mus., 1997–. Pres., Polynesian Soc., 1993–. Patron, Pitt-Rivers Mus. Soc., Oxford, 1991–. *Publications:* Orakei, a Ngati Whatua Community, 1975; Maori Land Tenure, 1977; (ed. and co-author): Administration in New Zealand's Multiracial Society, 1967; Conflict and Compromise, 1975; Trends in Ethnic Group Relations in Asia and Oceania, 1979; Waitangi: Maori and Pakeha Perspectives of the Treaty of Waitangi, 1989; contrib. to 10 vols of Waitangi Tribunal reports. *Recreation:* music. *Address:* University of Auckland, Private Bag 92019, Auckland, New Zealand. *T:* (9) 3737999.
Died 19 Sept. 2006.

KAY, Prof. Humphrey Edward Melville, MD, FRCP, FRCPath; Haematologist, Royal Marsden Hospital, 1956–84; Professor of Haematology. University of London, 1982–84 (Professor Emeritus, since 1984); *b* 10 Oct. 1923; *s* of late Rev. Arnold Innes and Winifred Julia Kay; *m* 1st, 1950, April Grace Lavinia Powlett (*d* 1990); one *s* two *d*; 2nd, 1996, Sallie Diana (*née* Charlton), *widow* of Roy Perry, RI. *Educ:* Bryanston Sch.; St Thomas's Hospital. MB, BS 1945. RAFVR, 1947–49; junior appts at St Thomas's Hosp., 1950–56. Sec., MRC Cttee on Leukaemia, 1968–84; Dean, Inst. of Cancer Research, 1970–72. Editor, Jl Clinical Pathology, 1972–80. Member: Council, Wiltshire Wildlife Trust (formerly Wiltshire Trust for Nature Conservation), 1983–96; Nat. Badger Adv. Panel, 1988–98. Christopher Cadbury Medal, Wildlife Trusts, 1996. *Publications:* Poems Polymorphic, 2002; Survey of Wiltshire Hedgehogs, 2002; papers and chapters on blood diseases, etc. *Recreation:* natural history including gardening. *Address:* New Mill Cottage, Pewsey, Wilts SN9 5LD.
Died 20 Oct. 2009.

KAYE, Michael, OBE 1991; General Administrator, Young Concert Artists Trust, 1983–92; Festival Director, City of London Festival, 1984–94; *b* 27 Feb. 1925; *s* of Harry Kaye and Annie Steinberg; *m* 1st, 1950, Muriel Greenberg (marr. diss. 1959); one *d*; 2nd, 1962, Fay Bercovitch. *Educ:* Malmesbury Road, Bow; Cave Road, Plaistow; Water Lane, Stratford; West Ham Secondary

Sch., E15. Served in Army, REME and Intelligence Corps, 1943–47. Journalism and Public Relations, 1947–53; Marketing and Public Relations in tobacco industry, 1953–61; PR Manager, later PR Director, Carreras-Rothmans, 1961–76; Director, Peter Stuyvesant Foundation, 1963–76; General Administrator, Rupert Foundn, 1972–76; Man. Dir, London Symphony Orchestra, 1976–80; Arts Dir, GLC, and Gen. Administrator, S Bank Concert Halls, 1980–83. Chm., Educn Cttee, British Assoc. of Concert Agents, 1989–92; Member: Exec. Cttee, Carl Flesch Internat. Violin Competition, 1984–95; Council, Centre for Study of Judaism and Jewish/Christian Relations, 1989–94. Trustee: Whitechapel Art Gallery, 1964–75; Youth & Music, 1970–78; A. M. Purnell Charitable Trust, 1994– (Trustee, 1994–, Chm., 1997–2001, Bath Mozartfest). Vice-Pres., Piano Trio Soc., 2000–02. *Recreations*: photography, music (clarinet). *Address*: 3 Coppice Way, E18 2DU. *T*: (020) 8989 1281. *Died 3 May 2008.*

KAYSEN, Prof. Carl; David W. Skinner Professor of Political Economy, Massachusetts Institute of Technology, 1977–90, then Emeritus (Director, Program in Science, Technology, and Society, 1981–87); *b* 5 March 1920; *s* of Samuel and Elizabeth Kaysen; *m* 1st, 1940, Annette Neutra (*d* 1990); two *d*; 2nd, 1994, Ruth Butler. *Educ*: Philadelphia Public Schs; Overbrook High Sch., Philadelphia; Pennsylvania, Columbia and Harvard Univs. AB Pa 1940; MA 1947, PhD 1954, Harvard. Nat. Bureau of Economic Research, 1940–42; Office of Strategic Services, Washington, 1942–43; Intelligence Officer, US Army Air Force, 1943–45; State Dept, Washington, 1945. Dep. Special Asst to President, 1961–63. Harvard University, 1947–66: Teaching Fellow in Econs, 1947; Asst Prof. of Economics, 1950–55; Assoc. Prof. of Economics 1955–57; Prof. of Economics. 1957–66; Assoc. Dean, Graduate Sch. of Public Administration, 1960–66; Lucius N. Littauer Prof. of Political Economy, 1964–66; Jr Fellow, Soc. of Fellows, 1947–50, Actg Sen. Fellow, 1957–58, 1964–65; Syndic, Harvard Univ. Press, 1964–66; Dir, Inst. for Advanced Study, Princeton, NJ, 1966–76, Dir Emeritus, 1976; Vice Chm., and Dir of Research, Sloan Commn on Govt and Higher Educn, 1977–79. Sen. Fulbright Res. Schol., LSE, 1955–56. Trustee: Pennsylvania Univ., 1967–; Russell Sage Foundn, 1979–89. *Publications*: United States *v* United Shoe Machinery Corporation, an Economic Analysis of an Anti-Trust Case, 1956; The American Business Creed (with others), 1956; Anti-Trust Policy (with D. F. Turner), 1959; The Demand for Electricity in the United States (with F. M. Fisher), 1962; The Higher Learning, The Universities, and The Public, 1969; (contrib.) Nuclear Energy Issues and Choices, 1979; A Program for Renewed Partnership (Sloan Commn on Govt and Higher Educn Report), 1980; (ed jtly and contrib.) Emerging Norms of Justified Intervention, 1995; (ed) The American Corporation Today, 1996; numerous articles on economic theory, applied economics, higher education, military strategy and arms control. *Address*: E38–614, Massachusetts Institute of Technology, Cambridge, MA 02139, USA. *Died 8 Feb. 2010.*

KEANE, Major Sir Richard (Michael), 6th Bt *cr* 1801; farmer; *b* 29 Jan. 1909; *s* of Sir John Keane, 5th Bart, DSO, and Lady Eleanor Hicks-Beach (*d* 1960), *e d* of 1st Earl St Aldwyn; *S* father, 1956; *m* 1939, Olivia Dorothy Hawkshaw (*d* 2002); two *s* one *d*. *Educ*: Sherborne Sch.; Christ Church, Oxford. Diplomatic Correspondent to Reuters 1935–37; Diplomatic Corresp. and Asst to Editor, Sunday Times, 1937–39. Served with County of London Yeomanry and 10th Royal Hussars, 1939–44; Liaison Officer (Major) with HQ Vojvodina, Yugoslav Partisans, 1944; attached British Military Mission, Belgrade, 1944–45. Publicity Consultant to Imperial Chemical Industries Ltd, 1950–62. *Publications*: Germany: What Next?, (Penguin Special), 1939; Modern Marvels of Science (editor), 1961. *Recreation*: fishing. *Heir*: *s* John Charles Keane [*b* 16 Sept. 1941; *m* 1977, Corinne, *d* of Jean Everard de Harzir; two *s* one *d*]. *Address*: Cappoquin

House, Cappoquin, County Waterford, Ireland. *T*: (58) 54004. *Club*: Kildare Street and University (Dublin). *Died 28 Dec. 2010.*

KEATINGE, Prof. William Richard, PhD; FRCP; Professor of Physiology, Queen Mary and Westfield College, 1990–96, then Emeritus (Dean of Basic Medical Sciences, 1991–94); Emeritus Professor, University College London; *b* 18 May 1931; *s* of Sir Edgar Keatinge, CBE; *m* 1st, 1955, M. E. Annette Hegarty (*d* 2000); one *s* two *d*; 2nd, 2005, Lynette Nelson. *Educ*: Upper Canada Coll.; Rugby Sch.; Cambridge Univ. (MA); St Thomas's Hospital (MB BChir). FRCP 1991. House Phys., St Thomas's Hospital, 1955–56; Surg.-Lt RN (Nat. Service), 1956–58; Dir of Studies in Medicine, Pembroke Coll., Cambridge, 1958–60; Fellow, Cardiovascular Research Inst., San Francisco, 1960–61; MRC appt Radcliffe Infirmary, Oxford, 1961–68; Fellow of Pembroke Coll., Oxford, 1965–68; Reader in Physiology, 1968–71, Prof. of Physiol., 1971–90, London Hosp. Med. Coll. *Publications*: Survival in Cold Water, 1969; Local Mechanisms Controlling Blood Vessels, 1980; chapters in textbooks of physiology and medicine; papers in physiological and medical jls on temperature regulation and on control of blood vessels. *Recreations*: dinghy sailing, archaeology. *Address*: University College London, Hampstead Campus, Rowland Hill Street, NW3 2PF. *Died 11 April 2008.*

KEEBLE, Sir (Herbert Ben) Curtis, GCMG 1982 (KCMG 1978, CMG 1970); HM Diplomatic Service, retired; Ambassador at Moscow, 1978–82; *b* 18 Sept. 1922; *s* of Herbert Keeble and Gertrude Keeble, BEM; *m* 1947, Margaret Fraser; two *d* (and one *d* decd). *Educ*: Clacton County High Sch.; London University. Served HM Forces, 1942–47. Entered HM Foreign (subsequently Diplomatic) Service, 1947; served in Jakarta, 1947–49; Foreign Office, 1949–51; Berlin, 1951–54; Washington, 1954–58; Foreign Office, 1958–63; Counsellor and Head of European Economic Organisations Dept, 1963–65; Counsellor (Commercial), Berne, 1965–68; Minister, Canberra, 1968–71; Asst Under-Sec. of State, FCO, 1971–73; HM Ambassador, German Democratic Republic, 1974–76; Dep. Under Sec. of State (Chief Clerk), FCO, 1976–78. Special Adviser, H of C Foreign Affairs Cttee, 1985–86. A Governor, BBC, 1985–90. Chairman: Britain-Russia Centre (formerly GB-USSR Assoc.), 1985–95 (Vice Pres., 1995–2000); Foundn for Accountancy and Financial Management, 1993–2000; Thames Ditton Hosp. Foundn, 1996–2000; Member Council: RIIA, 1985–90; SSEES, 1985–90. *Publications*: (ed) The Soviet State, 1985; Britain and The Soviet Union, 1917–1989, 1990; (contrib.) Harold Macmillan: aspects of a political life, 1999; Britain, Russia and the Soviet Union, 2000. *Recreations*: sailing, painting. *Address*: Dormers, St Leonards Road, Thames Ditton, Surrey KT7 0RR. *T*: (020) 8398 7778. *Club*: Royal Over-Seas League. *Died 6 Dec. 2008.*

KEIR, James Dewar; QC 1980; Director, Open University Educational Enterprises Ltd, 1983–88; Chairman, City and East London Family Practitioner Committee, 1985–89; part-time Member, Monopolies and Mergers Commission, 1987–92; *b* 30 Nov. 1921; *s* of David Robert Keir and Elizabeth Lunan (*née* Ross); *m* 1948, Jean Mary, *e d* of Rev. and Mrs E. P. Orr; two *s* two *d*. *Educ*: Edinburgh Acad.; Christ Church, Oxford (MA 1948). Served War, 1941–46: ME, Italy; Captain, The Black Watch (RHR). Called to the Bar, Inner Temple, 1949; Yarborough-Anderson Scholar, Inner Temple, 1950. Legal Adviser, United Africa Co. Ltd, 1954–66, Sec., 1966; Dep. Head of Legal Services, Unilever Ltd, 1973; Jt Sec., Unilever PLC and Unilever NV, 1976–84; Dir, UAC Internat. Ltd, 1973–77. Chm., 1969–72, Pres., 1980–82, Bar Assoc. for Commerce, Finance and Industry; Member: Bar Council, 1971–73; Senate of Inns of Ct and Bar, 1973–78. Chairman: Pharmacists Rev. Panel, 1986–97; Professional Cttee, Royal Coll. of Speech and Language Therapists,

1993–2001. *Recreations:* watching Rugby and ski-ing, active in opera, reading. *Address:* 15 Clays Close, East Grinstead, West Sussex RH19 4DJ. *T:* (01342) 323189. *Club:* Caledonian. *Died 18 Oct. 2009.*

KELLAS, Arthur Roy Handasyde, CMG 1964; HM Diplomatic Service, retired; High Commissioner in Tanzania, 1972–74; *b* 6 May 1915; *s* of Henry Kellas and Mary Kellas (*née* Brown); *m* 1952, Katharine Bridget, *d* of Sir John Le Rougetel, KCMG, MC; two *s* one *d. Educ:* Aberdeen Grammar Sch.; Aberdeen Univ.; Oxford Univ.; Ecole des Sciences Politiques. Passed into Diplomatic Service, Sept. 1939. Commissioned into Border Regt, Nov. 1939. War of 1939–45: Active Service with 1st Bn Parachute Regt and Special Ops, Africa and Greece, 1941–44 (despatches twice). Third Sec., HM Embassy, Tehran, 1944–47; First Sec., HM Legation, Helsingfors, 1948–50; First Sec. (press), HM Embassy, Cairo, 1951–52; First Sec., HM Embassy, Baghdad, 1954–58; Counsellor, HM Embassy, Tehran, 1958–62; Imperial Defence Coll., 1963–64; Counsellor, HM Embassy and Consul-Gen., Tel Aviv, 1964–65; Ambassador to Nepal, 1966–70, to Democratic Yemen, 1970–72. Pres., Britain-Nepal Soc., 1975–79. *Publications:* Down to Earth (war memoir of parachute subaltern), 1990; Ready Steady Go (pre-war reminiscences), 1999. *Recreations:* reading, reviewing books. *Address:* Inverockle, Achateny, Acharacle, Argyll PH36 4LG. *T:* (01972) 510265. *Club:* Oxford and Cambridge. *Died 6 March 2007.*

KELLY, Rt Hon. Sir Basil; *see* Kelly, Rt Hon. Sir J. W. B.

KELLY, Edward Ronald; journalist and trout farmer; *b* 14 Oct. 1928; *s* of late William Walter Kelly and of Millicent Kelly; *m* 1954, Storm Massada. *Educ:* Honiton Sch. Journalist: Bath Evening Chronicle, 1952; East African Standard, 1953; Sunday Post, Kenya, 1954; Reuters, 1956; Central Office of Information, 1958–84: Editor in Chief, Overseas Press Services Div., 1964; Asst Overseas Controller, 1968; Dir, Publications and Design Services Div., 1970; Home Controller, 1976; Overseas Controller, 1978–84. Chm., Assoc. of Stillwater Game Fishery Managers, 1993–96. *Recreations:* fishing, fly-tying, carpentry. *Address:* Windover House, Runcton Lane, Runcton, near Chichester, West Sussex PO20 1PT. *T:* (01243) 783069. *Club:* Flyfishers'. *Died 15 Feb. 2010.*

KELLY, Rt Hon. Sir (John William) Basil, Kt 1984; PC 1984; PC (NI) 1969; a Lord Justice of Appeal, Supreme Court of Judicature, Northern Ireland, 1984–95; a Judge of the High Court of Justice in Northern Ireland, 1973–84; *b* 10 May 1920; *o s* of late Thomas William Kelly and late Emily Frances (*née* Donaldson); *m* 1957, Pamela, *o d* of late Thomas Colmer and Marjorie Colthurst; one step *d. Educ:* Methodist Coll., Belfast; Trinity Coll., Dublin. BA (Mod.) Legal Science, 1943; LLB (Hons) 1944. Called to Bar: Inn of Court of N Ireland, 1944 (Bencher, 1968); Middle Temple, 1970 (Bencher, 2002). QC (N Ireland) 1958. MP (U) Mid-Down, Parliament of Northern Ireland, 1964–72; Attorney-Gen. for Northern Ireland, 1968–72. Chairman: Council of Legal Educn, NI, 1989–93; Judicial Studies Bd, NI, 1993–95; Mem., Law Adv. Cttee, British Council, 1982–92. *Recreations:* golf, music. *Died 5 Dec. 2008.*

KELLY, Peter (John); Under-Secretary for Atomic Energy, United Kingdom Department of Energy, 1980–82; *b* 26 Nov. 1922; *s* of Thomas and Lucy Kelly; *m* 1949, Gudrun Kelly (*née* Falck); two *s* three *d* (and one *s* decd). *Educ:* Downside; Oxford Univ. (BA). RNVR, 1942–46. 3rd Secretary, Moscow Embassy, 1948–49; journalism, 1950; rejoined public service, 1956; posts in Foreign Office, Defence Dept, Dept of Trade and Industry; Asst Secretary for Internat. Atomic Affairs, 1969–71; Counsellor, Office of UK Permanent Representative to the European Communities, Brussels, 1972–75; Director, Internat. Energy Agency, 1976–79.

Publications: Safeguards in Europe, 1985. *Recreations:* walking, music. *Address:* 2 The Crouch, Seaford, Sussex BN25 1PX. *T:* (01323) 896881. *Died 9 May 2009.*

KELSALL, William, OBE 1971; QPM 1969; DL; Chief Constable of Cheshire, 1974–77; *b* 10 Jan. 1914. DL Cheshire, 1979. CStJ 1983. *Address:* Three Keys Cottage, Quarry Bank, Utkinton, Tarporley, Cheshire CW6 0LA. *T:* (01829) 732328. *Died 19 May 2006.*

KELVEDON, Baron *cr* 1997 (Life Peer), of Ongar in the co. of Essex; **Henry Paul Guinness Channon;** PC 1980; *b* 9 Oct. 1935; *o s* of late Sir Henry Channon, MP, and of late Lady Honor Svejdar (*née* Guinness), *e d* of 2nd Earl of Iveagh, KG; *m* 1963, Ingrid Olivia Georgia Guinness (*née* Wyndham); one *s* one *d* (and one *d* decd). *Educ:* Lockers Park, Hemel Hempstead; Eton Coll., Christ Church, Oxford. 2nd Lieut Royal Horse Guards (The Blues), 1955–56. Pres. of Oxford Univ. Conservative Association, 1958. MP (C) Southend W, Jan. 1959–1997; PPS, to Minister of Power, 1959–60, to Home Sec., 1960–62, to First Sec. of State, 1962–63, to the Foreign Sec., 1963–64; Opposition Spokesman on Arts and Amenities, 1967–70; Parly Sec., Min. of Housing and Local Govt, June–Oct. 1970; Parly Under-Sec. of State, DoE, 1970–72; Minister of State, Northern Ireland Office, March–Nov. 1972; Minister for Housing and Construction, DoE, 1972–74; Opposition Spokesman on: Prices and Consumer Protection, March–Sept. 1974; environmental affairs, Oct. 1974–Feb. 1975; Minister of State, CSD, 1979–81; Minister for the Arts, 1981–83; Minister for Trade, 1983–86; Sec. of State for Trade and Industry, 1986–87; Sec. of State for Transport, 1987–89. Chairman: Finance and Services Cttee, H of C, 1992–97; Transport Select Cttee, 1993–97. Dep. Leader, Cons. Delegn to WEU and Council of Europe, 1976–79. Chm., British Assoc. for Central and Eastern Europe, 1992–97. Mem., Gen. Adv. Council to ITA, 1964–66. President: Southend West Cons. Assoc.; Brentwood and Ongar Cons. Assoc.; Old Etonian Assoc., 1999–2000. *Address:* c/o Iveagh Trustees Ltd, 41 Harrington Gardens, SW7 4JU. *Died 27 Jan. 2007.*

KEMP, Sir (Edward) Peter, KCB 1991 (CB 1988); Executive, Foundation for Accountancy and Financial Management, 1993–2000; *b* 10 Oct. 1934; *s* of late Thomas Kemp and Nancie (*née* Sargent); *m* 1961, Enid van Popta; three *s* one *d. Educ:* Millfield Sch.; Royal Naval Coll., Dartmouth. FCA (ACA 1959). Principal, later Asst Sec., Min. of Transport, 1967–73; HM Treasury, 1973, Under-Sec., 1978, Dep. Sec., 1983; Second Perm. Sec. and Next Steps Project Manager, Cabinet Office (OMCS), 1988–92. Comr, Audit Commission, 1993–99. Trustee, Action for Blind People, 2001–04. Gov., Millfield Sch., 1993–2005. *Publications:* Beyond Next Steps: a civil service for the twenty-first century, 1993; (with David Walker) A Better Machine: government for the twenty-first century, 1996; articles and pieces. *Address:* 2 Longton Avenue, SE26 6QJ. *Died 24 June 2008.*

KEMP, Rt Rev. Eric Waldram, DD; Bishop of Chichester, 1974–2001; *b* 27 April 1915; *o c* of Tom Kemp and Florence Lilian Kemp (*née* Waldram), Grove House, Waltham, Grimsby, Lincs; *m* 1953, Leslie Patricia, 3rd *d* of late Rt Rev. K. E. Kirk, sometime Bishop of Oxford; one *s* four *d. Educ:* Brigg Grammar Sch., Lincs; Exeter Coll., Oxford (MA); St Stephen's House, Oxford (Hon. Fellow 2005). Deacon 1939; Priest 1940; Curate of St Luke, Southampton, 1939–41; Librarian of Pusey House, Oxford, 1941–46; Chaplain of Christ Church Oxford, 1943–46; Actg Chap., St John's Coll., Oxford, 1943–45; Fellow, Chaplain, Tutor, and Lectr in Theology and Medieval History, Exeter Coll., Oxford, 1946–69, Emeritus Fellow, 1969; Dean of Worcester, 1969–74. Exam. Chaplain: to Bp of Mon, 1942–45; to Bp of Southwark, 1946–50; to Bp of St Albans, 1946–69; to Bp of Exeter, 1944–69; to Bp of Lincoln, 1950–69. Proctor in Convocation for University of Oxford, 1949–69. Bp of Oxford's Commissary for Religious Communities, 1952–69; Chaplain to the Queen,

1967–69. Canon and Prebendary of Caistor in Lincoln Cathedral, 1952–2001; Hon. Provincial Canon of Cape Town, 1960–; Canon of Honour, Chartres Cathedral, 1998. Bampton Lecturer, 1959–60. FRHistS 1951. Hon. Fellow, University Coll., Chichester, 2002. Hon. DLitt Sussex, 1986; Hon. DD Berne, 1987. *Publications:* (contributions to) Thy Household the Church, 1943; Canonization and Authority in the Western Church, 1948; Norman Powell Williams, 1954; Twenty-five Papal Decretals relating to the Diocese of Lincoln (with W. Holtzmann), 1954; An Introduction to Canon Law in the Church of England, 1957; Life and Letters of Kenneth Escott Kirk, 1959; Counsel and Consent, 1961; The Anglican-Methodist conversations: A Comment from within, 1964; (ed) Man: Fallen and Free, 1969; Square Words in a Round World, 1980; Shy But Not Retiring (memoirs), 2006; contrib. to English Historical Review, Jl of Ecclesiastical History. *Recreations:* music, travel. *Address:* 5 Alexandra Road, Chichester PO19 7LX. *Club:* National Liberal (Pres., 1994–).   *Died 28 Nov. 2009.*

KEMP, Kenneth Reginald; Hon. Life President, Smith & Nephew plc, 1990 (Chairman, 1976–90); *b* 13 Nov. 1921; *s* of Philip R. Kemp and Siew Pukalanan of Thailand; *m* 1949, Florence M. Hetherington (marr. diss.); *m* 1996, Frances M. Kemp-Bell; one *s* one *d*. *Educ:* Bradfield College, Berks. FCA. Joined Leeds Rifles, 1939; commissioned Royal Artillery, 1940–46; served in France, Germany, India, Far East (Captain). Peat, Marwick Mitchell & Co., 1947; qualified CA, 1950; Smith & Nephew: Company Sec., 1953, later Finance Dir; Dir, 1962; Chief Exec., 1968–76. Mem., Ct of Patrons, RCS, 1984–. *Recreation:* unlimited. *Address:* Smith & Nephew, Heron House, 15 Adam Street, WC2N 6LA. *T:* (020) 7401 7646.
                                        Died 17 Dec. 2010.

KEMP, Leslie Charles, CBE 1982; Chairman, Griffiths McGee Ltd, Demolition Contractors, 1982–87; Proprietor, Leslie Kemp Associates, 1976–97; *b* 10 Oct. 1920; *s* of Thomas and Violet Kemp; *m* (Patricia) Ann. *Educ:* Hawkhurst Moor Boys' School. Apprentice blacksmith, 1934–39; served War, 1939–46: Infantry, N Africa and Italy. Civil Engrg Equipment Operator, 1947–51; served in Korea, 1951; District Organiser, 1951–57, Regional Organiser, 1958–63, Nat. Sec. (Construction), TGWU, 1963–76. Jt Registrar, 1975–76, Dep. Chm., 1976–81, Demolition and Dismantling Industry Registration Council. Member, Nat. Jt Council for Building Industry, 1957–76; Operatives Sec., Civil Engrg Construction Conciliation Bd for GB, 1963–76; Mem., 1964–73, Dep. Chm., 1973–76, Chm., 1976–85, Construction Industry Trng Bd (Chm., Civil Engrg Cttee, 1964–76); Member: EDC for Civil Engrg, 1964–76; Construction Ind. Liaison Gp, 1974–76; Construction Ind. Manpower Bd, 1976; Bragg Adv. Cttee on Falsework, 1973–75; Vice Pres., Construction Health and Safety Gp. Chm., Corby Develt Corp., 1976–80; Dep. Chm., Peterborough Develt Corp., 1974–82. Member, Outward Bound Trust, 1977–88; Pres., W Norfolk Outward Bound Assoc., 1983–88. Chm., Syderstone Parish Council, 1983–87. Construction News Man of the Year Award, 1973; in recognition of services to trng, Leslie Kemp Eur. Prize for Civil Engrg trainees to study in France, instituted 1973. CompICE; FCMI. *Recreations:* travel, bird-watching, fishing. *Address:* Lamberts Yard, Syderstone, King's Lynn, Norfolk PE31 8SF. *Clubs:* Lighthouse; Fakenham Golf (Pres., 1985–88).   *Died 28 July 2009.*

KEMP, Sir Peter; *see* Kemp, Sir E. P.

KEMPE, John William Rolfe, CVO 1980; Headmaster of Gordonstoun, 1968–78; *b* 29 Oct. 1917; *s* of late William Alfred Kempe and Kunigunda Neville-Rolfe; *m* 1957, Barbara Nan Stephen, *d* of late Dr C. R. Huxtable, MC, FRCS and of Mrs Huxtable, OAM, Sydney, Australia; two *s* one *d*. *Educ:* Stowe; Clare Coll., Cambridge (Exhibitioner in Mathematics). Served war of 1939–45, RAFVR Training and Fighter Command; CO 153 and 255 Night Fighter Squadrons. Board of Trade,

1945; Firth-Brown (Overseas) Ltd, 1946–47; Head of Maths Dept, Gordonstoun, 1948–51; Principal, Hyderabad Public Sch., Deccan, India, 1951–54; Headmaster, Corby Grammar School, Northants, 1955–67. Chm., Round Square Internat. Service Cttee, 1979–87; Vice-Chm., The European Atlantic Movement, 1982–92 (Vice-Pres., 1992–). Exploration and mountaineering, Himalayas, Peru, 1952–56; Member: Cttee, Mount Everest Foundation, 1956–62; Cttee, Brathay Exploration Group, 1964–73; Foundn Trustee, Univ. of Cambridge Kurt Hahn Trust, 1986–89; Trustee: Thornton Smith Trust, 1981–96; Plevins Charity, 1987–96. *Publications:* A Family History of the Kempes, 1991; articles in Alpine Jl, Geographical Jl, Sociological Review. *Address:* 6 Marlpit Gardens, Ticehurst, E Sussex TN5 7BB. *T:* (01580) 201445. *Clubs:* Royal Air Force, Alpine.   *Died 10 May 2010.*

KENDALL, Prof. David George, DSc, ScD; FRS 1964; Professor of Mathematical Statistics, University of Cambridge, 1962–85 and Fellow of Churchill College, since 1962; *b* 15 Jan. 1918; *s* of Fritz Ernest Kendall and Emmie Taylor, Ripon, Yorks; *m* 1952, Diana Louise Fletcher; two *s* four *d*. *Educ:* Ripon GS; Queen's Coll., Oxford (MA, 1943; Hon. Fellow 1985); DSc Oxford, 1977; ScD Cambridge, 1988. Fellow Magdalen Coll., Oxford, and Lectr in Mathematics, 1946–62 (Emeritus Fellow, 1989). Visiting Lecturer: Princeton Univ., USA, 1952–53 (Wilks Prize, 1980); Zhong-shan Univ., Guangzhou; Xiangtan Univ.; Changsha Inst. Rlwys; Jiaotong Univ., Xian, 1983. Lectures: Larmor, Cambridge Philos. Soc., 1980; Milne, Wadham Coll., Oxford, 1983; Hotelling, Univ. of N Carolina, 1985; Rietz, Inst. of Math. Stats, 1989; Kolmogorov, Bernoulli Soc., 1990. Member: Internat. Statistical Inst.; Academia Europaea, 1991; Council, Royal Society, 1967–69, 1982–83; President: London Mathematical Soc., 1972–74; Internat. Assoc. Statist. in Phys. Sci., 1973–75; Bernoulli Soc. for Mathematical Stats and Probability, 1975; Section A (Math.) and Section P (Physics), BAAS, 1982. Chm. Parish Reg. Sect., Yorks Archaeol. Soc., 1974–79. Hon. Mem., Romanian Acad., 1992. Hon. D. de l'U Paris (René Descartes), 1976; Hon. DSc Bath, 1986. Guy Medal in Silver, Royal Statistical Soc., 1955; Weldon Meml Prize and Medal for Biometric Science, 1974; Sylvester Medal, Royal Soc., 1976; Whitehead Prize, London Math. Soc., 1980; Guy Medal in Gold, Royal Statistical Soc., 1981; De Morgan Medal, London Math. Soc., 1989. *Publications:* (jt ed) Mathematics in the Archaeological and Historical Sciences, 1971; (jt ed) Stochastic Analysis, 1973; (jt ed) Stochastic Geometry, 1974; (ed) Analytic and Geometric Stochastics, 1986; (jtly) Shape and Shape Theory, 1999.
                                        Died 23 Oct. 2007.

KENNEDY, Prof. Arthur Colville, CBE 1992; FRCPE, FRCPGlas, FRCP; FRSE 1984; Muirhead Professor of Medicine, Glasgow University, 1978–88; *b* 23 Oct. 1922; *s* of Thomas and Johanna Kennedy; *m* 1947, Agnes White Taylor; two *d* (one *s* decd). *Educ:* Whitehill Sch., Glasgow; Univ. of Glasgow. MB ChB 1945; MD 1956. FRCPE 1960; FRCPGlas 1964; FRCP 1977; FRCPI 1988. Hon. Consultant in Medicine, Royal Infirmary, Glasgow, 1959–88; Titular Professor, Univ. of Glasgow, 1969–78. Former External Examiner to Univs of Edinburgh, Dundee, Manchester, Dublin, West Indies, Hong Kong, Kuwait, Malaysia. Member: Greater Glasgow Health Bd, 1985–89; GMC, 1989–92 (Chm., Professional and Linguistic Bd, 1987–89). President: RCPSG, 1986–88; BMA, 1991–92; Royal Medico-Chirurgical Soc. of Glasgow, 1971–72; Eur. Dialysis and Transplant Assoc., 1972–75; Scottish Soc. of Physicians, 1983–84; Harveian Soc. of Edinburgh, 1985. Hon. FACP 1987; Hon. FRACP 1988. *Publications:* various papers on renal disease. *Recreations:* gardening, walking, reading, photography. *Address:* 16 Boclair Crescent, Bearsden, Glasgow G61 2AG. *T:* (0141) 942 5326. *Club:* Royal Over-Seas League.   *Died 30 Dec. 2009.*

KENNEDY, Edward Moore, Hon. KBE 2009; US Senator (Democrat) from Massachusetts, since 1962; *b* Boston, Mass, 22 Feb. 1932; *y s* of late Joseph Patrick Kennedy and Rose Kennedy (*née* Fitzgerald); *m* 1958, Joan Bennett (marr. diss. 1982); two *s* one *d*; *m* 1992, Victoria Anne Reggie. *Educ:* Milton Acad.; Harvard Univ. (BA 1956); Internat. Law Inst., The Hague; Univ. of Virginia Law Sch. (LLB 1959). Served US Army, 1951–53. Called to Massachusetts Bar, 1959; Asst Dist Attorney, Suffolk County, Mass, 1961–62. Senate majority whip, 1969–71; Chairman: Judiciary Cttee, 1979–81; Labor and Human Resources Cttee, later Health, Educn, Labor and Pensions Cttee, 1987– (Ranking Democrat, 1981–86 and 1995–2006); Member: Senate Armed Forces Cttee; Senate Jt Economic Cttee. Pres., Joseph P. Kennedy Jr Foundn, 1961–; Trustee: John F. Kennedy Lib.; John F. Kennedy Center for the Performing Arts; Robert F. Kennedy Meml Foundn. Holds numerous hon. degrees, foreign decorations and awards. *Publications:* Decisions for a Decade, 1968; In Critical Condition, 1972; Our Day and Generation, 1979; (with Senator Mark Hatfield) Freeze: how you can help prevent nuclear war, 1982; America Back on Track, 2006; My Senator and Me, 2006. *Address:* United States Senate, Washington, DC 20510–2101, USA.
Died 25 Aug. 2009.

KENNEDY, Graham Norbert, CVO 1993; Chairman: Walker Crips Weddle Beck, since 2000; Anglo Pacific Resources, 1989–97; Dwyer plc, 1993–97; *b* 21 Oct. 1936; *s* of Ernest Norbert Kennedy and Joan Foster Kennedy; *m* 1960, Dinah Mary Berrill. *Educ:* St Andrews Coll., Grahamstown, S Africa; Millfield. Union Acceptances Ltd, 1964–70; James Capel & Co., 1971–96: Partner, 1974–96; Dir of Moneybroking, 1986–90; Dir, 1990–96; Consultant, 1993–95. Dir, Ockham Hldgs, subseq. Highway Insce Hldgs, 1995–2003. Mem., Council and Bd, London Stock Exchange, 1980–92. *Recreations:* shooting, golf, bridge, ski-ing, music. *Address:* Hatchetts, Church Lane, Worting, Basingstoke, Hants RG23 8PX. *Clubs:* Boodle's, City of London; Rand (Johannesburg); Berkshire Golf, Swinley Forest Golf.
Died 28 Feb. 2007.

KENNEDY, Sir Ludovic (Henry Coverley), Kt 1994; FRSL; writer and broadcaster; *b* Edinburgh, 3 Nov. 1919; *o s* of Captain E. C. Kennedy, RN (killed in action, 1939, while commanding HMS Rawalpindi against German battle-cruisers Scharnhorst and Gneisenau), and Rosalind, *d* of Sir Ludovic Grant, 11th Bt of Dalvey; *m* 1950, Moira Shearer King, ballerina (*d* 2006); one *s* three *d*. *Educ:* Eton; Christ Church, Oxford (MA; Hon. Student, 2003). Served War, 1939–46, RNVR. Priv. Sec. and ADC to Gov. of Newfoundland, 1943–44. Librarian, Ashridge (Adult Education) Coll., 1949; Rockefeller Foundation Atlantic Award in Literature, 1950; Winner, Open Finals Contest, English Festival of Spoken Poetry, 1953; Editor, feature, First Reading (BBC Third Prog.), 1953–54; Lecturer for British Council, Sweden, Finland and Denmark, 1955; Belgium and Luxembourg, 1956. Lectures: Voltaire Meml, 1985; Stevens, RSocMed, 1993. Mem. Council, Navy Records Soc., 1957–60. Contested (L) Rochdale, By-elecn, 1958 and Gen. Elecn, 1959; Pres., Nat. League of Young Liberals, 1959–61; Mem., Lib. Party Council, 1965–67. Pres., Sir Walter Scott Club, Edinburgh, 1968–69; Patron, Russian Convoy Club, 1989–. Pres., Dignity in Dying (formerly Voluntary Euthanasia Soc.), 1995–. Columnist: Newsweek International, 1974–75; Sunday Standard, 1981–82. Chm., Royal Lyceum Theatre Co. of Edinburgh, 1977–84. Dir, The Spectator, 1988–90. Chm. of Judges, NCR Book Award, 1990–91. FRSA 1974–76; FRSL 1998. Hon. LLD: Strathclyde, 1985; Southampton, 1993; Dr *hc* Edinburgh, 1990; DUniv Stirling, 1991. Richard Dimbleby BAFTA Award, 1988. Cross, First Class, Order of Merit, Fed. Repub. of Germany, 1979. *TV and radio:* Introd. Profile, ATV, 1955–56; Newscaster, Independent Television News, 1956–58; Introducer of AR's feature On Stage, 1957; Introducer of AR's, This Week, 1958–59; Chm. BBC features: Your Verdict, 1962; Your Witness, 1967–70;

Commentator: BBC's Panorama, 1960–63; Television Reporters Internat., 1963–64 (also Prod.); Introducer, BBC's Time Out, 1964–65, World at One, 1965–66; Presenter: Lib. Party's Gen. Election Television Broadcasts, 1966; The Middle Years, ABC, 1967; The Nature of Prejudice, ATV, 1968; Face the Press, Tyne-Tees, 1968–69, 1970–72; Against the Tide, Yorkshire TV, 1969; Living and Growing, Grampian TV, 1969–70; 24 Hours, BBC, 1969–72; Ad Lib, BBC, 1970–72; Midweek, BBC, 1973–75; Newsday, BBC, 1975–76; Tonight, BBC, 1976–78; A Life with Crime, BBC, 1979; Change of Direction, BBC, 1979; Lord Mountbatten Remembers, 1980; Did You See?, 1980–88; Timewatch, 1984; Indelible Evidence, 1987 and 1990; A Gift of the Gab, 1989; Portrait, 1989. *Television films include:* The Sleeping Ballerina; The Singers and the Songs; Scapa Flow; Battleship Bismarck; Life and Death of the Scharnhorst; U-Boat War; Target Tirpitz; The Rise of the Red Navy; Lord Haw-Haw; Coast to Coast; Who Killed the Lindbergh Baby; Elizabeth: the first thirty years; Happy Birthday, dear Ma'am; Consider The End; From Princess to Queen. *Publications:* Sub-Lieutenant, 1942; Nelson's Band of Brothers, 1951; One Man's Meat, 1953; Murder Story (play, with essay on Capital Punishment), 1956; play: Murder Story (Cambridge Theatre), 1954; Ten Rillington Place, 1961; The Trial of Stephen Ward, 1964; Very Lovely People, 1969; Pursuit: the chase and sinking of the Bismarck, 1974; A Presumption of Innocence: the Amazing Case of Patrick Meehan, 1975; Menace: the life and death of the Tirpitz, 1979; The Portland Spy Case, 1979; Wicked Beyond Belief, 1980; (ed) A Book of Railway Journeys, 1980; (ed) A Book of Sea Journeys, 1981; (ed) A Book of Air Journeys, 1982; The Airman and the Carpenter, 1985 (republished in USA as Crime of the Century, 1996; filmed as Crime of the Century, 1996); On My Way to the Club (autobiog.), 1989; Euthanasia: the good death, 1990; Truth to Tell (collected writings), 1991; In Bed with an Elephant: a journey through Scotland's past and present, 1995; All In The Mind: a farewell to God, 1999; Thirty-Six Murders and Two Immoral Earnings, 2002; Gen. Editor, The British at War, 1973–77. *Address:* c/o Rogers, Coleridge and White, 20 Powis Mews, W11 1JN. *Clubs:* Brooks's, Army and Navy.
Died 18 Oct. 2009.

KENNEDY, Moira, (Lady Kennedy); *see* Shearer, M.

KENNEDY MARTIN, (Francis) Troy; writer; *b* 15 Feb. 1932; *s* of Frank Martin and Kathleen Flanagan; *m* 1967, Diana Aubrey (marr. diss.); one *s* one *d*. *Educ:* Finchley Catholic Grammar Sch.; Trinity Coll., Dublin (BA (Hons) History). Following nat. service with Gordon Highlanders in Cyprus, wrote Incident at Echo Six, a TV play, 1959; *television:* The Interrogator, 1961; Z Cars, 1962; Diary of a Young Man, 1964; Man Without Papers, 1965; Reilly, Ace of Spies, 1983; Edge of Darkness, 1985; Hostile Waters, 1998; Race Dust, 2005; *films:* The Italian Job, 1969; Kelly's Heroes, 1970. Jt Screenwriters' Guild Award, 1962; BAFTA Scriptwriter's Award, 1962. *Publications:* Beat on a Damask Drum, 1961. *Recreation:* collecting marine models. *Address:* 6 Ladbroke Gardens, W11 2PT.
Died 15 Sept. 2009.

KENNET, 2nd Baron *cr* 1935; **Wayland Hilton Young;** author and politician; *b* 2 Aug. 1923; *s* of 1st Baron Kennet, PC, GBE, DSO, DSC, and of Kathleen Bruce (who *m* 1st, Captain Robert Falcon Scott, CVO, RN, and died 1947); *S* father, 1960; *m* 1948, Elizabeth Ann, *d* of late Captain Bryan Fullerton Adams, DSO, RN; one *s* five *d*. *Educ:* Stowe; Trinity Coll., Cambridge. Served in RN, 1942–45. Foreign Office, 1946–47, and 1949–51. Correspondent in Rome and N Africa, Observer, 1953–54; theatre critic, Tribune, 1957–58; founding Sec., campaign to abolish theatre censorship, 1958; columnist, The Guardian, 1959–64. Deleg., Parly Assemblies, WEU and Council of Europe, 1962–65; Parly Sec., Min. of Housing and Local Govt, 1966–70; Opposition Spokesman on Foreign Affairs and Science Policy, 1971–74; SDP Chief Whip in H of L, 1981–83; SDP spokesman in H of L on foreign affairs and defence,

1981–90. Co-founder, POST, 1988. Chairman: Adv. Cttee on Oil Pollution of the Sea, 1970–74; Commonwealth Human Ecology Council, 1970–72; CPRE, 1971–72; Internat. Parly Confs on the Environment, 1972–78; Dir, Europe Plus Thirty, 1974–75; Member: Polar Cttee, NERC; Internat. Bioethics Cttee, UNESCO, 1994–98. Member: European Parlt, 1978–79; North Atlantic Assembly, 1997–99; Vice Pres., Parly and Scientific Cttee, 1989–98. Pres., Architecture Club, 1983–93; Mem., Redundant Churches Fund, 1978–84. Former Chairman, later President: Avebury Soc., 1990–; Stonehenge Alliance, 1995–; Pres., then Patron, Action for River Kennet, 1995–. Hon. FRIBA 1970. Editor of Disarmament and Arms Control, 1962–65. *Publications:* (as Wayland Young): The Italian Left, 1949; The Deadweight, 1952; Now or Never, 1953; Old London Churches (with Elizabeth Young), 1956; The Montesi Scandal, 1957; Still Alive Tomorrow, 1958; Strategy for Survival, 1959; The Profumo Affair, 1963; Eros Denied, 1965; Thirty-Four Articles, 1965; (ed) Existing Mechanisms of Arms Control, 1965; (as Wayland Kennet) Preservation, 1972; The Futures of Europe, 1976; The Rebirth of Britain, 1982; (with Elizabeth Young) London's Churches, 1986; (with Elizabeth Young) Northern Lazio, 1990 (trans. Italian 1993); Parliaments and Screening, 1995; (contrib.) Enciclopedia Treccani (The Italian Encyclopedia), 1998; Fabian and SDP pamphlets on defence, disarmament, environment, multinational companies, etc. *Heir: s* Hon. William Aldus Thoby Young [*b* 24 May 1957; *m* 1987, Hon. Josephine, *yr d* of 2nd Baron Keyes; two *s* one *d*]. *Address:* 100 Bayswater Road, W2 3HJ.
Died 7 May 2009.

KENYON, Sir George (Henry), Kt 1976; DL; JP; LLD; *b* 10 July 1912; *s* of George Henry Kenyon and Edith (*née* Hill); *m* 1938, Christine Dorey (*née* Brentnall) (*d* 1996); two *s* one *d*. *Educ:* Radley; Manchester Univ. Director: William Kenyon & Sons Ltd, 1942–92 (Chm., 1961–82); Tootal Ltd, 1971–79 (Chm., 1976–79); Manchester Ship Canal, 1972–86; Williams & Glyn's Bank, 1972–83 (Chm., 1978–83); Royal Bank of Scotland, 1978–83; Chm., Vuman Ltd, 1982–88. Gen. Comr, Inland Revenue, 1957–73. Manchester University: Chm. Bldgs Cttee, 1962–70; Treas., 1970–72, 1980–82; Chm. Council, 1972–80. Hon. Treas., Civic Trust, NW, 1962–78, Vice Pres., 1978; Member: NW Adv. Cttee, Civil Aviation, 1967–72; Manchester Reg. Hosp. Bd, 1962–68; NW Reg. Econ. Planning Council, 1970–73. Pres., Arkwright Soc., Cromford, 1995– (Vice-Pres., 1988–94). JP Cheshire, 1959; Chm., S Tameside Bench, 1974–82; DL Chester, 1969, Greater Manchester, 1983. High Sheriff, Cheshire, 1973–74. Hon. LLD Manchester, 1980. *Recreations:* reading, talking. *Address:* 11 Brookview, Brook Lane, Alderley Edge, Cheshire SK9 7QG.
Died 2 June 2008.

KENYON, Ian Roy; HM Diplomatic Service, retired; Executive Secretary, Preparatory Commission for Organisation for Prohibition of Chemical Weapons, The Hague, 1993–97; *b* 13 June 1939; *s* of late S. R. Kenyon and Mrs E. M. Kenyon; *m* 1962, Griselda Rintoul; one *s* one *d*. *Educ:* Lancaster Royal Grammar School; Edinburgh University (BSc Hons). Lever Bros, 1962–68; Birds Eye Foods, 1968–74; First Secretary, FCO, 1974–76; Geneva, 1976–78; Head of Chancery, Bogota, 1979–81; FCO, 1982–83; Head of Nuclear Energy Dept, FCO, 1983–85; Overseas Inspectorate, 1986–88; Dep. Leader, UK Delegn to Conf. on Disarmament, Geneva, 1988–92. Visiting Senior Research Fellow: Mountbatten Centre for Internat. Studies, Southampton Univ., 1997–; Sci. and Technol. Policy Res. Unit, Sussex Univ., 2003–. *Recreation:* carriage driving. *Died 7 Aug. 2008.*

KERMODE, Sir (John) Frank, Kt 1991; MA; FBA 1973; *b* 29 Nov. 1919; *s* of late John Pritchard Kermode and late Doris Pearl Kermode; *m* 1st, 1947, Maureen Eccles (marr. diss. 1970; she *d* 2004); twin *s* and *d*; 2nd, 1976, Anita Van Vactor (marr. diss.). *Educ:* Douglas High

Sch.; Liverpool Univ. (BA 1940; MA 1947). War Service (Navy), 1940–46. Lectr, King's Coll., Newcastle, in the University of Durham, 1947–49; Lectr, Univ. of Reading, 1949–58; John Edward Taylor Prof. of English Literature, Univ. of Manchester, 1958–65; Winterstoke Prof. of English, Univ. of Bristol, 1965–67; Lord Northcliffe Prof. of Modern English Lit., UCL, 1967–74, Hon. Fellow, 1996; King Edward VII Prof. of English Literature, Cambridge Univ., 1974–82; Fellow, King's Coll., Cambridge, 1974–87, Hon. Fellow, 1988. Charles Eliot Norton Prof. of Poetry at Harvard, 1977–78. Co-editor, Encounter, 1966–67. Editor: Fontana Masterguides and Modern Masters series; Oxford Authors. FRSL 1958. Mem. Arts Council, 1968–71; Chm., Poetry Book Soc., 1968–76. For. Hon. Mem., Amer. Acad. of Arts and Scis; For. Mem., Accademia dei Lincei, 2002; Hon. Mem. AAAL. Hon. DHL Chicago, 1975; Hon. DLitt: Liverpool, 1981; Newcastle, 1993; London, 1997; Hon. Dr: Amsterdam, 1988; Yale, 1995; Wesleyan, 1997; Sewanee, 1999; Columbia, 2003; Harvard, 2004. Officier de l'Ordre des Arts et des Sciences. *Publications:* (ed) Shakespeare, The Tempest (Arden Edition), 1954; Romantic Image, 1957; John Donne, 1957; The Living Milton, 1960; Wallace Stevens, 1960; Puzzles & Epiphanies, 1962; The Sense of an Ending, 1967; Continuities, 1968; Shakespeare, Spenser, Donne, 1971; Modern Essays, 1971; Lawrence, 1973; (ed, with John Hollander) Oxford Anthology of English Literature, 1973; The Classic, 1975; (ed) Selected Prose of T. S. Eliot, 1975; The Genesis of Secrecy, 1979; Essays on Fiction, 1971–82, 1983; Forms of Attention, 1985; (ed jtly) The Literary Guide to the Bible, 1987; History and Value, 1988; An Appetite for Poetry, 1989; Poetry, Narrative, History, 1990; (ed with Keith Walker) Andrew Marvell, 1990; Uses of Error, 1991; (ed with Anita Kermode) The Oxford Book of Letters, 1995; Not Entitled (memoirs), 1996; Shakespeare's Language, 2000; Pleasing Myself, 2001; Pieces of My Mind, 2003; The Age of Shakespeare, 2004; Pleasure and Change, 2004; Concerning E. M. Forster, 2009; Bury Place Papers: essays from the London Review of Books, 2009; contrib. New Republic, Partisan Review, New York Review, New York Times, New Statesman, London Rev. of Books, etc. *Address:* 9 The Oast House, Grange Road, Cambridge CB3 9AP. *T:* (01223) 357931.
Died 17 Aug. 2010.

KERNOHAN, Thomas Hugh, CBE 1978 (OBE 1955); Founder, 1959, and Chairman, 1961–80 and 1987–93, Kernohans Joinery Works Ltd (family joinery and plastic firm); *b* 11 May 1922; *s* of Thomas Watson Kernohan and Caroline Kernohan; *m* 1948, Margaret Moore; one *s* one *d*. *Educ:* Carrickfergus Model Sch.; Carrickfergus Technical Sch. On staff (admin), Harland & Wolff Ltd, Belfast, 1940–44; Engineering Employers' NI Association: Asst Sec., 1945; Sec., 1953; Dir, 1966–80; Parly Comr for Admin and Comr for Complaints, NI, 1980–87. *Address:* 103 Maritime Drive, Rodgers Bay, Carrickfergus, Co. Antrim, N Ireland BT38 8GQ.
Died 3 Dec. 2007.

KERR, Dr David Leigh; *b* 25 March 1923; *s* of Myer Woolf Kerr and Paula (*née* Horowitz); *m* 1st, 1944, Aileen Saddington (marr. diss. 1969); two *s* one *d*; 2nd, 1970, Margaret Dunlop; one *s* two *d*. *Educ:* Whitgift Sch., Croydon; Middlesex Hosp. Med. Sch., London. Hon. Sec., Socialist Medical Assoc., 1957–63; Hon. Vice-Pres., 1963–72. LCC (Wandsworth, Central), 1958–65, and Coun., London Borough of Wandsworth, 1964–68; Mem., Herts CC (Welwyn Garden City S), 1989–2001. Contested (Lab) Wandsworth, Streatham (for Parlt), 1959; MP (Lab) Wandsworth Central, 1964–70; PPS to Minister of State, FCO, 1967–69. Vis. Lectr in Medicine, Chelsea Coll., 1972–82. War on Want: Dir, 1970–77; Vice-Chm., 1973–74; Chm., 1974–77. Family Doctor, Tooting, 1946–82; Chief Exec., Manor House Hosp., London, 1982–87. Member: Inter-departmental Cttee on Death Certification and Coroners; E Herts CHC, 1992–2000 (Vice-Chm., 1998–2000); Med. Assessor, Registered Homes Tribunals, 1986–93. Hon. Vice-Pres.,

Community Practitioners & Health Visitors' Assoc. (formerly Health Visitors' Assoc.), 1969–2005; Trustee, CPHVA Charitable Trust, 1996–2005. FRSocMed. Governor, British Film Inst., 1966–71. *Recreations:* reading other people's biographies, refusing to write own. *Address:* 19 Homewood Avenue, Cuffley, Herts EN6 4QG. *T:* (01707) 872150.   *Died 12 Jan. 2008.*

KERR, Deborah Jane, (Deborah Kerr Viertel), CBE 1998; actress; *b* 30 Sept. 1921; *d* of Capt. Arthur Kerr-Trimmer; *m* 1st, 1945, Sqdn Ldr A. C. Bartley, DFC (marr. diss. 1959; he *d* 2001); two *d*; 2nd, 1960, Peter Viertel. *Educ:* Northumberland House, Clifton, Bristol. Open Air Theatre, Regent's Park, 1939, Oxford Repertory, 1939–40; after an interval of acting in films, appeared on West End Stage; Ellie Dunn in Heartbreak House, Cambridge Theatre, 1943; went to France, Belgium, and Holland for ENSA, playing in Gaslight, 1945. *Films:* Major Barbara, 1940; Love on the Dole, 1940–41; Penn of Pennsylvania, 1941; Hatter's Castle, 1942; The Day Will Dawn, 1942; Life and Death of Colonel Blimp, 1942–43; Perfect Strangers, 1944; I See a Dark Stranger, 1945; Black Narcissus, 1946; The Hucksters and If Winter Comes, 1947 (MGM, Hollywood); Edward My Son, 1948; Please Believe Me, 1949 (MGM, Hollywood); King Solomon's Mines, 1950; Quo Vadis, 1952; Prisoner of Zenda, Julius Caesar, Dream Wife, Young Bess (MGM), 1952; From Here to Eternity, 1953; The End of the Affair, 1955; The Proud and Profane, The King and I, 1956; Heaven Knows, Mr Allison, An Affair to Remember, Tea and Sympathy, 1957; Bonjour Tristesse, 1958; Separate Tables, The Journey, Count Your Blessings, 1959; The Sundowners, The Grass is Greener, The Naked Edge, The Innocents, 1961; The Chalk Garden, The Night of the Iguana, 1964; Casino Royale, 1967; Eye of the Devil, Prudence and the Pill, 1968; The Arrangement, 1970; The Assam Garden, 1985. *Stage:* Tea and Sympathy, NY, 1953; The Day After the Fair, London, 1972, tour of US, 1973–74; Seascape, NY, 1975; Candida, London, 1977; The Last of Mrs Cheyney, tour of US, 1978–79; The Day After the Fair, Melbourne and Sydney, 1979; Overheard, Haymarket, 1981; The Corn is Green, Old Vic, 1985. BAFTA Special Award, 1991; Hon. Oscar, Acad. of Motion Picture Arts and Scis, 1994.   *Died 16 Oct. 2007.*

KERSHAW, Sir (John) Anthony, Kt 1981; MC 1943; DL; Barrister-at-Law; *b* 14 Dec. 1915; *s* of Judge J. F. Kershaw, Cairo and London, and Anne Kershaw, Kentucky, USA; *m* 1939, Barbara, *d* of Harry Crookenden; two *s* two *d*. *Educ:* Eton; Balliol Coll., Oxford (BA). Called to the Bar 1939. Served War, 1940–46: 16th/5th Lancers. Mem. LCC, 1946–49; Westminster City Council, 1947–48. MP (C) Stroud Div. of Gloucestershire, 1955–87. Parly Sec., Min. of Public Building and Works, June–Oct. 1970; Parliamentary Under-Secretary of State: FCO, 1970–73; for Defence (RAF), 1973–74; Chm., H of C Select Cttee on Foreign Affairs, 1979–87; Mem. Exec., 1922 Cttee, 1983–87. Vice-Chm., British Council, 1974–87. DL 1989, Vice Lord-Lieut, 1990–93, Glos. *Address:* West Barn, Didmarton, Badminton, Glos GL9 1DT. *Club:* White's.   *Died 29 April 2008.*

KERSHAW, Joseph Anthony; *b* 26 Nov. 1935; *s* of Henry and Catherine Kershaw, Preston; *m* 1959, Ann Whittle; three *s* two *d*. *Educ:* Ushaw Coll., Durham; Preston Catholic Coll., SJ. Short service commn, RAOC, 1955–58; Unilever Ltd, 1958–67; Gp Marketing Manager, CWS, 1967–69; Managing Director: Underline Ltd, 1969–71; Merchant Div., Reed International Ltd, 1971–73; Head of Marketing, Non-Foods, CWS, 1973–74; (first) Director, Nat. Consumer Council, 1975; independent management consultant, 1975–91; Chairman: Antonian Investments Ltd, 1985–87; Organised Business Data Ltd, 1987–89; Director: John Stork & Partners Ltd, 1980–85; Allia (Holdings) Ltd, 1984–88; Associate Director: Foote, Cone & Belding Ltd, 1979–84; Phoenix Advertising, 1984–86. *Recreations:*

turning, woodcarving, water colour painting, fishing, cooking, gardening, RHS, NACF. *Address:* Westmead, Meins Road, Blackburn, Lancs BB2 6QF. *T:* (01254) 55915.   *Died 11 Feb. 2009.*

KEYNES, Prof. Richard Darwin, CBE 1984; MA, PhD, ScD Cantab; FRS 1959; Professor of Physiology, University of Cambridge, 1973–87; Fellow of Churchill College, since 1961; *b* 14 Aug. 1919; *e s* of Sir Geoffrey Keynes, MD, FRCP, FRCS, FRCOG, and late Margaret Elizabeth, *d* of Sir George Darwin, KCB; *m* 1945, Anne Pinsent Adrian, *e d* of 1st Baron Adrian, OM, FRS, and Dame Hester Agnes Adrian, DBE, *o d* of Hume C. and Dame Ellen Pinsent, DBE; three *s* (and one *s* decd). *Educ:* Oundle Sch. (Scholar); Trinity Coll., Cambridge (Scholar). Temporary experimental officer, HM Anti-Submarine Establishment and Admiralty Signals Establishment, 1940–45. 1st Class, Nat. Sci. Tripos Part II, 1946; Michael Foster and G. H. Lewes Studentships, 1946; Research Fellow of Trinity Coll., 1948–52; Gedge Prize, 1948; Rolleston Memorial Prize, 1950. Demonstrator in Physiology, University of Cambridge, 1949–53; Lecturer, 1953–60; Fellow of Peterhouse, 1952–60 (Hon. Fellow, 1989); Head of Physiology Dept and Dep. Dir, 1960–64, Dir, 1965–73, ARC Inst. of Animal Physiology. Sec.-Gen., Internat. Union for Pure and Applied Biophysics, 1972–78, Vice-Pres., 1978–81, Pres., 1981–84; Chairman: Internat. Cell Research Orgn, 1981–83; ICSU/Unesco Internat. Biosciences Networks, 1982–93; Pres., Eur. Fedn of Physiol Socs, 1991–94; a Vice-Pres., Royal Society, 1965–68, Croonian Lectr, 1983. Fellow of Eton, 1963–78. Foreign Member: Royal Danish Acad., 1971; American Philosophical Soc., 1977; Amer. Acad. of Arts and Scis, 1978; Amer. Physiolog. Soc., 1994; Acad. Brasileira de Ciencias, 1994. Dr *hc:* Brazil, 1968; Rouen, 1996; Nairobi, 1999. Order of Scientific Merit (Brazil), 1997. *Publications:* The Beagle Record, 1979; (with D. J. Aidley) Nerve and Muscle, 1981, 3rd edn 2001; (ed) Charles Darwin's Beagle Diary, 1988; (co jtly) Lydia and Maynard: the letters of Lydia Lopokova and John Maynard Keynes, 1989; (ed) Charles Darwin's Zoology Notes and Specimen Lists from HMS Beagle, 2000; Fossils, Finches and Fuegians: Charles Darwin's adventures and discoveries on the Beagle 1832–1836, 2002; papers in Journal of Physiology, Proceedings of Royal Soc., etc. *Recreations:* writing, pre-Columbian antiquities. *Address:* 4 Herschel Road, Cambridge CB3 9AG. *T:* (01223) 353107.   *Died 13 June 2010.*

KHABRA, Piara Singh; JP; MP (Lab) Ealing, Southall, since 1992; *b* Punjab, India, 20 Nov. 1924; *m* 1st; one *s*; 2nd, 1990, Beulah Marian. *Educ:* Punjab Univ., India (BA Social Scis, BEd); Whitelands Coll., London (DipEd). Chm., Co-op. Bank and Sarpanch of village Panchayat, Dist Hoshiarpur, Punjab; sch. teacher and later Head of a middle sch.; arrived in UK, 1959; factory work, 1959–61; clerical work, British Oxygen, 1961–64; teacher, ILEA 1964–78; community worker, 1978–86. Councillor (Lab), London Borough of Ealing, 1978–82; Gen. Cttee Delegate, Ealing/Southall CLP, 1989–90; Member: Exec. Cttee, Ealing, 1989; Local Govt Cttee, Ealing, 1989–90. Mem., Select Cttee on Internat. Develt, 1997–. Founder Mem. and Treas., Ealing CRC (Chm., Finance Cttee); Chairman: Southall Community Law Centre, 1982–; Community Prog. Agency, Southall, 1984–88; Member: Unified Community Action; Community Action Policy Gp, Ealing; Indian Workers' Association, Southall: Educn Sec., 1959–63; Gen. Sec., 1963–65 and 1977–79; Chm., 1979–. Trustee, Dominion Centre, Southall (Vice-Chm., Management Cttee). Gov., various schs in Ealing, incl. Featherstone High Sch. JP Ealing 1977. *Address:* House of Commons, SW1A 0AA.   *Died 19 June 2007.*

KHAN, Ghulam Ishaq; President of Pakistan, 1988–93; *b* 20 Jan. 1915; *m* 1950; one *s* five *d*. *Educ:* Islamia Coll., Peshawar; Punjab Univ. Indian Civil Service, 1940–47; NWFP service, 1947–56; Government of West Pakistan: Sec. for Develt and Irrigation, 1956–58; Chm., Water and Power Develt Authy, 1961–66; Chm., Land Reforms Commn, 1978; Sec., Finance, 1966–70; Cabinet Sec.,

1970; Sec.-Gen., Ministry of Defence, 1975–77; Sec.-Gen.-in-Chief, Adviser for Planning and Co-ordination, 1977–78; Adviser to Chief Martial Law Administrator, 1978; Minister for Finance and Co-ordination, 1978–79, for Finance, Econ. Affairs, Commerce and Co-ordination, 1979–85; Chairman of Senate, 1985–88. Governor, State Bank of Pakistan, 1971–75; Chm., Jt Ministerial Cttee, Board of Governors of World Bank and IMF, 1982–88. Life Pres., Soc. for Promotion of Engrg Scis and Technology in Pakistan, 1988–; Pres., Bd of Govs, Gulam Ishaq Khan Inst. of Engrg Scis and Technology, 1988–. Millennium Gold Medal, Sarhad Arts Soc., NWFP, Pakistan, 2000. *Address:* 3–B Jamrud Road, University Town, Peshawar, NWFP, Pakistan.
Died 27 Oct. 2006.

KIDD, Prof. Frank Forrest; Partner, Coopers & Lybrand, Chartered Accountants, 1979–97; *b* 4 May 1938; *s* of Frank F. Kidd and Constance Mary Kidd (*née* Godman); *m* 1961, Beryl Ann (*née* Gillespie); two *s* two *d*. *Educ:* George Heriot's Sch., Ballards. CA; Mem. Inst. of Taxation. CA apprentice, 1955–60; Partner, Wylie & Hutton, 1962–79; Partner, Coopers & Lybrand, 1979 (following merger of Coopers & Lybrand with Wylie & Hutton). Pres., Inst. of Chartered Accountants of Scotland, 1988–89. Hon. Prof., Dept of Accountancy and Business Law, Univ. of Stirling, 1987–94. Master, Co. of Merchants of City of Edinburgh, 1995–97. *Recreations:* squash, golf, walking. *Address:* 17 Merchiston Park, Edinburgh EH10 4PW. *T:* (0131) 229 3577. *Clubs:* New (Edinburgh); Luffness New Golf (Gullane).
Died 15 March 2008.

KIDWELL, Raymond Incledon; QC 1968; a Recorder, 1972–95; a Deputy High Court Judge, 1976–95; *b* 8 Aug. 1926; *s* of late Montague and Dorothy Kidwell; *m* 1st, 1951, Enid Rowe (marr. diss. 1975); two *s*; 2nd, 1976, Carol Evelyn Beryl Maddison, *d* of late Warren G. Hopkins, Ontario. *Educ:* Whitgift Sch.; Magdalen Coll., Oxford. RAFVR, 1944–48. BA (Law) 1st cl. 1950; MA 1951; BCL 1st cl. 1951; Vinerian Law Schol., 1951; Eldon Law Schol., 1951; Arden Law Schol., Gray's Inn, 1952; Birkenhead Law Schol., Gray's Inn, 1955. Called to Bar, 1951; Bencher, 1978. Lectr in Law, Oriel Coll., Oxford, 1952–55; Mem., Winn Commn on Personal Injuries, 1966–68. Member: Bar Council, 1967–71; Senate, 1981–85. *Address:* Sanderstead House, Rectory Park, Sanderstead, Surrey CR2 9JR. *T:* (020) 8657 4161; 2 Crown Office Row, Temple, EC4Y 7HJ. *T:* (020) 7797 8100, *Fax:* (020) 7797 8101.
Died 3 Oct. 2007.

KILBRACKEN, 3rd Baron *cr* 1909, of Killegar; **John Raymond Godley,** DSC 1945; journalist and author; *b* 17 Oct. 1920; *er s* of 2nd Baron Kilbracken, CB, KC, and Elizabeth Helen Monteith, *d* of Vereker Hamilton and *widow* of Wing Commander N. F. Usborne, RNAS; *S* father, 1950; *m* 1st, 1943, Penelope Anne (marr. diss. 1949), *y d* of Rear-Adm. Sir C. N. Reyne, KBE; one *s* (and one *s* decd); 2nd, 1981, Susan Lee (marr. diss. 1989), *yr d* of N. F. Heazlewood, Melbourne, Australia; one *s*. *Educ:* Eton; Balliol Coll., Oxford (MA). Served in RNVR (Fleet Air Arm), as pilot, 1940–46; commissioned 1941; Lieut-Comdr (A) 1945; commanded Nos 835 and 714 Naval Air Sqdns. A reporter for: Daily Mirror, 1947–49; Sunday Express, 1949–51; freelance contributor as writer and photographer to many UK and foreign magazines and newspapers, 1951–96. TV documentaries: The Yemen, 1965; Morgan's Treasure, 1965; Kurdistan, 1966. Joined Parly Liberal Party, 1953; transferred to Labour, 1966; Ind., 1999–. Hon. Sec., Connacht Hereford Breeders' Assoc., 1973–76. Pres., British-Kurdish Friendship Soc., 1975–90. *Publications:* Even For An Hour (poems), 1940; Tell Me The Next One, 1950; The Master Forger, 1951; (ed) Letters From Early New Zealand, 1951; Living Like a Lord, 1955; A Peer Behind the Curtain, 1959; Shamrocks and Unicorns, 1962; Van Meegeren, 1967; Bring Back My Stringbag, 1979; The Easy Way to Bird Recognition, 1982 (TES Sen. Information Book Award, 1983); The Easy Way to Tree Recognition, 1983; The Easy Way to Wild Flower Recognition, 1984. *Recreations:* bird-watching, chess. *Heir: s* Hon. Christopher John Godley [*b* 1 Jan. 1945; *m* 1969, Gillian Christine, *yr d* of late Lt-Comdr S. W. Birse OBE, DSC, RN retd, Alverstoke; one *s* one *d*. *Educ:* Rugby; Reading Univ. (BSc Agric.)]. *Address:* Killegar, Co. Leitrim, Ireland. *T:* and *Fax:* (49) 4334309; *e-mail:* johnkilbracken@aol.com. *Died 14 Aug. 2006.*

KILBY, Michael Leopold; *b* 3 Sept. 1924; *s* of Guy and Grace Kilby; *m* 1952, Mary Sanders; three *s*. *Educ:* Luton College of Technology. General Motors, 1942–80: Apprentice; European Planning and Govt and Trade Regulations Manager; European Sales, Marketing and Service Ops Manager; Plant Manager, Southampton, 1966–71; internat. management consultant, 1980–84. Mayor of Dunstable, 1963–64. MEP (C) Nottingham, 1984–89; contested (C) Nottingham, Eur. parly elecn, 1989. Member: SE Economic Planning Council, 1969; Industry and Economic Cttee, British Assoc. of Chambers of Commerce. *Publications:* The Man at the Sharp End, 1983, 2nd edn 1991; Mammon's Ladder, 1993; technical and political papers. *Recreations:* all sports; first love cricket; former Minor Counties cricketer. *Address:* Hall House, Moor Hill, Hawkhurst, Kent TN18 4QB.
Died 9 Sept. 2008.

KILGOUR, Dr John Lowell, CB 1987, Occupational Health consultant, 1994–2002; *b* 26 July 1924; *s* of Ormonde John Lowell Kilgour and Catherine (*née* MacInnes); *m* 1955, Daphne (*née* Tully); two *s*. *Educ:* St Christopher's Prep. Sch., Hove; Aberdeen Grammar Sch.; Aberdeen Univ. MB, ChB 1947, MRCGP, FFCM. Joined RAMC, 1948; served in: Korea, 1950–52; Cyprus, 1956; Suez, 1956; Singapore, 1961–64 (Brunei, Sarawak); comd 23 Para. Field Amb., 1954–57; psc 1959; ADMS GHQ FARELF, 1961–64; jssc 1964; Comdt, Field Trng Sch., RAMC, 1965–66. Joined Min. of Health, 1968, Med. Manpower and Postgrad. Educn Divs; Head of Internat. Health Div., DHSS, 1971–78; Under-Sec. and Chief Med. Advr, Min. of Overseas Develt, 1973–78; Dir of Co-ordination, WHO, 1978–83; Dir, Prison Medical Services, Home Office, 1983–89; Chairman: CS Commn Recruitment Bds, 1989–91; Industrial Injuries and War Pensions Med. Bds, 1989–94; Med. Examnr, Benefits Agency, DSS, 1989–94. UK Deleg. to WHO and to Council of Europe Public Health Cttees; Chm., European Public Health Cttee, 1976; Mem. WHO Expert Panel on Communicable Diseases, 1972–78, 1983; Chm., Cttee for Internat. Surveillance of Communicable Diseases, 1976; Consultant, WHO Special Programme on AIDS, 1987. Vis. Lectr, 1976–89, Governor, 1987–89, LSHTM; Mem. Governing Council, Liverpool Sch. of Tropical Medicine, 1973–87; Mem. Council, 1983–89, Mem. Exec. Cttee, 1987–90, Royal Commonwealth Society for the Blind. Winner, Cons. Constituency Speakers' Competition for London and the SE, 1968. Cantacucino Medal, for services to internat. health, Medical Inst. of Bucharest, Romania, 1980. *Publications:* chapter in, Migration of Medical Manpower, 1971; chapter in, The Global Impact of AIDS, 1988; contrib. The Lancet, BMJ, Hospital Medicine, Health Trends and other med. jls. *Recreations:* horse racing, reading, gardening, travel. *Address:* Stoke House, 22 Amersham Road, Chesham Bois, Bucks HP6 5PE.
Died 26 Sept. 2008.

KILLEN, Hon. Sir (Denis) James, AC 2004; KCMG 1982; *b* 23 Nov. 1925; *s* of James W. Killen, Melbourne; *m* 1st, 1949, Joyce Claire Buley (*d* 2000); two *d* (and one *d* decd); 2nd, 2001, Benise Atherton. *Educ:* Brisbane Grammar Sch.; Univ. of Queensland (LLB). Barrister-at-Law. Jackaroo; RAAF (Flight Serjeant); Mem. staff, Rheem (Aust.) Pty Ltd. MP (L) Moreton, Queensland, 1955–83; Minister for the Navy, 1969–71; Opposition Spokesman: on Educn, 1973–74; on Defence, 1975; Minister for Defence, 1975–82; Vice-Pres. of Exec. Council and Leader, House of Representatives, Commonwealth of Australia, 1982–83. Foundn Pres., Young Liberals Movement (Qld); Vice-Pres., Lib. Party,

Qld Div., 1953–56. *Recreations:* horseracing, golf. *Address:* 253 Chapel Hill Road, Chapel Hill, Qld 4069, Australia. *Clubs:* Tattersall's, Irish Association, QTC (Brisbane).
Died 12 Jan. 2007.

KILMARNOCK, 7th Baron *cr* 1831; **Alastair Ivor Gilbert Boyd;** Chief of the Clan Boyd; *b* 11 May 1927; *s* of 6th Baron Kilmarnock, MBE, TD, and Hon. Rosemary Guest (*d* 1971), *er d* of 1st Viscount Wimborne; *S* father, 1975; *m* 1st, 1954, Diana Mary (marr. diss. 1970, she *d* 1975), *o d* of D. Grant Gibson; 2nd, 1977, Hilary Ann, *yr d* of Leonard Sidney and Margery Bardwell; one *s. Educ:* Bradfield; King's Coll., Cambridge. Lieutenant, Irish Guards, 1946; served Palestine, 1947–48. Mem. SDP, 1981–92; Chief SDP Whip, House of Lords, 1983–86; Dep. Leader, SDP Peers, 1986–87. Chm., All-Party Parly Gp on AIDS, 1987–96. *Publications:* Sabbatical Year, 1958; The Road from Ronda, 1969; The Companion Guide to Madrid and Central Spain, 1974, revised edn 2002; (ed) The Radical Challenge: the response of social democracy, 1987; The Essence of Catalonia, 1988; The Sierras of the South, 1992; The Social Market and the State, 1999; Rosemary: a memoir, 2005. *Heir: b* Dr the Hon. Robin Jordan Boyd, MB BS, MRCP, MRCPEd, DCH, *b* 6 June 1941. *Address:* Apartado 445, 29400 Ronda (Málaga), Spain.
Died 19 March 2009.

KILMISTER, Prof. Clive William; Professor of Mathematics, King's College, London, 1966–84; *b* 3 Jan. 1924; *s* of William and Doris Kilmister; *m* 1955, Peggy Joyce Hutchins; one *s* two *d. Educ:* Queen Mary Coll., Univ. of London. BSc 1944, MSc 1948, PhD 1950. King's Coll. London: Asst Lectr, 1950; Lectr, 1953; Reader, 1959; FKC 1983. Gresham Prof. of Geometry, 1972–88. President: British Soc. for History of Mathematics, 1973–76; Mathematical Assoc., 1979–80; British Soc. for Philos. of Science, 1981–83. *Publications:* (with G. Stephenson) Special Relativity for Physicists, 1958; (with B. O. J. Tupper) Eddington's Statistical Theory, 1962; Hamiltonian Dynamics, 1964; The Environment in Modern Physics, 1965; (with J. E. Reeve) Rational Mechanics, 1966; Men of Physics: Sir Arthur Eddington, 1966; Language, Logic and Mathematics, 1967; Lagrangian Dynamics, 1967; Special Theory of Relativity, 1970; The Nature of the Universe, 1972; General Theory of Relativity, 1973; Philosophers in Context: Russell, 1984; (ed) Schrödinger: centenary celebration of a polymath, 1987; Eddington's search for a fundamental theory, 1995; (with Ted Bastin) Combinatorial Physics, 1995; (with Ted Bastin) Origin of Discrete Particles, 2009. *Recreation:* opera going. *Address:* Red Tiles Cottage, High Street, Barcombe, Lewes, East Sussex BN8 5DH. *Died 2 May 2010.*

KILVINGTON, Frank Ian; Headmaster of St Albans School, 1964–84; *b* West Hartlepool, 26 June 1924; *e s* of H. H. Kilvington; *m* 1949, Jane Mary, *d* of late Very Rev. Michael Clarke and of Katharine Beryl (*née* Girling); one *s* one *d. Educ:* Repton (entrance and foundn scholar); Corpus Christi, Oxford (open class. scholar). 2nd cl. Lit.Hum., 1948; MA 1950. Served War of 1939–45: RNVR, 1943–46 (Lt); West Africa Station, 1943–45; RN Intelligence, Germany, 1945–46. Westminster School: Asst Master, 1949–64; Housemaster of Rigaud's House, 1957–64. Chairman: St Albans Marriage Guidance Council, 1968–74; St Albans CAB, 1981–86; Herts Record Soc., 1985–90; St Albans Hospice Care Team, 1988–93. Pres., St Albans and Herts Architectural and Archæological Soc., 1974–77. *Publications:* A Short History of St Albans School, 1970. *Recreations:* music, local history. *Address:* 122 Marshalswick Lane, St Albans, Herts AL1 4XD. *Died 11 Oct. 2009.*

KIM DAE-JUNG; President of Republic of Korea, 1998–2003; *b* 3 Dec. 1925; *m* Lee Lee Ho; three *s. Educ:* Mokpo Commercial High Sch.; Korea Univ.; Kyunghee Univ.; Diplomatic Acad. of Foreign Ministry, Russia. Pres., Mokpo Merchant Shipping Co., 1948; arrested by N Korean Communists, escaped from jail, 1950; Pres., Mokpo Daily News, 1950; Dep. Comdr, S

Cholla Region, Maritime Defence Force, 1950; Pres., Heungkuk Merchant Shipping Co., 1951; Pres., Daeyang Shipbldg Co., 1951. Mem., Nat. Assembly of Republic of Korea (S Korea), 1961–72, 1988–97; held posts with Democratic Party, People's Party and New Democratic Party; periods of house-arrest, imprisonment and exile; returned from exile in USA to co-lead New Korea Democratic Party, 1985; Pres., Peace and Democracy Party, 1987; Pres., New Democratic Party, later Democratic Party, 1991; Founder, Nat. Congress for New Politics, 1995, which formed alliance with United Liberal Democrats, 1997. Founder and Chm., Kim Dae-Jung Peace Foundn for Asia-Pacific Region, 1994. Nobel Peace Prize, 2000. *Publications include:* Conscience in Action, 1985; Prison Writings, 1987; Building Peace and Democracy, 1987; Kim Dae-Jung's Views on International Affairs, 1990; In the Name of Justice and Peace, 1991; Korea and Asia, 1994; The Korean Problem: nuclear crisis, democracy and reunification, 1994; Unification, Democracy and Peace, 1994; Mass Participatory Economy: Korea's road to world economic power, 1996. *Address:* c/o Chong Wa Dae, 1 Sejong-no, Chongno-ku, Seoul, Republic of Korea. *Died 18 Aug. 2009.*

KIMBER, Sir Charles Dixon, 3rd Bt *cr* 1904; *b* 7 Jan. 1912; *o* surv. *s* of Sir Henry Dixon Kimber, 2nd Bt, and Lucy Ellen, *y d* of late G. W. Crookes; *S* father, 1950; *m* 1st, 1933, Ursula (marr. diss. 1949; she *d* 1981), *er d* of late Ernest Roy Bird, MP; three *s*; 2nd, 1950, Margaret Bonham (marr. diss. 1965), writer; one *d* (one *s* decd). *Educ:* Eton; Balliol Coll., Oxford (BA). Co Founder and Gen. Sec., Federal Union, 1938–41; Market Gardener, 1941–47; Diploma in Social Anthropology, 1948; collaborated in survey of Banbury, 1949–52; small holder, 1952–60; Landlord, Three Pigeons, Drayton St Leonard, 1962–65; apptd to undertake review of Parish Charities in Oxfordshire for Oxfordshire CC, 1967–77. *Heir: s* Timothy Roy Henry Kimber, DL [*b* 3 June 1936; *m* 1960, Antonia Kathleen Brenda (marr. diss. 1974), *d* of Sir Francis Williams, 8th Bt; two *s*; *m* 1979, Susan, *widow* of Richard North, Newton Hall, near Carnforth]. *Address:* Lower End Farm, Great Comberton, Pershore, Worcs WR10 3DU. *T:* (01386) 710230.
Died 10 April 2008.

KIMBLE, Dr David (Bryant), OBE 1962; Editor, Journal of Modern African Studies, 1972–97; *b* 12 May 1921; *s* of John H. and Minnie Jane Kimble; *m* 1st, 1949, Helen Rankin (marr. diss.); three *d* (and one *d* decd); 2nd, 1977, Margareta Westin. *Educ:* Eastbourne Grammar Sch.; Reading Univ. (BA 1942, DipEd 1943, Pres. Students Union, 1942–43); London Univ. (PhD 1961). Lieut RNVR, 1943–46. Oxford Univ. Staff Tutor in Berks, 1946–48, and Resident Tutor in the Gold Coast, 1948–49; Dir, Inst. of Extra-Mural Studies, Univ. of Ghana, 1949–62, and Master of Akuafo Hall, 1960–62; Prof. of Political Science, Univ. Coll., Dar es Salaam, Univ. of E Africa, and Dir, Inst. of Public Admin, Tanzania, 1962–68; Research Advr in Public Admin and Social Sciences, Centre africain de formation et de recherche administratives pour le développement, Tanger, Morocco, 1968–70, and Dir of Research, 1970–71; Prof. of Govt and Admin, Univ. of Botswana, Lesotho, and Swaziland, 1971–75, and Nat. Univ. of Lesotho, 1975–77; Prof. Emeritus, 1978; Tutor in Politics to King Moshoeshoe II, 1975, and Queen 'MaMohato, 1977; Vice-Chancellor, Univ. of Malaŵi, and Chm., Malaŵi Certificate Exam. and Testing Bd, 1977–86. Trustee, Malaŵi Against Polio, and Gov., Kamuzu Acad., 1977–86. Chm., Malaŵi/German/UK Study for Estabt of Med. Sch. in Stages, 1986. Founder and Joint Editor (with Helen Kimble), West African Affairs, 1949–51, Penguin African Series, 1953–61, and Jl of Modern African Studies, 1963–71. Officier, Ordre des Palmes Académiques, 1982. *Publications:* Public Opinion and Government, 1950; The Machinery of Self-Government, 1953; (with Helen Kimble) Adult Education in a Changing Africa, 1955; A Political History of Ghana, Vol. I, The Rise of Nationalism in the Gold Coast, 1850–1928, 1963; nine University Congregation

Addresses, 1978–86; (with Margareta Kimble) Jl of Modern African Studies: indexed bibliography of contents 1963–97, vols 1–35, 1999. *Recreations:* cricket, photography, editing. *Address:* Huish, Chagford, Devon TQ13 8AR. *Died 8 March 2009.*

KING, Alexander, CMG 1975; CBE 1948; Co-Founder, 1968, and Hon. President, Club of Rome (President, 1984–91); *b* Glasgow, 26 Jan. 1909; *s* of J. M. King; *m* 1933, Sarah Maskell Thompson (*d* 1999); two *d* (and one *d* decd). *Educ:* Highgate Sch.; Royal College of Science, London (DSc; FIC 1992); University of Munich. Demonstrator, 1932, and later Sen. Lectr, until 1940, in physical chemistry, Imperial Coll. of Science; Dep. Scientific Advr, Min. of Production, 1942; Head of UK Scientific Mission, Washington, and Scientific Attaché, British Embassy 1943–47; Head of Lord President's Scientific Secretariat, 1947–50; Chief Scientific Officer, Dept of Scientific and Industrial Research, 1950–56; Dep. Dir, European Productivity Agency, 1956–61; Dir for Scientific Affairs, OECD, 1961–68, Dir-Gen., 1968–74. Chm., Internat. Fedn of Insts for Advanced Study, 1974–84. Advr, Govt of Ontario. Assoc. Fellow, Center for the Study of Democratic Instns, Santa Barbara, Calif; Visiting Professor: Brandeis Univ., 1978; Univ. of Montréal, 1979. Mem. Council, RGS, 1939–41; Hon. Sec., Chemical Soc., 1948–50, Leader Imperial Coll. Expedition to Jan Mayen, 1938. Harrison Prize of Chemical Soc., 1938; Gill Meml Prize, RGS, 1938; Erasmus Prize, 1987; Great Medal of Paris, 1988. DSc (*hc*): Ireland, 1974; Guelph, 1987; Bucharest, 1993; DUniv Open, 1976; Hon. LLD Strathclyde, 1982. US Medal of Freedom, 1946. *Publications:* The International Stimulus, 1974; The State of the Planet, 1980; The First Global Revolution, 1991; various chemistry textbooks, and papers in Jl of Chemical Soc., Faraday Soc.; numerous articles on education, science policy and management. *Address:* 5 Chartwell House, 12 Ladbroke Terrace, W11 3PG; La Negronne, Callian, 83440 Fayence, France. *Club:* Athenæum. *Died 28 Feb. 2007.*

KING, Rt Rev. Brian Franklin Vernon; Bishop of Western Sydney (formerly Bishop in Parramatta) and an Assistant Bishop of Sydney, 1993–2003; *b* 3 Jan. 1938; *s* of Francis Brindley King and Merle Florence King; *m* 1965, Pamela Diane Gifford; three *s. Educ:* Sydney Boys' High Sch.; Univ. of NSW (BComm 1961); Univ. of London (BDiv 1964); Fuller Theol Seminary, Pasadena (DMin 1985); Moore Coll., NSW (Diploma); Aust. Coll. of Theol. (DipRE). ACA (Sydney) 1959. Chartered Accountant, 1959–61; theology student, 1961–64; ordained deacon, 1964, priest, 1965; Curate, Manly Anglican Church, 1964–67; Rector: Dural, 1967–73; Wahroonga, 1973–87; Manly, 1987–93; Canon, St Andrew's Cathedral, Sydney, 1989–93; Anglican Bishop to the Aust Defence Force, 1994–2001; Priest-in-charge, S Malling, dio. Chichester, 2003–04, retired. *Recreations:* travel, gardening, sport, family. *Address:* 38 Warringah Street, North Balgowlah, Sydney, NSW 2093, Australia. *Clubs:* Gordon Rugby (Chatswood, Sydney); City Tattersalls (Sydney). *Died 22 Nov. 2006.*

KING, Charles Martin M.; *see* Meade-King.

KING, Dr John William Beaufoy; Director, Advanced Breeders Ltd, since 1988; Head of AFRC Animal Breeding Liaison Group, 1982–87; *b* 28 June 1927; *s* of late John Victor Beaufoy and Gwendoleen Freda King; *m* 1951, Pauline Margaret Coldicott; four *s. Educ:* Marling Sch., Stroud; St Catharine's Coll., Cambridge; Edinburgh Univ. BA Cantab 1947, MA Cantab 1952; PhD Edinburgh 1951. FIBiol 1974; FRSE 1975. ARC Animal Breeding Res. Organisation, 1951–82. Kellogg Foundn Schol. to USA, 1954; Genetics Cons. to Pig Industry Develt Authority, 1959; Nuffield Foundn Fellowship to Canada, 1970; Vis. Lectr, Göttingen Univ., 1973. David Black Award (services to pig industry), 1966. *Publications:* papers in scientific jls. *Recreations:* gardening, dog training. *Address:* Cottage Farm, West Linton, Peeblesshire EH46 7AS. *T:* (01968) 660448. *Died 12 Jan. 2006.*

KING, Mark Baxter B.; *see* Barty-King.

KING, His Honour Michael Gardner; a Circuit Judge, 1972–87; *b* 4 Dec. 1920; *s* of late David Thomson King and Winifred Mary King, Bournemouth; *m* 1951, Yvonne Mary Lilian, *d* of late Lt-Col M. J. Ambler; two *s* one *d. Educ:* Sherborne Sch.; Wadham Coll., Oxford (MA). Served in RN, Lieut RNVR, 1940–46. Called to Bar, Gray's Inn, 1949. Dep. Chm., IoW QS, 1966–72; Dep. Chm., Hants QS, 1968–72. *Recreations:* sailing, shooting, golf. *Clubs:* Royal Naval Sailing Association, Royal Lymington Yacht (Cdre, 1986–88). *Died 7 Oct. 2008.*

KING, Rev. Canon Philip David; Secretary, Church of England Board of Mission, 1991–2000 (Secretary, Board for Mission and Unity, 1989–91); *b* 6 May 1935; *s* of Frank Harman King and Gladys Winifred King; *m* 1963, Margaret Naomi Rivers Pitt; two *s* two *d. Educ:* Keble College, Oxford (MA Jurisp.); Tyndale Hall, Bristol. Curate, Holy Trinity, Redhill, 1960–63; Minister in charge, St Patrick's, Wallington, 1963–68; Vicar, Christ Church, Fulham, 1968–74; Gen. Sec., S American Missionary Soc., 1974–86; Vicar, Christ Church and St Peter, Harrow, 1986–89. *Publications:* Leadership Explosion, 1987; Making Christ Known, 1992; Good News For A Suffering World, 1996; Leading a Church, 1997. *Recreation:* hill-walking. *Address:* 31 Myrtle Avenue, Ruislip, Middlesex HA4 8SA. *T:* and *Fax:* (020) 8429 0636. *Died 26 April 2006.*

KING, Dame Thea, (Dame Thea Thurston), DBE 2001 (OBE 1985); FRCM, FGSM; freelance musician; Professor, Guildhall School of Music, since 1988; *b* 26 Dec. 1925; *m* Jan. 1953, Frederick John Thurston (*d* Dec. 1953). *Educ:* Bedford High Sch.; Royal College of Music (FRCM 1975; ARCM 1944 and 1947), FGSM 1992. Prof. of Clarinet, RCM, 1961–87. Sadler's Wells Orchestra, 1950–52; Portia Wind Ensemble, 1955–68; London Mozart Players, 1956–84; Member: English Chamber Orchestra, Vesuvius Ensemble, Robles Ensemble. Frequent soloist, broadcaster, recitalist; recordings include Mozart, Brahms, Spohr, Finzi, Bruch, Mendelssohn, Stanford and 20th Century British music. Hon. RAM 1998. *Publications:* clarinet solos, Chester Woodwind series, 1977; arrangement of J. S. Bach, Duets for 2 Clarinets, 1979; Schumann for the Clarinet, 1991; Mendelssohn for the Clarinet, 1993; The Romantic Clarinet, Vol. 1, 1994, Vol. 2, 1995. *Recreations:* cows, pillow lace, painting, ski-ing, piano-playing. *Address:* 16 Milverton Road, NW6 7AS. *T:* (020) 8459 3453. *Died 26 June 2007.*

KING-HAMILTON, His Honour (Myer) Alan (Barry); QC 1954; an additional Judge of the Central Criminal Court, 1964–79; a Deputy Circuit Judge, 1979–83; *b* 9 Dec. 1904; *o s* of Alfred King-Hamilton; *m* 1935, Rosalind Irene Ellis (*d* 1991); two *d. Educ:* York House Prep. Sch.; Bishop's Stortford Grammar Sch.; Trinity Hall, Cambridge (BA 1927, MA 1929; Hon. Fellow, 2003). President: Cambridge Univ. Law Soc., 1926–27; Cambridge Union Soc., 1927. Called to Bar, Middle Temple, 1929 (Bencher, 1961); served War of 1939–45, RAF, finishing with rank of Squadron Leader; served on Finchley Borough Council, 1938–39 and 1945–50. Recorder of Hereford, 1955–56; Recorder of Gloucester, 1956–61; Recorder of Wolverhampton, 1961–64; Dep. Chm. Oxford County Quarter Sessions, 1955–64, 1966–71; Leader of Oxford Circuit, 1961–64. Elected to General Council of Bar, 1958. Pres., West London Reform Synagogue, 1967–75, 1977–83 (Hon. Life Pres., 1995); Vice-Pres., World Congress of Faiths, 1967–. Legal Member: Med. Practices Cttee, Min. of Health, 1946–64; ABTA Appeal Bd, 1980–95; Mem., Arts and Library Cttee, MCC, 1985–89; first Chm., Pornography and Violence Res. Trust (formerly Mary Whitehouse Res. and Educn Trust), 1986–96 (Mem. Cttee, 1996–2003). President: Weston Housing Assoc., 1995–97 (Founder Mem. and first Chm., 1975–95; Hon. Life Pres., 1998); Birnbeck Housing Assoc., 1995–98 (Founder Mem. and Mem. Cttee, 1982–95; Hon. Life

Pres., 1998). Trustee, Barnet Community Trust, 1986–89. Co-founder, Refreshers CC, 1935. Freeman of City of London; Master, Needlemakers' Co., 1969. *Publications:* And Nothing But the Truth (autobiog.), 1982. *Recreations:* cricket, gardening, the theatre. *Clubs:* Royal Air Force, MCC. *Died 23 March 2010.*

KINGHORN, William Oliver; Chief Agricultural Officer, Department of Agriculture and Fisheries for Scotland, 1971–75; *b* 17 May 1913; *s* of Thomas Kinghorn, Duns, and Elizabeth Oliver; *m* 1943, Edith Johnstone; one *s* two *d. Educ:* Berwickshire High Sch.; Edinburgh Univ. BSc (Agr) Hons, BSc Hons. Senior Inspector, 1946; Technical Develt Officer, 1959; Chief Inspector, 1970. SBStJ. *Publications:* contrib. Annals of Applied Biology, 1936. *Address:* Strachan House, 93 Craigcrook Road, Edinburgh EH4 3PE. *T:* (0131) 336 0050. *Died 22 Oct. 2008.*

KINGSLAND, Baron *cr* 1994 (Life Peer), of Shrewsbury in the County of Shropshire; **Christopher James Prout,** Kt 1990; TD 1987; PC 1994; QC 1988; DL; barrister-at-law; a Deputy High Court Judge, since 2005; *b* 1 Jan. 1942; *s* of late Frank Yabsley Prout, MC and bar, and Doris Lucy Prout (*née* Osborne); *m* Carolyn; four step *c. Educ:* Sevenoaks Sch.; Manchester Univ. (BA); The Queen's Coll., Oxford (Scholar; BPhil, DPhil; Hon. Fellow 2006). TA Officer (Major): OU OTC, 1966–74; 16/5 The Queen's Royal Lancers, 1974–82; 3rd Armoured Div., 1982–88; RARO, 1988–97. Called to the Bar, Middle Temple, 1972 (Bencher, 1996; Master of the Garden, 1999–); an Asst Recorder, Wales and Chester Circuit, 1997–99; a Recorder, 2000–05. English-Speaking Union Fellow, Columbia Univ., NYC, 1963–64; Staff Mem., IBRD (UN), Washington DC, 1966–69; Leverhulme Fellow and Lectr in Law, Sussex Univ., 1969–79. MEP (C) Shropshire and Stafford, 1979–94; contested (C) Herefordshire and Shropshire, Eur. parly elecns, 1994. Leader, British Cons. MEPs, 1987–94; Dep. Whip, 1979–82, Chief Whip, 1983–87, Chairman and Leader, 1987–92, EDG; Vice Chm., Eur. People's Party Parly Gp, 1992–94; Chm., Parlt Cttee on Legal Affairs, 1987. Rapporteur, Revision of Eur. Parlt's Rules of Procedure, 1987 and 1993. Shadow Lord Chancellor, 1997–2008. Chm. Sub-Cttee F, H of L Select Cttee on EC, 1996–97. Chm., Jersey Competition Regulatory Authy, 2004–. Vice Chm., Justice, 2006–. Chm., Plymouth Marine Lab., 2002–. Pres., Shropshire and W Midlands Agricl Soc., 1993. Master, Shrewsbury Drapers' Co., 1995. DL Shropshire, 1997. Grande Médaille de la Ville de Paris, 1988; Schuman Medal, EPP, 1995. *Publications:* Market Socialism in Yugoslavia, 1985; (contrib.) vols 8, 51 and 52, Halsbury's Laws of England, 4th edn; various lectures, pamphlets, chapters and articles. *Recreations:* boating, gardening, musical comedy, the turf. *Address:* c/o House of Lords, SW1A 0PW. *Clubs:* White's, Pratt's, Beefsteak, Buck's (Hon. Mem.), Royal Ocean Racing; Royal Yacht Squadron. *Died 12 July 2009.*

KINGSLEY, Roger James, OBE 1992; FREng, FIChemE; Director, Kingsley Process & Management, retired 2000; Consultant and Director, CAPCIS Ltd, retired 1999; *b* 2 Feb. 1922; *s* of Felix and Helene Loewenstein; changed name to Kingsley, 1942; *m* 1949, Valerie Marguerite Mary (*née* Hanna); one *s* two *d. Educ:* Manchester Grammar Sch.; Faculty of Technol., Manchester Univ. (BScTech); Harvard Business Sch. (Internat. Sen. Managers Program). Served War, Royal Fusiliers, 1940–46; Commando service, 1942–45; Captain; mentioned in despatches, 1946. Chemical Engr, Petrocarbon Ltd, 1949–51; technical appts, ultimately Tech. Dir, Lankro Chemicals Ltd, 1952–62; gen. management appts, Lankro Chemicals Group Ltd, 1962–77; Man. Dir, Lankro Chemicals Group Ltd, 1972–77; Director: ICI-Lankro Plasticisers Ltd, 1972–77; Fallek-Lankro Corp., Tuscaloosa, Ala, 1976–77; Dep. Chm., Diamond Shamrock Europe, 1977–82; Chairman: Duolite Internat., 1978–84; LMK Engrg, 1985–89; Freeman Process Systems, 1986–92; UMIST Ventures,

1988–94. Pres., IChemE, 1974–75. Member: Court of Governors, UMIST, 1969–79, 1985–. Hon. DEng UMIST, 1998. *Publications:* contrib. Chem. Engr, and Proc. IMechE. *Recreations:* ski-ing, riding, music. *Club:* Royal Anglo-Belgian. *Died 2 Jan. 2008.*

KINGTON, Miles Beresford; humorous columnist; *b* 13 May 1941; *s* of William Beresford Nairn Kington and Jean Anne Kington; *m* 1st, 1964, Sarah Paine (marr. diss. 1987); one *s* one *d;* 2nd, 1987, Mrs Hilary Caroline Maynard; one *s. Educ:* Trinity College, Glenalmond; Trinity College, Oxford (BA Mod Langs). Plunged into free-lance writing, 1963; took up part-time gardening while starving to death, 1964; jazz reviewer, The Times, 1965; joined staff of Punch, 1967, Literary Editor, 1973, left 1980; free-lance, 1980–; daily Moreover column in The Times, 1981–86; columnist, The Independent, 1986–; ex-member, musical group Instant Sunshine on double bass; jazz player, 1970–; *television:* various programmes incl. Three Miles High (Great Railway Journeys of the World series), 1980, Steam Days, 1986, and The Burma Road, 1989; In Search of the Holy Foreskin, 1996; writer and presenter, Fine Families, 1998; *radio:* co-presenter with Edward Enfield, Double Vision, 1996–; presenter of BBC Radio 4 documentaries on de Gaulle, Brezhnev, Franco, Django Reinhardt, etc., 2004–05. Stage play, Waiting for Stoppard, Bristol New Vic, 1995; stage shows with Simon Gilman, Edinburgh Festival: Bizarre, 1995; Death of Tchaikovsky - a Sherlock Holmes Mystery, 1996. *Publications:* World of Alphonse Allais, 1977, repr. as A Wolf in Frog's Clothing, 1983; 4 Franglais books, 1979–82; Moreover, 1982; Miles and Miles, 1982; Nature Made Ridiculously Simple, 1983; Moreover, Too…, 1985; The Franglais Lieutenant's Woman, 1986; Welcome to Kington, 1989; Steaming Through Britain, 1990; (ed) Jazz: an anthology, 1992; Motorway Madness, 1998; (ed) The Pick of Punch, 1998; Someone Like Me: tales from a borrowed childhood, 2005. *Recreations:* mending punctures, rehabilitating Clementi's piano works, falsifying personal records to mystify potential biographers. *Address:* Lower Hayes, Limpley Stoke, Bath BA2 7FR. *T:* (01225) 722262. *Clubs:* 100, Ronnie Scott's. *Died 30 Jan. 2008.*

KINNEAR, Ian Albert Clark, (Tim), CMG 1974; HM Diplomatic Service, retired; *b* 23 Dec. 1924; *s* of late George Kinnear, CBE and Georgina Lilian (*née* Stephenson), Nairobi; *m* 1966, Rosemary, *d* of late Dr K. W. D. Hartley, Cobham; two *d. Educ:* Pembroke House, Gilgil, Kenya; Marlborough Coll.; Lincoln Coll., Oxford (MA). HM Forces, 1943–46 (1st E Africa Reconnaissance Regt). Colonial Service (later HMOCS): Malayan Civil Service, 1951–56: District Officer, Bentong, then Alor Gajah, Asst Sec. Econ. Planning Unit; Kenya, 1956–63: Asst Sec., then Sen. Asst Sec., Min. of Commerce and Industry; 1st Sec., CRO, later Commonwealth Office, 1963–66; 1st Sec. (Commercial), British Embassy, Djakarta, 1966–68; 1st Sec. and Head of Chancery, British High Commn, Dar-es-Salaam, 1969–71; Chief Sec., later Dep. Governor, Bermuda, 1971–74; Senior British Trade Comr, Hong Kong, 1974–77; Consul-Gen., San Francisco, 1977–82. *Recreation:* painting. *Address:* Castle Hill Cottage, Crook Road, Brenchley, Tonbridge, Kent TN12 7BN. *T:* (01892) 723782. *Died 29 Oct. 2008.*

KIRBY, David Donald, CBE 1988; formerly railway manager and transport consultant; Chairman, Halcrow Transmark (formerly Transmark), 1994–97; *b* 12 May 1933; *s* of Walter Donald Kirby and Margaret Irene (*née* Halstead); *m* 1955, Joan Florence (*née* Dickins); one *s* one *d. Educ:* Royal Grammar Sch., High Wycombe; Jesus Coll., Oxford (MA). FCILT. British Rail and its subsidiaries: Divisional Shipping Manager, Dover, 1964; Operations Manager, Shipping and Continental, 1965; Asst Gen. Man., Shipping and International Services, 1966; Continental Traffic Man., BR, 1968; Gen. Man., Shipping and Internat. Services, 1974; Man. Dir, Sealink UK Ltd, 1979; Dir, London and SE, 1982–85; Mem.,

1985–89, Jt Man. Dir (Rlys), 1985–87, Vice-Chm., 1987–89, BRB. *Recreations:* painting, choral singing. *Address:* 25 East Street, Martlock, Somerset TA12 6NG.
Died 12 April 2008.

KIRBY, Gwendolen Maud, LVO 1969; Matron, The Hospital for Sick Children, Great Ormond Street, 1951–69; *b* 17 Dec. 1911; 3rd *d* of late Frank M. Kirby, Gravesend, Kent. *Educ:* St Mary's Sch., Calne, Wilts. State Registered Nurse: trained at Nightingale Training Sch., St Thomas' Hosp., SE1, 1933–36; The Mothercraft Training Soc., Cromwell House, Highgate, 1936; State Certified Midwife: trained at General Lying-in Hosp., York Road, Lambeth, 1938–39; Registered Sick Children's Nurse: trained at the Hospital for Sick Children, Great Ormond Street, WC1, 1942–44. Awarded Nightingale Fund Travelling Scholarship, 1948–49, and spent 1 year in Canada and United States. Member: RCN, 1936–; Gen. Nursing Council, 1955–65. *Address:* Brackenfield, Winsford, Minehead, Som TA24 7JL. *Died 30 March 2007.*

KIRBY, Louis Albert Francis; Editor, UK Mail, 1993–2003; *b* 30 Nov. 1928; 2nd *s* of late William Kirby and Anne Kirby; *m* 1st, 1952, Marcia Teresa Lloyd (marr. diss. 1976); two *s* three *d*; 2nd, 1976, Heather Veronica (*née* Nicholson); one *s* one *d*; 3rd, 1983, Heather McGlone; two *d*. *Educ:* Coalbrookdale High Sch. Daily Mail: Gen. Reporter, subseq. Courts Corresp., and Polit. Corresp., 1953–62; Daily Sketch: Chief Reporter, subseq. Leader Writer and Polit. Editor, Asst Editor, Exec. Editor, and, Actg Editor, 1962–71; Dep. Editor, Daily Mail (when relaunched), 1971–74; Editor, Evening News, 1974–80; Vice-Chm., Evening News Ltd, 1975–80; Editor, Evening Standard, 1980–86; Editl Dir, Mail Newspapers plc, 1986–88; Political Consultant, Daily Mail, 1988–93. *Recreations:* theatre, reading. *Address:* Northcliffe House, Derry Street, W8 5TT. *Club:* Special Forces. *Died 14 Oct. 2006.*

KIRKPATRICK, Gavin Alexander Yvone, FCIPD, FBCS, CITP; Chief Executive, The British Computer Society, 1991–95; *b* 8 July 1938; *s* of late Yvone Kirkpatrick, OBE, TD, MA and Margaret (*née* Sclanders); *m* 1961, Susan Ann Frances Parselle; two *s* one *d*. *Educ:* Cheltenham Coll. Nat. Service, RN, 1957–59. John Trundell & Partners, Publishers, 1959–61; International Computers Ltd: Technical Sales, Personnel Officer, 1961–67; Personnel Manager Internat., 1967–70; Sperry Univac Division of Sperry Rand Corporation: Personnel Dir, Europe, 1970–76; Dir, Worldwide Personnel, Planning and Develt (USA), 1976–78; International Computers Plc, 1978–91: Gp Personnel Manager, 1978–81; Ops Personnel Manager, HQ, 1981–92; on secondment to Brit. Computer Soc. as Programme Dir, Europe, 1989–91. Member: European Movt, 1990– (Vice Chm., Outer London Europe Gp, 1991–95; Sec., 1996–99, Chm., 1999–2004, Central & W Dorset Br.; Vice Chm., Branches Assoc., 1997–99; Mem. Mgt Bd, 1998–2000; Chm., Branches Council, 1999–2000); British-German Assoc., 1992–. Friend, London Bach Soc., 1989– (Mem. Cttee, 1996–2001). FCIPD 1990; FBCS 1992; CITP 2004; MInstD 1970. FRSA 1992. Liveryman, Co. of Information Technologists, 1994–2006. *Recreations:* music, sailing, travel, photography, other Europeans. *Address:* West Walks House, Dorchester, Dorset DT1 1RE. *T:* (01305) 269946, *Fax:* (01305) 269986; *e-mail:* gavin@west-walks.demon.co.uk. *Died 9 Feb. 2007.*

KIRKPATRICK, William Brown, OBE 1998; Member: Gaming Board for Great Britain, 1990–99; National Lottery Charities Board, 1994–98; *b* 27 April 1934; *s* of late Joseph and Mary Kirkpatrick, Thornhill, Dumfriesshire; *m* 1990, Joan L. Millar. *Educ:* Morton Acad., Thornhill; George Watson's Coll., Edinburgh; Univ. of Strathclyde (BScEcon); Columbia Business Sch., NY (MS and McKinsey Scholar); Stanford Executive Program. After three years in manufacturing industry in Glasgow, Dundee and London, served Finance for Industry, later 3i plc, 1960–85, latterly at

director level; worked in London, Scotland and Australia in investment capital, corporate finance, fixed interest capital markets, on secondment as Industrial Dir, Industry Dept for Scotland, in shipping finance and as a nominee director; company dir and corporate advr with various cos, 1985–95 (incl. appt within DoE on water privatisation). JP Inner London, 1985–92. *Recreations:* Scottish paintings, porcelain pigs, current affairs. *Address:* Roughhills, Sandyhills, Dalbeattie, Kirkcudbrightshire DG5 4NZ. *T:* (01387) 780239. *Club:* Caledonian.
Died 19 March 2010.

KIRKUP, James; travel writer, poet, novelist, playwright, translator, broadcaster; *b* 23 April 1918; *o s* of James Harold Kirkup and Mary Johnson. *Educ:* South Shields High Sch.; Durham Univ. (BA; Hon. Fellow, Grey Coll., 1992). FRSL 1964. Gregory Fellow in Poetry, University of Leeds, 1950–52; Visiting Poet and Head of English Dept, Bath Academy of Art, Corsham Court, Wilts, 1953–56; Lectr in English, Swedish Ministry of Education, Stockholm, 1956–57; Prof. of Eng. Lang. and Lit., University of Salamanca, 1957–58, of English, Tohoku Univ., Sendai, Japan, 1958–61; Lecturer in English Literature, University of Malaya in Kuala Lumpur, 1961–62; Literary Editor, Orient/West Magazine, Tokyo, 1963–64; Prof., Japan Women's Univ., 1964–; Poet in Residence and Visiting Prof., Amherst Coll., Mass, 1968–; Prof. of English Literature, Nagoya Univ., 1969–72; Arts Council Fellowship in Creative Writing, Univ. of Sheffield, 1974–75; Morton Vis. Prof. of Internat. Literature, Ohio Univ., 1975–76; Playwright in Residence, Sherman Theatre, University Coll., Cardiff, 1976–77; Prof. of English Lit., Kyoto Univ. of Foreign Studies, Kyoto, Japan, 1977–89. President: Poets' Soc. of Japan, 1969; British Haiku Soc., 1990; Sponsor, Inst. of Psychophysical Res., 1970. Atlantic Award in Literature (Rockefeller Foundn), 1950; Mabel Batchelder Award, 1968; Keats Prize for Poetry, 1974; Scott-Moncrieff Prize for Translation, 1997. *Plays performed:* Upon this Rock (perf. Peterborough Cathedral), 1955; Masque, The Triumph of Harmony (perf. Albert Hall), 1955; The True Mistery of the Nativity, 1957; Dürrenmatt, The Physicists (Eng. trans.), 1963; Dürrenmatt, The Meteor (Eng. trans.); Dürrenmatt, Play Strindberg (Eng. trans.), 1972; The Magic Drum, children's play, 1972, children's musical, 1977; Dürrenmatt, Portrait of a Planet, 1972; Dürrenmatt, The Conformer, 1974; Schiller, Don Carlos, 1975; Cyrano de Bergerac, 1975; *operas:* An Actor's Revenge, 1979; Friends in Arms, 1980; The Damask Drum, 1982; *television plays performed:* The Peach Garden, Two Pigeons Flying High, The Prince of Homburg, etc. Contributor to BBC, The Listener, The Spectator, Times Literary Supplement, The Independent, Modern Poetry in Translation, Time and Tide, New Yorker, Botteghe Oscure, London Magazine, Japan Qly, English Teachers' Magazine (Tokyo), etc. *Publications:* The Drowned Sailor, 1948; The Cosmic Shape, 1947; The Creation, 1950; The Submerged Village, 1951; A Correct Compassion, 1952; A Spring Journey, 1954; Upon This Rock, 1955; The True Mistery of the Nativity, 1957; The Descent into the Cave, 1957; Sorrows, Passions and Alarms, 1959; These Horned Islands, A Journal of Japan, 1962; frères Gréban, The True Mistery of the Passion, 1962; Refusal to Conform, 1963; Tropic Temper: a Memoir of Malaya, 1963; Japan Industrial, 1964–65 (2 vols); Daily Life in the French Revolution, 1964; Tokyo, 1965; England, Now, 1965; Japan, Now, 1966; Frankly Speaking, I–II, 1968; Bangkok, 1968; One Man's Russia, 1968; Filipinescas, 1968; Streets of Asia, 1969; Japan Physical, 1969; Aspects of the Short Story, 1969; Hong Kong, 1970; Japan Behind the Fan, 1970; Heaven, Hell and Hara-Kiri, 1974; (with Birgit Skiöld) Zen Gardens, 1974; Scenes from Sesshu, 1977; Zen Contemplations, 1979; (with Birgit Skiöld) The Tao of Water, 1980; Folktales Japanesque, 1982; Modern American Myths, 1982; I Am Count Dracula, 1982; I Am Frankenstein's Monster, 1983; Miniature Masterpieces of Kawabata Yasunari, 1983; When I was a Child: a study of nursery-rhymes, 1983; My Way-USA, 1984; The Glory that was Greece, 1984; The Mystery & Magic of Symbols, 1987; The Cry of the Owl:

Native Folktales & Legends, 1987; (ed) A Certain State of Mind: an anthology of modern and contemporary Japanese haiku poets, 1995; (ed) Burning Giraffes: modern and contemporary Japanese poets, 1995; *poems:* The Prodigal Son, 1959; Paper Windows: Poems from Japan, 1968; Shepherding Winds (anthol.), 1969; Songs and Dreams (anthol.), 1970; White Shadows, Black Shadows: Poems of Peace and War, 1970; The Body Servant; poems of exile, 1971; A Bewick Bestiary, 1971; Modern Japanese Poetry (anthol.), 1978; Dengonban Messages (one–line poems), 1980; To the Ancestral North: poems for an autobiography, 1983; The Sense of the Visit: new poems, 1984; The Guitar-Player of Zuiganji, 1985; Fellow Feelings, 1986; Shooting Stars (haiku), 1992; First Fireworks (haiku), 1992; Short Takes (one-line poems), 1993; Words for Contemplation, 1993; Look at it this way! (for children), 1993; Blue Bamboo: haiku, senryu and tanka, 1994; Formulas for Chaos, 1994; Strange Attractors, 1995; An Extended Breath: collected longer poems, 1995; Selected Shorter Poems, vol. 1 Omens of Disaster, vol. 2 Once and for All, 1995; Noems, Koans and a Navel Display, 1995; Counting to 9,999: haiku and tanka, 1995; Utsusemi: tanka, 1996; The Patient Obituarist: new poems, 1996; A Book of Tanka (Japan Fest. Foundn Award), 1997; Figures in a Setting, 1997; He Dreamed he was a Butterfly: tanka, 1997; One-Man Band: poems without words, 1999; A Crack in the Wall: an anthology of modern Arab poetry, 2000; Tokonoma, 2000; TankAlphabet, 2001; A Tiger in your Tanka, 2001; Shields Sketches, 2002; An Island in the Sky: poems for Andorra, 2004; The Authentic Touch, 2007; Marsden Bay, 2008; *poems and translations:* Ecce Homo: My Pasolini, 1982; No More Hiroshimas, new edn 2004; *autobiography:* vol. 1, The Only Child, 1957 (trans. Japanese, 1986, reprinted with vol. 2 as A Child of the Tyne, 1997); vol. 2, Sorrows, Passions and Alarms, 1987 (trans. Japanese); vol. 3, I, of All People: an Autobiography of Youth, 1990; vol. 4, A Poet could not But be Gay: some Legends of my Lost Youth, 1991; vol. 5, Me All Over: memoirs of a misfit, 1993; Throwback: poems towards an autobiography, 1992; *novels:* The Love of Others, 1962; Insect Summer (for children), 1971; The Magic Drum (for children), 1973; Gaijin on the Ginza, 1991; Queens have Died Young and Fair, 1993; *essays:* Eibungaku Saiken, 1980; The Joys of Japan, 1985; Lafcadio Hearn (biog.), 1985; James Kirkup's International Movie Theatre, 1985; Trends and Traditions, 1986; Portraits & Souvenirs (biog.), 1987; *opera:* The Damask Drum, 1982; An Actor's Revenge, 1989 (also complete music score of adaptation); The Genius of Haiku: essays on R. H. Blyth, 1994; *translations:* Camara Laye, The Dark Child, 1955; Ancestral Voices, 1956; Camara Laye, The Radiance of the King, 1956; Simone de Beauvoir, Memoirs of a Dutiful Daughter, 1958; The Girl from Nowhere, 1958; It Began in Babel, 1961; The Captive, 1962; Sins of the Fathers, 1962; The Gates of Paradise, 1962; The Heavenly Mandate, 1964; Daily Life of the Etruscans, 1964; Erich Kästner, The Little Man, 1966; Erich Kästner, The Little Man and The Little Miss, 1969; Heinrich von Kleist, Michael Kohlhaas, 1966; E. T. A. Hoffmann, Tales of Hoffmann, 1966; Camara Laye, A Dream of Africa, 1967; The Eternal Virgin (Eng. trans. of Valéry's La Jeune Parque), 1970; (with C. Fry) The Oxford Ibsen, vol III, Brand and Peer Gynt, 1972; Selected Poems of Kyozo Takagi, 1973, rev. edn as How to Cook Women, 1997; Camara Laye, The Guardian of the Word, 1980; Cold Mountain Poems (trans. Han Shan), 1980; Petru Dimitriu, To the Unknown God, 1982; Michel Kpomassié, An African in Greenland, 1982; Tierno Monénembo, The Bush Toads, 1982; Margherita Guidacci, This Little Measure, 1990; Patrick Drevet, A Room in the Woods, 1991; Marc Rigaudis, Ito-san, 1991; Jean-Baptiste Niel, Painted Shadows, 1991; Jean-Noël Pancrazi, Vagabond Winter, 1992; Pascal Quignard, All the World's Mornings, 1992; Patrick Drevet, My Micheline, 1993; Hervé Guibert, The Man in the Red Hat, The Compassion Protocol, 1993; Georges-Arthur Goldschmidt, Worlds of Difference, 1993; Hervé Guibert, Blindsight, Paradise, 1995; Tahar Ben Jelloun, State of Absence, 1995; Marcelle Lagesse,

Isabelle, 1995; Patrick Drevet, Auvers-sur-Oise, 1997; Saito Fumi, In Thickets of Memory (700 tanka poems), 2002; Fumiko Miura, Pages from the Seasons, 2002; Takahashi Mutsuo, Myself as an Anatomical Love-making Chart and other poems, 2004; We of Zipangu: poems of Takahashi Mutsuo (trans. with Makoto Tamaki), 2007; A Pilgrimage in Hell: poems by Iwan Gilkin, 2007; Nakahara Michiu, Collected Haiku, 2009; *translation and adaptation:* The Best Way to Travel, from The Works of Zhuangzi, 2004; *festschrift:* Diversions: Festschrift for James Kirkup's 80th Birthday, 1998. *Recreation:* living. *Died 10 May 2009.*

KITAJ, R. B., RA 1991 (ARA 1984); artist; *b* Ohio, 29 Oct. 1932; *m* 1953, Elsi (*d* 1969); two *c, m* 1983, Sandra Fisher (*d* 1994); one *s. Educ:* Cooper Union Inst., NY; Acad. of Fine Art, Vienna; Ruskin Sch. of Art, Oxford; RCA (ARCA). Part-time teacher: Camberwell Sch. of Art, 1961–63; Slade Sch., 1963–67; Visiting Professor: Univ. of Calif. at Berkeley, 1968; UCLA, 1971. Lived in Los Angeles and London. *One-man exhibitions:* Marlborough New London Gall., 1963, 1970; Marlborough Gall., NY, 1965, 1974, 1994, 2000, 2005; Los Angeles County Museum of Art, 1965; Stedelijk Mus., Amsterdam, 1967; Mus. of Art, Cleveland, 1967; Univ. of Calif, Berkeley, 1967; Kestner Gesellschaft, Hanover, 1970; Boymans-van-Beuningen Mus., Rotterdam, 1970; Cincinnati Art Mus., Ohio, 1973; Marlborough Fine Art, 1977, 1980, 1985; Hamburger Kunsthalle, 1990–91; National Gall., London, 2001. *Retrospective exhibitions:* Hirshhorn Museum, Washington, 1981; Cleveland Museum of Art, Ohio, 1981; Kunsthalle, Düsseldorf, 1982; Tate Gall. and LA County Mus., 1994; Metropolitan Mus., NY, 1994–95. Member: US Acad. (formerly Inst.) of Arts and Letters, NY, 1982; Nat. Acad. of Design, NY, 1982. Hon. DLit London, 1982; Hon. DLitt Durham, 1996; Hon. Dr: RCA, 1991; Calif Coll. of Art, 1995. Grand Prize for Painting (Golden Lion), Venice Biennale, 1995. Order of Arts & Letters (France), 1996. *Publications:* First Diasporist Manifesto, 1989; *relevant publication:* R. B. Kitaj by M. Livingstone, 1985. *Address:* c/o Marlborough Fine Art (London) Ltd, 6 Albemarle Street, W1X 3HF. *Died 21 Oct. 2007.*

KITCATT, Sir Peter (Julian), Kt 1992; CB 1986; Speaker's Secretary, House of Commons, 1986–93; *b* 5 Dec. 1927; *s* of late Horace Wilfred Kitcatt and Ellen Louise Kitcatt (*née* Julian); *m* 1952, Audrey Marian Aylen; three *s* two *d. Educ:* Borden Grammar Sch., Sittingbourne; King's Coll., Cambridge (Scholar). RASC (2nd Lt) 1948. Asst Principal, Colonial Office, 1950–53; Asst Private Sec. to Sec. of State for the Colonies, 1953–54; Principal, Colonial Office, 1954–64; Sec. to HRH The Princess Royal on Caribbean Tour, 1960; Sec., E African Econ. and Fiscal Commn, 1960; HM Treasury: Principal, 1964; Asst Sec., 1966; RCDS, 1972; Under Sec., 1973, seconded to DHSS, 1975–78. *Recreation:* golf. *Club:* Croham Hurst Golf (Croydon). *Died 25 March 2007.*

KITSON, George McCullough; Principal, Central School of Speech and Drama, London, 1978–87; *b* Castlegore, Ireland, 18 May 1922; *s* of George Kitson and Anna May McCullough-Kitson; *m* 1951, Jean Evelyn Tyte; four *s. Educ:* early educn in Ireland; London Univ. (Dip. in Child Develt, 1947); Trent Park Coll. (Teachers' Cert., 1949). Associate, Cambridge Inst. of Educn, 1956; MEd Leicester, 1960. Served War, RAF, 1940–45; Navigator, Coastal Comd. Asst Master, schs in Herts, 1949–54; Dep. Headmaster, Broadfield Sch., Hemel Hempstead, Herts, 1954–56; Lectr in Educn, Leicester Coll. of Educn, 1956–66; Tutor i/c Annexe for Mature Teachers, Northampton, 1966–71; Dep. Principal, Furzedown Coll., London, 1971–76; Vice-Principal, Philippa Fawcett and Furzedown Coll., 1976–78. Member: Nat. Council for Drama Trng, 1978–88; Conference of Drama Schs, 1980– (Chm., 1980–87; Pres., 1999–); Hon. Mem., GSMD, 1998. *Publications:* (contrib.) Map of Educational Research, 1969; articles on educn, social psychol., and interprofessionalism in Forum, New Era, Educn for Teaching, and Brit. Jl of Educnl

Psychol. *Recreations:* book collecting (first editions), sailing, walking, music, theatre. *Address:* 11 Bates Close, Burnmill Grange, Market Harborough, Leics LE16 7NT. *Club:* Arts.   *Died 10 June 2010.*

KLEIN, Prof. Dan Victor; Director, Dan Klein Associates, consultants in contemporary glass, since 1994; Research Professor in Glass, University of Sunderland, since 1996; *b* 4 Nov. 1938; *s* of Frederick Klein and Bianka Breitmann. *Educ:* Westminster Sch.; Wadham Coll., Oxford (BA Hons Greats). Guest soloist, Sadler's Wells Opera, 1966; Member, English Opera Group, 1968–73; freelance singer performing in operas and recitals, also founded and perf. with own ensemble, 1973–77; owner, 20th Century Decorative Arts Gall., Belgravia, 1978–84; Dir, 20th Century Decorative Arts, Christie's, London, 1985–95; Vice-Pres., Christie's, Switzerland, 1990–95; Chm., Adv. Bd, North Lands Creative Glass, 1995–; Internat. Exec. Dir, Phillips Internat. Auctioneers, 1998–2001. Regular lectr in Britain, USA, Switzerland, Sweden and Australia; orgnr, Venezia Aperto Vetro, first Internat. Biennale of Contemporary Glass, Venice, 1996. Pres., Scottish Glass Soc., 2009. Trustee, Nat. Glass Centre, Sunderland, 2002–; Patron, Guild of Glass Engravers, 2006–. Mem. Bd, Pilchuck Glass Sch., USA, 1985–. *Publications:* All Colour Book of Art Deco, 1974; (ed jtly) The History of Glass, 1985; (jtly) Decorative Arts from 1880 to the Present Day, 1986, 2nd edn, 1998; (jtly) In the Deco Style, 1986; Glass: a contemporary art, 1989; (contrib.) L'Art Décoratif en Europe, vol. III, 1994; (ed jtly) Venezio Aperto Vetro (catalogue), 1996; Artists in Glass: late twentieth century masters in glass, 2001; (jtly) 21st Century British Glass (catalogue), 2005; articles in jls. *Recreations:* collecting 20th Century Decorative Arts, contemporary British glass. *Address:* Dan Klein Associates, 43 Hugh Street, SW1V 1QJ. *T:* (020) 7821 6040.
                                                 Died 28 June 2009.

KLEPSCH, Dr Egon Alfred; President, European Parliament, 1992–94; *b* 30 Jan. 1930; *m* 1952, Anita Wegehaupt; three *s* three *d*. *Educ:* Marburg Univ. (DPhil 1954). Mem., CDU, 1951– (Mem. of Bureau, 1977–94); Fed. Chm., Young Christian Democrats, 1963–69; Chm., European Young Christian Democrats, 1964–70; Mem. for Koblenz-St Goar, Bundestag, 1965–80; European Parliament: Member, 1973–79, elected Mem. (EPP/CDU), 1979–94; Vice-Pres., 1982–84; Mem., Political Affairs and other Cttees, 1989–92; Vice-Pres., EPP, 1977–92; Chm., EPP Gp, 1977–82, 1984–92; Mem. Bureau, EPP, 1992–94. Chm., Europa-Union Deutschland, 1989–97 (Hon. Chm., 1997–); Vice-Chm., German Council of Eur. Movement, 1990–99 (Hon. Mem., 1999–). Hon. LLD Sunderland; Dr *hc* Buenos Aires. Grosses Verdienstkreuz mit Stern und Schulterband (Germany), 1986; orders from Italy, Luxembourg, Argentina and Chile. *Publications:* Die Deutsche Russlandpolitik unter dem Reichsminister des Auswärtigen Dr Gustav Stresemann, 1955; Der Kommunismus in Deutschland, 1964; Der Europäische Abgeordnete, 1978; Programme für Europa, 1978; Die Abgeordneten Europas, 1984.   *Died 18 Sept. 2010.*

KNEALE, George Victor Harris, CBE 1989; Speaker, House of Keys, Isle of Man, 1990–91; *b* 12 Jan. 1918; *s* of James Kneale and Ellen (*née* Harris); *m* 1940, Thelma Eugenie Creer; two *d*. *Educ:* Demesne Road Elementary Sch.; Douglas High Sch. for Boys. Served RHA, 1940–46, ME and Italy. Photo-process engraver, 1935–40 and 1946–57. Mem., IOM Educn Authy, 1951–62; Chm., Bd of Educn, 1962–72, 1981–86; Minister for Educn, 1986–90; Member: House of Keys, 1962–74, 1981–91; Legislative Council, 1974–81; Founder Chm., IOM PO Authy, 1972–81. President: IOM Art Soc., 1988–; IOM Br., Royal Artillery Assoc., 1989–; Manx Gateway Club, 1992–; IOM Scout Assoc., 1994–2001. Hon. MA Salford, 1990. Boy Scouts Awards: Medal of Merit; Silver Acorn; Silver Wolf. *Recreations:* drawing, painting, photography, Boy Scouts.
                                                 Died 8 April 2007.

KNIGHT, Edmund Alan; Commissioner of Customs and Excise, 1971–77; *b* 17 June 1919; *s* of Arthur Philip and Charlotte Knight; *m* 1953, Annette Ros Grimmitt (*d* 1998); one *d*. *Educ:* Drayton Manor Sch.; London Sch. of Economics. Entered Exchequer and Audit Dept, 1938; HM Customs and Excise, 1948; Asst Sec., 1957; Sec. to Cttee on Turnover Taxation, 1963–64; seconded to Inland Revenue, 1969–71; returned to Customs and Excise, 1971; Eur. Affairs Adviser to BAT Co., 1978–85; consultant on indirect taxation, 1985–87. Mem., SITPRO Bd, 1971–76. *Recreations:* local history and environment, gardening. *Address:* 40 Park Avenue North, Harpenden, Herts AL5 2ED. *Club:* Royal Commonwealth Society.   *Died 18 Oct. 2006.*

KNOWLES, Prof. Jeremy Randall, CBE 1993; FRS 1977; Amory Houghton Professor of Chemistry and Biochemistry (formerly of Chemistry), Harvard University, since 1974 (Dean of Faculty of Arts and Sciences, 1991–2002, 2006–07); *b* 28 April 1935; *s* of late Kenneth Guy Jack Charles Knowles and of Dorothy Helen Swingler; *m* 1960, Jane Sheldon Davis; three *s*. *Educ:* Magdalen College Sch.; Balliol Coll. (Hon. Fellow 1984), Merton Coll. and Christ Church, Oxford (MA, DPhil). Sir Louis Stuart Exhibr, Balliol Coll., Oxford, 1955–59; Harmsworth Schol., Merton Coll., Oxford, and Research Lectr, Christ Church, Oxford, 1960–62; Research Associate, Calif. Inst. of Technology, 1961–62; Fellow of Wadham Coll., Oxf., 1962–74 (Hon. Fellow 1990); Univ. Lectr, Univ. of Oxford, 1966–74. Visiting Prof., Yale Univ., 1969, 1971; Sloan Vis. Prof., Harvard Univ., 1973; Newton-Abraham Vis. Prof., Oxford Univ., 1983–84. Fellow, Amer. Acad. of Arts and Scis, 1982; Foreign Associate, Nat. Acad. of Scis, USA, 1988; Mem., Amer. Philosophical Soc., 1988. Hon. FRSC 1993. Dr *hc*: Edinburgh, 1992; ETH Zürich, 2001. Charmian Medal, RSC, 1980; Prelog Medal, ETH, 1989; Bader Award and Cope Scholar Award, 1989, Repligen Award, 1993, Nakanishi Award, 1999, Amer. Chemical Soc.; Davy Medal, Royal Soc., 1991; Robert A. Welch Award in Chemistry, Robert A. Welch Foundn, USA, 1995; Harvard Medal, 2002. *Publications:* research papers and reviews in learned jls. *Address:* 67 Francis Avenue, Cambridge, MA 02138, USA. *T:* (617) 8768469.
                                                 Died 3 April 2008.

KNOWLES, Sir Richard (Marchant), Kt 1989; Lord Mayor of Birmingham, 1994–95; Member, Birmingham City Council, 1972–74 and 1978–2000 (Leader, 1984–93); Chairman, Northfield Area Regeneration Initiative, since 1993; *b* 20 May 1917; *s* of William and Charlotte Knowles; *m* 1st, 1941, Dorothy Forster (*d* 1979); one *s*; 2nd, 1981, Anne Little (*née* Macmenemey). *Educ:* village schools in Kent; WEA; technical school. Building industry, 1931–39; served RE, 1940; building and shipbuilding, 1941–50; Labour Organiser, Sevenoaks, Dover, Leeds and Birmingham, 1950–72; Nat. Organiser, Co-op Party, 1971–83. Mem., W Midlands County Council, 1973–77; Chm., Planning Cttee, Birmingham CC, 1972–74, 1980–82. Mem., Policy Cttee, 1974–77, 1984–94, Sec., Lab Gp, 1992–94, AMA. Dir, Nat. Exhibition Centre Ltd, 1982–94. Vice Chm., Governing Body, Univ. Hosp. Birmingham NHS Trust, 1993– (Mem., New Hosp. Partnership Adv. Team, 2000–). Member: Council, Birmingham Univ., 1996–; Bd, S Birmingham Coll., 2001–05. Hon. LLD Birmingham, 1996. *Publications:* UNIP Election Manual, 1964; ABC of Organisation, 1977; A Voice for your Neighbourhood, 1977; contribs to local govt jls, planning and political pamphlets. *Recreations:* cycling, travel, rough gardening. *Address:* 64 Woodgate Lane, Bartley Green, Birmingham B32 3QY. *T:* (0121) 422 8061.   *Died 18 Feb. 2008.*

KNOWLES, Winifred, (Wyn); Editor, Woman's Hour, BBC, 1971–83; *b* 30 July 1923; *d* of Frederick Knowles and Dorothy Ellen Knowles (*née* Harrison). *Educ:* St Teresa's Convent, Effingham; Convents of FCJ in Ware and Switzerland; Polytechnic Sch. of Art, London. Cypher Clerk, War Office, 1941–45. Secretarial work, 1948–57; joined BBC, 1951; Asst Producer, Drama Dept,

1957–60; Woman's Hour: Producer, Talks Dept, 1960–65; Asst Editor, 1965–67; Dep. Editor, 1967–71. *Publications*: (ed with Kay Evans) The Woman's Hour Book, 1981. *Recreations*: travel, cooking, writing, painting. *Died 13 July 2010.*

KNOX-MAWER, Ronald; *b* 3 Aug. 1925; *s* of George Robert Knox-Mawer and Clara Roberts; *m* 1951, June Ellis (*d* 2006), writer and broadcaster; one *s* one *d*. *Educ*: Grove Park Sch. (Denbighshire County Exhibnr); Emmanuel Coll., Cambridge (Exhibitioner; MA). Royal Artillery, 1943–47. Called to Bar, Middle Temple; Wales and Chester Circuit, 1947–52; Chief Magistrate and Actg Chief Justice, Aden, 1952–58; Sen. Magistrate, Puisne Judge, Justice of Appeal, Actg Chief Justice, Fiji, and conjointly Chief Justice, Nauru and Tonga, 1958–71; Northern Circuit, 1971–75; Metropolitan Stipendiary Magistrate, 1975–84; Dep. Circuit Judge, London, 1979–84. Various series of humorous reminiscences broadcast on BBC Radio: Tales from a Palm Court, 1984; Islands of Hope and Glory, 1985; Wretchedness in Wrexham, 1986; More Tales from a Palm Court, 1987–88; Tales of a Man called Father, 1989; The Queen Goes West, 1990; A Case of Bananas, 1992; Family Failings, 1994; Tales from Land of My Father, 1998; A Man Called Father (new series), 1999. *Publications*: Palm Court, 1979 (as Robert Overton); Tales from a Palm Court, 1986; Tales of a Man Called Father, 1989; A Case of Bananas and other South Sea Trials, 1992; Land of My Father, 1994; Are You Coming or Going?, 1999; (contrib.) Wales: a celebration, 2000; (contrib.) Young and Easy: childhood in Wales, 2004; short stories and features (under different pseudonyms) in Punch, Cornhill, Argosy, The Times, Sunday Express, Blackwoods, Listener, Weekend Telegraph, Times Saturday Review, Sunday Telegraph; various contribs to legal jls. *Recreation*: countryside. *Address*: c/o HSBC, Ruabon, N Wales LL14. *Died 7 Feb. 2009.*

KOGAN, Prof. Maurice; Professor of Government and Social Administration, 1969–95, then Emeritus, and Director, Centre for the Evaluation of Public Policy, since 1990, Brunel University; *b* 10 April 1930; *s* of Barnett and Hetty Kogan; *m* 1960, Ulla Svensson; two *s*. *Educ*: Stratford Grammar Sch.; Christ's Coll., Cambridge (MA). Entered Civil Service, admin. cl. (1st in open examinations), 1953; Harkness Fellow of Commonwealth Fund, 1960–61; Secretary: Secondary Sch. Exams Council, 1961; Central Advisory Council for Educn (England), 1963–66; Asst Sec., DES, 1966. Brunel University: Head of Sch. of Social Scis, 1971–74; Dean, Faculty of Soc. Scis, 1987–89; Acting Vice-Chancellor, 1989–90. Member: Educn Sub-Cttee, UGC, 1972–75; SSRC, 1975–77; Davies Cttee on Hosp. Complaints' Procedure, 1971; Houghton Cttee on Teachers' Pay, 1974; Genetic Manipulation Adv. Gp, 1979–80; Chm., Adv. Gp, Cttee of award, Harkness Fellowship, 1989–. George A. Miller Vis. Prof., Univ. of Illinois, 1976; Vis. Scholar, Univ. of Calif, Berkeley, 1981; Leverhulme Emeritus Fellow, 1996–98. Founder AcSS 2000. Hon. DSc (Econ) Hull, 1987; DUniv Brunel, 1991. *Publications*: The Organisation of a Social Services Department, 1971; Working Relationships within the British Hospital Service, 1971; The Government of Education, 1971; The Politics of Education, 1971; (ed) The Challenge of Change, 1973; County Hall, 1973; Advisory Councils and Committees in Education, 1974; Educational Policy-Making, 1975; The Politics of Educational Change, 1978; The Working of the National Health Service, 1978; (with T. Becher) Process and Structure in Higher Education, 1980, 2nd edn 1992; The Government's Commissioning of Research, 1980; (with T. Bush) Directors of Education, 1982; (with D. Kogan) The Battle for the Labour Party, 1982; (jtly) Government and Research, 1983, 2nd edn 2006; (with D. Kogan) The Attack on Higher Education, 1983; (with T. Husen) Educational Research and Policy: how do they relate?, 1984; (with D. Johnson and others) School Governing Bodies, 1984; Education Accountability, 1986; (jtly) The Use of Performance

Indicators in Higher Education, 1988, 2nd edn 1990; (jtly) Higher Education and Employment, 1988; (ed) Evaluating Higher Education, 1989; (jtly) Directors of Education Facing Reform, 1989; (jtly) Evaluation as Policy Making, 1990; (jtly) Encyclopaedia of Government and Politics, 1992, 2nd edn 2003; (jtly) In Support of Education: the functioning of local government, 1993; (jtly) Graduate Education in Britain, 1994; (jtly) Making Use of Clinical Audit, 1995; Advancing Quality, 1995; Higher Education and Work, 1995; Reforming Higher Education, 2000; (jtly) Transforming Higher Education, 2000, 2nd edn 2006; contribs to TES, THES, Jl of Social Policy. *Recreations*: reading, listening to music. *Address*: 48 Duncan Terrace, Islington, N1 8AL. *T*: (020) 7226 0038. *Died 6 Jan. 2007.*

KOHNSTAMM, Max, Groot Officier, Order of Orange-Nassau, 1988; Comdr of the Order of House of Orange, 1949; Hon. Secretary-General, Action Committee for Europe, since 1989 (Sec.-Gen., 1985–88); Senior Fellow, European Policy Centre, Brussels, since 1991; *b* 22 May 1914; *s* of Dr Philip Abraham Kohnstamm and Johanna Hermana Kessler; *m* 1944, Kathleen Sillem; two *s* three *d*. *Educ*: Univ. of Amsterdam (Hist. Drs); American Univ., Washington. Private Sec. to Queen Wilhelmina, 1945–48; subseq. Head of German Bureau, then Dir of European Affairs, Netherlands FO; Sec. of High Authority, 1952–56; 1st Rep. of High Authority, London, 1956; Sec.-Gen. (later Vice-Pres.), Action Cttee for United States of Europe, 1956–75; Pres., European Community Inst. for Univ. Studies, 1958–75; Principal, Eur. Univ. Inst. of Florence, 1975–81. Co-Chm., Cttee on Soc. Develt and Peace, World Council of Churches and Pontifical Commn for Justice and Peace, 1967–75; European Pres., Trilateral Commn, 1973–75. Grande Ufficiale dell' Ordine Al Merito della Repubblica Italiana, 1981; Grosse Verdienstkreuz, 1982, mit Stern, 1989, Bundesrepublik Deutschland. *Publications*: The European Community and its Role in the World, 1963; (ed jtly) A Nation Writ Large?, 1972; (jtly) Europe: l'impossible statu quo, 1996. *Recreation*: walking. *Address*: 24 Fenffe, 5560 Houyet, Belgium. *T*: (84) 377183, *Fax*: (84) 377113. *Died 20 Oct. 2010.*

KOLAKOWSKI, Leszek, PhD; FBA 1980; Senior Research Fellow, All Souls College, Oxford, 1970–95; *b* 23 Oct. 1927; *s* of Jerzy and Lucyna (*née* Pietrusiewicz); *m* 1949, Dr Tamara Kołakowska (*née* Dynenson); one *d*. *Educ*: Łódź Univ., Poland 1945–50; Warsaw Univ. (PhD 1953). Asst in Philosophy: Łódź Univ., 1947–49; Warsaw Univ., 1950–59; Prof. and Chm., Section of History of Philosophy, Warsaw Univ., 1959–68, expelled by authorities for political reasons; Visiting Professor: McGill Univ., 1968–69; Univ. of California, Berkeley, 1969–70; Yale Univ., Conn, 1975; Univ. of Chicago, 1981–94. McArthur Fellowship, 1983. MAE; Member: Internat. Inst. of Philosophy, 1969; Académie Universelle des Cultures, 1993; Polish Acad. of Scis, 1997; Foreign Mem., Amer. Academy of Arts and Science, 1977; Mem.-correspondent, Bayerische Akademie der Künste, 1977. Hon. Dr Lit. Hum. Bard Coll., 1984; Hon. LLD Reed Coll., 1985; Hon. DHum: Adelphi, and NY State, USA; Hon. DPhil: Wrocław, 2001; Łódź, Gdansk, and Szczecin, Poland. Friedenpreis des Deutschen Buchhandels, 1977; Jurzykowski Foundn award, 1968; Charles Veillou Prix Européen d'Essai, 1980; (jtly) Erasmus Prize, 1984; Jefferson Award, 1986; Prix Tocqueville, Assoc. Alexis de Tocqueville, 1993; Kluge Prize, Library of Congress, 2003. *Publications*: about 30 books, some of them only in Polish; trans. of various books in 21 languages; *in English*: Marxism and Beyond, 1968; Conversations with the Devil, 1972; Positivist Philosophy, 1972; Husserl and the Search for Certitude, 1975; Main Currents of Marxism, 3 vols, 1978 (trans. from Polish); Religion, 1982; Bergson, 1985; Metaphysical Horror, 1988; Modernity on Endless Trial, 1990; God Owes Us Nothing: a brief remark on Pascal's religion and the spirit of Jansenism, 1995; Freedom, Fame, Lying and Betrayal (essays), 1999; The Two Eyes of Spinoza, 2004; My Correct Views on Everything, 2005; *in French*: Chrétiens sans Eglise, 1969; *in German*: Traktat über die Sterblichkeit der Vernunft, 1967; Geist und Ungeist christlicher Traditionen, 1971; Die Gegenwärtigkeit des Mythos, 1973; Der revolutionäre Geist, 1972; Leben trotz Geschichte Lesebuch, 1977; Zweifel um die Methode, 1977. *Died 17 July 2009.*

KOMOROWSKI, Dr Stanislaw Jerzy, Hon. KCVO 2004; Ambassador; Under-Secretary of State for Policy, Ministry of National Defence, Poland, since 2007; *b* 18 Dec. 1953; *s* of Henryk Komorowski and Helena Komorowska (*née* Krokowska); *m* 1st, 1976, Irena Kwiatkowska (marr. diss. 1987); two *s*; 2nd, 1989, Maria Wegrzecka (marr. diss. 1997); one *s*; 3rd, 2001, Ewa Minkowska. *Educ:* Inst. of Physics, Univ. of Warsaw (MSc 1978); Inst. of Physical Chem., Polish Acad. of Scis (PhD 1985). Research Fellow, Physical Chem. Inst., Polish Acad. of Scis, 1978–90; Post-doctoral Fellow, Univ. of Utah, Salt Lake City, 1986–87; Adjunct, Physical Chem. Inst., 1987–89; Asst Prof., Univ. of Utah, 1989–90; Ministry for Foreign Affairs, Poland: Head of Section and Asst Head, Personnel Dept, 1991; Asst Head, 1991–92, Head, 1992–94, Eur. Dept; Ambassador to the Netherlands, 1994–98; Head, Office of Minister for Foreign Affairs, 1998–99; Ambassador to UK, 1999–2004; Dir, Asia and Pacific Dept, 2004–05, Under-Sec. of State for European Affairs, 2005–06, Ministry of Foreign Affairs, Warsaw. Grand Cross, Order of Orange Nassau (Netherlands), 1998. *Publications:* articles in American, French and Dutch physical chemistry jls. *Recreations:* tennis, ski-ing, photography, gardening. *Address:* Ministry of National Defence, Al. Niepodlegości 218, 00–911 Warsaw, Poland. *Died 10 April 2010.*

KORNBERG, Prof. Arthur; Professor of Biochemistry, Stanford University, 1959–88, then Professor Emeritus; *b* Brooklyn, 3 March 1918; *m* 1943, Sylvy Ruth Levy (*d* 1986); three *s*; *m* 1988, Charlene Walsh Levering (*d* 1995); *m* 1998 Carolyn Frey Dixon. *Educ:* College of the City of New York (BSc 1937); University of Rochester, NY (MD 1941). Strong Memorial Hospital, Rochester, 1941–42; National Insts of Health, Bethesda, Md, 1942–52; Professor of Microbiology, Washington Univ., and Head of Dept of Microbiology, 1953–59; Head of Dept of Biochemistry, Stanford Univ., 1959–69. MNAS; MAAS; Mem. Amer. Phil Soc. Foreign Mem., Royal Soc., 1970. Many honours and awards, including: Paul Lewis Award in Enzyme Chemistry, 1951; Nobel Prize (joint) in Medicine, 1959; Nat Medal of Science, 1979. *Publications:* DNA Synthesis, 1974; DNA Replication, 1980 (Suppl., 1982); articles in scientific jls. *Address:* Stanford University Medical Center, Palo Alto, CA 94305–5307, USA. *Died 26 Oct. 2007.*

KREBS, Prof. Edwin Gerhard, MD; Professor, Departments of Pharmacology and Biochemistry, University of Washington, Seattle, 1983–88, then Professor Emeritus (Professor and Chairman, Department of Pharmacology, 1977–83); *b* Iowa, 6 June 1918; *m* 1945, Virginia French; one *s* two *d*. *Educ:* Univ. of Illinois (AB Chem. 1940); Washington Univ. Sch. of Med., St Louis, Mo (MD 1943). Intern and Asst Resident in Internal Med., Barnes Hosp., St Louis, Mo, 1944–45; Res. Fellow, Washington Univ. Sch. of Med., St Louis, 1946–48; University of Washington, Seattle: Asst Prof. of Biochem., 1948–52; Associate Prof., 1952–57; Prof., 1957–68; Asst Dean for Planning, Sch. of Med., 1966–68; Prof. and Chm., Dept of Biol Chem., Sch. of Med., Univ. of Calif, Davis, 1968–76; Howard Hughes Medical Institute: Investigator, 1977–80; Sen. Investigator, 1980–90, Emeritus, 1991–. Member: Editl Bd, Jl Biol Chem., 1965–70 (Associate Ed., 1972–93); Editl Adv. Bd, Biochem., 1971–76; Editl and Adv. Bd, Molecular Pharmacol., 1972–77; Editl Advr, Molecular and Cellular

Biochem., 1987–. Member: Amer. Soc. for Biochem. and Molecular Biol., 1951–; Amer. Acad. Arts and Scis, 1971–; Nat. Acad. Scis, 1973–; Amer. Soc. Pharmacology and Exptl Therapeutics, 1980–. Hon. DSc Geneva, 1979. Numerous awards; (jtly) Nobel Prize in Physiology or Medicine, 1992. *Address:* Department of Biochemistry, Box 357370, University of Washington, Seattle, WA 98195–7370, USA. *Died 21 Dec. 2009.*

KROHN, Dr Peter Leslie, FRS 1963; Professor of Endocrinology, University of Birmingham, 1962–66; *b* 8 Jan. 1916; *s* of Eric Leslie Krohn and Doris Ellen Krohn (*née* Wade); *m* 1941, Joanna Mary French; two *s*. *Educ:* Sedbergh; Balliol Coll., Oxford (BA 1st Cl. Hons Animal Physiol., 1937; BM, BCh Oxon, 1940). Wartime Research work for Min. of Home Security, 1940–45; Lectr, then Reader in Endocrinology, University of Birmingham, 1946–53; Nuffield Sen. Gerontological Research Fellow and Hon. Prof. in University, 1953–62. *Publications:* contrib. to scientific jls on physiology of reproduction, transplantation immunity and ageing. *Recreations:* scuba diving, mountain walking. *Address:* Coburg House, New St John's Road, St Helier, Jersey, Channel Islands JE2 3LD. *T:* (01534) 874870. *Died 25 May 2008.*

KUMAR, Dr Ashok; MP (Lab) Middlesbrough South and East Cleveland, since 1997; *b* 28 May 1956; *s* of Jagat Ram Saini and late Santosh Kumari. *Educ:* Univ. of Aston in Birmingham (BSc ChemEng 1978; MSc Process Control 1980; PhD Fluid Mechanics 1982). Res. Officer, British Steel Research, 1978–79; Res. Fellow, Imperial Coll. of Science and Technology, 1982–85; Sen. Res. Investigator, Teesside Labs, British Steel, 1985–91; Res. Officer, British Steel Technical, 1992–97. Mem., Middlesbrough BC, 1987–97: Chair, Equal Opportunities Sub-Cttee, 1995–97; Vice Chair, Educn Cttee, 1995–97. MP (Lab) Langbaurgh, Nov. 1991–1992; contested (Lab) Langbaurgh, 1992. PPS to Sec. of State for Internat. Devel t, 2003–07, to Sec. of State for Envmt, Food and Rural Affairs, 2007–. Member: Sci. and Technol Select Cttee, 1997–2001; Trade and Industry Select Cttee, 2001–03. Chairman: Parly Gp for Energy Studies, 1999–2002 (Vice-Chm., 2002–); All Party Parly British-Bahrain Gp, 1999–; All Party Parly Gp for Chemical Industry, 2000–03 (Jt Sec., 1997–2000); All Party British-Indo Parly Gp, 2006–. Chairman: Chem. Eng. Soc., 1981–82; Labour Club, Univ. of Aston, 1980–81. *Publications:* articles in scientific and mathematical jls. *Recreations:* reading, listening to music, cricket, badminton. *Address:* House of Commons, SW1A 0AA. *Clubs:* Reform; Easterside and Beechwood Social; Marton Cricket. *Died 15 March 2010.*

KUNCEWICZ, Eileen, (Mrs Witold Kuncewicz); *see* Herlie, E.

KYRLE POPE, Rear-Adm. Michael Donald, CB 1969; MBE 1946; DL; *b* 1 Oct. 1916; *e s* of late Comdr R. K. C. Pope, DSO, OBE, RN retd, and of Mrs A. J. Pope (*née* Macdonald); *m* 1947, Angela Suzanne Layton; one *s* one *d*. *Educ:* Wellington Coll., Berks. Joined RN, 1934; Submarine Service, 1938; HMS Vanguard, 1946–47; BJSM, Washington, 1951–53; Naval Intelligence: Germany, 1955–57, FE, 1958–60; Sen. Naval Off., Persian Gulf, 1962–64; MoD (Naval Intell.), 1965–67; Chief of Staff to C-in-C Far East, 1967–69; retd 1970. Comdr 1951; Capt. 1958; Rear-Adm. 1967. Gen. Manager, Middle East Navigation Aids Service, Bahrain, 1971–77. Dean's Administrator, St Alban's Abbey, 1977–80. Dir, Jerusalem and East Mission Trust, 1978–92. County Pres., Royal British Legion, 1987–95. DL Herts 1983. *Address:* Mayfield House, 2 Tidcombe Lane, Tiverton EX16 4DZ. *T:* (01884) 255917. *Club:* Army and Navy. *Died 14 Sept. 2008.*

L

LABOUISSE, Eve, (Mrs H. R. Labouisse); *see* Curie, E.

LACY, Sir John (Trend), Kt 1992; CBE 1983; General Director of Party Campaigning, Conservative Central Office, 1989–92; *b* 15 March 1928; *s* of Rev. Hubert Lacy and Mrs Gertrude Lacy (*née* Markham); *m* 1956, Pamela Guerin; one *s*. *Educ:* King's Sch., Ely, Cambs. Served RN, 1945–48. Harvey & Clark (Manufrs), 1948–50; Conservative Party: London, 1950–56; Aylesbury, 1956–61; W Midlands area, 1961–64; Northern area, 1964–71; S Eastern area, 1971–85; Dir of Campaigning, 1985–89. *Recreations:* racing, fishing, philately. *Address:* 18 Windmill Close, Milford-on-Sea, Hants SO41 0SX. *T:* (01590) 643984. *Clubs:* Carlton, St Stephen's (Vice Chm., 1988–93). *Died 5 Nov. 2009.*

LADDIE, Prof. Sir Hugh (Ian Lang), Kt 1995; Professor of Intellectual Property Law, University College London, since 2005; consultant to Rouse & Co. International, solicitors, since 2005; *b* 15 April 1946; *s* of late Bertie Daniel Laddie and of Rachel Laddie; *m* 1970, Stecia Elizabeth (*née* Zamet); two *s* one *d*. *Educ:* Aldenham Sch.; St Catharine's Coll., Cambridge (MA). Called to the Bar, Middle Temple, 1969 (Blackstone Pupillage Award; Bencher, 1993); Jun. Counsel to HM Treasury in Patent Matters, 1981–86; QC 1986; Judge of the High Ct of Justice, Chancery Div., 1995–2005. Jun. Bar Rep., Patents Procedure Cttee, 1976. Sec., 1971–75, Chm., 1993–94, Patent Bar Assoc.; Mem. Cttee, Chancery Bar Assoc., 1991–92. Chm., Vet. Code of Practice Cttee, Nat. Office of Animal Health; Dep. Chm., Copyright Tribunal, 1993–95; Dep. Ind. Chm., London Theatre Council and Provincial Theatre Council, 1993–95. Vice-Pres., Intellectual Property Inst., 1997–. Vis. Prof., Queen Mary, Univ. of London, 2005– (Mem. Council, 2000–05; Vice-Chm., 2005). Asst Ed.-in-Chief, Annual of Industrial Property Law, 1975–79; UK Correspondent, European Law Rev., 1978–83; Editor, Supreme Court Practice, 1995–2000; Ed.-in-Chief, In Context, 1998. *Publications:* (jtly) Patent Law of Europe and the United Kingdom, 1978; (jtly) The Modern Law of Copyright, 1980, 3rd edn 2000. *Recreations:* music, fishing, grandchildren. *Died 29 Nov. 2008.*

LAIDLAW, Sir Christophor (Charles Fraser), Kt 1982; Chairman: BP Oil, 1977–81; BP Oil International, 1981; *b* 9 Aug. 1922; *m* 1952, Nina Mary Prichard; one *s* three *d*. *Educ:* Rugby Sch.; St John's Coll., Cambridge (MA; Hon. Fellow, 1996). Served War of 1939–45: Europe and Far East, Major on Gen. Staff; Intelligence Corps, 1941–46. Joined British Petroleum, 1948: BP Rep. in Hamburg, 1959–61; Gen. Manager, Marketing Dept, 1963–67; Dir, BP Trading, 1967; Dir (Ops), 1971–72; a Man. Dir, 1972–81, and Dep. Chm., BP, 1980–81; Dir, Soc. Française BP, 1964–85; President, BP: Belgium, 1967–71; Italiana, 1972–73; Deutsche BP, 1972–83; Chm., Boving & Co. Ltd, 1984–86. Chm., ICL plc, 1981–84; Pres., ICL France, 1983; Chm., Bridon, 1985–90. Director: Commercial Union Assurance, 1978–83; Barclays Bank International, 1980–87; Barclays Bank plc, 1981–88; Barclays Merchant Bank Ltd, 1984–86; Equity Capital for Industry Ltd, 1983–86; Amerada Hess Corp., 1983–94; Amerada Hess Ltd, 1986–99; Dalgety, 1984–92; Redland, 1984–92; TWIL Ltd, 1985–89; Mercedes-Benz (UK) Ltd, 1986–93; Daimler-Benz (UK) Ltd, 1994–99; Daimler-Chrysler (UK) Hldgs Ltd, 1999–2001. Pres., German Chamber of Industry and Commerce, 1983–86; Vice Pres., British-German Assoc., 1996–2002. Institut Européen d'Administration des Affaires: Mem., Internat. Council, 1980–96; Chm. UK Adv. Bd, 1984–91; Dir, 1987–94. Trustee, Internat. Spinal Res. Trust, 1991–2002 (Patron,

2002–). FRSA 1996. Master, Tallow Chandlers' Co., 1988–89. *Address:* 49 Chelsea Square, SW3 6LH. *Clubs:* Buck's, Garrick. *Died 27 Nov. 2010.*

LAING OF DUNPHAIL, Baron *cr* 1991 (Life Peer), of Dunphail in the District of Moray; **Hector Laing,** Kt 1978; Life President, United Biscuits (Holdings) plc, 1990 (Director, 1953; Managing Director, 1964; Chairman, 1972–90); *b* 12 May 1923; *s* of Hector Laing and Margaret Norris Grant; *m* 1950, Marian Clare, *d* of Maj.-Gen. Sir John Laurie, 6th Bt, CBE, DSO; three *s*. *Educ:* Loretto Sch., Musselburgh, Scotland; Jesus Coll., Cambridge (Hon. Fellow, 1988). Served War, Scots Guards, 1942–47 (American Bronze Star, despatches, 1944); final rank, Captain. McVitie & Price: Dir, 1947; Chm., 1963. Mem. Bd, Royal Insurance Co., 1970–78; Director: Allied-Lyons, 1979–82; Exxon Corp. (USA), 1984–94. A Dir, Bank of England, 1973–91. Chairman: Food and Drink Industries Council, 1977–79; Scottish Business in the Community, 1982–91; Business in the Community, 1987–91; Dir, Grocery Manufrs of America, 1984–90; President: Eur. Catering Assoc., 1990–93; Inst. of Business Ethics, 1991–94. Treas., Cons. Party, 1988–93. Chm. Trustees, Lambeth Fund, 1983–97; Trustee: The Duke of Edinburgh's Commonwealth Study Conf., 1986–93; Royal Botanic Gardens Kew Foundn, 1990–94. Mem., St George's Council, Windsor, 1989–93 and 1995–2002; Gov., Wycombe Abbey Sch., 1981–94. FRSE 1989. DUniv Stirling, 1985; Hon. DLitt Heriot-Watt, 1986. Businessman of the Year Award, 1979; National Free Enterprise Award, 1980. *Recreations:* gardening, walking. *Address:* High Meadows, Windsor Road, Gerrards Cross, Bucks SL9 8ST. *T:* (01753) 882437. *Club:* White's. *Died 21 June 2010.*

LAING, Prof. John Archibald, PhD; Professor Emeritus, University of London, since 1984 (Courtauld Professor of Animal Husbandry and Hygiene, at Royal Veterinary College, University of London, 1959–84); *b* 27 April 1919; *s* of late John and Alexandra Laing; *m* 1946, June Margaret Lindsay Smith, *d* of Hugh Lindsay Smith, Downham Market; one *s* two *d*. *Educ:* Johnston Sch., Durham; Royal (Dick) School of Veterinary Studies, Edinburgh University (BSc); Christ's Coll., Cambridge (PhD). CBiol, FIBiol; MRCVS 1941. Aleen Cust Scholar, Royal Coll. of Veterinary Surgeons. Research Officer, 1943–46, Asst Veterinary Investigation Officer, 1946–49, Ministry of Agriculture; Univ. of Bristol, 1949–59 (Reader in Veterinary Science, 1957–59). Anglo-Danish Churchill Fellowship, Univ. of Copenhagen, 1954; Visiting Professor, Univs of: Munich, 1967; Mexico, 1967; Queensland, 1970 (and John Thompson Memorial Lectr); Ankara, 1977; Assiut, 1980; Consultant to FAO, UN, 1955–57; Representative of FAO in Dominican Republic, 1957–58; Consultant to UNESCO in Central America, 1963–65; Mem., British Agricultural Mission to Peru, 1970. Member: EEC Veterinary Scientific Cttee, 1981–84; Dairy Product Quota Tribunal for England and Wales, 1984. Hon. Mem., Internat. Congress on Animal Reproduction, 1988 (Sec., 1961–80; Pres., 1980–84). Chm., Melrose Meml Trust, 1984–91; Member: Governing Body, Houghton Poultry Research Station, 1968–74; Council, Royal Veterinary Coll., 1975–84; Vice-Pres., University Fedn for Animal Welfare, 1977–84 (Treasurer, 1969–75; Chm., 1975–77). Pres., World Assoc. for Transport Animal Welfare Studies, 1996–98. Hon. Fellow, Veterinary Acad., Madrid. Editor, British Veterinary Journal, 1960–84. *Publications:* Fertility and Infertility in the Domestic Animals, 1955, 4th edn 1988; papers on animal breeding and husbandry in various scientific journals. *Address:* Lower Meadow, Ayot St Lawrence, Herts AL6 9BW. *T:* (01438) 820413. *Club:* Athenæum. *Died 12 July 2009.*

LAING, Sir (John) Maurice, Kt 1965; Director, John Laing plc (formerly John Laing & Son Ltd), 1939–88 (Deputy Chairman, 1966–76, Chairman, 1976–82); *b* 1 Feb. 1918; *s* of Sir John Laing, CBE, and late Beatrice Harland; *m* 1940, Hilda Violet Richards; one *s. Educ:* St Lawrence Coll., Ramsgate. RAF, 1941–45; seconded to Glider Pilot Regt, 1945 for Rhine crossing. Dir, Bank of England, 1963–80. Member: UK Trade Missions to Middle East, 1953, and to Egypt, Sudan and Ethiopia, 1955; Economic Planning Bd, 1961; Export Guarantees Adv. Council, 1959–63; Min. of Transport Cttee of Inquiry into Major Ports of Gt Brit. (Rochdale Cttee), 1961–62; NEDC, 1962–66. First Pres., CBI, 1965–66; President: British Employers Confederation, 1964–65; Export Group for the Constructional Industries, 1976–80; Fedn of Civil Engrg Contractors, 1977–80. Visiting Fellow, Nuffield Coll., 1965–70; Governor: Administrative Staff Coll., 1966–72; Nat. Inst. of Economic and Social Research, 1964–82. Pres., London Bible Coll., 1993–99. Admiral, Royal Ocean Racing Club, 1976–82; Rear-Cdre, Royal Yacht Squadron, 1982–86 (Trustee, 1996–); Pres., Royal Yachting Assoc., 1983–87; Admiral, Island Sailing Club, 1997–2001. Hon. FCGI 1978; Hon. FCIOB 1981. Hon. LLD Strathclyde, 1967; Hon. DSc Exeter, 1996. Winner, Aims of Industry Free Enterprise Award, 1979. Keen interest in Church activities at home and abroad. *Recreations:* sailing, swimming. *Address:* Laing Family Trusts, 33 Bunns Lane, Mill Hill, NW7 2DX. *Clubs:* Royal Ocean Racing; Royal Yacht Squadron. *Died 22 Feb. 2008.*

LAING, Sir Kirby; *see* Laing, Sir W. K.

LAING, Sir Maurice; *see* Laing, Sir J. M.

LAING, Peter Anthony Neville Pennethorne; Founding Director, ActionAid Spain, since 1982; *b* 12 March 1922; *s* of late Lt-Col Neville Ogilvie Laing, DSO, 4th QO Hussars, and Zara Marcella (*née* Pennethorne), Fleet, Hants; *m* 1958, Penelope Lucinda, *d* of Sir William Pennington-Ramsden, 7th Bt; two *d. Educ:* Eton; Paris Univ. Served War: volunteer, French Army, 1939–40, Free French Forces, 1942–44; Grenadier Guards, 1944–46. Attaché, British Embassy, Madrid, 1946; internat. marketing consultant in Western Europe, USA, Caribbean and Latin America; UN, 1975–76, Dir of ITC proj. for UNDP in the Congo; Dir, Help the Aged internat. charity, 1976–82. Advr, European Affairs, Internat. Centre of Social Gerontology, 1982–87. Creator, Mediterranean Retirement Inc. (wardened housing villages for ageing Europeans of ind. means), 1985–. *Recreations:* people, foreign travel, riding any horse, fine arts. *Address:* Turweston Manor, near Brackley, Northants NN13 5JX. *T:* (01280) 703498, 700049. *Club:* Turf. *Died 21 April 2007.*

LAING, Sir (William) Kirby, Kt 1968; JP; DL; MA; FREng, FICE; Chairman, Laing Properties plc, 1978–87; President, 1987–90; *b* 21 July 1916; *s* of Sir John Laing, CBE, and Lady Laing (*née* Beatrice Harland); *m* 1st, 1939, Joan Dorothy Bratt (*d* 1981); three *s*; 2nd, 1986, Dr (Mary) Isobel Lewis, *yr d* of late Edward C. Wray. *Educ:* St Lawrence Coll., Ramsgate; Emmanuel Coll., Cambridge (Hon. Fellow, 1983). FREng (FEng 1977). Served with Royal Engineers, 1943–45. Dir, John Laing plc (formerly John Laing & Son Ltd), 1939–80 (Chm., 1957–76). President: London Master Builders Assoc., 1957; Reinforced Concrete Assoc., 1960; Nat. Fedn of Building Trades Employers (later Building Employers' Confedn) 1965, 1967 (Hon. Mem., 1975); ICE, 1973–74 (a Vice-Pres., 1970–73); Construction Industry Res. and Inf. Assoc., 1984–87 (Chm., 1978–81); Chm., Nat. Jt Council for Building Industry, 1968–74. Member, Board of Governors: St Lawrence Coll. (Chm., 1977–89, Life Pres., 1979); Princess Helena Coll., 1984–87; Member: Court of Governors, The Polytechnic of Central London, 1963–82; Council, Royal Albert Hall, 1970–92 (Pres., 1979–92; Life Vice-Pres., 2000); RAEng, 1977; Royal Instn of GB, 1989; Ct of Benefactors, Oxford Univ.; Ct of Benefactors, RSM, 2008. Dist. Mem., Amer. Assoc. of Civil Engineers, 2008. Mem., Smetonian Soc., 1969

(Pres., 1988). Master, Paviors' Co., 1987–88. DL Greater London, 1978–91. Hon. Fellow, UCNW, 1988. Hon. DTech, Poly. of Central London, 1990; Dr *hc* Edinburgh, 1991. *Publications:* papers in Proc. ICE and other jls concerned with construction. *Recreations:* flyfishing, travelling, listening to music. *Clubs:* Piscatorial Society; Royal Fowey Yacht. *Died 12 April 2009.*

LAKER, Sir Frederick Alfred, (Sir Freddie), Kt 1978; Chairman and Managing Director, Laker Airways (Bahamas) Ltd, since 1992; *b* 6 Aug. 1922; British; *m* 1st, 1942, Joan (marr. diss. 1968); one *d* (one *s* decd); 2nd, 1968, Rosemary Belfrage Black (marr. diss. 1975); 3rd, 1975, Patricia Gates (marr. diss. 1982); one *s* (and one *s* decd); 4th, 1985, Jacqueline Anne Harvey. *Educ:* Simon Langton Sch., Canterbury. Short Brothers, Rochester, 1938–40; General Aircraft, 1940–41; Air Transport Auxiliary, 1941–46; Aviation Traders, 1946–65; Man. Dir, British United Airways, 1960–65; Chm. and Man. Dir, Laker Airways Ltd, 1966–82; Dir, Freddie Laker's Skytrain Ltd, 1982–83; creator of Skytrain Air Passenger Service to USA; Partner, Laker Airways Inc., 1995–98. Hon. Fellow, UMIST, 1978. Hon. DSc: City, 1979; Cranfield Inst. of Technol., 1980; Hon. LLD Manchester, 1981. *Recreations:* horse breeding, racing, sailing. *Address:* Princess Tower, West Sunrise, Box F40207, Freeport, Grand Bahama, Bahamas. *Clubs:* Eccentric, Little Ship, Jockey. *Died 9 Feb. 2006.*

LAKES, Major Gordon Harry, CB 1987; MC 1951; Deputy Director General, Prison Service, 1985–88; *b* 27 Aug. 1928; *s* of Harry Lakes and Annie Lakes; *m* 1950, Nancy (*née* Smith) (*d* 1992); one *d. Educ:* Army Technical School, Arborfield; RMA Sandhurst. Commissioned RA 1948; service in Tripolitania, Korea, Japan, Hong Kong, Gold Coast (RWAFF), Ghana (Major), 1959–60. Middle Temple, 1960–61. Prison Service College, 1961–62; IIM Borstal Feltham, 1962–65; Asst Principal, Officers' Training Sch., Leyhill, 1965–68; Governor, HM Remand Centre, Thorp Arch, 1968–70; Prison Service HQ, 1970–74; HM Prisons: Pentonville, 1974–75; Gartree, 1975–77; Prison Service HQ, 1977–82; HM Dep. Chief Inspector of Prisons, 1982–85. Mem., Parole Bd, 1989–92; Comr, Mental Health Act, 1991–2002 (Mem. Mgt Bd, 1996–2002, Actg Chm. 1998–99). Non-exec. Dir, HM Prison, Buckley Hall, 2000–04. Chm., Nat. AIDS and Prisons Forum, 1989–98. Consultant to 8th UN Congress on Prevention of Crime and Treatment of Offenders, 1989–90; Assessor to Lord Justice Woolf's Inquiry into Prison Disturbances, 1990–91; Consultant on prison staffing and ops, Min. of Justice, Dublin, 1998–. Council of Europe: Mem., Cttee for Co-operation in Prison Affairs, 1986–91; Expert Witness, Cttee for Prevention of Torture, 1990–2000; Advr, Themis Plan (Prisons Proj.), 1993–2000; Co-Chm., Nord-Balt Prison Project, 1996–2004; Chm., Steering Cttee for Reform of Ukranian Prison System, 1997–2004. *Recreations:* golf, photography. *Died 23 April 2006.*

LAKING, Sir George (Robert), KCMG 1985 (CMG 1969); Chief Ombudsman, New Zealand, 1977–84; retired; *b* Auckland, NZ, 15 Oct. 1912; *s* of R. G. Laking; *m* 1940, Patricia (*d* 2004), *d* of H. Hogg; one *s* one *d. Educ:* Auckland Grammar Sch.; Auckland Univ.; Victoria Univ. of Wellington (LLB). Prime Minister's and Ext. Affairs Depts, 1940–49; New Zealand Embassy, Washington: Counsellor, 1949–54; Minister, 1954–56; Dep. Sec. of Ext. Affairs, Wellington, NZ, 1956–58; Acting High Comr for NZ, London, 1958–61, and NZ Ambassador to European Economic Community, 1960–61; New Zealand Ambassador, Washington, 1961–67; Sec. of Foreign Affairs and Permanent Head, Prime Minister's Dept, NZ, 1967–72; Ombudsman, 1975–77; Privacy Comr, 1977–78. Member: Human Rights Commn, 1978–84; Public and Administrative Law Reform Cttee, 1980–85. Chairman: NZ–US Educnl Foundn, 1976–78; NZ Oral History Archive Trust, 1985–90; Wellington Civic Trust, 1985–86; Legislation Adv. Cttee, 1986–91; Pres., NZ Inst. of Internat. Affairs 1980–84. Mem. Internat. Council, Asia Soc., NY,

1985–92. Hon. LLD Victoria Univ. of Wellington, 2001. *Address:* 3 Wesley Road, Wellington 1, New Zealand. *T:* (4) 4728454. *Died 10 Jan. 2008.*

LAMB, Prof. Christopher John, CBE 2009; PhD; FRS 2008; Director, John Innes Centre, and John Innes Professor of Biology, University of East Anglia, since 1999; *b* 19 March 1950; *s* of late John Mungall Lamb and Eileen Blanche Lamb (*née* Marley); *m* 1970, Jane Susan Wright; two *s* one *d. Educ:* Fitzwilliam Coll., Cambridge (BA 1972, PhD 1976, in Biochemistry). Oxford University: ICI Postdoctoral Fellow, Sch. of Botany, 1975–77; Deptl Demonstr, Dept of Biochemistry, 1977–82; Browne Res. Fellow, Queen's Coll., 1977–82; Dir and Prof., Plant Biology Lab., Salk Inst. for Biol Studies, Calif, 1982–98; Adjunct Prof., UCSD, 1988–98; Regius Prof. of Plant Sci., Univ. of Edinburgh, 1999. Founder, Akkadix Inc., 1998; Dir, Plant Bioscience Ltd, 1999–. Mem., EMBO, 2001. FAAAS 1992. McKnight Schol., 1983, Herman Frasch Award, 1986, ACS. *Publications:* numerous articles in Nature, Science, Cell and other learned jls. *Recreations:* fell walking, swimming, cycling, wine, sushi. *Address:* John Innes Centre, Norwich Research Park, Colney, Norwich NR4 7UH. *T:* (01603) 450000. *Died 21 Aug. 2009.*

LAMB, Prof. Willis E(ugene), Jr; Professor of Physics and Optical Sciences, University of Arizona, 1974–2003, then Emeritus, and Regents' Professor, 1989–2003, then Regents' Professor Emeritus, Arizona Research Laboratories; *b* Los Angeles, California, USA, 12 July 1913; *s* of Willis Eugene Lamb and Marie Helen Metcalf; *m* 1939, Ursula Schaefer (*d* 1996); *m* 1996, Bruria Kaufman (marr. diss. 2007); *m* 2008, Elsie A. Wattson. *Educ:* Los Angeles High Sch.; University of California (BS, PhD). Columbia Univ.: Instructor in Physics, 1938–43, Associate, 1943–45, Asst Prof., 1945–47, Associate Prof., 1947–48, Prof. of Physics, 1948–52; Prof. of Physics, Stanford Univ., California, 1951–56; Wykeham Prof. of Physics and Fellow of New Coll., University of Oxford, 1956–62; Yale University: Ford Prof. of Physics, 1962–72; Gibbs Prof. of Physics, 1972–74. Morris Loeb Lectr, Harvard Univ., 1953–54; Lectr, University of Colorado, Summer, 1959; Shrum Lectr, Simon Fraser Univ., 1972; Vis. Prof., Tata Institute of Fundamental Research, Bombay, 1960; Guggenheim Fellow, 1960–61; Vis. Prof., Columbia Univ., 1961; Fulbright Lectr, University of Grenoble, Summer, 1964. MNAS, 1954. Hon. Mem., Optical Soc. of Amer., 2000; Hon. Fellow, Institute of Physics and Physical Society, 1962; Hon. FRSE 1981. Hon. DSc: Pennsylvania, 1954; Gustavus Adolphus Coll., 1975; Columbia, 1990; MA (by decree), Oxford, 1956; Hon. MA Yale, 1961; Hon. LHD Yeshiva, 1965; Dr rer. nat. *hc* Ulm, 1997. Res. Corp Award, 1954; Rumford Medal, American Academy of Arts and Sciences, 1953; (jointly) Nobel Prize in Physics, 1955; Guthrie Award, Physical Society, 1958; Yeshiva University Award, 1962. *Publications:* (with M. Sargent and M. O. Scully) Laser Physics, 1974; contributions to The Physical Review, Physica, Science, Journal of Applied Physics, etc. *Died 15 May 2008.*

LAMBERT, Sir Anthony (Edward), KCMG 1964 (CMG 1955); HM Diplomatic Service, retired; *b* 7 March 1911; *o s* of late R. E. Lambert, Pensbury House, Shaftesbury, Dorset; *m* 1948, Ruth Mary (*d* 1998), *d* of late Sir Arthur Fleming, CBE; two *d. Educ:* Harrow; Balliol Coll., Oxford (scholar). Entered HM Foreign (subseq. Diplomatic) Service, 1934, and served in: Brussels, 1937; Ankara, 1940; Beirut and Damascus, 1942; Brussels, 1944; Stockholm, 1949; Athens, 1952; HM Minister to Bulgaria, 1958–60; HM Ambassador to: Tunisia, 1960–63; Finland, 1963–66; Portugal, 1966–70. *Died 28 April 2007.*

LAMBERT, Patricia, OBE 1981; Member, Consumer Panel, Personal Investment Authority, 1995–96; retired; *b* 16 March 1926; *d* of Frederick and Elsie Burrows; *m* 1949, George Richard Lambert (marr. diss. 1983); one *s* one *d. Educ:* Malet Lambert High Sch., Hull; West Bridgford Grammar Sch., Nottingham; Nottingham and

Dist Technical Coll. Served Royal Signals, Germany, 1944–46; medical technician, 1946–49. British Standards Institution: Member: BSI Bd, 1980–86; Quality Assce Bd, 1986–91; Chm., Consumer Standards Adv. Council, 1980–86; chm. of several technical cttees; Public Interest Dir, Lautro, 1986–94. Member: National Consumer Council, 1978–82; National House Bldg Council, 1980–91; Consumer Affairs Panel, Unit Trust Assoc., 1981–96; Direct Mail Services Standards Bd, 1983–96; Consumer Cttee, PIA, 1994–96. Dir and Vice-Chm., Invest in Britain, 1983–94. Local Govt Councillor, 1959–78. *Recreations:* driving, music, glass engraving. *Address:* 100 Wolds Drive, Keyworth, Nottingham NG12 5FS. *Died 6 July 2008.*

LAMBERT, Verity Ann, OBE 2002; independent film and television producer; Director, Cinema Verity Productions Ltd, since 1985; *b* 27 Nov. 1935; *d* of Stanley Joseph Lambert and Ella Corona Goldburg; *m* 1973, Colin Michael Bucksey (marr.diss. 1987). *Educ:* Roedean; La Sorbonne, Paris. Joined BBC Television as drama producer, 1963; first producer of Dr Who; also produced: The Newcomers, Somerset Maugham Short Stories (BAFTA Award, 1969), Adam Adamant, Detective; joined LWT as drama producer, 1970: produced Budgie and Between the Wars; returned to BBC, 1973: produced and co-created Shoulder to Shoulder; joined Thames Television as Controller of Drama Dept, 1974 (Dir of Drama, 1981–82; Dir, Thames Television, 1982–85): responsible for: Rock Follies, Rooms, Rumpole of the Bailey, Edward and Mrs Simpson, The Naked Civil Servant (many awards), Last Summer, The Case of Cruelty to Prawns, No Mama No; made creatively responsible for Euston Films Ltd, 1976 (Chief Executive, 1979–82): developed series which included Out and Danger UXB; responsible for: Minder (three series), Quatermass, Fox, The Flame Trees of Thika, Reilly: ace of spies; single films include: Charlie Muffin, Stainless Steel and the Star Spies, The Sailor's Return, The Knowledge; Dir of Prodn, THORN EMI Screen Entertainment, 1982–85: responsible for: Morons from Outer Space, Dreamchild, Restless Natives, Link, Clockwise. Executive Producer: American Roulette, 1987; May to December (6 series, 1989–94); So Haunt Me (3 series), 1992–94; Producer: A Cry in the Dark, 1988; Coasting, 1990; GBH, 1991; The Boys from the Bush, 1991, 1992; Sleepers, 1991; Comics, 1993; Class Act, 1994, Class Act II, 1995; She's Out, 1995; Heavy Weather, 1995; A Perfect State, 1996; Jonathan Creek, series II, 1998, III, 1999 and IV, 2002–03, Christmas Specials, 1999 and 2001; (jtly) The Cazalets, 2001; Love Soup, 2005, series II, 2006–07. McTaggart Lect., Edinburgh TV Fest., 1990. Governor: BFI, 1981–86 (Fellow, 1998; Chairperson, Prodn Bd, 1981–82); Nat. Film and Television Sch., 1984–. Hon. LLD Strathclyde, 1988. Veuve-Clicquot Businesswoman of 1982; Woman's Own Woman of Achievement, 1983; Alan Clarke Award, BAFTA, 2002. *Recreations:* reading, eating. *Address:* 11 Addison Avenue, W11 4QS. *Died 22 Nov. 2007.*

LAMBTON, Viscount; Antony Claud Frederick Lambton; *b* 10 July 1922; *s* of 5th Earl of Durham (*d* 1970) and Diana (*d* 1924), *o d* of Granville Farquhar; disclaimed peerages for life, 1970 but allowed by Mr Speaker Lloyd to continue to sit in Parliament using courtesy title; *m* 1942, Belinda (*d* 2003), *d* of Major D. H. Blew-Jones, Westward Ho!, North Devonshire; one *s* five *d.* MP (C) Berwick upon Tweed Div. of Northumberland, 1951–73; Parly Under-Sec. of State, MoD, 1970–May 1973; PPS to the Foreign Secretary, 1955–57. *Publications:* Snow and Other Stories, 1983; Elizabeth and Alexandra, 1985; The Abbey in the Wood, 1986; The Mountbattens, 1989; Pig and Other Stories, 1990. *Heir to disclaimed peerages:* *s* Hon. Edward Richard Lambton (Baron Durham) [*b* 19 Oct. 1961; *m* 1st, 1983, Christabel (marr. diss.), *y d* of late Rory McEwen and of Mrs McEwen, Bardrochat; one *s*; 2nd, 1995, Catherine, *e* *d* of D. J. V. Fitz-Gerald, 29th Knight of Glin]. *Address:* Villa Cetinale, Sovicille, Siena, Italy; Biddick Hall, Chester-le-Street, Co. Durham. *Died 30 Dec. 2006.*

LAMBTON, Prof. Ann Katharine Swynford, OBE 1942; FBA 1964; Professor of Persian, University of London, 1953–79, then Emeritus; *b* 8 Feb. 1912; *d* of late Hon. George Lambton, 5th *s* of 2nd Earl of Durham, and Cicely, *d* of Sir John Francis Fortescue Horner, KCVO. *Educ:* Sch. of Oriental Studies, London Univ. (BA; PhD 1939; DLit 1953). Press Attaché, British Embassy (formerly Legation), Tehran, 1939–45; Senior Lecturer in Persian, School of Oriental and African Studies, 1945–48; Reader in Persian, University of London, 1948–53. Reader Emeritus, dio. of Newcastle, 1988. Hon. Fellow: New Hall, Cambridge, 1973; SOAS, Univ. of London, 1983. Hon. DLit Durham, 1971; Hon. LittD Cambridge, 1973. *Publications:* Three Persian Dialects, 1938; Landlord and Peasant in Persia, 1953; Persian Grammar, 1953; Persian Vocabulary, 1964; The Persian Land Reform 1962–66, 1969; (ed, with others) The Cambridge History of Islam, vols 1–11, 1971; Theory and Practice in Medieval Persian Government, 1980; State and Government in Medieval Islam, 1981; Qajar Persia, 1987; Continuity and Change in Medieval Persia, 1988. *Died 19 July 2008.*

LAMBURN, Patricia, (Mrs Donald Derrick), CBE 1985; Editorial Director, IPC Magazines Ltd, 1981–86; Director, IPC, 1968–86; *er d* of Francis John Lamburn and Nell Winifred (*née* Kennedy); *m* 1949, Donald G. E. Douglas Derrick, DDS, LDSRCS, FRCD(Can.), FACD; *one s one d. Educ:* Queen's Gate Sch., S Kensington. Amalgamated Press, 1943–49; Curtis Publishing Co., USA, 1949–50; joined George Newnes Ltd, 1950; during ensuing yrs, edited, developed and was associated creatively with wide range of women's and teenage magazines; Dir, George Newnes Ltd, 1966–68; Gp Dir, Young Magazines Gp, 1968–71; Publishing Dir, Women's Magazines Gp, 1971–76; Asst Man. Dir (Editorial), 1976–81. Mem., Interim Licensing Authority for In Vitro Fertilisation and Embryology, 1986–91. Chm., Gen. Adv. Council, IBA, 1982–85 (Mem., 1980–82); Member: Health Educn Council, 1973–78; Editl Cttee, PPA, 1975–87; Information Cttee, British Nutrition Foundn, 1979–85; Periodical Publishing Trng Cttee, PPITB, 1980–82; Public Relations Cttee, RCP, 1981–88; Press Council, 1982–87; HFEA Inspectorate, 1991–94. Trustee, CancerBACUP, 1993–2000 (Mem. Exec. Cttee, 1986–93). Mem., Chelsea Crime Prevention Panel, 1990–95. *Address:* Chelsea, London. *Died 8 Dec. 2006.*

LAMER, Rt Hon. Antonio, CC 2000; PC (Can.) 1990; Chief Justice of Canada, 1990–2000; Senior Adviser, Stikeman Elliott, Barristers and Solicitors, since 2000; *b* 8 July 1933; *m*; one *s*; *m* 1987, Danièle Tremblay; one step *s* one step *d. Educ:* Univ. of Montreal. Called to the Bar, Quebec, 1957; private practice, Cutler, Lamer, Bellemare & Associates; Prof., Faculty of Law, Univ. of Montreal; Judge, Superior Court and Queen's Bench, Province of Quebec, 1969–78; Chm., Law Reform Commn of Canada, 1976 (Vice-Chm., 1971); Justice, Quebec Court of Appeal, 1978–80; Justice, Supreme Court of Canada, 1980–90. Associate Prof. of Law, Univ. of Montreal, 2000–. Dir, Canadian Human Rights Foundn, 1974. Pres., Soc. de Criminologie, Québec, 1974. Chairman: Adv. Council, Historica Foundn, 2000–; Bd of Dirs, Les Rendez-vous de la francophonie, 2000–. Hon. Col, 2nd Field Regt of Canada; Pres., Nat. Council of Hon. Cols and Lt-Cols, 2002– (Pres., Land Force, Quebec Area). DU Saint Paul, 2001. KStJ 1993. Order of Merit, Univ. of Montreal, 1991. Silver Jubilee Medal, 1977; Canadian Confedn 125th Anniv. Medal, 1992. *Address:* Stikeman Elliott, 50 O'Connor Street, Suite 1600, Ottawa, ON K1P 6L2, Canada. *Died 24 Nov. 2007.*

LAMMIMAN, Surg. Rear Adm. David Askey, CB 1993; LVO 1978; FFARCS; Medical Director General (Naval), 1990–93; Deputy Surgeon General: Health Services, 1990–91; Operations and Plans, 1991–93;

Consultant Anaesthetist, London Fertility Centre, since 1992; *b* 30 June 1932; *s* of Herbert Askey Lammiman and Lilian Elsie (*née* Park); *m* 1st, 1957, Sheila Mary Graham (marr. diss. 1984); three *s* one *d*; 2nd, 1984, Caroline Dale Brooks. *Educ:* Wyggeston Sch., Leicester; St Bartholomew's Hosp. (MB, BS 1957). DA 1962; DObstRCOG 1962; FFARCS 1969. Resident House Officer, Redhill County Hosp. and St Bartholomew's Hosp., 1957–58; joined RN, 1959; gen. service and hosp. appts at home and abroad; Clinical Asst, Southampton Gp of Hosps, Alder Hey Children's Hosp., Liverpool, and Radcliffe Infirmary, Oxford, 1966–69; served in: HMS Chaplet, 1959; HMS Eagle, 1967–68; HMY Britannia, 1976–78; Consultant Anaesthetist, RN Hospital: Malta, 1969–71; Haslar, 1971–73; Gibraltar, 1973–75; Plymouth, 1975–76; Haslar, 1978–82; Dir of Med. Personnel, MoD, 1982–84; Medical Officer i/c RN Hospital: Plymouth, 1984–86; Haslar, 1986–88; Surg. Rear Adm. (Support Med. Services), 1989–90. QHS 1987–93. *Recreations:* fly fishing, golf, tennis. *Club:* Flyfishers'. *Died 27 Jan. 2009.*

LAMOND, James Alexander; JP, DL; *b* Burrelton, Perthshire, 29 Nov. 1928; *s* of Alexander N. G. Lamond and Christina Lamond (*née* Craig); *m* 1954, June Rose Wellburn; three *d. Educ:* Burrelton Sch.; Coupar Angus Sch. Draughtsman. Mem., Aberdeen City Council, 1959–71; Lord Provost of Aberdeen, 1970–71; Lord Lieutenant of the County of the City of Aberdeen, 1970–71. MP (Lab) Oldham East, 1970–83, Oldham Central and Royton, 1983–92; Mem., Chairmen's Panel, 1979–92. Member (Lab): Grampian Regl Council, 1994–96; Aberdeen CC, 1995–2007 (Convenor: Planning and Strategic Develt Cttee, 1995–99; Standards and Scrutiny Cttee, 1999–2003). Chairman: Aberdeen Exhibition and Conf. Centre Ltd, 1996–2003; Royal Aberdeen Workshops for the Blind and Disabled, 2002–04. Mem., Unite (formerly TASS, then MSF, subseq. Amicus), 1944– (Chm., No 1 Divisional Council of DATA, 1965–70); Sec., Aberdeen Trades Council, 1994–98 (Pres., 1969). JP Aberdeen, 1967; DL Aberdeen, 1995. *Recreations:* golf, travel, reading, thinking. *Address:* 15 Belvidere Street, Aberdeen AB25 2QS. *T:* (01224) 638074. *Died 20 Nov. 2007.*

LANCASTER, Margaret Elizabeth; *see* Douglas, M. E.

LANDON, Howard Chandler Robbins; author and music historian; *b* 6 March 1926; *s* of late William Grinnell Landon and Dorothea LeBaron Robbins; *m* 1949, Christa Fuhrmann (marr. diss.; she *d* 1977); *m* 1977, Else Radant. *Educ:* Aiken Preparatory Sch.; Lenox Sch.; Swarthmore Coll.; Boston Univ., USA (BMus). European rep. of Intercollegiate Broadcasting System, 1947; founded Haydn Soc. (which recorded and printed music of Joseph Haydn), 1949; became a Special Correspondent of The Times, 1957 and contrib. to that newspaper until 1961. Visiting Prof., Queen's Coll., NYC, 1969; Regents Prof. of Music, Univ. of California (Davis), 1970, 1975, 1979; John Bird Prof. of Music, UC Cardiff, 1978–; Christian Johnson Prof. of Music, Middlebury Coll., Vermont, USA, 1980–. Advr, Prague Mozart Foundn, 1992–. Hon. Professorial Fellow, University Coll., Cardiff, 1971–79; Hon. Fellow, Lady Margaret Hall, Oxford, 1979–. Hon. DMus: Boston Univ., 1969; Queen's Univ., Belfast, 1974; Bristol, 1982. Verdienstkreuz für Kunst und Wissenschaft from Austrian Govt, 1972; Gold Medal, City of Vienna, 1987; Haydn Prize, Govt of Burgenland, Austria, 1990. Co-editor, The Haydn Yearbook, 1962–. *Publications:* The Symphonies of Joseph Haydn, 1955; The Mozart Companion (co-ed with Donald Mitchell), 1956; The Collected Correspondence and London Notebooks of Joseph Haydn, 1959; Essays on Eighteenth-Century Music, 1969; Ludwig van Beethoven: a documentary study, 1970; critical edn of the 107 Haydn Symphonies, (completed) 1968; five-vol. biog. of Haydn: vol. 3, Haydn in England, 1976; vol. 4, Haydn: The Years of The Creation, 1977; vol. 5, Haydn: The Late Years, 1977; vol. 1, Haydn: The Early Years, and vol. 2, Haydn

in Eszterhaza, 1978–80; Haydn: a documentary study, 1981; Mozart and the Masons, 1982; Handel and his World, 1984; 1791: Mozart's Last Year, 1988; (with David Wyn Jones) Haydn: his life and music, 1988; Mozart: the golden years, 1989; (ed) The Mozart Compendium, 1990; Mozart and Vienna, 1991; Five Centuries of Music in Venice, 1991; Vivaldi: voice of the Baroque, 1993; The Mozart Essays, 1995; Horns in High C: a memoir of musical discoveries and adventures, 1999; scholarly edns of eighteenth-century music (various European publishing houses). *Recreations:* swimming, cooking, walking. *Address:* Château de Foncoussières, 81800 Rabastens, Tarn, France. *T:* 563406145.
Died 20 Nov. 2009.

LANE OF HORSELL, Baron *cr* 1990 (Life Peer), of Woking in the County of Surrey; **Peter Stewart Lane,** Kt 1984; JP; FCA; Senior Partner, Binder Hamlyn, Chartered Accountants, 1979–92; *b* 29 Jan. 1925; *s* of Leonard George Lane; *m* Doris Florence (*née* Botsford) (*d* 1969); two *d. Educ:* Sherborne Sch., Dorset. Served RNVR (Sub-Lieut), 1943–46. Qualified as chartered accountant, 1948; Partner, Binder Hamlyn or predecessor firms, 1950–92. Chairman: Brent Internat., 1985–95; Elswick, 1993–94; Attwoods, 1994; Automated Security (Hldgs), 1994–96; Dep. Chm., More O'Ferrall, later More Gp, 1985–97. National Union of Conservative Associations: Vice Chm., 1981–83; Chm., 1983–84; Chm., Exec. Cttee, 1986–91. Chm., Nuffield Hosps, 1993–96 (Dep. Chm., 1990–93). Chm., Action on Addiction, 1991–94. JP Surrey, 1976–; Freeman, City of London. *Address:* c/o House of Lords, SW1A 0PW. *Clubs:* Boodle's, Beefsteak, MCC.
Died 9 Jan. 2009.

LANE, Ronald Anthony Stuart, CMG 1977; MC 1945; Deputy Chairman, Chartered Trust Ltd, 1979–83; *b* 8 Dec. 1917; 2nd *s* of late Wilmot Ernest Lane and F. E. Lane (*née* Blakey); *m* 1948, Anne Brenda, 2nd *d* of E. Walsh; one *s* one *d. Educ:* Lancing College. FIB. Served War, 1940–45, 7th Light Cavalry, Indian Army, India and Burma (Major). Joined Chartered Bank of India, Australia & China, 1937; served in Far East, 1939–60; Gen. Manager, 1961, Chief Gen. Manager, 1972, Man. Dir, 1973–77, Vice-Chm., 1977–83, Standard Chartered Bank Ltd. Mem., Export Guarantees Adv. Council, 1973–78 (Dep. Chm., 1977–78). *Recreations:* sailing, gardening. *Address:* West Hold, By the Church, West Mersea, Essex CO5 8QD. *T:* (01206) 382563. *Clubs:* East India; West Mersea Yacht. *Died 15 Jan. 2007.*

LANG, Prof. Andrew Richard, FRS 1975; Professor of Physics, University of Bristol, 1979–87, then Emeritus; Senior Research Fellow, University of Bristol, since 1995; *b* 9 Sept. 1924; *s* of late Ernest F. S. Lang and Susannah (*née* Gueterbock); unmarried. *Educ:* University College of South-West, Exeter, (BSc Lond. 1944; MSc Lond. 1947); Trinity Coll., Cambridge (PhD 1953). Research Dept, Lever Bros, Port Sunlight, 1945–47; Research Asst, Cavendish Laboratory, 1947–48; North American Philips, Irvington-on-Hudson, NY, 1952–53; Instructor, Harvard Univ., 1953–54; Asst Professor, Harvard Univ., 1954–59; Lectr in Physics, 1960–66, Reader, 1966–79, Univ. of Bristol. FInstP. Mem. Geol Assoc.; Mem. Soc. Sigma Xi. Foreign Associate, RSSAf 1996. Hon. DSc Exeter, 1994. Charles Vernon Boys Prize, Inst. of Physics, 1964; Hughes Medal, Royal Soc., 1997; Ernst Mach Medal, Acad. of Scis of Czech Rep., 2005. *Publications:* contribs to learned jls. *Address:* 1B Elton Road, Bristol BS8 1SJ. *T:* (0117) 973 9784. *Died 30 June 2008.*

LANGDON-DOWN, Antony Turnbull; Volunteer Consultant, Sevenoaks Citizens' Advice Bureau, 1995–2003; Clerk to Merchant Taylors Company, 1980–85; *b* 31 Dec. 1922; *s* of Dr Reginald Langdon-Down and Ruth Langdon-Down (*née* Turnbull); *m* 1954, Jill Elizabeth Style (*née* Caruth) (*d* 2001); one *s* one *d. Educ:* Harrow School. Member of Lincoln's Inn, 1940–60, called to the Bar, 1948; enrolled as a solicitor, 1960; practised as solicitor, 1961–80. Pt-time Chm., Social Security Appeals Tribunal, 1985–95. Pilot, Royal

Air Force, 1942–47 (finally Flt Lieut). Master of Merchant Taylors Company, 1979–80. *Recreations:* bridge, music, art. *Address:* Drumard, The Street, Plaxtol, Sevenoaks, Kent TN15 0QP. *T:* (01732) 810720. *Clubs:* Savile, MCC. *Died 8 Jan. 2010.*

LANGLEY, Maj.-Gen. Sir (Henry) Desmond (Allen), KCVO 1983; MBE 1967; Governor and Commander-in-Chief of Bermuda, 1988–92; *b* 16 May 1930; *s* of late Col Henry Langley, OBE, and Winsome Langley; *m* 1950, Felicity Joan, *d* of Lt-Col K. J. P. Oliphant, MC; one *s* one *d. Educ:* Eton; RMA Sandhurst. Commissioned The Life Guards, 1949; Adjt, Household Cavalry Regt, 1953–54; GSO3 HQ 10th Armoured Div., 1956–57; Regtl Adjt, Household Cavalry, 1959–60; psc 1961; GSO2(Ops) HQ Far East Land Forces, 1963–65; Bde Major, Household Bde, 1965–67; Comdg Officer, The Life Guards, 1969–71; Asst Sec., Chiefs of Staff Secretariat, 1971–72; Lt-Col Comdg Household Cavalry and Silver Stick-in-Waiting, 1972–75; Comdr 4th Guards Armoured Bde, 1976–77; RCDS 1978; BGS HQ UK Land Forces, 1979; GOC London District and Maj.-Gen. Comdg Household Div., 1979–83; Administrator, Sovereign Base Areas and Comdr, British Forces, Cyprus, 1983–85; retired, 1986. Gov., Church Lads' and Church Girls' Brigade, 1986–2005. Freeman, City of London, 1983. KStJ 1989. *Died 14 Feb. 2008.*

LANGRIDGE, Philip Gordon, CBE 1994; FRAM, FRCM; concert and opera singer (tenor), since 1964; *b* 16 Dec. 1939; *m* 1962, Margaret Hilary Davidson; one *s* two *d; m* 1981, Ann Murray, Hon. DBE, mezzo-soprano; one *s. Educ:* Maidstone Grammar Sch.; Royal Academy of Music, London. ARAM 1977; FRAM 1985; FRCM 1997. Glyndebourne Festival début, 1964; BBC Promenade Concerts, 1970–; Edinburgh Fest., 1970–; Netherlands Opera, Scottish Opera, Handel Opera etc. Covent Garden: L'Enfant et les Sortilèges, Rossignol, Boris, Jenufa, Idomeneo, Peter Grimes, Death in Venice, Rheingold, Palestrina, The Tempest, Le Nozze di Figaro, The Minotaur; ENO: Turn of the Screw, Osud (Olivier Award, Outstanding Individual Performer in a New Opera Production, 1984), The Mask of Orpheus, Billy Budd, Beatrice and Benedict, Makropoulos Case; Peter Grimes; Oedipus Rex; Glyndebourne, 1977–: Don Giovanni, Idomeneo, Fidelio, Jenufa, La Clemenza di Tito; The Second Mrs Kong; La Scala, 1979–: Rake's Progress, Wozzeck, Boris Godunov, Il Sosia, Idomeneo, Oberon, Peter Grimes; Frankfurt Opera: Castor and Pollux, Rigoletto, Die Entführung; Bavarian State Opera: Peter Grimes, Midsummer Marriage, La Clemenza di Tito, Rheingold; Zurich Opera: Poppea, Lucio Silla; Don Giovanni; La Fenice: Janacek's Diary; Palermo: Otello (Rossini); Pesaro: La Donna del lago; Maggio Musicale: Peter Grimes; Boris Godunov; Aix en Provence: Alcina, Les Boriades; Metropolitan Opera, NY: Così fan Tutte, Boris Godunov, Das Rheingold, Billy Budd, Peter Grimes, Moses und Aron, Hansel and Gretel; Vienna State Opera: Wozzeck; Salzburg Festival: Moses und Aron, Idomeneo, From the House of the Dead, Poppea, Boris Godunov; Amsterdam: Poppea, Idomeneo, Il Barbiere di Siviglia, Dorian Gray, Pelléas et Mélisande; Los Angeles: Peter Grimes; Barcelona: Billy Budd; Boris Godunov. Concerts with major, international orchestras and conductors including: Berlin Phil. (Abbado, Ozawa), Boston (Previn), Chicago (Solti, Abbado), Los Angeles (Christopher Hogwood), Sydney (Mackerras), Vienna Phil. (Previn), Orchestre de Paris (Barenboim, Mehta), and all major British orchestras; recitals with Pollini, Schiff, Donohoe, Norris. Many first performances of works, some dedicated to and written for him. Master classes on communication through singing. Made over 100 records of early, baroque, classical, romantic and modern music (Grammy Awards: for Schönberg's Moses und Aron, 1985; for Peter Grimes, 1996). Mem., Music Panel, Arts Council of GB, 1983–86. Singer of the Year, RPS/Heidsieck Award, 1989; Santay Award, Co. of Musicians; Making Music/ Sir Charles Groves Award, 2001; Helpmann Award, 2006. *Recreation:* collecting water colour paintings and

Victorian postcards. *Address:* c/o Allied Artists Agency, 42 Montpelier Square, SW7 1JZ. *T:* (020) 7589 6243. *Died 5 March 2010.*

LANGRIDGE, Richard James, CVO 1992; HM Diplomatic Service, retired; Consul-General, Bordeaux, 1990–92; *b* 29 Oct. 1932; *m* 1965, Jeannine Louise Joosen; one *d.* HM Forces, 1951–53; joined FO 1953; served NY, Leopoldville, Athens, Dakar, Paris and FCO; Ambassador to Madagascar, 1979–84; FCO, 1985; Dep. High Comr, Colombo, 1985–89. *Died 15 July 2009.*

LARMINIE, (Ferdinand) Geoffrey, OBE 1971; Director, British Geological Survey, 1987–90; *b* 23 June 1929; *s* of late Ferdinand Samuel Larminie and of Mary Larminie (*née* Willis); *m* 1956, Helena Elizabeth Woodside Carson; one *s* one *d. Educ:* St Andrews Coll., Dublin; Trinity Coll., Dublin (BA 1954, MA 1972; Hon. Fellow, 1989). Asst Lectr in Geology, Univ. of Glasgow, 1954–56; Lectr in Geology, Univ. of Sydney, 1956–60; joined British Petroleum Co. Ltd, 1960: Exploration Dept in Sudan, Greece, Canada, Libya, Kuwait, California, New York, Thailand and Alaska, 1960–74; Scientific Advr, Inf. Dept, London, 1974–75; Gen. Manager, Public Affairs and Inf. Dept, London, 1975–76; Gen. Manager, Environmental Control Centre, London, 1976–84; External Affairs Co-ordinator, Health, Safety and Environmental Services, BP plc, 1984–87. Chm., Cambridge Arctic Shelf Prog., 1996–98 (Vice-Chm., 1993–96). Member: Royal Commn on Environmental Pollution, 1979–83; NERC, 1983–87. Council Mem. 1984–90, Vice-Pres., 1987–90, RGS. President: Alaska Geol Soc., 1969; Soc. of Underwater Technol., 1987–89 (Hon. Fellow, 1992). Trustee, 1978–91, Life Trustee, 1991, Bermuda Biol Station; Member: Bd of Management, Inst. of Offshore Engrg, Heriot-Watt Univ., 1981–90; Polar Res. Bd, Nat. Res. Council, Washington, DC, 1984–88. Mem., IBA Gen. Adv. Council, 1980–85. Mem. of numerous scientific and professional socs. *Publications:* papers in scientific and technical jls on oil ind., and occasional reviews. *Recreations:* archaeology, natural history, reading, shooting. *Address:* Lane End, Lanes End, Tring, Herts HP23 6LF. *T:* (01296) 624907. *Died 16 Oct. 2008.*

LATHE, Prof. Grant Henry; Professor of Chemical Pathology, University of Leeds, 1957–77, then Emeritus Professor; *b* 27 July 1913; *s* of Frank Eugene and Annie Smith Lathe; *m* 1st, 1938, Margaret Eleanore Brown; one *s*; 2nd, 1950, Joan Frances Hamlin; one *s* two *d. Educ:* McGill Univ.; Oxford Univ. ICI Research Fellow: Dept. of Biochemistry, Oxford Univ., 1946; Dept. of Chemical Pathology, Post Graduate Medical School of London, 1948; Lecturer in Chemical Pathology, Guy's Hospital Medical School, 1948; Biochemist, The Bernhard Baron Memorial Research Laboratories, Queen Charlotte's Maternity Hospital, London, 1949. John Scott Award (with C. R. J. Ruthven), 1971, for invention of gel filtration. *Publications:* papers in medical and biochemical journals. *Recreations:* fell-walking, campaigning against nuclear weapons. *Address:* 12A The Avenue, Leeds LS8 1EH. *T:* (0113) 266 1507. *Died 2 July 2007.*

LATIMER, Sir (Courtenay) Robert, Kt 1966; CBE 1958 (OBE 1948); *b* 13 July 1911; *er s* of late Sir Courtenay Latimer, KCIE, CSI; *m* 1st, 1944, Elizabeth Jane Gordon (*née* Smail) (*d* 1989); one *s* one *d*; 2nd, 1990, Frederieka Jacoba Blankert (*née* Witteween). *Educ:* Rugby; Christ Church, Oxford. ICS, 1934 (Punjab); IPS, 1939; Vice-Consul, Bushire, 1940–41; Sec. Foreign Publicity Office, Delhi, 1941–42; Sec. Indian Agency Gen., Chungking, 1944; in NW Frontier Prov., as Asst Political Agent N Waziristan, Dir of Civil Supplies, Sec. to Governor and District Comr, Bannu, 1942–43 and 1945–47. HM Overseas Service, 1948; served in Swaziland, 1948–49; Bechuanaland Protectorate, 1951–54; Office of High Comr for Basutoland, the Bechuanaland Protectorate and Swaziland, as Asst Sec., 1949–51; Sec. for Finance, 1954–60; Chief Sec., 1960–64; Minister, British Embassy, Pretoria, 1965–66;

Registrar, Kingston Polytechnic, 1967–76. *Recreation:* photography. *Address:* Benedicts, Old Avenue, Weybridge, Surrey KT13 0PS. *Died 8 April 2010.*

LAUDERDALE, 17th Earl of, *cr* 1624; **Patrick Francis Maitland;** Baron Maitland, 1590; Viscount Lauderdale, 1616; Viscount Maitland, Baron Thirlestane and Boltoun, 1624; Bt of Nova Scotia, 1680; Hereditary Bearer of the National Flag of Scotland, 1790 and 1952; Chief of the Clan Maitland; *b* 17 March 1911; *s* of Rev. Hon. Sydney G. W. Maitland and Ella Frances (*née* Richards); *S* brother, 1968; *m* 1936, Stanka (*d* 2003), *d* of Professor Milivoje Lozanitch, Belgrade Univ.; two *s* two *d. Educ:* Lancing Coll., Sussex; Brasenose Coll., Oxford. BA Hons Oxon, 1933. Journalist 1933–59. Appts include: Balkans and Danubian Corresp., The Times, 1939–41; Special Corresp. Washington, News Chronicle, 1941; War Corresp., Pacific, Australia, New Zealand, News Chronicle, 1941–43. Foreign Office, 1943–45. MP (U) for Lanark Div. of Lanarks, 1951–Sept. 1959 (except for period May–Dec. 1957 when Ind. C). Founder and Chairman, Expanding Commonwealth Group, House of Commons, 1955–59; re-elected Chairman, Nov. 1959. Chm., Sub-Cttee on Energy, Transport and Res., House of Lords Select Cttee on EEC Affairs, 1974–79; Vice Chm. and Co-founder, Parly Gp for Energy Studies, 1980–99. Dir, Elf Petroleum (UK). Editor of The Fleet Street Letter Service, and of The Whitehall Letter, 1945–58. Mem., Coll. of Guardians of National Shrine of Our Lady of Walsingham, Norfolk, 1955–82 (Guardian Emeritus, 1982–). President, The Church Union, 1956–61. FRGS. *Publications:* European Dateline, 1945; Task for Giants, 1957. *Heir: s* The Master of Lauderdale, Viscount Maitland, *b* 4 Nov. 1937. *Address:* 10 Ovington Square, SW3 1LH. *T:* (020) 7589 7451; 12 St Vincent Street, Edinburgh EH3 6SH. *T:* (0131) 556 5692. *Club:* New (Edinburgh). *Died 2 Dec. 2008.*

LAURENCE, Dan Hyman; Literary and Dramatic Advisor, Estate of George Bernard Shaw, 1973–90; *b* 28 March 1920. *Educ:* New York City public schs; Hofstra Univ. (BA 1946); New York Univ. (MA 1950). First went on the stage as child actor, 1932; radar specialist with Fifth Air Force, USA, in S Pacific, 1942–45; wrote and performed for Armed Forces Radio Service in New Guinea and the Philippines during World War II, and subseq. for radio and television in USA and Australia; began teaching in 1950 as graduate asst, New York Univ.; Instr of English, Hofstra Univ., 1953–58; Editor, Readex Microprint Corp., 1959–60; Associate Prof. of English, New York Univ., 1962–67, Prof., 1967–70. Vis. Professor: Indiana Univ., 1969; Univ. of Texas at Austin, 1974–75; Tulane Univ., 1981 (Mellon Prof. in the Humanities); Univ. of BC, Vancouver, 1984; Adjunct Prof. of Drama, Univ. of Guelph, 1986–91 (Dist. Vis. Prof. of Drama, 1983); Vis. Fellow, Inst. for Arts and Humanistic Studies, Pennsylvania State Univ., 1976. John Simon Guggenheim Meml Fellow, 1960, 1961 and 1972; Montgomery Fellow, Dartmouth Coll., 1982. Literary Advr, 1982–90, Associate Dir, 1987–2000, Shaw Fest., Ont. Series Ed., Penguin edn works of Shaw, 2000–. Associate Mem., RADA, 1979. Phi Beta Kappa (hon.), 1967. President's Medal, Hofstra Univ., 1990. *Publications:* Henry James: a bibliography (with Leon Edel), 1957 (3rd edn 1981); Robert Nathan: a bibliography, 1960; (ed) Collected Letters of Bernard Shaw, vol. 1, 1874–1897, 1965, vol. 2, 1898–1910, 1972, vol. 3, 1911–1925, 1985, Vol. 4, 1926–1950, 1988; (ed) Bernard Shaw, Collected Plays with their Prefaces, 1970–74; Shaw, Books, and Libraries, 1976; Shaw: an exhibit, 1977; (dramatization) The Black Girl in Search of God, 1977; (ed) Shaw's Music, 1981, 2nd edn 1989; Bernard Shaw: a bibliography, 1983; A Portrait of the Author as a Bibliography (Engelhard Lecture on the Book, L of C, 1982), 1983; (Uncollected Writings of Shaw): How to Become a Musical Critic, 1960 (2nd edn 1968); Platform and Pulpit, 1961; (ed with David H. Greene) The Matter with Ireland, 1962, 2nd edn 2001; (ed with Daniel J. Leary) Flyleaves, 1977; (Gen. Editor) Bernard Shaw: Early Texts, Play Manuscripts in

Facsimile, 12 vols, 1981; (with James Rambeau) Agitations: letters to the Press 1875–1950, 1985; (with Martin Quinn) Shaw on Dickens, 1985; (with Nicholas Grene) Shaw, Lady Gregory, and the Abbey, 1993; (ed with Daniel J. Leary) Shaw, Complete Prefaces, vol. I, 1993, vol. II, 1995, vol. III, 1997; (ed) Bernard Shaw, Theatrics, 1995; (ed with Margot Peters) Unpublished Shaw, 1996; (ed with Fred D. Crawford) Bibliographical Shaw, 2000. Recreations: theatre-going, music, mountain climbing. Address: 101 Arcadia Place, Apt 403, San Antonio, TX 78209, USA.   Died 5 Feb. 2008.

LAURENCE, Sir Peter (Harold), KCMG 1981 (CMG 1976); MC 1944; DL; HM Diplomatic Service, retired; Vice-President of Council, British Institute of Archaeology, Ankara, since 1995 (Chairman, 1984–95); b 18 Feb. 1923; s of late Ven. George Laurence, MA, BD and Alice (née Jackson); m 1948, Elizabeth Aïda Way; two s (one d decd). Educ: Radley Coll.; Christ Church, Oxford. 60th Rifles, 1941–46 (Major). Entered Foreign Service, 1948; Western Dept, FO, 1948–50; Athens, 1950–53; Asst Political Adviser, Trieste, 1953–55; 1st Sec., Levant Dept, FO, 1955–57; Prague, 1957–60; Cairo, 1960–62; North and East African Dept, FO, 1962–65; Personnel Dept, DSAO, 1965–67; Counsellor, 1965; Political Adviser, Berlin, 1967–69; Visiting Fellow, All Souls Coll., 1969–70; Counsellor (Commercial), Paris, 1970–74; Chief Inspector, HM Diplomatic Service (Asst Under-Sec. of State), 1974–78; Ambassador to Ankara, 1980–83. Chairman: Foreign Anglican Church and Educnl Assoc. Ltd, 1976–2003; Community Council of Devon, 1986–92; Fellow, Woodard Corp. (W Div.), 1985. Mem. Council, Univ. of Exeter, 1989–99. Chm. of Governors, Grenville Coll., Bideford, 1988–95. DL Devon, 1989. Address: Trevilla, Beaford, Winkleigh, N Devon EX19 8NS. Club: Army and Navy.
                                        Died 26 Nov. 2007.

LAURISTON, Richard Basil; a Permanent Chairman of Industrial Tribunals, 1976–89; formerly Senior Partner, Alex Lauriston & Son, Solicitors, Middlesbrough; b 26 Jan. 1917; s of Alexander Lauriston, MBE, and Nellie Lauriston; m 1944, Monica, d of Wilfred Leslie Deacon, BA, Tonbridge, and Dorothy Louise Deacon; three s. Educ: Sir William Turner's Sch., Redcar; St John's Coll., Cambridge (MA, LLM). Solicitor, 1948; a Recorder of the Crown Court, 1974–82. Commnd and served in War of 1939–45, Royal Corps of Signals. Recreations: fishing, travelling. Address: Auchlochan House, 19 The Courtyard, New Trows Road, Lesmahagow, Lanarks ML11 0JS.   Died 5 Nov. 2010.

LAUTERBUR, Prof. Paul Christian, PhD; Professor, Center for Advanced Study, since 1987 and Center for Biophysics and Computational Biology, since 1988, and Distinguished University Professor, College of Medicine, since 1990, University of Illinois at Urbana-Champaign; b 6 May 1929; s of Edward and Gertrude Lauterbur; m 1st, 1962, Rose Mary Caputo (marr. diss.); one s one d; 2nd, 1984, Joan Dawson; one d. Educ: Case Inst. of Technol., Cleveland (BS Chem.); Univ. of Pittsburgh (PhD Chem. 1962). Res. Asst and Res. Associate, Mellon Inst., Pittsburgh, 1951–53; Mil. Service, Army Chem. Center Med. Labs, 1953–55; Fellow, Mellon Inst., 1955–63; State University of New York at Stony Brook: Associate Prof. of Chem., 1963–69; on sabbatical leave as Vis. Schol. at Dept of Chem., Stanford Univ., 1969–70; Prof. of Chem., 1969–83; Res. Prof. of Radiol., 1978–85; Leading Prof. of Chem., 1983–84; Univ. Prof., 1984–85; Adjunct Univ. Prof., 1985–; Prof., Coll. of Medicine, Univ. of Ill at Chicago, 1985–90; University of Illinois at Urbana-Champaign: Prof., Dept of Chemistry, 1985–; Dir, Biomed. Magnetic Resonance Lab., 1985–2001; Leader, MRI and Spectroscopy Gp, Beckman Inst., 1991–2003; College of Medicine: Res. Prof., Dept of Radiol., 1991–; Prof., 1985–2001, Actg Hd, 1995–96, Hd, 1996–2001, Dept of Med. Inf. Scis. Hon. Mem., Editl Bd, Magnetic Resonance in Medicine, 1992–. Mem., NAS, 1985. Hon. Member: Soc. for MRI, 1988; Amer. Assoc. of Physicists in Medicine, 2004. Hon.

Member: Deutsche Akad. der Naturforscher Leopoldina, 1992; Internat. Soc. for Magnetic Resonance in Medicine, 2004 (Fellow, 1994). FAAAS 1988; Fellow: APS, 1979; AIMBE, 1996. Holds numerous hon. degrees. US and internat. awards include: Gold Medal, Soc. of Magnetic Resonance in Medicine, 1982; Prize in Biol Physics, APS, 1983; Albert Lasker Clin. Res. Award, 1984; Gairdner Foundn Internat. Award, 1985; Harvey Prize in Sci. and Technol., Technion, 1986; Roentgen Medal, 1987; Medal of Honor, IEEE, 1987; Fiuggi Internat. Prize, 1987; Nat. Medal of Sci., 1987; Gold Medal, Radiol Soc. of N America, 1987; Nat. Medal of Technol., 1988; Alfred Heineken Prize for Medicine, 1989; Bower Award and Prize for Achievement in Sci., Benjamin Franklin Nat. Meml Commn, Franklin Inst., 1990; Internat. Soc. of Magnetic Resonance Award, 1992; Kyoto Prize for Advanced Technol., Inamori Foundn, 1994; Millennium Medal of Honor, IEEE, 2000; Award for Chem. in Service to Society, NAS, 2001; Technol. Award, Eduard Rhein Foundn, 2003; Nobel Prize in Physiol. or Medicine, 2003. Publications: (with Z. P. Liang) Principles of Magnetic Resonance Imaging: a signal processing perspective, 1999; numerous contribs to learned jls. Address: Department of Chemistry, Box 51–6, University of Illinois at Urbana-Champaign, Urbana, IL 61801, USA. T: (217) 2440445, Fax: (217) 2443186; e-mail: pcl@uiuc.edu.   Died 27 March 2007.

LAVAN, Hon. Sir John Martin, Kt 1981; retired 1981 as Senior Puisne Judge of the Supreme Court of Western Australia; b 5 Sept. 1911; s of late M. G. Lavan, KC; m 1st, 1939, Leith Harford (decd); one s three d; 2nd, 1984, Dorothy Bell (decd). Educ: Aquinas Coll., Perth; Xavier Coll., Melbourne. Barrister in private practice, 1934–69; a Judge of the Supreme Court of WA, 1969–81. Chm., Parole Bd, WA, 1969–79. Mem., Barristers' Bd, WA, 1960–69; Pres., Law Soc. of WA, 1964–66. KStJ. Club: Weld (Perth).   Died 1 Dec. 2006.

LAVER, Frederick John Murray, CBE 1971; Member, Post Office Corporation, 1969–73, retired; b 11 March 1915; er s of late Clifton F. Laver and Elsie Elizabeth Palmer, Bridgwater; m 1948, Kathleen Amy Blythe; one s two d. Educ: Plymouth Coll.; BSc London. Entered PO Engrg Dept, 1935; PO Research Stn, 1935–51; Radio Planning, 1951–57; Organization and Efficiency, 1957–63; Asst Sec., HM Treasury, 1963–65; Chief Scientific Officer, Min. of Technology, 1965–68; Dir, National Data Processing Service, 1968–70; Mem., NRDC, 1974–80. Vis. Prof., Computing Lab., Univ. of Newcastle upon Tyne, 1975–79. Mem. Council: IEE, 1966–69, 1972–73; British Computer Soc., 1969–72; Nat. Computing Centre, 1966–68, 1970–73; IEE Electronic Divl Bd, 1966–69, 1970–73. Mem. Council, 1979–87, Chm., 1985–87, Pro-Chancellor, 1981–87, Exeter Univ. Pres., Devonshire Assoc., 1990–91. CEng, FIET; Hon. FBCS. Hon. DSc Exeter, 1988. Publications: nine introductory books on physics and computing; several scientific papers. Recreations: reading, writing, and watching the sea. Address: The Old Vicarage, Otterton, Devon EX9 7JF.   Died 23 Nov. 2008.

LAVER, Graeme; see Laver, W. G.

LAVER, Patrick Martin; HM Diplomatic Service, retired; Director of Research, Foreign and Commonwealth Office, 1980–83; b 3 Feb. 1932; s of late James Laver, CBE, RE, FRSL, and Veronica Turleigh; m 1st, 1966, Marianne Ford (marr. annulled); one d; 2nd, 1979, Dr Elke Maria Schmitz, d of Thomas and Anneliese Schmitz. Educ: Ampleforth Coll., Yorks; New Coll., Oxford. Third Sec., Foreign Office, 1954; Second Sec., Djakarta, 1956; FO, 1957; Paris, 1958; Yaoundé, 1961; UK Delegn to Brussels Conf., 1962; First Sec., FO, 1963; UK Mission to UN, New York, 1964; Diplomatic Service Admin., 1965; Commercial Sec., Nairobi, 1968; FCO, 1970; Counsellor (Economic), Pretoria, 1973; UK Delegn to Conf. on Security and Co-operation in Europe, Geneva, 1974; Head of Rhodesia Dept, FCO, 1975–78; Counsellor, Paris, 1979–80. Address: The

Coach House, Keldholme, Kirkbymoorside, N Yorks YO62 6LZ. *T:* (01751) 432648. *Club:* Athenæum. *Died 11 Feb. 2006.*

LAVER, (William) Graeme, PhD; FRS 1987; Head, Influenza Research Unit, Australian National University, 1983–2001; *b* 3 June 1929; *s* of Lawrence and Madge Laver; *m* 1954, Judith Garrard Cahn; one *s* two *d. Educ:* Ivanhoe Grammar Sch., Melbourne; Univ. of Melbourne (BSc, MSc); Univ. of London (PhD). Technical Asst, Walter & Eliza Hall Inst. of Med. Res., Melbourne, 1947–52; Res. Asst, Dept of Biochemistry, Melbourne Univ., 1954–55; Res. Fellow, 1958–62, Fellow, 1962–64, Senior Fellow, 1964–90, Special Prof., 1990–2002, John Curtin Sch. of Med. Res., ANU. International Meetings: Rougemont, Switzerland, 1976; Baden, Vienna, 1977; Thredbo, Australia, 1979; Beijing, China, 1982; Banbury Center, Cold Spring Harbor, NY, 1985; Kona, Hawaii, 1989. (Jtly) Australia Prize, 1996. *Publications:* papers on structure of influenza virus antigens, molecular mechanisms of antigenic shift and drift in type A influenza viruses and develt of anti-influenza drugs; numerous research articles. *Recreations:* raising beef cattle, viticulture, wine-making, ski-ing, climbing volcanoes. *Address:* 3047 Barton Highway, Murrumbateman, NSW 2582, Australia. *T:* (2) 62270061. *Died 26 Sept. 2008.*

LAVERICK, Elizabeth, OBE 1993; PhD, CEng, FIET; CPhys, FInstP, FIEEE (US); Project Director, Advanced Manufacturing in Electronics, 1985–88; *b* 25 Nov. 1925; *d* of William Rayner and Alice Garland; *m* 1st, 1946 (marr. diss. 1960); no *c*; 2nd, 2004, Peter Ogden (*d* 2004). *Educ:* Dr Challoner's Grammar Sch., Amersham; Durham Univ. (PhD 1950). Research at Durham Univ., 1946–50; Section Leader at GEC, 1950–53; Microwave Engineer at Elliott Bros, 1954; Head of Radar Research Laboratory of Elliott-Automation Radar Systems Ltd, 1959; Jt Gen. Manager, Elliott-Automation Radar Systems Ltd, 1968–69, Technical Dir, 1969–71; Dep. Sec., IEE, 1971–85; Electronics CADMAT (Computer Aided Design, Manufacture and Test) Project Dir, 1982–85. Mem. Electronics Divisional Bd, 1967–70, Mem. Council, 1969–70, IEE. Chm., Engrg Careers Co-ordinating Cttee, 1983–85; Member: DE Adv. Cttee on Women's Employment, 1970–82; Adv. Cttee on Electronic and Electrical Engrg, Sheffield Univ., 1984–87; Nat. Electronics Council, 1986–98; Chm., Ninth Internat. Conf. of Women Engrs and Scientists, 1989–91; Hon. Sec., Women's Engrg Soc., 1991–95 (Pres., 1967–69). Member Council: Inst. of Physics, 1970–73 (Chm., Women in Physics Cttee, 1985–90); City and Guilds of London Inst., 1984–87 (Hon. Mem., 1991; Fellow, 1998); Member Court: Brunel Univ., 1985–88; City Univ., 1991–95. Mem. Ct of Govs, IEE Benevolent Fund, 1991–99. Liveryman, Co. of Engrs, 1985–88. FRSA 1991. Hon. FUMIST, 1969. Editor, Woman Engr (Jl of Women's Engrg Soc.), 1984–90. *Publications:* contribs to IEE and IEEE Jls. *Recreations:* music, tapestry. *Died 12 Jan. 2010.*

LAVERS, Patricia Mae, (Mrs H. J. Lavers); Executive Director, Bond Street Association, 1961–76, and Regent Street Association, 1972–76; *b* 12 April 1919; *d* of Edric Allan Jordan and May Holdcraft; *m* 1st, 1945, Frederick Handel Hayward (*d* 1965); one *s*; 2nd, 1966, John Harold Ellen, OBE; 3rd, 1976, Lt-Comdr Herbert James Lavers. *Educ:* Sydenham High School. Clerk, Securities Dept, National Provincial Bank, 1938–45; Export Dir, Perth Radios, 1955–60. Alderman, St Pancras Council, 1960–66 (Libraries/Public Health). Elected to Executive of Westminster Chamber of Commerce, 1971, Chm. City Affairs Cttee, 1971–75. Pres., Sandwich Soc., 1983–. FZS. *Recreations:* swimming, collecting first editions and press books, walking. *Address:* Horse Pond Sluice, Delf Street, Sandwich, Kent CT13 9HD. *Clubs:* Arts, Lansdowne, Naval. *Died 19 Feb. 2007.*

LAW, Francis Stephen, (Frank Law), CBE 1981; *b* 31 Dec. 1916; *s* of Henry and Ann Law-Lowensberg; *m* 1959, Nicole Vigne (*née* Fesch); one *s*, and one *d* from previous marriage. *Educ:* on the Continent. War service, 1939–45. Wills Law & Co., 1947; Truvox Engrg, 1960, subseq. Dir of Controls and Communications; Dep. Chm., NFC, 1982–85 (Dir, Consortium and its predecessors, 1969–87). Chairman: Varta Gp UK, 1971–2001; Rubis Investment & Cie, 1990–2001 (Pres., 2001–); Aegis (formerly WRCS) Gp plc, 1992–2000 (Dir, 1982–92); Director: B. Elliott Plc, 1968–86; BMW (GB) Ltd, 1978–88; Siemens, 1984–98; NFC Internat. Hldgs, 1985–92; Celab Ltd, 1991–2001; Mem. Adv. Bd, Berliner Bank, 1988–92. Chm., Social Responsibilities Council, NFC, 1988–92; Member: Org. Cttee, NFC, 1968; Economic and Social Cttee, EEC, 1978–86. Life Governor, RSC, 1985–. Kt Comdr, Royal Order of Al-Alaoui (Morocco), 2004. *Recreations:* music, theatre, swimming. *Address:* La Clergie, St Sulpice de Roumagnac, 24600 Riberac, France. *Clubs:* Boodle's; Pilgrims. *Died 18 May 2009.*

LAW, Peter John; JP; MP (Ind.) Blaenau Gwent, since 2005; Member (Lab, 1999–2005, Ind., since 2005) Blaenau Gwent, National Assembly for Wales; *b* 1 April 1948; *s* of John Law and Rita Mary Law; *m* 1976, Patricia Bolter; two *s* three *d. Educ:* Llanfoist Primary Sch.; Grofield Secondary Sch. Self-employed grocer, 1965–80; retail develt, 1980–90; self-employed consultant in local govt and public authorities, 1990–99. Chm., Gwent Healthcare NHS Trust, 1999. Mem. (Lab) Blaenau Gwent CBC, 1974–99. Envmt and Local Govt Sec., Nat Assembly for Wales, 1999–2000. MCIPR (MIPR 1997). Mem., Welsh Lang. Bd, 1990–95. JP Gwent, 1985. *Recreations:* walking, Land Rovers, countryside. *Address:* (office) 1A Bethcar Street, Ebbw Vale, Blaenau Gwent NP23 6HH. *T:* (01495) 304569; House of Commons, SW1A 0AA. *Clubs:* Nant-y-glo Rugby Football, Ebbw Vale Rugby Football. *Died 25 April 2006.*

LAW, Phillip Garth, AC 1995 (AO 1975); CBE 1961; MSc, FAIP, FTSE, FAA, FRSV; scientist, Antarctic explorer, educationist; *b* 21 April 1912; *s* of Arthur James Law and Lillie Lena Chapman; *m* 1941, Nellie Isabel Allan (*d* 1990); no *c. Educ:* Hamilton High Sch.; Ballarat Teachers' Coll.; Melbourne Univ. FAIP 1948; FTSE 1976; FAA 1978. Science master, State secondary schs, Vic., 1933–38; Tutor in Physics, Newman Coll., Melbourne Univ., 1940–47; Lectr in Physics, 1943–48. Research Physicist and Asst Sec. of Scientific Instrument and Optical Panel of Austr. Min. of Munitions, 1940–45. Sen. Scientific Officer, ANARE, 1947–48; cosmic ray measurements in Antarctica and Japan, 1948; Dir, Antarctic Div., Dept of External Affairs, Aust., and Leader, ANARE, 1949–66; Expedition relief voyages to Heard I. and Macquarie I., 1949, 1951, 1952, 1954. Australian observer with Norwegian-British-Swedish Antarctic Expedn, 1950; Leader of expedition: to establish first permanent Australian station in Antarctica at Mawson, MacRobertson Land, 1954; which established second continental station at Davis, Princess Elizabeth Land, 1957; which took over Wilkes station from USA, 1959; to relieve ANARE stations and to explore coast of Australian Antarctic Territory, annually, 1955–66. Chm., Australian Nat. Cttee for Antarctic Research, 1966–80. Exec. Vice-Pres., Victoria Inst. of Colls, 1966–77; Pres., Victorian Inst. of Marine Scis, 1978–80. Member: Council of Melbourne Univ., 1959–78; Council, La Trobe Univ., 1964–74; Chm., RMIT Foundn, 1995–98; President: Royal Soc. of Victoria, 1967, 1968; Aust. and NZ Schs Exploring Soc., 1977–82. Dep. Pres., Science Museum of Victoria, Melbourne, 1979–82 (Trustee, 1968–83). Pres., Grad. Union, Melbourne Univ., 1972–77. Patron, British Schs Exploring Soc. Fellow, Aust. Inst. of Physics; ANZAAS; Foundn FRSV 1995. Hon. Fellow, Royal Melbourne Inst. of Technology. Hon. DAppSc Melbourne, 1962; Hon. DEd Victoria Inst. of Colls, 1978; Hon. DSc La Trobe, 1995. Founder's Gold Medal, RGS, 1960; Gold Medal, Aust. Geographic Soc., 1988; Clunies Ross Nat. Sci. and Technol. Award, 2001. *Publications:* (with John Béchervaise) ANARE, 1957; Antarctic Odyssey, 1983; The Antarctic Voyage of HMAS Wyatt Earp, 1995; You Have to be Lucky, 1995;

chapters in: It's People that Matter, ed Donald McLean, 1969; Search for Human Understanding, ed M. Merbaum and G. Stricker, 1971; Australian Antarctic Science, ed Marchant, Lugg and Quilty, 2003; ed series of ANARE scientific reports; numerous papers on Antarctica and education. *Recreations:* tennis, ski-ing, music, photography. *Address:* Unit 3 Balwyn Manor, 23 Maleela Avenue, Balwyn, Vic 3103, Australia. *Clubs:* Melbourne, Kelvin, Melbourne Cricket, Royal South Yarra Lawn Tennis (Melbourne). *Died 28 Feb. 2010.*

LAWRENCE, Michael Hugh, CMG 1972; Head of the Administration Department, House of Commons, 1972–80; retired 1980; *b* 9 July 1920; *s* of late Hugh Moxon Lawrence and Mrs. L. N. Lawrence; *m* 1948, Rachel Mary (MA Cantab), *d* of late Humphrey Gamon, Gt Barrow, Cheshire; one *s* two *d*. *Educ:* Highgate (Scholar); St Catharine's Coll., Cambridge (Exhibnr; MA). Served Indian Army, 1940–45. Indian Civil Service, 1945–46; Asst Clerk, House of Commons, 1947; Senior Clerk, 1948; Deputy Principal Clerk, 1962; Clerk of the Overseas Office, 1967–72; Clerk Administrator, 1972–76; Mem., Bd of Management, House of Commons, 1979–80. Sec., History of Parliament Trust, 1959–66. *Recreations:* hound work, walking, looking at churches, gardening. *Address:* 28 Stradbroke Road, Southwold, Suffolk IP18 6LQ. *T:* (01502) 722794.
Died 11 Nov. 2006.

LAWSON, Sir Christopher (Donald), Kt 1984; management consultant; Director, Communications Centre, since 1984; *b* 31 Oct. 1922; *s* of James Lawson and Ellen de Verrine; *m* 1945, Marjorie Bristow; two *s* one *d*. *Educ:* Magdalen Coll., Oxford. Served RAF, 1941–49: Pilot, Sqdn Leader. Thomas Hedley (Proctor and Gamble), 1949–57; Cooper McDougal Robertson, 1958–61; Managing Dir, TMC, 1961–63; Director: Mars Ltd, 1965–81; Mars Inc., USA, 1975–82; Pres., Mars Snackmaster, USA, 1977–82; Chm. and Man. Dir, Goodblue Ltd, 1981–; Chm., Spearhead Ltd, 1983–; Dir of Marketing, 1982–83, Dir of Special Services, 1986–87, Cons. and Unionist Party. *Recreations:* collecting antiques and new artists' work; all sport, particularly golf, cricket, hockey. *Address:* Pound Corner, Buckland, Oxon SN7 8QN. *Clubs:* Royal Air Force, MCC; Lillybrook Golf (Cheltenham); Doublegate Country (Ga, USA).
Died 5 March 2007.

LAWSON, Edmund James; QC 1988; *b* 17 April 1948; *s* of late Donald Lawson and of Veronica Lawson; *m* 1st, 1973, Jennifer Cleary (marr. diss. 2002); three *s*; 2nd, 2003, Christina Russell; three *s* one *d*, and one step *s*. *Educ:* City of Norwich Sch.; Trinity Hall, Cambridge (BA Hons Law). Called to the Bar, Gray's Inn, 1971, Bencher, 1998; in chambers of: Dr F. Hallis, 1971–76; Sir Arthur Irvine, QC, subseq. Gilbert Gray, QC, 1976–2006; Head of Chambers, 1990–98; Founder Mem., Cloth Fair Chambers, 2006. *Recreations:* music, Rugby. *Address:* 39–40 Cloth Fair, EC1A 7NT.
Died 26 March 2009.

LAWSON, Rear-Adm. Frederick Charles William, CB 1971; DSC 1942 and Bar, 1945; Chief Executive, Royal Dockyards, Ministry of Defence, 1972–75; *b* 20 April 1917; *s* of M. L. Lawson, formerly of Public Works Dept, Punjab, India; *m* 1945, Dorothy (*née* Norman) (*d* 1986), Eastbourne; one *s* three *d*. *Educ:* Eastbourne Coll.; RNEC. Joined RN, 1935; specialised in engrg; Comdr 1949; Captain 1960; Cdre Supt Singapore, 1965–69; Rear-Adm. 1969; Flag Officer, Medway and Adm. Supt, HM Dockyard, Chatham, 1969–71. *Address:* Hillcrest House, Avon Park, Limpley Stoke, Bath BA2 7JS.
Died 25 Jan. 2010.

LAWSON, John David, ScD; FRS 1983; Deputy Chief Scientific Officer, Rutherford Appleton Laboratory, Science and Engineering Research Council, Chilton, Oxon, 1978–87, retired, then Hon. Scientist; *b* 4 April 1923; *s* of Ronald L. Lawson and Ruth (*née* Houseman); *m* 1949, Kathleen (*née* Wyllie); two *s* one *d*. *Educ:* Wolverhampton Grammar Sch.; St John's Coll.,

Cambridge (BA, ScD). FInstP. TRE Malvern, Aerials group, 1943; AERE Malvern Br., Accelerator gp, 1947; AERE Harwell, Gen. Physics Div., 1951–62; Microwave Laboratory, Stanford, USA, 1959–60; Rutherford Laboratory (later Rutherford Appleton Laboratory), Applied Phys. Div., and later Technology Div., 1962–87, except, Vis. Prof., Dept of Physics and Astronomy, Univ. of Maryland, USA, 1971; Culham Lab., Technology Div., 1975–76. *Publications:* The Physics of Charged Particle Beams, 1977, 2nd edn 1988; papers on various topics in applied physics in several jls. *Recreations:* travel, walking, collecting old books. *Address:* 7 Clifton Drive, Abingdon, Oxon OX14 1ET. *T:* (01235) 521516.
Died 16 Jan. 2008.

LAWSON-TANCRED, Sir Henry, 10th Bt *cr* 1662; JP; *b* 12 Feb. 1924; *e* surv. *s* of Major Sir Thomas Lawson-Tancred, 9th Bt, and Margery Elinor (*d* 1961), *d* of late A. S. Lawson, Aldborough Manor; *S* father, 1945; *m* 1st, 1950, Jean Veronica (*d* 1970), 4th and *y* *d* of late G. R. Foster, Stockeld Park, Wetherby, Yorks; five *s* one *d*; 2nd, 1978, Mrs Susan Drummond, *d* of Sir Kenelm Cayley, 10th Bt. *Educ:* Stowe; Jesus Coll., Cambridge. Served as Pilot in RAFVR, 1942–46. JP West Riding, 1967. *Heir:* *s* Andrew Peter Lawson-Tancred [*b* 18 Feb. 1952; *m* 2004, Julia, *d* of John Murray; one *s* one *d*]. *Address:* Flat 1, Aldborough Manor, Boroughbridge, York YO51 9EP.
Died 28 March 2010.

LAWTHER, Prof. Patrick Joseph, CBE 1978; DSc; FRCP; Professor of Environmental and Preventive Medicine, University of London, at St Bartholomew's Hospital Medical College, 1968–81, also at London Hospital Medical College, 1976–81, then Professor Emeritus; Member, Medical Research Council Scientific Staff, 1955–81; *b* 9 March 1921; *s* of Joseph and Winefride Lawther; *m* 1944, Kathleen May Wilkowski, MB BS (*d* 1998); two *s* (one *d* decd). *Educ:* Carlisle and Morecambe Grammar Schs; King's Coll., London; St Bartholomew's Hosp. Med. Coll. MB BS 1950; DSc London 1971. FRCP 1963 (MRCP 1954); FFOM 1981 (MFOM 1980). St Bartholomew's Hospital: Ho. Phys., Med. Professorial Unit, 1950; Cooper & Coventson Res. Schol., 1951–53; Associate Chief Asst, 1952–62; Hon. Cons. and Phys.-in-Charge, Dept of Envir. and Prev. Med., 1962–81; Consulting Physician, 1981–. Director, MRC Air Pollution Unit (later Envir. Hazards Unit), 1955–77; Head of Clinical Sect., MRC Toxicology Unit, 1977–81. Cons. Expert, WHO, 1960–; Civilian Cons. in Envir. Medicine, RN, 1975–90, then Emeritus. Chairman: DHSS Cttee on Med. Aspects of Contamination of Air and Soil, 1973–83; DHSS Working Party on Lead and Health, 1978–80; Environmental Dirs Gp, MRC, 1981–85; Cttee on Environmental and Occupational Health, MRC, 1985–89; Assessor, Inquiry on Lorries, People and Environment, (Armitage Inquiry), 1979–80. Pres., Nat. Soc. for Clean Air, 1975–77. Sir Arthur Thomson Vis. Prof., Univ. of Birmingham, 1975–76; RCP Marc Daniels Lectr, 1970; Harben Lectr, RIPH&H, 1970; Guymer Meml Lectr, St Thomas' Hosp., 1979. RSA Silver Medal, 1964; Acad. Nat. de Médecine Bronze Medal, 1972; RCP Bissett Hawkins Medal, 1974; RSM Edwin Stevens Gold Medal, 1975. *Publications:* various papers and chapters in books relating to environmental and occupational medicine. *Recreation:* almost everything. *Address:* Dawson Lodge, Botley Road, West End, Southampton SO30 2RS. *T:* (020) 8660 6398.
Died 6 June 2008.

LAZARIDIS, Stefanos, RDI 2003; freelance opera, ballet and theatre designer and director in UK and abroad, since 1967; Artistic Director and General Manager, Greek National Opera, 2006–07; *b* Ethiopia, 28 July 1942; *s* of Nicholas Lazaridis and Alexandra Cardovillis. *Educ:* Greek Sch., Addis Ababa; Ecole Internationale, Geneva; Byam Shaw Sch. of Art; Central Sch. of Speech and Drama. Professional début, Eccentricities of a Nightingale, Yvonne Arnaud Theatre, Guildford, 1967; *ballet:* El Amor Brujo, 1969, Knight Errant, 1975, Royal Ballet, Covent Garden; *theatre:* London (Almeida, Barbican and

West End), Stratford-upon-Avon, Chichester Fest., Oxford, Guildford, Watford, Milan, Bologna, Paris, Athens, 1967–95; *opera*: prodns for ENO incl. Doctor Faust, The Mikado (SWET Award, for Doctor Faust and The Mikado, 1986), Hansel and Gretel, Lady Macbeth of Mtsensk, Italian season (Laurence Olivier Award, 2000); prodns for Royal Opera incl. The Greek Passion (Laurence Olivier Award, 2001), Wozzeck (Laurence Olivier Award, 2002), Wagner's Ring cycle, 2004–06; directed and designed: Oedipus Rex, Opera North; Duke Bluebeard's Castle, Oedipus Rex, Maria Stuarda, Scottish Opera; Orphée et Eurydice, Australian Opera, 1994; The Ark of Life, by Dimitriadis, world première, Athens, 1995; *arena prodn:* Carmen, Earl's Court, 1988, also internat. tour; *rock show:* Duran Duran, US tour, 1993; designs for opera houses of Paris, Berlin, Frankfurt, Munich, Stuttgart, Brussels, Zurich, La Scala Milan, Florence, Bologna, Venice, Tel Aviv, Amsterdam, Copenhagen, Moscow, St Petersburg, Tokyo, Vancouver, Sydney, Melbourne, Houston, Los Angeles, NY and San Francisco; also Bregenz, Pesaro, and Bayreuth Festivals. Laurence Olivier and Evening Standard Awards for Most Outstanding Achievement in Opera, 1987; German Critics' Award, Designer of the Year, 1998; Diploma of Honour, Internat. Exhibn of Stage Design, Prague Quadrennial, 1999; Martinu Foundn Medal, for outstanding services to Martinu's operas, 2000. *Recreations:* reading, travel. *Address:* Kydathinaion 9, 10558 Athens, Greece; *e-mail:* stefanos_lazaridis@hotmail.com. *Died 8 May 2010.*

LEA, Rev. His Honour Christopher Gerald, MC; Assistant Curate (non-stipendiary), parish of Stratfield Mortimer, since 1992; a Circuit Judge, 1972–90; *b* 27 Nov. 1917; *y s* of late George Perry Lea, Franche, Kidderminster, Worcs; *m* 1952, Susan Elizabeth Dorrien Smith, *d* of Major Edward Pendarves Dorrien Smith, Greatwood, Restronguet, Falmouth, Cornwall; two *s* one *d* (and one *d* decd). *Educ:* Charterhouse; RMC, Sandhurst; St Stephen's House, Oxford. Commissioned into XX The Lancashire Fusiliers, 1937, and served with Regt in UK until 1939. Served War of 1939–45 (despatches, MC): with Lancashire Fusiliers, No 2 Commando, 11th SAS Bn, and Parachute Regt in France, Italy and Malaya. Post-war service in Indonesia, Austria and UK; retired, 1948. Called to Bar, Inner Temple, 1948; Oxford Circuit. Mem. Nat. Assistance Bd Appeal Tribunal (Oxford Area), 1961–63; Mem. Mental Health Review Tribunal (Oxford Region), 1962–68, 1983–92. A Metropolitan Magistrate, 1968–72; Dep. Chm., Berks QS, 1968–71. Ordained deacon, 1992, priest, 1993. *Address:* Simms Farm House, Mortimer, Berks RG7 2JP. *T:* (0118) 933 2360. *Club:* English-Speaking Union. *Died 1 June 2006.*

LEACH, Prof. Donald Frederick, CBE 1996; Principal, 1985–96, and Vice Patron, 1993–96, Queen Margaret College, Edinburgh; *b* 24 June 1931; *s* of Frederick John Mansell Leach and Annie Ivy Foster; *m* 1st, 1952, June Valentine Reid (*d* 1997); two *s* one *d*; 2nd, 1999, Marilyn Annette Jeffcoat. *Educ:* John Ruskin Grammar Sch., Croydon; Norwood Tech. Coll.; Dundee Tech. Coll.; Univ. of London (Ext. Student, BSc); Jordanhill Coll. of Educn, MInstP, CPhys, 1960; FIMA, CMath, 1969; MBCS, CEng, 1968. Pilot Officer, RAF, 1951–53. Physicist, British Jute Trade Res. Assoc., Dundee, 1954–65; Tech. Dir., A. R. Bolton & Co., 1965–66; Napier College: Lectr and Sen. Lectr in Maths, 1966–68; Head, Dept of Maths and Computing, 1968–74; Asst Principal/Dean, Faculty of Science, 1974–85. Interim Chief Exec., Edinburgh's Lifelong Learning Partnership, 1998. Chairman: Creative Edge Software Ltd, 1999–2002; D. M. Vaughan & Co. Ltd, 1999–2004. Member: Council for Professions Supplementary to Medicine, 1985–97; Exec. Cttee, Scottish Council Develt and Indust., 1987–96; Boards of: Edinburgh Chamber of Commerce and Manufactures, 1991–98 (Sen. Vice-Pres., 1996; Pres., 1996–98); Leith Chamber of Commerce, 1991–96 (Pres., 1994–96); British Chambers of Commerce, 1997–99; Higher Educn Quality Council,

1992–96; The Capital Enterprise Trust, 1993–98. Director: Businessweb Ltd, 1999–; Mull Theatre Ltd, 2004–. Trustee, Mendelssohn on Mull Trust, 2005–. Vice Convenor, One Parent Families Scotland, 1998–99. Contested: (L) W Edinburgh, 1959; (L) E Fife by-election, 1961; (Lab) Kinross and W Perthshire, 1970. Hon. Prof., Queen Margaret Coll., 1993. Hon. Fellow, Soc. of Chiropodists and Podiatrists, 1994. FRSA. Hon. DEd Queen Margaret UC, 2003. *Publications:* Future Employment and Technological Change (jtly), 1986; papers in sci., tech. and eductl jls on textile physics, electronic instrumentation, maths and statistics, higher educn. *Recreations:* music, Scrabble, walking, cooking. *Address:* 18 Rothesay Terrace, Edinburgh EH3 7RY. *T:* (0131) 226 7166. *Clubs:* New, Scottish Arts (Edinburgh). *Died 25 Feb. 2009.*

LEACH, Paul Arthur; General Consultant to The Law Society, 1980–81, retired; *b* 10 July 1915; *s* of Rev. Edward Leach and Edith Swannell Leach; *m* 1st, 1949, Daphne Copeland (marr. diss. 1957); one *s* one *d*; 2nd, 1958, Rachel Renée Lachmann. *Educ:* West House Sch., Edgbaston; Marlborough Coll.; Keble Coll., Oxford (1st Cl. Hons BA Mod. Hist., 1937; MA 1945); Birmingham Univ. (2nd Cl. Hons LLB 1940). Law Soc. Finals, 1940; admitted Solicitor, 1946. Served War, RA, 1940–45: Staff Captain 1st AA Bde; attached SO II, RAEC, 1945–46. Private practice as solicitor, 1946–48; Talks Producer, BBC Home Talks, 1949; joined Law Soc. staff, 1950; Clerk and later Sec., Professional Purposes Cttee, 1950–71; Secretary: Future of the Profession Cttee, 1971–80; Internat. Relations Cttee, 1975–80; Dep. Sec. Gen., 1975–80; removed from Roll of Solicitors, at own request, 1991. Secretary: UK Delegn to Commn Consultative des Barreaux de la Communauté Européenne, 1975–81; Inter-Professional Gp, 1978–81; UK Vice-Pres., Union Internationale des Avocats, 1978–81. *Publications:* (ed) Guide to Professional Conduct of Solicitors, 1974; articles in Law Society's Gazette. *Recreations:* foreign travel, history, listening to classical music. *Address:* 19 Lavant Court, Charles Street, Petersfield, Hants GU32 3EQ. *Died 20 Oct. 2006.*

LEADBETTER, Michael; consultant in children's and adult care services; Founder and Managing Director, Leadbetter Ltd, since 2003; Chairman, Children's Workforce Development Council, since 2007; *b* 25 July 1946; *s* of Robert Leadbetter and Edna (*née* Garlic); *m* Pamela Corti; two *s*. *Educ:* Ladybarn Secondary Mod. Sch.; Manchester Coll. of Sci. and Technol.; Manchester Coll., of Art and Design (DA); Manchester Univ. Extra Mural Dept (CQSW); MA (Econ) Manchester Univ. 1982. Works and prodn manager, 1971–72; Manchester Social Services: Social Worker, then Sen. Social Worker, 1972–82; Residential and Day Care Services Manager, 1982–86; Director of Social Services: Tameside, 1986–92; Essex, 1993–2003. Pres., Assoc. of Dirs of Social Services, 2001–02. Mem. Bd, General Social Care Council, 2007–. Chairman: Voice; Parentline Plus; Founder Mem., British Inst. of Transactional Analysis, 1974. England International, Rugby Union, 1970; 35 appearances for Lancs, 1968–74; Rugby League professional, Rochdale Hornets, 1974–76. *Recreations:* weight training, ski-ing, food, wine, opera. *Club:* England Internationals. *Died 17 April 2009.*

LEASOR, (Thomas) James; author; *b* 20 Dec. 1923; *s* of late Richard and Christine Leasor, Erith, Kent; *m* 1951, Joan Margaret Bevan, BA, LLB, Barrister-at-law, *o d* of late Roland and Dora Bevan, Crowcombe, Somerset; three *s*. *Educ:* City of London Sch.; Oriel Coll., Oxford. Kentish Times, 1941–42. Served in Army in Burma, India, Malaya, 1942–46, Capt. Royal Berks Regt. Oriel Coll., Oxford, 1946–48, BA 1948; MA 1952; edited The Isis. On staff Daily Express, London, 1948–55, as reporter, foreign correspondent, feature writer. Contrib. to many American and British magazines, newspapers and periodicals; scriptwriter for TV series The Michaels in Africa. FRSA. OStJ. *Publications: novels:* Not Such a Bad Day, 1946; The Strong Delusion, 1951; NTR-

Nothing to Report, 1955; Passport to Oblivion, 1964; Spylight, 1966; Passport in Suspense, 1967; Passport for a Pilgrim, 1968; They Don't Make Them Like That Any More, 1969; A Week of Love, 1969; Never had a Spanner on Her, 1970; Love-all, 1971; Follow the Drum, 1972; Host of Extras, 1973; Mandarin Gold, 1973; The Chinese Widow, 1974; Jade Gate, 1976; Love and the Land Beyond, 1979; Open Secret, 1982; Ship of Gold, 1984; Tank of Serpents, 1986; Frozen Assets, 1989; Love Down Under, 1991; as *Andrew MacAllan*: Succession, 1989; Generation, 1990; Diamond-Hard, 1991; Fanfare, 1992; Speculator, 1993; Traders, 1994; *non-fiction*: Author by Profession, The Monday Story, 1951; Wheels to Fortune, The Serjeant Major, 1954; The Red Fort; (with Kendal Burt) The One That Got Away, 1956; The Millionth Chance, 1957; War at the Top, 1959; (with Peter Eton) Conspiracy of Silence, 1959; Bring Out Your Dead, 1961; Rudolf Hess: The Uninvited Envoy, 1961; Singapore: The Battle that Changed the World, 1968; Green Beach, 1975; Boarding Party, 1977; The Unknown Warrior, 1980; Who Killed Sir Harry Oakes?, 1983; The Marine from Mandalay, 1988; Rhodes & Barnato: the Premier and the Prancer, 1997. *Recreation*: vintage sports cars. *Address*: Swallowcliffe Manor, Salisbury, Wilts SP3 5PB. *Club*: Garrick.   *Died 10 Sept. 2007.*

LE BAILLY, Vice-Adm. Sir Louis (Edward Stewart Holland), KBE 1972 (OBE 1952); CB 1969; DL; Director-General of Intelligence, Ministry of Defence, and Vice Chairman, Joint Intelligence Committee, 1973–75; *b* 18 July 1915; *s* of Robert Francis Le Bailly and Ida Gaskell Le Bailly (*née* Holland); *m* 1946, Pamela Ruth Berthon; three *d*. *Educ*: RNC Dartmouth. HMS Hood, 1932; RNEC, 1933–37; HMS Hood, 1937–40; HMS Naiad, 1940–42; RNEC, 1942–44; HMS Duke of York, 1944–46; Admiralty, 1946–52 (Schs Liaison Officer, 1946–47; Birmingham Univ., 1947–48; Sec. to Lord Geddes' Admiralty Oil Cttee and Chm., NATO Fuels and Lubricants Standardisation Cttee, 1948–52); HMS Bermuda, 1952–53; Dept of Second Sea Lord, 1953–55; RNEC, 1955–58; Admiralty: Staff Officer to Dartmouth Review Cttee, 1958; Asst Engineer-in-Chief, 1958–60; Naval Asst to Controller of the Navy, 1960–63; IDC, 1963; Dep. Dir of Marine Engineering, 1963–67; Naval Attaché, Washington, DC, and Comdr, British Navy Staff, 1967–69; Vice-Adm. 1970; Min. of Defence, 1970–72. DCDS (Intelligence), 1972–73. Chm., civil service, police and fire service selection bds, 1976–82. Mem. Council, Research Inst. for Study of Conflict and Terrorism, 1976–85. Chm. of Govs, Rendcomb Coll., 1979–85. DL Cornwall, 1982. FIMechE; FInstPet; FIMarEST. Hon. DSc Plymouth, 1994. *Publications*: The Man Around the Engine, 1990; From Fisher to the Falklands, 1991; Old Loves Return, 1993; We Should Look to Our Moat, 2007.   *Died 3 Oct. 2010.*

LeBLANC, Rt Hon. Roméo; PC (Can.) 1974; CC 1995; CMM 1995; CD 1995; Governor General and Commander-in-Chief of Canada, 1995–99; *b* 18 Dec. 1927; *s* of Philias and Lucie LeBlanc; *m* 1966, Joslyn Carter; one *s* one *d*; *m* Diana Fowler; two step *c*. *Educ*: Université St-Joseph, Memramcook (BA 1948; BEd 1951); Paris Univ. Teacher, New Brunswick, 1951–59; corresp. for Radio-Canada, in Ottawa, UK and US, 1960–67; Press Sec. to Prime Minister of Canada, 1967–71; Asst to Pres. and Dir of Public Relns, Moncton Univ., 1971–72. MP (L) Westmorland-Kent, 1972–84; Minister of State, Fisheries, 1974–76; Minister of: Fisheries and the Envmt, 1976–79; Fisheries and Oceans, 1980–82; Public Works, 1982–84; served on various Cabinet cttees; Mem., Senate, 1984–94; served on various Senate cttees; Speaker, 1993–94. Hon. DCL Mt Allison, 1977; Hon. Dr in Public Admin Moncton, 1979; Hon. LLD: Sainte-Anne, 1995; St Thomas, 1997; Meml, 1997; McGill, 1997; Hon. DLitt Ryerson, 1996; DUniv Ottawa, 1996. *Address*: PO Box 5254, Shediac, NB E4P 8T9, Canada.   *Died 24 June 2009.*

LEBLOND, Prof. C(harles) P(hilippe), CC 1999 (OC 1977); GOQ 2001; MD, PhD, DSc; FRSC 1951; FRS 1965; Professor of Anatomy, McGill University, Canada, since 1948; *b* 5 Feb. 1910; *s* of Oscar Leblond and Jeanne Desmarchelier; *m* 1936, Gertrude Elinor Sternschuss; three *s* one *d*. *Educ*: Sch. St Joseph, Lille, France; Univs. of Lille, Paris, Montreal. L-ès-S, Nancy 1932; MD Paris 1934; PhD Montreal 1942; DSc Sorbonne 1945. Asst in Histology, Med. School, Univ. of Paris, 1934–35; Rockefeller Fell., Sch. of Med., Yale Univ., 1936–37; Asst, Laboratoire de Synthése Atomique, Paris, 1938–40; McGill University: Lectr in Histology and Embryology, 1941–42; Asst Prof. of Anatomy, 1942–43; Assoc. Prof. of Anatomy, 1946–48; Chm. of Dept of Anatomy, 1957–75. Mem. Amer. Assoc. of Anatomists; Fellow, Amer. Acad. of Arts and Scis. Hon. DSc: Acadia, 1972; McGill, 1982; Montreal, 1985; York, 1986. *Publications*: over 300 articles, mainly on radio-autography and cell dynamics, in anatomical journals. *Recreation*: country. *Address*: (home) 68 Chesterfield Avenue, Westmount, Montreal, QC H3Y 2M5, Canada. *T*: (514) 4864837; (office) Department of Anatomy and Cell Biology, McGill University, 3640 University Street, Montreal, QC H3A 2B2, Canada. *T*: (514) 3986340.   *Died 10 April 2007.*

LE CHEMINANT, Peter, CB 1976; Director-General, General Council of British Shipping, 1985–91; consultant on government administration; *b* 29 April 1926; *s* of William Arthur Le Cheminant and Agnes Ann Le Cheminant (*née* Wilson); *m* 1959, Suzanne Elisabeth Horny; three *s*. *Educ*: Holloway Sch.; London Sch. of Economics. Sub-Lt, RNVR, 1944–47. Min. of Power, 1949; Cabinet Office, 1950–52 and 1964–65; UK Delegn to ECSC, 1962–63; Private Sec. to Prime Minister, 1965–68; Min. of Power, later Min. of Technology, 1968–71; Under-Sec., DTI, 1971–74; Deputy Secretary: Dept of Energy, 1974–77; Cabinet Office, 1978–81; CSD, subseq. HM Treas., 1981–83; Second Perm. Sec., Cabinet Office (MPO), 1983–84. Mem. Council, Inst. of Employment Studies (formerly Manpower), 1983–97; Trustee, King George's Fund for Sailors, 1987–2003. Freeman, City of London, 1987; Liveryman, Worshipful Co. of Shipwrights, 1987. CCMI (CBIM 1984); FCIT 1987. *Publications*: Beautiful Ambiguities: an inside view of the heart of government, 2001. *Recreations*: reading, walking, history. *Address*: 23 Weylea Avenue, Burpham, Guildford, Surrey GU4 7YN. *Club*: Reform.   *Died 25 July 2006.*

LECHMERE, Sir Reginald Anthony Hungerford, 7th Bt *cr* 1818, of The Rhydd, Worcestershire; *b* 24 Dec. 1920; *s* of Anthony Hungerford Lechmere, 3rd *s* of 3rd Bt, and Cicely Mary Lechmere; *S* cousin, 2001; *m* 1956, Anne Jennifer Dind; three *s* one *d*. *Educ*: Charterhouse; Trinity Hall, Cambridge. Served Army, 1940–47, 5th Royal Inniskilling Dragoon Guards, HQ6 Armoured Div. Publicity Manager, Penguin Books, 1950–51; journalist, 1952–56; antiquarian bookseller, 1955–87. *Heir*: *s* Nicholas Anthony Hungerford Lechmere [*b* 24 April 1960; *m* 1991, Caroline Gahan; three *s* one *d*].   *Died 8 Jan. 2010.*

LEDERBERG, Prof. Joshua, PhD; Sackler Scholar, Rockefeller University, since 1995 (President, 1978–90; University Professor, 1990–95); consultant; *b* Montclair, NJ, USA, 23 May 1925; *s* of Zwi H. Lederberg and Esther Lederberg (*née* Goldenbaum); *m* 1st, 1946 (marr. diss. 1966); 2nd, 1968, Marguerite Stein Kirsch, MD; one *d*; one step *s*. *Educ*: Stuyvesant High Sch., NYC; Columbia Coll. (BA); Yale Univ. (PhD). Assistant Professor of Genetics, University of Wisconsin, 1947; Associate Professor, 1950; Professor, 1954; Fulbright Vis. Prof. of Bacteriology, Univ. of Melbourne, Aust., 1957; Prof. and Exec. Head, Dept of Genetics, Sch. of Medicine, Stanford Univ., 1959–78. Shared in discoveries concerning genetic re-combination, and organization of genetic material of bacteria, contributing to cancer research; discovered a method of artificially introducing new genes into bacteria in investigation of hereditary

substance. Chm., President's Cancer Panel (US), 1980–81. Member: Adv. Cttee for Med. Res., WHO, 1971–76; Defense Sci. Bd, USA, 1979–; Chief of Naval Ops Exec. Panel, USN, 1981–; Tech. Assessment Adv. Cttee, Office of Technology Assessment, US Congress, 1988–; Adv. Cttee to Dir, NIH, 1993–; Ellison Med. Foundn, 1997–; Member Board: Chemical Industry Inst. for Toxicology, 1980–2002; Dreyfus Foundn, 1983–; Revson Foundn, 1986–93; Proctor and Gamble Co., Cincinnati, 1984–95; Carnegie Corp., NYC, 1985–93. Columnist, Science and Man (Washington Post Syndicate), 1966–71. Mem., National Academy of Sciences, United States, 1957. For. Mem., Royal Society, 1979. Hon. degrees include: ScD: Yale Univ.; Columbia Univ.; Univ. of Wisconsin; Rockefeller Univ.; MD Tufts Univ. (jointly) Nobel Prize in Medicine, 1958. US Nat. Medal of Science, 1989; Benjamin Franklin Award, Amer. Phil. Soc., 2002. *Publications:* (ed) Emerging Infections, 1992; (ed) Biological Weapons: containing the threat, 1999; (Ed. in Chief) Encyclopedia of Microbiology, 1992, 2nd edn 2000; contribs to learned journals on genetics, bacteria and general biological problems. *Address:* Rockefeller University, 1230 York Avenue, New York, NY 10021, USA. *T:* (212) 3277809.
Died 2 Feb. 2008.

LEE, Brig. Sir Henry, *see* Lee, Brig. Sir L. H.

LEE, Jong-wook, Order of Moran (Republic of Korea), 2002; MD; Director-General, World Health Organization, since 2003; *b* 12 April 1945; *s* of Myung-se Lee and Sang-kan Lee; *m* 1976, Reiko Kaburaki; one *s.* *Educ:* Sch. of Medicine, Seoul Nat. Univ. (MD 1976); Sch. of Public Health, Univ. of Hawaii (MPH 1981). World Health Organization: Team Leader, Leprosy Control in the S Pacific, 1984 86; Dir, Disease Prevention and Control, Western Pacific Regl Office, 1986–90; Head of polio eradication initiatives in the Western Pacific, 1990–94; Dir, Global Prog. for Vaccines and Immunization, and Exec. Sec., Children's Vaccine Initiative, 1994–98; Sen. Policy Advr to Dir-Gen., 1998–99; Special Rep. of Dir-Gen., 1999–2000; Dir, Stop TB, 2000–03. *Publications:* articles in Lancet, Science, Internat. Jl of Leprosy. *Recreations:* tennis, scuba diving, ski-ing. *T:* (Switzerland) (22) 7912111.
Died 22 May 2006.

LEE, Brig. Sir (Leonard) Henry, Kt 1983; CBE 1964 (OBE 1960); Deputy Director, Conservative Board of Finance, 1970–92; *b* 21 April 1914; *s* of late Henry Robert Lee and Nellie Lee; *m* 1949, Peggy Metham (*d* 2000). *Educ:* Portsmouth Grammar Sch.; Southampton Univ. (Law). Served War, 1939–45; with BEF in France, ME and NW Europe (despatches, 1945); Royal Scots Greys, Major; Staff Lt-Col 1954: Chief of Intelligence to Dir of Ops, Malaya, 1957–60; Mil. and Naval Attaché, Saigon, S Vietnam, 1961–64; Chief of Personnel and Admin, Allied Land Forces Central Europe, France, 1964–66; Chief of Intelligence, Allied Forces Central Europe, Netherlands, 1966–69; retd 1969. Chm. Trustees, Royal Cambridge Home for Soldiers' Widows, 1970–2006. *Recreation:* gardening. *Address:* Fairways, Sandy Lane, Kingswood, Surrey KT20 6ND. *T:* (01737) 832577.
Died 13 Dec. 2008.

LEE, Rt Rev. Patrick Vaughan, DD; Bishop of Rupert's Land, 1994–99; *b* 20 June 1931; *s* of William Samuel Lee and Elizabeth Miriam (*née* Struthers); *m* 1958, Mary Thornton; four *d.* *Educ:* Univ. of Manitoba (BA 1953); St John's Coll., Winnipeg (LTh 1957; DD 1978). Missioner, Interlake/Eriksdale, Manitoba, 1956–59; Rector: St Bartholomew, Winnipeg, 1959–67; St Mary la Prairie, Portage la Prairie, Manitoba, 1967–75; District Dean, Portage and Pembina Deaneries, 1970–75; Dean of Cariboo and Rector, St Paul's Cathedral, Kamloops, BC, 1975–84; Dean of Training and Educn Sec., Dio. of W Buganda, 1984–90; Exec. Archdeacon of Rupert's Land, 1990–94. *Recreations:* cross country ski-ing, cycling, woodworking, reading, stamp collecting. *Address:* 137 Mile Point Road, RR 5, Perth, ON K7H 3C7, Canada. *T:* (613) 2670174. *Died 26 Sept. 2010.*

LEEDS, Sir Christopher (Anthony), 8th Bt *cr* 1812; researcher; *b* 31 Aug. 1935; *s* of Geoffrey Hugh Anthony Leeds (*d* 1962) (*b* of 6th Bt) and Yoland Thérèse Barré (*d* 1944), *d* of James Alexander Mitchell; *S* cousin, 1983; *m* 1974, Elaine Joyce (marr. diss. 1981), *d* of late Sqdn Ldr C. H. A. Mullins. *Educ:* King's School, Bruton; LSE, Univ. of London (BSc Econ. 1958); Univ. of Southern California (Fulbright Travel Award; Sen. Herman Fellow in Internat. Relations, MA 1966). Assistant Master: Merchant Taylors' School, Northwood, 1966–68; Christ's Hospital, 1972–75; Stowe School, 1978–81. Publisher, 1975–78. University of Nancy 2: Sen. Lectr, 1982; Assoc. Prof., 1988–2000; Researcher, 2002–; Vis. Lectr, Univ. of Strasbourg 1, 1983–87; Vis. Res. Fellow, Univ. of Kent at Canterbury, 2000–01. *Publications:* Political Studies, 1968, 3rd edn 1981; European History 1789–1914, 1971, 2nd edn 1980; Italy under Mussolini, 1972; Unification of Italy, 1974; Historical Guide to England, 1976; (with R. S. Stainton and C. Jones) Management and Business Studies, 1974, 3rd edn 1983; Basic Economics Revision, 1982; Politics in Action, 1986; World History—1900 to the present day, 1987; Peace and War, 1987; English Humour, 1989; contrib to learned jls incl. Peacekeeping, Internat. Business Rev., Internat. Jl of Peace Studies. *Recreations:* hill-walking, modern art, travel. *Heir: cousin* John Charles Leeds [*b* 25 Dec. 1941; *m* 1965, Eileen Rose, *d* of Joseph Francis Shalka; one *s* two *d*]. *Address:* 6 Hurlingham Lodge, 14 Manor Road, Eastcliff, Bournemouth BH1 3EY; 7 rue de Turique, 54000 Nancy, France. *Died 18 Nov. 2009.*

LEES, Prof. Dennis Samuel, CBE 1980; Emeritus Professor of Industrial Economics, University of Nottingham, since 1983 (Professor, 1968–82); *b* 20 July 1924; *s* of late Samuel Lees and Evelyn Lees (*née* Withers), Borrowash, Derbyshire; *m* 1950, Elizabeth Dictisch, London (*d* 1992); two *s* (one *d* decd). *Educ:* Derby Technical Coll.; Nottingham Univ. BSc(Econ). PhD. Lecturer and Reader in Economics, Keele Univ., 1951–65; Prof. of Economics, University Coll., Swansea, 1965–67. Exchange Lectr, Reed Coll., Portland, Ore, 1958–59; Visiting Prof. of Economics: Univ. of Chicago, 1963–64; Univ. of California, Berkeley, 1971; Univ. of Sydney, 1975. Chairman: Nat. Ins. Advisory Committee, 1972–80; Industrial Injuries Advisory Council, 1973–78; Mem., Adv. Council, Inst. of Econ. Affairs, 1974–93 (Hon. Fellow, 1994). Freeman, City of London, 1973. *Publications:* Local Expenditure and Exchequer Grants, 1956; Health Thru Choice, 1961; Economic Consequences of the Professions, 1966; Economics of Advertising, 1967; Financial Facilities for Small Firms, 1971; Impairment, Disability, Handicap, 1974; Economics of Personal Injury, 1976; Solicitors' Remuneration in Ireland, 1977; articles on industrial and social policy in: Economica, Jl of Political Economy, Amer. Econ. Rev., Jl of Law and Econ., Jl Industrial Econ., Jl Public Finance. *Recreation:* cricket and pottering. *Address:* 8 Middleton Crescent, Beeston, Nottingham NG9 2TH. *T:* (0115) 925 8730. *Died 11 Feb. 2008.*

LEES, Dr William, CBE 1970; TD 1962; FRCOG; Medical Manpower Consultant to South West Thames Regional Health Authority, 1981–87, retired; *b* 18 May 1924; *s* of William Lees and Elizabeth Lees (*née* Massey); *m* 1947, Winifred Elizabeth (*née* Hanford); three *s.* *Educ:* Queen Elizabeth's, Blackburn; Victoria Univ., Manchester. MB ChB; LRCP; MRCS; MRCOG; FRCOG; DPH; MFCM. Obstetrics and Gynaecology, St Mary's Hosps, Manchester, 1947–58; Min. of Health, later DHSS, 1959–81; Under Sec., (SPMO) 1977–81. QHP, 1969–72. Col, 10th, later no 257, Gen. Hosp., TAVR RAMC, 1966–71; Col Comdt, NW London Sector, ACF, 1971–76; Mem. for Greater London, TA&VRA, 1966–. OStJ 1967. *Publications:* numerous contribs on: intensive therapy, progressive patient care, perinatal mortality, day surgery, district general hospital. *Recreations:* music, golf, travel. *Address:* 13 Hall Park Hill, Berkhamsted, Herts HP4 2NH. *T:* (01442) 863010. *Clubs:* Athenæum, St John's. *Died 9 April 2009.*

LE FANU, Sir (George) Victor (Sheridan), KCVO 1987; Serjeant at Arms, House of Commons, 1982–89; *b* 24 Jan. 1925; *s* of late Maj.-Gen. Roland Le Fanu, DSO, MC, and Marguerite (*née* Lumsden); *m* 1956, Elizabeth, *d* of late Major Herbert Hall and Kitty (*née* Gauvain); three *s. Educ*: Shrewsbury School. Served Coldstream Guards, 1943–63; Asst-Adjt, Royal Military Academy, Sandhurst, 1949–52; Adjt 2nd Bn Coldstream Guards, 1952–55; sc Camberley, 1959; Staff Captain to Vice-Quartermaster-General to the Forces, War Office, 1960–61; GSO2, Headquarters London District, 1961–63; Dep. Asst Serjeant at Arms, House of Commons, 1963–76; Asst Serjeant at Arms, 1976–81; Deputy Serjeant at Arms, 1981–82. Casework for SSAFA, 2001–. Chm., Morley Coll., 1992–2000. Trustee, Wall Trust, 1991–2003. *Address*: 29 Cranmer Court, Whitehead's Grove, SW3 3HN. *Died 5 Feb. 2007.*

LEFEVER, Kenneth Ernest, CB 1974; Deputy Chairman, Civil Service Appeal Board, 1978–80 (Official Side Member, 1975–78); *b* 22 Feb. 1915; *s* of E. S. Lefever and Mrs E. E. Lefever; *m* 1939, Margaret Ellen Bowley; one *s* one *d. Educ*: County High Sch., Ilford. Board of Customs and Excise: joined Dept as Officer, 1935; War Service, 1942–46 (Captain, RE); Principal Inspector, 1966; Dep. Chief Inspector, 1969; Collector, London Port, 1971; Chief Inspector, 1972; Dir of Organisation and Chief Inspector, 1974; Comr, Bd of Customs and Excise, 1972–75, retd. *Recreations*: gardening, walking, cricket. *Address*: Trebarwith, 37 Surman Crescent, Hutton Burses, Brentwood, Essex CM13 2PW. *T*: (01277) 212110. *Clubs*: MCC, Civil Service. *Died 8 July 2006.*

LEGGE-SCHWARZKOPF, Dame Elisabeth; see Schwarzkopf.

LEGHARI, Farooq Ahmed Khan; President of Pakistan, 1993–97; *b* 2 May 1940; *s* of Nawab Sardar Muhammad Khan Leghari; *m*; two *s* two *d. Educ*: Aitchison Coll., Lahore; Punjab Univ. (BA Hons); St Catherine's Coll., Oxford (BA Hons PPE, MA). Civil Servant, 1964–73; Mem., Pakistan People's Party, 1973–93; Senate of Pakistan, 1975; Mem. for Dera Ghazi Khan, Nat. Assembly, 1977; Minister for Production, 1977; jailed on numerous occasions, 1977–88; Sec.-Gen. and Mem. Exec. Cttee, Pakistan People's Party, 1978–83; Mem., Nat. Assembly, and Minister for Water and Power, 1989–90; re-elected 1990 and 1993; Dep. Leader of Opposition, 1990–93; Finance Minister, later Minister for Foreign Affairs, 1993. Chief, Baluchi Leghari Tribe. *Died 10 Oct. 2010.*

LEHANE, Maureen, (Mrs Peter Wishart); concert and opera singer, then teaching privately; *d* of Christopher Lehane and Honor Millar; *m* 1966, Peter Wishart (*d* 1984), composer. *Educ*: Queen Elizabeth's Girls' Grammar Sch., Barnet; Guildhall Sch. of Music and Drama. Studied under Hermann Weissenborn, Berlin (teacher of Fischer Dieskau); also under John and Aida Dickens (Australian teachers of Joan Sutherland); gained Arts Council award to study in Berlin. Speciality was Handel; numerous leading roles (operas incl. Ezio, Ariadne and Pharamondo) with Handel opera societies of England and America, in London, and in Carnegie Hall, New York, also in Poland, Sweden and Germany; gave master classes on the interpretation of Handel's vocal music (notably at s'Hertogenbosch Festival, Holland, July 1972; invited to repeat them in 1973); master classes on Handel and Purcell, The Hague and Maastricht, 1991; taught at GSMD, Reading Univ. and WCMD. Debut at Glyndebourne, 1967. Festival appearances include: Stravinsky Festival, Cologne; City of London; Aldeburgh; Cheltenham; Three Choirs; Bath; Oxford Bach; Göttingen Handel Festival, etc; toured N America; also 3-month tour of Australia at invitation of ABC and 2-month tour of Far East and ME, 1971; sang in Holland, and for Belgian TV, 1978; visits also to Berlin, Lisbon, Poland and Rome, 1979–80, to Warsaw, 1981. Title and lead rôles in: Purcell's Dido and Aeneas, Netherlands Opera, 1976; Peter Wishart's operas, Clytemnestra and The Lady of the Inn; Mozart's Marriage of Figaro, Cologne Opera; Rossini's La Cenerentola; 13 of Handel's operas. Cyrus in first complete recording of Handel's Belshazzar. Appeared regularly on BBC; also in promenade concerts. Made numerous recordings (Bach, Haydn, Mozart, Handel, etc). Mem. Jury, Internat. Singing Comp., s'Hertogenbosch Fest., Holland, 1982–; Adjudicator, Llangollen Internat. Eisteddfod 1991–93 and 1997. Founder and Music Dir, Great Elm Music Festival, 1987–98; Founder and Artistic Dir, Jackdaws Educnl Trust, 1993–2010. *Publications*: (ed with Peter Wishart) Songs of Purcell. *Recreations*: cooking, gardening, reading. *Address*: Ironstone Cottage, Great Elm, Frome, Somerset BA11 3NY. *T*: (01373) 812383. *Died 27 Dec. 2010.*

LEHMANN, Prof. Andrew George; Emeritus Professor, University of Buckingham; *b* 17 Feb. 1922; *m* 1942, Alastine Mary (*d* 2000), *d* of late K. N. Bell; two *s* one *d. Educ*: Dulwich Coll.; The Queen's Coll., Oxford. MA, DPhil Oxon. Served with RCS and Indian Army, 6th Rajputana Rifles (invalided). Fenced for England (Sabre), 1939. Asst lecturer and lecturer, Manchester Univ., 1945–51; Prof. of French Studies, 1951–68, Dean of Faculty of Letters and Soc. Scis, Univ. of Reading, 1960–66. Hon. Prof., Univ. of Warwick, 1968–78; various industry posts, 1968–78; Prof. and Dir, Inst. of European Studies, Hull Univ., 1978–83; Rank Foundn Prof. of European Studies, and Dean, Sch. of Humanities, Univ. of Buckingham, 1983–88. Mem., Hale Cttee on University Teaching Methods, 1961–63; Chm., Industrial Council for Educnl and Trng Technology, 1974–76 (Pres., 1979–81, Vice-Pres., 1981–85); Mem., Anglo-French Permanent Mixed Cultural Commission, 1963–68. Adviser: Chinese Univ. of Hong Kong, 1964; Haile Sellassie I Univ., Ethiopia, 1965. Member: Hong Kong Univ. Grants Cttee, 1966–73; Academic Planning Board and Academic Adv. Cttee, New Univ. of Ulster, 1966–77; Planning Bd, 1970–72, Acad. Adv. Cttee, 1974–83, UC at Buckingham; Court and Council, Bedford Coll., London Univ., 1971–78; British Library Adv. Cttee (Reference), 1975–78; Princeton Univ. Academic Adv. Council, 1975–81. Shakespeare Prize Cttee, FVS Foundn, Hamburg, 1984–90. Governor, Ealing Tech. Coll., 1974. *Publications*: the Symbolist Aesthetic in France, 1950 and 1967; Sainte-Beuve; a portrait of the Critic, 1962; The European Heritage, 1984; articles in various periodicals and learned reviews. *Recreations*: music, gardening. *Address*: Westway Cottage, West Adderbury, Banbury, Oxon OX17 3EU. *T*: (01295) 810272. *Died 9 July 2006.*

LEISHMAN, Frederick John, CVO 1957; MBE 1944; *b* 21 Jan. 1919; *s* of Alexander Leishman and Freda Mabel (*née* Hood); *m* 1945, Frances Webb, Evanston, Illinois, USA; two *d. Educ*: Oundle; Corpus Christi, Cambridge. Served RE, 1940–46, and with Military Government, Germany, 1945–46; Regular Commission, 1945; resigned 1946. Joined Foreign Service, 1946; FO, 1946–48; Copenhagen, 1948–51; CSSB, 1951; Asst Private Sec. to Foreign Sec., 1951–53; First Sec., Washington, 1953–58; First Sec. and Head of Chancery, Teheran, 1959–61; Counsellor, 1961; HM Consul-General, Hamburg, 1961–62; FO, 1962–63. Dir, Hill Samuel & Co. Ltd, 1965–80; Dep. Chm. and Chief Exec., Hill Samuel Gp (SA) Ltd, 1969–72; Partner and Chm., Hill Samuel & Co. oHG, Germany, 1975–77; Dir and Exec. Vice-Pres., Saehan Merchant Banking Corp., Seoul, 1977–80. Vice-Pres., The Friends of the Bowes Museum, 1992– (Chm., 1985–90). FRSA. *Recreations*: dreaming about golf, fishing, hill walking. *Address*: Saltoun House, Cotherstone, Barnard Castle, Co. Durham DL12 9PF. *T*: (01833) 650671. *Clubs*: Hawks (Cambridge); Cambridge University Rugby Union Football; London Scottish Football; Barnard Castle Rugby (Pres., 1987–99). *Died 27 Sept. 2006.*

LEMKIN, James Anthony, CBE 1986; Consultant, Field Fisher Waterhouse, Solicitors, 1990–91 (Senior Partner, 1985–90); *b* 21 Dec. 1926; *s* of late William Lemkin, CBE, and Rachel Irene (*née* Faith); *m* 1960, Joan Dorothy Anne Casserley, FFARCS, MRCPsych (*d* 2003); two *s* two *d*. *Educ:* Charterhouse; Merton Coll., Oxford (MA). Admitted solicitor, 1953; RN, 1945–47. Greater London Council: Additional Mem., 1970–73; Mem. for Hillingdon, Uxbridge, 1973–86; Chm., Legal and Parly Cttee, 1977–78; Chm., Scrutiny Cttee, 1978–81; Cons. spokesman on police, 1981–82; Opposition Chief Whip, 1982–86. Contested: (C and NL) Chesterfield, 1959; (L) Cheltenham, 1964. Bow Gp, 1952, 1956, 1957 (Founder Chm., Crossbow, 1957–60); a Vice-Pres., Soc. of Cons. Lawyers. Member: NW Thames RHA, 1980–84; Royal Marsden Hosp. SHA, 1982–89; Appeal Cttee, Cancer Res. Campaign, 1967–81; Chm., Barnet FPC, 1985–90. Governor: Westfield Coll., London Univ., 1970–83; Commonwealth Inst., 1985–92. Trustee, Whitechapel Art Gall., 1983–93; Chm., Hampstead Wells and Campden Trust, 1995–98. Co-founder, Africa Confidential, 1960. High Sheriff, Gtr London, 1992–93. *Publications:* (ed) Race and Power, 1956. *Recreation:* umpiring cricket. *Address:* 4 Frognal Close, NW3 6YB. *T:* (020) 7435 6499. *Club:* Athenæum.
Died 12 May 2008.

LENG, Gen. Sir Peter (John Hall), KCB 1978 (CB 1975); MBE 1962; MC 1945; Master-General of the Ordnance, 1981–83, retired; *b* 9 May 1925; *s* of J. Leng; *m* 1st, Virginia Rosemary Pearson (marr. diss. 1981); three *s* two *d*; 2nd, 1981, Mrs Flavia Tower, *d* of late Gen. Sir Frederick Browning and Lady Browning (Dame Daphne du Maurier, DBE). *Educ.* Bradfield Coll. Served War of 1939–45: commissioned in Scots Guards, 1944; Guards Armoured Div., Germany (MC). Various post-war appts; Guards Independent Parachute Company, 1949–51; commanded: 3rd Bn Royal Anglian Regt, in Berlin, United Kingdom and Aden, 1964–66; 24th Airportable Bde, 1968–70; Dep. Military Sec., Min. of Defence, 1971–73; Comdr Land Forces, N Ireland, 1973–75; Dir, Mil. Operations, MoD, 1975–78; Comdr 1 (Br) Corps, 1978–80. Colonel Commandant: RAVC, 1976–83; RMP, 1976–83. Fund Raising Dir, Jubilee Sailing Trust, 1984–85. Chm., Racecourse Assoc., 1985–89. *Recreations:* fishing, gardening. *Address:* c/o Barclays Bank, 1 Brompton Road, SW3 1EB. *Died 11 Feb. 2009.*

LENNARD, Rev. Sir Hugh Dacre B.; see Barrett-Lennard.

LEONARD, Rt Rev. Mgr and Rt Hon. Graham Douglas, KCVO 1991; PC 1981; *b* 8 May 1921; *s* of late Rev. Douglas Leonard, MA; *m* 1943, Vivien Priscilla, *d* of late M. B. R. Swann, MD, Fellow of Gonville and Caius Coll., Cambridge; two *s*. *Educ:* Monkton Combe Sch.; Balliol Coll., Oxford (Hon. Fellow, 1986). Hon. Sch. Nat. Science, shortened course. BA 1943, MA 1947. Served War, 1941–45; Captain, Oxford and Bucks Light Infantry; Army Operational Research Group (Ministry of Supply), 1944–45. Westcott House, Cambridge, 1946–47. Deacon 1947, Priest 1948; Vicar of Ardleigh, Essex, 1952–55; Director of Religious Education, Diocese of St Albans, 1955–58; Hon. Canon of St Albans, 1955–57; Canon Residentiary, 1957–58; Canon Emeritus, 1958; General Secretary, Nat. Society, and Secretary, C of E Schools Council, 1958–62; Archdeacon of Hampstead, Exam. Chaplain to Bishop of London, and Rector of St Andrew Undershaft with St Mary Axe, City of London, 1962–64; Bishop Suffragan of Willesden, 1964–73; Bishop of Truro, 1973–81; Bishop of London, 1981–91; received into RC Ch and ordained priest *sub conditione*, 1994. Prelate of Honour to HH The Pope, 2000. Dean of the Chapels Royal, 1981–91; Prelate of the Order of the British Empire, 1981–91; Prelate of the Imperial Soc. of Knights Bachelor, 1986–91. Chairman: C of E Cttee for Social Work and the Social Services, 1967–76; C of E Board for Social Responsibility, 1976–83; Churches Main Cttee, 1981–91; C of E Board of Education, 1983–88; BBC and IBA Central Religious

Adv. Cttee, 1984–89. Member: Churches Unity Commn, 1977–78, Consultant 1978; Churches Council for Covenanting, 1978–82; PCFC, 1989–93. An Anglican Mem., Commn for Anglican Orthodox Jt Doctrinal Discussions, 1974–81; one of Archbp of Canterbury's Counsellors on Foreign Relations, 1974–81. Pres., Path to Rome Internat. Convention (Miles Jesu), 1997–2001. Elected delegate, 5th Assembly WCC, Nairobi, 1975. House of Lords, 1977–91. Select Preacher to University of Oxford, 1968, 1984 and 1989; Hensley Henson Lectr, Univ. of Oxford, 1991–92. Lectures: John Findley Green Foundn, Fulton, Missouri, 1987; Earl Mountbatten Meml, Cambridge Union, 1990. Freeman, City of London, 1970. President: Middlesex Assoc., 1970–73; Corporation of SS Mary and Nicholas (Woodard Schools), 1973–78, Hon. Fellow, 1978. Fellow, Sion Coll., 1991–. Member Court of City Univ., 1981–91. Hon. Bencher, Middle Temple, 1982. Hon. DD: Episcopal Seminary, Kentucky, 1974; Westminster Coll., Fulton, Missouri, 1987; Hon. DCnL Nashotah, USA, 1983; STD Siena Coll., USA, 1984; Hon. LLD, Simon Greenleaf Sch. of Law, USA, 1987; Hon. DLitt CNAA, 1989. Episcopal Canon of Jerusalem, 1982–91. *Publications:* Growing into Union (Jt author), 1970; The Gospel is for Everyone, 1971; God Alive: Priorities in Pastoral Theology, 1981; Firmly I Believe and Truly, 1985; Life in Christ, 1986; (jtly) Let God be God, 1990; contrib. to: The Christian Religion Explained, 1960; Retreats Today, 1962; Communicating the Faith, 1969; A Critique of Eucharistic Agreement, 1975; Is Christianity Credible?, 1981; The Price of Peace, 1983; The Cross and the Bomb, 1983; Unholy Warfare, 1983; Synod of Westminster, 1986; After the Deluge, 1987; (ed) Faith and the Future, 1988; Tradition and Unity, 1991; Families for the Future, 1991; Challenge: spreading the faith, 1997; The Path to Rome, 1999. *Recreations:* reading, especially biographies; music. *Address:* 25 Woodlands Road, Witney, Oxon OX28 2DR.
Died 6 Jan. 2010.

LEONARD, Hugh, (John Keyes Byrne); playwright, since 1959; Programme Director, Dublin Theatre Festival, since 1978; Literary Editor, Abbey Theatre, 1976–77; *b* 9 Nov. 1926; *m* 1st 1955, Paule Jacquet (*d* 2000); one *d*; 2nd, 2000, Kathy Hayes. *Educ:* Presentation College, Dun Laoghaire. Hon. DHL Rhode Island, 1980; Hon. DLitt TCD, 1988. *Stage plays:* The Big Birthday, 1956; A Leap in the Dark, 1957; Madigan's Lock, 1958; A Walk on the Water, 1960; The Passion of Peter Ginty, 1961; Stephen D, 1962; The Poker Session, and Dublin 1, 1963; The Saints Go Cycling In, 1965; Mick and Mick, 1966; The Quick and the Dead, 1967; The Au Pair Man, 1968; The Barracks, 1969; The Patrick Pearse Motel, 1971; Da, 1973; Thieves, 1973; Summer, 1974; Times of Wolves and Tigers, 1974; Irishmen, 1975; Time Was, 1976; A Life, 1977; Kill, 1982; Scorpions (3 stage plays), 1983; The Mask of Moriarty, 1985; Moving, 1991; Senna for Sonny, 1994; The Lily Lally Show, 1994; Chamber Music (2 plays), 1994; Magic, 1997; Love in the Title, 1998; Fillums, 1999; Colquhoun and MacBryde, 2000; *adaptations:* Great Expectations, 1995; A Tale of Two Cities, 1996; Uncle Varrick, 2004. *TV plays:* Silent Song (Italia Award, 1967); The Last Campaign, 1978; The Ring and the Rose, 1978; A Life, 1986; Hunted Down, 1989; The Celadon Cup, 1993. *TV serials:* Nicholas Nickleby, 1977; London Belongs to Me, 1977; Wuthering Heights, 1978; Strumpet City, 1979; The Little World of Don Camillo, 1980; Good Behaviour, 1983; O'Neill, 1983; The Irish RM, 1985; Troubles, 1987; Parnell and the Englishwoman, 1991. *Films:* Herself Surprised, 1977; Da, 1988; Widows' Peak, 1994; Banjaxed, 1995. *Publications:* Home Before Night (autobiog.), 1979; Out After Dark (autobiog.), 1988; Parnell and the Englishwoman (novel), 1990; Rover and other cats (memoir), 1992; The Off-Off-Shore Island (novel), 1993; The Mogs (for children), 1995; A Wild People (novel), 2000; Fillums (novel), 2004. *Recreations:* travel (esp. French canals and waterways), vintage films, lunch, dinner, friendships. *Address:* 6 Rossaun, Pilot View, Dalkey, Co. Dublin. *T:* 2809590. *Died 12 Feb. 2009.*

LESLIE, Sir (Colin) Alan (Bettridge), Kt 1986; Commissioner, Foreign Compensation Commission, 1986–90; *b* 10 April 1922; *s* of Rupert Colin Leslie and Gladys Hannah Leslie (*née* Bettridge); *m* 1st, 1953, Anne Barbara (*née* Coates) (*d* 1982) (two *d*; 2nd, 1983, Jean Margaret (Sally), widow of Dr Alan Cheatle. *Educ:* King Edward VII School, Lytham; Merton College, Oxford (MA Law). Solicitor. Commissioned, The Royal Scots Fusiliers, 1941–46. Legal practice, Stafford Clark & Co., Solicitors, 1948–60; Head of Legal Dept and Company Secretary, British Oxygen Co., later BOC International, then BOC Group, 1960–83. Law Society: Vice-Pres., 1984–85; Pres., 1985–86. Adjudicator, Immigration Appeals, 1990–94. *Recreation:* fishing. *Address:* Tye Cottage, Alfriston, E Sussex BN26 5TD. *T:* (01323) 870518; 36 Abingdon Road, W8 6AS. *T:* (020) 7937 2874. *Club:* Oxford and Cambridge. *Died 1 Oct. 2008.*

LESLIE, Rt Rev. (Ernest) Kenneth, OBE 1972; *b* 14 May 1911; *s* of Rev. Ernest Thomas Leslie and Margaret Jane Leslie; *m* 1941, Isabel Daisy Wilson (*d* 1994); two *s* one *d* (and one *s* decd). *Educ:* Trinity Gram. Sch., Kew, Vic; Trinity Coll., University of Melbourne (BA); Aust. Coll. of Theology (ThL, 2nd Cl. 1933, Th School. 1951, 2nd Cl. 1952). Deacon, 1934; priest, 1935; Asst Curate, Holy Trinity, Coburg, 1934–37; Priest-in-Charge, Tennant Creek, Dio. Carpentaria, 1937–38; Alice Springs with Tennant Creek, 1938–40; Rector of Christ Church, Darwin, 1940–44; Chaplain, AIF, 1942–45; Rector of Alice Springs with Tennant Creek, 1945–46; Vice-Warden, St John's Coll., Morpeth, NSW, 1947–52; Chap. Geelong C of E GS, Timbertop Branch, 1953–58; Bishop of Bathurst, 1959–81. Hon. DLitt Charles Sturt, 1996. *Recreations:* walking, woodwork. *Address:* Hostel B4, Ilumba Gardens, Kelso, NSW 2795, Australia. *Died 6 Jan. 2010.*

LESLIE, Sir Peter (Evelyn), Kt 1991; Chairman, Commonwealth Development Corporation, 1989–95; *b* 24 March 1931; *s* of late Patrick Holt Leslie, DSc and Evelyn (*née* de Berry); *m* 1975, Charlotte, former wife of William Nigel Wenban-Smith, CMG and *d* of Sir Edwin Chapman-Andrews, KCMG, OBE and of Lady Chapman-Andrews; two step *s* two step *d*. *Educ:* Dragon Sch., Oxford; Stowe Sch.; New Coll., Oxford (Exhibnr; MA). Commnd Argyll and Sutherland Highlanders, 1951; served 7th Bn (TA), 1952–56. Entered Barclays Bank DCO, 1955; served in Sudan, Algeria, Zaire, Kenya and the Bahamas, 1956–71; Gen. Manager, Barclays Bank and Barclays Bank Internat., 1973–81, Sen. Gen. Manager, 1981–84; Dir, 1980–91, Chief Gen. Man., 1985–87, Man. Dir, 1987–88, Dep. Chm., 1987–91, Barclays Bank plc. Dep. Chm., Midland Bank plc, 1991–92; Chm., NCM Credit Insurance Ltd, 1995–98; Mem., Supervisory Bd, NCM Holding NV, 1995–2000. Mem., Bd of Banking Supervision, Bank of England, 1989–94. Chm., Export Guarantees Adv. Council, 1987–92 (Mem., 1978–81, Dep. Chm., 1986–87); Mem., Matthews Cttee on ECGD, 1983. Chairman: Exec. Cttee, British Bankers Assoc., 1978–79; Cttee, London and Scottish Clearing Bankers, 1986–88; Overseas Develt Inst., 1988–95. Member: Council for Ind. and Higher Educn, 1987–91; CARE Britain Bd, 1988–95; Council, RIIA, 1991–97; Ranfurly Liby Service, 1991–94. Chm. Council, Queen's Coll., London, 1989–94; Curator of Univ. Chest, Oxford, 1990–95; Chm., Audit Cttee, Oxford Univ., 1992–2001. Governor: Stowe Sch., 1983–2001 (Chm., 1994–2001); National Inst. of Social Work, 1973–83. *Publications:* Chapman-Andrews and the Emperor, 2005; articles in local and family history jls. *Recreations:* natural history, historical research. *Died 27 Sept. 2007.*

LETTS, John Campbell Bonner, OBE 1980; Founder and Chairman, Trollope Society, since 1987; *b* 18 Nov. 1929; *s* of C. Francis C. Letts and Ereleen F. C. Letts; *m*

1957, Sarah, *d* of E. Brian O'Rorke, RA; three *s* one *d*. *Educ:* Oakley Hall, Cirencester; Haileybury Coll.; Jesus Coll., Cambridge (English Schol.; BA 1953). Trainee, S. H. Benson, 1954–59; Publicity Manager, Penguin Books, 1959; Copywriter, J. Walter Thompson, 1960–64; General Manager: Sunday Times Publications, 1964–66; Book Club Associates, 1966–69; Mktg Dir, Hutchinsons, 1969–71; Jt Chm. (Editorial and Mktg), Folio Soc., 1971–87. Founder Trustee, Empire Mus., 1987–; Founder and Dir, Earth Centre, Doncaster, 1988–2000; Chairman: Nat. Heritage, 1971–98 (Life Pres., 1999); Empire Museum Ltd, 1989–; European Museums Trust, 1994–. FRSA. *Publications:* A Little Treasury of Limericks, 1975. *Recreations:* buying plants, walking in Scotland, listening to music, reading, keeping in touch with the past. *Address:* 83 West Side, Clapham Common, SW4 9AY. *T:* (020) 7228 9448. *Club:* Reform. *Died 25 March 2006.*

LEUCHARS, Maj.-Gen. Peter Raymond, CBE 1966; Chief Commander, St John Ambulance, 1980–89 (Commissioner-in-Chief, 1978–80 and 1985–86); *b* 29 Oct. 1921; *s* of late Raymond Leuchars and Helen Inez Leuchars (*née* Copland-Griffiths); *m* 1953, Hon. Gillian Wightman Nivison, *d* of 2nd Baron Glendyne; one *s*. *Educ:* Bradfield College. Commnd in Welsh Guards, 1941; served in NW Europe and Italy, 1944–45; Adjt, 1st Bn Welsh Guards, Palestine, 1945–48; Bde Major, 4 Guards Bde, Germany, 1952–54; GSO1 (Instr.), Staff Coll., Camberley, 1956–59; GSO1 HQ 4 Div. BAOR, 1960–63; comd 1st Bn Welsh Guards, 1963–65; Principal Staff Off. to Dir of Ops, Borneo, 1965–66; comd 11 Armd Bde BAOR, 1966–68; comd Jt Operational Computer Projects Team, 1969–71; Dep. Comdt Staff Coll., Camberley, 1972–73; GOC Wales, 1973–76. Col, The Royal Welch Fusiliers, 1974–84. Pres., Guards' Golfing Soc., 1977–2001. Chairman: St John Fellowship, 1989–95 (Vice-Pres., 1996–); Lady Grover's Fund for Officers' Families, 1991–98. FRGS 1996. BGCStJ 1989 (Bailiff of Egle, 2001). Order of Istiqlal (Jordan), 1946. *Recreations:* golf, shooting, travel, photography. *Address:* 5 Chelsea Square, SW3 6LF. *T:* (020) 7352 6187. *Clubs:* Royal and Ancient Golf; Sunningdale Golf (Captain 1975). *Died 17 July 2009.*

LEVER, His Honour (John) Michael; QC 1977; a Circuit Judge, 1981–97; *b* 12 Aug. 1928; *s* of late John and Ida Donaldson Lever; *m* 1st, 1964, Elizabeth Marr (*d* 1998); two *s*; 2nd, 2002, Eileen Cheetham (*née* Micallef) (*d* 2006). *Educ:* Bolton Sch.; Gonville and Caius Coll., Cambridge (Schol.; BA (1st cl. hons Law Tripos) 1949). Flying Officer, RAF, 1950–52. Called to Bar, Middle Temple, 1951 (Blackstone Schol.); practised Northern Circuit from 1952; Asst Recorder, Salford, 1969–71; a Recorder of the Crown Court, 1972–81. Gov., Bolton Sch., 1972–2003. *Recreations:* theatre, books, (watching) sport of all kinds. *Address:* Lakelands, Rivington, near Bolton, Lancs BL6 7RT. *T:* (01204) 468189. *Died 16 Feb. 2006.*

LEVEY, Sir Michael (Vincent), Kt 1981; LVO 1965; MA Oxon and Cantab; FRSL; FBA 1983; Director of the National Gallery, 1973–86 (Deputy Director, 1970–73); *b* 8 June 1927; *s* of O. L. H. Levey and Gladys Mary Milestone; *m* 1954, Brigid Brophy (*d* 1995), FRSL; one *d*. *Educ:* Oratory Sch.; Exeter Coll., Oxford (Hon. Fellow, 1973). Served with Army, 1945–48; commissioned, KSLI, 1946, and attached RAEC, Egypt. National Gallery: Asst Keeper, 1951–66, Dep. Keeper, 1966–68, Keeper, 1968–73. Slade Professor of Fine Art, Cambridge, 1963–64; Supernumerary Fellow, King's Coll., Cambridge, 1963–64; Slade Professor of Fine Art, Oxford, 1994–95; Hon. Fellow, Royal Acad., 1986; Foreign Mem., Ateneo Veneto, 1986. Hon. DLitt Manchester, 1989. *Publications:* Six Great Painters, 1956; National Gallery Catalogues: 18th Century Italian Schools, 1956; The German School, 1959; Painting in 18th Century Venice, 1959, 3rd edn 1994; From Giotto to Cézanne, 1962; Dürer, 1964; The Later Italian Paintings in the Collection of HM The Queen, 1964, rev.

edn 1991; Canaletto Paintings in the Royal Collection, 1964; Tiepolo's Banquet of Cleopatra (Charlton Lecture, 1962), 1966; Rococo to Revolution, 1966; Bronzino (The Masters), 1967; Early Renaissance, 1967 (Hawthornden Prize, 1968); Fifty Works of English Literature We Could Do Without (co-author), 1967; Holbein's Christina of Denmark, Duchess of Milan, 1968; A History of Western Art, 1968; Painting at Court (Wrightsman Lectures), 1971; 17th and 18th Century Italian Schools (Nat. Gall. catalogue), 1971; The Life and Death of Mozart, 1971, 2nd edn 1988; The Nude: Themes and Painters in the National Gallery, 1972; (co-author) Art and Architecture in 18th Century France, 1972; The Venetian Scene (Themes and Painters Series), 1973; Botticelli (Themes and Painters Series), 1974; High Renaissance, 1975; The World of Ottoman Art, 1976; Jacob van Ruisdael (Themes and Painters Series), 1977; The Case of Walter Pater, 1978; Sir Thomas Lawrence (Nat. Portrait Gall. exhibn), 1979; The Painter Depicted (Neurath Lect.), 1981; Tempting Fate (fiction), 1982; An Affair on the Appian Way (fiction), 1984; (ed) Pater's Marius the Epicurean, 1985; Giambattista Tiepolo, 1986 (Banister Fletcher Prize, 1987); The National Gallery Collection: a selection, 1987; Men at Work (fiction), 1989; (ed) The Soul of the Eye: anthology of painters and painting, 1990; Painting and Sculpture in France 1700–1789, 1992; Florence: a portrait, 1996; The Chapel is on Fire (memoir), 2000; (ed) The Burlington Magazine: a centenary anthology, 2003; Sir Thomas Lawrence, 2005; contribs to Burlington Magazine, Apollo, etc. *Address:* 36 Little Lane, Louth, Lincs LN11 9DU.　　　　　　　　　　　*Died 28 Dec. 2008.*

LÉVI-STRAUSS, Claude; Grand Croix de la Légion d'Honneur, 1991; Commandeur, Ordre National du Mérite, 1971; Member of French Academy, since 1973; Professor, Collège de France, 1959–82, Hon. Professor, since 1983; *b* 28 Nov. 1908; *s* of Raymond Lévi-Strauss and Emma Lévy; *m* 1st, 1932, Dina Dreyfus; 2nd, 1946, Rose-Marie Ullmo; one *s*; 3rd, 1954, Monique Roman; one *s*. *Educ:* Lycée Janson-de-Sailly, Paris; Sorbonne. Prof., Univ. of São Paulo, Brazil, 1935–39; Vis. Prof., New School for Social Research, NY, 1941–45; Cultural Counsellor, French Embassy, Washington, 1946–47; Associate Curator, Musée de l'Homme, Paris, 1948–49. Corresp. Member: Royal Acad. of Netherlands; Norwegian Acad.; British Acad.; Nat. Acad. of Sciences, USA; Amer. Acad. and Inst. of Arts and Letters; Amer. Philos. Soc.; Royal Anthrop. Inst. of Great Britain; London Sch. of African and Oriental Studies. Hon. Dr: Brussels, 1962; Oxford, 1964; Yale, 1965; Chicago, 1967; Columbia, 1971; Stirling, 1972; Univ. Nat. du Zaïre, 1973; Uppsala, 1977; Johns Hopkins, 1978; Laval, 1979; Mexico, 1979; Visva Bharati, India, 1980; Harvard, 1986; Montreal, 1998. *Publications:* La Vie familiale et sociale des Indiens Nambikwara, 1948; Les Structures élémentaires de la parenté, 1949 (The Elementary Structures of Kinship, 1969); Race et histoire, 1952; Tristes Tropiques, 1955 (A World on the Wane, 1961; complete English edn as Tristes Tropiques, 1973); Anthropologie structurale, Vol. 1, 1958, Vol. 2, 1973 (Structural Anthropology, Vol. 1, 1964, Vol. 2, 1977); Le Totémisme aujourd'hui, 1962 (Totemism, 1963); La Pensée sauvage, 1962 (The Savage Mind, 1966); Le Cru et le cuit, 1964 (The Raw and the Cooked, 1970); Du Miel aux cendres, 1967 (From Honey to Ashes, 1973); L'Origine des manières de table, 1968 (The Origin of Table Manners, 1978); L'Homme nu, 1971 (The Naked Man, 1981); La Voie des masques, 1975 (The Way of the Masks, 1982); Le Regard éloigné, 1983 (The View from Afar, 1985); Paroles Données, 1984 (Anthropology and Myth, 1987); La Potière Jalouse, 1985 (The Jealous Potter, 1988); (with D. Eribon) De Près et de loin, 1988 (Conversations with Claude Lévi-Strauss, 1991); Histoire de Lynx, 1991 (The Story of Lynx, 1995); Regarder écouter lire, 1993 (Look, Listen, Read, 1997); Saudades do Brasil, 1994 (A Photographic Memoir, 1995); *relevant publications:* Entretiens avec Lévi-Strauss (ed G. Charbonnier), 1962; Claude Lévi-Strauss and the Making of Structural Anthropology, by Marcel Henaff, 1998; by Octavio Paz: On Lévi-Strauss, 1970; Claude

Lévi-Strauss: an introduction, 1972. *Address:* 2 rue des Marronniers, 75016 Paris, France. *T:* (1) 42883471.
　　　　　　　　　　　　　　　　　　　　Died 1 Nov. 2009.

LEVINSKY, Prof. Roland Jacob, MD; FRCP, FMedSci; Vice-Chancellor, University of Plymouth, since 2002; *b* Bloemfontein, 16 Oct. 1943; *m* 1971, Beth Brigden; one *s* two *d*. *Educ:* Univ. of London (BSc 1965; MB, BS 1968; MD 1980). FRCP 1982. Hon. Sen. Registrar in Paediatrics, then Hon. Consultant Paediatrician, Great Ormond Street Hosp. for Children; Sen. Lectr in Immunol., subseq. Reader in Paediatric Immunol., then Hugh Greenwood Prof. of Immunol., 1985–99 and Dean, 1989–99, Inst. of Child Health, London; Vice-Provost for Biomedicine and Head of Graduate Sch., UCL, 1999–2002. Fellow, UCL, 2000; Hon. Fellow, Inst. of Child Health, 2004. FMedSci 1998; Hon. FRCPCH 2001. *Publications:* (ed) Immunoglobulin Subclass Deficiencies, 1988. *Recreations:* theatre, ceramics, sailing. *Address:* University of Plymouth, Drake Circus, Plymouth PL4 8AA.　　　　　　　*Died 1 Jan. 2007.*

LEWEN, John Henry, CMG 1977; HM Diplomatic Service, retired; Ambassador to the People's Republic of Mozambique, 1975–79; *b* 6 July 1920; *s* of Carl Henry Lewen and Alice (*née* Mundy); *m* 1945, Emilienne Alette Julie Alida Galant (*d* 2005); three *s*. *Educ:* Christ's Hospital; King's Coll., Cambridge. Royal Signals, 1940–45. HM Foreign (subseq. Diplomatic) Service, 1946; HM Embassy: Lisbon, 1947–50; Rangoon, 1950–53; FO, 1953–55; HM Embassy: Rio de Janeiro, 1955–59; Warsaw, 1959–61; FO, 1961–63; Head of Chancery, HM Embassy, Rabat, 1963–67; Consul-General, Jerusalem, 1967–70; Inspector of HM Diplomatic Estabts, 1970–73; Dir, Admin and Budget, Secretariat-Gen. of Council of Ministers of European Communities, 1973–75. OStJ 1969. *Recreations:* singing, history. *Address:* 1 Brimley Road, Cambridge CB4 2DQ. *T:* (01223) 359101.　　　　　　　*Died 10 March 2008.*

LEWIS, Maj.-Gen. (Alfred) George, CBE 1969; *b* 23 July 1920; *s* of Louis Lewis; *m* 1946, Daye Neville, *d* of Neville Greaves Hunt; two *s* two *d*. *Educ:* St Dunstan's Coll.; King's Coll., London. Served War of 1939–45, India and Burma. Commanded 15th/19th Hussars, 1961–63; Dir, Defence Operational Requirements Staff, MoD, 1967–68; Dep. Comdt, Royal Mil. Coll. of Science, 1968–70; Dir Gen., Fighting Vehicles and Engineer Equipment, 1970–72, retired 1973. Man. Dir, 1973–80, Dep. Chm., 1980–81, Alvis Ltd; Dep. Chm., Self Changing Gears Ltd, 1976–81; Company Secretary: Leyland Vehicles, 1980–81; Bus Manufacturers (Hldgs), 1980–84; Staff Dir, BL plc, 1981–84. Mem., Governing Bd, St Dunstan's Coll. Educational Foundn, 1976–87. Hon. Col, Queen's Own Mercian Yeomanry, 1977–82. Mem., St John Council for Warwickshire, 1973–97; OStJ 1996. *Recreations:* gardening, writing, making things, croquet.　　　　　　　　　　　*Died 1 Sept. 2010.*

LEWIS, Very Rev. Bertie; Vicar of Nevern with Eglwyswrw, Meline, Eglwyswen and Llanfair Nant-gwyn, 1994–96; *b* 24 Aug. 1931; *m* 1958, Rayann Pryce; one *s* three *d*. *Educ:* St David's Coll., Lampeter (BA); St Catherine's Coll., Oxford (MA); Wycliffe Hall, Oxford. Ordained deacon 1957; priest 1958; Curate: Cwmaman, 1957–60; Aberystwyth St Michael, 1960–62; Vicar: Llanddewibrefi, 1962–65; Henfynyw with Aberaeron, 1965–75; Lampeter, 1975–80; Canon, St Davids Cathedral, 1978–86; Rector, Rectorial Benefice of Aberystwyth, 1980–88; Archdeacon of Cardigan, 1986–90; Vicar of Nevern, 1988–90; Dean of St Davids Cathedral, 1990–94, Hon. Canon, 1994–96. *Recreations:* Rugby, music, books. *Address:* Bryn Golau, Llanfarian, Aberystwyth, Ceredigion SY23 4BT.
　　　　　　　　　　　　　　　　　　　Died 3 April 2006.

LEWIS, Prof. Dan, PhD; DSc; FRS 1955; Quain Professor of Botany, London University, 1957–78, then Emeritus; Hon. Research Fellow, University College, London, since 1978; *b* 30 Dec. 1910; *s* of Ernest Albert and Edith J. Lewis; *m* 1933, Mary Phœbe Eleanor Burry (*d* 2003); one *d*. *Educ:* High Sch., Newcastle-under-Lyme, Staffs; Reading University (BSc); PhD, DSc (London). Research Scholar, Reading Univ., 1935–36; Scientific Officer, Pomology Dept, John Innes Hort. Inst., 1935–48; Head of Genetics Dept, John Innes Horticultural Institution, Bayfordbury, Hertford, Herts, 1948–57. Rockefeller Foundation Special Fellowship, California Inst. of Technology, 1955–56; Visiting Prof. of Genetics, University of Calif, Berkeley, 1961–62; Royal Society Leverhulme Visiting Professor: University of Delhi, 1965–66; Singapore, 1970; Vis. Prof., QMC, 1978–. Pres., Genetical Soc., 1968–71; Mem., UGC, 1969–74. *Publications:* Sexual Incompatibility in Plants, 1979; Editor, Science Progress; scientific papers on Genetics and Plant Physiology. *Recreation:* music. *Address:* Flat 2, 56/57 Myddelton Square, EC1R 1YA. *T:* (020) 7278 6948. *Died 30 Sept. 2009.*

LEWIS, Sir David Courtenay M.; *see* Mansel Lewis.

LEWIS, (David) Ralph; QC 1999; a Recorder, since 2000; a Deputy High Court Judge, since 2008; *b* 29 June 1956; *s* of David Ieuan Lewis and late (Annie Mary) Eunice Lewis (*née* Evans); *m* Elizabeth Shelley; two *s* one *d*. *Educ:* Dudley Grammar Sch.; Jesus Coll., Oxford (MA). Called to the Bar, Middle Temple, 1978; an Asst Recorder, 1996–2000; Head, No 5 Chambers, 2007–. Mem., Bar Council, 1999–2002. *Recreations:* shooting, travel, ski-ing. *Address:* 5 Fountain Court, Steelhouse Lane, Birmingham B4 6DR. *T:* (0121) 606 0500. *Club:* Oxford and Cambridge. *Died 4 July 2010.*

LEWIS, Donald Gordon, OBE 1988; Director, National Exhibition Centre, 1982–84; *b* 12 Sept. 1926; *s* of late Albert Francis Lewis and Nellie Elizabeth Lewis; *m* 1950, Doreen Mary (*née* Gardner); one *d*. *Educ:* King Edward's Sch., Birmingham; Liverpool Univ. Dairy Industry, 1947–91; Gen. Sales Manager, Birmingham Dairies, 1961–91. Councillor (C) Birmingham CC, Selly Oak Ward, 1959, Alderman 1971–74; past Chairman, Transport and Airport Committees; West Midlands County Council: Mem., 1974–81; Chm., 1980–81; Chairman, Airport Cttee, 1974–80; Sec., Conservative Group, 1974–80; City of Birmingham District Council: Mem., 1982–95; Hon. Alderman, 1995–; Chm., Nat. Exhibn Centre Cttee, 1982–84; Chm., Birmingham Housing Cttee, 1983–84. Mem., W Midlands PTA, 1984–95; Director: Birmingham International Airport plc, 1994–96; Broader Choices for Old People, 1999–; W Midlands Special Needs Transport Ltd, 2000–; Nat. Exhibn Centre (Develts) PLC, 2005–. Gov., Heart of England NHS Foundn Trust, 2005–. Chm., Selly Oak (Birmingham) Constituency Conservative Assoc., 1975–80, Pres., 1980; Vice-Pres., Birmingham Cons. Assoc., 1987– (Chm., 1984–87). *Recreation:* eating out. *Address:* 25 Albany Gardens, Hampton Lane, Solihull B91 2PT. *T:* (0121) 705 7661. *Died 22 Feb. 2008.*

LEWIS, Ernest Gordon, (Toby), CMG 1972; OBE 1958; HM Diplomatic Service, retired; *b* New Zealand, 26 Sept. 1918; *s* of George Henry Lewis; *m* 1949, Jean Margaret (*d* 2003), *d* of late A. H. Smyth. *Educ:* Otago Boys' High Sch.; Otago Univ., NZ. Served War, Army, with 2nd NZ Div., Middle East, 1939–46 (Lt-Col; despatches, MBE); Staff Coll., Haifa, 1943. Joined Colonial Service, Nigeria, 1947; Administrator, Turks and Caicos Is, 1955–59; Permanent Sec., to Federal Govt of Nigeria, 1960–62; First Sec., Pakistan, 1963–66; Foreign and Commonwealth Office, 1966–69; Kuching, Sarawak, 1969–70; Governor and C-in-C, Falkland Islands, and High Comr, British Antarctic Territory, 1971–75; Head of Gibraltar and General Dept, FCO, 1975–77. *Address:* 5 Smith Street, Chelsea, SW3 4EE. *Died 29 Dec. 2006.*

LEWIS, Prof. Geoffrey Lewis, CMG 1999; FBA 1979; Professor of Turkish, University of Oxford, 1986, then Emeritus; Fellow, St Antony's College, Oxford, 1961, then Emeritus; *b* 19 June 1920; *s* of Ashley Lewis and Jeanne Muriel (*née* Sintrop); *m* 1941, Raphaela Rhoda Bale Seideman; one *s* (one *d* decd). *Educ:* University Coll.

Sch.; St John's Coll., Oxford (MA 1945, DPhil 1950; James Mew Arabic Scholar, 1947; Hon. Fellow, 2000). RAF, 1940–45. Lectr in Turkish, 1950–54, Sen. Lectr in Islamic Studies, 1954–64, Sen. Lectr in Turkish, 1964–86, Oxford Univ. Visiting Professor: Robert Coll., Istanbul, 1959–68; Princeton Univ., 1970–71, 1974; UCLA, 1975; British Acad. Leverhulme Vis. Prof., Turkey, 1984. Gunnar Jarring Lectr, Stockholm, 2002. Vice-Pres., 1972–2003, Pres., 2003–, Anglo-Turkish Soc.; Mem., British-Turkish Mixed Commn, 1975–95; Pres., British Soc. for Middle Eastern Studies, 1981–83 (award for outstanding contribs for many yrs to ME studies in UK, 2005). Corresp. Mem., Turkish Language Soc., 1953–. DUniv: Univ. of the Bosphorus, Istanbul, 1986; Univ. of Istanbul, 1992. Turkish Govt Cert. of Merit, 1973; Turkish Min. of For. Affairs Exceptional Service Plaque, 1991; Order of Merit (Turkish Republic), 1998. *Publications:* Teach Yourself Turkish, 1953, rev. edn 1989; Modern Turkey, 1955, 4th edn 1974; (trans., with annotations) Katib Chelebi, The Balance of Truth, 1957; Plotiniana Arabica, 1959; (with Barbara Hodge) A Study in Education for International Misunderstanding (Cyprus School History Textbooks), 1966; Turkish Grammar, 1967, rev. edn 2000; (with M. S. Spink) Albucasis on Surgery and Instruments, 1973; The Book of Dede Korkut, 1974; The Atatürk I Knew, 1981; Thickhead and other Turkish Stories, 1988; Just a Diplomat, 1992; Turkish Language Reform: a catastrophic success, 1999 (trans. Turkish, 2004); articles on Turkish language, history and politics, and on Arab alchemy and medicine. *Recreations:* bodging, etymology. *Address:* St Antony's College, Oxford OX2 6JF. *Died 12 Feb. 2008.*

LEWIS, Maj.-Gen. George; *see* Lewis, Maj.-Gen. A. G.

LEWIS, Graham D.; *see* Dixon-Lewis.

LEWIS, Michael ap Gwilym; QC 1975; a Recorder of the Crown Court, 1976–97; *b* 9 May 1930; *s* of Rev. Thomas William Lewis and Mary Jane May Selway; *m* 1959, Audrey Thomas; three *s* one *d*; *m* 1988, Sarah Turvill; two *d*. *Educ:* Mill Hill; Jesus Coll., Oxford (Scholar). MA (Mod. History). Commnd 2nd Royal Tank Regt, 1952–53. Called to Bar, Gray's Inn, 1956, Bencher, 1986; Mem., Senate, 1979–82; South Eastern Circuit. Mem., Criminal Injuries Compensation Bd, 1993–2002. *Address:* 33 Canonbury Park North, N1 2JU. *T:* (020) 7226 6440. *Died 12 Nov. 2010.*

LEWIS, Naomi, FRSL; writer, poet, critic and broadcaster; *b* coastal Norfolk, 3 Sept. 1911. Contributor at various times to Observer, New Statesman, New York Times, Listener, Encounter, TLS, TES, etc. FRSL 1981. Eleanor Farjeon Prize, Children's Book Circle, 1975. *Publications:* A Visit to Mrs Wilcox, 1957; A Peculiar Music, 1971; Fantasy, 1977; The Silent Playmate, 1979; Leaves, 1980; Come Wit h Us (poems), 1982; Once upon a Rainbow, 1981; A Footprint on the Air (poems), 1983; Messages (poems), 1985; A School Bewitched, 1985; Arabian Nights, 1987; Cry Wolf!, 1988; Proud Knight, Fair Lady, 1989; Johnny Longnose, 1989; The Mardi Gras Cat (poems), 1994; Classic Fairy Tales, 1996; Elf Hill, 1999; Rockinghorse Land, 2000; *translations* include: Hans Christian Andersen's Fairy Tales, 1981; The Snow Queen, 1988; The Frog Prince, 1990; The Emperor's New Clothes, 1997; Tales of Hans Christian Andersen, 2005; numerous introductory essays. *Recreations:* trying in practical ways to alleviate the lot of horses, camels, bears, sheep, wolves, cows, pigs and other ill-used mortals of the animal kind. *Address:* 13 Red Lion Square, WC1R 4QF. *Died 5 July 2009.*

LEWIS, Ralph; *see* Lewis, D. R.

LEWIS, Toby; *see* Lewis, E. G.

LEWISOHN, Neville Joseph; Director of Dockyard Manpower and Productivity (Under Secretary), Ministry of Defence, 1979–82; *b* 28 May 1922; *s* of Victor and Ruth Lewisohn; *m* 1944, Patricia Zeffertt; two *d* (and one *d* decd). *Educ:* Sutton County Sch., Surrey. Entered Admiralty as Clerical Officer, 1939; promoted through intervening grades to Principal, 1964; Dir of Resources and Progs (Ships), 1972 (Asst Sec.); Head of Civilian Management (Specialists), 2 Div., 1976. *Recreations:* music, drama. *Died 13 March 2007.*

LEWITTER, Prof. Lucjan Ryszard; Professor of Slavonic Studies, 1968–84, and Fellow of Christ's College, since 1951, University of Cambridge; *b* Krakow, 1 June 1922. *Educ:* schools in Poland; Perse Sch., Cambridge; Christ's Coll., Cambridge (BA; PhD 1951). Cambridge University: Asst Lectr in Polish, 1948; Univ. Lectr in Slavonic Studies (Polish), 1953–68; Christ's College: Dir of Studies in Modern Languages, 1951–64; Tutor, 1960–68; Vice-Master, 1977–80. *Publications:* (ed with A. P. Vlasto) Ivan Pososhkov, The Book of Poverty and Wealth, 1987; articles, mostly on Russo-Polish relations, in learned jls. *Address:* Christ's College, Cambridge CB2 3BU. *T:* (01223) 357320. *Club:* Oxford and Cambridge. *Died 19 Sept. 2007.*

LICHFIELD, Prof. Nathaniel; Professor Emeritus, University of London, since 1978; Partner, Lichfield Planning (formerly Dalia and Nathaniel Lichfield Associates), urban and environmental planners and economists, since 1992; *b* 29 Feb. 1916; 2nd *s* of Hyman Lichman and Fanny (*née* Grecht); *m* 1st, 1942, Rachel Goulden (*d* 1968), two *d*; 2nd, 1970, Dalia Kadury; one *s* one *d*. *Educ:* Raines Foundn Sch.; University of London. BSc (EstMan), DSc (Econ), PhD (Econ); PPRTPI, FRICS. Sen. Partner, 1962–89, Chm., 1989–92, Nathaniel Lichfield & Partners Ltd, planning, devlt, urban design and econ. consultants; from 1945 worked continuously in urban and regional planning, specialising in econs of planning from 1950, with particular reference to social cost-benefit in planning, impact assessment, land policy and urban conservation; worked in local and central govt depts and private offices. Consultant commns in UK and all continents. Special Lectr, UCL, 1950; Prof. of Econs of Environmental Planning, UCL, 1966–79. Visiting Professor: Univ. of California, 1976–78; Univ. of Tel Aviv, 1959–60, 1966; Technion—Israel Inst. of Technol., 1972–74; Hebrew Univ., Jerusalem, 1980–; Univ. of Naples, 1986–; Special Prof., Univ. of Nottingham, 1989–. Chm., Econs Cttee, ICOMOS, 1988–95 (Conservation Econs Cttee report published 1993); Member: Exec. Cttee, Internat. Centre for Land Policy Studies, 1975–85; Council, Tavistock Inst. of Human Relations, 1968–93 (Vice Pres., 1993–2001); formerly Member: SSRC; CNAA; SE Econ. Planning Council; Chairman: Economics of Urban Villages Cttee, Urban Villages Forum (report published 1995); Land Assembly Cttee, DETR/Urban Villages Forum, 1998–99 (summary report 2001). Hon. Fellow, Centre for Social and Econ. Res. on Global Envmt, 1992–. Lifetime Achievement Award, RTPI, 2004. *Publications:* Economics of Planned Development, 1956; Cost Benefit Analysis in Urban Redevelopment, 1962; Cost Benefit Analysis in Town Planning: a case study of Cambridge, 1966; Israel's New Towns: a development strategy, 1971; (with Prof. A. Proudlove) Conservation and Traffic: a case study of York, 1975; (with Peter Kettle and Michael Whitbread) Evaluation in the Planning Process, 1975; (with Haim Darin-Drabkin) Land Policy in Planning, 1980; (with Leslie Lintott) Period Buildings: evaluation of development-conservation options, 1985; (with Prof. J. Schweid) Conservation of the Built Heritage, 1986; Economics in Urban Conservation, 1988; Community Impact Evaluation, 1996; papers in Urban Studies, Regional Studies, Land Economics, Town Planning Review, Restauro, Built Environment, Project Appraisal, Planning and Envmtl Law, Chartered Surveyor, Planner, Envmt and Planning, Transport and Econ. Policy. *Recreations:* finding out less and less about more and more, countering advancing age, singing. *Address:* 13 Chalcot Gardens, England's Lane, NW3 4YB. *T:* (020) 7586 0461. *Died 27 Feb. 2009.*

LICHTER, Dr Ivan, ONZ 1997; FRCS, FRACS; Medical Director, Te Omanga Hospice, Lower Hutt, New Zealand, 1986–94; *b* 14 March 1918; *s* of Goodman Lichter and Sarah (*née* Mierowsky); *m* 1951, Heather Lloyd; three *s* one *d*. *Educ:* Univ. of Witwatersrand, Johannesburg (MB BCh). FRCS 1949; FRACS 1964. Capt., SAMC in Madagascar, Egypt, Italy and Hosp. Ship Amra, 1942–45. Postgrad. Registrar, Guy's Hosp., London, 1946; Resident Surgical Officer: Queen Mary's Hosp., London, 1947; Wembley Hosp., Middx, 1948; Registrar, and Chief Asst, Thoracic Surgical Unit, Harefield Hosp., Middx, 1948–51; Thoracic Surgeon: Johannesburg, SA, 1952–60; Otago Hosp. Bd, and Associate Prof. of Surgery, Univ. of Otago, Dunedin, 1961–84. NZ Postgrad. Travelling Fellow, 1976. Examr in Cardio-Thoracic Surgery, RACS, 1974–84. Estabd and developed palliative care services in NZ and undertook teaching and research in palliative medicine, 1974–94. Hon. FAChPM 2000. *Publications:* Palliative Care: the management of far advanced illness, 1981; Communication in Cancer Care, 1987; Ethical Dilemmas in Cancer Care, 1989; (contrib.) Oxford Textbook of Palliative Medicine, 1993, 2nd edn 1997; numerous contribs to learned jls, esp. on aspects of palliative care. *Recreations:* reading, music, walking. *Address:* 41 Kitchener Road, Milford, Auckland, New Zealand. *T:* (9) 4895340. *Died 12 June 2009.*

LIGETI, Prof. György Sándor; Member, Order of Merit, Germany, 1975; music composer; Professor for Composition, Hamburg Academy of Music, 1973–89; *b* 28 May 1923; *s* of Dr Sándor Ligeti and Dr Ilona Somogyi; *m* 1957, Dr Vera Spitz; one *s*. *Educ:* Budapest Academy of Music (Dipl. in composition). Lecturer for harmony and counterpoint, Budapest Acad. of Music, 1950–56; Guest Prof., Stockholm Acad. of Music, 1961–71; composer in residence, Stanford Univ., Calif, 1972. Member: Swedish Royal Acad. of Music, 1964; Acad. of Arts, Berlin, 1968; Free Acad. of Arts, Hamburg, 1971; Bavarian Acad. of Fine Arts, Munich, 1978. Hon. Mem., Amer. Acad. and Inst. of Arts and Letters, 1984. Dr *hc* Hamburg, 1988. Numerous prizes and awards, incl. Grawemeyer Award, 1986. *Main compositions:* Romanian concerto, 1950; Apparitions, for orch., 1959; Atmosphères, for orch., 1961; Aventures, for 3 singers and 7 instrumentalists, 1962; Requiem, for 2 soli, chorus and orch., 1965; Cello concerto, 1966; Chamber concerto, 1970; Melodien, for orch., 1971; Le Grand Macabre, opera, 1977; Trio, for violin, horn, piano, 1982; Piano études, 1985–2002; Piano concerto, 1986; Nonsense madrigals, for 6-part choir a cappella, 1988; Violin concerto, 1991; Viola sonata, 1996; Sippal, Dobbal, Nádihegedüvel, for low mezzo-soprano and 4 percussionists, 2000; Hamburg concerto, for horn and chamber orch., 2001. *Address:* Himmelhofgasse 34, 1130 Vienna, Austria. *Died 12 June 2006.*

LIGGINS, Sir Graham (Collingwood), Kt 1991; CBE 1983; FRCSE, FRACS, FRCOG; FRS 1980; FRSNZ 1976; Professor of Obstetrics and Gynaecological Endocrinology, University of Auckland, New Zealand, 1968–87, then Professor Emeritus (formerly Senior Lecturer); Consultant to National Women's Hospital, Auckland; *b* 24 June 1926; *m* 1954, Dr Cecilia Margaret Ward; two *s* two *d*. *Educ:* Univ. of NZ (MB, ChB, 1949); PhD Univ. of Auckland, 1969. MRCOG 1956; FRCSE 1958; FRACS 1960; FRCOG 1970. Distinguished for his work on the role of foetal hormones in the control of parturition. Hon. FAGS, 1976; Hon. FACOG, 1978. Hon. MD Lund, 1983; Hon. DSc Edinburgh, 1996. Hector Medal, RSNZ, 1980. *Publications:* approx. 200 published papers. *Recreations:* forestry, sailing, fishing. *Address:* 3/38 Awatea Road, Parnell, Auckland 1, New Zealand. *Died 24 Aug. 2010.*

LINDSAY, Rt Rev. Hugh; Bishop of Hexham and Newcastle, (RC), 1974–92; *b* 20 June 1927; *s* of William Stanley Lindsay and Mary Ann Lindsay (*née* Warren). *Educ:* St Cuthbert's Grammar Sch., Newcastle upon Tyne; Ushaw Coll., Durham. Priest 1953; Assistant Priest: St Lawrence's, Newcastle upon Tyne, 1953; St Matthew's, Ponteland, 1954; Asst Diocesan Sec., 1953–59, Diocesan Sec., 1959–69, Hexham and

Newcastle; Chaplain, St Vincent's Home, West Denton, 1959–69; Auxiliary Bishop of Hexham and Newcastle and Titular Bishop of Chester-le-Street, 1969–74. *Recreations:* walking, swimming. *Address:* Boarbank Hall, Grange-over-Sands, Cumbria LA11 7NH. *T:* (015395) 35591. *Died 19 Jan. 2009.*

LINDSAY, Sir James Harvey Kincaid Stewart, Kt 1966; Chairman, Kanbay Resources International (UK) Ltd, 1994–98; *b* 31 May 1915; *s* of Arthur Harvey Lindsay and Doris Kincaid Lindsay; *m* 1948, Vina Roy (marr. diss.); one *s* one *d*; *m* Marguerite Phyllis Boudville. *Educ:* Highgate Sch. Joined Metal Box Co. Ltd, 1934; joined Metal Box Co. of India Ltd, 1937; Man. Dir., 1961; Chm., 1967–69; Dir of Internat. Programmes, Admin. Staff Coll., Henley-on-Thames, 1970–79. Vis. Lectr, Univ. of Buckingham, 1984–89. President: Bengal Chamber of Commerce and Industry; Associated Chambers of Commerce and Industry of India, 1965; Rotary Club of Calcutta, 1965. Director: Indian Oxygen Co., 1966; Westinghouse, Saxby Farmer Ltd, Hindusthan Pilkington, 1966. Pres., Calcutta Management Association, 1964; Pres. (and elected Life Mem., 1984), All India Management Assoc., 1964–69; Mem. of Governing Body: Indian Inst. of Management, Calcutta, 1964; Administrative Staff Coll. of India, 1965; Indian Institutes of Technology, 1966; National Council of Applied Economic Research, 1966; All-India Board of Management Studies, 1964; Indian Inst. of Foreign Trade, 1965; Member: BoT, Central Adv. Council of Industries, Direct Taxes Adv. Cttee, 1966; National Council on Vocational and Allied Trades, 1963. Convener, Internat. Exposition of Rural Develt, 1981–85; Pres., Inst. of Cultural Affairs Internat., Brussels, 1982–89. Trustee, Inst. of Family and Environmental Research, 1971–92. Mem. Council, Inst. of Organizational Mgt, 1988–92. FInstD (Hon. Life Mem., 2005); CCMI (FBIM 1971). *Recreation:* music. *Died 22 April 2007.*

LINDSAY, (John) Maurice, CBE 1979; TD 1946; Consultant, The Scottish Civic Trust, 1983–2002, then Hon. Trustee (Director, 1967–83); *b* 21 July 1918; *s* of Matthew Lindsay and Eileen Frances Brock; *m* 1946, Aileen Joyce Gordon; one *s* two *d* (and one *d* decd). *Educ:* Glasgow Acad.; Scottish National Acad. of Music (later Royal Scottish Acad. of Music, Glasgow). Drama Critic, Scottish Daily Mail, Edinburgh, 1946–47; Music Critic, The Bulletin, Glasgow, 1946–60; Prog. Controller, 1961–62, Prodn Controller, 1962–64, and Features Exec. and Chief Interviewer, 1964–67, Border Television, Carlisle. Mem., Historic Buildings Council for Scotland, 1976–87; Pres., Assoc. for Scottish Literary Studies, 1988–91; Trustee: National Heritage Meml Fund, 1980–84; New Lanark Conservation Trust, 1987–94; Hon. Vice-Pres., Scottish Envmtl Educn Council, 1984–86; Hon. Sec.-Gen., Europa Nostra, 1983–91. Hon. Gov., Glasgow Acad., 2003. Hon. FRIAS 1985. Hon. DLitt Glasgow, 1982. Atlantic Rockefeller Award, 1946. Editor: Scots Review, 1949–50; The Scottish Review, 1975–85. *Publications: poetry:* The Advancing Day, 1940; Perhaps To-morrow, 1941; Predicament, 1942; No Crown for Laughter: Poems, 1943; The Enemies of Love: Poems 1941–1945, 1946; Selected Poems, 1947; Hurlygush: Poems in Scots, 1948; At the Wood's Edge, 1950; Ode for St Andrews Night and Other Poems, 1951; The Exiled Heart: Poems 1941–1956, 1957; Snow Warning and Other Poems, 1962; One Later Day and Other Poems, 1964; This Business of Living, 1969; Comings and Goings: Poems, 1971; Selected Poems 1942–1972, 1973; The Run from Life, 1975; Walking Without an Overcoat, Poems 1972–76, 1977; Collected Poems, 1979; A Net to Catch the Winds and Other Poems, 1981; The French Mosquitoes' Woman and Other Diversions and Poems, 1985; Requiem for a Sexual Athlete and Other Poems and Diversions, 1988; Collected Poems 1940–1990, 1990; On the Face of It: Collected Poems, vol. 2, 1993; News of the World: last poems, 1995; Speaking Likenesses: a postscript, 1997; Worlds Apart, 2000;

Looking Up Where Heaven Isn't, 2004; *prose:* A Pocket Guide to Scottish Culture, 1947; The Scottish Renaissance, 1949; The Lowlands of Scotland: Glasgow and the North, 1953, 3rd edn 1979; Robert Burns: The Man, His Work, The Legend, 3rd edn 1980; Dunoon: The Gem of the Clyde Coast, 1954; The Lowlands of Scotland: Edinburgh and the South, 1956, 3rd edn 1979; Clyde Waters: Variations and Diversions on a Theme of Pleasure, 1958; The Burns Encyclopedia, 1959, 4th edn 1995; Killochan Castle, 1960; By Yon Bonnie Banks: A Gallimaufry, 1961; Environment: A Basic Human Right, 1968; Portrait of Glasgow, 1972, rev. edn 1981; Robin Philipson, 1977; History of Scottish Literature, 1977, rev. edn 1992; Lowland Scottish Villages, 1980; Francis George Scott and the Scottish Renaissance, 1980; (with Anthony F. Kersting) The Buildings of Edinburgh, 1981, 2nd edn 1987; Thank You For Having Me: a personal memoir, 1983; (with Dennis Hardley) Unknown Scotland, 1984; The Castles of Scotland, 1986, rev. edn 1994; Count All Men Mortal—A History of Scottish Provident 1837–1987, 1987; Victorian and Edwardian Glasgow, 1987; Glasgow 1837, 1989; (with David Bruce) Edinburgh Past and Present, 1990; (with Joyce Lindsay) Chambers Guide to Good Scottish Gardens, 1995; Glasgow: fabric of a city, 2004; *editor:* Poetry Scotland One, Two, Three, 1943, 1945, 1946, (with Hugh MacDiarmid) Scottish Poetry Four, 1949; Sailing Tomorrow's Seas: An Anthology of New Poems, 1944; Modern Scottish Poetry: An Anthology of the Scottish Renaissance 1920–1945, 1946, 4th edn 1986; (with Fred Urquhart) No Scottish Twilight: New Scottish Stories, 1947; Selected Poems of Sir Alexander Gray, 1948; Poems, by Sir David Lyndsay, 1948; (with Hugh MacDiarmid) Poetry Scotland Four, 1949; (with Helen Cruickshank) Selected Poems of Marion Angus, 1950; John Davidson: A Selection of His Poems, 1961; (with Edwin Morgan and George Bruce) Scottish Poetry One to Six 1966–72; (with Alexander Scott and Roderick Watson) Scottish Poetry Seven to Nine, 1974, 1976, 1977; (with R. L. Mackie) A Book of Scottish Verse, 1967, 3rd edn 1983; The Discovery of Scotland: Based on Accounts of Foreign Travellers from the 13th to the 18th centuries, 1964, 2nd edn 1979; The Eye is Delighted: Some Romantic Travellers in Scotland, 1970; Scotland: An Anthology, 1974, 2nd edn 1989; As I Remember, 1979; Scottish Comic Verse 1425–1980, 1980; (with Alexander Scott) The Comic Poems of William Tennant, 1990; Thomas Hamilton, The Youth and Manhood of Cyril Thornton, 1991; (with Lesley Duncan) The Edinburgh Book of 20th Century Scottish Poetry, 2005; with Joyce Lindsay: The Scottish Dog, 1989; The Scottish Quotation Book, 1991; A Pleasure of Gardens, 1991; The Music Quotation Book, 1992; The Theatre and Opera Lovers' Quotation Book, 1993; A Mini-Guide to Scottish Gardens, 1994; The Robert Burns Quotation Book, 1994. *Recreations:* enjoying and adding to compact disc collection, cooking. *Address:* Park House, 104 Dumbarton Road, Bowling, Dunbartonshire G60 5BB. *T:* (01389) 606662. *Died 30 April 2009.*

LINE, Maurice Bernard, FCLIP; Director General (Science, Technology and Industry), British Library, 1985–88 (Deputy Director General, 1973–74, Director General, 1974–85, Lending Division); *b* 21 June 1928; *s* of Bernard Cyril and Ruth Florence Line; *m* 1954, Joyce Gilchrist; one *s* one *d*. *Educ:* Bedford Sch.; Exeter Coll., Oxford (MA). Library Trainee, Bodleian Library, 1950–51; Library Asst, Glasgow Univ., 1951–53; Sub-Librarian, Southampton Univ., 1954–65; Dep. Librarian, Univ. of Newcastle upon Tyne, 1965–68; Librarian: Univ. of Bath, 1968–71; Nat. Central Library, 1971–73; Project Head, DES Nat. Libraries ADP Study, 1970–71. Prof. Associate, Sheffield Univ., 1977–; External Prof., Loughborough Univ., 1986–92. Member: Library Adv. Council for England, 1972–75; British Library Board, 1974–88; Pres., Library Assoc., 1990. Editor, Alexandria, 1988–2002; Gen. Editor, Librarianship and Information Work Worldwide, 1990–2000. Mem. Bd of Dirs, Engineering Information Inc., 1990–98. Fellow, Birmingham Polytech., 1992. CCMI. Hon. DLitt Heriot

Watt, 1980; Hon. DSc Southampton, 1988. *Publications:* A Bibliography of Russian Literature in English Translation to 1900, 1963; Library Surveys, 1967, 2nd edn 1982; (ed jtly) Essays on Information and Libraries, 1975; (ed with Joyce Line) National Libraries, 1979; (jtly) Universal Availability of Publications, 1983; (jtly) Improving the Availability of Publications, 1984; (ed) The World of Books and Information, 1987; (ed with Joyce Line) National Libraries II, 1987; (jtly) The Impact of New Technology on Document Availability and Access, 1988; Line on Interlending, 1988; A Little Off Line, 1988; (ed) Academic Library Management, 1990; (ed with Joyce Line) National Libraries III, 1995; contribs to: Jl of Documentation; Aslib Proc.; Jl of Librarianship and Information Science, etc. *Recreations:* music, walking, other people. *Address:* 10 Blackthorn Lane, Burn Bridge, Harrogate, North Yorks HG3 1NZ. *T:* (01423) 872984.
Died 21 Sept. 2010.

LINKIE, William Sinclair, CBE 1989; Controller, Inland Revenue (Scotland), 1983–90; *b* 9 March 1931; *s* of late Peter Linkie and Janet Black Linkie (*née* Sinclair; she *m* 2nd, John McBryde); *m* 1955, Elizabeth Primrose Marion Reid (*d* 2003); one *s* one *d. Educ:* George Heriot's Sch., Edinburgh. Dept of Agriculture and Fisheries for Scotland, 1948; Inland Revenue (Scotland), 1952–90; HM Inspector of Taxes, 1961; Dist Inspector, Edinburgh 6, 1964; Principal Inspector i/c Centre 1, 1975; Dist Inspector, Edinburgh 5, 1982. Pres., Inland Revenue Sports Assoc. (Scotland), 1983–90. Elder, Church of Scotland. *Recreations:* art, theatre, travel.
Died 22 Jan. 2010.

LINNELL, David George Thomas, CBE 1987; Chairman, 1993–96, Deputy Chairman, 1996–98, Hiscox Dedicated Insurance Fund plc, later Hiscox plc; *b* 28 May 1930; *s* of George and Marguerite Linnell; *m* 1953, Margaret Mary Paterson; one *s* one *d. Educ:* Leighton Park School, Reading. Managing Dir, Thomas Linnell & Sons, 1964–75; Chief Exec., Linfood Holdings, 1975–79; Chm., Spar Food Holdings, 1975–81; Chm., Eggs Authority, 1981–86; Chairman: Neighbourhood Stores, 1983–87; Birkdale Group, 1987–95; Kendell, 1994–97. Pres., Inst. of Grocery Distribution, 1980–82. Gov., St Andrew's Hosp., Northampton, 1992–2007. *Address:* The Old Rectory, Titchmarsh, Kettering, Northants NN14 3DG.
Died 20 Nov. 2010.

LIPSTEIN, Prof. Kurt; Professor of Comparative Law, Cambridge University, 1973–76; Fellow of Clare College, Cambridge, since 1956; *b* 19 March 1909; *e s* of Alfred Lipstein, MD and Hilda (*née* Sulzbach); *m* 1944, Gwyneth Mary Herford (*d* 1998); two *d. Educ:* Goethe Gymnasium, Frankfurt on Main; Univs of Grenoble and Berlin; Trinity Coll., Cambridge. Gerichtsreferendar 1931; PhD Cantab 1936; LLD 1977. Called to Bar, Middle Temple, 1950, Hon. Bencher, 1966. Univ. Lectr, Cambridge, 1946; Reader in Conflict of Laws, Cambridge Univ., 1962–73. Dir of Research, Internat. Assoc. Legal Science, 1954–59. Vis. Professor: Univ. of Pennsylvania, 1962; Northwestern Univ., Chicago, 1966, 1968; Paris I, 1977. Mem., Inst. de Droit Internat., 1999. Hon. QC 1998. Hon. Fellow, Wolfson Coll., Cambridge, 2000. Hon. Dr jur. Würzburg, 1995. Humboldt Prize, Alexander von Humboldt Stiftung, Bonn, 1981. *Publications:* The Law of the EEC, 1974; Principles of the Conflict of Laws, National and International, 1981; joint editor and contributor: Dicey's Conflict of Laws, 6th edn, 1948—8th edn, 1967; Leske-Loewenfeld, Das Eherecht der europäischen Staaten, 1963; (ed) International Encyclopaedia of Comparative Law, vol. Private International Law, 1972; Harmonization of Private International Law by the EEC, 1978; contrib. English and foreign legal periodicals. *Address:* Clare College, Cambridge CB2 1TL. *T:* (01223) 333200; 7 Barton Close, Cambridge CB3 9LQ. *T:* (01223) 357048; Maitland Chambers, 7 Stone Buildings, Lincoln's Inn, WC2A 3ST. *T:* (020) 7406 1200.
Died 2 Dec. 2006.

LIPTON, Prof. Peter, DPhil; Professor of the History and Philosophy of Science, since 1997, and Fellow of King's College, since 1994, Cambridge University; *b* NYC, 9 Oct. 1954; *s* of Louis Lipton and Lini Lipton (*née* Strauss); *m* 1984, Diana Warner; two *s. Educ:* Fieldston Sch., NY; Wesleyan Univ., Connecticut (BA 1976); New Coll., Oxford (BPhil 1978; DPhil 1985). Asst Res. Prof., Clark Univ., Mass, 1982–85; Asst Prof., Williams Coll., Mass, 1985–91; Univ. Asst Lectr, 1991–94, Univ. Lectr, 1994–97, Cambridge Univ. Mem., Nuffield Council on Bioethics, 2003–. FMedSci 2006. *Publications:* Inference to the Best Explanation, 1991, 2nd edn 2004; (ed) Theory, Evidence and Explanation, 1995; contribs to philosophical jls. *Recreation:* pilpul. *Address:* King's College, Cambridge CB2 1ST; *e-mail:* peter.lipton@kings.cam.ac.uk.
Died 25 Nov. 2007.

LISTER, Very Rev. John Field, MA; Provost of Wakefield, 1972–82; *b* 19 Jan. 1916; *s* of Arthur and Florence Lister. *Educ:* King's Sch., Worcester; Keble Coll., Oxford; Cuddesdon Coll., Oxford. Ordained deacon, 1939, priest, 1941; Asst Curate, St Nicholas, Radford, Coventry, 1939–44; Asst Curate, St John Baptist, Coventry, 1944–45; Vicar of St John's, Huddersfield, 1945–54; Vicar of Brighouse, 1954–72; Asst Rural Dean of Halifax, 1955–61; Archdeacon of Halifax, 1961–72; RD of Wakefield, 1972–80. Examng Chaplain to Bishop of Wakefield, 1972–78 Hon. Canon of Wakefield Cathedral, 1961, Canon, 1968. Chaplain to The Queen, 1966–72. *Address:* College of St Barnabas, Blackberry Lane, Lingfield, Surrey RH7 6NJ.
Died 23 Aug. 2006.

LITTLE, John Philip Brooke B.; *see* Brooke-Little.

LITTLE, Most Rev. Thomas Francis, KBE 1977; DD, STD; Archbishop of Melbourne (RC), 1974–96; *b* 30 Nov. 1925; *s* of Gerald Thompson Little and Kathleen McCormack. *Educ:* St Patrick's Coll., Ballarat; Corpus Christi Coll., Werribee; Pontifical Urban Univ., Rome. STD Rome, 1953. Priest 1950; Asst Priest, Carlton, 1953–55; Secretary, Apostolic Deleg. to Aust., NZ and Oceania, 1955–59; Asst Priest, St Patrick's Cathedral, Melbourne, 1959–65; Dean, 1965–70; Episcopal Vicar for Lay Apostolate, 1969–74; Pastor, St Ambrose, Brunswick, 1971–73; Auxiliary Bishop, Archdiocese of Melbourne, 1973. STD *hc*, Melbourne Coll. of Divinity, 1992; DU Australian Catholic Univ., 1997. OM (Poland), 1999. *Address:* 21 Trafalgar Road, Camberwell, Vic 3124, Australia. *T:* (3) 98130291, *Fax:* (3) 98130296.
Died 7 April 2008.

LITTLEJOHN, William Hunter, RSA 1973 (ARSA 1966); Head of Fine Art Department, 1982–85, Head of Drawing and Painting Department, 1970–85, Gray's School of Art, Aberdeen, (Lecturer, 1966–70); *b* Arbroath, 16 April 1929; *s* of late William Littlejohn and Alice Morton King. *Educ:* Arbroath High Sch.; Dundee Coll. of Art (DA). National Service, RAF, 1951–53; taught Art at Arbroath High Sch. until 1966. *One man exhibitions:* The Scottish Gallery, Edinburgh, 1962, 1967, 1972, 1977, 1984, 1989; Bohun Gall., Henley-on-Thames, 1991. Exhibits in RA, RSA, SSA, etc. *Address:* 43 Viewfield Road, Arbroath, Angus, Scotland DD11 2DW. *T:* (01241) 874402.
Died 5 Sept. 2006.

LITTLER, Sir (James) Geoffrey, KCB 1985 (CB 1981); Director, Montanaro UK Smaller Companies Investment Trust plc, 1995–2000; *b* 18 May 1930; *s* of late James Edward Littler and Evelyn Mary Littler (*née* Taylor); *m* 1958, Shirley Marsh (*d* 2009); one *s. Educ:* Manchester Grammar Sch.; Corpus Christi Coll., Cambridge (MA; Hon. Fellow, 1994). Asst Principal, Colonial Office, 1952–54; transf. to Treasury, 1954; Principal 1957; Asst Sec. 1966; Under-Sec. 1972; Dep. Sec., 1977; Second Permanent Sec. (Overseas Finance), 1983–88. Chairman: EC Monetary Cttee Deputies, 1974–77; Working Party 3, OECD, 1985–88; EC Monetary Cttee, 1987–88. Chairman: TR European Growth Trust plc, 1990–98; County NatWest Group Ltd, 1991–92; Director: NatWest Investment Bank, 1989–91; National

Westminster Bank PLC, 1991–92; Chm., Israel Fund plc, 1994–99; Dir, Maritime Transport Services Ltd, 1990–93; Sen. Advr, BZW Ltd, 1993–98. *Recreation:* music. *Club:* Reform.   *Died 15 June 2010.*

LITTLER, Shirley, (Lady Littler); Chairman, Gaming Board for Great Britain, 1992–98; *b* 8 June 1932; *d* of late Sir Percy William Marsh, CSI, CIE, and Joan Mary Beecroft; *m* 1958, Sir (James) Geoffrey Littler, KCB; one *s*. *Educ:* Headington Sch., Oxford; Girton Coll., Cambridge (MA; Barbara Bodichon Fellow, 2005). Assistant Principal, HM Treasury, 1953; Principal: HM Treasury, 1960; Dept of Trade and Industry, 1964; HM Treasury, 1966; Asst Secretary, National Board for Prices and Incomes, 1969; Secretary, V&G Tribunal, 1971; transf. to Home Office, 1972, Asst Under-Sec. of State, 1978–83. Joined IBA, 1983; Dep. Dir Gen., 1986–89; Dir Gen., 1990. Chm., Gaming Regulators Eur. Forum, 1996–98. Chm., Nat. Adv. Body for Health Depts' Confidential Enquiry into Stillbirths and Deaths in Infancy, 1992–99. Trustee, Police Foundn, 1992–2001. *Recreations:* history, reading.   *Died 28 March 2009.*

LIVERMAN, John Gordon, CB 1973; OBE 1956; Deputy Secretary, Department of Energy, 1974–80; *b* London, 21 Oct. 1920; *s* of late George Gordon Liverman and Hadassah Liverman; *m* 1952, Peggy Earl; two *s* one *d*. *Educ:* St Paul's Sch.; Trinity Coll., Cambridge (MA). Served with RA, 1940–46. Civil servant in various government departments, 1947–80. *Address:* 12 The Stream Edge, Fisher Row, Oxford OX1 1HT. *T:* (01865) 725004.   *Died 10 Jan. 2009.*

LIVSEY OF TALGARTH, Baron *cr* 2001 (Life Peer), of Talgarth in the County of Powys; **Richard Arthur Lloyd Livsey,** CBE 1994; DL; *b* 2 May 1935; *s* of Arthur Norman Livsey and Lilian Maisie (*née* James); *m* 1964, Irene Martin Earsman; two *s* one *d*. *Educ:* Talgarth County Primary Sch.; Bedales Sch.; Seale-Hayne Agricl Coll.; Reading Univ. (MSc Agric.). Develt Officer, Agric. Div., ICI, 1961–67; Farm Manager, Blairdrummond, 1967–71; farmer at Llanon; Sen. Lectr in Farm Management, Welsh Agricl Coll., Aberystwyth, 1971–85; Develt Manager, ATB Landbase Wales, 1992–95. Joined Liberal Party, 1960; contested (L): Perth and E Perth, 1970; Pembroke, 1979; Brecon and Radnor, 1983; MP (L July 1985–1988, Lib Dem 1988–92) Brecon and Radnor; MP (Lib Dem) Brecon and Radnorshire, 1997–2001. Liberal Party spokesman on agric., 1985–87; Alliance spokesman on the countryside and on agric. in Wales, and on Wales, 1987; Leader, Welsh Liberal Democrats and Party Spokesman on Wales, 1988–92 and 1997–2001; Lib Dem spokesman in H of L on agric. and rural affairs, 2002–06, on Wales, 2004–. Mem., EU Select Cttee (D) on Agric. and the Envmt, H of L, 2002–06. Pres., Wales European Movt, 2003–06. Mem. Bd, Prime Cymru; Trustee, CPRW. Chm., Brecon Jazz Fest., 1993–96; Mem., Talgarth Male Voice Choir, 1993–; President: Brecon and Dist Disabled Club, 1986–; Brecknock Fedn of Young Farmers' Clubs, 2003–; Talgarth CC, 2005–; Keith Morris Fund; Vice-Pres., Cor Meibion Ystradgynlais, 2005–. Associate, BVA, 2005. DL Powys, 2004. *Recreations:* cricket, fishing. *Address:* House of Lords, SW1A 0PW.   *Died 15 Sept. 2010.*

LLEWELLYN, Sir David St Vincent, (Sir Dai), 4th Bt *cr* 1922, of Bwllfa, Aberdare, co. Glamorgan; impresario, writer and broadcaster; *b* 2 April 1946; *er s* of Sir Harry Llewellyn, 3rd Bt, CBE and Hon. Christine Saumarez, 2nd *d* of 5th Baron de Saumarez; *S* father, 1999; *m* 1980, Vanessa Mary Theresa Hubbard (marr. diss. 1987); two *d*. *Educ:* Eton; Univ. d'Aix-Marseille. Presenter, Cordially Invited, US TV show, 2002. Chevalier, l'Ordre des Côteaux de Champagne, 1992. KLJ 2000 (CLJ 1995). *Recreations:* equestrian sports, wildlife conservation. *Heir:* b Roderic Victor Llewellyn [*b* 9 Oct. 1947; *m* 1981, Tatiana Manora Caroline Soskin; three *d*]. *Address:* Studio Two, 2 Lansdowne Row, W1J 6HL. *T:* (020) 7413 9533.   *Died 13 Jan. 2009.*

LLOYD OF HIGHBURY, Baroness *cr* 1996 (Life Peer), of Highbury in the London Borough of Islington; **June Kathleen Lloyd,** DBE 1990; FRCP, FRCPE, FRCGP; Nuffield Professor of Child Health, British Postgraduate Medical Federation, London University, 1985–92, then Emeritus Professor; *b* 1 Jan. 1928; *d* of Arthur Cresswell Lloyd and Lucy Bevan Lloyd. *Educ:* Royal School, Bath; Bristol Univ. (MD); Durham Univ. (DPH). FRCP 1969; FRCPE 1989; FRCGP 1990. Junior Hosp. appts, Bristol, Oxford and Newcastle, 1951–57; Res. Fellow and Lectr in Child Health, Univ. of Birmingham, 1958–65; Sen. Lectr, Reader in Paediatrics, Inst. of Child Health, 1965–73; Prof. of Paediatrics, London Univ., 1973–75; Prof. of Child Health, St George's Hosp. Med. Sch., London Univ., 1975–85. Vis. Examr in Paediatrics in Univs in UK and abroad. Scientific Advr, AMRC, 1990–95. Chm., DoH Adv. Cttee on Gene Therapy, 1990–95; Member: Council, RCP, 1982–85, 1986–88 (Paediatric Vice Pres., 1992–95); MRC, 1984–88; ABRC, 1989–90. Pres., British Paediatric Assoc., 1988–91; Mem., Finnish, French, Swiss, German, Amer. and Sri Lankan Paediatric Assocs; Hon. Mem., Paediatric Res. Soc. of Australia. Hon. DSc: Bristol, 1991; Birmingham, 1993. *Publications:* research articles, reviews and leading articles in sci. jls. *Recreations:* cooking, gardening, walking. *Address:* Chilton House, Chilton, Aylesbury HP18 9SX.   *Died 28 June 2006.*

LLOYD, Dr Brian Beynon, CBE 1983; Director, International Nutrition Foundation, 1990–95; Chairman of Directors, Oxford Gallery, 1967–97; Chairman, Trumedia Study Oxford Ltd, since 1985; *b* 23 Sept. 1920; *s* of David John Lloyd, MA Oxon and Olwen (*née* Beynon); *m* 1949, Reinhild Johanna Engeroff; four *s* three *d* (incl. twin *s* and twin *d*). *Educ:* Newport High Sch.; Winchester Coll. (Schol.); Balliol Coll., Oxford (Domus and Frazer Schol.; Special Certif. for BA (War) Degree in Chem., 1941; took degrees BA and MA, 1946; Theodore Williams Schol. and cl. I in Physiology, 1948); DSc Oxon 1969. Joined Oxford Nutrition Survey after registration as conscientious objector, 1941; Pres., Jun. Common Room, Balliol Coll., 1941–42; Chm., Oxford Univ. Undergraduate Rep. Council, 1942; Biochemist: SHAEF Nutrition Survey Team, Leiden, 1945; Nutrition Survey Group, Düsseldorf, 1946. Fellow of Magdalen by exam. in Physiology, 1948–52, by special election, 1952–70; Senior Tutor, 1963–64; Vice-Pres., 1967 and 1968; Emeritus Fellow, 1970–; Chemist, Laboratory of Human Nutrition, later Univ. Lectr in Physiology, Univ. of Oxford, 1948–70; Senior Proctor, 1960–61; Dir, Oxford Polytechnic, 1970–79 (Hon. Fellow, 1991; opened Lloyd Bldg, 1984). Chairman: CNAA Health and Med. Services Bd, 1975–80; Health Educn Council, 1979–82 (Mem., 1975–82); Mem., Adv. Council on Misuse of Drugs, 1978–81. Vis. Physiologist, New York, 1963. Pres., Section I, 1964–65, Section X, 1980, British Assoc. for the Advancement of Science. Chm. of Govs, Oxford Coll. of Technology, 1963–69. Chairman: Oxford-Bonn Soc., 1973–81; Oxford Management Club, 1979–80; Pullen's Lane Assoc., 1985–95; Pres., Oxford Polytechnic Assoc., 1984–90 (Hon. Mem., 1992). *Publications:* Gas Analysis Apparatus, 1960; (jt ed) The Regulation of Human Respiration, 1962; Cerebrospinal Fluid and the Regulation of Respiration, 1965; (jt ed) Sinclair (biog.), 1990; articles in physiological and biochemical jls. *Recreations:* Klavarskribo, Correggio, round tables, the analysis of athletic records, slide rules, ready reckoners, soldering irons, home computing, collecting pictures. *Address:* High Wall, Pullen's Lane, Oxford OX3 0BX. *T:* (01865) 763353.
                                                      Died 28 June 2010.

LLOYD, Christopher, OBE 2000; VMH 1979; writer on horticulture; regular gardening correspondent, Country Life, since 1963; *b* 2 March 1921; *s* of late Nathaniel Lloyd and Daisy (*née* Field). *Educ:* Wellesley House, Broadstairs, Kent; Rugby Sch.; King's Coll., Cambridge (MA Mod Langs); Wye Coll., Univ of London (BSc Hort.). Asst Lectr in Decorative Horticulture, Wye Coll., 1950–54. Then returned to family home at Great Dixter

and started Nursery in clematis and uncommon plants. DUniv Open, 1996. *Publications:* The Mixed Border, 1957; Clematis, 1965, rev. edn (with Tom Bennett), 1989; Shrubs and Trees for Small Gardens, 1965; Hardy Perennials, 1967; Gardening on Chalk and Lime, 1969; The Well-Tempered Garden, 1970, rev. edn 2001; Foliage Plants, 1973, rev. edn 1985; The Adventurous Gardener, 1983; The Well-Chosen Garden, 1984; The Year at Great Dixter, 1987; (with Richard Bird) The Cottage Garden, 1990; (with Graham Rice) Garden Flowers from Seed, 1991; Christopher Lloyd's Flower Garden, 1993; In My Garden, 1993; Other People's Gardens, 1995; Gardener Cook, 1997; (with Beth Chatto) Dear Friend and Gardener, 1998; Christopher Lloyd's Gardening Year, 1999; Lloyd's Garden Flowers, 2000; Colour for Adventurous Gardeners, 2001; Meadows, 2004; Succession Planting for Adventurous Gardeners, 2005; regular gardening contributor to The Guardian, Country Life. *Recreations:* walking, entertaining and cooking for friends. *Address:* Great Dixter, Northiam, Rye, East Sussex TN31 6PH. *T:* (01797) 253107.
Died 27 Jan. 2006.

LLOYD, David Graham, PhD; FRS 1992; FRSNZ; Professor of Plant Science, University of Canterbury, Christchurch, New Zealand, 1986–93, then Emeritus; *b* 20 June 1937; *m* 1st, 1973, Jacqueline Mary Renouf (marr. diss. 1985); two adopted *s* one adopted *d*; 2nd, 1994, Linda Eileen Newstrom. *Educ:* Univ. of Canterbury, NZ (BSc 1st Cl. Hons 1959); Harvard Univ. (PhD 1964). University of Canterbury: Postdoctorate Fellow, 1964–67; Lectr, 1967–71; Sen. Lectr, 1971–75; Reader, 1975–86. FRSNZ 1984. Foreign Mem., Amer. Acad. of Arts and Scis, 1993. *Publications:* (ed jtly) Floral Biology, 1996; numerous res. papers. *Recreation:* reading.
Died 30 May 2006.

LLOYD, (George) Peter, CMG 1965; CVO 1983; Governor, Cayman Islands, 1982–87, retired; *b* 23 Sept. 1926; *er s* of late Sir Thomas Ingram Kynaston Lloyd, GCMG, KCB; *m* 1957, Margaret Harvey; two *s* one *d*. *Educ:* Stowe Sch.; King's Coll., Cambridge. Lieut, KRRC, 1945–48; ADC to Governor of Kenya, 1948; Cambridge, 1948–51 (MA; athletics blue); District Officer, Kenya, 1951–60; Principal, Colonial Office, 1960–61; Colonial Secretary, Seychelles, 1961–66; Chief Sec., Fiji, 1966–70; Defence Sec., Hong Kong, 1971–74; Dep. Governor, Bermuda, 1974–81. Chm., Bermuda Fest., 1987–99; Trustee, Bermuda Maritime Mus., 1987–97. *Address:* 5 The Wharf, 1 Harbour Road, Paget PG01, Bermuda.
Died 18 June 2007.

LLOYD, Sir Ian (Stewart), Kt 1986; *b* 30 May 1921; *s* of late Walter John Lloyd and Euphemia Craig Lloyd; *m* 1951, Frances Dorward Addison, *d* of late Hon. W. Addison, CMG, OBE, MC, DCM; three *s*. *Educ:* Michaelhouse; University of the Witwatersrand; King's Coll., Cambridge (President, Cambridge Union, and Leader, Cambridge tour of USA, 1947; MA 1951; MSc 1952). Served War of 1939–45, Flying Instructor, then No 7 Sqdn, SAAF; RAFVR (Cambridge Univ. Air Sqdn), 1945–49. Econ. Adviser, Central Mining and Investment Corporation, 1949–52; Member, SA Board of Trade and Industries, 1952–55; Director, Acton Soc. Trust, 1956; Dir of Res., 1956–64, Economic Advr, 1956–83, British and Commonwealth Shipping. Chairman, UK Cttee and Vice-Chairman, International Exec., International Cargo Handling Co-ordination Assoc., 1961–64. MP (C): Portsmouth, Langstone, 1964–74; Havant and Waterloo, 1974–83; Havant, 1983–92. Chairman: Cons. Parly Shipping and Shipbuilding Cttee, 1974–77; Select Cttee on Sci. Sub-Cttee, 1975–77; Select Cttee on Sci. Sub-Cttee on Technological Innovation, 1977–79; Select Cttee on Energy, 1979–89; All-Party Cttee on Information Technology, 1979–87; Pres., Parly and Scientific Cttee, 1990–92 (Vice-Pres., 1983–87; Vice-Chm., 1988–90); Chm. Bd, Parly Office of Science and Technology. Member, UK Delegation, Council of Europe, Western European Union, 1968–72; UK rep., Internat. Parly

Conf., Bucharest, 1975; Leader: UK Delegn, OECD Conf. on Energy, 1981; Parly and Scientific Cttee delegn to China, 1991. Member of Council: Save British Sci., 1992; Sci. Policy Support Gp, 1992–2000 (Chm., 2000–02). Trustee: Kasanka Trust, 1986–96; New Era Schs Trust, 1990–97. *Publications:* Rolls-Royce, 3 vols, 1978; contribs to various journals on economics, politics and information technology. *Recreations:* genealogy, good music. *Clubs:* Army and Navy, Royal Yacht Squadron.
Died 26 Sept. 2006.

LLOYD, Peter; *see* Lloyd, G. P.

LLOYD, Peter Gordon, CBE 1976 (OBE 1965); British Council Representative, Greece, 1976–80; *b* 20 Feb. 1920; *s* of Peter Gleave Lloyd and Ellen Swift; *m* 1952, Edith Florence (*née* Flurey) (*d* 2005); two *s* one *d*. *Educ:* Royal Grammar Sch., Newcastle upon Tyne; Balliol Coll., Oxford (Horsley Exhibnr, 1939; BA, MA 1948). RA (Light Anti-Aircraft), subseq. DLI, 1940–46, Captain. British Council, 1949–80: Brit. Council, Belgium and Hon. Lector in English, Brussels Univ., 1949–52; Reg. Dir, Mbale, Uganda, 1952–56; Dep. Dir Personnel, 1956–60; Representative: Ethiopia, 1960–68; Poland, 1969–72; Nigeria, 1972–76. *Publications:* (introd) Huysmans, A Rebours, 1946; The Story of British Democracy, 1959; Perspectives and Identities, 1989; Destinations Over Water, 2005; critical essays on literature in periodicals. *Recreations:* literature, music. *Address:* 111 Sussex Road, Petersfield, Hants GU31 4LB. *T:* (01730) 262007. *Club:* Oxford and Cambridge.
Died 22 Sept. 2010.

LLOYD GEORGE OF DWYFOR, 3rd Earl *cr* 1945; **Owen Lloyd George;** DL; Viscount Gwynedd, 1945; *b* 28 April 1924; *s* of 2nd Earl Lloyd George of Dwyfor, and Roberta Ida Freeman, 5th *d* of Sir Robert McAlpine, 1st Bt; *S* father, 1968; *m* 1st, 1949, Ruth Margaret (marr. diss. 1982; she *d* 2003), *o d* of Richard Coit; two *s* one *d*; 2nd, 1982, Cecily Josephine, *d* of late Sir Alexander Gordon Cumming, 5th Bt, MC, and of Elizabeth Countess Cawdor, *widow* of 2nd Earl of Woolton and former wife of 3rd Baron Forres. *Educ:* Oundle. Welsh Guards, 1942–47. Italian Campaign, 1944–45. Formerly Captain Welsh Guards. Carried the Sword at Investiture of HRH the Prince of Wales, Caernarvon Castle, 1969. Mem., Historic Buildings Council for Wales, 1971–94. DL Dyfed 1993. *Publications:* A Tale of Two Grandfathers, 1999. *Recreations:* shooting, gardening. *Heir:* *s* Viscount Gwynedd, *b* 22 Jan. 1951. *Address:* Ffynone, Boncath, Pembrokeshire SA37 0HQ; 47 Burton Court, SW3 4SZ. *Clubs:* White's, Pratt's.
Died 29 July 2010.

LLOYD-HUGHES, Sir Trevor Denby, Kt 1970; former consultant in Government/industry relations; Chairman, Lloyd-Hughes Associates Ltd, International Consultants in Public Affairs, 1970–89; *b* 31 March 1922; *er s* of late Elwyn and Lucy Lloyd-Hughes, Bradford, Yorks; *m* 1st, 1950, Ethel Marguerite Durward (marr. diss. 1971), *o d* of late J. Ritchie, Dundee and Bradford; one *s* one *d*; 2nd, 1971, Marie-Jeanne, *d* of late Marcel and Helene Moreillon, Geneva; one *d* (one *s* decd, and one adopted *d*, a Thai girl). *Educ:* Woodhouse Grove Sch., Yorks; Jesus Coll., Oxford (MA). Commissioned RA, 1941; served with 75th (Shropshire Yeomanry) Medium Regt, RA, in Western Desert, Sicily and Italy, 1941–45. Asst Inspector of Taxes, 1948; freelance journalist, 1949; joined staff of Liverpool Daily Post, 1949; Political Corresp., Liverpool Echo, 1950, Liverpool Daily Post, 1951. Press Secretary to the Prime Minister, 1964–69; Chief Information Adviser to Govt, 1969–70. Dir, Trinity International Holdings plc (formerly Liverpool Daily Post and Echo Ltd), 1978–91. Member of Circle of Wine Writers, 1961, Chm., 1972–73. *Publications:* The Euro Trap, or Future Choices for Britain, 1999; newspaper and magazine articles on political affairs and on wine. *Recreations:* yoga, reading, listening to classical and Spanish guitar music, contemplation. *Address:* 52 Glen Road, Castle Bytham,

Grantham, Lincs NG33 4RJ. *T:* (01780) 410001, *Fax:* (01780) 410001; *e-mail:* sirtrevorlloyd@aol.com.
Died 15 Feb. 2010.

LLOYD-JACOB, David Oliver, CBE 1984; Director, UK Sponsorships, Mountbatten Internship Programme, 2002–07; *b* 30 March 1938; *s* of Sir George and Lady Lloyd-Jacob; *m* 1st, 1961, Clare Bartlett; two *d*; 2nd, 1982, Carolyn Howard. *Educ:* Westminster; Christ Church, Oxford. Pres., Azcon Corp., USA, 1974–79; Man. Dir, Consolidated Gold Fields plc, 1979–81; Chm., Amcon Group Inc., USA, 1979–82; Chm. and Chief Exec. Officer, Levinson Steel Co., Pittsburgh, 1983–90; Chairman: Butte Mining plc, 1991–2000; Fibaflo Ltd, 1998–2003; Fibagroup Ltd, 2002–03; Kemp Town Enclosures Ltd, 2002–07; Fibaflo Composites Ltd, 2003–04. Chm., Britain Salutes NY, 1981–83. *Recreations:* opera, theatre, restoring old houses. *Address:* 28 Lewes Crescent, Brighton BN2 1GB. *T:* (01273) 692908. *Clubs:* Garrick; Leander (Henley-on-Thames).
Died 6 Aug. 2009.

LLOYD-JONES, Sir (Peter) Hugh (Jefferd), Kt 1989; FBA 1966; Regius Professor of Greek in the University of Oxford and Student of Christ Church, 1960–89, then Emeritus Professor and Emeritus Student; *b* 21 Sept. 1922; *s* of Major W. Lloyd-Jones, DSO, and Norah Leila, *d* of F. H. Jefferd, Brent, Devon; *m* 1st, 1953, Frances Elisabeth Hedley (marr. diss. 1981); two *s* one *d*; 2nd, 1982, Mary Lefkowitz (Andrew W. Mellon Professor Emeritus in the Humanities, Wellesley College, Mass), *d* of Harold and Mena Rosenthal, New York. *Educ:* Lycée Français du Royaume Uni, S Kensington; Westminster Sch.; Christ Church, Oxford. Served War of 1939–45, 2nd Lieut, Intelligence Corps, India, 1942; Temp. Captain, 1944. 1st Cl. Classics (Mods), 1941; MA 1947; 1st Cl., Lit.Hum., 1948; Chancellor's Prize for Latin Prose, 1947; Ireland and Craven Schol., 1947; Fellow of Jesus Coll., Cambridge, 1948–54; Asst Lecturer in Classics, University of Cambridge, 1950–52, Lecturer, 1952–54; Fellow and E. P. Warren Praelector in Classics, Corpus Christi Coll., Oxford, 1954–60; J. H. Gray Lecturer, University of Cambridge, 1961; Visiting Prof., Yale Univ., 1964–65, 1967–68; Sather Prof. of Classical Literature, Univ. of California at Berkeley, 1969–70; Alexander White Vis. Prof., Chicago, 1972; Vis. Prof., Harvard Univ., 1976–77. Fellow, Morse Coll., Yale Univ. Hon. Mem., Greek Humanistic Soc., 1968; Corresponding Member: Acad. of Athens, 1978 (Fellow, 2001); Nordrhein-Westfälische Akad. der Wissenschaften, 1983; Accademia di Archeologia Lettere e Belle Arti, Naples, 1984; Bayerische Akad. der Wissenschaften, 1992; Hon. Foreign Mem., Amer. Acad. of Arts and Scis, 1978; Mem., Amer. Philos. Soc., 1992. Hon. DHL Chicago, 1970; Hon. DPhil: Tel Aviv, 1984; Göttingen, 2002; Hon. PhD Thessalonica, 1999. *Publications:* Appendix to Loeb Classical Library edn of Aeschylus, 1957; Menandri Dyscolus (Oxford Classical Text), 1960; (trans.) Paul Maas, Greek Metre, 1962; (ed) The Greeks, 1962; Tacitus (in series The Great Historians), 1964; (trans.) Aeschylus: Agamemnon, The Libation-Bearers, and The Eumenides, 1970, 2nd edn 1979; The Justice of Zeus, 1971, 2nd edn 1983; (ed) Maurice Bowra, 1974; Females of the Species: Semonides of Amorgos on Women, 1975; (with Marcelle Quinton) Myths of the Zodiac, 1978; (with Marcelle Quinton) Imaginary Animals (US edn as Mythical Beasts), 1979; Blood for the Ghosts, 1982; Classical Survivals, 1982; (with P. J. Parsons) Supplementum Hellenisticum, 1983; (with N. G. Wilson) Sophoclis Fabulae, 1990; (with N. G. Wilson) Sophoclea, 1990; Academic Papers, vols 1 and 2, 1990, vol. 3, 2005; Greek in a Cold Climate, 1991; Sophocles I–II, 1994; Sophocles III, 1996; (with N. G. Wilson) Sophocles: second thoughts, 1997; Supplementum Supplementi Hellenistici, 2005; contribs to periodicals. *Recreations:* cats, remembering past cricket. *Address:* 15 West Riding, Wellesley, MA 02482, USA. *T:* (781) 2372212, *Fax:* (781) 2372246; Christ Church, Oxford OX1 1DP. *T:* (01865) 791063. *Club:* Oxford and Cambridge.
Died 5 Oct. 2009.

LLOYD-NEWSTROM, David Graham; *see* Lloyd, D. G.

LOANE, Most Rev. Marcus Lawrence, KBE 1976; *b* 14 Oct. 1911; *s* of K. O. A. Loane; *m* 1937, Patricia Evelyn Jane Simpson Knox; two *s* two *d*. *Educ:* The King's School, Parramatta, NSW; Sydney University (MA). Moore Theological College, 1932–33; Australian College of Theology (ThL, 1st Class, 1933; Fellow, 1955). Ordained deacon, 1935, priest, 1936; Resident Tutor and Chaplain, Moore Theological College, 1935–38; Vice-Principal, 1939–53; Principal, 1954–59. Chaplain AIF, 1942–44. Canon, St Andrew's Cathedral, 1949–58; Bishop-Coadjutor, Diocese of Sydney, 1958–66; Archbishop of Sydney and Metropolitan of Province of NSW, 1966–82; Primate of Australia, 1978–82. Hon. DD Wycliffe College, Toronto, 1958. *Publications:* Oxford and the Evangelical Succession, 1950; Cambridge and the Evangelical Succession, 1952; Masters of the English Reformation, 1955, repr. 2005; Life of Archbishop Mowll, 1960; Makers of Religious Freedom, 1961; Pioneers of the Reformation in England, 1964; Makers of Our Heritage, 1966; The Hope of Glory, 1968; This Surpassing Excellence, 1969; They Were Pilgrims, 1970; Hewn from the Rock, 1976; Men to Remember, 1987; *relevant publication:* Marcus L. Loane: a biography, by J. R. Reid, 2004. *Address:* 18 Harrington Avenue, Warrawee, NSW 2074, Australia. *T:* (2) 94892975.
Died 14 April 2009.

LOCKHART, His Honour Frank Roper; a Circuit Judge, 1988–2004; *b* 8 Dec. 1931; *s* of Clement and Betsy Lockhart; *m* 1958, Brenda Harriett Johnson; one *s* one *d*. *Educ:* King Edward VI Sch., Retford; Doncaster Grammar Sch.; Univ. of Leeds (LLB Hons). Asst Town Clerk, Southend-on-Sea, 1960–65; Partner, Jefferies, Solicitors, 1965–87. Chairman: Industrial Tribunal, 1983–87; Social Security Tribunal, 1970–87; a Recorder, 1985–88. *Recreations:* golf, Rack II. *Club:* Thorpe Hall Golf.
Died 28 Dec. 2008.

LODGE, Oliver Raymond William Wynlayne; Regional Chairman of Industrial Tribunals, London South Region, 1980–92; *b* Painswick, Glos, 2 Sept. 1922; *e s* of Oliver William Foster Lodge and Winifred, (Wynlayne), *o d* of Sir William Nicholas Atkinson, ISO, LLD; *m* 1953, Charlotte (*d* 1990), *o d* of Col Arthur Davidson Young, CMG; one *s* two *d*. *Educ:* Bryanston Sch.; King's Coll., Cambridge. BA 1943, MA 1947. Officer-cadet, Royal Fusiliers, 1942. Called to the Bar, Inner Temple, 1945; admitted *ad eundem*, Lincoln's Inn, 1949 (Bencher, 1973; Treas., 1995); practised at Chancery Bar, 1945–74; Permanent Chairman of Industrial Tribunals, 1975–92, part-time Chm., 1992–94. Member: Bar Council, 1952–56, 1967–71; Supreme Court Rules Cttee, 1968–71. Gen. Comr of Income Tax, Lincoln's Inn, 1983–91. *Publications:* (ed) Rivington's Epitome of Snell's Equity, 3rd edn, 1948; (ed) Fraudulent and Voidable Conveyances, article in Halsbury's Laws of England, 3rd edn, 1956; contribs to legal periodicals. *Recreations:* freemasonry, walking, reading history, formerly sailing. *Address:* Southridge House, Hindon, Salisbury, Wilts SP3 6ER. *T:* (01747) 820238. *Clubs:* Garrick; Bar Yacht.
Died 26 Jan. 2009.

LOFTHOUSE, John Alfred, (Jack), OBE 1967; Member, British National Oil Corporation, 1980–82; *b* 30 Dec. 1917; *s* of John Duncan Lofthouse and Clara Margaret Smith; *m* 1950, Patricia Ninette Mann (*d* 1956); one *d*. *Educ:* Rutlish Sch., Merton; St Catharine's Coll., Cambridge (BA Hons, MA). Joined ICI Ltd as engr, 1939; Engrg Manager, Petrochemicals Div., 1958; Technical Dir, Nobel Div., 1961; Chm., Petrochems Div., 1967; Dir, Main Bd of ICI Ltd, 1970–80; responsibilities included Personnel Dir, Petrochems, Oil, and Explosives businesses, and Chm., ICI Americas Ltd; Dir, Britoil, 1983–88. *Publications:* contrib. Geographical Jl and engrg jls. *Recreations:* gardening, hill-walking, music. *Address:* c/o Longfield House, Mill Bank, Fladbury, Pershore, Worcs WR10 2QA.
Died 6 May 2007.

LOGAN, Sir Donald (Arthur), KCMG 1977 (CMG 1965); HM Diplomatic Service, retired; *b* 25 Aug. 1917; *s* of late Arthur Alfred Logan and Louise Anne Bradley; *m* 1957, Irène Jocelyne Angèle, *d* of Robert Everts (Belgian Ambassador at Madrid, 1932–39) and Alexandra Comnène; one *s* two *d*. *Educ*: Solihull. Fellow, Chartered Insurance Institute, 1939. War of 1939–45: Major, RA; British Army Staff, Washington, 1942–43; Germany, 1945. Joined HM Foreign (subseq. Diplomatic) Service, Dec. 1945; Foreign Office, 1945–47; HM Embassy, Tehran, 1947–51; Foreign Office, 1951–53; Asst Political Agent, Kuwait, 1953–55; Asst Private Sec. to Sec. of State for Foreign Affairs, 1956–58; HM Embassy, Washington, 1958–60; HM Ambassador to Guinea, 1960–62; Foreign Office, 1962–64; Information Counsellor, British Embassy, Paris, 1964–70; Ambassador to Bulgaria, 1970–73; Dep. Permanent UK Rep. to NATO, 1973–75; Ambassador and Permanent Leader, UK Delegn to UN Conf. on Law of the Sea, 1976–77. Leader, UK delegn to Conf. on Marine Living Resources of Antarctica, Buenos Aires and Canberra, 1978–80. Dir, GB/E Europe Centre, 1980–87. Gov., St Clare's Coll., Oxford, 1982–2000 (Chm., 1984–93). Chairman: Jerusalem and the East Mission Trust Ltd, 1981–93; Brompton Assoc., 1986–97; Friends of Bulgaria, 1991–. Vice-Pres., Internat. Exhibitions Bureau, Paris, 1963–67. *Address*: 8 Melton Court, Onslow Crescent, SW7 3JQ. *Clubs*: Brooks's, Royal Automobile. *Died 23 Oct. 2009.*

LOMER, Dennis Roy, CBE 1984; Member, Central Electricity Generating Board, 1977–83; *b* 5 Oct. 1923; *s* of Bertie Cecil Lomer and Agnes Ellen Coward; *m* 1949, Audrey May Bick; one *s* one *d*. With Consulting Engineers, 1948–50; joined Electricity Supply Industry, 1950; Project Engr, Transmission Div., 1961, Asst Chief Transmission Engr, 1965; Generation Construction Div. (secondment at Dir level), 1972; Dep. Dir-Gen. (Projects), 1973; Dir-Gen., Transmission Div., 1975; Mem., Technical Review Gp for Eurotunnel, 1988–92. Dir, Davidson Gp Ltd, 1983–88. Pres., 1985–87, non-exec. Dir, 1988–94, Welding Inst.; Hon. FWeldI. FIET; CIMgt. *Address*: Henley House, Heathfield Close, Woking, Surrey GU22 7JQ. *T*: (01483) 764656. *Died 23 Oct. 2010.*

LONG, Hubert Arthur, CBE 1970; Deputy Secretary, Exchequer and Audit Department, 1963–73; *b* 21 Jan. 1912; *s* of Arthur Albert Long; *m* 1937, Mary Louise Parker; three *s*. *Educ*: Taunton's Sch., Southampton. Entered Exchequer and Audit Department, 1930. *Address*: 2A Hawthorndene Road, Hayes, Kent BR2 7DY. *T*: (020) 8462 4373. *Died 11 Oct. 2009.*

LONG, Ian Andrew; Director, Housing and City Support Services, Brighton and Hove City Council, 2003–07; *b* 8 Nov. 1952; *s* of late Peter Long and Jean Long; *m* 2000, Sasha Cockrell; three *s* two *d*. *Educ*: Univ. of Portsmouth (BSc Social Policy 1974); Univ. of Southampton (CQSW 1977). Social Services Depts, LBCs of Haringey and Brent, 1996–83, E Sussex CC, 1983–96; Asst Dir, Adult Social Care, Brighton and Hove CC, 1996–2000; Dir, Community Care, S Downs Health NHS Trust, 2000–03. *Recreations*: various sports, reading, music, family activities. *Address*: (office) PO Box 2501, King's House, Grand Avenue, Hove, E Sussex BN3 2SS. *Fax*: (01273) 295114; *e-mail*: ian.long@brighton-hove.gov.uk. *Died 26 Sept. 2008.*

LONG, Ven. John Sanderson, MA; Archdeacon of Ely, Hon. Canon of Ely, and Rector of St Botolph's, Cambridge, 1970–81; Archdeacon Emeritus, 1981; *b* 21 July 1913; *s* of late Rev. Guy Stephenson Long and Ivy Marion Long; *m* 1948, Rosamond Mary (*d* 1999), *d* of Arthur Temple Forman; one *s* three *d*. *Educ*: St Edmund's Sch., Canterbury; Queens' Coll., Cambridge; Cuddesdon Theological Coll. Ordained Deacon, 1936; Priest, 1937; Curate, St Mary and St Eanswythe, Folkestone, 1936–41. Chaplain, RNVR, 1941–46. Curate, St Peter-in-Thanet, 1946; Domestic Chaplain to the Archbishop of Canterbury, 1946–53; Vicar of: Bearsted, 1953–59;

Petersfield with Sheet, 1959–70; Rural Dean of Petersfield, 1962–70. *Recreations*: walking, gardening. *Address*: 23 Thornton Road, Girton, Cambridge CB3 0NP. *T*: (01223) 276421. *Died 4 June 2008.*

LONG, Captain Rt Hon. William Joseph, OBE 1985; PC (N Ireland) 1966; JP; Minister of Education, Northern Ireland, 1969–72; *b* 23 April 1922; *s* of James William Long and Frederica (Walker); *m* 1st, 1942, Dr (Elizabeth) Doreen Mercer (*d* 2007); one *s*; 2nd, 2007, Valerie Marion Bryans. *Educ*: Friends' Sch., Great Ayton, Yorks; Edinburgh Univ.; RMC, Sandhurst. Served Royal Inniskilling Fusiliers, 1940–48. Secretary: NI Marriage Guidance Council, 1948–51; NI Chest and Heart Assoc., 1951–62. Parliament of Northern Ireland: MP (Unionist) Ards, 1962–72; Parly Sec., Min. of Agriculture, 1964–66; Sen. Parly Sec., Min. of Development, Jan.-Oct. 1966; Minister of Educn, 1966–68; Minister of Home Affairs, Dec. 1968–March 1969; Minister of Devel, March 1969–May 1969. Owner/skipper, fishing industry, 1972–87; Chief Exec., NI Fish Producers Orgn, 1973–84; Chm., UK Assoc. of Fish Producers Orgns, 1982. *Recreations*: cricket, ornithology, model engineering, wood turning and carving. *Address*: 8 Castle Court, Helmsley, N Yorkshire YO62 5AZ. *Died 10 Feb. 2008.*

LONGRIGG, John Stephen, CMG 1973; OBE 1964; HM Diplomatic Service, retired; *b* 1 Oct. 1923; *s* of late Brig. Stephen Hemsley Longrigg, OBE; *m* 1st, 1953, Lydia Meynell (marr. diss. 1965); one *s* one *d*; 2nd, 1966, Ann O'Reilly; one *s* decd. *Educ*: Rugby Sch.; Magdalen Coll., Oxford (BA). War Service, Rifle Bde, 1942–45 (despatches). FO, 1948; Paris, 1948; Baghdad, 1951; FO, 1953; Berlin, 1955; Cabinet Office, 1957; FO, 1958; Dakar, 1960; Johannesburg, 1962; Pretoria, 1962; Washington, 1964; FO, 1965–67; Bahrain, 1967–69; FCO, 1969–73; seconded to HQ British Forces, Hong Kong, 1974–76; FCO, 1976–82; Administrator, Common Law Inst. of Intellectual Property, 1983–88. *Recreations*: reading, opera, theatre. *Address*: 45A Blackheath Park, Blackheath, SE3 9SQ. *T*: (020) 8852 4007. *Clubs*: Reform; Royal Blackheath Golf. *Died 12 March 2007.*

LONSDALE, 7th Earl of, *cr* 1807 (UK); **James Hugh William Lowther**; Viscount and Baron Lowther, 1797; Bt 1764; *b* 3 Nov. 1922; *er s* of Anthony Edward, Viscount Lowther (*d* 1949), and Muriel Frances, Viscountess Lowther (*d* 1968), 2nd *d* of late Sir George Farrar, Bt, DSO, and Lady Farrar; *S* grandfather, 1953; *m* 1st, 1945, Tuppina Cecily Bennet (marr. diss. 1954; she *d* 1984); one *s* one *d*; 2nd, 1954, Hon. Jennifer Lowther (marr. diss. 1962); one *s* two *d*; 3rd, 1963, Nancy Ruth (marr. diss.; she *d* 1999), *d* of late Thomas Cobbs, Pacific Palisades, Calif; one *s*, and three step *s*; 4th, 1975, Caroline, *y d* of Sir Gerald Ley, 3rd Bt, TD; one *s* one *d*. *Educ*: Eton. Armed Forces, 1941–46; RAC and East Riding Yeo. (despatches, Captain). Structural engrg, 1947–50; farmer and forester; formerly Chm. of family co., Lakeland Invesments Ltd and of three subsids. CCMI; FRSA 1984. *Heir*: *s* Viscount Lowther, *b* 27 May 1949. *Address*: Askham Hall, Penrith, Cumbria CA10 2PF. *T*: (01931) 712208. *Clubs*: Brooks's, Turf. *Died 23 May 2006.*

LONSDALE, Robert Henry H.; *see* Heywood-Lonsdale.

LORD, William Burton Housley, CB 1979; scientist; *b* 22 March 1919; *s* of Arthur James Lord and Elsie Lord (*née* Housley); *m* 1942, Helena Headon Jaques; two *d*. *Educ*: King George V Sch., Southport; Manchester Univ.; London Univ. (External MSc); Trinity Coll., Cambridge (MA). Enlisted Royal Fusiliers, commn S Lancs Regt (served Middle East and N Africa), 1941–46. Cambridge Univ., 1946. Entered Civil Service, 1949; joined Atomic Weapons Res. Estab., 1952; Head of Metallurgy Div., AWRE, 1958; moved to MoD, 1964; Asst Chief Scientific Adviser (Research), 1965; Dep. Chief Scientist (Army), 1968–71; Dir Gen., Establishments, Resources and Programmes (B), MoD, 1971–76; Dir, RARDE,

1976–79. Award for wartime invention of radio proximity fuse, 1952. *Recreations:* going to concerts, lectures and art galleries. *Address:* 2 Orchard Brae, Edinburgh EH4 1NY.   *Died 28 July 2008.*

LOSTY, Howard Harold Walter, FREng, FIET; Secretary, Institution of Electrical Engineers, 1980–89; *b* 1 Aug. 1926; *s* of Patrick J. Losty and Edith E. Wilson; *m* 1950, Rosemary L. Everritt; two *d. Educ:* Harvey Grammar Sch., Folkestone; Sir John Cass Coll., London. BSc. GEC Research Laboratories, 1942–53; GEC Nuclear Power Programme, 1953–66; Head of Engineering Div., GEC Research Centre, 1966–71; Dir, GEC Hirst Research Centre, 1971–77; Man. Dir, GEC Electronic Devices Ltd, 1977–80. Hon. DEng Bradford, 1986. *Publications:* (co-author) Nuclear Graphite, 1962; some forty technical papers. *Recreations:* walking, listening to music (opera), reading history. *Address:* Shandon, 14 Wyatts Road, Chorleywood, Herts WD3 5TE. *T:* (01923) 283568.   *Died 16 Oct. 2006.*

LOVEGROVE, His Honour Geoffrey David; QC 1969; a Circuit Judge (formerly County Court Judge), 1971–92; *b* 22 Dec. 1919; *s* of late Gilbert Henry Lovegrove; *m* 1959, Janet, *d* of John Bourne; one *s* two *d. Educ:* Haileybury; New College, Oxford (MA). Army, 1940–46. Called to the Bar, Inner Temple, 1947; Dep. Chairman, W Sussex Quarter Sessions, 1965–71. Master, Innholders' Company, 1980–81.   *Died 21 Jan. 2008.*

LOVERIDGE, Sir John (Warren), Kt 1988; JP; ARBS 2001; partner and director of businesses in education, farming and property; painter, and modern sculptor, since 1997; *b* 9 Sept. 1925; *s* of C. W. Loveridge and Emily (Mickie), *d* of John Malone; *m* 1954, Jean Marguerite, *d* of E. J. Chivers; three *s* two *d. Educ:* St John's Coll., Cambridge (MA). Mem., Hampstead BC, 1953–59. Contested (C) Aberavon, 1951, Brixton (LCC), 1952. MP (C) Hornchurch, 1970–74, Upminster, 1974–83. Member: Parly Select Cttee on Expenditure (Mem. General Purposes Sub-Cttee); Procedure Cttee; Chm., Cons. Smaller Business Cttee, 1979–83). Treasurer/Trustee, Hampstead Conservative Assoc., 1959–74; President: Hampstead and Highgate Conservative Assoc., 1986–91; Upminster Conservative Assoc., 1992–2002 (Patron, 2002–); Vice-Pres., Greater London Area Conservatives, 1984–93 (Pres., 1993–96). Exhibitions: one man: RSBS, 2000; Norwich Cathedral, 2001; permanent, E Devon; various shared exhibns incl. paintings. Vice-Pres., Nat. Council for Civil Protection (formerly Civil Defence), 1980–. Pres., Dinosaurs Club (former Cons. MPs), 1999–2004 (Chm., 1993–98). JP West Central Division, 1963. FRAS; FRAgS; MRIIA. Liveryman, Girdlers' Co.; Mem., Guild of Freemen of City of London. *Publications:* (jtly) Moving Forward: small businesses and the economy, 1983; New Sculpture in Stone, Metal, Wood and Glass, 2000; To Seek is to Find, 2005; *poetry:* God Save the Queen: Sonnets of Elizabeth I, 1981; Hunter of the Moon, 1983; Hunter of the Sun, 1984. *Recreations:* writing, historic houses, shooting. *Address:* c/o The Private Office, 2 Arkwright Road, NW3 6AE. *Clubs:* Buck's, Carlton, Hurlingham.
                              Died 13 Nov. 2007.

LOWE, His Honour David Bruce Douglas; a Circuit Judge, 1983–98; *b* 3 April 1935; *o s* of late Douglas Gordon Arthur Lowe, QC, and of Karen, *e d* of Surgeon Einar Thamsen; *m* 1978, Dagmar, *o d* of Horst and Anneliese Bosse; one *s* three *d,* and one *s* one *d* by a previous marriage. *Educ:* Winchester College; Pembroke Coll., Cambridge (MA). National service, RN, 1953–55. Called to the Bar, Inner Temple, 1960 (Profumo Scholar); Midland and Oxford (formerly Midland) Circuit; Prosecuting Counsel to Dept of Trade, 1975–83; a Recorder of the Crown Court, 1980–83. *Recreations:* music, tennis, gardening (formerly rackets and real tennis). *Address:* Marsh Green Cottage, Marsh, Aylesbury, Bucks HP17 8SP. *Club:* Hawks (Cambridge).   *Died 7 March 2006.*

LOWE, John Evelyn, MA; FSA, FRSA; cultural consultant and author, since 1978; foreign travel specialist, journalist and photographer; *b* 23 April 1928; *s* of late Arthur Holden Lowe; *m* 1st, 1956, Susan Helen Sanderson (marr. diss. 1981); two *s* one *d;* 2nd, 1989, Yukiko Nomura; one *d. Educ:* Wellington Coll., Berks; New Coll., Oxford. Served in RAEC, 1947–49 (Sgt Instructor). Victoria and Albert Museum, Dept of Woodwork, 1953–56; Deputy Story Editor, Pinewood Studios, 1956–57; Victoria and Albert Museum: Dept of Ceramics, 1957–61; Assistant to the Director, 1961–64; Dir, City Museum and Art Gall., Birmingham, 1964–69; Dir, Weald and Downland Open Air Museum, 1969–74; Principal, West Dean College, Chichester, West Sussex, 1972–78. Vis. Prof. in British Cultural Studies, Doshisha Univ., Japan, 1979–81; Vis. Prof., Internat. Res. Centre for Japanese Studies, Kyoto, 2001–02. Literary Editor, Kansai Time Out, 1983–88. Hofer-Hecksher Bibliographical Lectr, Harvard, 1974. Pres., Midlands Fedn of Museums, 1967–69. Member: Exec. Cttee, Midland Arts Centre for Young People, 1964–69; Council of the British School at Rome, 1968–70; Crafts Adv. Cttee, 1973–78. Consultant to: Seibu Ltd, Tokyo, 1968–72; Specialtours, London, 1969–74. Trustee: Sanderson Art in Industry Fund, 1968–2005; Edward James Foundn, 1972–73; Idlewild Trust, 1972–78. Hon. Fellow, RCA, 1988. Asst Ed., Collins Crime Club, 1953–54; Founding Ed., Faber Furniture Series, 1954–56. Library of European books about Japan acquired by Nichibunken, Kyoto, 1987; eponymous collection of Japanese arts and crafts presented to Pitt Rivers Mus., 1996. *Publications:* Thomas Chippendale, 1955; Cream Coloured Earthenware, 1958; Japanese Crafts, 1983; Into Japan, 1985; Into China, 1986; Corsica: a traveller's guide, 1988; A Surrealist Life—Edward James—Poet, Patron & Eccentric, 1991; Glimpses of Kyoto Life, 1996; The Warden: a portrait of John Sparrow, 1998; Old Kyoto, 1999; major contribs to Encyclopædia Britannica and OUP Junior Encyclopedia; articles on applied arts, foreign travel, social history and Japan. *Recreations:* Japan, music, reading, book-collecting, travel. *Address:* 2 rue Jean Guiton, 47300 Villeneuve sur Lot, France. *T:* 0553417253.   *Died 10 Aug. 2010.*

LOWE, Prof. Kenneth Gordon, CVO 1982; MD; FRCP, FRCPE, FRCPGlas; Physician to the Queen in Scotland, 1971–82; formerly Consultant Physician, Royal Infirmary and Ninewells Hospital, Dundee; Hon. Professor of Medicine, Dundee University, since 1969; *b* 29 May 1917; *s* of Thomas J. Lowe, MA, Arbroath, and Flora MacDonald Gordon, Arbroath; *m* 1942, Nancy Young, MB, ChB (*d* 1999), twin *d* of Stephen Young, Logie, Fife; two *s* one *d. Educ:* Arbroath High Sch.; St Andrews Univ. (MD Hons). Served with RAMC, 1942–46; Registrar, Hammersmith Hosp., Royal Postgrad. Med. Sch., 1947–52; Sen. Lectr in Medicine, St Andrews Univ., 1952–61. Hon. DSc St Andrews, 2003. *Publications:* (jtly) Regional Anatomy Illustrated, 1983; contribs to med. and scientific jls, mainly on renal, metabolic and cardiac disorders. *Recreations:* reading, fishing. *Address:* 36 Dundee Road, West Ferry, Dundee DD5 1HY. *T:* (01382) 778787. *Club:* Flyfishers'.
                              Died 13 Aug. 2010.

LOWNIE of Largo, His Honour Ralph Hamilton; Baron of Largo; a Circuit Judge, 1986–95; *b* 27 Sept. 1924; *yr s* of James H. W. Lownie and Jesse H. Aitken; *m* 1960, Claudine Therese, *o d* of Pierre Lecrocq, Reims; one *s* one *d. Educ:* George Watson's Coll.; Edinburgh Univ. (MA, LLB, Dip. Admin. Law and Practice); Univ. of Kent (PhD). Royal Engineers, 1943–47, NW Europe. WS 1952; enrolled as solicitor, 1953; Mem. Faculty of Advocates 1959; called to Bar, Inner Temple, 1962. Dep. Registrar, Supreme Court of Kenya, 1954–56; Resident Magistrate, 1956–61, Sen. Resident Magistrate, 1961–63, Dep. Registrar-Gen., Kenya, 1963–65; Sen. Magistrate, Bermuda, 1965–72; a Metropolitan Stipendiary Magistrate, 1974–86; a Deputy Circuit Judge, 1976–82; a Recorder, 1983–86. Chm. of Juvenile Courts, 1976–85. Lectr, Kenya Sch. of Law, 1963–65. *Publications:* Auld

Reekie: an Edinburgh anthology, 2004. *Recreation:* historical research. *Address:* 57 Greenhill Road, Otford, Kent TN14 5RR. *Died 28 Nov. 2007.*

LOWRY, John Christopher, CBE 2003; FDSRCSE, FDSRCS, FRCSE, FRCS, FFGDP(UK), FRCA; Consultant Maxillofacial and Oral Surgeon, Royal Bolton Hospital, since 1976; Dean, Faculty of Dental Surgery, Royal College of Surgeons of England, 2001–04; *b* 6 June 1942; *s* of Leslie and Betty Lowry; *m* 1968, Valerie Joyce Smethurst; one *s* one *d*. *Educ:* Altrincham Grammar Sch.; Univ. of Manchester (BDS 1963, MB ChB 1970). FDSRCS 1968; FRCSE 1984; MHSM 1994; FDSRCSE 1999; FRCS 2002; FFGDP(UK) 2005; FRCA 2007. Sen. Registrar, Manchester RHA, 1972–76; Lectr (pt-time), Univ. of Manchester, 1976–2001. Vis. Prof. of Surgery, Univ. of Central Lancs, 2004–. Hon. Consultant to the Army, 2004–. Leverhulme Travelling Fellow, 1974–75. Ed., Nat. Speciality Guidelines, 1994–97. Chairman: Central Cttee, Hosp. Dental Services, 1998–2001; Standing Dental Adv. Cttee, DoH, 2000–. Chairman: Senate of Dental Specialities, 2001–04; Jt Meeting Dental Faculties, 2001–04; Cosmetic Surgery Interspecialty Cttee, Senate of Surgery GB and Ire., 2005–08. Sec. Gen., Eur. Assoc. for Craniomaxillofacial Surgery, 1998–; Chm., British Acad. of Cosmetic Practice, 2008; President: British Assoc. of Oral and Maxillofacial Surgeons, 2001; Manchester Medical Soc., 2004–05 (Vice-Pres., 2003–04). Member: Acad. of Med. Royal Colls, 2001–04; Council, RCS, 2001–. Hon. Prof., Univ. of Bucharest, 2007. Dr *hc* Univ. of Iasi, 2006. *Publications:* (contrib.) Operative Maxillofacial Surgery, 1998; anonymous official documents for professional assocs; contrib. papers on maxillofacial reconstruction, oncology, salivary diseases and trauma, telemedicine specialisation and conscious sedation. *Recreations:* music (traditional jazz), cross-training, motor sport, walking. *Address:* The Valley House, 50 Ravens Wood, Bolton BL1 5TL. *T:* (01204) 848815, *Fax:* (01204) 845821; *e-mail:* secretary-general@eacmfs.org, johnlowry1@btinternet.com. *Club:* Royal Society of Medicine. *Died 29 Sept. 2008.*

LOYD, Sir Francis Alfred, KCMG 1965 (CMG 1961); OBE 1954 (MBE 1951); *b* 5 Sept. 1916; *s* of Major A. W. K. Loyd, Royal Sussex Regt; *m* 1st, 1946, Katharine Layzell (*d* 1981), *d* of Lt Col S. C. Layzell, MC, Mwatati, Kenya; two *d*; 2nd, 1984, Helen Monica (*d* 2005), *widow* of Lt Col C. R. Murray Brown, DSO. *Educ:* Eton; Trinity Coll., Oxford (Kitchener Schol.; MA). District Officer, Kenya, 1939; Mil. Service, E Africa, 1940–42; Private Secretary to Governor of Kenya, 1942–45; HM Consul, Mega, Ethiopia, 1945; District Comdr, Kenya, 1947–55; Commonwealth Fund Fellowship to USA, 1953–54; Provincial Commissioner, 1956; Permanent Secretary, Governor's Office, 1962–63; HM Commissioner for Swaziland, 1964–68. Dir, London House for Overseas Graduates, 1969–79; Chm., Oxfam Africa Cttee, 1979–85. *Recreations:* golf, gardening. *Address:* 53 Park Road, Aldeburgh, Suffolk IP15 5EN. *T:* (01728) 452478. *Club:* Vincent's (Oxford). *Died 13 Dec. 2006.*

LUCAS, (Charles) Vivian; Chief Executive, Devon County Council, 1974–79; solicitor; *b* 31 May 1914; *s* of Frank and Mary Renshaw Lucas, Malvern, Worcs; *m* 1941, Oonah Holderness; two *s* two *d*. *Educ:* Malvern Coll.; abroad; London Univ. (LLB). Clerk, Devon County Council, 1972–74; Clerk to the Lieutenancy of Devon, 1972–79. *Recreations:* sport, bridge. *Address:* Flat 25, Hamilton Court, Salterton Road, Exmouth EX8 2BR. *Died 16 March 2009.*

LUDDINGTON, Sir Donald (Collin Cumyn), KBE 1976; CMG 1973; CVO 1974; Governor, Solomon Islands, 1973–76; *b* 18 Aug. 1920; *s* of late F. Norman John Luddington, Ceylon Civil Service, and late M. Myrtle Amethyst Payne; *m* 1945, Garry Brodie Johnston (*d* 2002); one *s* one *d*. *Educ:* Dover Coll.; St Andrews Univ. (MA). Served War, Army, 1940–46, KOYLI and RAC, Captain. Hong Kong Govt, 1949–73; Sec. for Home Affairs, 1971–73. Chm., Public Services Commn,

Hong Kong, 1977–78; Comr, Ind. Commn against Corruption, Hong Kong, 1978–80. *Recreation:* reading. *Clubs:* Royal Commonwealth Society; Hong Kong (Hong Kong). *Died 26 Jan. 2009.*

LUFT, His Honour Arthur Christian, CBE 1988; Member, Legislative Council, Isle of Man, 1988–98; *b* 21 July 1915; *e s* of late Ernest Christian Luft and late Phoebe Luft; *m* 1950, Dorothy, *yr d* of late Francis Manley; two *s*. *Educ:* Bradbury Sch., Cheshire. Served Army, 1940–46. Admitted to Manx Bar, 1940; Attorney-Gen., IOM, 1972–74; Second Deemster, 1974–80; HM's First Deemster, Clerk of the Rolls, and Dep. Governor, IOM, 1980–88. Chairman: IOM Criminal Injuries Compensation Tribunal, 1974–80; Prevention of Fraud (Unit Trust) Tribunal, 1974–80; IOM Licensing Appeal Court, 1974–80; Wireless Telegraphy Appeal Bd for IOM, 1974–80; IOM Income Tax Appeal Comrs, 1980–88; IOM Gaming Control Comrs, 1988–90; Rivers Pollution Cttee, 1989–92; Data Protection Tribunal, 1990–92; IOM Arts Council, 1992–98; Member: Dept of Local Govt and Envmt, IOM, 1988–93; Dept of Agric., Fisheries and Forestry, IOM, 1993–98; Public Accounts Cttee, 1988–98; Ecclesiastical Cttee of Tynwald, 1992–98; Standing Orders Cttee of Legislative Council, 1995–98. Chm., Legislative Cttee, Diocesan Synod., 1989–98. Pres., Youth Adv. Gp, 1991–94. Pres., Manx Deaf Soc., 1975–. Pres., IOM Cricket Club, 1980–98. *Recreations:* theatre, watching cricket, gardening. *Address:* Leyton, Victoria Road, Douglas, Isle of Man IM2 6AQ. *T:* (01624) 621048. *Died 21 June 2009.*

LUSTIGER, His Eminence Cardinal (Aaron) Jean-Marie; Archbishop of Paris, 1981–2005, then Emeritus; *b* Paris, 17 Sept. 1926; *s* of Charles and Giselle Lustiger. *Educ:* Carmelite Seminary; Institut Catholique de Paris; Sorbonne (Lèsl, LenThéol). Ordained priest, 1954. Chaplain to students, Sorbonne, Paris; Dir, Centre d'étudiants Richelieu, Paris, 1959–69; Parish Pastor, Sainte Jeanne de Chantal, Paris, 1969–79; Bishop of Orléans, 1979–81. Cardinal, 1983. Mem., Académie Française, 1995–. *Publications:* Sermons d'un curé de Paris, 1978; Pain de vie, peuple de Dieu, 1981; Osez croire, 1985 (trans. Dare to Believe, 1986); Osez vivre, 1985 (trans. Dare to Live, 1989); Freude der Weihnacht, 1985, revd and enlarged edn as Petites Paroles de Nuit de Noël, 1992; Premiers pas dans la prière, 1986 (trans. First Steps in Prayer, 1988); Six sermons aux élus de la nation, 1987; The Mass, 1987 (abridged edn of La Messe, 1988); Le choix de Dieu, 1987 (trans. Choosing God, Chosen by God, 1990); The Lord's Prayer, 1988; Le Sacrement de l'onction des malades, 1990; Dieu merci, les droits de l'homme, 1990; Dare to Rejoice, 1990; Nous avons rendez-vous avec l'Europe, 1991; Devenez dignes de la condition humaine, 1995; Le Baptême de votre enfant, 1997; Soyez heureux, 1997; Pour l'Europe, un nouvel art de vivre, 1999; Les prêtres que Dieu donne, 2000; Comme Dieu vous aime, 2001; La Promesse, 2002; Comment Dieu ouvre les portes de la Foi, 2004; (contrib.) Apocalypse, 2005. *Address:* Maison diocésaine, 7 rue Saint-Vincent, 75018 Paris, France. *Died 5 Aug. 2007.*

LUSTY, Prof. James Richard, PhD; CSci, CChem, FRSC; Vice-Chancellor, University of Wales, Newport (formerly University of Wales College, Newport), 2002–06, Professor Emeritus, since 2007; *b* 27 March 1951; *s* of Frank James and Myrtle Gladys Lusty; *m* 1974, Jacqueline Ann Currell; one *s* two *d*. *Educ:* Queen Elizabeth Coll., London Univ. (BSc 1st cl. Hons (Chem.) 1973; PhD (Inorganic Chem.) 1976). CChem 1978; FRSC 1991; CSci 2004. Asst Prof. of Inorganic Chem., Univ. of Petroleum and Minerals, Saudi Arabia, 1978–81; Lectr in Inorganic Chem., 1981–83; Sen. Lectr, 1983–84; Nat. Univ. of Singapore; Lecturer: (temp.) in Inorganic Chem., Univ. of Keele, 1984–85; in Bioinorganic Chem., Robert Gordon's Inst. of Technol., Aberdeen, 1985–86; Lancashire Polytechnic, later University of Central Lancashire: Hd, Dept of Chemistry, 1987–90; Dir of Progs, 1990–93; Prof. of

Chemistry, 1991; Dean, Inter-Faculty Studies, 1993–95; Pro-Vice-Chancellor, 1995–2000; Sen. Pro-Vice-Chancellor, 2000–01. *Publications:* articles in scientific jls incl. Jl Chem. Soc., Dalton Trans and Inorganic Chem. *Recreations:* football, running, swimming. *Address:* c/o University of Wales, Newport, Caerleon Campus, Newport NP18 3YG. *T:* (01633) 432111, *Fax:* (01633) 432002. *Died 4 Feb. 2008.*

LUTHER, Rt Rev. Arthur William; Bishop of Bombay, 1970–73; *b* 21 March 1919; *s* of William and Monica Luther; *m* 1946, Dr Kamal Luther; one *s* two *d.* *Educ:* Nagpur University; India (MA, BT); General Theological Seminary, New York (STD 1957). Deacon, 1943; Priest, 1944; in USA and Scotland for study and parish work, 1952–54; Chaplain to Bishop of Nagpur, 1954; Head Master, Bishop Cotton School, Nagpur, 1954–57; Bishop of Nasik, 1957–70; held charge of Kolhapur Diocese concurrently with Bombay Diocese, Dec. 1970–Feb. 1972; Bishop, Church of North India, and Reg. Sec. of the Leprosy Mission, 1973–80; Promotional Sec., 1980–84. *Address:* Shripad-B, Flat 1, 60 Tulshibagwale Colony, Lane 3, Sahakar Nagar 2, Pune 411009, Maharashtra, India. *T:* 24222576. *Died 25 Jan. 2009.*

LUTTRELL, Col Sir (Geoffrey) Walter (Fownes), KCVO 1993; MC 1945; JP; Lord-Lieutenant of Somerset, 1978–94; *b* 2 Oct. 1919; *s* of late Geoffrey Fownes Luttrell of Dunster Castle, Somerset; *m* 1942, Hermione Hamilton, *er d* of late Capt. Cecil Gunston, MC, and Lady Doris Gunston. *Educ:* Eton; Exeter Coll., Oxford. Served War of 1939–45, with 15th/19th King's Royal Hussars, 1940–46; North Somerset Yeomanry, 1952–57; Lt-Col 1955; Hon. Col, 6th Bn LI, TAVR, 1977–87; Col 1987. Liaison Officer, Ministry of Agriculture, 1965–71. Regional Dir, Lloyds Bank, 1972–83. Member: National Parks Commn, 1962–66; Wessex Regional Cttee, Nat. Trust, 1970–85; SW Electricity Bd, 1969–78; UGC, 1973–76. Pres., Royal Bath and West and Southern Counties Soc., 1983. DL Somerset, 1958–68, Vice Lord-Lieutenant, 1968–78; High Sheriff of Somerset, 1960; JP 1961. Hon. Col Somerset ACF, 1982–89. KStJ. *Address:* Court House, East Quantoxhead, Bridgwater, Somerset TA5 1EJ. *T:* (01278) 741242. *Club:* Cavalry and Guards. *Died 3 April 2007.*

LYELL OF MARKYATE, Baron *cr* 2005 (Life Peer), of Markyate, in the county of Hertfordshire; **Nicholas Walter Lyell,** Kt 1987; PC 1990; QC 1980; *b* 6 Dec. 1938; *s* of late Sir Maurice Legat Lyell and Veronica Mary Lyell; *m* 1967, Susanna Mary Fletcher; two *s* two *d. Educ:* Stowe Sch.; Christ Church, Oxford (MA Hons Mod. Hist.). National Service, commnd Royal Artillery, 1957–59; Walter Runciman & Co., 1962–64; called to the Bar, Inner Temple, 1965, Bencher, 1986; private practice, London (Commercial and Public Law), 1965–86, 1997–2005; a Recorder, 1985–86 and 1997–2002. MP (C): Hemel Hempstead, 1979–83; Mid Bedfordshire, 1983–97; NE Bedfordshire, 1997–2001. Jt Sec., Constitutional Cttee, 1979; PPS to the Attorney General, 1979–86; Parly Under-Sec. of State (Social Security), DHSS, 1986–87; Solicitor General, 1987–92; Attorney General, 1992–97. Exec. Chm., 1985–86, Chm., 2002–, Soc. of Cons. Lawyers. Chm., Fedn of British Artists, Mall Galleries, 2007–. Vice-Chm., BFSS, 1983–86. Governor, Stowe Sch., 1990–2007 (Chm., 2001–07). *Recreations:* gardening, shooting, drawing. *Address:* House of Lords, SW1A 0PW. *Clubs:* Brooks's, Pratt's. *Died 30 Aug. 2010.*

LYMBERY, His Honour Robert Davison; QC 1967; a Circuit Judge (formerly Judge of County Courts), 1971–93; Common Serjeant in the City of London, 1990–93; *b* 14 Nov. 1920; *s* of late Robert Smith Lymbery and Louise Lymbery; *m* 1952, (Pauline) Anne, *d* of late John Reginald and of Kathleen Tuckett; three *d. Educ:* Gresham's Sch.; Pembroke Coll., Cambridge. Served Army, 1940–46; commissioned 17/21 Lancers, 1941; Middle East, Italy, Greece (Royal Tank Regt),

1942–46, Major. Pembroke Coll., 1939–40, 1946–48 (MA, LLB 1st class hons). Foundation Exhibn. 1948; called to Bar, Middle Temple, 1949, Bencher, 1991; Harmsworth Law Scholar, 1949; practice on Midland Circuit, 1949–71. Recorder of Grantham, 1965–71; Chairman: Rutland QS, 1966–71 (Dep. Chm., 1962–66); Bedfordshire QS, 1969–71 (Dep. Chm., 1961–69); Commissioner of Assize, 1971. Freeman, City of London, 1983; Liveryman, Cutlers' Co., 1992–. *Recreation:* various. *Address:* c/o Central Criminal Court, EC4M 7EH. *Club:* Hawks (Cambridge). *Died 13 Oct. 2008.*

LYNTON, Norbert Casper, OBE 2006; Professor of the History of Art, 1975–89, and Dean of the School of European Studies, 1985–88, University of Sussex, then Professor Emeritus; *b* 22 Sept. 1927; *s* of Paul and Amalie Christiane Lynton; *m* 1st, 1949, Janet Irving; two *s*; 2nd, 1969, Sylvia Anne Towning; two *s. Educ:* Douai Sch.; Birkbeck Coll., Univ. of London (BA Gen.); Courtauld Inst., Univ. of London (BA Hons). Lectr in History of Art and Architecture, Leeds Coll. of Art, 1950–61; Sen. Lectr, then Head of Dept of Art History and Gen. Studies, Chelsea Sch. of Art, 1961–70. London Corresp. of Art International, 1961–66; Art Critic, The Guardian, 1965–70; Dir of Exhibitions, Arts Council of GB, 1970–75; Vis. Prof. of History of Art, Open Univ., 1975; Vis. Tutor in Painting, RCA, 1989–92. Trustee, National Portrait Gallery, 1985–99; Chm., Charleston Trust, 1998–2006. Responsible for many exhibns and catalogues, including: Marc Vaux, NY, 1989; Victor Pasmore, NY, 1989; Ben Nicholson, Tokyo and Japanese tour, 1992–93; for British Council: Henry Moore, Delhi, 1987; Picturing People, Kuala Lumpur, Hong Kong and Singapore, 1989–90; Henry Moore: the human dimension, Leningrad, Moscow, Helsinki, 1991–92. *Publications:* (jtly) Simpson's History of Architectural Development, vol. 4 (Renaissance), 1962; Kenneth Armitage, 1962; Paul Klee, 1964; The Modern World, 1968; The Story of Modern Art, 1980, 2nd edn 1989; Looking at Art, 1981; (jtly) Looking into Paintings, 1985; Victor Pasmore, paintings and graphics 1980–92, 1992; Ben Nicholson, 1993; Jack Smith, 2000; William Tillyer: against the grain, 2000; (jtly) Yale Dictionary of Art and Artists, 2000; William Scott, 2004; Marc Vaux, 2005; articles in Burlington Mag., TLS, Studio International, Architectural Design, Art in America, Smithsonian, Leonardo, Modern Painters, Prospect, etc. *Recreations:* art, people, music, travel. *Address:* 4/14 Clifton Terrace, Vine Place, Brighton BN1 3HA. *T:* (01273) 328078. *Died 30 Oct. 2007.*

LYON, Hon. Sterling Rufus Webster, PC 1982; OC 2009; OM 2002; a Judge of the Manitoba Court of Appeal, 1986–2002; *b* 30 Jan. 1927; *s* of David Rufus Lyon and Ella May (*née* Cuthbert); *m* 1953, Barbara Jean Mayers (*d* 2006); two *s* three *d. Educ:* Portage La Prairie Collegiate (Governor-General's Medal); United College (BA 1948); Univ. of Manitoba Law Sch. (LLB 1953). Crown Attorney, Manitoba, 1953–57; QC (Canada) 1960. Member, Manitoba Legislative Assembly, and Executive Council, 1958–69; Attorney-General, 1958–63 and 1966–69; Minister of: Municipal Affairs, 1960–61; Public Utilities, 1961–63; Mines and Natural Resources, 1963–66; Tourism and Recreation, Commissioner of Northern Affairs, 1966–68; Govt House Leader, 1966–69; Leader, Progressive Cons. Party of Manitoba, 1975–83; MLA: for Fort Garry, 1958–69; for Souris-Killarney, 1976–77; for Charleswood, 1977–86; Leader of the Opposition, Manitoba, 1976–77 and 1981–83; Premier of Manitoba and Minister of Dominion-Provincial Affairs, 1977–81. *Recreations:* hunting, fishing. *Club:* Albany (Toronto). *Died 16 Dec. 2010.*

LYONS, Bernard, CBE 1964; JP; DL; Chairman: UDS Group PLC, 1972–82 (Director, 1954–83; Joint Managing Director, 1966; Managing Director, 1972–79); Colmore Trust Ltd, since 1984; *b* 30 March 1913; *s* of Samuel H. Lyons; *m* 1938, Lucy Hurst (*d* 2001); three *s*

one *d*. *Educ*: Leeds Grammar Sch. Chairman: Yorkshire and City Properties Ltd, 1956–73; Glanfield Securities, 1958–74. Chm., Yorkshire and NE Conciliation Cttee, Race Relations Bd, 1968–70; Member: Leeds City Council, 1951–65; Community Relations Commn, 1970–72; Govt Adv. Cttee on Retail Distribution, 1970–76. Mem. Court and Council, Univ. of Leeds, 1953–58; Chm., Swarthmore Adult Educn Centre Appeal for Building Extensions, 1957–60. Chm., Leeds Judean Youth Club, 1955–70; Jt Chm., Leeds Br., CCJ, 1955–60; Life Pres., Leeds Jewish Representative Council, 1960–. JP Leeds, 1960; DL West Riding, Yorks, 1971. Hon. LLD Leeds, 1973. *Publications*: The Thread is Strong, 1981; The Narrow Edge, 1985; Tombola, 1996. *Recreations*: farming, forestry, travel, writing. *Address*: Upton Wood, Fulmer, Bucks SL3 6JJ. *T*: (01753) 662404. *Died 12 April 2008.*

LYONS, Charles Albert; General Secretary, Transport Salaried Staffs' Association, 1982–89, retired; *b* Liverpool, 13 Aug. 1929; *s* of Maurice Lyons and Catherine Jones; *m* 1958, Judith Mary Robinson; three *s*. *Educ*: St Mary's RC Secondary Modern Sch., Fleetwood. Wages Clerk, fishing industry, 1943–47; National Service, RAPC, 1947–49; Clerical Officer, British Rail, 1950–59; Transport Salaried Staffs' Association: Clerical Asst, 1959–64; Scottish Sec., 1965–68; London Midland Div. Officer, 1968–73; Asst Gen. Sec., 1973–77; Senior Asst Gen. Sec., 1977–82; Member: TUC Gen. Council, 1983–89 (Mem. Committees: Finance and Gen. Purposes; Equal Rights; Transport; Public Enterprise; Social Insurance and Indust. Welfare; Employment, Policy and Orgn); Hotels and Catering Industrial Training Bd, 1982–84; Railway Industry Adv. Cttee, 1982–86; Jt Council for Railways, EEC; Vice-Chm., ITF Travel Bureau Section, 1979–89; individual Mem., Labour Party, 1950–. *Died 1 Jan. 2008.*

LYONS, Edward; QC 1974; LLB, BA; a Recorder of the Crown Court, 1972–98; *b* 17 May 1926; *s* of late A. Lyons and Mrs S. Taylor; *m* 1955, Barbara, *d* of Alfred Katz; one *s* one *d*. *Educ*: Roundhay High Sch.; Leeds Univ. (LLB Hons 1951; BA Hons (European Studies) 2003). Served Royal Artillery, 1944–48; Combined Services Russian Course, Cambridge Univ., 1946; Interpreter in Russian, Brit. CCG, 1946–48. Called to Bar, Lincoln's Inn, 1952, Bencher, 1983. MP (Lab 1966–81, SDP 1981–83) Bradford E, 1966–74, Bradford W, 1974–83; PPS at Treasury, 1969–70; SDP spokesman: on home affairs, 1981–82; on legal affairs, 1982–83. Member: H of C Select Cttee on European Legislation, 1975–83; SDP Nat. Cttee, 1984–87; Chairman: PLP Legal and Judicial Gp, 1974–77; PLP Home Office Gp, 1974–79 (Dep. Chm., 1970–74). Contested: (Lab) Harrogate, 1964; (SDP) Bradford W, 1983; (SDP) Yorkshire West, European Parly Elecn, 1984. Mem., Exec. of Justice, 1974–89. *Recreations*: history, opera. *Address*: 59 Westminster Gardens, Marsham Street, SW1P 4JG. *T*: (020) 7834 1960; 4 Primley Park Lane, Leeds LS17 7JR. *T*: (0113) 268 5351. *Died 23 April 2010.*

LYONS, (Isidore) Jack; Chairman: J. E. London Properties Ltd, since 1986; Natural Nutrition Company Ltd, 1989–91; Advisor, Cranbury Group, 1981–89; Director of other companies; *b* 1 Feb. 1916; *s* of Samuel H. Lyons and Sophia Niman; *m* 1943, Roslyn Marion Rosenbaum; two *s* two *d*. *Educ*: Leeds Grammar Sch. Director: UDS Gp, 1955–80; Adv. Bd, Bain Capital, USA, 1981–87; Advr for Guinness plc, Bain & Co., USA, 1981–87. Chm., Leeds Musical Festival, 1955–72, Vice-Pres., 1973; Jt Founder, 1961, and former Chm., Leeds Internat. Pianoforte Competition; Chm., London Symphony Orchestra Trust, 1970–91 (Jt Chm., 1963–70), Trustee, 1970– (Hon. Mem., LSO, 1973); Jt Chm., Southwark Rehearsal Hall Trust, 1974–95; Chm.,

Shakespeare Exhibn (quatercentenary celebrations Stratford-upon-Avon), 1964; Mem. Exec. Cttee, Royal Acad. of Dancing, 1964; Life Trustee, Shakespeare Birthplace Trust, 1967; Mem., Culture Adv. Cttee, UNESCO, 1973, Dep. Chm., Fanfare for Europe, 1972–73; Chm., FCO US Bicentennial Cttee for the Arts, 1973–; Mem., Adv. Cttee of Honour, Britain's Salute to NY 1983 Bicentennial. Chairman: Sir Jack Lyons Charitable Trust; Musical Therapy Charity, 1984–85; Trustee, Heslington Foundn for Music and Associated Arts, 1987–; Dir, Wolf Trap Foundn, USA. Vice-Pres., Anglo-Italian Chamber of Commerce, 1977–. Vice-Pres., Jt Israel Appeal, 1972– (Dep. Chm. 1957); Chm., Fedn of Jewish Relief Organisations, 1958–86. Member: Canadian Veterans' Assoc., 1964; Pilgrims, 1965. Mem. Council, Internat. Triangle Res. Inst., 1983–. Patron: St Gemma's Hospice; ORT, 1997–; Sponser Patron: British Osteoporosis Soc., 1989–93; Univ. of York Music Res. Dept, 2002. Dep. Chm., Governors of Carmel Coll., 1961–69; Mem. Ct, York Univ., 1965. FRSA 1973 Hon. FRAM 1972. DUniv York, 1975. CBE 1967, Kt 1973, both cancelled and annulled 1991. *Recreations*: music, the arts and swimming. *Died 18 Feb. 2008.*

LYTHGOE, Prof. Basil, FRS 1958; Professor of Organic Chemistry, Leeds University, 1953–78, then Emeritus; *b* 18 Aug. 1913; 2nd *s* of Peter Whitaker and Agnes Lythgoe; *m* 1946, Kathleen Cameron (*d* 2003), *er d* of H. J. Hallum, St Andrews; two *s*. *Educ*: Leigh Grammar Sch.; Manchester Univ. Asst Lectr, Manchester Univ., 1938; Univ. Lectr, Cambridge Univ., 1946. Fellow of King's Coll., Cambridge, 1950. *Publications*: papers on chemistry of natural products, in Jl of Chem. Soc. *Recreation*: hill walking. *Died 18 April 2009.*

LYTTELTON, Humphrey Richard Adeane; musician; band-leader (specializing in Jazz); journalist; *b* Eton, Bucks, 23 May 1921; *s* of late Hon. George William Lyttelton; *m* 1st, 1948, Patricia Mary Braithwaite (marr. diss. 1952); one *d*; 2nd, 1952, Elizabeth Jill (*d* 2006), *d* of Albert E. Richardson; two *s* one *d*. *Educ*: Sunningdale Sch.; Eton Coll.; Camberwell Sch. of Art; self-taught as regards musical educn. Served War of 1939–45: Grenadier Guards, 1941–46. Cartoonist, Daily Mail, 1949–53. Formed his own band, 1948; leader of Humphrey Lyttelton's Band, and free-lance journalist, 1953–; founded: own record label, Calligraph, 1984; own music publishers, Humph Music. Composed over 200 original works for his band; numerous recordings and television appearances; jazz festival appearances, Nice, Bracknell, Zürich, Camden, Montreux, Newcastle, Warsaw, Edinburgh, and Glasgow. Compère, BBC radio jazz programmes: Jazz Scene, Jazz Club, The Best of Jazz, etc., Chm., I'm Sorry I Haven't a Clue, BBC R4, 1972–. Pres., Soc. for Italic Handwriting, 1990–. Hon. Prof. of Music, Keele Univ., 1993. Hon. DLitt: Warwick, 1987; Loughborough, 1988; Hon. DMus: Durham, 1989; Keele, 1992. Walpole Medal of Excellence, 2007. *Publications*: I Play as I Please, 1954; Second Chorus, 1958; Take It from the Top (autobiog.), 1975; The Best of Jazz: Basin Street to Harlem, 1978, The Best of Jazz 2—Enter the Giants, 1981, both books repr. as one vol. 1997; Humphrey Lyttelton's Jazz and Big Band Quiz, 1979; Why No Beethoven? the diary of a vagrant musician, 1984; It Just Occured to Me… the reminiscences and thoughts of chairman Humph, 2007; contributor: Melody Maker, 1954–2001; Reynolds News, 1955–62; Sunday Citizen, 1962–67; Harper's & Queen's, Punch, The Field, High Life. *Recreations*: birdwatching, calligraphy. *Address*: BBC, Broadcasting House, Portland Place, W1A 1AA. *T*: (020) 7580 4468; (home) Alyn Close, Barnet Road, Arkley, Herts EN5 3LJ. *Died 25 April 2008.*

M

MABBS, Alfred Walter, CB 1982; Keeper of Public Records, 1978–82; *b* 12 April 1921; *e s* of James and Amelia Mabbs; *m* 1942, Dorothy Lowley; one *s. Educ:* Hackney Downs Sch. Served War, RAF, 1941–46. Asst Keeper, Public Record Office, 1950–66; Principal Asst Keeper, 1967–69; Records Admin. Officer, 1970–73; Dep. Keeper of Public Records, 1973–78. Pres., Internat. Council on Archives, 1980–82. Gen. Editor, Herts Record Soc., 1991–96. FRHistS 1954. FSA 1979. *Publications:* Guild Stewards Book of the Borough of Calne (vol. vii, Wilts Arch. and Record Soc.), 1953; The Records of the Cabinet Office to 1922, 1966; Guide to the Contents of the Public Record Office, vol. iii (main contributor), 1968; Exchequer of the Jews, vol. iv (jt contrib.), 1972; The Organisation of Intermediate Records Storage (with Guy Duboscq), 1974; articles and reviews in various jls. *Recreation:* retirement. *Address:* 32 The Street, Wallington, Baldock, Herts SG7 6SW.
Died 29 Jan. 2009.

MABON, Rt Hon. (Jesse) Dickson; PC 1977; company director and physician; Chairman, Gem and Ashtree Ltd, since 1988; *b* 1 Nov. 1925; *s* of Jesse Dickson Mabon and Isabel Simpson Montgomery; *m* 1970, Elizabeth, *o d* of Maj. William Zinn; one *s. Educ:* Possilpark, Cumbrae, North Kelvinside Schools. Worked in coalmining industry before Army service, 1944–48. MB, ChB (Glasgow); DHMSA; FFHom; Visiting Physician, Manor House Hospital, London, 1958–64. Political columnist, Scottish Daily Record, 1955–64; studied under Dr Kissinger, Harvard, 1963. President: Glasgow University Union, 1951–52; Scottish Union of Students, 1954–55; Chairman: Glasgow Univ. Labour Club, 1948–50; National Assoc. of Labour Students, 1949–50. Contested: (Lab) Bute and N Ayrshire, 1951; (Lab and Co-op) W Renfrewshire, 1955; Renfrew W and Inverclyde (SDP) 1983, (SDP/Alliance) 1987; (SDP) Lothians, European Parly Election, 1984. MP (Lab and Co-op 1955–81, SDP 1981–83) Greenock, Dec. 1955–1974, Greenock and Port Glasgow, 1974–83; Joint Parly Under-Sec. of State for Scotland, 1964–67; Minister of State, Scottish Office, 1967–70; Dep. Opposition Spokesman on Scotland, 1970–72 (resigned over Labour's attitude to Common Mkt); Minister of State, Dept of Energy, 1976–79. Chairman: UK Labour Cttee for Europe, 1974–76; Scottish Parly Labour Party, 1972–73, 1975–76; Member: Council of Europe, 1970–72 and 1974–76; Assembly, WEU, 1970–72 and 1974–76; North Atlantic Assembly, 1980–82; Chm., European Movement, 1975–76, Dep. Chm., 1979–83. Founder Chm., Manifesto Gp, Parly Lab. Party, 1974–76. Founder Mem., SDP, 1981; Mem., SDP Nat. Cttee, 1984–88; rejoined Labour Party, 1991. Chm., Young Volunteer Force Foundn, 1974–76. Mem., Energy Saving Trust, 1992–96; Chm., Labour Finance and Industry Gp Energy Gp, 1993–98. Fellow: Inst. of Petroleum; Inst. of Directors; Faculty of History of Medicine (Pres. 1990–94); Soc. of Apothecaries; FRSA. Freeman of City of London. *Recreations:* gardening, theatre. *Address:* 7 Kepplestone, Staveley Road, Meads, Eastbourne, E Sussex BN20 7JY. *T:* (01323) 438565, *Fax:* (01323) 438659. *Died 10 April 2008.*

MacALISTER, Very Rev. Randal George Leslie; Dean of St Andrews, Dunkeld and Dunblane, 1998–2006; Rector, St Kessog's, Auchterarder and St James', Muthill, 1998–2006; *b* 31 Dec. 1941; *s* of James Daniel Beaton MacAlister and Doreen MacAlister (*née* Thompson); *m* 1964, Valerie Jane Letitia Nelson; three *s. Educ:* Royal Sch., Armagh; Trinity Coll., Dublin (BA 1963; MA 1966; Divinity Testimonium 1964). Ordained deacon, 1964, priest 1966; Curate, St Mark's, Portadown, 1964–67; Rector: St Matthew's, Keady and Armaghbreague, 1967–74, and St John's, Derrynoose, 1973–74; St Mary's,

Kirriemuir, 1974–81; St John's, Greenock, 1981–87; St John's, Forfar, 1987–95; Canon, St Ninian's Cathedral, Perth, 1993–95; Chaplain, St Mark's, Sophia Antipolis, France, 1995–98. *Recreations:* gardening, hill-walking, languages, music. *Address:* Auld Mill, Dykehead Cortachy, Kirriemuir, Angus DD8 4QN. *T:* (01575) 540216.
Died 19 June 2009.

MacALLAN, Andrew; *see* Leasor, T. J.

McALPINE, (Robert Douglas) Christopher, CMG 1967; HM Diplomatic Service, retired; Director: Baring Brothers, 1969–79; H. Clarkson (Holdings) plc, 1980–87; *b* 14 June 1919; *s* of late Dr Douglas McAlpine, FRCP and Elizabeth Meg Sidebottom; *m* 1943, Helen Margery Frances Cannan; two *s* one *d* (and one *d* decd). *Educ:* Winchester; New Coll., Oxford. RNVR, 1939–46. Entered Foreign Service, 1946. FO, 1946–47; Asst Private Sec. to Sec. of State, 1947–49; 2nd Sec. and later 1st Sec., UK High Commn at Bonn, 1949–52; FO, 1952–54; Lima, 1954–56; Moscow, 1956–59; FO, 1959–62; Dep. Consul-Gen. and Counsellor, New York, 1962–65; Counsellor, Mexico City, 1965–68. Town Councillor, Tetbury, 1987–91. *Recreation:* travel. *Address:* Longtree House, Cutwell, Tetbury, Glos GL8 8EB.
Died 1 Sept. 2008.

McARDLE, Rear-Adm. Stanley Lawrence, CB 1975; LVO 1952; GM 1953; JP; Flag Officer, Portsmouth, and Port Admiral, Portsmouth, 1973–75; retired; *b* 27 Sept. 1922; *s* of Theodore McArdle, Lochmaben, Dumfriesshire; *m* 1st, 1945, (Helen) Joyce (marr. diss. 1960), *d* of Owen Cummins, Wickham, Hants; one *d*; 2nd, 1962, Jennifer, *d* of Walter Talbot Goddard, Salisbury, Wilts; one *d. Educ:* Royal Hospital Sch., Holbrook, Suffolk. Joined RN, 1938; served War, 1939–45. Lieut 1945; Comdr 1956; Captain 1963. Comd HMS Mohawk, 1965; Directorate of Naval Operations and Trade, 1969; Comd HMS Glamorgan, 1970; Dir Naval Trng, Director General, Personal Services and Trng (Naval), 1971–73; Rear Admiral 1972. Dir, Endless Holdings Ltd, 1985–94. JP Wilts, 1977. *Address:* The Coach House, Church Road, Farley, Salisbury, Wilts SP5 1AH. *Died 4 Dec. 2007.*

MACARTHUR, Rev. Arthur Leitch, OBE 1981; MA, MLitt; inducted, Christ Church, Marlow-on-Thames, 1980, retired 1986; *b* 9 Dec. 1913; *s* of Edwin Macarthur and Mary Macarthur (*née* Leitch); *m* 1950, Doreen Esmé Muir; three *s* one *d. Educ:* Rutherford Coll.; Armstrong Coll., Durham Univ. (MA, MLitt Dunelm); Westminster Coll., Cambridge. Ordained, 1937; inducted, Clayport, Alnwick, 1937; served with YMCA in France, 1940. Inducted: St Augustine's, New Barnet, 1944; St Columba's, North Shields, 1950. Gen. Sec., Presbyterian Church of England, 1960–72; Moderator, Presbyterian Church of England, 1971–72; Jt Gen.-Sec., URC, 1972–74; Moderator, URC, 1974–75; Gen. Sec., URC, 1975–80; Moderator, Free Church Federal Council, 1980–81. Vice-Pres., BCC, 1974–77 (Chm., Admin. Cttee, 1969–74). *Publications:* Setting up Signs, 1997. *Recreations:* gardening, golf, walking. *Address:* 4 Hoopers Court, West Way, Cirencester, Glos GL7 1GS.
Died 1 Sept. 2008.

MacARTHUR, Ian, OBE 1988; Hon. Treasurer, 1991–98, and Vice-Chairman, 1992–98, Texprint Ltd, charity; *b* 17 May 1925; *yr s* of late Lt-Gen. Sir William MacArthur, KCB, DSO, OBE, MD, DSc, FRCP, KHP; *m* 1957, Judith Mary (RGN 1976), *d* of late Francis Gavin Douglas Miller; four *s* three *d. Educ:* Cheltenham Coll.; The Queen's Coll., Oxford (Scholar, MA). Served War of 1939–45, with RN (Ord. Seaman) and RNVR, 1943–46 (King's Badge; Flag Lieut to C-in-C Portsmouth, 1946).

Contested (U), Greenock, 1955, also by-election, Dec. 1955; MP (C) Perth and E Perthshire, 1959–Sept. 1974; an Asst Government Whip (unpaid), 1962–63; a Lord Comr of the Treasury and Govt Scottish Whip, 1963–64; Opposition Scottish Whip, 1964–65; an Opposition Spokesman on Scottish Affairs, 1965–70 (Opposition front bench, 1965–66, 1969–70). Former Member: Speaker's Conf. on Electoral Law; Select Cttees on European Legislation, on Scottish Affairs, and on Members' Interests. Chm., Scottish Cons. Mems' Cttee, 1972–73. Introduced, as Private Member's Bills: Law Reform (Damages and Solatium) (Scotland) Act, 1962; Interest on Damages (Scotland) Act, 1971; Social Work (Scotland) Act, 1972; Domicile and Matrimonial Proceedings Act, 1973. Personal Asst to the Prime Minister, Rt Hon. Sir Alec Douglas-Home, Kinross and W Perthshire By-Election, Nov. 1963. Hon. Pres., Scottish Young Unionists, 1962–65; Vice-Chm., Cons. Party in Scotland, 1972–75. Formerly Dir of Administration, J. Walter Thompson Co. Ltd. Dir, British Textile Confederation, 1977–89. FRSA 1984. Gold Cross of Merit, Polish Govt in Exile, 1971. *Address:* 15 Old Palace Lane, Richmond, Surrey TW9 1PG.
Died 30 Nov. 2007.

McCALL, John Armstrong Grice, CMG 1964; *b* 7 Jan. 1913; 2nd *s* of Rev. Canon J. G. McCall; *m* 1951, Kathleen Mary Clarke; no *c. Educ:* Glasgow Academy; Trinity Coll., Glenalmond; St Andrews Univ.; St John's Coll., Cambridge. MA 1st class hons Hist. St Andrews, 1935. Colonial Administrative Service (HMOCS), Nigeria, 1935–67; Cadet, 1936; Class I, 1956; Staff Grade, 1958. Chm., Mid-Western Nigeria Development Corp., Benin City, 1966–67, retired 1967. Asst Chief Admin. Officer, East Kilbride Develt Corp., 1967–76. Scottish Rep., Executive Cttee, Nigerian British Chamber of Commerce, 1977–88. Mem. 1969, Vice-Chm. 1971, S Lanarkshire Local Employment Cttee; Mem. Panel, Industrial Tribunals (Scotland), 1972–74; Gen. Sec., Scotland, Royal Over-Seas League, 1978–80. Sec., West Linton Community Council, 1980–83. *Recreations:* golf, walking. *Address:* Burnside, West Linton, Peeblesshire EH46 7EW. *T:* (01968) 660488. *Clubs:* Caledonian, Royal Over-Seas League (Hon. Life Mem.); Old Glenalmond (Chm., 1978–81); Royal and Ancient (St Andrews). *Died 6 Dec. 2006.*

McCALLUM, Ian; *see* McCallum, R. I.

McCALLUM, John Neil, AO 1992; CBE 1971; Chairman and Executive Producer, Fauna Films, Australia, since 1967, and John McCallum Productions, since 1976; actor and producer; *b* 14 March 1918; *s* of John Neil McCallum and Lilian Elsie (*née* Dyson); *m* 1948, Georgette Lizette Withers (Googie Withers, AO, CBE, actress); one *s* two *d. Educ:* Oatlands Prep. Sch., Harrogate; Knox Grammar Sch., Sydney; C of E Grammar Sch., Brisbane; RADA. Served War, 2/5 Field Regt, AIF, 1941–45. Actor, English rep. theatres, 1937–39; Stratford-on-Avon Festival Theatre, 1939; Old Vic Theatre, 1940; British films and theatre, 1946–58; films include: It Always Rains On Sunday; Valley of Eagles; Miranda; London stage plays include: Roar Like a Dove; Janus; Waiting for Gillian; J. C. Williamson Theatres Ltd, Australia: Asst Man. Dir, 1958; Jt Man. Dir, 1959–65; Man. Dir, 1966. Appeared in: (with Ingrid Bergman) The Constant Wife, London, 1973–74; (with Googie Withers) The Circle, London, 1976–77, Australia, 1982–83; (with Googie Withers) The Kingfisher, Australia, 1978–79; The Skin Game, The Cherry Orchard, and Dandy Dick, theatrical tour, England, 1981; The School for Scandal, British Council European tour, 1984; (with Googie Withers, and dir.) Stardust, tours England, 1984, Australia, 1984–85; The Chalk Garden, Chichester Fest., 1986; Hay Fever, Chichester Fest., 1988; The Royal Baccarat Scandal, Chichester Fest., 1988, Haymarket, 1989; (with Googie Withers) The Cocktail Hour, Australian and UK tour, 1989–90; (with Googie Withers) High Spirits, Australia, 1991; On Golden Pond, UK tour, 1992; The Chalk

Garden, Sydney, 1995; An Ideal Husband, Old Vic, 1996, Australia, 1997–98; Lady Windermere's Fan, Chichester, 1997, Haymarket, 2002; A Busy Day, Bristol Old Vic and Lyric, London, 2000. Author of play, As It's Played Today, produced Melbourne, 1974. Produced television series, 1967–: Boney; Barrier Reef; Skippy; Bailey's Bird. Prod., Attack Force Z (feature film), 1980; Exec. Prod., The Highest Honor (feature film), 1982. Pres., Aust. Film Council, 1971–72. *Publications:* Life with Googie, 1979. *Recreation:* golf. *Address:* 5/19 Annam Road, Bayview, NSW 2104, Australia. *T:* (2) 99976879. *Clubs:* Melbourne (Melbourne); Australian, Elanora Country (Sydney). *Died 3 Feb. 2010.*

McCALLUM, Prof. (Robert) Ian, CBE 1987; MD, DSc; FRCP, FRCPEd, FFOM; Professor of Occupational Health and Hygiene, University of Newcastle upon Tyne, 1981–85, then Emeritus; Hon. Consultant, Institute of Occupational Medicine, Edinburgh, 1985–2003; *b* 14 Sept. 1920; *s* of Charles Hunter McCallum and Janet Lyon Smith; *m* 1952, Jean Katherine Bundy Learmonth (MBE 1997), *d* of Sir James Rögnvald Learmonth, KCVO, CBE; two *s* two *d. Educ:* Dulwich Coll., London; Guy's Hosp., London Univ. (MD 1946; DSc 1971). FRCP 1970; FRCPEd 1985; FFOM 1979. House physician, house surgeon, Guy's Hosp., 1943; house physician, Brompton Hosp., 1945. Rockefeller Travelling Fellowship in Medicine (MRC), USA, 1953–54. Reader in Industrial Health, Univ. of Newcastle upon Tyne, 1962–81. Hon. Physician, Industrial Medicine, Royal Victoria Infirmary, Newcastle upon Tyne, 1958–85; Hon. Consultant in Occ. Health to the Army, 1980–86. Mem., MRC Decompression Sickness Panel, 1962– (Chm., 1982–85). British Council: Vis. Consultant, USSR, 1977; Vis. Specialist, Istanbul, 1987; Vis. Lectr, Faculty of Medicine, Baghdad, 1987. Stanley Melville Meml Lectr, Coll. of Radiographers, 1983; Sydenham Lectr, Soc. of Apothecaries, London, 1983; Ernestine Henry Lectr, RCP, 1987. Dean, Faculty of Occ. Medicine, RCP, 1984–86; President: Sect. of Occ. Medicine, RSM, 1976–77; Soc. of Occ. Medicine, 1979–80; British Occ. Hygiene Soc., 1983–84; Mem., Adv. Cttee on Pesticides, 1975–87. Hon. Dir, North of England Industrial Health Service, 1975–84. Editor, British Jl of Industrial Medicine, 1973–79. FSAScot 1997. *Publications:* Antimony in Medical History, 1999; papers on Scottish alchemists, pneumoconiosis, decompression sickness, dysbaric bone necrosis, and antimony toxicology. *Recreation:* gardening. *Address:* 4 Chessels Court, Canongate, Edinburgh EH8 8AD. *T:* (0131) 556 7977. *Club:* Royal Society of Medicine. *Died 15 Feb. 2009.*

McCARTHY, (Patrick) Peter; Regional Chairman, London North, Industrial Tribunals, 1987–90; Part-time Chairman, Industrial Tribunals, 1990–92; *b* 10 July 1919; *er s* of late William McCarthy, OBE, and Mary McCarthy; *m* 1945, Isabel Mary (*d* 1994), *y d* of late Dr Joseph Unsworth, St Helens; two *s* three *d. Educ:* St Francis Xavier's Coll., Liverpool; Liverpool Univ. LLB 1940, LLM 1942. Admitted Solicitor, 1942; in private practice until 1974. Part-time Chm., 1972–74, full-time Chm., 1975–90, Regl Chm., Liverpool, 1977–87, Industrial Tribunals; part-time Chm., Rent Assessment Cttee, 1972–74. JP Liverpool, 1968–74. *Address:* Brook Cottage, Sham Castle Lane, Bath BA2 6JH. *Died 11 Dec. 2008.*

McCARTNEY, Hugh; Director, East Dunbartonshire Initiative for Creative Therapy and Social Care, 1997–99; *b* 3 Jan. 1920; *s* of John McCartney and Mary Wilson; *m* 1949, Margaret McDonald; one *s* two *d. Educ:* Royal Technical Coll., Glasgow; John Street Senior Secondary School. Apprentice in textile industry, 1934–39; entered aircraft engrg industry, Coventry, 1939; joined Rolls Royce, Glasgow, 1941; joined RAF as aero-engine fitter, 1942 and resumed employment with Rolls Royce, 1947; representative with company (later one of GKN group) specialising in manufacture of safety footwear, 1951. Joined Ind. Labour Party, 1934; joined Labour Party,

1936. Town Councillor, 1955–70 and Magistrate, 1965–70, Kirkintilloch; Mem., Dunbarton CC, 1965–70. MP (Lab): Dunbartonshire E, 1970–74; Dunbartonshire Central, 1974–83; Clydebank and Milngavie, 1983–87. Scottish Regional Whip, 1979–83; Mem., Speaker's Panel of Chairmen, 1984–87. Chm., TGWU Parly Group, 1986–87. Mem., Rent Assessment Panel for Scotland, 1968–70. Mem., Scottish Council, RoSPA, 1965–70. *Address:* 23 Merkland Drive, Kirkintilloch, Glasgow G66 3PG.   *Died 28 Feb. 2006.*

McCLAY, Sir Allen (James), Kt 2006; CBE 2000 (OBE 1994); Founder and Chairman, Almac Group, since 2001; *b* 21 March 1932; *m* 2009, Heather Topping. *Educ:* Cookstown High Sch.; Belfast Coll. of Technology. Sales rep., Glaxo, 1955–68; founder, Galen Ltd, 1968; retired as Pres., Galen Hldgs plc, 2001; acquired Chemical Synthesis Services from Galen, 2001, and other cos, to form Almac Gp; acquired Galen Ltd, 2004. *Address:* Almac Group, Almac House, 20 Seagoe Industrial Estate, Craigavon BT63 5QD.   *Died 12 Jan. 2010.*

McCONVILLE, Michael Anthony, MBE 1958; writer; *b* 3 Jan. 1925; *s* of late Lt-Col James McConville, MC and Winifred (*née* Hanley); *m* 1952, Beryl Anne (*née* Jerrett); two *s* four *d.* *Educ:* Mayfield Coll.; Trinity Coll., Dublin. Royal Marines, 1943–46. Malayan Civil Service, 1950–61: served in Perak, Johore, Trengganu, Negri Sembilam, Pahang and Kedah; retd as Chm., Border War Exec. Cttee. CRO (later HM Diplomatic Service), 1961–77: Colombo, 1963–64; Kingston, Jamaica, 1966–67; Ottawa, 1967–71; Consul-Gen., Zagreb, 1974–77. Kesatria Mankgu Negara (Malaya), 1962. *Publications:* (as Anthony McCandless): Leap in the Dark, 1980; The Burke Foundation, 1985; (as Michael McConville) Ascendancy to Oblivion: the story of the Anglo-Irish, 1986; A Small War in the Balkans: the British in war time Yugoslavia, 1986; Nothing Much to Lose, 1993; (ed) Tell it to the Marines, 1994; (as Miles Noonan): Tales from the Mess, 1983; More Tales from the Mess, 1984. *Recreations:* gardening, watching Rugby. *Address:* 72 Friarn Street, Bridgwater, Som TA6 3LJ.   *Died 30 May 2008.*

McCORKELL, Col Sir Michael (William), KCVO 1994; OBE 1964; TD 1954; JP; Lord-Lieutenant, County Londonderry, 1975–2000; *b* 3 May 1925; *s* of late Captain B. F. McCorkell, Templeard, Culmore, Co. Londonderry and of Mrs E. M. McCorkell; *m* 1950, Aileen Allen, OBE 1975, 2nd *d* of late Lt-Col E. B. Booth, DSO, Darver Castle, Dundalk, Co. Louth, Eire; three *s* one *d.* *Educ:* Aldenham. Served with 16/5 Lancers, 1943–47; Major (TA) North Irish Horse, 1951; Lt-Col 1961; comd North Irish Horse (TA); retd, 1964. T&AVR Col, NI, 1971–74; Brevet Col, 1974; Pres., T&AVR, NI, 1977–88; ADC to the Queen, 1972. Hon. Col, N Irish Horse, 1975–81. Co. Londonderry: High Sheriff 1961; DL 1962; JP 1980. *Recreations:* fishing, shooting. *Address:* Ballyarnett, 50 Beragh Hill Road, Londonderry, Northern Ireland BT48 8LY. *T:* (028) 7135 1239. *Club:* Cavalry and Guards.   *Died 13 Nov. 2006.*

MacCORMICK, Sir (Donald) Neil, Kt 2001; FBA 1986; Regius Professor of Public Law, University of Edinburgh, 1972–2008 (on leave of absence, 1999–2004); *b* 27 May 1941; *yr s* of J. M. MacCormick, MA, LLD (Glasgow) and Margaret I. Miller, MA, BSc (Glasgow); *m* 1st, 1965, Caroline Rona Barr (marr. diss. 1992); three *d*; 2nd, 1992, Flora Margaret Britain (*née* Milne), Edinburgh. *Educ:* High School, Glasgow; Univ. of Glasgow (MA, 1st cl. Philos. and Eng. Lit.); Balliol Coll., Oxford (BA, 1st cl. Jurisprudence; MA; Hon. Fellow, 2008); LLD Edinburgh, 1982. Pres., Oxford Union Soc., 1965. Called to the Bar, Inner Temple, 1971. Lecturer, St Andrew's Univ. (Queen's Coll., Dundee), 1965–67; Fellow and Tutor in Jurisprudence, Balliol Coll., Oxford, 1967–72, and CUF Lectr in Law, Oxford Univ., 1968–72; Pro-Proctor, Oxford Univ., 1971–72; University of Edinburgh: Dean of Faculty of Law, 1973–76 and 1985–88; Provost, Faculty Gp of Law and Social Scis, 1993–97; Leverhulme Personal Res. Prof., 1997–99; Vice

Principal (Internat.), 1997–99. Visiting Professor: Univ. of Sydney, 1981; Univ. of Uppsala, 1991; Anne Green Vis. Prof., Univ. of Texas, 1990; Higgins Visitor, NW Sch. of Law, Oregon, 1987. Lectures: Corry, Queen's Univ., Kingston, Ont, 1981; Dewey, NY Univ., 1982; Or Emet, Osgoode Hall, 1988; Chorley, LSE, 1992; Hart, Oxford, 1993; Stevenson, Glasgow, 1994. Contested (SNP): Edinburgh North, 1979; Edinburgh, Pentlands, 1983, 1987; Argyll and Bute, 1992, 1997; MEP (SNP) Scotland, 1999–2004. President: Assoc. for Legal and Social Philosophy, 1974–76; Soc. of Public Teachers of Law, 1983–84; Vice-President: Internat. Assoc. for Phil. of Law and Social Phil., 1991–95; RSE, 1991–94. Member: Houghton Cttee on Financial Aid to Political Parties, 1975–76; Broadcasting Council for Scotland, 1985–89; ESRC, 1995–99. Hon. QC 1999. MAE, 1995; For. Mem., Finnish Acad. of Scis, 1994. FRSE 1986. Hon. LLD: Uppsala, 1986; Saarland, 1994; Queen's Univ., Kingston, Ont, 1996; Macerata, 1998; Glasgow, 1999; Hon. DLitt Queen Margaret UC, Edinburgh, 2003. Hon. DSc (SocSci) Edinburgh, 2008. *Publications:* (ed) The Scottish Debate: Essays on Scottish Nationalism, 1970; (ed) Lawyers in their Social Setting, 1976; Legal Reasoning and Legal Theory, 1978; H. L. A. Hart, 1981; Legal Right and Social Democracy: essays in legal and political philosophy, 1982; (with O. Weinberger) Grundlagen des Institutionalistischen Rechtspositivismus, 1985; An Institutional Theory of Law, 1986 (trans. Italian, 1991); (ed jtly) Enlightenment, Right and Revolution, 1989; (ed jtly) Interpreting Statutes, 1991; Interpreting Precedents, 1997; Questioning Sovereignty, 1999; Who's Afraid of a European Constitution, 2005; Rhetoric and the Rule of Law, 2005; Institutions of Law, 2007; Practical Reason in Law and Morality, 2009; contribs to various symposia, jls on law, philosophy and politics. *Recreations:* hill walking, bagpiping, sailing. *Address:* 19 Pentland Terrace, Edinburgh EH10 6HA.   *Died 5 April 2009.*

McCORMICK, Prof. James Stevenson, FRCPI, FRCGP; FFPH; Professor of Community Health, Trinity College Dublin, 1973–91 (Dean of School of Physic, 1974–79); *b* 9 May 1926; *s* of Victor Ormsby McCormick and Margaretta Tate (*née* Stevenson); *m* 1954, Elizabeth Ann Dimond; three *s* one *d.* *Educ:* The Leys Sch., Cambridge; Clare Coll., Cambridge (BA, MB); St Mary's Hospital, W2. Served RAMC, 1960–62; St Mary's Hosp., 1963; general practice, 1964–73. Chairman: Eastern Health Board, 1970–72; Nat. Health Council, 1984–86. Pres., Irish Coll. of General Practitioners, 1986–87. Hon. MCFP 1982. *Publications:* The Doctor—Father Figure or Plumber, 1979; (with P. Skrabanek) Follies and Fallacies in Medicine, 1989; papers, espec. on General Practice and Ischaemic Heart Disease. *Recreation:* open air. *Address:* The Barn, Windgates, Bray, Co. Wicklow, Ireland. *T:* (1) 2874113.   *Died 2 Jan. 2007.*

MacCORMICK, Sir Neil; *see* MacCormick, Sir D. N.

MacDIARMID, Prof. Alan Graham, ONZ 2002; PhD; FRS 2003; Blanchard Professor of Chemistry, University of Pennsylvania, since 1988; *b* Masterton, NZ, 14 April 1927; *s* of late Archibald and Ruby MacDiarmid; *m* 1st, 1954, Marian Mathieu (*d* 1990); one *s* three *d*; 2nd, 2005, Gayl Gentile. *Educ:* Hutt Valley High Sch.; Victoria University Coll. (MSc 1950); Univ. of Wisconsin (Fulbright Schol.; PhD 1953); Sidney Sussex Coll., Cambridge (PhD 1955; Hon. Fellow, 2003). With Univ. of Pennsylvania, 1955–; pioneered work on conductive polymers. James Von Ehr Dist. Prof. of Sci. and Technol., Univ. of Texas, Dallas. (Jtly) Nobel Prize for Chemistry, 2000; Rutherford Medal, Royal Soc. of NZ, 2001. *Publications:* research papers. *Address:* Department of Chemistry, University of Pennsylvania, 231 South 34th Street, Philadelphia, PA 19104–6323, USA.   *Died 7 Feb. 2007.*

McDONALD, David Wylie, CMG 1978; DA, RIBA, ARIAS, FHKIA; Secretary for Lands and Works, Hong Kong, 1981–83; MLC Hong Kong, 1974–83; *b* 9 Oct.

1927; *s* of William McDonald and Rebecca (*née* Wylie); *m* 1951, Eliza Roberts Steele; two *d*. *Educ*: Harris Acad., Dundee; School of Architecture, Dundee Coll. of Art (Lorimer Meml Prize, RIAS, 1950; City Coronation Design Prize, Corporation of Dundee, 1953; DA 1953). Architect with Gauldie, Hardie, Wright and Needham, Chartered Architects, Dundee, 1953–55; Public Works Department, Hong Kong: Architect, 1955; Sen. Architect, 1964; Chief Architect, 1967; Govt Architect, 1970; Principal Govt Architect, 1972; Dir of Building Develt, 1973; Dir of Public Works, 1974. Member: Legislative Council, 1974–83; Commonwealth Parly Assoc., 1974–83. Director: Mass Transit Railway Corp., Hong Kong, 1975–83; Ocean Park Ltd, Hong Kong, 1976–83; Hong Kong Industrial Estate Corp., 1981–83; Mem., Hong Kong Housing Auth., 1982–83. Mem. Exec. Cttee: Girl Guides Assoc. (Hong Kong Br.), 1977–83; Hong Kong Red Cross, 1981–83. Mem., Margaret Blackwood Hsg Assoc., 1984–2002; Trustee, Scottish Trust for Physically Disabled, 1984–2002. Mem., Mensa, 1968–2002. JP Hong Kong, 1972–83. Silver Jubilee Medal, 1977. *Recreations*: swimming (Coach and Manager, Hong Kong Swimming Team at Commonwealth Games, Christchurch, NZ, 1974), drawing, painting and calligraphy. *Address*: 5 Kincraig Way, South Duncraig, WA 6023, Australia. *T*: (8) 94483303. *Clubs*: Hong Kong (Hong Kong) (Chairman, 1977); Hong Kong Jockey (Hong Kong).
Died 8 March 2007.

McDONALD, (Edward) Lawson, MA, MD Cantab; FRCP; FACC, FAHA; Hon. Consultant Cardiologist: National Heart Hospital, since 1983 (Consultant Cardiologist, 1961–83); Canadian Red Cross Memorial Hospital, Taplow, 1960–83; Consultant Cardiologist: King Edward VII's Hospital for Officers, London, 1968–88; to King Edward VII Hospital, Midhurst, 1970–92, Emeritus, 1992; Senior Lecturer to the Institute of Cardiology, 1961–83; *b* 8 Feb. 1918; *s* of late Charles Seaver McDonald and Mabel Deborah (*née* Osborne); *m* 1953, Ellen Greig Rattray (marr. diss. 1972); one *s*. *Educ*: Felsted Sch.; Clare Coll., Cambridge; Middlesex Hospital; Harvard Univ. House appointments Middlesex Hospital, 1942–43. Temp. Surgeon-Lt, RNVR, 1943–46; served War of 1939–45, in N Atlantic and Normandy Campaigns (HMS Glasgow). RMO, Nat. Heart Hosp., 1946–47; Asst Registrar, Inst. of Cardiology, 1947–48; Med. Registrar, Middlesex Hosp., 1948–49; studied in Stockholm, 1949; Asst to Prof. of Medicine, Middlesex Hosp., 1949–52; Rockefeller Travelling Fellow in Medicine, 1952–53; Asst in Medicine, Med. Dept, Peter Bent Brigham Hosp., Boston, Mass, and Research Fellow in Medicine, Harvard Univ., 1952–53; Clinical and Research Asst, Dept of Cardiology, Middlesex Hosp., 1953–55; Asst Dir, Inst. of Cardiology and Hon. Asst Physician, Nat. Heart Hosp., 1955–61; Physician, and Physician to Cardiac Dept, London Hosp., 1960–78. Member: Cardiology Cttee, RCP, 1963–76 (Chm. Jt Adv. Cttee, RCP and British Cardiac Soc., 1973–75); Bd of Governors, National Heart and Chest Hosps, 1975–82; Council, British Heart Foundn, 1975–83. Visiting Lecturer: American Coll. of Cardiology; American Heart Assoc.; Univ. of Toronto, Queen's Univ., Kingston, Ont; Univ. of Bombay; University of Barcelona, Eliseo Migoya Inst. of Cardiology, Bilbao, Spain; Istanbul Univ., Turkey; Univs of Chicago, Cincinnati and Kansas; Harvard Univ.; Mayo Foundation, USA; Univs of Belgrade, Ljubljana and Zagreb, Yugoslavia; Nat. Univ. of Cordoba, Argentine; Univ. of Chile, and Catholic Univ., Santiago; Nat. Univ. of Colombia; Nat. Inst. of Cardiology, Mexico; Nat. Univ. of Mexico; University of San Marcos and University of Cayetano Heredia, Peru; Nat. Univ. of Venezuela; Vis. Prof., Univ. of Oregon Med. Sch.; has addressed numerous cardiac societies in Europe, Africa, Australia, Canada, NZ, USA, People's Republic of China, USSR, and South America, 1961–; St Cyres Lecturer, 1966; First Charles A. Berns Meml Lectr, Albert Einstein Coll. of Medicine, NY, 1973; Vth World Congress of Cardiology Souvenir Orator and Lectr's Gold Medallist, 1977. Advisor to the Malaysian Govt on Cardiac Services. Editorial Bd, New Istanbul Contribution to Clinical Science. Member: British Cardiac Soc. (Mem. Council, 1967–71; Chm., 1979); Assoc. of Physicians of Great Britain and Ireland, and other societies; Fellow Emeritus: Amer. Coll. of Cardiology, 1998; Amer. Heart Assoc., 2001; Corresp. Mem. or Hon. Mem. of various socs of Cardiology or Angiology in S America. Hon. Fellow, Turkish Med. Soc.; Internat. Fellow, Council on Clinical Cardiol., Amer. Heart Assoc.; Mem., Italian Soc. of Cardiology; Hon. Member: Pakistan Cardiac Soc.; Scientific Council, Revista Portuguesa de Cardiologia. Member, Most Honourable Order of the Crown of Johore, 1980. *Publications*: (ed) Pathogenesis and Treatment of Occlusive Arterial Disease, 1960; Medical and Surgical Cardiology, 1969; (ed) Very Early Recognition of Coronary Heart Disease, 1978; numerous contribs to learned jls; also papers and addresses. *Recreations*: art, ski-ing, mountain walking, sailing. *Address*: 9 Bentinck Mansions, Bentinck Street, W1U 2ER. *T*: (020) 7935 7101.
Died 13 Jan. 2007.

McDONALD, Iverach; Associate Editor, The Times, 1967–73; Director, The Times Ltd, 1968–73; *b* 23 Oct. 1908; *s* of Benjamin McDonald, Strathcool, Caithness, and Janet Seel; *m* 1935, Gwendoline (*d* 1993), *o d* of late Captain Thomas R. Brown; one *s* one *d*. *Educ*: Leeds Grammar Sch. Asst Editor, Yorkshire Post, 1933; sub-editor, The Times, 1935; correspondent in Berlin, 1937; diplomatic correspondent 1938; Asst Editor, 1948; Foreign Editor, 1952; Managing Editor, 1965. War of 1939–45: Capt., Gen. Staff, 1939–40; travelled extensively in Soviet Union, Far East and America; reported all allied conferences after the war, including San Francisco, 1945, Paris, 1946 and 1947, Moscow, 1947, Colombo, 1950, and Bermuda, 1953. Sen. Associate Mem., St Antony's Coll., Oxford, 1976–. *Publications*: A Man of the Times, 1976; The History of The Times, vol. V, 1939–1966, 1984; chapters in: Walter Lippmann and His Times, 1959; The Times History of our Times, 1971. *Address*: Strathallan Care Home, 77 West Haugh Road, Stirling FK9 5GF.
Died 14 Dec. 2006.

McDONALD, Lawson; *see* McDonald, E. L.

McDONNELL, Christopher Thomas, CB 1991; Deputy Under-Secretary of State, Ministry of Defence, 1988–91; *b* 3 Sept. 1931; *s* of Christopher Patrick McDonnell and Jane McDonnell; *m* 1955, Patricia Anne (*née* Harvey) (*d* 1967); three *s* one *d*. *Educ*: St Francis Xavier's Coll., Liverpool; Corpus Christi Coll., Oxford (MA). WO, 1954; HM Treasury, 1966–68; RCDS, 1973; Asst Under-Sec. of State, MoD, 1976–88.
Died 31 March 2008.

MacDOUGALL, John William; JP; MP (Lab) Glenrothes, since 2005 (Fife Central, 2001–05); *b* 8 Dec. 1947; *m* 1968, Catherine; one *s* one *d*. *Educ*: Templehall Secondary Modern Sch., Kirkaldy, Fife; Rosyth Dockyard Coll.; Fife Coll.; Glenrothes Coll. Former Chm., Burntisland Initiative Recreational Trust Ltd; Chm., Community Business Fife Ltd, 1988–92. Trustee, 1996–98, Vice-Chm., 1998–, St Andrews Links Trust. Mem. (Lab) Fife Regl Council, 1982–96; Fife Council, 1995–2001 (Leader of Admin, 1987–96; Convenor, 1996–2001). Mem., Admin Select Cttee, H of C, 2002–05. Former Mem. Court, St Andrews Univ. JP Fife, 1983. *Address*: (office) 5 Hanover Court, Glenrothes, Fife KY7 5SB; c/o House of Commons, SW1A 0AA.
Died 13 Aug. 2008.

MacDOWELL, Prof. Douglas Maurice, DLitt; FRSE; FBA 1993; Professor of Greek, University of Glasgow, 1971–2001, then Emeritus; *b* 8 March 1931; *s* of Maurice Alfred MacDowell and Dorothy Jean MacDowell (*née* Allan). *Educ*: Highgate Sch.; Balliol Coll., Oxford (1st Cl. Classical Mods 1952, 1st Cl. Lit. Hum. 1954; MA, DLitt). FRSE 1991. Classics Master: Allhallows Sch., 1954–56; Merchant Taylors' Sch., 1956–58; University of Manchester: Asst Lectr, Lectr and Sen. Lectr, 1958–70;

Reader in Greek and Latin, 1970–71. Vis. Fellow, Merton Coll., Oxford, 1969. Sec., Council of University Classical Depts, 1974–76; Chm. Council, Classical Assoc. of Scotland, 1976–82. *Publications:* Andokides: On the Mysteries, 1962; Athenian Homicide Law, 1963; Aristophanes: Wasps, 1971; The Law in Classical Athens, 1978; Spartan Law, 1986; Demosthenes: Against Meidias, 1990; Aristophanes and Athens, 1995; (with M. Gagarin) Antiphon and Andocides, 1998; Demosthenes: On the False Embassy, 2000; Demosthenes: speeches 27–38, 2004. *Address:* 2 Grosvenor Court, 365 Byres Road, Glasgow G12 8AU. *T:* (0141) 334 7818. *Club:* Oxford and Cambridge. *Died 16 Jan. 2010.*

McEACHERN, Allan; Chief Justice of British Columbia, 1988–2001; *b* 20 May 1926; *s* of John A. and L. B. McEachern; *m* 1st, 1953, Gloria L. (*d* 1997); two *d*; 2nd, 1999, Hon. Mary Newbury, Judge of Court of Appeal, BC. *Educ:* Univ. of British Columbia (BA 1949; LLB 1950). Called to the Bar of British Columbia, 1951. Partner, Russell and DuMoulin, Barristers, 1950–79; Chief Justice, Supreme Court of BC, 1979–88. Associate Counsel, Fasken Martineau DuMoulin, barristers, Vancouver, 2002–. Chancellor, University of BC, 2002–. Hon. LLM Univ. of BC, 1990. *Recreations:* walking, sailing, gardening. *Address:* c/o Fasken Martineau DuMoulin LLP, 2100–1075 West Georgia Street, Vancouver, BC V6E 3G2, Canada. *Died 11 Jan. 2008.*

McENERY, John Hartnett; author, consultant and conceptual analyst, since 1981; *b* 5 Sept. 1925; *y s* of late Maurice Joseph and Elizabeth Margaret McEnery (*née* Maccabe); *m* 1977, Lilian Wendy, *yr d* of late Reginald Gibbons and Lilian Gibbons (*née* Cox). *Educ:* St Augustine's Sch., Coatbridge; St Aloysius Coll., Glasgow; Glasgow Univ. (MA(Hons)). Served War of 1939–45: RA, 1943–47; Staff Captain, Burma Command, 1946–47. Glasgow Univ., 1947–49. Asst Principal, Scottish Educn Dept, 1949; Principal, 1954; Cabinet Office, 1957; HM Treasury, 1959; Min. of Aviation, 1962; UK Delegn to NATO, 1964; Counsellor (Defence Supply), British Embassy, Bonn, 1966; Asst Sec., Min. of Technology, 1970; Dept of Trade and Industry, 1970–72; Under-Sec. and Regional Dir for Yorks and Humberside, DTI, 1972, Dept of Industry, 1974–76; Under Sec., Concorde and Nationalisation Compensation Div., Dept of Industry, 1977–81. *Publications:* Manufacturing Two Nations—the sociological trap created by the bias of British regional policy against service industry, 1981; Towards a New Concept of Conflict Evaluation, 1985; Epilogue in Burma 1945–48: the military dimension of British withdrawal, 1990; Fortress Ireland: the story of the Irish coastal forts and the River Shannon defence line, 2006; articles in Jl of Economic Affairs. *Recreations:* various games and sports, chess, travel. *Address:* 37 Leinster Avenue, East Sheen, SW14 7JW. *Club:* Hurlingham. *Died 14 Dec. 2006.*

MacEWEN, Ann Maitland, RIBA (DisTP), MRTPI; retired planning consultant; *b* 15 Aug. 1918; *d* of Dr Maitland Radford, MD, DPH, MOH St Pancras, and Dr Muriel Radford; *m* 1st, 1940, John Wheeler, ARIBA, AADip (Hons), Flt-Lt, RAF (killed on active service, 1945); two *d*; 2nd, 1947, Malcolm MacEwen, MA, LLB, Hon. FRIBA (*d* 1996); one *d*. *Educ:* Howell's Sch., Denbigh, N Wales; Architectural Assoc. Sch. of Architecture (AA Dip., RIBA); Assoc. for Planning and Regional Reconstruction Sch. of Planning (SP Dip., MRTPI). Architectural Asst, 1945–46; Planning Asst, Hemel Hempstead New Town Master Plan, 1946–47; Architect-Planner with LCC, 1949–61; Mem., Colin Buchanan's Gp, Min. of Transport, which produced official report, Traffic in Towns, 1961–63; res. work, Transport Section, Civil Engineering Dept, Imperial Coll., 1963–64; Partner, Colin Buchanan and Partners, 1964–73. Senior Lectr, Bristol Univ. Sch. of Advanced Urban Studies, 1974–77; Hon. Res. Fellow, UCL, 1977–87. Mem., Noise Adv. Council, 1971–73. RIBA Distinction in Town Planning, 1967. *Publications:*

National Parks—Conservation or Cosmetics? (with M. MacEwen), 1982; (with Joan Davidson) The Livable City, 1983; (with M. MacEwen) Greenprints for the Countryside? the story of Britain's National Parks, 1987. *Address:* Greathed Lodge, 41 Abbey Road, NW8 0AA. *Died 20 Aug. 2008.*

MACFADYEN, Rt Hon. Lord; Donald James Dobbie Macfadyen; PC 2002; a Senator of the College of Justice in Scotland, since 1995; *b* 8 Sept. 1945; *er s* of late Donald James Thomson Macfadyen and Christina Dick Macfadyen; *m* 1971, Christine Balfour Gourlay Hunter; one *s* one *d*. *Educ:* Hutchesons' Boys' Grammar Sch., Glasgow; Glasgow Univ. (LLB 1967). Admitted to Faculty of Advocates, 1969, Vice-Dean 1992–95. Advocate Depute, 1979–82; Standing Jun. Counsel to Dept of Agric. and Fisheries for Scotland, 1977–79, to SHHD, 1982–83; QC (Scot.) 1983. Part-time Chm., Med. Appeal Tribunals and Vaccine Damage Tribunals, 1989–95; Temp. Judge, Court of Session, 1994–95. Chm., Judges' Forum, Internat. Bar Assoc., 2005– (Vice Chm., 2000–04). Chm. Council, Cockburn Assoc. (Edinburgh Civic Trust), 2001–. FCIArb 1993. *Publications:* (ed and contrib.) Court of Session Practice, 2005. *Address:* 66 Northumberland Street, Edinburgh EH3 6JE. *T:* (0131) 556 6043. *Club:* New (Edinburgh). *Died 11 April 2008.*

MACFARLANE, Sir George (Gray), Kt 1971; CB 1965; BSc; Dr Ing (Dresden); FREng; retired; Member of the Board, British Telecommunications Corporation, 1981–84; Corporate Director, British Telecom plc, 1984–87; *b* 8 Jan. 1916; *s* of late John Macfarlane, Airdrie, Lanarks; *m* 1941, Barbara Grant, *d* of Thomas Thomson, Airdrie, Lanarks; one *s* one *d*. *Educ:* Airdrie Academy; Glasgow Univ.; Technische Hochschule, Dresden, Germany. FREng (FEng 1976); FIMA; FInstP. On scientific staff, Air Ministry Research Establishment, Dundee and Swanage, 1939–41; Telecommunications Research Establishment (TRE), Malvern, 1941–60; Deputy Chief Scientific Officer (Individual Merit Post), 1954–60; Deputy Director, National Physical Laboratory, 1960–62; Director, Royal Radar Establishment, 1962–67; Controller (Research), Min. of Technology and Min. of Aviation Supply, 1967–71; Controller, Research and Develt Establishments and Research, MoD, 1971–75. Member: PO Review Cttee, 1976–77; PO Bd, 1977–81; NEB, 1980–85 and NRDC, 1981–85 (subseq. British Technology Gp). Mem., Bd of Trustees, Imperial War Museum, 1978–86. Deputy-Pres., IEE, 1976–78 (Vice-Pres., 1972–74), Hon. FIET (Hon. FIEE, 1988); Hunter Meml Lecturer, IEE, 1966; Council Mem., Fellowship of Engrg, 1982–87 (Vice-Pres. 1983–86). Hon. LLD Glasgow. Glazebrook Medal and Prize, Inst. of Physics, 1978. *Publications:* papers in IEE, Proc. Phys. Society, Phys. Review. *Recreations:* walking, gardening. *Address:* Red Tiles, 17 Orchard Way, Esher, Surrey KT10 9DY. *T:* (01372) 463778. *Club:* Athenæum. *Died 20 May 2007.*

McFARLANE, Sir Ian, Kt 1984; Chairman and Managing Director, Trans Pacific Petroleum NL, since 1964; *b* 25 Dec. 1923; *s* of Stuart Gordon McFarlane, CMG, MBE and Mary Grace McFarlane; *m* 1956, Ann, *d* of M. A. Shaw, Salt Lake City, USA; one *s* two *d*. *Educ:* Melbourne Grammar School; Harrow; Sydney Univ. (BSc, BE); MIT (MS). Served War of 1939–45. RANVR. Morgan Stanley & Co., 1949–59; Mem., Sydney Stock Exchange, 1959–64; Partner, Ord, Minnett, T. J. Thompson & Partners, 1959–64; Dep. Chm., Magellan Petroleum, 1964–70; Chairman and Managing Director: Southern Pacific Petroleum NL, 1968–2001; Central Pacific Minerals NL, 1968–2001; Director: Trans City Discount Ltd, 1960–64; Consolidated Rutile Ltd, 1964–68; International Pacific Corp., 1967–73; Aust. Gen. Insurance Co., 1968–74; Mercantile Mutual Insurance Co., 1969–74; Concrete Construction, 1972–74; International Pacific Aust. Investments, 1972–73; Morgan Stanley Internat., NYC, 1976–80. Mem. Council, Imperial Soc. of Knights

Bachelor, 1985–. Founder, Sir Ian McFarlane Travelling Professorship in Urology, 1980. Chm., Royal Brisbane Hosp. Res. (formerly Hosp.) Foundn, 1985–93; Mem., Appeal Bd, Pain and Mgt Res. Centre. Royal North Shore Hosp., 1994–2003; Mem., 1997–2000, Vice Patron, 2001–, Nat. Trust St John's Cathedral Completion Fund, Brisbane. Co-Founder and Dep. Chm., Great Barrier Reef Res. Foundn, Brisbane, 2000–04. Life Governor, Royal Prince Alfred Hosp., Sydney, 1982; Founding Governor, St Luke's Hosp. Foundn, Sydney, 1982–. Fellow Commoner, Christ's Coll., Cambridge, 1987. Founder: Sir Ian McFarlane Scholarship for Excellence, Christ's Coll., Cambridge, 1989; Sir Ian McFarlane's Nurses' award, Royal Brisbane Hosp., 1994. Fellow, Aust. Inst. of Mining and Metallurgy, 1993. Hon. Col Kentucky, 1984–. KCGSJ 1999. *Address:* 40 Wentworth Road, Vaucluse, NSW 2030, Australia. *Clubs:* Australian (Sydney); Commonwealth (Canberra); University (NY); Royal Sydney Golf; Rose Bay Surf (Sydney).
Died 22 Oct. 2008

McFETRICH, (Charles) Alan; Deputy Chairman, Tenon Group PLC, since 2000; Managing Partner, External Affairs, Coopers & Lybrand, 1994–96; *b* 15 Dec. 1940; *s* of late Cecil McFetrich, OBE, FCA and Kathleen M. McFetrich (*née* Proom); *m* 1990, Janet Elizabeth Henkel (*née* Munro); two *s* one *d* from previous marriage. *Educ:* Oundle Sch., Magdalene Coll., Cambridge. FCA. Trainee Accountant, Graham Proom & Smith, 1959–61 and 1964–66; Deloitte Haskins & Sells: Accountant, 1966–68; Consultant, 1968–73; Consultancy Partner, 1973–80; seconded to Dept of Industry, 1981–82; Nat. Operations Partner, 1983–85; Nat. Managing Partner, 1985–90; Coopers & Lybrand Deloitte, later Coopers & Lybrand: Man. Partner, 1990–92; Exec. Partner, 1992–94. FRSA 1989. *Recreations:* travel, theatre.
Died 6 Sept. 2009.

McGAHERN, John, FRSL; author; *b* 12 Nov. 1934; *s* of Francis McGahern and Susan McManus; *m* 1st, 1965, Annikki Laaksi; 2nd, 1973, Madeline Green. *Educ:* University Coll., Dublin. Research Fellow, Univ. of Reading, 1968–71; O'Connor Prof., Colgate Univ., 1969, 1972, 1977, 1979 and 1983. Member: Aosdana Irish Acad of Letters. British Northern Arts Fellow, 1974–76. McCauley Fellowship, 1964; British Arts Council Award, 1967; Soc. of Authors Award, 1975; Amer. Irish Foundn Literary Award, 1985; Irish Times/Aer Lingus Award, 1990; GPA Award, 1992. Hon. LitD TCD, 1991. Chevalier de l'Ordre des Arts et des Lettres (France), 1989. *Publications:* The Barracks, 1962 (AE Meml Award, 1962); The Dark, 1965; Nightlines, 1970; The Leavetaking, 1975; Getting Through, 1978; The Pornographer, 1979; High Ground, 1985; The Rockingham Shoot, 1987; Amongst Women, 1990; The Power of Darkness, 1991; The Collected Stories, 1992; That They May Face The Rising Sun, 2002; By the Lake, 2002; Memoir, 2005. *Address:* c/o Faber & Faber, 3 Queen Square, WC1N 3AU.
Died 30 March 2006.

McGEOCH, Vice-Adm. Sir Ian (Lachlan Mackay), KCB 1969 (CB 1966); DSO 1943; DSC 1943; Director, Midar Systems Ltd, since 1986; *b* 26 March 1914; 3rd *s* of L. A. McGeoch; *m* 1937, Eleanor Somers, *d* of Rev. Canon Hugh Farrie; two *s* two *d. Educ:* Pangbourne Coll. Joined RN, 1931. Comd HM Submarine Splendid, 1942–43; Staff Officer (Ops) 4th Cruiser Sqdn, 1944–45; Comd: HMS Fernie, 1946–47; 4th Submarine Squadron, 1949–51; 3rd Submarine Squadron, 1956–57; Dir of Undersurface Warfare, Admiralty, 1959; IDC 1961; Comd HMS Lion 1962–64; Admiral Pres., RNC, Greenwich, 1964–65; Flag Officer Submarines, 1965–67; Flag Officer, Scotland and Northern Ireland, 1968–70. Trustee, Imperial War Mus., 1977–87. Member: The Queen's Body Guard for Scotland, Royal Co. of Archers, 1969–2003; Hon. Co. of Master Mariners, 1999–. MPhil Edinburgh, 1975. FNI 1986; FRIN 2001. Editor, The Naval Review, 1972–80. *Publications:* (jtly) The Third World War: a future history, 1978; (jtly) The Third

World War: the untold story, 1982; An Affair of Chances, 1991; The Princely Sailor, 1996. *Recreations:* sailing, the arts. *Address:* c/o Coutts and Co., 440 Strand, WC2R 0QS. *Clubs:* Army and Navy, Special Forces; Royal Yacht Squadron, Royal Naval Sailing Association (Cdre 1968–70).
Died 12 Aug. 2007.

MacGILLIVRAY, Barron Bruce, FRCP; Consultant in Clinical Neurophysiology and Neurology, Royal Free Hospital, 1964–93 (Dean, School of Medicine, 1975–89); Consultant in Clinical Neurophysiology, National Hospital for Nervous Diseases, 1971–93; *b* 21 Aug. 1927; *s* of late John MacGillivray and of Doreene (*née* Eastwood), S Africa; *m* 1955, Ruth Valentine; two *s* one *d. Educ:* King Edward VII Sch., Johannesburg; Univ. of Witwatersrand (BSc Hons 1949); Univ. of Manchester; Univ. of London (MB, BS 1962). FRCP 1973. House Surg., House Phys., Manchester Royal Infirm., 1955–56; RMO, Stockport and Stepping Hill Hosp., 1957–59; Registrar, subseq. Sen. Registrar, Nat. Hosp. for Nervous Diseases, Queen Sq., London, 1959–64; Res. Fellow, UCLA, 1964–65. Pro Vice Chancellor, Medicine, Univ. of London, 1985–87. Member: Camden and Islington AHA(T), 1975–78; NE Thames RHA, 1979–84; CVCP, 1983–87; Senate, Collegiate Council, Univ. of London; Univ. rep., Council, Sch. of Pharmacy, St George's Hosp. Med. Sch. (Treasurer, 1996–2000), and British Postgraduate Med. Fedn; Examr and Teacher, Univ. of London. Mem., Complaints Review Cttee, DHSS, 1993–94. Pres., Electrophys. Technicians Assoc., 1976–82. MRI 1975; FRSocMed; FRSA. *Publications:* papers in sci. jls on cerebral electrophysiol., epilepsy, computing and cerebral death. *Recreations:* sailing, photography. *Address:* 45 Eustace Building, 372 Queenstown Road, SW8 4NT. *T:* (020) 7498 5568; *e-mail:* bmacg@btinternet.com. *Died 17 Dec. 2010.*

McGILLIVRAY, Robert, CEng, FICE, FCIWEM; Chairman, Fisheries (Electricity) Committee (formerly Fisheries Committee for Hydro-Electric Schemes), Scotland, 1992–2002; Chief Engineer and Under Secretary, Scottish Development Department, 1987–91; *b* 11 May 1931; *o s* of late William Gilchrist McGillivray and of Janet Love Jamieson; *m* 1955, Pauline, *e d* of late Alexander Davie; one *s. Educ:* Boroughmuir Sch., Edinburgh; Univ. of Edinburgh (BSc CivEng.). National Service, 1949–51. Training with J. & A. Leslie & Reid, CE, 1955–57; Asst Engr, Midlothian CC, 1957–60; CE, Dept of Agric. & Fisheries for Scotland, 1960–72; Scottish Development Department: Prin. CE, 1972–75; Engrg Inspector, 1976–80; Asst Chief Engr, 1980–85; Dep. Chief Engr, 1985–87. *Publications:* A History of the Clan MacGillivray (with George B. Macgillivray), 1973; The Clan MacGillivray, 2004. *Recreations:* music, genealogy. Highland history. *Address:* Fairview, 88/3 Barnton Park View, Edinburgh EH4 6HJ. *T:* (0131) 339 1667. *Club:* Royal Scots (Edinburgh). *Died 18 April 2009.*

McGLASHAN, John Reid Curtis, CBE 1974; HM Diplomatic Service, retired 1979; *b* 12 Dec. 1921; *s* of late John Adamson McGlashan and Emma Rose May McGlashan; *m* 1947, Dilys Bagnall (*née* Buxton Knight); one *s* two *d. Educ:* Fettes; Christ Church, Oxford (Rugger Blue, 1945). RAF (Bomber Command), 1940–45 (POW, 1941–45). Entered Foreign Service, 1953; Baghdad, 1955; Tripoli, 1963; Madrid, 1968; Counsellor, FCO, 1970–79. *Recreations:* gardening, reading. *Address:* Allendale, Selsey Bill, West Sussex PO20 9DB.
Died 14 Aug. 2010.

McGREGOR, Sir Ian (Alexander), Kt 1982; CBE 1968 (OBE 1959); FRS 1981; FRSE; Visiting Professor (formerly Professorial Fellow), Department of Tropical Medicine, Liverpool School of Tropical Medicine, 1981–94; *b* 26 Aug. 1922; *s* of John McGregor and Isabella (*née* Taylor), Cambuslang, Lanarks; *m* 1954, Nancy Joan, *d* of Frederick Small, Mapledurham, Oxon; one *s* one *d. Educ:* Rutherglen Academy; St Mungo Coll., Glasgow. LRCPE, LRCSE, LRFPS(G) 1945; DTM&H 1949; MRCP 1962; FRCP 1967; FFCM 1972; Hon. FRCPGlas 1984. Mil. Service, 1946–48 (despatches).

Mem. Scientific Staff, Human Nutrition Research Unit, MRC, 1949–53; Dir, MRC Laboratories, The Gambia, 1954–74, 1978–80; Head of Laboratory of Trop. Community Studies, Nat. Inst. for Med. Research, Mill Hill, 1974–77; Mem., External Staff, MRC, 1981–84. Chm., WHO Expert Cttee on Malaria, 1985–89; Member: WHO Adv. Panel on Malaria, 1961–99; Malaria Cttee, MRC, 1962–71; Cttee on Nutrition Surveys, Internat. Union of Nutrition Sciences, 1971–75; Tropical Medicine Res. Bd, MRC, 1974–77, 1981–83; Steering Cttee on Immunology of Malaria, WHO, 1978–89; Council, Liverpool Sch. of Trop. Medicine, 1982–95; Steering Cttee on Applied Field Res. in Malaria, WHO, 1984–90; Council, Royal Soc., 1985–87. Lectures: Heath Clark, London Sch. of Hygiene and Tropical Medicine, 1983–84; Fred Soper, Amer. Soc. of Trop. Medicine and Hygiene, 1983; Lord Cohen History of Medicine, Liverpool Univ., 1989; Albert Norman Meml, Inst. of Med. Lab. Scis, 1992; Manson Orator, RSTM&H, 1994. Pres., Royal Soc. of Trop. Medicine and Hygiene, 1983–85 (Vice-Pres., 1981–83; Hon. Fellow, 1995). FRSE 1987. Hon. Fellow: Liverpool Sch. of Trop. Medicine, 1980; RSTM&H, 1995; Hon. Member: Amer. Soc. of Trop. Medicine and Hygiene, 1983; British Soc. for Parasitology, 1988. Hon. LLD Aberdeen, 1983; Hon. DSc Glasgow, 1984. Chalmers Medal, Royal Soc. Trop. Med. and Hygiene, 1963; Stewart Prize, BMA, 1970; Darling Foundn Medal, WHO, 1974; Laveran Medal, Société de Pathologie Exotique de Paris, 1983; Glaxo Prize for Medical Writing, 1989; Mary Kingsley Medal, Liverpool Sch. of Trop. Medicine, 1994. *Publications:* (ed with W. Wernsdorfer) Malaria: the principles and practice of malariology, 1988; scientific papers on infections, nutrition, immunity, child health and community medicine in tropical environments. *Recreations:* ornithology, golf, fishing. *Address:* Greenlooms House, Homington, Salisbury, Wilts SP5 4NL.
Died 1 Feb. 2007.

McGRIGOR, Captain Sir Charles Edward, 5th Bt *cr* 1831; DL; Rifle Brigade, retired; Member, Royal Company of Archers (HM Body Guard for Scotland); *b* 5 Oct. 1922; *s* of Lieut-Colonel Sir Charles McGrigor, 4th Bt, OBE, and Lady McGrigor, *d* of Edward Lygon Somers Cocks, Bake, St Germans, Cornwall; *S* father, 1946; *m* 1948, Mary Bettine, *e d* of Sir Archibald Charles Edmonstone, 6th Bt; two *s* two *d. Educ:* Eton. War of 1939–45 (despatches); joined Army, 1941, from Eton; served with Rifle Bde, N. Africa, Italy, Austria. ADC to Duke of Gloucester, 1945–47, in Australia and England. Exon, Queen's Body Guard, Yeoman of the Guard, 1970–85. Mem. Cttee of Management, and Dep. Chm., RNLI. DL Argyll and Bute, 1987. *Recreations:* fishing, gardening. *Heir: s* James Angus Rhoderick Neil McGrigor, *b* 19 Oct. 1949. *Address:* Upper Sonachan, Dalmally, Argyll PA33 1BJ. *Died 1 Oct. 2007.*

McGUINNESS, Rt Rev. James Joseph; Bishop of Nottingham, (RC), 1974–2000, then Emeritus; *b* 2 Oct. 1925; *s* of Michael and Margaret McGuinness. *Educ:* St Columb's College, Derry; St Patrick's College, Carlow; Oscott College, Birmingham. Ordained, 1950; Curate of St Mary's, Derby, 1950–53; Secretary to Bishop Ellis, 1953–56; Parish Priest, Corpus Christi Parish, Clifton, Nottingham, 1956–72; Vicar General of Nottingham Diocese, 1969; Coadjutor Bishop of Nottingham and Titular Bishop of St Germans, 1972–74. *Recreation:* gardening. *Address:* St Mary's Nursing Home, Ednaston, Brailsford, Derby DE6 3BY. *Died 6 April 2007.*

McILWAIN, Alexander Edward, CBE 1985; WS; President, Law Society of Scotland, 1983–84; Consultant, Leonards, Solicitors, Hamilton, 1995–97 (Partner, 1963–95, Senior Partner, 1984–95); *b* 4 July 1933; *s* of Edward Walker McIlwain and Gladys Edith Horne or McIlwain; *m* 1961, Moira Margaret Kinnaird; three *d. Educ:* Aberdeen Grammar Sch.; Aberdeen Univ. MA 1954; LLB 1956. Pres., Students Representative Council, Univ. of Aberdeen, 1956–57. Commnd RCS, 1957–59,

Lieut. Admitted Solicitor in Scotland, 1957; SSC, 1966. Burgh Prosecutor, Hamilton, 1966–75; District Prosecutor, Hamilton, 1975–76; Dean, Soc. of Solicitors of Hamilton, 1981–83; Vice Pres., Law Soc. of Scotland, 1982–83; Hon. Sheriff, Sheriffdom of South Strathclyde, Dumfries and Galloway at Hamilton, 1982; Temp. Sheriff, 1984. WS 1985. Chairman: Legal Aid Central Cttee, 1985–87; Hamilton Sheriff Court Project, 1991–94 and 1996–99; Member: Lanarkshire Health Bd, 1981–91; Central Adv. Cttee on Justices of the Peace, 1987–96; Supreme Court (formerly Review) Cttee, Scottish Legal Aid Bd, 1987–93; Cameron Cttee on Shrieval Trng, 1994–96; Criminal Injuries Compensation Appeal Panel, 1997–2006; Judicial Studies Cttee, 1997–2000; Criminal Injuries Compensation Bd, 1998–2000. Pres., Temporary Sheriffs' Assoc., 1995–98 (Vice Pres., 1993–95). Chm., Lanarkshire Scout Area, 1981–91; Mem. Council, Scout Assoc., 1987–97. Founder Fellow, Inst. of Contemp. Scotland, 2000. Hon. Mem., Amer. Bar Assoc., 1983. *Recreations:* gardening, listening to music. *Address:* Craigievar, Bothwell Road, Uddingston, Glasgow G71 7EY. *T:* (01698) 813368.
Died 18 July 2008.

McINTOSH OF HARINGEY, Baron *cr* 1982 (Life Peer), of Haringey in Greater London; **Andrew Robert McIntosh;** PC 2002; Chairman, Committee on Culture, Science and Education, Council of Europe Parliamentary Assembly, since 2006; President, GamCare (National Association for Gambling Care, Educational Resources and Training), since 2005; Member, Gambling Commission, since 2006; *b* 30 April 1933; *s* of late Prof. A. W. McIntosh and Jenny (*née* Britton); *m* 1962, Naomi Ellen Sargant (*d* 2006); two *s. Educ:* Haberdashers' Aske's Hampstead Sch.; Royal Grammar Sch., High Wycombe; Jesus Coll., Oxford (MA); Ohio State Univ. (Fellow in Econs, 1956–57). Gallup Poll, 1957–61; Hoover Ltd, 1961–63; Market Res. Manager, Osram (GEC) Ltd, 1963–65; IFF Research Ltd: Man. Dir, 1965–81; Chm., 1981–88; Dep. Chm., 1988–97. Chm., SVP United Kingdom Ltd, 1983–92. Member: Hornsey Bor. Council, 1963–65; Haringey Bor. Council, 1964–68 (Chm., Develt Control); Greater London Council: Member for Tottenham, 1973–83; Chm., NE Area Bd, 1973–74, W Area Bd, 1974–76, and Central Area Bd, 1976; Opposition Leader on Planning and Communications, 1977–80; Leader of the Opposition, 1980–81. House of Lords: Opposition spokesman on educn and science, 1985–87, on industry matters, 1983–87, on the environment, 1987–92, on home affairs, 1992–97; Dep. Leader of the Opposition, 1992–97; Captain of the Yeomen of the Guard (Dep. Govt Chief Whip), 1997–2003; Minister for the Media and Heritage, DCMS, 2003–05. Chm., Computer Sub-Cttee, H of L Offices Cttee, 1984–92; Member: Council of Europe Parly Assembly, 2005 (Chm., Media Sub-Cttee, 2008–); Parly Assembly of Western EU, 2005. Vis. Res. Fellow, Policy Studies Inst., Univ. of Westminster, 2007–; Hon. Prof. of Applied Social Res., Univ. of Salford, 2008–. Mem., Metrop. Water Bd, 1967–68. Market Research Society: Ed. of Jl, 1963–67; Chm., 1972–73; Pres., 1995–98. Vice-Pres., Royal Television Soc., 2006–10. Chairman: Assoc. of Neighbourhood Councils, 1974–80; Fabian Soc., 1985–86 (Mem., NEC, 1981–87). Principal, Working Men's Coll., NW1, 1988–97; Governor, Drayton Sch., Tottenham, 1967–83. *Publications:* Industry and Employment in the Inner City, 1979; (ed) Employment Policy in the UK and United States, 1980; Women and Work, 1981; jl articles on theory, practice and findings of survey research. *Recreations:* cooking, reading, music. *Address:* 27 Hurst Avenue, N6 5TX. *T:* (020) 8340 1496, *Fax:* (020) 8348 4641.
Died 27 Aug. 2010.

MACINTOSH, Dr Farquhar, CBE 1982; Rector (Headmaster), The Royal High School, Edinburgh, 1972–89; *b* 27 Oct. 1923; *s* of John Macintosh and Kate Ann Macintosh (*née* MacKinnon); *m* 1959, Margaret Mary Inglis, Peebles; two *s* two *d. Educ:* Elgol Primary Sch.; Portree High Sch., Skye; Edinburgh Univ. (MA);

Glasgow Univ. (DipEd). Served RN, 1943–46; commnd RNVR, 1944. Headmaster, Portree High Sch., 1962–66; Rector, Oban High Sch., 1967–72. Member: Highlands and Islands Develt Consultative Council, 1965–82; Broadcasting Council for Scotland, 1975–79; Chairman: BBC Secondary Programme Cttee, 1972–80; School Broadcasting Council for Scotland, 1981–85; Scottish Examination Bd, 1977–90; Scottish Assoc. for Educnl Management and Admin, 1979–82; Highlands and Is Educn Trust, 1988–97 (Chm., Educn Cttee, 1973–97); Gaelic Educn Action Gp, 1994–2004; European Movt (Scotland), 1996–2004 (Chm., Educn Cttee, 1993–96). Chm. of Governors, Jordanhill Coll. of Educn, 1970–72; Mem. Court, Edinburgh Univ., 1975–91; Chm., Sabhal Mor Ostaig (Gaelic Coll.), Skye, 1991–2007; Mem., Foundn and Bd of Govs (formerly Bd of Dirs), Univ. of Highlands and Islands, 1996–2007 (Chm., Forum, 1999–2004). Governor: Aberdeen Coll. of Educn, 1961–66; St Margaret's Sch., Edinburgh, 1989–98 (Vice-Chm., Bd of Govs, 1996–98); Royal Blind Sch., 1990–2006 (Chm. Educn Exec. Cttee, 1994–2005; Vice-Chm. Bd of Dirs, 2004–). Member, Board of Management: Skye Hosps, 1963–66; Oban Hosps, 1968–72. Pres., St Andrew Soc., Edinburgh, 1996–2000. Elder, Church of Scotland. FEIS 1970; FScotvec 1990; Fellow, UHI, 2003. Hon. DLitt Heriot-Watt, 1980; Dr hc Edinburgh, 1992. Publications: (contrib.) Celtic Connections, vol. I, 1999; regular contribs to TES Scotland; contrib. to European Jl of Educn. Recreations: hill-walking, Gaelic, travel. Address: 12 Rothesay Place, Edinburgh EH3 7SQ. T: (0131) 225 4404. Clubs: East India; Rotary of Murrayfield and Cramond (Edinburgh).
Died 18 Nov. 2007.

McINTOSH, Prof. Naomi Ellen Sargant, (Lady McIntosh of Haringey); see Sargant, N. E.

McINTYRE, Prof. Alasdair Duncan, CBE 1994; FRSE 1975; Emeritus Professor of Fisheries and Oceanography, Aberdeen University, since 1986; b 17 Nov. 1926; s of Alexander Walker McIntyre and Martha Jack McIntyre; m 1967, Catherine; one d. Educ: Hermitage Sch., Helensburgh; Glasgow Univ. BSc (1st class Hons Zoology) 1948; DSc 1973. Scottish Home Department (from 1960, DAFS) Marine Laboratory, Aberdeen: Develt Commn Grant-aided Student, 1948–49; Scientific Officer, 1950; Head, Lab. Environmental Gp, 1973; Dep. Dir, 1977; Dir, 1983. Dir of Fisheries Res. Services for Scotland, Dept of Agric. and Fisheries for Scotland, 1983–86. UK Co-ordinator, Fisheries Res. and Develt, 1986. President: Scottish Marine Biological Assoc., later Scottish Assoc. for Marine Sci., 1988–93; Estuarine and Coastal Scis Assoc., 1992–96; Sir Alister Hardy Foundn for Ocean Sci., 1992–99; Chairman: UN Gp of Experts on Scientific Aspects of Marine Pollution (GESAMP), 1981–84; Adv. Cttee on Marine Pollution, Internat. Council for the Exploration of the Sea, 1982–84; Marine Forum for Envmtl Issues, 1988–98; Atlantic Frontier Envmtl Forum, 1996–; Falkland Is Exploration and Production Envmtl Forum, 1997–; Assessor: Donaldson Inquiry into protection of UK coastline from pollution by merchant shipping, 1993–94; Donaldson Review of Salvage and Intervention Command and Control, 1997–99. Member: NCC for Scotland, 1991; Res. Bd, Scottish Natural Heritage, 1992–96. Hon. Res. Prof., Aberdeen Univ., 1983–86. Chm., Trustees of Buckland Foundn, 1994–99 (Vice Chm., 1988–94). Ed., Fisheries Research, 1988–. DUniv Stirling, 1997; Hon. DSc Napier, 2005. Publications: over 100 articles in scientific jls on marine ecology and pollution. Recreations: cooking, wine, walking. Address: 63 Hamilton Place, Aberdeen AB15 5BW. T: (01224) 645633.
Died 15 April 2010.

McINTYRE, Prof. Donald Ian; Professor of Education, University of Cambridge, 1996–2004 (Head of School of Education, 1997–2002); Fellow of Hughes Hall, Cambridge, 1996–2004, then Life Fellow; b 3 Jan. 1937; s of George McIntyre and Mary Gladys McIntyre (née

Bell); m 1964, Anne Roberta Brown; two s one d. Educ: George Watson's Coll., Edinburgh; Edinburgh Univ. (MA; MEd). Math. Teacher, Dunfermline High Sch., 1960–61; Lectr in Educn, Moray House Coll., Edinburgh, 1961–65, 1967–69; Res. Tutor in Math. Educn, Univ. of Hull, 1965–67; Sen. Res. Fellow, subseq. Lectr, and Sen. Lectr, Reader in Educn, Univ. of Stirling, 1969–85; Reader in Educnl Studies, Univ. of Oxford, 1986–95. Pres., British Educnl Res. Assoc., 1996–97. Fellow, Scottish Council for Res. in Educn, 1998. Hon. LLD Dundee, 2002; Hon. DEd Edinburgh, 2006. Publications: jointly: Teachers and Teaching, 1969; Schools and Socialization, 1971; Investigations of Microteaching, 1977; Making Sense of Teaching, 1993; The School Mentor Handbook, 1993; Effective Teaching and Learning, 1996; Learning Without Limits, 2004; Learning Teaching from Teachers, 2006. Recreations: writing, golf, walking, visiting Scotland and France. Address: Faculty of Education, University of Cambridge, 184 Hills Road, Cambridge CB2 2PQ. T: (01223) 767600.
Died 16 Oct. 2007.

MacINTYRE, Prof. Iain, FMedSci; FRS 1996; Professor and Research Director, William Harvey Research Institute, Bart's and The London, Queen Mary's School of Medicine and Dentistry (formerly St Bartholomew's and the Royal London School of Medicine and Dentistry, Queen Mary and Westfield College), University of London, since 1995; b 30 Aug. 1924; s of John MacIntyre, Tobermory, Mull, and Margaret Fraser Shaw, Stratherick, Inverness-shire; m 1947, Mabel Wilson Jamieson, MA (d 2003), y d of George Jamieson and J. C. K. K. Bell, Largs, Ayrshire; one d. Educ: Jordanhill Coll. Sch., Glasgow; Univ. of Glasgow (MB, ChB 1947); PhD 1960, DSc 1970, London. MRCPath 1963 (Founder Mem.), FRCPath 1971; FRCP 1977 (MRCP 1969). Asst Clinical Pathologist, United Sheffield Hosps, and Hon. Demonstrator in Biochem., Sheffield Univ., 1948–52; Royal Postgraduate Medical School: Registrar in Chemical Pathology, 1952–54; first Sir Jack Drummond Meml Fellow, 1954–56; Asst Lectr in Chem. Path., 1956–59; Reader in Chem. Path., 1963–67; Dir, Endocrine Unit, 1967–89; Chm., Academic Bd, 1985–89; Sen. Res. Fellow, Dept of Medicine, 1989–91; Prof., Chem. Path., London Univ., 1967–89, then Emeritus; Res. Dir, William Harvey Res. Inst., St Bartholomew's Hosp. Med. Coll., 1991–94. Director: Dept of Chem. Path., Hammersmith Hosp., 1982–89; Chelsea Hosp. for Women, Queen Charlotte's Hosp. for Women, 1986–89. Vis. Scientist, Nat. Insts of Health, Bethesda, 1960–61; Commonwealth Fund Schol., Australia, 1968; Visiting Professor: San Francisco Medical Center, 1964; Melbourne Univ., 1979–80; St George's Hosp. Med. Sch., 1989–; Vis. Lectr, Insts of Molecular Biol. and Cytol., USSR Acad. of Scis, 1978. Lectures: A. J. S. McFadzean, Univ. of Hong Kong, 1981; Transatlantic, Amer. Endocrine Soc., 1987; Per Edman Meml, St Vincent's Inst. of Medical Res., Australia, 1990. Mem., Hammersmith and Queen Charlotte's SHA, 1982–89. Chm. Organizing Cttee, Hammersmith Internat. Symposium on Molecular Endocrinology, 1967–81; Member: Org Cttee, Hormone and Cell Regulation Symposia, 1976–79; Adv. Council, Workshop on Vitamin D, 1977–79. Pres., Bone and Tooth Soc., 1984–87; Member: Cttee, Soc. for Endocrinology, 1978–80; Biochem. Soc.; NIH Alumni Assoc.; Assoc. of Amer. Physicians, 1998; Amer. Endocrine Soc.; Amer. Soc. for Bone and Mineral Res.; European Calcified Tissue Soc.; Assoc. of Clin. Biochemists. Vice-Pres., English Chess Assoc., 1989–. Member Editorial Board: Clinical Endocrinology, 1975–79; Molecular and Cellular Endocrinology, 1975–80; Jl of Endocrinological Investigation; Jl of Mineral and Electrolyte Metabolism; Jl of Investigative and Cell Pathol.; Jl of Metabolic Bone Disease and Related Res. Hon. Mem., Assoc. of American Physicians, 1998. Founder FMedSci 1998. Hon. MD: Turin, 1985; Sheffield, 2002. (Jtly) Gairdner Internat. Award for the discovery of the existence and origin of calcitonin, Toronto, 1967; Elsevier Award, Internat. Confs on

Calcium Regulating Hormones, Inc., 1992; John B. Johnson Award, Paget Foundn, 1995; Buchanan Medal, Royal Soc., 2006. *Publications:* articles in endocrinology. *Recreations:* tennis, chess, music. *Address:* Great Broadhurst Farm, Broad Oak, Heathfield, East Sussex TN21 8UX. *T:* (01435) 883515. *Clubs:* Athenæum; Queen's, Hurlingham.   *Died 18 Sept. 2008.*

McINTYRE, William Ian Mackay, CBE 1990; PhD; FRCVS; Professor Emeritus of Veterinary Medicine, University of Glasgow, since 1991 (Senior Lecturer, 1951–61, Professor, 1961–83); *b* 7 July 1919; *s* of George John and Jane McIntyre; *m* 1st, 1948, Ruth Dick Galbraith (*d* 2007); three *s*; 2nd, 2007, Elizabeth Margaret Hunter. *Educ:* Altnaharra Primary and Golspie Secondary Sch., Sutherland; Royal (Dick) Veterinary Coll. (MRCVS); University of Edinburgh (PhD). FRCVS 1983. Clinical Asst, Royal (Dick) Veterinary Coll., 1944–48; Lectr, Vet. Med., Royal (Dick) Vet. Coll., 1948–51. Seconded to University of East Africa, University Coll., Nairobi, as Dean, Faculty of Veterinary Science, and Prof., Clinical Studies, 1963–67. Dir, International Trypanotolerance Centre, The Gambia, 1984–89. Hon. DVM Justus Liebig Univ., Giessen, 1987. *Publications:* various, on canine nephritis, parasitic diseases and vaccines, clinical communications, and African Trypanosomiasis. *Address:* Stuckenduff, Shandon, Helensburgh G84 8NW. *T:* (01436) 820571.   *Died 20 March 2008.*

MACKANESS, George Bellamy, MB, BS, DPhil; FRS 1976; President, Squibb Institute for Medical Research and Development, 1976–87, retired; *b* Sydney, Australia, 20 Aug. 1922; *s* of James V. Mackaness and Eleanor F. Mackaness; *m* 1945, Gwynneth Patterson; one *s*. *Educ:* Sydney Univ. (MB, BS Hons 1945); London Univ. (DCP 1948); Univ. of Oxford (Hon. MA 1949, DPhil 1953). Resident MO, Sydney Hosp., 1945–46; Resident Pathologist, Kanematsu Inst. of Pathology, Sydney Hosp., 1946–47; Dept of Path., Brit. Postgrad. Med. Sch., London Univ., 1947–48 (DCP); ANU Trav. Scholarship, Univ. of Oxford, 1948–51; Demonstrator and Tutor in Path., Sir William Dunn Sch. of Path., Oxford, 1949–53; Dept of Experimental Pathology, Australian National University: Sen. Fellow, 1954–58; Associate Prof. of Exp. Path., 1958–60; Professorial Fellow, 1960–63; Vis. Investigator, Rockefeller Univ., NY, 1959–60; Prof. of Microbiology, Univ. of Adelaide, 1963–65; Dir, Trudeau Inst. for Med. Res., NY, 1965–76; Adjunct Prof. of Path., NY Univ. Med. Center, 1969–. Director: Josiah Macy Jr Foundn, 1982–86; Squibb Corp., 1984–87. Member: Allergy and Immunol. Study Sect., Nat. Insts of Health, 1967–71; Bd of Sci. Counsellors, Nat. Inst. of Allergy and Infect. Diseases, 1971–75; Armed Forces Epidemicol Bd, 1967–73; Bd of Governors, W. Alton Jones Cell Science Center, 1970–72; Council, Tissue Culture Assoc., 1973–; Bd of Sci. Consultants, Sloan-Kettering Inst. Member: Amer. Assoc. of Immunologists; Amer. Assoc. for Advancement of Science; Reticuloendothelial Soc.; Lung Assoc.; Internat. Union Against Tuberculosis; Amer. Soc. of Microbiologists. Fellow, Amer. Acad. of Arts and Scis, 1978. Paul Ehrlich-Ludwig Darmstaedter Prize, 1975; Novartis Prize, 1998. *Address:* 677 Lake Frances Drive, St Michael's Place, James Island, SC 29412, USA. *T:* (843) 7623951.   *Died 4 March 2007.*

McKAY, Prof. Alexander Gordon, OC 1988; FRSC 1965; Professor of Classics, McMaster University, 1957–90, then Emeritus; Adjunct Professor of Humanities, 1990–96, and Fellow, Vanier College, since 1992, York University; President, Royal Society of Canada, 1984–87; *b* 24 Dec. 1924; *s* of Alexander Lynn McKay and Marjory Maude Redfern Nicoll McKay; *m* 1964, Helen Jean Zulauf; two step *d*. *Educ:* Trinity Coll., Toronto (Hons BA Classics 1946); Yale Univ. (MA 1947); Princeton Univ. (AM 1948; PhD 1950). Classics faculty: Wells Coll., NY, 1949–50; Univ. of Pennsylvania, 1950–51; Univ. of Manitoba, 1951–52; Mount Allison Univ., 1952–53; Waterloo Coll., Ont.,

1953–55; Univ. of Manitoba, 1955–57; McMaster Univ., 1957–90: Chm. of Dept, 1962–68, 1976–79; Founding Dean of Humanities, 1968–73; Senator, 1968–73, 1985–87. Dist. Vis. Prof., Univ. of Colorado, 1973; Prof. i/c, Intercollegiate Center for Classical Studies in Rome (Stanford Univ.), 1975; Mem. Inst. for Advanced Study, Princeton, 1979, 1981; Vis. Schol., Univ. of Texas, Austin, 1987; Vis. Fellow Commoner, Trinity Coll., Cambridge, 1988; Distinguished Vis. Lectr, 1992–93, Prof. Emeritus, 1999–, Concordia Univ., Montreal. Dir, Internat. Union of Academies, 1980–83, 1986–90 (Vice-Pres., 1983–86). Vice-Pres., Bristol Inst. of Hellenic and Roman Studies, 1998–. Hon. LLD: Manitoba, 1986; Brock Univ., Ont, 1990; Queen's Univ., Kingston, 1991; Hon. DLitt: McMaster, 1992; Waterloo, 1993. KStJ 1986. Silver Jubilee Medal, 1977; 125th Anniversary of the Confederation of Canada Medal, 1992; Golden Jubilee Medal, 2002. *Publications:* Naples and Campania: texts and illustrations, 1962; Roman Lyric Poetry: Catullus and Horace, 1962; Vergil's Italy, 1970; Cumae and the Phlegraean Fields, 1972; Naples and Coastal Campania, 1972; Houses, Villas and Palaces in the Roman World, 1975, German edn 1980; Roman Satire, 1976; Vitruvius, Architect and Engineer, 1978; Roma Antiqua: Latium and Etruria, 1986; Selections from Vergil's Aeneid Books I, IV, VI: Dido and Aeneas, 1988; Tragedy, Love and Change, 1994; Arma Virumque: heroes at war, 1998; Classics at McMaster 1890–2000, 2000; A Song of War: readings from Vergil's Aeneid, 2003. *Recreations:* pianoforte, travel. *Address:* 15 Inglewood Drive, Hamilton, ON L8P 2T2, Canada. *T:* (905) 5261331, *Fax:* (905) 5269245; *e-mail:* ag.mckay@sympatico.ca. *Clubs:* Yale (NY); Tamahaac (Ancaster, Hamilton); Arts and Letters, X (Toronto); University (McMaster Univ.).   *Died 31 Aug. 2007.*

MACKAY, Eric Beattie; Editor of The Scotsman, 1972–85; *b* 31 Dec. 1922; *s* of Lewis Mackay and Agnes Johnstone; *m* 1954, Moya Margaret Myles Connolly (*d* 1981); two *s* one *d* (and one *s* decd). *Educ:* Aberdeen Grammar Sch.; Aberdeen Univ. (MA). Aberdeen Bon-Accord, 1948; Elgin Courant, 1949; The Scotsman, 1950; Daily Telegraph, 1952; The Scotsman, 1953: London Editor, 1957; Dep. Editor, 1961. *Recreations:* travel, reading, theatre.   *Died 16 May 2006.*

McKEE, Dr Robert Andrew; Chief Executive, Chartered Institute of Library and Information Professionals (formerly Library Association), since 1999; *b* 16 Aug. 1950; *s* of Rev. Harry McKee and Nancy McKee; *m* 1976, Victoria Alexandra Lippman; one *s* one *d*. *Educ:* Bury Grammar Sch.; St Catherine's Coll., Oxford (BA 1971); Shakespeare Inst., Univ. of Birmingham (MA 1972; PhD 1976); Birmingham Poly. (DipLib 1977). MCLIP (ALA 1979; MIInfSc 1986). Trainee and Resources Librarian, Birmingham Liby Service, 1974–79; Tutor Librarian, Solihull Coll. of Technol., 1979–84; Principal Lectr, Dept of Liby and Inf. Studies, Birmingham Poly., 1984–88; Dir, Libraries and Arts, 1988–96, Asst Chief Exec., 1996–99, Solihull MBC. Hon. Prof., Univ. of Worcester, 2006–. Member: Council, MLA, 2003–06; PLR Adv. Cttee, 2003–; Governing Bd, IFLA, 2005–. FRSA 1991. *Publications:* The Information Age, 1985; Public Libraries into the 1990s, 1987; Planning Library Service, 1989; contribs to jl literature of liby and inf. studies. *Recreations:* walking, music, watching football (Bury FC) and cricket, enjoying the company of family and friends. *Address:* Chartered Institute of Library and Information Professionals, 7 Ridgmount Street, WC1E 7AE. *T:* (020) 7255 0691; *e-mail:* bob.mcKee@cilip.org.uk.   *Died 13 Aug. 2010.*

McKEE, Dr William James Ernest, MD; Regional Medical Officer and Advisor, Wessex Regional Health Authority, 1976–89; *b* 20 Feb. 1929; *s* of John Sloan McKee, MA, and Mrs Annie Emily McKee (*née* McKinley); *m* Josée Tucker; three *d*. *Educ:* Queen Elizabeth's, Wakefield; Trinity Coll., Cambridge; Queen's Coll., Oxford. MA, MD, BChir (Cantab);

LRCP, MRCS, FFCM. Clinical trng and postgrad. clinical posts at Radcliffe Infirmary, Oxford, 1952–57; med. res., financed by Nuffield Provincial Hosps Trust, 1958–61; successive posts in community medicine with Metrop. Regional Hosp. Bds, 1961–69; Sen. Admin. Med. Officer, Liverpool Regional Hosp. Bd, 1970–74; Regional Med. Officer, Mersey RHA, 1974–76. Chairman: Regional Med. Officers' Gp, 1984–86; Wessex Regl Working Party to review policy for Mental Handicap Services, 1979; UK Head of Delegation, EEC Hosp. Cttee, 1988–89 (Mem., 1985–89); Member: Council for Postgrad. Med. Educn in England and Wales, 1975–85; Hunter Working Party on Med. Admin, 1972–83; DHSS Adv. Cttee on Med. Manpower Planning, 1982–85; DHSS Jt Planning Adv. Cttee on Med. Manpower, 1985–89; Bd of Faculty of Medicine, Univ. of Southampton, 1976–89. QHP 1987–90. *Publications:* papers on tonsillectomy and adenoidectomy in learned jls. *Recreations:* fly-fishing, golf. *Address:* 22a Borowecke Avenue, Winchester SO22 6BH. *T:* (01962) 861369.   *Died 17 Oct. 2009.*

MACKENZIE, Ian Clayton, CBE 1962; HM Diplomatic Service, retired; Ambassador to Korea, 1967–69; *b* 13 Jan. 1909; *m* 1948, Anne Helena Tylor (*d* 2006); one *s* one *d*. *Edu.* Bedford Sch.; King's Coll., Cambridge. China Consular Service, 1932–41; Consul, Brazzaville, 1942–45, Foreign Office, 1945; 1st Sec., Commercial, Shanghai, 1946–49; Santiago, Chile, 1949–53; Commercial Counsellor: Oslo, 1953–58; Caracas, 1958–63; Stockholm, 1963–66. *Address:* Koryo, Armstrong Road, Brockenhurst, Hants SO42 7TA. *T:* (01590) 623453.   *Died 17 Oct. 2009.*

MACKENZIE, James, BSc; CEng, FIMMM; a Managing Director, British Steel Corporation, 1976–85; *b* 2 Nov. 1924; *s* of James Mackenzie and Isobel Mary Chalmers; *m* 1950, Elizabeth Mary Ruttle; one *s* one *d*. *Educ:* Queen's Park Sch., Glasgow; Royal Technical Coll., Glasgow (BSc). The United Steel Companies Ltd, Research and Develt Dept, 1944–67; British Steel Corporation, 1967–85. Chm., Wade Building Services Ltd, 1987–99; former Dir, Geo. Cohen Sons & Co. Ltd; Dir, Lloyds Register Quality Assce Ltd, 1985–98. President: Inst. of Ceramics, 1965–67; Metals Soc., 1983–85. *Address:* Westhaven, Beech Waye, Gerrards Cross, Bucks SL9 8BL. *T:* (01753) 886461.   *Died 29 Oct. 2007.*

McKENZIE, Sir Roy (Allan), ONZ 1995; KBE 1989; Director, Rangatira Ltd, 1946–93; *b* 7 Nov. 1922; *s* of John Robert McKenzie and Ann May McKenzie (*née* Wrigley); *m* 1949, Shirley Elizabeth Howard; two *s* one *d*. *Educ:* Timaru Boys' High Sch. ACA 1948. Executive, 1949–70, Exec. Dir, 1955, McKenzie NZ Ltd; Chairman: Rangatira Investment Co. Ltd, 1968–85; J. R. McKenzie Trust, 1970–87. Chairman and Founder: McKenzie Educn Foundation; Roy McKenzie Foundn, Chm., J. R. McKenzie Youth Educn Fund, 1947–2002. Patron: Te Omanga Hospice, 1995– (Chm., 1979–95); Outward Bound Trust NZ, 1977– (Chm., 1968). Hon. DLitt Massey, 1992; Hon. DCom Victoria Univ. of Wellington, 2004. Rotary Internat. Service Above Self Award, 1995; Rotary Paul Harris Five Jewel Award, 1997. *Publications:* The Roydon Heritage, 1978; Footprints: harnessing an inheritance into a legacy, 1998. *Recreations:* tennis, ski-ing, tramping, breeding standardbreds (horses). *Address:* 221 Marine Drive, Lowry Bay, Eastbourne, New Zealand. *T:* (4)684492.
                              Died 1 Sept. 2007.

MACKERRAS, Sir (Alan) Charles (MacLaurin), AC 1997; CH 2003; Kt 1979; CBE 1974; Musical Director, Welsh National Opera, 1987–92, then Conductor Emeritus; Principal Guest Conductor: Scottish Chamber Orchestra, 1992–95, then Conductor Laureate; Philharmonia Orchestra, since 2002; President, Trinity College of Music, since 2000; *b* Schenectady, USA, 17 Nov. 1925; *s* of late Alan Patrick and Catherine Mackerras, Sydney, Australia; *m* 1947, Helena Judith (*née* Wilkins); one *d* (and one *d* decd). *Educ:* Sydney Grammar Sch.; Sydney Conservatorium of Music; student with

Vaclav Talich, Prague Acad. of Music. Principal Oboist, Sydney Symphony Orchestra, 1943–46; Staff Conductor, Sadler's Wells Opera, 1948–54; Principal Conductor BBC Concert Orchestra, 1954–56; freelance conductor with most British and many continental orchestras; concert tours in USSR, S Africa, USA, 1957–66; First Conductor, Hamburg State Opera, 1966–69; Musical Dir, Sadler's Wells Opera, later ENO, 1970–77; Chief Guest Conductor, BBC SO, 1976–79; Chief Conductor, Sydney Symphony Orch., ABC, 1982–85; Principal Guest Conductor: Royal Liverpool Philharmonic Orch., 1986–88 (Conductor Emeritus, 2009); San Francisco Opera, 1993–96 (then Conductor Emeritus); RPO, 1993–96; Czech Philharmonic Orch., 1997–2003; Mus. Dir, Orch. of St Luke's, NY, 1998–2001 (then Mus. Dir Emeritus); Conductor Laureate, Brno Philharmonic Orch., 2007; Conductor Emeritus, Orch. of the Age of Enlightenment, 2007; Guest Conductor: Vienna State Opera; Paris Opera; Munich Opera; Opera Australia; Royal Opera House Covent Garden; Metropolitan Opera: frequent radio and TV broadcasts; many commercial recordings, notably Handel, Janáček, Mozart operas and symphonies, Brahms, Dvořák, Schubert, Mahler and Beethoven symphonies; appearances at many internat. festivals and opera houses. Hon. Pres., Edinburgh Internat. Festival, 2008–. Hon. Fellow: St Peter's Coll., Oxford, 1999; Cardiff Univ., 2003. Hon. RAM 1969; Hon. FRCM 1987; Hon. FRNCM 1999; Hon. FTCL 1999; Hon. FRWCMD 2005; Hon. GSM 2007. Hon. DMus: Hull, 1990; Nottingham, 1991; York, Brno, Brisbane, 1994; Oxford, 1997; Prague Acad. of Music, 1999; Napier Univ., 2000; Melbourne, 2003; Sydney, 2003; Janáček Acad., Brno, 2004; London, 2005. Evening Standard Award for Opera, 1977; Janáček Medal, 1978; Gramophone Record of the Year, 1977, 1980, 1999; Gramophone Operatic Record of the Year Award, 1983, 1984, 1994, 1999; Gramophone Best Choral Record, 1986; Grammy Award for best opera recording, 1981, 2007; Chocs de l'Année Award, Le Monde de la Musique, 1998; Edison Award, 1999; Lifetime Achievement Award and Chopin Prize, Cannes, 2000; Assoc. of British Orchestras Award, 2001; Dist. Musicians Award, ISM, 2002; Gold Medal, Royal Philharmonic Soc., 2005; Queen's Medal for Music, 2005; Silver Medal, Musicians' Co., 2006; Classic FM Gramophone Lifetime Achievement Award, 2006; Orchestral Award, Midem Classical Music Awards, 2009; Critics Award, Classical BRIT Awards, 2009; Orchestral Award, Disc of the Year, BBC Music Mag. Awards, 2009. Medal of Merit (Czech Republic), 1996; Centenary Medal (Australia), 2003. *Publications:* ballet arrangements of Pineapple Poll (Sullivan), 1951 and of The Lady and the Fool (Verdi), 1954; reconstruction of Arthur Sullivan's lost Cello Concerto, 1986; contrib. 4 appendices to Charles Mackerras: a musicians' musician, by Nancy Phelan 1987; articles in Opera Magazine, Music and Musicians and other musical jls. *Recreations:* languages, yachting. *Address:* 10 Hamilton Terrace, NW8 9UG.   *Died 14 July 2010.*

MACKIE, Eric Dermott, OBE 1987; Executive Chairman, Swansea Dry Docks Ltd, 1995–2000; *b* 4 Dec. 1924; *s* of James Girvan and Ellen Dorothy Mackie; *m* 1950, Mary Victoria Christie; one *s* one *d*. *Educ:* Coll. of Technology, Belfast. CEng; MIMechE, FIMarEST, FRINA. 1st Class MoT Cert. (Steam and Diesel). Trained with James Mackie & Son (Textile Engrs), 1939–44; Design draughtsman, Harland & Wolff, Belfast, 1944–48; 2nd Engineer (sea-going) in both steam and diesel ships for Union Castle Mail Steamship Co., 1948–53; Harland & Wolff, Belfast, 1953–75: Test Engr; Manager, Shiprepair Dept; Gen. Manager i/c of Southampton branch; Gen. Manager i/c of ship prodn and ship repair, Belfast; Man. Dir, James Brown Hamer, S Africa, 1975–79; Chief Exec. and Man. Dir of Shiprepair in UK, British Shipbuilders, 1979–81; Chm. and Man. Dir, Govan Shipbuilders, later Govan Kvaerner Ltd, 1979–90. Former Mem., Governing Bd, British Marine Technology; Mem., Lloyds Gen. Cttee, 1979–, laterly Hon. Member. Denny Gold Medal, IMarE, 1987.

Publications: articles for marine engrg instns on various subjects pertaining to marine engrg and gen. engrg. *Recreations:* golf, swimming, reading. *Address:* No 3 Castle Meadow, Whittingham, near Alnwick, Northumberland NE66 4SH. *T:* (01665) 574648. *Clubs:* Caledonian; Durban, Rand (Johannesburg). *Died 13 May 2010.*

McKINNEY, Her Honour (Sheila Mary) Deirdre; a Circuit Judge, 1981–2001; *b* 20 Oct. 1928; *d* of Patrick Peter McKinney and Mary Edith (*née* Conoley). *Educ:* Convent of the Cross, Boscombe, Bournemouth. Called to the Bar, Lincoln's Inn, 1951; a Recorder of the Crown Court, 1978–81. *Died 9 Oct. 2009.*

MACKINNON, Dame (Una) Patricia, DBE 1977 (CBE 1972); *b* Brisbane, 24 July 1911; *d* of Ernest T. and Pauline Bell; *m* 1936, Alistair Scobie Mackinnon; one *s* one *d*. *Educ:* Glennie School and St Margaret's School, Queensland. Member Cttee of Management, Royal Children's Hospital, Melbourne, 1948–79; Vice-President, 1958; President, 1965–79; Chm., Research Bd, 1967–85. *Recreations:* gardening, reading history and biographies. *Address:* Lisson Manor, 12 Lisson Grove, Hawthorn, Vic 3122, Australia. *Club:* Alexandra (Melbourne). *Died 17 May 2009.*

McLACHLAN, Gordon, CBE 1967; BCom; FCA; Secretary, Nuffield Provincial Hospitals Trust, 1956–86; *b* 12 June 1918; *s* of late Gordon McLachlan and Mary McLachlan (*née* Baird); *m* 1951, Monica Mary Griffin (*d* 2002); two *d*. *Educ:* Leith Academy; Edinburgh Univ. Served with RNVR, 1938–46; Gunnery Specialist, 1943–46. Accountant, Edinburgh Corp., 1946–48; Dep. Treas., NW Met. Regional Hosps Bd, 1948–53; Accountant Nuffield Foundn, Nuffield Provincial Hosps Trust, Nat. Corp. for Care of Old People, 1953–56. Asst Dir, Nuffield Foundn, 1955–56. Henry Cohen Lectr, Univ. of Jerusalem, 1969; Parker B. Francis Foundn Distinguished Lectr, Amer. Coll. of Hosp. Admin, 1976; Sir David Bruce Lectr, RAMC, 1982; Rock Carling Fellow, 1989–90. Consultant, American Hospitals Assoc. and American Hospitals Research and Educational Trust, 1964–65; Member Council, American Hospitals Research and Educational Trust, 1965–74 (citation for meritorious service, AHA, 1976); Mem., Inst. of Medicine, Nat. Acad. of Sciences, Washington DC, 1974–. General Editor, Nuffield Provincial Hospitals Trust publications, 1956–86; Consulting Editor, Health Services Research Journal (US), 1966–74. Hon. FRCGP 1978. Hon. LLD Birmingham, 1977. *Publications:* What Price Quality?, 1990; A History of the Nuffield Provincial Hospitals Trust 1940–90, 1992; editor of many publications on Nuffield Provincial Hospitals Trust list; contrib. to Lancet, Practitioner, Times, Twentieth Century, etc. *Recreations:* reading, watching ballet, theatre, Rugby football. *Address:* 95 Ravenscourt Road, W6 0UJ. *T:* (020) 8748 8211. *Club:* Caledonian. *Died 13 Aug. 2007.*

McLAREN, (Dame) Anne Laura, (Dr Anne McLaren), DBE 1993; DPhil; FRCOG, FMedSci; FRS 1975; Principal Research Associate, Wellcome Trust/ Cancer Research UK Gurdon Institute; Hon. Fellow, King's College, Cambridge, since 1996; *b* 26 April 1927; *d* of 2nd Baron Aberconway; *m* 1952, Donald Michie, *qv* (marr. diss. 1959); one *s* two *d*. *Educ:* Lady Margaret Hall, Oxford (MA, DPhil). FRCOG *ad eund* 1986. Post-doctoral research, UCL, 1952–55 and Royal Vet. Coll., London, 1955–59; joined staff of ARC Unit of Animal Genetics at Edinburgh Univ., 1959; Dir, MRC Mammalian Develt Unit, 1974–92; Principal Res. Associate, Wellcome/CRC Inst., then Wellcome Trust/ Cancer Res. Inst. UK, subseq. Wellcome Trust CR UK Gurdon Inst., 1992–; Res. Fellow, King's Coll., Cambridge, 1992–96. Fullerian Prof. of Physiology, Royal Instn, 1990–95; Professorial Fellow, Univ. of Melbourne, 1998–. Mem., ARC, 1978–83; Mem., HFEA, 1990–2001. Vice-Pres., Royal Soc., 1992–96 (Mem. Council, 1985–87; Foreign Sec., 1991–96); Pres., BAAS, 1993–94. Mem., Cttee of Managers, Royal Instn, 1976–81; Chm., Governing Body, Lister Inst. of

Preventive Medicine, 1994–2002; Trustee, Natural Hist. Mus., 1994–2003. Founder MAE 1988; Founder FMedSci 1998. Hon. Fellow, UCL, 1993. Scientific Medal, Zool Soc. London, 1967; Royal Medal, Royal Soc., 1990; Japan Prize, Sci. and Technol. Foundn of Japan, 2002; (jtly) March of Dimes Prize in Develtl Biol., 2007. *Publications:* Mammalian Chimaeras, 1976; Germ Cells and Soma, 1980; papers on reproductive biology, embryology, genetics and immunology in sci. jls. *Address:* Wellcome Trust/Cancer Research UK Gurdon Institute, Tennis Court Road, Cambridge CB2 1QN; 21 Dunollie Road, NW5 2XN. *Died 7 July 2007.*

McLAREN, Sir Robin (John Taylor), KCMG 1991 (CMG 1982); HM Diplomatic Service, retired; Director: Invesco Asia Trust, 1995–2009; Fidelity Asian Values, 1997–2009; *b* 14 Aug. 1934; *s* of late Robert Taylor McLaren and of Marie Rose McLaren (*née* Simond); *m* 1964, Susan Ellen Hatherly; one *s* two *d*. *Educ:* Richmond and East Sheen County Grammar Sch. for Boys; Ardingly Coll.; St John's Coll., Cambridge (Schol.; MA). Royal Navy, 1953–55. Entered Foreign Service, 1958; language student, Hong Kong, 1959–60; Third Sec., Peking, 1960–61; FO, 1962–64; Asst Private Sec. to Lord Privy Seal (Mr Edward Heath), 1963–64; Second, later First Sec., Rome, 1964–68; seconded to Hong Kong Govt as Asst Political Adviser, 1968–69; First Sec., FCO, 1970–73; Dep. Head of Western Organisations Dept, 1974–75; Counsellor and Head of Chancery, Copenhagen, 1975–78; Head of Hong Kong and Gen. Dept, 1978–79, of Far Eastern Dept, 1979–81, FCO; Political Advr, Hong Kong, 1981–85; Ambassador to Philippines, 1985–87; Asst Under Sec. of State, FCO, 1987–90; Sen. British Rep., Sino-British Jt Liaison Gp, 1987–89; Dep. Under Sec. of State, FCO, 1990–91; Ambassador to People's Republic of China, 1991–94. Director: Batey Burn Ltd (Hong Kong), 1995–2008; Govett Asian Recovery Trust, then Gartmore Asia Pacific Trust, later Aberdeen All Asia Investment Trust, 1998–2009. Member Council: Ardingly Coll., 1996–2004 (Chm., 1999–2004); RHBNC, 1997–2004 (Chm., 1999–2004; Hon. Fellow, 2006). *Recreations:* music, reading, grandchildren. *Address:* 11 Hillside, Wimbledon, SW19 4NH. *Clubs:* Oxford and Cambridge; Hong Kong (Hong Kong). *Died 20 July 2010.*

McLAUCHLAN, Derek John Alexander, CBE 1998; CEng, FIET; FRAeS; FInstP; Secretary-General, Civil Air Navigation Services Organisation, Geneva, 1997–2001; *b* 5 May 1933; *s* of Frederick William McLauchlan and Nellie (*née* Summers); *m* 1960, Dr Sylvia June Smith; two *d*. *Educ:* Queen Elizabeth's Hospital, Bristol; Bristol Univ. (BSc). CEng, FIET (FIEE 1988); FRAeS 1993; FInstP 1997. BAC, 1954–66; European Space Technol. Centre, 1966–70; Marconi Space and Defence Systems, 1970–76; ICL, 1976–88; Renishaw Research, 1988–89; Dir Gen., Projects and Engrg, CAA, 1989–91; Chief Exec., NATS, 1991–97; Mem. Bd, CAA, 1991–97. Non-exec. Chm., Architecture Projects Management Ltd, 1994–96. Chm., Jt Air Navigation Services Council, 1996–97; Mem. Council, Air League, 1994–2004. Gold Medal, Czech Air Navigation Services, 2000. *Recreations:* music, theatre, walking. *Address:* 7 Holmwood Close, East Horsley, Leatherhead, Surrey KT24 6SS. *T:* (01483) 285144. *Died 7 Oct. 2009.*

McLEAN, Colin, CMG 1977; MBE 1964; HM Diplomatic Service, retired; UK Permanent Representative to the Council of Europe (with the personal rank of Ambassador), 1986–90; *b* 10 Aug. 1930; *s* of late Dr L. G. McLean and H. I. McLean; *m* 1953, Huguette Marie Suzette Leclerc; one *s* one *d*. *Educ:* Fettes; St Catharine's Coll., Cambridge (MA). 2RHA, 1953–54. District Officer, Kenya, 1955–63; Vice-Principal, Kenya Inst. of Administration, 1963–64; HM Diplomatic Service, 1964; served Wellington, Bogotá and FCO, 1964–77; Counsellor, Oslo, 1977–81; Head of Trade Relations and Export Dept, FCO, 1981–83; High Comr in Uganda, 1983–86. *Recreation:* sailing. *Address:* 28 The Heights, Foxgrove Road, Beckenham, Kent BR3 5BY. *T:* (020) 8650 9565. *Died 14 June 2007.*

MACLEAN, Sir Donald (Og Grant), Kt 1985; optometrist, practising in Ayr, 1965–2001; *b* 13 Aug. 1930; *s* of Donald Og Maclean and Margaret Maclean (*née* Smith); *m* 1st, 1958, Muriel Giles (*d* 1984); one *s* one *d*; 2nd, 2002, Mrs Margaret Ross. *Educ:* Morrison's Academy, Crieff; Heriot-Watt Univ. FBOA; FCOptom. RAMC, 1952–54. Optical practice: Newcastle upon Tyne, 1954–57; Perth, 1957–65. Chm., Ayr Constituency Cons. Assoc., 1971–75; Scottish Conservative and Unionist Association: Vice-Pres., 1979–83; Pres., 1983–85; Chm., W of Scotland Area, 1977–79; Exec. Mem., Nat. Union, 1979–89; Scottish Conservative Party: Dep. Chm., 1985–89; Vice-Chm., 1989–91; Chm., Carrick, Cumnock and Doon Valley Cons. Assoc., 1998–2000. Chm., Ayrshire and Arran Local Optical Cttee, 1986–88. Chm., Ayrshire Medical Support Ltd, 1995–. Chm., Bell Hollingworth Ltd, 1996–99. Freeman: Spectacle Makers' Co., 1986 (Liveryman, 1989–); City of London, 1987. Dean of Guildry, Royal Burgh of Ayr, 1993–95. *Recreations:* coastal shipping, reading, photography, philately. *Died 1 May 2010.*

McLEAN, Geoffrey Daniel, CBE 1988; QPM 1981; Assistant Commissioner (Territorial Operations), Metropolitan Police, 1984–90; *b* 4 March 1931; *s* of late William James McLean and Matilda Gladys (*née* Davies); *m* 1959, Patricia Edna Pope; two *s* two *d*. Following service in RA, joined Metropolitan Police, 1951; Chief Supt, 1969; Staff Officer to HMCIC, Home Office, 1970–72; Comdr, 1975; Graduate, RCDS, 1978; Dep. Asst Comr, 1979; Dep. Comdt, Police Staff Coll., 1981–83. *Recreations:* Met. Police Athletics Assoc. (Chm., 1984); Met. Police Football Club (Chm., 1984); Met. Police Race-Walking Club (Chm., 1978); riding. *Died 24 Oct. 2008.*

McLEAN, (John David) Ruari (McDowall Hardie), CBE 1973; DSC 1943; freelance typographer and author; *b* 10 June 1917; *s* of late John Thomson McLean and late Isabel Mary McLean (*née* Ireland); *m* 1945, Antonia Maxwell Carlisle (*d* 1995); two *s* one *d*. *Educ:* Dragon Sch., Oxford; Eastbourne Coll. First studied printing under B. H. Newdigate at Shakespeare Head Press, Oxford, 1936. Industrial printing experience in Germany and England, 1936–38; with The Studio, 1938; Percy Lund Humphries, Bradford, 1939. Served Royal Navy, 1940–45. Penguin Books, 1945–46; Book Designer (freelance), 1946–53; Tutor in Typography, Royal College of Art, 1948–51; Typographic Adviser to Hulton Press, 1953; Founder Partner, Rainbird, McLean Ltd, 1951–58; Founder Editor, and Designer, Motif, 1958–67. Typographic Consultant to The Observer, 1960–64; Hon. Typographic Adviser to HM Stationery Office, 1966–80. Sandars Reader in Bibliography, Univ. of Cambridge, 1982–83; Alexander Stone Lectr in Bibliophily, Univ. of Glasgow, 1984. Member: Nat. Council for Diplomas in Art and Design, 1971; Vis. Cttee of RCA, 1977–83; Academic Adv. Cttee, Heriot-Watt Univ. for Edinburgh Coll. of Art, 1978–96. Crown Trustee, Nat. Library of Scotland, 1981–2001. American Printing History Assoc. Individual Award, 1993. Croix de Guerre (French), 1942. *Publications:* George Cruikshank, 1948; Modern Book Design, 1958; Wood Engravings of Joan Hassall, 1960; Victorian Book Design, 1963, rev. edn 1972; Tschichold's Typographische Gestaltung (trans.), 1967; (ed) The Reminiscences of Edmund Evans, 1967; Magazine Design, 1969; Victorian Publishers' Book-bindings in Cloth and Leather, 1973; Jan Tschichold, Typographer, 1975; Joseph Cundall, 1976; (ed) Edward Bawden: A Book of Cuts, 1979; Thames and Hudson Manual of Typography, 1980; Victorian Publishers' Book-Bindings in Paper, 1983; The Last Cream Bun (drawings by Roger Pettiward), 1984; Benjamin Fawcett, Engraver and Colour Printer, 1988; (ed) Edward Bawden, War Artist, 1989; Nicolas Bentley

drew the Pictures, 1990; Tschichold's Die neue Typographie (trans.), 1994; (ed) Typographers on Type, 1995; Jan Tschichold: a life in typography, 1997; True to Type, 2000; How Typography Happens, 2000; Half Seas Under, 2001. *Recreations:* reading, acquiring books. *Address:* 9 Kirk Court, Tillicoultry, Clackmannshire FK13 6QN. *T:* (01259) 753204. *Clubs:* Double Crown; New (Edinburgh). *Died 27 March 2006.*

MacLEAN, Kenneth Smedley, MD, FRCP; Consultant Physician to Guy's Hospital, 1950–79, then Emeritus; *b* 22 Nov. 1914; *s* of Hugh MacLean and Ida Smedley; *m* 1939, Joan Hardaker (*d* 2002); one *s* one *d* (and one *s* decd). *Educ:* Westminster; Clare Coll., Cambridge. MRCS, LRCP, 1939; House appts at Guy's, 1939; MB, BChir 1939. RNVR, 1939–46, Surg.-Lt and Surg.-Lt-Comdr. MRCP 1946; House Officer and Medical Registrar, Guy's Hosp., 1946–48; MD Cantab 1948; FRCP 1954; elected to Assoc. of Physicians of Great Britain and Ireland, 1956. Assistant Director, Dept of Medicine, Guy's Hospital Medical Sch., 1949, Director, 1961–63. Chm., University Hosps Assoc., 1975–78. Pres., Assurance Medical Soc., 1985–87. *Publications:* Medical Treatment, 1957. *Recreation:* golf. *Address:* Flat 1 Brackenhill, 16 Westerham Road, Limpsfield, Oxted, Surrey RH8 0ER. *T:* (01883) 716652. *Died 4 Dec. 2009.*

McLEAN, Ruari; *see* McLean, J. D. R. McD. H.

MacLEOD, John; Chairman, British Beet Research Organisation, since 2000; Professor of Horticulture, Royal Horticultural Society, since 2001; *b* 16 Aug. 1939; *s* of James Rae MacLeod and Mollie McKee MacLeod (*née* Shaw); *m* 1966, Janet Patricia Beavan (*d* 2009), sculptor; one *s* (and one *s* decd). *Educ:* Nicolson Inst., Stornoway; Univ. of Glasgow (BSc Hons Agr. 1962); Michigan State Univ. (MS 1964). FRAgS 2003. NAAS, later ADAS, MAFF, 1964–90. Director: Arthur Rickwood Exptl Farm, 1982–85; ADAS Exptl Farms, MAFF, 1985–90; NIAB, Cambridge, 1990–99. Non-exec. Dir, Nat. Non Food Crops Centre, 2006–. Pres., Groupe Consultatif Internat. de Recherche sur le Colza, Paris, 1993–97; Vice-Chm., BCPC, 2000–07. Mem. Admin. Council, Internat. Inst. for Beet Res., 2003– (Vice Pres., 2009–). Chm., BASIS (Registration) Ltd, 2004–09. *Recreations:* long term restoration of a 16th century farmhouse and garden, sculpture, early music. *Address:* British Beet Research Organisation, The Research Station, Great North Road, Thornhaugh, Peterborough PE8 6HJ; Church Farm House, Over, Cambs CB24 5NX. *Died 19 June 2010.*

MacLEOD OF MacLEOD, John; 29th Chief of MacLeod; *b* 10 Aug. 1935; 2nd *s* of late Captain Robert Wolrige-Gordon, MC, and Joan, *d* of Hubert Walter and Dame Flora MacLeod of MacLeod, DBE; officially recognised in name of MacLeod of MacLeod by decree of Lyon Court, 1951; *S* grandmother, 1976; *m* 1st, 1961, Drusilla Shaw (marr. diss. 1971); 2nd, 1973, Melita Kolin (marr. diss. 1992); one *s* one *d*; 3rd, 2004, Ulrika Tham. *Educ:* Eton. *Heir: s* Hugh Magnus MacLeod, younger of MacLeod, *b* 1973. *Address:* Dunvegan Castle, Isle of Skye. *T:* (01470) 521206. *Died 12 Feb. 2007.*

McLEOD, Keith Morrison, CBE 1975; Financial Controller, British Airports Authority, 1971–75; *b* 26 May 1920; *yr s* of John and Mary McLeod; *m* 1943, Patricia Carter; two *s* one *d*. *Educ:* Bancroft's School. Asst Auditor, Exchequer and Audit Dept, 1939; served RAF, 1941–46; Asst Principal, Min. of Supply, 1948; Principal, 1950; BJSM, Washington, 1955–57; Asst Sec., Min. of Supply, 1957; Cabinet Office, 1962; Finance Dir, British Airports Authority, 1966. *Address:* 24 Grange Close, Goring-on-Thames, Reading, Berks RG8 9DY. *T:* (01491) 871167. *Died 4 Dec. 2006.*

McLINTOCK, Sir (Charles) Alan, Kt 1999; CA; President, Woolwich Building Society, 1995–97 (Director, 1970–95; Deputy Chairman, 1980–84; Chairman, 1984–95); Chairman: Allchurches Trust,

1986–2003 (Director, 1975–2003); Central Board of Finance of the Church of England, 1992–98; *b* 28 May 1925; *s* of late Charles Henry McLintock, OBE, and Alison McLintock; *m* 1955, Sylvia Mary Foster Taylor; one *s* three *d*. *Educ:* Rugby School. Served Royal Artillery, 1943–47; commnd 1945; Captain RHA 1946. With Thomson McLintock & Co., Chartered Accountants, 1948–87; qualified, 1952; Partner, 1954; Sen. Partner, KMG Thomson McLintock, 1982–87; Partner, Klynveld Main Goerdeler (KMG), 1979–87. Chairman: Grange Trust, 1973–81 (Dir, 1958–81); Border and Southern Stockholders Investment Trust, subseq. Govett Atlantic Investment Trust, 1978–92; Ecclesiastical Insce Office, subseq. Ecclesiastical Insce Gp, 1981–93 (Dir, 1972–93); Director: Trust Houses Ltd, 1967–71; Lake View Investment Trust, later Govett Oriental Investment Trust, 1971–90 (Chm., 1975–90); National Westminster Bank, 1979–90 (Adv. Bd, 1990–91); M & G Gp, 1982–94; AJ's Family Restaurants, 1987–96; Acxiom UK (formerly Southwark Computer Services), 1988–90; Royal Artillery Mus Ltd, 1996–2004; Cheltenham & Gloucester Coll. Develt Trust, 1996–2003. Mem., Archbishops' Commn on organisation of C of E, 1994–96. Vice-Pres., Metropolitan Assoc. of Building Socs, 1985–90. Trustee, Church Urban Fund, 1990–98. Chairman of Governors: Rugby Sch., 1988–95 (Gov., 1973–95); Westonbirt Sch., 1991–2000 (Gov., 1977–2000); Vice-Pres., Clergy Orphan Corp., 1984–97 (Mem., Cttee of Management, 1963–84); Member: Royal Alexandra and Albert Sch. Bd of Management, 1965–88; Council, London Univ., 1987–99. Hon. DBA Greenwich, 1994. *Recreations:* music, family pursuits. *Address:* Manor House, Westhall Hill, Fulbrook, Burford, Oxon OX18 4BJ. *T:* (01993) 822276. *Club:* Army and Navy.
Died 28 March 2007.

McMANNERS, Rev. Prof. John, CBE 2000; DLitt; FBA 1978; Fellow and Chaplain, All Souls College, Oxford, 1984–2001 (Hon. Fellow, 2001); *b* 25 Dec. 1916; *s* of Rev. Canon Joseph McManners and Mrs Ann McManners; *m* 1951, Sarah Carruthers Errington; two *s* two *d*. *Educ:* St Edmund Hall, Oxford (BA 1st cl. hons Mod. History, 1939; Hon. Fellow, 1983); Durham Univ. (DipTheol 1947; Hon. Fellow, St Chad's Coll., 1992); DLitt Oxon, 1980. Military Service, 1939–45 in Royal Northumberland Fusiliers (Major). Priest, 1948; St Edmund Hall, Oxford: Chaplain, 1948; Fellow, 1949–56; Dean, 1951; Prof., Univ. of Tasmania, 1956–59; Prof., Sydney Univ., 1959–66; Professorial Fellow, All Souls Coll., Oxford, 1965–66; Prof. of History, Univ. of Leicester, 1967–72; Canon of Christ Church and Regius Prof. of Ecclesiastical History, Oxford Univ., 1972–84. Lectures: Birkbeck, 1976, Trevelyan, 1989, Cambridge; John Coffin Meml, London Univ., 1982; Sir Owen Evans, Univ. of Wales, 1984; F. D. Maurice, King's Coll., London, 1985; Zaharoff, 1985, Hensley Henson, 1986, A.B. Emden Meml, 1992, Oxford. Dir d'études associé, Ecole Pratique des Hautes Etudes, sect. IV, Paris, 1980–81. Mem., Doctrinal Commn of C of E, 1978–82. Trustee, Nat. Portrait Gallery, 1970–78; Mem. Council, R.HistS, 1971; Pres., Ecclesiastical Hist. Soc., 1977–78. FAHA 1970. Hon. DLitt Durham, 1984. Officer, Order of King George I of the Hellenes, 1945; Comdr, Ordre des Palmes académiques (France), 1991; Comdr, Ordre Nat. du Mérite (France), 2001. *Publications:* French Ecclesiastical Society under the Ancien Régime: a study of Angers in the 18th Century, 1960; (ed) France, Government and Society, 1965, 2nd edn 1971; Lectures on European History 1789–1914: Men, Machines and Freedom, 1966; The French Revolution and the Church, 1969; Church and State in France 1870–1914, 1972; Death and the Enlightenment, 1981 (Wolfson Literary Award, 1982); (ed) The Oxford Illustrated History of Christianity, 1990; Church and Society in 18th Century France, 2 vols, 1998; Fusilier: 1939–1945: recollections and reflexions, 2001; All Souls and the Shipley Case, 1808–1810, 2002; contrib.: New Cambridge Modern History vols VI and VIII; Studies in

Church History, vols XII, XV and XXII. *Recreation:* conversation. *Address:* All Souls College, Oxford OX1 4AL.
Died 4 Nov. 2006.

McNAB JONES, Robin Francis, FRCS; Consultant Otolaryngologist, 1959–99; Surgeon: ENT Department, St Bartholomew's Hospital, 1961–87; Royal National Throat, Nose and Ear Hospital, 1962–83; *b* 22 Oct. 1922; *s* of late E. C. H. Jones, CBE, and M. E. Jones, MBE; *m* 1950, Mary Garrett; one *s* three *d*. *Educ:* Manchester Grammar Sch.; Dulwich Coll.; Med. Coll., St Bartholomew's Hosp. (MB BS 1945); FRCS 1952. House Surg., St Bart's, 1946–47; MO, RAF, 1947–50; Demonstrator of Anatomy, St Bart's, 1950–52; Registrar, Royal Nat. Throat, Nose and Ear Hosp., 1952–54; Sen. Registrar, ENT Dept, St Bart's, 1954–59; Lectr, Dept of Otolaryngology, Univ. of Manchester, 1959–61; Dean, Inst. of Laryngology and Otology, Univ. of London, 1971–76; Vice-Pres., St Bart's Hosp. Med. Coll., 1984–87. Mem., Court of Examiners, 1972–78, and Mem. Council (for Otolaryngology), 1982–87, RCS; External Examiner, RCSI, 1980–83, 1988–91. Hon. Sec., Sect. of Otology, 1965–68, Pres., Sect. of Laryngology, 1981–82, RSocMed. *Publications:* various chapters in standard med. textbooks; contribs to med. jls. *Recreations:* tennis, ski-ing, golf, fishing, gardening. *Address:* 91 Barnfield Wood Road, Beckenham, Kent BR3 6ST. *T:* (020) 8650 0217.
Died 15 June 2009.

MACNAGHTEN, Sir Patrick (Alexander), 11th Bt *cr* 1836; farmer; *b* 24 Jan. 1927; *s* of Sir Antony Macnaghten, 10th Bt, and Magdalene, *e d* of late Edmund Fisher; *S* father, 1972; *m* 1955, Marianne, *yr d* of Dr Erich Schaefer and Alice Schaefer, Cambridge; three *s*. *Educ:* Eton; Trinity Coll., Cambridge (BA Mechanical Sciences). Army (RE), 1945–48. Project Engineer, Cadbury Bros (later Cadbury Schweppes), 1950–69; in General Management, Cadbury-Schweppes Ltd, 1969–84. *Recreations:* fishing, shooting. *Heir: s* Malcolm Francis Macnaghten, *b* 21 Sept. 1956. *Address:* Dundarave, Bushmills, Co. Antrim, Northern Ireland BT57 8ST. *T:* (028) 2073 1215.
Died 22 Aug. 2007.

McNAMARA, Robert Strange; Medal of Freedom with Distinction; *b* San Francisco, 9 June 1916; *s* of Robert James McNamara and Clara Nell (*née* Strange); *m* 1st, 1940, Margaret McKinstry Craig (*d* 1981); one *s* two *d*; 2nd, 2004, Diana Masieri Byfield. *Educ:* University of California (AB); Harvard Univ. (MBA). Asst Professor of Business Administration, Harvard, 1940–43. Served in USAAF, England, India, China, Pacific, 1943–46 (Legion of Merit); released as Lieut-Colonel. Joined Ford Motor Co., 1946; Executive, 1946–61; Controller, 1949–53; Asst General Manager, Ford Div., 1953–55; Vice-President, and General Manager, Ford Div., 1955–57; Director, and Group Vice-President of Car Divisions, 1957–61, President, 1960–61; Secretary of Defense, United States of America, 1961–68; Pres., The World Bank, 1968–81; Director: Royal Dutch Petroleum, 1981–87; Bank of America, 1981–87; Corning, 1981–90; The Washington Post, 1981–89. Trustee: Urban Inst.; Trilateral Commn. Hon. degrees from: Harvard, Calif, Mich, Columbia, Ohio, Princeton, NY, Notre Dame, George Washington, Aberdeen, St Andrews, Fordham and Oxford Univs; Williams, Chatham and Amherst Colls. Phi Beta Kappa. Albert Pick Jr Award, Univ. of Chicago (first recipient), 1979; Albert Einstein Peace Prize, 1983; Franklin D. Roosevelt Freedom from Want Medal, 1983; Amer. Assembly Service to Democracy Award; Dag Hammarskjöld Hon. Medal; Entrepreneurial Excellence Medal, Yale Sch. of Organization and Management; Olive Branch Award for Outstanding Book on subject of World Peace, 1987; Sidney Hillman Foundn Award, 1987; Onassis Athinai Prize, 1988. *Publications:* The Essence of Security, 1968; One Hundred Countries, Two Billion People: the dimensions of development, 1975; The McNamara Years at the World Bank, 1981; Blundering into Disaster, 1987; Out of the

Cold, 1990; In Retrospect: the tragedy and lessons of Vietnam, 1995; Argument Without End, 2000; Wilson's Ghost, 2001. *Died 6 July 2009.*

MACNEIL OF BARRA, Prof. Ian Roderick; The Macneil of Barra; Chief of Clan Macneil and of that Ilk; Wigmore Professor of Law, Northwestern University, 1980–99, then Emeritus; *b* 20 June 1929; *s* of Robert Lister Macneil of Barra and Kathleen, *d* of Orlando Paul Metcalf, NYC, USA; *m* 1952, Nancy, *e d* of James Tilton Wilson, Ottawa, Canada; two *s* one *d* (and one *s* decd). *Educ:* Univ. of Vermont (BA 1950); Harvard Univ. (LLB 1955). Lieut, Infty, Army of US, 1951–53 (US Army Reserve, 1950–69). Clerk, US Court of Appeals, 1955–56; law practice, Concord, NH, USA, 1956–59. Cornell Univ., USA: Asst Prof. of Law, 1959–62; Associate Prof., 1962–63; Prof. of Law, 1962–72 and 1974–76; Ingersoll Prof. of Law, 1976–80; Prof. of Law, Univ. of Virginia, 1972–74. Visiting Professor of Law: Univ. of East Africa, Dar es Salaam, Tanzania, 1965–67; Harvard Univ., 1988–89; Guggenheim Fellow, 1978–79; Vis. Fellow, Wolfson Coll., Oxford, 1979. Hon. Vis. Fellow, Faculty of Law, Edinburgh Univ., 1979 and 1987. Member: Scottish Medievalists; Standing Council of Scottish Chiefs. FSAScot; Fellow, American Acad. of Arts and Scis. *Publications.* Bankruptcy Law in East Africa, 1966; (with R. B. Schlesinger, *et al*) Formation of Contracts: A Study of the Common Core of Legal Systems, 1968; Contracts: Instruments of Social Co-operation-East Africa, 1968; (with R. S. Morison) Students and Decision Making, 1970; Contracts: Exchange Transactions and Relations, 1971, 3rd edn (with P. Gudel) 2001; The New Social Contract, 1980; American Arbitration Law, 1992; (jtly) Federal Arbitration Law, 1994; The Relational Theory of Contract: selected works of Ian Macneil, ed D. Campbell, 2001. *Heir:* s Roderick Wilson Macneil, Younger of Barra [*b* 22 Oct. 1954; *m* 1988, Sau Ming, *d* of Chun Kwan, Hong Kong]. *Address:* Carlton Grange, 95/6 Grange Loan, Edinburgh EH9 2ED. *T:* (0131) 667 6068; Taigh A'Mhonaidh, Garrygall, Castlebay, Isle of Barra, Scotland HS9 5UH. *T:* (01871) 810300; (seat) Kisimul Castle, Isle of Barra. *Died 16 Feb. 2010.*

MACPHAIL, Hon. Lord; Iain Duncan Macphail, FRSE; a Senator of the College of Justice in Scotland, since 2005; *b* 24 Jan. 1938; *o s* of late Malcolm John Macphail and Mary Corbett Macphail (*née* Duncan); *m* 1970, Rosslyn Graham Lillias, *o d* of E. J. C. Hewitt, MD, TD, Edinburgh; one *s* one *d*. *Educ:* George Watson's Coll.; Edinburgh and Glasgow Univs. MA Hons History Edinburgh 1959, LLB Glasgow 1962. FRSE 2005. Admitted to Faculty of Advocates, 1963; in practice at Scottish Bar, 1963–73; Faulds Fellow in Law, Glasgow Univ., 1963–65, Lectr in Evidence and Procedure, Strathclyde Univ., 1968–69 and Edinburgh Univ., 1969–72; Standing Jun. Counsel to Scottish Home and Health Dept and to Dept of Health and Social Security, 1971–73; Extra Advocate-Depute, 1973; QC (Scot.) 1990; Sheriff: of Lanarks, later Glasgow and Strathkelvin, 1973–81; of Tayside, Central and Fife, 1981–82; of Lothian and Borders, 1982–89, 1995–2002; Sheriff Principal of Lothian and Borders, and Sheriff of Chancery, 2002–05. Member: Scottish Law Commn, 1990–94; Judicial Studies Cttee for Scotland, 2003–05; Chm., Sheriff Court Rules Council, 2003–05. Chm., Scottish Assoc. for Study of Delinquency, 1978–81. Arthur Goodhart Prof. in Legal Sci., Cambridge Univ., 2001–02. Comr, Northern Lighthouse Bd, 2002–05. Mem., Editl Bd, Criminal Law Review, 2001–. Hon. LLD Edinburgh, 1992. *Publications:* Law of Evidence in Scotland (Scottish Law Commn), 1979; Evidence, 1987; Sheriff Court Practice, 1988; articles and reviews in legal jls. *Address:* Court of Session, Parliament House, Parliament Square, Edinburgh EH1 1RQ. *Club:* New (Edinburgh). *Died 21 Oct. 2009.*

MACPHERSON OF DRUMOCHTER, 2nd Baron *cr* 1951; **(James) Gordon Macpherson;** Chairman and Managing Director of Macpherson, Train & Co. Ltd, and

Subsidiary and Associated Companies, since 1964; Chairman, A. J. Macpherson & Co. Ltd (Bankers), since 1973; founder Chairman, Castle Dairies (Caerphilly) Ltd; *b* 22 Jan. 1924; *s* of 1st Baron Macpherson of Drumochter and Lucy Lady Macpherson of Drumochter (*d* 1984); *S* father, 1965; *m* 1st, 1947, Dorothy Ruth Coulter (*d* 1974); two *d* (one *s* decd); 2nd, 1975, Catherine, *d* of Dr C. D. MacCarthy; one *s* two *d*. *Educ:* Loretto; Wells House, Malvern. Served War of 1939–45, with RAF; 1939–45 Campaign medal, Burma Star, Pacific Star, Defence Medal, Victory Medal. Founder Chm. and Patron, British Importers Confedn, 1968–72. Member: Council, London Chamber of Commerce, 1958–73 (Gen. Purposes Cttee, 1959–72); East European Trade Council, 1969–71; PLA, 1973–76; Exec. Cttee, W India Cttee, 1959–83 (Dep. Chm. and Treasurer, 1971, Chm. 1973–75); Highland Soc. of London, 1975–. Freeman of City of London, 1969; Mem., Butchers' Co., 1969–. Governor, Brentwood Sch. JP Essex, 1961–76; Dep. Chm., Brentwood Bench, 1972–76; Mem. Essex Magistrates Court Cttee, 1974–76. Hon. Game Warden for Sudan, 1974; Chief of Scottish Clans Assoc. of London, 1972–74; Member: Macpherson Clan Assoc. (Chm., 1963–64); Sen. Golfers' Soc., 1981–91. Life Managing Governor, Royal Scottish Corp., 1975–. Founder Mem., WWF, 1961. FRSA 1971; FRES 1940; TZS 1965. *Recreations:* shooting, fishing, golf, bridge. *Heir: s* Hon. James Anthony Macpherson, *b* 27 Feb. 1979. *Address:* Kyllachy, Tomatin, Inverness-shire IV13 7YA. *T:* (01808) 511212. *Clubs:* Boodle's, Shikar; Royal and Ancient (St Andrews); Thorndon Park Golf (capt. 1962–63); Hartswood Golf (Founder Pres., 1970–74). *Died 7 Sept. 2008.*

MACQUARRIE, Rev. Prof. John, TD 1962; FBA 1984; Lady Margaret Professor of Divinity, University of Oxford, and Canon of Christ Church, 1970–86; *b* 27 June 1919; *s* of John Macquarrie and Robina Macquarrie (*née* McInnes); *m* 1949, Jenny Fallow (*née* Welsh); two *s* one *d*. *Educ:* Paisley Grammar Sch.; Univ. of Glasgow. MA 1940; BD 1943; PhD 1954; DLitt 1964; DD Oxon 1981. Royal Army Chaplains Dept, 1945–48; St Ninian's Church, Brechin, 1948–53; Lecturer, Univ. of Glasgow, 1953–62; Prof. of Systematic Theology, Union Theological Seminary, NY, 1962–70. Consultant, Lambeth Conf., 1968 and 1978. Hon. degrees: STD: Univ. of the South, USA, 1967; General Theological Seminary, NY, 1968; DD: Glasgow, 1969; Episcopal Seminary of SW, Austin, Texas, 1981; Virginia Theol Seminary, 1981; Univ. of Dayton, 1994; DCnL, Nashotah House, Wisconsin, 1986. *Publications:* An Existentialist Theology, 1955; The Scope of Demythologising, 1960; Twentieth Century Religious Thought, 1963, 5th edn 2001; Studies in Christian Existentialism, 1965; Principles of Christian Theology, 1966; God-Talk, 1967; God and Secularity, 1967; Martin Heidegger, 1968; Three Issues in Ethics, 1970; Existentialism, 1972; Paths in Spirituality, 1972; The Faith of the People of God, 1972; The Concept of Peace, 1973; Thinking about God, 1975; Christian Unity and Christian Diversity, 1975; The Humility of God, 1978; Christian Hope, 1978; In Search of Humanity, 1982; In Search of Deity (Gifford Lectures), 1984; Theology, Church and Ministry, 1986; Jesus Christ in Modern Thought, 1990 (HarperCollins Religious Book Prize, 1991); Mary for All Christians, 1991, new edn 2001; Heidegger and Christianity, 1994; Invitation to Faith, 1995; The Mediators, 1995; A Guide to the Sacraments, 1997; Christology Revisited, 1998; On Being a Theologian, 1999; Stubborn Theological Questions, 2003; Two Worlds Are Ours: an introduction to Christian mysticism, 2004. *Address:* 206 Headley Way, Headington, Oxford OX3 7TA. *T:* (01865) 761889. *Died 28 May 2007.*

McQUEEN, Alexander, CBE 2003; fashion designer; *b* Lee McQueen, 17 March 1969. *Educ:* Rokeby Comp. Sch. for Boys; Central St Martin's Coll. of Art and Design (MA 1992). Worked successively for Anderson and Sheppard, and Gieves and Hawkes (Savile Row tailors),

Angels and Bermans (theatrical costumiers), Koji Tatsuno (Japanese designer), Romeo Gigli (Italian designer); est. own label, 1992; men's and ladies' collections retailed worldwide; Chief Designer, Givenchy, 1996–2001; Creative Dir, Alexander McQueen label, 2001– (Gucci acquired 51%, 2001). British Designer of the Year, British Fashion Awards, 1996, (jtly) 1997, 2000, 2001. *Address:* 1st Floor, 10 Amwell Street, EC1R 1UQ.
Died 11 Feb. 2010.

McQUILLAN, William Rodger; HM Diplomatic Service, retired; *b* 18 March 1930; *s* of late Albert McQuillan and Isabella Glen McQuillan; *m* 1970, Sheriell May Fawcett; one *s* two *d. Educ:* Royal High Sch., Edinburgh; Edinburgh Univ.; Yale Univ. Served RAF, 1954–57. Asst Sec., Manchester Univ. Appointments Board, 1957–65; HM Diplomatic Service, 1965–83: First Sec., CRO, 1965; Lusaka, 1968, Head of Chancery, 1969; First Sec. (Commercial), Santiago, Chile, 1970; Counsellor and HM Consul, Guatemala City, 1974; Head of Inf. Policy Dept, FCO, 1978–81; Ambassador to Iceland, 1981–83. *Address:* Lidston House, Edderton, Ross-shire IV19 1LF.
Died 19 Sept. 2007.

MACROSSAN, Hon. John Murtagh, AC 1993; Chancellor, Griffith University, 1988–2000; *b* 12 March 1930; *m* 1961, Margery Newton; one *s. Educ:* St Columban's Coll., Brisbane; Univ. of Queensland; Univ. of Oxford. Admitted Qld Bar, 1951; QC 1967; Judge, 1980–89, Chief Justice, 1989–98, of Supreme Court, Qld. *Address:* c/o Queensland Club, Alice Street, Brisbane, Qld 4000, Australia. *Died 5 Aug. 2008.*

McWATTERS, George Edward; Director of Corporate Affairs, HTV Group plc, 1989–91; Chairman: TVMM, 1988–91; HTV West, 1969–88; *b* India, 17 March 1922; *s* of Lt-Col George Alfred McWatters and Ellen Mary Christina McWatters (*née* Harvey); *m* 1st, 1946, Margery Robertson (*d* 1959); 2nd, 1960, Joy Anne Matthews (*d* 2006); one *s. Educ:* Clifton Coll., Bristol. Vintners' Scholar, 1947. Served War of 1939–45: enlisted ranks Royal Scots, 1940; commissioned 14th Punjab Regt, Indian Army, 1941–46. John Harvey & Sons (family wine co.): joined, 1940; Dir, 1951; Chm., 1956–66; estab. a holding co. (Harveys of Bristol Ltd), 1962, but Showerings took over, 1966, and he remained Chm. until resignation, Aug. 1966; Chm., John White Footwear Holdings Ltd, later Ward White Gp Ltd, 1967–82; Actg Chm., HTV Group plc, 1985–86; Chm., HTV Ltd, 1986–88 (Vice-Chm., 1969–86). Chm., Bristol Avon Phoenix, 1987–90; Director: Bristol and West Bldg Soc., 1985–92 (Vice-Chm., 1988–92); Martins Bank, 1960–70; Local Adv. Dir (Peterborough), Barclays Bank, 1970–82; Local Dir (Northampton), Commercial Union Assce Co., 1969–82; Dir, Bain Clarkson Ltd, 1982–95. Mem., CBI Grand Council, 1970–82. Mem. Cttee, Automobile Assoc., 1962–89. Chairman: Council, Order of St John, Avon, 1983–93; Bishop of Bristol's Urban Fund, 1989–95; Millennium Appeal, RWEA, 1996–2000; Vice-Pres., Avon Wildlife Trust, 1989–2000 (Chm., Appeal Cttee, 1982). Pres., Avon and Bristol Fedn of Boys Clubs, 1985–94. Governor: Clifton Coll., 1958–; Kimbolton Sch., 1970–82. Master, Soc. of Merchant Venturers, 1986. City Councillor, Bristol, 1950–53. JP, Bristol, 1960–67; JP, Marylebone, 1969–71; High Sheriff, Cambridgeshire, 1979. *Recreation:* swimming. *Address:* 135 Torriano Avenue, NW5 2RX. *T:* (020) 7267 2920. *Club:* MCC. *Died 19 Dec. 2007.*

McWATTERS, Stephen John; Headmaster, The Pilgrims' School, Winchester, 1976–83, retired; *b* 24 April 1921; *er s* of late Sir Arthur Cecil McWatters, CIE and Mary McWatters (*née* Finney); *m* 1957, Mary Gillian, *o d* of late D. C. Wilkinson and Mrs G. A. Wilkinson; one *s* two *d. Educ:* Eton (Scholar); Trinity Coll., Oxford (Scholar; 1st Cl. Class. Mods 1941; MA). Served in The King's Royal Rifle Corps, 1941–45. Distinction in Philosophy section of Litterae Humaniores, Oxford, 1946. Asst Master, Eton Coll., 1947–63 (Master in Coll., 1949–57, Housemaster, 1961–63); Headmaster, Clifton Coll., 1963–75. Governor: Clifton Coll., 1977–; Milton

Abbey Sch., 1978–94. *Recreations:* music, bird-watching. *Address:* 4 St Michael's Gardens, Winchester SO23 9JD. *T:* (01962) 867523. *Died 12 March 2006.*

MACWHINNIE, Sir Gordon (Menzies), Kt 1992; CBE 1984 (OBE 1977); JP; FCA; Chairman: Allied Group Ltd, since 1998; Allied Properties Ltd, since 1998; *b* 13 Nov. 1922; *s* of Arthur William Philip Macwhinnie and Nellie Evelyn (*née* Rand); *m* 1948, Marjorie Grace Benwell; two *s. Educ:* Westminster Sch. FCA 1958 (ACA 1948). War Service, 1941–46: Capt., No 1 Commando, Burma and FE. Joined Peat Marwick Mitchell & Co., 1948, Sen. Partner, Hong Kong, 1968–78; chm. and dir of cos, 1978–; consultant in private practice, 1978–. Chm. and Mem., Govt cttees, 1978–98. Mem. Ct, Hong Kong Univ. of Science and Technol., 1998– (Mem. Council, 1988–98). Hon. DLitt Hong Kong Poly., 1991; Hon. DBA Hong Kong Univ. of Sci. and Technol., 1995. *Recreations:* golf, horse-racing, watching cricket, football, athletics, etc. *Address:* Apt 703, de Ricou, The Repulse Bay, 109 Repulse Bay Road, Hong Kong. *T:* 28031302, *Fax:* 28129874. *Clubs:* Oriental; Royal & Ancient Golf (St Andrews); Piltdown Golf; Hong Kong Golf (Pres.), Hong Kong, Royal Hong Kong Golf (Chm.), Hong Kong, Royal Hong Kong Jockey (Chm., 1989–91). *Died 18 July 2007.*

McWILLIAM, John David; *b* 16 May 1941; *s* of Alexander and Josephine McWilliam; *m* 1st, 1965, Lesley Mary Catling (marr. diss. 1991); two *d*; 2nd, 1994, Mary McLoughlin (marr. diss. 1997); 3rd, 1998, Helena Lovegreen. *Educ:* Leith Academy; Heriot Watt Coll.; Napier College of Science and Technology. Post Office Engineer, 1957–79. Councillor, Edinburgh CC, 1970–75 (last Treasurer of City of Edinburgh and only Labour one, 1974–75); Commissioner for Local Authority Accounts in Scotland, 1974–78. Mem., Scottish Council for Technical Educn, 1973–85. MP (Lab) Blaydon, 1979–2005. Dep. to Shadow Leader of H of C, 1983; Opposition Whip, 1984–87. Member: Select Cttee on Educn, Science and the Arts, 1980–83; Select Cttee on Procedure, 1984–87; Services Cttee (Chm., Computer sub-cttee, 1983–87); Select Cttee on Defence, 1987–99; Speaker's Panel of Chairmen, 1988–2005; Dep. Speaker, 2000–05. Mem., Gen. Adv. Council, BBC, 1984–89. JP Edinburgh, 1973. *Recreations:* reading, listening to music, angling. *Died 14 Nov. 2009.*

MADDEN, Sir Peter John, 3rd Bt *cr* 1919, of Kells, co. Kilkenny; *b* 10 Sept. 1942; *s* of Lt-Col John Wilmot Madden, MC, RA, *yr s* of 1st Bt, and Beatrice Catherine (*née* Sievwright); *S* uncle, 2001; *m* 1993, Mrs Vellie Laput Co (decd); three step *d. Educ:* Blundell's; RMA Sandhurst. Late Captain, RA. *Heir: b* Charles Jonathan Madden [*b* 11 Aug. 1949; *m* 1980, Kirsteen Victoria Noble; one *s* one *d*]. *Died 20 Nov. 2006.*

MADDISON, Prof. Angus; Professor of Economics, University of Groningen, Netherlands, 1978–96, then Emeritus; *b* 6 Dec. 1926; *s* of Thomas Maddison and Jane (*née* Walker); *m* 1st, Carol Hopkins; two *s*; 2nd, Penelope Pearce; one *d. Educ:* Darlington Grammar Sch.; Selwyn Coll., Cambridge (BA, MA; Hon. Fellow 1999); McGill Univ., Montreal; Johns Hopkins Univ.; Univ. Aix-en-Provence (docteur d'état). Pilot Officer, RAF, 1948–49. Lectr in Econ. Hist., Univ. of St Andrews, 1951–52; Head of Econs Div., later Dir, Develt Assistance, then Fellow, Develt Centre, OEEC and OECD, Paris, 1953–66; Dir, Res. Project on Econ. Growth, Twentieth Century Fund, NY, 1966–69; Res. Fellow and Econ. Advr, Harvard Univ. Centre for Internat. Affairs, 1969–71; Head, Central Analysis Div., OECD, Paris, 1971–78. Visiting Lecturer or Professor: Univ. of Calif, Berkeley, 1968; Nuffield Coll., Oxford, 1975; Université Paris Dauphine, 1981; ANU, 1982; St Antony's Coll. Oxford, 1988; Internat. Develt Centre, Japan, 1989; Universitá Ca' Foscari, Venice, 1990; Univ. of Turin, 1993; NY Univ., 1993; SOAS, London Univ., 1996–99; ASERI, Univ. del Sacro Cuore, Milan, 1997; Keio Univ., Fujisawa, 1998. Lectures: Kuznets Meml, Yale Univ., 1998; Wendt, Amer. Enterprise Inst., Washington, 2001;

Abramovitz Meml, Stanford Univ., 2001; Colin Clark, Univ. of Qld, 2003; Ruggles, Internat. Assoc. for Res. in Income and Wealth, Cork, 2004; Arndt Meml, ANU, 2006. Consultant: EU, ECAFE, ECE, ECLAC, FAO, GATT, IADB, UNESCO, UN, UNIDO; World Bank; govts of Brazil, Ghana, Greece, Mexico and Pakistan. Corresp. FBA 1994. Foreign Hon. Member: Amer. Econ. Assoc., 1989; Amer. Acad. of Arts and Scis, 1996; Foreign Mem., Russian Acad. of Scis in Econs and Business, 1992. Hon. Dr Econs Hitotsubashi, Japan, 2007. Medal, Univ. of Helsinki, 1986. Comdr, Order of Orange Nassau (Netherlands), 2006. *Publications:* Economic Growth in the West, 1964; Foreign Skills and Technical Assistance in Economic Development, 1965; Economic Growth in Japan and the USSR, 1969; Economic Progress and Policy in Developing Countries, 1970; Class Structure and Economic Growth: India and Pakistan since the Moghuls, 1971; Phases of Capitalist Development, 1982; Two Crises: Latin America and Asia 1929–38 and 1973–83, 1985; The World Economy in the Twentieth Century, 1989; Dynamic Forces in Capitalist Development, 1991; The Political Economy of Poverty, Equity and Growth: Brazil and Mexico, 1992; Explaining the Economic Performance of Nations: essays in time and space, 1995; Monitoring the World Economy, 1995; Chinese Economic Performance in the Long Run 1–2030, 1998, rev. 2nd edn 2007; The World Economy: a millennial perspective, 2001; The Asian Economics in the Twentieth Century, 2002; The World Economy: historical statistics, 2003; Growth and Interaction in the World Economy: the roots of modernity, 2004; Contours of the World Economy 1–2030: essays in macroeconomic history, 2007; numerous articles in econ. and financial jls. *Recreations:* collecting furniture, books and hats. *Address:* Chevincourt, 60150, France. *T:* 344760532, *Fax:* 344766514. *Died 24 April 2010.*

MADDOCKS, Rt Rev. Morris Henry St John; Adviser on the Ministry of Health and Healing to Archbishops of Canterbury and York, 1983–95; Hon. Assistant Bishop, Diocese of Chichester, since 1987; *b* 28 April 1928; *s* of late Rev. Canon Morris Arthur Maddocks and Gladys Mabel Sharpe; *m* 1955, Anne Miles (*d* 2006); no *c. Educ:* St John's Sch., Leatherhead; Trinity Coll., Cambridge (BA 1952; MA 1956); Chichester Theological Coll. Ordained in St Paul's Cathedral, London, 1954; Curate: St Peter's, Ealing, 1954–55; St Andrews, Uxbridge, 1955–58; Vicar of: Weaverthorpe, Helperthorpe and Luttons Ambo, 1958–61; St Martin's on the Hill, Scarborough, 1961–71; Bishop Suffragan of Selby, 1972–83. Preb., Chichester Cathedral, 1992–2002. Chm., Churches' Council for Health and Healing, 1982–85 (Co-Chm., 1975–82); Co-Founder, with wife, of Acorn Christian Healing Trust (then Acorn Christian Healing Foundation), 1983. *Publications:* The Christian Healing Ministry, 1981; The Christian Adventure, 1983; Journey to Wholeness, 1986; A Healing House of Prayer, 1987; Twenty Questions about Healing, 1988; The Vision of Dorothy Kerin, 1991. *Recreations:* music, walking, reading. *Address:* 3 The Chantry, Cathedral Close, Chichester, W Sussex PO19 1PZ. *T:* (01243) 788888. *Died 19 Jan. 2008.*

MADDOX, Sir John (Royden), Kt 1995; writer and broadcaster; Editor, Nature, 1966–73 and 1980–95; *b* 27 Nov. 1925; *s* of A. J. and M. E. Maddox, Swansea; *m* 1st, 1949, Nancy Fanning (*d* 1960); one *s* one *d*; 2nd, 1960, Brenda Power Murphy, (Brenda Maddox, writer); one *s* one *d. Educ:* Gowerton Boys' County Sch.; Christ Church, Oxford; King's Coll., London. Asst Lecturer, then Lecturer, Theoretical Physics, Manchester Univ., 1949–55; Science Correspondent, Guardian, 1955–64; Affiliate, Rockefeller Institute, New York, 1962–63; Asst Director, Nuffield Foundation, and Co-ordinator, Nuffield Foundation Science Teaching Project, 1964–66; Man. Dir, Macmillan Journals Ltd, 1970–72; Dir, Macmillan & Co. Ltd, 1968–73; Chm., Maddox Editorial Ltd, 1972–74; Dir, Nuffield Foundn, 1975–80.

Member: Royal Commn on Environmental Pollution, 1976–81; Genetic Manipulation Adv. Gp, 1976–80; British Library Adv. Council, 1976–81; Council on Internat. Develt, 1977–79; Chm. Council, Queen Elizabeth Coll., 1980–85; Mem. Council, King's Coll. London, 1985–89. Mem., Crickadarn and Gwendwr Community Council, 1981–. Hon. FRS 2000. Hon. DTech Surrey, 1982; Hon. DSc: UEA, 1992; Liverpool, 1994; Glamorgan, 1997; Hon. DLitt Nottingham Trent, 1996. *Publications:* (with Leonard Beaton) The Spread of Nuclear Weapons, 1962; Revolution in Biology, 1964; The Doomsday Syndrome, 1972; Beyond the Energy Crisis, 1975; What Remains to be Discovered, 1998. *Address:* 9 Pitt Street, W8 4NX. *T:* (020) 7937 9750; *e-mail:* john.maddox@btopenworld.com. *Club:* Athenæum. *Died 12 April 2009.*

MADGE, James Richard, CB 1976; Deputy Secretary, Department of the Environment, on secondment as Chief Executive, Housing Corporation, 1973–84; *b* 18 June 1924; *s* of James Henry Madge and Elisabeth May Madge; *m* 1955, Alice June Annette (*d* 1975), *d* of late Major Horace Reid, Jamaica; two *d. Educ:* Bexhill Co. Sch.; New Coll., Oxford. Pilot in RAFVR, 1942–46. Joined Min. of Civil Aviation, 1947; Principal Private Secretary: to Paymaster-General, 1950–51; to Minister of Transport, 1960–61; Asst Secretary, Min. of Transport, 1961–66; Under-Sec., Road Safety Gp, 1966–69; Head of Policy Planning, 1969–70; Under-Sec., Housing Directorate, DoE, 1971–73. Churchwarden, St Mary Abbots, Kensington, 1987–2000. *Died 2 Aug. 2010.*

MAGGS, Air Vice-Marshal William Jack, CB 1967; OBE 1943; Fellow and Domestic Bursar, Keble College, Oxford, 1969–77, Emeritus Fellow since 1981; *b* 2 Feb. 1914; *s* of late Frederick Wilfrid Maggs, Bristol; *m* 1940, Margaret Grace, *d* of late Thomas Liddell Hetherington, West Hartlepool; one *s* one *d. Educ:* Bristol Grammar Sch.; St John's Coll., Oxford (MA). Mgt Trainee, 1936–38. Joined RAF, 1939; Unit and Training duties, 1939–42; Student, Staff Coll., 1942; Planning Staffs, and participated in, Algerian, Sicilian and Italian landings, 1942–44; SESO Desert Air Force, 1944; Jt Admin. Plans Staff, Cabinet Offices, Whitehall, 1945–48; Instructor, RAF Coll., Cranwell, 1948–50; comd No 9 Maintenance Unit, 1950–52; exchange officer at HQ, USAF Washington, 1952–54; student, Jt Services Staff Coll., 1954–55; No 3 Maintenance Unit, 1955–57; Dep. Dir of Equipment, Air Ministry, 1958–59; SESO, HQ, NEAF, Cyprus, 1959–61; student, Imperial Defence Coll., 1962; Dir of Mech. Transport and Marine Craft, Air Ministry, 1963–64; Dir of Equipment, MoD (Air), 1964–67; SASO, RAF Maintenance Comd, 1967–69. Group Captain, 1958; Air Commodore, 1963; Air Vice-Marshal, 1967. Governor, Bristol Grammar Sch., 1980–89. *Recreations:* golf, gardening. *Club:* Royal Air Force. *Died 25 Feb. 2006.*

MAGNUSSON, Magnus, Hon. KBE 1989; MA (Oxon); FRSE; writer and broadcaster; *b* 12 Oct. 1929; *s* of late Sigursteinn Magnusson, Icelandic Consul-Gen. for Scotland, and Ingibjorg Sigurdardottir; *m* 1954, Mamie Baird; one *s* three *d* (and one *s* decd). *Educ:* Edinburgh Academy; Jesus Coll., Oxford (MA; Hon. Fellow, 1990). Subseq. Asst Editor, Scottish Daily Express and Asst Editor, The Scotsman. Presenter, various television and radio programmes including: Chronicle, 1966–80; Mastermind, 1972–97; Pebble Mill at One; BC, The Archaeology of the Bible Lands; Tonight; Cause for Concern; All Things Considered; Living Legends; Vikings!; Birds For All Seasons. Editor: The Bodley Head Archaeologies; Popular Archaeology, 1979–80. Chairman: Ancient Monuments Bd for Scotland, 1981–89; Cairngorms Working Party, 1991–93; NCC for Scotland, 1991–92; Scottish Natural Heritage, 1992–99. Stewards, York Archaeol Trust; Scottish Churches Architectural Heritage Trust, 1978–85; Scottish Youth Theatre, 1976–78; Member: Bd of Trustees, Nat. Museums of Scotland, 1985–89; UK Cttee for European

Year of the Environment, 1987; Pres., RSPB, 1985–90; Hon. Vice-President: Age Concern Scotland; RSSPCC. Rector, Edinburgh Univ., 1975–78; Chancellor, Glasgow Caledonian Univ., 2002–. FSAScot 1974; FRSE 1980; FRSA 1983; Hon. FRIAS 1987; FSA 1991; FRSGS 1991. Dr *hc* Edinburgh, 1978; DUniv: York, 1981; Paisley, 1993; Hon. DLitt: Strathclyde, 1993; Napier Univ., 1994; Glasgow, 2001; Glasgow Caledonian, 2001. Scottish Television Personality of the Year, 1974; Iceland Media Award, 1985; Medlicott Medal, HA, 1989. Knight of the Order of the Falcon (Iceland), 1975, Knight Commander, 1986; Silver Jubilee Medal, 1977. *Publications*: Introducing Archaeology, 1972; Viking Expansion Westwards, 1973; The Clacken and the Slate (Edinburgh Academy, 1824–1974), 1974; Hammer of the North (Norse mythology), 1976, 2nd edn, Viking Hammer of the North, 1980; BC, The Archaeology of the Bible Lands, 1977; Landlord or Tenant? a view of Irish history, 1978; Iceland, 1979; Vikings!, 1980; Magnus on the Move, 1980; Treasures of Scotland, 1981; Lindisfarne: The Cradle Island, 1984; Iceland Saga, 1987, 2nd edn 2005; I've Started, So I'll Finish, 1997; Rum: nature's island, 1997; Magnus Magnusson's Quiz Book, 2000; Scotland: the story of a nation, 2000; Magnus Magnusson's Family Quiz Book, 2002; Fakers, Forgers and Phoneys, 2006; *translations*: The Icelandic Sagas, Vol. I, 1999, Vol. II, 2002; (all with Hermann Pálsson): Njal's Saga, 1960; The Vinland Sagas, 1965; King Harald's Saga, 1966; Laxdaela Saga, 1969; (all by Halldor Laxness): The Atom Station, 1961; Paradise Reclaimed, 1962; The Fish Can Sing, 1966; World Light, 1969; Christianity Under Glacier, 1973; (by Samivel) Golden Iceland, 1967; *contributor*: The Glorious Privilege, 1967; The Future of the Highlands, 1968; Strange Stories, Amazing Facts, 1975; Pass the Port, 1976; Book of Bricks, 1978; Chronicle, 1978; Discovery of Lost Worlds, 1979; Pass the Port Again, 1981; Second Book of Bricks, 1981; *introduced*: Ancient China, 1974; The National Trust for Scotland Guide, 1976; Karluk, 1976; More Lives Than One?, 1976; Atlas of World Geography, 1977; Face to Face with the Turin Shroud, 1978; Modern Bible Atlas, 1979; Living Legends, 1980; The Hammer and the Cross, 1980; Household Ghosts, 1981; Great Books for Today, 1981; The Voyage of Odin's Raven, 1982; Robert Burns: Bawdy Verse & Folksongs, 1982; Mastermind 4, 1982; Northern Voices, 1984; The Village, 1985; Secrets of the Bible Seas, 1985; Beowulf, 1987; Complete Book of British Birds, 1988; Trustlands, 1989; The Wealth of a Nation, 1989; The Return of Cultural Treasures, 1990; William Morris: Icelandic Journals, 1996; *edited*: Echoes in Stone, 1983; Readers Digest Book of Facts, 1985; Chambers Biographical Dictionary, 5th edn 1990; The Nature of Scotland, 1991, 2nd edn 1997. *Recreation*: digging and delving. *Address*: Blairskaith House, Balmore-Torrance, Glasgow G64 4AX. *T*: (01360) 620226.
Died 7 Jan. 2007.

MAGUIRE, John Joseph; QC (Scot.) 1990; Sheriff Principal of Tayside, Central and Fife, 1990–98; *b* 30 Nov. 1934; *y s* of Robert Maguire, Solicitor, Glasgow, and Julia Maguire; *m* 1962, Eva O'Hara, Tralee, Co. Kerry; two *s* two *d*. *Educ*: St Mary's Coll., Blairs; Pontifical Gregorian Univ., Rome (PhL 1955); Edinburgh Univ. (LLB 1958). Mem., Faculty of Advocates, 1958; Standing Junior to MPBW, 1963–68; Sheriff Substitute: Airdrie, 1968; Glasgow, 1973; Sheriff Principal *ai*, S Strathclyde, Dumfries and Galloway, 2003. Member: Deptl Cttee on Alternatives to Prosecution, 1977–82; Parole Bd for Scotland, 2000–05. Pres., Sheriffs' Assoc., 1989–90 (Sec., 1982–87). *Recreations*: reading, pottering in the garden. *Address*: Spring Lodge, Hatton Way, Perth PH2 7DP. *T*: (01738) 636260. *Club*: Royal Perth Country and City. *Died 28 April 2007.*

MAHFOUZ, Naguib; Egyptian novelist; *b* Gamallya, Cairo, 11 Dec. 1911; *s* of Abdel Aziz Ibrahim and Fatma Mostapha Mahfouz; *m* 1954, Attiyah-Allah; two *d*. *Educ*: King Fuad I Univ. (later Cairo Univ.). Civil servant, 1934; Sec., King Fuad I Univ., 1936–38; Min. of Religious Affairs, 1939–54; Dept Arts and Censorship Bd,

1954–59; Dir, Foundn for Cinema, State Cinema Orgn, Cairo, 1959–69; cons. cinema affairs, Min. of Culture, 1969–71. Staff mem., Ar-Risala; contribs to Al-Hilal, Al-Ahram. Hon. Mem., Amer. Acad. and Inst. of Arts and Letters. Nat. Prize for Letters, Egypt, 1970. Collar of the Republic, 1972; Nobel Prize for Literature, 1988. *Publications: fiction*: Hams al-junun, 1938; 'Abath al-aqdar (Games of Fate), 1939; Radubis (Radobis), 1943; Kifah Tibah (The Struggle of Thebes), 1944; Al-Qahira al-jadida (New Cairo), 1945; Khan al-Khalili, 1946; Zuqaq al-middaq (Midaq Alley), 1947; Al-Sarab (The Mirage), 1948; Bidaya wa nihaya (The Beginning and the End), 1949; trilogy, Al-thulathiya: vol. 1, Bayn al-qasrayn (Palace Walk), 1956 (Egyptian State Prize); vol. 2, Qasr al-shawq (Palace of Desire), 1957; vol. 3, Al-Sukkariyya (Sugar Street), 1957; Awlad haritna (Children of Our Alley), 1959; Al-Liss wa'l-kilab (The Thief and the Dogs), 1961; Al-Samman wa'l-kharif (Autumn Quail), 1962; Dunya Allah (God's World), 1962; Al-Tariq (The Search), 1964; Al-Shahhaz (The Beggar), 1965; Bayt sayyi'al-sum'a, 1965; Tharthara fawq al-nil (Adrift on the Nile), 1966; Miramar, 1967; Khammarat al-qitt al-aswad, 1969; Taht al-midhalla, 1969; Hikaya a bi-la bidaya wa-la nihaya, 1971; Shahr al-'asal, 1971; Al-Maraya (Mirrors), 1972; Al-Hubb taht al-matar, 1973; Al-jarima, 1973; Al-Karnak, 1974; Hikayat haratina (Fountain and Tomb), 1975; Qalb al-layl, 1975; Hadrat al-muhtaram (Respected Sir), 1975; Malhamat al-harafish (The Harafish), 1977; Al-hubb fawqa Hadabat al-Haram, 1979; Al-shaytan ya'iz, 1979; Asr al Hubb, 1980; Afrah al-qubba (Wedding Song), 1981; Layali alf layla (Arabian Nights and Days), 1982; Ra'aytu fima yara al-na'im, 1982; Al-Baqi min al-zaman saa, 1982; Amama al'arsh, 1982; Rihlat Ibn Fattuma (The Journey of Ibn Fattouma), 1983; Al-tandhim al-sirri, 1984; Yawm qutila al-zaim (The Day the Leader was Killed), 1985; Al-Aish fi-l-haqiqa (Akhenaton: Dweller in Truth), 1985; Hadith al sabah wa-al-masa, 1987; Sabah al-ward, 1987; Qushtumor, 1988; Al-Fajr al-Kadhib, 1988; Asda al-sira al dhatiyya (Echoes of an Autobiography), 1996. *Address*: (agent) c/o The American University in Cairo Press, 113 Kasr al-Aini Street, Cairo 11511, Egypt. *Fax*: (2) 7941440. *Died 30 Aug. 2006.*

MAHLER, Prof. Robert Frederick, FRCP, FRCPE; Editor, Journal of Royal College of Physicians, 1987–94, Editor Emeritus, 1994–2005; Consultant Physician, Clinical Research Centre, Northwick Park Hospital, Harrow, 1979–90, retired; *b* 31 Oct. 1924; *s* of Felix Mahler and Olga Lowy; *m* 1951, Maureen Calvert; two *s*. *Educ*: Edinburgh Academy; Edinburgh Univ. (BSc; MB, ChB). Research fellowships and univ. posts in medicine, biochemistry and clinical pharmacology at various med. schs and univs: in Gt Britain: Royal Postgrad. Med. Sch., Guy's Hosp., Manchester, Dundee, Cardiff; in USA: Harvard Univ., Univ. of Indiana; in Sweden: Karolinska Inst., Stockholm; Prof. of Med., Univ. of Wales, 1970–79. Royal College of Physicians: Mem. Council, 1974–76; Censor, 1976–78; Bradshaw Lectr, 1977. Member: MRC, 1977–81; Commonwealth Scholarship Commn, 1980–93; Council, Imperial Cancer Res. Fund, 1984–94; Res. Cttee, British Diabetic Assoc., 1984–87; Scientific Co-ord. Cttee, Arthritis and Rheumatism Council, 1986–91. Hon. Fellow, UWCM, 2003. *Publications*: contribs to British and Amer. med. and scientific jls. *Recreations*: opera, music, theatre. *Address*: 14 Manley Street, NW1 8LT. *Club*: Royal Society of Medicine. *Died 29 May 2006.*

MAILER, Norman Kingsley; *b* 31 Jan. 1923; *s* of Isaac Barnett Mailer and Fanny Schneider; *m* 1st, 1944, Beatrice Silverman (marr. diss., 1951); one *d*; 2nd, 1954, Adèle Morales (marr. diss., 1962); two *d*; 3rd, 1962, Lady Jeanne Campbell (marr. diss., 1963; she *d* 2007); one *d*; 4th, 1963, Beverly Bentley (marr. diss. 1979); two *s*; 5th, 1980, Carol Stevens (marr. diss. 1980); one *d*; 6th, 1980, Norris Church; one *s*. *Educ*: Harvard. Infantryman, US Army, 1944–46. Co-founder of Village Voice, 1955; an Editor of Dissent, 1953–63. Democratic Candidate, Mayoral Primaries, New York City, 1969. Directed films:

Wild 90, 1967; Beyond the Law, 1967; Maidstone, 1968; Tough Guys Don't Dance, 1988. Pulitzer Prize for Fiction, 1980. *Publications:* The Naked and the Dead, 1948; Barbary Shore, 1951; The Deer Park, 1955 (dramatized, 1967); Advertisements for Myself, 1959; Deaths For The Ladies, 1962; The Presidential Papers, 1963; An American Dream, 1964; Cannibals and Christians, 1966; Why Are We In Vietnam?, 1967 (a novel); The Armies of the Night, 1968 (Pulitzer Prize, 1969); Miami and the Siege of Chicago, 1968 (National Book Award, 1969); Of a Fire on the Moon, 1970; The Prisoner of Sex, 1971; Existential Errands, 1972; St George and the Godfather, 1972; Marilyn, 1973; The Faith of Graffiti, 1974; The Fight, 1975; Some Honorable Men, 1975; Genius and Lust, 1976; A Transit to Narcissus, 1978; The Executioner's Song, 1979; Of a Small and Modest Malignancy, Wicked and Bristling with Dots, 1980; Of Women and Their Elegance, 1980; The Essential Mailer, 1982; Ancient Evenings, 1983; Tough Guys Don't Dance, 1984; Harlot's Ghost, 1991; Oswald's Tale: an American mystery, 1995; Picasso: portrait of Picasso as a young man, 1996; The Gospel According to the Son, 1997; The Time of Our Time, 1998; The Spooky Art, 2003; The Castle in the Forest, 2007. *Address:* c/o Random House Inc., 1745 Broadway, New York, NY 10019, USA.					*Died 10 Nov. 2007.*

MAIN, Sir Peter (Tester), Kt 1985; ERD 1964, Chairman, The Boots Company PLC, 1982–85; *b* 21 March 1925; *s* of late Peter Tester Main and Esther Paterson (*née* Lawson); *m* 1st, 1952, Dr Margaret Fimister, MB, ChB (*née* Tweddle) (*d* 1984); two *s* one *d*; 2nd, 1986, May Hetherington Anderson (*née* McMillan). *Educ:* Robert Gordon's Coll., Aberdeen; Univ. of Aberdeen (MB, ChB 1948, MD 1963; Hon. LLD 1986). MRCPE 1981, FRCPE 1982. Captain, RAMC, 1949–51; MO with Field Ambulance, Suez, 1956; Lt-Col RAMC (AER), retd 1964. House Surg., Aberdeen Royal Infirmary, 1948; House Physician, Woodend Hosp., Aberdeen, 1949; Demonstrator in Anatomy, Univ. of Durham, 1952; gen. practice, 1953–57; joined Res. Dept, Boots, 1957; Dir of Res., 1968; Man. Dir, Industrial Div., 1979–80; Dir, 1973–85, Vice-Chm., 1980–81, The Boots Company PLC. Chm., Inveresk Res. Internat., 1986–89; Dir, W. A. Baxter and Sons Ltd, 1985–91. Chm., Cttee of Inquiry into Teachers' Pay and Conditions, Scotland, 1986; Member: NEDC, 1984–85; Scottish Health Service Policy Board, 1985–88; SDA, 1986–91. Governor, Henley Management Coll., 1983–86; Chm., Grantown Heritage Trust, 1987–91; Trustee, Univ. of Aberdeen Develt Trust, 1988–97. Elder, C of S, Chirnside. CCMI (FBIM 1978). *Recreation:* fly fishing. *Address:* Ninewells House, Chirnside, Duns, Berwickshire TD11 3XF.					*Died 17 May 2008.*

MAINGARD de la VILLE ès OFFRANS, Sir (Louis Pierre) René, (Sir René Maingard), Kt 1982; CBE 1961; company chairman and director, Mauritius; *b* 9 July 1917; *s* of Joseph René Maingard de la Ville ès Offrans and Véronique Hugnin; *m* 1946, Marie Hélène Françoise Raffray; three *d*. *Educ:* St Joseph's Coll.; Royal Coll. of Mauritius; Business Training Corp., London. Rogers & Co. Ltd: Clerk, 1936; Dir, 1948–2002; Man. Dir, 1948; Chm., 1956–82. Chairman: Mauritius Portland Cement Co. Ltd, 1960–; Mauritius Steam Navigation Co. Ltd, 1964–; De Chazal du Mée Associates Ltd, 1982–. Director: New Mauritius Dock Co. Ltd, 1948–; Mauritius Commercial Bank Ltd, 1956–. Formerly, Consul for Finland in Mauritius. Chevalier 1st Cl., Order of the White Rose, Finland, 1973. *Recreations:* golf, fishing, boating. *Address:* Rogers & Co. Ltd, PO Box 60, Port Louis, Mauritius. *T:* 086801. *Clubs:* Royal Air Force; Dodo, Mauritius Naval & Military Gymkhana (Mauritius).					*Died Nov. 2006.*

MAIR, Prof. William Austyn, CBE 1969; MA; FREng; Francis Mond Professor of Aeronautical Engineering, University of Cambridge, 1952–83; Head of Engineering Department, 1973–83; Fellow of Downing College, Cambridge, 1953–83, Hon. Fellow, 1983; *b* 24 Feb.

1917; *s* of William Mair, MD; *m* 1944, Mary Woodhouse Crofts; two *s*. *Educ:* Highgate Sch.; Clare Coll., Cambridge. Aerodynamics Dept, Royal Aircraft Establishment, Farnborough, 1940–46; Dir, Fluid Motion Laboratory, Univ. of Manchester, 1946–52. Mem. various cttees, Aeronautical Research Council, 1946–80. Dir, Hovercraft Development Ltd, 1962–81. John Orr Meml Lectr, S Africa, 1983. Chm., Editorial Bd, Aeronautical Qly, 1975–81. FRAeS (Silver Medal 1975); FREng (FEng 1984). Hon. DSc Cranfield, 1990. *Publications:* (with D. L. Birdsall) Aircraft Performance, 1992; papers on aerodynamics. *Address:* c/o 11 Milton Court, Milton Malsor, Northants NN7 3AX. *T:* (01604) 858530.					*Died 17 Jan. 2008.*

MAISNER, Air Vice-Marshal Aleksander, CB 1977; CBE 1969; AFC 1955; *b* 26 July 1921; *s* of Henryk Maisner and Helene Anne (*née* Brosin); *m* 1946, Mary (*née* Coverley) (*d* 1997); one *s* one *d*. *Educ:* High Sch. and Lyceum, Czestochowa, Poland; Warsaw Univ. Labour Camps, USSR, 1940–41; Polish Artillery, 1941–42; Polish Air Force, 1943–16; joined RAF, 1946; Flying Trng Comd, 1946–49; No 70 Sqdn Suez Canal Zone, 1950–52; No 50 Sqdn RAF Binbrook, 1953–55; No 230 (Vulcan) OCU, RAF Waddington, 1955–59; psa 1960; OC Flying Wing, RNZAF Ohakea, 1961–62; Dirg Staff, RAF Staff Coll., Andover, 1963–65; DD Air Plans, MoD, 1965–68; CO, RAF Seletar, Singapore, 1969–71; Asst Comdt, RAF Coll., Cranwell, 1971–73; Dir, Personnel (Policy and Plans), MoD, 1973–75; Asst Air Sec., 1975; Dir-Gen. of Personnel Management, RAF, 1976. Personnel Exec., Reed Internat. Ltd, 1977–82; Dir, Industry and Parlt Trust, 1984–87. Governor, Shiplake Coll., 1978–96. Pres., Polish Air Force Assoc., 1982–. Comdr's Cross with Star, Order of Polonia Restituta (Poland), 1990; Comdr's Cross, OM (Poland), 1992; OM with Star (Poland), 1998.					*Died 21 Dec. 2008.*

MAITLAND, Sir Donald (James Dundas), GCMG 1977 (CMG 1967); Kt 1973; OBE 1960; Permanent Under-Secretary of State, Department of Energy, 1980–82; Visiting Professor, Bath University, since 2000; *b* 16 Aug. 1922; *s* of Thomas Douglas Maitland and Wilhelmina Sarah Dundas; *m* 1950, Jean Marie Young, *d* of Gordon Young; one *s* one *d*. *Educ:* George Watson's Coll.; Edinburgh Univ. (MA). Served India, Middle East, and Burma, 1941–47 (Royal Scots; Rajputana Rifles). Joined Foreign Service, 1947; Consul, Amara, 1950; British Embassy, Baghdad, 1950–53; Private Sec. to Minister of State, Foreign Office, 1954–56; Director, Middle East Centre for Arab Studies, Lebanon, 1956–60; Foreign Office, 1960–63; Counsellor, British Embassy, Cairo, 1963–65; Head of News Dept, Foreign Office, 1965–67; Principal Private Sec. to Foreign and Commonwealth Secretary, 1967–69; Ambassador to Libya, 1969–70; Chief Press Sec., 10 Downing St, 1970–73; UK Permanent Rep. to UN, 1973–74; Dep. Under-Sec. of State, FCO, 1974–75; UK Mem., Commonwealth Group on Trade, Aid and Develt, 1975; Ambassador and UK Perm. Rep. to EEC, 1975–79; Dep. to Perm. Under-Sec. of State, FCO, Dec. 1979–June 1980. Chairman: Independent Commn for World-Wide Telecommunications Develt (Maitland Commn), 1983–85; UK Nat. Cttee for World Communications Year, 1983; HEA, 1989–94. Govt Dir, Britoil, 1983–85; Director: Slough Estates, 1983–92; Northern Engrg Industries, 1986–89. Dep. Chm., IBA, 1986–89. Chm., Charlemagne Inst. (formerly Christians for Europe), 1984–97. Mem., Commonwealth War Graves Commn, 1983–87. President: Bath Inst. for Rheumatic Diseases, 1986–95 and 1997–2004; Federal Trust for Educn and Res., 1987–2003; Vice-Pres., Centre Européen de Prospective et de Synthèse, Paris, 1990–95; Governor, Westminster Coll., Oxford, 1990–97 (Chm., 1994–97); Pro-Chancellor, Bath Univ., 1996–2000. Private pilot, 1969–79. Hon. Fellow, Bath Spa UC, 2000. Hon. LLD Bath, 1995; Hon. DLitt UWE, 2000. *Publications:* Diverse Times, Sundry Places (autobiog.), 1996; The Boot and Other Stories, 1999; The Running Tide, 2000; Edinburgh: seat of learning, 2001; articles on internat.

affairs, sovereignty, world telecommunications, public health. *Recreation:* music. *Address:* 2 Rosemary Walk, Church Street, Bradford-on-Avon BA15 1BP. *T:* (01225) 863063. *Died 22 Aug. 2010.*

MAITLAND-MAKGILL-CRICHTON, Maj.-Gen. Edward; *see* Crichton.

MAKEPEACE-WARNE, Maj.-Gen. Antony, CB 1992; MBE 1972; Director, Army Museums Ogilby Trust, 1996–2002; Commandant, Joint Service Defence College, 1990–92; *b* 3 Sept. 1937; *e s* of late Keith Makepeace-Warne and Nora (*née* Kelstrup); *m* 1966, Jill Estelle Seath; two *d. Educ:* Taunton School; Open Univ. (BA Hons 1990). Commissioned Intelligence Corps, 1958, KOYLI, 1960; served BAOR, Malaya, Aden, Berlin, MoD, to 1969; Staff College, 1970; 2nd Bn LI, 1971–72; 24 Airportable Bde, 1972–74; Instructor, Staff Coll., 1975–77; CO 1st Bn LI, 1977–80; Col ASD2, MoD, 1980–82; Comdr, Berlin Inf. Bde, 1982–84; RCDS 1985; ACOS HQ UKLF, 1986–88; GS Study of Indiv. Trg Orgn, 1988–89. Dep. Col, LI (Somerset and Cornwall), 1987–89; Colonel, The Light Infantry, 1990–92. Member: Council, Assoc. of Independent Museums, 1996–2002; Council, Museums Assoc., 1997–2002. *Publications:* Exceedingly Lucky: a history of the Light Infantry 1968–1993, 1993; The British Army Today and Tomorrow 1993/94, 1993; Brassey's Companion to the British Army, 1995. *Address:* c/o Lloyds TSB, Cox's & King's, 7 Pall Mall, SW1Y 5NA. *Club:* Army and Navy. *Died 16 May 2007.*

MALIM, Rear-Adm. Nigel Hugh, CB 1971; LVO 1960; DL; *b* 5 April 1919; *s* of late John Malim, Pebmarsh, and Brenda Malim; *m* 1944, Moonyeen, *d* of late William and Winefride Maynard; two *s* one *d. Educ:* Weymouth Coll.; RNEC Keyham. Cadet, RN, 1936; HMS Manchester, 1940–41; HMS Norfolk, 1942; RNC Greenwich, 1943–45; HMS Jamaica, 1945–47; Staff of RNEC, 1948–50; Admty, 1951–54; HMS Triumph, 1954–56; Admty, 1956–58; HM Yacht Britannia, 1958–60; District Overseer, Scotland, 1960–62; Asst, and later Dep., Dir Marine Engrg, 1962–65; idc 1966; Captain, RNEC Manadon, 1967–69; Chief Staff Officer Technical to C-in-C, W Fleet, 1969–71, retd. Man. Dir, Humber Graving Dock & Engrg Co. Ltd, 1972–82. Chm., Fabric Council, Lincoln Cathedral, 1985–91. DL Lincoln, 1987. *Recreation:* offshore racing and cruising. *Address:* The Old Vicarage, Caistor, Lincoln LN7 6UG. *Clubs:* Royal Ocean Racing; Royal Naval Sailing Association. *Died 23 Aug. 2006.*

MALLET, Sir (William) George, GCSL 1996; GCMG 1997; CBE 1989; Governor-General of St Lucia, 1996–97; *b* 24 July 1923; *m* Beryl Bernadine Leonce (*d* 2003); two *c. Educ:* RC Boys' Sch.; Castries Intermediate Sch. Mem., Castries City Council, 1952–64; MLC, 1958–79, MHA, 1979–96, St Lucia; Minister for Trade, Industry, Agric. and Tourism, 1964–79; Minister for Trade, Industry and Tourism, 1982–92; Dep. Prime Minister, Minister for For. Affairs, and Minister for Caribbean Community Affairs, 1992–96. *Address:* The Morne, Castries, St Lucia. *Died 20 Oct. 2010.*

MALLETT, Francis Anthony, CBE 1984; Chief Executive, South Yorkshire County Council, 1973–84; Clerk of the Lieutenancy, South Yorkshire, 1974–84; solicitor; *b* 13 March 1924; *s* of Francis Sidney and Marion Mallett; *m* 1956, Alison Shirley Melville, MA; two *s* one *d. Educ:* Mill Hill; London Univ. (LLB). Army, 1943–47: commissioned, Royal Hampshire Regt, 1944; served in Middle East, Italy and Germany; Staff Capt. A 160(SW) Inf. Bde, 4th Guards Bde, 1946–47. Second Dep. Clerk, Herts CC, 1966–69; Dep. Clerk, West Riding CC, 1969–74. Chairman: Assoc. of Local Authority Chief Execs, 1979–84; Crown Prosecution Service Staff Commn, 1985–87; Mem., W Yorks Residuary Body, 1985–91. *Recreations:* gardening, fishing. *Address:* Lurley Manor, Tiverton, Devon EX16 9QS. *T:* (01884) 255363. *Club:* Lansdowne. *Died 13 Nov. 2008.*

MALLINSON, Anthony William; Senior Partner, Slaughter and May, 1984–86; *b* 1 Dec. 1923; *s* of Stanley Tucker Mallinson and Dora Selina Mallinson (*née* Burridge); *m* 1955, Heather Mary Gardiner (*d* 1999). *Educ:* Cheam School; Marlborough College; Gonville and Caius College, Cambridge (Exhibnr 1948, Tapp Post-Graduate Scholar, 1949, BA, LLM). Served RA, 1943–47, Major. Admitted solicitor, England and Wales, 1952, Hong Kong, 1978; Partner, Slaughter and May, 1957–86; Solicitor to Fishmongers' Co., 1964–86. Mem. London Bd, Bank of Scotland, 1985–93; Director: Baring Stratton (formerly Stratton) Investment Trust, 1986–94; Morgan Grenfell Asset Management Ltd, 1986–91. Mem., BoT Cttee examining British Patent System (Banks Cttee), 1967–70; Chm., Cinematograph Films Council, 1973–76. Hon. Legal Adviser to Accounting Standards Cttee, 1982–86; Member: Council, Section on Business Law, Internat. Bar Assoc., 1984–90; (co-opted) Law Soc. Co. Law Cttee, 1986–92; Financial Services Tribunal, 1988–97; Financial Reporting Review Panel, 1991–95; Registration Cttee, TCCB, 1986–96; Trustee, Essex CCC, 1990–2001 (Mem. Exec. Cttee, 1986–92). *Recreations:* watching sport, particularly cricket. *Address:* 21 Cottesmore Court, Stanford Road, W8 5QN. *T:* (020) 7937 2739. *Clubs:* Royal Commonwealth Society, MCC. *Died 14 Aug. 2006.*

MALLINSON, William Arthur, CBE 1978; FREng; Vice Chairman, Smiths Industries PLC, 1978–85; *b* 12 June 1922; *s* of Arthur Mallinson and Nellie Jane Mallinson; *m* 1948, Muriel Ella Parker (*d* 2003); two *d. Educ:* William Hulme's Grammar Sch., Manchester; Faculty of Technol., Manchester Univ. (BScTech 1st Cl. Hons). MIEE, MIMechE, MRAeS; FREng (FEng 1985). Electrical Officer, Tech. Br., RAFVR, 1943–47; Elec. Designer, Electro-Hydraulics Ltd, 1947–51; Ferranti Ltd: Proj. Engr, GW Dept, 1951–55; Chief Engr, Aircraft Equipment Dept, 1955–68; Smiths Industries Ltd, 1968–85: Technical Dir, then Gen. Man., Aviation Div.; Divl Man. Dir; Main Bd Dir; Corporate Man. Dir. Member: Airworthiness Requirements Bd, CAA, 1981–85; Electronics and Avionics Requirements Bd, DTI, 1983–85 (Chm., Aviation Cttee, 1984–85). FCMI (FBIM 1976). *Recreations:* music, horticulture. *Address:* 3 Wayewood Lodge, Branksome Park Road, Camberley, Surrey GU15 2AE. *T:* (01276) 692694. *Died 17 Nov. 2006.*

MALLON, Rt Rev. Mgr Joseph Laurence; Parish Priest, St Brendan, Harwood, Bolton, since 1995; *b* 8 Aug. 1942; *s* of John Mallon and Mary (*née* O'Neill). *Educ:* St Nathy's Coll., Ballaghaderreen; St Kiernan's Coll., Kilkenny. Ordained priest, Dio. of Salford, 1966; Curate: St Joseph's, Bury, 1966–67; St Anne's, Stretford, 1967–73; commnd into RAChD, 1973; service in England, NI, Germany and Cyprus; Sen. RC Chaplain, BAOR, 1988; Prin. RC Chaplain and VG (Army), 1989–93, retired; Parish Priest, St Anne's, Ancoats, Manchester, 1993–95. Prelate of Honour, 1989. *Recreations:* bridge, golf, recreational mathematics, The Times crossword. *Address:* St Brendan's Presbytery, 171 Longsight, Harwood, Bolton, Lancs BL2 3JF. *Died 31 Oct. 2007.*

MALLON, Most Rev. Peter Joseph; Archbishop of Regina, (RC), 1995–2005, then Archbishop Emeritus; *b* 5 Dec. 1929; *s* of Joseph P. Mallon and Sheila (*née* Keenan). *Educ:* Christ the King Seminary, Mission, BC, Canada. Ordained priest, 1956; Asst Priest, Holy Rosary Cathedral, Vancouver, 1956–64; Chancellor, Archdio. of Vancouver, 1964–65; Administrator, Guardian Angels Parish, Vancouver, 1965–66; Rector of Holy Rosary Cathedral, 1966–82; Dir of Religious Educn, 1971–73; Pastor, St Anthony's Parish, W Vancouver, 1982–89; Bishop of Nelson, BC, 1989–95. *Address:* 445 Broad Street North, Regina, SK S4R 2X8, Canada. *T:* (306) 352 1651. *Died 3 Feb. 2007.*

MALLOWS, Surg. Rear-Adm. (Harry) Russell; Senior Medical Officer, Shell Centre, 1977–85; *b* 1 July 1920; *s* of Harry Mallows and Amy Mallows (*née* Law); *m* 1st,

1942, Rhona Frances Wyndham-Smith (*d* 1997); one *s* two *d*; 2nd, 1999, Jean Richardson. *Educ:* Wrekin Coll.; Christ's Coll., Cambridge (MA, MD); UCH, London. FFPH, FFOM, DPH, DIH. SMO, HM Dockyards at Hong Kong, Sheerness, Gibraltar and Singapore, 1951–67; Naval MO of Health, Scotland and NI Comd, and Far East Stn, 1964–68; Dir of Environmental Medicine, Inst. of Naval Medicine, 1970–73; Comd MO, Naval Home Comd, 1973–75; QHP, 1974–77; Surgeon Rear-Adm. (Ships and Estabts), 1975–77; retd 1977. CStJ 1976. *Publications:* articles in BMJ, Royal Naval Med. Service Jl, Proc. RSM. *Recreations:* music, travel. *Address:* 1 Shear Hill, Petersfield, Hants GU31 4BB. *T:* (01730) 263116. *Died 19 April 2007.*

MAMO, Sir Anthony (Joseph), Kt 1960; OBE 1955; Companion of Honour, National Order of Merit (Malta), 1990; *b* 8 Jan. 1909; *s* of late Joseph Mamo and Carla (*née* Brincat); *m* 1939, Margaret Agius; one *s* two *d*. *Educ:* Royal Univ. of Malta. BA 1931; LLD 1934. Mem. Statute Law Revision Commn, 1936–42; Crown Counsel, 1942–51; Prof., Criminal Law, Malta Univ., 1943–57; Dep. Attorney-Gen., 1952–54, Attorney-Gen., 1955, Malta; Chief Justice and President, Court of Appeal, Malta, 1957–71; President, Constitutional Court, Malta, 1964–71; Governor-General, Malta, 1971–74; President, Republic of Malta, 1974–76. QC (Malta) 1957. Hon. DLitt Malta, 1969; Hon. LLD Libya, 1971. KStJ 1969. Gieh ir-Repubblika (Malta), 1992; Gieh Birkirkara (Malta), 1996. *Address:* Casa Arkati, Constitution Street, Mosta, Malta. *T:* 434342. *Clubs:* Casino, Maltese. *Died 1 May 2008.*

MANDELSTAM, Prof. Joel, FRS 1971; Emeritus Professor, University of Oxford, and Emeritus Fellow, Linacre College, since 1987; *b* S Africa, 13 Nov. 1919; *s* of Leo and Fanny Mandelstam; *m* 1954, Dorothy Hillier (*d* 1996); one *s* one *d*; *m* 1975, Mary Maureen Dale. *Educ:* Jeppe High Sch., Johannesburg; University of Witwatersrand. Lecturer, Medical Sch., Johannesburg, 1942–47; Queen Elizabeth Coll., London, 1947–51; Scientific Staff, Nat. Institute for Med. Research, London, 1952–66; Iveagh Prof. of Microbiology, and Fellow of Linacre College, Univ. of Oxford, 1966–87; Deptl Demonstrator, Sir William Dunn Sch. of Pathology, Univ. of Oxford, 1987–90. Fulbright Fellow, US, 1958–59; Vis. Prof., Univ. of Adelaide, 1971. Mem., ARC, 1973–83. Leeuwenhoek Lectr, Royal Soc., 1975. Editorial Board, Biochemical Journal, 1960–66. *Publications:* Biochemistry of Bacterial Growth (with K. McQuillen and I. Dawes), 1968; articles in journals and books on microbial biochemistry. *Address:* 13 Cherwell Lodge, Water Eaton Road, Oxford OX2 7QH. *Died 20 Dec. 2008.*

MANDER, Sir Charles (Marcus), 3rd Bt *cr* 1911; Underwriting Member of Lloyd's, 1957–92; Director: Manders (Holdings) Ltd, 1951–58; Mander Brothers Ltd, 1948–58; Headstaple Ltd, since 1977; *b* 22 Sept. 1921; *o s* of Sir Charles Arthur Mander, 2nd Bt, and late Monica Claire Cotterill, *d* of G. H. Neame; *S* father, 1951; *m* 1945, Maria Dolores Beatrice, *d* of late Alfred Brodermann, Hamburg; two *s* one *d*. *Educ:* Eton Coll., Windsor; Trinity Coll., Cambridge. Commissioned Coldstream Guards, 1942; served War of 1939–45, Canal Zone, 1943; Italy, 1943; Germany, 1944; War Office (ADC to Lieut-General R. G. Stone, CB), 1945. Chairman: Arlington Securities Ltd, 1977–83; London & Cambridge Investments Ltd, 1984–91. High Sheriff of Staffordshire, 1962–63. *Recreations:* shooting, music. *Heir: s* Charles Nicholas Mander [*b* 23 March 1950; *m* 1972, Karin Margareta, *d* of Arne Norin; four *s* one *d*]. *Address:* Little Barrow Farm, Moreton-in-Marsh, Glos GL56 0XU. *T:* (01451) 830265. *Died 9 Aug. 2006.*

MANN, Patricia Kathleen Randall, (Mrs Pierre Walker), OBE 1996; Consultant, J. Walter Thompson Co. Ltd, and Director, JWT Trustees; *b* 26 Sept. 1937; *d* of late Charles Mann and of Marjorie Mann (*née* Heath); *m* 1962, Pierre George Armand Walker (*d* 1997); one *d*. *Educ:* Clifton High School, Bristol. FCAM, FIPA. Joined

J. Walter Thompson Co., 1959, Copywriter, 1959–77; Head of Public Affairs, 1978; Dir of External Affairs, J. Walter Thompson Gp, and Vice Pres. Internat., JWT, 1981–97. Director: Yale and Valor plc, 1985–91; Woolwich (formerly Woolwich Equitable) Building Soc., 1983–96; British Gas plc, 1995–97; Centrica plc, 1997–2006 (Sen. Non-exec. Dir, 2001–06); Hill & Knowlton Internat. (Brussels), 1998–2001. Non-exec. Dir, Nat. Trust Enterprises, 2003–. Mem., Monopolies and Mergers Commn, 1984–93. Member: Council, Inst. of Practitioners in Advertising, 1965–97 (Hon. Sec., 1979–83); Advertising Creative Circle, 1965–; Council, Nat. Advertising Benevolent Soc., 1973–77; Council, Advertising Standards Authy, 1973–86; Board, European Advertising Tripartite, 1981–97; Board, European Assoc. of Advertising Agencies, 1984–97; Gas Consumers Council, 1981–90; Board, UK CEED, 1984–; Food Adv. Cttee, MAFF, 1986–95; Kingman Cttee on English, DES, 1987; EC Commerce and Distribution Commn, 1989–2001; Sen. Salaries Rev. Body, 1994–2000; CBI Europe Cttee, 1996–2004; Mgt Council, Canada-UK Colloquia, 2001–. Vice President, History of Advertising Trust, 1997–; Eur. Food Law Assoc. UK, 1998–. Chm., Debating Gp, 2000–. Member, Advisory Board: Centre of Internat. Studies, Univ. of Cambridge, 2001–04; Consumer Policy Inst., 2002–05. Governor: CAM Educn Foundn, 1971–77; Admin. Staff Coll., Henley, 1976–92; ESU, 1999–2005; Mem. Ct, Brunel Univ., 1976–2004 (Council, 1976–86). Vice-Pres., RSAS Age Care, 2003–. Editor, Consumer Affairs, 1978–98. Mem., Awards Nomination Panel, RTS, 1974–78; Judge, Eur. Women of Achievement, 1999–. Mackintosh Medal, Advertising Assoc., 1977. CCMI; FRSA. DUniv Brunel, 1996. *Publications:* 150 Careers in Advertising, 1971; Advertising, 1979; (ed) Advertising and Marketing to Children, 1980; various articles. *Recreation:* words. *Address:* 269 Lonsdale Road, Barnes, SW13 9QL. *T:* (020) 8748 8345, *Fax:* (020) 8255 4313. *Clubs:* Reform, Women's Advertising, London Cornish Association. *Died 15 Sept. 2006.*

MANNERS, 5th Baron *cr* 1807; **John Robert Cecil Manners;** DL; Consultant, Osborne, Clarke & Co., Solicitors, Bristol (Partner, 1952–84); *b* 13 Feb. 1923; *s* of 4th Baron Manners, MC, and of Mary Edith, *d* of late R.t Rev. Lord William Cecil; *S* father, 1972; *m* 1949, Jennifer Selena (*d* 1996), *d* of Ian Fairbairn; one *s* two *d*. *Educ:* Eton; Trinity College, Oxford. Served as Flt-Lieut, RAFVR, 1941–46. Solicitor to the Supreme Court, 1949. Official Verderer of the New Forest, 1983–92. DL Hampshire, 1987. *Recreation:* hunting and shooting. *Heir: s* Hon. John Hugh Robert Manners [*b* 5 May 1956; *m* 1st, 1983, Lanya Mary Jackson (marr. diss.), *d* of late Dr H. E. Heitz and of Mrs Ian Jackson; two *d*; 2nd, 2007, Juliet McMyn]. *Address:* Sabines, Ringwood Road, Avon, Christchurch, Dorset BH23 7BQ. *Club:* Brooks's. *Died 28 May 2008.*

MANNERS, Prof. Gerald, OBE 2005; Professor of Geography, University College London, 1980–97, then Emeritus; Chairman, Association of Charitable Foundations, 2003–07; *b* 7 Aug. 1932; *s* of George William Manners and Louisa Hannah Manners; *m* 1st, 1959, Anne (*née* Sawyer) (marr. diss. 1982); one *s* two *d*; 2nd, 1982, Joy Edith Roberta (*née* Turner); one *s*. *Educ:* Wallington County Grammar School; St Catharine's College, Cambridge (MA). Lectr in Geography, University Coll. Swansea, 1957–67; Reader in Geography, UCL, 1967–80. Vis. Schol., Resources for the Future, Inc., Washington DC, 1964–65; Vis. Associate, Jt Center for Urban Studies, Harvard and MIT, 1972–73; Vis. Fellow, ANU, 1990. Dir, Economic Associates Ltd, 1964–74. Member: Council, Inst. of British Geographers, 1967–70; LOB 1970–80; SE Economic Planning Council, 1971–79; Council, TCPA, 1980–89; Subscriber, Centre for Environmental Studies Ltd, 1981–99. Specialist Advisor to: H of C Select Cttee on Energy, 1980–92; H of L Select Cttee on Sustainable Develt, 1994–95; H of C Envmtl Audit Cttee, 1999–2001; Advr to Assoc. for Conservation of Energy,

1981–; Chairman: Regl Studies Assoc., 1981–84; RSA Panel of Inquiry into regl problem in UK, 1982–83. Trustee: City Parochial Foundn and Trust for London, 1977–2007 (Chm., Estate Cttee, 1987–2001; Chm., 1996–2004); Chelsea Physic Garden, 1980–83; Eaga Partnership Charitable Trust, 1993–. Sadler's Wells Foundn (formerly Sadler's Wells Foundn and Trust): Gov., 1978–95; Vice-Chm., 1982–86; Chm. Theatre Bd, 1986–93; Chm., 1986–95; Vice-Pres., 1995–99; Mem. Council, ENO Works, 1996–99. Mem., Investment Adv. Cttee, St Paul's Cathedral, 2000–. Mem. Court, City Univ., 1985–. *Publications:* Geography of Energy, 1964, 2nd edn 1971; South Wales in the Sixties, 1964; Changing World Market for Iron Ore 1950–1980, 1971; (ed) Spatial Policy Problems of the British Economy, 1971; Minerals and Man, 1974; Regional Development in Britain, 1974, 2nd edn 1980; Coal in Britain, 1981; Office Policy in Britain, 1986; contribs to edited volumes and learned jls. *Recreations:* music, dance, theatre, walking, undergardening. *Address:* 338 Liverpool Road, Islington, N7 8PZ. *T:* (020) 7607 7920.   *Died 16 Feb. 2009.*

MANNING, Dr Geoffrey, CBE 1986; FInstP; Visiting Professor, Department of Physics and Astronomy, University College London, since 1987; Chairman, Eazi-Way Ltd, since 2005; *b* 31 Aug. 1929; *s* of Jack Manning and Ruby Frances Lambe; *m* 1951, Anita Jacqueline Davis; two *s* one *d*. *Educ:* Tottenham Grammar Sch.; Imperial Coll., London Univ. BSc, PhD; ARCS. FRAS 2005. Asst Lectr in Physics, Imperial Coll., 1953–55; Research worker: English Electric Co., 1955–56; Canadian Atomic Energy Co., 1956–58; Calif Inst. of Technol., 1958–59; AERE, 1960–65; Rutherford Laboratory, Science Research Council: Gp Leader, 1965–69; Dep. Dir, 1969–79; Head of High Energy Physics Div., 1969–75; Head of Atlas Div., 1975–79; Dir. Rutherford (Rutherford & Appleton Labs), 1979–81; Dir, Rutherford Appleton Lab., SERC, 1981–86 (Hon. Scientist, 1995–); Chairman: Active Memory Technology Ltd, 1986–92; Galore Park Ltd, 2001–; Man. Dir, Eazi-Way Ltd, 2000–; non-exec. Dir, Recogniton Res., 1991–94; Consultant: to UFC on formation of UKERNA, 1991–93; Cambridge Parallel Processing, 1992–94. Mem., Visiting Cttee, Physics Dept, Imperial Coll., 1988–92. Vis. Scientist, Fermi Nat. Accelerator Lab., 1994–95. Chairman: Parallel and Novel Architectures Sub Cttee, DTI, 1988–91; Systems Architecture Cttee, DTI/SERC, 1991–92 (Mem., 1988–91); Mem., IT Adv. Bd, DTI/SERC, 1991–92. Glazebrook Medal and Prize, Inst. of Physics, 1986. *Recreations:* playing bridge, chess and Go. *Address:* 10 Parklands, Eynsham Road, Farmoor, Oxon OX2 9TA. *T:* (01865) 864755.   *Died 21 Dec. 2006.*

MANSEL LEWIS, Sir David (Courtenay), KCVO 1995; JP; Lord-Lieutenant of Dyfed, 1979–2002 (Lieutenant, 1974–79; HM Lieutenant for Carmarthenshire, 1973–74); *b* 25 Oct. 1927; *s* of late Charlie Ronald Mansel Lewis and Lillian Georgina Warner, *d* of Col Sir Courtenay Warner, 1st Bt, CB; *m* 1953, Lady Mary Rosemary Marie-Gabrielle Montagu-Stuart-Wortley, OBE, JP, 4th *d* of 3rd Earl of Wharncliffe; one *s* two *d*. *Educ:* Eton; Keble Coll., Oxford (BA). Served in Welsh Guards, 1946–49; Lieut 1946, RARO. Chairman: SW Div., Royal Forestry Soc., 1963–93; S Wales Woodlands, 1969–85; Founder Chm., Carmarthen-Cardigan Cttee, 1968–, Regl Chm., S Wales, 1985–, STA. Member, Court: Nat. Mus. of Wales, 1974–91 (Mem. Council, 1987–91); UCW Aberystwyth, 1974–2002. President: Llanelli Art Soc., 1956–; Carmarthen-Cardigan Br., 1977–91, Dyfed Br., 1991–, CLA; Dyfed Wildlife Trust, 1978–2002; Gŵyl Llanelli Fest., 1979–; Dyfed Br., Magistrates' Assoc., 1979–2002; Burry Port RNLI, 1982–; Welsh Assoc. of Male Voice Choirs, 1997–; Chm., Llanelli Millennium Coastal Park Trustees, 1999–. Patron: Carmarthen RBL, 1974–; Tall Ships Council of Wales, 1991–; Commonwealth Games Council for Wales, 1996–98; Wales Gurkha Villages Aid Trust, 1999–. Pres. of Trustees, Llandovery Coll., 2006– (Trustee, 1985–2001,

Chm., 2001–06). President: W Wales, 1979–90, Wales. 1995–99, TAVRA; Dyfed SSAFA, 1986–2003. FRSA; Hon. Fellow, Trinity Coll., Carmarthen, 1997. High Sheriff, Carmarthenshire, 1965; JP 1969; DL 1971. KStJ (Sub Prior for Wales, 1998–2002). *Recreations:* music, sailing. *Address:* Stradey Castle, Llanelli, Dyfed SA15 4PL. *T:* (01554) 774626. *Clubs:* Cavalry and Guards, Lansdowne; Royal Yacht Squadron (Cowes); Burry Port Yacht (Founder Cdre, 1966; Pres., 1975–).
          Died 17 April 2009.

MANSELL, Gerard Evelyn Herbert, CBE 1977; Managing Director, External Broadcasting, BBC, 1972–81; Deputy Director-General, BBC, 1977–81; *b* 16 Feb. 1921; 2nd *s* of late Herbert and Anne Mansell, Paris; *m* 1956, Diana Marion Sherar; two *s*. *Educ:* Lycée Hoche, Versailles; Lycée Buffon, Paris; Ecole des Sciences Politiques, Paris; Chelsea Sch. of Art. Joined HM Forces, 1940; served in Western Desert, Sicily and NW Europe, 1942–45 (despatches). Joined BBC European Service, 1951; Head, Overseas Talks and Features Dept, 1961; Controller, BBC Radio 4 (formerly Home Service), and Music Programme, 1965–69; Dir of Programmes, BBC, Radio, 1970. Chairman: British Cttee, Journalists in Europe, 1978–95; Jt Adv. Cttee on Radio Journalism Trng, 1981–87; Sony Radio Awards Organising Cttee, 1983–87; Communications Adv. Cttee, UK Nat. Commn for UNESCO, 1983–85; Friends of UNESCO, 1986–88; Member: Communication and Cultural Studies Bd, CNAA, 1982–87; Exec. Cttee, GB-China Centre, 1986–96 (Vice-Chm., 1988–96); Franco-British Council, 1990–2002; Sandford St Martin Trust, 1991–2003. Governor, Falmouth Sch. of Art and Design, 1988–97; Chairman: New Hampstead Garden Suburb Trust, 1984–90, 1992–93; Burgh House Trust, Hampstead, 1995–98, 1999–2004. FRSA 1979. Sony Gold Award for Services to Radio, 1988. French Croix de Guerre, 1945. *Publications:* Tragedy in Algeria, 1961; Let Truth be Told, 1982. *Address:* 15 Hampstead Hill Gardens, NW3 2PH.
          Died 18 Dec. 2010.

MANSFIELD, Rear-Adm. David Parks, CB 1964; *b* 26 July 1912; *s* of Comdr D. Mansfield, RD, RNR; *m* 1939, Jean Craig Alexander (*d* 1984); one *s* one *d*. *Educ:* RN Coll., Dartmouth; RN Engineering Coll., Keyham. Lt (E) 1934; HMS Nelson, 1934–36; Staff of C-in-C Med., 1936–39; HMS Mauritius, 1939–42; Lt-Comdr (E) 1942; HMS Kelvin, 1942–43; Chatham Dockyard, 1943–46; Comdr (E) 1945; Admty (Aircraft Maintenance Dept), 1946–49; Staff of FO Air (Home), 1949–51; HMS Kenya, 1951–53; RN Engrg Coll., 1953–55; Captain 1954; RNAS Anthorn (in command), 1955–57; RN Aircraft Yard, Fleetlands (Supt.), 1957–60; Admty Dir of Fleet Maintenance, 1960–62; Rear-Adm. 1963; Rear-Adm. Aircraft, on Staff of Flag Officer Naval Air Command, 1963–65. *Recreation:* family affairs. *Address:* The Lawn, Holybourne, Alton, Hants GU34 4ER.   *Died 2 Jan. 2008.*

MANSFIELD, Vice-Adm. Sir (Edward) Gerard (Napier), KBE 1974; CVO 1981; retired 1975; *b* 13 July 1921; *s* of late Vice-Adm. Sir John Mansfield, KCB, DSO, DSC, and Alice Talbot Mansfield; *m* 1943, Joan Worship Byron, *d* of late Comdr John Byron, DSC and Bar, and late Frances Byron; two *d*. *Educ:* RNC, Dartmouth. Entered Royal Navy, 1935. Served War of 1939–45 in destroyers and Combined Ops (despatches), taking part in landings in N Africa and Sicily. Comdr. 1953; comd HMS Mounts Bay, 1956–58; Captain 1959; SHAPE, 1960–62; Captain (F) 20th Frigate Sqdn, 1963–64; Dir of Defence Plans (Navy), 1965–67; Cdre Amphibious Forces, 1967–68; Senior Naval Member, Directing Staff, IDC, 1969–70; Flag Officer Sea Training, 1971–72; Dep. Supreme Allied Comdr, Atlantic, 1973–75. Chm., Assoc. of RN Officers, 1975–86; Chm. Council, Operation Raleigh, 1984–89. Chm., Crondall Parish Council, 1977–81. Mem. Admin. Council, Royal Jubilee Trusts, 1978–81. *Recreations:* golf, gardening.

Address: White Gate House, Heath Lane, Ewshot, Farnham, Surrey GU10 5AH. *T:* (01252) 850325. *Club:* Army and Navy. *Died 27 June 2006.*

MANTELL, Rt Hon. Sir Charles (Barrie Knight), Kt 1990; PC 1997; a Surveillance Commissioner, since 2006; a Lord Justice of Appeal, 1997–2004; *b* 30 Jan. 1937; *s* of Francis Christopher Knight Mantell and Elsie Mantell; *m* 1960, Anne Shirley Cogger; two *d. Educ:* Manchester Grammar Sch.; Manchester Univ. (LLM). Called to the Bar, Gray's Inn, 1960, Bencher, 1990. Flying Officer, RAF, 1958–61. In practice at Bar, London and Manchester, 1961–82; a Recorder of the Crown Court, 1978–82; QC 1979; Judge of Supreme Court, Hong Kong, 1982–85; a Circuit Judge, 1985–90; Judge, High Court of Justice, QBD, 1990–97; Presiding Judge, Western Circuit, 1993–96; Judge of Courts of Appeal, Jersey and Guernsey, 2004–07; Justice of Appeal, Bermuda, 2005–07. Alternative Chm., Security Commn, 1999–2010; Chairman: Proscribed Orgns Appeal Commn, 2002–10; Pathogens Access Appeal Commission, 2002–10. *Recreations:* reading, watching cricket. *Club:* Hong Kong (Hong Kong). *Died 1 May 2010.*

MANTLE, Rt Rev. John Ambrose Cyril, PhD; FRHistS; Bishop of Brechin, 2005–10; *b* 3 April 1946; *s* of Rupert Mantle and Jean (*née* Bailey); *m* 1969, Gillian Armstrong; one *s* one *d. Educ:* Grove Acad., Broughty Ferry, Dundee; St Andrews Univ. (MTheol 1974); Dundee Coll. of Educn (PGCE 1975); Univ. of Kent (MA 1990); Leeds Univ. (PhD 1998). FRHistS 2001. Ordained deacon, 1969, priest, 1970; Curate: Broughty Ferry, 1969–71; All Saints, St Andrews, 1971–75; SS Philip and James, Edinburgh, 1975–77; Master, Royal High Sch., Edinburgh, 1975–77; Anglican Chaplain, St Andrews Univ., 1977–80; Priest-in-charge: Pittenweem, 1978–80; Elie and Earlsferry, 1978–80; Chaplain, Fitzwilliam Coll., Cambridge, 1980–86 (Fellow, 1984–86); Hon. Curate, Ascension, Cambridge, 1980–86; Staff Tutor and Vice-Principal, Canterbury Sch. of Ministry, 1986–94; Curate, Bexley with Detling, 1986–93; Adult Educn Advr, dio. Chichester, 1994–99; Archbishops' Advr for Bishops' Ministry, 1999–2005. *Publications:* Britain's First Worker-Priests, 2000; contribs to jls. *Recreations:* walking, travel, drawing, painting, film, jazz. *Died 29 Nov. 2010.*

MANWARING, Randle (Gilbert), DSL; poet and author; company director; *b* 3 May 1912; *s* of late George Ernest and Lilian Manwaring; *m* 1st, 1941, Betty Violet (*d* 2001), *d* of H. P. Rout, Norwich; three *s* one *d*; 2nd, 2002, Mary Ratcliffe (*née* Blackburn). *Educ:* private schools; Keele Univ. (MA 1982); Mellen Univ. (DSL 2002). Joined Clerical, Medical and Gen. Life Assce Soc., 1929. War service, RAF, 1940–46. W/Cdr; comd RAF Regt in Burma, 1945. Clerical, Medical & Gen. Pensions Rep., 1950; joined C. E. Heath & Co. Ltd, 1956: Asst Dir, 1960, Dir, 1964, Man. Dir, 1969; Founder Dir (Man.), C. E. Heath Urquhart (Life and Pensions), 1966–71, and a Founder Dir, Excess Life Assce Co., 1967–75; Dir, Excess Insce Gp, 1975–78; Insce Advr, Midland Bank, 1971; first Man. Dir, Midland Bank Insce Services, 1972–74, Vice-Chm., 1974–77, Dir, 1977–78. Chm., Life Soc., Corp. of Insce Brokers, 1965–66; Dep. Chm., Corp. of Insce Brokers, 1970–71; Pres., Soc. of Pensions Consultants, 1968–70. Chairman of Governors: Luckley-Oakfield Sch., 1972–83; Northease Manor Sch., 1972–84. Diocesan Reader (Chichester), subseq. Emeritus, 1968–; Mem., C of E Evangelical Council, 1980–82; Lay Pres., Chichester Diocesan Evangelical Union, 1989–91; Mem., Diocesan Synod, 1985–98; Lay Chm., Uckfield Deanery Synod, 1993–99; Churchwarden, St Peter-upon-Cornhill, London, 1985–90. Chm., Vine Books Ltd; Dir, Crusaders Union Ltd, 1960–91 (Vice-Pres., 1983–). Vice-Pres., RAF Regt, 1990–. Chm. of Trustees, Careforce, 1980–87. Chm., Probus Club, Uckfield, 1989–90. *Publications:* The Heart of this People, 1954; A Christian Guide to Daily Work, 1963;

Thornhill Guide to Insurance, 1976; The Run of the Downs, 1984; From Controversy to Co-existence, 1985; The Good Fight, 1990; A Study of Hymnwriting and Hymnsinging in the Christian Church, 1991; (for children) The Swallows, the Fox and the Cuckoo, 1998; Songs of the spirit in Poetry and Hymnology, 2004; On the Road to Mandalay, 2006; *poems:* Posies Once Mine, 1951; Satires and Salvation, 1960; Under the Magnolia Tree, 1965; Slave to No Sect, 1966; Crossroads of the Year, 1975; From the Four Winds, 1976; In a Time of Unbelief, 1977; Poem Prayers for Growing People, 1980; The Swifts of Maggiore, 1981; In a Time of Change, 1983; Collected Poems, 1986; Some Late Lark Singing, 1992; Love So Amazing, 1995; Trade Winds, 2001; Poems of the Spirit, 2004; The Making of a Minor Poet, 2007; contrib. poems and articles to learned jls in GB and Canada; contrib. hymns to several hymn books. *Recreations:* music, reading, following cricket. *Address:* Marbles Barn, Newick, Lewes, East Sussex BN8 4LG. *T:* (01825) 723845. *Clubs:* Royal Air Force, MCC; Sussex County Cricket, Sussex Martlets. *Died 31 Dec. 2010.*

MARCEAU, Marcel; Officier de la Légion d'Honneur; Grand Officier de l'Ordre National du Mérite; Commandeur des Arts et des Lettres de la République Française; mime; Founder, Compagnie de Mime Marcel Marceau, 1949 (Director, 1949–64); Director: International School of Mime of Paris Marcel Marceau, since 1978; New Mimodrama Co., since 1993; *b* Strasbourg, 22 March 1923; *s* of Charles and Anne Mangel; two *s* two *d. Educ:* Ecole des Beaux Arts; Arts Décoratifs, Limoges; Ecole Etienne Decroux; Ecole Charles Dullin. First stage appearance, in Paris, 1946; with Barrault/Renaud Co., 1946–49; founded his company, 1949; then toured constantly, playing in 65 countries. Created about 100 pantomimes (most famous are The Creation of the World, The Cage, The Maskmaker, The Tree, Bip Liontamer, Bip hunts Butterfly, Bip plays David and Goliath, Bip at a Society Party, Bip in the Modern and Future Life, Bip Soldier, etc), and 26 mimodrames, and in particular the character 'Bip' (1947); *Mimodrames:* Bip et la fille des rues, 1947; Bip et L'Oiseau, 1948; Death Before Dawn, 1948; The Fair, 1949; The Flute Player, 1949; The Overcoat, 1951; Moriana and Galvan, Pierrot of Montmartre, 1952; Les Trois Perruques, 1953; Un Soir aux Funambules, 1953; La Parade en bleu et noir, 1956; le 14 juillet, 1956; Le Mont de Piété, 1956; Le Loup de Tsu Ku Mi, 1956; Le Petit Cirque, 1958; Les Matadors, 1959; Paris qui rit, Paris qui pleure, 1959; Don Juan, 1964; Candide, 1970, with Ballet de l'Opéra de Hambourg; Le Chapeau Melon, 1997; *films:* The Overcoat, 1951; Barbarella, 1967; Scrooge (BBC London), 1973; Shanks, US, 1973; Silent Movie, 1976. Made frequent TV appearances and many short films for TV, incl. Pantomimes, 1954, A Public Garden, 1955; Le mime Marcel Marceau, 1965, The World of Marcel Marceau, 1966, 12 short films with Enc. Brit., NY, 1974. Member: Acad. of Arts and Letters (DDR); Akad. der schönen Künste, Munich; Acad. des Beaux Arts, Paris. Emmy Awards (US), 1955, 1968. Hon. Dr, Univ. of Oregon; Dr *hc* Univ. of Princeton, 1981. Gold Medal of Czechoslovak Republic (for contribution to cultural relations). *Publications:* Les 7 Péchés Capitaux (lithographs); Les Rêveries de Bip (lithographs); La Ballade de Paris et du Monde (text, lithographs, watercolours, drawings in ink and pencil); Alphabet Book; Counting Book; L'Histoire de Bip (text and lithographs); The Third Eye (lithoprint); Pimporello. *Recreations:* painting, poetry, fencing. *Died 22 Sept. 2007.*

MARCHANT, Ven. George John Charles; Archdeacon Emeritus and Canon Emeritus of Durham, since 1983; *b* 3 Jan. 1916; *s* of late T. Marchant, Little Stanmore, Mddx; *m* 1944, Eileen Lillian Kathleen, *d* of late F. J. Smith, FCIS; one *s* three *d. Educ:* St John's Coll., Durham (MA, BD); Tyndale Hall, Bristol. Ordained deacon 1939, priest 1940, London; Curate of St Andrew's, Whitehall Park, N19, 1939–41; Licence to officiate, London dio., 1941–44 (in charge of Young Churchmen's Movt);

Curate of St Andrew-the-Less, Cambridge (in charge of St Stephen's), 1944–48; Vicar of Holy Trinity, Skirbeck, Boston, 1948–54; Vicar of St Nicholas, Durham, 1954–74; Rural Dean of Durham, 1964–74; Hon. Canon of Durham Cathedral, 1972–74; Archdeacon of Auckland and Canon Residentiary, Durham Cathedral, 1974–83. Pre-Retirement Advr, Dio. Norwich Clergy, 1990–2000. Member of General Synod, 1970–80 (Proctor in Convocation for Dio. Durham). Chm. Editorial Bd, Anvil, 1983–91. *Publications:* (ed) Moving Forward to Retirement, 1996; contributed to: Baker's Dictionary of Theology, 1960; Bishops in the Church, 1966; articles in Evangelical Qly, Churchman, and Anvil; book reviews. *Recreations:* reading, music, bird watching, gardening. *Address:* 28 Greenways, Eaton, Norwich NR4 6PE. *T:* (01603) 458295. *Died 3 Feb. 2006.*

MARJORIBANKS, Prof. Kevin McLeod, PhD; FSS; FASSA; FACE; Professor of Education, University of Adelaide, 1975–86 and 1994–2005, then Emeritus (Vice-Chancellor, 1987–93); *b* 25 July 1940; *s* of Hugh and Irene Marjoribanks; *m* 1962, Janice Humphreys; one *s* one *d. Educ:* Universities of: New South Wales (BSc); New England (BA); Harvard (MA); Toronto (PhD). FSS 1977; FASSA 1982; FACE 1983. Asst Prof., Univ. of Toronto, 1969; Lectr, Univ. of Oxford, 1970–74; Pro Vice-Chancellor, Univ. of Adelaide, 1986. Visiting Professor: Stanford Univ., 1979; Haifa Univ., 1983; (in Educn) Oxford Univ., 1994–95; Harvard Univ., 1994–95. *Publications:* Environments for Learning, 1974; Families and their Learning Environments, 1979; Ethnic Families and Children's Achievements, 1980; The Foundations of Children's Learning, 1989; Families, Schools and Learning: a study of children's learning environments, 1993; Australian Education: a review of research, 1999; Family and School Capital: towards a context theory of students' school outcomes, 2002. *Recreations:* writing, music listening, walking. *Address:* 81 Molesworth Street, North Adelaide, SA 5006, Australia. *Club:* Adelaide. *Died 29 April 2006.*

MARK, Janet Marjorie; freelance writer, since 1976; *b* 22 June 1943; *d* of Colin Denis Brisland and Marjorie Léa Brisland (*née* Harrow); *m* 1969, Neil Mark (marr. diss. 1989); one *s* one *d. Educ:* Ashford (Kent) Grammar Sch.; Canterbury Coll. of Art. (NDD 1965). Secondary Sch. teacher, 1965–71. *Publications* include: Thunder and Lightnings, 1976 (Penguin/Guardian Award, Carnegie Medal); The Ennead, 1978; Divide and Rule, 1979; Nothing to be Afraid of, 1980; Aquarius, 1982; Feet, 1983 (Angel Award); Handles, 1983 (Carnegie Medal); Zeno was Here, 1987 (Angel Award); A Can of Worms, 1990; The Hillingdon Fox, 1991; Great Frog and Mighty Moose, 1992; They Do Things Differently There, 1994; A Fine Summer Knight, 1995; The Tale of Tobias, 1995; God's Story, 1997; The Sighting, 1997; The Eclipse of the Century, 1999; Heathrow Nights, 2000; Something in the Air, 2003; Stratford Boys, 2003; Useful Idiots, 2004; Riding Tycho, 2005; reviews and articles for Signal Magazine, The Guardian and TES; *posthumous publication:* Turbulence, 2006. *Recreation:* gardening. *Address:* 98 Howard Street, Oxford OX4 3BG. *T:* (01865) 727702. *Died 15 Jan. 2006.*

MARK, Sir Robert, GBE 1977; Kt 1973; QPM 1965; Commissioner, Metropolitan Police, 1972–77 (Deputy Commissioner, 1968–72); *b* Manchester, 13 March 1917; *y s* of late John Mark and Louisa Mark (*née* Hobson); *m* 1941, Kathleen Mary Leahy (*d* 1997); one *s* one *d. Educ:* William Hulme's Grammar Sch., Manchester. Constable to Chief Superintendent, Manchester City Police, 1937–42, 1947–56; Chief Constable of Leicester, 1957–67; Assistant Commissioner, Metropolitan Police, 1967–68. Vis. Fellow, Nuffield Coll., Oxford, 1970–78 (MA Oxon 1971). Member: Standing Advisory Council of Penal System, 1966; Adv. Cttee on Police in Northern Ireland, 1969; Assessor to Lord Mountbatten during his Inquiry into Prison Security, 1966. Royal Armoured Corps, 1942–47: Lieut, Phantom (GHQ Liaison Regt), North-West Europe, 1944–45; Major, Control

Commission for Germany, 1945–47. Lecture tour of N America for World Affairs Council and FCO, Oct. 1971; Edwin Stevens Lecture to the Laity, RCM, 1972; Dimbleby Meml Lecture (BBC TV), 1973. Director: Phoenix Assurance Co. Ltd, 1977–85; Control Risks Ltd, 1982–87. Mem. Cttee, AA, 1977–87; Governor and Mem. Admin. Bd, Corps of Commissionaires, 1977–86; Hon. Freeman, City of Westminster, 1977. Hon. LLM Leicester Univ., 1967; Hon. DLitt Loughborough, 1976; Hon. LLD: Manchester, 1978; Liverpool, 1978. KStJ 1977. *Publications:* Policing a Perplexed Society, 1977; In the Office of Constable, 1978. *Address:* Esher, Surrey KT10 8LU. *Died 30 Sept. 2010.*

MARKHAM, Sir Charles (John), 3rd Bt *cr* 1911; *b* 2 July 1924; *s* of Sir Charles Markham, 2nd Bt, and Gwladys, *e d* of late Hon. Rupert Beckett; *S* father, 1952; *m* 1949, Valerie (*d* 1998), *o d* of Lt-Col E. Barry-Johnston, Makuyu, Kenya; two *s* one *d. Educ:* Eton. Served War of 1939–45, Lieut in 11th Hussars (despatches). Vice-Chm., Nairobi Co. Council, 1953–55; MLC Kenya, 1955–60. Pres., Royal Agricultural Soc., Kenya, 1958. KStJ 1973. *Heir: s* Arthur David Markham [*b* 6 Dec. 1950; *m* 1977, Carolyn, *yr d* of Captain Mungo Park; two *d*]. *Address:* PO Box 42263, Nairobi, Kenya, East Africa. *Club:* MCC. *Died 5 June 2006.*

MARKS, Dr Louis Frank; film and television producer; *b* 23 March 1928; *s* of Michael Marks and Sarah Abrahams; *m* 1957, Sonia Herbstman (*d* 2006); two *d. Educ:* Christ's Coll., London; Balliol Coll., Oxford (MA, BLitt, DPhil 1957). Sen. History teacher, Beltane Sch., 1951–53; founder and editor, Books and Bookmen, 1956; freelance scriptwriter, TV series, 1958–69; joined BBC, 1970; Script Editor, Series Dept, 1970; Plays Dept, 1972; Drama Producer, 1974; producer, film and TV Drama, 1976–; over 60 productions, including: The Lost Boys (RTS Award, 1979); Play of the Month, later Festival, 1979–86, incl. Lady Windermere's Fan and Ghosts (ACE Awards, 1988, 1992); Loving, 1996; Plotlands (serial), 1997; *films* include: Silas Marner (Banff Film Fest. Award, 1986); Memento Mori (Writers' Guild Award, 1992); The Trial, 1993; *television adaptations:* Middlemarch (serial), 1994 (Writers' Guild Award, BPG TV Award for best serial, Voice of the Listener and Viewer Award for excellence in broadcasting and best TV prog., 1994); Daniel Deronda (serial), 2002 (BPG TV Award for best drama serial, 2002; Banff TV Fest. Award for best mini-series, 2003). *Publications:* (ed and trans.) Antonio Gramsci: the modern prince, 1957; articles in Archivio Storico Italiano and Italian Renaissance Studies. *Address:* Woodhall Farm, Woodhall Drive, Pinner HA5 4TG. *T:* (020) 8428 4268. *Died 17 Sept. 2010.*

MARKUS, Prof. Robert Austin, OBE 2000; FBA 1985; Professor of Medieval History, Nottingham University, 1974–82, then Emeritus; *b* 8 Oct. 1924; *s* of Victor Markus and Lily Markus (*née* Elek); *m* 1955, Margaret Catherine Bullen; two *s* one *d. Educ:* Univ. of Manchester (BSc 1944; MA 1948; PhD 1950). Mem., Dominican Order, 1950–54; Asst Librarian, Univ. of Birmingham, 1954–55; Liverpool University: Sub-Librarian, 1955–59; Lectr, Sen. Lectr, Reader in Medieval Hist., 1959–74. Mem., Inst. for Advanced Study, Princeton, 1986–87; Distinguished Professor of Early Christian Studies: Catholic Univ. of America, Washington, 1988–89; Univ. of Notre Dame, 1993. Pres., Assoc. Internationale d'Etudes Patristiques, 1991–95. *Publications:* Christian Faith and Greek Philosophy (with A. H. Armstrong), 1964; Saeculum: history and society in the theology of St Augustine, 1970; Christianity in the Roman world, 1974; From Augustine to Gregory the Great, 1983; The End of Ancient Christianity, 1990; Gregory the Great and his World, 1997; Christianity and the Secular, 2005; contribs to Jl of Ecclesiastical Hist., Jl of Theol Studies, Byzantion, Studies in Church Hist., etc. *Recreation:* music. *Address:* Apt 11, The Lace Mill, Wollaton Road, Beeston, Nottingham NG9 2NN. *T:* (0115) 925 5965. *Died 8 Dec. 2010.*

MARLAND, Michael, CBE 1977; FCP; General Editor, Heinemann School Management Series, since 1971; *b* 28 Dec. 1934; *m* 1st, 1955, Eileen (*d* 1968); three *s* one *d* (and one *s* decd); 2nd, 1971, Rose (marr. diss. 1977); 3rd, 1989, Linda; one *s*. *Educ*: Christ's Hospital Sch.; Sidney Sussex Coll., Cambridge (MA). Head of English, Abbey Wood Sch., 1961–64; Head of English and subseq. Dir of Studies, Crown Woods Sch., 1964–71; Headmaster, Woodberry Down Sch., 1971–79; founder Headteacher, N Westminster Community Sch., 1980–99. Hon. Prof., Dept of Educn, Univ. of Warwick, 1980–92. Member: many educn cttees, incl. Bullock Cttee, 1972–75; Commonwealth Inst. Educn Cttee, 1982–; Arts Council of GB Educn Cttee, 1988–92; Educn and Human Develt Cttee, ESRC (formerly SSRC), 1983–88; Nat. Assoc. for Educn in the Arts, 1986–; Nat. Book League Council, 1984; Finniston Cttee on Technol. in Educn, 1985–88; Video Adv. Cttee, British Bd of Film Classification, 1989–; Educn Cttee, ESU; Careers Cttee, ICE; Bd, Young Persons' Concert Foundn; Nat. Adv. Forum, DIVERT. Chairman: Schools Council English Cttee, 1978–81; Books in Curriculum Res. Project, 1982–; Royal Ballet Educn Adv. Council, 1983–2008; Nat. Assoc. for Pastoral Care in Educn, 1982–86; Royal Opera House Educnl Adv. Council, 1984–95; Nat. Textbook Ref. Library Steering Cttee, 1984–92; Exec., City of Westminster Arts Council; Vice-Chair, City of Westminster Race Equality Council. Mem., Paddington and N Kensington DHA, 1982–84. Patron, Tagore Foundn. FCP 1999; Fellow, British Educnl Leadership, Mgt and Admin Soc., 2005. Hon. Fellow, Inst. of Educn, London Univ., 2002. Hon. DEd Kingston, 2000; DUniv Surrey Roehampton, 2001. *Publications:* Towards the New Fifth, 1969; The Practice of English Teaching, 1970; Peter Grimes, 1971; Head of Department, 1971; Pastoral Care, 1974; The Craft of the Classroom, 1975, 3rd edn 2003; Language Across the Curriculum, 1977; Education for the Inner City, 1980; Departmental Management, 1981; Sex Differentiation and Schooling, 1983; Short Stories for Today, 1984; Meetings and Partings, 1984; School Management Skills, 1985; The Tutor and the Tutor Group, 1990; Marketing the School, 1991; (with Peter Ribbins) Leadership in the Secondary School: portraits of headship, 1994; Scenes from Plays, 1996; (with Rick Rogers) The Art of the Tutor, 1997; Managing the Arts in the Curriculum, 2002; (with Rick Rogers) How to be a Successful Form Tutor, 2004; General Editor of: The Student Drama Series; Longman Imprint Books; The Times Authors; Heinemann Organisation in Schools Series; Longman Tutorial Resources; English Poetry Plus; Series Editor of: Cambridge Collections; contrib. Times Educnl Supplement. *Recreations:* music, literature. *Address:* 22 Compton Terrace, N1 2UN. *T:* (020) 7226 0648; The Green Farmhouse, Cranmer Green, Walsham-le-Willows, Bury St Edmunds, Suffolk IP31 3BJ. *T:* (01359) 259483.   *Died 3 July 2008.*

MARQUIS, James Douglas, DFC 1945; Managing Director, Irvine Development Corporation, 1972–81; *b* 16 Oct. 1921; *s* of James Charles Marquis and Jessica Amy (*née* Huggett); *m* 1945, Brenda Eleanor (decd), *d* of Robert Reyner Davey; two *s*. *Educ*: Shooters Hill Sch., Woolwich. Local Govt, 1938–41. Served War: RAF: 1941–46 (RAF 1st cl. Air Navigation Warrant, 1945; Navigation Officer, 177 Sqdn, 224 Gp, and AHQ Malaya (Sqdn Ldr 1945). Local Govt, 1946–56; Harlow Develt Corp., 1957–68; Irvine Develt Corp.: Chief Finance Officer, 1968–72; Dir of Finance and Admin, 1972. Pres., Ayrshire Chamber of Industries, 1979–80. FRMetS 1945; CPFA (IPFA 1950); FCIS 1953. *Publications:* An Ayrshire Sketchbook, 1979. *Recreation:* sketching and painting (five one-man exhibns, incl. one in Sweden; works in collections: Japan, Sweden, Norway, Denmark, Australia, USA, Canada). *Address:* 34 Malins Court, Maidens, Girvan, Ayrshire KA26 9PB. *T:* (01655) 334334.   *Died 19 Oct. 2010.*

MARRIS, Stephen Nicholson; *b* 7 Jan. 1930; *s* of Eric Denyer Marris, CB, and Phyllis May Marris (*née*

Lapthorn); *m* 1955, Margaret Swindells; two *s* one *d*. *Educ*: Bryanston School; King's College, Cambridge. MA, PhD. Nat. Inst. of Economic and Social Research, 1953–54; economist and international civil servant; with Org. for European Economic Co-operation, later Org. for Economic Co-operation and Development (OECD), 1956–83: Dir, Economics Branch, 1970; Economic Advr to Sec.-Gen., 1975; Sen. Fellow, Inst. for Internat. Econs, Washington, 1983–88. Vis. Res. Prof. of Internat. Economics, Brookings Instn, Washington DC, 1969–70; Vis. Prof., Institut d'Etudes Politiques, Paris, 1986. Hon. Dr Stockholm Univ., 1978. *Publications:* Deficits and the Dollar: the World Economy at Risk, 1985. *Address:* 8 Sentier des Pierres Blanches, 92190 Meudon, France. *T:* 146269812.   *Died 28 March 2010.*

MARSDEN, Frank; JP; *b* Everton, Liverpool, 15 Oct. 1923; *s* of Sidney Marsden and Harriet Marsden (*née* Needham); *m* 1943, Muriel Lightfoot (*d* 2001); three *s*. *Educ*: Abbotsford Road Sec. Mod. Sch., Liverpool. Served War, with RAF Bomber Command, 115 Sqdn (Warrant Officer), 1941–46. Joined Lab Party and Co-op. Movement, 1948. MP (Lab) Liverpool, Scotland, Apr. 1971–Feb. 1974. Local Councillor: Liverpool St Domingo Ward, May 1964–67; Liverpool Vauxhall Ward, 1969–71; Knowsley DC, 1976–. Chm. Liverpool Markets, 1965–67; Past Mem. Exec. Cttee: Liverpool Trades Council; Liverpool Lab Party. JP City of Liverpool, 1969. *Recreations:* jazz music, gardening. *Address:* 2 Thunderbolt Cottage, 6 Alder Lane, Knowsley, Prescot, Merseyside L34 9EQ. *T:* (0151) 546 8666.   *Died 5 Nov. 2006.*

MARSDEN, Prof. Jerrold Eldon, PhD; FRS 2006; FRSC; Carl F. Braun Professor of Engineering, Control and Dynamical Systems, and Applied and Computational Mathematics, California Institute of Technology, since 2009 (Professor of Control and Dynamical Systems, 1995–2003; Braun Professor of Applied and Computational Mathematics and Computer Science, 2003–09); *b* British Columbia, Canada, 17 Aug. 1942. *Educ*: Univ. of Toronto (BSc 1965); Princeton Univ. (PhD 1968). FRSC 1991. Lectr, latterly Prof., Univ. of Calif, Berkeley, 1968–95. *Publications:* (with Michael Hoffman) Elementary Classical Analysis, 1974, 2nd edn 1993; (with Anthony Tromba) Vector Calculus, 1976, 5th edn 2003; Calculus, 2nd edn 1985; (with Alan Weinstein) Calculus Unlimited, 1981; (with Anthony Tromba and Alan Weinstein) Basic Multivariable Calculus, 1992; (with Michael Hoffman) Basic Complex Analysis, 3rd edn 1998. *Address:* Division of Engineering and Applied Science, California Institute of Technology, 1200 E California Boulevard, Pasadena, CA 91125–8100, USA.   *Died 21 Sept. 2010.*

MARSDEN, Dr John Christopher, MBE 2006; Executive Secretary, Linnean Society, 1999–2004; *b* 4 March 1937; *s* of Ewart and May Marsden; *m* 1962, Jessany Margaret Hazel Macdonald; two *s*. *Educ*: Bristol Grammar Sch.; Keble Coll., Oxford (MA, DPhil). FRSC; FIBiol. Lectr in Biology, Univ. of York, 1965–71; Sen. Res. Fellow, Inst. of Child Health, 1971–72; Reader in Cell Physiology, City of London Polytechnic, 1972–74; Polytechnic of Central London: Head of Life Scis, 1974–86; Dean, Faculty of Engrg and Sci., 1986–88, retired. Hon. FLS 2005. *Publications:* Enzymes and Equilibria (with C. F. Stoneman), 1974; numerous contribs to biol. jls. *Recreations:* book collecting, cookery. *Address:* 7 Surrey Close, Tunbridge Wells, Kent TN2 5RF. *T:* (01892) 533784; *e-mail:* taxon@pavilion.co.uk.   *Died 19 Aug. 2008.*

MARSH, Gordon Victor, MA; FHSM; Member, Police Complaints Authority, 1989–94 and 1995–96; *b* 14 May 1929; *s* of late Ven. Wilfred Carter Marsh, Devil's Lake, North Dakota, USA and Rosalie (*née* Holliday); *m* Millicent, *e d* of late Christopher Thomas and Edith Rowsell; one *s* one *d*. *Educ*: Grammar Schs, Swindon; Keble Coll., Oxford (MA); Inst. of Health Service Administrators (FHA 1964); Sloan Business Sch., Cornell Univ., USA. NHS admin. posts, England and Wales,

1952–72; Administrator and Sec., Bd of Governors, UCH, 1972–74; Area Administrator, Lambeth, Southwark and Lewisham AHA(T), 1974–82; Dep. Health Service Comr, 1982–89, retd. Vice-Chm., Assoc. of Chief Administrators of Health Authorities, 1980–82; Member: Council, National Assoc. of Health Authorities, 1979–82; Adv. Bd, Coll. of Occupational Therapists, 1974–95. Chm., Trelawn Cttee of Richmond Fellowship, 1970–83; Hon. Sec. to Congregational Meeting and Wandsman, St Paul's Cathedral, 1980–2005. *Publications:* articles in professional jls. *Recreations:* music, gardening. *Address:* 61 Abingdon Road, Didcot, Oxon OX11 9BY. *T:* (01235) 519197; *e-mail:* g.marsh@homecall.co.uk. *Clubs:* Oxford and Cambridge, Nikaean. *Died 15 Aug. 2007.*

MARSH, Norman Stayner, CBE 1977; QC 1967; Law Commissioner, 1965–78; Member, Royal Commission on Civil Liability and Compensation for Personal Injury, 1973–78; *b* 26 July 1913; 2nd *s* of Horace Henry and Lucy Ann Marsh, Bath, Som; *m* 1939, Christiane Christinnecke (*d* 2000), 2nd *d* of Professor Johannes and Käthe Christinnecke, Magdeburg, Germany; two *s* two *d*. *Educ:* Monkton Combe Sch.; Pembroke Coll., Oxford (2nd Class Hons, Final Honour Sch. of Jurisprudence, 1935; 1st Cl. Hons BCL; Hon. Fellow, 1978). Vinerian Scholar of Oxford Univ., Harmsworth Scholar of Middle Temple, called to Bar, 1937; practice in London and on Western Circuit, 1937–39; Lieut-Col Intelligence Corps and Control Commission for Germany, 1939–46. Stowell Civil Law Fellow, University Coll., Oxford, 1946–60; University Lecturer in Law, 1947–60; Estates Bursar, University Coll., 1948–56; Secretary-General, International Commission of Jurists, The Hague, Netherlands, 1956–58. Member: Bureau of Conference of Non-Governmental Organisations with Consultative Status with the United Nations, 1957–58; Internat. Cttee of Legal Science (Unesco), 1960–63. Dir of British Institute of International and Comparative Law, 1960–65. Mem., Younger Cttee on Privacy, 1970–72. Hon. Vis. Prof. in Law, KCL, 1972–77. Vice-Chm., Age Concern, England, 1979–86. General editor, International and Comparative Law Quarterly, 1961–65, Mem., Editorial Board, 1965–93. *Publications:* The Rule of Law as a supra-national concept, in Oxford Essays in Jurisprudence, 1960; The Rule of Law in a Free Society, 1960; Interpretation in a National and International Context, 1974; (editor and part-author) Public Access to Government-held Information, 1987; articles on common law and comparative law in English, American, French and German law jls. *Address:* 10 Trinity Close, The Pavement, Clapham, SW4 0JD. *Died 15 Oct. 2008.*

MARSHALL, Sir Arthur Gregory George, Kt 1974; OBE 1948; DL; Life President, Marshall of Cambridge (Holdings), 1990; *b* 4 Dec. 1903; *s* of David Gregory Marshall, MBE, and Maude Edmunds Wing; *m* 1931, Rosemary Wynford Dimsdale (*d* 1988), *d* of Marcus Southwell Dimsdale; two *s* one *d*. *Educ:* Tonbridge Sch.; Jesus Coll., Cambridge (Engrg, MA; Hon. Fellow, 1990). Joined Garage Company of Marshall (Cambridge) Ltd, 1926, which resulted in estabt of Aircraft Company, now Marshall of Cambridge (Aerospace) Ltd, 1929, Chm. and Jt Man. Dir, 1942–89. Chm., Aerodrome Owners Assoc., 1964–65; Member: Air Cadet Council, 1951–59 and 1965–76; Adv. Council on Technology, 1967–70. Liveryman, GAPAN, 1958– (Guild Award of Honour, 2000). Hon. Old Cranwellian, 1979; CRAeS 1980; Companion, Air League, 1997. JP Linton, 1951–61; DL 1968, High Sheriff of Cambridgeshire and Isle of Ely, 1969–70. Eponymous Inst. for Aeronautics estabd within Cambridge Univ. Engrg Dept, 2001. Hon. FRAeS 2001. Hon. Freeman, City of Cambridge, 2004. Hon. DSc Cranfield, 1992; Hon. LLD Cantab, 1996. Masefield Gold Medal, British Assoc. of Aviation Consultants, 1998; Air League Founders' Medal, 2003; Lifetime Achievement Award, Cambridge News, 2005. Order of Istiqlal, First Class (Jordan), 1990. *Publications:* The Marshall Story: a century of wheels and wings, 1994; No

104 (City of Cambridge) Squadron Air Training Corps 1939–1994, 1995. *Recreations:* Cambridge Athletics Blue, Olympic Team Reserve, 1924; flying. *Address:* Horseheath Lodge, Linton, Cambridge CB1 6PT. *T:* (01223) 891318. *Clubs:* Royal Air Force (Hon. Mem., 1969); Hawks (Cambridge). *Died 16 March 2007.*

MARSHALL, Daniel; see Marshall, T. D.

MARSHALL, Sir Denis (Alfred), Kt 1982; solicitor; with Barlow Lyde & Gilbert, 1937–83; *b* 1 June 1916; *s* of Frederick Herbert Marshall and Winifred Mary Marshall; *m* 1st, 1949, Joan Edith Straker (*d* 1974); one *s*; 2nd, 1975, Jane Lygo (*d* 2002). *Educ:* Dulwich Coll. Served War: HAC, 1939; XX Lancs Fusiliers (Temp. Major), 1940–46. Articled to Barlow Lyde & Gilbert, Solicitors, 1932–37; admitted Solicitor, 1937. Mem. Council, Law Soc., 1966–86, Vice-Pres., 1980–81, Pres., 1981–82. Member: Insurance Brokers Registration Council, 1979–91; Criminal Injuries Compensation Bd, 1982–90; Council, FIMBRA, 1986–90. *Recreation:* gardening. *Address:* 15 Coombe Road, Dartmouth, Devon TQ6 9PQ. *Died 17 Nov. 2009.*

MARSHALL, Howard Wright; retired; Under Secretary, Department of Transport, 1978–82; *b* 11 June 1923; *s* of Philip Marshall, MBE, and Mary Marshall; *m* 1st (marr. diss.); two *s*; 2nd, 1963, (Carol) Yvonne (*née* Oddy); one *d*. *Educ:* Prudhoe West Elementary, Northumberland; Queen Elizabeth Grammar Sch., Hexham. Served War, RAF, 1941–46; POW, 1943–45. Min. of Health, Newcastle upon Tyne, 1940; Regional Offices, Ministries of Health, Local Govt and Planning, Housing and Local Govt, 1948–55; HQ, Min. of Housing and Local Govt, 1955–59; National Parks Commn, 1959–62; Min. of Housing and Local Govt, later DoE, 1962; Asst Sec., 1968; Under Sec., 1976; Regl Dir, Eastern Region, Depts of Environment and Transport, 1976–78; Chm., East Anglia Regl Economic Planning Bd, 1976–78. *Recreations:* gardening, sport. *Address:* Brackenwood, Farthing Green Lane, Stoke Poges, Bucks SL2 4JH. *T:* (01753) 662974. *Clubs:* Caterpillar; Wexham Park Golf and Leisure. *Died 6 May 2006.*

MARSHALL, Jeremy; see Marshall, John J. S.

MARSHALL, John, MA; Headmaster, Robert Gordon's College, Aberdeen, 1960–77; *b* 1 July 1915; *s* of Alexander Marshall and Margaret Nimmo Carmichael; *m* 1940, May Robinson Williamson; two *d*. *Educ:* Airdrie Acad.; Glasgow Univ. MA (1st cl. hons Classics), 1935; Medley Memorial Prizeman, History 1934; John Clark Schol., Classics, 1935. Asst Master: Bluevale Sch., 1937–39; Coatbridge Sec. Sch., 1939–41; Principal Teacher of Classics, North Berwick High Sch., 1941–50; Rector, North Berwick High Sch., 1950–60. Mem., Adv. Coun. on Educn for Scotland, 1955–57; Trustee, Scottish Sec. Schools Travel Trust, 1960–78 (Chm., 1971–78; Sec., 1978–80); Pres., Headmasters' Assoc. of Scotland, 1962–64; Member: HMC, 1960–77; Gen. Teaching Coun. for Scotland, 1966–70; Exec. Cttee, UCCA, 1970–78; Co-ordinator, Scottish Scheme of Oxford Colls' Admissions, 1978–84. Trustee, Gordon Cook Foundn, 1974– (Chm., 1992–93). JP City of Aberdeen, 1967–95. *Publications:* Off the Beaten Track in Switzerland, 1989; The Visitor's Guide to Switzerland, 1990, 2nd edn 1995; The Visitor's Guide to The Rhine and Mosel, 1992; numerous articles on educational and travel subjects. *Recreations:* photography, writing, language studies, travel. *Address:* 11 Hazledene Road, Aberdeen AB15 8LB. *T:* (01224) 318003. *Club:* Royal Northern and University (Aberdeen). *Died 23 Jan. 2007.*

MARSHALL, (John) Jeremy (Seymour); DL; Chairman, Trans Siberian Gold plc, 2001–06; *b* 18 April 1938; *s* of late Edward Pope Marshall and Nita Helen Marshall (*née* Seymour); *m* 1962, Juliette Butterley; one *s* two *d*. *Educ:* Sherborne Sch.; New Coll., Oxford (MA Chem.). Nat. Service, Royal Signals, 1956–58. Wiggins Teape, 1962–64; Riker Labs, 1964–67; CIBA

Agrochemicals, 1967–71; Hanson Trust: Managing Director: Dufaylite Developments, 1971–76; SLD Olding, 1976–79; Chief Executive: Lindustries, 1979–86; Imperial Foods, 1986–87; BAA plc, 1987–89; De La Rue Co. plc, 1989–98. Director: John Mowlem & Co., 1991–97; Camelot Gp, 1993–98; BTR plc, 1995–98; Hillsdown Holdings, 1998–2000. Dir, Fleet Exec. Bd, RN, 2002–05. Hon. Treas., Design Museum, 2000–06 (Trustee, 1996–2006). Chm., Varrier-Jones Foundn, 2006–. Chm., St John Council, Cambs, 2007–. Mem. Council, Sch. of Mgt Studies, Oxford Univ., 1995–2002. High Sheriff 2006–07, DL 2007, Cambs. CCMI (CBIM 1991); FCILT 1989. *Recreations:* squash, lawn tennis, shooting, music. *Address:* Willow House, Bourn, Cambridge CB23 2SQ. *T:* (01954) 719435. *Club:* Royal Automobile. *Died 31 Dec. 2008.*

MARSHALL, Dr John Walton, CBE 2004; DL; former Chairman, Cardea Group; Regional Appointments Commissioner, Northern and Yorkshire Region, NHS Executive, 2001–03; *b* 3 Feb. 1931; *s* of Harry and Gladys Marshall; *m* 1958, Glenison Mills; three *s*. *Educ:* University of Manchester (BSc 1952, PhD 1955). Scientific Officer, UKAEA, 1955–58; Tech. Officer, ICI, 1958–65; Vice-Pres., 1965–68, Pres., 1968–74, Katalco Corp.; Business Area Manager, ICI, 1974–78; Director: ICI Agricl Div., 1978–89; Durham Univ. Business Sch., 1989–94; Chm. (pt-time), Magneco-Metrel UK Ltd, 1994–2001. Part-time Chairman: S Durham HA, 1994–96, Co. Durham HA, 1996–2001. Chm. (pt-time), Darlington CAB. Hon. Chairman of Governors: Macmillan CTC, 1998–2004; Durham Sch., 2001–. DL Co. Durham, 2002. *Recreations:* mountaineering, music, theatre. *Address:* Lea Close, Roman Way, Middleton-St-George, Co. Durham DL2 1DG. *T:* (01325) 332215, *Fax:* (01325) 332632. *Clubs:* Farmers; Rucksack (Manchester). *Died 3 Nov. 2008.*

MARSHALL, Sir Michael; see Marshall, Sir R. M.

MARSHALL, Noël Hedley, CMG 1986; HM Diplomatic Service, retired; *b* 26 Nov. 1934; *s* of late Arthur Hedley Marshall, CBE, and Margaret Louise Marshall (*née* Longhurst). *Educ:* Leighton Park Sch.; Lawrenceville Sch., NJ (E-SU Exchange Scholar, 1953–54); St John's Coll., Cambridge (BA 1957, MA 1992; Sir Joseph Larmor Award, 1957). Pres., Cambridge Union Soc., 1957. Entered Foreign (later Diplomatic) Service; FO, 1957–59; Third Sec., Prague, 1959–61; FO, 1961–63; Second (later First) Sec., Moscow, 1963–65; CRO, 1965–66; First Sec. (Economic): Karachi, 1966–67; Rawalpindi, 1967–70; Chargé d'affaires *ai*, Ulan Bator, 1967; FCO, 1970–74; First Sec. (later Counsellor) Press, Office of UK Permanent Rep. to European Communities, Brussels, 1974–77; NATO Defence Coll., Rome, 1977–78; Counsellor, UK Delegn to Cttee on Disarmament, Geneva, 1978–81; Head of N America Dept, FCO, 1982–85; Overseas Inspector, 1985–86; Minister, Moscow, 1986–89; Co-ordinator, British Days in the USSR, Kiev, 1990; UK Perm. Rep. to Council of Europe (with personal rank of Ambassador), 1990–93. Skippered own yacht Sadko on circumnavigation of world, 1994–97 (Challenge Cup, Royal Cruising Club; Rose Medal, Ocean Cruising Club; Lacey Trophy, Cruising Assoc.); sailed new yacht, Sadko, to White Sea, 2003 and to N America and Greenland, 2004 (Romola Cup, Royal Cruising Club), to the Pacific Ocean, round S America to Argentina, 2005–06 (Irish Cruising Club Decanter, Royal Cruising Club) and to Antarctica, 2007 (Goldsmith Exploration Award, Challenge Cup and Replica, Royal Cruising Club). FRGS 1998. *Publications:* contrib. to sailing jls. *Recreations:* sailing, the theatre. *Clubs:* Royal Ocean Racing, Royal Cruising. *Died 16 Aug. 2008.*

MARSHALL, Peter, QPM 1979; Commissioner of Police for the City of London, 1978–85; *b* 21 June 1930; *s* of late Christopher George Marshall and Sylvia Marshall; *m* 1954, Bridget Frances Humphreys; three *s* one *d*. *Educ:* St Clement Danes Holborn Estate Grammar Sch. Trooper, 8th Royal Tank Regt, 1948–50. Police Officer,

Metropolitan Police, 1950–78. *Recreations:* reading, gardening. *Address:* The Cottage, Cock Lane, Elham, Canterbury, Kent CT4 6TL. *Died 20 Feb. 2007.*

MARSHALL, Peter Izod; Chairman, Ocean Group (formerly Ocean Transport and Trading), 1987–97; *b* 16 April 1927; *s* of Charles and Gwendoline Marshall; *m* 1955, Davina Mary (*née* Hart); one *s* one *d*. *Educ:* Buxton College. FCA; LRAM. Commercial Dir, EMI Electronics, 1962–67; Dir of Finance, Norcros, 1967–77; Dep. Chief Exec., Plessey Co., 1977–87; Dir, Hogg Robinson plc, 1987–96; Dep. Chm., Astec (BSR) plc, 1989–99; Chm., Plessey Pension Trust Ltd, 1990–97. *Recreations:* music, swimming, golf. *Address:* The Shrubbery, Badgers Hill, Wentworth Estate, Virginia Water, Surrey GU25 4SB. *T:* (01344) 842118. *Club:* Wentworth. *Died 24 Oct. 2007.*

MARSHALL, Robert Leckie, OBE 1945; Principal, Co-operative College, and Chief Education Officer, Co-operative Union Ltd, 1946–77; *b* 27 Aug. 1913; *s* of Robert Marshall and Mary Marshall; *m* 1944, Beryl Broad; one *s*. *Educ:* Univ. of St Andrews (MA Mediaeval and Modern History; MA 1st Cl. Hons English Lit.); Commonwealth Fellow, Yale Univ. (MA Polit. Theory and Govt). Scottish Office, 1937–39. Served War, 1939–46: RASC and AEC; finally Comdt, Army Sch. of Educn. Pres., Co-op. Congress, 1976. Missions on Co-op. develt to Tanganyika, Nigeria, India, Kenya, S Yemen and Thailand. Member: Gen. Adv. Council, and Complaints Rev. Bd, IBA, 1973–77; Monopolies and Mergers Commn, 1976–82; Distributive Studies Bd, Business Educn Council, 1976–79; Treas., Council for Educnl Advance, 1974–77; Chm., Quest House, Loughborough, 1980–86; Vice-Chm., Charnwood Community Council, 1980–90. Mem. Court, Loughborough Univ. of Technol., 1981–91. Hon. MA Open Univ., 1977; Hon. DLitt Loughborough Univ. of Technol., 1977. Jt Editor, Jl of Soc. for Co-operative Studies, 1967–95. *Publications:* Lippen on Angus—a celebration of North Angus Co-operative Society, 1983; contribs to educnl and co-op jls. *Recreations:* walking, reading, sharing in community life. *Address:* c/o 28 Denmark Road, Ealing, W13 8RG. *Died 20 Oct. 2008.*

MARSHALL, Sir (Robert) Michael, Kt 1990; DL; company director, author, and retired politician; *b* 21 June 1930; *s* of late Robert Ernest and Margaret Mary Marshall, Hathersage; *m* 1972, Caroline Victoria Oliphant, *d* of late Alexander Hutchison, Strathairly, Scotland; two step *d*. *Educ:* Bradfield Coll.; Harvard Univ. (MBA 1960); Stanford Univ. Joined United Steel Cos Ltd, 1951; Branch Man., Calcutta, 1954–58; Man. Dir, Bombay, 1960–64; Commercial Dir, Workington, 1964–66; Man. Dir, Head Wrightson Export Co. Ltd, 1967–69; Management Consultant, Urwick Orr & Partners Ltd, 1969–74. MP (C) Arundel, Feb. 1974–1997; Parly Under-Sec. of State, DoI, 1979–81. Chairman: Parly Space Cttee, 1982–97; IPU, 1987–90 (Vice Chm., 1985–87); Parly IT Cttee, 1986–97 (Vice-Chm., 1982–86); Vice-Chairman: Cons. Party Parly Industry Cttee, 1976–79; All Party Parly Cttee on Management, 1974–79; Member: Select Cttee on Defence, 1982–87; Procedure Cttee, 1994–95. Adviser: British Aerospace, 1982–97; Cable and Wireless, 1982–98; SWET, subseq. SOLT, 1984–97; Williams Hldgs, 1988–97; Matra Marconi Space Ltd, then Astrium, 1997–2001; Chairman, Advisory Board: Lava Systems Inc. (Canada), 1992–98; MCI/SHL Systemhouse (Europe) Ltd, 1992–98. Non-executive Director: General Offshore (UK) Ltd, 1992–98; Pathlore Software Corp. (USA), 1995–2006; Impatica.Inc. (Canada), 1998–2004; Catholic Herald, 2003–. Visiting Lecturer: Judge Inst. of Mgt Studies, Cambridge, 1997; Chief Execs Orgn, USA, Toronto, Hong Kong, 1998; Bristol Univ., 2001; Cunard/Oxford Univ., 2004. Member Council: Assoc. of MBAs, 1990–95; British Assoc. for Central and Eastern Europe, 1994–97; RIIA, 1997–99; Foundn for Mgt Educn; Mem. Adv. Panel, Data Protection Registrar,

1995–98. Chm., Arundel and S Downs Cons. Patrons Club, 1997–. Life Member: Equity; BAFTA; RSL. Trustee, Theatres Trust, 1987–99; Chm., Chichester Fest. Theatre Trust Co., 1997–. Trustee, UC, Chichester (Hon. Fellow, 2004). Liveryman, Information Technologists' Co. DL W Sussex, 1990. FRSA. Hon. DL New England Coll., 1982. *Publications:* Top Hat and Tails: the story of Jack Buchanan, 1978; (ed) The Stanley Holloway Monologues, 1979; More Monologues and Songs, 1980; The Book of Comic and Dramatic Monologues, 1981; The Timetable of Technology, 1982; No End of Jobs, 1984; Gentlemen and Players, 1987; (contrib.) A Celebration of Lords and Commons Cricket, 1989; (contrib.) My Lord's, 1990; Cricket at the Castle, 1995; (contrib.) The Planetary Interest, 1998; More Sussex Seams, 1999. *Recreations:* writing, travel, cricket, commentating, golf. *Address:* Old Inn House, Slindon, Arundel, W Sussex BN18 0RB. *Clubs:* Garrick, Beefsteak, MCC, Lord's Taverners, Cricket Writers'; Sussex (Worthing); Royal & Ancient Golf (St Andrews); Arundel Castle Cricket. *Died 6 Sept. 2006.*

MARSHALL, Stephen; Deputy Minister of Education, Ontario, 2008; *b* Adelaide, 3 March 1954; *s* of late Frank and Barbara Marshall; *m* 1981, Karyn Thompson; two *s* one *d. Educ:* Deakin Univ., Geelong (MEducAdmin, MBA); South Australia Coll. of Educn (Dip. Teaching (Primary), Grad. Dip. Curr. Develt, Grad. Dip. Professional Develt, Cert. Human Achievement Skills). Teacher, Elizabeth Vale Primary Sch., 1977–85; Project Officer, Primary Educn Review, 1986–87; Primary Educn, 1988–89, SA Dept of Educn; Principal (Class 1), Murray Bridge S Primary Sch., 1989–92; Dist Supt of Educn, Murrylands, SA Dept of Educn, 1992–94; Asst Gen. Manager, Central Highlands/Wimmera Reg., 1994–96; Gen. Manager Schs, Loddon/Campaspe/Mallee Reg., 1998–99; Gen. Manager, Sch. and Regl Ops, SA Dept of Educn, 1999–2001; Regl Dir, Western Metropolitan Reg., Victoria Dept of Educn, Employment and Trng, 2001–02; CEO, Dept of Educn and Children's Services, S Australia, 2002–06; Welsh Assembly Government: Member: Mgt Bd, 2006; Ministerial Adv. Gp for Educn, Lifelong Learning and Skills, 2006; Dir, Educn, Lifelong Learning and Skills, subseq. Children, Educn, Lifelong Learning and Skills, 2006–08. Mem., Govt Adv. Cttee, Internat. Baccalaureate Orgn, 2006–. *Died 7 March 2010.*

MARSHALL, (Thomas) Daniel; Member (Lab), Newcastle City Council, 1986–2004; Lord Mayor of Newcastle, 1998–99; *b* 6 Nov. 1929; *s* of James William and Leonora Mary Marshall; *m* 1st, 1953, Eileen James (*d* 1995); one *s*; 2nd, 2000, Catherine Fix, San Diego. *Educ:* St George's RC Elementary Sch., Bell's Close, Newcastle upon Tyne; Ruskin Coll.; Open Univ. Post Office, then Nat. Assistance Board, 1960; DHSS, 1966. Councillor, Newburn UDC, 1967; Mem., Tyne and Wear CC, 1974–86 (Chm., 1978–79). Chairman: Newburn Riverside Recreation Assoc. Ltd, 1980–; Tyne and Wear Enterprise Trust, 1981–2006; Nat. Resource for Innovative Trng, Res. and Employment Ltd, 1985–; Throckley Community Hall Ltd, 1991–; Tyne and Wear PTA, 1995–2004 (Mem., 1986–2004); Grange Day Centre Ltd, 1994–; Director: Bowes Railway Co., 1982–2005; Newburn Sports Services Ltd, 1984–; Managed Business Services, 2003–. Trustee: Grange Welfare Assoc., 1970–; Building Preservation Trust Ltd, 1978–2007 (Vice Chm.). DL Tyne and Wear, 1999. Hon. Alderman, Newcastle CC, 2005. *Recreation:* reading. *Address:* 7 Hallow Drive, Throckley, Newcastle upon Tyne NE15 9AQ. *T:* (0191) 267 0956. *Clubs:* Grange Welfare; Newburn Memorial (Newcastle). *Died 16 July 2008.*

MARTEN, Francis William, CMG 1967; MC 1943; formerly Counsellor, Foreign and Commonwealth Office; *b* 8 Nov. 1916; *er s* of late Vice-Adm. Sir Francis Arthur Marten and Lady Marten (*née* Phyllis Raby Morgan); *m* 1940, Hon. Avice Irene Vernon (*d* 1964); one *s* one *d*; 2nd, 1967, Miss Anne Tan; one *s. Educ:*

Winchester Coll.; Christ Church, Oxford. Served HM Forces, 1939–46. Entered HM Foreign Service, 1946; served FO, 1946–48; Washington, 1948–52; FO, 1952–54; Teheran, 1954–57; NATO Defence Coll., Paris, 1957–58; Bonn, 1958–62; Leopoldville, 1962–64; Imperial Defence Coll., 1964–65; Dep. High Comr, Eastern Malaysia, 1965–67; ODM, 1967–69. *Recreation:* gardening. *Address:* 113 Pepys Road, SE14 5SE. *T:* (020) 7639 1060. *Died 9 Dec. 2007.*

MARTIN, (Francis) Troy K.; *see* Kennedy Martin.

MARTIN, Prof. Geoffrey Haward, CBE 1986; DPhil; FSA, FRHistS; Research Professor of History, University of Essex, since 1990; *b* 27 Sept. 1928; *s* of late Ernest Leslie Martin and Mary H. Martin (*née* Haward); *m* 1953, Janet, *d* of late Douglas Hamer, MC and Enid Hamer; three *s* one *d. Educ:* Colchester Royal Grammar Sch.; Merton Coll., Oxford (MA, DPhil); Univ. of Manchester. FSA 1975; FRHistS 1958. University of Leicester (formerly University Coll. of Leicester): Lectr in Econ. History, 1952–65; Reader in History, 1966–73; Prof. of History, 1973–82; Public Orator, 1971–74; Pro-Vice-Chancellor, 1979–82; Hon. Archivist, 1989–. Keeper of Public Records, 1982–88. Vis. Prof. of Medieval History, Carleton Univ., Ottawa, 1958–59 and 1967–68; Vis. Res. Fellow, 1971, Sen. Res. Fellow, 1990–93, Merton Coll., Oxford; Sen. Vis. Res. Fellow, Loughborough Univ. of Technol., 1987–95; Hon. Res. Fellow, Dept of Library and Archive Studies, UCL, 1987–; Dist. Vis. Prof. of History, Univ. of Toronto, 1989; Emeritus Fellow, Leverhulme Trust, 1989–91. Evelyn Wrench Lectr, ESU, 1992. Chairman: Board of Leicester University Press, 1975–82; Selection Cttee, Miners' Welfare National Educn Fund, 1978–84; British Records Assoc., 1982–91 (Vice-Pres., 1992–); Commonwealth Archivists' Assoc., 1984–88; Arts and Humanities Res. Degrees Sub-Cttee, CNAA, 1986–92; Mem., RCHM, 1987–94. Vice-Pres., RHistS, 1984–88; Mem. Council, Soc. of Antiquaries, 1989–91; Pres., Cumberland and Westmorland Antiquarian and Archaeological Soc., 1999–2002. Gov., Museum of London, 1989–95. Hon. Gen. Editor, Suffolk Record Soc., 1956–94. Res. Associate, Oxford DNB, 1997–. Dist. Mem., Sistema Nacional de Archivos, Mexico, 1988. Proposed the Immortal Memory, Portsmouth Mess, 21 Oct. 1986. DUniv Essex, 1989. Besterman Medal, Library Assoc., 1972. *Publications:* The Town: a visual history, 1961; Royal Charters of Grantham, 1963; (with Sylvia McIntyre) Bibliography of British and Irish Municipal History, vol. 1, 1972; Ipswich Recognizance Rolls: a calendar, 1973; (with Philomena Connolly) The Dublin Guild Merchant Roll *c* 1190–1265, 1992; Portsmouth Royal Charters 1194–1974, 1995; Knighton's Chronicle 1337–96, 1995; (with J. R. L. Highfield) History of Merton College, Oxford, 1997; contribs to learned jls, etc. *Recreations:* fell-walking at low altitudes, bibliophily. *Address:* Church View Cottage, Finsthwaite, Ulverston, Cumbria LA12 8BJ. *Club:* Oxford and Cambridge. *Died 20 Dec. 2007.*

MARTIN, Leslie Vaughan; Directing Actuary (Superannuation and Research), Government Actuary's Department, 1974–79; *b* 20 March 1919; *s* of late Hubert Charles Martin and late Rose Martin (*née* Skelton); *m* 1949, Winifred Dorothy Hopkins; one *s* one *d. Educ:* Price's Sch., Fareham. FIA 1947. Served with RAMC and REME, 1940–46. Deptl Clerical Officer, Customs and Excise, 1936–38; joined Govt Actuary's Dept, 1938; Asst Actuary, 1949; Actuary, 1954; Principal Actuary, 1962. Mem. Council, Inst. of Actuaries, 1971–76; Vice-Chm., CS Medical Aid Assoc., 1976–79. Churchwarden, St Barnabas, Dulwich, 1965–70, 1977–79, Vice-Chm. of PCC, 1970–79; Treasurer: Morchard Bishop Parochial Church Council, 1980–83; Cadbury Deanery Synod, 1981–88; Chulmleigh Deanery Synod, 1989–97; Lapford PCC, 1991–93. *Recreations:* crosswords, mathematical puzzles. *Address:* Pickwick House, Down St Mary, Crediton, Devon EX17 6EQ. *T:* (01363) 84581. *Died 11 Nov. 2009.*

MARTIN, His Honour Oliver Samuel; QC 1970; a Circuit Judge, 1975–93; *b* 26 Nov. 1919; *s* of Sidney Edward Martin and Nita Martin; *m* 1st, 1954, Marion Eve (marr. diss. 1982); two *s*; 2nd, 1982, Gloria Audrey (*d* 2006). *Educ:* King's College Sch., Wimbledon; London University. Served RNVR, 1939–46. Called to Bar, Gray's Inn, 1951. Dep. Chm. E Sussex QS, 1970–71; a Recorder of the Crown Court, 1972–75. *Recreations:* golf, music, reading, writing, holidays. *Died 2 July 2007.*

MARTIN, Maj.-Gen. Peter Lawrence de Carteret, CBE 1968 (OBE 1964); President, Lady Grover's Hospital Fund for Officers' Families, since 1989 (Chairman, 1975–85); Vice President, 1985–89); President, Normandy Veterans' Association, since 1995 (Vice President, 1989–95); *b* 15 Feb. 1920; *s* of late Col Charles de Carteret Martin, MD, ChD, IMS and of Helen Margaret Hardinge Grover; *m* 1st, 1949, Elizabeth Felicia (marr. diss. 1967), *d* of late Col C. M. Keble; one *s* one *d*; 2nd, 1973, Mrs Valerie Singer (marr. diss. 1997). *Educ:* Wellington Coll.; RMC Sandhurst. Commnd Cheshire Regt, 1939; BEF (Dunkirk), 1940; Middle East, 1941; N Africa 8th Army, 1942–43 (despatches); invasion of Sicily, 1943; Normandy landings and NW Europe, 1944 (despatches); Palestine, 1945–47; GSO2 (Int.), HQ British Troops Egypt, 1947, Instructor, RMA Sandhurst, 1948–50; psc 1951; Bde Major 126 Inf. Bde (TA), 1952–53; Chief Instructor MMG Div. Support Weapons Wing, Sch. of Infantry, 1954–56; Malayan Ops, 1957–58 (despatches); DAAG GHQ FARELF, 1958–60; CO 1 Cheshire, N Ireland and BAOR, 1961–63; AA&QMG Cyprus District, 1963–65; comd 48 Gurkha Inf. Bde, Hong Kong, 1966–68; Brig. AQ HQ Army Strategic Comd, 1968–71; Dir, Personal Services (Army), 1971–74. Col The 22nd (Cheshire) Regt, 1971 78; Col Comdt, Mil. Provost Staff Corps, 1972–74. Services Advr, Variety Club of GB, 1976–86. Member: Ex-Services Mental Welfare Soc., 1977–91; Nat. Exec. Cttee, Forces Help Soc., 1975–97. FCMI (MBIM 1970, FBIM 1979). *Recreations:* golf, ski-ing, ex-Services associations. *Address:* 17 Station Street, Lymington, Hants SO41 3BA. *T:* and *Fax:* (01590) 672620. *Club:* Army and Navy. *Died 10 Feb. 2006.*

MARTINDALE, Air Vice-Marshal Alan Rawes, CB 1984; Royal Air Force, retired; *b* 20 Jan. 1930; *s* of late Norman Martindale and Edith (*née* Rawes); *m* 1952, Eileen Alma Wrenn; three *d*. *Educ:* Kendal Grammar Sch.; University Coll., Leicester (BA History, London Univ., 1950). Commissioned RAF, 1951; served, 1951–71: RAF Driffield, Oakington, Eindhoven, Stafford, Wickenby, Faldingworth and Marham; Instructor, RAF Coll., Cranwell; Staff AHQ Malta; RAF Staff Coll., Bracknell, MoD, Jt Services Staff Coll. (student and Directing Staff), and HQ Maintenance Comd; Dep. Dir of Supply Management, MoD, Harrogate, 1971–72; Comd Supply Officer, RAF Germany, 1972–74; Dir of Supply Management, MoD, Harrogate, 1974–75; RCDS, 1976; Air Cdre Supply and Movements, RAF Support Comd, 1977; Dep. Gen. Man., NAMMA, 1978–81; Dir of Supply Policy (RAF), MoD, 1981–82; Dir Gen. of Supply (RAF), 1982–84; retd 1985. Dist Gen. Manager, Hastings HA, 1985–90; Census Area Manager, S Kent and Hastings, 1990–91. Chm., Battle Festival, 1991–96. *Recreations:* golf, grandchildren, gardening. *Address:* Stores Barn, The Old Stable Yard, Radway, Warwicks CV35 0UQ. *Club:* Royal Air Force. *Died 29 Jan. 2006.*

MARTYN, (Charles) Roger (Nicholas); Master of the Supreme Court, 1973–95; part-time Adjudicator, Immigration Appellate Authority, 1991–95; *b* 10 Dec. 1925; *s* of Rev. Charles Martyn; *m* 1960, Helen, *d* of Frank and Florence Everson; two *s* one *d*. *Educ:* Charterhouse, 1939–44; Merton Coll., Oxford, 1947–49. MA (Hons) Mod. Hist. Joined Regular Army, 1944; commissioned 60th Rifles (KRRC), 1945; CMF, 1946–47; special release, 1947. Articles, 1950–52, and admitted as solicitor, 1952. Sherwood & Co., Parly Agents (Partner), 1952–59; Lee, Bolton & Lee,

Westminster (Partner), 1961–73; Notary Public, 1969. Mem. and Dep. Chm., No 14 Legal Aid Area Cttee, 1967–73; Hon. Legal Adviser to The Samaritans (Inc.), 1955–73. Chairman: Family Welfare Assoc., 1973–78 (Chief Trustee of 129 public charities and 6 almshouses); NHS Complaints Panel for Gtr London, 1999–2004; Member: Gtr London Citizens' Advice Bureaux Management Cttee, 1974–79; Council, St Gabriel's Coll. (Further Education), Camberwell, 1973–77 (Vice-Chm.); Council, Goldsmiths' Coll., Univ. of London, 1988–94 (Mem., Delegacy, 1977–88). Freeman, City of London, 1995. *Recreations:* walking, sailing (Vice-Cdre, Thames Barge Sailing Club, 1962–65), observing people, do-it-yourself, nigrology. *Address:* 29 St Albans Road, NW5 1RG. *T:* (020) 7267 1076. *Died 15 Nov. 2009.*

MARWICK, Prof. Arthur John Brereton, FRHistS; Professor of History, The Open University, 1969–2001, Emeritus Professor, 2004; *b* 29 Feb. 1936; *s* of William Hutton Marwick and Maeve Cluna Brereton; unmarried; one *d*. *Educ:* George Heriot's School, Edinburgh; Edinburgh Univ. (MA, DLitt); Balliol Coll., Oxford (BLitt). Asst Lectr in History, Univ. of Aberdeen, 1959–60; Lectr in History, Univ. of Edinburgh, 1960–69; Dean and Dir of Studies in Arts, Open Univ., 1978–84. Vis. Prof. in History, State Univ. of NY at Buffalo, 1966 67; Vis. Scholar, Hoover Instn and Vis. Prof., Stanford Univ., 1984–85; Directeur d'études invité, l'Ecole des Hautes Etudes en Sciences Sociales, Paris, 1985; Visiting Professor: Rhodes Coll., Memphis, 1991; Univ. of Perugia, 1991. FRSA 1999. *Publications:* The Explosion of British Society, 1963; Clifford Allen, 1964; The Deluge, 1965, new edn 1991; Britain in the Century of Total War, 1968; The Nature of History, 1970, 3rd edn 1989; War and Social Change in the Twentieth Century, 1974; The Home Front, 1976; Women at War 1914–1918, 1977; Class: image and reality in Britain, France and USA since 1930, 1980, rev. edn 1990; (ed) Illustrated Dictionary of British History, 1980; British Society since 1945, 1982, 4th edn 2003; Britain in Our Century, 1984; (ed) Class in the Twentieth Century, 1986; Beauty in History: society, politics and personal appearance *c* 1500 to the present, 1988; (ed) Total War and Social Change, 1988; (ed) The Arts, Literature and Society, 1990; Culture in Britain since 1945, 1991; The Sixties: cultural revolution in Britain, France, Italy and the United States *c*. 1958–*c*. 1974, 1998; (ed) Windows on the Sixties: exploring key texts of media and culture, 2000; A History of the Modern British Isles 1914–1999: circumstances, events and outcomes, 2000; The New Nature of History: knowledge, evidence, language, 2001; The Arts in the West since 1945, 2002; It: a history of human beauty, 2004; contribs to English Hist. Review, Amer. Hist. Review, Jl of Contemporary Hist. *Recreation:* tennis. *Address:* 67 Fitzjohns Avenue, Hampstead, NW3 6PE. *T:* (020) 7794 4534. *Died 27 Sept. 2006.*

MASEFIELD, Sir Peter (Gordon), Kt 1972; CEng; Hon. FRAeS; President: Brooklands Museum Trust, since 1993 (Chairman, 1987–93); Croydon Airport Society, since 1962; aviation historian; *b* Trentham, Staffs, 19 March 1914; *e s* of late Dr W. Gordon Masefield, CBE, MRCS, and Marian A. Masefield (*née* Lloyd-Owen); *m* 1936, Patricia Doreen, 3rd *d* of late Percy H. Rooney, Wallington, Surrey; three *s* one *d*. *Educ:* Westminster Sch.; Chillon Coll., Switzerland; Jesus Coll., Cambridge (BA (Eng) 1935; MA). On Design Staff, The Fairey Aviation Co. Ltd, 1935–37; Pilot's licence, 1937–77; joined The Aeroplane newspaper, 1937, Technical Editor, 1939–43; Air Correspondent Sunday Times, 1940–43; War Corresp. with RAF and US Army Eighth Air Force on active service, 1939–43; Editor, The Aeroplane Spotter, 1941–43; Chm. Editorial Cttee, The Inter-Services Journal on Aircraft Recognition, MAP, 1942–45; Personal Adviser to the Lord Privy Seal (Lord Beaverbrook) and Sec. of War Cabinet Cttee on Post War Civil Air Transport, 1943–45; first British Civil Air Attaché, British Embassy, Washington, DC, 1945–46 (Signator to Anglo-American Bermuda Air Agreement, 1946); Dir-Gen. of Long Term Planning and Projects,

Ministry of Civil Aviation, 1946–48; Chief Executive and Mem. of Board of BEA, 1949–55; Managing Dir, Bristol Aircraft Ltd, 1956–60; Man. Dir, Beagle Aircraft Ltd, 1960–67, Chm., 1968–70; Dir, Beagle Aviation Finance Ltd, 1962–71. Chm., British Airports Authority, 1965–71. Chm., Nat. Jt Council for Civil Air Transport, 1950–51; Member: Cairns Cttee on Aircraft Accident Investigation, 1960; Min. of Aviation Advisory Cttees on Civil Aircraft Control and on Private and Club Flying and Gliding; Aeronautical Research Council, 1958–61; Board, LTE, 1973–82 (Chm. and Chief Exec., London Transport, 1980–82); CAA Flight Time Limitations Bd, 1986–91. Mem., Cambridge Univ. Appointments Bd, 1956–69. Director: Pressed Steel Co. Ltd, 1960–68; Worldwide Estates Ltd, 1972–88; Nationwide Building Soc., 1973–86; British Caledonian Aviation Gp Plc, 1975–88 (Dep. Chm., 1978–87); LRT Internat., 1982–91; Chm., Project Management Ltd, 1972–88. President: RAeS, 1959–60 (Mem. Council, 1945–65); Inst. of Travel Managers, 1967–71; Duxford Aviation Soc., 1970–; British Assoc. of Aviation Consultants, 1972–84 (Patron, 1984–); IRTE, 1979–81; Internat. Fedn of Airworthiness, 1980–83 (Patron, 1983–88); Bd Mem., Imperial War Mus. and HMS Belfast, 1942–44; Chm., Bd of Trustees, Imperial War Museum, 1977–78; Mem. Council, Royal Aero Club (Chm., Aviation Cttee, 1960–65; Chm., 1968–70). Liveryman, GAPAN; Freeman, City of London. Chm., Bd of Governors, Reigate Grammar Sch., 1979–91; Governor, Ashridge Mgt Coll., 1981–91. FRSA (Chm. Council, 1977–79; Vice-Pres., 1979, then Vice-Pres. Emeritus); CCMI. Hon. FAIAA; Hon. FCASI; Hon. DSc Cranfield, 1977; Hon. DTech Loughborough, 1977. Publications: To Ride the Storm, 1982; articles on aviation, transport, management, and First World War. Recreations: reading, writing, gardening. Address: Kitley Lodge, Lewes Road, Laughton, Lewes, East Sussex BN8 6BQ. Clubs: Athenæum, Royal Aero; National Aviation (Washington). Died 14 Feb. 2006.

MASON, Sir Frederick (Cecil), KCVO 1968; CMG 1960; HM Diplomatic Service, retired; b 15 May 1913; s of late Ernest Mason and Sophia Charlotte Mason (née Dodson); m 1941, Karen Rørholm; two s one d (and two d decd). Educ: City of London Sch.; St Catharine's Coll., Cambridge. Vice-Consul: Antwerp, 1935–36; Paris, 1936–37; Leopoldville, 1937–39; Elisabethville, 1939–40; Consul at Thorshavn during British occupation of Faroes, 1940–42; Consul, Colon, Panama, 1943–45; First Sec., British Embassy, Santiago, Chile, 1946–48; First Sec. (Information), Oslo, 1948–50; Asst Labour Adviser, FO, 1950–53; First Sec. (Commercial), UK Control Commission, Bonn, 1954–55; Counsellor (Commercial), HM Embassy, Athens, 1955–56; Counsellor (Economic), HM Embassy, Tehran, 1957–60; Head of Economic Relations Dept, Foreign Office, 1960–64; Under-Sec., Ministry of Overseas Development, 1965, and CRO, 1966; Ambassador to Chile, 1966–70; Under-Sec. of State, FCO, Oct. 1970–Apr. 1971; Ambassador and Perm. UK Rep. to UN and other Internat. Orgns, Geneva, 1971–73. Dir, New Court Natural Resources, 1973–83. British Mem., Internat. Narcotics Control Bd, Geneva, 1974–77. Chm., Anglo-Chilean Soc., 1978–82. Grand Cross, Chilean Order of Merit, 1968. Publications: Ropley Past and Present, 1989. Recreations: walking, painting. Address: The Forge, Ropley, Hants SO24 0DS. T: (01962) 772285. Club: Canning. Died 18 Jan. 2008.

MASON, His Honour (George Frederick) Peter; QC 1963; FCIArb 1986; a Circuit Judge, 1970–87; b 11 Dec. 1921; s of George Samuel and Florence May Mason, Keighley, Yorks; m 1st, 1950, Faith Maud Bacon (marr. diss. 1977); two s two d (and one d decd); 2nd, 1981, Sara, er d of Sir Robert Ricketts, 7th Bt. Educ: Lancaster Royal Grammar Sch.; St Catharine's Coll., Cambridge. Open Exhibnr St Catharine's Coll., 1940. Served with 78th Medium Regt RA (Duke of Lancaster's Own Yeo.) in Middle East and Italy, 1941–45, latterly as Staff Capt. RA, HQ 13 Corps. History Tripos Pt 1, 1st cl. hons with

distinction, 1946; called to Bar, Lincoln's Inn, 1947; MA 1948; Cholmeley Schol., 1949. Asst Recorder of Huddersfield, 1961; Dep. Chairman: Agricultural Land Tribunal, W Yorks and Lancs, 1962; West Riding of Yorks Quarter Sessions, 1965–67; Recorder of York, 1965–67; Dep. Chm., Inner London QS, 1970; Dep. Chm., NE London QS, 1970–71; Senior Judge: Snaresbrook Crown Ct, 1974–81; CCC, 1982; Inner London Crown Court, 1983–87. Member: Council, Assoc. of Futures Brokers and Dealers, 1987–91; London Court of Internat. Arbitration, 1990–2000; Bd, Securities and Futures Authy, 1991–93; Amer. Arbitration Assoc., 1992–2002; Bd, Internat. Petroleum Exchange, 1993–98; Special Cttee, London Metal Exchange, 1995–2006. Freeman, City of London, 1977. Liveryman, Wax Chandlers' Co., 1980–. Publications: Next Please: a judge's daybook, 2001. Recreations: reflection, survival. Address: Lane Cottage, Amberley, Glos GL5 5AB. T: (01453) 872412, Fax: (01453) 878557; e-mail: peter@masonamberley.co.uk. Clubs: Athenæum; Hawks (Cambridge). Died 11 April 2009.

MASON, Sir Gordon (Charles), Kt 1993; OBE 1982; JP; b 8 Nov. 1921; s of Joseph Henry Mason and May Louisa Mason; m 1944, Tui Audrey King; two s one d. Educ: Kaipara Flats. In local government, New Zealand, 1960–92: Dep. Chm., 1965–72, Co. Chm., 1972–89; Mayor, Rodney DC, 1989–92. Chm., Local Govt Trng Bd, 1981–89; Pres., NZ Counties Assoc., 1984–87. Past Master: Rodney Masonic Lodge; Rotary; Lions. JP NZ, 1968. Recreations: travel, gardening. Address: 40 Alnwick Street, Warkworth, New Zealand. T: (9) 4258878. Clubs: Bowling (NZ); RSA (Warkworth, NZ). Died 20 July 2010.

MASON, Sir John (Charles Moir), KCMG 1980 (CMG 1976); Chairman, Pirelli Cables Australia Ltd, 1993–99 (Director, 1987–99); b 13 May 1927; o s of late Charles Moir Mason, CBE and Madeline Mason; m 1954, Margaret Newton; one s one d. Educ: Manchester Grammar Sch.; Peterhouse, Cambridge. Lieut, XX Lancs Fusiliers, 1946–48; BA 1950, MA 1955, Cantab; Captain, Royal Ulster Rifles, 1950–51 (Korea); HM Foreign Service, 1952; 3rd Sec., FO, 1952–54; 2nd Sec. and Private Sec. to Ambassador, British Embassy, Rome, 1954–56; 2nd Sec., Warsaw, 1956–59; 1st Sec., FO, 1959–61; 1st Sec. (Commercial), Damascus, 1961–65; 1st Sec. and Asst Head of Dept, FO, 1965–68; Dir of Trade Develt and Dep. Consul-Gen., NY, 1968–71; Head of European Integration Dept, FCO, 1971–72; seconded as Under-Sec., ECGD, 1972–75; Asst Under-Sec. of State (Economic), FCO, 1975–76; Ambassador to Israel, 1976–80; High Commissioner to Australia, 1980–84. Chairman: Thorn-EMI (Australia), 1985–94; Lloyd's Bank (NZA), Sydney, 1985–90; Lloyds International Ltd, 1985–90; Vickers Shipbuilders (Australia), 1985–92; Bd of Advice, Spencer Stuart and Associates, Sydney, 1985–96; Multicon, 1987–92; Prudential (Australia and NZ), later Prudential Corp. Australia, 1987–92; Prudential Assets Management, 1987–92; Prudential Funds Management, 1987–92; Director: Nat. Bank of NZ, 1984–90; Wellcome (Australia) Ltd, 1985–90; Fluor Daniel (Australia) Ltd, 1985–93; Sen. Internat. Advr, Fluor Corp., USA, 1989–93. Public Mem., Australia Press Council, 1992–99; Member: Professional Conduct Cttees, NSW Bar Assoc., 1992–99; NSW Law Soc., 1994–99. Chairman: North Shore Heart Foundn, Sydney, 1986–92; Bequests Cttee, RACP, 1992–95; Mem., Finance Cttee, State Cancer Council, NSW, 1993–95. Nat. Dep. Chm., Churchill Meml Trust, Aust., 1995–2001. Publications: Diplomatic Despatches From a Son to his Mother, 1998. Address: 51/543 New South Head Road, Double Bay, NSW 2028, Australia; c/o Lloyds TSB, 7 Pall Mall, SW1Y 5NA. Club: Union (Sydney). Died 16 March 2007.

MASON, Peter; see Mason, G. F. P.

MASON, Peter Geoffrey, MBE 1946; High Master, Manchester Grammar School, 1962–78; b 22 Feb. 1914; o s of Harry Mason, Handsworth, Birmingham; m 1st,

1939, Mary Evelyn Davison (marr. diss.); three *d*; 2nd, 1978, Elizabeth June Bissell (*d* 1983); 3rd, 1985, Marjorie Payne. *Educ:* King Edward's Sch., Birmingham; Christ's Coll., Cambridge (Scholar). Goldsmith Exhibitioner, 1935; Porson Scholar, 1936; 1st Class, Classical Tripos, Pts 1 and 2, 1935, 1936. Sixth Form Classical Master, Cheltenham Coll., 1936–40, Rugby Sch., 1946–49; Headmaster, Aldenham Sch., 1949–61. War Service, 1940–46: commissioned into Intelligence Corps, 1940; various staff appointments including HQ 21 Army Group; later attached to a dept of the Foreign Office. Member: Advisory Cttee on Education in the Colonies, 1956; ITA Educnl Adv. Council, 1964–69; Council, University of Salford, 1969–87; Council, British Volunteer Programme (Chm., 1966–74); Chairman: Council of Educn for World Citizenship, 1966–83; Reg. Conf. on IVS, 1972–82; (first), Eur. Council of Nat. Assocs of Ind. Schs, 1988–94, Hon. Life Pres., 1994; Hon. Dir of Research, ISCis (formerly ISIS), 1981–. *Publications:* Private Education in the EEC, 1983; Private Education in the USA and Canada, 1985; Private Education in Australia and New Zealand, 1987; Independent Education in Southern Africa, 1990; Independent Education in Western Europe, 1992, 2nd edn 1997; articles and reviews in classical and educational journals. *Recreations:* travel, fly-fishing, walking. *Address:* Leeward, Longborough, Moreton-in-Marsh, Glos GL56 0QR. *T:* and *Fax:* (01451) 830147; *e-mail:* xbf15@dial.pipex.com. *Club:* East India. *Died 29 July 2009.*

MASON, Rachel Anne, (Mrs A. T. Mason); *see* Squire, R. A.

MASON, Prof. Stephen Finney, FRS 1982; FRSC; Emeritus Professor of Chemistry, University of London; *b* 6 July 1923; *s* of Leonard Stephen Mason and Christine Harriet Mason; *m* 1955, Joan Banus; three *s*. *Educ:* Wyggeston Sch., Leicester; Wadham Coll., Oxford. MA, DPhil, DSc. Demonstrator, Mus. of Hist. of Sci., Oxford Univ., 1947–53; Research Fellow in Med. Chemistry, ANU, 1953–56; Reader in Chemical Spectroscopy, Univ. of Exeter, 1956–64; Professor of Chemistry: Univ. of East Anglia, 1964–70; KCL, 1970–87. Fellow, Wolfson Coll., Cambridge, 1988–90; FKC 1997. *Publications:* A History of the Sciences: main currents of scientific thought, 1953; Molecular Optical Activity and the Chiral Discriminations, 1982; Chemical Evolution: origin of the elements, molecules and living systems, 1991; articles in Jl Chem. Soc., 1945–. *Recreation:* history and philosophy of science. *Address:* 12 Hills Avenue, Cambridge CB1 7XA. *T:* (01223) 247827. *Died 11 Dec. 2007.*

MASSINGHAM, John Dudley, CMG 1986; HM Diplomatic Service, retired; Consul General and Director of Trade Promotion, Johannesburg, 1987–90; *b* 1 Feb. 1930; *yr s* of Percy Massingham and Amy (*née* Sanders); *m* 1952, Jean Elizabeth Beech (*d* 1995); two *s* two *d*. *Educ:* Dulwich Coll.; Magdalene Coll., Cambridge (MA); Magdalen Coll., Oxford. HM Overseas Civil Service, N Nigeria, 1954–59; BBC, 1959–64; HM Diplomatic Service, 1964–90: First Secretary, CRO, 1964–66; Dep. High Comr and Head of Chancery, Freetown, 1966–70; FCO, 1970–71; seconded to Pearce Commn, Jan.–May 1972; First Sec. (Information), later Aid (Kuala Lumpur), 1972–75; First Sec. and Head of Chancery, Kinshasa, 1976–77; Chief Sec., Falkland Islands Govt, 1977–79; Consul-General, Durban, June–Dec. 1979; Counsellor (Economic and Commercial), Nairobi, 1980–81; Governor and C-in-C, St Helena, 1981–84; High Comr to Guyana and non-resident Ambassador to Suriname, 1985–87. *Recreations:* bird watching, nature conservation work. *Address:* 24 Cherry Orchard, Pershore, Worcs WR10 1EL. *Died 16 March 2009.*

MATHER, Sir (David) Carol (Macdonell), Kt 1987; MC 1944; *b* 3 Jan. 1919; *s* of late Loris Emerson Mather, CBE; *m* 1951, Hon. Philippa Selina Bewicke-Copley, *o d* of 5th Baron Cromwell, DSO; one *s* three *d*. *Educ:* Harrow; Trinity Coll., Cambridge. War of 1939–45: commissioned Welsh Guards, 1940; served in Western

Desert Campaigns, Commandos, SAS, 1941–42; Liaison Officer to Montgomery at Alamein, 1942, and NW Europe; PoW, 1942; escaped, 1943; NW Europe, 1944–45 (despatches); wounded, 1945; Palestine Campaign, 1946–48. Asst Mil. Attaché, British Embassy, Athens, 1953–56; GSO 1, MI Directorate, War Office, 1957–61; Mil. Sec. to GOC-in-C, Eastern Command, 1961–62; retd as Lt-Col, 1962. Conservative Research Dept, 1962–70; contested (C) Leicester (NW), 1966. MP (C) Esher, 1970–87. An Opposition Whip, 1975–79; a Lord Comr of HM Treasury, 1979–81; Vice-Chamberlain of HM Household, 1981–83; Comptroller of HM Household, 1983–86. FRGS. *Publications:* Aftermath of War: everyone must go home, 1992; When the Grass Stops Growing, 1997. *Club:* Brooks's. *Died 3 July 2006.*

MATHESON, Very Rev. James Gunn; Moderator of General Assembly of Church of Scotland, 1975–76; *b* 1 March 1912; *s* of Norman Matheson and Henrietta Gunn; *m* 1937, Janet Elizabeth Clarkson (*d* 1997); three *s* one *d* (and one *d* decd). *Educ:* Inverness Royal Academy; Edinburgh Univ. (MA, BD). Free Church of Olrig, Caithness, 1936–39; Chaplain to HM Forces, 1939–45 (POW Italy, 1941–43); St Columba's Church, Blackhall, Edinburgh, 1946–51; Knox Church, Dunedin, NZ, 1951–60; Sec. of Stewardship and Budget Cttee of Church of Scotland, 1961–73; Parish Minister, Portree, Isle of Skye, 1973–79; retired 1979. Hon. DD Edinburgh, 1975. *Publications:* Do You Believe This?, 1960; Saints and Sinners, 1975; contrib. theol jls. *Recreations:* gardening, walking. *Died 28 Oct. 2007.*

MATTHEWMAN, His Honour Keith; QC 1979; a Circuit Judge, 1983–2001; *b* 8 Jan. 1936; *e s* of late Lieut Frank Matthewman and Elizabeth Matthewman; *m* 1962, Jane (*née* Maxwell); one *s*. *Educ:* Long Eaton Grammar Sch.; University College London (LLB). Called to the Bar, Middle Temple, 1960. School teacher, Barking, Essex, 1958–59, and Heanor, Derbys, 1960–61; Commercial Assistant, Internat. Div., Rolls-Royce Ltd, 1961–62; practice at the Bar, 1962–83, Midland Circuit, later Midland and Oxford Circuit; a Recorder of the Crown Court, 1979–83. Newspaper columnist, Beeston Express (Notts), 2004–06. Mem. Cttee, Council of HM's Circuit Judges, 1984–89. Member: Notts Probation Cttee, 1986–2001; Parole Bd, 1996–2002 (Judge Appraiser, 2002–04). A Pres., Mental Health Review Tribunals, 1993–99. Ext. Examr, Bar vocational course, Nottingham Trent Univ., 2000–03. Inaugural Pres., Friends of the Galleries of Justice (Nottingham), 1998–2007. Patron, Criminal Justice Assoc., 2003–. Patron, Nottingham Cartoon Fest., 2002–. Mem. (Lab), Heanor UDC, 1960–63. TV appearances include Crimestalker, Central TV, 1993. *Recreations:* gardening, reading. *Address:* c/o Crown Court, Nottingham NG1 7EJ. *Club:* Beeston Fields Golf (Bramcote). *Died 23 Dec. 2008.*

MATTHEWS, Edwin James Thomas, TD 1946; Chief Taxing Master of the Supreme Court, 1979–83 (Master, 1965–78); *b* 2 May 1915; *s* of Edwin Martin Matthews (killed in action, 1916); *m* 1939, Katherine Mary Hirst, BA (Oxon), DipSocSc (Leeds); two *d*. *Educ:* Sedbergh Sch., Yorks. Admitted as Solicitor of Supreme Court, 1938; practice on own account in Middlesbrough, 1938–39. Served in Royal Artillery, 1939–46, UK, France and Belgium (Dunkirk 1940); released with rank of Major. Partner, Chadwick Son & Nicholson, Solicitors, Dewsbury, Yorks, 1946–50; Area Sec., No 6 (W Midland) Legal Aid Area Cttee of Law Soc., 1950–56; Sec. of Law Soc. for Contentious Business (including responsibility for administration of Legal Aid and Advice Schemes), 1956–65. Toured Legal Aid Offices in USA for Ford Foundation and visited Toronto to advise Govt of Ontario, 1963. Mem., Council, British Academy of Forensic Sciences, 1965–68. Special Consultant to NBPI on Solicitors' Costs, 1967–68; General Consultant, Law Soc., 1983–84. Member: Lord Chancellor's Adv. Cttee on Legal Aid, 1972–77; Working Party on Legal Aid

Legislation, 1974–76; Working Party on the Criminal Trial, 1980–83; Supreme Ct Procedure Cttee, 1982–83. Lectr, mainly on costs and remuneration for solicitors and counsel, for Coll. of Law, Legal Studies and Services Ltd and to various provincial Law Socs, 1983–89. *Publications:* contrib. Halsbury's Laws of England, 1961 and Atkin's Encyclopaedia of Forms and Precedents, 1962; (with Master Graham-Green) Costs in Criminal Cases and Legal Aid, 1965; (jointly) Legal Aid and Advice Under the Legal Aid and Advice Acts, 1949 to 1964, 1971; (ed jtly) Supreme Court Practice; contribs to legal journals. *Recreations:* trout fishing, theatre, gardening, French wines. *Address:* 11 Old Parsonage Court, Otterbourne, Winchester, Hants SO21 2EP. *T:* (01962) 714956.
Died 29 March 2006.

MATTHEWS, Dr John Duncan, CVO 1989; FRCPE; retired; Consultant Physician, Royal Infirmary, Edinburgh, 1955–86; Hon. Senior Lecturer, University of Edinburgh, 1976–86; *b* 19 Sept. 1921; *s* of Joseph Keith Matthews and Ethel Chambers; *m* 1945, Constance Margaret Moffat; two *s*. *Educ:* Shrewsbury; Univ. of Cambridge (BA); Univ. of Edinburgh (MB, ChB). FRCPE 1958. Surgeon, High Constables and Guard of Honour, Holyroodhouse, 1961–87, Moderator, 1987–89. Hon. Consultant in Medicine to the Army in Scotland, 1974–86; Examr in Medicine, Edinburgh and Cambridge Univs and Royal Colleges of Physicians. Vice-Pres., RCPE, 1982–85; Mem./Chm., various local and national NHS and coll. cttees. Sec., Edinburgh Medical Angling Club, 1963–86. *Publications:* occasional articles in med. jls on diabetes and heart disease. *Recreations:* cricket (Free Foresters, Grange, and Scotland), fishing, golf, gardening. *Address:* 3 Succoth Gardens, Edinburgh EH12 6BR. *Died 22 Jan. 2009.*

MATTHEWS, Percy; *b* 24 July 1921; *s* of Samuel and Minnie Matthews; *m* 1946, Audrey Rosenthal; one *s* two *d*. *Educ:* Parmiters Sch., London. Jt Man. Dir, First Nat. Finance Corp., 1963; Dir, Phoenix Assce Co. Ltd, 1971; Overseas Associate, J. O. Hambro & Co. Former Chm., Whitechapel Art Gall.; Trustee, Ravenswood Foundn; Mem. Mgt Cttee, RPMS, Hammersmith Hosp. Pres., Aston Villa FC. Freeman, City of London. Hon. Fellow, St Peter's Coll., Oxford. *Recreations:* painting, golf. *Address:* 20 Pavilion Court, Frognal Rise, NW3 6PZ. *Died 11 Aug. 2006.*

MATTHEWS, Sir Peter (Alec), Kt 1975; AO 1980; *b* 21 Sept. 1922; *s* of Major Alec Bryan Matthews and Elsie Lazarus Barlow; *m* 1946, Sheila Dorothy Bunting; four *s* one *d*. *Educ:* Shawnigan Lake Sch., Vancouver Island; Oundle Sch. Served Royal Engineers (retired as Major), 1940–46. Joined Stewarts and Lloyds Ltd, 1946; Director of Research and Technical Development, 1962; Member for R&D, BSC, 1968–70, Dep. Chm., 1973–76; Vickers PLC: Man. Dir, 1970–79; Chm., 1980–84; Chm., Pegler-Hattersley plc, 1979–87 (Dir, 1977–87); Director: Lloyds Bank, 1974–91 (Chm., Central London Regl Bd, 1978–91); British Electric Traction Plc, 1976–87; Sun Alliance and London Insurance, 1979–89; Lead Industries Gp, then Cookson Gp, 1980–91; Hamilton Oil GB, 1981–91; Lloyds & Scottish, 1983–86. Chm., Armed Forces Pay Review Body, 1984–89; Mem., Top Salaries Review Body, 1984–89. Member: BOTB, 1973–77; Export Guarantees Adv. Council, 1973–78; Status Review Cttee, ECGD, 1983–84; Pres., Sino-British Trade Council, 1983–85. Member: NRDC, 1974–80; Engineering Industries Council, 1976–84 (Chm., 1980–84); Adv. Council for Applied R&D, 1976–80. Pres., Engineering Employers Fedn, 1982–84; Chm., Council, University Coll., London, 1980–89 (Hon. Fellow, 1982). CCMI, FRSA. *Recreations:* sailing, gardening. *Address:* Chalkwell, Nether Wallop, Stockbridge, Hants SO20 8HE. *T:* (01264) 782136. *Club:* Royal Yacht Squadron (Cowes). *Died 20 May 2006.*

MATTHEWS, Prof. Robert Charles Oliver, (Robin), CBE 1975; FBA 1968; Master, Clare College, Cambridge, 1975–93, then Emeritus; Professor of Political Economy, Cambridge University, 1980–91, then Emeritus; *b* 16 June 1927; *s* of Oliver Harwood Matthews, WS, and Ida Finlay; *m* 1948, Joyce Hilda Lloyds (*d* 2006); one *d*. *Educ:* Edinburgh Academy; Corpus Christi Coll., Oxford (Hon. Fellow, 1976). Student, Nuffield Coll., Oxford, 1947–48; Lectr, Merton Coll., Oxford, 1948–49; University Asst Lectr in Economics, Cambridge, 1949–51, and Univ. Lectr, 1951–65; Fellow of St John's Coll., Cambridge, 1950–65; Drummond Prof. of Political Economy, Oxford, and Fellow of All Souls Coll., 1965–75. Vis. Prof., Univ. of California, Berkeley, 1961–62. Chm., SSRC, 1972–75. A Managing Trustee, Nuffield Foundn, 1975–96; Trustee, Urwick Orr and Partners Ltd, 1978–86. Pres., Royal Econ. Soc., 1984–86; Mem., OECD Expert Group on Non-inflationary Growth, 1975–77. Chm., Bank of England Panel of Academic Consultants, 1977–93. FIDE Internat. Master of chess composition, 1965. For. Hon. Mem., Amer. Acad. of Arts and Scis, 1985; Hon. Mem., Amer. Econ. Assoc., 1993. Hon. DLitt: Warwick, 1980; Abertay Dundee, 1996. *Publications:* A Study in Trade Cycle History, 1954; The Trade Cycle, 1958; (with M. Lipton and J. M. Rice) Chess Problems: introduction to an art, 1963; (with F. H. Hahn) Théorie de la Croissance Economique, 1972; (ed) Economic Growth: trends and factors, 1981; (with C. H. Feinstein and J. C. Odling-Smee) British Economic Growth 1856–1973, 1982; (ed with G. B. Stafford) The Grants Economy and Collective Consumption, 1982; (ed) Slower Growth in the Western World, 1982; (ed with J. R. Sargent) Contemporary Problems of Economic Policy: essays from the CLARE Group, 1983; (ed) Economy and Democracy, 1985; Mostly Three-Movers: collected chess problems, 1995; articles in learned journals. *Address:* Clare College, Cambridge CB2 1TL. *Club:* Reform. *Died 19 June 2010.*

MATTHÖFER, Hans; Member of the Bundestag (Social Democrat), 1961–87; *b* Bochum, 25 Sept. 1925; *m* 1951, Traute Mecklenburg (*d* 2008). *Educ:* primary sch.; studied economics and social sciences in Frankfurt/Main and Madison, Wis, USA, 1948–53 (grad. Economics). Employed as manual and clerical worker, 1940–42; Reich Labour Service, 1942; conscripted into German Army, 1943 (Armoured Inf.), final rank NCO. Joined SPD (Social Democratic Party of Germany), 1950; employed in Economics Dept, Bd of Management, IG Metall (Metalworkers' Union) and specialized in problems arising in connection with automation and mechanization, 1953 (Head of Educn Dept, 1961). Member, OEEC Mission in Washington and Paris, 1957–61; Vice-Pres., Gp of Parliamentarians on Latin American Affairs (Editor of periodical Esprés Español until end of 1972); Mem., Patronage Cttee of German Section of Amnesty Internat.; Pres., Bd of Trustees, German Foundn for Developing Countries, 1971–73; Parly State Sec. in Federal Min. for Economic Co-operation, 1972; Federal Minister for Research and Technology, 1974, of Finance, 1978–82, for Posts and Telecommunications, 1982. Mem. of Presidency and Treasurer, SPD, 1985–87. Chm., Exec. Bd, Beteiligungsges. der Gewerkschaften (formerly für Gemeinwirtschaft) AG, trade union holding, 1987–97. Counsellor to Govt of Bulgaria, 1997–2000. Publisher, Vorwärts, 1985–88. *Publications:* Der Unterschied zwischen den Tariflöhnen und den Effektivverdiensten in der Metallindustrie der Bundesrepublik, 1956; Technological Change in the Metal Industries (in two parts), 1961–62; Der Beitrag politischer Bildung zur Emanzipation der Arbeitnehmer—Materialien zur Frage des Bildungsurlaubs, 1970; Streiks und streikähnliche Formen des Kampfes der Arbeitnehmer im Kapitalismus, 1971; Für eine menschliche Zukunft—Sozialdemokratische Forschungs—und Technologiepolitik, 1976; Humanisierung der Arbeit und Produktivität in der Industriegesellschaft, 1977, 1978, 1980; Agenda 2000: Vorschläge zur Wirtschafts-und Gesellschaftspolitik, 1993; numerous articles on questions of trade union, development, research and finance policies. *Relevant publication*: Hans Matthöfer: Gewerkschafter, Politiker, Unternehmer, by W. Abelshauser, 2007. *Address*: Augustinum, Appartment 306, Georg Rückert Strasse 2, 65812 Bad Soden am Taunus, Germany. *Died 15 Nov. 2009.*

MAUGHAN, Air Vice-Marshal Charles Gilbert, CB 1976; CBE 1970; AFC; Independent Panel Inspector, Department of the Environment, 1983–94; *b* 3 March 1923; *m* 1947, Pamela Joyce (*d* 2007), *d* of Christopher Wicks; one *s* one *d*. *Educ*: Sir George Monoux Grammar Sch.; Harrow County Sch. Served War, Fleet Air Arm (flying Swordfishes and Seafires), 1942–46. Joined RAF, 1949, serving with Meteor, Vampire and Venom sqdns in Britain and Germany; comd No 65 (Hunter) Sqdn, Duxford, Cambridgeshire (won Daily Mail Arch-to-Arc race, 1959). Subseq. comd: No 9 (Vulcan) Sqdn; flying bases of Honington (Suffolk) and Waddington (Lincs); held a staff post at former Bomber Comd, Air Staff (Ops), Strike Command, 1968–70; Air Attaché, Bonn, 1970–73; AOA Strike Command, 1974–75; SASO RAF Strike Command, 1975–77. Gen. Sec., Royal British Legion, 1978–83. *Address*: Whitestones, Tresham, Wotton-under-Edge, Glos GL12 7RW. *Died 1 Dec. 2009.*

MAUNDRELL, Rev. Canon Wolseley David; Canon and Prebendary of Chichester Cathedral, 1981–89; Priest in-charge (NSM), Stonegate, 1989–94; *b* 2 Sept. 1920; *s* of late Rev. William Herbert Maundrell, RN, and Evelyn Helen Maundrell; *m* 1950, Barbara Katharine Simmons (*d* 1985); one *s* one *d*. *Educ*: Radley Coll.; New Coll., Oxford. Deacon, 1943; Priest, 1944; Curate of Haslemere, 1943; Resident Chaplain to Bishop of Chichester, 1949; Vicar of Sparsholt and Lainston, Winchester, 1950; Rector of Weeke, Winchester, 1956; Residentiary Canon of Winchester Cathedral, 1961–70 (Treasurer, 1961–70; Vice-Dean, 1966–70); Examining Chaplain to Bishop of Winchester, 1962–70; Asst Chaplain of Holy Trinity Church, Brussels, 1970–71; Vicar of Icklesham, E Sussex, 1972–82; Rural Dean of Rye, 1978–84; Rector of Rye, 1982–89. Chm., Chichester DAC for Care of Churches, 1977–90. *Address*: 13 North Walls, Chichester, West Sussex PO19 1DA. *T*: (01243) 537359. *Died 23 Sept. 2006.*

MAVOR, Michael Barclay, CVO 1983; MA; Headmaster, Loretto School, 2001–08; *b* 29 Jan. 1947; *s* of late William Ferrier Mavor and Sheena Watson Mavor (*née* Barclay); *m* 1970, Jane Elizabeth Sucksmith; one *s* one *d*. *Educ*: Loretto School; St John's Coll., Cambridge (Exhibn and Trevelyan Schol.; Pres., Johnian Soc., 2000). MA (English); CertEd. Woodrow Wilson Teaching Fellow, Northwestern Univ., Evanston, Ill, 1969–72; Asst Master, Tonbridge Sch., 1972–78; Course Tutor (Drama), Open Univ., 1977–78; Headmaster, Gordonstoun Sch., 1979–90; Head Master, Rugby Sch., 1990–2001. Chm., HMC, 1997. Mem., Queen's Body Guard for Scotland, Royal Co. of Archers, 1997–. Gov., Oundle Sch., 2008–. Trustee, E Lothian Pipes and Drums Charitable Trust, 2008–. *Recreations*: theatre, writing, archery, golf, fishing. *Clubs*: Hawks (Cambridge); New (Edinburgh). *Died 8 Dec. 2009.*

MAVOR, Ronald Henry Moray, CBE 1972; *b* 13 May 1925; *s* of late Dr O. H. Mavor, CBE (James Bridie) and Rona Bremner; *m* 1959, Sigrid Bruhn (marr. diss. 1989); one *s* one *d* (and one *d* decd). *Educ*: Merchiston Castle Sch.; Glasgow Univ. MB, ChB 1948; MRCPGlas 1955, FRCPGlas 1989. In medical practice until 1957, incl. periods in RAMC, at American Hosp., Paris, and Deeside Sanatoria. Drama Critic, The Scotsman, 1957–65; Dir, Scottish Arts Council, 1965–71. Prof., 1981–90, and Head, 1983–90, Dept of Drama, Univ. of Saskatchewan (Vis. Prof., 1977–78, 1979–81), Prof. Emeritus. Vice-Chm., Edinburgh Festival Council, 1975–81 (Mem., 1965–81); Mem. Gen. Adv. Council, BBC, 1971–76; Mem. Drama Panel, British Council, 1973–79. Vis. Lectr on Drama, Guelph, Ontario, and Minneapolis, 1976. *Plays*: The Keys of Paradise, 1959; Aurelie, 1960; Muir of Huntershill, 1962; The Partridge Dance, 1963; A Private Matter (originally A Life of the General), 1973; The

Quartet, 1980; A House on Temperance, 1981; The Grand Inquisitor, 1990. *Publications*: Art the Hard Way, in, Scotland, 1972; A Private Matter (play), 1974; Dr Mavor and Mr Bridie, 1988. *Address*: 19 Falkland Street, Glasgow G12 9PY. *T*: (0141) 339 3149; *e-mail*: bingo@bingomavor.co.uk; 5 place de la Halle Aux Grains, 46800 Montcuq, France. *Died 9 Aug. 2007.*

MAW, (John) Nicholas; composer; *b* 5 Nov. 1935; *s* of Clarence Frederick Maw and Hilda Ellen (*née* Chambers); *m* 1960, Karen Graham; one *s* one *d*. *Educ*: Wennington Sch., Wetherby, Yorks; Royal Academy of Music. Studied in Paris with Nadia Boulanger and Max Deutsch, 1958–59. Fellow Commoner in Creative Arts, Trinity Coll., Cambridge, 1966–70; Visiting Professor of Composition: Yale Music Sch., 1984–85, 1989; Boston Univ., 1986; Prof. of Music, Milton Avery Grad. Sch. of Arts, Bard Coll., NY, 1990–99; Prof. of Composition, Peabody Conservatory of Music, Baltimore, 1999–2008. Midsummer Prize, Corp. of London, 1980; Konssevitsky Foundn Award, 1990; Sudler Internat. Wind Band Prize, John Philip Sousa Soc., 1992; Stoeger Prize for Chamber Music, Chamber Music Soc., Lincoln Center, 1993. *Compositions include*: operas: One-Man Show, 1964; The Rising of The Moon, 1970; Sophie's Choice, 2002; *for orchestra*: Sinfonia, 1966; Sonata for Strings and Two Horns, 1967; Serenade, for small orchestra, 1973, 1977; Life Studies, for 15 solo strings, 1973; Odyssey, 1974–86; Summer Dances, 1981; Spring Music, 1983; The World in the Evening, 1988; Shahnama, 1992; Dance Scenes, 1995; Variations in Old Style, 1995, subseq. retitled Voices of Memory; Concert Suite from Sophie's Choice, 2004; *for instrumental soloist and orchestra*: Sonata Notturna, for cello and string orchestra, 1985; Little Concert, for oboe and chamber orchestra, 1987; Violin Concerto, 1993; Cor Anglais Concerto, 2001; *for voice and orchestra*: Nocturne, 1958; Scenes and Arias, 1962; *for wind band*: American Games, 1991; *chamber music*: String Quartet, no 1, 1965, no 2, 1983, no 3, 1994, no 4, 2005; Chamber Music for wind and piano quintet, 1962; Flute Quartet, 1981; Ghost Dances, for chamber ensemble, 1988; Piano Trio, 1991; String Sextet, 2006; *instrumental music*: Sonatina for flute and piano, 1957; Essay for organ, 1961; Personae for piano, nos I–III, 1973, IV–VI, 1985; Music of Memory, for solo guitar, 1989; Sonata for solo violin, 1997; Narration for solo cello, 2001; *vocal music*: The Voice of Love, for mezzo soprano and piano, 1966; Six Interiors, for high voice and guitar, 1966; La Vita Nuova, for soprano and chamber ensemble, 1979; Five American Folksongs, for high voice and piano, 1988; Roman Canticle, for mezzo soprano, flute, viola and harp, 1989; *choral music*: Five Epigrams, for chorus, 1960; Round, for chorus and piano, 1963; Five Irish Songs, for mixed chorus, 1973; Reverdie, five songs for male voices, 1975; Te Deum, for treble and tenor soli, chorus, congregation and organ, 1975; Nonsense Rhymes; songs and rounds for children, 1975–76; The Ruin, for double choir and solo horn, 1980; Three Hymns, for mixed choir and organ, 1989; One Foot in Eden Still, I Stand (motet for choir and soloists), 1990; Hymnus, for chorus and orch., 1996. *Address*: c/o Faber Music Ltd, Bloomsbury House, 74–77 Great Russell Street, WC1B 3DA. *Died 19 May 2009.*

MAWER, Ronald K.; *see* Knox-Mawer.

MAWSON, Stuart Radcliffe; Consultant Surgeon, Ear Nose and Throat Department, King's College Hospital, London, 1951–79, Head of Department, 1973–79, Hon. Consultant, 1979; *b* 4 March 1918; *s* of late Alec Robert Mawson, Chief Officer, Parks Dept, LCC, and Ena (*née* Grossmith), *d* of George Grossmith Jr, Actor Manager; *m* 1948, June Irene (*d* 2006), *d* of George Percival; two *s* two *d*. *Educ*: Canford Sch.; Trinity Coll., Cambridge; St Thomas's Hosp., London. BA Cantab 1940, MA 1976; MRCS, LRCP 1943; MB, BChir Cantab 1946; FRCS 1947; DLO 1948. House Surg., St Thomas's Hosp., 1943; RMO XIth Para. Bn, 1st Airborne Div., Arnhem, POW, 1944–45; Chief Asst, ENT Dept, St Thomas's Hosp., 1950; Consultant ENT Surgeon: King's Coll.

Hosp., 1951; Belgrave Hosp. for Children, 1951; Recog. Teacher of Oto-Rhino-Laryngology, Univ. of London, 1958. Chm., KCH Med. Cttee and Dist Management Team, 1977–79. FRSocMed (Pres. Section of Otology, 1974–75); Liveryman, Apothecaries' Soc.; former Mem. Council, Brit. Assoc. of Otolaryngologists. *Publications:* Diseases of the Ear, 1963, 6th edn 1998; (jtly) Essentials of Otolaryngology, 1967; (contrib.) Scott-Brown's Diseases of the Ear, Nose and Throat, 4th edn 1979; (contrib.) Modern Trends in Diseases of the Ear, Nose and Throat, 1972; Arnhem Doctor, 1981, repr. 2000; Doctor After Arnhem, 2006; numerous papers in sci. jls. *Clubs:* Aldeburgh Golf, Aldeburgh Yacht.
Died 20 Feb. 2008.

MAXWELL-HYSLOP, Sir Robert John, (Sir Robin), Kt 1992; *b* 6 June 1931; 2nd *s* of late Capt. A. H. Maxwell-Hyslop, GC, RN, and late Mrs Maxwell-Hyslop; *m* 1968, Joanna Margaret, *er d* of Thomas McCosh; two *d*. *Educ:* Stowe; Christ Church, Oxford (MA). Hons Degree in PPE Oxon, 1954. Joined Rolls-Royce Ltd Aero Engine Div., as graduate apprentice, Sept. 1954; served 2 years as such, then joined Export Sales Dept; PA to Sir David Huddie, Dir and GM (Sales and Service), 1958; left Rolls-Royce, 1960. Contested (C) Derby (North), 1959; MP (C) Tiverton Div. of Devon, Nov. 1960–1992. Member: Trade and Industry Select Cttee, 1971–92; Standing Orders Cttee, 1977–92; Procedure Select Cttee, 1978–92. Former Chm., Anglo-Brazilian Parly Gp. Politician of the Year Award (first recipient), Nat. Fedn of Self-employed and Small Businesses, 1989. Hon. Member, BVA, 2008 (Hon. Associate, 1977–2008). *Publications:* (ed) Secretary to the Speaker: Ralph Verney's correspondence, 1999. *Recreation:* naval and South American history. *Address:* 2 Lime Tree Mead, Tiverton, Devon EX16 4PX.
Died 13 Jan. 2010.

MAY, 3rd Baron *cr* 1935, of Weybridge; **Michael St John May;** Bt 1931; late Lieut, Royal Corps of Signals; *b* 26 Sept. 1931; *o s* of 2nd Baron May and of Roberta, *d* of George Ricardo Thoms; *S* father, 1950; *m* 1st, 1958, Dorothea Catherine Ann (marr. diss. 1963), *d* of Charles McCarthy, Boston, USA; 2nd, 1963, Jillian Mary, *d* of Albert Edward Shipton, Beggars Barn, Shutford, Oxon; one *s* one *d*. *Educ:* Wycliffe Coll., Stonehouse, Glos; Magdalene Coll., Cambridge. 2nd Lieut, Royal Signals, 1950. *Recreations:* sailing, travel. *Heir: s* Hon. Jasper Bertram St John May, *b* 24 Oct. 1965. *Address:* Gautherns Barn, Sibford Gower, Oxon OX15 5RY; 10 Rabbit Row, W8 4DX.
Died 22 Sept. 2006.

MAY, Prof. Brian Albert, FREng; independent development adviser; Professor of Agricultural Engineering, 1982–91, and Head, Cranfield Rural Institute, 1989–91, Cranfield Institute of Technology; Emeritus Professor, 1992; *b* 2 June 1936; *s* of Albert Robert and Eileen May; *m* 1961, Brenda Ann Smith; three *s*. *Educ:* Faversham Grammar Sch.; Aston Univ., Birmingham. Design Engineer, Massey Ferguson, 1958–63; National College of Agricultural Engineering: Lectr, 1963–68; Sen. Lectr, 1968–72; Principal Lectr, 1972–75; Head of Environmental Control and Processing Dept, 1972–75; Cranfield Institute of Technology: Prof. of Environmental Control and Processing, 1975–82; Head, Nat. Coll. of Agricl Engrg, later Silsoe Coll., 1976–89; Dean, Faculty of Agricl Engrg, Food Prodn and Rural Land Use, 1977–86. Dir, British Agricl Export Council, 1985–88. Member: Res. Requirements Bd on Plants and Soils, AFRC, 1980–86; Engrg Adv. Cttee, AFRC, 1984–88; Standing Cttee on University Entrance Requirements, 1984–91; Agric. and Vet. Cttee, 1985–91, Engrg and Technol. Adv. Cttee, 1991–95, British Council. Pres., IAgrE, 1984–86; FRAgS (Mem. Council, 1984–91); FREng (FEng 1990; Member: Overseas Affairs Cttee, 1991–95; Undergrad. Adv. Gp, 1993–). Governor, British Soc. for Res. in Agricl Engrg, 1979–90. Chm., Kent History Fedn, 2002–03 (Vice-Chm., 1999–2002); Pres., Ramsgate Soc., 2002– (Chm., 1995–2002). Chm. of Govs, Thanet Coll., 1997–2003. *Publications:* Power on

the Land, 1974; The Ramsgate Millennium Book, 2001; papers in agricl and engrg jls. *Recreations:* reading, travel, community affairs. *Address:* Fairfield Cottage, 6 Grafton Road, Yardley Gobion, Northants NN12 7UE. *T:* (01908) 542544; *e-mail:* brian.may6@btinternet.com. *Club:* Farmers'.
Died 17 Nov. 2007.

MAY, Charles Alan Maynard, FREng, FIET; lately Senior Director, Development and Technology, British Telecom; retired 1984; *b* 14 April 1924; *s* of late Cyril P. May and Katharine M. May; *m* 1947, Daphne, *o d* of late Bertram Carpenter; one *s* two *d*. *Educ:* The Grammar Sch., Ulverston, Cumbria; Christ's Coll., Cambridge (Mech. Sciences tripos 1944, MA). FIET (FIEE 1967); FREng (FEng 1982). Served REME and Indian Army, 1944–47. Entered Post Office Engrg Dept, 1948; Head of Electronic Switching Gp, 1956; Staff Engr, Computer Engrg Br., 1966; Dep. Dir (Engrg), 1970; Dir of Research, Post Office, later British Telecom, 1975–83. Dir, SIRA Ltd, 1982–89. Chm., IEE Electronics Divl Bd, 1977–78; Member: Council, IEE, 1970–72 and 1976–80; BBC Engrg Adv. Cttee, 1978–84; Adv. Cttee on Calibration and Measurement, 1978–83; Adv. Cttee, Dept of Electronic and Electrical Engrg, Sheffield Univ., 1979–82; Communications Systems Adv. Panel, Council of Educnl Technology, 1980–83; Ind. Adv. Bd, Sch. of Eng. and Applied Scis, Sussex Univ., 1981–84; Council, ERA Technology, 1983–88. Graham Young Lectr, Glasgow Univ., 1979. Vis. Examr, Imperial Coll., Univ. of London, 1980–82; External Examnr, NE London Polytechnic, 1982–86. Governor, Suffolk Coll. of Higher and Further Educn, 1980–83. *Publications:* contribs on telecommunications to learned jls. *Recreations:* gardening, snooker, bridge. *Address:* Corner Cottage, High Park Avenue, East Horsley, Leatherhead, Surrey KT24 5DD. *T:* (01483) 282521.
Died 2 April 2010.

MAYFIELD, Lt-Col Richard, DSO 1972; LVO 2000; Lieutenant, HM Body Guard of the Honourable Corps of Gentlemen-at-Arms, 1998–2000; *b* 2 Nov. 1930; *s* of Col Bryan Mayfield (formerly Scots Guards) and Rowena Lucy (*née* Hordern); *m* 1964, Rosemary Elisabeth Carlton, *d* of Col and Mrs Donald Matheson; one *s* two *d*. *Educ:* Radley Coll. Commnd Scots Guards, 1949; served FE, ME and Europe; Lt-Col 1971; in comd 1st Bn, Scots Guards, 1971–74; retd 1974. Mem., HM Body Guard of Hon. Corps of Gentlemen-at-Arms, 1981–2000 (Clerk of the Cheque and Adjutant, 1994–98). *Recreations:* shooting, collecting watercolours. *Address:* Home Farm House, Ewhurst Park, Ramsdell, Tadley, Hants RG26 5RQ. *T:* (01256) 850051. *Club:* Army and Navy.
Died 30 Nov. 2007.

MAYNARD, Edwin Francis George; Overseas Business Consultant; Member, Export Council Advisory Panel; HM Diplomatic Service, retired; Deputy High Commissioner, Calcutta, 1976–80; *b* 23 Feb. 1921; *s* of late Edwin Maynard, MD, FRCS, DPH, and Nancy Frances Tully; *m* 1945, Patricia Baker; one *s* one *d*; *m* 1963, Anna McGettrick; two *s*. *Educ:* Westminster. Served with Indian Army (4/8th (PWO) Punjab Regt and General Staff) (Major, GSO II), Middle East and Burma, 1939–46. BBC French Service, 1947; Foreign Office, 1949; Consul and Oriental Sec., Jedda, 1950; Second, later First, Sec., Benghazi, 1952; FO 1954; Bogota, 1956; Khartoum, 1959; FO, 1960; Baghdad, 1962; Founder Dir, Diplomatic Service Language Centre, 1966; Counsellor, Aden, 1967; Counsellor, New Delhi, 1968–72; Minister (Commercial), 1972–76, Chargé d'Affaires, 1974–75, Buenos Aires. *Recreations:* shooting, fishing, languages, gardening. *Address:* Littlebourne Court, Littlebourne, Canterbury, Kent CT3 1TU. *Club:* Brooks's.
Died 9 March 2006.

MAYNE, Very Rev. Michael Clement Otway, KCVO 1996; Dean of Westminster, 1986–96, then Dean Emeritus; Dean of the Order of the Bath, 1986–96; *b* 10 Sept. 1929; *s* of late Rev. Michael Ashton Otway Mayne and Sylvia Clementina Lumley Ellis; *m* 1965, Alison Geraldine McKie; one *s* one *d*. *Educ:* King's Sch., Canterbury; Corpus Christi Coll., Cambridge (MA);

Cuddesdon Coll., Oxford. Curate, St John the Baptist, Harpenden, 1957–59; Domestic Chaplain to the Bishop of Southwark, 1959–65; Vicar of Norton, Letchworth, 1965–72; Head of Religious Progs, BBC Radio, 1972–79; Vicar of Great St Mary's, Cambridge (the University Church), 1979–86. Select Preacher: Univ. of Cambridge, 1988; Univ. of Oxford, 1989, 1993. Chairman: London Ecumenical AIDS Forum, 1992–96; Sandford St Martin Trust, 1993–99. Trustee: Royal Foundn of Grey Coat Hosp., 1986–96; King George VI and Queen Elizabeth Foundn of St Catherine's, Cumberland Lodge, 1992–2005. Vice-Pres., St Christopher's Hospice, 2005– (Mem. Council, 1988–2004). Chm. Governors, Westminster Sch., 1986–96. *Publications:* Prayers for Pastoral Occasions, 1982; (ed) Encounters, 1985; A Year Lost and Found, 1987; This Sunrise of Wonder, 1995; Pray, love, remember, 1998; Learning to Dance, 2001; The Enduring Melody, 2006. *Recreations:* theatre, bird-watching, books, pottery, silence. *Address:* 37 St Mark's Road, Salisbury, Wilts SP1 3AY. *T:* (01722) 331069.
Died 22 Oct. 2006.

MAYNE, Richard (John); writer; broadcaster; *b* 2 April 1926; *s* of John William Mayne and Kate Hilda (*née* Angus); *m* 1st, Margot Ellingworth Lyon; 2nd, Jocelyn Mudie Ferguson; two *d*. *Educ:* St Paul's Sch., London; Trinity Coll., Cambridge (1st Cl. Hons Pts I and II, Hist. Tripos; MA and PhD). War service, Royal Signals, 1944–47. Styring, Sen., and Res. Scholar, and Earl of Derby Student, Trinity Coll., Cambridge, 1947–53; Leverhulme European Scholar, Rome, and Rome Corresp., New Statesman, 1953–54; Asst Tutor, Cambridge Inst. of Educn, 1954–56; Official: ECSC, Luxembourg, 1956–58; EEC, Brussels, 1958–63; Dir of Documentation Centre, Action Cttee for United States of Europe, and Personal Asst to Jean Monnet, Paris, 1963–66; Encounter: Paris Corresp., 1966–71; Co-Editor, 1985–90; Contributing Editor, 1990–91. Vis. Prof., Univ. of Chicago, 1971; Dir of Federal Trust for Educn and Res., 1971–73; Head of UK Offices, 1973–79; Special Advr, 1979–80, EEC. Hon. Professorial Fellow, UCW, Aberystwyth, 1986–89. Film critic: Sunday Telegraph, 1987–89; The European, 1990–98. Officier, Ordre des Arts et des Lettres (France), 2002. *Publications:* The Community of Europe, 1962; The Institutions of the European Community, 1968; The Recovery of Europe, 1970, rev. edn 1973; The Europeans, 1972; (ed) Europe Tomorrow, 1972; (ed) The New Atlantic Challenge, 1975; (trans.) The Memoirs of Jean Monnet, 1978 (Scott-Moncrieff Prize, 1979); Postwar: the dawn of today's Europe, 1983; (ed) Western Europe: a handbook, 1986; Federal Union: the pioneers, 1990; (trans.) Europe: a history of its peoples, 1990; (trans.) A History of Civilisations, 1993; (trans.) Illustrated History of Europe, 1993; The Language of Sailing, 2000; In Victory Magnanimity, in Peace Goodwill: a history of Wilton Park, 2003; (ed) Cross Channel Currents, 2004; Nuances, 2006. *Recreations:* travel, sailing, singing. *Address:* Albany Cottage, 24 Park Village East, Regent's Park, NW1 7PZ. *T:* (020) 7387 6654. *Clubs:* Groucho; Les Misérables (Paris).
Died 29 Nov. 2009.

MAYNE, William; writer; *b* 16 March 1928; *s* of William and Dorothy Mayne. *Educ:* Cathedral Choir Sch., Canterbury, 1937–42 (then irregularly). Pursued a career as novelist and published a large number of stories for children and young people—about 120 altogether, beginning in 1953. Lectr in Creative Writing, Deakin Univ., Geelong, Vic, Aust., academic years, 1976 and 1977; Fellow in Creative Writing, Rolle Coll., Exmouth, 1979–80. Library Assoc.'s Carnegie Medal for best children's book of the year (1956), 1957; Guardian Award for Children's Fiction, 1993; (jtly) Kurt Maschler Award, 1997. *Address:* c/o David Higham Associates, 5–8 Lower John Street, Golden Square, W1F 9HA.
Died 24 March 2010.

MAYO, 10th Earl of, *cr* 1785; **Terence Patrick Bourke;** Baron Naas, 1766; Viscount Mayo, 1781; Lieut RN (retired); Managing Director, Irish Marble Ltd, Galway, 1965–82; *b* 26 Aug. 1929; *s* of Hon. Bryan Longley Bourke (*d* 1961) and Violet Wilmot Heathcote Bourke (*d* 1950); *S* uncle, 1962; *m* 1st, 1952, Margaret Jane Robinson Harrison (marr. diss. 1987; she *d* 1992); three *s*; 2nd, 1987, Sally Anne, *o d* of F. G. Matthews; one *s*. *Educ:* St Aubyns, Rottingdean; RNC Dartmouth. Lieut, RN, 1952; Fleet Air Arm, 1952; Suez, 1956; Solo Aerobatic Displays, Farnborough, 1957; invalided, 1959. Mem., Gosport Borough Council, 1961–64; Pres., Gosport Chamber of Trade, 1962; Gov., Gosport Secondary Schs, 1963–64. Mem., Liberal Party, 1963–65; contested (L) Dorset South, 1964. *Heir: s* Lord Naas, *b* 11 June 1953.
Died 22 Sept. 2006.

MAYO, Rear-Adm. Robert William, CB 1965; CBE 1962; *b* 9 Feb. 1909; *s* of late Frank Mayo, Charminster; *m* 1st, 1942, Sheila (*d* 1974), *d* of late John Colvill, JP, of Campbeltown; one *s*; 2nd, 1980, Mrs Betty Washbrook. *Educ:* Weymouth Coll.; HMS Conway. RNR and officer with Royal Mail Steam Packet Co., 1926–37; Master's Certificate; transferred to Royal Navy, 1937; qualified Anti-Submarine Specialist, 1938; served Hong Kong and Malayan Area, 1939–41; Fleet Destroyers Atlantic and N Russian Convoys, 1942–44; commanded: HMS Aberdeen and Escort Gp 56, Atlantic, 1944–45; HMS Chevron, Mediterranean, 1947–48; HMS Theseus, 1951–52; served Korean War; Capt., HMS Osprey, 1956–58; Capt. i/c Clyde (US submarines), 1959–61; Capt., HMS St Angelo, 1961–63, and Cdre, Malta Naval Base, 1962–63; Rear-Adm. and Naval Dep. to C-in-C AFNORTH, 1964–66; retired, 1966.
Died 6 July 2007.

MEADE-KING, Charles Martin, MA; Headmaster, Plymouth College, 1955–73, retired; *b* 17 Aug. 1913; *s* of late G. C. Meade-King, solicitor, Bristol; *m* 1948, Mary (*née* Frazer); one *s* one *d*. *Educ:* Clifton Coll.; Exeter Coll., Oxford (Stapeldon Scholar). Asst Master, King's Sch., Worcester, 1935–38; Asst Master, Mill Hill Sch., 1938–40. Intelligence Corps, 1940–45. Housemaster, Mill Hill Sch., 1945–55. *Recreations:* history, arts, games. *Address:* Mistledown, Iron Mine Lane, Dousland, Yelverton, Devon PL20 6NA. *T:* (01822) 852237.
Died 27 April 2008.

MEAGHER, Most Rev. Anthony Giroux; Archbishop (RC) of Kingston (Ontario), since 2002; *b* 17 Nov. 1940; *s* of Frank Meagher and Lillian Meagher (*née* Giroux). *Educ:* Univ. of Toronto (BA 1963, BEd 1963); St Augustine's Seminary, Toronto; St Paul's Univ., Ottawa (STB (Theol.) 1972). Ordained priest, 1972; Associate Pastor and Rector: St Michael's Cathedral, Toronto, 1972–76; St John the Evangelist, Whitby, Ont, 1976–81; Pastor: Blessed Trinity, Willowdale, Ont, 1981–92; St Anthony of Padua, Brampton, Ont, 1992–97; Auxiliary Bp of Toronto and Vicar for Religious, Archdio. Toronto, 1997–2002. Titular Bp of Dura, 1997. Pres., Council, World Youth Day 2002, 1999–2006. *Address:* 390 Palace Road, Kingston, ON K7L 4T3, Canada. *T:* (613) 548 4461, *Fax:* (613) 548 4744; *e-mail:* archbishop@romancatholic.kingston.on.ca.
Died 14 Jan. 2007.

MEDD, David Leslie, OBE 1964; Consultant Architect, Department for Education (formerly Department of Education and Science), since 1978; *b* 5 Nov. 1917; *s* of Robert Tate Medd and Dorothy (*née* Rogers); *m* 1949, Mary Beaumont Crowley, OBE, architect (*d* 2005). *Educ:* Oundle; Architectural Assoc. (AA Dip. Hons). ARIBA 1941. Architects' Dept, Herts CC, 1946–49. Develt Gp, Architects and Building Br., Min. of Educn, later DES, 1949–78; private architectural work, 1978–. Commonwealth Fund Fellowship, 1958–59. Hon. DSc: Edinburgh, 1987; Hull, 1993. SADG Medal (France), 1941; Distinguished Service Certificate, BSI, 1992. *Publications:* School Furniture, 1981; contrib. to numerous learned jls, incl. HMSO building bulletins. *Recreations:* art, music, furniture making, gardening. *Address:* 5

Pennyfathers Lane, Harmer Green, Welwyn, Herts AL6 0EN. *T:* (01438) 714654. *Club:* Royal Over-Seas League.
Died 7 April 2009.

MEGAHY, Thomas, MBE 1979; *b* 16 July 1929; *s* of Samuel and Mary Megahy; *m* 1954, Jean (*née* Renshaw); three *s. Educ:* Wishaw High Sch.; Ruskin Coll., Oxford, 1953–55; College of Educn (Technical), Huddersfield, 1955–56 and 1968–69; London Univ. (external student), 1959–63. BScEcon London; DipEcon and PolSci Oxon; DipFE Leeds. Left school at 14 to work on railway; National Service, RN, 1947–49; railway signalman, 1950–53. Lecturer: Rotherham Coll. of Technology, 1956–59; Huddersfield Technical Coll., 1960–65; Park Lane Coll., Leeds, 1965–79. MEP (Lab) SW Yorks, 1979–99. European Parliament: Vice Pres., 1987–89; Dep. Leader, British Labour Group of MEPs, 1985–87; Member: Social Affairs Cttee, 1984–99; Transport and Tourism Cttee, 1989–99; Hungarian Jt Cttee, 1992–99; Substitute Mem., Social Affairs Cttee, 1984. Active member of Labour Party, 1950–; Chm., Scottish Labour League of Youth; Executive Mem., Dewsbury CLP, 1962–. Councillor, Mirfield UDC, 1963–74; Leader, Kirklees Metropolitan Borough Council, 1973–76; Opposition Leader, 1976–78. Member, Yorks and Humberside REPC, 1974–77; Vice-President: AMA, 1979–97; Yorks and Humberside Develt Assoc., 1981–. *Address:* 6 Lady Heton Grove, Mirfield, West Yorks WF14 9DY. *T:* (01924) 492680. *Died 5 Oct. 2008.*

MEGARRY, Rt Hon. Sir Robert (Edgar), Kt 1967; PC 1978; FBA 1970; a Judge of the Chancery Division of the High Court of Justice, 1967–76; the Vice-Chancellor: of that Division, 1976–81; of the Supreme Court, 1982–85; *b* 1 June 1910; *e s* of late Robert Lindsay Megarry, OBE, MA, LLB, Belfast, and Irene, *d* of Maj.-Gen. E. G. Clark; *m* 1936, Iris (*d* 2001), *e d* of late Elias Davies, Neath, Glam; three *d. Educ:* Lancing Coll.; Trinity Hall, Cambridge (MA, LLD; Hon. Fellow, 1973). Music Critic, Varsity, 1930–32. Solicitor, 1935–41; taught for Bar and Solicitors' exams, 1935–39; Mem., Faculty of Law, Cambridge Univ., 1939–40; Certificate of Honour, and called to Bar, Lincoln's Inn, 1944, in practice, 1946–67; QC 1956–67; Bencher, Lincoln's Inn, 1962, Treasurer 1981. Principal, 1940–44, and Asst Sec., 1944–46, Min. of Supply; Book Review Editor and Asst Ed., Law Quarterly Review, 1944–67; Dir of Law Society's Refresher Courses, 1944–47; Sub-Lector, Trinity Coll., Cambridge, 1945–46; Asst Reader, 1946–51, Reader, 1951–67, Hon. Reader, 1967–71 in Equity in the Inns of Court (Council of Legal Educn); Member: Gen. Council of the Bar, 1948–52; Lord Chancellor's Law Reform Cttee, 1952–73; Senate of Inns of Court and Bar, 1966–70, 1980–82; Adv. Council on Public Records, 1980–85; Consultant to BBC for Law in Action series, 1953–66; Chairman: Notting Hill Housing Trust, 1967–68; Bd of Studies, and Vice-Chm., Council of Legal Educn, 1969–71; Friends of Lancing Chapel, 1969–93; Incorporated Council of Law Reporting, 1972–87; Comparative Law Sect., British Inst. of Internat. and Comp. Law, 1977–89; President: Soc. of Public Teachers of Law, 1965–66; Lancing Club, 1974–98; Selden Soc., 1976–79. Visiting Professor: New York Univ. Sch. of Law, 1960–61; Osgoode Hall Law Sch., Toronto, 1964; Regents' Prof., UCLA, 1983; Lectures: John F. Sonnett, Fordham Univ., 1982; Tyrrell Williams, Washington Univ., St Louis, 1983; Leon Ladner, Univ. of British Columbia, 1984. Visitor: Essex Univ., 1983–90; Clare Hall, Cambridge, 1984–89. Hon. LLD: Hull, 1963; Nottingham, 1979; Law Soc. of Upper Canada (Osgoode Hall), 1982; London, 1988; DU Essex, 1991. Hon. Life Member: Canadian Bar Assoc., 1971; Amer. Law Inst., 1985. *Publications:* The Rent Acts, 1939, 11th edn: Vols 1 and 2, 1988; Vol. 3, 1989, 2nd edn as Megarry's Assured Tenancies by T. M. Fancourt, 1999; A Manual of the Law of Real Property, 1946, 8th edn (ed A. J. Oakley), 2002; Lectures on the Town and Country Planning Act, 1947, 1949; Miscellany-at-Law, 1955; (with Prof. Sir William Wade QC) The Law of Real Property, 1957, 6th edn (ed C. Harpum) 2000; Lawyer

and Litigant in England (Hamlyn Lectures, 1962); Arabinesque-at-Law, 1969; Inns Ancient and Modern, 1972; A Second Miscellany-at-Law, 1973; Editor, Snell's Equity, 23rd edn 1947, (with P. V. Baker, QC) 24th edn 1954 to 27th edn 1973; A New Miscellany-at-Law, 2005; contrib. to legal periodicals. *Recreation:* heterogeneous. *Address:* 5 Stone Buildings, Lincoln's Inn, WC2A 3XT. *T:* (020) 7242 8607. *Died 11 Oct. 2006.*

MEGAW, Arthur Hubert Stanley, (Peter), CBE 1951; FSA; *b* Dublin, 14 July 1910; *s* of late Arthur Stanley Megaw; *m* 1937, Elene Elektra (*d* 1993), *d* of late Helias Mangoletsi, Koritsa, Albania; no *c. Educ:* Campbell Coll., Belfast; Peterhouse, Cambridge (Walston Student, 1931; MA). Macmillan Student, British School of Archæology at Athens, 1932–33, Asst Dir, 1935–36; Dir of Antiquities, Cyprus, 1936–60; Field Dir, Byzantine Institute, Istanbul, 1961–62; Dir, British Sch. of Archæology, Athens, 1962–68. CStJ 1967. *Publications:* (with A. J. B. Wace) Hermopolis Magna-Ashmunein, Alexandria, 1959; (with E. J. W. Hawkins) The Church of the Panagia Kanakariá in Cyprus, its Mosaics and Frescoes, 1977; various papers in archæological journals. *Recreation:* travel. *Address:* 27 Perrins Walk, NW3 6TH. *Died 28 June 2006.*

MEGGESON, Michael; Solicitor and Notary Public; Senior Partner, Warner, Goodman & Streat, 1986–94; a Recorder of the Crown Court, 1981–92; *b* 6 Aug. 1930; *s* of Richard Ronald Hornsey Meggeson and Marjorie Meggeson; *m* 1975, Alison Margaret (*née* Wood). *Educ:* Sherborne; Gonville and Caius Coll., Cambridge (BA 1953; MA 1963). Nat. Service, RA, 1949–50; 5th Bn Royal Hampshire Regt, TA, 1950–63. Admitted a Solicitor, 1957; Asst Solicitor, 1957–59, Partner, 1959–94, Warner & Sons, subseq. Warner Goodman & Co., and Warner, Goodman & Streat; Dep. Circuit Judge, 1978–81. Mem. Cttee, Solicitors Staff Pension Fund, 1980–2004 (Chm., Cttee of Management, 1988–92); Pres., Hampshire Incorp. Law Soc., 1981–82. *Recreations:* sailing, golf, gardening, music. *Address:* Church Farm, Langrish, near Petersfield, Hants GU32 1RQ. *T:* (01730) 264470. *Clubs:* Royal Southern Yacht (Hamble); Hayling Island Golf, Liphook Golf. *Died 22 Aug. 2010.*

MELDRUM, Maj.-Gen. Bruce, CB 1991; OBE 1986; Chief of New Zealand General Staff, 1989–92; *b* 15 March 1938; *s* of late Ian Maitland Meldrum and of Vivienne Meldrum; *m* 1960, Janet Louise Boyling; one *s* one *d. Educ:* Feilding Agricl High Sch., NZ; RMC Duntroon. Lieut, RNZAC, 1959; Troop Comdr, Queen Alexandra's Regt, 1960–62; RAC Sch. of Tank Technol., UK, 1962–63; Sen. Instructor, then Chief Instructor, Sch. of Armour, Waiouru, 1963–66; OC 1 Armoured Sqdn, 1966–68; with US 11th Armoured Cavalry Regt, S Vietnam, Nov.–Dec. 1966; Staff Officer, Trng Directorate, Army HQ, 1968–69; HQ NZ Force Far East, Singapore, 1969–71; HQ NZ V Force, Saigon, 1971–72; Australian Comd and Staff Coll., 1972; Bde Maj., HQ 1 Inf. Bde, 1972–74; Lt-Col 1974; Staff Officer, HQ Field Force Comd, 1974–76; Dir, Ops and Plans, Army Gen. Staff, 1976–78; Australian JSSC, 1978; Special Projects Officer, 1978–80; Col 1980; Defence Advr, NZ High Commn, Kuala Lumpur, 1980–83; Comdr, Army Trng Gp, 1983–85; rcds, 1985–86; DCGS, 1986–89; Brig. 1987; Maj.-Gen. 1989. *Recreations:* golf, walking, reading. *Club:* Northern (Auckland). *Died 14 June 2006.*

MELLERS, Prof. Wilfrid Howard, OBE 1982; DMus; author; composer; Professor of Music, University of York, 1964–81, then Emeritus; *b* 26 April 1914; *s* of Percy Wilfrid Mellers and Hilda Maria (*née* Lawrence); *m* 1st, 1940, Vera Muriel (*née* Hobbs) (marr. diss.); 2nd, 1950, Peggy Pauline (*née* Lewis) (marr. diss. 1975); two *d*; 3rd, 1987, Robin Hildyard. *Educ:* Leamington Coll.; Downing Coll., Cambridge (Hon. Fellow 2001); BA Cantab 1939; MA Cantab 1945; DMus Birmingham 1962. FGSM 1982. Supervisor in English and College Lecturer in Music, Downing Coll., Cambridge, 1945–48;

Staff Tutor in Music, Extra Mural Dept, University of Birmingham, 1949–60; Visiting Mellon Prof. of Music, University of Pittsburgh, USA, 1960–62; Vis. Prof., City Univ., 1984–87. Hon. DPhil City, 1981. *Publications:* Music and Society, 1946; Studies in Contemporary Music, 1948; François Couperin and the French Classical Tradition, 1950, 2nd edn 1987; Music in the Making, 1951; Man and his Music, 1957; Harmonious Meeting, 1964; Music in a New Found Land, 1964, 2nd edn 1987; Caliban Reborn: renewal in 20th-century music, 1967 (US), 1968 (GB); Twilight of the Gods: the Beatles in retrospect, 1973; Bach and the Dance of God, 1981; Beethoven and the Voice of God, 1983; A Darker Shade of Pale: a backdrop to Bob Dylan, 1984; Angels of the Night: popular female singers of our time, 1986; The Masks of Orpheus, 1987; Vaughan Williams and the Vision of Albion, 1989, 2nd edn 1997; Le Jardin Parfumé: homage to Federico Mompou, 1990; The Music of Percy Grainger, 1992; The Music of Francis Poulenc, 1993; New Worlds and Old (selected music journalism), 1997; Singing in the Wilderness, 2001; Celestial Music: some masterpieces of European religious music, 2001; *compositions* include: Requiem Canticle; Cloud Canticle; Canticum Incarnationi, 1960; Chants and Litanies of Carl Sandburg, 1960; Missa Brevis, 1961; Aubade, for recorder and piano, 1961, for strings, 2001; Alba in 9 Metamorphoses, 1962; Rose of May, for voice, flute, clarinet and string quartet, 1964; Life-Cycle, 1967; Yeibichai, 1968; Canticum Resurrectionis, 1968; Natalis Invicti Solis, for piano, 1969; The Word Unborn, 1970; The Ancient Wound, 1970; De Vegetabilis et Animalibus, 1971; Venery for Six Plus, 1971; Sun-flower: the Quaternity of William Blake, 1972–73; Opus Alchymicum, for organ, 1972, revd 1995; The Key of the Kingdom, 1976; Rosae Hermeticae, 1977; A Blue Epiphany, for guitar, 1977; Shaman Songs, 1980, The Wellspring of Loves, for strings, 1981; Hortus Rosarium, 1986; The Echoing Green, for voice and recorders, 1995; A Fount of Fair Dances, for solo recorder and strings, 2003. *Address:* Oliver Sheldon House, 17 Aldwark, York YO1 7BX. *T:* (01904) 638686.   *Died 16 May 2008.*

MELLOR, David, CBE 2001 (OBE 1981); DesRCA; RDI 1962; FCSD; designer, manufacturer and retailer; Chairman, Crafts Council, 1982–84; *b* 5 Oct. 1930; *s* of Colin Mellor; *m* 1966, Fiona MacCarthy; one *s* one *d*. *Educ:* Sheffield College of Art; Royal College of Art (DesRCA and Silver Medal, 1953, Hon. Fellow 1966); British School at Rome. Set up silver-smithing workshop, Sheffield, 1954; designer and maker of silver for Worshipful Co. of Goldsmiths, Cutlers' Co., Southwell Minster, Essex Univ., Darwin Coll., Cambridge, among others, and range of silver tableware for use in British embassies; designer of fountain in bronze for Botanic Gdns, Cambridge, 1970; concurrently opened industrial design office. Consultancies, 1954–, include: Walker & Hall, Abacus Municipal, Glacier Metal, ITT, Post Office, British Rail, James Neill Tools; Magis Furniture; Cons. to DoE on design of traffic signals, 1965–70. Trustee: V&A Museum, 1984–88; Peak Park Trust, 1992–96. Work in collections: Goldsmiths' Co., V&A, Millennium Galls, Sheffield, Mus. of Modern Art, NY; retrospective exhibn, Design Mus., 1998; permanent exhibn, David Mellor Design Mus., Hathersage, 2006. Liveryman, Goldsmiths' Co., 1980; Freeman, Cutlers' Co. of Hallamshire, 1981. FCSD (FSIAD 1964; CSD Medal 1988). Hon. Fellow, Sheffield City Polytechnic, 1979; Hon. DLitt Sheffield Univ., 1986; Hon. DDes De Montfort, 1997; Hon. Dr RCA, 1999; Hon. DTech Loughborough, 2006. Awards: Design Centre: 1957, 1959, 1962, 1965, 1966; Design Council: 1974, 1977; RSA Presidential Award for Design Management, 1981; V&A Lifetime Achievement Award, 2006. *Address:* The Round Building, Hathersage, Sheffield S32 1BA. *T:* (01433) 650220.   *Died 7 May 2009.*

MELLY, (Alan) George (Heywood); professional jazz singer; with John Chilton's Feetwarmers, 1974–2002; *b* 17 Aug. 1926; *s* of Francis Heywood and Edith Maud Melly; *m* 1955, Victoria Vaughan (marr. diss. 1962); one *d*; *m* 1963, Diana Margaret Campion Dawson; one *s* and one step *d*. *Educ:* Stowe School. Able Seaman, RN, 1944–47. Art Gallery Asst, London Gallery, 1948–50; sang with Mick Mulligan's Jazz Band, 1949–61. Wrote Flook strip cartoon balloons (drawn by Trog (Wally Fawkes)), 1956–71. Critic, The Observer: pop music, 1965–67; TV, 1967–71; films, 1971–73. Film scriptwriter: Smashing Time, 1968; Take a Girl Like You, 1970. Pres., British Humanist Assoc., 1972–74. Critic of the Year, IPC Nat. Press Awards, 1970. *Publications:* I Flook, 1962; Owning Up, 1965; Revolt into Style, 1970; Flook by Trog, 1970; Rum Bum and Concertina, 1977; (with Barry Fantoni) The Media Mob, 1980; Tribe of One: Great Naive and Primitive Painters of the British Isles, 1981; (with Walter Dorin) Great Lovers, 1981; Mellymobile, 1982; (ed) Edward James, Swans Reflecting Elephants: my early years, 1982; Scouse Mouse, 1984; It's All Writ Out for You: the life and work of Scottie Wilson, 1986; (with Michael Woods) Paris and the Surrealists, 1991; Don't tell Sybil: an intimate memoir of E. L. T. Mesens, 1997; Hooked, fishing memories, 2000; Slowing Down, 2005. *Recreations:* trout fishing, singing and listening to blues of 1920s, collecting modern paintings. *Address:* 81 Frithville Gardens, Shepherds Bush, W12 7JQ. *Clubs:* Colony Room, Chelsea Arts.   *Died 5 July 2007.*

MELMOTH, Christopher George Frederick Frampton, CMG 1959; South Asia Department, International Bank for Reconstruction and Development, 1962–75, retired; *b* 25 Sept. 1912; *s* of late George Melmoth and Florence Melmoth; *m* 1946, Maureen Joan (*née* Brennan); three *d*. *Educ:* Sandringham Sch., Forest Gate. Accountant Officer, Co-ordination of Supplies Fund, Malta, 1942–45; Administrative Officer, Hong Kong, 1946–55; Minister of Finance, Uganda, 1956–62. *Recreation:* choral music. *Address:* Hoptons Cottage, Kemerton, Tewkesbury, Glos GL20 7JE.   *Died 27 April 2006.*

MELROSE, Prof. Denis Graham; Professor of Surgical Science, Royal Postgraduate Medical School, 1968–83, Emeritus since 1983; *b* 20 June 1921; *s* of late Thomas Robert Gray Melrose, FRCS and Floray Collings; *m* 1945, Ann, *d* of late Kathleen Tatham Warter; two *s*. *Educ:* Sedbergh Sch.; University Coll., Oxford; UCH London. MA, BM, BCh, MRCP, FRCS. Junior appts at Hammersmith Hosp. and Redhill County Hosp., Edgware, 1945; RNVR, 1946–48; subseq. Lectr, later Reader, Royal Postgrad. Med. Sch.; Nuffield Travelling Fellow, USA, 1956; Fulbright Fellow, 1957; Associate in Surgery, Stanford Univ. Med. Sch., 1958. Fellow: RPMS, 1993; ICSM, 1999. *Publications:* numerous papers and chapters in books, particularly on heart surgery, heart lung machine and med. engrg. *Recreations:* sailing, ski-ing. *Address:* Ses Roques Port, G4 Attico, Calle del Mar 14, Santa Eulalia del Rio, 07840 Ibiza, Baleares, Spain. *T:* (971) 338045, *Fax:* (971) 336902. *Club:* Royal Naval Sailing Association.   *Died 2 July 2007.*

MENDL, His Honour James Henry Embleton; a Circuit Judge at Knightsbridge Crown Court, 1974–93; *b* 23 Oct. 1927; *s* of late R. W. S. Mendl, barrister and author, and Dorothy Williams Mendl (*née* Burnett), and *g s* of late Sir S. F. Mendl, KBE; *m* 1971, Helena Augusta Maria Schrama, *d* of late J. H. and H. H. Schrama-Jekat, The Netherlands. *Educ:* Harrow; University Coll., Oxford (MA). Called to Bar, Inner Temple, 1953; South Eastern Circuit. Commissioned. Worcestershire Regt, 1947; served: Egypt, with 2nd N Staffs, 1947–48; with Royal Signals (TA), 1952–54, and Queen's Royal Regt (TA) (Captain, 1955), 1954–56. Councillor, Royal Borough of Kensington and Chelsea, 1964–74 (Vice-Chm., Town Planning Cttee, 1969; Chm. (Vice-Chm. 1970), Libraries Cttee, 1971). Contested (C) Gateshead East, 1966. Liveryman, Musicians' Co., 1997–.

Recreations: music (incl. singing with Noblemen and Gentlemen's Catch Club), reading, theatre. *Clubs:* Garrick, Lansdowne. *Died 13 July 2008.*

MENDOZA, Vivian P.; *see* Pereira-Mendoza.

MENOTTI, Gian Carlo; composer; Founder, Spoleto Festivals, Italy and Charleston, USA; *b* Cadegliano, Italy, 7 July 1911. *Educ:* The Curtis Institute of Music, Philadelphia, Pa. Resident in the United States since 1928. Teacher of Composition at Curtis Inst. of Music, 1948–55. First performances of works include: Amelia Goes to the Ball (opera), 1936; The Old Maid and the Thief (radio opera), 1939 (later staged); The Island God, 1942; Sebastian (Ballet), 1943; Piano Concerto in F, 1945; The Medium (opera), 1946 (later filmed); The Telephone (opera), 1947; Errand into the Maze (ballet), 1947; The Consul (opera), 1950 (Pulitzer Prize); Apocalypse (orchestral), 1951; Amahl and the Night Visitors (television opera), 1951; Violin Concerto in A Minor, 1952; The Saint of Bleeker Street (opera), 1954 (Pulitzer Prize); The Unicorn, The Gorgon, and the Manticore, 1956; Maria Golovin (television opera), 1958; The Last Savage (opera), 1963; The Death of the Bishop of Brindisi (oratorio), 1963; Martin's Lie (opera), 1964; Canti della Lontananza (song cycle), 1967; Help, Help, the Globolinks (opera), 1968; The Leper (drama), 1970; Triplo Concerto a Tre (symphonic piece), 1970; The Most Important Man (opera), 1971; Fantasia for 'cello and orch., 1971; Tamu-Tamu (opera), 1973; The Egg (opera), 1976; The Trial of the Gypsy (opera), 1976; Landscapes & Remembrances, for chorus and orch., 1976; Symphony no 1, 1976; Chip & his Dog (opera), 1978; Juana la Loca (opera), 1979; Mass, O Pulchritudo, 1979; Song of Hope (cantata), 1980; A Bride from Pluto (opera), 1982; St Teresa (cantata), 1982; The Boy Who Grew Too Fast (opera), 1982; Goya (opera), 1986; Giorno di Nozze (opera), 1988; wrote libretto for Vanessa (opera, by Samuel Barber), 1958. Internationally recognised as a producer; has worked at the greatest opera houses, including La Scala, Metropolitan, Paris Opéra, Vienna Staatsoper. Guggenheim Award, 1946, 1947; Kennedy Centre Award, 1984; NYC Mayor's Liberty Award; Hon. Association, Nat. Inst. of Arts and Letters. *Publications:* his major works have been published, also some minor ones; author of all his libretti, most of which in English. *Address:* c/o Thea Dispeker, 59 East 54th Street, New York, NY 10022, USA; Yester House, Gifford, Haddington, East Lothian EH41 4JF. *Died 1 Feb. 2007.*

MENTER, Sir James (Woodham), Kt 1973; PhD; ScD; FRS 1966; CPhys, FInstP; Principal, 1976–86, Fellow, 1986, Queen Mary College, London University; *b* 22 Aug. 1921; *s* of late Horace Menter and Jane Anne Lackenby; *m* 1947, Marjorie Jean, *d* of late Thomas Stodart Whyte-Smith, WS and Jean Witherow (*née* Gilchrist); two *s* one *d*. *Educ:* Dover Grammar Sch.; Peterhouse, Cambridge (MA; PhD 1949; ScD 1960). Experimental Officer, Admty, 1942–45; Research, Cambridge Univ., 1946–54 (ICI Fellow, 1951–54; Sir George Beilby Mem. Award, 1954); Tube Investments Research Labs, Hinxton Hall, 1954–68; Dir of R & D, Tube Investments Ltd, 1965–76. Director: Tube Investments Res. Labs, 1961–68; Tube Investments Ltd, 1965–86; Round Oak Steelworks Ltd, 1967–76; British Petroleum Co., 1976–87; Steetley Co., 1981–85. Member: SRC, 1967–72; Cttee of Inquiry into Engrg Profession, 1977–79; a Vice-Pres., Royal Society, 1971–76, Treasurer, 1972–76; Royal Institution: a Manager, 1982–84; a Vice-Pres., 1983–85; Chm. Council, 1984–85. Fellow, Churchill Coll., Cambridge, 1966–88. President: Inst. of Physics, 1970–72; Metals Soc., 1976; Dep. Chm., Adv. Council Applied R&D, 1976–79. Mem. (part-time), BSC, 1976–79. Member: Bd of Govs, London Hosp. Med. Coll.; Ct of Governors, City of London Polytechnic, 1982–85; Court, Stirling Univ., 1988–94. Hon. FRMS 1974; Hon. FRSE 1992. Hon. DTech Brunel, 1974; DUniv Stirling, 1995. Bessemer Medal, Iron and Steel Inst., 1973;

Glazebrook Medal and Prize, Inst. of Physics, 1977. *Publications:* scientific papers in Proc. Royal Society, Advances in Physics, Jl Iron and Steel Inst., etc. *Recreation:* fishing. *Address:* Strathlea, Taybridge Terrace, Aberfeldy, Perthshire PH15 2BS. *Died 18 July 2006.*

MENTETH, Sir James (Wallace) Stuart-, 6th Bt *cr* 1838; *b* 13 Nov. 1922; *e s* of 5th Bt and Winifred Melville (*d* 1968), *d* of Daniel Francis and *widow* of Capt. Rupert G. Raw, DSO; *S* father, 1952; *m* 1949, Dorothy Patricia, *d* of late Frank Greaves Warburton; two *s*. *Educ:* Fettes; St Andrews Univ.; Trinity Coll., Oxford (MA). Served War of 1939–45, with Scots Guards, 1942–44; on active service in North Africa and Italy (Anzio) (severely wounded). *Recreations:* gardening, ornithology. *Heir: s* Charles Greaves Stuart-Menteth [*b* 25 Nov. 1950; *m* 1976, Nicola St Lawrence; four *d* (one *s* decd)]. *Died 9 Oct. 2008.*

MENZIES, John Maxwell; Life President, John Menzies, since 1997 (Chairman, 1952–97); *b* 13 Oct. 1926; *s* of late John Francis Menzies, and of Cynthia Mary Graham; *m* 1953, Patricia Eleanor, *d* of late Comdr Sir Hugh Dawson, Bt, CBE and Lady Dawson; four *d*. *Educ:* Eton. Lieut Grenadier Guards. Berwickshire CC, 1954–57. Director: Scottish American Mortgage Co., 1959–63; Standard Life Assurance Co., 1960–63; Vidal Sassoon Inc., 1969–80; Gordon & Gotch plc, 1970–85; Atlantic Assets Trust, 1973–88 (Chm., 1983–88); Ivory & Sime Enterprise Capital plc (formerly Independent Investment Co. plc), 1973–96 (Chm., 1983–96); Ivory & Sime plc, 1980–83; Personal Assets Trust PLC, 1981–92; Bank of Scotland, 1984–94; Guardian Royal Exchange, 1985–96; Malcolm Innes Gallery (formerly Malcolm Innes & Partners), 1989–2000; Kames Dairies Ltd, 1995–. Trustee, Newsvendors' Benevolent Instn, 1974–95 (Pres., 1968–74; Life Vice Pres., 1996). Mem. Bd of Trustees, Nat. Library of Scotland, 1991–99. Mem., Royal Co. of Archers, HM's Body Guard for Scotland. Landowner. *Recreations:* shooting, reading, travel. *Address:* Kames, Duns, Berwickshire. *T:* (01890) 840202. *Clubs:* Boodle's, Beefsteak; New (Edinburgh); Lyford Cay (Nassau). *Died 21 Feb. 2007.*

MERCHANT, Piers Rolf Garfield; *b* 2 Jan. 1951; *s* of Garfield Frederick Merchant and Audrey Mary Rolfe-Martin; *m* 1977, Helen Joan Burrluck; one *s* one *d*. *Educ:* Nottingham High Sch.; Univ. of Durham (BA (Hons) Law and Politics, MA Political Philosophy). Reporter, Municipal Correspondent, Chief Reporter, Dep. News Editor, 1973–80, News Editor, 1980–82, The Journal; Editor, Conservative Newsline, 1982–84. Dir of Corporate Publicity, NEI plc, 1987–90; Dir of Public Affairs, The Advertising Assoc., 1990–92; Man. Dir, Cavendish Gp plc, 1998–2000 (non-exec. Dir, 2000–01); Exec. Dir, Made in London, 2000–04; Dir of Campaigns, LCCI, 2001–04; Actg Chief Exec., UKIP, 2004. Contested (C) Newcastle upon Tyne Central, 1979. MP (C): Newcastle upon Tyne Central, 1983–87; Beckenham, 1992–Oct. 1997. PPS to Sec. of State for Social Security, 1992–97. Co-Chm., Freeflow of Information Cttee, Internat. Parly Gp, 1986–91; Vice-Chm., All-Party Parly Cttee on AIDS, 1987. Contested (UK Ind), North-East, EP, 2004. Pol Advr to Roger Knapman, Ldr of UKIP, 2002–06. Non-executive Director: Eur. Public Health Foundn, 1993–2004; Tyne and Wear Waste Saver Ltd, 1996–98; London Asset Mgt Ltd, 2000–04; 91 St George's Drive Co. Ltd, 2006–. Member: London Business Bd, 2001–02; London Sports Bd, 2001–03; Team London, 2002–04; London Fund Manager's Adv. Bd, 2002–04; Econs Res. Adv. Bd, GLA, 2003–04. Mem., Sen. Common Room. UC. Durham. *Publications:* newspaper articles and features. *Recreations:* swimming, walking, genealogy, electronics, computers. *Address: e-mail:* pmerchant@yahoo.co.uk. *Died 21 Sept. 2009.*

MERI, Lennart; President, Republic of Estonia, 1992–2001; *b* Tallinn, 29 March 1929; *s* of Georg-Peeter Meri and Alice-Brigitta Meri (*née* Engmann); *m* 1st, Regina Ojavere; two *s*; 2nd, Helle Pihlak; one *d*. *Educ:*

schs in Berlin, Paris, Yaransk and Tallinn; Tartu Univ., Siberia (grad *cum laude* in hist. 1953). Family deported to Siberia, 1941–46. Hd, MS Section, and dramatist, Vanemuine Theatre, 1953–55; producer, Estonian Radio, 1955–61; scriptwriter, 1963–68, and producer, 1968–71, 1986–88, Tallinnfilm (*films* depicting the history of Finno-Ugric people include: Veelinnurahvas, 1970; Linnutee tuuled, 1977; Kaleva hääled, 1986; Toorumi pojad, 1989; Šamaan, 1997). For. Relns Sec., Estonian Writers Union, 1985–87; Founder and Dir, Estonian Inst., 1988–90; Minister of Foreign Affairs, 1990–92; Ambassador to Finland, April–Oct. 1992. Active in Estonian Popular Front and Nat. Heritage Preservation Assoc., during 1980s. Member: Internat. Council, Meml Foundn for Victims of Communism, 1995–; Inter-Parly Council against Antisemitism, 1997–. Member: Estonian Writers Union, 1963; Estonian Cinematographers Union, 1966; Eur. Acad. of Arts, Scis and Humanities (Co-Pres., Cttee of Honour, 1993–); Estonian Acad. of Scis, 2001. For. Mem., Kalevala Soc., Finland, 1975; Corresp. Mem., Finnish Literary Soc., 1976; Hon. Mem., Writers' Union, Finland, 1982. Hon. DLitt: Helsinki, 1986; Lapland (Finland), 1999; Turku, 2000; St Olaf, 2000. East-West Liberty Award, Inst. for East-West Studies, New York, 1996; Coudenhove-Kalergi European Award, Coudenhove-Kalergi Foundn, 1996; Crans Montana Universal Forum Foundn Award, 1997. Holds foreign decorations. *Publications:* Kobrade ja karakurtide jälgedes (Following the trails of cobras and black widows), 1959; Laevapoisid rohelisel ookeanil (Shipmates on the Green Ocean), 1961; Tulemägede maale (To the land of fiery mountains), 1964; Virmaliste väraval (At the gate of Northern Lights), 1974; Hõbevalge (Silverwhite), 1976; Lähenevad rannad (Approaching coasts), 1977; Hõbevalgem (Silverwhiter), 1984; (jtly) 1940 Eestis (1940 in Estonia: documents and materials), 1989; Tulen maasta, jonka nimi on Viro (Coming from the country called Estonia), 1995; Presidential Speeches, 1996 (trans. German); Riigmured (State Worries), 2001; translations of works by Remarque, Vercors, Greene, Boulle and Solzhenitsyn. *Recreations:* history, literature, maps. *Address:* 74001 Haabneeme, Tallinn, Estonia. *T:* (2) 6931986.　　　　　　　　　　*Died 14 March 2006.*

MERLYN-REES, Baron *cr* 1992 (Life Peer), of Morley and South Leeds in the County of West Yorkshire and of Cilfynydd in the County of Mid Glamorgan; **Merlyn Merlyn-Rees;** PC 1974; *b* Cilfynydd, South Wales, 18 Dec. 1920; *s* of late L. D. and E. M. Rees; name changed to Merlyn-Rees by deed poll, 1992; *m* 1949, Colleen Faith (*née* Cleveley); three *s. Educ:* Elementary Schools, S Wales and Wembley, Middx; Harrow Weald Grammar School; London School of Economics; London Univ. Institute of Education. Nottingham Univ. Air Sqdn; Served RAF, 1941–46; demobilised as Sqdn Ldr. Teacher in Economics and History, Harrow Weald Grammar School, 1949–60. Organised Festival of Labour, 1960–62. Lecturer in Economics, Luton Coll. of Technology, 1962–63; contested (Lab) Harrow East, Gen. Elections 1955 and 1959 and by-election, 1959. MP (Lab) South Leeds, June 1963–83, Morley and Leeds South, 1983–92. PPS to Chancellor of the Exchequer, 1964; Parly Under-Sec. of State, MoD (Army), 1965–66; MoD (RAF), 1966–68; Home Office, 1968–70; Mem., Shadow Cabinet, 1972–74; Opposition spokesman on NI affairs, 1972–74; Sec. of State for NI, 1974–76; Home Sec., 1976–79; Shadow Home Sec., 1979–80; Opposition spokesman on Energy, 1980–83. Member: Cttee to examine operation of Section 2 of Official Secrets Act, 1971; Falklands Is Inquiry Cttee, 1982. Pres., Video Standards Council, 1990–. Pres., South Leeds Groundwork Trust, 2001– (Chm., 1987–97). Chancellor, Univ. of Glamorgan, 1994–2001. Hon. Fellow, Goldsmiths' Coll., London Univ., 1984. Hon. LLD: Wales, 1987; Leeds, 1992; DUniv Glamorgan, 2002. *Publications:* The Public Sector in the Mixed Economy, 1973; Northern Ireland: a personal perspective, 1985. *Recreation:* reading. *Address:* c/o House of Lords, SW1A 0PW.　　　　　　　　　　　　*Died 5 Jan. 2006.*

MERRIFIELD, Prof. (Robert) Bruce; Professor, since 1966, John D. Rockefeller Jr Professor, since 1984, Rockefeller University; *b* 15 July 1921; *s* of George and Lorene Merrifield; *m* 1949, Elizabeth L. Furlong; one *s* five *d. Educ:* Univ. of California, Los Angeles (BA 1943, Chemistry; PhD 1949, Biochemistry). Chemist, Philip R. Park Research Foundn, 1943–44; Research Asst, UCLA Med. Sch., 1948–49; Asst to Associate Prof., Rockefeller Inst. for Med. Research, 1949–66. Nobel Guest Prof., Uppsala, 1968. Member: Amer. Chem. Soc.; Amer. Soc. of Biological Chemists; Amer. Inst. of Chemists; Nat. Acad. of Sciences. Associate Editor, Internat. Jl of Peptide and Protein Research; Mem. Editl Bd of Analytical Biochemistry. Numerous hon. degrees from Amer. univs and colls. Lasker Award for Basic Med. Research, 1969; Gairdner Award, 1970; Intra-Science Award, 1970; Amer. Chem. Soc. Award for Creative Work in Synthetic Organic Chemistry, 1972; Nichols Medal, 1973; Instrument Specialties Co. Award, Univ. of Nebraska, 1977; Alan E. Pierce Award, 1979; Nobel Prize in Chemistry, 1984; Hirschmann Award in Peptide Chem., ACS, 1990; Josef Rudinger Award, Eur. Peptide Soc., 1990. Order of San Carlos (Columbia), 1984. *Publications:* numerous papers in sci. jls, esp. on peptide chemistry, solid phase peptide synthesis. *Address:* The Rockefeller University, 1230 York Avenue, New York, NY 10021, USA. *T:* (212) 3278244.　　　　　*Died 14 May 2006.*

MERRIVALE, 3rd Baron *cr* 1925, of Walkhampton, Co. Devon; **Jack Henry Edmond Duke;** *b* 27 Jan. 1917; *o s* of 2nd Baron Merrivale, OBE, and Odette, *d* of Edmond Roger, Paris; *S* father, 1951; *m* 1st, 1939, Colette (marr. diss. 1974), *d* of John Douglas Wise, Bordeaux, France; one *s* one *d*; 2nd, 1975, Betty (*d* 2002), *widow* of Paul Baron. *Educ:* Brightlands Sch.; Dulwich; private tuition, SW France; Ecole des Sciences Politiques, Paris. Served War of 1939–45, RAF, 1940; Flight-Lieut, 1944 (despatches). Formerly Chm., Scotia Investments Plc; Chm., Grecian Investments (Gibraltar) Ltd (formerly Leisure Investments (Gibraltar) Ltd), 1990–; Pres., Inst. of Traffic Administration, 1953–70; Chm., 1961–86, Pres., 1986–96, Anglo-Malagasy Soc.; Chairman: British Cttee for Furthering of Relations with French-speaking Africa, 1973; GB-Senegal Friendship Assoc., 1990. Founder Mem., Club de Dakar, 1974. Freeman, City of London, 1979; Hon. Freedom, City of Gibraltar, 2001. FRSA 1964. Chevalier, Nat. Order (Madagascar), 1968; Commander, Nat. Order of the Lion (Senegal), 1992. *Recreations:* sailing, photography. *Heir: s* Hon. Derek John Philip Duke, *b* 16 March 1948. *Address:* 16 Brompton Lodge, SW7 2JA. *T:* and *Fax:* (020) 7581 5678.　　　　　　　*Died 1 Nov. 2007.*

MERSEY, 4th Viscount *cr* 1916, of Toxteth; **Richard Maurice Clive Bigham;** Lord Nairne 1681; Baron Mersey 1910; film director; *b* 8 July 1934; *e s* of 3rd Viscount Mersey, and 12th Lady Nairne (*d* 1995); *S* father, 1979; *m* 1961, Joanna, *d* of late John A. R. G. Murray, CBE; one *s. Educ:* Eton; Balliol Coll., Oxford. Irish Guards, 1952–54 (final rank Lt). Films incl. documentaries for Shell, LEPRA and Government (various awards, London and Venice). President: SIESO, 1987–91; Combined Heat and Power Assoc., 1989–92. FRGS. Hon. FRAM 1995. *Publications:* The Hills of Cork and Kerry, 1987; Pole Power: changing the face of Poland's energy for the European Union, 2001. *Heir: s* Hon. Edward John Hallam Bigham, Master of Nairne [*b* 23 May 1966; *m* 1st, 1994, Claire Haigh (marr. diss. 1996); 2nd, 2001, Clare, *d* of late Robert Schaw Miller; one *d*]. *Address:* Bignor Park, Pulborough, West Sussex RH20 1HG. *T:* (01798) 869214.　　　*Died 5 Aug. 2006.*

MESSMER, Pierre Auguste Joseph; Grand Croix de la Légion d'Honneur; Compagnon de la Libération; Croix de Guerre, 1939–45; Médaille de la Résistance; Member, Académie Française, 1999; Député (RPR) from Moselle, 1968–88; *b* Vincennes (Seine), 20 March 1916; *s* of Joseph Messmer, industrialist, and of Marthe (*née* Farcy); *m* 1947, Gilberte Duprez (*d* 1991); *m* 1999, Christiane Terrail. *Educ:* Lycées Charlemagne and Louis-le Grand; Faculty of Law, Paris; Ecole Nationale de la France d'Outre-Mer. Pupil Administrator of Colonies, 1938. Served War of 1939–45: Free French Forces, 1940; African Campaigns (Bir-Hakeim), France, Germany; parachuted Tonkin; PoW of Vietminh, 1945. Sec.-Gen., Interministerial Cttee of Indochina, 1946; Dir of Cabinet of E. Bollaert (High Commissioner, Indochina), 1947–48; Administrator-in-Chief of France Overseas, 1950; Governor of Mauritania, 1952, of Ivory Coast, 1954–56; Dir of Cabinet of G. Defferre (Minister, France Overseas), Jan.–April 1956; High Commissioner: Republic of Cameroon, 1956–58; French Equatorial Africa, 1958; French West Africa, July 1958–Dec. 1959; Minister of Armed Forces: (Cabinets: M. Debré, 5 Feb. 1958–14 April 1962; G. Pompidou, April–Nov. 1962, 6 Dec. 1962–7 Jan. 1966, 8 Jan. 1966–1 April 1967, 7 April 1967–10 July 1968; M. Couve de Murville, 12 July 1968–20 June 1969); Minister of State in charge of Depts and Territories Overseas, Feb. 1971–72; Prime Minister, 1972–74; Mem. European Parliament, 1979–80. Pres., RPR Federal Cttee, Moselle, 1968–88. Mayor of Sarrebourg, 1971–89. Mem., l'Institut (Académie des Sciences Morales et Politiques), 1988; Secrétaire perpétuel, Acad. des Sciences Morales et Politiques, 1995–98. Officer, American Legion. *Publications:* (jtly) Les écrits militaires de Charles de Gaulle: essai d'analyse thématique, 1986; Après tant de batailles, 1992; Les Blancs s'en vont, 1998; La Patrouille perdue, 2002; La part de France, 2003. *Recreations:* tennis, sailing. *Address:* 23 quai de Conti, 75006 Paris, France. *Died 29 Aug. 2007.*

METFORD, Prof. John Callan James; Professor of Spanish, 1960–81, then Emeritus Professor, Head of Department of Hispanic and Latin American Studies, 1973–81, University of Bristol; *b* 29 Jan. 1916; *s* of Oliver Metford and Florence Stowe Thomas; *m* 1944, Edith Donald; one *d*. *Educ:* Porth Grammar Sch.; Universities of Liverpool, Yale and California. Commonwealth Fund Fellow, 1939–41; British Council Lecturer in Brazil, 1942–44; Regional Officer, Latin American Department of the British Council, 1944–46; Lectr in Latin American Studies, Univ. of Glasgow, 1946–55; Bristol University: Head of Dept of Spanish and Portuguese, 1955–73; Prof., 1960–81; Dean of Faculty of Arts, 1973–76; Chm., Sch. of Modern Langs, 1976–79. Vis. Prof., Lehigh Univ., USA, 1968–69. Chm., Council of Westonbirt Sch., 1976–83; Mem., Central Cttee of Allied Schs, 1970–83; Governor, Coll. of St Matthias, Bristol, 1960–79; Mem., St Matthias Trust, 1979–96; Professorial Mem., Council of Univ. of Bristol, 1972–74; Founder Trustee, The Octagon, Univ. of West England (formerly Bristol Poly.), 1993–96. Mem., Diocesan Adv. Cttee, Bristol, 1984–93. *Publications:* British Contributions to Spanish and Spanish American Studies, 1950; San Martín the Liberator, 1950, 2nd edn 1970; Modern Latin America, 1964; Falklands or Malvinas?, rev. edn of J. Goebel: The Struggle for the Falkland Islands, 1982; Dictionary of Christian Lore and Legend, 1983 (trans. Lithuanian, 2001); The Christian Year, 1991; articles in Bull. of Spanish Studies, Bull. of Hispanic Studies, Liverpool Studies in Spanish, International Affairs, Contemporary Review, etc. *Recreations:* opera, iconography. *Address:* 58 Westfield House, Cote Lane, Westbury-on-Trym, Bristol BS9 3TJ. T: (0117) 949 4858. *Died 29 March 2007.*

METHUEN, Very Rev. John Alan Robert; Dean of Ripon, 1995–2005; *b* 14 Aug. 1947; *s* of late Rev. Alan Robert Methuen and Ruth Josephine Tyrrell Methuen; *m* 1970, Bridget Mary (*née* Andrews); two *d*. *Educ:* Upton Prep. Sch., Windsor; Eton Coll. Choir Sch.; St John's Sch., Leatherhead; Brasenose Coll., Oxford (Colquitt Exhibnr 1966; BA 1969; MA 1972); Cuddesdon Coll., Oxford. Asst Curate, Fenny Stratford and Water Eaton Team Ministry, Milton Keynes, 1971–74; Asst Chaplain, Eton Coll., 1974–77; Priest-in-Charge, St James, Dorney and Warden of Dorney Parish-Eton Coll. Conf. Centre, 1974–77; Vicar, St Mark, Reading, 1977–83; Rector, The Ascension, Hulme, Manchester, 1983–95. Church Comr, 1998–2004. Master, Ripon Hosps of St John the

Baptist and St Mary Magdalen, 1995–2005. Member: Egypt Exploration Soc., 1991–; N Yorks Ancient Egyptian Soc., 1996–; Thames Valley Ancient Egypt Soc., 2005–; Actors Church Union, 2006–; Nat. Exec., Christian CND. Writer and Dir, The Christian Life (series of 8 educnl videos), 1990–93; lecturer: Interchurch Travel, 1975–95; Swan Hellenic Cruises, 1996–; Voyages of Discovery, 2007–; Ancient World Tours, 2007–; Saga Holidays 2008–; Petrie Museum, 2008–. Gerald Avery Near Eastern Archaeol. Prize, Oxford Univ., 1965. *Publications:* various lectures, reviews and papers. *Recreations:* drama and theatre, opera, concerts and music-making; film-making, directing, writing and broadcasting; history and archaeology; pilgrimage and travel (especially as leader and lecturer). *Address:* Dean's Lodge, 108 Honeypot Lane, NW9 9QX. *Clubs:* Leeds City (Leeds); Ripon City (Ripon). *Died 18 July 2010.*

METZGER, Rev. Prof. Bruce Manning; George L. Collord Professor of New Testament Language and Literature, Princeton Theological Seminary, 1964–84, then Emeritus; *b* Middletown, Pa, 9 Feb. 1914; *o s* of late Maurice R. Metzger and Anna Manning Metzger; *m* 1944, Isobel Elizabeth, *e d* of late Rev. John Alexander Mackay, DD; two *s*. *Educ:* Lebanon Valley Coll. (BA 1935); Princeton Theol Seminary (ThB 1938, ThM 1939); Princeton Univ. (MA 1940, PhD 1942, Classics). Ordained, United Presbyterian Church, USA, 1939; Princeton Theological Seminary: Teaching Fellow in NT Greek, 1938–40; Instr. in NT, 1940–44; Asst Prof., 1944–48; Associate Prof., 1948–54; Prof., 1954–84. Dist. Vis. Prof., Fuller Theol Sem., 1970; Visiting Professor: Gordon–Conwell Theol Sem., 1978; Caribbean Grad. Sch. of Theol., Jamaica, 1990; Seminario Internacional Teológico Bautista, Buenos Aires, 1991; Schol. in Residence, Tyndale Hse, Cambridge, 1969; Visiting Fellow: Clare Hall, Cambridge, 1974; Wolfson Coll., Oxford, 1979; Vis. Lectr, Sem. Theol. Presbyt. do Sul, Campinas, Brazil, 1952; Lectr, New Coll. for Advanced Christian Studies, Berkeley, 1978; many lectures to some 100 other academic instns on 5 continents. Chairman, Amer. Cttee on Versions, Internat. Greek NT Project, 1950–; Secretary: Panel of Translators, Rev. Standard Version of Apocrypha, 1952–57; Amer. Textual Criticism Seminar, 1954–56; Member: Kurat. of Vetus Latina Inst., Beuron, 1959–; Adv. Cttee, Inst. of NT Textual Res., Münster, Germany, 1961–; Inst. for Advanced Study, Princeton, 1964 and 1974; Chairman: Cttee on Trans., Amer. Bible Soc., 1964–70; Amer. Exec. Cttee, Internat. Greek NT Project, 1970–88; Cttee of Translators, New RSV of the Bible, 1977–90. President: Soc. of Biblical Lit., 1971; Stud. Novi Test. Soc., 1971–72; N Amer. Patristic Soc., 1972; Soc. for Textual Scholarship, 1995; Corresp. Fellow Brit. Acad., 1978; Hon. Fellow and Corresp. Mem., Higher Inst. of Coptic Studies, Cairo, 1955; Mem., Amer. Philosophical Soc., 1986–. Hon. DD: Lebanon Valley Coll., 1951 (also Dist. Alumnus award of Alumni Assoc. 1961); St Andrews, 1964; Hon. DTheol Münster, 1971; Hon. LHD Findlay Coll., 1962; Hon. DLitt Potchefstroom, 1985. Burkitt Medal for Biblical Studies, British Acad., 1994. *Publications:* The Saturday and Sunday Lessons from Luke in the Greek Gospel Lectionary, 1944; Lexical Aids for Students of New Testament Greek, 1946, enlarged edn 1955 (trans. Malagasy, Portuguese, Korean); A Guide to the Preparation of a Thesis, 1950, 2nd edn 1961; Index of Articles on the New Testament and the Early Church Published in Festschriften, 1951, Supplement 1955; Annotated Bibliography of the Textual Criticism of the New Testament, 1955; (jtly) The Text, Canon, and Principal Versions of the Bible, 1956; An Introduction to the Apocrypha, 1957 (trans. Korean); Index to Periodical Literature on the Apostle Paul, 1960, 2nd edn 1970; Lists of Words Occurring Frequently in the Coptic New Testament (Sahidic Dialect), 1961; (jtly) The Oxford Concise Concordance to the Revised Standard Version of the Holy Bible, 1962; (jtly) The Oxford Annotated Bible, 1962; Chapters in the History of New Testament Textual

Criticism, 1963; The Text of the New Testament, its Transmission, Corruption, and Restoration, 1964 (trans. German, Japanese, Korean, Chinese, Italian, Russian), 4th enlarged edn 2005; The Oxford Annotated Apocrypha, 1965; The New Testament, its Background, Growth, and Content, 1965, 3rd edn 2003 (trans. Chinese, Korean); Index to Periodical Literature on Christ and the Gospels, 1966; (ed jtly) The Greek New Testament, 1966, 4th edn 1993; Historical and Literary Studies, Pagan, Jewish, and Christian, 1968; A Textual Commentary on the Greek New Testament, 1971, 2nd edn 1994; The New Oxford Annotated Bible with the Apocrypha, expanded edn 1977; The Early Versions of the New Testament, their Origin, Transmission, and Limitations, 1977 (trans. Russian); New Testament Studies, Philological, Versional, and Patristic, 1980; Manuscripts of the Greek Bible, an Introduction to Greek Palaeography, 1981 (trans. Japanese); (general editor) Reader's Digest Condensed Bible, 1982 (trans Italian, French, Korean); The Canon of the New Testament, its Origin, Development, and Significance, 1987 (trans. Italian, Russian, Korean, German); (jtly) The Making of the New Revised Standard Version of the Bible, 1991; Breaking the Code, Understanding the Book of Revelation, 1993 (trans. Chinese, Korean); (ed) The Oxford Companion to the Bible, 1993 (trans. Polish); Reminiscences of an Octogenarian, 1997; (ed) The Oxford Guide to People and Places of the Bible, 2001; (ed) The Oxford Guide to Ideas and Issues of the Bible, 2001; The Bible in Translation, Ancient and English Versions, 2001; (ed) New Testament Tools and Studies, thirty two vols, 1960–2004; numerous articles in learned jls and encycs. *Recreations:* reading, woodworking. *Address:* 20 Cleveland Lane, Princeton, New Jersey 08540, USA. *T:* (609) 9244060. *Club:* Nassau (Princeton, New Jersey).

Died 13 Feb. 2007.

MEYNELL, Benedict William; Hon. Director-General, Commission of the European Communities, since 1981; *b* 17 Feb. 1930; *s* of late Sir Francis Meynell, RDI, and of Lady (Vera) Meynell, MA; *m* 1st, 1950, Hildamarie (*née* Hendricks) (marr. diss. 1965); two *d*; 2nd, 1967, Diana (*née* Himbury) (marr. diss. 1971). *Educ:* Beltane Sch.; Geneva Univ. (Licencié-ès-sciences politiques); Magdalen Coll., Oxford (Doncaster schol.; MA). Asst Principal, Bd of Inland Revenue, 1954–56; Asst Principal, BoT, 1957–59, Principal, 1959–68; Principal British Trade Commissioner, Kenya, 1962–64; Board of Trade: Principal Private Sec. to Pres., 1967–68; Asst Sec., 1968–70; Commercial Counsellor, Brit. Embassy, Washington, DC, 1970–73; a Dir, EEC, responsible for relations with Far East, and for commercial safeguards and textiles negotiations, 1973–77, for relations with N America, Japan and Australasia, 1977–81. *Publications:* (paper) International Regulation of Aircraft Noise, 1971; contribs: Japan and Western Europe, ed Tsoukalis and White, 1982; A Survey of External Relations, in Yearbook of European Law 1982; Servir l'Etat, 1987 (Cahiers de l'Homme series). *Address:* New Cottage, Greatham Lane, Pulborough, West Sussex RH20 2ES. *T:* (01798) 872688. *Club:* Savile. *Died 14 Nov. 2009.*

MICHIE OF GALLANACH, Baroness *cr* 2001 (Life Peer), of Oban in Argyll and Bute; **Janet Ray Michie;** *b* 4 Feb. 1934; *d* of Baron Bannerman of Kildonan, OBE and Lady Bannerman of Kildonan; *m* 1957, Dr Iain Michie, MB, FRCPE, *s* of Malcolm and Margaret Michie; two *d* (and one *d* decd). *Educ:* Aberdeen High Sch. for Girls; Lansdowne House Sch., Edinburgh; Edinburgh Coll. of Speech Therapy. MCST. Area Speech Therapist, Argyll and Clyde Health Board, 1977–87. Chm., Argyll Lib. Assoc., 1973–76; Vice-Chm., Scottish Lib. Party, 1977–79; Chair, Scottish Lib. Democrats, 1992–93. Contested (L): Argyll, 1979; Argyll and Bute, 1983. MP Argyll and Bute, 1987–2001 (L 1987–88, Lib Dem 1988–2001). Lib Dem spokesman on transport and rural develt, 1987–88, on Scotland, 1988–97, on women's issues, 1988–94. Member: Select Cttee on Scottish Affairs, 1992–97; Chairmen's Panel, 1997–2001.

Jt Vice Chm., All Party Parly Gp on Whisky Industry, 1990–2001. Member: Scottish NFU; Scottish Crofting Foundn. Vice-Pres., Coll., subseq. Royal Coll., of Speech and Language Therapists, 1991–2001, 2002–. Hon. Pres., Clyde Fishermen's Assoc. Hon. Associate, Nat. Council of Women of GB. *Recreations:* golf, swimming, gardening, watching Rugby. *Address:* House of Lords, SW1A 0PW. *Club:* National Liberal. *Died 6 May 2008.*

MICHIE, Prof. Donald, DPhil (Oxon), DSc (Oxon); Professor of Machine Intelligence, Edinburgh University, 1967–84, Professor Emeritus, since 1984; *b* 11 Nov. 1923; *s* of late James Kilgour Michie and Marjorie Crain Michie; *m* 1st, 1949, Zena Margaret Davies (marr. diss.); one *s*; 2nd, 1952, Hon. Anne Laura McLaren (*see* (Dame) A. L. McLaren) (marr. diss. 1959); one *s* two *d*; 3rd, 1971, Jean Elizabeth Hayes (*née* Crouch) (*d* 2002). *Educ:* Rugby Sch.; Balliol Coll., Oxford (Schol., MA). FRSE 1969; FBCS 1971. War Service in FO, Bletchley, 1942–45; Res. Associate, Univ. of London, 1952–58; University of Edinburgh: Sen. Lectr, Surg. Science, 1958; Reader in Surg. Science, 1962; Dir of Expermtl Programming Unit, 1965; Chm. of Dept of Machine Intelligence and Perception, 1966; Dir, Machine Intelligence Res. Unit, 1974–84; Prof., Computer Sci., Univ. of Strathclyde, 1984–92; Turing Institute, Glasgow: Dir of Res., 1984–86; Chief Scientist, 1986–92; Sen. Fellow, 1992–94. Technical Dir, Intelligent Terminals Ltd (Knowledgelink), 1984–92. Royal Soc. Lectr in USSR, 1965; Wm Withering Lectr, Univ. of Birmingham, 1972; Vis. Lectr, USSR Acad. Sci., 1973, 1985; Geo. A. Miller Lectr, Univ. of Illinois, 1974, 1984; Herbert Spencer Lectr, Univ. of Oxford, 1976; Samuel Wilks Meml Lectr, Princeton Univ., 1978; S. L. A. Marshall Lectr, US Army Res. Inst. for the Behavioural and Soc. Scis, 1990; C. C. Garvin Lectr, Virginia Polytech. Inst. and State Univ., 1992. Chief Editor, Machine Intelligence series, 1967–. Chm., A. M. Turing Trust, 1975–97. Treas., Human-Computer Learning Foundn, 1995–. Foreign Hon. Member: American Acad. of Arts and Sci., 2001; Slovenian Acad. of Arts and Sci., 2005. Fellow, Amer. Assoc. Artificial Intell., 1990. Hon. DSc: CNAA, 1991; Salford, 1992; Aberdeen, 1999; DUniv: Stirling, 1996; York, 2000. (With A. McLaren) Pioneer Award, Internat. Embryo Transfer Soc., 1988; Achievement Award, IEE, 1995; Feigenbaum Medal, World Congress on Expert Systems, 1996; Res. Excellence Award, Internat. Jt Conf. on Artificial Intelligence, 2001. *Publications:* (jtly) An Introduction to Molecular Biology, 1964; On Machine Intelligence, 1974, 2nd edn 1986; Machine Intelligence and Related Topics, 1982; (jtly) The Creative Computer, 1984; papers in tech. and sci. jls. *Recreation:* writing. *Address:* 24 Corinne Road, N19 5EY. *Clubs:* Chelsea Arts; New (Edinburgh). *Died 7 July 2007.*

MIDDLETON, Michael Humfrey, CBE 1975; Director, Civic Trust, 1969–86; *b* 1 Dec. 1917; *s* of Humfrey Middleton and Lilian Irene (*née* Tillard); *m* 1954, Julie Margaret Harrison (*d* 2003); one *s* two *d*. *Educ:* King's Sch., Canterbury. Art Critic, The Spectator, 1946–56; Art Editor and Asst Editor, Picture Post, 1949–53; Exec. Editor, Lilliput, 1953–54; Editor, House and Garden, 1955–57; Sec. and Dep. Dir, Civic Trust, 1957–69; Mem. Council, Soc. of Industrial Artists and Designers, 1953–55, 1968–70; UK Sec.-Gen., European Architectural Heritage Year, 1972–75. Member: Adv. Cttee on Trunk Road Assessment, 1977–80; UK Commn for UNESCO, 1976–80. Hon. Fellow: RIBA, 1974; Landscape Inst., 1986. Film scripts include A Future for the Past, 1972. Council of Europe Pro Merito Medal, 1976. *Publications:* Soldiers of Lead, 1948; Group Practice in Design, 1967; Man Made the Town, 1987; Cities in Transition, 1991; contributor to many conferences and jls, at home and abroad, on art, design and environmental matters. *Recreation:* looking. *Address:* c/o 47 Tunley Road, SW17 7QH. *T:* (020) 8673 7221. *Died 6 Aug. 2009.*

MIDDLETON, Stanley; novelist; *b* Bulwell, Nottingham, 1 Aug. 1919; *y s* of Thomas and Elizabeth Ann Middleton; *m* 1951, Margaret Shirley, *y d* of Herbert and Winifred Vera Welch; two *d. Educ:* High Pavement Sch.; University Coll., Nottingham (later Univ. of Nottingham). Served Army (RA and AEC), 1940–46. Head of English Dept, High Pavement Coll., Nottingham, 1958–81. Judith E. Wilson Vis. Fellow, Emmanuel Coll., Cambridge, 1982–83. FRSL 1998. Hon. MA Nottingham, 1975; MUniv Open, 1995; Hon. DLitt: De Montfort, 1998; Nottingham Trent, 2000. *Publications:* novels: A Short Answer, 1958; Harris's Requiem, 1960; A Serious Woman, 1961; The Just Exchange, 1962; Two's Company, 1963; Him They Compelled, 1964; Terms of Reference, 1966; The Golden Evening, 1968; Wages of Virtue, 1969; Apple of the Eye, 1970; Brazen Prison, 1971; Cold Gradations, 1972; A Man Made of Smoke, 1973; Holiday (jtly, Booker Prize), 1974; Distractions, 1975; Still Waters, 1976; Ends and Means, 1977; Two Brothers, 1978; In A Strange Land, 1979; The Other Side, 1980; Blind Understanding, 1982; Entry into Jerusalem, 1983; The Daysman, 1984; Valley of Decision, 1985; An After Dinner's Sleep, 1986; After a Fashion, 1987; Recovery, 1988; Vacant Places, 1989; Changes and Chances, 1990; Beginning to End, 1991; A Place to Stand, 1992; Married Past Redemption, 1993; Catalysts, 1994; Toward the Sea, 1995; Live and Learn, 1996; Brief Hours, 1997; Against the Dark, 1998; Necessary Ends, 1999; Small Change, 2000; Love in the Provinces, 2002; Brief Garlands, 2004; Sterner Stuff, 2005; Mother's Boy, 2006; Her Three Wise Men, 2008. *Recreations:* music, listening, argument, water-colour painting. *Address:* 42 Caledon Road, Sherwood, Nottingham NG5 2NG. *T:* (0115) 962 3085. *Club:* PEN. *Died 25 July 2009.*

MILES, Prof. Albert Edward William, LRCP; MRCS; FDS; DSc; Professor of Dental Pathology at The London Hospital Medical College, 1950–76, retired; Hon. Curator, Odontological Collection, Royal College of Surgeons of England, 1955–89; *b* 15 July 1912; *m* 1st, 1939, Sylvia Stuart (one *s* decd); 2nd, 1979, Diana Cross (*d* 2005). *Educ:* Stationers' Company Sch.; Charing Cross and Royal Dental Hosps. John Tomes Prize, RCS, 1954–56. Part-time Lectr, Anatomy Dept, London Hosp. Med. Coll., 1977–85; Hon. Researcher, Dept of Palaeontology, Nat. Hist. Museum, 1993–99. Charles Tomes Lecturer, RCS, 1957; Evelyn Sprawson Lectr, London Hosp. Med. Coll., 1977. Hunterian Trustee, 1978–98. Hon. FRSocMed 1988. Howard Mummery Meml Prize, BDA, 1976; Colyer Gold Medal, RCS, 1978; Sir Arthur Keith Medal, RCS, 1990; Wood Jones Medal, RCS, 1993; G. L. Slack Medal, London Hosp. Med. Coll., 1997. Exec. Editor, Archives of Oral Biology, 1969–88. *Publications:* Structural and Chemical Organization of Teeth, 1967; Teeth and Their Origins, 1972; An Early Christian Chapel and Burial Ground in the Outer Hebrides, with a Study of the Skeletal Remains, 1989; (with Caroline Grigson) Colyer's Variations and Diseases of the Teeth in Animals, 1990; contrib. to scientific literature, latterly on physical anthropology and age changes in shoulder joint. *Clubs:* Tetrapods, Zoo. *Died 7 March 2008.*

MILES, Mrs Caroline Mary; Founder, Chairman, 1996–2006, and Trustee, since 1999, The Ethox Foundation, The Oxford Foundation (formerly Institute) for Ethics and Communication in Health Care Practice; *b* 30 April 1929; *d* of Brig. A. J. R. M. Leslie, OBE. *Educ:* numerous schools; Somerville Coll., Oxford. HM Treasury, 1953–54; NIESR, 1954–56 and 1964–67; attached to UN Secretariat, NY, 1956–63. Associate Mem., Nuffield Coll., Oxford, 1972–74; Ian Ramsey Fellow, St Cross Coll., Oxford, 1988–94. Market Develt Consultant, Harwell Res. Lab., 1981–86. Chm., Oxfordshire HA, 1984–92. Member: Textile Council, 1968–71; Inflation Accounting Cttee (Sandilands Cttee), 1974–75; Monopolies and Mergers Commn, 1975–84; NEB, 1976–79; Nuffield Council on Bioethics, 1991–96. Trustee: The Tablet, 1982–98; APT Design and Develt,

then APT Enterprise Develt Ltd, 1992–2000 (Chm., 1994–98); Nuffield Dominions Trust, 1994–2004; Opus Anglicanum Trust, 2001–03; Radcliffe Medical Foundation: Trustee, 1986–2000; Hon. Treas., 1996–99; Patron, 2000–03. Governor: Ditchley Foundn, 1983–2003; Oxford Polytechnic, 1988–92. *Publications:* Lancashire Textiles, A Case Study of Industrial Change, 1968; numerous papers and articles. *Recreations:* music, picnics, poohsticks. *Address:* Flat 5, Blenheim Court, 316 Woodstock Road, Oxford OX2 7DG. *T:* (01865) 456295. *Died 21 Nov. 2006.*

MILES, Dillwyn, FSA, FRGS, FRHistS; The Herald Bard, 1966–96; Director, Dyfed Rural Council, 1975–81; Chairman, National Association of Local Councils, 1977–87, Vice-President, since 1987; *b* 25 May 1916; *s* of Joshua Miles and Anne Mariah (*née* Lewis), Newport, Pembrokeshire; *m* 1944, Joyce Eileen (*d* 1976), *d* of Lewis Craven Ord, Montreal and London; one *s* one *d. Educ:* Fishguard County Sch.; University College of Wales, Aberystwyth. Served War of 1939–45, Middle East, Army Captain. National Organiser Palestine House, London, 1945–48; Extra-mural Lectr, Univ. of Wales, 1948–51; Community Centres Officer, Wales, 1951–54; Gen. Sec., Pembrokeshire Community Council, 1954–75. Founder: Jerusalem Welsh Soc., 1940; W Wales Tourist Assoc., 1962; Assoc. of Trusts for Nature Conservation in Wales, 1973; Hon. Sec., W Wales Naturalists Trust, 1958–75 (Vice-Pres., 1975–). Grand Sword Bearer, Gorsedd of Bards of Isle of Britain, 1959–67 (Mem. Bd, 1945–96). Member: Pembrokeshire CC, 1947–63; Cemaes RDC, 1947–52; Newport Parish Council, 1946–52; Haverfordwest Bor. Council, 1957–63; Pembrokeshire Coast Nat. Park Cttee, 1952–75; Exec. Cttee, Council for Protection of Rural Wales, 1946–64; Nature Conservancy's Cttee for Wales, 1966–73; Council, Soc. for Promotion of Nature Reserves, 1961–73; Countryside in 1970 Cttee for Wales, 1969–70; Sports Council for Wales, 1965–69; Mental Health Rev. Tribunal for Wales, 1959–71; Rent Trib. for Wales, 1966–87; Court of Govs, Nat. Libr. of Wales, 1963–64; Court of Govs, Univ. of Wales, 1957–66; Pembroke TA Assoc., 1956–59; Council for Small Industries in Wales, 1968–72; Age Concern Wales, 1972–77; Exec. Cttee, Nat. Council for Social Service, 1978–81; Exec. Cttee, NPFA, 1977–81; Council, Royal Nat. Eisteddfod of Wales, 1967–97; Prince of Wales Cttee, 1971–80 (former Chm., Dyfed Projects Gp); Welsh Environment Foundn, 1971–80; Heraldry Soc., 1974–; Rural Voice, 1980–87. Former Chairman: Further Educn and Libraries and Museums Cttees, Pembs CC; Pembs Cttee, Arthritis and Rheumatism Council; Pembs Jun. Ch. of Commerce; Pembs Community Health Council; Policy and Welsh Cttees, Nat. Assoc. of Local Councils. Chairman: Wales Playing Fields Assoc., 1965–81; Pembs PO and Telecom Adv. Cttee, 1984–94 (Vice-Chm., 1971–84); Pembs Wildlife Appeal, 1988–89. President: Pembs Histl Soc., 1994–; Haverfordwest Shrievalty Assoc., 1996–99. Editor: The Pembrokeshire Historian, 1955–81; Nature in Wales, 1970–80. Mayor of Newport, Pembs, 1950, 1966, 1967, 1979, and Sen. Alderman. Mayor and Adm. of the Port, Haverfordwest, 1961, Sheriff 1963, Burgess Warden 1974–. FRGS 1946; FSA 1997; FRHistS 2000. Broadcaster, TV and radio, 1936–. *Publications:* (ed) Pembrokeshire Coast National Park, 1973, 3rd edn 2001; (jtly) Writers of the West, 1974; The Sheriffs of the County of Pembroke, 1975; The Royal National Eisteddfod of Wales, 1978; A Pembrokeshire Anthology, 1982, 2nd edn 2000; The Castles of Pembrokeshire, 1979, 3rd edn 1988; Portrait of Pembrokeshire, 1984, 2nd edn 2003; The Pembrokeshire Coast National Park, 1987; The Secret of the Bards, 1992; The Description of Pembrokeshire, 1994; The Ancient Borough of Newport, 1995; The Lords of Cemais, 1997; A Book on Nevern, 1998; A Mingled Yarn, 2000; Lieutenant John George, Royal Marines: letters 1799–1808, 2002; Llwyngwair and the Bowen Family, 2002; The Mariners of Newport, 2006. *Recreations:* natural history, local history, books, food and wine. *Address:* 9 St Anthony's Way, Haverfordwest, Pembrokeshire SA61 1EL. *T:* (01437) 765275. *Died 1 Aug. 2007.*

MILES, Sir William (Napier Maurice), 6th Bt *cr* 1859; architect; *b* 19 Oct. 1913; *s* of Sir Charles William Miles, 5th Bt, OBE; *S* father, 1966; *m* 1946, Pamela, *d* of late Capt. Michael Dillon; one *s* two *d. Educ:* Stowe; University of Cambridge (BA). Architectural Assoc. Diploma, 1939; RIBA 1940. Mem., Dignity in Dying (formerly Voluntary Euthanasia Soc.). *Recreation:* surviving. *Heir: s* Philip John Miles, *b* 10 Aug. 1953. *Address:* Old Rectory House, Walton-in-Gordano, near Clevedon, North Somerset BS21 7AW. *T:* (01275) 873365. *Died 29 Dec. 2010.*

MILKINA, Nina, (Mrs A. R. M. Sedgwick), Hon. RAM; concert pianist; *b* Moscow, 27 Jan. 1919; *d* of Jacques and Sophie Milkine; *m* 1943, Alastair Robert Masson Sedgwick; one *s* one *d. Educ:* privately. Studied in France with Leon Conus of the Moscow Conservatoire, and composition with Alexander Glazunov; also with Profs Harold Craxton and Tobias Matthay in London; first public appearance at age of 11 with Lamoureux Orchestra, Paris, and first compositions published by Boosey and Hawkes in same year; commissioned by BBC to broadcast series of all Mozart's piano sonatas; invited to give Mozart recital for bicentenary celebration of Mozart's birth, Edinburgh Festival. Major works recorded: Mozart piano concertos K271 and K467; Mozart recitals; complete Chopin Mazurkas; Chopin 24 Preludes; Scarlatti Sonatas; Mozart and Haydn Sonatas; works by Rachmaninov, Prokofiev, Scriabin. Widely noted for interpretation of Mozart's piano works. *Recreations:* swimming, chess, fly fishing. *Address:* 17 Montagu Square, W1H 2LE; Casa delle Colonne, San Pietro, Sardinia. *Died 29 Nov. 2006.*

MILLAR, Sir Oliver Nicholas, GCVO 1988 (KCVO 1973; CVO 1963; MVO 1953); FBA 1970; Director of the Royal Collection, 1987–88; Surveyor of the Queen's Pictures, 1972–88, Surveyor Emeritus, since 1988; *b* 26 April 1923; *er s* of late Gerald Millar, MC and late Ruth Millar; *m* 1954, Delia Mary (CVO 1996) (*d* 2004), two *d* of late Lt-Col Cuthbert Dawnay, MC; one *s* three *d. Educ:* Rugby; Courtauld Institute of Art, University of London (Academic Diploma in History of Art). Unable, for medical reasons, to serve in War of 1939–45. Asst Surveyor of the King's Pictures, 1947–49, Dep. Surveyor 1949–72. Trustee, Nat. Portrait Gallery, 1972–95. Member: Reviewing Cttee on Export of Works of Art, 1975–87; Exec. Cttee, Nat. Art Collections Fund, 1986–98. Visitor, Ashmolean Mus., 1987–93. Trustee, Nat. Heritage Meml Fund, 1988–92. A Dir, Friends of the Tate Gall., 1989–2002; Chm., Patrons of British Art, 1989–97. Pres., Walpole Soc., 1998–. FSA. Corresponding Fellow: Ateneo Veneto, Venice; Koninklijke Academie voor Wetenschappen, Letteren en Schone Kunsten, Belgium. *Publications:* Gainsborough, 1949; William Dobson, Tate Gallery Exhibition, 1951; English Art, 1625–1714 (with Dr M. D. Whinney), 1957; Rubens's Whitehall Ceiling, 1958; Abraham van der Doort's Catalogue, 1960; Tudor, Stuart and Early Georgian Pictures in the Collection of HM the Queen, 1963; Zoffany and his Tribuna, 1967; Later Georgian Pictures in the Collection of HM the Queen, 1969; Inventories and Valuations of the King's Goods, 1972; The Age of Charles I (Tate Gallery Exhibn), 1972; The Queen's Pictures, 1977; Sir Peter Lely (Nat. Portrait Gall. Exhibn), 1978; Van Dyck in England (Nat. Portrait Gall. Exhibn), 1982; Victorian Pictures in the Collection of HM the Queen, 1992; (jtly) Van Dyck, A Complete Catalogue of the Paintings, 2004; articles in the Burlington Magazine, etc; numerous catalogues, principally for The Queen's Gallery. *Recreations:* grandchildren, drawing, gardening, reading, listening to music. *Address:* The Cottage, Ray's Lane, Penn, Bucks HP10 8LH. *T:* (01494) 812124. *Clubs:* Brooks's, MCC. *Died 10 May 2007.*

MILLER, Alan John McCulloch, DSC 1941; VRD 1950; Chairman, Miller Insulation Ltd, 1975–86; *b* 21 April 1914; *s* of late Louis McEwan Miller and Mary McCulloch; *m* 1940, Kirsteen Ross Orr (*d* 1995); three *s* one *d. Educ:* Kelvinside Academy; Strathclyde Univ. CEng, MRINA, MIESS, FBIM, FRSA. Family engrg business, 1933–39. Commnd RNVR (Clyde Div.), 1938; served RN, 1939–45: Far East, Indian Ocean, S Atlantic, HMS Dorsetshire, then destroyers; in comd, HMS Fitzroy, Wolverine, Holderness, St Nazaire, Dieppe raids, Russian convoys, 1943–44; psc 1944. Rejoined family business, 1945, until sold to Bestobell Ltd, 1951; Dir, Bestobell Ltd, 1951–73, Chm. and Man. Dir, 1965–73; Chm. and Man. Dir, Wm Simons & Co. Ltd, Shipbuilders, 1956–60; Dir, Truckline Ferries Ltd, 1972–88; Chairman: Antigua Slipway Ltd, 1966–86; Dev West Ltd, 1973–76; Low & Bonar, 1977–82. Chm., BNEC Southern Africa Cttee, 1970. Member: Sports Council, 1973–80; Central Council of Physical Recreation. *Publications:* Over the Horizon 1939–45, 1999. *Recreations:* sailing, golf, ski-ing, shooting. *Address:* Dalruadh, 17 Victoria Terrace, Crieff, Perthshire PH7 4AA. *T:* (01764) 652299. *Clubs:* Royal Thames Yacht, Royal Ocean Racing, Royal Cruising; Western (Glasgow); Royal and Ancient (St Andrews); Helensburgh Golf; Sunningdale Golf. *Died 2 Feb. 2008.*

MILLER, David Ivimey, OBE 1991; HM Diplomatic Service, retired; Senior Consultant, MEC International Ltd, since 2003; *b* 26 March 1937; *y s* of late Reginald James Miller and Helen Joyce (*née* Leech), Cambridge; *m* 1966, Caroline Ethel Jackson; two *d. Educ:* Aldenham Sch.; Sch. of Slavonic and East European Studies, London Univ.; Magdalen Coll., Oxford. Served FO, subseq. FCO, and Moscow, 1964–72; Berlin, 1972–74; CSCE, Geneva, 1974, Belgrade, 1977; First Sec. and Head of Chancery, Belgrade, 1978–81; seconded to Cabinet Office, 1982–85, to NATO Secretariat, Brussels, 1985–90; Asst Dir of Research, FCO, 1990–95; Ambassador to Armenia, 1995–97. Political Advr, OSCE, Tirana, 2000. Associate Fellow, RUSI, 1997. *Address:* 60 Grove Road, Sonning Common RG4 9RL. *Club:* Travellers. *Died 30 Nov. 2010.*

MILLER, G(eorge) William; Chairman, G. William Miller & Co., Inc., Merchant Banking, since 1983; *b* Oklahoma, USA, 9 March 1925; *s* of James Dick Miller and Hazle Deane Miller (*née* Orrick); *m* 1946, Ariadna Rogojarsky. *Educ:* Borger High Sch.; Amarillo Junior Coll.; US Coast Guard Acad. (BS 1945); School of Law, Univ. of California, Berkeley (JD 1952). Served as US Coast Guard Officer, Pacific Area, 1945–49, stationed (one year) in China. Admitted to Bar of California, 1952, New York Bar 1953; law practice with Cravath, Swaine & Moore, NYC, 1952–56. Joined Textron Inc., Providence, RI, 1956; Vice Pres. 1957; Treas. 1958; Pres. 1960; Chief Exec. 1968–78, also Chm., 1974–78; Dir, Federal Reserve Bank of Boston, 1970–78; Chm., Bd of Governors of Federal Reserve System of US, 1978–79; Sec. of the Treasury, USA, 1979–81. Regent Lectr, Univ. of Calif at Berkeley, 1983–84; Lloyd Bentsen Prof. of Govt-Business Relations, Lyndon B. Johnson Sch. of Public Affairs, Univ. of Texas at Austin, 1984; Fannie Wilson Smith Eminent Scholars Chair, Florida State Univ., 1989; Fellow, Univ. of Calif at Berkeley. Chm. and Chief Exec. Officer, Federated Stores, Inc., 1990–92; Director: Repligen Corp., 1982–2005; Simon Property Gp, Inc., 1996–2005. Chairman: Indust. Adv. Council, President's Cttee on Equal Employment Opportunity, 1963–65; The Conference Board, 1977–78; National Alliance of Business, 1978; US Industrial Payroll Savings Cttee, 1977; President's Cttee on HIRE, 1977; Co-Chairman: US-USSR Trade and Econ. Council; Polish–US Econ. Council; President's Circle, Nat. Acad. of Scis, 1989–92. Mem. Bd, Washington Opera. Treasurer, Amer. Red Cross, 1983–87. Mem., State Bar, California. Phi Delta Phi. *Publications:* (ed) Regrowing the American Economy, 1983. *Recreations:* music, golf. *Address:* 1100 Connecticut

Avenue NW, Suite 725, Washington, DC 20036, USA. *T:* (202) 4291780. *Clubs:* Chevy Chase (Maryland); The Brook (NY); Burning Tree (Bethesda, Md); Acoaxet (Westport, Mass); Sailfish Point Golf (Fla); Lyford Cay (Bahamas). *Died 17 March 2006.*

MILLER, Sir Harry, 12th Bt *cr* 1705, of Chichester, Sussex; hill country farmer, New Zealand, 1942–89; *b* 15 Jan. 1927; *yr s* of Sir Ernest Henry John Miller, 10th Bt and Netta Mehalah Miller (*née* Bennett) (*d* 1980); *S* brother, 1995; *m* 1954, Gwynedd Margaret Sheriff; one *s* two *d*. RNZAF 1945 (volunteer pilot). *Recreations:* mountain climbing, golf, forestry management. *Heir: s* Anthony Thomas Miller [*b* 4 May 1955; *m* 1990, Barbara Battersby (*née* Kensington); two *s*, and two step *s* one step *d*]. *Address:* 53 Koha Road, Taupo, New Zealand. *T:* (7) 3780905. *Died 28 Dec. 2007.*

MILLER, Lt-Col Sir John (Mansel), GCVO 1987 (KCVO 1974; CVO 1966); DSO 1944; MC 1944; Crown Equerry, 1961–87, an Extra Equerry since 1987; *b* 4 Feb. 1919; 3rd *s* of Brig.-Gen. Alfred Douglas Miller, CBE, DSO, DL, JP, Royal Scots Greys, and of Ella Geraldine Fletcher, Saltoun, E Lothian. *Educ:* Eton; RMA, Sandhurst. 2nd Lieut Welsh Guards, 1939; Adjt 1942–44; ADC to F-M Lord Wilson, Washington, DC, 1945–47; Regtl Adjt, 1953–56; Brigade Major 1st Guards Brigade, 1956–58; comd 1st Bn Welsh Guards, 1958–61. President: Royal Internat. Horse Show, 1993–; Coaching Club, 1975–82; Hackney Horse Soc., 1978–79, 1994–95; Nat. Light Horse Breeding Soc. (HIS), 1982; British Driving Soc., 1982–; Royal Windsor Horse Show Club, 1985–90; Horse Rangers Assoc., 1985–; Cleveland Bay Horse Soc., 1986–88; BSJA, 1988–93; BHS, 1992–94; Rare Breeds Survival Trust, 1995–; Vice-Pres., Irish Draught Horse Soc., GB, 1990–. Patron: Side Saddle Assoc., 1984–; Coloured Horse and Pony Soc., 1988; Caspian Horse Soc., 1999. President: Wheatley Br., RNLI, 1982–; Wheatley Scouts, 1982–. *Recreations:* hunting, shooting, polo, driving. *Address:* Shotover House, Wheatley, Oxon OX9 1QS. *T:* (01865) 872450. *Clubs:* Pratt's, White's; Constitutional (Windsor). *Died 17 May 2006.*

MILLER, Dame Mary Elizabeth H.; *see* Hedley-Miller.

MILLER, Michael, RD 1966; QC 1974; *b* 28 June 1933; 2nd *s* of late John Bryan Peter Duppa-Miller, GC; *m* 1st, 1958, Mary Elizabeth (marr. diss. 1991), *e d* of late Donald Spiers Monteagle Barlow, FRCS; two *s* two *d*; 2nd, 1991, Prof. Barbara Lepine Goodwin (Prof. of Politics, UEA), *d* of late Thomas Goodwin. *Educ:* Dragon Sch., Oxford; Westminster Sch. (King's Scholar); Christ Church, Oxford (Westminster Scholar; BA Lit. Hum. 1955; MA 1958). Ord. Seaman, RNVR, 1950; Sub-Lt 1956; qual. submarines, 1956; Lt-Comdr RNR. Called to Bar, Lincoln's Inn, 1958, Bencher 1984; practice at Chancery Bar, 1958–97; Mem. Bar Council, 1972–74 and 1988–92; Mem. Senate of Inns of Court and Bar, 1974–76. Author and editor of computer programs incl. expert systems; founder of Clarendon Software. *Recreations:* sailing, music, chess, football, gardening. *Address:* Fairfield House, Norwich NR2 2NQ. *Died 20 Feb. 2008.*

MILLER, William; *see* Miller, G. W.

MILLINGTON, Wing Comdr Ernest Rogers, DFC 1945; advisor on training, Youth Training Scheme, 1980–90; Teacher in charge of Teachers' Centre, London Borough of Newham, 1967–80, retired; Founder, and Editor, Project, 1967–80; *b* 15 Feb. 1916; *s* of Edmund Rogers Millington and Emily Craggs; *m* 1st, 1937, Gwen Pickard (marr. diss. 1974); four *d*; 2nd, 1975, Ivy Mary Robinson. *Educ:* Chigwell Sch., Essex; College of S Mark and S John, Chelsea; Birkbeck Coll., London Univ. Clerk; Accountant; Company Sec.; served War of 1939–45, soldier, gunner officer, pilot RAF, instructor and heavy bomber, CO of a Lancaster Sqdn. MP (Commonwealth) for Chelmsford, 1945–50. Re-joined Royal Air Force, 1954–57. Head of Social Educn, Shoreditch Comprehensive Sch., London, 1965–67.

Publications: (edited): A Study of Film, 1972; The Royal Group of Docks, 1977; A Geography of London, 1979; National Parks, 1980; Was That Really Me? (autobiog.), 2005. *Recreation:* healthy living – ambition to survive to 100! *Address:* Villa Martine, Couze St Front, 24150 Lalinde, France. *T:* 553249431. *Died 9 May 2009.*

MILLS, Vice-Adm. Sir Charles (Piercy), KCB 1968 (CB 1964); CBE 1957; DSC 1953; Lieutenant-Governor and Commander-in-Chief, Guernsey, 1969–74; *b* 4 Oct. 1914; *s* of late Capt. Thomas Piercy Mills, Woking, Surrey; *m* 1944, Anne Cumberlege; two *d*. *Educ:* RN College, Dartmouth. Joined Navy, 1928; Comdr 1947; Capt. 1953; Rear-Adm. 1963; Vice-Adm. 1966. Served War of 1939–45, Home Waters, Mediterranean and Far East; Korea, 1951–52; Flag Officer, Second in Command, Far East Fleet, 1966–67; C-in-C Plymouth, 1967–69. KStJ 1969. US Legion of Merit, 1955. *Recreation:* golf. *Address:* Aldewaye, Aldeburgh, Suffolk IP15 5ER. *Died 27 July 2006.*

MILLS, Sir Frank, KCVO 1983; CMG 1971; HM Diplomatic Service, retired; Chairman of Council, Royal Commonwealth Society for the Blind (Sight Savers), 1985–91; *b* 3 Dec. 1923; *s* of Joseph Francis Mills and Louisa Mills; *m* 1953, Trilby Foster; one *s* two *d*. *Educ:* King Edward VI Sch., Nuneaton; Emmanuel Coll., Cambridge. RAFVR, 1942–45. CRO, 1948; served in: Pakistan, 1949–51; S Africa, 1955–58; Malaysia, 1962–63; Singapore, 1964–66; India, 1972–75; High Comr, Ghana, 1975–78; Private Sec. to Sec. of State, 1960–62; RCDS, 1971; Dir of Communications, FCO, 1978–81; High Comr, Bangladesh, 1981–83. Chairman: Camberwell HA, 1984–89; Chichester CHC, 1993–95. *Recreations:* water colours, pastels. *Club:* Royal Commonwealth Society. *Died 11 May 2006.*

MILNE, Ian Innes, CMG 1965; OBE 1946; a Senior Clerk, House of Commons, 1969–76; *b* 16 June 1912; *e s* of Kenneth John Milne, CBE, and Maud Innes; *m* 1939, Marie Mange (*d* 1989); one *d*. *Educ:* Westminster Sch.; Christ Church, Oxford. Advertising, 1935–40; RE, 1940–46 (Lt-Col). FO, 1946–68; 2nd Sec., Teheran, 1948–51; 1st Sec., Berne, 1955–56; 1st Sec., Tokyo, 1960–63; retired 1968. US Legion of Merit (Off.), 1946. *Recreations:* gardening, music. *Died 17 Feb. 2010.*

MILNER, Prof. (Arthur John) Robin (Gorell), FRS 1988; FRSE; Professor of Computer Science, 1995–2001, then Professor Emeritus, and Fellow of King's College, since 1995, Cambridge University; *b* 13 Jan. 1934; *s* of John Theodore Milner and Muriel Emily (*née* Barnes-Gorell); *m* 1963, Lucy Petronella Moor (*d* 2010); one *s* one *d* (and one *s* decd). *Educ:* Eton Coll.; King's Coll., Cambridge (BA Maths, 1957). FRSE 1993. Maths teacher, Marylebone Grammar Sch., 1959–60; Ferranti Ltd, London, 1960–63; Lectr in Maths and Computing, City Univ., London, 1963–68; Research Fellow: University Coll., Swansea, 1968–70; Artificial Intelligence Lab., Stanford Univ., Calif, 1970–72; Edinburgh University: Lectr, 1973–75; Sen. Lectr, 1975–78; Reader, 1978–84; Prof. of Computation Theory, 1984–94. Founder Mem., Academia Europaea, 1988; For. Mem., French Acad. of Scis, 2007. Hon. DSc(Eng) Chalmers Univ., Gothenburg, Sweden, 1988. A. M. Turing Award, ACM, 1991; Royal Medal, RSE, 2004. *Publications:* A Calculus of Communicating Systems, 1980; Calculus for Communication and Concurrency, 1989; The Definition of Standard ML, 1990, 2nd edn 1997; Commentary on Standard ML, 1990; Communicating and Mobile Systems: the π calculus, 1999; The Space and Motion of Communicating Agents, 2009; contribs to Computer Science on mechanised logic of computation and on calculus of communicating systems. *Recreations:* music, carpentry, walking. *Address:* 24 Lyndewode Road, Cambridge CB1 2HN. *Died 20 March 2010.*

MILNER, Joseph, CBE 1975; QFSM 1962; Chief Officer of the London Fire Brigade, 1970–76; *b* 5 Oct. 1922; *e s* of Joseph and Ann Milner; *m* 1943, Bella Grice (*d* 1976), *e d* of Frederick George Flinton; one *s* one *d*; *m* 1976, Anne Cunningham, *e d* of J. Cunningham. *Educ:* Ladybarn Sch., Manchester. Served King's Regt (Liverpool), 1940–46: India/Burma, 1943–46 (Wingate's Chindits). Nat. Fire Service, 1946–48; North Riding Fire Bde, 1948–50; Manchester Fire Bde, 1950–51; Hong Kong Fire Bde, 1951–60; Dep. Dir, Hong Kong Fire Services, 1961–65; Dir, Hong Kong Fire Services, and Unit Controller, Auxiliary Fire Service, 1965–70. Mem., Hong Kong Council, Order of St John, 1965–70; JP Hong Kong, 1965–70. Regional Fire Commander (designate), London, 1970–76. Mem. Bd, Fire Service College, 1970–76; Mem., Central Fire Brigades Adv. Council, 1970–76; Adviser, Nat. Jt Council for Local Authority Fire Brigades, 1970–76; Chm., London Fire Liaison Panel, 1970–76; Mem., London Local Adv. Cttee, IBA, 1974–78; Fire Adviser, Assoc. of Metrop. Authorities, 1970–76. Vice-President: Fire Services Nat. Benevolent Fund (Chm., 1975–77); GLC Br., Royal British Legion, 1977–. Mem., Caston Parish Council, 1980–2002; Community Controller, Civil Defence, 1981–2005; Fellow, Instn of Fire Engineers, 1971; Associate Mem., Inst. of British Engineers, 1953–95; Associate, LCSP, 1987. OStJ 1971. *Publications:* To Blazes with Glory: a Chindit's war, 1995. *Recreations:* walking, poetry, hacking, horse management, remedial therapies, oil painting. *Address:* Lam Low, Caston, Attleborough, Norfolk NR17 1DD. *T:* (01953) 483697. *Club:* Hong Kong (Hong Kong). *Died 13 Jan. 2007.*

MILTON, Peter James Denis, MD; FRCOG; Consultant Obstetrician and Gynaecologist, Addenbrooke's Hospital, Cambridge, and Associate Lecturer, University of Cambridge, 1976–2002, then Consultant Emeritus; Internal Professional Advisor, NHS Ombudsman, 2002, then Emeritus Internal Clinical Advisor; *b* 17 Jan. 1938; *s* of James Hugh Milton, CEng, FInstMarE, and Dorothy Winifred Milton (*née* Nelson); *m* 1968, Rosemary Jane Phillips; two *s* one *d*. *Educ:* Merchant Taylors' Sch., Crosby, Liverpool; King's Coll., London; St George's Hosp. Med. Sch., Univ. of London (MB BS 1964; MD 1978); MA Cantab 1978. MRCS, LRCP 1963; DA 1969; MRCOG 1970, FRCOG 1983. Jun. med. and surgical posts, St George's, Winchester, Canterbury and St Thomas' Hosps, 1963–70; Ships Surgeon, Blue Star Line, 1968; Registrar, Obstetrics and Gynaecology, St Thomas' Hosp. and Groote Schuur Hosp., Cape Town, 1970–72; Lectr and Sen. Registrar, St Thomas' Hosp., 1972–76; Res. Associate, Imperial Cancer Res. Lab., Lincoln's Inn, 1972–76. Editor and reviewer, obstetric and gynaecological specialist books and jls. Royal College of Obstetricians and Gynaecologists: Fellows' Rep., Council, 1993–98; Chm., Continuing Med. Educn Cttee, 1995–98; Mem., various cttees; Sen. Vice Pres., 1998–2001. Pres., Sect. Obstetrics and Gynaecol., RSocMed, 2004–05 (Hon. Sec, 1992–93; Vice-Pres., 1993–96). Examiner: RCOG; Univs of Cambridge, London, Edinburgh, Liverpool, Manchester, Glasgow, W Indies, Colombo and Khartoum. *Publications:* papers and chapters on pre-natal diagnosis, pre-malignant disease, menopause and other obstetric and gynaecol topics in British and overseas specialist jls. *Recreations:* sailing, ski-ing, second-hand bookshops, walking dogs and more distant travel. *Address:* King's Head House, Duxford, Cambridge CB22 4RP. *T:* (01223) 832238. *Clubs:* Athenæum, Royal Society of Medicine; Royal Fowey Yacht; Aldeburgh Yacht; Gynaecological Travellers of UK and Ireland. *Died 5 July 2010.*

MILWARD, Prof. Alan Steele, FBA 1987; Official Historian, Cabinet Office, 1993–2007; Professor of Economic History, London School of Economics, 1986–96, then Emeritus; *b* 19 Jan. 1935; *s* of Joseph Thomas Milward and Dorothy Milward (*née* Steele); *m* 1st, 1963, Claudine Jeanne Amélie Lemaître (marr. diss. 1994); one *d*; 2nd, 1998, Frances M. B. Lynch; one *d*; one *d*. *Educ:* University College London (BA 1956); LSE (PhD 1960); MA Manchester 1981. Asst Lectr in Indian Archaeology, Univ. of London, 1959; Lectr in Economic

History, Univ. of Edinburgh, 1960; Sen. Lectr in Social Studies, Univ. of East Anglia, 1965; Associate Prof. of Economics, Stanford Univ., 1969; Prof. of European Studies, UMIST, 1971; Prof. of Contemp. Hist., Eur. Univ. Inst., 1983–86 and 1996–2002. Visiting Professor: Stanford Univ., 1966; Ecole Pratique des Hautes Etudes, 1977, 1990; Univ. of Illinois, 1978; Univ.-Gesamthochschule, Siegen, 1980; Oslo Univ., 1990; Aarhus Univ., 1992; Trondheim Univ., 1993–2000; Sen. Vis. Fellow, St John's Coll., Oxford, 2002–03. Hon. Fellow, Royal Norwegian Acad. of Scis and Letters, 1994. *Publications:* The German Economy at War, 1965; The New Order and the French Economy, 1970; The Social and Economic Effects of the Two World Wars on Britain, 1971, 2nd edn 1984; The Fascist Economy in Norway, 1972; (with S. B. Saul) The Economic Development of Continental Europe 1780–1870, 1973; (with S. B. Saul) The Development of the Economies of Continental Europe 1870–1914, 1977; War, Economy and Society, 1977; The Reconstruction of Western Europe 1945–1951, 1984, 2nd edn 1987; (with B. Martin) Landwirtschaft und Ernährung im Zweiten Weltkrieg, 1984; The European Rescue of the Nation-State, 1992; The Frontier of National Sovereignty, 1993; (with G. Brennan) Britain's Place in the World: a historical enquiry into import controls 1945–60, 1996; The Rise and Fall of a National Strategy 1945–1963, 2002. *Recreation:* theatre. *Address:* 5 Richmond Crescent, N1 0LZ. *Died 28 Sept. 2010.*

MINGHELLA, Anthony, CBE 2001; writer and film director; *b* 6 Jan. 1954; *s* of Edward Minghella and Gloria Alberta Minghella, MBE; *m* Carolyn Choa; one *s*, and one *d* by previous *m*. *Educ:* Hull Univ. (BA). Lectr in Drama, Hull Univ., 1976–81. Chm., BFI, 2003–. *Plays include: theatre:* Two Planks and a Passion, Exeter, 1983, Greenwich, 1984; A Little Like Drowning, Hampstead, 1984; Made in Bangkok, Aldwych, 1986; *television* includes: Whale Music; What If It's Raining, 1986; Inspector Morse (various episodes); *films:* (wrote and dir.) Truly, Madly, Deeply, 1991 (BAFTA and Writers' Guild Awards for best original screenplay, 1992); (dir.) Mr Wonderful, 1993; (adapted and dir.) The English Patient, 1997 (Academy Award for best dir; BAFTA Award for best adapted screenplay); (adapted and dir.) The Talented Mr Ripley, 2000; (adapted and dir.) Cold Mountain, 2003; (wrote and dir.) Breaking and Entering, 2006; *radio:* Hang Up, 1987; Cigarettes and Chocolate, 1988; *opera:* (dir.) Madam Butterfly, ENO, 2005 (Olivier Award, 2006). First Hon. Freeman, IoW, 1997. Hon. DLit Hull, 1997. *Publications:* Whale Music, 1983; Made in Bangkok, 1986; Jim Henson's Storyteller, 1988; Interior—Room; Exterior—City, 1989; Plays: One, 1992; Driven to Distraction: a case for Inspector Morse, 1994; Plays: Two, 1997, The English Patient (screenplay), 1997; Minghella on Minghella, ed T. Bricknell, 2005. *Died 18 March 2008*

MINGINS, Rev. Canon Marion Elizabeth; Canon Residentiary, 1993–2002, Canon Pastor, 1999–2002, St Edmundsbury Cathedral, then Canon Emeritus; Chaplain to the Queen, since 1996; *b* 12 July 1952; *d* of George and Marion Mingins. *Educ:* Univ. of Birmingham (BSocSci and Social Admin); Univ. of Leicester (CQSW); Church Army Training Coll. (Cambridge Dip. Religious Studies). Warden, Church Army Old People's Home, 1979; Selection Sec., later Sen. Selection Sec., ACCM, Gen. Synod of C of E, 1983–89; ordained deacon, 1987; Novice, Order of Holy Paraclete, Whitby, 1989; Diocesan Vocations Advr and Asst Diocesan Dir of Ordinands, 1991–92, Diocesan Dir of Ordinands, 1992–99, St Edmundsbury and Ipswich; ordained priest, 1994. *Recreations:* analytical psychology, reading novels, politics. *Address:* 54 College Street, Bury St Edmunds, Suffolk IP33 1NH. *T:* (01284) 753396. *Died 26 June 2006.*

MINOGUE, Maj.-Gen. Patrick John O'Brien; Commander, Base Organisation, Royal Army Ordnance Corps, 1975–78; *b* 28 July 1922; *s* of Col M. J.

Minogue, DSO, MC, late East Surrey Regt, and Mrs M. V. E. Minogue; *m* 1st, 1950, June Elizabeth (*née* Morris) (*d* 2000); one *s* two *d*; 2nd, 2005, Carol Lee; three step *d*. *Educ*: Brighton Coll.; RMCS. FBCS, FIWSP, FIMH; jssc, psc, ato. Indian Army, 1942–46; East Surrey Regt, 1947; RAOC, 1951; served UK, BAOR, USA, Cyprus; Col, 1969; Brig., 1971; Insp. RAOC, 1971–73; Comdt, Central Ord. Depot, Bicester, 1973–75; Maj.-Gen. 1975. Hon. Col, RAOC (TAVR), 1975–78; Col Comdt, RAOC, 1980–87. Group Systems Controller, Lansing Bagnall Ltd, 1978–81; Chm., LT Electronics, 1979–81. Mem., Sandhurst Foundn, 2008–. Mem., Spanish Golf Fedn, 1982–. CCMI (FBIM 1976, CBIM 1980). *Recreations*: cricket, sailing (Cdre Wayfarer Class, UK, 1975; RYA Coach), golf, shooting, gun-dogs, athletics, lawn bowling. *Address*: 26 Pegasus Court, South Street, Yeovil BA20 1ND. *Clubs*: MCC; Army Sailing Association; Royal Logistic Corps Yacht; Milocarian Athletic; Staff College (Camberley); Yeovil Golf; Cabrera Lawn Bowling (Pres., 1987–92). *Died 31 Oct. 2010.*

MIRVISH, Edwin, OC 1987; CBE 1989; *b* 24 July 1914; *s* of David and Anna Mirvish; *m* 1941, Anne Maklin; one *s*. *Educ*: Toronto. Proprietor: Ed Mirvish Enterprises and other cos; Honest Ed's World Famous Bargain Shopping Centre, 1948–; Mirvish Village; Royal Alexandra Theatre, Toronto, 1962–; Old Vic Theatre, 1982–98; Princess of Wales Theatre, Toronto, 1993–. Hon. LLD: Trent Univ., 1967; Univ. of Waterloo, 1969; Fellow, Ryerson Technical Inst., 1981. Freeman, City of London, 1984. Award of Merit, City of Toronto. *Recreation*: ballroom dancing. *Address*: 581 Bloor Street West, Toronto, ON M6G 1K3, Canada. *T*: (416) 5372111. *Clubs*: Empire, Canadian, Arts and Letters, Variety (Toronto). *Died 11 July 2007.*

MISCAMPBELL, Norman Alexander; QC 1974; barrister; a Recorder of the Crown Court, 1977–95; *b* 20 Feb. 1925; *s* of late Alexander and Eileen Miscampbell; *m* 1961, Margaret Kendall; two *s* two *d*. *Educ*: St Edward's Sch., Oxford; Trinity Coll., Oxford. Called to Bar, Inner Temple, 1952, Bencher 1983; N Circuit. Mem., Criminal Injuries Compensation Bd, 1993–2000. Mem., Hoylake UDC, 1955–61. Contested (C) Newton, 1955, 1959; MP (C) Blackpool North, 1962–92. *Address*: 1 Temple Gardens, Temple, EC4Y 9BB. *Died 16 Feb. 2007.*

MISCHLER, Norman Martin; Chairman: Hoechst UK Ltd, 1975–84; Hoechst Ireland Ltd, 1976–84; Berger Jenson & Nicholson Ltd, 1979–84; *b* 9 Oct. 1920; *s* of late Martin Mischler and Martha Sarah (*née* Lambert); *m* 1949, Helen Dora Sinclair (*d* 2007); one *s* one *d*. *Educ*: St Paul's Sch., London; St Catharine's Coll., Cambridge (MA). Cricket Blue, 1946. Indian Army, 1940; served in Burma Campaign; released, rank of Major, 1946. Joined Burt, Boulton & Haywood, 1947, Vice-Chm. 1963; Dep. Man. Dir, Hoechst UK Ltd, 1966; Chairman: Harlow Chemical Co. Ltd, 1972–74; Kalle Infotec Ltd, 1972–74; Director: Berger, Jenson & Nicholson Ltd, 1975–84; Ringsdorff Carbon Co. Ltd, 1968–84; Vice-Chm., German Chamber of Industry and Commerce in London, 1974–84; Mem. Council, Chemical Industries Assoc. Ltd, 1975–84. Freeman, City of London. Officer's Cross, German Order of Merit, 1985. *Recreations*: cricket, opera, and theatre. *Address*: Scott House, Earsham Street, Bungay, Suffolk NR35 1AF. *Club*: Hawks (Cambridge). *Died 10 Sept. 2009.*

MISHCON, Baron *cr* 1978 (Life Peer), of Lambeth in Greater London; **Victor Mishcon;** DL; Solicitor; Senior Partner, Mishcon de Reya (formerly Victor Mishcon & Co.), 1988–92, then Consultant; *b* 14 Aug. 1915; *s* of Rabbi Arnold and Mrs Queenie Mishcon; *m* 1st, 1940, Jean Marie Hydleman (*d* 1943); 2nd, 1945, Beryl Honor Posnansky (marr. diss. 1959); two *s* one *d*; 3rd, 1967, Doreen Segal (*née* Hayden (marr. diss.); 4th, 1976, Joan Estelle Conrad (marr. diss. 2001). *Educ*: City of London Sch. Mem. Lambeth Borough Coun., 1945–49 (Chm. Finance Cttee, 1947–49); Mem. London CC for Brixton,

1946–65 (Chairman: Public Control Cttee, 1947–52; Gen. Purposes Cttee, 1952–54; Council, April 1954–55; Supplies Cttee, 1956–57; Fire Brigade Cttee, 1958–65); Mem. GLC for Lambeth, 1964–67 (Chm., Gen. Purposes Cttee, 1964–67); Mem., ILEA, 1964–67. Member: Jt Cttee with House of Commons on Consolidation of Bills, 1983–85; Law Sub-Cttee, House of Lords European Communities Cttee, 1978–86; House of Lords Select Cttee on Procedure, 1981–83; House of Lords Select Cttee on Med. Ethics, 1993; Opposition spokesman, House of Lords, on home affairs, 1983–90, on legal affairs, 1983–92. Vice Chm., Lords and Commons Solicitors Gp, 1983–. Chm. Governors, Cormont and Loughborough Secondary Schools, 1947–60; Governor: Stockwell Manor Sch., 1960–78 (Chm. of Governors, 1960–67, 1970–78); JFS Comprehensive Sch., 1970–85; Philippa Fawcett Coll. of Educn, 1970–80. Member: Standing Joint Cttee, Co. of London Sessions, 1950–65 (Vice-Chm. 1959–61); Nat. Theatre Board, 1965–67, 1968–90; South Bank Theatre Board, 1977–82; London Orchestra Bd, 1966–67; Exec. Cttee, London Tourist Board, 1965–67; Government Cttee of Enquiry into London Transport, 1953–54; Departmental Cttee on Homosexual Offences and Prostitution, 1954–57. Vice-Chm., Council of Christians and Jews, 1976–77; Vice-Pres., Bd of Deputies of British Jews, 1967–73; Hon. President, Brit. Technion Soc.; Vice-Pres. (Past Pres.) Assoc. of Jewish Youth; Pres., British Council of the Shaare Zedek Hosp., Jerusalem. Contested (Lab) NW Leeds, 1950, Bath, 1951, Gravesend, 1955, 1959. DL Greater London, 1954. Hon. QC 1992. Hon. Fellow, UCL, 1993. Hon. LLD Birmingham, 1991. Comdr Royal Swedish Order of North Star, 1954; Star of Ethiopia, 1954; Star of Jordan, 1995. *Address*: House of Lords, SW1A 0PW. *Died 27 Jan. 2006.*

MISKIN, Raymond John, CEng, FIMechE, FIEE, MRAeS, FIQA; Chief Executive, Certification Authority for Dental Laboratories and Suppliers, 1989–93; *b* 4 July 1928; *s* of late Sydney George Miskin and Hilda (*née* Holdsworth); *m* 1st, 1951, Betty Tavener (marr. diss. 1981); one *d* (one *s* decd); 2nd, 1991, Brenda (*née* Mills). *Educ*: Woking Grammar Sch.; Southall Technical Coll. The Fairey Aviation Co. Ltd: apprentice, 1945–49; develt engr, 1949–59; Dep. Chief Inspector, 1959–63; Quality Control Manager and Chief Inspector, Graviner Ltd, 1963–69; Sec., Inst. of Qual. Assurance, 1969–73; Dep. Sec., 1973–76, Sec., 1976–87, IProdE; Dir, IPRODE Ltd, 1976–87. Mem. Council and Hon. Treasurer, Inst. of Qual. Assurance, 1963–69; Mem., Bd, Nat. Council for Qual. and Reliability, 1969–81 (Chm., 1975–77). Hon. Mem., Amer. Inst. of Industrial Engrs, 1985. FSME 1994. Hon. FIIPE 1979. Freeman, City of London, 1985. Internat. Industrial Management Award, San Fernando Valley Engineers Council, USA, 1978; Internat. Achievement Award, Los Angeles Council of Engrs, 1981; GTE (Hungary) Technical Achievement Medal, 1984. *Publications*: articles in technical pubns. *Recreation*: golf. *Address*: 36 Hayes Drive, Mosborough, Sheffield S20 4TR. *Club*: Renishaw Park Golf. *Died 9 April 2006.*

MITCHELL, Adrian; writer; *b* 24 Oct. 1932; *s* of James Mitchell and Kathleen Fabian; *m* 1st, Maureen Bush (marr. diss. 1963); two *s* one *d*; 2nd, Celia Hewitt; two *d*. *Educ*: Greenways Sch.; Dauntsey's Sch.; Christ Church, Oxford. Worked as reporter on Oxford Mail, Evening Standard, 1955–63; subseq. free-lance journalist for Daily Mail, Sun, Sunday Times, New Statesman; Granada Fellow, Univ. of Lancaster, 1968–69; Fellow, Center for Humanities, Wesleyan Univ., 1972; Resident Writer, Sherman Theatre, Cardiff, 1974–75; Vis. writer, Billericay Comp. Sch., 1978–80; Judith E. Wilson Fellow, Cambridge Univ., 1980–81; Resident writer, Unicorn Theatre for Children, 1982–83; Fellow in Drama, Nanyang Univ., Singapore, 1995; Dylan Thomas Fellow, UK Festival of Literature, 1995. Poetry Editor, New Statesman and Society, 1994–96. FRSL 1987. Hon. DArts N London, 1997. Apptd shadow poet laureate by Red Pepper mag., 2003. *Plays*: Marat/Sade (stage adaptation), RSC, 1964; Tyger, NT Co. at New Theatre, 1971; Man Friday, 7:84 Theatre Co., 1973 (TV 1972, Screenplay 1975); Mind Your Head, Liverpool Everyman, 1973; Daft as a Brush (TV), 1975; A Seventh Man, Hampstead, 1976; White Suit Blues, Nottingham, Edinburgh and Old Vic, 1977; Houdini, Amsterdam, 1977; Glad Day (TV), 1978; Uppendown Mooney, Welfare State Theatre Co., 1978; The White Deer, Unicorn Theatre, 1978; Hoagy, Bix and Wolfgang Beethoven Bunkhaus, King's Head Theatre, 1979; In the Unlikely Event of an Emergency, Bath, 1979; Peer Gynt (adaptation), Oxford Playhouse, 1980; You Must Believe All This (TV), 1981; The Tragedy of King Real, Welfare State Theatre Co., 1982; Mowgli's Jungle, Contact Theatre, Manchester, 1982; A Child's Christmas in Wales (with Jeremy Brooks), Great Lakes Fest., 1983; The Wild Animal Song Contest, Unicorn Theatre, 1983; Life's a Dream (adaptation with John Barton), RSC Stratford, 1983, Barbican, 1984; C'Mon Everybody, Tricycle Theatre, 1984; The Great Theatre of the World (adaptation), Mediaeval Players, 1984; Satie Day/Night, Lyric Studio, Hammersmith, 1986; Mirandolina (adaptation), Bristol Old Vic, 1987; The Last Wild Wood in Sector 88, Rugby Music Centre, 1987; Anna on Anna, Th. Workshop, Edinburgh, 1988; Woman Overboard, The Patchwork Girl of Oz, Palace Th., Watford, 1988; The Snow Queen, NY, 1990; Vasilisa The Fair (adaptation), NY, 1991; Pieces of Peace (TV), 1991; Unicorn Island, Dartington, 1992; The Blue, Walk the Plank, Fitzcarraldo Theatre Ship, Glasson Dock, Lancs and other UK ports, 1992; A New World and The Tears of the Indians (adaptation), Nuffield Theatre, Southampton, 1992; Meet the Baron, Dartington, 1993; Sir Fool's Quest, Dartington and nat. tour, 1994; Tyger Two, Boston, USA, 1995; Tom Kitten and his Friends, Unicorn Th., 1995; The Siege, Nat. Playwright Commissioning Gp, 1996–97; The Little Violin (adaptation), Tricycle Th., 1998; The Lion, the Witch and the Wardrobe (adaptation), RSC, 1998; Start Again, Morecambe, 1998; Jemima Puddleduck and her Friends, Unicorn Th., 1998; The Heroes (trilogy), Kageboushi Th., Japan, 1999; The Mammoth Sails Tonight, Dream Factory, Warwick, 1999; All Shook Up, Tricycle Th., 2001; Alice in Wonderland (adaptation), RSC, 2001; Peter Rabbit and his Friends, Unicorn Th., 2002; Aladdin, Doublejoint, Belfast, 2005; King of Shadows, NY, 2005; Nobody Rides the Unicorn, Puppetcraft, Devon, 2005; Perseus and the Gorgon's Head, Puppetcraft, Devon, 2006; The Fear Brigade, Global Village, Kent, 2006; Maudie and the Green Children, Playhouse, 2008; To the River (radio), 2008; National Theatre: The Mayor of Zalamea (adaptation), 1981; Animal Farm (lyrics), 1984; The Government Inspector, 1985; The Pied Piper, 1986; Love Songs of World War Three, 1987; Fuente Ovejuna (adaptation), 1989; Triple Threat, 1989. Publications: novels: If You See Me Comin', 1962; The Bodyguard, 1970; Wartime, 1973; poetry: Poems, 1964; Out Loud, 1968; Ride the Nightmare, 1971; The Apeman Cometh, 1975; For Beauty Douglas, (Collected Poems 1953–1979), 1982; On the Beach at Cambridge, 1984; Nothingmas Day, 1984; Love Songs of World War Three, 1988; All My Own Stuff, 1991; Adrian Mitchell's Greatest Hits—The Top Forty, 1991; Blue Coffee, 1996; Heart on the Left, 1997; All Shook Up, 2000; (ed) Blackbird Singing: lyrics and poems of Paul McCartney, 2001; The Shadow Knows, 2004; for children: The Baron Rides Out, 1985; The Baron on the Island of Cheese, 1986; The Baron All At Sea, 1987; Leonardo the Lion from Nowhere, 1987; Our Mammoth, 1987; Our Mammoth Goes to School, 1987; Our Mammoth in the Snow, 1988; The Pied Piper, 1988; Strawberry Drums, 1989; The Thirteen Secrets of Poetry, 1993; (ed) The Orchard Book of Poems, 1993; Maudie and the Green Children, 1996; Gynormous!, 1996; Balloon Lagoon, 1997; Robin Hood and Marian, 1998; Twice My Size, 1998; My Cat Mrs Christmas, 1998; Nobody Rides the Unicorn, 1999; (ed) Dancing in the Street, 1999; Zoo of Dreams, 2001; (ed) A Poem A Day,

2001; Daft as a Doughnut, 2004; also plays. *Address:* c/o United Agents, 12–26 Lexington Street, W1F 0LE. *Club:* Chelsea Arts. *Died 20 Dec. 2008.*

MITCHELL, Angelica Elizabeth; Her Honour Judge Angelica Mitchell; a Circuit Judge, since 1998; b 21 Aug. 1948; o d of Sir George Mitchell, CB, QC (Scot.) and Elizabeth Mitchell (née Leigh Pemberton); m 1981, (James) Nicholas Browne, QC; two d. *Educ:* Putney High Sch.; Inns of Court Sch. of Law. Called to the Bar, Gray's Inn, 1972 (Bencher, 2005); an Asst Recorder, 1992–95; a Recorder, 1995–98. Mem., Steering Gp Adv. Cttee for Diploma in Forensic Psychotherapy, Portman Clinic, 1998–. Mem. Bd, 1999–2004, Mem. Adv. Gp, 2004–, Hampstead Theatre. Trustee, Noel Buxton Trust, 1990–2005. Patron, Art Room, Oxford, 2002–. *Recreations:* reading, opera, watching cricket, theatre, being with family and friends. *Died 7 Feb. 2006.*

MITCHELL, Sir Derek (Jack), KCB 1974 (CB 1967); CVO 1966; Second Permanent Secretary (Overseas Finance), HM Treasury, 1973–77; b 5 March 1922; s of late Sidney Mitchell, Schoolmaster, and Gladys Mitchell; m 1944, Miriam (d 1993), d of late F. E. Jackson; one s two d. *Educ:* St Paul's Sch.; Christ Church, Oxford. Served War of 1939–45: Royal Armoured Corps and HQ London District, 1942–45. Asst Principal HM Treasury, 1947; Private Sec to Economic Sec., 1948–49; Private Sec. to Permanent Sec. and Official Head of Civil Service (Sir Edward Bridges), 1954–56; Principal Private Secretary to: Chancellor of Exchequer (Mr Reginald Maudling), 1962–63; The Prime Minister (Mr Harold Wilson, previously Sir Alec Douglas-Home), 1964–66; Under-Sec., 1964; Dep Under Sec. of State, DEA, 1966–67; Dep. Sec., MAFF, 1967–69; Economic Minister and Head of UK Treasury and Supply Delegn, Washington, (also UK Exec. Dir for IMF and IBRD), 1969–72. Director: Guinness Mahon & Co., 1977–78; Bowater Corp., 1979–84; Bowater Industries, 1984–89; Bowater Inc., 1984–93; Standard Chartered, 1979–89; Ind. Dir, The Observer Ltd, 1981–93; Sen. Advr, Shearson Lehman Brothers Internat., 1979–88; Chm., Jocelyn Burton Silversmith & Goldsmith Ltd, 1991–98. Mem., PLA, 1979–82. Dir, Peter Hall Production Co. Ltd, 1989–90; Mem. Bd, NT, later RNT, 1977–95; Chm., Royal Nat. Theatre Foundn, 1989–2002 (Treas., 1982–89); Bd Mem., French Theatre Season, London 1997, 1996–99. Mem. Council, University Coll. London, 1978–82; Governing Trustee, Nuffield Trust (formerly Nuffield Provincial Hospitals Trust), 1978–98; Trustee, Royal Nat. Theatre Endowment Fund, 1990–2000. *Recreations:* opera, theatre, music, motoring on minor roads. *Died 16 Aug. 2009.*

MITCHELL, Douglas Svärd; Controller of Personnel and Administrative Services, Greater London Council, 1972–78; b 21 Aug. 1918; er s of late James Livingstone Mitchell and Hilma Josefine (née Svärd); m 1943, Winifred Thornton Paterson (d 2002), d of late William and Ellen Paterson; one s two d. *Educ:* Morgan Academy, Dundee. Royal Ordnance Factories, 1937–51; Principal, Min. of Supply, 1951–55; Dir of Personnel and Admin, in Industrial, Production and Engineering Groups, UKAEA, 1955–63; Authority Personnel Officer for UKAEA, 1963–64; Dir of Establishments, GLC, 1964–72. *Address:* The Manor House, Horncastle, Lincolnshire LN9 5HF. *T:* (01507) 523553. *Died 16 Nov. 2009.*

MITCHELL, Helen Josephine, (Mrs Michael Mitchell); see Watts, H. J.

MITCHELL, John Wesley, PhD, DSc; FRS 1956; Senior Research Fellow and Emeritus Professor, University of Virginia, since 1979; b 3 Dec. 1913; s of late John Wesley Mitchell and Lucy Ruth Mitchell; m 1976, Virginia Hill; one step d of former marriage. *Educ:* Canterbury University Coll., Christchurch, NZ; Univ. of Oxford. BSc 1934. MSc 1935, NZ; PhD 1938, DSc 1960, Oxford. Reader in Experimental Physics in the Univ. of Bristol, 1945–59; Prof. of Physics, Univ. of Virginia, 1959–63; Dir of the National Chemical

Laboratory, Oct. 1963–Aug. 1964; William Barton Rogers Prof. of Physics, Univ. of Virginia, 1964–79. Hon. FRPS 1995. Commonwealth of Virginia Lifetime Achievement Award in Science, 1993; Progress Medal, RPS, 1995. *Publications:* various on photographic sensitivity and on plastic deformation of crystals in scientific journals. *Recreation:* colour photography. *Address:* Department of Physics, University of Virginia, PO Box 400714, Charlottesville, VA 22904–4714, USA. *Clubs:* Athenæum; Cosmos (Washington, DC). *Died 12 July 2007.*

MITCHELL, Keith Kirkman, OBE 1979; Lecturer in Physical Education, University of Leeds, 1955–90; *b* 25 May 1927; *s* of John Stanley Mitchell and Annie Mitchell; *m* 1950, Hannah Forrest; two *s. Educ:* Loughborough Coll. (Hons Dip. in Physical Educn). Phys. Educn Master, Wisbech Grammar Sch., 1950–52; Dir of Phys. Recreation, Manchester YMCA, 1952–55. Chm. Exec. Cttee, CCPR, 1981–87; Mem., Sports Council, 1976–87. Dir, 1953–84, Pres., 1985, then Pres. Emeritus and Patron, England Basketball (formerly English Basketball Assoc.). *Recreations:* basketball, photography, gardening, golf. *Address:* 6 Kirkbourne Grove, Baildon, Shipley BD17 6HW. *T:* (01274) 584907. *Died 12 Jan. 2010.*

MITCHELL, Prof. Ross Galbraith, MD, FRCPE, FRCPCH; Professor of Child Health, University of Dundee and Pædiatrician, Ninewells Hospital, Dundee, 1973–85, then Emeritus; *b* 18 Nov. 1920; *s* of late Richard Galbraith Mitchell, OBE and Ishobel, *d* of late James Ross, Broadford, Skye; *m* 1950, June Phylis Butcher; one *s* three *d. Educ:* Kelvinside Acad.; University of Edinburgh (MB, ChB 1944); DCH. Surg-Lt, RNVR, 1944–47; Jun. hosp. posts, Liverpool, London, Edinburgh, 1947–52; Rockefeller Res. Fellow, Mayo Clinic, USA, 1952–53; Lectr in Child Health, Univ. of St Andrews, 1952–55; Cons. Pædiatrician, Dundee Teaching Hosps, 1955–63; Prof. of Child Health, Univ. of Aberdeen, Pædiatrician, Royal Aberdeen Children's and Aberdeen Maternity Hosps, 1963–72; Univ. of Dundee: Dean, Faculty of Medicine and Dentistry, 1978–81; Mem. Court, 1982–85. Chairman: Scottish Adv. Council on Child Care, 1966–69; Specialist Adv. Cttee on Pædiatrics, 1975–79; Academic Bd, British Pædiatric Assoc., 1975–78; Spastics Internat. Med. Pubns, 1981–85; Mac Keith Press, London, 1986–95; Mem., GMC, 1983–86. President: Harveian Soc., Edinburgh, 1982–83; Scottish Paediatric Soc., 1982–84. For. Corresp. Mem., Amer. Acad. of Cerebral Palsy and Developmental Medicine, 1965–. Jt Editor, Developmental Medicine and Child Neurology, 1968–80. *Publications:* Disease in Infancy and Childhood, 7th edn, 1973; Child Life and Health, 5th edn, 1970; Child Health in the Community, 2nd edn, 1980; contribs to textbooks of paediatrics, medicine and obstetrics and articles in scientific and medical jls. *Recreations:* Celtic language and literature, oil painting. *Address:* Craigard, Abertay Gardens, Broughty Ferry, Dundee DD5 2RR. *Died 14 Aug. 2006.*

MITCHELL, Rev. Mgr William Joseph; Parish Priest, St Michael's, Tetbury, since 2001; *b* 4 Jan. 1936; *s* of late William Ernest and Catherine Mitchell. *Educ:* St Brendan's Coll., Bristol; Corpus Christi Coll., Oxford (MA); Séminaire S Sulpice, Paris; Gregorian Univ., Rome (LCL). Ordained Priest, Pro-Cathedral, Bristol, 1961; Curate, Pro-Cathedral, Bristol, 1963–64; Secretary to Bishop of Clifton, 1964–75; Parish Priest, St Bernadette, Bristol, 1975–78; Rector, Pontifical Beda Coll., Rome, 1978–87; VG, 1987–2001; Judicial Vicar, 2002–07, Dio. Clifton; Parish Priest: St John's, Bath, 1988–90; St Antony's, Bristol, 1990–96; St Mary's, Bristol, 1996–97; Adminr, subseq. Dean, Clifton Cathedral, Bristol, 1997–2001. Canon, Clifton Cathedral Chapter, 1987–. Prelate of Honour, 1978. KHS 2003. *Address:* St Michael's Presbytery, 31 Silver Street,

Tetbury, Glos GL8 8DH. *T:* (01666) 502367; *e-mail:* billmitchell@tetbury31.freeserve.co.uk. *Died 29 Aug. 2008.*

MITHEN, Dallas Alfred, CB 1983; Chairman, Forestry Training Council, 1984–93; Commissioner for Harvesting and Marketing, Forestry Commission, 1977–83; *b* 5 Nov. 1923; *m* 1st, 1947, Peggy (*née* Clarke) (decd); one *s* one *d*; 2nd, 1969, Avril Teresa Dodd (*née* Stein). *Educ:* Maidstone Grammar Sch.; UC of N Wales, Bangor (BSc Forestry). Fleet Air Arm, 1942–46. Joined Forestry Commission as District Officer, 1950; Dep. Surveyor, New Forest and Conservator SE (England), 1968–71; Senior Officer (Scotland), 1971–75; Head of Forest Management Div., Edinburgh, 1975–76. Pres., Inst. of Chartered Foresters, 1984–86; Pres., Forestry Section, BAAS, 1985. Trustee, Central Scotland Woodland Trust, 1985–95. *Recreations:* gardening, swimming, walking. *Address:* 12 Stanehead Park, Biggar, South Lanarkshire ML12 6PU. *T:* (01899) 221308. *Died 20 Feb. 2006.*

MITRA, Dr Ashesh Prosad, FRS 1988; FNA; Hon. Scientist of Eminence, National Physical Laboratory, New Delhi, since 1997; Bhatnagar Fellow, Council of Scientific and Industrial Research, 1991–96; *b* 21 Feb. 1927; *s* of late A. C. Mitra and Subarna Prova Mitra; *m* 1956, Sunanda Mitra; two *d. Educ:* University of Calcutta (DPhil 1955). FNA 1963. Res. Assistant, Calcutta Univ., 1949–51; Colombo Plan Fellow, CSIRO, Sydney, 1951; Vis. Asst Prof. of Engrg Res., 1952–53, Vis. Prof., 1953–54, Penn. State Univ.; National Physical Laboratory, New Delhi: Sec., Radio Res. Cttee, 1954–56; Head, Radio Propagation Unit, later Radio Sci. Div., 1956–86; Director-level Scientist, 1974–82; Dir., 1982–86; Sec. to Govt of India, Dept of Industrial & Scientific Res., and Dir-Gen., Council of Scientific and Industrial Res., 1986–91. Mem., Indian Acad. of Astronautics, 1974–; Fellow, Third World Acad. of Scis, Trieste, 1988. Hon. DSc: Manipur, 1988; Calcutta; Jadavpur; Vidyasagar; N Bengal. *Publications:* (ed) Proceedings of the International Geophysical Year Symposium, vols 1 & 2, 1962; The Chemistry of the Ionosphere, 1970; Advances in Space Exploration, vol. 6, 1979; 50 Years of Radio Science in India, 1984; (ed jtly) Handbook on Radio Propagation for Tropical and Subtropical Countries, 1987; 165 papers. *Recreation:* music. *Address:* National Physical Laboratory, Dr K. S. Krishnan Marg, New Delhi 110012, India. *T:* (11) 25745298. *Clubs:* Delhi Gymkhana, India International Centre (New Delhi); Calcutta (Calcutta). *Died 3 Sept. 2007.*

MOELWYN-HUGHES, Edmwnd Goronwy; Vice Judge Advocate General, 1994–2004; a Recorder, 1990–2003; *b* 29 Aug. 1937; twin *s* of late Dr E. A. Moelwyn-Hughes and Mair Elen Moelwyn-Hughes (*née* Evans); *m* 1964, Carolyn, *o d* of late John Sanders and Beryl (*née* Hobday); one *s* two *d. Educ:* The Leys Sch., Cambridge; Trinity Hall, Cambridge (MA). Nat. Service, 1956–58, 2nd Lieut Royal Welch Fusiliers. Called to the Bar, Inner Temple, 1968; practised Wales and Chester Circuit, 1968–73. Dep. Judge Advocate, 1973–78; Asst JAG, 1978–94; Standing Civilian Court Magistrate, 1982–96; an Asst Recorder, 1984–90; DJAG, British Forces in Germany, 1989–91. Governor: The Leys Sch., 1996–2001; St Faith's Sch., Cambridge, 1996–2001. *Recreations:* reading, music, walking, theatre. *Clubs:* Army and Navy, Royal Commonwealth Society. *Died 27 July 2010.*

MONCKTON OF BRENCHLEY, 2nd Viscount *cr* 1957; **Maj.-Gen. Gilbert Walter Riversdale Monckton,** CB 1966; OBE 1956; MC 1940; DL; FSA; Chief of Staff, HQ British Army of the Rhine, 1965–67; *b* 3 Nov. 1915; *o s* of 1st Viscount Monckton of Brenchley, PC, GCVO, KCMG, MC, QC, and Mary A. S. (*d* 1964), *d* of Sir Thomas Colyer-Fergusson, 3rd Bt; *S* father, 1965; *m* 1950, Marianna Laetitia (Dame of Honour and Devotion, SMO Malta (also Cross of Merit), OStJ, Pres., St John's Ambulance, Kent, 1975–80, High

Sheriff of Kent, 1981–82), 3rd *d* of late Comdr Robert T. Bower; four *s* one *d*. *Educ*: Harrow; Trinity Coll., Cambridge (BA 1939, MA 1942). 2/Lt 5th Royal Inniskilling Dragoon Guards, SR 1938; Reg. 1939; France and Belgium, 1939–40; Staff Coll., 1941; Bde Major Armd Bde, 1942; Comd and Gen. Staff Sch., USA, 1943; Sqdn Ldr, 3rd King's Own Hussars, 1944, Italy and Syria; Sqdn Ldr, 5th Royal Inniskilling Dragoon Gds, 1945. RAF Staff Coll., 1949; GSO2, 7th Armd Div., 1949; Sqdn Ldr and 2 i/c 5th Royal Inniskilling Dragoon Gds, Korea and Egypt, 1951–52; GSO1, Mil. Ops, WO, 1954–56; Mil. Adv., Brit. Delegn, Geneva Confs on Indo-China and Korea, 1954; transf. 12th Royal Lancers and comd, 1956–58; Comdr Royal Armd Corps, 3rd Div., 1958–60; psc, idc 1961; Dep. Dir, Personnel Admin., WO, 1962; Dir of Public Relations, WO (subseq. MoD), 1963–65. Col 9th/12th Royal Lancers (Prince of Wales's), 1967–73; Hon. Col, Kent and Sharpshooters Yeomanry Sqdn, 1974–79. President: Kent Assoc. of Boys' Clubs, 1965–78; Inst. of Heraldic and Genealogical Studies, 1965–2000; Kent Archæological Soc., 1968–75; Medway Productivity Assoc., 1968–72; Kent Co. Rifle Assoc., 1970–75; Anglo-Belgian Union, 1973–83; Chm., Thurnham Parish Council, 1968–70. FSA 1987. DL Kent, 1970. Liveryman, Broderers' Co. (Master, 1978). KStJ; Chm., Council of Order of St John for Kent, 1969–75; SMO Malta: Bailiff, Grand Cross of Obedience (Chancellor of the British Assoc., 1963–68, Vice-Pres., 1968–74, Pres., 1974–83); Grand Cross of Merit, 1980; Comdr, Order of Crown (Belgium), 1965; Grand Officer, Order of Leopold II (Belgium), 1978. *Recreation*: archaeology. *Heir*: *s* Hon. Christopher Walter Monckton, *b* 14 Feb. 1952. *Address*: Runhams Farm, Runham Lane, Harrietsham, Maidstone, Kent ME17 1NJ. *T*: (01622) 850313. *Clubs*: Brooks's, MCC; Casino Maltese (Valetta).   *Died 22 June 2006*.

MONEY, Hon. George Gilbert, CHB 1986; FCIB; Director, Barclays Bank International Ltd, 1955–81 (Vice-Chairman, 1965–73); *b* 17 Nov. 1914; 2nd *s* of late Maj.-Gen. Sir A. W. Money, KCB, KBE, CSI and Lady Money (*née* Drummond). *Educ*: Charterhouse Sch. Clerk, L. Behrens & Soehne, Bankers, Hamburg, 1931–32; Clerk, Barclays Bank Ltd, 1932–35, Dir 1972–73; joined Barclays Bank DCO (later Barclays Bank PLC), London, 1935; served in Egypt, Palestine, Cyprus, Ethiopia, Cyrenaica, E Africa, 1936–52; Local Dir, W Indies, 1952; Director: Barclays Bank of California, 1965–75; Bermuda Provident Bank Ltd, 1969–89; Barclays Bank of the Netherlands, Antilles NV, 1970–86; Republic Finance Corp. Ltd, 1972–88; Republic Bank Ltd, 1972–88; Barclays Bank of Jamaica Ltd, 1972–77; Barclays Australia Ltd, 1972–75; New Zealand United Corp., 1972–75; Chairman: Bahamas Internat. Trust Co. Ltd, 1970–72; Cayman Internat. Trust Co. Ltd, 1970–72; Mem., Caribbean Bd, Barclays Bank PLC, 1952–88. *Publications*: Nine Lives of a Bush Banker, 1990. *Recreations*: water skiing, fishing, bridge. *Address*: Saltram, St Joseph, Barbados.   *Died 23 Oct. 2008*.

MONK, Rear-Adm. Anthony John, CBE 1973; Appeals Organizer, The Royal Marsden Hospital Cancer Fund, 1984–87; *b* 14 Nov. 1923; *s* of Frank Leonard and Barbara Monk; *m* 1951, Elizabeth Ann Samson; four *s* (one *d* decd). *Educ*: Whitgift Sch.; RNC Dartmouth; RNEC Keyham. MSc, BScEng, CEng, FIMarEST, FRAeS, FIMechE. Engr Cadet, 1941; served War of 1939–45, Pacific Fleet; flying trng, Long Air Engrg Course, Cranfield, 1946; RN Air Stn Ford; RNEC Manadon, 1950; Prodn Controller and Man., RN Aircraft Yard, Belfast, 1953–56; Mem. Dockyard Work Measurement Team, subseq. Engr Officer HMS Apollo, Techn. Asst to Dir-Gen. Aircraft, Sqdn Engr Officer to Flag Officer Aircraft Carriers, 1963–65; Asst Dir of Marine Engrg, 1965–68; Dir of Aircraft Engrg, 1968; Comd Engrg Officer to Flag Officer Naval Air Comd; Naval Liaison Officer for NI and Supt RN Aircraft Yard, Belfast, 1970; Port Admiral, Rosyth, 1974–76; Rear-Adm. Engineering to Flag Officer Naval Air Comd, 1976–78. Comdr 1956; Captain 1964; Rear-Adm. 1974. Dir Gen., Brick Develt

Assoc., 1979–84. Liveryman, Co. of Engrs, 1998–. MRI. FRSA. *Recreation*: swimming (ASA teacher). *Address*: Morning Glory, Kingsdown, Deal, Kent CT14 8AT.
          Died 5 July 2010.

MONRO OF LANGHOLM, Baron *cr* 1997 (Life Peer), of Westerkirk in Dumfries and Galloway; **Hector Seymour Peter Monro,** Kt 1981; AE; PC 1995; JP; DL; *b* 4 Oct. 1922; *s* of late Capt. Alastair Monro, Cameron Highlanders, and Mrs Monro, Craigcleuch, Langholm, Scotland; *m* 1st, 1949, (Elizabeth) Anne Welch (*d* 1994), Longstone Hall, Derbys; two *s*; 2nd, 1994, Mrs Doris Kaestner, Baltimore, USA. *Educ*: Canford Sch.; King's Coll., Cambridge. RAF, 1941–46, Flight Lt; RAuxAF, 1946–53 (AE 1953). Mem. of Queen's Body Guard for Scotland, Royal Company of Archers. Dumfries CC, 1952–67 (Chm. Planning Cttee, and Police Cttee). Chm. Dumfriesshire Unionist Assoc., 1958–63. MP (C) Dumfries, 1964–97. Scottish Cons. Whip, 1967–70; a Lord Comr of HM Treasury, 1970–71; Parly Under-Sec. of State, Scottish Office, 1971–74; Opposition Spokesman on: Scottish Affairs, 1974–75; Sport, 1974–79; Parliamentary Under-Secretary of State: (with special responsibility for sport), DoE, 1979–81; Scottish Office, 1992–95. Member, Select Committee: on Scottish Affairs, 1983–86; on Defence, 1987. Chairman: Scottish Cons Members Cttee, 1983–92; Cons. Parly Cttee on Sport, 1984–85. Vice Chm., Cons. Members Agricl Cttee, 1983–87. Mem. Dumfries T&AFA, 1959–67; Hon. Air Cdre, No 2622 RAuxAF Regt Sqdn, 1982–2000; Hon. Insp. Gen., RAuxAF, 1990–2000. Member: Area Executive Cttee, Nat. Farmers' Union of Scotland; Nature Conservancy Council, 1982–91; Council, Nat. Trust for Scotland, 1983–92. President: Auto-cycle Union, 1983–90; NSRA, 1987–92. JP 1963, DL 1973, Dumfries. *Recreations*: Rugby football (Mem. Scottish Rugby Union, 1958–77, Vice-Pres., 1975, Pres., 1976–77); golf, flying, country sports, vintage sports cars. *Address*: Williamwood, Kirtlebridge, Dumfriesshire DG11 3LN. *T*: (01461) 500213. *Clubs*: Royal Air Force, MCC.
          Died 30 Aug. 2006.

MONTAGU-DOUGLAS-SCOTT, Douglas Andrew; *see* Scott.

MONTGOMERY, Hugh Bryan Greville; non-executive Director, Andry Montgomery group of companies (organisers, managers and consultants in exhibitions), since 1994 (Managing Director, 1952–88; Chairman, 1988–94); *b* 26 March 1929; *s* of Hugh Roger Greville Montgomery, MC, and Molly Audrey Montgomery, OBE (*née* Neele). *Educ*: Repton; Lincoln Coll., Oxford (MA PPE; Fleming Fellow, 1996). Founder member, Oxford Univ. Wine and Food Soc. Consultant and adviser on trade fairs and developing countries for UN; Consultant, Internat. Garden Festival, Liverpool, 1984. Chairman: Brit. Assoc. of Exhibn Organisers, 1970; Internat. Cttee, Amer. Nat. Assoc. of Exposition Managers, 1980–82 and 1990–93; British Exhibn Promotion Council, 1982–83; World Trade Centers Assoc., NY, 2000– (Founder, World Trade Center, Novosibirsk, Russia, 1993); Pres., Union des Foires Internat., 1994–97 (Vice Pres., 1987–94). Member: Adv. Bd, Hotel Inst. for Management, Montreux, 1986–2002; London Regl Cttee, CBI, 1987–90; BOTB, 1991–94. Mem. Council, Design and Industries Assoc., 1983–85. Chm. of Trustees of ECHO (Supply of Equipment to Charity Hosps Overseas), 1978–89; Chairman: Interbuild Fund, 1972–2006; The Building Museum, 1988–2000; British Architectural Library Trust, 1989–2000; Vice-Pres., Bldg Conservation Trust, 1992–94 (Vice-Chm., 1979–92); Trustee: The Cubitt Trust, 1982–99; Music for the World, 1990–92; Hon. Treas., Contemporary Art Soc., 1980–82; Councillor, Acad. of St Martin-in-the-Fields Concert Soc., 1988–2000. Member Executive Committee: CGLI, 1974–2003; Nat. Fund for Research into Crippling Diseases, 1970–92. Common Councilman, Dowgate Ward, City of London, 1999–2004. Mem. Court, Co. of

World Traders, 1992–2003 (Master, 1995); Liveryman, 1952, Master, 1980–81, Co. of Tylers and Bricklayers (Trustee, Charitable and Pension Trusts, 1981–2000). Hon. FRIBA 2001; Hon. FCGI 2002. Hon. DHL Endicott Coll., Mass, 2003. Silver Jubilee Medal, 1977; Pro Cultura Hungaria Medal, 1991; Brooch, City of Utrecht, 1992; Gold Medal, Belgrade Fair, 1995; Leadership Award, Internat. Council for Caring Communities, UN, 2000. *Publications:* Industrial Fairs and Developing Countries (UNIDO), 1975; Going into Trade Fairs (UNCTAD/GATT), 1982; Exhibition Planning and Design, 1989 (Russian edn 1991, Chinese edn 2001); The Montgomery Painting Collection at Museum of Fine Art in Budapest, 1999; contrib. to Internat. Trade Forum (ITC, Geneva). *Recreation:* commissioning contemporary sculpture. *Address:* 9 Manchester Square, W1U 3PL. *T:* (020) 7886 3123; Snells Farm, Amersham Common, Bucks HP7 9QN. *Clubs:* Oxford and Cambridge, City Livery, Guildhall. *Died 14 Dec. 2008.*

MONTGOMERY, Col John Rupert Patrick, OBE 1979; MC 1943; *b* 25 July 1913; *s* of George Howard and Mabella Montgomery; *m* 1st, 1940, Alice Vyvyan Patricia Mitchell (*d* 1976); one *s* two *d*; 2nd, 1981, Marguerite Beatrice Chambers (*née* Montgomery). *Educ:* Wellington Coll.; RMC, Sandhurst. Commissioned, Oxfordshire and Buckinghamshire LI, 1933; Regimental Service in India, 1935–40 and 1946–47. Served War in Middle East, N Africa and Italy, 1942–45. Commanded 17 Bn Parachute Regt (9 DLI), 1953–56; SHAPE Mission to Portugal, 1956–59; retired, 1962. Sec., Anti-Slavery Soc., 1963–80. Silver Medal, RSA, 1973. *Club:* Army and Navy. *Died 27 June 2008.*

MONTGOMERY WATT, William; see Watt.

MOODY, Leslie Howard; General Secretary, Civil Service Union, 1977–82; *b* 18 Aug. 1922; *s* of George Henry and Edith Jessie Moody; *m* 1944, Betty Doreen Walton; two *s*. *Educ:* Eltham College. Telephone Engineer, General Post Office, 1940–53. Served Royal Signals, Far East, 1944–47. Asst Sec., Civil Service Union, 1953, Dep. Gen. Sec., 1963. A Dep. Chm., Civil Service Appeal Bd, 1990–92. *Recreation:* reading. *Club:* Civil Service. *Died 28 April 2008.*

MOOLLAN, Sir Cassam (Ismael), Kt 1982; Chief Justice, Supreme Court of Mauritius, 1982–88; Acting Governor-General, several occasions in 1984, 1985, 1986, 1987, 1988; Commander-in-Chief of Mauritius, 1984; *b* 26 Feb. 1927; *s* of Ismael Mahomed Moollan and Fatimah Nazroo; *m* 1954, Rassoulbibie Adam Moollan; one *s* two *d*. *Educ:* Royal Coll., Port Louis and Curepipe; London Sch. of Econs and Pol Science (LLB 1950). Called to the Bar, Lincoln's Inn, 1951. Private practice, 1951–55; Dist Magistrate, 1955–58; Crown Counsel, 1958–64; Sen. Crown Counsel, 1964–66; Solicitor Gen., 1966–70; QC (Mauritius) 1969; Puisne Judge, Supreme Court, 1970; Sen. Puisne Judge, 1978. Editor, Mauritius Law Reports, 1982–84. Chevalier, Légion d'Honneur (France), 1986. *Recreations:* bridge, Indian classical and semi-classical music. *Address:* Chambers, 43 Sir William Newton Street, Port Louis, Mauritius. *T:* 2120794, 2083881, *Fax:* 2088351; 22 Hitchcock Avenue, Quatre Bornes, Mauritius. *T:* 4546949. *Died 15 Nov. 2010.*

MOORE OF WOLVERCOTE, Baron *cr* 1986 (Life Peer), of Wolvercote in the City of Oxford; **Philip Brian Cecil Moore,** GCB 1985 (KCB 1980; CB 1973); GCVO 1983 (KCVO 1976); CMG 1966; QSO 1986; PC 1977; Private Secretary to the Queen and Keeper of the Queen's Archives, 1977–86; a Permanent Lord-in-Waiting to the Queen, since 1990; *b* 6 April 1921; *s* of late Cecil Moore, Indian Civil Service; *m* 1945, Joan Ursula Greenop; two *d*. *Educ:* Dragon Sch.; Cheltenham Coll. (Scholar); Oxford Univ. Classical Exhibitioner, Brasenose Coll., Oxford, 1940. RAF Bomber Command, 1940–42 (prisoner of war, 1942–45). Brasenose Coll., Oxford, 1945–46 (Hon. Fellow 1981). Asst Private Sec. to First Lord of Admiralty, 1950–51; Principal Private Sec. to

First Lord of Admiralty, 1957–58; Dep. UK Commissioner, Singapore, 1961–63; British Dep. High Comr in Singapore, 1963–65; Chief of Public Relations. MoD, 1965–66; Asst Private Secretary to the Queen. 1966–72, Dep. Private Secretary, 1972–77. Dir, General Accident, Fire and Life Assurance Corp., 1986–91. Chm., King George VI and Queen Elizabeth Foundn of St Catharine's, Cumberland Lodge, 1986–97. Vice-Pres., SPCK. *Recreations:* golf, Rugby football (Oxford Blue, 1945–46; International, England, 1951), hockey (Oxford Blue, 1946), cricket (Oxfordshire). *Address:* Hampton Court Palace, East Molesey, Surrey KT8 9AU. *Club:* MCC. *Died 7 April 2009.*

MOORE, Prof. Derek William, FRS 1990; Professor of Applied Mathematics, Imperial College, London, 1973–96, then Professor Emeritus and Senior Research Fellow; *b* 19 April 1931; *s* of William McPherson Moore and Elsie Marjorie Moore (*née* Patterson). *Educ:* Jesus Coll., Cambridge (MA, PhD). Asst Lectr and Lectr in Maths, Bristol, 1958–64; Sen. Postdoctoral Res. Fellow, Nat. Acad. of Scis, USA, 1964; Imperial College London: Sen. Lectr, Dept of Maths, 1967; Reader in Theoretical Fluid Mechanics, 1968. Sherman Fairchild Dist. Scholar, CIT, 1986. Foreign Hon. Mem., Amer. Acad. of Arts and Scis, 1985. Sen. Whitehead Prize, LMS, 2001. *Recreation:* jazz tenor saxophone. *Address:* 71 Boileau Road, W5 3AP. *T:* (020) 8998 8572. *Died 15 July 2008.*

MOORE, Maj.-Gen. Sir Jeremy; see Moore, Maj.-Gen. Sir John J.

MOORE, Captain John Evelyn, RN; Editor: Jane's Fighting Ships, 1972–87; Jane's Naval Review, 1982–87; *b* Sant Ilario, Italy, 1 Nov. 1921; *s* of William John Moore and Evelyn Elizabeth (*née* Hooper); *m* 1st, 1945, Joan Pardoe (marr. diss. 1967); one *s* two *d*; 2nd, 1970, Barbara (*née* Kerry) (*d* 2008). *Educ:* Sherborne Sch., Dorset. Served War: entered Royal Navy, 1939; specialised in hydrographic surveying, then submarines, in 1944. Commanded HM Submarines: Totem, Alaric, Tradewind, Tactician, Telemachus. RN Staff course, 1950–51; Comdr, 1957; attached to Turkish Naval Staff, 1958–60; subseq. Plans Div., Admty; 1st Submarine Sqdn, then 7th Submarine Sqdn in comd; Captain, 1967; served as: Chief of Staff, C-in-C Naval Home Command; Capt. DI3 (Navy), Defence Intell. Staff; retired list at own request, 1972. FRGS 1942. Hon. Professor: Aberdeen Univ., 1987–90; St Andrews Univ., 1990–92. *Publications:* Jane's Major Warships, 1973; The Soviet Navy Today, 1975; Submarine Development, 1976; (jtly) Soviet War Machine, 1976; (jtly) Encyclopaedia of World's Warships, 1978; (jtly) World War 3, 1978; Seapower and Politics, 1979; Warships of the Royal Navy, 1979; Warships of the Soviet Navy, 1981; (jtly) Submarine Warfare: today and tomorrow, 1986; (ed) The Impact of Polaris, 1999. *Address:* 1 Ridgelands Close, Eastbourne, East Sussex BN20 8EP. *T:* (01323) 638836. *Died 8 July 2010.*

MOORE, Maj.-Gen. Sir (John) Jeremy, KCB 1982 (CB 1982); OBE (mil.) 1973; MC 1952, Bar 1962; *b* 5 July 1928; *s* of Lt-Col Charles Percival Moore, MC, and Alice Hylda Mary (*née* Bibby); *m* 1966, Veryan Julia Margaret Acworth; one *s* two *d*. *Educ:* Brambletye Sch.; Cheltenham Coll. Joined RM as Probationary 2/Lt, 1947; training until 1950 (HMS Sirius, 1948); Troop subaltern, 40 Commando RM, 1950–53 (MC Malayan Emergency 1952); Housemaster, RM School of Music, 1954; ADC to MGRM Plymouth Gp, 1954–55; Instructor, NCO's Sch., RM, 1955–57; Adjt, 45 Cdo RM, 1957–59; Instr, RMA Sandhurst, 1959–62; Adjt and Company Comdr, 42 Cdo RM, 1962–63 (Bar to MC Brunei Revolt 1962); Australian Staff Coll., 1963–64; GSO2 Operations, HQ 17 Gurkha Div., 1965; Asst Sec., Chiefs of Staff Secretariat, MoD, 1966–68; HMS Bulwark, 1968–69; Officer Comdg, Officers Wing Commando Trng Centre RM, 1969–71; CO 42 Cdo RM, 1972–73 (OBE operational, NI 1973); Comdt RM School of Music (Purveyor of Music to the Royal Navy), 1973–75; RCDS 1976; Comdr 3rd Cdo Bde RM,

1977–79; Maj. Gen. Commando Forces, RM, 1979–82; Comdr, Land Forces, Falkland Islands, May–July 1982; MoD, 1982–83, retired. Col Comdt, RM, 1990–93. Hon. Col, Wilts ACF, 1991–94. Director-General: Food Manufacturers' Fedn, 1984–85; Food and Drink Fedn, 1984–85. *Recreations:* music (no performing ability except on a gramophone), painting, Wells Cathedral. *Died 15 Sept. 2007.*

MOORE, Noel Ernest Ackroyd; Under-Secretary, Management and Personnel Office (formerly Civil Service Department), 1975–86, and Principal of Civil Service College, 1981–86, retired; *b* 25 Nov. 1928; *s* of late Rowland H. Moore and Hilda Moore (*née* Ackroyd); *m* 1954, Mary Elizabeth Thorpe (*d* 2008); two *s*. *Educ:* Penistone Grammar Sch., Yorks; Gonville and Caius Coll., Cambridge (MA; Major Scholar; Half-Blue for chess). Asst Principal, Post Office, 1952; Asst Private Sec. to Postmaster General, 1955–56; Private Sec. to Asst PMG, 1956–57; Principal, 1957; Sec., Cttee of Inquiry on Decimal Currency, 1961–63; Treasury, 1966; Asst Sec., 1967; Sec., Decimal Currency Bd, 1966–72; Civil Service Dept, 1972. Official Side Mem., Civil Service Appeal Bd, 1987–98. Mem., Barking and Havering FHSA, 1992–96. Consultant to EC and other bodies on relevance of UK currency decimalisation for introduction of Euro. FIPM 1985; FITD 1985. *Publications:* The Decimalisation of Britain's Currency (HMSO), 1973. *Address:* 30 Spurgate, Hutton, Brentwood, Essex CM13 2LA. *Died 30 May 2008.*

MOORE, Prof. Peter Gerald, TD 1963; PhD; FIA; Principal, London Business School, 1984–89 (Professor of Statistics, 1965–93, then Emeritus; Fellow, 1993); *b* Richmond, Surrey, 5 April 1928; *s* of late Leonard and Ruby Moore; *m* 1958, Sonja Enevoldsen Thomas, Dulwich; one *s* one *d* (and one *s* decd). *Educ:* King's College Sch., Wimbledon; University Coll. London (BSc (1st Cl. Hons Statistics), PhD; Rosa Morison Meml Medal 1949; Fellow, 1988). Served with 3rd Regt RHA, 1949–51, TA, 1951–65, Major 1963. Lectr, UCL, 1951–57; Commonwealth Fund (Harkness) Fellow, Princeton, NJ, 1953–54; Asst to Economic Adviser, NCB, 1957–59; Head of Statistical Services, Reed Paper Gp, 1959–65; Dep. Principal, London Business Sch., 1972–84. Director: Shell UK, 1969–72; Copeman Paterson Ltd, 1978–87; Martin Paterson Associates, 1984–88; Elf Petroleum UK plc, 1989–94; Partner, Duncan C. Fraser, 1974–77. Consultant, Pugh-Roberts Associates Inc., US, 1989–94. Gresham Prof. of Rhetoric, 1992–95. Member: Review Body on Doctors' and Dentists' Pay, 1971–89; Cttee on 1971 Census Security, 1971–73; UGC, 1979–84 (Vice-Chm., 1980–83); Cons. to Wilson Cttee on Financial Instns, 1977–80. Pres., Royal Statistical Soc., 1989–91 (Mem. Council, 1966–78, 1988–97; Hon. Sec., 1968–74; Guy Medal, 1970; Chambers Medal, 1995); Pres., Inst. of Actuaries, 1984–86 (Mem. Council, 1966–90; Vice-Pres., 1973–76); Member: Internat. Stat. Inst., 1972– (Council, 1985–91); Council, Internat. Actuarial Assoc., 1984–87; Industry and Employment Cttee, ESRC, 1983–88; Jarratt Cttee on Univ. Efficiency, 1984–85; Council, Hong Kong Univ. of Science and Technology, 1986–91; Acad. Council, China Europe Management Inst., Beijing, 1986–94; Univ. of London Senate, 1988–92; Council, UCL, 1989– (Vice-Chm., 1998–2000); Court, Cranfield Inst. of Technology, 1989–96; Court, City Univ., 1990–; Chm., Council of Univ. Management Schs, 1974–76; a Governor: London Business Sch., 1968–89; NIESR, 1985–; Sevenoaks Sch., 1984–90. Freeman, City of London, 1964; Mem., Court of Assts, 1987–, Master, 1994–95, Tallow Chandlers' Co. CCMI (CBIM 1986). Hon. DSc Heriot-Watt, 1985. J. D. Scaife Medal, Instn of Prodn Engrs, 1964. *Publications include:* Principles of Statistical Techniques, 1958, 2nd edn 1969; (with D. E. Edwards) Standard Statistical Calculations, 1965; Statistics and the Manager, 1966; Basic Operational Research, 1968, 3rd edn 1986; Risk and Business Decisions, 1972; (jtly) Case Studies in Decision Analysis, 1975; (with H. Thomas) Anatomy of

Decisions, 1976, 2nd rev. edn 1988; Reason by Numbers, 1980; The Business of Risk, 1983; numerous articles in professional jls. *Recreations:* cricket, opera, walking, travel. *Address:* 3 Chartway, Sevenoaks, Kent TN13 3RU. *T:* (01732) 451936. *Clubs:* Athenæum, Ward of Cordwainer. *Died 14 June 2010.*

MOORHOUSE, Geoffrey, FRSL; writer; *b* Bolton, Lancs, 29 Nov. 1931; *s* of William Heald and Gladys Heald (*née* Hoyle, subseq. Moorhouse) and step *s* of Richard Moorhouse; *m* 1st, 1956, Janet Marion Murray; two *s* one *d* (and one *d* decd); 2nd, 1974, Barbara Jane Woodward (marr. diss. 1978); 3rd, 1983, Marilyn Isobel Edwards (marr. diss. 1996). *Educ:* Bury Grammar School. Nat. Service, Royal Navy (Coder), 1950–52; editorial staff: Bolton Evening News, 1952–54; Grey River Argus (NZ), Auckland Star (NZ), Christchurch Star-Sun (NZ), 1954–56; News Chronicle, 1957; (Manchester) Guardian, 1958–70 (Chief Features Writer, 1963–70). Rode camels 2000 miles across Sahara, 1972–73; deep-sea fisherman, Gloucester, Mass, 1976–77. FRGS 1972–95; FRSL 1982. Hon. DLitt Warwick, 2006. *Publications:* in numerous editions and translations: The Other England, 1964; The Press, 1964; Against All Reason, 1969; Calcutta, 1971; The Missionaries, 1973; The Fearful Void, 1974; The Diplomats, 1977; The Boat and The Town, 1979; The Best-Loved Game, 1979 (Cricket Soc. Award); India Britannica, 1983; Lord's, 1983; To the Frontier, 1984 (Thomas Cook Award, 1984); Imperial City: the rise and rise of New York, 1988; At the George (essays), 1989; Apples in the Snow, 1990; Hell's Foundations: a town, its myths and Gallipoli, 1992; Om: an Indian pilgrimage, 1993; A People's Game: the centenary history of Rugby League football 1895–1995, 1995; Sun Dancing: a medieval vision, 1997; Sydney, 1999; The Pilgrimage of Grace: the rebellion that shook Henry VIII's throne, 2002; Great Harry's Navy: how Henry VIII gave England seapower, 2005; The Last Office: 1539 and the dissolution of a monastery, 2008. *Recreations:* music, gardening, hill-walking, looking at buildings, watching cricket, and Bolton Wanderers FC. *Address:* Park House, Gayle, near Hawes, North Yorkshire DL8 3RT. *T:* (01969) 667456. *Club:* Lancashire County Cricket. *Died 26 Nov. 2009.*

MORAN, Air Chief Marshal Sir Christopher (Hugh), KCB 2009; OBE 1997; MVO 1993; Commander-in-Chief Headquarters Air Command, since 2009; Air Aide-de-Camp to the Queen, since 2009; *b* 28 April 1956; *s* of late Edward Moran and Margaret Moran (*née* Hewitt); *m* 1980, Elizabeth Jane Goodwin; one *s* two *d*. *Educ:* Ullathorne Sch., Coventry; UMIST (BSc Hons 1977); KCL (MA 2000). Pilot Trng, RAF Coll., Cranwell, 1977–78; IV (Army Co-op.) Sqdn, Gütersloh, 1980–85; qualified Weapons Instructor (Harrier), 1983; Exchange Service, USMC, Sqdn VMA 542, 1985–87; 233 (Harrier) OCU, 1987–91; OC, IV (Army Co-op.) Sqdn, Laarbruch, 1994–96; acsc RAF Coll., Bracknell, 1991; Equerry to Duke of Edinburgh, 1992–93; OC, RAF Wittering, 1997–98; HCSC, JSCSC, Bracknell, 1999; Divl Dir, JSCSC, Bracknell, 1999–2000; Dir of Air Staff, MoD, 2000–02; AOC No 1 Gp, 2003–05; ACAS, 2005–07; Dep. Comdr, Allied Jt Force Comd, Brunssum, 2007–09. *Recreations:* ski-ing, sailing, triathlon. *Address:* c/o RAF High Wycombe, Bucks HP14 4UE. *Clubs:* Royal Air Force; Yealm Yacht. *Died 26 May 2010.*

MORDUE, Richard Eric; Director of Economics and Statistics, Ministry of Agriculture, Fisheries and Food, 1989–96, retired; *b* 14 June 1941; *s* of Ralph Yielder Mordue and Helen Mary Mordue; *m* 1979, Christine Phillips; one *s* one *d*. *Educ:* Royal Grammar Sch., Newcastle upon Tyne; King's Coll., Univ. of Durham (BSc); Michigan State Univ. (MS). Joined MAFF as Asst Economist, 1964; Sen. Economic Advr, 1978; Head of Horticulture Div., 1982. *Recreations:* golf, bridge. *Died 19 June 2008.*

MORGAN, David Gethin; County Treasurer, Avon County Council, 1973–94; *b* 30 June 1929; *s* of Edgar and Ethel Morgan; *m* 1st, 1955, Marion Brook (*d* 2001); 2nd,

2002, José Hall. *Educ:* Jesus Coll., Oxford (MA Hons English). CPFA, FInstAM(AdvDip). Accountant, Staffordshire CC, 1952–58; Computer Officer, Sen. O&M Officer, Cheshire CC, 1958–62; County Management Services Officer, Durham CC, 1962–65; Leicestershire CC: Asst County Treasurer, 1965–68; Dep. County Treasurer, 1968–73. Chm., Local Govt Finance Exec., CIPFA, 1991–92 (Vice Chm., 1987–91); Pres., Soc. of County Treasurers in England and Wales, 1988–89. Mem. Bd, UK Transplant Authy, 1996–2001. Hon. Freeman, City of London, 1989. Hon. MA UWE, 1994. *Publications:* Vol. XV Financial Information Service (IPFA). *Recreations:* local history, church architecture, tai chi. *Address:* 6 Wyecliffe Road, Henleaze, Bristol BS9 4NH. *T:* (0117) 962 9640. *Died 29 Aug. 2010.*

MORGAN, His Honour David Glyn; a Circuit Judge, 1984–2001; *b* 31 March 1933; *s* of late Dr Richard Glyn Morgan, MC, and Nancy Morgan; *m* 1959, Ailsa Murray Strang; three *d*. *Educ:* Mill Hill Sch.; Merton Coll., Oxford (MA). Called to Bar, Middle Temple, 1958; practised Oxford Circuit, 1958–70; Wales and Chester Circuit, 1970–84. A Recorder of the Crown Court, 1974–84; Assigned Judge, Newport County Court, 1987; a Designated Family Judge and Dep. High Court Judge, 1990. 2nd Lieut, The Queen's Bays, 1955; Dep. Col, 1st The Queen's Dragoon Guards, 1976. An Hon. Pres., Royal Nat. Eisteddfod of Wales, Casnewydd, 1988. *Recreations:* fishing, Rugby football, opera. *Clubs:* Cavalry and Guards; Cardiff and County (Cardiff). *Died 25 March 2010.*

MORGAN, Sir David John H.; *see* Hughes-Morgan.

MORGAN, Prof. Edwin (George), OBE 1982; Titular Professor of English, University of Glasgow, 1975–80, then Emeritus; Poet Laureate for Glasgow, 1999–2005; National Poet for Scotland, since 2004; *b* 27 April 1920; *s* of Stanley Lawrence Morgan and Margaret McKillop Arnott. *Educ:* Rutherglen Academy; High Sch. of Glasgow; Univ. of Glasgow (MA 1st Cl. Hons, Eng. Lang. and Lit., 1947). Served War, RAMC, 1940–46. University of Glasgow: Asst, 1947, Lectr, 1950, Sen. Lectr, 1965, Reader, 1971, in English. Vis. Prof., Strathclyde Univ., 1987–90; Hon. Prof., UCW, 1991–95. Visual/concrete poems in many internat. exhibns, 1965–. Opera librettos (unpublished): The Charcoal-Burner, 1969; Valentine, 1976; Columba, 1976; Spell, 1979. HRSA 1997. Hon. DLitt: Loughborough, 1981; Glasgow, 1990; Edinburgh, 1991; St Andrews, 2000; Heriot-Watt, 2000; DUniv: Stirling, 1989; Waikato, 1992; MUniv Open, 1992. Cholmondeley Award for Poets, 1968; Hungarian PEN Meml Medal, 1972; Scottish Arts Council Book Awards, 1968, 1973, 1975, 1977, 1978, 1983, 1985, 1991 and 1992; Soros Translation Award, NY, 1985; Queen's Gold Medal for Poetry, 2000. Order of Merit (Republic of Hungary), 1997. *Publications: poetry:* The Vision of Cathkin Braes, 1952; The Cape of Good Hope, 1955; (ed) Collins Albatross Book of Longer Poems, 1963; Starryveldt, 1965; Emergent Poems, 1967; Gnomes, 1968; The Second Life, 1968; Proverbfolder, 1969; Penguin Modern Poets 15, 1969; Twelve Songs, 1970; The Horseman's Word, 1970; (co–ed) Scottish Poetry 1–6, 1966–72; Glasgow Sonnets, 1972; Instamatic Poems, 1972; The Whittrick, 1973; From Glasgow to Saturn, 1973; The New Divan, 1977; Colour Poems, 1978; Star Gate, 1979; (ed) Scottish Satirical Verse, 1980; Poems of Thirty Years, 1982; Grafts/Takes, 1983; Sonnets From Scotland, 1984; Selected Poems, 1985; From the Video Box, 1986; Newspoems, 1987; Themes on a Variation, 1988; Tales from Limerick Zoo, 1988; Collected Poems, 1990; Hold Hands Among the Atoms, 1991; (ed) James Thomson, The City of Dreadful Night, 1993; Sweeping out the Dark, 1994; Virtual and Other Realities, 1997; Demon, 1999; New Selected Poems, 2000; Cathures, 2002; Love and a Life, 2003; Tales from Baron Munchausen, 2005; The Play of Gilgamesh, 2005; Thirteen Ways of Looking at Rillie, 2006; A Book of Lives, 2007; Beyond the Sun, 2007; Dreams and Other

Nightmares, 2010; *play:* A.D., a Trilogy, 2000; *prose:* Essays, 1974; East European Poets, 1976; Hugh MacDiarmid, 1976; Twentieth Century Scottish Classics, 1987; Nothing Not Giving Messages (interviews), 1990; Crossing the Border: essays in Scottish Literature, 1990; Language, Poetry, and Language Poetry, 1990; Evening Will Come They Will Sew the Blue Sail, 1991; *translations:* Beowulf, 1952; Poems from Eugenio Montale, 1959; Sovpoems, 1961; Mayakovsky, Wi the Haill Voice, 1972; Fifty Renascence Love Poems, 1975; Rites of Passage (selected poetic translations), 1976; Platen: selected poems, 1978; Master Peter Pathelin, 1983; Rostand, Cyrano de Bergerac: a new verse translation, 1992; Collected Translations, 1996; Doctor Faustus, 1999; Phaedra, 2000; Attila József, Sixty Poems, 2001; The Battle of Bannockburn, 2004. *Recreations:* photography, scrapbooks, walking in cities. *Address:* Clarence Court, 234 Crow Road, Glasgow G11 7PD. *T:* (0141) 357 7229. *Died 19 Aug. 2010.*

MORGAN, Gemmell; *see* Morgan, H. G.

MORGAN, George Lewis Bush; Chief Registrar, Bank of England, 1978–83; *b* 1 Sept. 1925; *s* of late William James Charles Morgan and Eva Averill Morgan (*née* Bush); *m* 1949, Mary Rose (*née* Vine); three *s*. *Educ:* Cranbrook Sch., Kent. Captain, Royal Sussex Regt, 1943–47. Entered Bank of England, 1947; Asst Chief Accountant, 1966; Asst Sec., 1969; Dep. Sec., 1973. Mem. Bd of Govs, Holmewood House Prep. Sch., Tunbridge Wells, 1983–98 (Chm., 1986–98). *Recreations:* golf, gardening. *Address:* Irvings Cottage, Fletching Street, Mayfield, East Sussex TN20 6TJ. *Club:* Piltdown Golf. *Died 30 March 2010.*

MORGAN, Gwyn; *see* Morgan, J. G.

MORGAN, Prof. (Henry) Gemmell; Professor of Pathological Biochemistry, University of Glasgow, 1965–88, then Professor Emeritus, and Hon. Senior Research Fellow, since 1988; *b* 25 Dec. 1922; *s* of John McIntosh Morgan, MC, MD, FRCPE, and Florence Ballantyne; *m* 1949, Margaret Duncan, BSc, MB, ChB; one *d*. *Educ:* Dundee High Sch.; Merchiston Castle Sch., Edinburgh; Univ. of St Andrews at University Coll., Dundee; BSc 1943; MB, ChB (distinction), 1946. FRCPE 1962; FRCPGlas 1968; FRCPath 1970; FRSE 1971. Res. Fellow, Endocrinology, Johns Hopkins Univ., USA, 1956–57. Hon. Consultant, Royal Hosp. for Sick Children, Glasgow, 1965–67. Hon. Consultant and Dir, Inst. of Clin. Biochem., Royal Infirmary, Glasgow, 1966–88; Chm., Med. Cttee, Royal Infirmary, Glasgow, 1984–87. Hon. Life Mem., Assoc. of Clinical Biochemists (UK), 1990 (Chm., 1982–85; Pres., 1985–87); Member: NY Acad. of Scis; British Hyperlipidaemia Assoc. Academic Advr, Univ. of London, 1970–72; External Examiner: in Biochem., Univ. of Dundee, 1974–77; Final in Pathology, Charing Cross and Westminster Med. Sch., 1985–88; UMDS of Guy's and St Thomas' Hosps, London, 1987–89; MSc and PhD Clinical Chemistry, Newcastle, 1972–74, Leeds, 1977–80, Dublin, 1979–82; Examnr in FRCS, RCPGlas, 1970–94. Chm., Scottish Br., Nutrition Soc., 1967–68. Adviser to Greater Glasgow Health Bd and Scottish Health Dept. MInstD. *Publications:* chapters; papers in medical jls on calcium, and lipoproteins. *Recreations:* golf, foreign travel, history. *Address:* Firwood House, 8 Eaglesham Road, Newton Mearns, Glasgow G77 5BG. *T:* (0141) 639 4404; *e-mail:* profmorgan@gem9.demon.co.uk. *Club:* Athenæum. *Died 31 Oct. 2006.*

MORGAN, (John) Gwyn(fryn), OBE 1999; private consultant; Head, South-East Asia, Directorate-General of External Relations, European Commission, 1995–99; Head, European Union Election Observation Team, Ivory Coast, 2000; *b* 16 Feb. 1934; *s* of Arthur G. Morgan, coal miner, and Mary Walters; *m* 1st, 1960, Joan Margaret Taylor (marr. diss. 1974); one *d*; 2nd, 1979, Colette Anne Rumball (marr. diss. 1989); two *s* one *d*; 3rd, 1990, Margery Sue Greenfield (marr. diss. 1999). *Educ:* Aberdare Boys' Grammar Sch.; UCW

Aberystwyth; MA Classics 1957; Dip. Educn 1958. Senior Classics Master, The Regis Sch., Tettenhall, Staffs, 1958–60; Pres., National Union of Students, 1960–62; Sec.-Gen., Internat. Student Conf. (ISC), 1962–65; Head of Overseas Dept, British Labour Party, 1965–69; Asst Gen. Secretary, British Labour Party, 1969–72; Chef de Cabinet to Rt Hon. George Thomson, EC Comr, 1973–75; Head of Welsh Inf. Office, EEC, 1975–79; a Dir, Development Corp. for Wales, 1976–81, Hon. Consultant in Canada 1981–83; Head of EEC Press and Inf. Office for Canada, 1979–83; EEC Rep. in Turkey, 1983–86; Hd, Delegn of EEC to Israel, West Bank and Gaza, 1987–92; Ambassador-Head of Delegn of EC to Thailand, Vietnam, Laos, Cambodia, Myanmar and Malaysia, 1993–95. Vice-Chm., European Inst. for Asian Studies, Brussels, 2000–. Mem., Hansard Commn on Electoral Reform, 1975–76. Head, EU Election Observation Unit, Indonesia, 1999. *Publications:* contribs to numerous British and foreign political jls. *Recreations:* cricket, Rugby football, crosswords, wine-tasting. *Address:* 14 Ravenscroft Road, Chiswick, W4 5EQ. *T:* (020) 8994 4218, *Fax:* (office) (020) 7460 7091. *Clubs:* Reform, Royal Commonwealth Society, MCC; Cardiff and County. *Died 21 April 2010.*

MORGAN-OWEN, John Gethin, CB 1984; MBE 1945; QC 1981; Judge Advocate General, 1979–84; *b* 22 Aug. 1914; *s* of late Maj.-Gen. Ll. I. G. Morgan-Owen, CB, CMG, CBE, DSO, West Dene, Beech, Alton; *m* 1950, Mary, *d* of late F. J. Rimington, MBE, Master Mariner; two *s* one *d*. *Educ:* Shrewsbury; Trinity Coll., Oxford (BA). Called to Bar, Inner Temple, 1938; Wales and Chester Circuit, 1939; practised at Cardiff, 1939–52. 2nd Lieut Suppl. Reserve, S Wales Borderers, 1939; served 2nd Bn SWB, 1939–44: N Norway, 1940; NW Europe, 1944–45; DAA&QMG, 146 Inf. Bde, 1944–45; Hon. Major. Dep. Judge Advocate, 1952: Germany, 1953–56; Hong Kong, 1958–60; Cyprus, 1963–66; AJAG, 1966; DJAG, Germany, 1970–72; Vice JAG, 1972–79. Jt Chm., Disciplinary Appeals Cttee, ICA, 1985–87. *Recreations:* bad tennis, inland waterways, beagling, croquet. *Died 17 Jan. 2008.*

MORISON, Air Vice-Marshal Richard Trevor, CBE 1969 (MBE 1944); RAF retired; President, Ordnance Board, 1971–72; *b* 20 Aug. 1916; *s* of late Oscar Colin Morison and Margaret Valerie (*née* Cleaver); *m* 1964, Rosemary June Brett; one *s* one *d*. *Educ:* Perse Sch., Cambridge; De Havilland Sch. of Aeronautical Engineering. Commnd in RAF, 1940; RAF Staff Coll., 1952; Sen. Techn. Officer, RAF Gaydon, 1955–57; HQ Bomber Comd, 1958–60; STSO HQ 224 Group, Singapore, 1960–61; Dir of Techn. Services, Royal NZ Air Force, 1961–63; Comd Engrg Officer, HQ Bomber Comd, 1963–65; Air Officer i/c Engrg, HQ Flying Training Comd, 1966–68; Air Officer i/c Engrg, HQ Training Comd RAF, 1968–69; Vice-Pres. (Air) Ordnance Bd, 1969–70. *Recreation:* cabinet making. *Address:* Meadow House, Chedgrave, Loddon, Norfolk NR14 6BS. *Died 23 April 2008.*

MORLEY, Prof. David Cornelius, CBE 1989; MD; FRCP; Founder and President, Teaching-aids At Low Cost (TALC), since 1964; *b* 15 June 1923; *s* of Rev. John Arthur Morley and Ruth Elwell Morley (*née* Potter); *m* 1952, Aileen Leyburn; two *s* one *d*. *Educ:* Marlborough Coll. (Foundn Schol.); Clare Coll., Cambridge (BA 1944; MB BChir 1947; MD 1955; St Thomas' Hosp. MRCS, LRCP 1947; DCH 1955; MRCP 1972, FRCP 1977. Nat. Service, Captain RAMC, Malaya, 1948–50. Gen. Practice, Yallourn, Vic, Australia, 1950–51; studied paediatrics, Newcastle-upon-Tyne, 1951–56; Paediatrician to Methodist Hosp., Ilesha, Nigeria, and Lectr, Univ. of Ibadan, 1956–61; Lectr, Dept of Human Nutrition, LSHTM, 1961–65; Institute of Child Health, London University: Sen. Lectr i/c UNICEF/WHO course for sen. paediatricians, 1965–72; Reader, 1972–78; Prof. of Tropical Child Health, 1978–88, then Prof. Emeritus. Initiated concept of Under Fives Clinics, 1961; with a colleague in Inst. of Educn, started Child-to-Child

prog., 1978, which subseq. spread worldwide; designed Growth Charts for small children. Lectured and travelled worldwide. Hon. MD Uppsala, 1986. King Faisal Award for Internat. Health, 1982; James Spence Medal, RCPCH, 1989; Leon Bernard Prize, WHO, 1992; Beacon Fellow for Lifetime in Philanthropy, 2003. *Publications:* Paediatric Priorities in the Developing World, 1978; See How They Grow, 1979; Practising Health for All, 1983; Reaching Health for All, 1993; My Name is Today, 1986 (French, Arabic and Thai edns); contribs to jls on Under Fives Clinics, Growth Charts, severe measles, diarrhoea and malnutrition. *Recreation:* gardening. *Address:* 51 Eastmoor Park, Harpenden, Herts AL5 1BN. *T:* and *Fax:* (01582) 712199; *e-mail:* david@ morleydc.demon.co.uk. *Died 2 July 2009.*

MORLEY, Herbert, CBE 1974; Director and General Works Manager, Samuel Fox & Co. Ltd, 1959–65; Director, United Steel Cos, 1966–70; *b* 19 March 1919; *s* of George Edward and Beatrice Morley; *m* 1st, 1942, Gladys Hardy (*d* 1991); one *s* one *d*; 2nd, 1994, Mrs Frances H. Suagee, Cincinnati, Ohio. *Educ:* Almondbury Grammar Sch., Huddersfield; Sheffield Univ. (Assoc. Metallurgy); Univ. of Cincinnati (Post-Grad. Studies in Business Admin). Dir and Gen. Man., Steel Peech Tozer, 1965–68; British Steel Corporation: Dir, Northern Tubes Gp, 1968–70; Man. Dir, Gen. Steel Div., 1970–73; Man. Dir, Planning and Capital Develt, 1973–76. Chm., Templeborough Rolling Mills Ltd, 1977–82; Dep. Chm. and Dir, Ellison Circlips Gp Ltd, 1990–92; Director: Ellison-Morlock, 1985–92; Bridon Ltd, 1973–85. *Recreations:* music, cricket lover, weekend golfer. *Address:* 11120 Springfield Pike, Apt A211, Cincinnati, OH 45246, USA. *T:* (513) 7822557. *Died 11 Dec. 2009.*

MORLEY, Sheridan Robert; author, journalist and broadcaster; Drama Critic, Daily Express; Drama Critic, Spectator, 1990–2005; London Drama Critic, International Herald Tribune, 1979–2005; *b* Ascot, Berks, 5 Dec. 1941; *s* of late Robert Morley, CBE and Joan Morley (*née* Buckmaster); *m* 1st, 1965, Margaret Gudejko (marr. diss. 1990); one *s* two *d*; 2nd, 1995, Ruth Leon. *Educ:* Sizewell Hall, Suffolk; Merton Coll., Oxford (MA (Hons) 1964). Newscaster, reporter and scriptwriter, ITN, 1964–67; interviewer, Late Night Line Up, BBC2, 1967–71; Presenter, Film Night, BBC2, 1972; Dep. Features Editor, The Times, 1973–75; Arts Editor, 1975–88, Drama Critic, 1975–89, Punch; Arts Diarist and TV Critic, The Times, 1989–90; Film Critic, Sunday Express, 1992–95; Regular presenter: Kaleidoscope, BBC Radio 4; Theatreland, LWT, 1995–96; Meridian, BBC World Service; Melodies for You, BBC Radio 2, 2000–; frequent radio and TV broadcasts on the performing arts, incl. Broadway Babes, Song by Song by Sondheim, Morley at the Musicals, and the Arts Programme (Radio 2), Sheridan Morley Meets (BBC1) and Countdown (C4). Mem., Drama Panel, British Council, 1982–89. Narrator: Side by Side by Sondheim, Guildford and Norwich, 1981–82; (also devised): Noël and Gertie (Coward anthology), King's Head, London, 1983; Sonning, 1985, Warehouse, London, 1986, Sydney, 1988, Comedy, London, 1989, NY, 1999; Spread a Little Happiness (Vivian Ellis anthology), King's Head and Whitehall, London, 1992; director: Song at Twilight, Gielgud, 1999; Jermyn Street Revue, 2000, Noël Coward Tonight, 2001, The Lodger, 2002, Jermyn Street Theatre; Where are the Songs we Sung?, King's Head, London, 2002; cabaret seasons, Pizza on the Park, 1992, 1994, 1995 and 1998. BP Arts Journalist of the Year, 1989. *Publications:* A Talent to Amuse: the life of Noël Coward, 1969; Review Copies, 1975; Oscar Wilde, 1976; Sybil Thorndike, 1977; Marlene Dietrich, 1977; Gladys Cooper, 1979; (with Cole Lesley and Graham Payn) Noël Coward and his Friends, 1979; The Stephen Sondheim Songbook, 1979; Gertrude Lawrence, 1981; (ed, with Graham Payn) The Noël Coward Diaries, 1982; Tales from the Hollywood Raj, 1983; Shooting Stars, 1983; The Theatregoers' Quiz Book, 1983; Katharine Hepburn, 1984; The Other Side of the Moon, 1985; (ed) Bull's Eyes, 1985; Ingrid Bergman, 1985; The Great Stage

Stars, 1986; Spread a Little Happiness, 1986; Out in the Midday Sun, 1988; Elizabeth Taylor, 1988; Odd Man Out: the life of James Mason, 1989; Our Theatres in the Eighties, 1990; Robert My Father, 1993; Audrey Hepburn, 1993; Ginger Rogers, 1995; Faces of the 90s, 1995; Dirk Bogarde: rank outsider, 1996; (with Ruth Leon): Gene Kelly, 1996; Marilyn Monroe, 1998; Hey Mr Producer!: the musicals of Cameron Mackintosh, 1999; Beyond the Rainbow: Judy Garland, 1999; Oberon Theatre Century, 1999; John G: the authorised biography of John Gielgud, 2001; Asking for Trouble (memoir), 2003; Brits in Hollywood, 2006; ed, series of theatre annuals and film and theatre studies, incl. Punch at the Theatre, 1980, Methuen Book of Theatrical Short Stories, 1992 and Methuen Book of Movie Stories, 1993; contribs to The Times, Sunday Telegraph, Evening Standard, Radio Times, Mail on Sunday, Playbill (NY), High Life, Sunday Times, Variety, and The Australian. *Recreations:* talking, swimming, eating, narrating Spread a Little Happiness and Gertie. *Address:* 7 Coral Row, Plantation Wharf, SW11 3UF; (office) 7 Ivory Square, Plantation Wharf, SW11 3UF. *Club:* Garrick.
Died 16 Feb. 2007.

MORRELL, Frances Maine; Joint Chief Executive, Arts Inform, since 1997 (Chair, 1993–97); *b* 28 Dec. 1937; *d* of Frank and Beatrice Galleway; *m* 1964, Brian Morrell (*d* 2009); one *d*. *Educ:* Queen Anne Grammar Sch., York; Hull Univ. (BA (Hons) English Lang. and Lit.); MA (Distinction) Goldsmiths Coll., Univ. of London 1995. Secondary Sch. Teacher, 1960–69; Press Officer, Fabian Soc. and NUS, 1970–72; Research into MPs' constituency role, 1973; Special Adviser to Tony Benn, as Sec. of State for Industry, then as Sec. of State for Energy, 1974–79. Dep. Leader, 1981–83, Leader, 1983–87, ILEA; Mem. for Islington S and Finsbury, GLC, 1981–86; Sec., Speaker's Commn on Citizenship, 1988–91; Exec. Dir, Inst. for Citizenship Studies, 1992–93; Dir of Studies, Practising Citizenship Project, 1994–98. Sen. Res. Fellow, Federal Trust for Educn and Res., 1993–; Mem., LSE Grad. Sch., 1996–. Member: Oakes Cttee, Enquiry into Payment and Collection Methods for Gas and Electricity Bills (report publ. 1976); Exec., Campaign for Labour Party Democracy, 1979–; Co-Founder: Labour Co-ordinating Cttee, 1978; Women's Action Cttee, 1980–. Contested (Lab) Chelmsford, Feb. 1974. Chair: NCVQ Performing Arts Adv. Cttee, 1994–; London Schs Newspaper Project, 1994–; London Schs Arts Service, 2005–; Member: Bd of Dirs, Sadler's Wells Theatre, 1982–88; Bd, King's Head Theatre, 2000–; Bd, Islington Internat. Fest., 2000– (Dep. Chm., 2001–). Hon. FRIBA 2005. *Publications:* (with Tony Benn and Francis Cripps) A Ten Year Industrial Strategy for Britain, 1975; (with Francis Cripps) The Case for a Planned Energy Policy, 1976; From the Electors of Bristol: the record of a year's correspondence between constituents and their Member of Parliament, 1977; (jtly) Manifesto—a radical strategy for Britain's future, 1981; Children of the Future: the battle for Britain's schools, 1989; The Community Sphere, 2002. *Recreations:* reading, cooking, gardening. *Address:* 91 Hemingford Road, N1 1BY.
Died 10 Jan. 2010.

MORRICE, Norman; choreographer; Director: the Royal Ballet, 1977–86; Choreographic Studies, Royal Ballet School, 1987–2000; Royal Ballet Choreographic Group, 1987–96; *b* Mexico, 10 Sept. 1931; of British parents. *Educ:* Rambert School of Ballet. Joined the Ballet Rambert in early 1950s as a dancer; notably danced Dr Coppélius, in Coppélia, and subseq. also choreographer; first considerable success with his ballet, Two Brothers, in America, and at first London perf., Sept. 1958; première of his 2nd ballet, Hazaña, Sadler's Wells Theatre, 1958; the New Ballet Rambert Company was formed in 1966 and he was Co-Dir with Marie Rambert, to create new works by unknown and established choreographers; his ballet, Hazard, was danced at Bath Festival, 1967; he composed 10 new ballets by 1968 and had taken his place with leading choreographers; *ballets include:* 1–2–3, Them

and Us and Pastorale Variée, which were staged at the Jeanetta Cochrane Theatre, 1968–69; Ladies, Ladies!, perf. by Ballet Rambert at Young Vic, 1972; Spindrift, at Round House, 1974, etc. Danced frequently overseas.
Died 11 Jan. 2008.

MORRIS, Rev. David Richard; *b* 28 Jan. 1930; *m* (separated); one *s* one *d*; partner, Shirley. *Educ:* Stebonheath Central Sch., Llanelli; Ruskin Coll., Oxford; University Coll., Swansea; Theological Coll., Aberystwyth. Former foundry labourer; Minister, Mid-Wales and Newport, Presbyterian Church of Wales, 1958–62; former district and county councillor; Educnl Advisor, Gwent CC, 1974–84. Contested (Lab) Brecon and Radnor, 1983. MEP (Lab) Mid and West Wales, 1984–94, South Wales West, 1994–99. Formerly: Member, European Parliament Committees: Social Affairs; Transport and Tourism (substitute); Full Mem., ACP/EEC Assembly; Mem., EU-Romania delegn. Vice-Pres., Welsh Parlt Campaign. Contributor, Low Pay Unit. Member: TGWU; Socialist Educnl Assoc.; Tribune Gp; CND (Chm., CND Wales); Socialist Health Assoc. *Address:* 65 Harlech Crescent, Sketty, Swansea SA2 9LL.
Died 24 Jan. 2007.

MORRIS, Gareth (Charles Walter); flautist; Professor of the Flute, Royal Academy of Music, 1945–85; *b* Clevedon, Som, 13 May 1920; *e s* of late Walter and Enid Morris; brother of Jan Morris, CBE, FRSL; *m* 1954; one *d*; *m* 1975, Patricia Mary, *y d* of Neil and Sheila Murray, Romsey, Hampshire; one *s* two *d*. *Educ:* Bristol Cathedral Sch.; Royal Academy of Music, London. First studied the flute at age of twelve under Robert Murchie and later won a scholarship to RAM. Career since then has been as soloist, chamber music and symphonic player, teacher and lecturer; Principal Flautist, 1949–72, Chm., 1966–72, Philharmonia Orch. Gave first British performances of works by Alwyn, Bowen, Gerhard, Ghedini, Honegger, Ibert, Jacob, Koechlin, Martin, Martinu, Piston, Poulenc, Prokofiev, Rawsthorne, Reizenstein, Roussel, Seiber, Wellesz. Has been mem. Arts Council Music Panel, and Warden of Incorporated Soc. of Musicians Soloists Section; Adjudicator, International Flute playing Competitions, Geneva, 1973, 1978, Munich, 1974, Leeds, 1977, 1980, Ancona, 1978, 1979, 1984. Played at Her Majesty's Coronation in Westminster Abbey in 1953. Gov., RSM; Trustee, Loan Fund for Musical Instruments. Mem. Council of Honour, RAM, 1999–. ARAM 1945; FRAM 1950; FRSA 1967 (Mem. Council, 1977–83; Chm., Music Cttee, 1981–83). *Publications:* Flute Technique, 1991. *Recreations:* reading and collecting books, astronomy, antiquarian horology. *Address:* 4 West Mall, Clifton, Bristol BS8 4BH. *T:* (0117) 973 4966. *Club:* Royal Over-Seas League.　　*Died 14 Feb. 2007.*

MORRIS, Sir (James) Richard (Samuel), Kt 1992; CBE 1985; FREng; Chairman and Managing Director, 1980–90, non-executive Chairman, 1990–92, Brown and Root Ltd; *b* 20 Nov. 1925; *o s* of James John Morris and Kathleen Mary Morris (*née* McNaughton); *m* 1958. Marion Reid Sinclair; two *s* two *d*. *Educ:* Ardingly Coll.; Birmingham Univ. BSc, 1st cl. hons Chem. Engrg; Vice-Chancellor's Prize, 1955; FIChemE. Captain Welsh Guards, 1944–48. Courtaulds Ltd, 1950–78: Man. Dir. National Plastics Ltd, 1959–64; Dep. Chm., British Cellophane Ltd, 1967–70; Chm., British Celanese Ltd, 1970–72; Chm., Northgate Gp Ltd, 1971–76; Chm., Meridian Ltd, 1972–76; Dir, 1967–78, Gp Technical Dir. 1976–78, Courtaulds Ltd. Chairman: Devonport Management Ltd, 1987–91; Devonport Royal Dockyard plc, 1987–91; UK Nirex, 1989–97; Dresser Kellogg Energy Services, 1997–98; Independent Power Corp. plc, 2002–; Dir, British Nuclear Fuels Ltd, 1971–85; non-exec. Dir, OGC International plc, 1994–96; Chairman: M40 Trains Ltd, 1997–2003; Spectron Ltd, 1999–2002; Adv. Bd, Consort Resources Ltd, 1999–2003; Laing Rail Ltd, 2000–03. Vis. Prof. of Chem. Engrg, Univ. of Strathclyde, 1979–88; Pro-Chancellor, 1982–86, Sen. Pro-Chancellor and Chm. of Council, 1986–95, Loughborough Univ. Chm., Cttee of Chairmen of Univ.

Councils and Boards, 1991–94. Member: Nuclear Power Adv. Bd, 1973; Adv. Council for Energy Conservation, 1974–80; Adv. Bd for Res. Councils, 1981–90, Dep. Chm., 1988–90; Dep. Chm., NEB, 1978–79; Industrial Adviser to Barclays Bank, 1980–85; Dep. Chm., Foundn for Science and Technology, 1994–98. Mem. Council, 1974, Vice-Pres., 1976, Pres., 1977, IChemE; Vice-Pres., Soc. of Chem. Industry, 1978–81; Hon. Sec., 1979–82, Hon. Sec. for Educn and Training, 1984–91, Vice Pres., 1987–91, Royal Acad. of Engrg; President: Pipeline Industries Guild, 1983–85; Engrg Sect., BAAS, 1989; Soc. for Underwater Technology, 1989–91; Assoc. of Science Educn, 1990. Chm. British Cttee, Det Norske Veritas, 1983–98. Chm., Bd of Govs, Repton Sch., 1997–2003 (Gov., 1987–97). Chm., Derby Cathedral Council, 2000–03. FRSA 1986. Hon. DSc: Leeds, 1981; Bath, 1981; Birmingham, 1985; Loughborough, 1991. *Recreations:* gardening, music. *Address:* Field House, Breadsall, Derby DE21 5LL. *T:* (01332) 831368. *Club:* Athenæum. *Died 1 July 2008.*

MORRIS, James Shepherd, RSA 1989 (ARSA 1975); RIBA, FRIAS; Partner, Morris & Steedman, Architects and Landscape Architects; *b* 22 Aug. 1931; *s* of Thomas Shepherd Morris and Johanna Sime Malcolm; *m* 1959, Eleanor Kenner Smith; two *s* one *d. Educ:* Daniel Stewart's Coll.; Edinburgh Sch. of Architecture (DipArch); Univ. of Pennsylvania (MLA). ALI. *Architectural works:* Edinburgh Univ., Strathclyde Univ., Princess Margaret Rose Hosp., Countryside Commn for Scotland. Member, Arts Council of Gt Britain, 1973–80; Vice-Chm., Scottish Arts Council, 1976–80 (Chm., Art Cttee, 1976–80; Mem., Enquiry into Community Arts, 1974); Mem., Council, RSA, 1991–2003 (Hon. Treas., 1992–99); Mem. Council, RIAS and Edinburgh AA, 1969–71; Past Member: Council of Cockburn Assoc.; Edinburgh; Cttee of Management, Traverse Theatre, Edinburgh. Convenor, Fellowship Cttee, RIAS, 1985–87. Trustee, Nat. Mus. of Antiquities, 1980–86. Trustee, Chec-Nigeria, 2003–. RIBA Award, 1974; 10 Civic Trust Awards, 1962–75; British Steel Award, 1971; European Architectural Heritage Award, 1975; European Heritage Business & Industry Award, 1975. *Publications:* contribs to RIBA Jl. *Recreations:* golf, tennis, ski-ing, painting. *Address:* (office) 7 Great Stuart Street, Edinburgh EH3 7TP. *T:* (0131) 226 6563. *Clubs:* New (Edinburgh); Philadelphia Cricket (Philadelphia); Valderrama, Real de Golf Sotogrande (Sotogrande, Spain). *Died 16 Aug. 2006.*

MORRIS, Prof. Jeremy Noah, CBE 1972; FRCP; Professor of Public Health, University of London, at London School of Hygiene and Tropical Medicine, 1967–78, Hon. Research Officer, since 1978; *b* 6 May 1910; *s* of Nathan and Annie Morris; *m* 1939, Galina Schuchalter (*d* 1997); one *s* one *d. Educ:* Hutcheson's Grammar Sch., Glasgow; Univ. of Glasgow; University Coll. Hosp., London; London School of Hygiene and Tropical Medicine (Hon. Fellow 1979). MA, DSc, DPH. Qual., 1934; hosp. residencies, 1934–37; general practice, 1937–38; Asst MOH, Hendon and Harrow, 1939–41; Med. Spec., RAMC, 1941–46 (Lt-Col 1944–46); Rockefeller Fellow, Prev. Med., 1946–47; Dir, MRC Social Med. Unit, 1948–75; Prof., Social Med., London Hosp., 1959–67. Visiting Professor: Yale, 1957; Berkeley, 1963; Jerusalem, 1968, 1980; Adelaide, 1983. Consultant, Cardiology, WHO, 1960–2003. Lectures: Ernestine Henry, RCP London; Chadwick Trust; Gibson, RCP Edinburgh; Fleming, RCPS Glasgow; Carey Coombs, Univ. of Bristol; Brontë Stewart, Univ. of Glasgow; St Cyres, Nat. Heart Hosp.; Alumnus, Yale; Delamar, Johns Hopkins Univ.; Wade Hampton Frost, APHA; George Clarke, Univ. of Nottingham. Member: Royal Commission on Penal Reform; Cttee, Personal Social Services, Working Party Med. Admin, 1964–72; Health Educn Council, 1978–80; Chairman: Nat. Adv. Cttee on Nutrition Educn, 1979–83; Fitness and Health Adv. Gp, Sports Council and Health Educn Authority, 1980–. Hon. Member: Amer. Epid. Soc., 1976; Soc. for Social Medicine, 1978; British Cardiac Soc., 1982;

Swedish Soc. for Sports Medicine, 1984. JP Middx, 1956–66. Hon. FFPH (Hon. FFCM 1977); Hon. FRSocMed 1991. Hon. MD Edinburgh, 1974; Hon. DSc: Hull, 1982; Loughborough, 2002. Bisset Hawkins Medal, RCP, 1980; Honor Award, Amer. Coll. of Sports Medicine, 1985; Jenner Medal, RSM, 1987; Alwyn Smith Medal, FPHM, 1996; Internat. Olympic Gold Medal and Prize in Exercise Sci., 1996; Chadwick Medal, LSHTM, 2002; Medal, British Geriatric Soc., 2008. *Publications:* Uses of Epidemiology, 1957, 3rd edn 1975 (trans. Japanese, Spanish); papers on coronary disease and exercise, and in social medicine. *Recreations:* walking, swimming, piano music. *Address:* 3 Briardale Gardens, NW3 7PN. *T:* (020) 7435 5024; *e-mail:* Jerry.Morris@LSHTM.ac.uk. *Died 28 Oct. 2009.*

MORRIS, Max; educational propagandist and reformer; pioneer of the Comprehensive School; Headmaster, Willesden High School, 1967–78, retired; *b* 15 Aug. 1913; *s* of Nathan and Annie Morris; *m* 1961, Margaret Saunders (*née* Howard), historian. *Educ:* Hutcheson's, Glasgow; Kilburn Grammar Sch., Middx; University Coll., Univ. of London (BA 1st cl. Hons History); Inst. of Education, Univ. of London (DipEd); LSE. Began teaching, 1936, in Willesden. Served War, 1941–46, demobilised as Captain RASC. Sen. Lectr, Colls of Education, 1946–50; Dep. Head, Tottenham, 1960, after nine years of political discrimination in Middlesex; Headmaster, Chamberlayne Wood Secondary Sch., Willesden, 1962–67. NUT: Mem. Exec., 1966–79; Pres., 1973–74; Chm. Action Cttee, 1976–79. Chairman: Middx Regional Examining Bd, 1975–79; London Regional Examining Bd, 1979–90; Vice-Chairman: Centre for Information and Advice on Educnl Disadvantage, 1975–80; London and E Anglian Gp, GCSE; Member: Schools Council Cttees, 1967–84; Burnham Cttee, 1970–79; Board of NFER, 1970–80; CLEA/School Teachers Cttee, 1972–79; Schools Broadcasting Council, 1972–80; Nat. Adv. Cttee on Supply and Trng of Teachers, 1973–78; Sub-Cttee on Educn, Labour Party NEC, 1978–83; Council, Inst. of Educn; Jt Council, GCE and CSE Boards; Univ. of London Exams and Assessment Council. Mem. (Lab) Haringey Borough Council, 1984–86. Chm., Socialist Educnl Assoc., 1995–98. *Publications:* The People's Schools, 1939; From Cobbett to the Chartists, 1948; Your Children's Future, 1953; (with Jack Jones) An A to Z of Trade Unionism and Industrial Relations, 1982, 2nd edn 1986; (ed jtly) Education: the wasted years 1973–1986?, 1988; contribs on educnl and historical subjects in newspapers, weeklies and jls. *Recreations:* baiting the bigwigs of educational policy making; tasting malt whisky. *Address:* 44 Coolhurst Road, N8 8EU. *T:* (020) 8348 3980. *Died 27 Aug. 2008.*

MORRIS, Prof. Norman Frederick, MD; FRCOG, FFFP; Professor of Obstetrics and Gynæcology, University of London, Charing Cross and Westminster Medical School (formerly Charing Cross Hospital Medical School), 1958–85, then Emeritus; Dean, Faculty of Medicine, University of London, 1971–76; Deputy Vice-Chancellor, University of London, 1976–80; *b* Luton, 26 Feb. 1920; *s* of F. W. Morris, Luton; *m* 1944, Lucia Xenia Rivlin; two *s* two *d. Educ:* Dunstable Sch., Dunstable; St Mary's Hospital Medical Sch. MRCS, LRCP 1943; MRCOG 1949; MB, BS (London) 1943; MD (London) 1949; FRCOG 1959; FFFP 1993. House appts St Mary's Hosp., Paddington and Amersham, 1943–44; Res. Obstetrician and Surg. Officer, East Ham Memorial Hosp., E6, 1944–46; Surg. Specialist RAF (Sqdn Ldr), 1946–48; Registrar, St Mary's Hosp., W2, and East End Maternity Hosp., E1, 1948–50; Sen. Registrar (Obst. and Gynæcol.), Hammersmith Hosp., 1950–52; First Asst, Obstetric Unit, Univ. Coll. Hosp., WC1, 1953–56; Reader, Univ. of London in Obst. and Gynæcol., Inst. of Obstetrics and Gynæcology, 1956–58; Med. Dir, IVF Unit, 1986–97, Dir, Dept of Postgrad. Medicine, 1997–2005, Cromwell Hosp. Dep. Chm., NW Thames RHA, 1974–80; Chm., NW Thames Reg. Res. Cttee, 1981–86. External Examiner, Univs of

Sheffield, Leeds, Dundee and Liverpool. President: (founder) Internat. Soc. of Psychosomatic Obstetrics and Gynaecology, 1972–80; Section of Obstetrics and Gynaecology, RSocMed, 1978–79; W London Medico-Chirurgical Soc., 1982; Chairman: Assoc. of Profs of Obstets and Gynaecol. of UK, 1981–86; British Soc. of Psychosomatic Obstets, Gynaecol. and Andrology, 1988–96 (Pres., 1996–); Treas., Internat. Soc. for Investigation of Stress, 1990–2000. Mem., Academic Forum, DHSS, 1981–84; Chm., Commonwealth Health Develt Prog., Commonwealth Secretariat, 1990–2000; Sec. Gen., Commonwealth Health Foundn, 1994–. Mem., Hammersmith and Fulham HA, 1983–84. Mem. Ct and Senate, Univ. of London, 1972–80; Governor: Wye Coll., 1973–76; St Paul's Sch., 1976–91. Trustee, Little Foundn, 1992– (Chm., Scientific Cttee, 1993–). Fellow, Soc. Gyn. et Obst., Italy, 1970–; Hon. FFFP 1993. Formerly Chm., Assoc. of University Clinical Academic Staff. Editor, Midwife and Health Visitor Jl. *Publications:* Sterilisation, 1976; Contemporary Attitudes to Care in Labour (The Psychosomatic Approach), 1986; Factors Influencing Population Control, 1986; articles in medical jls related to obstetric and gynaecological problems, 1952–. *Recreations:* travelling, collecting glass, music. *Address:* Flat 3, The Etons, 13 Eton Avenue, NW3 3EL. *Clubs:* Athenæum, 1942. *Died 29 Feb. 2008.*

MORRIS, Sir Richard; *see* Morris, Sir J. R. S.

MORRIS, Prof. Trevor Raymond; Professor of Animal Production, University of Reading, 1984–95, then Professor Emeritus; *b* 11 April 1930; *s* of Ivor Raymond Morris and Dorothy May Morris; *m* 1st, 1954, Elisabeth Jean (*née* Warren) (*d* 1992); three *s* two *d*; 2nd, 1994, Mary (*née* Gillett). *Educ:* Rendcomb Coll., Glos; Reading Univ. (BSc, PhD, DSc). University of Reading: Asst Lectr, 1952–54, 1956–57; Lectr in Agric., 1957–69; Reader in Agric., 1969–81; Prof. of Agriculture, 1981–84; Hd of Dept of Agriculture, 1984–91. *Publications:* over 200 articles in sci. jls. *Recreations:* music, gardening. *Address:* Rowan Trees, Beech Road, Tokers Green, Oxfordshire RG4 9EH. *T:* (0118) 9470758. *Died 2 Feb. 2009.*

MORRIS, Wyn, FRAM; conductor; Principal Conductor, New Queen's Hall Orchestra; *b* 14 Feb. 1929; *s* of late Haydn Morris and Sarah Eluned Phillips; *m* 1962, Ruth Marie McDowell (decd); one *s* one *d*. *Educ:* Llanelli Grammar Sch.; Royal Academy of Music; Mozarteum, Salzburg. August Mann's Prize, 1950; Apprentice Conductor, Yorkshire Symph. Orch., 1950–51; Musical Dir, 17th Trng Regt, RA Band, 1951–53; Founder and Conductor of Welsh Symph. Orch., 1954–57; Koussevitsky Memorial Prize, Boston Symph. Orch., 1957; (on invitation George Szell) Observer, Cleveland Symph. Orch., 1957–60; Conductor: Ohio Bell Chorus, Cleveland Orpheus Choir and Cleveland Chamber Orch., 1958–60; Choir of Royal National Eisteddfod of Wales, 1960–62; London debut, Royal Festival Hall, with Royal Philharmonic Orch., 1963; Conductor: Royal Choral Society, 1968–70; Huddersfield Choral Soc., 1969–74; Ceremony for Investiture of Prince Charles as Prince of Wales, 1969; Royal Choral Soc. tour of USA, 1969; former Chief Conductor and Musical Dir, Symphonica of London. FRAM 1964. Specialised in conducting of Mahler; recorded Des Knaben Wunderhorn (with Dame Janet Baker and Sir Geraint Evans), Das Klagende Lied, Symphonies 1, 2, 5, 8 and 10 in Deryck Cooke's final performing version. Mahler Memorial Medal (of Bruckner and Mahler Soc. of Amer.), 1968. *Recreations:* chess, Rugby football, climbing, cynghanedd and telling Welsh stories. *Died 23 Feb. 2010.*

MORRIS WILLIAMS, Christine Margaret; *see* Puxon, C. M.

MORRISON, Sir Howard (Leslie), Kt 1990; OBE 1976; entertainer, self-employed, since 1957; Youth Development Director for Maori Affairs, 1978–91; *b* 18 Aug. 1935; *s* of late Temuera Leslie Morrison and Gertrude Harete Morrison (*née* Davidson); *m* 1957, Rangiwhata Anne (*née* Manahi); two *s* one *d*. *Educ:* Huiarau Primary Sch.; Rotorua Primary Sch.; Rotorua High Sch.; Te Aute College. Surveyor's Asst, 1954–59; performer with Maori concert party groups from childhood; formed Howard Morrison Quartet, 1957 (part-time, later full-time); numerous recordings, TV, national tours; quartet disbanded 1965; solo entertainer, 1965–; tours in NZ, S Pacific, SE Asia; TV and films; Royal Command perfs, 1963, 1974, 1981. Patron, Life Educn Trust, NZ, 1996. Hon. Dr Waikato. Entertainer of the Year, 1966, 1990; Life Achievement Award, Entertainer of the Year, 1996. *Recreations:* golf, swimming. *Address:* Korokai Street, Ohinemutu Village, Rotorua, New Zealand. *T:* (7) 3485735, *Fax:* (7) 3480910; *e-mail:* Sir.H@xtra.co.nz. *Club:* Carbine (Auckland, NZ). *Died 24 Sept. 2009.*

MORROW, Sir Ian (Thomas), Kt 1973; CA; FCMA; FIEE; Chairman: MAI (formerly Mills and Allen International) plc, 1974–93 (Director, 1974–94); Additional Underwriting Agencies (No 3) Ltd, since 1985; Scotia Pharmaceuticals Ltd, Scotia (formerly Efamol) Holdings plc, 1986–95; Thurne Group Ltd, 1993–99; *b* 8 June 1912; *er s* of late Thomas George Morrow and Jamesina Hunter, Pilmour Links, St Andrews; *m* 1940, Elizabeth Mary Thackray (marr. diss. 1967); one *s* one *d*; *m* 1967, Sylvia Jane Taylor; one *d*. *Educ:* Dollar Academy, Dollar. JDipMA. Chartered Accountant 1936; FCMA 1945; Asst Accountant, Brocklehurst-Whiston Amalgamated Ltd, 1937–40; Partner, Robson, Morrow & Co., 1942–51; Financial Dir, 1951–52, Dep. Man. Dir, 1952–56, Joint Man. Dir, 1956–57, Man. Dir, 1957–58, The Brush Electrical Engineering Co. Ltd (then The Brush Group Ltd); Jt Man. Dir, H. Clarkson & Co. Ltd, 1961–72; Chairman: UKO International plc (formerly UK Optical & Industrial Holdings Ltd), 1959–86 (former Man. Dir and Chm. of subsidiary cos); Hector Whaling Ltd, 1959–64; Rowe Bros & Co. (Holdings) Ltd, 1960–70; Kenwood Manufacturing Co. Ltd, 1961–68; Crosfield Electronics Ltd, 1963–72; W. M. Still & Sons Ltd, 1964–86; Associated Fire Alarms Ltd, 1965–70; Crane Fruehauf Trailers Ltd, 1969–71; Martin-Black PLC, 1977–86; Collett, Dickenson, Pearce Internat. Ltd, 1979–83; Scotia DAF Trucks Ltd, 1979–83; Agricultural Holdings Co. Ltd, 1981–84; Strong & Fisher (Hldgs), 1981–90 (Dir, 1981–90); Argunex Ltd, 1985–89; Insport Consultants, 1988–93; Beale Dobie & Co. Ltd, 1989–97; Walbrook Insce Co., 1990–92; Brightstone Estates, 1990–92; Deputy Chairman, Rolls Royce Ltd, 1970–71, Rolls Royce (1971) Ltd, 1971–73 (Man. Dir, 1971–72); Director: Hambros Industrial Management Ltd, 1965–91; Hambros PLC, 1972–90 (Dep. Chm., 1983–86); The Laird Gp, 1973–92 (Chm., 1975–87); DAF Trucks (GB), 1977–83; Zeus Management Ltd, 1985–93; Psion PLC, 1987–98; C. E. Heath Public Ltd Co., 1988–97. Led Anglo-American Council on Productivity Team on Management Accounting to US, 1950. Council Member: British Electrical & Allied Manufacturers' Assoc., 1957–58; British Internal Combustion Engine Manufacturers' Assoc., 1957–58; Member: Grand Council, FBI, 1953–58; Council, Production Engineering Research Assoc., 1955–58; Council, Inst. of Cost and Works Accountants (later Inst. of Management Accountants), 1952–70 (Pres. 1956–57, Gold Medallist 1961); Performing Right Tribunal, 1968–74; Council, Inst. of Chartered Accountants of Scotland, 1968–72, 1979–82 (Vice-Pres. 1970–72, 1979–80, 1980–81, Pres., 1981–82); Inflation Accounting Steering Gp, 1976–79; Lay Member, Press Council, 1974–80; Freeman, City of London; Liveryman, Worshipful Co. of Spectaclemakers. FIMgT. DUniv Stirling, 1979; Hon. DLitt Heriot-Watt, 1982. *Publications:* papers and addresses on professional and management subjects. *Recreations:* reading, music, golf, ski-ing. *Address:* Broadacres, Seven Devils Lane, Saffron Walden CB11 4BB. *T:* (01799) 521358. *Clubs:* National Liberal, Royal Automobile; Royal and Ancient (St Andrews); Saffron Walden Golf. *Died 19 April 2006.*

MORROW, Martin S.; Stipendiary Magistrate, Glasgow, 1972–88; *b* 16 Nov. 1923; *s* of late Thomas Morrow and Mary Lavery; *m* 1952, Nancy May, BMus, LRAM; one *s* two *d*. *Educ:* St Aloysius' Coll., Glasgow; Glasgow Univ. Solicitor. Private practice, 1951–56; Asst Procurator Fiscal, 1956–72. *Recreations:* music, golf, reading. *Address:* 33 Leicester Avenue, Glasgow G12 0LU. *T:* (0141) 334 1324.   *Died 10 Nov. 2006.*

MORTIMER, Clifford Hiley, DSc, DrPhil; FRS 1958; Distinguished Professor in Zoology, University of Wisconsin-Milwaukee, 1966–81, then Distinguished Professor Emeritus, *b* Whitchurch, Som, 27 Feb. 1911; *er s* of Walter Herbert and Bessie Russell; *m* 1936, Ingeborg Margarete Closs (*d* 2000), Stuttgart, Germany; two *d*. *Educ:* Sibford and Sidcot Schs; Univ. of Manchester. BSc (Manchester) 1932, DSc (Manchester) 1946; Dr Phil (Berlin) 1935. Served on scientific staff of Freshwater Biological Assoc., 1935–41 and 1946–56. Seconded to Admiralty scientific service, 1941–46. Sec. and Dir, Scottish Marine Biological Assoc., 1956–66; Dir, Center for Great Lakes Studies, Univ. of Wisconsin-Milwaukee, 1966–79. Hon. DSc Wisconsin-Milwaukee, 1985; DèsSc *hc* Ecole Polytechnique Fédérale de Lausanne, 1987. *Publications:* Lake Michigan in Motion, 2004; scientific papers on lakes and the physical and chemical conditions which control life in them. *Recreation:* music. *Address:* Milwaukee Catholic Home, 2462 N Prospect Avenue, Milwaukee, WI 53211, USA.   *Died 11 May 2010.*

MORTIMER, Sir John (Clifford), Kt 1998; CBE 1986; QC 1966; FRSL; barrister; playwright and author; *b* 21 April 1923, *s* of Clifford Mortimer and Kathleen May (*née* Smith); *m* 1st, 1949, Penelope Ruth Fletcher (marr. diss. 1972; she *d* 1999); one *s* one *d*; 2nd, Penelope (*née* Gollop); two *d*; one *s*. *Educ:* Harrow; Brasenose Coll., Oxford (Hon. Fellow, 2006). Called to the Bar, 1948; Master of the Bench, Inner Temple, 1975. Mem. Nat. Theatre Bd, 1968–88. Chm. Council, RSL, 1989–99; Chm., 1990–2000, Vice-Pres., 2004–, Royal Court Theatre. Pres., Howard League for Penal Reform, 1991–2003. Pres., Berks, Bucks and Oxon Naturalists' Trust, 1984–90. Chm., Cttee to advise on vacant plinth, Trafalgar Square, 1999–2001. FRSL 1973. Hon. DLitt: Susquehanna Univ., 1985; St Andrews, 1987; Nottingham, 1989; Hon. LLD: Exeter, 1986; Brunel, 1990. Won the Italia Prize with short play, The Dock Brief, 1958; another short play What Shall We Tell Caroline, 1958. Full-length plays: The Wrong Side of the Park, 1960; Two Stars for Comfort, 1962; (trans.) A Flea in Her Ear, 1966; The Judge, 1967; (trans.) Cat Among the Pigeons, 1969; Come as You Are, 1970; A Voyage Round My Father, 1970 (filmed, 1982); (trans.) The Captain of Köpenick, 1971; I, Claudius (adapted from Robert Graves), 1972; Collaborators, 1973; Mr Luby's Fear of Heaven (radio), 1976; Heaven and Hell, 1976; The Bells of Hell, 1977; (trans.) The Lady from Maxim's, 1977; (trans.) A Little Hotel on the Side, 1984; opera (trans.) Die Fledermaus, 1988; A Christmas Carol (adapted from Dickens), 1994; Summer of a Dormouse (radio), 1999; Naked Justice, 2001; Hock and Soda Water, 2001; Full House, 2002; The Hairless Diva (adapted from Ionesco), 2002; Legal Fictions, 2008. Film Scripts: John and Mary, 1970; Brideshead Revisited (TV), 1981; Edwin (TV), 1984; Cider with Rosie (TV), 1998; Tea with Mussolini, 1999. British Acad. Writers Award, 1979; Life Achievement Award, Banff Television Fest., 1998; Lifetime Achievement Award, British Book Awards, 2005. *Publications: novels:* Charade, 1947; Rumming Park, 1948; Answer Yes or No, 1950; Like Men Betrayed, 1953, reissued 1987; Three Winters, 1956; Will Shakespeare: an entertainment, 1977; Rumpole of the Bailey, 1978 (televised; BAFTA Writer of the Year Award, 1980); The Trials of Rumpole, 1979; Rumpole's Return, 1980 (televised); Regina v Rumpole, 1981; Rumpole for the Defence, 1982; Rumpole and the Golden Thread, 1983 (televised); Paradise Postponed, 1985 (televised 1986); Rumpole's Last Case, 1987 (televised); Rumpole and the Age of Miracles, 1988 (televised); Summer's Lease, 1988 (televised 1989);

Titmuss Regained, 1990 (televised 1991); Rumpole à la Carte, 1990; Dunster, 1992; Rumpole on Trial, 1992; Under the Hammer, 1994 (televised); Rumpole and the Angel of Death, 1995; Felix in the Underworld, 1997; The Sound of Trumpets, 1998; Rumpole Rests His Case, 2001; Rumpole and the Primrose Path, 2002; Rumpole and the Penge Bungalow Murders, 2004; Quite Honestly, 2005; Rumpole and the Reign of Terror, 2006; The Anti-Social Behaviour of Horace Rumpole, 2007; *travel:* (in collab. with P. R. Mortimer) With Love and Lizards, 1957; *plays:* The Dock Brief and Other Plays, 1959; The Wrong Side of the Park, 1960; Lunch Hour and Other Plays, 1960; Two Stars for Comfort, 1962; (trans.) A Flea in Her Ear, 1965; A Voyage Round My Father, 1970; (trans.) The Captain of Köpenick, 1971; Five Plays, 1971; Collaborators, 1973; Edwin and Other Plays, 1984; (trans.) Die Fledermaus, 1989; Naked Justice, 2001; Hock and Soda Water, 2001; *interviews:* In Character, 1983; Character Parts, 1986; *autobiography:* Clinging to the Wreckage (Book of the Year Award, Yorkshire Post), 1982; Murderers and Other Friends, 1994; Summer of a Dormouse, 2000; Where There's a Will, 2003, TV plays (incl. six Rumpole series); contribs to periodicals. *Recreations:* working, gardening, going to opera. *Address:* United Agents, 12–26 Lexington Street, W1F 0LE. *Club:* Garrick.   *Died 16 Jan. 2009.*

MORTIMER, Katharine Mary Hope, (Mrs Robert Dean); financial sector consultant, mainly to aid agencies; *b* 28 May 1946; *d* of late Rt Rev. Robert Cecil Mortimer and Mary Hope (*née* Walker); *m* 1st, 1973, John Noel Nicholson (marr. diss. 1986); one *s*; 2nd, 1990, Robert Michael Dean. *Educ:* School of SS Mary and Anne, Abbots Bromley; Somerville Coll., Oxford. MA, BPhil Oxon. Head 1969–72; Central Policy Review Staff, 1972–78; N. M. Rothschild Asset Management Ltd, 1978–84; Dir, N. M. Rothschild & Sons (International Corporate Finance, subseq. Internat. Asset Management), 1984–88; seconded as Dir of Policy, SIB, 1985–87; Chief Exec., Walker Books, 1988–89; Consultant/Financial Advr, Know How Fund for Eastern Europe, 1990–97. Member: Bd, Crown Agents, 1990–97; Crown Agents Foundn Council, 1997–; non-executive Director: National Bus Company, 1979–91; Inst. of Development Studies, 1983–95; Mast Develt Co., 1989–93; Crown Agents Bank Ltd (formerly Crown Agents Financial Services Ltd), 1990–2007; Crown Agents Asset Mgt Ltd, 1990–2007; IQI Ltd, 1991–92; British Nuclear Fuels plc, 1993–2000; Pennon Gp plc, 2000–. Member: ESRC, 1983–86; Competition (formerly Monopolies and Mergers) Commn, 1995–2001. Mem., Royal Commn for Exhibn of 1851, 1988–2002. Member, Governing Body: Centre for Economic Policy Res., 1986–91; Imperial Coll., 1987–90. Trustee, Inst. for Public Policy Res., 1989–92. Church Warden, St Andrew's, Sampford Courtenay, 2000–. *Address:* Lower Corscombe, Okehampton, Devon EX20 1SD.   *Died 15 July 2008.*

MORTON, Admiral Sir Anthony (Storrs), GBE 1982; KCB 1978; DL; King of Arms, Order of the British Empire, 1983–97; Vice Admiral of the United Kingdom, 1990–94; *b* 6 Nov. 1923; *s* of late Dr Harold Morton. *Educ:* Loretto School. Joined RN 1941; war service in Atlantic, Mediterranean and Far East (despatches, HMS Wrangler, 1945); Commander 1956; Comd HMS Appleton and 100th MSS 1957–58; HMS Undine 1960; HMS Rocket 1960–62; Captain 1964; Captain (F) 20th Frigate Squadron, 1964–66; Chief Staff Officer, Plans and Policy, to Commander Far East Fleet, 1966–68; Senior Naval Officer, Northern Ireland, 1968–70; Senior Naval Mem., RCDS, 1971–72; ACDS (Policy), 1973–75; Flag Officer, First Flotilla, 1975–77; Vice-Chief of Defence Staff, 1977–78; Vice-Chief of Naval Staff, 1978–80; UK Mil. Rep. to NATO, 1980–83. Rear Adm. of the UK, 1988–90. Chairman: Govs, Royal Star and Garter Home, 1986–91 (Vice-Pres., 1992–); Trustees, RN Museum, Portsmouth, 1985–94; Vice Pres., King George's Fund for Sailors, 1993– (Chm., 1986–93). DL Hants, 1989. OStJ 1990. *Recreations:* fishing, sailing, shooting,

watching Association football. *Address:* c/o Barclays Bank, Winchester, Hants SO23 8RG. *Clubs:* Royal Cruising; Royal Yacht Squadron; Irish Cruising.
Died 6 May 2006.

MOSDELL, Lionel Patrick; Judge of the High Court of Kenya, 1966–72, Tanganyika, 1960–64; *b* 29 Aug. 1912; *s* of late William George Mosdell and Sarah Ellen Mosdell (*née* Gardiner); *m* 1945, Muriel Jean Sillem; one *s* one *d.* *Educ:* Abingdon Sch.; St Edmund Hall, Oxford (MA). Solicitor, England, 1938. Served War of 1939–45, Gunner, Sussex Yeomanry RA, 1939–41; Commnd Rifle Bde, 1941; Libyan Arab Force; Force 133; No 1 Special Force; Egypt, Cyrenaica, Eritrea, Abyssinia, Italy (Capt.). Registrar of Lands and Deeds, N Rhodesia, 1946; Resident Magistrate, 1950; Senior Resident Magistrate, 1956; Barrister, Gray's Inn, 1952; Asst Solicitor, Law Soc., 1964–66. Part-time Chairman: Surrey and Sussex Rent Assessment Panel, 1972–82; Nat. Insce Local Tribunal, London S Region, 1974–84; Immigration Appeal Tribunal, 1975–84; Pensions Appeal Tribunals, 1976–86. Volunteer, SSAFA, 1988–2002. *Recreation:* reading. *Clubs:* Special Forces, Royal Commonwealth Society. *Died 18 July 2008.*

MOSES, Eric George Rufus, CB 1973; Solicitor of Inland Revenue, 1970–79; *b* 6 April 1914; *s* of Michael and Emily Moses; *m* 1940, Pearl Lipton; one *s. Educ:* University Coll. Sch., London; Oriel Coll., Oxford. Called to Bar, Middle Temple, 1938, Hon. Bencher, 1979. Served Royal Artillery, 1940–46 (Major). Asst Solicitor, Inland Revenue, 1953–65, Principal Asst Solicitor, 1965–70. *Address:* Broome Cottage, Castle Hill, Nether Stowey, Bridgwater, Somerset TA5 1NB.
Died 7 Aug. 2008.

MOSS, Very Rev. Basil Stanley; Provost of Birmingham Cathedral, 1973–85; Rector, Cathedral parish of St Philip, 1973–85; *b* 7 Oct. 1918; *e s* of Rev. Canon Harry George Moss and Daisy Violet (*née* Jolly); *m* 1950, Rachel Margaret, *d* of Dr Cyril Bailey and Gemma (*née* Creighton); three *d. Educ:* Canon Slade Grammar Sch., Bolton; Queen's Coll., Oxford; Lincoln Theol Coll. Ordained deacon, 1943, priest, 1944; Asst Curate, Leigh Parish Church, 1943–45; Sub-Warden, Lincoln Theological Coll., 1946–51; Sen. Tutor, St Catharine's Cumberland Lodge, Windsor Gt Pk, 1951–53; Vicar of St Nathanael with St Katharine, Bristol, 1953–60; Dir, Ordination Training, Bristol Dio., 1956–66; Residentiary Canon of Bristol Cath., 1960–66, Hon. Canon, 1966–72; Chief Secretary, Advisory Council for the Church's Ministry, 1966–72; Chaplain to Church House, Westminster, 1966–72; Examining Chaplain to Bishop of Bristol, 1956–72, to Bishop of Birmingham, 1985–. Chm., Birmingham Community Relations Council, 1973–81. *Publications:* Clergy Training Today, 1964; (ed) Crisis for Baptism, 1966; (contrib.) Living the Faith, 1980. *Recreation:* walking. *Address:* Engelberg, Ash Hill, Compton, Wolverhampton WV3 9DR. *T:* (01902) 420613. *Club:* Stourbridge Rotary. *Died 24 March 2006.*

MOSS, Charles James, CBE 1977; Director, National Institute of Agricultural Engineering, 1964–77; *b* 18 Nov. 1917; *s* of James and Elizabeth Moss; *m* 1939, Joan Bernice Smith; two *d. Educ:* Queen Mary Coll., London Univ. (BSc 1938, Sir John William Lubbock Meml Prize 1938). Rotol Ltd, Gloucester, 1939–43; RAE Farnborough, 1943–45; CIBA Ltd, Cambridge, 1945–51; ICI Ltd, Billingham, 1951–58; Central Engineering Estabt, NCB, Stanhope Bretby, 1958–61; Process Develt Dept, NCB, London, 1961–63; Vis. Prof., Dept of Agric. Engrg, Univ. of Newcastle upon Tyne, 1972–75; Head of Agr. Engineering Dept, Internat. Rice Res. Inst., Philippines, 1977–80; Liaison scientist and agr. engineer, Internat. Rice Res. Inst., Cairo, 1980–81. *Publications:* papers in learned jls, confs, etc. *Recreations:* gardening, walking. *Address:* 1 Laurel Court, Endcliffe Vale Road, Sheffield, South Yorks S10 3DU. *Died 7 Aug. 2010.*

MOSS, Dr Christopher Michael; Astronomer, Liverpool John Moores University, since 2000; *b* 6 Nov. 1946; *s* of Joseph Moss and Hilda Moss (*née* Wilder). *Educ:* Heythrop Coll. (Bacc Phil 1969); MA Oxon 1972; BD London 1979; MA Cantab; DPhil Sussex 1976. Entered Jesuit Order, 1964; ordained priest, 1979; Staff Mem., Vatican Observatory, Rome and Vatican Observatory Res. Gp, Univ. of Arizona, 1980–85; Dean, 1986–92, Fellow, 1986–97, St Edmund's Coll., Cambridge; Postdoctoral Staff Mem., Inst. of Astronomy, Univ. of Cambridge, 1986–97; Principal, Heythrop Coll., London Univ., 1997–98; Associate Faculty Mem., Univ. of Arizona, 1998–2000; resigned from SJ, 2003. *Publications:* papers in astrophysical and astronomical jls. *Recreations:* walking, sketching, foreign travel. *Address:* Astrophysics Research Institute, Twelve Quays House, Egerton Wharf, Birkenhead CH41 1LD. *Died 12 May 2010.*

MOSS, (James) Richard (Frederick), OBE 1955; FRINA; RCNC; Founder, Chairman, 1978–94, and President, since 1994, Polynous, Cambridge; Chief Executive, Balaena Structures (North Sea), 1974–77; *b* 26 March 1916; *s* of late Lt-Cdr J. G. Moss, RN, and late Kathleen Moss (*née* Steinberg); *m* 1941, Celia Florence Lucas (*d* 2008); three *d. Educ:* Marlborough College; Trinity Coll., Cambridge (1st Cl. Hons Mech. Sci. Tripos and Maths Pt I, MA); RCNC, 1941. Constructor Comdr to C-in-C, Far East Fleet, 1949–52; Chief Constructor, HM Dockyard, Singapore, 1955–58; Supt, Naval Construction Research Estab., Dunfermline, 1965–68; Dir, Naval Ship Production, 1968–74. Hon. Life Member: RINA, 2009; Cambridge Soc. for Application of Res., 2009. *Recreations:* yachting, music, bell ringing. *Address:* 13 Beaufort Place, Thompsons Lane, Cambridge CB5 8AG. *T:* (01223) 328583; *e-mail:* j.richard26@btinternet.com. *Club:* Royal Naval Sailing Association.
Died 15 July 2010.

MOSS, Martin Grenville, CBE 1975; Director of National Trust Enterprises Ltd, 1985–89; *b* 17 July 1923; *s* of late Horace Grenville Moss and Gladys Ethel (*née* Wootton); *m* 1953, Jane Hope Bown, CBE; two *s* one *d. Educ:* Lancing Coll. Served RAF, 1942–46 (Sqdn Ldr, pilot). Managing Director: Woollands Knightsbridge, 1953–66; Debenham & Freebody, 1964–66; Simpson (Piccadilly) Ltd, 1966–73, 1981–85; Chm. and Chief Exec. Officer, May Department Stores Internat., USA, 1974–80. Member: Export Council of Europe, 1960–64; Design Council, 1964–75 (Dep. Chm., 1971–75); Council, RCA, 1953–58; Royal Fine Art Commn, 1982–84; Council, RSA, 1977–94 (Chm., 1983–85). Formerly Governor: Sevenoaks Sch.; Ravensbourne Coll. of Art and Design; W Surrey Coll. of Art and Design. Order of the Finnish Lion, 1970. *Recreations:* gardening, painting, classic cars. *Address:* Old Mill House, 50 Broad Street, Alresford, Hants SO24 9AN. *T:* (01962) 732419. *Club:* Royal Air Force.
Died 19 Nov. 2007.

MOSS, Richard; *see* Moss, J. R. F.

MOSTYN, Gen. Sir (Joseph) David (Frederick), KCB 1984; CBE 1974 (MBE 1962); Adjutant General, 1986–88; Aide de Camp General to the Queen, 1987–89; *b* 28 Nov. 1928; *s* of late J. P. Mostyn, Arundel; *m* 1952, Diana Patricia Sheridan; four *s* two *d. Educ:* Downside; RMA Sandhurst; psc, rcds. Commnd Oxf. and Bucks LI, 1948; served BAOR, Greece, Cyprus, UK, 1948–58; Canadian Army Staff Coll., 1958; WO, 1959–61; Coy Comdr 1st Green Jackets, Malaya, Brunei, Borneo, 1962–63 (despatches); Instructor, Staff Coll., Camberley, 1964–67; MoD, 1967–69; CO 2 RGJ, BAOR and NI, 1969–71; Comdt Tactics Wing, Sch. of Infantry, 1972; Comdr 8 Inf. Bde, NI, 1972–74; Dep. Dir Army Training, 1974–75; RCDS 1976; BGS, HQ BAOR, 1977; Dir Personal Services (Army), 1978–80; GOC Berlin and Comdt British Sector, 1980–83; Military Sec., 1983–86. Col Commandant: The Light Div., 1983–86; Army Legal Corps, 1983–88. Chm., Army Beagling Assoc., 1979–89; President: Army Boxing Assoc., 1986–89; Army Swimming Assoc., 1986–89. Special

Comr, Duke of York's Royal Mil. Sch., Dover, 1989–97. Chairman: Lyme Regis Hosp. Trust, 1990–95; Council, Dorset Respite and Hosp. Trust, 1990–99. President: Uplyme and Lym Valley Soc., 1990–; Devon County Royal British Legion, 1992–98. Kt SMO Malta, 1974. *Recreations:* maintaining a home for the family; all field sports. *Address:* c/o Lloyds TSB Plc, 54 Broad Street, Lyme Regis, Dorset DT7 3QR. *Died 20 Jan. 2007.*

MOTTERSHEAD, Frank William, CB 1957; Deputy Secretary, Department of Health and Social Security (formerly Ministry of Health), 1965–71; *b* 7 Sept. 1911; *o s* of late Thomas Hastings and Adeline Mottershead; unmarried. *Educ:* King Edward's Sch., Birmingham; St John's Coll., Cambridge (BA 1933, MA 1973). Entered Secretary's Dept of Admiralty, 1934; Principal Private Sec. to First Lord, 1944–46; idc 1949; Under Sec., 1950; transferred to Ministry of Defence, 1956; Deputy Sec., 1958. *Address:* Old Warden, Grevel Lane, Chipping Campden, Glos GL55 6HS. *T:* (01386) 840548. *Club:* Oxford and Cambridge. *Died 17 May 2006.*

MOULE, Rev. Prof. Charles Francis Digby, CBE 1985; FBA 1966; Lady Margaret's Professor of Divinity in the University of Cambridge, 1951–76; Fellow of Clare College, Cambridge, since 1944; Canon Theologian (non-residentiary) of Leicester, 1955–76; Honorary Member of Staff, Ridley Hall, Cambridge, 1976–80; *b* Hangchow, China, 3 Dec. 1908; *s* of late Rev. Henry William Moule and Laura Clements Pope; unmarried. *Educ:* Weymouth Coll., Dorset; Emmanuel Coll., Cambridge (scholar) (Hon. Fellow 1972); Ridley Hall, Cambridge. 1st Cl. Classical Tripos Part I, 1929; BA (1st Cl. Classical Tripos Part II), 1931; Evans Prize, 1931; Jeremie Septuagint Prize, 1932; Crosse Scholarship, 1933; MA 1934. Deacon, 1933, priest, 1934; Curate, St Mark's, Cambridge, and Tutor of Ridley Hall, 1933–34; Curate, St Andrew's, Rugby, 1934–36; Vice-Principal, Ridley Hall, 1936–44, and Curate of St Mary the Great, Cambridge, 1936–40. Dean of Clare Coll., Cambridge, 1944–51; Faculty Asst Lecturer in Divinity in the Univ. of Cambridge, 1944–47; Univ. Lecturer, 1947–51. Burkitt Medal for Biblical Studies, British Acad., 1970. Hon. DD: St Andrews, 1958; Cambridge, 1988. *Publications:* An Idiom Book of New Testament Greek, 1953; The Meaning of Hope, 1953; The Sacrifice of Christ, 1956; Colossians and Philemon (Cambridge Greek Testament Commentary), 1957; Worship in the New Testament, 1961; The Birth of the New Testament, 1962, 3rd edn 1981; The Phenomenon of the New Testament, 1967; (co-editor) Christian History and Interpretation, 1968; The Origin of Christology, 1977 (Collins Theological Book Prize, 1977); The Holy Spirit, 1978; Essays in New Testament Interpretation, 1982; (co-editor) Jesus and the Politics of His Day, 1984; Forgiveness and Reconciliation and other New Testament Themes, 1998; contrib., Encyclopædia Britannica, Interpreter's Dictionary of the Bible, Biblisch-Historisches Handwörterbuch. *Address:* The Old Vicarage, Leigh, Sherborne, Dorset DT9 6HL. *Died 30 Sept. 2007.*

MOULSON, (Roger) Harry; company director; adviser, consultant and lecturer to major firms and universities, on how to run a business, deal with massive change events, culture, and energy, since 1997; *b* 25 Jan. 1944; *s* of Frank and Mary Moulson; *m* Elaine Ann Douthwaite; one *s* one *d*. *Educ:* Harvard Business Sch. (AMP). CEng. British Gas: Engineer, then Manager, 1962–69; Service Management/Dir and Computer Dir, 1971–81; Marketing Dir and New Business Develt Dir, 1981–92; Regl Chm., Wales Reg., 1991–93; Chief Exec., TransCo, 1993–97; Dir, 1995–97. *Recreations:* music, antiques, DIY, sport. *Address:* Sedgecombe House, Broad Campden, Chipping Campden, Glos GL55 6UX. *Died 27 Aug. 2006.*

MOULTON, Air Vice-Marshal Leslie Howard, CB 1971; DFC 1941; with The Plessey Co., 1971–82, retired; *b* 3 Dec. 1915; *s* of late Peter Moulton, Nantwich, Cheshire; *m* 1943, Lesley, *d* of late P. C. Clarke, Ilford; two *s* two *d*. *Educ:* Nantwich and Acton School. FIEE, CEng, 1959. Joined RAF, 1932; served War of 1939–45,

Pilot; Operations with 14 Sqdn in Africa, 1940–42; CFS, 1942–44; specialised in Signals, 1945; Staff Coll., 1950; USAF, Strategic Air Comd, 1954–56; Dep. Dir Radio, Air Min., 1958–61; Comdt RAF Cosford, 1961–63; CSO Fighter Comd, 1963–65; Min. of Technology, 1965–68. Wing Comdr 1955; Gp Captain 1959; Air Cdre 1964; Air Vice-Marshal 1969; AOC No 90 (Signals) Group, RAF, 1969–71; retired 1971. *Recreations:* gardening, golf, hill walking. *Address:* No 14 The Paddock, Willaston House, Willaston, Nantwich, Cheshire CW5 7EP. *T:* (01270) 665308. *Club:* Royal Air Force. *Died 8 May 2006.*

MOWBRAY (26th Baron *cr* 1283), **SEGRAVE** (27th Baron *cr* 1283), **AND STOURTON,** of Stourton, Co. Wilts (23rd Baron *cr* 1448); **Charles Edward Stourton,** CBE 1982; *b* 11 March 1923; *s* of William Marmaduke Stourton, 25th Baron Mowbray, 26th Baron Segrave and 22nd Baron Stourton, MC, and Sheila (*d* 1975), *er d* of Hon. Edward Gully, CB; *S* father, 1965; *m* 1952, Hon. Jane de Yarburgh Bateson (*d* 1998), *o c* of 5th Baron Deramore, and of Nina Lady Deramore, OBE, *d* of Alastair Macpherson-Grant; two *s*; *m* 1999, Joan, Lady Holland, *widow* of Sir Guy Holland, 3rd Bt. *Educ:* Ampleforth; Christ Church, Oxford. Joined Army, 1942; Commissioned Gren. Guards, 1943; served with 2nd Armd Bn Gren. Gds, as Lt, 1943–44 (wounded, France, 1944; loss of eye and invalided, 1945). Mem. of Lloyd's 1952; Mem. Securicor, 1961–64; Chairman: Ghadeco (UK) Ltd, 1986–; Thames Estuary Airport Co. Ltd, 1993–; Director: Securicor (Scotland) Ltd, 1964–70; General Development Co. Ltd (Ghana), 1980–; EIRC Ghana Ltd, 1982–; EIRC Hldgs Ltd (Jersey), 1986–. Mem., Nidderdale RDC, 1954–58. A Conservative Whip in House of Lords, 1967–70, 1974–78; a Lord in Waiting (Govt Whip), and spokesman for DoE, 1970–74; Dep. Chief Opposition Whip in House of Lords, 1978–79; a Lord in Waiting (Govt Whip), and spokesman for the arts, envt and transport, 1979–80; elected Mem., H of L, 1999. Chm., Govt Picture Buying Cttee, 1972–74; Mem., British Parly Delegn to Bicentennial Celebrations, Washington, 1976. Trustee, College of Arms Trust, 1975–. Chancellor, Primrose League, 1974–80, 1981–83. Life Governor, Cancer Res. UK (formerly ICRF), 1983–. Patron, Tayside and Mearns Normandy Veterans Assoc., 1992–. Bicentennial Year Award of Baronial Order of Magna Charta, USA, 1976. Kt of Hon. and Devotion, SMO Malta, 1947 (Vice-Pres., British Assoc., 2001–); Bailiff Grand Cross and Senaitor, Constantinian Order of St George (Parma), 2001. *Recreations:* reading, shooting, gardening. *Heir:* *s* Hon. Edward William Stephen Stourton [*b* 17 April 1953; *m* 1980, Penelope, *e d* of Dr Peter Brunet; one *s* four *d*]. *Address:* Marcus, by Forfar, Angus DD8 3QH. *T:* (01307) 850219. *Clubs:* Turf, White's, Pratt's, Pilgrims, Roxburghe. *Died 12 Dec. 2006.*

MOYES, Christopher, OBE 2006; Chief Executive, Go-Ahead Group plc, 2005–06; *b* 26 July 1949; *s* of Gilbert Moyes and Eileen Lucy Moyes (*née* Williams); *m* 1975, Jan King; three *d*. *Educ:* Birkenhead Sch.; Univ. of Liverpool (BEng Civil Engrg 1970); Univ. of Salford (MSc Transport Engrg 1971). FCILT 1993. Various mgt posts, National Bus Co., 1971–87; Commercial Dir, Go-Ahead Northern Ltd, 1987–93; Go-Ahead Group plc: Commercial Dir, 1993–99; Dep. Chief Exec., 1999–2005. Chm., GoSkills, 2003–. University of Durham: Mem. Council, 1992– (Vice Chm., 2001–02); Chm., 2002–); Chm., Audit Cttee, 1996–2001. FRSA; CCMI 2003. *Recreations:* theatre, travel, classic/vintage vehicles. *Address:* Heathcroft, Potters Bank, Durham City DH1 3RR. *T:* (0191) 386 9096, *Fax:* (0191) 383 1855. *Club:* Royal Commonwealth Society. *Died 12 Sept. 2006.*

MOYES, Lt-Comdr Kenneth Jack, MBE (mil.) 1960; RN retd; Under-Secretary, Department of Health and Social Security, 1975–78; *b* 13 June 1918; *s* of Charles Wilfrid and Daisy Hilda Moyes; *m* 1943, Norma Ellen Outred Hillier; one *s* two *d*. *Educ:* Portsmouth Northern

Grammar Sch. FCIS. Royal Navy, 1939–63. Principal, Dept of Health and Social Security, 1963; Asst Secretary, 1970. *Recreations:* gardening, bridge. *Address:* Garden House, Darwin Road, Birchington, Kent CT7 9JL. *T:* (01843) 842015. *Died 17 Aug. 2009.*

MOYNIHAN, Martin John, CMG 1972; MC; HM Diplomatic Service, retired; *b* 17 Feb. 1916; *e s* of late William John Moynihan and Phebe Alexander; *m* 1946, Monica Hopwood (*d* 2003); one *s* one *d*. *Educ:* Birkenhead Sch.; Magdalen Coll., Oxford (MA). India Office, 1939. Punjab Frontier Force, IA, N-W Frontier and Burma, 1940–45. Commonwealth Service: Delhi, Madras, Bombay and London, 1946–54; Deputy High Commissioner: Peshawar, 1954–56; Lahore, 1956–58; Kuala Lumpur, 1961–63; Port of Spain, 1964–66; HM Consul-General, Philadelphia, 1966–70; Ambassador to Liberia, 1970–73; High Comr in Lesotho, 1973–76. Administering Officer, Kennedy Meml Trust, 1977–79. Mem., Council, Hakluyt Soc., 1976–90. Associate Mem. in S African Studies, Clare Hall, Cambridge, 1977–78. Hon. Knight Grand Band of Humane Order of African Redemption (Liberia), 1973. *Publications:* The Strangers, 1946; South of Fort Hertz, 1956; The Latin Letters of C. S. Lewis, 1987; Letters: C. S. Lewis and Don Giovanni Calabria, 1988; Europe Videos in Verse, 1999. *Address:* Heathland Court, 56 Parkside, SW19 5NJ. *Died 28 July 2007.*

MUIR, Sir Laurence (Macdonald), Kt 1981; VRD 1954; company director; Deputy Chairman, National Science and Technology Centre Advisory Committee, 1986–96; Founding Chairman, Canberra Development Board, 1979–86; *b* 3 March 1925; *s* of Andrew Muir and Agnes Campbell Macdonald; *m* 1948, Ruth Richardson; two *s* two *d*. *Educ:* Yallourn State Sch.; Scotch Coll., Melbourne; Univ. of Melbourne (LLB). Served RAN, 1942–46 (Lieut); Lt-Comdr, RANR, 1949–65. Admitted Barrister and Solicitor, Supreme Court of Victoria, 1950. Sharebroker, 1950–80; Mem., Stock Exchange of Melbourne, 1960–80; Partner, 1962–80, Sen. Partner, 1976–80, Potter Partners. Director: ANZ Banking Gp, 1980–91; ACI Internat. Ltd (formerly ACI Ltd), 1980–88; Nat. Commercial Union Assce Co. of Aust. Ltd (formerly Commercial Union Assce Co. of Aust.), 1979–91; Wormald Internat. Ltd, 1980–88; Herald and Weekly Times Ltd, 1982–87; ANZ Pensions Ltd, 1982–91; Alcoa of Australia Ltd, 1982–96; Hudson Conway Ltd (formerly Australian Asset Management Ltd), 1987–2000; Templeton Global Growth Fund, 1987–99; Greening Australia, 1985–90; Australian Consolidated Press Group, subseq. Publishing and Broadcasting Ltd, 1992–2006; Member Board: Focus Books Pty Ltd, 1990–2006; Crown Ltd, 2003–; Chairman: Aust. Biomedical Corp. Ltd, 1983–87; Liquid Air Australia Ltd, 1982–95; Elders Austral Chartering Pty Ltd, 1984–90; University Paton Ltd, 1986–90; State Development Fund Ltd, 2002–06. Chm., John Curtin Sch. of Medical Res. Adv. Bd, 1982–88; Member: Parlt House Construction Authority (Chm., Artworks Adv. Cttee), 1979–89; Council, Gen. Motors, Aust., 1977–94; L'Air Liquide World Adv. Cttee, 1983–95; Victoria Garden State Cttee, Anti-Cancer Council; Commn for the Future, 1991–; Bd, Royal Soc. of Victoria Foundn, 2006–; Consultant, Alfred Hosp. Bd, 1983–88. Patron: Baker Med. Res. Inst.; Microsurgery Foundn; Earthwatch Australia; Trustee and Bd Mem., Sir Robert Menzies Meml Trust, 1984–96; Founder and Trustee, Delta Soc. Aust.; Trustee, Aust. Scout Educn & Trng Foundn; Life Trustee, Cttee for Economic Develt of Aust. Mem. Exec. Cttee, World Athletic Cup 1985; Council Mem., HRH Duke of Edinburgh's 6th Commonwealth Study Conf. (Chm., Aust. Finance Cttee). Fellow: Securities Inst. of Australia, 1962; Australian Inst. of Dirs, 1967; FAIM 1965. Centenary Medal Australia, 2003. *Recreations:* gardening, walking. *Address:* Unit 3, 61 Black Street, Brighton, Vic 3186, Australia. *Club:* Melbourne Cricket (Melbourne). *Died 21 April 2010.*

MUIR WOOD, Sir Alan (Marshall), Kt 1982; FRS 1980; FREng, FICE; Consultant, Halcrow Group (Partner, 1964–84, Senior Partner, 1979–84, Sir William Halcrow & Partners); *b* 8 Aug. 1921; *s* of Edward Stephen Wood and Dorothy (*née* Webb); *m* 1943, Winifred Leyton Lanagan, (Dr W. L. Wood, mathematician); three *s. Educ:* Abbotsholme Sch.; Peterhouse, Cambridge Univ. (MA; Hon. Fellow 1982). FICE 1957. Engr Officer, RN, 1942–46. Asst Engr, British Rail, Southern Reg., 1946–50; Res. Asst, Docks and Inland Waterways Exec., 1950–52; Asst Engr, then Sen. Engr, Sir William Halcrow & Partners, 1952–64. Principally concerned with studies and works in fields of tunnelling, geotechnics, coastal engrg, energy, roads and railways; major projects include: (Proj. Engr) Clyde Tunnel and Potters Bar railway tunnels; (Partner) Cargo Tunnel at Heathrow Airport, and Cuilfail Tunnel, Lewes; studied and worked for Channel Tunnel (intermittently, 1958–98); Dir, Orange-Fish Consultants, resp. for 80 km irrigation tunnel. Member: ACARD, 1980–84; SERC, 1981–84; Governing Body, Inst. of Development Studies, 1981–87; Council, ITDG, 1981–84; Chairman: SERC/ESRC Jt Cttee, 1983–85; Res. Councils Individual Merit Promotion Panel, 1989–94. Mem. Council, Royal Soc., 1983–84, a Vice-Pres., 1983–84; President: Internat. Tunnelling Assoc., 1975–77 (Hon. Life Pres., 1977); ICE, 1977–78; FREng (FEng 1977; a Vice-Pres., 1984–87). FIC 1981. Foreign Member, Royal Swedish Acad. of Engrg Sci., 1980; Hon. Fellow, Portsmouth Polytech., 1984. Hon. DSc: City, 1978; Southampton, 1986; Hon. LLD Dundee, 1985; Hon. DEng Bristol, 1991. Telford Medal, ICE, 1976; James Alfred Ewing Medal, ICE and Royal Soc., 1984; Gold Medal, ICE, 1998. *Publications:* Coastal Hydraulics, 1969, (with C. A. Fleming) 2nd edn 1981; Tunnelling: management by design, 2000; Civil Engineering in Context, 2004; papers, mainly on tunnelling, coastal engrg and wider aspects of engrg, in Proc. ICE and elsewhere. *Address:* Franklands, Bere Court Road, Pangbourne, Berks RG8 8JY. *T:* (0118) 984 2833. *Club:* Athenæum. *Died 1 Feb. 2009.*

MULLENS, Lt-Gen. Sir Anthony (Richard Guy), KCB 1989; OBE 1979 (MBE 1973); Associate, Varley Walker & Partners, since 1992; *b* 10 May 1936; *s* of late Brig. Guy John de Wette Mullens, OBE, and Gwendoline Joan Maclean; *m* 1964, Dawn Elizabeth Hermione Pease. *Educ:* Eton; RMA Sandhurst. Commnd 4th/7th Royal Dragoon Guards, 1956; regtl service, BAOR, 1956–58; ADC to Comdr 1st British Corps, 1958–60; Adjt 1962–65; sc 1967, psc; MA to VCGS, MoD, 1968–70; regtl service, 1970–72; Bde Major, 1972–73; Directing Staff, Staff Coll., 1973–76; CO 4/7 DG, BAOR, 1976–78; HQ BAOR, 1978–80; Comdr 7th Armd Bde, 1980–82; MoD (DMS(A)), 1982–85; Comdr 1st Armoured Div., 1985–87; ACDS (Operational Requirements), Land Systems, MoD, 1987–89; DCDS (Systems), MoD, 1989–92, retd. Consultant, BR, 1992–95. Col, Royal Dragoon Guards, 1994–99; Hon. Col, Eton Coll. CCF, 2001–07. Trustee, Army Museums Ogilby Trust, 1997–2007; President: 7th Armoured Div. Thetford Forest Meml Assoc., 1999–; 7th Armoured Div. Officers Club, 2000–05. Liveryman: Armourers' and Braziers' Co., 1974 (Mem., Ct of Assts, 1993–97; Renter Warden, 1996–97); Coachmakers' and Coach Harness Makers' Co., 1976. Member: Alpheton Parish Council, 2000–03; Alpheton PCC, 1989–2006; Church Warden, St Peter and St Paul, Alpheton, 1997–2003. Dir, Cranmer Ct (Chelsea) Tenants Ltd, 2009–. MInstD 1992–2002. Niedersachsen Verdienstkreuz am Bande, 1982, Erste Klasse, 1987. *Recreations:* travel, shooting. *Address:* 138 Cranmer Court, Sloane Avenue, SW3 3HE. *Club:* Cavalry and Guards. *Died 27 Nov. 2009.*

MULLER, Dr Ralph Louis Junius, FIBiol; Hon. Senior Lecturer, London School of Hygiene and Tropical Medicine, since 2001; Director, International Institute of Parasitology, CAB International, 1981–93; *b* 30 June 1933; *s* of Carl and Sarah Muller; *m* 1st, 1959, Gretta Shearer; one *s* one *d*; 2nd, 1979, Annie Badilla Delgado (*d*

1998); one *s* one *d. Educ:* Summerhill Sch., Suffolk; London Univ. (BSc, PhD, DSc). Res. Fellow, KCL, 1958–59; ODM, 1959–61; Lectr, Univ. of Ibadan, 1961–66; Sen. Lectr, LSHTM, 1966–80. Pres., European Fedn of Parasitologists, 1988–92; Hon. Sec., British Soc. for Parasitology, 1995–98. Editor: Advances in Parasitology, 1978–; Jl of Helminthology, 1986–95. *Publications:* Worms and Disease, 1975, 3rd edn 2002; Onchocerciasis, 1987; Medical Parasitology, 1989. *Recreations:* beekeeping, writing instruments, photography. *Address:* 22 Cranbrook Drive, St Albans, Herts AL4 0SS. *T:* and *Fax:* (01727) 769322; *e-mail:* ralphmuller@hotmail.co.uk. *Died 11 Oct. 2007.*

MULLETT, Leslie Baden; consultant; *b* 22 Aug. 1920; *s* of Joseph and Edith Mullett; *m* 1st, 1945, Katharine Lear (marr. diss. 1968); no *c*; 2nd, 1971, Gillian Pettit. *Educ:* Gram. Sch., Hales Owen, Worcs; Birmingham Univ. (BSc (Hons Physics) 1941). Telecommunications Research Estab., 1941–46; AEA, 1946–60 (Head of Accelerator Div., 1958); Asst Dir, Rutherford High Energy Lab., SRC, 1960–68; on secondment to Res. Gp, Min. of Technology, 1966–68; CSO, Min. of Transport, 1968; CSO, Res. Requirements, DoE, 1970–74; Dep. Dir, Transport and Road Res. Lab., DoE/Dept of Transport, 1974–80. Vis. Prof., Univ. of Reading, 1982–90. *Publications:* A Guide to Transport for Disabled People, 1982; papers in learned jls on particle accelerators and solar energy. *Recreation:* gardening. *Address:* 42 Grosvenor Avenue, Grosvenor Park, Bourne, Lincs PE10 9HU. *T:* (01778) 423054. *Died 13 March 2008.*

MULLIN, Prof. John William, DSc, PhD; FREng, FRSC, FIChemE; Ramsay Memorial Professor of Chemical Engineering, University College London, 1985–90, then Emeritus Professor; Hon. Research Fellow, University College London, since 1990; *b* Rock Ferry, Cheshire, 22 Aug. 1925; *er s* of late Frederick Mullin and Kathleen Nellie Mullin (*née* Oppy); *m* 1952, Averil Margaret Davies, Carmarthen; one *s* one *d. Educ:* Hawarden County Sch.; UCW Cardiff (Fellow, 1981); University Coll. London (Fellow, 1981). Served RAF, 1945–48. 8 yrs in organic fine chemicals industry; University College London: Lectr, 1956; Reader, 1961; Prof., 1969; Dean, Faculty of Engrg, 1975–77; Vice-Provost, 1980–86; Crabtree Orator, 1993; Dean, Faculty of Engrg, London Univ., 1979–85. Vis. Prof., Univ. New Brunswick, 1967. Chm. Bd of Staff Examrs, Chem. Engrg, Univ. London, 1965–70. Hon. Librarian, IChemE, 1965–77 (Mem. Council, 1973–76); Mem., Materials Sci. Working Gp, European Space Agency, 1977–81; Founder Mem., Brit. Assoc. for Crystal Growth; Chairman: Process Engrg Gp, SCI, 1996–99; BS and ISO cttees on industrial screens, sieves, particle sizing, etc. Mem., Parly Gp for Engrg Develt, 1994–2004. Member: Cttee of Management, Inst. of Child Health, 1970–83; Court of Governors, University Coll., Cardiff, 1982–99; Council, Sch. of Pharmacy, Univ. of London, 1983–2000 (Vice-Chm., 1988–2000; Hon. Fellow, 1998). Liveryman, Engineers' Co., 1984–. Moulton Medal, IChemE, 1970; Kurnakov Meml Medal, Inst. of Gen. and Inorganic Chem., USSR Acad. of Scis, 1991. Dr *hc* Inst Nat. Polytechnique de Toulouse, 1989. *Publications:* Crystallization, 1961, 4th edn 2001; (ed) Industrial Crystallization, 1976; papers in Trans IChemE, Chem. Engrg Sci., Jl Crystal Growth, etc. *Address:* 12 Church Place, Ickenham, Middx UB10 8XB. *T:* (01895) 634950. *Club:* Athenæum. *Died 11 March 2009.*

MUMFORD, Prof. Enid; Professor of Organizational Behaviour, Manchester Business School, 1979–88, then Emeritus; *b* 6 March 1924; *d* of Arthur McFarland and Dorothy Evans; *m* 1947, Jim Mumford; one *s* one *d. Educ:* Wallasey High Sch.; Liverpool Univ. (BA, MA); Manchester Univ. (PhD). CIPM; FBCS. Personnel Officer, Rotol Ltd, 1946–47; Production Supervisor, J. D. Francis Ltd, 1947–48; Research Associate: Dept of Social Science, Liverpool Univ., 1948–56; Bureau of Public Health Economics, Univ. of Michigan, USA, 1956–57; Res. Lectr, Dept of Social Science, Liverpool

Univ., 1957–65; Lectr, then Sen. Lectr and Reader, Manchester Business Sch., 1966–79. LEO Award for Lifetime Exceptional Achievement in Inf. Systems, 1999. *Publications:* Chester Royal Infirmary 1856–1956, 1956; Living with a Computer, 1964; Computers Planning and Personnel Management, 1969; Systems Design for People, 1971; Job Satisfaction: a study of computer specialists, 1972; (with others) Coal and Conflict, 1963; (with O. Banks) The Computer and the Clerk, 1967; (with T. B. Ward) Computers: planning for people, 1968; (with A. Pettigrew) Implementing Strategic Decisions, 1975; (ed, with H. Sackman) Human Choice and Computers, 1975; (ed, with K. Legge) Designing Organizations for Efficiency and Satisfaction, 1978; (with D. Henshall) A Participative Approach to Computer Systems Design, 1978; (with M. Weir) Computer Systems in Work Design, 1979; (ed. with C. Cooper) The Quality of Working Life, 1979; (with others) The Impact of Systems Change in Organizations, 1980; Values, Technology and Work, 1980; Designing Secretaries, 1983; Designing Human Systems for New Technology, 1983; Designing Human Systems for Health Care, 1993; Using Computers for Business Success, 1986; (with W. B. MacDonald) XSEL's Progress, 1989; Tools for Change, 1994; Effective Systems Design and Requirements Analysis, 1995; System Design: ethical tools for ethical change, 1996; Dangerous Decisions: problem solving in tomorrow's world, 1999; Redesigning Human Systems, 2003; contribs to books and journals. *Address:* 4 Windmill Close, Appleton, Warrington, Cheshire WA4 5JS. *T:* (01925) 601039. *Died 7 April 2006.*

MUNN, Sir James, Kt 1985; OBE 1976; MA; *b* 27 July 1920; *s* of Douglas H. Munn and Margaret G. Dunn; *m* 1946, Muriel Jean Millar Moles; (one *d* decd). *Educ:* Stirling High Sch.; Glasgow Univ (MA (Hons)). Entered Indian Civil Service, 1941; served in Bihar, 1942–47. Taught in various schools in Glasgow, 1949–57; Principal Teacher of Modern Languages, Falkirk High Sch., 1957–62, Depute Rector, 1962–66; Rector: Rutherglen Acad., 1966–70; Cathkin High Sch., Cambuslang, Glasgow, 1970–83. Univ. Comr, 1988–95; Chairman: Manpower Services Cttee for Scotland, 1984–88; MSC, subseq. Training Commn, 1987–88; Scottish Adv. Bd, Open Coll., 1989–91; Pres., Inst. of Trng and Develt, 1989–92 (Fellow, 1989). Member: Consultative Cttee on Curriculum, 1968–80 (Chm., 1980–87); University Grants Cttee, 1973–82; Chm., Cttee to review structure of curriculum at SIII and SIV, 1975–77. Mem. Court, Strathclyde Univ., 1983–91. Fellow: Paisley Coll. of Technology, 1988; SCOTVEC, 1989; FIPD 1995. Chevalier des Palmes Académiques, 1967. DUniv Stirling, 1978; Hon. LLD Strathclyde, 1988; Hon. DEd Napier Polytechnic, 1989. *Address:* 4 Kincath Avenue, High Burnside, Glasgow G73 4RP. *T:* (0141) 634 4654. *Died 4 Aug. 2009.*

MUNRO, Dame Alison, DBE 1985 (CBE 1964); Chairman, Chichester Health Authority, 1982–88; *b* 12 Feb. 1914; *d* of late John Donald, MD; *m* 1939, Alan Lamont Munro (killed on active service, 1941); one *s. Educ:* Queen's Coll., Harley Street; Wynberg Girls' High Sch., South Africa; St Paul's Girls' Sch.; St Hilda's Coll., Oxford (MA). Ministry of Aircraft Production, 1942–45; Principal, Ministry of Civil Aviation, 1945; Asst Sec., 1949; Under-Sec., Ministry of Transport and Civil Aviation, 1958; Under-Sec., Ministry of Aviation, 1960; High Mistress, St Paul's Girls' Sch. Hammersmith, 1964–74. Chm., Merton, Sutton and Wandsworth AHA(T), 1974–82. Chairman: Training Council for Teachers of the Mentally Handicapped, 1966–69; Cttee of Inquiry into Children's Footwear, 1972; Central Transport Consultative Cttee, 1980–85; Maternity Services Adv. Cttee, 1981–85; Code Monitoring Cttee on Infant Formulae, 1985–89; Member: Board, BEA, 1966–73; Board, British Library, 1973–79; British Tourist Authority, 1973–81. Pres., Chichester and Dist Caledonian Soc., 1992–96. Governor: Charing Cross Group of Hospitals, 1967–74; Chichester High Sch. for Girls, 1990–94. Chm., St Richard's Hosp. Equipment

Appeal, 1994–98. *Recreation:* conservation. *Address:* Heathfield Care Home, Chichester Road, West Wittering, West Sussex PO20 8QA. *T:* (01243) 511083. *Club:* West Wittering Sailing (Cdre, 1986–88). *Died 2 Sept. 2008.*

MUNRO, Kenneth Alexander; Member, Royal Commission on Reform of the House of Lords, 1999; *b* 17 Dec. 1936; *s* of James Gibb Munro and Jean Ralston (*née* McKay); *m* 1961, Elizabeth Coats Forrest McCreanor; two *d*. *Educ:* Hutchesons' Boys' Grammar Sch., Glasgow; Univ. of Glasgow (MA 1963). Served Intelligence Corps, 1955–57. Worked in family business, 1957–59; Scottish American Investment Co. Ltd, 1963–66; Electrical Trades Union, 1966–67; NEDO, 1967–69; Ford Motor Co. Ltd, 1969–74 (on secondment to Pay Bd, 1973–74); European Commission, 1974–98: responsible for employment policy in transport and Asst to Dir Gen. for Transport, Brussels, 1974–82; Press Officer and Dep. Head of Office, London, 1982–88; Head of Commn Office, Edinburgh, 1988–98. Chm., Centre for Scottish Public Policy, 1997–2008. Member: Equal Opportunities Adv. Cttee for Scotland, 1993–2006; BP (formerly BP-Amoco) Adv. Bd for Scotland, 1997–2003. Mem. (Lab), Brentwood DC, Essex, 1971–74. Convenor, Children in Scotland, 1999–2003. Hon. Sec., 1991–2000, Vice Chm., 2000–04, Chm., 2004–07, Scottish Council, Eur. Movement; Convenor, Scotland in Europe, 2000–06. Hon. Fellow, Faculty of Law, Univ. of Edinburgh, 1998. Contested: (Lab) W Aberdeenshire, 1964; (New Scottish Lab) Lothian, Scottish Parlt elecns, 1999. Vice-Chm., John Smith Meml Trust, 1994–2005 (Vice-Chm., Adv. Bd, 2005–07). Convenor, Internat. Cttee, Saltire Soc., 2005–08. Mem., Campaigns Cttee, Queen Margaret UC, 1999–2003. Mem., Scotch Malt Whisky Soc. FRSA. *Recreations:* theatre, cinema, swimming, walking. *Address:* 23 Greenhill Gardens, Edinburgh EH10 4BL. *T:* (0131) 447 2284. *Club:* New (Edinburgh). *Died 23 Sept. 2008.*

MUNRO, Sir Sydney Douglas G.; *see* Gun-Munro.

MURPHY, Rear-Adm. Anthony Albert, CBE 1976; Special Project Executive, Ministry of Defence, 1977–82; retired, 1983; *b* 19 May 1924; *s* of Albert Edward Murphy and Jennie (*née* Giles); *m* 1954, Antonia Theresa (*née* Rayner); four *s*. *Educ:* Sir George Monoux Grammar Sch. National Provincial Bank, 1940–42; joined RN, 1942; commnd, 1944; Western Approaches, 1944–45; HMS Vanguard (Royal Tour of S Africa), 1945–49; HMS Bulwark (Suez); Comdr 1960; HMS Yarmouth/6th Frigate Sqdn, Kuwait, 1961–63; HMS Eagle, 1965–67; Captain 1967; Dir, Naval Guided Weapons, 1970–73; in comd HMS Collingwood, 1973–76; Rear-Adm. 1977; Vice-Pres., and Senior Naval Mem., Ordnance Board, 1977. *Recreations:* cricket, soccer (Chm. RNFA, 1973–76), country activities. *Died 9 Aug. 2008.*

MURPHY, Sir Leslie (Frederick), Kt 1978; Chairman, National Enterprise Board, 1977–79 (Deputy Chairman, 1975–77); *b* 17 Nov. 1915; *s* of Frederick Charles and Lillian Annie Murphy; *m* 1st, 1940, Marjorie Iris Cowell (*d* 1991); one *s* one *d*; 2nd, 1993, Dorothy Anne Murray (*d* 2002). *Educ:* Southall Grammar Sch.; Birkbeck Coll., Univ. of London. Principal Private Sec. to Minister of Fuel and Power, 1947–49; Asst Sec., Min. of Fuel and Power, 1949–52; Chm., Mobil Supply Co. Ltd and Mobil Shipping Co. Ltd, 1955–59; Finance Dir, Iraq Petroleum Co. Ltd, 1959–64; Director: J. Henry Schroder Wagg & Co. Ltd, 1964–75 (Dep. Chm. 1972–73); Schroders plc, 1979–90 (Dep. Chm., 1973–75); Unigate Ltd, 1968–75; Simon Engrg Ltd, 1980–85; Folksam International Insurance (UK) Ltd, 1980–90; Petroleum Economics Ltd, 1980–94 (Chm. 1980–87). Mem., NEDC, 1977–79. Mem. Royal Commn on Distribution of Income and Wealth, 1974–76; Board Mem., Church Army, 1964–94; Chm., Church Army Housing Ltd, 1973–82, Pres., 1982–84. Trustee, SDP, 1981–90. *Recreations:* music, golf. *Address:* Hedgerley, Barton Common Road, Barton-on-Sea, Hants BH25 5PR. *Died 29 Sept. 2007.*

MURPHY, Thomas A(quinas); Chairman, General Motors Corporation, 1974–80; *b* Hornell, NY, 10 Dec. 1915; *s* of John Joseph Murphy and Alma (*née* O'Grady); *m* 1941, Catherine Rita Maguire; one *s* two *d*. *Educ:* Leo High Sch., Chicago; Univ. of Illinois. US Naval Reserve, 1943–46. Joined General Motors Corporation, 1938; Asst Treas., 1959; Comptroller, 1967; Treas., 1968–70; Vice-Pres. and Gp Exec., Car and Truck Div., 1970–72; Vice-Chm., 1972–74. *Died 18 Jan. 2006.*

MURRAY, Charles Henry; Chairman, National Irish Bank (formerly Northern Bank (Ireland)) Ltd, 1986–89; *b* 29 Jan. 1917; *s* of Charles and Teresa Murray; *m* 1942, Margaret Ryan; one *s* four *d*. *Educ:* Christian Brothers Sch., Synge Street, Dublin; London Univ. (BCom). Asst Secretary, Dept of Finance (Ireland), 1961, Secretary, 1969–76; Dir, 1969–76, Governor, 1976–81, Central Bank of Ireland. Dir, Northern Bank, 1982–88. Hon. LLD, NUI, 1977. *Recreations:* reading, theatre, golf. *Address:* 6 Washington Park, Dublin 14, Ireland. *T:* 4947781. *Died 31 Jan. 2008.*

MURRAY, Iain Richard, OBE 1991; HM Diplomatic Service, retired; Consul-General, Houston, 2001–04; *b* 13 Aug. 1944; *s* of William Potts Murray and Barbara (*née* Beard); *m* 1st, 1967, Victoria Crew Gee (marr. diss.); one *s* one *d*; 2nd, 1984, Judith Wilson (marr. diss. 1991); 3rd, 1993, Norma Wisden (*née* Hummel). *Educ:* King Alfred's Grammar Sch., Wantage; Univ. of Kent at Canterbury (BA Hons 1968); Univ. of London (BSc Hons Econs (ext.)). Exec. Officer, CRO, 1963–65; re-joined FCO, 1968: Econ./Commercial Attaché, Accra, 1970–72; Second Sec., Addis Ababa, 1972–75; Vice-Consul (Commercial), Rio de Janeiro, 1975–79; Consul, Oporto, 1979–83; on secondment to Press Office, 10 Downing Street, 1983–85; FCO, 1985–87; Chargé d'Affaires, San Salvador, 1987–91; Asst Hd, Jt Export Promotion Directorate, FCO/DTI, 1992–94; Commercial/Econ. Counsellor, Kuala Lumpur, 1994–96; Consul-Gen., São Paulo, and Dir, Trade Promotion, Brazil, 1997–2000. Man. Dir, Q Publications Ltd, 2005–08; Dir, Search Oil and Gas, 2008–; Advr, 2005–06, Dir, Energy Practice, 2006–07, Norman Broadbent. Mem., Keepers of the Quaich, 2000–. Hon. FEI 2004. *Recreations:* hill-walking, history through travel and reading, losing golf balls. *Club:* Farmers. *Died 2 May 2009.*

MURRAY, Sir James, KCMG 1978 (CMG 1966); HM Diplomatic Service, retired; Ambassador and Permanent UK Representative to UN and other International Organisations at Geneva, 1978–79; *b* 3 Aug. 1919; *er s* of late James Hamilton Murray, King's Cross, Isle of Arran, and Hester Macneill Buie; *m* 1982, Mrs Jill Charmian Chapuisat, *d* of Maj.-Gen. Frederick William Gordon-Hall, CB, CBE; two step *d*. *Educ:* Bellahouston Acad.; Glasgow Univ. Royal Regt of Artillery, 1939; served India and Burma, 1943–45; Staff Coll., Quetta, 1945; Bde Major (RA) 19 Ind. Div.; GSO II (RA) ALFSEA; GSO II War Office. HM Foreign (subseq. Diplomatic) Service, 1947; Foreign Office, 1947–49; First Sec. (Information), HM Embassy, Cairo, 1949–54; Foreign Office, 1954–56; attached National Defence Coll. of Can., 1956–57; First Sec., HM Embassy, Paris, 1957–61; HM Consul in Ruanda-Urundi, 1961–62; Special Ambassador for Independence celebrations in Ruanda, July 1962, and in Burundi, Sept. 1962; Ambassador to Rwanda and Burundi, 1962–63; Deputy Head of UK Delegation to European Communities, 1963–65; Counsellor, Djakarta, 1965–67; Head of Far Eastern Dept, FCO, 1967–70; Consul-Gen., San Francisco, 1970–73; Asst Under-Sec. of State, FCO, 1973–74; Dep. Perm. Representative to UN, 1974–78 (Ambassador, 1976). Special Envoy of 5 Western Govts for negotiations on Namibia, 1979–80. Withrow Prof. of Govt, Deep Springs Coll., Calif, 1990; Adviser: Trade Policy Res. Centre, London, 1981–89; to Chm., Hanson Industries, NY, 1983–92; Nat. Bd of Dirs, Congressional Award Foundn, 1985–; Internat. Advr, Assoc. for a Better New York, 1990–. *Recreations:* horses, lawn tennis. *Address:* 220 Columbia Heights, Brooklyn

Heights, New York, NY 11201, USA. *T*: (718) 8523320. *Clubs*: Brooks's, Beefsteak, Pratt's; Brook (New York).
Died 28 Nov. 2007.

MURSELL, Sir Peter, Kt 1969; MBE 1941; Vice Lord-Lieutenant, West Sussex, 1974–90; *b* 20 Jan. 1913; *m* 1938, Cicely, *d* of late Mr and Mrs M. F. North; two *s* two *d. Educ*: Bedales Sch.; Downing Coll. Cambridge. Fruit growing, 1934. War Service: Air Transport Auxiliary, 1940–44, Sen. Comdr. West Sussex County Council: Mem., 1947–74; Chm., 1962–67 and 1969–74. Member: Cttee on Management in Local Govt, 1965–66; Royal Commn on Local Govt in England, 1966–69; Water Space Amenity Commn, 1973–76; Inland Waterways Amenity Adv. Council, 1974–77. DL West Sussex, 1962. *Recreations*: sailing, mountain walking, skiing, squash, canal cruising. *Address*: Taints Orchard, The Street, Washington, West Sussex RH20 4AS. *T*: (01903) 893062.
Died 23 Aug. 2008.

MURTON OF LINDISFARNE, Baron *cr* 1979 (Life Peer), of Hexham in the County of Northumberland; **(Henry) Oscar Murton,** OBE 1946; TD 1947 (Clasp 1951); PC 1976; JP; a Deputy Chairman of Committees, 1981–2004 and a Deputy Speaker, 1983–2004, House of Lords; *b* 8 May 1914; *o s* of late H. E. C. Murton, and of E. M. Murton (*née* Renton), Hexham, Northumberland; *m* 1st, 1939, Constance Frances (*d* 1977), *e d* of late F. O'L. Connell; one *s* (one *d* decd); 2nd, 1979, Pauline Teresa (Freeman, City of London, 1980), *y d* of late Thomas Keenan, JP, Johannesburg. *Educ*: Uppingham Sch. Commissioned, TA, 1934; Staff Capt., 149 Inf. Bde, TA, 1937–39; Staff Coll., Camberley, 1939; tsc; active service, Royal Northumberland Fusiliers, 1939–46; Lt-Col. Gen. Staff, 1942–46 (C-in-C's commendation for special service, 1942, 1944). Managing Dir, Henry A. Murton Ltd, Departmental Stores, Newcastle-upon-Tyne and Sunderland, 1949–57. MP (C) Poole, 1964–79; Sec., Cons. Parly Cttee for Housing, Local Government and Land, 1964–67, Vice-Chm., 1967–70; Chm., Cons. Parly Cttee for Public Building and Works, 1970; PPS to Minister of Local Government and Development, 1970–71; an Asst Govt Whip, 1971–72; a Lord Comr, HM Treasury, 1972–73; Second Dep. Chm., 1973–74, First Dep. Chm., 1974–76, Dep. Speaker and Chm. of Ways and Means, House of Commons, 1976–79. Member: Exec. Cttee, Inter-Parliamentary Union British Group, 1970–71; Panel of Chairmen of Standing Cttees, 1970–71; Jt Select Cttee of Lords and Commons on Private Bill Procedure, 1987–88. Introduced: The Highways (Amendment) Act 1965; The Access to Neighbouring Land Act, 1992. Mem., Poole BC, 1961–63; Pres., Poole Cons. Assoc., 1983–95; a former Vice-Pres., Assoc. of Municipal Corporations; Mem. Herrison (Dorchester) Hosp. Group Management Cttee, 1963–74. Governor, Canford Sch., 1972–76. Chancellor, Primrose League, 1983–88. Freeman, City of London, 1977; Freeman, Wax Chandlers' Co.; Past Master, Clockmakers' Co. JP, Poole, 1963. *Recreations*: painting, naval and military history from 17th century onwards. *Address*: 49 Carlisle Mansions, Carlisle Place, SW1P 1HY. *T*: (020) 7834 8226.
Died 5 July 2009.

MUSGRAVE, Prof. William Kenneth Rodgerson, PhD, DSc (Birmingham); Professor of Organic Chemistry, 1960–83, then Emeritus, and Head of Department of Chemistry, 1968–71, 1974–77, 1980–81, University of Durham; *b* 16 Sept. 1918; *s* of late Charles Musgrave and Sarah Alice Musgrave; *m* 1944, Joyce

Cadman (decd); two *s. Educ*: Stanley Grammar Sch., Co. Durham; Univ. of Birmingham. Mem., Tube Alloys, Birmingham Univ., 1940–44; British-Canadian Atomic Energy Project, 1944–45; Univ. of Durham: Lecturer in Chemistry, 1945–56; Senior Lecturer, 1956–60; Personal Readership in Organic Chem., 1960; Second Pro-Vice-Chancellor, 1970–73; Pro-Vice-Chancellor and Sub-Warden, 1973–78; Acting Vice-Chancellor, 1979. *Publications*: (joint) Advances in Fluorine Chemistry, vol. I, edited by Stacey, Tatlow and Sharpe, 1960; Rodd's Chemistry of Carbon Compounds, vols Ia and IIIa, edited by Coffey; scientific papers in chemical journals. *Recreations*: gardening, rough shooting. *Address*: Apt 43, Pegasus Court, 61–63 Broad Road, Sale, Greater Manchester M33 2ES.
Died 14 Nov. 2010.

MUSSON, Gen. Sir Geoffrey (Randolph Dixon), GCB 1970 (KCB 1965; CB 1959); CBE 1945; DSO 1944; BA; *b* 9 June 1910; *s* of late Robert Dixon Musson, Yockleton, Shrewsbury; *m* 1939, Hon. Elspeth L. Bailey, *d* of late Hon. Herbert Crawshay Bailey; one *s* (one *d* decd). *Educ*: Shrewsbury; Trinity Hall, Cambridge. 2nd Lt KSLI, 1930. Served War of 1939–45, North Africa and Italy; Comdr 2nd Bn DCLI, 1943–44; Comdr 36th Infantry Bde, 1944–46. Comdr Commonwealth Forces in Korea, 1954–55; Comdt Sch. of Infantry, 1956–58, Comdr 7th Armoured Div., BAOR, 1958; Maj.-Gen. 1958; Comdr, 5th Div., 1958–59. Chief of Staff, GHQ, Near East Land Forces, 1959–62; Vice-Adjutant-Gen., War Office, subseq. Min. of Defence, 1963–64; GOC-in-C, N Command, 1964–67; Adjutant-General, 1967–70, retired. Colonel: King's Shropshire Light Infantry, 1963–68; The Light Infantry, 1968–72. A Vice-Chm., Nat. Savings Cttee, 1970–78; Chairman: HM Forces Savings Cttee, 1970–78; Regular Forces Employment Assoc., 1978–80; Vice-Pres., Royal Patriotic Fund Corporation, 1974–83; Pres., Victory Services Club, 1970–80. *Address*: Barn Cottage, Hurstbourne Tarrant, Andover, Hants SP11 0BD. *T*: (01264) 736354.
Died 10 Jan. 2008.

MUSTOE, Anne, MA; travel writer and lecturer; *b* 24 May 1933; *d* of H. W. Revill; *m* 1960, Nelson Edwin Mustoe, QC (*d* 1976); three step *s. Educ*: Girton Coll., Cambridge (BA Classical Tripos 1955, MA 1958). DipIPM 1959. Guest, Keen & Nettlefolds Ltd, 1956–60; Head of Classics, Francis Holland School, NW1, 1965–69; independent travel agent, 1969–73; Dep. Headmistress, Cobham Hall, Kent, 1975–78; Headmistress, St Felix School, Southwold, 1978–87. Chm., ISIS, 1986–87; President, Girls' Schools Assoc., 1984–85; Mem., Board of Managers of Girls' Common Entrance Examinations, 1983–86. Mem., CS Final Selection Bd, 1980–92. Chm. Trustees, National Byway, 2005–. Governor: Hethersett Old Hall Sch., 1981–86; Cobham Hall, 1986–99; James Allen's Girls' Sch., 1991–97; Thornton Coll., 1992–97. FRGS 1996. JP Suffolk, 1981–85. *Publications*: A Bike Ride: 12,000 miles around the world, 1991; Escaping the Winter, 1993, 2nd edn 2003; Lone Traveller, 1998; Two Wheels in the Dust, 2001; Cleopatra's Needle, 2003; Amber, Furs and Cockleshells, 2005; Che Guevara and the Mountain of Silver, 2007. *Recreations*: music, cycling (world cycling tours, 1987–88, 1994–95, 2009–). *Address*: 12 Melcombe Court, Dorset Square, NW1 6EP. *T*: (020) 7262 1701.
Died 10 Nov. 2009.

MYLLENT, Peter; *see* Hamylton Jones, K.

N

NABARRO, Prof. Frank Reginald Nunes, MBE 1946; FRS 1971; Professor of Physics, University of the Witwatersrand, 1953–84, then Hon. Professorial Research Fellow; Fellow, South African Council for Scientific and Industrial Research, 1994–2005; *b* 7 March 1916; *s* of late Stanley Nunes Nabarro and Leah Nabarro; *m* 1948, Margaret Constance (*d* 1997), *d* of late James Dalziel, ARAM; three *s* two *d*. *Educ:* Nottingham High Sch.; New Coll., Oxford (MA, BSc); DSc Birmingham. Sen. Exper. Officer, Min. of Supply, 1941–45; Royal Soc. Warren Research Fellow, Univ. of Bristol, 1945–49; Lectr in Metallurgy, Univ. of Birmingham, 1949–53; University of Witwatersrand: Prof. and Head of Dept of Physics, 1953–77, City of Johannesburg Prof. of Physics, 1970–77; Dean, Faculty of Science, 1968–70; Representative of Senate on Council, 1967–77; Deputy Vice-Chancellor, 1978–80. Vis. Prof., Nat. Research Council, Ottawa, 1956; Republic Steel Vis. Prof., Dept of Metallurgy, Case Inst. of Techn., Cleveland, Ohio, 1964–65; Overseas Fellow of Churchill Coll., Cambridge, 1966–67; Gauss Prof., Akademie der Wissenschaften, Göttingen, 1970; Professeur-associé, Univ. Paris-Sud, 1971, Montpellier II, 1973; Vis. Prof., Dept of Material Science, Univ. of Calif., Berkeley, 1977; Vis. Fellow, Robinson Coll., Cambridge, 1981 and 1999; Vis. Prof., Dept of Materials Engrg, Technion, Haifa, 1983. Founder Mem., Acad. of Sci. of S Africa, 1996; For. Associate, US NAE, 1996. Hon. Member: S African Inst. of Physics, 1992 (Vice-Pres., 1956–57); Microscopy Soc. of S Africa, 1998; Hon. FRSSAf 1973 (Pres., 1989–92). Hon. Pres., Johannesburg Musical Soc., 1999–. Hon. DSc: Witwatersrand, 1987; Natal, 1988; Cape Town, 1988; Pretoria, 2003. Order of Mapungubwe (Silver) (SA), 2005. Beilby Memorial Award, 1950; South Africa Medal, 1972; De Beers Gold Medal, 1980; Claude Harris Leon Foundn Award of Merit, 1983; J. F. W. Herschel Medal, 1989; R. F. Mehl Award, 1995; Platinum Medal, Inst. of Materials, 1997. *Publications:* Theory of Crystal Dislocations, 1967, repr. 1987; (jtly) Physics of Creep, 1995; scientific papers, mainly on solid state physics. *Recreation:* gardening. *Address:* 32 Cookham Road, Auckland Park, Johannesburg 2092, South Africa. *T:* (11) 7267745.
Died 20 July 2006.

NATHAN, 2nd Baron *cr* 1940; **Roger Carol Michael Nathan;** *b* 5 Dec. 1922; *s* of 1st Baron Nathan, PC, TD, and Eleanor Joan Clara (*d* 1972), *d* of C. Stettauer; S father, 1963; *m* 1950, Philippa Gertrude, *d* of Major Joseph Bernard Solomon, MC, Pulborough, Sussex; one *s* two *d*. *Educ:* Stowe Sch.; New Coll., Oxford (MA). Served War of 1939–45: Capt., 17/21 Lancers (despatches, wounded twice). Admitted Solicitor (Hons), 1950; Senior Partner, Herbert Oppenheimer Nathan & Vandyk, 1978–86; Consultant, Denton Hall Burgin & Warrens, 1989–92. Chm., Arbitration Panel, The Securities Assoc., 1988–92. Hon. Associate Mem., Bar Assoc. of City of New York. FSA; FRSA; FRGS. Pres., Jewish Welfare Board, 1967–71; Chairman: Central British Fund for Jewish Relief and Rehabilitation, 1971–77 (Hon. Pres., 1977–); Exec. Cttee, Cancer Research Campaign (formerly British Empire Cancer Campaign), 1970–75 (Hon. Treasurer, 1979–87); Working Party on Energy and the Envmt (reported 1974); Animal Procedures Cttee, 1990–93; Wkg Party on Efficiency and Effectiveness in Voluntary Sector, 1989–90; Court of Discipline, Cambridge Univ., 1989–92; Vice Chm., Cttee on Charity Law and Practice (reported 1976); Mem., Royal Commn on Envmtl Pollution, 1979–89. Mem., H of L Select Cttee on European Communities, 1983–88 and 1990–92 (Chm., *ad hoc* Sub-Cttee on European Co. Statute, 1989–90; Chm., Sub-Cttee F (Envmt), 1983–87 and 1990–92), on

Science and Technology, 1994–99; Chm., H of L Select Cttee on Murder and Life Imprisonment, 1988–89. Chm., RSA, 1975–77, Vice-Pres., 1977–. Chairman: Inst. of Envmtl Assessment, 1990–91; South Downs Conservation Bd, 1992–97; President: UK Envmtl Law Assoc., 1987–92; Nat. Soc. for Clean Air, 1987–89; Soc. of Sussex Downsmen, 1987–92; Weald and Downland Open Air Mus., 1995–97; Mem., Court and Council, Sussex Univ., 1989–98. Chm., City Festival of Flowers, 1964; Master, Worshipful Company of Gardeners, 1963–64. Hon. LLD Sussex, 1988. *Publications:* Spice of Life (memoir), 2003. *Heir:* *s* Hon. Rupert Harry Bernard Nathan [*b* 26 May 1957; *m* 1987, Ann Hewitt (marr. diss. 1997); *m* 1997, Jane, *d* of D. Cooper]. *Address:* Collyers Farm, Lickfold, Petworth, West Sussex GU28 9DU. *T:* (01798) 861284. *Clubs:* Athenæum, Cavalry and Guards.
Died 19 July 2007.

NATHAN, Michael Bernard; *see* Wharton, M. B.

NAYLOR, Prof. Malcolm Neville, RD 1967; DL; BSc, BDS, PhD; FDSRCS; Hon. Senior Research Fellow: Forsyth Institute, Boston, since 1984; Institute of Dental Surgery, since 1991; Professor of Preventive Dentistry, University of London, 1970–91, then Professor Emeritus; Head of Department of Periodontology and Preventive Dentistry, Guy's Hospital Dental School, 1980–91; *b* 30 Jan. 1926; *er s* of late Roland B. Naylor, MBE and Mabel L. (*née* Neville), Walsall, Staffs; *m* 1956, Doreen Mary (*d* 2006), *d* of late H. E. Jackson, CBE; one *s*. *Educ:* Queen Mary's Sch., Walsall; Univ. of Glasgow; Univ. of Birmingham (BSc 1951, BDS 1955; Nuffield Scholar, 1949–51); Univ. of London (PhD 1963). FDSRCS 1958; Hon. FDSRCPSGlas 1992. Hosp. appts, Birmingham and Dundee, 1955–59; Guy's Hosp. Dental School: Res. Fellow, 1959–62; mSen. Lectr in Preventive Dentistry, 1962–66; Reader in Preventive Dentistry, 1966–70; Hon. Consultant Dental Surgeon, Guy's Hosp., 1966–91, Consultant Emeritus, 1991. William Waldorf Astor Fellow, USA, 1963. President: British Div., IADR, 1990–92 (Hon. Treas., 1975–90); Odontol Sect., RSocMed, 1984–85; Mem., FDI Commn, 1992–95; Trustee and Treas., Oral and Dental Res. Trust, 1992–2006; Patron, Soc. of Cosmetic Scientists, 1995–. Served RNVR and RNR, retiring as Surg. Captain (D), 1943–76; Civil Consultant Dental Surgeon, RN, 1974–91; Hon. Dental Surgeon to the Queen, 1976; Hon. Col, Univ. of London OTC, 1979–94; Sec., 1978–82, Chm., 1982–89, COMEC; Pres., 50F (Lambeth) Sqn, ATC, 1999–2002; Chairman: Mil. Educn Cttee, Univ. of London, 1979–91; Sea Cadet Assoc., Sports Council, 1975–; Mem., Services Liaison Cttee, Sussex Univ., 1988–. Governor: Roehampton Inst. for Higher Educn, 1978–96; Whitelands Coll., 1975–96; Bacons Sch., Bermondsey, 1979–90 (Vice Chm., 1981–90); St Saviour's and St Olave's Sch., 1980– (Chm., 1988–2004); Wye Coll., Univ. of London, 1992–2000; Member: Council of Govs, UMDS, 1987–91; Ct of Govs, Brunel Univ., 1994–98. Trustee: Sino-British Fellowship Trust, 1978– (Dep. Chm., 1995–98; Chm., 1998–); Walter St John Educn Trust, 1991–; Mem., St Olave's and St Saviour's Foundn, 1985– (Warden, 1997–99). Lay Reader, C of E, 1974–. Mem., Southwark Diocesan Synod, 1983–92. Freeman, City of London, 1983; Liveryman, Bakers' Co., 1983–. DL Greater London, 1992 (Rep. DL Lambeth, 1994–2005). Hon. FDSRCPSGlas 1992. Colgate Prize, IADR, 1961; Silver Medal, Soc. of Cosmetics Scientists, 1975; Tomes Medal, BDA, 1987. *Publications:* papers and articles in prof. and scientific jls. *Recreations:* off-shore sailing, music, golf, watercolour painting, family and home. *Address:* Rosedale,

18 Apple Grove, Aldwick Bay, W Sussex PO21 4NB. *T*: (01243) 266646. *Clubs*: Royal Society of Medicine; Royal Naval Sailing Assoc.; Chichester Golf. *Died 15 April 2008.*

NAYLOR, Peter Brian, CBE 1987; Representative, British Council, Greece, 1983–86; *b* 10 July 1933; *s* of late Eric Sydney Naylor and Phyllis Marian Jolly; *m* 1st, 1958, Barbara Pearson (*d* 1995); two *s* one *d* (and one *s* decd); 2nd, 2005, Heather Margaret Fibbens (*née* White). *Educ*: Grange High Sch., Bradford; Selwyn Coll., Cambridge (Open Exhibnr; BA 1957). Wool Top Salesman, Hirsch, Son & Rhodes, Bradford, 1957; British Council: Asst Rep., Bangkok, 1959; Courses Dept and E Europe Dept, London, 1962; Asst Rep., Warsaw, 1967; Reg. Rep., Dacca, E Pakistan, 1969; Actg Rep., Athens, 1971; Rep., Argentina, 1972, Brazil, 1975; Controller, European Div., 1978–83. *Publications*: contrib. Blood Sweat and Tears, 1992. *Recreations*: reading, writing, drawing, salukis. *Address*: 3 Farmadine Court, Saffron Walden, Essex CB11 3HT. *T*: (01799) 527708. *Club*: Saffron Walden Golf. *Died 25 March 2009.*

NEAL, Sir Leonard (Francis), Kt 1974; CBE 1971; FCIT; CIPM; Industrial Relations Consultant to number of industrial and commercial companies; *b* 27 Aug. 1913; *s* of Arthur Henry Neal and Mary Neal; *m* 1939, Mary Lilian Puttock; one *s* one *d*. *Educ*: London School of Economics; Trinity College, Cambridge (MA). Labour Manager, Esso, 1956; Employee Relations Manager, Fawley Refinery, 1961; Labour Relations Adviser, Esso Europe Inc. Mem., British Railways Board, 1967–71; Chm., Commn on Industrial Relations, 1971–74. Prof. (part-time) of Industrial Relations, UMIST, 1970–76; Chairman: MAT International Op Ltd, 1974–85; Employment Conditions Abroad Ltd, 1977–84; Dir (non-exec.), Pilkington Bros, 1976–83. *Publications*: (with A. Robertson) The Managers Guide to Industrial Relations. *Recreations*: reading, gardening, motoring. *Address*: Towcester, Northants. *Died 4 May 2008.*

NEAME, Ronald, CBE 1996; film producer and director; *b* 23 April 1911; *s* of Elwin Neame and Ivy Close; *m* 1933, Beryl Yolanda Heanly (marr. diss. 1992; she *d* 1999); one *s*; *m* 1993, Donna Bernice Friedberg. *Educ*: University College School; Hurstpierpoint College. Entered film industry, 1928; became Chief Cameraman, 1934. In charge of production on: In Which We Serve, This Happy Breed, Blithe Spirit, Brief Encounter, 1942–45; produced: Great Expectations, Oliver Twist, The Magic Box; directed: Take My Life, The Card, 1945–51; The Million Pound Note, 1953; Windom's Way, 1957; The Horse's Mouth, 1958; Tunes of Glory, 1960; I Could Go On Singing, 1962; The Chalk Garden, 1963; Mr Moses, 1964; Gambit, 1966; The Prime of Miss Jean Brodie, 1968; Scrooge, 1970; The Poseidon Adventure, 1972; Odessa File, 1973; Meteor, 1978; Hopscotch, 1979; First Monday in October, 1980; Foreign Body, 1985; The Magic Balloon, 1989. *Publications*: Straight from the Horse's Mouth: an autobiography, 2003. *Address*: 2317 Kimridge, Beverly Hills, CA 90210, USA. *Died 16 June 2010.*

NEAVE, Julius Arthur Sheffield, CBE 1978 (MBE (mil.) 1945); JP; DL; General Manager, since 1966, Director since 1977, Mercantile & General Reinsurance Co. Ltd (Managing Director, 1980–82); *b* 17 July 1919; *s* of Col Richard Neave and Helen Mary Elizabeth (*née* Miller); *m* 1951, Helen Margery, *d* of Col P. M. Acton-Adams, DSO, Clarence Reserve, Marlborough, NZ; three *d*. *Educ*: Sherborne School. Joined Mercantile & General Reinsurance Co. Ltd, 1938. Served War, 1939–46: called as Territorial, commnd 13th/18th Royal Hussars, Adjt 3 years, final rank Major (despatches 1945). Returned to Mercantile & General, 1946; Asst Gen. Manager, 1964. Dir, Prudential Corp., 1982–92. (First) Chairman, Reinsurance Offices Assoc., 1969–74, Hon. Pres., 1974–82; Chm., Reinsurance Panel, British Insce Assoc., 1971–82; representative, Gt Britain: Cttee, annual internat. meeting of reinsurers, Monte Carlo, 1969–82; Vice-Pres., Assoc. Internat. pour l'Etude de l'Assurance,

Geneva, 1976–83, Pres., 1983. Dir and Governor, Internat. Insce Seminars, 1977–82 (Founder's Gold Medal, 1977); President: Insce Inst. of London, 1976–77, 1983–84; Chartered Insce Inst., 1983–84 (Mem. Council, 1975–); Mem. Court, Insurers' Co., 1979– (Master, 1984–85). Hon. Fellow, RSA, 1975. Essex: JP (Brentwood), 1975; DL, 1983; High Sheriff, 1987–88. OStJ 1988. *Publications*: Speaking of Reinsurance, 1980; Still Speaking of Reinsurance, 1983. *Recreations*: shooting, fishing, golf, needlework. *Address*: Mill Green Park, Ingatestone, Essex CM4 0JB. *T*: (01277) 353036. *Club*: Cavalry and Guards. *Died 30 Oct. 2008.*

NEEDHAM, Karen Ida Boalth; *see* Spärck Jones, K. I. B.

NEGUS, Her Honour Norma Florence, (Mrs D. J. Turner-Samuels); a Circuit Judge, 1990–97; *b* 31 July 1932; *d* of late George David Shellabear and Kate (*née* Calvert); *m* 1st, 1956, Richard Negus (marr. diss. 1960); 2nd, 1976, David Jessel Turner-Samuels, QC. *Educ*: Malvern Girls' Coll., Malvern, Worcs. Fashion promotion and advertising in UK, Canada and USA, 1950–61; Merchandise Editor, Harper's Bazaar, 1962–63; Asst Promotion Manager, Vogue and House & Garden, 1963–65; Unit Manager, Trends Merchandising and Fashion Promotion Unit, 1965–67; Export Marketing Manager and Advertising Manager, Glenoit (UK) Ltd, 1967–68. Called to the Bar, Gray's Inn, 1970; Mem., Middle Temple, 1984. In practice on SE Circuit, 1971–84; a Metropolitan Stipendiary Magistrate, 1984–90; a Recorder, 1987–90. Member: Parole Bd, 1991–94; Mental Health Review Tribunal, 1996–97. Mem., Central Criminal Court Bar Mess, 1978–84. *Recreations*: reading, writing, theatre, music, travel, swimming. *Address*: c/o Cloisters, 1 Pump Court, Temple, EC4Y 7AA. *Died 17 Aug. 2009.*

NEIL, Matthew, CBE 1976; Secretary and Chief Executive, Glasgow Chamber of Commerce, 1954–83; *b* 19 Dec. 1917; *er s* of John Neil and Jean Wallace. *Educ*: John Neilson High Sch., Paisley; Glasgow Univ. (MA, LLB). Served War, 1939–46: Far East, ME, Mediterranean and Western Europe; RHA, RA and Air Observation Post; RAuxAF, 1950–57. Admitted solicitor, 1947; Hon. Sheriff, Renfrew and Argyll, later N Strathclyde, 1973–. Mem., British Overseas Trade Adv. Council, 1975–82. Hon. LLD Glasgow, 1983. *Recreations*: golf, music. *Address*: 39 Arkleston Road, Paisley PA1 3TH. *T*: (0141) 889 4975. *Clubs*: East India, Devonshire, Sports and Public Schools; Lamlash Golf, Prestwick Golf. *Died 19 Sept. 2008.*

NELDER, John Ashworth, DSc; FRS 1981; Visiting Professor, Imperial College of Science, Technology and Medicine (formerly Imperial College of Science and Technology), 1971–2009; Head of Statistics Department, 1968–84, and of Division of Biomathematics, Jan.–Oct. 1984, Rothamsted Experimental Station; *b* 8 Oct. 1924; *s* of Reginald Charles and Edith May Ashworth Nelder; *m* 1955, Mary Hawkes; one *s* one *d*. *Educ*: Blundell's Sch., Tiverton; Cambridge Univ. (MA); DSc Birmingham. Head, Statistics Section, National Vegetable Research Station, 1950–68. Pres., Royal Statistical Soc., 1985–86. Hon. DSc Paul Sabatier, Toulouse, 1981. *Publications*: Computers in Biology, 1974; (with P. McCullagh) Generalized Linear Models, 1983, 2nd edn 1989; (jtly) Generalized Linear Models with Random Effects, 2006; responsible for statistical programs (computer), Genstat and GLIM; numerous papers in statistical and biological jls. *Recreations*: piano-playing, music, natural history. *Address*: Cumberland Cottage, 33 Crown Street, Redbourn, St Albans, Herts AL3 7JX. *T*: (01582) 792907. *Died 7 Aug. 2010.*

NELSON, 9th Earl *cr* 1805, of Trafalgar and of Merton; Peter John Horatio Nelson; Baron Nelson of the Nile and of Hilborough, Norfolk, 1801; Viscount Merton, 1805; *b* 9 Oct. 1941; *s* of Captain Hon. John Marie Joseph Horatio Nelson (*y s* of 5th Earl) and of Kathleen Mary, *d* of William Burr, Torquay; *S* uncle, 1981; *m* 1st, 1969, Maureen Diana (marr. diss. 1992), *d* of Edward

Patrick Quinn, Kilkenny; one *s* one *d*; 2nd, 1992, Tracy Cowie; one *s*. Chm., Retainacar Ltd, 1988–94. Vice-Pres., Jubilee Sailing Trust; Hon. Life Member: Royal Naval Assoc.; Royal Naval Museum. *Heir: s* Viscount Merton, *b* 21 Sept. 1971.   *Died 28 March 2009.*

NELSON OF STAFFORD, 3rd Baron *cr* 1960; **Henry Roy George Nelson;** Bt 1955; Managing Director, TIB Mercantile Ltd, since 1998; *b* 26 Oct. 1943; *er s* of 2nd Baron Nelson of Stafford and Pamela Roy, *yr d* of Ernest Roy Bird, MP; *S* father, 1995; *m* 1968, Dorothy, *yr d* of Leslie Caley; one *s* one *d*. *Educ:* Ampleforth; King's Coll., Cambridge (MA). CEng, FIMechE, MIEE. Joined RHP Bearings, 1970: Gen. Manager, transmission bearings, 1973–78, automotive bearings, 1978–81; Manufacturing Dir, industrial bearings, 1981–83; Man. Dir, Hopkinsons Ltd, 1983–85; Man. Dir, industrial and distribution divs, Pegler-Hattersley plc, 1985–86; Gp Man. Dir, GSPK Ltd, 1986–90; Man. Dir, power transmission div., Fenner plc, 1991–92; Ops Dir, TIB plc, 1993–97 (non-exec. Dir, 1998–2000). Mem., Govt Cttee of Enquiry into Engrng Profession, 1978–80. *Heir: s* Hon. Alistair William Henry Nelson, *b* 3 June 1973. *Address:* Eastlands, Tibthorpe, Driffield, E Yorks YO25 9LD. *Club:* Farmers'.
                                     Died 22 Sept. 2006.

NELSON, Bertram James, OBE 1984; HM Diplomatic Service, retired; Consul-General, Antwerp, 1983–85; *b* 7 Dec. 1925; *s* of Herbert James Nelson and Adelaide Mabel Nelson (*née* Newton); *m* 1958, Constance Dangerfield; one *s* one *d*. *Educ:* North Kensington Central School. Grenadier Guards, 1944–47; Post Office and Cable and Wireless, 1947–54; Foreign Office, 1954; served Cairo, Budapest, Athens, Asunción, Zagreb, DSAO, 1966–69; Vice-Consul, Tokyo, 1969–71; Vice-Consul, Tehran, 1972–75; FCO, 1975–79; First Sec. and Consul, Brussels, 1979–83. *Recreations:* theatre, bridge, gardening. *Address:* 6 Craigweil Manor, Aldwick, Bognor Regis, West Sussex PO21 4AP.   *Died 24 Feb. 2008.*

NERINA, Nadia, (Mrs Charles Gordon); Prima Ballerina; Ballerina with Royal Ballet, 1951–69; *b* Cape Town, 21 Oct. 1927; *née* Nadine Judd; *m* 1955, Charles Gordon. Joined Sadler's Wells Sch., 1946; after two months joined Sadler's Wells Theatre Ballet; transferred Sadler's Wells Ballet, Royal Opera House (later Royal Ballet), as soloist, then (1952) principal. *Rôles:* Princess Aurora in The Sleeping Beauty; Ondine; Odette-Odile in Swan Lake; Swanhilda in Coppelia; Sylvia; Giselle; Cinderella; Firebird; Can Can Dancer in La Boutique Fantasque; Ballerina in Petrushka; Colombine in Carnaval; Mazurka, Little Waltz, Prelude, in Les Sylphides; Mam'zelle Angot; Ballet Imperial; Scènes de Ballet; Flower Festival of Genzano; Les Rendezvous; Polka in Façade; The Girl in Spectre de la Rose; Casse Noisette; Laurentia; Khadra; Vagabonds; The Bride in A Wedding Bouquet; *creations:* Circus Dancer in Mardi Gras; Fairy Spring in Cinderella; Queen of the Earth in Homage to the Queen; Faded Beauty in Noctambules; Variation on a Theme; Birthday Offering; Lise in La Fille Mal Gardée; Electra; The Girl in Home; Clorinda in Tancredi. Appeared with Royal Ballet: Europe; South Africa; USA; Canada; USSR; Bulgaria; Romania. Recital Tours with Alexis Rassine: South Africa, 1952–55; England, 1956–57; concert performances, Royal Albert Hall and Royal Festival Hall, 1958–60. *Guest appearances include:* Turkish Nat. Ballet, 1957; Bolshoi Ballet, Kirov Ballet, 1960; Munich Ballet, 1963; Nat. Finnish Ballet, Royal Danish Ballet, 1964; Stuttgart Ballet, 1965; Ballet Theatre, Opera House Chicago, 1967; Royal Command Variety Performances, 1963–66. Mounted, dir. and prod three Charity Gala performances, London Palladium, 1969, 1971, 1972. Many TV appearances, UK and USA. Hon. Consultant on Ballet, Ohio Univ., 1967–69. British Jury Member: 3rd Internat. Ballet Competition, Moscow, 1977; Benois de la Danse Competition, Moscow, 1993, Paris, 1996. Fellow, 1959, Patron, 1964, Cecchetti Soc. Mem. Council, RSPCA, 1969–74. *Publications:* contrib.: La Fille

Mal Gardée, 1960; Ballet and Modern Dance, 1974; *relevant publication:* Ballerina, ed Clement Crisp, 1975.
                                     Died 6 Oct. 2008.

NEWBY, (George) Eric, CBE 1994; MC 1945; FRSL 1972; FRGS 1975; writer; *b* 6 Dec. 1919; *o s* of George Arthur Newby and Hilda Pomeroy, London; *m* 1946, Wanda, *d* of Viktor Skof and Gisella Urdih, Trieste; one *s* one *d*. *Educ:* St Paul's School. With Dorland Advertising, London, 1936–38; apprentice and merch. seaman, 4-masted Finnish barque, Moshulu, 1938–39; served War of 1939–45, Special Boat Section, POW 1942–45; Women's Fashion Business, 1946–56 (with Worth Paquin, 1955–56); explored in Nuristan and made unsuccessful attempt to climb Mir Samir, Afghan Hindu Kush, 1956; with Secker & Warburg, 1956–59; with John Lewis Partnership (Central Buyer, Model Dresses), 1959–63; descended Ganges with wife, 1963. Travel Editor, The Observer, and Gen. Editor, Time Off Books, 1964–73. Mem., Assoc. of Cape Horners. Hon. DLitt Bournemouth, 1994; DUniv Open, 1996. *Publications:* The Last Grain Race, 1956; A Short Walk in the Hindu Kush, 1958; Something Wholesale, 1962; Slowly Down the Ganges, 1966; Time Off in Southern Italy, 1966; Grain Race: Pictures of Life Before the Mast in a Windjammer, 1968; (jointly) The Wonders of Britain, 1968; (jointly) The Wonders of Ireland, 1969; Love and War in the Apennines, 1971; (jointly) The World of Evelyn Waugh, 1973; Ganga (with photographs by Raghubir Singh), 1973; World Atlas of Exploration, 1975; Great Ascents, 1977; The Big Red Train Ride, 1978; A Traveller's Life, 1982; On the Shores of the Mediterranean, 1984; A Book of Travellers' Tales, 1985; Round Ireland in Low Gear, 1987; What the Traveller Saw, 1989; A Small Place in Italy, 1994; A Merry Dance Around the World, 1995; Learning the Ropes, 1999; Departures and Arrivals, 1999; Around the World in Eighty Years, 2000; A Book of Lands and Peoples, 2003. *Recreations:* walking, reading. *Address:* Pine View House, 4 Pine View Close, Chilworth, Surrey GU4 8RS. *T:* (01483) 571430. *Club:* Travellers (Hon. Mem.).   *Died 20 Oct. 2006.*

NEWIS, Kenneth, CB 1967; CVO 1970 (MVO 1958); FRSAMD; *b* 9 Nov. 1916; *o s* of late H. T. and G. Newis, Manchester; *m* 1943, Kathleen, *o d* of late John Barrow, Davenport, Cheshire; two *d*. *Educ:* Manchester Grammar Sch.; St John's Coll., Cambridge (Scholar). BA 1938, MA 1942. Entered HM Office of Works, 1938; Private Sec. to Minister of Works (Rt Hon. C. W. Key), 1948–49; Asst Sec., 1949; Under-Sec., 1959; Dir of Management Services, MPBW, 1969–70; Under-Sec., Scottish Develt Dept, 1970–73, Sec., 1973–76. Hon. Pres., Queen's Hall (Edinburgh) Ltd, 1991– (Chm., 1977–91). Vice-Chm., Cockburn Assoc., 1986–94; Member: Historic Buildings Council for Scotland, 1978–88; Bd, Methodist Homes for the Aged, and Vice-Chm., MHA Housing Assoc., 1977–91; Bd, RSAMD, 1977–88 (FRSAMD 1995); Scottish Churches' Council, 1984–87 (Chm., Friends of Scottish Churches' Council, 1984–87). Conservator of Wimbledon and Putney Commons, 1963–70. Governor: Farrington's School, 1964–70; Richmond College, 1964–70. *Recreation:* music. *Address:* 10/9 St Margaret's Place, Thirlestane Road, Edinburgh EH9 1AY. *T:* (0131) 447 4138. *Club:* New (Edinburgh).   *Died 19 Nov. 2006.*

NEWMAN, Dr Barry Hilton; Director, Propellants, Explosives and Rocket Motor Establishment, and Head of Rocket Motor Executive, Ministry of Defence, 1980–84, retired; *b* 16 Sept. 1926; *s* of Charles Ernest Newman and Kathleen (*née* Hilton); *m* 1950, Dorothy Ashworth Truesdale; one *s* one *d*. *Educ:* Bishop Vesey's Grammar Sch., Sutton Coldfield; Univ. of Birmingham (BSc (Hons) 1947, PhD 1950). Joined Scientific Civil Service, 1950; Explosives R&D Estabt, 1950–63; Defence Research Staff, Washington, 1963–66; Supt Explosives Br., Royal Armament R&D Estabt, 1966–71; Asst Dir, Directorate General Weapons (Army), 1971–72; Dir, Research Armaments, 1972–74; RCDS 1975; Head of

Terminal Effects Dept, RARDE, 1976–77; Dep. Dir, RARDE, 1977–80. *Publications:* official reports. *Recreations:* France, cricket, bridge, history, theatre. *Address:* c/o Barclays Bank, 80 High Street, Sevenoaks, Kent. *Club:* MCC. *Died 12 July 2008.*

NEWMAN, Paul; American actor and director; *b* 26 Jan. 1925; *s* of Arthur Newman and Theresa (*née* Fetzer); *m* 1st, 1949, Jacqueline Witte (marr. diss. 1958); two *d* (one *s* decd); 2nd, 1958, Joanne Woodward; three *d*. *Educ:* Kenyon Coll. (BA); Yale Drama Sch. Mil. Service, USNR, 1943–46. Chairman: Newman's Own; Salad King. Team owner, and formerly driver, IndyCar racing. *Stage appearances include:* Picnic, 1953–54; Sweet Bird of Youth, 1959; Our Town, NY, 2002; *films include:* Somebody Up There Likes Me, 1956; Cat on a Hot Tin Roof, 1958; The Hustler, 1961; Sweet Bird of Youth, 1962; Hud, 1963; Torn Curtain, 1966; Cool Hand Luke, 1967; Butch Cassidy and the Sundance Kid, 1969; The Sting, 1973; Drowning Pool, 1975; Quintet, 1979; Fort Apache, the Bronx (also dir), 1980; Absence of Malice, 1981; The Verdict, 1982; Harry and Son (also wrote and directed), 1984; The Color of Money, 1986 (Academy Award, 1987); Blaze, 1990; Shadow Makers, 1990; Mr and Mrs Bridge, 1991; The Hudsucker Proxy, 1994; Nobody's Fool, 1995; Twilight, 1998; Message in a Bottle, 1999; Where the Money Is, 2000; Road to Perdition, 2002; *films directed include:* Rachel, Rachel, 1968; When Time Ran Out, 1980; The Glass Menagerie, 1987; *TV mini-series:* Empire Falls, 2005. Hon. Academy Award for career achievement, 1986. *Address:* Newman Haas Racing, 500 Tower Parkway, Lincolnshire, IL 60069, USA. *Died 26 Sept. 2008.*

NEWMARCH, Michael George, (Mick); Chief Executive, Prudential Corporation plc, 1990–95; *b* 19 May 1938; *s* of late George Langdon Newmarch and Phyllis Georgina Newmarch; *m* 1959, Audrey Clarke; one *s* two *d*. *Educ:* Univ. of London (BSc (Econs) external). Joined Prudential, 1955, Econ. Intelligence Dept; Exec. Dir, Prudential Corp., 1985–95; Chairman: Prudential Money Funds, 1983–95; Prudential Holborn, 1986–89; Prudential Financial Services, 1987–95 (Chief Exec., 1987–89); Prudential Currency Fund, 1987–95; Prudential Assce Co., 1990–95; Prudential Portfolio Managers, 1990–95 (Chief Exec., 1982–89); Prudential Nominees, 1990–95; Prudential Services, 1990–95; Mercantile and Gen. Gp., 1990–95. Non-executive Chairman: Transacsys, 2000–02; Weston Medical, 2001–03; non-exec. Dir, Celltech Gp (formerly Celltech plc), 1996–2004. Chm., Princess Royal Trust for Carers, 2004–07 (Vice-Chm., 1989); Trustee, Berks Community Foundn, 1998–2002 (Chm. Trustees, 1999–2002). Member: Adv. Bd, Orchestra of the Age of Enlightenment, 1992–2005; Council, Univ. of Reading, 1999–2007. *Recreations:* salmon and trout fishing, flytying, bridge, theatre, concerts. *Club:* Flyfishers'. *Died 2 April 2010.*

NEWSOM-DAVIS, Prof. John Michael, CBE 1996; MD; FRCP; FRS 1991; Professor of Clinical Neurology, University of Oxford, 1987–98, then Emeritus; *b* 18 Oct. 1932; *s* of late John Kenneth and Dorothy Eileen Newsom-Davis; *m* 1963, Rosemary Elisabeth (*née* Schmid); one *s* two *d*. *Educ:* Sherborne Sch.; Pembroke Coll., Cambridge (BA 1957 Nat. Scis); Middlesex Hosp. Med. Sch. (MB BChir 1960, MD 1966); FRCP 1973. RAF, 1951–53 (Pilot). Lectr, Univ. Dept of Clinical Neurology, Nat. Hosp. for Nervous Diseases, 1967–69; Neurological Research Fellow, Cornell Med. Center, New York Hosp., 1969–70; Consultant Neurologist, Royal Free Hosp. and Nat. Hosp. for Nervous Diseases, 1970–80; MRC Clinical Res. Prof. of Neurology, Royal Free Hosp. Med. Sch. and Inst. of Neurology, 1980–87; Hon. Consultant, Nat. Hosp. for Nervous Diseases, 1987–. Department of Health: consultant advr in neurology, 1985–94; Mem., Central R & D Cttee, 1991–95. Mem., MRC, 1983–87 (Mem., Neurosciences Grants Cttee, 1978–80; Mem., 1980–83, 1992–, Chm., 1983–85, Neuroscis Bd); President: Biomedical Section,

BAAS, 1982–83; Assoc. of British Neurologists, 1999–2000 (Hon. Sec., 1981–84); Vice-Pres., Internat. Soc. for Neuroimmunology, 1987–95; Chairman: Med. Adv. Cttee, British Council, 1995–99; Chairs and Prog. Grants Cttee, BHF, 1996–97; Med. Res. Cttee, Muscular Dystrophy Group UK, 1996–99. Mem. Council, Royal Soc., 1996–97. Founder FMedSci 1998. Hon. Mem., Amer. Acad. of Neurology; For. Associate Mem., Inst. of Medicine Nat. Acad. of Scis, USA, 2001. Assoc. of British Neurologists Medal, 1999; Galen Medal, Soc. of Apothecaries, 2004. Editor, Brain, 1997–2004. *Publications:* (with E. J. M. Campbell and E. Agostoni) Respiratory Muscles: mechanics and neural control, 1970; numerous papers in Neurol. and Immunol. jls. *Recreation:* music. *Address:* Department of Clinical Neurology, University of Oxford, West Wing, John Radcliffe Hospital, Oxford OX3 9DU. *Died 24 Aug. 2007.*

NEWSTROM, Prof. David Graham L.; see Lloyd-Newstrom.

NEWTON, Sir (Harry) Michael (Rex), 3rd Bt *cr* 1900; *b* 7 Feb. 1923; 2nd and *e* surv. *s* of Sir Harry K. Newton, 2nd Bt, OBE, DL, and Myrtle Irene (*d* 1977), *e d* of W. W. Grantham, Balneath Manor, Lewes; *S* father, 1951; *m* 1958, Pauline Jane (*d* 2002), *o d* of late R. J. F. Howgill, CBE; one *s*, and three adopted *d*. *Educ:* Eastbourne College. Served War of 1939–45, with KRRC, in 8th Army and Middle East, 1941–46 (wounded). Master, Girdlers' Company, 1975–76; Freeman of City of London. *Recreation:* sailing (winner of 1953 Fastnet Race). *Heir: s* Rev. George Peter Howgill Newton [*b* 26 March 1962; *m* 1988, Jane, twin *d* of John Rymer; two *d*]. *Address:* c/o 2 Cranmore Lane, Aldershot, Hants GU11 3AS. *T:* (01252) 320618. *Club:* Royal Ocean Racing. *Died 29 Feb. 2008.*

NEWTON, Sir Kenneth (Garnar), 3rd Bt *cr* 1924; OBE 1970 (MBE 1944); TD; Chairman, Garnar Booth plc, 1972–87 (Managing Director, 1961–83); *b* 4 June 1918; *s* of Sir Edgar Henry Newton, 2nd Bt, and Gladys Maud (*d* 1966), *d* of late Sir James Garnar; *S* father, 1971; *m* 1944, Margaret Isabel (*d* 1979), *d* of Rev. Dr George Blair, Dundee; two *s*. *Educ:* Wellington College, Berks. Served War of 1939–45 (MBE); Lt-Col, RASC (TA). Chm. Governors, Colfe's Sch., 1982–93. Pres., Internat. Council of Tanners, 1972–78; Past President, British Leather Federation (1968–69); Liveryman and Member of Court of Assistants, Leathersellers' Company (Master, 1977–78) and Feltmakers' Company (Master, 1983–84). *Heir: s* John Garnar Newton [*b* 10 July 1945; *m* 1972, Jacynth A. K. Miller; three *s* (incl. twins)]. *Address:* Oaklands, Harborough Gorse, West Chiltington, West Sussex RH20 2RU. *Died 12 Aug. 2008.*

NEWTON, Sir Michael; see Newton, Sir H. M. R.

NICHOLLS, Air Marshal Sir John (Moreton), KCB 1978; CBE 1970; DFC 1953; AFC 1965; non-executive Director, James Paget Hospital NHS Trust, 1993–95; *b* 5 July 1926; *s* of Alfred Nicholls and Elsie (*née* French); *m* 1st, 1946, Enid Jean Marjorie Rose (*d* 1975); two *d*; 2nd, 1977, Shelagh Joyce Hall (*née* Strong). *Educ:* Liverpool Collegiate; St Edmund Hall, Oxford. RAF Coll., 1945–46; No 28 Sqdn and No 257 Sqdn; 335th Ftr Sqdn USAF, Korea, 1952; Fighter Leader Sch.; 435th and 83rd Ftr Sqdns USAF, 1956–58; attached British Aircraft Co., Lightning Project, 1959–61; psa 1961; Comd, Air Fighting Develt Sqdn; jssc 1964; a Dep. Dir, Air Staff Briefing, MoD, 1965–67; comd RAF Leuchars, 1967–70; idc 1970; SASO 11 Gp, 1971; Principal Staff Officer to CDS, 1971–73; SASO, Strike Comd, 1973–75; ACAS (Op. Requirements), 1976–77; Air Mem. for Supply and Orgn, 1977–79; Vice-Chief of the Air Staff, 1979–80. Dir i/c, British Aircraft Co. (British Aerospace), Saudi Arabia, 1980–82. CCMI. DFC (USA) and Air Medal (USA), 1953. *Club:* Royal Air Force. *Died 17 May 2007.*

NICHOLLS, Philip, CB 1976; *b* 30 Aug. 1914; *yr s* of late W. H. Nicholls, Radlett; *m* 1955, Sue, *yr d* of late W. E. Shipton; two *s*. *Educ:* Malvern; Pembroke Coll.,

Cambridge. Asst Master, Malvern, 1936; Sen. Classical Master, 1939; resigned, 1947. Served in Army, 1940–46: 8th Bn, The Worcestershire Regt; HQ, East Africa Command; Allied Commn for Austria. Foreign Office (German Section), 1947; HM Treasury, 1949; a Forestry Commissioner (Finance and Administration), 1970–75. Mem. Council, Malvern Coll., 1960–90 (Vice-Chm., 1963–88). *Address:* Barnards Green House, Barnards Green, Malvern, Worcs WR14 3NQ. *T:* (01684) 574446. *Died 7 Oct. 2010.*

NICHOLS, William Henry, CB 1974; *b* 25 March 1913; *s* of William and Clara Nichols. *Educ:* Owens School. Entered Inland Revenue, 1930; Exchequer and Audit Dept, 1935, Secretary, 1973–75, retired. *Address:* 23 Church View, Haughley, Stowmarket, Suffolk IP14 3NU. *Died 3 Sept. 2006.*

NICHOLS, William Reginald, CBE 1975; TD; MA; Clerk of the Worshipful Company of Salters, 1946–75, Master, 1978–79; *b* 23 July 1912; *s* of late Reginald H. Nichols, JP, FSA, Barrister-at-Law; *m* 1946, Imogen (*d* 2001), *d* of late Rev. Percy Dearmer, DD, Canon of Westminster, and Nancy (who *m* 1946, Sir John Sykes, KCB; he *d* 1952); one *s* one *d*. *Educ:* Harrow; Gonville and Caius Coll., Cambridge (Sayer Classical Scholar; MA 1938). Called to the Bar, Gray's Inn, 1937. Served War of 1939–45 with Hertfordshire Regt (despatches) and on staff 21st Army Group. Former Jt Hon. Sec., CGLI; Governor of Christ's Hospital; former Governor of Grey Coat Hospital Foundation. *Address:* Ashley Grange, Lode Hill, Downton, Salisbury, Wilts SP5 3PP. *Died 19 March 2006.*

NICHOLSON, Air Cdre Angus Archibald Norman, CBE 1961; AE 1945; Deputy Secretary-General, International Shipping Secretariat, 1971–80; *b* 8 March 1919; *s* of Major Norman Nicholson and Alice Frances Nicholson (*née* Salvidge), Hoylake, Cheshire; *m* 1943, Joan Mary, *d* of Ernest Beaumont, MRCVS, DVSM; one *s* one *d*. *Educ:* Eton; King's Coll., Cambridge. Cambridge Univ. Air Sqn, 1938–39; commissioned RAFVR, 1939; served War 1939–45: flying duties in Bomber Command and Middle East; tranf. RAF, 1945; Air Cdre, 1966; Dir of Defence Plans (Air), Min. of Defence, 1966–67; Defence Adviser to British High Comr in Canada and Head of British Defence Liaison Staff, 1968–70; retired from RAF, 1970. FCMI (MBIM 1967, FBIM 1980). *Recreations:* sailing, music. *Clubs:* Leander (Henley); Royal Lymington Yacht. *Died 1 June 2007.*

NICHOLSON, (Charles) Gordon (Brown), CBE 2002; QC (Scot.) 1982; Temporary Judge of the High Court and Court of Session, since 2002; Sheriff Principal of Lothian and Borders and Sheriff of Chancery, 1990–2002; *b* 11 Sept. 1935; *s* of late William Addison Nicholson, former Director, Scottish Tourist Board, and Jean Brown; *m* 1963, Hazel Mary Nixon; two *s*. *Educ:* George Watson's Coll., Edinburgh; Edinburgh Univ. (Hon. Fellow, Faculty of Law, 1988). MA Hons (English Lit.) 1956, LLB 1958. 2nd Lieut Queen's Own Cameron Highlanders, 1958–60. Admitted Faculty of Advocates, Edinburgh, 1961; in practice at Bar; Standing Junior Counsel, Registrar of Restrictive Trading Agreements, 1968; Advocate-Depute, 1968–70; Sheriff of: South Strathclyde, Dumfries and Galloway, 1970–76; Lothian and Borders, 1976–82; Mem., Scottish Law Commn, 1982–90. Vice-Pres., Sheriffs' Assoc., 1979–82 (Sec., 1975–79); Convener, Sheriffs Principal, 1991–2002. Member: Scottish Council on Crime, 1972–75; Dunpark Cttee on Reparation by Offenders, 1974–77; May Cttee of Inquiry into UK Prison Service, 1978–79; Kincraig Review of Parole in Scotland, 1988–89; Judicial Studies Cttee, 1997–2002; Criminal Justice Forum, 2000–02; Chm., Cttee on Licensing Law in Scotland, 2001–03. Hon. President: Victim Support Scotland (formerly Scottish Assoc. of Victim Support Schemes), 1989–2005 (Chm., 1987–89); Scottish Assoc. for Study of Delinquency, 1988–2002 (Chm., 1974–79; Hon. Vice-Pres., 1982–88); Jt Patron, Children Law UK (formerly British Juvenile and Family Courts Soc.), 1995–2003.

Chm., Edinburgh CAB, 1979–82. Comr, Northern Lighthouse Bd, 1990–2002 (Vice Chm., 1993–94; Chm., 1994–95). *Publications:* The Law and Practice of Sentencing in Scotland, 1981, 2nd edn 1992; (ed jtly) Sheriff Court Practice by I. Macphail, 2nd edn 1999; contrib. to legal periodicals. *Recreation:* music. *Address:* Back o'Redfern, 24C Colinton Road, Edinburgh EH10 5EQ. *T:* (0131) 447 4300. *Club:* New (Edinburgh). *Died 26 Aug. 2009.*

NICHOLSON, David; former racehorse trainer, National Hunt; *b* 19 March 1939; *s* of Herbert Charles Denton, (Frenchie), Nicholson and Diana Nicholson; *m* 1962, Dinah Caroline Pugh; two *s*. *Educ:* Oakley Hall Prep. Sch.; Haileybury Coll. Professional National Hunt jockey, 1951–74 (won Whitbread Gold Cup, 1967, with Mill House); racehorse trainer, 1968–99 (won Gold Cup, 1988, with Charter Party); Champion National Hunt Trainer, seasons 1993–94, 1994–95. *Recreation:* watching sport. *Address:* Halloween Cottage, Nether Westcote, Chipping Norton, Oxon OX7 6SD. *T:* (01993) 830297, *Fax:* (01993) 831573. *Clubs:* MCC; Gloucester County Cricket. *Died 27 Aug. 2006.*

NICHOLSON, Gordon; *see* Nicholson, C. G. B.

NICHOLSON, Michael Constantine; a Recorder of the Crown Court, 1980–95; *b* 3 Feb. 1932; *m* 1960, (Kathleen) Mary Strong; two *d*. *Educ:* Wycliffe Coll., Stonehouse; University Coll. of Wales, Aberystwyth (LLB). Called to the Bar, Gray's Inn, 1957; Crown Counsel, Nyasaland, 1960–63; Wales and Chester circuit, 1963–94. *Recreations:* opera, cinema, theatre. *Address:* c/o 33 Park Place, Cardiff CF10 3TN. *Died 2 Feb. 2006.*

NICOLLE, Anthony William, OBE 1991; formerly consultant on banking supervision; *b* 13 April 1935; *s* of late Roland Nicolle and Dorothy May Pearce; *m* 1960, Josephine Anne (*née* Read); one *s* one *d*. *Educ:* Tiffin Sch.; King's Coll., London (LLB). Served RA, 1956–58. Joined Bank of England, 1958; seconded to NEDO, 1968–70; Econ. Intelligence Dept, 1970–77; seconded to Royal Commn on Distribn of Income and Wealth, 1974–75; banking supervision, 1977–80; Banking Dept, 1980–83; banking supervision, 1983–87; Comr of Banking, Hong Kong, 1987–91; Gen. Man. for Hong Kong and China, Standard Chartered Bank, 1991–94. Trustee, Psychiatry Res. Trust, 2000–06. *Recreations:* walking (a little), gardening (occasionally). *Address:* Upper Folds, Little Bognor, Fittleworth, Pulborough, W Sussex RH20 1JT. *Club:* Oriental. *Died 8 June 2008.*

NICOLLE, Dr Hilary Ann; Schools Adjudicator for England, Department for Education and Skills (formerly Department for Education and Employment), since 1999; *b* 12 April 1945; *d* of A. H. and E. V. Upton; *m* 1st, 1970, Noël Leo Nicolle (marr. diss. 1978); two *s*; 2nd, 1985, Paul Newman Hudson Clokie; one step *s* one step *d*. *Educ:* Bromley High Sch.; St Hilda's Coll., Oxford (BA 1st Class Hons; MA); London Sch. of Economics (PhD); PGCE London Univ. 1977. HM Diplomatic Service, 1967–70; PhD research and univ. lecturing, 1970–76; school teacher, 1977–82; Headmistress, Tiffin Girls' Sch., Kingston upon Thames, 1982–88; Dep. Dir of Educn, London Borough of Wandsworth, 1988–92; Chief Exec., Sch. Examinations and Assessment Council, 1992–93; Dir of Educn, London Bor. of Islington, 1993–98. JP Kent, 1999–2004. Trustee, Rochester Cathedral, 2001–. *Recreations:* history, choral music, National Trust, gardening. *Address:* Gibbet Oak, Appledore Road, Tenterden, Kent TN30 7DH. *Died 2 May 2006.*

NIELSEN, Hon. Erik H., DFC; PC (Can.) 1984; QC (Can.) 1962; Principal, Solar Electric Engineering Distributors, Canada, since 1992; President: Solar Electric Engineering Hawaii Inc., since 1993; Electricycle Inc., since 1994; *b* 24 Feb. 1924; *m* 1st, 1945, Pamela Hall (*d* 1969); two *s* one *d*; 2nd, 1983, Shelley Coxford. *Educ:* Dalhousie Univ. (LLB). Royal Canadian Air Force, 1942–51; flew Lancaster bombers, War of 1939–45.

Called to the Bar of Nova Scotia, 1951; legal practice in Whitehorse, Yukon, 1952–. MP (PC) Yukon, 1957–87; Minister of Public Works, 1979–80; Dep. Opposition House Leader, Opposition House Leader, Leader of the Opposition, and Dep. Leader of the Opposition, 1980–84; Dep. Leader, Progressive Cons. Party, 1983; Dep. Prime Minister and Pres. of the Queen's Privy Council for Canada, 1984–85; Minister of Nat. Defence, 1985–86. Pres., Canadian Transport Commn, 1987; Chm., Nat. Transportation Agency of Canada, 1987–92. Dep. House Leader, 1980–81; Opposition appts, 1981–83. Caucus Chm., Cttee on Govt Planning and Orgn, 1983–84. Chm., Ministerial Task Force on Program Review (report published, 1985). Member: Canadian Bar Assoc.; Yukon Law Soc.; NS Barristers' Soc.; Hon. Mem., Whitehorse Chamber of Commerce; Hon. Life Mem., Yukon Chamber of Mines, 1987. Hon. Fellow, Canadian Sch. of Mgt, 1984. Hon. Life Mem., Royal Canadian Mounted Police Veterans' Assoc., 1990. *Publications:* The House is Not a Home, 1989. *Address:* MSPO PO Box 31024, Whitehorse, YT Y1A 5P7, Canada. *Died 4 Sept. 2008.*

NIND, Philip Frederick, OBE 1979; TD 1946; Director, Foundation for Management Education, 1968–83; Secretary, Council of Industry for Management Education, 1969–83; *b* 2 Jan. 1918; *s* of W. W. Nind, CIE; *m* 1944, Fay Allardice Crofton (*née* Errington) (*d* 1991); two *d*. *Educ:* Blundell's Sch.; Balliol Coll., Oxford (MA). War service, 1939–46, incl. Special Ops in Greece and Albania (despatches), 1943–44, Mil. Govt Berlin, 1945–46 (Major). Shell Gp of Cos in Venezuela, Cyprus, Lebanon, Jordan and London, 1939–68. Educn and Trng Cttee, CBI (formerly FBI), 1961–68; OECD Working Gp on Management Educn, 1966–69; Nat. Adv. Council on Educn for Industry and Commerce, 1967–70; UGC Management Studies Cttee, 1968–83; NEDO Management Educn Trng and Develt Cttee, 1968–83; Chm., NEDO Management Teacher Panel, 1969–72; Member: Council for Techn. Educn and Trng for Overseas Countries, 1970–75; CNAA Management Studies Bd, 1971–83; Vice-Pres., European Foundn for Management Develt, 1978–83. Member: Oxford Univ. Appts Cttee, 1967–83; Grand Council, Royal Academy of Dancing, 1988– (Mem. Exec. Cttee, 1970–88); Governor: Univ. of Keele, 1961–; Bedford Coll., London Univ., 1967–85. Hon. Fellow, London Business School, 1988. FRSA. Chevalier, Order of Cedars of Lebanon, 1959; Grand Cross, Orders of St Mark and Holy Sepulchre, 1959. *Publications:* (jtly) Management Education and Training Needs of Industry, 1963; Fourth Stockton Lecture, 1973; A Firm Foundation, 1985; Never a Dull Moment, 1991; articles in various jls. *Club:* Special Forces. *Died 27 May 2008.*

NIRENBERG, Dr Marshall Warren; Research Biochemist; Chief, Laboratory of Biochemical Genetics, National Heart, Lung and Blood Institute, National Institutes of Health, Bethesda, Md, since 1966; *b* New York, 10 April 1927; *m* 1st, 1961, Perola Zaltzman (*d* 2001); 2nd, 2006, Myrna Weissman. *Educ:* Univs of Florida (BS, MS) and Michigan (PhD). Univ. of Florida: Teaching Asst, Zoology Dept, 1945–50; Res. Associate, Nutrition Lab., 1950–52; Univ. of Michigan: Teaching and Res. Fellow, Biol Chemistry Dept, 1952–57; Nat. Insts of Health, Bethesda: Postdoctoral Fellow of Amer. Cancer Soc., Nat. Inst. Arthritis and Metabolic Diseases, 1957–59, and of Public Health Service, Section of Metabolic Enzymes, 1959–60; Research Biochemist, Section of Metabolic Enzymes, 1960–62 and Section of Biochem. Genetics, 1962–66. Member: Amer. Soc. Biol Chemists; Amer. Chem. Soc.; Amer. Acad. Arts and Sciences; Biophys. Soc.; Nat. Acad. Sciences; Washington Acad. Sciences; Sigma Xi; Soc. for Study of Development and Growth; (Hon.) Harvey Soc.; Leopoldina Deutsche Akademie der Naturforscher; Neurosciences Research Program, MIT; NY Acad. Sciences; Pontifical Acad. Science, 1974. Robbins Lectr, Pomona Coll., 1967; Remsden Mem. Lectr, Johns Hopkins Univ., 1967. Numerous awards and prizes, including Nobel Prize in

Medicine or Physiology (jtly), 1968. Hon. Dr Science: Michigan, Yale, and Chicago, 1965; Windsor, 1966; Harvard Med. Sch., 1968; Hon. PhD, Weitzmann Inst. of Science, Israel, 1978. *Publications:* numerous contribs to learned jls and chapters in symposia. *Address:* NIH Laboratory of Biochemical Genetics, 10 Center Drive, Building 10, Bethesda, MD 20892–1654, USA. *Died 15 Jan. 2010.*

NIVEN, John Robertson, (Ian); Under-Secretary, Department of the Environment, formerly Ministry of Housing and Local Government, 1974–79; *b* 11 May 1919; *s* of Robert Niven and Amelia Mary Hill; *m* 1946, Jane Bicknell; three *s*. *Educ:* Glasgow Academy; Jesus Coll., Oxford. Entered Min. of Town and Country Planning, 1946; Sec., Royal Commn on Local Govt in Greater London, 1957–60. *Address:* White Gates, Parham, Woodbridge, Suffolk IP13 9AA. *Died 18 May 2007.*

NIXON, Sir Edwin (Ronald), Kt 1984; CBE 1974; DL; Deputy Chairman, National Westminster Bank PLC, 1987–96 (Director, 1975–96); Chairman: Amersham International plc, 1988–96 (Director, 1987–96); Natwest Pension Trustees Ltd, 1992–98; Leicester BioSciences Ltd, 1997–2000; *b* 21 June 1925; *s* of William Archdale Nixon and Ethel (*née* Corrigan); *m* 1st, 1952, Joan Lilian (*née* Hill) (*d* 1995); one *s* one *d*; 2nd, 1997, Bridget Diana, *er d* of late Reginald and of Lenna Rogers. *Educ:* Alderman Newton's Sch., Leicester; Selwyn Coll., Cambridge (MA; Hon. Fellow 1983). Man. Accountant, Dexion Ltd, 1950–55; IBM United Kingdom Ltd, 1955–90; Chm., IBM UK Hldgs Ltd, 1986–90 (Man. Dir, 1965–78; Chm. and Chief Exec., 1979–86); Director: Royal Insurance PLC, 1980–88; International Westminster Bank PLC, 1987–96; UK-Japan 2000 Gp Ltd, 1987–96; Partnership Sourcing, 1990–96; Natwest Bancorp Inc., 1991–96; Natwest Bank USA, 1992–96; Alternate Dir, BCH Property Ltd, 1988–96. Member Council: Foundn for Automation and Employment, 1967–77; Electronic Engineering Assoc., 1965–76; CBI, 1971–96 (Chm. Standing Cttee on Marketing and Consumer Affairs, 1971–78; Mem., Cttee on Industrial Policy, 1978–85; President's Cttee, 1986–88); Foundn for Management Educn, 1973–84. Member: British Cttee of Awards for Harkness Fellowships, 1976–82; Adv. Council, Business Graduates Assoc., 1976–87; Board of Governors, United World Coll. of Atlantic, 1977–; Bd of Trustees, Internat. Inst. for Management Develt, 1990–96; Chm. Council, Leicester Univ., 1992–98; Member Council: Manchester Business Sch., 1974–86 (Chm., 1979–86); Business in the Community, 1981–88 (Companion, 1992); Westfield Coll., London, 1969–82 (Vice Chm., 1980–82; Hon. Fellow 1983); William Temple Coll., Manchester, 1972–80; Oxford Centre for Management Studies, 1973–83; Open Univ., 1986–92. Member: The Civil Service Coll., 1979–91; Adv. Council, New Oxford English Dictionary, 1985–89; Council for Industry and Higher Educn, 1986–97. Trustee, Inst. of Econ. Affairs, 1986–92 (Hon. Trustee, 1992). Trustee, Boxgrove Priory Trust, 2003–; Dir, Boxgrove Priory Enterprises Ltd, 2003–. Member: Chichester Cathedral Develt Trust, 1986–96; The Prince's Youth Business Trust, 1987–2001; Lloyd's of London Tercentenary Foundn, 1987–2005. Pres., Nat. Assoc. for Gifted Children, 1980–91 (Hon. Mem., 1991); Vice-Pres., Opportunities for People with Disabilities (formerly Opportunities for the Disabled), 1980–2003; Chm., Jt Bd for Pre-Vocational Educn, 1983–87; Mem., Study Commn on the Family, 1979–83. Chm. of Bd of Trustees and a Dir, Royal Opera House, Covent Garden, 1984–87 (Trustee, 1980–87); Chm., Bd of Trustees, Monteverdi Choir and Orch., 1988–2001 (Trustee, 1980–); Vice-Pres., London Internat. String Quartet Competition. Patron, Assoc. Internationale des Etudiantes en Sciences Economiques et Commerciales, 1980–2002. DL Hampshire, 1987. Hon. Fellow: Inst. of Marketing, 1982 (Hon. Vice-Pres., 1980–96); Portsmouth Polytechnic, subseq. Portsmouth Univ., 1986; Leeds Polytechnic, subseq. Leeds Metropolitan

Univ., 1991. Hon. DSc Aston, 1985; DUniv Stirling, 1985; Hon. DTech Brunel, 1986; Hon. LLD: Manchester, 1987; Leicester, 1990; Hon. DTech CNAA, 1991. *Recreations:* music, golf, reading. *Address:* Starkes Heath, Rogate, Petersfield, Hants GU31 5EJ. *T:* (01730) 821504. *Club:* Athenæum. *Died 17 Aug. 2008.*

NOAKES, Rt Rev. George; Archbishop of Wales, 1987–91; Bishop of St Davids, 1982–91; *b* 13 Sept. 1924; *s* of David John and Elizabeth Mary Noakes; *m* 1957, Jane Margaretta Davies. *Educ:* Tregaron Secondary School; University Coll. of Wales, Aberystwyth (BA); Wycliffe Hall, Oxford. Curate of Lampeter, 1950–56; Vicar: Eglwyswrw, 1956–59; Tregaron, 1959–67; Dewi Sant, Cardiff, 1967–76; Rector of Aberystwyth, 1976–79; Canon of St Davids Cathedral, 1977–79; Archdeacon of Cardigan, 1979–82; Vicar of Llanychaearn, 1980–82. Hon. DD Wales, 1989. *Recreations:* cricket, angling. *Address:* 1 Ger-y-Llan, The Parade, Carmarthen, Dyfed SA31 1LY. *T:* (01267) 253302. *Died 14 July 2008.*

NOBLE, Sir Iain (Andrew), 3rd Bt *cr* 1923, of Ardkinglas and Eilean Iarmain; OBE 1988; businessman and entrepreneur, historian and writer; Proprietor, Fearann Eilean Iarmain estate, Isle of Skye, since 1972, and Hotel Eilean Iarmain; Chairman, Pràban na Linne Ltd (The Gaelic Whiskies), since 1976; Chairman and Chief Executive, Sir Iain Noble & Partners Ltd, since 2000; *b* 8 Sept. 1935; *s* of Sir Andrew Napier Noble, 2nd Bt, KCMG and Sigrid, 2nd *d* of Johan Michelet, Norwegian Diplomatic Service; *S* father, 1987; *m* 1990, Lucilla Charlotte James, *d* of late Col H. A. C. Mackenzie, OBE, MC, TD, DL, JP, Dalmore. *Educ:* China; Argentina; Eton; University Coll., Oxford (MA 1959). Matthews Wrightson, London, 1959–64; Scottish Council (Devel and Industry), Edinburgh, 1964–69; Jt Founder and Jt Man. Dir, Noble Grossart Ltd, merchant bankers, Edinburgh, 1969–72; Jt Founder and Chm., Seaforth Maritime Ltd, Aberdeen, 1972–78; Founder and Chairman: Lennox Oil Co. plc, Edinburgh, 1980–85; Noble Gp Ltd, merchant bankers, 1980–2000; non-exec. Chm., Skye Bridge Ltd, 1994–96; Founder and Dir, Adam and Co. plc, Edinburgh, 1983–93; Dir, Premium Investment Trust, 1993–2002. Dep. Chm., Traverse Theatre, Edinburgh, 1966–68; Mem., Edinburgh Univ. Court, 1970–73; Founder, first Chm., 1973–74, and Trustee, 1974–84, College of Sabhal Mor Ostaig, Isle of Skye; Trustee, Nat. Museums of Scotland, 1987–91 (Trustee, Charitable Trust, 1991–). Founder, and first Chm., Scots Australian Council, 1991–99; Pres., Saltire Soc., 1992–96. Keeper of the Quaich, 2000–. Visits to Faroe Isles, 1969–75. Hotel Eilean Iarmain awarded Hotel of the Year, Relais Routier, 2001. Scotsman of the Year Award, 1981. *Publications:* (ed) Sources of Finance, 1968. *Recreations:* Comhradh, beul-aithris is ceol le deagh chompanaich. *Heir: b* Timothy Peter Noble [*b* 21 Dec. 1943; *m* 1976, Elizabeth Mary, *d* of late Alexander Wallace Aitken; two *s* one *d*]. *Address:* An Lamraig, Eilean Iarmain, An t-Eilean Sgitheanach IV43 8QR; 20 Great Stuart Street, Edinburgh EH3 7TN. *T:* (offices) (01471) 833266 and (0131) 220 2400. *Club:* New (Edinburgh). *Died 25 Dec. 2010.*

NOEL-BAKER, Hon. Francis Edward; Director, North Euboean Enterprises Ltd, since 1973; *b* 7 Jan. 1920; *o s* of Baron Noel-Baker, PC, and late Irene, *o d* of Frank Noel, British landowner, of Achmetaga, Greece; *m* 1st, 1947, Ann Lavinia Saunders (marr. diss. 1955); one *s* (and one *s* decd); 2nd, 1957, Barbara Christina (*d* 2004), *yr d* of late Joseph Sonander, Sweden; three *s* one *d*. *Educ:* Westminster Sch.; King's Coll., Cambridge (Exhibitioner; 1st cl. hons History). Founder and Chm., CU Lab. Club, 1939; left Cambridge to join Army, summer 1940, as Trooper, Royal Tank Regt; Commissioned in Intelligence Corps and served in UK, Force 133, Middle East (despatches). Editor, United Nations World/World Horizon, 1945–47, Go! magazine, 1947–48; BBC European Service, 1950–54. MP (Lab) Brentford and Chiswick Div. of Middx, 1945–50; PPS Admiralty, 1949–50; MP (Lab) Swindon, 1955–68; sent

by Prime Minister to mediate in Cyprus, 1956; Sec., 1955–64, Chm., 1964–68, UN Parly Cttee; resigned from Lab. Party, 1969; Vice-Chm., Lab. Cttee for Europe, 1976–78; Member: SDP 1981–83; NUJ, 1946–81. Chm., Advertising Inquiry Council, 1951–68. Chairman: North Euboean Foundation Ltd, 1965–; Candili Craft Centre, Philip Noel-Baker Centre, Euboea, 1983–; Dir, Fini Fisheries, Cyprus, 1976–90; Founder Pres., European Council for Villages and Small Towns, 1984–; Hon. Pres., Union of Forest Owners of Greece, 1968–. Member: Parochial Church Council, St Martin in the Fields, 1960–68; Freedom from Hunger Campaign UK Cttee Exec. Cttee, 1961; Ecology Party, 1978–; Soil Assoc., 1979–. Governor, Campion Sch., Athens, 1973–78. Archives Fellow Commoner, Churchill Coll., Cambridge, 1989. Wine Constable, Guyenne, 1988–. *Publications:* Greece, the Whole Story, 1946; Spanish Summary, 1948; The Spy Web, 1954; Land and People of Greece, 1957; Nansen, 1958; Looking at Greece, 1967; My Cyprus File, 1985; Book Eight: a taste of hardship, 1987; Three Saints and Poseidon, 1988. *Recreation:* gardening. *Address:* Achmetaga Estate, 340–04 Procopi, Greece. *T:* (22270) 41204, *Fax:* (22270) 41190. *Club:* Special Forces. *Died 25 Sept. 2009.*

NOKES, Prof. David Leonard, PhD; FRSL; Professor of English, King's College, London, since 1998; *b* 11 March 1948; *s* of Anthony John Nokes and Ethel Murray Nokes; *m* 1997, Margaret Andrée Marie Denley (*née* Riffard); one *d*. *Educ:* King's Coll., Wimbledon; Christ's Coll., Cambridge (BA 1st Cl. 1969; MA 1972; PhD 1974). Lectr, 1973–86, Reader, 1986–98, King's Coll., London. FRSL 1994. Mem., Johnson Club. *Adaptations for television:* Clarissa, 1991; The Count of Solar, 1992; The Tenant of Wildfell Hall, 1996; *radio play:* The Man on the Heath, 2005. *Publications include:* Jonathan Swift: a hypocrite reversed (James Tait Black Meml Prize), 1985; Raillery and Rage, 1987; John Gay, 1995; Jane Austen, 1997; The Nightingale Papers (novel), 2005; Samuel Johnson: a life, 2009. *Recreations:* reading, writing, painting. *Address:* 3 Hobson's Acre, Great Shelford, Cambridge CB2 5XB; *e-mail:* DavidLNokes@aol.com. *Died 19 Nov. 2009.*

NOLAN, Baron *cr* 1994 (Life Peer), of Brasted in the County of Kent; **Michael Patrick Nolan,** Kt 1982; PC 1991; DL; a Lord of Appeal in Ordinary, 1994–98; *b* 10 Sept. 1928; *yr s* of James Thomas Nolan and Jane (*née* Walsh); *m* 1953, Margaret, *yr d* of Alfred Noyes, CBE, and Mary (*née* Mayne); one *s* four *d*. *Educ:* Ampleforth; Wadham Coll., Oxford (Hon. Fellow, 1992). Served RA, 1947–49; TA, 1949–55. Called to Bar, Middle Temple, 1953 (Bencher, 1975); QC 1968; called to Bar, NI, 1974; QC (NI) 1974; a Recorder of the Crown Court. 1975–82; Judge, High Court of Justice, QBD, 1982–91; Presiding Judge, Western Circuit, 1985–88; a Lord Justice of Appeal, 1991–93. Member: Bar Council, 1973–74; Senate of Inns of Court and Bar, 1974–81 (Treasurer, 1977–79). Mem., Sandilands Cttee on Inflation Accounting, 1973–75; Chairman: Cttee on Standards in Public Life, 1994–97; Review on Child Protection in the Catholic Church in England and Wales, 2000–01. Chm. Bd, Inst. of Advanced Legal Studies, 1994–2000. DL Kent, 2001. Mem. Governing Body, Convent of the Sacred Heart, Woldingham, 1973–83; Governor, Combe Bank Sch., 1974–83. Chancellor, Essex Univ., 1997–2002. DU: Essex, 1996; Middlesex, 1999; DUniv Surrey, 1996; Hon. LLD: Warwick, 1998; Exeter, 1998; Bournemouth, 2000. KSG 2002. *Recreation:* fishing. *Address:* House of Lords, SW1A 0PW. *Clubs:* Army and Navy, MCC. *Died 22 Jan. 2007.*

NORCROSS, Lawrence John Charles, OBE 1986; Headmaster, Highbury Grove School, 1975–87; *b* 14 April 1927; *s* of Frederick Marshall Norcross and Florence Kate (*née* Hedges); *m* 1958, Margaret Wallace (*d* 2009); three *s* one *d*. *Educ:* Ruskin Coll., Oxford; Univ. of Leeds (BA Hons English). Training Ship, Arethusa, 1941–42; RN, 1942–49 (E Indies Fleet, 1944–45); clerical asst, 1949–52; Asst Teacher: Singlegate Sch., 1957–61; Abbey

Wood Sch., 1961–63; Housemaster, Battersea County Sch., 1963–74; Dep. Headmaster, Highbury Grove Sch., 1974–75. Member: NAS/UWT, 1970–86; Secondary Heads' Assoc., 1975–87; HMC, 1985–87; Trustee and Mem. Exec. Cttee, Nat. Council for Educnl Standards, 1976–89; Trustee: Educnl Res. Trust, 1986–; Ind. Primary and Secondary Educn Trust, 1987–93; Grant Maintained Schools Trust, 1988–94; Nat. Cttee for Educnl Standards, 1997–; Director: Choice in Educn, 1989–94; Grant-Maintained Schs Foundn, 1994–97; Member: Educn Study Gp, Centre for Policy Studies, 1980–; Univ. Entrance and Schs Examinations Council, Univ. of London, 1980–84; Steering Cttee, Campaign for a Gen. Teaching Council. Mem., Adv Council, Educn Unit, IEA, 1986–90. Founder and Hon. Sec., John Ireland Soc., 1960–; former Chm., Contemp. Concerts Co-ordination. *Publications:* (with F. Naylor) The ILEA: a case for reform, 1981; (with F. Naylor and J. McIntosh) The ILEA after the Abolition of the GLC, 1983; (contrib.) The Wayward Curriculum, 1986; GCSE: the Egalitarian Fallacy, 1990; occasional articles. *Recreations:* talking to friends, playing bridge badly, watching cricket, listening to music. *Address:* Amberley, Cotswold Close, Tredington, Shipston-on-Stour, Warwicks CV36 4NR. *T:* (01608) 661628. *Club:* Surrey County Cricket.
Died 31 Jan. 2010

NORFOLK, Leslie William, CBE 1973 (OBE 1944); TD 1946; CEng; Chief Executive, Royal Dockyards, Ministry of Defence, 1969–72; *b* 8 April 1911; *e s* of late Robert and Edith Norfolk, Nottingham; *m* 1944, A. I. E. W. (Nancy) Watson (then WRNS), *d* of late Sir Hugh Watson, IFS (retd); two *s* one *d*. *Educ:* Southwell Minster Grammar Sch., Nottm; University Coll., Nottingham (BSc). MICE; MIMechE; MIEE. Assistant and later Partner, E. G. Phillips, Son & Norfolk, consulting engineers, Nottingham, 1932–39. 2nd Lieut 1931, 5 Foresters TA, transferred and served with RE. France, Gibraltar, Home Forces, 1939–45, Lt-Col. Engineer, Dyestuffs Div., ICI Ltd, 1945–53; Resident Engineer, ICI of Canada, Kingston, Ont., 1953–55; Asst Chief Engr, Metals Div., ICI Ltd, 1955–57; Engineering Manager, Severnside Works, ICI Ltd, 1957–59; Engineering Director, Industrias Quimicas Argentinas Duperial SAIC, Buenos Aires, 1959–65; Director, Heavy Organic Chemicals Div., ICI Ltd, 1965–68; retired from ICI, 1968. *Recreations:* home workshop, industrial archaeology. *Club:* Bath & County (Bath).
Died 25 Aug. 2006.

NORMAN, Andrew John; international sports marketing consultant, since 1994; *b* 21 Sept. 1943; *m* 1997, Fatima Whitbread, MBE; one *s*. Metropolitan Police Officer, 1962–84; Promotions Dir, British athletics, BAAB, 1984–91, British Athletics Fedn, 1991–94; agent for many top British athletes, 1994–. Principal Dir, European Athletics Championships, Budapest, 1998; Consultant, S African Athletics Fedn, 1994–2003; Meeting Dir, Budapest IAAF, 1994–; Special Projs Consultant, Eur. Athletics Assoc., 1999–2004; Competition Develt Consultant, IAAF, 2000–06. Member: Grand Prix Commn, and Mkting Commn, IAAF, 1984–99; Mkting Commn, European Athletics Assoc., 1992–99. *Recreations:* sport, theatre. *Address:* Javel Inn, Mill Hill, Shenfield, Essex CM15 8EU. *T:* (01277) 213957.
Died 24 Sept. 2007.

NORMAN, Geoffrey, OBE 1995; Deputy Secretary of Commissions (Training), Lord Chancellor's Department, 1990–95; *b* 25 March 1935; *s* of late William Frederick Trafalgar Norman and Vera May Norman (*née* Goodfellow); *m* 1st, 1958, Dorothy Frances King (*d* 1978); two *s* two *d*; 2nd, 2006, Miriam Debora Ivy Hanbury. *Educ:* Harrow County Sch.; Brasenose Coll., Oxford (MA). Admitted Solicitor, 1959. Deputy Clerk to the Justices, Uxbridge, 1961–66; Clerk to the Justices, N Hertfordshire and Stevenage, 1966–77; Sec., Magistrates' Assoc., 1977–86; Asst Sec. of Commns (Trng), Lord Chancellor's Dept, 1986–90. Member: Duty Solicitor Scheme-making Cttee, 1984–86; Magisterial Cttee,

Judicial Studies Bd, 1986–95; Magistrates' Courts Rules Cttee, 1989–93. JP Inner London, 1982–90. Freeman. City of London, 1981; Liveryman, Curriers' Co., 1983. *Publications:* The Magistrate as Chairman (with Lady Ralphs), 1987; Benchmarks, 1997. *Address:* Easter Cottage, Gosmore, Hitchin, Herts SG4 7QH. *T:* (01462) 450783.
Died 10 Feb. 2008.

NORMAN, Sir Robert (Henry), Kt 1989; OBE 1957; Chairman, Cairns Campus Co-ordinating Committee, James Cook University of North Queensland, since 1987; *b* 30 Jan. 1914; *s* of Robert Moreton Norman and Dora Muriel Hoole; *m* 1942, Betty Merle Kimmins; one *s* three *d*. *Educ:* Christian Brothers' Coll. Joined RAAF, 1941; Dep. Flt Lieut, 1942; 459 Sqdn, 1943; discharged, 1945. Founded Bush Pilot Airways, 1952, retd 1984. Cairns Centenary Co-ordinator, 1976. Past Pres., Rotary Club of Cairns, Marlin Coast; Dist Gov., Dist 9550, Rotary Internat., 1991–92. Hon. DLitt James Cook Univ. of N Qld, 1994. *Publications:* Bush Pilot, 1976. *Recreations:* motoring, reading. *Address:* c/o 21 East Park Ridge Drive, Brinsmead, Qld 4870, Australia.
Died 3 April 2007.

NORRIS, Rt Rev. Mgr David Joseph; Protonotary Apostolic to the Pope; Vicar General of Westminster Diocese, 1972–99; General Secretary to RC Bishops' Conference of England and Wales, 1967–83; *b* 17 Aug. 1922; *s* of David William and Anne Norris. *Educ:* Salesian Coll., Battersea; St Edmund's Coll., Ware; Christ's Coll., Cambridge (MA). Priest, 1947; teaching at St Edmund's Coll., Ware, 1948–53; Cambridge, 1953–56; Private Secretary to Cardinal Godfrey, 1956–64; National Chaplain to Catholic Overseas Students, 1964–65; Private Secretary to Cardinal Heenan, 1965–72. *Recreations:* reading, music, sport. *Address:* Cathedral Clergy House, 42 Francis Street, SW1P 1QW. *T:* (020) 7798 9055.
Died 9 June 2010.

NORRIS, Col Graham Alexander, OBE (mil.) 1945; JP; Vice Lord-Lieutenant of County of Greater Manchester, 1975–87; *b* 14 April 1913; *er s* of late John O. H. Norris and Beatrice H. Norris (*née* Vlies), Manchester; *m* 1st, 1938, Frances Cicely, *d* of late Walter Gorton, Minchinhampton, Glos; one *d*; 2nd, 1955, Muriel, *d* of late John Corris, Manchester. *Educ:* William Hulme's Grammar Sch.; Coll. of Technology, Manchester; Regent St Polytechnic, London; Merchant Venturers Techn. Coll., Bristol. CEng, FIMechE. Trng as automobile engr, Rolls Royce Ltd, Bristol Motor Co. Ltd; Joseph Cockshoot & Co. Ltd: Works Man., 1937, Works Dir 1946, Jt Man. Dir 1964, Chm. and Man. Dir, 1968; Dir, Lex Garages Ltd, 1968–70; Dir, Red Garages (N Wales) Ltd, 1973–88. War service, RAOC and REME, UK, ME and Italy, 1940–46 (Lt-Col); Comdr REME 22 (W) Corps Tps (TA), 1947–51; Hon. Col. 1957–61. Mem., NEDC for Motor Vehicle Distribn and Repair, 1966–74; Pres., Motor Agents Assoc., 1967–68; Vice-Pres., Inst. of Motor Industry, 1973–76; Mem., Industrial Tribunal Panel, 1976–82. Pres., Manchester and Dist Fedn of Boys' Clubs, 1968–74; Vice-Pres., NABC, 1972–98; Chm. Council, UMIST, 1971–83; Member Court: Univ. of Manchester; UMIST. Master, Worshipful Co. of Coachmakers and Coach Harness Makers, 1961–62; Freeman, City of London, 1938. JP, Lancashire 1963; DL Co. Palatine of Lancaster, 1962. *Recreations:* walking, social service activities. *Address:* c/o Croft of Greenbog, Glenkindle, Alford, Aberdeenshire AB33 8SE.
Died 18 July 2010.

NORTH, Prof. John David, FBA 1992; Senior Research Associate, Museum of the History of Science, University of Oxford, since 2003; Professor of History of Philosophy and the Exact Sciences, University of Groningen, Netherlands, 1977–99, then Emeritus; *b* 19 May 1934; *s* of late J. E. and G. A. North, Cheltenham; *m* 1957, Marion Pizzey; one *s* two *d*. *Educ:* Grammar Sch., Batley; Merton Coll., Oxford (BA 1956, MA 1960, DPhil 1964, DLitt 1993); London Univ. (BSc 1958). University of Oxford: Nuffield Foundn Res. Fellow, 1963–68; Asst Curator, Mus. of Hist. of Sci., 1968–77; University of

Groningen, 1977–: Dean, Central Inter-Faculty, 1981–84; Dean of Faculty, 1991–93. Vis. Prof., Univs in Germany, Denmark and USA. Member: Council, Mus. Boerhaave, Leiden, 1986–94; Comité Scientifique, CNRS, Paris, 1985–99; Acad. internat. d'histoire des scis, 1967– (Hon. Permanent Sec., 1983–); IAU, 1977 (Pres., Hist. Commn, 1988–92). Member: Royal Netherlands Acad., 1985 (Mem Council, 1990–93); Acad. Leopoldina, 1992; Foreign Mem., Royal Danish Acad., 1985. Editor: Archives internat. d'hist. des scis, 1971–84; Travaux de l'Académie, 1984–97. Kt, Order of Netherlands Lion, 1999. Publications: The Measure of the Universe, 1965, 2nd edn 1990; Isaac Newton, 1967; (ed) Mid-Nineteenth Century Scientists, 1969; Richard of Wallingford, 3 vols, 1976; (ed with J. Roche) The Light of Nature, 1985; Horoscopes and History, 1986; Chaucer's Universe, 1988, 2nd edn 1990; Stars, Minds and Fate, 1989; The Universal Frame, 1989; Fontana History of Astronomy and Cosmology, 1994; Stonehenge, 1996; The Ambassadors' Secret, 2002, 2nd edn 2004; God's Clockmaker: Richard of Wallingford and the invention of time, 2005; Cosmos: an illustrated history of astronomy and cosmology, 2008. Recreation: archaeology. Address: 28 Chalfont Road, Oxford OX2 6TH. T: (01865) 558458. Died 31 Oct. 2008.

NORTHCOTE, His Honour Peter Colston; a Circuit Judge 1973–89; b 23 Oct. 1920; s of late William George Northcote and Edith Mary Northcote; m 1947, Patricia Bickley; two s. Educ: Ellesmere Coll.; Bristol Univ. Called to Bar, Inner Temple, 1948. Chm., Nat. Insce Tribunal; Chm., W Midland Rent Tribunal; Dep. Chm., Agric. Land Tribunal. Commnd KSLI, 1940; served 7th Rajput Regt, Far East (Major). Recreations: music, travel, ski-ing. Address: Pendil House, Pendil Close, Wellington, Salop TF1 2PQ. T: (01952) 641160. Died 28 June 2009.

NORTHESK, 14th Earl of, cr 1647; David John MacRae Carnegie; Lord Rosehill and Inglismaldie 1639; estate manager/owner; b 3 Nov. 1954; s of 13th Earl of Northesk, and Jean Margaret (d 1989), yr d of Captain (John) Duncan George MacRae; S father, 1994; m 1979, Jacqueline Reid, d of Mrs Elizabeth Reid, Sarasota, Florida, USA; three d (one s decd). Educ: West Hill Park, Titchfield; Eton; Brooke House, Market Harborough; UCL. Elected Mem., H of L, 1999; an Opposition Whip, 1999–2002. Heir: kinsman Patrick Charles Carnegie, b 23 Sept. 1940. Address: House of Lords, SW1A 0PW. Died 27 March 2010.

NORTON, Donald; Regional Administrator, Oxford Regional Health Authority, 1973–80, retired; b 2 May 1920; s of Thomas Henry Norton and Dora May Norton (née Prentice); m 1945, Miriam Joyce, d of Herbert and Florence Mann; two s one d. Educ: Nether Edge Grammar Sch., Sheffield; Univs of Sheffield and London. LLB, DPA; FHA. Senior Administrator, Sheffield Regional Hosp. Bd, 1948–51; Sec. Supt, Jessop Hosp. for Women and Charles Clifford Dental Hosp., Sheffield, 1951–57; Dep. Sec., Archway Gp of Hosps, London, 1957–60; Gp Sec., Dudley Road Gp of Hosps, Birmingham 1960–70; Sec., Oxford Regional Hosp. Bd, 1970–73. Recreations: marriage, gardening. Address: Room 108, Sunrise of Edgbaston, 5 Church Road, Birmingham B15 3SH. Died 4 March 2009.

NOTTAGE, Raymond Frederick Tritton, CMG 1964; Chairman, Bobath Centre for Children with Cerebral Palsy, 1987–2002; Deputy Chairman, Association of Lloyd's Members, 1985–91; Treasurer, Arkwright Arts Trust, Hampstead, 1975–92; b 1 Aug. 1916; s of Frederick and Frances Nottage; m 1941, Joyce Evelyn, d of Sidney and Edith Philpot; three d. Educ: Hackney Downs Secondary Sch. Civil servant, Post Office Headquarters, 1936–49; Editor of Civil Service Opinion, and Member Exec. Cttee, Soc. of Civil Servants, 1944–49; Dir-Gen., RIPA, 1949–78. Mem. Hornsey Borough Council, 1945–47. Mem. Cttee on Training in Public Admin for Overseas Countries, 1961–63; Vice-Pres. Internat. Inst. of Admin. Sciences, 1962–68; Mem. Governing Body,

Inst. of Development Studies, Univ. of Sussex, 1966–76; travelled abroad as Consultant and Lectr. Publications: Sources of Local Revenue (with S. H. H. Hildersley), 1968; Financing Public Sector Pensions, 1975; (with Gerald Rhodes) Pensions: a plan for the future, 1986; articles on public administration. Recreations: music, reading. Died 19 Feb. 2010.

NOWELL-SMITH, Prof. Patrick Horace; Professor of Philosophy, York University, Toronto, 1969–85, then Emeritus; b 17 Aug. 1914; s of Nowell Charles Smith; m 1st, 1946, Perilla Thyme (marr. diss. 1968), d of Sir Richard Vynne Southwell; three s one d; 2nd, 1968, Felicity Margret (marr. diss. 1986), d of Dr Richard Leonard Ward; two d. Educ: Winchester Coll.; New College, Oxford (MA); Harvard Univ. (AM). Commonwealth Fellow, Harvard Univ., 1937–39. Served War of 1939–45, in Army, 1939–45. Fellow and Lecturer, 1946–57, Estates Bursar, 1951–57, Trinity Coll., Oxford; Professor of Philosophy: Univ. of Leicester, 1957–64; Univ. of Kent, 1964–69. Publications: Ethics, 1954; articles in Mind, Proc. Aristotelian Soc., Theoria, etc. Died 16 Feb. 2006.

NUGENT, Sir John (Edwin Lavallin), 7th Bt cr 1795; b 16 March 1933; s of Sir Hugh Charles Nugent, 6th Bt, and Margaret Mary Lavallin, er d of late Rev. Herbert Lavallin Puxley; S father, 1983; m 1959, Penelope Anne, d of late Brig. Richard Nigel Hanbury, CBE, TD; one s one d. Educ: Eton. Short service commn, Irish Guards, Lieut, 1953–56. PA to William Geoffrey Rootes (later 2nd Baron Rootes), Chm. of Rootes Gp, 1957–59; joined board of Lambourn group of cos, 1959, Chm., 1980–90. High Sheriff of Berks, 1981–82; JP Berks 1962–87. Recreation: garden and fishing. Heir: s Nicholas Myles John Nugent [b 17 Feb. 1967; m 1999, Alice, d of Peter Player; two d]. Address: The Steward's House, Ballinlough Castle, Clonmellon, Navan, Co. Meath, Ireland. T: (046) 9433135. Died 9 Oct. 2009.

NUGENT, Sir Robin (George Colborne), 5th Bt cr 1806; b 11 July 1925; s of Sir Guy Nugent, 4th Bt and Maisie, Lady Nugent (d 1992), d of J. A. Bigsby; S father, 1970; m 1st, 1947, Ursula Mary (marr. diss. 1967), d of late Lt-Gen. Sir Herbert Fothergill Cooke, KCB, KBE, CSI, DSO; two s one d; 2nd, 1967, Victoria Anna Irmgard, d of late Dr Peter Cartellieri. Educ: Eton; RWA School of Architecture. Lt Grenadier Guards, 1943–48; served Italy, 1944–45. ARIBA 1959. Recreation: fishing. Heir: s Christopher George Ridley Nugent [b 5 Oct. 1949; m 1985, Jacqueline Vagba; three s]. Died 26 Nov. 2006.

NUNN, Rear-Adm. John Richard Danford, CB 1980; Bursar and Official Fellow, Exeter College, Oxford, 1981–88; b 12 April 1925; s of Surg. Captain Gerald Nunn and Edith Florence (née Brown); m 1951, Katharine Mary (née Paris); three d. Educ: Epsom Coll. CEng, FIMechE; MPhil Cantab, 1981; MA Oxon, 1982. Entered RN, 1943; RN Engrg Coll., Keyham, 1943–47; HMS Devonshire, Second Cruiser Sqdn, 1945; HMS Vengeance, 1947; Advanced Engineering Course, RNC Greenwich, 1949–51. HMS Amethyst, Korea, 1952–53; HMS Tiger, 1957–59; Commander, 1960; HMS Glamorgan, 1967–68; Captain, 1969; Sea Dart and Seaslug Chief Engineer, 1970–72; Cabinet Office, 1973–74; Staff of SACLANT, 1975–77; Rear-Adm., 1978; Port Adm., Rosyth, 1977–80. Fellow Commoner, Downing Coll., Cambridge, 1980–. Vice Chm. of Govs, Peter Symonds VI Form Coll., Winchester, 1996–99. Editor, The Naval Review, 1980–83. Recreations: sailing, tennis, gliding, travel. Address: No 4 Godfrey Pink Way, Bishops Waltham, Hants SO32 1PB. Club: Royal Naval Sailing Association (Portsmouth). Died 22 Dec. 2009.

NUTTALL, Prof. Anthony David, FBA 1997; Professor of English, Oxford University, 1992–2004 (Reader, 1990–92); Fellow of New College, Oxford, 1984–2004, then Emeritus; b 25 April 1937; s of Kenneth and Hilda Mary Nuttall; m 1960, Mary Donagh; one s one d. Educ:

Hereford Cathedral Sch.; Merton Coll., Oxford. Sussex University: Asst Lectr, 1962–70; Reader in English, 1970–73; Prof. of English, 1973–84; Pro-Vice-Chancellor, 1978–81. *Publications:* Shakespeare: The Winter's Tale, 1966; Two Concepts of Allegory, 1967; A Common Sky: philosophy and the literary imagination, 1974; Dostoevsky's Crime and Punishment: murder as philosophical experiment, 1978; Overheard by God, 1980; A New Mimesis, 1983; Pope's Essay on Man, 1984; Timon of Athens, 1989; The Stoic in Love, 1989; Openings, 1992; Why Does Tragedy Give Pleasure?, 1996; The Alternative Trinity: Gnostic heresy in Marlowe, Milton and Blake, 1998; Dead From the Waist Down: scholars and scholarship in literature and the popular imagination, 2003; *posthumous publication:* Shakespeare the Thinker, 2007. *Recreations:* walking, looking at architecture. *Address:* New College, Oxford OX1 3BN. *Died 24 Jan. 2007.*

NUTTALL, Dr Geoffrey Fillingham, FBA 1991; ecclesiastical historian, retired; Visiting Professor, King's College, London, 1977–80; *b* Colwyn Bay, Wales, 8 Nov. 1911; *s* of Harold Nuttall and Muriel Fillingham (*née* Hodgson); *m* 1944, Mary (*née* Preston) (*d* 1983), *widow* of George Philip Powley. *Educ:* Bootham Sch., York; Balliol Coll., Oxford (MA 1936); Mansfield Coll., Oxford (BD 1938, DD 1945). Ordained Congregational Minister, 1938; Warminster, Wilts, 1938–43; Fellow, Woodbrooke, Selly Oak Colls, Birmingham, 1943–45; Lectr in Church Hist., New Coll. (Sch. of Divinity), London Univ., 1945–75; Chm., Bd of Studies in Theol., Univ. of London, 1957–59; Dean, Faculty of Theol., 1960–64; FKC 1977. University Preacher: Leeds, 1950; Cambridge, 1958; London, 1968; Oxford, 1972, 1980. Lectures: Friends of Dr Williams's Library, 1951, Drew, New Coll., London, 1956; Hibbert, 1962; W. M. Llewelyn, Memorial Coll., Swansea, 1966; Charles Gore, Westminster Abbey, 1968; Owen Evans, Aberystwyth, 1968; F. D. Maurice, King's Coll., London, 1970; R. T. Jenkins, Bangor, 1976; Ethel M. Wood, London, 1978; Dr Williams Meml, Swansea, 1978. External Examiner: Belfast, Birmingham, Cambridge, Canterbury, Durham, Edinburgh, Leeds, McMaster, Manchester, Nottingham, Oxford, Salford, St Andrews, Wales. President: Friends' Hist. Soc., 1953; Congregational Hist. Soc., 1965–72; London Soc. for Study of Religion, 1966; Eccles. History Soc., 1972; United Reformed Church History Soc., 1972–77. Trustee, Dr Daniel Williams's Charity, 1948–98. A Vice-Pres., Hon. Soc. of Cymmrodorion, 1978–. Mem., Adv. Editorial Bd, Jl of Eccles. History, 1950–86. For. Hon. Mem., Kerkhistorisch Gezelschap, 1981–. Hon. DD Wales, 1969. *Publications:* (ed) Letters of John Pinney 1679–1699, 1939; The Holy Spirit in Puritan Faith and Experience, 1946 (2nd edn 1947; 3rd edn (with new foreword), 1992); The Holy Spirit and Ourselves, 1947 (2nd edn 1966); Studies in Christian Enthusiasm illustrated from Early Quakerism, 1948; (ed) Philip Doddridge 1702–1751: his contribution to English religion, 1951; Richard Baxter and Philip Doddridge: a study in a tradition, 1951; The Reality of Heaven, 1951; James Nayler: a fresh approach, 1954; (contrib.) Studies in Christian Social Commitment, 1954; Visible Saints: the Congregational Way 1640–1660, 1957, 2nd edn 2001; The Welsh Saints 1640–1660: Walter Cradock, Vavasor Powell, Morgan Llwyd, 1957; Christian Pacifism in History, 1958 (2nd edn 1971); (ed with Owen Chadwick) From Uniformity to Unity 1662–1962, 1962; Better Than Life: the lovingkindness of God, 1962; (contrib.) Man's Faith and Freedom: the theological influence of Jacobus Arminius, 1962; (contrib.) The Beginnings of Nonconformity, 1964; (contrib.) Choose your Weapons, 1964; Richard Baxter (Leaders of Religion), 1965; Howel Harris 1714–1773: the last enthusiast, 1965; The Puritan Spirit: essays and addresses, 1967; Congregationalists and Creeds, 1967; (contrib.) A Declaration of Faith (Congregational Church in England and Wales), 1967; The Significance of Trevecca College

1768–91, 1969; The Faith of Dante Alighieri, 1969; Christianity and Violence, 1972; (contrib.) Violence and Oppression: a Quaker Response, 1973; New College, London and its Library, 1977; The Moment of Recognition: Luke as story-teller, 1978; contrib. Studies in Church History: Vol. VII, 1971; Vol. X, 1973; (contrib.) Pietismus und Réveil, 1978; (ed) Calendar of the Correspondence of Philip Doddridge, DD 1702–1751, 1979; (contrib.) Philip Doddridge, Nonconformity and Northampton, 1981; Handlist of the Correspondence of Mercy Doddridge 1751–1790, 1984; (with J. van den Berg) Philip Doddridge (1702–1751) and the Netherlands, 1987; (ed with N. H. Keeble) Calendar of the Correspondence of Richard Baxter, 1991; Studies in English Dissent, 2002; Early Quaker Studies and the Divine Presence, 2003; contrib. to Festschriften for: Gordon Rupp, 1975; Martin Schmidt, 1975; C. W. Dugmore, 1979; A. G. Dickens, 1980; R. Buick Knox, 1985; R. Tudur Jones, 1986; J. van den Berg, 1987; H. Barbour, 1992; B. R. White, 1999; contrib. Dict. of Nat. Biog., Encyc. Brit., Dict. d'Histoire et de Géog. Eccls., Evang. Kirchenlexikon; articles and revs in Jl Eccles. History and Jl Theol Studies; *Festschrift:* Reformation, Conformity and Dissent: essays in honour of Geoffrey Nuttall, 1977. *Recreations:* genealogy, languages. *Address:* Burcot Grange, Bromsgrove, Worcs B60 1BJ. *T:* (0121) 445 2700. *Died 24 July 2007.*

NUTTALL, Sir Nicholas Keith Lillington, 3rd Bt *cr* 1922; *b* 21 Sept. 1933; *s* of Lieut-Colonel Sir E. Keith Nuttall, 2nd Bt, RE (who died on active service, Aug. 1941), and Gytha Primrose Harrison (*d* 1967), *e d* of Sidney H. Burgess, of Heathfield, Bowdon, Cheshire; *S* father, 1941; *m* 1st, 1960, Rosemary Caroline (marr. diss. 1971; she *d* 2007), *e d* of late Christopher York; one *s* (one *d* decd); 2nd, 1971, Julia Jill Beresford (marr. diss. 1975), *d* of Thomas Williamson; 3rd, 1975, Miranda (marr. diss. 1983), *d* of Richard St John Quarry and Diana Elizabeth (who *m* subseq. 2nd Baron Mancroft, KBE, TD); three *d*; 4th, 1983, Eugenie Marie Alicia, *e d* of William Thomas McWeeney; one *s*. *Educ:* Eton; Royal Military Academy, Sandhurst. Commissioned Royal Horse Guards, 1953; Captain, 1959; Major 1966; retd 1968. *Heir: s* Harry Nuttall [*b* 2 Jan. 1963; *m* 1st, 1996, Kelly Marie (marr. diss. 1999), *o d* of Anthony E. Allen, Raleigh, N Carolina; 2nd, 2002, Dalit, *o d* of late Isaac Cohen, Stockholm; one *s* one *d*]. *Address:* PO Box N7776, Nassau, Bahamas. *T:* (242) 3626982. *Club:* White's. *Died 29 July 2007.*

NYE, Peter Hague, FRS 1987; Reader in Soil Science, University of Oxford, 1961–88; Fellow of St Cross College, Oxford, 1966–88 (Senior Fellow, 1982–83), then Emeritus Fellow; *b* 16 Sept. 1921; *s* of Haydn Percival Nye and Jessie Mary (*née* Hague); *m* 1953, Phyllis Mary Quenault; one *s* one *d* (and one *d* decd). *Educ:* Charterhouse; Balliol Coll., Oxford (MA, BSc (Domus Exhibnr)); Christ's Coll., Cambridge. Agricl Chemist, Gold Coast, 1947–50; Lectr in Soil Science, University Coll. of Ibadan, Nigeria, 1950–52; Sen. Lectr in Soil Science, Univ. of Ghana, 1952–60; Res. Officer, Internat. Atomic Energy Agency, Vienna, 1960–61. Vis. Professor, Cornell Univ., 1974, 1981, Messenger Lectures, 1989; Commonwealth Vis. Prof., Univ. of Western Aust., 1979; Vis. Prof., Royal Vet. and Agricl Univ., Copenhagen, 1990; Hon. Res. Prof., Scottish Crops Res. Inst., 1995–2000. Pres., British Soc. Soil Science, 1968–69; Mem. Council, Internat. Soc. Soil Science, 1968–74. Governor, Nat. Vegetable Res. Station, 1972–87. *Publications:* (with D. J. Greenland) The Soil under Shifting Cultivation, 1961; (with P. B. Tinker) Solute Movement in the Soil-Root System, 1977, 2nd edn as Solute Movement in the Rhizosphere, 2000; articles, mainly in Jl of Soil Science, Plant and Soil, Jl of Agricl Science. *Recreations:* formerly cycling, cricket, tennis, squash. *Address:* 15 Stourwood Road, Southbourne, Bournemouth BH6 3QP. *T:* and *Fax:* (01202) 269092. *Died 13 Feb. 2009.*

O

OAKES, Joseph Stewart; barrister-at-law; *b* 7 Jan. 1919; *s* of Laban Oakes and Mary Jane Oakes; *m* 1950, Irene May Peasnall (*d* 1995). *Educ:* Royal Masonic Sch., Bushey; Stretford Grammar Sch.; Manchester Univ., 1937–40 (BA Hons). Royal Signals, 1940–48, Captain. Called to Bar, Inner Temple, 1948; practised on Northern Circuit, 1948–91; a Recorder, 1975–82. Presiding Legal Mem., Mental Health Review Tribunal, 1971–91. *Recreations:* horticulture, photography, music, freemasonry. *Died 25 April 2009.*

OBASI, Godwin Olu Patrick, OFR 1983; Secretary-General, World Meteorological Organization, 1984–2004, then Secretary-General Emeritus; *b* 24 Dec. 1933; *s* of Albert B. Patrick Obasi and Rhoda A. Akande; *m* 1967, Winifred O. Akande; one *s* five *d*. *Educ:* McGill Univ., Canada (BSc Hons Maths and Physics); Massachusetts Inst. of Technology (MSc, DSc Meteorology). Mem., Inst. of Statisticians. University of Nairobi: WMO/UNDP Expert and Sen. Lectr, 1967–74; Acting Head of Dept of Meteorology, 1972–73; Dean, Faculty of Science, Prof. of Meteorology and Chm., Dept of Meteorology, 1974–76; Adviser in Meteorology to Nigerian Govt and Head of Nigerian Inst. for Met. Res. and Training, 1976–78; Dir, Educn and Training Dept, WMO, 1978–83. Chm., New Sun Foundn. Cons. Ed., *Weatherwise* (Amer. Met. Soc.). Fellow: African Acad. of Scis, 1993; Third World Acad. of Scis, 1996 (Vice-Pres., 1999); Internat. Energy Foundn, 1998; FSS; meteorol socs of USA, Africa, Nigeria, Dominican Republic, Ecuador and Colombia. Hon. Fellow, meteorol socs of India, Cuba and Burkina Faso; Hon. Member: Acad. of Agricl and Forestry Scis, Romania, 1995; Kenya Meteorol Soc. Dr of Physics *hc* Bucharest, 1991; Hon. LLD Philippines, 1992; Hon. DSc: Federal Univ. of Technology, Akure, Nigeria, 1992; Alpine Geophys. Res. Inst., Nal-Chik, 1993; Nairobi, 1998. Carl Rossby Award, MIT, 1963; Gold plaque merit award medal, Czechoslovakian Acad. of Sciences, 1986; Medal, Inst. of Meteorol. and Water Management, Poland, 1989; Ogori Merit Award, Nigeria, 1991; Climate Inst. Award, Washington, 1990; Direccion Nacional de Aeronautica Civil Honour of Merit Award, Paraguay, 1992; Gold Medal Award, African Meteorological Soc., 1993; Medal of Merit, Slovak Hydrometeorol Inst., 1994; Gold Medal, Balkan Physical Union, 1997; Award for Promotion of Hydromet., Viet Nam, 1998; Nat. Roll of Honour for envmtl achievement, Nigeria, 1999; Plaque of Appreciation, Iran, 1999; Head of State Commendation Award, Kenya, 1999; First Internat. Prize on water and agriculture, Italy, 2002. Gold Medal, Govt of Paraguay, 1988; Air Force Cross, Venezuela, 1989; Freedom of Ho Chi Minh City, Viet Nam, 1990; Commander, National Order: Côte d'Ivoire, 1992; Niger, 1994; Senegal, 1995; Benin, 1997; Burkina Faso, 1997; Medal, Order of Gediminas, Lithuania, 1998; Presidential Medal of Friendship, Viet Nam, 1998; Order of Grand Warrior, Kenya, 2000; First Class, Order of Saman de Aragua, Venezuela, 2001; Commander, Légion d'Honneur, France, 2002; Oman Civil Order, 2002; Officer's Cross, Order of Merit, Poland, 2003. *Publications:* numerous contribs to learned jls. *Recreations:* tennis, gardening. *Address:* c/o World Meterological Organisation, 7 bis avenue de la Paix, PO Box 2300, 1211 Geneva 2, Switzerland. *Died 3 March 2007.*

O'BRIEN, Charles Michael, MA; FIA, FPMI; General Manager (formerly Manager), and Actuary, 1957–84; Council Member, 1984–99, Royal National Pension Fund for Nurses; *b* 17 Jan. 1919; *s* of late Richard Alfred O'Brien, CBE, MD, and Nora McKay; *m* 1950, Joy, *d* of late Rupert Henry Prebble and Phyllis Mary Langdon; two *s*. *Educ:* Westminster Sch.; Christ Church, Oxford (MA). Commissioned, Royal Artillery, 1940 (despatches,

1945). Asst Actuary, Equitable Life Assce Soc., 1950; Asst Manager, Royal National Pension Fund for Nurses, 1953–57. Director: M & G Assurance Gp Ltd, 1984–91; M & G Life Assurance Co. Ltd, 1991–94. Institute of Actuaries: Fellow, 1949; Hon. Sec., 1961–62; Vice-Pres., 1965–68; Pres., 1976–78. Mem., Governing Body, 1970–95, Hon. Fellow, 1998, Westminster Sch. *Address:* The Boundary, Goodley Stock, Crockham Hill, Edenbridge, Kent TN8 6TA. *T:* (01732) 866349. *Died 26 April 2010.*

O'BRIEN, Conor Cruise; Contributing Editor, The Atlantic, Boston; Editor-in-Chief, The Observer, 1979–81; Pro-Chancellor, University of Dublin, 1973; *b* 3 Nov. 1917; *s* of Francis Cruise O'Brien and Katherine Sheehy; *m* 1st, 1939, Christine Foster (marr. diss. 1962); one *s* one *d* (and one *d* decd); 2nd, 1962, Máire Mac Entee; one adopted *s* one adopted *d*. *Educ:* Sandford Park School, Dublin; Trinity College, Dublin (BA, PhD). Entered Department of External Affairs of Ireland, 1944; Counsellor, Paris, 1955–56; Head of UN section and Member of Irish Delegation to UN, 1956–60; Asst Sec., Dept of External Affairs, 1960; Rep. of Sec.-Gen. of UN in Katanga, May–Dec. 1961; resigned from UN and Irish service, Dec. 1961. Vice-Chancellor, Univ. of Ghana, 1962–65; Albert Schweitzer Prof. of Humanities, New York Univ., 1965–69. TD (Lab) Dublin North-East, 1969–77; Minister for Posts and Telegraphs, 1973–77. Mem. Senate, Republic of Ireland, 1977–79. Vis. Fellow, Nuffield Coll., Oxford, 1973–75; Fellow, St Catherine's Coll., Oxford, 1978–81; Vis. Prof. and Montgomery Fellow, Dartmouth Coll., USA, 1984–85; Sen. Res. Fellow, Nat. Humanities Center, N Carolina, 1993–94. Member: Royal Irish Acad.; Royal Soc. of Literature. Hon. DLitt: Bradford, 1971; Ghana, 1974; Edinburgh, 1976; Nice, 1978; Coleraine, 1981; QUB, 1984. Valiant for Truth Media Award, 1979. *Publications:* Maria Cross (under pseud. Donat O'Donnell), 1952 (reprinted under own name, 1963); Parnell and his Party, 1957; (ed) The Shaping of Modern Ireland, 1959; To Katanga and Back, 1962; Conflicting Concepts of the UN, 1964; Writers and Politics, 1965; The United Nations: Sacred Drama, 1967 (with drawings by Felix Topolski); Murderous Angels, 1968; (ed) Power and Consciousness, 1969; Conor Cruise O'Brien Introduces Ireland, 1969; (ed) Edmund Burke, Reflections on the Revolution in France, 1969; Camus, 1969; A Concise History of Ireland, 1972; (with Máire Cruise O'Brien) The Suspecting Glance, 1972; States of Ireland, 1972; Herod, 1978; Neighbours: the Ewart-Biggs memorial lectures 1978–79, 1980; The Siege: the saga of Israel and Zionism, 1986; Passion and Cunning, 1988; God Land: reflections on religion and nationalism, 1988; The Great Melody: a thematic biography and commented anthology of Edmund Burke, 1992; Ancestral Voices, 1994; On the Eve of the Millennium, 1996; The Long Affair: Thomas Jefferson and the French Revolution, 1996; Memoir: my life and themes, 1998. *Recreation:* travelling. *Address:* Whitewater, Howth Summit, Dublin, Ireland. *T:* (1) 8322474. *Club:* Athenæum. *Died 18 Dec. 2008.*

O'BRIEN, Rt Rev. James Joseph; Auxiliary Bishop of Westminster, (R.C), 1977–2005; Titular Bishop of Manaccenser; *b* 5 Aug. 1930; *s* of John and Mary Elizabeth O'Brien. *Educ:* St Ignatius College, Stamford Hill; St Edmund's Coll., Ware. Priest, 1954; Assistant, St Lawrence's, Feltham, 1954–62; Catholic Missionary Society, 1962–68; Director of Catholic Enquiry Centre, 1967–68; Rector of Allen Hall, 1968–77; Bishop in Hertfordshire, 1977–2001. Bishops' Conference of England and Wales: Chm., Dept for Internat. Affairs, 1984–88; Chm., Cttee for Ministerial Formation, 1988–. Hon. DLitt Herts, 2001. Prelate of Honour, 1969. *Address:*

The Gate House, All Saints Pastoral Centre, London Colney, St Albans, Herts AL2 1AG. *T:* (01727) 824664.
Died 11 April 2007.

O'BRIEN, (Michael) Vincent; racehorse trainer, 1943–94, retired; *b* 9 April 1917; *s* of Daniel P. O'Brien and Kathleen (*née* Toomey); *m* 1951, Jacqueline (*née* Wittenoom), Perth, Australia; two *s* three *d*. *Educ:* Mungret Coll., Ireland. Started training in Co. Cork, 1944; moved to Co. Tipperary, 1951. Champion trainer: Nat. Hunt, 1952–53 and 1954–55; Flat, 1966 and 1967. Won all major English and Irish hurdle and steeple-chases, incl. 3 consecutive Grand Nationals, Gold Cups and Champion Hurdles. From 1959 concentrated on flat racing and trained winners of 44 Classics, incl. 6 Epsom Derbys, 6 Irish Derbys and 1 French Derby; also 3 Prix de l'Arc de Triomphe, Breeders Cup Mile, and Washington International; trainer of Nijinsky, first triple crown winner since 1935. Hon. LLD NUI, 1983; Hon. DSc Ulster, 1995. *Relevant publication:* Vincent O'Brien, the Official Biography, by Jacqueline O'Brien and Ivor Herbert, 2005. *Recreations:* fishing, golf. *Address:* Ballydoyle House, Cashel, Co. Tipperary, Ireland. *T:* (62) 62615, *Fax:* (62) 61217. *Died 1 June 2009.*

O'BRIEN, Raymond Francis, CBE 2000; Chairman, Liverpool Land Development Co., 2002–05; *b* 13 Feb. 1936; *s* of late Ignatius and Anne O'Brien; *m* 1959, Mary Agnes, (Wendy), *d* of late James and Agnes Alcock; two *s* two *d*. *Educ:* St Mary's Coll., Great Crosby, Liverpool; St Edmund Hall, Oxford (BA Hons 1959; MA 1962). IPFA. Accountant, Cheshire CC, 1959–65; Head of Data Processing, Staffs CC, 1965–67; Asst County Treas., Notts CC, 1967–70; Dep. Clerk, Notts CC, 1970–73; Clerk of CC and Chief Executive, Notts, 1973–77; Chief Exec., Merseyside MCC, and Clerk to Lord Lieut, Merseyside, 1978–86; Chief Exec. and Bd Mem., Severn-Trent Water Authy, 1986–87; Chief Exec., FIMBRA, 1987–90. Chm., Speke/Garston Development Co., 1995–2003. Consultant, Information Corp. (UK) Ltd, 1993. Mem., Merseyside Area Bd, MSC, 1980–86; Director: Merseyside Economic Development Co. Ltd, 1981–86; Merseyside Cablevision Ltd, 1982–86; Anfield Foundation, 1983–92. Chm., Midlands Reg. Electricity Consumers Cttee, 1996–2000. DL Merseyside, 1980–86. *Recreations:* sports critic, gardening, music, reading. *Address:* Cornerways, 12 Selworthy Road, Birkdale, Southport, Merseyside PR8 2NS. *T:* and *Fax:* (01704) 551780. *Died 3 May 2010.*

O'BRIEN, Sir Richard, Kt 1980; DSO 1944, MC 1942 (Bar 1944); Chairman, Manpower Services Commission, 1976–82; *b* 15 Feb. 1920; *s* of late Dr Charles O'Brien and of Marjorie Maude O'Brien; *m* 1951, Elizabeth M. D. Craig; two *s* three *d*. *Educ:* Oundle Sch.; Clare Coll., Cambridge (MA). Served, 1940–45, with Sherwood Foresters and Leicesters, N Africa, ME, Italy and Greece; Personal Asst to Field Marshal Montgomery, 1945–46. Develt Officer, Nat. Assoc. of Boys' Clubs, 1946–48; Richard Sutcliffe Ltd, Wakefield (latterly Prodn Dir), 1948–58; Dir and Gen. Man., Head Wrightson Mineral Engrg Ltd, 1958–61; Dir, Industrial Relns, British Motor Corp., 1961–66; Industrial Adviser (Manpower), DEA, 1966–68; Delta Metal Co. Ltd (subseq. Dir of Manpower, and Dir, 1972–76), 1968–76. Chairman: CBI Employment Policy Cttee, 1971–76; Crown Appointments Commn, 1979; Engineering Industry Trng Bd, 1982–85; Archbishop's Commn on Urban Priority Areas, 1983–85; Industrial Participation Assoc., 1983–86; Policy Studies Inst., 1984–90 (Jt Pres., 1991–98); Employment Inst. and Charter for Jobs, 1985–87; Community Educn Develt Centre, 1989–94; People for Action, 1991–98 (Pres., 1994–); Deputy Chairman: AMARC, 1988–91; Church Urban Fund, 1988–94. Member: NEDC, 1977–82; Engrg Council, 1985–88; President: British Inst. of Industrial Therapy, 1982–87; Inst. of Trng and Develt, 1983–84; Nat. Assoc. of Colls of Further and Higher Educn, 1983–85; Concordia (Youth Service Volunteers), 1987–91 (Chm., 1981–87); Campaign for Work, 1988–92; Employment Policy Inst.,

1992–95. Mem. Bd, Community Industry, 1991–96; Member Council: Industrial Soc., 1962–86; Univ. of Birmingham, 1969–88; Hymns Ancient & Modern, 1984–2000. Mem. Ct of Governors, ASC, 1977–83. Chm., Chiswick House Friends, 1997–2000. Hon. DSc Aston, 1979; Hon. LLD: Bath, 1981; Liverpool, 1981; Birmingham, 1982; Hon. DLitt: Warwick, 1983; CNAA (Coll. of St Mark and St John), 1988; DCL Lambeth, 1987; Hon. Fellow Sheffield City Polytech., 1980. JP Wakefield, 1955–61. *Publications:* contrib: Conflict at Work (BBC pubn), 1971; Montgomery at Close Quarters, 1985; Seekers and Finders, 1985; articles in various jls. *Recreations:* reading, theatre, cinema. *Address:* 54 Abbotsbury Close, W14 8EQ. *T:* (020) 7371 1327. *Died 11 Dec. 2009.*

O'BRIEN, Terence John, CMG 1971; MC 1945; HM Diplomatic Service, retired; *b* 13 Oct. 1921; *s* of Joseph O'Brien; *m* 1950, Phyllis Mitchell (*d* 1952); *m* 1953, Rita Emily Drake Reynolds; one *s* two *d*. *Educ:* Gresham's Sch., Holt; Merton Coll., Oxford. Ayrshire Yeo., 1942–45. Dominions Office, 1947; CRO, 1947–49; British High Comr's Office, Ceylon, 1950–52; Princ., Treasury, 1953–56; 1st Sec. (Financial), Canberra, 1956–58; Planning Officer, CRO, 1958–60; 1st Sec., Kuala Lumpur, 1960–62; Sec. to Inter-Governmental Cttee, Jesselton, 1962–63; Head of Chancery, New Delhi, 1963–66; Imp. Def. Coll., 1967; Counsellor, FCO (formerly FO), 1968–70; Ambassador: Nepal, 1970–74; Burma, 1974–78; Indonesia, 1978–81. *Address:* 6 Marlow Close, Wallingford, Oxon OX10 0PF. *Died 22 Dec. 2006.*

O'BRIEN, Vincent; *see* O'Brien, M. V.

O'CONNOR HOWE, Mrs Josephine Mary; HM Diplomatic Service, retired; *b* 25 March 1924; *d* of late Gerald Frank Claridge and Dulcie Agnes Claridge (*née* Waldegrave); *m* 1947, John O'Connor Howe (decd); one *d*. *Educ:* Wychwood Sch., Oxford; Triangle Coll. (course in journalism). Inter-Allied Information Cttee, later, United Nations Information Office, 1942–45; Foreign Office: The Hague, 1945–46; Internat. News Service and freelance, 1946–50; FO, 1952; Counsellor, FCO, 1974–79. Reader's Digest, 1979–83; Dir, Council for Arms Control, 1983–84; Exec. Editor, Inst. for the Study of Conflict, 1985–89; Freelance Editor specialising in internat. affairs, arms control, etc., 1985–. *Publications:* (ed) Armed Peace—the search for world security, 1984. *Recreations:* theatre, gardening, grandchildren. *Address:* 56 High Street, Charing, Kent TN27 0LS. *T:* (01233) 714762. *Died 5 May 2010.*

O'DEA, Sir Patrick Jerad, KCVO 1974; New Zealand Secretary to the Queen, 1969–78; Extra Gentleman Usher to the Queen, since 1981; *b* 18 April 1918; 2nd *s* of late Patrick O'Dea; *m* 1945, Jean Mary, *d* of Hugh Mulholland; one *s* three *d*. *Educ:* St Paul's Coll. and Univ. of Otago, Dunedin, NZ; Victoria Univ., Wellington, NZ. Joined NZ Public Service, 1936; served in Agriculture Dept, 1936–47. Served War in Royal New Zealand Artillery of 2 NZEF, 1941–45. With Industries and Commerce Dept, 1947–49; subseq. served with Dept of Internal Affairs in various posts interrupted by 2 years' full-time study at Victoria Univ. of Wellington (DPA). Group Exec. Officer, Local Govt, 1959–64; Dep. Sec., 1964–67; Sec. for Internal Affairs, NZ, 1967–78; formerly Secretary for: Local Govt; Civil Defence; Recreation and Sport; Clerk of the Writs; reapptd as NZ Sec. to the Queen, 1981, for visit of Queen and Duke of Edinburgh to NZ. Nat. Co-ordinator and Chm., Duke of Edinburgh Award in NZ, 1975–90; Chm., Duke of Edinburgh NZ Foundn, 1988–92; Mem., Vicentian Foundn. *Publications:* several papers on local govt in New Zealand. *Recreations:* gardening, golf, bowls. *Address:* 8 Cranbrook Grove, Waikanae, Kapiti Coast, New Zealand. *T:* (4) 2931235. *Club:* Waikanae Golf. *Died 28 Aug. 2010.*

ODELL, John William, (Jack), OBE 1969; *b* 19 March 1920. Chairman, Lledo (London) Ltd, 1982–99. Lesney Products & Co. Ltd, Diecasting Engineers, London E9:

Joint Managing Director, 1947–73; Deputy Chairman, 1973–81; Jt Vice-Chm., 1981–82. Inventor of Matchbox toys, 1952. *Died 7 July 2007.*

ODGERS, Paul Randell, CB 1970; MBE (mil.) 1945; TD 1949; Deputy Secretary, Department of Education and Science, 1971–75; *b* 30 July 1915; *e s* of late Dr P. N. B. Odgers and Mrs M. A. Odgers (*née* Higgins); *m* 1944, Diana, *d* of late R. E. F. Fawkes, CBE; one *s* one *d*. *Educ:* Rugby; New Coll., Oxford. Entered CS, Board of Education, 1937. Army Service, UK, Malta, Sicily, Italy, NW Europe, 1939–45 (despatches three times). Asst Secretary: Min. of Educn, 1948; Cabinet Office, 1956; Under-Secretary: Min. of Educn, 1958; Office of First Secretary of State, 1967; Office of Lord President of the Council, 1968; Office of Sec. of State for Social Services, 1968; Cabinet Office, 1970. Mem. Council, GPDST, 1976–89. *Address:* Stone Walls, Aston Road, Haddenham, Bucks HP17 8AF. *T:* (01844) 291830. *Club:* Oxford and Cambridge. *Died 24 Dec. 2007.*

O'DONOGHUE, His Honour Michael; a Circuit Judge, 1982–94; *b* 10 June 1929; *s* of late Dr James O'Donoghue, MB, ChB and Vera O'Donoghue (*née* Cox). *Educ:* Rhyl Grammar School; Univ. of Liverpool (LLB (Hons) 1950). Called to the Bar, Gray's Inn, 1951; National Service as Flying Officer, RAF, 1951–53; practised at the Chancery Bar, 1954–82; Lectr in Law (part time), Univ. of Liverpool, 1966–82. Mem. (part-time), Lands Tribunal, 1990–94. *Recreations:* music, sailing, photography. *Club:* Royal Welsh Yacht (Caernarfon) (Commodore, 1980–82; Pres., 1994–). *Died 13 March 2010.*

O'FERRALL, Very Rev. Basil Arthur, CB 1979; Dean of Jersey, and Rector of St Helier, Jersey, 1985–93; Hon. Canon of Winchester, 1986–93, then Emeritus; permission to officiate, diocese of Chichester, since 1993; *b* 25 Aug. 1924; *s* of Basil James and Mabel Violet O'Ferrall, Dublin; *m* 1952, Joyce Forbes (*née* Taylor); one *s* two *d*. *Educ:* St Patrick's Cathedral Grammar Sch., Dublin; Trinity Coll., Dublin (BA 1948, MA 1966). Ordained deacon, 1948, priest, 1949; Curate Assistant, St Patrick's, Coleraine, 1948; Chaplain RN, 1951; served: HMS Victory, 1951; Ganges, 1952; Gambia, 1952–54; Curlew, 1955; Daedalus, 1956; Amphibious Warfare Sqdn, 1956–58; HMS Adamant, 1958–60 (3rd Submarine Sqn); CTC, RM, 1960; 40 Commando, RM, 1960–62; RN Hosp., Bighi, 1962; HMS Victorious, 1963–64; Condor, 1964–66; HMS Maidstone, 1966–68 (3rd and 10th Submarine Sqns); St Vincent, 1968; Commando Training Centre, RM, 1969–71; HM Naval Base, Portsmouth, 1971–74; CTC, RM, 1975; Chaplain of the Fleet and Archdeacon of the Royal Navy, 1975–80; QHC 1975–80; Vicar of Ranworth with Panxworth and Woodbastwick (Norwich) and Bishop's Chaplain for the Broads, 1980–85; Chaplain to the Queen, 1980–85. Hon. Canon of Gibraltar, 1977–80. Anglican Advr, Channel TV, 1985–93. Mem., Gen. Synod of C of E, 1990–93. Pres., Jersey Br., Missions to Seamen, 1987–93. *Recreations:* sailing, ornithology. *Address:* The Stone House, Barrack Square, Winchelsea, East Sussex TN36 4EG. *T:* (01797) 223458. *Died 23 June 2006.*

O'HIGGINS, Prof. Paul; Fellow, Christ's College, Cambridge, since 1959 (Vice-Master, 1992–95); Professor of Law, King's College London, 1987–92, then Emeritus; *b* 5 Oct. 1927; *s* of Richard Leo O'Higgins, MC, MRCVS and Elizabeth O'Higgins, MA (*née* Deane); *m* 1952, Rachel Elizabeth Bush; one *s* three *d*. *Educ:* St Ignatius' Coll., Galway; St Columba's Coll., Rathfarnham; Trinity Coll., Dublin (MA, LLB, LLD; Hon. Fellow, 1996); MA, PhD, LLD Cantab. MRIA 1986. Called to the Bar, King's Inns, 1957, and Lincoln's Inn, 1959. University of Cambridge: Dir of Studies in Law, Peterhouse, 1960–74; Steward, Christ's Coll., 1964–68; Tutor for Advanced Students, Christ's, 1970–79; University Lectr, 1965–79; Reader in Labour Law, 1979–84; Regius Prof. of Laws, TCD, 1984–87 (Hon. Prof., 1992–). Co-founder, Cambridge Law Surgery, 1969. Lectr in Labour Law, Inns of Court Sch.

of Law, 1976–84; Visiting Professor: Univ. of Kent at Canterbury, 1973–74; City Univ., 1992–96. Mem. Bureau, European Inst. of Social Security, 1970–95; Mem., Staff Side Panel, Civil Service Arbitration Tribunal, 1972–84; Vice-Pres., Inst. of Shops, Health and Safety Acts Admin, 1973–; Pres., Irish Soc. for Labour Law, 1985–87 (Hon. Life Mem., 1997); Mem., Exec. Cttee, Internat. Soc. for Labour Law and Social Security, 1985–. Patron, Cambridge Univ. Graduate Union, 1973–84; Trustee, Cambridge Union Soc., 1973–84; Vice-Pres., Haldane Soc., 1976–; President: Ireland Br., Cambridge Soc., 1999–; Cambridge Br., TCD Assoc., 2003–. Gov., British Inst. of Human Rights, 1988–93; Vice-Pres., Inst. of Employment Rights, 1989–; Mem., Acad. of European Private Lawyers, 1994. Hon. Treas., Alan Bush Music Trust, 1997–. Mem. Editl Bd, Bibliography of Nineteenth Century Legal Lit., 1991–. Hon. Mem., Grotian Soc., 1968. Gilbert Murray Prize (jt), 1968; Joseph L. Andrews Bibliographical Award, Amer. Assoc. of Law Libraries, 1987. Grand Consul honorifique du consulat de la Vinée de Bergerac, 1983. *Publications:* Bibliography of Periodical Literature relating to Irish Law, 1966, 2nd supp. 1983; (with B. A. Hepple) Public Employee Trade Unionism in the UK: the legal framework, 1971; (with B. A. Hepple) Employment Law, 1971, 4th edn 1981; Censorship in Britain, 1972; Workers' Rights, 1976, 2nd edn 1986; Cases and Materials on Civil Liberties, 1980; Bibliography of Irish Trials, 1986; (with A. D. Dubbins and J. Gennard) Fairness at Work: even-handed industrial relations, 1986; (with M. Partington) Bibliography of Social Security Law, 1986; (ed jtly) The Common Law Tradition: Essays in Irish Legal History, 1990; (ed jtly) Lessons from Northern Ireland, 1991; British and Irish Labour Law, 1979–88: a bibliography, 1993. *Recreations:* wine, talking and travelling, particularly in France and Italy. *Address:* Christ's College, Cambridge CB2 3BU. *T:* (01223) 232659. *Club:* Royal Dublin Society (Dublin). *Died 13 March 2008.*

O'LEARY, Michael; barrister; District Court Judge, 1997–2006; *b* 8 May 1936; *s* of John O'Leary and Margaret McCarthy. *Educ:* Presentation Coll., Cork; University Coll., Cork; Columbia Univ., NY. Called to the Bar, King's Inns, Dublin, 1979. Educn Officer, Irish TUC, 1962–65. TD: (Lab) Dublin N Central, 1965–82; (FG) Dublin SW, 1982–87; Minister for Labour, 1973–77; Dep. Leader, Labour Party, 1977–81, Leader, 1981–82 (resigned); Tánaiste (Dep. Prime Minister) and Minister for Industry and Energy, 1981–82; joined Fine Gael, 1982. President, ILO, 1976. Mem. for Ireland, European Parlt, 1979–81. *Address:* Áras Uí Dhálaigh, Inns Quay, Dublin 7, Ireland. *Died 11 May 2006.*

O'LEARY, Terence Daniel, CMG 1982; MA; HM Diplomatic Service, retired 1988; *b* 18 Aug. 1928; 2nd *s* of late Daniel O'Leary and Mary (*née* Duggan); *m* 1960, Janet Douglas Berney (*d* 1997), *d* of Dr H. B. Berney, Masterton, NZ; twin *s* one *d*. *Educ:* Dulwich; St John's Coll., Cambridge (MA). Army, commnd Queen's Royal Regt, 1946–48. Commerce, 1951–53; Asst Principal, CRO, 1953; 2nd Sec., British High Commn, Wellington, 1956–58; Principal, PSO's Dept, CRO, 1958; 1st Sec., New Delhi, 1960–63; 1st Sec., Dar es Salaam, 1963–64; CRO, 1964–65; 1st Sec. and Defence Sec., Canberra, 1965–68; Actg Head, S Asia Dept, FCO, 1969; Asst Sec., Cabinet Office, 1970–72; Counsellor, Pretoria/Cape Town, 1972–74; Dep. High Comr, Wellington, 1974–78; Senior Civil Mem., Directing Staff, Nat. Defence Coll., 1978–81; High Comr in Sierra Leone, 1981–84; High Comr in New Zealand and concurrently to Western Samoa, and Governor of Pitcairn, 1984–87. Mem., EC Monitoring Mission, Yugoslavia, 1991–92. Parish Councillor (Ind.), Petworth, 1993–97. *Recreations:* cutting grass, croquet. *Address:* 25 Cooper Street, Karori, Wellington, New Zealand. *T:* (4) 763959. *Club:* Wellington (NZ). *Died 11 July 2006.*

OLIVER OF AYLMERTON, Baron cr 1986 (Life Peer), of Aylmerton in the County of Norfolk; **Peter Raymond Oliver,** Kt 1974; PC 1980; a Lord of Appeal in Ordinary, 1986–92; b 7 March 1921; s of David Thomas Oliver, Fellow of Trinity Hall, Cambridge, and Alice Maud Oliver; m 1st, 1945, Mary Chichester Rideal (d 1985), d of Sir Eric Keightley Rideal, MBE, FRS; one s one d; 2nd, 1987, Wendy Anne, widow of I. Lewis Lloyd Jones. Educ: The Leys, Cambridge; Trinity Hall, Cambridge (Hon. Fellow, 1980). Military Service, 1941–45, 12th Bn RTR (despatches). Called to Bar, Lincoln's Inn, 1948, Bencher 1973; QC 1965; Judge of the High Ct of Justice, Chancery Div., 1974–80; a Lord Justice of Appeal, 1980–86. Mem., Restrictive Practices Court, 1976–80; Chm., Review Body on Chancery Div. of High Court, 1979–81. Hon. LLD: City of London Poly., 1989; UEA, 1991; Cambridge, 1995. Recreations: gardening, music. Address: House of Lords, SW1A 0PW.
Died 17 Oct. 2007.

OLIVER, Dr John Andrew, CB 1968; b 25 Oct. 1913; s of Robert John Oliver, Limavady, Co. Londonderry and Martha Sherrard, Magilligan, Co. Londonderry; m 1943, Stella Ritson; five s. Educ: Royal Belfast Academical Institution; Queen's Univ., Belfast (BA 1936); Bonn Univ.; Königsberg Univ.; Zimmern School of International Studies, Geneva; Imperial Defence Coll., London (idc 1954); DrPhil 1951. Ministry of Development, NI: Second Sec., 1964–71; Permanent Sec., 1971–74; Permanent Sec., Housing, Local Govt and Planning, NI, 1974–75; Chief Adviser, NI Constitutional Convention, 1975–76. Hon. Sec., Assoc. of Governing Bodies of Voluntary Grammar Schs in NI, 1964–77; Chm., Bd of Governors, Royal Belfast Academical Instn, 1970–77. UK Election Supervisor, Que Que, Rhodesia, 1980. Chm. Management Review, Royal Victoria Hosp. Gp, Belfast, 1981–82. Chm., S Lakeland Council for Voluntary Action, 1980; Vice-Chm., Voluntary Action Cumbria, 1980–. Proposer and interim Governor, new Dallam Schs, Cumbria, 1983–84. Retired deliberately from all cttees and exec. positions on reaching 70. Hon. MRTPI, 1964; Hon. Member, Assoc. for Housing and Town Planning, W Germany, 1966. Rhodesia Medal, 1980; Zimbabwe Independence Medal, 1980. Publications: Ulster Today and Tomorrow, 1978; Working at Stormont, 1978; Aspects of Ulster (essays), 1994; short stories; many articles in learned jls on Ulster Admin and on family history; posthumous publication: Come Away With Me, 2006. Recreations: swimming, maps, languages, family history. Address: 28 Ashleigh Court, Arnside, Cumbria LA5 0JH. T: (01524) 761948. Club: Royal Over-Seas League. *Died 28 May 2006.*

OLLARD, Richard Laurence, FRSL; author and editor; b 9 Nov. 1923; s of Rev. Dr 3. L. Ollard and Mary Ollard (née Ward); m 1954, Mary, d of Sir Walter Buchanan Riddell, 12th Bt; two s one d. Educ: Eton College; New College, Oxford. MA. Lectr in History and English, Royal Naval College, Greenwich, 1948–59; Senior Editor, Collins, 1960–83. Caird Medal, Nat. Maritime Mus., 1992; (jtly) Heywood Hill Lit. Prize, 1998. Publications: The Escape of Charles II, 1966; Man of War: Sir Robert Holmes and the Restoration Navy, 1969; Pepys: a biography, 1974, 2nd edn 1991; This War Without an Enemy, 1976; The Image of the King: Charles I and II, 1979; An English Education: a perspective of Eton, 1982; (ed jtly) For Veronica Wedgwood These: studies in Seventeenth-Century History, 1986; Clarendon and his Friends, 1987; (ed) Clarendon's Four Portraits, 1989; Fisher and Cunningham: a study in the personalities of the Churchill era, 1991; Cromwell's Earl: a life of Edward Mountagu, 1st Earl of Sandwich, 1994; Dorset: a Pimlico county history guide, 1995; The Sayings of Samuel Pepys, 1996; A Man of Contradictions: a life of A. L. Rowse, 1999; (ed) The Diaries of A. L. Rowse, 2003. Address: Norchard Farmhouse, Morcombelake, Bridport, Dorset DT6 6EP; c/o Curtis Brown Ltd, 28–29 Haymarket, SW1 4SP.
Died 21 Jan. 2007.

ONSLOW, Sir John (Roger Wilmot), 8th Bt cr 1797; Captain, Royal Yacht of Saudi Arabia; b 21 July 1932; o s of Sir Richard Wilmot Onslow, 7th Bt, TD, and Constance (d 1960), o d of Albert Parker; S father, 1963; m 1955, Catherine Zoia (marr. diss. 1973), d of Henry Atherton Greenway, The Manor, Compton Abdale, near Cheltenham, Gloucestershire; one s one d; m 1976, Susan Fay (d 1998), d of E. M. Hughes, Frankston, Vic, Australia. Educ: Cheltenham College. Heir: s Richard Paul Atherton Onslow [b 16 Sept. 1958; m 1984, Josephine Anne Dean (marr. diss. 2003); one s one d].
Died 14 Oct. 2009.

OPPÉ, Prof. Thomas Ernest, CBE 1984; FRCP; Professor of Paediatrics, University of London at St Mary's Hospital Medical School, 1969–90, then Emeritus Professor; b 7 Feb. 1925; s of late Ernest Frederick Oppé and Ethel Nellie (née Rackstraw); m 1948, Margaret Mary Butcher; three s one d. Educ: University Coll. Sch., Hampstead; Guy's Hosp. Med. Sch. (MB BS, hons dist. in Medicine, 1947). DCH 1950, FRCP 1966. Sir Alfred Fripp Meml Fellow, Guy's Hosp., 1952; Milton Res. Fellow, Harvard Univ., 1954; Lectr in Child Health, Univ. of Bristol, 1956–60; Consultant Paediatrician, United Bristol Hosps, 1960; Asst Dir, 1960–64, Dir, 1964–69, Paediatric Unit, St Mary's Hosp. Med. Sch.; Consultant Paediatrician, St Mary's Hosp., 1960–90. Consultant Adviser in Paediatrics, DHSS, 1971–86; Member, DHSS Committees: Safety of Medicines, 1974–79; Med. Aspects of Food Policy, 1966–88 (Chm., Panel on Child Nutrition); Child Health Services, 1973–76. Royal College of Physicians: Chm., Cttee on Paediatrics, 1970–74; Pro-Censor and Censor, 1975–77; Sen. Censor and Sen. Vice-Pres., 1983–84; University of London: Mem., Bd of Studies in Medicine, 1964–90 (Chm., 1978–80); elected Mem. of Senate, 1981 89; Dean, Faculty of Medicine, 1984–86; Mem. of Court, 1984–89. Member: BMA (Dep. Chm., Bd of Sci. and Educn, 1974–82); British Paediatric Assoc. (Hon. Sec., 1960–63); European Soc. for Paediatric Res., 1969–; GMC, 1984–88; sometime Mem., Governing Bodies, St Mary's Hosp., Inst. of Med. Ethics, Paddington Coll.; Examiner in Paediatrics, Univs of Glasgow, Leicester, Liverpool, London, Sheffield, Wales, Colombo, Singapore. Publications: Modern Textbook of Paediatrics for Nurses, 1961; Neurological Examination of Children (with R. Paine), 1966; chapters in books and papers on paediatrics and child health. Address: 160A Kew Road, Richmond, Surrey TW9 2AU. T: (020) 8948 0116.
Died 25 June 2007.

ORCHARD, Edward Eric, CBE 1966 (OBE 1959); b 12 Nov. 1920. Educ: King's Sch., Grantham; Jesus Coll., Oxford (MA). War Service, 1941–46; FO and HM Embassy, Moscow, 1948–51; Lectr in Russian, Oxford, 1951–52; HM Embassy Moscow and FCO, 1953–70 (Dir of Research, 1970–76). Mem., Waverley Borough Council, 1978–87; Mayor, Haslemere, 1987. Publications: articles and reviews. Recreations: swimming, gardening, local government and welfare. Address: Sturt Meadow House, Haslemere, Surrey GU27 3RT. T: (01428) 643034. *Died 26 Feb. 2006.*

ORGEL, Prof. Leslie Eleazer, DPhil Oxon, MA; FRS 1962; Senior Fellow and Research Professor, Salk Institute, La Jolla, California, USA, and Adjunct Professor, University of California, San Diego, Calif, since 1964; b 12 Jan. 1927; s of Simon Orgel; m 1950, Hassia Alice Levinson; two s one d. Educ: Dame Alice Owen's Sch., London. Reader, University Chemical Laboratory, Cambridge, 1963–64, and Fellow of Peterhouse, 1957–64. Fellow, Amer. Acad. of Arts and Sciences, 1985; Mem., Nat. Acad. of Scis, USA, 1990. Publications: An Introduction to Transition-Metal Chemistry, Ligand-Field Theory, 1960; The Origins of Life: molecules and natural selection, 1973; (with Stanley L. Miller) The Origins of Life on the Earth, 1974. Address: Salk Institute, PO Box 85800, San

Diego, CA 92186–5800, USA. *T*: (858) 4534100, ext. 1321. *Fax*: (858) 5509959; *e-mail*: orgel@salk.edu.
Died 27 Oct. 2007.

ORR, Sir David (Alexander), Kt 1977; MC and bar 1945; LLB; Chairman, Unilever Ltd, 1974–82; *b* 10 May 1922; *s* of late Canon Adrian William Fielder Orr and Grace (*née* Robinson); *m* 1949, Phoebe Rosaleen Davis; three *d*. *Educ*: High Sch., Dublin; Trinity Coll., Dublin (Hon. LLD 1978). Served Royal Engineers attached QVO Madras Sappers and Miners, 1941–46. With various Unilever companies, 1948–82; Hindustan Lever, 1955–60; Mem. Overseas Cttee, Unilever, 1960–63; Lever Bros Co., New York, 1963, Pres. 1965–67; Dir, 1967–82, Vice-Chm. 1970–74, Unilever Ltd; Vice-Chm., Unilever NV, 1974–82; Chm., 1983–86, 1991–92, Inchcape (Dep. Chm., 1986–91); Director: Rio Tinto-Zinc Corp., 1981–92; Shell Transport & Trading Co., 1982–92; Mem. Court, Bank of Ireland, 1982–90. Chm., British Council, 1985–92. Chm., Armed Forces Pay Review Body, 1982–84; Member: Cttee to Review Functioning of Financial Instns, 1977–80; Top Salaries Review Body, 1982–85; Adv. Cttee on Business Appointments of Crown Servants, 1984–92. Chairman: Leverhulme Trust, 1982–92; Shakespeare Globe Theatre Trust, 1982–93; Charles Wallace (India) Trust, 1991–98; Jt Chm., Anglo-Irish Encounter, 1983–87. Dir, Five Arrows Chile Fund, 1990–96; Pres., Children's Medical Charity, 1991–96. Chancellor, QUB, 1992–99; President: Liverpool Sch. of Tropical Medicine, 1981–89; Coll. of Speech Therapists, 1992–96; Governor, LSE, 1980–96. FRSA. Hon. LLD: TCD, 1978; Liverpool, 1989; NUI, 1993; DUniv Surrey, 1981. Comdr, Order of Oranje Nassau, 1979. *Recreations*: golf, Rugby, travel. *Address*: 81 Lyall Mews West, SW1X 8DJ; Home Farm House, Shackleford, near Godalming, Surrey GU8 6AH. *Clubs*: Athenæum; Sunningdale Golf. *Died 2 Feb. 2008.*

ORR, James Bernard Vivian, CVO 1968 (MVO 1962); Secretary, Medical Commission on Accident Prevention, 1970–82; *b* 19 Nov. 1917; *s* of Dr Vivian Bernard Orr and Gladys Constance Orr (*née* Power); unmarried. *Educ*: Harrow; Gordonstoun; RMC, Sandhurst. British South Africa Police, Southern Rhodesia, 1939–46. Attached Occupied Enemy Territory Administration in Ethiopia and Eritrea Police Forces, 1941–49; Kenya Police, 1954–57. Private Secretary to HRH The Duke of Edinburgh, 1957–70, an Extra Equerry, 1970–. *Recreations*: horse racing, watching cricket. *Died 14 June 2008.*

ORR, Prof. Robert Kemsley, (Robin), CBE 1972; MusD; FRCM; Hon. RAM; Hon. FRSAMD; Hon. DMus, Hon. LLD; Composer; Professor of Music, Cambridge University, 1965–76, now Professor Emeritus; Fellow of St John's College, Cambridge, 1965–76, Hon. Fellow 1987; *b* Brechin, Scotland, 2 June 1909; *s* of Robert Workman Orr and Florence Mary Kemsley; adopted, additionally, Swiss nationality, 1995; *m* 1st, 1937, Margaret (marr. diss. 1979), *er d* of A. C. Mace; one *s* one *d* (and one *d* decd); 2nd, 1979, Doris Winny-Meyer, *d* of Leo Meyer-Bechtler, Zürich. *Educ*: Loretto Sch.; Royal Coll. of Music; Pembroke Coll., Cambridge (Organ Scholar; BA, MusB 1932; Hon. Fellow, 1988); MA 1938, MusD 1951, Cantab; Accademia Musicale Chigiana, Siena. Studied privately with Casella and Nadia Boulanger. Dir of Music, Sidcot Sch., Somerset, 1933–36; Asst Lecturer in Music, Univ. of Leeds, 1936–38. Served War of 1939–45, RAFVR, Photographic Intelligence (Flight Lieut). Organist and Dir of Studies in Music, St John's Coll., 1938–51, and Fellow, 1948–56, Univ. Lecturer in Music, 1947–56, Cambridge; Prof. of Theory and Composition, RCM, 1950–56; Gardiner Prof. of Music, Univ. of Glasgow, 1956–65. Mem., Carl Rosa Trust, 1953–70; Chm., Scottish Opera, 1962–76; Director: Arts Theatre, Cambridge, 1970–75; Welsh Nat. Opera, 1977–83. Mem., Assoc. Suisse des Musiciens, 1997. Compositions include: Sonatina for violin and piano, 1941; Three Chinese Songs, 1943;

Sonata for viola and piano, 1947; Winter's Tale (Incidental Music), BBC, 1947; Overture, The Prospect of Whitby, 1948; Oedipus at Colonus (Cambridge Univ. Greek Play), 1950; Four Romantic Songs (for Peter Pears), 1950; Festival Te Deum, 1950; Three Pastorals for soprano, flute, viola and piano, 1951; Deirdre of the Sorrows (Incidental Music), BBC, 1951; Italian Overture, 1952; Te Deum and Jubilate in C, 1953; Motet, I was glad, 1955; Spring Cantata, 1955; Sonata for violin and clavier, 1956; Rhapsody for string orchestra, 1956; Antigone (Bradfield College Greek Play), 1961; Symphony in one movement, 1963; Full Circle (opera), 1967; From the Book of Philip Sparrow, 1969; Journeys and Places (mezzo-sop. and strings), 1971; Symphony No 2, 1971; Hermiston (opera), 1975; Symphony No 3, 1978; Versus from Ogden Nash for medium voice and strings, 1978; Songs of Zion (choir), 1978; On the Razzle (opera), 1986; Sinfonietta Helvetica, 1990; Rondeau des Oiseaux for recorder, 1993; Three Lyric Pieces for piano, 1994; O Gracious Light (choir), 1999; A Carol for Christmas (choir), 2001. Hon. DMus Glasgow, 1972; Hon. LLD Dundee, 1976. Silver Medal, Musicians' Co., 2002. *Publications*: Musical Chairs (autobiog.), 1998. *Recreations*: gardening, mountain walks. *Address*: 16 Cranmer Road, Cambridge CB3 9BL. *T*: (01223) 352858. *Died 9 April 2006.*

ORTOLI, François-Xavier; Hon. Chairman, Total, since 1990 (Président Directeur Général, 1984–90); *b* 16 Feb. 1925; *m* 1945, Yvonne Calbairac; one *s* three *d*. *Educ*: Hanoi Faculty of Law; Ecole Nationale d'Administration. Inspector of Finances, 1948–51; Tech. Adv., Office of Minister of Econ. Affairs and Information, 1951–53; Asst Dir to Sec. of State for Econ. Affairs and Sec.-Gen., Franco-Italian Cttee of EEC, 1955; Head, Commercial Politics Service of Sec. of State for Econ. Affairs, 1957; Dir-Gen., Internal Market Div., EEC, 1958; Sec.-Gen., Inter-Ministerial Cttee for Questions of European Econ. Co-operation, Paris, 1961; Dir of Cabinet to Prime Minister, 1962–66; Comr-Gen. of the Plan, 1966–67; Minister: of Works, 1967–68; of Educn, 1968; of Finance, 1968–69; of Industrial and Scientific Develt, 1969–72; Pres., EEC, 1973–76, a Vice-Pres., with responsibility for econ. and financial affairs, 1977–84. Hon. Fellow, Worcester Coll., Oxford, 1991. Hon. DCL Oxon, 1975; Hon. Dr Sch. of Political Scis, Athens, 1975. Grand Officier de la Légion d'Honneur, 2001; Médaille Militaire; Croix de Guerre, 1945; Médaille de la Résistance. *Address*: 18 rue de Bourgogne, 75007 Paris, France. *Died 30 Nov. 2007.*

ORTON, Peter Charles, CVO 2007; Founder, 1989, and non-executive Chairman, 2003–05, HIT Entertainment plc (Chief Executive, 1989–2001; Executive Chairman, 2001–02); *b* 17 June 1943; *s* of Harold Charles Orton and Eva Lillian Orton; *m* 1972, Susan Virginia Stevenson; one *s*. *Educ*: Portsmouth Tech. Coll.; Westlane Grammar Sch. Gen. salesman, Scholl Medical Co., 1962–67; Programme Exec., TIE, 1967–69; Internat. Dir of Programming, Children's TV Workshop, NY, 1969–72; Founder, Sport on TV (TV Sports Packaging Co.), 1972–74; Vice-Pres., Worldwide Distribn, Children's TV Workshop, NY, 1974–82; CEO, Henson Internat. TV, 1982–89. Hon. DArt De Montfort, 2002. Lifetime Achievement Awards: BAFTA, 2002; Marche Internat. de Programmes TV, 2005. *Recreations*: breeding steeplechase race horses, shooting, golf, most other country pursuits. *Address*: Lower Greenhill Farm, Wootton Bassett, Wilts SN4 7QP. *Clubs*: White's, Turf; Wootton Bassett Rugby. *Died 5 Dec. 2007.*

OSBORNE, Col Robert; Director, Tree Council, 1991–2001; *b* 14 March 1936; *s* of Kenneth George Hulbert Osborne and Mary Irene (*née* Daymond); *m* 1st, 1961, Sybil Kathi Gisela Hudson (*née* von Knobloch) (marr. diss. 1988); two *s*; 2nd, 1988, Claudia Downing (*née* Radok); one step *d*. *Educ*: Cheltenham Coll.; RMA, Sandhurst. Commnd RTR, 1955; served BAOR and UK, 1956–72; Staff Coll., Camberley, 1968; US Army, 1972–75; UN Force in Cyprus, 1977–80; Defence and

Military Attaché, Cairo, 1983–86; NATO Defence Coll., Rome, 1987; HQ NATO, Brussels, 1987–90. Hon. Citizen, State of Texas, USA, 1974. *Recreations:* antiquities, the countryside, plain cookery. *Address:* Unwin's House, Waterbeach Road, Landbeach, Cambridge CB25 9FA. *T:* (01223) 861243.
Died 26 Sept. 2009.

OSMOND, Sir Douglas, Kt 1971; CBE 1968 (OBE 1958); QPM 1962; DL; Chief Constable, Shropshire, 1946–62, Hampshire, 1962–77; *b* 27 June 1914. *Educ:* University Coll., London. Metropolitan Police Coll., Metropolitan Police, RN, Control Commn for Germany (Public Safety Branch); Dep. Asst Inspector Gen., 1944–46. Pres., Assoc. of Chief Police Officers of England and Wales, 1967–69; Chm., Police Council for UK, 1972, 1974; Provincial Police Representative, Interpol, 1968–70; Member: Inter-Deptl Cttee on Death Certification and Coroners, 1964–71; Bd of Governors, Police Coll., 1968–72 (Adv. Cttee, 1959–77); Royal Commn on Criminal Procedure, 1978–81. DL Hants, 1981. OStJ 1971. *Address:* 12 Hays Park, Sedgehill, Shaftesbury, Dorset SP7 9JR. *T:* (01747) 830881.
Died 20 April 2006.

OSMOND, Michael William Massy, CB 1977; Solicitor to the Department of Health and Social Security, and to the Office of Population Censuses and Surveys, and the General Register Office, 1974–78; *b* 1918; *s* of late Brig. W. R. F. Osmond, CBE, and Mrs C. R. E. Osmond; *m* 1943, Jill Ramsden (*d* 1989); one *s* one *d*. *Educ:* Winchester; Christ Church, Oxford. 2nd Lieut Coldstream Guards, 1939–40. Called to Bar, Inner Temple, 1941; Asst Principal, Min. of Production, 1941–43; Housemaster, HM Borstal Instn, Usk, 1943–45; Legal Asst, Min. of Nat. Insce, 1946; Sen. Legal Asst, 1948; Asst Solicitor, Min. of Pensions and Nat. Insce, 1958; Principal Asst Solicitor, DHSS, 1969. *Recreation:* music. *Address:* Hunters, Cherry Tree Lane, Cirencester, Glos GL7 5DT. *T:* (01285) 653707. *Club:* Oxford and Cambridge.
Died 22 Nov. 2010.

O'SULLIVAN, (Carrol Austin) John (Naish), CB 1973; Public Trustee, 1971–75; *b* Plaistow, 24 Jan. 1915; *s* of late Dr Carrol Naish O'Sullivan and Stephanie O'Sullivan (*née* Manning); *m* 1939, Lillian Mary (*d* 2000), *y d* of Walter Frank Yate Molineux, Ulverston; one *s* one *d*. *Educ:* Mayfield College. LLB (London). Admitted Solicitor, 1936. Served War of 1939–45, Gordon Highlanders and HQ Special Force SEAC (Captain). Joined Public Trustee Office, 1945; Chief Administrative Officer, 1963–66; Asst Public Trustee, 1966–71. Pres., Holborn Law Soc., 1965–66. Chm. of Governors of St Thomas More High Sch. for Boys, Westcliff-on-Sea, 1964–66. *Publications:* articles in legal jls; short stories. *Recreations:* television, reading, The Times crosswords. *Address:* 62 Hullbridge Road, South Woodham Ferrers, Chelmsford CM3 5LJ. *T:* (01245) 322749.
Died 15 Jan. 2007.

OSWALD, Dr Neville Christopher, TD 1946; MD; FRCP; retired 1975; formerly: Consultant Physician: St Bartholomew's Hospital; Brompton Hospital; King Edward VII's Hospital for Officers, London; King Edward VII's Hospital, Midhurst; *b* 1 Aug. 1910; *s* of late Col Christopher Percy Oswald, CMG; *m* 1st, 1941, Patricia Rosemary Joyce Cooke (*d* 1947); one *s* one *d*; 2nd, 1948, Marjorie Mary Sinclair; one *d*. *Educ:* Clifton Coll.; Queens' Coll., Cambridge (MD 1946). FRCP 1947. Research Fellow, USA, 1938–39. Royal Army Medical Corps, 1939–45. Hon. Physician to the Queen, 1956–58; Hon. Consultant in Diseases of the Chest to the Army, 1972–75. Hon. Col, 17th (London) General Hospital RAMC (TA), 1963–70, 217 (Eastern) General Hospital RAMC (V), 1967–70. President: British Tuberculosis Assoc., 1965–67; Thoracic Soc., 1974. Mitchell Lectr, and Tudor Edwards Lectr, RCP. DL Greater London, 1973–78. *Publications:* Recent Trends in Chronic Bronchitis, 1958; Diseases of the Respiratory System, 1962; many articles upon respiratory diseases.

Recreations: travel, golf. *Address:* 4 St Martins Square, Chichester, West Sussex PO19 1NT. *T:* (01243) 784457.
Died 19 April 2006.

OTTEWILL, Prof. Ronald Harry, OBE 1989; PhD; FRS 1982; FRSC; Leverhulme Professor of Physical Chemistry, 1982–92, then Emeritus, and Senior Research Fellow, since 1996, University of Bristol; *b* 8 Feb. 1927; *m* Ingrid Geraldine Roe; one *s* one *d*. *Educ:* Southall Grammar Sch.; Queen Mary Coll., London (BSc 1948; PhD 1951); Fitzwilliam Coll., Cambridge (MA 1955; PhD 1956). Sen. Asst in Res., 1955–58, Asst Dir of Res., 1958–63, Dept of Colloid Sci., Cambridge Univ.; Bristol University: Lectr, 1964–66; Reader, 1966–70; Prof. of Colloid Science, 1970–82; Head of Dept of Physical Chem., 1973–92; Dean, Faculty of Science, 1988–90; Head, Sch. of Chem., 1990–92. Chm., SERC Neutron Beam Res. Cttee, 1982–85. Vice Pres., Faraday Soc., 1986–89, 1991–99 (Pres., 1989–91; Hon. Treas., 1985–89). Lectures: A. E. Alexander, RACI, 1982; Liversidge, RSC, 1985–86; Canadian High Polymer Forum, 1987; Langmuir, ACS, 1988; Rideal, RSC/SCI, 1990; Orica, Melbourne Univ., 1999. Medal for Surface and Colloid Chemistry, RSC, 1972; Wolfgang Ostwald Medal, Kolloid Gesellschaft, W Germany, 1979; Bude Medal, Collège de France, Paris, 1981; Colloid and Interface Science Gp Medal, Faraday Div., RSC, 1993. *Publications:* contribs to learned jls. *Address:* School of Chemistry, The University, Bristol BS8 1TS.
Died 4 June 2008.

OUNSTED, John, MA Cantab; HM Inspector of Schools, 1971–81, retired; *b* London, 24 May 1919; *e s* of late Rev. Laurence J. Ounsted, Dorchester Abbey, Oxon (ordained 1965; formerly with Sun Life Assurance) and Vera, *d* of E. S. Hopkins, India Office; *m* 1940, Irene (*d* 2007), 3rd *d* of late Rev. Alfred Newns; one *s* four *d*. *Educ:* Winchester (Scholar); Trinity College, Cambridge (Major Scholar). Math. Tripos Part I, 1st Class; Science Tripos Part II, 1st Class; Senior Scholarship, Trinity College. Assistant Master, King Edward's School, Birmingham, 1940–48; Headmaster, Leighton Park School, 1948–70. First layman ever to be Select Preacher, Oxford Univ., 1964. Page Scholarship to visit USA, 1965. Vice-Pres., Botanical Soc. of British Isles, 1989–93 (Hon. Mem., 1997). Liveryman, Worshipful Company of Mercers (Trustee, Educnl Trust Fund, 1957–2001). *Publications:* verses from various languages in the 2 vols of Translation, 1945 and 1947; contributions to Watsonia, The Proceedings of the Botanical Society of the British Isles, and various other educational and botanical periodicals. *Recreations:* botany, camping, being overtaken when motoring. *Address:* Apple Tree Cottage, Woodgreen Common, Fordingbridge, Hants SP6 2BD. *T:* (01725) 512271.
Died 2 Dec. 2007.

OWEN, His Honour Aron Leslie, PhD; a Circuit Judge, 1980–92 (Resident Judge, Clerkenwell County Court, 1986–92); Deputy Judge, Clerkenwell County Court, and Family Division, Royal Courts of Justice, 1992–94; *b* 16 Feb. 1919; *m* 1946, Rose (*née* Fishman), JP; one *s* two *d*. *Educ:* Tredegar County Grammar Sch.; Univ. of Wales (BA Hons, PhD). Called to the Bar, Inner Temple, 1948. Freeman, City of London, 1963. *Recreations:* travel, gardening. *Address:* 44 Brampton Grove, Hendon, NW4 4AQ. *T:* (020) 8202 8151.
Died 23 Sept. 2009.

OWEN, Gerald Victor; QC 1969; a Recorder of the Crown Court, 1979–95; *b* London, 29 Nov. 1922; *m* 1946, Phyllis (*née* Ladsky); one *s* one *d*. *Educ:* Kilburn Grammar Sch.; St Catharine's Coll., Cambridge (exhibnr, 1940; 1st cl. Maths Tripos I, 1941; Sen. Optimes Tripos II, 1942; BA 1943, MA 1946); Drapers' Co. Sci. Schol., Queen Mary Coll., London, 1940; Royal Statistical Soc. Certif., 1947; LLB London (Hons) 1949. Research Ballistics, Min. of Supply, 1942–45; Statistical Officer, LCC, 1945–49. Called to Bar, Gray's Inn, 1949; *ad eundem* Inner Temple, 1969. A Dep. Circuit Judge, 1971. Chairman: Dairy Produce Quota Tribunal, 1984–85; Medical Appeals Tribunal, 1984–94. Member, Cttees of Justice on: Legal Aid in Criminal Cases; Complaints against Lawyers, 1970; False Witness, the problem of perjury, 1973. *Address:* 11 Wellington House, Eton Road, NW3 4SY. *T:* (020) 7586 1596.   *Died 24 July 2007.*

OWEN, Griffith; *see* Owen, S. G.

OWEN, Hon. Sir John (Arthur Dalziel), Kt 1986; a Judge of the High Court of Justice, Queen's Bench Division, 1986–2000; Dean, Arches Court of Canterbury and Auditor, Chancery Court of York, and Master of the Faculty Office, 1980–2000; *b* 22 Nov. 1925; *s* of late R. J. Owen and Mrs O. B. Owen; *m* 1952, Valerie, *d* of W. Ethell; one *s* one *d. Educ:* Solihull Sch.; Brasenose Coll., Oxford (MA, BCL 1949); LLM Wales, 1996. RN, 1944; commnd 2nd King Edward VII's Own Goorkha Rifles, 1946. Called to Bar, Gray's Inn, 1951, Bencher, 1980. Dep. Chm., Warwickshire QS, 1967–71; QC 1970; a Recorder, 1972–84; Dep. Leader, Midland and Oxford Circuit, 1980–84; a Circuit Judge, CCC, 1984–86; a Presiding Judge, Midland and Oxford Circuit, 1988–92. Mem. Senate of the Inns of Court and the Bar, 1977–80. Chm., West Midlands Area Mental Health Review Tribunal, 1972–80. Mem., General Synod of Church of England, Dio. Coventry, 1970–80; Chancellor, Dio. Derby, 1973–80, Dio. Coventry, 1973–80, Dio. Southwell, 1979–80. DCL Lambeth, 1993. *Club:* Garrick.
                                                         Died 9 Dec. 2010.

OWEN, John Gethin M.; *see* Morgan-Owen.

OWEN, John Halliwell, OBE 1975; HM Diplomatic Service, retired; *b* 16 June 1935; *e s* of late Arthur Llewellyn Owen, OBE and Doris Spencer (*née* Halliwell); *m* 1st, 1963 (marr. diss. 1971); one *s* (one *d* decd); 2nd, 1972, Dianne Elizabeth (*née* Lowry); one *d. Educ:* Sedbergh School; The Queen's Coll., Oxford (Hastings Scholar). MA. 2nd Lieut, RA, 1954–56; HMOCS, Tanganyika Govt Service, 1960; Dist Officer, Provincial Administration, 1960–61; Dist Comr, 1962; Dist Magistrate and Regional Local Courts Officer, 1963–65; HM Diplomatic Service, 1966; Second Sec., Dar-es-Salaam, 1968–70; FCO, 1970–73; First Sec., Dhaka, 1973–75; FCO 1976; First Sec., Accra, 1976–80; FCO, 1980–82; Counsellor, Pretoria, 1982–86; Counsellor, FCO, 1986–90; Trng Consultant, FCO, 1990–98; conservation res., Kenya, 2000–01; Advr to Govt of Sierra Leone, 2003–04. *Recreations:* music, travel, wildlife, gardening, tennis. *Club:* Dar es Salaam Yacht.
                                                        Died 29 Nov. 2006.

OWEN, (Samuel) Griffith, CBE 1977; MD, FRCP; Second Secretary, Medical Research Council, 1968–82; *b* 3 Sept. 1925; *e s* of late Rev. Evan Lewis Owen and Marjorie Lawton; *m* 1954, Ruth, *e d* of late Merle W. Tate, Philadelphia, Pa, USA; two *s* two *d. Educ:* Dame Allan's Sch.; Durham Univ. (MB, BS Dunelm 1948; MD 1954). MRCP 1951, FRCP 1965. Clinical and research

appts at Royal Victoria Infirmary, Newcastle upon Tyne, 1948–49 and 1950–53; RAMC, SMO, HM Troopships, 1949–50; Med. Registrar, Nat. Heart Hosp., 1953–54; Instr in Pharmacology, Univ. of Pennsylvania Sch. of Med., 1954–56; Reader in Med., Univ. of Newcastle upon Tyne, 1964–68 (First Asst, 1956, Lectr, 1960, Sen. Lectr, 1961); Hon. Cons. Physician, Royal Victoria Infirmary, Newcastle upon Tyne, 1960–68; Clin. Sub-Dean of Med. Sch., Univ. of Newcastle upon Tyne, 1966–68 (Academic Sub-Dean, 1964–66); Examr in Med., Univ. of Liverpool, 1966–68; Examr in Membership, 1967–68 and Mem., Research Cttee, 1968–76, RCP; Member: Brit. Cardiac Soc., 1962–82; Assoc. of Physicians of GB, 1965–; European Molec. Biol. Conf., 1971–82; European Molec. Biol. Lab., 1974–82; Exec. Council, European Science Foundn, 1974–78; Comité de la Recherche Médicale et de la Santé Publique, EEC, 1977–82; Scientific Coordinating Cttee, Arthritis and Rheumatism Council, 1978–82; NW Thames RHA, 1978–82. Consultant to WHO, SE Asia, 1966 and 1967–68; Commonwealth Fund Fellow, Univ. of Illinois, 1966; Fellow, Hunterian Soc., 1978. Chm., Feldberg Foundn, 1974–78; Governor, Queen Charlotte's Hosp. for Women, 1979–82. Liveryman, Soc. of Apothecaries, 1976–. *Publications:* Essentials of Cardiology, 1961, 2nd edn 1968; Electrocardiography, 1966, 2nd edn 1973; contribs to med. jls on heart disease, cerebral circulation, thyroid disease, med. research, etc. *Recreations:* gastronomy, music, theatre. *Address:* Flat 17, 9 Devonhurst Place, Heathfield Terrace, Chiswick, W4 4JB. *T:* (020) 8995 3228. *Club:* Royal Society of Medicine.   *Died 5 June 2010.*

OWEN, Prof. Walter Shepherd, PhD, DEng; Professor Emeritus of Materials Science, Massachusetts Institute of Technology; *b* 13 March 1920; *s* of Walter Lloyd and Dorothea Elizabeth Owen; *m*; one *d. Educ:* Alsop High Sch.; University of Liverpool. Metallurgist, D. Napier and Sons and English Electric Co., 1940–46; Asst Lecturer and Lecturer in Metallurgy, Univ. of Liverpool, 1946–54; Commonwealth Fund Fellow, Metallurgy Dept, Mass Inst. of Technol., 1951–52; on research staff, 1954–57, and Henry Bell Wortley Professor of Metallurgy, 1957–66, Univ. of Liverpool; Thomas R. Briggs Prof. of Engineering and Dir of Materials Science and Engineering, Cornell Univ., 1966–70; Dean of Technological Inst., Northwestern Univ., 1970–71; Vice Pres. for Science and Research, Northwestern Univ., 1971–73; Head of Dept, 1973–82, and Prof. of Physical Metallurgy, 1973–85, Mass Inst. of Technol. Mem., Nat. Acad. of Engineering, USA, 1977. *Publications:* papers in British and American journals on aspects of physical metallurgy. *Recreation:* reading. *Address:* 100 Memorial Drive, Apt 5–5A, Cambridge, MA 02142, USA. *Club:* St Botolph (Boston).   *Died 10 Oct. 2007.*

P

PADOA-SCHIOPPA, Tommaso; banker and economist; President, Notre Europe, since 2005; *b* Belluno, Italy, 23 July 1940; *m* Fiorella Kostoris (marr. diss.); one *s* two *d*. *Educ:* Luigi Bocconi Univ., Milan; Massachusetts Inst. Technol. (MSc). C. & A. Brenninkmeyer, 1966–68; Economist, Res. Dept, Banca d'Italia, 1970–79; Dir Gen. for Econ. and Financial Affairs, CEC, Brussels, 1979–83; Central Dir for Econ. Res., 1983, Dep. Dir Gen., 1984–97, Banca d'Italia; Pres., Commissione Nazionale per le Società e la Borsa, 1997–98; Mem., Exec. Bd, European Central Bank, 1998–2005; Minister of Economy and Finance, Italy, 2006–08. Mem., Bd of Dirs, EID, 1979 83. Jt Sec, Delors Cttee for Study of Eur. Econ. and Monetary Union, 1988–89; Chm., Banking Adv. Cttee, CEC, 1988–91; Member: G-7 Deputies; G-10 Deputies; G-20 Deputies; Chairman: Eur. Regl Cttee, IOSCO, 1997–98; FESCO, 1997–98; Internat. Monetary and Financial Cttee, IMF, 2007–08; Mem., Wkg Party 3, Econ Policy Cttee, OECD. Hon. Prof., Univ. of Frankfurt am Main, 1999. Alternate Mem. Council, Eur. Monetary Inst., 1995–97; Member, Advisory Board: Inst. for Internat. Econs; Eur. Univ. Inst. Hon. Dr Trieste, 1999. *Publications:* include: (with F. Modigliani) The Management of an Open Economy with 100% plus Wage Indexation, 1978; (with F. Padoa-Schioppa) Agenda e Non Agenda: limiti o crisi della politica economica?, 1984; Money, Economic Policy and Europe, 1985; Efficiency, Stability and Equity: a strategy for the evolution of the economic system of the European Community, 1987; La moneta e il sistema dei pagamenti, 1992; The Road to Monetary Union in Europe: The Emperor, the Kings and the Genies, 1994; Europe: the impossible status quo, 1997; Il governo dell'economia, 1997; Che cosa ci ha insegnato l'avventura europea, 1998. *Died 18 Dec. 2010.*

PAGE, Sir (Arthur) John, Kt 1984; Chairman, Three Valleys Water, 1986–2001; *b* 16 Sept. 1919; *s* of Sir Arthur Page, QC (late Chief Justice of Burma), and Lady Page, KiH; *m* 1950, Anne, MA (Cantab), *d* of Charles Micklem, DSO, JP, DL, Longcross House, Surrey; four *s*. *Educ:* Harrow; Magdalene College, Cambridge. Joined RA as Gunner, 1939, commissioned, 1940; served War of 1939–45, Western Desert (wounded), France, Germany; demobilised as Major, comdg 258 Battery Norfolk Yeomanry, 1945; various positions in industry and commerce, 1946–. Chm. Bethnal Green and E London Housing Assoc., 1957–70; contested (C) Eton and Slough, Gen. Election, 1959. MP (C) Harrow W, March 1960–1987. PPS to Parly Under-Sec. of State, Home Office, 1961–63; Conservative Parly Labour Affairs Cttee: Sec., 1960–61, 1964–67, Vice-Chm., 1964–69, Chm., 1970–74; Sec., Conservative Broadcasting Cttee, 1974–76. Pres., Cons. Trade Unionists Nat. Adv. Council, 1967–69; Member: Parly Select Cttee on Race Relations and Immigration, 1970–71; British Delegn to Council of Europe and WEU, 1972–87 (Chm. Budget Cttee, 1973–74, Social and Health Cttee, 1975–78). Mem. Exec., IPU, British Gp, 1970 (Treasurer, 1974–77; Vice-Chm., 1977–79; Chm., 1979–82); Acting Internat. Pres., IPU, 1984 (Dep. Internat. Pres., 1982–84). Vice-Pres., British Insurance Brokers Assoc., 1980–; President: Water Companies Assoc., 1986–89 (Dep. Pres., 1984–86); Independent Schools Assoc., 1971–78; Chm., Council for Ind. Educn, 1974–80. *Recreations:* painting, politics, defending the Monarchy. *Address:* Hitcham Lodge, Taplow, Maidenhead, Berks SL6 0HG. *T:* (01628) 605056. *Clubs:* Brooks's, MCC. *Died 31 Oct. 2008.*

PAGE, Rt Rev. Dennis Fountain; *b* 1 Dec. 1919; *s* of Prebendary Martin Fountain Page and Lilla Fountain Page; *m* 1946; Margaret Bettine Clayton; two *s* (one *d* decd). *Educ:* Shrewsbury Sch.; Gonville and Caius Coll.,

Cambridge (MA); Lincoln Theological Coll.; BSc Open Univ., 1996. Curate, Rugby Parish Church, 1943; Priest-in-Charge, St George's Church, Hillmorton, Rugby, 1945; Rector of Hockwold, Vicar of Wilton and Rector of Weeting, Norfolk, 1949; Archdeacon of Huntingdon and Vicar of Yaxley, 1965–75; Hon. Canon of Ely Cathedral, 1968; Bishop Suffragan of Lancaster, 1975–85. *Publications:* Reflections on the Reading for Holy Communion in the Alternative Service Book 1980, 1983. *Recreations:* music, astronomy, gardening. *Address:* Larkrise, Hartest Hill, Hartest, Bury St Edmunds, Suffolk IP29 4ES. *Died 19 Jan. 2009.*

PAGE, Sir John, see Page, Sir A J

PAGE, Sir John (Joseph Joffre), Kt 1979; OBE 1959; Chairman, Christie Hospital NHS Trust, 1991–92; *b* 7 Jan. 1915; 2nd *s* of late William Joseph and Frances Page; *m* 1939, Cynthia Maynard (decd), *d* of late L. M. Swan, CBE; two *s*. *Educ:* Emanuel School. RAF, 1933–38 and 1939–46 (despatches, 1943); Group Captain. Iraq Petroleum Group of Cos, 1938–39 and 1946–70; served in Palestine, Jordan, Lebanon, Syria, Iraq, Qatar, Bahrain and Abu Dhabi; Head Office, London, 1958–61; Gen. Man., 1955–58; Chief Representative, 1961–70. Chm., 1972–77 and 1980–84, Chief Exec., 1975–77, Mersey Docks and Harbour Co.; Dep. Chm., British Ports Assoc., 1974–77; Chm., Nat. Ports Council, 1977–80. Chairman: Chester DHA, 1981–82, North Western RHA, 1982–88. Hon. Fellow, Manchester Metropolitan Univ., 1993. *Recreations:* photography, fishing, music. *Club:* Royal Air Force. *Died 5 Feb. 2006.*

PAGEL, Prof. Bernard Ephraim Julius, FRS 1992; Professor of Astrophysics, NORDITA (Nordic Institute for Theoretical Physics), Copenhagen, 1990–98; Visiting Professor of Astronomy, University of Sussex, since 1970; *b* 4 Jan. 1930; *s* of Walter T. U. Pagel and Magdalene M. E. Pagel; *m* 1958, Annabel Ruth Tuby; two *s* one *d*. *Educ:* Merchant Taylors' Sch., Northwood; Sidney Sussex Coll., Cambridge (MA, PhD). Res. Fellow, Sidney Sussex Coll., 1953–56; Radcliffe Student, Pretoria, 1955; PSO, Royal Greenwich Observ., 1955–61; Astrophysicist, Sacramento Peak Observ., New Mexico, 1960; SPSO, 1961–71, DCSO, 1971–89, Royal Greenwich Observ. Vis. Reader in Astronomy, Univ. of Sussex, 1966–70. Kelvin Lectr, BAAS, 1962; Vice-Pres. and For. Corresp., RAS, 1974–75. Gold Medal, RAS, 1990. *Publications:* Théorie des Atmosphères Stellaires, 1971; Nucleosynthesis and Chemical Evolution of Galaxies, 1997; articles in Nature, Encycl. Britannica, Monthly Notices of RAS, New Scientist, and procs of astronomical confs. *Recreations:* music, ski-ing, bicycling. *Address:* Groombridge, Lewes Road, Ringmer, East Sussex BN8 5ER. *T:* (01273) 812729; *e-mail:* bejp@ sussex.ac.uk. *Died 14 July 2007.*

PAICE, Karlo Bruce; Assistant Under-Secretary of State, Home Office, 1955–66; *b* 18 Aug. 1906; *s* of H. B. Paice, Horsham, Sussex; *m* 1st, 1935, Islay (*d* 1965), *d* of late Paymaster Comdr Duncan Cook; four *s*; 2nd, 1966, Mrs Gwen Morris (*née* Kenyon) (*d* 1991). *Educ:* Collyer's School, Horsham; Jesus Coll., Cambridge (MA). Second Clerk, Metropolitan Police Courts, 1928; Assistant Principal, Home Office, 1929; Asst Sec. to the Poisons Bd, 1933–35; Private Sec. to successive Parliamentary Under-Secretaries of State for Home Affairs, 1935–39; Principal, 1936; Assistant Secretary, 1941, serving in London Civil Defence Region, Fire Service Department, and Aliens Department; Secretary to the Prison Commission and a Prison Commissioner, 1949–55. *Recreations:* history, music. *Address:* 38 Gretton Court, Girton, Cambridge CB3 0QN. *T:* (01223) 277442. *Died 6 Jan. 2007.*

PAKENHAM, Henry Desmond Verner, CBE 1964; HM Diplomatic Service, retired; *b* 5 Nov. 1911; *s* of Hamilton Richard Pakenham and Emilie Willis Stringer; *m* 1st, 1946, Crystal Elizabeth Brooksbank (marr. diss.. 1960); one *s* one *d* (and one *s* decd); 2nd, 1963, Venetia Maude; one *s* one *d*. *Educ:* Monkton Combe; St John Baptist College, Oxford. Taught modern languages at Sevenoaks School, 1933–40. Served in HM Forces, 1940–45. Entered Foreign Service, 1946; served in Madrid, Djakarta, Havana, Singapore, Tel Aviv, Buenos Aires and Sydney; retired 1971. Chm., Suffolk Preservation Soc., 1979–82. Asst Editor, Satow's Guide to Diplomatic Practice, 5th edn, 1979. *Address:* The Mill House, Lavenham, Suffolk CO10 9RD. *Died 17 April 2010.*

PALADE, Prof. George Emil; scientist, USA; Professor, Department of Cellular and Molecular Medicine and Dean for Scientific Affairs, School of Medicine, University of California at San Diego, 1990–2000, Emeritus Professor and Emeritus Dean for Scientific Affairs, since 2001; *b* Iassy, Romania, 19 Nov. 1912; *s* of Emil Palade and Constanta Cantemir; *m* 1st, 1941, Irina Malaxa (*d* 1969); one *s* one *d*; 2nd, 1970, Dr Marilyn Farquhar. *Educ:* Liceul Al. Hasdeu, Buzau, Romania; Med. Sch., Univ. of Bucharest (MD). Arrived in US, 1946; naturalized US citizen, 1952. Instructor, Asst Prof., then Lectr in Anatomy, Sch. of Med., Univ. of Bucharest, 1940–45; Visiting Investigator, Rockefeller Inst. for Med. Research, 1946–48; continuing as an Assistant (later the Inst. became Rockefeller Univ., NYC); promoted to Associate, 1951, and Associate Mem., 1953; Prof. of Cell Biology, Rockefeller Univ. and full Member of Rockefeller Inst., 1956; Prof. of Cell Biology, Yale Univ. Med. Sch., 1973; Sen. Res. Scientist, Yale Univ., 1983–90. Fellow, Amer. Acad. of Arts and Sciences; Member: Nat. Acad. of Sciences; Pontifical Acad. of Sciences; Leopoldina Acad.; Romanian Acad.; For. Mem., Royal Soc., 1984. Awards include: Albert Lasker Basic Research, 1966; Gairdner Award, 1967; Hurwitz Prize, 1970; Nobel Prize for Medicine, 1974; Nat. Medal of Science, USA, 1986. *Publications:* Editor: Annual Review of Cell Biology, 1985–95; Jl of Cell Biology (co-founder); Jl of Membrane Biology; numerous contribs med. and sci. jls on structure, biochemistry and function of sub-cellular components. *Address:* School of Medicine, University of California, San Diego, 9500 Gilman Drive, La Jolla, CA 92093–0602, USA. *T:* (858) 5347708, *Fax:* (858) 5346573. *Died 7 Oct. 2008.*

PALETHORPE-TODD, Richard Andrew; see Todd.

PALMAR, Sir Derek (James), Kt 1986; FCA; President, Bass PLC, 1987–89 (Chairman, 1976–87; Chairman and Chief Executive, 1976–84; Director, 1970–76); Chairman: Yorkshire Television, 1981–93; Yorkshire–Tyne Tees Television Holdings, 1992–93; Vice President, Brewers' Society, since 1982 (Chairman, 1980–82); *b* 25 July 1919; *o s* of late Lt-Col Frederick James Palmar and Hylda (*née* Smith); *m* 1st, 1946, Edith Brewster (*d* 1990); one *s* one *d*; 2nd, 1992, Shuna, *o d* of late Keith Pyman and Peggy (*née* Hare). *Educ:* Dover College. FCA 1957 (ACA 1947). Served RA and Staff, 1941–46; psc; Lt-Col 1945. Peat, Marwick, Mitchell & Co., 1937–57; Director: Hill Samuel Group, 1957–70; Grindlays Bank, 1970–85. Adviser, Dept of Economic Affairs, 1965–67; Mem., British Railways Bd, 1969–72; Chm., BR Southern Regional Adv. Bd, 1972–79. Chm., Readyhigh, 1986–94; Director: Drayton Consolidated Trust, 1982–93; Consolidated Venture Trust, 1984–93; CM Group Holdings, 1985–92; United Newspapers, 1986–93; Chm., NEDC for Food and Drink Packaging Equipment, 1986–87. Chairman: Zool Soc. of London Develt Trust, 1986–89; Leeds Univ. Foundn, 1986–89; Member: Accounting Standards Cttee, 1982–84; Alcohol Educn and Res. Council, 1982–87. Director: Business in the Community, 1984–; Centre for Policy Studies, 1983–88; Mem., Adv. Council, Prince's Trust, 1984–. Trustee, Develt Trust, Queen Elizabeth's Foundn for Disabled People,

1993–96. Freeman, City of London; Mem., Ct, Brewers' Co., 1982–89. *Recreation:* gardening. *Address:* Church Farm, Naunton, Cheltenham, Glos GL54 3AJ. *Died 17 Aug. 2006.*

PALMER, Edward Hurry, CB 1972; retired Civil Servant; *b* 23 Sept. 1912; *s* of late Harold G. Palmer and late Ada S. Palmer; *m* 1940, Phyllis Eagle; no *c*. *Educ:* Haileybury. Dep. Chief Surveyor of Lands, Admty, 1942; Chief Surveyor of Lands, Admty, 1950; Chief Surveyor of Defence Lands, MoD, 1964; Comptroller of Defence Lands and Claims, MoD, 1968–72; Property Services Agency, Department of the Environment: Dir, Defence Lands Services, 1972–73; Dir, Estate Surveying Services, 1973–74. *Recreation:* walking. *Address:* 4 Barrowdene Close, Pinner, Middlesex HA5 3DD. *T:* (020) 8866 5961. *Died 21 Feb. 2006.*

PALMER, Most Rev. Norman Kitchener, CMG 1981; MBE 1975; *b* 2 Oct. 1928; *s* of Philip Sydney and Annie Palmer; *m* 1960, Elizabeth Lucy Gorringe; three *s* one *d*. *Educ:* Kokeqolo, Pawa, Solomon Is; Te Aute, NZ; Ardmore, NZ (Teachers' Cert,); St John's Theological Coll., NZ (LTh; ordained deacon, 1964). Appts in Solomon Islands: Asst Master and Chaplain, All Hallows' Sch., Pawa, 1965–67; Deacon/Teacher, Pawa Secondary (Anglican), 1966; priest, Pawa, 1966; Priest/Headmaster: Alanguala Primary, 1967–69; St Nicholas Primary, 1970–72; Dean, St Barnabas Cathedral, 1973–75; Bishop of Central Melanesia, 1975–87; Archbishop of Melanesia, 1975–87. Member, Public Service Advisory Bd, 1971–75. *Address:* Varei Village, Bauro District, General Post Office, Kira Kira, Makira Province, Solomon Islands. *Died 13 Nov. 2008.*

PANTLIN, Sir Dick (Hurst), Kt 1993; CBE 1977 (OBE 1970); Partner, 1946–52, Co-Managing Director, 1952–68, Henrijean International Insurance Brokers; *b* 8 Dec. 1919; *s* of Albert Ralph Pantlin and Gwendolyn Clara Thomas; *m* 1946, Janine Henrijean; two *s*. *Educ:* Felsted; Alliance Française, Paris. ACIB. War service, Royal Marines, 1940–46, Major (despatches 1944). Founder and Chairman: British Sch., Brussels, 1969–95 (Hon. Pres., 1995–); Council of British Ind. Schs in EC, 1980–95 (Hon. Pres., 1995–); Trustee, St George's English Sch., Rome, 1988–97; Pres., British Chamber of Commerce, Belgium and Luxembourg, 1975–77; Vice-Pres., Royal Belgo-British Union, 1975–2000; Founder and first Pres., Council of British Chambers of Commerce in Continental Europe, 1975–78. Chevalier: Ordre de la Couronne (Belgium), 1959; Ordre de Léopold (Belgium), 1969. *Publications:* articles for expatriates on educn, British nationality and voting legislation. *Recreations:* golf, travel, politics, ancestral research. *Address:* Les Jardins de Longchamp, Avenue Winston Churchill 255, 1180 Brussels, Belgium. *T:* and *Fax:* (2) 3752721; *e-mail:* dpantlin@voo.be. *Clubs:* Army and Navy; Royal Golf de Belgique. *Died 30 Oct. 2008.*

PAPADOPOULOS, Tassos; President of Cyprus, 2003–08; *b* 7 Jan. 1934; *m* Fotini Michaelides; two *s* two *d*. Called to the Bar, Gray's Inn. Founder and Man. Partner, Tassos Papadopoulos & Co., law firm, Nicosia, until 2003. Mem., House of Reps, 1970–2003 (Pres.. 1976). Former Minister: of the Interior; of Finance; of Labour and Social Insurance; of Health; of Agriculture and Natural Resources. Leader, Democratic Party, 2000. *Address:* c/o Presidential Palace, Dem. Severis Avenue, 1400 Nicosia, Cyprus. *Died 12 Dec. 2008.*

PAPOULIAS, George Dimitrios; Commander, Order of Phoenix; Order of George I; Greek Ambassador to the Court of St James's and (non-resident) to Iceland, 1990–93; *b* 19 May 1927; *s* of Dimitrios G. Papoulias and Caterina Kontopoulou; *m* 1974, Emily Pilavachi; one *d*. *Educ:* Athens Univ. (Law degree; Econ. and Comm. Scis degree). Military service, 2nd Lieut, 1950–51. Entered Greek Diplomatic Service, 1955; served Athens, New Delhi, Bonn; Dep. Perm. Deleg. to UN and to Internat. Orgns, Geneva, 1964–69; Counsellor, 1967; Dir, Political Affairs, Min. of N

Greece, 1969–70; Minister, Paris and Perm. Rep. to Unesco, 1971–74; Mem., Bd of Dirs, Resettlement Fund, Council of Europe, 1971–74; Ambassador to UN, NY, 1975–79, to Turkey, 1979–83, to USA, 1983–89; Alternate Minister and Minister for Foreign Affairs, 1989, 1990; special envoy of Greek govt to UN talks on former Yugoslav Republic of Macedonia, 1993. Foreign orders and decorations. *Recreations:* archaeology, history. *Address:* Rigillis 16, Athens 10674, Greece. *T:* 7229888. *Club:* Athenian (Greece). *Died 11 Sept. 2009.*

PARENT, Hon. Gilbert; PC (Can.) 2001; Ambassador for the Environment, Department of Foreign Affairs and International Trade, Canada, 2000–04; Vice Chairman, Protocol Energy International; Head, Gilbert Parent Consultants, 2005; *b* 25 July 1935; *s* of Joseph Nelson Parent and Marie Delina (*née* Boulanger); *m* 1958, Joan Davis; four *d*. *Educ:* St Joseph's Coll., Rensselear, Ind. (BSc); Niagara Univ., NY (MA); State Univ. of NY (MEd). French teacher: Notre Dame High Sch., Welland, Ont, 1957–59; Dennis Morris High Sch., St Catharines, Ont, 1959–70; Vice-Principal, Thorold Secondary Sch., 1970–74; history teacher, Niagara South Bd of Educn, 1985–89. MP (L) Welland-St Catharines-Thorold, 1974–85 and 1988–2001. Speaker of H of C, Canada, 1994–2000. Hon. LLD: St Joseph's Coll., Ind., 1995; Niagara Univ., NY, 1995; Brock Univ., Ont, 1996. *Recreations:* reading, playing golf, spending time with grand-children, promoting greater awareness of Parliament among young people. *Address:* 110 Bloor Street West, Toronto, ON M5S 2W4, Canada. *Died 3 March 2009.*

PARK OF MONMOUTH, Baroness *cr* 1990 (Life Peer), of Broadway in the County of Hereford and Worcester; **Daphne Margaret Sybil Désirée Park,** CMG 1971; OBE 1960; HM Diplomatic Service, retired; Principal of Somerville College, Oxford, 1980–89; *b* England, 1 Sept. 1921; British parents; unmarried. *Educ:* Rosa Bassett Sch.; Somerville Coll., Oxford (Hon. Fellow, 1990). WTS (FANY), 1943–47 (Allied Commn for Austria, 1946–48). FO, 1948; UK Delegn to NATO, 1952; 2nd Sec., Moscow, 1954; FO, 1956; Consul and 1st Sec., Leopoldville, 1959; FO, 1961; Lusaka, 1964; FO, 1967; Consul-Gen., Hanoi, 1969–70; Hon. Res. Fellow, Univ. of Kent, 1971–72, on sabbatical leave from FCO; Chargé d'Affaires *ai*, Ulan Bator, Apr.–June 1972; FCO, 1973–79. Gov., BBC, 1982–87. Chm., Legal Aid Adv. Cttee to the Lord Chancellor, 1985–91. Chm., RCHME, 1989–94. Member: British Library Bd, 1983–89; Sheffield Develt Corp. Bd, 1989–92; RIIA; Royal Asiatic Soc.; Forum UK; Mem. Council, VSO, 1981–84; Mem. Council, GB-Sasakawa Foundn, 1994–2001 (Patron, 2002–); Dir, Zoo Develt Trust, 1989–90. Pro-Vice-Chancellor, Univ. of Oxford, 1985–89. Pres., Soc. for Promotion of Training of Women, 1995–2006. Mem., Thatcher Foundn, 1992–; Trustee: Royal Armouries Develt Trust, 1991–92; Jardine Educnl Trust, 1991–98; Phoenix-Zimbabwe Trust, 2007–. Vice-Patron, Atlantic Council Appeal, 2001–. MRSA. Hon. LLD: Bristol, 1988; Mount Holyoke Coll., 1992. *Recreations:* good talk, politics, and difficult places. *Address:* House of Lords, SW1A 0PW. *Clubs:* Oxford and Cambridge, Naval and Military, Royal Over-Seas League, Royal Commonwealth Society, Special Forces. *Died 24 March 2010.*

PARKER, Christopher William Oxley, MA; JP; DL; *b* 28 May 1920; *s* of late Lieut-Col John Oxley Parker, TD, and Mary Monica (*née* Hills); *m* 1947, Jocelyn Frances Adeline (decd), *d* of late Colonel C. G. Arkwright, Southern Rhodesia; one *s* two *d*. *Educ:* Eton; Trinity Coll., Oxford. Served War of 1939–45, 147th Field Regt (Essex Yeomanry) RA, 1939–42. Director: Strutt and Parker (Farms) Ltd; Local Dir, Chelmsford Bd, Barclays Bank, 1951–83. Mem., Nat. Trust Properties Cttee, 1974–89; Mem. Exec. Cttee, CLA, 1959–73; Pres., Essex CLA, 1987–. JP Essex, 1952; High

Sheriff of Essex, 1961; DL Essex 1972. *Address:* Faulkbourne Hall, Witham, Essex CM8 1SP. *T:* (01376) 513385. *Died 23 April 2009.*

PARKER, Sir Douglas D.; *see* Dodds-Parker.

PARKER, Hugh; Industrial Liaison Officer, Massachusetts Institute of Technology, since 1996; *b* 12 June 1919; *s* of Ross Parker and Ruth Baker Parker; *m* 1957, Elsa del Carmen Mijares Osorio (*d* 2003); one *s* one *d*. *Educ:* Tabor Academy; Trinity Hall, Cambridge; Massachusetts Inst. of Technology. North Carolina Shipbuilding Co., 1941–43; General Electric Co., 1945–46; Ludlow Manufacturing Co., 1947–50; McKinsey & Co. Inc., 1951–84 (Sen. Dir, 1974–84). Pres., American Chamber of Commerce (UK), 1976–79. Vis. Lectr, Sloan Sch. of Mgt, MIT, 1992–96. Governor, Ditchley Foundn. *Publications:* Letters to a New Chairman, 1979; numerous articles on management and corporate governance. *Recreations:* reading, writing, cooking. *Address:* Zero Redstone Lane, Marblehead, MA 01945, USA. *Clubs:* Oxford and Cambridge; Leander; Eastern Yacht (Mass). *Died 16 June 2008.*

PARKER, James Roland Walter, CMG 1978; OBE 1968; HM Diplomatic Service, retired; Governor and Commander-in-Chief, Falkland Islands and Dependencies, and High Commissioner, British Antarctic Territory, 1976–80; *b* 20 Dec. 1919; *s* of late Alexander Roland Parker, ISM; *m* 1941, Deirdre Mary Ward (*d* 2001). Served War of 1939–45: 1st London Scottish, 1940–41. Ministry of Labour, 1938–57; Labour Attaché, Tel Aviv, 1957–60; Labour Adviser: Accra, 1960–62; Lagos, 1962–64; seconded to Foreign Office, 1965–66; Dep. High Comr, Enugu, 1966–67; Commonwealth Office (later FCO), 1968–70; Head of Chancery, Suva, Fiji, 1970–71; High Comr in The Gambia, 1972–75; Consul-Gen., Durban, 1976. *Address:* 7 Elliscombe Park, Higher Holton, Wincanton, Som BA9 8EA. *Died 17 Nov. 2009.*

PARKES, Margaret, (Lady Parkes), CBE 1990; JP; President, Christian Education Movement, 1992–2000; a Governor of the BBC, 1984–89; *b* 26 Sept. 1925; *d* of John and Dorothy Parr; *m* 1950, Sir Edward Walter Parkes; one *s* one *d*. *Educ:* Perse School for Girls, Cambridge; Leicester Univ. (MEd). Homerton Coll., Cambridge, 1965–74. Pres., Leeds Marriage and Personal Counselling Service, 1987–91; Chairman: London Diocesan Bd of Educn, 1976–80; Colleges Adv. Cttee, Gen. Synod Bd of Educn, 1982–86; Radio London Adv. Council, 1979–83; Ripon Diocesan Bd of Educn, 1988–91; Leeds Parish Church Commn, 1988. Member: Press Council, 1978–84; Secondary Exams Council, 1983–88; Voluntary Sector Consultative Council, 1984–88; Chairman: Design and Technology Wkg Gp for Nat. Curriculum, 1988–89; NCET, 1991–92. Chm. of Governors, Whitelands Coll., London, 1981–87. JP Inner London, 1977. *Address:* The Cottage, Headington Hill, Oxford OX3 0BT. *Died 23 Aug. 2007.*

PARKIN, John Mackintosh; Administrator, Royal Courts of Justice, 1982–85; *b* 18 June 1920; *s* of Thomas and Emily Cecilia Parkin; *m* Biancamaria Giuganino, Rome; two *d*. *Educ:* Nottingham High Sch.; Emmanuel Coll., Cambridge (Sen. Schol.; MA). Royal Artillery, 1939–46 (Captain). Asst Principal, WO, 1949; Registrar, RMCS, 1957–60; Principal Private Sec. to Sec. of State for War, 1960–62; Asst Sec. 1962; Sen. Fellow, Harvard Univ., 1966–67; Comd Sec., BAOR, 1967–70; Asst Under-Sec. of State, MoD, 1974–80. Mem., Royal Patriotic Fund Corp., 1977–80. *Recreation:* history of architecture and art. *Address:* 18 Dulwich Mead, 48–50 Half Moon Lane, SE24 9HS. *T:* (020) 7274 7581. *Died 9 March 2010.*

PARKINSON, Graham Edward, CBE 2001; a District Judge (Magistrates' Courts) (formerly Metropolitan Stipendiary Magistrate), 1982–2002, Deputy District Judge, 2002–07; Chief Metropolitan Stipendiary Magistrate, 1997–2000; *b* 13 Oct. 1937; *s* of Norman

Edward Parkinson and late Phyllis (née Jaquiss); *m* 1963, Dinah Mary Pyper; one *s* one *d*. *Educ*: Loughborough Grammar Sch. Admitted Solicitor of the Supreme Court, 1961. Articled to J. Tempest Bouskell, Leicester, 1955–60; Asst Solicitor: Slaughter & May, 1961–63; Amery Parkes & Co., 1963–67; Partner, Darlington and Parkinson, Ealing, 1967–82. A Recorder, 1989–2000; Chm., Inner London Magistrates' Courts Cttee, 1997–2001; a Chairman: Inner London Youth Court, 2000; City and Family Proceedings Court, 2001. Pres., Central and S Middx Law Soc., 1978–79; Mem. Cttee, London Criminal Courts Solicitors Assoc., 1978–80; Chm., Legal Cttee, Magistrates' Assoc., 1992–97; Mem., Lord Chancellor's Adv. Cttee for Inner London, 1997–99. *Recreations*: opera, reading, playing piano and church organ. *Address*: The Old Stables, Melchbourne Park, Melchbourne, Bedford MK44 1BD.
Died 8 Feb. 2010.

PARKINSON, Dr James Christopher, MBE 1963; TD 1962; Deputy Director, Brighton Polytechnic, 1970–83, retired; *b* 15 Aug. 1920; *s* of late Charles Myers Parkinson, Pharmacist, Blackburn, Lancs; *m* 1950, Gwyneth Margot, *d* of late Rev. John Raymond Harrison, Macclesfield, Ches; three *s*. *Educ*: Queen Elizabeth's Gram. Sch., Blackburn; Univ. Coll., Nottingham. BPharm, PhD (London), FRPharmS. Served in Mediterranean area, Parachute Regt, 1943–46; Parachute Regt TA: 16 AB Div. and 44 Parachute Bde, 1949–63 (Major). Lectr, Sch. of Pharmacy, Univ. of London, 1948–54; Head of Sch. of Pharmacy, Brighton Coll. of Technology, 1954–64; Dep. Sec., Pharmaceutical Soc. of Gt Britain, 1964–67; Principal, Brighton Coll. of Technology, 1967–70. Mem. various pharmaceutical cttees of British Pharmacopœia, British Pharmaceutical Codex and British Veterinary Codex, 1956–64; Examr, Pharmaceutical Soc. of Gt Britain, 1954–64; Mem. Bds of Studies in Pharmacy and Librarianship, CNAA, 1965–75. Mem., Mid-Downs DHA, 1984–87. Member, Gen. Synod of Church of England, 1970–85. *Publications*: research papers on applied microbiology in Jl Appl. Bact. and Jl Pharm. (London) and on pharmaceutical education in Pharm. Jl. *Recreation*: do-it-yourself. *Address*: 5 Marchants Close, Hurstpierpoint, West Sussex BN6 9XB. *T*: (01273) 833369.
Died 6 Sept. 2007.

PARKYN, Brian (Stewart); General Manager, Training Services, British Caledonian Airways Ltd, 1981–88; *b* 28 April 1923; *o s* of Leslie and Gwen Parkyn, Whetstone, N20; *m* 1951, Janet Anne, *o d* of Charles and Jessie Stormer, Eastbourne; one *s* one *d*. *Educ*: King Edward VI Sch., Chelmsford; technical colleges. Principal, Glacier Inst. of Management (Associated Engineering Ltd), 1976–80. Director: Scott Bader Co. Ltd, 1953–83; Hunting Industrial Plastics Ltd, 1979–83; Halmatic Ltd, 1983–88. British Plastics Federation: Chm., Reinforced Plastics Gp, 1961–63; Mem. Council, 1959–75. Vice Pres., Rubber and Plastics Inst., 1972–75. Has travelled widely and lectured in N and S America, Africa, Australasia, India, Japan, USSR and China, etc.; Plastics Lectr, Worshipful Co. of Horners, 1967. Contested (Lab) Bedford, 1964; MP (Lab) Bedford, 1966–70; Mem., Select Cttee on Science and Technology, 1967–70; Chm., Sub-Cttee on Carbon Fibres, 1969; contested (Lab) Bedford, Oct. 1974. Member: Council, 1970–94, Ct, 1970–, Cranfield Univ. (formerly Inst. of Technology); Council, RSA, 1976–82 (Hon. Treas., 1977–82). FIMMM. *Publications*: Democracy, Accountability and Participation in Industry, 1979; various papers and books on polyester resins and reinforced plastics. *Recreations*: writing, industrial democracy. *Address*: 4 Meadow Road, Southam, Warwicks CV47 1EN. *T*: (01926) 815133.
Died 22 March 2006.

PARMOOR, 4th Baron *cr* 1914; **Milo Cripps;** *b* 18 June 1929; *s* of 3rd Baron Parmoor, DSO, TD, DL, and Violet Mary Geraldine, *d* of Sir William Nelson, 1st Bt; *S* father, 1977. *Educ*: Ampleforth; Corpus Christi College, Oxford.

Heir: *cousin* (Michael Leonard) Seddon Cripps [*b* 18 June 1942; *m* 1971, Elizabeth Anne Millward Shennan; one *s* one *d* (and one *s* decd)]. *Address*: Dairy, Sutton Veny, Wilts BA12 7AL.
Died 12 Aug. 2008.

PARRY, Margaret Joan; Headmistress of Heathfield School, Ascot, 1973–82; *b* 27 Nov. 1919; *d* of W. J. Tamplin, Llantrisant, Glamorgan; *m* 1946, Raymond Howard Parry (*d* 2005); two *s* one *d*. *Educ*: Howell's Sch., Llandaff, Cardiff; Univ. of Wales. Hons English Cl I. Married to a schoolmaster at Eton; taught and coached interesting people from time to time; Examiner for: Civil Service, LCC, Schools Examination Boards. Patron, Univ. of Buckingham, 1983. *Recreations*: books, music, tapestry. *Address*: Carreg Gwaun, 23a Murray Court, Ascot, Berks SL5 9BP. *T*: (01344) 626299.
Died 30 Jan. 2008.

PARRY, Prof. William, PhD; FRS 1984; Professor of Mathematics, University of Warwick, 1970–99, then Emeritus; *b* 3 July 1934; *s* of late Richard Parry and Violet Irene Parry; *m* 1958, Benita (née Teper); one *d*. *Educ*: University Coll. London (BSc 1956); Univ. of Liverpool (MSc 1957); Imperial Coll. of Science and Technol., London (PhD 1960). Lectr, Univ. of Birmingham, 1960–65; Sen. Lectr, Univ. of Sussex, 1965–68; Reader, Univ. of Warwick, 1968–70. Member: Labour Party; NCCL. *Publications*: Entropy and Generators in Ergodic Theory, 1969; Topics in Ergodic Theory, 1981; (with S. Tuncel) Classification Problems in Ergodic Theory, 1982; articles in Trans Amer. Math. Soc., Amer. Jl of Maths, and Annals of Maths. *Recreations*: theatre, concerts, walking. *Address*: Manor House, High Street, Marton CV23 9RR. *T*: (01926) 632501.
Died 20 Aug. 2006.

PARRY BROWN, Arthur Ivor; *see* Brown.

PARSONS, Alan; *see* Parsons, T. A.

PARSONS, Alfred Roy, AO 1986; High Commissioner for Australia in the UK, 1984–87; *b* 24 May 1925; *s* of W. G. R. Parsons and R. E. Parsons; *m* 1958, Gillian Tryce Pigot; two *s* one *d*. *Educ*: Hobart High School; Univ. of Tasmania (postgraduate research; BCom); Canberra University College. Dept of Foreign Affairs, 1947; Djakarta, 1950–53, Rangoon, 1956–58, Berlin, 1961–62; Aust. Mission to UN, NY, 1962–64; Counsellor, Djakarta, 1964–66; High Comr, Singapore, 1967–70; First Asst Sec., Canberra, 1970–73; High Comr, Kuala Lumpur, 1973–76; Dep. Sec., periodically Acting Sec., Dept of Foreign Affairs, 1978–83. Chm., Commonwealth Observer Gp on Namibia, 1989. Member: Australia Japan Foundn, 1978–83; Australia China Council. Centenary Medal, Australia, 2003. *Recreations*: golf, reading. *Address*: 11 Hotham Crescent, Deakin, Canberra, ACT 2600, Australia. *Clubs*: Commonwealth (Canberra); Royal Canberra Golf, Canberra Wine and Food.
Died 19 June 2010.

PARSONS, Graham Colin; a District Judge (Magistrates' Courts), since 2004; *b* 8 May 1953; *s* of late Jack Rowland Parsons and of Davina Evelyn Parsons. *Educ*: Worthing High Sch. for Boys; Guildford Coll. of Law. Admitted solicitor, 1978; Prosecuting Solicitor, Hampshire Police Authy, 1979–85; private practitioner specialising in criminal defence work, 1985–2004; Actg Stipendiary Magistrate, 1998–2000, subseq. Dep. Dist Judge (Magistrates' Courts), 2000–04. *Recreations*: sailing, travel, choral music. *Address*: Brighton Magistrates' Court, Edward Street, Brighton, East Sussex BN2 2LG.
Died 5 Dec. 2010.

PARSONS, Sir (John) Michael, Kt 1970; Deputy Chairman and Chief Executive, 1979–81, Senior Managing Director, 1976–81, Director, 1971–81, Inchcape & Co. Ltd; *b* 29 Oct. 1915; *s* of late Rt Rev. Richard Godfrey Parsons, DD, Bishop of Hereford; *m* 1st, 1946, Hilda Mary Frewen (marr. diss. 1964); one *s* two *d*; 2nd, 1964, Caroline Inagh Margaret Frewen. *Educ*: Rossall Sch.; University Coll., Oxford. Barry & Co., Calcutta, 1937. Served in Royal Garhwal Rifles (Indian Army), 1939–45: Bde Major, 1942; POW, Singapore,

1942. Macneill & Barry Ltd, Calcutta, 1946–70; Chm. & Managing Dir, 1964–70; Chm., Macdonald Hamilton & Co. Pty Ltd, 1970–72; Chairman and Director: Assam Investments, 1976–81; Paxall Investments Ltd, 1982–84; Dep. Chm. and Dir, Inchcape Insurance Hldgs Ltd, 1979–83; Dir, Commonwealth Develt Finance Co. Ltd, 1973–86. Vice-Chm., Indian Jute Mills Assoc., 1960–61; President: Bengal Chamber of Commerce, 1968–69; Associated Chambers of Commerce of India, 1969; Chm., UK Cttee, Fedn of Commonwealth Chambers of Commerce, 1974; Mem., Advisory Council on Trade, Bd of Trade, India, 1968–69. Chm. Council, Royal Commonwealth Soc., 1976–80, Vice Pres., 1980–; Pres., India, Pakistan and Bangladesh Assoc., 1973–78, Vice Pres., 1978. Dep. Chm., Internat. Bd, United World Colls, 1981–86. *Publications:* Room to Swing a Cat (autobiog.), 2003. *Recreation:* golf. *Address:* Garrett House, Park Road, Aldeburgh, Suffolk IP15 5EN. *T:* (01728) 452917. *Club:* Oriental. *Died 19 April 2009.*

PARSONS, (Thomas) Alan, CB 1984; LLB; Chief Adjudication Officer, Department of Health and Social Security, 1984–86; *b* 25 Nov. 1924; *s* of late Arthur and Laura Parsons; *m* 1st, 1947, Valerie Vambeck; one *s*; 2nd, 1957, Muriel Lewis; two *s. Educ:* Clifton Coll.; Bristol Univ. (LLB). Called to the Bar, Middle Temple, 1950. Served, Royal Marines, 1943–46. Legal Asst, Min. of Nat. Insurance, 1950; Sen. Legal Asst, Min. of Pensions and Nat. Insurance, 1955; Asst Solicitor, 1968, Principal Asst Solicitor, 1977, DHSS. *Recreations:* walking, listening to music. *Address:* 18 Alpine Grove, E9 7SX. *T:* (020) 8986 0930. *Died 17 Oct 2008.*

PASHLEY, Prof. Donald William, FRS 1968; Professor of Materials, Imperial College of Science, Technology and Medicine, 1979–92, then Professor Emeritus and Senior Research Fellow; *b* 21 April 1927; *s* of late Harold William Pashley and Louise Pashley (*née* Clarke); *m* 1954, Glenys Margaret Ball; one *s* one *d. Educ:* Henry Thornton Sch., London; Imperial Coll., London (BSc). 1st cl. hons Physics, 1947; PhD 1950. Research Fellow, Imp. Coll., 1950–55; TI Res. Labs, Hinxton Hall: Res. Scientist, 1956–61; Gp Leader and Div. Head, 1962–67; Asst Dir, 1967–68; Dir, 1968–79 (also Dir of Research, TI Ltd, 1976–79); Imperial College: Hd, Dept of Materials, 1979–90; Dean, Royal Sch. of Mines, 1986–89; Mem. Governing Body, 1986–89. Mem. Council, Royal Soc., 1981–83. Rosenhain Medal, Inst. of Metals, 1968. *Publications:* (jtly) Electron Microscopy of Thin Crystals, 1965; numerous papers on electron microscopy and diffraction, thin films and epitaxy in Phil. Mag., Proc. Roy. Soc., etc. *Address:* 11 Birch Court, The Gables, Oxshott, Leatherhead, Surrey KT22 0SD. *T:* (01372) 844518; Department of Materials, Imperial College, SW7 2AZ. *Died 16 May 2009.*

PATERSON, James Veitch; Sheriff of the Lothian and Borders (formerly Roxburgh, Berwick and Selkirk) at Jedburgh, Selkirk and Duns, 1963–2000; *b* 16 April 1928; *s* of late John Robert Paterson, ophthalmic surgeon, and Jeanie Gouinlock; *m* 1st, 1956, Ailie (*d* 2003), *o d* of Lt-Comdr Sir (George) Ian Clark Hutchison, RN; one *s* (one *d* decd); 2nd, 2004, Elspeth, widow of William Marshall Colledge. *Educ:* Peebles High School; Edinburgh Academy; Lincoln College, Oxford; Edinburgh University. Admitted to Faculty of Advocates, 1953. *Recreations:* fishing, shooting, gardening. *Address:* Sunnyside, Melrose, Roxburghshire TD6 9BE. *T:* (01896) 822502. *Club:* New (Edinburgh). *Died 7 May 2010.*

PATERSON, Very Rev. John Munn Kirk; Minister Emeritus of St Paul's Parish Church, Milngavie (Minister, 1970–87); Moderator of the General Assembly of the Church of Scotland, 1984–85; *b* 8 Oct. 1922; *s* of George Kirk Paterson and Sarah Ferguson Paterson (*née* Wilson); *m* 1946, Geraldine Lilian Parker; two *s* one *d. Educ:* Hillhead High School, Glasgow; Edinburgh Univ. MA, BD. RAF, 1942–46 (Defence and Victory medals, Italy Star, 1945). Insurance Official, 1940–58 (ACII 1951); Assistant Minister, 1958–64; Ordained Minister of

Church of Scotland, 1964–. Hon. DD Aberdeen, 1986. *Recreations:* fishing, hill walking. *Club:* Royal Over-Seas League (Edinburgh). *Died 6 Aug. 2009.*

PATERSON-BROWN, Dr June, CVO 2007; CBE 1991; JP; Lord-Lieutenant of Roxburgh, Ettrick and Lauderdale, 1998–2007; Chief Commissioner, Girl Guides Association, and Commonwealth Chief Commissioner, 1985–90; *b* 8 Feb. 1932; *d* of Thomas Clarke Garden and Jean Martha (*née* Mallace); *m* 1957, Dr Peter N. Paterson-Brown; three *s* one *d. Educ:* Esdaile Sch.; Edinburgh Univ. (MB, ChB). MO in Community Health, 1960–85. Scottish Chief Comr, Girl Guides Assoc., 1977–82; Vice-Pres., Guide Assoc., 1992–; Pres., Roxburghshire, Guide Assoc., 1993–. Non-exec. Dir, Border Television, 1980–2000; Chm., Borders Children's Panel Adv. Cttee, 1982–85; Trustee: Prince's Trust, 1982–94 (Vice-Chm., 1982–92); MacRobert Trusts, 1987–2002; Chm., Scottish Standing Conf. Voluntary Youth Organisations, 1982–85. Chm. Cttee, Duke of Edinburgh's Award Scheme, Roxburgh, 1970–85. DL 1990, JP 1999, Roxburgh, Ettrick and Lauderdale. Paul Harris Fellow, Rotary Internat., 1990. Silver Jubilee Medal, 1977; Golden Jubilee Medal, 2002. *Recreations:* golfing, fishing, tennis, music, reading. *Address:* Norwood, Hawick, Roxburghshire TD9 7HR. *T:* (01450) 372352. *Club:* Lansdowne. *Died 6 Dec. 2009.*

PATHAK, Raghunandan Swarup; Member: Indian Council of Arbitration, since 1991; Permanent Court of Arbitration, The Hague, since 1997; *b* 25 Nov. 1924; *s* of Gopal Swarup Pathak and Prakashwati; *m* 1955, Asha Paranjpe; three *s. Educ:* St Joseph's Coll., Allahabad; Ewing Christian Coll., Allahabad; Allahabad Univ. (BSc 1945; LLB 1947, MA (Pol. Sci.) 1948; Sastri Medal in Internat. Law, 1947). Enrolled Advocate: Allahabad High Court, 1948; Supreme Court of India, 1957; Additional Judge, 1962, Judge, 1963, Allahabad High Court; Chief Justice, Himachal Pradesh High Court, 1972; Judge, Supreme Court of India, 1978; Chief Justice of India, 1986–89; Judge, Internat. Court of Justice, The Hague, 1989–91. Chm., All India Univ. Professors' Internat. Law Res. Gp, 1969–89; Visitor, Nat. Law Sch. of India, Bangalore, 1986–89; Pro-Chancellor, Univ. of Delhi, 1986–89; Distinguished Vis. Prof., Inst. of Advanced Studies in the Humanities, Edinburgh Univ. President: Indian Law Inst., 1986–89; Indian Council of Legal Aid and Advice; Indian Soc. of Internat. Law, 1989–93; International Law Association, London: Mem., 1952–; Pres., India Regl Br., 1986–89; Mem., Cttee on Space Law, and Cttee on Enforcement of Human Rights; Vice-Pres., Indian Acad. of Environmental Law and Research; Pres., Centre for Res. on Envmt, Ecol. and Develt, New Delhi, 1995–. Chairman: World Congress on Law and Medicine, New Delhi, 1985; Indian Nat. Steering Cttee, Leadership in Envmt and Develt Prog., 1991–; Indian Nat. Cttee for Promotion of Social and Economic Welfare; Sarvodaya Internat. Trust, Bangalore. Member: Indo-Soviet Internat. Law Confs; Indo-W German Internat. Law Colloquia; UN Univ. project on Internat. Law, Common Patrimony and Intergenerational Equity; UN Univ. project on Internat. Law and Global Change, 1989; UN High-level Adv. Bd on Sustainable Develt, 1993–95. Hon. Mem., Indian Social Security Foundn Mem., Internat. Council of Arbitration for Sport, 1994–; Court of Arbitration for Sport *ad hoc* Division: Co-Pres., Olympic Games, Atlanta, 1996, Nagano, 1998, Sydney, 2000; Pres., Commonwealth Games, Kuala Lumpur, 1998, Winter Olympic Games, Salt Lake City, 2002. Pres., Nehru Trust for Indian Collections at V&A Mus. (London), India, 1991–; Trustee, Bd of Trustees, The Tribune, Chandigarh, 1994– (Pres., 2002–). Mem. Exec. Council, Univ. of Delhi. Lectured worldwide on human rights, envmtl law and sustainable develt, commercial arbitration, constitutional law, internat. law. Hon. Bencher, Gray's Inn, 1988. Hon. LLD: Agra; Panjab; Hon. DLitt Kashi Vidyapeeth, Varanasi. *Publications:* papers on internat. law, law of the sea, etc, in learned jls. *Recreations:* golf, photography. *Address:* 7 Sardar Patel

Marg, New Delhi 110021, India. *T:* (11) 3017161, *Fax:* (11) 3017170. *Clubs:* Delhi Gymkhana, India International Centre, Delhi Golf (New Delhi).
Died 17 Nov. 2007.

PATTINSON, Rev. Sir (William) Derek, Kt 1990; Secretary-General, General Synod of Church of England, 1972–90; *b* 31 March 1930; *s* of late Thomas William and Elizabeth Pattinson; partner, Barnaby Miln. *Educ:* Whitehaven Grammar Sch.; Queen's Coll., Oxford (Stanhope Historical Essay Prize, 1951; BA 1952; MA 1956); St Deiniol's Liby, Hawarden; Coll. of Resurrection, Mirfield. Entered Home Civil Service, 1952; Inland Revenue Dept, 1952–62 and 1965–68; HM Treasury, 1962–65 and 1968–70; Assoc. Sec.-Gen., General Synod, 1970–72. Chm., William Temple Assoc., 1966–70; Member: Archbishops' Commn on Church and State, 1966–70; British Council of Churches, 1972–90; London Diocesan Synod, 1972–91. Ordained deacon, 1991, priest, 1992; Asst Curate, St Gabriel's Pimlico, 1991–2000. Principal, Soc. of the Faith, 1992–2001. Vice-Chm., Grosvenor Chapel Cttee, 1973–81; Vice-Pres., SPCK; Chm. of Governors, Liddon House, 1972–2001; Chm., English Friends of Anglican Centre in Rome, 1985–2001; Gov., Sir John Cass Foundn, 1973–92; Vice Chm., Greycoat Hosp., 1988–97. Freeman, City of London, 1973; Mem., Parish Clerks' Co. (Master, 1986–87). Member: Alcuin Club; Nikaean Club. Parish Clerk, St Luke's, Old Street, 1972–; Churchwarden, St Michael's Cornhill, 1988–91. *Address:* 48 Boundary Road, NW8 0HJ. *T:* (020) 7644 2930.
Died 10 Oct. 2006.

PAUL, Hugh Glencairn B.; *see* Balfour-Paul.

PAUL, Rev. Canon John Douglas; Dean of Moray, Ross and Caithness, 1991–92; *b* 13 Sept. 1928; *s* of George Anson Moncreiff Paul and Vivian (*née* Ward); *m* 1969, Mary Susan Melody Woodhouse. *Educ:* Winchester Coll.; Edinburgh Univ. (MA); Ely Theol Coll. Asst Curate, Portsmouth, 1954–56; Missionary Priest, Mozambique, 1956–70; Archdeacon, Mozambique, 1965–70; Rector: Castle Douglas, 1970–75; Portobello, 1975–80; Holy Trinity, Elgin, with St Margaret's, Lossiemouth, 1980–92. Hon. Canon and Synod Clerk, Dio. of Moray, Ross and Caithness, 1989–91; Hon. Canon, St Andrew's Cathedral, Inverness, 1992–. *Publications:* Mozambique: Memoirs of a Revolution, 1975. *Recreation:* travel. *Address:* 2 The Avenue, Gifford EH41 4QX. *T:* (01620) 810547. *Club:* Royal Scots (Edinburgh). *Died 23 Sept. 2009.*

PAUL, Robert Cameron, CBE 1996; FREng; Chief Executive, Albright & Wilson plc, 1995–97; *b* 7 July 1935; *s* of late Dr F. W. Paul, MB, ChB, and Maureen K. Paul (*née* Cameron); *m* 1st, 1965, Diana Kathleen Bruce (*d* 2001); two *d*; 2nd, 2003, Catherine Frances Young. *Educ:* Rugby Sch.; Corpus Christi Coll., Cambridge (BA 1958; MEng 1992); UCL (Dip Astronomy 2006). Nat. Service. 2nd Lieut RE, 1953–55. Chemical Engineer, ICI, Runcorn, 1959; Dir, ICI Fibres, 1976; Dep. Chm., Mond Div., ICI, 1979; Dep. Chm. and Man. Dir, Albright & Wilson, 1986–95. Non-exec. Dir, Courtaulds plc, 1994–98. President: IChemE, 1990–91; Chemical Industries Assoc., 1995–97. FREng (FEng 1990); FRAS 2006. Hon. DEng Birmingham, 1990. *Recreations:* music (piano), astronomy. *Address:* 2 Devonshire Place, Kensington, W8 5UD. *Died 23 Sept. 2008.*

PAUNCEFORT, Bernard Edward, OBE 1983; HM Diplomatic Service, retired 1986; Administrator, Tristan da Cunha, South Atlantic, 1989–92; *b* 8 April 1926; *o s* of Frederick George Pauncefort and Eleanor May (*née* Jux); *m* 1956, Patricia Anne (*d* 2004), *yr d* of Charles Ernest Leah and Alice (*née* Kendal-Banks). *Educ:* Wandsworth School. RAFVR 1942–44; transf. and commnd into Royal Fusiliers (service in Egypt and Palestine), 1944–48. Metropolitan Police Civil Staff, 1948–53; HM Colonial Service, 1953; Malaya, 1953–56; Tanganyika, 1956–63; CRO, 1963–67; First Sec., Zambia, 1967–68; Consul, Cape Town, 1969–72; Lord

Pearce's staff, Rhodesia, 1971–72; Head of Chancery, Madagascar, 1972–73; FCO, 1973–76; Sec. to Seychelles Electoral Review Commn, 1976; Head of Chancery, Burma, 1976–78; Dir, British Inf. Services, S Africa. 1978–80; Lord Soames' staff, Rhodesia–Zimbabwe, 1979–80; Administrator, Ascension Island, 1980–82; FCO, 1982–83; Counsellor and Chief Sec., Falkland Is, 1983–85; Counsellor, FCO, 1985–86; Under-Sec., Govt of the Turks & Caicos Is, W Indies, 1986–88. Zimbabwe Medal, 1980. *Recreations:* dogs, birds, waterways. *Address:* 10 New Church Road, Uphill, Weston-super-Mare BS23 4UY. *Died 14 July 2010.*

PAVAROTTI, Luciano; Italian tenor; *b* 12 Oct. 1935; *s* of late Fernando Pavarotti and Adele (*née* Venturi); *m* 1961, Adua Veroni (marr. diss. 2001); three *d*; *m* 2003, Nicoletta Mantovani; one *d* (one (twin) *s* decd). *Educ:* Istituto Magistrale. Teacher, 1955–57. Professional début, Teatro Municipale, Reggio Emilia, 1961; sang throughout Europe, 1961–64; US début and Australian tour 1965; rôles include Rodolfo in La Bohème, Cavaradossi in Tosca, Duke of Mantua in Rigoletto, Radames in Aïda, Ernani, Alfredo in La Traviata, Manrico in Il Trovatore, Rodolfo in Luisa Miller, Arturo in I Puritani, Elvino in La Sonnambula, Nemorino in L'Elisir d'Amore, Idomeneo, Enzo in La Gioconda, Riccardo (Gustavo) in Un Ballo in Maschera, Don Carlos, Chevalier des Grieux in Manon. Grammy Award for best classical vocal soloist, 1978, 1979, 1981, 1988, 1990. *Publications:* (jtly) Pavarotti: my own story, 1981; Grandissimo Pavarotti, 1986; (jtly) Pavarotti: My World, 1995. *Address:* c/o Terri Robson, 63–64 Leinster Square, W2 4PS. *Died 6 Sept. 2007.*

PAYNE, Rev. James Richmond, MBE 1982; ThL; General Secretary, Bible Society in Australia, 1968–88; Chairman, United Bible Societies World Executive Committee, 1976–88; *b* 1 June 1921; *s* of late R. A. Payne, Sydney, New South Wales; *m* 1943, Joan *d* of late C. S. Elliott; three *s*. *Educ:* Drummoyne High School; Metropolitan Business College, Moore Theological College, Sydney. Served War of 1939–45: AIF, 1941–44. Catechist, St Michael's, Surry Hills, NSW, 1944–47; Curate, St Andrew's, Lismore, NSW, 1947–50; Rector, St Mark's, Nimbin, NSW, 1950–52; Chaplain, RAAF, Malta and Amberley, Qld, 1952–57; Rector, St Stephen's, Coorparoo, Qld, 1957–62; Dean of Perth, Western Australia, 1962–68. Hon. Commissary in Australia for Anglican Bp of Central Tanganyika, E Africa, 1988–. JP, ACT, 1969. *Publications:* Around the World in Seventy Days, 1965; And Now for the Good News, 1982. *Recreations:* sport, walking, reading, family. *Address:* 10/42 Jinka Street, Hawker, ACT 2614. Australia. *T:* (2) 62546722. *Died 26 Jan. 2008.*

PAYNE, Sir Norman (John), Kt 1985; CBE 1976 (OBE 1956; MBE (mil.) 1944); FREng; Chairman, BAA plc (formerly British Airports Authority), 1977–91 (Chief Executive, 1972–77); *b* 9 Oct. 1921; *s* of late F. Payne, Folkestone; *m* 1946, Pamela Vivien Wallis (separated; she *d* 2006); four *s* one *d*. *Educ:* John Lyon Sch., Harrow; City and Guilds Coll., London. BSc Eng Hons. FCGI, FICE, FCIT; FREng (FEng 1984). Royal Engrs (Captain), 1939–45 (despatches twice); Imperial Coll. of Science and Technology London (Civil), 1946–49; Sir Frederick Snow & Partners, 1949, Partner 1955; British Airports Authority: Dir of Engrg, 1965; Dir of Planning, 1969, and Mem. Bd 1971. Pres., West European Airports Assoc., 1975–77; Chairman: Airports Assoc. Co-ordinating Council, 1976; Aerodrome Owners' Assoc., 1983–84. Chm., British Sect., Centre for European Public Enterprise, 1979–82. Chm., NICG, 1982–83; Comr. Manpower Services Commn, 1983–85. Pres., CIT, 1984–85. CBIM (FBIM 1975); RAeS 1987. FIC 1989; FRSA 1990. Hon. FIStructE, 1988; Hon. FR.IBA 1991. Hon. DTech Loughborough, 1985. *Publications:* various papers on airports and air transport. *Address:* L'Abri, La route des Merriennes, St Martin, Guernsey, CI GY4 6NS. *Died 7 Feb. 2010.*

PAYNE-GALLWEY, Sir Philip (Frankland), 6th Bt *cr* 1812; Director, British Bloodstock Agency plc, 1968–97; *b* 15 March 1935; *s* of late Lt-Col Lowry Philip Payne-Gallwey, OBE, MC and Janet (*d* 1996), *d* of late Albert Philip Payne-Gallwey; *S* cousin, 1964. *Educ:* Eton; Royal Military Academy, Sandhurst. Lieut, 11th Hussars, 1957. *Recreations:* hunting, shooting, golf. *Heir:* none. *Address:* The Little House, Boxford, Newbury, Berks RG20 8DP. *T:* (01488) 608315; 160 Cranmer Court, Whiteheads Grove, SW3 3HF. *T:* (020) 7589 4231. *Clubs:* Cavalry and Guards, White's. *Died 3 Feb. 2008 (ext).*

PAYNTER, Prof. John Frederick, OBE 1985; Professor of Music, 1982–97, and Head of Department of Music, 1983–94, University of York, then Professor Emeritus; *b* 17 July 1931; *s* of late Frederick Albert Paynter and Rose Alice Paynter; *m* 1st, 1956, Elizabeth Hill (*d* 1998); one *d*; 2nd, 2003, Joan Minnetta Burrows (*née* Lee). *Educ:* Emanuel Sch., London; Trinity Coll. of Music, London (GTCL 1952). DPhil York, 1971. Teaching appts, primary and secondary schs, 1954–62; Lectr in Music, City of Liverpool C. F. Mott Coll. of Educn, 1962–65; Principal Lectr (Head of Dept of Music), Bishop Otter Coll., Chichester, 1965–69; Lectr, Dept of Music, Univ. of York, 1969, Sen. Lectr, 1974–82. Composer and writer on music-educn. Dir, Schs Council Proj., Music in the Secondary School Curriculum, 1973–82. Gen. Editor, series, Resources of Music, 1969–93; Jt Editor, British Jl of Music Educn, 1984–97. FRSA 1987. Hon. GSM 1985. Leslie Boosey Award, Royal Philharmonic Soc./PRS, 1998. *Publications:* (with Peter Aston) Sound and Silence, 1970; Hear and Now, 1972; (with Elizabeth Paynter) The Dance and the Drum, 1974; All Kinds of Music, vols 1–3, 1976, vol. 4, 1979; Sound Tracks, 1978; Music in the Secondary School Curriculum: trends and developments in class music teaching, 1982; Sound and Structure, 1992; Thinking and Making, 2008; editor and contributor to: A Companion to Contemporary Musical Thought, 1992; Between Old Worlds and New: occasional writings on music by Wilfrid Mellers, 1997; contributor to: How Music Works, 1981; Musik og Skola, 1981; Musikalische Erfahrung: Wahrnehmen, Erkennen, Aneignen, 1992; Zwischen Aufklärung & Kulturindustrie, 1993; Music Education: international viewpoints, 1994; Mellers at 80/Popular Music, 1994; Powers of Being: David Holbrook and his work, 1995; Settling the Score, 1999; articles in Internat. Jl of Music Educn, British Jl of Music Educn, La Discussione, Popular Music, Música Arte y Proceso, beQuadro, Musica Domani, Psychol. of Music; scripts and commentaries for radio and TV; *musical compositions:* choral and instrumental works including: Landscapes, 1972; The Windhover, 1972; May Magnificat, 1973; God's Grandeur, 1975; Sacraments of Summer, 1975; Galaxies for Orchestra, 1977; The Voyage of St Brendan, 1978; The Visionary Hermit, 1979; The Inviolable Voice, 1980; String Quartet no 1, 1981; Cantata for the Waking of Lazarus, 1981; The Laughing Stone, 1982; Contrasts for Orchestra, 1982; Variations for Orchestra and Audience, 1983; Conclaves, 1984; Piano Sonata, 1987; Time After Time, 1991; String Quartet no 2, 1991; Four Sculptures of Austin Wright (for solo viola and orch.), 1991–94; Melting (for solo piano), 1997; Holding On (for viola and piano), 1998; Breakthrough (double piano duet), 2000; Memorials (unacc. choir), 2000; Ouverture d'Urgence (double piano duet), 2002; Binsey Poplars (voice and prepared piano), 2004; The Habit of Perfection (voice and piano), 2004; Of Time and Place (soprano, recorder and piano), 2004; Sequela (recorder and optional percussion), 2004; Inscape (unacc. choir), 2005; When the Time Comes (piano), 2007; The Oxen (choir and piano), 2007. *Died 1 July 2010.*

PEACOCKE, Rev. Canon Arthur Robert, MBE 1993; DSc, ScD, DD; SOSc; Hon. Canon, Christ Church Cathedral, Oxford, 1995–2004, then Canon Emeritus (Hon. Chaplain, 1988–96 and 2001–04); Director, Ian Ramsey Centre, Oxford, 1985–88, and 1995–99; *b* 29 Nov. 1924; *s* of Arthur Charles Peacocke and Rose Elizabeth (*née* Lilly); *m* 1948, Rosemary Winifred Mann; one *s* one *d*. *Educ:* Watford Grammar Sch.; Exeter Coll., Oxford (Scholar; BA Chem., BSc 1946; MA, DPhil 1948); DSc Oxon, 1962; ScD Cantab (incorp.), 1973; DD Oxon, 1982; DipTh 1960, BD 1971, Birmingham. Asst Lectr, Lectr and Sen. Lectr in Biophys. Chemistry, Univ. of Birmingham, 1948–59; Lectr in Biochem., Oxford Univ., and Fellow and Tutor in Chem., subseq. in Biochem., St Peter's Coll., 1959–73; Lectr in Chem., Mansfield Coll., Oxford, 1964–73; Dean and Fellow, Clare Coll., Cambridge, 1973–84; Fellow, St Cross Coll., 1985–88; Catechist, Exeter Coll., Oxford, 1989–93. Rockefeller Fellow, Univ. of Calif at Berkeley, and Univ. of Wis, 1951–52; Vis. Fellow, Weizmann Inst., Israel, 1956; Prof. of Judeo-Christian Studies, Tulane Univ., 1984; J. K. Russell Fellow in Religion and Science, Center for Theology and Natural Sci., Berkeley, 1986; Royden Davis Prof., Georgetown Univ., 1994; Select Preacher, Oxford Univ., 1973, 1985; Hulsean Preacher, Cambridge Univ., 1976; Lectures: Bampton, Oxford Univ., 1978; Bishop Williams Meml, Rikkyo (St Paul's) Univ., Japan, 1981; Shann, Univ. of Hong Kong, 1982; Mendenhall, DePauw Univ., Indiana, 1983; McNair, Univ. of N Carolina, 1984; Nina Booth Bricker Meml, Tulane Univ., 1986, 1989; Norton, Southern Baptist Seminary, Louisville, 1986; Sprigg, Virginia Theol Seminary, 1987; Rolf Buchdahl, N Carolina State Univ., 1987; Drawbridge, KCL, 1987; Alister Hardy Meml, 1989; Gifford, St Andrews Univ., 1993; Idreos, Oxford, 1997; Witherspoon, Princeton Center of Theol Inquiry, 1999; Washington Univ., 2002. Lay Reader, Oxford Dio., 1960–71; ordained, 1971; Mem., Archbps' Commn on Christian Doctrine, 1969–76 (Mem. sub-gp on Man and Nature, 1972–74); Chm., Science and Religion Forum, 1972–78 (Vice-Pres., 1981–95, Hon. Pres., 1995–2001), Vice Pres, Inst, of Religion in an Age of Science, USA, 1984–87 (Academic Fellow, 1987); Warden, SOSc, 1987–92, then Emeritus. Judge, Templeton Foundn Prize, 1979–82. Meetings Sec., Sec. and Chm., Brit. Biophys. Soc., 1965–69. Mem. Editorial Bd, Biochem. Jl, and Biopolymers, 1966–71, Zygon, 1973–; Editor, Monographs in Physical Biochemistry (OUP), 1967–82. Hon. Fellow, St Peter's Coll., Oxford, 2005; Hon. DSc DePauw Univ., Indiana, 1983; Hon. DLitHum Georgetown Univ., Washington, 1991. Lecomte du Noüy Prize, 1973; Templeton Prize for Progress in Religion, 2001. *Publications:* Molecular Basis of Heredity (with J. B. Drysdale), 1965 (repr. 1967); Science and the Christian Experiment, 1971; (with M. P. Tombs) Osmotic Pressure of Biological Macromolecules, 1974; (with J. Dominian) From Cosmos to Love, 1977; Creation and the World of Science, 1979, 2nd edn 2004; (ed) The Sciences and Theology in the Twentieth Century, 1982; The Physical Chemistry of Biological Organization, 1983; Intimations of Reality, 1984; (ed) Reductionism in Academic Disciplines, 1985; God and the New Biology, 1986; (ed with G. Gillett) Persons and Personality, 1987; (ed with S. Andersen) Evolution and Creation: a European perspective, 1987; Theology for a Scientific Age, 1990, new edn 1993 (Templeton Prize, 1995); (ed with R. Russell and N. Murphy) Chaos and Complexity, 1995; From DNA to Dean, 1996; God and Science, 1996; Paths from Science towards God, 2001; The Palace of Glory: God's world and science, 2005; (with Ann Pederson) The Music of Creation, 2005; articles and papers in scientific and theol jls, and symposia vols. *Recreations:* piano, music, visual arts, churches. *Address:* 55 St John Street, Oxford OX1 2LQ; Exeter College, Oxford OX1 3DP. *T:* (01865) 512041, *Fax:* (01865) 554791; *e-mail:* arthur.peacocke@theology.oxford.ac.uk. *Died 21 Oct. 2006.*

PEARCE, (Ann) Philippa, (Mrs M. J. G. Christie), OBE 1997; freelance writer of children's fiction, since 1967; *b* 23 , Jan. 1920; *d* of Ernest Alexander Pearce and Gertrude Alice (*née* Ramsden); *m* 1963, Martin James Graham Christie (*d* 1965); one *d*. *Educ:* Perse Girls' Sch., Cambridge; Girton Coll., Cambridge (MA Hons English Pt I, History Pt II). Temp. civil servant, 1942–45;

Producer/Scriptwriter, Sch. Broadcasting, BBC Radio, 1945–58; Editor, Educn Dept, Clarendon Press, 1958–60; Children's Editor, André Deutsch Ltd, 1960–67. Also lectures. FRSL 1994. Hon. DLitt Hull, 1995. *Publications:* Minnow on the Say, 1955 (3rd edn 1974); Tom's Midnight Garden, 1958 (3rd edn 1976; Carnegie Medal, 1959; filmed and staged, 2000); Mrs Cockle's Cat, 1961 (2nd edn 1974); A Dog So Small, 1962 (2nd edn 1964); (with Sir Harold Scott) From Inside Scotland Yard, 1963; The Strange Sunflower, 1966; (with Sir Brian Fairfax-Lucy) The Children of the House, 1968 (2nd edn 1970) (reissued as The Children of Charlecote, 1989); The Elm Street Lot, 1969 (enlarged edn, 1979); The Squirrel Wife, 1971 (2nd edn 1992); What the Neighbours Did and other stories, 1972 (2nd edn 1974); (ed) Stories from Hans Christian Andersen, 1972; Beauty and the Beast (re-telling), 1972; The Shadow Cage and other stories of the supernatural, 1977; The Battle of Bubble and Squeak, 1978 (Whitbread Award, 1978); Wings of Courage (trans. and adapted from George Sand's story), 1982; The Way to Sattin Shore, 1983; Lion at School and other stories, 1985; Who's Afraid? and other strange stories, 1986; The Toothball, 1987; Emily's Own Elephant, 1987; Freddy, 1988; Old Belle's Summer Holiday, 1989; Here comes Tod, 1992; (ed) Dread and Delight: a century of children's ghost stories (anthology), 1995; The Little White Hen, 1996; The Rope and other stories, 2000; The Ghost in Annie's Room, 2001; Amy's Three Best Things, 2003; The Little Gentleman, 2004; reviews in TLS and Guardian. *Address:* c/o Penguin Children's Books, 80 Strand, WC2R 0RL.   *Died 21 Dec. 2006.*

PEARCE, Howard Spencer; Director for Wales, Property Services Agency, Department of Environment, 1977–85; *b* 23 Sept. 1924; *s* of Ivor Stanley Pearce and Evelyn Pearce; *m* 1951, Enid Norma Richards (*d* 1994); one *s*. *Educ:* Barry County Sch.; College of Estate Management. MRICS. Armed Services, Major RE, 1943–47. Ministry of Works: Cardiff, 1953–61; Salisbury Plain, 1961–64; Ministry of Public Building and Works: Sen. Quantity Surveyor, Hong Kong, 1964–67, Abingdon, 1967–70; Area Officer, Abingdon, 1970–72; Regional Works Officer, SW Region, Bristol, PSA, Dept of Environment, 1972–77. *Recreations:* music, playing golf and watching Rugby football. *Address:* 2 Longhouse Close, Lisvane, Cardiff CF14 0XR. *T:* (029) 2076 2029. *Club:* Cardiff Golf.   *Died 30 May 2006.*

PEARCE, Philippa; see Pearce, A. P.

PEARS, David Francis, FBA 1970; Student of Christ Church, Oxford, 1960–88, then Emeritus; Professor of Philosophy, Oxford University, 1985–88; *b* 8 Aug. 1921; *s* of late Robert and Gladys Pears; *m* 1963, Anne Drew; one *s* one *d*. *Educ:* Westminster Sch.; Balliol Coll., Oxford. Research Lecturer, Christ Church, 1948–50; Univ. Lectr, Oxford, 1950–72; Reader, 1972–85; Fellow and Tutor, Corpus Christi Coll., 1950–60. Visiting Professor: Harvard, 1959; Univ. of Calif, Berkeley, 1964; Rockefeller Univ., 1967; UCLA, 1979; Hill Prof., Univ. of Minnesota, 1970; Humanities Council Res. Fellow, Princeton, 1966. Mem., l'Institut Internat. de Philosophie, 1978– (Prés., 1988–90); For. Corresp. Fellow, Amer. Acad. of Arts and Scis, 1998. *Publications:* (trans. with B. McGuinness), Wittgenstein, Tractatus Logico-Philosophicus, 1961, repr. 1975; Bertrand Russell and the British Tradition in Philosophy, 1967, 2nd edn 1972; Ludwig Wittgenstein, 1971; What is Knowledge?, 1971; (ed) Russell's Logical Atomism, 1973; Some Questions in the Philosophy of Mind, 1975; Motivated Irrationality, 1984; The False Prison: a study of the development of Wittgenstein's philosophy, vol. I, 1987, vol. II, 1988; Hume's System, 1990; Paradox and Platitude in Wittgenstein's Philosophy, 2006. *Address:* 7 Sandford Road, Littlemore, Oxford OX4 4PU. *T:* (01865) 778768.   *Died 1 July 2009.*

PEARSON, Derek Leslie, CB 1978; Deputy Secretary, Overseas Development Administration (formerly Ministry of Overseas Development), 1977–81; *b* 19 Dec. 1921; *s* of late George Frederick Pearson and Edith Maud

Pearson (*née* Dent); *m* 1956, Diana Mary (*d* 2005), *d* of late Sir Ralph Freeman; no *c*. *Educ:* William Ellis Sch.; London Sch. of Economics (BSc (Econ)). Served War of 1939–45; Lieut (A) (O) RNVR and subseq. Channel Air Div.; Lt-Comdr (A) RNVR, 1956. Colonial Office, 1947; seconded to Kenya, 1954–56; Principal Private Sec. to Sec. of State for Colonies, 1959–61; Dept of Technical Cooperation, 1961; Asst Sec., 1962; ODM, 1964; Under Secretary: CSD, 1970–72; Min. of Overseas Develt, 1972–75; Dep. Sec., Cabinet Office, 1975–77. *Address:* Langata, Little London Road, Horam, Heathfield, East Sussex TN21 0BG. *Clubs:* Naval, Civil Service.   *Died 14 Oct. 2009.*

PEARSON, Captain John William, CBE 1981; Regional Administrator, Mersey Regional Health Authority, 1977–81; *b* 19 Sept. 1920; *s* of Walter and Margaret Jane Pearson; *m* 1945, Audrey Ethel Whitehead; two *s*. *Educ:* Holloway Sch. FCIS, FHA, FCCA, IPFA. Served War, RA (Field), 1939–46. Hospital Service, LCC, 1947–48; NW Metropolitan Regional Hosp. Bd, 1948–49; Northern Gp, HMC, Finance Officer, 1949–62; Treasurer: St Thomas' Bd of Governors, 1962–73; Mersey Regional Health Authority, 1973–77. Pres., Assoc. of Health Service Treasurers, 1970–71. *Recreations:* tennis, golf, gardening, snooker. *Address:* 20 Weare Gifford, Shoeburyness, Essex SS3 8AB. *T:* (01702) 585039.   *Died 10 May 2009.*

PEASE, Sir (Alfred) Vincent, 4th Bt *cr* 1882; *b* 2 April 1926; *s* of Sir Alfred (Edward) Pease, 2nd Bt (*d* 1939), and his 3rd wife, Emily Elizabeth Pease (*d* 1979); *S* half-brother, 1963; unmarried. *Educ:* Bootham School, York; Durham Sch. of Agric., Houghall. *Heir: b* Joseph Gurney Pease [*b* 16 Nov. 1927; *m* 1953, Shelagh Munro, *d* of C. G. Bulman; one *s* one *d*]. *Address:* The Roseberry, Flatts Lane, Nunthorpe, Middlesbrough, Cleveland TS7 0PQ. *T:* (01287) 636453.   *Died 23 Sept. 2008.*

PEASE, Robert John Claude; HM Diplomatic Service, retired; Counsellor (Administration) and Consul-General, British Embassy, Moscow, 1977–80; *b* 24 April 1922; *s* of Frederick Robert Hellier Pease and Eileen Violet Pease (*née* Beer); *m* 1945, Claire Margaretta Whall; one *s* two *d*. *Educ:* Cattedown Road Sch., Plymouth; Sutton High Sch., Plymouth. Served War of 1939–45; Telegraphist, RN, 1942; commnd Sub Lt RNVR, 1944. Clerk, Lord Chancellor's Dept, Plymouth County Court, 1939, Truro County Court, 1946; Foreign Office, 1948; Moscow, 1952; HM Consul, Sarajevo, 1954; 2nd Sec., Bangkok, 1958; HM Consul, Gdynia, 1959, Düsseldorf, 1961; 1st Sec., Pretoria, 1964, Bombay, 1966; FCO, 1969; Dep. High Commissioner, Mauritius, 1973. *Recreations:* golf, opera. *Address:* Palmetto, Kiln Close, Prestwood, Bucks HP16 9DJ.   *Died 14 Sept. 2010.*

PEASE, Sir Vincent; see Pease, Sir A. V.

PECK, His Honour David (Edward); a Circuit Judge (formerly Judge of County Courts), 1969–85; *b* 6 April 1917; *m* 1st, 1950, Rosina Seton Glover Marshall (marr. diss.); one *s* three *d*; 2nd, 1973, Frances Deborah Redford (*née* Mackenzie) (marr. diss.); one *s*; 3rd, 1983, Elizabeth Charlotte Beale (*née* Boost). *Educ:* Charterhouse School; Balliol College, Oxford. Served Army (Cheshire Regiment), 1939–46. Called to Bar, Middle Temple, 1949. Mem., County Court Rule Cttee, 1978–84 (Chm., 1981–84); Jt Editor, County Court Practice, 1982–90. *Address:* 2/3 Gray's Inn Square, WC1R 5JH.   *Died 22 Dec. 2007.*

PECK, Sir Edward (Heywood), GCMG 1974 (KCMG 1966; CMG 1957); HM Diplomatic Service, retired; *b* 5 Oct. 1915; *s* of Lt-Col Edward Surman Peck, IMS, and Doris Louise Heywood; *m* 1948, Alison Mary MacInnes (*d* 2009); one *s* two *d* (and one *d* decd). *Educ:* Clifton College; The Queen's College, Oxford. 1st Cl. Hons (Mod. Langs), 1937; Laming Travelling Fellow, 1937–38. Entered Consular Service, 1938; served in Barcelona, 1938–39; Foreign Office, 1939–40; Sofia, 1940; Ankara, 1940–44; Adana, 1944; Iskenderun, 1945; Salonica,

1945–47; with UK Deleg. to UN Special Commn on the Balkans, 1947; Foreign Office, 1947–50; seconded to UK High Commissioner's Office, Delhi, 1950–52; Counsellor, Foreign Office, 1952–55; Dep. Comdt, Brit. Sector, Berlin, 1955–58; on staff of UK Commissioner-General for S-E Asia, 1959–60; Assistant Under-Secretary of State, Foreign Office, 1961–66; British High Commissioner in Kenya, 1966–68; Dep. Under-Secretary of State, FCO, 1968–70; British Perm. Rep. to N Atlantic Council, 1970–75. Dir, Outward Bound (Loch Eil), 1976–90; Mem. Council, Nat. Trust for Scotland, 1982–87. Hon. Vis. Fellow in Defence Studies, Aberdeen Univ., 1976–85. Hon. LLD Aberdeen, 1997. *Publications:* North-East Scotland (Bartholomew's Guides Series), 1981; Avonside Explored, 1983; The Battle of Glenlivet, 1994. *Recreations:* hill-walking, travel, reading history. *Address:* Easter Torrans, Tomintoul, Banffshire AB37 9HJ. *Club:* Alpine.   *Died 24 July 2009.*

PEDDIE, Peter Charles, CBE 1983; Adviser to the Governor, and Head of Legal Unit, Bank of England, 1992–96; *b* 20 March 1932; *s* of Ronald Peddie and Vera Peddie (*née* Nicklin); *m* 1960, Charlotte Elizabeth Ryan; two *s* two *d*. *Educ:* Canford Sch., Wimborne; St John's Coll., Cambridge (BA 1954; MA 1977). Admitted Solicitor, 1957; Freshfields: articled, 1954–57; Asst Solicitor, 1957–60; Partner, 1960–92; Consultant, 1992. Mem., Standing Cttee on Company Law, Law Soc., 1972–92. Mem. Council, Middlesex Hosp. Med. Sch., 1977–88; Special Trustee, Middlesex Hosp., 1977–92. Gov., Canford Sch., 1981–94. Hon. QC 1997. *Recreations:* gardening, foreign travel. *Address:* Bannisters Farmhouse, Mattingley Green, Hook, Hants RG27 8LA. *T:* (0118) 932 6570. *Clubs:* Athenæum, City of London.   *Died 3 Feb. 2009.*

PEDELTY, Sir Mervyn (Kay), Kt 2005; FCA, FCIB; Chief Executive: Co-operative Bank, 1997–2004; Co-operative Insurance Society, 2002–04 (Director, 1998–2004); Co-operative Financial Services, 2002–04; *b* 16 Jan. 1949; *s* of late William Hopper Pedelty and Muriel Pedelty; *m* 1st, 1983, Carol (decd); 2nd, 1988, Jill Wesson (*née* Hughes); one *s*, and one step *d*. *Educ:* Felixstowe GS; AMP, Harvard Business Sch. ACA 1971, FCA 1976. Scrutton, Goodchild & Sanderson, 1966–71; Whinney Murray & Co., 1971–73; British Leyland Ltd, 1973–76; Divl Finance Dir, 1976–80, Divl Man. Dir, 1980, Plantation Hldgs, then Phicom plc; Divl Man. Dir, Gould Inc., 1981–83; Finance Dir and Asst Man. Dir, Abacus Electronics Hldgs plc, 1983–87; Finance Dir, TSB Banking and Insurance, 1987–92; Chief Exec., Commercial Ops, TSB Gp plc, 1992–95; Partner, LEK Consulting LLP, 1995–97. Dir and Dep. Chm., Unity Trust Bank plc, 1997–2004; Exec. Cttee, Co-operative Gp (CWS) Ltd, 1997–2004. Non-executive Director: Hiscox plc, 2005–06; Hiscox Insurance Co. Ltd, 2005–; Hiscox plc (incorp. Bermuda), 2006–; Friends Provident plc, 2006– (Chm., 2009–); Sen. Advr, Permira Advrs LLP, 2005–. Member: The Co-operative Commn, 2000–02; Employer Task Force on Pensions, DWP, 2003–05. Chairman: Sustainability NW, 1998–2003; Manchester Investment and Development Agency Service, 1999–2003; FTSE4Good Policy Cttee, 2001–; Manchester Enterprises Ltd, 2002–05 (Dir, 2000–); Dep. Chm., NW Business Leadership Team, 1997–2005. Vice-Pres., Community Foundn for Gtr Manchester, 2000–05. Mem., Chief Exec.'s Cttee, BBA, 1999–2005; Director: BITC, 2002–07; ABI, 2003–05. Trustee: Triumph over Phobia, 1995–; Symphony Hall, Birmingham, subseq. Performances Birmingham, 1996–. FCIB 1992; FRSA 1997. Freeman, City of London, 1996; Liveryman, Tin Plate Workers' Alias Wire Workers' Co., 1997; Mem., Guild of Internat. Bankers, 2002. *Recreations:* charity and community work, the countryside and the environment, music, art, ski-ing. *Address:* PO Box 50416, London, W8 7YU. *Club:* Royal Automobile.   *Died 26 Jan. 2010.*

PEEK, Vice-Adm. Sir Richard (Innes), KBE 1972 (OBE 1944); CB 1971; DSC 1945; *b* 30 July 1914; 2nd *s* of late James Norman and Kate Ethel Peek; *m* 1943,

Margaret Seinor (*née* Kendall) (*d* 1946); one *s*; *m* 1952, Mary Catherine Tilley (*née* Stops) (*d* 2005); two *d*. *Educ:* Royal Australian Naval College. Joined RAN, 1928; served War of 1939–45 in HMS Revenge, HMAS Cerberus, Hobart, Australia, Navy Office; Korean War Service in HMAS Tobruk, 1951; Flag Officer Comdg HMA Fleet, 1967–68; Chief of Naval Staff, Australia, 1970–73. Legion of Merit (US), 1951. *Recreation:* gardening. *Address:* 10 Galway Place, Deakin, ACT 2600, Australia. *Clubs:* Royal Automobile (Sydney); Royal Commonwealth Society (Canberra).   *Died 28 Aug. 2010.*

PEGG, Michael Anstice, PhD; University Librarian and Director, John Rylands University Library, University of Manchester, 1981–90; *b* 3 Sept. 1931; *s* of Benjamin and Rose Pegg; *m* 1st, 1955, Jean Williams; three *s*; 2nd, 1986, Margaret Rae. *Educ:* Burton-on-Trent Grammar Sch.; Univ. of Southampton. BA (London); PhD (Southampton); MA (Manchester) 1985. Captain, Royal Army Education Corps, Educn Officer, SHAPE, Paris, 1958–61; Asst Keeper, Nat. Library of Scotland, Edinburgh, 1961–67; Sec. and Estabt Officer, Nat. Library of Scotland, Edinburgh, 1967–76; Librarian, Univ. of Birmingham, 1976–80. Vis. Fellow, Beinecke Library, Yale Univ., 1989. Member: British Library Bd, 1981–84; Standing Conference of Nat. and Univ. Libraries' Council, 1981–83. *Publications:* Les Divers Rapports d'Eustorg de Beaulieu (édn critique), 1964 (Geneva); Catalogue of German Reformation Pamphlets in Libraries of Great Britain and Ireland, 1973 (Baden Baden); Catalogue of Sixteenth-century German Pamphlets in Collections in France and England, 1977 (Baden Baden); Catalogue of Reformation Pamphlets in Swiss Libraries, 1983; Catalogue of Sixteenth-century German and Dutch books in the Royal Library Copenhagen, 1989; Catalogue of German Reformation Pamphlets in Swedish Libraries, 1994; Catalogue of German Reformation pamphlets in libraries of Belgium and the Netherlands, 1999; Catalogue of German Reformation Pamphlets in Libraries of Alsace, Pt 1: Colmar, 2000, Pt 2: Strasbourg, 2003, Pt 3: Haguenau, Sélestat, Mulhouse, 2004; occasional papers to learned jls. *Recreations:* travel, wine, reading, railways. *Address:* c/o John Rylands University Library, University of Manchester, Oxford Road, Manchester M13 9PP.   *Died 23 Nov. 2006.*

PEMBERTON, Col Alan Brooke, CVO 1988; MBE 1960; *b* 11 Sept. 1923; *s* of Eric Harry Pemberton (Canadian by birth) and Phyllis Edith Pemberton (*née* Brooke-Alder); *m* 1952, Pamela Kirkland Smith, of Winnipeg, Canada; two *s*. *Educ:* Uppingham School; Trinity College, Cambridge. Commissioned Coldstream Guards, 1942; war service in Italy and NW Europe; ADC to Earl Alexander of Tunis, Governor-General of Canada, 1951–52; ADC to Gen. Sir Gerald Templer, High Comr to Malaya, 1952–53; Commanded 1st Bn Coldstream Guards, 1963–66; Regtl Lt-Col, 1966–67; retired 1967 (Hon. Col). Queen's Body Guard, Yeomen of the Guard: Exon, 1967; Ensign; Clerk of the Cheque; Lieutenant, 1985–93. Chm. and Man. Dir, Diversified Corporate Services Ltd, 1970–85. Special Constable, A Div., Metropolitan Police, 1975–76. *Recreations:* reading, travel. *Address:* Searchers, Wildmoor, Sherfield-on-Loddon, Hook, Hants RG27 0HQ. *Club:* Boodle's.   *Died 1 April 2010.*

PEMBERTON, Prof. John, MD; FRCP, FFPH; Professor of Social and Preventive Medicine, The Queen's University, Belfast, 1958–76; *b* 18 Nov. 1912; British; *m* 1937, Winifred Ethel Gray (decd); three *s*. *Educ:* Christ's Hospital; University College and UCH, London (MD); DPH Leeds. House Physician and House Surgeon, University College Hospital, 1936–37; Rowett Research Institute under the late Lord Boyd Orr, 1937–39; Rockefeller Travelling Fellow in Medicine, Harvard, Mass., USA, 1954–55; Director of MRC Group for research on Respiratory Disease and Air Pollution, and Reader in Social Medicine, University of Sheffield,

1955–58. Mem., Health Educn Council, DHSS, 1973–76. Co-founder, Internat. Epidemiol Assoc., 1957. Milroy Lectr, RCP, 1976. *Publications:* (with W. Hobson) The Health of the Elderly at Home, 1954; (ed) Recent Studies in Epidemiology, 1958; (ed) Epidemiology: Reports on Research and Teaching, 1963; Will Pickles of Wensleydale, 1970; articles in Lancet, BMJ, etc. *Recreations:* reading, TV, walking, painting. *Address:* Iona, Cannon Fields, Hathersage, Hope Valley S32 1AG.
Died 7 Feb. 2010.

PENDER, Comr Dinsdale Leslie; Territorial Commander in United Kingdom and Republic of Ireland, Salvation Army, 1993–97; *b* 22 March 1932; *s* of William Leslie Pender and Florence Lilian Pender (*née* Widdowson); *m* 1955, Winifred Violet Dale; one *s* two *d*. *Educ:* Colfe's Grammar Sch., Lewisham; Bradford Grammar Sch.; William Booth Meml Trng Coll. Served RAF, 1949–51. Commnd and ordained as Salvation Army Officer, 1953; CO, Manchester, Bath, Coventry and London, 1953–73; Divl Comdr, Northern Div., 1973–77; Asst Field Sec., Nat. HQ, 1977–80; Chief Sec., NZ and Fiji, 1980–82; Territorial Commander: Southern Africa, 1982–86; Scotland, 1986–90; Australia Southern, 1990–93. Chm., Bd, Salvation Army Housing Assoc., 1997–2002; Res. Consultant, Salvation Army Internat. Heritage Centre, 1997–2002. *Recreations:* music, walking. *Address:* 4 Old School Court, Wraysbury, Berks TW19 5BP.
Died 3 Dec. 2006.

PENDERED, Richard Geoffrey; Chairman, Bunge & Co., 1987–90; *b* 26 Sept. 1921; *s* of Richard Dudley Pendered and Adèle Pendered (*née* Hall); *m* 1953, Jennifer Preston Mead; two *s* two *d*. *Educ:* Winchester College (Scholar); Magdalene College (Scholar). GCCS Bletchley, 1940–52 (renamed GCHQ); Bunge & Co., 1952–90, Dir, 1957, Man. Dir, 1963–86. *Recreations:* fishing, shooting, golf. *Address:* Wildcroft, The Hollow, West Chiltington, Pulborough, W Sussex RH20 2QA.
Died 19 Nov. 2010.

PENMAN, Alistair, PhD; Chairman, Leatherhead Food International, since 2005; *b* 25 Oct. 1943; *s* of late Archibald Penman and Jean Penman; *m* 1968, Gina Hawthorn. *Educ:* Musselburgh Grammar Sch.; Univ. of Edinburgh (BSc Hons 1966; PhD 1969). Unilever: joined as Res. Scientist, 1969; Hd, Food Res., Rotterdam, 1989–95; Dir, Colworth House Lab., 1996–2003. Mem., BBSRC, 2002–08 (Chm., Audit Cttee, 2004–08; Chm., Diet and Health Res. Industry Club, 2007–). Chm. Governing Body, Inst. of Food Res., 1998–2002. Non-exec. Dir, E Malling Res., 2009–; Trustee, E Malling Trust for Horticl Res., 2004–. Hon. Prof., Tea Res. Inst., Hangzhou, 1999. FIFST 1999. *Publications:* several scientific papers and patents. *Recreations:* golf, reading, walking. *Address:* Tregenna, Bubnell Lane, Baslow, Derbys DE45 1RL; *e-mail:* alistair@penman2510.freeserve.co.uk. *Clubs:* Sickleholme Golf, Chatsworth Golf.
Died 3 Aug. 2010.

PENNINGTON, Prof. Robert Roland; Professor of Commercial Law, Birmingham University, 1968–94, subseq. Professor Emeritus; *b* 22 April 1927; *s* of R. A. Pennington; *m* 1965, Patricia Irene; one *d*. *Educ:* Birmingham Univ. (LLB, LLD). Solicitor. Reader, Law Soc.'s Sch. of Law, 1951–62; Mem. Bd of Management, Coll. of Law, 1962; Sen. Lectr in Commercial Law, 1962–68 and Dean, Faculty of Law, Birmingham Univ., 1979–82. Vis. Prof., QMW, 1995–96 and 1999–2002. Govt Adviser on Company Legislation, Trinidad, 1967 and Seychelles, 1970; UN Adviser on Commercial Law, 1970–; Special Legal Adviser to EEC, 1972–79. Editor, European Commercial Law Library, 1974–. *Publications:* Company Law, 1959, 8th edn 2001; Companies in the Common Market, 1962, 3rd edn as Companies in the European Communities, 1982; The Investor and the Law, 1967; Stannary Law: A History of the Mining Law of Cornwall and Devon, 1973; Commercial Banking Law, 1978; Gesellschaftsrecht des Vereinigten Königreichs, 1981 (in Jura Europae: Gesellschaftsrecht);

The Companies Acts 1980 and 1981: a practitioners' manual, 1983; Stock Exchange Listing: the new regulations, 1985; Directors' Personal Liability, 1987; Company Liquidations: the substantive law: the procedure (2 vols), 1987; The Law of the Investment Markets, 1990; Pennington's Corporate Insolvency Law, 1991, 2nd edn 1997; Small Private Companies, 1998; The Reorganisation of Public and Private Companies' Share Capital, 1999. *Recreations:* travel, walking, history, archaeology. *Address:* Gryphon House, Langley Road, Claverdon, Warwicks CV35 8QA.
Died 12 Feb. 2008.

PEPPARD, Nadine Sheila, CBE 1970; race relations consultant, 1983–2003; *b* 16 Jan. 1922; *d* of late Joseph Anthony Peppard and May Peppard (*née* Barber). *Educ:* Macclesfield High Sch.; Manchester Univ. (BA, Teacher's Dip.). French teacher, Maldon Grammar Sch., 1943–46; Spanish Editor, George G. Harrap & Co. Ltd, 1946–55; Trng Dept, Marks and Spencer, 1955–57; Dep. Gen.-Sec., London Council of Social Service, 1957–64; Nat. Advisory Officer for Commonwealth Immigrants, 1964–65; Gen. Sec., Nat. Cttee for Commonwealth Immigrants, 1965–68; Chief Officer, Community Relations Commn, 1968–72; Adviser on Race Relations, Home Office, 1972–83, retd. *Publications:* (trans.) Primitive India, 1954; (trans.) Toledo, 1955; various professional articles. *Address:* 321 The Cedars, Abbey Foregate, Shrewsbury SY2 6BY. *T:* (01743) 235124.
Died 26 Aug. 2010.

PERCIVAL, Prof. John, OBE 2003; FSA; Professor and Head of School of History and Archaeology, University of Wales College of Cardiff, 1988–96; Pro Vice-Chancellor, Cardiff University, 1996–2002; *b* 11 July 1937; *s* of Walter William Percival and Eva Percival (*née* Bowers); *m* 1st, 1962, Carole Ann Labrum (*d* 1977); two *d*; 2nd, 1988, Jacqueline Anne Gibson (*née* Donovan). *Educ:* Colchester Royal Grammar Sch.; Hertford Coll., Oxford (Lucy Schol.; 1st Cl. Lit. Hum.; MA; DPhil). FSA 1977. Harmsworth Sen. Schol., Merton Coll., Oxford, 1961; University College, Cardiff: Asst Lectr in Ancient History, 1962; Lectr, 1964; Sen. Lectr, 1972; Reader, 1979; Dean of Faculty of Arts, 1977–79; Dep. Principal, UWCC, 1987–90. Vice-Pres., 1989–, Chm. Council, 1990–95, Classical Assoc. (Jt Sec., 1979–89). Mem. Ct of Govs, Nat. Library of Wales, 1991–2002. Hon. Fellow, Cardiff Univ., 2004. *Publications:* The Reign of Charlemagne (with H. R. Loyn), 1975; The Roman Villa, 1976, 2nd edn 1988; articles in historical and archaeol jls. *Recreations:* music, gardening. *Address:* 26 Church Road, Whitchurch, Cardiff CF14 2EA. *T:* (029) 2061 7869.
Died 8 Jan. 2007.

PERCY, His Honour Rodney Algernon; a Circuit Judge, 1979–93; caravan site operator, 1993–99; general handyman on the site, since 2000; *b* 15 May 1924; 3rd *s* of late Hugh James Percy, Solicitor, Alnwick; *m* 1948, Mary Allen (*d* 2002), *d* of late J. E. Benbow, Aberystwyth; one *s* three *d*. *Educ:* Uppingham; Brasenose Coll., Oxford (MA). Lieut, Royal Corps of Signals, 1942–46, served in Burma, India, Malaya, Java. Called to Bar: Middle Temple, 1950; Lincoln's Inn, 1987 (*ad eund*). Dep. Coroner, N Northumberland, 1957; Asst Recorder, Sheffield QS, 1964; Dep. Chm., Co. Durham QS, 1966–71; a Recorder of the Crown Court, 1972–79. Pres., Tyneside Marriage Guidance Council, 1983–87; Founder Mem., Family Conciliation Service for Northumberland and Tyneside, 1982–93 (Pres., 1988–93). *Publications:* (ed) Charlesworth on Negligence, 4th edn 1962 to 6th edn 1977, 7th edn (Charlesworth & Percy on Negligence) 1983 to 9th edn 1997, consultant ed., 10th edn 2001 to 11th edn 2006; (contrib.) Atkin's Court Forms, 2nd edn, Vol. 20, 1982, rev. edn 1987, 1993 (title Health and Safety at Work), and Vol. 29, 1983, rev. edn 1991 (title Negligence). *Recreations:* golf, gardening, hill walking, King Charles Cavalier spaniels, beach-combing. *Address:* Brookside, Lesbury, Alnwick, Northumberland NE66 3AT. *T:* (01665) 830326/830000.
Died 17 May 2008.

PEREIRA, Most Rev. Simeon Anthony; Archbishop of Karachi, (RC), 1994–2002, then Archbishop Emeritus; *b* 19 Oct. 1927. Ordained priest, 1951; consecrated Bishop, 1971; Bishop of Islamabad-Rawalpindi, 1973–93; Co-adjutor Bishop of Karachi, 1993–94. *Address:* c/o Monastery of Angels, Plot No 213, Deh Landhi, Karachi 75120, Pakistan.   *Died 21 Aug. 2006.*

PEREIRA-MENDOZA, Vivian, CEng, FIEE; Director, Polytechnic of the South Bank, 1970–80; *b* 8 April 1917; *o s* of Rev. Joseph Pereira-Mendoza, Manchester; *m* 1942, Marjorie, *y d* of Edward Lichtenstein; two *d. Educ:* Manchester Central High Sch.; Univ. of Manchester (MScTech). Asst Lectr, Univ. of Manchester, 1939. Served War, 1940–45, in Royal Corps of Signals; Major, and GSO II (War Office). Sen. Lectr, Woolwich Polytechnic, 1948; Head of Department: of Electrical Engrg, NW Kent Coll. of Technology, 1954; of Electrical Engrg and Physics, Borough Polytechnic, 1957; Vice-Principal, 1964, Principal, 1966–70, Borough Polytechnic. Mem. Council, Chelsea Coll., Univ. of London, 1972–85.   *Died 19 April 2006.*

PERKINS, Maj.-Gen. Kenneth, CB 1977; MBE 1955; DFC 1953; Commander, Sultan's Armed Forces, Oman, 1975–77 (successfully concluded Dhofar War); *b* 15 Aug. 1926; *s* of George Samuel Perkins and Arabella Sarah Perkins (*née* Wise); *m* 1st, 1949, Anne Theresa Barry (marr. diss. 1984); three *d*; 2nd, 1985, Hon. Celia Sandys, *d* of Rt Hon. Lord Duncan-Sandys, CH, PC and Diana, *d* of Rt Hon. Sir Winston Churchill, KG, OM, CH, FRS; one *s* one *d. Educ:* Lewes County Sch. for Boys; New Coll., Oxford. Enlisted 1944; commnd RA 1946; various appts in Middle and Far East, BAOR and UK until 1965, incl. air OP pilot in Korean War, Malayan Emergency, and Staff Coll. Quetta 1958; Instructor, Staff Coll. Camberley, 1965–66; CO 1st Regt Royal Horse Artillery, 1967–69; GSO 1 Singapore, 1970; Comdr 24 Bde, 1971–72; RCDS 1973; Central Staff, MoD, 1974; Maj.-Gen., 1975; Asst Chief of Defence Staff (Ops), 1977–80; Dir, Military Assistance Office, MoD, 1980–82. Defence Advr, BAe, 1982–85. Col Comdt, RA, 1980–85. Vice Pres., Sultan of Oman's Armed Forces Assoc., 1994– (Chm., 1987–94). Mem. Council, Res. Inst. for Study of Conflict, 1992–2000. Mil. Advr, The Sun newspaper, 1991–2006. Chm., Politicians' Complaints Commn, 1992–93. Trustee, Battlefield Trust, 1998–2001. Selangor Distinguished Conduct Medal (Malaya), 1955; Hashemite Order of Independence, first class, 1975; Order of Oman, 1977. *Publications:* Weapons and Warfare, 1987; A Fortunate Soldier (autobiog.), 1988; Khalida (novel), 1991; articles in press and professional jls. *Recreations:* writing, painting (exhibited RA), cycling. *Address:* 88 Church Street, Great Bedwyn, Marlborough, Wilts SN8 3PF.   *Died 23 Oct. 2009.*

PERRETT, His Honour Desmond Seymour; QC 1980; a Circuit Judge, 1992–2005; Resident Judge, Shrewsbury Crown Court, 2001–05; *b* 22 April 1937; *s* of His Honour John Perrett and Elizabeth Mary Perrett (*née* Seymour); *m* 1961, Pauline Merriel (*d* 2005), *yr d* of late Paul Robert Buchan May, ICS, and of Esme May; one *s* one *d. Educ:* Westminster Sch. National Service, RN, 1955–57: midshipman RNVR, 1955; Suez, 1956, and Cyprus, 1957. Called to the Bar, Gray's Inn, 1962, Bencher, 1989; Oxford Circuit, 1963–72; Midland and Oxford Circuit, 1972–; a Recorder, 1978–92; Mem., Senate of the Inns of Court and of the Bar, 1983–87. Chm. Disciplinary Appeals Cttee, Cricket Council, 1986–97. *Recreations:* cricket, fishing, shooting. *Address:* The Old Bakehouse, Cartway, Bridgnorth, Shropshire WV16 4BG. *Clubs:* MCC; Band of Brothers Cricket (Kent); IZ, Arabs Cricket.   *Died 18 March 2010.*

PERRY, Sir (David) Norman, Kt 1977; MBE 1962; *b* 25 July 1914; *s* of Frederick and Letitia Perry; *m* 1939, Phyllis Ruth Conway (decd); two *s* three *d.* Served War, 1942–44, 2nd NZEF, 28th (Maori) Bn. Engaged in tribal affairs, 1938–50; former Maori Welfare Dist Officer; Advr, 1961–62, then Sec., and Consultant, NZ Maori Council; Chm., Mahi Tahi Charitable Trust, reformative

prog. Maori prison inmates, 1990–; advr to rural industries and tribal trusts. Lay Moderator, Presbyterian Church, 1965. Knighthood awarded for services to the community and the Maori people, New Zealand.
                    Died 2 Aug. 2006.

PERRY, Prof. Samuel Victor, BSc (Liverpool), PhD, ScD (Cantab); FRS 1974; Professor of Biochemistry, 1959–85, then Emeritus, and Head of Department of Biochemistry, 1968–85, University of Birmingham; *b* 16 July 1918; *s* of late Samuel and Margaret Perry; *m* 1948, Maureen Tregent Shaw; one *s* two *d. Educ:* King George V Sch., Southport; Liverpool Univ.; Trinity Coll., Cambridge. Served in War of 1939–45, home and N Africa; Royal Artillery, 1940–46, Captain; POW 1942–45. Research Fellow, Trinity Coll., Cambridge, 1947–51; Commonwealth Fund Fellow, University of Rochester, USA, 1948–49; University Lecturer, Dept of Biochemistry, Cambridge, 1950–59. Member: Standing Cttee for Research on Animals, ARC, 1965–72; Biol Scis and Enzyme Cttees, SRC, 1968–71; Medical Res. Cttee, Muscular Dystrophy Gp of GB, 1970–90; Systems Bd, MRC, 1974–77; Research Funds Cttee, British Heart Foundn, 1974–82; British Nat. Cttee for Biochemistry, 1978–87 (Chm., 1982–87); Council, Royal Soc., 1986–88; Chairman: Cttee of Biochemical Soc., 1980–83; Adv. Bd, Meat Res. Inst., 1980–85. Croonian Lectr, Royal Soc., 1984. FAAAS 1987. Hon. Mem., Amer. Soc. of Biol Chemists, 1978; Corresponding Mem., Société Royale des Sciences, Liège, 1978; Mem., Accad. Virgiliana, Mantova, 1979; Foreign Mem., Accademia Nazionale dei Lincei, 1989. CIBA Medal, Biochemical Soc., 1977. *Publications:* scientific papers in Biochemical Journal, Nature, Biochemica Biophysica Acta, etc. *Recreations:* gardening, building stone walls, Rugby football (Cambridge, 1946, 1947, England, 1947, 1948). *Address:* Cae Bach, Fishguard Road, Dinas Cross, Newport, Pembrokeshire SA42 0XB. *T:* (01348) 811447.
                    Died 17 Dec. 2009.

PERRYMAN, (Francis) Douglas; Corporate Director for Finance (formerly Board Member), British Telecommunications, 1981–86; *b* 23 April 1930; *s* of Frank Smyth Perryman and Caroline Mary Anderson; *m* 1955, Margaret Mary Lamb; two *d. Educ:* West Hartlepool Grammar School; Durham Univ. BCom (Hons); FCA. Articled Clerk, 1951–55; Nat. Service, commnd RAPC, 1955–57; National Coal Board: Area Chief Accountant, Fife and Scottish South Areas, 1963–72; Finance Dir, Opencast Exec., 1972; Dir Gen. of Finance, 1978–81; Board Mem. for Finance, PO, 1981; Corporate Commercial Dir, BT, 1986–88. Mem. Council, CBI, 1987–88; Dir, Homes Assured Corp., 1989–90. *Recreations:* golf, Rugby football, music, Francophile. *Address:* 8 Henrietta Villas, Bath BA2 6LX. *T:* (01225) 460952.   *Died 21 Sept. 2007.*

PETERKIEWICZ, Prof. Jerzy; novelist and poet; Professor of Polish Language and Literature, University of London, 1972–79; *b* 29 Sept. 1916; *s* of late Jan Pietrkiewicz and Antonina (*née* Politowska). *Educ:* Dlugosz Sch., Włocławek; Univ. of Warsaw; Univ. of St Andrews (MA 1944); King's Coll., London (PhD 1947). Freelance writer until 1950; Reader (previously Lectr) in Polish Language and Literature, Sch. of Slavonic and East European Studies, Univ. of London, 1952–72, Head of Dept of E European Lang. and Lit., 1972–77. Comdr's Cross, Order of Polonia Restituta (Poland), 1995. *Publications:* Prowincja, 1936; Wiersze i poematy, 1938; Pogrzeb Europy, 1946; The Knotted Cord, 1953; Loot and Loyalty, 1955; Polish Prose and Verse, 1956; Antologia liryki angielskiej, 1958; Future to Let, 1958; Isolation, 1959; (with Burns Singer) Five Centuries of Polish Poetry, 1960 (enlarged edn 1970); The Quick and the Dead, 1961; That Angel Burning at my Left Side, 1963; Poematy londynskie, 1965; Inner Circle, 1966; Green Flows the Bile, 1969; The Other Side of Silence (The Poet at the Limits of Language), 1970; The Third Adam, 1975; (ed and trans.) Easter Vigil and other Poems, by Karol Wojtyla (Pope John Paul II), 1979; Kula

magiczna (Poems 1934–52), 1980; (ed and trans.) Collected Poems, by Karol Wojtyla (Pope John Paul II), 1982; Poezje wybrane (Selected Poems), 1986; Literatura polska w perspektywie europejskiej (Polish Literature in its European context; essays trans. from English), 1986; Messianic Prophecy: a case for reappraisal, 1991; In the Scales of Fate (autobiog.), 1993; Wiersze dobrzynskie (early poems), 1994; (ed and trans.) The Place Within: the poetry of Pope John Paul II, 1994; Metropolitan Idyll (bilingual edn), 1998; Slowa sa bez poreczy (Selected Poems), 1998; (trans.) Poezje—poems by Karol Wojtyla (Pope John Paul II) (bilingual edn), 1998; (ed and trans.) Cyprian Norwid: poems, letters, drawings, 2000; (ed and trans.) Roman Triptych, by Pope John Paul II, 2003; essays, poems and articles in various periodicals; radio plays, BBC Radio 3. *Recreations:* travels, outward and inward. *Address:* 7 Lyndhurst Terrace, NW3 5QA.
Died 26 Oct. 2007.

PETERS, Alan George, OBE 1990; furniture maker, since 1962; *b* 17 Jan. 1933; *s* of George Peters, BEM and Evelyn Gladys Amy Peters (*née* Weeks); *m* 1962, Laura Robinson; one *s* one *d*. *Educ:* Petersfield and Cowplain schools; Shoreditch Teacher Trng Coll., Egham (Dip. with distinction); Central Sch. of Arts and Crafts, London. Apprenticed to Edward Barnsley, CBE, 1949–56. Crafts Council Bursary, Japan, 1975; Winston Churchill Fellow, S Korea and Taiwan, 1980; Guest Advr, NZ Crafts Council, 1984. Vice-Pres., Devon Guild of Craftsmen, 1987–2003 (Hon. Vice-Pres., 2003–). Founder Academician, SW Acad. of Fine and Applied Arts, 2000. Trustee, Crafts Study Centre, Bath, 1990–99. *Exhibitions:* Alan Peters Furniture, Cheltenham and touring, 1985–86; 30 Pieces for 30 Years, Bedales Gall., Petersfield, 1992; Crafts Council nat. and touring exhibns, 1973–; work exhibited in: museums, incl. V&A, Cheltenham, Bristol, Leicester, Plymouth, Portsmouth and Bath; Crafts Council Collection; seating for Earth Gall., Gall. of Modern Art, Glasgow, 1996. Fellow, Soc. of Designer-Craftsmen, 1968 (Centennial Medal, 1988; Hon. Fellow, 2005). Hon. Fellow, Somerset Guild of Craftsmen, 2006. Award of Distinction, Furniture Soc., USA, 2002; Gane Trust Award, 2005. *Publications:* Cabinetmaking: the professional approach, 1984; (ed) The Technique of Furniture Making, by Ernest Joyce, 1987, 4th edn 1997. *Recreations:* cycling, walking, real ale. *Address:* Aller Studio, 3 Mart Road, Minehead, Somerset TA24 5BJ.
Died 11 Oct. 2009.

PETERS, Theophilus, CMG 1967; HM Diplomatic Service, retired; freelance lecturer on Chinese Art and History; *b* 7 Aug. 1921; *er s* of late Mark Peters and Dorothy Knapman; *m* 1953, Lucy Bailey Summers, *d* of late Lionel Morgan Summers, Winter Park, Fla; two *s* three *d*. *Educ:* Exeter Sch.; St John's Coll., Cambridge (MA). Served War of 1939–45: 2nd Lieut, Intelligence Corps, 1942; Captain, 8 Corps HQ, 1944; Normandy, 1944; Holland, 1944–45 (despatches); Germany; Major. Entered HM Foreign (subseq. Diplomatic) Service; Vice-Consul/2nd Secretary, Peking, 1948; FO, 1951–52; Tripoli and Benghazi (Libya), 1953; FO, 1956; Dep. Secretary-General, Cento, 1960; Head of Chancery, Manila, 1962; Counsellor (Commercial), Peking, 1965; Dir, Diplomatic Service Language Centre, 1968–71, and Head of Training Dept, FCO, 1969–71; Counsellor and Consul-Gen., Buenos Aires, 1971–73; Consul-Gen., Antwerp, 1973–78. Dir, Theophilus Knapman & Co., 1979–87. *Address:* King's Mill, St Peter's Vale, Stamford, Lincs PE9 2QT.
Died 9 Feb. 2008.

PETERSEN, Sir Jeffrey (Charles), KCMG 1978 (CMG 1968); HM Diplomatic Service, retired; *b* 20 July 1920; *s* of Charles Petersen and Ruby Petersen (*née* Waple); *m* 1st, 1944, Catherine Judith Bayly (marr. diss. 1959); one *s* one *d*; 2nd, 1962, Karin Kristina Hayward; one *s* three *d*. *Educ:* Westcliff High Sch.; London School of Economics. Served RN (Lieut, RNVR), 1939–46. Joined Foreign Office, 1948; 2nd Secretary, Madrid, 1949–50; 2nd Secretary, Ankara, 1951–52; 1st Secretary, Brussels,

1953–56; NATO Defence College, 1956–57; FO, 1957–62; 1st Secretary, Djakarta, 1962–64; Counsellor, Athens, 1964–68; Minister (Commercial), Rio de Janeiro, 1968–71; Ambassador to: Republic of Korea, 1971–74; Romania, 1975–77; Sweden, 1977–80. Chairman: Barclays Bank SAE (Spain), 1981–87; GVA Internat. Ltd, 1983–89; North Sea Assets PLC, 1989–94; Ake Larson Ltd, 1990–93. Chm., British Materials Handling Bd, 1981–95. Pres., Anglo-Korean Soc.; Vice President: Anglo Swedish Soc.; Swedish Chamber of Commerce for UK. Knight Grand Cross, Order of Polar Star (Sweden), 1984; Order of Diplomatic Merit (Republic of Korea), 1985. *Recreations:* painting, making things, totting. *Address:* 32 Longmoore Street, SW1V 1JF. *T:* (020) 7834 8262; Crofts Wood, Petham, Kent CT4 5RX. *T:* (01227) 700537. *Clubs:* Travellers; Kent and Canterbury.
Died 14 Oct. 2006.

PETERSON, Oscar Emmanuel, CC (Canada) 1984 (OC 1972); OOnt 1992; concert jazz pianist; *b* 15 Aug. 1925; *s* of Daniel Peterson and Olivia Peterson; *m* 1st, 1947, Lillian Alice Ann Fraser (marr. diss.); two *s* three *d*; 2nd, 1966, Sandra Cythia, *d* of H. A. King (marr. diss. 1976); 3rd, 1977, Charlotte Huber (marr. diss.); one *s*; 4th, 1990, Kelly Ann Green; one *d*. *Educ:* (academic) Montreal High Sch.; (music) private tutors. 1st prize, amateur show, 1940; Carnegie Hall debut, 1950; 1950–: numerous jazz awards; TV shows; composer and arranger; yearly concert tours in N America, Europe, GB and Japan; performed also in S America, Mexico, WI, Australia, NZ and Russia. *Television series:* (Canada): Oscar Peterson Presents, 1974; Oscar Peterson and Friends, 1980; (BBC) Oscar Peterson's Piano Party, 1974. Chancellor, York Univ., Ontario, 1991–94. Mem., Bd of Govs, Credit Valley Hosp., Mississauga, Ont., 1984–. Oscar Peterson scholarship established, Berklee Coll. of Mus., 1982. Grammy award, 1974, 1975, 1977, 1978, 1979, 1990, 1991; Grammy lifetime achievement award, 1997. Hon. LLD: Carleton Univ., 1973; Queen's Univ., Kingston, 1976; Concordia, 1979; MacMaster, 1981; Victoria, 1981; York, 1982; Toronto, 1985; Hon. DMus: Sackville, 1980; Laval, 1985; Hon. DFA: Northwestern, Ill, 1983; Niagara Univ., NY, 1996. Civic Award of Merit, Toronto, 1972, second mention, 1983; Diplôme d'Honneur, Canadian Conf. of the Arts, 1974; Toronto Arts Awards, Lifetime Achievement, 1991; Gov. General's Award, Lifetime Achievement, 1992; Glenn Gould Prize, 1993; Praemium Imperiale, Japan, 1999. Officer, Order of Arts and Letters (France), 1989; Chevalier, Order of Quebec, 1991. *Publications:* Oscar Peterson New Piano Solos, 1965; Jazz Exercises and Pieces, 1965; Jazz Playbook, vol. 1A, 1991, vol. 1B, 1993; A Jazz Odyssey (autobiog.), 2002. *Recreations:* audio, photography, boating, fishing. *Address:* Regal Recordings Ltd, 2421 Hammond Road, Mississauga, ON L5K 1T3, Canada. *T:* (905) 8552370, *Fax:* (905) 8551773.
Died 23 Dec. 2007.

PETO, Sir Michael (Henry Basil), 4th Bt *cr* 1927; *b* 6 April 1938; *s* of Brig. Sir Christopher Henry Maxwell Peto, 3rd Bt, DSO, and Barbara (*d* 1992), *yr d* of Edwyn Thomas Close; S father, 1980; *m* 1st, 1963, Sarah Susan (marr. diss. 1970), *y d* of Major Sir Dennis Stucley, 5th Bt; one *s* two *d*; 2nd, 1971, Lucinda Mary (marr. diss. 2001), *yr d* of Major Sir Charles Douglas Blackett, 9th Bt; two *s*. *Educ:* Eton; Christ Church, Oxford (MA). Called to the Bar, Inner Temple, 1960. *Heir: s* Henry Christopher Morton Bampfylde Peto [*b* 8 April 1967; *m* 1998, Louise Imogen, *y d* of Christopher Balck-Foote; one *s* two *d*]. *Address:* 12 St Helen's Terrace, Spittal, Berwick upon Tweed TD15 1RJ.
Died 2 Aug. 2008.

PETTIT, Sir Daniel (Eric Arthur), Kt 1974; Chairman, PosTel Investment Management (formerly Post Office Staff Superannuation Fund), 1979–83; *b* Liverpool, 19 Feb. 1915; *s* of Thomas Edgar Pettit and Pauline Elizabeth Pettit (*née* Kerr); *m* 1940, Winifred (*d* 2004), *d* of William and Sarah Bibby; two *s*. *Educ:* Quarry Bank High Sch., Liverpool; Fitzwilliam Coll., Cambridge (MA; Hon. Fellow, 1985). School Master, 1938–40 and 1946–47;

War Service, Africa, India, Burma, 1940–46 (Major, RA); Unilever: Management, 1948–57; Associated Company Dir and Chm., 1958–70. Chm., Nat. Freight Corp., 1971–78 (part-time Mem. Bd, 1968–70); Member: Freight Integration Council, 1971–78; National Ports Council, 1971–80; Bd, Foundn of Management Educn, 1973–84; Waste Management Adv. Council, 1971–78; Chm., EDC for Distributive Trades, 1974–78. Chairman: Incpen, 1979–90; RDC Properties, 1987–2004; Director: Lloyds Bank Ltd, 1977–78 (Chm., Birmingham & W Midlands Bd, 1978–85; Lloyds Bank (UK) Ltd, 1979–85; Bransford Partnership, 1979–; Black Horse Life Assurance Co. Ltd, 1983–85; Lloyds Bank Unit Trust Managers Ltd, 1981–85. Mem. Council, British Road Fedn Ltd. Hon. Col, 162 Regt RCT (V). Freeman, City of London, 1971; Liveryman, Worshipful Co. of Carmen, 1971. CCMI; FCILT (Pres. 1971–72); FRSA; FIMMM; MIPD. *Publications:* various papers on transport and management matters. *Recreations:* cricket, Association football (Olympic Games, 1936; Corinthian FC, 1935–); fly-fishing. *Address:* Bransford Court Farm, Worcester WR6 5JL. *Clubs:* Farmers; MCC; Hawks (Cambridge).
Died 28 July 2010.

PEYTON OF YEOVIL, Baron *cr* 1983 (Life Peer), of Yeovil in the County of Somerset; **John Wynne William Peyton;** PC 1970; Chairman, British Alcan Aluminium, 1987–91; *b* 13 Feb. 1919; *s* of late Ivor Eliot Peyton and Dorothy Helen Peyton; *m* 1st, 1947, Diana Clinch (marr. diss., 1966); one *s* one *d* (and one *s* decd); 2nd, 1966, Mrs Mary Cobbold. *Educ:* Eton; Trinity College, Oxford. Commissioned 15/19 Hussars, 1939; Prisoner of War, Germany, 1940–45. Called to the Bar, Inner Temple, 1945. MP (C) Yeovil, 1951–83; Parly Secretary, Ministry of Power, 1962–64; Minister of Transport, June–Oct. 1970; Minister for Transport Industries, DoE, 1970–74. Chm., Texas Instruments Ltd, 1974–90. Treas., Zoological Society of London, 1984–91. *Publications:* Without Benefit of Laundry, 1997; Solly Zuckerman: a scientist out of the ordinary, 2001. *Address:* The Old Malt House, Hinton St George, Somerset TA17 8SE. *T:* (01460) 73618. *Clubs:* Boodle's, Beefsteak.
Died 22 Nov. 2006.

PHELPS, Richard Wintour, CBE 1986; General Manager, Central Lancashire New Town Development Corporation, 1971–86; *b* 26 July 1925; *s* of Rev. H. Phelps; *m* 1955, Pamela Marie Lawson (*d* 2006); two *d*. *Educ:* Kingswood Sch.; Merton Coll., Oxford (MA). 14th Punjab Regt, IA, 1944–46. Colonial Admin. Service, Northern Region and Fed. Govt. of Nigeria, 1948–57 and 1959–61; Prin., HM Treasury, 1957–59 and 1961–65; Sen. Administrator, Hants CC, 1965–67; Gen. Manager, Skelmersdale New Town Develt Corp., 1967–71. Consultant: in mgt of urban develt and housing, 1986–98; on housing policy to Falkland Is Govt, 1988–89; Advr (part-time) on housing to Govt of Vanuatu, 1986–89. Chm., Examn in Public Replacement Structure Plan, Derbys CC, 1989, Notts CC and Northants CC, 1990, West Sussex CC, 1991, Leics CC, 1992, Cambs CC, 1994, Hants CC, 1996. Conducted indep. inquiry into possible abuses of planning system, Bassetlaw DC, 1996; Chm., Countryside movement inquiry into hunting with hounds, 1996–97. Contested (SDP) Barrow and Furness, 1987. Winston Churchill Trust Travelling Fellowship, 1971. *Recreations:* reading, living in Spain. *Address:* 38 Wharncliffe Road, Christchurch, Dorset BH23 5DE. *T:* (01425) 272242. *Club:* Royal Commonwealth Society.
Died 17 April 2008.

PHILLIPS, Prof. Dewi Zephaniah; Rush Rhees Research Professor, University of Wales, Swansea, 1996–2001, then Emeritus; Danforth Professor of the Philosophy of Religion, Claremont Graduate School, California, since 1992; *b* 24 Nov. 1934; *s* of David Oakley Phillips and Alice Frances Phillips; *m* 1959, Margaret Monica Hanford; three *s*. *Educ:* Swansea Grammar Sch.; UC Swansea (MA); St Catherine's Society, Oxford (BLitt). Asst Lectr, Queen's Coll.,

Dundee, Univ. of St Andrews, 1961–62; Lectr: at Queen's Coll., Dundee, 1962–63; UC Bangor, 1963–65; University College, Swansea, later University of Wales, Swansea: Lectr, 1965–67; Sen. Lectr, 1967–71; Prof. of Philosophy, 1971–96; Dean of the Faculty of Arts, 1982–85; Vice-Principal, 1989–92. Visiting Professor: Yale Univ., 1985; Claremont Graduate Sch., 1986. Hintz Meml Lectr, Univ. of Arizona, Tucson. 1975; Vis. Prof. and McMartin Lectr, Univ. of Carleton, 1976; Agnes Cuming Visitor, Univ. Coll. Dublin, 1982; Lectures: William James, Lousiana State Univ., 1982; Marett, Oxford, 1983; Riddell Meml, Newcastle, 1986; Aquinas, Oxford, 1987; Cardinal Mercier, Leuven, 1988; R. I. Aaron, Aberystwyth, 1993; Leibniz, Calif State Univ., 1995; McManis, Wheaton Coll., 1996; Tanner McMurrin, Westminster Coll., 2004; Suarez, Fordham, 2006. Pres., British Soc. for the Philosophy of Religion, 2001–. Editor, Philosophical Investigations, 1982–. Hon. PhD Åbo Akademi, Finland, 1998. *Publications:* The Concept of Prayer, 1965; (ed) Religion and Understanding, 1967; (ed) Saith Ysgrif Ar Grefydd, 1967; (with H. O. Mounce) Moral Practices, 1970; Death and Immortality, 1970; Faith and Philosophical Enquiry, 1970; (with Ilham Dilman) Sense and Delusion, 1971; Athronyddu Am Grefydd, 1974; Religion Without Explanation, 1976; Through A Darkening Glass: Philosophy, Literature and Cultural Change, 1981; Dramau Gwenlyn Parry, 1981; Belief, Change and Forms of Life, 1986; R. S. Thomas: poet of the hidden God, 1986; Faith after Foundationalism, 1988; (ed jtly) Wittgenstein: attention to particulars, 1989; From Fantasy to Faith, 1991; Interventions in Ethics, 1992; Wittgenstein and Religion, 1993; Writers of Wales: J. R. Jones, 1995; Introducing Philosophy, 1996; (ed) Religion and Morality, 1996; (ed) Can Religion Be Explained Away?, 1996; (ed jtly) Religion Without Transcendence, 1997; (ed) On Religion and Philosophy, by Rush Rhees, 1997; (ed) Wittgenstein and the Possibility of Discourse, by Rush Rhees, 1998; Religion and Hume's Legacy, 1999; Philosophy's Cool Place, 1999; (ed) Moral Questions, by Rush Rhees, 1999; (ed) Discussions of Simone Weil, by Rush Rhees, 1999; Recovering Religious Concepts, 2000; (ed jtly) Kant and Kierkegaard on Religion, 2000; (ed jtly) Philosophy of Religion and the 21st Century, 2001; Religion and the Hermeneutics of Contemplation, 2001; The Problem of Evil and the Problem of God, 2004; Religion and Friendly Fire, 2004; (ed jtly) Biblical Concepts and Our World, 2004; (ed jtly) Language and Spirit, 2004; (ed) In Dialogue with the Greeks, by Rush Rhees, 2 vols, 2004; (ed jtly) Religion and Wittgenstein's Legacy, 2005; General Editor: Studies in Ethics and the Philosophy of Religion, 1968–74; Values and Philosophical Enquiry, 1976–86; Swansea Studies in Philosophy, 1989–; Claremont Studies in the Philosophy of Religion, 1993–; Wittgensteinian Studies, 2003–; papers in philosophical jls. *Recreation:* lawn tennis and supporting Swansea City AFC. *Address:* Department of Philosophy, University of Wales Swansea, Singleton Park, Swansea SA2 8PP. *T:* (01792) 295189.
Died 25 July 2006.

PHILLIPS, Eric Lawrance, CMG 1963; Secretary, Monopolies Commission, 1969–74; consultant to Monopolies and Mergers Commission, 1974–75; *b* 23 July 1909; *s* of L. Stanley Phillips and Maudie Phillips (*née* Elkan), London, NW1; *m* 1938, Phyllis Bray (*d* 1991), artist; two *s*, and one step *d*; one *d* by Pauline Sharpe. *Educ:* Haileybury Coll.; Balliol Coll., Oxford (Scholar, BA). With Erlangers Ltd, 1932–39. Served War of 1939–45, Captain, RA. Principal, Bd of Trade, 1945, Monopolies Commn, 1949; Asst Secretary, Monopolies Commn, 1951, Bd of Trade, 1952; Under-Sec., Bd of Trade, 1964–69. Hon. Chm., Abbeyfield West London Soc., 1980–86. *Recreations:* looking at pictures, places and buildings. *Address:* The Old Prebendal House, Station Road, Shipton-under-Wychwood, Chipping Norton OX7 6BQ.
Died 11 Jan. 2010.

PHILLIPS, Prof. the Hon. John Harber, AC 1998; QC (Vic.) 1975; Chief Justice of Victoria, 1991–2003; Provost, Sir Zelman Cowen Centre, Victoria University, Melbourne, since 2003; *b* 18 Oct. 1933; *s* of Anthony and I. Muriel Phillips; *m* 1962, Helen Isobel Rogers; two *s* one *d*. *Educ:* De La Salle Coll., Malvern; Univ. of Melbourne (LLB). Called to the Bar: Victoria, 1959; Middle Temple, 1979; practised at Victorian Bar, 1959–84; Justice: Supreme Court of Victoria, 1984–90; Federal Court of Australia, 1990–91. Mem., Victorian Bar Council, 1974–84; Chairman: Criminal Bar Assoc., 1982, 1983; Nat. Crime Authy, 1990–91; Chm., Nat. Inst. of Forensic Sci., 1991–. Pres., French Australian Lawyers Soc., 2000–. Vis. Prof. of Advocacy, Monash Univ., 1988–89. Hellenic Dist. for Service to Greek community of Victoria, 1992, 2000; Australian Hellenic Council Award, 2003. *Publications:* (jtly) Forensic Science and the Expert Witness, 1985; Advocacy with Honour, 1986; The Trial of Ned Kelly, 1987; Poet of the Colours: the life of John Shaw Neilson, 1988; *plays:* By a Simple Majority: the trial of Socrates, 1990; Conference with Counsel, 1991; The Cab Rank Rule, 1995; Starry Night with Cypresses: the last hours of Vincent van Gogh, 2003; (for sch. children) Murder at Blue Hills, 2003; *poetry:* Wounds, 2001 (trans. Italian); Lament for an Advocate, 2005. *Address:* Sir Zelman Cowen Centre, Victoria University, Level 2, 295 Queen Street, Melbourne, Vic 3000, Australia. *Died 7 Aug. 2009.*

PHILLIPS, Prof. Owen Martin, FRS 1968; Decker Professor of Science and Engineering, Johns Hopkins University, 1975–98, then Emeritus; *b* 30 Dec. 1930; *s* of Richard Keith Phillips and Madeline Lofts; *m* 1953, Merle Winifred Simons; two *s* two *d*. *Educ:* University of Sydney; Trinity Coll., Cambridge (Hon. Fellow, 1997). ICI Fellow, Cambridge, 1955–57; Fellow, St John's Coll., Cambridge, 1957–60; Asst Prof., 1957–60, Assoc. Prof., 1960–63, Johns Hopkins Univ.; Asst Director of Research, Cambridge, 1961–64; Prof. of Geophysical Mechanics, Johns Hopkins Univ., 1963–68, of Geophysics, 1968–75. Mem. Council, Nat. Center of Atmospheric Research, Boulder, Colorado, 1964–68; Member: US Nat. Cttee Global Atmospheric Research Project, 1968; Res. Co-ord. Panel, Gas Research Inst., 1981–85; Principal Staff, Applied Phys. Lab., 1982–90. Associate Ed., Jl of Fluid Mechanics, 1964–95; Regl Ed., Proc. of Royal Soc. series A, 1992–98; Mem. Adv. Cttee, Annual Review of Fluid Dynamics, 1995–98. Mem.-at-large, Amer. Meteorol. Soc. Publications Commn, 1971–75; Pres., Maryland Acad. of Scis, 1979–85. Sec., Bd of Trustees, Chesapeake Res. Consortium, 1973–74 (Trustee, 1972–75); Vis. Cttees, Univ. of Michigan Res. Initiatives, 1990–93, 1994–97. Vis. Prof., Japan Soc. for the Promotion of Sci., 1982. Mem., US NAE, 1996. Adams Prize, Univ. of Cambridge, 1965; Sverdrup Gold Medal, Amer. Meteorol. Soc., 1975. *Publications:* The Dynamics of the Upper Ocean, 1966, 3rd edn 1976, Russian edn 1968, Chinese edn 1983; The Heart of the Earth, 1968, Italian edns 1970, 1975; The Last Chance Energy Book, 1979, Japanese edn 1983; (ed) Wave Dynamics and Radio Probing of the Ocean Surface, 1985; Flow and Reactions in Permeable Rocks, 1990; Geological Fluid Dynamics: sub-surface flow and reactions, 2009; various scientific papers in Jl Fluid Mechanics, Proc. Cambridge Philos. Soc., Jl Marine Research, Proc. Royal Society, Deep Sea Research, Journal Geophys. Research. *Address:* 462 Heron Point, Chestertown, MD 21620–1681, USA. *T:* (410) 7787579. *Clubs:* Johns Hopkins (Baltimore); Quissett Yacht (Mass). *Died 13 Oct. 2010.*

PHILLIS, Sir Robert (Weston), Kt 2004; Chief Executive, Guardian Media Group, 1997–2006; Chairman: Guardian Newspapers Ltd, 1997–2006; Greater Manchester Newspapers Ltd, 1997–2006; Trader Media Group Ltd, 2000–06; All3Media, since 2004; *b* 3 Dec. 1945; *s* of Francis William Phillis and Gertrude Grace Phillis; *m* 1966, Jean (*née* Derham); three *s*. *Educ:* John Ruskin Grammar Sch.; Nottingham Univ. (BA Industrial Econs 1968). Apprentice, printing industry,

1961–65; Thomson Regional Newspapers Ltd, 1968–69; British Printing Corp. Ltd, 1969–71; Lectr in Industrial Relations, Edinburgh Univ. and Scottish Business Sch., 1971–75; Vis. Fellow, Univ. of Nairobi, 1974; Personnel Dir, later Man. Dir, Sun Printers Ltd, 1976–79; Managing Director: Independent Television Publications Ltd, 1979–82 (Dir, 1979–87); Central Independent Television plc, 1981–87 (non-exec. Dir, 1987–91); Gp Man. Dir, Carlton Communications, 1987–91; Chief Exec., ITN, 1991–93; Dep. Dir-Gen., BBC, 1993–97; Man. Dir, BBC World Service, 1993–94; Chm., BBC Enterprises Ltd, 1993–94; Chm., later Chief Exec., BBC Worldwide, 1994–97. Chairman: Zenith Productions Ltd, 1984–91; GMG Endemol Entertainment, 1997–2000; GMG Radio Hldgs, 1999–2003. Director: ITN Ltd, 1982–87 and 1991–93; Worldwide Television News Corp., 1991–93; Jazz FM, 1999–2006; Radio Investments, 1999–2004; Artsworld Channels, 2000–02; Elizabeth Phillips Hughes Hall Co., 2001–; ITV plc, 2005–07. Chm., Ind. Rev. of Govt Communications, 2003–04; Mem., Ind. Rev. of Crime Statistics, 2006. Director: Periodical Publishers Assoc., 1979–82; ITCA, 1982–87; Internat. Council, Nat. Acad. of Television Arts and Scis, 1985– (Vice Chm. (Internat.), 1994–97; Life Fellow, 1997); LTA, 2005–; Vice-Pres., EBU, 1996–97. Dir and Trustee, Television Trust for the Environment, 1985–2006; Dir, Teaching Awards Trust, 2001–. Hon. Prof., Stirling Univ., 1997; City Fellow, Hughes Hall, Univ. of Cambridge, 2002–06 (MA 2006). FRSA 1984; FRTS 1988 (Chm., 1989–92; Vice Pres., 1994–2004; Pres., 2004–). Hon. Fellow: Cardiff Univ., 2004; Univ. of the Arts, London, 2006. Hon. DLitt: Salford, 1999; City, 2000; Nottingham, 2003. *Recreations:* ski-ing, golf, military and political history. *Clubs:* Garrick, Reform, Groucho. *Died 22 Dec. 2009.*

PHILO, Gordon Charles George, CMG 1970; MC 1944; HM Diplomatic Service, retired; *b* 8 Jan. 1920; *s* of Charles Gilbert Philo and Nellie Philo (*née* Pinnock); *m* 1952, Mavis (Vicky) Ella (*d* 1986), *d* of John Ford Galsworthy and Sybel Victoria Galsworthy (*née* Strachan). *Educ:* Haberdashers' Aske's Hampstead Sch.; Wadham Coll., Oxford (Methuen Schol. in Modern History, 1938). Served War, HM Forces, 1940–46: Royal West African Frontier Force, 1942–43; Airborne Forces, Normandy and Europe, 1944–45; India 1945–46. Alexander Korda Scholar, The Sorbonne, 1948–49; Lectr in Modern History, Wadham Coll., 1949–50; Foundn Mem., St Antony's Coll., Oxford, 1950–51. Foreign Office, 1951; Russian course, Christ's Coll., Cambridge, 1952–53; Istanbul, Third Sec., 1954–57; Ankara, Second Sec., 1957–58; FO, 1958–63; Kuala Lumpur, First Sec., 1963–67; FO, 1968; Consul-Gen., Hanoi, 1968–69; FCO, 1969–78. Extended Interview Assessor, Home Office Unit, CSSB, 1978–90. Chm. Council, Kipling Soc., 1986–88, 1997–99. Kesatria Mangku Negara (Hon.), Order of Malaysia, 1968. *Publications:* (jtly with wife, as Charles Forsyte): Diplomatic Death, 1960; Diving Death, 1962; Double Death, 1965; Murder with Minarets, 1968; The Decoding of Edwin Drood, 1980; articles in various jls. *Recreations:* travel, writing. *Address:* 10 Abercorn Close, NW8 9XS. *Club:* Athenæum. *Died 24 Jan. 2009.*

PHIPPS, Colin Barry, PhD; Chairman, Desire Petroleum plc, since 1996; *b* 23 July 1934; *s* of Edgar Reeves Phipps and Winifred Elsie Phipps (*née* Carroll); *m* 1956, Marion May Phipps (*née* Lawrey); two *s* two *d*. *Educ:* Townfield Elem. Sch., Hayes, Middx; Acton County; Swansea Grammar; University Coll. London (BSc 1st cl. Hons Geol. 1955); Birmingham Univ. (PhD Geol. 1957). Royal Dutch/Shell Geologist: Holland, Venezuela, USA, 1957–64; Consultant Petroleum Geologist, 1964–79; Dep. Chm. and Chief Exec., 1979–83, Chm., 1983–95, Clyde Petroleum. Chairman: Greenwich Resources plc, 1989–2002; Recycling Services Gp Ltd, 1996–2004. Chm., Brindex (Assoc. of British Independent Oil Exploration Cos), 1983–86. MP (Lab) Dudley W, Feb. 1974–1979. Mem., Council of Europe/WEU, 1976–79. Contested: (Lab) Walthamstow E, 1969; (SDP/L

Alliance) Worcester, 1983; (SDP/L Alliance) Stafford, 1987. Founder mem., SDP; Mem. SDP Nat. Cttee, 1984–89; Chm., W Midland Regional council, SDP, 1986–89. FGS 1956; FInstPet 1972; CGeol 1991; CSci 2005; Mem. Instn of Geologists, 1978. Chairman: Twentieth Century British Art Fair, 1988–93; Falklands Conservation (formerly Falkland Islands Foundn), 1990–92 (Trustee, 1983–99); English String Orch., 1990–92 (Dir, 1985–92). *Publications:* (co-ed) Energy and the Environment: democratic decision-making, 1978; What Future for the Falklands?, 1977 (Fabian tract 450); contrib.: Qly Jl Geol Sci., Geol. Mag., Geol. Jl, etc. *Recreation:* playing with my grandchildren. *Address:* Mathon Court, Mathon, Malvern WR13 5NZ. *T:* (01684) 892267. *Clubs:* Reform, Chelsea Arts; Oporto Cricket and Tennis. *Died 10 Jan. 2009.*

PICCARD, Dr Jacques; scientist; President, Foundation for the Study and Preservation of Seas and Lakes; *b* Belgium, 28 July 1922; Swiss Citizen; *s* of late Prof. Auguste Piccard (explorer of the stratosphere, in lighter-than-air craft, and of the ocean depths, in vehicles of his own design); *m* 1953, Marie Claude (*née* Maillard); two *s* one *d.* *Educ:* Brussels; Switzerland. Grad., Univ. of Geneva, 1946; Dip. from Grad. Inst. of Internat. Studies. Asst Prof., Univ. of Geneva, 1946–48. With his father, he participated in design and operation of the first deep diving vessels, which they named the bathyscaph (deep ship); this vessel, like its successor, operated independently of a mother ship; they first constructed the FNRS-2 (later turned over to the French Navy) then the Trieste (ultimately purchased by US Navy); Dr J. Piccard piloted the Trieste on 65 successive dives (the last, 23 Jan. 1960, was the record-breaking descent to 35,800 feet in the Marianas Trench, off Guam in the Pacific Ocean). He built in 1963, the mesoscaph Auguste Piccard, the first civilian submarine, which made, in 1964–65, over 1,100 dives carrying 33,000 people into the depths of Lake Geneva; built (with Grumman) 2nd mesoscaph, Ben Franklin, and in 1969 made 1.500 miles/30 days drift dive in Gulf Stream. Founded: Fondation pour l'Etude et la Protection de la Mer et des Lacs, 1966 (built research submersible, F. A.-FOREL, 1978); Institut International d'Ecologie, 1972. Hon. doctorate in Science, Amer. Internat. Coll., Springfield, Mass, 1962; Hon. DSc Hofstra Univ., 1970. Holds Distinguished Public Service Award, etc. *Publications:* The Sun beneath the Sea, 1971; technical papers and a popularized account (trans. many langs) of the Trieste, Seven Miles Down (with Robert S. Dietz). *Address:* (office) Fondation pour l'Etude et la Protection de la Mer et des Lacs, 1096 Cully, Switzerland. *T:* (21) 7992565. *Died 1 Nov. 2008.*

PICKARD, Hon. Neil Edward William; Agent General for New South Wales, 1991–92; *b* 13 Feb. 1929; *s* of Edward Henry Pickard and Ruby (*née* McGilvray); *m* 1983, Sally Anne Egan. *Educ:* Sydney Univ. (BA, MEd, DipEd); Leigh Coll. (LTh). Mem., World Student Conf., Strasbourg, 1960. Minister, Methodist Ch., 1952–65; High Sch. teacher, 1966–69; Chm., Far W Ambulance Service, 1969–70; Sydney University: Lectr in Educn, 1970–73; Member: House Cttee, Wesley Coll.; Univ. Educn Res. Cttee. Alderman: Peak Hill Council, 1964–65; Dubbo CC, 1968–70. Liberal Party: Western Regl Chm., 1966–72; Mem., Central Exec., NSW, 1966–72; Chm., Educn and Agenda Cttees, 1966–72. New South Wales Parliament: MP (Lib) Hornsby, 1973–91; Chm., Parly Educn Cttee; Mem., Select Cttee on NSW Sch. Cert. Assessment Procedures, 1979–81; Minister for Educn, 1976; Shadow Minister for Educn, Develt, Mineral Resources and Energy, 1976–88; Minister for Minerals and Energy, 1988–91. Freeman, City of London, 1992. *Recreations:* music, international relations, travel, tennis, cricket, bowls, soccer. *Address:* 11 Woolcott Avenue, Wahroonga, NSW 2076, Australia. *Clubs:* Royal Automobile, East India; Australian (Sydney). *Died 13 April 2007.*

PICKEN, Dr Laurence Ernest Rowland, FBA 1973; Fellow of Jesus College, Cambridge, 1944–76, then Emeritus (Hon. Fellow, 1989); *b* 16 July 1909. *Educ:* Oldknow Road and Waverley Road, Birmingham; Trinity Coll., Cambridge (BA 1931; PhD 1935; Hon. Fellow 1991); ScD Cantab 1952. Asst Dir of Research (Zoology), Cambridge Univ., 1946–66; Asst Dir of Research (Oriental Music), Cambridge Univ., 1966–76. Editor: Musica Asiatica, 1977–84; Music from the Tang Court, 1981–. FIBiol. Hon. Fellow, SOAS, 1991. DUP *hc* 1988. Trail Award, Linnean Soc., 1960; Curt Sachs Award, Amer. Musical Instrument Soc., 1995. *Publications:* The Organization of Cells and Other Organisms, 1960; Folk Musical Instruments of Turkey, 1975; contribs to many learned jls. *Address:* Jesus College, Cambridge CB5 8BL. *Died 16 March 2007.*

PICKERING, Ven. Fred; Archdeacon of Hampstead, 1974–84, then Archdeacon Emeritus; *b* 18 Nov. 1919; *s* of Arthur and Elizabeth Pickering; *m* 1948, Mabel Constance Threlfall; one *s* one *d.* *Educ:* Preston Grammar Sch.; St Peter's Coll., Oxford; St Aidan's Theol Coll., Birkenhead. BA 1941 (PPE), MA 1945. Curate: St Andrew's, Leyland, 1943–46; St Mary's, Islington, 1946–48; Organising Sec. for Church Pastoral Aid Soc. in NE England, 1948–51; Vicar: All Saints, Burton-on-Trent, 1951–56; St John's, Carlisle, 1956–63; St Cuthbert's, Wood Green, 1963–74; Rural Dean of East Haringey, 1968–73; Examng Chaplain to Bp of Edmonton, 1973–84. *Address:* Flat 8, Fosbrooke House, Clifton Drive, Lytham St Annes, Lancs FY8 5RQ. *T:* (01253) 667018. *Died 22 Jan. 2010.*

PICKFORD, David Michael, FRICS; Chairman, Committee of Management, Lionbrook (formerly Lilliput) Property Unit Trust, 1984–2002; *b* 25 Aug. 1926; *s* of Aston Charles Corpe Pickford and Gladys Ethel Pickford; *m* 1956, Elizabeth Gwendoline Hooson (decd); one *s* two *d.* *Educ:* Emanuel Sch., London; Coll. of Estate Management. FRICS 1953. Hillier Parker May & Rowden, 1943–46; LCC, 1946–48; London Investment & Mortgage Co., 1948–57; Haslemere Estates plc, 1957–86: Man. Dir, 1968–83; Chm., 1983–86; Dir, City & Metropolitan Building Soc., 1986–90; Chairman: Exeter Park Estates, 1986–91; Luis Palau Europe Ltd, 1980–2001; Dabet Ltd, 1986–2004; Compco Hldgs PLC, 1987–2002; Louth Estates (No 2) Ltd, 1989–2000; Brushfield Properties Ltd, 1990–2000; Stonechange Ltd, 1990–97; Wigmore Property Investment Trust Plc, 1993–96; Chairman, Committee of Management: Gulliver Develts Property Unit Trust, 1987–2000; Swift Balanced Property Unit Trust, 1993–97. President: London Dist, The Boys' Bde, 1967–86 (Hon. Life Pres., 1986); Christians in Property, 1990– (Chm., 1978–90); Chm., Drug and Alcohol Foundn, 1987–90 (Vice-Pres., 1990–92); Director: Mission to London, 1980–2000; London and Nationwide Missions, 1982–; Billy Graham Evangelistic Assoc., 1986–; Youth with a Mission, 1986–95; CARE Campaigns Ltd (also Trustee), 1987–; Trustee: David Pickford Charitable Foundn, 1968–; Pickford Trust, 1972–; Prison Fellowship, 1989–2001 (Chm. Trustees, 1990–93); London Prison Creative and Counselling Trust, 1991–93; Genesis Arts Trust, 1994–96. *Recreations:* sheep farming, youth work, gardening. *Address:* Elm Tree Farm, Mersham, near Ashford, Kent TN25 7HS. *T:* (01233) 720200, *Fax:* (01233) 720522. *Died 20 Sept. 2009.*

PICKLES, His Honour James; a Circuit Judge, 1976–91; *b* 18 March 1925; *s* of Arthur Pickles, OBE, JP and Gladys Pickles; *m* 1948, Sheila Ratcliffe (*d* 1995); two *s* one *d.* *Educ:* Worksop Coll.; Leeds Univ. (LLB); Christ Church, Oxford (MA). Called to the Bar, Inner Temple, 1946. Practised at Bradford, 1949–76; a Recorder of the Crown Court, 1972–76. Mem., Brighouse BC, 1956–62. Contested (L) Brighouse and Spenborough, 1964. *Publications:* Straight from the Bench, 1987; Judge for Yourself, 1992; Off the Record (novel), 1993. *Address:* Hazelwood, Heath Road, Halifax, West Yorks HX3 0BA. *Died 18 Dec. 2010.*

PIERRE, Abbé; *see* Grouès, Henri Antoine.

PIHL, Brig. Hon. Dame Mary Mackenzie, DBE 1970 (MBE 1958); Director, Women's Royal Army Corps, 1967–70, retired; *b* 3 Feb. 1916; *d* of Sir John Anderson, later 1st Viscount Waverley, PC, GCB, OM, GCSI, GCIE, FRS, and Christina Mackenzie Anderson; *m* 1973, Frithjof Pihl (*d* 1988). *Educ:* Sutton High Sch.; Villa Brillantmont, Lausanne. Joined Auxiliary Territorial Service, 1941; transferred to Women's Royal Army Corps, 1949. Hon. ADC to the Queen, 1967–70.
Died 18 June 2006.

PILE, Colonel Sir Frederick (Devereux), 3rd Bt *cr* 1900; MC 1945; *b* 10 Dec. 1915; *s* of Gen. Sir Frederick Alfred Pile, 2nd Bt, GCB, DSO, MC; *S* father, 1976; *m* 1st, 1940, Pamela (*d* 1983), *d* of late Philip Henstock; two *d*; 2nd, 1984, Mrs Josephine Culverwell (*neé* Cowper). *Educ:* Weymouth; RMC, Sandhurst. Joined Royal Tank Regt, 1935; served War of 1939–45, Egypt and NW Europe; commanded Leeds Rifles, 1955–56; Colonel GS, BJSM, Washington, DC, 1957–60; Commander, RAC Driving and Maintenance School, 1960–62. Secretary, Royal Soldiers' Daughters' School, 1965–71. *Publications:* Better than Riches, 1993. *Recreations:* fishing, cricket, travelling. *Heir: nephew* Anthony John Devereux Pile [*b* 7 June 1947; *m* 1977, Jennifer Clare Youngman; two *s* one *d*]. *Club:* MCC. *Died 1 Nov. 2010.*

PILKINGTON, (Richard) Godfrey; Partner and Director, Piccadilly Gallery, since 1953; *b* 8 Nov. 1918; *e s* of Col Guy R. Pilkington, DSO and Margery (*née* Frost); *m* 1950, Evelyn Edith (Eve) Vincent; two *s* two *d*. *Educ:* Clifton; Trinity Coll., Cambridge (MA). Lieut, RA, N Africa and Central Mediterranean, 1940–46. Joined Frost & Reed, art dealers, 1947; edited Pictures and Prints, 1951–60; founded Piccadilly Gallery, 1953. Master, Fine Art Trade Guild, 1964–66; Chm., Soc. of London Art Dealers, 1974–77. Governor, Wimbledon Sch. of Art, 1990–2000. *Publications:* numerous exhibn catalogues and magazine articles. *Recreations:* walking, boating, tennis, golf. *Address:* 45 Barons Court Road, W14 9DZ. *Clubs:* Athenæum, Garrick, Hurlingham.
Died 8 July 2007.

PIMLOTT, Steven Charles, OBE 2007; stage director; Joint Artistic Director, Chichester Festival Theatre, 2003–05; *b* 18 April 1953; *m* 1991, Daniela Bechly; two *s* one *d*. *Educ:* Manchester Grammar Sch.; Sidney Sussex Coll., Cambridge (MA). Staff Producer, ENO, 1976–78; Associate Dir, Sheffield Crucible, 1987–88; Company Dir, 1996, Associate Dir, 1996–2002, Associate Artist, RSC, Stratford; Artistic Dir, Savoy Theatre Opera, 2004. *Productions* include: *operas:* Opera North, 1978–80: La Bohème; Tosca; Nabucco; Werther; The Pearl Fishers, Scottish Opera; Don Giovanni, Victoria State Opera; Manon Lescaut, Australian Opera; La Traviata, Jerusalem Fest.; Samson et Dalila, Bregenz Fest., 1988; Carmen, 1989; Un Ballo in Maschera, Flanders Opera; Eugene Onegin, New Israeli Opera, 1991, Royal Opera House, 2006; La Bohème, ENO, 1993; Macbeth, Hamburg, 1997; L'Incoronazione di Poppea, ENO, 2000; *theatre:* Royal Exchange, Manchester: Ring Round the Moon, 1983; Carousel; Leeds Playhouse: On the Razzle; A Patriot for Me; York Mystery Plays, 1988; Sheffield Crucible: Carmen Jones; Twelfth Night, A Winter's Tale, 1987; The Park, 1988; Royal National Theatre: Sunday in the Park with George, 1990; The Miser, 1991; Royal Shakespeare Company: Julius Caesar, 1991; Murder in the Cathedral, 1993; Unfinished Business, Measure for Measure, 1994; Richard III, 1995; As You Like It, The Learned Ladies, 1996; Camino Real, 1997; Bad Weather, 1998; Antony and Cleopatra, 1999; Richard II, 2000; Hamlet, 2001; Chichester Festival Theatre: Nathan the Wise, The Seagull, 2003; The Master and Margarita, 2004; King Lear, 5/11 (world première), 2005; other productions include: Joseph and the Amazing Technicolor Dreamcoat, Palladium, 1991, and tour of UK, Canada, Australia, USA; Never Land, Royal Court, 1998; Doctor Doolittle, Apollo Hammersmith, 1998; Ion, Almeida, 2000; Bombay Dreams, Apollo Victoria

(world première), 2002, NY, 2004; And Then There Were None, Gielgud, 2005; *film:* Joseph and the Amazing Technicolor Dreamcoat, 1999. *Recreation:* playing the oboe. *Address:* c/o Cruickshank Cazenove Ltd, 97 Old South Lambeth Road, SW8 1XU. *T:* (020) 7735 2933.
Died 14 Feb. 2007.

PINA-CABRAL, Rt Rev. Daniel (Pereira dos Santos) de; an Assistant Bishop, Diocese of Europe (formerly Auxiliary Bishop, Diocese of Gibraltar in Europe), since 1976; Archdeacon of Gibraltar, 1986–94; *b* 27 Jan. 1924; *m* 1951, Ana Avelina Pina-Cabral; two *s* two *d*. *Educ:* University of Lisbon (Licentiate in Law). Archdeacon of the North in the Lusitanian Church, 1965; Suffragan Bishop of Lebombo (Mozambique), Church of the Province of Southern Africa, 1967; Diocesan Bishop of Lebombo, 1968; Canon of Gibraltar, 1976–. *Address:* Rua Henrique Lopes de Mendonça 253–4° Dto-Hab. 42, 4150 Porto, Portugal. *T:* (22) 6177772. *Died 23 June 2008.*

PINKER, Sir George (Douglas), KCVO 1990 (CVO 1983); FRCS, FRCSEd, FRCOG; Surgeon-Gynaecologist to the Queen, 1973–90; Consulting Gynaecological Surgeon and Obstetrician, St Mary's Hospital, Paddington and Samaritan Hospital, 1958–89; Consulting Gynaecological Surgeon, Middlesex and Soho Hospitals, 1969–80; Consultant Gynæcologist, King Edward VII Hospital for Officers, 1974–89; *b* 6 Dec. 1924; *s* of late Ronald Douglas Pinker and of Queenie Elizabeth Pinker (*née* Dix); *m* Dorothy Emma (*née* Russell) (*d* 2003); three *s* one *d* (incl. twin *s* and *d*). *Educ:* Reading Sch.; St Mary's Hosp., London Univ. MB BS London 1947; DObst 1949; MRCOG 1954; FRCS(Ed) 1957; FRCOG 1964; FRCS 1989. Late Cons. Gyn. Surg., Bolingbroke Hosp., and Res. Off., Nuffield Dept of Obst., Radcliffe Infirmary, Oxford; late Cons. Gyn. Surg., Queen Charlotte's Hosp. Arthur Wilson Orator, 1972 and 1989, Turnbull Scholar, and Hon. Consultant Obstetrician and Gynaecologist, 1972, Royal Women's Hosp., Melbourne. Examiner in Obst. and Gynae.: Univs of Cambridge, Dundee, London, and FRCS Edinburgh; formerly also in RCOG, and Univs of Birmingham, Glasgow and Dublin. Sims Black Travelling Prof., RCOG, 1979; Vis. Prof., SA Regional Council, RCOG, 1980. Pres., RCOG, 1987–90 (Hon. Treas., 1970–77; Vice-Pres., 1980–83). Pres., British Fertility Soc., 1987; Mem. Council, Winston Churchill Trust, 1979–95; Mem., Blair Bell Res. Soc.; FRSocMed (Pres., 1992–95); Hon. Mem., British Paediatric Assoc., 1988. Hon. FRCSI 1987; Hon. FRACOG 1989; Hon. FACOG 1990; Hon. Fellow, S African Soc. of Obstetricians and Gynaecologists, 1990; Hon. FCMSA 1991. Chm., Editorial Bd, Modern Medicine (Obs. and Gynae.), 1989–91 (Mem., 1980–91). *Publications:* (all jtly) Ten Teachers Diseases of Women, 1964; Ten Teachers Obstetrics, 1966; A Short Textbook of Obstetrics and Gynaecology, 1967. *Recreations:* music, gardening, sailing, ski-ing, fell walking. *Address:* Sycamore House, Willersey, Broadway, Worcs WR12 7PJ. *Club:* Garrick.
Died 29 April 2007.

PINNER, Hayim, OBE 1989; consultant, administrator, linguist, educator, lecturer, journalist, broadcaster; Director, Sternberg Charitable Trust, 1991–96; *b* London, 25 May 1925; *s* of late Simon Pinner and Annie Pinner (*née* Wagner); *m* 1956, Rita Reuben, Cape Town (marr. diss. 1980); one *s* one *d*. *Educ:* Davenant Foundation School; London University; Yeshivah Etz Hayim; Bet Berl College, Israel. Served RAOC, 1944–48; Editor, Jewish Vanguard, 1950–74; Exec. Dir, B'nai B'rith, 1957–77; Sec. Gen., Board of Deputies of British Jews, 1977–91. Hon. Vice-Pres., Zionist Fedn of GB and Ireland, 1975– (Hon. Treasurer, 1971–75); Vice-Pres., Labour Zionist Movement (former Nat. Chm.); Hon. Sec., CCJ; Member: Jewish Agency and World Zionist Orgn; Adv. Council, World Congress of Faiths; Trades Adv. Council; Hillel Foundn; Jt Israel Appeal; Lab. Party Middle East Cttee; 'B' List of Lab. Parly Candidates; UNA; Founder Mem. Exec., Inter-Faith.

FRSA. Freeman, City of London. Contribs to Radio 4, Radio London, London Broadcasting, BBC TV. Encomienda de la Orden del Mérito Civil (Spain), 1993. *Publications:* contribs to UK and foreign periodicals, Isra-Kit. *Recreations:* travelling, swimming, reading, talking.
Died 5 Nov. 2007.

PINTER, Harold, CH 2002; CBE 1966; CLit 1998; FRSL; actor, playwright and director; Associate Director, National Theatre, 1973–83; *b* 10 Oct. 1930; *s* of Jack and Frances Pinter; *m* 1st, 1956, Vivien Merchant (marr. diss. 1980; she *d* 1982); one *s*; 2nd, 1980, Lady Antonia Fraser, CBE, FRSL. *Educ:* Hackney Downs Grammar Sch. Actor (mainly repertory), 1949–57. *Directed:* The Collection (co-dir with Peter Hall), Aldwych, 1962; The Birthday Party, Aldwych, 1964; The Lover, The Dwarfs, Arts, 1966; Exiles, Mermaid, 1970; Butley, Criterion, 1971; Butley (film), 1973; Next of Kin, Nat. Theatre, 1974; Otherwise Engaged, Queen's, 1975, NY 1977; Blithe Spirit, Nat. Theatre, 1977; The Rear Column, Globe, 1978; Close of Play, Nat. Theatre, 1979; The Hothouse, Hampstead, 1980 (for TV, 1982); Quartermaine's Terms, Queen's, 1981; Incident at Tulse Hill, Hampstead, 1982; The Trojan War Will Not Take Place, Nat. Theatre, 1983; The Common Pursuit, Lyric Hammersmith, 1984; Sweet Bird of Youth, Haymarket, 1985; Circe and Bravo, Wyndham's, 1986; Vanilla, Lyric, 1990; The New World Order, Royal Court, 1991; Party Time, Almeida, 1991 (for TV, 1992); Oleanna, Royal Court, 1993; Taking Sides, Criterion, 1995; Twelve Angry Men, Comedy, 1996; The Late Middle Classes, Watford, 1999; Celebration, and The Room, Almeida, 2000; No Man's Land, RNT, 2001; The Old Masters, Birmingham Rep., transf. Comedy, 2004. Fellow, BAFTA, 1997. Hon. DLitt: Reading, 1970; Birmingham, 1971; Glasgow, 1974; East Anglia, 1974; Stirling, 1979; Brown, 1982; Hull, 1986; Sussex, 1990; E London, 1994; Sofia, 1995; Bristol, 1998; London, 1999; Univ. of Aristotle, Thessaloniki, 2000; Florence, 2001; Turin, 2002; Nat. Univ. of Ireland, 2004; Leeds, 2007; Cambridge, 2008; Kragujevac, Serbia, 2008. Shakespeare Prize, Hamburg, 1970; Austrian State Prize for European Literature, 1973; Pirandello Prize, 1980; Donatello Prize, 1982; Elmer Holmes Bobst Award, 1984; David Cohen British Literary Prize, 1995; Laurence Olivier Special Award, 1996; Molière d'Honneur, Paris, 1997; Award for Literary Excellence, Sunday Times, 1997; Critics' Circle Award, 2000; Brianza Poetry Prize, 2000; South Bank Show Award, 2001; World Leaders Award, Canada, 2001; Hermann Kesten Medallion, 2001; Teatro Filodrammatici, 2004; 50th Anniversary Special Award, Evening Standard Theatre Awards, 2004; Wilfred Owen Poetry Prize, 2005; Kafka Prize, 2005; Nobel Prize for Literature, 2005; European Theatre Prize, 2006. Chevalier, Légion d'Honneur (France), 2007. *Plays:* The Room (stage 1957, television 1965); The Birthday Party, 1957 (stage 1958, television 1960 and 1987, film 1968); The Dumb Waiter, 1957 (stage 1960, television 1964 and 1987); The Hothouse, 1958 (stage 1980, television 1981); A Slight Ache, 1958 (radio 1959, stage 1961, television 1966); A Night Out, 1959 (radio and television, 1960); The Caretaker, 1959 (stage 1960 and 1991, film 1963, television 1966 and 1982); Night School, 1960 (television 1960 and 1982, radio 1966); The Dwarfs (radio 1960, stage 1963); The Collection (television 1961 and 1979, stage 1962); The Lover (television 1962 (Italia Prize) and 1977, stage 1963); Tea Party, 1964 (television 1965, stage 1970); The Homecoming, 1964 (stage 1965, film 1973); The Basement, 1966 (television 1967, stage 1970); Landscape, 1967 (radio 1968, stage 1969); Silence, 1968 (stage 1968); Night, 1969; Old Times, 1970 (stage 1971, television 1975); Monologue, 1972 (television 1973); No Man's Land, 1974 (stage 1975 and 1992, television 1978); Betrayal (stage 1978 (SWET Award, 1979) and 1991, film 1983); Family Voices, 1980 (radio 1981 (Giles Cooper Award, 1982), stage 1981); A Kind of Alaska, 1982 (stage and television 1984); Victoria Station (stage 1982); One for the Road (stage and television 1984); Mountain Language (stage 1988); The New World Order (stage 1991); Party Time (stage 1991, television 1992);

Moonlight (stage 1993); Ashes to Ashes (stage 1996); Celebration (stage 2000); Sketches, 2002. *Screenplays:* The Caretaker, The Servant, 1962; The Pumpkin Eater, 1963; The Quiller Memorandum, 1966; Accident, 1967; The Birthday Party, The Homecoming, 1968; The Go-Between, 1969; Langrishe, Go Down, 1970 (adapted for television, 1978); A la Recherche du Temps Perdu, 1972; The Last Tycoon, 1974; The French Lieutenant's Woman, 1981; Betrayal, 1981; Victory, 1982; Turtle Diary, 1985; The Handmaid's Tale, 1987; The Heat of the Day, 1988; Reunion, 1989; The Trial, 1989; The Comfort of Strangers, 1990; Sleuth, 2007. *Publications:* The Caretaker, 1960; The Birthday Party, and other plays, 1960; A Slight Ache, 1961; The Collection, 1963; The Lover, 1963; The Homecoming, 1965; Tea Party, and, The Basement, 1967; (co-ed) PEN Anthology of New Poems, 1967; Mac, 1968; Landscape, and, Silence, 1969; Five Screenplays, 1971; Old Times, 1971; Poems, 1971; No Man's Land, 1975; The Proust Screenplay: A la Recherche du Temps Perdu, 1978; Betrayal, 1978; Poems and Prose 1949–1977, 1978; I Know the Place, 1979; Family Voices, 1981; Other Places, 1982; French Lieutenant's Woman and other screenplays, 1982; One For The Road, 1984; Collected Poems and Prose, 1986; (co-ed) 100 Poems by 100 Poets, 1986; Mountain Language, 1988; The Heat of the Day, 1989; The Dwarfs (novel), 1990; Party Time, 1991; Moonlight, 1993; (ed jtly) 99 Poems in Translation, 1994; Ashes to Ashes, 1996; Various Voices: prose, poetry, politics 1948–1998, 1998; Celebration, 2000. *Recreation:* cricket. *Address:* c/o Judy Daish Associates Ltd, 2 St Charles Place, W10 6EG.
Died 24 Dec. 2008.

PIPPARD, Prof. Sir (Alfred) Brian, Kt 1975; FRS 1956; Cavendish Professor of Physics, University of Cambridge, 1971–82, then Emeritus; *b* 7 Sept. 1920; *s* of late Prof. A. J. S. Pippard; *m* 1955, Charlotte Frances Dyer; three *d*. *Educ:* Clifton Coll.; Clare Coll., Cambridge (BA 1941; MA 1945; PhD 1949; ScD 1966; Hon. Fellow 1973). Scientific Officer, Radar Research and Development Establishment, Great Malvern, 1941–45; Stokes Student, Pembroke Coll., Cambridge, 1945–46; Demonstrator in Physics, University of Cambridge, 1946; Lecturer in Physics, 1950; Reader in Physics, 1959–60; John Humphrey Plummer Prof. of Physics, 1960–71; Pres., Clare Hall, Cambridge, 1966–73 (Hon. Fellow, 1993). Visiting Prof., Institute for the Study of Metals, University of Chicago, 1955–56. Fellow of Clare Coll., Cambridge, 1947–66. Cherwell-Simon Memorial Lectr, Oxford, 1968–69; Eddington Meml Lectr, Cambridge, 1988. Pres., Inst. of Physics, 1974–76 (FInstP 1970, Hon. FInstP 1995). Hughes Medal of the Royal Soc., 1959; Holweck Medal, 1961; Dannie-Heineman Prize, 1969; Guthrie Prize, 1970; Lars Onsager Medal, Norwegian Univ. of Sci. and Technol., Trondheim, 2005. *Publications:* Elements of Classical Thermodynamics, 1957; Dynamics of Conduction Electrons, 1962; Forces and Particles, 1972; The Physics of Vibration, vol. 1, 1978, vol. 2, 1983; Response and Stability, 1985; Magnetoresistance, 1989; (ed and contrib.) 20th Century Physics, 1995; papers in Proc. Royal Soc., etc. *Recreation:* music. *Address:* 30 Porson Road, Cambridge CB2 8EU. *T:* (01223) 358713.
Died 21 Sept. 2008.

PIRELLI, Leopoldo; Knight, Order of Labour Merit, 1977; engineer; Hon. President, Pirelli & Co., since 1999 (Partner, 1957–99, and Chairman, 1995–99); *b* 27 Aug. 1925; *s* of Alberto Pirelli and Ludovica Zambeletti; *m* 1947, Giulia Ferlito; one *s* one *d*. *Educ:* Milan University (Politecnico); graduated in Mech. Eng. 1950. Mem., Bd of Dirs, 1954, Vice-Chm., 1956, Chm., 1965–96, Pirelli SpA; Mem., Bd of Dirs, 1956–65, Vice-Chm., 1979–99, Soc. Internat. Pirelli. Mem., Exec. Council, Confedn of Italian Industries, 1957– (Dep. Chm., 1974–80; Mem. Bd, 1974–82). *Address:* Via Gaetano Negri 10, 20123 Milan, Italy. *Clubs:* Clubino, Rotary, Unione (Milan); Yacht Club Italiano (Genoa). *Died 23 Jan. 2007.*

PIRIE, Iain Gordon; Sheriff of Glasgow and Strathkelvin, 1982–99; part time Sheriff, 2000–03; *b* 15 Jan. 1933; *s* of Charles Fox Pirie and Mary Ann Gordon; *m* 1960, Sheila Brown Forbes, MB, ChB; two *s* one *d*. *Educ*: Harris Acad., Dundee; St Andrews Univ. (MA, LLB). Legal Asst, Stirling, Eunson & Belford, Solicitors, Dunfermline, 1958–60; Depute Procurator Fiscal, Paisley, 1960–67; Sen. Depute Procurator Fiscal, Glasgow, 1967–71; Procurator Fiscal: Dumfries, 1971–76; Ayr, 1976–79; Sheriff of S Strathclyde, Dumfries and Galloway, 1979–82. *Recreations*: golf, tennis, reading, gardening, playing the violin. *Died 17 March 2006.*

PITCHFORD, His Honour Charles Neville; a Circuit Judge, Wales and Chester Circuit, 1972–87; *b* 18 Feb. 1921; *m* Emily; one *s*. *Educ*: Oxford Univ. (MA). Served War of 1939–45, RAF (Flt Lt). Called to the Bar, Middle Temple, 1948. *Address*: Llanynant, Kennel Lane, Coed Morgan, Abergavenny, Gwent NP7 9UR. *Died 19 July 2006.*

PITMAN, Sir Brian (Ivor), Kt 1994; Chief Executive, 1983–97, Chairman, 1997–2001, Lloyds TSB Group plc (formerly Lloyds Bank Plc); Senior Adviser, Morgan Stanley, since 2001; Chairman, Virgin Money, since 2010; *b* 13 Dec. 1931; *s* of late Ronald Ivor Pitman and Doris Ivy Pitman (*née* Short); *m* 1954, Barbara Mildred Ann (*née* Darby); two *s* one *d*. *Educ*: Cheltenham Grammar School. Entered Lloyds Bank, 1952, Jt Gen. Manager, 1975; Exec. Dir, Lloyds Bank International, 1976, Dep. Chief Exec., 1978; Dep. Group Chief Exec., 1982, Dir, 1983–2001, Lloyds Bank Plc, subseq. Lloyds TSB Gp plc. Chm., Lloyds First Western Corp., 1983–94; Director: Lloyds Bank California, 1982–86; Nat. Bank of New Zealand Ltd, 1982–97; Lloyds and Scottish Plc, 1983; Lloyds Bank International Ltd, 1985–87; Lloyds Merchant Bank Holdings Ltd, 1985–88; NBNZ Holdings Ltd, 1990–97; Carlton Communications Plc, 1998–2004; Tomkins PLC, 2000–07; Carphone Warehouse Gp, 2001–; Singapore Airlines Ltd, 2003–09; ITV plc, 2003–08; Chm., Next plc, 1998–2002. Mem., Internat. Adv. Panel, Monetary Authy of Singapore, 1999–2001. President: BBA, 1996–97; CIB, 1997–98. Gov., Ashridge Mgt Coll., 1997–. FCIB. Master, Guild of Internat. Bankers, 2002–03. Hon. DSc: City, 1996; UMIST, 2000. *Recreations*: golf, cricket, music. *Address*: Morgan Stanley, 20 Bank Street, Canary Wharf, E14 4AD. *Clubs*: MCC; Yorkshire CC; Gloucestershire CC; St George's Hill Golf. *Died 11 March 2010.*

PITT, Barrie (William Edward); author and editor of military histories; *b* Galway, 7 July 1918; *y s* of John Pitt and Ethel May Pitt (*née* Pennell); *m* 1st, 1943, Phyllis Kate (*née* Edwards); one *s* (decd); 2nd, 1953, Sonia Deirdre (*née* Hoskins) (marr. diss., 1971); 3rd, 1983, Frances Mary Crook (*née* Moore). *Educ*: Portsmouth Southern Grammar Sch. Bank Clerk, 1935. Served War of 1939–45, in Army. Surveyor, 1946. Began writing, 1954. Information Officer, Atomic Energy Authority, 1961; Historical Consultant to BBC Series, The Great War, 1963; Editor, Purnell's History of the Second World War, 1964; Editor-in-Chief: Ballantine's Illustrated History of World War 2, 1967 (US Book Series); Ballantine's Illustrated History of the Violent Century, 1971; Editor: Purnell's History of the First World War, 1969; British History Illustrated, 1974–78; Consultant Editor, The Military History of World War II, 1986. *Publications*: The Edge of Battle, 1958; Zeebrugge, St George's Day, 1918, 1958; Coronel and Falkland, 1960; 1918 The Last Act, 1962; The Battle of the Atlantic, 1977; The Crucible of War: Western Desert 1941, 1980; Churchill and the Generals, 1981; The Crucible of War: Year of Alamein 1942, 1982; Special Boat Squadron, 1983; (with Frances Pitt) The Chronological Atlas of World War II, 1989; contrib. to: Encyclopaedia Britannica; The Sunday Times. *Recreations*: reading, listening to classical music. *Address*: 10 Wellington Road, Taunton, Somerset TA1 4EG. *T*: (01823) 337188. *Club*: Savage. *Died 15 April 2006.*

PITTILO, Prof. (Robert) Michael, MBE 2010; PhD; FSB; Principal and Vice-Chancellor, Robert Gordon University, Aberdeen, since 2005; *b* 7 Oct. 1954; *s* of Robert Dawson Pittilo and Betsy Brown Pittilo (*née* Baird); *m* 1987, Dr Carol Margaret Blow. *Educ*: Kelvinside Acad., Glasgow; Univ. of Strathclyde (BSc Hons Biol.); NE London Poly. (PhD Biol. 1981). FSB (FIBiol 1994). Postdoctoral Res. Asst, Middx Hosp. Med. Sch., 1981–85; Hon. Res. Associate, University Coll. and Middx Sch. of Medicine, 1985–94; Kingston Polytechnic, subsequently Kingston University: Lectr, Sen. Lectr, then Reader, 1985–92; Prof. of Biomed. Scis and Hd, Dept of Life Scis, 1992–94; Dean: Faculty of Health and Social Care Scis, Kingston Univ. and St George's Hosp. Med. Sch., Univ. of London, 1995–2001; for Multiprofessional Educn, 1996–2001, and for Taught Postgrad. Courses, 1999–2001, St George's Hosp. Med. Sch., Univ. of London; Pro Vice-Chancellor, Univ. of Herts, 2001–05. Chm., Regulatory Wkg Gps for Herbal Medicine and Acupuncture, DoH, 2002–03 and 2006–09; Mem., various nat. health cttees, 1997–. FLS 1980; FRSPH (FRSH 1993); FIBMS 1997; FRMS 2008. FRSA 2001. *Publications*: book chapters, articles, papers and reviews on the electron microscopy of parasitic protozoa, smoking, atherosclerosis and endothelial injury and health policy. *Recreations*: photography, mountain walking, motorcycling, cinema, music, clay shooting. *Address*: Office of the Principal and Vice-Chancellor, Robert Gordon University, Schoolhill, Aberdeen AB10 1FR. *T*: (01224) 262001, *Fax*: (01224) 262626; *e-mail*: R.M.Pittilo@rgu.ac.uk. *Clubs*: Royal Society of Medicine; Royal Northern and University (Aberdeen). *Died 16 Feb. 2010.*

PITTS, Sir Cyril (Alfred), Kt 1968; Governor, University of Westminster (formerly Polytechnic of Central London), 1984–95 (Chairman of Governors, 1985–93); *b* 21 March 1916; *m* 1942, Barbara; two *s* one *d*. *Educ*: St Olave's; Jesus Coll., Cambridge. Chairman of ICI Companies in India, 1964–68; Chm., ICI (Export) Ltd and Gen. Manager, Internat. Coordination, ICI Ltd, 1968–78; Dir, ICI Americas Ltd, 1974–77; Dep. Chm., Ozalid Gp Holdings Ltd, 1975–77. Chairman: Process Plant EDC, 1979–83; Peter Brotherhood, 1980–83. President: Bengal Chamber of Commerce and Industry, and Associated Chambers of Commerce and Industry of India, 1967–68; British and S Asian Trade Assoc., 1978–83. Councillor, RIIA, 1968–77. Hon. DLitt Westminster, 1993. *Address*: 11 Middle Avenue, Farnham, Surrey GU9 8JL. *T*: (01252) 715864. *Clubs*: Oriental; Bengal (Calcutta). *Died 8 March 2009.*

PITTS CRICK, Ronald; *see* Crick.

PLATER, Alan Frederick, CBE 2005; FRSL 1985; freelance writer, since 1960; *b* 15 April 1935; *s* of Herbert Richard Plater and Isabella Scott Plater; *m* 1st, 1958, Shirley Johnson (marr. diss. 1985); two *s* one *d*; 2nd, 1986, Shirley Rubinstein; three step *s*. *Educ*: Pickering Road Jun. Sch., Hull; Kingston High Sch., Hull; King's Coll., Newcastle upon Tyne. ARIBA. Trained as architect and worked for short time in the profession before becoming full-time writer in 1960; wrote extensively for radio, television, films and theatre, also for The Guardian, Listener, New Statesman, etc. Vis. Prof., Univ. of Bournemouth, 2002–09. Pres., Writers' Guild of GB, 1991–95 (Co-chair, 1986–87). Works include: *theatre*: A Smashing Day (also televised); Close the Coalhouse Door (Writers' Guild Radio Award, 1972); And a Little Love Besides; Swallows on the Water; Trinity Tales; The Fosdyke Saga; Fosdyke Two; On Your Way, Riley!; Skyhooks; A Foot on the Earth; Prez; Rent Party (musical); Sweet Sorrow; Going Home; I Thought I Heard a Rustling; Shooting the Legend; All Credit to the Lads; Peggy for You; Tales from the Backyard; Only a Matter of Time; Barriers; The Last Days of the Empire; Charlie's Trousers; Blonde Bombshells of 1943; Confessions of a City Supporter; Sweet William; Tales from the Golden Slipper; Looking for Buddy; *films*: The Virgin and the Gypsy; It Shouldn't Happen to a Vet;

Priest of Love; Keep the Aspidistra Flying; *television:* plays: So Long Charlie; See the Pretty Lights; To See How Far It Is (trilogy); Land of Green Ginger; Willow Cabins; The Party of the First Part; The Blacktoft Diaries; Thank You, Mrs Clinkscales; Doggin' Around; The Last of the Blonde Bombshells; Belonging; The Last Will and Testament of Billy Two Sheds; Joe Maddison's War; biographies: The Crystal Spirit; Pride of our Alley; Edward Lear—at the edge of the sand; Coming Through; series and serials: Z Cars; Softly Softly; Shoulder to Shoulder; Trinity Tales; The Good Companions; The Consultant; Barchester Chronicles (adaptation of The Warden, and Barchester Towers, by Trollope); The Beiderbecke Affair; The Beiderbecke Tapes; The Fortunes of War (adaptation of Balkan and Levant trilogies by Olivia Manning); A Very British Coup (International Emmy; Golden Fleece of Georgia (USSR); Best Series BAFTA Award; Best Series RTS Award; Best Series Broadcasting Press Guild Award; Best Series and Grand Prix, Banff Internat. TV Fest., Canada); The Beiderbecke Connection; Campion (adapted from Margery Allingham); A Day in Summer (adaptation of J. L. Carr novel); Misterioso; A Few Selected Exits (adapted from Gwyn Thomas; Cymru Writing Award, BAFTA, Regl Programme Award, RTS, 1993); Oliver's Travels; Dalziel & Pascoe (from Reginald Hill); Lewis; *radio:* The Journal of Vasilije Bogdanovic (Sony Radio Award, 1983); All Things betray Thee (from Gwyn Thomas); The Lower Depths (from Gorky); Only a Matter of Time; Time Added On For Injuries; The Devil's Music; Abandoned Projects; Stories for Another Day; The Gallery. FRSA 1991. Hon. Fellow, Humberside Coll. of Higher Educn, 1983; Hon. DLitt: Hull, 1985; Newcastle, 2005; Hon. DCL Northumbria, 1997; DUniv Open, 2004. RTS Writer's Award, 1984/85; Broadcasting Press Guild Award, 1987; Writer's Award, BAFTA, 1988; Northern Personality Award, Variety Club of GB, 1989; Dennis Potter Award, BAFTA, 2005; Writer's Guild Lifetime Achievement Award, 2007. *Publications:* The Beiderbecke Affair, 1985; The Beiderbecke Tapes, 1986; Misterioso, 1987; The Beiderbecke Connection, 1992; Oliver's Travels, 1994; Doggin' Around, 2006; plays and shorter pieces in various anthologies. *Recreations:* reading, theatre, snooker, jazz, grandchildren, talking and listening. *Address:* c/o Alexandra Cann Representation, 52 Beauchamp Place, SW3 1NY. *T:* (020) 7584 9047. *Club:* Dramatists'.
Died 25 June 2010.

PLATT, Sir Harold (Grant), Kt 1995; Chairman, Uganda Law Reform Commission, 1995–2000; *b* 11 March 1925; *s* of Rev. Harold George Platt and Frances Eaton Platt; *m* 1971, Eleonore Magdolna Gräfin Meran; one *d. Educ:* Ootacamund, S India; St Peter's Coll., Oxford. Called to the Bar, Middle Temple, 1952; joined Colonial Legal Service, 1954: Puisne Judge: Tanzania, 1965–73; Kenya, 1973–84; Judge of Court of Appeal, Kenya, 1984–89; Judge of Supreme Court, Uganda, 1989–95. *Recreations:* golf, tennis, gardening. *Address:* Johann Fuxgasse 8, 8010 Graz, Austria. *T:* (316) 323462. *Club:* Muthaiga Country (Kenya). *Died 2 Sept. 2010.*

PLOWDEN, William Julius Lowthian, PhD; independent consultant; *b* 7 Feb. 1935; *s* of Lord Plowden, GBE, KCB, and Lady Plowden, DBE; *m* 1960, Veronica Gascoigne; two *s* two *d. Educ:* Eton; King's Coll., Cambridge (BA, PhD); Univ. of Calif, Berkeley (Commonwealth Fund Fellow). Staff Writer, Economist, 1959–60; BoT, 1960–65; Lectr in Govt, LSE, 1965–71; Central Policy Review Staff, Cabinet Office, 1971–77; Under Sec., Dept of Industry, 1977–78; Dir-Gen., RIPA, 1978–88; Exec. Dir, UK Harkness Fellowships, NY, 1988–91; Sen. Advr, Harkness Fellowships, London, 1991–98; UK Dir, Atlantic Fellowships, 1995–98. Hon. Prof., Dept of Politics, Univ. of Warwick, 1977–82; Vis. Prof. in Govt, LSE, 1982–88, 2002–; Vis. Prof., Univ. of Bath, 1992–95; Sen. Res. Associate, IPPR, 1992–94; Vis. Sen. Res. Fellow, London Business Sch., 1993–94; Vis. Res. Fellow, Constitution Unit, UCL, 1999–2002. Member: W Lambeth DHA, 1982–87; QCA,

1999–2002. Trustee: CSV, 1984–2004; Southern Africa Advanced Educn Project, 1986–95; Public Mgt Foundn, 1992–98. Mem. Ct of Govs, LSE, 1987–2006, Council, 2000–03. *Publications:* The Motor Car and Politics in Britain, 1971; (with Tessa Blackstone) Inside the Think Tank: advising the Cabinet 1971–1983, 1988; Mandarins and Ministers, 1994; (with Kate Jenkins) Governance and Nation-Building: the failure of international intervention, 2006. *Address:* 49 Stockwell Park Road, SW9 0DD. *T:* (020) 7274 4535. *Died 26 June 2010.*

PLOWRIGHT, David Ernest, CBE 1996; Chairman, Granada Television Ltd, 1987–92; Deputy Chairman, Channel Four Television, 1992–97; Visiting Professor in Media Studies, Salford University, since 1992; *b* 11 Dec. 1930; *s* of late William Ernest Plowright and of Daisy Margaret Plowright; *m* 1953, Brenda Mary (née Key); one *s* two *d. Educ:* Scunthorpe Grammar Sch.; on local weekly newspaper and during National Service, Germany. Reporter, Scunthorpe Star, 1950; freelance corresp. and sports writer, 1952; Reporter, Feature Writer and briefly Equestrian Corresp., Yorkshire Post, 1954; Granada Television: News Editor, 1957; Producer, Current Affairs, 1960; Editor, World in Action, 1966; Head of Current Affairs, 1968; Controller of Programmes, 1969–79; Jt Man. Dir, 1975–81; Man. Dir, 1981–87; Director: Granada Internat., 1975–92; Granada Gp, 1981–92. Chm., Network Programme Cttee, ITV, 1980–82. Chm., ITCA, 1984–86. Director: Superchannel, 1986–89; Merseyside Tourism Board, 1986–88; British Satellite Broadcasting, 1987–90; British Screen, 1988–92; Tate Gall., Liverpool, 1988–91. Vice Pres., RTS, 1982–94; Member: Steering Cttee, European Film and TV Forum, 1988–91; Internat. Council, Nat. Acad. for TV Arts and Scis, 1988–92; Manchester Olympic Bid Cttee, 1980, Chm. Develt Cttee, Manchester City of Drama 1994, 1992–94. Trustee, BAFTA (Fellow, 1992). Gov., Manchester Polytechnic, 1988–90. Hon. DLitt Salford, 1989; Hon. DArt Liverpool Poly., 1991. *Recreations:* television, watching sport, messing about in a boat. *Address:* Westways, Wilmslow Road, Mottram St Andrew, Cheshire SK10 4QT. *T:* (01625) 820948. *Died 24 Aug. 2006.*

PLOWRIGHT, Walter, CMG 1974; DVSc; FRS 1981; FRCVS; Head, Department of Microbiology, ARC Institute for Research on Animal Diseases, Compton, Berks, 1978–83; *b* 20 July 1923; 2nd *s* of Jonathan and Mahala Plowright, Holbeach, Lincs; *m* 1959, Dorothy Joy (née Bell). *Educ:* Moulton and Spalding Grammar Schs; Royal Veterinary Coll., London. DVSc (Pret.) 1964; MRCVS 1944; FRCVS 1977; FRVC 1987. Commissioned, RAVC, 1944–48; Colonial Service, 1950–64; Animal Virus Research Inst., Pirbright, 1964–71 (seconded E Africa, 1966–71); Prof. of Vet. Microbiology, RVC, 1971–78. Hon. Mem., Acad. Royale des Sciences d'Outre-Mer, Brussels, 1986. Hon. DSc: Univ. of Nairobi, 1984; Reading, 1986. J. T. Edwards Memorial Prize, 1964; R. B. Bennett Commonwealth Prize of RSA, 1972; Bledisloe Vet. Award, RASE, 1979; King Baudouin Internat. Develt Prize, 1984; Dalrymple-Champneys Cup, BVA, 1984; Gold Award, Office Internat. des Epizooties, Paris, 1988; Outstanding Scientific Achievement Award, Animal Health Trust, 1991; Theiler Meml Trust Award, South Africa, 1994; World Food Prize, World Food Prize Foundn, Iowa, 1999. Moran, Order of the Burning Spear (Kenya), 2000. *Publications:* numerous contribs to scientific jls relating to virus diseases of animals. *Recreations:* gardening, reading on wine and investment, African history. *Address:* The Garage, Grange Close, Goring-on-Thames, Reading RG8 9EA. *T:* (01491) 872891. *Died 20 Feb. 2010.*

PLUMMER OF ST MARYLEBONE, Baron *cr* 1981 (Life Peer), of the City of Westminster; **(Arthur) Desmond (Herne) Plummer,** Kt 1971; TD 1950; JP; DL; President, Portman Building Society, 1990–2007 (Chairman, 1983–90); *b* 25 May 1914; *s* of late Arthur Herne Plummer and Janet (née McCormick); *m* 1941,

Pat Holloway (Pres., Cons. Women's Adv. Cttee, Greater London Area, 1967–71) (*d* 1998); one *d. Educ:* Hurstpierpoint Coll.; Coll. of Estate Management. FAI 1948; FRICS 1970. Served 1938–46, Royal Engineers, Field and Staff. Member: TA Sports Bd, 1953–79; London Electricity Consultative Council, 1955–66; St Marylebone Borough Council, 1952–65 (Mayor, 1958–59); LCC, for St Marylebone, 1960–65; Inner London Educn Authority, 1964–76. Greater London Council: Mem. for Cities of London and Westminster, 1964–73, for St Marylebone, 1973–76; Leader of Opposition, 1966–67 and 1973–74; Leader of Council, 1967–73. Member: South Bank Theatre Board, 1967–74; Standing Conf. on SE Planning, 1967–74; Transport Co-ordinating Council for London, 1967–69; Local Authorities Conditions of Service Adv. Bd, 1967–71; Exec. Cttee, British Section of Internat. Union of Local Authorities, 1967–74; St John Council for London, 1971–94; Exec. Cttee, Nat. Union Cons. and Unionist Assocs, 1967–76; Chm., St Marylebone Conservative Assoc., 1965–66. Chm., Horserace Betting Levy Bd, 1974–82. Chm., Nat. Employers' Life Assce, 1983–89; Pres., Met. Assoc. of Bldg Socs, 1983–89. Mem. Court, Univ. of London, 1967–77. Chairman: Epsom and Walton Downs Trng Grounds Mgt Bd, 1974–82; National Stud, 1975–82; President: London Anglers' Assoc., 1976–; Thames Angling Preservation Soc., 1970–99. Liveryman, Worshipful Co. of Tin Plateworkers. FRSA 1974; Hon. FASI (Hon. FFAS 1966). JP, Co. London, 1958; DL Greater London, 1970. KStJ 1986. *Publications:* Time for Change in Greater London, 1966; Report to London, 1970; Planning and Participation, 1973. *Recreations:* swimming (Capt. Otter Swimming Club, 1952–53); horse racing. *Address:* 4 The Lane, Marlborough Place, St Johns Wood, NW8 0PN. *Clubs:* Carlton (Chm., Political Cttee, 1979–84; Pres., 1984–98), Royal Automobile, MCC. *Died 2 Oct. 2009.*

PLUMMER, Peter Edward; Deputy Director, Department for National Savings, 1972–79; *b* 4 Nov. 1919; *s* of Arthur William John and Ethel May Plummer; *m* 1949, Pauline Wheelwright; one *s* one *d. Educ:* Watford Grammar Sch. Served War, REME, 1941–46. Customs and Excise, 1936–38; Dept for National Savings, 1938–79; Principal, 1956; Assistant Sec., 1964; seconded to Nat. Giro, 1970–71; Under-Sec., 1972. *Recreations:* gardening, photography. *Address:* Old Timbers, Farm Lane, Nutbourne, Chichester, W Sussex PO18 8SA. *T:* (01243) 377450. *Died 14 Dec. 2009.*

POCOCK, Air Vice-Marshal Donald Arthur, CBE 1975 (OBE 1957); Director, British Metallurgical Plant Constructors Association, 1980–85; *b* 5 July 1920; *s* of late A. Pocock and of E. Broad; *m* 1947, Dorothy Monica Griffiths (*d* 2006); two *s* three *d. Educ:* Crouch End. Served War of 1939–45: commissioned, 1941; Middle East, 1941–48. Transport Command, 1948–50; commanded RAF Regt Sqdn, 1950–52; Staff Coll., 1953; Staff Officer, HQ 2nd Allied TAF, 1954–57; comd RAF Regt Wing, 1957–58; MoD, 1958–59; HQ Allied Air Forces Central Europe, 1959–62; Sen. Ground Defence SO, NEAF, 1962–63; MoD, 1963–66; Sen. Ground Defence SO, FEAF, 1966–68; ADC to the Queen, 1967; Commandant, RAF Catterick, 1968–69; Dir of Ground Defence, 1970–73; Comdt-Gen. RAF Regt, 1973–75. Gen. Man., Iran, British Aerospace Dynamics Gp, 1976–79. *Address:* 16 Dence Park, Herne Bay, Kent CT6 6BQ. *T:* (01227) 374773. *Club:* Royal Air Force. *Died 30 July 2008.*

PODRO, Prof. Michael Isaac, CBE 2001; PhD; FBA 1992; Professor, Department of Art History and Theory, University of Essex, 1973–97, then Emeritus; *b* 13 March 1931; *s* of Joshua Podro and Fanny Podro; *m* 1961, Charlotte Booth; two *d. Educ:* Berkhamsted Sch.; Jesus Coll., Cambridge (MA); University Coll. London (PhD). Hd of Dept of Art History, Camberwell Sch. of Art and Crafts, 1961–67; Lectr in the Philosophy of Art, Warburg Inst., Univ. of London, 1967–69; Reader, Dept of Art History and Theory, Univ. of Essex, 1969–73. Trustee, V&A Mus., 1987–96. DU Essex, 2000. *Publications:* Manifold in Perception: theories of art from Kant to Hildebrand, 1972; Critical Historians of Art, 1982; Depiction, 1998. *Died 28 March 2008.*

POLANI, Prof. Paul Emanuel, MD; FRCP, FRCOG; FRCPCH; FRS 1973; Prince Philip Professor of Pædiatric Research in the University of London, 1960–80, then Professor Emeritus; Geneticist, Division of Medical and Molecular Genetics (formerly Pædiatric Research Unit) of Guy's, King's and St Thomas' Hospitals' Medical School, King's College, London at Guy's Hospital; Children's Physician, and Consultant Emeritus, Guy's Hospital; Geneticist, Italian Hospital; Director, SE Thames Regional Genetics Centre, 1976–82; *b* 1 Jan. 1914; first *s* of Enrico Polani and Elsa Zennaro; *m* 1944, Nina Ester Sullam (*d* 1999); no *c. Educ:* Trieste, Siena and Pisa (Scuola Normale Superiore, Italy). CM; MD (Pisa) 1938; DCH 1945; MRCP 1948, FRCP 1961; FRCOG *ad eund* 1979; FRCPCH 1997. Surg. Lieut, MN (aux.), 1939–40. National Birthday Trust Fund Fellow in Pædiatric Research, 1948; Assistant to Director, Dept of Child Health, Guy's Hos. Med. Sch., 1950–55; Res. Physician on Cerebral Palsy and Dir, Med. Res. Unit, Nat. Spastic Soc., 1955–60; Dir, Paediatric Res. Unit, Guy's Hosp. Med. Sch., 1960–83. Consultant to WHO (Regl Office for Europe) on Pregnancy Wastage, 1959; Consultant, Nat. Inst. Neurol. Disease and Blindness, NIH, USA, 1959–61. Chm., Mutagenesis Cttee, UK, 1975–86. Vis. Prof. of Human Genetics and Develt, Columbia Univ., 1977–86. Harveian Orator, 1988. FKC 1998. Hon. FRCPath 1985; Hon. FRCPI 1989; Hon. Fellow, UMDS of Guy's and St Thomas' Hospital, 1994. Sanremo Internat. Award and Prize for Genetic Res., 1984; Baly Medal, RCP, 1985; Gold Medal, International Cerebral Palsy Society, 1988; City of Florence Golden Florin Award, 1994; Gold Medal for Genetic Res., Univ. of Modena, Breggio Emilia, 2005. Commendatore, Order of Merit of the Republic, Italy, 1981. *Publications:* The Impact of Genetics on Medicine, 1990; chapters in books on human genetics, mental deficiency, psychiatry and pædiatrics; papers on human genetics, cytogenetics, experimental meiosis, congenital malformations and neurological disorders of children; historical reviews. *Recreations:* reading, riding, ski-ing. *Address:* Little Meadow, West Clandon, Surrey GU4 7TL. *T:* (01483) 222436. *Club:* Athenæum. *Died 18 Feb. 2006.*

POLE, Prof. Jack Richon, PhD; FBA 1985; FRHistS; Rhodes Professor of American History and Institutions, Oxford University, 1979–89; Fellow of St Catherine's College, since 1979; *b* 14 March 1922; *s* of Joseph Pole and Phœbe (*née* Rickards); *m* 1952, Marilyn Louise Mitchell (marr. diss. 1988); one *s* two *d. Educ:* King Alfred Sch.; Queen's Coll., Oxford Univ. (BA 1949); Princeton Univ. (PhD 1953). MA Cantab 1963. FRHistS 1970. Instr in History, Princeton Univ., 1952–53; Asst Lectr/ Lectr in Amer. History, UCL, 1953–63; Cambridge University: Reader in Amer. History and Govt, 1963–79; Fellow, Churchill Coll., 1963–79 (Vice-Master, 1975–78); Mem., Council of Senate, 1970–74. Vis. Professor: Berkeley, 1960–61; Ghana, 1966; Chicago, 1969; Beijing, 1984. Commonwealth Fund Amer. Studies Fellowship, 1956; Fellow, Center for Advanced Study in Behavioral Sciences, 1969–70; Guest Schol., Wilson Internat. Center, Washington, 1978–79; Golieb Fellow, NY Univ. Law Sch., 1990; Sen. Res. Fellow, Coll. of William & Mary, Va, 1991; Leverhulme Trust Emeritus Fellow, 1991–93. Jefferson Meml Lectr, Berkeley, 1971; Richard B. Russell Lectr, Ga, 1981. Vice-Pres., Internat. Commn for History of Representative and Parly Instns, 1990–2000; Member: Council, Inst. for Early Amer. History and Culture, 1973–76; Acad. Européenne d'Histoire, 1981; Council, King Alfred Sch. Soc., 1981–84 (Hon. Fellow). Hon. Vice-Pres., British Amer. Nineteenth Century Historians, 2000–; Hon. Foreign Mem., Amer. Hist. Assoc., 2003. Hon. Fellow, Hist. Soc. of Ghana. *Publications:* Abraham

Lincoln and the Working Classes of Britain, 1959; Abraham Lincoln, 1964; Political Representation in England and the Origins of the American Republic, 1966, 2nd edn 1971 (both edns also USA); (ed) The Advance of Democracy, USA 1967; The Seventeenth Century: the origins of legislative power, USA 1969; (ed jtly) The Meanings of American History, USA, 1971; (ed) The Revolution in America: documents of the internal development of America in the revolutionary era, 1971 (also USA); Foundations of American Independence 1763–1815, 1973 (USA 1972); The Decision for American Independence, USA 1975; (Gen. Ed.) American Historical Documents (ed, Slavery, Secession and Civil War), 1975; The Idea of Union, USA 1977; The Pursuit of Equality in American History, USA 1978, 2nd edn 1993; Paths to the American Past, 1979 (also USA); The Gift of Government: political responsibility from the English Restoration to American Independence, USA 1983, 2nd edn 2008; (co-ed) Colonial British America: essays in the new history of the early modern era, USA 1983; (ed) The American Constitution: For and Against: the Federalist and Anti-Federalist papers, USA 1987; (co-ed) The Blackwell Encyclopedia of the American Revolution, 1991 (also USA), rev. edn as A Companion to the American Revolution, 2000; Freedom of Speech: right or privilege?, 1998; (ed) The Federalist, 2005; articles in Amer. Hist. Rev., William and Mary Qly, Jl of Southern Hist., etc., Enc. Brit., Enc. of Amer. Congress. *Recreations:* cricket, painting (exhibn Wolfson Coll., Oxford, 2001), writing. *Address:* 20 Divinity Road, Oxford OX4 1LJ; St Catherine's College, Oxford OX1 3UJ. *Clubs:* MCC; Trojan Wanderers Cricket (Co-founder, 1957).　　　　　　　　　*Died 30 Jan. 2010.*

POLE, Sir Peter Van Notten, 5th Bt *cr* 1791; FASA; ACIS; accountant; *b* 6 Nov. 1921; *s* of late Arthur Chandos Pole and Marjorie, *d* of late Charles Hargrave, Glen Forrest, W Australia; *S* kinsman, 1948; *m* 1949, Jean Emily, *d* of late Charles Douglas Stone, Borden, WA; one *s* one *d*. *Educ:* Guildford Grammar Sch. *Recreations:* reading, travel. *Heir: s* Peter John Chandos Pole [*b* 27 April 1952; *m* 1973, Suzanne Norah, BAppSc(MT), *d* of late Harold Raymond Hughes; two *s* one *d*]. *Address:* 249 Dartnell Parade, Cambrai Village, 85 Hester Avenue, Merriwa, WA 6030, Australia.　　　　　*Died 31 Jan. 2010.*

POLGE, Prof. (Ernest John) Christopher, CBE 1992; FRS 1983; Director, Mastercalf Ltd, since 1994; Hon. Professor of Animal Reproductive Biotechnology, University of Cambridge, since 1989; Fellow, Wolfson College, Cambridge, since 1984; *b* 16 Aug. 1926; *s* of late Ernest Thomas Ella Polge and Joan Gillet Polge (*née* Thorne); *m* 1954, Olive Sylvia Kitson; two *s* two *d*. *Educ:* Bootham Sch., York; Reading Univ. (BSc Agric.); PhD London 1955. Dept of Agricl Econs, Bristol Univ., 1947–48; Nat. Inst. for Med. Res., London, 1948 54; ARC Unit of Reproductive Physiology and Biochem., later Animal Res. Station, 1954–86, Officer-in-Charge, 1979–86; Scientific Dir, Animal Biotechnology Cambridge Ltd, Animal Res. Stn, Cambridge, 1986–93. Lalor Foundn Fellow, Worcester Foundn for Exptl Biol., Shrewsbury, Mass and Univ. of Illinois, 1967–68. Consultant: WHO, Geneva, 1965; FAO, Rome, 1983 and 1987. Member Committee: Soc. for Study of Fertility, 1955–64, 1976–83 (Sec., 1960–63; Chm., 1978–81); Soc. for Low Temp. Biol., 1974–79 (Chm., 1976–79). Chm. Journals of Reproduction and Fertility Ltd, 1982–87 (Mem., Council of Management and Exec. Cttee, 1972–79). Lectures: Sir John Hammond Meml, Soc. for Study of Fertility, 1974; Blackman, Oxford, 1979; Cameron-Gifford, Newcastle, 1984; E. H. W. Wilmott, Bristol, 1986; Clive Behrens, Leeds, 1988; Sir John Hammond Meml, British Soc. of Animal Production, 1989. Foreign Associate, US Nat. Acad. of Sci., 1997. FRAgS 1991; Hon. FRASE 1984; Hon. ARCVS 1986. Prof. *hc* and Dr *hc*, Ecological Univ. of Romania, 1991; Hon. DSc: Univ. of Illinois, 1990; Guelph, 1994. (Jtly) John Scott Award, City of Philadelphia, 1969; Sir John Hammond Meml Prize, British Soc. of Animal Prodn, 1971; Pioneer Award,

Internat. Embryo Transfer Soc., 1986; Marshall Medal, Soc. for Study of Fertility, 1988; Internat. Prize for Agriculture, Wolf Foundn, 1988; Japan Prize for Science and Technology for Biological Prodn, 1992; first Lazzaro Spallanzani Internat. Award for Animal Reprodn, Italy, 1995; Bertebos Prize, Royal Swedish Acad. of Agric. and Forestry, 1997. *Publications:* papers on reproduction in domestic animals and low temp. biol., in biological jls. *Recreations:* gardening, fishing. *Address:* The Willows, 137 Waterbeach Road, Landbeach, Cambridge CB4 8EA. *T:* (01223) 860075, *Fax:* (01223) 861248.
　　　　　　　　　　　　　　　　　　　Died 17 Aug. 2006.

POLLOCK, Adm. of the Fleet Sir Michael (Patrick), GCB 1971 (KCB 1969; CB 1966); LVO 1952; DSC 1944; *b* 19 Oct. 1916; *s* of late C. A. Pollock and Mrs G. Pollock; *m* 1st, 1940, Margaret Steacy (*d* 1951), Bermuda; two *s* one *d*; 2nd, 1954, Marjory Helen Reece (*née* Bisset) (*d* 2001); one step *d*. *Educ:* RNC Dartmouth. Entered Navy, 1930; specialised in Gunnery, 1941. Served War of 1939–45 in Warspite, Vanessa, Arethusa and Norfolk, N Atlantic, Mediterranean, Arctic and Indian Ocean (despatches thrice). Captain, Plans Div. of Admiralty and Director of Surface Weapons; comd HMS Vigo and Portsmouth Sqdn, 1958–59; comd HMS Ark Royal, 1963–64; Asst Chief of Naval Staff, 1964–66; Flag Officer Second in Command, Home Fleet, 1966–67; Flag Officer Submarines and Nato Commander Submarines, Eastern Atlantic, 1967–69; Controller of the Navy, 1970–71; Chief of Naval Staff and First Sea Lord, 1971 74; First and Principal Naval Aide-de-Camp to the Queen, 1972–74. Comdr, 1950; Capt., 1955; Rear-Adm., 1964; Vice-Adm., 1968; Adm., 1970. Bath King of Arms, 1976–85. Chm., Naval Insurance Trust, 1976–81; Liddle Hart Trustee, 1976–81. *Address:* Hurst Manor Residential and Nursing Home, Hurst, Martock, Somerset TA12 6JU.　　　　　　　　　　　　　*Died 27 Sept. 2006.*

PONSONBY, Sir Ashley (Charles Gibbs), 2nd Bt *cr* 1956; KCVO 1993; MC 1945; Director, J. Henry Schroder, Wagg & Co. Ltd, 1962–80; Lord–Lieutenant of Oxfordshire, 1980–96; *b* 21 Feb. 1921; *o s* of Col Sir Charles Edward Ponsonby, 1st Bt, TD, and Hon. Winifred (*d* 1984), *d* of 1st Baron Hunsdon; *S* father, 1976; *m* 1950, Lady Martha Butler, *yr d* of 6th Marquess of Ormonde, CVO, MC; four *s*. *Educ:* Eton; Balliol College, Oxford. 2nd Lieut Coldstream Guards, 1941; served war 1942–45 (North Africa and Italy, wounded); Captain 1943; on staff Bermuda Garrison, 1945–46. A Church Commissioner, 1963–80; Mem., Council of Duchy of Lancaster, 1977–92. DL Oxon, 1974–80. Hon. DArts Oxford Brookes, 1995; Hon. MA Oxon, 1996. *Heir: e s* Charles Ashley Ponsonby [*b* 10 June 1951; *m* 1983, Mary P., *yr d* of late A. R. Bromley Davenport and of Mrs A. R. Bromley Davenport, Over Peover, Knutsford, Cheshire; two *s* one *d*]. *Address:* Grim's Dyke Farm, Woodleys, Woodstock, Oxon OX20 1HJ. *T:* (01993) 811422. *Club:* Pratt's.　　　　　*Died 15 June 2010.*

POOLE, Hon. Sir David (Anthony), Kt 1995; **Hon. Mr Justice Poole;** a Judge of the High Court of Justice, Queen's Bench Division, since 1995; *b* 8 June 1938; *s* of late William Joseph Poole and Lena (*née* Thomas); *m* 1974, Pauline Ann O'Flaherty; four *s*. *Educ:* Ampleforth; Jesus Coll., Oxford (Meyricke Exhibnr in Classics; MA; Hon. Fellow, 1997); Univ. of Manchester Inst. of Science and Technology (DipTechSc). Called to the Bar, Middle Temple, 1968 (Bencher, 1992); QC 1984; a Recorder, 1983–95. Chm., Assoc. of Lawyers for the Defence of the Unborn, 1985–92. *Address:* Royal Courts of Justice, Strand, WC2A 2LL. *Clubs:* London Irish Rugby Football, Vincent's.　　　　　　　　　　　　　*Died 18 June 2006.*

POOLE, Richard John; Director, Defence Operational Analysis Establishment, Ministry of Defence, 1986–89, retired; *b* 20 Feb. 1929; *s* of Leonard Richard Poole and Merrie Wyn Poole; *m* 1st, 1953, Jean Doreena Poole (*née* Welch) (*d* 1991); two *d*; 2nd, 1993, Jane Amelia (*née* Allen). *Educ:* Univ. of Adelaide, SA (BEng 1st Cl. Hons). Long Range Weapons Estabt, Aust. Dept of Defence, 1951; Ministry of Defence, UK: Admiralty Signals and

Radar Estabt, 1957; Head of Div., 1971; Scientific Adviser, 1980, Dir Gen. (Estabts), 1984. *Recreations*: radio, cars, photography, computing. *Died 6 Aug. 2006.*

POOLE-WILSON, Prof. Philip Alexander, MD; FRCP, FMedSci; British Heart Foundation Simon Marks Professor of Cardiology, National Heart and Lung Institute (formerly Cardiothoracic Institute), Faculty of Medicine, Imperial College London (formerly Imperial College School of Medicine), since 1988; *b* 26 April 1943; *s* of late Denis Smith Poole-Wilson, CBE, MCh, FRCS and Monique Michelle Poole-Wilson; *m* 1969, Mary Elizabeth, *d* of late William Horrocks Tattersall, MA, MD and Joan Tattersall; two *s* one *d*. *Educ*: Marlborough Coll.; Trinity Coll., Cambridge (Major Scholar; MA, MD); St Thomas's Hosp. Med. Sch. FRCP 1983; FACC 1992. House appts, St Thomas' Hosp., Brompton Hosp., Hammersmith Hosp.; Lectr, St Thomas' Hosp.; British-American Travelling Fellowship from British Heart Foundn at UCLA, 1973–74; Cardiothoracic Institute, London University: Senior Lectr and Reader, 1976–83; Vice-Dean, 1981–84; apptd Prof. of Cardiology, 1983; Hon. Consultant Physician, Royal Brompton Hosp. (formerly at Nat. Heart Hosp.), 1976–. Chm., Cardiac Muscle Research Group, 1984–87; Mem. Council, British Heart Foundn, 1985–97; Founding Chm., British Soc. for Heart Failure, 1999–2001; World Heart Federation: Pres.-elect, 2001–03; Pres., 2003–04; European Society of Cardiology: Fellow, 1988; Mem. Bd, 1988–98; Sec., 1990–92; Pres.-elect, 1992–94; Pres., 1994–96. Strickland-Goodall Lectr, 1983, Bradshaw Lectr, 1993, Paul Wood Lectr, 1999, British Cardiac Soc. Founder FMedSci 1998. Le Prix Europe et Medicine, 2001. *Publications*: articles and contribs to books on physiology and biochemistry of normal and diseased heart. *Recreations*: sailing, gardening, opera. *Address*: Cardiac Medicine, National Heart and Lung Institute, Dovehouse Street, Imperial College London, SW3 6LY. *T*: (020) 7351 8179, *Fax*: (020) 7351 8113. *Clubs*: Athenæum; Parkstone Yacht. *Died 4 March 2009.*

POPE, Rear-Adm. Michael Donald K.; *see* Kyrle Pope.

PORTEOUS, James; DL; FREng, FIET; Chairman and Chief Executive, Yorkshire Electricity Group plc, 1990–92; *b* 29 Dec. 1926; *e s* of James and Isabella Porteous; *m* 1960, Sheila Beatrice (*née* Klotz); two *d*. *Educ*: Jarrow Grammar School; King's College, Durham University (BSc Hons). FREng (FEng 1986). NESCo Ltd, NE Electricity Bd, NE Div., BEA, 1945–62; Central Electricity Generating Board: Operations Dept, HQ, 1962–66; System Op. Eng., Midlands Region, 1966–70; Dir, Operational Planning, SE Region, 1970–72; NE Region, 1972–75; Dir-Gen., Midlands Region, 1975–84; Chm., Yorks Electricity Bd, 1984–90. Mem., Electricity Council, 1984–90; Director: Electricity Association Ltd, 1990–92; National Grid Company (Holdings) plc, 1990–92. Chm., BR (Eastern) Board, 1990–92 (Mem., 1986–90); Mem., E Midlands Economic Planning Council, 1976–79. Director: Peter Peregrinus Ltd, 1981–92, 1993–96; Merz and McLellan Ltd, 1992–96; Parsons Brinckerhoff Ltd, 1995–98; Nuclear Liabilities (formerly Nuclear Generation Decommissioning) Fund Ltd, 1996–2008; PB Power Ltd, 1998–2002. Vice-Pres., IEE, 1992–93 (Hon. FIET (Hon. FIEE 1997)). National Vice-President: Opportunities for People with Disabilities, 1990–92; Nat. Energy Action, 1992–2008. Hon. DSc Aston, 1990; Hon. DEng Bradford, 1991. DL N Yorks, 1991. *Recreations*: highland life, railways. *Club*: Caledonian. *Died 18 March 2009.*

PORTER, Prof. Arthur, OC 1983; MSc, PhD (Manchester); FIEE; FCAE; FRSC 1970; Professor of Industrial Engineering, and Chairman of Department, University of Toronto, Toronto, 1961–76, then Emeritus Professor; President, Arthur Porter Associates Ltd, since 1973; Associate, Institute for Environmental Studies, University of Toronto, since 1981; *b* 8 Dec. 1910; *s* of late John William Porter and Mary Anne Harris; *m* 1941, Phyllis Patricia Dixon; one *s*. *Educ*: The Grammar Sch., Ulverston; University of Manchester. Asst Lecturer,

University of Manchester, 1936–37; Commonwealth Fund Fellow, Massachusetts Inst. of Technology, USA, 1937–39; Scientific Officer, Admiralty, 1939–45; Principal Scientific Officer, National Physical Laboratory, 1946; Prof. of Instrument Technology, Royal Military Coll. of Science, 1946–49; Head, Research Division, Ferranti Electric Ltd, Toronto, Canada, 1949–55; Professor of Light Electrical Engineering, Imperial College of Science and Technology, University of London, 1955–58; Dean of the College of Engineering, Saskatchewan Univ., Saskatoon, 1958; Acting Dir, Centre for Culture and Technology, Toronto Univ., 1967–68; Academic Comr, Univ. of W Ontario, 1969–71. Dir and Founding Chm., Scientists and Engineers for Energy and Environment Inc., 1981–84. Chairman: Canadian Environmental Adv. Council, 1972–75; Ontario Royal Commn on Electric Power Planning, 1975–80. Hon. DSc Manchester, 2004. *Publications*: An Introduction to Servomechanisms, 1950; Cybernetics Simplified, 1969; Towards a Community University, 1971; So Many Hills to Climb, 2004 (autobiog.); articles in Trans. Royal Society, Proc. Royal Society, Phil. Mag., Proc. Inst. Mech. Eng, Proc. IEE, Nature, etc. *Recreations*: travel, energy conservation. *Address*: 3314 Bermuda Village, Advance, NC 27006–9479, USA. *Club*: Bermuda Run Country (Advance, NC). *Died 26 Feb. 2010.*

PORTER, John Andrew, TD; JP; DL; Partner, Porter and Cobb, as Chartered Surveyor, 1940–81; *b* 18 May 1916; *s* of late Horace Augustus Porter, DFC, JP, and Vera Marion Porter; *m* 1941, Margaret Isobel Wisnom; two *d*. *Educ*: Radley Coll.; Sidney Sussex Coll., Cambridge (MA). Commissioned RA, TA, 1938; served War, 1939–46, Lt-Col. Director: Kent County Building Soc., 1947 (Chm., 1965–68); Hastings and Thanet Building Soc., 1968–78 (Chm., 1972–78); Anglia, Hastings and Thanet, later Anglia, Building Soc., 1978–87 (Chm., 1978–81). JP Gravesham PSD, 1952, Chm., Gravesham Div., 1976–83, Dep. Chm., 1983–85. Pres., Gravesend Cons. Assoc., 1965–77. Chm., Bd of Govs, Cobham Hall Sch., 1987–91. General Commissioner of Taxes, 1970–90. DL Kent, 1984. *Recreations*: cricket, reading, golf. *Address*: Flat 23, Beech Court, Willicombe Park, Tunbridge Wells, Kent TN2 3UX. *T*: (01892) 615529. *Clubs*: MCC; Hawks (Cambridge); Kent CC (Pres., 1985–86). *Died 10 Nov. 2006.*

PORTER, Prof. Rev. Canon (Joshua) Roy; Professor of Theology, University of Exeter, 1962–86 (Head of Department, 1962–85), then Professor Emeritus; *b* 7 May 1921; *s* of Joshua Porter and Bessie Evelyn (*née* Earlam). *Educ*: King's Sch., Macclesfield; Merton Coll., Oxford (Exhibnr; BA: Mod. Hist. (Cl. I), Theology (Cl. I); MA; Liddon Student, 1942); St Stephen's House, Oxford. Ordained deacon 1945, priest 1946; Curate of St Mary, Portsea, 1945–47; Resident Chaplain to Bp of Chichester, 1947–49 (Hon. Chaplain, 1949–50; Examining Chaplain, 1950–2002); Fellow, Chaplain and Lectr, Oriel Coll., Oxford, 1949–62; Tutor, 1950–62; Kennicott Hebrew Fellow, 1955; Sen. Denver and Johnson Schol., 1958; Select Preacher: Univs of Oxford, 1953–55, Cambridge, 1957, TCD, 1958; Canon and Preb. of Wightring and Theol Lectr in Chichester Cath., 1965–88; Wiccamical Canon and Preb. of Exceit, 1988–2001, then Canon Emeritus; Vis. Prof., Southeastern Seminary, Wake Forest, N Carolina, 1967; Dean of Arts, Univ. of Exeter, 1968–71; Proctor in Convocation of Canterbury for dio. of Exeter, 1964–75; for Other Univs (Canterbury), 1975–90; Examining Chaplain to Bps of Peterborough, 1973–86, of Truro, 1973–81, of London, 1981–91, and of Gibraltar in Europe, 1989–93. Ethel M. Wood Lectr, Univ. of London 1979; Michael Harrah Wood Lectr, Univ. of the South, Sewanee, Tenn, 1984; Lectr in Old Testament Studies, Holyrood Seminary, NY, 1987–95. Member: Gen. Synod, 1970–90 (Panel of Chairmen, 1984–86); ACCM, 1975–86; Council of Management, Coll. of St Mark and St John, 1980–85; Vice-Pres., Folklore Soc.,

1979–83 (Pres., 1976–79; Hon. Mem., 1983); President: SOTS, 1983; Anglican Assoc., 1986–2001; Vice-Chm., Prayer Book Soc., 1987–96. FAMS. *Publications:* World in the Heart, 1944; Moses and Monarchy, 1963; The Extended Family in the Old Testament, 1967; Proclamation and Presence, 1970, 2nd rev. edn, 1983; The Non-Juring Bishops, 1973; Leviticus, 1976, Japanese edn 1984; Animals in Folklore, 1978; The Crown and the Church, 1978; Folklore and the Old Testament, 1981; trans. C. Westermann, The Living Psalms, 1989; Synodical Government in the Church of England, 1990; The Illustrated Guide to the Bible, 1995; Jesus Christ: the Jesus of history, the Christ of faith, 1999; The Lost Bible: forgotten scriptures revealed, 2001; The New Illustrated Companion to the Bible, 2003; *contributor to:* Promise and Fulfilment, 1963; A Source Book of the Bible for Teachers, 1970; The Journey to the Other World, 1975; Tradition and Interpretation, 1979; A Basic Introduction to the Old Testament, 1980; Divination and Oracles, 1981; Folklore Studies in the Twentieth Century, 1981; The Folklore of Ghosts, 1981; Israel's Prophetic Tradition, 1982; Tracts for Our Times, 1983; The Hero in Tradition and Folklore, 1984; Harper's Bible Dictionary, 1985, 2nd edn 1996; Arabia and the Gulf: from traditional society to modern states, 1986; The Seer in Celtic and Other Traditions, 1989; Schöpfung und Befreiung, 1989; A Dictionary of Biblical Interpretation, 1990; Christianity and Conservatism, 1990; The Oil of Gladness, 1993; Boundaries and Thresholds, 1993; The Oxford Companion to the Bible, 1993; World Mythology, 1993; The First and Second Prayer Books of Edward VI, 1999; Dictionary of Biblical Interpretation, 1999; Reconsidering Israel and Judah, 2000; Supernatural Enemies, 2001; Bell of Chichester, 2004; numerous articles in learned jls and dictionaries. *Recreations:* theatre and opera, book-collecting, travel. *Address:* 36 Theberton Street, Barnsbury, N1 0QX. *T:* (020) 7354 5861; 68 Sand Street, Longbridge Deverill, near Warminster, Wilts BA12 7DS. *T:* (01985) 840311.   *Died 31 Dec. 2006.*

PORTER, Peter Neville Frederick, CLit 2006; FRSL; freelance writer, poet; *b* Brisbane, 16 Feb. 1929; *s* of William Ronald Porter and Marion Main; *m* 1st, 1961, Jannice Henry (*d* 1974); two *d*; 2nd, 1991, Christine Berg. *Educ:* Church of England Grammar Sch., Brisbane; Toowoomba Grammar Sch. Worked as journalist in Brisbane before coming to England in 1951; clerk, bookseller and advertising writer, before becoming full-time poet, journalist, reviewer and broadcaster in 1968. Chief work done in poetry and English literature. Hon. DLitt: Melbourne, 1985; Loughborough, 1987; Sydney, 1999; Queensland, 2001. Queen's Gold Medal for Poetry, 2002. *Publications:* Once Bitten, Twice Bitten, 1961; Penguin Modern Poets No 2, 1962; Poems, Ancient and Modern, 1964; A Porter Folio, 1969; The Last of England, 1970; Preaching to the Converted, 1972; (trans.) After Martial, 1972; (with Arthur Boyd) Jonah, 1973; (with Arthur Boyd) The Lady and the Unicorn, 1975; Living in a Calm Country, 1975; (jt ed) New Poetry 1, 1975; The Cost of Seriousness, 1978; English Subtitles, 1981; Collected Poems, 1983 (Duff Cooper Prize); Fast Forward, 1984; (with Arthur Boyd) Narcissus, 1985; The Automatic Oracle, 1987 (Whitbread Poetry Award, 1988); (with Arthur Boyd) Mars, 1988; A Porter Selected, 1989; Possible Worlds, 1989; The Chair of Babel, 1992; Millennial Fables, 1995; (ed) Oxford Book of Modern Australian Verse, 1996; (ed jtly) New Writing 5, 1996, 6, 1997; Dragons in their Pleasant Palaces, 1997; Collected Poems 1961–1999, 2 vols, 1999; Saving from the Wreck: essays on poetry, 2001; Max is Missing (poems), 2001 (Forward Prize, 2002); Afterburner, 2004; Better than God, 2009. *Recreations:* buying records and listening to music; travelling in Italy. *Address:* 42 Cleveland Square, W2 6DA. *T:* (020) 7262 4289.   *Died 23 April 2010.*

PORTER, Robert Stanley, CB 1972; OBE 1959; Deputy Secretary (Chief Economist), Overseas Development Administration, Foreign and Commonwealth Office (formerly Ministry of Overseas Development), 1980–84; retired; *b* 17 Sept. 1924; *s* of S. R. Porter; *m* 1st, 1953, Dorothea Naomi (marr. diss. 1967), *d* of Rev. Morris Seale; one *d*; 2nd, 1967, Julia Karen (*d* 1992), *d* of late Edmund A. Davies; 3rd, 1993, Mary Napiorkowska (*née* Woolley) (*d* 2001). *Educ:* St Clement Danes, Holborn Estate, Grammar Sch.; New Coll., Oxford. Research Economist, US Economic Cooperation Administration Special Mission to the UK, 1949; British Middle East Development Division: Asst Statistical Adviser, Cairo, 1951; Statistical Adviser and Economist, Beirut, 1955; Min. of Overseas Development: Dir, Geographical Div., Economic Planning Staff, 1965; Dep. Dir-Gen. of Economic Planning, 1967; Dir-Gen. of Economic Planning, 1969. Vis. Prof., David Livingstone Inst. for Overseas Develt Studies, 1984–87. *Publications:* articles in Oxford Economic Papers, Kyklos, Review of Income and Wealth, ODI Development Policy Review. *Recreations:* music, theatre. *Address:* Lower Saunders, Cheriton Fitzpaine, Crediton, Devon EX17 4JA. *T:* (01363) 866645. *Club:* Athenæum.   *Died 30 July 2007.*

PORTER, Rev. Canon Roy; *see* Porter, Rev. Canon J. R.

PORTERFIELD, Dr James Stuart; Reader in Bacteriology, Sir William Dunn School of Pathology, Oxford University, and Senior Research Fellow, Wadham College, Oxford, 1977–89; then Emeritus Fellow; *b* 17 Jan. 1924; *yr s* of late Dr Samuel Porterfield and Mrs Lilian Porterfield, Widnes, Lancs, and Portstewart, Co. Londonderry, NI; *m* 1950, Betty Mary Burch; one *d* (one *s* decd). *Educ:* Wade Deacon Grammar Sch., Widnes; King's Sch., Chester; Liverpool Univ. MB, ChB 1947, MD 1949. Asst Lectr in Bacteriology, Univ. of Liverpool, 1947–49; Bacteriologist and Virologist, Common Cold Res. Unit, Salisbury, Wilts, 1949–51; Pathologist, RAF Inst. of Pathology and Tropical Med., Halton, Aylesbury, Bucks, 1952–53; seconded to W African Council for Med. Res. Labs, Lagos, Nigeria, 1953–57; Mem. Scientific Staff, Nat. Inst. for Med. Res., Mill Hill, 1949–77; WHO Regional Ref. Centre for Arthropod-borne Viruses, 1961–65; WHO Collaborating Lab., 1965–89; Ref. Expert on Arboviruses, Public Health Lab. Service, 1967–76. Chm., Arbovirus Study Gp, Internat. Cttee for Nomenclature of Viruses, 1968–78; Meetings Sec., Soc. for General Microbiology, 1972–77; Vice-Pres., Royal Soc. for Tropical Med. and Hygiene, 1980–81 (Councillor, 1973–76); Secretary and Vice-Pres., Royal Institution, 1973–78. *Publications:* (ed) Andrewes' Viruses of Vertebrates, 5th edn, 1989; (ed) Exotic Viral Infections, 1995; contribs to Oxford DNB, medical and scientific jls. *Recreations:* fell-walking, gardening. *Address:* 8 Port Mill Court, Mills Way, Barnstaple, Devon EX31 1GW.   *Died 23 Nov. 2010.*

POSNER, Michael Vivian, CBE 1983; Secretary-General, European Science Foundation, 1986–93; *b* 25 Aug. 1931; *s* of Jack Posner; *m* 1953, Rebecca Reynolds (Prof. Rebecca Posner); one *s* one *d*. *Educ:* Whitgift Sch.; Balliol Coll., Oxford. Research Officer, Oxford Inst. of Statistics, 1953–57; University of Cambridge: Asst Lecturer, Lecturer, then Reader in Economics, 1958–79; Fellow, Pembroke Coll., 1960–83; Chm., Faculty Bd of Economics, 1974–75. Visiting Professor: Brookings Instn, Washington, 1971–72; Bristol Univ. Grad. Sch. of Internat. Business, 1996–. Director of Economics, Ministry of Power, 1966–67; Economic Adviser to Treasury, 1967–69; Economic Consultant to Treasury, 1969–71; Consultant to IMF, 1971–72; Energy Adviser, NEDO, 1973–74; Econ. Adviser, Dept of Energy, 1974–75; Dep. Chief Econ. Adviser, HM Treasury, 1975–76. Chm., SSRC, 1979–83; Econ. Dir, NEDO, 1984–86. Member: BRB, 1976–84; Post Office Bd, 1978–79; Member: Adv. Council for Energy Conservation, 1974–82; Standing Commn on Energy and the Environment, 1978–81; a Dir, British Rail, later Railways, Pension Trustee Co., 1986–98. Mem. Council, PSI, 1978–83 (Senior Res. Fellow, 1983–84).

DEd (*hc*) CNAA, 1989; Hon. LLD Bristol, 1992. *Publications:* (co-author) Italian Public Enterprise, 1966; Fuel Policy: a study in applied economics, 1973; (ed) Resource Allocation in the Public Sector, 1977; (ed) Demand Management, 1978; (co-author) Energy Economics, 1981; (ed) Problems of International Money 1972–1985, 1986; books and articles on economics. *Recreation:* country life. *Address:* Rushwood, Jack Straw's Lane, Oxford OX3 0DN. *T:* (01865) 763578.
Died 14 Feb. 2006.

POSNETT, Sir Richard (Neil), KBE 1980 (OBE 1963); CMG 1976; HM Diplomatic Service, retired; *b* 19 July 1919; *s* of Rev. Charles Walker Posnett, K-i-H, Medak, S India, and Phyllis (*née* Barker); *m* 1st, Elisabeth Stiebel (marr. diss.); two *s* one *d*; 2nd, 1959, Shirley Margaret Hudson (*d* 2005); two *s* one *d*. *Educ:* Kingswood; St John's Coll., Cambridge (won 120 yards hurdles for Cambridge *v* Oxford, 1940). BA 1940, MA 1947. Called to the Bar, Gray's Inn, 1951. HM Colonial Administrative Service in Uganda, 1941; Chm., Uganda Olympic Cttee, 1956; Colonial Office, London, 1958; Judicial Adviser, Buganda, 1960; Perm. Sec. for External Affairs, Uganda, 1962; Perm. Sec. for Trade and Industry, 1963; joined Foreign (subseq. Diplomatic) Service, 1964; FO, 1964; served on UK Mission to UN, NY, 1966–70; briefly HM Comr in Anguilla, 1969; Head of W Indian Dept, FCO, 1970–71; Governor and C-in-C of Belize, 1972–76; Special Mission to Ocean Island, 1977; Dependent Territories Adviser, FCO, 1977–79; British High Comr, Kampala, 1979. UK Comr, British Phosphate Comrs, 1978–81. Governor and C-in-C, Bermuda, 1981–83. Mem., Lord Chancellor's Panel of Ind. Inspectors, 1983–89. First ascent of South Portal Peak on Ruwenzori, 1942. Member: RIIA; Royal Forestry Soc.; Royal African Soc. President: Kingswood Assoc., 1980; Godalming Joigny Friendship Assoc., 1987– (Chm., 1984–87); Eddystone Housing Assoc., 2003–. Gov., Kingswood Sch., 1985–93. KStJ 1972. *Publications:* (contrib.) Looking Back at the Uganda Protectorate, 1996; The Scent of Eucalyptus (autobiog.), 2001; articles in Uganda Journal, World Today, Empire & After. *Recreations:* ski-ing, golf, trees. *Address:* Bahati, Old Kiln Close, Churt, Surrey GU10 2JH. *Clubs:* Royal Commonwealth Society, Achilles; Hankley Common Golf; Privateers Hockey. *Died 11 May 2009.*

POSTON, James, CBE 2002; HM Diplomatic Service, retired; Governor, Turks and Caicos Islands, 2002–05; *b* 19 June 1945; *m* 1st, 1976, Anna Caroline Bos (marr. diss. 1980); 2nd, Rosemary Fullerton; one *s* two *d*. Third Sec., FCO, and Third Sec. and Vice-Consul, Chad, 1970; Second Sec. and Private Sec. to Hd of UK Delegn to EC, Brussels, 1971; First Sec., Tel Aviv, 1973; FCO, 1978; First Sec. (Commercial), Lagos, 1982; FCO, 1985; Counsellor and Hd of Chancery, Pretoria, 1988; Counsellor, FCO, 1992; Consul-Gen., Boston, 1995–99; FCO, 1999–2002. *Died 13 Oct. 2007.*

POTTER, Prof. Allen Meyers, PhD; James Bryce Professor of Politics, University of Glasgow, 1970–84; *b* 7 March 1924; *s* of Maurice A. and Irene M. Potter; *m* 1949, Joan Elizabeth Yeo; two *d*. *Educ:* Wesleyan Univ., Conn (BA 1947, MA 1948); Columbia Univ., NY (PhD 1955). FSS 1967. Instructor, College of William and Mary, 1949–51; Lectr, then Sen. Lectr, Univ. of Manchester, 1951–62; Vis. Professor, Univ. of Texas, 1960; Professor: Univ. of Strathclyde, 1963–65; Univ. of Essex, 1965–70; Pro-Vice-Chancellor, Univ. of Essex, 1969–70; Vice-Principal, Univ. of Glasgow, 1979–82. Dir, SSRC Data Bank, 1967–70. Member, US-UK Educational Commn, 1979–84. Governor, Glasgow Sch. of Art, 1979–82. *Publications:* American Government and Politics, 1955, 2nd edn 1978; Organised Groups in British National Politics, 1961; articles in American and British social science jls. *Died 23 April 2010.*

POTTER, Donald Charles; QC 1972; *b* 24 May 1922; *s* of late Charles Potter, Shortlands, Kent. *Educ:* St Dunstan's Coll.; London Sch. of Economics. RAC (Westminster Dragoons), 1942–46 (Lieut); served

England, NW Europe (D-day), Germany; mentioned in despatches; Croix de Guerre (France). LLB London 1947; called to Bar, Middle Temple, 1948; Bencher, Lincoln's Inn, 1979. Asst Lectr in Law, LSE, 1947–49; practised at Bar, 1950–95. Chm., Revenue Bar Assoc., 1978–88. Special Comr of Income Tax (part-time), 1986–95; Chm. (part-time), VAT Tribunal, 1986–95. *Publications:* (with H. H. Monroe) Tax Planning with Precedents, 1954; (with K. J. Prosser) Tax Appeals, 1991. *Recreations:* music, theatre, reading. *Address:* 3 The Grove, Highgate, N6 6JU; Compass Cottage, East Portlemouth, Devon TQ8 8PE. *Club:* Garrick. *Died 8 March 2008.*

POTTS, Robin; QC 1982; barrister; *b* 2 July 1944; *s* of William and Elaine Potts; *m* 1968, Rebeca Giwercer; one *s*; *m* Helen Elizabeth Sharp; two *s* one *d*. *Educ:* Wolstanton Grammar Sch.; Magdalen Coll., Oxford (BA, BCL). Called to the Bar, Gray's Inn, 1968, Bencher, 1993. Head of Erskine Chambers. Consulting Ed., Gore-Browne on Companies, 43rd and 44th edns. *Address:* 2 Harley House, Brunswick Place, NW1 4PR. *T:* (020) 7486 0897. *Died 11 Aug. 2009.*

POUT, Harry Wilfrid, CB 1978; OBE 1959; CEng, FIET; Marconi Underwater Systems Ltd, 1982–86; Defence Consultant, since 1986; *b* 11 April 1920; British; *m* 1949, Margaret Elizabeth (*née* Nelson); three *d*. *Educ:* East Ham Grammar Sch.; Imperial Coll., London. BSc (Eng); ACGI 1940. RN Scientific Service, 1940; Admty Signal Estab. (later Admty Signal and Radar Estab.), 1940–54; Dept of Operational Research, Admty, 1954–59; idc 1959; Head of Guided Weapon Projects, Admty, 1960–65; Asst Chief Scientific Adviser (Projects), MoD, 1965–69; Dir, Admiralty Surface Weapons Estabt, 1969–72; Dep. Controller, Guided Weapons, 1973, Guided Weapons and Electronics, 1973–75, Air Systems, 1975–79, Aircraft Weapons and Electronics, 1979–80, MoD. Defence consultant, 1980–82. FCGI 1972; FCMI. *Publications:* (jtly) The New Scientists, 1971; (contrib.) Radar at Sea—the Royal Navy in World War 2, 1993; (contrib.) The Applications of Radar in the Royal Navy in World War 2, 1995; classified books; contribs to jls of IEE, RAeS, RUSI, Jl of Naval Sci., etc. *Recreations:* mountaineering, gardening and do-it-yourself activities, amateur geology. *Address:* c/o Mrs M. Pugh, 35 Regent Way, Frimley, Camberley, Surrey GU16 8NT.
Died 15 July 2006.

POWELL, Francis Turner, MBE 1945; Chairman, Laing & Cruickshank, Stockbrokers, 1978–80; *b* 15 April 1914; *s* of Francis Arthur and Dorothy May Powell; *m* 1940, Joan Audrey Bartlett (*d* 2003); one *s* one *d*. *Educ:* Lancing College. Served War, Queen's Royal Regt (TA), 1939–45 (Major). Joined L. Powell Sons & Co. (Stockbrokers), 1932, Partner, 1939; merged with Laing & Cruickshank, 1976. Mem. Council, Stock Exchange, 1963–78 (Dep. Chm., 1976–78). *Recreations:* golf, gardening. *Address:* 2 Horsley Court, East Horsley, Leatherhead, Surrey KT24 6QS.
Died 27 Oct. 2009.

POWELL, Air Vice-Marshal John Frederick, OBE 1956; Warden and Director of Studies, Moor Park College, 1972–77; *b* 12 June 1915; *y* *s* of Rev. Morgan Powell, Limpley Stoke, Bath; *m* 1939, Geraldine Ysolda (*d* 2003), *e* *d* of late Sir John Fitzgerald Moylan, CB, CBE; four *s*. *Educ:* Lancing; King's Coll., Cambridge (MA). Joined RAF Educnl Service, 1937; Lectr, RAF College, 1938–39; RAFVR (Admin. and Special Duties) ops room duties, Coastal Comd, 1939–45 (despatches); RAF Educn Br., 1946; Sen. Instructor in History, RAF Coll., 1946–49; RAF Staff Coll., 1950; Air Min., 1951–53; Sen. Tutor, RAF Coll., 1953–59; Educn Staff, HQ FEAF, 1959–62; MoD, 1962–64; Comd Educn Officer, HQ Bomber Comd, 1964–66; OC, RAF Sch. of Educn, 1966–67; Dir of Educational Services, RAF, 1967–72; Air Commodore, 1967; Air Vice-Marshal, 1968. *Recreations:* choral music, gardening. *Address:* Barker's Hill Cottage, Donhead St Andrew, Shaftesbury, Dorset SP7 9EB. *T:* (01747) 828505. *Club:* Royal Air Force.
Died 24 Nov. 2008.

POWELL, Prof. Percival Hugh, MA, DLitt, Dr Phil; Professor of German, Indiana University, 1970–83, then Emeritus; *b* 4 Sept. 1912; 3rd *s* of late Thomas Powell and Marie Sophia Roeser; *m* 1944, Dorothy Mavis Pattison (*née* Donald) (marr. diss. 1964); one *s* (and one *s* decd) one adopted *d*; *m* 1966, Mary Kathleen (*née* Wilson) (decd); one *s*. *Educ*: University College, Cardiff (Fellow 1981); Univs of Rostock, Zürich, Bonn. 1st Class Hons German (Wales), 1933; Univ. Teachers' Diploma in Education, 1934; MA (Wales) Dist. 1936; Dr Phil (Rostock) 1938. Research Fellow of Univ. of Wales, 1936–38; Modern Languages Master, Towyn School, 1934–36; Lektor in English, Univ. of Bonn, 1938–39; Asst Lectr, Univ. Coll., Cardiff, 1939–40; War Service, 1940–46 (Capt. Intelligence Corps; Lecturer in German, Univ. Coll., Leicester, 1946, Head of Department of German, 1954; Prof. of German, Univ. of Leicester, 1958–69. Barclay Acheson Prof. of Internat. Studies at Macalester Coll., Minn., USA, 1965–66. DLitt (Wales) 1962. British Academy Award, 1963; Fritz Thyssen Foundation Award, 1964; Leverhulme Trust Award, 1968. *Publications*: Pierre Corneilles Dramen in Deutschen Bearbeitungen, 1939; critical editions of dramas of Andreas Gryphius, 1955–72; critical edn of J. G. Schoch's Comœdia vom Studentenleben, 1976; Trammels of Tradition, 1988; Louise von Gall, 1993; Fervor and Fiction, 1996; Heinrich Burkart, 1997; (ed) Berliner Don Quixote, facsimile of 1832–33 edn, 2001; articles and reviews in English and foreign literary jls. *Recreation*: music. *Address*: c/o Department of Germanic Studies, Ballantine Hall, Indiana University, Bloomington, IN 47405, USA.
Died 31 Dec. 2009.

POWELL, Sir Richard (Royle), GCB 1967 (KCB 1961; CB 1951); KBE 1954; CMG 1946; Deputy Chairman, Permanent Committee on Invisible Exports, 1968–76; Chairman, Alusuisse (UK) Ltd and subsidiary companies, 1969–84; *b* 30 July 1909; *er s* of Ernest Hartley and Florence Powell; unmarried. *Educ*: Queen Mary's Grammar Sch., Walsall; Sidney Sussex Coll., Cambridge (Hon. Fellow, 1972). Entered Civil Service, 1931 and apptd to Admiralty; Private Sec. to First Lord, 1934–37; Member of British Admiralty Technical Mission, Canada, and of British Merchant Shipbuilding Mission, and later of British Merchant Shipping Mission in USA, 1940–44; Civil Adviser to Commander-in-Chief, British Pacific Fleet, 1944–45; Under-Secretary, Ministry of Defence, 1946–48. Dep. Sec., Admiralty, 1948–50; Dep. Sec., Min. of Defence, 1950–56; Permanent Secretary, Board of Trade, 1960–68 (Min. of Defence, 1956–59). Dir, Philip Hill Investment Trust, 1968–81; Director: GEC, 1968–79; Albright & Wilson, 1968–73 (Chm., 1969–73); Whessoe Ltd, 1968–88; Hill Samuel Group, 1970–79; Sandoz Gp of Cos, 1972–87 (Chm.); Clerical, Medical and General Life Assurance Soc., 1972–85; Wilkinson Match, 1973–80 (Chm., 1976–80); BPB Industries PLC, 1973–83; Ladbroke Gp, 1980–86; Bridgewater Paper Co. Ltd, 1984–90. Pres., Inst. for Fiscal Studies, 1970–78. *Address*: Thornbank, 6 Westerfield Road, Ipswich IP4 2UJ. *Club*: Athenæum.
Died 30 March 2006.

POWELL-COTTON, Christopher, CMG 1961; MBE 1951; MC 1945; JP; Uganda Civil Service, retired; *b* 23 Feb. 1918; *s* of Major P. H. G. Powell-Cotton and Mrs H. B. Powell-Cotton (*née* Slater); unmarried. *Educ*: Harrow School; Trinity College, Cambridge. Army Service, 1939–45: commissioned Buffs, 1940; seconded KAR, Oct. 1940; T/Major, 1943. Apptd to Uganda Administration, 1940, and released for mil. service; Dist Comr, 1950; Provincial Comr, 1955; Minister of Security and External Relations, 1961. Landowner in SE Kent; Chm., Quex Park Estates Co. Ltd, 1945–. Chm. of Govs, Powell-Cotton Museum. *Address*: Quex Park, Birchington, Kent CT7 0BH. *T*: (01843) 841836. *Club*: MCC.
Died 12 April 2006.

POWER, Mrs Brian St Quentin; *see* Stack, (Ann) Prunella.

POWER, Sir Noel (Plunkett), GBS 1999; Kt 1999; a Non-Permanent Judge: Hong Kong Court of Final Appeal, since 1997; Court of Appeal, Brunei Darussalam, since 2003 (President, since 2007); *b* 4 Dec. 1929; *s* of John Joseph Power and Hilda Power; *m* 1965, Irma Maroya; two *s* one *d*. *Educ*: Downlands Coll.; Univ. of Queensland (BA, LLB). Called to the Bar, Supreme Court of Queensland and High Court of Australia, 1955; Magistrate, Hong Kong, 1965–76; Pres., Lands Tribunal, Hong Kong, 1976–79; a Judge of the Supreme Court of Hong Kong, 1979–87; a Judge of Appeal, 1987–93; a Vice-Pres. of the Court of Appeal of the Supreme Court, then a Justice of Appeal, Appeal Court of the High Court, Hong Kong, 1993–99; Acting Chief Justice, Hong Kong, 1996–97. Chairman: Broadcasting Rev. Bd, HK, 1984–85; Univ. of HK Panel of Enquiry into allegations of political pressure, 2000. Chm., Hong Kong Island, 1984–99, Asia-Pacific Zone, 1994–99, Gold Coast, 1999–, Internat. Wine and Food Soc. Chm. Editl Bd, Hong Kong Law Reports, 1994–97. *Publications*: (ed) Lands Tribunal Law Reports, 1976–79. *Recreations*: travel, cooking, reading. *Address*: 44 Surfers Waters, 40 Cotlew Street, Southport, Qld 4215, Australia. *Clubs*: Hong Kong (Hong Kong); Queensland (Brisbane).
Died 19 Nov. 2009.

POWNALL, Leslie Leigh, MA, PhD; Chairman, NSW Planning and Environment Commission, 1974–77, retired; *b* 1 Nov. 1921; *y s* of A. de S. Pownall, Wanganui, New Zealand; *m* 1943, Judith, *d* of late Harold Whittaker, Palmerston North. *Educ*: Palmerston North Boys' High Sch.; Victoria University College, University of Canterbury, University of Wisconsin. Asst Master, Christchurch Boys' High Sch., 1941–46; Lecturer in Geography: Christchurch Teachers' Coll., 1946–47; Ardmore Teachers' Coll., 1948–49; Auckland University College, 1949–51; Senior Lecturer in Geography, 1951–60, Prof. of Geography, 1960–61, Vice-Chancellor and Rector, 1961–66, University of Canterbury; Clerk of the University Senate, Univ. of London, 1966–74. Consultant, Inter-University Council for Higher Educn Overseas, London, 1963; Consultant to Chm. of Working Party on Higher Educn in E Africa, 1968–69. Member Meeting, Council on World Tensions on Social and Economic Development (S Asia and Pacific), Kuala Lumpur, Malaysia, 1964; Governor, Internat. Students Trust, London, 1967–74; Member: Central Governing Body, City Parochial Foundation, London, 1967–74 (Mem., Grants Sub-Cttee; Chm., Finance and Gen. Purposes Cttee); UK Commonwealth Scholarship Commn, 1979–80. *Publications*: New Zealand, 1951 (New York); geographic contrib. in academic journals of America, Netherlands and New Zealand. *Recreations*: music, literature. *Club*: University (Christchurch, NZ).
Died 13 Oct. 2008.

PRAG, Derek Nathan; Member (C) Hertfordshire, European Parliament, 1979–94; *b* 6 Aug. 1923; *s* of late Abraham J. Prag and Edith Prag; *m* 1948, Dora Weiner; three *s*. *Educ*: Bolton Sch.; Emmanuel Coll., Univ. of Cambridge (Scholar; MA; Cert. of Competent Knowledge in Russian). Served War, Intelligence Corps, England, Egypt, Italy, Austria, 1942–47. Economic journalist with Reuters News Agency in London, Brussels and Madrid, 1950–55; Information Service of High Authority, European Coal and Steel Community, 1955–59; Head of Publications Div., Jt Information Service of European Communities, 1959–65; Dir, London Information Office of European Communities, 1965–73; ran own consultancy company on relations with EEC, 1973–79. Mem., 1982–94, Dep. Chm., 1989–94, Constitutional Cttee (EDG spokesman, 1982–84 and 1987–92; EPP dep. spokesman, and British Cons. spokesman, 1992–94; elected Chm., 1993, but stood down); Rapporteur, EU's internat. relns for European Parlt's draft treaty on European Union, adopted 1984; Prag report on seat of EC Instns and working place of European Parlt, adopted 1989. Political spokesman for European Democratic (Cons.) Group, 1984–87; Chm., European Parlt All-Party Disablement Gp, 1980–94;

Vice-Pres., Eur. Parlt-Israel Intergroup, 1990–94; Founder Mem., Cons. Gp for Europe (Dep. Chm., 1974–77, 1991–93). Member: Anglo-Spanish Soc.; Luxembourg Soc. Hon. Dir, EEC Commn, 1974; Hon. Mem., EP, 1994. Hon. DLitt Hertfordshire, 1993. Silver Medal of European Merit, Fondation du Mérite Européen, 1974. Comdr, Order of Leopold II (Belgium), 1996. *Publications:* (with E. D. Nicholson) Businessman's Guide to the Common Market, 1973; various reports on Europe's internat. role, and booklets and articles on European integration. *Recreations:* reading, theatre, music, swimming, gardening; speaker of seven languages. *Address:* 47 New Road, Digswell, Welwyn, Herts AL6 0AQ. *Clubs:* Royal Over-Seas League, Anglo-Belgian; Royal Automobile (Brussels). *Died 20 Jan. 2010.*

PRATT, Christopher Leslie; a District Judge (Magistrates' Courts) (formerly Metropolitan Stipendiary Magistrate), 1990–2007; *b* 15 Dec. 1947; *s* of late Leslie Arthur Cottrell Pratt and Phyllis Elizabeth Eleanor Pratt; *m* 1973, Jill Rosemary Hodges; two *s. Educ:* Highgate Sch. Admitted Solicitor, 1972. Court Clerk, Hendon, Harrow and Uxbridge Courts, 1967–72; Dep. Clerk to the Justices, Wimbledon and Uxbridge, 1972–76; Clerk to the Justices, Highgate, Barnet and S Mimms, 1976–90; Clerk to Barnet Magistrates' Courts Cttee and Trng Officer, Justices and staff, 1986–90. Mem. Council, Justices' Clerks' Soc., 1983–90 (Chm., Parly Cttee, Chm., Conf. and Social Cttee); Mem., Inner London Probation Cttee, 1996–2001. *Recreations:* conjuring (Vice Pres., The Magic Circle), cartophily. *Address:* c/o City of Westminster Magistrates' Court, 70 Horseferry Road, SW1P 2AX. *Club:* Magic Circle. *Died 11 Aug. 2008.*

PRENTICE, (Hubert Archibald) John, CEng; CPhys, FInstP; consultant on manufacturing and management strategies to several UK and USA companies; *b* 5 Feb. 1920; *s* of Charles Herbert Prentice and Rose Prentice; *m* 1947, Sylvia Doreen Elias; one *s. Educ:* Woolwich Polytechnic, London; Salford Univ. (BSc, MSc). MRAeS 1962, CEng 1970; FInstP 1967, CPhys 1985. Min. of Supply, 1939–56; R&D posts, res. estabts and prodn, MoD, 1956–60; Space Dept, RAE, Min. of Aviation, 1960–67; Head, Road User Characteristics Res., 1967–70, and Head, Driver Aids and Abilities Res., 1970–72, MoT; Head, Road User Dynamics Res., Dept, 1972–75; Counsellor (Sci. and Technol.), British Embassy, Tokyo, 1975–80. *Recreations:* walking, climbing. *Address:* 5 Foxhill Crescent, Camberley, Surrey GU15 1PR. *T:* (01276) 66373. *Died 18 Sept. 2008.*

PRENTICE, Thomas, MC 1945; Life President, Harrisons & Crosfield plc, then Elementis plc, since 1988 (Chairman, 1977–88); *b* 14 Oct. 1919; *s* of Alexander and Jean Young Prentice; *m* 1949, Peggy Ann Lloyd; two *s* two *d. Educ:* McLaren High Sch., Callander, Perthshire. Served Army, 1939–46. Harrisons & Crosfield (Sabah) Sdn Bhd, Malaysia, 1947–67; Harrisons & Crosfield plc, then Elementis plc, 1967–. *Recreations:* golf, gardening. *Clubs:* East India, Devonshire, Sports and Public Schools. *Died 17 Nov. 2007.*

PRENTICE, Dame Winifred (Eva), DBE 1977 (OBE 1972); SRN; President, Royal College of Nursing, 1972–76; *b* 2 Dec. 1910; *d* of Percy John Prentice and Anna Eva Prentice. *Educ:* Northgate Sch. for Girls, Ipswich; E Suffolk and Ipswich Hosp. (SRN); W Mddx Hosp. (SCM Pt I); Queen Elizabeth Coll., London Univ. (RNT); Dip. in Nursing, London Univ. Ward Sister: E Suffolk and Ipswich Hosp., 1936–39; Essex County Hosp., 1941–43; Nurse Tutor, King's Lynn Hosp., 1944–46; Principal Tutor, Stracathro Hosp., Brechin, Angus, 1947–61, Matron, 1961–72. *Publications:* articles in Nursing Times and Nursing Mirror. *Recreations:* music, amateur dramatics, gardening. *Address:* Marleish, 4 Duke Street, Brechin, Angus DD9 6JY. *T:* (01356) 622606. *Died 17 March 2007.*

PRESCOTT, Brig. Peter George Addington, MC 1944; Secretary, National Rifle Association, 1980–88; *b* 22 Sept. 1924; *s* of Col and Mrs John Prescott; *m* 1953, June Marian Louise Wendell; one *s* one *d. Educ:* Eton Coll.; Staff Coll. (psc 1957); Royal Coll. of Defence Studies (rcds 1973). Commnd Grenadier Guards, 1943; 2nd Armoured Bn Gren. Gds, 1944–45; comd 2nd Bn Gren. Gds, 1966–69; Comdr 51st Inf. Bde, 1970–72; Dep. Comdr NE Dist, 1974–77; Dep. Dir of Army Trng, 1977–79, retd. Chevalier, Royal Order of the Sword, Sweden, 1954. *Recreations:* sailing, painting, gardening. *Address:* West House, 66 High Street, Rolvenden, Kent TN17 4LW. *Died 31 Oct. 2007.*

PRESS, John Bryant, FRSL; author and poet; *b* 11 Jan. 1920; *s* of late Edward Kenneth Press and late Gladys (*née* Cooper); *m* 1947, Janet Crompton; one *s* one *d. Educ:* King Edward VI Sch., Norwich; Corpus Christi Coll., Cambridge, 1938–40 and 1945–46. Served War of 1939–45: RA, 1940–45. British Council, 1946–79: Athens, 1946–47; Salonika, 1947–50; Madras, 1950–51; Colombo, 1951–52; Birmingham, 1952–54; Cambridge, 1955–62; London, 1962–65; Paris, 1966–71 (also Cultural Attaché, British Embassy); Regional Dir, Oxford, 1972–78; Literature Advr, London, 1978–79. Mem. Council, RSL, 1961–88. Gave George Elliston Poetry Foundation Lectures at Univ. of Cincinnati, 1962; Vis. Prof., Univ. of Paris, 1981–82. *Publications:* The Fire and the Fountain, 1955; Uncertainties, 1956; (ed) Poetic Heritage, 1957; The Chequer'd Shade, 1958 (RSL Heinemann Award); Andrew Marvell, 1958; Guy Fawkes Night, 1959; Herrick, 1961; Rule and Energy, 1963; Louis MacNeice, 1964; (ed) Palgrave's Golden Treasury, Book V, 1964, Book VI, 1994; A Map of Modern English Verse, 1969; The Lengthening Shadows, 1971; John Betjeman, 1974; Spring at St Clair, 1974; Aspects of Paris, (with illus by Gordon Bradshaw), 1975; (with Edward Lowbury and Michael Riviere) Troika, 1977; Poets of World War I, 1983; Poets of World War II, 1984; A Girl with Beehive Hair, 1986; Poems, 2004; Sidney Keyes, 2005. Libretto, new version of Bluebeard's Castle, for Michael Powell's colour television film of Bartok's opera, 1963. *Recreations:* travel (especially in France), theatre, opera, concerts, cinema; architecture and visual arts. *Address:* 5 South Parade, Frome BA11 1EJ. *T:* (01373) 302166. *Died 26 Feb. 2007.*

PRESTON, Geoffrey Averill; Assistant Counsel to Chairman of Committees, House of Lords, 1982–89; *b* 19 May 1924; *s* of George and Winifred Preston; *m* 1953, Catherine Wright. *Educ:* St Marylebone Grammar Sch. Barrister-at-Law. Served, RNVR, 1942–46. Called to Bar, Gray's Inn, 1950. Treasury Solicitor's Dept, 1952–71; Solicitor's Department: Dept of Environment, 1971–74; Dept of Trade, 1974–75; Under-Sec. (Legal), Dept of Trade, 1975–82. *Recreations:* gardening, carpentry, chess. *Address:* Ledsham, Glaziers Lane, Normandy, Surrey GU3 2DQ. *T:* (01483) 811250. *Died 20 May 2010.*

PRESTON, Myles Park; HM Diplomatic Service, retired; *b* 4 April 1927; *s* of Robert and Marie Preston; *m* 1st, 1951, Ann Betten (marr. diss.); one *s* one *d;* 2nd, 1981, Joy Moore (*née* Fisher). *Educ:* Sudley Road Council Sch.; Liverpool Inst. High Sch.; Clare Coll., Cambridge. Instructor Lieut, RN, 1948–51; Asst Principal, Admty, 1951–53; CRO, 1953–54; 2nd Sec., British High Commn, New Delhi, 1954–56; 1st Sec., CRO, 1956–59; 1st Sec., Governor-General's Office and British High Commn, Lagos, 1959–62; CRO, 1962–64; 1st Sec., British High Commn, Kampala, 1964–67; Commonwealth Office and FCO, 1967–69; Counsellor and Consul-Gen., Djakarta, 1969–72; Canadian Nat. Defence Coll., 1972–73; FCO, 1973–77; Dep. Governor, Solomon Islands, 1977–78; Consul-Gen., Vancouver, 1978–79. *Address:* 20 Prince Edwards Road, Lewes, East Sussex BN7 1BE. *T:* (01273) 475809. *Died 4 May 2007.*

PRICE, Sir Norman (Charles), KCB 1975 (CB 1969); Member, European Court of Auditors, 1977–83; Chairman, Board of Inland Revenue, 1973–76 (Deputy Chairman, 1968–73); *b* 5 Jan. 1915; *s* of Charles William and Ethel Mary Price; *m* 1940, Kathleen Beatrice (*née* Elston); two *d*. *Educ:* Plaistow Grammar School. Entered Civil Service as Executive Officer, Customs and Excise, 1933; Inspector of Taxes, Inland Revenue, 1939; Secretaries' Office, Inland Revenue, 1951; Board of Inland Revenue, 1965. *Recreations:* crosswords, history. *Address:* 73 Linkswood, Compton Place Road, Eastbourne BN21 1EF. *T:* (01323) 725941.
Died 19 Feb. 2007.

PRICHARD-JONES, Sir John, 2nd Bt *cr* 1910; barrister; farmer and bloodstock breeder; *b* 20 Jan. 1913; *s* of Sir John Prichard-Jones, 1st Bt and Marie, *y d* of late Charles Read, solicitor; *S* father, 1917; *m* 1937, Heather, (from whom he obtained a divorce, 1950), *er d* of late Sir Walter Nugent, 4th Bt; one *s*; *m* 1959, Helen Marie Thérèse, *e d* of J. F. Liddy, dental surgeon, 20 Laurence Street, Drogheda; one *d*. *Educ:* Eton; Christ Church, Oxford (BA Hons; MA). Called to Bar, Gray's Inn, 1936. Commnd, Queen's Bays, 1939, and served throughout War. *Heir: s* David John Walter Prichard-Jones, BA (Hons) Oxon, *b* 14 March 1943. *Address:* Allenswood House, Lucan, Co. Dublin, Ireland.
Died 2 July 2007.

PRICKETT, Air Chief Marshal Sir Thomas (Other), KCB 1965 (CB 1957); DSO 1943; DFC 1942; Air Member for Supply and Organisation, Ministry of Defence, 1968–70; *b* 31 July 1913; *s* of late E. G. Prickett; *m* 1st, 1942, Elizabeth Gratian, (*d* 1984), *d* of late William Galbally, Laguna Beach, Calif, USA; one *s* one *d*; 2nd, 1985, Shirley Westerman. *Educ:* Stubbington House Sch., Haileybury Coll. Assistant, later Manager, sugar estates, India with Begg Sutherland Ltd, 1932–37. Served Bihar Light Horse, Indian Army (Auxiliary). Joined RAF, 1937; Desert Air Force, Bomber Comd, 1939–44; RAF Delegn, Washington; Dep. Dir Trng, 1944–45; commanded RAF Tangmere, 1949–51; Group Captain operations, HQ Middle East Air Force, 1951–54; commanded RAF Jever, 1954–55; attended Imperial Defence Coll., 1956; Chief of Staff Air Task Force, 1956; Director of Policy, Air Ministry, 1957–58; SASO, HQ No 1 Group, 1958–60; ACAS (Ops) Air Ministry, 1960–63; ACAS (Policy and Planning) Air Ministry, 1963–64; AOC-in-C, NEAF, Comdr British Forces Near East, and Administrator, Sovereign Base Area, 1964–66; AOC-in-C, RAF Air Support Command, 1967–68. Dir, Goodwood Estate, 1970–78; Man. Dir, Goodwood Terrena, 1970–78. *Recreations:* polo, sailing, golf. *Address:* 46 Kingston Hill Place, Kingston upon Thames KT2 7QY. *Club:* Royal Air Force. *Died 23 Jan. 2010.*

PRIESTMAN, John David; Clerk of the Parliamentary Assembly of the Council of Europe, 1971–86; *b* 29 March 1926; *s* of Bernard Priestman and Hermine Bréal; *m* 1951, Nada Valić (*d* 1999); two *s* two *d*. *Educ:* private sch. in Paris; Westminster Sch.; Merton Coll. and Christ Church, Oxford (Hon. Mods, Lit. Hum.). Served Coldstream Guards, 1944–47, Temp. Captain. Third, subseq. Second, Sec., Belgrade, 1949–53; Asst Private Sec. to Rt Hon. Anthony Eden, 1953–55; joined Secretariat, Council of Europe, 1955; Head of Sec. Gen's Private Office, 1961; Sec., Cttee of Ministers, 1966; Dep. Clerk of Parly Assembly, 1968–71. Hon. Life Mem., Assoc. of Secretaries General of Parlt, 1986. Rep. in Alpes Maritimes, French Nat. Assoc. of Prison Visitors, 1987–99. *Recreations:* off-piste Alpine ski-ing, music, competition bridge, gastronomic research. *Address:* 6 rue Adolphe Wurtz, 67000 Strasbourg, France. *T:* 388354049. *Died 12 March 2009.*

PRINCE-SMITH, Sir (William) Richard, 4th Bt *cr* 1911; *b* 27 Dec. 1928; *s* of Sir William Prince-Smith, 3rd Bt, OBE, MC, and Marjorie, Lady Prince-Smith (*d* 1970); *S* father, 1964; *m* 1st, 1955, Margaret Ann Carter; one *d* (one *s* decd); 2nd, 1975, Ann Christina Faulds. *Educ:* Charterhouse; Clare Coll.,

Cambridge (MA). BA (Agric.) 1951. *Recreations:* music, photography, travel. *Heir:* none. *Address:* 40–735 Paxton Drive, Rancho Mirage, CA 92270–3516, USA. *T:* (760) 3211975. *Club:* Springs Country (Rancho Mirage).
Died 28 June 2007 (ext).

PRITCHARD, Arthur Alan, CB 1979; JP; former Deputy Under Secretary of State, Ministry of Defence; *b* 3 March 1922; *s* of Arthur Henry Standfast Pritchard and Sarah Bessie Myra Pritchard (*née* Mundy); *m* 1949, Betty Rona Nevard (*née* Little); two *s* one *d*. *Educ:* Wanstead High Sch., Essex. Board of Trade, 1939. RAFVR Pilot, 1941–52; CFS Instr, 1946. Joined Admiralty, 1952; Asst Sec., 1964; Royal College of Defence Studies, 1972; Asst Under-Sec. of State, Naval Personnel and Op. Requirements, MoD, 1972–76, seconded as Dep. Sec., NI Office, 1976–78; Secretary to the Admiralty Bd, 1978–81. Management consultant, 1984–89. Pres., Fordingbridge and Dist Community Assoc., 1996–2002 (Chm., 1990–95); Chm., Sandleheath Parish Council, 2001–03. JP Ringwood, 1986 (Totton and New Forest, 1981–86; Chm., Ringwood Bench, 1991–92). *Recreation:* walking. *Died 30 Aug. 2010.*

PRITCHARD, Sir Neil, KCMG 1962 (CMG 1952); HM Diplomatic Service, retired; Ambassador in Bangkok, 1967–70; *b* 14 Jan. 1911; *s* of late Joseph and Lillian Pritchard; *m* 1943, Mary Burroughes (*d* 1988), Pretoria, S Africa; one *s*. *Educ:* Liverpool Coll.; Worcester Coll., Oxford. Dominions Office, 1933; Private Secretary to Permanent Under-Sec., 1936–38; Assistant Secretary, Rhodesia-Nyasaland Royal Commission, 1938; Secretary, Office of UK High Commissioner, Pretoria, 1941–45; Principal Secretary, Office of UK Representative, Dublin, 1948–49; Assistant Under-Secretary of State, Commonwealth Relations Office, 1951–54; Dep. UK High Commissioner: Canada, 1954–57; Australia, 1957–60; Actg Dep. Under-Sec. of State, CRO, 1961; British High Comr in Tanganyika, 1961–63; Deputy Under-Secretary of State, Commonwealth Office (formerly CRO), 1963–67. *Address:* Little Garth, Daglingworth, Cirencester, Glos GL7 7AQ. *Died 10 Oct. 2010.*

PROFUMO, John Dennis, CBE 1975 (OBE (mil.) 1944); 5th Baron of Italy (*cr* 1903); *b* 30 Jan. 1915; *e s* of late Baron Albert Profumo, KC; *m* 1954, Valerie Hobson, actress (*d* 1998); one *s*. *Educ:* Harrow; Brasenose College, Oxford. 1st Northamptonshire Yeomanry, 1939 (despatches); Brigadier, Chief of Staff UK Mission in Japan, 1945. MP (C): Kettering Division, Northamptonshire, 1940–45; Stratford-on-Avon Division of Warwickshire, 1950–63. Parliamentary Secretary, Ministry of Transport and Civil Aviation, Nov. 1952–Jan. 1957; Parliamentary Under-Secretary of State for the Colonies, 1957–58; Parliamentary Under-Sec. of State, Foreign Affairs, Nov. 1958–Jan. 1959; Minister of State for Foreign Affairs, 1959–60; Secretary of State for War, July 1960–June 1963; PC, 1960–63. Dir, Provident Life Assoc. of London, 1975– (Dep. Chm., 1978–82). Mem., Bd of Visitors, HM Prison, Grendon, 1968–75. Chm., Toynbee Hall, 1982–85, Pres. 1985– (Hon. Life Mem., 2001). Hon. Fellow, Queen Mary, Univ. of London, 2001. *Recreations:* fishing, gardening, DIY. *Heir: s* David Profumo [*b* 30 Oct. 1955; *m* 1980, Helen, *o d* of Alasdair Fraser; two *s* one *d*]. *Club:* Boodle's.
Died 9 March 2006.

PRYOR, His Honour Brian Hugh; QC 1982; a Circuit Judge, 1986–2001; *b* 11 March 1931; *s* of Lt-Col Ronald Ernest Pryor, Royal Sussex Regt, and Violet Kathleen Pryor (*née* Steele); *m* 1955, Jane Mary Smith (*d* 2007); one *s* two *d*. *Educ:* Chichester High Sch.; University Coll., Oxford (Open Exhibnr Mod. History; BA Jurisprudence). Called to the Bar, Lincoln's Inn, 1956; Sir Thomas More Bursary, Lincoln's Inn, 1958. Member: SE Circuit Bar Mess, 1957; Kent County Bar Mess, 1957; Chm., Kent Bar Mess, 1979–82; Mem., SE Circuit Bar Mess Wine Cttee, 1979–82. A Recorder, 1981–86; Resident Judge, Woolwich Crown Court, 1993–99.

Mem., Res. Ethics Cttee, Camberwell HA and King's Healthcare NHS Trust, 1990–95. *Recreation:* gardening.
Died 25 Jan. 2009.

PUGH, Charles Edward, (Ted), CBE 1988; Managing Director, National Nuclear Corporation Ltd, 1984–87; *b* 17 Sept. 1922; *s* of Gwilym Arthur and Elsie Doris Pugh; *m* 1945, Edna Wilkinson; two *s* one *d. Educ:* Bolton and Salford Technical Colleges. CEng, MIMechE; FInstE 1987. Lancashire Electric Power Co., 1942–48; CEGB Project Manager responsible for design and construction of 6 power stations, 1951–71; Chief Electrical and Control and Instrumentation Engineer, CEGB, Barnwood, 1971–73; Special Services, CEGB, 1973–76; Dir of Projects, CEGB, 1976–82, with responsibility for completion of the AGR prog. of reactors; PWR Project Dir, NNC, 1982–84. Pres., Inst. of Energy, 1988–89. Hon. FINucE 1984. *Recreations:* power stations, sculpture, painting, music, gardening, walking, secure energy supplies for the UK.   *Died 21 Sept. 2008.*

PUGH, Sir Idwal (Vaughan), KCB 1972 (CB 1967); Chairman, Chartered Trust Ltd, 1979–88; Director: Standard Chartered Bank, 1979–88; Halifax Building Society, 1979–88; *b* 10 Feb. 1918; *s* of late Rhys Pugh and Elizabeth Pugh; *m* 1946, Mair Lewis (*d* 1985); one *s* one *d. Educ:* Cowbridge Grammar Sch.; St John's Coll., Oxford (Hon. Fellow, 1979). Army Service, 1940–46. Entered Min. of Civil Aviation, 1946; Alternate UK Rep. at International Civil Aviation Organisation, Montreal, 1950–53; Asst Secretary, 1956; Civil Air Attaché, Washington, 1957–59; Under Secretary, Min. of Transport, 1959; Min. of Housing and Local Govt, 1961; Dep. Sec., Min. of Housing and Local Govt, 1966–69; Permanent Sec., Welsh Office, 1969–71; Second Permanent Sec., DoE, 1971–76. Parly Comr for Administration and Health Service Comr for England, Wales and Scotland, 1976–79. Chm., Develt Corp. of Wales, 1980–83. Chm., RNCM, 1988–92 (Hon. Mem., 1992); Vice-Pres., UC Swansea, 1988–94 (Hon. Fellow, 1995); President: Coleg Harlech, 1990–98; Cardiff Business Club, 1991–98. Hon. LLD Wales, 1988. *Address:* 5 Murray Court, 80 Banbury Road, Oxford OX2 6LQ. *Club:* Brooks's.   *Died 21 April 2010.*

PUGH, John Stanley; Corporate Affairs Executive, Wavertree Technology Park, Liverpool, 1982–99; *b* 9 Dec. 1927; *s* of John Albert and Winifred Lloyd Pugh; *m* 1953, Kathleen Mary; two *s* one *d. Educ:* Wallasey Grammar School. Editor: Liverpool Daily Post, 1969–78; Liverpool Echo, 1978–82. *Recreations:* golf, ornithology. *Address:* 21 Church Meadow Lane, Heswall, Wirral, Merseyside L60 4SB. *Club:* Royal Liverpool (Hoylake).
Died 12 April 2007.

PUGH, Ted; *see* Pugh, C. E.

PUMFREY, Rt Hon. Sir Nicholas (Richard), Kt 1997; PC 2007; **Rt Hon. Lord Justice Pumfrey;** a Lord Justice of Appeal, since 2007; *b* 22 May 1951; *s* of late Peter Pumfrey and of Maureen Pumfrey. *Educ:* St Edward's Sch., Oxford; St Edmund Hall, Oxford (BA Physics, 1972, Law, 1974). Called to the Bar, Middle Temple, 1975, Bencher, 1998; QC 1990; Jun. Counsel to HM Treasury (Patents), 1987–90; a Judge of the High Court of Justice, Chancery Div., 1997–2007. *Address:* Royal Courts of Justice, Strand, WC2A 2LL.
Died 24 Dec. 2007.

PUMPHREY, Sir (John) Laurence, KCMG 1973 (CMG 1963); HM Diplomatic Service, retired; Ambassador to Pakistan (formerly High Commissioner), 1971–76; *b* 22 July 1916; *s* of late Charles Ernest Pumphrey and Iris Mary (*née* Moberly-Bell); *m* 1945, Jean, *e d* of Sir Walter Buchanan Riddell, 12th Bt; four *s* one *d. Educ:* Winchester; New College, Oxford. Served War of 1939–45 in Army. Foreign Service from 1945. Head of Establishment and Organisation Department, Foreign Office, 1955–60; Counsellor, Staff of British Commissioner-General for SE Asia, Singapore, 1960–63; Counsellor, HM Embassy, Belgrade, 1963–65; Deputy

High Commissioner, Nairobi, 1965–67; British High Comr, Zambia, 1967–71. Military Cross, 3rd Class (Greece), 1941. *Address:* Caistron, Thropton, Morpeth, Northumberland NE65 7LG.   *Died 23 Dec. 2009.*

PURVES, Dame Daphne (Helen), DBE 1979; Senior Lecturer in French, Dunedin Teachers College, 1967–73, retired (Lecturer, 1963–66); *b* 8 Nov. 1908; *d* of Irvine Watson Cowie and Helen Jean Cowie; *m* 1939, Herbert Dudley Purves, CMG, FRSNZ (*d* 1993); one *s* two *d. Educ:* Otago Girls' High Sch., Dunedin, NZ; Univ. of Otago, Dunedin (MA 1st Cl. Hons English and French). Secondary sch. teacher, 1931–40 and 1957–63. Pres., NZ Fedn of University Women, 1962–64; Internat. Fedn of University Women: Mem., Cultural Relations Cttee, 1965–68, Convener, 1968–71; 3rd Vice-Pres., 1971–74; 1st Vice-Pres., 1974–77; Pres., 1977–80. Chm., National Theme Cttee, The Child in the World, NZ Nat. Commn for Internat. Year of the Child, 1978–80; Mem., Internat. Year of the Child Telethon Trust, 1978–81; Exec. Mem., NZ Cttee for Children (IYC) Inc., 1980–82. Mem., NZ Nat. Commn, Unesco, 1964–68. Pres., Friends of Olveston Inc., 1986–88. Mem., Theomin Gall. Management Cttee, 1986–91. *Relevant publication:* Nothing Like a Dame: a biography of Dame Daphne Purves, by Molly Anderson, 1998. *Recreations:* reading, croquet, bridge, travel, heraldry. *Clubs:* University (Dunedin); Punga Croquet (Pres., 1988–90); Dunedin Bridge, Otago Bridge.   *Died 14 Oct. 2008.*

PUSINELLI, (Frederick) Nigel (Molière), CMG 1966; OBE 1963; MC 1940; HM Overseas Civil Service, retired; *b* 28 April 1919; second *s* of late S. Jacques and T. May Pusinelli, Frettenham, Norfolk and Fowey, Cornwall; *m* 1941, Joan Mary Chaloner (*d* 1999), *d* of late Cuthbert B. and Mildred H. Smith, Cromer, Norfolk and Bexhill-on-Sea, Sussex; one *d* (one *s* decd). *Educ:* Aldenham School; Pembroke College, Cambridge (BA Hons in law). Commissioned RA 1939; served BEF, 1940; India/Burma, 1942–45; Major, 1942; Staff College, Quetta, 1945. Administrative officer, Gilbert and Ellice Islands Colony, 1946–57; transferred to Aden, 1958; Dep. Financial Sec. and frequently Actg Financial Sec. till 1962; Director of Establishments, 1962–68, and Assistant High Commissioner, 1963–68, Aden and Federation of South Arabia. Member E African Currency Board, 1960–62. Salaries Commissioner various territories in West Indies, 1968–70. Chm., Overseas Service Pensioners' Assoc., 1978–99 (Hon. Vice-Pres., 2004–). Chairman: Chichester Harbour Conservancy, 1987–90 (Vice-Chm., 1985–87; Mem., Adv. Cttee, 1971–2004); RYA Southern Region, 1979–96; Chichester Harbour Fedn of sailing clubs and yachting orgns, 1980–87. RYA Yachtsman's Award, 1996. *Publications:* Report on Census of Population of Gilbert and Ellice Islands Colony, 1947. *Recreation:* dinghy racing. *Address:* Mile End House, Westbourne, Emsworth, Hants PO10 8RP. *T:* (01243) 372915. *Clubs:* Royal Commonwealth Society; Royal Yachting Association; Cambridge University Cruising, Emsworth Sailing.   *Died 17 July 2010.*

PUTTFARKEN, Prof. Thomas Monrad, Dr phil; FBA 2003; Professor of the History and Theory of Art, University of Essex, since 1984; *b* 19 Dec. 1943; *s* of Franz Ferdinand and Traut Puttfarken; *m* 1st, 1969, Herma Zimmer (marr. diss. 1981); one *s* one *d*; 2nd, 1981, Elspeth Crichton Stuart. *Educ:* Gymnasium Blankenese, Hamburg; Univ. of Innsbruck; Univ. of Munich; Univ. of Hamburg (Dr phil 1969); Warburg Inst., Univ. of London. Lectr, Univ. of Hamburg, 1971–74; Sen. Lectr, 1974–77, Reader, 1977–84, Univ. of Essex. Visiting Professor: Univ. of Hamburg, 1990–91; Univ. of Freiburg, 1999. *Publications:* Masstabsfragen, 1972; Roger de Piles' Theory of Art, 1985; The Discovery of Pictorial Composition: theories of visual order in painting 1400–1800, 2000; Titian and Tragic Painting, 2005; articles in Jl of Warburg and Courtauld Insts, Burlington Mag., Art Hist., etc. *Recreations:* painting, walking, music. *Address:* Department of Art History and Theory,

University of Essex, Wivenhoe Park, Colchester CO4
3SQ. *T:* (01206) 873008, *Fax:* (01206) 873003; *e-mail:*
tomp@essex.ac.uk.   *Died 5 Oct. 2006.*

**PUXON, (Christine) Margaret, (Mrs Margaret
Williams);** QC 1982; MD, FRCOG; medical/legal
consultant; practising barrister, 1954–93; *b* 25 July 1915;
d of Reginald Wood Hale and Clara Lilian Hale;
m 1955, F. Morris Williams (*d* 1986), MBE; two *s*
one *d. Educ:* Abbey Sch., Malvern Wells;
Birmingham Univ. (MB, ChB; MD Obstetrics 1944).
MRCS, LRCP 1942; FRCOG 1976. Gynaecological
Registrar, Queen Elizabeth Hosp., Birmingham, and
later Consultant Gynaecologist, Essex CC, 1942–49.
Called to the Bar, Inner Temple, 1954. A Dep. Circuit
Judge, 1970–86; a Recorder, 1986–88. Privy
Council Member, Council of Royal Pharmaceutical
Soc., 1975–90; Member: Genetic Manipulation Adv.
Gp, 1979–84; Ethics Cttee, RCGP, 1981–93; Chm.,
Ethics Cttee, Lister Hosp. IVF Unit, 1983–. Consulting
Editor, Medical Law Reports, 1993–99. Liveryman,
Worshipful Soc. of Apothecaries, 1982–. *Publications:*
The Family and the Law, 1963, 2nd edn 1971;
contributed to: Progress in Obstetrics and Gynaecology,
1983; In Vitro Fertilisation: Past, Present and Future,
1986; Gynaecology (ed Shaw, Souter and Stanton),
1991; Safe Practice in Obstetrics and Gynaecology (ed
Clements), 1994; contrib. med. and legal jls, incl.
Proc. RSM, Practitioner, New Law Jl and Solicitors' Jl.
Address: 19 Clarence Gate Gardens, Glentworth Street,
NW1 6AY. *T:* (020) 7723 7922; *e-mail:* margaret
puxon@aol.com.   *Died 1 April 2008.*

PYBUS, William Michael; Chairman, AAH Holdings
plc, 1968–92; *b* 7 May 1923; *s* of Sydney James Pybus
and Evelyn Mary (*née* Wood); *m* 1959, Elizabeth Janet
Whitley; two *s* two *d. Educ:* Bedford Sch.; New College,
Oxford (1st cl. hons Jurisprudence). Served War,
1942–46: commissioned 1st King's Dragoon Guards;
Lieut attached XIth Hussars in Normandy (wounded);
King's Dragoon Guards, Egypt, Palestine, Syria,
Lebanon; Prosecutor, Mil. Courts, Palestine, 1946
(Major). Admitted Solicitor, 1950 (Scott Scholar, and
Grotius Prize, 1950); Partner, Herbert Oppenheimer,
Nathan & Vandyk, Solicitors, 1953–88. Consultant,
Denton Hall Burgin & Warrens, 1988–94. Chairman:
British Fuel Co., 1968–87; Inter-Continental Fuels Ltd,
1975–88; Siebe (formerly Siebe Gorman Hldgs),
1980–90 (Dir, 1972–97); Leigh Interests, 1982–89;
Homeowners Friendly Soc. Ltd, 1991–96 (Dir,
1980–96); Dep. Chm., R. Mansell Ltd, 1980–85;
Director: National Westminster Bank (Outer London
Region), 1977–88; Cornhill Insurance PLC, 1977–97;
Overseas Coal Developments Ltd, 1979–88; Bradford &
Bingley Building Soc., 1983–94; Vestric Ltd, 1985–91;
Conservation Foundn, 1991–97; Conservation Foundn
Enterprise Ltd, 1991–97. Part-time Member: British
Railways (London Midland) Bd, 1974; British Railways
(Midlands and West) Bd, 1975–77; Chm., BR (London
Midland) Bd, 1977–89. Pres., Coal Trade Benevolent
Assoc., 1998 (Dir, 1969–); Vice-Pres., Coal Industry
Soc., 1981– (Pres., 1976–81); Pres., Chagford Agricl and
Horticl Soc., 1992. Governor, Harpur Trust, 1979–87.
Master: Pattenmakers' Co., 1972–73; Fuellers' Co.,
1994–95. Chairman: Ashdown House School Trust Ltd,
1975–89; City Univ. Club, 1975–76; Devon
Community Foundn, 1997–2000. CCMI (CBIM 1974);
FCIM (FInstM 1974); FRSA 1984. *Recreation:* fishing.
Clubs: Cavalry and Guards, Royal Automobile, MCC;
Yorkshire CC.   *Died 2 June 2006.*

PYE, Prof. Norman; Professor of Geography, University
of Leicester, 1954–79, then Emeritus; Pro-Vice-
Chancellor, 1963–66; Dean, Faculty of Science,

1957–60; Chairman of Convocation, 1982–85; *b* 2 Nov.
1913; *s* of John Whittaker Pye and Hilda Constance (*née*
Platt); *m* 1940, Isabella Jane (*née* Currie) (*d* 2000); two *s*.
Educ: Wigan Grammar School; Manchester University.
Manchester University: BA Hons Geography Class I,
1935, Diploma in Education Class I, 1936. Asst Lecturer
in Geography, Manchester Univ., 1936–37 and
1938–46; Mem., Cambridge Univ. Spitsbergen Expedn,
1938. Seconded to Hydrographic Dept, Admiralty, for
War Service, 1940–46; pt-time lectr, Univ. of Bristol
Cttee on Educn in HM Forces, 1941–45. Lecturer in
Geography, 1946–53, Sen. Lecturer, 1953–54,
Manchester Univ; Mem. Expedn to US Sonora and
Mojave Deserts, 1952. Chm., Conf. of Heads of Depts
of Geography in British Univs, 1968–70. Vis. Professor:
Univ. of Ghana, 1958, 1960; Univ. of BC, 1964, 1983;
Univ. of Alberta, Edmonton, 1967, 1968, 1969, 1973,
1974, 1975, 1978; External Examnr: Univ. of E Africa,
1964–67; Univ. of Guyana, 1974–78. Editor,
"Geography", 1965–80. Member Corby Development
Corp., 1965–80. Governor, Up Holland Grammar Sch.,
1953–74; Member: Northants CC Educn Cttee,
1956–74; Court, Nottingham Univ., 1964–79; Standing
Conf. on Univ. Entrance, 1966–79; Schools Council,
1967–78. Member: Council, RMetS, 1953–56; Council,
Inst. of Brit Geographers, 1954, 1955; Council, RGS,
1967–70 (Hon. Fellow, 1991); Council for Urban
Studies Centres, 1974–81; Brit. Nat. Cttee for
Geography, 1970–75; Civic Trust Educn Gp (formerly
Heritage Educn Gp), 1976–90; Young Enterprise Leics
Area Bd, 1983–96; Hon. Mem., Geographical Assoc.,
1983– (Mem. Council, 1965–83; Hon. Vice-Pres.,
1979–83). *Publications:* The Land Utilisation Survey of
Britain: Part 44, Isle of Man, 1941; Leicester and its
Region (ed and contrib.), 1972; research papers, articles
and revs in learned journals. *Recreations:* travel, oenology,
music, gardening. *Address:* 2 Austen Avenue, Oliver's
Battery, Winchester SO22 4HP. *T:* (01962) 869052.
Club: Geographical.   *Died 16 March 2007.*

PYM, Baron *cr* 1987 (Life Peer), of Sandy in the County of
Bedfordshire; **Francis Leslie Pym,** MC 1945; PC 1970;
DL; *b* 13 Feb. 1922; *s* of late Leslie Ruthven Pym, MP,
and Iris, *d* of Charles Orde; *m* 1949, Valerie Fortune
Daglish; two *s* two *d. Educ:* Eton; Magdalene Coll,
Cambridge (Hon. Fellow 1979). Served War of 1939–45
(despatches, 1944 and 1945, MC): 9th Lancers, 1942–46;
African and Italian campaigns. Contested (C) Rhondda
West, 1959; MP (C): Cambridgeshire, 1961–83;
Cambridgeshire South East, 1983–87. Asst Govt Whip
(unpaid), Oct. 1962–64; Opposition Whip, 1964–67;
Opposition Dep. Chief Whip, 1967–70; Parly Sec. to the
Treasury and Govt Chief Whip, 1970–73; Sec. of State
for NI, 1973–74; Opposition spokesman on: agriculture,
1974–76; H of C affairs and devolution, 1976–78;
Foreign and Commonwealth affairs, 1978–79; Sec. of
State for Defence, 1979–81; Chancellor of the Duchy of
Lancaster and Paymaster Gen., and Leader of the House
of Commons, 1981; Lord Pres. of the Council and Leader
of the House of Commons, 1981–82; Sec. of State for
Foreign and Commonwealth Affairs, 1982–83.
Chairman: Diamond Cable Communications plc,
1995–99; Christie Brockbank Shipton Ltd, 1994–99.
Pres., Atlantic Treaty Assoc., 1985–87. Chm., E-SU,
1987–92. Member: Council, BESO, 1988–98; Bd, The
Landscape Foundn, 1993–98; Vice-Pres., Registered
Engineers for Disaster Relief, 1986–98. Mem.
Herefordshire County Council, 1958–61. DL Cambs,
1973. Mem. Council, Liverpool Univ., 1949–53.
Publications: The Politics of Consent, 1984; Sentimental
Journey: tracing an outline of family history, 1998.
Address: Everton Park, Sandy, Beds SG19 2DE.
                                                  Died 7 March 2008.

Q

QUANTRILL, Prof. Malcolm, RIBA; architect, author and critic; Distinguished Professor of Architecture, Texas A&M University, 1986–2007, then Distinguished Professor Emeritus; Co-Founder, 1990, and Director, since 1996, Center for the Advancement of Studies in Architecture; *b* Norwich, Norfolk, 25 May 1931; *s* of Arthur William Quantrill and Alice May Newstead; *m* 1971, Esther Maeve, *d* of James Brignell Dand and Winifred Dand, Chester; two *s* two *d*. *Educ:* City of Norwich Sch.; Liverpool Univ. (BArch); Univ. of Pennsylvania (MArch); Univ. of Wroclaw (Doc. Ing Arch, now redesignated DScEng). RIBA 1961. Fulbright Scholar and Albert Kahn Meml Fellow, Univ. of Pennsylvania, 1954–55; Asst Prof., Louisiana State Univ., 1955–60; Lecturer: Univ. of Wales, Cardiff, 1962–65; UCL, 1965–66; Asst to Dir, Architectural Assoc., 1966–67, Dir, 1967–69; Lectr, Univ. of Liverpool, 1970–73; Dean, Sch. of Environmental Design, Polytechnic of N London, 1973–80; Prof. of Architecture and Urban Design, Univ. of Jordan, Amman-Jordan, 1980–83. Vis. Professor: Univ. of Illinois, Chicago, 1973–75; Carleton Univ., Ottawa, 1978; Gastprofessor, Technische Universität, Wien, 1975–77; Fellow, Graham Foundn for Advanced Studies in the Fine Arts, Chicago, 1984; Distinguished Prof., Assoc. of Coll. Schs of Architecture, 1990. Lectures: Sir William Dobell Meml in Modern Art, Sydney, NSW, 1978; Thomas Cubitt, London, 1993; Kivett Meml, Kansas City, 1994. Haecker Award, Assoc. of Architectl Res. Councils Consortium of N. America, 2002–03. Knight Commander, Order of Finnish Lion (Finland), 1988. *Plays performed:* Honeymoon, 1968; Life Class, 1968 (TV); Dust, 1990; radio plays include: The Fence, 1964; Let's Get This Straight, 1977; Immortal Bite, 1982. *Publications:* The Gotobed Trilogy (novels), 1962–64; Ritual and Response in Architecture, 1974; Monuments of Another Age, 1975; On the Home Front (novel), 1977; The Art of Government and the Government of Art, 1978; Alvar Aalto—a critical study, 1983; Reima Pietilä—architecture, context and modernism, 1985; The Environmental Memory, 1987; Reima Pietilä: one man's odyssey in search of Finnish architecture, 1988; (ed) Constancy and Change in Architecture, 1991; (ed) Urban Forms, Suburban Dreams, 1993; Finnish Architecture and the Modernist Tradition, 1995; The Culture of Silence, 1998; The Norman Foster Studio, 1999; (ed) Latin American Architecture: six voices, 2000; Julia Leiviska and the Continuity of Finnish Modern Architecture, 2001; (with Alfonso Corona-Martinez) The Architectural Project, 2003; The Unmade Bed of Architecture, 2004; Plain Modern: the architecture of Brian MacKay Lyons, 2005; (ed) Space and Place in the Mexican Landscape, 2007; articles in RIBA Jl, Arch. Assoc. Qly, Arch. Design, Jl of Arch. Educn, and Art Internat. *Club:* Garrick.
Died 22 Sept. 2009.

QUAYLE, Prof. (John) Rodney, PhD; FRS 1978; Vice-Chancellor, University of Bath, 1983–92; *b* 18 Nov. 1926; *s* of John Martin Quayle and Mary Doris Quayle (*née* Thorp); *m* 1951, Yvonne Mabel (*née* Sanderson); one *s* one *d*. *Educ:* Alun Grammar Sch., Mold; University Coll. of North Wales, Bangor (BSc, PhD; Hon. Fellow, 1996); PhD Cantab; MA Oxon. Res. Fellow, Radiation Lab., Univ. of California, 1953–55; Sen. Scientific Officer, Tropical Products Institute, London, 1955–56; Mem. Scientific Staff, MRC Cell Metabolism Res. Unit, Univ. of Oxford, 1956–63; Lectr, Oriel Coll., Oxford, 1957–63; Sen. Lectr in Biochemistry, 1963–65, West Riding Prof. of Microbiol., 1965–83, Sheffield Univ. Vis. Res. Prof. of Gesellschaft für Strahlen und Umweltforschung, Institut für Mikrobiologie, Universität Göttingen, 1973–74; Walker-Ames Vis. Prof., Univ. of Washington, Seattle, 1981. Chm., British Nat. Cttee for Microbiol., 1985–90;

Member: AFRC, 1982–84; Adv. Council, RMCS, 1983–92; Council, Royal Soc., 1982–84; Biol Sciences Cttee, SERC, 1981–84; Pres., Soc. for General Microbiology, 1990–93. Member: Council of Management, Bath Festival Soc., 1992–93 (Trustee, 1984–89); Bd, Bath Festivals Trust, 1993–98; Bd, Bristol Exploratory, 1995–2000. Korrespondierendes Mitglied, Akademie der Wissenschaften, Göttingen, 1976. Hon. Dr rer. nat. Göttingen, 1989; Hon. DSc: Bath, 1992; Sheffield, 1992. Ciba Medal, Biochem. Soc., 1978. *Publications:* articles in scientific jls. *Recreations:* hill-walking, gardening, bread-making. *Address:* The Coach House, Vicarage Lane, Compton Dando, Bristol BS39 4LA. *T:* (01761) 490399.
Died 26 Feb. 2006.

QUENNELL, Joan Mary, MBE 1958; *b* 23 Dec. 1923; *o c* of late Walter Quennell, Dangstein, Rogate. *Educ:* Dunhurst and Bedales Schools. War Service, WLA and BRCS. Vice-Chairman, Horsham Division Cons. Assoc., 1949 (Chairman, 1958–61); W Sussex CC, 1951–61. Served on Finance, Local Government, Selection and Education Cttees, etc; also as Governor various schools and colleges; Governor, Crawley Coll., Further Education, 1956–69; Member: Southern Reg. Council for Further Education, 1959–61; Reg. Adv. Council, Technological Education (London and Home Counties), 1959–61. MP (C) Petersfield, 1960–Sept. 1974; PPS to the Minister of Transport, 1962–64; Member: Select Cttee on Public Accounts, 1970–74; Speaker's Panel of Temporary Chairmen of House of Commons, 1970–74; Cttee of Selection, House of Commons, 1970–74; Select Cttee on European Secondary Legislation, 1973–74. Chm., EUW, Hampshire, 1978–80. JP W Sussex, 1959–80. *Recreations:* reading, gardening. *Address:* Dangstein, Rogate, near Petersfield, Hants GU31 5BZ.
Died 2 July 2006.

QUICK, Anthony Oliver Hebert; Headmaster of Bradfield College, 1971–85, retired; *b* 26 May 1924; *er s* of late Canon O. C. Quick, sometime Regius Prof. of Divinity at Oxford, and Mrs F. W. Quick; *m* 1955, Eva Jean, *er d* of late W. C. Sellar and of Mrs Hope Sellar; three *s* one *d*. *Educ:* Shrewsbury Sch.; Corpus Christi Coll., Oxford (2nd cl. hons Mod. History); Sch. of Oriental and African Studies, Univ. of London (Govt Schol.). Lieut, RNVR, serving mainly on East Indies Stn, 1943–46. Asst Master, Charterhouse, 1949–61; Headmaster, Rendcomb Coll., Cirencester, 1961–71. *Publications:* (jtly) Britain 1714–1851, 1961; Britain 1851–1945, 1967; Twentieth Century Britain, 1968; Charterhouse: a history of the school, 1990; (contrib.) A History of Rendcomb College, vol. 2, 1995; James Carthew Quick and his Family, 2002. *Recreations:* walking, gardening, sailing. *Address:* Corbin, Scorriton, Buckfastleigh, Devon TQ11 0HU.
Died 27 Sept. 2006.

QUICKE, Sir John (Godolphin), Kt 1988; CBE 1978; DL; *b* 20 April 1922; *s* of Captain Noel Arthur Godolphin Quicke and Constance May Quicke; *m* 1953, Prudence Tinné Berthon, *d* of Rear-Adm. (E) C. P. E. Berthon; three *s* three *d*. *Educ:* Eton; New Coll., Oxford. Vice-Chm., North Devon Meat, 1982–86; Mem., SW Reg. Bd, National Westminster Bank, 1974–92. Chairman: Minister of Agriculture's SW Regional Panel, 1972–75; Agricl EDC, NEDO, 1983–88, Agricl Sector Gp, 1988–90; RURAL, 1983–96; Estates Panel, NT, 1984–92; Member: Consultative Bd for R&D in Food and Agric., 1981–84; Severn Barrage Cttee, 1978–80; Countryside Commn, 1981–88 (Chm., Countryside Policy Review Panel, 1986–87); Properties Cttee, NT, 1984–97. President: CLA, 1975–77; Royal Bath & West of England Soc., 1989–90. Mem. Bd of Governors, Univ. of Plymouth (formerly Polytechnic SW), 1989–93. DL Devon, 1985. Hon. FRASE, 1989. Hon. DSc: Exeter,

1989; Polytechnic South West, 1991. Bledisloe Gold Medal for Landowners, RASE, 1985. *Recreations:* reading, music, gardening. *Address:* Sherwood, Newton St Cyres, near Exeter, Devon EX5 5BT. *T:* (01392) 851216.
Died 16 Nov. 2009.

QUILTER, David (Cuthbert) Tudway; Vice Lord-Lieutenant of Somerset, 1978–96; Local Director, Barclays Bank, Bristol, 1962–84 (Director, Barclays Bank UK Ltd, 1971–81); *b* 26 March 1921; *o s* of Percy Cuthbert Quilter and Clare Tudway; *m* 1953, Elizabeth Mary, *er d* of Sir John Carew Pole, 12th Bt, DSO, TD; one *s* two *d. Educ:* Eton. Served War of 1939–45, Coldstream Guards, 1940–46. Dir, Bristol Evening Post, 1982–91. JP London Juvenile Courts, 1959–62. Mayor of Wells, 1974–75; Chm. of Trustees, Wells Cathedral Preservation Trust, 1976–; Chm., Somerset Gardens Trust, 1991–99; Treasurer, Bristol Univ., 1976–88; Governor, Wells Cathedral Sch., 1968–2005 (Life Pres.); Member: Council, Outward Bound Trust, 1959–92; Garden Soc., 1973–; Trustee, Carnegie UK Trust, 1981–2000. Master, Soc. of Merchant Venturers, 1984–85. DL 1970, High Sheriff 1974–75, Somerset. Hon. LLD Bristol, 1989. *Publications:* No Dishonourable Name, 1947; A History of Wells Cathedral School, 1985. *Recreations:* gardening, music. *Address:* The Flat, Milton Lodge, Wells, Somerset BA5 3AQ. *T:* (01749) 672168. *Clubs:* Boodle's, Army and Navy, Pratt's.
Died 6 Jan. 2007.

QUINLAN, Sir Michael (Edward), GCB 1991 (KCB 1985; CB 1980); Director, Ditchley Foundation, 1992–99; *b* 11 Aug. 1930; *s* of late Gerald and Roseanne Quinlan; *m* 1965, (Margaret) Mary Finlay; two *s* two *d. Educ:* Wimbledon Coll.; Merton Coll., Oxford. (1st Cl. Hon. Mods, 1st Cl. LitHum; MA; Hon. Fellow, 1989). RAF, 1952–54. Asst Principal, Air Ministry, 1954; Private Sec. to Parly Under-Sec. of State for Air, 1956–58; Principal, Air Min., 1958; Private Sec. to Chief of Air Staff, 1962–65; Asst Sec., MoD, 1968; Defence Counsellor, UK Delegn to NATO, 1970–73; Under-Sec., Constitution Unit, Cabinet Office, 1974–77; Dep. Under-Sec. of State (Policy), MoD, 1977–81; Dep. Sec. (Industry), HM Treasury, 1981–82; Perm. Sec., Dept of Employment, 1983–88; Perm. Under-Sec. of State, MoD, 1988–92. Special Advr to Parly Cttees, 2002–06. Vis. Prof., KCL, 1992–95 and 2002–; Public Policy Scholar, Woodrow Wilson Center, Washington, 2000; Consulting Sen. Fellow, IISS, 2004–. Director: Lloyds Bank, 1992–95; Lloyds TSB Gp, 1996–98; Pilkington, 1992–99. Chm., Tablet Trust, 2001–. Trustee, Science Mus., 1992–2001. Governor, Henley Mgt Coll., 1983–88. Chm., CS Sports Council, 1985–89; Pres., CS Cricket Assoc., 1992–98. Pres., Merton Soc., 1992–95. CCMI (CBIM 1983). *Publications:* Thinking About Nuclear Weapons, 1997; European Defence Co operation, 2001; (with Baron Guthrie of Craigiebank) Just War: the just war tradition: ethics in modern warfare, 2007; many articles on defence and public admin and ethics. *Recreations:* golf, watching cricket, listening to music. *Address:* 3 Adderbury Park, West Adderbury, Oxon OX17 3EN. *Clubs:* Royal Air Force, MCC, Lord's Taverners; Chipping Norton Golf. *Died 26 Feb. 2009.*

QUINN, James Charles Frederick; film producer and exhibitor; Chairman, The Minema, 1984–94; *b* 23 Aug. 1919; *y s* of Rev. Chancellor James Quinn and Muriel Alice May (*née* MaGuire); *m* 1942, Hannah (*d* 2002), 2nd *d* of Rev. R. M. Gwynn, BD (Sen. Fellow and Vice-Provost, TCD), and Dr Eileen Gwynn; one *s* one *d. Educ:* Shrewsbury Sch.; TCD (Classical Exhibnr); Christ Church, Oxford (MA; Dip. in Econ. and Polit. Sci.). Served War, Irish Guards, Italy, NW Europe;

British Army Staff, France, and Town Major, Paris, 1945–46. Courtaulds Ltd, 1949–55. Dir, BFI, 1955–64: National Film Theatre built; London Film Festival inaugurated; 1st Univ. Lectureship in Film Studies in UK estabd at Slade Sch. of Fine Art, University Coll., London; BFI's terms of ref. enld to incl. television; 1st world TV Fest., NFT, 1964. UK Mem. Jury, Cannes and Venice Internat. Film Fests, 1956; Chm. Jury, Berlin Film Fest., 1961. Council of Europe Fellowship, 1966. Chairman: Internat. Short Film Conf., 1971–78 (Life Pres., 1979); National Panel for Film Festivals, 1974–83. Member: Gen. Adv. Council, BBC, 1960–64; Bd, Gardner Arts Centre, Sussex Univ., 1968–71; British Council Film Television and Video Adv. Cttee, 1983–90. Trustee: Imperial War Museum, 1968–78; Grierson Meml Trust, 1975–2001; Nat. Life Story Collection, 1986–91. Invited to stand by New Ulster Movement as Indep. Unionist Parly candidate, S Down, 1968. Foreign Leader Award, US State Dept, 1962. Films: co-producer, Herostratus, 1966; Producer, Overlord, 1975. Silver Bear Award, Berlin Internat. Film Festival, 1975; Special Award, London Evening News British Film Awards, 1976. Chevalier de l'Ordre des Arts et des Lettres, France, 1979. *Publications:* Outside London, 1965; The Film and Television as an Aspect of European Culture, 1968; contrib. Chambers's Encyclopaedia (cinema), 1956–59. *Recreations:* lawn tennis; formerly Eton Fives. *Address:* Crescent Cottage, 108 Marine Parade, Brighton, E Sussex BN2 1AT. *Clubs:* Cavalry and Guards; Vincent's (Oxford).
Died 11 Feb. 2008.

QUINTON, Baron *cr* 1982 (Life Peer), of Holywell in the City of Oxford and County of Oxfordshire; **Anthony Meredith Quinton,** FBA 1977; Chairman of the Board, British Library, 1985–90; *b* 25 March 1925, *s* of late Richard Frith Quinton, Surgeon Captain, RN, and Gwenllyan Letitia Quinton; *m* 1952, Marcelle Wegier; one *s* one *d. Educ:* Stowe Sch.; Christ Church, Oxford (St Cyres Scholar; BA 1st Cl. Hons PPE 1949). Served War, RAF, 1943–46: flying officer and navigator. Fellow: All Souls Coll., Oxford, 1949–55; New Coll., Oxford, 1955–78 (Emeritus Fellow, 1980; Hon. Fellow, 1997); Pres., Trinity Coll., Oxford, 1978–87 (Hon. Fellow, 1987). Delegate, OUP, 1970–76. Mem., Arts Council, 1979–81; Vice Pres., British Acad., 1985–86. Visiting Professor: Swarthmore Coll., Pa, 1960; Stanford Univ., Calif, 1964; New Sch. for Social Res., New York, 1976–77; Brown Univ., 1994. Lecturer: Dawes Hicks, British Acad., 1971; Gregynog, Univ. of Wales, Aberystwyth, 1973; T. S. Eliot, Univ. of Kent, Canterbury, 1976; Robbins, Univ. of Stirling, 1987; Hobhouse, LSE, 1988; Tanner, Warsaw, 1988; R. M. Jones, QUB, 1988; Carter, Lancaster, 1989. President: Aristotelian Soc., 1975–76; Soc. for Applied Philosophy, 1988–91; Royal Inst. of Philosophy, 1990–2004; Assoc. of Ind. Libraries, 1991–97; Friends of Wellcome Inst., 1992–97. Chm., Kennedy Meml Trust, 1990–95. Governor, Stowe Sch., 1963–84 (Chm. Governors, 1969–75); Fellow, Winchester Coll., 1970–85. DHumLit NY Univ., 1987; DHum Ball State Univ., 1990. Order of Leopold II, Belgium, 1984. *Publications:* Political Philosophy (ed), 1967; The Nature of Things, 1973; Utilitarian Ethics, 1973; (trans.) K. Ajdukiewicz (with H. Skolimowski) Problems and Theories of Philosophy, 1973; The Politics of Imperfection, 1978; Francis Bacon, 1980; Thoughts and Thinkers, 1982; From Wodehouse to Wittgenstein, 1998. *Recreation:* sedentary pursuits. *Address:* A11 Albany, Piccadilly, W1J 0AL. *Club:* Garrick.
Died 19 June 2010.

R

RACE, Stephen Russell, (Steve), OBE 1992; broadcaster, musician and author; *b* Lincoln, 1 April 1921; *s* of Russell Tinniswood Race and Robina Race (*née* Hurley); *m* 1st, Marjorie Clair Leng (*d* 1969); one *d*; 2nd, Léonie Rebecca Govier Mather. *Educ:* Lincoln Sch. (later Christ's Hospital Sch.); Royal Academy of Music. FRAM 1978. Served War, RAF, 1941–46; free-lance pianist, arranger and composer, 1946–55; Light Music Adviser to Associated-Rediffusion Ltd, 1955–60; presenter, Our World (first global TV Prog.) from Beatles' recording studio, 1967; conductor for many TV series incl. Tony Hancock and Peter Sellers Shows. Appearances in radio and TV shows include: My Music, A Good Read, Jazz in Perspective, Any Questions?, Kaleidoscope, Musician at Large With Great Pleasure, Desert Island Discs, Steve Race Presents the Radio Orchestra Show, The Two Worlds of Joseph Race; radio reviews in The Listener, 1975–80; long-playing records and commentary for Nat. Gall., London, Glasgow Art Gall. and Nat. Mus. of Wales, 1977–80. Dep. Chm., PRS, 1973–76. Member: Council, Royal Albert Hall of Arts and Scis, 1976–95; Exec. Council, Musicians' Benevolent Fund, 1985–95. FRSA 1975. Freeman, City of London, 1982. Governor of Tokyo Metropolis Prize for Radio, 1979; Wavendon Allmusic Media Personality of the Year, 1987; Radio Prog. of the Year, TV and Radio Industries Club Awards, 1988; Gold Badge of Merit for services to British music, BASCA, 1991. *Principal compositions:* Nicola (Ivor Novello Award); Faraway Music; The Pied Piper; incidental music for Richard The Third, Cyrano de Bergerac, Twelfth Night (BBC); Cantatas: Song of King David; The Day of the Donkey; Songs of Praise; My Music—My Songs; misc. works incl. ITV advertising sound-tracks (Venice Award, 1962; Cannes Award, 1963); film scores include: Calling Paul Temple, Three Roads to Rome, Against The Tide, Land of Three Rivers. *Publications:* Musician at Large: an autobiography, 1979; My Music, 1979; Dear Music Lover, 1981; Steve Race's Music Quiz, 1983; You Can't be Serious, 1985; The Penguin Masterquiz, 1985; (contrib.) With Great Pleasure, 1986; The Two Worlds of Joseph Race, 1988; (contrib.) The Illustrated Counties of England, 1984; contribs to DNB, Punch, Literary Review, Times, Daily Telegraph (crossword compiler, 1998–2009), Daily Mail, Independent, Listener, Country Living. *Recreations:* avoiding smokers, trying to lip-read. *Address:* Martins End Lane, Great Missenden, Bucks HP16 9HS. *Died 22 June 2009.*

RADFORD, Rt Rev. Andrew John; Bishop Suffragan of Taunton, since 1998; *b* 26 Jan. 1944; *m* 1969, Christine Davis; two *d*. *Educ:* Kingswood Grammar Sch.; Trinity Coll., Bristol. Local govt service; jt founder and manager, building co., 1965–72; ordained deacon, 1974, priest, 1975; Curate: Shirehampton, 1974–78; Henleaze, 1978–80; producer, Religious Progs, BBC Radio Bristol, 1974–80; Vicar, St Barnabas with Englishcombe, Bath, 1980–85; Diocesan Communications Officer, Gloucester, 1985–93; Religious Progs Presenter, Severn Sound, 1985–93; Develt and Trng Officer, C of E Communications Unit, 1993–98; Archbishops' Advr for Bishops' Ministry, 1998. Hon. Canon, Gloucester Cathedral, 1991–98. Local Radio Personality of the Year, SONY Radio Award, 1987. *Address:* Bishop's Lodge, Monkton Heights, W Monkton, Taunton, Som TA2 8LU. *Died 21 May 2006.*

RADNOR, 8th Earl of, *cr* 1765; **Jacob Pleydell-Bouverie;** Bt 1713–14; Viscount Folkestone, Baron Longford, 1747; Baron Pleydell-Bouverie, 1765; *b* 10 Nov. 1927; *e s* of 7th Earl of Radnor, KG, KCVO, and Helen Olivia, *d* of late Charles R. W. Adeane, CB; *S* father, 1968; *m* 1st, 1953, Anne (marr. diss. 1962), *d* of Donald Seth-Smith, Njoro, Kenya and Whitsbury Cross,

near Fordingbridge, Hants; two *s*; 2nd, 1963, Margaret Robin (marr. diss. 1985), *d* of late Robin Fleming, Catter House, Drymen; four *d*; 3rd, 1986, Mary Jillean Gwenellan Pettit (*d* 2004). *Educ:* Harrow; Trinity Coll., Cambridge (BA Agriculture). *Heir: s* Viscount Folkestone, *b* 5 Jan. 1955. *Died 11 Aug. 2008.*

RAE, Dr John (Malcolm); Headmaster, Westminster School, 1970–86; author; *b* 20 March 1931; *s* of late Dr L. John Rae, radiologist, London Hospital, and Blodwen Rae; *m* 1955, Daphné Ray Simpson, JP, *d* of John Phimester Simpson; two *s* four *d*. *Educ:* Bishop's Stortford Coll.; Sidney Sussex Coll., Cambridge. MA Cantab 1958; PhD 1965. 2nd Lieut Royal Fusiliers, 1950–51. Asst Master, Harrow School, 1955–66; Dept of War Studies, King's Coll., London, 1962–65; Headmaster, Taunton School, 1966–70; Dir, Laura Ashley Foundn, 1986–89. Director: The Observer Ltd, 1986–93; Portman Gp, 1989–96. Gresham Prof. of Rhetoric, 1988–90. Robert Birley Meml Lectr, Charterhouse Sch., 1997. Chairman: HMC, 1977; Council for Educn in World Citizenship, 1983–87. Member: Nat. Bd for Crime Prevention, 1993–95; Council, Nat. Cttee for Electoral Reform; Council, King's Coll. London, 1981–84. Trustee: Children's Film Unit, 1979–; Imperial War Mus., 1980–85. Gov. Highgate Sch., 1989–2003. Judge, Whitbread Prize, 1980. Freeman, City of London, 1985. JP Middlesex, 1961–66. Hon. FCP 1982. *Publications:* The Custard Boys, 1960 (filmed 1979); (jtly, film) Reach for Glory (UN Award); Conscience and Politics, 1970; The Golden Crucifix, 1974; The Treasure of Westminster Abbey, 1975; Christmas is Coming, 1976; Return to the Winter Palace, 1978; The Third Twin: a ghost story, 1980; The Public School Revolution: Britain's independent schools, 1964–1979, 1981; Letters from School, 1987; Too Little, Too Late?, 1989; Delusions of Grandeur: a headmaster's life 1966–1986, 1993; Letters to Parents: how to get the best available education for your child, 1998; Sister Genevieve, 2001; articles in The Times, Encounter; columnist in Times Ed. Supp. *Recreations:* writing, swimming, cinema. *Address:* 2s Cedar Lodge, Lythe Hill Park, Haslemere, Surrey GU27 3TD. *T:* (01428) 652616. *Clubs:* East India, Devonshire, Sports and Public Schools; Hawks (Cambridge). *Died 16 Dec. 2006.*

RAE, Hon. Sir Wallace (Alexander Ramsay), Kt 1976; Agent-General for Queensland, in London, 1974–80; formerly grazier, Ramsay Park, Blackall, Queensland; *b* 31 March 1914; *s* of George Ramsay Rae and Alice Ramsay Rae. *Educ:* Sydney, Australia. Served War: RAAF Coastal Command, 1939; Pilot, Flt Lt, UK, then OC Test Flight, Amberley, Qld. Mem., Legislative Assembly (Nat. Party of Australia) for Gregory, Qld, 1957–74; Minister for: Local Govt and Electricity, 1969–74; Lands and Forestry, Qld, 1974. Founder Pres., Pony Club Assoc. of Queensland. *Recreations:* music, bowls. *Address:* 94 Garden Village, Findlay Avenue, Port Macquarie, NSW 2444, Australia. *Clubs:* United Service, Tattersall's (Brisbane); Longreach (Longreach). *Died 18 March 2006.*

RAEBURN, Prof. John Ross, CBE 1972; BSc (Agric.), PhD, MS; FRSE; FIBiol; Strathcona-Fordyce Professor of Agriculture, Aberdeen University, 1959–78; Principal, North of Scotland College of Agriculture, 1963–78; *b* 20 Nov. 1912; *s* of late Charles Raeburn and Margaret (*née* Ross); *m* 1941, Mary, *o d* of Alfred and Cathrine Roberts; one *s* three *d*. *Educ:* Manchester Grammar School; Edinburgh and Cornell Universities. Professor of Agricultural Economics, Nanking University, 1936–37; Research Officer, Oxford University, 1938–39; Ministry of Food Divisional statistician, 1939–41, Head Agricultural Plans Branch, 1941–46; Senior research officer, Oxford University, 1946–49; Reader in

Agricultural Economics, London University, 1949–59. Visiting Professor: Cornell, 1950; Wuhan, 1983. Consultant to UN. Member: Agricultural Mission to Yugoslavia, 1951; Mission of Enquiry into Rubber Industry, Malaya, 1954; Colonial Economic Research Committee, 1949–61; Scottish Agricultural Improvement Council, 1960–71; Scottish Agricultural Develt Council, 1971–76; Verdon-Smith Committee, 1962–64; Council, Scottish Agricultural Colls, 1974–78. Hon. MA Oxford, 1946. FRSE 1961; FIBiol 1968. Vice-President, International Association of Agricultural Economists, 1964–70 (Hon. Life Mem., 1976–); President, Agric. Econ. Society, 1966–67 (Hon. Life Mem., 1981–). *Publications:* Preliminary economic survey of the Northern Territories of the Gold Coast, 1950; (jtly) Problems in the mechanisation of native agriculture in tropical African Territories, 1950; Agriculture: foundations, principles and development, 1984; (jtly) History of the IAAE, 1990; research bulletins and contributions to agricultural economic journals. *Address:* Flat 15, Kilravock, 5 Oswald Road, Edinburgh EH9 2HE. *Died 9 July 2006.*

RAGLAN, 5th Baron *cr* 1852; **FitzRoy John Somerset;** Chairman, Cwmbran New Town Development Corporation, 1970–83; *b* 8 Nov. 1927; *er s* of 4th Baron Raglan and Hon. Julia Hamilton, CStJ (*d* 1971), *d* of 11th Baron Belhaven and Stenton, CIE; *S* father, 1964; *m* 1973, Alice Baily (marr. diss. 1981), *yr d* of Peter Baily, Great Whittington, Northumberland. *Educ:* Westminster; Magdalen College, Oxford; Royal Agricultural College, Cirencester. Captain, Welsh Guards, RARO. Crown Estate Comr, 1970–74. Mem., Agriculture and Consumer Affairs sub-cttee, House of Lords Select Cttee on the European Community, 1974–83, 1985–90 (Chm., 1975–77). President: UK Housing Trust, 1983–89 (Chm., S Wales Region, 1976–89); United Welsh Housing Trust, 1989–. Pres., Pre Retirement Assoc., 1970–77, Vice-Pres. 1977–90 (Hon. Treas., 1987). Chairman: Bath Preservation Trust, 1975–77; The Bath Soc., 1977–; Bugatti Owners' Club, 1988–97 (Patron, 1999–). President: Usk Civic Soc.; Bath Centre of Nat. Trust; Usk Rural Life Mus.; Monmouthshire Brecon and Abergavenny Canals Trust; Gwent Beekeepers Assoc.; S Wales Reg., RSMHCA, 1971–2008; Parity; Mem., Distinguished Members Panel, National Secular Soc.; Patron: Usk Farmers Club; The Raglan Baroque Players; Gwent County History Assoc.; Hospice of the Valleys; Mon Crossroads; Friends of Swanage Pier; Nat. Museums and Galleries of Wales; Trustee: Bugatti Trust; Cwmbran Arts Trust. JP 1958–97, DL 1971–97, Monmouthshire, then Gwent. *Recreation:* being mechanic to a Bugatti. *Heir: b* Hon Geoffrey Somerset [*b* 29 Aug. 1932; *m* 1956, Caroline Rachel, *d* of late Col E. R. Hill, DSO; one *s* two *d*]. *Address:* Cefntilla, Usk, Monmouthshire NP15 1DG. *T:* (01291) 672050. *Clubs:* Beefsteak, Vintage Sports Car; Usk Farmers. *Died 24 Jan. 2010.*

RAINBOW, (James) Conrad (Douglas), CBE 1979; Chairman, Sovereign Country House Ltd, 1979–96; *b* 25 Sept. 1926; *s* of Jack Conrad Rainbow and Winifred Edna (*née* Mears); *m* 1974, Kathleen Margaret (*née* Holmes); one *s* one *d. Educ:* William Ellis Sch., Highgate; Selwyn Coll., Cambridge (MA). Asst Master, St Paul's Sch., London, 1951–60; HM Inspector of Schools, 1960–69; Dep. Chief Educn Officer, Lancashire, 1969–74, Chief Educn Officer, 1974–79. Vis. Prof., Univ. of Wisconsin, 1979. Education Consultant: ICI, 1980–85; Shell Petroleum Co. Ltd, 1980–; Advr to H of C Select Cttee on Educn, 1980–82. Mem., Exec. Cttee, Council of British Internat. Schs in EEC, 1975–91. Chairman of Governors: Northcliffe Sch., Hants, 1984–90; Elmslie Sch., Blackpool, 1994–98. *Publications:* various articles in educnl jls. *Recreations:* rowing (later as an observer), music, reading. *Address:* 7 Seville Court, Clifton Drive, Lytham St Annes, Lancs FY8 5RG. *T:* (01253) 737245. *Club:* Leander. *Died 4 Dec. 2010.*

RAITT, Prof. Alan William, DPhil; FBA 1992; FRSL; Professor of French Literature, Oxford University, 1992–97, then Professor Emeritus; Fellow, Magdalen College, Oxford, 1966–97, then Fellow Emeritus; *b* 21 Sept. 1930; *s* of William Raitt, MBE, BSc and May (*née* Davison); *m* 1st, 1959, Janet Taylor (marr. diss. 1971); two *d*; 2nd, 1974, Lia Noémia Rodrigues Correia. *Educ:* King Edward VI Grammar Sch. Morpeth; Magdalen Coll., Oxford (MA 1955; DPhil 1957). Oxford University: Fellow (by Examn), Magdalen Coll., 1953–55; Fellow and Lectr in French, Exeter Coll., 1955–66; Lectr in French, Magdalen Coll., 1966–97; Reader in French Lit., 1979–92. Vis. Lectr, Univ. of Georgia, 1986; Vis. Prof., Sorbonne, Paris, 1987–88. Gen. Editor, French Studies, 1987–97. FRSL 1971. Médaille d'Argent, Grand Prix du Rayonnement de la Langue Française, French Acad., 1987. Commandeur, Ordre des Palmes Académiques, 1995. *Publications:* Villiers de l'Isle-Adam et le Mouvement symboliste, 1965; Life and Letters in France: the nineteenth century, 1966; Prosper Mérimée, 1970; The Life of Villiers de l'Isle-Adam, 1981; (ed jtly) Villiers de l'Isle-Adam: Œuvres complètes, 1986; Villiers de l'Isle-Adam exorciste du réel, 1987; Flaubert: Trois Contes, 1991; (ed) Mallarmé, Villiers de l'Isle-Adam, 1993; (ed) Villiers de l'Isle-Adam, L'Eve future, 1993; (ed) Flaubert, Pour Louis Bouilhet, 1994; A. C. Friedel et 'Le Nouveau Théâtre allemand': un intermédiaire méconnu, 1996; Flaubert et le théâtre, 1998; The Originality of Madame Bovary, 2002; Gustavus Flaubertus Bourgeoisophobus, 2005. *Recreation:* watching sport on television. *Address:* Magdalen College, Oxford OX1 4AU. *T:* (home) (01865) 515587. *Died 2 Sept. 2006.*

RAITZ, Vladimir Gavrilovich; airline and travel consultant; *b* 23 May 1922; *s* of Dr Gavril Raitz and Cecilia Raitz; *m* 1954, Helen Antonia (*née* Corkrey); three *d. Educ:* Mill Hill Sch.; LSE (BScEcon, Econ History, 1942). British United Press, 1942–43; Reuters, 1943–48; Chm., Horizon Holidays, 1949–74 (pioneered holidays by air). Dir, Scantours Ltd, 1999–2005. Member: NEDC for Hotels and Catering Industry, 1968–74; Cinematograph Films Council, 1969–74; Ct of Governors, LSE, 1971–95. Cavaliere Ufficiale, Order of Merit (Italy), 1971. *Publications:* (with Roger Bray) Flight to the Sun: the story of the holiday revolution, 2001. *Recreation:* watching grandchildren grow up. *Address:* 32 Dudley Court, Upper Berkeley Street, W1H 7PH. *T:* (020) 7262 2592. *Club:* Reform. *Died 31 Aug. 2010.*

RALLI, Sir Godfrey (Victor), 3rd Bt *cr* 1912; TD; *b* 9 Sept. 1915; *s* of Sir Strati Ralli, 2nd Bt, MC; *S* father, 1964; *m* 1st, 1937, Nora Margaret Forman (marr. diss. 1947; she *d* 1990); one *s* two *d*; 2nd, 1949, Jean (*d* 1998), *er d* of late Keith Barlow. *Educ:* Eton. Joined Ralli Bros Ltd, 1936. Served War of 1939–45 (despatches), Captain, Berkshire Yeomanry RA. Dir and Vice-Pres., Ralli Bros Ltd, 1946–62; Chm., Greater London Fund for the Blind, 1962–82. *Recreations:* fishing, golf. *Heir: s* David Charles Ralli [*b* 5 April 1946; *m* 1975, Jacqueline Cecilia, *d* of late David Smith; one *s* one *d*]. *Address:* Panworth Hall, Ashill, Thetford, Norfolk IP25 7BB. *Died 3 Jan. 2010.*

RAMSAY, Donald Allan, CM 1997; ScD; FRS 1978; FRSC 1966; Principal Research Officer, National Research Council of Canada, 1968–87, then Researcher Emeritus; *b* 11 July 1922; *s* of Norman Ramsay and Thirza Elizabeth Beckley; *m* 1946, Nancy Brayshaw (*d* 1998); four *d*; *m* 2000, Marjorie Craven Findlay. *Educ:* Latymer Upper Sch.; St Catharine's Coll., Cambridge. BA 1943, MA 1947, PhD 1947, ScD 1976 (all Cantab). Research Scientist, National Research Council of Canada: Div. of Chemistry, 1947–49; Div. of Physics, 1949–75; Herzberg Inst. of Astrophysics, 1975–94; Steacie Inst. of Molecular Scis, 1994–. Fellow, Amer. Phys. Soc., 1964; FCIC 1970 (CIC Medal, 1992); Vice-Pres., Acad. of Science, 1975–76; Hon. Treas., RSC, 1976–79, 1988–91 (Centennial Medal, 1982). Alexander von Humboldt Res. Award, 1993–95. Dr *hc* Reims,

1969; Fil.Hed. Stockholm, 1982. Silver Jubilee Medal, 1977; Commemorative Medal for 125th anniversary of Canadian Confederation, 1992. *Publications:* numerous articles on molecular spectroscopy and molecular structure, espec. free radicals. *Recreations:* sailing, fishing, organ playing. *Address:* 400 Laurier Avenue East, Apt 11, Ottawa, ON K1N 8Y2, Canada. *T:* (613) 2376667. *Club:* Leander (Henley). *Died 25 Oct. 2007.*

RAMSBOTHAM, Hon. Sir Peter (Edward), GCMG 1978 (KCMG 1972; CMG 1964); GCVO 1976; DL; HM Diplomatic Service, retired; *b* 8 Oct. 1919; *yr s* of 1st Viscount Soulbury, PC, GCMG, GCVO, OBE, MC; *S* brother, 2004 as 3rd Viscount Soulbury, but does not use the title; *m* 1st, 1941, Frances Blomfield (*d* 1982); two *s* (one *d* decd); 2nd, 1985, Dr Zaida Hall, *widow* of Ruthven Hall. *Educ:* Eton College; Magdalen College, Oxford (Hon. Fellow, 1991). Intelligence Corps, Europe, 1943–46 (Lt-Col; despatches; Croix de Guerre, 1945). Control Office for Germany and Austria from 1947; Regional Political Officer in Hamburg; entered Foreign Service, Oct. 1948; Political Division of Allied Control Commission, Berlin, Nov. 1948; transferred to Foreign Office, 1950; 1st Secretary, 1950; Head of Chancery, UK Delegation, New York, 1953; Foreign Office, 1957; Counsellor, 1961, Head of Western Organisations and Planning Dept; Head of Chancery, British Embassy, Paris, 1963–67; Foreign Office, 1967–69 (Sabbatical year, Inst. of Strategic Studies, 1968); High Comr, Cyprus, 1969–71; Ambassador to Iran, 1971–74; Ambassador to the United States, 1974–77; Governor and C-in-C of Bermuda, 1977–80. Director: Lloyds Bank, 1981–90; Lloyds Bank Internat., 1981–83; Southern Regl Bd, Lloyds Bank, 1981–90 (Chm., 1983–90); Commercial Union Assurance Co., 1981–90. Trustee, Leonard Cheshire Foundn, 1981–94; Chairman: Ryder-Cheshire Foundn for the Relief of Suffering, 1982–99; World Meml Fund for Disaster Relief, 1992–96 (Trustee, 1989–); Gov., Ditchley Foundn, 1978–2007. Pres., British-American-Canadian Associates, 1994–97. Governor, King's Sch., Canterbury, 1981–90. DL Hants, 1992. Hon. LLD: Akron Univ., 1975; Coll. of William and Mary, 1975; Maryland Univ., 1976; Yale Univ., 1977. KStJ 1976. *Recreations:* gardening, fishing. *Heir:* (to *Viscountcy*) *er s* Prof. the Hon. Oliver Peter Ramsbotham, *b* 27 Oct. 1943. *Address:* East Lane, Ovington, near Alresford, Hants SO24 0RA. *T:* (01962) 732515. *Club:* Garrick. *Died 9 April 2010.*

RANDALL, Col Charles Richard, OBE 1969; TD 1947; Vice Lord-Lieutenant for the County of Bedfordshire, 1978–91; *b* 21 Jan. 1920; *s* of Charles Randall and Elizabeth Brierley; *m* 1945, Peggy Dennis (*d* 1977); one *s* one *d*. *Educ:* Bedford Sch. Served War, 1939–45: commissioned Bedfordshire Yeomanry, 1939. Chm., Randalls Gp Ltd, 1965–81. High Sheriff, Bedfordshire, 1974–75. *Recreations:* shooting, fishing, gardening. *Died 24 Sept. 2006.*

RANDALL, Rev. Edmund Laurence, AM 1980; Warden, St Barnabas' Theological College, Adelaide, 1964–85, retired; Scholar in Residence, Diocese of Wangaratta, since 1986; *b* 2 June 1920; *s* of Robert Leonard Randall and Grace Annie Randall (*née* Young); unmarried. *Educ:* Dulwich College; Corpus Christi College, Cambridge (BA 1941; MA 1947); Wells Theological Coll. Served War, 1940–45, with Royal Artillery (AA). Corpus Christi Coll., 1938–40 and 1945–47; ordained deacon, 1949; priest, 1950; Assistant Curate at St Luke's, Bournemouth, 1949–52; Fellow of Selwyn College, Cambridge, 1952–57, Chaplain, 1953–57; Residentiary Canon of Ely and Principal of Ely Theological Coll., 1957–59; Chaplain, St Francis Theological Coll., Brisbane, 1960–64; Hon. Canon of Adelaide, 1979–86, of Wangaratta, 1989–. Pres., Adelaide Coll. of Divinity, 1984–85. Vis. Lectr, St Barnabas' Theol Coll., and Lectr in Theology, Flinders Univ. of SA, Feb.–July 1990. *Recreations:* reading biographies, doing

the Times crossword. *Address:* 44 Mackay Street, Wangaratta, Vic 3677, Australia. *T:* (3) 57219007. *Died 8 July 2006.*

RANDLE, Prof. Sir Philip (John), Kt 1985; MD, FRCP; FRS 1983; Professor of Clinical Biochemistry, University of Oxford, 1975–93, then Emeritus; Fellow of Hertford College, Oxford, 1975–93, then Emeritus; *b* 16 July 1926; *s* of Alfred John and Nora Anne Randle; *m* 1952, Elizabeth Ann Harrison (*d* 2004); two *d* (one *s* and one *d* decd). *Educ:* King Edward VI Grammar Sch., Nuneaton; Sidney Sussex Coll., Cambridge (MA, PhD, MD); UCH, London (Fellow, UCL, 1990). Med. and Surg. Officer, UCH, 1951; Res. Fellow in Biochem., Cambridge, 1952–55; Univ. Lectr, Biochem., Cambridge, 1955–64; Fellow of Trinity Hall and Dir of Med. Studies, 1957–64 (Hon. Fellow, Trinity Hall, 1988); Prof. of Biochem., Univ. of Bristol, 1964–75. Member: Board of Governors, United Cambridge Hospitals, 1960–64; Clinical Endocrinology Cttee, MRC, 1957–64; Chm., Grants Cttee, MRC, 1975–77; Pres., European Assoc. for Study of Diabetes, 1977–80; Chairman, Research Committee: British Diabetic Assoc., 1971–78; British Heart Foundn, 1987–92. DHSS: Mem. Cttee on Med. Aspects Food Policy, 1981–89; Chm., COMA Panel on Diet and Cardiovascular Disease, 1981–84; Consultant Adviser in Biochemistry to CMO, 1981–89. Member: General Medical Council, 1967–75; Gen. Dental Council, 1971–75; Council, Royal Soc., 1987–89 (Vice Pres., 1988–89). Pres., Biochemical Soc., 1995–2000. Lectures: Banting, British Diabetic Assoc., 1965; Minkowski, European Assoc. for Study of Diabetes, 1966; Copp, La Jolla, 1972; Humphry Davy Rolleston, RCP, 1983; Ciba Medal and Lectr, Biochem. Soc., 1984; Kroc, San Diego, 1992. Founder FMedSci 1998. Corresp. Mem. of many foreign medical and scientific bodies. Hon. DSc Oxford Brookes, 1997. *Publications:* numerous contribs to books and med. sci. jls on diabetes mellitus, control of metabolism and related topics. *Recreations:* travel, swimming, bricklaying. *Address:* 11 Fitzherbert Close, Iffley, Oxford OX4 4EN; Department of Clinical Biochemistry, Radcliffe Infirmary, Oxford OX2 6HE. *Died 26 Sept. 2006.*

RASHLEIGH BELCHER, John; *see* Belcher.

RAU, Johannes; President, Federal Republic of Germany, 1999–2004; *b* Wuppertal, 16 Jan. 1931; *s* of Ewald and Helene Rau; *m* 1982, Christina Delius; one *s* two *d*. Served apprenticeship as publisher and bookseller; publishing director, 1954–67. North Rhine-Westphalia Landtag: Mem. (SPD), 1958–99; Chm., SPD Parly Gp, 1967–70; Minister for Sci. and Res., 1970–78; Premier, 1978–98. Mem., Wuppertal City Council, 1964–78 (Lord Mayor, 1969–70). Joined SPD, 1957; Dep. Chm., 1982–99. Mem., Rhineland, Synod of Evangelical Church, 1965–99. *Died 27 Jan. 2006.*

RAWES, Francis Roderick, MBE 1944; MA; *b* 28 Jan. 1916; *e s* of late Prescott Rawes and Susanna May Dockery; *m* 1940, Dorothy Joyce (*d* 2004), *d* of E. M. Hundley, Oswestry; two *s* one *d*. *Educ:* Charterhouse; St Edmund Hall, Oxford. Served in Intelligence Corps, 1940–46; GSO3(I) 13 Corps; GSO1 (I) HQ 15 Army Group and MI14 WO. Asst Master at Westminster School, 1938–40 and 1946–64; Housemaster, 1947–64; Headmaster, St Edmund's School, Canterbury, 1964–78; Adminr, ISIS Assoc., 1979–83. C of E Lay Reader, 1979–96. Chm. Governing Body, Westonbirt Sch., 1983–91 (Governor, 1979–95). *Address:* Peyton House, Chipping Campden, Glos GL55 6AL. *Died 27 Sept. 2008.*

RAWLINSON OF EWELL, Baron *cr* 1978 (Life Peer), of Ewell in the County of Surrey; **Peter Anthony Grayson Rawlinson,** Kt 1962; PC 1964; QC 1959; QC (NI) 1972; *b* 26 June 1919; *o surv. s* of late Lt-Col A. R. Rawlinson, OBE, and Ailsa, *e d* of Sir Henry Mulleneux Grayson, 1st Bt, KBE; *m* 1st, 1940, Haidee Kavanagh (marr. diss.); two *d* (and one *d* decd); 2nd, 1954, Elaine Dominguez, Newport, Rhode Island, USA; two *s* one *d*.

Educ: Downside; Christ's Coll., Cambridge (Exhibitioner 1938, Hon. Fellow 1980). Officer Cadet Sandhurst, 1939; served in Irish Guards, 1940–46; N Africa, 1943 (despatches); demobilized with rank of Major, 1946. Called to Bar, Inner Temple, 1946, Bencher, 1962, Reader, 1983, Treas., 1984; Recorder of Salisbury, 1961–62; called to Bar, Northern Ireland, 1972; Recorder of Kingston upon Thames, 1975; Leader, Western Circuit, 1975–82; retired from practice at the Bar, 1985. Contested (C) Hackney South, 1951; MP (C) Surrey, Epsom, 1955–74; Epsom and Ewell, 1974–78. Solicitor-General, July 1962–Oct. 1964; Opposition Spokesman: for Law, 1964–65, 1968–70; for Broadcasting, 1965; Attorney-General, 1970–74; Attorney-General for NI, 1972–74. Chm., Parly Legal Cttee, 1967–70. Member of Council, Justice, 1960–62, 1964; Trustee of Amnesty, 1960–62; Member, Bar Council, 1966–68; Mem. Senate, Inns of Court, 1968, Vice-Chm., 1974; Vice-Chm., Bar, 1974–75; Chairman of the Bar and Senate, 1975 76; Pres., Senate of Inns of Court and Bar, 1986–87; Chm., Enquiry into Constitution of the Senate, 1985–86. Chm. of Stewards, RAC, 1985–2000. Director: Pioneer International (formerly Pioneer Concrete Services) Ltd, Sydney, 1985–91 (Chm., UK subsidiary); Daily Telegraph plc, 1985–; STC plc, 1986 91; Mem., London Adv. Cttee, Hongkong and Shanghai Banking Corp., 1984–90. Chm., London Oratory Appeal, 1983–94; Gov., London Oratory Sch., 1985–95. Hon. Fellow, Amer. Coll. of Trial Lawyers, 1973; Hon. Mem., Amer. Bar Assoc., 1976. SMO Malta. *Publications:* War Poems and Poetry today, 1943; Public Duty and Personal Faith—the example of Thomas More, 1978; A Price Too High (autobiog.), 1989; The Jesuit Factor, 1990; *novels:* The Colombia Syndicate, 1991; Hatred and Contempt (Rumpole Award, CWA), 1992; His Brother's Keeper, 1993; Indictment for Murder, 1994; The Caverel Claim, 1998; The Richmond Diary, 2001; articles and essays in law jls. *Recreations:* the theatre, painting. *Address:* House of Lords, SW1A 0PW. *Clubs:* White's, Royal Automobile, MCC. *Died 28 June 2006.*

RAY, Hon. Ajit Nath; Chief Justice of India, Supreme Court of India, 1973–77; *b* Calcutta, 29 Jan. 1912; *s* of Sati Nath Ray and Kali Kumari Debi; *m* 1944, Himani Mukherjee; one *s. Educ:* Presidency Coll., Calcutta; Calcutta Univ. (Hindu Coll. Foundn Schol., MA); Oriel College, Oxford (MA; Hon. Fellow, 1975). Called to Bar, Gray's Inn, 1939; practised at Calcutta High Court, 1940–57; Judge, Calcutta High Court, 1957–69; Judge, Supreme Court of India, 1969–73. Pres., Governing Body, Presidency Coll., Calcutta, 1959–70; Vice-President: Asiatic Soc., 1963–65 (Hon. Treas., 1960–63); Internat. Law Assoc., 1977– (Pres., 1974–76; Pres., Indian Br., 1973–77); Indian Law Inst., New Delhi, 1973–77; Mem., Internat. Court of Arbitration, 1976–. Vice-Pres., Ramakrishna Mission Inst. of Culture, 1981–2006; Chm., Guru Saday Folk Art Soc., Calcutta, 1986–2004; Pres., Soc. for Welfare of Blind, Narendrapur, 1959–80. Mem., Karma Samiti (Exec. Council), 1963–67 and 1969–72, and Samsad (Court), 1967–71, Visva-Bharati Univ., Santiniketan. *Address:* 15 Panditia Place, Calcutta 700029, India. *T:* (33) 24541452. *Club:* Calcutta (Calcutta). *Died 25 Dec. 2010.*

RAYMER, Michael Robert, OBE 1951; Assistant Secretary, Royal Hospital, Chelsea, 1975–82; *b* 22 July 1917; surv. *s* of late Rev. W. H. Raymer, MA; *m* 1948, Joyce Marion Scott; two *s* one *d. Educ:* Marlborough College (Foundation Scholar); Jesus College, Cambridge (Rustat Schol.). BA (Hons) 1939. Administrative Officer, Nigeria, 1940–49 and 1952–55. Served in Royal W African Frontier Force, 1940–43. Colonial Sec. to Govt of the Falkland Islands, 1949–52; Prin. Estab. Officer, N Nigeria, 1954; Controller of Organisation and Establishments, to Government of Fiji, 1955–62; retired, 1962; Principal, MoD, 1962–75. *Recreation:* gardening. *Address:* The Stable House, Manor Farm, Apethorpe, Northants PE8 5DG. *Died 13 May 2007.*

RAYNER, Claire Berenice, OBE 1996; writer and broadcaster; *b* 22 Jan. 1931; *m* 1957, Desmond Rayner; two *s* one *d. Educ:* City of London Sch. for Girls; Royal Northern Hosp. Sch. of Nursing, London (Gold Medal; SRN 1954); Guy's Hosp. (midwifery). Nurse, Royal Free Hosp.; Sister, Paediatric Dept, Whittington Hosp. Woman's Own: Med. Correspondent, as Ruth Martin, 1966–75, as Claire Rayner, 1975–87; advice column: The Sun, 1973–80; The Sunday Mirror, 1980–88; Today, 1988–91; columnist, Woman, 1988–92. Radio and television broadcasts included: family advice, Pebble Mill at One, BBC, 1972–74; (co-presenter) Kitchen Garden, ITV, 1974–77; Contact, BBC Radio, Wales, 1974–77; Claire Rayner's Casebook (series), BBC, 1980, 1983, 1984; TV-am Advice Spot, 1985–92; A Problem Shared, Sky TV Series, 1989; Good Morning with Anne and Nick, BBC, 1992–93. Non-exec. Dir, Northwick Park Hosp., 1991–98; Associate non-exec. Dir, Royal Hosps NHS Trust, 1995–2000. Member: Royal Commn on Long Term Care of the Elderly, 1997–98; Prime Minister's Commn on the Future of Nursing and Midwifery, 2009; Founder Mem., Forum on Children and Violence, later part of Children are Unbeatable. FRSocMed; FRSA. President: Gingerbread; Patients' Assoc.; Nat. Assoc. of Bereavement Counsellors; British Humanist Assoc., 1999–2003 (Vice Pres., 2003–); Patron: Terrence Higgins Trust; Turning Point; Royal Philanthropic Soc., and others. Freeman, City of London, 1981. Hon. Fellow, Poly. of N London, 1988. Hon. Dr: Oxford Brookes, 2000; Middlesex, 2002; Surrey, 2007. Med. Journalist of the Year, 1987; Best Specialist Consumer Columnist Award, 1988; Award for Lifetime Achievement, MJA, 2008. *Publications:* Mothers and Midwives, 1962; What Happens in Hospital, 1963; The Calendar of Childhood, 1964; Your Baby, 1965; Careers with Children, 1966; Essentials of Out-Patient Nursing, 1967; For Children, 1967; Shall I be a Nurse?, 1967; 101 Facts an Expectant Mother should know, 1967; 101 Key Facts of Practical Baby Care, 1967; Housework - The Easy Way, 1967; Home Nursing and Family Health, 1967; A Parent's Guide to Sex Education, 1968; People in Love, 1968 (subseq. publd as About Sex, 1972); Protecting Your Baby, 1971; Woman's Medical Dictionary, 1971; When to Call the Doctor - What to Do Whilst Waiting, 1972; The Shy Person's Book, 1973; Childcare Made Simple, 1973; Where Do I Come From?, 1975; (ed and contrib.) Atlas of the Body and Mind, 1976; (with Keith Fordyce) Kitchen Garden, 1976; (with Keith Fordyce) More Kitchen Garden, 1977; Family Feelings, 1977; Claire Rayner answers your 100 Questions on Pregnancy, 1977; (with Keith Fordyce) Claire and Keith's Kitchen Garden, 1978; The Body Book, 1978; Related to Sex, 1979; (with Keith Fordyce) Greenhouse Gardening, 1979; Everything your Doctor would Tell You if He Had the Time, 1980; Claire Rayner's Lifeguide, 1980; Baby and Young Child Care, 1981; Growing Pains, 1984; Claire Rayner's Marriage Guide, 1984; The Getting Better Book, 1985; Woman, 1986; When I Grow Up, 1986; Safe Sex, 1987; The Don't Spoil Your Body Book, 1989; Life and Love and Everything: children's questions, 1993; (autobiog.) How Did I Get Here From There, 2003; *fiction:* Shilling a Pound Pears, 1964; The House on the Fen, 1967; Starch of Aprons, 1967 (subseq. publd as The Hive, 1968); Lady Mislaid, 1968; Death on the Table, 1969; The Meddlers, 1970; A Time to Heal, 1972; The Burning Summer, 1972; Sisters, 1978; Reprise, 1980; The Running Years, 1981; Family Chorus, 1984; The Virus Man, 1985; Lunching at Laura's, 1986; Maddie, 1988; Clinical Judgements, 1989; Postscripts, 1991; Dangerous Things, 1993; First Blood, 1993; Second Opinion, 1994; Third Degree, 1995; Fourth Attempt, 1996; Fifth Member, 1997; The Performers: Book 1, Gower Street, 1973; Book 2, The Haymarket, 1974; Book 3, Paddington Green, 1975; Book 4, Soho Square, 1976; Book 5, Bedford Row, 1977; Book 6, Long Acre, 1978; Book 7, Charing Cross, 1979; Book 8, The Strand, 1980; Book 9, Chelsea Reach, 1982; Book 10, Shaftesbury Avenue, 1983; Book 11, Piccadilly, 1985; Book 12, Seven Dials, 1986; Poppy Chronicles: Book 1,

Jubilee, 1987; Book 2, Flanders, 1988; Book 3, Flapper, 1989; Book 4, Blitz, 1990; Book 5, Festival, 1992; Book 6, Sixties, 1992; Quentin Quartet: Book 1, London Lodgings, 1994; Book 2, Paying Guests, 1995; *as Sheila Brandon: fiction:* The Final Year, 1962; Cottage Hospital, 1963; Children's Ward, 1964; The Lonely One, 1965; The Doctors of Downlands, 1968; The Private Wing, 1971; Nurse in the Sun, 1972; *as Ann Lynton:* Mothercraft, 1967; contrib. Lancet, Med. World, Nursing Times, Nursing Mirror, and national newspapers and magazines, incl. Design. *Recreations:* talking, party-giving, theatre-going. *Address:* PO Box 125, Harrow, Middx HA1 3XE. *Died 11 Oct. 2010.*

RAYNER, Edward John, CBE 1990; Controller, Europe (formerly Europe and North Asia), British Council, 1986–89; *b* 27 Feb. 1936; *s* of Edward Harold Rayner and Edith Rayner; *m* 1960, Valerie Anne Billon; one *s* one *d*. *Educ:* Slough Grammar Sch.; London Univ. (BSc Econs). British Council: Asst Regional Rep., Lahore, Pakistan, 1959–62; Asst Rep., Lagos, Nigeria, 1962–65; Inspector, Complements Unit, 1965–67; Head, Overseas Careers, Personnel Dept, 1967–70; Dep. Rep., Pakistan, 1970–71; Regional Dir, Sao Paulo, Brazil, 1972–75; Controller, Estabts Div., 1975–78; Secretary, 1978–82; Rep., Brazil, 1983–86. *Recreations:* theatre, music. *Died 12 July 2008.*

READ, John Leslie, FCA; Chairman, Carvest Inc., since 1988; *b* 21 March 1935; *s* of Robert and Florence Read; *m* 1958, Eugenie Ida (*née* Knight); one *s* one *d*. *Educ:* Sir William Turner's School. Partner, Price Waterhouse & Co., 1966–75; Finance Dir, then Jt Chief Exec., Unigate plc, 1975–80; Chairman: Macarthy plc, 1989–92 (Dir, 1986–92); LEP Gp, 1982–91; Director: MB-Caradon Group (formerly Metal Box) plc, 1979–92; Equity Law Life Assurance Soc. plc, 1980–87; Border and Southern Stockholders Investment Trust, later Govett Strategic Investment Trust, 1985–92. Chm., Audit Commn for Local Authorities in England and Wales, 1983–86. *Recreations:* music, sport, reading, photography. *Address:* 2 Milbrook, Esher, Surrey KT10 9EJ. *Club:* Royal Automobile. *Died 31 Jan. 2010.*

REASON, John; journalist and author; Rugby Union correspondent, Daily Telegraph and Sunday Telegraph, 1964–94; Director, Rugby Football Books Ltd, since 1971; *s* of C. L. Reason and G. M. Reason; *m* Joan Wordsworth; two *s* (and one *s* decd). *Educ:* Dunstable Grammar Sch.; London Univ. Res. at ICI; local journalist, Watford and Dunstable; Sports Ed., West Herts Post, Watford, 1952; sports journalist: News Chronicle, Manchester, 1953; The Recorder, London, 1953–54; News of the World, Manchester, 1954; sports and feature writer: News of the World, London, 1955–63; Daily Telegraph, 1964–80; Sunday Telegraph, 1980–94; Asst Ed. and feature writer, The Cricketer, 1965–79. *Publications:* The 1968 Lions, 1968; The 1971 Lions, 1971, 5th edn 1973; The Lions Speak, 1972, 2nd edn 1973; The Unbeaten Lions, 1974, 2nd edn 1975; Lions Down Under, 1977; The World of Rugby, 1978 (TV series); Backs to the Wall, 1980; Six of the Best, 2004. *Recreations:* authorship, property enhancement, bemoaning our bog standard House of Commons, designing golf courses to eliminate metal drivers and resurrect shot-making, contemplating an English Parliament containing Frederick Forsyth and Kelvin McKenzie. *Clubs:* Royal Mid-Surrey Golf; Dunstablians Rugby Football. *Died 9 Feb. 2007.*

REDFERN, Philip, CB 1983; Deputy Director, Office of Population Censuses and Surveys, 1970–82; *b* 14 Dec. 1922; *m* 1951, Gwendoline Mary Phillips; three *d*. *Educ:* Bemrose Sch., Derby; St John's Coll., Cambridge. Wrangler, Mathematical Tripos, Cambridge, 1942. Asst Statistician, Central Statistical Office, 1947; Chief Statistician, Min. of Education, 1960; Dir of Statistics and Jt Head of Planning Branch, Dept of Educn and Science, 1967. *Recreation:* walking from Yorkshire to Wester Ross. *Died 1 June 2009.*

REDFORD, Donald Kirkman, CBE 1980; DL; President, The Manchester Ship Canal Company, since 1986 (Managing Director, 1970–80; Chairman, 1972–86); *b* 18 Feb. 1919; *er s* of T. J. and S. A. Redford; *m* 1942, Mabel (*née* Wilkinson), Humberstone, Lincs; one *s* one *d*. *Educ:* Culford Sch.; King's Coll., Univ. of London (LLB). Served, 1937–39, and War until 1945, in RAFVR (retd as Wing Comdr). Practice at the Bar until end of 1946, when joined The Manchester Ship Canal Company, with which Company has since remained. Chairman, Nat. Assoc. of Port Employers, 1972–74; Dep. Chm., British Ports Assoc., 1973–74, Chm. 1974–78. Member: Cttee of Management, RNLI, 1977– (Chm., Search and Research Cttee, 1984–89); Court, Manchester Univ., 1977– (Dep. Treas., 1980–82, Treas., 1982–83, Mem. of Council, 1977–92, Chm. of Council, 1983–87). DL Lancs 1983. Hon. LLD Manchester, 1988. *Recreations:* reading, history, golf. *Address:* North Cotes, 8 Harrod Drive, Birkdale, Southport PR8 2HA. *T:* (01704) 67406. *Club:* Union (Southport). *Died 25 June 2006.*

REDGRAVE, Corin William; actor and director; *b* 16 July 1939; *s* of Sir Michael Redgrave, CBE and Rachel Kempson; *m* 1st, 1962, Deirdre Hamilton-Hill (marr. diss. 1975; she *d* 1997); one *s* one *d*; 2nd, 1985, Kika Markham; two *s*. *Educ:* Westminster Sch.; King's Coll., Cambridge (Classical Schol.; BA 1st cl. Hons (English)). Joined Royal Court Th. as Asst Dir, 1962; Founder, Moving Th. at Riverside Studios, 1994; Associate Artist, Alley Th., Houston, 1996; launched Lichfield Garrick Th., 2003. With Royal Shakespeare Co., 1972–73, 1996–97 and 2004: *plays* include: The Romans, 1973; The General from America, 1996; King Lear, 2004, transf. Albery, 2005; Royal National Theatre: *plays* include: Marat/Sade, 1997; Not About Nightingales, 1998; The Cherry Orchard, 2000; De Profundis, 2000; No Man's Land, 2001; Honour, 2003; Pericles, Shakespeare's Globe, 2005; Trumbo, Jermyn St Th., 2009; *plays directed* include: Romeo and Juliet, Moscow; Lillian, Lyric Shaftesbury and Fortune, 1986; Real Writing, Moving Th., 1995; Ousama, USA, 1995; *films* include: A Man for All Seasons, 1966; The Charge of the Light Brigade, 1968; The Magus, 1968; Oh! What a Lovely War, 1969; When Eight Bells Toll, 1971; The Red Baron, 1971; Excalibur, 1981; In the Name of the Father, 1993; Four Weddings and a Funeral, 1994; Honest, 2000; Enigma, 2001; To Kill a King, 2003; Enduring Love, 2004; Glorious 39, 2009; *television* includes: Canterbury Tales, 1969; David Copperfield, 1969; Wagner, 1983; The Ice House, 1997; Trial and Retribution, 1997; The Woman in White, 1997; Trial and Retribution IV, 2000, VI, 2002; The Forsyte Saga, 2002; Shameless, 2004. *Plays written* for BBC Radio 4: Roy and Daisy; Fool for the Rest of his Life; Blunt Speaking; Saint Lucy. Ed., The Marxist, 1988–. *Publications:* Michael Redgrave: my father, 1995; Julius Caesar (Actors on Shakespeare series), 2003. *Recreations:* tennis, piano. *Address:* c/o Sadie Feast Management, 10 Primrose Hill Studios, Fitzroy Road, NW1 8TR. *Died 6 April 2010.*

REDGRAVE, Lynn Rachel, OBE 2002; actress; *b* 8 March 1943; *d* of Sir Michael Redgrave, CBE, and Rachel Kempson; *m* 1967, John Clark (marr. diss. 2000); one *s* two *d*. *Educ:* Queensgate Sch.; Central Sch. of Speech and Drama. Nat. Theatre of GB, 1963–66 (Tulip Tree, Mother Courage, Andorra, Hay Fever, Much Ado About Nothing, etc); Black Comedy, Broadway 1966; The Two of Us, Slag, Zoo Zoo Widdershins Zoo, Born Yesterday, London 1968–71; A Better Place, Dublin 1972; My Fat Friend, Knock Knock, Mrs Warren's Profession, Broadway 1973–76; The Two of Us, California Suite, Hellzapoppin, US tours 1976–77; Saint Joan, Chicago and NY 1977; Twelfth Night, Amer. Shakespeare Festival, Conn, 1978; Les Dames du Jeudi, LA, 1981; Sister Mary Ignatius Explains It All For You, LA, 1983; The King and I, N American Tour, 1983; Aren't We All, 1985, Sweet Sue, 1987, Love Letters, 1989, Broadway; Les Liaisons Dangereuses, Don Juan in Hell, LA, 1989–91; Three Sisters, Queen's, 1990; A Little

Hotel on the Side, The Master Builder, Broadway, 1991–92; The Notebook of Trigorin, Ohio, 1996; (also writer) The Mandrake Root, Conn, 2001; Noises Off, Piccadilly, 2001; Talking Heads, NY, 2003. One-woman show: Shakespeare for my Father, NY and US tour, 1993; Nightingale, LA 2006, Hartford, 2007, NY 2009. *Films include:* Tom Jones, Girl with Green Eyes, Georgy Girl (NY Film Critics, Golden Globe and IFIDA awards, Academy nomination Best Actress), Deadly Affair, Smashing Time, Virgin Soldiers, Last of the Mobile Hotshots, Every Little Crook and Nanny, National Health, Happy Hooker, Everything You Always Wanted to Know about Sex, The Big Bus, Sunday Lovers, Morgan Stewart's Coming Home, Getting it Right, Midnight, Shine, Gods and Monsters (Best Supporting Actress, Golden Globe award, 1999), Strike, The Simian Line, Touched, The Annihilation of Fish, The Next Best Thing, How to Kill Your Neighbor's Dog, My Kingdom, Unconditional Love, Anita and Me. *Television includes:* USA: Co-host of nationally televised talk-show, Not For Women Only, appearances in documentaries, plays, The Muppets, Centennial, Beggarman Thief, The Seduction of Miss Leona, Rehearsal for Murder, The Old Reliable, Jury Duty, Whatever Happened to Baby Jane?, Calling the Shots, Toothless, Indefensible: the truth about Edward Brannigan, White Lies, Different, and series: Housecalls (CBS); Teachers Only (NBC); Chicken Soup (ABC); Rude Awakening; BBC: A Woman Alone, 1988; Death of a Son, 1989; Calling the Shots, 1994. *Publications:* Diet for Life (autobiog.) (US as This is Living), 1991; Journal: a mother and daughter's recovery from breast cancer, 2004. *Recreations:* cooking, gardening, horse riding *Died 2 May 2010.*

REDMAN, Maj.-Gen. Denis Arthur Kay, CB 1963; OBE 1942; retired; Colonel Commandant, REME, 1963–68; Director, Electrical and Mechanical Engineering, War Office, 1960–63; *b* 8 April 1910; *s of* late Brig. A. S. Redman, CB; *m* 1943, Penelope (*d* 2007), *d* of A. S. Kay; one *s* one *d. Educ:* Wellington Coll.; London Univ. (BSc (Eng) 1st class Hons). CEng. Commissioned in RAOC, 1934; served in Middle East, 1936–43; transferred to REME, 1942; Temp. Brig., 1944; DDME 1st Corps, 1951; Comdt REME Training Centre 1957–59. Graduate of Staff Coll., Joint Services Staff Coll. and Imperial Defence Coll. Pres., Ramsbury RBL, 1985–96. FCGI. *Recreation:* normal. *Died 18 July 2009.*

REDMAYNE, Hon. Sir Nicholas (John), 2nd Bt *cr* 1964; *b* 1 Feb. 1938; *s of* Baron Redmayne, DSO, PC (Life Peer) and Anne (*d* 1982), *d* of John Griffiths; *S to* baronetcy of father, 1983; *m* 1st, 1963, Ann Saunders (marr. diss. 1976; she *d* 1985); one *s* one *d*; 2nd, 1978, Christine Diane Wood Hewitt (*née* Fazakerley); two step *s. Educ:* Radley College; RMA Sandhurst. Grenadier Guards, 1957–62. Joined Grieveson, Grant, later Kleinwort Benson Securities, 1963; Dir, 1987, Chief Exec., 1994–96, Kleinwort Benson Ltd; Dir, 1989–96, Dep. Chm., 1996, Kleinwort Benson Gp; Chairman: Kleinwort Benson Securities, 1990–96; Kleinwort Benson Investment Mgt, 1995–96. *Recreations:* shooting, ski-ing. *Heir: s* Giles Martin Redmayne [*b* 1 Dec. 1968; *m* 1994, Claire Ann O'Halloran; two *s*]. *Address:* Walcote Lodge, Walcote, Lutterworth, Leics LE17 4JR. *Died 18 Oct. 2008.*

REDMOND, Robert Spencer, TD 1953; Director and Chief Executive, National Federation of Clay Industries, 1976–84; *b* 10 Sept. 1919; *m* 1949, Marjorie Helen Heyes; one *s. Educ:* Liverpool Coll. Commissioned The Liverpool Scottish (TA), 1938; served War, Army and Special Ops Exec.; released, rank of Major, 1946. Conservative Agent, 1947–56 (Wigan, 1947–49, Knutsford, 1949–56). Managing Dir, Heyes & Co. Ltd, Wigan, 1956–66; Ashley Associates Ltd: Commercial Manager, 1966–69; Managing Dir, 1969–70; Dir, 1970–72. Dir, Manchester Chamber of Commerce, 1969–74. MP (C) Bolton West, 1970–Sept. 1974; Vice-Chm., Cons. Parly Employment Cttee, 1972–74 (Sec.,

1971–72). President: Alderley Edge RBL, 1968–76; Knutsford and Dist RBL, 2000–02 (Chm., 1990–99); Chm. (and Founder), NW Export Club, 1958–60. *Publications:* How to Recruit Good Managers, 1989; The Atrocities of the Pirates, 1997. *Address:* 194 Grove Park, Knutsford, Cheshire WA16 8QE. *T:* (01565) 632657. *Club:* Army and Navy. *Died 12 March 2006.*

REDPATH, John Thomas, CB 1969; MBE 1944; FRIBA; Director General of Research and Development, Department of the Environment, 1967–71; *b* 24 Jan. 1915; *m* 1st, 1939, Kate (*née* Francis) (*d* 1949); one *d*; 2nd, 1949, Claesina (*née* van der Vlerk); three *s* one *d. Educ:* Price's Sch.; Southern Coll. of Art. Served with RE, 1940–47. Asst Architect: Kent CC, 1936–38; Oxford City Coun., 1938–40; Princ. Asst Architect, Herts, CC, 1948–55; Dep. County Architect, Somerset CC, 1955–59; Chief Architect (Abroad), War Office, 1959–63; MPBW later DoE: Dir of Development, 1963–67; Dir Gen. of Develt, 1971–72; Dep. Chief Executive, PSA, 1972 75; Man. Dir, Millbank Technical Services Educn Ltd, 1975–77; architect in private practice, 1977–87. *Publications:* various articles in architectural jls. *Recreation:* golf. *Address:* Pines Edge, Sandy Lane, Cobham, Surrey KT11 2EU. *Club:* Arts. *Died 11 Sept. 2006.*

REECE, Sir Charles (Hugh), Kt 1988; Research and Technology Director, Imperial Chemical Industries, 1979 89; *b* 2 Jan. 1927; *s of* Charles Hugh Reece and Helen Youlle; *m* 1951, Betty Linford; two *d. Educ:* Pocklington Sch., E Riding; Huddersfield Coll.; Leeds Univ. (PhD, BSc Hons) FRSC 1981. ICI: joined Dyestuffs Div., 1949; Head of Medicinal Process Develt Dept, Dyestuffs Div., 1959; Manager, Works R&D Dept, 1965; Jt Research Manager, Mond Div., 1967; Dir, R&D, Mond Div., 1969; Dep. Chm., Mond Div., 1972; Chm., Plant Protection Div., 1975. Dir, Finnish Chemicals, 1971–75; Chm., Teijin Agricultural Chemicals, 1975–78; non-executive Director: APV plc (formerly APV Holdings), 1984–96; British Biotechnology Gp, 1989–95. Chm., Univ. of Surrey Robens Inst. of Indust. and Envmtl Health and Safety Cttee, 1985–92; Member: ACARD, 1983–87, ACOST, 1987–89; Adv. Cttee on Industry, Cttee of Vice-Chancellors and Principals, 1983–; Council, RSC, 1985–86; SERC, 1985–89; ABRC, 1989–91; UFC, 1989–93; Royal Instn of GB, 1979–92 (Mem. Council, 1985–88); SCI; Parly and Sci. Cttee, 1979– (Vice-Chm., 1986). Hon. DSc: St Andrews, 1986; Queen's, 1988; Bristol, 1989; South West Poly., 1991; DUniv Surrey, 1989. *Publications:* reports and papers in learned jls. *Recreations:* sailing, gardening. *Address:* Heath Ridge, Graffham, Petworth, W Sussex GU28 0PT. *Died 6 Nov. 2010.*

REED, Adrian Harbottle, CMG 1901; HM Diplomatic Service, retired; Consul-General, Munich, 1973–80; *b* 5 Jan. 1921; *s of* Harbottle Reed, MBE, FRIBA, and Winifred Reed (*née* Rowland); *m* 1st, 1947, Doris Davidson Duthie (marr. diss. 1975); one *s* one *d*; 2nd, 1975, Maria-Louise, *d* of Dr and Mrs A. J. Boekelman, Zeist, Netherlands. *Educ:* Hele's Sch., Exeter; Emmanuel Coll., Cambridge. Royal Artillery, 1941–47. India Office, 1947; Commonwealth Relations Office, 1947; served in UK High Commission: Pakistan, 1948–50; Fedn of Rhodesia and Nyasaland, 1953–56; British Embassy, Dublin, 1960–62; Hd Econ. Relns, 1962–65, Far East and Pacific Depts, 1966–68, CO; Counsellor (Commercial), and Consul-Gen., Helsinki, 1968–70; Economic Counsellor, Pretoria, 1971–73. Chairman: Cold Harbour Working Wool Mus., 1983–86; Devon and Exeter Instn, 1989–2001; SW Maritime Hist. Soc., 1994–97; Devon Hist. Soc., 1994–2003. Bavarian Order of Merit, 1980. *Publications:* From Past to Present (autobiog.), 2006; articles and reviews on historical (mainly maritime) subjects. *Recreations:* maritime history, the English countryside. *Address:* Old Bridge House, Uffculme, Cullompton, Devon EX15 3AX. *T:* (01884) 840595. *Died 27 Jan. 2010.*

REED, Dr John Langdale, CB 1993; FRCP, FRCPsych; Medical Inspector, HM Inspectorate of Prisons, 1996–2002; *b* 16 Sept. 1931; *s* of John Thompson Reed and Elsie May Abbott; *m* 1959, Hilary Allin; one *s* one *d. Educ:* Oundle Sch.; Cambridge Univ.; Guy's Hosp. Med. Sch. FRCP 1974; FRCPsych 1974 (Hon. FRCPsych 1992). Maudsley Hosp., 1960–67; Consultant Psychiatrist and Sen. Lectr in Psychol Medicine, St Bartholomew's Hosp., 1967–96. SPMO, Health Care Div. (Medical), DHSS, subseq. DoH, 1986–93. Special Advr in Forensic Psychiatry, DoH, 1993–96. Chairman: DoH/Home Office Rev. of Services for Mentally Disordered Offenders, 1991–92; DoH Wkg Gp on High Security Psychiatric Care, 1992–93; DoH Wkg Gp on Psychopathic Disorder, 1992–93; Adv. Cttee on Mentally Disordered Offenders, 1993–96. Chm., Vanguard Housing Assoc., 1992–96. QHP 1990–93. *Publications:* (with G. Lomas) Psychiatric Services in the Community, 1984; papers on psychiatric services, on drug abuse, and on health care in prisons. *Recreations:* genealogy, opera, bridge, walking (preferably in the Lake District). *Address:* Willow Tree House, Westleigh Drive, Bromley BR1 2PN. *Died 9 Oct. 2009.*

REES, Baron *cr* 1987 (Life Peer), of Goytre in the County of Gwent; **Peter Wynford Innes Rees;** PC 1983; QC 1969; chairman and director of companies; *b* 9 Dec. 1926; *s* of late Maj.-Gen. T. W. Rees, Indian Army, Goytre Hall, Abergavenny; *m* 1969, Mrs Anthea Wendell, *d* of late Major H. J. Maxwell Hyslop, Argyll and Sutherland Highlanders. *Educ:* Stowe; Christ Church, Oxford. Served Scots Guards, 1945–48. Called to the Bar, 1953, Bencher, Inner Temple, 1976; Oxford Circuit. Contested (C): Abertillery, 1964 and 1965; Liverpool, West Derby, 1966. MP (C): Dover, 1970–74 and 1983–87; Dover and Deal, 1974–83; PPS to Solicitor General, 1972; Minister of State, HM Treasury, 1979–81; Minister for Trade, 1981–83; Chief Sec. to HM Treasury, 1983–85. Dep. Chm., Leopold Joseph Holdings Plc, 1985–97; Dir, Fleming Mercantile Investment Trust, 1987–96; Chairman: LASMO, 1988–94; General Cable Ltd, 1990–95; CLM plc, 1994–99. Chm., Duty Free Confedn, 1987–99. Member: Council and Court of Governors, Museum of Wales, 1987–96; Museums and Galleries Commn, 1988–96. *Address:* 39 Headfort Place, SW1X 7DE; Goytre Hall, Abergavenny, Monmouthshire NP7 9DL. *Clubs:* Boodle's, Beefsteak, White's, Pratt's. *Died 30 Nov. 2008.*

REES, Prof. Charles Wayne, CBE 1995; DSc; FRS 1974; FRSC; Hofmann Professor of Organic Chemistry, Imperial College, London, 1978–93, then Emeritus Professor; *b* 15 Oct. 1927; *s* of Percival Charles Rees and Daisy Alice Beck; *m* 1953, Patricia Mary Francis; three *s. Educ:* Farnham Grammar Sch.; University Coll., Southampton (BSc, PhD). Lectr in Organic Chem.: Birkbeck Coll., Univ. of London, 1955–57; King's Coll., Univ. of London, 1957–63, Reader, 1963–65; Prof. of Organic Chem., Univ. of Leicester, 1965–69; Prof. of Organic Chem., 1969–77, Heath Harrison Prof. of Organic Chem., 1977–78, Univ. of Liverpool. Visiting Prof., Univ. of Würzburg, 1968. Royal Society of Chemistry (formerly Chemical Society): Tilden Lectr, 1973–74; Award in Heterocyclic Chem., 1980; Pres., Perkin Div., 1981–83; Pedler Lectr, 1984–85; Pres., 1992–94; Internat. Award in Heterocyclic Chem., 1995; Pres., Chemistry Sect., BAAS, 1984. FKC 1999. Hon. DSc: Leicester, 1994; Sunderland, 2000; London, 2003. *Publications:* Organic Reaction Mechanism (8 annual vols), 1965–72; Carbenes, Nitrenes, Arynes, 1969; (ed jtly) Comprehensive Heterocyclic Chemistry (8 vols), 1984, 2nd edn (10 vols), 1996; (ed jtly) Organic Functional Group Transformations (7 vols), 1995; about 450 research papers and reviews, mostly in jls of Chemical Soc. *Recreations:* music, theatre, London. *Address:* Department of Chemistry, Imperial College London, South Kensington, SW7 2AZ; *e-mail:* c.rees@imperial.ac.uk. *Died 21 Sept. 2006.*

REES, Prof. Graham Charles, OBE 2009; PhD; FBA 2005; Research Professor of English, Queen Mary, University of London, since 1998; *b* 31 Dec. 1944; *s* of Charles Rees and Margaret Fernie Rees; *m* Elizabeth Warren; one *d; m* 1995, Maria Eve Wakely; two step *c. Educ:* Univ. of Birmingham (BA 1966; MA 1968; PhD 1970). Asst Lectr in English, Shenstone New Coll., 1969–72; Lectr in English, 1972–74, Sen. Lectr, 1974–98, Wolverhampton Poly., subseq. Univ.; British Acad./Leverhulme Trust Sen. Res. Fellow, 1995–96. Part-time tutor, Open Univ., 1971–81. *Publications:* (ed) The Oxford Francis Bacon, vol. VI: philosophical studies c1611–c1619, 1996, vol. XIII: Instauratio Magna: last writings, 2000, vol. XI: Novum Organum, 2004. *Recreations:* book collecting, cats, gardens (but not gardening), Wagner, wine. *Address:* 14 Latchett Road, South Woodford, E18 1DJ. *T:* (020) 8505 9375; *e-mail:* g.c.rees@qmul.ac.uk. *Died 23 July 2009.*

REES, Prof. Hubert, DFC 1945; PhD, DSc; FRS 1976; Professor of Agricultural Botany, University College of Wales, Aberystwyth, 1968–91, then Emeritus; *b* 2 Oct. 1923; *s* of Owen Rees and Tugela Rees, Llangennech, Carmarthenshire; *m* 1946, Mavis Hill; one *s* two *d* (and one *s* decd). *Educ:* Llandovery and Llanelli Grammar Schs; University Coll. of Wales, Aberystwyth (BSc); PhD, DSc Birmingham. Served RAF, 1942–46. Student, Aberystwyth, 1946–50; Lectr in Cytology, Univ. of Birmingham, 1950–58; Sen. Lectr in Agric. Botany, University Coll. of Wales, Aberystwyth, 1958, Reader 1966. *Publications:* Chromosome Genetics, 1977; B Chromosomes, 1982; articles on genetic control of chromosomes and on evolutionary changes in chromosome organisation. *Recreation:* fishing. *Address:* Irfon, Llanbadarn Road, Aberystwyth, Dyfed SY23 1EY. *T:* (01970) 623668. *Died 13 Sept. 2009.*

REES, Peter Magnall; a Senior Clerk, House of Lords, 1981–84; *b* 17 March 1921; *s* of late Edward Saunders Rees and Gertrude Rees (*née* Magnall); *m* 1949, Moya Mildred Carroll. *Educ:* Manchester Grammar Sch.; Jesus Coll., Oxford. Served War, RA, 1941–46 (SE Asia, 1942–45). HM Overseas Service, Nigeria, 1948; Dep. Govt Statistician, Kenya, 1956; Dir of Economics and Statistics, Kenya, 1961; HM Treasury, 1964; Chief Statistician, 1966; Under-Sec., DTI later Dept of Industry, 1973–81. Consultant, OECD, 1981. *Publications:* articles in statistical jls. *Recreations:* choral singing, music, studying architecture. *Club:* Royal Commonwealth Society. *Died 16 Aug. 2006.*

REEVE, James Ernest, CMG 1982; HM Diplomatic Service, retired; international management consultant, since 1992; *b* 8 June 1926; *s* of Ernest and Anthea Reeve; *m* 1947, Lillian Irene Watkins; one *s* one *d. Educ:* Bishop's Stortford Coll. Vice-Consul, Ahwaz and Khorramshahr, Iran, 1949–51; UN General Assembly, Paris, 1951; Asst Private Sec. to Rt Hon. Selwyn Lloyd, Foreign Office, 1951–53; 2nd Secretary: Washington, 1953–57; Bangkok, 1957–59; FO, 1959–61; HM Consul, Frankfurt, 1961–65; 1st Secretary: Libya, 1965–69; Budapest, 1970–72; Chargé d'Affaires, Budapest, 1972; Counsellor (Commercial), East Berlin, 1973–75; Consul-Gen., Zurich and Principality of Liechtenstein, 1975–80; HM Minister and Consul-Gen., Milan, 1980–83. Secretariat, Internat. Primary Aluminium Inst., London, 1985–93. Dir, Sprester Investments Ltd, 1986–91. *Publications:* Cocktails, Crises and Cockroaches: a diplomatic trail. *Recreations:* theatre, tennis, travel. *Address:* 14 Century Court, Montpellier Grove, Cheltenham, Glos GL50 2XR. *T:* and *Fax:* (01242) 578033. *Clubs:* New, East Gloucestershire (Cheltenham). *Died 3 Jan. 2006.*

REEVES, Christopher Reginald; Senior Adviser, Merrill Lynch Holdings Ltd, since 2000; *b* 14 Jan. 1936; *s* of Reginald and Dora Reeves; *m* 1965, Stella, *d* of Patrick and Maria Whinney; three *s. Educ:* Malvern College. National Service, Rifle Bde, 1955–57. Bank of England, 1958–63; Hill Samuel & Co. Ltd, 1963–67; joined Morgan Grenfell & Co. Ltd, 1968; Dir, 1970; Gp Chief

Exec., 1980–87, and Dep. Chm., 1984–87, Morgan Grenfell Gp; Jt Chm., Morgan Grenfell & Co., 1984–87; Sen. Advr to Pres., Merrill Lynch, 1988–89; Vice Chm., Merrill Lynch Internat., 1989–93; Chm., Merrill Lynch Europe and Merrill Lynch International, 1993–98; Senior Adviser: Office of Dep. Chm., 1998–99, Office of Chm., 1999–2000, Merrill Lynch Inc.; Merrill Lynch Internat., 1999–2000. Director: London Board, Westpac Banking Corp. (formerly Commercial Bank of Australia Ltd) 1972–90 (Chm., 1976–82, Dep. Chm., 1982–89); Midland and International Banks Ltd, 1976–83; Balfour Beatty (formerly BICC), 1982–2003; Andrew Weir & Co., 1982–92; Allianz Cornhill Insurance PLC (formerly Allianz Internat. Insurance Co., subseq. Cornhill Insurance), 1983–; Oman Internat. Bank, 1984–2001; International Freehold Properties SARL, 1988–96; Smith Borkum Hare Pty Ltd, 1996–99; DSP Financial Consultants Ltd, 1995–; MGM Assurance, 1999– (Chm., 2000–); East India Hotels Ltd, 2002–. Chm., Mercury Energy Fund, 1998–2001. Dir, Exec. Cttee, Amer. Chamber of Commerce (UK), 1992–2001. Member, BESO, 1994–2003; Adv. Panel, City University Business Sch., 1972–81 (Chm., 1979–81); Council, City Univ. Business Sch., 1986–93; Council, Inst. for Fiscal Studies, 1982–87; Council, CBI, 1998–2002; Treas., Council, City Univ., 1992–2004; Governor: Stowe Sch., 1976–81; Dulwich College Prep. Sch., 1977–96; Mermaid Theatre Trust, 1981–85; Trustee, Chichester Fest. Theatre Trust, 1992–2001. Hon. DSc City, 2000. Recreations: sailing, shooting, ski-ing. Address: (office) 2 King Edward Street, EC1A 1HQ. Clubs: Boodle's; Royal Yacht Squadron; Royal Southern Yacht (Southampton); Itchenor Sailing.
Died 20 Nov. 2007.

REFSHAUGE, Maj.-Gen. Sir William (Dudley), AC 1980; Kt 1966; CBE 1959 (OBE 1944); ED 1965; Director-General, Army Medical Services, Australia, 1955–60; Secretary-General, World Medical Association, 1973–76; *b* 3 April 1913; *s* of late F. C. Refshauge, Melbourne; *m* 1942, Helen Elizabeth (*d* 2002), *d* of late R. E. Allwright, Tasmania; four *s* one *d*. *Educ:* Hampton High Sch.; Scotch Coll., Melbourne; Melbourne University. MB, BS (Melbourne) 1938; FRCOG 1961; FRACS 1962; FRACP 1963; Hon. FRSPH (Hon. FRSH 1967); FACMA 1967; FRACOG 1978. Served with AIF, 1939–46; Lt-Col, RAAMC (despatches four times). Medical Supt, Royal Women's Hosp., Melbourne, 1948–51; Col, and Dep. DGAMS, Aust., 1951–55; Maj.-Gen., 1955; QHP, 1955–64. Commonwealth Dir-Gen. of Health, Australia, 1960–73. Chairman: Council, Aust. Coll. of Nursing, 1958–60 (Chm. Educn Cttee, 1951–58); Nat. Health and MRC, 1960–73; Nat. Fitness Council, 1960–73; Nat. Tuberculosis Adv. Council, 1960–73; Prog. and Budget Cttee, 15th World Health Assembly, 1962; Admin., Fin. and Legal Cttee 19th World Health Assembly (Pres., 24th Assembly, 1971); Exec. Bd, WHO, 1969–70 (Mem., 1967–70). Member: Council, Aust. Red Cross Soc., 1954–60; Mem. Nat. Blood Transfusion Cttee, ARCS 1955–60; Nat. Trustee, Returned Services League Aust., 1961–73, 1976–; Mem. Bd of Management, Canberra Grammar Sch., 1963–68; Mem. Bd of Trustees, Walter and Eliza Hall Inst. of Med. Res., Melbourne, 1977–86 (Chm., Ethics Cttee, 1983–88); Chm., Governing Bd, Menzies Sch. of Health Research, Darwin, 1983–87. Chm., ACT Cttee, Mem., Nat. Cttee and Mem. Nat. Exec., Sir Robert Menzies Foundn, 1979–84; Chm., Australian-Hellenic Meml Cttee, 1986–88. Hon. Consultant, Australian Foundn on Alcoholism and Drugs of Dependence, 1979–. Hon. Life Mem., Australian Dental Assoc., 1966. Patron: Australian Sports Medicine Assoc., 1971–; ACT Br., Aust. Sports Medicine Fedn, 1980–; Totally and Permanently Incapacitated Assoc., ACT, 1982–; 2/2 (2nd AIF) Field Regtl Assoc., 1984–; Medical Assoc. for Prevention of War (MAPW), 1989–; ACT Hospice Soc., 1991–; 15 Field Ambulance Assoc., 1991–. Leader, Commemorative Tour of Europe for 60th anniversary, RSL. Nat. Pres., 1st Pan Pacific Conf. on alcohol and drugs, 1980. Hon MD Sydney, 1988. Anzac Peace Prize, 1990, Meritorious Medal, 1992, RSL.

Publications: contribs to Australian Med. Jl, NZ Med. Jl, etc. *Recreation:* reading. *Address:* 13/95 Groom Street, Hughes, Canberra, ACT 2605, Australia. *Clubs:* Royal Society of Medicine (London); Naval and Military, Cricket (Melbourne); Commonwealth (Canberra).
Died 27 May 2009.

REID, Sir (Harold) Martin (Smith), KBE 1987; CMG 1978; HM Diplomatic Service, retired; *b* 27 Aug. 1928; *s* of late Marcus Reid and late Winifred Mary Reid (*née* Stephens); *m* 1956, Jane Elizabeth Harwood; one *s* three *d*. *Educ:* Merchant Taylors' Sch.; Brasenose Coll., Oxford (Open Scholar). RN, 1947–49. Entered HM Foreign Service, 1953; served in: FO, 1953–54; Paris, 1954–57; Rangoon, 1958–61; FO, 1961–65; Georgetown, 1965 68; Bucharest, 1968–70; Dep. High Comr, Malawi, 1970–73; Private Sec. to successive Secs of State for NI, 1973–74; Head of Central and Southern Africa Dept, FCO, 1974–78; Minister, British Embassy, Pretoria/Cape Town, 1979–82; Resident Chm. (Dip. Service) CS Selection Bd, 1983–84; High Comr to Jamaica, and Ambassador (non-resident) to Haiti, 1984–87; Research Advr, FCO, 1987–88. Hon. Sec., Friends of Student Christian Movement, 1989–92. Paintings regularly exhibited, notably in one-man shows in Westminster, 1983, Kingston, 1987 and Dulwich, 1995, 1997 and 2002. *Publications:* Pissarro, 1993. *Recreation:* painting. *Address:* 43 Carson Road, SE21 8HT. *T:* (020) 8670 6151.
Died 20 June 2006.

REID, Ian George; Director, Centre for European Agricultural Studies, Wye College, University of London, 1974–86; *b* 12 May 1921; 2nd *s* of James John Reid and Margaret Jane Reid; *m* 1946, Peggy Eileen Bridgman. *Educ:* Merchant Taylors' Sch.; London Sch. of Econs (BScEcon); Christ's Coll., Cambridge (Dip. Agric.). Lectr, Reading Univ., 1945–53; Lectr, 1953–63, and Sen. Lectr, 1963–86, Wye Coll. Pres., Agricultural Econs Soc., 1981–82. *Recreations:* enjoying music, gardening, art. *Club:* Farmers'.
Died 6 July 2006.

REID, Sir Martin; *see* Reid, Sir H. M. S.

REID, Sir Norman (Robert), Kt 1970; DA (Edinburgh); FMA; FIIC; Director, the Tate Gallery, 1964–79; *b* 27 Dec. 1915; *o s* of Edward Daniel Reid and Blanche, *d* of Richard Drouet; *m* 1941, Jean Lindsay Bertram (*d* 2007); one *s* one *d*. *Educ:* Wilson's Grammar School; Edinburgh Coll. of Art; Edinburgh Univ. Served War of 1939–46, Major, Argyll and Sutherland Highlanders. Joined staff of Tate Gallery, 1946; Deputy Director, 1954; Keeper, 1959. Fellow, International Institute for Conservation (IIC) (Secretary General, 1963–65; Vice-Chm., 1966); British Rep. Internat. Committee on Museums and Galleries of Modern Art, 1963–79; President, Penwith Society of Arts; Member: Council, Friends of the Tate Gall., 1958–79 (Founder Mem.); Arts Council Art Panel, 1964–74; Inst. of Contemporary Arts Adv. Panel, 1965–; Contemporary Art Soc. Cttee, 1965–72, 1973–77; "Paintings in Hospitals" Adv. Cttee, 1965–69; British Council Fine Arts Cttee, 1965–77 (Chm. 1968–75); Culture Adv. Cttee of UK Nat. Commn for Unesco, 1966–70; Univ. of London, Bd of Studies in History of Art, 1968; Cttee, The Rome Centre, 1969–77 (Pres. 1975–77); Adv. Council, Paul Mellon Centre, 1971–78; Council of Management, Inst. of Contemp. Prints, 1972–78; Council, RCA, 1974–77. Mem. Bd, Burlington Magazine, 1971–75. Trustee, Graham and Kathleen Sutherland Foundn, 1980–85. Represented in collections: Scottish Nat. Gall. of Modern Art; Tate Gall. Hon. LittD East Anglia, 1970. Officer of the Mexican Order of the Aztec Eagle. *Club:* Arts.
Died 17 Dec. 2007.

REINERS, William Joseph; Director of Research Policy, Departments of the Environment and Transport, 1977–78, retired 1978; *b* 19 May 1923; *s* of late William and Hannah Reiners; *m* 1952, Catharine Anne Palmer; three *s* one *d*. *Educ:* Liverpool Collegiate Sch.; Liverpool Univ. RAE Farnborough, 1944–46; Min. of Works, 1946–50; Head, Building Operations and Economics

Div., Building Research Station, 1950–63; Dir of Research and Information, MPBW, 1963–71; Dir of Research Requirements, DoE, 1971–77. Chm., Aldwyck Housing Assoc., 1993–95 (Mem. Bd, 1980–97). *Publications:* various on building operations and economics. *Address:* Valais, 10 Berks Hill, Chorleywood, Herts WD3 5AQ. *T:* (01923) 448604.
Died 2 May 2009.

RENFREW, Glen McGarvie; Managing Director and Chief Executive, Reuters Ltd, 1981–91; *b* 15 Sept. 1928; *s* of Robert Renfrew and Jane Grey Watson; *m* 1954, Daphne Ann Hailey; one *s* two *d* (and one *d* decd). *Educ:* Sydney Univ., NSW, Australia (BA). Joined Reuters, London, 1952; reporting and/or management assignments in Asia, Africa and Europe, 1956–64; London management posts in computer and economic information services, 1964–70; Manager, Reuters N America, 1971–80. *Recreation:* sailing. *Club:* Manhasset Bay Yacht (Long Island, NY). *Died 29 June 2006.*

RENFREY, Rt Rev. Lionel Edward William; Dean of Adelaide, 1966–97; Assistant Bishop of Adelaide, 1969–89; *b* Adelaide, SA, 26 March 1916; *s* of late Alfred Cyril Marinus Renfrey and Catherine Elizabeth Rose Frerichs (*née* Dickson); *m* 1948, Joan Anne, *d* of Donald Smith, Cooke's Plains, SA; one *s* five *d*. *Educ:* Unley High School; St Mark's Coll., Univ. of Adelaide; St Barnabas' Theological Coll., Adelaide. BA (First Cl. Hons English), ThL (ACT) (Second Cl. Hons). Deacon 1940, priest 1941, Dio. Adelaide; Curate, St Cuthbert's, Prospect, 1940–43; Mission Chaplain, Mid Yorke Peninsula, 1943–44; Warden, Brotherhood of St John Baptist, 1944–47; Priest-in-charge: Berri-Barmera, 1948–50; Kensington Gardens, 1950–57; Rector, St James', Mile End, 1957–63; Rural Dean, Western Suburbs, 1962–63; Organising Chaplain, Bishop's Home Mission Soc., 1963–66; Editor, Adelaide Church Guardian, 1961–66; Archdeacon of Adelaide, 1965–66; Examining Chaplain to Bishop of Adelaide, 1965–85; Administrator (*sede vacante*), Diocese of Adelaide, 1974–75; Rector, Mallala and Two Wells, 1981–88. Patron: Prayer Book Soc. in Australia, 1980–; Monarchist League, 1994–. OStJ 1981 (SBStJ 1969). *Publications:* Father Wise: a Memoir, 1951; Short History of St Barnabas' Theological College, 1965; What Mean Ye By This Service?, 1978; (ed) Catholic Prayers, 1980; (ed) SS Peter and Paul Prayer Book, 1982; Arthur Nutter Thomas, Bishop of Adelaide 1906–1940, 1988; Their Happy Brotherhood: a history of the Dean and Chapter of the Diocese of Adelaide, 2006. *Recreation:* reading. *Address:* 13 Northcote Terrace, Medindie, SA 5081, Australia. *Club:* Adelaide (Adelaide). *Died 11 Nov. 2008.*

RENNELL, 3rd Baron *cr* 1933, of Rodd, Herefordshire; **John Adrian Tremayne Rodd;** *b* 28 June 1935; *s* of Hon. Gustaf Guthrie Rennell Rodd (*d* 1974) (*yr s* of 1st Baron) and Yvonne Mary Rodd (*d* 1982), *d* of late Sir Charles Murray Marling, GCMG, CB; *S* uncle, 1978; *m* 1977, Phyllis, *d* of T. D. Neill; one *s* three *d*. *Educ:* Downside; RNC, Dartmouth. Served Royal Navy, 1952–62. With Morgan Grenfell & Co. Ltd, 1963–66; free-lance journalist, 1966–67; Marks of Distinction Ltd, 1968–79; Dir, Tremayne Ltd, 1980–91. Team Leader for Vladimir Kramnik, World Championship Chess Match, 2000. *Recreations:* Scotland Rugby XV, 1958–65; golf, Real tennis. *Heir: s* Hon. James Roderick David Tremayne Rodd, *b* 9 March 1978. *Clubs:* White's; Sunningdale (Ascot). *Died 9 Dec. 2006.*

RENTON, Baron *cr* 1979 (Life Peer), of Huntingdon in the County of Cambridgeshire; **David Lockhart-Mure Renton,** KBE 1964; TD; PC 1962; QC 1954; DL; MA; BCL; a Deputy Speaker of the House of Lords, 1982–88; *b* 12 Aug. 1908; *s* of late Dr Maurice Waugh Renton, The Bridge House, Dartford, Kent, and Eszma Olivia, *d* of late Allen Walter Borman; *m* 1947, Claire Cicely Duncan (*d* 1986); two *d* (and one *d* decd). *Educ:* Stubbington; Oundle; University College, Oxford (BA Hons Jurisprudence, 1930; BCL, 1931; MA; Hon. Fellow, 1990). Called to Bar, Lincoln's Inn, 1933; South-

Eastern Circuit; elected to General Council of the Bar, 1939; Bencher, Lincoln's Inn, 1962, Treasurer, 1979. Commnd RE (TA), 1938; transferred to RA 1940; served throughout War of 1939–45; Capt. 1941; Major, 1943; served in Egypt and Libya, 1942–45. MP (Nat L) 1945–50, (Nat L and C) 1950–68, (C) 1968–79, Huntingdonshire; Parly Sec., Min. of Fuel and Power, 1955–57, Ministry of Power, 1957–58; Joint Parly Under-Sec. of State, Home Office, 1958–61; Minister of State, Home Office, 1961–62; Chm., Select Cttee for Revision of Standing Orders, House of Commons, 1963 and 1970; Dep. Chm., Special Select Cttee on H of C Procedure, 1976–78; Mem., Cttee of Privileges, 1973–79. Life Pres., Assoc. of Conservative Peers, H of L, 2003–. Recorder of Rochester, 1963–68, of Guildford, 1968–71; Vice-Chm., Council of Legal Educn, 1968–70, 1971–73. Member: Senate of Inns of Court, 1967–69, 1970–71, 1975–79; Royal Commn on the Constitution, 1971–73; Chm., Cttee on Preparation of Legislation, 1973–75. Pres., Statute Law Soc., 1980–2000. Pres., Mencap (Royal Soc. for Mentally Handicapped Children), 1982–88 (Hon. Treas., 1976–78; Chm., 1978–82). President: Conservation Soc., 1970–71; Nat. Council for Civil Protection (formerly Nat. Council for Civil Defence), 1980–91; Pres., All Party Arts and Heritage Gp, 1989–. Patron: Huntingdon Conservative Assoc., 1979–; Ravenswood Foundn, 1979–; Huntingdonshire RBL, 1984–; Gtr London Assoc. for the Disabled, 1986–; DEMAND (Design and Manufacture for Disablement), 1986–. DL Huntingdonshire, 1962, Huntingdon and Peterborough, 1964, Cambs, 1974. Coronation and Jubilee Medals. *Recreations:* outdoor sports and games, gardening. *Address:* Moat House, Abbots Ripton, Huntingdon, Cambs PE17 2PE. *T:* (01487) 773227; 16 Old Buildings, Lincoln's Inn, WC2A 3TL. *T:* (020) 7242 8986. *Clubs:* Carlton, Pratt's. *Died 24 May 2007.*

RENTON, Stuart, MBE 1973; RSA 1997 (ARSA 1983); Senior Partner, Reiach and Hall, architects, 1982–91; *b* 15 Sept. 1929; *s* of William Langlands Renton and Mary Renton (*née* Crighton); *m* 1953, Ethnie Sloan; one *s* one *d*. *Educ:* Royal High Sch., Edinburgh; Sch. of Architecture, Edinburgh Coll. of Art (DA 1952). ARIBA 1953, FRIBA 1971; ARIAS 1953, FRIAS 1985. Served RAF, 1953–55, RAFVR, 1955–65. Joined Alan Reiach's practice, 1955, Partner, 1959; Founding Partner: Reiach and Hall, 1965; Reiach Hall Blyth, 1973–83. Major projects include: New Club, Edinburgh (with Alan Reiach), 1969; Hugh Nisbet Building, Heriot-Watt Univ., 1973; Teesside Coll. of Educn, 1974; BSC Clydesdale and Airdrie, 1977 (British Steel and RIBA Awards, 1978); Life Association of Scotland: HQ, 1989 (Civic Trust Award, 1991), and 10 George Street, Edinburgh, 1992 (RIBA Award, 1994); Midlothian Council HQ, 1990 (Civic Trust Award, 1992); Strathclyde Grad. Business Sch., 1992 (RIBA Award, 1993). Vis. Prof., Strathclyde Univ., 1992–98. Gov., Edinburgh Coll. of Art, 1985–98 (Chm., 1992–98). Other architectural awards include: Construction Industry, 1990; Civic Trust, 1993. *Recreations:* ski-ing, gamefishing, Italian hill villages. *Address:* Grianan, Killichonan, Rannoch, Perthshire PH17 2QW. *T:* (01882) 633247. *Club:* New (Edinburgh). *Died 23 Jan. 2006.*

REYNOLDS, Prof. Philip Alan, CBE 1986; DL; Vice-Chancellor, University of Lancaster, 1980–85; *b* 15 May 1920; *s* of Harry Reynolds and Ethel (*née* Scott); *m* 1946, Mollie Patricia (*née* Horton); two *s* one *d*. *Educ:* Worthing High Sch.; Queen's Coll., Oxford (BA 1940, 1st Cl. Mod. Hist.; MA 1950). Served War, 1940–46: HAA and Staff, UK, ME and Greece; Major 1945. Asst Lectr, later Lectr in Internat. History, LSE, 1946–50; Woodrow Wilson Prof. of Internat. Politics, UCW Aberystwyth, 1950–64 (Vice-Principal, 1961–63); Prof. of Politics and Pro-Vice-Chancellor, Univ. of Lancaster, 1964–80. Vis. Professor: in Internat. Relations, Toronto, 1953; in Commonwealth History and Instns, Indian Sch. of Internat. Studies, New Delhi, 1958; Anspach Fellow,

Univ. of Pa, 1971; Vis. Res. Fellow, ANU Canberra, 1977. Vice-Chm., Cttee of Vice-Chancellors and Principals, 1984–85; Chm., Brit. Internat. Studies Assoc., 1976, Hon. Pres., 1981–84; Mem. Council, RIIA, 1975–80. DL Lancs, 1982. Hon. DLitt Lancaster, 1985; DUniv Open, 1994. *Publications:* War in the Twentieth Century, 1951; Die Britische Aussenpolitik zwischen den beiden Weltkriegen, 1952 (rev. edn, 1954, as British Foreign Policy in the Inter-War Years); An Introduction to International Relations, 1971, 3rd edn 1994 (Japanese edn 1977, Spanish edn 1978, Chinese edn 1997); (with E. J. Hughes) The Historian as Diplomat: Charles Kingsley Webster and the United Nations 1939–46, 1976; contrib. New Cambridge Mod. Hist., History, Slavonic Rev., Pol. Qly, Pol. Studies, Internat. Jl, Internat. Studies, Brit. Jl of Internat. Studies, Educn Policy Bulletin, Higher Educn, Univs Qly, Minerva. *Recreations:* music, bridge, eating and drinking. *Address:* Lattice Cottage, Borwick, Carnforth, Lancs LA6 1JR. *T:* (01524) 732518.
Died 11 Sept 2009.

RICE, Peter D.; *see* Davis-Rice.

RICHARDS, Denis Edward, CMG 1981; HM Diplomatic Service, retired; Ambassador to the United Republic of Cameroon and the Republic of Equatorial Guinea, 1979–81; *b* 25 May 1923; *m* 1947, Nancy Beryl Brown (*d* 2002); one *d* (and one *d* decd). *Educ:* Wilson's Grammar Sch., London; St Peter's Coll., Oxford. Lieut RNVR, 1941–46; Colonial Service (HMOCS), 1948–60: District Admin. and Min. of Finance, Ghana (Gold Coast); HM Diplomatic Service, 1960–81: CRO, 1960; Karachi, 1961–63; FO (News Dept), 1964–68; Brussels (NATO), 1969; Brussels (UK Negotiating Delegn), 1970–72; Counsellor, Kinshasa, 1972–74; Consul-Gen., Philadelphia, 1974–79. *Recreations:* music, watching cricket. *Address:* Tresco House, Spencer Road, Birchington, Kent CT7 9EY. *T:* (01843) 845637.
Died 27 April 2008.

RICHARDSON OF DUNTISBOURNE, Baron *cr* 1983 (Life Peer), of Duntisbourne in the County of Gloucestershire; **Gordon William Humphreys Richardson,** KG 1983; MBE (mil.) 1944; TD 1979; PC 1976; DL; Governor, Bank of England, 1973–83, Member, Court of the Bank of England, 1967–83; Senior International Adviser, Morgan Stanley & Co. Inc., since 1997; *b* 25 Nov. 1915; *er s* of John Robert and Nellie Richardson; *m* 1941, Margaret Alison (*d* 2005), *er d* of Canon H. R. L. Sheppard; one *s* one *d*. *Educ:* Nottingham High School; Gonville and Caius College, Cambridge (MA, LLB). Commnd S Notts Hussars Yeomanry, 1939; Staff Coll., Camberley, 1941; served until 1946. Called to Bar, Gray's Inn, 1946 (Hon. Bencher, 1973); Mem. Bar Council, 1951–55; ceased practice at Bar, Aug. 1955. Industrial and Commercial Finance Corp. Ltd, 1955–57; Director: J. Henry Schroder & Co., 1957; Lloyds Bank Ltd, 1960–67 (Vice-Chm., 1962–66); Legal and General Assurance Soc., Ltd, 1956–70 (Vice-Chm. 1959–70); Rolls Royce (1971) Ltd, 1971–73; ICI Ltd, 1972–73; Chairman: J. Henry Schroder Wagg & Co. Ltd, 1962–72; Schroders Ltd, 1966–73; Schroder Banking Corp. Inc. (NY), 1968–73; Morgan Stanley Internat. Inc., 1986–95. Mem., Adv. Bd, Morgan Stanley Dean Witter; Chm. and Vice-Chm., Internat. Adv. Bd, Chase Manhattan. Chm., Industrial Develt Adv. Bd, 1972–73. Mem. Company Law Amendment Committee (Jenkins Committee), 1959–62; Chm. Cttee on Turnover Taxation, 1963. Member: Court of London University, 1962–65; NEDC, 1971–73, 1980–83; Trustee, National Gallery, 1971–73; Chm., Pilgrim Trust, 1984–88. One of HM Lieutenants, City of London, 1974–83; High Steward of Westminster, 1985–89; DL Glos, 1983. Deputy High Steward, Univ. of Cambridge, 1982–2008; Hon. Fellow: Gonville and Caius Coll., 1977; Wolfson Coll., Cambridge, 1977. Hon. LLD Cambridge, 1979; Hon. DSc: City Univ., 1976; Aston, 1979; Hon. DCL East Anglia, 1984. Benjamin Franklin Medal, RSA, 1984. *Address:* 25 St Anselm's Place, W1K 5AF. *T:* (020) 7629 4448. *Clubs:* Brooks's, Pratt's.   *Died 22 Jan. 2010.*

RICHARDSON, Sir Eric; *see* Richardson, Sir J. E.

RICHARDSON, Ian William, CBE 1989; actor; *b* 7 April 1934; *s* of John Richardson and Margaret Drummond; *m* 1961, Maroussia Frank; two *s*. *Educ:* Tynecastle; Edinburgh; Univ. of Glasgow. Studied for stage at Coll. of Dramatic Art, Glasgow (James Bridie Gold Medal, 1957). FRSAMD 1971. Joined Birmingham Repertory Theatre Co. 1958 (leading parts incl. Hamlet); joined Shakespeare Meml Theatre Co. (later RSC), 1960; rôles, Stratford and Aldwych, 1960–: Arragon in Merchant of Venice; Sir Andrew Aguecheek, 1960; Malatesti in Duchess of Malfi, 1960; Oberon in A Midsummer Night's Dream, 1961; Tranio in Taming of the Shrew, 1961; the Doctor in The Representative, 1963; Edmund in King Lear, 1964; Antipholus of Ephesus in Comedy of Errors, 1964; Herald and Marat in Marat/Sade, 1964, 1965; Ithamore, The Jew of Malta, 1964; Ford, Merry Wives of Windsor, 1964, 1966, 1969; Antipholus of Syracuse in Comedy of Errors, 1965; Chorus, Henry V, 1965; Vindice, The Revengers Tragedy, 1965, 1969; Coriolanus, 1966; Bertram, All's Well That Ends Well, 1966; Malcolm, Macbeth, 1966; Cassius, Julius Caesar, 1968; Pericles, 1969; Angelo, Measure for Measure, 1970; Buckingham, Richard III, 1970; Proteus, Two Gentlemen of Verona, 1970; Prospero, The Tempest, 1970; Richard II/Bolingbroke, Richard II, 1973; Berowne, Love's Labour's Lost, 1973; Iachimo, Cymbeline, 1974; Shalimov, Summer Folk, 1974; Ford, Merry Wives of Windsor, 1975; Richard III, 1975; The Hollow Crown, 2002, 2003, 2004, also Australia and Canada; tours with RSC: Europe and USSR, NY, 1964; NY, 1965; USSR, 1966; Japan, 1970; NY, 1974, 1975; Tom Wrench in musical Trelawny, Sadler's Wells, 1971–72; Professor Higgins, My Fair Lady, NY, 1976 (Drama Desk Award, 1976); Jack Tanner, in Man and Superman, and Doctor in The Millionairess, Shaw Festival Theatre, Niagara, Ont; The Government Inspector, Old Vic, 1979; Romeo and Juliet, Old Vic, 1979; Lolita, NY, 1981; The Miser, Chichester, 1995; The Magistrate, Chichester, 1997, transf. Savoy, 1998; The Seven Ages of Man (one-man show), Guildford, 1999; The Alchemist, NT, 2006. *Films:* Captain Fitzroy in The Darwin Adventure, 1971; Priest in Man of la Mancha, 1972; Montgomery in Ike—the War Years, 1978; Charlie Muffin, 1979; The Sign of Four, 1982; Hound of the Baskervilles, 1982; Brazil, 1984; Whoops Apocalypse, 1987; The Fourth Protocol, 1987; Burning Secret, 1989; The Year of the Comet, 1992; M. Butterfly, 1994; Words upon the Window Pane, 1995; BAPS, 1997; From Hell, 2002. *Television: plays:* Danton's Death, 1978; Churchill and the Generals, 1979; A Cotswold Death, Passing Through, 1981; Russian Night, Kisch-Kisch, Beauty and the Beast, Salad Days, 1982; Slimming Down, 1984; Star Quality, 1985; The Devil's Disciple, 1987; The Winslow Boy, 1989; An Ungentlemanly Act, 1992; The Canterville Ghost, 1997; The Woman in White, 1997; *films:* Monsignor Quixote, 1985; Blunt, 1987; Rosencrantz and Guildenstern Are Dead, 1990; Baps, 1996; The Fifth Province, 1996; Dark City, 1996; *serials and series:* Eyeless in Gaza, 1971; Tinker, Tailor, Soldier, Spy, 1979; Private Schulz, 1981; The Woman in White, 1982; Ramsay Macdonald, in Number 10, 1982; The Master of Ballantrae, 1984; Six Centuries of Verse, 1984; Mistral's Daughter, 1985; Nehru, in Mountbatten—the last Viceroy, 1986; Porterhouse Blue, 1987; Troubles, 1988; Twist of Fate, 1989; Under a Dark Angel's Eye, 1989; Phantom of the Opera, 1990; The Plot to Kill Hitler, 1990; The Gravy Train, 1990; House of Cards, 1990 (BAFTA Best Actor Award, 1991); The Gravy Train Goes East, 1991; To Play the King, 1993; Remember, 1994; Catherine the Great, 1994; The Final Cut, 1995; The Magician's House, 1999; Gormenghast, 2000; Murder Rooms, 2000; Murder Rooms II, 2001; Strange, 2002; Nero, in Imperium, 2004; Bleak House, 2005; Booze Cruise 2, 2005; Booze Cruise 3, 2006. Hon. DDra RSAMD, 1999. RTS Award, 1982. *Publications:*

Preface to Cymbeline (Folio Soc.), 1976. *Recreations:* music, exploring churches and castles. *Address:* c/o Diamond Management, 31 Percy Street, W1T 2DD. *T:* (020) 7631 0400. *Died 9 Feb. 2007.*

RICHARDSON, Joanna Leah, DLitt; FRSL; author; *b* London, 8 Aug. 1925; *o d* of late Frederick Richardson and Charlotte Elsa (*née* Benjamin). *Educ:* The Downs School, Seaford, Sussex; St Anne's College, Oxford (MA; DLitt 2004). Contributions to BBC include: translated plays; interviews; numerous features for Radios 3 and 4. FRSL 1959 (Mem. Council, 1961–86). Chevalier de l'Ordre des Arts et des Lettres, 1987. *Publications include:* Fanny Brawne: a biography, 1952; Théophile Gautier: his Life and Times, 1958; Edward FitzGerald, 1960; (ed) FitzGerald: Selected Works, 1962; The Pre-Eminent Victorian: a study of Tennyson, 1962; The Everlasting Spell: a study of Keats and his Friends, 1963; (ed) Essays by Divers Hands (trans. Royal Soc. Lit.), 1963; introd. to Victor Hugo: Choses Vues (The Oxford Lib. of French Classics), 1964; Edward Lear, 1965; George IV: a Portrait, 1966; Creevey and Greville, 1967; Princess Mathilde, 1969; Verlaine, 1971; Enid Starkie, 1973; (ed and trans.) Verlaine, Poems, 1974; Stendhal: a critical biography, 1974; (ed and trans.) Baudelaire, Poems, 1975; Victor Hugo, 1976; Zola, 1978; Keats and his Circle: an album of portraits, 1980; (trans.) Gautier, Mademoiselle de Maupin, 1981; The Life and Letters of John Keats, 1981; Letters from Lambeth: the correspondence of the Reynolds family with John Freeman Milward Dovaston 1808–1815, 1981; Colette, 1983; Judith Gautier, 1987 (trans. French 1989; Prix Goncourt for Biography); Portrait of a Bonaparte: the life and times of Joseph-Napoléon Primoli 1851–1927, 1987; Baudelaire, 1994; contributed to The Times, The Times Literary Supplement, French Studies, French Studies Bulletin, Modern Language Review, Keats-Shelley Memorial Bulletin, etc. *Recreation:* antique-collecting. *Address:* c/o Curtis Brown Group, Haymarket House, 28–29 Haymarket, SW1Y 4SP. *T:* (020) 7396 6600. *Died 7 March 2008.*

RICHARDSON, Sir (John) Eric, Kt 1967; CBE 1962; PhD, DSc; CEng, FIEE, MIMechE, FBHI, FBOA, FPS; Director, The Polytechnic of Central London, 1969–70; *b* 30 June 1905; *e surv. s* of late William and Mary Elizabeth Richardson, Birkenhead; *m* 1941, Alice May, *d* of H. M. Wilson, Hull; one *s* two *d* (and one *d* decd). *Educ:* Birkenhead Higher Elementary Sch.; Liverpool Univ. (BEng 1st Cl. Hons, 1931; PhD 1933). Chief Lectr in Electrical Engineering, 1933–37, Head of Engineering Dept, 1937–41, Hull Municipal Technical Coll.; Principal: Oldham Municipal Technical Coll., 1942–44; Royal Technical Coll., Salford, 1944–47; Northampton Polytechnic, London, EC1, 1947–56; Dir, Nat. Coll. of Horology and Instrument Technology, 1947–56; Dir of Educn, Regent Street Polytechnic, W1, 1957–69. Hon. Sec., Assoc. of Technical Insts, 1957–67, Chm., 1967–68; Pres. Assoc. of Principals of Technical Instns, 1961–62; Dep. Chm., Council for Overseas Colls of Arts, Science and Technology, 1949–62; Member: Council for Tech. Educn and Trng in Overseas Countries, 1962–73 (Chm. Technical Educn Cttee, 1971–73); and Vice-Chm. Council and Cttees, London and Home Counties Regional Adv. Council for Technol Educn, 1972–84; Chm., Adv. Cttee on Educn for Management, 1961–66; Pres. and Chm., CICRIS, 1972–89; Member: Governing Council of Nigerian Coll. of Art, Science and Technology, 1953–61; Council, Univ. Coll., Nairobi, 1961–70; Provisional Council, Univ. of East Africa, 1961–63; Governing Body, College of Aeronautics, Cranfield, 1956–59; Council of British Horological Institute, 1951–56; Gen. Optical Council, 1959–78 (Chm., 1975–78); Assoc. of Optical Practitioners (Vice-Pres., 1983–84; Pres., 1984–95); Science and Technol Cttee of CNAA, 1965–71; Electrical Engrg Bd of CNAA (Chm.); Industrial Trg Bd for Electricity Supply Industry, 1965–71; Univ. and Polytechnic Grants Cttee, Hong Kong, 1972–77; Council, RSA, 1968–78 (FRSA; Chm. Exams Cttee, 1969–78, Hon. Treasurer, 1974–78);

Council and Exec. Cttee, Leprosy Mission, 1970–84 (Chm., 1974–84; Vice-Pres., 1984–98); Council and Exec. Cttee, City and Guilds of London Inst., 1969–80 (Chm. Policy and Overseas Cttees; Vice-Chm. Technical Educn Cttee; Jt Hon. Sec., 1970–80; Vice-Pres., 1979–82; Hon. FCGI 1981); Chm., Ealing Civic Soc., 1972–76. Chairman: Africa Evangelical Fellowship (SAGM), 1950–70; Nat. Young Life Campaign, 1949–64; Council, Inter-Varsity Fellowship of Evangelical Unions, 1966–69; Pres., Crusaders Union, 1972–86. Chm. Governors, Clarendon Sch., Abergele, 1971–75; Governor, London Bible Coll., 1968– (Chm., 1970–77; Pres., 1978–90). *Publications:* paper in IEE Jl (Instn Prize); various papers on higher technological education in UK and Nigeria. *Recreations:* gardening, photography. *Died 20 July 2006.*

RICHARDSON, Natasha Jane; actress; *b* 11 May 1963; *d* of late Tony Richardson and of Vanessa Redgrave, CBE; *m* 1st, 1990, Robert Michael John Fox (marr. diss. 1994); 2nd, 1994, William John, (Liam), Neeson, OBE, two *s*. *Educ:* Lycée Française de Londres; St Paul's Girls' Sch.; Central Sch. of Speech and Drama. Season at Leeds Playhouse; A Midsummer Night's Dream, New Shakespeare Co.; Ophelia in Hamlet, Young Vic; The Seagull, Lyric Hammersmith, tour and Queen's, 1985 (Most Promising Newcomer, London Drama Critics, 1986); China, Bush Th., 1986; High Society, Leicester Haymarket and Victoria Palace, 1987; Anna Christie, Young Vic, 1990 (Best Actress, London Drama Critics, 1992), NY, 1993 (Outer Critics Circle Award, 1993); Cabaret, NY (Tony, Outer Critics' Circle and Drama Desk Awards), 1998; Closer, NY, 1999; The Lady from the Sea, Almeida, 2003; A Streetcar Named Desire, NY, 2005. *Films:* Every Picture Tells a Story, 1985; Gothic; A Month in the Country, 1987; Patty Hearst, 1988; Fat Man and Little Boy, 1989; The Handmaid's Tale, The Comfort of Strangers, 1990 (Best Actress, London Evening Standard Awards, 1990); The Favour, the Watch and the Very Big Fish, 1992; Past Midnight; Widows Peak (Best Actress, Prague Film Fest., 1994), Nell, 1994; The Parent Trap, 1998; Blow Dry, 2001; Chelsea Walls, Wakin' up in Reno, 2002; Maid in Manhattan, 2003; Asylum, The White Countess, 2006; Evening, 2007; Wild Child, 2008. *Television:* In a Secret State, 1985; Ghosts, 1986; Hostages, 1992; Suddenly Last Summer, 1993; Zelda, 1993; Tales from the Crypt, 1996; Haven (series), 2000; The Mastersons of Manhattan, 2007. Most Promising Newcomer Award, Plays and Players, 1986; Best Actress: Evening Standard Film Awards, 1990; London Theatre Critics, 1990; Plays and Players, 1990. *Address:* c/o Independent Talent Group Ltd, Oxford House, 76 Oxford Street, W1D 1BS. *Died 18 March 2009.*

RICHINGS, Lewis David George; Deputy Director, National Radiological Protection Board, 1978–80 (Secretary, 1970–79); *b* 22 April 1920; *s* of Lewis Vincent Richings and Jessie Helen (*née* Clements); *m* 1944, Margaret Alice Hume (*d* 2005); three *d*. *Educ:* Battersea Grammar Sch.; Devonport High Sch.; Darlington Grammar Sch.; London Sch. of Econs and Polit. Science (part-time). Served War, Army, 1939–46: commnd 2 Lieut Inf., 1940; attached 8 DLI, 1940–41; seconded 11 KAR, 1941–45; Actg Major, 1945; various postings, UK, 1945–46. MAFF, 1937–58; attached MoD, 1958; Gen. Administrator, AWRE, 1958–65; Health and Safety Br., UKAEA, 1965–70. Mem., Radiol Protection and Public Health Cttee, Nuclear Energy Agency, OECD, 1966–80 (Chm., 1972–74). FRSA. *Publications:* articles in press and jls on admin and technical matters relating to common land, rural electrification, earthquakes, and radiological protection. *Recreation:* boats. *Address:* Cumberland View Hostel, 123–127 Whalley Drive, Vic 3150, Australia. *Died 28 April 2009.*

RICHMOND, Prof. John, CBE 1993; MD, FRCP, FRCPE; FRSE; President, Royal College of Physicians of Edinburgh, 1988–91; Emeritus Professor of Medicine, University of Sheffield, since 1989; *b* 30 May 1926; *er s* of late Hugh Richmond and Janet Hyslop Brown; *m* 1951, Jenny, 2nd *d* of T. Nicol; two *s* one *d*. *Educ:* Doncaster Grammar Sch.; Univ. of Edinburgh (MB, ChB 1948 (with Distinction in Medicine); MD 1963). FRCPE 1963; FRCP 1970; FRCPS 1988; FRCPI 1990; FCPS (Pak) 1990; FRCSE 1991; Hon. FACP 1990; Hon. FFPM 1990; Hon. FRACP 1991; Hon. FCP(SoAf) 1991; Hon. FFPH (Hon. FFPHM 1991). RAMC, Military Mission to Ethiopia, Captain 1st Bn King's African Rifles, N Rhodesia, 1949–50; Rural Gen. Practice, Galloway, Scotland, 1950–52; Res. Fellow, Meml Sloan Kettering Cancer Center, New York, 1958–59; Sen. Lectr, later Reader in Medicine, Univ. of Edinburgh, 1963–73; University of Sheffield: Prof. of Medicine, 1973–89; Chm., Academic Div. of Medicine, 1978–85; Dean of Medicine and Dentistry, 1985–88. Censor, 1981–82, Sen. Vice-Pres. and Sen. Censor, 1984–85, RCP; Mem. Council, RCPE, 1987–88. Chm., MRCP (UK) Part 2 Examining Bd, 1985–89. Member: Clin. Standards Adv. Gp, Dept of Health, 1991–94; Bd of Advisrs, London Univ., 1984–93; External Advr, Chinese Univ. of Hong Kong, 1984–96. Member: Scottish Adv. Cttee, British Council, 1991–97; Scottish Cttee, Marie Curie Meml Foundn, 1992–2001. Hon. MD Sheffield, 1994. *Publications:* contribs to books and papers in med. jls, mainly on haematology and oncology. *Address:* 15 Church Hill, Edinburgh EH10 4BG.   *Died 27 March 2008.*

RICKARD, Prof. Peter, DPhil, PhD, LittD; Drapers Professor of French, University of Cambridge, 1980–82, Emeritus since 1983; Fellow of Emmanuel College, Cambridge, 1953, Professorial Fellow, 1980, Life Fellow, since 1983; *b* 20 Sept. 1922; *yr s* of Norman Ernest Rickard and Elizabeth Jane (*née* Hosking); unmarried. *Educ:* Redruth County Grammar Sch., Cornwall; Exeter Coll., Oxford (Final Hons Mod. Langs (French and German), Cl. I, 1948; MA 1948); DPhil Oxon 1952; PhD Cantab 1952; LittD Cambridge 1982. Seaforth War, 1st Bn Seaforth Highlanders and Intell. Corps, India, 1942–46. Heath Harrison Travelling Scholar (French), 1948; Amelia Jackson Sen. Scholar, Exeter Coll., Oxford, 1948–49; Lectr in Mod. Langs, Trinity Coll., Oxford, 1949–52; Univ. of Cambridge: Asst Lectr in French, 1952–57, Lectr, 1957–74; Reader in French Lang., 1974–80; Mem., St John's Coll., 1952–; Tutor, Emmanuel Coll., 1954–65. *Publications:* Britain in Medieval French Literature, 1956; La langue française au XVIe siècle, 1968; (ed with T. G. S. Combe) The French Language: studies presented to Lewis Charles Harmer, 1970; (ed and trans.) Fernando Pessoa, Selected Poems, 1971; A History of the French Language, 1974; Chrestomathie de la langue française au XVe siècle, 1976; (ed with T. G. S. Combe) L. C. Harmer, Uncertainties in French Grammar, 1979; The Embarrassments of Irregularity, 1981; The French Language in the 17th Century: contemporary opinion in France, 1992; The Transferred Epithet in Modern English Prose, 1996; articles in Romania, Trans Phil. Soc., Neuphilologische Mitteilungen, Cahiers de Lexicologie, and Zeitschrift für Romanische Philologie. *Recreations:* travel, music. *Address:* Upper Rosevine, Portscatho, Cornwall TR2 5EW. *T:* (01872) 580582.   *Died 2 April 2009.*

RICKARDS, Prof. (Richard) Barrie, CGeol, FGS; Professor of Palaeontology and Biostratigraphy, University of Cambridge, 2000–05, then Emeritus Professor; Curator, Sedgwick Museum of Geology, 1969–2005, then Hon. Curator; Fellow, Emmanuel College, Cambridge, 1977–2004, then Life Fellow; Hon. Curator, Emmanuel College Museum, 1994–99; *b* 12 June 1938; *s* of Robert Rickards and Eva (*née* Sudborough); *m* 1960, Christine Townsley (marr. diss. 1991); one *s* decd. *Educ:* Goole Grammar Sch.; Univ. of Hull (BSc; PhD 1963; DSc 1990; MA Cantab, 1969; ScD Cantab, 1976. FGS 1960; Founder MIFM 1969; CGeol 1990. Reckitt Scholar, Univ. of Hull, 1960–63; Curator, Garwood Library, UCL, 1963; Asst in Research, Univ. of Cambridge, 1964–66; SSO, BM (Natural History), 1967; Lectr, TCD, 1967–69; University of

Cambridge: Lectr, 1969–90; Reader, 1990–2000; Official Lectr, Emmanuel Coll., 1977–2000. Founder and first Sec., Pike Anglers' Club; Founding Mem., Nat. Anglers' Council; Deleg., E Reg., 1987–2000, Mem., Gen. Purposes Cttee, 1989–2000, Nat. Fedn of Anglers; Mem. Council, Waterbeach Angling Club, 1980–84; first Fishery Manager, Leland Water, 1982–83. Consultant, Shakespeare Co. (UK) Ltd, 1988–. President: Lure Fishing Soc. of GB, 1992–; Nat. Assoc. of Specialist Anglers, 1993–2000; Specialist Anglers Alliance, 2001–; Trustee, Specialist Anglers' Conservation Gp, 1995–2000. Gov., Caldecote Co. Primary Sch., Cambs, 1994–95. Murchison Fund, 1982, Lyell Medal, 1997, Geol Soc.; John Phillips Medal, Yorks Geol Soc., 1988. *Publications:* Fishers on the Green Roads (novel), 2002; *angling:* (with R. Webb) Fishing for Big Pike, 1971, (sole author) 3rd edn, as Big Pike, 1986; Perch, 1974; (with R. Webb) Fishing for Big Tench, 1976, 2nd edn 1986; Pike, 1976; (with K. Whitehead) Plugs and Plug Fishing, 1976, and Spinners, Spoons and Wobbled Baits, 1977, rev. edn of both titles as A Textbook of Spinning, 1987; (with N. Fickling) Zander, 1979, 2nd edn 1990; (with K. Whitehead) Fishing Tackle, 1981; (with K. Whitehead) A Fishery of Your Own, 1984; Angling: fundamental principles, 1986; (with M. Gay) A Technical Manual of Pike Fishing, 1986; (ed) River Piking, 1987; (ed) Best of Pikelines, 1988; (with M. Gay) Pike, 1989; (with M. Bannister) The Ten Greatest Pike Anglers, 1991; (jtly) Encyclopaedia of Fishing, 1991; Success with Pike, 1992; Success with the Lure, 1993; (with M. Bannister) The Great Modern Pike Anglers, 2006; Richard Walker: biography of an angling legend, 2007; (with T. Baily) Nile Perch, 2008; Modern Lure Fishing, 2009; over 700 articles on angling in newspapers and magazines; *geology:* Graptolites: writing in the rocks, 1991; (ed with D. C. Palmer) H. B. Whittington, Trilobites, 1992; (ed with S. Rigby) Graptolites in Colour: a teaching aid, 1998; upwards of 200 scientific articles and monographs in internat. jls, mostly on fossils (graptolites) and evolution. *Recreations:* angling, marathon running, angling administration (from local to national). *Address:* Emmanuel College, Cambridge CB2 3AP. *T:* (01223) 334282.   *Died 5 Nov. 2009.*

RICKETTS, Sir (Robert) Tristram, 8th Bt *cr* 1828, of The Elms, Gloucestershire, and Beaumont Leys, Leicestershire; Chief Executive, Horserace Betting Levy Board, 1984–93 and since 2005; *b* 17 April 1946; *s* of Sir Robert Ricketts, 7th Bt, and Anne Theresa Ricketts, CBE (*d* 1998); *S* father, 2005; *m* 1969, Ann Lewis; one *s* one *d*. *Educ:* Winchester Coll.; Magdalene Coll., Cambridge (BA Hons 1968; MA 1972). Admin. Officer, GLC, 1968–72; Personal Asst to Leader of GLC, 1972–73; Horserace Betting Levy Board: Asst Principal Officer, 1974–76; Dep. Sec., 1976–79; Sec., 1980–84; Mem., 1993–98, 2000–05; Chief Exec., 1993–2000, Sec. Gen., 2000–05, British Horseracing Bd. Chm., British Horse Industry Confedn, 2002–05. *Recreations:* horseracing, theatre, cinema, making bonfires. *Heir:* s Stephen Tristram Ricketts, *b* 24 Dec. 1974. *Address:* 47 Lancaster Avenue, SE27 9EL. *T:* (020) 8670 8422. *Club:* Athenæum.   *Died 7 Nov. 2007.*

RICKMAN, Prof. Geoffrey Edwin, FBA 1989; Professor of Roman History, University of St Andrews, 1981–97, then Emeritus; *b* 9 Oct. 1932; *s* of Charles Edwin Rickman and Ethel Ruth Mary (*née* Hill); *m* 1959, Anna Rosemary Wilson; one *s* one *d*. *Educ:* Peter Symonds' Sch., Winchester; Brasenose Coll., Oxford (MA, DipClassArchaeol, DPhil). FSA 1966; FRSE 2001. Henry Francis Pelham Student, British Sch. at Rome, 1958–59; Jun. Res. Fellow, The Queen's Coll., Oxford, 1959–62; University of St Andrews: Lectr in Ancient History, 1962–68; Sen. Lectr, 1968–81; Master of the United Coll. of St Salvator and St Leonard, 1992–96; Pro-Vice-Chancellor, 1996–97. Vis. Fellow, Brasenose Coll., Oxford, 1981; Mem., IAS, Princeton, 1997–98. Mem., Faculty of Archaeol., History and Letters, 1979–87 (Chm., 1983–87), Chm. Council, 1997–2002, Hon. Fellow, 2002, British Sch. at Rome; Mem., Humanities

Res. Bd, British Acad., 1995–98. *Publications:* Roman Granaries and Storebuildings, 1971; The Corn Supply of Ancient Rome, 1980. *Recreations:* opera, swimming, walking beside the sea. *Address:* 56 Hepburn Gardens, St Andrews, Fife KY16 9DG. *T:* (01334) 472063.
Died 8 Feb. 2010.

RIDDELL, Sir John (Charles Buchanan), 13th Bt *cr* 1628; KCVO 2009 (CVO 1990); CA; Extra Equerry to HRH the Prince of Wales, since 1990; Lord-Lieutenant of Northumberland, 2000–09; Chairman, Northern Rock plc, 2000–04 (Director, 1981–85, and 1990–2004; Deputy Chairman, 1992–99); *b* 3 Jan. 1934; *o s* of Sir Walter Buchanan Riddell, 12th Bt, and Hon. Rachel Beatrice Lyttelton (*d* 1965), *y d* of 8th Viscount Cobham; *S* father, 1934; *m* 1969, Hon. Sarah (LVO 1993), *o d* of Baron Richardson of Duntisbourne, KG, MBE, TD, PC; three *s*. *Educ:* Eton; Christ Church, Oxford. 2nd Lieut Rifle Bde, 1952–54. With IBRD, Washington DC, 1969–71; Associate, First Boston Corp., 1972–75; Director: First Boston (Europe) Ltd, 1975–78; UK Provident Instn, 1975–85; Northumbrian Water Gp, 1992–97; Alpha Bank London Ltd, 1995–2004; Chm., Govett Strategic Investment Trust, 1995–2004; Dep. Chm., Credit Suisse First Boston Ltd, 1990–95 (Dir, 1978–85). Dep. Chm., IBA, 1981–85; Private Sec., 1985–90, and Treasurer, 1986–90, to TRH the Prince and Princess of Wales; Member, Prince's Council, 1985–90. Contested (C): Durham NW, Feb. 1974; Sunderland S, Oct. 1974. Mem., Bloomsbury DHA, 1982–85; Dir, Poplar Housing and Regeneration Community Assoc., 1998–2000. Trustee, Guinness Trust, 1998–2001; Mem., Winston Churchill Meml Trust, 2000–07. Chm., Northumbria Regl Cttee, NT, 1995–2003. FRSA 1990. DL Northumberland, 1990. *Heir: s* Walter John Buchanan Riddell [*b* 10 June 1974; *m* 2003, Lucy, *d* of Selwyn Awdry; one *s* three *d* (of whom one *s* one *d* are twins)]. *Address:* Hepple, Morpeth, Northumberland NE65 7LN; 11 Farm Place, W8 7SX. *Clubs:* Garrick; Northern Counties (Newcastle upon Tyne). *Died 24 July 2010.*

RIDDELSDELL, Dame Mildred, DCB 1972; CBE 1958; Second Permanent Secretary, Department of Health and Social Security, 1971–73 (Deputy Secretary, 1966–71); *b* 1 Dec. 1913; 2nd *d* of Rev. H. J. Riddelsdell. *Educ:* St Mary's Hall, Brighton; Bedford Coll., London. Entered Min. of Labour, 1936; Asst Sec., Min. of National Insurance, 1945; Under Secretary, 1950; On loan to United Nations, 1953–56; Secretary, National Incomes Commission, 1962–65; Ministry of Pensions and National Insurance, 1965, Social Security, 1966. Chm., CS Retirement Fellowship, 1974–77. *Recreation:* gardening. *Address:* The Old Prebendal House, Shipton-under-Wychwood, Oxon OX7 6BQ.
Died 25 July 2006.

RIDDLE, Hugh Joseph, (Huseph), RP 1960; artist; portrait painter; *b* 24 May 1912; *s* of late Hugh Howard Riddle and Christine Simons Brown; *m* 1936, Joan Claudia Johnson (*d* 1994); one *s* two *d*. *Educ:* Harrow; Magdalen Coll., Oxford; Slade School of Art; Byam Shaw School of Art and others. Specialises in portraits of children and adults; work includes HRH Prince Edward, aged 9, and HM the Queen. *Recreations:* sailing, swimming, gardening. *Address:* 18 Boulevard Verdi, Domaine du château de Tournon, Montauroux 83440, France. *Died 16 April 2009.*

RIDGE, Anthony Hubert; Director-General, International Bureau, Universal Postal Union, Bern, 1973–74 (Deputy Director-General, 1964–73); *b* 5 Oct. 1913; *s* of Timothy Leopold Ridge and Magdalen (*née* Hernig); *m* 1938, Marjory Joan Sage (*d* 2007); three *s* one *d*. *Educ:* Christ's Hospital; Jesus College, Cambridge. Entered GPO, 1937; seconded to Min. Home Security, 1940; GPO Personnel Dept, 1944; PPS to Postmaster General, 1947; Dep. Dir, London Postal Region, 1949; Asst Sec., Overseas Mails, 1951, Personnel, 1954, Overseas Mails, 1956; Director of Clerical Mechanization and Buildings, and Member of Post Office Board, GPO,

1960–63. Mem., Postling Parish Council, 1979–87. Governor, Christ's Hosp. *Recreations:* music, languages, transport, gardening. *Address:* 36 Pegasus Court, St Stephen's Road, Cheltenham, Glos GL51 3GB. *T:* (01242) 519804. *Clubs:* Christ's Hospital, Oxford and Cambridge, Cambridge Society. *Died 16 Oct. 2010.*

RIDLER, Vivian Hughes, CBE 1971; Printer to the University of Oxford, 1958–78; *b* 2 Oct. 1913; *s* of Bertram Hughes Ridler and Elizabeth Emmeline (*née* Best); *m* 1938, Anne Barbara Bradby, OBE, FRSL, poet (*d* 2001); two *s* two *d*. *Educ:* Bristol Gram. Sch.; MA Oxon 1958 (by decree; Corpus Christi College). Appren. E. S. & A. Robinson, Ltd, 1931–36. Works Manager University Press, Oxford, 1948; Assistant Printer, 1949–58. Pres., British Federation of Master Printers, 1968–69. Professorial Fellow, St Edmund Hall, 1966, Emeritus Fellow, 1978. *Recreations:* printing, theatre, cinema, cinematography. *Address:* 14 Stanley Road, Oxford OX4 1QZ. *T:* (01865) 247595.
Died 11 Jan. 2009.

RIDLEY, Gordon, OBE 1980; FICE, FIHT; retired; Director of Planning and Transportation, Greater London Council, 1978–80; *b* 1 Nov. 1921; *s* of Timothy Ridley and Lallah Sarah Ridley; *m* 1952, Doreen May Browning; one *s* one *d*. *Educ:* Selwyn Coll., Cambridge (MA). FICE 1965; FIMunE 1964; FInstHE 1966. Served War, Admiralty Signals Estab., 1941–46. Engrg appts, various local authorities, 1946–55; Bridges Br., MoT, 1955–58; AEA, 1958–63; LCC, 1963–65; engrg appts, GLC, 1965–78. *Publications:* papers on engrg topics presented to learned instns. *Recreation:* words. *Address:* 26 Greenacres, Preston Park Avenue, Brighton BN1 6HR. *T:* (01273) 559951. *Died 30 July 2006.*

RIDSDALE, Dame Victoire Evelyn Patricia, (Paddy), (Lady Ridsdale), DBE 1991; *b* 11 Oct. 1921; *d* of Col J. and Edith Marion Bennett; *m* 1942, Julian Errington Ridsdale (later Sir Julian Ridsdale, CBE; *d* 2004); one *d*. *Educ:* Sorbonne. Sec., DNI, 1939–42; Sec. to her husband, 1953–2004. Chm., Conservative MPs' Wives, 1978–91. British Gold Hero Award, ARP/050, 1998. *Address:* 12 The Boltons, SW10 9TD. *T:* (020) 7373 6159. *Died 16 Dec. 2009.*

RIGNEY, Howard Ernest; HM Diplomatic Service, retired; Consul-General, Lyons, 1977–82; *b* 22 June 1922; *o s* of late Wilbert Ernest and Minnie Rigney; *m* 1950, Margaret Grayling Benn (*d* 2002); one *s*. *Educ:* Univs of Western Ontario, Toronto and Paris. BA Western Ont. 1945, MA Toronto 1947. Lectr, Univ. of British Columbia, 1946–48; grad. studies, Paris Univ., 1948–50; COI, 1953–56; CRO, 1956; Regional Information Officer, Dacca, 1957–60, Montreal, 1960–63; CRO, 1963–65; FO/CO, 1965–67; Consul (Information), Chicago, 1967–69; Dep. Consul-Gen., Chicago, 1969–71; Head of Chancery and Consul, Rangoon, 1971–73; Head of Migration and Visa Dept, FCO, 1973–77. Hon. DLitt, Winston Churchill Coll., Ill, 1971. *Recreations:* opera, book-collecting, gardening. *Address:* The Old Forge, Frinstead, Sittingbourne, Kent ME9 0TF. *Died 12 Feb. 2009.*

RITCHIE OF DUNDEE, 5th Baron *cr* 1905; Harold Malcolm Ritchie; English and Drama Teacher, Bedgebury School, Kent, retired 1984; Social and Liberal Democrat (formerly Liberal) spokesman on education, House of Lords, 1985–92; *b* 29 Aug. 1919; 4th *s* of 2nd Baron Ritchie of Dundee and Sarah Ruth (*d* 1950), *d* of J. L. Jennings, MP; *S* brother, 1978; *m* 1948, Anne, *d* of late Col C. G. Johnstone, MC; one *s* one *d*. *Educ:* Stowe School; Trinity College, Oxford. MA 1940. Served in Middle East, Italy and Greece, Captain KRRC, 1940–46. Assistant Headmaster, Brickwall House School, Northiam, Sussex, 1952–65; Headmaster, 1965–72. President: Rye Meml Care Centre, 1990–; Arts Dyslexia Trust, 1998–. *Recreations:* gardening, drama, music. *Heir: s* Hon. Charles Rupert Rendall Ritchie [*b* 15 March 1958;

m 1984, Tara Van Tuyl Koch (marr. diss. 1992)]. *Address:* The Roundel, Spring Steps, Winchelsea, Sussex TN36 4EG. *Died 11 Jan. 2008.*

RITCHIE, Prof. J(oseph) Murdoch, PhD, DSc; FRS 1976; Eugene Higgins Professor of Pharmacology, Yale University, 1968–2000, then Emeritus; *b* 10 June 1925; *s* of Alexander Farquharson Ritchie and Agnes Jane (*née* Bremner); *m* 1951, Brenda Rachel (*née* Bigland); one *s* one *d. Educ:* Aberdeen Central Secondary Sch.; Aberdeen Univ. (BSc Maths); UCL (BSc Physiol., PhD, DSc; Fellow 1978). CPhys, FInstP, 1997. Res. in Radar, Telecommunications Res. Establt, Malvern, 1944–46; University Coll. London: Hon. Res. Asst, Biophysics Res. Unit, 1946–49; Lectr in Physiol., 1949–51; Mem. staff, Nat. Inst. for Med. Res., Mill Hill, 1951–55; Asst Prof. of Pharmacology, 1956–57, Associate Prof., 1958–63 and Prof., 1963–68, Albert Einstein Coll. of Medicine, NY; Overseas Fellow, Churchill Coll., Cambridge, 1964–65; Chm., Dept of Pharmacol., 1968–74, Dir, Div. of Biol Scis, 1975–78, Yale Univ. Hon. MA Yale, 1968; Hon. DSc Aberdeen, 1987. *Publications:* papers on nerve and muscle physiol. and biophysics in Jl of Physiol. *Recreations:* ski-ing, chess. *Address:* Apt 526, Whitney Center, Hamden, CT 06517, USA. *T:* (home) (203) 7770420, (office) (203) 7854567. *Club:* Yale (NYC). *Died 9 July 2008.*

RITCHIE, Robert Blackwood, (Robin); grazier running family sheep and cattle property, Western Victoria, 1958–2001; *b* 6 April 1937; *s* of Alan Blackwood Ritchie and Margaret Louise (*née* Whitcomb); *m* 1965, Eda Natalie Sandford Beggs; two *s* one *d. Educ:* Geelong Grammar Sch.; Corpus Christi Coll., Cambridge (MA; Rowing Blue, 1958). Dir, Agricl Investments Australia, 1968–89 (Chm., 1968–85). Exec. Mem., Graziers Assoc. of Vic, 1968–72; Mem., National Rural Adv. Council, 1974–75; Chairman: Exotic Animal Disease Preparedness Consultative Council, 1990–95; Renewable Energy Authority, Vic, 1993–98. Dir-Gen., Min. for Economic Develt, Vic, 1981–83. Geelong Grammar School: Mem. Council, 1966–78 (Chm., 1973–78); Chief Exec., 1979–80 (during period between Head Masters). *Recreation:* sailing. *Address:* 42 Griffith Street, Port Fairy, Vic 3284, Australia. *T:* (55) 681447. *Club:* Melbourne (Melbourne). *Died 9 May 2008.*

RIVETT-CARNAC, Sir Miles (James), 9th Bt *cr* 1836, of Derby; DL; Vice Lord-Lieutenant of Hampshire, 2000–07; *b* 7 Feb. 1933; *s* of Vice-Adm. James William Rivett-Carnac, CB, CBE, DSC (2nd *s* of 6th Bt) (*d* 1970), and Isla Nesta Rivett-Carnac (*d* 1974), *d* of Harry Officer Blackwood; *S* brother, 2004; *m* 1958, April Sally Villar; two *s* one *d. Educ:* Royal Naval College, Dartmouth, RN, 1950–70 (despatches 1965); Commander, 1965; US Staff Coll., 1966; Commanded HMS Dainty, 1967–68; MoD, 1968–70. Joined Barings, 1971; Dir, Baring Bros & Co., 1976; Pres., Baring Bros Inc., 1978; Managing Dir, Baring Bros & Co., 1981; Dep. Chm., Barings plc, 1988–93; Chairman: Baring Asset Management, 1989–93; Baring Securities, 1993–94. Chm., Tribune Investment Trust, 1985–99. Director: London Stock Exchange, 1991–94; Allied Domecq (formerly Allied Lyons) plc, 1992–97. Chm., Hampshire Boys' Clubs, 1982–90. Mem. Council, King George V Fund for Sailors, 1989. Elder Brother, Trinity House, 1992–. High Sheriff, Hants, 1995, DL Hants, 1996. *Recreations:* tennis, golf, shooting, philately (FRPS). *Heir: s* Jonathan James Rivett-Carnac, *b* 14 June 1962. *Address:* 47 Broad Street, Alresford, Hants SO24 9AS. *T:* (01962) 733640. *Clubs:* White's, Naval and Military; Links, Racquet (NY). *Died 15 Sept. 2009.*

RIX, Sir John, Kt 1977; MBE 1955; DL; FREng; Chairman, Seahorse International Ltd, 1986–89; Deputy Chairman, The Victorian Cruise Line Ltd, 1987–96; *b* 30 Jan. 1917; *s* of Reginald Arthur Rix; *m* 1953, Sylvia Gene Howe; two *s* one *d. Educ:* Southampton Univ. FRINA; FIMarEST; FREng (FEng 1979). Chm. and Chief Exec., Vosper Thornycroft (UK) Ltd, 1970–78; Chm. and Dir, Vosper PLC, 1978–85; Chairman: Vosper Shiprepairers

Ltd, 1977–78; David Brown Vosper (Offshore) Ltd, 1978–85; Vosper Hovermarine Ltd, 1980–85; David Brown Gear Industries Ltd, 1980–85; Mainwork Ltd, 1980–85; Director: Vosper Private Ltd, 1966–77 and 1978–85; Charismarine Ltd, 1976–88; Southampton Cable Ltd, 1986–88; Chilworth Centre Ltd, 1986–94. Liveryman, Shipwrights' Co., 1973–. DL Hants 1985. *Recreations:* sailing, tennis, golf, walking. *Address:* Lower Baybridge House, Owslebury, Winchester, Hants SO21 1JN. *T:* (01962) 777306. *Clubs:* Royal Thames Yacht; Hockley Golf. *Died 13 Oct. 2007.*

RIZK, Waheeb, CBE 1984 (OBE 1977); MA, PhD; FREng, FIMechE; Engineering Consultant, W R Associates, since 1986; *b* 11 Nov. 1921; *s* of Dr and Mrs I. Rizk; *m* 1952, Vivien Moyle, MA (Cantab); one *s* one *d* (and one *d* decd). *Educ:* Emmanuel College, Cambridge. MA, PhD. Joined English Electric Co., 1954, Chief Engineer, Gas Turbine Div., 1957, Gen. Manager, new div., combining gas turbines and industrial steam turbines, 1967; after merger with GEC became Man. Dir, GEC Gas Turbines Ltd, 1971; Chairman: GEC-Ruston Gas Turbines Ltd, 1983–86; GEC Diesels Ltd, 1983–86. Chm. of Bd, BSI, 1982–85. Pres., IMechE, 1984–85 (Mem. Council, 1978–89); Mem. Council, Fellowship of Engrg, 1982–85. Pres., Internat. Council on Combustion Engines (CIMAC), 1973–77. Chm., Smallpeice Trust, 1991–98. Mem. Council, Cranfield Inst. of Technology, 1985–95; Member Court: Brunel Univ., 1986–99; Cranfield Univ., 1986–. Liveryman, Worshipful Co. of Engineers. Gold Medal, CIMAC, 1983. *Publications:* technical papers to IMechE, Amer. Soc. of Mech. Engineers and CIMAC. *Recreations:* intelligent tinkering with any mechanism, photography, old motor cycles. *Address:* 231 Hillmorton Road, Rugby CV22 5BD. *T:* (01788) 565093. *Died 15 Aug. 2009.*

ROBBE-GRILLET, Alain; literary consultant, writer and cinéaste; Editions de Minuit, Paris, since 1955; *b* 18 Aug. 1922; *s* of Gaston Robbe-Grillet and Yvonne Canu; *m* 1957, Catherine Rstakian. *Educ:* Lycée Buffon, Paris; Lycée St Louis, Paris; Institut National Agronomique, Paris. Engineer: Institut National de la Statistique, 1945–49; Institut des Fruits et Agrumes Coloniaux, 1949–51. *Films:* L'Immortelle, 1963; Trans-Europ-Express, 1966; L'Homme qui ment, 1968; L'Eden et après, 1970; Glissements progressifs du plaisir, 1974; Le jeu avec le feu, 1975; La belle captive, 1983; Un Bruit qui rend fou, 1995; Gradiva, 2007. *Publications:* Les Gommes, 1953 (The Erasers, 1966); Le Voyeur, 1955 (The Voyeur, 1959); La Jalousie, 1957 (Jealousy, 1960); Dans le labyrinthe, 1959 (In the Labyrinth, 1967); L'Année dernière à Marienbad, 1961 (Last Year in Marienbad, 1962); Instantanés, 1962 (Snapshots, and, Towards a New Novel, 1965); L'Immortelle, 1963 (The Immortal One, 1971); Pour un nouveau roman, 1964; La Maison de rendezvous, 1965 (The House of Assignation, 1968); Projet pour une révolution à New York, 1970 (Project for a Revolution in New York, 1972); Glissements progressifs du plaisir, 1974; Topologie d'une cité fantôme, 1976 (Topology of a Phantom City, 1978); La Belle captive, 1976; Souvenirs du Triangle d'or, 1978 (Recollections of the Golden Triangle, 1985); Un Régicide, 1978; Djinn, 1981; Le Miroir qui revient (autobiog.), 1985 (Ghosts in the Mirror, 1988); Angélique ou l'enchantement (autobiog.), 1988; Les Derniers jours de Corinthe, 1994; La Reprise, 2001; Le Voyageur, 2001; Gradiva, 2003; Scenarios en rose et noir, 2004. *Address:* 18 Boulevard Maillot, 92200 Neuilly-sur-Seine, France. *T:* 47223122. *Died 18 Feb. 2008.*

ROBBINS, Dr (Raymond Frank) Michael, CBE 1987; Director, Polytechnic South West (formerly Plymouth Polytechnic), 1974–89; Hon. Fellow, 1989; *b* 15 Feb. 1928; *s* of Harold and Elsie Robbins; *m* 1955, Eirian Meredith Edwards; two *d. Educ:* Grove Park Grammar Sch., Wrexham; UCW Aberystwyth. PhD 1954; FRIC 1962. Research Chemist, Monsanto Chemicals Ltd, 1954–55; Research Fellow, Univ. of Exeter, 1955–56; Lectr, Nottingham Coll. of Technology, 1956–59; Sen.

Lectr, Hatfield Coll. of Technology, 1960–61; Head of Dept of Chem. Sciences, Hatfield Polytechnic, 1961–70; Dep. Dir, Plymouth Polytechnic, 1970–74. Chm., Sci. Prog. Adv. Gp, PCFC, 1989–92; Mem., British Accreditation Council, 1984–93. *Publications:* papers on organic chemistry in chem. jls, various reviews and articles in sci. and educnl press. *Recreations:* hill walking, creative gardening. *Died 29 Oct. 2008.*

ROBERTS, Angus Thomas; Director of Litigation and Prosecution, Post Office Solicitor's Office (formerly Principal Assistant Solicitor to General Post Office), 1965–74; *b* 28 March 1913; *s* of late Edward Roberts and Margaret (*née* Murray); *m* 1940, Frances Monica, *d* of late Frederick and Agnes Bertha Cane; two *s. Educ:* Felsted School. Admitted Solicitor, 1936. Entered Post Office Solicitor's Dept, 1939. Served in Royal Navy, 1941–46 (Lieut, RNVR). Asst Solicitor to GPO, 1951. *Recreations:* golf, fishing, gardening. *Address:* 8 Watermill Court, Bath Road, Woolhampton, Berks RG7 5RD. *T:* (0118) 971 3075. *Died 6 Oct. 2008.*

ROBERTS, Bertie; Director, Department of the Environment, 1971–79; *b* 4 June 1919; *y s* of late Thomas and Louisa Roberts, Blaengarw, S Wales; *m* 1st, 1946, Dr Peggy Clark (marr. diss.; she *d* 2002); one *s*; 2nd, 1962, Catherine Matthew (*d* 2003). *Educ:* Garw Grammar School. HM Forces, 1942–46, Captain RAOC (active service in France (Normandy), Belgium); leader of study gp on feasibility of using computers in Min. of Public Bldg and Works, 1958; formed and directed operational computer orgn, 1962; Comptroller of Accounts, 1963, also Dir of Computer Services, 1967; Head of Organisation and Methods, 1969; Dir of Estate Management Overseas, Dept of the Environment (with FCO), 1971; Reg. Dir (equiv. Maj.-Gen.), DoE, British Forces Germany, 1976–79. Mem., Community Health Council (Hastings Health Dist), 1982–90. *Recreations:* foreign travel, music. *Club:* Rotary of St Leonard's-on-Sea. *Died 28 Feb. 2007.*

ROBERTS, Maj.-Gen. David Michael, MD; FRCP, FRCPE; equestrian centre proprietor, 1990–95; *b* 9 Sept. 1931; *s* of James Henry and Agnes Louise Roberts; *m* 1964, Angela Louise Squire; one *s* two *d. Educ:* Emanuel Sch., London; Royal Free Hospital School of Medicine (MB, BS). Qualified in medicine, 1954; commissioned RAMC, 1955; service in field units, BAOR, 1955–59; Hon. Registrar in Medicine, Radcliffe Infirmary, Oxford, 1960; various medical specialty appts in military hosps in UK, BAOR and Hong Kong, 1960–75; graded consultant physician, 1968; Joint Professor of Military Medicine, RAMC and RCP, London, 1975–81; Command Cons. Physician, BAOR, 1981–84; Dir of Army Medicine and Cons. Physician to the Army, 1984–88, retired. Consulting Physician, Royal Hosp., Chelsea, 1984–88; MO (Res.), MoD, 1988–90. Lectr in Tropical Medicine, Mddx Hosp. Medical Sch., 1976–81; Examiner in Tropical Medicine for RCP, 1981–88. Mem., British Soc. of Gastroenterology, 1973–90. QHP 1984–88. *Publications:* many articles on gastroenterological subjects. *Recreation:* horse trials follower. *Died 4 Feb. 2006.*

ROBERTS, Denis Edwin, CBE 1974 (MBE (mil.) 1945); Managing Director, Posts, The Post Office, 1977–80; *b* 6 Jan. 1917; *s* of late Edwin and Alice G. Roberts; *m* 1940, Edith (*née* Whitehead) (*d* 2002); two *s. Educ:* Holgate Grammar Sch., Barnsley. Served War of 1939–45, Royal Signals, France, N Africa, Italy and Austria. Entered Post Office, Barnsley, 1933; various appts, 1933–71; Dir Postal Ops, 1971–75; Sen. Dir, Postal Services, 1975–77. Mem., Industrial Tribunal, 1982–86. Chm., British Philatelic Trust, 1981–85. *Address:* Room 7, Cottenham Court Care Home, High Street, Cottenham, Cambridge CB24 8SS. *Club:* City of London. *Died 7 April 2010.*

ROBERTS, Eirlys Rhiwen Cadwaladr, CBE 1977 (OBE 1971); Deputy Director, Consumers' Association (Which?), 1973–77 (Head of Research and Editorial Division, 1958–73); *b* 3 Jan. 1911; *d* of Dr Ellis James

Roberts and Jane Tennant Macaulay; *m* 1941, John Cullen (marr. diss.); no *c. Educ:* Clapham High School; Girton College, Cambridge (BA (Hons) Classics). Sub-editor in Amalgamated Press; Military, then Political Intelligence, 1943–44 and 1944–45; Public Relations in UNRRA, Albanian Mission, 1945–47; Information Division of the Treasury, 1947–57. Chief Exec., Bureau of European Consumer Orgns, 1973–78. Mem., Royal Commn on the Press, 1974–77. Mem., Economic and Social Cttee of EEC, 1973–82 (Chm., Environment and Consumer Protection section, 1978–82); Chm., European Res. into Consumer Affairs, 1978–97. *Publications:* Consumers, 1966. *Recreations:* walking, reading detective novels. *Died 18 March 2008.*

ROBERTS, Sir Gareth (Gwyn), Kt 1997; FRS 1984; FREng; President, Wolfson College, Oxford, since 2001; *b* 16 May 1940; *s* of Edwin and Meri Roberts; *m* 1st, 1962, Charlotte Standen (marr. diss. 1993); two *s* one *d*; 2nd, 1994, Carolyn Mary Butler; two step *d. Educ:* UCNW, Bangor (BSc, PhD, DSc; Hon. Fellow, 1989); MA Oxon 1987. Lectr in Physics, Univ. of Wales, 1963–66; Res. Physicist, Xerox Corp., USA, 1966–68; Sen. Lectr, Reader, and Professor of Physics, NUU, 1968–76; Prof. of Applied Physics and Head, Dept of Applied Physics and Electronics, Univ. of Durham, 1976–85; Chief Scientist, 1985, Dir of Research, 1986–90, Thorn EMI plc; Vice-Chancellor, Univ. of Sheffield, 1991–2000; University of Oxford: Fellow of Brasenose Coll., 1985–95 (Hon. Fellow, 1995) and Vis. Prof. of Electronic Engrg, 1985–93; Vis. Prof. of Sci. Policy, 2004–. BBC/Royal Instn Christmas Lectures, 1988. Member: UFC, 1989–92; HEFCE, 1997–; Bd, Retained Organs Commn, 2001–04; Bd, COPUS, 2001–03; Chairman: Defence Scientific Adv. Council, 1993–97; CVCP, 1995–97; Res. Careers Initiative, 1997–2003; Genome Valley Steering Gp, DTI, 2000–01; HM Treasury Review on Supply of Scientists and Engrg in UK, 2001–02; UK Funding Councils Review of Res. Assessment, 2002–03; Science Learning Networks, 2003–. Review, UK-USA Res. Partnership, Gatsby Foundn, 2006. Chairman: Medical Solutions plc, 2000–; Global Educn Mgt Systems, 2003–; Director: e-University Holding Co., 2001–02; Isis Innovations Ltd, 2001–. Director: Sheffield Develt Corp., 1992–97; DERA, 1994–97; Sheffield HA, 1996–99; Univs Superannuation Scheme, 1997–2001; Yorkshire Forward, 1999–2000; Foundn for Sci. and Technol., 2000–. President: Inst. of Physics, 1998–2000; Science Council, 2000–; Techniquest, 2002–; Assoc. for Sci. Educn, 2006–. Mem. Council, Foundn for Sci. and Technol., 2000–; Chairman: SETNET, 2005– (Mem. Bd, 2002–); Engrg and Technology Bd, 2006–; Trustee, HEFCE Higher Educn Policy Inst., 2002–. Gov., Wellington Coll., 1991–2005. FREng 2003. Hon. Fellow: UCNW, 1990; Univ. of Wales Coll. of Medicine, 1996; NE Wales Inst., 1997. Hon. LLD Wales, 1990; Hon. DSc: UWE, 1997; Sheffield, 2002; Ulster, 2003; Durham, Heriot-Watt, 2005. Holweck Gold Medal and Prize, Inst. of Physics, 1986. *Publications:* Insulating Films on Semiconductors, 1979; Langmuir-Blodgett Films, 1990; many publications and patents on physics of semiconductor devices and molecular electronics. *Recreations:* watching soccer and supporting Tottenham Hotspurs, listening to classical music, hosting town and gown functions. *Address:* Wolfson College, Oxford OX2 6UD. *Died 6 Feb. 2007.*

ROBERTS, Gillian Frances; Academic Registrar, University of London, 1983–2006; *b* 3 Nov. 1944; *d* of late Frank and Mabel Murray; *m* 1969, Andrew Clive Roberts. *Educ:* Sydenham High Sch.; Southampton Univ. (BA Hist., 1966). Academic Dept, London Univ., 1967–83. Trustee: City Parochial Foundn, 1993–2007; Resource Centre (London) Ltd (formerly London Vol. Sector Resource Centre), 1997– (Chm. Bd, 1997–2007). *Address:* Flat 601, 7 High Holborn, WC1V 6DR. *T:* (020) 7430 2369. *Died 9 Sept. 2010.*

ROBERTS, John Lewis, CMG 1987; Assistant Under-Secretary of State (Equipment Collaboration), Ministry of Defence, 1985–88; *b* 21 April 1928; *s* of Thomas Hubert and Meudwen Roberts; *m* 1952, Maureen Jocelyn (*née* Moriarty); two *s*. *Educ:* Pontardawe Grammar Sch.; Trinity Hall, Cambridge. BA (Hons) History. Joined Min. of Civil Aviation, 1950; Private Sec. to the Parly Sec., 1953; Principal: in Railways, then in Sea Transport; branches of MoT and Civil Aviation, 1954–59; Civil Air Attaché, Bonn Embassy, 1959–62; Defence Supply Counsellor, Paris Embassy, 1966–69; Ministry of Defence: Asst Sec., Internat. Policy Div., 1971–74; Assistant Under-Secretary of State: Air MoD PE, 1974–76; Sales, 1976–77; Personnel, (Air), 1977–80; Supply and Organisation, (Air), 1980–82; Internat. and Industrial Policy, PE, 1982–85. FRSA 1988. *Recreations:* angling, sailing. *Died 2 July 2007.*

ROBERTS, (Richard) Julian, FSA, Deputy Librarian, 1986–97, and Keeper of Printed Books, 1974–97, Bodleian Library, Oxford; Fellow of Wolfson College, Oxford, 1975–97, later Emeritus; *b* 18 May 1930; *s* of A. R. and K. M. Roberts; *m* 1957, Anne Ducé; one *s* one *d*. *Educ:* King Edward's Sch., Birmingham; Magdalen Coll., Oxford. MCLIP (ALA 1956); FSA 1983 Asst Keeper, BM, 1958–74. Vicegerent, Wolfson Coll., Oxford, 1983–85. Regents' Prof., UCLA, 1991. Pres., Bibliographical Soc., 1986–88. *Publications:* (ed) Beawty in Raggs: poems by Cardell Goodman, 1958; John Dee's Library Catalogue, 1990; (contrib.) Cambridge History of the Book in Britain, vol. 4, 2002, (contrib.) Cambridge History of Libraries in Britain and Ireland, vols 1 and 2, 2006; contrib. to Library, Book Collector, Bodleian Liby Record, Oxford DNB, etc. *Recreation:* antiquarianism *Address:* St John's Farm House, Tackley, Oxford OX5 3AT. *T:* (01869) 331249. *Died 20 Oct. 2010.*

ROBERTS, Robert Evan, CBE 1976; National General Secretary, National Council of YMCAs, 1965–75; *b* 16 July 1912; *s* of late Robert Thomas Roberts, Llanilar, Denbighshire; *m* 1939, Rhoda, *d* of late William Driver, Burnley, Lancs; one *s* one *d*. *Educ:* Cilcain, Flintshire; Liverpool. YMCA: Asst Sec.: Central YMCA Liverpool, 1933; Hornsey (N London), 1935; Asst Div. Sec., Lancs/Cheshire, 1937; Div. Sec., NW Div. (Cumberland, Westmorland, N Lancs), 1939; Dep. Dir, YMCA Welfare Services, NW Europe, 1944–46; Mem. 21st Army Gp, Council of Voluntary Welfare Work, Normandy, 1944–46 (mentioned in despatches). Nat. Sec., Ireland, 1946; Sec., Personnel Dept, Nat. Council of YMCAs, London, 1948; Nat. Sec., Nat. Council of YMCAs, Wales, 1956–65; Hon. Sec/Treasurer, Assoc. of Secs of YMCAs of Gt Brit. and Ireland, 1963–65; Dep. Chm., Welsh Standing Conf. of Nat. Vol. Youth Orgs. 1963–65. Past Member: Welsh Nat. Council of Social Service; Welsh Jt Educn Cttee; Nat. Inst. of Adult Educn. Member: Nat. Council of Social Service, 1965–75; Brit. Council of Churches (and its Exec.), 1965–74; Council of Voluntary Welfare Work, 1965–75; World Council of YMCAs (and its Finance Cttee), 1965–75; Vice-Pres., Welsh Nat. Council of YMCAs, 1975; Chm., Job Creation Programme, Barrow and S Lakeland, 1976–80; Exec. Member: SE Cumbria Community Health Council, 1977–82; S Lakeland Voluntary Action, 1978–85; S Cumbria Community Health Council, 1982–92 (Vice-Chm., 1986–89); S Cumbria DHA Ethics of Medical Research Cttee, 1983–92; Cumbria FHSA, 1990–92; CHC Observer, Cumbria FPC, 1984–90. Trustee, Framlington Trust, 1973–96. Age Concern: Mem., 1976–82, Vice Chm., 1981–82, Exec. Cttee, Cumbria; Chm., S Lakeland, 1977–82; Exec. Mem. and Trustee, Kendal and Ulveston. Meals on Wheels, 1975–86, Books on Wheels, 1986–97, S Cumbria Social Services Dept. Dist Judge, Cumbria Best Kept Village, 1977–85; Warden, Lakeland Horticultural Soc. Gardens, 1977–98. Fellow, Royal Commonwealth Soc., 1974. Silver Jubilee Medal, 1977. *Recreation:* trying to keep abreast with what's happening

in the world. *Address:* 19 Strand Court, The Esplanade, Grange over Sands, Cumbria LA11 7HH. *T:* (01539) 533277. *Died 10 Aug. 2006.*

ROBERTS, Thomas Somerville; JP; FCILT; Chairman, Milford Haven Conservancy Board, 1976–82; *b* Ruabon, N Wales, 10 Dec. 1911; *s* of Joseph Richard Roberts, Rhosllanerchrugog and Lily Agnes (*née* Caldwell); *m* 1st, 1936, Ruth Moira Teasdale; two *s*; 2nd, 1950, Margaret, (Peggy), Anderson (decd), Sunderland. *Educ:* Roath Park Elem. Sch., Cardiff; Cardiff High Sch.; Balliol Coll., Oxford (Domus Exhibnr). Traffic Apprentice, LNER, 1933; Docks Manager, Middlesbrough and Hartlepool, 1949; Chief Docks Manager: Hull, 1959; S Wales, 1962; Port Dir, S Wales Ports, 1970–75. Chm., S Wales Port Employers, 1962–75; Member: Nat. Jt Council for Port Transport Industry, 1962–75; Nat. Dock Labour Bd, 1970–75; Race Relations Bd, 1968–76. Dir, Develt Corp. for Wales, 1965–80, Vice-Pres. 1979–83; Dep. Chm., Welsh Develt Agency, 1976–80. Member: Court, Univ. of Wales; Pwyllgor Tywysog Cymru (Prince of Wales' Cttee), 1977–81; Exec. Cttee, Welsh Environment Foundn, 1977–. Hon. Fellow and Life Governor, Univ. of Wales Coll. Cardiff (formerly University Coll., Cardiff and UWIST). JP City of Cardiff, 1966. *Recreation:* TV. *Address:* Marcross Lodge, 9 Ely Road, Llandaff, Cardiff CF5 2JE. *T:* (029) 2056 1153. *Died 8 May 2006.*

ROBERTSON OF OAKRIDGE, 2nd Baron *cr* 1961; **William Ronald Robertson;** Bt 1919; Member of the London Stock Exchange, 1973–95; *b* 8 Dec. 1930; *s* of General Lord Robertson of Oakridge, GCB, GBE, KCMG, KCVO, DSO, MC, and Edith (*d* 1982), *d* of late J. B. Macindoe; *S* father, 1974; *m* 1972, Celia Jane, *d* of William P. Elworthy; one *s*. *Educ:* Hilton Coll., Natal; Charterhouse; Staff Coll., Camberley (psc). Served The Royal Scots Greys, 1949–69. Mem. Salters' Co. (Master, 1985–86). *Heir:* *s* Hon. William Brian Elworthy Robertson, *b* 15 Nov. 1975. *Died 18 Jan. 2009.*

ROBERTSON of Brackla, Maj.-Gen. Ian Argyll, CB 1968; MBE 1947; MA; DL; Vice-Lord-Lieutenant, Highland Region (Nairn), 1980–88; Representative in Scotland of Messrs Spink & Son, 1969–76; Chairman, Royal British Legion, Scotland, 1974–77 (Vice-Chairman, 1971–74); *b* 17 July 1913; 2nd *s* of John Argyll Robertson and Sarah Lilian Pitt Healing; *m* 1939, Marjorie Violet Isobel Duncan; two *d*. *Educ:* Winchester Coll.; Trinity Coll., Oxford. Brigade Major: 152 Highland Bde, 1943; 231 Infantry Bde, 1944; GSO2, Staff College, Camberley, 1944–45; AAG, 15 Indian Corps, 1945–46; GSO1, 51 Highland Div., 1952–54; commnd Seaforth Highlanders, 1954; Comdg 1st Bn Seaforth Highlanders, 1954–57; Comdg Support Weapons Wing, 1957–59; Comdg 127 (East Lancs) Inf. Bde, TA, 1959–61; Nat. Defence College, Delhi, 1962–63; Comdg School of Infantry, 1963–64; Commanding 51st Highland Division, 1964–66; Director of Army Equipment Policy, Ministry of Defence, 1966–68. Mem. Council, Nat. Trust for Scotland, 1972–75. DL Nairn 1973. *Recreation:* various in a minor way. *Address:* Gardeners Cottage, Brackla, Nairn IV12 5QY. *T:* (01667) 404220. *Clubs:* Army and Navy, MCC; Vincent's (Oxford). *Died 10 Jan. 2010.*

ROBERTSON, James Downie, MBE 2009; RSA 1989 (ARSA 1974); RSW 1962; RGI 1980; Senior Lecturer in Fine Art (Drawing and Painting), 1975–96, Painter in Residence, 1996–98, Glasgow School of Art; *b* 2 Nov. 1931; *s* of Thomas Robertson and Mary Welsh; *m* 1970, Ursula Orr Crawford (*d* 2009); two step *s* one step *d*. *Educ:* Hillhead High Sch., Glasgow; Glasgow Sch. of Art (DA). Taught at Keith Grammar Sch., 1957–58; Glasgow School of Art: part time Lectr, 1959; Lectr in Drawing and Painting, 1967. Vis. Lectr, Art Schools and Univs, Scotland, England and overseas; one-man exhibitions, 1961–, UK, Ireland, Spain, USA, including: Christopher Hull Gall., London, 1984, 1987, 1989; Jorgensen Fine Art Gall., Dublin, 1995, 2005; Roger Billcliffe Gall., Glasgow, 2000, 2006; retrospective,

Glasgow Sch. of Art, 2000; Scottish Gall., Edinburgh, 2008; numerous group exhibns; annual exhibns at RSA, RSW, RGI, RA; works in public collections of arts socs, art galleries (incl. RSA), corporations, banks, univs and in many private collections. Lectr, Sorbonne Univ., 2007. Hon. DLitt Glasgow, 2001. Awards: RGI, 1971, 1982, 1990; RSW, 1976, 1981, 1987, 1999; RSA, 1993 (Scottish Post Office Award); Shell Exploration and Production Award, 1985; Dunfermline Building Soc. Prize, RSA, 2001. *Recreations:* drawing, painting. *Address:* Carruthmuir, by Kilbarchan, Renfrewshire PA10 2QA. *T:* (01505) 613592. *Club:* Glasgow Art (Pres., 2001–03, 2004–06). *Died 7 Jan. 2010.*

ROBERTSON, Sir Lewis (Findlay), Kt 1991; CBE 1969; FRSE; industrialist, administrator, and corporate recovery specialist; Trustee, Carnegie Trust for Universities of Scotland, since 1963 (Member, Executive Committee, 1963–2003; Chairman, 1990–2003); *b* 28 Nov. 1922; *s* of John Farquharson Robertson and Margaret Arthur; *m* 1950, Elspeth Badenoch (*d* 2001); two *s* one *d* (and one *s* decd). *Educ:* Trinity Coll., Glenalmond. Accountancy training; RAF Intelligence, Bletchley Park. Chm., 1968–70, and Man. Dir, 1965–70, Scott & Robertson Ltd; Chief Executive, 1971–76, and Dep. Chm., 1973–76, Grampian Holdings plc; Director: Scottish and Newcastle Breweries plc, 1975–87; Whitman (International) SA (formerly IC Industries (International) SA), Geneva, 1987–90; Bank of Edinburgh Group (formerly Aristuein), 1990–94; EFM Income Trust plc, 1991–99; Scottish Financial Enterprise, 1991–93; Berkeley Hotel Co., 1995–97; Chairman: Girobank Scotland, 1984–90; Borthwicks (formerly Thomas Borthwick & Sons plc), 1985–89; F. J. C. Lilley, subseq. Lilley, 1986–93; Triplex Lloyd, 1987–90 (F. H. Lloyd Hldgs, 1982–87; Triplex, 1983–87); Havelock Europa plc, 1989–92; Stakis plc, 1991–95; Postern Exec. Gp Ltd, 1991–96. Mem., 1975–76, Dep. Chm. and Chief Exec., Scottish Develt Agency, 1976–81. Chm., Eastern Regional Hosp. Bd (Scotland), 1960–70; Member: Provincial Synod, Episcopal Church of Scotland, 1963–83 (Chm. Policy Cttee, 1974–76); (Sainsbury) Cttee of Enquiry, Pharmaceutical Industry, 1965–67; Court (Finance Convener), Univ. of Dundee, 1967–70; Monopolies and Mergers Commn, 1969–76; Arts Council of GB (and Chm., Scottish Arts Council), 1970–71; Scottish Economic Council, 1977–83; Scottish Post Office Bd, 1984–90; British Council (Chm., Scottish Adv. Cttee), 1978–87; Council, BESO, 1995–98 (Chm., Scotland, 1995–98); Council, Scottish Business School, 1978–82; Restrictive Practices Court, 1983–96; Edinburgh Univ. Press Cttee, 1985–88; Bd, Friends of Royal Scottish Acad., 1986–95; Chairman: Bd for Scotland, BIM, 1981–83; Scotland, Imperial Soc. of Kts Bachelor, 1994–99. Mem., Adv. Bd, Edinburgh edn of Waverley novels, 1984–. Trustee: Foundn for Study of Christianity and Society, 1980–88; RSE Scotland Foundn, 1996–2000 (Chm., 1999–2000); Foundn for Skin Res., 2000–04; Scottish Cancer Foundn, 2000–06; Trustee and Mem. Bd, Advanced Mgt Prog., Scotland, 1996–2003. FRSE 1978 (Mem. Council, 1992–99; Treasurer, 1994–99; Bicentenary Medal, 2001); CCMI (CBIM 1976). Hon. FRCSE 1999. Hon. LLD: Dundee, 1971; Aberdeen, 1999; Hon. DBA Napier, 1992; DUniv: Stirling, 1993; Glasgow, 2003. Lifetime achievement award, Soc. of Turnaround Practitioners, 2004. *Recreations:* foreign travel, computer use, music, reading, listmaking, things Italian. *Address:* Flat 5, 29 Inverleith Place, Edinburgh EH3 5QD. *T:* (0131) 552 3045; *e-mail:* lr32scp@talk21.com. *Clubs:* Athenæum; New (Edinburgh). *Died 24 Nov. 2008.*

ROBERTSON, Patrick Allan Pearson, CMG 1956; *b* 11 Aug. 1913; *s* of A. N. McI. Robertson; *m* 1st, 1939, Penelope Margaret Gaskell (*d* 1966); one *s* two *d*; 2nd, 1975, Lady Stewart-Richardson. *Educ:* Sedbergh School; King's College, Cambridge. Cadet, Tanganyika, 1936; Asst Dist Officer, 1938; Clerk of Exec. and Legislative Councils, 1945–46; Dist Officer, 1948; Principal Asst Sec., 1949; Financial Sec., Aden, 1951; Asst Sec.,

Colonial Office, 1956–57; Chief Sec., Zanzibar, 1958; Civil Sec., Zanzibar, 1961–64; Deputy British Resident, Zanzibar, 1963–64; retired, 1964. Associate Member, Commonwealth Parliamentary Association. *Recreations:* gardening, fishing. *Address:* Lynedale, Longcross, Chertsey, Surrey KT16 0DP. *T:* (01932) 872329. *Died 16 Dec. 2008.*

ROBERTSON, (Richard) Ross, RSA, FRBS; DA; sculptor; *b* Aberdeen, 10 Sept. 1914; *s* of Rev. R. R. Robertson; *m* Kathleen May Matts; two *d*. *Educ:* Glasgow School of Art; Gray's School of Art, Aberdeen (DA). Lectr, Gray's Sch. of Art, 1946–79. FRBS 1963 (ARBS 1951); RSA 1977 (ARSA 1969). *Recreation:* study of art. *Address:* Creaguir, Woodlands Road, Rosemount, Blairgowrie, Perthshire PH10 7JX. *Died 3 May 2007.*

ROBERTSON, Brig. Sidney Park, MBE 1962; TD 1967; JP; Vice Lord-Lieutenant of Orkney, 1987–90; Director, S. & J. D. Robertson Group Ltd (Chairman, 1965–79); *b* 12 March 1914; *s* of John Davie Manson Robertson and Elizabeth Park Sinclair; *m* 1940, Elsa Miller Croy (*d* 1997); one *s* one *d*. *Educ:* Kirkwall Grammar Sch.; Edinburgh Univ. (BCom 1939; Hon. Fellow 1996). MIBS 1936. Served War; commnd RA, 1940 (despatches, NW Europe, 1945). Managerial posts, Anglo-Iranian Oil Co., ME, 1946–51; Manager, Operation/Sales, Southern Div., Shell Mex and BP, 1951–54; founded Robertson firm, 1954. Chm., Orkney Hosps Bd of Management/Orkney Health Bd, 1965–79. Maj. comdg 861 (Ind.) LAA Batt., RA (Orkney and Zetland) TA, 1956–61; Lt-Col comdg Lovat Scouts, TA, 1962–65; CRA 51st Highland Div., TA, 1966–67 (Brig.); Hon. Col, 102 (Ulster and Scottish) Light Air Defence Regt, RA (TA), 1975–80; Hon. Col Comdt, RA, 1977–80; Chm., RA Council of Scotland, 1980–84; Vice Pres., Nat. Artillery Assoc., 1977–; Pres., RBL Scotland, Kirkwall Br., 1957–97; Hon. Vice Pres., RBL Scotland, Highlands and Is Area, 1975–; Hon. President: Orkney Bn, Boys' Bde, 1972–; Friends of St Magnus Cathedral, 1994; Orkney Family History Soc., 1996–2005; Orkney Norway Friendship Assoc., 1999–2005; Vice-Pres., 1985, Life Vice Pres., 1989, RNLI (Chm., 1972–97, Pres., 1997–, Kirkwall Stn Cttee); Hon. Life Vice Pres., Longhope Lifeboat Mus. Trust, 2002; Patron, N Ronaldsay Heritage Trust, 1995–. Pres., Villars Curling Club, 1978–80, 1986–88. DL Orkney, 1968; Hon. Sheriff, Grampian, Highlands and Islands, 1969–. Freedom of Orkney, 1990. Hon. DLitt Napier, 2002. *Recreations:* travel, hill walking, angling. *Address:* Daisybank, Kirkwall, Orkney KW15 1LX. *T:* (01856) 872085. *Clubs:* Army and Navy, Caledonian; New (Edinburgh). *Died 13 Dec. 2008.*

ROBERTSON, Prof. William Bruce, MD, FRCPath; Professor of Histopathology, St George's Hospital Medical School, 1969–84, then Emeritus; Director of Studies, Royal College of Pathologists, 1984–92; *b* 17 Jan. 1923; *s* of late William Bruce Robertson and Jessie Robertson (*née* McLean); *m* 1948, Mary Patricia Burrows (*d* 2003); two *d*. *Educ:* Forfar Academy; Univ. of St Andrews (BSc 1944, MB ChB 1947, MD 1959). MRCPath 1963, FRCPath 1969. Junior appts, Cumberland Infirm., Carlisle, 1947–48; RAMC, E Africa, 1948–50; Registrar Pathology, Cumberland Infirm., 1950–53; Demonstr Pathology, Royal Victoria Infirm., Newcastle upon Tyne, 1953–56; Sen. Lectr Pathology, Univ. of the West Indies, Jamaica, 1956–64; Reader in Morbid Anatomy, St George's Hosp. Med. Sch., Univ. of London, 1964–69. Visiting Professor: Louisiana State Univ., New Orleans, USA, 1961–62; Katholieke Universiteit te Leuven, Belgium, 1972–73. *Publications:* scientific papers and book chapters in various med. jls and publns. *Died 20 April 2008.*

ROBERTSON, Air Cdre William Duncan, CBE 1968; Royal Air Force, retired; Senior Air Staff Officer, HQ 38 Group, Royal Air Force, 1975–77; *b* 24 June 1922; *s* of William and Helen Robertson, Aberdeen; *m* 1st, 1952, Doreen Mary (*d* 1963), *d* of late Comdr G. A.

C. Sharp, DSC, RN (retd); one *s* one *d*; 2nd, 1968, Ute, *d* of late Dr R. Koenig, Wesel, West Germany; one *d*. *Educ*: Robert Gordon's Coll., Aberdeen. Sqdn Comdr, No 101 Sqdn, 1953–55, No 207 Sqdn, 1959–61. Gp Dir, RAF Staff Coll., 1962–65; Station Comdr, RAF Wildenrath, 1965–67; Dep. Dir, Administrative Plans, 1967; Dir of Ops (Plans), 1968; Dir of Ops Air Defence and Overseas, 1969–71; RCDS, 1971–72; SASO RAF Germany, 1972–74; SASO 46 Group, 1975. *Recreations*: golf, tennis. *Address*: Parkhouse Farm, Leigh, Surrey RH2 8QE. *Clubs*: Royal Air Force; Walton Heath Golf. *Died 24 Sept. 2010.*

ROBINS, Malcolm Owen, CBE 1978; Learned Societies Officer, Royal Society/British Academy, 1979–81; a Director, Science Research Council, 1972–78; *b* 25 Feb. 1918; *s* of late Owen Wilfred Robins and Amelia Ada (*née* Wheelwright); *m* 1944, Frances Mary (*d* 2001), *d* of late William and Frances Hand; one *s* one *d*. *Educ*: King Edward's Sch., Stourbridge; Queen's Coll., Oxford (Open Scholar in Science; MA 1943). On scientific staff of Royal Aircraft Establishment, 1940–57; a Div. Supt in Guided Weapons Dept, RAE, 1955–57; Asst Dir, Guided Weapons, Min. of Supply, London, 1957–58; UK Project Manager for jt UK/USA Space Research programme, and hon. Research Associate, University Coll. London, 1958–62; a Dep. Chief Scientific Officer and Head of Space Research Management Unit, Office of Minister for Science, later Dept of Educn and Science, 1962–65; Head of Astronomy, Space and Radio Div., SRC, 1965–68; a Research Planning post in Min. of Technology, later DTI, 1968–72. Vis. Prof., UCL, 1974–77. FInstP 1945; FRAS 1974. *Publications*: (with Sir Harrie Massey) History of British Space Science, 1986; (with K Proust and S. C. B. Gascoigne) The Creation of the Anglo-Australian Observatory, 1990; papers on space research in scientific jls. *Recreation*: reading. *Address*: 4 The Lindens, Great Austins, Farnham, Surrey GU9 8LA. *T*: (01252) 723186. *Died 27 March 2006.*

ROBINSON, Sir Albert (Edward Phineas), Kt 1962; Director, E. Oppenheimer and Son (Pty) Ltd, 1963–2000; *b* 30 Dec. 1915; *s* of late Charles Phineas Robinson (formerly MP Durban, S Africa) and Mabel V. Robinson; *m* 1st, 1944, Mary Judith Bertram (*née* Bertish) (*d* 1973); four *d*; 2nd, 1975, Mrs Madeleine L'Estrange Royston-Piggot (*née* Barrett) (*d* 2005). *Educ*: Durban High School; Universities of Stellenbosch, London (LSE), Cambridge (Trinity Coll.) and Leiden; MA (Cantab). Pres., Footlights Club, Cambridge, 1936–37. Barrister, Lincoln's Inn. Served War of 1939–45, in Imperial Light Horse, Western Desert, N Africa, 1940–43. Member Johannesburg City Council, 1945–48 (Leader United Party in Council, 1946–47); MP (United Party), S African Parlt, 1947–53; became permanent resident in Rhodesia, 1953. Dep. Chm., General Mining and Finance Corp. Ltd, 1963–71; Chairman: Johannesburg Consolidated Investment Co., 1971–80; Rustenburg Platinum Mines, 1971–80; Australian Anglo American Ltd, 1980–85; Director: Anglo American Corp., Zimbabwe Ltd, 1964–86; Founders Bldg Soc., 1954–86; Rand Mines Ltd, 1965–71; Anglo American Corp. of SA Ltd, 1965–88; Johannesburg Consolidated Investment Co., 1965–85; Standard Bank Investment Corp., 1972–86; Director, in Zimbabwe and South Africa, of various Mining, Financial and Industrial Companies. Chm. Central African Airways Corp., 1957–61. Member, Monckton Commission, 1960; High Commissioner in the UK for the Federation of Rhodesia and Nyasaland, 1961–63. Chancellor, Univ. of Bophuthatswana, 1980–91. Hon. DComm Univ. of Bophuthatswana, 1990. *Recreations*: people, music and conversation. *Address*: 43 St Mary Abbots Court, Warwick Gardens, W14 8RB. *Clubs*: Carlton; Country (Johannesburg); Country (Durban). *Died 17 Jan. 2009.*

ROBINSON, (Arthur) Geoffrey, CBE 1978; Chairman, Medway Ports Authority, 1978–87; *b* 22 Aug. 1917; *s* of Arthur Robinson and Frances M. Robinson; *m* 1st, 1943,

Patricia MacAllister (*d* 1971); three *s* one *d*; 2nd, 1973, Hon. Mrs Treves, *d* of Rt Hon. Lord Salmon; three step *s* one step *d*. *Educ*: Lincoln Sch.; Jesus Coll., Cambridge (MA); Sch. of Oriental and African Studies, London Univ. Served War, RA, 1939–46. Solicitor, 1948; Treasury Solicitor's Dept, 1954–62; PLA, 1962–66; Man. Dir, Tees and Hartlepool Port Authority, 1966–77; Chm., English Indust. Estates Corp., 1977–83. Member: National Dock Labour Bd, 1972–77; National Ports Council, 1980–81; Chm., British Ports Assoc., 1983–85. *Publications*: Hedingham Harvest, 1977; various articles. *Recreation*: music. *Died 30 Dec. 2009.*

ROBINSON, Ven. Neil; Archdeacon of Suffolk, 1987–94; *b* 28 Feb. 1929; *s* of James and Alice Robinson; *m* 1956, Kathlyn Williams; two *s* two *d*. *Educ*: Penistone Grammar School; Univ. of Durham (BA, DipTh). Curate of Holy Trinity Church, Hull, 1954–58; Vicar of St Thomas, South Wigston, Leicester, 1958–69; Rector and RD of Market Bosworth, Leicester, 1969–83; Residentiary Canon of Worcester Cathedral, 1983–87. *Recreation*: hill walking. *Address*: 16 Mallorie Court, Ripon, N Yorks HG4 2QG. *T*: (01765) 603075. *Died 4 Oct. 2009.*

ROBINSON, Oswald Horsley, CMG 1983; OBE 1977; HM Diplomatic Service, retired; *b* 24 Aug. 1926; *s* of Sir Edward Stanley Gotch Robinson, CBE, FSA, FBA, and Pamela, *d* of Sir Victor Horsley, CB, FRS; *m* 1954, Helena Faith, *d* of Dr F. R. Seymour; two *s* one *d*. *Educ*: Bedales Sch.; King's Coll., Cambridge. Served RE, 1943–48. Joined FO, 1951; served: Rangoon and Maymyo, 1954; FO, 1958; Mexico and Guatemala, 1961; Quito and Bogotá, 1963; FO (later FCO), 1965; Georgetown, Guyana, 1973; Bangkok, 1976; FCO, 1979–84. Dir, RCC Pilotage Foundn, 1985–95. PCC Medal, 1993. *Publications*: (compiled) Atlantic Spain and Portugal, 1988; *edited*: Ports and Anchorages of the Antilles, 1989; North Africa, 1991; A Baltic Guide, 1992; Faeroes, Iceland and Greenland, 1994; Cruising Notes on the South Atlantic Coast of South America, 1996; Chile: Atacama Desert to Tierra del Fuego, 1998; Mediterranean Spain: part 1, 1998, part 2, 1999. *Recreation*: sailing. *Address*: Dunn House, The Green, Long Melford, Suffolk CO10 9DU. *Clubs*: Royal Cruising, Royal Overseas League. *Died 5 Sept. 2009.*

ROBINSON, Peter; Director, Tootal Ltd, 1973–91; *b* 18 Jan. 1922; *s* of Harold Robinson and Lesley Anne, step *d* of Major J. M. May, TD; two *s* one *d* (and one *d* decd). *Educ*: Prince Henry's Sch., Otley; Leeds Coll. of Technology (Diploma in Printing); Mem., Inst. of Printing. Management Trainee, 1940–41; flying duties, RAFVR, 1942–46; Leeds Coll. of Technol., 1946–49; Asst Manager, Robinson & Sons Ltd, Chesterfield, 1949–53; Works Dir and Man. Dir, Taylowe Ltd, 1953–62; Dir, Hazell Sun, 1964; British Printing Corporation, subseq. BPC: Dir, 1966–68; Man. Dir, 1969–75; Chm. and Chief Exec., 1976–82; Director: Chromoworks Ltd; Petty & Sons Ltd; Purnell & Sons Ltd; Radio Times Ltd; Hazells Offset Ltd; Taylowe Ltd. Formerly Council Mem., PIRA. CCMI. *Recreations*: military history, cricket, golf. *Died 3 Oct. 2007.*

ROBINSON, Rev. Thomas Hugh, CBE 1989; Rector, St Peter's, Cleethorpes, 1998–99; *b* Murree, India, 11 June 1934; *s* of Lt-Col James Arthur Robinson, OBE and Maud Loney Robinson; *m* 1959, Mary Elizabeth Doreen Clingan; two *s* one *d*. *Educ*: Bishop Foy School, Waterford; Trinity Coll., Dublin (BA 1955, MA 1971). Pres., Univ. Philosophical Soc., 1955–56. Ordained deacon 1957, priest 1958; Curate, St Clement's, Belfast, 1957–60; Chaplain, Missions to Seamen, Mombasa, 1961–64; Rector of Youghal, Diocese of Cork, 1964–66; CF, 1966–89; DACG, 2 Armoured Div., 1977–80; Senior Chaplain: RMCS, 1980–82; Eastern Dist, 1982–84; 1st British Corps, 1984–85; BAOR, 1985–86; Dep. Chaplain Gen. to the Forces, 1986–89; Team Rector, Cleethorpes, 1990–98. QHC 1985–89. *Recreations*: travel, photography. *Address*: Brailes View

House, Landgate, Blockley, Moreton in Marsh, Glos GL56 9BX. *T:* (01386) 701189; *e-mail:* brailesview@ tiscali.co.uk. *Died 26 Aug. 2007.*

ROBSON, Prof. Sir (James) Gordon, Kt 1982; CBE 1977; MB, ChB; FRCS; FRCA; Professor of Anaesthetics, University of London, Royal Postgraduate Medical School and Hon. Consultant, Hammersmith Hospital, 1964–86, retired; Chairman, Advisory Committee on Distinction Awards, 1984–94; *b* Stirling, Scot, 18 March 1921; *o s* of late James Cyril Robson and Freda Elizabeth Howard; *m* 1st, 1945, Dr Martha Graham Kennedy (*d* 1975); one *s*; 2nd, 1984, Jennifer Kilpatrick. *Educ:* High Sch. of Stirling; Univ. of Glasgow. FRCS 1977. RAMC, 1945–48 (Captain). Sen. Registrar in Anaesthesia, Western Inf., Glasgow, 1948–52; First Asst, Dept of Anaesthetics, Univ. of Durham, 1952–54; Cons. Anaesth., Royal Inf., Edinburgh, 1954–56; Wellcome Res. Prof. of Anaesth., McGill Univ., Montreal, 1956–64. Consultant Advr in Anaesthetics to DHSS, 1975–84; Hon. Consultant in Anaesthetics to the Army, 1983–88. Royal College of Surgeons: Master, Hunterian Inst., 1982–88. Mem. Bd of Faculty of Anaesthetists, 1968–85 (Dean of Faculty, 1973–76); Mem. Council, 1973–81, 1982–88 (a Vice-Pres., 1977–79); Chm., Jt Cttee on Higher Trng of Anaesthetists, 1973–76; Member: AHA, Ealing, Hammersmith and Hounslow, 1974–77 (NW Met. RHB, 1971–74); Chief Scientists' Res. Cttee and Panel on Med. Res., DHSS, 1973–77; Neurosciences Bd, MRC, 1974–77; Clin. Res. Bd, MRC (Chm. Grants Cttee II), 1969–71; Mem. Council, RPMS (Vice-Chm. Academic Bd, 1973–76; Chm. 1976–80); Mem., Rock Carling Fellowship Panel, 1976–78; Vice-Chm., Jt Consultants' Cttee, 1974–79. Special Trustee, Hammersmith Hosp., 1974–77; Chm., Cttee of Management, Inst. of Basic Med. Scis, 1982–85; Hon. Sec., Conf. of Med. Royal Colls and Their Faculties, UK, 1976–82; Examiner, Primary FFARCS, 1967–73; Member: Editorial Bd (and Cons. Editor), British Jl of Anaesthesia, 1965–85; Edit. Bd, Psychopharmacology; Council, Assoc. of Anaesths of GB and Ire., 1973–84; Physiol. Soc., 1966–; Cttee of AA, 1979–91; Hon. Mem., Assoc. of Univ. Anaesths (USA), 1963–; President: Scottish Soc. of Anaesthetists, 1985–86; RSocMed, 1986–88. Royal National Life-boat Institution: Mem. Cttee of Mgt, 1988–; Life Vice-Pres., 1996 (a Vice-Pres., 1992–); Mem., Med. and Survival Cttee, 1981– (Chm., 1988–91). Sir Arthur Sims Commonwealth Trav. Prof., 1968; Visiting Prof. to many med. centres, USA and Canada; Lectures: Wesley Bourne, McGill Univ., 1965; First Gillies Meml, Dundee, 1978; 2nd Gilmartin, Faculty of Anaesthetists, RCSI, 1986; Morrell Mackenzie, Inst. of Laryngology, 1989; (first) J. D. Robertson Meml, Edinburgh Univ., 1992. Hon. FFARACS 1968; Hon. FFARCSI 1980; Hon. FDSRCS 1979; Hon. FRCP(C) 1988; Hon. FRSocMed 1989; Hon. FRCPSGlas 1993. Hon. DSc: McGill, 1984; Glasgow, 1991. Joseph Clover Medal and Prize, Fac. of Anaesths, RCS, 1972; John Snow Medal, Assoc. of Anaesthetists of GB and Ireland, 1986. *Publications:* on neurophysiol., anaesthesia, pain and central nervous system mechanisms of respiration, in learned jls. *Recreations:* computing, china restoration, writing. *Died 23 Feb. 2007.*

ROBSON, Prof. James Scott, MD; FRCP, FRCPE; Professor of Medicine, University of Edinburgh, 1977–86, then Emeritus; Consultant Physician, and Physician in charge, Medical Renal Unit, Royal Infirmary, Edinburgh, 1959–86; *b* 19 May 1921; *s* of William Scott Robson, FSA and Elizabeth Hannah Watt; *m* 1948, Mary Kynoch MacDonald, MB ChB, FRCPE, *d* of late Alexander MacDonald, Perth; two *s*. *Educ:* Edinburgh Univ. (Mouat Schol.). MB ChB (Hons) 1945, MD 1946; FRCPE 1960, FRCP 1977. Captain, RAMC, India, Palestine and Egypt, 1945–48. Rockefeller Student, NY Univ., 1942–44; Rockefeller Res. Fellow, Harvard Univ., 1949–50. Edinburgh University: Sen. Lectr in Therapeutics, 1959; Reader, 1961; Reader in Medicine, 1968. Hon. Associate Prof., Harvard Univ.,

1962; Merck Sharp & Dohme Vis. Prof., Australia, 1968. External examnr in medicine to several univs in UK and overseas. Mem., Biomed. Res. Cttee, SHHD, 1979–84; Chm., Sub-cttee in Medicine, Nat. Med. Consultative Cttee, 1983–85. Pres., Renal Assoc., London, 1977–80. Hon. Mem., Australasian Soc. of Nephrology. Sometime Mem. Editl Bd, and Dep. Chm., Clinical Science, 1969–73, and other med. jls. *Publications:* (ed with R. Passmore) Companion to Medical Studies, vol. 1, 1968, 3rd edn 1985; vol. 2, 1970, 2nd edn 1980; vol. 3, 1974; contribs on renal physiology and disease to med. books, symposia and jls. *Recreations:* gardening, theatre, reading, writing, contemporary art of Scotland. *Address:* 1 Grant Avenue, Edinburgh EH13 0DS. *T:* (0131) 441 3508. *Died 14 March 2010.*

ROBSON, Prof. Peter Neville, OBE 1983; FRS 1987; FREng; Professor of Electronic and Electrical Engineering, University of Sheffield, 1968–96, then Emeritus; *b* 23 Nov. 1930; *s* of Thomas Murton and Edith Robson; *m* 1957, Anne Ross Miller Semple; one *d*. *Educ:* Cambridge Univ. (BA); PhD Sheffield. FIET, FIEEE. Res. Engr, Metropolitan Vickers Electrical Co., Manchester, 1954–57; Lectr 1957–63, Sen. Lectr 1963–66, Sheffield Univ.; Res. Fellow, Stanford Univ., USA, 1966–67; Reader, University Coll. London, 1967–68. FREng (FEng 1983). *Publications:* Vacuum and Solid State Electronics, 1963; numerous papers on semiconductor devices and electromagnetic theory. *Address:* Department of Electronic and Electrical Engineering, Sheffield University, Mappin Street, Sheffield S1 3JD. *T:* (0114) 222 5131. *Died 10 Jan. 2010.*

ROBSON, Sir Robert William, Kt 2002; CBE 1991; Founder, The Sir Bobby Robson Foundation, 2008; International Football Consultant, Republic of Ireland Football Team, 2006–07; *b* 18 Feb. 1933; *s* of Philip and Lilian Robson; *m* 1955, Elsie Mary Gray; three *s*. *Educ:* Langley Park Primary Sch.; Waterhouses Secondary Mod. Sch., Co. Durham. Professional footballer: Fulham FC, 1950–56 and 1962–67; West Bromwich Albion FC, 1956–62; twenty appearances for England; Manager: Vancouver FC, 1967–68; Fulham FC, 1968–69; Ipswich Town FC, 1969–82 (FA Cup Winners, 1978; UEFA Cup Winners, 1981); England Assoc. Football Team, and Nat. Coach, 1982–90; Manager, PSV Eindhoven, Netherlands, 1990–92 (Dutch Champions, 1990–91, 1991–92); Head Coach: Sporting Lisbon, Portugal, 1992–93; Futebol Clube Do Porto, Portugal, 1994–96 (Portuguese Champions, 1994–95, 1995–96; Portuguese Cup Winners, 1995; Super Cup Winners, 1994, 1995); Coach, Barcelona FC, 1996–98 (Spanish Super Cup, 1996; Eur. Cup Winners Cup, 1997; Spanish Cup, 1997); Head Coach, PSV Eindhoven, Netherlands, 1998–99 (Super Cup Winners, 1999); Manager, Newcastle Utd FC, 1999–2004. Lifetime Achievement Award, BBC Sports Personality of the Year, 2007. Hon. MA UEA, 1997; Hon. DCL Newcastle, 2003. Hon. Freeman, Newcastle upon Tyne, 2005. *Publications:* Time on the Grass (autobiog.), 1982; Farewell But Not Goodbye; my autobiography, 2005; with Bob Harris: So Near and Yet So Far: Bobby Robson's World Cup diary, 1986; Against The Odds, 1990; An Englishman Abroad, 1998. *Recreations:* golf, squash, reading, gardening. *Address:* The Sir Bobby Robson Foundation, Metropolitan House, Longrigg, Swalwell, Newcastle upon Tyne NE16 3AS. *Died 31 July 2009.*

RODDICK, Dame Anita (Lucia), DBE 2003 (OBE 1988); Founder, 1976, and consultant, since 2006, The Body Shop (non-executive Director, 2002–06); *b* 23 Oct. 1942; *d* of Henry Perilli and Gilda de Vita; *m* 1970, (Thomas) Gordon Roddick; two *d*. *Educ:* Maude Allen Secondary Modern Sch. for Girls; Newton Park Coll. of Educn, Bath. 1962–76: worked in library of Internat. Herald Tribune, Paris; Teacher of History and English; worked in Women's Rights Dept, ILO, at UN, Geneva; owned and managed restaurant and hotel; opened first br. of The Body Shop, Brighton, 1976. Man. Dir, to

1994, Chief Exec., 1994–98; Co-Chm., 1998–2002. Trustee: The Body Shop Foundn, 1990–; New Acad. of Business, 1996–; Patron: START, 1987–; Schumacher Coll. for Human Scale Educn, 1991–; Assoc. for Creation Spirituality, 1994–; Findhorn Coll. of Internat. Educn, 1995–; Body and Soul, 1996. DUniv: Sussex, 1988; Open, 1995; Hon. LLD: Nottingham, 1990; New England Coll., 1991; Victoria, Canada, 1995; Hon. DSc Portsmouth, 1994; Hon. DBA Kingston, 1996. Veuve Clicquot Business Woman of the Year, 1984; County NatWest Retailer of the Year, 1988; Global 500 award, UNEP, 1989; World Vision Award, 1991; Internat. Banksia Envmtl Award, 1993; Botwinick Prize in Business Ethics, 1994. *Publications:* Body and Soul, 1991; Business as Unusual, 2000. *Address:* The Body Shop International PLC, Watersmead, Littlehampton, W Sussex BN17 6LS; *e-mail:* info@bodyshop.co.uk.
Died 10 Sept. 2007.

RODOTÀ, Antonio; Director General, European Space Agency, 1997–2003, *b* Cosenza, Italy, 24 Dec. 1935; *s* of Carlo Rodotà and Maria Cristofaro; *m* 1965, Barbara Salvini; one *s* two *d. Educ:* Rome Univ. (BSc Electronic Engrg 1959). Asst Lectr in Radio Engrg, Univ. of Rome, 1959–61; with SISPRE SpA (Italy), 1959–65; Italian delegate to NATO, Paris, 1965–66; Selenia: Head, Electronic Design Gp, 1966–71; i/c engrg, Radar and Systems Div., 1971–76, Head of Div., 1976–80; Dir Gen., CNS (Compagnia Nazionale Satelliti) SpA, 1980–83; Joint Managing Director: Selenia Spazio SpA, 1983–90; Alenia Spazio SpA, 1990–95 (Man. Dir, 1995–96); Alenia Spazio SpA incorporated into Finmeccanica, 1996; Head, Space Div., 1996–97 Chm. and Man. Dir, Quadrics Supercomputer World Ltd. Formerly Dir, several aerospace firms, incl. Arianespace. Vice-Chm., Defence and Space Gp, Italian Nat. Assoc. of Electrical Industries; Mem., Managing Cttee, Italian Aerospace Assoc. Mem., High-Performance Computer Gp, Italian Min. of Res. FRAeS 1997. *Recreations:* ski-ing, tennis, classical music. *Address:* c/o European Space Agency, 8–10 rue Mario Nikis, 75738 Paris Cedex, France.   *Died 23 Feb. 2006.*

RODRIGUES, Sir Alberto, Kt 1966; CBE 1964 (OBE 1960; MBE (mil.) 1948); ED; Senior Unofficial Member Executive Council, Hong Kong, 1964–74; former Pro-Chancellor and Chairman of Executive Council, University of Hong Kong; *b* 5 Nov. 1911; *s* of late Luiz Gonzaga Rodrigues and Giovanina Remedios; *m* 1940, Cynthia Maria da Silva; one *s* two *d. Educ:* St Joseph's College and University of Hong Kong. MB BS Univ. of Hong Kong, 1934; FRCPE 1988. Post graduate work, London and Lisbon, 1935–36; Medical Practitioner, 1937–40; also Medical Officer in Hong Kong Defence Force. POW, 1940–45. Medical Practitioner, 1945–50; Post graduate work, New York, 1951–52; Resident, Winnipeg Maternity Hosp. (Canada), 1952–53; General Medical Practitioner, Hong Kong, 1953. Member: Urban Council (Hong Kong), 1940–41; 1947–50; Legislative Council, 1953–60; Executive Council, 1960–74. Med. Superintendent, St Paul's Hospital, 1953. Director: Jardine Strategic Hldgs (formerly Jardine Securities), 1969; Lap Heng Co. Ltd, 1970; HK & Shanghai Hotels Ltd, 1969; Peak Tramways Co. Ltd, 1971; Li & Fung Ltd, 1973; HK Commercial Broadcasting Co. Ltd, 1974; Hong Kong and Shanghai Banking Corporation, 1974–76. Officer, Ordem de Cristo (Portugal), 1949; Chevalier, Légion d'Honneur (France), 1962; Knight Grand Cross, Order of St Sylvester (Vatican), 1966. *Recreations:* cricket, hockey, tennis, swimming, badminton. *Address:* c/o University of Hong Kong, Pokfulam Road, Hong Kong. *Clubs:* Hong Kong Jockey, Hong Kong Country, Lusitano, Recreio (all Hong Kong).   *Died 5 Feb. 2006.*

RODWELL, Sheila Anne; *see* Bingham, S. A.

ROGERS, General Bernard William; General, United States Army, retired; Supreme Allied Commander, Europe, 1979–87; *b* 16 July 1921; *s* of late Mr and Mrs W. H. Rogers; *m* 1944, Ann Ellen Jones; one *s* two *d. Educ:* Kansas State Coll.; US Mil. Acad. (BS); Oxford Univ. (Rhodes Scholar; BA, MA); US Army Comd Staff Coll., Fort Leavenworth, Kansas; US Army War Coll., Carlisle Barracks, Pa. CO 3rd Bn, 9th Inf. Regt, 2nd Inf. Div., Korea, 1952–53; Bn Comdr 1st Bn, 23rd Inf., 2nd Inf. Div., Fort Lewis, Washington, 1955–56; Comdr, 1st Battle Gp, 19th Inf., Div. COS, 24th Inf. Div., Augsburg, Germany, 1960–61; Exec. Officer to Chm., Jt Chiefs of Staff, Washington, DC, 1962–66; Asst Div. Comdr, 1st Inf. Div., Republic of Vietnam, 1966–67; Comdt of Cadets, US Mil. Acad., 1967–69; Comdg Gen., 5th Inf. Div., Fort Carson, Colo, 1969–70; Chief of Legislative Liaison, Office of Sec. to the Army, Washington, DC, 1971–72; Dep. Chief of Staff for Personnel, Dept of the Army, Washington, DC, 1972–74; Comdg Gen., US Army Forces Comd, Fort McPherson, Ga, 1974–76; Chief of Staff, US Army, Washington, DC, 1976–79. Hon. Fellow, University Coll., Oxford, 1979. Hon. LLD: Akron, 1978; Boston, 1981; Hon. DCL Oxon, 1983. Dist. Graduate Award, US Mil. Acad., 1995; George C. Marshall Medal, Assoc. of US Army, 1999. *Publications:* Cedar Falls-Junction City: a Turning Point, 1974; contribs to: Foreign Affairs, RUSI, 1982; Strategic Review, NATO's Sixteen Nations, 1983; Europa Archiv, Defense, NATO Review, 1984; Europäische Wehrkunde, Rivista Militaire, 1985; The Adelphi Papers, 1986; Soldat und Technik, 1987. *Recreations:* golf, reading. *Address:* 1467 Hampton Ridge Drive, McLean, VA 22101–6023, USA.   *Died 27 Oct. 2008.*

ROGERS, David Bryan, CB 1984; Deputy Secretary and Director General, Board of Inland Revenue, 1981–89; *b* 8 Sept. 1929; *s* of Frank Rogers and Louisa Rogers; *m* 1955, Marjory Geraldine Gilmour Horribine; one *s* two *d. Educ:* Grove Park, Wrexham; University Coll., London (BA Classics). Inspector of Taxes, 1953; Principal Inspector, 1968; Sen. Principal Inspector, 1976; Under Sec. and Dir of Operations, Bd of Inland Revenue, 1978–81. Mem. Council, UCL, 1983–93. *Recreations:* piano, organ, singing, reading.   *Died 6 Nov. 2006.*

ROGERS, Richard Ian; Director, Company Law and Investigations, Department of Trade and Industry, 1997–2003; *b* 10 June 1947; *s* of Charles Murray Rogers and Aileen Mary Seton Rogers (*née* Hole); *m* 1970, (Frances) Alice Monroe; one *s* one *d. Educ:* Monkton Combe Sch.; Queens' Coll., Cambridge (BA). Prison Asst Gov., 1969–72; Brent Family Service Unit, 1972–77; Civil Service, 1977–2003: Depts of Prices and Consumer Protection, of Trade, and of Industry; Department of Trade and Industry: British Steel Privatisation, 1986–88; Projects and Export Policy, 1989–92; Telecoms Policy, 1992–93; Sen. Staff Mgt, 1993–97; Chm., Company Law Review Steering Gp, 1998–2001. *Recreations:* mountains, music and opera, books, heavy gardening, motorcycling. *Address:* 21 Keyes Road, NW2 3XB.   *Died 30 Oct. 2009.*

ROHMER, Eric, (Maurice Henri Joseph Schérer); French film director and writer; *b* 21 March 1920; *s* of Désiré Schérer and Jeanne Monzat; *m* 1957, Thérèse Barbet; two *s. Educ:* Paris. Teacher, 1942–55; journalist, 1951–55. Film critic, Revue du cinéma, Arts, Temps Modernes, La Parisienne, 1949–63; Jt Founder, La Gazette du cinéma (also former Jt Editor). Dir of educnl films for French television, 1964–70. Co-Dir, Société des Films du Losange, 1964–. Films include (director and writer): Charlotte et son steak (short film), 1951; Le signe du lion, 1959; La boulangère de Monceau (short film), 1962; La collectionneuse, 1966; Ma nuit chez Maud, 1969 (prix Max Ophüls, 1970); Le genou de Claire, 1970 (prix Louis-Delluc, prix Méliès, 1971); L'amour l'après-midi, 1972; La Marquise d'O, 1976; Perceval le Gallois, 1978; Le beau mariage, 1982; Pauline à la plage, 1982; Les nuits de la pleine lune, 1984; Le rayon vert (Lion d'or, Venice Film Fest., prix de la critique internationale), 1986; L'ami de mon amie, 1988; Conte de Printemps, 1989; Conte d'Hiver, 1992; L'Arbre, le maire et la médiathèque, 1993; Rendezvous in Paris, 1996; Conte d'Eté, 1996; Conte d'Automne, 1999; L'Anglaise et le

Duc, 2001; Triple Agent, 2004; Les Amours d'Astrée et de Céladon, 2007. Best Dir Award, Berlin Film Fest., 1983; Lifetime Achievement Award, Venice Film Fest., 2001. *Publications:* Alfred Hitchcock, 1973; Charlie Chaplin, 1973; Six contes moraux, 1974; L'organisation de l'espace dans le "Faust" de Murnau, 1977; The Taste for Beauty (essays), 1992; De Mozart en Beethoven, 1996. *Address:* Les Films du Losange, 22 avenue Pierre 1er de Serbie, 75116 Paris, France.   *Died 11 Jan. 2010.*

ROLFE JOHNSON, Anthony, CBE 1992; tenor; *b* 5 Nov. 1940; *m* (marr. diss.); two *s*; *m* Elisabeth Jones Evans; one *s* two *d*. Performed at Glyndebourne, Covent Garden, Hamburg State Opera, La Scala Milan, Royal Albert Hall, Coliseum, Queen Elizabeth Hall, Aldeburgh Festival, Royal Festival Hall, Barbican Centre, Wigmore Hall, Salzburg Festival, Metropolitan NY. Appeared with all major British orchestras and with Chicago Symphony Orchestra, Boston Symphony Orchestra, New York Philharmonic Orchestra and others. *Rôles include:* Ulisse, Orfeo (Monteverdi), Idomeneo, Aschenbach, Peter Grimes, Lucio Silla, Tamino.   *Died 20 July 2010.*

ROMAIN, Roderick Jessel Anidjar; Metropolitan Stipendiary Magistrate, 1972–83; *b* 2 Dec. 1916; *s* of late Artom A. Romain and Winifred (*née* Rodrigues); *m* 1947, Miriam (*d* 1991), *d* of late Semtob Sequerra; one *s* one *d*. *Educ:* Malvern Coll.; Sidney Sussex Coll., Cambridge. Called to the Bar, Middle Temple, 1939. Commissioned from HAC to 27th Field Regt, RA, 1940. Served War of 1939–45; France and Belgium, also N Africa and Italy, JAG Staff, 1943–45; JA at Neuengamme War Crimes Trial. Admitted a Solicitor, 1949, in practice as Partner, in Freke Palmer, Romain & Gassman, until 1972; recalled to Bar, 1973; a Dep. Circuit Judge, 1975–78.   *Died 11 Sept. 2009.*

ROME, Alan Mackenzie, OBE 1997; FSA; architect in private practice, 1960–2002; *b* 24 Oct. 1930; *s* of John and Evelyn Rome; *m* 1956, Mary Lilyan Barnard; one *s* one *d*. *Educ:* King's Sch., Bruton; Royal West of England Academy Sch. of Architecture (DipArch 1955). FRIBA 1971; FSA 1979. Pupil in office of Sir George Oatley, 1947–49; Nat. Service, RE, 1949–50; Asst to Stephen Dykes Bower at Westminster Abbey, 1955–60; Associate Architect with Michael Torrens and Alan Crozier Cole, 1960–64. Architect to: Glastonbury Abbey, 1972–96; Bath Abbey, 1976–97; Lancing Coll. Chapel, 1984–98 (later Architect Emeritus); St Mary Redcliffe, Bristol, 1986–2001, and other churches in Somerset, Devon and Wilts; Deans, Chapters and Cathedrals of: Leicester, 1971–97 (Consultant); Salisbury, 1974–92; Peterborough, 1976–89; Wells, 1979–94; Bristol, 1986–2001; St Edmundsbury, 1991–98; Truro, 1992–2001 (later Architect Emeritus). Member: Council for the Care of Churches, 1972–96 (Mem., Organs Adv. Cttee, 1991–96); Churches Conservation Trust (formerly Redundant Churches Fund), 1980–99; Cttee of Hon. Consulting Architects, Historic Churches Preservation Trust, 1990–95; Bath and Wells DAC, 1978–. Occasional Lectr, Bath and Bristol Univs. *Publications:* (jtly) Bristol Cathedral - History and Architecture, 2000; papers and addresses on architectural subjects. *Recreations:* walking, sketching, music. *Address:* 11 Mayfair Avenue, Nailsea, N Somerset BS48 2LR. *T:* (01275) 853215.   *Died 24 Dec. 2010.*

RONAY, Egon; Founder of the Egon Ronay hotel and restaurant guides (taken over by the Automobile Association, 1985, purchased by Leading Guides Ltd, 1992, all publishing rights reverted to Egon Ronay, 1997); *b* July 1915; *m* 1967, Barbara Greenslade; one *s*, and two *d* of previous marr. *Educ:* School of Piarist Order, Budapest; Univ. of Budapest (LLD); Academy of Commerce, Budapest. Dip. Restaurateurs' Guild, Budapest; FIH. After univ. degree, trained in kitchens of family's five restaurants; continued training abroad, finishing at Dorchester Hotel, London; progressed to management within family concern of 5 restaurants, of which eventually he took charge; emigrated from Hungary, 1946; Gen. Manager, Princes Restaurant,

Piccadilly, then Society Restaurant, Jermyn Street, followed by 96 Restaurant, Piccadilly; opened own restaurant, The Marquee, SW1, 1952–55; started eating-out and general food, wine and tourism weekly column in Daily Telegraph and later Sunday Telegraph, 1954–60, also eating-out guide, 1957; weekly dining out column in Evening News, 1968–74; fortnightly gastronomic column, Sunday Times, 1986–92; Ed.-in-Chief, Egon Ronay Recommends (BAA Airports magazine), 1992–94. Constant team surveyance of catering and rating, BAA's 7 airports, 1992–2002. Founder and Pres., British Acad. of Gastronomes, 1983–; Mem. l'Académie des Gastronomes, France, 1979; Founder, Internat. Acad. of Gastronomy, 1985. Lifetime Achievement Award, Carlton London Restaurant Awards, 1999; Lifetime Achievement Award, Caterer and Hotelkeeper Award, 2001. Médaille de la Ville de Paris, 1983; Chevalier de l'Ordre du Mérite Agricole, 1987. *Publications:* Egon Ronay's Guide to Hotels and Restaurants, annually, 1956–85; Egon Ronay's Just A Bite, annually, 1979–85; Egon Ronay's Pub Guide, annually, 1980–85; Egon Ronay's Guide to 500 Good Restaurants in Europe's main cities, annually, 1983–85; The Unforgettable Dishes of My Life, 1989; Egon Ronay's Guide 2005 to the Top 200 Restaurants in the UK, 2005; Egon Ronay's 2006 Guide to the Best Restaurants and Gastropubs in the UK, 2005; various other guides to Britain and overseas, to ski resorts in Europe, to Scandinavian hotels and restaurants and to eating places in Greece.   *Died 12 June 2010.*

ROOKE, Daphne Marie; author; *b* 6 March 1914; *d* of Robert Pizzey and Marie Knevitt; *m* 1937, Irvin Rooke; one *d*. *Educ:* Durban, S Africa. Hon. DLit Univ. of Natal, 1997. *Publications:* A Grove of Fever Trees, 1950, repr. 2008; Mittee, 1951, repr. 2008; Ratoons, 1953, repr. 2008; The South African Twins, 1953; The Australian Twins, 1954; Wizards' Country, 1957, repr. 2008; The New Zealand Twins, 1957; Beti, 1959; A Lover for Estelle, 1961; The Greyling, 1962, repr. 2008; Diamond Jo, 1965; Boy on the Mountain, 1969; Double Ex!, 1970; Margaretha de la Porte, 1974; A Horse of his Own, 1976; Three Rivers: a memoir, 2003. *Recreation:* walking. *Address:* 4 Brookfield Road, Coton, Cambridge CB23 7PT. *T:* (01954) 210585.   *Died 21 Jan. 2009.*

ROOKE, Sir Denis (Eric), OM 1997; Kt 1977; CBE 1970; BSc (Eng.); FRS 1978; FREng; Chairman, British Gas plc (formerly The Gas Council, then British Gas Corporation), 1976–89 (Deputy Chairman, 1972–76); Chancellor, Loughborough University (formerly Loughborough University of Technology), 1989–2003; *b* 2 April 1924; *yr s* of F. G. Rooke; *m* 1949, Elizabeth Brenda, *d* of D. D. Evans, Ystradgynlais, Brecon; one *d*. *Educ:* Westminster City Sch.; Addey and Stanhope Sch.; University Coll., London (Fellow, 1972). FREng (FEng 1977). Served with REME, UK and India, 1944–48 (Major). Joined staff of S Eastern Gas Bd as Asst Mechanical Engr in coal-tar by-products works, 1949; Dep. Man. of works, 1954; seconded to N Thames Gas Bd, 1957, for work in UK and USA on liquefied natural gas; mem. technical team which sailed in Methane Pioneer on first voyage bringing liquefied natural gas to UK, 1959; S Eastern Gas Bd's Development Engr, 1959; Development Engr, Gas Council, 1960; Mem. for Production and Supplies, 1966–71. Chm., CNAA, 1978–83; Member: Adv. Council for R&D, 1972–77; Adv. Council for Energy Conservation, 1974–77; Offshore Energy Technology Bd, 1975–78; BNOC, 1976–82; NEDC, 1976–80; Energy Commn, 1977–79. President: IGasE, 1975; Assoc. for Science Educn, 1981; Fellowship of Engineering, 1986–91; BAAS, 1990; Inst. of Quality Assce, 1990–92. Foreign Associate, NAE, 1987. Chm., Science Museum, 1995 (Trustee, 1983–95); Comr, Royal Commn for Exhibn of 1851, 1984–2001 (Chm., 1987–2001). Hon. Sen. Fellow, RCA, 1991. Hon. DSc: Salford, 1978; Leeds, 1980; City, 1985; Durham, 1986; Cranfield Inst. of Technol., 1987; London, 1991; Loughborough Univ. of Technol., 1994; Cambridge, 2000; Hon. DTech CNAA, 1986; Hon. LLD Bath, 1987; Hon. DEng: Bradford, 1989; Liverpool,

1994; DUniv Surrey, 1990. KStJ 1989. Rumford Medal, Royal Soc., 1986; Prince Philip Medal, Royal Acad. of Engrg, 1992. *Publications:* papers to Instn of Gas Engrs, World Power Conf., World Petroleum Conf., etc. *Recreations:* photography, listening to music. *Address:* 23 Hardy Road, Blackheath, SE3 7NS. *Clubs:* Athenæum, English-Speaking Union. *Died 2 Sept. 2008.*

ROOKE, Brig. Vera Margaret, CB 1984; CBE 1980; RRC 1973; Matron-in-Chief (Army) and Director of Army Nursing Services, 1981–84; *b* 21 Dec. 1924; *d* of late William James Rooke and Lily Amelia Rooke (*née* Cole). *Educ:* Girls' County Sch., Hove, Sussex. Addenbrooke's Hosp., Cambridge (SRN); Royal Alexandra Children's Hosp., Brighton (RSCN); St Helier Hosp., Carshalton (Midwifery). Joined Queen Alexandra's Royal Army Nursing Corps, 1951; appointments include: service in military hospitals, UK, Egypt, Malta, Singapore; Staff Officer in Work Study; Liaison Officer, QARANC, MoD, 1973–74; Assistant Director of Army Nursing Services and Matron: Military Hosp., Hong Kong, 1975; Royal Herbert Hosp. and Queen Elizabeth Military Hosp., Woolwich, 1976–78; Dep. Dir, Army Nursing Services, HQ UKLF, 1979–80. QHNS, 1981–84. Lt-Col 1972, Col 1975, Brig. 1981. *Recreations:* gardening, walking, cookery, opera. *Address:* c/o Lloyds TSB, 74 Church Road, Hove, Sussex BN3 2EE. *Died 13 Sept. 2009.*

ROOME, Maj. Gen. Oliver McCrea, CBE 1973; Vice Lord-Lieutenant, Isle of Wight, 1987–95; *b* 9 March 1921; *s* of late Maj. Gen. Sir Horace Roome, KCIE, CB, CBE, MC, DL, late Royal Engineers; *m* 1947, Isobel Anstis (*d* 2003), *d* of Rev. A. B. Jordan; two *s* one *d. Educ:* Wellington Coll. Commissioned in Royal Engineers, 1940. Served War: UK, Western Desert, Sicily, Italy, 1939–45. Various appts, UK, Far and Middle East, Berlin, 1946–68; IDC, 1969; Director of Army Recruiting, 1970–73; Chief, Jt Services Liaison Organisation, Bonn, 1973–76. Col Comdt, RE, 1979–84. County Comr, Scouts, Isle of Wight, 1977–85. DL Isle of Wight, 1981–96; High Sheriff of the Isle of Wight, 1983–84. *Recreations:* sailing, youth activities. *Address:* The White Cottage, Hill Lane, Freshwater, Isle of Wight PO40 9TQ. *Clubs:* Royal Ocean Racing, Royal Cruising; Royal Solent Yacht. *Died 8 Nov. 2009.*

ROOT, Rev. Canon Howard Eugene; Preceptor of Malling Abbey, 1993–98; *b* Oak Park, Ill, 13 April 1926; *s* of Howard Root and Flora Hoskins; *m* 1952, Celia (MA Lambeth), *e d* of Col R. T. Holland, CBE, DSO, MC; two *s* two *d. Educ:* Univ. of Southern California (BA 1945; Fellow, 1945–47); St Catherine's Soc., Oxford (BA 1951; MA 1970); Magdalen Coll., Oxford; Ripon Hall, Oxford; Magdalene Coll., Cambridge (MA 1953). Instructor, American Univ., Cairo, 1947–49; Sen Demy, Magdalen Coll., Oxford, and Liddon Student, 1951–53. Deacon, 1953; Priest, 1954. Curate of Trumpington, 1953; Asst Lectr in Divinity, Cambridge, 1953–57; Lectr, 1957–66; Fellow, Emmanuel Coll., Cambridge, 1954–66, Chaplain, 1954–56, Dean, 1956–66; Prof. and Hd of Dept of Theology, Univ. of Southampton, 1966–81; Dir, Anglican Centre, Rome, and Counsellor on Vatican affairs to Archbishop of Canterbury, 1981–91; St Augustine Canon, Canterbury Cathedral, 1980–91, Canon Emeritus, 1991–. Wilde Lectr, Oxford Univ., 1957–60; Senior Denyer and Johnson Scholar, Oxford, 1963–64; Bampton Lectr, Univ. of Oxford, 1972; Pope Adrian VI Chair, Univ. of Louvain, 1979; Vis. Prof., Pontifical Gregorian Univ., Rome, 1984–91. Exam. Chaplain to Bishops of Ripon, 1959–76, Southwark, 1964–81, Bristol, 1965–81, Winchester, 1971–81, and Wakefield, 1977–81; Commissary to Bishop in Jerusalem, 1976–. Delegated Anglican Observer at Second Vatican Council, 1963–65; Consultant, Lambeth Conf., 1968 and 1988. Chm., Archbishops' Commn on Marriage, 1968–71; Member: Academic Council, Ecumenical Inst., Jerusalem, 1966–81; Anglican-RC Preparatory Commn, 1967–68; Archbishops' Commn on Christian Doctrine, 1967–74; Anglican-Roman Catholic Internat. Commn,

1969–81. Hon. Chaplain, Winchester Cathedral, 1966–67; Canon Theologian of Winchester, 1967–80. Mem., BBC/ITV Central Religious Adv. Cttee, 1971–75. Jt Editor, Jl of Theol Studies, 1969–74. Corresp. Fellow, 1993–97, Fellow, 1997–, Pontifical Internat. Marian Acad., Rome. *Address:* Flat 9, Lions Hall, St Thomas Street, Winchester, Hants SO23 9HW. *Club:* Brooks's. *Died 19 Nov. 2007.*

ROPER, Robert Burnell, CB 1978; Chief Land Registrar, 1975–83 (Deputy Chief Land Registrar, 1973–75); *b* 23 Nov. 1921; *s* of late Allen George and Winifred Roper; *m* 1948, Mary Brookes; two *s. Educ:* King's College Sch., Wimbledon; King's Coll., London (LLB (Hons) 1941). Called to Bar, Gray's Inn, 1948. Served War, RAF, 1942–46. Miners' Welfare Commn, 1946–48; Nat. Coal Bd, 1948–49; Treasury Solicitor's Dept, 1949–50; HM Land Registry, 1950–83. *Publications:* (Ruoff and Roper) The Law and Practice of Registered Conveyancing, 3rd edn 1972 to 7th (looseleaf) 2003; Consulting Editor on Land Registration matters for Encyclopaedia of Forms and Precedents (4th edn). *Recreations:* gardening, watching sport. *Address:* 11 Dukes Road, Lindfield, Haywards Heath, West Sussex RH16 2JH. *Died 23 April 2006.*

ROSE, Gerald Gershon, PhD; CChem, FRSC; Director, Thornton Research Centre, Shell Research Ltd, 1975–80; *b* 4 May 1921; *m* 1945, Olive Sylvia; one *s* two *d. Educ:* Hendon County Grammar Sch.; Imperial Coll. of Science and Technology (BSc, ARCS, DIC, PhD). Joined Shell Group, 1944; served in refineries, Stanlow, Trinidad, Singapore and South Africa; General Manager, Shell/BP South Africa Petroleum Refineries, 1963; Manufacturing and Supply Director, Shell/BP Service Co., 1968; Manager, Teesport Refinery, 1971. *Recreations:* golf, tennis, gardening. *Died 1 Feb. 2009.*

ROSE, Jack, CMG 1963; MBE 1954; DFC 1942; *b* 18 Jan. 1917; *s* of late Charles Thomas Rose; *m* 1st, 1940, Margaret Valerie (*d* 1966), 2nd *d* of late Alec Stuart Budd; two *s*; 2nd, 1967, Beryl Elizabeth, 4th *d* of late A. S. Budd. *Educ:* Shooters Hill School; London University. Served RAF, 1938–46 (Wing Commander); served in fighter, fighter/bomber and rocket firing sqdns; France, 1940 and 1944; Battle of Britain; Burma, 1944–45. Joined Colonial Administrative Service, N Rhodesia, 1947; Private Secretary to Governor of Northern Rhodesia, 1950–53; seconded to Colonial Office, 1954–56; Administrative posts, Northern Rhodesia, 1956–60; Administrator, Cayman Islands (seconded), 1960–63; Assistant to Governor, British Guiana, 1963–64 (Actg Governor and Dep. Governor for periods). Member: Professional and Technical 'A' Whitley Council for Health Services, 1965–75 (Chm., 1973–75); Gen. Whitley Council for Health Services, 1973–75; Secretary: Chartered Soc. of Physiotherapy, 1965–75; Salmon and Trout Assoc., 1975–79 (Vice-Pres., 1980–). Chm., Burford Charity Trustees, 1994–2002. *Address:* The Little House, 178 The Hill, Burford, Oxon OX18 4QY. *T:* (01993) 822553. *Died 10 Oct. 2009.*

ROSE, Col (Lewis) John, OBE 1990; Vice Lord-Lieutenant of Bedfordshire, 1991–98; *b* 18 Aug. 1935; *s* of Reginald George Rose and Mary Agnes Rose; *m* 1st, 1964, Aileen Beth Robertson (marr. diss. 1974); two *s*; 2nd, 1978, Gillian Mary King (marr. diss. 2005); one step *s* one step *d. Educ:* Bedford Sch.; College of Law. Served RA, 1954–56; Beds Yeomanry, later Herts & Beds Yeomanry, 1956–67. In practice as solicitor, 1962–. Comdt, Beds ACF, 1976–90; Chm., Beds TA&VR Cttee, 1991–94; Vice Chm. (Mil.), E Anglia TA&VRA, 1994–99. President: Beds Small-bore Shooting Assoc., 1992–2004; Bedford District Scout Council, 1975–2007. DL Bedfordshire, 1981. *Recreations:* shooting, rowing (Pres., Bedford Rowing Club, 1988–91). *Address:* 11 Woodlands Close, Cople, Beds MK44 3UE. *T:* (01234) 838210. *Club:* Leander (Henley on Thames). *Died 9 Jan. 2009.*

ROSE, Mark Willson; Agent General for British Columbia in London, 1992–95; *b* Vancouver, 5 March 1924; *s* of Mark C. Rose and Mildred Willson; *m* 1947, Isabel Phillips; three *d. Educ:* Univ. of British Columbia (BScA); Univ. of Western Washington, USA (MEd). Teacher in Okanagan, 1949; Dist Supervisor for New Westminster schools, 1958; University of British Columbia: Faculty of Educn, 1962 (Mem. Policy Council); Mem. Bd of Alumni Assoc. Exec.; Professor Emeritus 1983. Alderman, Coquitlam, 1966–67; MP (NDP) for Fraser Valley W, then Mission-Port Moody, 1968–83; Mem., standing and special cttees, incl. culture, communications, agriculture, the Constitution and alternative energy, to 1978; Chm., NDP Parly Caucus, 1979–83; MLA (NDP) for Coquitlam-Moody, British Columbia, 1983–91; Opposition House Leader, 1986–91; Mem., parly cttee to review and reform Standing Orders; Mem., Speaker's Bd of Internal Economy. Mem., Rotary Club, London. Freeman, City of London, 1993. *Recreations:* music, travel, handyman, renovations, landscaping. *Club:* University of British Columbia Faculty. *Died 8 March 2008.*

ROSE, William Michael; His Honour Judge Rose; a Circuit Judge, since 1998; *b* 12 July 1949; *s* of Laurence Melville Rose and Anita Rose; *m* 2002, Susan Lawe. *Educ:* Haberdashers' Aske's Sch., Elstree; Univ. of Southampton (LLB Hons). Called to the Bar, Middle Temple, 1972; Asst Recorder, 1992–94; a Recorder, 1994–98. Dir of Studies, Judicial Studies Bd, 2002–04. Mem., Bd of Examrs, Council of Legal Educn/Inns of Court Sch. of Law, 1990–2001. Hon. Vice Pres., Travel and Tourism Lawyers Assoc. Editl Advr, ICSL Manual on Civil Litigation, annually, 1990–; Mem. Editl Bd, Judicial Studies Board Jl, 2000–04; Ed., Blackstone's Civil Practice, 2000– (Ed. in Chief, 2005–). *Publications:* Pleadings Without Tears, 1990, 6th edn 2002; (ed) Blackstone's Guide to the Civil Procedure Rules, 1999; Blackstone's Civil Practice, 2006. *Recreations:* music, reading, su doku, computers, powerboating, James Bond movies, digital photography. *Address:* c/o Wandsworth County Court, 76–78 Upper Richmond Road, Putney, SW15 2SU. *Died 10 May 2007.*

ROSENBLUM, Prof. Robert; Professor of Fine Arts, New York University, USA, since 1967; Curator, Guggenheim Museum, New York, since 1996; *b* 24 July 1927; *m* 1977, Jane Kaplowitz; one *s* one *d. Educ:* Queens Coll., Flushing, NY (BA); Yale Univ. (MA); New York Univ. (PhD); Oxford Univ. (MA). Prof. of Art and Archaeology, Princeton Univ., USA, 1956–66; Slade Prof. of Fine Art, Oxford Univ., 1971–72. Fellow, Amer. Acad. of Arts and Scis, 1984. Frank Jewett Mather Award for Art Criticism, 1981. Chevalier de la Légion d'Honneur (France), 2002. *Publications:* Cubism and Twentieth-Century Art, 1960; Transformations in Late Eighteenth Century Art, 1967; Jean-Auguste-Dominique Ingres, 1967; Frank Stella, 1971; Modern Painting and the Northern Romantic Tradition: Friedrich to Rothko, 1975; French Painting, 1774–1830 (exhibn catalogue), 1975; Andy Warhol: Portraits of the Seventies, 1979; (with H. W. Janson) Nineteenth Century Art, 1984; The Dog in Art from Rococo to Post-Modernism, 1988; The Romantic Child from Runge to Sendak, 1988; Paintings in the Musée d'Orsay, 1989; The Jeff Koons Handbook, 1992; (with H. Geldzahler) Andy Warhol Portraits, 1993; Mel Ramos: Pop images, 1994; The Paintings of August Strindberg: the structure of chaos, 1995; On Modern American Art, 1999; 1900: art at the crossroads, 2000; Introducing Gilbert & George, 2004; articles in learned jls: Art Bulletin; Burlington Magazine; Jl of the Warburg and Courtauld Institutes; La Revue de l'Art, etc. *Address:* Department of Fine Arts, New York University, New York, NY 10003, USA. *T:* (212) 9988180. *Died 6 Dec. 2006.*

ROSENBROCK, Prof. Howard Harry, DSc; FRS 1976; FREng, FIET, FIChemE; Professor of Control Engineering, 1966–87, later Emeritus, Vice-Principal, 1977–79, University of Manchester Institute of Science and Technology, (UMIST); Science Research Council Senior Fellow, 1979–83; *b* 16 Dec. 1920; *s* of Henry Frederick Rosenbrock and Harriett Emily (*née* Gleed); *m* 1950, Cathryn June (*née* Press); one *s* two *d. Educ:* Slough Grammar Sch.; University Coll. London (BSc, PhD; Fellow 1978). Served War, RAFVR, 1941–46. GEC, 1947–48; Electrical Research Assoc., 1949–51; John Brown & Co., 1951–54; Constructors John Brown Ltd, 1954–62 (latterly Research Manager); ADR, Cambridge Univ., 1962–66. Mem. Council, IEE, 1966–70, Vice-Pres., 1977–78; Pres., Inst. of Measurement and Control, 1972–73; Member: Computer Bd, 1972–76; SRC Engineering Bd, 1976–78; SERC/ESRC Jt Cttee, 1981–85. Hon. FInstMC. Hon. DSc Salford, 1987. *Publications:* (with C. Storey) Computational Techniques for Chemical Engineers, 1966; (with C. Storey) Mathematics of Dynamical Systems, 1970; State-space and Multivariable Theory, 1970; Computer-aided Control System Design, 1974; (ed) Designing Human-centred Technology, 1989; Machines with a Purpose, 1990; contribs Proc. IEE, Trans IChemE, Proc. IEEE, Automatica, Internat. Jl Control, etc. *Recreations:* microscopy, photography, 17th and 18th Century literature. *Address:* Linden, Walford Road, Ross-on-Wye, Herefordshire HR9 5PQ. *T:* (01989) 565372. *Died 21 Oct. 2010.*

ROSLING, Peter Edward, CMG 1987; LVO 1972; HM Diplomatic Service, retired; *b* 17 June 1929; *s* of Peregrine Starr and Jessie Rosling; *m* 1950, Kathleen Nuell; three *s. Educ:* grammar school. Served Royal Navy, 1948–50. HM Diplomatic Service, 1946; Belgrade, Innsbruck, Cape Town, Rome (NATO Defence College), FCO; Consul-Gen., Zagreb, 1980–83; High Comr, Lesotho, 1984–88. EC Monitor, EC Monitoring Mission, Croatia, 1991. Mem. Council, British Commonwealth Ex-Services League, 1988–2002. *Recreations:* tennis, walking, bridge. *Address:* Southernhay, Vaughan Way, Dorking, Surrey RH4 3DR. *Died 8 Jan. 2007.*

ROSS, Rev. Dr Andrew Christian, FRHistS; Senior Lecturer in Ecclesiastical History, University of Edinburgh, 1966–99; Principal of New College and Dean of the Faculty of Divinity, 1978–84; *b* 10 May 1931; *s* of George Adams Ross and Christian Glen Walton; *m* 1953, Isabella Joyce Elder; four *s* (one *d* decd). *Educ:* Dalkeith High Sch.; Univ. of Edinburgh (MA, BD; PhD 1968; DLitt 1998); Union Theol Seminary, New York (STM). Served Royal Air Force, Pilot Officer, then FO, 1952–54. Ordained Minister of Church of Scotland, 1958; Minister, Church of Central Africa Presbyterian (Malaŵi), 1958–65; Chm., Lands Tribunal of Nyasaland, then Malaŵi Govt, 1963–65; Vice-Chm., Nat. Tenders Bd of Nyasaland, then Malaŵi, 1963–65. Sen. Studentship in African History, Univ. of Edinburgh, 1965–66; Mem. Court of Univ. of Edinburgh, 1971–73. Chm. Student Affairs Cttee of the Court, 1977–83. Kerr Lectr, Glasgow Univ., 1984; Coll. Lectr, Assembly's Coll., Belfast, 1985. Visiting Professor: Univ. of Witwatersrand, 1984; Dartmouth Coll., USA, 1992; Univ. of Malaŵi, 1997; Res. Fellow, Yale Univ., 1994. FRHistS 1996. *Publications:* chapter in: The Zambesian Past, 1965; Religion in Africa, 1965; Witchcraft and Healing, 1969; David Livingstone and Africa, 1973; Malaŵi, Past and Present, 1974; introd. and ed for micro film-prodn: Life and Work in Central Africa 1885–1914, 1969; The Records of the UMCA 1859–1914, 1971; John Philip: missions, race and politics in South Africa, 1986; A Vision Betrayed: the Jesuits in Japan and China 1542–1742, 1994; Blantyre Mission and Malaŵi, 1996; David Livingstone: mission and empire, 2002; contribs to Union Qly Rev., New Left Rev., Scottish Historical Rev. *Recreation:* watching soccer. *Address:* 20 Forbes Road, Edinburgh EH10 4ED. *T:* (0131) 228 8984. *Died 26 July 2008.*

ROSS GOOBEY, Alastair, CBE 2000; Senior Advisor, Morgan Stanley, since 2002; Chairman, Hermes Focus Asset Management Ltd, since 2002; *b* 6 Dec. 1945; *s* of late George Henry Ross Goobey and of Gladys Edith (née Menzies); *m* 1969, Sarah Georgina Mary Stille; one *s* one *d*. *Educ*: Marlborough Coll.; Trinity Coll., Cambridge (MA Econs). With Kleinwort Benson, 1968–72; Hume Holdings Ltd, 1972–77; Investment Manager, Pension Fund, Courtaulds Ltd, 1977–81; Dir, Geoffrey Morley & Partners Ltd, 1981–85; Special Advr to Chancellor of Exchequer, HM Treasury, 1986–87 and 1991–92; Chief Investment Strategist, James Capel & Co., 1987–93; Chief Exec., Hermes Pensions Mgt Ltd, 1993–2001. Director: Scottish Life, 1978–86; Cheltenham and Gloucester Building Soc., 1989–91 and 1992–97; TR Property Investment Trust plc, 1994–2004 (Chm., 2002–04); GCap Media plc. 2005–; Chm., John Wainwright & Co. Ltd, 1997–. Pres., Investment Property Forum, 1995–2004; Chairman: Private Finance Panel, 1996–97 (Mem., 1995–97); Internat. Corporate Governance Network, 2002–05. Member: Pensions Law Rev. Cttee (Goode Cttee), 1992–93; Council of Lloyd's, 1997–2003; Member: Adv. Cttee on Film Finance, 1995–96; Investment Cttee, Nat. Gallery, 1996–; Opera Bd, Royal Opera House, 1995–97; Council, Nat. Opera Studio Foundn, 1996–. Trustee: Royal Opera House Pension Fund, 1995–; Jean Sainsbury Royal Opera House Fund, 1997–; CancerBACUP, subseq. Cancerbackup, 1999–. Gov., Wellcome Trust, 2002–; Mem. Governing Body, RAM, 2002–. Liveryman, Gold and Silver Wyre Drawers' Co. FRSA. Contested (C) Leicester West, 1979. Hon. RICS 2000; Hon. FIA 2001; Hon. FSIA 2003. *Publications*: The Money Moguls, 1987; (ed jtly) Kluwer Handbook on Pensions, 1988; Bricks & Mortals, 1992, rev. edn 1993. *Recreations*: music, cricket, writing, broadcasting (The Board Game, Radio 4). *Address*: (office) Morgan Stanley, 25 Cabot Square, E14 4QA. *T*: (020) 7425 5111. *Clubs*: Reform, MCC, Bottesford Cricket (Leics). *Died 2 Feb. 2008.*

ROSTROPOVICH, Mstislav, Hon. KBE 1987; 'cellist; Music Director and Conductor, National Symphony Orchestra, Washington, 1977–94; *b* 27 March 1927; *m* 1955, Galina Vishnevskaya, soprano; two *d*. *Educ*: State Conservatoire, Moscow. Played in many concerts in Russia and abroad from 1942; first performance of Shostakovich's 'cello concerto (dedicated to him), Edinburgh Festival, 1960. Series of concerts with London Symphony Orchestra under Gennadi Rozhdestvensky, Festival Hall, 1965 (Gold Medal); first perf. Britten's third cello suite, Aldeburgh, 1974. Pres., Evian Fest., 1987–. Mem. Union of Soviet Composers, 1950–78, 1990–. Holds over 30 honorary degrees including Hon. MusD: St Andrews, 1968; Cambridge, 1975; Harvard, 1976; Yale, 1976; Oxon, 1980. Lenin Prize, 1964; Premium Imperiale (Japan), 1992. US Presidential Medal of Freedom, 1987; Commandeur de la Légion d'Honneur (France), 1987. *Address*: c/o Jonathan Brill, CAMI, 165 West 57th Street, New York, NY 10019, USA. *T*: (212) 8419599, *Fax*: (212) 8419525. *Died 27 April 2007.*

ROTA, Anthony Bertram; Chairman, Bertram Rota Ltd, antiquarian booksellers, since 2003 (Managing Director, 1967–2003); *b* 24 Feb. 1932; *s* of Cyril Bertram Rota and Florence Ellen Rota (née Wright); *m* 1957, Jean Mary Foster Kendall; two *s*. Entered family business, 1952. Vis. Distinguished Fellow, Univ. of Tulsa, 1988. President: Antiquarian Booksellers' Assoc., 1971–72; Internat. League of Antiquarian Booksellers, 1988–91. DeGolyer Medal, Southern Methodist Univ., 1988. *Publications*: Points at Issue, 1984; Life in a London Bookshop, 1989; The Changing Face of Antiquarian Bookselling 1950–2000 AD, 1995; Apart from the Text, 1998; Books in the Blood: memoirs, 2002; articles on book-collecting and bibliography in British and American jls. *Recreations*: cinema, opera, theatre, concerts, watching cricket, walking. *Address*: 31 Long Acre, WC2E 9LT. *T*: (020) 7836 0723. *Clubs*: Garrick; Grolier (New York). *Died 13 Dec. 2009.*

ROTH, Andrew; Director, Parliamentary Profiles, since 1955; *b* NY, 23 April 1919; *s* of Emil and Bertha Roth; *m* 1st, 1941, Renee Knitel (marr. annulled 1949); 2nd,

1949, Mathilda Anna Friederich (marr. diss. 1984); one *s* one *d*; 3rd, 2004, Antoinette Putnam. *Educ*: City Coll. of NY (BSS); Columbia Univ. (MA); Harvard Univ. Reader, City Coll., 1939; Res. Associate, Inst. of Pacific Relations, 1940; US Naval Intell., 1941–45 (Lieut, SG); Editorial Writer, The Nation, 1945–46; Foreign Corresp., Toronto Star Weekly, 1946–50; London Corresp., France Observateur, Sekai, Singapore Standard, 1950–60; Political Correspondent: Manchester Evening News, 1972–84; New Statesman, 1984–97. Editor: Parliamentary Profiles, 1953–; Westminster Confidential, 1955–; Obituarist, Guardian, 1996–. DUniv Open, 1993. *Publications*: Japan Strikes South, 1941; French Interests and Policies in the Far East, 1942; Dilemma in Japan, 1945 (UK 1946); The Business Background of MPs, 1959, 7th edn 1980; The MPs' Chart, 1967, 5th edn 1979; Enoch Powell: Tory Tribune, 1970; Can Parliament Decide…, 1971; Heath and the Heathmen, 1972; Lord on the Board, 1972; The Prime Ministers, Vol. II (Heath chapter), 1975; Sir Harold Wilson: Yorkshire Walter Mitty, 1977; Parliamentary Profiles, 4 vols, 1984–85, 6th series 2003–; New MPs of '92, 1992; Mr Nice Guy and His Chums, 1993; New MPs of '97, 1997; New MPs of '01, 2001. *Recreation*: sketching. *Address*: 34 Somali Road, NW2 3RL. *T*: (office) (020) 7435 6673, *T*: (020) 7794 5884, *Fax*: (020) 7794 5774; 25 rue des Sabotiers, Lanrivain, Bretagne 22480, France. *Died 12 Aug. 2010.*

ROTH, Prof. Sir Martin, Kt 1972; MD; FRCP; FRCPsych; FRS 1996; Professor of Psychiatry, University of Cambridge, 1977–85, then Emeritus; Fellow, Trinity College, Cambridge, since 1977; *b* Budapest, 6 Nov. 1917; *s* of late Samuel Simon and Regina Roth; *m* 1945, Constance Heller; three *d*. *Educ*: Davenant Foundn Sch.; University of London, St Mary's Hospital; DPM; MA Cantab; MD Cantab 1984. FRCP 1958. Formerly: Senior Registrar, Maida Vale, and Maudsley Hosps; Physician, Crichton Royal Hosp., Dumfries; Director of Clinical Research, Graylingwell Hosp.; Prof. of Psychological Medicine, Univ. of Newcastle upon Tyne, 1956–77. Royal College of Physicians' Examiner in Medicine, 1962–64, 1968–72; Mem. Council, 1968–71. Visiting Assistant Professor, in the Department of Psychiatry, McGill University, Montreal, 1954; Consultant, WHO Expert Cttee on Mental Health Problems of Ageing and the Aged, 1958; Member: Med. Cons. Cttee, Nuffield Provincial Hosp. Trust, 1962; Central Health Services Council, Standing Med. Adv. Cttee, Standing Mental Health Adv. Cttee, DHSS, 1966–75; Scientific Adv. Cttee, CIBA Foundn, 1970–; Syndic of Cambridge Univ. Press, 1980–87. Mayne Vis. Prof., Univ. of Queensland, 1968; Albert Sterne Vis. Prof., Univ. of Indiana, 1976; first Andrew Woods Vis. Prof., Univ. of Iowa, 1976; Vis. Prof., Swedish unıvs, 1979–80. Adolf Meyer Lectr, Amer. Psychiatric Assoc., 1971; Linacre Lectr, St John's Coll., Cambridge, 1984. Pres., Section of Psychiatry, RSM, 1968–69; Member: MRC, 1964–68; Clinical Research Board, MRC, 1964–70; Hon. Dir, MRC Group for study of relationship between functional and organic mental disorders, 1962–68. FRCPsych (Foundn Fellow; Pres., 1971–75; Hon. Fellow, 1975); Distinguished Fellow, Amer. Psychiatric Assoc., 1972; FMedSci 2001. Hon. FRCPSGlas. Corresp. Mem., Deutsche Gesellschaft für Psychiatrie und Nervenheilkunde; Hon. Mem., Société Royale de Médecine Mentale de Belgique. Hon. Fellow: Amer. Coll. Neuropsychopharmacology; Canadian Psychiatric Assoc., 1972; Australian and New Zealand College of Psychiatry, 1974. Hon. ScD TCD, 1977; Hon. DSc Indiana, 1993. Burlingame Prize, Royal Medico Psychol Assoc., 1951; First Prize, Anna Monika Foundn, 1977; Paul Hoch Prize, Amer. Psychopathological Assoc., 1979; Gold Florin, City of Florence, 1979; Gold Medal, Soc. of Biological Psychiatry, 1980; Kesten Prize, Univ. of Southern Calif, 1983; Sandoz Prize, Internat. Assoc. of Gerontology, 1985; Gold Medal, Max-Planck Inst., 1986; Camillo Golgi Award in Neuroscience, Italian

Acad. of Neuroscience, 1993; Lifetime Achievement Medal, Soc. of Biological Psychiatry, 1996. Hon. Citizen, Salamanca, Spain, 1975. Co-Editor: British Jl of Psychiatry, 1967; Psychiatric Developments, 1983–89. *Publications:* (with Mayer-Gross and Slater) Clinical Psychiatry, 1954, (with Slater) rev. 3rd edn 1977 (trans. Spanish, Italian, Portuguese, Chinese); (with L. Iversen) Alzheimer's Disease and Related Disorders, 1986; (with J. Kroll) The Reality of Mental Illness, 1986; (jtly) CAMDEX: the Cambridge examination for mental disorders of the elderly, 1988; (ed jtly) Handbook of Anxiety, Vols I–V, 1988, 1990, 1992; (Consultant Ed. and contrib.) The Oxford Companion to the Mind, 2nd edn 2004; papers on psychiatric aspects of ageing, depressive illness, anxiety states, in various psychiatric and medical journals. *Recreations:* music, literature, conversation, travel. *Address:* Trinity College, Cambridge CB2 1TQ. *Died 26 Sept. 2006.*

ROTHSCHILD, Edmund Leopold de, CBE 1997; TD; VMH; Partner, N M Rothschild & Sons Limited, 1946–70 (Senior Partner, 1960–70, Chairman, 1970–75); *b* 2 Jan. 1916; *s* of late Lionel Nathan de Rothschild and Marie Louise Beer; *m* 1st, 1948, Elizabeth Edith Lentner (*d* 1980); two *s* two *d*; 2nd, 1982, Anne, JP, *widow* of J. Malcolm Harrison, OBE. *Educ:* Harrow Sch.; Trinity Coll., Cambridge. Major, RA (TA). Served France, North Africa and Italy, 1939–46 (wounded). Deputy Chairman: Brit. Newfoundland Corp. Ltd, 1963–69; Churchill Falls (Labrador) Corp. Ltd, 1966–69. Mem., Asia Cttee, BNEC, 1970–71, Chm., 1971. Pres., Exbury Gardens Ltd, 2000–. Trustee, Queen's Nursing Inst.; Founder, Res. into Ageing. Pres., Assoc. of Jewish Ex-Servicemen and Women; Vice-Pres., Council of Christians and Jews. Governor, Tech. Univ. of Nova Scotia. Hon. LLD Memorial Univ. of Newfoundland, 1961; Hon. DSc Salford, 1983. VMH 2005. Order of the Sacred Treasure, 1st Class (Japan), 1973. *Publications:* Window on the World, 1949; A Gilt-Edged Life: memoir, 1998. *Recreations:* gardening, fishing. *Address:* Exbury House, Exbury, Southampton SO45 1AF. *Clubs:* White's, Portland, Cavalry and Guards. *Died 17 Jan. 2009.*

ROTHSCHILD, Baron Guy (Edouard Alphonse Paul) de; Officier de la Légion d'Honneur, 1959; *b* 21 May 1909; *s* of late Baron Edouard de Rothschild and Baronne de Rothschild (*née* Germaine Halphen); *m* 1st, 1937, Baronne Alix Schey de Koromla (marr. diss. 1956; she *d* 1982); one *s*; 2nd, 1957, Baronne Marie-Hélène de Zuylen de Nyevelt (who *m* 1st, Comte François de Nicolay; she *d* 1996); one *s*, and one step *s*. *Educ:* Lycées Condorcet et Louis le Grand, Facultés de Droit et des Lettres (Licencié en Droit). Served War of 1939–45 (Croix de Guerre). Associé de MM de Rothschild Frères, 1936–67; President: Compagnie du Chemin de Fer du Nord, 1949–68; Banque Rothschild, 1968–78; Société Imétal, 1975–79. Mem., Société d'Encouragement, 1950–92. Chevalier du Mérite Agricole, 1948. *Publications:* The Whims of Fortune (autobiog.), 1985; Mon ombre Siamoise, 1993; Le Fantôme de Léa, 1998; Les Surprises de la Fortune, 2002. *Recreations:* haras et écurie de courses, golf. *Address:* 2 rue Saint-Louis-en-l'Isle, 75004 Paris, France. *Died 12 June 2007.*

ROUGIER, Hon. Sir Richard George, Kt 1986; Judge of the High Court of Justice, Queen's Bench Division, 1986–2002; *b* 12 Feb. 1932; *s* of late George Ronald Rougier, CBE, QC, and Georgette Heyer, novelist; *m* 1st, 1962, Susanna Allen Flint (*née* Whitworth) (marr. diss. 1996); one *s*; 2nd, 1996, Mrs Judy Williams. *Educ:* Marlborough Coll.; Pembroke Coll., Cambridge (Exhibnr, BA). Called to Bar, Inner Temple, 1956, Bencher 1979. QC 1972; a Recorder, 1973–86; Presiding Judge, Midland and Oxford Circuit, 1990–94. *Recreations:* fishing, golf, bridge. *Clubs:* Garrick; Rye Golf; Burnham and Berrow Golf. *Died 25 Oct. 2007.*

ROUTLEDGE, Alan, CBE 1979; *b* 12 May 1919; *s* of late George and of Rose Routledge, Wallasey, Cheshire; *m* 1949, Irene Hendry, Falkirk, Stirlingshire; one *s* (and one *s* decd). *Educ:* Liscard High Sch., Wallasey. Served Army, Cheshire (Earl of Chester's) Yeomanry, 1939–46. Control Commn for Germany, 1946–51; Diplomatic Wireless Service of FO, later Foreign and Commonwealth Office, 1951–79: Head, Cypher and Signals Branch, 1962; Head, Commns Planning Staff, 1973; Head, Commns Ops Dept, 1979; retired FCO, 1979. *Recreations:* English history, cricket, golf. *Clubs:* Civil Service; Old Liscardians. *Died 25 July 2008.*

ROWE, Andrew John Bernard; DL; *b* 11 Sept. 1935; *s* of John Douglas Rowe and Mary Katharine Storr; *m* 1st, 1960, Alison Boyd (marr. diss.); one *s*; 2nd, 1983, Sheila L. Finkle, PhD; two step *d*. *Educ:* Eton Coll.; Merton Coll., Oxford (MA). Sub Lt RNVR, 1954–56. Schoolmaster, 1959–62; Principal, Scottish Office, 1962–67; Lectr, Edinburgh Univ., 1967–74; Consultant to Voluntary Services Unit, Home Office, 1974; Dir, Community Affairs, Cons. Central Office, 1975–79; self-employed consultant and journalist, 1979–83. MP (C) Mid Kent, 1983–97, Faversham and Mid Kent, 1997–2001. PPS to Minister for Trade, 1992–95. Chm., Parly Panel for Personal Social Services, 1986–92; Member: Public Accounts Cttee, 1995–97; Internat. Develt Cttee, 1997–2001. Chm. Steering Cttee, UK Youth Parlt, 1998–2001. Pres., Kent Youth. *Publications:* Democracy Renewed, 1975; pamphlets and articles incl. Somewhere to Start. *Recreations:* fishing, reading, theatre. *Address:* Knowle Cottage, The Green, Bearsted, Maidstone, Kent ME14 4DN. *Died 21 Nov. 2008.*

ROWE, Robert Stewart, CBE 1969; Director, Leeds City Art Gallery and Temple Newsam House, 1958–83 (and also of Lotherton Hall, 1968–83); *b* 31 Dec. 1920; *s* of late James Stewart Rowe and Mrs A. G. Gillespie; *m* 1953, Barbara Elizabeth Hamilton Baynes; one *s* two *d*. *Educ:* privately; Downing Coll., Cambridge; Richmond Sch. of Art. Served RAF, 1941–46. Asst Keeper of Art, Birmingham Museum and Art Gallery, 1950–56; Dep. Dir, Manchester City Art Galls, 1956–58. Pres., Museums Assoc., 1973–74; Member: Adv. Council, V&A Mus., 1969–74; Arts Council of GB, 1981–86; Fine Arts Adv. Cttee, British Council, 1972–84; Chm., Bar Convent Museum Trust, York, 1986–91; Trustee, Henry Moore Sculpture Trust, 1983–95. Liveryman, Worshipful Co. of Goldsmiths. Hon. LittD Leeds, 1983. *Publications:* Adam Silver, 1965; articles in Burlington Magazine, Museums Jl, etc. *Recreations:* gardening, reading. *Address:* Grove Lodge, Shadwell, Leeds LS17 8LB. *T:* (0113) 265 6365. *Died 27 June 2009.*

ROWE, Dr Roy Ernest, CBE 1977; FREng; consultant; Director General, Cement and Concrete Association, 1977–87; *b* 26 Jan. 1929; *s* of Ernest Walter Rowe and Louisa Rowe; *m* 1954, Lillian Anderson; one *d*. *Educ:* Taunton's Sch., Southampton; Pembroke Coll., Cambridge (MA, ScD). FICE, FIStructE; FREng (FEng 1979). Cement and Concrete Association, later British Cement Association: Research Engineer, 1952–57; Head, Design Research Dept, 1958–65; Dir, R&D, 1966–77. Chm., Engrg Res. Commn, SERC, 1991–93. President: IStructE, 1983–84; Comité Euro-Internat. du Béton, 1987–98. Hon. Mem., Amer. Concrete Inst., 1978; For. Associate, Nat. Acad. of Engineering, USA, 1980. Hon. DEng Leeds, 1984. *Publications:* Concrete Bridge Design, 1962, 3rd impr. 1972; numerous papers in technical and professional jls. *Recreations:* fell walking, listening to music, playing bridge. *Address:* 15 Hollesley Road, Alderton, Woodbridge, Suffolk IP12 3BX. *T:* (01394) 411096. *Died 18 Dec. 2008.*

ROWLAND, David Powys; Stipendiary Magistrate, Mid Glamorgan (formerly Merthyr Tydfil), 1961–89; *b* 7 Aug. 1917; *s* of late Henry Rowland, CBE, Weston-super-Mare; *m* 1st, 1946, Joan (*d* 1958), *d* of late Group Capt. J. McCrae, MBE, Weston-super-Mare; one *s* one *d*; 2nd, 1961, Jenny (marr. diss. 1977), *d* of late Percival Lance,

Swanage, and *widow* of Michael A. Forester-Bennett, Alverstoke; one *s* one *d,* and one step *d*; 3rd, 1980, Diana, *d* of late W. H. Smith, Cannock, and *widow* of Lt-Col W. D. H. McCardie, S Staffs Regt; two step *d. Educ:* Cheltenham Coll.; Oriel Coll., Oxford (BA). Lieut, Royal Welch Fusiliers, 1940–46. Called to Bar, Middle Temple, 1947. Deputy Chairman: Glamorgan QS, 1961–71; Breconshire QS, 1964–71. Mem. Nat. Adv. Council on Training of Magistrates, 1964–73. *Recreations:* fly-fishing, gardening. *Address:* Holmdale, Cwmdu, Crickhowell, Powys NP8 1RY. *T:* (01874) 730635.
Died 6 Oct. 2010.

ROWLANDS, Air Marshal Sir John (Samuel), GC 1943; KBE 1971 (OBE 1954); Consultant, Civil Aviation Administration, 1981–86; *b* 23 Sept. 1915; *s* of late Samuel and Sarah Rowlands; *m* 1942, Constance Wight; two *d. Educ:* Hawarden School; University of Wales (BSc Hons). Joined RAFVR, 1939; permanent commission in RAF, 1945. British Defence Staff, Washington, 1961–63; Imperial Defence College, 1964; Royal Air Force College, Cranwell, 1965–68; First Director General of Training, RAF, 1968–70; AOC-in-C, RAF Maintenance comd, 1970–73; Asst Principal, Sheffield Polytechnic, 1974–80. *Recreations:* photography, tennis, motoring. *Club:* Royal Air Force. *Died 4 June 2006*

ROWLEY, Sir Charles (Robert), 7th Bt *cr* 1836, of Hill House, Berkshire, and 8th Bt *cr* 1786, of Tendring Hall, Suffolk; *b* 15 March 1926; *s* of Sir William Joshua Rowley, 6th Bt and Beatrice Gwendoline, *d* of Rev. Augustus George Kirby; *S* father, 1971; claim proven to Rowley Baronetcy of Tendring Hall, dormant, since 1997, and entered on Official Roll of the Baronetage, 2002; *m* 1952, Astrid, *d* of Sir Arthur Massey, CBE; one *s* one *d. Educ:* Wellington. *Heir: s* Richard Charles Rowley [*b* 14 Aug. 1959; *m* 1989, Alison (marr. diss. 1999), *d* of late Henry Bellingham, and of Mrs Ian Baillie; two *s*]. *Address:* 21 Tedworth Square, SW3 4DR; Naseby Hall, Northamptonshire NN6 6DP. *Died 11 May 2008.*

ROWLEY, Geoffrey William, CBE 1989; Town Clerk, City of London, 1982–91; *b* 9 Sept. 1926; *s* of George Frederick Rowley and Ellen Mary Rowley; *m* 1950, Violet Gertrude Templeman (*d* 2008); one *s* one *d. Educ:* Owens School. FCIPD (FIPM 1974). Served War, Royal Marines, 1944–47. Corporation of the City of London, 1947–: Head, Personnel Sect., 1965–74; Dep. Town Clerk, 1974–82. Trustee, Jubilee Walkway Trust, 1992–. Liveryman, Basketmakers' Co. (Prime Warden, 1990–91). Hon. Fellow, City of London Poly., subseq. London Guildhall Univ., 1991. DCL *hc* City, 1989. Order of White Rose, Finland, 1969; Order of Orange Nassau, Holland, 1982; Légion d'Honneur, France, 1985. OStJ 1987. *Recreations:* sport: badminton, cricket and soccer as a spectator. *Address:* 3 Wensley Avenue, Woodford Green, Essex IG8 9HE. *T:* (020) 8504 6270. *Died 28 April 2010.*

ROXBURGH, Rt Rev. James William; Assistant Bishop, Diocese of Liverpool, since 1991; *b* 5 July 1921; *s* of James Thomas and Margaret Roxburgh; *m* 1st, 1949, Marjorie Winifred (*née* Hipkiss) (*d* 2002); one *s* one *d*; 2nd, 2003, Audrey Patricia (*née* Hawthorne), *widow* of John Howard Wood. *Educ:* Whitgift School; St Catharine's Coll., Cambridge (MA); Wycliffe Hall, Oxford. Deacon 1944, priest 1945; Curate: Christ Church and Holy Trinity, Folkestone, 1944–47; Handsworth, Birmingham, 1947–50; Vicar: St Matthew, Bootle, 1950–56; Drypool, Hull, 1956–65; Barking, 1965–77; Archdeacon of Colchester, 1977–83; Bishop Suffragan, later Area Bishop of Barking, 1983–90. Canon of Chelmsford, 1972–77. Pro-Prolocutor, Convocation of Canterbury, 1977–83. Pres. Barking Rotary Club, 1976–77. Hon. Freeman, Barking and Dagenham, 1990. *Recreations:* travel, philately. *Address:* 3 Grantham, 8 Park Road West, Southport, Merseyside PR9 0JS. *Died 10 Dec. 2007.*

ROYCE, David Nowill; Director-General, Institute of Export, 1980–85; *b* 10 Sept. 1920; *s* of late Bernard Royce and Ida Christine (*née* Nowill); *m* 1942, Esther Sylvia Yule (*d* 2001); two *s* one *d. Educ:* Reading School; Vienna University. Served HM Forces, 1940–46. Major, Intelligence Corps, 1946; Asst Principal, Foreign Office, German Section, 1948; Foreign Service, 1949; First Secretary: Athens, 1953; Saigon, 1955; Foreign Office, 1957; Head of Chancery, Caracas, 1960; Counsellor (Commercial), Bonn, 1963; Counsellor (Commercial) and Consul-Gen., Helsinki, 1967–68; Commercial Inspector, FCO, 1969–71; Dir for Co-ordination of Export Services, DTI, 1971–73; Under-Secretary: Overseas Finance and Planning Div., Dept of Trade, 1973–75; CRE 3 and Export Develt Divs, Dept of Trade, 1975–77; Export Develt Div., Dept of Trade, 1977–80. Hon. Fellow, Inst. of Export, 1985. *Publications:* Successful Exporting for Small Businesses, 1990. *Recreations:* croquet, bridge. *Address:* 5 Sprimont Place, SW3 3HT. *T:* (020) 7589 9148. *Club:* Hurlingham.
Died 31 Dec. 2009

ROZARIO, Most Rev. Michael, STL; Archbishop of Dhaka, (RC), 1978–2005; *b* Solepore, Dhaka, Bangladesh, 18 Jan. 1926; *s* of Urban Rozario. *Educ:* Little Flower Seminary, Dhaka, Bangladesh; St Albert's Seminary, Ranchi, India. Jagannath Coll., Dhaka, Bangladesh, 1948–50; Univ. of Notre Dame, USA, 1951–53; Urbano Univ., Rome, 1953–57. Ordained priest, 1956; Bishop of Dinajpur, 1968. Pres., Catholic Bishops' Conf. of Bangladesh. *Died 18 March 2007.*

RUBYTHON, Eric Gerald, CBE 1978; Member of Aerospace Board, British Aerospace, 1977–83, retired (Deputy Chief Executive of Aircraft Group, 1977–82); *b* 11 Feb. 1921; *s* of Reginald Rubython and Bessie Rubython; *m* 1943, Joan Ellen Mills. Joined Hawker Aircraft Ltd, 1948; Co. Sec., 1953; Exec. Dir, 1959; Dir and Gen. Man., 1960; Divl Dir and Gen. Man., Hawker Blackburn Div., 1963; Hawker Siddeley Aviation: Commercial Dir, 1965; Dir and Gen. Manager, 1970; Chm. and Man. Dir, 1977. *Recreations:* golf, gardening. *Address:* 1230 San Julian Drive, Lake San Marcos, CA 92078–4807, USA. *Died 25 Jan. 2007.*

RUDDOCK, Alan Stephen Dennis; columnist, Sunday Independent, since 2006; *b* 21 July 1960; *s* of John and Doreen Ruddock; *m* 1986, Jacqueline Kilroy; three *s. Educ:* Coll. of St Columba, Dublin; TCD (BA 1983). Reporter: Business Day, Johannesburg, 1984–86; Today newspaper, 1986–89; Business Editor, Sunday Tribune, Dublin, 1989–92; Sunday Times, 1992–96; Man. Editor, Sunday Express, 1996; Projects Editor, Mirror Gp Newspapers, 1996–98; Editor, The Scotsman, 1998–2000; columnist, The Sunday Times, 2004–06. *Publications:* Michael O'Leary: a life in full flight, 2007. *Recreations:* watching sport, ski-ing, tennis. *Address:* Rathmore Park, Tullow, Co. Carlow, Ireland. *T:* (5991) 61179. *Died 30 May 2010.*

RUDDUCK, Prof. Jean, PhD; Professor of Education, University of Cambridge, 2001–04, then Emeritus; Fellow, Homerton College, Cambridge, since 2001; *b* 11 Feb. 1939; *d* of Frank and Dorothy Rudduck; partner, 1971, Prof. Lawrence Stenhouse (*d* 1982); *m* 2005, Prof. John Michael Gray, FBA. *Educ:* Westfield Coll., London (BA 1st cl. Hons English); KCL (PGCE); UEA (PhD Educn). English teacher, Godolphin and Latymer Sch., London, 1961–65; Researcher: Schs Council, 1965–68; Humanities Curriculum Project, 1968–71; Founder Mem., Centre for Applied Res. in Educn, and Lectr, then Sen. Lectr in Educn, UEA, 1971–83; Prof. of Educn, Sheffield Univ., 1983–93; Dir of Res., Homerton Coll., Cambridge, 1994–2001. Pres., British Educnl Res. Assoc., 1995. AcSS 2002. Hon. FCP 1998. *Publications:* Dissemination of Innovation: the Humanities Curriculum Project, 1976; Learning Through Small Group Discussion, 1978; Making the Most of the Short In-Service Course, 1981; The Sixth Form and Libraries, 1984; Research as a Basis for

Teaching, 1985; A Room Full of Children Thinking, 1985; Co-operative Group Work, 1989; Innovation and Change, 1991; Dimensions of Discipline, 1993; Developing a Gender Policy in Secondary Schools, 1994; An Education that Empowers, 1995; School Improvement: what can pupils tell us?, 1996; Educational Research: the challenges facing us, 1999; How to Improve Your School: giving pupils a voice, 2004; Improving Learning through Consulting Pupils, 2007. *Recreations:* reading, music. *Address:* Scales Barn, 1 Pearces Yard, Grantchester, Cambridge CB3 9NZ; *e-mail:* jr10026@cam.ac.uk.   *Died 28 March 2007.*

RUFFLE, Mary, (Mrs Thomas Ruffle); *see* Dilnot, M.

RUGGLES-BRISE, Col Sir John Archibald, 2nd Bt *cr* 1935; CB 1958; OBE (mil.) 1945; TD; JP; Lord-Lieutenant of Essex, 1958–78; first Pro-Chancellor, University of Essex, 1964–79; *b* 13 June 1908; *er s* of Colonel Sir Edward Archibald Ruggles-Brise, 1st Bt, MC, TD, DL, JP, MP, and Agatha (*d* 1937), *e d* of J. H. Gurney, DL, JP, of Keswick Hall, Norfolk; *S* father, 1942. *Educ:* Eton. Served AA Comd, 1939–45 (comd 1st 450 Mixed HAA Regt, and 2nd AA Demonstration and User Trials Regt); formed and comd 599 HAA Regt, 1947. Member of Lloyd's. Pres., CLA, 1957–59 (helped promote Game Fair); Church Comr, 1959–64; Chm., Council of the Baronetage, 1958–63. Formerly Chm. Promotion Cttee, 1959, then Chm. Council, Univ. of Essex. Patron, Essex Agricl Soc., 1970–78. Liveryman, Spectacle Makers' Co., 1948–. DL 1945, JP 1946, Vice-Lieutenant, 1947, Co. Essex. Hon. Freeman of Chelmsford. Governor of Felsted and Chigwell Schools, 1950–75. DUniv Essex, 1980. KStJ. *Recreation:* shooting. *Heir: nephew* Timothy Edward Ruggles-Brise [*b* 11 April 1945; *m* 1975, Rosemary Craig; three *s* two *d*]. *Address:* Spains Hall, Finchingfield, Essex CM7 4PF. *T:* (01371) 810276.   *Died 20 Feb. 2007.*

RUMBOLD, Rt Hon. Dame Angela (Claire Rosemary), DBE 1992 (CBE 1981); PC 1991; a Vice Chairman, Conservative Party, 1995–97 (a Deputy Chairman, 1992–95); *b* 11 Aug. 1932; *d* of late Harry Jones, FRS; *m* 1958, John Marix Rumbold; two *s* one *d*. *Educ:* Perse Sch. for Girls; Notting Hill and Ealing High Sch.; King's Coll., London. Founder Member, National Assoc. for the Welfare of Children in Hospital, and National Chairman, 1974–76. Councillor, Royal Borough of Kingston upon Thames, 1974–83; Chm., Council, Local Educn Authorities, 1979–80. Mem., Doctors and Dentists Review Body, 1979–81. Co-Chm., Women's Nat. Commn, 1986–90. MP (C) Merton, Mitcham and Morden, June 1982–1983, Mitcham and Morden 1983–97; contested (C) Mitcham and Morden, 1997. PPS to Financial Sec. to the Treasury, 1983, to Sec. of State for Transport, 1983–85; Parly Under Sec. of State, DoE, 1985–86; Minister of State, DES, 1986–90, Home Office, 1990–92. Mem., Social Services Select Cttee, 1982–83. Chairman: Minerva Fund, GDST, 1993–2001; GBGSA, 2001–; United Learning Trust, 2002–; Co-Chm., Assoc. of Governing Bodies of Ind. Schs, 2001–07; Dir, United Church Schs Trust (formerly Church Schs Co.), 2000–. Chairman of Governors: Mill Hill Sch. Foundn, 1995–2004; Wimbledon High Sch., 1999–2005; Governor: Danes Hill Prep. Sch., 1998– (Chm., Vernon Educn Trust, 2005); More House Sch., 2000–02; Chm., Surbiton High Sch., 2006–. Freeman, City of London, 1988. *Recreations:* swimming, cinema, reading, ballet.   *Died 19 June 2010.*

RUNACRES, Eric Arthur; *b* 22 Aug. 1916; *s* of Arthur Selwyn Runacres and Mildred May (*née* Dye); *m* 1950, Penelope Jane Elizabeth Luxmoore; one *s* one *d*. *Educ:* Dulwich College; Merton College, Oxford (Postmaster; 1st cl. hons Lit. Hum. 1939). Commissioned Royal Engineers, Oct. 1939; served UK, Malta, Middle East, India, 1939–46 (Major). J. & P. Coats Ltd, 1946–48. Entered HM Foreign Service, 1948; First Secretary, 1951–53. British Productivity Council, 1954–71 (Deputy Director, 1959–71, and Secretary, 1962–71); Vice-Chm.,

OECD, Cttee on National Productivity Centres, 1960–66; Exec. Director, Commonwealth Agricultural Bureaux, 1973–77; Consultant, Industrial Facts & Forecasting Ltd, 1978–81. *Recreation:* European thought and literature. *Address:* Gables, Radbone Hill, Over Norton, Oxon OX7 5RA. *T:* (01608) 643264.
            Died 29 May 2006.

RUNGE, Charles David; Hon. Secretary, Royal Agricultural Society of the Commonwealth, since 2000; Chief Executive, Royal Agricultural Society of England, 1992–2000; *b* 24 May 1944; *s* of Sir Peter Runge and late Hon. Fiona Margaret Stewart (*née* Macpherson), *d* of 1st Baron Strathcarron, PC, KC; *m* 1st, 1969, Harriet (marr. diss. 1979), *d* of late John Bradshaw; one *s* one *d*; 2nd, 1981, Jil, *d* of late John Liddell, Greenock; one *d*. *Educ:* Eton; Christ Church, Oxford (MA Nat. Scis); Manchester Business Sch. Tate & Lyle: Man. Dir, Transport, 1977–79; Chief Exec., Refineries, 1979–81; Man. Dir, Agribusiness, 1983–86; Dir of Corporate Affairs, 1986–87; Chief Exec., MMB, 1988–92. *Recreations:* music, walking, fishing. *Address:* Little Finings, Lane End, High Wycombe, Bucks HP14 3LP; Royal Agricultural Society of the Commonwealth, 2 Grosvenor Gardens, SW1W 0DH. *Clubs:* Boodle's, Royal Commonwealth Society.   *Died 8 Feb. 2006.*

RUSHFORD, Antony Redfern, CMG 1963; consultant on constitutional, international and commonwealth law; *b* 9 Feb. 1922; *m* 1975, June Jeffrey, *widow* of Roy Eustace Wells; one step *s* one step *d*. *Educ:* Taunton Sch.; Trinity Coll., Cambridge (BA 1948; LLM (LLB 1948); MA 1951). RAFVR, 1942 (active service, 1943–47, reserve, 1947–59); Sqdn Ldr, 1946. Solicitor, 1944–57 (distinction in Law Soc. final exams, 1942); Called to the Bar, Inner Temple, 1983. Asst Solicitor, E. W. Marshall Harvey & Dalton, 1948. Home Civil Service, Colonial Office, 1949–68; joined HM Diplomatic Service, 1968; CO, later FCO, retd as Dep. Legal Advr (Asst Under-Sec. of State), 1982. Crown Counsel, Uganda, 1954; Principal Legal Adviser, British Indian Ocean Territory, 1983; Attorney-Gen., Anguilla, and St Helena, 1983; Legal Adviser for Commonwealth Sec.-Gen. to Governor-Gen. of Grenada, Mem. Interim Govt, Attorney-Gen., and JP, Grenada, 1983; consultancies: FCO (special duties), 1982; Commonwealth Sec.-Gen., St Kitts and Nevis independence, 1982–83, St Lucia treaties, 1983–85; E Caribbean courts, 1983; maritime legislation for Jamaica, Internat. Maritime Orgn, 1983 and 1985; constitutional advr, Govt of St Kitts and Nevis, and Govt of St Lucia, 1982–85. Drafted many constitutions for UK dependencies and Commonwealth countries attaining independence; presented paper on constitutional develt to meeting of Law Officers from Smaller Commonwealth Jurisdictions, IoM, 1983. UK deleg. or advr at many constitutional confs and discussions; CO Rep., Inst. of Advanced Legal Studies; participant, Symposium on Federalism, Chicago, 1962; Advr, Commonwealth Law Ministers Conf., 1973. Lectr, Overseas Legal Officers Course, 1964; Special Examnr, London Univ., 1963, 1987; a dir of studies, RIPA (Overseas Services Unit), and also associate consultant on statute law, 1982–86. Mem. Editl Bd, Inst. of Internat. Law and Econ. Develt, Washington, 1977–82. Co. Sec., Forwardstrike Ltd, 1997–. Foundn Mem. Exec. Council, Royal Commonwealth Soc. for the Blind, 1969–81, 1983–99 (Hon. Legal Counsellor, 1984–2001; Indiv. Mem., 1998–); Hon. Sec., Services Race Club, Hong Kong, 1946–47. Member: Glyndebourne Fest. Soc., 1950–96; Inst. of Advanced Motoring, 1959–73; Commonwealth Lawyers Assoc., 1982–90; Commonwealth Assoc. of Legislative Counsel, 1984–; Commonwealth Magistrates and Judges Assoc., 1986–90; Anglo-Arab Assoc., 1990–; Saudi-British Soc., 1990–. FRSA. Governor, Taunton Sch., 1948–. CStJ 1989 (Hon. Legal Counsellor, 1978–93; Mem., Chapter-Gen., 1983–94). *Address:* Flat 5, 50 Pont Street, Knightsbridge, SW1X 0AE. *T:* (020) 7589 4235; (chambers) 12 King's Bench Walk, Temple,

EC4Y 7EL. *T*: (020) 7353 5692/6. *Clubs*: Royal Commonwealth Society; Polish Air Force Association.
Died 24 Sept. 2009.

RUSSELL, Anna; International Concert Comedienne; *b* 27 Dec. 1911; *d* of Col C. Russell-Brown, CB, DSO, RE, and Beatrice M. Tandy; *m* 1st, 1936, John Law Denison, CBE (marr. diss. 1946; he *d* 1996); 2nd, Charles Goldhamer. *Educ*: St Felix School, Southwold; Royal College of Music, London. ARCM 1939. Folk singer, BBC, 1935–40; Canadian Broadcasting Corp. programmes, 1942–46; Radio interviewer, CBC, 1945–46; Debut, Town Hall, New York, as concert comedienne, 1948; Broadway show, Anna Russell and her Little Show, 1953; Towns of USA, Canada, Great Britain, Australia, New Zealand, the Orient and South Africa, 1948–60. Television, Radio Summer Theatre, USA; recordings, Columbia Masterworks. Resident in Australia, 1968–75. Mayfair Theatre, London, 1976. *Publications*: The Power of Being a Positive Stinker (NY), 1955; The Anna Russell Song Book, 1960; I'm Not Making This Up, You Know (autobiog.), 1985; *relevant publication*: Anna in a Thousand Cities, by Deirdre Prussak, 2002. *Recreation*: gardening. *Address*: 70 Anna Russell Way, Unionville, ON L3R 3X3, Canada. *Club*: Zonta International (USA, Toronto Branch, Internat. Mem.). *Died 18 Oct. 2006.*

RUSSELL, Cecil Anthony Francis; Director of Intelligence, Greater London Council, 1970–76; *b* 7 June 1921; *s* of late Comdr S. F. Russell, OBE, RN retd and Mrs M. E. Russell (*née* Sneyd-Kynnersley); *m* 1950, Editha May (*née* Birch); no *c*. *Educ*: Winchester Coll.; University Coll., Oxford (1940–41, 1945–47). RNVR, 1941–45. Civil Service, 1949–70: Road Research Lab., 1949–50; Air Min., 1950–62; Dep. Statistical Adviser, Home Office, 1962–67; Head of Census Div., General Register Office, 1967–70. FSS. *Recreation*: ocean sailing. *Address*: Pagan Hill, Whiteleaf, Princes Risborough, Bucks HP27 0LQ. *T*: (01844) 343655. *Clubs*: Cruising Association; Ocean Cruising. *Died 4 May 2009.*

RUSSELL, Rev. David Syme, CBE 1982; MA, DD, DLitt; President, Baptist Union of Great Britain and Ireland, 1983–84 (General Secretary, 1967–82); *b* 21 Nov. 1916; second *s* of Peter Russell and Janet Marshall Syme; *m* 1943, Marion Hamilton Campbell; one *s* one *d*. *Educ*: Scottish Baptist Coll., Glasgow; Trinity Coll., Glasgow; Glasgow Univ. (MA, BD, DLitt, Hon. DD); Regent's Park Coll., Oxford Univ. (MA, MLitt; Hon. Fellow, 1995). Minister of Baptist Churches: Berwick, 1939–41; Oxford, 1943–45; Acton, 1945–53. Principal of Rawdon Coll., Leeds, and lectr in Old Testament languages and literature, 1953–64; Joint Principal of the Northern Baptist College, Manchester, 1964–67. Moderator, Free Church Federal Council, 1974–75. Pres., European Baptist Fedn, 1979–81. Mem., Central Cttee, WCC, 1968–83; Vice-Pres., BCC, 1981–84. Hon. DD McMaster, 1991. *Publications*: Between the Testaments, 1960; Two Refugees (Ezekiel and Second Isaiah), 1962; The Method and Message of Jewish Apocalyptic, 1964; The Jews from Alexander to Herod, 1976; Apocalyptic: Ancient and Modern, 1978; Daniel (The Daily Study Bible), 1981; In Journeyings Often, 1982; From Early Judaism to Early Church, 1986; The Old Testament Pseudepigrapha: patriarchs and prophets in early Judaism, 1987; Daniel: an active volcano, 1989; Poles Apart: the Gospel in creative tension, 1990; Divine Disclosure: an introduction to Jewish apocalyptic, 1992; Prophecy and the Apocalyptic Dream: protest and promise, 1994; contrib. to Encyc. Britannica, 1963. *Recreation*: woodwork. *Address*: Abbots Leigh Manor, Manor Road, Abbots Leigh, Bristol BS8 3RP.
Died 8 Nov. 2010.

RUSSELL, Francis Mark; Chairman, B. Elliott plc, 1975–87 (Chief Executive, 1972–83); *b* 26 July 1927; *s* of W. Sidney and Beatrice M. Russell; *m* 1950, Joan Patricia Ryan (decd); two *s* three *d*. *Educ*: Ratcliffe Coll., Leicester; Clare Coll., Cambridge (MA). Palestine

Police, 1946–48; Director: S. Russell & Sons Ltd, 1959; B. Elliott & Co. Ltd, 1967; Chief Executive, 1969, Dir, 1969–88, Chm., 1975–87, Goldfields Industrial Corporation; Dep. Chm., B. Elliott & Co. Ltd, 1971; Dir, Johnson & Firth Brown plc, 1982–92. CCMI. *Recreations*: golf, gardening. *Address*: 16 St Mary's Court, Malthouse Square, Beaconsfield, Bucks HP9 2LG. *T*: (01494) 673854. *Clubs*: Aldeburgh Golf; Denham Golf.
Died 15 March 2007.

RUSSELL, Prof. James Knox, MD; ChB; FRCOG; Emeritus Professor of Obstetrics and Gynæcology, University of Newcastle upon Tyne, since 1982; Dean of Postgraduate Medicine, 1968–77; Consultant Obstetrician, Princess Mary Maternity Hospital, Newcastle upon Tyne, 1956–82, then Hon. Consultant; Consultant Gynæcologist, Royal Victoria Infirmary, Newcastle upon Tyne, 1956–82, then Hon. Consultant; *b* 5 Sept. 1919; *s* of James Russell, Aberdeen; *m* 1944, Cecilia V. Urquhart, MD, DCH, *o d* of Patrick Urquhart, MA; three *d*. *Educ*: Aberdeen Grammar School; University of Aberdeen. MB, ChB 1942, MD 1954, Aberdeen; MRCOG 1949; FRCOG 1958. Served War, 1943–46, as MO in RAF, UK and Western Europe. First Assistant to Prof. of Obstetrics and Gynæcology, Univ. of Durham, 1950; Senior Lecturer in Obstetrics and Gynæcology, Univ. of Durham, 1956; Prof., first at Durham, then at Newcastle upon Tyne, 1958–82. Hon. Obstetrician, MRC Unit on Reproduction and Growth; Examiner in Obstetrics and Gynæcology, Univs of London, Birmingham, Manchester, Belfast, Aberdeen, Liverpool, RCOG, CMB, Tripoli and Kuala Lumpur; Presiding Examiner, CMB, Newcastle upon Tyne; Consultant in human reproduction, WHO. Commonwealth Fund Fellow 1962. Visiting Professor: New York, 1974; South Africa, 1978; Kuala Lumpur, 1980, 1982; Oviedo, Spain, 1987; Graham Waite Meml Lectr, Amer. Coll. of Obstetricians and Gynaecologists, Dallas, 1982. *Publications*: Teenage Pregnancy: Medical, Social and Educational Aspects, 1982; various papers, editorials and articles on obstetrical and gynæcological subjects and medical education to learned journals, newspapers and magazines. *Recreations*: writing, gardening, curing and smoking bacon, eels, salmon, etc. *Address*: Newlands, Tranwell Woods, Morpeth, Northumberland NE61 6AG. *T*: (01670) 515666.
Died 27 Oct. 2006.

RUSSELL, John, CBE 1975; Art critic, The New York Times, 1974–2001 (Chief Art Critic, 1982–90); *b* 22 Jan. 1919; *o s* of Isaac James Russell and Harriet Elizabeth Atkins; *m* 1st, 1945, Alexandrine Apponyi (marr. diss. 1950); one *d*; 2nd, 1956, Vera Poliakoff (marr. diss. 1971; she *d* 1992); 3rd, 1975, Rosamond Bernier. *Educ*: St Paul's Sch.; Magdalen Coll., Oxford (MA). Hon. Attaché, Tate Gall., 1940–41; MOI, 1941–43; Naval Intell. Div., Admty, 1943–46. Regular contributor, The Sunday Times, 1945–, art critic, 1949–74. Mem. art panel, Arts Council, 1958–68. Organised Arts Council exhibns: Modigliani, 1964; Rouault, 1966 and Balthus, 1968 (all at Tate Gallery); Pop Art (with Suzi Gablik), 1969 (at the Hayward Gallery); organised Vuillard exhibn (Toronto, Chicago, San Francisco), 1971. Trustee, Hermitage Mus., St Petersburg, 2000–. Hon. Fellow, Royal Acad. of Arts, 1989; Mem., Amer. Acad. of Arts and Letters, 1996. Frank Jewett Mather Award (College Art Assoc.), 1979; Mitchell Prize for Art Criticism, 1984. Grand Medal of Honour (Austria), 1972; Officier de l'Ordre des Arts et des Lettres, 1975; Order of Merit, Fed. Repub. of Germany, 1982; Chevalier, Légion d'Honneur, 1986. *Publications*: books include: Shakespeare's Country, 1942; British Portrait Painters, 1945; Switzerland, 1950; Logan Pearsall Smith, 1950; Erich Kleiber, 1956; Paris, 1960, new and enlarged edn, 1983; Seurat, 1965; Private View (with Bryan Robertson and Lord Snowdon), 1965; Max Ernst, 1967; Henry Moore, 1968; Ben Nicholson, 1969; Pop Art Redefined (with Suzi Gablik), 1969; The World of Matisse, 1970; Francis Bacon, 1971; Edouard Vuillard, 1971; The Meanings of Modern Art, 1981, new and enlarged edn

1990; Reading Russell, 1989; London, 1994; Matisse: father and son, 1999. *Recreations:* reading, writing, Raimund (1790–1836). *Address:* 166 East 61st Street, New York, NY 10021, USA. *Club:* Century (New York). *Died 23 Aug. 2008.*

RUSSELL, Prof. Michael Anthony Hamilton, FRCP, FRCPsych; Hon. Consultant and Head of Tobacco Research Section, National Addiction Centre, Institute of Psychiatry, University of London, 1997–2002, then Emeritus Consultant (Professor of Addiction, 1992–98, then Emeritus); *b* 9 March 1932; *s* of late James Hamilton Russell and of Hon. Kathleen Mary (*née* Gibson); *m* 1962, Audrey Ann Timms; two *s. Educ:* Diocesan Coll., Cape Town; University Coll., Oxford (BA Physiol. 1954; MA); Guy's Hosp., London (BM BCh 1957). FCP (SA) 1963; MRCP 1964, FRCP 1982; DPM 1968; FRCPsych 1980. Junior hospital appointments: Guy's Hosp., 1957–58; in Medicine, Cardiology and Pathology, Groote Schuur Hosp., Cape Town and King Edward VII Hosp., Durban, 1959–63; Sen. Med. Registrar, Groote Schuur Hosp., 1963–64; travel, incl. 6 months as Med. Registrar, Ruttonjee TB Sanatorium, Hong Kong, 1964–65; Trainee Registrar in Psychiatry, 1965–68, Sen. Registrar, 1968–69, Maudsley Hosp.; Institute of Psychiatry: Res. Worker, 1969–71; Lectr, 1971–73; Sen. Lectr, 1973–85; Reader, 1985–92. Hon. Consultant Psychiatrist: Maudsley Hosp., 1973–2002; UCH, 1996–2002. Mem., Ext. Scientific Staff, MRC, 1978–98; built up ICRF Health Behaviour Unit at Inst. of Psychiatry, 1988–96, moved to UCL, 1996, Hon. Dir, 1988–97, Hon. Consultant, 1997–2002. Invited Lect., Royal Stat. Soc., 1974; Robert Philip Lect., RCPE, 1978. No-tobacco Medal, WHO, 1989; Alton Oschner Award, Amer. Coll. Chest Physicians, 1996; Ove Ferno Award, Soc. Res. on Nicotine and Tobacco, 1998. *Publications:* numerous contribs to scientific books and jls on: nicotine psychopharmacology, pharmacokinetics and dependence; regulation of nicotine intake by smokers; motivational typologies of smoking; effect of cigarette prices on consumption; smoking in children; passive smoking; less harmful cigarettes; nicotine replacement and other treatments in clinic, workplace, primary care and medical practice settings. *Recreations:* reading, travel, watersports, oil paintings. *Address:* 10 Alphen Drive, Constantia, 7806 Cape Town, South Africa. *Died 16 July 2009.*

RUSSELL, Prof. Sir Peter (Edward Lionel Russell), Kt 1995; DLitt; FBA 1977; King Alfonso XIII Professor of Spanish Studies, Oxford University, 1953–81; *b* 24 Oct. 1913; *er s* of Hugh Bernard Wheeler and late Rita Muriel (*née* Russell), Christchurch, NZ; adopted surname Russell by deed poll, 1929. *Educ:* Cheltenham College; Queen's College, Oxford (DLitt 1981; Hon. Fellow, 1990). Lecturer of St John's College, 1937–53 and Queen's College, 1938–45, Oxford. Enlisted, 1940; commissioned (Intelligence Corps) Dec. 1940; Temp. Lt-Col, 1945; specially employed in Caribbean, W Africa and SE Asia, 1942–46. Oxford University: Fellow of Queen's College, 1946–53; Univ. Lectr in Spanish Studies, 1946–53; Fellow of Exeter Coll., 1953–81, Emeritus Fellow, 1981; Taylorian Special Lectr, 1983. Visiting Professor: Univ. of Virginia, 1982; Univ. of Texas, 1983, 1987; Johns Hopkins Univ., 1986; Vanderbilt Univ., 1987. Member: Portuguese Academy of History, 1956; Real Academia de Buenas Letras, Barcelona, 1972; UGC Cttee on Latin-American Studies in British Univs, 1962–64. FRHistS. Premio Antonio de Nebrija, Univ. of Salamanca, 1989. Comdr, Order of Isabel the Catholic (Spain), 1989; Comdr, Order of the Infante Dom Henrique (Portugal), 1993. *Publications:* As Fontes de Fernão Lopes, 1941; The English Intervention in Spain and Portugal in the Time of Edward III and Richard II, 1955 (Portuguese edn 2000); Prince Henry the Navigator, 1960; (with D. M. Rogers) Hispanic Manuscripts and Books in the Bodleian and Oxford College Libraries, 1962; (ed) Spain: a Companion to Spanish Studies, 1973, Spanish edn, 1982; Temas de la Celestina y otros estudios (del Cid al Quijote), 1978;

Prince Henry the Navigator: the rise and fall of a culture hero, 1984; Traducción y traductores en la Península Ibérica 1400–1550, 1985; Cervantes, 1985; La Celestina, 1991; Portugal, Spain and the African Atlantic 1343–1490, 1995; Prince Henry the Navigator: a life, 2000 (Portuguese edn 2004); articles and reviews in Modern Language Review, Medium Aevum, Bulletin of Hispanic Studies, etc. *Recreation:* reading travel literature. *Address:* 23 Belsyre Court, Observatory Street, Oxford OX2 6HU. *T:* (01865) 556086. *Club:* Oxford and Cambridge. *Died 22 June 2006.*

RUSSELL, Robert Christopher Hamlyn, CBE 1981; Director, Hydraulics Research Station, Department of the Environment (formerly Ministry of Technology), 1965–81; *b* Singapore, 1921; *s* of late Philip Charles and Hilda Gertrude Russell; *m* 1950, Cynthia Mary Roberts; one *s* two *d. Educ:* Stowe; King's Coll., Cambridge. Asst Engineer: BTH Co., Rugby, 1944; Dunlop Rubber Co., 1946; Sen. Scientific Officer, later PSO, then SPSO, in Hydraulics Research Station, 1949–65. Visiting Prof., Univ. of Strathclyde, 1967. *Publications:* Waves and Tides, 1951; papers on civil engineering hydraulics. *Address:* 29 St Mary's Street, Wallingford, Oxfordshire OX10 0ET. *T:* (01491) 837323. *Died 18 Aug. 2010.*

RUSSELL-JOHNSTON, Baron *cr* 1997 (Life Peer), of Minginish in Highlands; **(David) Russell Russell-Johnston,** Kt 1985; *b* 28 July 1932; *s* of late David Knox Johnston and Georgina Margaret Gerrie Russell; name changed to Russell-Johnston by Deed Poll, 1997; *m* 1967, Joan Graham Menzies; three *s. Educ:* Carbost Public Sch.; Portree High Sch.; Edinburgh Univ. (MA). Commissioned into Intelligence Corps (Nat. Service), 1958; subseq., Moray House Coll. of Educn until 1961; taught in Liberton Secondary Sch., 1961–63. Research Asst, Scottish Liberal Party, 1963–64. MP (L 1964–88, LibDem 1988–97) Inverness, 1964–83, Inverness, Nairn and Lochaber, 1983–97. Mem., Select Cttee of Privileges, 1988–92; Lib Dem spokesman: on foreign affairs, 1988–89; on European Community affairs, 1988–97; on East-West relations, 1992–94; on Central and Eastern Europe, 1994–97. Chm., Scottish Liberal Party, 1970–74 (Vice-Chm., 1965–70), Leader, 1974–88; Dep. Leader, Social and Liberal Democrats, 1988–92; Pres., Scottish Liberal Democrats, 1988–94. Mem., UK Delegn to European Parlt, 1973–75 and 1976–79, Vice Pres., Political Cttee, 1976–79; Mem., UK Delegn to Council of Europe and WEU, 1988; Council of Europe: Chm., Cttee on Culture and Educn, 1996–97; Ldr, Liberal, Democrat and Reform Gp, 1994; Pres., Parly Assembly, 1999–2002. Contested (L) Highlands and Islands, European Parly elecn, 1979, 1984. Chm., All Party Scottish Gaelic Parly Gp; Vice Chm., Europe Gp; Vice-President: Liberal Gp; European Lib Dem and Reform Parties, 1990–92; Liberal Internat., 1994–; Secretary: UK-Falkland Is Parly Gp; British-Hong Kong Parly Gp; Treasurer, All Party Photography Gp. Mem., Royal Commission on Local Govt in Scotland, 1966–69. *Publications:* (pamphlet) Highland Development, 1964; (pamphlet) To Be a Liberal, 1972; Scottish Liberal Party Conf. Speeches, 1979 and 1987. *Recreations:* reading, photography, shinty (Vice Chief, Camanachd Assoc., 1987–90). *Address:* House of Lords, SW1A 0PW. *Club:* Scottish Liberal (Edinburgh). *Died 27 July 2008.*

RUSSELL VICK, Arnold Oughtred; *see* Vick.

RUSTON, Rt Rev. John Harry Gerald, OGS; Bishop of St Helena, 1991–99; *b* 1 Oct. 1929; *s* of late Alfred Francis Gerald Ruston and Constance Mary (*née* Symonds). *Educ:* Berkhamsted Sch.; Sidney Sussex Coll., Cambridge (BA 1952; MA 1956); Ely Theol Coll. Ordained deacon 1954, priest 1955; joined OGS, 1955; Asst Curate, St Andrew's, Leicester, 1954–57; Tutor, Cuddesdon Coll., Oxford, 1957–61; Asst Curate, All Saints, Cuddesdon, 1957–61; Asst Priest, St Francis, Sekhukhuniland, Transvaal, dio. of Pretoria, 1962–70; Principal, St Francis's Coll., Sekhukhuniland, 1967–70; Canon, Pretoria, 1968–76; Sub-Dean, Pretoria, 1970–76; Archdeacon of Bloemfontein, 1976–83;

Warden, Community of St Michael and All Angels, and Chaplain, St Michael's Sch., Bloemfontein, 1976–83; consecrated Bishop, 1983; Bishop Suffragan, Pretoria, 1983–91. *Recreation:* music (composition and adaptation for 3-part singing). *Address:* The College of St Barnabas, Blackberry Lane, Lingfield, Surrey RH7 6NJ.
Died 27 April 2010.

RUTTER, His Honour John Cleverdon; a Circuit Judge, 1972–92 (a Senior Circuit Judge, 1990–92); *b* 18 Sept. 1919; 2nd *s* of late Edgar John Rutter; *m* 1951, Jill (*d* 1993), *d* of late Maxwell Duncan McIntosh; one *s* one *d*. *Educ:* Cardiff High Sch.; Univ. Coll., of SW of England, Exeter (Open Schol.); Keble Coll., Oxford. MA Oxon; LLB London. Royal Artillery, 1939–46; commnd 1941; served overseas. Called to the Bar, Lincoln's Inn, 1948; practised Western Circuit, 1948–66, Stipendiary Magistrate for City of Cardiff, 1966–71. A Legal Member, Mental Health Review Tribunal for Wales Region, 1960–66. An Assistant Recorder of: Cardiff, 1962–66; Merthyr Tydfil, 1962–66; Swansea, 1965–66; Dep. Chm., Glamorgan QS, 1969–71. *Recreations:* reading, bridge. *Address:* Law Courts, Cardiff CF1 3PG. *T:* (029) 2041 4400.   *Died 14 May 2009.*

RYAN, Dr Thomas Anthony, (Tony); Chairman, Irelandia Investments, since 1994; Director, Ryanair, since 1996 (Chairman, 1996–98); *b* 2 Feb. 1936; *m*; three *s*. *Educ:* Christian Brothers Sch., Thurles, Co. Tipperary; North Western Univ., Chicago. Aer Lingus, 1956–75, incl. sen. mgt positions in Ireland and US; founder: GPA Gp, 1975–93; Ryanair Gp, 1985. Mem., Bd of Govs, Nat. Gall. of Ireland. Hon. Mem., Univ. of Limerick Foundn, 1986. Hon. LLD: TCD, 1987; NUI, 1987; Limerick, 1992. *Recreations:* farming, horse breeding in Co. Kildare.   *Died 3 Oct. 2007.*

RYDER, Eric Charles, MA, LLB; barrister; Professor of English Law in the University of London, at University College, 1960–82, then Professor Emeritus; *b* 28 July 1915; *er s* of late Charles Henry Ryder, solicitor, Hanley, Staffs, and of Ellen Ryder (*née* Miller); *m* 1941, Nancy Winifred Roberts (*d* 2006). *Educ:* Hanley High School; Gonville and Caius College, Cambridge (scholar; BA (Law Tripos Parts I and II, 1st Cl.), 1936; LLB (1st Cl.) 1937; MA 1940; Tapp Law Scholar, 1937). Called to Bar, Gray's Inn, 1937; practice at Chancery Bar. Ministry of Food, 1941–44; Lecturer in Law, King's College, Newcastle upon Tyne, 1944; Dean of Faculty of Law, Univ. of Durham, 1947–60; Professor of Law, Univ. of Durham (King's College), 1953–60. Practised as conveyancing counsel, Newcastle upon Tyne, 1944–53. *Publications:* Hawkins and Ryder on the Construction of Wills, 1965; contrib. to legal periodicals. *Address:* 9 Arlington Court, Kenton Avenue, Gosforth, Newcastle upon Tyne NE3 4JR. *T:* (0191) 285 1172.
Died 5 July 2008.

RYDILL, Prof. Louis Joseph, OBE 1962; FREng; RCNC, Consultant in Naval Ship Design, since 1986; Professor of Naval Architecture, University College London, 1981–85, then Emeritus Professor; *b* 16 Aug. 1922; *s* of Louis and Queenie Rydill; *m* 1949, Eve (*née* Newman); two *d*. *Educ:* HM Dockyard Sch., Devonport; RNEC Keyham; RNC Greenwich; Royal Corps of Naval Constructors. FRINA (Gold Medallist); FREng (FEng 1982). Asst Constructor, 1946–52; Constructor, 1952–62, incl. Asst Prof. of Naval Architecture, RNC Greenwich, 1953–57; Chief Constructor, 1962–72, incl. Prof. of Naval Architecture, RNC Greenwich and UCL, 1967–72; Asst Dir Submarines, Constructive, 1972–74; Dep. Dir Submarines (Polaris), 1974–76; Dir of Ship Design and Engrg (formerly Warship Design), MoD, 1976–81. Hon. Fellow, UCL, 2008; Vis. Prof., US Naval Acad., Annapolis, Md, 1985–86. Silver Jubilee Medal, 1977. *Publications:* (jtly) Concepts in Submarine Design, 1993. *Recreations:* literature, theatre, jazz and other music. *Address:* The Lodge, Entry Hill Drive, Bath BA2 5NJ. *T:* (01225) 427888.   *Died 21 March 2009.*

S

SACKLER, Dr Mortimer David, Hon. KBE 1999; philanthropist; Co-Chairman, Purdue Pharma Inc., Stamford, Connecticut, 1952–2007; *b* NYC, 7 Dec. 1916; *s* of Isaac Sackler and Sophie Greenberg; *m* 1980, Theresa Rowling; one *s* two *d*; one *s* three *d* (and one *s* decd) from previous marriages. *Educ:* Anderson Coll. of Medicine, Glasgow Univ.; Middlesex Univ. Sch. of Medicine, USA (MD 1944). FAPA 1952. Co-Founder and Associate Dir, Creedmoor Inst. for Psychobiologic Studies, NY, 1950–53. Mem., Chancellor's Court of Benefactors, Oxford Univ., 1993–; Benefactor, Univ. of Edinburgh, 2005. Fellow, Ashmolean Mus., Univ. of Oxford, 2006. Hon. Senator, Univ. of Salzburg, 1981; Hon. Fellow: KCL, 2001; UCL, 2003. Hon. PhD Tel Aviv, 1980; Hon. DSc Glasgow, 2001. Philanthropies include: universities and educational institutes: (jtly) Sackler Sch. for Biomed. Scis, Tufts Univ., Boston, 1980; (jtly) Sackler Inst. of Grad. Biomed. Scis, NY Univ. Sch. of Medicine, 1981; Sackler Inst. of Pulmonary Pharmacol., King's Coll. Sch. of Medicine and Dentistry, 1993; Sackler Liby of Humanities, Oxford Univ., 1996; Sackler Musculo-Skeletal Res. Centre, UCL, 2000; Sackler Labs, Reading Univ., 2000; Sackler Inst. of Psychobiological Res., Edinburgh and Glasgow Univs, 2003; galleries and museums: (jtly) Sackler Gall., Metropolitan Mus. of Art, NYC, 1985; Sackler Res. Fellowship at Ashmolean Mus., Worcester Coll., Oxford, 1993; Sackler Centre for Arts Education: Serpentine Gall., 1995; Dulwich Picture Gall., 1998; Guggenheim Mus., NY, 1995; Sackler Octagon, Tate Gall., 1990; Sackler Room, National Gall., London, 1992; Sackler Wing of Oriental Antiquities, Louvre Mus., 1995; Jewish Mus., Berlin, 2003; Sackler Seminar Rooms, Sadlers Wells Th., 1998; Sackler Sculpture Hall, National Gall. of Scotland, Edinburgh, 2001; (jtly) Educn Centre, V&A Mus., 2004; Sackler Crossing, Royal Botanic Gdns, 2006; Darwin Centre, Natural Hist. Mus., 2006; (jtly) Mus. of London, 2006; Sackler Centre for Arts Educn, V&A Mus., 2008. Hon. Mention for Scientific Res., Med. Soc. of State of NY, 1952. Officier, Légion d'Honneur, 1997 (Chevalier 1989). *Publications:* scientific papers. *Recreation:* tennis. *Clubs:* Eagle Ski (Gstaad); Gstaad Yacht.
Died 24 March 2010.

SAFFMAN, Prof. Philip Geoffrey, FRS 1988; Theodor von Kármán Professor of Applied Mathematics and Aeronautics, California Institute of Technology, since 1995 (Professor of Applied Mathematics, 1964–95); *b* 19 March 1931; *s* of Sam Ralph Saffman and Sarah Rebecca Leviten; *m* 1954, Ruth Arion; one *s* two *d*. *Educ:* Roundhay Sch., Leeds; Trinity Coll., Cambridge (BA, MA, PhD). Prize Fellow, Trinity Coll., Cambridge, 1955–59; Asst Lectr, Applied Math., Cambridge, 1958–60; Reader in Applied Math., King's Coll. London, 1960–64. Fellow, Amer. Acad. of Arts and Scis, 1978. *Publications:* Vortex Dynamics, 1992; numerous papers in sci. jls. *Recreations:* hiking, camping. *Address:* 399 Ninita Parkway, Pasadena, CA 91106–3514, USA.
Died 17 Aug. 2008.

ST CLAIR-FORD, Sir James (Anson), 7th Bt *cr* 1793, of Ember Court, Surrey; *b* 16 March 1952; *s* of Capt. Sir Aubrey St Clair-Ford, 6th Bt, DSO, RN and of Anne, *o d* of Harold Cecil Christopherson; *S* father, 1991; *m* 1st, 1977, Jennifer Margaret (marr. diss. 1984), *yr d* of Commodore Robin Grindle, RN; 2nd, 1987, Mary Anne, *er d* of His Honour Nathaniel Robert Blaker, QC. *Educ:* Wellington; Bristol Univ. *Heir: cousin* Colin Anson St Clair-Ford [*b* 19 April 1939; *m* 1964, Gillian Mary, *er d* of Rear Adm. Peter Skelton, CB; two *d*].
Died 3 Aug. 2009.

ST DAVIDS, 3rd Viscount *cr* 1918; **Colwyn Jestyn John Philipps;** Baron Strange of Knokin, 1299; Baron Hungerford, 1426; Baron de Moleyns, 1445; Bt 1621;

Baron St Davids, 1908; *b* 30 Jan. 1939; *s* of 2nd Viscount St Davids and Doreen Guinness (*d* 1956), *o d* of late Captain Arthur Jowett; *S* father, 1991; *m* 1965, Augusta Victoria Correa Larrain, *d* of late Don Estanislao Correa Ugarte; two *s*. *Educ:* Haverfordwest Grammar Sch.; Sevenoaks Sch.; King's Coll., London (Cert. Advanced Musical Studies, 1989). Nat. Service, 1958–60; commnd 2nd Lt Welsh Guards. Securities Agency Ltd, 1960–65; Mem., Stock Exchange, 1965–93; Maguire Kingsmill and Co., 1965–68; Partner, Kemp-Gee and Co., later Scrimgeour Kemp-Gee and Co., 1971; Director: Citicorp Scrimgeour Vickers (Securities) Ltd, 1985–88; Greig Middleton & Co. Ltd, 1989–90, 1994–99. Mem. Bd, Milford Haven Port Authority, 1997–2007. A Lord in Waiting (Govt Whip), 1992–94; a Dep. Speaker, H of L, 1995–99. Mem., Baden-Powell Fellowship, 1985–. Mem. Council, Univ. of Wales, Lampeter, 1995–99; Gov., WCMD, 1996–2000. Liveryman: Musicians' Co., 1971–; Welsh Livery Guild, 1997–2006. *Recreations:* music, literature, natural history. *Heir: s* Hon. Rhodri Colwyn Philipps [*b* 16 Sept. 1966; *m* 2003, Sarah, *o d* of late Dr Peter Butcher]. *Club:* Garrick. *Died 26 April 2009.*

ST JOHN WILSON, Sir Colin Alexander; *see* Wilson.

ST JOHNSTON, Sir Kerry, Kt 1988; Chairman, Tri Anchors Ltd, since 1993; *b* 30 July 1931; *s* of late George Eric St Johnston and Viola Rhona Moriarty; *m* 1st, 1960, Judith Ann Nichols; two *s* one *d*; 2nd, 1980, Charlotte Ann Taylor, *d* of late John Scott Limnell Lyon and Patricia Marjorie Hambro. *Educ:* Summer Fields, Oxford; Eton Coll.; Worcester Coll., Oxford (MA Jurisprudence). Lt, 11th Hussars, PAO, 1950–52. Joined Ocean Steamship Co. Ltd, 1955, Man. Dir 1963; Overseas Containers Ltd: Founder Dir, 1965; Commerical Dir, 1966; Jt Man. Dir, 1969; Dep. Chm., 1973; Pres. and Chief Exec. Officer, Private Investment Co. for Asia (PICA), SA, Singapore, 1977–82; Chm. and Chief Exec., P & O (formerly Overseas) Containers Ltd, 1982–89. Chairman: Wilrig AS, 1989–92; NM Funds Mgt (Europe) Ltd, 1993–95; Freightliner Ltd, 1996–2001. Director: Royal Insurance, 1973–76; TR Pacific, then Henderson TR Pacific, Investment Trust, 1982–2000; Lloyds Bank Internat. Ltd, 1983–85; P&OSNCo., 1986–89; Diehl and St Johnston Ltd, 1989–2002; OTAL Hldgs Ltd, 1997–99. President: Gen. Council of British Shipping, 1987–88; CIT, 1989–90. Chm., Children in Crisis, 1999–. *Recreations:* trout fishing, gardening. *Clubs:* Boodle's, White's.
Died 6 Nov. 2006.

SAINT LAURENT, Yves (Henri Donat); Officier de la Légion d'Honneur, 1995; couturier; *b* 1 Aug. 1936; *s* of Charles and Lucienne-Andrée (Wilbaux) Mathieu Saint Laurent. *Educ:* Lycée d'Oran. Collaborator, 1954, then successor of Christian Dior, 1957–60; Dir, Société Yves Saint Laurent, 1962–2002. *Exhibitions:* Metropolitan Mus. of Art, NY, 1983; Fine Arts Mus., Beijing, 1985; Musée des Arts de la Mode, Paris, 1986; House of Painters of the USSR, Moscow, 1986; Hermitage Mus., Leningrad, 1987; Art Gall. of NSW, Sydney, 1987; Sezon Mus. of Art, Tokyo, 1990. *Costume design: for theatre:* Le Mariage de Figaro, 1964; Delicate Balance, 1967; *for ballet:* Cyrano de Bergerac, 1959; Adage et Variations, 1965; Notre Dame de Paris, 1965; Scheherazade, 1973; *for films:* The Pink Panther, 1962; Belle de Jour, 1967; La Chamade, 1968; La Sirène du Mississippi (with Catherine Deneuve), 1969; L'affaire Stavisky, 1974; *stage sets and costumes:* Les Chants de Maldoror, 1962; Spectacle Zizi Jeanmaire, 1961, 1963, 1968; Revue Zizi Jeanmaire, 1970, 1972, 1977; L'Aigle à deux têtes, 1978. Celebration of 40 yrs of fashion creation with a show of 300 models at Stade de France before Football World Cup Final, 1998. Neiman-Marcus Award for fashion, 1958; Oscar from Harper's Bazaar, 1966; Council of Fashion Designers of America:

Internat. Award, 1982; Lifetime Achievement Award, 1999; Best Fashion Designer Oscar, 1985; Golden Rose, Palermo, 2001. *Publications:* La Vilaine Lulu, 1967, repr. 2002. *Died 1 June 2008.*

ST VINCENT, 7th Viscount *cr* 1801; **Ronald George James Jervis;** *b* 3 May 1905; *o* surv. *s* of 6th Viscount and Marion Annie (*d* 1911), *d* of James Brown, JP, Orchard, Carluke, Scotland; *S* father, 1940; *m* 1945, Phillida, *o d* of Lt-Col R. H. Logan, Taunton; two *s* one *d*. *Educ:* Sherborne. JP Somerset, 1950–55. *Heir: s* Hon. Edward Robert James Jervis [*b* 12 May 1951; *m* 1977, Victoria Margaret, *o d* of Wilton J. Oldham, St Peter, Jersey; one *s* one *d*]. *Address:* Les Charrieres House, Les Charrieres, St Ouen, Jersey, CI JE3 2LG. *Died 4 Sept. 2006.*

SALINGER, Jerome David; American author; *b* New York City, 1 Jan. 1919; *m* 1st, 1945, Sylvia (marr. diss. 1946); 2nd, 1955, Claire Douglas (marr. diss. 1967); one *s* one *d*; 3rd, 1988, Colleen O'Neill. *Educ:* Manhattan public schools; Military Academy, Paris. Served with 4th Infantry Division, US Army, 1942–46 (Staff Sergeant). Travelled in Europe, 1937–38. Started writing at age of 15; first story published, 1940. *Publications:* The Catcher in the Rye, 1951; Nine Stories, 1953; Franny and Zooey, 1962; Raise High the Roof Beam, Carpenters and Seymour: an Introduction, 1963. *Address:* c/o Harold Ober Associates, 425 Madison Avenue, New York, NY 10017–1110, USA. *Died 27 Jan. 2010.*

SALISSE, John Joseph, CBE 1986; Director, Marks and Spencer, 1968–85; *b* 24 March 1926; *s* of Joseph and Anne Salisse; *m* 1949, Margaret Horsfield; one *d*. *Educ:* Portsmouth Grammar Sch. Marks and Spencer, 1944–85. Chairman: CBI Distributive Trades Survey Cttee, 1983–86; St Enoch Management Centre Ltd, 1986–97; Jt London Tourism Forum, 1986–97; London Enterprise Agency, 1983–88; Retail Consortium, 1986–92; Director: London Tourist Bd, 1984–97 (Vice-Chm., 1989–97); City Shops, 1986–88; Fullemploy, 1984–86; Allied Internat. Designers, 1986–87. Jt Treas., European Movement, 1982–86; Member: CBI Council, 1984–89; Cttee, Amer. European Community Assoc., 1983–90; Nat. Employers' Liaison Cttee, 1987–92; Cttee on Commerce and Distribution, 1988–93; Council for Charitable Support, 1986–89; Inst. of Dirs; Trustee, London Educn Business Partnership, 1986–92; Dir, CECD, 1986–93 (Vice-Pres., 1989–93). Hon. Mem., RCP, 2004. Hon. Vice Pres., Magic Circle, 1975– (Hon. Sec., 1965–86); Hon. Life Mem., Acad. of Magical Arts and Scis, America, 1979. Freeman, City of London, 1992. *Publications:* (jtly) A Candid View of Maskelyne's 1916–17, 1995; History of St George's Hall, 2002; various contribs to Magic literature. *Recreations:* golf, theatre, history of magic, collecting Victorian theatre programmes. *Address:* 12 Hampstead Way, NW11 7LS. *Clubs:* Savage, Magic Circle, Highgate Golf; Magic Castle (Los Angeles). *Died 26 Sept. 2006.*

SALT, Rear-Adm. James Frederick Thomas George, CB 1991; Director of UK Ship Sales, Vosper Thornycroft, then VT Shipbuilding, 2001–05; *b* 19 April 1940; *s* of Lieut Comdr George Salt (lost in 1939–45 War in command HMS Triad, 1940) and Lillian Bridget Lamb; *m* 1975, Penelope Mary Walker; three *s* (and one *s* decd). *Educ:* Wellington College; RNC Dartmouth (1958–59). Served Far East, Mediterranean, South Atlantic and home waters; commanded HM Sub. Finwhale, 1969–71; 2 i/c HM Sub. Resolution (Polaris), 1973–74; Comd HM Nuclear Sub. Dreadnought, 1978–79; Comd HMS Sheffield, 1982 (sank Falklands); Comd HMS Southampton, 1983; ACOS Ops C-in-C Fleet, 1984–85; Dir, Defence Intell., 1986–87; Sen. Naval Mem., Directing Staff, RCDS, 1988–90; ACNS (Gulf War), 1990–91; Mil. Dep., Defence Export Services, 1992–97. Hd of Marketing, Colebrand Ltd, 1998–2000. Master, Cordwainers' Co., 2000–01. *Recreations:* sailing, stone engraving, painting, gardening. *Address:* Salterns, Birdham Pool, Chichester, West Sussex PO20 7BB. *Died 3 Dec. 2009.*

SALTON, Prof. Milton Robert James, FRS 1979; Professor and Chairman of Microbiology, New York University School of Medicine, 1964–90, then Emeritus Professor; *b* 29 April 1921; *s* of Robert Alexander Salton and Stella Salton; *m* 1951, Joy Marriott; two *s*. *Educ:* Univ. of Sydney (BSc Agr. 1945); Univ. of Cambridge (PhD 1951, ScD 1967). Beit Meml Res. Fellow, Univ. of Cambridge, 1950–52; Merck Internat. Fellow, Univ. of California, Berkeley, 1952–53; Reader, Univ. of Manchester, 1956–61; Prof. of Microbiology, Univ. of NSW, Australia, 1962–64. Hon. Mem., British Soc. for Antimicrobial Chemotherapy, 1983. Docteur en Médecine, Dhc, Université de Liège, 1967. *Publications:* Microbial Cell Walls, 1960; The Bacterial Cell Wall, 1964; Immunochemistry of Enzymes and their Antibodies, 1978; β-Lactam Antibiotics, 1981; (ed jtly) Antibiotic Inhibition of Bacterial Cell Surface Assembly and Function, 1988. *Address:* Department of Microbiology, New York University School of Medicine, 550 First Avenue, New York, NY 10016, USA. *Club:* Oxford and Cambridge. *Died 14 April 2008.*

SAMARANCH, Juan Antonio; Marqués de Samaranch, 1991; President, International Olympic Committee, 1980–2001 (Member, 1966; Hon. Life President, 2001); *b* 17 July 1920; *s* of Francisco Samaranch and Juana Torello; *m* 1955, Maria Teresa Salisachs Rowe (*d* 2000); one *s* one *d*. *Educ:* Instituto Superior Estudios de Empresas, Barcelona; German College; Higher Inst. of Business Studies, Barcelona. Industrialist, Bank Consultant; Pres., Barcelona Diputacion, 1973–77; Ambassador to USSR and to People's Republic of Mongolia, 1977–80. Mem., Spanish Olympic Cttee, 1954 (Pres., 1967–70); Nat. Deleg. for Physical Educn and Sport. Hon. Pres., Caja de Ahorros y de Pensiones de Barcelona Numerous decorations and honorary degrees from different univs. *Publications:* Deporte 2000, 1967; Olympic Message, 1980; Memorias Olímpicas, 2002; Olympic Review. *Recreation:* philately. *Address:* Diagonal 520-bajos, 08006 Barcelona, Spain. *Died 21 April 2010.*

SAMPLES, Reginald McCartney, (Mac), CMG 1971; DSO 1942; OBE 1963; HM Diplomatic Service, retired; *b* 11 Aug. 1918; *o s* of late William and Jessie Samples; *m* 1947, Elsie Roberts Hide (*d* 1999); two *s* one step *d*. *Educ:* Rhyl Grammar Sch.; Liverpool Univ. (BCom). Served, 1940–46; RNVR (Air Branch); torpedo action with 825 Sqn against German ships Scharnhorst, Gneisenau and Prinz Eugen in English Channel (wounded, DSO); Lieut (A). Central Office of Information (Economic Editor, Overseas Newspapers), 1947–48. CRO (Brit. Inf. Services, India), 1948; Economic Information Officer, Bombay, 1948–52; Editor-in-Chief, BIS, New Delhi, 1952; Dep.-Dir, BIS, New Delhi, 1952–56; Dir, BIS, Pakistan (Karachi), 1956–59; Dir, BIS, Canada (Ottawa), 1959–65, OBE; Counsellor (Information) to Brit. High Comr, India, and Dir, BIS, India (New Delhi), 1965–68; Asst Under-Sec. of State, Commonwealth Office, 1968; Head of British Govt Office, and Sen. British Trade Comr, Toronto, 1969; Consul-Gen., Toronto, 1974–78. Asst Dir, Royal Ontario Museum, 1978–83. Volunteer recording books for the blind, Canadian Nat. Inst. for the Blind, 1983–. *Recreations:* watching tennis, ballet. *Address:* 514W Belmont House, 55 Belmont Street, Toronto, ON M5R 1R1, Canada. *Clubs:* Naval; Queens (Toronto). *Died 31 July 2009.*

SAMUEL, Adrian Christopher Ian, CMG 1959; CVO 1963; *b* 20 Aug. 1915; *s* of late George Christopher Samuel and Alma Richards; *m* 1942, Sheila, *er d* of late J. C. Barrett, Killiney, Co. Dublin; three *s* one *d*. *Educ:* Rugby Sch.; St John's Coll., Oxford. Entered HM Consular Service, 1938; served at Beirut, Tunis and Trieste. Served War, 1940–44, in Royal Air Force. Returned to HM Foreign Service and served at HM Embassies in Ankara, Cairo and Damascus; First Secretary, 1947; Counsellor, 1956; Principal Private Secretary to the Secretary of State for Foreign Affairs, Oct. 1959–63; Minister at HM Embassy,

Madrid, 1963–65; resigned 1965. Director: British Chemical Engrg Contractors Assoc., 1966–69; British Agrochemicals Assoc., 1972–78; Dir-Gen., Groupement Internat. des Assocs Nats de Fabricants de Pesticides (GIFAP), 1978–79. *Publications:* An Astonishing Fellow: a life of Sir Robert Wilson, KMT, MP, 1986. *Recreation:* reading. *Address:* 6 The Meadows, St George's Park, Ditchling Common, Ditchling, East Sussex RH15 0SF. *T:* (01444) 247741. *Club:* Garrick.
Died 26 Dec. 2010.

SAMUELS, Hon. Gordon (Jacob), AC 1987; CVO 2000; Governor of New South Wales, 1996–2001; *b* 12 Aug. 1923; *s* of Harry Samuels and Zelda Selina (*née* Glass); *m* 1957, Jacqueline Kott; two *d. Educ:* University Coll. Sch., London; Balliol Coll., Oxford (Domus Scholar; Jenkins Law Prize; MA). Served War, 1942–46; Capt. 96th (Royal Devon Yeomanry) Field Regt, RA. Called to the Bar: Inner Temple, 1948; NSW, 1952; Teaching Fellow in Jurisprudence, Sydney Univ. Law Sch., 1952–56; QC NSW 1964, Vic, 1965; Challis Lectr in Pleading, Sydney Univ. Law Sch., 1964–70; Judge: Supreme Court of NSW, 1972–92; Court of Appeal, 1974–92; independent arbitrator, referee and mediator, 1992–96. Chairman: Law Reform Commn of NSW, 1993–96; Mediator Accreditation Bd, Australian Commercial Disputes Centre, 1994–96; Sen. Comr, Commn of Inquiry into Australian Secret Intelligence Service, 1994–95; Pres., Australian Security Appeals Tribunal, 1980–90. Mem., NSW Migrant Employment and Qualifications Bd, 1989–95 (Chm., 1992–95). President: NSW Bar Assoc., 1971–72; Acad. of Forensic Scis, 1974–76; Australian Soc. of Legal Phil., 1976–79. Chancellor, Univ. of NSW, 1976–94. Mem., Bd of Govs, Law Foundn of NSW, 1992–94 (Chm., 1992–93). Hon. LLD Sydney, 1994; Hon. DSc NSW, 1994. *Recreations:* reading, music, theatre. *Address:* 38 Evans Street, Bronte, NSW 2024, Australia. *Club:* Australian (Sydney).
Died 10 Dec. 2007.

SAMUELSON, Sir (Bernard) Michael (Francis), 5th Bt *cr* 1884; *b* 17 Jan. 1917; *s* of Sir Francis Henry Bernard Samuelson, 4th Bt, and Margaret Kendall (*d* 1980), *d* of H. Kendall Barnes; *S* father, 1981; *m* 1952, Janet Amy, *yr d* of Lt-Comdr L. G. Elkington, RN retd, Chelsea; two *s* two *d. Educ:* Eton. Served War of 1939–45 with RA and Leicestershire Regt (despatches). *Heir:* *s* James Francis Samuelson [*b* 20 Dec. 1956; *m* 1987, Caroline Anne Woodley; two *d*]. *Address:* Harborne, Hailsham Road, Stone Cross, Pevensey, East Sussex BN24 5AS. *T:* (01323) 760487.
Died 21 Nov. 2008.

SAMUELSON, Prof. Paul Anthony; Institute Professor, Massachusetts Institute of Technology, 1966–86, then Emeritus; Shinsei Bank (formerly Long-Term Credit Bank of Japan) Visiting Professor of Political Economy, Center for Japan-US Business and Economic Studies, New York University, since 1987; *b* Gary, Indiana, 15 May 1915; *m* 1st, 1938, Marion Crawford (*d* 1978); four *s* (incl. triplets) two *d;* 2nd, 1981, Risha Claypool. *Educ:* Univs of Chicago (BA) and Harvard (MA, PhD). SSRC Predoctoral Fellow, 1935–37; Soc. of Fellows, Harvard, 1937–40; Guggenheim Fellow, 1948–49; Ford Faculty Research Fellow, 1958–59; Hoyt Vis. Fellow, Calhoun Coll., Yale, 1962; Carnegie Foundn Reflective Year, 1965–66. MIT: Asst Prof. of Econs, 1940; Assoc. Prof. of Econs, 1944; Staff Mem., Radiation Lab., 1944–45; Prof. of Econs, 1947; Prof. of Internat. Economic Relations (part-time), Fletcher Sch. of Law and Diplomacy, 1945. Consultant: to Nat. Resources Planning Bd, 1941–43; to Rand Corp., 1948–75; to US Treasury, 1945–52, 1961–74; to Johnson Task Force on Sustained Prosperity, 1964; to Council of Econ. Advisers, 1960–68; to Federal Reserve Bd, 1965–; to Congressional Budget Office, 1974–. Economic Adviser to Senator, Candidate and President-elect John F. Kennedy, informal adviser to President Kennedy. Member: War Prodn Bd and Office of War Mobilization and Reconstruction, 1945; Bureau of the Budget, 1952; Adv. Bd of Nat Commn on Money and Credit, 1958–60; Research Adv. Panel to President's

Nat. Goals Commn, 1959–60; Research Adv. Bd Cttee for Econ. Develt, 1960; Nat. Task Force on Econ. Educn, 1960–61; Sen. Advr, Brookings Panel on Econ. Activity. Contrib. Editor and Columnist, Newsweek, 1966–81. Vernon F. Taylor Vis. Dist. Prof., Trinity Univ., Texas, 1989. Lectures: Stamp Meml, London, 1961; Wicksell, Stockholm, 1962; Franklin, Detroit, 1962; Gerhard Colm Meml, NYC, 1971; Davidson, Univ. of New Hampshire, 1971; 12th John von Neumann, Univ. of Wisconsin, 1971; J. Willard Gibbs, Amer. Mathematical Soc., 1974; 1st Sulzbacher, Columbia Law Sch., 1974; John Diebold, Harvard Univ., 1976; Alice Bourneauf, Boston Coll., 1981; Horowitz, Jerusalem and Tel Aviv, 1984; Marschak Meml, UCLA, 1984; Olin, Univ. of Virginia Law Sch., 1989; Joseph W. Martin Commemorative, Stonehill Coll., 1990; Lionel Robbins Meml, Claremont Coll., 1991. Corresp. Fellow, British Acad., 1960; Fellow: Amer. Philosoph. Soc.; Econometric Soc. (Mem. Council; Vice-Pres. 1950; Pres. 1951); Member: Amer. Acad. Arts and Sciences; Amer. Econ. Assoc. (Pres. 1961; Hon. Fellow, 1965); Phi Beta Kappa; Commn on Social Sciences (NSF), 1967–70; Internat. Econ. Assoc. (Pres. 1965–68; Hon. Pres. 1968–); Nat. Acad. of Sciences, 1970–; Omicron Delta Epsilon, Bd of Trustees (Internat. Honor Soc. in Econ.). Hon. Fellow: LSE; Peruvian Sch. of Economics, 1980. Hon. LLD: Chicago, 1961; Oberlin, 1961; Boston Coll., 1964; Indiana, 1966; Michigan, 1967; Claremont Grad. Sch., 1970; New Hampshire, 1971; Seton Hall, 1971; Keio, Tokyo, 1971; Harvard, 1972; Gustavas Adolphus Coll., 1974; Univ. of Southern Calif, 1975; Univ. of Rochester, 1976; Univ. of Pennsylvania, 1976; Emmanuel Coll., 1977; Stonehill Coll., 1978; Widener, 1982; Indiana Univ. of Pennsylvania, 1993; Hon. DLitt: Ripon Coll., 1962; Northern Michigan Univ., 1973; Valparaiso Univ., 1987; Columbia Univ., 1988; Hon DSc: E Anglia, 1966; Massachusetts, 1972; Rhode Is., 1972; City Univ. of London, 1980; Tufts Univ., 1988; Rensselaer Poly. Inst., 1998; Hon. LHD Williams Coll., 1971; *Dhc:* Université Catholique de Louvain, 1976; Catholic Univ. at Riva Aguero Inst., Lima, 1980; Universidad Nacional de Educación a Distancia, Madrid, 1989; Universidad Politécnica de Valencia, 1991; DUniv New Univ. of Lisbon, 1985; Hon. DSS Yale, 2005. David A. Wells Prize, Harvard, 1941; John Bates Clark Medal, Amer. Econ. Assoc., 1947; Medal of Honor, Univ. of Evansville, 1970; Nobel Prize in Econ. Science, 1970; Albert Einstein Commemorative Award, 1971; Alumni Medal, Chicago Univ., 1983; Britannica Award, 1989; Medal and Hon. Mem., Club of Economics and Management, Valencia, Spain, 1990; Gold Scanno Prize in Economy, Naples, Italy, 1990; Nat. Medal of Science, USA, 1996. *Publications:* Foundations of Economic Analysis, 1947, enlarged edn 1982; Economics, 1948, (with William D. Nordhaus) 12th edn 1985 to 18th edn 2005 (trans. 40 langs, 1948); (jtly) Linear Programming and Economic Analysis, 1958 (trans. French, Japanese); Readings in Economics, 1955; The Collected Scientific Papers of Paul A. Samuelson (ed J. E. Stiglitz), vols I and II, 1966, vol. III (ed R. C. Merton), 1972, vol. IV (ed H. Nagatani and K. Crowley), 1977, vol. V (ed K. Crowley), 1986; co-author, other books in field, papers in various jls, etc. *Recreation:* tennis. *Address:* Department of Economics, Massachusetts Institute of Technology E52–383C, 50 Memorial Drive, Cambridge, MA 02142, USA. *T:* (617) 2533368, *Fax:* (617) 2530560.
Died 13 Dec. 2009.

SANDBANK, Charles Peter, FREng; Deputy Director of Engineering, BBC, 1985–91; Broadcasting Technology Adviser, Department of Trade and Industry, 1993–2007; *b* 14 Aug. 1931; *s* of Gustav and Clare Sandbank; *m* 1955, Audrey Celia; one *s* two *d. Educ:* Bromley Grammar Sch.; London Univ. (BSc, DIC). FREng (FEng 1983); FIET, FInstP. Prodn Engr, 1953–55, Develt Engr, 1955–60, Brimar Valve Co.; Develt Section Head, STC Transistor Div., 1960–64; Head of Electron Devices Lab., 1964–68, Manager, Communication Systems Div., 1968–78, Standard Telecommunication Laboratories; Head of BBC Research Dept, 1978–84; Asst Dir of Engrg, 1984–85,

Asst to Dir of Engrg, 1991–93, BBC. Mem. Council: IEE, 1978–81, 1989–92 (Chairman: Electronics Divisional Bd, 1979–80; London Centre, 1991–92); Royal TV Soc., 1983–86, 1989–92; Chairman: EBU New Systems and Services Cttee, 1984–89; EBU High Definition TV Cttee, 1981–84; EUREKA High Definition Television Project Adv. Bd, 1988–94; Jt Technical Cttee, EBU/Eur. Telecommunications Standards Inst., 1990–93; DTI Cttee for Enhanced Definition TV, 1990–2007; DCMS/DTI Electronic Cinema Cttee, 2000; Founding Co-Chm., European Digital Cinema Forum, 2001–; Bureau mem., EBU Tech. Cttee, 1989–93. Ext. Examr, London Univ., 1982–89. Royal Acad. of Engrg Vis. Prof. of Information Systems Design, Univ. of Bradford, 1995–. Dir, Snell and Wilcox Ltd, 1993–97. Chm., Internal Cttee of Inquiry into Legionnaires Disease Outbreak at Broadcasting House, London, 1988. Liveryman, Scientific Instrument Makers' Co., 1988–. Fellow, SMPTE, 1989; FBKST3 1991, FRTS; FRSA DUniv Surrey, 1994; Hon. DEng Bradford, 2004. *Publications:* Optical Fibre Communication Systems, 1980; Digital Television, 1990; papers and patents (about 200) on semiconductor devices, integrated circuits, solid-state bulk effects, compound semiconductors, micro-waves, electron-phonon interactions, navigational aids, electro-optics and broadcasting technology. *Recreations:* boatbuilding, sailing, film-making, music, garden-watching. *Address:* Grailands, 30 Beech Road, Reigate, Surrey RH2 9NA. *Club:* Royal Norfolk and Suffolk Yacht.   *Died 15 Dec. 2008.*

SANDERS, Cyril Woods, CB 1959; *b* 21 Feb. 1912; *er s* of Cyril Sturgis Sanders and Dorothy (*née* Woods); *m* 1944, Kate Emily Boyes; one *s* three *d*. *Educ:* St Paul's Sch.; Queen's Coll., Oxford (BA 1934, Lit. Hum). Joined General Post Office as Assistant Principal, 1934; transferred to Board of Trade, 1935; retired from Dept of Trade and Industry (formerly Bd of Trade) as Under-Secretary, 1972.   *Died 3 March 2008.*

SANDERSON, Very Rev. (William) Roy; Parish Minister at Stenton and Whittingehame, 1963–73; Extra Chaplain to the Queen in Scotland, since 1977 (Chaplain, 1965–77); *b* 23 Sept. 1907; *er s* of late Arthur Watson Sanderson, Leith, and Ethel Catherine Watson, Dundee; *m* 1941, Annie Muriel Easton, Glasgow; three *s* one *d* (and one *d* decd). *Educ:* Cargilfield Sch.; Fettes Coll.; Oriel Coll., Oxford; Edinburgh University. BA 1929, MA 1933, Oxon. Ordained, 1933. Asst Minister, St Giles' Cath., Edin., 1932–34; Minister: at St Andrew's, Lochgelly, 1935–39; at the Barony of Glasgow, 1939–63. Moderator: Glasgow Presbytery, 1958; Haddington and Dunbar Presbytery, 1972–74; Convener of Assembly Cttees: on Religious Instruction of Youth, 1950–55; on Deaconesses, 1956–61; Panel of Doctrine, 1960–65; on Gen. Administration, 1967–72. Convener of Business Cttee and Leader of General Assembly of the Church of Scotland, 1965–66, 1968–72. Moderator of Gen. Assembly of the Church of Scotland, 1967–68. Chm., BBC Scottish Religious Advisory Committee, 1961–71; Member Central Religious Advisory Cttee of BBC and ITA, 1961–71. Governor, Fettes Coll., Edinburgh, 1967–76. Hon. DD Glasgow, 1959. *Publications:* Responsibility (Moderatorial address), 1967. *Recreations:* cooking, reading. *Address:* 20 Craigleith View, Station Road, North Berwick, East Lothian EH39 4BF. *T:* (01620) 892780.   *Died 19 June 2008.*

SANDFORD, 2nd Baron *cr* 1945, of Banbury; **Rev. John Cyril Edmondson,** DSC 1942; *b* 22 Dec. 1920; *e s* of 1st Baron Sandford; *S* father, 1959; *m* 1947, Catharine Mary Hunt; two *s* two *d*. *Educ:* Eton Coll.; Royal Naval Coll., Dartmouth; Westcott House, Cambridge. Served War of 1939–45: Mediterranean Fleet, 1940–41; Home Fleet, 1942; Normandy Landings, 1944 (wounded); Mediterranean Fleet, HMS Saumarez, 1946 (wounded). Staff of RN Coll., Dartmouth, 1947–49; HMS Vengeance, 1950; HMS Cleopatra, 1951–52; Staff Commander-in-Chief Far East, 1953–55;

Commander of Home Fleet Flagship, HMS Tyne, 1956; retired 1956. Ordained in Church of England, 1958; Parish of St Nicholas, Harpenden, 1958–63; Exec. Chaplain to Bishop of St Albans, 1965–68. Conservative Peer in H of L, 1959–99; Opposition Whip, 1966–70; Parly Sec., Min. of Housing and Local Govt, June–Oct. 1970; Parliamentary Under-Secretary of State: DoE, 1970–73; DES, 1973–74. Dir, Ecclesiastical Insce Office, 1977–89. Chairman: Cttee to review the condition and future of National Parks in England and Wales, 1971; Standing Conf. of London and SE Regl Planning Authorities, 1981–89. A Church Comr, 1982–89. Chairman: Hertfordshire Council of Social Service, 1969–70; Church Army, 1969–70; Community Task Force, 1975–82; Redundant Churches Cttee, 1982–88; Founder Chm., Pilgrims Assoc., 1982–88; Mem., Adv. Council on Penal Reform, 1968–70. President: Anglo-Swiss Soc., 1974–84; Council for Environmental Educn, 1974–84; Assoc. of District Councils, 1980–86; Offa's Dyke Assoc., 1980–84; Countrywide Holidays Assoc., 1982–86; Vice-Pres., YHA, 1979–90; Founder Trustee, WaterAid, 1981 (Council Mem., 1984; Vice Pres., 1991). Founder, Sandford Award for Heritage Educn in Monuments, Stately Homes, Museums and Cathedrals, 1978; inaugurated Heritage Educn Trust, 1982. Hon. Fellow, Inst. of Landscape Architects, 1971. *Heir: s* Hon. James John Mowbray Edmondson [*b* 1 July 1949; *m* 1st, 1973, Ellen Sarah, *d* of Jack Shapiro, Toronto; one *d*; 2nd, 1986, Linda, *d* of Mr and Mrs Wheeler, Nova Scotia; one *s*]. *Address:* 27 Ashley Gardens, Ambrosden Avenue, Westminster, SW1P 1QD. *T:* (020) 7834 5722. *Clubs:* Ski of Great Britain, Camping and Caravan.
                    Died 13 Jan. 2009.

SANGER, David John, FRAM, FRCO; organ recitalist, composer, teacher; consultant on organ building and restoration; *b* 17 April 1947; *s* of Stanley Charles Sanger and Ethel Lillian Florence Sanger (*née* Woodgate). *Educ:* Eltham Coll.; Royal Acad. of Music, London (FRAM). ARCM; FRCO. Royal Academy of Music: Prof. of Organ, 1982–89; Chm., Organ Dept, 1987–89; Vis. Prof. of Organ, 1989–96; freelance teaching at Cambridge and Oxford Univs, 1976–. Guest Prof., Royal Danish Acad. of Music, 1991–93; Vis. Tutor in Organ Studies, RNCM, 1991–; Cons. Tutor in Organ, Birmingham Conservatoire of Music, 2010–. Pres., RCO, 2008–. Perfs at the Proms and RFH; internat. tours as soloist, notably in Scandinavia; masterclasses, lectures and seminars. Jury Mem., internat. organ competitions in St Albans, Paisley, Speyer, Biarritz, Alkmaar and Odense. Consultant: new organ, Exeter Coll., Oxford; restoration of Usher Hall organ, Edinburgh. Numerous recordings. Winner, international organ competition: St Albans, 1969; Kiel, 1972. *Publications:* Play the Organ, vol. 1, 1990, vol. 2, 1993; (ed) organ works of Willan, 1990, Pepusch, 1991, and Lefébure-Wély, 2 vols, 1994; Complete Organ Works of Louis Vierne, 13 vols, 2008; numerous compositions for organ and choir; articles for Organists' Review, The Organ. *Recreations:* racquet sports, swimming, fell-walking. *Address:* Old Wesleyan Chapel, Embleton, Cumbria CA13 9YA. *T:* (01768) 776493; *e-mail:* david.sanger@virgin.net; *web:* www.davidsanger.co.uk.   *Died May 2010.*

SAPPER, Alan Louis Geoffrey; Founder and Chief Executive, Interconnect AV, 1991–2000; General Secretary, Association of Cinematograph, Television and Allied Technicians, 1969–91; *b* 18 March 1931; *y s* of late Max and Kate Sapper; *m* 1959, Helen Rubens; one *s* one *d*. *Educ:* Upper Latymer Sch.; Univ. of London. Botanist, Royal Botanic Gardens, Kew, 1948–58; Asst Gen. Sec., 1958–64, Dep. Gen. Sec., 1967–69, Assoc. of Cinematograph, Television and Allied Technicians; Gen. Sec., Writers' Guild of Great Britain, 1966–67. Mem. General Council, Trades Union Congress, 1970–84 (Chm., 1982). President: Confedn of Entertainment Unions, 1970–91; Internat. Fedn of Audio-Visual Workers, 1974–94; Sec., Fedn of Film Unions, 1968–91; Treas., Fedn of Broadcasting Unions, 1968–91; Member: British Copyright Council, 1964–74; British Screen Adv.

Council, 1985–. Governor: BFI, 1974–94; Nat. Film School, 1980–95; Hammersmith Hosp., 1965–72; Ealing Coll. of Higher Educn, 1976–78. Dir, Ealing Studios, 1994–2000. Chm., League for Democracy in Greece, 1970–2000. *Publications:* articles, short stories; stage plays, On Licence, Kith and Kin; TV play, The Return, 1961. *Recreations:* taxonomic botany, hill walking, politics and human nature. *Address:* 3 Boston Gardens, Chiswick, W4 2QJ. *T:* (020) 8742 8313.   *Died 19 May 2006.*

SARAMAGO, José; writer; *b* Azinhaga, Portugal, 16 Nov. 1922; *s* of José de Sousa and Maria da Piedade; *m* 1st, 1944, Ilda Reis (marr. diss. 1970; she *d* 1998); one *d*; 2nd, 1998, Pilar de Río. Formerly car mechanic, admin. civil servant, and metal co. worker; with Estúdios Cor until 1971; translator of Colette, Tolstoy, Maupassant, Baudelaire, etc, 1955–81; political commentator and cultural editor, Diário de Lisboa, 1972–75; Asst Ed., Diário de Notícias, 1975. Nobel Prize for Literature, 1998. *Publications: fiction:* Terra do Pecado, 1947; Manual de Pintura e Caligrafia, 1977 (trans. Manual of Painting and Calligraphy); Objecto Quase (short stories), 1978; Levantado do Chão, 1980; Memorial do Convento, 1982 (trans. Baltasar and Blimunda); O Ano da Morte de Ricardo Reis, 1984 (The Year of the Death of Ricardo Reis); A Jangada de Pedra, 1986 (The Stone Raft); História do Cerco de Lisboa, 1989 (The History of the Siege of Lisbon); O Evangelho Segundo Jesus Cristo, 1991 (The Gospel According to Jesus Christ); Ensaio Sobrea a Cegueira, 1995 (Blindness); O Conto da ilha desconhecida, 1996 (The Tale of the Unknown Island); Todos os Nomes, 1997 (All the Names); El Amor Posible, 1998; La Caverna (The Cave, 2002); El Hombre Duplicado (The Double, 2004); Ensaio Sobre a Lucidez, 2004 (Seeing, 2006); As Intermitências da Morte, 2005 (Death at Intervals, 2008); A Viagem do Elefante, 2008; *poetry:* Os Poemas Possíveis, 1966; Provavelmente Alegria, 1970; O Ano de 1993, 1975; *plays:* A Noite, 1979; Que Farei com este Livro?, 1980; A Segunda Vida de Francisco de Assis, 1987; In Nomine Dei, 1993; *essays:* Deste Mundo e do Outro, 1971; A Bagagem do Viajante, 1973; Os Opiniões que o D. L. Teve, 1974; Os Apontamentos, 1976; Viagem a Portugal, 1981; *journals:* Cadernos de Lanzarote, 5 Vols, 1994–; *memoir:* As Pequenas Memórias, 2006 (Small Memories). *Address:* c/o Literarische Agentur Mertin, Taunusstrasse 38, 60329 Frankfurt am Main, Germany.   *Died 18 June 2010.*

SARGANT, Naomi Ellen, (Lady McIntosh of Haringey); writer and consultant; *b* 10 Dec. 1933; *d* of late Tom Sargant, OBE, and of Marie Cerny (*née* Hlouskova); *m* 1st, 1954, Peter Joseph Kelly; one *s*; 2nd, 1962, Andrew Robert McIntosh (later Baron McIntosh of Haringey); two *s*. *Educ:* Friends' Sch., Saffron Walden, Essex; Bedford Coll., London (BA Hons Sociology). Social Surveys (Gallup Poll) Ltd, 1955–67; Sen. Lectr in Market Res., Enfield Coll. of Technol., 1967–69; Open University: Sen. Lectr in Res. Methods, 1970–75; Reader in Survey Research, 1975–78; Head, Survey Res. Dept, Inst. of Educnl Technol., 1972–81; Pro Vice-Chancellor (Student Affairs), 1974–78; Prof. of Applied Social Research, 1978–81; Sen. Commng Editor for Educnl Programming, Channel 4, 1981–89; Acting Chief Exec., Open Poly., 1990. Vis. Prof. in Higher Educn (part-time), Univ. of Mass, Amherst, 1974–75; Vis. Prof., Open Univ. Quality Support Centre, 1995–. Councillor. and Chm. Children's Cttee, London Bor. of Haringey, 1964–68; Vice-Chm., London Boroughs Trng Cttee (Social Services), 1966–68. Chm., National Gas Consumers' Council, 1977–80. Pres., Nat. Soc. for Clean Air, 1981–83. Member: Council and Exec. Cttee, Social Work Adv. Service, 1966–68; Local Govt Trng Bd, 1967–68; Energy Commn, 1978–79; Commn on Energy and the Environment, 1978–81; Nat. Consumer Council, 1978–81; Adv. Council for Adult and Continuing Educn, 1977–83; Council, Bedford Coll., Univ. of London, 1977–83; Council, Polytechnic of the South Bank, 1982–86; Bd, Nat. Inst. of Adult Continuing Educn, 2003– (Mem., Exec. Cttee, 1986–89, 1992–2003); Gov., Haringey Coll., 1984–87; Pro-Chancellor, Univ. of E

London HEC, 1992–94 (Vice-Chm., Poly. of E London HEC, 1989–92); Gov., NE London Poly., 1987–89. Vice Chm., Film, TV and Video Panel, Arts Council of GB, 1986–90; Vice-Chair, NCVO, 1992–98; Vice-Chair, 1998–2001, Pres., 2001–, Open Coll. of the Arts. Chm., Great Ormond Street Hosp. for Children NHS Trust, 1997–2000. Chair, Harington Scheme, 2003–. Trustee: Nat. Extension Coll., 1975–97; Charities Aid Foundn, 1992–2001 (Vice Chm., Grants Council, 1995–2000). Mem. RTS, 1982– (Hall of Fame, 1996). FRSA 1991. Hon. Fellow RCA, 1988. DUniv Open, 2005. *Publications:* A Degree of Difference, 1976 (New York 1977); (with A. Woodley) The Door Stood Open, 1980; Learning and 'Leisure', 1991; Learning for a Purpose, 1993; (with A. Tuckett) Pandora's Box, 1997; The Learning Divide, 1997; The Learning Divide Revisited, 2000; (with Fiona Aldridge) Adult Learning and Social Division, vol. 1, 2002, vol. 2, 2003. *Recreation:* gardening. *Address:* 27 Hurst Avenue, N6 5TX. *T:* (020) 8340 1496, *Fax:* (020) 8348 4641.   *Died 23 July 2006.*

SARGEANT, Frank Charles Douglas, CMG 1972; HM Diplomatic Service, retired 1977; *b* 7 Nov. 1917; *s* of late John Sargeant and Anna Sargeant; *m* 1946, Joan Adene Bickerton (*d* 2005); one *s* one *d. Educ:* Lincoln; St Catharine's Coll., Cambridge. MA Cantab, Natural Sciences. Cadbury Bros. Ltd, 1939. Served War: Army, 1939–46; Lt-Col, Royal Signals. Imperial Chemical Industries Ltd, 1947–48. HM Diplomatic Service: Curacao, 1948; The Hague, 1951; Kuwait, 1954; Foreign Office, 1957 (First Sec. 1958); First Sec., Head of Chancery and Consul, Mogadishu, 1959; First Sec. (Commercial) Stockholm, 1962–66; First Sec., Head of Chancery, Colombo, and Consul for the Maldive Islands, 1967; Counsellor, 1968; Consul-General, Lubumbashi, 1968–70; Dep. High Comr, Dacca, 1970–71; Sen. Officers' War Course, RN Coll., Greenwich, 1971–72; Consul Gen., Lyons, 1972–77 (Doyen of the Consular Corps). *Recreation:* birdwatching. *Address:* Rue Joseph Kessel, 47150 Lacapelle-Biron, France.   *Died 4 March 2007.*

SARGESON, Prof. Alan McLeod, FRS 1983; Professor of Inorganic Chemistry, Australian National University, 1978–95, then Emeritus; *b* 13 Oct. 1930; *s* of late H. L. Sargeson; *m* 1959, Marietta, *d* of F. Anders; two *s* two *d. Educ:* Maitland Boys' High Sch.; Sydney Univ. (BSc, PhD, DipEd). FRACI; FAA. Lectr, Chem. Dept, Univ. of Adelaide, 1956–57; Res. Fellow, John Curtin Sch. of Med. Research, ANU, 1958, Fellow 1960; Sen. Fellow, then Professorial Fellow, 1969–78, Res. Sch. of Chemistry, ANU. For. Mem., Royal Danish Acad. of Science, 1976; Mem., Royal Physiographic Soc., Lund, 2002; For. Hon. Mem., Amer. Acad. of Arts and Sci., 1998; For. Associate, US Nat. Acad. of Science, 1996. DSc *hc*: Sydney, 1990; Copenhagen, 1996; Bordeaux, 1997. *Address:* Research School of Chemistry, Australian National University, Canberra, ACT 0200, Australia.   *Died 29 Dec. 2008.*

SAUNDERS, Albert Edward, CMG 1975; OBE 1970; HM Diplomatic Service, retired; Ambassador to the United Republic of Cameroon and the Republic of Equatorial Guinea, 1975–79; *b* 5 June 1919; *s* of late Albert Edward and Marie Marguerite Saunders; *m* 1945, Dorothea Charlotte Mary Whittle (*d* 1985); one *s* one *d. Educ:* yes. Westminster Bank Ltd, 1937. Royal Navy, 1942–45: last appt, Asst Chief Port Security Officer, Middle East. Apptd to British Embassy, Cairo, 1938 and 1945; Asst Information Officer, Tripoli, 1949; Asst Admin. Officer, Athens, 1951; MECAS, 1952; Third Sec., Office of UK Trade Comr, Khartoum, 1953; Third Sec. (Information), Beirut, 1954; POMEF, Cyprus, 1956; FO, 1957; Second Sec. (Oriental), Baghdad, 1958; FO, 1959; Vice-Consul, Casablanca, 1963; Second Sec. (Oriental), Rabat, 1963; Consul, Jerusalem, 1964; First Sec., FO, 1967; Chancery, Baghdad, 1968; Head of Chancery and Consul, Rabat, 1969; Counsellor and Consul General in charge British Embassy, Dubai, 1972; Chargé d'Affaires, Abu Dhabi, 1972 and 1973; RN War

Coll., Greenwich, 1974, sowc, 1975. *Recreation:* iconoclasm (20th Century). *Address:* 3 Deanhill Road, SW14 7DQ. *Died 2 Oct. 2009.*

SAUNDERS, Andrew Downing; Chief Inspector of Ancient Monuments and Historic Buildings, Department of the Environment, then English Heritage, 1973–89; Hon. Curator, Cranbrook Museum, since 2004; *b* 22 Sept. 1931; *s* of Lionel Edward Saunders; *m* 1st, 1961, Hilary Jean (*née* Aikman) (marr. diss. 1980); two *s* one *d*; 2nd, 1985, Gillian Ruth Hutchinson; one *d*. *Educ:* Magdalen Coll. Sch., Oxford; Magdalen Coll., Oxford (MA). FSA, FRHistS, FSAScot, MIFA. Joined Ancient Monuments Inspectorate, 1954; Inspector of Ancient Monuments for England, 1964. President: Cornwall Archaeol Soc., 1968–72; Royal Archaeol Inst., 1993–96; Vice-Pres., Hendon and Dist Archaeol Soc.; Chairman: Internat. Fortress Council, 1995–98; Fortress Study Gp, 1995–2001; Member: Exec. Cttee, Council for British Archaeology, 1996–2002; Scientific Council, Europa Nostra/Internat. Castles Inst. Chm. Adv Panel, Defence of Britain Project, Council for British Archaeology, 1996–2002. Hon. Res. Fellow, Exeter Univ., 2000–01. Editor, Fortress: the Castles and Fortifications Qly, 1989–94. *Publications:* ed jtly and contrib., Ancient Monuments and their Interpretation, 1977; Fortress Britain, 1989; Devon and Cornwall, 1991; Channel Defences, 1997; Fortress Builder: Bernard de Gomme, Charles II's military engineer, 2004; Excavations at Launceston Castle, Cornwall, 2006; excavation reports on various Roman and Medieval sites and monuments, papers on castles and artillery fortification in various archæological and historical jls, guidebooks to ancient monuments. *Address:* The Crest, The Hill, Cranbrook, Kent TN17 3AH. *Club:* Athenæum. *Died 13 March 2009.*

SAUNDERS, David Martin St George; HM Diplomatic Service, retired; *b* 23 July 1930; *s* of late Hilary St George Saunders and Helen (*née* Foley); *m* 1960, Patricia, *d* of James Methold, CBE; one *s* one *d*. *Educ:* Marlborough Coll.; RMA Sandhurst; Staff Coll., Quetta, Pakistan. Commnd Welsh Guards, 1950; Staff Captain Egypt, 1954–56; Asst Adjt, RMA Sandhurst, 1956–58; Adjt 1st Bn Welsh Guards, 1958–60; GSO III War Office, 1960–62; sc Quetta, Pakistan, 1963; Company Comdr 1st Bn Welsh Guards, 1964; GSO II British Defence Liaison Staff, Canberra, 1965–67; Guards Depot, Pirbright, 1967–68; joined Foreign Service, 1968; Consul (Economic), Johannesburg, 1970–73; First Secretary: FCO, 1973–74; Dakar, 1974–76; FCO, 1976–77; Pretoria, 1977–79; The Hague, 1979–83; Counsellor, FCO, 1983–90. *Recreations:* military history, shooting, cinema, bridge, the wines of Burgundy. *Address:* 18 Garfield Road, SW11 5PN. *Died 2 Feb. 2009.*

SAUNDERS, Prof. Derek William, CBE 1986; Professor of Polymer Physics and Engineering, Cranfield Institute of Technology, 1967–87, retired 1988, Emeritus Professor, since 1989; Director, Science and Engineering Research Council/Department of Industry Teaching Company Scheme, 1981–88; *b* 4 Dec. 1925; *s* of Alfred and Elizabeth Hannah Saunders; *m* 1949, Mahalah Harrison; three *s* two *d*. *Educ:* Morley Grammar Sch.; Imperial Coll., Univ. of London. PhD, ARCS, FInstP, FIMMM, CEng, CPhys. Building Res. Stn, Garston, 1945–47; British Rubber Producers Res. Assoc., 1947–51; Royal Instn, 1951–54; British Rayon Res. Assoc., 1954–60; Cranfield Inst. of Technology: Sen. Lectr 1960, subseq. Reader; Head of Materials Dept, 1969–81; Pro-Vice-Chancellor, 1973–76. Chm. Council, Plastics Inst., 1973–75; Chm. Council, 1975–76, Pres., 1983–85 and 1990–91, Plastics and Rubber Inst.; Vice-Pres., Inst. of Materials, 1992–94. Mem. Harpur Trust (Bedford Charity), 1968–88. Hon. DTech CNAA, 1990. *Publications:* chapters in several books on polymeric materials; sci. papers in various learned jls. *Address:* 98 Topcliffe Road, Thirsk, N Yorks YO7 1RY. *T:* (01845) 523344. *Died 12 June 2008.*

SAUNDERS, Kenneth Herbert; Chief Architect, Commission for the New Towns, 1976–82, retired; *b* 5 April 1915; *s* of William James Saunders and Anne Elizabeth Baker; *m* 1940, Kathleen Bettye Fortune (*d* 1981); one *s* one *d*. *Educ:* elementary sch., Worthing; Sch. of Art, Worthing; Brighton Coll. of Art. ARIBA 1940. Served War: RA Iraq and Persia; OCTU Bengal Sappers and Miners, India and Burma; Major RE ALFSEA, SORE II, 1940 (mentioned in despatches). Articled pupil, 1933; Dept of Architecture, Bor. of Worthing, 1936; City Architect's Dept, Portsmouth, 1937–39, 1946–49; Crawley Develt Corporation: Architect, 1949; Sen. Architect, 1952; Asst Chief Architect, 1958; Commission for New Towns: Asst Chief Architect, 1962; Exec. Architect, 1965; Manager (Crawley), 1978–80. *Recreations:* architecture, buildings. *Address:* Longthorpe, 22 Goffs Park Road, Crawley, West Sussex RH11 8AY. *T:* (01293) 521334. *Died 5 Jan. 2006.*

SAUNDERS, Prof. Wilfred Leonard, CBE 1982; FCLIP; Director, University of Sheffield Postgraduate School of Librarianship and Information Science, 1963–82, then Professor Emeritus; *b* 18 April 1920; *s* of Leonard and Annie Saunders; *m* 1946, Joan Mary Rider, *er d* of late Major W. E. Rider; two *s*. *Educ:* King Edward's Grammar Sch. for Boys, Camp Hill, Birmingham; Fitzwilliam House, Univ. of Cambridge (MA). FCLIP (FLA 1952). Served War: France, 1940; N Africa, 1942–43; Italy, 1943–46; Captain Royal Signals. Library Asst, Birmingham Reference Library, 1936–39; Dep. Lib., Inst. of Bankers, 1948–49; Lib., Univ. of Birmingham Inst. of Educn, 1949–56; Dep. Lib., Univ. of Sheffield, 1956–63; 12 months' secondment to UNESCO as Expert in Educnl Documentation, Uganda, 1962; Univ. of Sheffield: Prof. of Librarianship and Inf. Science, 1968; Dean, Faculty of Educnl Studies, 1974–77. Visiting Professor: Pittsburgh Univ. Grad. Sch. of Library and Inf. Sciences, 1968; UCLA, 1985; Commonwealth Vis. Fellow, Australia, 1969; (1st) Elsie O. and Philip Sang Internat. Lectr, Rosary Grad. Sch. of Library Science, USA, 1974. UK Rep., Internat. Fedn for Documentation/Training of Documentalists Cttee, 1966–70; Hon. Consultant, E Africa Sch. of Librarianship, Makerere Univ., 1967–73; numerous overseas consultancy and adv. missions. Mem. Council, Library Assoc., 1979–83 (Pres. 1980); Member: Council, ASLIB, 1965–71, 1972–78; British Council, 1970 (Mem., Libraries Adv. Panel, 1970–87, Chm. 1975–81); Bd of Librarianship, CNAA, 1966–79; Library Adv. Council (England), 1970–73; Adv. Cttee, British Library Ref. Div., 1975–80; *ad hoc* Cttee on Educn and Trng (Gen. Inf. Prog.), UNESCO, 1978–85; Adv. Cttee, British Library R&D Dept, 1980–88; British Library Adv. Council, 1981–84; Adv. Council on Public Records, 1986–91; Chairman: Jt Consultative Cttee of Library Assoc., Aslib, SCONUL, Soc. of Archivists and IInfSc, 1980–81; Library and Information Services Council (formerly Library Adv. Council for Eng.), 1981–84. Hon. FIInfSc 1977; Hon. FCP 1983. Hon. LittD Sheffield, 1989. *Publications:* (ed) The Provision and Use of Library and Documentation Services, 1966; (ed) Librarianship in Britain Today, 1967; (with H. Schur and Lisbeth J. Pargeter) Education and Training for Scientific and Technological Library and Information Work, 1968; (ed) University and Research Library Studies, 1968; (with W. J. Hutchins and Lisbeth J. Pargeter) The Language Barrier: a study in depth of the place of foreign language materials in the research activity of an academic community, 1971; (ed) British Librarianship Today, 1977; (with E. M. Broome) The Library and Information Services of the British Council, 1977; Guidelines for Curriculum Development in Information Studies, 1978; Professional Education for Library and Information Work in the Socialist Republic of Macedonia, 1982; Postgraduate Training for Information Specialists (Venezuela), 1984; An Evaluation of Education for Librarianship in New Zealand, 1987; Towards a Unified Professional Organization for Library and Information Science and Services, 1989; Dunkirk Diary of a Very Young Soldier (autobiog.), 1989 (contrib., TV film, Dunkirk, 2004); jl articles and res. reports. *Recreations:* gardening, walking, listening to music, book collecting. *Address:* 30 Endcliffe Glen Road, Sheffield S11 8RW.   *Died 27 July 2007.*

SAVILE, 3rd Baron *cr* 1888; **George Halifax Lumley-Savile**; DL; JP; *b* 24 Jan. 1919; *s* of 2nd Baron Savile, KCVO and Esme Grace Virginia (*d* 1958), *d* of J. Wolton; *S* father, 1931. *Educ:* Eton. Served in 1939–45 War in Duke of Wellington's Regiment, and attached Lincolnshire Regiment during the Burma Campaigns. DL W Yorks, 1954. Patron of two livings. Owned about 18,000 acres. JP Borough of Dewsbury, 1955. CStJ 1982. *Recreations:* music, walking. Heir: *nephew* John Anthony Thornhill Lumley-Savile [*b* 10 Jan. 1947; *m* 1986, Barbara Ann Holmes (*née* Toms)]. *Address:* Gryce Hall, Shelley, Huddersfield HD8 8LP. *T:* (01484) 602774; Walshaw, Hebden Bridge, Yorks HX7 7AX. *T:* (01422) 842275. *Clubs:* Brooks's, Sloane.   *Died 2 June 2008.*

SAVILL, Colonel Kenneth Edward, CVO 1976; DSO 1945; DL; Member, HM Bodyguard of Hon. Corps of Gentlemen at Arms, 1955–76 (Lieutenant, 1973–76; Standard Bearer, 1972–73); *b* 8 Aug. 1906; *o s* of Walter Savill, Chilton Manor, Alresford and May, *d* of Major Charles Marriott; *m* 1935, Jacqueline (*d* 1980), *o d* of Brig. John Salusbury Hughes, MC; two *d* (and one *d* decd). *Educ:* Winchester College; RMC Sandhurst. Commissioned, 12th Royal Lancers, 1926; 1st King's Dragoon Guards, 1936; The Queen's Bays, 1947. Served War of 1939–45, France, 1939–40; N Africa and Italy, 1943–45; Col 1950; retd 1953. High Sheriff of Hampshire, 1961; DL Hampshire, 1965. Col, 1st The Queen's Dragoon Guards, 1964–68. *Address:* Chilton Manor, Alresford, Hants SO24 9TX. *T:* (01256) 389246. *Club:* Cavalry and Guards.   *Died 29 Dec. 2007.*

SAVILLE, Prof. John; Emeritus Professor of Economic and Social History, University of Hull; *b* 2 April 1916; *o s* of Orestes Stamatopoulos, Volos, Greece, and Edith Vessey (name changed by deed poll to that of step-father, 1937); *m* 1943, Constance Betty Saunders (*d* 2007); three *s* one *d*. *Educ:* Royal Liberty Sch.; London Sch. of Economics. 1st Cl. Hons BSc (Econ) 1937. Served War, RA, 1940–46; Chief Scientific Adviser's Div., Min. of Works, 1946–47; Univ. of Hull, 1947–82, Prof. of Economic and Social History, 1972–82. Leverhulme Emeritus Fellow, 1984–86. Mem., British Communist Party, 1934–56; Chm., Oral Hist. Soc., 1976–87; Convenor, Northern Marxist Historians Gp, 1986–95; Vice-Chm., and later Chm., Soc. for Study of Labour Hist., 1974–82; Mem. Exec. Cttee and Founder-Mem., Council for Academic Freedom and Democracy, 1971–81, Chm. 1982–89; Chm., Economic and Social Hist. Cttee, SSRC, 1977–79. Trustee, Michael Lipman Trust, 1977–93. Vice-Chm., Friends of the Brynmor Jones Library, Hull Univ., 1988–2000. FRHistS 1973. *Publications:* Ernest Jones, Chartist, 1952; Rural Depopulation in England and Wales 1851–1951, 1957; 1848, The British State and the Chartist Movement, 1987; The Labour Movement in Britain: a commentary, 1988; The Politics of Continuity: British Foreign Policy and the Labour Government 1945–46, 1993; The Consolidation of the Capitalist State, 1994; Memoirs from the Left, 2003; numerous articles; Co-Editor: (with E. P. Thompson) Reasoner and New Reasoner, 1956–59; (with Asa Briggs) Essays in Labour History, 1960, 1971, 1977; (with Ralph Miliband) Socialist Register (annual, 1964–90); (with Joyce M. Bellamy) Dictionary of Labour Biography, 1972–2000. *Recreations:* working for socialism, looking at churches. *Address:* 152 Westbourne Avenue, Hull HU5 3HZ. *T:* (01482) 343425.   *Died 13 June 2009.*

SAY, Rt Rev. Richard David, KCVO 1988; DD (Lambeth) 1961; an Assistant Bishop, diocese of Canterbury, since 1988; *b* 4 Oct. 1914; *s* of Commander Richard Say, OBE, RNVR, and Kathleen Mary (*née* Wildy); *m* 1943, Irene Frances (OBE 1980, JP 1960) (*d* 2003), *e d* of Seaburne and Frances Rayner, Exeter; one *s* two *d* (and one *s* decd). *Educ:* University Coll. Sch.; Christ's College, Cambridge (MA); Ridley Hall,

Cambridge. Ordained deacon, 1939; priest, 1940. Curate of Croydon Parish Church, 1939–43; Curate of St Martin-in-the-Fields, London, 1943–50; Asst Sec. Church of England Youth Council, 1942–44; Gen. Sec., 1944–47; Gen. Sec. British Council of Churches, 1947–55; Church of England delegate to World Council of Churches, 1948, 1954 and 1961. Select Preacher, University of Cambridge, 1954 and University of Oxford, 1963; Rector of Bishop's Hatfield, 1955–61; Hon. Canon of St Albans, 1957–61; Bishop of Rochester, 1961–88; High Almoner to HM the Queen, 1970–88. Domestic Chaplain to Marquess of Salisbury and Chaplain of Welfield Hospital, 1955–61; Hon. Chaplain of The Pilgrims, 1968–2002 (Vice Pres., 2001–). Entered House of Lords, 1969. Chaplain and Sub-Prelate, Order of St John, 1961. Church Comr, 1981–88 (Dep. Chm., Bd of Govs, 1981–88). Member: Commn on Deployment and Payment of the Clergy, 1965–67; Court of Ecclesiastical Causes Reserved, 1984–93; Chm., Cttee for State Aid for historic churches in use, 1971–91. Dep. Pro-Chancellor, 1977–83, Pro-Chancellor, 1983–93, Kent Univ.; Governor, University Coll. Sch., 1980–88. A Vice-Pres., UNA of GB, 1986–; Pres., Friends of Kent Churches, 1988–. Chm., Age Concern, England, 1986–89 (Vice Pres., 1990–94; Patron, 1994–). Freeman of City of London, 1953; Hon. Freeman: of Tonbridge and Malling, 1987; of Rochester upon Medway, 1988. Hon. Member: Smeatonian Soc., 1977; Instn of Royal Engineers, 1987. Hon. DCL Kent, 1987. *Recreations:* history, grandchildren. *Address:* 23 Chequers Park, Wye, Ashford, Kent TN25 5BB. *T:* (01233) 812720. *Club:* Oxford and Cambridge.   *Died 15 Sept. 2006.*

SAYCE, Roy Beavan, FRICS, FAAV; FRAC; Director, RPS Group (formerly Rural Planning Services) PLC, Didcot, 1980–88; *b* 19 July 1920; *s* of Roger Sayce, BScAgric, NDA, and Lilian Irene Sayce; *m* 1949, Barbara Sarah (*née* Leverton) (marr. diss. 1990); two *s*. *Educ:* Culford, Royal Agricultural Coll. (MRAC; Silver Medal 1948; FRAC 1999). FRICS 1949; FAAV 1978. Univ. of London, 1938–40. Served War, Intell., RAFVR, 1940–46. Agricultural Land Service: Asst Land Comr, Chelmsford, 1949–50; Sen. Asst Land Comr, Norwich, 1950–63; Divl Land Comr, Oxford, 1963–71; Reg. Surveyor, Land Service, Agric. Develt and Adv. Service, Bristol, 1971–76; Chief Surveyor, Land Service, Agric. Develt and Adv. Service, MAFF, 1977–80. Royal Instn of Chartered Surveyors: Mem., Gen. and Divl Councils, 1970–80; Divl Pres., Land Agency and Agric. Div., 1973–74. Chm., Farm Buildings Information Centre, 1980–85. Governor, Royal Agric. Coll., Cirencester, 1975–88. Fellow, RAC, 1999. Hon. Mem., CAAV, 1978. *Publications:* Farm Buildings, 1966; (contrib.) Walmsley's Rural Estate Management, 1969; The History of the Royal Agricultural College, 1992, and Supplement, 2003; A Rural Surveyor, 2000. *Recreation:* historical writing. *Address:* 48 Park Lane East, Reigate, Surrey RH2 8HR. *T:* (01737) 215227. *Club:* Civil Service.   *Died 11 March 2008.*

SAYEED, Dr (Abulfatah) Akram, OBE 1976; FRCPE, FRCGP; author and writer; General Medical Practitioner in Leicester, 1964–2003; Hon. Adviser in UK to Ministry of Health, Government of Bangladesh, 1991–2004; Chairman, Overseas Doctors' Association in UK, 1993–96; *b* Bangladesh, 23 Nov. 1935; *s* of late Mokhles Ahmed, school teacher; registered British; *m* 1959, Hosne-ara Ali, *d* of M. S. Ali; two *s* one *d*. *Educ:* St Joseph's Sch., Khulna; Dacca Univ. MB, BS 1958. FCPS (Bangladesh) 1991; FRCPE 1994; FRCGP 1997 (MRCGP 1992). Editor, Dacca Med. Coll. Jl and Magazines, 1957–58; Lit. Sec., Students Union. Went to USA, 1960; resident in Britain from 1961. Mem. Staff, Leicester Royal Infirmary, 1964–89; Member: Leics Local Medical Cttee, 1979–2003; Leics Family Practitioner Cttee, 1982–87; Leics Med. Adv. and Audit Gp. Member: DHSS Working Party on Asian Health Gp, 1979; DHSS Adv. Council on Violence Against NHS Staff, 1986–89; Home Office Statutory Adv. Council on Community and Race Relations, 1983–88; Health Care

Planning Team, Leics HA, 1984–86; Policy Planning (formerly Unit Management) Team, Leics Central Unit, 1986–89; Gen. Optical Council, 1994–98. British Medical Association: Mem., 1961–; Mem. Gen. Med. Services Cttee, 1993–97; Pres., Leics Div., 1993–94; Fellow, 1995; Visitor, Council, 1994–96; Mem., GMC, 1999–2003. Co-founder, Nat. Fedn of Pakistani Assocs in GB, 1963; Adviser, NCCI, 1965–68; Founder Member: Leicester Council for Community Relations, 1965; British-Bangladesh Soc.; Member: Community Relations Commn, 1968–77; E Midlands Adv. Cttee, CRE, 1978–80; RCGP Inner City Task Force, 1991–97; Stop Rickets Campaign (Chm., Leicester Campaign); Central Exec. Council, Bangladesh Med. Assoc. in UK; Chm., Standing Conf. of Asian Orgns in UK, 1973–77 (Vice-Chm., 1970–73; Pres., 1977–90); Hon. Sec., Inst. of Transcultural Health Care, 1985–93; Pres., Pakistan Assoc., Leics, 1965–71. Pres., Leicester Med. Soc., 2001–02. Mem., BBC Asian Programme Adv. Cttee, 1972–77. Special interest in problems of Asians; initiated study of problems of second generation Asians (CRE report Between Two Cultures); Overseas Doctors' Association: Founder Chm., 1975, Sponsor Chm., 1975; Gen. Sec., 1975–77; Vice-Pres., 1979–84; Vice-Chm., 1984–90; Chm., Annual Reps Meeting, 1990–93; Nat. Chm., 1993–96; Fellow, 1985; Member Editorial Board: ODA News Review, 1976–96; Ethnicity and Health, 1992–2000. FRSocMed 1981; Associate Mem., MJA. Attended First World Conf. on Muslim Educn, Mecca, 1977; did much work with disaster funds, etc. Joint Editor, Asian Who's Who, 1974–. *Publications:* Letters from Leicester, vol. 1, 2004, vol. 2, 2005, vol. 3, 2007; Shesher Adhaya (novel), 2005; Rahu Grash, 2006; In the Shadow of my Taqdir, 2006; contribs on socio-med. aspects of Asians in Britain to various jls. *Recreations:* being blind, confined to only fictional writing. *Address:* Ramna, 2 Mickleton Drive, Leicester LE5 6GD. *T:* (0116) 241 6703.   *Died 18 Jan. 2008.*

SAYER, Guy Mowbray, CBE 1978; JP; retired banker; *b* 18 June 1924; *yr s* of late Geoffrey Robley and Winifred Lily Sayer; *m* 1951, Marie Anne Sophie, *o d* of late Henri-Marie and Elisabeth Mertens; one *s* two *d Educ:* Mill Mead Prep. Sch.; Shrewsbury School. FCIB (FIB 1971). Royal Navy, 1942–46. Joined Hongkong & Shanghai Banking Corp., 1946; Gen. Man. 1969; Exec. Dir 1970; Dep. Chm. 1971; Chm., 1972–77. Treas., Hong Kong Univ., 1972–77. Mem., Exchange Fund Adv. Cttee, Hong Kong, 1971–77. MLC, 1973–74; MEC, 1974–77, Hong Kong. JP Hong Kong, 1971. Hon. LLD Hong Kong, 1978. Liveryman, Innholders' Co., 1963– (Master, 2000–01). *Recreations:* golf, walking. *Address:* 5 Pembroke Gardens, W8 6HS. *T:* (020) 7602 4578. *Clubs:* Oriental, MCC; Royal Wimbledon Golf; West Sussex Golf; Hong Kong, Shek O Country (Hong Kong).   *Died 14 April 2009.*

SAYERS, Prof. Bruce McArthur, PhD, DScEng; FREng, FIET; Professor Emeritus of Computing Applied to Medicine, and Senior Research Fellow, Imperial College of Science, Technology and Medicine, since 1993; *b* 6 Feb. 1928; *s* of John William McArthur Sayers and Mabel Florence Sayers (*née* Howe); *m* 1951, R. Woolls Humphery. *Educ:* Melbourne Boys' High School; Univ. of Melbourne (MSc); Imperial College, Univ. of London (PhD, DIC, DScEng; FIC 1996). FREng (FEng 1990). Biophysicist, Baker Med. Research Inst. and Clinical Research Unit, Alfred Hosp., Melbourne, 1949–54; Imperial College, London: Research Asst, 1955–56; Philips Elec. Ltd Research Fellow, 1957; Lectr, 1958; Senior Lectr, 1963; Reader, 1965; Prof. of Electrical Engrg Applied to Medicine, 1968–84; Head of Dept of Electrical Engrg, 1979–84; Prof. of Computing Applied to Medicine and Head of Dept of Computing, 1984–89; Kobler Prof. of the Management of IT, and Dir, Centre for Cognitive Systems, 1990–93; Dean, City and Guilds Coll., 1984–88, and 1991–93, Fellow, 1996. Pres., Section of Measurement in Medicine, Royal Soc. of Medicine, 1971–72; Hon. Consultant, Royal Throat, Nose and Ear Hosp., 1974–93; UK rep., Bio-engineering

Working Group, EEC Cttee for Med. Res., 1976–80; Temp. Adviser, WHO, 1970–76, 1981–87 and 1995–2001; Member: WHO Adv. Cttee for Health Res., 1988–94 and 1997–2000 (Vice Chm., 1990–92); Engrg Adv. Cttee, Science Mus., 1987–93. Consultant: Data Laboratories, 1968–80; Data Beta, 1981–93; Advent Eurofund, 1981–89; Shinan Investment Services SA, Switzerland, 1984–87; Advent Capital Ltd, 1985–89; Neuroscience Ltd, 1985–90; Transatlantic Capital (Biosciences) Fund, 1985–93; Director: Imperial Software Technology Ltd, 1984–90; Imperial Information Technology Ltd, 1986–90. Former Visiting Prof., Univs of Melbourne, Rio de Janeiro, McGill, Toronto. Travelling Lectr: Nuffield Foundn-Nat. Research Council, Canada, 1971; Inst. of Electron. and Radio Engrs, Australia, 1976. Member: (PC nominee), Academic Adv. Council, 1988–96, Council, 1994–96, Buckingham Univ.; Internat. Academic Cttee on Energy Studies, Ecole Polytechnique Fédérale de Lausanne, 1989–98; Scientific Council, Internat. Center of Biocybernetics, Warsaw, 1993–99; Steering Gp, Internat. Centre for Advanced Studies in Health Sci., Univ. of Ulm, 2000–; Vice-Pres., Internat. Commn on Theme: Health and Medical Scis, UNESCO on-line Encyclopaedia of Life Support Systems, 2004–. Fellow, World Innovation Foundn, 2002; FCGI 1983 (Pres., City and Guilds Coll. Assoc., 1995–96). Hon Fellow, British Cybernetics Soc., 1986. Hon. Foreign Mem., Medico-Chirurgical Soc. of Bologna, 1965; Hon. Member, Eta Kappa Nu (USA), 1980. Freeman of the City of London, 1986; Liveryman, Scientific Instrument Makers' Co., 1986. *Publications:* (ed jtly and contrib.) Understanding the Global Dimensions of Health, 2004; papers, mainly on biomedical signals and control systems, epidemiology, cardiology and audiology. *Recreations:* lazing around the Languedoc, music. *Address:* Lot's Cottage, Compton Abbas, Dorset SP7 0NQ. *T:* (01747) 811406; La Payrastrié, 81360 Montredon-Labessonnié, France. *T:* 563751018. *Club:* Athenæum.   *Died 12 May 2008.*

SCANNELL, Vernon, FRSL; free-lance author, poet and broadcaster, since 1962; *b* 23 Jan. 1922; *m* 1954, Josephine Higson; two *s* two *d* (and one *s* decd). *Educ:* elementary schools; Leeds Univ. Served with Gordon Highlanders (51st Highland Div.), ME and Normandy, 1940–45; Leeds Univ. (reading Eng. Lit.), 1946–47; various jobs incl. professional boxer, 1945–46, English Master at Hazelwood Prep. Sch., 1955–62. Southern Arts Assoc. Writing Fellowship, 1975–76; Vis. Poet, Shrewsbury Sch., 1978–79; Res. Poet, King's Sch. Canterbury, Michaelmas Term 1979. FRSL 1960. Granted a civil list pension, 1981, for services to literature. *Publications: novels:* The Fight, 1953; The Wound and the Scar, 1953; The Big Chance, 1960; The Face of the Enemy, 1961; The Shadowed Place, 1961; The Dividing Night, 1962; The Big Time, 1965; The Dangerous Ones (for children), 1970; A Lonely Game (for younger readers), 1979; Ring of Truth, 1983; Feminine Endings, 2000; *poetry:* The Masks of Love, 1960 (Heinemann Award, 1960); A Sense of Danger, 1962; Walking Wounded: poems 1962–65, 1968; Epithets of War: poems 1965–69, 1969; Mastering the Craft (Poets Today Series) (for children), 1970; (with J. Silkin) Pergamon Poets, No 8, 1970; Selected Poems, 1971; The Winter Man: new poems, 1973; The Apple Raid and other poems (for children), 1974 (Cholmondeley Poetry Prize, 1974); The Loving Game, 1975 (also in paperback); New and Collected Poems 1950–80, 1980; Winterlude and other poems, 1982; Funeral Games and other poems, 1987; The Clever Potato (for children), 1988; Soldiering On: poems of military life, 1989; Love Shouts and Whispers (for children), 1990; A Time for Fires, 1991; Travelling Light (for children), 1991; Collected Poems 1950–93, 1994; The Black and White Days, 1996; Views and Distances, 2000; Of Love and War: new and selected poems, 2002; *edited:* (with Ted Hughes and Patricia Beer) New Poems: a PEN anthology, 1962; Sporting Literature: an anthology, 1987; *criticism:* Not Without Glory: poets of World War II, 1976; How to Enjoy Poetry, 1982; How to Enjoy Novels, 1984; *autobiography:* The Tiger and

the Rose, 1971; A Proper Gentleman, 1977; Argument of Kings, 1987; Drums of Morning, 1992. *Recreations:* listening to radio (mainly music), drink, boxing (as a spectator), films, reading, learning French. loathing Tories and New Labour. *Address:* 51 North Street, Otley, W Yorks LS21 1AH. *T:* (01943) 467176.
Died 16 Nov. 2007.

SCHERMERS, Prof. Dr Henry Gerhard; Professor of Law, University of Leiden, 1978–2002; *b* 27 Sept. 1928; *s* of Petrus Schermers and Amelia M. Gooszen; *m* 1957, Hotsche A. C. Tans; one *s* two *d. Educ:* Leiden Univ. (LLM 1953; LLD 1957). Ministry of Foreign Affairs: Internat. Orgns Dept, 1953–56; Asst Legal Advr, 1956–63; University of Amsterdam: Lectr in Internat. Law, 1963–65; Prof. of Law, 1965–78. Visiting Professor: Ann Arbor, Michigan, 1968; Louisiana, 1981; QMC, 1988; Oxford, 1996. Mem., Eur. Commn of Human Rights, 1981–96. Corresp. Fellow, British Acad., 1990; Mem., Inst. de Droit Internat., 1989. Chief Editor, Common Market Law Review, 1978–93. Dr *(hc):* Edinburgh, 1993; Osnabrück, 1994. Kt of Netherlands Lion, 1984; Comdr, Order of Oranje Nassau, 1993; Officer: Crown of Belgium, 1962; Ordre des Palmes Académiques (France), 1998. *Publications:* International Institutional Law, 1972, 4th edn 2003; Judicial Protection in the European Communities, 1976, 6th edn 2001; numerous articles in Common Market Law Review and professional jls. *Recreations:* hiking, ski-ing, carpentry. *Address:* Schouwenhove 226, 2332 DV Leiden, Netherlands. *T:* (71) 5124294. *Died 31 Aug. 2006.*

SCHLESINGER, Arthur (Meier), Jr, Hon. CMG 2000; writer, educator; Schweitzer Professor of the Humanities, City University of New York, 1966–95, then Emeritus; *b* Columbus, Ohio, 15 Oct. 1917; *s* of late Arthur Meier and of Elizabeth Bancroft Schlesinger; *m* 1st, 1940, Marian Cannon (marr. diss. 1970); two *s* two *d;* 2nd, 1971, Alexandra Emmet; one *s. Educ:* Phillips Exeter Acad. AB (Harvard), 1938; Henry Fellow, Peterhouse, Cambridge, 1938–39. Soc. of Fellows, Harvard, 1939–42; US Office of War Information, 1942–43; US Office of Strategic Services, 1943–45; US Army, 1945. Mem. Adlai Stevenson Campaign Staff, 1952, 1956. Professor of History, Harvard University, 1954–61 (Associate, 1946–54); Special Assistant to President Kennedy, 1961–63. Film Reviewer: Show, 1962–65; Vogue (US), 1966–70; Saturday Review, 1977–80; Amer. Heritage, 1981. Member of Jury, Cannes Film Festival, 1964. Holds 35 honorary doctorates, incl. DLitt Oxford, 1987. Mem. of numerous Socs and Instns; Pres., Amer. Acad. of Arts and Letters, 1981–84; Chancellor, Amer. Acad., 1985–88. Pulitzer Prize: History, 1946; Biography, 1966; Nat. Book Award for Biog., 1966 (for A Thousand Days: John F. Kennedy in the White House), 1979 (for Robert Kennedy and His Times); Amer. Acad. of Arts and Letters, Gold Medal for History, 1967; US Nat. Humanities Medal, 1998; U Thant Award for Internat. Understanding, 1998. Commander, Order of Orange-Nassau (Netherlands), 1987; Ordem del Libertador (Venezuela), 1995. *Publications:* Orestes A. Brownson: a Pilgrim's Progress, 1939; The Age of Jackson, 1945; The Vital Center, 1949, (in UK) The Politics of Freedom, 1950; The General and the President (with R. H. Rovere), 1951; (co-editor) Harvard Guide to American History, 1954; The Age of Roosevelt: I: The Crisis of the Old Order, 1957; II: The Coming of the New Deal, 1958; III: The Politics of Upheaval, 1960; Kennedy or Nixon, 1960; The Politics of Hope, 1963; (ed with Morton White) Paths of American Thought, 1963; A Thousand Days: John F. Kennedy in the White House, 1965; The Bitter Heritage: Vietnam and American Democracy 1941–1966, 1967; The Crisis of Confidence: ideas, power & violence in America, 1969; (ed with F. L. Israel) History of American Presidential Elections, 1971; The Imperial Presidency, 1973; (ed) History of US Political Parties, 1973; Robert Kennedy and His Times, 1978; The Cycles of American History, 1986; The

Disuniting of America, 1991; A Life in the 20th Century: vol. I, Innocent Beginnings, 2000; War and the American Presidency, 2004; articles to magazines and newspapers. *Recreations:* theatre, movies, tennis. *Address:* 455 E 51st Street, New York, NY 10022–6474, USA. *Clubs:* Century, Knickerbocker (New York).
Died 28 Feb. 2007.

SCHOLES, Hubert, CB 1977; a Commissioner of Customs and Excise, 1978–81; *b* 22 March 1921; *s* of late Hubert Scholes and Lucy (*née* Carter); *m* 1949, Patricia Caldwell (*d* 1999); one *s. Educ:* Shrewsbury Sch.; Balliol Coll., Oxford. Served RA, 1940–45. Asst Principal, Min. of Fuel and Power, 1946; Principal, 1950; Ministry of Housing and Local Govt, 1956–57; Principal Private Sec. to Minister of Power, 1959–62; Asst Sec., 1962; Under-Sec., Min. of Power, subseq. Min. of Technol., DTI and Dept of Industry, 1968–78. Specialist Advr to H of C Employment Cttee, 1981–82. *Address:* 5A Lancaster Avenue, Farnham, Surrey GU9 8JY. *T:* (01252) 723992.
Died 11 May 2006.

SCHOLES, Rodney James; QC 1987; *b* 26 Sept. 1945; *s* of late Henry Scholes and Margaret Bower; *m* 1977, Katherin Elizabeth (*née* Keogh); two *s* (and one *s* decd). *Educ:* Wade Deacon Grammar Sch., Widnes; St Catherine's Coll., Oxford (scholar) (BA; BCL); Univ. of Cape Town (MPhil Criminology 2007). Lincoln's Inn: Hardwicke Schol., 1964; Mansfield Schol., 1967; called to the Bar, 1968, Bencher, 1997; a Recorder, 1986–2004. Mem., Northern Circuit, 1968–. *Recreations:* watching Rugby football, gazing at Table Mountain. *Address:* 706 Witsand, Beach Boulevard, Bloubergrand, Cape Town 7441, S Africa. *T:* (21) 5575442; *e-mail:* rjsqc@ scholes.co.za. *Died 16 Nov. 2009.*

SCHRAMEK, Sir Eric (Emil) von; *see* von Schramek.

SCHUSTER, Rt Rev. James Leo; Assistant Bishop of George, since 1980; *b* 18 July 1912; *s* of Rev. Harold Vernon Schuster and Elsie Jane (*née* Roberton); *m* 1951, Ilse Henriette Emmy Gottschalk; three *s* two *d* (and one *s* decd). *Educ:* Lancing; Keble Coll., Oxford. Ordained deacon, 1937; priest, 1938; Asst Missioner, Clare Coll. Mission, Rotherhithe, 1937–38; Chaplain, St Stephen's House, Oxford, 1938–40 and 1946–49; CF (EC), 1940–46; wounded, 1942; despatches, 1943; Principal, St Bede's Coll., Umtata, 1949–56; Bishop of St John's, 1956–79; Archdeacon of Riversdale, 1980–86; Rector of Swellendam, 1980–87. *Address:* PO Box 285, 19 Aanhuizen Street, Swellendam 6740, South Africa.
Died 28 Feb. 2006.

SCHWARTZ, Melvin, PhD; I. I. Rabi Professor of Physics, Columbia University, New York, 1994, then Emeritus; *b* 2 Nov. 1932; *s* of Harry Schwartz and Hannah Schwartz (*née* Shulman); *m* 1953, Marilyn Fenster; one *s* two *d. Educ:* Columbia College, NY (AB 1953); Columbia Univ., NY (PhD 1958). Associate Physicist, Brookhaven Nat. Lab., 1956–58; Asst Prof., Associate Prof. and Prof. of Physics, Columbia Univ., 1958–66; Prof. of Physics, 1966–83, Consulting Prof., 1983–, Stanford Univ.; Associate Dir for High Energy and Nuclear Physics, Brookhaven Nat. Lab., NY, 1991–94. Chief Exec. Officer, Digital Pathways Inc., 1970–91. Mem., Nat. Acad. of Scis, 1975. Hughes Prize, 1964; (jtly) Nobel Prize in Physics, 1988. *Publications:* Principles of Electrodynamics, 1972. *Recreations:* ski-ing, photography, woodworking. *Address:* PO Box 5068, Ketchum, ID 83340–5068, USA.
Died 28 Aug. 2006.

SCHWARZ-BART, André; French writer; *b* Metz, Lorraine, France, 23 May 1928; *né* Abraham Szwarcbart; 2nd *s* of parents from Poland; *m* 1961, Simone Schwarz-Bart; two *c. Educ:* self-educated; Trades Sch., Sillac; Sorbonne. Joined French Resistance at 15. Has worked in factories as a fitter and in Les Halles, Paris, while writing; has travelled to Israel, Africa and to the West Indies. *Publications:* Le Dernier des Justes, 1959 (Prix Goncourt, 1959; Eng. trans., 1960); (with Simone

Schwarz-Bart) Un plat de porc aux bananes vertes, 1967 (Jerusalem Prize, 1967); La Mulâtresse Solitude, 1972 (Eng. trans., A Woman Named Solitude, 1973); Hommage à la femme noire, 6 vols, 1988 (Eng. trans., In Praise of Black Women, 2001). *Address:* c/o Editions du Seuil, 27 rue Jacob, 75261 Paris Cedex 06, France.
Died 30 Sept. 2006.

SCHWARZKOPF, Dame Elisabeth Friederike Marie Olga, (Dame Elisabeth Legge-Schwarzkopf), DBE 1992; soprano; *b* Jarotschin/Poznan, 9 Dec. 1915; *o d of* Oberschulrat Friedrich Schwarzkopf and Elisabeth (*née* Fröhlich); held dual UK/Austrian nationality; *m* 1953, Walter Legge (*d* 1979). *Educ:* High School for Music, Berlin; studied with Lula Mysz-Gmeiner, Dr Heinrich Egenolf and Maria Ivogün-Raucheisen. Début at Deutsches Opernhaus, Berlin, 1938; has appeared at Vienna State Opera, 1943–49 and 1958–65; Royal Opera House, Covent Garden, 1948–50; La Scala, Milan, 1948–63; San Francisco Opera, 1955, Chicago Opera, etc; at reopening of Bayreuth Festival, 1951, Salzburg Festival, 1947–64. Film, Der Rosenkavalier (Salzburg Festival), 1961. *Roles:* Rosina (Barber of Seville), Blondchen, Konstanze (Entführung aus dem Serail), Susanna, Contessa (Le Nozze di Figaro), Donna Elvira (Don Giovanni), Fiordiligi (Così fan Tutte), Pamina (Die Zauberflöte), Marzelline, Leonore (Fidelio), Violette (Traviata), Gilda (Rigoletto), Alice (Falstaff), Musetta, Mimi (Bohème), Cio-sio-san (Madam Butterfly), Liù (Turandot), Manon (Manon), Eva (Meistersinger), Elsa (Lohengrin), Elisabeth (Tannhäuser), Mélisande (Pelléas and Mélisande), Iole (Herakles), Anne (Rake's Progress), Margarethe (Faust), Mařenka (Bartered Bride), Ännchen, Agathe (Freischütz), Nedda (Pagliacci), Zerbinetta (Ariadne auf Naxos), Sophie, Marschallin (Rosenkavalier), Madeleine (Capriccio). Many recordings incl. 16 complete operas, six complete operettas, symphonies, lieder and arias. Hon. Member: Royal Swedish Acad. for Arts and Sciences; Accad. S Cecilia, Roma; RAM; Wiener Staatsoper; Corres. Mem., Bayerischer Akad. der Künste. Hon. Senator, Carl Maria von Weber Music Soc., Dresden. Hon. Prof., Baden-Württemberg. MusD (*hc*) Cambridge, 1976; Hon. DMus Amer. Univ. Washington, DC, 1982; Hon. DMus Glasgow, 1990. Lilli Lehmann Medal, Salzburg, 1950; first Premio Orfeo d'oro, Mantua; Hugo Wolf Ges. Medal, Vienna, 1973; Premio Viotti, Vercelli, 1991; UNESCO Mozart Medal, Paris, 1991; Litteris et Artibus Medal, Sweden; Kammersängerin, Austria; Mozart Medal, Frankfurt; Grosses Bundesverdienstkreuz with star, Germany, 1995; Order of Merit for Sci. and the Arts (Germany), 1983; 1st class Order of Danneborg, Denmark; Commandeur, Ordre des Arts et des Lettres, France. *Publications:* (ed) On and Off the Record: a memoire of Walter Legge, 1982. *Died 3 Aug. 2006.*

SCOFIELD, (David) Paul, CH 2001; CBE 1956; actor; *b* 21 Jan. 1922; *s* of Edward H. and M. Scofield; *m* 1943, Joy Parker, actress; one *s* one *d. Educ:* Varndean Sch. for Boys, Brighton. Theatre training, Croydon Repertory, 1939; London Mask Theatre School, 1940. Shakespeare with ENSA, 1940–41; Birmingham Repertory Theatre, 1942; CEMA Factory tours, 1942–43; Whitehall Theatre, 1943; Birmingham Repertory, 1943–45; Stratford-upon-Avon, 1946–48. Mem., Royal Shakespeare Directorate, 1966–68. Associate Dir, Nat. Theatre, 1970–71. London theatres: Arts, 1946; Phoenix, 1947; Adventure Story, and The Seagull, St James's, 1949; Ring Round the Moon, Globe, 1950; Much Ado About Nothing, Phœnix, 1952; The River Line, Edin. Fest., Lyric (Hammersmith), Strand, 1952; John Gielgud's Company, 1952–53; Richard II, The Way of the World, Venice Preserved, etc; A Question of Fact, Piccadilly, 1953–54; Time Remembered, Lyric, Hammersmith, New Theatre, 1954–55; Hamlet, Moscow, 1955; Paul Scofield-Peter Brook Season, Phœnix Theatre, 1956; Hamlet, The Power and the Glory, Family Reunion; A Dead Secret, Piccadilly Theatre, 1957; Expresso Bongo, Saville Theatre, 1958; The Complaisant Lover, Globe Theatre, 1959; A Man For All Seasons, Globe Theatre, 1960, New

York, 1961–62; Coriolanus and Love's Labour's Lost, at Shakespeare Festival Season, Stratford, Ont., 1961; King Lear: Stratford-on-Avon, Aldwych Theatre, 1962–63, Europe and US, 1964; Timon of Athens, Stratford-on-Avon, 1965; The Government Inspector, also Staircase, Aldwych, 1966; Macbeth, Stratford-on-Avon, 1967, Russia, Finland, 1967, Aldwych, 1968; The Hotel in Amsterdam, Royal Court, 1968; Uncle Vanya, Royal Court, 1970; Savages, Royal Court and Comedy, 1973; The Tempest, Wyndhams, 1975; Dimetos, Comedy, 1976; The Family, Royal Exchange, Manchester, and Haymarket, 1978; I am Not Rappaport, Apollo, 1986–87; Exclusive, Strand, 1989; Heartbreak House, Haymarket, 1992; *National Theatre:* The Captain of Kopenick, The Rules of the Game, 1971; Volpone, The Madras House, 1977; Amadeus, 1979; Othello, 1980; Don Quixote, A Midsummer Night's Dream, 1982; John Gabriel Borkman, 1996. *Films:* The Train, 1964; A Man for All Seasons, 1966 (from the play); Bartleby, King Lear, 1971; Scorpio, 1973; A Delicate Balance, 1974; Nineteen Nineteen, 1985; When the Whales Came, 1989; Henry V, 1989; Hamlet, 1991; Utz, 1992; Quiz Show, 1995; The Little Riders, 1995; The Crucible, 1997; *TV films:* Anna Karenina, 1985; The Attic, 1988; *TV serial:* Martin Chuzzlewit, 1994. Hon. LLD Glasgow, 1968; Hon. DLit Kent, 1973; Hon. DLitt: Sussex, 1985; St Andrews, 1998; Oxon 2002. Shakespeare prize, Hamburg, 1972; Shakespeare Birthday Award, Shakespeare Birthday Celebrations Cttee, Stratford upon-Avon, 1999. *Relevant publications:* Paul Scofield, by J. C. Trewin, 1956; Paul Scofield - The Biography, by Garry O'Connor, 2002. *Address:* The Gables, Balcombe, W Sussex RH17 6ND. *Club:* Athenæum. *Died 19 March 2008.*

SCOTHORNE, Prof. Raymond John, BSc, MD Leeds; MD Chicago; FRSE; FRCSGlas; Regius Professor of Anatomy, University of Glasgow, 1972–90, then Emeritus; *b* 1920; *s* of late John and Lavinia Scothorne; *m* 1948, Audrey, *o d* of late Rev. Selwyn and Winifred Gillott; one *s* two *d. Educ:* Royal Grammar School, Newcastle upon Tyne; Universities of Leeds and Chicago, BSc (Hons) 1st cl. (Leeds), 1941; MD (Chicago), Rockefeller Student, 1941–43; MB (Hons) 1st cl. (Leeds), 1944; MD (with Distinction) (Leeds), 1951. Demonstrator and Lecturer in Anatomy, 1944–50, Univ. of Leeds; Sen. Lecturer in Anatomy, 1950–60, Univ. of Glasgow; Prof., Univ. of Newcastle upon Tyne, 1960–72. Hon. Sec., Anat. Soc. of Great Britain and Ireland, 1967–71, Pres., 1971–73; Hon. Fellow, British Assoc. of Clinical Anatomists (Pres., 1986–88); Mem., Med. Sub-Cttee, UGC, 1967–76. Hon. Member: Assoc. des Anatomistes; Amer. Assoc. of Clinical Anatomists. Struthers Prize and Gold Medal in Anatomy, Univ. of Glasgow, 1957. Anatomical Editor, Companion to Medical Studies; British Editor, Clinical Anatomy, 1987–2001. *Publications:* chapter on Peripheral Nervous System in Hamilton's Textbook of Anatomy, 2nd edn, 1975; chapters on Early Development, on Tissue and Organ Growth, on Skin and on the Nervous System in Companion to Medical Studies, 3rd edn, 1985; chapter on Development and Structure of Liver in Pathology of the Liver, 1979, 4th edn 2002; chapter on Respiratory System in Cunningham's Textbook, 12th edn, 1981; chapter on Development of Spinal Cord and Vertebral Column in Surgery of the Spine, 1992; papers on embryology, histology and tissue transplantation. *Address:* Southernknowe, Linlithgow, West Lothian EH49 6BQ. *T:* (01506) 842463. *Died 11 Sept. 2007.*

SCOTT, Prof. Alastair Ian, FRS 1978; FRSE 1981; Distinguished Professor and Director, Center for Biological NMR, since 1981, Derek Barton Professor of Chemistry and Robert Welch Chair in Chemistry, since 2002, Texas A & M University; *b* 10 April 1928; *s* of William Scott and Nell Florence (*née* Newton); *m* 1950, Elizabeth Wilson (*née* Walters); one *s* one *d. Educ:* Glasgow Univ. (BSc, PhD, DSc). Postdoctoral Fellow, Ohio State Univ., 1952–53; Technical Officer, ICI (Nobel Div.), 1953–54; Postdoctoral Fellow, London and Glasgow Univs, 1954–57; Lectr, Glasgow Univ.,

1957–62; Professor: Univ. of British Columbia, 1962–65; Univ. of Sussex, 1965–68; Yale Univ., 1968–77; Texas A&M Univ., 1977–80; Edinburgh Univ., 1980–83 (Forbes Prof., 1980–81); Davidson Prof. of Chem. and Biochem., Texas A & M Univ., 1981–2002. Lectures: Karl Folkers, Wisconsin Univ., 1964; Burger, Virginia Univ., 1975; Benjamin Rush, Pennsylvania Univ., 1975; 5 colls, Mass, 1977; Andrews, NSW Univ., 1979; Dreyfus, Indiana Univ., 1983; Centenary, RSC, 1994; Gottlieb Meml, Univ. of Illinois, 1995; Bakerian, Royal Soc., 1996. FAAAS 1988. Hon. Mem., Pharmaceutical Soc. of Japan, 1985. Hon. MA Yale, 1968; Hon. DSc: Coimbra, 1990; Paris, 1992. Corday-Morgan Medallist, Chemical Soc., 1964; Natural Products Res. Award, Royal Soc. Chem., 1995; Ernest Guenther Medallist, 1976, Cope Scholar Award, 1992, Nakanishi Prize, 2003, Amer. Chem. Soc.; Res. Achievement Award, Amer. Soc. of Pharmacognosy, 1993; Tetrahedron Prize, Pergamon, 1995; Robert A. Welch Award in Chem., R. A. Welch Foundn, Houston, Tex, 2000; Davy Medal, Royal Soc., 2001; Royal Medal, RSE, 2001; Texas Scientist of the Year, Texas Acad. of Sci., 2002. *Publications*: Interpretation of Ultraviolet Spectra of Natural Products, 1964; (with T. K. Devon) Handbook of Naturally Occurring Compounds, 1972; numerous pubns in learned jls. *Recreations*: music, gardening. *Address*: Department of Chemistry, Texas A & M University, 3255 TAMU College Station, TX 77843–3255, USA. *T*: (979) 8453243. *Club*: Athenæum.   *Died 18 April 2007.*

SCOTT, Sir David; see Scott, Sir W. D. S.

SCOTT, Sir David (Aubrey), GCMG 1979 (KCMG 1974; CMG 1966); HM Diplomatic Service, retired; *b* 3 Aug. 1919; *s* of late Hugh Sumner Scott and Barbara E. Scott, JP; *m* 1941, Vera Kathleen (*d* 2010), *d* of late Major G. H. Ibbitson, MBE, RA; two *s* one *d*. *Educ*: Charterhouse; Birmingham University (Mining Engrg). Served War of 1939–45, Royal Artillery, 1939–47; Chief Radar Adviser, British Military Mission to Egyptian Army, 1945–47, Major. Appointed to CRO, 1948; Asst Private Secretary to Secretary of State, 1949; Cape Town/Pretoria, 1951–53; Cabinet Office, 1954–56; Malta Round Table Conf., 1955; Secretary-General, Malaya and Caribbean Constitutional Confs, 1956; Singapore, 1956–58; Monckton Commn, 1960; Dep. High Comr, Fedn of Rhodesia and Nyasaland, 1961–63; Imperial Defence College, 1964; Dep. High Comr, India, 1965–67; British High Comr to Uganda, and Ambassador (non-resident) to Rwanda, 1967–70; Asst Under-Sec. of State, FCO, 1970–72; British High Comr to New Zealand, and Governor, Pitcairn Is., 1973–75; HM Ambassador to Republic of S Africa, 1976–79. Chairman: Ellerman Lines plc, 1982–83; Nuclear Resources Ltd, 1984–88; Director: Barclays Bank International Ltd, 1979–85; Mitchell Cotts plc, 1980–86; Delta Metal Overseas Ltd, 1980–83; Bradbury Wilkinson plc, 1984–86; Consultant, Thomas De La Rue & Co. Ltd, 1986–88. Pres., Uganda Soc. for Disabled Children, 1984–2000; Vice-Pres., UK South Africa Trade Assoc., 1980–85. Mem., Manchester Olympic Bid Cttee, 1989–93. Gov., Sadler's Wells Trust, 1984–89. Trustee, John Ellerman Foundn, 1979–2000 (Chm., 1997–2000). Freeman, City of London, 1982; Liveryman, Shipwrights' Co., 1983. *Publications*: Ambassador in Black and White, 1981; Window into Downing Street, 2003; contrib. DNB. *Recreations*: music, birdwatching. *Address*: Birtley House, Birtley Road, Bramley, Guildford, Surrey GU5 0LB. *Club*: Royal Over-Seas League (Chm., 1981–86; Vice-Pres., 1986–98, 2005–; Pres., 1998–2002).   *Died 27 Dec. 2010.*

SCOTT, Douglas Andrew Montagu-Douglas-, OBE 1994; Chief Executive and Director, Cancer Relief Macmillan Fund, 1987–95; *b* 21 June 1930; *s* of late Col C. A. Montagu-Douglas-Scott, DSO and Lady Victoria Haig, *d* of Field Marshal 1st Earl Haig, KT, GCB, OM, GCVO, KCIE; *m* 1st, 1954, Bridget George (marr. diss. 1976), *d* of Air Vice-Marshal Sir Robert George, KCMG,

KCVO, KBE, CB, MC; two *d* (one *s* decd); 2nd, 1977, Daphne Shortt (marr. diss. 2000), *d* of Dr Cyril Shortt, Winchcombe; 3rd, 2005, Monica, former wife of Sir Dallas Bernard, 2nd Bt; one step *d*. *Educ*: Eton; RMA, Sandhurst. Commnd Irish Guards, 1950. ADC to Gov. of S Australia, 1953–55; Tubemakers of Australia, 1955–63; TI Group, 1963–83: Dir, Accles & Pollock Ltd, 1966–76; Man. Dir, TI Chesterfield Ltd, 1976–81; Dir, TI Gp Overseas Ops, 1981–83; Recruitment Consultant, PE Internat. plc, 1984–87. Director: S Warwicks Gen. Hosps NHS Trust, 1995–97; Global Cancer Concern, 1995–2000; CLIC, 1997–2000; Compton Hospice, 1995–99. Douglas Haig Fellow, 2004. *Publications*: (ed) The Preparatory Prologue: Douglas Haig, diaries and letters 1861–1914, 2006. *Recreations*: painting, gardening, fishing, opera. *Address*: Stonefield, Bemersyde, Melrose TD6 9DP. *T*: (01835) 824123. *Clubs*: Pratt's, MCC, New (Edinburgh).   *Died 30 June 2010.*

SCOTT, Prof. Douglas Frederick Schumacher; Professor of German in the University of Durham (late Durham Colleges), 1958–75, then Emeritus Professor; *b* Newcastle under Lyme, Staffs, 17 Sept. 1910; *o s* of Frederick Scott and Magdalena (*née* Gronbach); *m* 1942, Margaret (*d* 1972), *o d* of late Owen Gray Ellis, Beaumaris, Anglesey, and Helen (*née* Gibbs); two *d*. *Educ*: Queen Mary's Grammar School, Walsall, Staffs; Dillman-Realgymnasium Stuttgart, Germany; University of Tübingen, Göttingen (Dr phil); University College, London (MA). Part-time Assistant, German Dept, University Coll. London, 1935–37; Lecturer in charge German Dept, Huddersfield Technical Coll., 1937–38; Lecturer in German, King's Coll., Newcastle, 1938–46; released for service with Friends' Ambulance Unit, 1940–46; Lecturer in German, King's Coll., London, 1946–49; Reader and Head of Dept of German, The Durham Colls, 1949–58. *Publications*: Some English Correspondents of Goethe, 1949; W. v. Humboldt and the Idea of a University, 1960; Luke Howard: his correspondence with Goethe and his continental journey of 1816, 1976; articles and reviews on German lit. and Anglo-German literary relations in various English and German journals. *Recreations*: music, travel. *Address*: 6 Fieldhouse Terrace, Durham DH1 4NA. *T*: (0191) 386 4518.   *Died 15 April 2006.*

SCOTT, Esme, (Lady Scott), CBE 1985; WS; Chair, Volunteer Centre UK, 1993–96; *b* 7 Jan. 1932; *d* of David Burnett, SSC and Jane Burnett (*née* Thornton); *m* 1st, 1956, Ian Macfarlane Walker, WS (*d* 1988); one *s*; 2nd, 1990, Sir Kenneth Bertram Adam Scott, KCVO, CMG; one step *s* one step *d*. *Educ*: St George's School for Girls, Edinburgh; Univ. of Edinburgh (MA, LLB). NP; Vice-Pres., Inst. of Trading Standards Admin. Lectr in Legal Studies, Queen Margaret College, Edinburgh, 1977–83. Voluntary worker, Citizens' Advice Bureau, 1960–85; Chm., Scottish Assoc. of CABx, 1986–88. Comr, Equal Opportunities Commn, 1986–90. Chm., Scottish Consumer Council, 1980–85; Vice-Chm., Nat. Consumer Council, 1984–87; Chm., Volunteer Development Scotland, 1989–92; Member: Expert Cttee, Multiple Surveys and Valuations (Scotland), 1982–84; Working Party on Procedure for Judicial Review of Admin. Action, 1983–84; Cttee on Conveyancing, 1984; Scottish Cttee, Council on Tribunals, 1986–92; Social Security Adv. Cttee, 1990–96; Direct Mail Services Standards Bd, 1990–95; Privacy Adv. Cttee, Common Services Agency, 1990–95; SIB, 1991–93; Monopolies and Mergers Commn, 1992–95; Exec. Cttee, NCVO, 1993–95. Member: Court, Edinburgh Univ., 1989–92; Council, St George's Sch. for Girls, 1989–96. FRSA. *Recreation*: crosswords. *Address*: 13 Clinton Road, Edinburgh EH9 2AW. *T*: (0131) 447 5191.   *Died 24 July 2010.*

SCOTT, James Steel; Professor of Obstetrics and Gynæcology, 1961–89, and Dean of Faculty of Medicine, 1986–89, University of Leeds, Emeritus Professor; *b* 18 April 1924; *s* of late Dr Angus M. Scott and late Margaret Scott; *m* 1958, Olive Sharpe; two *s*. *Educ*: Glasgow

Academy; University of Glasgow. MB, ChB 1946, MD 1959; FRCSEd 1959; FRCOG 1962 (MRCOG 1953); FRCS (ad eund) 1986. Service in RAMC, 1947–49. Liverpool University: Obstetric Tutor, 1954; Lecturer, 1958; Senior Lecturer, 1960. Publications: contrib. to New Engl. Jl of Medicine, Lancet, BMJ, Jl of Obst. and Gynæc. of Brit. Empire, Amer. Jl of Obstetrics and Gynæcology, etc. Recreations: ski-ing, biography. Address: Byards Lodge, Boroughbridge Road, Knaresborough, N Yorks HG5 0LT.   Died 17 Sept. 2006.

SCOTT, John James, PhD; medical research consultant, since 2003; b 4 Sept. 1924; s of late Col John Creagh Scott, DSO, OBE and Mary Elizabeth Marjory (née Murray of Polmaise); m 1st, Katherine Mary (née Bruce); twin d; 2nd, Heather Marguerite (née Douglas Brown); 3rd, June Rose (née Mackie); twin s. Educ: Radley (Schol.); Corpus Christi Coll., Cambridge (Schol.); National Inst. for Medical Research, London. War Service, Captain, Argyll and Sutherland Highlanders, 1944–47. BA 1st cl. hons Nat. Sci. Tripos, Pts I and II, 1950, MA 1953, Cantab; PhD London 1954. Senior Lectr in Chem. Pathology, St Mary's Hosp., 1955–61; Mem. Editorial Bd, Biochem. Jl, 1956–61; Mem. Cttee of Biochem. Soc., 1961; Vis. Scientist, Nat. Insts of Health, Bethesda, Md, 1961. Joined Govt Service: Singapore, 1961–66; London, 1966–71; Rio de Janeiro and Brasilia, 1971–74; NI (Stormont), 1974–76; London, 1976–80. Asst Managing Dir, later Commercial Dir, Industrial Engines (Sales) Ltd, Elbar Group, 1980; Man. Dir, Dudmass Ltd, 1983–93; Associate: Trident Life, 1984–85; Save & Prosper Group, 1985–95; Financial Advr, Allied Dunbar, 1995–96. Sir Nicholas Bacon Prize, Cambridge, 1950. Publications: papers in Biochem. Jl, Proc. Royal Soc. and other learned jls. Recreations: botany, photography, music. Address: Moat Cottage, Northbeck, Scredington, Sleaford, Lincs NG34 0AD. Clubs: Carlton, Institute of Directors; Leander (Henley-on-Thames); Hawks (Cambridge); Ski Club of GB.   Died 14 May 2006.

SCOTT, Kenneth Farish, MC 1943 and Bar, 1944; FREng, FICE; Senior Partner, 1977–84, Senior Consultant, 1984–87, Sir Alexander Gibb & Partners; b 21 Dec. 1918; s of Norman James Stewart and Ethel May Scott; m 1945, Elizabeth Mary Barrowcliff (d 2004); one s one d. Educ: Stockton Grammar School; Constantine Tech. Coll. Served Royal Engineers, 1939–46. Joined Sir Alexander Gibb & Partners, 1946; Resident Engineer, Hydro-Electric Works, Scotland, 1946–52; Chief Rep., NZ, 1952–55, Scotland, 1955–59; Partner 1959, Senior Partner 1977; responsible for design and supervision of construction of major water resource develt projects, incl. Latiyan Dam, 1959–67, Lar Dam 1968–82, Greater Tehran Water Supply, 1959–82; major maritime works incl. modernisation Devonport Dockyard, 1970–80; internat. airports at Tripoli, 1966–70, Bahrain, 1970–72. Pres., Soc. des Ingénieurs et Scientifiques de France (British Section), 1975; Vice-Pres., ICE, 1985–87. Chm., Assoc. of Consulting Engineers, 1976. FREng (FEng 1979). Hon. Mem., Instn of RE, 1982. Publications: papers to ICE and International Congress of Large Dams. Recreations: sailing, golf, wood working. Address: Forest House, Brookside Road, Brockenhurst, Hants SO42 7SS. T: (01590) 623531. Clubs: Special Forces, Royal Over-Seas League; Royal Southampton Yacht.   Died 25 Dec. 2007.

SCOTT, Maurice FitzGerald, FBA 1990; Official Fellow in Economics, Nuffield College, Oxford, 1968–92, then Emeritus Fellow; b 6 Dec. 1924; s of Colonel G. C. Scott, OBE and H. M. G. Scott; m 1953, Eleanor Warren (née Dawson) (d 1989); three d. Educ: Wadham Coll., Oxford (MA), Nuffield Coll., Oxford (BLitt). Served RE, 1943–46. OEEC, Paris, 1949–51; Paymaster-General's Office (Lord Cherwell), 1951–53; Cabinet Office, 1953–54; NIESR, London, 1954–57; Tutor in Economics and Student of Christ Church, Oxford, 1957–68; NEDO, London, 1962–63; OECD, Paris, 1967–68. Publications: A Study of U.K. Imports, 1963;

(with I. M. D. Little and T. Scitovsky) Industry and Trade in Some Developing Countries, 1970; (with J. D. MacArthur and D. M. G. Newbery) Project Appraisal in Practice, 1976; (with R. A. Laslett) Can We get back to Full Employment?, 1978; (with W. M. Corden and I. M. D. Little) The Case against General Import Restrictions, 1980; A New View of Economic Growth, 1989; Peter's Journey, 1998. Recreation: walking. Address: 11 Blandford Avenue, Oxford OX2 8EA. T: (01865) 559115.   Died 2 March 2009.

SCOTT, Michael John; broadcaster; b 8 Dec. 1932; s of Tony and Pam Scott; m 1956, Sylvia Hudson; one d. Educ: Latymer Upper Sch., Hammersmith; Clayesmore, Iwerne Minster, Dorset. National Service, RAOC, 1951–53. Stagehand with Festival Ballet, and film extra, 1954; TV production trainee, Rank Organization, 1955; Granada TV: joined as floor manager, 1956; Prog. Dir, 1957; Producer/Performer, daily magazine prog., 1963–65; Presenter, Cinema, 1965–68; Exec. Producer, local progs, 1968–73; World in Action interviewer, and producer/performer of other progs, 1974–75; Exec. Producer and Reporter, Nuts and Bolts of the Economy, 1975–78; Dep. Prog. Controller, 1978–79; Prog. Controller, 1979–87; returned to active broadcasting, via live daily programme The Time... The Place, 1987–93. Director: Channel 4 Television Co., 1984–87; Granada TV, 1978–87. Recreations: watching the box, jogging, a 1932 Lagonda, a garden.   Died 30 May 2008.

SCOTT, Peter Francis, CBE 1982; Chairman, Provincial Insurance Company Ltd, 1957–77; b 21 Sept. 1917; s of Francis C. Scott and Frieda Jager; m 1953, Prudence Mary Milligan (marr. diss. 1974); one s three d. Educ: Winchester; Oriel Coll., Oxford (BA). Commnd 1st Bn, KRRC; Capt.; served War, 1939–46: with 8th Army in N Africa, Sicily and Italy; with 21st Army Gp in NW Europe. Joined Provincial Insurance Co. Ltd, 1946: Dir, 1946–77; Pres., 1977; Pres., Sand Aire Ltd, 1997. Former Member: Northern Econ. Planning Council; Careers Res. Adv. Council; Standing Cttee on Museums and Galleries. Former Chairman: Trustees, Brathay Hall; Lake Dist Art Gall. Trust; Kendal Brewery Arts Centre Trust; Mem., Lake Dist Mus. Trust. Chm., Lake Dist Cttee, NT. Dir, National Theatre (Mem., Exec. Cttee); Mem., Council, Northern Arts Assoc. DL, High Sheriff 1963, Westmorland. Freeman of Kendal. Hon. LLD Lancaster. Clubs: Brooks's, Garrick, Royal Automobile.   Died 13 Nov. 2010.

SCOTT, His Honour Roger Martin; a Circuit Judge, 1993–2009; b 8 Sept. 1944; s of Hermann Albert and Sarah Margaret Scott; m 1966, Diana Elizabeth Clark; two s one d. Educ: Mill Hill Sch.; St Andrews Univ. (LLB). Called to the Bar, Lincoln's Inn, 1968. Recreations: golf, cricket, walking, theatre. Address: North Eastern Circuit Administrator's Office, West Riding House, Albion Street, Leeds LS1 5AA. T: (0113) 244 1841. Club: Yorkshire County Cricket (Leeds).   Died 8 May 2010.

SCOTT, Rear-Adm. Sir (William) David (Stewart), KBE 1977; CB 1974; b 5 April 1921; yr s of Brig. Henry St George Stewart Scott, CB, DSO and bar and Ida Christabel Trower Scott (née Hogg); m 1952, Pamela Dorothy Whitlock; one s two d. Educ: Tonbridge. Naval Cadet, 1938; comd HM Submarines: Umbra, 1944; Vulpine, Satyr, 1945; Andrew, 1953; Thermopylae, 1955; comd HM Ships: Gateshead, 1951; Surprise, 1960; Adamant, 2nd Submarine Sqdn, 1963; Fife, 1969; Trng Comdr, BRNC, Dartmouth, 1956; Fleet Ops Officer, Home Fleet, 1958; US Naval War Coll., 1962; Dep. Dir of Defence Plans, Navy, 1965; Chief of British Navy Staff, Washington, UK Rep. to SACLANT, and Naval Attaché to USA, 1971–73; Deputy Controller, Polaris, 1973–76; Chief Polaris Executive, 1976–80, retd; Comdr 1956; Captain 1962; Rear-Adm. 1971. Address: c/o Lloyds TSB, Pall Mall Branch, 8–10 Waterloo Place, SW1Y 4BE.   Died 20 Jan. 2006.

SCOTT-JAMES, Anne Eleanor, (Lady Lancaster); author and journalist; *b* 5 April 1913; *d* of R. A. Scott-James and Violet Brooks; *m* 1st, 1939, Derek Verschoyle (marr. diss.); 2nd, 1944, Macdonald Hastings (marr. diss. 1962; he *d* 1982); one *s* one *d*; 3rd, 1967, Sir Osbert Lancaster, CBE (*d* 1986). *Educ:* St Paul's Girls' Sch.; Somerville Coll., Oxford (Class. Schol.). Editorial staff of *Vogue*, 1934–41; Woman's Editor, *Picture Post*, 1941–45; Editor, *Harper's Bazaar*, 1945–51; Woman's Editor, *Sunday Express*, 1953–57; Woman's Adviser to Beaverbrook Newspapers, 1959–60; Columnist, *Daily Mail*, 1960–68; freelance journalist, broadcasting, TV, 1968–. Member: Council, RCA, 1948–51, 1954–56; Council, RHS, 1978–82. *Publications:* In the Mink, 1952; Down to Earth, 1971; Sissinghurst: The Making of a Garden, 1975; (with Osbert Lancaster) The Pleasure Garden, 1977; The Cottage Garden, 1981; (with Christopher Lloyd) Glyndebourne—the Gardens, 1983; The Language of the Garden: a personal anthology, 1984; (introd.) Our Village, by Mary Russell Mitford, 1987; The Best Plants for your Garden, 1988; (with Ray Desmond) The British Museum Book of Flowers, 1989; (with Clare Hastings) Gardening Letters to My Daughter, 1990; Sketches from a Life (autobiog.), 1993. *Recreations:* reading, gardening, travelling, looking at churches and flowers. *Died 13 May 2009.*

SCOTT WRIGHT, Prof. Margaret, PhD; Dean, 1979–84, and Professor, 1979–86, then Emeritus, Faculty of Nursing, University of Calgary; *b* 10 Sept. 1923; *d* of Ebenezer Wright and Margaret Greig Masson. *Educ:* Wallington County Grammar Sch.; Univ. of Edinburgh; St George's and Queen Charlotte's Hosps, London. MA Hons Hist., PhD and Dipl. Med. Services Admin, Edinburgh; SRN and SCM. Research Asst, Unilever Ltd, 1947–50; Student Nurse, St George's Hosp., 1950–53; Student Midwife, Queen Charlotte's Hosp. and E Sussex CC, 1954–55; Staff Nurse and Sister, St George's Hosp., London, 1955–57; Boots Research Fellow in Nursing, Dept of Social Medicine, Univ. of Edinburgh, 1957–61; Rockefeller Fellow, USA, 1961–62; Deputy Matron, St George's Hosp., 1962–64; Matron, Middlesex Hosp., 1965–68; Dir, Dept of Nursing Studies, Univ. of Edinburgh, 1968–71; Prof. of Nursing Studies, Univ. of Edinburgh, 1972–76; Dir and Prof. of Sch. of Nursing, Dalhousie Univ., Nova Scotia, 1976–79. Second Vice-Pres., Internat. Council of Nurses, 1973–77. Margaret Scott Wright Annual Lecture in Nursing Research established in Faculty of Nursing, Univ. of Alberta, 1984. Silver Jubilee Medal, 1977. *Publications:* Experimental Nurse Training at Glasgow Royal Infirmary, 1963; Student Nurses in Scotland, 1968. *Recreations:* walking, music, reading, travel. *Address:* 11 Victoria Street, Norwich NR1 3QX. *Died 11 March 2008.*

SCOURFIELD, Edward Grismond Beaumont D.; *see* Davies-Scourfield.

SCROGGIE, Alan Ure Reith, CBE 1973 (OBE 1961); QPM 1968; one of HM's Inspectors of Constabulary, 1963–75; *b* 10 March 1912; *s* of late Col William Reith John Scroggie, CIE, IMS, Callander, Perthshire; *m* 1940, Shiela Catherine (*d* 2003), *d* of late Finlay Mackenzie, Elgin, Morayshire; two *s*. *Educ:* Cargilfield Preparatory Sch.; Fettes Coll.; Edinburgh Univ. (BL). Joined Edinburgh City Police, 1930; Asst Chief Constable of Bucks, 1947–53; Chief Constable of Northumberland, 1953–63. OStJ 1955. *Recreations:* golf, country pursuits, gardening. *Address:* 8 Mackie House, Bank Street, Elie, Fife K19 1BL. *Clubs:* Royal and Ancient (St Andrews); Golf House (Elie). *Died 8 June 2006.*

SEABROOK, Air Vice-Marshal Geoffrey Leonard, CB 1965; *b* 25 Aug. 1909; *s* of late Robert Leonard Seabrook; *m* 1949, Beryl Mary (*née* Hughes); one *s* one *d*. *Educ:* King's Sch., Canterbury. Commissioned in RAF (Accountant Branch), 1933; served in: Middle East, 1935–43; Bomber Command, 1943–45; Transport Command, 1945–47; Iraq, 1947–49; Signals Command, 1949–51; Air Ministry Organisation and Methods, 1951–53; Home Command Group Captain Organisation,

1953–56; Far East Air Force, 1957–59; idc 1960; Director of Personnel, Air Ministry, 1961–63; Air Officer Administration, HQ, RAF Tech. Trng Comd, 1963–66; retired June 1966. Air Cdre 1961; Air Vice-Marshal, 1964. Head of Secretarial Branch, Royal Air Force, 1963–66. FCA 1957 (Associate, 1932). *Recreations:* sailing, golf. *Address:* Long Pightle, Piltdown, Uckfield, E Sussex TN22 3XB. *T:* (01825) 722322. *Clubs:* Royal Air Force; Piltdown Golf. *Died 16 June 2008.*

SEARBY, Philip James, CBE 1981; Secretary and Authority Finance Officer, UK Atomic Energy Authority, 1976–84; *b* 20 Sept. 1924; *s* of Leonard James and Lillian Mary Searby; *m* 1955, Mary Brent Dudley; two *s*. *Educ:* Bedford Sch.; Wadham Coll., Oxford (MA). Entered Civil Service, Min. of Nat. Insurance, 1949; Prime Minister's Statistical Branch, 1951; Private Sec. to Paymaster Gen. (Lord Cherwell), 1952; Principal, Atomic Energy Office, 1954. Joined UK Atomic Energy Authority, 1956; Dep. Gen. Sec., Harwell, 1959; Principal Economics and Programmes Officer, 1965; Authority Finance and Programmes Officer, 1971. St Albans Diocesan Reader, 1950. *Recreation:* reading. *Address:* 5 Borodale, Kirkwick Avenue, Harpenden, Herts AL5 2QW. *T:* (01582) 760837. *Died 23 June 2007.*

SEATON, Prof. Michael John, FRS 1967; Professor of Physics, Department of Physics and Astronomy, University College London, 1963–88, then Emeritus; Senior Fellow, Science and Engineering Research Council, 1984–88; *b* 16 Jan. 1923; *s* of late Arthur William Robert Seaton and Helen Amelia Seaton; *m* 1st, 1943, Olive May (*d* 1959), *d* of Charles Edward Singleton; one *s* one *d*; 2nd, 1960, Joy Clarice, *d* of Harry Albert Balchin; one *s*. *Educ:* Wallington Co. Sch., Surrey; University Coll., London (Fellow, 1972). BSc 1948, PhD 1951, London. Dept of Physics, UCL: Asst Lectr, 1950; Lectr, 1953; Reader, 1959; Prof., 1963. Chargé de Recherche, Institut d'Astrophysique, Paris, 1954–55; Univ. of Colorado, 1961; Fellow-Adjoint, Jt Inst. for Laboratory Astrophysics (Nat. Inst. of Standards and Technology and Univ. of Colorado), Boulder, Colo, 1964–. Hon. Mem., Amer. Astronomical Soc., 1983; For. Associate, Amer. Nat. Acad. of Scis, 1986. Pres., RAS, 1979–81, Gold Medal, 1983; Guthrie Medal and Prize, Inst. of Physics, 1984; Hughes Medal, Royal Soc., 1992. Dr *hc* Observatoire de Paris, 1976; Hon. DSc QUB, 1982. *Publications:* papers on atomic physics and astrophysics in various jls. *Address:* Chatsworth, Bwlch, Powys LD3 7RQ. *T:* (01874) 730652. *Died 29 May 2007.*

SEDDON, (Edward) Jeremy; Chief Executive, British Invisibles, 1997–2001; *b* 14 April 1941; *s* of Col Roland Nelson Seddon, OBE and Dorothy Ida Kathleen Seddon (*née* Canning); *m* 1975, Prudence Mary Clarke; one *s* two *d*. *Educ:* King's Sch., Bruton; Southampton Univ. (BScEng). Associated Electrical Industries, 1958–68; Dalgety Ltd, 1968–73; Barclays Merchant Bank, then BZW Ltd, 1973–97: Dir, Barclays Development Capital, 1978–87; Head, BZW Privatisation and Govt Adv. Practice, 1987–95; Chm., BZW & Barclays India, 1995–97. Mem., Competition Commn, 1998–. Chm., Chilworth Sci. Park, 2004– (Dir, 2001–). Council Mem., Chartered Soc. of Queen Square, 1996–. *Recreations:* gardening, music, sailing. *Address:* The Meadow House, Toys Hill, Westerham, Kent TN16 1QE. *T:* (01732) 750699. *Clubs:* Royal Thames Yacht, Special Forces. *Died 9 Nov. 2006.*

SEDGWICK, Nina, (Mrs A. R. M. Sedgwick); *see* Milkina, N.

SEGAL, Prof. Erich; Adjunct Professor of Classics, Yale University, 1981–88; *b* 16 June 1937; *s* of Samuel M. Segal, PhD, DHL and Cynthia Shapiro Segal; *m* 1975, Karen James; two *d* (one *s* decd). *Educ:* Harvard (Boylston Prize 1957, Bowdoin Prize 1959; AB 1958, AM 1959, PhD 1965, Guggenheim Fellowship, 1968). Teaching Fellow, Harvard, 1959–64; Lectr in Classics, Yale, 1964, Asst Prof., 1965–68, Associate Prof., 1968–73; Vis. Prof.

in Classics: Munich, 1973; Princeton, 1974–75; Tel Aviv, 1976–77; Vis. Prof. in Comp. Lit., Dartmouth, 1976–78; Wolfson College, Oxford: Vis. Fellow, 1979–80; Supernumerary Fellow, 1982–88; Mem. Common Room, 1984–; Hon. Fellow, 1999. Member: Acad. of Literary Studies, USA, 1981; Nat. Adv. Council, 1970–72, Exec. Cttee, 1971–72, Peace Corps, USA (Presidential Commendation for Service to Peace Corps, 1971). Lectures: Amer. Philological Assoc., 1971, 1972; Amer. Comparative Lit. Assoc., 1971; German Classical Assoc., 1974; Boston Psychoanalytic Inst., 1974; Istituto Nazionale del Dramma Antico, Sicily, 1975; Brit. Classical Assoc., 1977; William Kelley Prentice Meml, Princeton, 1981; Inaugural Andrea Rosenthal Meml, Brown Univ., 1992. Author and narrator, The Ancient Games, 1972; TV commentator, ABC-TV, US, radio commentator in French, RTL Paris, Olympic Games, 1972 and 1976. Screenplays include: The Beatles' Yellow Submarine, 1968; The Games, 1969; Love Story, 1970 (Golden Globe Award, 1970), Oliver's Story, 1978; Man, Woman and Child, 1983. Mem., Authors Guild, 1970–. (With Mother Teresa and Peter Ustinov) Premio San Valentin di Terni, 1989. Chevalier de l'Ordre des Arts et des Lettres (France), 1998. *Publications:* Roman Laughter: the comedy of Plautus, 1968, rev. edn 1987; (ed) Euripides: a collection of critical essays, 1968; (ed and trans.) Plautus: Three Comedies, 1969, rev. edn 1985; (ed) Oxford Readings in Greek Tragedy, 1983; (ed with Fergus Millar) Caesar Augustus: seven aspects, 1984; (ed) Plato's Dialogues, 1985; Oxford Readings in Aristophanes, 1996; (ed and trans.) Plautus: Four Comedies, 1996; Death of Comedy, 2001; Oxford Readings in Menander, Plautus and Terence, 2002; *novels:* Love Story, 1970; Fairy Tale (for children), 1973; Oliver's Story, 1977; Man, Woman and Child, 1980, The Class, 1985 (Prix Deauville, France, and Premio Bancarella Selezione, Italy, 1986); Doctors, 1988; Acts of Faith, 1992; Prizes, 1995; Only Love, 1997; articles and reviews in Amer. Jl of Philology, Classical World, Harvard Studies in Classical Philology, Classical Review, Greek, Roman and Byzantine Studies, TLS, New York Times Book Review, New Republic, The Independent, Washington Post. *Recreations:* swimming, walking. *Address:* Wolfson College, Oxford OX2 6UD. *T:* (01865) 274100. *Club:* Athenæum. Died 17 Jan. 2010.

SELLORS, Sir Patrick (John) Holmes, KCVO 1999 (LVO 1990); FRCS, FRCOphth; Surgeon-Oculist to the Queen, 1980–99; Ophthalmic Surgeon, King Edward VIIth Hospital for Officers, 1975–99; *b* 11 Feb. 1934; *s* of Sir Thomas Holmes Sellors, DM, MCh, FRCP, FRCS; *m* 1961, Gillian Gratton Swallow; two *s* one *d*. *Educ:* Rugby Sch.; Oriel Coll., Oxford (MA; BM, BCh 1958); Middlesex Hosp. Med. Sch. FRCS 1965; FRCOphth 1990. Registrar, Moorfields Eye Hosp., 1962–65; recognised teacher in Ophthalmology, St George's Hosp.; 1966; Ophthalmic Surgeon: St George's Hosp., 1965–82 (Hon., 1983); Croydon Eye Unit, 1970–94; Surgeon-Oculist to HM Household, 1974–80; Hon. Consultant Ophthalmic Surgeon, St Luke's Hosp. for the Clergy, 1983–96. Sec. to Ophthalmic Soc. of UK, 1970–72; Examr for Diploma of Ophthalmology, 1974–77; Pres., Ophthalmology Section, RSocMed, 1992–94; Vice-Pres., Coll. of Ophthalmologists, 1992–96 (Mem. Council, 1988–96); Member, Council: Faculty of Ophthalmologists, 1977–88; Med. Defence Union, 1977–2003; Gen. Optical Council, 1978–96. Dep. Master, Oxford Congress, 1991. *Publications:* (jtly) Outline in Ophthalmology, 1985, 2nd edn 1994; articles in BMJ and Trans OSUK. *Recreations:* gardening, golf. *Address:* The Summer House, Sandy Lane, West Runton, Cromer, Norfolk NR27 9NB. Died 30 Sept. 2010.

SENIOR, (Alan) Gordon, CBE 1981; CEng, FICE, FIStructE; Managing Partner, Gordon Senior Associates, Engineering and Management Consultants, since 1980; *b* 1 Jan. 1928; *s* of late Oscar Senior and Helen Senior (*née* Cooper); *m* 1st, 1955, Sheila Lockyer (marr. diss. 1961); 2nd, 1968, Lawmary Mitchell (marr. diss. 1978); one *s*. *Educ:* Normanton Grammar School; Leeds Univ. (BSc

1948, MSc 1949). J. B. Edwards (Whyteleafe) Ltd, 1949–51; Oscar Faber & Partners, Consulting Engineers, 1951–54; W. S. Atkins & Partners, Consulting Engineers, 1954–80: Technical Dir, 1967; Man. Dir of Atkins Research and Development, 1972; Director, W. S. Atkins & Partners, 1976. Chairman: Surface Engineering and Inspection Ltd, 1983–86; Masta Corp. Ltd, 1987–92; Aptech Ltd, 1988–89; Industrial Science and Technology Ltd, 1997–2005; Director: Ansen Offshore Consultants Ltd and McMillan Sloan & Partners, 1981–84; Armstrong Technology Services Ltd, 1986; Quest Central Europe, 1991–2002; MARIS Fish Ranches Ltd, 2004–. Member, Navy Dept Advisory Cttee on Structural Steels, 1967–71. Science and Engineering Research Council: Mem., Engineering Bd, 1974–78; Chm., Transport and Civil Engineering Cttee, 1974–78; Chm., Marine Technology Management Cttee, 1980–83. Department of Trade and Industry: Mem., Ship and Marine Technology Requirements Bd, and Chm., Marine Technology Cttee, 1976–81; Mem., Maritime Technology Cttee, 1981–86; Chm., Adv. Cttee on Resources from the Sea, 1983–86. Member: Dept of Energy Programme Cttee, Offshore Energy Technology Bd, 1978–85; HSE Offshore Safety and Tech. Bd, 1985–92. Chm., Greenwich Forum, 1991–; Pres., Soc. for Underwater Technology, 2003–05 (Vice-Pres. and Chm. of Council, 1979–81). *Publications:* (co-author) Brittle Fracture of Steel Structures, 1970; papers on welding, fatigue, brittle fracture, design of steel structures, computer aided design, renewable energy from the sea, and future developments offshore and in the oceans. *Recreations:* food and wine, travel, music, opera, ski-ing. *Address:* 3 Briar Patch, Charterhouse, Godalming, Surrey GU7 2JB. *T:* (01483) 417781, *Fax:* (01483) 427781; *e-mail:* agsenior@btinternet.com. *Club:* Athenæum Died 24 Jan. 2007.

SERIÈS, Sir (Joseph Michel) Emile, Kt 1978; CBE 1974; FCIS, FAIA, FSCA, FREconS, FInstD, FRSA; Chairman, Flacq United Estates Ltd and WEAL Group (West East Ltd), 1968–99 (General Manager, 1968–96); *b* 29 Sept. 1918; *s* of late Emile Seriès and Julie (*née* Langlois); *m* 1942, Rose-Aimée Jullienne; two *s* two *d*. *Educ:* Royal Coll., Mauritius; London Univ. MCom Delhi Commercial Univ., 1967. FCCS 1958. Accounts Dept, General Electric Supply Co. of Mauritius Ltd, 1936–52 (final position, Chief Acct); Chief Acct and Econ. Adviser, Union Flacq Sugar Estate Ltd and Flacq United Estates Ltd, 1952–61; Manager, Union Flacq Sugar Estate Ltd, 1961–68. Chairman: Rogers & Co. Ltd; Alcohol & Molasses Co. Ltd; Compagnie Mauricienne de Commerce Ltd. Director: Maur. Commercial Bank Ltd; Anglo-Maur. Assurance Society Ltd, and other cos in Mauritius. Past President: Maur. Chamber of Agriculture; Maur. Sugar Industry Research Inst. Member: Maur. Sugar Producers' Assoc.; Maur. Sugar Syndicate; Amer. Management Assoc., New York; National Assoc. of Accts, New York. FCMI. Chevalier de l'Ordre National du Mérite (France), 1978; Chevalier de la Légion d'Honneur, 1988. *Recreations:* sailing, photography, classical music. *Address:* c/o Weal House, 2 Queen Street, Port Louis, Mauritius. *Clubs:* Dodo, Mauritius Turf, Mauritius Gymkhana, Le Morne Anglers', Grand'Baie Yacht (Mauritius). Died 2006.

SERPELL, Sir David Radford, KCB 1968 (CB 1962); CMG 1952; OBE 1944; Member, British Railways Board, 1974–82; *b* 10 Nov. 1911; 2nd *s* of Charles Robert and Elsie Leila Serpell, Plymouth; *m* 1st, 1938, Alice Ann Dooley (marr. diss.); three *s*; 2nd, 1972, Doris Farr (*d* 2004). *Educ:* Plymouth Coll.; Exeter Coll., Oxford (Hon. Fellow, 1992); Univ. of Toulouse (DèsL); Syracuse University, USA; Fletcher School of Law and Diplomacy, USA. (Fell.) Imp. Economic Cttee, 1937–39; Min. of Food, 1939–42; Min. of Fuel and Power, 1942–45; Under-Sec., HM Treasury, 1954–60; Dep. Sec., MoT, 1960–63; Second Sec., BoT, 1963–66; Second Permanent Sec., 1966–68; Second Sec., Treasury, 1968; Permanent Secretary: MoT, 1968–70; DoE, 1970–72. Private Sec. to Parly Sec., Ministry of Food, 1941–42; Principal Private Sec. to Minister of Fuel and Power,

1942–45. Chairman: Nature Conservancy Council, 1973–77; Ordnance Survey Review Cttee, 1978–79; Cttee on the Review of Railway Finances, 1982; Member: NERC, 1973–76; Council, National Trust, 1973–77. *Recreation:* walking. *Address:* Hyne Town House, Strete, Dartmouth, Devon TQ6 0RU. *T:* (01803) 770420.   *Died 28 July 2008.*

SERVAN-SCHREIBER, Prof. Jean-Jacques; engineer, author, politician; Professor of Strategic Thinking and Chairman, International Committee, Carnegie-Mellon University, 1985; *b* Paris, 13 Feb. 1924; *s* of late Emile Servan-Schreiber, journalist, and Denise Bresard; *m* 1960, Sabine de Fouquières; four *s. Educ:* Ecole Polytechnique, Paris. Served as US-trained fighter pilot, Free French Air Force, World War II. Diplomatic Editor of Le Monde, 1948–53; Founder and Editor of weekly news-magazine, L'Express, 1953–73. Deputy for Lorraine, French National Assembly, 1970–78; Minister of Reforms, June 1974. Pres., Region of Lorraine, 1975–78. Pres., Radical Party, 1971–79; Chm., World Center for Computer Literacy, Paris, 1981–85. Holds military cross for valour, with bar. *Publications:* Lieutenant en Algérie, 1957 (Lieutenant in Algeria); Le Défi américain, 1967 (The American Challenge); Le Manifeste Radical, 1970 (The Radical Alternative); Le Défi mondial, 1980 (The World Challenge); The Chosen and the Choice, 1988; Passions, 1992; Les Fossoyeurs, 1993 (The Gravediggers). *Address:* 37 avenue du Roule, Neuilly/Seine 92200, France.
                                  Died 7 Nov. 2006.

SESSIONS, His Honour John Lionel; a Circuit Judge, 1992–2007; Judge Advocate of the Fleet, 1995–2007; *b* 8 Jan. 1941; *s* of Geoffrey and Anita Sessions; *m* 1st, 1967, Patrizia Corinna Sanminiatelli (*d* 2005); one *s* two *d*; 2nd, 2006, Averil Harrison. *Educ:* King Edward's Sch., Birmingham; BRNC, Dartmouth. Joined RN, 1959; served in HM Ships incl. Venus, Roebuck, Protector, Agincourt and Leopard; Naval interpreter in Italian, 1966; Comdr, 1976; retd 1981. Called to the Bar, Middle Temple, 1972; in practice (Common Law), 1981–92; Recorder, 1989–92. Mem., Parole Bd, 2005–08. Member: Civil and Family Cttee, 1996–99, Criminal Cttee, 2002–06, Judicial Studies Bd; Civil Justice Council, 1998–2000. Grand Registrar, United Grand Lodge of England, 1996–98. Chm., Arun Choral Soc., 2007–09. *Publications:* Naval Interpreters' Handbook (Italian), 1974. *Recreations:* sailing, music. *Address:* Henderson Chambers, 2 Harcourt Buildings, Temple, EC4Y 9DB. *Clubs:* Anchorites; Bar Yacht; Royal London Yacht (Cowes); Itchenor Sailing.
                                  Died 16 June 2010.

SETON, Lady, (Julia), OBE 1989; VMH; (Julia Clements, professionally); author, speaker, international floral art judge; flower arrangement judge for RHS and National Association of Flower Arrangement Societies; *b* 10 April 1906; *d* of late Frank Clements; *m* 1962, Sir Alexander Hay Seton, 10th Bt, of Abercorn (*d* 1963); no *c. Educ:* Isle of Wight; Zwicker College, Belgium. Organised and conducted first Judges' School in England at Royal Horticultural Society Halls; subseq. conducted many other courses for judges all over Europe. VMH, RHS, 1974. *Publications:* Fun with Flowers; Fun without Flowers; 101 Ideas for Flower Arrangement; Party Pieces; Flower Arranging for All Occasions, 1993; Flower Arrangements in Stately Homes; Julia Clements' Gift Book of Flower Arranging; Flowers in Praise; The Art of Arranging a Flower, etc; My Life with Flowers, 1993. *Address:* c/o Pepperwood, Hare Lane End, Little Kingshill, Great Missenden, Bucks HP16 0EX.
                                  Died 1 Nov. 2010.

SEVERN, David; see Unwin, David Storr.

SEWARD, Guy William; QC 1982; *b* 10 June 1916; *s* of late William Guy Seward and Maud Peacock; *m* 1946, Peggy Dearman (*d* 2003). *Educ:* Stationers' Sch. Called to the Bar, Inner Temple, 1956. FRVA 1948. Chairman: Medical Service Cttee, 1977–81; Examination in Public, Devon Structure Plan, 1980; E Herts Health Authority,

1982–90; Member: Mid-Herts HMC, 1966–70; Napsbury HMC, 1970–74 (Chm., 1972–74); Bd of Governors, UCH, 1970–74; Herts AHA, 1974–82 (Vice Chm., 1980–82); Herts FPC, 1974–82; Council, Rating and Valuation Assoc., 1983. Freeman, City of London, 1949. Grand Officer, United Grand Lodge of England (Asst Grand Registrar, 1978; Past Jun. Grand Deacon, 1987). *Publications:* (jtly) Enforcement of Planning Control, 1956; (jtly) Local Government Act, 1958; Howard Roberts Law of Town and Country Planning, 1963; (jtly) Rent Act, 1965; (jtly) Land Commission Act, 1967; (jtly) Leasehold Reform, 1967. *Recreations:* travel, gardening. *Address:* Stocking Lane Cottage, Ayot St Lawrence, Welwyn, Herts AL6 9BW. *Club:* Garrick.
                                  Died 2 July 2009.

SEWARD, William Richard, RCNC; General Manager, HM Dockyard, Portsmouth, 1975–79, retired; *b* 7 Feb. 1922; *s* of William and Gertrude Seward, Portsmouth; *m* 1946, Mary Deas Ritchie; one *d. Educ:* Portsmouth Dockyard Techn. Coll.; RNC Greenwich; Royal Corps of Naval Constructors. Asst Constructor, HM Dockyard, Rosyth, 1945–47; Constructor, Naval Construction Dept, Admty, 1947–58; Admty Constructor Overseer, Birkenhead, 1958–63; Chief Constructor, MoD (N), 1963–70; Prodn Man., HM Dockyard, Chatham, 1970–73, Gen. Manager, 1973–75. *Recreations:* reading, music, caravanning, hill walking. *Club:* Civil Service.
                                  Died 12 April 2008.

SHACKLETON, Sir Nicholas (John), Kt 1998; PhD; FRS 1985; Director, Institute for Quaternary Research, Department of Earth Sciences, 1995–2004, and Professor of Quaternary Palaeoclimatology, 1991–2004, University of Cambridge, then Professor Emeritus; Fellow of Clare Hall, Cambridge, 1980–2004, then Fellow Emeritus; *b* 23 June 1937; *s* of Prof. Robert Millner Shackleton, FRS; *m* 1st, 1967, Judith Carola Murray (marr. diss. 1977); 2nd, 1986, Vivien Anne Law, PhD, FBA (*d* 2002). *Educ:* Cranbrook Sch.; Clare Coll., Cambridge (BA, PhD); ScD Cantab 1984. Cambridge University: Senior Asst in Research, 1965–72, Asst Dir of Res., 1972–87, Reader, 1987–91, Dir, 1988–95, Sub-Dept of Quaternary Res.; Research Fellow, 1974–80, Official Fellow, 1980–2004, Clare Hall. Sen. Vis. Res. Fellow, Lamont Doherty Geol Observatory of Columbia Univ., 1974–75. Founding Mem., Academia Europaea, 1988; Foreign Mem., Royal Netherlands Soc. of Arts and Scis, 2001. Hon. LLD Dalhousie, 1996; Hon. DPhil Stockholm, 1997. Hon. Dr Geol. Padova, 2002. Carus Medal, Deutsche Akad. der Naturforscher Leopoldina, 1985; Sheppard Medal, SEPM, 1985; Lyell Medal, Geol Soc. of London, 1987; Huntsman Award, Bedford Inst. of Oceanography, Canada, 1991; Crafoord Prize, Royal Swedish Acad. of Scis, 1995; Wollaston Medal, Geol Soc. of London, 1996; Milankovitch Medal, European Geophysical Soc., 1999; Ewing Medal, Amer. Geophysical Union, 2002; Urey Medal, Eur. Assoc. of Geochemistry, 2003; Royal Medal, Royal Soc., 2003; Vetlesen Prize, Lamont-Doherty Earth Observatory, Columbia Univ., 2004; Founder's Medal, RGS, 2005; Blue Planet Prize, Asahi Glass Foundn, Tokyo, 2005. *Publications:* numerous articles on marine geology, geological history of climate, etc; articles in New Grove Dictionary of Music and Musicians. *Recreations:* clarinet playing, researching history of clarinet, Thai food. *Address:* 12 Tenison Avenue, Cambridge CB1 2DY. *T:* (01223) 311938; Department of Earth Sciences, University of Cambridge, Downing Street, Cambridge CB2 3EQ.   *Died 24 Jan. 2006.*

SHAND, Major Bruce Middleton Hope, MC 1940, and Bar 1942; Vice Lord-Lieutenant, East Sussex, 1974–92; *b* 22 Jan. 1917; *s* of late P. Morton Shand; *m* 1946, Rosalind Maud (*d* 1994), *d* of 3rd Baron Ashcombe; one *s* two *d. Educ:* Rugby; RMC, Sandhurst. 2nd Lieut 12th Royal Lancers, 1937; Major 1942; wounded and PoW 1942; retd 1947. Exon, Queen's Body Guard of the Yeomen of the Guard, 1971, Ensign, 1978–85, Adjutant and Clerk of the Cheque, 1985–87. Joint or Acting Master, Southdown Fox Hounds,

1956–75. DL Sussex, 1962. *Publications:* Previous Engagements, 1991. *Recreation:* gardening. *Address:* Stourpaine Cottage, Stourpaine, near Blandford, Dorset DT11 8TQ. *T:* (01258) 459436. *Club:* Cavalry and Guards. *Died 11 June 2006.*

SHAPLAND, Maj.-Gen. Peter Charles, CB 1977; MBE 1960; MA; Senior Planning Inspector, Department of the Environment, 1980–93; *b* 14 July 1923; *s* of late F. C. Shapland, Merton Park, Surrey; *m* 1954, Joyce Barbara Shapland (*née* Peradon); two *s. Educ:* Rutlish Sch., Merton Park; St Catharine's Coll., Cambridge. Served War: commissioned Royal Engineers, 1944; QVO Madras Sappers and Miners, Indian Army, 1944–47. Served United Kingdom, Middle East (Canal Zone) and Cyprus, 1948–63. Attended Staff Coll., 1952; jssc, 1960. Lt-Col, 1965; comd in Aden, 1965–67; Brig., Dec. 1968; comd 30 Engineer Bde. Attended Royal Coll. of Defence Studies, 1971. Dep. Comdr and Chief of Staff, HQ SE Dist, 1972–74; Maj.-Gen. 1974; Dir, Volunteers Territorials and Cadets, MoD (Army), 1974–78, retired. Hon. Col, 73 Engineer Regt, TA, 1979–89; Col Comdt, RE, 1981–86. Vice Pres., CCF Assoc., 1997–2003 (Chm., 1982–96). Pres., Instn of Royal Engrs, 1982–87. Mem., Worshipful Co. of Painter-Stainers, 1983–. *Publications:* contribs to Royal Engineers' Jl. *Recreations:* sailing, swimming. *Clubs:* Royal Ocean Racing; Royal Engineer Yacht (Chatham). *Died 24 May 2007.*

SHARP, Dr John, OBE 1994; Headmaster of Rossall School, 1973–87; *b* 18 Dec. 1927; *o s* of late Alfred and May Sharp, North Ives, Oxenhope, Keighley; *m* 1950, Jean Prosser; one *s* two *d. Educ:* Boys' Grammar Sch., Keighley; Brasenose Coll., Oxford (MA, MSc, DPhil). RAF Educn Br., 1950–52; research at Oxford, 1952–54; Marlborough College: Asst Master, 1954–56; Senior Chemistry Master, 1956–62; Senior Science Master, 1959–62; Headmaster, Christ Coll., Brecon, 1962–72. Co-opted Mem., Oxford and Cambridge Schools Examn Bd, 1966–74; Selected Mem., Breconshire Educn Cttee, 1966–72; Co-opted Mem., Lancs Educn Cttee, 1974–81; Divisional Chm., HMC, SW 1971 and NW 1977–78; Chm., HMC Acad. Policy Sub-Cttee, 1982–85. Chm., Independent Schs' Jt Council Accreditation and Consultancy Service, 1987–93; Founder Gov., City Technology Coll., Kingshurst, Solihull, 1989–96; Gov., Christ Coll., Brecon, 1992–99 (Chm., 1993–99). *Publications:* contrib. Anal. Chim. Acta. *Recreations:* fishing, photography, roses and shrubs. *Address:* Wood End Cottage, St Michael's, Tenbury Wells, Worcs WR15 8TG. *Club:* East India. *Died 24 Nov. 2006.*

SHARP, Sir Kenneth (Johnston), Kt 1984; TD 1960; Partner, Baker, Tilly & Co. (formerly Howard, Tilly), Chartered Accountants, 1983–89; *b* 29 Dec. 1926; *s* of late Johnston Sharp and Ann Sharp (*née* Routledge); *m* 1955, Barbara Maud Keating; one *s. Educ:* Shrewsbury Sch.; St John's Coll., Cambridge (MA). ACA 1955, FCA 1960. Partner, Armstrong, Watson & Co., Chartered Accountants, 1955–75; Head, Govt Accountancy Service and Accountancy Advr to DoI, 1975–83. Indian Army, 1945–48; TA, 251st (Westmorland and Cumberland Yeo.) Field Regt RA, 1948–62; 2nd-in-Comd, 1959–62. Inst. of Chartered Accountants: Mem. Council, 1966–83; Vice-Pres., 1972–73; Dep. Pres., 1973–74; Pres., 1974–75. Master, Co. of Chartered Accountants in England and Wales, 1979–80. Mem., Governing Body, Shrewsbury Sch., 1976–95. JP Carlisle, 1957–73. *Publications:* The Family Business and the Companies Act 1967, 1967; articles in professional accountancy press. *Recreation:* gardening. *Address:* Lower Bohella House, The Square, St Mawes, Truro TR2 5AG. *Died 28 April 2009.*

SHARP, Robert Charles, CMG 1971; Director of Public Works, Tasmania, 1949–71; *b* 20 Sept. 1907; *s* of Robert George Sharp and Gertrude Coral (*née* Bellette); *m* 1st, 1935, Margaret Fairbrass Andrewartha (*d* 1976); one *d*; 2nd, 1978, Marie, *widow* of Alan C. Wharton, St Albans, Herts. *Educ:* Univ. of Tasmania. BE 1929. Bridge Engr, Public Works, 1935. Enlisted RAE (Major): comd 2/4

Aust. Field Sqdn RAE, 1942; 1 Aust. Port Mtce Co. RAE, 1943; HQ Docks Ops Gp, 1944. Chief Engr, Public Works, 1946; State Co-ordinator of Works, 1949–71. *Address:* The Coach House, Wickwood Court, Sandpit Lane, St Albans, Herts AL1 4BP; 594 Sandy Bay Road, Hobart, Tasmania 7005, Australia. *Club:* Athenæum. *Died 25 April 2007.*

SHATTOCK, Sir Gordon, Kt 1985; Vice-Chairman, VDC plc, since 1990 (Director, 1982–98); Divisional Bursar, Western Division, and Hon. Fellow, Woodard Schools, since 1988; *b* 12 May 1928; *s* of Frederick Thomas and Rose May Irene Shattock; *m* 1952, Jeanne Mary Watkins (*d* 1984); one *s* one *d*; *m* 1988, Mrs Wendy Sale. *Educ:* Hele's Sch., Exeter; Royal Veterinary Coll., London. MRCVS. Senior Partner, St David's Vet. Hosp., Exeter, 1954–84. Mem., Exeter HA, 1987–93. Fellow of Woodard Corp., 1973–88; Executive Member: Animal Health Trust, 1978–99; GBA, 1986–89; Mem. of Council, Guide Dogs for the Blind, 1985–97; Chairman: Grenville Coll., 1982–88; Exeter Cathedral Music Foundn Trust, 1987–2004 (Trustee, 2004–). Pres., Old Heleans' Soc., 1999–2008. FRSocMed 1987; FRSA 1990. Hon. FRVC 1994; Hon. Mem., BVA, 1989. Farriers' Company: Liveryman, 1978–; Mem. Ct of Assistants, 1986–; Master, 1992. Jun. Grand Warden, United Grand Lodge of England, 1997–98. *Publications:* contrib. to Jl Small Animal Practice; papers to British Veterinary Assoc. *Recreation:* gardening. *Address:* Bowhill, Riverside Road, Topsham, Exeter EX3 0LR. *T:* (01392) 876655, *Fax:* (01392) 875588. *Died 10 April 2010.*

SHAUGHNESSY, 4th Baron *cr* 1916 of Montreal and of Ashford, Limerick; **Michael James Shaughnessy;** *b* 12 Nov. 1946; *s* of 3rd Baron Shaughnessy, CD and Mary (*née* Whitley); S father, 2003. *Heir: cousin* Charles George Patrick Shaughnessy [*b* 9 Feb.1955; *m* 1983, Susan Fallender; two *d*]. *Died 9 Dec. 2007.*

SHAW, Sir (Charles) Barry, Kt 1980; CB 1974; QC 1964; DL; Director of Public Prosecutions for Northern Ireland, 1972–89; *b* 12 April 1923; *s* of late Ernest Hunter Shaw and Sarah Gertrude Shaw, Mayfield, Balmoral, Belfast; *m* 1950, Jean Boyd (marr. diss.); *m* 1964, Jane (*née* Phillips) (*d* 2010). *Educ:* Inchmarlo House, Belfast; Pannal Ash Coll., Harrogate; The Queen's Univ. of Belfast (LLB). Served War: commissioned RA, 97 A/Tk Regt RA, 15th (Scottish) Div., 1942–46. Called to Bar of Northern Ireland, 1948, Bencher 1968; called to Bar, Middle Temple, 1970, Hon. Bencher, 1986. DL Co. Down, 1990. *Address:* 20 Larch Hill, Holywood, Co. Down BT18 0JN. *Died 30 Sept. 2010.*

SHAW, Dr Gavin Brown, CBE 1981; FRCP, FRCPE, FRCPGlas; Consultant Physician, Southern General Hospital, Glasgow, 1956–84, Hon. Consultant, since 1984; *b* 24 May 1919; *s* of Gavin Shaw and Christian Douglas Cormack; *m* 1943, Margaret Mabon Henderson (*d* 1990); one *d* (and one *s* one *d* decd). *Educ:* Glasgow Academy; Glasgow Univ., 1936–42 (BSc, MB ChB). President, Students' Representative Council, 1940–41. House Phys. to Sir J. W. McNee, 1942; Temporary Surg.-Lieut, RNVR, 1942–45; Asst Phys., Southern Gen. Hosp., Glasgow, 1948–56. Actg post-Grad. Dean., Glasgow Univ., 1983–84. Royal College of Physicians and Surgeons of Glasgow: Hon. Sec., 1957–65; Visitor, 1977–78; Pres., 1978–80. Mem., West Regional Hosp. Bd, 1971–74; Chairman: Greater Glasgow Med. Adv. Cttee, 1973–76; Jt Cttee for Higher Med. Trng, 1979–83; Specialty Adviser in Medicine, W of Scotland Post-Graduate Cttee, 1971–83. Mem., GMC, 1982–89. Hon. FACP 1979; Hon. FRCPI 1979; Hon. FRCPsych 1980; Hon. FRCGP 1980. *Publications:* (ed jtly) Cardiac Resuscitation and Pacing, 1964; occasional contributor to BMJ, Brit. Heart Jl, Lancet, Practitioner, Amer. Heart Jl, Scottish Med. Jl. *Recreations:* walking, gardening, bird watching and one-time sailor, listening to music, painting, reading. *Address:* c/o 14 Murrayfield Drive, Edinburgh EH12 6EB. *Died 11 Nov. 2007.*

SHAW, Roy Edwin, OBE 1991; Council Member, London Borough of Camden, 1964–2007 (Hon. Alderman, 2007); Mayor of Camden, 1999–2000; *b* 21 July 1925; *s* of Edwin Victor and Edith Lily Shaw. Hampstead Borough Council, 1956–62; St Pancras Borough, 1962–65; Camden Borough Council: Chm., Planning Cttee, 1967–68; Chm., Finance Cttee, 1971–74; Chief Whip and Dep. Leader, 1965–73; Leader, 1975–82; Dep. Leader, 1990–94. Vice-Chm., AMA, 1979–83; Dep. Chm. and Leader of Labour Party, London Boroughs Assoc.; Dep. Leader, London Fire and Civil Defence Authy, 1999–2000; Mem., London Fire and Emergency Planning Authy, 2000–07 (Vice Chm., 2000–03; Dep. Chm., 2003–04). Part-time Mem., London Electricity Bd, 1977–83; Member: Transport Users Consultative Cttee for London, 1974–80; Adv. Cttee on Local Govt Audit, 1979–82; Audit Commn, 1983–91; Consult. Council on Local Govt Finances, 1978–84. Chm., Camden Trng Centre, 1990–99. *Recreations:* listening to music; entertaining attractive women. *Address:* Town Hall, Euston Road, NW1 2RU. *T:* (020) 7278 4444.   *Died 4 Jan. 2008.*

SHEA, Michael Sinclair MacAuslan, CVO 1987 (LVO 1985); DL; PhD; author and broadcaster; *b* 10 May 1938; *s* of late James Michael Shea and Mary Dalrymple Davidson MacAuslan, North Berwick; *m* 1968, Mona Grec Stensen, Oslo; two *d. Educ:* Gordonstoun Sch.; Edinburgh Univ. (MA, PhD Econs). FO, 1963; Inst. of African Studies, Accra, Ghana, 1963; FO, 1964; Third, later Second Sec., CRO, 1965; Second, later First Sec. (Econ.), Bonn, 1966; seconded to Cabinet Office, 1969; FO, 1971; Head of Chancery, Bucharest, 1973; Dep. Dir Gen., Brit. Inf. Services, New York, 1976; Press Sec. to the Queen, 1978–87; Dir of Public Affairs, Hanson PLC, 1987–92; Chairman: Connoisseurs Scotland, 1992–98; Scottish Nat. Photography Centre, subseq. Hill Adamson Centre, 2002–; non-executive Director: Caledonian Newspaper Publishing, 1993–96. Scottish Mem., ITC, 1996–2003. Vis. Prof., Strathclyde Univ. Grad. Business Sch., 1991–99. Trustee, Nat. Galls of Scotland, 1992–99; Chm., Royal Lyceum Theatr Co., 1998–2004. Gov., Gordonstoun Sch., 1988–99. Vice-Chm., Foundn for Skin Res., 1993–2004. DL Edinburgh, 1996. *Publications:* Britain's Offshore Islands, 1981; Maritime England, 1981; Tomorrow's Men, 1982; Influence: how to make the system work for you, 1988; Leadership Rules, 1990; Personal Impact: the art of good communication, 1993; Spin Doctor, 1995; To Lie Abroad, 1996; The British Ambassador, 1996; State of the Nation, 1997; Berlin Embassy, 1998; The Primacy Effect, 1998; Spin off, 2000; A View from the Sidelines, 2003; The Freedom Years, 2006; (as Michael Sinclair): Sonntag, 1971; Folio Forty-One, 1972; The Dollar Covenant, 1974; A Long Time Sleeping, 1976; The Master Players, 1978; (with David Frost): The Mid-Atlantic Companion, 1986; The Rich Tide, 1986. *Recreations:* writing, sailing. *Address:* 1A Ramsay Garden, Edinburgh EH1 2NA. *Club:* Garrick.
Died 17 Oct. 2009.

SHEARER, Janet Sutherland; *see* Avonside, Lady.

SHEARER, Magnus MacDonald; JP; Lord-Lieutenant of Shetland, 1982–94; Managing Director, J. & M. Shearer Ltd (Est. 1919), 1960–85; *b* 27 Feb. 1924; *s* of late Lt-Col Magnus Shearer, OBE, TD, JP, and Flora MacDonald Stephen; *m* 1949, Martha Nicolson Henderson (*d* 2003), *d* of late Captain John Henderson, DSM, and Martha Nicolson; one *s. Educ:* Anderson Educational Institute, Shetland; George Watson's Coll., Edinburgh. Served RN in Atlantic, Mediterranean and Far East, 1942–46. 2nd Lieut, RA (TA), 1949; Captain, TARO, 1959. Hon. Consul: for Sweden in Shetland and Orkney, 1958–94; for Federal Republic of Germany in Shetland, 1972–87. Mem., Lerwick Harbour Trust, 1960–75 (Chm., 1967–72); Hon. Sec., RNLI Lerwick Stn, 1968–92; Mem. Lerwick Town Council, 1963–69; JP 1969, DL 1973, Shetland. Knight 1st Class, Royal Order of Vasa (Sweden), 1969; Officer 1st Class, Order of Merit (Federal Republic of Germany), 1983; Officer 1st

Class, Order of Polar Star (Sweden), 1983. *Recreations:* reading, bird watching, ships. *Address:* 4 Queen's Place, Lerwick, Shetland ZE1 0BZ. *T:* (01595) 696612.
Died 22 July 2007.

SHEARER, Moira, (Lady Kennedy); writer; *b* Dunfermline, Fife, 17 Jan. 1926; *d* of Harold King; *m* 1950, Ludovic Henry Coverley Kennedy (later Sir Ludovic Kennedy); one *s* three *d. Educ:* Dunfermline High School; Ndola, N Rhodesia; Bearsden Acad., Scotland. Professional training: Mayfair Sch.; Nicolas Legat Studio. Début with International Ballet, 1941; joined Sadler's Wells Ballet, 1942, during following ten years danced all major classic roles and full repertoire of revivals and new ballets; first ballerina rôle in Sleeping Beauty, Royal Opera House, Covent Gdn, 1946; created rôle of Cinderella, 1948; Carmen, with Roland Petit, Théâtre Marigny, 1950; George Balanchine's Ballet Imperial, Covent Garden, 1950; Titania in Old Vic production of A Midsummer Night's Dream (Edin. Festival, 1954, and tour of US and Canada); American tours with Sadler's Wells Ballet, 1949, 1950–51. Toured as Sally Bowles in I am a Camera, 1955; joined Bristol Old Vic, 1955; Major Barbara, Old Vic, 1956; Man of Distinction, Edin. Fest., 1957; Madame Ranevskaya in The Cherry Orchard, Royal Lyceum, Edin., 1977; Judith Bliss in Hay Fever, Royal Lyceum, 1978; Elizabeth Lowry, in A Simple Man (Gillian Lynne's ballet for L. S. Lowry's centenary), BBC TV, 1987; Juliana Bordereau in The Aspern Papers, Citizens Th., Glasgow, 1994. Recorded: Thomas Hardy's Tess of the D'Urbervilles, 1977; Muriel Spark's The Ballad of Peckham Rye, BBC Radio 4, 1982; Dame Ninette de Valois' short stories, Acad. of Sound and Vision, 1990. Member: Scottish Arts Council, 1971–73; BBC Gen. Adv. Council, 1970–77; Dir, Border TV, 1977–82. Toured US, lecturing on history of ballet and Sergei Diaghilev, 1973; regular lecturing in England and Wales; lectured and gave recitals on three world cruises, Queen Elizabeth II; poetry and prose recitals, Edinburgh Festivals, 1974 and 1975; regular performance with Ludovic Kennedy, and harpist Gillian Tingay. *Films:* Ballerina in The Red Shoes (première, 1948); Tales of Hoffmann, 1950; Story of Three Loves, 1952; The Man Who Loved Redheads, 1954; Peeping Tom, 1960; Black Tights, 1961. Formerly regular book reviewer for Daily and Sunday Telegraphs. *Publications:* Balletmaster: a dancer's view of George Balanchine, 1986 (USA 1987); Ellen Terry (biog.), 1998.   *Died 31 Jan. 2006.*

SHEFFIELD, John Vincent, CBE 1984; Chairman, Norcros Ltd, 1956–81; *b* 11 Nov. 1913; *y s* of Sir Berkeley Sheffield, 6th Bt; *m* 1st, 1936, Anne (*d* 1969), *d* of Sir Lionel Faudel-Phillips, 3rd Bt; one *s* three *d*; 2nd, 1971, Mrs France Crosthwaite (*d* 2005), *d* of Brig.-Gen. Goland Clarke, CMG, DSO. *Educ:* Eton; Magdalene College, Cambridge (MA). Private Secretary to Minister of Works, 1943–44; Chairman: Portals Ltd, 1968–78; Atlantic Assets Trust Ltd, 1972–83. Chm., BEC, 1980–83; Vice-Chm., BTEC, 1983. High Sheriff of Lincolnshire, 1944–45. *Address:* New Barn House, Laverstoke, Whitchurch, Hants RG28 7PF. *T:* (01256) 893187. *Club:* White's.   *Died 9 May 2008.*

SHELDON, Bernard, CB 1981; *b* 14 June 1924; *s* of Gerald Walter Sheldon and Doris Sheldon (*née* Hopkins); *m* 1951, Dorothy Kirkland (*d* 1999); one *s* two *d. Educ:* Hurstpierpoint Coll. (Scholar). War service, N Atlantic and Pacific, 1943–46 (Lieut RNVR). Called to the Bar, Middle Temple, 1949. Joined Colonial Legal Service, 1951; Federal Counsel and Dep. Public Prosecutor, Fedn of Malaya, 1951–59; Legal Adviser: Pahang, 1953; Kedah and Perlis, 1955–59; War Office, 1959–67; MoD, 1967–87, retired 1987. Badlishah Decoration for Loyalty, Kedah, 1959. *Recreation:* chess. *Address:* c/o Lloyds TSB, 64 High Street, Epsom, Surrey KT19 8AT.   *Died 19 Feb. 2008.*

SHEPARD, Giles Richard Carless, CBE 1994; Chairman, Searcy Tansley & Co. Ltd, since 1995; *b* 1 April 1937; *er s* of late Richard S. H. Shepard, MC, TD;

m 1966, Peter Carolyn Fern Keighley; one *s* one *d*. *Educ:* Heatherdown, Ascot; Eton (King's Scholar); Harvard Business School (PMD 1967). Commissioned Coldstream Guards, 1955–60. Director: Charrington & Co., 1960–64; H. P. Bulmer & Co., 1964–70; Managing Director: Findlater Mackie, Todd, 1967–70; Westminster & Country Properties, 1970–76; Savoy Hotel plc, 1979–94; Ritz Hotel (London) Ltd, 1995–2004. Director: Dorchester Hotel, 1972–76; Savoy Hotel, 1976–79; Guinness Mahon & Co. Ltd, 1994–98; Longshot Ltd, 1994–; Kleinwort Develt Fund, 1990–2005; Omenport Develts Ltd, 2004–. Mem., Adv. Council for the Royal Parks, 1993–98; Hon. Catering Advr to the Army, 1994–2002. Member Council: Union Jack Club, 1980–; King Edward VII's Hosp. (Sister Agnes) (formerly King Edward VII's Hosp. for Officers), 1995–; RUSI, 1995–97. Chairman: City and Guilds of London Art Sch., 1982–2002; Heritage of London Trust, 1996; Trustee, St James's Conservation Trust, 1999–. Mem., Court of Assistants, Fishmongers' Co. (Prime Warden, 1987–88); High Sheriff of Greater London, 1986–87. Governor, Gresham's School, Holt, 1980–2005. *Recreations:* gardening, shooting, embroidery. *Address:* Wallop House, Nether Wallop, Hants SO20 8HE. *Clubs:* White's, Beefsteak, Boodle's.
Died 21 April 2006.

SHEPHERD-BARRON, John Adrian, OBE 2005; Chairman, Ross and Cromarty Enterprise, 1990–95; *b* 23 June 1925; *s* of Wilfrid and Dorothy Shepherd-Barron; *m* 1953, (Jane Patricia) Caroline Murray; three *s*. *Educ:* Stowe Sch.; Trinity Coll., Cambridge. Served War, 159 Parachute Light Regt, 6th Airborne Div. and 2nd Indian Airborne Div. (Captain). Mgt trainee, De La Rue, 1950; set up original op. in USA, 1957–59; Chm., Security Express, 1963 (took co. into Courier Express, Britain's first overnight parcels co.); Man. Dir, De La Rue Instruments, 1964, led team that invented the cash-dispenser (Automated Teller Machine); Dir N America, De La Rue, 1979–85. *Recreations:* shooting, fishing. *Address:* Mains of Geanies, Portmahomack, Ross-shire IV20 1TW. *T:* and *Fax:* (01862) 871443. *Clubs:* Sloane; All England Lawn Tennis. *Died 15 May 2010.*

SHEPPERD, Sir Alfred (Joseph), Kt 1989; Chairman and Chief Executive: Wellcome plc, 1986–90; The Wellcome Foundation Ltd, 1977–90; Chairman, Burroughs Wellcome Co., 1986–90; *b* 19 June 1925; *s* of Alfred Charles Shepperd and Mary Ann Williams; *m* 1950, Gabrielle Marie Yvette Bouloux; two *d*. *Educ:* Archbishop Tenison's Sch.; University Coll., London (BSc Econ; Fellow, 1986). Rank Organisation, 1949; Selincourt & Sons Ltd, 1963; Chamberlain Group, 1965; Managing Director, Keyser Ullmann Industries Ltd, 1967; Dir, Keyser Ullmann Ltd, 1967, Financial Dir, Laporte Industries Ltd, 1971, Wellcome Foundation Ltd, 1972; Director: Anglia Maltings (Holdings) Ltd, 1972–97; Mercury Asset Management Group (formerly Holdings) Ltd, 1987–96; Isoscelles plc, 1991–93; Oxford Instruments plc, 1991–95; National Transcommunications Ltd, 1992–96; Dep. Chm., Zoo Ops Ltd, 1988–91. Mem., ACOST, 1989–93. Member: Adv. Bd, British-Amer. Chamber of Commerce, 1988–96; Governing Body, Internat. Chamber of Commerce UK, 1988–96. Mem. and Gov., Adv. Panel, Inst. of Intellectual Property, 1986–96; Governor: NIESR, 1981–90; Royal Agricl Soc. of England, 1977–90. Chm., Barts NHS Trust, 1991–93. Commendatore della Repubblica, Italy, 1983; Encomienda al Merito de Sanidad, Spain, 1988; Comdr, Order of Leopold II, Belgium, 1989. *Club:* County (Guildford). *Died 15 Oct. 2007.*

SHERFIELD, 2nd Baron *cr* 1964, of Sherfield-on-Loddon, Southampton; **Christopher James Makins;** President, Atlantic Council of the United States, 1999–2005; *b* 23 July 1942; *er s* of 1st Baron Sherfield, GCB, GCMG, FRS and Alice Brooks (*d* 1985), *e d* of Hon. Dwight Davis; *S* father, 1996; *m* 1975, Wendy Cortesi; one *d*. *Educ:* Winchester; New Coll., Oxford. Fellow, All Souls Coll.,

Oxford, 1963–77; HM Diplomatic Service, 1964–75; Carnegie Endowment for Internat. Peace, 1977–79; Sci. Applications Internat. Corp., 1979–89; Partner, Washington Center for Pol Security and Review, 1981–94; Vice-Pres., 1989–93, Exec. Vice-Pres., 1993–97, Aspen Inst.; Sen. Advr, German Marshall Fund, USA, 1997–99. *Heir: b* Hon. Dwight William Makins [*b* 2 March 1951; *m* 1983, Penelope Jane, *d* of D. R. L. Massy Collier]. *Address:* 3034 P Street NW, Washington, DC 20007, USA. *Died 28 Jan. 2006.*

SHERMAN, Sir Alfred, Kt 1983; journalist; public affairs advisor in private practice; co-founder, Centre for Policy Studies, 1974 (Director of Studies until 1984); *b* 10 Nov. 1919; *s* of Jacob Vladimir Sherman and Eva (*née* Goldental); *m* 1st, 1958, Zahava (*d* 1993), *d* of Dr Gideon Levin; one *s*; 2nd, 2001, Angela Valentina Martin. *Educ:* Hackney Downs County Secondary Sch.; London Sch. of Econs (BScEcon). Served in International Brigade, Spanish Civil War, 1937–38; war of 1939–45 in field security and occupied enemy territory administration. Mem., economic adv. staff of Israeli Govt, in 1950s; leader writer, Jewish Chronicle, 1959–70; leader writer, subseq. London corresp., Haaretz newspaper, 1961–75; various appts with Daily Telegraph, 1965–86, as leader writer 1977–86. Consultant to Pres. Radovan Karadžic of the Serbian Republic in Bosnia-Herzogovina, 1993–94. Chm., Lord Byron Foundn for Balkan Studies, Arizona, 1995–. Vis. Fellow, LSE, 1983–85. Broadcaster. Councillor, RBK&C, 1971–78. FRSA 1996. *Publications:* Local Government Reorganisation and Industry, 1970; Councils, Councillors and Public Relations, 1973; Local Government Reorganization and the Salary Bill, 1974; (with D. Mallam) Waste in Wandsworth, 1976; Crisis Calls for a Minister for Denationalization, 1980; The Scott Report, 1981; (introd.) The Grenada Documents, ed Brian Crozier, 1987; Paradoxes of Power: reflections on the Thatcher interlude, 2005; (contrib.) Revisionism, 1961; Communism and Arab Nationalism: a reappraisal; Capitalism and Liberty; Our Complacent Satirists; Political Violence in Britain; contribs to newspapers and periodicals. *Address:* 14 Malvern Court, Onslow Square, SW7 3HU. *T:* (020) 7581 4075; *e-mail:* shermania@aol.com. *Died 26 Aug. 2006.*

SHERRIN, Edward George, (Ned), CBE 1997; film, theatre and television producer, presenter, director and writer; *b* Low Ham, Som, 18 Feb. 1931; *s* of late T. A. Sherrin and D. F. Sherrin (*née* Drewett). *Educ:* Sexey's Sch., Bruton; Exeter Coll., Oxford; Gray's Inn. Producer: ATV, Birmingham, 1955–57; BBC TV, 1957–66 (prod. and dir. That Was The Week That Was). Produced films: The Virgin Soldiers (with Leslie Gilliat) 1968; Every Home Should Have One, 1969; (with Terry Glinwood) Up Pompeii, 1971; Up the Chastity Belt, 1971; Girl Stoke Boy, 1971; Rentadick, 1971; Up the Front, 1972; The National Health, 1972; acted in film: Orlando, 1993; TV plays (with Caryl Brahms) include: Little Beggars; Benbow was his Name; Take a Sapphire; The Great Inimitable Mr Dickens; Feydeau Farces; plays (with Caryl Brahms): No Bed for Bacon; Cindy-Ella or I Gotta Shoe, 1962–63; The Spoils, 1968; Nicholas Nickleby, 1969; Sing a Rude Song, 1970; Fish out of Water, 1971; Liberty Ranch, 1972; Nickleby and Me, 1975; Beecham, 1980; The Mitford Girls, 1981; Oh, Kay! (new book with Tony Geiss), 1984; directed: Come Spy with Me, Whitehall, 1967; (and appeared in) Side by Side by Sondheim, Mermaid, 1976, NY 1977; Only in America (with D. Yakir), Roundhouse, 1980; Noël, Goodspeed, USA, 1981; Mr & Mrs Nobody, Garrick, 1986; Jeffrey Bernard is Unwell, Apollo, 1989, Old Vic, 1999, Garrick, 2006; Same Old Moon, Nuffield, Southampton, 1990; Bookends, Apollo, 1990; Our Song, Apollo, 1992; A Passionate Woman, Comedy, 1994; Salad Days, Vaudeville, 1996; Good Grief, touring, 1998; Bing Bong, touring, 1999; A Saint She Ain't, King's Head, Islington, 1999, Apollo, 2000; directed and co-adapted: The Ratepayers' Iolanthe, QEH, 1984 (Olivier Award); The Metropolitan Mikado, QEH, 1985; Small Expectations, QEH, 1986; dir, The Sloane Ranger

Revue, Duchess, 1985; scripted (with A. Beaton) Ziegfeld, London Palladium, 1988. TV appearances include: Song by Song, BBC and Yorkshire TV series; Quiz of the Week, BBC; The Rather Reassuring Programme, ITV; We Interrupt this Week, PBS, NY; Friday Night Saturday Morning, BBC-2; Countdown, Channel 4; radio appearances: Midweek (host), Medium Dry Sherrin, Extra Dry Sherrin, And So to Ned; Loose Ends; Counterpoint. Governor, BFI, 1980–84. Guild of TV Producers and Directors' Awards; Ivor Novello Award, 1966. *Publications:* (with Caryl Brahms) Cindy-Ella or I Gotta Shoe, 1962; Rappell 1910, 1964; Benbow was his Name, 1967; Ooh la! la! (short stories), 1973; After You Mr Feydeau, 1975; A Small Thing—Like an Earthquake (memoirs), 1983; (with Caryl Brahms) Song by Song, 1984; Cutting Edge, 1984; (with Neil Shand) 1956 and all that, 1984; (with Caryl Brahms) Too Dirty for the Windmill, 1986; Loose Neds, 1990; Theatrical Anecdotes, 1991; Ned Sherrin in his Anecdotage, 1993; (ed) The Oxford Dictionary of Humorous Quotations, 1995, 2nd edn 2001; Scratch an Actor (novel), 1996; Sherrin's Year (diary), 1996; (ed) I Wish I'd Said That, 2004; The Autobiography, 2005; many songs. *Address:* c/o Casarotto Ramsay Ltd, Waverley House, 7–12 Noel Street, W1F 8GQ. *T:* (020) 7287 4450.   *Died 1 Oct. 2007.*

SHERWOOD, (Peter) Louis (Michael); Chairman, Govett European Technology and Income Trust plc (formerly First Ireland Investment Co.), 1999–2003; Director, HBOS, 2001–04; *b* 27 Oct. 1941; *s* of Peter Louis Sherwood and Mervyn Sherwood (*née* de Toll); *m* 1970, Nicole Dina; one *s* two *d*. *Educ:* New Coll., Oxford (BA 1963; MA 1966). Stanford Univ. (MBA 1965). Morgan Grenfell & Co., Corporate Finance Officer, 1965–68; Asst to Chm., Fine Fare (Supermarkets), 1968–69; Man. Dir, Melias (Fine Fare subsid.), 1969–72; Dir, Anglo-Continental Investment & Finance Co., 1972–79; Sen. Vice-Pres. for Development, Grand Union Co., USA, 1979–85; Pres., Great Atlantic & Pacific Tea Co., USA, 1985–88; Chm. and Chief Exec., Gateway Foodmarkets, 1988–89; Chairman: HTV Gp, 1991–97 (Dir, 1990–97); HTV West, 1997–99. Director: ROK (formerly EBC Gp, then ROK property solutions) plc, 2001–2006; Clerical Medical Investment Group (formerly Clerical Medical & General Life Assurance Soc.), 1990–2004 (Dep. Chm., 1996–2000; Chm., 2000–01); Halifax Bldg Soc., subseq. Halifax Gp plc, 1997–2001; Wessex Water Services Ltd, 1998–2006; Insight Investment Mgt Ltd, 2001–. Master, Soc. of Merchant Venturers, Bristol, 2003–04. *Recreations:* mountain walking, collecting fine wine. *Address:* 10 College Road, Clifton, Bristol BS8 3HZ. *Clubs:* Garrick, Lansdowne.   *Died 26 March 2009.*

SHEUMACK, Rt Rev. Colin Davies; Bishop of Gippsland, 1987–94; *b* 9 Feb. 1929; *s* of Joseph Sheumack and Gwladys (*née* Davies); *m* 1951, Ena Beryl Dickson (*d* 1994); one *s* three *d*, and one adopted *d*. *Educ:* Tingha Central and Inverell High School; Moore Theological Coll. (ThL 2nd cl. Hons). Deacon 1952, priest 1953, Canberra Goulburn; Rector: Kemeruka, 1954–59; Kyabram, Vic., 1959–67; Archdeacon of Bendigo, 1967–83; Vicar General, 1968–83; Dean of Bathurst, 1983–87. Registrar of Melbourne, 1994; Administrator, Dio. Carpentaria, 1995–96. Chairman: SPCK Aust., 1992–2002; Nat. Anglican Men's Soc., 1994–2005; Nat. Home Missions Fund, 1997–99; Samaritan Foundn, 1997–2004. *Recreations:* gardening, fishing. *Address:* 3 Iron Bark Close, Trinity Heights, Kelso, NSW 2795, Australia. *Clubs:* Nat. Roads and Motoring Assoc. (Sydney); Royal Automobile of Victoria (Melbourne); Avoca Beach Bowling.   *Died 5 Jan. 2006.*

SHIELD, Leslie, TD; DL; a Recorder of the Crown Court, 1980–91; *b* 8 May 1916; *s* of Tom Shield and Annie Maud Shield; *m* 1941, Doris Leather; one *s*. *Educ:* Cowley Sch., St Helens; Univ. of Liverpool (LLB 1936, LLM 1938). Qualified solicitor, 1939, admitted 1945. Served War, 1939–46: commnd 5th Bn Prince of Wales'

Volunteers (S Lancs) Regt; demob., Major. Entered into gen. practice as solicitor, 1946. DL Merseyside, 1976. *Recreations:* gardening (particular interest, orchids), music. *Address:* Flat 2, School House Court, Cross Pit Lane, Rainford, St Helens, Merseyside WA11 8AH. *T:* (01744) 882708.   *Died 16 June 2008.*

SHIELDS, Sir Robert, Kt 1990; DL; MD, FRCS, FRCPS, FRCSE, FRCPS, FRCPE; Professor of Surgery, University of Liverpool, 1969–96; Consultant Surgeon, Royal Liverpool Hospital and Broadgreen Hospital, 1969–96; President, Royal College of Surgeons of Edinburgh, 1994–97; *b* 8 Nov. 1930; *o s* of late Robert Alexander Shields and Isobel Dougall Shields; *m* 1957, Grace Marianne Swinburn; one *s* two *d*. *Educ:* John Neilson Institution, Paisley; Univ. of Glasgow. MB, ChB 1953 (Asher-Asher Medal and MacLeod Medal); MD (Hons and Bellahouston Medal) 1965; FRCSE 1959; FRCS 1966; FRCPS 1993; FRCPE 1996. House appts, Western Infirmary, Glasgow, 1953–54; RAMC, Captain attached 1 Bn Argyll and Sutherland Highlanders, 1954–56; RAMC (TA), Major (Surg. Specialist) attached 7 Bn A and SH, 1956–61. Hall Fellow, Univ. of Glasgow, 1957–58; Mayo Foundn Fellow, 1959–60; Lectr in Surgery, Univ. of Glasgow, 1960–63; Sen. Lectr and Reader in Surgery, Welsh Nat. Sch. of Medicine, 1963–69; Dean, Faculty of Medicine, Univ. of Liverpool, 1982–85. Mem., GMC, 1982–94. Royal College of Surgeons: Mem., Ct of Examrs, 1980–86; Mem. Bd, Hunterian Inst., 1986–94; Zachary Cope Lectr, 1992; Vice Chm., Royal Liverpool Univ. Hosp. Trust, 1992–95 (non-exec. Trustee, 1991–95); Member: Liverpool AHA (T) (Chm., Area/Univ. Liaison Cttee), 1974–78; Mersey RHA, 1982–85 (Vice-Chm., 1985; Regl Advr, 1986–94); Liverpool Med. Instn (Vice-Pres., 1983–84; Pres., 1988–89); Council, RCSE, 1985–98 (Regent, 1999–); MRC, 1987–91 (Member: Cell Bd, 1974–77; Strategy Cttee, 1987–91); Exec. Cttee, Council of Military Educn Cttees of Univs of UK, 1990–94; Vice-Chm., Specialist Trng Authy, Med. Royal Colls, 1996–97. Member: Surgical Research Soc. (Hon. Sec. 1972–76 and Pres. 1983–85); British Soc. of Gastroenterology (Mem. Council, 1984–86; Pres., 1990–91; Hon. Mem., 1998–); N of England Gastroent. Soc. (Pres., 1981–83); Internat. Surgical Gp; James IV Assoc. of Surgeons, 1986– (Dir, 1991–96; Pres., 1994–96); Assoc. of Surgs of GB and Ire. (Mem. Council 1966–69; Pres., 1986–87); Council, European Surgical Assoc., 1995–98; Chm., Med. Adv. Cttee, British Liver Trust (formerly British Liver Foundn), 1991–94; Vice-Chm., Brit. Jl of Surgery Soc., 1989–95; Pres., Travelling Surgical Soc., 2002–03. Member: Panel of Assessors, Nat. Health and Med. Res. Council of Commonwealth and Australia, 1983–; List of Assessors for Cancer Grants, Anti-Cancer Council of Vic, Australia, 1986–. Chm., Merseyside, Lancashire and Cheshire Council on Alcoholism, 1992–94. Marjorie Budd Prof., Univ. of Bristol, 1983; Wilson Wang Vis. Prof., Chinese Univ. of Hong Kong, 1990; Wellcome Prof., Coll. of Medicine of S Africa, 1991. Former Visiting Prof., Univs of Toronto, Virginia, Witwatersrand, Rochester (NY), Hong Kong, Calif, Yale, and Examiner in Surgery, Univs of Glasgow, Edinburgh, Dundee, Leicester, Sheffield, Cambridge, Lagos, Amman, Riyadh, Malta; Dist. Lectr, Alpha Omega Alpha Assoc., 1994; Hon. Sen. Res. Fellow, Univ. of Glasgow, 1998–2001. Mem. Bd of Advrs in Surgery, London Univ., 1983–. Member: Editorial Board: Gut, 1969–76; Brit. Jl of Surgery, 1970–85, 1989–95; Internat. Editl Bd, Current Practice in Surgery, 1989–. Hon. Col Liverpool Univ. OTC, 1994–2001. DL Merseyside, 1991. Founder FMedSci 1998. Hon. FACS 1990; Hon. FCSSA 1991; Hon. FCSHK 1995; Hon. FRCSI 1996; Hon. FRACS 1997; Hon. Fellow: Amer. Surgical Assoc., 1993; Acad. Medicine of Singapore, 1996; Japanese Council for Med. Trng, 2002; Hon. Mem., Indian Assoc. of Surgeons, 1993. Hon. DSc Wales, 1990. Moynihan Medal, Assoc. of Surgs of GB and Ire., 1966. *Publications:* (ed jtly): Surgical Emergencies II, 1979; Textbook of Surgery, 1983; Gastrointestinal Emergencies, 1992; contribs to medical and surgical jls relating to surgery and gastroenterology. *Recreations:* sailing, walking. *Address:* 81 Meols Drive, West Kirby, Wirral CH48 5DF. *T:* (0151) 632 3588. *Club:* Army and Navy. *Died 3 Oct. 2008.*

SHINNIE, Prof. Peter Lewis; Professor of Archæology, in the University of Calgary, 1970–80, then Emeritus; *b* 18 Jan. 1915; *s* of late Andrew James Shinnie, OBE; *m* 1st, 1940, Margaret Blanche Elizabeth Cloake (marr. diss. 1970; she *d* 1995); one *s* one *d* (and one *s* decd); 2nd, 1971, Ama Nantwi. *Educ:* Westminster Sch.; Christ Church, Oxford. Served War with RAF, 1939–45. Temp. Asst Keeper, Ashmolean Museum, 1945; Asst Commissioner for Archæology, Sudan Government, 1946; Commissioner for Archæology, Sudan Govt, 1948; Director of Antiquities, Uganda, 1956; Prof. of Archæology: Univ. of Ghana, 1958–66; Univ. of Khartoum, 1966–70. Corresp. FBA 1999; FSA. Hon. LLD Calgary, 1983. Order of the Two Niles (Sudan), 2006. *Publications:* Excavation at Soba, 1955; Medieval Nubia, 1954; Ghazali: A Monastery in Northern Sudan, 1960; Meroe-Civilization of the Sudan, 1967; The African Iron Age, 1971; Debeira West, 1978; (with R. J. Bradley) The Capital of Kush, 1980; (ed with R. Haaland) African Iron Working: ancient and traditional, 1985; (with F. J. Kense) Archaeology in Gonja: excavations at Daboya, 1989; Early Asante, 1995; Ancient Nubia, 1996; (ed with J. R. Anderson) The Capital of Kush 2: Meroë Excavations 1973–4, 2004; articles in Journal of Egyptian Archæology, Sudan Notes and Records, Kush. *Recreations:* reading, photography, travelling in Greece. *Address:* Department of Archæology, University of Calgary, Calgary, AB T2N 1N4 Canada. *T:* (403) 2205227. *Died 9 July 2007.*

SHIPTON, Sidney Lawrence, OBE 2004; Co-ordinator, Three Faiths Forum (Muslim, Christian, Jewish Trialogue), since 1997; *b* 25 July 1929; *s* of Harold and Rose Shipton; *m* 1974, Judith Ackerman; one step *s* one step *d*. *Educ:* Central Foundn Sch.; Univ. of London (LLB ext. 1951); Middlesex Univ. (MBA 1985). Admitted solicitor, 1955; in private practice as a solicitor, 1954–77; Exec. Dir, Sephardi Fedn and Taali, 1987–97. Executive Member: CCJ; Bd of Deputies of British Jews; United Religious Initiative. Hon. Sec. and Vice Chm., British Section, World Jewish Congress; Hon. Sec. British Section, Internat. Assoc. Jewish Lawyers and Jurists. Hon. Exec. Dir, Business Against Drugs. Mem., Exec. and Council, London Civic Forum. Mem., Exec., Faith in Europe. Mem. Council, Jewish Histl Soc. Mem. Council, Wyndham Place Charlemagne Trust. Chm. Govs, Simon Marks Day Sch. Pres., Leo Baeck B'nai B'rith Lodge, 2000–02. Member: RIIA; Law Soc.; Medico-Legal Soc.; British Acad. Forensic Sci.; MENSA. FCMI (FBIM 1980); FRSA. Freeman, City of London, 1991. Kt 1st Cl., Royal Order of Francis I, 2006. *Publications:* Unity in Diversity, 1996; Visions of a Just Society, 2006; presentations to internat. confs; book reviews and articles in jls. *Recreations:* book collecting, international politics, criminology, cinema, travel. *Address:* Three Faiths Forum, Star House, 104–108 Grafton Road, NW5 4BA. *T:* (020) 7482 9549, *Fax:* (020) 7485 4512; *e-mail:* Sidney@threefaithsforum.org.uk. *Died 12 Jan. 2008.*

SHIVAS, Mark; film and television producer; Chairman, Headline Pictures, since 2004; *b* Banstead, Surrey, 24 April 1938; *s* of James Dallas Shivas and Winifred Alice Lighton (*née* Bristow). *Educ:* Whitgift School; Merton College, Oxford (MA Law). Asst Editor, Movie Magazine, 1962–64; freelance journalist; joined Granada TV, 1964, Director-Producer, 1965–68; Producer of Drama, 1969–88, Head of Drama, 1988–93, Head of Films, 1993–97, BBC TV; Creative Dir, Southern Pictures, 1979–81. Productions include: The Six Wives of Henry VIII (BAFTA awards, Prix Italia), The Evacuees (BAFTA and Emmy awards), Casanova, The Glittering Prizes, Rogue Male, Professional Foul (BAFTA award), Telford's Change, On Giant's Shoulders (Emmy award), Talking Heads 2, Telling Tales, Cambridge Spies; for Channel 4: The Price, What if it's Raining?, The Storyteller (Emmy award); feature films include:

Moonlighting, 1982; A Private Function, 1984; The Witches, 1988; Truly, Madly, Deeply, 1991; Enchanted April, 1991; The Snapper, 1993; Priest, 1995; Small Faces, 1996; Jude, 1996; Regeneration, 1997; Hideous Kinky, 1998; I Capture the Castle, 2002. *Publications:* articles in art jls. *Recreations:* Italy, gardens, swimming, cycling, movie-going. *Address:* 38 Gloucester Mews, W2 3HE. *T:* (020) 7723 4678, *Fax:* (020) 7262 1415. *Died 11 Oct. 2008.*

SHORE, David Teignmouth, OBE 1982; FREng; Director (Technical), APV PLC, 1984–88; *b* 15 Nov. 1928; *e s* of Geoffrey and Cecilia Mary Shore; *m* 1950, Pamela Goodge; one *s* two *d*. *Educ:* Tiffin Boys' Sch., Kingston; Imperial Coll., London (MSc(Eng)). FIMechE 1967; FIChemE 1970; FIFST 1970; FCGI 1979; FREng (FEng 1979). Engrg apprenticeship, 1944–47; Thermal Engr, Foster Wheeler Ltd, 1953–54; APV Co. Ltd: Research Engr, 1950–52; Process Develt Engr, 1954–65; Research Dir, 1965–77; Man. Dir, 1977–82; Chm., 1982–84; Divisional Dir, APV Holdings PLC, 1982–84. Chm., British Food Manufg Industries Res. Assoc., 1984–87; Chm. Engrg Bd, 1985–89 and Mem. Council, 1985–89, SERC; Member: Bd of Advisers in Chemical Engrg, Univ. of London, 1983–; Bd of Food Studies, Univ. of Reading, 1984–93; Jt Delegacy for Food Res. Inst., Reading, 1985–; Council, Univ. of Reading, 1987–93. *Publications:* technical articles on rheology, heat transfer and food process engrg in learned jls. *Recreations:* walking, astronomy, wine-making. *Address:* Hembury, Garratts Lane, Banstead, Surrey SM7 2EA. *T:* (01737) 353721. *Died 7 July 2007.*

SHORE, Jack; President, Royal Cambrian Academy of Art, 1977–83; *b* 17 July 1922; *s* of Frank and Maggie Shore; *m* 1970, Olive Brenda Williams; one *s* one *d*. *Educ:* Accrington and Manchester Schools of Art. Lectr, Blackpool School of Art, 1945–60; Head, Chester Sch. of Art, 1960–81. Paintings in public and private collections, including USA. RCamA 1962–2003 (ARCamA 1961). Jubilee Medal, 1977. *Recreations:* gardening, enjoyment of music. *Address:* 11 St George's Crescent, Queens Park, Chester CH4 7AR. *T:* (01244) 675017. *Died 7 Feb. 2009.*

SIDEY, Thomas Kay Stuart, CMG 1968; Founder Patron, Wickliffe Press Ltd, since 1993 (Managing Director, 1961–83; Executive Chairman, 1983–93); Barrister and Solicitor, NZ, since 1932; *b* 8 Oct. 1908; *s* of Sir Thomas Kay Sidey; *m* 1933, Beryl, *d* of Harvey Richardson Thomas, Wellington, NZ; one *s* one *d*. *Educ:* Otago Boys' High School; Univ. of Otago (LLM; Hon LLD, 1978). Served War of 1939–45 (despatches): 2nd NZEF; 4 years, Middle East and Italy, rank of Major. Dunedin City Council, 1947–50, 1953–65, 1968–83; Dep. Mayor, 1956–59, 1968–77; Mayor, 1959–65. Mem., Univ. of Otago Council, 1947–83, Pro Chancellor, 1959–70, Chancellor, 1970–76. Past President: Dunedin Chamber of Commerce; Automobile Assoc., Otago; Trusteebank Otago; NZ Library Assoc.; Otago Old People's Welfare Council; Otago Boys' High Sch. Old Boys' Soc. *Recreations:* fishing, boating. *Address:* 190 Beacon Point Road, Wanaka 9305, New Zealand. *T:* (3) 4438471. *Club:* Dunedin (Dunedin, NZ). *Died 28 Oct. 2007.*

SIEGBAHN, Prof. Kai Manne Börje; Professor of Physics, University of Uppsala, 1954–84; *b* 20 April 1918; *s* of Manne Siegbahn (Nobel Prize for Physics, 1924) and Karin Siegbahn (*née* Högbom); *m* 1944, Anna-Brita (*née* Rhedin); three *s*. *Educ:* Univ. of Uppsala (BSc 1939; Licentiat of Philosophy 1942); Univ. of Stockholm (Dr of Philosophy 1944). Research Associate, Nobel Inst. of Physics, 1942–51; Prof. of Physics, Royal Inst. of Technology, Stockholm, 1951–54. Founder, and Editor 1957, Internat. Jl of Nuclear Instruments and Methods in Physics Res. Member: Roy. Swedish Acad. of Sci.; Roy. Swedish Acad. of Engrg Scis; Roy. Soc. of Sci.; Roy. Acad. of Arts and Sci. of Uppsala; Roy. Physiographical Soc. of Lund; Societas Scientiarum Fennica; Norwegian Acad. of Sci.; Roy. Norwegian

Soc. of Scis and Letters; Nat. Acad. of Sciences; Pontifical Acad. of Sci.; European Acad. of Arts, Scis and Humanities. Hon. Mem. Amer. Acad. of Arts and Scis; Membre de Comité des Poids et Mesures, Paris; Pres., IUPAP, 1981–84. Dr of Science, hc Durham, 1972; Basel, 1980; Liège, 1980; Upsala Coll., East Orange, NJ, 1982; Sussex, 1983. Lindblom Prize, 1945; Björkén Prize, 1955, 1977; Celsius Medal, 1962; Sixten Heyman Award, 1971; Harrison Howe Award, 1973; Maurice F. Hasler Award, 1975; Charles Frederick Chandler Medal, 1976; Torbern Bergman Medal, 1979; (jtly) Nobel Prize for Physics, 1981; Pittsburgh Award of Spectroscopy, 1982; Röntgen Medal, 1985; Fiuggi Award, 1986; Humboldt Award, 1986; Premio Castiglione Di Sicilia, 1990. *Publications:* Beta- and Gamma-Ray Spectroscopy, 1955; Alpha-, Beta- and Gamma-Ray Spectroscopy, 1965; ESCA—Atomic, Molecular and Solid State Structure Studied by Means of Electron Spectroscopy, 1967; ESCA Applied to Free Molecules, 1969; Some Current Problems in Electron Spectroscopy, 1983; around 400 scientific papers. *Recreations:* tennis, ski-ing, music. *Address:* Department of Materials Science, University of Uppsala, Box 534, 751 21 Uppsala, Sweden. *T:* (18) 4713559. *Died 20 July 2007.*

SIEGERT, Air Vice-Marshal Cyril Laurence, CB 1979; CBE 1975; MVO 1954; DFC 1944; AFC 1954; *b* 14 March 1923; *s* of Lawrence Siegert and Julia Ann Siegert; *m* 1948, Shirley Berenice Dick (*d* 2007); two *s* two *d*. *Educ:* Fairlie High School; St Kevin's Coll., Oamaru; Victoria Univ. of Wellington. Joined RNZAF, 1942; served in UK with Nos 299 and 190 Sqdns; on loan to BOAC, 1945–47; Berlin airlift, 1949; NZ, 1952–54; NZ Defence Staff, Washington, 1954–56; RAF Staff Coll., 1957; NZ, 1958–62; Comdt, RNZAF's Command and Staff Sch., 1962; RAF Coll. of Air Warfare, 1963; Singapore, 1963–65; CO, No 3 Battlefield Support Sqdn and RNZAF Transport Wing, 1965–69; AOC RNZAF Ops Group, 1969–70; IDC 1970; RNZAF Air Staff, 1971; Chief of Staff, ANZUK Joint Force HQ, Singapore, 1971–73; Dep. Chief of Defence Staff (Policy), 1973–76; Chief of Air Staff, RNZAF, 1976–79. Gen. Manager, Marine Air Systems, 1980–84; Mem., Air Services Licensing Authority, 1980–87. *Recreations:* fishing, tramping, gardening. *Address:* Townhouse 60, 66 Mabey Road, Lower Hutt, New Zealand. *Died 17 Sept. 2007.*

SILLITOE, Alan; writer, since 1948; *b* 4 March 1928; *s* of Christopher Sillitoe and Sabina (*née* Burton); *m* 1959, Ruth Fainlight, poet; one *s* one *d*. *Educ:* various elementary schools in Nottingham. Raleigh Bicycle Factory, 1942; air traffic control asst, 1945–46; wireless operator, RAF, 1946–49. Lived in France and Spain, 1952–58. Vis. Prof. of English, De Montfort Univ., 1994–97. FRGS. Hon. Fellow, Manchester Polytechnic, 1977. Hon. DLitt: Nottingham Poly., 1990; Nottingham Univ., 1994; De Montfort Univ., 1998. Freedom, City of Nottingham, 2008. *Publications: novels:* Saturday Night and Sunday Morning, 1958 (Authors' Club Award for best first novel of 1958; filmed, 1960, play, 1964); The General, 1960 (filmed 1967 as Counterpoint); Key to the Door, 1961; The Death of William Posters, 1965; A Tree on Fire, 1967; A Start in Life, 1970; Travels in Nihilon, 1971; Raw Material, 1972; The Flame of Life, 1974; The Widower's Son, 1976; The Storyteller, 1979; Her Victory, 1982; The Lost Flying Boat, 1983; Down from the Hill, 1984; Life Goes On, 1985; Out of the Whirlpool, 1987; The Open Door, 1989; Last Loves, 1990; Leonard's War: a love story, 1991; Snowstop, 1993; The Broken Chariot, 1998; The German Numbers Woman, 1999; Birthday, 2001; A Man of His Time, 2004; *stories:* The Loneliness of the Long Distance Runner, 1959 (Hawthornden Prize; filmed, 1962); The Ragman's Daughter, 1963 (filmed, 1972); Guzman, Go Home, 1968; Men, Women and Children, 1973; The Second Chance, 1981; The Far Side of the Street, 1988; Collected Stories, 1995; Alligator Playground, 1997; New and Collected Stories, 2003; *poetry:* The Rats and Other Poems, 1960; A Falling Out of Love, 1964; Love in the

Environs of Voronezh, 1968; Storm and Other Poems, 1974; Snow on the North Side of Lucifer, 1979; Sun before Departure, 1984; Tides and Stone Walls, 1986; Collected Poems, 1993; *for children:* The City Adventures of Marmalade Jim, 1967; Big John and the Stars, 1977; The Incredible Fencing Fleas, 1978; Marmalade Jim at the Farm, 1980; Marmalade Jim and the Fox, 1985; *travel:* Road to Volgograd, 1964; (with Fay Godwin) The Saxon Shore Way, 1983; (with David Sillitoe) Nottinghamshire, 1987; Leading the Blind, 1995; Gadfly in Russia, 2007; *plays:* (with Ruth Fainlight) All Citizens are Soldiers, 1969; Three Plays, 1978; *essays:* Mountains and Caverns, 1975; A Flight of Arrows, 2003; *autobiography:* Life Without Armour, 1994; *miscellanea:* Every Day of the Week, 1987. *Recreations:* travel, shortwave wireless telegraphy listening. *Address:* 14 Ladbroke Terrace, W11 3PG. *Died 24 April 2010.*

SILLS, Beverly, (Mrs P. B. Greenough); Chairman, Lincoln Center for the Performing Arts, 1994–2002; Director, New York City Opera, 1979–88; former leading soprano, New York City Opera and Metropolitan Opera; *b* 25 May 1929; *d* of late Morris Silverman and of Sonia Bahn; *née* Belle Miriam Silverman; *m* 1956, Peter B. Greenough (*d* 2006); one *s* one *d*. *Educ:* Professional Children's Sch., NYC; privately. Vocal studies with Estelle Liebling, piano with Paulo Gallico. Operatic debut, Philadelphia Civic Opera, 1947; San Francisco Opera, 1953; New York City Opera, 1955; Vienna State Opera, 1967; Teatro Colón, Buenos Aires, 1968; La Scala, Milan, 1969; Teatro San Carlo, Naples, 1970; Royal Opera, Covent Garden, London, 1970; Deutsche Oper, W Berlin, 1971; NY Metropolitan Opera, 1975, etc. Repeated appearances as soloist with major US symphony orchestras; English orchestral debut with London Symphony Orch., London, 1971; Paris debut, orchestral concert, Salle Pleyel, 1971. Repertoire includes title roles of Norma, Manon, Lucia di Lammermoor, Maria Stuarda, Daughter of Regiment, Anna Bolena, Traviata, Lucrezia Borgia, Thais, Louise, Cleopatra in Giulio Cesare, Elizabeth in Roberto Devereux, Tales of Hoffmann, Elvira in Puritani, Rosina in Barber of Seville, Norina in Don Pasquale, Pamira in Siege of Corinth; created title role, La Loca, San Diego Opera, 1979. Subject of BBC-TV's Profile in Music (Nat. Acad. of TV Arts and Sciences Emmy Award, 1975); other TV includes: Sills and Burnett at the Met, 1976; Hostess/Commentator for Young People's Concerts, NY Philharmonic, 1977; Moderator/Hostess, Lifestyles with Beverly Sills, 1976, 1977 (Emmy 1978). Hon. DMus: Temple Univ., 1972; New York Univ., 1973; New England Conservatory, 1973; Harvard Univ., 1974. Woman of the Year, Hasty Pudding Club, Harvard, 1974; Handel Medallion, NYC: US Presidential Medal of Freedom. *Publications:* Bubbles: a self-portrait, 1976; (autobiog. with Lawrence Linderman) Beverly, 1987. *Recreations:* fishing, bridge. *Address:* c/o Edgar Vincent, Vincent & Farrell Associates Inc., 157 West Street, Suite 502, New York, NY 10019, USA. *Died 2 July 2007.*

SIMMONS, Jean Merilyn, OBE 2003; film actress; *b* London, 31 Jan. 1929; *m* 1950, Stewart Granger (marr. diss. 1960; he *d* 1993); one *d*; *m* 1960, Richard Brooks (marr. diss. 1977; he *d* 1992); one *d*. *Educ:* Orange Hill Sch.; Aida Foster School of Dancing. First film appearance in Give Us the Moon, 1942; minor parts in Cæsar and Cleopatra, The Way to the Stars, etc., 1942–44; from then appeared in numerous British films, including: Great Expectations, 1946; Black Narcissus, Hungry Hill, Uncle Silas, 1947; Hamlet, 1948 (Best Actress Award, Venice Film Festival, 1950); The Blue Lagoon, Adam and Evalyn, 1949; So Long at the Fair, Trio, 1950; Clouded Yellow, 1951; The Grass is Greener, 1960; Life at the Top, 1965; Say Hello to Yesterday, 1971; began American film career, 1950; American films include: Androcles and the Lion, 1952; Young Bess, The Actress, 1953; Desirée, 1954; Footsteps in the Fog, Guys and Dolls, 1955; This Could be the Night, 1957; Spartacus, Elmer Gantry, 1960; All the Way Home, 1963;

Divorce American Style, 1967; The Happy Ending, 1970; How to Make an American Quilt, 1996; American television includes: Beggarman, Thief, 1979; A Small Killing, 1981; Down at the Hydro, 1982; The Thorn Birds, 1982 (Emmy Award, 1983); Murder She Wrote, 1984; North and South, 1985; Perry Mason, Star Trek: The New Generation, 1987; Dark Shadows, 1991; UK television: December Flower, 1984; The Dawning, 1988; Great Expectations, 1989; They Do it with Mirrors, 1991; Daisies in December, 1995; Winter Solstice, 2003. Musical: A Little Night Music, Adelphi, 1975. Outstanding Film Achievement Award, Italy, 1989. Comdr, Order of Arts and Letters (France), 1990.
Died 22 Jan. 2010.

SIMMONS, Marion Adèle; QC 1994; a Recorder, since 1998; *b* 11 , April 1949; *d* of late Sidney Simmons and Bella Simmons (*née* Byer). *Educ:* Hendon County Grammar Sch.; Queen Mary Coll., Univ. of London (LLB Hons, LLM). Called to the Bar, Gray's Inn, 1970 (Bencher, 1993); Asst Recorder, 1990–98. Asst Boundary Comr, 2000–; Legal Mem., Restricted Cases Panel, Mental Health Review Tribunal, 2000–; Chm. (pt-time), Competition Appeal Tribunal, 2004–. Vice Chm., Appeals Cttee, ICAEW, 2000–05; Mem., Chm. Panel, Accountancy Investigation and Disciplinary Bd, 2004–; Chm., Disciplinary Cttee, Taxation Disciplinary Bd, 2006–. *Club:* Athenæum. *Died 2 May 2008.*

SIMON OF GLAISDALE, Baron *cr* 1971 (Life Peer), of Glaisdale, Yorks; **Jocelyn Edward Salis Simon,** Kt 1959; PC 1961; DL; a Lord of Appeal in Ordinary, 1971–77; *b* 15 Jan. 1911; *s* of Frank Cecil and Claire Evelyn Simon, 51 Belsize Pk, NW3; *m* 1st, 1934, Gwendolen Helen (*d* 1937), *d* of E. J. Evans; 2nd, 1948, Fay Elizabeth Leicester, JP, *d* of Brig. H. G. A. Pearson; three *s*. *Educ:* Gresham's School, Holt; Trinity Hall, Cambridge (Exhibitioner; Hon. Fellow, 1963). Called to Bar, Middle Temple, 1934 (Blackstone Prizeman). Served War of 1939–45; commissioned RTR, 1939; comd Spec. Service Sqn, RAC, Madagascar, 1942; Burma Campaign, 1944; Lieut-Col 1945. Resumed practice at Bar, 1946; KC 1951. MP (C) Middlesbrough West, 1951–62; Mem. of the Royal Commission on the Law relating to Mental Illness and Mental Deficiency, 1954–57. Jt Parly Under-Sec. of State, Home Office, 1957–58; Financial Sec. to the Treasury, 1958–59; Solicitor-General, 1959–62. President, Probate, Divorce and Admiralty Div. of the High Court of Justice, 1962–71. Elder Brother, Trinity House, 1975. DL NR (later North) Yorks, 1973. Hon. Dr en Droit Laval, 1961; Hon. LLD Cambridge, 1994. *Publications:* Change is Our Ally, 1954 (part); Rule of Law, 1955 (part); The Church and the Law of Nullity, 1955 (part). *Address:* c/o House of Lords, SW1A 0PW.
Died 7 May 2006.

SIMPLE, Peter; *see* Wharton, Michael B.

SIMPSON, Dr Diana, FEI, FFSSoc, FIFST, CEng, FIMMM, EurChem, CSci, CChem, FRSC; Forensic Scientist (civil and criminal); Principal Consultant, Analysis Industry, since 1975; *b* 26 Sept. 1929; *d* of Simon and Leah Caplan; *m* 1960, W. Gordon Simpson (*d* 1999). *Educ:* Oldham Municipal High Sch.; Manchester and Salford Polys; Northern Poly. (MPhil 1970, PhD 1974, London Univ.). CChem, FRSC 1979; FRMS 1987; FIFST 1988; CEng 1989; EurChem 1993; FIM 1997; CSci 2004; FFSSoc 2006. Asst Tech. Officer, ICI Pharmaceutical Div., 1953; Dep. to Control and Develt Dir, Pfizer Ltd, 1953–60; Hd, Analytical Services, Bakelite Xylonite Ltd, 1960–75. Member of Council and Trustee: RSC; Analytical Chem. Trust Fund, RSC; Inst. Food Sci. and Technol.; Soc. Chem. Industry. Life MInstD, 1980. Distinguished Service Award: Soc. Analytical Chem., 1984; RSC, 1994. *Publications:* (with W. G. Simpson) An Introduction to Applications of Light Microscopy to Analysis, 1988; (ed with W. G. Simpson) The COSHH Regulations: a practical guide, 1991; contrib. jls incl. British Plastics, The Analyst, Trends in Analytical Chem., Analysis and Chromatography. *Recreations:* children and animal charities, reading, light microscopy, perpetuance of the use of correct English, attempting to persuade people that English and American are two different languages, word and mathematical puzzles, trying to out-predict the FTSE, watching cricket. *T:* (01206) 851775. *Died 15 March 2009.*

SIMPSON, His Honour Keith Taylor; a Circuit Judge, 1990–2005; *b* 8 May 1934; *m* 1961, Dorothy Preece; two *s* one *d*. *Educ:* privately; Jesus Coll., Oxford (MA). Called to the Bar, Middle Temple, 1958; joined SE Circuit; general Common Law practice. *Recreations:* walking, gardening, reading, opera. *Died 5 May 2008.*

SIMSON, Michael Ronald Fraser, OBE 1966; Secretary of the National Corporation for the Care of Old People, 1948–73; *b* 9 Oct. 1913; *er s* of Ronald Stuart Fraser Simson and Ethel Alice Henderson; *m* 1939, Elizabeth Joan Wilkinson; one *s*. *Educ:* Winchester Coll.; Christ Church, Oxford. OUAFC 1936 and 1937. Asst Master, West Downs Sch., 1938–40; RNVR, 1941–46; Asst Sec., Nat. Fedn of Housing Socs, 1946–48. Member: Min. of Labour Cttee on Employment of Older Men and Women, 1953–55; Cttee on Local Authority and Allied Personal Social Services (Seebohm Cttee), 1966–68; Supplementary Benefits Commn, 1967–76; Adv. Cttee on Rent Rebates and Rent Allowances, 1973–75, resigned 1975; Personal Social Services Council, 1973–78. *Recreation:* interested in all forms of sport. *Address:* Beauchamp House, Hatch Beauchamp, Taunton, Somerset TA3 6SG. *T:* (01823) 481508. *Died 28 March 2009.*

SINCLAIR, Hon. Ian David, QC 1979; QC (Can.) 1961; Member, Senate of Canada, 1983–88; *b* Winnipeg, 27 Dec. 1913; *s* of late John David Sinclair and Lillian Sinclair; *m* 1942, Ruth Beatrice, *d* of Robert Parsons Drennan, Winnipeg; two *s* two *d*. *Educ:* public schs, Winnipeg; Univ. of Manitoba (BA Econs 1937); Manitoba Law School (LLB 1941). Barrister, Guy Chappell & Co., Winnipeg, 1937–41; Lectr in Torts, Univ. of Manitoba, 1942–43; joined Canadian Pacific Law Dept as Asst Solicitor, Winnipeg, 1942; Solicitor, Montreal, 1946; Asst to General Counsel, 1951; General Solicitor, 1953; Vice-Pres. and Gen. Counsel, 1960; Vice-Pres., Law, 1960; Canadian Pacific Railway Co.: Vice-Pres., Dir and Mem. Exec. Cttee, 1961; Pres., 1966; Chief Exec. Officer, 1969; Chm. and Chief Exec. Officer: Canadian Pacific Ltd, 1972–81; Canadian Pacific Enterprises Ltd, 1972–82 (Chm.), 1982–84); Dir, Canadian Investment Fund, Ltd, 1972–89; Public Dir, Investment Dealers Assoc. of Canada, 1984–88; Public Gov., Car Investors Protection Fund, 1990–2000; Mem., Internat. Adv. Cttee, Chase Manhattan Bank, N America, 1973–87. Hon. LLD Manitoba, 1967; Hon. DBA Laval, 1981; Hon. DCL Acadia, 1982. Mem., Canadian Business Hall of Fame. *Address:* 35 Cameo Street, Oakville, ON L6J 5X9, Canada. *Club:* Toronto (Toronto). *Died 7 April 2006.*

SINCLAIR, Prof. John McHardy; Professor of Modern English Language, University of Birmingham, 1965–2000; President, Tuscan Word Centre, since 1996; *b* 14 June 1933; *s* of late George Ferguson Sinclair and Isabella (*née* Palmer); *m* 1st, 1956, Margaret Myfanwy Lloyd; two *s* one *d*; 2nd, 1996, Elena Tognini Bonelli; one *s* one *d*. *Educ:* George Heriot's Sch., Edinburgh; Edinburgh Univ. (MA). Served Royal Air Force (Flt-Lt), 1955–58. Lectr, Edinburgh Univ., 1959–65. Adjunct Prof., Shanghai Jiao Tong Univ., 1986–; Hon. Prof. Res. Fellow, Univ. of Glasgow, 1997–. Pres., Trans-European Language Resources Infrastructure, 1997–2001. MAE. Hon. Life Mem., Linguistics Assoc. of GB, 2000. Hon. DPhil Gothenburg, 1998. *Publications:* A Course in Spoken English—Grammar, 1972; (with R. M. Coulthard) Towards an Analysis of Discourse, 1975, 2nd edn 1978; (with D. C. Brazil) Teacher Talk, 1982; Corpus, Concordance, Collocation, 1991; Reading Concordances, 2003; Trust the Text, 2004; Founding Editor in Chief, Cobuild: Collin's Cobuild English Language Dictionary, 1987; Collins Cobuild English

Grammar, 1990. *Address:* Via Pandolfini 27, 50122 Florence, Italy. *T:* and *Fax:* (055) 295470; *e-mail:* jms@twc.it.   *Died 13 March 2007.*

SINCLAIR, Michael; *see* Shea, M. S. MacA.

SINGER, Aubrey Edward, CBE 1984; Managing Director, White City Films, 1984–96 (Chairman, 1984–94); *b* 21 Jan. 1927; *s* of Louis Henry Singer and late Elizabeth (*née* Walton); *m* 1949, Cynthia Hilda Adams; one *s* two *d* (and one *d* decd). *Educ:* Giggleswick; Bradford Grammar School. Joined film industry, 1944; directed various films teaching armed forces to shoot; worked extensively in Africa, 1946–48; worked on children's films in Austria, 1948–49; joined BBC TV Outside Broadcasts, 1949; TV Producer Scotland, 1951; BBC New York Office, 1953; returned to London as Producer, 1956; produced many scientific programmes; Asst Head of Outside Broadcasts, 1959; Head of Science and Features, 1961; Head of Features Gp, BBC TV, 1967; Controller, BBC 2, 1974–78; Man. Dir, BBC Radio, 1978–82; Dep. Dir-Gen., and Man. Dir, Television, BBC, 1982–84. Chm., Soc. of Film and Television Arts, 1971–73. President: TV and Radio Industries Club, 1984–85; Council, Nat. Mus. of Photography, Film and TV, 1984–96. FRTS 1978 (a Vice-Pres., 1982–88); FRAS; FRSA. Hon. DLitt Bradford, 1984. *Publications:* The Lion and the Dragon, 1992. *Recreations:* walking, talking, archery.   *Died 26 May 2007.*

SINGER, Sir Hans (Wolfgang), Kt 1994; PhD; Professorial Fellow, Institute of Development Studies, University of Sussex, since 1969, Emeritus Professor, since 1980; *b* 29 Nov. 1910; *s* of Heinrich and Antonia Singer; *m* 1934, Ilse Lina Plaut (*d* 2001); one *s* (and one *s* decd). *Educ:* Univ. of Bonn (Econ. Dip. 1931); King's Coll., Cambridge (PhD 1936). Pilgrim Trust Unemployment Enquiry, 1936–38; Manchester Univ., 1938–44; Min. of Town and Country Planning, 1945–46; Glasgow Univ., 1946–47; with United Nations Secretariat, 1947–69: Dir, Econ. Div., UNIDO, 1967–69. Hon. Fellow, Inst. of Social Studies, The Hague, 1978. Hon. DLitt: Sussex, 1990; Santa Fe, Argentina, 1989; Glasgow, 1994; Lisbon, 1994; Innsbruck, 1997. *Publications:* numerous books including: (jtly) Men Without Work, 1938; International Development, Growth and Change, 1964; (with J. Ansari) Rich and Poor Countries, 1977 (trans. Portuguese, 1979, Spanish, 1982), 4th edn 1988; (jtly) Food Aid: the challenge and the opportunity, 1987; (ed jtly) New World Order Series, 12 vols, 1987–92; (with S. Roy) Economic Progress and Prospects in the Third World: lessons of development experience since 1945, 1993; (with K. Raffer) The Foreign Aid Business, 1996; also articles in learned jls. *Recreations:* walking, music, chess. *Address:* Institute of Development Studies, University of Sussex, Brighton, E Sussex BN1 9RE; 18 The Vale, Ovingdean, Brighton, E Sussex BN2 7AB. *T:* (01273) 303567.   *Died 26 Feb. 2006.*

SINGH, Vishwanath Pratap; Prime Minister of India, 1989–90; *b* 25 June 1931; *s* of Raja Bahadur Ram Gopal Singh; *m* 1955, Sita Kumari; two *s*. *Educ:* Poona Univ.; Allahabad Univ. (Vice-Pres., Students Union; LLB); Udip Pratap College, Varanasi (Pres., Students Union). Participated in Bhoodan Movement, 1957, and donated farm, Pasna, Allahabad; Mem. Exec., Allahabad Univ., 1969–71; founded Gopal Vidyalaya, Intermediate Coll., Koraon, Allahabad. Uttar Pradesh appointments: MLA, 1969–71 and 1981–83; Whip, Congress Legislature Party, 1970–71; MLC, 1980–81; Chief Minister, 1980–82; Pres., UP Congress Cttee, 1984. Mem., Lok Sabha, 1971–77, 1980, 1988–89 and 1989–94; Mem., Rajya Sabha, 1983–88; Union Dep. Minister (Commerce), 1974–76; Union Minister of State (Commerce), 1976–77; Union Minister (Commerce), 1983 (also i/c Dept of Supply); Union Finance Minister, 1984–87; Defence Minister, Jan.–April 1987. Founded Jan Morcha, 1987; Pres., Janata Dal, 1988; Convenor, Nat. Front, 1988. *Address:* 1 Teen Murti Marg, New Delhi 110001, India.   *Died 27 Nov. 2008.*

SINGHVI, Dr Laxmi Mall; Senior Advocate, Supreme Court of India, since 1967 (Advocate, 1951–67); *b* 9 Nov. 1931; *s* of D. M. Singhvi and Akal Kaur Singhvi; *m* 1957, Kamla Baid, author; one *s* one *d*. *Educ:* Allahabad Univ. (BA); Rajasthan Univ. (LLB); Harvard Univ. Law Sch. (LLM); Cornell Univ. Law Sch. (SJD). MP, Independent, Lok Sabha, 1962–67; Senior Standing Counsel, State of UP, Union of India, 1967–71; Advocate-Gen., 1972–77. High Comr for India in UK, 1991–97. MP (BJP) Rajasthan, Rajya Sabha, 1998–2004. Mem., Perm. Court of Arbitration, The Hague, 2000; Comr of Inquiry into admin of justice, Trinidad and Tobago, 2000. Dep. Leader, Indian Parly Delegn to CPA, 1964, Leader Parly Delegn, 1966; Chm. and Founder, Inst. of Constitutional and Parly Studies, 1964–. Chairman: Indian Fedn of Unesco Assocs, 1974–; World Colloquium on Legal Aid, 1975; State Bar Council, 1975–77; Indian Nat. Cttee for Abolition of Death Penalty, 1977–; Nat. Sch. of Drama, 1978–82; Supreme Court Law Reforms Cttee, 1981–82; Asian Conf. on Approaches to Human Rights, 1985; Govt of India Cttee on Revitalisation of Rural Local Self-Govt, 1986–87; Govt of India Task Force on Child Labour; Govt of India Cttee on Brain Death and Organ Transplantation, 1991; Founder Chm., 1972, Hon. Patron, 1983, Commonwealth Legal Educn Assoc.; Founder-Pres., Indian Centre for Human Rights Educn and Research, 1980; Pres., World Congress on Human Rights, 1990; Member: UN Human Rights Sub-Commn, Geneva, 1978–82 (Vice-Chm.); Nat. Commn for Unesco; Govt of India Expert Cttee on Legal Aid, 1971–73; Commn on Inf. and Broadcasting, 1964–68; Internat. Forum on Freedoms and Rights of Man, Paris, 1985–. Co-Chm., Bharatiya Vidya Bhavan Internat.; President: Supreme Court Bar Assoc., 1977, 1978, 1980, 1982; Supreme Court Bar Trust, 1981–; Nat. Legal Aid Assoc., 1970–; Indian Centre for Independence of Judges and Lawyers, 1979–; Indira Gandhi Nat. Centre for Arts, 2000–; UN Special Rapporteur on Independence of Judges and Lawyers, 1979–; Hon. Mem. and Adv. Panelist, Comparative Const. Law Project and Bicentennial of Amer. Constitution, Amer. Council of Learned Socs, 1986–88. Chm., Pravara Mandals for Jamna Lal Bajaj and Jnan Peeth Awards; Trustee and Mem. Jury, G. D. Birla Award on Humanism. Life Trustee and Pres., India Internat. Centre; Pres. Emeritus, Authors Guild of India (Pres., 1986–90). Hon. Tagore Law Prof., 1975–; Visiting Professor and Fellow: Univ. of Leicester, 1991–; Univ. of Hull, 1994–. Rede Lectr, Univ. of Cambridge, 1993. Hon. Bencher, Middle Temple, 1987. Hon. LLD: Jabalpur, 1983; Banaras Hindu, 1984; Tamil, Tamilnadu, 1991; Buckingham, 1993; N London, 1993; Osmania, 1994; De Montfort, 1994. Hon. Nyayavacaspati, Gurukul, 1968. *Publications:* Horizons of Freedom, 1969; (ed) Law and Poverty, 1970; Indian Federalism, 1974; Legal Aid, 1985; Law Day, 1985; Independence of Justice, 1985; Jain Declaration on Nature, 1990; Freedom on Trial, 1991; The Evening Sun (poems), 1991; A Third International Covenant for the Prevention of Ecocide, 1991; Jain Temples in India and Around the World, 2002; A Diplomatic Sojourn, 2002; Democracy & Rule of Law: towards global togetherness, 2002; Bharat Aur Hamara Samaya: towards a new global order. *Recreations:* theatre, poetry, chess, gardening, classical Indian dance appreciation, archaeology. *Address:* 18 Willingdon Crescent, New Delhi 110001, India. *Club:* Athenæum.   *Died 6 Oct. 2007.*

SITWELL, Sir (Sacheverell) Reresby, 7th Bt *cr* 1808, of Renishaw; DL; *b* 15 April 1927; *s* of Sir Sacheverell Sitwell, 6th Bt, CH and Georgia Louise (*d* 1980), *d* of Arthur Doble; *S* father, 1988; *m* 1952, Penelope, *yr d* of late Col Hon. Donald Alexander Forbes, DSO, MVO; one *d*. *Educ:* Eton College; King's Coll., Cambridge (schol.). Served Grenadier Guards, 1945–48, mainly as Lieut, 2nd Bn, BAOR. Advertising and PR executive, 1948–63; operated vending machines and wholesale wine business, 1963–73. Took over Renishaw and family estates from late uncle, Sir Osbert, 1965. High Sheriff of Derbyshire, 1983; DL Derbyshire 1984. Freedom of City of London, 1984. Hon. Fellow, Grey Coll., Durham,

2001. Hon. LittD Sheffield, 2004. *Publications:* (with John Julius Norwich and A. Costa) Mount Athos, 1964; Hortus Sitwellianus (epilogue), 1984; Robin Hood's Bow, 2007. *Recreations:* art and architecture, music, travel, photography, racing. *Heir: nephew* George Reresby Sacheverell Sitwell, *b* 22 April 1967. *Address:* Renishaw Hall, Sheffield S21 3WB; 4 Southwick Place, W2 2TN. *T:* (020) 7262 3939. *Clubs:* White's, Brooks's, Pratt's, Society of Dilettanti; Pitt (Cambridge); Derby County.
Died 31 March 2009.

SIZER, Prof. John, CBE 1989; DLitt; higher education consultant, since 2002; Chief Executive and Member: Scottish Higher Education Funding Council, 1992–2001; Scottish Further Education Funding Council, 1999–2001; *b* 14 Sept. 1938; *s* of Mary and John Robert Sizer; *m* 1965, (Valerie) Claire Davies; three *s. Educ:* Grimsby Coll. of Technology; Univ. of Nottingham (BA); DLitt Loughborough, 1989. FCMA. Teaching Fellow, later Lectr, Univ. of Edinburgh, 1965; Sen. Lectr, London Graduate Sch. of Business Studies, 1968; Loughborough University of Technology: Prof. of Financial Mgt, 1970–96; Vis. Prof., 1996–2005; Emeritus Prof., 2005–; Founding Head of Dept of Management Studies, 1971–84; Dean of Sch. of Human and Environmental Studies, 1973–76; Sen. Pro Vice-Chancellor, 1980–82; Dir, Business Sch., 1991–92. Chm., Directing Group, OECD/CERI Programme on Institutional Management in Higher Educn, 1980–84; Mem., UGC, 1984–89 (Chm., Business and Management Studies Sub-Cttee, 1984–89); Advr on Business and Management Studies, and Mem., NI Cttee, UFC, 1989–93; Member: Council, CIMA, 1981–88 (Chairman: Internat. Cttee, 1982–86; Finance Cttee, 1986–88); Nat. Forum for Management Educn and Develt, 1989–95 (Chm., Finance and Resourcing Cttee, 1989–95; Mem., Exec. Cttee, 1989–95); Sci. and Engrg Base Co-ordinating Cttee, 1993–2001; Foresight Prog. Steering Gp, 1995–2001; Chm., Soc. for Res. into Higher Educn, 1992–93 (Vice Pres., 1995–). Member: Public Sector and Not-for-Profit Cttee, Accounting Standards Bd, 1994–98; Sec. of State for Scotland's Scottish Parlt Financial Issues Adv. Gp, 1998–99. Trustee, and Chm. Audit Cttee, Nat. Centre for Social Res., 2007. FCMI; FRSA. Hon. Dr Laws: St Andrews, 2002; Abertay Dundee, 2002; Hon. DSc(Econ) Hull, 2005. *Publications:* An Insight into Management Accounting, 1969, 1979, 1989; Case Studies in Management Accounting, 1974; Perspectives in Management Accounting, 1981; (ed jtly) Resources and Higher Education, 1983; (jtly) A Casebook of British Management Accounting, vol. 1, 1984, vol. 2, 1985; Institutional Responses to Financial Reductions in the University Sector, 1987; numerous articles in accounting, economics, higher educn and management jls. *Recreations:* enjoying Scotland, walking. *Address:* Charnwood, 15 Selwyn Road, The Pavillions, Burntwood, Staffs WS7 9HU. *T:* (01543) 674361.   *Died 22 March 2008.*

SKEET, Muriel Harvey; Chief Nursing Officer and Nursing Adviser, British Red Cross Society, and St John of Jerusalem and British Red Cross Society Joint Committee, 1970–78; *b* 12 July 1926; *y d* of late F. W. C. Skeet, Suffolk. *Educ:* privately; Endsleigh House; Middlesex Hosp. SRN, MRSH; FRCN. Gen. Nursing Trg at Middx Hosp., 1946–49; also London Sch. of Hygiene and Tropical Med.; Ward Sister and Admin. Sister, Middx Hosp., 1949–60; Field Work Organiser, Opl Res. Unit, Nuffield Provincial Hosps Trust, 1961–64; Res. Org., Dan Mason Nursing Res. Cttee of Nat. Florence Nightingale Memorial Cttee of Gt Britain and N Ire., 1965–70; Internat. Health Services advr and consultant, WHO HQ, 1971–96. WHO Res. Consultant, SE Asia, 1970; European Deleg. and First Chm. of Bd of Commonwealth Nurses' Fed., 1971. Leverhulme Fellowship, 1974–75. Member: Hosp. and Med. Services Cttee, 1970; Ex-Services War Disabled Help Cttee, 1970; British Commonwealth Nurses War Memorial Fund Cttee and Council, 1970; Council of Management of Nat. Florence Nightingale Memorial Cttee, 1970; Council of Queen's Inst. of District Nursing,

1970; Royal Coll. of Nursing and Nat. Council of Nurses; RSM, 1980. Fellow RCN, 1977. *Publications:* Waiting in Outpatient Departments (Nuffield Provincial Hospitals Trust), 1965; Marriage and Nursing (Dan Mason NRC), 1968; Home from Hospital (Dan Mason NRC), 1970; Home Nursing, 1975; Manual: Disaster Relief Work, 1977; Back to Our Basic Skills, 1977; Health needs Help, 1977; (jtly) Health Auxiliaries in the Health Team, 1978; Self Care for the People of Developing Countries, 1979; Discharge Procedures, 1980; Notes on Nursing 1860 and 1980, 1980; Emergency Procedures and First Aid for Nurses, 1981; The Third Age, 1982; Providing Continuing Care for Elderly People, 1983; First Aid for Developing Countries, 1983; Protecting the Health of the Elderly, 1983; Know Your Own Body, 1987; Add Life to Years, 1989; Tropical Health: concise notes, 1989; Better Opportunities for Disabled People, 1989; Care and Maintenance of Hospital Equipment, 1995; various articles in professional jls. *Recreations:* music, opera, painting, reading. *Club:* Sloane.   *Died 22 Nov. 2006.*

SKINNER, James John; QC; Social Security Commissioner, 1986–96; a Child Support Commissioner, 1993–96; *b* 24 July 1923; *o s* of late William Skinner, Solicitor, Clonmel, Ireland; *m* 1950, Regina Brigitte Reiss; three *s* two *d. Educ:* Clongowes Wood Coll.; Trinity Coll., Dublin; King's Inns, Dublin. Called to Irish Bar, 1946; joined Leinster Circuit; called to English Bar, Gray's Inn, 1950; called to Bar of Northern Rhodesia, 1951; QC (Northern Rhodesia) 1964; MP (UNIP) Lusaka East, 1964–68; Minister of Justice, 1964–65; Attorney-General, 1965–69 (in addition, Minister of Legal Affairs, 1967–68); Chief Justice of Zambia, March–Sept. 1969; Chief Justice of Malaŵi, 1970–85. Grand Comdr, Order of Menelik II of Ethiopia, 1965. *Recreation:* reading. *Address:* 12A Ashley Court, Ashley Road, Epsom, Surrey KT18 5AJ. *T:* (01372) 728299.
Died 21 Oct. 2008.

SKINNER, Joyce Eva, CBE 1975; *b* 5 Sept. 1920; *d* of Matthew and Ruth Eva Skinner. *Educ:* Christ's Hosp.; Girls' High Sch., Lincoln; Somerville Coll., Oxford (BA 1941, MA 1945). Teacher: Bridlington Girls' High Sch., 1942–45; Perse Girls' Sch., 1946–50 (Hd of History); Keswick Sch., 1950–52 (Sen. Mistress); Sen. Lectr, then Dep. Principal, Homerton Coll., Cambridge, 1952–64; Vis. Prof., Queen's Coll., NY, 1955–56; Principal, Bishop Grosseteste Coll., Lincoln, 1964–74; Dir, Cambridge Inst. of Educn, 1974–80; Academic Sec., Universities' Council for Educn of Teachers, 1979–84. Fellow: Hughes Hall, Cambridge, 1974–85; Worcester Coll. of Higher Educn, 1985. Hon. FCP 1971. Hon. DEd CNAA, 1989; Hon. DLitt Hull, 1997. *Publications:* (jtly) Growing up Downhill, 1998. *Recreation:* conversation. *Address:* 26 Rasen Lane, Lincoln LN1 3EY. *T:* (01522) 529483.   *Died 31 Oct. 2010.*

SKIPPER, David John; Director: Westminster Centre for Education, Independent Schools Joint Council, 1991–96; Secondary Post Graduate Certificate of Education Course by Distance Learning, South Bank University (formerly Polytechnic), 1991–97; *b* 14 April 1931; *s* of late Herbert G. and Edna Skipper; *m* 1955, Brenda Ann Williams; three *s* one *d. Educ:* Watford Grammar Sch.; Brasenose Coll., Oxford (2nd Cl. Hons Nat. Science (Chemistry)). Royal Air Force (Short Service Commn) (Education), 1954–57; Assistant Master: Radley Coll., 1957–63; Rugby Sch., 1963–69; Headmaster: Ellesmere Coll., Shropshire, 1969–81; Merchant Taylors' Sch., Northwood, 1982–91. Chairman: ISJC Special Educnl Needs, 1983–91; Soc. of Schoolmasters, 1985–97; Pres., Soc. of Schoolmasters and Schoolmistresses, 1998–. Trustee: Confide-Shropshire Counselling, 2000– (Chm., 2002–05); Ellesmere Community Care Centre, 2000– (Chm., 2004–); Founding Chm., Ellesmere Patient Gp, 2004–08. Chm. Governors, Quainton Sch., Harrow, 1993–2001. Fellow, Midland Div., Woodard Corp., 1996–2002. Treas., Welshampton PCC, 2000–; Churchwarden, 2007–.

Freeman, City of London, 1991; Liveryman, Merchant Taylors' Co., 1991–. *Recreations:* drawing, music, gardening, books. *Address:* 4 St Michael's Green, Lyneal Lane, Welshampton, Ellesmere, Shropshire SY12 0QT. *T:* (01948) 710899. *Died 17 April 2009.*

SLABBERT, Dr Frederik Van Zyl; political consultant; Chairman: Adcorp Holdings, since 1998; Metro Cash&Carry, since 2000; *b* 2 March 1940; *s* of Petrus Johannes and Barbara Zacharia Slabbert; *m* 1965, Marié Jordaan (marr. diss. 1983); one *s* one *d*; *m* 1984, Jane Catherine Stephens. *Educ:* Univ. of Stellenbosch. BA, BA (Hons), MA 1964, DPhil 1967. Lectr in Sociology, Stellenbosch Univ., 1964–68; Senior Lecturer: Rhodes Univ., 1969; Stellenbosch Univ., 1970–71; Cape Town Univ., 1972–73; Prof. of Sociology, Univ. of the Witwatersrand, 1973–74. MP (Progressive Federal Party) Claremont, 1974–86; Leader, Official Opposition, S African Parlt, 1979–86. Founder and Dir, Inst. for a Democratic Alternative for South Africa, 1987; Chm., Open Soc. Initiative for Southern Africa. Vis. Prof., Univ. of the Witwatersrand Business Sch., 1988–. *Publications:* South African Society: its central perspectives, 1972; (jtly) South Africa's Options: strategies for sharing power, 1979; The Last White Parliament (autobiog.), 1986; (jtly) Comrades in Business: post-liberation politics in South Africa, 1998; Afrikaner Afrikaan, 1999; contributions to: Change in Contemporary South Africa, 1975; Explorations in Social Theory, 1976; various SPROCAS (Study Project of a Christian in an Apartheid Society) publications. *Recreations:* jogging, swimming, squash, chess. *Address:* Khula Consulting (Pty) Ltd, PO Box 2817, Houghton, 2041, South Africa. *Died 14 May 2010.*

SLADE, Brian John, FCIPS; Director General of Defence Contracts, Ministry of Defence, 1986–91; *b* 28 April 1931; *s* of late Albert Edward Victor Slade and Florence Elizabeth (*née* Eveleigh); *m* 1955, Grace, *d* of late W. McK. Murray and Mary Murray, Ayr; one *s* one *d*. *Educ:* Portsmouth Northern Grammar School; London University. Joined Min. of Supply, 1951; Private Sec. to Permanent Sec., Min. of Aviation, 1962–64; Hed of Industrial Personnel Branch, Min. of Technology, 1968–73; Principal Dir of Contracts, Air, MoD, 1982–86. Director: SERCO Gp plc, 1991–94; A & P Gp, 1993–2006. Pres., Shipbuilders and Ship Repairers Assoc., 2002–; Chm., Shipbuilding and Marine Industries Forum, 2002–. *Recreations:* cricket, downs walking. *Address:* Doonbank, 16 Greenway, Great Bookham, Surrey KT23 3PA. *T:* (01372) 454359. *Died 20 March 2007.*

SLADE, Julian Penkivil; author and composer since 1951; *b* 28 May 1930; *s* of G. P. Slade, KC. *Educ:* Eton College; Trinity College, Cambridge (BA). Went to Bristol Old Vic Theatre School, 1951; wrote incidental music for Bristol Old Vic production of Two Gentlemen of Verona, 1952; joined Bristol Old Vic Co. as musical director, 1952; wrote and composed Christmas in King St (with Dorothy Reynolds and James Cairncross), Bristol, 1952; composed music for Sheridan's The Duenna, Bristol, 1953; transferred to Westminster Theatre, London, 1954; wrote and composed The Merry Gentleman (with Dorothy Reynolds), Bristol, 1953; composed incidental music for The Merchant of Venice (1953 Stratford season); wrote musical version of The Comedy of Errors for TV, 1954, and for Arts Theatre, London, 1956, revd version for 400th anniv. of first perf. at Gray's Inn, 1994; wrote (with Dorothy Reynolds) Salad Days, Bristol, Vaudeville, 1954, Duke of York's, 1976, Bristol Old Vic, 1994 (adaptation for Yorks TV, 1983, and for 40th birthday recording, BBC, 1994), Vaudeville, 1996; Free as Air, Savoy, London, 1957; Hooray for Daisy!, Bristol, 1959, Lyric, Hammersmith, 1960; Follow that Girl, Vaudeville, London, 1960, revived Theatre Mus., 2000; Wildest Dreams, 1960; Vanity Fair (with Alan Pryce-Jones and Robin Miller), Queen's Theatre, London, 1962, revived Theatre Mus., 2001; Nutmeg and Ginger, Cheltenham, 1963, revived Orange Tree Theatre, Richmond, 1991; Sixty Thousand

Nights (with George Rowell), Bristol, 1966; The Pursuit of Love, Bristol, 1967; composed music for songs in: As You Like It, Bristol, 1970; A Midsummer Night's Dream and Much Ado About Nothing, Regent's Park, 1970; adapted A. A. Milne's Winnie The Pooh, Phoenix Theatre, 1970, 1975; (music and lyrics with Aubrey Woods and George Rowell) Trelawny (based on Pinero's Trelawny of the Wells), Bristol, then London West End, 1972; Out of Bounds (book, music and lyrics, based on Pinero's The Schoolmistress), 1973. Composed incidental music for Nancy Mitford's Love in a Cold Climate, Thames TV, 1980; (with Veronica Flint-Shipman and Kit Hesketh-Harvey) musical stage adaptation of J. M. Barrie's Dear Brutus, 1985; (with Gyles Brandreth) Now We Are Sixty (musical play based on works of A. A. Milne), Arts Theatre, Cambridge, 1986; (with Elizabeth Seal) concert performances of own songs, Easy to Sing, 1986–87; played and sang, gala concert to launch Questfest, Buxton Opera House Festival of Musicals, 1992; (with Eden Phillips) musical stage adaptation of Nancy Mitford's Love in a Cold Climate, 1997; 70th birthday celebration concert, Theatre Mus., 2000. Played and sang for solo record album of own songs, Looking for a Piano, 1981; played for vocal album, Salad Days, 1982. Gold Badge of Merit, British Acad. of Songwriters, Composers and Authors, 1987. *Publications:* Nibble the Squirrel (children's book), 1946; music of: The Duenna, 1954; Salad Days, 1954; Free as Air, 1957; Follow That Girl, 1967; Trelawny, 1974; The Merry Gentleman, 1985. *Recreations:* drawing, going to theatres and cinemas, listening to music. *Address:* 86 Beaufort Street (Ground Floor/Basement), SW3 6BU. *T:* (020) 7376 4480. *Died 17 June 2006.*

SLATER, John Christopher Nash; QC 1987; FCIArb; a Recorder, since 1990; *b* 14 June 1946; *er s* of late Lt-Col Leonard Slater, CBE and Olga Patricia Slater (*née* George); *m* 1971, Jane Schapiro; two *s* one *d*. *Educ:* Sedbergh School; University College, Oxford (MA Hon. Classical Mods 1966 and Jurisprudence 1968). FCIArb 2006. Called to the Bar, Middle Temple, 1969 (Harmsworth Scholar; Bencher, 1996); Hd of Chambers, 1996–99. Assistant Recorder, 1987–90. *Recreations:* golf, acting, travel. *Address:* Crown Office Chambers, 2 Crown Office Row, Temple, EC4Y 7HJ. *T:* (020) 7797 8100; 41 Wood Vale, N10 3DJ. *T:* (020) 8442 0689. *Clubs:* Hampstead Golf; Hampstead Cricket. *Died 11 Nov. 2007.*

SLEE, Very Rev. Colin Bruce, OBE 2001; Dean (formerly Provost) of Southwark, since 1994; *b* 10 Nov. 1945; *s* of late Herbert Samuel Slee and of Miriam Clara May Slee; *m* 1971, Edith Tryon; one *s* two *d*, and one adopted *s* one adopted *d*. *Educ:* Ealing Grammar Sch.; King's Coll., London (BD, AKC; FKC 2001); St Augustine's Coll., Canterbury. Ordained deacon, 1970, priest, 1971; Curate, St Francis, Heartsease, 1970–73; Curate, Great St Mary's, Cambridge, and Chaplain, Girton Coll., Cambridge, 1973–76; Chaplain and Tutor, KCL, 1976–82; Sub-Dean and Canon Residentiary, St Alban's Abbey, 1982–94. Member: General Synod, C of E, 1995–; Crown Nominations Cttee, 2006–. Hon. Chaplain, Shakespeare's Globe Theatre, 1997–2000. Mem., Cttee of Visitors, Harvard Univ., 2002–07. Chm., Tutu Foundn UK, 2004–. Trustee: Crisis, 1995–2005; Parents for Children, 1995–2006; Millennium Footbridge, 1996–2001; Borough Market, 2000–10. Governor, INFORM, 1985–. Patron: Southwark Fest., 1994–2001; Home Start, 1994–; British Sch. of Osteopathy, 1997–. Winston Churchill Meml Trust Fellowship, 2003. *Publications:* (ed) Honest to God: 40 years on, 2005. *Recreations:* rowing (purple, London Univ., 1967, 1968), gardening, bee keeping. *Address:* Southwark Cathedral, London Bridge, SE1 9DA. *T:* (020) 7367 6731; *Fax:* (020) 7367 6725; Provost's Lodging, 51 Bankside, SE1 9JE. *T:* (020) 7928 6414; *e-mail:* colin.slee@southwark.anglican.org. *Died 25 Nov. 2010.*

SLEEMAN, His Honour (Stuart) Colin; a Circuit Judge, 1976–86; *b* 10 March 1914; *s* of Stuart Bertram Sleeman and Phyllis Grace (*née* Pitt); *m* 1944, Margaret Emily, *d* of late William Joseph Farmer; two *s* one *d*. *Educ:* Clifton Coll.; Merton Coll., Oxford (BA 1936, MA 1963). Called to the Bar, Gray's Inn, 1938, Bencher, 1974. War of 1939–45: Admin. Officer, Prize Dept, Min. of Economic Warfare, 1939–40; Lt-Col 16th–5th Lancers; Staff Captain: RAC Wing, Combined Trng Centre, 1941; 6th Armoured Div., 1942; Adjt, RAC Range, Minehead, 1942–44; Asst Judge Advocate Gen., HQ Allied Land Forces, SE Asia, 1945. London Corresp., Scottish Law Rev., 1949–54; a Recorder, 1975–76. *Publications:* The Trial of Gozawa Sadaichi and Nine Others, 1948; (with S. C. Silkin) The 'Double Tenth' Trial, 1950. *Recreations:* travel, genealogy. *Address:* West Walls, Cotmandene, Dorking, Surrey RH4 2BL. *T:* (01306) 883616.   *Died 27 May 2006.*

SLOAN, Sir Andrew (Kirkpatrick), Kt 1991; QPM 1983; Chief Constable of Strathclyde, 1985–91; *b* 27 Feb. 1931; *s* of Andrew Kirkpatrick Sloan and Amelia Sarah (*née* Vernon), Kirkcudbright; *m* 1953, Agnes Sofie Storvik, Trondheim, Norway; three *d*. *Educ:* Kirkcudbright Acad.; Dumfries Acad., Open Univ. (BA). Joined RN as boy seaman, 1947; served at home and abroad in cruisers and submarines, and worked in industry in Norway, 1947–55; joined W Riding Constab., 1955; apptd to CID, 1963; Det. Sgt, Barnsley, 1964; Det. Insp., Reg. Crime Squad, Leeds, 1966; Det. Chief Insp., Goole and Pontefract, 1969; Det. Supt, Reg. Crime Squad, Wakefield, 1970; Chief Supt, Toller Lane Div., Bradford, 1975; Asst Chief Constable, Operations, Lincolnshire Police, 1976–79; National Co-ordinator, Regional Crime Squads of England and Wales, 1979–81; Dep. Chief Constable, Lincs, 1981–83; Chief Constable, Beds, 1983–85. Pres., ACPO (Scotland), 1987–88. *Recreations:* reading, travel, walking, conversation.   *Died 11 Nov. 2009.*

SLYNN OF HADLEY, Baron *cr* 1992 (Life Peer), of Eggington in the County of Bedfordshire; **Gordon Slynn,** GBE 2009; Kt 1976; PC 1992; arbitrator and accredited mediator, since 2002; President, Civil Mediation Council, since 2008; a Lord of Appeal in Ordinary, 1992–2002; *b* 17 Feb. 1930; *er s* of John and Edith Slynn; *m* 1962, Odile Marie Henriette Boutin. *Educ:* Sandbach Sch.; Goldsmiths' Coll., Univ. of London (BA; Hon. Fellow, 1993); Trinity Coll., Cambridge (Sen. Schol.; Sub-Lector, 1956–61; MA, LLB; Hon. Fellow, 2001). Called to Bar, Gray's Inn, 1956, Bencher, 1970, Treas., 1988. Junior Counsel: Min. of Labour, 1967–68; to the Treasury (Common Law), 1968–74; QC 1974; Leading Counsel to the Treasury, 1974–76. Recorder of Hereford, 1971; a Recorder, and Hon. Recorder of Hereford, 1972–76; a Judge of the High Ct of Justice, QBD, 1976–81; Pres., Employment Appeal Tribunal, 1978–81; an Advocate Gen., 1981–88, a Judge, 1988–92, Court of Justice of EC, Luxembourg; Pres., Court of Appeal, Solomon Islands, 2001–. Chairman: H of L Select Sub-Cttee on Eur. Law and Instns, 1992–95; H of L Select Cttee on Public Service, 1996–98; Jt Parly Cttee on Corruption Bill, 2003. Dist. Global Fellow, NY Univ., 1999; Singhvi Fellow, Raj Loomba Foundn, India, 1999; Lectures include: Bloomfield, Montreal, 1980; Irvine, Cornell, 1984; Leon Ladner, Univ. of BC, 1987; Hamlyn, 1992; Tanner, 1993, Romanes, 1994, Oxford Univ.; Presidential, Roumania, 1995; M. K. Nambyar, India, 1996; Sakkar, India, 1998; John E. James, Mercer, 2001. Chief Steward of Hereford, 1978–2008 (Freedom of the City, 1996). Chm., Exec. Council, Internat. Law Assoc., 1988–2008; Hon. Vice-Pres., Union Internat. des Avocats, 1976– (Vice-Pres., 1973–76). Mem., Exec. Cttee, Pilgrims, 1992–98, 1999–2005. Fellow, Internat. Soc. of Barristers, USA; Mem., American Law Inst.; Hon. Member: Canadian Bar Assoc.; Georgia Trial Lawyers' Assoc.; SPTL. Governor: Internat. Students' Trust, 1979–85, and 1992– (Fellow, 1986–); Sadler's Wells Theatre, 1988–95; Chm. Ct of Governors, Mill Hill Sch., 1989–95; Visitor: Mansfield Coll., Oxford, 1995–2002;

Univ. of Essex, 1995–2000. President: Bentham Club, 1992; Holdsworth Club, 1993. Master, Broderers' Co., 1994–95. FCIArb 1995. FKC 1995; Hon. Fellow: UC at Buckingham, 1982; St Andrews Coll., Univ. of Sydney, 1991; Amer. Coll. of Trial Lawyers, 1992; Liverpool John Moores, 1993; U C Northampton, 2001. Hon. LLD: Birmingham, Buckingham, 1983; Exeter, 1985; Univ. of Technol., Sydney, 1991; Bristol Poly. (CNAA), Sussex, 1992; Stetson, USA, 1993; Staffordshire, 1994; Pace, NY, 1995; Pondicherry, Kingston, 1997; Strathclyde, London, 1999; Hertfordshire, 2003; Szeged, Hungary, 2003 Hon. DCL: Durham, 1989; City 1994; Hon. Dr Juris Saarlandes, 1994; DUniv: Univ. del Museo Social Argentino, 1994; Essex, 2001; Mercer, Ga, 2001; Münster, 2004. Cordell Hull Medal, Samford Univ., Ala, USA, 1993. Chevalier du Tastevin; Commandeur, Confrérie de St Cunibert; Commandeur d'Honneur, Commanderie du Bon Temps du Médoc et des Graves. KStJ 1998 (OStJ 1992; Prior, England and the Islands, 1999–2004). Grande Croix de l'Ordre de Mérite (Luxembourg), 1998; Knight Cross, Order of Merit (Poland), 1999; Grand Cross, Order of Merit (Malta), 2001; Officer's Cross, Order of Merit (Hungary), 2002; Cross of Solomon Islands, 2007. *Address:* House of Lords, SW1A 0PW. *Clubs:* Beefsteak, Garrick, White's.
                    Died 7 April 2009.

SMALL, (Charles) John; development consultant, 1985–94; economist; *b* Chengdu, Sichuan, China, 19 Dec. 1919; *s* of Rev. and Mrs Walter Small; *m* 1946, Jean McNeel; four *d*. *Educ:* Ontario Agricultural Coll. (BSA); Univ. of Toronto (BA). Royal Canadian Navy service, 1941–46, in N Atlantic, Mediterranean, Normandy and Australia. Mem., Dept of Trade and Commerce, 1949–55; serving in The Hague as Commercial Sec. (Agriculture), 1950–55; Dept of External Affairs, 1955–84; Chinese studies at Univ. of Toronto, 1956–57; seconded to Dept of Trade and Commerce, and apptd Canadian Govt Trade Comr, Hong Kong, 1958–61; Ottawa, 1961–63; Counsellor, Canadian High Commn, Karachi, 1963–65; Perm. Rep. of Canada to OECD, Paris, concurrently Canadian observer, Council of Europe, Strasbourg, 1965–69; Amb. to Pakistan, 1969–72, concurrently Amb. to Afghanistan; Amb. to People's Repub. of China, 1972–76, concurrently to Socialist Repub. of Viet-Nam, 1975–76; Dep. Sec.-Gen. of the Commonwealth, 1978–83; High Comr to Malaysia and concurrently to Brunei, 1983–84; retd from Foreign Service, 1984. Administrator, Code of Conduct concerning employment practices of Canadian cos operating in South Africa, 1986–90. Chm., Presbyterian World Service and Develt Cttee, 1989–91. Patron, Ex Terra Foundn (Canada/China Dinosaur Project), 1987–. Member: CIIA; Agricl Inst. of Canada; Royal Commonwealth Society, Ottawa. Hon. LLD Guelph, 1975. *Recreations:* tennis, golf, swimming.
                    Died 24 May 2006.

SMALLWOOD, John Frank Monton, CBE 1991; a Church Commissioner, 1966–98 (Member, Board of Governors, 1966–98, and Member, General Purposes Committee, 1968–98); *b* 12 April 1926; *s* of late Frank Theodore and Edith Smallwood; *m* 1952, Jean Margaret Lovell; one *s* two *d*. *Educ:* City of London Sch.; Peterhouse, Cambridge, 1948–51 (MA Classics). Served RAF, 1944–48 (Japanese translation and interrogation). Joined Bank of England, 1951; Private Sec. to Governors, 1959–62; Adviser, 1967; Auditor, 1969; Dep. Chief Accountant, 1974–79. Member: Church Assembly / General Synod, 1965–2000 (Standing Cttee, 1971–96); numerous *ad hoc* Cttees, etc, over years, incl. Wkg Party on State Aid for Churches in use, 1971–96; Central Bd of Finance, 1965–98 (Dep. Vice-Chm. 1972–82); Pensions Bd, 1985–96; Anglican Consultative Council, 1975–87 (Trinidad, 1976, Lambeth Conf., 1978, Canada, 1979, Newcastle, 1981, Singapore, 1987). A Trustee: City Parochial Foundn, 1969–99 (Vice-Chm., 1977–81; Chm., 1981–92); Trust for London, 1986–99 (Chm., 1986–92); Overseas Bishoprics Fund, 1977–99 (Chm., 1992–99); Lambeth Palace Library, 1978–98. Member:

Southwark Dio. Bd of Finance, 1962–2000 (Chm. 1975–2000); Southwark Ordination Course Council, 1960–74 and 1980–94 (Vice-Chm., 1980–94); Corp. of Church House Council, 1986–96; Churches' Main Cttee, 1987–96; BCC 1987–90. Lee Abbey Council, 1969–74; Lay Reader, 1983–. *Recreations:* writing episcopal biographies, church finances, family, music, cathedrals, old churches, historic houses, gardens. *Address:* 54 Linters Court, London Road, Redhill, Surrey RH1 2JN. *T:* (01737) 767268. *Died 14 Dec. 2007.*

SMART, Andrew, CB 1981; defence consultant, retired 1991; Director, Royal Signals and Radar Establishment, Malvern, 1978–84; *b* 12 Feb. 1924; *s* of late Mr and Mrs William S. Smart; *m* 1949, Pamela Kathleen Stephens; two *s* two *d*. *Educ:* Denny; High Sch. of Stirling; Glasgow Univ. MA 1944. TRE Malvern, 1943; Science 2 Air Min., 1950–53; Guided Weapons Gp, RRE, Malvern, 1953–70 (Head, 1968–70); Dep. Dir (Scientific B), DOAE, 1970; RAE, Farnborough: Head of Weapons Res. Gp, 1972; Head of Weapons Dept, 1973; Dep. Dir (W), 1974–77. *Recreations:* gardening, reading. *Address:* Shelsley, Redland Drive, Colwall, Malvern, Worcs WR13 6ES. *T:* (01684) 540664. *Died 26 Oct. 2008.*

SMART, Sir Jack, Kt 1982; CBE 1976; JP; DL; Chairman, Wakefield District Health Authority, 1982–88; *b* 25 April 1920; *s* of James and Emily Smart; *m* 1941, Ethel King; one *d*. *Educ:* Altofts Colliery Sch. Miner, 1934–59; Branch Sec., Glasshoughton Colliery, NUM, 1949–59; Mem., Castleford Municipal Borough Council, 1949–74; Mayor of Castleford, 1962–63; Mem., Wakefield City Council, 1973–86 (Leader, 1973–86). Chm., Assoc. of Metropolitan Authorities, 1977–78, 1980–84; Leader of the Opposition Group, AMA, 1978–80. Chm., Wakefield AHA, 1977–81; Mem., Layfield Cttee of Enquiry into Local Govt Finance, 1974–76. Pres., Yorkshire Soc. (1980), 1988–. Hon. Fellow, Bretton Coll., 1983. Hon. Freeman, City of Wakefield, 1985. JP Castleford, 1960; DL West Yorks, 1987. FRSA. *Recreations:* golf, music. *Address:* Churchside, Weetworth, Pontefract Road, Castleford, West Yorks WF10 4BW. *T:* (01977) 554880. *Died 4 March 2010.*

SMART, William Norman H.; *see* Hunter Smart.

SMEDLEY, Sir (Frank) Brian, Kt 1995; a Judge of the High Court, Queen's Bench Division, 1995–2000; *b* 28 Nov. 1934. *Educ:* West Bridgford Grammar Sch.; London Univ. LLB Hons, 1957. Called to the Bar, Gray's Inn, 1960; Midland Circuit; a Recorder, 1972; QC 1977; a Circuit Judge, 1987–95; Sen. Judge, Sovereign Base Areas, Cyprus, 1991–95 (Dep. Sen. Judge, 1989–91). Judicial Mem., Proscribed Organisations Appeal Commn, 2001–. Mem., Senate of the Inns of Court and the Bar, 1973–77. Freeman, City of London, 1990. *Recreations:* travel, music. *Club:* Garrick. *Died 6 April 2007.*

SMITH; *see* Delacourt-Smith.

SMITH, Prof. Alexander Crampton, (Alex Crampton Smith); Nuffield Professor of Anaesthetics, Oxford University, and Fellow of Pembroke College, Oxford, 1965–79; then Emeritus Professor; *b* 15 June 1917; *s* of William and Mary Elizabeth Crampton Smith; *m* 1953, Marjorie (*née* Mason); three *s*; two *d* by a former marriage. *Educ:* Inverness Royal Acad.; Edinburgh University; MA Oxon 1961. FFARCS 1953. Medical student, Edinburgh Univ., 1935–41. Served War of 1939–45 (Croix de Guerre, despatches), RNVR, 1942–46. Consultant Anaesthetist, United Oxford Hospitals, 1951–65; Clinical Lectr in Anaesthetics, Oxford Univ., 1961–65. Civilian Consultant Anaesthetist to Royal Navy, 1968–73. Mem. Bd, Faculty of Anaesthetists, 1965–80. Mem. Trustees, Nuffield Medical Benefaction, 1973–92. *Publications:* Clinical Practice and Physiology of Artificial Respiration (with J. M. K. Spalding), 1963; contribs to anaesthetic, medical and

physiological jls. *Recreations:* bird watching, art galleries. *Address:* 1/15 Rawlinson Road, Oxford OX2 6UE. *T:* (01865) 512954. *Died 20 March 2010.*

SMITH, Brian, CMG 1993; OBE 1975; HM Diplomatic Service, retired; High Commissioner to Trinidad and Tobago, 1991–94; *b* 15 Sept. 1935; *s* of Charles Francis Smith and Grace Amelia (*née* Pope); *m* 1955, Joan Patricia Rivers; one *s* two *d*. *Educ:* Hull Grammar School; BSc Open Univ. 1994. Foreign Office, 1952; HM Forces, 1954–57; Bahrain, 1957; Doha, 1959; Vice-Consul, Luxembourg, 1960, Casablanca, 1962; Tehran, 1964; Berne, 1967; FCO, 1969; Kampala, 1973; Tehran, 1975; FCO, 1977; New York, 1979; Counsellor (Commercial), Bonn, 1982; Overseas Inspector, FCO, 1986; High Comr, Botswana, 1989. *Recreations:* photography, music, handicrafts. *Address:* Bancroft, Castle Walk, Wadhurst, E Sussex TN5 6DB. *Died 17 Nov. 2009.*

SMITH, (Charles) Russell, CBE 1984; Chairman, Allied Textile Companies PLC, 1983–91 (Chief Executive, 1963–86); Director, Lloyds Bank plc, 1985–95 (Regional Chairman, Yorkshire and Humberside, 1984–91; Regional Director, 1973–91); *b* 19 Aug. 1925; *m* 1951, Jean Rita Thomas; one *s* three *d*. *Educ:* Rastrick Grammar Sch., Brighouse, W Yorks. Served War, RNVR, 1943–46 (commnd). Armitage and Norton, Chartered Accountants, Huddersfield, 1941–50; Dir, subseq. Man. Dir, R. Beanland and Co. Ltd, 1950–63. Director: Yorkshire Bank PLC, 1978–84; Lloyds Bank UK Management Ltd, 1984–85; Lloyds & Scottish PLC, 1985–86; Lloyds Abbey Life PLC (formerly Abbey Life Gp), 1988–96; Lloyds Merchant Bank (Hldgs) Ltd, 1989–93; Heywood Williams Gp, 1990–96. Pres., British Textile Confedn, 1982 and 1983; Chm., Wakefield Diocesan Bd of Finance, 1974–90; Mem., Yorks and Humberside Regional Develt Bd, 1975–79. *Recreation:* too few. *Address:* Tabara, 12 Wheatcroft Avenue, Scarborough, North Yorks YO11 3BN. *T:* (01723) 376266. *Died 24 May 2006.*

SMITH, Sir Cyril, Kt 1988; MBE 1966; DL; Managing Director, Smith Springs (Rochdale) Ltd, 1963–87; *b* 28 June 1928; unmarried. *Educ:* Rochdale Grammar Sch. for Boys. Civil Service, 1944–45; Wages Clerk, 1945–48; Liberal Party Agent, Stockport, 1948–50; Labour Party Agent, Ashton-under-Lyne, 1950–53; Heywood and Royton 1953–55; rejoined Liberal Party, 1967; MP Rochdale, Oct. 1972–1992 (L, 1972–88, Lib Dem, 1988–92); Liberal Chief Whip, 1975–76. Newsagent (own account), 1955–58; Production Controller, Spring Manufacturing, 1958–63; founded Smith Springs (Rochdale) Ltd, 1963. Director: Ratcliffe Springs, 1987–90; Robert Riley Springs. Councillor, 1952–66, Alderman, 1966–74, Mayor, 1966–67, Co. Borough of Rochdale (Chm., Education Cttee, 1966–72); Councillor, Rochdale Metropolitan DC, 1973–75. A Dep. Pro-Chancellor, Lancaster Univ., 1978–86. Freeman, Borough of Rochdale, 1992. DL Greater Manchester, 1991. Hon. LLD Lancaster, 1993; Hon. DEd Manchester Metropolitan, 1996. OStJ 1976. *Publications:* Big Cyril (autobiog.), 1977; Industrial Participation, 1977. *Recreations:* music (listener), reading, charitable work, local government. *Address:* 14 Emma Street, Rochdale, Lancs OL12 6QW. *T:* (01706) 648840. *Died 3 Sept. 2010.*

SMITH, Prof. David; *see* Smith, N. J. D.

SMITH, Derek Edward H.; *see* Hill-Smith.

SMITH, Douglas; *see* Smith, I. D.

SMITH, Prof. Edwin, PhD; FRS 1996; Emeritus Professor, Manchester University School of Materials (formerly Materials Science Centre), since 2004 (Consultant and Hon. Fellow, Manchester University-UMIST Materials Science Centre, 1988–2004); *b* 28 July 1931; *s* of late Albert Edwin Smith and Sarah Ann Smith (*née* Toft); *m* 1958, Patricia Georgina Gale (*d* 2009). *Educ:* Chesterfield Grammar Sch.; Nottingham Univ. (BSc); Sheffield Univ. (PhD); MSc Manchester. CEng,

FIMMM. AEI Res. Lab., Aldermaston, 1955–61; CEGB Res. Lab., Leatherhead, 1961–68. Manchester University: Prof. of Metallurgy, UMIST Materials Science Centre, 1968–88; Dean, Faculty of Science, 1983–85; Pro-Vice-Chancellor, 1985–88. Vis. Scientist, Battelle Meml Inst., Columbus, Ohio, 1968. Consultant to industrial organisations in UK, USA, Canada. *Publications:* contribs to learned jls on materials science and engineering. *Recreations:* interest in various sports; when young, played cricket for Derbyshire Under 21s, ran 14 marathons (personal best, 2 hrs 47 mins, 1957). *Address:* Manchester University School of Materials, Grosvenor Street, Manchester M1 7HS. *T:* (0161) 306 3556. *Died 4 July 2010.*

SMITH, Prof. Frederick Viggers; Professor of Psychology, University of Durham, 1950–77, then Emeritus; *b* Hamilton, New South Wales, 24 Jan. 1912; *s* of Frederick Thomas Smith and Agnes (*née* Viggers), unmarried. *Educ:* Newcastle (NSW) High School; Sydney and London Universities. BA 1938, MA 1941, Lithgow Schol., Sydney; PhD London 1948. FBPsS, 1950 (Pres., British Psychological Society, 1959–60). Research Office, Dept of Educ., NSW, 1936; Lecturer in Psychology, The Teachers' Coll., Sydney, 1938; Lectr, Birkbeck Coll., Univ. of London, 1946; Lectr, Univ. of Aberdeen, 1948. Visiting Prof., Cornell Univ., USA, 1957, Christchurch and Wellington Univs, NZ, 1960. Consultant, Council of Europe Sub-Cttee on Crime Problems, 1973; Unesco Consultant, Univ. of Riyadh, 1973. Hon. Research Associate, Univ. of Newcastle, NSW, 1980. *Publications:* The Child's Point of View (Sydney), 1946 (under pseudonym Victor Southward); Explanation of Human Behaviour (London), 1951, 1960; Attachment of the Young: Imprinting and Other Developments, 1969; Purpose in Animal Behaviour, 1971; papers to psychological and philosophical jls. *Recreations:* walking, swimming, photography, music, golf. *Address:* 58 Harbourside Haven, Shoal Bay, Port Stephens, NSW 2315, Australia. *Died 6 July 2006.*

SMITH, Rt Hon. Sir Geoffrey J.; *see* Johnson Smith.

SMITH, Gordon E.; *see* Etherington-Smith, R. G. A.

SMITH, Gordon Edward C.; *see* Connell-Smith.

SMITH, Hedworth Cunningham, CBE 1972; Chairman: Medical Appeal Tribunals, England and Scotland, 1973–84; Pensions Appeal Tribunals, England, 1973–85; Judge of the Supreme Court of the Bahama Islands, 1965–72, retired; *b* 12 May 1912; *s* of James Smith and Elizabeth (*née* Brown); unmarried. *Educ:* George Watson's Coll., Edinburgh; Edinburgh Univ. MA 1933; LLB 1936. Solicitor, Scotland, 1937–40; Barrister at Law, Gray's Inn, London, 1950. Served War of 1939–45: commnd 1940; Staff Officer, GHQ India Command, 1943–46 (Major). District Magistrate, 1946, Senior District Magistrate, 1950, Gold Coast; Judge of Supreme Court of Ghana, 1957; retd from Ghana Govt service, 1961; Legal Adviser, Unilever Ltd Gp of Cos in Ghana, 1962–64. *Recreation:* golf. *Address:* The Old (Police) House, Main Street, Aberlady, E Lothian. *T:* (01875) 870420. *Clubs:* East India, Devonshire, Sports and Public Schools; Kilspindie Golf. *Died 15 March 2007.*

SMITH, Ian Douglas, GCLM 1979; ID 1970; MP (Cons. Alliance, formerly Republican Front), Zimbabwe, 1980–88; *b* Selukwe, S Rhodesia, 8 April 1919; *m* Janet Watt (*d* 1994); one *s* one *d* (and one *s* decd). *Educ:* Selukwe Sch.; Chaplin Sch., Gwelo, S Rhodesia; Rhodes Univ., Grahamstown, S Africa (BCom). Served War of 1939–45 in 237 (Rhodesia) Sqdn and 130 Sqdn, RAF. Farmer. Member: Southern Rhodesia Legislative Assembly, 1948–53; Parliament of Fedn of Rhodesia & Nyasaland, 1953–61; former Chief Whip (United Federal Party), 1958; resigned from United Federal Party, 1961; Foundn Mem. and Vice-Pres., Republican Front (formerly Rhodesian Front), 1962, President, 1964–87; Dep. Prime Minister and Minister of the Treasury, S Rhodesia, 1962–64; Prime

Minister of Rhodesia, 1964–79; delivered Rhodesia's Unilateral Declaration of Independence, Nov. 1965; Minister Without Portfolio in Bishop Muzorewa's Govt, 1979; Mem., Transitional Exec. Council to prepare for transfer of power in Rhodesia, 1978–79. *Address:* Gwenoro Farm, Shurugwi, Zimbabwe; Box 8198, Causeway, Harare, Zimbabwe. *Clubs:* Harare, Harare Sports (Zimbabwe). *Died 20 Nov. 2007.*

SMITH, Jack Stanley, CMG 1970; Professor, and Chairman, Graduate School of Business Administration, University of Melbourne, 1973–77, retired; *b* 13 July 1916; *s* of C. P. T. Smith, Avoca, Victoria; *m* 1940, Nancy, *d* of J. C. Beckley, Melbourne; one *s* two *d*. *Educ:* Ballarat Grammar Sch.; Melbourne Univ. Construction Engineer, Australasian Petroleum Co., 1938–41. Served in Australian Imperial Forces, 1942–45, Lieut. Project Engineer, Melbourne & Metropolitan Bd of Works, 1946–48. P.A. Management Consultants, UK and Australia, 1949–72, Managing Dir, 1964–72. Hon. LLD Melbourne, 1987. *Recreations:* golf, tennis. *Address:* 12 Lisson Grove, Hawthorn, Vic 3122, Australia. *Clubs:* Melbourne (Melbourne); Lawn Tennis Association of Victoria, Metropolitan Golf (Vic.). *Died 30 Aug. 2006.*

SMITH, James Andrew Buchan, CBE 1959; DSc; FRSE 1952; Director of the Hannah Dairy Research Institute, Ayr, Scotland, 1951–70 (Acting Director, 1948–51); *b* 26 May 1906; *yr s* of late Dr James Fleming Smith, JP, MB, CM, Whithorn, Wigtownshire; *m* 1933, Elizabeth Marion (*d* 2003), *d* of James Kerr, Wallasey, Cheshire; three *d* (and one *d* decd). *Educ:* Leamington College, Warwicks; Univ. of Birmingham. PhD (Birmingham) 1929; DSc (London) 1940. Graduate Research Asst: at UCL, 1929–30; at Imperial College, London, 1930–32; Lectr in Biochemistry, Univ. of Liverpool, 1932–36; Biochemist, Hannah Dairy Research Inst., 1936–46; Lectr in Biochemistry, Univ. of Glasgow, 1946–47. President: Society of Dairy Technology, 1951–52; Nutrition Society, 1968–71; Treasurer, Internat. Union of Nutritional Sciences, 1969–75. Hon. LLD Glasgow, 1972. *Publications:* scientific papers in Biochemical Jl, Jl of Dairy Research, Proc. Nutrition Soc., etc. *Recreation:* gardening. *Address:* Creggan Bahn Court, 2 Seafield Road, Ayr KA7 4AA. *T:* (01292) 264865. *Died 25 April 2006.*

SMITH, James Ian, CB 1974; Secretary, Department of Agriculture and Fisheries for Scotland, 1972–84; *b* 22 April 1924; *s* of late James Smith, Ballater, Aberdeenshire, and of Agnes Michie; *m* 1947, Pearl Myra Fraser (*d* 2003); one *s*; *m* 2005, Jill Madge Weightman Smith (*née* Bell). *Educ:* Alderman Newton's Sch., Leicester; St Andrews Univ. Served War of 1939–45: India and Burma; RA (attached Indian Mountain Artillery), Lieut, 1943–46. Entered Dept of Agriculture for Scotland, 1949; Private Sec. to Parly Under-Sec. of State, Scottish Office, 1953; Dept of Agriculture for Scotland: Principal, 1953; Asst Sec., 1959; Asst Sec., Scottish Development Dept, 1965–67; Under-Sec., Dept of Agriculture and Fisheries for Scotland, 1967–72. Mem., ARC, 1967–72, 1983–84; Mem., Potato Marketing Bd, 1985–87. Mem., St Andrews Links Trust, 1985–90 (Chm., 1989–90). *Recreation:* golf. *Died 1 Dec. 2007.*

SMITH, Dr John, OBE 1945; TD 1950; Deputy Chief Medical Officer, Scottish Home and Health Department, 1963–75; *b* 13 July 1913; *e s* of late John Smith, DL, JP, Glasgow and Symington, and Agnes Smith; *m* 1942, Elizabeth Fleming (*d* 1981), twin *d* of late A. F. Wylie, Giffnock; three *s* one *d* (and one *s* decd). *Educ:* High Sch., Glasgow; Sedbergh Sch.; Christ's Coll., Cambridge; Glasgow Univ. BA 1935; MA 1943; MB, BChir Cantab 1938; MB, ChB Glasgow 1938; MRCPG 1965; FRCPG 1967; FRCPE 1969; FFPH (FFCM 1972). TA (RA from 1935, RAMC from 1940); War Service, 1939–46; ADMS Second Army, DDMS (Ops and Plans) 21 Army Group (despatches); OC 155 (Lowland) Fd Amb., 1950–53; ADMS 52 (Lowland) Div., 1953–56; Hon. Col 52 Div. Medical Service, 1961–67. House appts Glasgow

Victoria and Western Infirmaries; joined Dept of Health for Scotland, 1947; Medical Supt, Glasgow Victoria Hosps, 1955–58; rejoined Dept of Health for Scotland, 1958; specialised in hospital planning. QHP 1971–74. Deacon, Incorp. of Bakers of Glasgow, 1956–57. Officier, Ordre de Leopold I (Belgium), 1947. *Publications:* articles on medical administration and hospital services in various medical jls. *Recreations:* rifle shooting (shot in Scottish and TA representative teams), hill walking, reading. *Address:* 7 Oswald Road, Edinburgh EH9 2HE.   *Died 10 Aug. 2010.*

SMITH, Sir John (Lindsay Eric), Kt 1988; CH 1994; CBE 1975; Director, Coutts & Co., 1950–93; *b* 3 April 1923; *s* of Captain E. C. E. Smith, MC, LLD and Helen Smith (*née* Williams); *m* 1952, Christian Margaret, (OBE 2005), *d* of late Col U. E. C. Carnegy of Lour, DSO, MC; two *s* two *d* (and one *d* decd). *Educ:* Eton (Fellow, 1974–89); New Coll., Oxford (MA; Hon. Fellow, 1979). Served Fleet Air Arm 1941–45 (Lieut RNVR). MP (C) Cities of London and Westminster, Nov. 1965–1970; Member: Public Accounts Cttee, 1968–69; Exec., 1922 Cttee, 1968–70. National Trust: Mem., Historic Bldgs Cttee, 1952–61; Mem. Exec. Cttee, 1959–85; Mem. Council, 1961–95; Dep. Chm., 1980–85. Member: Standing Commission on Museums and Galleries, 1958–66; Inland Waterways Redevelopment Cttee, 1959–62; Historic Buildings Council, 1971–78; Redundant Churches Fund, 1972–74; Nat. Heritage Memorial Fund, 1980–82. Director: Financial Times Ltd, 1959–68; Rolls Royce Ltd, 1955–75; Dep. Governor, Royal Exchange Assurance, 1961–66. Founder, Manifold Charitable Trust, 1962 and Landmark Charitable Trust, 1965. High Steward of Maidenhead, 1966–75. Freeman of Windsor and Maidenhead, 1975. FSA; Hon. FRIBA 1973; Hon. FRIAS 1983. JP Berks, 1964; DL 1978, Lord-Lieut, 1975–78, Berks. Hon. LLD: Exeter, 1989; Portsmouth, 1994. *Address:* Shottesbrooke Park, Maidenhead, Berks SL6 3SW; 1 Smith Square, SW1P 3PA. *Clubs:* Athenæum, Pratt's, Beefsteak, Brooks's.
                    Died 28 Feb. 2007.

SMITH, Prof. Joseph Victor, FRS 1978; Louis Block Professor of Physical Sciences, 1977–2005, then Emeritus, and Co-ordinator of Scientific Programs, since 1992 (Executive Director, 1988–91), Consortium for Advanced Radiation Sources, University of Chicago (Professor of Mineralogy and Crystallography, 1960–76); *b* 30 July 1928; *s* of Henry Victor Smith and Edith (*née* Robinson); *m* 1951, Brenda Florence Wallis; two *d. Educ:* Cambridge Univ. (MA, PhD). Fellow, Carnegie Instn of Washington, 1951–54; Demonstrator in Mineralogy and Petrology, Cambridge Univ., 1954–56; Asst then Associate Prof., Pennsylvania State Univ., 1956–60. Editor, Power Diffraction File, 1959–69. Visiting Prof., California Inst. of Technology, 1965. Consultant: Union Carbide Corp., 1956–85; UOP, 1985–99. Member, US Nat. Acad. of Scis, 1986. Murchison Medal, Geol Soc., 1980; Roebling Medal, Mineralogical Soc. of America, 1982. *Publications:* Feldspar Minerals, Vols 1 and 2, 1975, 2nd edn 1987; Geometrical and Structural Crystallography, 1982; numerous articles on crystallography, inorganic chemistry, mineralogy, petrology and planetology. *Recreations:* music, art. *Address:* Department of the Geophysical Sciences, University of Chicago, 5734 S Ellis Avenue, Chicago, IL 60637–1434, USA. *T:* (773) 7028110.   *Died 6 April 2007.*

SMITH, Hon. Kenneth George, OJ 1973; Justice of Appeal, Bahamas, 1985–90; *b* 25 July 1920; *s* of Franklin C. Smith; *m* 1942, Hyacinth Whitfield Connell; two *d. Educ:* Primary schs; Cornwall Coll., Jamaica; Inns of Court Sch. of Law, London. Barrister-at-Law, Lincoln's Inn. Asst Clerk of Courts, 1940–48; Dep. Clerk of Courts, 1948–53; Clerk of Courts, 1953–56; Crown Counsel, 1956–62; Asst Attorney-Gen., 1962–65; Supreme Court Judge, 1965–70; Judge of Appeal, Jamaica, 1970–73; Chief Justice of Jamaica, 1973–85; Judge, Admin. Tribunal, Inter-American Develt Bank,

1987–92 (Pres., 1990–92). *Recreations:* swimming, gardening. *Address:* 5 Wagner Avenue, Kingston 8, Jamaica.   *Died 21 Dec. 2009.*

SMITH, Sir Leslie (Edward George), Kt 1977; Director, The BOC Group plc (formerly The British Oxygen Co. Ltd), 1966–92 (Chairman, 1972–85); *b* 15 April 1919; *m* 1st, 1943, Lorna Bell Pickworth; two *d*; 2nd, 1964, Cynthia Barbara Holmes (*d* 2005); one *s* one *d. Educ:* Christ's Hospital, Horsham, Sussex. FCA. Served War, Army (Royal Artillery, Royal Fusiliers), 1940–46. Variety of activities, 1946–55. Joined British Oxygen as Accountant, 1956, Group Man. Dir, 1969–72, Group Chm. and Chief Exec., 1972–79, Chm., 1979–85. Dir, British Gas plc (formerly British Gas Corp.), 1982–90. Mem., Exec. Cttee, King Edward VII Hospital for Officers, 1978–88. *Recreation:* unremarkable. *Address:* Woolstaplers' House, High Street, Chipping Campden, Glos GL55 6HB.   *Died 4 July 2006.*

SMITH, Dame Margôt, DBE 1974; *b* 5 Sept. 1918; *d* of Leonard Graham Brown, MC, FRCS, and Margaret Jane Menzies; *m* 1st, 1938, Bertram Aykroyd (marr. diss. 1947; he *d* 1983), *y s* of Sir Frederic Aykroyd, 1st Bt; one *s* (one *d* decd); 2nd, 1947, Roy Smith, MC, TD (*d* 1983); one *s. Educ:* Westonbirt. Chm., Nat. Conservative Women's Adv. Cttee, 1969–72; Chm., Nat. Union of Conservative and Unionist Assocs, 1973–74. Mem., NSPCC Central Exec. Cttee, 1969–86. *Address:* 85 Dale Grove, Wensleydale Grange, Leyburn, N Yorks DL8 5GA. *T:* (01969) 623621.   *Died 8 May 2007.*

SMITH, Prof. (Norman John) David, FRCR; Professor of Dental Radiology, University of London, 1978–96, then Emeritus; *b* 2 Feb. 1931; *s* of late Norman S. Smith; *m* 1st, 1954, Regina Eileen Lugg (marr. diss.); one *s*; 2nd, 1983, Mary Christine Pocock; one *d. Educ:* King's Coll. Sch., Wimbledon; King's Coll., London; KCH Dental Sch. (BDS 1963; MPhil 1969); Royal Free Hosp. Sch. of Medicine (MSc 1966). FRCR 1997. Apprenticed to Pacific Steam Navigation Co., 1948–51; Officer Service, Royal Mail Lines, 1952–58 (Master Mariner, 1957); part-time posts at KCH Dental Sch., Guy's Hosp. Dental Sch. and in gen. dental practice, 1966–69; Sen. Lectr in Dental Surg., KCH Dental Sch., 1969–72; Hd of Dept of Dental Radiol., KCH Dental Sch., later King's Coll. Sch. of Medicine and Dentistry, 1972–96; Reader in Dental Radiol., Univ. of London, 1973–78; Course Dir, 1996–2002, Project Dir, 2002–04, Unit of Distance Educn, Guy's, King's and St Thomas' (formerly King's) Dental Inst., KCL. Civil Consultant to RAF, 1990–96. Member: Southwark Bor. Council, 1974–78; GLC for Norwood, 1977–86 (Leader of Opposition, ILEA 1979–86); Thames Water Authority, 1977–83; SE Thames RHA, 1978–86; Council, Open Univ., 1978–81, 1982–91; Court, Univ. of London, 1982–87; Governor, Bethlem Royal and Maudsley Hosps, 1980–82; Mem., Bethlem Royal and Maudsley SHA, 1982–86. Vis. Prof. and lectr worldwide. Gov., King's Coll. Sch., Wimbledon, 1998–2003. Liveryman, Hon. Co. of Master Mariners. Hon. Mem., Polish Radiol Soc., 1989. DUniv Open, 1993. Sir Charlton Briscoe Res. Prize, KCH Med. Sch., 1969. *Publications:* Simple Navigation by the Sun, 1974; Dental Radiography, 1980; articles in dental jls. *Recreations:* oral history, wildlife photography. *Address:* Beechwood, Old Lane, Tatsfield, Westerham, Kent TN16 2LH. *T:* (01959) 577661. *Club:* Athenæum.   *Died 15 Feb. 2010.*

SMITH, Patrick Horace N.; *see* Nowell-Smith.

SMITH, Peter Anthony, CBE 2003; General Secretary, Association of Teachers and Lecturers (formerly Assistant Masters and Mistresses Association), 1988–2002; *b* 25 June 1940; *s* of Charles George and Margaret Patricia Smith; *m* 1961, Anne Elizabeth; one *s* one *d. Educ:* Haberdashers' Aske's Boys' Sch., Hatcham; Brasenose Coll., Oxford (MA). Graduate trainee, Midland Bank, 1961–63; teacher: LCC, 1963–66; Whitgift Foundn, 1966–74; Asst Sec., 1974–82, Dep. Gen. Sec., 1982–88, Asst Masters and Mistresses Assoc. Member: Equal

Opportunities Commn, 1994–2000; Gen. Council, TUC, 2000–02. Mem. Council, Specialist Schs Trust, 2000–02; Trustee, Teaching Awards Trust, 2000–. Governor, Haberdashers' Aske's City Technol. Coll., 2002–05. FRSA 1991. *Recreations:* cooking, listening to music, living in France, dolls' houses. *Address:* 19 Woodstock Road, Croydon CR0 1JS. *T:* (020) 8686 6726. *Club:* Royal Commonwealth Society.
Died 10 Feb. 2006.

SMITH, Dr Peter Graham, CB 1988; Director General Guided Weapons and Electronics, Ministry of Defence (Procurement Executive), 1982–88; *b* 12 June 1929; *s* of James A. and Florence L. Smith; *m* 1952, Doreen Millicent (*née* Wyatt) (*d* 2000); two *d. Educ:* Wellington Grammar Sch., Shropshire; Birmingham Univ. (BSc, PhD). Radar Res. Estab., 1953–75: seconded to British Defence Staff, Washington, 1966–68; Supt, Airborne Defensive Radar Div., 1970–75; Dir Defence Science 8, MoD, 1975–78; Dir Surveillance and Instrument Projs, MoD (PE), 1978–82. *Recreations:* gardening, reading, modelling. *Address:* c/o Lloyd's Bank, High Street, Harpenden AL5 2TA. *Died 17 June 2008.*

SMITH, (Raymond) Gordon (Antony) E.; *see* Etherington-Smith.

SMITH, Sir Richard P.; *see* Prince-Smith, Sir W. R.

SMITH, Roger Bonham; Chairman and Chief Executive Officer, General Motors, 1981–90 (Member, Board of Directors, 1974–92); *b* Columbus, Ohio, 12 July 1925; *m* 1954, Barbara Rasch; two *s* two *d. Educ:* Detroit University Sch.; Univ. of Michigan (BBA, MBA). Served US Navy, 1944–46. General Motors: Sen. Clerk, subseq. Director, general accounting, Detroit Central Office, 1949–58; Dir, financial analysis sect., NY Central Office, 1960, later Asst Treas.; transf. to Detroit as Gen. Asst Comptroller, then Gen. Asst Treas., 1968; Treasurer, 1970; Vice-Pres. i/c Financial Staff, 1971, also Mem. Admin Cttee, 1971–90; Vice-Pres. and Gp Exec. i/c Nonautomotive and Defense Gp, 1972; Exec. Vice-Pres., Mem. Bd of Dirs and Mem. Finance Cttee, 1974, also Mem. Exec. Cttee, 1974–90; Vice-Chm. Finance Cttee, 1975–80, Chm., 1981–90. Conceived GM Cancer Res. Awards, 1978 (Trustee); Member: Business Council, 1981–; Soc. of Automotive Engrs, 1978–. Hon. degrees from several univs. Hon. Dr DePauw, 1979; Hon. Dr Albion Coll., 1982. *Address:* General Motors Corporation, 31 Judson Street, Pontiac, MI 48342–2230, USA; (home) Bloomfield Hills, MI 48304, USA. *Clubs:* Economic, Detroit, Detroit Athletic (Detroit); Links (NY). *Died 29 Nov. 2007.*

SMITH, Russell; *see* Smith, C. R.

SMITHERS, Sir Peter (Henry Berry Otway), Kt 1970; VRD with clasp; DPhil; Lt-Comdr RNR, retired; *b* 9 Dec. 1913; *o s* of late Lt-Col H. O. Smithers, JP, Hants, and Ethel Berry; *m* 1943, Dojean, *d* of late T. M. Sayman, St Louis, Mo; two *d. Educ:* Hawtrey's; Harrow Sch.; Magdalen Coll., Oxford (Demyship in History, 1931; 1st cl. Hons Modern History, 1934); DPhil Oxon 1953. Called to Bar, Inner Temple, 1936; joined Lincoln's Inn, 1937. Commn, London Div. RNVR, 1939; British Staff, Paris, 1940; Naval Intelligence Div., Admiralty; Asst Naval Attaché, British Embassy, Washington; Actg Naval Attaché, Mexico, Central Amer. Republics and Panama. Mem., Winchester RDC, 1946–49. MP (C) Winchester Div. of Hampshire, 1950–64; PPS to Minister of State for Colonies, 1952–56 and to Sec. of State for Colonies, 1956–59; Deleg., Consultative Assembly of Council of Europe, 1952–56 and 1960; UK Deleg. to UN Gen. Assembly, 1960–62; Parly Under-Sec. of State, FO, 1962–64; Sec.-Gen., Council of Europe, 1964–69; Senior Research Fellow, UN Inst. for Trng and Research, 1969–72; General Rapporteur, European Conf. of Parliamentarians and Scientists, 1970–77. Chairman: British-Mexican Soc., 1952–55; Conservative Overseas Bureau, 1956–59; Vice-Chm., Conservative Party Foreign Affairs Cttee,

1958–62; Vice-Pres., European Assembly of Local Authorities, 1959–62. 22 one-man photographic exhibitions in museums and institutions in England, USA, France and Italy. Master, Turners' Co., 1955; Liveryman, Goldsmiths' Co. Hon. FRHS 1996. Dr of Law *hc* Zürich, 1969. Marzotto Prize, Marzotto Foundn, Italy, 1969; Alexander von Humboldt Gold Medal, 1969; Medal of Honour, Parly Assembly, Council of Europe, 1984; Gold Medal (for photography), RHS, 1981, 1983, 1990, 1991, 1992, Gold Medal and Grenfell Medal, 1985, Veitch Meml Gold Medal, 1993, Lyttel Cup, for breeding lilies, 2001; Herbert Medal, Internat. Bulb Soc., 1997; Gold Medal pro merito, Council of Europe, 1999; Schulthess Prize, best garden in Switzerland, 2001. Hon. Citizen, Commune of Vico Morcote, Switzerland, 1995. Chevalier de la Légion d'Honneur; Orden Mexicana del Aguila Azteca. *Publications:* Life of Joseph Addison, 1954, 2nd edn, 1966; Adventures of a Gardener, 1995; L'Avventura di un Giardinere, 2005. *Recreations:* gardening, computer. *Address:* 6921 Vico Morcote, Switzerland; *e-mail:* ps@vico.to. *Clubs:* Carlton; The Everglades. *Died 8 June 2006.*

SMITHSON, Rt Rev. Alan; Hon. Assistant Bishop, diocese of Glasgow and Galloway, since 2002, and diocese of Edinburgh, since 2007; Hon. Assistant Curate, All Saints, Challock, 2002–08; *b* 1 Dec. 1936; *s* of Herbert and Mary Smithson; *m* 1964, Margaret Jean McKenzie; two *s* two *d. Educ:* Queen's Coll., Oxford (BA 1962; MA 1968); Queen's Coll., Birmingham (DipTh 1964). Deacon 1964, priest 1965; Curate: Christ Church, Skipton, 1964–68; St Mary the Virgin with St Cross and St Peter, Oxford, 1968–72; Chaplain: Queen's Coll., Oxford, 1969–72; Reading Univ., 1972–77; Vicar of Bracknell, 1977–84; Residentiary Canon, Carlisle Cathedral and Dir of Training and Diocesan Training Inst., 1984–90; Bp Suffragan of Jarrow, 1990–2001. External Moderator: Ministry Div., NE Oecumenical Course, 2002–05; Theol Inst. of Scottish Episcopal Ch, 2003–06. Chm., Pastoral Cttee, Mission to Seafarers, 1991–2006. Brigade Chaplain, Church Lads and Church Girls' Bde, 1997–2007. *Recreations:* water colour painting, travel, camping, fell walking, 'cello playing. *Address:* 4 Eskside East, Musselburgh EH21 7RS.
Died 17 June 2010.

SMYTH, His Honour (James) Robert Staples; a Circuit Judge, 1986–97; *b* 11 July 1926; *s* of late Major Robert Smyth, Gaybrook, Co. Westmeath, and Mabel Anne Georgiana (*née* MacGeough-Bond); *m* 1971, Fenella Joan Mowat; one *s. Educ:* St Columba's, Dublin; Merton Coll., Oxford (BA 1948, MA). Served RAF, 1944–46. Called to Bar, Inner Temple, 1949. Resident Magistrate, Northern Rhodesia, 1951–55; a Dep. Circuit Judge, 1974; Stipendiary Magistrate, W Midlands, 1978–86; a Recorder, 1983–86. Dep. Chm., Agricl Land Tribunal, 1974. *Recreations:* shooting, fishing, English literature. *Address:* Leys, Shelsley Beauchamp, Worcs WR6 6RB. *Died 2 Sept. 2009.*

SNEDDON, Hutchison Burt, CBE 1983 (OBE 1968); JP; Lord-Lieutenant of Lanarkshire, 1992–99; former Scottish Divisional Director, Nationwide Anglia Building Society (formerly Nationwide Building Society); *b* 17 April 1929; *s* of Robert and Catherine Sneddon; *m* 1960, Elizabeth Jardine; one *s* two *d. Educ:* Wishaw High School. Chm., Cumbernauld Develt Corp., 1979–83; Regl Sales Manager (Special Projects), Scottish Gas, 1983–88. Dir, Motherwell Enterprise Develt Co., 1996–. Dir, National Bldg Agency, 1973–82; Vice-Chm., Scottish National Housing and Town Planning Council, 1965–71; Member: Bd, Housing Corp., 1977–83; Consultative Cttee, Scottish Develt Agency, 1979–83; Scottish Adv. Commn on Housing Rents, 1973–74; Anderson Cttee on Commercial Rating, 1972–74; Western Regional Hosp. Bd, 1968–70; Scottish Tourist Bd, 1969–83; Chm., Burns Heritage Trail, 1971–83; Sen. Vice Pres., 1988–89, Pres., 1989–90, World Fedn of Burns Clubs (Jun. Vice Pres., 1987–88). Dep. Pres., Convention of Scottish Local Authorities, 1974–76;

Chairman: Gas Higher Managers Assoc., Scotland, 1984–88; Gas Higher Managers Assoc., GB, 1987–88. Motherwell and Wishaw Burgh Council: Councillor, 1958–77; Bailie, 1960–64; Chm., Housing Cttee, 1960–71; Chm., Policy and Resources Cttee, 1974–77; Leader, 1960–77; Chm., Motherwell DC, 1974–77; Provost, Burgh of Motherwell and Wishaw, 1971–75. Pres., Lanarks Multiple Sclerosis Assoc., 1998–. Gov., Erskine Hosp., 1993–. Hon. Pres., Royal Marines, Lanarks, 1993–. JP North Motherwell District, 1974 (Mem. JP Adv. Cttee); DL Motherwell, Hamilton, Monklands, E Kilbride and Clydesdale Districts, 1989. Gold Medal of Schweinfurt, Bavaria, 1977 (Internat. Relations). *Recreations:* football (watching), philately. *Address:* 36 Shand Street, Wishaw, Lanarks ML2 8HN. *Died 7 Nov. 2009.*

SNELL, Rt Rev. George Boyd, DD, PhD; Bishop of Toronto, 1966–72; *b* Toronto, Ontario, 17 June 1907; *s* of John George Snell and Minnie Alice Boyd (*née* Finnie); *m* 1934, Esther Mary Hartley (decd). *Educ:* Trinity College, Toronto (BA 1929, MA 1930, PhD 1937, Hon. DD 1948). Ordained deacon, Toronto, 1931, priest, Niagara (for Tor.), 1932; Curate of St Michael and All Angels, Toronnto, 1931–39; Rector, 1940–48; Private Chaplain to Bp of Toronto, 1945–48; Rector of Pro-Cathedral, Calgary, and Dean of Calgary, 1948–51; Exam. Chaplain to Bp of Calgary, 1948–51; Rector of St Clement Eglinton, Toronto, 1951–56; Archdeacon of Toronto, 1953–56; Exam. Chaplain to Bp of Toronto, 1953–55; consecrated Bp Suffragan of Toronto, 1956; elected Bp-Coadjutor of Toronto, 1959. Hon. DD: Wycliffe Coll., Toronto, 1959; Huron Coll., Ontario, 1968. *Address:* 1210 Glen Road, Mississauga, ON L5H 3K8, Canada. *Clubs:* National, Albany (Toronto). *Died 26 Dec. 2006.*

SNODGRASS, John Michael Owen, CMG 1981; HM Diplomatic Service, retired; *b* 12 Aug. 1928; *e s* of Major W. M. Snodgrass, MC, RAMC; *m* 1957, Jennifer James; three *s.* *Educ:* Marlborough Coll.; Trinity Hall, Cambridge (MA, Maths and Moral Scis). Diplomatic Service: 3rd Sec., Rome, 1953–56; FO, 1956–60; 1st Sec., Beirut, 1960–63; S Africa, 1964–67; FCO, 1967–70; Consul-Gen., Jerusalem, 1970–74; Counsellor, South Africa, 1974–77; Hd of South Pacific Dept, FCO, 1977–80; Ambassador: to Zaire, 1980–83 (also to Burundi, Rwanda and Congo); to Bulgaria, 1983–86. CStJ 1975. *Recreation:* bridge. *Address:* 5 Luddington Road, Stratford-upon-Avon, Warwicks CV37 9SF. *T:* (01789) 267171. *Died 4 Feb. 2008.*

SOEHARTO, General Mohamed, Hon. GCB 1974; President of Indonesia, 1968–98; *b* 8 June 1921; *s* of Kertosudiro and Sukirah; *m* 1947, Siti Hartinah (*d* 1996); three *s* three *d.* *Educ:* Elementary Sch., Puluhan Village; Junior High Sch., Wonogiri and Yogyakarta; Senior High Sch., Semarang. Military Basic Training Course and Non Commissioned Officers' Sch., 1940; Asst Police Chief, Yogyakarta (Japanese Police Unit Keibuho), 1941; Platoon Leader, Volunteer Corps, Wates, 1943; Co. Comdrs Sch., 1944; Mem., People's Security Army during Physical Revolution's counter insurgency ops against Indonesian Communist Party, 1945–50; crushed rebellion of Andi Aziz, Ujung Pandang, 1950; ops against Moslem rebels, Central Java, 1951–59; Comdg Gen., Liberation of W Irian (Western New Guinea), 1962; ops against Indonesian Communist Party, 1965; took measures to control the country, 1966; Acting President, 1967–68. Awarded numerous decorations. *Address:* c/o Office of the President, Jakarta, Indonesia. *Died 27 Jan. 2008.*

SOLZHENITSYN, Alexander Isayevitch; author; Hon. Fellow, Hoover Institution on War, Revolution and Peace, 1975; *b* 11 Dec. 1918; *m* 1940, Natalya Reshetovskaya (marr. diss. 1951; remarried 1957; marr. diss. 1973; she *d* 2003); *m* 1973, Natalya Svetlova; three *s.* *Educ:* Univ. of Rostov (degree in maths and physics); Moscow Inst. of History, Philosophy and Literature (correspondence course). Joined Army, 1941; grad. from

Artillery School, 1942; in comd artillery battery and served at front until 1945 (twice decorated); sentenced to eight years' imprisonment, 1945, released, 1953; exile in Siberia, 1953–56; officially rehabilitated, 1957; taught and wrote in Ryazan and Moscow; expelled from Soviet Union, 1974; Soviet citizenship restored, 1990. Member Union of Soviet writers, 1962, expelled 1969; Member: Amer. Acad. of Arts and Sciences, 1969; Russian Acad. of Scis, 1997. Awarded Nobel Prize for Literature, 1970; Templeton Prize for Progress in Religion, 1983; Russian State Literature Prize, 1990. *Publications:* in English: One Day in the Life of Ivan Denisovich, 1962, new edn 1991, filmed 1971; An Incident at Krechetovka Station, and Matryona's House (publ. US as We Never Make Mistakes, 1969), 1963; For the Good of the Cause, 1964; The First Circle, 1968; Cancer Ward, part 1, 1968, part 2, 1969 (Prix du Meilleur Livre Etranger, Paris); Stories and Prose Poems, 1970; August 1914, 1972; One Word of Truth: the Nobel speech on literature, 1972; The Gulag Archipelago: an experiment in literary investigation, vol. 1, 1973, vol. 2, 1974, vol. 3, 1976 (first Russian edn, 1989); The Oak and the Calf (autobiog.), 1975; Lenin in Zurich, 1975; Prussian Nights (poem), 1977; The Red Wheel: August 1914, 1983 (revd edn of 1972 publication); October 1916, 1985; March 1917 (4 vols); April 1917 (2 vols); How to Reconstruct Russia, 1991; The Russian Question at the End of the Twentieth Century, 1995; Invisible Allies, 1997; Russia in Collapse, 1998; Le Grain entre deux meules (autobiog.), 1998; November 1916: the Red Wheel/Knot II, 1999; Two Hundred Years Together, vol. 1, 2001; *plays:* trilogy: The Love Girl and the Innocent, 1969, Victory Celebrations, Prisoners, 1983. *Address:* c/o Claude Durand, Editions Fayard, 13 rue du Montparnasse, 75278 Paris Cedex 06, France. *Died 3 Aug. 2008.*

SOMERVILLE, Sir Quentin Charles Somerville A.; *see* Agnew-Somerville.

SORRIE, George Strath, CB 1993; Medical Adviser and Director, Civil Service Occupational Health Service, 1987–93; *b* 19 May 1933; *s* of Alexander James Sorrie and Florence Edith Sorrie (*née* Strath); *m* 1959, Gabrielle Ann Baird; three *d.* *Educ:* Woodside Sch., Aberdeen; Robert Gordon's Coll., Aberdeen; Univ. of Aberdeen (MB ChB); Univs of London and Dundee. FFOM, DPH, DIH. Medical Branch, RAF, 1958–61; Lectr in Epidemiology, London Sch. of Hygiene and Tropical Medicine, 1965–67; GP, Rhynie, Aberdeenshire, 1967–72; Health and Safety Exec., 1972, Dep. Dir of Med. Services, 1980–87. *Address:* 30 Irvine Crescent, St Andrews, Fife KY16 8LG. *T:* (01334) 474510. *Died 5 June 2007.*

SOULBURY, 3rd Viscount; *see* Ramsbotham, Hon. Sir P. E.

SOUTHERTON, Thomas Henry, BSc (Eng); CEng, MIET; Senior Director, Data Processing, Post Office, 1975–78, retired; *b* 1 July 1917; *s* of C. H. Southerton, Birmingham; *m* 1st, 1945, Marjorie Elizabeth Sheen (*d* 1979); one *s;* 2nd, 1981, Joyce Try (*d* 2008). *Educ:* Bemrose Sch., Derby; Northampton Coll., London (BSc(Eng)). PO Apprentice, Derby, 1933–36; Engineering Workman, Derby and Nottingham, 1936–40; Inspector, Engineer-in-Chief's Office, 1940–45; Engineer, 1945–50; Sen. Exec. Engr, 1950–53; Factory Manager, PO Provinces, 1953–56; Dep. Controller, Factories Dept, 1956–64; Controller, Factories Dept, 1964–67; Dir, Telecommunications Management Services, 1967–73; Sen. Dir Telecommunications Personnel, 1973–75. Mem., Industrial Tribunals, 1978–86. *Recreations:* art, architecture, music. *Died 27 June 2008.*

SOUTHWORTH, Jean May; QC 1973; a Recorder of the Crown Court, 1972–93; *b* 20 April 1926; *o c* of late Edgar and Jane Southworth, Clitheroe. *Educ:* Queen Ethelburga's Sch., Harrogate; St Anne's Coll., Oxford (MA; Hon. Fellow, 2004). Served in WRNS, 1944–45. Called to Bar, Gray's Inn, 1954; Bencher, 1980. Standing

Counsel to Dept of Trade and Industry for Central Criminal Court and Inner London Sessions, 1969–73. Fellow, Woodard Corporation (Northern Div.), 1974–90. *Recreations:* music, travel. *Address:* 21 Caroline Place, W2 4AN. *Died 13 Jan. 2010.*

SPACKMAN, Christopher John, FCIOB; Chairman, Bovis Construction Ltd, 1989–96 (Managing Director, 1985–93); Director, Bovis Ltd, 1997–99; *b* 21 May 1934; *s* of Eric Dickens Spackman, MB and Kathleen (*née* Crisp); *m* 1967, Marilyn Ann Rowland; one *s* two *d*. *Educ:* Sherborne Sch., Dorset; Brixton Sch. of Building (HND Building 1959); London Business Sch. FCIOB 1980. Commnd RA, 1952–54. Joined Bovis as trainee, 1955; Asst Contract Manager, then Contract Manager, 1959–64; Regl Dir, 1964; i/c Bovis Bristol Office, 1964–69; Harrow Office, 1969–73; Dir, Bovis Construction Ltd, 1973–99; Asst Man. Dir, 1983–85; Man. Dir, Bovis Europe, 1994 96; Vice-Chm, Bovis Construction Gp, 1996–97; retired 2002. Chm., Deregulation Task Force for Construction, 1993. FRSA 1996. *Recreations:* squash, tennis. *Clubs:* Knotty Green Cricket; Jordans Tennis. *Died 23 July 2010.*

SPANTON, (Harry) Merrik, OBE 1975; CEng; Chairman, British Coal Enterprise Ltd (formerly NCB (Enterprise) Ltd), 1984–91; *b* 27 Nov. 1924; *s* of late Henry Broadley Spanton and Edith Jane Spanton; *m* 1945, Mary Margaret Hawkins; one *s*. *Educ:* Eastbourne Coll.; Royal Sch. of Mines (BSc (Min) (Eng) 1945; ARSM). CEng, FIMinE 1957 (Hon. FIMinE 1986). Colliery Manager, 1950; Agent, 1954; Gp Man., 1956; Dep. Prodn Man., 1958; Dep. Prodn Dir, 1960; Asst Gen. Man., 1962; Gen. Man., 1964; Area Dir, 1967 80; Mem., NCB, 1980–85. Chairman: J. H. Sankey & Son, 1982–83; Coal Industry (Patents) Ltd, 1982–85; Director: British Mining Consultants Ltd, 1980–87 (Chm., 1981–83); Overseas Coal Develts Ltd, 1980–83; Compower, 1981–85 (Chm., 1984–85); NCB (Coal Products) Ltd, 1981–83; Coal Processing Consultants, 1981–83; Staveley Chemicals Ltd, 1981–83; NCB (Ancillaries) Ltd, 1982–85; British Fuel Co., 1983–87; Berry Hill Investments Ltd, 1984–85; CIBT Insurance Services Ltd, 1984–85; CIBT Developments Ltd, 1984–85; Coal Industry Social Welfare Orgn, 1983–85. Member: W European Coal Producers Assoc., 1980–85; CBI Overseas Cttee, 1981–85. Vice-Pres., Coal Trade Benevolent Assoc., 1979– (Chm., 1978). CCMI (CBIM 1979). *Publications:* articles in prof. jls. *Recreations:* travel, shooting, genealogy. *Address:* 4 Roselands Gardens, Canterbury, Kent CT2 7LP. *T:* (01227) 769356. *Died 11 Nov. 2007.*

SPÄRCK JONES, Prof. Karen Ida Boalth, PhD; FBA 1995; Professor of Computers and Information, Computer Laboratory, University of Cambridge, 1999–2002, then Emeritus; Fellow, Wolfson College, Cambridge, 2000–02, then Hon. Fellow; *b* 26 Aug. 1935; *d* of A. Owen Jones and Ida Spärck; *m* 1958, Prof. Roger Michael Needham, CBE, FRS, FREng (*d* 2003). *Educ:* Girton Coll., Cambridge (BA, PhD). Cambridge University: Research Fellow, Newnham Coll., 1965–68; Royal Society Res. Fellow, 1968–73; Sen. Res. Associate, 1974–88; GEC Fellow, 1983–88; Asst Dir of Res., 1988–94; Reader in Computers and Information, Computer Lab., 1994–99. Vice-Pres., British Acad., 2000–02. Fellow: Amer. Assoc. for Artificial Intelligence, 1993; Eur. Co-ordinating Cttee for Artificial Intelligence, 1999. Hon. DSc City, 1997. Lifetime Achievement Award, Assoc. for Computational Linguistics, 2004. *Publications:* Automatic Keyword Classification for Information Retrieval, 1971; (jtly) Linguistics and Information Science, 1973; (ed) Information Retrieval Experiment, 1981; (ed jtly) Automatic Natural Language Parsing, 1983; Synonymy and Semantic Classification, 1986; (ed jtly) Readings in Natural Language Processing, 1986; (jtly) Evaluating Natural Language Processing Systems, 1996; (ed jtly) Readings in Information Retrieval, 1997; (ed jtly) Computer Systems: theory, technology, and applications, 2004; numerous papers.

Recreation: art. *Address:* Computer Laboratory, University of Cambridge, William Gates Building, J J Thomson Avenue, Cambridge CB3 0FD. *T:* (01223) 763500. *Died 4 April 2007.*

SPARK, Dame Muriel (Sarah), DBE 1993 (OBE 1967); CLit 1991; writer; *b* Edinburgh, 1 Feb. 1918; *d* of Bernard Camberg and Sarah Elizabeth Maud (*née* Uezzell); *m* 1937, Sidney Oswald Spark (marr. diss.); one *s*. *Educ:* James Gillespie's School for Girls, Edinburgh; Heriot Watt Coll., Edinburgh. FO, 1944; General Secretary, The Poetry Society, Editor, The Poetry Review, 1947–49. FRSL 1963; FRSE 1995. Hon. Mem., Amer. Acad. of Arts and Letters, 1978. Hon. DLitt: Strathclyde, 1971; Edinburgh, 1989; Aberdeen, 1995; St Andrews, 1998; Oxford, 1999; London, 2001; DUniv Heriot-Watt, 1995; Hon. DHL Amer. Univ. of Paris, 2005. David Cohen British Literature Prize, 1997; Gold Pen Award, Internat. PEN, 1998. Commandeur de l'Ordre des Arts et des Lettres, France, 1996. *Publications: critical and biographical:* (ed) Selected Poems of Emily Brontë, 1952; Child of Light: a Reassessment of Mary Shelley, 1951, rev. edn, Mary Shelley, 1988; John Masefield, 1953, repr. 1992; (joint) Emily Brontë: her Life and Work, 1953; (ed) The Brontë Letters, 1954; (ed jointly) Letters of John Henry Newman, 1957; The Essence of the Brontës, 1993; *poems:* The Fanfarlo and Other Verse, 1952; Collected Poems I, 1967; Going Up to Sotheby's and other poems, 1982; All the Poems of Muriel Spark, 2004; *fiction:* The Comforters, 1957; Robinson, 1958; The Go-Away Bird, 1958; Memento Mori, 1959 (adapted for stage, 1964; televised, BBC, 1992); The Ballad of Peckham Rye, 1960 (Italia prize, for dramatic radio, 1962); The Bachelors, 1960; Voices at Play, 1961; The Prime of Miss Jean Brodie, 1961 (adapted for stage, 1966, filmed 1969, and BBC TV, 1978); Doctors of Philosophy (play), 1963; The Girls of Slender Means, 1963 (adapted for radio, 1964, and BBC TV, 1975); The Mandelbaum Gate, 1965 (James Tait Black Memorial Prize); Collected Stories I, 1967; The Public Image, 1968; The Very Fine Clock (for children), 1969; The Driver's Seat, 1970 (filmed 1974); Not to Disturb, 1971; The Hothouse by the East River, 1973; The Abbess of Crewe, 1974 (filmed 1977); The Takeover, 1976; Territorial Rights, 1979; Loitering with Intent, 1981; Bang-Bang You're Dead and other stories, 1982; The Only Problem, 1984; The Stories of Muriel Spark, 1987 (Scottish Book of Year Award); A Far Cry from Kensington, 1988; Symposium, 1990; Curriculum Vitae (autobiog.), 1992; The French Window and The Small Telephone (for children), 1993; Omnibus I, 1993; Omnibus II, 1994; Reality and Dreams, 1996; Omnibus III, 1996; Omnibus IV, 1997; Aiding and Abetting, 2000; The Complete Short Stories, 2001; The Ghost Stories of Muriel Spark, 2003; The Finishing School, 2004. *Recreations:* reading, travel. *Address:* c/o David Higham Associates Ltd, 5–8 Lower John Street, Golden Square, W1F 9HA. *Died 13 April 2006.*

SPARKES, Sir Robert Lyndley, Kt 1979; State President, National Party of Australia (formerly Country Party), Queensland, 1970–90; Managing Partner, Lyndley Pastoral Co., since 1974; *b* 30 May 1929; *s* of late Sir James Sparkes, Jandowae, Queensland; *m* 1953, June (*d* 1999), *d* of M. Morgan; two *s*. *Educ:* Southport Sch., Queensland. Chairman: National Party (formerly Country Party) Lands Cttee, Queensland, 1966–90; NPA Nominees Pty Ltd. Mayor (formerly Chm.), Wambo Shire Council, 1967–99 (Mem., 1952–55 and 1964–67). *Recreation:* reading. *Address:* Dundonald, PO Box 117, Jandowae, Qld 4410, Australia. *T:* (7) 46685196. *Died 6 Aug. 2006.*

SPARKS, Arthur Charles; Under-Secretary, Ministry of Agriculture, Fisheries and Food, 1959–74; *b* 1914; *s* of late Charles Herbert and Kate Dorothy Sparks; *m* 1939, Betty Joan (*d* 1978), *d* of late Harry Oswald and Lilian Mary Simmons; three *d*. *Educ:* Selhurst Grammar Sch.; London School of Economics (BSc (Econ)). Clerk, Ministry of Agriculture and Fisheries, 1931;

Administrative Grade, 1936; National Fire Service, 1942–44; Principal Private Secretary to Minister of Agriculture and Fisheries, 1946–47; Asst Secretary, Ministry of Agriculture and Fisheries, 1947–49 and 1951–59; Asst Secretary, Treasury, 1949–51. Chm., Internat. Wheat Council, 1968–69. *Recreations:* reading, walking.												*Died 16 Dec. 2008.*

SPEAR, Prof. Walter Eric, PhD, DSc; FRS 1980; FRSE; Harris Professor of Physics, University of Dundee, 1968–90, then Emeritus Professor; *b* 20 Jan. 1921; *s* of David and Eva Spear; *m* 1952, Hilda Doris King; two *d. Educ:* Musterschule, Frankfurt/Main; Univ. of London (BSc 1947, PhD 1950, DSc 1967). Lecturer, 1953, Reader, 1967, in Physics, Univ. of Leicester; Vis. Professor, Purdue Univ., 1957–58. FRSE 1972; FInstP 1962. Max Born Prize and Medal, 1977; Europhysics Prize, 1977; Makdougal-Brisbane Medal, RSE, 1981; Rank Prize, 1988; Mott Award, Jl of Non-crystalline Solids, 1989; Rumford Medal, Royal Soc., 1990. *Publications:* numerous research papers on electronic and transport properties in crystalline solids, liquids and amorphous semiconductors. *Recreations:* literature, music (particularly chamber music), languages. *Address:* 20 Kelso Place, Dundee DD2 1SL. *T:* (01382) 667649.												*Died 21 Feb. 2008.*

SPEARING, George David; Technical Adviser, Institution of Highways and Transportation, 1984–86, retired; *b* 16 Dec. 1927; *s* of late George Thomas and Edith Lydia Anna Spearing; *m* 1951, Josephine Mary Newbould; two *s* one *d. Educ:* Rotherham Grammar Sch.; Sheffield Univ. BEng; MICE, FIHE. RAF, Airfield Construction Br., 1948. Asst Divl Surveyor, Somerset CC, 1951; Asst Civil Engr, W Riding of Yorks CC, 1953; Asst Engr, MoT, 1957; Supt. Engr, Midland Road Construction Unit, 1967; Asst Chief Engr, MoT, 1969; Regional Controller (Roads and Transportation), West Midlands, 1972; Dep. Chief Engr, DoE, 1973; Under Sec., DoE, 1974; Under Sec., Dept of Transport, and Dir Highways Planning and Management, 1974–78; Regional Dir, Eastern Reg., Depts of the Environment and Transport, and Chm., E Anglia Regional Bd, 1978–83. *Publications:* papers in Proc. Instn CE and Jl Instn HE. *Address:* 23 Colburn Avenue, Caterham, Surrey CR3 6HW. *T:* (01883) 347472.												*Died 9 Feb. 2007.*

SPEIGHT, Hon. Sir Graham (Davies), Kt 1983; Judge of the High Court of New Zealand, 1966–98; *b* 21 July 1921; *s* of Henry Baxter and Anna May Speight; *m* 1947, Elisabeth Muriel Booth; one *s* one *d. Educ:* Auckland Grammar Sch.; Univ. of Auckland (LLB). Qualified barrister and solicitor, 1942; served 2nd NZ Expeditionary Force, Middle East and Italy, 1943–46: Lieut Royal NZ Artillery, 1943–46; Aide-de-Camp, General B. C. Freyberg, VC (later 1st Baron Freyberg), 1944–45; practising barrister, 1946–66. Justice of Appeal, Fiji, 1980–87; Chief Justice, Cook Is, 1982–87. Chairman: Eden Park Bd, 1988–94; Rothman Foundn, 1988–95; NZ Sports Drug Agency, 1990–2000. Chancellor, Univ. of Auckland, 1973–79; Hon. LLD Auckland, 1983. *Publications:* (ed jtly) Adams: criminal law in New Zealand, 1986. *Recreations:* golf, yachting. *Clubs:* Auckland Golf, Royal New Zealand Yacht Squadron (Auckland) (Cdre 1961–63).												*Died 17 July 2008.*

SPEIRS, William MacLeod; General Secretary, Scottish Trades Union Congress, 1998–2006; *b* 8 March 1952; *s* of late Ronald Speirs and of Mary Speirs (*née* MacKenzie); *m* 1st, 1975, Lynda Speirs (marr. diss. 1990); one *s* one *d*; 2nd, 2002, Patricia Grieve. *Educ:* Univ. of Strathclyde (BA 1st Cl. Hons Politics). Univ. researcher, Strathclyde, 1974–76; Lectr, Cardonald Coll., Glasgow, 1977; bar steward, Paisley, 1977–78; researcher, Paisley Coll. of Technol., 1978–79; Asst Sec., 1979–88, Dep. Gen. Sec., 1988–98, Scottish TUC. Member: Central Arbitration Cttee; Employment Appeal Tribunal; Bd, Scottish Low Pay Unit; Scottish One Fund For All; Bd, Scottish Enterprise Glasgow; Chm. Bd, Workbase Trng (Scotland); TUC nominee, Nat. Employers' Adv. Bd for the Reserve Forces. Mem. Bd, 7:84 Theatre Co. FRSA

1993. DUniv Paisley, 1999. *Publications:* (contrib.) The Manpower Services Commission in Scotland, ed Brown and Fairley, 1989; contrib. to Scottish Trade Union Rev. *Recreations:* folk music, reading, watching St Mirren FC, cricket, losing money on horses. *Club:* Daft Watty's Ramblers (Paisley).												*Died 23 Sept. 2009.*

SPENCE, Gabriel John; Under Secretary, Department of Education and Science, 1973–81; *b* 5 April 1924; *s* of G. S. and D. A. Spence, Hope, Flints; *m* 1950, Averil Kingston (*née* Beresford) (*d* 1998); (one *s* decd). *Educ:* Arnold House; King's Sch., Chester (King's Schol., Head of School); Wadham Coll., Oxon (Schol.). MA 1949; Stanhope Prize and Proxime, Gibbs Schol., Oxon, 1947; Haldane Essay Prize, Inst. Public Admin, 1959. Joined Civil Service 1949 (Min. of Works, Science Office, Min. of Housing and Local Govt, DES); Jt Sec., Adv. Council on Scientific Policy, 1959–62; Asst Sec., DES, 1964–73; Sec., Council for Scientific Policy, 1964–67; Dep. Sec., UGC, 1978–81. Admin. Staff Coll., Henley, 1957. Trustee, The Oates Meml and Gilbert White Library and Museum, 1982–. *Recreations:* natural history, photography, golf. *Address:* Old Heath, Hillbrow Road, Liss, Hants GU33 7QD. *T:* (01730) 893235.												*Died 17 Feb. 2009.*

SPENCER, Prof. Anthony James Merrill, FRS 1987; Professor of Theoretical Mechanics, University of Nottingham, 1965–94, then Emeritus; *b* 23 Aug. 1929; *s* of James Lawrence Spencer and Gladys Spencer; *m* 1955, Margaret Bosker; three *s. Educ:* Queen Mary's Grammar Sch., Walsall; Queens' Coll., Cambridge (MA, PhD, ScD). Research Associate, Brown Univ., USA, 1955–57; Senior Scientific Officer, UKAEA, 1957–60; Lectr, Reader, Prof., Univ. of Nottingham, 1960–94. Visiting Professor: Brown Univ., 1966 and 1971; Lehigh Univ., 1978; Univ. of Queensland, 1982; Erskine Fellow, Univ. of Canterbury, 1995; Leverhulme Emeritus Fellow, 1995–97. Foreign Hon. Mem., Amer. Acad. of Arts and Scis, 2004. *Publications:* Deformations of Fibre-reinforced Materials, 1972; (jtly) Engineering Mathematics, Vols I and II, 1977; Continuum Mechanics, 1980; Continuum Theory of the Mechanics of Fibre-reinforced composites, 1984; numerous articles in math. and eng. jls. *Address:* 43 Stanton Lane, Stanton-on-the-Wolds, Keyworth, Nottingham NG12 5BE. *T:* (0115) 937 3134; School of Mathematical Sciences, The University, Nottingham NG7 2RD. *T:* (0115) 951 3838.												*Died 26 Jan. 2008.*

SPENCER, Ivor, MBE 2002; DL; professional toastmaster, since 1956; Chairman and Managing Director, Ivor Spencer Enterprises Ltd, since 1965; *b* 20 Nov. 1924; *s* of Barnet and Dora Isaacs; named Ivan, name changed to Ivor Spencer by Deed Poll, 1955; *m* 1948, Estella Spencer; one *s* one *d. Educ:* Rochells Sch., London. Principal: Ivor Spencer Sch. for Professional Toastmasters, 1975–; Ivor Spencer Internat. Sch. for Butler Administrators/Personal Assistants, UK and USA, 1981–. Founder and Life President: Guild of Professional Toastmasters, 1967–98; Guild of Internat. Professional Toastmasters, 1990– (Lifetime Achievement Award, 1998; Toastmaster of the Year 2000); President: Toastmasters for Royal Occasions, 1975–; Toastmasters of GB, 1976–; Toastmasters of England, 1978–. Dir, Guild of British Butlers, 1980–; Chief Executive: British Professional Toastmasters Authority, 1995–; Ivor Spencer Professional Toastmasters Authority, 1998–. AMInstD 1997. DL Greater London, 1985. *Publications:* A Toastmaster's Story, 1975; Speeches and Toasts, 1980. *Recreations:* after-dinner speaking, organising special events worldwide. *Address:* 12 and 14 Little Bornes, Dulwich, SE21 8SE. *T:* (020) 8670 5585, *Fax:* (020) 8670 0055; *e-mail:* ivor@ivorspencer.com.												*Died 10 Jan. 2009.*

SPICKERNELL, Rear-Adm. Derek Garland, CB 1974; CEng, FIMechE, FIET, FIMarEST; Chairman, Ritec Ltd, 1987–2004; Director General, British Standards Institution, 1981–86 (Technical Director, 1976–81); *b* 1 June 1921; *s* of late Comdr Sidney Garland Spickernell, RN, and Florence Elizabeth (*née*

March); *m* 1st, 1946, Ursula Rosemary Sheila Money (*d* 1997); one *s* one *d* (and one *s* decd); 2nd, 1998, Carolyn Mary Jenkins. *Educ:* RNEC, Keyham. Served War, HM Ships Abdiel, Wayland, and Engr Officer HM Submarine Statesman, 1943–45. Engr Officer HM Submarines Telemachus, Tudor and Alcide, 1945–50; Submarine Trials Officer, 1950–51; Engrg Dept, HM Dockyard, Portsmouth, 1951–53; SEO: Portsmouth Frigate Sqdn, 1954–55; 2nd Submarine Sqdn, 1956–57; Supt, ULE, Bournemouth, 1958–59; Dep. Captain Supt, AUWE, Portland, 1959–62; Dep. Manager, Engrg Dept, HM Dockyard, Portsmouth, 1962–64; in command, HMS Fisgard, 1965–66; Dep. Dir, Naval Ship Production, 1967–70; Dep. Chief Exec., Defence Quality Assurance Bd, 1970–71; Dir-Gen., Quality Assurance, MoD (PE), 1972–75. Dir, James Martin Associates PLC, 1986–90; Bd Mem., Southern Water, 1987–89; Chm., Jeniva Landfill, 1987–92. Chm., Nat. Council for Quality and Reliability, 1973–75; A Vice-President: Inst. of Quality Assurance, 1974– (Hon. FCQI); Inst. of Trading Standards Admin, 1986–; Vice-Pres., Internat. Orgn for Standardisation, 1985–87; Bd Mem. for Internat. Affairs, BSI, 1986–87; Dir, Turkish Standards Inst., 1987–90; Member: Internat. Acad. of Quality Assurance, 1977–97; Design Council, 1984–87; Council, Cranfield Inst. of Technol. FRSA; CCMI. *Publications:* papers on Quality Assurance. *Club:* Royal Fowey Yacht. *Died 14 May 2009.*

SPIERS, Ven. Graeme Hendry Gordon; Archdeacon of Liverpool, 1979–91, Archdeacon Emeritus, since 1991; *b* 15 Jan. 1925, *s* of Gordon and Mary Spiers; *m* 1958, Ann Chadwick; two *s*. *Educ:* Mercers Sch.; London College of Divinity. Westminster Bank, 1941–49; served RNVR, 1943–47. Deacon 1952, Priest 1953; Curate of Addiscombe, 1952–56; Succentor of Bradford Cathedral, 1956–58; Vicar of Speke, 1958–66; Vicar of Aigburth, 1966–80 and Rural Dean of Childwall, 1975–79. Hon. Canon, Liverpool Cathedral, 1977. *Recreation:* gardening. *Address:* 19 Barkfield Lane, Formby, Merseyside L37 1LY. *T:* (01704) 872902. *Died 20 June 2007.*

SPINNER, Bruno Max; Ambassador of Switzerland to the Republic of Italy, and to Malta and San Marino, since 2004; *b* 9 Jan. 1948; *s* of Max Spinner and Ruth Spinner-Schaffner; *m* 1976, Madelon Blaser-Giroud; two *s*. *Educ:* Univ. of Zurich (LLM); Univ. of Geneva. Entered Swiss Diplomatic Service, 1976: Attaché, Ankara, 1977; Diplomatic Sec., Mission to EC, Brussels, 1978–82; Dep. Hd of Mission, Ottawa, 1982–85; Hd, Div. of Internat. Law, Federal Dept of Foreign Affairs, Berne, 1985–89 (Legal Advr to Swiss chief negotiator at GATT negotiations (Uruguay Round), 1987–89; Pres., EFTA Cttee of Legal Experts, 1988–89); Minister, Dep. Hd of Mission to EC, Brussels, 1989–91; Mem., Delegn to EEA negotiations, and Vice-Pres., editl cttee, 1990–92; Ambassador and Hd, Integration Office, Federal Dept of Foreign Affairs and Federal Dept of the Economy, Berne, 1992–99; Ambassador to the UK, 2000–04. Hon. Prof. of European Law, Zurich Univ., 1993–2000. FRPSL 2003 (Mem., 2000). *Recreations:* sports, philately, art. *Address:* Embassy of Switzerland, Via Barnaba Oriani 61, 00197 Rome, Italy. *T:* (06) 80957322. *Club:* Garrick. *Died 25 July 2009.*

SPINNEY, Ronald Richard, CBE 2004; FRICS; Chairman, Hammerson plc, 1999–2005 (Chief Executive, 1993–99); *b* 1 April 1941; *m* 1st, Julia (*d* 1996); two *d*; 2nd, 1999, Lu; two step *s* two step *d*. *Educ:* Clayesmore Sch.; Coll. of Estate Mgt. Jt Founder, Greycoat plc, 1976, Jt Man. Dir and Dep. Chm., 1983–92. A Crown Estate Comr, 1999–2006. Chm., Unicorn Children's Theatre, 1992–; Deputy Chairman: Rentokil Initial plc, 1997–2006; Think London (formerly London First Centre), 1998–2006 (Chm., 2001); non-executive Director: Fuller Smith & Turner, 2000–; J P Morgan Cazenove, 2005–. Chm. Govs, Clayesmore Sch., 1997–2004. Trustee, Theatres Trust, 2003–. *Address:* 22 Dartmouth Hill, SE10 8AJ. *Clubs:* Garrick, RAC. *Died 13 July 2008.*

SPOONER, Prof. Frank Clyffurde, MA, PhD, LittD; Professor of Economic History, University of Durham, 1966–85, then Emeritus; *b* 5 March 1924; *s* of Harry Gordon Morrison Spooner. *Educ:* Bromley Grammar Sch.; Christ's Coll., Cambridge. Hist. Tripos, 1st cl., Pt I 1947 and Pt II 1948; MA 1949; PhD 1953; LittD 1985. War Service, Sub-Lt (S) RNVR, 1943–46; Bachelor Research Scholar, 1948; Chargé de Recherches, CNRS, Paris, 1949–50; Allen Scholar, 1951; Fellow, Christ's Coll., Cambridge, 1951–57; Commonwealth Fund Fellow, 1955–57 at Chicago, Columbia, New York, and Harvard Univs; Ecole Pratique des Hautes Etudes, VI Section, Sorbonne, 1957–61; Lectr, Univ. of Oxford, 1958–59; Vis. Lectr in Econs, Harvard Univ., 1961–62; Irving Fisher Research Prof. of Econs, Yale Univ., 1962–63; Univ. of Durham: Lectr, 1963; Reader, 1964; Resident Tutor-in-charge, Lumley Castle, 1965–70; Dir, Inst. of European Studies, 1969–76; Leverhulme Fellow, 1976–78; Leverhulme Emeritus Fellow, 1985–86. FRHistS 1970; FSA 1983. Prix Limantour de l'Académie des Sciences Morales et Politiques, 1957; West European Award, British Academy, 1979; Ernst Meyer Award, 1983. *Publications:* L'économie mondiale et les frappes monétaires en France, 1493–1680, 1956, rev. edn The International Economy and Monetary Movements in France, 1493–1725, 1972; Risks at Sea: Amsterdam insurance and maritime Europe 1766–1780, 1983; contribs to joint works and to jls. *Recreations:* music, photography, walking. *Club:* Oxford and Cambridge. *Died 23 June 2007.*

SPRIGGE, Prof. Timothy Lauro Squire, PhD; FRSE; Professor Emeritus, University of Edinburgh, since 1989; *b* 14 Jan. 1932; *s* of Cecil and Katriona Sprigge; *m* 1959, Giglia Gordon; one *s* twin *d*. *Educ:* Gonville and Caius Coll., Cambridge (MA, PhD). FRSE 1993. Lecturer in Philosophy, University Coll. London, 1961–63; Lectr in Philosophy, 1963–70, Reader in Philosophy, 1970–79, Univ. of Sussex; Prof. of Logic and Metaphysics, 1979–89, Endowment Fellow, 1989–98, Univ. of Edinburgh. Visiting Associate Professor, Univ. of Cincinnati, 1968–69. Member: Aristotelian Soc., 1960– (Pres., 1991–92); Mind Assoc., 1955–; Assoc. for the Advancement of Amer. Philosophy, 1978–; Scots Philosophical Club, 1979–. Vice-Chm., Advocates for Animals, 1994–2004. *Publications:* ed, Correspondence of Jeremy Bentham, vols 1 and 2, 1968; Facts, Words and Beliefs, 1970; Santayana: an examination of his philosophy, 1974; The Vindication of Absolute Idealism, 1983; Theories of Existence, 1985; The Rational Foundations of Ethics, 1988; James and Bradley: American truth and British reality, 1993; The God of Metaphysics, 2006; contribs to various vols of philosophical essays and to periodicals, incl. Mind, Philosophy, Inquiry, Nous. *Recreation:* backgammon. *Address:* Saffrons, 5 King Henry's Road, Lewes, East Sussex BN7 1BT. *T:* (01273) 487541; *e-mail:* lauro@ squire1.demon.co.uk. *Died 11 July 2007.*

SPRIGGS, Elizabeth; actress; *b* 18 Sept. 1929; *m* 1st, Kenneth Spriggs (marr. diss.); one *d*; 2nd, Marshall Jones (marr. diss.); 3rd, Murry Manson. *Educ:* Royal Sch. of Music. Early repertory experience with Bristol Old Vic and Birmingham Rep.; joined RSC, 1962; *stage* includes: Royal Shakespeare Company: Hamlet; Romeo and Juliet; Julius Caesar, The Merry Wives of Windsor, 1968; A Delicate Balance, 1969; Twelfth Night, Major Barbara, and London Assurance, 1970; Much Ado about Nothing, 1971; Othello, 1971; Misalliance, 1986; National Theatre: Blithe Spirit, 1976; Volpone, and The Country Wife, 1977; Macbeth, and Love Letters on Blue Paper (SWET Award for best supporting actress), 1978; When We Are Married, Whitehall, 1986; Arsenic and Old Lace, Chichester, 1991; *television* includes: series: The Glittering Prizes, 1976; Shine on Harvey Moon, 1982–85, 1995; Simon and the Witch; Watching; Lovejoy; Sherlock Holmes; Jeeves and Wooster; Boon; Heartbeat; Ruth Rendel Mysteries; Inspector Alleyn, 1993; Midsomer Murders; Playing the Field, 1997–99; serials: Strangers and Brothers, 1986; Oranges are not the only fruit, 1990;

The Old Devils, 1991; Anglo-Saxon Attitudes, 1991; Middlemarch, 1994; Taking Over the Asylum, 1994; Martin Chuzzlewit, 1994; Wives and Daughters, 1999; plays: Able's Will, 1977; Afternoon Off, 1979; We, the Accused, 1980; The Merry Wives of Windsor, 1983; Henry IV, 1996; *films* include: Impromptu, 1992; Sense and Sensibility, 1996; The Secret Agent; Paradise Road; Alice in Wonderland, 1998; A Christmas Carol, 1999. *Address:* c/o Fionna McCullock, Independent Talent Group Ltd, Oxford House, 76 Oxford Street, W1D 1BS. *Died 2 July 2008.*

SPRINGFORD, John Frederick Charles, CBE 1980 (OBE 1970); British Council Officer; *b* 6 June 1919; *s* of Frederick Charles Springford and Bertha Agnes Springford (*née* Trenery); *m* 1945, Phyllis Wharton; one *s* two *d*. *Educ:* Latymer Upper Sch.; Christ's College, Cambridge (MA). Served War 1940–46, RAC; seconded Indian Armoured Corps, 1942; Asst Political Agent II in Mekran, 1945. British Council Service, Baghdad and Mosul, Iraq, 1947–51; Isfahan, Iran, 1951–52; British Council Representative: Tanzania, 1952–57; Sudan, 1957–62; Dir, Overseas Students Dept, 1962–66; Representative: Jordan, 1966–69; Iraq, 1969–74; Canada, 1974–79, and Counsellor, Cultural Affairs, British High Commission, Ottawa. Mem. Council, British Sch. of Archaeology in Iraq, 1980–86. Hon. Sec., Sussex Heritage Trust, 1980–83; Chm., Sussex Eastern Sub-Area, 1981–85, Sussex Area, 1985–92, RSCM. Organist: St Mary's Church, Battle, 1986–99; St Laurence Ch, Guestling, 2001–06. *Recreations:* archaeology, music. *Died 1 Nov. 2010.*

SQUIRE, Rachel Anne; MP (Lab) Dunfermline and Fife West, since 2005 (Dunfermline West, 1992–2005); *b* 13 July 1954; *d* of Louise Anne Squire (*née* Binder) and step *d* of Percy Garfield Squire; *m* 1984, Allan Lee Mason. *Educ:* Godolphin and Latymer Girls' Sch.; Durham Univ. (BA Hons); Birmingham Univ. (CQSW). Social worker, Birmingham, 1975–81; trade union officer, 1981–92. *Recreations:* reading, cooking, archaeology. *Address:* (office) Music Hall Lane, Dunfermline, Fife KY12 7NG. *T:* (01383) 622889, *Fax:* (01383) 623500. *Died 5 Jan. 2006.*

SRISKANDAN, Kanagaretnam, CEng, FICE, FIStructE, FCIHT; Divisional Director, Mott, MacDonald Group (formerly Mott, Hay and Anderson), Consulting Engineers, 1988–93; consultant in highway and bridge engineering, 1993–2000; *b* 12 Aug. 1930; *s* of Kathiravelu Kanagaretnam and Kanmanyammal Kumaraswamy; *m* 1956, Dorothy (*née* Harley); two *s* one *d*. *Educ:* Royal College, Colombo; Univ. of Ceylon. BSc Hons London 1952. Junior Asst Engineer, PWD, Ceylon, 1953; Asst Engr, Sir William Halcrow and Partners, Cons. Engrs, London, 1956; Section Engr, Tarmac Civil Engineering Ltd, 1958; Asst Engr, West Riding of Yorkshire CC, 1959, left as Principal Engr; Department of Transport: Superintending Engr, Midland Road Construction Unit, 1968; Asst Chief Engr, 1971; Deputy Chief Highway Engr, 1976; Chief Highway Engr, 1980–87. *Publications:* papers on various engrg topics. *Recreation:* golf. *Died 21 April 2010.*

STACK, (Ann) Prunella, (Mrs Brian St Quentin Power), OBE 1980; President, The Fitness League (formerly Women's League of Health and Beauty), since 1982 (Member of Council, since 1950); *b* 28 July 1914; *d* of Capt. Hugh Bagot Stack, 8th Ghurka Rifles, and Mary Meta Bagot Stack, Founder of The Women's League of Health and Beauty; *m* 1st, 1938, Lord David Douglas-Hamilton (*d* 1944); two *s*; 2nd, 1950, Alfred G. Albers, FRCS (*d* 1951), Cape Town, S Africa; 3rd, 1964, Brian St Quentin Power (*d* 2008). *Educ:* The Abbey, Malvern Wells. Mem. of the National Fitness Council, 1937–39. Vice-Pres., Outward Bound Trust, 1980–. *Publications:* The Way to Health and Beauty, 1938; Movement is Life, 1973; Island Quest, 1979; Zest for Life, 1988; Style for Life, 1990; If I Were to Tell

You (poems), 1994; Then and Now (poems), 2003. *Recreations:* poetry, music, travel. *Address:* 14 Gertrude Street, SW10 0JN. *Died 30 Dec. 2010.*

STALLARD, Baron *cr* 1983 (Life Peer), of St Pancras in the London Borough of Camden; **Albert William Stallard;** *b* 5 Nov. 1921; *m* 1944, Sheila (*d* 2004), *d* of W. C. Murphy; one *s* one *d*. *Educ:* Low Waters Public School; Hamilton Academy, Scotland. Engineer, 1937–65; Technical Training Officer, 1965–70. Councillor, St Pancras, 1953–59, Alderman, 1962–65; Councillor, Camden, 1965–70, Alderman, 1971–78. MP (Lab) St Pancras N, 1970–83; PPS to: Minister of State, Agriculture, Fisheries and Food, 1974; Minister of State for Housing and Construction, 1974–76; an Asst Govt Whip, 1976–78; a Lord Comr, HM Treasury, 1978–79. Chairman: Camden Town Disablement Cttee (Mem., 1951); Camden Assoc. for Mental Health. Mem., Inst. of Training Officers, 1971. AEU Order of Merit, 1968. *Died 29 March 2008.*

STANBURY, Richard Vivian Macaulay; HM Diplomatic Service, retired; *b* 5 Feb. 1916; *s* of late Gilbert Vivian Stanbury and Doris Marguerite (*née* Smythe); *m* 1953, Geraldine Anne, *d* of late R. F. W. Grant and Winifred Helen Grant; one *s* one *d*. *Educ:* Shrewsbury Sch. (exhibnr); Magdalene Coll., Cambridge (exhibnr, 1st cl. Hons in Classical Tripos). Sudan Political Service, 1937–50 (District Comr in 12 districts, and Magistrate); HM Foreign (subseq. Diplomatic) Service, 1951–71: 2nd Sec., Cairo, 1951; FO 1954; Bahrain, Persian Gulf, 1956; FO 1959; Counsellor, Buenos Aires, 1968. Peach farm in Portugal, 1971–80. *Recreations:* golf, writing, watching cricket (played for Somerset), poetry. *Address:* Shepherds House, Peasmarsh, near Rye, East Sussex TN31 6TF. *Clubs:* Royal Over-Seas League; Hawks (Cambridge); Rye Golf; Hurlingham (Buenos Aires). *Died 29 June 2008.*

STANIER, Field Marshal Sir John (Wilfred), GCB 1982 (KCB 1978); MBE 1961; DL; Constable, HM Tower of London, 1990–96; *b* 6 Oct. 1925; *s* of late Harold Allan Stanier and Penelope Rose Stanier (*née* Price); *m* 1955, Cicely Constance Lambert; four *d*. *Educ:* Marlborough Coll.; Merton Coll., Oxford. FRGS. Commd in 7th Queen's Own Hussars, 1946; served in N Italy, Germany and Hong Kong; comd Royal Scots Greys, 1966–68; comd 20th Armd Bde, 1969–70; GOC 1st Div., 1973–75; Comdt, Staff Coll., Camberley, 1975–78; Vice Chief of the General Staff, 1978–80; C-in-C, UKLF, 1981–82; CGS, 1982–85. ADC General to the Queen, 1981–85. Col, The Royal Scots Dragoon Guards, 1979–84; Col Comdt, RAC, 1982–85. Chm., RUSI, 1986–89. Pres., Hampshire Br., British Red Cross Soc., 1986–94. Mem. Council, Marlborough Coll., 1984–96. DL Hampshire, 1987. *Publications:* (jtly) War and the Media, 1997. *Recreations:* fishing, sailing, talking. *Address:* The Old Farmhouse, Hazeley Bottom, Hartley Wintney, Hook, Hants RG27 8LU; *e-mail:* johnw.stanier@virgin.net. *Club:* Cavalry and Guards. *Died 10 Nov. 2007.*

STANLEY, Derek Peter; His Honour Judge Stanley; a Circuit Judge, since 1994; *b* 7 Aug. 1947; *s* of Peter Stanley and Vera Stanley (*née* Sterry-Cooper); *m* 1971, Gabrielle Mary Tully; one *s* two *d*. *Educ:* Solihull Sch.; Inns of Court Sch. of Law. Called to the Bar, Gray's Inn, 1968; practised on Midland and Oxford Circuit, 1969–94; a Recorder, 1988–94. Member: Bar Council, 1989–91; Cttee, Council of Circuit Judges, 1999–. Chm., W Midlands Criminal Justice Strategy Cttee, 2001–03. *Recreations:* tennis, sailing, church music. *Address:* Birmingham Crown Court, Newton Street, Birmingham B4 7NA. *T:* (0121) 681 3300. *Died 9 Oct. 2006.*

STANTON, Prof. Graham Norman, PhD; Lady Margaret's Professor of Divinity, 1998–2007, then Emeritus, and Chairman, Faculty Board of Divinity, 2001–03, University of Cambridge; Fellow of Fitzwilliam College, Cambridge, 1998–2007; *b* 9 July 1940; *s* of Norman Schofield Stanton and Gladys Jean Stanton (*née*

McGregor); *m* 1965, (Valerie) Esther Douglas, MA; two *s* one *d*. *Educ*: Univ. of Otago, NZ (BA 1960; MA 1961; BD 1964); Fitzwilliam Coll., Cambridge (PhD 1969). Temp. Lectr, Princeton Theological Seminary, 1969; Naden Res. Student, St John's Coll., Cambridge, 1969–70; King's College, London: Lectr in New Testament Studies, 1970–77; Prof. of New Testament Studies, 1977–98; Head of Department: Biblical Studies, 1982–88; Theology and Religious Studies, 1996–98. Gresham Prof. of Divinity, 1982–86. Humboldt Stiftung Res. Fellow, Tübingen, 1974; lectures on NT and Early Christianity, in Australia, NZ, Singapore, Ireland, Canada, Finland, Netherlands, Switzerland, Belgium, Israel, US and UK. Chm., British SNTS, 1989–92; Pres., SNTS, 1996–97 (Sec., 1976–82). FKC 1996. Hon. DD Otago, 2000. Burkitt Medal for Biblical Studies, British Acad., 2006. Editor: New Testament Studies, 1982–90; SNTS Monograph Series, 1982–91; Gen. Editor, International Critical Commentaries, 1984–2008. *Publications*: Jesus of Nazareth in New Testament Preaching, 1974, repr. 2004; (ed) The Interpretation of Matthew, 1983, 2nd edn 1994; The Gospels and Jesus, 1989 (trans. Japanese and Korean), 3rd edn 2010; A Gospel for a New People: studies in Matthew, 1992; (ed jtly) Resurrection, 1994; Gospel Truth? new light on Jesus and the Gospels, 1995 (trans. French, Dutch, Italian and Spanish); (ed jtly) Tolerance and Intolerance in Early Judaism and Christianity, 1998; (ed jtly) Reading Texts, Seeking Wisdom: scripture and theology, 2003; (jtly) Lady Margaret Beaufort and her Professors of Divinity at Cambridge, 2003; Jesus and Gospel, 2004 (trans. French, Italian and Spanish); (ed jtly) The Holy Spirit and Christian Origins, 2004; *festschrift*: The Written Gospel, ed M. Bockmuehl and D. A. Hagner, 2005; contrib. learned jls and symposia in UK, Europe and USA. *Recreations*: music, cricket, gardening. *Address*: 11 Dane Drive, Cambridge CB3 9LP. *T*: (01223) 740560; *e-mail*: gns23@cam.ac.uk. *Died 18 July 2009.*

STAPLE, Rev. David, OBE 1995; General Secretary, 1986–96, General Secretary Emeritus, 1996–2002, Free Church Federal Council; *b* 30 March 1930; *s* of William Hill Staple and Elsie Staple; *m* 1955, Margaret Lilian Berrington; one *s* three *d*. *Educ*: Watford Boys' Grammar Sch.; Christ's Coll., Cambridge (MA); Regent's Park Coll., Oxford; Wadham Coll., Oxford (MA); BD London (external). Baptist Minister: West Ham Central Mission, 1955–58; Llanishen, Cardiff, 1958–74; College Road, Harrow, 1974–86. Chm., Baptist Missionary Soc., 1981–82; Mem. Council, Baptist Union of GB, 1970–96 (Ecumenical Rep. to Gen. Synod of C of E, 1995–2001). Co-Pres., CCBI, 1995–99; Mem. Exec., CCJ, 1986–98. Life Mem. of Council, Regent's Park Coll., Oxford, 2004 (Gov., 1965–2002); Gov., Westhill Coll., Birmingham, 1986–96. *Recreation*: music. *Address*: 1 Althorp Road, St Albans, Herts AL1 3PH. *T*: (01727) 810009, *Fax*: (01727) 867888. *Died 26 Sept. 2007.*

STARK, Sir Andrew (Alexander Steel), KCMG 1975 (CMG 1964); CVO 1965; DL; HM Diplomatic Service, retired; Director, The Maersk Co., 1978–90 (Chairman, 1978–87); Adviser on European Affairs, Society of Motor Manufacturers and Traders, 1977–89; *b* 30 Dec. 1916; *yr s* of late Thomas Bow Stark and Barbara Black Stark (*née* Steel), Fauldhouse, West Lothian; *m* 1944, Helen Rosemary, *er d* Lt-Col J. Oxley Parker, TD, and Mary Monica (*née* Hills); two *s* (and one *s* decd). *Educ*: Bathgate Acad.; Edinburgh Univ. (MA (Hons) Eng. Lit. 1938). Served War of 1939–45, Green Howards and Staff appts. Major 1945. Entered Foreign Service, 1948, and served in Foreign Office until 1950; 1st Secretary, Vienna, 1951–53; Asst Private Sec. to Foreign Secretary, 1953–55; Head of Chancery: Belgrade, 1956–58; Rome, 1958–60; Counsellor: FO, 1960–64; Bonn, 1964–68; attached to Mission to UN with rank of Ambassador, Jan. 1968; British Mem., Seven Nation Cttee on Reorganisation of UN Secretariat; seconded to UN, NY, as Under-Secretary-General, Oct. 1968–1971; HM Ambassador to Denmark, 1971–76; Dep. Under-Sec. of State, FCO, 1976–78. Director: Scandinavian Bank Ltd, 1978–88;

Carlsberg Brewery Ltd, 1980–87. Mem., CBI Europe Cttee, 1980–85. Chairman: Anglo-Danish Soc., 1983–95 (Hon. Pres., 1995–2005); Anglo-Danish Trade Adv. Bd, 1983–93. President: British Assoc. of Former UN Civil Servants, 1989–94; Essex Disabled People's (formerly Essex Physically Handicapped) Assoc., 1979–99; Chm., Rural Community Council of Essex, 1990–93. DL Essex, 1981. University of Essex: Mem. Council, 1978–2005 (Chm. Council, 1983–89); Pro-Chancellor, 1983–95; DU 1990. Grosses Verdienstkreuz, German Federal Republic, 1965; Grand Cross, Order of the Dannebrog, Denmark, 1974. *Address*: Fambridge Hall, White Notley, Witham, Essex CM8 1RN. *T*: (01376) 583117. *Club*: Travellers (Chm., 1978–81). *Died 3 April 2006.*

STAVELEY, Sir John (Malfroy), KBE 1980 (OBE 1972); MC 1941; FRCP; FRACPath; Haematologist, Auckland Hospital Board, 1950–64; Director, Auckland Blood Transfusion Service, 1965–76; *b* 30 Aug. 1914; *s* of William Staveley and Annie May Staveley (*née* Malfroy); *m* 1940, Elvira Cliafe Wycherley (*d* 1992); one *s* one *d*. *Educ*: Univ. of Otago, Dunedin (MB ChB); Univ. of Edinburgh. FRCP 1958; FRACPath 1965. House Surgeon, Auckland Hosp., 1939; war service with 2NZEF, Middle East, 1940–45; post graduate educn, UK, 1946–47; Pathologist, Auckland Hosp., 1948–50. Landsteiner Award, USA, for medical research, 1980. *Publications*: papers in medical and scientific jls (British, American and NZ). *Recreations*: mountaineering, fishing, music. *Address*: 11 Matanui Street, Northcote, Auckland 9, New Zealand. *Died 14 May 2006.*

STEAD, Rev. Canon (George) Christopher, LittD; FBA 1980; Fellow, King's College, Cambridge, 1938–49 and 1971–85 (Professorial Fellow, 1971–80); Emeritus Fellow, Keble College, Oxford, since 1981; *b* 9 April 1913; *s* of Francis Bernard Stead, CBE, and Rachel Elizabeth, *d* of Rev. Canon G. C. Bell; *m* 1958, (Doris) Elizabeth Odom; two *s* one *d*. *Educ*: Marlborough Coll.; King's Coll., Cambridge (scholar). 1st cl. Classical Tripos Pt I, 1933; Pitt Scholar, 1934; 1st cl. Moral Science Tripos Pt II, 1935; BA 1935, MA 1938, LittD Cantab 1978; New Coll., Oxford (BA 1935); Cuddesdon Coll., Oxford, 1938. Ordained, 1938; Curate, St John's, Newcastle upon Tyne, 1939; Lectr in Divinity, King's Coll., Cambridge, 1938–49; Asst Master, Eton Coll., 1940–44; Fellow and Chaplain, Keble Coll., Oxford, 1949–71 (MA Oxon 1949); Ely Professor of Divinity, Cambridge, and Canon Residentiary of Ely Cathedral, 1971–80, Canon Emeritus, 1981. *Publications*: Divine Substance, 1977; Substance and Illusion in the Christian Fathers, 1985; Philosophie und Theologie I, 1990; Philosophy in Christian Antiquity, 1994 (trans. Portuguese, 1999, Hungarian, 2002); Doctrine and Philosophy in Early Christianity: Arius, Athanasius, Augustine, 2000; The Birth of the Steam Locomotive, 2002; contributor to: Faith and Logic, 1957; New Testament Apocrypha, 1965; A New Dictionary of Christian Theology, 1983; Dizionario di Patristica, 1983; Theologische Realenzyklopädie, vol. 13 1985, vol. 21 1991; Augustinus-Lexikon, 1986–93; Reallexikon für Antike und Christentum, 1992; Dictionnaire Critique de Théologie, 1998; Routledge Encyclopedia of Philosophy, 1998; about 30 major articles in Jl of Theol Studies, Vigiliae Christianae, and various Festschriften; *Festschriften*: Christian Faith and Greek Philosophy in Late Antiquity, 1993; A Voice in the Octagon, Ely Cathedral, 2007. *Recreations*: walking, sailing, music, industrial archaeology. *Address*: 9 Bishop Laney Drive, Ely, Cambs CB6 1BZ. *Died 28 May 2008.*

STEELE, Dr Bernard Robert; Development and Property Director (formerly Property Secretary), Methodist Homes for the Aged, 1987–91; *b* 21 July 1929; *s* of late Robert Walter and Phyllis Mabel Steele; *m* 1953, Dorothy Anne Newman; one *s* two *d*. *Educ*: Oakham Sch.; Selwyn Coll., Cambridge (MA, PhD). Scientific Officer, Min. of Supply, 1953–55; Section Leader, UKAEA, Springfields, 1955–66; Building Research Station: Head, Materials Div., 1966–69; Asst Dir,

1969–72; Dep. Dir, Building Res. Estabt, 1972–75; Borough Housing Officer, Haringey, 1975–78; Dir, Science and Research Policy, DoE, 1978–82; Head, Housing Services, GLC, 1982–86. Vis. Prof., Bartlett Sch. of Architecture and Planning, UCL, 1987–89. Chm., Environment Cttee, SRC, later SERC, 1978–81. Pres., RILEM (Internat. Union of Testing and Res. Labs for Materials and Structures), 1974–75. Chm., Watford Churches Housing Assoc., 1975–78. *Publications:* contrib. numerous scientific publications on chemistry, materials science and building. *Recreations:* travelling, photography. *Address:* 1 Broom Grove, Watford WD17 4RY. *T:* (01923) 447584. *Died 15 Aug. 2010.*

STEELE, Kenneth Walter Lawrence, CBE 1980 (OBE 1967); KPM 1936; Chief Constable, Avon and Somerset Constabulary, 1974–79; *b* 28 July 1914; *s* of Walter and Susan Steele, Godalming, Surrey; *m* 1940, Ursula Biggs Davison (marr. diss.); *m* 1987, Irene Koh, Malaysia. *Educ:* Wellington Sch., Wellington, Somerset. Served War: with Somerset LI and Royal Northumberland Fusiliers, 1942–45. Asst Chief Constable, Buckinghamshire, 1953–55; Chief Constable: Somerset, 1955–66; Somerset and Bath, 1966–74. *Address:* Lloyds TSB, 31 Fore Street, Taunton, Somerset TA1 1HN. *Died 14 April 2008.*

STEELE-BODGER, Prof. Alasdair, CBE 1980; FRCVS; FRAgS, FRASE; freelance consultant in forensic veterinary medicine; Professor of Veterinary Clinical Studies, University of Cambridge, 1979–90; *b* 1 Jan. 1924; *s* of late Harry Steele-Bodger, MRCVS, and Mrs K. Steele-Bodger (*née* MacDonald); *m* 1948, Anne, 2nd *d* of late Captain A. W. J. Finlayson, RN, and Mrs Nancy Finlayson; three *d. Educ:* Shrewsbury Sch.; Caius Coll., Cambridge (BA 1945, MA); Royal 'Dick' Veterinary Coll., Edinburgh Univ. (BSc, MRCVS 1948). Hon. FRCVS 1975; Scientific FZS 1989. Gen. vet. practice, Lichfield, Staffs, 1948–77; consultant practice, Fordingbridge, Hants, 1977–79. Hon. Vet. Consultant to British Agricl Export Council, 1967–88. Vis. Prof., Univ. of Toronto, 1973. Pres., British Small Animal Vet. Assoc., 1962; Member: Horserace Scientific Adv. Cttee (formerly Jockey Club's Horserace Anti-Doping Cttee), 1973–92; UGC's Agricl and Vet. Sub-Cttee, 1973–81; Council: BVA, 1957–85 (Pres., 1966; Hon. Mem., 1985); RCVS, 1960–90 (Pres., 1972); Jt RCVS/BVA Cttee on Eur. Vet. Affairs, 1967–90; Eur. Liaison Gp for Agriculture, 1972–90; Cttee of Inquiry on Experiments on Animals, 1963–65; Council, RASE, 1967–98 (Hon. Fellow, 1993; Hon. Vice-Pres., 1996); Animal Feedingstuffs Industry/BVA/ADAS HQ Liaison Cttee, 1967–85. UK Deleg. to Fedn of Veterinarians of EEC, 1967–90; EEC Official Vet. Expert, 1974–98; Member: EEC Adv. Cttee on Vet. Trng, 1981–90; Home Office Panel of Assessors under Animals (Scientific Procedures) Act, 1986–98. Vice-Pres., Inst. of Animal Technology, 1988–2000. Dir, B & K Universal Ltd (formerly Bantin & Kingman Ltd), 1980–2000. Hon. Vet. Consultant, Nat. Cattle Breeders' Assoc., 1979–99. Mem. Bd of Advisers, Univ. of London, 1984–98. Gov., Cambs Coll. of Agric. and Hort., 1989–90. Gen. Comr to Bd of Inland Revenue, 1969–81. Chairman: Editorial Bd, Veterinary Times (formerly Veterinary Drug), 1978–88; Adv. Bd, British Veterinary Formulary, 1987–96. Ehrenbürger, Tierärztlich Hochschule, Hannover, 1992. FRASE 1986; ARAgS 1996, FRAgS 1998. Crookes' Prize, 1970; Dalrymple-Champneys Cup and Medal, 1972. Cambridge Triple Blue. *Publications:* Society of Practising Veterinary Surgeons Economics Report, 1961, and papers in vet. jls on clinical subjects and vet. econs. *Recreations:* swimming, travel. *Address:* The Little Rectory, Grosmont, Monmouth, Wales NP7 8LW. *Clubs:* Farmers'; Hawks (Cambridge). *Died 17 Sept. 2008.*

STEER, Kenneth Arthur, CBE 1978; MA, PhD, FSA, FSAScot; Secretary, Royal Commission on the Ancient and Historical Monuments of Scotland, 1957–78; *b* 12 Nov. 1913; *o s* of Harold Steer and Emily Florence Thompson; *m* 1st, 1941, Rona Mary Mitchell (*d* 1983); one *d*; 2nd, 1985, Eileen Alice Nelson (*d* 1999). *Educ:*

Wath Grammar School; Durham University. Research Fellowship, 1936–38. Joined staff of Royal Commission on Ancient and Historical Monuments of Scotland, 1938. Intelligence Officer in Army, 1941–45 (despatches twice). Monuments, Fine Arts and Archives Officer, North Rhine Region, 1945–46. Corresponding Member, German Archæological Inst.; Horsley Memorial Lectr, Durham University, 1963; Rhind Lectr, Edinburgh, 1968. Pres., Soc. of Antiquaries of Scotland, 1972–75. Arts Council Literary Award, 1978. *Publications:* Late Medieval Monumental Sculpture in the West Highlands (with J. W. M. Bannerman), 1976; numerous articles in archæological journals. *Address:* 2 Morningside Courtyard, Idsall Drive, Prestbury, Cheltenham, Glos GL52 3BU. *Died 20 Feb. 2007.*

STEINBERG, Baron *cr* 2004 (Life Peer), of Belfast in the County of Antrim; **Leonard Steinberg;** Founding Chairman, Stanley Leisure plc (formerly L. Stanley), 1958–2006, then Life President; *b* 1 Aug. 1936; *m* 1962, Beryl Cobden; one *s* one *d. Educ:* Royal Belfast Academical Inst. Founded L. Stanley, Belfast, 1958; expanded group by acquisition of betting shops and casinos, incl. Mecca chain, 1989; Chairman: Stanley Casinos Ltd; Stanley Racing Ltd. Dep. Treas., Cons. Party, 1994–2002. *Address:* Stanley Leisure plc, Stanley House, 151 Dale Street, Liverpool L2 2JW. *Died 2 Nov. 2009.*

STENHAM, Anthony William Paul, (Cob); Chairman: Telewest Global Inc., since 2004 (Chairman, 1999–2004, Deputy Chairman, 1994–99, Telewest Communications plc); Ashtead Group, since 2004; Deputy Chairman, NTL Inc., since 2005; *b* 28 Jan. 1932; *s* of Bernard Basil Stenham and Annie Josephine (*née* Naylor); *m* 1st, 1966, Hon. Sheila Marion Poole (marr. diss.); 2nd, 1983, Anne Martha Mary O'Rawe (marr. diss.); two *d. Educ:* Eton Coll.; Trinity Coll., Cambridge (MA). Qualified Accountant FCA 1958–98. Mem., Inner Temple, 1955. Price Waterhouse, 1955–61; Philip Hill Higginson Erlanger, 1962–64; William Baird & Co., 1964–69: Finance Dir and Jt Man. Dir; Unilever, 1969–86: Financial Dir, 1970–86, Corporate Develt Dir, 1984–86, Unilever PLC and Unilever NV; Chm., Unilever United States Inc., 1978–79; a Man. Dir, Bankers Trust Co. of NY, 1986–90 (Chm., Bankers Trust UK and Europe); Chm., Wiggins Teape Appleton, subseq. Arjo Wiggins Appleton plc, 1990–97. Director: Equity Capital for Industry, 1976–81; Capital Radio, 1982–94; Virgin Gp, 1986–89; Rank Organisation, subseq. Rank Gp, 1987–2000; VSEL plc, 1987–95 (Dep. Chm., 1989–); Rothmans Internat., 1988–99; Unigate, 1989–98; STC, 1990–91; Arjomari Prioux, 1990–93; Colonial Mutual Gp (UK Hldgs), 1987–92; Standard Chartered, 1991–2003; Worms et Cie, 1991–96; Trafalgar House, 1993–96; Jarrold & Sons Ltd, 1997–2003; Hawkpoint Partners, 1999–2002; Hebridean Cruises plc (formerly Altanamara Shipping), 1999–2004; Proudfoot Consulting plc (formerly The Consulting Gp), 2000–; Chairman: Darfield Investments Ltd, 1997–; Whatsonwhen, 2000–; IFonline, 2000–. Sen. Industrialist Advr to DG of Water Services, 1998–2002. Institute of Contemporary Arts: Chm. Council, 1977–87; Chm., Adv. Bd, 1987–89; Dir, Adv. Bd, Roundhouse Trust, 2001–; Mem. Council, Architectural Assoc., 1982–84; Royal Coll. of Art: Mem. Court, 1978–; Mem. Council, 1978–81; Chm. Council and Pro-Provost, 1979–81; Hon. Fellow, 1980. Governor: Museum of London, 1986–92; Theatres Trust, 1989–96. Trustee, Design Mus., 1992–96. FRCA 1958; FRSA. *Recreations:* cinema, opera, painting. *Address:* Telewest Global Inc., 160 Great Portland Street, W1W 5QA. *T:* (020) 7299 5562, *Fax:* (020) 7299 5495; *e-mail:* cob_stenham@flextech.co.uk; 4 The Grove, Highgate, N6 6JU. *T:* (020) 8340 2266, *Fax:* (020) 8341 7987. *Clubs:* White's, Beefsteak. *Died 22 Oct. 2006.*

STERN, Linda Joy; QC 1991; **Her Honour Judge Stern;** a Circuit Judge, since 2001; *b* 21 Dec. 1941; *d* of late Mrs L. R. Saville; *m* 1st, 1961, Michael Brian Rose (decd); two *s*; 2nd, 1978, Nigel Maurice Stern. *Educ:* St

Paul's Girls' Sch. Called to the Bar, Gray's Inn, 1971. A Recorder, 1990–2001. FRSA 1993. *Recreations:* music, theatre, reading, travel. *Address:* The Law Courts, Lordship Lane. Wood Green, N22 5LF. *Died 7 Sept. 2006.*

STEVENS, Prof. Kenneth William Harry; Professor of Theoretical Physics, 1958–87, then Emeritus, and Senior Research Fellow, 1987–88, University of Nottingham; *b* 17 Sept. 1922; *s* of Harry and Rose Stevens; *m* 1949, Audrey A. Gawthrop; one *s* one *d. Educ:* Magdalen College School, Oxford; Jesus and Merton Colleges, Oxford. MA 1947, DPhil 1949. Pressed Steel Company Ltd Research Fellow, Oxford University, 1949–53; Research Fellow, Harvard University, 1953–54, Reader in Theoretical Physics, University of Nottingham, 1953–58. Leverhulme Emeritus Fellow, 1990. Mem., IUPAP Commn on Magnetism, 1984–87. (Jtly) Maxwell Medal and Prize, 1968. *Publications:* Magnetic Ions in Crystals, 1997; contrib. to learned journals. *Recreations:* music, tennis, walking. *Address:* The University, Nottingham NG7 2RD. *Died 16 July 2010.*

STEVENS, Sir Laurence (Houghton), Kt 1983; CBE 1979; company director and business consultant; Chairman Emeritus, Sir George Elliot Charitable Trust; *b* 9 Jan. 1920; *s* of Laurence Stevens and Annie (*née* Houghton); *m* 1943, Beryl J. Dickson; one *s* two *d. Educ:* Auckland Boys' Grammar Sch.; Auckland Univ. (BCom). FCA NZ 1969; CMA 1966. Served War, Pacific (Tonga Defence Force) and ME (2NZEF). Joined Auckland Knitting Mills Ltd, 1946; Man. Dir., 1952; retd 1980. Chairman: Thorn EMI Gp of Cos, NZ, 1980–93; Chambard Property Develt (formerly Les Mills Corporation) Ltd, 1985–91; Fay Richwhite & Co. (formerly Capital Markets Ltd), 1986–96; Ascent Corp. Ltd, 1986–88; Auckland Internat. Airport Ltd, 1988–96 (Dir, 1988–98); Marker Ltd, 1990; CMI Screws & Fasteners Ltd, 1992–97; Hawk Packaging Ltd, 1993–98 (Dir, 1998–2000); Director: Guardian Royal Exchange, 1983–90; Wormald International NZ Ltd, 1983–90; Reserve Bank of New Zealand, 1978–86; Petroleum Corp. of New Zealand Ltd, 1984–88; R. W. Saunders Ltd, 1984–87; Petralgas Chemicals NZ Ltd, 1986–87; Wormald Pacific Ltd, 1987–90. Past President and Life Member: NZ Knitting Industries Fedn; Textile and Garment Fedn of NZ; Auckland Manufrs' Assoc.; Pres., NZ Manufrs' Fedn, 1970–71 and 1980–81; Chm., Auckland Agricl, Pastoral and Indust. Shows Bd, 1976–86; Mem., Melanesian Trust Bd, 1977–93. Laureate, NZ Business Hall of Fame, 1999. *Recreation:* tennis (Pres., Auckland Lawn Tennis Assoc., 1983–84). *Address:* Apt S508, Grace Joel Retirement Village, 184 St Heliers Bay Road, St Heliers, Auckland 5, New Zealand. *T:* (9) 5755682. *Club:* Northern (Auckland). *Died 28 Sept. 2006.*

STEVENSON, Dr Jim; Chief Executive, Educational Broadcasting Services Trust, since 1988; *b* 9 May 1937; *s* of George Stevenson and Frances Mildred Groat; *m* 1963, Brenda Cooley; one *s* one *d. Educ:* Kirkham Grammar Sch.; Univ. of Liverpool (BSc, PhD). NATO Res. Fellow, Univ. of Trondheim, 1963–65; Lectr in Biochemistry, Univ. of Warwick, 1965–69; BBC Open Univ. Production Centre: Producer, 1969–75; Exec. Producer, 1975–76; Editor (Science), 1976–79; Head of Programmes, 1979–82; Dep. Sec., BBC, 1982–83; Head of Educnl Broadcasting Services and Educn Sec., BBC, 1983–89. *Publications:* contribs to sci. jls and communications jls. *Recreations:* television, history. *Address:* 34 Vallance Road, N22 7UB. *T:* (020) 8889 6261. *Died 25 Feb. 2007.*

STEVENSON, John, CBE 1987; Deputy Licensing Authority: South East Traffic Area, 1987–95; Metropolitan Traffic Area, 1989–95; Eastern Traffic Area, 1990–95; Western Traffic Area, 1991–95; *b* 15 June 1927; *s* of John and Harriet Esther Stevenson; *m* 1956, Kathleen Petch; one *s* one *d. Educ:* Durham Univ. (LLB); MA Oxon 1982. Solicitor. Legal Asst, Borough of Hartlepool, 1951; Junior Solicitor, County Borough

of Sunderland, 1952; Solicitor, Hertfordshire CC, 1953. Asst Clerk, 1964; Clerk of the Peace and County Solicitor, Gloucestershire CC, 1969; Chief Executive. Buckinghamshire CC, 1974; Sec., ACC, 1980–87. Hon. Fellow, Inst. Local Govt Studies, Birmingham Univ., 1981–; Vis. Fellow, Nuffield Coll., Oxford, 1982–90. Vice President, Inst. of Trading Standards Administration, 1988. *Address:* Mark Two, Abbots Worthy, Winchester, Hants SO21 1DR. *T:* (01962) 886766. *Died 20 April 2006.*

STEVENSON, William Trevor, CBE 1985; DL; Founder President, Elite association of companies, 1987; *b* 21 March 1921; *o s* of late William Houston Stevenson and Mabel Rose Stevenson (*née* Hunt); *m* 1948, Alison Wilson (*née* Roy). *Educ:* Edinburgh Acad. Apprentice mechanical engineer, 1937–41; engineer, 1941–45; entered family food manufacturing business, Cottage Rusks, 1945; Man. Dir, 1948–54; Chm., 1954–59; Chief Executive, Cottage Rusks Associates, (following merger with Joseph Rank Ltd), 1959–69; Reg. Dir., Ranks Hovis McDougall, 1969–74; Dir, various cos in food, engrg, medical, hotel and aviation industries, 1974–; Chairman: Gleneagles Hotels, 1981–83; Scottish Transport Gp, 1981–86; Hodgson Martin Ventures, 1982–98; Alexander Wilkie, 1977–90; Founder, Elite Gp of cos, 2000. Master, Co. of Merchants of City of Edinburgh, 1978–80. FCILT (FILT 1981). DL City of Edinburgh, 1984. *Recreations:* flying, sailing, curling. *Club:* Caledonian. *Died 22 April 2008.*

STEWART, Sir Edward (Jackson), Kt 1980; Chairman, Stewarts Hotels Pty Ltd, 1956–96; *b* 10 Dec. 1923; *s* of Charles Jackson Stewart and Jessie Stewart (*née* Dobbie); *m* 1956, Shirley Patricia Holmes; four *s. Educ:* St Joseph's College, Brisbane. Fellow Catering Inst. of Australia; FAIM. Served with Australian Army, RAA, 1942–44. Chairman: Castlemaine Perkins Ltd, 1977–80 (Dir, 1970); Castlemaine Tooheys Ltd, 1980–85; Director: Birch Carroll & Coyle Ltd, 1967–92; Roadshow (Qld) Pty Ltd, 1970–92; Darwin Cinemas Pty Ltd, 1972–92; G. R. E. (Australia) Ltd, 1980–92; Besser (Qld) Ltd, 1981–87; Bank of Queensland Ltd, 1986–96; QUF Industries Ltd, 1986–95. President: Queensland Hotels Assoc., 1963–69; Aust. Hotels Assoc., 1966–69. Mem. Totalisator Administration Bd of Queensland, 1977–81. Chm., Queensland Inst. of Medical Research Trust, 1980–88. *Recreations:* reading, fishing and thoroughbred breeding. *Address:* PO Box 88, Clayfield, Qld 4011, Australia. *Clubs:* Australian (Sydney); Brisbane, Tattersall's (Past Pres.) (Brisbane); Queensland Turf. *Died 24 Feb. 2006.*

STEWART, James Cecil Campbell, CBE 1960; consultant; *b* 25 July 1916; *s* of late James Stewart and Mary Campbell Stewart; *m* 1946, Pamela Rouselle, *d* of William King-Smith; one *d. Educ:* Armstrong College and King's College, Durham University (BSc Physics). Telecommunications Research Establishment, 1939–46; Atomic Energy Research Establishment, Harwell, 1946–49; Industrial Group, UKAEA, 1949–63; Dep. Chm., British Nuclear Design and Construction, 1969–75; Member: UKAEA, 1963–69; Central Electricity Generating Bd, 1965–69; Dep. Chm., Nuclear Power Co. Ltd, 1975–80; Dir, National Nuclear Corp. Ltd, 1980–82. Chairman: British Nuclear Forum, 1974–92; Nuclear Power Co. Pension Trustee Ltd, 1979–92. Consultant, Internat. Adv. Cttee Concord, Denver, 1986–94. *Recreation:* tending a garden. *Address:* White Thorns, Higher Whitley, Cheshire WA4 4QJ. *T:* (01925) 730377. *Clubs:* East India, Devonshire, Sports and Public Schools; Les Ambassadeurs. *Died 22 May 2008.*

STEWART, Hon. Kevin James, AO 1989; *b* 20 Sept. 1928; *m* 1952, Jean, *d* of late F. I. Keating; two *s* five *d. Educ:* Christian Brothers School, Lewisham, NSW; De La Salle College, NSW. Officer, NSW Govt Rlys, 1944–62 (Regional Pres., Aust. Transport Officers' Assoc. and Fedn, 1959–62). MLA for Canterbury, NSW, 1962–85; Exec., NSW Parly Labor Party and Spokesman on Health

Matters, 1967; NSW State Exec., Aust. Labor Party, 1968; Minister, NSW: for Health, 1976–81; for Youth and Community Services, 1981–83; for Mineral Resources, 1983–84; for Local Govt, 1984–85. Mem., Labor Transport Cttee, 1965–76; Chm., Labor Health Cttee, 1968–76; Mem., Jt Cttee, Legislative Council upon Drugs. Agent General for NSW in UK, 1986–88. Vice-Chm., Federal Govt Sydney Area Consultant Cttee, 1993–. Life Mem., British-Australia Soc., 1988. Chm., Bd of Canterbury Hosp., 1955–76 (Dir, 1954). FRSA 1988. Freeman, City of London, 1987. Hon. Citizen of Tokyo, Japan, 1985. *Recreations:* supporter of community services, Rugby Football League, swimming, bowls. *Address:* 44 Chalmers Street, Belmore, NSW 2192, Australia. *T:* (2) 97597777. *Club:* Bulldogs League (Pres., 2002–) (Sydney). *Died 22 Aug. 2006.*

STEWART, Sir Robertson (Huntly), Kt 1979; CBE 1970; CEng, FIProdE, FPRI, FNZIM, FInstD; Founder President: PDL Holdings Ltd (manufacturers of electrical and plastic products), since 1995 (Chairman and Managing Director, 1957–82; Executive Chairman, 1982–95); PDL (Asia), since 1995 (Executive Chairman, 1975–95); *b* 21 Sept. 1913; *s* of Robert McGregor Stewart and Ivy Emily (*née* Grigg); *m* 1st, 1937, Ada Gladys Gunter; two *s* one *d*; 2nd, 1970, Ellen Adrienne Cansdale (ONZM 2006, QSM, FInstD, FNZIM); two *s*. *Educ:* Christchurch Boys' High Sch.; Christchurch Technical Inst. CEng, FIET (FIProdE 1967); FPRI 1960; FNZIM 1962; FInstD 1970. Introd plastics industry to NZ, 1936; commenced manuf. of electrical products in NZ, 1937; estabd PDL Gp of Cos, 1947. Led NZ Trade Missions, 1962, 1964, 1966, 1967, 1970 and 1972. Pres., NZ Manufrs Fedn, 1963–64. Hon. DEng Canterbury, 1999. Hon. Malaysian Consul. Hon. JSM 1998. *Recreations:* motor racing, tennis, fishing. *Address:* 52 Wroxton Terrace, Fendalton, Christchurch 8014, New Zealand. *T:* (3) 3510660. *Club:* Canterbury (Christchurch). *Died 13 Aug. 2007.*

STEWART, Victor Colvin, FCA; Registrar General for Scotland, 1978–82; *b* 12 April 1921; *s* of Victor Stewart and Jean Cameron; *m* 1949, Aileen Laurie; one *s*. *Educ:* Selkirk High Sch.; Edinburgh Univ. (BCom). FCA 1954. Served War in RAF, Africa and ME, 1942–46. Joined Dept of Health for Scotland, 1938; Chief Exec. Officer, 1959; Principal, 1963, Asst Sec., 1971, SHHD; Dep. Registrar Gen. for Scotland, 1976. *Recreations:* golf, walking, reading. *Address:* Tynet, Lodgehill Road, Nairn IV12 4QL. *T:* (01667) 452050. *Club:* Royal Commonwealth Society. *Died 23 April 2006.*

STIBBS, Prof. Douglas Walter Noble, MSc Sydney, DPhil Oxon; FRAS; FRSE; Visiting Professor, Mathematical Sciences Institute, Centre for Mathematics and its Applications, 1990–2009, Hon. Librarian to the Institute, 1996–2008, and Visiting Fellow, 2005–09, Australian National University; *b* 17 Feb. 1919; 2nd *s* of Edward John Stibbs, Sydney, NSW; *m* 1949, Margaret Lilian Calvert, BSc, DipEd (Sydney), er *d* of Rev. John Calvert, Sydney, NSW; two *d*. *Educ:* Sydney High Sch.; Univ. of Sydney; New College, Oxford. Deas Thomson Scholar, Sch. of Physics, Univ. of Sydney, 1940; BSc (Sydney), 1st Class Hons, Univ. Medal in Physics, 1942; MSc (Sydney), 1943; DPhil (Oxon), 1954. Johnson Memorial Prize and Gold Medal for Advancement of Astronomy and Meteorology, Oxford Univ., 1956. Res. Asst, Commonwealth Solar Observatory, Canberra, ACT, 1940–42; Asst Lectr, Dept of Mathematics and Physics, New England University Coll., Armidale, NSW (later Univ. of New England), 1942–45; Scientific Officer and Sen. Scientific Officer, Commonwealth Observatory, Canberra, ACT, 1945–51; Radcliffe Travelling Fellow in Astronomy, Radcliffe Observatory, Pretoria, S Africa, and Univ. Observatory, Oxford, 1951–54; PSO, UKAEA, 1955–59; University of St Andrews: Napier Prof. of Astronomy, and Dir, Univ. Observatory, 1959–89; Sen. Prof. Senatus Academicus, 1987–89; Napier Prof. Emeritus, 1990–; Vis. Fellow, ANU Res. Sch. of Astronomy and Astrophysics, 1990–2005. Vis. Prof. of

Astrophysics, Yale Univ. Observatory, 1966–67; British Council Vis. Prof., Univ. of Utrecht, 1968; Prof., Collège de France, 1975–76 (Médaille du Collège, 1976). University College, London: External Expert (appts and promotions), 1970–74 and 1976–80; External Examr (BSc Astronomy), 1977–81. Member: Internat. Astronomical Union, 1951– (Chm. Finance Cttee, 1964–67, 1973–76, 1976–79); Amer. Astronomical Soc., 1956–73; Adv. Cttee on Meteorology for Scotland, 1960–69, 1972–75, 1978–80; Board of Visitors, Royal Greenwich Observatory, 1963–65; Council RAS, 1964–67, 1970–73 (Vice-Pres., 1972–73), Editorial Board, 1970–73; Council, RSE, 1970–72; National Cttee for Astronomy, 1964–76; SRC Cttees for Royal Greenwich Observatory, 1966–70, and Royal Observatory, Edinburgh, 1966–76, Chm., 1970–76; SRC Astronomy, Space and Radio Bd, 1970–76; SRC, 1972–76; S African Astron. Observatory Adv. Cttee, 1972–76; Chairman: Astronomy Policy and Grants Cttee, 1972–74; Northern Hemisphere Observatory Planning Cttee, 1972–75; Astronomy II Cttee, 1974–75; Mem., Centre National de la Recherche Scientifique Cttee, Obs. de Haute Provence, 1973–82. Life Member: Sydney Univ. Union, 1942; New Coll. Soc., 1953; New England Univ. Union, NSW, 1957. Mem., Western Province Masters Athletics Assoc., Cape Town, 1983–. Marathon Medals: Paris, Caithness, Edinburgh (3hrs 59mins), Flying Fox (British Veterans Championships), Honolulu, 1983; London, Loch Rannoch, Aberdeen (Veterans Trophy Winner), 1984; Stoke-on-Trent (Potteries), Athens, Honolulu, 1985; London, Edinburgh (Commonwealth Games Peoples Marathon), Stoke-on-Trent (Potteries), Berlin, Honolulu, 1986; Boston, 1987; Half-marathons: 13 events incl. Windsor Great Park, Dundee, Dunfermline, Wagga (Australian Veterans Games, 1991, Gold Medallist), Canberra. *Publications:* The Outer Layers of a Star (with Sir Richard Woolley), 1953; contrib. Theoretical Astrophysics and Astronomy in Monthly Notices of RAS and other jls. *Recreations:* music, ornithology, photography, golf, coaching (long-distance running). *Address:* Mathematical Sciences Institute, Australian National University, Canberra, ACT 0200, Australia. *Club:* Royal and Ancient (St Andrews). *Died 12 April 2010.*

STIRLING of Fairburn, Captain Sir Roderick William Kenneth, KCVO 2007; TD 1965; JP; Lord Lieutenant of Ross and Cromarty and Skye and Lochalsh, since 1988; *b* 17 June 1932; *s* of late Major Sir John Stirling, KT, MBE and Lady Marjory Kythé, *d* of Sir Kenneth Mackenzie, 7th Bt of Gairloch; *m* 1963, Penelope Jane Wright; four *d*. *Educ:* Wellesley House; Harrow. National Service, Scots Guards, 1950–52; commissioned 1951; TA Seaforth Highlanders and Queen's Own Highlanders (Seaforth and Cameron), 1953–69. Member: Ross and Cromarty County Council, 1970–74 (Chm. of Highways, 1973–74); Ross and Cromarty District Council, 1984–96. Mem., Red Deer Commn, 1984–89 (Vice-Chm., 1975–89); Chm., S Ross Deer Mgt Gp, 1997–2002; Director: Moray Firth Salmon Fishing Co., 1973–91; Scottish Salmon and Whitefish Co., 1972–91 (Chm., 1980–). Mem., Scottish Council, NPFA, 1971–91 (Chm., Highland Cttee); President: Ross and Cromarty CVS, 1990–95; Ross and Sutherland Scout Council, 1990–; Highlands, Islands and Moray Br., Scots Guards Assoc., 1994–; Jun. Vice-Pres., Scottish Accident Prevention Council, 1991–92. JP Ross and Cromarty, 1975. *Recreations:* stalking, shooting, fishing, gardening, curling. *Address:* Fearnach, Urray, Muir of Ord, Ross and Cromarty IV6 7QD. *T:* (01997) 433207. *Club:* New (Edinburgh). *Died 24 March 2007.*

STOATE, Isabel Dorothy; HM Diplomatic Service, retired; Counsellor, Foreign and Commonwealth Office, 1980–82; *b* 31 May 1927; *d* of late William Maurice Stoate and Dorothy Evelyn Stoate (*née* French). *Educ:* Talbot Heath Sch., Bournemouth; St Andrews Univ. Athlone Press, London Univ., 1950–52; joined HM Diplomatic Service, 1952; served Cyprus, Vienna, Buenos Aires, Tokyo, Athens, Rio de Janeiro and FCO,

1952–80. *Recreations:* travel, tapestry. *Address:* 177 Gloucester Street, Cirencester, Glos GL7 2DP.
Died 22 Sept. 2010.

STOCKHAUSEN, Karlheinz; composer and conductor; *b* 22 Aug. 1928; *s* of late Simon and Gertrud Stockhausen; *m* 1st, 1951, Doris Andreae (marr. diss.); one *s* three *d*; 2nd, 1967, Mary Bauermeister (marr. diss.); one *s* one *d*. *Educ:* Hochschule für Musik, and Univ., Cologne, 1947–51; studied with: Messiaen, 1952–53; Prof. Werner Meyer-Eppler, Bonn Univ., 1954–56. With Westdeutscher Rundfunk Electronic Music Studio, 1953–, Artistic Dir, 1963–77, Artistic Consultant, 1977–90. Lectr, Internat. Summer Sch. for New Music, Darmstadt, 1953–74; Dir, Interpretation Group for live electronic music, 1964–; Founder, and Artistic Dir, Kölner Kurse für Neue Musik, 1963–68; Visiting Professor: Univ. of Pa, 1965; Univ. of Calif, 1966–67; Prof. of Composition, Cologne State Conservatory, 1971–77. Co-Editor, Die Reihe, 1954–59. First annual tour of 30 concerts and lectures, 1958, USA and Canada, then throughout world. Composed over 316 individually performable works and made more than 120 records of his own works; since 1991, involved with production of complete issue of his works on CD. Member or Foreign Member: Akad. der Künste, Hamburg, 1968; Kungl. Musikaliska Akad., Sweden, 1970; Akad. der Künste, Berlin, 1973; Amer. Acad. and Inst. of Arts and Letters, 1977; Acad. Filarmonica Romana, 1979; Acad. Européenne des Sciences, des Arts et des Lettres, 1980; Associate Mem., Acad. Royale des sciences, des lettres et des beaux-arts, Belgium, 2004; Hon. RAM 1987. Hon. DPhil QUB, 2004. Awards and Prizes from France, Germany, Italy and USA; Prix Ars Electronica, Cluiz, Austria, 1990; Picasso Medal, UNESCO, 1992; Edison Prize, Holland, 1996; Polar Prize, Swedish Royal Acad. of Arts, 2001. Bundesverdienstkreuz 1st class, 1974; Verdienstorden des Landes Nordrhein-Westfalen, 1992. *Publications:* Texte, 10 vols, 1963–91; Stockhausen on Music, 1989; Karlheinz Stockhausen bei den Internationalen Ferienkursen für Neue Musik in Darmstadt 1951–1996, 2001; *compositions:* Chöre für Doris, Drei Lieder, Choral, 1950–51; Sonatine, Kreuzspiel, Formel, 1951; Schlagtrio, Spiel für Orchester, Etude, 1952; Punkte, 1952, rev. 1962; Klavierstücke I–XI, 1952–56; Kontra-Punkte, 1953; Elektronische Studien I and II, 1953–54; Zeitmasze, Gesang der Jünglinge, 1956; Gruppen, 1957; Zyklus, Refrain, 1959; Carré, Kontakte für elektronische Klänge, Kontakte für elektronische Klänge, Klavier und Schlagzeug, 1960; Originale (musical play with Kontakte), 1961; Plus Minus, 1963; Momente, 1962–64, completed, 1969; Mixtur (new arr. 1967), Mikrophonie I, 1964; Mikrophonie II, Stop (new arr. 1969), 1965; Telemusik, Solo, Adieu, 1966, Hymnen, Prozession, Ensemble, 1967; Kurzwellen, Stimmung, Aus den sieben Tagen, Spiral, Musik für ein Haus, 1968; Für Kommende Zeiten, 1968–70; Hymnen mit Orchester, Fresco, Dr K-Sextett, 1969; Pole, Expo, Mantra, 1970; Sternklang, Trans, 1971; Alphabet für Liège, Am Himmel wandre ich, (Indianerlieder), Ylem, 1972; Inori, 1973–74; Vortrag über Hu, Herbstmusik, Atmen gibt das Leben..., 1974; Musik im Bauch, Harlekin, Der Kleine Harlekin, 1975; Tierkreis, 1975–76; Sirius, 1975–77; Amour, 1976; Jubiläum, In Freundschaft, 1977; Licht, die sieben Tage der Woche (an operatic cycle for solo voices, solo instruments, solo dancers/choirs, orchestras, ballet and mimes/electronic and concrete music), 1977–2004: Donnerstag 1978–80 (Donnerstags-Gruss, or Michaels-Gruss, 1978; Unsichtbare Chöre, 1978–79; Michaels Jugend, 1979; Michaels Reise um die Erde, 1978; Michaels Heimkehr, 1980; Donnerstags-Abschied, 1980); Samstag, 1981–84 (Samstags-Gruss or Luzifers-Gruss, 1983; Luzifers Traum or Klavierstück XIII, 1981; Kathinkas Gesang als Luzifers Requiem, 1982–83; Luzifers Tanz, 1983; Luzifers Abschied, 1982); Montag, 1984–88 (Montags-Gruss or Eva-Gruss, 1984/88; Evas Erstgeburt, 1987; Evas Zweitgeburt, 1984/87; Evas Zauber, 1986; Montags-Abschied, or Eva-Abschied, 1988); Dienstag, 1977/1990–91 (Dienstags-Gruss,

1987–88; Jahreslauf, 1977–91; Invasion-Explosion mit Abschied, 1990–91); Freitag, 1991–94 (Freitags-Gruss, 1991; Freitag-Versuchung, 1991; Freitags-Abschied, 1994); Mittwoch, 1993–98 (Mittwochs-Gruss, 1998; Welt-Parlament, 1995; Orchester-Finalisten, 1995; Helikopter-Streichquartett, 1993; Michaelion, 1997–98; Mittwochs-Abschied, 1996); Sonntag, 1998–2003 (Lichter-Wasser, 1999; Engel-Prozessionen, 2000; Licht-Bilder, 2002; Düfte-Zeichen, 2002; Hoch-Zeiten, 2001–02; Sonntags-Abschied, 2001–03); Refrain, 2000; STOP und START (for six instrumental gps), 2001 (German Music Publishers Soc. Award, 2004); Mixtur (for five instrumental gps), 2003; Klang, 2005. *Address:* Stockhausen-Verlag, Kettenberg 15, 51515 Kürten, Germany.
Died 5 Dec. 2007.

STODDART, Sir Kenneth (Maxwell), KCVO 1989; AE 1942; JP; DL; Lord-Lieutenant, Metropolitan County of Merseyside, 1979–89; *b* 26 May 1914; *s* of late Wilfrid Bowring Stoddart and Mary Hyslop Stoddart (*née* Maxwell); *m* 1940, Jean Roberta Benson Young, DL; two *d. Educ:* Sedbergh; Clare Coll., Cambridge. Chairman: Cearns and Brown Ltd, 1973–84; United Mersey Supply Co. Ltd, 1978–81. Commissioned No 611 (West Lancashire) Sqdn, Auxiliary Air Force, 1936; served War, UK and Europe; comd W Lancashire Wing, Air Trng Corps, 1946–54; Vice-Chm. (Air) W Lancashire T&AFA, 1954–64. Pres., Merseyside Wing, ATC, 1991–99. Chairman, Liverpool Child Welfare Assoc., 1965–81. DL Lancashire 1958 (transf. to Metropolitan County of Merseyside, 1974); JP Liverpool 1952; High Sheriff of Merseyside, 1974. Hon. Fellow, Liverpool John Moores Univ. (formerly Liverpool Poly.), 1989. Hon. LLD Liverpool, 1986. KStJ 1979. *Recreation:* gardening. *Address:* Dunlins, 8 Hadlow Lane, Willaston, Neston CH64 2UH. *T:* (0151) 327 5183.
Died 26 Dec. 2008.

STOICHEFF, Prof. Boris Peter, OC 1982; FRS 1975; FRSC 1965; Professor of Physics, 1964–89, then Emeritus, and University Professor, 1977–89, then Emeritus, University of Toronto; *b* 1 June 1924; *s* of Peter and Vasilka Stoicheff; *m* 1954, Lillian Joan Ambridge; one *s. Educ:* Univ. of Toronto, Faculty of Applied Science and Engineering (BASc), Dept of Physics (MA, PhD). McKee-Gilchrist Fellowship, Univ. of Toronto, 1950–51; National Research Council of Canada: Fellowship, Ottawa, 1952–53; Res. Officer in Div. of Pure Physics, 1953–64; Mem. Council, 1978–83. Exec. Dir, Ontario Laser and Lightware Res. Centre, 1988–91. Visiting Scientist, Mass Inst. of Technology, 1963–64. Chm., Engrg Science, Univ. of Toronto, 1972–77. Izaak Walton Killam Meml Scholarship, 1977–79; Senior Fellow, Massey Coll., Univ. of Toronto, 1979– Dist Vis Prof., Univ. of Central Florida, 2000. H. L. Welsh Lecture, Univ. of Toronto, 1984; Elizabeth Laird Meml Lecture, Univ. Western Ontario, 1985; UK/Canada Rutherford Lectr, 1989. Pres., Canadian Assoc. of Physicists, 1983–84; Council Mem., Assoc. of Professional Engrs of Ontario, 1985–91; Vice-Pres., IUPAP, 1994–96. For. Co-Sec., RSC, 1995–2000. Fellow, Optical Soc. of America, 1965 (Pres. 1976); Fellow, Amer. Phys. Soc., 1969; Geoffrey Frew Fellow, Australian Acad. of Science, 1980. Hon. Fellow: Indian Acad. of Scis, 1971; Macedonian Acad. of Sci. and Arts, 1981; Foreign Hon. Fellow, Amer. Acad. of Arts and Scis, 1989. Hon. DSc: York, Canada, 1982; Skopje, Yugoslavia, 1982; Windsor, Canada, 1989; Toronto, 1994; Western Ontario, 2007. Gold Medal for Achievement in Physics of Canadian Assoc. of Physicists, 1974; William F. Meggers Award, Optical Soc. of America, 1981; Frederic Ives Medal, Optical Soc. of America, 1983; Henry Marshall Tory Medal, RSC, 1989; Dist. Service Award, Optical Soc. of America, 2002. Centennial Medal of Canada, 1967; Golden Jubilee Medal, 2002. *Publications:* Gerhard Herzberg: an illustrious life in science, 2002; numerous scientific contribs to phys. and chem. jls. *Address:* Department of

Physics, University of Toronto, 60 St George Street, Toronto, ON M5S 1A7, Canada. *T:* (416) 9782948.
Died 15 April 2010.

STOKES, Baron *cr* 1969 (Life Peer), of Leyland; **Donald Gresham Stokes,** Kt 1965; TD; DL; FREng, FIMechE; MSAE; FIMI; FICE; Chairman, KBH Communications, 1987–95; Chairman and Managing Director, 1968–75, Chief Executive, 1973–75, British Leyland Motor Corporation Ltd; President, BL Ltd, 1975–79; Consultant to Leyland Vehicles, 1979–81; *b* 22 March 1914; *o s* of Harry Potts Stokes; *m* 1939, Laura Elizabeth Courteney Lamb (*d* 1995); one *s; m* 2000, Patricia June Pascall. *Educ:* Blundell's School; Harris Institute of Technology, Preston. Started Student Apprenticeship, Leyland Motors Ltd, 1930. Served War of 1939–45: REME (Lt-Col). Rejoined Leyland as Exports Manager, 1946; General Sales and Service Manager, 1950; Director, 1954; Managing Director, and Deputy Chairman, Leyland Motor Corp., 1963, Chm. 1967; Chm. and Man. Dir, British Leyland Ltd, 1973. Director: National Westminster Bank, 1969–81; London Weekend Television Ltd, 1967–71; Opus Public Relations Ltd, 1979–84; Scottish & Universal Investments Ltd, 1980–92; Dovercourt Motor Co. Ltd, 1982–90; Beherman Auto-Transport SA, 1983–89; GWR Gp, 1990–94. Vice-President, Empresa Nacional de Autocamiones SA, Spain, 1959–73. Chairman: British Arabian Adv. Co. Ltd, 1977–85; Two Counties Radio Ltd, 1978–84, 1990–94 (Pres., 1984–90); Jack Barclay Ltd, 1980–90; British Arabian Technical Co-operation Ltd, 1981–85; Reliant Group, 1990; Dutton Forshaw Motor Gp, 1980–90. Vice-Pres., Engineering Employers Fedn, 1967–75; President: SMMT, 1961–62; Motor Industry Res. Assoc., 1965–66; Manchester Univ. Inst. of Science and Technology, 1972–76 (Vice-Pres., 1967–71); IMechE, 1972 (Vice-Pres., 1971); Chm., EDC for Electronics Industry, 1966–67; Member: NW Economic Planning Council, 1965–70; IRC, 1966–71 (Dep. Chm. 1969); EDC for the Motor Manufacturing Industry, 1967–; Council, Public Transport Assoc.; Worshipful Co. of Carmen. Fellow, IRTE (Pres., 1983–84), Hon. FIRTE. DL Lancs 1968. Hon. Fellow, Keble Coll., Oxford, 1968. Hon. LLD Lancaster, 1967; Hon. DTech Loughborough, 1968; Hon. DSc: Southampton, 1969; Salford, 1971. Officier de l'Ordre de la Couronne (Belgium), 1964; Commander de l'ordre de Leopold II (Belgium), 1972. *Recreation:* sailing. *Address:* 2 Branksome Cliff, Westminster Road, Poole, Dorset BH13 6JW. *Clubs:* Army and Navy; Royal Motor Yacht (Commodore, 1979–81).   *Died 21 July 2008.*

STOKES, John Fisher, MA, MD, FRCP; Physician. University College Hospital, since 1947; *b* 19 Sept. 1912; *e s* of late Dr Kenneth Stokes and Mary (*née* Fisher); *m* 1940, Elizabeth Joan (*d* 2010), *d* of Thomas Rooke and Elizabeth Frances (*née* Pearce); one *s* one *d. Educ:* Haileybury (exhibitioner); Gonville and Caius Coll., Cambridge (exhibitioner); University Coll. Hosp. (Fellowes Silver Medal for clinical medicine). MB BChir (Cambridge) 1937; MRCP 1939; MD (Cambridge) 1947 (proxime accessit, Horton Smith prize); FRCP 1947; FRCPE 1975; Thruston Medal, Gonville and Caius Coll., 1948. Appointments on junior staff University Coll. Hosp. and Victoria Hosp. for Children, Tite St, 1937–42; RAMC 1942–46; served in Far East, 1943–46, Lt-Col (despatches). Examiner in Medicine, various Univs, 1949–70. Member of Council, Royal Soc. of Med., 1951–54, 1967–69. Vice-Pres., RCP, 1968–69; Harveian Orator, RCP, 1981. Trustee, Leeds Castle Foundn, 1984–. Amateur Squash Rackets Champion of Surrey, 1935, of East of England, 1936, Runner-up of British Isles, 1937; English International, 1938; Technical Adviser to Squash Rackets Assoc., 1948–52; Chm. Jesters Club, 1953–59. *Publications:* Examinations in Medicine (jtly), 1976; contrib. on liver disease and general medicine in medical journals. *Recreations:* music, tennis, painting. *Address:* 24 Gypsy Lane, Hunton Bridge, Kings Langley, Herts WD4 8PR.   *Died 11 May 2010.*

STONE, Richard Frederick; QC 1968; *b* 11 March 1928; *s* of Sir Leonard Stone, OBE, QC, and Madeleine Marie (*née* Scheffler); *m* 1st, 1957, Georgina Maxwell Morris (decd); two *d;* 2nd, 1964, Susan van Heel; two *d. Educ:* Lakefield College Sch., Canada; Rugby; Trinity Hall, Cambridge (MA). Lt, Worcs Regt, 1946–48. Called to Bar, Gray's Inn, 1952, Bencher, 1974, Treasurer, 1992; retired, 2006. Member: Panel of Lloyd's Arbitrators in Salvage Cases, 1968–99; Panel of Wreck Comrs, 1968–98. *Recreation:* sea fishing. *Address:* 18 Wittering Road, Hayling Island, Hants PO11 9SP. *T:* (023) 9246 3645; Flat N, Rectory Chambers, Old Church Street, Chelsea, SW3 5DA. *T:* (020) 7351 1719.
Died 24 Oct. 2008.

STONEFROST, Maurice Frank, CBE 1983; DL; Director General and Clerk, Greater London Council, 1984–85; *b* 1 Sept. 1927; *s* of Arthur and Anne Stonefrost, Bristol; *m* 1953, Audrey Jean Fishlock; one *s* one *d. Educ:* Merrywood Grammar Sch., Bristol (DPA). IPFA. Nat. Service, RAF, 1948–51; local govt finance: Bristol County Borough, 1951–54; Slough Borough, 1954–56; Coventry County Borough, 1956–61; W Sussex CC, 1961–64; Sec., Inst. of Municipal Treasurers and Accountants, 1964–73; Comptroller of Financial Services, GLC, 1973–84; Chief Exec., BR Pension Fund, 1986–90; Chairman: Municipal Mutual Insce, 1990–93; CLF Municipal Bank, 1993–98. Dep. Pro Chancellor, and Vice-Chm. Council, City Univ., 1992–99. President: Soc. of County Treasurers, 1982–83; CIPFA, 1984–85. Chm., Commn on Citizenship, 1989–90; Member: Layfield Cttee on Local Govt Finance, 1976; Marre Cttee on Future of Legal Profession, 1989–90; Review Cttee of Finances of C of E, 1993; Chm., Cttee on Finance of Liverpool CC, 1985. Member: Architectural Heritage Fund, 1990–96 (Vice Chm., 1996–98); Foundn for Accountancy and Financial Management, Eastern Europe, 1993–2000; London Pensions Fund Authority, 1996–2001. Chm., Dolphin Sq. Trust, 1993–2001. DL Greater London, 1986. Hon. DSc City Univ., 1987. *Recreation:* gardening.   *Died 25 Oct. 2008.*

STONES, Sir William (Frederick), Kt 1990; OBE 1980; Managing Director, China Light & Power Co., Hong Kong, 1984–92 (Director, 1975–93); Chairman, Hong Kong Nuclear Investment Co., 1985–93; *b* 3 March 1923; *s* of Ralph William Stones and Ada Stones (*née* Armstrong); *m* 1st, 1946, Irene Mary Punter (marr. diss.); one *s* one *d;* 2nd, 1968, Margaret Joy Catton. *Educ:* Rutherford Coll., Newcastle upon Tyne. Chief Chemist, Michie & Davidson, 1948–51; Regional Res. Dir, CEGB NE Region, 1951–63; Supt, Ferrybridge Power Station, 1963–66; CEGB NE Region: Group Manager, 1966–68; Dir, Operational Planning, 1968–71; Dir, Generation, and Dep. Dir-Gen., 1971–75; Gen. Manager, China Light & Power Co., 1975–83. Dep. Chm., Guangdong Nuclear Power Joint Venture Co., 1985–93; Sen. Advr. West Merchant Bank, 1993–2000. Commander, Order of Leopold II (Belgium), 1986. *Recreations:* fishing, country life.   *Died 3 Dec. 2008.*

STORMONTH DARLING, Robin Andrew; Chairman: Capital Opportunities (formerly Voyageur European Smaller Companies) Trust, 1994–2004; Dumyat Investment Trust, 1995–2001; Intrinsic Portfolio Fund PCC Ltd, 2000–03; *b* 1 Oct. 1926; *s* of Patrick Stormonth Darling and Edith Mary Ormston Lamb; *m* 1st, 1956, Susan Marion Clifford-Turner (marr. diss. 1970); three *s* one *d;* 2nd, 1974, Harriet Heathcoat-Amory (*née* Nye) (marr. diss. 1978); 3rd, 1981, Carola Marion Brooke, *er d* of Sir Robert Erskine-Hill, 2nd Bt. *Educ:* Abberley Hall; Winchester Coll. Served Fleet Air Arm (Pilot), 1945; 9th Queen's Royal Lancers, 1946–54: ADC to GOC-in-C Scotland, 1950–52; Officer Cadet Instr, 1952–54. Alexanders Laing & Cruickshank (formerly Laing & Cruickshank), 1954–87, Chm., 1980–87; Director: Austin Motor Co., 1959; British Motor Corp., 1960–68; British Leyland, 1968–75. Chm., Tranwood Gp, subseq. Tranwood, 1987–91. Director: London Scottish Bank (formerly London Scottish Finance

Corp.), 1984–92; Mercantile House Holdings, 1984–87 (non-exec. Dep. Chm., 1987); GPI Leisure Corp. (Australia), 1986–90; Ptarmigan Internat. Capital Trust, 1993–2003. Stock Exchange: Mem., 1956–87; Mem. Council, 1978–86; Chairman: Quotations Cttee, 1981–85; Disciplinary Appeals Cttee, 1985–90. Dep. Chm., Panel on Take-Overs and Mergers, 1985–87; Mem., Securities and Investments Bd, 1985–87. Hon. Consul of Mexico at Edinburgh, 1992–2007. *Recreations:* shooting, ski-ing, flying, swimming. *Address:* Balvarran, Enochdhu, Blairgowrie, Perthshire PH10 7PA. *T:* (01250) 881248. *Clubs:* White's, MCC, Hurlingham; Perth Hunt.   *Died 17 Oct. 2009.*

STOTT, Richard Keith; journalist; Political and Current Affairs Columnist, Sunday Mirror, since 2001; *b* 17 Aug. 1943; *s* of late Fred B. Stott and Bertha Stott; *m* 1970, Penny, *yr d* of Air Vice-Marshal Sir Colin Scragg, KBE, CB, AFC; one *s* two *d. Educ:* Clifton College, Bristol. Bucks Herald, 1963–65; Ferrari Press Agency, 1965–68; Daily Mirror: Reporter, 1968–79; Features Editor, 1979–81; Asst Editor, 1981; Editor: Sunday People, 1984; Daily Mirror, 1985–89; The People, 1990–91; Daily Mirror, 1991–92; Today, 1993–95; columnist: News of the World, 1997–2000; Microsoft Network, 1997–2001. Dir, People Publishing Co., 1990–91. Reporter of the Year, British Press Awards, 1977; Editor of the Year, What the Papers Say Awards, 1993. *Publications:* Dogs and Lampposts, 2002; (ed) The Blair Years: extracts from Alastair Campbell's diaries, 2007. *Recreations:* theatre, reading.   *Died 30 July 2007.*

STOYLE, Roger John B.; *see* Blin-Stoyle.

STRABOLGI, 11th Baron *cr* 1318, of England; **David Montague de Burgh Kenworthy;** a Deputy Speaker and Deputy Chairman of Committees, House of Lords, 1986–2001; an Extra Lord in Waiting to the Queen, since 1998; *b* 1 Nov. 1914; *e s* of 10th Baron Strabolgi and Doris Whitley (*d* 1988), *o c* of late Sir Frederick Whitley-Thomson, MP; *S* father, 1953; a co-heir to Baronies of Cobham and Burgh; *m* 1st, 1939, Denise Godefroi (marr. diss. 1946); 2nd, 1947, Angela Street (marr. diss. 1951); 3rd, 1955, Myra Sheila Litewka (marr. diss. 1961); 4th, 1961, Doreen Margaret, *e d* of late Alexander Morgan, Ashton-under-Lyne, and Emma Morgan (*née* Mellor). *Educ:* Gresham's School; Chelsea Sch. of Art. Served with HM Forces, BEF, 1939–40; MEF, 1940–45, as Lt-Col RAOC. Mem. Parly Delegations to USSR, 1954, SHAPE, 1955, and France, 1981, 1983 and 1985; PPS to Minister of State, Home Office, 1968–69; PPS to Leader of the House of Lords and Lord Privy Seal, 1969–70; Asst Opposition Whip, and spokesman on the Arts, House of Lords, 1970–74; Captain of the Queen's Bodyguard of the Yeomen of the Guard (Dep. Govt Chief Whip), and Govt spokesman on Energy and Agriculture, 1974–79, Opposition spokesman on arts and libraries, 1979–85. Member: Jt Cttee on Consolidation Bills, 1986–2001; Select Cttee for Privileges, 1987–2008; Private Bills Cttee, 1987–96; Ecclesiastical Jt Cttee, 1991–2001; Select Cttee on Procedure, 1993–96, 1998–2001; Franco-British Parly Relations Cttee (Hon. Treas., 1991–96); Vice Pres., All-Pty Arts and Amenities Gp; elected Mem., H of L, 1999. Pres., Franco-British Soc.; Member: British Sect., Franco-British Council, 1981–98; Council, Alliance Française in GB, 1972–97. Dir, Bolton Building Soc., 1958–74, 1979–87 (Dep. Chm., 1983, Chm., 1986–87). Hon. Life Mem., RPO, 1977. Freeman, City of London, 1960. Officier de la Légion d'Honneur, 1981. *Heir-pres.:* nephew Andrew David Whitley Kenworthy, *b* 11 Feb. 1967. *Address:* House of Lords, SW1A 0PW. *Club:* Reform.   *Died 24 Dec. 2010.*

STRAKER, Rear-Adm. Bryan John, CB 1980; OBE 1966; Area Appeal Manager, Cancer Relief Macmillan Fund, 1993–94; *b* 26 May 1929; *s* of late George and Marjorie Straker; *m* 1954, Elizabeth Rosemary, *d* of Maj.-Gen. C. W. Greenway, CB, CBE, and Mrs C. W. Greenway; two *d. Educ:* St Albans Sch. Cadet, RNC Dartmouth, 1946; Flag Lieut to Flag Officer, Malayan Area, 1952–53; qual. in communications, 1955; CO:

HMS Malcolm, 1962–63; HMS Defender, 1966–67; Asst Dir, Naval Operational Requirements, MoD, 1968–70; CO HMS Fearless, 1970–72; Dir of Naval Plans, MoD, 1972–74; Comdr British Forces Caribbean Area and Island Comdr, Bermuda, 1974–76; Asst Chief of Naval Staff (Policy), 1976–78; Sen. Naval Mem., DS, RCDS, 1978–80; RN retd, 1981. Hd of Personnel Services, ICRF, 1981–89; Appeal Dir, Macmillan (Cancer Relief) Service, Midhurst, 1990–93. FCMI (FBIM 1978). Freeman, City of London. *Recreation:* gardening. *Address:* The Cottage, Durford Court, Petersfield, Hants GU31 5AR.   *Died 25 Dec. 2007.*

STRATFORD, Baron *cr* 2005 (Life Peer), of Stratford in the London Borough of Newham; **Anthony Louis Banks;** 8 April 1943; *m* Sally Jones. *Educ:* St John's Primary Sch., Brixton; Archbishop Tenison's Grammar Sch., Kennington; York Univ. (BA); London School of Economics. Former trade union research worker; Head of Research, AUEW, 1969–75; an Asst Gen. Sec., Assoc. of Broadcasting and Allied Staffs, 1976–83. Political Advr to Minister for Overseas Develt, 1975. Joined Labour Party, 1964; Greater London Council: Mem. for Hammersmith, 1970–77, for Tooting, 1981–86; Chairman: Gen. Purposes Cttee, 1975–77; Arts and Recreation Cttee, 1981–83; GLC, 1985–86. Contested (Lab): E Grinstead, 1970; Newcastle upon Tyne N, Oct. 1974; Watford, 1979. MP (Lab) Newham NW, 1983–97, West Ham, 1997–2005. Parly Under-Sec. of State, DCMS, 1997–99. Member: Select Cttee, HM Treasury, 1986–87; Select Cttee on Procedure, 1987–97; Select Cttee on Accommodation and Works, 2000–05; Jt Lords/ Commons Cttee on Private Bill Procedure, 1987–88; former Chm., Adv. Cttee on Works of Art; Mem., Council of Europe Parly Assembly and WEU, 1989–2005; former Chm., Sport and Youth Cttee, Council of Europe. Chm., London Gp, Labour MP's, 1987–91. Member: ENO Bd, 1981–83; London Festival Ballet Bd, 1981–83; Nat. Theatre Bd, 1981–85. *Publications:* (jtly) Out of Order, 1993. *Address:* House of Lords, SW1A 0PW.   *Died 6 Jan. 2006.*

STRATHCARRON, 2nd Baron, *cr* 1936, of Banchor; **David William Anthony Blyth Macpherson;** Bt, *cr* 1933; Partner, Strathcarron & Co.; Director: Kirchhoff (London) Ltd; Seabourne World Express Group plc; *b* 23 Jan. 1924; *s* of 1st Baron Strathcarron and Jill (*d* 1956), *o d* of Sir George Rhodes, 1st Bt; *S* father, 1937; *m* 1st, 1947, Valerie Cole (marr. annulled on his petition, 1947); 2nd, 1948, Mrs Diana Hawtrey Curle (*d* 1973), *o d* of Comdr R. H. Deane; two *s*; 3rd 1991, Mrs Eve Samuel (*d* 1999), *o d* of late J. C. Higgins, CIE; 4th, 1999, Diana, *widow* of Hugo Nicholson. *Educ:* Eton; Jesus College, Cambridge. Served War of 1939–45, RAFVR, 1942–47. Motoring Correspondent of The Field, 1954–2002. Member, British Parly Delegn to Austria, 1964. President: Inst. of Freight Forwarders, 1974–75; Guild of Motoring Writers, 1971–; Guild of Experienced Motorists, 1980–86; National Breakdown Recovery Club, 1982–96; Driving Instructors' Assoc., 1982–2002; Vehicle Builders' and Repairers' Assoc., 1983–; IRTE, 1990–2000; Order of the Road, 1994– (Chm., 1974–94); Fellowship of the Motor Industry, 1994–. FIMI 1989; FCILT (FCIT 1991); Fellow, Inst. of Advanced Motorists, 1993; Fellow, Motor Industry, 1995. *Publications:* Motoring for Pleasure, 1963. *Recreations:* motor-racing, sailing, motorcycling. *Heir: s* Hon. Ian David Patrick Macpherson, *b* 31 March 1949. *Address:* 3 Elizabeth Court, Milmans Street, SW10 0DA. *T:* (020) 7351 3224; Otterwood, Beaulieu, Hants SO42 7YS. *T:* (01590) 612334. *Clubs:* Boodle's, Royal Air Force.   *Died 31 Aug. 2006.*

STRAUSS, Claude L.; *see* Levi-Strauss.

STRAWSON, Sir Peter (Frederick), Kt 1977; FBA 1960; Fellow of Magdalen College, Oxford, 1968–87, Hon. Fellow, 1989; Waynflete Professor of Metaphysical Philosophy in the University of Oxford, 1968–87 (Reader, 1966–68); Fellow of University College, Oxford, 1948–68, Hon. Fellow since 1979; *b* 23 Nov. 1919; *s* of late Cyril Walter and Nellie Dora Strawson; *m*

1945, Grace Hall Martin; two s two d. *Educ:* Christ's College, Finchley; St John's College, Oxford (scholar; Hon. Fellow, 1973). Served War of 1939–45, RA, REME, Capt. Asst Lectr in Philosophy, UCNW, 1946; John Locke Schol., Univ. of Oxford, 1946; Lectr in Philosophy, 1947, Fellow and Praelector, 1948, University Coll., Oxford. Vis. Prof., Duke Univ., N Carolina, 1955–56; Fellow of Humanities Council and Vis. Associate Prof., Princeton Univ., 1960–61, Vis. Prof., 1972; Woodbridge Lectr, Columbia Univ., NY, 1983; Immanuel Kant Lectr, Munich, 1985; Vis. Prof., Collège de France, 1985. MAE 1990; For. Hon. Mem., Amer. Acad. Arts and Scis, 1971. Hon. DPhil: Munich, 1998; Sofia, 2003. Internat. Kant Prize, Berlin, 2000. *Publications:* Introduction to Logical Theory, 1952; Individuals, 1959; The Bounds of Sense, 1966; (ed) Philosophical Logic, 1967; (ed) Studies in the Philosophy of Thought and Action, 1968; Logico-Linguistic Papers, 1971; Freedom and Resentment, 1974; Subject and Predicate in Logic and Grammar, 1974; Scepticism and Naturalism: some varieties, 1985; Analyse et Métaphysique, 1985; Analysis and Metaphysics, 1992; Entity and Identity, 1997; The Philosophy of P. F. Strawson (autobiog. and replies to critics), 1998; contrib. to Mind, Philosophy, Proc. Aristotelian Soc., Philosophical Review, etc. *Address:* 25 Farndon Road, Oxford OX2 6RT. *T:* (01865) 515026. *Club:* Athenæum. *Died 13 Feb. 2006.*

STREET, John Edmund Dudley, CMG 1966; retired; *b* 21 April 1918; *er s* of late Philip Edmund Wells Street and of Elinor Gladys Whittington-Ince; *m* 1st, 1940, Noreen Mary (*d* 1984), *o d* of Edward John Griffin Comerford and Mary Elizabeth Winstone; three s one d; 2nd, 1983, Mrs Patricia Curzon. *Educ:* Tonbridge School; Exeter College, Oxford. Served War of 1939–45, HM Forces, 1940–46. Entered Foreign Service, 1947; First Secretary: British Embassy, Oslo, 1950; British Embassy, Lisbon, 1952; Foreign Office, 1954; First Secretary and Head of Chancery, British Legation, Budapest, 1957–60; HM Ambassador to Malagasy Republic, 1961–62, also Consul-General for the Island of Réunion and the Comoro Islands, 1961–62; Counsellor, FO, 1963–67; Asst Sec., MoD, 1967–76; Asst Under-Sec. of State, MoD, 1976–78. *Recreation:* reading. *Address:* Cornerways, High Street, Old Woking, Surrey GU22 9JH. *T:* (01483) 764371. *Died 19 March 2006.*

STUART, Joseph B.; *see* Burnett-Stuart.

STUART, Michael Francis Harvey; Treasury Adviser, UK Mission to the United Nations, 1974–82, retired; *b* 3 Oct. 1926; *s* of late Willoughby Stuart and Ethel Candy; *m* 1961, Ruth Tennyson-d'Eyncourt; one *s* one *d*. *Educ:* Harrow; Magdalen Coll., Oxford (Demy). Air Min., 1950–65; DEA, 1965–69; HM Treasury, 1969–74. Mem., UN Adv. Cttee on Administrative and Budgetary Questions, 1975–80. *Recreations:* music, golf. *Address:* Bourne House, Chertsey Road, Chobham, Woking, Surrey GU24 8NB. *T:* (01276) 857954. *Died 29 June 2008.*

STUART-MENTETH, Sir James; *see* Menteth.

STUBBS, John Francis Alexander H.; *see* Heath-Stubbs.

STURDEE, Rear-Adm. (Arthur) Rodney (Barry), CB 1971; DSC 1945; Flag Officer, Gibraltar, 1969–72; *b* 6 Dec. 1919; *s* of Comdr Barry V. Sturdee, RN, and Barbara (*née* Sturdee); *m* 1st, 1953, Marie-Claire Amstoutz (*d* 1995), Mulhouse, France; one s one d; 2nd, 2001, Joyce (*née* Jeacock), *widow* of Major James Hunter. *Educ:* Canford Sch. Entered Royal Navy as Special Entry Cadet, 1937. Served War of 1939–45: Midshipman in HMS Exeter at Battle of the River Plate, 1939; Lieut, 1941; specialised in Navigation, 1944; minesweeping in Mediterranean, 1944–45 (DSC). Lt-Comdr, 1949; RN Staff Coll., 1950–51; Staff of Navigation Sch., 1951–52; Comdr, 1952; JSSC, 1953; BJSM, Washington, 1953–55; Fleet Navigating Officer, Medit., 1955–57; Exec. Officer,

RNAS, Culdrose, 1958–59; Captain 1960; NATO Defence Coll., 1960–63; Queen's Harbour-Master, Singapore, 1963–65; Staff of Chief of Defence Staff, 1965–67; Chief of Staff to C-in-C, Portsmouth (as Cdre), 1967–69; Rear-Adm. 1969. ADC to the Queen, 1969. *Address:* Cider Mill Cottage, Hancocks Lane, Castlemorton Common, Malvern, Worcestershire WR13 6LG. *T:* (01684) 573627. *Died 6 Oct. 2009.*

STYLES, Lt-Col (Stephen) George, GC 1972; company director and consultant, 1974–86, retired; *b* 16 March 1928; *s* of Stephen Styles and Grace Lily Styles (*née* Preston); *m* 1952, Mary Rose Styles (*née* Woolgar); one s two d. *Educ:* Collyers Sch., Horsham; Royal Military Coll. of Science. Ammunition Technical Officer, commissioned RAOC, Nov. 1947; seconded to 1 Bn KOYLI, 1949–51 (despatches, 1952); RMCS, 1952–56; HQ Ammunition Organisation, 1956–58; OC 28 Commonwealth Bde, Ordnance Field Park, Malaya, 1958–61; 2i/c 16 Bn RAOC, Bicester, 1961–64; OC Eastern Command Ammunition Inspectorate, 1964–67; Sen. Ammo Tech. Officer, 3 BAPD, BAOR, 1967–68; OC 1(BR) Corps Vehicle Company, 1968–69; Sen. Ammo Tech. Officer, Northern Ireland, 1969–72; Chief Ammo Tech. Officer (EOD), HQ DOS (CILSA), 1972–74. Member: Royal Soc. of St George; NRA; NSRA. *Publications:* Bombs Have No Pity, 1975; contrib. Proc. ICE, Jl of Forensic Science Soc. *Recreations:* rifle and game shooting, cataloguing a huge cartridge collection. *Address:* c/o Barclays Bank, Abingdon. *Died 1 Aug. 2006.*

SUDDABY, Arthur, CBE 1980; PhD; MSc; CChem; FRSC; CEng, MIChemE; scientific consultant on the carriage of goods by sea, until 1990; Provost, City of London Polytechnic, 1970–81; *b* 26 Feb. 1919; *e s* of George Suddaby, Kingston-upon-Hull, Yorks; *m* 1944, Elizabeth Bullin Vyse (*d* 1988), *d* of Charles Vyse; two s. *Educ:* Riley High Sch., Kingston-upon-Hull; Hull Technical Coll.; Chelsea Polytechnic; Queen Mary Coll. London. Chemist and Chemical Engr, in industry, 1937–47; Lectr in Physical Chemistry, and later Sen. Lectr in Chem. Engrg, West Ham Coll. of Technology, 1947–50; Sir John Cass Coll.: Sen. Lectr in Physics, 1950–61; Head of Dept of Physics, 1961–66; Principal, 1966–70. Chm., Cttee of Directors of Polytechnics, 1976–78; Member: Chem. Engrg Cttee, 1948–51; London and Home Counties Regional Adv. Council, 1971–; Bd of Examrs and Educn Cttee, Inst. of Chem. Engrs, 1948–51; Oakes Cttee on Management of Public Sector Higher Educn, 1977–78; CNAA: Chem. Engrg Bd, 1969–75; Nautical Studies Bd, 1972–75; Chm., Standing Conf. of Approved Coll. Res. Deg. Cttees, 1979–81; Court of the City University, 1967–81; Vis. Cttee, Cranfield Inst. of Technology, 1979–85; Chm., Assoc. of Navigation Schs, 1972. *Publications:* various original research papers in theoretical physics, in scientific jls; review articles. *Recreations:* country sports, music. *Address:* Castle Hill House, Godshill Wood, near Fordingbridge, Hants SP6 2LU. *T:* (01425) 652234. *Club:* Athenæum. *Died 23 Jan. 2008.*

SUGG, Aldhelm St John, CMG 1963; retired as Provincial Commissioner, Southern Province of Northern Rhodesia, August 1963; *b* 21 Oct. 1909; *s* of H. G. St J. Sugg; *m* 1935, Jessie May Parker (*d* 1994); one s one d. *Educ:* Colchester Royal Grammar School. Palestine Police, 1930–31; Northern Rhodesia Police, 1932–43; Colonial Administrative Service, in N Rhodesia, 1943–63. Retired to England, 1963. *Recreations:* sailing, field sports. *Club:* Royal Commonwealth Society. *Died 6 July 2006.*

SUHARTO, Gen. Mohamed; *see* Soeharto.

SUMMERHAYES, David Michael, CMG 1975; HM Diplomatic Service, retired; Disarmament Adviser, Foreign and Commonwealth Office, 1983–92; *b* 29 Sept. 1922; *s* of Sir Christopher Summerhayes, KBE, CMG and Anna (*née* Johnson); *m* 1959, June van der Hardt Aberson; two s one d. *Educ:* Marlborough;

Emmanuel Coll., Cambridge. Served War of 1939–45 in Royal Artillery (Capt.) N Africa and Italy. 3rd Sec., FO, 1948; Baghdad, 1949; Brussels, 1950–53; 2nd Sec., FO, 1953–56; 1st Sec. (Commercial), The Hague, 1956–59; 1st Sec. and Consul, Reykjavik, 1959–61; FO, 1961–65; Consul-General and Counsellor, Buenos Aires, 1965–70; Head of Arms Control and Disarmament Dept, FCO, 1970–74; Minister, Pretoria/Cape Town, 1974–78; Ambassador and Leader, UK Delegn to Cttee on Disarmament, Geneva, 1979–82. Hon. Officer, Order of Orange Nassau. *Recreations:* golf, walking. *Address:* Ivy House, South Harting, Petersfield, Hants GU31 5QQ. *Clubs:* Oxford and Cambridge; Liphook Golf.
Died 12 Nov. 2008.

SUMPTION, Anthony James Chadwick, DSC 1944; *b* 15 May 1919; *s* of late John Chadwick Sumption and Winifred Fanny Sumption; *m* 1946, Hedy Hedigan (marr. diss. 1979); two *s* two *d. Educ.* Cheltenham Coll.; London Sch. of Economics. Served RNVR, 1939–46; HM Submarines, 1941–45: comd Varangian, 1944; Upright, 1945; Flag Lieut to Flag Officer Gibraltar and Mediterranean Approaches, 1945–46. Solicitor, 1946; called to the Bar, Lincoln's Inn, 1971; a Recorder of the Crown Court, 1980–85. Member (C): LCC, 1949–52; Westminster City Council, 1953–56. Contested (C): Hayes and Harlington, March 1953; Middlesbrough W, 1964. *Publications:* Taxation of Overseas Income and Gains, 1973, 4th edn 1982; Tax Planning, (with Philip Lawton) 6th edn 1973–8th edn 1979, (with Giles Clarke) 9th edn 1981–10th edn 1982; Capital Gains Tax, 1981. *Recreations:* painting, angling. *Club:* Garrick.
Died 8 Jan. 2008.

SUMRAY, Monty, CBE 1989; Chairman, FII Group, 1965–95 (Managing Director, 1965–95); *b* 12 Oct. 1918; *m* 1939, Catherine Beber; one *s* one *d. Educ:* Upton House, London. Royal Berkshire Regt, 1939–46; served in Burma (Captain). UK footwear manufacturing, 1934–95; Dir, FII Group. Pres., British Footwear Manufacturers' Fedn, 1976–77, formerly: Member: Footwear Industry Study Steering Gp (Chm., Home Working Cttee); Footwear Economic Develt Cttee (4 years); Pres., London Footwear Manufacturers' Assoc.; Chm., London Branch, British Boot & Shoe Instn. FCFI 1974; FInstD 1981; FRSA 1993. *Recreations:* bowls, reading, social and charitable work. *Address:* 6 Inverforth House, North End Way, NW3 7EU. *T:* (020) 8458 2788.
Died 2 June 2008.

SUNDERLAND, Prof. Eric, CBE 2005 (OBE 1999); PhD; FSB; Principal, later Vice-Chancellor, University College of North Wales, Bangor, 1984–95, then Emeritus Professor, University of Wales; Lord-Lieutenant of Gwynedd, 1999–2006; *b* 18 March 1930; *s* of Leonard Sunderland and Mary Agnes (*née* Davies); *m* 1957, Jean Patricia (*née* Watson); two *d. Educ:* Amman Valley Grammar Sch.; Univ. of Wales (BA, MA); Univ. of London (PhD). FSB (FIBiol 1975). Commnd Officer, RA, 1955–56. Res. Asst, UCL, 1953–54; Res. Scientist, NCB, 1957–58; University of Durham: Lectr, 1958–66; Sen. Lectr, 1966–71; Prof. of Anthropology, 1971–84; Pro Vice-Chancellor and Sub-Warden, 1979–84; Vice-Chancellor, Univ. of Wales, 1989–91. Welsh Supernumerary Fellow, Jesus Coll., Oxford, 1987–88 and 1992–93. Chm., Gypsy-Traveller Accommodation Res. Steering Gp, Welsh Assembly Govt, 2005–06. Sec.-Gen., Internat. Union of Anthropol and Ethnol Sciences, 1978–98 (Pres., 1998–2003); President, Royal Anthropol Inst., 1989–91 (Hon. Sec., 1978–85; Hon. Treasurer, 1985–89); Chm., Biosocial Soc., 1981–85; Pres., N Wales Br., Inst. Biol., 2005–. Member: Welsh Language Bd, 1988–91; Ct of Govs, Nat. Mus. of Wales, 1991–94; Gen. Cttee, ICSU, 1993–99; Bd, British Council, 1996–2001 (Chm., Welsh Cttee, 1996–2001); BBC Broadcasting Council for Wales, 1996–2000; Vice Pres., Internat. Social Sci. Council, 1994; Chairman: Welsh Language Educn Develt Cttee, 1987–94; Local Govt Boundary Commn for Wales, 1994–2001; Adv. Cttee for Wales, Environment Agency, 1996–2001; Wetlands for Wales

Project, 2001–09; Commn on Local Govt Electoral Arrangements in Wales, 2001–02; CILT Cymru (Centre for Inf. on Language Teaching and Res.), 2002–06; Vice-Pres., Sefydliad (Community Foundn in Wales), 2003–07. Vice-Patron, Atlantic Council of UK, 2002–. Chm. Bd, Welsh Chamber Orch., 2003–; Vice-Pres., Welsh Music Guild, 2005–. Pres., Univ. of Wales, Lampeter, 1998–2002. Area Pres., Scouts Assoc., Anglesey, Conwy and Gwynedd, 2002–; Pres., Anglesey Bd, SSAFA, 2005–. Hon. Col, 6th Cadet Bn, RWF (Gwynedd), ACF, 2003–07. Mem., Welsh Livery Guild, 2001– (Mem. Court, 2008–). Hon. Mem., The Gorsedd, 1985. High Sheriff, 1998–99, DL 1998, Gwynedd. Hon. Fellow: Univ. of Wales, Lampeter, 1995; Univ. of Wales. Bangor, 1996. Hon. LLD Wales, 1997. CStJ 2000. Golden Jubilee Medal, 2002. *Publications:* Elements of Human and Social Geography: some anthropological perspectives, 1973; (ed jtly) Genetic Variation in Britain, 1973; (ed jtly) The Operation of Intelligence: biological preconditions for the operation of intelligence, 1980; (ed jtly) Genetic and Population Studies in Wales, 1986; contrib. Annals of Human Biol., Human Heredity, Man, Human Biol., Nature, Amer. Jl of Phys. Anthropol., and Trans Royal Soc. *Recreations:* travel, gardening, book collecting, reading. *Address:* The Old Custom House, Townsend, Beaumaris, Anglesey LL58 8BH. *Club:* Athenæum.
Died 24 March 2010.

SUTHERLAND, Dame Joan, OM 1991; AC 1975; DBE 1979 (CBE 1961); soprano; *b* 7 Nov. 1926; *d* of McDonald Sutherland, Sydney, NSW, and Muriel Alston Sutherland; *m* 1954, Richard Bonynge, AO, CBE; one *s. Educ:* St Catherine's, Waverley, Sydney. Début as Dido in Purcell's Dido and Aeneas, Sydney, 1947; subsequently concerts, oratorios and broadcasts throughout Australia. Came to London, 1951; joined Covent Garden, 1952, where she remained resident soprano for 7 years; won international fame with début as Lucia di Lammermoor, Covent Garden, 1959, and by early 1960s had sung throughout the Americas and Europe; later ROH rôles included Amina in La Sonnambula, Marie in La Fille du Régiment and title rôles in Norma and Maria Stuarda. Specialised throughout her career in the popular and lesser-known bel canto operatic repertoire of 18th and 19th centuries, and made many recordings. Hon. DMus: Sydney, 1984; Oxon, 1992. *Publications:* The Joan Sutherland Album (autobiog., with Richard Bonynge), 1986; A Prima Donna's Progress: the autobiography of Joan Sutherland, 1997; *relevant publications:* Joan Sutherland, by R. Braddon, 1962; Joan Sutherland, by E. Greenfield, 1972; La Stupenda, by B. Adams, 1980; Joan Sutherland, by Norma Major, 1987. *Recreations:* reading, gardening, needlepoint. *Address:* c/o Ingpen & Williams, 7 St George's Court, 131 Putney Bridge Road, SW15 2PA.
Died 11 Oct. 2010.

SUZMAN, Mrs Helen, OM (Gold) South Africa, 1997; Hon. DBE 1989; Member, South African Human Rights Commission, 1996–98; *b* 7 Nov. 1917; *d* of late Samuel Gavronsky; *m* 1937, Dr M. M. Suzman, FRCP (*d* 1994); two *d. Educ:* Parktown Convent, Johannesburg; Univ. of Witwatersrand (BCom). Lectr in Economic History, Univ. of Witwatersrand, 1944–52. Elected MP for Houghton, RSA, 1953 (United Party, 1953–61; Progressive Party (later Progressive Reform Party and Progressive Federal Party), 1961–89); Inaugural Mem. Progressive Party, 1959; sole rep. of Progressive Party in Parlt, 1961–74; returned unopposed as Progressive Federal Party MP, 1977. Mem., Ind. Electoral Commn, 1994. Pres., SA Inst. of Race Relns, 1991–93. Hon. Fellow: St Hugh's Coll., Oxford, 1973; London Sch. of Economics, 1975; New Hall, Cambridge, 1990. Hon. DCL Oxford, 1973; Hon. LLD: Harvard, Witwatersrand, 1976; Columbia, Smith Coll., 1977; Brandeis, 1981; Cape Town, Jewish Theological Seminary, NY, 1986; Ohio, Western Ontario, 1989; Rhodes, S Africa, Cambridge, Glasgow, Nottingham, Warwick, Ulster, 1990; Indiana, Rutgers, 1992; Toronto, 1993; De Montfort, 1994; Wales, 1996; KCL, 2008; Hon. DHL: Denison, 1982; New Sch. for Social Res., NY, Sacred

Heart Univ., USA, 1984; DUniv Brunel, 1991; Hon. Dr: Yale, 1999; Stellenbosch, 2006. UN Human Rights Award, 1978; Roger E. Joseph Award, Hebrew Union Coll., NY, 1986; Moses Mendelssohn Prize, Berlin Senate, 1988; B'Nai B'Rith Dor L'Dor Award, 1992; Notre Dame Univ., Indiana, Award, 1995; Liberal Internat. Prize for Freedom, 2002. Freedom of Sandton, 1989. *Publications:* In No Uncertain Terms (autobiog.), 1993. *Recreations:* swimming, fishing, bridge. *Address:* 52 2nd Avenue, Illovo, Sandton, Gauteng 2196, South Africa. *T:* and *Fax:* (11) 7882833; *e-mail:* helen01@icon.co.za. *Clubs:* Lansdowne; Inanda, Wanderers (Johannesburg).   *Died 1 Jan. 2009.*

SWANSON, Dr Kenneth Macgregor; JP; farmer, since 1991; Vice Lord-Lieutenant for Caithness, 1996–2005; *b* 14 Feb. 1930; *s* of Magnus Houston Swanson and Margaret Swanson (*née* Macgregor); *m* 1956, Elspeth Janet Will Paton; two *s* one *d*. *Educ:* Wick High Sch.; St Andrews Univ. (BSc 1st cl. Hons Natural Philosophy 1951; PhD 1959). Nat. service, FO (Pilot), RAF, 1952–54; St Andrews Univ. Air Sqn, RAFVR, 1954–58. Lectr in Physics, UCNW, Bangor, 1955–58; United Kingdom Atomic Energy Authority, Dounreay: SSO, Fast Reactor Fuel Develt, 1958–61; PSO, 1961–71; Res. Manager, Fuels, 1971–86; Asst Dir, 1986–91. Chm., European Cttee on Fast Reactor Fuel Develt, 1987–90; Mem. Bd, NW Reg., 1992–97, Northern Areas, 1997–99, Scottish Natural Heritage; Chm., Caithness Jobs Commn, 1988–98; Dir, Caithness and Sutherland Enterprise, 1990–99 (Vice Chm., 1995–99). JP, 1970, DL, 1977, Caithness. *Publications:* papers and patents on develt of plutonium fuels for electricity production. *Recreations:* enjoying the countryside, sailing. *Address:* Knockglass, Westfield, Thurso, Caithness KW14 7QN. *T:* (01847) 871201.   *Died 15 Oct. 2009.*

SWARTZ, Rt Rev. George Alfred; Bishop of Kimberley and Kuruman, 1983–91; *b* 8 Sept. 1928; *s* of Philip and Julia Swartz; *m* 1957, Sylvia Agatha (*née* George); one *s* one *d*. *Educ:* Umbilo Road High Sch., Durban; Univ. of the Witwatersrand, Johannesburg; Coll. of the Resurrection, Mirfield, Yorks; St Augustine's Coll., Canterbury. BA, Primary Lower Teacher's Cert., Central Coll. Dip. (Canterbury). Asst Teacher, Sydenham Primary Sch., 1951–52; Deacon, 1954; Priest, 1955; Asst Curate, St Paul's Church, Cape Town, 1955–56; Priest in Charge, Parochial Dist of St Helena Bay, Cape, 1957–60; St Augustine's Coll., Canterbury, 1960–61; Dir, Cape Town Dio. Mission to Muslims, 1962–63; Dir, Mission to Muslims and Rector St Philip's Church, Cape Town, 1963–70; Regional Dean of Woodstock Deanery, 1966–70; Priest in Charge, Church of the Resurrection, Bonteheuwel, Cape, 1971–72; a Bishop Suffragan of Cape Town, 1972–83; Canon of St George's Cathedral, Cape Town, 1969–72. Dean of the Province, Church of the Province of Southern Africa, 1986–89. *Recreations:* cinema, music (traditional jazz; instruments played are guitar and saxophone). *Address:* 11 Tanglin, Thomas Road, Kenilworth, Cape Town, 7708, Republic of South Africa. *T:* (21) 7979079.   *Died 31 Dec. 2006.*

SWARTZ, Col Hon. Sir Reginald (William Colin), KBE 1972 (MBE (mil.) 1948); ED; FAIM, FAICD; retired parliamentarian and company director (director of nine companies, 1973–83); *b* 14 April 1911; *s* of late J. Swartz, Toowoomba, Qld; *m* 1st, 1936, Hilda (*d* 1995), *d* of late G. C. Robinson; two *s* one *d*; 2nd, 1998, Muriel McKinstry. *Educ:* Toowoomba and Brisbane Grammar Schs. Commonwealth Military Forces, 1928–40, Lieut, 1934. Served War of 1939–45: Captain 2–26 Bn, 8 Div., AIF, 1940; Malaya (PoW): Singapore, Malaya, Thailand (Burma–Thailand Rly); CMF, in Darling Downs Regt, Lt-Col, AQMG, CMF, N Comd, Col (RL), 1961. Hon. Col Australian Army Aviation Corps, 1969–75. MHR (L) Darling Downs, Qld, 1949–72; Parly Under-Sec. for Commerce and Agric., 1952–56; Parly Sec. for Trade, 1956–61; Minister: (of State) for Repatriation, Dec. 1961–Dec. 1964; for Health, 1964–66; for Social Services, 1965; for Civil Aviation, 1966–69; for Nat.

Develt, 1969–72; Leader, House of Representatives, Canberra, 1971–72. Leader of many delegns overseas incl. Aust. Delegn to India, 1967, and Trade Mission to SE Asia, 1958; Parly Delegn to S and SE Asia, 1966. Patron and/or Vice-Pres. or Mem. of numerous public organizations. Chm. of Trustees, Australian Army Aviation Corps, 1978–91. Past Chm., Inst. of Dirs (Queensland). Member, RSL. *Recreation:* bowls. *Address:* 56 Immanuel Gardens, 10 Magnetic Drive, Buderim, Qld 4556, Australia. *Clubs:* United Service (Brisbane); Twin Towns Services (Tweed Head); Darling Downs Aero; Probus (Doncaster) (Life Mem., Foundation Pres.); Templestowe Bowling (Life Mem.) (Melbourne).
                                 Died 2 Feb. 2006.

SWINGLAND, Owen Merlin Webb; QC 1974; Barrister-at-Law; *b* 26 Sept. 1919; *er s* of Charles and Maggie Eveline Swingland; *m* 1941, Kathleen Joan Eason (*née* Parry), Newport, Mon; one *s* one *d* (and one *d* decd). *Educ:* Haberdashers' Aske's Hatcham Sch.; King's Coll., London (LLB 1941, AKC). Called to Bar, Gray's Inn, 1946, Bencher, 1985; practice at Chancery Bar, 1948–88; Barrister of Lincoln's Inn, 1977. A Church Comr, 1982–90. Past Pres., British Insurance Law Assoc. Freeman, City of London; Mem., Court of Assts, Haberdashers' Co. (Master, 1987–88). *Recreations:* music, theatre, fishing, reading; interested in competitive sports. *Address:* Warberry Park Gardens, Bishops Down Road, Tunbridge Wells, Kent TN4 8GJ. *T:* (01892) 535277.
                                 Died 1 Sept. 2006.

SWINTON, 2nd Earl of, *cr* 1955; **David Yarburgh Cunliffe-Lister;** JP; DL; Viscount Swinton, 1935; Baron Masham, 1955; *b* 21 March 1937; *s* of Major Hon. John Yarburgh Cunliffe-Lister (*d* of wounds received in action, 1943) and Anne Irvine (*d* 1961), *yr d* of late Rev. Canon R. S. Medlicott (she *m* 2nd, 1944, Donald Chapple-Gill); *S* grandfather, 1972; *m* 1959, Susan Lilian Primrose Sinclair (later Baroness Masham of Ilton); one *s* one *d* (both adopted). *Educ:* Winchester; Royal Agricultural College. Member: N Riding Yorks CC, 1961–74; N Yorks CC, 1973–77. Captain of the Yeoman of the Guard (Dep. Govt Chief Whip), 1982–86. Dir, Leeds Permanent Building Soc., 1987–93. Mem., Countryside Commn, 1987–93. JP North (formerly NR) Yorks, 1971; DL North Yorks, 1978. *Heir:* *b* Hon. Nicholas John Cunliffe-Lister [*b* 4 Sept. 1939; *m* 1966, Hon. Elizabeth Susan (marr. diss.), *e d* of Viscount Whitelaw, KT, CH, MC, PC; two *s* one *d*; *m* 1996, Pamela Sykes]. *Address:* Dykes Hill House, Masham, N Yorks HG4 4NS. *T:* (01765) 689241; 46 Westminster Gardens, SW1P 4JG. *T:* (020) 7834 0700. *Clubs:* White's, Pratt's; Leyburn Market (N Yorks).   *Died 26 March 2006.*

SYKES, Prof. Alfred Geoffrey, PhD, DSc; FRS 1999; CChem, FRSC; Professor of Inorganic Chemistry, University of Newcastle upon Tyne, 1980–99, then Emeritus; *b* 12 Jan. 1934; *s* of Alfred H. Sykes and Edith A. (*née* Wortley); *m* 1963, Elizabeth Blakey; two *s* one *d*. *Educ:* Huddersfield Coll.; Univ. of Manchester (BSc; PhD 1958; DSc 1973); Univ. of Princeton; Univ. of Adelaide. CChem, FRSC 1972. Lectr, 1961–70, Reader, 1970–80, Univ. of Leeds. Vis. Scientist, Argonne Nat. Labs, USA, 1968; Visitor or Visiting Professor: Heidelberg Univ., 1975; Northwestern Univ., 1978; Univ. of Berne, 1981; Univ. of Sydney, 1984; Univ. of Kuwait, 1989; Univs of Adelaide and Melbourne, 1992; Univ. of Newfoundland, 1995; Univs of the W Indies, 1997; Univ. of Lausanne, 1998; Univs of Stellenbosch, Cape Town and Bloemfontein, 1999; Univ. La Laguna, Spain, 2000; City Univ., Hong Kong, 2001, 2002; Denmark Technical Univ., 2002; Troisième Cycle Lectr, Les Rasses, 1971, Les Diablerets, 1987, Champéry, 2000, French-speaking Swiss Univs. Editor: Advances in Inorganic and Bioinorganic Mechanisms (vols 1–4), 1982–86; Advances in Inorganic Chem. (vols 32–53), 1988–2002. Tilden Lectr (Medal and Prize), RSC, 1984. Fellow, Japanese Soc. for Promotion of Sci., 1986; Royal Soc. Kan Tong Po Fellow, HK, 2002–03. Hon. DSc Free State Univ., SA, 2003. *Publications:* Kinetics of Inorganic Reactions, 1966;

contrib. over 470 papers and reviews in chemistry jls. *Recreations:* travel, birdwatching, classical music, sport. *Address:* Department of Chemistry, University of Newcastle, Newcastle upon Tyne NE1 7RU; 73 Beech Court, Darras Hall, Newcastle upon Tyne NE20 9NE.
Died 10 July 2007.

SYKES, (James) Richard; QC 1981; Chairman, Financial Reporting Review Panel, 2000–04; *b* 28 May 1934; *s* of late Philip James and Lucy Barbara Sykes; *m* 1959, Susan Ethne Patricia Allen, *d* of late Lt-Col J. M. and Mrs E. M. B. Allen, Morrinsville, NZ; three *d* (one *s* decd). *Educ:* Charterhouse; Pembroke Coll., Cambridge (BA 1957; MA 1971). Nat. Service, 2nd Lieut RASC, 1952–54. Called to the Bar, Lincoln's Inn, 1958, Bencher, 1989; in practice at Bar, 1958–99. CEDR Accredited Mediator, 1999. Member: City Company Law Cttee, 1974–79; City Capital Markets Cttee, 1980–94; Steering Gp, Govt Review of Company Law, 1998–2001; Chairman: Judging Panel, Accountant and Stock Exchange Annual Awards, 1982–90; Judging Panel, Stock Exchange and Inst. of Chartered Accountants Awards, 1990–99. Mem. Mgt Cttee, Internat. Exhibn Co-operative Wine Soc. Ltd, 1986–2003; Maître, Commanderie de Bordeaux, London, 2005–. Mem. Council, VSO, 1987–99 (Mem. Exec., 1987–93). *Publications:* (Consultant Editor) Gore-Browne on Companies, 42nd edn 1972, 43rd edn 1977, 44th edn 1986; (ed jtly) The Conduct of Meetings, 20th edn 1966, 21st edn 1975. *Address:* c/o Erskine Chambers, 33 Chancery Lane, WC2A 1EN. *T:* (020) 7242 5532.
Died 17 July 2007.

SYKES, Joseph Walter, CMG 1962; CVO 1953; Chairman, Fiji Public Service Commission, 1971–80, retired 1981; *b* 10 July 1915; *s* of Samuel Sykes and Lucy M. Womack; *m* 1940, Elima Petrie, *d* of late Sir Hugh Hall Ragg; three *s* two *d. Educ:* De La Salle Coll., Sheffield; Rotherham Gram. Sch.; Jesus Coll., Oxford. Colonial Administrative Service, Fiji; Cadet, 1938; Dist Officer, 1940; District Commissioner, 1950; Deputy Secretary for Fijian Affairs, 1952; Assistant Colonial Secretary, 1953; transferred to Cyprus as Dep. Colonial Sec., Nov. 1954; Admin. Sec., Cyprus. 1955–56; Colonial Sec., Bermuda, 1956–68; Chief Sec., Bermuda, 1968–71; retired. *Publications:* The Royal Visit to Fiji 1953, 1954. *Recreations:* gardening, carpentry. *Address:* 8 Dorking Road, City Beach, Perth, WA 6015, Australia.
Died 4 April 2007.

SYKES, Richard; see Sykes, J. R.

SYMINGTON, Prof. Sir Thomas, Kt 1978; MD; FRSE; Director, 1970–77, and Professor of Pathology, 1970–77, Institute of Cancer Research, Royal Cancer Hospital; *b* 1 April 1915; *m* 1943, Esther Margaret Forsyth, MB, ChB; two *s* one *d. Educ:* Cumnock Academy; Glasgow Univ. BSc 1936; MB ChB, 1941; MD 1950. Maj., RAMC (Dep. Asst Dir Pathology, Malaya, 1947–49). St Mungo (Notman) Prof. of Pathology, Univ. of Glasgow, 1954–70. Visiting Prof. of Pathology, Stanford Univ., Calif., 1965–66. Member, Medical Research Council, 1968–72. FRSE 1956; FRIC 1958 (ARIC 1951); FRCP(G) 1963; FRFPS (G) 1958; FRCPath 1964. Hon. MD Szeged Univ., Hungary, 1971; Hon. DSc McGill Univ., Canada, 1983. *Publications:* Functional Pathology of the Human Adrenal Gland, 1969; Scientific Foundations of Oncology, 1976; A Chance to Remember: my life in medicine (autobiog.), 2003; numerous papers on problems of adrenal glands in Journals of Endocrinology and Pathology. *Recreation:* golf.
Died 30 April 2007.

SYMONDS, (John) Richard (Charters); Senior Research Associate, Queen Elizabeth House, Oxford, since 1979; *b* 2 Oct. 1918; *s* of Sir Charles Putnam Symonds, KBE, CB, DM, FRCP, and Janet (*née* Poulton); *m* 1st, 1948, Juanita Ellington (*d* 1979); one *s* (and one *s* decd); 2nd, 1980, Ann Hazel Spokes (A. H. Spokes Symonds). *Educ:* Rugby Sch.; Corpus Christi Coll., Oxford (Scholar in Mod. History, MA); Secretary Elect, Oxford Union, 1939. Friends Amb. Unit, 1939–44; Dep. Dir Relief and Rehab., Govt of Bengal, 1944–45; UNRRA, Austria, 1946–47; Friends Service Unit, Punjab and Kashmir, 1947–48; UN Commn for India and Pakistan (Kashmir), 1948–49; UN Technical Assistance Board: New York, 1950–51; Liaison Officer in Europe, 1952–53; Resident Rep., Ceylon, 1953–55; Yugoslavia, 1955–58; Rep. in Europe, 1959–62; Reg. Rep., E Africa, 1961. Sen. Res. Officer, Oxford Univ. Inst. of Commonwealth Studies, 1962–65; Reg. Rep. in Southern Africa, UNTAB, 1964–65; Professorial Fellow, IDS, Univ. of Sussex, 1966–69, later Vis. Prof.; Consultant, UN Population Div., 1968–69; Rep. in Europe, UNITAR, 1969–71; UNDP Resident Rep. in Greece, 1972–75, and in Tunisia, 1975–78; Sen. Adviser, UNDP and UN Fund for Population Activities, NY, 1978–79; Sen. Associate Mem., St Antony's Coll., Oxford, 1979–92; Hon. Dir, UN Career Records Project, 1989–92; Consultant: Commonwealth Foundn, 1980; WHO, 1981. Mem. Council, Royal Commonwealth Soc., 1983–86. *Publications:* The Making of Pakistan, 1950; The British and their Successors, 1966; (ed) International Targets for Development, 1970; (with M. Carder) The United Nations and the Population Question, 1973; Oxford and Empire—the last lost cause?, 1986; Alternative Saints: the post Reformation British people commemorated by the Church of England, 1988; Far Above Rubies: the women uncommemorated by the Church of England, 1993; Inside the Citadel: men and the emancipation of women 1850–1920, 1999; In the Margins of Independence: a relief worker in India and Pakistan 1942–49, 2001; The Fox, The Bees and The Pelican: worthies and noteworthies of Corpus Christi College, Oxford, 2002; Daring To Be Wise: more worthies and noteworthies of Corpus Christi College, Oxford, 2004. *Recreations:* walking, travel. *Address:* 43 Davenant Road, Oxford OX2 8BU. *Club:* Royal Over-Seas League.
Died 15 July 2006.

SYMONS, Prof. Robert Henry, FRS 1988; FAA 1983; Professor, Department of Plant Science, University of Adelaide, 1991–99, Emeritus Professor, since 2000; *b* 20 March 1934; *s* of Irene Olivette Symons (*née* Wellington) and Henry Officer Symons; *m* 1958, Verna Helen Lloyd; two *s* two *d. Educ:* Univ. of Melbourne (BAgSc 1956; PhD 1963), Senior Demonstrator, Univ. of Melbourne, 1958–60; Post-Doctoral Fellow, UK, 1961–62; Lectr, Sen. Lectr, Reader, Prof., Dept of Biochemistry, Univ. of Adelaide, 1962–90. Hon. DSc Macquarie, 1992. Lemberg Medal, Aust. Biochem. Soc., 1985; Centenary Medal, Australia, 2003. *Publications:* papers to learned jls on nucleic acid biochemistry and allied subjects. *Recreations:* gardening, wine, managing wine grape vineyard.
Died 4 Oct. 2006.

SYSONBY, 3rd Baron *cr* 1935, of Wonersh; **John Frederick Ponsonby;** *b* 5 Aug. 1945; *s* of 2nd Baron Sysonby, DSO and Sallie Monkland, *d* of Dr Leonard Sanford, New York; *S* father, 1956. *Address:* c/o Friars, White Friars, Chester CH1 1XS.
Died 23 Oct. 2009 (ext).

T

TAFTI, Rt Rev. Hassan Barnaba D.; *see* Dehqani-Tafti.

TAHOURDIN, John Gabriel, CMG 1961; HM Diplomatic Service, retired; *b* 15 Nov. 1913; *s* of late John St Clair Tahourdin; *m* 1957, Margaret Michie (*d* 2004); one *s* one *d*. *Educ*: Merchant Taylors' School; St John's College, Oxford. Served HM Embassy, Peking, 1936–37; Private Secretary to HM Ambassador at Shanghai, 1937–40; BoT, 1940–41; Vice-Consul, Baltimore, 1941; Foreign Office, 1942; Private Secretary to Parliamentary Under-Secretary of State, 1943, and to Minister of State, 1945; Athens, 1946; returned to Foreign Office, 1949; Counsellor, British Embassy, The Hague, 1955; Foreign Office, 1957; Minister, UK Delegn to 18 Nation Disarmament Conf., Geneva, 1963–66; HM Ambassador to: Senegal, 1966–71, and concurrently to Mauritania, 1968–71, to Mali, 1969–71, and to Guinea, 1970–71; Bolivia, 1971–73. Mem., Internat. Inst. for Strategic Studies. Price Commission, 1975–77; Kleinwort Benson, 1977–79. *Recreations*: music cinematography, foreign languages, travel. *Address*: Diana Lodge, Little Kineton, Warwick CV35 0DL. *T*: (01926) 640276.   *Died 11 Feb. 2007.*

TAIT, Dr Alan Anderson; Director, International Monetary Fund in Geneva, 1995–98; *b* 1 July 1934; *s* of Stanley Tait and Margaret Ruth (*née* Anderson); *m* 1963, Susan Valerie Somers; one *s*. *Educ*: Heriot's Sch., Edinburgh; Univ. of Edinburgh (MA); Trinity Coll., Dublin (PhD; Hon. Fellow, 1996). Lectr, Trinity Coll., Dublin, 1959–71 (Fellow, 1968, Sen. Tutor, 1970); Visiting Prof., Univ. of Illinois, 1969. Economic adviser to Irish Govt on industrial develt and taxation and chief economic adviser to Confedn of Irish Industry, 1967–71; Prof. of Money and Finance, Univ. of Strathclyde, 1971–77; economic consultant to Sec. of State for Scotland, 1972–77; International Monetary Fund: Visiting Scholar, 1972; Consultant, 1973, 1974, 1999, 2001; Chief, Fiscal Analysis Div., 1976–79; Asst Dir, 1979–82; Dep. Dir, Fiscal Affairs Dept, 1982–94. Hon. Prof., Univ. of Kent at Canterbury, 2000–. Co-Chm., Wkg Gp on Financing Health, Commn on Macroeconomics and Health, 2000–02. *Publications*: The Taxation of Personal Wealth, 1967; (with J. Bristow) Economic Policy in Ireland, 1968; (with J. Bristow) Ireland: some problems of a developing economy, 1971; The Value Added Tax, 1972; The Value Added Tax: international practice and problems, 1988; (ed) Value Added Tax: administrative and policy issues, 1991; articles on public finance in Rev. of Economic Studies, Finanzarchiv, Public Finance, Staff Papers, etc. *Recreation*: painting and gardening. *Address*: Cramond House, Harnet Street, Sandwich, Kent CT13 9ES. *T*: (01304) 621038.   *Club*: Cosmos   (Washington,   DC).
                                                       Died 19 Oct. 2009.

TANCRED, Sir Henry L.; *see* Lawson-Tancred.

TANGAROA, Hon. Sir Tangaroa, Kt 1987; MBE 1984; Queen's Representative, Cook Islands, 1984–90; *b* 6 May 1921; *s* of Tangaroa and Mihiau; *m* 1941; two *s* seven *d*. *Educ*: Avarua Primary School, Rarotonga. Radio operator, 1939–54; Shipping Clerk, A. B. Donald Ltd and J. & P. Ingram Ltd, 1955–63; MP for Penrhyn, 1958–84; Minister of Educn, Works, Survey, Printing and Electric Power Supply; Minister of Internal Affairs, 1978–80; retired from politics, 1984. Pres., Cook Is Crippled Children's Soc., 1966–; Deacon, Cook Is Christian Church (served 15 years in Penrhyn, 28 years in Avarua); former community positions: Mem., Tereora Coll. Sch. Cttee for 20 years and 10 as Sec./Treasurer; Pres., Cook Is Boys Brigade for 15 years; delegate to Cook Is Sports

Assoc. Silver Jubilee Medal, 1977; Commemoration Medal (NZ), 1990. *Address*: PO Box 870, Avarua, Rarotonga, Cook Islands.   *Died 23 May 2009.*

TANNER, John W., CBE 1983; FRIBA, FRTPI; Director, United Nations Relief and Works Agency for Palestine Refugees, Jordan, 1971–83 (accorded rank of Ambassador to Hashemite Kingdom of Jordan, 1973); *b* 15 Nov. 1923; *s* of Walter George Tanner and Elizabeth Wilkes Tanner (*née* Humphreys); *m* 1st, 1948, Hazel Harford Harford-Jones (*d* 1996); one *s* two *d*; 2nd, 1999, Jacqueline Mary Richards (*née* Hands). *Educ*: Clifton Coll.; Liverpool Univ. Sch. of Architecture and Dept of Civic Design. MCD, BArch (Hons). Sen. Planning Officer, Nairobi, 1951; Architect, Nairobi, 1953; Hon. Sec., Kenya Chapter of Architects, 1954; UN Relief and Works Agency: Architect and Planning Officer, Beirut, 1955; Chief Techn. Div., 1957. Past Mem. Cttee, Fedn of Internat. Civil Servants Assoc., 1968–70. *Buildings*: vocational and teacher training centres (Damascus, Syria; Siblin, Lebanon; Ramallah; Wadi Seer; Amman, Jordan); schools; low cost housing and health centres; E African Rugby Union HQ, Nairobi. *Publications*: The Colour Problem in Liverpool: accommodation or assimilation, 1951; Building for the UNRWA/UNESCO Education and Training Programme, 1968. *Recreations*: formerly: Rugby football (Waterloo, Lancs, 1950; Kenya Harlequins, Kenya and E Africa); ski-ing, squash, board sailing. *Address*: 69B La Pleta, Ordino, Andorra.
                                                       Died 19 Sept. 2009.

TAPP, David Robert George; District Judge (Magistrates' Courts) (formerly Provincial Stipendiary Magistrate): County of Merseyside, 1992–2002; Greater Manchester Magistrates' Court, 2002; *b* 13 Oct. 1948; *s* of Victor George Tapp and May Allen Tapp. *Educ*: Stockport Sch.; Manchester Univ. (LLB Hons). Solicitor. Articled Clerk, Wigan Magistrates' Court, 1971–73; Principal Asst, Eccles Magistrates' Court, 1973–80; Dep. Justices' Clerk, 1980–83, Justices' Clerk, 1983–92, Stoke-on-Trent Magistrates' Court. Mem., British Pottery Manufrs' Fedn Club. *Recreations*: watching sport, waterfowl, music, Manchester City FC, Lancashire CCC.   *Died 2008.*

TARJANNE, Pekka Johannes; Chairman, Futurice Ltd, Finland, 2002–08; *b* 19 Sept. 1937; *s* of P. K. Tarjanne and Annu Tarjanne; *m* 1962, Aino Kairamo; two *s* one *d* (and one *d* decd). *Educ*: Helsinki Univ. of Technology (Dr Tech. 1962). Prof. of Theoretical Physics, Univ. of Oulu, 1965–66, Univ. of Helsinki, 1967–77. MP, Finland, 1970–77; Minister of Communications, 1972–75; Dir Gen., Posts and Telecommunications, 1977–89; Sec. Gen., ITU, UN, 1989–99; Vice-Chm., Project Oxygen, 1999–2000; Exec. Co-ordinator, ICT Task Force, UN, 2001–03. Chm., Internat. Selection Bd, Millennium Technology Prize, Finland, 2003–07. Commander, Order of White Rose of Finland, 1977; Grand Cross, Order of Finnish Lion, 1998; Comdr, Legion of Honour (France), 1999.   *Died 24 Feb. 2010.*

TATLOW, John Colin, PhD, DSc (Birmingham); CChem; FRSC; consultant; Professor of Organic Chemistry, University of Birmingham, 1959–82, then Emeritus; *b* 19 Jan. 1923; *s* of Thomas George and Florence Annie Tatlow, Cannock, Staffs; *m* 1946, Clarice Evelyn Mabel, *d* of Eric Millward and Mabel Evelyn Joiner, Sutton Coldfield; two *d*. *Educ*: Rugeley Grammar School, Staffs; University of Birmingham. Scientific Officer, Min. of Supply, 1946–48; University of Birmingham: Lectr in Chemistry, 1948–56; Sen. Lectr, 1956–57; Reader in Organic Chemistry, 1957–59; Head of Dept of Chemistry, 1974–81. Council of Chemical Society, 1957–60. Examiner, Royal Inst. of Chemistry, 1963–67. Journal of Fluorine Chemistry: Founding Ed.,

1971; Jt Ed., 1971–97; Hon. Ed., 1997. ACS Award for creative work in fluorine chemistry, 1990. *Publications:* over 300 scientific papers on fluorine chemistry, mainly in Jl of Chem. Soc., Tetrahedron, Nature, and Jl of Fluorine Chem. *Died 9 April 2008.*

TAVARÉ, Andrew Kenneth; Special Commissioner of Income Tax, 1976–88 (Deputy Special Commissioner, April–Oct. 1988); *b* 10 Jan. 1918; *s* of late L. A. Tavaré, Bromley, Kent; *m* 1950, June Elinor Attwood, Beckenham, Kent; three *s*. *Educ:* Chatham House School, Ramsgate; King's College, London (LLB). Solicitor of the Supreme Court. Served War with 79th HAA Regt (Hertfordshire Yeomanry), RA, 1940–45; N Africa and Italy, rank of Captain. Admitted Solicitor, 1948; Solicitor's Office, Inland Revenue, 1953–; Assistant Solicitor, 1965–75. Consultant Editor of Sergeant on Stamp Duties, 4th edition 1963, to 8th edition 1982. *Publications:* (contrib.) Simon's Taxes, 2nd edn, 1965, and 3rd edn, 1970. *Died 24 June 2006.*

TAYLOR, Claire Mavis, RRC 1994 (ARRC 1977); Matron-in-Chief, 1994–97, and Captain (formerly Principal Naval Nursing Officer), Queen Alexandra's Royal Naval Nursing Service, 1990–97; *b* 26 May 1943; *d* of late William Taylor and Sybil (*née* Matthews). *Educ:* George Dixon Grammar Sch., Edgbaston. SRN 1964; SCM 1967; RNT 1977. Served QARNNS, 1967–73; Nursing Sister, Papua New Guinea, 1973–74; rejoined QARNNS 1975; QHNS, 1994–97. OStJ. *Recreations:* travel, reading. *Address:* c/o Lloyds TSB, 20–24 High Street, Gosport, Hants PO12 1DE. *Club:* Army and Navy. *Died 23 Feb. 2010.*

TAYLOR, David George Pendleton, CBE 1993; Governor of Montserrat, West Indies, 1990–93; *b* 5 July 1933; *s* of George James Pendleton Taylor and Dorothy May Taylor (*née* Williams). *Educ:* Clifton College; Clare College, Cambridge (MA). Nat. Service as Sub-Lieut (Special) RNVR, 1952–54; Admin. Officer, HMOCS Tanganyika, 1958–63; joined Booker McConnell, 1964; Chm. and Chief Exec., Bookers (Malawi) Ltd, 1976–77; Director: Consumer Buying Corp. of Zambia, 1978; National Drug Co., Zambia, 1978; Bookers (Zambia), 1978; Minvielle & Chastanet Ltd, St Lucia, 1979; United Rum Merchants Ltd, 1981; Estate Industries Ltd, Jamaica, 1981; seconded full time to Falkland Is Govt, Dec. 1983; Chief Exec., Falkland Islands Govt and Exec. Vice Chm., FI Develt Corp., 1983–87 and 1988–89 (sometime acting Governor). Dir, Booker Agric. Internat., 1987–88. Member: Royal African Soc., 1986–; RIIA, 1988–. Mem., Commonwealth Election Observer Mission to Tanzania, 1995. Mem. Council, Book Aid Internat., 1996–2001; Trustee: Falklands Conservation, 1996–2001; Montserrat Foundn, 1997–; Overseas Territories Envmtl Forum, 1998–2006. Governor, Clifton Coll., 1987–; Pres., Old Cliftonian Soc., 1993–95; Mem., Gen. Purposes Cttee, Clifton Coll. Foundn, 2003–. FRGS 1990–2002. *Recreations:* water colour painting, travel, rural France, writing about colonial administration. *Address:* 17 Cholmeley Lodge, Cholmeley Park, N6 5EN. *Clubs:* Oxford and Cambridge, MCC. *Died 8 Nov. 2007.*

TAYLOR, David Leslie; MP (Lab and Co-op) Leicestershire North West, since 1997; *b* 22 Aug. 1946; *s* of late Leslie Taylor and of Eileen Mary Taylor; *m* 1969, Pamela (*née* Caunt); four *d* (one *s* decd). *Educ:* Ashby-de-la-Zouch Boys' Grammar Sch.; Leicester Poly.; Lanchester Poly. (CPFA); Open Univ. (BA Maths and Computing). Accountant and computer manager, Leics CC, 1977–97. Mem. (Lab) NW Leics DC, 1981–87, 1992–95. Contested (Lab) Leics NW, 1992. JP Ashby-de-la-Zouch, 1985. *Address:* House of Commons, SW1A 0AA. *Died 26 Dec. 2009.*

TAYLOR, Eric; a Recorder of the Crown Court, 1978–98; *b* 22 Jan. 1931; *s* of Sydney Taylor and Sarah Helen (*née* Lea); *m* 1958, Margaret Jessie Taylor, OBE. *Educ:* Wigan Grammar Sch.; Manchester Univ. (LLB 1952; Dauntesey Sen. Legal Scholar; LLM 1954).

Admitted solicitor, 1955. Partner, Temperley Taylor (formerly Temperley Taylor Chadwick), Middleton, Manchester, 1957–2001, Consultant (full-time), 2001–05. Part-time Lectr in Law, Manchester Univ., 1958–80, Hon. Special Lectr in Law, 1980–2005. Examr, (Old) Law Soc. Final Exams, 1968–81, Chief Examr, (New) Law Soc. Final Exams, 1978–83; External Examiner, Qualified Lawyers' Transfer Test, 1990–2002; Chief Examr for solicitors qualifying to appear as advocates, 1993–97. President: Oldham Law Assoc., 1970–72; Rochdale Law Assoc., 1998–99. Chairman: Manchester Young Solicitors' Gp, 1963; Manchester Nat. Insurance Appeal Tribunal, 1967–73; Disciplinary Cttee, Architects Registration Council, 1989–95. Member: Council, Law Soc., 1972–91 (Chm., Educn and Trng Cttee, 1980–83; Chm., Criminal Law Cttee, 1984–87); CNAA Legal Studies Bd, 1975–84; Lord Chancellor's Adv. Cttee on Trng of Magistrates, 1974–79. Governor: Coll. of Law, 1984–2000; Bd, Common Professional Examn, 1990–2002. *Publications:* Modern Conveyancing Precedents, 1964, 2nd edn 1989; Modern Wills Precedents, 1969, 3rd edn 1997; contrib. legal jls. *Recreation:* equestrian sports. *Address:* 10 Mercers Road, Heywood, Lancs OL10 2NP. *T:* (01706) 366630. *Died 22 Nov. 2010.*

TAYLOR, Henry George, DSc(Eng); Director of Electrical Research Association, 1957–69, retired; *b* 4 Nov. 1904; *m* 1931, Gwendolyn Hilda Adams; one *s* two *d*. *Educ:* Taunton School, Battersea Polytechnic Inst., City and Guilds Engineering College. Metropolitan Vickers, 1929–30; Electrical Research Assoc., 1930–38; Copper Development Assoc., 1938–42; Philips Lamps Ltd, 1942–47; British Welding Research Assoc., 1947–57. *Publications:* contribs to: Instn of Electrical Engineers Jl, Jl of Inst. of Physics, etc. *Recreation:* walking. *Died 9 March 2007.*

TAYLOR, His Honour Ivor Ralph; QC 1973; a Circuit Judge, 1976–94; *b* 26 Oct. 1927; *s* of late Abraham and Ruth Taylor; *m* 1st, 1954, Ruth Cassel (marr. diss. 1974); one *s* one *d* (and one *d* decd); 2nd, 1974, Jane Elisabeth Ann Gibson (marr. diss. 1978); 3rd, 1984, (Audrey) Joyce Goldman (*née* Wayne). *Educ:* Stand Grammar Sch., Whitefield; Manchester Univ. Served War of 1939–45, AC2 in RAF, 1945. Called to Bar, Gray's Inn, 1951. Standing Counsel to Inland Revenue, N Circuit, 1969–73; a Recorder of the Crown Court, 1972–76. Chm., Inquiry into Death of Baby Brown at Rochdale Infirmary, 1974. Chm., PTA, Dept of Audiology, Manchester Univ., 1966–67. Pres., Manchester and District Medico Legal Soc., 1974, 1975. Gov., Royal Manchester Children's Hosp., 1967–70; Mem. Management Cttee, Salford Hosp., 1967–70. *Died 1 July 2006.*

TAYLOR, Keith Breden, MA, DM; FRCP; Vice-Chancellor for International Development, St George's University (formerly St George's University School of Medicine), since 1998 (Vice-Chancellor, 1989–90 and 1992–98); George de Forest Barnett Professor of Medicine, Stanford University, 1966–81 and 1982–89, then Emeritus; *b* 16 April 1924; *yr s* of Francis Henry Taylor and Florence (*née* Latham); *m* 1st, 1949, Ann Gaynor Hughes Jones (marr. diss. 1971); three *s* one *d* (and one *s* decd); 2nd, 1972, Kym Williams (*d* 1992), Adelaide, Aust. *Educ:* King's College Sch., Wimbledon; Magdalen Coll., Oxford (Exhibnr; BA Hons Physiology 1946, BM BCh 1949). Member, SHAEF Nutrition Survey Team, 1945; RAMC (Major), 1951–53; Dir Gen., Health Educn Council, 1981–82. Late Hon. Consultant, Central Middlesex Hosp.; Mem., MRC Gastroenterology Research Unit; Asst in Nuffield Dept Clin. Med., Oxford. Radcliffe Travelling Fellow, 1953; Rockefeller Foundn Fellow, 1959; Guggenheim Fellow, 1971; Fogarty Sen. Fellow, USPHS, 1978–79. Cons., US National Insts of Health; Mem., USPHS Trng Grants Cttee in Gastroenterology and Nutrition, 1965–70; Chm., Stanford Univ. Cttee on Human Nutrition, 1974–81; Vis. Professorships include: Rochester, NY, 1966; Columbia-Presbyterian, NY, 1969; Univ. of

Adelaide, 1971; Academic Medical Unit, Royal Free Hosp., 1978–79. *Publications:* contribs to scientific jls, also texts, espec. in biochemistry and physiology of vitamin B12, immunological and other aspects of gastrointestinal disease and nutrition. *Recreations:* theatre, tennis, walking, gardening. *Address:* St George's International School of Medicine, Grenada, Kingdon's Yard, Parchment Street, Winchester, Hampshire SO23 8AT. *Club:* Athenæum.
Died 31 Dec. 2006.

TAYLOR, Sir Robert (Richard), KCVO 2006; OBE 1989 (MBE (mil.) 1972); JP; Lord Lieutenant, County of West Midlands, 1993–2006; *b* 14 June 1932; *s* of Sydney Arthur Taylor and Edith Alice Taylor; *m* 1957, Sheila Welch. *Educ:* Yardley Grammar Sch., Birmingham. Pilot then Sqdn Leader, RAF, 1950–73. Progressive Properties, Birmingham, 1973–74; Asst Dir, 1974–76, Airport Dir, 1976–86, Man. Dir, 1986–94, Birmingham Airport plc. Chm., Airport Operators Assoc., 1987–88. Council Mem., Birmingham Chamber of Commerce, 1989–94; Dir, Central England TEC, 1990–94. Chm., BRMB Radio Ltd, 1994–2000; Director: Capital Radio plc, 1994–2000; Maersk Air Ltd, 1994–2003. Chairman: Solihull Crime Concern, 1989–94; Disabled Persons Transport Adv. Cttee, 1993–98; Tourism For All Consortium, 1997–2002. Freeman, City of London, 1998. JP W Midlands, 1994. DUniv Central England, 1993; Hon. LLD Birmingham, 1998. KStJ 1994. QCVSA 1966. *Recreations:* literature, people. *Address:* Holly Cottage, 43 Fieldgate Lane, Kenilworth, Warwicks CV8 1BT. *T:* (01926) 853113. *Club:* Royal Air Force.
Died 7 June 2008.

TAYLOR, Ronald George, CBE 1988; Director-General, British Chambers of Commerce (formerly Association of British Chambers of Commerce), 1984–98; *b* 12 Dec. 1935; *s* of Ernest and May Taylor; *m* 1960, Patricia Stoker; one *s* two *d*. *Educ:* Jesus College, Oxford (BA Modern Langs). Commnd Royal Signals, 1957–59. Leeds Chamber of Commerce and Industry: joined, 1959; Asst Sec., 1964–74; Director, 1974–84. *Recreations:* family history, Rugby Union, bridge. *Address:* 2 Holly Bush Lane, Harpenden, Herts AL5 4AP. *T:* (01582) 712139. *Died 28 Sept. 2009.*

TE ATAIRANGIKAAHU, Arikinui, ONZ 1987; DBE 1970; Arikinui and Head of Maori Kingship, since 1966; *b* 23 July 1931; *o d* of King Koroki V; *m* 1952, Whatumoana; two *s* five *d*. *Educ:* Waikato Diocesan School, Hamilton, NZ. Elected by the Maori people as Head of the Maori Kingship on the death of King Koroki, the fifth Maori King, with title of Arikinui (Queen), in 1966. Hon. Dr Waikato, 1979; Hon. LLD Victoria Univ., Wellington, 1999. OStJ 1986. Gold and Silver Star, Order of Sacred Treasure (Japan), 1996. *Recreation:* the fostering of all aspects of Maori culture and traditions. *Address:* Turongo House, Turangawaewae Marae, PO Box 63, Ngaruawahia 2171, New Zealand.
Died 15 Aug. 2006.

TEBBIT, Sir Donald (Claude), GCMG 1980 (KCMG 1975; CMG 1965); HM Diplomatic Service, retired; *b* 4 May 1920; *er s* of Richard Claude Tebbit and Edith Magdalen Tebbit (*née* Dixon); *m* 1947, Barbara Margaret Olson, *d* of Rev. Norman Matheson and Henrietta Matheson (*née* Gunn); one *s* two *d* (and one *d* decd). *Educ:* Perse School; Trinity Hall, Cambridge (MA). Served War of 1939–45, RNVR. Joined Foreign (later Diplomatic) Service, 1946; Second Secretary, Washington, 1948; transferred to Foreign Office, 1951; First Secretary, 1952; transferred to Bonn, 1954; Private Secretary to Minister of State, Foreign Office, 1958; Counsellor, 1962; transferred to Copenhagen, 1964; Commonwealth Office, 1967; Asst Under-Sec. of State, FCO, 1968–70; Minister, British Embassy, Washington, 1970–72; Chief Clerk, FCO, 1972–76; High Comr in Australia, 1976–80. Chairman: Diplomatic Service Appeals Bd, 1980–87; E-SU, 1983–87; Mem., Appeals Bd, Council of Europe, 1981–90. Dir, RTZ Corp., 1980–90. Dir Gen., British Property Fedn, 1980–85. Pres. (UK), Australian-British Chamber of Commerce,

1980–90; Chairman: Zimbabwe Tech. Management Training Trust, 1983–91; Marshall Aid Commemoration Commn, 1985–95; Jt Commonwealth Socs Council, 1987–93. Governor, Nuffield Hospitals, 1980–90, Dep. Chm., 1985–90. President: Old Persean Soc., 1981–82; Trinity Hall Assoc., 1984–85. *Address:* Morningside, 38 Chapel Street, Ely, Cambs CB6 1AD. *Club:* Travellers.
Died 25 Sept. 2010.

TELFORD, Sir Robert, Kt 1978; CBE 1967; DL; FREng, FIET; Life President, The Marconi Company Ltd, 1984 (Managing Director, 1965–81; Chairman, 1981–84, retired); *b* 1 Oct. 1915; *s* of Robert and Sarah Annie Telford; *m* 1st, 1941 (marr. diss. 1950); one *s*; 2nd, 1958, Elizabeth Mary (*née* Shelley); three *d*. *Educ:* Quarry Bank Sch., Liverpool; Queen Elizabeth's Grammar Sch., Tamworth; Christ's Coll., Cambridge (MA). FREng (FEng 1978). Manager, Hackbridge Works, The Marconi Co. Ltd, 1940–46; Man. Dir, Companhia Marconi Brasileira, 1946–50; The Marconi Company Ltd: Asst to Gen. Manager, 1950–53; Gen. Works Manager, 1953–61; Gen. Manager, 1961–65; Man. Dir, GEC-Marconi Electronics Ltd, 1968–84; Chm., GEC Avionics Ltd, 1982–86; Director: The General Electric Co., 1973–84; Canadian Marconi Co., Montreal, 1968–84; Ericsson Radio Systems AB (formerly SRA Communications, AB), Stockholm, 1969–85. Chairman: DRI Hldgs Ltd, 1984–88; Prelude Technology Investments, 1985–91; CTP Investments, 1987–90; Diametric, 1988–89; Dir, BAJ Hldgs, 1985–87. Visitor, Hatfield Polytech., 1986–91. President: Electronic Engrg Assoc., 1963–64; IProdE, 1982–83; Chairman: Electronics and Avionics Requirement Bd, DTI, 1980–85; Alvey Steering Cttee, 1983–88; SERC Teaching Company Management Cttee, 1984–87; Commonwealth Engineers' Council, 1989–93; Member: Electronics EDC, 1964–67, 1981–85; Engrg Industry Trng Bd, 1968–82; Council, Industrial Soc., 1982–86; Council, Fellowship of Engrg, 1983–86; BTEC, 1984–86; SERC Engrg Bd, 1985–88; Engrg Council, 1985–89; IT Adv. Gp, DTI, 1985–88. Advr to Comett Programme of European Community, 1987–95; Mem., Industrial R & D Adv. Cttee to European Community, 1988–92. Mem., Council of Sen. Advrs to Internat. Assoc. of Univ. Presidents, 1992. Mem., Council, 1981–88, and Court, 1981–, Univ. of Essex. DL Essex, 1981. Freeman, City of London, 1984. CCMI; FRSA. Hon. FIMechE 1983; Hon. FIET (Hon. FIEE 1987); Hon. FICE 1992. Hon. Fellow, Hatfield Poly., 1991. Hon. DSc: Salford, 1981; Cranfield, 1983; Bath, 1984; Aston, 1985; Hon. DEng: Bradford, 1986; Birmingham, 1986; Hon. DTech Anglia Inst., 1989. Leonardo da Vinci Medal, SEFI, 1992. *Address:* Rettendon House, Rettendon, Chelmsford, Essex CM3 8DW. *T:* (01268) 733131. *Club:* Royal Air Force.
Died 10 March 2008.

TELLO, Manuel, Hon. CMG 1975; Permanent Representative of Mexico to the United Nations, 1993–94 and 1995–2000; *b* 15 March 1935; *s* of late Manuel Tello and Guadalupe M. de Tello; *m* 1959, Sonia D. de Tello; *m* 1983, Rhonda M. de Tello (*née* Mosesman); three step *d*. *Educ:* schools in Mexico City; Georgetown Univ.; Sch. for Foreign Service, Washington, DC; Escuela Libre de Derecho; Institut de Hautes Etudes Internationales, Geneva. Equivalent of BA in Foreign Service Studies; post-grad. studies in Internat. Law. Joined Mexican Foreign Service, 1957; Asst Dir Gen. for Internat. Organizations, 1967–70, Dir Gen., 1970–72; Dir for Multilateral Affairs, 1972–74; Dir for Political Affairs, 1975–76; Ambassador to UK, 1977–79; Under Sec., Dept of Foreign Affairs, Mexico, 1979–82; Perm. Rep. of Mexico to Internat. Orgns, Geneva, 1983–89; Ambassador to France, 1989–92; Minister of Foreign Affairs, 1994–95. Alternate Rep. of Mexico to: OAS, 1959–63; Internat. Orgs, Geneva, 1963–65; Conf. of Cttee on Disarmament, Geneva, 1963–66; Rep. of Mexico to: Org. for Proscription of Nuclear Weapons in Latin America, 1970–73; 3rd UN Conf. on Law of the Sea, 1971–76 and 1982. Attended several Sessions of UN Gen. Assembly. Pres., Matías

Romeros Inst. of Diplomatic Studies, 2002–04. Decorations from Chile, Ecuador, Egypt, France, Italy, Jordan, Panama, Senegal, Sweden, Venezuela, Yugoslavia. *Publications:* contribs to learned jls in the field of international relations. *Recreations:* reading, theatre, music.   *Died 23 March 2010.*

TEMPANY, Myles McDermott, OBE 1984; Vice-Principal (External Affairs), King's College London, 1986–88; *b* 31 March 1924; *y s* of late Martin Tempany and Margaret (*née* McDermott); *m* 1951, Pamela Allan; one *s* one *d. Educ:* St Muredach's College, Ballina, Co. Mayo; Intermediate and University College, Dublin. Military service, 1944–47. King's College London: Asst Acct, 1948–70; Acct, 1970–73; Finance Officer and Acct, 1973–77; FKC 1975; Bursar, 1977–81; Head of Admin and Bursar, 1981–83; Secretary, 1983–85; Mem. Council, 1986–89. Mem. Delegacy, King's Coll. Sch. of Medicine and Dentistry, 1986–88; Founder Chm., St Raphael's Training Centre Develt Trust, 1978–83; Mem., Governing Body, Univ. of Hertfordshire (formerly Hatfield Polytechnic), 1985–96; Chm., Bd of Governors, Pope Paul Sch., Potters Bar, 1986–96. KHS 1972, KCHS 1978; KSG 1983, KCSG 1996. President's Award, Develt Bd, Univ. of Texas Health Science Center, Houston, 1986. *Recreations:* golf, watching Association Football. *Address:* 18 Tiverton Road, Potters Bar, Herts EN6 5HY. *T:* (01707) 656860. *Club:* Brookman's Park Golf.   *Died 14 March 2008.*

TEMPLE, Reginald Robert, CMG 1979; HM Diplomatic Service, retired; *b* 12 Feb. 1922; *s* of Lt-Gen. R. C. Temple, CB, OBE, RM, and Z. E. Temple (*née* Hunt); *m* 1st, 1952, Julia Jasmine Anthony (marr. diss. 1979); one *s* one *d*; 2nd, 1979, Susan McCorquodale (*née* Pick); one *d* (one step *s* one step *d*). *Educ:* Wellington College; Peterhouse, Cambridge. HM Forces, 1940–46, RE and Para Regt; Stockbroking, 1947–51; entered HM Foreign Service, 1951; Office of HM Comr Gen. for SE Asia, 1952–56; 2nd Sec., Beirut, 1958–62; 1st Sec., Algiers, 1964–66, Paris, 1967–69; FCO, 1969–79; Counsellor 1975; Sultanate of Oman Govt Service, 1979–85. Dir, Shearwater Securities Ltd, I of M, 1989–92. American Silver Star, 1944; Order of Oman, 3rd Class, 1985. *Recreations:* sailing, fishing. *Address:* Scarlett House, near Castletown, Isle of Man IM9 1TB. *Clubs:* Army and Navy, Royal Cruising.   *Died 25 Nov. 2009.*

TEMPLE, Sir Richard Anthony Purbeck, 4th Bt, *cr* 1876; MC 1941; *b* 19 Jan. 1913; *s* of Sir Richard Durand Temple, 3rd Bt, DSO; *S* father, 1962; *m* 1st, 1936, Lucy Geils (marr. diss. 1946), 2nd *d* of late Alain Joly de Lotbinière, Montreal; two *s*; 2nd, 1950, Jean, *d* of late James T. Finnie, and *widow* of Oliver P. Croom-Johnson; one *d. Educ:* Stowe; Trinity Hall, Cambridge; Lausanne University. Served War of 1939–45 (wounded, MC) Sometime Major, KRRC. *Recreation:* sailing. *Heir: s* Richard Temple [*b* 17 Aug. 1937; *m* 1964, Emma Rose, 2nd *d* of late Maj.-Gen. Sir Robert Laycock, KCMG, CB, DSO; three *d*].   *Died 5 Dec. 2007.*

TEMPLETON, Edith; author, since 1950; *b* Prague, 7 April 1916; *m* 1939, William Stockwell Templeton; *m* Edmund Ronald, MD (*d* 1984); one *s. Educ:* Prague and Paris; Prague Medical University. During War of 1939–45 worked in American War Office, in office of Chief Surgeon. Conference Interpreter for British Forces in Germany, 1945–46, rank of Capt. *Publications:* Summer in the Country, 1950 (USA 1951), repr. 1985; Living on Yesterday, 1951, repr. 1986; The Island of Desire, 1952, repr. 1985; The Surprise of Cremona, 1954 (USA 1957), repr. 1988; This Charming Pastime, 1955; (as Louise Walbrook) Gordon, 1966 (US edn as The Demon's Feast, 1968), repr. 2003; Three (USA 1971); Murder in Estoril, 1992; The Darts of Cupid and Other Stories, 2003; contributor to The New Yorker, Holiday, Atlantic Monthly, Vogue, Harper's Magazine, Abroad, The Gourmet's Companion, The Compleat Imbiber, Italian Pleasures. *Recreations:* travel, with the greatest comfort possible. *Address:* 76 Corso Europa, 18012 Bordighera, Italy.   *Died 2006.*

TEMPLETON, Sir John (Marks), Kt 1987; Secretary, John Templeton Foundation, since 1985; Chairman, Templeton, Galbraith and Hansberger Ltd, 1986–92; Chairman Emeritus, Templeton International, Inc.; chartered financial analyst, 1965–92; *b* 29 Nov. 1912; *s* of Harvey Maxwell Templeton and Vella Templeton (*née* Handly); *m* 1st, 1937, Judith Dudley Folk (*d* 1950); two *s* (and one *d* decd); 2nd, 1958, Irene Reynolds Butler (*d* 1993); one step *s* one step *d. Educ:* Yale Univ. (BA *summa cum laude*); Balliol Coll., Oxford (MA; Rhodes Scholar). Vice Pres., Nat. Geophysical Co., 1937–40; President: Templeton Dobbrow and Vance Inc., 1940–60; Templeton Growth Fund Ltd, 1954–85; Templeton Investment Counsel Ltd of Edinburgh, 1976–92; Templeton World Fund Inc., 1978–87; Founder: Templeton Prizes for Progress in Religion, 1972; Templeton UK Project Trust, 1984; Trustee, Templeton Educn and Charity Trust, 1991–; Pres., Bd of Trustees, Princeton Theol Seminary, 1967–73 and 1979–85; Mem., Bd of Trustees, Westminster Abbey Trust, 1991–96. Mem. Council, Templeton College (formerly Oxford Centre for Management Studies), 1983–95 (Hon. Fellow, 1991). Hon. LLD: Beaver Coll., 1968; Marquette Univ., 1980; Jamestown Coll., 1983; Maryville Coll., 1984; Moravian Coll., 1994; Stone Hill Coll., 1995; Hon. LHD: Wilson Coll., 1974; Brigham Young Univ., 1998; Hon. DD Buena Vista Coll., 1979; Hon. DCL Univ. of the South, 1984; Hon. DLitt Manhattan Coll., 1990; Hon. DHL: Campbell Univ., 1993; Johns Hopkins Univ., 2006; Hon. DH Furman Univ., 1995; Hon. PhD: Rhodes Coll., Babson Coll., Florida Southern Coll., Univ. of Dubuque, and Univ. of Rochester, 1992; Notre Dame Univ., 1995. Benjamin Franklin Award, RSA, 1993; Lifetime Achievement Award, Laymans Nat. Bible Assoc., 1995; Nat. Business Hall of Fame Award, Jun. Achievement Assoc., 1996; Interfaith Gold Medallion, Internat. CCJ, 1997; Abraham Lincoln Award, Union League of Philadelphia, 1997; Indep. Award, Brown Univ., 1998; Alexis de Tocqueville Award, Independent Inst. of Calif., 1998; Faith and Freedom Award, Acton Inst., 2000; Adam Smith Award, Excellence in Free Market Educn Entrepreneurship, 2005. KStJ 1995. *Publications:* The Humble Approach, 1981; Riches for the Mind and Spirit, 1990; (jtly) The God Who Would Be Known, 1990; Is God the Only Reality, 1993; (ed) Evidence of Purpose, 1994; Future Agenda, 1995; Discovering the Laws of Life, 1994; Worldwide Laws of Life, 1998; Possibilities, 2000; (ed) Worldwide Worship, 2001; articles in professional jls. *Recreations:* swimming, gardening. *Address:* Box N7776, Lyford Cay, Nassau, Bahamas. *T:* 3624295. *Clubs:* Athenæum, White's, Oxford and Cambridge; University (NY); Lyford Cay (Bahamas).   *Died 8 July 2008.*

TENNANT, Sir Iain (Mark), KT 1986; JP; Lord-Lieutenant of Morayshire, 1963–94; Crown Estate Commissioner, 1970–90; Lord High Commissioner to General Assembly, Church of Scotland, 1988–89; *b* 11 March 1919; *e s* of late Col Edward Tennant, Innes, Elgin and Mrs Georgina Tennant; *m* 1946, Lady Margaret Helen Isla Marion Ogilvy, 2nd *d* of 12th Earl of Airlie, Kt, GCVO, MC; one *s* one *d* (and one *s* decd). *Educ:* Eton College; Magdalene College, Cambridge. Scots Guards, 1939–46. Caledonian Cinemas, 1947; Chm., Grampian Television Ltd, 1968–89; Director: Times Publishing Co. Ltd, 1962–66; Clydesdale Bank Ltd, 1968–89; The Seagram Co. Ltd, Montreal, 1978–81; Moray Enterprise Trust Ltd, 1986–94; Chairman: The Glenlivet Distillers Ltd, 1964–84; Seagram Distillers, 1979–84. Mem. Newspaper Panel, Monopolies and Mergers Commn, 1981–86. Chm. Bd of Governors, Gordonstoun School, 1954–71. Lieut, Queen's Body Guard for Scotland (Royal Company of Archers), 1981–2002. FRSA 1971; CCMI (CBIM 1983). DL Moray, 1954; JP Moray, 1961. Freeman, Dist of Moray, 1994. Hon. LLD Aberdeen, 1990. *Recreations:* shooting, fishing; formerly rowing (rowed for Eton, 1937). *Address:* Lochnabo, Lhanbryde, Moray IV30 3QY. *T:* (01343) 842228, *Fax:* (01343) 842696.   *Died 25 Sept. 2006.*

TENNYSON, 5th Baron *cr* 1884; **Comdr Mark Aubrey Tennyson,** DSC 1943; RN retd; *b* 28 March 1920; *s* of 3rd Baron and Hon. Clarissa Tennant (*d* 1960), *o d* of 1st Baron Glenconner; *S* brother, 1991; *m* 1964, Deline Celeste Budler (*d* 1995). *Educ:* RNC Dartmouth. RN, 1937–60; served war 1939–45 on destroyers in action in Atlantic and Mediterranean (despatches 1945). Production Manager, Rowntree-Mackintosh (S Africa), 1960–67; Export Sales Dir, Joseph Terry & Sons (UK), 1968–82. Skied for RN, 1947–51; Captain, RN Cresta Run team, 1951–54. *Heir: cousin* David Harold Alexander Tennyson, *b* 4 June 1960. *Address:* 304 Grosvenor Square, Duke Road, Rondebosch, Cape Town 7700, South Africa. *Clubs:* White's, Royal Automobile. *Died 3 July 2006.*

TERLEZKI, Stefan, CBE 1992; *b* Ukraine, 29 Oct. 1927; *s* of late Oleksa Terlezki and Olena Terlezki; *m* 1955, Mary; two *d. Educ:* Cardiff Coll. of Food Technol. and Commerce. Member: Hotel and Catering Inst., 1965–80; Chamber of Trade, 1975–80. Member: Cardiff CC, 1968–83 (Press Officer, 1970–83; Chairman: Licensing Cttee, 1975–78; Environment Services Cttee, 1978–80; Housing Liaison Cttee, 1978–80); S Glam CC, 1973–85; S Wales Police Authy, 1975–80; Welsh Jt Educn Cttee, 1975–85; Chm., Jt Consultative Cttee, S Glam HA, 1978–79; Member: Educn Authority for Cardiff CC and S Glam CC, 1969–85; Planning, Finance and Policy Cttee, 1965–83. Member: Welsh Tourist Council, 1965–80; Welsh Games Council, 1974–80; Cardiff Wales Airport Authy, 1979–83; Adv. Bd of Internat. Politics, Univ. of Wales, Aberystwyth, 1993–. Contested (C): Cardiff South East, Feb. and Oct. 1974; Cardiff West, 1987; South Wales, European Parly elecn, 1979. MP (C) Cardiff West, 1983–87. Mem., Parly Select Cttee on Welsh Affairs, 1983–87. Chairman: Keep Britain in Europe Campaign, 1973–75; Cons. Gp for European Movement, 1973–75; Foreign Affairs Forum, 1974–; European Freedom Council, 1986–91. Vice-Pres., Wales Area Young Conservatives, 1975–80; Member: Central Council, CPC, 1979–83; Official Nat. Speaking Panels of Cons. Party, European Movement, and Eur. Parlt; British delegn, Council of Europe, 1985–87 (UK Rep. Mem., Convention Cttee for the Prevention of Torture and In-Human or Degradation Treatment and Punishment, 1989–); WEU, 1985–87; Industry and Parlt Trust; IPU, 1987– (Life Mem., British Parly Gp); UN Temple of Peace, Cardiff, 1979–87; Rapporteur, Assembly of Western European Community for Parly and Public Relns, 1986–87. Vice Pres., Cardiff Business Club, 1993–. Life Mem., CPA; Mem., Primrose League. Mem. Gen. Council, Ukrainian Assoc. in GB, 1949–. Consultant on econ. and public affairs to Embassy of Ukraine in the UK. Chairman: Cardiff City Football Club, 1975–77; Cardiff High Sch. Bd of Governors, 1975–83; Mem. Ct of Governors, Univs of Swansea and Aberystwyth, 1975–83. Liveryman, Welsh Livery Guild, 1996. Radio and television broadcasts; occasional journalism. Languages: Ukrainian, Polish, Russian, German (basic). Interested in foreign affairs, East/West relations, European union, international trade organisation, tourism, public relations, human rights, glasnost, perestroika, environment and defence. Silver Jubilee Medal, 1977. *Publications:* From War to Westminster (autobiog.), 2005. *Recreations:* sport, travel, theatre, documentaries, historical and Hollywood films. *Address:* 16 Bryngwyn Road, Cyncoed, Cardiff CF23 6PQ. *T:* (029) 2075 9524. *Club:* Dinosaurs. *Died 21 Feb. 2006.*

TERRY, Nicholas John, RIBA; Chairman, BDP South, since 2006; *b* 12 Nov. 1947; *s* of John Edmund Terry and Winifred Nina Terry (*née* White); *m* 1970, Dorothy Atkins; one *d. Educ:* Peveril Sch., Nottingham; Bilborough Grammar Sch., Nottingham; Univ. of Bath Sch. of Architecture (BSc Hons; BArch Hons). RIBA 1973; MAIBC, MRAIC 1976. Architect: Terry Associates, Bath, 1970–72; Building Design Partnership, Manchester, 1972–75; Arthur Erickson Architects, Canada, 1975–77; J. S. Bonnington Partnership, St Albans, 1978–81; Man. Dir, Heery Architects & Engrs,

1981–89; joined Building Design Partnership, London, 1990: Equity Partner, 1995–97, Dir, 1997–; Chm., 2002–06; Chairman: Dixon Jones BDP, 1996–; BDP Design Ltd, 1996–. *Projects include:* Durham Millburngate, 1972–75 (RIBA award, 1977, Europa Nostra medal and Civic Trust award, 1978); Citibank HQ, London, 1981, Frankfurt, 1983; Cribbs Causeway Regional Shopping Centre, 1997 (BCSC and ICSC (USA) awards, 2000); Niketown, London, 1998; Royal Opera House, 1999 (RIBA and RICS awards, 2000; Europa Nostra dip., 2001); Jubilee Place, Canary Wharf, 2003; Royal Albert Hall, 2004 (Civic Trust and Europa Nostra awards). *Exhibitions:* Royal Acad. Summer Exhibns, 1974 (Durham Millburngate), 1975 (Albert Dock); MOMA, NY, 1979; RIBA, 1982 (Kuwait Stock Exchange). Member: IoD, 1988; British Council of Offices, 1990–; British Council of Shopping Centres, 1995–; Internat. Council of Shopping Centres, 1995–. Chairman: Internat. Alliance for Interoperability, 2001– (Chm., UK Chapter, 2001–; Vice Chm., Internat. Council, 2005–); European Enterprise Interoperability Centre, 2006–; Bldg and Civil Engrg Sector Policy 4 Strategy Cttee, BSI, 2007–. FRSA 2005. *Publications:* numerous articles in architecture/design press and jls. *Recreations:* walking, gardening, reading, architecture and design. *Address:* Building Design Partnership, 16 Brewhouse Yard, Clerkenwell, EC1V 4LJ. *T:* (020) 7812 8071; *e-mail:* nj-terry@bdp.co.uk; Lansdown, 26A Middle Street, Thriplow, Royston, Herts SG8 7RD. *Died 30 Nov. 2008.*

TETLEY, Glen; choreographer, since 1948; *b* 3 Feb. 1926; *s* of Glenford Andrew Tetley and Mary Eleanor (*née* Byrne). *Educ:* Franklyn and Marshal Coll., Lancaster, USA (pre-med); New York Univ. (BSc). Studied medicine; then dance with Hanya Holm, Antony Tudor, Martha Graham. Danced with Holm's Co., 1946–51; New York City Opera, 1952–54; John Butler Dance Theatre, 1955; Joffrey Ballet, 1956–57; Martha Graham Co., 1958; American Ballet Theatre, 1960; Robbins Ballets USA, 1961. Joined Netherlands Dance Theatre as dancer and choreographer, 1962, eventually becoming artistic co-director; directed own company, 1969; Dir, Stuttgart Ballet, 1974–76. *Choreography:* Pierrot Lunaire, own company, 1962, Ballet Rambert, 1985; Netherlands Dance Theatre: The Anatomy Lesson, 1964; Fieldmass, 1965; Circles, 1968; Arena, 1969; Imaginary Film, 1970; Mutations, 1970; Small Parades, 1972; Summer's End, 1980; American Ballet Theatre: Ricercare, 1966; Nocturne, 1977; Sphinx, 1977; Contredances, 1979; Ballet Rambert: Freefall, 1967; Ziggurat, 1967; Embrace Tiger and Return to Mountain, 1968; Rag Dances, 1971; Praeludium, 1978; The Tempest, first full-length work, 1979; Murderer, Hope of Women, 1983; Royal Ballet: Field Figures, 1970; Laborintus, 1972; Dances of Albion, 1980; Amores, 1997; Stuttgart Ballet: Voluntaries, 1973; Daphnis and Chloe, 1975; Greening, 1975; National Ballet of Canada: Alice, 1986; La Ronde, 1987; Tagore, 1989; Oracle, 1994; also: Mythical Hunters, Batsheva Dance Co., 1965; Le Sacre du Printemps, Munich State Opera Ballet, 1974; Tristan, Paris Opera, 1974; Firebird, Royal Danish Ballet, 1981; Revelation and Fall, Australian Dance Theatre, 1984; Pulcinella, Festival Ballet, 1984; Dream Walk of the Shaman, Aterballetto, 1985; Orpheus, Australian Ballet, 1987; Dialogues, Dance Theatre of Harlem, 1991; Lux in Tenebris, Houston Ballet, 1999. Hon DFA Franklin and Marshall Coll., Penn, 2001. Queen Elizabeth Coronation Award, Royal Acad. of Dancing, 1980; Prix Italia, 1982; Ohioana Career Medal, 1986; NY Univ. Achievement Award, 1988. Kt, Order of Merit (Norway), 1997. *Address:* 860 United Nations Plaza, Apt 10G, New York, NY 10017, USA. *T:* (212) 3711835. *Died 26 Jan. 2007.*

THAIN, Eric Malcolm, PhD; FRSC; Director, Tropical Development and Research Institute (formerly Tropical Products Institute), Overseas Development Administration, 1981–86; Hon. Research Fellow, Chemistry Department, University College London, since 1986; *b* 29 Nov. 1925; *s* of late Arthur Robert Thain and Olive Grace (*née* Parsons); *m* 1954, Nancy Garbutt

Key, *d* of late Mr and Mrs T. G. Key; one *s* one *d*. *Educ:* St Dunstan's Coll., Catford; Univ. of London (BSc, PhD). Lister Institute of Preventive Medicine, 1949: ICI Research Fellow, 1953–54; Royal Society/National Academy of Science Research Fellow, Univ. of California, Berkeley, 1954–55; ICI Research Fellow, University Coll. London, 1955–57; Tropical Products Institute: Member, Scientific Staff, 1957; Asst Director, 1963; Dep. Director, 1969. Member: WHO and FAO Expert Committees on Pesticides, 1961–; Executive Cttee, Essex Bird Watching and Preservation Soc., 1950–85 (Chm. 1970–73); Queckett Microscopical Club (Pres., 1980 81). Mem. Council, Norfolk and Norwich Naturalists' Soc., 1994–97. *Publications:* research papers on organic chemistry and pesticides in jls of various learned societies. *Recreations:* natural history, visiting museums, painting. *Address:* 36 Friars Quay, Norwich, Norfolk NR3 1ES. *T:* (01603) 625017.   *Died 7 July 2007.*

THATCHER, Arthur Roger, CB 1974; Director, Office of Population Censuses and Surveys, and Registrar General for England and Wales, 1978–86; *b* 22 Oct. 1926; *s* of Arthur Thatcher and Edith Mary Ruth (*née* Dobson); *m* 1950, Mary Audrey Betty (*née* Street); two *d*. *Educ:* The Leys Sch.; St John's Coll., Cambridge (MA). Instr Lieut, Royal Navy, 1947–49. North Western Gas Board, 1949–52; Admiralty, 1952 61; Cabinet Office, 1961–63; Ministry of Labour, 1963–68; Director of Statistics, Dept of Employment, 1968–78, Dep. Sec., 1972–78. *Publications:* (jtly) The Force of Mortality at Ages 80 to 120, 1998; official publications, articles in jls. *Address:* 35 Thetford Road, New Malden, Surrey KT3 5DP. *Club:* Army and Navy.   *Died 13 Feb. 2010.*

THICKETT, Michael Godfrey, CMG 1995; HM Diplomatic Service, retired; Counsellor, Foreign and Commonwealth Office, 1986–2007; *b* 22 Oct. 1940; *s* of Stanley Thickett and Margery Louvain Thickett (*née* Fletcher); *m* 1970, Heather Caroline Fraser; two *s* one *d*. *Educ:* Univ. of Birmingham (BSocSc); Faculté de Droit and Sorbonne, Univ. of Paris (Dip. Droit Internat. Publique). NUS, 1962–63; Programme Manager, Internat. Student Conf., Leiden, Netherlands, 1964–66; Dir, Internat. Dept, NUS, 1967–69; joined FCO, 1970; Lusaka, 1971–75; Hamburg, 1978–80; Bonn, 1980–83; Pretoria, 1986–90. *Recreations:* fishing, gardening, reading, watching football, Rugby and cricket, writing, DIY—woodworking.   *Died 20 June 2008.*

THICKNESSE, John Dacres; Cricket Correspondent, Evening Standard, 1967–96; *b* 30 July 1931; *s* of late Very Rev. Cuthbert Carroll Thicknesse, Dean of St Albans, and Rhoda Thicknesse (*née* Pratt); *m* 1957, Anne Margaret Hardie; two *s* one *d*. *Educ:* Summer Fields, Oxford; Harrow; Trinity Coll., Oxford. News and sports reporter, sports sub-editor, sports diarist, cricket writer: Daily Express, 1957–58; Daily Telegraph, 1958–61 and 1965–66; Sunday Telegraph, 1961–65; occasional county cricket matches for The Times, 1996–. *Recreations:* bridge, golf, racing, hallucinating that England are holders of the Ashes. *Address:* 17 Silver Street, Warminster, Wilts BA12 8PS. *T:* (01985) 213443. *Clubs:* Somerset Stragglers, IZ, Arabs; West Wilts Golf.   *Died 26 Feb. 2006.*

THODAY, Prof. John Marion, BSc Wales, PhD, ScD Cantab; FRS 1965; Arthur Balfour Professor of Genetics, Cambridge University, 1959–83, then Emeritus; Life Fellow of Emmanuel College, 1983 (Fellow, 1959); *b* 30 Aug. 1916; *s* of Professor D. Thoday, FRS; *m* 1950, Doris Joan Rich, PhD (Emeritus Fellow, Lucy Cavendish College); one *s* one *d*. *Educ:* Bootham School, York; University Coll. of N Wales, Bangor; Trinity College, Cambridge. Photographic Intelligence, Royal Air Force, 1941–46; Cytologist, Mount Vernon Hospital, 1946–47; Asst Lectr, then Lectr for Cytogenetics, Departments of Botany and Zoology, University of Sheffield, 1947–54; Head of Department of Genetics: Sheffield, 1954–59; Cambridge, 1959–82. Director, OECD Project for reform of secondary school Biology teaching 1962, 1963. Chm., UK Nat. Cttee for Biology, 1982–88. Pres., Genetical Soc., 1975–78.

Publications: (with J. N. Thompson) Quantitive Genetics, 1979; articles on radiation cytology, experimental evolution, the genetics of continuous variables, biological progress and on genetics and society. *Address:* 7 Clarkson Road, Cambridge CB3 0EH; *e-mail:* thoday@waitrose.com; *web:* www.jmthodaygeneticist.com.
          Died 25 Aug. 2008.

THOMAS OF GWYDIR, Baron *cr* 1987 (Life Peer), of Llanrwst in the county of Gwynedd; **Peter John Mitchell Thomas;** PC 1964; QC 1965; a Recorder of the Crown Court, 1974–88; *b* 31 July 1920; *o s* of late David Thomas, Solicitor, Llanrwst, Denbighshire, and Anne Gwendoline Mitchell; *m* 1947, Frances Elizabeth Tessa (*d* 1985), *o d* of late Basil Dean, CBE and Lady Mercy Greville; two *d* (and two *s* decd). *Educ:* Epworth College, Rhyl; Jesus College, Oxford (MA; Hon. Fellow, 2001). Served War of 1939–45, in RAF (Bomber Comd); Prisoner of War (Germany), 1941–45. Called to Bar, Middle Temple, 1947 (Master of the Bench 1971, Emeritus 1991); Member of Wales and Chester Circuit; Deputy Chairman: Cheshire QS, 1966–70; Denbighshire QS, 1968–70. Arbitrator, Court of Arbitration, Internat. Chamber of Commerce, Paris, 1974–88. MP (C): Conway Div. of Caernarvonshire, 1951–66; Hendon South, 1970–87; PPS to the Solicitor-General, 1954–59; Parly Secretary, Min. of Labour, 1959–61; Parly Under-Sec. of State, Foreign Office, 1961–63; Minister of State for Foreign Affairs, 1963–64; Oppn. Front Bench Spokesman on Foreign Affairs and Law, 1964–66; Sec. of State for Wales, 1970–74. Member: Select Cttee on Conduct of Members, 1976–77, Select Cttee on Procedure (Supply), 1981–83 (Chm.); Select Cttee on Foreign Affairs, 1983–87 (Dep. Chm.); Select Cttee on Privileges, 1984–87; Chairman: Select Cttee on Members' Salaries, 1981–82; Select Cttee on Revision of Standing Orders, 1982–83. Chm., Cons. Party Organisation, 1970–72. Pres., Nat. Union of Conservative and Unionist Assocs, 1974 and 1975. Mem., Council of Europe and WEU, 1957–59. Member, Historic Buildings Council for Wales, 1965–67. *Address:* 37 Chester Way, SE11 4UR. *T:* (020) 7735 6047; Millicent Cottage, Elstead, Surrey GU8 6IID. *T:* (01252) 702052. *Club:* Carlton.   *Died 4 Feb. 2008.*

THOMAS, Aneurin Morgan; Director, Welsh Arts Council, 1967–84; *b* 3 April 1921; *s* of Philip Thomas and Olwen Amy Thomas (*née* Davies); *m* 1947, Mary Dineen (*d* 2005); one *s* one *d*. *Educ:* Ystalyfera Intermediate Sch., Glamorgan; Swansea School of Art and Crafts. British and Indian Armies, 1941–46 (Major). Lecturer, later Vice-Principal, Somerset College of Art, 1947–60; Vice-Principal, Hornsey College of Art, 1960–67. Member, Board of Governors: Loughborough Coll. of Art and Design, 1980–89; S Glamorgan Inst of Higher Educn, 1985–89 (Chm., Faculty of Art and Design Adv. Cttee, 1985–90); Carmarthenshire Coll. of Tech. and Art, 1985– (Chm., Faculty of Art and Design Adv. Cttee, 1985–); Vice-President: Nat. Soc. for Art Educn, 1967–68; Llangollen Internat. Music Eisteddfod, 1970–. Chm., Assoc. of Art Instns, 1977–78. *Publications:* periodic contribs to books and professional jls. *Recreations:* observing with interest and humour, but with increasing bewilderment. *Address:* Netherwood, 8 Lower Cwrt-y-vil Road, Penarth, Vale of Glamorgan CF64 3HQ. *T:* (029) 2070 2239.   *Died 16 Jan. 2009.*

THOMAS, Cedric Marshall, CBE 1991 (OBE 1983); Director and Chief Executive, Engineering Employers' West Midlands Association, 1984–91; *b* 26 May 1930; *s* of David J. Thomas and Evis (*née* Field); *m* 1st, 1954, Dora Ann Pritchard (*d* 1975); one *s* one *d*; 2nd, 1976, Margaret Elizabeth (*née* Crawley); one step *s* three step *d*. *Educ:* King Edward's Sch., Birmingham; Univ. of Birmingham (BSc Hons, PhD). CEng; FIMMM; FMES (Pres., 1969–71). NCB, 1954–60; Johnson Progress Group, 1961–77 (Chief Exec., 1970–77); Business Consultant, 1977–80; Benjamin Priest Group, 1980–84 (Chief Exec., 1983); Chm., Jesse Shirley & Son, then Jesse Shirley, Ltd, 1991–99 (Dir, 1999–2005); Dir, Poplars Resource

Management Co. Ltd, 1992–99; Dep. Chm., Thomas William Lench Hldgs Ltd, 1993-2004 (Dir, 1991–2004). Member: Management Bd, Engrg Employers' Fedn, 1974–80, 1983–84; HSC, 1980–90; Engrg Employers' Fedn Council, 1992–95. Non-executive Director: Staffs Ambulance Service NHS Trust, 1995–2001 (Vice Chm., 1999–2001); Staffordshire Environmental Fund Ltd, 1997–2005 (Chm., 2000–05). Chairman: Special Programmes Area Bd, 1978–83; Area Manpower Bd, 1986–88. Pres., Engineering Employers' W Midlands Assoc., 1976–78. Governor, N Staffs Polytechnic, 1973–80. FRSA; CCMI. Hon. FFOM 1992. *Recreations:* Rugby football (spectator), tennis, theatre, walking. *Address:* Parkfields House, Tittensor, Staffs ST12 9HQ. *T:* (01782) 373677.   *Died 26 Feb. 2008.*

THOMAS, Colin Agnew; *b* 14 Feb. 1921; *s* of Harold Alfred Thomas and Nora (*née* Williams); *m* 1947, Jane Jardine Barnish, *d* of Leonard Barnish, FRIBA; one *s* one *d*. *Educ:* Oundle School. Lieut, RNVR, 1941–46. Chartered Accountant; Finance Comptroller, Lloyd's, 1964–75, Sec.-Gen., 1976–79. Mem., Cirencester Art Soc. *Recreations:* gardening, sketching. *Address:* Spinet Cottage, 35 Cheltenham Road, Cirencester GL7 2HU. *T:* (01285) 653978; 15 Ravenspoint, Trearddur Bay, Anglesey LL65 2AJ. *T:* (01407) 860091. *Club:* Trearddur Bay Sailing.   *Died 24 June 2008.*

THOMAS, David Hamilton Pryce, CBE 1977; solicitor, retired; Chairman, Land Authority for Wales, 1980–86 (Deputy Chairman, 1975–80); President, Rent Assessment Panel for Wales, 1971–89 (Member, 1966); *b* 3 July 1922; *s* of Trevor John Thomas and Eleanor Maud Thomas; *m* 1948, Eluned Mair Morgan; two *s* one *d*. *Educ:* Barry County Sch.; University College, Cardiff. Served War of 1939–45; British and Indian Armies, terminal rank T/Captain (GSO III), 1941–46. Qualified as Solicitor, 1948, with hons; Partner in J. A. Hughes & Co., Solicitors, Barry, 1950–75; Notary Public, 1953. Director 1962–67, Vice-Chm. 1967–71, Chm. 1971–78, Barry Mutual Building Society; Vice Chm., 1978, Chm., 1982–84, Glam. Building Soc.; Chm., Wales Area Bd, Bradford and Bingley Bldg Soc., 1984–87; Vice-Chm., Building Socs Assoc. for Wales, 1983; Mem., Adv. Cttee on Fair Rents, 1973; Chm., E Glam. Rent Tribunal, 1967–71; District Comr of Scouts, Barry and District, 1963–70; Chm., Barry District Scout Assoc. 1971–81; Vice-Chm., S Glam. Scout Council, 1975–81. *Recreations:* books, music. *Address:* 34 Camden Road, Brecon, Powys LD3 7RT.   *Died 1 Sept. 2008.*

THOMAS, David Owen; QC 1972; a Recorder of the Crown Court, 1972–98; *b* 22 Aug. 1926; *s* of late Emrys Aeron Thomas and Dorothy May Thomas; *m* 1967, Mary Susan Atkinson; three *d* (and one *d* decd). *Educ:* Queen Elizabeth's, Barnet; John Bright Sch., Llandudno; Queen's Univ., Belfast. Served War, HM Forces, 1943–45 and to 1948. Called to the Bar, Middle Temple, 1952, Bencher, 1980; Dep. Chairman, Devon QS, 1971. Mem., Criminal Injuries Compensation Bd, 1987. Freeman, City of London; Liveryman, Needlemakers' Co. *Recreations:* acting, cricket, Rugby football. *Address:* 2 King's Bench Walk, Temple, EC4Y 7DE. *Clubs:* Garrick, MCC; Western (Glasgow).   *Died 16 April 2007.*

THOMAS, Kenneth Rowland, OBE 1995; General Secretary, Civil and Public Services Association, 1976–82; *b* 7 Feb. 1927; *s* of William Rowland Thomas and Anne Thomas; *m* 1955, Nora (*née* Hughes); three *s* (and one *s* decd). *Educ:* St Joseph's Elementary Sch., Penarth; Penarth Grammar Sch. Trainee Reporter, South Wales Echo and Western Mail, 1943–44; Civil Servant, 1944–54; Asst Sec., Civil and Public Services Assoc., 1955, Dep. Gen. Sec., 1967. Mem., TUC Gen. Council, 1977–82. Member: Occupational Pensions Bd, 1981–97; CSAB, 1984–91; Law Soc. Professional Purposes Cttee, 1984–86; Solicitors Complaints Bureau, 1986–92; Trustee: Post Office Pension Fund, 1969–84; London Develt Capital Fund, 1984–99; British Telecommunications Fund, 1983–97; Charity Aid Foundn, 1982–92; Director: Postel, 1982–95; W

Midlands Enterprise Bd, 1982–; Univ. of Warwick Sci. Park, 1986–, Sci. Park Foundn, 1998–, and Sci. Park Innovation Centre, 1998–; Warwickshire Venture Capital Fund, 1988–91; Coventry Venture Capital Fund, 1988–91; W Midlands Growth Fund, 1990–2005; W Midlands Technol. Transfer Co., 1997–99. Chm. Trustees, CPSA Pensions Fund, 2005–. Governor and Chm. Audit Cttee, Coleg Harlech, 1997–2002; Chm., Bangor Civic Soc., 2002–. *Recreations:* music, anything Welsh. *Address:* Pen-y-Bryn House, Penybryn, Bangor, Gwynedd LL57 1PX. *T:* (01248) 353289.
                                    Died 12 Aug. 2008.

THOMPSON, Charles Norman, CBE 1978; CChem; FRSC; Head of Research and Development Liaison, and Health, Safety and Environment Administration, Shell UK Ltd, 1978–82; Consultant to Shell UK Ltd, since 1982; *b* 23 Oct. 1922; *s* of Robert Norman Thompson and Evelyn Tivendale Thompson (*née* Wood); *m* 1946, Pamela Margaret Wicks; one *d*. *Educ:* Birkenhead Institute; Liverpool Univ. (BSc Hons 1943). Research Chemist, Thornton Research Centre (Shell Refining & Marketing Co. Ltd), 1943; Lectr, Petroleum Chemistry and Technology, Liverpool Coll. of Technology, 1947–51; Personnel Supt and Dep. Associate Manager, Thornton Research Centre, Shell Research Ltd, 1959–61; Dir (Res. Admin), Shell Research Ltd, 1961–78. Mem. Council, 1976–82, Vice Pres., 1977–80, 1981–82, Inst. of Petroleum (Chm., Res. Adv. Cttee, 1973–82). Pres., RIC, 1976–78. Chairman: Professional Affairs Bd, 1980–84, Water Chemistry Forum, 1987–90, RSC; Council of Science and Technology Insts, 1981–83 (Chm., Health Care Scientific Adv. Cttee, 1986–94); Bd Mem., Thames Water Authority, 1980–87; Member: Technician Educn Council, 1980–83; Ct, Univ. of Surrey, 1980–; Parly and Scientific Cttee, 1976–. *Publications:* Reviews of Petroleum Technology, vol. 13: insulating and hydraulic oils, 1953; numerous papers in Jl Inst. Petroleum, Chem. and Ind., Chem. in Brit., on hydrocarbon dielectrics, insulating oils, diffusion as rate-limiting factor in oxidation, antioxidants in the oil industry, mechanism of copper catalysis in insulating oil oxidation, scientific manpower, etc. *Recreations:* golf, bowls. *Address:* Delamere, Horsell Park, Woking, Surrey GU21 4LW. *T:* (01483) 714939.   *Died 12 Oct. 2010.*

THOMPSON, Maj.-Gen. Christopher Noel, CB 1988; *b* 25 Dec. 1932; *s* of late Brig. William Gordon Starkey Thompson and Kathleen Elizabeth (*née* Craven); *m* 1964, Margaret (*née* Longsworth); one *s* twin *d*. *Educ:* Wellington College; RMA Sandhurst; Sidney Sussex College, Cambridge (BA); University College London. Commissioned RE, 1953; served BAOR, 1957–59; Bomb Disposal, UK, 1959–62; Aden, 1963–66; Canada, 1966–68; OC 13 Field Survey Sqn, 1969–70; USA, 1971–75; CO 42 Survey Engr Regt, 1975–77; Dep. Dir. Planning and Develt, Ordnance Survey, 1978–79; Dir. Surveys and Production, Ordnance Survey, 1980–83; Dir of Mil. Survey, MoD, 1984–87. Col Comdt, RE, 1987–92. Pres., Commission D, European Organisation for Experimental Photogrammetric Research, 1980–87. *Publications:* articles on surveying and mapping in Chartered Surveyor, Photogrammetric Record. *Recreations:* photography, IT, gardening, house restoration. *Address:* Burgh House, Burgh-by-Sands, Carlisle CA5 6AN.   *Died 9 Dec. 2007.*

THOMPSON, Colin Edward, CBE 1983; FRSE 1978; Director, National Galleries of Scotland, 1977–84; *b* 2 Nov. 1919; *s* of late Edward Vincent Thompson, CB, and Jessie Forbes Cameron; *m* 1950, Jean Agnes Jardine O'Connell; one *s* one *d*. *Educ:* Sedbergh Sch.; King's College, Cambridge; Chelsea Polytechnic Sch. of Art. MA (Cantab). FMA. FS Wing CMP, 1940–41; Foreign Office (Bletchley Park), 1941–45. Lectr, Bath Acad. of Art, Corsham, 1948–54; Asst Keeper, 1954, Keeper, 1967, National Gall. of Scotland. Sen. Adviser, Res. Centre in Art Educn, Bath Acad. of Art, 1962–65; Chm., Scottish Museums Council, 1984–87; Member: Scottish

Arts Council, 1976–83; Edinburgh Fest. Council, 1979–82; Bd of Governors, Edinburgh Coll. of Art, 1985–91 (Chm., 1989–91); Scottish Mining Museum Trust. 1987– (Chm., 1992–97); Expert Panel on Museums, Nat. Heritage Lottery Fund, 1995–98. DUniv Edinburgh, 1985. *Publications:* (with Lorne Campbell) Hugo van der Goes and the Trinity Panels in Edinburgh, 1974; Exploring Museums: Scotland, 1990; guide books, catalogues and a history of the National Gallery of Scotland; articles in Burlington Magazine, Museums Jl, etc. *Address:* Edenkerry, Lasswade, Midlothian EH18 1LW. *T:* (0131) 663 7927. *Died 5 Oct. 2007.*

THOMPSON, Hon. David John Howard; MP (DLP) St John, Barbados, since 1987; Prime Minister of Barbados, since 2008; Minister of Finance, Investment, Energy, Labour and Telecommunications, since 2008; *b* London, 25 Dec. 1961; *s* of Charles F. H. Thompson and Margaret Thompson (*née* Knight); *m* 1989, Marie-Josephine Mara Graudy; three *d. Educ:* Combermere Sch.; Univ. of W Indies (LLB Hons); Hugh Wooding Law Sch., Trinidad (Legal Educn Cert.). Called to the Barbados Bar, 1986; Partner, Thompson & Patterson, later Thompson Associates, 1994–2008. Minister of Community Develt and Culture, 1991–93; Minister of Finance, 1993–94; Leader of Opposition, 1994–2003 and 2006–08. Pres. and Political Leader, DLP, 1994– . Mem., Combermere Sch. Old Scholars Assoc. *Recreations:* cooking, cricket, football. *Address:* Prime Minister's Office, Bay Street, St Michael, Barbados. *T:* 4263179, *Fax:* 4365811; *e-mail:* thompson@caribsurf.com. *Clubs:* Families First (St John, Barbados); Sussex Cricket; St John's Cultural Cricket, St John Sonnets Football. *Died 23 Oct. 2010.*

THOMPSON, Donald Henry, MA; Headmaster, Chigwell School, Essex, 1947–71; *b* 29 Aug. 1911; *s* of H. R. Thompson, solicitor, Swansea; *m* 1942, Helen Mary Wray; four *s. Educ:* Shrewsbury School; Merton College, Oxford (Postmaster in Classics, 1930; 1st Class Hon. Mod., 1932; 1st Class Literae Humaniores, 1934; MA 1939). Asst Master, Haileybury Coll., Hertford, 1934–46. Served War of 1939–45, RA, 1940–45. JP Essex, 1955–81. *Recreations:* cricket, bird-watching, conservation. *Address:* Glasses Farm, Holcombe, Bath, Somerset BA3 5EQ. *T:* (01761) 232322. *Died 13 March 2006.*

THOMPSON, Dr Frank Derek, FRCP; Senior Consultant Nephrologist, St Peter's Hospital, 1981–2003; Dean, Institute of Urology and Nephrology, London University, 1985–98, at Royal Free and University College Medical School; *b* 18 May 1939; *s* of Frank and Irene Thompson; *m* 1964, Elizabeth Ann Sherwood; two *s* one *d. Educ:* St Catharine's College, Cambridge (MA, MB BChir); St Mary's Hosp., London. FRCP 1983. Sen. Lectr, Inst. of Urology, 1974; Consultant Nephrologist to Harefield Hosp., 1979–2004, to Mount Vernon Hosp., 1979–2003; Hon. Consultant Nephrologist to Nat. Heart Hosp., 1980–2003; Vice-Dean, Faculty of Clinical Science, University College and Middx Sch. of Medicine, 1990. *Publications:* Disorders of the Kidney and Urinary Tract, 1987; contribs to BMJ, Clinical Nephrology. *Recreations:* golf, gardening, ornithology. *Address:* 27 Moor Park Road, Northwood, Middx HA6 2DL. *T:* (01923) 827361. *Club:* Moor Park Golf. *Died 15 July 2006.*

THOMPSON, Rev. Ian Malcolm; Dean, King's College, Cambridge, since 2005; *b* 24 June 1959; *s* of Ernest Henry Thompson and Kathleen Joyce (*née* Cavanagh); *m* 1980, Ann Perry. *Educ:* Harris Acad., Dundee; William Booth Meml Coll., London (CertEd 1979); Univ. of Aberdeen (BTh 1998). Officer, Salvation Army, 1979–93; ordained deacon, 1994, priest, 1995; Curate in charge, Central Buchan, 1994–96; Rector, St Mary's Aberdeen, 1996–99; Chaplain and Dean of Chapel, Selwyn Coll., Cambridge, 1999–2005; Hon. Asst Priest, Little St Mary's, Cambridge, 2004–06. *Recreations:*

swimming, rowing. *Address:* King's College, Cambridge CB2 1ST. *T:* (01223) 331419, *Fax:* (01223) 331315; *e-mail:* dean@kings.cam.ac.uk. *Died 24 Sept. 2009.*

THOMPSON, John Keith Lumley, CMG 1982; MBE (mil.) 1965; TD 1961; President, Lumley Associates, since 1983; *b* 31 March 1923; *s* of late John V. V. and Gertrude Thompson; *m* 1950, Audrey Olley; one *s. Educ:* Wallsend Grammar Sch.; King's Coll., Durham Univ. (BSc). MSAE 1983. Served War of 1939–45: Officer in REME, 1942–47, NW Europe; BEME 44 Para Bde (V), 1948–70. Dep. Inspector, REME (V) Southern Comd, 1970–72 (Lt-Col); Dep. Comdr, 44 Para Bde (V), 1972–75 (Col). Road Research Lab., DSIR, 1948–55; AWRE, Aldermaston, 1955–64; Staff of Chief Scientific Adviser, MoD, 1964–65; Head of E Midlands Regional Office, Min. Tech., 1965–70; Head, Internat. Affairs, Atomic Energy Div., Dept of Energy, 1972–74; Regional Dir, W Midlands and Northern Regional Offices, DoI, 1970–72 and 1974–78; Counsellor (Sci. and Tech.), Washington, 1978–83. ADC to the Queen (TAVR), 1974–78. FCMI (FBIM; MBIM 1975). *Publications:* papers on vehicle behaviour, crash helmets and implosion systems; numerous articles on American science and technology. *Recreations:* outdoor activities, reading. *T:* (01778) 560374. *Died 20 Dec. 2010.*

THOMPSON, Hon. Lindsay Hamilton Simpson, AO 1990; CMG 1975; Premier of Victoria, 1981–82; Leader of the Opposition, Victoria, 1982, *b* 15 Oct. 1923; *s* of Arthur K. Thompson and Ethel M. Thompson; *m* 1950, Joan Margaret Poynder; two *s* one *d. Educ:* Caulfield Grammar Sch., Victoria (Captain and Dux 1941); Melbourne Univ. (BA Hons, BEd; Hon. LLD 2002). MACE. AIF, New Guinea, 1942–45. MP (Lib.) in Victorian Legislative Council: Higinbotham Prov., 1955–67; Monash Prov., 1967–70; MLA Malvern, 1970–82; Member of Cabinet, 1956–82; Parly Sec. of Cabinet, 1956–58; Asst Chief Sec. and Asst Attorney-Gen., 1958–61; Asst Minister of Transport, 1960–61; Minister of Housing and Forests, 1961–67; Dep. Leader of Govt in Legislative Council, 1962–70; Minister in charge of Aboriginal Welfare, 1965–67; Minister of Educn, 1967–79 (longest term ever in this portfolio); Leader of Legislative Assembly, 1972–79; Dep. Premier of Victoria, 1972–81; Minister for Police and Emergency Services, 1979–81; Treasurer, 1979–82; served longest period as Cabinet Minister in history of Victoria. Director: Mutual Friendly Soc., 1986–; Composite Benefits Soc., 1986–92. State Govt Rep., Melbourne Univ. Council, 1955–59. Dep. Chm., Aust. Advertising Standards Council, 1990–97 (Mem., 1988–90). Pres., Royal Life Saving Soc., 1970–96. Trustee: Melb. Cricket Ground, 1967–2000 (Chm., 1987–99); Nat. Tennis Centre Trust, 1986–96 (Chm., 1994–96); Patron: Victorian Cricket Assoc., 1978–92; Prahran CC; Aust. Quadriplegic Assoc.; Richmond FC; Australian Children's Choir. Bronze Medal, Royal Humane Soc., 1974. *Publications:* Australian Housing Today and Tomorrow, 1965; Looking Ahead in Education, 1969; A Fair Deal for Victoria, 1981; I Remember, 1989. *Recreations:* cricket, golf, tennis. *Address:* 19 Allenby Avenue, Glen Iris, Vic 3146, Australia. *T:* (3) 98856191. *Clubs:* Kingston Heath Golf, Sorrento Golf. *Died 16 July 2008.*

THOMPSON, Nicolas de la Mare; Chairman, Heinemann Educational Books, 1985–91; *b* 4 June 1928; *s* of Rupert Spens Thompson and Florence Elizabeth Thompson (*née* de la Mare); *m* 1st, 1956, Erica Pennell (*d* 1993); two *s* one *d*; 2nd, 1997, Caroline Graham (*née* Middleton). *Educ:* Eton; Christ Church, Oxford (MA). Managing Director, George Weidenfeld and Nicolson, 1956–70; Publishing Dir, Pitman, 1970–85; Managing Dir, Heinemann Gp of Publishers, 1985–87; Director: Octopus Publishing Gp, 1985–92; Reed Internat. Books, 1990–93; Internat. Book Develt Ltd, 1991–2004; Chairman: Ginn & Co., 1985–91; Heinemann Professional Publishing, 1986–90; George Philip & Son, 1988–90; Mitchell Beazley, 1988–90; Copyright

Licensing Agency Ltd, 1994–96. Chairman: Book Development Council, 1984–86; Publishers Licensing Soc., 1992–96; Treas., Publishers Assoc., 1986–88. Dir, Almeida Theatre Co. Ltd, 1993–2001. *Address:* 5 Walham Grove, SW6 1QP. *Died 25 April 2010.*

THOMPSON, Dr Noel Brentnall Watson, CEng; education and training consultant; Councillor (Lab), London Borough of Brent, 1999–2006; *b* 11 Dec. 1932; *s* of George Watson Thompson and Mary Henrietta Gibson; *m* 1957, Margaret Angela Elizabeth Baston; one *s*. *Educ:* Manchester Grammar School; Cambridge Univ. (MA); Imperial College, London (MSc Eng, PhD). National Service, RN (Sub-Lieut), 1951–53. Research, Imperial Coll., 1958–61; Lectr in Physical Metallurgy, Univ. of Birmingham, 1961–65; Dept of Education and Science, 1966–67, 1969–77 and 1979–88 (Under Sec., 1980–88; Head of Higher and Further Educn III Br., 1980–86; Head of Schools 2 Br. and Internat. Relations, 1986–88); Secretary, National Libraries Cttee, 1967–69; Cabinet Office, 1977–79; Chief Exec., Nat. Council for Educnl Technol., 1988–92. Consultant and Vis. Prof. of Educnl Develt, Luton Univ., 1993–98. Chief Exec., English Folk Dance and Song Soc., 1995–97. *Publications:* papers in professional journals. *Recreations:* railways of all sizes, mechanics, music, traditional dance, modern history, photography, walking. *Address:* 101 Woodcock Hill, Kenton, Harrow HA3 0JJ. *T:* (020) 8907 1716; *e-mail:* nbwt@waitrose.com. *Died 18 Aug. 2007.*

THOMPSON, (William) Pratt; consultant and director, various companies; *b* 9 Feb. 1933; *s* of Philip Amos Thompson and Regina Beatrice (*née* Kirby); *m* 1963, Jenny Frances Styles; two *d*. *Educ:* Princeton Univ.; Columbia Univ. (BA Econ *magna cum laude*, Phi Beta Kappa); Centre d'Etudes Industrielles, Geneva (MBA). AMF Incorporated, 1959–73: executive assignments in NYC, Geneva, Tokyo, Hong Kong and London; Vice Pres., 1968; Dep. Managing Director, Bowthorpe Holdings Ltd, 1973–78; BL Limited, 1978–81: Man. Dir, Jaguar Rover Triumph Ltd, 1978–79; Chm., BL Internat. Ltd, 1979–81; Dir, Metalurgica de Santa Ana SA (Madrid), 1978–81; Vice-Chm., Colbert Gp (Geneva), 1981–84; Chairman: AIDCOM International plc, 1983–86 (Dir, 1982–); AIDCOM Technology Ltd, 1982–86; Husky Computers Ltd, 1982–86; Gallex Ltd, 1989–91; Dir, 1987–93, Man. Dir, 1989–93, Unitech plc. Member: Council, SMM&T, 1978–81; Council on Foreign Relations (USA), 1980–89. *Recreation:* various. *Address:* Trinity Hall, Castle Hedingham, Essex CO9 3EY. *Clubs:* Brooks's; Hong Kong (Hong Kong). *Died 9 May 2007.*

THOMSON OF FLEET, 2nd Baron *cr* 1964; **Kenneth Roy Thomson;** art collector; Director (formerly Chairman), The Thomson Corporation; *b* Toronto, Ont, 1 Sept. 1923; *s* of 1st Baron Thomson of Fleet, GBE, founder of Thomson Newspapers, and Edna Annis (*d* 1951), *d* of John Irvine, Drayton, Ont.; *S* father, 1976; *m* 1956, Nora Marilyn, *d* of A. V. Lavis; two *s* one *d*. *Educ:* Upper Canada Coll.; St John's Coll., Cambridge, England (MA). Served War of 1942–45 with RCAF. Began in editorial dept of Timmins Daily Press, Timmins, Ont., 1947; Advertising Dept, Galt Reporter, Cambridge, Ont, 1948–50, General Manager, 1950–53; returned to Toronto Head Office of Thomson Newspapers to take over direction of Company's Canadian and American operations. Pres., Thomson Works of Art Ltd; Dep. Chm., 1966–67, Chm., 1968–70, Co-Pres., 1971–81, Times Newspapers Ltd; Chm., The Woodbridge Co. Ltd. *Recreations:* collecting paintings and works of art, walking, golf. *Heir: s* Hon. David Kenneth Roy Thomson, *b* 12 June 1957. *Address:* (home) 8 Castle Frank Road, Toronto, ON M4W 2Z4, Canada; 8 Kensington Palace Gardens, W8 4QP; (office) The Thomson Corporation, 65 Queen Street West, Toronto, ON M5H 2M8, Canada; The Thomson Corporation plc, The Quadrangle, PO Box 4YG, 180 Wardour Street, W1A 4YG. *Clubs:* Granite, Hunt, Toronto, York, York Downs (Toronto). *Died 12 June 2006.*

THOMSON OF MONIFIETH, Baron *cr* 1977 (Life Peer), of Monifieth, Dundee; **George Morgan Thomson,** KT 1981; PC 1966; Chairman, Independent Broadcasting Authority, 1981–88 (Deputy Chairman, 1980); Chancellor, Heriot Watt University, 1977–91; *b* 16 Jan. 1921; *s* of late James Thomson, Monifieth; *m* 1948, Grace Jenkins; two *d*. *Educ:* Grove Academy, Dundee. Served War of 1939–45, in Royal Air Force, 1940–46. Assistant Editor, Forward, 1946, Editor, 1948–53. Contested (Lab) Glasgow, Hillhead, 1950; MP (Lab) Dundee East, July 1952–72. Joint Chm., Council for Education in the Commonwealth, 1959–64; Adviser to Educational Institute of Scotland, 1960–64. Minister of State, Foreign Office, 1964–66; Chancellor of the Duchy of Lancaster, 1966–67; Joint Minister of State, Foreign Office, 1967; Secretary of State for Commonwealth Affairs, Aug. 1967–Oct. 1968; Minister Without Portfolio, 1968–69; Chancellor of the Duchy of Lancaster, 1969–70; Shadow Defence Minister, 1970–72. Chm., Labour Cttee for Europe, 1972–73; Commissioner, EEC, 1973–Jan. 1977. Mem., Lib Dems, 1989– (spokesman on foreign affairs and broadcasting, H of L, 1990–98). Chairman: European Movement in Britain, 1977–80; Advertising Standards Authority, 1977–80; European TV and Film Forum, 1989–91. First Crown Estate Comr, 1978–80. Director: Royal Bank of Scotland Gp, 1977–90; ICI plc, 1977–89; Woolwich Equitable Building Soc., 1979–91 (Dep. Chm., 1988–91); Chairman: Value and Income Trust, 1988–2000; Grant Leisure, 1990–94; Woolwich Europe, 1990–92. President: Hist. of Advertising Trust, 1985–99; Prix Italia, 1989–91; Dir, ENO, 1987–93. Chm., Suzy Lamplugh Trust, 1990–93; Dep. Chm., Ditchley Foundn, 1983–87; Pilgrims Trustee, 1977–97; Trustee: Thomson Foundn, 1977–; Leeds Castle Foundn, 1978–2001 (Chm., 1994–2001). FRSE 1985; FRTS 1990 (Vice-Pres., 1982–89). Hon. LLD Dundee, 1967; Hon. DLitt: Heriot-Watt, 1973; New Univ. of Ulster, 1984; Hon. DSc Aston, 1976. *Address:* House of Lords, SW1A 0PW. *Died 3 Oct. 2008.*

THOMSON, Brian Harold, TD 1947; DL; Director, D. C. Thomson & Co. Ltd, since 1947 (Chairman, 1974–2005); *b* 21 Nov. 1918; *e s* of late William Harold Thomson of Kemback and Helen Irene, *d* of Sir Charles Ballance; *m* 1947, Agnes Jane Patricia Cunninghame (*d* 1991); one *s* four *d*. *Educ:* Charterhouse. Served War of 1939–45: 1st Fife and Forfar Yeomanry, and on Staff, DAQMG 1st Armoured Div., N Africa and Italy, 1943–44. GS02 Instructor, Staff Coll., Haifa, 1944–46; Lt-Col Comdg Fife and Forfar Yeomanry TA, 1953–56. Entered D. C. Thomson & Co. Ltd, 1937. Director: John Leng & Co. Ltd, 1948–; Southern Television, 1959–88; Alliance Trust and Second Alliance Trust, 1961–89. DL Fife, 1988. Hon. DLitt Abertay Dundee, 2002. *Recreations:* golf, shooting. *Club:* Royal and Ancient Golf (St Andrews). *Died 7 Nov. 2006.*

THOMSON, Garry, CBE 1983; Scientific Adviser to the Trustees and Head of the Scientific Department, National Gallery, London, 1960–85; *b* 13 Sept. 1925; *s* of late Robert Thomson and Mona Spence; *m* 1954, M. R. Saisvasdi Svasti; four *s*. *Educ:* Charterhouse; Magdalene College, Cambridge (MA). Editorial Staff of A History of Technology, 1951; Research Chemist, National Gallery, 1955; Hon. Editor, Studies in Conservation, 1959–67; Pres., Internat. Inst. for Conservation of Historic and Artistic Works, 1983–86. Vice-Pres., Buddhist Soc., London, 1978–88. Trustee, Nat. Museums and Galls on Merseyside, 1986–91. (First) Plowden Gold Medal, Royal Warrant Holders Assoc., 1999 (for achievement in field of conservation). *Publications:* Recent Advances in Conservation (ed); 1963; Museum Climatology (ed), 1967; The Museum Environment, 1978; Reflections on the Life of the Buddha, 1982; The Sceptical Buddhist, 1995. *Address:* Squire's Hill, Tilford, Surrey GU10 2AD. *T:* (01252) 782206. *Died 23 May 2007.*

THOMSON, Sir John Sutherland, (Sir Ian), KBE 1985 (MBE (mil.) 1944); CMG 1968; retired, 1987; *b* 8 Jan. 1920; *s* of late William Sutherland Thomson and of Jessie McCaig Malloch; *m* 1st, 1945, Nancy Marguerite Kearsley (*d* 1988), Suva, Fiji; seven *s* one *d*; 2nd, 1989, Nancy Caldwell (*née* McColl). *Educ:* High Sch. of Glasgow; Univ. of Glasgow (MA Hons). Served War of 1939–45: Black Watch, 1940; Fiji Military Forces, 1941–45 (Captain). Appointed Cadet, Colonial Administrative Service, Fiji and Western Pacific, 1941; District Administration and Secretariat, Fiji, 1946–54; Seconded to Colonial Office, 1954–56; Dep. Comr, Native Lands and Fisheries, Fiji, 1957–58; Comr of Native Reserves and Chairman, Native Lands and Fisheries Commission, Fiji, 1958–62; Divisional Commissioner, Fiji, 1963–66; Administrator, British Virgin Islands, 1967–71; Acting Governor-Gen., Fiji, 1980–83 on occasions. Indep. Chm., Fiji Sugar Industry, 1971–84; Chairman: Fiji Coconut Bd, 1973–83; Economic Develt Bd, Fiji, 1980–86; Fiji Liquor Laws Review Cttee, 1985; Fiji Nat. Tourism Assoc., 1984–87. Chairman: Sedgwick (Fiji) Ltd, 1984–87; Air Pacific Ltd, 1984–87; Thomson Pacific Resources Ltd, 1988–92. *Publications:* Fiji in the Forties and Fifties, 1994. *Recreations:* golf, gardening. *Address:* 1/4 Fettes Rise, Edinburgh EH4 1QH. *T:* (0131) 552 6421.
Died 13 March 2008.

THOMSON, Robert Howard Garry; *see* Thomson, Garry.

THORN, E. Gaston; Politician, Luxembourg; President: Banque Internationale, Luxembourg, since 1985; Mouvement Européen International, since 1985; President-Director General, RTL Luxembourg, since 1987; *b* 3 Sept. 1928; *s* of Edouard Thorn and Suzanne Weber; *m* 1957, Liliane Petit; one *s*. *Educ:* Univs of Montpellier, Lausanne, and Paris. DenD. Admitted to Luxembourg Bar; Pres., Nat. Union of Students, Luxembourg, 1959; Member, European Parlt, 1959–69, Vice-Pres., Liberal Group; Pres., Democratic Party, Luxembourg, 1969; Minister of Foreign Affairs and of Foreign Trade, also Minister of Physical Educn and Sport, 1974–77; Prime Minister and Minister of State, 1974–79; Minister of Nat. Econ. and Middle Classes, 1977; of Justice, 1979; Dep. Prime Minister, and Minister of Foreign Affairs, July 1979–1980; Pres., EEC, 1981–85. Pres., 30th Session of UN Gen. Assembly, 1975–76. President: Liberal International, 1970–82; Fedn of Liberal and Democratic Parties of European Community, 1976–80. Mem., Public Review Board, Arthur Andersen & Co. Decorations include Grand Cross of Orders of Adolphe de Nassau, Couronne de Chêne, and Mérite (Luxembourg), Grand Cross of Légion d'Honneur (France), GCVO and GCMG (GB) and other Grand Crosses. *Recreations:* tennis, reading. *Address:* 1 rue de la Forge, Luxembourg. *Died 26 Aug. 2007.*

THORN, Sir John (Samuel), Kt 1984; OBE 1977; Mayor, Port Chalmers Borough Council, 1956–89 (Member, 1938–41, 1947–50 and 1950–53); *b* 19 March 1911; *s* of J. S. Thorn; *m* 1936, Constance Maud (*d* 1997), *d* of W. T. Haines; one *s*. *Educ:* Port Chalmers School; King Edward Technical College. Served 1939–45 war, 3rd Div. Apprentice plumber, later plumbing contractor and land agent; Manager, Thorn's Bookshop, 1950–80. Chairman: Municipal Insce Co.; Coastal N Otago United Council. Pres., Municipal Assoc., 1974–; Dep. Chm., Nat. Roads Board, 1974–83. *Address:* 94C Stevenson Avenue, Sawyers Bay, Dunedin, New Zealand.
Died 27 Sept. 2008.

THORNE, Stanley George; *b* 22 July 1918; *s* of postman and dressmaker; *m* 1952, Catherine Mary Rand; two *s* three *d*. *Educ:* Ruskin Coll., Oxford; Univ. of Liverpool. Dip. Social Studies Oxon 1968; BA Hons Liverpool 1970. 30 yrs in industry and commerce: coal-miner, semi-skilled fitter, chartered accountant's clerk, railway signalman, office manager, auditor, commercial manager, etc; lectr in govt and industrial sociology. MP (Lab):

Preston South, Feb. 1974–1983; Preston 1983–87. *Recreations:* chess, bridge, golf. *Address:* 26 Station Road, Gateacre, Liverpool L25 3PZ. *Died 26 Nov. 2007.*

THORNELY, Gervase Michael Cobham; Headmaster of Sedbergh School, 1954–75; *b* 21 Oct. 1918; *er s* of late Major J. E. B. Thornely, OBE, and Hon. Mrs M. H. Thornely; *m* 1954, Jennifer Margery, *d* of late Sir Hilary Scott, Knowle House, Addington, Surrey; two *s* two *d*. *Educ:* Rugby Sch.; Trinity Hall, Cambridge (Organ Scholar; 2nd Cl. Hons, Modern and Mediæval Languages Tripos; BA 1940; MA 1944). Assistant Master, Sedbergh School, 1940. FRSA 1968. *Recreations:* music, fly-fishing. *Address:* High Stangerthwaite, Killington, Sedbergh, Cumbria LA10 5EP. *T:* (01539) 620444. *Died 13 Oct. 2009.*

THORNEYCROFT, Lady; Carla Thorneycroft, DBE 1995; Founder Member, Trustee and Vice-Chairman, 1971–96, President, since 1996, Venice in Peril Fund; *b* 12 Feb. 1914; *e d* of late Count Malagola Cappi and Alexandra Dunbar-Marshall; *m* 1st, 1934, Count Giorgio Roberti (marr. annulled 1946); one *d* (one *s* decd); 2nd, 1949, Major George Edward Peter Thorneycroft, MP, later Baron Thorneycroft of Dunston, CH, PC (*d* 1994); one *d*. *Educ:* privately. Fashion Editor, Vogue, 1946–51; political campaign with husband, 1949–66. Pres. and Founder, League of Friends of Italian Hosp., 1956–89; Vice-Pres., British-Italian Soc., 1957–; Founder Mem., Trustee and Patron, Rosehill Arts Theatre, 1959–77; Founder Mem. and Trustee, Chichester Fest. Theatre Trust, 1962–88; Trustee, Royal Sch. of Needlework, 1964–76; Vice-Chm., Italian Art and Archives Rescue Fund, 1966–69; Vice-Pres., Council of Friends of Westminster Cathedral, 1993– (Mem. Council, 1976–); Trustee, Conservative Winter Ball (Pres., 1984–94). Order of Merit (Italy), 1967. *Recreations:* arts, politics, travel, charity work. *Died 7 March 2007.*

THORNTON, Peter Kai, CBE 1996; FSA 1976; Curator of Sir John Soane's Museum, 1984–95; *b* 8 April 1925; *s* of Sir Gerard Thornton, FRS, and of Gerda, *d* of Kai Nørregaard, Copenhagen; *m* 1st, 1950, Mary Ann Rosamund (marr. diss. 2001), *d* of E. A. P. Helps, Cregane, Rosscarbery, Co. Cork; three *d*; 2nd, 2002, Lena Spindler, Stockholm. *Educ:* Bryanston Sch.; De Havilland Aeronautical Technical Sch.; Trinity Hall, Cambridge. Served with Army, Intelligence Corps, Austria, 1945–48; Cambridge, 1948–50; Voluntary Asst Keeper, Fitzwilliam Museum, Cambridge, 1950–52; Joint Secretary, National Art-Collections Fund, London, 1952–54; entered Victoria and Albert Museum as Asst Keeper, Dept of Textiles, 1954; transf. to Dept of Woodwork, 1962; Keeper, Dept of Furniture and Woodwork, 1966–84. Sen. Vis. Res. Fellow, St John's Coll., Oxford, 1985–86; Leverhulme Emeritus Res. Fellow, 1988–89. Chm., Furniture History Soc., 1974–84; Member: Council, Nat. Trust, 1983–85; London Adv. Cttee, English Heritage, 1986–88. Iris Foundn award, Bard Center, NY, 1999. *Publications:* Baroque and Rococo Silks, 1965; Seventeenth Century Interior Decoration in England, France and Holland, 1978 (Alice Davis Hitchcock Medallion, Soc. of Architectural Historians of GB, 1982); (jtly) The Furnishing and Decoration of Ham House, 1981; Musical Instruments as Works of Art, 1982; Authentic Decor: the domestic interior 1620–1920, 1984, rev. edn 2000 (Sir Bannister Fletcher Prize, RIBA, 1985); The Italian Renaissance Interior 1400–1600, 1992 (Prix Vasari International du Livre d'Art for French edn, 1992); (jtly) A Miscellany of Objects from Sir John Soane's Museum, 1992; Form and Decoration: innovation in the decorative arts 1470–1870, 1998. *Address:* 4 Staveley Gardens, Chiswick, W4 2SA. *Died 8 Feb. 2007.*

THORNTON, Robert Ribblesdale, CBE 1973; DL; solicitor; Deputy Chairman, Local Government Boundary Commission for England, 1982 (Member, 1976–82); *b* 2 April 1913; *s* of Thomas Thornton and Florence Thornton (*née* Gatenby); *m* 1940, Ruth Eleonore Tuckson (decd); one *s* one *d*. *Educ:* Leeds

Grammar Sch.; St John's Coll., Cambridge (MA, LLM). Asst Solicitor, Leeds, 1938–40 and 1946–47. Served War, 1940–46. Asst Solicitor, Bristol, 1947–53; Dep. Town Clerk, Southampton, 1953–54; Town Clerk: Salford, 1954–66; Leicester, 1966–73; Chief Exec., Leicestershire CC, 1973–76. Pres., Soc. of Town Clerks, 1971. DL Leicestershire, 1974–85. Treasurer, Leicester Univ., 1980–85. Hon. LLD Leicester, 1987. French Croix de Guerre, 1946. *Recreations:* music, sport. *Address:* 16 St Mary's Close, Winterborne Whitechurch, Blandford Forum, Dorset DT11 0DJ. *T:* (01258) 880980.
Died 25 July 2006.

THOROGOOD, Kenneth Alfred Charles; company director; *b* 1924; *s* of Albert Jesse and Alice Lucy Thorogood; *m* 1st, 1947, José Patricia Smith; two *d*; 2nd, 1979, Mrs Gaye Lambourne. *Educ:* Highbury County Grammar School. Pilot, RAF, 1941–46. Chm., Tozer Kemsley & Millbourn (Holdings) plc, 1972–82; Dep. Chm. and Dir, Felixstowe Dock and Railway Co., 1976–81; Director: Alexanders Discount Co. Ltd, to 1983; Royal Insurance Co. Ltd; Abelson Plant (Holdings) Ltd; Spicer-Firgos Ltd; Welbeck Finance plc, 1984–88. Chairman, Brit. Export Houses Assoc., 1968–70; Mem., Cttee of Invisibles, 1968–70. *Recreations:* aviation, music. *Address:* 1 Chiswick Mall, W4 2QH. *Clubs:* Travellers, City of London, Royal Air Force, MCC; Wanderers (Johannesburg). *Died 9 May 2006.*

THOURON, Sir John (Rupert Hunt), KBE 1976 (CBE 1967); *b* 10 May 1908; *m* 1st, 1930, Lorna Ellett (marr. diss. 1939; she *d* 2000); (one *s* decd); 2nd, 1953, Esther duPont (*d* 1984). *Educ:* Sherborne School, Dorset. Served War of 1939–45; Major, Black Watch. With Lady Thouron, Founder of the Thouron University of Pennsylvania Fund for British-American Student Exchange, 1960. *Recreations:* shooting, fishing, golf, gardening. *Address:* Unionville, Chester County, PA 19375, USA. *T:* (610) 3845542; (winter) 416 South Beach Road, Hobe Sound, FL 33455, USA. *T:* (561) 5463577. *Clubs:* White's; Brook (NY); Sunningdale Golf; Royal St George Golf; Wilmington, Wilmington Country, Vicmead (all Delaware); Pine Valley, British Officers Club of Philadelphia (Pennsylvania); Seminole Golf, Island Club of Hobe Sound (Florida).
Died 6 Feb. 2007.

THRING, Prof. Meredith Wooldridge, ScD; FREng; Professor of Mechanical Engineering, Queen Mary College, London University, 1964–81; *b* 17 Dec. 1915; *s* of Captain W. H. C. S. Thring, CBE, RN, and Dorothy (*née* Wooldridge); *m* 1940, Alice Margaret Hooley (*d* 1986); two *s* one *d*. *Educ:* Malvern Coll., Worcs; Trinity Coll., Cambridge (Senior Scholar, 1937; BA Hons Maths and Physics, 1937; ScD 1964). Student's Medal, Inst. of Fuel, for work on producer gas mains, 1938; British Coal Utilisation Research Assoc.: Asst Scientific Officer, 1937; Senior Scientific Officer and Head of Combustion Research Laboratory, 1944; British Iron and Steel Research Assoc.: Head of Physics Dept, 1946; Superintendent, 1950; Assistant Director, 1953; Prof. of Fuel Technology and Chemical Engineering, Sheffield Univ., 1953–64. General Superintendent International Flame Radiation Research Foundn, 1951–76. Visitor: Production Engineering Research Assoc., 1967; Machine Tool Industry Research Assoc., 1967. Member Clean Air Council, 1957–62; Fuel Research Board, 1957–58; Fire Research Board, 1961–64; BISRA Council, 1958–60; President, Inst. of Fuel, 1962–63 (Vice-President, 1959–62); Member: Adv. Council on Research and Development, Ministry of Power, 1960–66; Acad. Adv. Council, University of Strathclyde, 1962–67; Education Cttee, RAF, 1968–76; Unesco Commn to Bangladesh, 1979. FInstP 1944; FInstF 1951; FIChemE 1972 (MIChemE 1956); FIMechE 1968 (MIMechE 1964); FIET (FIEE 1968; MIEE 1964); FREng (a Founder Fellow, 1976); FRSA 1964; MRI 1965; FRAeS 1969. Elected Mem., Royal Norwegian Scientific Soc., 1974; Mem., NY Acad. of Scis, 1998; Corresp. Mem., Nat. Acad. of Engineering of Mexico, 1977. Lectures: Parsons

Meml on Magnetohydrodynamics, 1961; First Wenca. Lagos, 1989. DUniv Open, 1982. Sir Robert Hadfield medal of Iron and Steel Inst. for studies on open hearth furnaces, 1949. *Publications:* The Science of Flames and Furnaces, 1952, 2nd edn, 1960; (with J. H. Chesters) The Influence of Port Design on Open Hearth Furnace Flames (Iron and Steel Institute Special Report 37), 1946; (with R. Edgeworth Johnstone) Pilot Plants, Models and Scale-up Methods in Chemical Engineering, 1957; (ed.) Air Pollution, 1957; Nuclear Propulsion, 1961; Man, Machines and Tomorrow, 1973; Machines—Masters or Slaves of Man?, 1973; (ed with R. J. Crookes) Energy and Humanity, 1974; (with E. R. Laithwaite) How to Invent, 1977; The Engineer's Conscience, 1980; Robots and Telechirs, 1983; Quotations from G. I. Gurdjieff's Teachings, 1998; The Seven Riddles of the Universe, 2005. *Recreations:* arboriculture, wood-carving. *Address:* Cranford Nursing Home, 15 Cranford Avenue, Exmouth, Devon EX8 2HS. *Club:* Athenæum.
Died 15 Sept. 2006.

THURNHAM, Peter Giles; Chairman, WR Group Holdings Ltd (formerly First and Third Securities Ltd, then Wathes Group of Cos), 1972–2002; *b* 21 Aug. 1938; *s* of late Giles Rymer Thurnham and Marjorie May (*née* Preston); *m* 1963, Sarah Janet Stroude (marr. diss. 2004); one *s* three *d* and one adopted *s*; *m* 2008, Carole Emery. *Educ:* Oundle Sch.; Peterhouse, Cambridge (MA 1967); Cranfield Inst. of Technol. (Dip. in Advanced Engrg, 1967); SRC/NATO Scholarship, Harvard Business Sch., Harvard Univ. (MBA 1969). CEng 1967; FIMechE 1985. Design Engr, NEI Parsons Ltd, 1957–66; Divl Dir, British Steam Specialties Ltd, 1967–72. MP Bolton North East, 1983–97 (C, 1983–96, Ind, 1996, Lib Dem, 1996–97). Parliamentary Private Secretary: to Sec. of State for Employment, 1987–90; to Eric Forth, MP and Robert Jackson, MP, 1991–92; to Sec. of State for the Envmt, 1992–93. Lib Dem spokesman on social services, 1996–97. Member: Select Cttee on Employment, 1983–87; Public Accounts Cttee, 1995–97. Treas., All-Party Parly Gp, Chemical Industry, 1985–87; Vice Chairman: All-Party Parly Gp for Children, 1986–97; All Party Disability Gp, 1992–97. Conservative Back Bench 1922 Committees: Vice-Chairman: Smaller Business Cttee, 1985–87; Home Improvement Sub-Cttee, 1986–87; Secretary: Employment Cttee, 1986–87; Social Security Cttee, 1990–91; Founder and Chm., Cons. Disability Gp, 1989–96. Mem. Council, PSI, 1985–89. Dir, Rathbone, 1997–2001. Founder Mem., 1985 and Mem. Cttee, 1985–2001, Progress, Campaign for Res. into Reproduction; Founder and Vice Pres., Campaign for Inter Country Adoption, 1991 (Pres., 1995); Vice-President: Croft Care Home, 1995–2001; Adoption Forum, 1997–2001. Patron, Stork, Assoc. of Families who have Adopted from Abroad, 1991–2001. *Publications:* discussion papers; contrib. technical jls. *Recreations:* country life, restoring classic British engineering. *Address:* Fourstones House, Bentham, Lancaster LA2 7DL. *T:* (01524) 264876, *Fax:* (01524) 264877; *e-mail:* peter@ fourstoneshouse.co.uk. *Died 10 May 2008.*

THURSTON, Dame Thea; *see* King, Dame T.

TICKELL, Maj.-Gen. Marston Eustace, CBE 1973 (MBE 1955); MC 1945; CEng, FICE; Commandant Royal Military College of Science, 1975–78, retired; *b* 18 Nov. 1923; *er s* of late Maj.-Gen. Sir Eustace Tickell, KBE, CB, MC, and Mary Violet Tickell; *m* 1961, Pamela Vere, *d* of Vice-Adm. A. D. Read, CB; no *c. Educ:* Wellington Coll.; Peterhouse, Cambridge (MA). Commnd in RE, 1944; NW Europe Campaign and Middle East, 1944–45; psc 1954; Mil. Ops, MoD, 1955–57; served in Libya, Cyprus and Jordan, 1958–59; US Armed Forces Staff Coll. and Instructor RMCS and Staff Coll., 1959–62; Defence Planning Staff, MoD, 1962–64; CRE 4th Div., 1964–66; comd 12 Engr Bde, 1967–69; Indian Nat. Defence Coll., 1970; COS Northern Ireland, 1971–72; E-in-C, MoD, 1972–75. Col Comdt, RE, 1978–83. Hon. Col, Engr and Transport Staff Corps, 1983–88. Lord Chancellor's Panel of

Independent Inspectors, 1979–93. Pres., Instn of Royal Engrs, 1979–82. FICE 1974. *Recreation:* sailing. *Address:* The Old Vicarage, Branscombe, Seaton, Devon EX12 3DW. *Clubs:* Army and Navy; Royal Ocean Racing. *Died 8 Sept. 2009.*

TICKLE, Brian Percival, CB 1985; Senior Registrar of the Family Division, High Court of Justice, 1982–88 (Registrar, 1970–88); *b* 31 Oct. 1921; *s* of late William Tickle and Lucy (*née* Percival); *m* 1945, Margaret Alice Pendrey (*d* 1994); one *s* one *d. Educ:* The Judd Sch., Tonbridge. Entered Civil Service, 1938. Served War, Royal Signals, 1941–46. Civil Service, 1946–70. Member: Matrimonial Causes Rules Cttee, 1982–88; Independent Schs Tribunal, 1988–93. Vice Pres., Nevill Golf Club, 1997–. *Publications:* Rees Divorce Handbook, 1963; Atkin's Court Forms and Precedents (Probate), 2nd edn 1974, rev. edn 1984. *Recreations:* watching golf, cricket and Rugby. *Address:* Hillbrow Court, 1A Royal Chase, Tunbridge Wells, Kent TN4 8AX. *Died 18 May 2008.*

TIERNEY, Sydney; JP; President, 1977–81, and 1983–91, and National Officer, 1979–91, Union of Shop, Distributive and Allied Workers; Chairman, Labour Party, 1986–87 (Vice-Chairman, 1985–86); *b* 16 Sept. 1923; *m* 1985, Margaret Olive (*née* Hannah); two *d. Educ:* Secondary Modern Sch., Dearne; Plater Coll., Oxford. Mem., Co-operative Party; an Official and Member, USDAW. Vice-Chm., W Midlands Labour Gp of MPs, 1974–79; Mem., Labour Party NEC, to 1990. MP (Lab) Birmingham, Yardley, Feb. 1974–1979; PPS to Min. of State for Agriculture, 1976–79. JP Leicester, 1966. *Address:* Rocklands, 56 Priory Lane, Kents Bank, Grange Over Sands, Cumbria LA11 7BJ. *Died 6 March 2010.*

TINDALL, Prof. Victor Ronald, CBE 1992; MD; FRCS, FRCOG; Professor of Obstetrics and Gynaecology, University of Manchester at St Mary's Hospital, 1972–93, then Emeritus; *b* 1 Aug. 1928; *m* 1955, Brenda Fay; one *s* one *d. Educ:* Wallasey Grammar Sch.; Liverpool Univ. (MB ChB; MD); Manchester Univ. (MSc). Sen. Lectr and Consultant, Welsh Nat. Sch. of Medicine, Cardiff, 1965–70; Consultant Obstetrician and Gynaecologist, Univ. Hosp. of Wales, 1970–72. Sen. Vice-Pres., RCOG, 1990–93. FRCS by election, 1991. *Publications:* MCQ Tutor, MRCOG Part I, 1977, 2nd edn 1985, combined edn 1987; (jtly) Practical Student Obstetrics, 1980; Colour Atlas of Clinical Gynaecology, 1981; Essential Sciences for Clinicians, 1981; Clinical Gynaecology, 1986; (ed) Jeffcoates' Principles of Gynaecology, 5th edn 1987; Diagnostic Picture Tests in Obstetrics and Gynaecology, 1986; (ed jtly) Current Approaches to Endometrial Carcinoma, 1988; (jtly) Preparations and Advice for the Members of the Royal College of Obstetricians and Gynaecologists, 1989; Illustrated Textbook of Gynaecology, 1991; (ed jtly) Self Assessment Picture Tests: obstetrics and gynaecology, 1996; reports for DHSS on maternal deaths in the UK. *Recreations:* ex-England Rugby international, international sporting activities. *Address:* 4 Planetree Road, Hale, Altrincham, Cheshire WA15 9JJ. *T:* (0161) 980 2680, (office) (0161) 904 8222. *Died 11 June 2010.*

TINKER, Dr Jack, FRCP, FRCSGlas; Emeritus Consultant, University College Hospitals, since 1996; Dean, Royal Society of Medicine, 1998–2002, then Emeritus; *b* 20 Jan. 1936; *s* of Lawrence and Jessie Tinker; *m* 1961, Maureen Ann Crawford; two *s. Educ:* Manchester Univ. (BSc (Hons), MB ChB); DIC. Dir, Intensive Therapy Unit, Middlesex Hosp., 1974–88; Hon. Cons. Physician, Middlesex Hosp., 1988–96; Hon. Sen. Clin. Lectr, UCL Med. Sch. (formerly UCMSM), 1988–96; Hon. Sen. Lectr, St Bartholomew's Hosp. Med. Coll., 1991–96; Dean of Postgrad. Medicine, Univ. of London and N Thames RHA, 1988–96. Sen. Med. Consultant, Sun Life of Canada, 1983–2000; Med. Advr, Rio Tinto plc (formerly RTZ Gp), 1986–2006; Med. Dir, Health Screening Unit, London Clinic, 1994–2006.

Chm., Dr Foster Ethics Cttee, 2001–08. Gov., Expert Witness Inst., 2003–07. FRSocMed 1989 (Hon. Sub-Dean, 1996–98). FRSA 1997. Editor in Chief, British Jl of Hospital Medicine, 1985–; Man. Editor, Intensive Care Medicine, 1973–88. *Publications:* A Course in Intensive Therapy Nursing, 1980; Care of the Critically Ill Patient, 1982, 2nd edn 1991; A Pocket Book for Intensive Care, 1986, 2nd edn 1990; Critical Care, Standards, Audit and Ethics, 1996; contribs to intensive care and cardiological jls. *Recreation:* watching soccer and cricket. *Address:* 1 Rectory Road, Barnes, SW13 0DU. *T:* (020) 8878 0159. *Clubs:* Royal Automobile, MCC; Scarborough. *Died 14 April 2010.*

TIPPET, Vice-Adm. Sir Anthony (Sanders), KCB 1984; *b* 2 Oct. 1928; *s* of W. K. R. Tippet and H. W. P. Kitley (*née* Sanders); *m* 1950, Lola Bassett; two *s* one *d* (and one *s* decd). *Educ:* West Buckland Sch., Devon. Called to the Bar, Gray's Inn, 1959. Entered RN, 1946; Lieut 1950; HM Ships Ceres, Superb, Staff C-in-C Mediterranean; Lt Comdr 1958; HMS Trafalgar, Britannia RNC; Comdr 1963; Secretary: to Director of Naval Intelligence; to Flag Officer Middle East; CO HMS Jufair, Supply Officer, HMS Eagle; Captain 1970: Asst Director Naval Plans (Warfare), 1970–72; CSO (Administration) to Flag Officer Plymouth, 1972–74; Director of Naval Officers' Appointments (Supply and WRNS Officers), 1974–76; Captain HMS Pembroke and Flag Captain to Flag Officer Medway, 1976–79; Rear-Adm. 1979; Asst Chief of Fleet Support, MoD, 1979–81; Flag Officer and Port Admiral, Portsmouth, and Chief Naval Supply and Secretariat Officer, 1981–83; Chief of Fleet Support and Mem., Admiralty Bd, 1983–86. Gen. Manager, Hospitals for Sick Children, London, 1987–94; Chief Exec., Gt Ormond Street Hosp. for Children NHS Trust, 1994–95. Chairman: Funding Agency for Schs, 1997–99; Halifax Learning Zone, 1998–2003; Bradford Educn Policy Partnership, 2001–02. Chairman: RN Benevolent Soc. for Officers, 1993–98; Children in Hospital, 1990–98; Write Away, 1990–97; Nat. Appeal for Music Therapy, 1995–97. Trustee, Sea Cadet Assoc., 1999–2003. Pres., West Buckland Sch., 2000–06 (Gov., 1979–2001; Chm., 1989–96). CCMI. Hon. Fellow, Inst. of Child Health, 1995; Hon. Fellow, S Bank Univ., 1995. *Recreations:* sailing, hill walking. *Clubs:* Royal Naval Sailing Association; Anchorites. *Died 13 Oct. 2006.*

TITHERIDGE, Roger Noel; QC 1973; a Recorder of the Crown Court 1972–99; Barrister-at-Law; *b* 21 Dec. 1928; *s* of Jack George Ralph Titheridge and Mabel Titheridge (*née* Steains); *m* 1963, Annabel Maureen (*née* Scott-Fisher); two *d. Educ:* Midhurst Grammar Sch.; Merton Coll., Oxford (Exhibnr; MA (History and Jurisprudence)). Called to the Bar, Gray's Inn, 1954; Holker Sen. Scholar, Gray's Inn, 1954; Bencher, Gray's Inn, 1985; Dep. High Court Judge, QBD, 1984–98; Leader, Western Circuit, 1989–92. *Recreations:* tennis, sailing. *Address:* 1 Paper Buildings, Temple, EC4Y 7EP. *T:* (020) 7353 3728; 13 The Moat, Traps Lane, New Malden, Surrey KT3 4SB. *T:* (020) 8942 2747. *Died 10 Nov. 2010.*

TODD, Rev. Andrew Stewart; Minister of St Machar's Cathedral, Old Aberdeen, 1967–93; Extra Chaplain to the Queen in Scotland, since 1996 (Chaplain, 1991–96); *b* 26 May 1926; *s* of late William Stewart Todd and Robina Victoria Fraser; *m* 1953, Janet Agnes Brown Smith (decd), *d* of late John Smith, JP, DL, and Agnes Brown, Glasgow and Symington; two *s* one *d* (and one *d* decd). *Educ:* High Sch. of Stirling; Edinburgh Univ. (MA Hons, Classics 1947); New Coll., Edinburgh (BD 1950); Basel Univ. Asst Minister, St Cuthbert's, Edinburgh, 1951–52; ordained, 1952; Minister: Symington, Lanarkshire, 1952–60; North Leith, 1960–67. Convener, Gen. Assembly's Cttee on Public Worship and Aids to Devotion, 1974–78; Moderator, Aberdeen Presbytery, 1980–81; Convener, Panel on Doctrine, 1990–95; Member: Church Hymnary Cttee, 1963–73; Church Hymnary Trust, 1965–2008. Hon. President: Church Service Soc.; Scottish Church Soc. Hon. DD Aberdeen, 1982. *Publications:* jt translator, Oscar Cullmann, Early

Christian Worship, 1953; translator: Ludwig Koehler, Old Testament Theology, 1957; Ernst Lohmeyer, Lord of the Temple, 1961; contributions to liturgical jls. *Recreations:* music, gardening. *Address:* Fentoun House, 11 Bedford Place, Alloa, Clackmannanshire FK10 1LJ. *Club:* Royal Over-Seas League. *Died 2 Sept. 2009.*

TODD, Richard, (Richard Andrew Palethorpe-Todd), OBE 1993; actor; *b* 11 June 1919; *s* of Major A. W. Palethorpe-Todd, MC, Castlederg, Co. Tyrone, and Marvil Agar-Daly, Ballymalis Castle, Kerry; *m* 1st, 1949, Catherine Stewart Crawford Grant-Bogle (marr. diss. 1970); one *d* (one *s* decd); 2nd, 1970, Virginia Anne Rollo Mailer (marr. diss. 1992); one *s* (and one *s* decd). *Educ:* Shrewsbury; privately; RMC Sandhurst, 1940–41. Entered the theatre in 1937. Served in King's Own Yorkshire Light Infantry and The Parachute Regt, 1940–46; GSO iii (Ops), 6 Airborne Div., 1944–45. *Films from War of 1939–45* include: The Hasty Heart, 1949; Stage Fright, 1950; Robin Hood, 1952; Rob Roy, 1953; A Man Called Peter, 1954; The Dambusters, 1954; The Virgin Queen, 1955; Yangtse Incident, 1957; Chase a Crooked Shadow, 1957; The Long and the Short and the Tall, 1960; The Hellions, 1961; The Longest Day, 1962; Operation Crossbow, 1964; Coast of Skeletons, 1964; The Love-Ins (USA), 1967; Subterfuge, 1968; Dorian Grey, 1969; Asylum, 1972; Secret Agent 008, 1976; The House of the Long Shadows, 1982; The Olympus Force, 1988. *Stage* appearances include: An Ideal Husband, Strand, 1965–66; Dear Octopus, Haymarket, 1967; USA tour, The Marquise, 1972; Australia tour, Sleuth, 1973; led RSC N American tour, 1974; Equus, Australian Nat. Theatre Co., 1975; On Approval (S Africa), 1976; nat. tour of Quadrille, and The Heat of the Moment, 1977; Nightfall (S Africa), 1979; This Happy Breed (nat. tour), 1980; The Business of Murder, Duchess, 1981, Mayfair, 1982–88; The Woman in Black, Sydney Opera House, Liverpool Playhouse, 1991; nat. tour of Sweet Revenge, 1993; nat. tour of Brideshead Revisited, 1995; An Ideal Husband, Old Vic and tour, 1997, Gielgud and Albery, 1998, Theatre Royal, Haymarket and Lyric, 1999. *Television:* Heathcliffe, in Wuthering Heights, 1960; Carrington VC, 1964; H. G. Wells, in Beautiful Lies, 1991; series, Virtual Murder, 1992; Dr Newman, in Silent Witness, 2000; Midsomer Murders, 2002; The Royal, 2002; Heartbeat, 2007. Formed Triumph Theatre Productions, 1970. Pres., Age Concern, Birmingham, 1990–. Past Grand Steward, Past Master, Lodge of Emulation No 21. *Publications:* Caught in the Act (autobiog.), 1986; In Camera (autobiog.), 1989. *Recreations:* fishing, gardening. *Address:* Chinham Farm, Faringdon, Oxon SN7 8EZ; Sandal Cottage, Little Humby, Grantham, Lincs NG33 4HW. *Club:* Army and Navy. *Died 3 Dec. 2009.*

TOLER, Maj.-Gen. David Arthur Hodges, OBE 1963; MC 1945; DL; General Officer Commanding East Midland District, 1970–73; *b* 13 Sept. 1920; *s* of Major Thomas Clayton Toler, DL, JP, Swettenham Hall, Congleton; *m* 1951, Judith Mary *(d* 2000), *d* of James William Garden, DSO, Aberdeen; one *s* one *d. Educ:* Stowe; Christ Church, Oxford (MA). 2nd Lieut Coldstream Guards, 1940; served War of 1939–45, N Africa and Italy; Regimental Adjt, Coldstream Guards, 1952–54; Bde Major, 4th Gds Bde, 1956–57; Adjt, RMA Sandhurst, 1958–60; Bt Lt-Col 1959; Br Liaison Officer, US Continental Army Comd (Col), 1960–62; comd 2nd Bn Coldstream Guards, 1962–64; comd Coldstream Guards, 1964–65; comd 4th Guards Bde, 1965–68; Dep. Comdt, Staff Coll., Camberley, 1968–69; Dep. Comdr Army, NI, 1969–70. Dep. Hon. Col, Royal Anglian Regt (Lincolnshire) TAVR, 1979–84. Emergency Planning Officer, Lincolnshire CC, 1974–77. Chm., Lincoln Dio. Adv. Cttee, 1981–86. Pres., SSAFA, Lincs, 1978–98. DL Lincs, 1982. *Recreation:* gardening. *Address:* Rutland Farm, Fulbeck, Grantham, Lincs NG32 3LG. *Club:* Army and Navy. *Died 19 Nov. 2009.*

TOMKINS, Sir Edward Emile, GCMG 1975 (KCMG 1969; CMG 1960); CVO 1957; Grand Officiér, Légion d'Honneur, 1984; HM Diplomatic Service, retired; HM Ambassador to France, 1972–75; *b* 16 Nov. 1915; *s* of late Lt-Col E. L. Tomkins; *m* 1955, Gillian Benson *(d* 2003); one *s* two *d. Educ:* Ampleforth Coll.; Trinity Coll., Cambridge. Foreign Office, 1939. Military service, 1940–43. HM Embassy, Moscow, 1944–46; Foreign Office, 1946–51; HM Embassy, Washington, 1951–54; HM Embassy, Paris, 1954–59; Foreign Office, 1959–63; HM Embassy, Bonn, 1963–67; HM Embassy, Washington, 1967–69; Ambassador to the Netherlands, 1970–72. Mem., Bucks CC, 1977–85. *Address:* Winslow Hall, Winslow, Bucks MK18 3HL. *T:* (01296) 712323. *Died 20 Sept. 2007.*

TONGA, HM the King of; **King Taufa'ahau Tupou IV,** Hon. GCMG 1977 (Hon. KCMG 1968); Hon. GCVO 1970; Hon. KBE 1958 (Hon. CBE 1951); *b* 4 July 1918; *s* of Prince Uiliami Tupoulahi Tungi and Queen Salote Tupou of Tonga; *S* mother, 1965; *m* 1947, Halaevalu Mata'aho 'Ahome'e; three *s* one *d. Educ:* Tupou College, Tonga; Newington College, Sydney; Wesley College, Sydney University. Minister for Health and Education, Tonga, 1943–50; Prime Minister, 1950–65. *Heir: s* HRH Prince Tupouto'a, *b* 4 May 1948. *Address:* The Palace, Nukualofa, Tonga. *T:* 21000. *Died 10 Sept. 2006.*

TOPHAM, Surgeon Captain Lawrence Garth; RN (Retd); Consultant Physician in Geriatric Medicine, Central Hampshire District Winchester and Andover Hospitals, 1974–83; *b* 14 Nov. 1914; *s* of late J. Topham and late Mrs Topham; *m* 1943, Olive Barbara Marshall (VAD), *yr d* of late J. Marshall and late Mrs Marshall; one *s* one *d. Educ:* Bradford Grammar Sch.; Univ. of Leeds. MB, ChB 1937; MD 1946; MRCPE 1957; FRCPE 1967; MRCP 1969. Joined RN 1938. Served War: HMS Newcastle and HMS Milford, 1939–41; USN Flight Surgeon's Wings, 1943; RN Fleet Air Arm Pilot's Wings, 1944. Pres., Central Air Med. Bd, 1949; HMS Sheffield, 1951; Med. Specialist and Consultant in Medicine, at RN Hosps, Trincomalee, Haslar and Plymouth, 1952–66; Prof. of Med., RN, and RCP, 1966–71; QHP 1970; retd at own request, from RN, 1971. House Governor and Medical Superintendent, King Edward VII Convalescent Home for Officers, Osborne, IoW, 1971–74. Member: British Nat. Cttee, Internat. Soc. of Internal Medicine; British Geriatric Soc.; Wessex Physicians Club. OStJ (Officer Brother) 1970. *Publications:* several articles in med. jls, especially on subject of diseases of the chest. *Recreations:* Rugby football refereeing, rowing, photography, Oriental cookery. *Address:* Tilings, 3 Holt Close, Wickham, Hants PO17 5EY. *T:* (01329) 832072. *Died 3 June 2006.*

TOPLEY, Kenneth Wallis Joseph, CMG 1976; Secretary for Education and Manpower, Hong Kong, 1981–83, retired; *b* 22 Oct. 1922; *s* of William Frederick Topley, MC and Daisy Elizabeth (*née* Wellings); *m* 1st, 1949, Marjorie Doreen Wills (marr. diss.); two *s* two *d*; 2nd, 1989, Barbara Newman Hough. *Educ:* Dulwich Coll.; Aberdeen Univ.; London Sch. of Econs and Pol. Science (BScEcon 1949). Served War, RAFVR, 1941–46 (Flt Lieut). Westminster Bank, 1939–41; Mass-Observation, 1941; Malayan Civil Service, 1950–55: Econ. Affairs Secretariat, Comr Gen.'s Office, and Labour Dept; Hong Kong Civil Service, 1955–83: various appts, 1955–62; Comr for Co-operative Develt and Fisheries, 1962–64; Sec., UGC, 1965–67; Comr for Census and Statistics, 1970–73; Dir of Social Welfare, 1973–74; Dir of Educn, 1974–80; Chm., Cttee to Review Post-Secondary and Technical Educn, 1980–81. Secretary: Univ. of E Asia, Macau, 1984–88; E Asia Open Inst., 1988–90. Commandeur de l'Ordre des Arts et des Lettres (France), 1987. *Recreations:* walking, study of philosophy. *Address:* 10 The Grange, Glebe Road, Cambridge CB1 7TL. *Club:* Hong Kong Jockey (Hong Kong). *Died 22 March 2007.*

TORRANCE, Very Rev. Prof. Thomas Forsyth, MBE 1945; DLitt, DTh, DThéol, Dr Teol, DD, DSc; FRSE 1979; FBA 1983; Professor of Christian Dogmatics, University of Edinburgh, and New College, Edinburgh, 1952–79; Moderator of General Assembly of

Church of Scotland, 1976–77; *b* 30 Aug. 1913; *e s* of late Rev. Thomas Torrance, then of Chengtu, Szechwan, China; *m* 1946, Margaret Edith, *y d* of late Mr and Mrs G. F. Spear, The Brow, Combe Down, Bath; two *s* one *d*. *Educ*: Chengtu Canadian School; Bellshill Academy; Univs of Edinburgh, Oxford, Basel. MA Edinburgh 1934; studies in Jerusalem and Athens, 1936; BD Edinburgh 1937; post-grad. studies, Basel, 1937–38; DLitt Edinburgh 1971. Prof. of Theology, Auburn, NY, USA, 1938–39; post-grad. studies, Oriel Coll., Oxford, 1939–40; ordained minister of Alyth Barony Parish, 1940; Church of Scotland chaplain (with Huts and Canteens) in MEF and CMF, 1943–45; returned to Alyth; DTh Univ. of Basel, 1946; minister of Beechgrove Church, Aberdeen, 1947; Professor of Church History, Univ. of Edinburgh, and New Coll., Edinburgh, 1950–52. Participant, World Conf. on Faith and Order, Lund, 1952; Evanston Assembly of WCC, 1954; Faith and Order Commn of WCC, 1952–62; Participant in Conversations between: Church of Scotland and Church of England, 1950–58; World Alliance of Reformed Churches and Greek Orthodox Church, 1979–. Lectures: Hewett, 1959 (NY, Newton Center and Cambridge, Mass); Harris, Dundee, 1970; Anderson, Presbyterian Coll., Montreal, 1971; Taylor, Yale, 1971; Keese, Univ. of Chattanooga, 1971; Cummings, McGill Univ., Montreal, 1978; Richards, Univ. of Virginia at Charlottesville, 1978; Staley, Davidson Coll., NC, 1978; Cosgrove, Glasgow, 1981; Warfield, Princeton, 1981; Payton, Pasadena, 1981; Didsbury, Manchester, 1982; Staley, Regent Coll., Vancouver, 1982; William Lyall Meml, Montreal, 1990; Warburton, Lincoln's Inn, 1995. Mem., Académie Internationale des Sciences Religieuses, 1965 (Pres., 1972–81); For. Mem., Société de l'Histoire du Protestantisme Français, 1968; Mem. Soc. Internat. pour l'Etude de la Philosophie Médiévale, 1969; Hon. President: Soc. for Study of Theology, 1966–68; Church Service Soc. of the Church of Scotland, 1970–71; New Coll. Union, 1972–73. Vice-Pres., Inst. of Religion and Theology of GB and Ireland, 1973–76 (Pres., 1976–78); Mem., Center of Theol Inquiry, Princeton, 1982–. Protopresbyter of Greek Orthodox Church (Patriarchate of Alexandria), 1973. Curator: Deutsches Institut für Bildung und Wissen, 1982–; Europäische Akademie für Umweltfragen, 1986–. Membre d'honneur, Acad. Internat. de Philosophie des Scis, 1976. Hon. DD: Presbyterian Coll., Montreal, 1950; St Andrews, 1960; Edinburgh, 1997; Hon. DThéol: Geneva, 1959; Paris, 1959; Dr Teol (*hc*) Oslo, 1961; Hon. DSc Heriot-Watt, 1983; Dr Th (*hc*) Debrecen, 1988. Templeton Foundn Prize, 1978. Cross of St Mark (first class), 1970. *Publications*: The Modern Theological Debate, 1942; The Doctrine of Grace in the Apostolic Fathers, 1949; Calvin's Doctrine of Man, 1949; Royal Priesthood, 1955, 2nd edn 1993; Kingdom and Church, 1956, When Christ Comes and Comes Again, 1957; The Mystery of the Lord's Supper (Sermons on the Sacrament by Robert Bruce), 1958; ed Calvin's Tracts and Treatises, Vols I–III, 1959; The School of Faith, 1959; Conflict and Agreement in the Church, Vol. I, Order and Disorder, 1959; The Apocalypse Today, 1959; Conflict and Agreement in the Church, Vol. II, The Ministry and the Sacraments of the Gospel, 1960; Karl Barth: an Introduction to his Early Theology, 1910–1930, 1962; ed (with D. W. Torrance) Calvin's NT Commentaries, 1959–73; Theology in Reconstruction, 1965; Theological Science, 1969 (Collins Religious Book Award; trans. French, 1990); Space, Time and Incarnation, 1969; God and Rationality, 1971, 2nd edn 1998; Theology in Reconciliation: Essays towards Evangelical and Catholic Unity in East and West, 1975; The Centrality of Christ, 1976; Space, Time and Resurrection, 1976; The Ground and Grammar of Theology, 1980; Christian Theology and Scientific Culture, 1980; (ed) Belief in Science and in Christian Life, 1980; (ed) The Incarnation: ecumenical studies in the Nicene Constantinopolitan Creed, 1981; Divine and Contingent Order, 1981; Reality and Evangelical Theology, 1982; Juridical Law and Physical Law, 1982; (ed) James Clerk Maxwell: A Dynamical Theory of the

Electromagnetic Field, 1982; The Meditation of Christ, 1983, 2nd edn 1992; Transformation and Convergence in the Frame of Knowledge, 1984; The Christian Frame of Mind, 1985, 2nd enlarged edn (subtitled Reason, Order and Openness in Theology and Natural Science), 1989; Reality and Scientific Theology, 1985; (ed) Theological Dialogue between Orthodox and Reformed Churches, vol. 1, 1985, vol. 2, 1993; The Trinitarian Faith: the Evangelical Theology of the Ancient Catholic Church, 1988; The Hermeneutics of John Calvin, 1988; (ed) Thomas Torrance, China's First Missionaries, Ancient Israelites, 1988; Karl Barth, Biblical and Evangelical Theologian, 1990; Senso del divino e scienza moderna, 1992; Divine Meaning: studies in Patristic Hermaneutics, 1993; Trinitarian Perspectives: towards doctrinal agreement, 1993; Preaching Christ Today: the Gospel and scientific thinking, 1994; Divine Meaning: studies in patristic hermeneutics, 1995; The Christian Doctrine of God, One Being, Three Persons, 1996; Scottish Theology, 1996; (ed) H R, Mackintosh, The Person of Jesus Christ, 2000; The Doctrine of Jesus Christ, 2002; Theological and Natural Science, 2002; Editor, Theology and Science at the Frontiers of Knowledge, series, 1985–91; Jt Editor, Church Dogmatics, Vols 1, 2, 3 and 4, by Karl Barth, 1956–69; Emeritus Editor: Scottish Jl Theology; SJT Monographs. *Address*: 37 Braid Farm Road, Edinburgh EH10 6LE. *T. and Fax*: (0131) 447 3224; *e-mail*: ttorr@globalnet.co.uk.
Died 2 Dec. 2007.

TOTTLE, Prof. Charles Ronald; Professor of Medical Engineering, 1975–78, then Emeritus, and a Pro Vice-Chancellor, 1973–77, University of Bath; Director, Bath Institute of Medical Engineering, 1975–78; Editor, Materials Science, Research Studies Press, 1977–94; *b* 2 Sept. 1920; *m* 1944, Eileen P. Geoghegan; (one *s* one *d* decd). *Educ*: Nether Edge Grammar School; University of Sheffield (MMet). English Electric Co. Ltd, 1941–45; Lecturer in Metallurgy, University of Durham, King's College, 1945–50; Ministry of Supply, Atomic Energy Division, Springfields Works, 1950–51; Culcheth Laboratories, 1951–56 (UKAEA); Head of Laboratories, Dounreay, 1956–57; Deputy Director, Dounreay, 1958–59; Prof. of Metallurgy, 1959–67, Dean of Science, 1966, Univ. of Manchester; Prof. and Head of School of Materials Science, Univ. of Bath, 1967–75; Man. Dir, South Western Industrial Research Ltd, 1970–75. Resident Research Associate, Argonne Nat. Laboratory, Illinois, USA, 1964–65. Vice-Pres., Instn of Metallurgists, 1968–70; Jt Editor, Institution of Metallurgists Series of Textbooks, 1962–70. Governor, Dauntsey's Sch., 1979–88. CEng 1978; FIMMM; FInstP 1958, CPhys 1985. Hon. MSc Manchester. *Publications*: The Science of Engineering Materials, 1965; An Encyclopaedia of Metallurgy and Materials, 1984; various contribs to metallurgical and engineering jls. *Recreations*: music, model making, gardening, restoration of old metal artefacts. *Address*: 47 Queens Road, Devizes, Wilts SN10 5HP.
Died 13 Feb. 2006.

TOULMIN, Prof. Stephen Edelston, MA, PhD; University Professor, since 2002, Professor of Anthropology and International Relations, University of Southern California, since 1993; Avalon Foundation Professor in the Humanities, Northwestern University, 1986–92, then Emeritus; *b* 25 March 1922; *s* of late G. E. Toulmin and Mrs E. D. Toulmin; *m* 1st, 1945, Margaret Alison Coutts (marr. diss. 1960); two *s* two *d*; 2nd, 1960, Gwyneth June Goodfield; *m* 3rd; 4th, Donna. *Educ*: Oundle School; King's College, Cambridge. BA 1943; MA 1946; PhD 1948; MA (Oxon) 1948. Junior Scientific Officer, Ministry of Aircraft Production, 1942–45; Fellow of King's College, Cambridge, 1947–51; University Lecturer in the Philosophy of Science, Oxford, 1949–55; Acting Head of Department of History and Methods of Science, University of Melbourne, Australia, 1954–55; Professor of Philosophy, University of Leeds, 1955–59; Visiting Prof. of Philosophy, NY Univ. and Stanford Univ. (California) and Columbia Univ. (NY), 1959–60; Director, Nuffield Foundation Unit for History of Ideas,

1960–64; Prof. of Philosophy, Brandeis Univ., 1965–69; Michigan State Univ., 1969–72; Provost, Crown College, Univ. of California, Santa Cruz, 1972–73; Prof. in Cttee on Social Thought, Univ. of Chicago, 1973–86; Henry R. Luce Foundn Prof., Center for Multiethnic and Transnat. Studies, USC, 1993–2001. Counsellor, Smithsonian Institution, 1966–75. Thomas Jefferson Lectr, Nat. Endowment for the Humanities, Washington, 1997; Tanner Lectr, Clare Hall, Cambridge, 1998. Hon. DTech Royal Inst. of Technol., Stockholm, 1991. *Publications:* The Place of Reason in Ethics, 1950; The Philosophy of Science: an Introduction, 1953; Metaphysical Beliefs (3 essays: author of one of them), 1957; The Uses of Argument, 1958; Foresight and Understanding, 1961; The Ancestry of Science, Vol. I (The Fabric of the Heavens) 1961, Vol. II (The Architecture of Matter), 1962, Vol. III (The Discovery of Time), 1965; Night Sky at Rhodes, 1963; Human Understanding, vol. 1, 1972; Wittgenstein's Vienna, 1973; Knowing and Acting, 1976; An Introduction to Reasoning, 1979; The Return to Cosmology, 1982; The Abuse of Casuistry, 1987; Cosmopolis, 1989; Beyond Theory, 1996; Return to Reason, 2001; also films, broadcast talks and contribs to learned jls and weeklies. *Address:* School of International Relations, University of Southern California, Los Angeles, CA 90089, USA.
Died 4 Dec. 2009.

TOWER, Maj.-Gen. Philip Thomas, CB 1968; DSO 1944; MBE 1942; National Trust Administrator, Blickling Hall, 1973–82; *b* 1 March 1917; *s* of late Vice-Admiral Sir Thomas Tower, KBE, CB and Mrs E. H. Tower; *m* 1943, Elizabeth, *y d* of late Thomas Ralph Sneyd-Kynnersley, OBE, MC and Alice Sneyd-Kynnersley. *Educ:* Harrow; Royal Military Acad., Woolwich. 2nd Lt Royal Artillery, 1937; served in India, 1937–40; served War of 1939–45 (despatches); Middle East, 1940–42; POW Italy, 1942–43; escaped, 1943; Arnhem, 1944; Norway, 1945; Staff Coll., 1948; Instructor at RMA Sandhurst, 1951–53; comd J (Sidi Rezegh) Bty RHA in Middle East, 1954–55; Joint Services Staff Coll., 1955–56; GSO1 Plans, BJSM Washington, DC, 1956–57; comd 3rd Regt RHA, 1957–60; Imperial Defence Coll., 1961; Comd 51 Inf. Bde Gp, 1961–62; Comd 12 Inf. Bde Gp, BAOR, 1962–64; Director of Public Relations (Army), 1965–67; GOC Middle East Land Forces, 1967 (despatches); Comdt, RMA Sandhurst, 1968–72, retd 1972. Col Comdt, Royal Regt of Artillery, 1970–80. County Comr (Norfolk), SJAB, 1975–78. OStJ 1977. *Recreations:* reading, gardening. *Address:* Chilton House, Chilton, Aylesbury, Bucks HP18 9LR. *Club:* Army and Navy.
Died 8 Dec. 2006.

TOWNDROW, Ven. Frank Noel; Archdeacon of Oakham, 1967–77, then Archdeacon Emeritus; Residentiary Canon of Peterborough, 1966–77, then Canon Emeritus; a Chaplain to the Queen, 1975–81; *b* 25 Dec. 1911; *e s* of F. R. and H. A. Towndrow, London; *m* 1947, Olive Helen Weinberger (*d* 1978); one *d* (one *s* decd). *Educ:* St Olave's Grammar Sch.; King's Coll., Cambridge; Coll. of Resurrection, Mirfield. Curate, Chingford, E4, 1937–40; Chaplain, RAFVR, 1940–47; Rector of Grangemouth, Stirlingshire, 1947–51; Vicar of Kirton Lindsey, Lincs, 1951–53; Rector of Greenford, Middx, 1953–62; Vicar of Ravensthorpe, E Haddon and Rector of Holdenby, 1962–66. *Recreation:* modern history. *Address:* R10, 14 Dundee Road, Perth PH2 7EY. *T:* (01738) 441543.
Died 7 April 2007.

TOWNSEND, Albert Alan, FRS 1960; PhD; Reader (Experimental Fluid Mechanics), Cavendish Laboratory, University of Cambridge, 1961–85 (Assistant Director of Research, 1950–61); Fellow of Emmanuel College, Cambridge, since 1947; *b* 22 Jan. 1917; *s* of A. R. Townsend and D. Gay; *m* 1950, Valerie Dees; one *s* two *d*. *Educ:* Telopea Park IHS; Melbourne and Cambridge Universities. PhD 1947. *Publications:* The Structure of Turbulent Shear Flow, 1956; papers in technical journals. *Address:* c/o Emmanuel College, Cambridge CB2 3AP.
Died 31 Aug. 2010.

TOWNSEND, Prof. Peter Brereton, FBA 2004; Professor of International Social Policy, London School of Economics and Political Science, since 1999; Professor of Social Policy, University of Bristol, 1982–93, then Emeritus; *b* 6 April 1928; *s* of late Philip Brereton Townsend and Alice Mary Townsend (*née* Southcote); *m* 1st, 1949, Ruth (*née* Pearce); four *s*; 2nd, 1977, Joy (*née* Skegg); one *d*; 3rd, 1985, Jean Ann Corston (later Baroness Corston); one step *s* one step *d*. *Educ:* Fleet Road Elementary Sch., London; University Coll. Sch., London; St John's Coll., Cambridge Univ.; Free Univ., Berlin. Research Sec., Political and Economic Planning, 1952–54; Research Officer, Inst. of Community Studies, 1954–57; Research Fellow and then Lectr in Social Administration, London Sch. of Economics, 1957–63; Prof. of Sociology, 1963–81, Pro-Vice-Chancellor (Social Policy), 1975–78, Univ. of Essex; Dir, Sch. of Applied Social Studies, Bristol Univ., 1983–85 and 1988–93. Vis. Prof. of Sociology, Essex Univ., 1982–86; Michael Harrington Distinguished Vis. Prof. of Social Sci., CUNY, 1991–92; Vis. Prof. of Social Policy, 1998–99, Acting Dir, Centre for Study of Human Rights, 2002, LSE; Vis. Prof. of Internat. Social Policy, Univ. of Wales, Swansea, 1998–2003 (Hon. Prof., 2008–). Vice Pres., 1989–, and Trustee, 2005–, Fabian Society (Chm., 1965–66; Chairman: Social Policy Cttee, 1970–82; Res. and Pubns Cttee, 1983–86). President: Psychiatric Rehabilitation Assoc., 1968–83; Child Poverty Action Gp, 1989– (Chm., 1969–89); SW Region, MENCAP, 1989–93; Disability Alliance, 1999– (Chm., 1974–99). Member: Chief Scientist's Cttee, DHSS, 1976–78; Govt Working Gp on Inequalities and Health, 1977–80; MSC Working Gp on Quota Scheme for Disabled, 1983–85; Chm., Steering Gp, 2000–02, Standing Cttee, 2002–05, on Allocation of NHS Resources, Nat. Assembly for Wales. UNESCO consultant on poverty and development, 1978–80; Consultant: to GLC on poverty and the labour market in London, 1985–86; to Northern RHA on Inequalities of Health, 1985–86; to a consortium of 7 metropolitan boroughs on deprivation and shopping centres in Greater Manchester, 1987–88; to Islington Borough Council on deprivation and living standards, 1987–88; to UN for world summit on social devell, 1994–95; to UNDP on social safety net in Georgia, 1994; to UNDP and IILS on patterns and causes of social exclusion, 1994; to Ministry of Foreign Affairs, Denmark, 1997–2000; to EC on Eur. Social Policy Forum, 1998; to DFID, 2005–06; to ILO, 2006–07. Chm., C4 Commn on Poverty, 1996. AcSS 1999. DU Essex, 1990; Hon. DLitt: Teesside, 1994; NUI, 2006; DUniv: Open, 1995; York, 2000; Stirling, 2002; Hon. DSc Edinburgh, 1996; Hon. DArts Lincolnshire and Humberside, 1997; Hon. DSSc Baptist Univ. of HK, 2005. Lifetime Achievement Award, Social Policy Assoc., 2008. *Publications:* The Family Life of Old People, 1957; National Superannuation (co-author), 1957; Nursing Homes in England and Wales (co-author), 1961; The Last Refuge: a survey of residential institutions and homes for the aged in England and Wales, 1962; The Aged in the Welfare State (co-author), 1965; The Poor and the Poorest (co-author), 1965; Old People in Three Industrial Societies (co-author), 1968; (ed) The Concept of Poverty, 1970; (ed) Labour and Inequality, 1972; The Social Minority, 1973; Sociology and Social Policy, 1975; Poverty in the United Kingdom: a survey of household resources and standards of living, 1979; (ed) Labour and Equality, 1980; Inequalities in Health (co-author), 1980; Manifesto (co-author), 1981; (ed jtly) Disability in Britain, 1981; The Family and Later Life, 1981; (ed jtly) Responses to Poverty: lessons from Europe, 1984; (jtly) Inequalities of Health in the Northern Region, 1986; Poverty and Labour in London, 1987; (jtly) Health and Deprivation: inequalities and the North, 1987; (jtly) Service Provision and Living Standards in Islington, 1988; (jtly) Inequalities in Health: the Black report and the health divide, 1988, 3rd edn 1993; The International Analysis of Poverty, 1993; A Poor Future, 1996; (jtly)

Poverty and Social Exclusion in Britain, 2000; (ed jtly) Breadline Europe: the measurement of poverty, 2001; Targeting Poor Health, 2001; (ed jtly) World Poverty: new policies to defeat an old enemy, 2002; (jtly) Child Poverty in the Developing World, 2003; Inequalities of Health: the Welsh dimension, 2005; The Right to Social Security and National Development: lessons of OECD experience for low-income countries, 2007; (ed) Building Decent Societies: re-thinking the role of social security in development, 2009. *Recreations:* writing, gardening.
Died 7 June 2009.

TOWNSHEND, 7th Marquess *cr* 1787; **George John Patrick Dominic Townshend;** Bt 1617; Baron Townshend of Lynn Regis, 1661; Viscount Townshend of Raynham, 1682; *b* 13 May 1916; *s* of 6th Marquess Townshend and Gladys Ethel Gwendolen Eugenie (*d* 1959), *e d* of late Thomas Sutherst, barrister; *S* father, 1921; *m* 1st, 1939, Elizabeth (marr. diss. 1960; she *m* 1960, Brig. Sir James Gault, KCMG, MVO, OBE; she *d* 1989), *o d* of Thomas Luby, ICS; one *s* two *d*; 2nd, 1960, Ann Frances (*d* 1988), *d* of Arthur Pellew Darlow; one *s* one *d*; 3rd, 2004, Philippa Sophia Swire, *d* of Col George Jardine Kidston-Montgomerie of Southannan, DSO, MC. Norfolk Yeomanry TA, 1936–40; Scots Guards, 1940–45. Chairman: Anglia Television Gp plc, 1971–86; Anglia Television Ltd, 1958–86; Survival Anglia, 1971–86; Anchor Enterprises Ltd, 1967–88; AP Bank Ltd, 1975–87; East Coast Grain Ltd, 1982–90; D. E. Longe & Co. Ltd, 1982–90; Norfolk Agricultural Station, 1973–87; Raynham Farm Co. Ltd, 1957–; Vice-Chairman: Norwich Union Life Insurance Society Ltd, 1973–86; Norwich Union Fire Insurance Society Ltd, 1975–86; Director: London Merchant Securities plc, 1964–95; Napak Ltd, 1982–90; Riggs Nat. Corp., Washington, 1987–89. Chairman, Royal Norfolk Agricultural Association, 1978–85. Hon. DCL East Anglia, 1989. DL Norfolk, 1951–61. *Heir: s* Viscount Raynham, *b* 26 Sept. 1945. *Address:* Raynham Hall, Fakenham, Norfolk NR21 7EP. *T:* (01328) 862133. *Clubs:* White's, MCC; Norfolk (Norwich).
Died 23 April 2010.

TOY, Sam, OBE 1994; Chairman and Managing Director, Ford Motor Co. Ltd, 1980–86; Chairman, Norman Cordiner Ltd, Inverness, 1991–96; *b* 21 Aug. 1923; *s* of Edward and Lillian Toy; name changed from Samuel Edward Glenwood Toy by Deed Poll; *m* 1st, 1944, Jean Balls; one *s*; 2nd, 1950, Joan Franklin Rook (marr. diss. 1984; she *d* 2002); two *s* one *d*; 3rd, 1984, Janetta McMorrow. *Educ:* Falmouth Grammar Sch.; Fitzwilliam Coll., Cambridge (MA; Hon. Fellow, 1984). Pilot (Flt Lieut), RAF, 1942–48. Graduate trainee, Ford Motor Co. Ltd, 1948; thereafter, all business career with Ford Motor Co. Ltd Mem. Council, SMMT, 1975– (Vice-Pres., 1982–86; Pres., 1986–87; Dep. Pres., 1987–88). Chm., UK 2000 Scotland, 1988–96. *Recreations:* trout and salmon fishing, golf. *Address:* 4 Millbrook Close, Liss, Hants GU33 7SR. *T:* (01730) 892631. *Clubs:* Lord's Taverners, Eccentric.
Died 24 March 2008.

TOYE, Wendy, CBE 1992; theatrical and film director; choreographer, actress, dancer; *b* 1 May 1917; *née* Beryl May Jessie Toye; *m* 1940, Edward Selwyn Sharp (marr. diss. 1950). First professional appearance as Peasblossom in A Midsummer Night's Dream, Old Vic, 1929; principal dancer in Hiawatha, Royal Albert Hall, 1931; Marigold, Phoebe in Toad of Toad Hall and produced dances, Royalty, Christmas, 1931–32. Trained with Euphen MacLaren, Karsavina, Dolin, Morosoff, Legat, Rambert. In early 1930s performed and choreographed for the very distinguished Carmargo Society of Ballet; guest artist with Sadler's Wells Ballet and Mme Rambert's Ballet Club; went to Denmark as principal dancer with British Ballet, organized by Adeline Genée, 1932; danced in C. B. Cochran's The Miracle, Lyceum, 1932; masked dancer in Ballerina, Gaiety, 1933; member of Ninette de Valois' original Vic Wells Ballet, principal dancer for Ninette de Valois in The Golden Toy, Coliseum, 1934; toured with Anton Dolin's ballet (choreog. for divertissements and short ballets), 1934–35; in Tulip

Time, Alhambra, then Markova-Dolin Ballet as principal dancer and choreog., 1935; in Love and How to Cure It, Globe, 1937. Arranged dances and ballets for many shows and films including most of George Black's productions for next 7 years, notably Black Velvet in which also principal dancer, 1939. Shakespearean season, Open Air Theatre, 1939. *Theatre productions:* Big Ben, Bless the Bride, Tough at the Top (for C. B. Cochran), Adelphi; The Shephard Show, Prince's; Co-Director and Choreographer, Peter Pan, New York; And So To Bed, New Theatre; Co-Director and Choreographer, Feu d'Artifice, Paris; Night of Masquerade, Q; Second Threshold, Vaudeville; Choreography for Three's Company in Joyce Grenfell Requests the Pleasure, Fortune; Wild Thyme, Duke of York's; Lady at the Wheel, Lyric, Hammersmith; Majority of One, Phoenix; Magic Lantern, Saville; As You Like It, Old Vic; Virtue in Danger, Mermaid and Strand; Robert and Elizabeth, Lyric; On the Level, Saville; Midsummer Night's Dream, Shakespeare quatercentenary Latin American tour, 1964; Soldier's Tale, Edinburgh Festival, 1967; Boots with Strawberry Jam, Nottingham Playhouse, 1968; The Great Waltz, Drury Lane, 1970; Showboat, Adelphi, 1971; She Stoops to Conquer, Young Vic, 1972; Cowardy Custard, Mermaid, 1972; Stand and Deliver, Roundhouse, 1972; R loves J, Chichester, 1973; The Confederacy, Chichester, 1974; The Englishman Amused, Young Vic, 1974; Follow The Star, Chichester, 1974; Westminster Theatre, 1976; Made in Heaven, Chichester, 1975; Make Me a World, Chichester, 1976; Once More with Music (with Cicely Courtneidge and Jack Hulbert), 1976; Oh, Mr Porter, Mermaid, 1977; Dance for Gods, Conversations, 1979; Colette, Comedy, 1980; Gingerbread Man, Watermill, 1981; This Thing Called Love, Ambassadors, 1983; (Associate Prod.) Singin' in the Rain, Palladium, 1983; (dir and narr.) Noel and Gertie, Monte Carlo and Canada; (Associate Prod.) Barnum, Manchester, 1984, Victoria Palace, 1985; Birds of a Feather, 1984, and Mad Woman of Chaillot, 1985, Niagara-on-the-Lake; Gala for Joyce Grenfell Tribute, 1985; (Associate Prod.) Torvill and Dean World Tour, 1985; Once Upon a Mattress, Watermill, 1985; Kiss Me Kate, Aarhus and Copenhagen, 1986; Unholy Trinity, Stephenville Fest., 1986; Laburnam Grove, Palace Th. Watford, 1987; Miranda, Chichester Fest., 1987; Get the Message, Molecule, 1987; Songbook, Watermill, 1988; Mrs Dot, Watford, 1988; When That I Was, Manitoba, 1988; Oh! Coward, Hong Kong, 1989; Cinderella, Palace Th., Watford, 1989; Penny Black, Wavendon, 1990; Moll Flanders, Watermill, 1990; Heaven's Up, Playhouse, 1990; Mrs Pat's Profession (workshop with Cleo Laine), Wavendon, 1991; The Drummer, Watermill, 1991; Sound of Music, Sadler's Wells, 1992; See How They Run, Watermill, 1992; Vienna, 1993; Under their Hats, King's Head, 1994, Vienna, 1995; The Anastasia File, 1994, Lloyd George Knew My Father, 1995, Warts and All, Rogues to Riches, 1996, Watermill; Finale Gala, Sadler's Wells, 1996; *opera productions:* Bluebeard's Castle (Bartok), Sadler's Wells and Brussels; The Telephone (Menotti), Sadler's Wells; Rusalka (Dvořák), Sadler's Wells; Fledermaus, Coliseum and Sadler's Wells; Orpheus in the Underworld, Sadler's Wells and Australia; La Vie Parisienne, Sadler's Wells; Seraglio, Bath Festival, 1967; The Impresario, Don Pasquale (for Phoenix Opera Group), 1968; The Italian Girl in Algiers, Coliseum, 1968; La Cenerentola; Merry Widow, 1979, Orpheus in the Underworld, 1981, ENO North; The Mikado, Nat. Opera Co., Ankara, 1982; Italian Girl in Algiers, ENO, 1982; La Serva Padrona and Der Apotoker, Aix-en-Provence Fest., 1991. *Films directed:* The Stranger Left No Card; The Teckman Mystery; Raising a Riot; The Twelfth Day of Christmas; Three Cases of Murder; All for Mary; True as a Turtle; We Joined the Navy; The King's Breakfast; Cliff in Scotland; A Goodly Manor for a Song; Girls Wanted—Istanbul; Trial by Jury (TV). Retrospectives of films directed: Festival de Films des Femmes International, Créteil, Paris, 1990; Tokyo Film Fest., 1991. Productions for TV, etc, inc. Golden Gala, ATV, 1978; Follow the Star, BBC2, 1979; Stranger in Town, Anglia, 1981. Dir concert, Till We Meet Again,

RFH, 1989. Advisor, Arts Council Trng Scheme, for many years; Member: Council, LAMDA; (original) Accreditation Bd instig. by Nat. Council of Drama Training for acting courses, 1981–84; Grand Council, Royal Acad. of Dancing. Committee Member: Wavendon Allmusic Scheme; Vivian Ellis Award Scheme; Richard Stilgoe Award Scheme. Hon. DLitt City, 1996. Silver Jubilee Medal, 1977. *Address:* c/o Jean Diamond, London Management, Noel House, 2–4 Noel Street, W1V 3RB. *Died 27 Feb. 2010.*

TRACY, Rear-Adm. Hugh Gordon Henry, CB 1965; DSC 1945; *b* 15 Nov. 1912; *e s* of Comdr A. F. G. Tracy, RN; *m* 1938, Muriel (*d* 2005), *d* of Maj.-Gen. Sir R. B. Ainsworth, CB, DSO, OBE; two *s* one *d. Educ:* Nautical Coll., Pangbourne. Joined RN, 1929; Lieut, 1934; served in HMS Shropshire, Hawkins and Furious, in Admiralty and attended Advanced Engineering course before promotion to Lt-Comdr, 1942; Sen. Engineer, HMS Illustrious, 1942–44; Asst to Manager, Engineering Dept, HM Dockyard Chatham, 1944–46; Comdr 1946; served in HMS Manxman, Admiralty, RN Engineering Coll. and HM Dockyard Malta; Captain, 1955; Asst Director of Marine Engineering, Admiralty, 1956–58; CO HMS Sultan, 1959–60; Imperial Defence Coll., 1961; CSO (Tech.) to Flag Officer, Sea Training, 1962–63; Rear-Admiral, 1963; Director of Marine Engineering, Ministry of Defence (Navy), 1963–66; retired, 1966. Pres., Wilts Gardens Trust, 1992–97 (Chm., 1985–89). *Recreations:* gardening, plant ecology, assorted collections. *Address:* 21a Sion Hill, Bath BA1 2UL; *e-mail:* hughtracy@googlemail.com. *Died 7 Sept. 2009.*

TRAFFORD; *see* de Trafford.

TRAIN, Christopher John, CB 1986; Deputy Under Secretary of State, Home Office, and Director-General, Prison Service, 1983–91; *b* 12 March 1932; *s* of late Keith Sydney Sayer Train and Edna Ashby Train; *m* 1957, Sheila Mary Watson; one *s* one *d. Educ:* Nottingham High Sch.; Christ Church, Oxford (BA Lit. Hum., MA). Served Royal Navy, 1955–57; Assistant Master, St Paul's Sch., W Kensington, 1957–67; Principal, Home Office, 1968; Asst Sec., Home Office, 1972; Secretary, Royal Commn on Criminal Procedure, 1978–80; Asst Under Sec. of State, Home Office, 1980–83. Vis. Prof., Dept of Management Sci., Strathclyde Univ., 1992–95. Pres., Suffolk Horse Soc., 1989–90. *Publications:* Quietest Under the Sun: a history of Clunbury in the Clun Valley, 1996; The Walls and Gates of Ludlow: their origin and early days, 1999; A Country Education: a history of the schools at Clunbury, 1999; Of Steam and Sheep: the story of Craven Arms, 2000; The Higglers of Horderley: the J. P. Wood story, 2001; The Sheepe Hath Payed For All: the Ludlows of Stokesay, 2005. *Recreations:* collecting cricket books, jogging, local history. *Clubs:* MCC; Vincent's (Oxford). *Died 7 May 2007.*

TRANT, Gen. Sir Richard (Brooking), KCB 1982 (CB 1979); DL; Chairman: Hunting Engineering Ltd, 1988–93; Defence Division, Hunting Plc, 1989–96; Irvin Aerospace Ltd, 1993–96; Deputy Chairman, Wilson's Hogg Robinson Ltd, 1988–96; *b* 30 March 1928; *s* of Richard Brooking Trant and Dora Rodney Trant (*née* Lancaster); *m* 1957, Diana Clare, 2nd *d* of Rev. Stephen Zachary and Ruth Beatrice Edwards; one *s* two *d.* Commissioned DCLI, 1947, later RA; served Korean War, 1952–53; Defence Services Staff Coll., India, 1961–62; S Arabia, 1962–65; Jt Services Staff Coll., 1965; commanded 3rd Regt RHA, 1968–71, 5th Airportable Brigade, 1972–74; Dep. Mil. Sec., MoD (Army), 1975–76; Comdr Land Forces, NI, 1977–79; Dir, Army Staff Duties, 1979–82; GOC South East District, 1982–83, Land Dep. C-in-C Fleet during S Atlantic Campaign, 1982; QMG, 1983–86. Col Comdt: RAEC, 1979–86; RA, 1982–87; RAOC, 1984–88; HAC (TA), 1984–92. Special Comr, Duke of York's Royal Mil. Sch., Dover, 1987–93; Comr, Royal Hosp. Chelsea, 1988–94. Defence Advisor, Short Bros, 1987–88; Dir, Eastern Region Technology Centre, 1989–93. Member: Armed Forces Pay Rev. Body, 1988–94; Council, SBAC,

1988–96; Vice Pres., Defence Manufacturers' Assoc., 1989–96. Pres., Beds Chamber of Commerce and Industry, 1993–96; Dir, S Beds Community Health Trust, 1991–95. Pres., RA Hunt and RA Saddle Club, 1984–90; Admiral, Army Sailing Assoc., 1984–87. Chm., RA Museums Ltd, 1991–96. Pres., Cornwall Heritage Trust, 2005–. DL Cornwall, 1997. Bard, Cornish Gorsedd, 2000. Mem. Court, Cranfield Univ., 1996–2005; Hon. DSc Cranfield, 1995. CIMgt (CBIM 1985); MInstD 1987. Freeman, City of London, 1984. Order of South Arabia, 3rd Class, 1965. *Recreations:* golf, field sports, natural history, sailing. *Address:* Benbole House, Lostwithiel, Cornwall PL22 0DT. *Club:* Army and Navy. *Died 3 Oct. 2007.*

TRASENSTER, Michael Augustus Tulk, CVO 1954; ARPS 1979; photographer; *b* 26 Jan. 1923; *er s* of late Major William Augustus Trasenster, MC, and Brenda de Courcy Trasenster; *m* 1950, Fay Norrie Darley, *d* of late Thomas Bladworth Darley, Cantley Hall, Yorkshire; two *d. Educ:* Winchester. Served with 4th/7th Royal Dragoon Guards, 1942–52; NW Europe (Tanks, D-Day to V-E Day; Comdr, first support tank to cross Seine at Giverney, from which bridgehead Brussels was liberated), 1944; Middle East, 1946; ADC to Governor of South Australia, 1947–49; School of Tank Technology, 1951; Military Secretary and Comptroller to the Governor General of New Zealand, 1952–55. Chevalier of Order of Leopold II of Belgium, with palm, 1944; Belgian Croix de Guerre, with palm, 1944. *Recreations:* painting, reading. *Address:* c/o Royal Bank of Scotland, High Street, Winchester, Hants SO23 9DA. *Died 17 July 2008.*

TRAVERS, John Richard Lewis, FRICS; Chief Executive Officer (formerly Senior Partner), Cushman & Wakefield EMEA (formerly Healey & Baker, then Cushman & Wakefield Healey & Baker), 1999–2006; Chairman (non-executive), Cushman & Wakefield Asia, since 2007; *b* 20 Aug. 1946; *s* of Edward Arthur Reginald Travers and Dorothy May Travers; *m* 1967, Jennifer Auronwyn Williams; two *s* one *d. Educ:* King Edward VI Sch., Aston; BSc Estate Mgt London Univ. Laing Develt Co. Ltd, Manchester, 1973–75; Healey & Baker: retail negotiator, 1975–79, head of Belgian operation, 1979–2006, Brussels; Mem., Main Bd, 1992–2006; Dep. Sen. Partner, 1997–99. Non-exec. Dir, British Land, 2007–. *Recreations:* golf, tennis, travel. *Address:* 31 Thames Quay, Chelsea Harbour, SW10 0UY. *Died 21 June 2007.*

TREADWELL, Charles James, CMG 1972; CVO 1979; HM Diplomatic Service, retired; *b* 10 Feb. 1920; *s* of late C. A. L. Treadwell, OBE, Barrister and Solicitor, Wellington, NZ; *m* 1946, Philippa Perkins; three *s. Educ:* Wellington Coll., NZ; University of New Zealand (LLB). Served with HM Forces, 1939–45. Sudan Political Service and Sudan Judiciary, 1945–55; FO, 1955–57; British High Commn, Lahore, 1957–60; HM Embassy, Ankara, 1960–62; HM Embassy, Jedda, 1963–64; British Dep. High Comr for Eastern Nigeria, 1965–66; Head of Joint Information Services Department, Foreign Office/Commonwealth Office, 1966–68; British Political Agent, Abu Dhabi, 1968–71; Ambassador, United Arab Emirates, 1971–73; High Comr to Bahamas, 1973–75; Ambassador to Oman, 1975–79. *Address:* Cherry Orchard Cottage, Buddington Lane, Midhurst, W Sussex GU29 0QP. *Died 7 Jan. 2010.*

TREGEAR, Mary, FBA 1985; Keeper of Eastern Art, Ashmolean Museum, Oxford, 1987–91; *b* 11 Feb. 1924; *d* of late Thomas R. and Norah Tregear. *Educ:* Sidcot Sch., Somerset; West of England Coll. of Art (ATD 1946); London Univ. (BA); MA Oxon. Taught Art, Wuhan, China, 1947–50; Curator/Lectr, Hong Kong Univ., 1956–61; Sen. Asst Keeper, Chinese, Ashmolean Museum, 1961–87. *Publications:* Arts of China, vol. 1 (co-ordinating ed.), 1968; Catalogue of Chinese Greenwares in the Ashmolean Museum, 1976; Chinese Art, 1980 (trans. French and Spanish), 2nd edn 1997; Song Ceramics, 1982; Tesori d'Arte in Cina, 1994 (trans. English, French and Spanish). *Died 17 Dec. 2010.*

TRELAWNY, Sir John Barry Salusbury-, 13th Bt *cr* 1628; Director, Goddard Kay Rogers and Associates Ltd, 1984–95; Chairman, GKR Group Ltd, 1993–95; *b* 4 Sept. 1934; *s* of Sir John William Robin Maurice Salusbury-Trelawny, 12th Bt and of his 1st wife, Glenys Mary (*d* 1985), *d* of John Cameron Kynoch; *S* father, 1956; *m* 1958, Carol Knox, *yr d* of late C. F. K. Watson, The Field, Saltwood, Kent; one *s* three *d*. *Educ*: HMS Worcester; Univ. of Kent (MA 2007). Sub-Lt RNVR (National Service). Dir, The Martin Walter Group Ltd, 1971–74; various directorships, 1974–83; Dir, 1978–83, Jt Dep. Man. Dir 1981–83, Korn/Ferry Internat. Inc. Pres., London Cornish Assoc., 1997–2005. Pres., Folkestone & Hythe Dist Scout Council, 1980–. FInstM 1974. JP 1973–78. *Heir*: *s* John William Richard Salusbury-Trelawny [*b* 30 March 1960; *m* 1st, 1980, Anita (marr. diss. 1986), *d* of Kenneth Snelgrove; one *s* one *d*; 2nd, 1987, Sandra (marr. diss. 1993), *d* of Joseph Thompson; one *s*, 3rd, 2001, Laurian, *d* of Rev. Peter Adams; two *s*]. *Address*: Beavers Hill, Rectory Lane, Saltwood, Kent CT21 4QA. *T*: (01303) 266476. *Club*: Royal Cinque Ports Yacht.   *Died 29 July 2009.*

TRENCH, Sir Peter (Edward), Kt 1979; CBE 1964 (OBE (mil.) 1945); TD 1949; *b* 16 June 1918; *s* of James Knights Trench and Grace Sim; *m* 1940, Mary St Clair Morford (*d* 2004); one *s* one *d*. *Educ*: privately; London Sch. of Economics, London Univ.; St John's Coll., Cambridge Univ. BSc (Econ.) Hons. Served in The Queen's Royal Regt, 1939–46: Staff Coll., 1942; AAG, HQ 21 Army Gp, 1944–45 (OBE). Man. Dir, Bovis Ltd, 1954–59; Director: Nat. Fedn of Bldg Trades Employers, 1959–64; Nat. Bldg Agency, 1964–66; Part-time Mem., Nat. Bd for Prices and Incomes, 1965–68. Chm., Y. J. Lovell (Holdings) plc, 1972–83; Director, 1970–83: LEP plc; Haden plc; Capital & Counties plc; Builder Gp plc; Crendon Ltd; Nationwide Building Soc. Vis. Prof. in Construction Management, Reading Univ., 1981–88. Chm., Construction and Housing Res. Adv. Council, 1973–79; Pres., Construction Health Safety Gp, 1974–80; Vice-President: NHBC, 1984– (Chm., 1978–84); Building Centre, 1976–; Member: Review of Housing Finance Adv. Gp, 1975–76; Council, CBI, 1981–83; Council, RSA, 1981–83. Mem. Court of Governors, LSE; Hon. Mem., Architectural Assoc.; Hon. Treasurer, St Mary's Hosp. Med. Sch. JP Inner London, 1963–71. Hon. FCIOB; Hon. FFB; FCIArb; FRSA; CCMI; Hon. FRIBA; Hon. Mem. CGLI. Hon. DSc Reading, 1986. *Recreations*: tennis, swimming, travelling. *Address*: 4 Napier Close, Kensington, W14 8LX. *T*: (020) 7602 3936. *Club*: MCC.   *Died 10 Sept. 2006.*

TRESS, Ronald Charles, CBE 1968; Director, The Leverhulme Trust, 1977–84; *b* Upchurch, Sittingbourne, Kent, 11 Jan. 1915; *er s* of S. C. Tress, *m* 1942, Josephine Kelly (*d* 1993), *d* of H. J. Medland; one *s* two *d*. *Educ*: Gillingham (Kent) County School; University College, Southampton. BSc (Econ.) London; DSc Bristol. Gladstone Student, St Deiniol's Library, Hawarden, 1936–37; Drummond Fraser Research Fellow, Univ. of Manchester, 1937–38; Asst Lecturer in Economics, Univ. Coll. of the S West, Exeter, 1938–41; Economic Asst, War Cabinet Offices, 1941–45; Economic Adviser, Cabinet Secretariat, 1945–47; Reader in Public Finance, Univ. of London, 1947–51; Prof. of Political Economy, Univ. of Bristol, 1951–68; Master of Birkbeck Coll., 1968–77, Fellow, 1977–; Mem., Univ. of London Senate, 1968–77, and Court, 1976–77. Managing Editor, London and Cambridge Economic Service, 1949–51; Member: Reorganisation Commn for Pigs and Bacon, 1955–56; Nigeria Fiscal Commn, 1957–58; Departmental Cttee on Rating of Charities, 1958; Develt Commn, 1959–81; Financial Enquiry, Aden Colony, 1959; East Africa Economic and Fiscal Commn, 1960; Uganda Fiscal Commn, 1962; Kenya Fiscal Commn (Chm.), 1962–63; National Incomes Commn, 1963–65; Chm., SW Economic Planning Council, 1965–68; Mem., Cttee of Inquiry into Teachers' Pay, 1974; Chm., Cttee for Univ. Assistance to Adult Educn in HM Forces, 1974–79; Lay Mem., Solicitors' Disciplinary Tribunal,

1975–79; Chm., Lord Chancellor's Adv. Cttee on Legal Aid, 1979–84. Trustee, City Parochial Foundn, 1974–77, 1979–89; Governor, Christ Church Coll., Canterbury, 1975–91; Mem. Council, Kent Univ., 1977–92. Royal Economic Society: Council, 1960–70, Sec.-Gen., 1975–79, Vice-Pres., 1979–. Hon. LLD: Furman Univ., S Carolina, 1973; Exeter, 1976; DUniv Open Univ., 1974; Hon. DSc (SocSc) Southampton, 1978; Hon. DCL Kent, 1984. *Publications*: articles and reviews in Economic Journal, Economica, LCES Bulletin, etc. *Address*: 211 Whiteley House, North Avenue, Whiteley Village, Walton on Thames KT12 4EJ. *T*: (01932) 843306.
Died 28 Sept. 2006.

TREW, Francis Sidney Edward, CMG 1984; HM Diplomatic Service, retired; Ambassador to Bahrain, 1984–88; *b* 22 Feb. 1931; *s* of Harry Francis and Alice Mary Trew; *m* 1958, Marlene Laurette Regnery; three *d*. *Educ*: Taunton's Sch., Southampton. Served Army, 1949–51, 2nd Lieut, Royal Hampshire Regt. FO, 1951; Lebanon, 1952; Amman, 1953; Bahrain, 1953–54; Jedda, 1954–56; Vice-Consul, Philadelphia, 1956–59; Second Sec., Kuwait, 1959–62; FO, 1962; seconded as Sec., European Conf. on Satellite Communications, 1963–65; Consul, Guatemala City, 1965–70; First Sec., Mexico City, 1971–74; FCO, 1974–77; Consul, Algeciras, 1977–79; FCO, 1980–81; High Comr at Belmopan, Belize, 1981–84. Mem. Bd, Devon Community Housing Soc., 1994–2004. Order of Aztec Eagle (Mexico), 1975. *Recreations*: carpentry, fishing. *Address*: The Orchard, Higher Trickeys, Morebath, Devon EX16 9AL.
Died 8 Feb. 2006.

TROTTER, Sir Ronald (Ramsay), Kt 1985; FCA; New Zealand business executive; Chairman, Fletcher Challenge Ltd, 1981–95 (Chief Executive, 1981–87); *b* Hawera, 9 Oct. 1927; *s* of Clement George Trotter, CBE and Annie Euphemia Trotter (*née* Young); *m* 1955, Margaret Patricia, *d* of James Rainey; three *s* one *d*. *Educ*: Collegiate School, Wanganui; Victoria Univ. of Wellington; Lincoln Coll., Canterbury (BCom, Cert. in Agric.). FCA 1976. Wright Stephenson & Co., 1958–72: Dir, 1962–68; Man. Dir, 1968–70; Chm. and Man. Dir, 1970–72; Chm. and Man. Dir, Challenge Corp., 1972–81. Chairman: Telecom Corp. of New Zealand Ltd, 1987–90; Post Office Bank, 1989; Ciba-Geigy New Zealand Ltd, 1990–96; Wrightson Ltd, 1993–98; Toyota New Zealand Ltd, 1994–2001 (Dir, 1990–94); Director: Reserve Bank of NZ, 1986–88; Australia and New Zealand Banking Gp, 1988–97 (Inaugural Mem., Internat. Bd of Advice, 1986–93); Air New Zealand Ltd, 1989–98; Ciba-Geigy Australia Ltd, 1991–96; Wrightson Farmers Finance Ltd, 1993–98; Mem., Internat. Adv. Bd, Proudfoot plc, 1992–95. Trustee and Chm., NZ Inst. of Economic Research, 1973–86; Chairman: Overseas Investment Commn, 1974–77; NZ Business Roundtable, 1985–90; Pacific Basin Econ. Council, 1985–90 (Internat. Pres., 1986–88); Museum of NZ, 1995–2001 (Mem., Project Develt Bd, 1988–92). Pres., NZ Equestrian Fedn, 2001–04. Hon. LLD Victoria Univ. of Wellington, 1984; Hon. DCom Lincoln, 1999. Bledisloe Medal, Lincoln Coll., 1988. NZ Business Hall of Fame, 1999. Silver Jubilee Medal, 1977; NZ Commemoration Medal, 1990. *Address*: Te Kowhai Road, RD1 Otaki, New Zealand. *T*: (4) 2933947, *Fax*: (4) 2937339. *Club*: Wellington (Wellington, NZ).   *Died 11 Aug. 2010.*

TROUNSON, Rev. Ronald Charles, MA; Rector (non-stipendiary), Easton-on-the-Hill, 1994–99 (Rector, Easton-on-the-Hill and Collyweston with Duddington and Tixover, 1989–94); Rural Dean of Barnack, 1991–94; *b* 7 Dec. 1926; *s* of Edwin Trounson and Elsie Mary Trounson (*née* Bolitho); *m* 1952, Leonora Anne Keate (*d* 2008); two *s* three *d*. *Educ*: Plymouth Coll.; Emmanuel Coll., Cambridge (Schol.); Ripon Hall, Oxford (MA). Deacon, 1956; Priest, 1957. National Service, RAF, 1948–50. Asst Master, Scaitcliffe Sch., Englefield Green, Surrey, 1950–52; Sixth Form Classics Master, Plymouth Coll., 1953–58; Asst Curate, St Gabriel's, Plymouth, 1956–58; Chaplain, Denstone Coll.,

1958–76; Second Master, 1968–76, Bursar, 1976–78; Principal of St Chad's College and Lectr in Classics, Univ. of Durham, 1978–88. Chm. of Governors, Durham High Sch., 1990–94. Fellow, Woodard Corporation, 1983. FRSA 1984. *Address:* Belmont Grange, Broomside Lane, Belmont, Durham DH1 2QW.   *Died 10 May 2009.*

TROUP, Vice-Adm. Sir (John) Anthony (Rose), KCB 1975; DSC and Bar; *b* 18 July 1921; *s* of late Captain H. R. Troup, RN and N. M. Troup (*née* Milne-Thompson); *m* 1st, 1943, B. M. J. Gordon-Smith (marr. diss. 1952); two *s* one *d*; 2nd, 1953, Cordelia Mary Hope; two *s* one *d*. *Educ:* Naut. Trng Coll., HMS Worcester, 1934; RNC Dartmouth, 1936. War service includes: Submarines Turbulent and Strongbow, 1941–45 (dispatches, 1942); HMS Victorious, 1956–59; Comd 3rd Submarine Sqdn, 1961–63; HMS Intrepid, 1966–68; Flag Officer Sea Training, 1969–71; Comdr Far East Fleet, 1971; Flag Officer Submarines and NATO Comdr Submarines, Eastern Atlantic, 1972–74; Flag Officer, Scotland and NI, and NATO Comdr Norlant, 1974–77. *Recreations:* sailing, shooting, gardening. *Address:* Bridge Gardens, Hungerford, Berks RG17 0DL. *Club:* Royal Yacht Squadron.   *Died 8 July 2008.*

TROYAT, Henri; Grand-Croix, Légion d'Honneur; writer; Member of the French Academy, 1959; *b* Moscow, 1 Nov. 1911; *né* Lev Aslanovitch Tarassoff; *m* 1948, Marguerite Saintange (decd); one *s*, and one step *d*. *Educ:* Paris. *Publications: novels:* Faux jour (Prix Populiste), 1935; Le Vivier, 1935; Grandeur Nature, 1936; L'Araigne (Prix Goncourt), 1938 (The Web, 1984); Le mort saisit le vif, 1938; Le signe du taureau, 1938; Tant que la terre durera (3 vols), 1947–50; La tête sur les épaules, 1951; La neige en deuil, 1952; Les semailles et les moissons (5 vols), 1953–58; La lumière des justes (5 vols), 1959–63 (televised); Une extrême amitié, 1963; Les Eygletière (3 vols), 1965–67 (televised); Les héritiers de l'avenir (3 vols), 1968–70; La pierre, la feuille et les ciseaux, 1972; Anne Prédaille, 1973; Le Moscovite (3 vols), 1974–75; Grimbosq, 1976; Le front dans les nuages, 1976; Le prisonnier n° 1, 1978; Viou (3 vols), 1980; Le pain de l'etranger, 1982 (The Children, 1983); La dérision, 1983; Marie Karpovna, 1984; Le Bruit solitaire du Coeur, 1985; A demain, Sylvie, 1986; Le troisième bonheur, 1987; Toute ma vie sera mensonge, 1988; La gouvernante française, 1989; La femme de David, 1990; Aliocha, 1991; Youri, 1992; Le chant des insensés, 1993; Le marchand de masques, 1994; Le défi d'Olga, 1995; Votre très humble et très obéissant serviteur, 1996; L'affaire Cremonnière, 1997; Le fils du satrape, 1998; Namouna ou la chaleur animale, 1999; La ballerine du Saint-Petersbourg, 2000; La fille de l'écrivain, 2001; L'étage des bouffons, 2002; La fiancée de l'ogre, 2004; *short stories:* La clef de voûte, 1938; La fosse commune, 1938; Le jugement de Dieu, 1939; Du philantrope à la rouquine, 1939; Le geste d'Eve, 1964; Les ailes du Diable, 1966; L'éternel contretemps, 2003; *plays include:* Les vivants, 1946; *non-fiction:* Les ponts de Paris, 1946; La case de l'oncle Sam, 1948; De gratte-ciel en cocotier, 1955; Sainte-Russie: reflexions et souvenirs, 1956; Naissance d'une dauphine, 1958; La vie quotidienne en Russie au temps du dernier tsar, 1959; Un si long chemin (memoirs), 1976; *biographies:* Dostoievsky, 1940; Pushkin, 1946; L'étrange destin de Lermontov, 1952; Tolstoi, 1965; Gogol, 1971; Catherine la Grande, 1978; Pierre le Grand, 1979; Alexandre 1er, 1981; Ivan le Terrible, 1982; Tchekhov, 1984; Turgenev, 1985; Gorki, 1986; Flaubert, 1988; Maupassant, 1989; Alexandre II, 1990; Nicolas II, 1991; Zola, 1992; Verlaine, 1993; Baudelaire, 1994; Balzac, 1995; Rasputin, 1996; Juliette Drouet, 1997; Terribles Tsarines, 1999; Les turbulences d'une grande famille, 1999; Nicolas Ier, 2000; Marina Tsvetaeva, 2001; Paul Ier, 2002; La baronne et le musicien, 2003; Alexandre III, 2004; Alexandre Dumas, 2005; La Traque, 2006. *Address:* Académie Française, Quai de Conti, 75006 Paris, France.   *Died 4 March 2007.*

TRUEMAN, Frederick Sewards, OBE 1989; writer and broadcaster; *b* Stainton, Yorks, 6 Feb. 1931; *s* of late Alan Thomas Trueman; *m* 1st, 1955, Enid Chapman (marr. diss. 1972); one *s* two *d* (incl. twin *s* and *d*); 2nd, 1973, Veronica Wilson (*née* Lundy). *Educ:* Maltby Secondary Sch. Apprentice bricklayer, 1946; worked in tally office of Maltby Main pit, 1948–51; nat. service, RAF, 1951–53. Played club cricket, 1945–48; Yorks Fedn cricket tour, 1948; played for Yorks CCC, 1949–68 (took 2304 wickets in first class games, incl. 100 wickets in a season twelve times; also made 3 centuries); county cap, 1951; captained Yorkshire 31 times, 1962–68; played 6 one day matches for Derby CCC, 1972; first Test series, against India, 1952; MCC tours to WI, 1953–54, 1959–60, and to Australia, 1958–59, 1962–63 (took a total of 307 Test wickets, 1952–65, incl. 10 in a match and 7 in an innings three times, and was first bowler to take 300 Test wickets, 1963). Journalist, Sunday People, 1957–; anchorman, Indoor League series, Yorks TV; cricket commentator for BBC. *Publications:* Fast Fury, 1961; Cricket, 1963; Book of Cricket, 1964; The Freddie Trueman Story, 1966; Ball of Fire (autobiog.), 1976; (with John Arlott) On Cricket, 1977; Thoughts of Trueman Now, 1978; (with Frank Hardy) You Nearly Had Him That Time, 1978; My Most Memorable Matches, 1982; (with Trevor Bailey) From Larwood to Lillee, 1983; (with Don Mosey) Fred Trueman's Yorkshire, 1984; (with Trevor Bailey) The Spinners' Web, 1988; (with Peter Grosvenor) Fred Trueman's Cricket Masterpieces: classic tales from the pavilion, 1990; (with Don Mosey) Champion Times, 1994; (with Don Mosey) Talking Cricket: with friends past and present, 1997; Fred Trueman's Dales Journey, 1998. *Recreations:* ornithology, working for children's charities. *Address:* c/o BBC, Broadcasting House, W1A 1AA. *Clubs:* Yorkshire County Cricket (Hon. Life Mem.), MCC (Hon. Life Mem.), Lord's Taverners, Variety of GB, Forty; Ilkley Golf.   *Died 1 July 2006.*

TRYTHALL, Maj.-Gen. Anthony John, CB 1983; Director of Army Education, 1980–84; Director: Brassey's (UK) Ltd (formerly Brassey's Defence Publishers Ltd), 1984–97 (Managing Director, 1984–87; Executive Deputy Chairman, 1988–95); Brassey's (US) Inc., 1984–95; *b* 30 March 1927; *s* of Eric Stewart Trythall and Irene (*née* Hollingham); *m* 1952, Celia Haddon; two *s* one *d*. *Educ:* Lawrence Sheriff Sch., Rugby; St Edmund Hall, Oxford (BA Hons Mod. Hist., 1947, DipEd 1951); Institute of Education, London Univ. (Academic DipEd 1962); King's College, London (MA in War Studies, 1969). National Service as RAEC Officer, UK, Egypt and Akaba, 1947–49; teaching, 1951–53; Regular RAEC Officer, 1953; seconded to Malay Regt for service at Fedn Mil. Coll., Port Dickson, 1953–56; WO, 1957–62; BAOR, 1962–66; Inspector, 1967–68; Educn Adviser, Regular Commns Bd, 1969–71; Head of Officer Educn Br., 1971–73; Chief Inspector of Army Educn, and Col Res., 1973–74; MoD, 1974–76; Chief Educn Officer, UKLF, 1976–80. Col Comdt, RAEC, 1986–89. Member: Council, Royal United Services Instn for Def. Studies, 1978–84; London Univ. Bd of War Studies, 1983–95; Chm. Bd, British Military Studies Gp, 1996 (Mem., 1984–99). Chm., Gallipoli Meml Lecture Trust, 1986–89, 1999–2000 (Trustee, 1984–2000). Chm. Bd of Govs, Selwyn Sch., Glos, 1997–2003. 1st Prize, Trench-Gascoigne Essay Competition, 1969. *Publications:* Boney Fuller: the intellectual general, 1977 (USA, as Boney Fuller: soldier, strategist and writer); (contrib.) The Downfall of Leslie Hore-Belisha in the Second World War, 1982; Fuller, the Tanks in Home Fires and Foreign Fields, 1985; J. F. C. Fuller: Staff Officer Extraordinary in the British General Staff, 2002; articles in Army Qly, Jl of RUSI, British Army Rev., and Jl of Contemp. Hist. *Address:* c/o Royal Bank of Scotland, Holt's Branch, Lawrie House, Victoria Road, Farnborough, Hants GU14 7NR. *Club:* Naval and Military.   *Died 2 Dec. 2006.*

TSUJI, Yoshifumi; Consultant, Nissan Motor Co. Ltd, since 2000 (Chairman, 1996–2000); *b* Kagawa Prefecture, Japan, 6 Feb. 1928; *m*. *Educ:* Faculty of Engrg, Univ. of Tokyo. Joined Nissan Motor Co. Ltd,

1954: General Manager: Prodn Control and Engrg Dept No 1, Yokohama Plant, 1978–80; Engrg Dept No 1, 1980–83; Engrg Dept No 1 and Cost Mgt Office, 1983–84; Tochigi Plant, 1984–87 (Gen. Manager Mfg Dept No 4, 1985–87); Dir and Mem. Bd, 1985–; Man. Dir i/c Product Planning, Marketing Gp No 1, 1987–89; Exec. Man. Dir, 1989–90; Exec. Vice Pres., 1990–92; Pres., 1992–96. Chm., Japan Automobile Manufactures Assoc. Inc., 1996. Vice Chm., Fedn of Econ. Orgn, 1997. Blue Ribbon Medal (Japan), 1995; Order of Queen Isabel la Católica (Spain), 1995. *Recreations*: golf, reading. *Address*: Nissan Motor Co. Ltd, 17–1 Ginza 6-chome, Chuo-ku, Tokyo 104–0061, Japan. *T*: (3) 35435523. *Died 11 Feb. 2007.*

TUCK, Prof. Ronald Humphrey; Professor of Agricultural Economics, University of Reading, 1965–86 (part-time, 1982–86), then Emeritus; *b* 28 June 1921; *s* of Francis Tuck and Edith Ann Tuck (*née* Bridgewater); *m* 1942, Margaret Sylvia Everley (*d* 1990); one *s* two *d*. *Educ*: Harrow County Sch.; Corpus Christi Coll., Oxford. War Service, RAOC and REME, mainly N Africa and Italy, 1941–45 (despatches). Univ. of Reading, Dept of Agric. Economics: Research Economist, 1947–49; Lecturer, 1949–62; Reader, 1962–65; Head of Dept of Agricultural Economics and Management, Univ. of Reading, and Provincial Agricultural Economist (Reading Province), 1965–81; Dean, Faculty of Agriculture and Food, Univ. of Reading, 1971–74. *Publications*: An Essay on the Economic Theory of Rank, 1954; An Introduction to the Principles of Agricultural Economics, 1961 (Italian trans., 1970); reviews etc in Jl of Agric. Economics and Economic Jl. *Recreations*: reading, music, drawing, walking. *Address*: 211 Kidmore Road, Caversham, Reading RG4 7NW. *T*: (0118) 954 6563. *Died 2 April 2007.*

TUDOR, Rev. Dr (Richard) John, BA; Chaplain to the Regents, Harris Manchester College, Oxford, since 2000; *b* 8 Feb. 1930; *s* of Charles Leonard and Ellen Tudor; *m* 1956, Cynthia Campbell Anderson; one *s* one *d*. *Educ*: Clee Grammar Sch., Grimsby; Queen Elizabeth's, Barnet; Univ. of Manchester, 1951–54 (BA Theology). Served RAF, 1948–51. Junior Methodist Minister, East Ham, London, 1954–57; Ordained, Newark, 1957; Minister, Thornton Cleveleys, Blackpool, 1957–60; Superintendent Minister: Derby Methodist Mission, 1960–71 (Chaplain to Mayor of Derby, Factories and Association with Derby Football Club); Coventry Methodist Mission, 1971–75 (Chaplain to Lord Mayor); Brighton Dome Mission, 1975–81; Westminster Central Hall, London, 1981–95; Free Church Chaplain, Westminster Hosp., 1982–93; Chaplain to Ancient Order of Foresters, 1989–, to Lord Mayor of Westminster, 1993–94. Hon. DD Texas Wesleyan Univ., Fort Worth, USA, 1981; Hon. Texan, 1965; Freeman of Fort Worth, 1970. *Publications*: Word for all Seasons, 1992. *Recreations*: motoring, cooking, photography, the delights of family life. *Address*: Harris Manchester College, Oxford OX1 3TD. *T*: (01865) 271007. *Died 29 Oct. 2009.*

TUDWAY QUILTER, David Cuthbert; *see* Quilter.

TUITA, Sir Mariano (Kelesimalefo), KBE 1992 (OBE 1975); Cross of Solomon Islands, 1985; Managing Director, L. K. P. Hardware Ltd, since 1985; *b* Solomon Is, 12 Nov. 1932; *s* of late Joachim Alick and Ann Maria Tangoia Hagota; *m* 1957, Luisa Mae; three *s* six *d*. *Educ*: St Joseph's Sch., Tenaru on Guadalcanal. Mem. for Lau, Malaita Local Govt Council, 1958–60; Pres., Malaita Council, 1960–68; Member: first Solomon Is Legislative Council, 1960–65; for N Malaita Constituency, 1965–67; for NE Malaita Constituency, 1967–69; Governing Council for Lau and Baelelea, 1970–73; for Lau and Baelelea, Legislative Assembly, Solomon Is Nat. Parlt, 1976–80. *Address*: L. K. P. Hardware Ltd, PO Box 317, Honiara, Solomon Islands. *T*: 22594 and 23848. *Died Dec. 2009.*

TUMIM, Winifred Letitia, (Lady Tumim), CBE 2003 (OBE 1992); Chair, National Council for Voluntary Organisations, 1996–2001; Chairman, National Registers of Communication Professionals Working with Deaf and Deafblind People, since 2009; *b* 3 June 1936; *d* of Algernon Malcolm Borthwick and Edith Wylde Borthwick (*née* Addison); *m* 1962, Sir Stephen Tumim (*d* 2003); three *d*. *Educ*: Lady Margaret Hall, Oxford (PPE Hons 1958; MA); SOAS, London Univ. (Dip. Linguistics 1979). Non-exec. Dir, Parkside Health NHS Trust, 1992–98. Chairman: Sec. of State's Youth Treatment Service Gp, 1991–95; Ind. Adv. Gp on Teenage Pregnancy, 2000–; Mem., Warnock Cttee of Enquiry on Educn of Handicapped Children, 1974–78. Member: Council, Vol. Council for Handicapped Children, 1981–87; GMC, 1996–2003 (Associate Mem., 2003–); Council for Charitable Support, 1996–; Vice-Chm., Family Housing Assoc., 1983–88; Chairman: RNID, 1985–92; NCVO/Charity Commn On Trust Wkg Party, 1992; Council for Advancement of Communication with Deaf People, 1994–97. Gov., Mary Hare Grammar Sch. for The Deaf, 1974–90; Trustee, United Westminster Schs, 2003–. Trustee: Nat. Portrait Gall., 1992–99; City Parochial Foundn, 1989–2001; Charities Aid Foundn, 1996–2001; Adapt, 2007–09; Chm., Foyer Fedn, 2001–04. FRSA 1989. *Recreations*: painting watercolours, gardening, classical music, modern ceramics, tribal rugs. *Club*: Athenæum. *Died 5 Nov. 2009.*

TUNNELL, Hugh James Oliver Redvers; HM Diplomatic Service, retired; Ambassador to Bahrain, 1992–95; *b* 31 Dec. 1935; *s* of late Oliver and Heather Tunnell; *m* 1st, 1958, Helen Miller (marr. diss.); three *d*; 2nd, 1979, Margaret, *d* of Sir Richard John Randall; two *d*. *Educ*: Chatham House Grammar School, Ramsgate. Royal Artillery, 1954–56. FO, 1956–59; Amman, 1959–62; Middle East Centre for Arab Studies, 1962–63; served FO, Aden, CRO, Damascus and FO, 1964–67; UK Delegn to European Communities, 1968–70; FCO, 1970–72; Kuwait, 1972–76; FCO, 1976–79; Head of Chancery, Muscat, 1979–83; Consul Gen., Brisbane, 1983–88; Comr-Gen., British Section, EXPO 88, 1987–88; Consul Gen., Jedda, 1989–92. Mem. Cttee, Bahrain Soc., 1996–2000. *Recreations*: water sports, tennis. *Address*: 44 Fernberg Road, Paddington, Qld 4064, Australia. *T*: (7) 33697892; *e-mail*: tunnell@optushome.com.au. *Club*: Brisbane (Brisbane). *Died 20 April 2009.*

TUOHY, Thomas, CBE 1969; Managing Director, British Nuclear Fuels Ltd, 1971–73; *b* 7 Nov. 1917; *s* of late Michael Tuohy and Isabella Tuohy, Cobh, Eire; *m* 1940, Una Goodacre (marr. diss.); two *s*; *m* 1949, Lilian May Barnes (*d* 1971); one *s* one *d*; *m* Shirley de Bernardo, Calif. *Educ*: St Cuthberts Grammar Sch., Newcastle; Reading Univ. (BSc). Chemist in various Royal Ordnance Factories, 1939–46. Manager: Health Physics, Springfields Nuclear Fuel Plant, Dept Atomic Energy, 1946; Health Physics, Windscale Plutonium Plant, 1949; Plutonium Piles and Metal Plant, Windscale, 1950; Works Manager: Springfields, 1952; Windscale, UKAEA, 1954; Windscale and Calder Hall: Dep. Gen. Manager, 1957; Gen. Manager, 1958; Man. Dir, Production Gp, UKAEA, 1964–71. Managing Director: Urenco, 1973–74; Vorsitzender der Geschäftsführung Centec GmbH, 1973–74; Dep. Chm., Centec, 1973–74; former Dir, Centec-Algermann Co. Mem. Council, Internat. Inst. for Management of Technology, 1971–73. *Publications*: various technical papers on reactor operation and plutonium manufacture. *Recreations*: gardening, travel. *Address*: Ingleberg, Beckermet, Cumbria CA21 2XX. *T*: (01946) 841226. *Died 12 March 2008.*

TURNER, Prof. Cedric Edward, CBE 1987; FREng; Emeritus Professor and Senior Research Fellow, Imperial College, London, since 1991; *b* 5 Aug. 1926; *s* of Charles Turner and Mabel Evelyn (*née* Berry); *m* 1953, Margaret Dorothy (*née* Davies); one *s* two *d*. *Educ*: Brockenhurst Grammar Sch.; University Coll., Southampton (BScEng); DScEng, PhD London. CEng, FIMechE, FREng (FEng

1989). Res. Asst, Imperial Coll., 1948–52; Academic Staff, Imperial Coll., 1952–76 and 1979–: Prof. of Materials in Mech. Engrg, 1975–91; seconded NPL and Brit. Aerospace, 1976–78. Hon. Prof., Shenyang Inst. of Aeronautical Engrg, Shenyang, China, 1987; Leverhulme Emeritus Fellow, 1990–92. Silver Medal, Plastics Inst., 1963; James Clayton Prize, IMechE, 1981. *Publications:* Introduction to Plate and Shell Theory, 1965; (jtly) Post Yield Fracture Mechanics, 1979, 2nd edn 1984; contribs to Proc. Royal Soc., Proc. IMechE, Jl Strain Anal., Amer. Soc. Test & Mat., etc. *Recreations:* Meccano modelling of old machines, reading, friend of Kirkaldy Testing Museum, London. *Address:* The Corner House, 17 Meadway, Epsom, Surrey KT19 8JZ. *T:* (01372) 722989.
Died 13 Feb. 2010.

TURNER, Donald William, CEng, FICE; *b* 17 Aug. 1925; *s* of William John Turner and Agnes Elizabeth Jane (*née* Bristow); *m* 1947, Patricia (*née* Stuteley); one *s* one *d*. *Educ:* Wanstead County High Sch.; Birmingham Univ. Served War, Army, 1943–45. Subseq. completed engrg trng in Britain; then took up post in Australia with Qld Railways, 1949. Left Qld, 1954; joined firm of UK consulting engrs and then worked in W Africa on rly and highway construction until 1960. Returned to UK, but remained with consultants until 1966, when joined BAA; Chief Engr, Heathrow Airport, 1970; Dir of Planning and Bd Mem., 1973; Dir of Privatisation, 1985–86; Chm., British Airports International, 1984–87. Dir, London Underground, 1985–93. *Address:* 27 Kingsway Court, Hove, Sussex BN3 2LP. *Died 1 Dec. 2006.*

TURNER, Captain Ernest John Donaldson, CBE 1968; DSO 1942; DSC 1941; RN retd; Vice Lord-Lieutenant of Dunbartonshire, since 1986; *b* 21 March 1914; *s* of Ernest Turner (*d* 1916, HMS Hampshire) and Margaret Donaldson; *m* 1940, Catherine Chalmers; one *d*. *Educ:* Hermitage Academy; Glasgow Technical College; Royal Navy; sowc, IDC. Joined Merchant Navy as Cadet, 1930; RN from RNR, 1937; specialised in submarines, 1939; served in submarines, 1941–68; Commodore, Submarines, 1964; Captain i/c Clyde, 1965–68, during building of Faslane Polaris Base; officer recruitment (after retiring), 1968–80; PA to Chm., Whyte & Mackay Distillers Ltd, 1980–82. Croix de Guerre (France), 1941. *Recreations:* hockey and golf, holidays abroad. *Died 2 March 2007.*

TURNER, Prof. Martin John Leslie, CBE 2004; FRAS; Principal Research Fellow, since 1995, and Professor, 2004–08, then Professor Emeritus, Department of Physics and Astronomy, University of Leicester; *b* 7 Oct. 1942; *s* of late Edward Charles Turner and Betsy Turner (*née* Richardson); *m* 1966, Josephine Anne Ward; two *s* one *d*. *Educ:* Harwich Co. High Sch.; Univ. of Durham (BSc 1965; PhD 1969; DSc 1992). FRAS 1990. Foreign Res. Fellow, Inst. of Physics, Univ. degli Studi di Milano, 1969–72; Department of Physics and Astronomy, University of Leicester: Res. Associate, 1973–80; Res. Fellow, 1980–88; Sen. Res. Fellow, 1988–95. Vis. Fellow, Inst. of Space and Astronautical Sci., Japan, 1987; Vis. Prof., Dept of Physics, Univ. of Tokyo (To Dai), 1988. European Space Agency: Principal Investigator, EPIC instrument on ESA space observatory XMM-Newton; Chm., Xeus Sci. Adv. Gp, 1997–; Member: Astronomy Wkg Gp, 1992–94; Astro-E Sci. Wkg Gp, Inst. of Space and Astronautical Sci., Japan, 1995–; European Photon Imaging Camera Internat. Mgt Gp, 1996–; Space Sci. Cttee, ESF, 1999–2003; Particle Physics and Astronomy Research Council: Member: Space Sci. Adv. Cttee, 1996–98; Project Peer Review Panel, 2001–04. *Publications:* Rocket and Spacecraft Propulsion, 2000, 3rd edn 2008; Expedition Mars, 2004; numerous papers in learned jls on instrumentation for space astronomy and x-ray astronomy. *Recreations:* growing vegetables, singing English choral music, walking, fly fishing, old scientific instruments, old books. *Address:* 63 Elms Road, Leicester LE2 3JD. *T:* (0116) 270 7070; *e-mail:* mjlt@star.le.ac.uk. *Died 6 May 2009.*

TURNER, Michael Ralph, FRSA; Group Managing Director, 1976–88, Chief Executive, 1982–88, Associated Book Publishers PLC; Chairman, Associated Book Publishers (UK) Ltd, 1977–90; *b* 26 Jan. 1929; *s* of Ralph Victor Turner and May Turner; *m* 1955, Ruth Baylis (*d* 1997); two adopted *s* two adopted *d*. *Educ:* Newport Sch., Essex; Trinity Coll., Cambridge (BA Hons). Served RAF, Transport Comd, 1947–49. Jun. Editor, J. M. Dent & Sons, 1949–50; Methuen & Co.: Jun. Editor, 1953; subseq. Publicity and Promotion Manager, and Dir; Associated Publishers Ltd: Marketing Dir, 1973; Asst Gp Man. Dir, 1975; Gp Man. Dir, 1976. Chm., Methuen Inc., New York, 1981–88; Pres., Carswell Co. Ltd, Toronto, 1982–84; Dir, ABP Investments (Aust.) Pty Ltd, 1976–88; Sen. Vice-Pres., Publishing Information Gp, Internat. Thomson Orgn Ltd, 1987–89. Chairman: Book Marketing Council, 1981–84; Book Trust, 1990–92; Member: Book Trade Working Party, 1973–74; Council, Publishers Assoc., 1981–90 (Vice-Pres., 1985–87 and 1989–90; Pres., 1987–89); Chm., Home Trade and Services Council, 1989–90); National Council and Exec., NBL, 1980–87; British Library Adv. Council, 1989–94; Centre for the Book Adv. Cttee, 1990–95; Publishing Bd, Design Council, 1991–94. Mem. Adv. Cttee, Book Trade Lives, Nat. Life Story Collection at BL Sound Archive, 1988–2007. Chm., Soc. of Bookmen, 1992–94. FRSA 1984. *Publications:* The Bluffer's Guide to the Theatre, 1967; Parlour Poetry, 1967; (with Antony Miall) The Parlour Song Book, 1972; (with Antony Miall) Just a Song at Twilight, 1975; (with Antony Miall) The Edwardian Song Book, 1982; (with Michael Geare) Gluttony, Pride and Lust and Other Sins from the World of Books, 1984; Do You Scratch Your Bottom in the Bath?, 1998; (with Leslie Lonsdale-Cooper) translations of Hergé's Tintin books, 1958–2005. *Recreations:* reading, music, theatre, maritime painting and models. *Address:* c/o 5 Grove Road, Alton, Hants GU34 1NP. *T:* (01420) 88701. *Club:* Garrick. *Died 10 July 2009.*

TURNER, Norman Henry, CBE 1977; Official Solicitor to the Supreme Court of Judicature, 1970–80; *b* 11 May 1916; *s* of late Henry James Turner, MA and Hilda Gertrude Turner; *m* 1st, 1939, Dora Ardella (*née* Cooper) (*d* 1990); three *s* two *d*; 2nd, 1991, Mona Florence Mackenzie. *Educ:* Nottingham High School. Articled, Nottingham, 1933; admitted Solicitor (Hons), 1938; joined Official Solicitor's Dept, 1948; Asst Official Solicitor, 1958. *Died 8 Dec. 2007.*

TURNER-SAMUELS, Norma Florence, (Mrs D. J. Turner-Samuels); *see* Negus, N. F.

TURNEY, Alan Harry, CB 1991; Assistant Under Secretary of State, Fire and Emergency Planning Department, Home Office, 1986–92; *b* 20 Aug. 1932; *s* of late Harry Landry Turney and Alice Theresa Turney (*née* Bailey); *m* 1957, Ann Mary Dollimore. *Educ:* St Albans Grammar Sch.; London School of Economics (BScEcon). Asst Principal, Home Office, 1961; Asst Private Sec. to Home Sec., 1962–65; Principal, 1965; Asst Sec., Broadcasting Dept, 1976; Rayner Review of Forensic Science Service, 1981; Criminal Dept, 1981–82; Prison Dept, 1982–86. *Recreations:* Rugby Union football, touring provincial France, enjoying the garden. *Address:* Brookfield Cottage, Bury End, Nuthampstead, Royston, Herts SG8 8NG. *T:* (01763) 848935. *Died 4 Aug. 2009.*

TURPIN, James Alexander, CMG 1966; HM Diplomatic Service, retired; *b* 7 Jan. 1917; *s* of late Samuel Alexander Turpin; *m* 1942, Kathleen Iris Eadie; one *d*. *Educ:* King's Hosp., Dublin; Trinity Coll., Dublin (schol., 1st cl. Hons, Gold Medal, MA). Asst Lectr, Trinity College, Dublin, 1940. Served Army (Royal Irish Fusiliers), 1942–46. Joined Foreign Service, 1947; Mem., UK Delegn to OEEC, Paris, 1948; 1st Sec., 1949; FO, 1950; Warsaw, 1953; Tokyo, 1955; Counsellor, 1960; seconded to BoT, 1960–63; Counsellor (Commercial), The Hague, 1963–67; Minister (Economic and Commercial), New Delhi, 1967–70; Asst Under-Sec. of State, FCO, 1971–72;

Ambassador to the Philippines, 1972–76; retired, 1977. Chm., British-Philippine Soc., 1986–88. *Publications:* New Society's Challenge in the Philippines, 1980; The Philippines: problems of the ageing New Society, 1984. *Recreations:* tennis, music, swimming, wine, cookery. *Address:* 12 Grimwood Road, Twickenham, Middlesex TW1 1BX.   *Died 3 Oct. 2006.*

TUTI, Rt Rev. Dudley, KBE 1988 (OBE 1974); Paramount Chief of Santa Ysabel, since 1975; Chairman: Solomon Islands Credit Union, since 1982; Ysabel Timber Co. Ltd, since 1991; Chairman, Santa Ysabel Council of Chiefs, since 1984; *b* 1919; *s* of John Tariniu and Daisy Mele Pago; *m* 1957, Naomi Tate; one *s* seven *d* (and one *s* decd). *Educ:* St John's Coll., Auckland, NZ. Deacon, 1946; priest, 1954. Headmaster, Vureas Boys' Sch., 1954–56; District Priest and Rural Dean of Santa Ysabel, 1956–63; consecrated Bishop (by the Archbishop of NZ), 1963; Asst Bishop, dio. of Melanesia, 1963–75; Bishop and Archdeacon, Central Solomons, 1968–75; Vicar-General, dio. of Melanesia, 1971–75; Bishop of Santa Ysabel, 1975–82. Mem., Law Reform Commn, Solomon Is, 1995–98. Chm., Ysabel Community Trust, 1991–96. *Address:* PO Box 35, Jejevo, Buala, Santa Ysabel, Solomon Islands. *T:* 35005.   *Died 31 Jan. 2006.*

TUTIN, Mrs Winifred Anne, (Winifred Pennington), PhD; FRS 1979; Principal Scientific Officer, Freshwater Biological Association, 1967–81, retired; *b* 8 Oct. 1915; *d* of Albert R. Pennington and Margaret S. Pennington; *m* 1942, Thomas Gaskell Tutin, FRS (*d* 1987); one *s* three *d*. *Educ:* Barrow-in-Furness Grammar Sch., Reading Univ. (BSc, PhD). Research posts with Freshwater Biological Assoc., 1940–45; Demonstrator and Special Lectr, Univ. of Leicester, 1947–67; Hon. Reader in Botany, Univ. of Leicester, 1971–79, Hon. Professor, 1980–. Foreign Member, Royal Danish Academy, 1974. *Publications:* (as Winifred Pennington): The History of British Vegetation, 1969, 2nd edn 1974; (with W. H. Pearsall) The Lake District, 1973; papers in New Phytologist, Jl of Ecology, Phil. Trans of Royal Society, and others. *Recreations:* gardening, plain cooking. *Address:* Priory Cottage, North Street, Kingsclere, Newbury, Berks RG20 5QY.   *Died 1 May 2007.*

TWEEDSMUIR, 3rd Baron *cr* 1935, of Elsfield, Oxford; **William de l'Aigle Buchan;** *b* 10 Jan. 1916; 2nd *s* of 1st Baron Tweedsmuir, PC, GCMG, GCVO, CH and Susan Charlotte (*d* 1977), *d* of Hon. Norman Grosvenor; *S* brother, 1996; *m* 1st, 1939, Nesta Crozier (marr. diss. 1946); one *d*; 2nd, 1946, Barbara (marr. diss. 1960; she *d* 1969), 2nd *d* of E. N. Ensor; three *s* three *d* (incl. twin *d*); 3rd, 1960, Sauré Cynthia Mary, *y d* of Maj. G. E. Tatchell; one *s*. *Educ:* Eton; New Coll., Oxford. Sqdn Leader, RAFVR. *Publications:* John Buchan: a memoir, 1982; The Rags of Time (autobiog.), 1990; *novels:* Kumari, 1955; Helen All Alone, 1961; The Blue Pavilion, 1966. *Heir: s* Hon. John William Howard de l'Aigle Buchan [*b* 25 May 1950; *m* 1977, Amanda Jocelyn, *d* of Sir Gawain Westray Bell, KCMG, CBE; two *s*]. *Club:* Travellers.   *Died 29 June 2008.*

TWITCHETT, Prof. Denis Crispin, FBA 1967; Gordon Wu Professor of Chinese Studies, Princeton University, 1980–94; *b* 23 Sept. 1925; *m* 1956, Umeko Ichikawa (*d* 1993); two *s*. *Educ:* St Catharine's Coll., Cambridge. Lectr in Far-Eastern History, Univ. of London, 1954–56; Univ. Lectr in Classical Chinese, Univ. of Cambridge, 1956–60; Prof. of Chinese, SOAS, London Univ., 1960–68; Prof. of Chinese, Univ. of Cambridge, 1968–80. Vis. Prof., Princeton Univ., 1973–74, 1978–79. Principal Editor, Cambridge History of China, 1977–. *Publications:* (ed with A. F. Wright) Confucian Personalities, 1962; The Financial Administration under the T'ang dynasty, 1963, 2nd edn 1971; (ed with A. F. Wright) Perspectives on the T'ang, 1973; (ed with P. J. M. Geelan) The Times Atlas of China, 1975; (ed) Cambridge History of China, Vol. 10 1978, Vol. 3 1979, Vol. 11 1980, Vol. 12 1983, Vol. 1

1986, Vol. 13 1986, Vol. 7 1987, Vol. 14 1987, Vol. 15 1990, Vol. 6 1994, Vol. 8 1998, Vol. 9A 2002; Printing and Publishing in Medieval China, 1983; Reader in T'ang History, 1986; The Writing of Official History in T'ang China, 1992; The Historian, his Readers, and the Passage of Time, 1997. *Address:* 24 Arbury Road, Cambridge CB4 2JE.   *Died 24 Feb. 2006.*

TYACKE, Maj.-Gen. David Noel Hugh, CB 1970; OBE 1957; Controller, Army Benevolent Fund, 1971–80; *b* 18 Nov. 1915; *s* of Capt. Charles Noel Walker Tyacke (killed in action, March 1918) and late Phoebe Mary Cicely (*née* Coulthard), Cornwall; *m* 1940, Diana (*d* 2004), *d* of Aubrey Hare Duke; one *s*. *Educ:* Malvern Coll.; RMC Sandhurst. Commissioned DCLI, 1935; India, 1936–39; France and Belgium, 1939–40; India and Burma, 1943–46; Instructor, Staff Coll., Camberley, 1950–52; CO 1st Bn DCLI, 1957–59; Comdr 130 Inf. Bde (TA), 1961–63; Dir of Administrative Planning (Army), 1963–64; Brig. Gen. Staff (Ops), Min. of Defence, 1965–66; GOC Singapore Dist, 1966–70. Col, The Light Infantry, 1972–77. Mem., Malvern Coll. Council, 1978–88. *Recreations:* walking, motoring, bird-watching. *Address:* c/o Lloyds TSB, Cox's & King's Branch, 7 Pall Mall, SW1Y 5NA.   *Died 10 Feb. 2010.*

TYLER, Ven. Leonard George; Rector of St Michael and St Mary Magdalene, Easthampstead, 1973–85; *b* 15 April 1920; *s* of Hugh Horstead Tyler and Mabel Adam Stewart Tyler; *m* 1946, Sylvia May Wilson; one *s* two *d*. *Educ:* Darwen Grammar School; Liverpool University; Christ's College, Cambridge; Westcott House. Chaplain, Trinity College, Kandy, Ceylon, 1946–48; Principal, Diocesan Divinity School, Colombo, Ceylon, 1948–50; Rector, Christ Church, Bradford, Manchester, 1950–55; Vicar of Leigh, Lancs, 1955–66 (Rural Dean, 1955–62); Chaplain, Leigh Infirmary, 1955–66; Archdeacon of Rochdale, 1962–66; Principal, William Temple College, Manchester, 1966–73. Anglican Adviser to ABC Television, 1958–68. *Publications:* contributor to Theology. *Address:* 11 Ashton Place, Kintbury, Hungerford, Berks RG17 9XS. *T:* (01488) 658510.   *Died 21 Sept. 2010.*

TYNDALL, Nicholas John; Chief Officer, National Marriage Guidance Council, 1968–86; *b* 15 Aug. 1928; *s* of Rev. Edward Denis Tyndall and Nora Mildred Tyndall; *m* 1953, Elizabeth Mary (*née* Ballard); two *s* two *d*. *Educ:* Marlborough College; Jesus College, Cambridge (BA). HM Prison and Borstal Service, 1952–68; Training Officer, Cruse-Bereavement Care, 1987–91, retd. Dir, Council of Europe Co-ordinated Research Fellowship on Marriage Guidance and Family Counselling, 1973–75; Mem., Home Office/DHSS Working Party on Marriage Guidance, 1976–78; Chairman: British Assoc. for Counselling, 1976–78; Marriage and Marriage Guidance Commn of Internat. Union of Family Organisations, 1971–86; Training Cttee, Nat. Assoc. of Bereavement Socs, 1993–99. Mem., Gen. Synod of Church of England, 1981–88. Fellow, British Assoc. for Counselling, 1997. *Publications:* Counselling in the Voluntary Sector, 1993. *Recreation:* Morris dancing (Squire, Icknield Way Morris Men, 1998–2000). *Address:* 4 Folly View Road, Faringdon, Oxon SN7 7DH.   *Died 19 April 2006.*

TYSON, Monica Elizabeth; Editor, A La Carte, 1986–87, retired; *b* 7 June 1927; *d* of F. S. Hill and E. Hill; *m* 1st, 1950, P. M. Lyon (marr. diss. 1958); one *d*; 2nd, 1960, R. E. D. Tyson. *Educ:* George Watson's Ladies Coll.; Edinburgh Coll. of Domestic Science (Dip. in Domestic Sci.). Asst Home Editor, Modern Woman, 1958–60; Ideal Home: Domestic Planning Editor, 1960–64; Asst Editor, 1964–68; Editor, 1968–77; Editor: Woman's Realm, 1977–82; Special Assignments, IPC Magazines, 1982–84; Mother, 1984–86. *Recreations:* travelling, reading. *Address:* Ramsgate, Kent.   *Died 18 March 2009.*

U

ULLMANN, (Frederick) Ralph, MA; JP; Headmaster, Wellingborough School, 1993–2004; *b* 29 July 1945; *s* of late Prof. Walter Ullmann, FBA and Elizabeth Ullmann (*née* Knapp); *m* 1980, Alison Kemp; two *s* one *d. Educ:* Trinity Coll., Cambridge (schol.; MA; PGCE). FCollP (ACP). History Teacher, and Head of Gen. Studies, Bishop's Stortford Coll., 1968–72; Head of History and Sen. Housemaster, Bloxham Sch., 1972–85; Headmaster, Ruthin Sch., 1986–93. Member: ASCL (formerly SHA), 1986– (Mem. Council, 1997–); HMC, 1993–2004 (Member: Community Service Cttee, 1995–2001; Professional Develt Cttee, 1997–2004; Cttee, 1998–99; Sec., 1998, Chm., 1999, Midland Div.); Gen. Teaching Council, 2001– (Initial Teacher Trng Cttee, 2001–03; Audit Monitoring and Review Cttee, 2001–07; Professional Develt Adv. Cttee, 2003–04; Co-ordinating Cttee, 2006–07; Exec. Cttee, 2007–; Chm., Policy Services Gp, 2004–07). Founding Dir, Bd, Castle Theatre and Arts Centre, Wellingborough, 1994–98. Mem. Adv. Bd, 2000–04, Chm., 2004–09, Rudolf Kempe Soc. JP Leicester, 2007. *Recreations:* photography, music, wine. *Address:* 7 School Lane, Braybrooke, Market Harborough LE16 8LS. *Club:* East India. *Died 26 Sept. 2010.*

UNSWORTH, Sir Edgar (Ignatius Godfrey), Kt 1963; CMG 1954; QC (N Rhodesia) 1951; *b* 18 April 1906; *yr s* of John William and Minnie Unsworth; *m* 1964, Eileen, *widow* of Raymond Ritzema. *Educ:* Stonyhurst Coll.; Manchester Univ. (LLB Hons). Barrister-at-Law, Gray's Inn, 1930; private practice, 1930–37. Parly Cand. (C) for Farnworth, General Election, 1935. Crown Counsel: Nigeria, 1937; N Rhodesia, 1942; Solicitor-General: N Rhodesia, 1946; Fedn of Malaya, 1949; Chm. of Cttees, N Rhodesia, 1950; Attorney-General, N Rhodesia, 1951–56. Acting Chief Sec. and Dep. to Governor of N Rhodesia for periods during 1953, 1954 and 1955; Attorney-General, Fedn of Nigeria, 1956–60; Federal Justice of Federal Supreme Court of Nigeria, 1960–62; Chief Justice, Nyasaland, 1962–64; Director of a Course for Government Officers from Overseas, 1964–65; Chief Justice of Gibraltar, 1965–76; Justice of Appeal, Gibraltar, 1976–81. Member Rhodesia Railways Arbitration Tribunal, 1946; Chm., Commn of Enquiry into Central African Airways Corp., 1947; Mem., British Observers' Group, Independence Elections, Rhodesia, 1980 (submitted independent report). *Publications:* Laws of Northern Rhodesia, rev. edn, 1949. *Recreations:* gardening, bridge. *Address:* Pedro El Grande 9, Sotogrande, San Roque, 11310 Cadiz, Spain. *Clubs:* Bath and County (Bath); Royal Gibraltar Yacht. *Died 15 March 2006.*

UNWIN, David Storr; author; *b* 3 Dec. 1918; *e s* of Sir Stanley Unwin, KCMG, and Alice Mary Storr; *m* 1945, Periwinkle, *yr d* of late Captain Sidney Herbert, RN; twin *s* and *d. Educ:* Abbotsholme. League of Nations Secretariat, Geneva, 1938–39; George Allen & Unwin Ltd, Publishers, 1940–44. *Publications:* The Governor's Wife, 1954 (Authors' Club First Novel Award, 1955); A View of the Heath, 1956; Fifty Years with Father: a Relationship (autobiog.), 1982; *for children:* (under pen name David Severn) Rick Afire!, 1942; A Cabin for Crusoe, 1943; Waggon for Five, 1944; Hermit in the Hills, 1945; Forest Holiday, 1946; Ponies and Poachers, 1947; Dream Gold, 1948; The Cruise of the Maiden Castle, 1948; Treasure for Three, 1949; My Foreign Correspondent through Africa, 1950; Crazy Castle, 1951; Burglars and Bandicoots, 1952; Drumbeats!, 1953; The Future Took Us, 1958; The Green-eyed Gryphon, 1958; Foxy-boy, 1959; Three at the Sea, 1959; Clouds over the Alberhorn, 1963; Jeff Dickson, Cowhand, 1963; The Girl in the Grove, 1974; The Wishing Bone, 1977. *Recreations:* travel, gardening. *Address:* Garden Flat, 31 Belsize Park, NW3 4DX. *Club:* PEN. *Died 11 Feb. 2010.*

UPDIKE, John Hoyer; freelance writer; *b* 18 March 1932; *s* of late Wesley R. and Linda G. Updike; *m* 1st, 1953, Mary E. Pennington (marr. diss. 1976); two *s* two *d;* 2nd, 1977, Martha Ruggles Bernhard. *Educ:* Harvard Coll. Worked as journalist for The New Yorker magazine, 1955–57. *Publications: poems:* Hoping for a Hoopoe (in America, The Carpentered Hen), 1958; Telephone Poles, 1968; Midpoint and other poems, 1969; Tossing and Turning, 1977; Facing Nature, 1985; Collected Poems, 1993; Americana and other poems, 2001; Endpoint, 2009 (published posthumously); *novels:* The Poorhouse Fair, 1959; Rabbit, Run, 1960; The Centaur, 1963; Of the Farm, 1966; Couples, 1968; Rabbit Redux, 1972; A Month of Sundays, 1975; Marry Me, 1976; The Coup, 1979; Rabbit Is Rich (Pulitzer Prize), 1982; The Witches of Eastwick, 1984 (filmed 1987); Roger's Version, 1986; S., 1988; Rabbit at Rest, 1990 (Pulitzer Prize 1991); Memories of the Ford Administration, 1993; Brazil, 1994; Rabbit Angstrom: a tetralogy, 1995; In the Beauty of the Lilies, 1996; Toward the End of Time, 1998; Gertrude and Claudius, 2000; Seek My Face, 2003; Villages, 2004; Terrorist, 2006; The Widows of Eastwick, 2008; *short stories:* The Same Door, 1959; Pigeon Feathers, 1962; The Music School, 1966; Bech: A Book, 1970; Museums and Women, 1973; Problems, 1980; Bech Is Back, 1982; (ed) The Year's Best American Short Stories, 1985; Trust Me, 1987; The Afterlife and other stories, 1995; Bech at Bay: a quasi-novel, 1998; Licks of Love, 2001; The Early Stories: 1953–1975, 2004; My Father's Tears and Other Stories, 2009 (published posthumously); *miscellanies:* Assorted Prose, 1965; Picked-Up Pieces, 1976; Hugging the Shore, 1983; Just Looking: essays on art, 1989; Odd Jobs: essays and criticism, 1991; Golf Dreams, 1997; More Matter, 1999; Still Looking: essays on American art, 2006; Due Considerations: essays and criticism, 2007; *autobiography:* Self-Consciousness: Memoirs, 1989; *play:* Buchanan Dying, 1974. *Address:* Beverly Farms, MA 01915, USA. *Died 27 Jan. 2009.*

USBORNE, Richard Alexander; writer; *b* 16 May 1910; *s* of Charles Frederick Usborne, ICS, and Janet Muriel (*née* Lefroy); *m* 1938, Monica (*d* 1986), *d* of Archibald Stuart MacArthur, Wagon Mound, New Mexico, USA; one *s* one *d. Educ:* Summer Fields Preparatory Sch.; Charterhouse; Balliol Coll., Oxford (BA Mods and Greats; MA 1981). Served War, 1941–45: Army, SOE and PWE. Middle East, Major, Gen. List. Advertising agencies. 1933–36; part-owner and Editor of What's On, 1936–37; London Press Exchange, 1937–39; BBC Monitoring Service, 1939–41; Asst Editor, Strand Magazine, 1946–50; Dir, Graham & Gillies Ltd, Advertising, retd, 1970; Custodian, National Trust, 1974–81. *Publications:* Clubland Heroes, 1953, rev. 1975, 1983; (ed) A Century of Summer Fields, 1964; Wodehouse at Work, 1961, rev. edn as Wodehouse at Work to the End, 1977; (ed) Sunset at Blandings, 1977; (ed) Vintage Wodehouse, 1977; A Wodehouse Companion, 1981; (ed) Wodehouse 'Nuggets', 1983; (ed) The Penguin Wodehouse Companion, 1988; After Hours with P. G. Wodehouse, 1991; adaptations of Wodehouse novels and stories for BBC radio serials. *Recreations:* reading, writing light verse. *Address:* The Charterhouse, Charterhouse Square, EC1M 6AN. *T:* (020) 7608 0140. *Died 21 March 2006.*

V

VACHON, His Eminence Cardinal Louis-Albert, CC (Canada) 1969; OQ 1985; FRSC 1974; Officier de l'Ordre de la fidélité française, 1963; Archbishop (RC) of Quebec and Primate of Canada, 1981–90, then Emeritus; *b* 4 Feb. 1912; *s* of Napoléon Vachon and Alexandrine Gilbert. *Educ:* Laval Univ. (PhD Philosophy, 1947); PhD Theology, Angelicum, Rome, 1949. Ordained priest, 1938; Prof. of Philosophy, 1941–47, Prof. of Theology, 1949–55, Laval Univ. Superior, Grand Séminaire de Québec, 1955–59; Superior General, 1960–77; Auxiliary Bishop of Quebec, 1977–81; Cardinal, 1985. Vice-Rector of Laval Univ., 1959–60, Rector, 1960 72. Mem , Royal Canadian Soc. of Arts. Hon. FRCP&S (Canada), 1972. Hon. doctorates: Montreal, McGill and Victoria, 1964; Guelph, 1966; Moncton, 1967; Queen's, Bishop's and Strasbourg, 1968; Notre-Dame (Indiana), 1971; Carleton, 1972, Laval, 1982. Centennial Medal, 1967. KHS 1985; KM 1987. *Publications:* Espérance et Présomption, 1958, Vérité et Liberté, 1962; Unité de l'Université, 1962; Apostolat de l'universitaire catholique, 1963; Mémorial, 1963; Communauté universitaire, 1963; Progrès de l'université et consentement populaire, 1964; Responsabilité collective des universitaires, 1964; Les humanités aujourd'hui, 1966, Excellence et loyauté des universitaires, 1969; Pastoral Letters, 1981. *Recreations:* reading, beaux arts. *Address:* 1 rue des Remparts, Quebec, QC G1R 5L7, Canada. *Died 29 Sept. 2006*

VAEA, Baron of Houma; **'Alipate Halakilangi Tau'alupeoko Tupou;** Chairman: National Reserve Bank Board, since 1989; Shipping Corporation of Polynesia; *b* 15 May 1921; *s* of Viliami Vilai Tupou and Tupou Seini Vaea; *m* 1952, Tuputupu Ma'afu; two *s* three *d*, and one adopted *d* (and one *s* decd). *Educ:* Wesley College, Auckland, NZ. RNZAF, 1942–45; Tonga Civil Service, 1945–53; ADC to HM Queen Salote, 1954–59; Governor of Ha'apai, 1959–68; Commissioner and Consul in UK, 1969; High Comr in UK, 1970–72; Minister for Labour, Commerce and Industries, 1973–91; Actg Dep. Prime Minister, 1986; Prime Minister of Tonga, 1991–2000; Minister of Agric. and Forestry, for Marine and Ports, responsible for Telecommunications, 1991–2000. Chairman: Tonga Telecommunications Commn, 1991–2000; Tonga Broadcasting Commn, 1991–2000; Chm., Tonga Investment Ltd, 1991–. Given the title Baron Vaea of Houma by HM The King of Tonga, 1970. *Recreations:* fishing, tennis. *Heir: e s* Albert Tu'ivanuavou Vaea, *b* 19 Sept. 1957. *Address:* PO Box 262, Nuku'alofa, Tonga. *Died 7 June 2009.*

VALENTINE, Rt Rev. Barry, MA, BD, LTh, DD; Rector, Parish of Salt Spring Island, British Columbia, 1989–95; *b* 26 Sept. 1927; *s* of Harry John Valentine and Ethel Margaret Purkiss; *m* 1st, 1952, Mary Currell Hayes; three *s* one *d*; 2nd, 1984, Shirley Carolyn Shean Evans. *Educ:* Brentwood Sch.; St John's Coll., Cambridge; McGill Univ., Montreal. Curate, Christ Church Cath., Montreal, 1952; Incumbent, Chateauguay-Beauharnois, 1954; Dir, Religious Educn, Dio. Montreal, 1957; Rector of St Lambert, PQ, 1961; Exec. Officer, Dio. Montreal, 1965; Dean of Montreal, 1968; Bishop Coadjutor of Rupert's Land, 1969; Bishop of Rupert's Land, 1970–82; Chaplain, Univ. of British Columbia, 1984–85; Asst Bishop of Maryland, 1986–89. Interim Rector, St Paul's Parish, Washington, 1997. Chancellor, 1970, Res. Fellow, 1983, St John's Coll., Winnipeg. Hon. DD: St John's Coll., Winnipeg, 1969; Montreal Dio. Theol Coll., 1970. *Publications:* The Gift that is in you, 1984. *Recreations:* music, theatre, walking, reading. *Address:* 111 Carlin Avenue, Salt Spring Island, BC V8K 2J5, Canada. *Died 16 Oct. 2009.*

VALENTINE, (Christopher) Robert; former Executive Director, Learning and Skills Council, Nottinghamshire; *b* 28 March 1948; *s* of Robert and Barbara Valentine; *m* 1969, Aline Margaret Wielding; one *s* one *d*. *Educ:* Sheffield Univ. (BA Hons, CertEd, MPhil). Lectr, Granville Coll., Sheffield, 1969; Lectr and Sen. Lectr, Stannington Coll., Sheffield, 1970–81; seconded to Manpower Services Commn, 1981; seconded to Further Education Staff Coll., 1983; joined Notts LEA, 1985; Dep. Dir of Educn, 1991–94, Dir of Educn, 1994–2000, Notts CC. *Recreations:* wildfowling, rough shooting, game shooting, trout fishing, Manchester United FC. *Died 20 Dec. 2007.*

VALLAT, Prof. Sir Francis Aimé, GBE 1982; KCMG 1962 (CMG 1955); QC 1961; Barrister-at-Law; Emeritus Professor of International Law, University of London; *b* 25 May 1912; *s* of Col Frederick W. Vallat, OBE; *m* 1st, 1939, Mary Alison Cockell (marr. diss. 1973; she *d* 2004); one *s* one *d*; 2nd, 1988, Patricia Maria Morton Anderson (*d* 1995); 3rd, 1996, Joan Olive Parham. *Educ:* University College, Toronto (BA Hons); Gonville and Caius Coll., Cambridge (LLB). Called to Bar, Gray's Inn, 1935, Bencher, 1971; Assistant Lecturer, Bristol Univ., 1935–36; practice at Bar, London, 1936–39; RAFVR (Flt Lieut), 1941–45; Asst Legal Adviser, Foreign Office, 1945–50; Legal Adviser, UK Permanent Deleg. to UN, 1950–54; Deputy Legal Adviser, FO, 1954–60, Legal Adviser, 1960–68; Dir of Internat. Law Studies, 1968–76, Reader, 1969–70, Prof., 1970–76, KCL; practice in internat. law, 1968–2001. (On leave of absence) Actg Director, Inst. of Air and Space Law, and Vis. Prof. of Law, McGill Univ., 1965–66. Dir of Studies, Internat. Law Assoc., 1969–73. UK Mem., UN Fact Finding Panel, 1969–. Associate Mem., Institut de Droit International, 1965, elected Mem. 1977, Emeritus Mem., 1999; Member: Internat. Law Commn, 1973–81 (Chm. 1977–78); Permanent Court of Arbitration, 1980–92; Curatorium, Hague Acad., 1982–98 (Vice-Pres., 1993–98). Jt Vice-Pres., David Davies Meml Inst. of Internat. Relations Studies, 1982–2001. Expert Consultant, UN Conf. on Succession of States in respect of Treaties, 1977–78. Dr en dr. *hc*, Lausanne Univ., 1979. *Publications:* International Law and the Practitioner, 1966; Introduction to the Study of Human Rights, 1972; articles in British Year Book of International Law and other journals. *Recreations:* reading, music. *Address:* The Coach House, Church Road, West Lavington, Midhurst, West Sussex GU29 0EH. *Club:* Hurlingham. *Died 6 April 2008.*

VALLINGS, Vice-Adm. Sir George (Montague Francis), KCB 1986; Secretary, Chartered Institute of Management Accountants, 1987–95; *b* 31 May 1932; *s* of Robert Archibald Vallings and Alice Mary Joan Vallings (*née* Bramsdon); *m* 1964, Tessa Julia Cousins; three *s*. *Educ:* Belhaven Hill, Dunbar; Royal Naval College, Dartmouth. Midshipman, HMS Theseus, 1950–51; HMS Scarborough, 1961–63; HMS Defender, 1967–68; HMS Bristol, 1970–73; Naval Adviser and RNLO Australia, 1974–76; Captain F2, HMS Apollo, 1977–78; Dir, Naval Ops and Trade, 1978–80; Commodore, Clyde, 1980–82; Flag Officer: Gibraltar, 1983–85; Scotland and NI, 1985–87. Chm., STA Race Cttee, 1988–96. *Recreation:* family and sport. *Address:* Meadowcroft, 25 St Mary's Road, Long Ditton, Surrey KT6 5EU. *Clubs:* Royal Ocean Racing; Woking Golf. *Died 25 Dec. 2007.*

VAN ALLEN, Prof. James Alfred; Professor of Physics and Head of Department of Physics (of Physics and Astronomy, 1959–85), 1951–85, Carver Professor of Physics, 1972–85, then Regent Distinguished Professor, University of Iowa, USA; *b* Iowa, 7 Sept. 1914; *s* of Alfred Morris and Alma Olney Van Allen; *m* 1945, Abigail Fithian Halsey II; two *s* three *d*. *Educ:* Public

High School, and Iowa Wesleyan Coll., Mount Pleasant, Iowa (BSc); University of Iowa, Iowa City (MSc, PhD). Research Fellow, then Physicist, Carnegie Instn of Washington, 1939–42; Physicist, Applied Physics Lab., Johns Hopkins Univ., Md, 1942. Ordnance and Gunnery Officer and Combat Observer, USN, 1942–46, Lt-Comdr 1946. Supervisor of High-Altitude Research Group and of Proximity Fuze Unit, Johns Hopkins Univ., 1946–50. Leader, various scientific expeditions to Central and S Pacific, Arctic and Antarctic, for study of cosmic rays and earth's magnetic field, using Aerobee and balloon-launched rockets, 1949–57. Took part in promotion and planning of International Geophysical Year, 1957–58; developed radiation measuring equipment on first American satellite, Explorer I, and subseq. satellites (discoverer of Van Allen Radiation Belts of the earth, 1958); has continued study of earth's radiation belts, aurorae, cosmic rays, energetic particles in interplanetary space, planetary magnetospheres. Research Fellow, Guggenheim Memorial Foundation, 1951; Research Associate (controlled thermonuclear reactions), Princeton Univ., Project Matterhorn, 1953–54; Regents' Fellow, Smithsonian Inst., 1981. Acting Ed., Jl of Geophysical Research—Space Physics, 1991–92. Mem., Space Science Bd of Nat. Acad. of Sciences, 1958–70, 1980–83; Fellow: American Phys. Society; Amer. Geophysical Union (Pres., 1982–84), etc; Member: Nat. Acad. of Sciences; RAS; Royal Swedish Acad. of Sciences; Founder Member, International Acad. of Astronautics, etc. Holds many awards and hon. doctorates; Gold Medal, RAS, 1978; US Nat. Medal of Sci., 1987; Crafoord Prize, Royal Swedish Acad. of Scis, 1989; Nansen Award and Prize, Norwegian Acad. of Sci. and Letters, 1990. *Publications:* (ed and contrib.) Scientific Uses of Earth Satellites, 1956, 2nd edn 1958; (jtly) Pioneer: first to Jupiter, Saturn and beyond, 1980; Origins of Magnetospheric Physics, 1983; (ed) Cosmic Rays, the Sun, and Geomagnetism: the works of Scott E. Forbush, 1993; 924 Elementary Problems and Answers in Solar System Astronomy, 1993; numerous articles in learned journals and contribs to scientific works. *Address:* Department of Physics and Astronomy, University of Iowa, Iowa City, IA 52242, USA; 5 Woodland Mounds Road, Iowa City, IA 52245, USA.
Died 9 Aug. 2006.

VAN ALLAN, Richard, CBE 2002; principal bass; Director, National Opera Studio, 1986–2001; *b* 28 May 1935; *s* of Joseph Arthur and Irene Hannah Van Allan; *m* 1976, Elisabeth Rosemary (marr. diss. 1986); one *s* one *d* (and one *s* decd). *Educ:* Worcester College of Education (DipEd Science); Birmingham School of Music. Glyndebourne, 1964; Welsh National Opera, 1968; English National Opera, 1969 (Mem. Bd of Dirs, 1995–98); Royal Opera House, Covent Garden, 1971; performances also: l'Opéra de Paris, Bordeaux, Nice, Toulouse, Rome, Brussels; USA: Boston, San Diego, Phoenix, Houston, Austin, San Antonio, New Orleans, NY; Argentina: Buenos Aires; Spain: Madrid and Barcelona; Hong Kong; Victoria State Opera, Melbourne. Recordings incl. Don Giovanni, Cosi fan tutte (Grammy Award), Luisa Miller, L'Oracolo, Britten's Gloriana. Hon. RAM 1987; Hon. FBC (FBSM 1991). Sir Charles Santley Memorial Award, Musicians' Co., 1996. *Recreation:* shooting. *Died 4 Dec. 2008.*

VANDERFELT, Sir Robin (Victor), KBE 1973 (OBE 1954); Secretary-General, Commonwealth Parliamentary Association, 1961–86; *b* 24 July 1921; *y s* of late Sydney Gorton Vanderfelt, OBE, and Ethel Maude Vanderfelt (*née* Tremayne); *m* 1962, Jean Margaret Becker (*d* 1996), *d* of John and Eve Steward; two *s* (and one step *s* one step *d*). *Educ:* Haileybury; Peterhouse, Cambridge. Served War in India and Burma, 1941–45. Asst Secretary, UK Branch, CPA, 1949–59; Secretary, 1960–61. Secretary, UK Delegn, Commonwealth Parly Conf., India, 1957; as Sec.-Gen., CPA, served as Secretary to Parliamentary Conferences throughout Commonwealth, 1961–85, also attended many area and regional confs and Confs of Commonwealth Speakers

and Clerks. Mem. Internat. Services Bd, RIPA, 1986–89; Governor: Queen Elizabeth House, Oxford, 1980–87; E-SU, 1984–89. *Recreation:* gardening. *Address:* No 6 Saddler's Mead, Wilton, Salisbury, Wilts SP2 0DE. *T:* (01722) 742637. *Clubs:* Royal Commonwealth Society, Royal Over-Seas League, English-Speaking Union. *Died 29 Oct. 2007.*

VANDYK, Neville David, PhD; Editor, Solicitors' Journal, 1968–88; *b* 6 Sept. 1923; *yr s* of late Arthur Vandyk, solicitor, and Constance Vandyk (*née* Berton); *m* 1956, Paula (*née* Borchert); one *d*. *Educ:* St Paul's Sch.; London School of Economics, Univ. of London (BCom 1947, PhD 1950). Admitted Solicitor, 1957. HM Forces, incl. service in India, Burma and Japan, 1942–46; research asst, LSE, 1951–52; with Herbert Oppenheimer, Nathan & Vandyk, Solicitors, 1953–58; Asst Editor, 1958, Managing Editor, 1963, Solicitors' Journal; Member for its duration, Law Society's Constitution Cttee prior to the adoption in 1969 of their revised Bye-Laws, 1966–68. Founder Mem., W London Law Soc. (Pres., 1970–71); Mem. Council, Medico-Legal Soc., 1963–66, Vice-Pres. 1966–67, and 1985–90, Hon. Treas. 1967–85; Founder Mem., Assoc. of Disabled Professionals, Vice-Chm. 1972–80; Mem. for its duration, RBKC's Working Gp on the Disabled and their Families, 1980–81. Governor (nominated by Univ. of London) William Blake County Secondary Sch., 1957–70. Freeman 1962, Liveryman 1963, Worshipful Co. of Solicitors of City of London. Founder's Meml Lecture, British Council for Rehabilitation of the Disabled, 1971; Hon. Prof. of Legal Ethics, Univ. of Birmingham, 1981–83. Life Member: Burma Star Assoc., RAFA; Hon. Life Mem., British Legal Assoc., 1989. *Publications:* Tribunals and Inquiries, 1965; Accidents and the Law, 1975, 2nd edn 1979; (title) National Health Service, in Halsbury's Laws of England, 3rd edn 1959, 4th edn 1982. *Address:* c/o Law Society Records Office, Ipsley Court, Berrington Close, Redditch, Worcs B98 0TD. *Died 22 Aug. 2006.*

VAN MIERT, Karel; President, Nyenrode University, Netherlands Business School, 2000–03; *b* 17 Jan. 1942; *m* 1971, Annegret Sinner; one *s*. *Educ:* Univ. of Ghent; European Univ. Centre, Nancy. With Sicco Mansholt, 1968–70; Asst in Internat. Law, New Univ. of Brussels, 1971–73; Office of Vice-Pres. of EC, 1973–75; Head of Private Office of Minister of Economic Affairs, Belgium, 1977; part-time Lectr on European Instns, Free Univ. of Brussels, 1978; Mem., European Parlt, 1979–85; Mem., Belgian Chamber of Reps, 1985–88; Mem., CEC, later EC, responsible for tranport, 1989–92, for competition, 1993–99; Chm., EU high-level gp on transeuropean networks, 2003. Vice-Chm., Socialist Internat., 1986–89. *Publications:* papers on European integration. *Address:* Puttestraat 10, 1650 Beersel, Belgium. *Died 22 June 2009.*

VANN, (William) Stanley, DMus; *b* 15 Feb. 1910; *s* of Frederick and Bertha Vann; *m* 1934, Frances Wilson (decd); one *s* one *d*. *Educ:* Alderman Newton's Grammar Sch. BMus London; FRCO; ARCM. Asst Organist, Leicester Cath., 1931–33; Chorus Master, Leicester Phil. Soc., 1931–36; Organist and Choirmaster, Gainsborough Parish Ch., Dir of Music, Queen Elizabeth Grammar Sch. and High Sch., Gainsborough, Conductor, Gainsborough Mus. and Orch. Socs, also Breckin Choir, Doncaster, 1933–39; Organist and Choirmaster, Holy Trinity PC, Leamington Spa, Founder-Conductor, Leamington Bach Choir and Warwicks Symph. Orch., and Dir of Music, Emscote Lawn Sch., Warwick, 1939–49. Served War of 1939–45, RA, final rank Captain. Master of Music, Chelmsford Cath., Conductor, Chelmsford Singers, Founder Conductor, Essex Symph. Orch., Prof., Trinity Coll. of Music, London, 1949–53; Master of Music, Peterborough Cath., Conductor, Peterborough Phil. Choir and Orch., 1953–77. Conductor, St Mary's Singers, 1984–2002. Examiner, TCL, 1953–77; Mem. Council and Examr RCO, 1972–98; Mem., ISM; Adjudicator, Brit. Fed. of Festivals, Canadian Fed. Fest. and Hong Kong Fest., 1950–84; Chairman: Peterborough

Music Fest., 1953–2002; Eastern Area Council, British Fedn of Music Festivals, 1982–90; President: Essex Symph. Orch., 1990–; Peterborough Children's Choir, 1994–2002; Gildenburgh Choir, 1997–. Patron, Precincts Soc., 1985–. DMus Lambeth 1971 (for eminent services to church music); Hon. FTCL 1953. *Publications*: twelve settings of Missa Brevis and Missa Sancti Pauli; Billingshurst Mass; three settings of Rite A Communion Service; two settings of Rite B Communion Service; Evening Services in E minor and C major and for Rochester, Gloucester, Hereford, Lincoln, Lichfield, Peterborough, Chester, Salisbury, York, Chichester, Ripon and Worcester Cathedrals; over 100 anthems, motets, carols, organ works and choral arrangements of folk-songs and of Handel; five sets of Preces and Responses and a Collection of Anglican Chants. *Recreations*: railway modelling, painting.
Died 27 March 2010.

van RIEMSDIJK, John Theodore; Keeper of Mechanical and Civil Engineering, Science Museum, 1976–84; author and broadcaster; *b* 13 Nov. 1924; *s* of late Adrianus Kors van Riemsdijk and Nora Phyllis van Riemsdijk (*née* James); *m* 1957, Jocelyn Kilma Afron-Price. *Educ*: University College Sch.; Birkbeck Coll. (BA). Served SOE, 1943–46. Manufacturer of gearing, 1946–54; Science Museum: Asst, 1954; Lectr, 1961; Educn Officer, 1969. Curator i/c setting up Nat. Railway Mus., York, 1973–75. *Publications*: Pregrouping Railways, 1972; Pictorial History of Steam Power, 1980; Compound Locomotives, 1982, 2nd edn 1994; John van Riemsdijk's Contribution (selected articles for Gauge One Model Railway Assoc. journal), 2005; Science Museum Books; contribs to: DDC Publications; Newcomen Soc. Trans, Procs of IMechE. *Recreations*: oil painting, making models. *Address*: Le Moulin du Gavot, St Maximin, 30700 Uzès, Gard, France. *T*: 466227378.
Died 31 Aug. 2008.

VARAH, Rev. Dr (Edward) Chad, CH 2000; CBE 1995 (OBE 1969); Rector, Lord Mayor's Parish Church of St Stephen Walbrook, in the City of London, 1953–2003; Senior Prebendary of St Paul's Cathedral, 1997–2003 (a Prebendary, 1975–97); Founder, The Samaritans (to befriend the suicidal and despairing), 1953, President of London Branch, 1974–86 (Director, 1953–74); President, Befrienders International (Samaritans Worldwide), 1983–86 (Chairman 1974–83); *b* 12 Nov. 1911; *e s* of Canon William Edward Varah, Vicar of Barton-on-Humber, and Mary (*née* Atkinson); *m* 1940, Doris Susan Whanslaw, OBE (*d* 1993); three *s* one *d* (and one *s* decd). *Educ*: Worksop Coll., Notts; Keble Coll., Oxford (Hon. Fellow 1981); Lincoln Theol. Coll.; Exhibnr in Nat. Sci. (Keble); BA Oxon (Hons in PPE), 1933, MA 1943. Secretary: OU Russian Club, 1931; OU Slavonic Club, 1932; Founder Pres., OU Scandinavian Club, 1931–33. Ordained deacon, 1935, priest, 1936; Curate of: St Giles, Lincoln, 1935–38; Putney, 1938–40; Barrow-in-Furness, 1940–42; Vicar of: Holy Trinity, Blackburn, 1942–49; St Paul, Clapham Junction, 1949–53. Staff Scriptwriter-Visualiser for Eagle and Girl, 1950–61; Sec., Orthodox Churches Aid Fund, 1952–69; Pres., Cttee for Publishing Russian Orthodox Church Music, 1960–76; Chm., The Samaritans (Inc.), 1963–66; Pres., Internat. Fedn for Services of Emergency Telephonic Help, 1964–67. Consultant: Forum Magazine, 1967–87, 1998–; Assoc. for Crisis Intervention, China, 1994–. Patron, Outsiders' Club, 1984–2002; Terrence Higgins Trust, 1987–99; Founder, Men Against Genital Mutilation of Girls, 1992. Hon. Liveryman, Worshipful Co. of Carmen, 1977, Worshipful Co. of Grocers, 1994. Freedom, City of Lincoln, 1999. Hon. LLD: Leicester, 1979; St Andrews, 1993; Leeds, 1995; Hon. DSc City, 1993; Hon. DLitt De Montfort, 1998; Hon. DArts Lincs and Humberside, 2000. Roumanian Patriarchal Cross, 1968. Albert Schweitzer Gold Medal, 1972; Louis Dublin Award, Amer. Assoc. Suicidology, 1974; with Befrienders International, Prix de l'Institut de la Vie, 1978; Honra ao Mérito Medal, São Paulo TV, Brazil, 1982; Pride of

Britain Award for Lifetime Achievement, 2000. *Publications*: Notny Sbornik Russkogo Pravoslavnogo Tserkovnogo Peniya, vol. 1 Bozhestveniya Liturgia, 1962, vol. 2 Pt 1 Vsenoshchnaya, 1975; (ed) The Samaritans, 1965; Samariter: Hilfe durchs Telefon, 1966; Vänskap som hjälp, 1971; (TV play) Nobody Understands Miranda, 1972; (ed) The Samaritans in the 70s, 1973, rev. edn 1977; Telephone Masturbators, 1976; (ed) The Samaritans in the 80s, 1980, rev. edn as The Samaritans: befriending the suicidal, 1984, 2nd edn 1988; Before I Die Again (autobiog.), 1992; Limp, 1993. *Recreations*: reading, listening to music, watching videos of science and nature programmes on television. *Clubs*: Athenæum; Oxford Union.
Died 8 Nov. 2007.

VARLEY, Baron *cr* 1990 (Life Peer), of Chesterfield in the County of Derbyshire; **Eric Graham Varley;** PC 1974; DL; Director: Ashgate Hospice Ltd, 1987–96; Cathelco Ltd, 1989–99; Laxgate Ltd, 1991–92; *b* 11 Aug. 1932; *s* of Frank Varley, retired miner, and Eva Varley; *m* 1955, Marjorie Turner; one *s*. *Educ*: Secondary Modern and Technical Schools; Ruskin Coll., Oxford. Apprentice Engineer's Turner, 1947–52; Engineer's Turner, 1952–55; Mining Industry (Coal) Craftsman, 1955–64. National Union of Mineworkers: Branch Sec., 1955–64; Mem. Area Exec. Cttee, Derbyshire, 1956–64. Chm., and Chief Exec., Coalite Gp, 1984–89; N and E Midlands Regl Dir, 1987–89, Midlands and N Wales Regl Dir, 1989–91, Lloyds Bank PLC. MP (Lab) Chesterfield, 1964–84; Asst Govt Whip, 1967–68; PPS to the Prime Minister, 1968–69; Minister of State, Min. of Technology, 1969–70; Chm., Trade Union Gp of Labour MPs, 1971–74; Secretary of State: for Energy, 1974–75; for Industry, 1975–79; Principal Opposition Spokesman on employment, 1979–83; Treasurer, Labour Party, 1981–83. Mem., H of L European Communities Select Cttee, 1991–96. Vis. Fellow, Nuffield Coll., 1977–81. DL Derbys, 1989. *Recreations*: reading, gardening, music, sport. *Address*: c/o House of Lords, SW1A 0PW.
Died 29 July 2008.

VAUGHAN, Prof. Leslie Clifford, FRCVS; Professor of Veterinary Surgery, 1974–91, then Emeritus, and Vice-Principal, 1982–91, Royal Veterinary College; *b* 9 Jan. 1927; *s* of Edwin Clifford and Elizabeth Louise Vaughan; *m* 1951, Margaret Joyce Lawson; one *s* one *d*. *Educ*: Bishop Gore Grammar School, Swansea; Royal Veterinary College, Univ. of London (DVR 1967; DSc 1970; FRVC 1995). FRCVS 1957. Lectr in Veterinary Surgery, RVC, 1951; Reader, London Univ., 1968; Prof. of Vet. Orthopaedics, 1972. Junior Vice-Pres., 1986, Pres., 1987–88, Senior Vice-Pres., 1988–89, 1989–90, RCVS. Vice-Chm., Dogs Home Battersea, 2002–04. Francis Hogg Prize for contribs to small animal medicine and surgery, RCVS, 1962; Simon Award for small animal surgery, 1966; Bourgelat Prize, 1975, British Small Animal Vet. Assoc.; Victory Medal, Central Vet. Soc., 1982; Dalrymple-Champneys Cup and Medal, BVA, 1995. *Publications*: papers in sci jls. *Recreations*: gardening, watching rugby football. *Address*: 26 Burywick, Harpenden, Herts AL5 2AH.
Died 14 Nov. 2008.

VAUGHAN, Prof. Peter Rolfe, FREng; FICE; Professor of Ground Engineering, Imperial College, London, 1987–94, then Emeritus; *b* 10 March 1935; *s* of Ernest Alfred Vaughan and Clarrice Marjorie Vaughan. *Educ*: Luton Grammar Sch.; Imperial Coll., London (BSc Eng, PhD, DSc). FREng (FEng 1991). Industry; postgraduate studies; work on Kainji Dam, Nigeria, 1964–67; academic staff, Imperial Coll., 1969–. Dir, 1982–99, Sen. Consultant, 1999–, Geotechnical Consulting Group. *Publications*: numerous technical papers. *Recreation*: growing old. *Address*: 101 Angel Street, Hadleigh, Ipswich, Suffolk IP7 5DE.
Died 16 May 2008.

VEAL, Group Captain John Bartholomew, CBE 1956; AFC 1940; Civil Aviation Safety Adviser, Department of Trade and Industry, 1972–74, retired; *b* 28 Sept. 1909; *er s* of John Henry and Sarah Grace Veal; *m* 1933, Enid Marjorie Hill (*d* 1987); two *s*. *Educ*: Christ's Hosp. Special trainee, Metropolitan-Vickers, 1926–27; commissioned in RAF as pilot officer, 1927; served in Nos 4 and 501 Squadrons and as flying Instructor at Central Flying School, transferring to RAFO, 1932; Flying-Instructor, Chief Flying Instructor, and Test Pilot, Air Service Training Ltd, 1932–39; recalled to regular RAF service, 1939; commanded navigation and flying training schools, 1939–43; Air Staff No. 46 Transport Group, 1944 and Transport Command, 1945–46 (despatches); released from RAF, 1946, to become Deputy Director of Training, Ministry of Civil Aviation; Director of Air Safety and Training, 1947; Director of Operations, Safety and Licensing, 1952; Deputy Director-General of Navigational Services, Ministry of Transport and Civil Aviation, 1958; Director-General of Navigational Services, Ministry of Aviation, 1959–62; Chief Inspector of Accidents, Civil Aviation Department, Board of Trade (formerly Min. of Aviation), 1963–68; Dir Gen. of Safety and Operations, DTI (formerly BOT), 1968–72. FRAeS 1967 (AFRAeS 1958). *Address:* Woodacre, Horsham Road, Cranleigh, Surrey GU6 8DZ. *T:* (01483) 274490. *Club:* Royal Air Force. *Died 5 Feb. 2009.*

VEALE, Sir Alan (John Ralph), Kt 1984; FREng; Chairman: Rossmore Warwick Ltd, 1986–88; RFS Industries Ltd, 1987–92; Exeter Enterprise Ltd, since 1990; *b* 2 Feb. 1920; *s* of Leslie H. Veale and Eleanor Veale; *m* 1946, Muriel Veale; two *s* (and one *s* decd). *Educ:* Exeter School; Manchester College of Technology (AMCT). FIMechE, FIEE; FREng (FEng 1980). Manufacturing Dir, AEI Turbine Generators Ltd, 1963; Director and General Manager: Heavy Plant Div., AEI, 1966; Motor Control Group, AEI, 1967; Managing Director: GEC Diesels Ltd, 1969; GEC Power Engineering Ltd, 1970–85; Dir, GEC plc, 1973–85; Chm., Fairey Gp, 1987; Dir, Throgmorton Trust PLC, 1986–90. Pres., IProdE, 1985–86. CCMI. Hon. DSc Salford, 1984. *Recreations:* sailing, walking. *Address:* 41 Northumberland Road, Leamington Spa CV32 6HF. *T:* (01926) 424349. *Died 29 March 2006.*

VENKATARAMAN, Ramaswamy; President of India, 1987–92 (Vice-President, 1984–87); *b* 4 Dec. 1910; *s* of Ramaswami Iyer; *m* 1938, Janaki; three *d*. *Educ:* Madras Univ. (MA, LLB). Formerly in practice as a lawyer, Madras High Court and Supreme Court; prominent trade union leader, also political and social worker. Mem., Provisional Parlt, 1950; Mem., Lok Sabha, 1952–57 and (for Madras S), 1977–84; Leader of the House, Madras Legislative Council, and Minister of Industries, 1957–67; Mem., Planning Commn, Madras, 1967–71. Minister of: Finance and Industry, 1980–82; Defence, 1982–84. Sec., Madras Provincial Bar Fedn, 1947–50. Chm., Nat. Research and Develt Corp. Leader, Indian delegation to ILO, 1958, and delegate, UN Gen. Assembly, 1953–61. Chm., Kalakshetra Foundn; Mem. Internat. Jury, Gandhi Peace Prize Award; Trustee: Jawaharlal Nehru Meml Fund; Indira Gandhi Nat. Centre for the Arts. *Address:* 5 Safdarjang Road, New Delhi 110011, India. *T:* (11) 3794366, *Fax:* (11) 3014925. *Died 27 Jan. 2009.*

VERCOE, Rt Rev. Whakahuihui, PCNZM 2000; MBE 1970; Primate and Archbishop of Aotearoa, New Zealand and Polynesia, 2004–06 (Bishop of Aotearoa, 1981–2006); *b* 4 June 1928; *s* of Joseph and Wyness Vercoe; *m* 1951, Dorothy Eivers; three *s*. *Educ:* Torere Primary; Feilding Agricultural High School; College House Theological Coll.; Canterbury Univ. (Cert Soc. Studies, 1975); BTS, LTh 1985; DipSocServ Wellington, 1992. Curate, St John's Church, Feilding, 1951–53; Priest-in-Charge, Wellington Pastorate, 1953–54; Pastor: Wairarapa, 1954–57; Rangitikei, 1957–61; Chaplain: Armed Forces, Malaya, 1961–64; Papakura Military Camp, 1964–65; ANZAC Brigade, Vietnam, 1968–69; Burnham Mil. Camp, 1965–71; Principal, Te Waipounamu Girls' School, 1971–76; Vicar: Ohinemutu Pastorate, 1976–78; Ruatoki-Whakatane, 1978–81; Archdeacon of Tairawhiti and Vicar-General to Bishopric of Aotearoa, 1978–81. Mem., Central Cttee, WCC, Geneva, 1983–90. *Publications:* Te Aomarama series, 1993; (contrib.)

Dictionary of New Zealand Biography, 1995; profiles and Orders of Services. *Recreations:* Rugby, golf, reading, tennis, cricket, fishing. *Died 13 Sept. 2007.*

VERNEY, Rt Rev. Stephen Edmund, MBE 1945; Assistant Bishop, diocese of Oxford, since 1991; *b* 17 April 1919; 2nd *s* of Sir Harry Verney, 4th Bt, DSO and Lady Rachel Verney (*née* Bruce); *m* 1st, 1947, Priscilla Avice Sophie Schwerdt (*d* 1974); one *s* three *d*; 2nd, 1981, Sandra Ann Bailey; (one *s* decd). *Educ:* Harrow School; Balliol College, Oxford (MA). Curate of Gedling, Nottingham, 1950; Priest-in-charge and then first Vicar, St Francis, Clifton, Nottingham, 1952; Vicar of Leamington Hastings and Diocesan Missioner, Dio. Coventry, 1958; Canon Residentiary, Coventry Cathedral, 1964; Canon of Windsor, 1970; Bishop Suffragan of Repton, 1977–85. *Publications:* Fire in Coventry, 1964; People and Cities, 1969; Into the New Age, 1976; Water into Wine, 1985; The Dance of Love, 1989. *Recreations:* conversation and aloneness; music, gardening, travel. *Address:* Cherry Patch, Church Road, Blewbury, Didcot, Oxon OX11 9PY. *Club:* English-Speaking Union. *Died 9 Nov. 2009.*

VERNON, Sir Nigel (John Douglas), 4th Bt *cr* 1914; Director, Bain Hogg Ltd UK Division, subseq. Aon Risk Services UK, 1987–99; *b* 2 May 1924; *s* of Sir (William) Norman Vernon, 3rd Bt, and Janet Lady Vernon (*d* 1973); *S* father, 1967; *m* 1947, Margaret Ellen (*née* Dobell) (*d* 1999); one *s* one *d* (and one *s* decd). *Educ:* Charterhouse. Royal Naval Volunteer Reserve (Lieutenant), 1942–45. Spillers Ltd, 1945–65; Director: Castle Brick Co. Ltd, 1965–71; Deeside Merchants Ltd, 1971–74; Travel Finance Ltd, 1971–87. *Recreations:* golf, shooting, gardening. *Heir:* *s* James William Vernon, FCA [*b* 2 April 1949; *m* 1981, Davinia, *er d* of Christopher David Howard, Ryton, Shrewsbury; two *s* one *d*]. *Address:* Top-y-Fron Hall, Kelsterton, near Flint, N Wales CH6 5TF. *T:* (01244) 830010. *Clubs:* Naval, Army and Navy. *Died 4 Sept. 2007.*

VESTEY, Edmund Hoyle; DL; Director, Vestey Group Ltd, 1993–2000; *b* 19 June 1932; *o s* of late Ronald Arthur Vestey and Florence Ellen McLean, *e d* of Col T. G. Luis, VD; *m* 1960, Anne Moubray (*d* 2007), *yr d* of Gen. Sir Geoffry Scoones, KCB, KBE, CSI, DSO, MC; four *s*. *Educ:* Eton. 2nd Lieut Queen's Bays, 1951; Lieut, City of London Yeomanry. Chairman: Blue Star Line, 1971–96; Associated Container Transportation (Australia), 1979–82, 1985–88. Pres., Gen. Council of British Shipping, later Chamber of Shipping, 1981–82, 1992–94. FRSA. Joint Master, Thurlow Foxhounds; Chm., Masters of Foxhounds Assoc., 1992–96. President: Essex County Scout Council, 1979–87; E of England Agricl Soc., 1995. High Sheriff, Essex, 1977; DL Essex, 1978; DL Suffolk, 1991. *Address:* Little Thurlow Hall, Haverhill, Suffolk CB9 7LQ; Iolaire Lodge, Lochinver, Sutherland IV27 4LU; Sunnyside Farmhouse, Hawick, Roxburghshire TD9 9SS. *Clubs:* Cavalry and Guards, Carlton. *Died 23 Nov. 2007.*

VICARY, Rev. Douglas Reginald; Canon Residentiary and Precentor of Wells Cathedral, 1975–88; *b* 24 Sept. 1916; *e s* of R. W. Vicary, Walthamstow; *m* 1947, Ruth, *y d* of late F. J. L. Hickinbotham, JP, and of Mrs Hickinbotham, Edgbaston; two *s* two *d*. *Educ:* Sir George Monoux Grammar Sch., Walthamstow; Trinity Coll., Oxford (Open Scholar), Wycliffe Hall, Oxford. 1st Class Nat. Sci. 1939; BSc 1939, MA 1942; Diploma in Theology with distinction, 1940. Deacon, 1940; priest, 1941. Curate of St Peter and St Paul, Courteenhall, and Asst Chaplain and House Master, St Lawrence Coll., Ramsgate, while evacuated at Courteenhall, Northampton, 1940–44; Chaplain, Hertford Coll., Oxford, 1945–48; Tutor at Wycliffe Hall, 1945–47; Chaplain 1947–48; Dir of Religious Education, Rochester Diocese, 1948–57; Sec., CACTM Exams Cttee and GOE, 1952–57; Dir, Post-Ordination Training, 1952–57; Headmaster of King's School, Rochester, 1957–75; Chaplain to HM the Queen, 1977–86. Minor Canon, Rochester Cathedral, 1949–52;

Canon Residentiary and Precentor, 1952–57; Hon. Canon, 1957–75. Exam. Chaplain to Bishop of Rochester, 1950–88, to Bishop of Bath and Wells, 1975–87. Mem., Archbishops' Liturgical Commn. 1955–62. Mem. Court, Kent Univ., 1965–75. FRSA 1970. *Publications:* (contrib.) Canterbury Chapters, 1976; contrib. DNB. *Recreations:* music, architecture, walking, reading. *Address:* 8 Tor Street, Wells, Somerset BA5 2US. T: (01749) 679137.   *Died 27 Feb. 2007.*

VICK, His Honour Arnold Oughtred Russell; QC 1980; a Circuit Judge, 1982–2001; a Designated Family Judge, 1991–2001; *b* 14 Sept. 1933; *yr s* of late His Honour Judge Sir Godfrey Russell Vick, QC and Lady Russell Vick, JP, *d* of J. A. Compston, KC; *m* 1959, Zinnia Mary, *e d* of Thomas Brown Yates, Godalming; two *s* one *d. Educ:* The Leys Sch., Cambridge; Jesus Coll., Cambridge (MA). Pilot, RAF, 1952–54. Called to Bar, Inner Temple, 1950, Mem. Gen Council of the Bar, 1964–68; Prosecuting Counsel to the Post Office, 1964–69; Dep. Recorder, Rochester City QS, 1971; a Recorder of the Crown Court, 1972–82; Principal Judge for Civil Matters in Kent, 1990–98. Mem., Lord Chancellor's County Court Rules Cttee, 1972–80; Recorder, SE Circuit Bar Mess, 1978–80. Gov., New Beacon Sch., Sevenoaks, 1982–2000. Master, Curriers' Co., 1976–77. *Publications:* A Hundred Years of Golf at Wildernesse, 1990. *Recreations:* golf, cricket, bridge, flying. *Address:* Little Hermitage, Wildernesse Avenue, Seal, Sevenoaks, Kent TN15 0ED. T: (01732) 761686. *Clubs:* MCC; Hawks (Cambridge); Wildernesse (Captain 1978) (Sevenoaks); Senior Golfers.   *Died 18 Sept. 2008.*

VICKERS, James Oswald Noel, OBE 1977; General Secretary, Civil Service Union, 1963–77 (Deputy General Secretary, 1960–62); *b* 6 April 1916; *s* of Noel Muschamp and Linda Vickers; *m* 1940, Winifred Mary Lambert; one *s* one *d. Educ:* Stowe Sch.; Queens' Coll., Cambridge (Exhibnr, BA Hons Hist., MA). Served War, HM Forces, 1939–45. Warden, Wedgwood Memorial Coll., 1946–49; Educn Officer, ETU, and Head of Esher Coll., 1949–56. Member: Civil Service Nat. Whitley Council, 1962–77 (Chm. Staff Side, 1975–77); TUC Inter-Union Disputes Panel, 1970–77; TUC Non-Manual Workers Adv. Cttee, 1973–75; Fabian Soc. Trade Union and Industrial Relations Cttee, 1964–81 (Chm. 1973–78; Vice-Chm., 1978–79); UCL Coll. Cttee, 1974–79; Council, Tavistock Inst., 1976–80; Employment Appeal Tribunal, 1978–86; CS Appeal Bd, 1978–86. *Publications:* contrib. to Fabian pamphlets. *Recreations:* bird-watching, gardening, travel. *Address:* Heathmount, Rake, near Liss, Hants GU33 7PG. T: (01730) 894029   *Died 1 June 2008.*

VICKERS, Prof. Michael Douglas Allen, OBE 2000; Professor of Anaesthetics, University of Wales College of Medicine (formerly Welsh National School of Medicine), 1976–95, then Emeritus; Vice Provost, University of Wales College of Medicine, 1990–93; *b* 11 May 1929; *s* of George and Freda Vickers; *m* 1959, Ann Hazel Courtney; one *s* one *d* (and one *s* decd). *Educ:* Abingdon Sch.; Guy's Hosp. Med. Sch. (MB, BS). FFARCS. Lectr, RPMS, 1965–68; Consultant Anaesthetist, Birmingham AHA, 1968–76. Chm., N Glamorgan NHS Trust, 1996–2000. Mem. Bd, Faculty of Anaesthetists, 1971–85; President: Assoc. of Anaesthetists of GB and Ireland, 1982–84 (Hon. Sec., 1974–76; John Snow Lectr, 1982); European Acad. of Anaesthesiology, 1988–91 (Sec., 1982–84); World Fedn of Socs of Anaesthesiologists, 1996–2000 (Chm., Exec. Cttee, 1988–92; Sec. Gen., 1992–96). Chm., Retired Members' Forum, BMA, 2004–05. FRSocMed (Pres., Sect. of Anaesthetics, 1998–99; Mem. Council, 2003–06). Hon. FANZCA. Editor: European Journal of Anaesthesiology, 1983–94; Today's Anaesthetist, 1994–2001. *Publications:* (jtly) Principles of Measurement for Anaesthetists, 1970 (2nd edn, as Principles of Measurement, 1981, 3rd edn 1991); (jtly) Drugs in Anaesthetic Practice, 3rd edn 1968, to 8th edn 1999; Medicine for Anaesthetists, 1977, 4th edn 1999; (jtly)

Ethical Issues in Anaesthesia, 1994; (jtly) Objective Structured Clinical Examinations for Anaesthetists, 1995. *Recreations:* music, theatre. *Address:* North Pines, 113 Cyncoed Road, Cardiff CF23 6AD. T: (029) 2075 3698.   *Died 16 Nov. 2007.*

VICKERY, Prof. Brian Campbell, FCLIP; Professor of Library Studies and Director, School of Library Archive and Information Studies, University College London, 1973–83, then Professor Emeritus; *b* 11 Sept. 1918; *s* of Adam Cairns McCay and Violet Mary Watson; *m* 1st, 1945, Manuletta McMenamin; one *s* one *d;* 2nd, 1970, Alina Gralewska. *Educ:* King's Sch., Canterbury; Brasenose Coll., Oxford. MA. Chemist, Royal Ordnance Factory, Somerset, 1941–45; Librarian, ICI Ltd, Welwyn, 1946–60; Principal Scientific Officer, Nat. Lending Library for Sci. and Technology, 1960–64; Librarian, UMIST, 1964–66; Head of R&D, Aslib, 1966–73. *Publications:* Classification and Indexing in Science, 1958, 3rd edn 1975; On Retrieval System Theory, 1961, 2nd edn 1965; Techniques of Information Retrieval, 1970; Information Systems, 1973; Information Science, 1987, 3rd edn 2004; Online Search Interface Design, 1993; (ed) Fifty Years of Information Progress, 1994; Scientific Communication in History, 2000; A Long Search for Information, 2004; articles in professional jls. *Recreations:* reading history, poetry, philosophy; music and theatre; personal computing. *Address:* 9 Clover Close, Cumnor Hill, Oxford OX2 9JH. T: (01865) 863306.   *Died 17 Oct. 2009.*

VIERTEL, Deborah Kerr; *see* Kerr, D. J.

VILJOEN, Marais, DMS 1976; State President of the Republic of South Africa, 1979–84; *b* 2 Dec. 1915; *s* of Gabriel François Viljoen and Magdalena Debora (*née de* Villiers); *m* 1940, Dorothea Maria Brink (*d* 2005); one *d. Educ:* Jan van Riebeeck High Sch., Cape Town; Univ. of Cape Town. After leaving school, employed in Dept of Posts and Telegraphs, 1932–37; on editorial staff, Die Transvaler newspaper, 1937–40; manager, Transvaler book trade business, Potchefstroom, 1940; co-founder and provincial leader of Nat. Youth League, 1940–45; organiser of Transvaal National Party, 1945–49; Member, Provincial Council, Transvaal, 1949–53; Information Officer, Transvaal National Party, several years from 1951; Chairman, Inf. Service of Federal Council, National Party of S Africa, 1969–74; Dep. Chm., Nat. Party, Transvaal, 1966–75. MP Alberton, 1953–76; Dep. Minister of Labour and of Mines, 1958–61; various other ministerial offices, incl. Interior and Immigration, until 1966; Cabinet appointments, 1966–76: Minister of Labour and of Coloured Affairs, 1966–69, also of Rehoboth Affairs, 1969–70; Minister of Labour and of Posts and Telecommunications, 1970–76. President of the Senate, 1976–79. Special Cl., Grand Collar, Order of Good Hope, Republic of S Africa, 1981. *Recreations:* golf, bowls, reading. *Address:* PO Box 5555, Pretoria, 0001, Republic of South Africa.   *Died 4 Jan. 2007.*

VINCENT, Leonard Grange, CBE 1960; FRIBA;; formerly architect and town planner, and Principal Partner, Vincent and Gorbing, Architects and Planning Consultants; *b* 13 April 1914; *s* of late Godfrey Grange Vincent; *m* 1942, Evelyn (*née* Gretton) (*d* 1998); twin *s* one *d. Educ:* Forest House School. FRTPI, Distinction Town Planning (RIBA). Trained as architect in London, 1933, and subsequently as a town planner; experience in private practice and local government. Served War of 1939–45: Royal Engineers (Major); mostly overseas, in Western Desert, and Italian campaigns with 8th Army, 1940–45. Formerly Chief Architect and Planner, Stevenage Development Corporation. *Publications:* various technical and planning articles in technical press. *Recreations:* archaeology, painting. *Address:* Medbury, Rectory Lane, Stevenage, Hertfordshire SG1 4BX. T: (01438) 351175.   *Died 30 April 2007.*

VINE, David Martin; broadcaster and promotions consultant, since 1960; Presenter, ESPN, since 2006; *b* 3 Jan. 1935; *s* of Dorothy and Harold Vine; *m* 1st, 1958,

Shirley (d 1970); one s two d; 2nd, 1972, Mandy; one s. *Educ:* Barnstaple Grammar Sch. Journalist: North Devon Journal-Herald, 1953; Western Morning News, 1956; Westward Television, 1960; presenter, 1965–2001, consultant, 2001–06, BBC TV; programmes include: The Superstars, Question of Sport, Wimbledon, Horse of Year Show, World Snooker Championships, 1976–2000, Ski Sunday, 1977–97, fourteen Summer and Winter Olympic Games, Miss World, Eurovision Song Contest, Jeux Sans Frontières. *Publications:* The Superstars, 1984. *Recreation:* relaxing. *Died 11 Jan. 2009.*

VINELOTT, Sir John (Evelyn), Kt 1978; Judge of the High Court of Justice, Chancery Division, 1978–95; *b* 15 Oct. 1923; *s* of George Frederick Vine-Lott and Vera Lilian Vine-Lott (*née* Mockford); *m* 1956, Sally Elizabeth, *d* of His Honour Sir Walker Kelly Carter, QC; two *s* one *d*. *Educ:* Queen Elizabeth's Grammar Sch., Faversham, Kent; Queens' Coll., Cambridge (MA). War Service, Sub-Lieut RNVR, 1942–46. Called to Bar, Gray's Inn, 1953 (Atkin Scholar; Bencher, 1974; Treas., 1993); QC 1968; practised at the Chancery Bar. Chairman: Insolvency Rules Adv. Cttee, 1984–92; Trust Law Cttee, 1995–. Vice-Pres., Selden Soc., 2002–. *Publications:* essays and articles on Revenue and Administration Law, in specialist periodicals. *Address:* 22 Portland Road, W11 4LG. *T:* (020) 7727 4778. *Club:* Garrick. *Died 22 May 2006.*

VINER, Her Honour Monique Sylvaine, (Mrs M. S. Gray), CBE 1994; QC 1979; a Circuit Judge, 1990–99; *b* 3 Oct. 1926; *d* of late Hugh Viner and Eliane Viner; *m* 1958, Dr Pieter Francis Gray; one *s* three *d*. *Educ:* Convent of the Sacred Heart, Roehampton; St Hugh's Coll., Oxford (MA; Hon. Fellow, 1990). In teaching, publishing, factory and shop work, 1947–50. Called to the Bar, Gray's Inn, 1950, Bencher, 1988. A Recorder, 1986–90. Chm. of five Wages Councils, 1952–94; Mem., Industrial Court, 1976. *Recreations:* talking, reading, tennis, music, piano, walking, gardening, cooking, bird watching, history. *Address:* Old Glebe, Waldron, Heathfield, East Sussex TN21 0RB. *T:* (01435) 863865, *Fax:* (01435) 862599. *Died 10 Oct. 2006.*

VINEY, Hon. Anne Margaret, (Hon. Mrs Viney); JP; barrister; part-time Chairman, Social Security Appeal Tribunals, 1987–96; *b* 14 June 1926; *d* of late Baron Morton of Henryton, PC, MC, and Lady Morton of Henryton; *m* 1947, Peter Andrew Hopwood Viney (*d* 2005); one *s* two *d*. *Educ:* Priorsfield, Godalming, Surrey. Called to the Bar, Lincoln's Inn, 1979. Councillor, Kensington and Chelsea BC, 1960–62. Helped to found London Adventure Playground Assoc., 1962 (Sec. 1962–69); Chm., Consumer Protection Adv. Cttee, 1973–82. JP, 1961; Mem., Inner London Juvenile Court panel, 1961–87 (Chm. 1970). *Recreations:* conversation, playing poetry game. *Address:* Worth House, Worth Matravers, near Swanage, Dorset BH19 3LQ. *Died 4 Oct. 2006.*

VIS, Dr Rudolf Jan; *b* 4 April 1941; *s* of late Laurens and Helena Vis; *m* 1st, 1968, Dr Joan Hanin (marr. diss. 1984); one *s*; 2nd, 2001, Jacqueline Suffling; twin *s*. *Educ:* Univ. of Maryland (BSc Econ 1970); LSE (MSc Econ 1972); Brunel Univ. (PhD Econ 1976). Dutch military service, 1960–64; USAF Base, Spain, 1964–65; Hotel Fleissig, Amsterdam, 1966; Fox Language Inst., USA, 1967; Lectr in Econs, Poly. of East London, later Univ. of East London, 1971–97. MP (Lab) Finchley and Golders Green, 1997–2010. Mem., Council of Europe and WEU, 1997. *Recreations:* walking through London, bridge. *Died 30 May 2010.*

VIVIAN, Michael Hugh; full-time Board Member, 1974–80, and Deputy Chairman, 1978–80, Civil Aviation Authority; *b* 15 Dec. 1919; *s* of Hugh Vivian and Mary (*née* Gilbertson); *m* 1st, 1951, June Stiven (*d* 1980); one *s* one *d*; 2nd, Joy D. Maude. *Educ:* Uppingham; Oxford. Served War: RAF (139 Sqdn), Flying Instructor, Test Pilot, 1940–44. Min. of Civil Aviation, 1945; Private Sec. to Parly Sec. for Civil Aviation, 1945–46; various

operational appts, 1947–61; Dep. Dir of Flight Safety, 1961–66; Dir of Flight Safety, 1966–67; Dir of Advanced Aircraft Ops, 1967–71; Civil Aviation Authority, 1972: Dir-Gen. Safety Ops, 1972–74; Gp Dir, Safety Services, 1974–78; Dir, CSE Aviation Ltd, 1980–82. *Recreations:* golf, vintage cars. *Address:* Willow Cottage, The Dickredge, Steeple Aston, Bicester, Oxfordshire OX25 4RS. *T:* (01869) 347171. *Club:* Royal Air Force. *Died 21 June 2007.*

VONNEGUT, Kurt, Jr; writer; *b* Indianapolis, 11 Nov. 1922; *m* 1st, 1945, Jane Marie Cox (marr. diss. 1979; decd); one *s* two *d*; 2nd, 1979, Jill Krementz. *Educ:* Cornell Univ.; Carnegie Inst. of Technol.; Univ. of Chicago. Served War, US Army, 1942–45 (POW). Reporter, Chicago City News Bureau, 1945–47; PRO, GEC, Schenectady, 1947–50; freelance writer, 1950–65; Lectr, Writers' Workshop, Univ. of Iowa, 1965–67; Guggenheim Fellow, 1967–68; Lectr in English, Harvard, 1970; Dist. Prof., City Coll., New York, 1973–74. Mem., National Inst. of Arts and Letters. *Publications:* Player Piano, 1951; The Sirens of Titan, 1959; Mother Night, 1961; Cat's Cradle, 1963; God Bless You, Mr Rosewater, 1964; Welcome to the Monkey House (short stories), 1968; Slaughterhouse-Five, 1969; Happy Birthday, Wanda June (play), 1970; Between Time and Timbuktu or Prometheus-5 (TV script), 1972; Breakfast of Champions, 1973; Wampeters, Foma and Granfalloons (essays), 1974; Slapstick, or Lonesome No More, 1976; Jailbird, 1979; (with Ivan Chermayeff) Sun Moon Star, 1980; Palm Sunday (autobiog.), 1981; Deadeye Dick, 1982; Galapagos, 1985; Bluebeard, 1988; Hocus Pocus, 1990; Fates Worse Than Death (essays and speeches), 1991; Timequake, 1997; Bagombo Snuff Box, 1999; A Man Without a Country, 2006. *Address:* c/o Donald C. Farber Esq., 14 East 75th Street, #2E, New York, NY 10021, USA. *Died 11 April 2007.*

von SCHRAMEK, Sir Eric (Emil), Kt 1982; architect; Chairman, von Schramek and Dawes Pty Ltd, 1963–91; Consultant to Hames Sharley International, Architects and Planners, 1989–97; *b* 4 April 1921; *s* of Emil and Annie von Schramek; *m* Edith, *d* of Dipl. Ing. W. Popper; one *s* two *d*. *Educ:* Stefans Gymnasium, Prague; Technical Univ., Prague. DiplIngArch; Life Fellow: RAIA; Inst. of Arbitrators and Mediators of Aust. Town Planner, Bavaria, 1946–48; Sen. Supervising Architect, Dept of Works and Housing, Darwin, NT, 1948–51; Evans, Bruer & Partners (later von Schramek and Dawes), 1951–91: work included multi-storey office buildings in Adelaide (Nat. Mutual Centre; State Govt Insce Bldg; Wales House; Qantas Bldg, etc); Wesley House, Melbourne; Westpac House, Hobart; AMP Bldg and Qantas Bldg, Darwin; numerous churches throughout Australia and New Guinea. National Pres., Building Science Forum of Aust., 1970–72; President: RAIA (SA Chapter), 1974–76; Inst. of Arbitrators, Aust. (SA Chapter), 1977–80. Vis. Lectr, Univ. of Adelaide; former Vis. Lectr, S Australian Inst. of Technol. Past National Dep. Chm., Austcare; past Councillor, Council of Professions; past Chm., Commn on Worship and other Depts, Lutheran Church of Australia. Hon. Associate (Arch.), SA Inst. of Technology, 1989. KCSJ 2001 (KSJ 1995). *Publications:* Remembrances: Eric von Schramek and his churches, 2007; contribs and articles in architectural pubns. *Recreations:* music, reading, golf. *Address:* 48 Coopers Avenue, Leabrook, SA 5068, Australia. *T:* (8) 84315263. *Died 6 April 2010.*

von WECHMAR, Baron Rüdiger, Hon. GCVO 1986; Member (FDP) for Germany, European Parliament, 1989–94; *b* 15 Nov. 1923; *s* of Irnfried von Wechmar and Ilse (*née* von Binzer); *m* 1961, Dina-Susanne (Susie) (*née* Woldenga); one *d* (one *s* one *d* of previous marr.). *Educ:* Oberrealschule, Berlin; Univ. of Minnesota, USA (as prisoner of war). MA Journalism. Army, 3rd Reconnaissance Battalion, Western Desert and PoW Camp, 1941–46. Journalist, 1946–58; joined German Foreign Service as Consul, New York, 1958; Dir, German Inf. Centre, NY; Dep. Head, Govt Press and Inf.

Office, Bonn, 1969; State Sec. and Chief Govt Spokesman, 1972; Perm. Rep. to UN, 1974–81; Pres., UN Security Council, 1977–78; Pres., 35th Gen. Assembly, UN, 1980–81; Ambassador to Italy, 1981–83; Ambassador to UK, 1983–88. Commander's Cross, Order of Merit (FRG), 1980; decorations from UK, Sweden, Norway, Japan, Netherlands, Egypt, Mexico, Italy, Romania. Paul Klinger Award, DAG, 1973; UN Peace Gold Medal, 1980. *Address:* Hiltenspergerstrasse 15, 80798 München, Germany.   *Died 17 Oct. 2007.*

von WEIZSÄCKER, Freiherr Carl-Friedrich, Dr Phil; University Professor Emeritus; *b* Kiel, 28 June 1912; *s* of late Baron Ernst von Weizsäcker; *m* 1937, Gundalena (*née* Wille); three *s* one *d. Educ:* Universities of Berlin, Leipzig, Göttingen, Copenhagen, 1929–33. Dr.phil 1933, Dr.phil.habil, 1936, Univ. Leipzig; Asst., Inst. of Theor. Physik, Univ. of Leipzig, 1934–36; Wissenschaftl. Mitarb., Kaiser Willielm Inst., Berlin, 1936–42; Dozent, Univ. of Berlin, 1937–42; pl. ao. Prof. Theor. Physik, Univ. of Strassburg, 1942–44; Kaiser-Wilhelm-Inst., Berlin and Hechingen, 1944–45; Hon. Prof., Univ. Göttingen and Abt. Leiter, Max Planck Inst. für Physik, Göttingen, 1946–57; Ord. Prof. of Philosophy, Univ. of Hamburg, 1957–69. Hon. Prof., Univ. of Munich, and Dir, Max-Planck-Institut on the preconditions of human life in the modern world, 1970–80. Gifford Lecturer, Glasgow Univ., 1959–61. Member: Deutsche Akademie der Naturforscher Leopoldina, Halle; Akademie der Wissenschaften, Göttingen; Joachim-Jungius-Gesellschaft der Wissenschaften, Hamburg; Bayerische Akademie der Wissenschaften, München; Österreichische Akademie der Wissenschaften, Wien; Sächsische Akademie der Wissenschaften zu Leipzig. Hon. Dr theol. Univ. Tübingen, 1977; Univ. Basel, 1989; Hon. Dr iur Free Univ., Amsterdam, 1977; Hon. LLD: Alberta, Canada, 1981; Aberdeen, 1989; Hon. Dr rer. nat. Karl-Marx-Univ., Leipzig, 1987. Dr.phil *hc*: Technische Univ., Berlin, 1987; Aachen, 1988. Max Planck Medal, 1957; Goethe Prize (Frankfurt) 1958; Friedenspreis des deutschen Buchhandels, 1963; Erasmus Prize (with Gabriel Marcel), 1969; Templeton Prize for Progress in Religion (jtly), 1989. Verdienstorden der Bundesrepublik Deutschland, 1959–73; Orden Pour le Mérite für Wissenschaften und Künste, 1961. *Publications:* Die Atomkerne, 1937; Zum Weltbild der Physik, 11th edn, 1970 (English, London, 1952); Die Geschichte der Natur, 7th edn, 1970 (English, Chicago, 1949); Physik der Gegenwart (with J. Juilfs), 2nd edn, 1958 (Engl., 1957); Die Verantwortung der Wissenschaft im Atomzeitalter, 5th edn, 1969; Atomenergie und Atomzeitalter, 3rd edn, 1958; Bedingungen des Friedens, 1963, 5th edn, 1970; Die Tragweite der Wissenschaft, 1964; Der ungesicherte Friede, 1969; Die Einheit der Natur, 1971, 3rd edn, 1972; (ed) Kriegsfolgen und Kriegsverhütung, 1970, 3rd edn, 1971; Voraussetzungen der naturwissenschaftlichen Denkens, 1972, 2nd edn, 1972; Fragen zur Weltpolitik, 1975; Wege in der Gefahr, 1976; Der Garten des Menschlichen, Beiträge zur geschichtlichen Anthropologie, 1977; Deutlichkeit, Beiträge zu politischen und religiösen Gegenwartsfragen, 1978; Der bedrohte Friede, 1981; Wahrnehmung der Neuzeit, 1983; Aufbau der Physik, 1985; Die Zeit drängt. Eine Weltversammlung der Christen für Gerechtigkeit, Frieden und die Bewahrung der Schöpfung, 1986; Bewusstseinswandel, 1988; Bedingungen der Freiheit, 1990; Der Mensch in seiner Geschichte, 1991; Zeit und Wissen, 1992; Der bedrohte Friede-heute, 1994; Wohin gehen wir?, 1994; Grosse Physiker, 1999; *Festschrift:* Einheit und Vielheit, ed Scheibe and Süssmann, 1973. *Recreations:* hiking, chess. *Address:* Alpenstrasse 15, 82319 Starnberg, Germany.   *Died 28 April 2007.*

VREDELING, Hendrikus, (Henk); Member, and Vice-President (responsible for Employment and Social Affairs), Commission of European Communities, 1977–80; *b* 20 Nov. 1924. *Educ:* Agricultural Univ., Wageningen. Member. Second Chamber of States-General, Netherlands, 1956–73; European Parliament, 1958–73; Socio-Economic Adviser to Agricultural Workers' Union, Netherlands, 1950–73; Minister of Defence, Netherlands, 1973–76. Member: Dutch Emancipation Council, 1981–85; Dutch Council on Peace and Security, 1987–94. *Address:* Rembrandtlaan 13A, 3712 AJ Huis ter Heide, Netherlands.   *Died 27 Oct. 2007.*

W

WADDINGTON, Very Rev. Robert Murray; Dean of Manchester, 1984–93, then Emeritus; *b* 24 Oct. 1927; *s* of Percy Nevill Waddington and Dorothy Waddington. *Educ:* Dulwich Coll.; Selwyn Coll., Cambridge (BA 2nd cl. Theol.; MA); Ely Theological Coll. Ordained deacon 1953, priest 1954; Asst Curate, St John's, Bethnal Green, 1953–55; Chaplain, Slade Sch., Warwick, Qld, Aust., 1955–59; Curate, St Luke's, Cambridge, 1959–61; Headmaster, St Barnabas Sch., Ravenshoe, N Qld, Aust., 1961–70; Oxford Univ. Dept of Education, 1971–72; Residentiary Canon, Carlisle Cathedral, and Bishop's Adviser for Education, 1972–77; Gen. Sec., C of E Bd of Education and Nat. Soc. for Promoting Religious Education, 1977–84. Superior, Oratory of the Good Shepherd, 1987–90. *Recreations:* cooking, films, sociology. *Address:* 10B Selsey Court, Selsey Avenue, Bognor Regis, W Sussex PO21 2QZ. *T:* (01243) 862668.
Died 15 March 2007.

WADDY, Rev. Lawrence Heber; Lecturer in Classics, University of California, San Diego, 1969–80; *b* 5 Oct. 1914; *s* of late Archdeacon Stacy Waddy, Secretary of SPG, and Etheldred (*née* Spittal); *m* 1st, 1944, Natalie Robinson; three *d*; 2nd, Laurie. *Educ:* Marlborough Coll.; Balliol Coll., Oxford (Domus Exhibitioner in Classics, Balliol, 1933; 1st Class Hon. Mods., Oxford, 1935; de Paravicini Scholar, 1935; Craven Scholar, 1935; 2nd Class Lit. Hum., 1937; BA 1937; MA 1945). Deacon, 1940; Priest, 1941; Chaplain, RNVR, 1942–46; Assistant Master: Marlborough Coll., 1937–38; Winchester Coll., 1938–42 and 1946–49 (Chaplain, 1946); Headmaster, Tonbridge Sch., 1949–62; Education Officer, School Broadcasting Council, 1962–63; Chaplain to The Bishop's School, La Jolla, California, 1963–67; Headmaster, Santa Maria Internat. Acad., Chula Vista, Calif, 1967–69; Vicar, Church of the Good Samaritan, University City, 1970–74; Hon. Asst, St James', La Jolla, 1974–94. Examining Chaplain to the Bishop of Rochester, 1959–63; Hon. Canon of Rochester, 1961–63; Hon. Canon of San Diego, 1997. Select Preacher: Cambridge Univ., 1951; Oxford Univ., 1954–56. *Publications:* Pax Romana and World Peace, 1950; The Prodigal Son (musical play), 1963; The Bible as Drama, 1974; Faith of Our Fathers, 1975; Symphony, 1977; Drama in Worship, 1978; Mayor's Race, 1980; A Parish by the Sea, 1988; First Bible Stories, 1994; Shakespeare Remembers, 1994; Florence Nightingale, 1995; Jonah, 1995; Bible Drama, 2005. *Address:* 5910 Camino de la Costa, La Jolla, CA 92037, USA; *e-mail:* lawrencewaddy@yahoo.com. *Died 21 March 2010.*

WADE, Prof. Owen Lyndon, CBE 1983; MD; FRCP; FRCPI; FFPM; Professor of Therapeutics and Clinical Pharmacology, 1971–86, then Emeritus, and Pro-Vice-Chancellor and Vice-Principal, 1985–86, University of Birmingham; *b* 17 May 1921; *s* of J. O. D. Wade, MS, FRCS, and Kate Wade, Cardiff; *m* 1948, Margaret Burton, LDS; three *d*. *Educ:* Repton; Emmanuel Coll., Cambridge (Sen. Scholar, 1941); University College Hospital, London (Achison and Atkinson Morley Schol., 1945). Resident Medical Officer, UCH, 1946; Clinical Assistant, Pneumoconiosis Research Unit of the Medical Research Council, 1948–51; Lecturer and Sen. Lecturer in Medicine, Dept of Medicine, University of Birmingham, 1951–57; Whitla Prof. of Therapeutics and Pharmacology, Queen's Univ., Belfast, 1957–71; Dean, Faculty of Medicine and Dentistry, Univ. of Birmingham, 1978–84. Research Fellow, Columbia Univ. at Department of Medicine, Presbyterian Hospital, New York, 1953–54; Rockefeller Travelling Fellowship in Medicine, 1954–55; Consultant, WHO. Chm., Cttee on the Review of Medicines, 1978–84; Chm., Jt Formulary Cttee for British Nat. Formulary, 1978–86.

Mem. GMC, 1981–84. Hon. MD QUB, 1989. *Publications:* (with J. M. Bishop) The Cardiac Output and Regional Blood Flow, 1962; Adverse Reactions to Drugs, 1970, 2nd edn with L. Beeley, 1976; The Romance of Remedies, 1996; When I Dropped the Knife, 1996. *Recreations:* books, travel and sailing. *Address:* 26 West Street, Stratford upon Avon, Warwicks CV37 6DN. *Club:* Athenæum. *Died 10 Dec. 2008.*

WAKEFIELD, Sir Peter (George Arthur), KBE 1977; CMG 1973; HM Diplomatic Service, retired; art management consultant; Life President, Asia House, London, since 2006 (Chairman of Trustees, 1993–2003; Trustee, since 2003); *b* 13 May 1922; *s* of John Bunting Wakefield and Dorothy Ina Stace; *m* 1951, Felicity Maurice-Jones; four *s* one *d*. *Educ:* Cranleigh Sch.; Corpus Christi Coll., Oxford. Army Service, 1942–47; Military Govt, Eritrea, 1946–47; Hulton Press, 1947–49; entered Diplomatic Service, 1949; Middle East Centre for Arab Studies, 1950; 2nd Sec., Amman, 1950–52; Foreign Office, 1953–55; 1st Sec., British Middle East Office, Nicosia, 1955–56; 1st Sec. (Commercial), Cairo, 1956; Administrative Staff Coll., Henley, 1957; 1st Sec. (Commercial), Vienna, 1957–60; 1st Sec. (Commercial), Tokyo, 1960–63; SE Asia Dept, FO, 1964–66; Consul-General and Counsellor, Benghazi, 1966–69; Econ. and Commercial Counsellor, Tokyo, 1970–72; Econ. and Commercial Minister, Tokyo, 1973; seconded as Special Adviser on the Japanese Market, BOTB, 1973–75; Ambassador to the Lebanon, 1975–78, to Belgium, 1979–82. Director: NACF, 1982–92; UK, Trust for Mus. Exhibns, 1992–99. Chairman: Richmond Theatre Trust, 1989–2001; Heritage Co-ordination Gp, 1992–98. *Recreations:* looking at paintings, collecting pots, restoring ruins. *Address:* Lincoln House, 28 Montpelier Row, Twickenham, Middx TW1 2NQ. *T:* (020) 8892 6390; Cortijo Rosa, Periana 29710, Provincia de Malaga, Spain. *T:* (951) 230229. *Club:* Travellers. *Died 1 Dec. 2010.*

WAKEFORD, Air Marshal Sir Richard (Gordon), KCB 1976; LVO 1961; OBE 1958; AFC 1952; Director, RAF Benevolent Fund, Scotland, 1978–89; *b* 20 April 1922; *s* of Charles Edward Augustus Wakeford; *m* 1948, Anne Butler (*d* 2002); two *s* one *d* (and one *d* decd). *Educ:* Montpelier Sch., Paignton; Kelly Coll., Tavistock. Joined RAF, 1941; flying Catalina flying boats, Coastal Comd, operating out of India, Scotland, N Ireland, 1942–45; flying Liberator and York transport aircraft on overseas routes, 1945–47; CFS 1947; Flying Instructor, RAF Coll. Cranwell; CFS Examining Wing; ground appts, incl. 2½ years on staff of Dir of Emergency Ops in Malaya, 1952–58; comdg Squadron Flight, 1958–61; Directing Staff, RAF Staff Coll., 1961–64; subseq.: comdg RAF Scampton; SASO, HQ 3 Group Bomber Comd; Asst Comdt (Cadets), RAF Coll. Cranwell; idc 1969; Comdr N Maritime Air Region, and Air Officer Scotland and N Ireland, 1970–72; Dir of Service Intelligence, MoD, 1972–73; ANZUK Force Comdr, Singapore, 1974–75; Dep. Chief of Defence Staff (Intell.), 1975–78; HM Comr, Queen Victoria Sch., Dunblane; Vice-Chm. (Air), Lowland T&AVR. Trustee, MacRobert Trusts (Chm., 1982–94); Director: Thistle Foundn; Cromar Nominees. President's Medal, Fellowship of Engrg, 1987. CStJ 1986. *Recreations:* golf, fishing. *Address:* Sweethome Cottage, Inchberry Road, Fochabers, Moray IV32 7QA. *T:* (01343) 820436. *Clubs:* Flyfishers', Royal Air Force. *Died 13 Feb. 2007.*

WAKEMAN, Sir Edward Offley Bertram, 6th Bt *cr* 1828, of Perdiswell Hall, Worcestershire; *b* 31 July 1934; *s* of Captain Sir Offley Wakeman, 4th Bt, CBE and his 2nd wife, Josceline Ethelreda (*d* 1996), *e d* of Maj.-Gen.

Bertram Revely Mitford, CB, CMG, DSO; *S* half-brother, 1991, but his name does not appear on the Official Roll of the Baronetage. *Heir:* none.
Died 25 Nov. 2008 (ext).

WALBANK, Frank William, CBE 1993; FBA 1953; MA; Rathbone Professor of Ancient History and Classical Archæology in the University of Liverpool, 1951–77, then Professor Emeritus; Dean, Faculty of Arts, 1974–77; *b* 10 Dec. 1909; *s* of A. J. D. and C. Walbank, Bingley, Yorks; *m* 1935, Mary Woodward (*d* 1987), *e d* of O. C. A. and D. Fox, Shipley, Yorks; one *s* two *d*. *Educ:* Bradford Grammar School; Peterhouse, Cambridge (Hon. Fellow, 1984). Scholar of Peterhouse, 1928–31; First Class, Parts I and II Classical Tripos, 1930–31; Hugo de Balsham Research Student, Peterhouse, 1931–32; Senior Classics Master at North Manchester High School, 1932–33; Thirlwall Prize, 1933; Asst Lecturer, 1934–36, Lecturer, 1936–46, in Latin, Professor of Latin, 1946–51, University of Liverpool; Public Orator, 1956–60; Hare Prize, 1939. J. H. Gray Lectr, Univ. of Cambridge, 1957; Andrew Mellon Vis. Prof., Univ. Pittsburgh, 1964; Myres Memorial Lectr, Univ. of Oxford, 1964–65; Sather Prof., Univ. of Calif (Berkeley), 1971. Pres., Cambridge Phil Soc., 1982–84; Member Council: Classical Assoc., 1944–48, 1958–61 (Pres. 1969–70); Roman Soc., 1948–51 (Vice-Pres., 1953–; Pres., 1961–64); Hellenic Soc., 1951–54, 1955–56; Classical Journals Bd, 1948–66; British Acad., 1960–63; British Sch. at Rome, 1979–87. Mem., Inst. for Advanced Study, Princeton, 1970–71; Foreign Mem., Royal Netherlands Acad. of Arts and Sciences, 1981–; Corresp. Mem., German Archaeol Inst., 1987–. Hon. Mem., Israel Soc. for Promotion of Classical Studies, 1992–; Foreign Hon. Mem., Amer. Acad. of Arts and Scis, 2002. Hon. DLitt Exeter, 1988; Hon. DHL Louisville, 1996. Kenyon Medal, British Acad., 1989; Steven Runciman Prize, Anglo-Hellenic Soc., 1989. Kentucky Col, 1995. *Publications:* Aratos of Sicyon, 1933; Philip V of Macedon, 1940; Latin Prose Versions contributed to Key to Bradley's Arnold, Latin Prose Composition, ed J. F. Mountford, 1940; The Decline of the Roman Empire in the West, 1946; A Historical Commentary on Polybius, Vol. i, 1957, Vol. ii, 1967, Vol. iii, 1979; The Awful Revolution, 1969; Polybius, 1972; The Hellenistic World, 1981; Selected Papers: Studies in Greek and Roman history and historiography, 1985; (with N. G. L. Hammond) A History of Macedonia, Vol. III: 336–167 BC, 1988; Polybius, Rome and the Hellenistic World, 2002; chapters in: The Cambridge Economic History of Europe, Vol. II, 1952, 2nd edn 1987; A Scientific Survey of Merseyside, 1953; (ed jtly and contrib.) Cambridge Ancient History, Vol VII pt 1, 1984, pt 2, 1989, Vol VIII 1989; contribs to: the Oxford Classical Dictionary, 1949; Chambers' Encyclopædia, 1950; Encyclopædia Britannica, 1960 and 1974; English and foreign classical books and periodicals. *Address:* 64 Grantchester Meadows, Cambridge CB3 9JL. T: (01223) 364350. *Died 23 Oct. 2008.*

WALCOTT, Sir Clyde (Leopold), KA 1993; GCM 1991; OBE 1966; Chairman, 1993–97, Chairman of Cricket Committee, 1997–2000, International Cricket Council; *b* 17 Jan. 1926; *s* of late Frank Eyre Walcott and Ruth Walcott (*née* Morris); *m* 1951, Muriel Edith Ashby; two *s*. *Educ:* Harrison Coll., Barbados. Début for Barbados Cricket IX, 1942; played for Barbados, 1942–55, for British Guiana, 1955–64 (record highest score of 314 not out for Barbados *v* Trinidad, 1946); 44 caps for WI, 1947–60 (scored record 5 centuries in single Test series, *v* Australia, 1955). Chief Personnel Officer and Dir, Barbados Shipping and Trading Co. Ltd, 1980–91, retd. Mem., Barbados Public Service Commn, 1982–87. Barbados Employers' Confederation: Pres., 1978–81; Trustee, 1987–91; President: Guyana Cricket Bd of Control, 1968–70; WI Cricket Bd of Control, 1988–93 (Chm., Selection Cttee, 1973–88); Hon. Life Vice-Pres., Barbados Cricket Assoc. *Publications:* Island Cricketers, 1958; Sixty Years on the Backfoot, 1999. *Recreations:* cricket, football. *Address:* Wildey Heights, St

Michael, Barbados, WI. *T:* 4294638. *Clubs:* MCC (Hon. Life Mem.), Surrey (Hon. Life Mem.); Melbourne (Hon. Cricket Mem.). *Died 26 Aug. 2006.*

WALDHEIM, Dr Kurt, Hon. GCMG 1969; President of the Republic of Austria, 1986–92; *b* 21 Dec. 1918; *m* 1944, Elisabeth Ritschel Waldheim; one *s* two *d*. *Educ:* Consular Academy, Vienna; Univ. of Vienna (Dr Jr 1944). Entered Austrian foreign service, 1945; served in Min. for Foreign Affairs; Mem., Austrian Delegn to Paris, London and Moscow for negotiations on Austrian State Treaty, 1945–47; 1st Sec., Embassy, Paris, 1948–51; apptd Counsellor and Head of Personnel Div., Min. of Foreign Affairs, 1951–55; Permanent Austrian Observer to UN, 1955–56; Minister Plenipotentiary to Canada, 1956–58; Ambassador to Canada, 1958–60; Dir-Gen. for Political Affairs, Min. of Foreign Affairs, 1960–64; Permanent Rep. of Austria to UN, 1964–68 (Chm., Outer Space Cttee of UN 1965–68 and 1970–71); Federal Minister for Foreign Affairs, 1968–70, Candidate for the Presidency of Republic of Austria, 1971; Permanent Rep. of Austria to UN, 1970–Dec. 1971; Sec.-Gen. of UN, 1972–81. Guest Prof. of Diplomacy, Georgetown Univ., Washington, 1982–84. Chm., InterAction Council for Internat. Co-operation, 1983–85. Hon. LLD: Chile, Carleton, Rutgers, Fordham, 1972; Jawaharlal Nehru, Bucharest, 1973; Wagner Coll., NY, Catholic Univ. of America, Wilfrid Laurier, 1974; Catholic Univ. of Leuven, Charles Univ., Hamilton Coll., Clinton, NY, 1975; Denver, Philippines, Nice, 1976; American Univ., Kent State, Warsaw, Moscow State Univ., Mongolian State Univ., 1977; Atlanta Univ., Humboldt Univ., Univ. of S Carolina, 1979; Notre Dame, USA, 1980. George Marshall Peace Award, USA, 1977; Dr Karl Renner Prize, City of Vienna, 1978. *Publications:* The Austrian Example, 1971, English edn 1973; The Challenge of Peace, 1977, English edn 1980; Building the Future Order, 1980; In the Eye of the Storm, 1985; Die Antwort, 1996. *Recreations:* sailing, swimming, ski-ing, horseback riding. *Address:* 1 Lobkowitz-Platz, 1010 Vienna, Austria. *Died 14 June 2007.*

WALFORD, John Howard; President, Solicitors' Disciplinary Tribunal, 1979–88; Senior Legal Officer, Office of the Banking Ombudsman, 1991–96; *b* 16 May 1927; *s* of Henry Howard Walford and Marjorie Josephine Solomon; *m* 1953, Peggy Ann Jessel; two *s* two *d*. *Educ:* Cheltenham College; Gonville and Caius College, Cambridge; MA (Hons). Solicitor, 1950; Bischoff & Co.: Senior Partner, 1979–88; Consultant, 1988–91. Mem. Council, Law Society, 1961–69; Governor, College of Law, 1967–88; Senior Warden, City of London Solicitors' Co., 1980–81, Master, 1981–82. Governor, St John's Hosp. for Diseases of the Skin, 1967–82; Chairman: Appeal Cttee, Skin Disease Research Fund, 1974–93; Bd of Management, Petworth Cottage Nursing Home, 1988–93. Mem., Arbitration Panel, The Securities and Futures Authority Consumer Arbitration Scheme, 1988–94. Hon. Mem., British Assoc. of Dermatologists, 1993. Commander, Order of Bernardo O'Higgins, Chile, 1972. *Address:* 75 Onslow Square, SW7 3LS. *Clubs:* Garrick, City Law. *Died 3 Feb. 2008.*

WALKER OF WORCESTER, Baron *cr* 1992 (Life Peer), of Abbots Morton in the County of Hereford and Worcester; **Peter Edward Walker;** MBE 1960; PC 1970; *b* 25 March 1932; *s* of Sydney and Rose Walker; *m* 1969, Tessa, *d* of G. I. Pout; three *s* two *d*. *Educ:* Latymer Upper Sch. Member, National Executive of Conservative Party, 1956–70; Nat. Chairman, Young Conservatives, 1958–60; contested (C) Dartford, 1955 and 1959. MP (C) Worcester, March 1961–1992. PPS to Leader of House of Commons, 1963–64; Opposition Front Bench Spokesman: on Finance and Economics, 1964–66; on Transport, 1966–68; on Local Government, Housing, and Land, 1968–70; Minister of Housing and Local Govt, June–Oct. 1970; Secretary of State for: the Environment, 1970–72; Trade and Industry, 1972–74; Opposition Spokesman on Trade, Industry and

Consumer Affairs, Feb.–June 1974, on Defence, June 1974–Feb. 1975; Minister of Agric., Fisheries and Food, 1979–83; Sec. of State for Energy, 1983–87, for Wales, 1987–90. Chairman: Thornton & Co., 1991–97; Allianz Cornhill Insurance plc (formerly Cornhill Insurance), 1992–2006; English Partnerships, 1992–98; Kleinwort Benson, 1997–99; Vice Chm., Dresdner Kleinwort (formerly Dresdner Kleinwort Benson, later Dresdner Kleinwort Wasserstein), 1999–2009; non-executive Director: British Gas, 1990–96; Dalgety, 1990–96; Tate & Lyle, 1990–2001; LIFFE, 1995–2009; ITM Power plc, 2004–. Pres., British German Chamber of Commerce, 1999–2002 (Vice-Pres., 2002–). *Publications:* The Ascent of Britain, 1977; Trust The People, 1987; Staying Power (autobiog.), 1991. *Address:* Abbots Morton Manor, Gooms Hill, Abbots Morton, Worcester WR7 4LT. *Clubs:* Carlton (Chm., 1998–2004); Worcestershire County Cricket; Worcester Rugby Football. *Died 23 June 2010.*

WALKER, Sir (Alfred) Cecil, Kt 2002; JP; *b* 17 Dec. 1924; *s* of Alfred George Walker and Margaret Lucinda Walker; *m* 1953, Ann May Joan Verrant; two *s*. *Educ:* Methodist Coll. Senior Certificate. In timber business with James P. Corry & Co. Ltd, Belfast, 1941–83, Departmental Manager, 1952. MP (UU) Belfast N, 1983–2001 (resigned seat Dec. 1985 in protest against Anglo-Irish Agreement; re-elected Jan. 1986); contested same seat, 2001. JP Belfast, 1966. *Recreations:* sailing, sea angling. *Address:* 1 Wynnland Road, Newtownabbey, Northern Ireland BT36 6RZ. *T:* (028) 9083 8146. *Club:* Down Cruising. *Died 3 Jan. 2007.*

WALKER, Catherine Marguerite Marie-Therese; French couturier; Founder: The Chelsea Design Company Ltd, 1977; Catherine Walker Ltd, 2003; *b* Pas de Calais, 27 June 1945; *d* of Remy Baheux and Agnes (*née* Lefèbvre); *m* 1st, John Walker (*d* 1975); two *d*; 2nd, Saïd Ismael. *Educ:* Univ. of Lille; Univ. of Aix-en-Provence. Dir, Film Dept, French Inst., London, 1970; Lecture Dept, French Embassy, London, 1971. Hon. Bd Mem., 1999–, and Donor Patron, Gilda's Club; Founder Sponsor, Haven Trust, Catherine Walker Tree of Life (fund-raising mural/sculpture). FRSA 2000. Designer of the Year Award: for British Couture, 1990–91; for Glamour, 1991–92. *Publications:* Catherine Walker, An Autobiography by the Private Couturier to Diana, Princess of Wales, 1998; Catherine Walker, 25 Years 1977–2002, British Couture, 2002. *Address:* Catherine Walker Ltd, 65 Sydney Street, Chelsea, SW3 6PX. *T:* (020) 7352 4626; *e-mail:* catwalk@catherinewalker.com. *Died 23 Sept. 2010.*

WALKER, Sir Cecil; *see* Walker, Sir A. C.

WALKER, Guy; *see* Walker, W. G.

WALKER, James Findlay, QPM 1964; Commandant, National Police College, 1973–76; *b* 20 May 1916; *m* 1941, Gertrude Eleanor Bell (*d* 1993); one *s*. *Educ:* Arbroath High Sch., Angus, Scotland. Joined Metropolitan Police, 1936. Served War, 1943–46: commissioned Black Watch; demobilised rank Captain. Served in Metropolitan Police through ranks to Chief Supt, 1963; Staff of Police Coll., 1963–65; Asst Chief Constable: W Riding Constabulary, 1965–68; W Yorks Constabulary, 1968–70; Dep. Chief Constable, W Yorks Constabulary, 1970–73. *Recreations:* gardening, golf. *Died 2 Oct. 2007.*

WALKER, Patricia Kathleen Randall; *see* Mann, P. K. R.

WALKER, Rt Rev. Peter Knight, MA; Bishop of Ely, 1977–89; an Hon. Assistant Bishop, diocese of Oxford, 1989–95; *b* 6 Dec. 1919; *s* of late George Walker and Eva Muriel (*née* Knight); *m* 1973, Mary Jean, JP 1976, *yr d* of late Lt-Col J. A. Ferguson, OBE. *Educ:* Leeds Grammar Sch. (Schol.); The Queen's Coll., Oxford (Hastings schol., 1938; Cl. 2 Classical Hon. Mods. 1940, Cl. 1 Lit. Hum. 1947; MA Oxon 1947; Hon. Fellow, 1981); Westcott House, Cambridge; MA Cantab by

incorporation, 1958. Served in RN (Lieut, RNVR, Atlantic, Indian Ocean, Mediterranean), 1940–45. Asst Master: King's Sch., Peterborough, 1947–50; Merchant Taylors' Sch., 1950–56. Ordained, 1954; Curate of Hemel Hempstead, 1956–58; Fellow, Dean of Chapel and Lectr in Theology, Corpus Christi Coll., Cambridge, 1958–62 (Asst Tutor, 1959–62), Hon. Fellow, 1978; Principal of Westcott House, Cambridge, 1962–72; Commissary to Bishop of Delhi, 1962–66; Hon. Canon of Ely Cathedral, 1966–72; Bishop Suffragan of Dorchester, and Canon of Christ Church, Oxford, 1972–77. Entered H of L, 1984. Select Preacher: Univ. of Cambridge, 1962, 1967 (Hulsean), 1986; Univ. of Oxford, 1975, 1980, 1990, 1996; Examining Chaplain to Bishop of Portsmouth, 1962–72. Chm., Hosp. Chaplaincies Council, 1982–86. Pres., British Sect., Internat. Bonhoeffer Soc., 1987–96. A Governor, St Edward's Sch., Oxford, 1975–96. Hon. Fellow, St John's Coll., 1989, St Edmund's Coll., 1989, Peterhouse, 2010, Cambridge. Hon. DD Cantab, 1978. *Publications:* The Anglican Church Today: rediscovering the middle way, 1988; contrib. to: Classical Quarterly; Theology, Expository Times, etc. *Address:* Flat 24, Lammas Court, 14 Grantchester Street, Cambridge CB3 9HY. *T:* (01223) 363041. *Died 28 Dec. 2010.*

WALKER, Prof. Peter Martin Brabazon, CBE 1976; FRSE; Hon. Professor and Director, MRC Mammalian Genome Unit, 1973–80; *b* 1 May 1922; *e s* of Major Ernest Walker and Mildred Walker (*née* Heaton-Ellis), Kenya; *m* 1st, 1943, Violet Norah Wright (*d* 1985); one *s* three *d*; 2nd, 1986, Joan Patricia Taylor; one *d*. *Educ:* Haileybury Coll.; Trinity Coll., Cambridge, 1945. BA, PhD. Tool and instrument maker, 1939 (during War); Scientific Staff, MRC Biophysics Research Unit, King's Coll., London, 1948; Royal Society Research Fellow, Edinburgh, 1958; Univ. of Edinburgh: Lectr in Zoology, 1962; Reader in Zoology, 1963; Professor of Natural History, 1966–73. Member: Biological Research Bd, MRC, 1967 (Chm., 1970–72); MRC, 1970–72; Ext. Scientific Staff, MRC, 1980–84; Chief Scientist Cttee, Scottish Home and Health Dept, 1973–85; Chm., Equipment Res. Cttee, Scottish Home and Health Dept, 1973–79; Mem. Council, Imp. Cancer Res. Fund, 1971–94; Chm., Imp. Cancer Res. Fund Scientific Adv. Cttee, 1975–85; Mem., Scientific Adv. Cttee of European Molecular Biology Lab., 1976–81. General Editor: Chambers Science & Technology Dictionary, 1985–94; Chambers Biology Dictionary, 1989; Chambers Air and Space Dictionary, 1990; Chambers Earth Sciences Dictionary, 1991; Larousse Dictionary of Science and Technology, 1994–95; Chambers Dictionary of Science and Technology, 1998–99. *Publications:* contribs to the molecular biology of the genetic material of mammals in: Nature; Jl of Molecular Biology, etc. *Recreations:* gardening, design of scientific instruments, railway history. *Address:* Drumlaggan, The Ross, Comrie, Perthshire PH6 2JT. *T:* (01764) 670303. *Died 16 Jan. 2006.*

WALKER, Raymond Augustus; QC 1988; a Recorder, since 1993; *b* 26 Aug. 1943; *s* of Air Chief Marshal Sir Augustus Walker, GCB, CBE, DSO, DFC, AFC and Lady Walker; *m* 1976, June Rose Tunesi; one *s*. *Educ:* Radley; Trinity Hall, Cambridge (MA). Called to the Bar, Middle Temple, 1966. *Recreations:* golf, tennis, ski-ing, sailing, opera. *Address:* Lombard Chambers, 1 Sekforde Street, Clerkenwell, EC1R 0BE. *T:* (020) 7107 2100. *Clubs:* Garrick; Royal West Norfolk Golf, Sunningdale Golf. *Died 10 April 2009.*

WALKER, Richard John Boileau, CVO 2000; MA; FSA; picture cataloguer; *b* 4 June 1916; *s* of Comdr Kenneth Walker and Caroline Livingstone-Learmonth; *m* 1946, Margaret, *d* of Brig. Roy Firebrace, CBE; one *s* two *d*. *Educ:* Harrow; Magdalene Coll., Cambridge (MA); Courtauld Institute of Art. Active service, RNVR, 1939–45. British Council, 1946; Tate Gallery, 1947–48; Min. of Works Picture Adviser, 1949–76; Curator of the Palace of Westminster, 1950–76; Nat.

Portrait Gallery Cataloguer, 1976–85; Royal Collection Cataloguer, 1985–91; Nat. Trust Cataloguer, 1990–2001. Trustee: Nat. Maritime Museum, 1977–84; Army Museums Ogilby Trust, 1979–90. *Publications:* Catalogue of Pictures at Audley End, 1950 and 1973; Old Westminster Bridge, 1979; Regency Portraits, 1985; Palace of Westminster: a catalogue, 4 vols, 1988; Royal Collection: the 18th century miniatures, 1992; Miniatures in the Ashmolean Museum, 1997; The Nelson Portraits, 1998 (Anderson Prize, Soc. for Nautical Res.); (with Hugh Tait) The Athenæum Collection, 2000; (with Alastair Laing) Miniatures in National Trust Houses, vol. 1, 2003, vol. 2, 2005. *Recreation:* looking at pictures. *Address:* Quint Ash, Chagford, Newton Abbot, Devon TQ13 8EJ. *Clubs:* Athenæum, Oxford and Cambridge.   *Died 6 May 2010.*

WALKER, Sir Robert Cecil, 5th Bt *cr* 1906, of Pembroke House, City of Dublin; *b* 26 Sept. 1974; *s of* Major Sir Hugh Ronald Walker, 4th Bt and of Norna, *er d of* Lt-Comdr R. D. Baird, RNR; *S* father, 2004, but his name does not appear on the Official Roll of the Baronetage. *Heir: b* Roy Edward Walker, *b* 10 Aug. 1977.
                                Died 28 Feb. 2006.

WALKER, (William) Guy, CBE 1993; Chairman, Van den Bergh Foods Ltd, 1985–98; UK National Manager, Unilever plc, 1995–98; *b* 1 March 1936; *s* of Arthur and Margaret Walker; *m* 1st, 1960, Elizabeth Barbette Lawrence (*d* 1980); one *s* two *d*; 2nd, 1983, Marian Farrow Norric, (Her Honour Judge Norrie); two step *d*. *Educ:* Cheltenham Coll.; St John's Coll., Cambridge (MA 1958). Salesman, W. M. Sowry, S Africa, 1960; Trainee, Unilever, 1961–64; Manager: Batchelor Foods, 1964–78; Unilever, Rotterdam, 1978–82; Chm., Batchelor Foods, 1982–85. Mem., BBSRC, 1997–2000. Pres., Food and Drink Fedn, 1995–97. Mem. (C), Sheffield CC, 1967–71. Dir and Treas., Britain in Europe Campaign, 2000–05. Chm., Brighton Festival Trust, 2000–04. Gov., Varndean Coll., Brighton, 2001–. *Recreations:* golf, skiing. *Address:* c/o Van den Bergh Foods Ltd, Manor Royal, Crawley, West Sussex RH10 2RQ. *Club:* Sussex CC (Mem. Cttee).   *Died 26 April 2007.*

WALL, Sir John (Anthony), Kt 2000; CBE 1994; Chairman, Royal National Institute for the Blind, 1990–2000; Partner, Lawrence Graham, solicitors, 1977–93 (Consultant, 1993–95); *b* 4 June 1930; *s* of George and Edith Wall; *m* 1st, 1956, Joan Reeve (*d* 1991); four *s*; 2nd, 1996, Friedel Lawrence (*d* 1999). *Educ:* Worcester Coll. for the Blind; Balliol Coll., Oxford (MA). Legal Officer, NALGO, 1956–74; Partner, Middleton Lewis, 1974–77; Dep. Master of High Court, Chancery Div., 1990–2002. Mem., Supreme Ct Rule Cttee, 1993–99. Pres., European Blind Union, 1996–2003 (Mem. Bd, 1990–2003; Sec.-Gen., 1992–96); Hon. Sec., Soc. of Visually Impaired Lawyers (formerly Blind Lawyers), 1993–. Vice-Pres., British Chess Fedn, 1991–. Hon. DBA Kingston, 2001; DUniv Open, 2003. Gold Medal, IBCA Correspondence Chess Olympiad, 1987. *Publications:* articles in learned periodicals. *Recreation:* chess (Oxford *v* Cambridge 1949 and 1951). *Address:* 36 Broadmead Avenue, Worcester Park, Surrey KT4 7SW. *T:* (020) 8330 2309. *Club:* Reform.
                                Died 1 Dec. 2008.

WALL, Maj.-Gen. Robert Percival Walter, CB 1978; Member, North East Thames Regional Health Authority, 1990–94; Chairman, Essex Family Health Services Authority, 1990–96; *b* 23 Aug. 1927; *s* of Frank Ernest and Ethel Elizabeth Wall; *m* 1st, 1953, Patricia Kathleen O'Brien (marr. diss. 1985); two *s* one *d*; 2nd, 1986, Jennifer Hilary Anning. Joined Royal Marines, 1945; regimental soldiering in Commandos, followed by service at sea and on staff of HQ 3 Commando Bde RM, 1945–58; psc(M) 1959; jssc 1961; Asst Sec., Chiefs of Staff Secretariat, 1962–65; 43 Commando RM, 1965–66; Naval Staff, 1966–68; Directing Staff, JSS Coll., 1969–71; Col GS Commando Forces and Dept of Commandant General RM, 1971–74; course at RCDS 1975; Chief of Staff to Commandant General, RM,

1976–79. Dir, Land Decade Educnl Council, 1982–90. Chm., Essex FPC, 1985–90. Vice-Pres., River Thames Soc., 1983– (Chm., 1978–83); Mem. Council, Thames Heritage Trust, 1980–83; Pres., Blackheath Football Club (RFU), 1983–85; Council, Officers' Pension Soc., 1980–91. Freeman of City of London, 1977; Freeman, Co. of Watermen and Lightermen of River Thames, 1979. FCMI; FRSA 1985. JP: City of London, 1982–92; Essex, 1992. *Recreations:* cricket, rugby, walking, reading. *Address:* c/o Barclays Bank, Metropolitan Essex Group, Barking, Essex IG11 8GY. *Clubs:* Army and Navy, MCC.   *Died 1 April 2007.*

WALL, Sir Robert (William), Kt 1987; OBE 1980; DL; Pro-Chancellor, University of Bristol, 1990–98; *b* 27 Sept. 1929; *s* of William George and Gladys Perina Wall; *m* 1968, Jean Ashworth; one *d* (and one *s* decd). *Educ:* Monmouth School; Bristol Coll. of Technology. HND MechEng; AMRAeS, TechEng. Student apprentice, Bristol Aeroplane Co., 1947–52; commissioned RAF Eng. Branch, and Mountain Rescue Service, 1955–57; management posts with British Aircraft Corp., 1957–67, Chief Ratefixer, 1969–75, Manager, Cost Control, 1975–88. Bristol City Council: Councillor 1959; Alderman 1971; re-elected Councillor 1974; Leader, Cons. Gp, 1974–97; Chm., Public Works Cttee, 1968–72; Dep. Leader, 1971–72, Council Leader, 1983–84. Mem., Bristol Develt Corp., 1993–96. Chairman: Bristol Cons. Assoc., 1979–88; Western Area Provincial Council, Nat. Union of Cons. and Unionist Assocs, 1988–91. Mem. Council, Univ. of Bristol, 1974–98 (Chairman: GP Cttee, 1979–87; Buildings Cttee, 1987–91; Audit Cttee, 1991–98); Governor, Bristol Old Vic Theatre Trust, 1974–87, and 1988–93; Mem. Council, SS Great Britain Project, 1975–; Chm., Rail Users' Cons. Cttee for W England, 1982–98. Mem., Audit Commn, 1986–94. Pres., Bristol Soc. of Model and Experimental Engrs, 1972–2000. FCILT (FCIT 1990). DL Bristol, 2002. Freeman, Co. of Watermen and Lightermen. Hon. MA Bristol, 1982; Hon. DEng Bristol, 1999. *Publications:* Bristol Channel Pleasure Steamers, 1973; Ocean Liners, 1978 (trans. German, French, Dutch), 2nd edn 1984; Air Liners, 1980; Bristol: maritime city, 1981; The Story of HMS Bristol, 1986; Quayside Bristol, 1992; Ocean Liner Postcards, 1998; Brabazon, 1999; Bristol Aircraft, 2000; Shipsides Bristol, 2001; Shipsides Slow Boat to Bristol, 2003. *Recreations:* writing maritime history, collecting postcards, hill walking. *Address:* The Glebe, Winsford, Somerset TA24 7JF. *Clubs:* Bristol Savages, Clifton (Bristol).   *Died 3 Oct. 2009.*

WALLACE, Ian Bryce, OBE 1983; Hon. RAM; Hon. RCM; singer, actor and broadcaster; *b* London, 10 July 1919; *o s* of late Sir John Wallace, Kirkcaldy, Fife (onetime MP for Dunfermline), and Mary Bryce Wallace (*née* Temple), Glasgow; *m* 1948, Patricia Gordon Black, Edenwood, Cupar, Fife; one *s* one *d*. *Educ:* Charterhouse; Trinity Hall, Cambridge (MA). Served War of 1939–45, (invalided from) RA, 1944. London stage debut in The Forrigan Reel, Sadler's Wells, 1945. Opera debut, as Schaunard, in La Bohème, with New London Opera Co., Cambridge Theatre, London, 1946. Sang principal roles for NLOC, 1946–49, incl. Dr Bartolo in Il Barbiere di Siviglia. Glyndebourne debut, Masetto, Don Giovanni, Edin. Fest., 1948. Regular appearances as principal *buffo* for Glyndebourne, both in Sussex and at Edin. Fest., 1948–61, incl. perfs as Don Magnifico in La Cenerentola, at Berlin Festwoche, 1954. Italian debut: Masetto, Don Giovanni, at Parma, 1950; also Don Magnifico, La Cenerentola, Rome, 1955, Dr Bartolo, Il Barbiere di Siviglia, Venice, 1956, and Bregenz Fest., 1964–65. Regular appearances for Scottish Opera, 1965–, incl. Leporello in Don Giovanni, Pistola in Falstaff, Duke of Plaza Toro in The Gondoliers. Don Pasquale, Welsh Nat. Opera, 1967, Dr Dulcamara, L'Elisir d'Amore, Glyndebourne Touring Opera, 1968. Devised, wrote and presented three series of adult education programmes on opera, entitled Singing For Your Supper, for Scottish Television (ITV), 1967–70. Recordings include: Gilbert

and Sullivan Operas with Sir Malcolm Sargent, and humorous songs by Flanders and Swann. Theatrical career includes: a Royal Command Variety Perf., London Palladium, 1952; Cesar in Fanny, Theatre Royal, Drury Lane, 1956; 4 to the Bar, Criterion, 1960; Toad in Toad of Toad Hall, Queen's, 1964. Regular broadcaster, 1944–: radio and TV, as singer, actor and compere; a regular panellist on radio musical quiz game, My Music; acted in series, Porterhouse Blue, Channel 4 TV, 1987. President: ISM, 1979–80; Council for Music in Hosps, 1987–99. Hon. DMus St Andrews, 1991. Sir Charles Santley Meml Award, Musicians' Co., 1984. *Publications:* Promise Me You'll Sing Mud (autobiog.), 1975; Nothing Quite Like It (autobiog.), 1982; Reflections on Scotland, 1988. *Recreations:* reading, sport watching, going to the theatre, singing a song about a hippopotamus to children of all ages. *Address:* c/o Peters, Fraser & Dunlop, Drury House, 34–43 Russell Street, WC2B 5HA. *T:* (020) 7344 1010. *Clubs:* Garrick, MCC; Stage Golfing Society.
Died 12 Oct. 2009.

WALLACE, Sir Ian (James), Kt 1982; CBE 1971 (OBE (mil.) 1942); Director, Coventry Motor and Sundries Co. Ltd, 1986–92; Chairman, SNR Bearings (UK) Ltd, 1975–85; *b* 25 Feb. 1916; *s* of John Madder Wallace, CBE; *m* 1942, Catherine Frost Mitchell, *e d* of Cleveland S. Mitchell; one *s* (one *d* decd). *Educ:* Uppingham Sch.; Jesus Coll., Cambridge (BA). Underwriting at Lloyd's, 1935–39. War Service, Fleet Air Arm: Comdr (A) RNVR, 1939–46. Harry Ferguson Ltd from 1947: Dir 1950; later Massey Ferguson Ltd, Dir Holdings Board until 1970. Coventry Conservative Association: Treas., 1956–68; Chm., 1968–88; Pres., 1988–92; Pres., S Worcs Cons. Assoc., 1992–96; Life Pres., Mid Worcs Cons. Assoc., 1996–; Chm., W Midlands Cons. Council, 1967–70 (Treas., 1962–67); Pres., W Midlands Area Cons. Council. Member: Severn-Trent Water Authority, 1974–82; W Midlands Econ. Planning Council, 1965–75; Vice-Chm., Midland Regional Council, CBI, 1964, Chm., 1967–69; President: Coventry Chamber of Commerce, 1972–74; Birmingham and Midland Inst., 1992–93. Pres., Hereford and Worcester (formerly Worcs County) Rifle Assoc., 1983–2004. *Recreations:* rifle shooting, horology. *Address:* Little House, 156 High Street, Broadway, Worcs WR12 7AJ. *T:* (01386) 852414. *Club:* North London Rifle. *Died 14 May 2009.*

WALLACE, Ian Norman Duncan; QC 1973; *b* 21 April 1922; *s* of late Duncan Gardner Wallace, HBM Crown Advocate in Egypt, Paymaster-Comdr RNR and Eileen Agnes Wallace. *Educ:* Loretto; Oriel Coll., Oxford (MA). Served War of 1939–45: Ordinary Seaman RN, 1940; Lieut RNVR, 1941–46. Called to Bar, Middle Temple, 1948; Western Circuit, 1949. Vis. Scholar, Berkeley Univ., Calif, 1977–; Vis. Prof., Centre of Construction Law and Management, KCL, 1987–. Mem. Editl Bd, Construction Law Jl, 1984–. Medallist, Soc. of Construction Law, 1994. *Publications:* (ed) Hudson on Building and Civil Engineering Contracts, 8th edn 1959, to 11th edn 1995, supplement, 2003; Building and Civil Engineering Standard Forms, 1969; Further Building and Engineering Standard Forms, 1973; The International Civil Engineering Contract, 1974, supplement 1980; The ICE Conditions (5th edn), 1978; Construction Contracts: principles and policies in Tort and Contract, vol. I 1986, vol. II 1996; draftsman, Singapore Institute of Architects Forms of Contract, 1980, and subseq. revisions; contrib. Law Qly Review, Jl of Internat. Law and Commerce, Construction Law Jl, Internat. Construction Law Rev., Arbitration Internat., Singapore Acad. of Law Jl. *Recreations:* keeping fit, foreign travel. *Address:* 53 Holland Park, W11 3RS. *T:* (020) 7727 7640. *Club:* Hurlingham.
Died 2 Aug. 2006.

WALLACE, Lawrence James, OC 1972; CVO 1983; OBC 1990; Deputy Minister to the Premier of British Columbia, 1980–81; *b* Victoria, BC, Canada, 24 April 1913; *s* of John Wallace and Mary Wallace (*née* Parker); *m* 1942, Lois Leeming; three *d. Educ:* Univ. of British Columbia (BA); Univ. of Washington, USA (MEd).

Served War, Lt-Comdr, Royal Canadian Navy Voluntary Reserve, 1941–45. Joined British Columbia Govt, as Dir of Community Programmes and Adult Educn, 1953; Dep. Provincial Sec., 1959–77, Dep. to Premier, 1969–72; Agent-General for British Columbia in UK and Europe, 1977–80. General Chairman: four centennial celebrations, marking founding of Crown Colony of British Columbia in 1858, union of Crown Colonies of Vancouver Is. and British Columbia, 1866, Canadian Confedn, 1867, and joining into confedn by British Columbia in 1871. Former Dir, Provincial Capital Commn; Vice Chm., BC Press Council; Past Chm., Inter-Provincial Lottery Corp., Queen Elizabeth II Schol. Cttee, and Nancy Green Schol. Cttee; Hon. Trustee, British Columbia Sports Hall of Fame. Director: Sen. Citizens Lottery; BC Forest Museum; Adv. Bd, Salvation Army; Canadian Council of Christians and Jews; President: Duke of Edinburgh Awards Cttee, BC; McPherson Playhouse Foundn; Hon. Pres., Univ of Victoria Alumni; Hon. Co-Chm., Operation Eye Sight, BC; Chm., Historic Royal Theatre Renovations and Restoration; Hon. Member: BC High Sch. Basketball Assoc.; BC Recreation Assoc.; Hon. Life Mem., BC Legislative Press Gallery, 1984. Freeman of City of London, 1978. Hon. LLD: British Columbia, 1978; Royal Roads Military Coll., 1994. British Columbia Man of the Year, 1958; Greater Vancouver Man of the Year, 1967; Canadian Centennial Medal, 1967; City of Victoria Citizenship Award, 1971; Silver Jubilee Medal, 1977; 125 Confederation Medal; Good Servant Award, Canadian Council of Christians and Jews, 1980; Peakes Meml Citizenship Award, 1991; (jtly) Canadian and BC Tourism William Van Horne Visionary Award (for Expo '86), 1999. Hon. Chief: Alberni, Gilford and Southern Vancouver Is Indian Bands. Comdr Brother, OStJ, 1969. *Recreations:* gardening, community activities. *Address:* 1345 Fairfield Road, Victoria, BC V8S 1E4, Canada.
Died 12 Jan. 2006.

WALLEY, Keith Henry, FREng, FIChemE; Managing Director, Shell Chemicals UK Ltd, 1978–84; *b* 26 June 1928; *s* of Eric Henry James Walley and Rose Walley; *m* 1950, Betty Warner; one *s* one *d. Educ:* Hinckley Grammar School; Loughborough College (Dip. Chem. 1949, Dip. Chem. Eng. 1952). FIChemE 1972, FREng (FEng 1981). Commissioned RAOC 1949–51. Joined Royal Dutch/Shell Group, 1952; served in Holland, 1952–69; Works Manager, Shell Chemicals, Carrington, 1970–71; Head, Manufacturing Economic and Ops, The Hague, 1972–73; Gen. Man., Base Chemicals Shell International Chemicals, 1974–77; Jt Man. Dir, Shell UK Ltd, 1978–84; Chm., International Military Services, 1985–91 (Dir, 1984–91); Dep. Chm., Johnson Matthey, 1986–91 (Dir, 1985–91). Non-executive Director: John Brown plc, 1984–86; Reckitt & Colman plc, 1986–90. Vis. Prof., UCL, 1986–. Pres., Soc. of Chemical Industry, 1984–86 (Vice-Pres., 1981–84); Member Council: Chem. Ind. Assoc., 1978–84 (Chm., Educn and Sci. Policy Cttee, 1980–84); IChemE, 1983– (Vice-Pres., 1985; Pres., 1987); Royal Acad. (formerly Fellowship) of Engineering, 1984–. CCMI (CBIM 1982). Hon. DSc Loughborough, 1989. *Publications:* papers in chem. jls and planning jls. *Recreations:* the Pyrenees, opera, tennis, ski-ing. *Club:* Athenæum. *Died 15 May 2006.*

WALLS, Prof. Eldred Wright; Emeritus Professor of Anatomy in the University of London at Middlesex Hospital Medical School (Dean, Medical School, 1967–74); Hon. Consultant Anatomist, St Mark's Hospital; *b* 17 Aug. 1912; 2nd *s* of late J. T. Walls, Glasgow; *m* 1939, Jessie Vivien Mary Robb, MB, ChB, DPH (*d* 1999), *o d* of late R. F. Robb and M. T. Robb; one *s* one *d. Educ:* Hillhead High Sch.; Glasgow Univ. BSc, 1931; MB, ChB (Hons), 1934; MD (Hons), 1947, FRSE, FRCS, FRCSE; Struthers Medal and Prize, 1942. Demonstrator and Lectr in Anatomy, Glasgow Univ., 1935–41; Senior Lectr in Anatomy, University Coll. of S Wales and Monmouthshire, 1941–47; Reader in Anatomy, Middlesex Hospital Medical Sch. 1947–49, S. A. Courtauld Prof. of Anatomy, 1949–74; Lectr in

Anatomy, Edinburgh Univ., 1975–82. Past President: Anatomical Soc. of GB and Ireland; Chartered Soc. of Physiotherapy. Lectures: West., UC Cardiff, 1965; Osler, Soc. of Apothecaries, 1967; Astor, Middx Hosp., 1975; Gordon Taylor, RCS, 1976; Struthers, RCSE, 1983. Farquharson Award, RCSE, 1988. *Publications:* (co-editor) Rest and Pain (by John Hilton) (6th edn), 1950; (co-author) Sir Charles Bell, His Life and Times, 1958; contrib. Blood-vascular and Lymphatic Systems, to Cunningham's Textbook Anat., 1981; contrib. to Journal of Anatomy, Lancet, etc. *Recreation:* annual visit to Lord's. *Address:* 19 Dean Park Crescent, Edinburgh EH4 1PH. *T:* (0131) 332 7164. *Clubs:* MCC; New (Edinburgh).
Died 24 March 2008.

WALLWORK, John Sackfield, CBE 1982; Director, Daily Mail and General Trust PLC, 1982–91; Managing Director, Northcliffe Newspapers Group Ltd, 1972–82 (General Manager, 1967–71); *b* 2 Nov. 1918; *s* of Peter Wallwork and Clara Cawthorne Wallwork; *m* 1945, Bessie Bray; one *s* one *d*. *Educ:* Leigh Grammar Sch., Leigh, Lancs. FCIS. General Manager, Scottish Daily Mail, Edinburgh, 1959–62; Asst Gen. Man., Associated Newspapers Gp Ltd, London, 1962–66, Dir, 1973–82. Chm., Press Association Ltd, 1973–74 (Dir, 1969–76); Director: Reuters Ltd, 1973–76; Reuters Founders Share Co. Ltd, 1984–87; Reuters Trustee, 1978–84; Member Press Council, 1974–75; Newspaper Society: Mem. Council, 1967–85; Jun. Vice-Pres. 1975; Sen. Vice-Pres., 1976, Pres., 1977–78. Commander, Order of Merit, Republic of Italy, 1973. *Recreations:* reading, music. *Address:* 14 Bowling Green Court, 2 Brook Street, Chester CH1 3DP. *T:* (01244) 350299.
Died 9 July 2008.

WALTERS, Sir Alan (Arthur), Kt 1983; Professor of Economics, Johns Hopkins University, Maryland, 1976–91; *b* 17 June 1926; *s* of James Arthur Walters and Claribel Walters (*née* Heywood); *m* 1950, Audrey Elizabeth Claxton; one *d*; *m* 1975, Margaret Patricia (Paddie) Wilson. *Educ:* Alderman Newton's Sch., Leicester; University Coll., Leicester (BSc (Econ) London); Nuffield Coll., Oxford (MA). Lectr in Econometrics, Univ. of Birmingham, 1951; Visiting Prof. of Economics, Northwestern Univ., Evanston, Ill, USA, 1958–59; Prof. of Econometrics and Social Statistics, Univ. of Birmingham, 1961; Cassel Prof. of Economics, LSE, 1968–76. Vis. Prof. of Econs, MIT, 1966–67; Vis. Fellow, Nuffield Coll., Oxford, 1982–84; Sen. Fellow, Amer. Enterprise Inst., 1983– (Boyer Lectr, 1983). Vice-Chm. and Dir, AIG Trading Gp Inc., 1991–2003. Economic Adviser to World Bank, 1976–80, 1984–88; Chief Econ. Advr to the Prime Minister (on secondment), 1981–84, 1989. Mem. Commission on Third London Airport (the Roskill Commission), 1968–70. Contested (Referendum) Cities of London and Westminster, 1997. Fellow, Econometric Soc., 1971. Hon. Fellow, Cardiff Univ., 2001. Hon. DLitt Leicester, 1981; Hon. DSocSc: Birmingham, 1984; Francisco Marroquin Univ., Guatemala, 1994. *Publications:* Growth Without Development (with R. Clower and G. Dalton), 1966 (USA); Economics of Road User Charges, 1968; An Introduction to Econometrics, 1969 (2nd edn 1971); Economics of Ocean Freight Rates (with E. Bennathan), 1969 (USA); Money in Boom and Slump, 1970 (3rd edn 1971); Noise and Prices, 1974; (with R. G. Layard) Microeconomic Theory, 1977; (with Esra Bennathan) Port Pricing and Investment Policy for Developing Countries, 1979; Britain's Economic Renaissance, 1986; Sterling in Danger, 1990; The Economics and Politics of Money, 1998. *Recreations:* music, Thai porcelain. *Address:* 3 Chesterfield Hill, W1J 5BJ. *Club:* Political Economy.
Died 3 Jan. 2009.

WALTERS, Rear-Adm. John William Townshend, CB 1984; Chairman, Industrial Tribunals, 1984–98; Deputy Chairman, Data Protection Tribunal, 1985–98; *b* 23 April 1926; *s* of William Bernard Walters and Lilian Martha Walters (*née* Hartridge); *m* 1949, Margaret Sarah Patricia Jeffkins; two *s* one *d*. *Educ:* John Fisher Sch.,

Purley, Surrey. Called to Bar, Middle Temple, 1956. Special Entry to RN, 1944; Secretary: to Flag Officer Middle East, 1962–64; to Naval Secretary, 1964–66; jssc 1967; Supply Officer, HMS Albion, 1967–69; Secretary to Chief of Fleet Support, 1969–72; Chief Naval Judge Advocate, 1972–75; Captain Naval Drafting, 1975–78; Director Naval Administrative Planning, 1978–80; Defence Deleg., UN Law of the Sea Conf., 1980–81; ACDS (Personnel and Logistics), 1981–84, retired. *Address:* 60 Chiltley Way, Liphook, Hants GU30 7HE. *T:* (01428) 723222. *Club:* Royal Naval Sailing Association.
Died 7 May 2008.

WALTERS, Sir Roger (Talbot), KBE 1971 (CBE 1965); RIBA, FIStructE; architect in private practice, 1979–87; *b* 31 March 1917; 3rd *s* of Alfred Bernard Walters, Sudbury, Suffolk; *m* 1st, 1946, Gladys Evans (marr. diss.); 2nd, 1976, Claire Myfanwy Chappell. *Educ:* Oundle; Architectural Association School of Architecture; Liverpool University; Birkbeck Coll., London Univ. (BA 1980, BSc 2000). Diploma in Architecture, 1939. Served in Royal Engineers, 1943–46. Office of Sir E. Owen Williams, KBE, 1936; Directorate of Constructional Design, Min. of Works, 1941–43; Architect to Timber Development Assoc., 1946–49; Principal Asst Architect, Eastern Region, British Railways, 1949–59; Chief Architect (Development), Directorate of Works, War Office, 1959–62; Dep. Dir-Gen., R&D, MPBW, 1962–67; Dir-Gen., Production, 1967–69; Controller General, 1969–71; Architect and Controller of Construction Services, GLC, 1971–78. Hon. FAIA. *Address:* 46 Princess Road, NW1 8JL. *T:* (020) 7722 3740. *Club:* Reform.
Died 11 Sept. 2010.

WALTON, Arthur Halsall, FCA; Partner in Lysons, Haworth & Sankey, 1949–85; *b* 13 July 1916; *s* of Arthur Walton and Elizabeth Leeming (*née* Halsall); *m* 1958, Kathleen Elsie Abram; three *s*. *Educ:* The Leys School. Articled in Lysons & Talbot, 1934; ACA 1940. Military Service, 1939–48: commnd Lancs Fusiliers, 1940. Institute of Chartered Accountants: Mem. Council, 1959; Vice-Pres., 1969; Dep. Pres., 1970; Pres., 1971. *Recreation:* reading. *Address:* 17 Langdale Avenue, Formby, Liverpool L37 2LB.
Died 8 Jan. 2009.

WALTON, David Robert; Member, Monetary Policy Committee, Bank of England, since 2005; *b* 30 May 1963; *s* of Norman Walton and Jean Walton; *m* 1991, Nicola Reeves; two *s*. *Educ:* Durham Univ. (BA); Warwick Univ. (MA). Economist, HM Treasury, 1984–86; Economist, Man. Dir, then Chief European Economist, Goldman Sachs, 1987–2005. Vis. Res. Prof. of Econs, Oxford Univ., 2005–. Chm., Soc. of Business Economists, 2003–. *Address:* External MPC Unit, Bank of England, Threadneedle Street, EC2R 8AH. *T:* (020) 7601 3235, *Fax:* (020) 7601 4610; *e-mail:* david.walton@bankofengland.co.uk.
Died 21 June 2006.

WARBURTON, Col Alfred Arthur, CBE 1961; DSO 1945; DL; JP; Chairman, SHEF Engineering Ltd, 1970–75; Company Director since 1953; *b* 12 April 1913; *s* of late A. V. Warburton. *Educ:* Sedbergh. Served War of 1939–45, with Essex Yeomanry; Lt-Col comdg South Notts Hussars Yeomanry, 1953–58; Hon. Col 1966–76; Col DCRA 49th Inf. Div. TA, 1958–60; ADC to the Queen, 1961–66; Chm., Notts Cttee TA&VR Assoc. for E Midlands, 1970–78. Director, John Shaw Ltd, Worksop, 1953–66. President: East Midlands Area, Royal British Legion, 1976–77, 1981–82, 1986–87, 1991–92; Notts County Royal British Legion, 1979–95. DL 1966, High Sheriff 1968, JP 1968, Notts. *Recreations:* shooting, fishing, gardening. *Address:* Wigthorpe House, Wigthorpe, Worksop, Notts S81 8BT. *T:* (01909) 730357. *Club:* Cavalry and Guards.
Died 17 Jan. 2006.

WARBURTON, Prof. Geoffrey Barratt, FREng; Hives Professor of Mechanical Engineering, University of Nottingham, 1982–89; *b* 9 June 1924; *s* of Ernest McPherson and Beatrice Warburton; *m* 1952, Margaret Coan; three *d*. *Educ:* William Hulme's Grammar School,

Manchester; Peterhouse, Cambridge (Open Exhibition in Mathematics, 1942; 1st cl. Hons in Mechanical Sciences Tripos, 1944; BA 1945; MA 1949); PhD Edinburgh, 1949. FREng (FEng 1985). Junior Demonstrator, Cambridge Univ., 1944–46; Asst Lecturer in Engineering, Univ. Coll. of Swansea, 1946–47; Dept of Engineering, Univ. of Edinburgh: Assistant, 1947–48, Lecturer, 1948–50 and 1953–56; ICI Research Fellow, 1950–53; Head of Post-graduate School of Applied Dynamics, 1956–61; Nottingham University: Prof. of Applied Mechanics, 1961–82; a Pro-Vice-Chancellor, 1984–88. Vis. Prof., Dept of Civil Engrg, Imperial Coll., 1990–97. FRSE 1960; FIMechE 1968. Rayleigh Medal, Inst. of Acoustics, 1982. Editor, Earthquake Engineering and Structural Dynamics, 1988–96 (Associate Editor, 1972–88); Member, Editorial Boards: Internat. Jl of Mechanical Sciences, 1967–92; Internat. Jl for Numerical Methods in Engineering, 1969–96; Jl of Sound and Vibration, 1971–96. *Publications:* The Dynamical Behaviour of Structures, 1964, 2nd edn 1976; research on mechanical vibrations, in several scientific journals. *Address:* 18 Grangewood Road, Wollaton, Nottingham NG8 2SH. *Died 1 Aug. 2009.*

WARD, Prof. Alan Gordon, CBE 1972 (OBE 1959); Procter Professor of Food and Leather Science, Leeds University, 1961–77, then Emeritus; *b* 18 April 1914; *s* of Lionel Howell Ward and Lily Maud Ward (*née* Morgan); *m* 1938, Cicely Jean Chapman (*d* 2004); one *s* two *d*. *Educ:* Queen Elizabeth's Grammar Sch., Wimborne; Trinity Coll., Cambridge (schol.; BA 1935; MA 1940). FInstP 1946; FIFST 1966 (Hon. FIFST 1979); CPhys; FSLTC 1986. Lectr in Physics and Mathematics, N Staffs Technical Coll., 1937–40; Experimental Officer, Min. of Supply, 1940–46; Sen. Scientific Officer, Building Research Station, 1946–48; Principal Scientific Officer, 1948–49; Dir of Research, The British Gelatine and Glue Research Assoc., 1949–59; Prof. of Leather Industries, Leeds Univ., 1959–61. Chm., Food Standards Cttee set up by Minister of Agriculture, 1965–79. Hon. FAIFST 1979. *Publications:* Nature of Crystals, 1938; Colloids, Their Properties and Applications, 1945; The Science and Technology of Gelatin, 1977; papers in Trans. Far. Soc., Jl Sci. Instr, Biochem. Jl, etc. *Recreations:* music, gardening. *Address:* 35 Templar Gardens, Wetherby, West Yorkshire LS22 7TG. *T:* (01937) 584177. *Died 3 Oct. 2007.*

WARD, Most Rev. John Aloysius, OFM Cap; Archbishop of Cardiff, (RC), 1983–2001, then Archbishop Emeritus; *b* 24 Jan. 1929; *s* of Eugene Ward and Hannah Ward (*née* Cheetham). *Educ:* Prior Park College, Bath. Entered Franciscan Friary, 1945; first vows 1946; solemn profession, 1950; ordained Priest, 1953; Diocesan Travelling Mission, Menevia, 1954–60; Guardian and Parish Priest, Peckham, London, 1960–66; Provincial Definitor (Councillor), 1963–69; Provincial Dir of Vocations, 1963–69; Provincial Deleg. to Secular Order of Franciscans, 1966–69; Minister Provincial, 1969–70; General Definitor (Councillor), Rome, 1970–80; Bishop Coadjutor of Menevia, 1980–81; Bishop of Menevia, 1981–83. *Address:* Assisi, 11 Badgers Brook Drive, Ystradowen, Cowbridge, Glamorgan CF71 7TX. *Died 27 March 2007.*

WARD, Sir John (Devereux), Kt 1997; CBE 1973; BSc; CEng, FICE, FIStructE; *b* 8 March 1925; *s* of late Thomas Edward and Evelyn Victoria Ward; *m* 1955, Jean Miller Aitken; one *s* one *d*. *Educ:* Romford County Technical Sch.; Univ. of St Andrews (BSc). Navigator, RAF, 1943–47; student, 1949–53. Employed, Consulting Engineers, 1953–58, Taylor Woodrow Ltd, 1958–79; Man. Dir, Taylor Woodrow Arcon, Arcon Building Exports, 1976–78. MP (C) Poole, 1979–97. PPS to: Financial Sec. to Treasury, 1984–86; Sec. of State for Social Security, 1987–89; Prime Minister, 1994–97. UK Rep. to Council of Europe and WEU, 1983–87, 1989–94. Chm., British Gp, IPU, 1993–94 (Mem., Exec. Cttee, 1982–94). Chm., Wessex Area Conservatives, 1966–69; Conservative Party: Mem., Nat. Union Exec.,

1965–78 (Mem., Gen. Purposes Cttee, 1966–72, 1975–78); Mem., Central Bd of Finance, 1969–78; Vice-Chm., Cons. Trade and Industry Cttee, 1983–84. *Died 26 June 2010.*

WARD, John Stanton, CBE 1985; NEAC; RP 1952; artist and portrait painter; *b* 10 Oct. 1917; *s* of Russell Stanton and Jessie Elizabeth Ward; *m* 1950, Alison Christine Mary Williams; four *s* twin *d*. *Educ:* St Owen's School, Hereford; Royal College of Art. Royal Engineers, 1939–46. Vogue Magazine, 1948–52. ARA 1956, RA 1966, resigned 1997; former Vice-Pres., Royal Soc. of Portrait Painters. Mem. Exec., Nat. Art-Collections Fund, 1976–87. Trustee, Royal Acad. Held exhibitions at Agnews Gallery, Maas Gallery, and at Hazlitt Gooden & Fox, 1994, 1996, 1998. Freeman: City of Hereford, 1991; City of Canterbury. Hon. DLitt Kent, 1982. *Recreation:* book illustration. *Address:* Bilting Court, Bilting, Ashford, Kent TN25 4HF. *T:* (01233) 812478. *Clubs:* Athenæum, Harry's Bar. *Died 14 June 2007.*

WARD, Michael John; Chairman, Charlton Triangle Homes Ltd, 1999–2004 (Director, 1999–2006); *b* 7 April 1931; *s* of late Stanley and Margaret Ward; *m* 1953, Lilian Lomas; two *d*. *Educ:* Mawney Road Jun. Mixed Sch., Romford; Royal Liberty Sch., Romford; Bungay Grammar Sch.; Univ. of Manchester (BA (Admin)). FCIPR. Education Officer, RAF, 1953–57; Registrar, Chartered Inst. of Secretaries, 1958–60; S. J. Noel-Brown & Co. Ltd: O&M consultant to local authorities, 1960–61; Local Govt Officer to Labour Party, 1961–65; Public Relns consultant to local authorities, 1965–70; Press Officer, ILEA, 1970–74 and 1979–80; Public Relns Officer, London Borough of Lewisham, 1980–84; Dir of Information, ILEA, 1984–86; Public Affairs Officer, Gas Consumers Council, 1986–88; Exec. Officer to Rt Hon. Paddy Ashdown, MP, 1988–89; Asst Gen. Sec., Public Relations, Assoc. of Chief Officers of Probation, 1989–95. Administrator, Blackheath Cator Estate Residents Ltd, 1995–2001. Contested: (Lab) Peterborough, 1966, 1970, Feb. 1974; (SDP/Alliance) Tonbridge and Malling, 1987. MP (Lab) Peterborough, Oct. 1974–1979; PPS to Sec. of State for Educn and Science, 1975–76, to Minister for Overseas Develt, 1976, to Minister of State, FCO, 1976–79. Sponsored Unfair Contract Terms Act, 1977. Councillor, Borough of Romford, 1958–65; London Borough of Havering: Councillor, 1964–78; Alderman, 1971–78; Leader of Council, 1971–74. Labour Chief Whip, London Boroughs Assoc., 1968–71; Member: Essex River Authority, 1964–71; Greenwich DHA, 1982–85; Greenwich and Bexley FPC, 1982–85; SE London Valuation Tribunal, 1997–2003; Gov., Medway NHS Foundn Trust, 2007–08. FRSA 1992. *Recreations:* gardens, music, aviation history. *Address:* 55 Bridge House, Valetta Way, Rochester, Kent ME1 1LQ. *Died 25 March 2009.*

WARD, Prof. (William) Reginald, DPhil; FBA 2009; Professor of Modern History, University of Durham, 1965–86, then Emeritus; *b* Chesterfield, Derbys, 23 March 1925; *s* of William Cromwell Gilmour Ward and Clarice Ward (*née* Bowmer); *m* 1949, Barbara Elizabeth Uridge; two *s* one *d*. *Educ:* Devonport High Sch. for Boys; University Coll., Oxford (BA 1946; DPhil 1952). Resident Tutor, Ruskin Coll., Oxford, 1946–49; University of Manchester: Asst Lectr, Lectr, then Sen. Lectr in Modern Hist., 1949–65; Warden, Needham Hall, 1959–65. President: Chetham Soc., 1970–75; Ecclesiastical Hist. Soc., 1972; Vice-Pres., RHistS, 1988–92. Hon. DTheol Basel, 1992. *Publications:* The English Land Tax in the 18th Century, 1952; Georgian Oxford, 1958; Victorian Oxford, 1965; The Early Correspondence of Jabez Bunting, 1972; Religion and Society in England 1790–1850, 1972; Early Victorian Methodism, 1976; Theology, Sociology and Politics: the German Protestant social conscience 1890–1933, 1979; (with R. P. Heitzenrater) The Journal and Diaries of John Wesley, 7 vols, 1988–2003; The Protestant Evangelical Awakening, 1992, 3rd edn 2002; Faith and Faction, 1993;

Parson and Parish in 18th Century Surrey, 1994; Parson and Parish in 18th Century Hampshire, 1995; Christianity under the Ancien Regime, 1999; Kirchengeschichte Grossbritanniens vom 17. bis zum 20. Jahrhundert, 2000; Early Evangelicalism 1670–1789: a global intellectual history, 2006; trans., Besier, The Holy See and Hitler's Germany, 2007; contrib. papers in biographical and theol dictionaries, Festschriften and collective works; contrib. many articles in learned jls incl. English Histl Rev., Jl of Ecclesiastical Hist., Studies in Church Hist., Jl of Modern Hist., etc. *Recreation:* hill walking. *Address:* 21 Grenehurst Way, Petersfield, Hants GU31 4AZ. *T:* (01730) 267834; *e-mail:* w.b.ward@ntlworld.com.   *Died 2 Oct. 2010.*

WARD-JONES, Norman Arthur, CBE 1990; VRD 1959; Chairman, Gaming Board for Great Britain, 1986–92 (Member, 1984–92); *b* 19 Sept. 1922; *s* of Alfred Thomas Ward-Jones and Claire Mayall Lees; *m* 1962, Pamela Catherine Ainslie (*née* Glessing). *Educ:* Oundle Sch.; Brasenose Coll., Oxford. Solicitor 1950. War service, Royal Marines (Captain), 1941–46; RM Reserve, 1948–64, Lt-Col and CO RMR (City of London), 1961–64; Hon. Col 1968–74. Solicitor, Lawrance Messer & Co., Sen. Partner, 1981–85, retired 1989. Hon. Solicitor, Magistrates' Assoc., 1960–85. Chm., East Anglian Real Property Co. Ltd, 1970–80, non-exec. Dir, 1980–89. Pres., Brasenose Soc., 1991–92. JP N Westminster PSD, 1966–92. *Recreation:* wine drinking. *Address:* The Cottage, Barnhorn Manor, 75 Barnhorn Road, Little Common, Bexhill-on-Sea, East Sussex TN39 4QU. *Club:* East India.
Died 24 June 2009.

WARNE, Maj.-Gen. Antony M.; *see* Makepeace-Warne.

WARNER, Prof. Sir Frederick (Edward), Kt 1968; FRS 1976; FREng; Visiting Professor, Essex University, since 1983; *b* 31 March 1910; *s* of Frederick Warner; *m* 1st, Margaret Anderson McCrea; two *s* two *d*; 2nd, Barbara Ivy Reynolds. *Educ:* Bancroft's Sch.; University Coll., London. Pres., Univ. of London Union, 1933. Chemical Engr with various cos, 1934–56; self-employed, 1956–. Joined Cremer and Warner, 1956, Senior Partner 1963–80. Inst. of Chemical Engrs: Hon. Sec., 1953; Pres., 1966; Mem. Council, Engrg Instns, 1962; President: Fedn Européenne d'Assocs nationales d'Ingénieurs, 1968–71 (European Engr, 1987); Brit. Assoc. for Commercial and Industrial Educn, 1977–89; Inst. of Quality Assurance, 1987–90; Vice-Pres., BSI, 1976–80 and 1983–89 (Chm., Exec Bd, 1973–76; Pres., 1980–83). Missions and Consultations in India, Russia, Iran, Egypt, Greece, France. Assessor, Windscale Inquiry, 1977. Chairman: Cttee on Detergents, 1970–74; Process Plant Working Party, 1971–77; Sch. of Pharmacy, Univ. of London, 1971–79; CSTI, 1987–90; Member: Royal Commn on Environmental Pollution, 1973–76; Adv. Council for Energy Conservation, 1974–79; Treasurer, SCOPE (Scientific Cttee on Problems of Environment), 1982–88 (Chm., Environmental Consequences of Nuclear Warfare, 1983–88). Visiting Professor: Imperial Coll., 1970–78 and 1993–2001; UCL, 1970–86; Pro-Chancellor, Open Univ., 1974–79; Member Court: Cranfield Inst. of Technology; Essex Univ.; Fellow UCL, 1967. FREng (FEng 1976). Hon. FRSC 1991; Hon. FICE 1998; Hon. Fellow: UMIST, 1986; Sch. of Pharmacy, 1979. Ordinario, Accademia Tiberina, 1969. Hon. DTech, Bradford, 1969; Hon. DSc: Aston, 1970; Cranfield, 1978; Heriot-Watt, 1978; Newcastle, 1979; DUniv: Open, 1980; Essex, 1992. Gold Medal, Czecho-Slovak Soc. for Internat. Relations, 1969; Medal, Insinöö-riliitto, Finland, 1969; Leverhulme Medal, Royal Soc., 1978; Buchanan Medal, 1982; Environment Medal, Technical Inspectorate of the Rheinland, 1984; Gerard Piel Award, 1991; World Fedn of Engrg Organs Medal for World Engrg Excellence, 1993. Hon. Mem., Koninklijk Instituut van Ingenieurs, 1972; Academico Correspondiente, AI Mexico, 1972. *Publications:* Problem in Chemical Engineering Design (with J. M. Coulson), 1949; Technology Today (ed de Bono), 1971; Standards

in the Engineering Industries, NEDO, 1977; Risk Assessment, Royal Soc., 1982; (ed jtly) Treatment and Handling of Wastes, 1992; (ed jtly) Radioecology since Chernobyl, 1992; (ed) Risk Analysis, Perception and Assessment, 1992; (ed) Quality 2000, 1992; (ed jtly) Nuclear Test Explosions, 1998; papers on Kuwait oil fires, nuclear winter, underground gasification of coal, air and water pollution, contracts, planning, safety, professional and continuous education. *Recreations:* monumental brasses, ceramics, gardens. *Address:* Essex University, Colchester CO4 3SQ. *T:* (01206) 873370. *Club:* Athenæum.   *Died 3 July 2010.*

WARRELL, Ernest Herbert, MBE 1991; Organist: King's College, London, 1980–91; Harrow and Wembley Liberal and Progressive Synagogue, since 1992; St Paul's, Deptford, since 2000; *b* 23 June 1915; *er s* of Herbert Henry Warrell and Edith Peacock; *m* 1952, Jean Denton Denton; two *s* one *d*. *Educ:* Loughborough School. Articled pupil (Dr E. T. Cook), Southwark Cath., 1938; Asst Organist, Southwark Cath., 1946–54; Lectr in Music, KCL, 1953–80; Organist, St Mary's, Primrose Hill, 1954–57; Lectr in Plainsong, RSCM, 1954–59; Organist, St John the Divine, Kennington, SW9, 1961–68; Organist and Dir of Music, Southwark Cathedral, 1968–76; Musical Dir, Gregorian Assoc., 1969–82; Conductor, Lynne Singers, St Paul's, Covent Gdn, 1989–2006. Chief Examiner in Music, Internat. Baccalaureate, 1984–89; Examinations Sec., Guild of Church Musicians, 1991–97. Hon. FTCL 1977; FKC 1979; Hon. FGCM 1988. MA Lambeth, 2006. *Publications:* Accompaniments to the Psalm Tones, 1942; Plainsong and the Anglican Organist, 1943; (ed jtly) An English Kyriale, 1988; (ed jtly) Seriously Silly Hymns, 1999. *Recreation:* sailing. *Address:* 41 Beechhill Road, Eltham, SE9 1HJ. *T:* (020) 8850 7800. *Clubs:* Special Forces, Little Ship; Royal Scots (Edinburgh).
Died 17 Aug. 2010.

WARREN, Alastair Kennedy, TD 1953; Editor, Dumfries and Galloway Standard, 1976–86; *b* 17 July 1922; *s* of John Russell Warren, MC, and Jean Cousin Warren; *m* 1952, Ann Lindsay Maclean; two *s*. *Educ:* Glasgow Acad.; Loretto; Glasgow Univ. (MA Hons). Served War of 1939–45; HLI, 1940–46; Major, 1946. Served 5/6th Bn HLI (TA) 1947–63. Sales Clerk, Stewarts & Lloyds Ltd, 1950–53; joined editorial staff of The Glasgow Herald as Sub-Editor, 1954; Leader Writer, 1955–58; Features Editor, 1958–59; Commercial Editor, 1960–64; City Editor, 1964–65; Editor, 1965–74; Regional Editor, Scottish and Universal Newspapers Ltd, 1974–76. Provost of New Galloway and Kells Community Council, 1978–81; Chairman: Loch Arthur Village Community (Camphill Movt), 1985–92; Nithsdale Council of Voluntary Service, 1988–91 (Pres., 1992–). Hon. Pres., Galloway Community Coll *Publications:* Pebbles on the Beach (poems), 1999; Then and Now and Next (poems), 2000; Haiku for All Seasons, 2001; contribs to various periodicals. *Recreations:* swimming, hill walking, marathon running. *Address:* Rathan, New Galloway, Castle Douglas DG7 3RN. *T:* (01644) 420257.   *Died 25 March 2006.*

WARREN, Sir (Brian) Charles (Pennefather), 9th Bt *cr* 1784; *b* 4 June 1923; *o s* of Sir Thomas Richard Pennefather Warren, 8th Bt, CBE; *S* father, 1961; *m* 1st, 1976, Cola (marr. diss. 1983), *d* of Captain E. L. Cazenove, Great Dalby, Leics; 2nd, 1996, Rosemary, *d* of B. W. Day, OBE, Hovingham, Yorks. *Educ:* Wellington College. Served War of 1939–45; Lt, 1943–45, 2nd Bn Irish Guards. *Recreation:* gardening. *Address:* Saffron Hill, Doneraile, Co. Cork, Ireland.
Died 24 June 2006 (dormant)

WARREN, Jack Hamilton, OC 1982; Principal Trade Policy Advisor, Government of Quebec, 1986–94; *b* 10 April 1921; *s* of Tom Hamilton Warren and Olive Sykes (*née* Horsfall); *m* 1953, Hilary Joan Titterington; two *s* two *d*. *Educ:* Queen's Univ., Kingston, (BA). Served War, with Royal Canadian Navy. Public Service, 1945–79: Dept of External Affairs; Dept of Finance; diplomatic

postings in Ottawa, London, Washington, Paris and Geneva; Asst Dep. Minister of Trade and Commerce, 1958; Chm., Council of Representatives, 1960, and Chm., Contracting Parties, 1962 and 1964, GATT; Dep. Minister: Dept of Trade and Commerce, 1964; Dept of Industry, Trade and Commerce, 1969; High Comr for Canada in London, 1971–74; Ambassador to USA, 1975–77; Ambassador, and Canadian Co-ordinator for the Multilateral Trade Negotiations, 1977–79; Vice-Chm., Bank of Montreal, 1979–86; Director: Royal Insurance Co. of Canada, 1980–91; Pratt and Whitney, Canada, 1983–91; PACCAR of Canada Ltd, 1984–91. Dep. Chm. (N America), Trilateral Commn, 1985–91. Hon. LLD Queen's, Ont, 1974. Outstanding Achievement Award, Public Service of Canada, 1975. *Recreations:* fishing, gardening, ski-ing. *Address:* Apt 301C, 999 North River Road, Ottawa, ON K1K 3V5, Canada. *Clubs:* Rideau (Ottawa); White Pine Fishing (Canada).
Died 2 April 2008.

WASSERSTEIN, Bruce Jay; Chief Executive, since 2001, and Chairman, since 2005, Lazards; *b* 25 Dec. 1947; *s* of Morris and Lola Wasserstein; *m* 1st, Laura (marr. diss. 1974); 2nd, Christine Parrott (marr. diss. 1992); two *s* one *d*; 3rd, 1996, Claude Elizabeth Becker (marr. diss. 2008); two *s* and one adopted *d*; one *d*; 4th, 2009, Angela Chao. *Educ:* Univ. of Michigan (BA Hons 1967); Harvard Univ. (MBA with high distinction 1971; JD cl 1971); Darwin Coll., Cambridge (Dip. Law 1972). Associate, Cravath, Swaine and Moore, 1972–77; Man. Dir, First Boston Corp., 1977–88; Chm. and CEO, Wasserstein Perella & Co., 1988–2000; Exec. Chm., Dresdner Kleinwort Wasserstein, 2000–01. *Publications:* Corporate Finance Law: a guide for the executive, 1978; Big Deal: 2000 and beyond, 2000. *Address:* Lazards, 30 Rockefeller Plaza, New York, NY 10020, USA. *T:* (212) 6326000. *Died 14 Oct. 2009.*

WATERHOUSE, Keith Spencer, CBE 1991; FRSL; writer; *b* 6 Feb. 1929; 4th *s* of Ernest and Elsie Edith Waterhouse; *m* 1984, Stella Bingham (marr. diss. 1989); one *s* one *d* (and one *d* decd) from previous marriage. *Educ:* Leeds. Journalist in Leeds and London, 1950–; Columnist with: Daily Mirror, 1970–86; Daily Mail, 1986–; Contributor to various periodicals; Mem. Punch Table, 1979. Mem., Kingman Cttee on Teaching of English Language, 1987–88. Hon. Fellow, Leeds Metropolitan Univ. (formerly Poly.), 1991. Granada Columnist of the Year Award, 1970; IPC Descriptive Writer of the Year Award, 1970; IPC Columnist of the Year Award, 1973; British Press Awards Columnist of the Year, 1978, 1991; Granada Special Quarter Century Award, 1982; Edgar Wallace Trophy, London Press Club, 1996; Gerald Barry Lifetime Achievement Award, What the Papers Say awards, 2000. *Films* (with Willis Hall) include: Billy Liar; Whistle Down the Wind; A Kind of Loving; Lock Up Your Daughters. Plays: Mr and Mrs Nobody, 1986; Jeffrey Bernard is Unwell, 1989 (Evening Standard Best Comedy Award, 1990), revived 1999; Bookends, 1990; Our Song, 1992; Good Grief, 1998; Bing-Bong!, 1999; The Last Page, 2007; *plays* with Willis Hall include: Billy Liar, 1960 (from which musical Billy was adapted, 1974); Celebration, 1961; All Things Bright and Beautiful, 1963; Say Who You Are, 1965; Whoops-a-Daisy, 1968; Children's Day, 1969; Who's Who, 1972; The Card (musical), 1973; Saturday, Sunday, Monday (adaptation from de Filippo), 1973; Filumena (adaptation from de Filippo), 1977; Worzel Gummidge, 1981; Budgie (musical), 1988. *TV series:* Budgie, Queenie's Castle, The Upper Crusts, Billy Liar, The Upchat Line, The Upchat Connection, Worzel Gummidge, West End Tales, The Happy Apple, Charters and Caldicott, Andy Capp; *TV films:* Charlie Muffin, 1983; This Office Life, 1985; The Great Paper Chase, 1988. *Publications: novels:* There is a Happy Land, 1957; Billy Liar, 1959; Jubb, 1963; The Bucket Shop, 1968; Billy Liar on the Moon, 1975; Office Life, 1978; Maggie Muggins, 1981; In the Mood, 1983; Thinks, 1984; Our Song, 1988; Bimbo, 1990; Unsweet Charity, 1992; Good Grief, 1997; Soho, 2001; Palace Pier, 2003; *plays:* Jeffrey

Bernard Is Unwell and other plays, 1991; (with Willis Hall) include: Billy Liar, 1960; Celebration, 1961; All Things Bright and Beautiful, 1963; Say Who You Are, 1965; Who's Who, 1974; Saturday, Sunday, Monday (adaptation from de Filippo), 1974; Filumena (adaptation from de Filippo), 1977; *general:* (with Guy Deghy) Café Royal, 1956; (ed) Writers' Theatre, 1967; The Passing of The Third-floor Buck, 1974; Mondays, Thursdays, 1976; Rhubarb, Rhubarb, 1979; Daily Mirror Style, 1980, rev. and expanded edn, Newspaper Style, 1989; Fanny Peculiar, 1983; Mrs Pooter's Diary, 1983; Waterhouse At Large, 1985; Collected Letters of a Nobody, 1986; The Theory and Practice of Lunch, 1986; The Theory and Practice of Travel, 1989; English Our English, 1991; Sharon & Tracy & The Rest, 1992; City Lights, 1994; Streets Ahead, 1995. *Recreation:* lunch. *Address:* 84 Coleherne Court, Old Brompton Road, SW5 0EE. *Club:* Garrick. *Died 4 Sept. 2009.*

WATERLOW, Prof. John Conrad, CMG 1970; MD; ScD; FRCP; FRS 1982; FRGS; Professor of Human Nutrition, London School of Hygiene and Tropical Medicine, 1970–82, then Emeritus; *b* 13 June 1916; *o s* of Sir Sydney Waterlow, KCMG, CBE, HM Diplomatic Service; *m* 1939, Angela Pauline Cecil Gray; two *s* one *d*. *Educ:* Eton Coll.; Trinity Coll., Cambridge (MD, ScD); London Hosp. Med. College. Mem., Scientific Staff, MRC, 1942; Dir, MRC Tropical Metabolism Research Unit, Univ. of the West Indies, 1954–70. For. Associate Mem., Nat. Acad. of Scis, USA, 1992. *Publications:* numerous papers on protein malnutrition and protein metabolism. *Recreation:* mountain walking. *Address:* 15 Hillgate Street, W8 7SP. *Club:* Savile. *Died 19 Oct. 2010.*

WATERTON, Sqdn Leader William Arthur, AFC 1942, Bar 1946; GM 1952; *b* Edmonton, Canada, 18 March 1916. *Educ:* Royal Military College of Canada; University of Alberta. Cadet Royal Military College of Canada, 1934–37; Subaltern and Lieut, 19th Alberta Dragoons, Canadian Cavalry, 1937–39; served RAF, 1939–46: Fighter Squadrons; Training Command; Transatlantic Ferrying Command; Fighter Command; Meteorological Flight; Fighter Experimental Unit; CFE High Speed Flight World Speed Record. Joined Gloster Aircraft Co. Ltd, 1946. 100 km closed circuit record, 1947; Paris/London record (618.5 mph), 1947; "Hare and Tortoise" Helicopter and jet aircraft Centre of London to Centre of Paris (47 mins), 1948. Chief Test Pilot Gloster Aircraft Co. Ltd, 1946–54. Prototype trials on first Canadian jet fighter, Canuck and British first operational delta wing fighter, the Javelin. *Publications:* The Comet Riddle, 1956; The Quick and The Dead, 1956; aeronautical and meteorological articles. *Recreations:* sailing, riding, photography, motoring, shooting. *Address:* RR #4, Owen Sound, ON N4K 5N6, Canada. *Club:* Royal Military College of Canada (Kingston, Ont.). *Died 17 April 2006.*

WATKINS, Alan (Rhun); journalist; Political Columnist, Independent on Sunday, since 1993; *b* 3 April 1933; *o c* of late D. J. Watkins, teacher, Tycroes, Carmarthenshire, and Violet Harris, teacher; *m* 1955, Ruth Howard (*d* 1982); one *s* one *d* (and one *d* decd). *Educ:* Amman Valley Grammar Sch., Ammanford; Queens' Coll., Cambridge (MA, LLM). Chm., Cambridge Univ. Labour Club, 1954. National Service, FO, Educn Br., RAF, 1955–57. Called to Bar, Lincoln's Inn, 1957. Research Asst to W. A. Robson, LSE, 1958–59; Editorial Staff, Sunday Express, 1959–64 (New York Corresp., 1961; Actg Political Corresp., 1963; Crossbencher Columnist, 1963–64); Political Columnist: Spectator, 1964–67; New Statesman, 1967–76; Sunday Mirror, 1968–69; Observer, 1976–93; Columnist, Evening Standard, 1974–75; Rugby Columnist: Field, 1984–86; Independent, 1986–2006; Drink Columnist, Observer Magazine, 1992–93. Scriptwriter, BBC 3 and The Late Show, 1966–67. Mem. (Lab) Fulham Bor. Council, 1959–62. Dir, The Statesman and Nation Publishing Co. Ltd, 1973–76. Chm., Political Adv. Gp, British Youth Council, 1978–81. Hon. Fellow,

Univ. of Wales, Lampeter, 1999. Awards: Political Columnist, 1973, Gerald Barry, 2007, What the Papers Say; British Press, Columnist, 1982, commended 1984; Edgar Wallace, London Press Club, 2005. *Publications:* The Liberal Dilemma, 1966; (contrib.) The Left, 1966; (with A. Alexander) The Making of the Prime Minister 1970, 1970; Brief Lives, 1982, reissued 2004; (contrib.) The Queen Observed, 1986; Sportswriter's Eye, 1989; A Slight Case of Libel, 1990; A Conservative Coup, 1991, 2nd edn 1992; (contrib.) The State of the Nation, 1997; The Road to Number 10, 1998; (contrib.) Secrets of the Press, 1999; A Short Walk Down Fleet Street, 2000; (contrib.) Roy Jenkins, 2004; contrib. Oxford DNB. *Recreation:* watching cricket. *Address:* 54 Barnsbury Street, N1 1ER. *T:* (020) 7607 0812. *Clubs:* Beefsteak, Garrick.
Died 8 May 2010.

WATKINS, Rt Hon. Sir Tasker, VC 1944; GBE 1990; Kt 1971; PC 1980; DL; a Lord Justice of Appeal, 1980–93; Deputy Chief Justice of England, 1988–93; *b* 18 Nov. 1918; *s* of late Bertram and Jane Watkins, Nelson, Glam; *m* 1941, Eirwen Evans; one *d* (one *s* decd). *Educ:* Pontypridd Grammar Sch. Served War, 1939–45 (Major, the Welch Regiment). Called to Bar, Middle Temple, 1948, Bencher 1970; QC 1965; Deputy Chairman: Radnor QS, 1962–71; Carmarthenshire QS, 1966–71; Recorder: Merthyr Tydfil, 1968–70, Swansea, 1970–71; Leader, Wales and Chester Circuit, 1970–71; Judge of the High Court of Justice, Family Div., 1971–74, QBD, 1974–80; Presiding Judge, Wales and Chester Circuit, 1975–80; Sen. Presiding Judge for England and Wales, 1983–91. Counsel (as Deputy to Attorney-General) to Inquiry into Aberfan Disaster, 1966. Chairman: Mental Health Review Tribunal, Wales Region, 1960–71; Judicial Studies Bd, 1979–80. Pres., Univ. of Wales Coll. of Medicine, 1987–98. Pres., British Legion, Wales, 1947–68; Mem., TA Assoc., Glamorgan and Wales, 1947–. Chm., Welsh RU Charitable Trust, 1975–; Pres., Welsh RU, 1993–2004 (Hon. Life Vice Patron, 2004). DL Glamorgan, 1956. Hon. Freeman, City of Cardiff, 2006. Hon. FRCS 1992. Hon. Fellow, Amer. Coll. of Trial Lawyers, 1985. Hon. LLD: Wales, 1979; Glamorgan, 1996. KStJ 2000. *Address:* Fairwater Lodge, Fairwater Road, Llandaff, Glamorgan CF5 2LE. *T:* (029) 2056 3558. *Clubs:* Army and Navy, East India; Cardiff and County (Cardiff); Glamorgan Wanderers Rugby Football (Pres., 1968–). *Died 9 Sept. 2007.*

WATSON, Adam; *see* Watson, John Hugh A.

WATSON, Rear-Adm. Alan George, CB 1975; *b* 27 May 1922; *m* Dolores (*d* 2008). Served Royal Navy, 1941–77; Asst Chief of Naval Staff, 1974–77, retired. Pres., Church of England Soldiers', Sailors' and Airmen's Clubs, 1997–. *Died 25 Feb. 2008.*

WATSON, Sir Bruce (Dunstan), AC 2004; Kt 1985; Chairman, M.I.M. Holdings Limited, 1983–91 (Chief Executive Officer, 1981–90); *b* 1 Aug. 1928; *s* of James Harvey and Edith Mary (Crawford); *m* 1952, June Kilgour; one *s* two *d. Educ:* University of Queensland (BE (Elec) 1949, BCom 1957). Engineer, Tasmanian Hydro Electricity Commn, 1950–54, Townsville Regional Electricity Board, 1954–56; MIM Group of Companies: Engineer, Copper Refineries Pty Ltd, Townsville, 1956–69; Mount Isa Mines Ltd, 1970–73; Group Industrial Relations Manager, MIM Group, Brisbane, 1973–75; First Gen. Manager, Agnew Mining Co., WA, 1975–77; M.I.M. Holdings Ltd, Brisbane: Director, 1977; Man. Dir, 1980; Man. Dir and Chief Exec. Officer, 1981. Director: Asarco Inc., 1985–90; National Australia Bank, 1984–91, 1992–98; Boral, 1990–99; Mem., Supervisory Bd, Metallgesellschaft AG, 1988–93. Member: Business Council of Australia, 1983–90; Exec. Cttee, Australian Mining Industry Council, 1980–90 (Pres., 1985–87); President: Australian Inst. of Mining and Metallurgy, 1992; Australian Inst. of Co. Dirs, 1992–95. Mem., Qld Corrective Services Commn, 1997–99 (Chm., 1998–99); Chm. Council, Qld Inst. of Med. Res., 1998–. Bd Mem., Australian Management Coll., Mt Eliza, 1980–91. Pres., Qld Art

Gall. Foundn, 1985–2008. Hon. DEng Queensland, 1989; DUniv Griffith 1992. *Recreation:* golf. *Address:* 272 Jesmond Road, Fig Tree Pocket, Brisbane, Qld 4069, Australia. *T:* (7) 33781536. *Died 1 Nov. 2008.*

WATSON, John, FRCS, FRCSE; Consultant Plastic Surgeon to: Queen Victoria Hospital, East Grinstead, 1950–77, then Hon. Consultant; King Edward VII Hospital for Officers, 1963–87; London Hospital, 1963–82; *b* 10 Sept. 1914; *s* of late John Watson; *m* 1941, June Christine Stiles (*d* 2008); one *s* three *d. Educ:* Leighton Park, Reading; Jesus Coll., Cambridge; Guy's Hospital. MRCS, LRCP 1938; MA, MB, BChir (Cantab) 1939; FRCS(Ed.) 1946; FRCS 1963. Served as Sqdn Ldr (temp.) RAF, 1940–46 (despatches twice). Marks Fellow in Plastic Surgery, Queen Victoria Hosp., E Grinstead, 1947–50; Consultant Plastic Surgeon, Queen Victoria Hospital, East Grinstead, and Tunbridge Wells Gp of Hospitals, 1950–77. Gen. Sec., Internat. Confedn for Plastic and Reconstructive Surgery, 1971–75; Hon. Mem. Brit. Assoc. of Plastic Surgeons, 1979– (Hon. Sec., 1960–62, Pres., 1969); Hon. MRSocMed. *Publications:* numerous articles on plastic surgery in techn. jls and scientific periodicals. Chapters in: Textbook of Surgery, Plastic Surgery for Nurses, Modern Trends in Plastic Surgery, Clinical Surgery. *Recreations:* fishing, astronomy. *Address:* Iddons, Henley's Down, Catsfield, Battle, East Sussex TN33 9BN. *T:* (01424) 830226. *Died 14 Jan. 2009.*

WATSON, Sir John Forbes I.; *see* Inglefield-Watson.

WATSON, (John Hugh) Adam, CMG 1958; Professor, Center for Advanced Studies, University of Virginia, 1980–95; *b* 10 Aug. 1914; *er s* of Joseph Charlton Watson and Alice (*née* Tate); *m* 1950, Katharine Anne Campbell; two *s* one *d. Educ:* Rugby; King's Coll., Camb. Entered the Diplomatic Service, 1937; Brit. Legation, Bucharest, 1939; Cairo, 1940; Moscow, 1944; FO, 1947; Washington, 1950; Head of African Dept, Foreign Office, 1956–59; Minister for African Affairs, Paris, 1959–62; British Consul-General at Dakar, 1959; Ambassador: to the Federation of Mali, 1960–61; to Senegal, Mauritania and Togo, 1960–62; to Cuba, 1963–66; Under-Secretary, Foreign Office, 1966–68; Diplomatic Adviser, British Leyland Motor Corp., 1968–73. Gwilym Gibbon Fellow, Nuffield Coll., Oxford, Oct. 1962–Oct. 1963. Vis. Fellow, ANU, 1973; Vis. Prof., Univ. of Virginia, 1978. Dir Gen., Internat. Assoc. for Cultural Freedom, 1974–78. *Publications:* The War of the Goldsmith's Daughter, 1964; Nature and Problems of Third World, 1968; (ed) The Origins of History, 1981; Diplomacy: the dialogue between States, 1982; (with Hedley Bull) The Expansion of International Society, 1984; The Evolution of International Society, 1992; The Limits of Independence, 1997; Hegemony and History, 2007; various plays broadcast by BBC. *Address:* Sharnden Old Manor, Mayfield, East Sussex TN20 6QA. *T:* (01435) 872441; 1871 Field Road, Charlottesville, VA 22903, USA. *T:* (434) 2958295. *Club:* Brooks's.
Died 21 Aug. 2007.

WATSON, Vice-Adm. Sir Philip (Alexander), KBE 1976; LVO 1960; Chief Naval Engineer Officer, 1974–77; *b* 7 Oct. 1919; *yr s* of A. H. St C. Watson; *m* 1948, Jennifer Beatrice Tanner; one *s* two *d. Educ:* St Albans School. FIET (FIEE 1963). Sub-Lt RNVR, 1940; qual. Torpedo Specialist, 1943; transf. to RN, 1946; Comdr 1955; HM Yacht Britannia, 1957–59; Captain 1963; MoD (Ship Dept), 1963; Senior Officers' War Course, 1966; comd HMS Collingwood, 1967; Dep. Dir of Engrg (Ship Dept), MoD, 1969; Dir Gen. Weapons (Naval), MoD, 1970–77. Rear-Adm. 1970; Vice-Adm. 1974. Director: Marconi International Marine Co. Ltd, 1977–86; Marconi Radar Systems Ltd, 1981–86 (Chm., 1981–85); Consultant, GEC-Marconi Ltd, 1986–87. Mem. Council, IEE, 1975–78, 1982–91, Chm. South East Centre, 1982–83. Adm. Pres., Midland Naval

Officers Assoc., 1979–85, Vice Pres., 1985–. CCMI (CBIM 1973). *Address:* The Hermitage, Bodicote, Banbury, Oxon OX15 4BZ. *T:* (01295) 263300.
Died 8 Dec. 2009.

WATSON, Prof. William, CBE 1982; FBA 1972; FSA; Professor of Chinese Art and Archaeology in the University of London, at the School of Oriental and African Studies, 1966–83, then Emeritus, and Head of the Percival David Foundation of Chinese Art, 1966–83; *b* 9 Dec. 1917; *s* of Robert Scoular Watson and Lily Waterfield; *m* 1940, Katherine Sylvia Mary, *d* of Mr and Mrs J. H. Armfield, Ringwood, Hants; four *s. Educ:* Glasgow High Sch.; Herbert Strutt Sch.; Gonville and Caius Coll., Cambridge (Scholar; tripos in Modern and Medieval Langs; MA). Served Intelligence Corps, 1940–46, Egypt, N Africa, Italy, India, ending as Major. Asst Keeper, British Museum, first in Dept of British and Medieval Antiquities, then in Dept of Oriental Antiquities, 1947–66. Slade Prof. of Fine Art, Cambridge University, 1975–76. Trustee, BM, 1980–90. Pres., Oriental Ceramic Soc., 1981–84. Hon. DLitt Chinese Univ. of Hong Kong, 1984. Sir Percy Sykes Meml Medal, 1973. *Publications:* The Sculpture of Japan, 1959; Archaeology in China, 1960; China before the Han Dynasty, 1961; Ancient Chinese Bronzes, 1961; Jade Books in the Chester Beatty Library, 1963; Cultural Frontiers in Ancient East Asia, 1971; The Genius of China (catalogue of Burlington House exhibn), 1973; Style in the Arts of China, 1974; L'Art de l'Ancienne Chine, 1980; (ed) Catalogue of the Great Japan Exhibition (at Burlington House 1981–82); Tang and Liao Ceramics, 1984; Pre-Tang Ceramics of China, 1991; The Arts of China to AD 900, 1995; Collected Papers, 2 vols, 1997, 1998; The Arts of China 900–1620, 2000. *Recreations:* exploring N Wales, Romanesque France and Spain. *Address:* Cefn y Maes, Parc, Bala, Gwynedd LL23 7YS. *T:* (01678) 540302.   *Died 15 March 2007.*

WATT, Charlotte Joanne, (Mrs G. L. Watt); *see* Erickson, C. J.

WATT, Surgeon Vice-Adm. Sir James, KBE 1975; MS, FRCS; Medical Director-General (Navy), 1972–77; *b* 19 Aug. 1914; *s* of Thomas Watt and Sarah Alice Clarkson. *Educ:* King Edward VI Sch., Morpeth; Univ. of Durham. MB, BS 1938; MS 1949; FRCS 1955; MD 1972; FRCP 1975. Served War, RN, FE and N Atlantic, 1941–46 (despatches, 1945). Surgical Registrar, Royal Vic. Infirm., Newcastle upon Tyne, 1947; Surgical Specialist: N Ire., 1949; RN Hosp., Hong Kong, 1954; Consultant in Surgery, RN Hospitals: Plymouth, 1956; Haslar, 1959; Malta, 1961; Haslar, 1963; Jt Prof. of Naval Surgery, RCS and RN Hosp., Haslar, 1965–69; Dean of Naval Medicine and MO i/c, Inst. of Naval Medicine, 1969–72. Chm. Bd of Trustees, Naval Christian Fellowship, 1968–75; President: Royal Naval Lay Readers Soc., 1973–83; Inst. of Religion and Medicine, 1989–91. QHS 1969–77. Surg. Comdr 1956; Surg. Captain 1965; Surg. Rear-Adm. 1969; Surg. Vice-Adm. 1972. Thomas Vicary Lectr, RCS, 1974; Vis. Prof. in Naval History, Univ. of Calgary, 1985; University House Vis. Fellow, ANU, 1986. FICS 1964; Fellow: Assoc. of Surgeons of GB and Ire.; Med. Soc. of London (Mem. Council, 1976; Lettsomian Lectr, 1979; Pres., 1980–81; Vice-Pres., 1981–83); RSocMed (Pres., 1982–84; Hon. FRSocMed 1998); Hon. FRCSE; Hon. Fellow, Royal Acad. of Medicine in Ireland, 1983; Member: Brit. Soc. for Surgery of the Hand; Internat. Soc. for Burns Injuries; Corresp. Mem., Surgical Research Soc., 1966–77. FSA 1982; FRGS 1982; Mem. Council, RGS, 1985–88. Pres., ECHO, 1989–2003; Vice-Pres., Churches' Council for Health and Healing, 1987–99. Mem., Archival Res. Task Force, Canada, 1992–99. Trustee: Marylebone Centre Trust, 1989–93; Medical Soc. of London, 1986–. Gov., Epsom Coll., 1990–2001 (Vice Pres., 2001–). Pres., Smeatonian Soc. of Civil Engineers, 1996 (Hon. Mem., 1978–). Hon. Freeman, Co. of Barbers, 1978. Hon. DCh Newcastle, 1978. Errol-Eldridge Prize, 1968; Gilbert Blane Medal, 1971. CStJ 1972. *Publications:* edited:

Starving Sailors, 1981; Talking Health, 1988; What is Wrong with Christian Healing?, 1993; The Church, Medicine and the New Age, 1995; contributions to: Meta Incognita: a discourse of discovery - Martin Frobisher's Arctic Expeditions (ed T. Symons), 1999; Notable Barber Surgeons (ed Ian Burn), 2008; papers on: burns, cancer chemotherapy, peptic ulceration, hyberbaric oxygen therapy, naval medical history, contemporary Christianity. *Recreations:* mountain walking, music. *Address:* 3 Otterbourne House, Otterbourne, Hants SO21 2EQ. *Clubs:* Royal Over-Seas League, Naval and Military.   *Died 28 Dec. 2009.*

WATT, Prof. W(illiam) Montgomery; Professor of Arabic and Islamic Studies, University of Edinburgh, 1964–79; *b* Ceres, Fife, 14 March 1909; *o c* of late Rev. Andrew Watt; *m* 1943, Jean Macdonald, *er d* of late Prof. Robert Donaldson; one *s* four *d. Educ:* George Watson's Coll., Edinburgh; University of Edinburgh (MA, PhD); Balliol Coll., Oxford (Warner Exhibition, 1930; Ferguson Schol. in Classics, 1931; MA, BLitt); University of Jena; Cuddesdon Coll. Asst Lecturer, Moral Philosophy, University of Edinburgh, 1934–38; Curate, St Mary Boltons, London, 1939–41; Curate, Old St Paul's, Edinburgh, 1941–43; Arabic specialist to Bishop in Jerusalem, 1943–46; Lectr, Ancient Philosophy, 1946–47, Lectr, Sen. Lectr and Reader in Arabic, 1947–64, Univ. of Edinburgh. Visiting Professor: of Islamic Studies, University of Toronto, 1963; Collège de France, Paris, 1970; of Religious Studies, Univ. of Toronto, 1978; of Arab Studies, Georgetown Univ., 1978–79. Chairman, Assoc. of British Orientalists, 1964–65. Editor, series, Islamic Surveys, 1961–79. Hon. DD Aberdeen, 1966; Hon. DLitt Hamdard Univ., Karachi, 1998. Levi Della Vida Medal, Los Angeles, 1981. *Publications:* Free Will and Predestination in Early Islam, 1949; The Faith and Practice of al-Ghazali, 1953; Muhammad at Mecca, 1953; Muhammad at Medina, 1956; The Reality of God, 1958; The Cure for Human Troubles, 1959; Islam and the Integration of Society, 1961; Muhammad Prophet and Statesman, 1961; Islamic Philosophy and Theology, 1962, new enlarged edn, 1986; Muslim Intellectual, 1963; Truth in the Religions, 1963; Islamic Spain, 1965; Islam (in Propyläen Weltgeschichte, XI), 1965; A Companion to the Qur'an, 1967; What is Islam?, 1968; Islamic Political Thought, 1968; Islamic Revelation and the Modern World, 1970; Bell's Introduction to the Qur'an, 1970; The Influence of Islam on Medieval Europe, 1972; The Formative Period of Islamic Thought, 1973; The Majesty that was Islam, 1974; Der Islam, i, 1980, ii, 1985; Islam and Christianity Today, 1984; Muhammad's Mecca, 1988; Islamic Fundamentalism and Modernity, 1988; Early Islam, 1991; Muslim-Christian Encounters, 1991; Islamic Creeds: a selection, 1994; Religious Truth for Our Time, 1995; A Short History of Islam, 1995; A Christian Faith for Today, 2002; contribs learned journals. *Address:* 2 Bridgend, Dalkeith, Midlothian EH22 1JT. *T:* (0131) 663 3197.   *Died 24 Oct. 2006.*

WATTS, Sir Arthur (Desmond), KCMG 1989 (CMG 1977); QC 1988; barrister and international arbitrator; *b* 14 Nov. 1931; *o s* of Col A. E. Watts, MA (Cantab); *m* 1957, Iris Ann Collier, MA (Cantab); one *s* one *d. Educ:* Haileybury and Imperial Service College; Royal Military Academy, Sandhurst; Downing Coll., Cambridge (Schol.). BA 1954; LLM (First Cl.) 1955; MA; Whewell Schol. in Internat. Law, 1955; Hon. Fellow, 1999). Called to Bar, Gray's Inn, 1957, Bencher, 1996. Legal Asst, Foreign Office, 1956–59; Legal Adviser, British Property Commn (later British Embassy), Cairo, 1959–62; Asst Legal Adviser, FO, 1962–67; Legal Adviser, British Embassy, Bonn, 1967–69; Asst Solicitor, Law Officers Dept, 1969–70; Legal Counsellor, FCO, 1970–73; Counsellor (Legal Advr), Office of UK Permanent Rep. to EEC, 1973–77; Legal Counsellor, 1977–82, Dep. Legal Advr, 1982–87, Legal Advr, 1987–91, FCO. High Rep's Special Negotiator on Succession Issues, former Yugoslavia, 1996–2001; Member: Panel of Arbitrators, UN Law of the Sea Convention, 1998–; UK Nat. Gp, Permanent Ct of Arbitration, 2003–; Eritrea-Ethiopia

Boundary Commn, 2001–; Ireland-UK Arbitral Tribunal, 2002–; Malaysia-Singapore Arbitral Tribunal, 2003–05; Barbados-Trinidad and Tobago Arbitral Tribunal, 2004–06; Pres. or Mem. of, and Counsel before, various internat. foreign investment arbitral tribunals; Counsel before ICJ for France, Nigeria, Indonesia, Slovak Republic, Colombia, Ukraine and Jordan. Member: Bd, Inst. of Advanced Legal Studies, 1988–91; Adv. Bd, Inst für Internationales Recht, Kiel Univ., 1989–2002; Inst de Droit Internat., 1991– (Assoc. Mem., 1991–97); Adv. Council, Liechtenstein Inst. for Self-Determination, Princeton Univ., 2003–07; Adv. Council, British Inst. of Internat. and Comparative Law, 2006– (Mem., Bd of Mgt, 1987–2006). Pres., British Br., Internat. Law Assoc., 1992–98 (Hon. Pres., 1998–). Mem. Editl Cttee, British Year Book of International Law, 1991–. Trustee, Sussex Heritage Trust, 2002– (Chm., 2006–). Order of Independence (Jordan), 2007. *Publications:* Legal Effects of War, 4th edn (with Lord McNair), 1966; (with C. and A. Parry and J. Grant) Encyclopaedic Dictionary of International Law, 1986; (with Sir Robert Jennings) Oppenheim's International Law, vol. 1, 9th edn 1992; International Law and the Antarctic Treaty System, 1992; (with W. F. Danspeckgruber) Self-Determination and Self-Administration, 1997; The International Law Commission 1949–1998 (3 vols), 1999–2000; contribs to: British Year Book of Internat. Law; Internat. and Comparative Law Quarterly, and other internat. law publications. *Recreations:* cricket (County Cap, Shropshire, 1955; in Antarctica, 1985), Tortington Priory (West Sussex). *Address:* 20 Essex Street, WC2R 3AL. *Died 16 Nov. 2007.*

WATTS, Helen Josephine, (Mrs Michael Mitchell), CBE 1978; concert, lieder and opera singer (contralto); *b* 7 Dec. 1927; *d* of Thomas Watts and Winifred (*née* Morgan); *m* 1980, Michael Mitchell (decd). *Educ:* Sch. of St Mary and St Anne, Abbots Bromley; Royal Academy of Music. Began career with Glyndebourne Fest. Chorus and BBC Chorus; Proms début, 1958; with Royal Opera, Covent Gdn, 1965–71; with WNO, 1969–83; worked with world's leading conductors, notably Solti, Giulini, Haitink and von Karajan; sang in all major cities in Europe and USA; toured Australia, 1967, NZ, 1972; many recordings of oratorio, opera and songs (Grand Prix du Disque, 1959); retired 1985. Hon. FRAM 1961. *Recreations:* gardening, reading. *Died 7 Oct. 2009.*

WATTS, Col John Cadman, OBE 1959; MC 1946; FRCS 1949; first Professor of Military Surgery, Royal College of Surgeons, 1960–64; *b* 13 April 1913; *s* of John Nixon Watts, solicitor, and Amy Bettina (*née* Cadman); *m* 1938, Joan Lilian (*née* Inwood) (*d* 2009); two *s* one *d* (and one *s* decd). *Educ:* Merchant Taylors' Sch.; St Thomas's Hospital. MRCS, LRCP, 1936; MB, BS, 1938. Casualty Officer, Resident Anæsthetist, House Surgeon, St Thomas's Hospital, 1937; Surgical Specialist, RAMC, 1938–60, served in Palestine, Egypt, Libya, Syria, Tunisia, Italy, France, Holland, Germany, Malaya, Java, Japan, and Cyprus. Hunterian Professor, RCS, 1960; Conslt Surgeon, Bedford Gen. Hosp., 1966–76. Co. Comr, St John Ambulance Brigade, 1970. British Medical Association: Chm., N Beds Div., 1971; Mem. Council, 1972–74; Chm., Armed Forces Cttee, 1978–82; Pres., Ipswich Div., 1982–83. OStJ 1970. *Publications:* Surgeon at War, 1955; Clinical Surgery, 1964; Exploration Medicine, 1964. *Recreations:* sailing, gardening. *Address:* Grove Court, 17 Beech Way, Woodbridge, Suffolk IP12 4BW. *T:* (01394) 382618. *Clubs:* Deben Yacht (Woodbridge); United Hospitals Sailing (Burnham-on-Crouch). *Died 17 Dec. 2009.*

WATTS, John Francis, BA; educational writer; Principal, Countesthorpe College, Leicestershire, 1972–81; *b* 18 Oct. 1926; *s* of John Weldon Watts and Norah K. Watts; *m* 1st, 1950, Elizabeth Hamilton (marr. diss.); four *s* one *d*; 2nd, 1985, Madeleine Marshall. *Educ:* West Buckland Sch.; Univ. of Bristol (BA). First Headmaster, Les Quennevais Sch., Jersey, CI, 1964–69; Lectr, Univ. of

London, 1969–72. Chm., Nat. Assoc. for Teaching of English (NATE), 1974–76. *Publications:* Encounters, 1965, 2nd edn 1983; Contact, 1970 (Australia); Interplay, 1972; Teaching, 1974; The Countesthorpe Experience, 1977; Towards an Open School, 1980; Hearings, 1994; contrib. to various publications. *Address:* Kingfisher Barn, Kings Lane, Weston, Beccles, Suffolk NR34 8TX. *Died 14 May 2007.*

WEATHERALL, Miles, DM, DSc; FIBiol; medical scientist; *b* 14 Oct. 1920; *s* of Rev. J. H. and Mary Weatherall; *m* 1944, Josephine A. C. Ogston (*d* 2006); three *d*. *Educ:* Dragon School and St Edward's School, Oxford; Oriel College, Oxford (Open Schol. in Nat. Sci., 1938; BA, BSc 1941; BM 1943; MA 1945; DM 1951; DSc 1966). FIBiol 1972. Lectr in Pharmacology, Edinburgh Univ., 1945; Head, Dept of Pharmacology, London Hosp. Med. Coll., 1949–66; Prof. of Pharmacology, Univ. of London, 1958–66; Wellcome Research Laboratories: Head, Therapeutic Res. Div., 1967–75; Dep. Dir, 1969–74; Dir of Estabt, 1974–79. Member: Adv. Cttee on Pesticides and other Toxic Chemicals, 1964–66; Council, Pharmaceutical Soc., 1966–70; Council, Roy. Soc. Med., 1972–82 (Hon. Sec. 1974–82); Comr, Medicines Commn, 1979–81. Chm., Sci. Co-ord. Cttee, Arthritis and Rheumatism Council, 1983–88. Chm., Council, Chelsea Coll., Univ. of London, 1970–83. Hon. Lecturer: UCL, 1968–89; KCL, 1979–82; Hon. Fellow: Chelsea Coll., London, 1984; KCL, 1985. Mem. Cttee, Wine Soc., 1964–72. *Publications:* Statistics for Medical Students (jointly with I. Bernstein), 1952; Scientific Method, 1968; (ed jtly) Safety Testing of New Drugs, 1984; In Search of a Cure, 1990; papers in scientific and medical journals; *fiction:* The Search and the Girl, 2001; The Green Ointment, 2001; Mistmagic Castle, 2002; My Friend at Last, 2004. *Recreations:* writing, gardening, cooking. *Address:* Willows, Charlbury, Oxford OX7 3PX. *Club:* Royal Society of Medicine. *Died 8 March 2007.*

WEATHERILL, Baron *cr* 1992 (Life Peer), of North East Croydon in the London Borough of Croydon; **(Bruce) Bernard Weatherill;** PC 1980; DL; *b* 25 Nov. 1920; *s* of late Bernard Weatherill, Spring Hill, Guildford, and Annie Gertrude (*née* Creak); *m* 1949, Lyn, *d* of late H. T. Eatwell; two *s* one *d*. *Educ:* Malvern College. Served War of 1939–45; commissioned 4/7th Royal Dragoon Guards, 1940; transferred to Indian Army, 1941 and served with 19th King George V's Own Lancers, 1941–45 (Captain). Man. Dir, Bernard Weatherill Ltd, 1957–70, President, 1992–. First Chm., Guildford Young Conservatives, 1946–49; Chm., Guildford Cons. Assoc., 1959–63; Vice-Chm., SE Area Prov. Council, 1962–64; Member National Union of Cons. Party, 1963–64. MP (C) Croydon NE, 1964–83 (when elected Speaker); MP Croydon NE and Speaker of The House of Commons, 1983–92; an Opposition Whip, 1967; a Lord Comr of HM Treasury, 1970–71; Vice-Chamberlain, HM Household, 1971–72; Comptroller of HM Household, 1972–73; Treasurer of HM Household and Dep. Chief Govt Whip, 1973–74; Opposition Dep. Chief Whip, 1974–79; Chm. of Ways and Means and Dep. Speaker, 1979–83. Convenor, Cross Bench Peers, 1995–99. Chairman: Commonwealth Speakers and Presiding Officers, 1986–88; Industry and Parlt Trust, 1994–2002. Pres., CPA, 1986. High Bailiff of Westminster Abbey, 1989–99. Freeman of City of London, 1949; Freeman of Borough of Croydon, 1983. Hon. Bencher, Lincoln's Inn, 1988. DL Kent, 1992. Hon. LLD Coll. of William and Mary, Va, 1989; Hon. DCL: Kent, 1990; Denver, 1992; DUniv Open, 1993. KStJ 1992; Vice-Chancellor, Order of St John of Jerusalem, 1992–99. Hilal-e-Pakistan 1993. *Recreation:* playing with grandchildren. *Address:* 15 St Michaels, Wolf's Row, Limpsfield, Surrey RH8 0QL. *Died 6 May 2007.*

WEATHERSTONE, Sir Dennis, KBE 1990; Chairman and Chief Executive Officer, J. P. Morgan & Co., New York, 1990–94; *b* 29 Nov. 1930; *s* of Henry and Gladys Weatherstone; *m* 1959, Marion Blunsum; one *s* three *d*.

Educ: Northwestern Polytechnic, London. Morgan Guaranty Trust Co., subseq. J. P. Morgan & Co.: Sen. Vice-Pres., 1972–77; Exec. Vice-Pres., 1977–79; Treas., 1977–79; Vice-Chm., 1979–80; Chm., Exec. Cttee, 1980–86; Pres., 1987–89. *Address:* J. P. Morgan Chase & Co., 270 Park Avenue, 32nd Floor, New York, NY 10017, USA. *Died 13 June 2008.*

WEATHERSTONE, (Robert) Bruce, TD 1962; CA; Chairman, Lothian Health Board, 1986–90; *b* 14 May 1926; *s* of Sir Duncan Mackay Weatherstone, MC, TD, and late Janet Pringle; *m* 1954, (Agnes) Elaine Jean Fisher; one *s* one *d. Educ:* Edinburgh and Dollar Academies. CA 1951. Served Royal Marines, 44 Commando, 1944–47. Dir/Sec., J. T. Salvesen Ltd, 1954–62; Dir and Mem., Management Cttee, Christian Salvesen Ltd, 1962–83; Dir, Lothian Region Transport plc, 1986–92. Chm., Leith Enterprise Trust, 1983–88; Vice-Pres., Leonard Cheshire Foundn, 1996– (Trustee, 1973–96). *Recreations:* hill-walking, ornithology. *Address:* Strachan House, 93 Craigcrook Road, Edinburgh EH4 3PE. *Club:* New (Edinburgh). *Died 30 Oct. 2009.*

WEAVER, Leonard John, CBE 1990; Chairman, The Engineering Link, 1996–2002; *b* 10 June 1936; *s* of A. W. Weaver, HMOCS, and B. I. M. Weaver (*née* Geleyns); *m* 1st, 1963, Penelope Ann Sturge-Young (marr. diss. 2004); five *s* one *d*; 2nd, 2004, Gillian Margaret Woolcock (*née* Fayers). *Educ:* St Mary's Sch.; Battersea Coll. of Advanced Technology (Surrey Univ.); MA London. CEng, FIEE, FIMMM, FIMechE, FCMC. Served Kenya Regt, 1955–57. AEI, 1962–64; PYE-TMC, 1964–66; Consultant, Dir and Man. Dir, P-E Internat., 1966–82; Chairman: Polymark Internat., 1982–92; Manifold Industries, 1982–95; Pearson Engineering, 1985–88; Jones & Shipman, 1988–98; Eutech Engrg Servs, 1995–2001. Member: NEDO Prod. Control Adv. Gp (Chm., 1980–82); NEDO Advanced Manfg Systems Gp, 1983–86; SERC Teaching Co. Mangt Cttee, 1983–86; Jt DTI/SERC Advanced Manfg Tech. Cttee, 1983–91 (Chm., 1987–91); SERC Engrg Bd, 1987–91; Indust. Develt Adv. Bd, 1989–95; Innovation Adv. Bd, 1991–93; Steering Bd, NPL, 1993–95. Member Council: Inst. of Mgt (formerly BIM), 1978–83, 1991–98 (Vice Chm., 1993–97); Inst. of Mgt Consultants, 1978–86 (Pres., 1983–84); IProdE, 1980–91 (Pres., 1990–91); IEE, 1991–96. Mem. Bd of Dirs, Soc. of Manfg Engrs, USA, 1998–99 (Hon. Mem., 1990). Freeman, City of London, 1984; Master, Engrs' Co., 2000–01. CCMI (CBIM 1980); FRSA, FSME, FCGI. DUniv Surrey, 1991; Hon. DSc Greenwich, 2003. Sandforth Smith Award, Inst. of Management Consultants, 1984; Internat. Engineer of the Year, San Fernando Valley Engrs Council, 1985; Calif. State Legis. Commend., 1985. *Publications:* contribs to professional jls. *Recreations:* book collecting, cricket. *Address:* Crab Apple Court, Oxshott Road, Leatherhead, Surrey KT22 0DQ. *T:* (01372) 843647. *Clubs:* Reform, MCC. *Died 24 June 2006.*

WEAVER, Oliver; QC 1985; *b* 27 March 1942; *s* of late Denis Weaver and Kathleen (*née* Lynch); *m* 1964, Julia Mary (*née* MacClymont); one *s* two *d. Educ:* Friends' Sch., Saffron Walden; Trinity Coll., Cambridge (MA, LLM). President, Cambridge Union Society, 1963. Called to the Bar, Middle Temple, 1965; Lincoln's Inn, 1969. Mem. Bar Council, 1981–84; Vice-Chm., Bar Law Reform Cttee, 1987–89; Member: Incorporated Council of Law Reporting, 1987–93; Panel of Chairmen of Authorisation and Disciplinary Tribunals, Securities and Futures Authy (formerly Securities Assoc., then Securities and Futures Assoc.), 1988–93. Retired due to ill-health, 1993. *Recreations:* fishing, racing, gun dogs. *Address:* Kennel Farm, Albury End, Ware, Herts SG11 2HS. *T:* (01279) 771331. *Died 18 April 2008.*

WEBB, Rear-Adm. Arthur Brooke, CB 1975; Flag Officer, Admiralty Interview Board, 1973–75; *b* 13 June 1918; 2nd *s* of late Captain A. B. H. Webb and Mrs G. Webb; *m* 1949, Rachel Marian Gerrish; three *d. Educ:* St John's Coll., Southsea, Hants. Joined Royal Navy, 1936;

served in Alexandria, 1939–42, HMS Howe, 1942–46, Egypt, 1946–48. Secretary: to Dep. Chief of Naval Personnel (Manpower) Admiralty, 1951–53; to Flag Officer Germany, 1953–55; to Dir of Naval Intelligence, 1955–58; HM Ships: Belfast, 1958–60; Hermes, 1962–64; Staff of Chief of Defence Staff, 1964–67; Chief Staff Officer (Admin) to Fleet Commander, Far East Fleet, 1967–69, and Flag Officer, Plymouth, 1970–72. Comdr 1954, Captain 1963, Rear-Adm. 1973. *Recreations:* gardening, walking, survival. *Died 25 Sept. 2008.*

WEBB, Prof. Edwin Clifford; Emeritus Professor, University of Queensland and Macquarie University; Vice-Chancellor, Macquarie University, 1976–86; *b* 21 May 1921; *s* of William Webb and Nellie Webb; *m* 1st, 1942, Violet Sheila Joan (*née* Tucker) (marr. diss. 1987); one *s* four *d* (and one *s* decd); 2nd, 1988, Miriam Margaret Therese (*née* Armstrong). *Educ:* Poole Grammar Sch.; Clare Coll., Cambridge (BA, MA; PhD 1947). FRACI 1968. Cambridge University: Beit Meml Res. Fellow, 1944–46; Univ. Demonstrator in Biochem., 1946–50; Univ. Lectr in Biochem., 1950–62; University of Queensland: Foundn Prof. of Biochem. and Head of Dept, 1962–70; Dep. Vice-Chancellor (Academic), 1970–76. Pres., Australasian Council on Chiropractic and Osteopathic Educn, 1991–93. Hon. DSc: Queensland, 1978; Macquarie, 1988. *Publications:* Enzymes, 1959, 3rd edn 1979; 56 scientific papers. *Recreations:* music, theatre. *Address:* 97A Buderim Gardens Village, 405 Mooloolaba Road, Buderim, Qld 4556, Australia. *Died 17 Jan. 2006.*

WEBB, George Hannam, CMG 1984; OBE 1974; HM Diplomatic Service, retired; *b* 24 Dec. 1929; *s* of George Ernest Webb, HM Colonial Service, Kenya, and Mary Hannam (*née* Stephens); *m* 1956, Josephine, *d* of late Richard Chatterton, Horncastle; two *s* two *d. Educ:* Malvern Coll.; King's Coll., Cambridge (MA). Served 14/20th King's Hussars, 1948–49; Parachute Regt (TA), 1950–53. Joined Colonial Administration, Kenya, 1953: District Officer, Central Nyanza, 1954–56; N Nyanza, 1956–57; District Commissioner, Moyale, 1958–60; Secretariat, Nairobi, 1960–62; retired 1963 and joined HM Diplomatic Service; First Sec., Bangkok, 1964–67; Accra, 1969–73; Counsellor, Tehran, 1977–79, Washington, 1980–82; retd 1985. Dir, Management Develt, 1985–89, Sen. Fellow, 1989–93, City Univ. Editor, *Kipling Journal,* 1980–2001. *Publications:* The Bigger Bang: growth of a financial revolution, 1987; (ed with Sir Hugh Cortazzi) Kipling's Japan, 1988; contribs to learned jls. *Recreation:* books. *Club:* Travellers. *Died 9 Dec. 2007.*

WEBB, Prof. John Stuart, FREng; Professor of Applied Geochemistry in the University of London, 1961–79, then Emeritus, and Senior Research Fellow, 1979–89, Imperial College of Science and Technology; *b* 28 Aug. 1920; *s* of Stuart George Webb and Caroline Rabjohns Webb (*née* Pengelly); *m* 1946, Jean Millicent Dyer; one *s. Educ:* Westminster City School; Royal School of Mines, Imperial College of Science and Technology (BSc, ARSM, 1941; PhD, DIC, in Mining Geology, 1947; DSc, 1967). Served War of 1939–45, Royal Engineers, 1941–43. Geological Survey of Nigeria, 1943–44; Royal School of Mines, Imperial Coll., 1945–89; Beit Scientific Res. Fellow, 1945–47; Lectr in Mining Geology, 1947–55; Reader in Applied Geochemistry, 1955–61. Mem., Home Office Forensic Science Cttee, 1969–75. Institution of Mining and Metallurgy: Mem. Council, 1964–71, and 1974–83; Vice Pres., 1971–73; Pres., 1973–74. Mem. Bd, Council Engineering Instns. 1973–74; Regl Vice-Pres. (Europe), Soc. of Econ. Geologists, USA, 1979–81. Mem., Royal Soc. Wkg Pty on Envmtl Geochem. and Health, 1979–83. FREng (FEng 1979). Hon. Mem., Assoc. Exploration Geochemists, USA, 1977; Hon. FIMMM (Hon. FIMM 1980). Consolidated Goldfields of SA Gold Medal, IMM, 1953; William Smith Medal, Geol. Soc. of London, 1981. *Publications:* (with H. E. Hawkes) Geochemistry in Mineral Exploration, 1962, 2nd edn (with A. W. Rose)

1979; (jtly) Geochemical Atlas of Northern Ireland, 1973; (jtly) Wolfson Geochemical Atlas of England and Wales, 1978; contrib. to scientific and technical jls. *Recreations:* amateur radio, meteorology. *Died 2 April 2007.*

WEBSTER, Very Rev. Alan Brunskill, KCVO 1988; Dean of St Paul's, 1978–87, then Dean Emeritus; *b* 1 July 1918; *s* of Rev. J. Webster; *m* 1951, Margaret C. F. Falconer; two *s* two *d. Educ:* Shrewsbury School; Queen's College, Oxford (MA, BD). Ordained deacon 1942, priest 1943; Curate of Attercliffe Parishes, Sheffield, 1942; Curate of St Paul's, Arbourthorne, Sheffield, 1944; Chaplain and Vice Principal, Westcott House, 1946; Vicar of Barnard Castle, 1953; Warden, Lincoln Theol Coll., 1959–70; Dean of Norwich, 1970–78. Founder, Norwich Night Shelter, 1973. Pres., Cathedral Camps, 1981–2000. Hon. DD City Univ., 1983. *Publications:* Joshua Watson, 1954; Broken Bones May Joy, 1968; Julian of Norwich, 1974, rev. edn 1980; Reaching for Reality, 2002; contributed: The Historic Episcopate, 1954; Living the Faith, 1980; Strategist for the Spirit, 1985; Preaching from the Cathedrals, 1998. *Recreations:* gardening, writing. *Address:* Rocket Lodge, High Street, Cley-next-the-Sea, Norfolk NR25 7RB. *T:* (01263) 741022. *Died 3 Sept. 2007.*

WEBSTER, Alec, FCCA; CIGEM; Regional Chairman, British Gas Wales, 1989–92; *b* 22 March 1934; *s* of Clifford Webster and Rose Webster (*née* Proctor); *m* 1958, Jean Thompson; one *s* two *d. Educ:* Hull Univ. (BScEcon Hons). Chief Accountant, British Gas Southern, 1974; Controller of Audit and Investigations, British Gas, 1979; Treas., British Gas, 1981; Reg. Dep. Chm., British Gas Southern, 1984. Pres., Chartered Assoc. of Certified Accountants, 1989–90. Chairman: Hendref Building Preservation Trust, 1992–2000; Darwin Centre for Biology and Medicine, 1993–2000. FRSA 1990. *Recreations:* sailing, mountaineering, wood carving. *Address:* Tŷ Carreg, 2 Maillards Haven, Penarth, S Glam CF64 5RF. *Died 20 Oct. 2008.*

WEBSTER, Dr Cyril Charles, CMG 1966; Chief Scientific Officer, Agricultural Research Council, 1971–75 (Scientific Adviser, 1965–71); *b* 28 Dec. 1909; *s* of Ernest Webster; *m* 1947, Mary, *d* of H. R. Wimhurst; one *s* one *d. Educ:* Beckenham County Sch.; Wye Coll.; Selwyn Coll., Cambridge; Imperial Coll. of Tropical Agriculture, Trinidad. Colonial Agricultural Service, 1936–57: Nigeria, 1936–38; Nyasaland, 1938–50; Kenya (Chief Research Officer), 1950–55; Malaya (Dep. Dir of Agriculture), 1956–57; Prof. of Agriculture, Imperial Coll. of Tropical Agriculture, Univ. of W Indies, 1957–60; Dir, Rubber Research Inst. of Malaya, subseq. of Malaysia, 1961–65; Dir-Gen., Palm Oil Research Inst. of Malaysia, 1978–80. JMN, 1965. *Publications:* (with P. N. Wilson) Agriculture in the Tropics, 1966, 3rd edn 1998; (with W. J. Baulkwill) Rubber, 1989; scientific papers in agricultural jls. *Address:* The Croft Cottage, Hawksworth Road, Syerston, Newark, Notts NG23 5NB. *T:* (01636) 525280. *Died 8 Aug. 2007.*

WEBSTER, Henry George, CBE 1974; FSAE; Chairman, SKF Steel UK, 1982–87; retired; *b* Coventry, 27 May 1917; *s* of William George Webster; *m* 1943, Margaret (*d* 2003), *d* of H. C. Sharp; (one *d* decd). *Educ:* Welshpool County Sch.; Coventry Technical Coll. Standard Motor Co. Ltd: apprenticed, 1932; Asst Technl Engr, 1938–40; Dep. Chief Inspector, 1940–46; Asst Technl Engr, 1946–48; Chief Chassis Engr, 1948–55; Chief Engr, 1955–57; Dir and Chief Engr, Standard-Triumph Internat., 1957–68; Technical Dir, Austin Morris Div., British Leyland UK Ltd, 1968–74; Group Engineering Dir, Automotive Products, 1974–83. Joined original Instn of Automobile Engrs, as a grad., 1937 (Sec. of Grad. Section, Coventry Br. of Instn, 1941–45); transf. to Associate Mem., 1946, Mem., 1964. MSAE 1958; FSAE 1976; FRSA. Freeman, City of Coventry. *Recreation:* golf. *Address:* The Old School House, Barrowfield Lane, Kenilworth, Warwickshire CV8 1EP. *T:* (01926) 853363. *Died 6 Feb. 2007.*

WEBSTER, John Lawrence Harvey, CMG 1963; *b* 10 March 1913; *s* of late Sydney Webster, Hindhead, and Elsie Gwendoline Webster (*née* Harvey); *m* 1st, 1940, Elizabeth Marshall Gilbertson (marr. diss. 1959); two *d*; 2nd, 1960, Jessie Lillian Royston-Smith. *Educ:* Rugby Sch.; Balliol College, Oxford (MA). District Officer, Colonial Administrative Service, Kenya, 1935–49; Secretary for Development, 1949–54; Administrative Sec., 1954–56; Sec. to Cabinet, 1956–58; Permanent Sec., Kenya, 1958–63; on retirement from HMOCS, with the British Council, 1964–80, in Thailand, Sri Lanka, Hong Kong, Istanbul and London. *Recreations:* travel, reading, swimming. *Clubs:* Royal Commonwealth Society; Leander; Nairobi (Kenya). *Died 19 Sept. 2009.*

WEBSTER, Sir Peter (Edlin), Kt 1980; a Judge of the High Court of Justice, Queen's Bench Division, 1980–92; *b* 16 Feb. 1924; *s* of Herbert Edlin Webster and Florence Helen Webster; *m* 1955, Susan Elizabeth Richards (marr. diss. 1967); one *s* two *d*; *m* 1968, Avril Carolyn Simpson, *d* of Dr John Ernest McCrae Harrisson. *Educ:* Haileybury; Merton Coll., Oxford (MA). RNVR, 1943–46 and 1950, Lieut (A). Imperial Tobacco Co., 1949; Lectr in Law, Lincoln Coll., Oxford, 1950–52; called to Bar, Middle Temple, 1952; Bencher, 1972; Standing Jun. Counsel to Min. of Labour, 1964–67; QC 1967; a Recorder of the Crown Court, 1972–80. Mem., Council of Justice, 1955–60, 1965–70; Mem., General Council of the Bar, 1967–74, and of Senate of the Inns of Court and the Bar, 1974–81 (Vice-Chm. 1975–76; Chm., 1976–77); Chairman: London Common Law Bar Assoc., 1975–79; Judicial Studies Bd, 1980–83 (Mem. 1979–83); Review Bd for Govt Contracts, 1993–; Mem., City Disputes Panel, 1994–. Dir, Booker McConnell, 1978–79. FCIArb 1993. *Address:* West Stowell Place, Oare, Marlborough SN8 4JU. *Died 10 April 2009.*

WEDGWOOD, Sir (Hugo) Martin, 3rd Bt *cr* 1942, of Etruria, Co. Stafford; *b* 27 Dec. 1933; *s* of Sir John Hamilton Wedgwood, 2nd Bt, TD and Diana Mildred (*d* 1976), *d* of late Col Oliver Hawkshaw, TD; *S* father, 1989; *m* 1963, Alexandra Mary Gordon Clark, *er d* of late Judge Alfred Gordon Clark; one *s* two *d. Educ:* Eton; Trinity Coll., Oxford. European Sales Manager, Josiah Wedgwood & Sons Ltd, 1962–68. Mem., Stock Exchange, 1973–91; Partner, Laurence, Prust and Co., 1973–84; Dir, Smith New Court Far East Ltd, 1986–91. *Recreation:* ceramics. *Heir: s* Ralph Nicholas Wedgwood, *b* 10 Dec. 1964. *Club:* Athenæum. *Died 12 Oct. 2010.*

WEEDON, Dudley William, CEng, FIEE; retired; *b* 25 June 1920; *s* of Reginald Percy Weedon and Ada Kate Weedon; *m* 1951, Monica Rose Smith; one *s* one *d* (and one *s* decd). *Educ:* Colchester Royal Grammar Sch.; Northampton Polytechnic (BSc(Eng)). Marconi's Wireless Telegraph Co., 1937–48; Cable & Wireless Ltd, 1949–82 (Dir, 1979–82); Chm., Energy Communications Ltd, 1980–82. *Recreation:* sailing. *Address:* 103 Lexden Road, Colchester, Essex CO3 3RB. *Died 15 Feb. 2006.*

WEINBERGER, Caspar Willard, Hon. GBE 1988; Secretary of Defense, United States of America, 1981–87; Chairman, Forbes Magazine, since 1993 (Publisher, 1989–93); *b* San Francisco, Calif, 18 Aug. 1917; *s* of Herman and Cerise Carpenter (Hampson) Weinberger; *m* 1942, Jane Dalton; one *s* one *d. Educ:* Harvard Coll. (AB *magna cum laude*); Harvard Law Sch. (LLB). Member: Phi Beta Kappa; Amer. Bar Assoc.; State Bar of Calif; Dist of Columbia Bar. Served in Infantry, Private to Captain, AUS, 1941–45 (Bronze Star). Law Clerk to US Ct of Appeals Judge William E. Orr, 1945–47; with law firm Heller, Ehrman, White & McAuliffe, 1947–69, Partner, 1959–69. Member, Calif Legislature from 21st Dist, 1952–58; Vice-Chm., Calif Republican Central Cttee, 1960–62, Chm. 1962–64; Chm., Commn on Calif State Govt Organization and Economy, 1967–68; Dir of Finance, Calif, 1968–69; Chm., Fed. Trade Commn, 1970; Dep. Dir, 1970–72, Dir 1972–73, Office of Management and Budget; Counsellor to the President, 1973; Sec., HEW, 1973–75. Gen. Counsel, Vice-Pres., Dir, Bechtel gp of companies, 1975–81; Counsel, Rogers & Wells Internat. Law Firm, 1988–94; former Dir, Pepsi Co. Inc., Quaker Oats Co. Distinguished Vis. Prof., Edinburgh Univ., 1988. Formerly staff book reviewer, San Francisco Chronicle; moderator weekly TV prog., Profile, Bay area, station KQED, San Francisco, 1959–68; host, World Business Review, public TV, 1996–99. Frank Nelson Doubleday (Smithsonian) Lectr, 1974; Chm., Pres.'s Commn on Mental Retardation, 1973–75; Chm., USA-Republic of China Economic Council, 1991–94; Member: Nat. Econ. Commn, 1988–89; Pres's For. Intelligence Adv. Bd, 1988–90; Chatham House Foundn Inc., 1999–; former Member: Trilateral Commn; Adv. Council, Amer. Ditchley Foundn; Bd of Trustees, St Luke's Hosp., San Francisco; Trustee, Winston Churchill Meml Trust, 1994–; former Nat. Trustee, Nat. Symphony, Washington, DC; former Treas., Episcopal Dio. of California. Hon. LLD Leeds, 1989; Hon. DLitt Buckingham, 1995. Medal of Freedom, with Distinction (USA), 1987; Grand Cordon, Order of Rising Sun (Japan), 1988; Order of Brilliant Star, with Grand Cordon (China), 1988; Hilal-i-Pakistan (Pakistan), 1989. *Publications:* Fighting for Peace: seven critical years in the Pentagon, 1990; (with P. Schweizer) The Next War, 1996; In the Arena: a memoir of the 20th Century, 2001; (with P. Schweizer) Chain of Command, 2005; contributed a semi-weekly column for a number of Calif newspapers. *Address:* Forbes Magazine, 1101 17th Street NW, Suite 406, Washington, DC 20036, USA; Forbes Magazine, 60–5th Avenue, New York, NY 10011, USA. *Clubs:* Century (NY); Bohemian (San Francisco); Harvard (San Francisco/Washington DC). *Died 28 March 2006.*

WEIR, Sir Michael (Scott), KCMG 1980 (CMG 1974); HM Diplomatic Service, retired; Director, 21st Century Trust, 1990–2000; *b* 28 Jan. 1925; *s* of Archibald and Agnes Weir; *m* 1953, Alison Walker; two *s* two *d*; *m* 1976, Hilary Reid (OBE 1998); two *s*. *Educ:* Dunfermline High School; Balliol College, Oxford. Served RAF (Flt Lt), 1944–47; subseq. HM Diplomatic Service; Foreign Office, 1950; Political Agent, Trucial States, 1952–54; FO, 1954–56; Consul, San Francisco, 1956–58; 1st Secretary: Washington, 1958–61; Cairo, 1961–63; FO, 1963–68; Counsellor, Head of Arabian Dept, 1966; Dep. Political Resident, Persian Gulf, Bahrain, 1968–71; Head of Chancery, UK Mission to UN, NY, 1971–73; Asst Under-Sec. of State, FCO, 1974–79; Ambassador, Cairo, 1979–85. Pres., Egypt Exploration Soc., 1988–; Chm., British Egyptian Soc., 1990–. Officer's Cross, Order of Merit (Germany), 2002. *Recreations:* golf, music. *Address:* 37 Lansdowne Gardens, SW8 2EL. *Clubs:* Rye Golf, Royal Wimbledon Golf. *Died 22 June 2006.*

WEISSMÜLLER, Alberto Augusto, FCIB; President and Chief Executive Officer, A. A. Weissmüller Ltd, since 1992; General Partner, The Stillwaters Group, Washington, since 1992; *b* 2 March 1927; *s* of late Carlos Weissmüller and Michela Cottura; *m* 1976, Joan Ann Freifrau von Süsskind-Schwendi (*née* Smithson); one *s* one *d* by previous *m*. *Educ:* Univ. of Buenos Aires, Argentina; Illinois Inst. of Technol., Chicago, USA. Civil Engr, 1952; FCIB (FIB 1977). The Lummus Co., New York, 1958–59; Office of Graham Parker, NY, 1960–62; Bankers Trust Co., NY, 1962–71: Edge Act subsid., 1962–64; Asst Treasurer, and Mem., Bd of Corporation Financiera Nacional, Colombia, 1964–65; Asst Vice-Pres., 1965–67; Vice-Pres., 1967–71; Rome Rep., 1968–71; Man. Dir, Bankers Trust Finanziaria, SpA, Rome, 1970–71; Crocker National Bank, San Francisco, seconded to United Internat. Bank (subseq. Unibank Ltd), London, as Chief Exec., 1971–79; Chief Adviser, Bank of England, 1979–81; Chief Exec. (UK), Banca Commerciale Italiana, 1981–82; Chm., BCI Ltd, London, 1981–83; Dir, N American Bancorp Inc. (a subsid. of Banca Commerciale Italiana), 1982–87; Rep. of Banca Commerciale Italiana in Washington, 1983–92 and in Mexico City, 1987–92. *Publications:* Castles from the

Heart of Spain, 1977; Palladio in Venice, 2005. *Recreations:* medieval fortified and Palladian architecture, photography (architectural). *Address:* A. A. Weissmüller Ltd, 13801 Deakins Lane, Germantown, MD 20874, USA. *Died 12 Oct. 2007.*

WELLER, Dr Thomas Huckle; Richard Pearson Strong Professor of Tropical Public Health, Harvard University, 1954–85, Emeritus 1985 (Head, Department of Tropical Public Health, 1954–81); Director, Center for Prevention of Infectious Diseases, Harvard School of Public Health, 1966–81; *b* 15 June 1915; *s* of Carl V. and Elsie H. Weller; *m* 1945, Kathleen R. Fahey; two *s* two *d*. *Educ:* University of Michigan (AB, MS); Harvard (MD). Fellow, Departments of Comparative Pathology and Tropical Medicine and Bacteriology, Harvard Medical School, 1940–41; Intern, Children's Hosp., Boston, 1941–42. Served War, 1942–45: 1st Lieut to Major, Medical Corps, US Army. Asst Resident in Medicine, Children's Hosp., 1946; Fellow, Pediatrics, Harvard Medical School, 1947; Instructor, Dept Tropical Public Health, Harvard School of Public Health, 1948; Assistant Professor, 1949; Associate Professor, 1950. Asst Director, Research Div. of Infectious Diseases, Children's Medical Center, Boston, 1949–55; Dir, Commission on Parasitic Diseases, Armed Forces Epidemiological Bd, 1953–59, Mem. 1959–72; Mem. Trop. Med. and parasitology study sect., US Public Health Service, 1953–56. Diplomate, American Board of Pediatrics, 1948; Amer. Acad. of Arts and Sciences, 1955; National Academy of Sciences, USA. Consultant on tropical medicine and infectious diseases to foundations and industries, 1985–. Hon. FRSTM&H, 1987. Hon. LLD Michigan, 1956; Hon. DSc: Gustavus Adolphus Coll., 1975; Univ. of Mass Med. Sch., 1986; Hon. LHD Lowell, 1977. Mead Johnson Award of Amer. Acad. of Pediatrics (jointly), 1954; Kimble Methodology Award (jointly), 1954; Nobel Prize for Physiology or Medicine (jointly), 1954; Ledlie Prize, 1963; United Cerebral Palsy Weinstein-Goldenson Award, 1974; Bristol Award, Infectious Diseases Soc. of America, 1980; First Scientific Achievement Award, VZV Res. Foundn, 1993; Walter Reed Medal, Amer. Soc. of Tropical Medicine and Hygiene, 1996. *Publications:* numerous scientific papers on *in vitro* cultivation of viruses and on helminth infections of man. *Recreations:* gardening, photography. *Address:* 56 Winding River Road, Needham, MA 02492–1025, USA. *Club:* Harvard (Boston). *Died 23 Aug. 2008.*

WELLINGS, Sir Jack (Alfred), Kt 1975; CBE 1970; Chairman, 1968–87, Managing Director, 1963–84, The 600 Group Ltd; *b* 16 Aug. 1917; *s* of Edward Josiah and Selina Wellings; *m* 1946, Greta (*d* 2005), *d* of late George Tidey; one *s* two *d*. *Educ:* Selhurst Grammar Sch.; London Polytechnic. Vice-Pres., Hawker Siddeley (Canada) Ltd, 1954–62; Dep. Man. Dir, 600 Group Ltd, 1962. Member: NCB, 1971–77; NEB, 1977–79; part-time Mem., British Aerospace, 1980–87; non-exec. Dir, Clausing Corp., USA, 1982–84. *Address:* F115, Sunrise of Chorleywood, High View, Chorleywood, Rickmansworth, Herts WD3 5TQ. *Died 9 April 2010.*

WELLS, Ronald Alfred, OBE 1965; FRSC, FIMMM; industrial consultant, 1983–87; *b* 11 Feb. 1920; *s* of Alfred John Wells and Winifred Jessie (*née* Lambert); *m* 1953, Anne Brebner Lanshe; two *s*. *Educ:* Birkbeck College, London; Newport Technical College; BSc. Service with Government Chemist, 1939–40; Royal Naval Scientific Service, 1940–47; Joined Nat. Chemical Laboratory, 1947; Mem. UK Scientific Mission, Washington, 1951–52; Head of Radio-chemical Group, 1956; Head of Div. of Inorganic and Mineral Chemistry, 1963; Deputy Director, Nov. 1963; Director of National Chemical Laboratory, 1964; Dir of Research, TBA Industrial Products Ltd, 1965–70, Jt Man. Dir, 1970–77; Man. Dir, AMFU Ltd (Turner & Newall), 1977–81; Gp Scientist, Turner & Newall, 1981–83. Director: Salford Univ. Industrial Centre Ltd, 1981–82; Rochdale Private Surgical Unit, 1975–81; non-exec. Dir, Eversave (UK)

Ltd, 1984–85. Mem. Council, Royal Inst. Chemistry, 1965–68. *Publications:* numerous contribs to Inorganic Chromatography and Extractive Metallurgy. *Recreations:* gardening, golf, mineralogy. *Address:* Westbury, 19 First Avenue, Charmandean, Worthing, Sussex BN14 9NJ. *T:* (01903) 233844.   *Died 13 Aug. 2006.*

WEMYSS, 12th Earl of *cr* 1633, **AND MARCH,** 8th Earl of *cr* 1697; **Francis David Charteris,** KT 1966; Lord Wemyss of Elcho, 1628; Lord Elcho and Methil, 1633; Viscount Peebles, Baron Douglas of Neidpath, Lyne and Munard, 1697; Baron Wemyss of Wemyss (UK), 1821; President, The National Trust for Scotland, 1967–91, then President Emeritus (Chairman of Council, 1946–69); Lord Clerk Register of Scotland and Keeper of the Signet, 1974–2007; *b* 19 Jan. 1912; *s* of late Lord Elcho (killed in action, 1916) and Lady Violet Manners (she *m* 2nd, 1921, Guy Holford Benson (decd), and *d* 1971), 2nd *d* of 8th Duke of Rutland; *S* grandfather, 1937; *m* 1st, 1940, Mavis Lynette Gordon, BA (*d* 1988), *er d* of late E. E. Murray, Hermanus, Cape Province; one *s* one *d* (and one *s* and one *d* decd); 2nd, 1995, Shelagh Kathleen Kennedy, *d* of George Ernest Thrift, Vancouver. *Educ:* Eton; Balliol College, Oxford. Assistant District Commissioner, Basutoland, 1937–44. Served with Basuto Troops in Middle East, 1941–44. Lieut, Queen's Body Guard for Scotland, Royal Company of Archers; Lord High Comr to Gen. Assembly of Church of Scotland, 1959, 1960, 1977; Chairman: Scottish Cttee, Marie Curie Meml Foundn, 1952–86; Royal Commn on Ancient and Historical Monuments, Scotland, 1949–84; Scottish Churches Council, 1964–71; Hon. Pres., The Thistle Foundn; Mem., Central Cttee, WCC, 1961–75; Mem., Royal Commn on Historical Manuscripts, 1975–85. Consultant, Wemyss and March Estates Management Co. Ltd; formerly Director: Standard Life Assurance Co. Ltd; Scottish Television Ltd. Lord-Lieut, E Lothian, 1967–87. Hon. LLD St Andrews, 1953; DUniv Edinburgh, 1983. *Heir: s* Lord Neidpath, *b* 22 June 1948. *Address:* Gosford House, Longniddry, East Lothian EH32 0PX. *Club:* New (Edinburgh).   *Died 12 Dec. 2008.*

WERNER, Alfred Emil Anthony; Chairman, Pacific Regional Conservation Center, 1975–82; *b* 18 June 1911; *o s* of late Professor Emil Alphonse Werner, Dublin; *m* 1939, Marion Jane Davies (*d* 1973); two *d. Educ:* St Gerard's School, Bray; Trinity College, Dublin (MSc 1936; MA 1937); Univ. of Freiburg im Breisgau (DPhil 1937). ARIC 1936. Lecturer in Chemistry, TCD, 1937; Reader in Organic Chemistry, TCD, 1946; Research Chemist, National Gallery, 1948; Principal Scientific Officer, British Museum Research Laboratory, 1954, Keeper, 1959–75. Prof. of Chemistry, Royal Acad., 1962–75. FSA 1958; FMA 1959 (President, 1967); MRIA 1963. Pres., International Institute for the Conservation of Artistic and Historic Works, 1971 (Hon. Treasurer, 1962). Hon. ScD Dublin, 1971. *Publications:* The Scientific Examination of Paintings, 1952; (with H. Roosen-Runge) Codex Lindisfarnensis, Part V, 1961; (with H. J. Plenderleith) The Conservation of Antiquities and Works of Art, 1972; articles in scientific and museum journals. *Recreations:* chess, travelling. *Address:* 11/73 South Street, Bellerive, Tas 7018, Australia. *T:* (3) 62446959. *Clubs:* Athenæum; Tasmanian (Hobart).   *Died 21 Jan. 2006.*

WESIL, Dennis; Senior Director, Posts, 1971–75, and Member, 1975, Post Office Management Board; *b* 18 Feb. 1915; *e s* of Jack and Polly Wesil, London; *m* 1941, Kathleen, *d* of H. S. McAlpine; two *d. Educ:* Central Foundation Sch.; University Coll., London. Entered London telephone service as Asst Supt of Traffic, 1937; PO Investigation Branch, 1941; Asst Postal Controller, 1947; Principal, GPO Headqrtrs, 1953; Dep. Chief Inspector of Postal Services, 1961; Asst Sec., head of Postal Mechanisation Branch (in charge of develt of UK postcode system, admin. responsibility for security of mails and post offices), 1963; Dep. Dir, NE Region (GPO), 1966; Director: NE Postal Region, 1967; London Postal Region, 1970–71. *Recreations:* reading,

lunching out. *Address:* 2 Stoneleigh, 17 Martello Road South, Poole, Dorset BH13 7HQ. *T:* (01202) 707304.   *Died 7 April 2008.*

WEST, David Thomson, CBE 1982; *b* 10 March 1923; *m* 1958, Marie Sellar; one *s* one *d. Educ:* Malvern Coll.; St John's Coll., Oxford. Served in RNVR, 1942–45; HM Diplomatic Service, 1946–76; served in Foreign Office, Office of Comr General for UK in SE Asia, HM Embassies, Paris, Lima, and Tunis; Counsellor, 1964; Commercial Inspector, 1965–68; Counsellor (Commercial) Berne, 1968–71; Head of Export Promotion Dept, FCO, 1971–72; seconded to Civil Service Dept as Head of Manpower Div., 1972–76; transf. to Home Civil Service, 1976, retired 1983. *Publications:* Admiral Edward Russell and the Rise of British Naval Supremacy, 2005. *Address:* 14 Newbiggen Street, Thaxted CM6 2QR. *T:* (01371) 830228.   *Died 16 Dec. 2008.*

WEST, Michael Charles B.; *see* Berestord-West.

WEST, Norman; Member (Lab) Yorkshire South, European Parliament, 1984–98; *b* 26 Nov. 1935; *m* Shirley; two *s. Educ:* Barnsley; Sheffield Univ. Miner. Mem., South Yorks CC (Chm., Highways Cttee; Mem., anti-nuclear working party). Member: NUM; CND. Mem., Energy, Research and Technology Cttee, European Parlt, 1984–98. *Address:* 43 Coronation Drive, Birdwell, Barnsley, South Yorks S70 5RJ.   *Died 7 Sept. 2009.*

WEST, Prof. Richard John, FRCP, FRCPCH; Medical Postgraduate Dean to South West Region, Hon. Professor of Postgraduate Medical Education, University of Bristol, and Hon. Consultant Paediatrician, Royal Hosp. for Sick Children, Bristol, 1991–99; *b* 8 May 1939; *s* of late Cecil J. West and of Alice B. West (*née* Court); *m* 1962, Jenny Winn Hawkins; one *s* two *d. Educ:* Tiffin Boys' Sch.; Middlesex Hospital Medical School (MB, BS); Inst. of Child Health, London (MD 1975). MRCP 1967, FRCP 1979; FRCPCH 1997. Research Fellow, Inst. of Child Health, London, 1971–73; Sen. Registrar, Hosp. for Sick Children, London, 1973–74; Lectr, Inst. of Child Health, 1974–75; Sen. Lectr, 1975–91, Dean, 1982–87, St George's Hosp. Med. Sch.; Consultant Paediatrician, St George's Hosp., 1975–91. Member: Wandsworth HA, 1981–82, 1989–90; SW Thames RHA, 1982–88. Member: DoH Clinical Outcomes Gp, 1991–96; Steering Gp on Undergraduate Med. and Dental Educn and Res., 1992–97. Mem. Governing Body, Inst. of Med. Ethics, 1985–96 (Gen. Sec., 1989–96); Governor: Tiffin Boys' Sch., 1983–86; Wimbledon High Sch., 1988–91. *Publications:* Family Guide to Children's Ailments, 1983; Royal Society of Medicine Child Health Guide, 1992; research papers on metabolic diseases, incl. lipid disorders. *Recreations:* windmills, medical history, travel, archaeology.   *Died 1 March 2010.*

WEST, Prof. Thomas Summers, CBE 1988; FRS 1989; FRSE, FRSC; Director, Macaulay Institute for Soil Research, Aberdeen, 1975–87; Honorary Research Professor, University of Aberdeen, 1983–87, then Emeritus; *b* 18 Nov. 1927; *s* of late Thomas West and Mary Ann Summers; *m* 1952, Margaret Officer Lawson, MA; one *s* two *d. Educ:* Tarbat Old Public Sch., Portmahomack; Royal Acad., Tain; Aberdeen Univ. (BSc 1st Cl. Hons Chemistry, 1949); Univ. of Birmingham (PhD 1952, DSc 1962). FRSC (FRIC 1962); FRSE 1979. Univ. of Birmingham: Sen. DSIR Fellow, 1952–55; Lectr in Chem., 1955–63; Imperial Coll., London: Reader in Analytical Chem., 1963–65; Prof. of Analytical Chem., 1965–75. Royal Society: Mem., British National Cttee for Chem., and Chm., Analytical Sub-cttee, 1965–82; Mem., Internat. Cttee, 1990–92; Mem., Internat. Exchanges Cttee, 1992– (Chm. Panel III). Sec. Gen., IUPAC, 1983–91 (Pres., Analytical Div., 1977–79); Pres., Soc. for Analytical Chem., 1969–71; Chm., Finance Cttee, ICSU, 1990–92; Mem., British Nat. Cttee for IUPAC, RSC, 1990–98;

Hon. Sec., Chemical Soc., 1972–75 (Redwood Lectr, 1974); Hon. Member: Bunseki Kagakukai (Japan), 1981; Fondation de la Maison de la Chimie (Paris), 1985. Meldola Medal, RIC, 1956; Instrumentation Medal, 1976, and Gold Medal, 1977, Chemical Soc.; Johannes Marcus Medal for Spectroscopy, Spectroscopic Soc. of Bohemia, 1977. *Publications:* Analytical Applications of Diamino ethane tetra acetic acid, 1958, 2nd edn 1961; New Methods of Analytical Chemistry, 1964; Complexometry with EDTA and Related Reagents, 1969. *Recreations:* gardening, motoring, reading, music, family history research. *Address:* 31 Baillieswells Drive, Bieldside, Aberdeen AB15 9AT. *T:* (01224) 868294.
Died 9 Jan. 2010.

WESTON, John William, CB 1979; Principal Assistant Solicitor, Board of Inland Revenue, 1967–80; *b* 3 Feb. 1915; *s* of Herbert Edward Weston, MA, and Emma Gertrude Weston; *m* 1943, Frances Winifred (*née* Johnson); two *s* one *d. Educ:* Berkhamsted Sch., Herts. Solicitor, 1937. Joined Inland Revenue, 1940; Sen. Legal Asst, 1948; Asst Solicitor, 1954. *Recreation:* golf. *Address:* 5 Dickerage Road, Kingston Hill, Surrey KT1 3SP.
Died 1 Dec. 2006.

WHALE, John Hilary; journalist; Editor, Church Times, 1989–95; *b* 19 Dec. 1931; *s* of late Rev. Dr John Seldon Whale and Mary Whale (*née* Carter); *m* 1957, Judith Laurie Hackett; one *s. Educ:* Winchester; Corpus Christi College, Oxford. BA Lit Hum 1955, MA 1958. Lieut, Intelligence Corps, 1950–51 (Nat. Service). Writing, acting and teaching, 1954–58; Section Anglaise, French radio, Paris, 1958–59; ITN, 1960–69: Political Corresp., 1963–67; US Corresp., Washington, 1967–69; Sunday Times, 1969–84: political staff, 1969–79; Religious Affairs Corresp., 1979–84; Asst Editor, 1981–84; leader-writer throughout; Head of Religious Programmes, BBC TV, 1984–89. Dir, London programme, Univ. of Missouri Sch. of Journalism, 1980–83. Churchwarden, St. Mary's, Barnes, 1976–81. *Publications:* The Half-Shut Eye, 1969; Journalism and Government, 1972; The Politics of the Media, 1977; One Church, One Lord, 1979 (Winifred Mary Stanford Prize, 1980); (ed) The Pope from Poland, 1980; Put it in Writing, 1984; (contrib.) Why I am Still an Anglican, 1986; The Future of Anglicanism, 1988; contribs to books, quarterlies, weeklies. *Address:* 45 Shakespeare Road, W3 6SE. *T:* (020) 8993 7952.
Died 17 June 2008.

WHARTON, Michael Bernard; author and journalist; 'Peter Simple' Columnist, Daily and Sunday Telegraph, since 1957; *b* 19 April 1913; *s* of Paul Nathan and Bertha Wharton; *m* 1st, 1936, Joan Atkey (marr. diss. 1947); one *s*; 2nd 1952, Catherine Mary Derrington (marr. diss. 1972; she *d* 1992); one *d*; 3rd, 1974, Susan Moller. *Educ:* Bradford Grammar Sch.; Lincoln Coll., Oxford. Army service, Royal Artillery and General Staff, 1940–46. Scriptwriter and Producer, BBC, 1946–56; (with Colin Welch) writer of Peter Simple column, Daily Telegraph, 1957–60. *Publications: as Michael Wharton:* (ed) A Nation's Security, 1955; Sheldrake (novel), 1958; The Missing Will (autobiog.), 1984; A Dubious Codicil (autobiog.), 1991; editor and mainly writer of anthologies of Peter Simple column, 1963, 1965, 1969, 1971, 1973, 1975, 1978, 1980, 1984, 1987; Far Away is Close at Hand: 40 years of Peter Simple, 1995; Peter Simple's Century, 1999; Peter Simple's Domain, 2003; *under pseudonym Simon Crabtree:* Forgotten Memories, 1941; Hector Tumbler Investigates, 1943.
Died 23 Jan. 2006.

WHEELER, Sir Charles (Cornelius-), Kt 2006; CMG 2001; journalist and broadcaster, since 1940; *b* 26 March 1923; *s* of late Wing-Comdr Charles Cornelius-Wheeler, RFC, RAF and RAFVR, and Winifred (*née* Rees); *m* 1962, Dip Singh; two *d. Educ:* Cranbrook School. Began journalism as tape-boy, Daily Sketch, 1940. Served War, Royal Marines, 1942–46; Captain 1944 (despatches NW Europe). Sub-editor, BBC Latin American Service, 1947–49; German Service Correspondent in Berlin, 1950–53; Talks writer, European Service, 1954–56; Producer, Panorama, 1956–58; S Asia Correspondent,

1958–62; Berlin Corresp., 1962–65; Washington Corresp., 1965–68; Chief Correspondent: USA, 1969–73; Europe, 1973–76; BBC Television News, 1977; Panorama, 1977–79; Newsnight, 1980–95. Documentaries include: The Kennedy Legacy, 1970; Battle for Berlin, 1985; The Road to War (series), 1989; Bloody Sunday in Tbilisi, 1989; Beyond Reasonable Doubt, 1990; The Legacy of Martin Luther King, 1993; D-Day, 1994; The Battle of Normandy, 1994; Burma: the forgotten war, 1995; Wheeler on America (series), 1996; The LBJ Tapes, 1997; Why Stephen?, 1999; The White House Tapes (series), 1999; The Evacuation (series), 1999; The Peacetime Conscripts (series), 2000; The Nationbuilders (series), 2001; Death Row on Trial, 2001; The Child Migrants (series), 2003; From Dunkirk to D-Day, 2004; Coming Home (series), 2006. DUniv Open, 1992; Hon. DLitt Sussex, 1995. TV Journalist of the Year, RTS, 1988; Internat. Documentary Award, RTS, 1989; James Cameron Meml Award, City Univ., 1990; RTS Special Commendation, 1992; Cyril Bennett Award, RTS, 1993; Harvey Lee Award, BPG, 1995; TV Journalist of the Year, BPG, 1996; RTS Judges' Award, 1996; BAFTA Special Award, 1997; Home Documentary Award, RTS, 1999; Sony Radio Speech Award, 2000; Media Soc. Award, 2003; Radio Award, Voice of the Listener and Viewer, 2005. *Publications:* The East German Rising (with Stefan Brant), 1955. *Recreations:* gardening, travel. *Address:* 10A Portland Road, W11 4LA.
Died 4 July 2008.

WHEELER, Air Chief Marshal Sir (Henry) Neil (George), GCB 1975 (KCB 1969; CB 1967); CBE 1957 (OBE 1949); DSO 1943; DFC 1941 (Bar 1943); AFC 1954; *b* 8 July 1917; *s* of late T. H. Wheeler, South African Police; *m* 1942, Elizabeth, *d* of late W. H. Weightman, CMG; two *s* one *d. Educ:* St Helen's College, Southsea, Hants. Entered Royal Air Force College, Cranwell, 1935; Bomber Comd, 1937–40; Fighter and Coastal Comds, 1940–45; RAF and US Army Staff Colls, 1943–44; Cabinet Office, 1944–45; Directing Staff, RAF Staff Coll., 1945–46; FEAF, 1947–49; Directing Staff, JSSC, 1949–51; Bomber Comd, 1951–53; Air Min., 1953–57. Asst Comdt, RAF Coll., 1957–59; OC, RAF Laarbruch, 1959–60; IDC, 1961; Min. of Defence, 1961–63; Senior Air Staff Officer, HQ, RAF Germany (2nd TAF), Sept. 1963–66; Asst Chief of Defence Staff (Operational Requirements), MoD, 1966–67, Deputy Chief of Defence Staff, 1967–68; Commander, FEAF, 1969–70; Air Mem. for Supply and Organisation, MoD, 1970–73; Controller, Aircraft, MoD Procurement Exec., 1973–75. ADC to the Queen, 1957–61. Director: Rolls-Royce Ltd, 1977–82; Flight Refuelling (Holdings) Ltd, 1977–85. Chm., Anglo-Ecuadorian Soc., 1986–88. Vice-Pres., Air League; Liveryman, GAPAN, 1980, Master, 1986–87. FRAeS; CCMI. *Address:* Boundary Hall, Cooksbridge, Lewes, East Sussex BN8 4PT. *Clubs:* Royal Air Force, Flyfishers'.
Died 9 Jan. 2009.

WHEELER, Sir (Selwyn) Charles (Cornelius-); *see* Wheeler, Sir C. C.

WHEELER-BENNETT, Richard Clement; Chairman of the Council, Marie Curie Cancer Care (formerly Marie Curie Memorial Foundation), 1990–2000; *b* 14 June 1927; *s* of Dr Clement Wheeler-Bennett and Enid Lucy (*née* Boosey); *m* 1st, 1954, Joan Ellen Havelock (marr. diss. 2000); two *d* (one *s* decd); 2nd, 2001, Hon. Lady Smith-Ryland. *Educ:* Radley; Christ Church, Oxford (MA); Harvard Business Sch. Served Royal Marines, 1944–48. First Nat. City Bank of NY, 1951–66, Manager 1960–66; Australia and New Zealand Banking Group, 1966–80; Exec. Dir, 1967–78; Gen. Manager Europe, 1978–80; Chm., Thomas Borthwick & Sons Ltd, 1980–85; Director: Fleming Technology Trust, 1983–90; Fleming Internat. High Income Investment Trust, 1990–92; ANZ Grindlays Bank, 1993–96. Pres. Dir Gen., Boucheries Bernard SA, Paris, 1980–85. Chm., British Overseas and Commonwealth Banks Assoc., 1980. Founder Chm., Prospect Housing Assoc., 1965–77.

Chm. of Govs, Springfields Sch., Calne, 1991–2007. Chm., Roehampton Club Ltd, 1988–92. Freeman, City of London; Liveryman, Butchers' Co. *Recreations:* flyfishing, golf, shooting, viticulture. *Address:* The Old Hall, Medbourne, Market Harborough, Leics LE16 8DZ. *T:* (01858) 565543. *Clubs:* Brooks's, Pratt's, MCC.
Died 17 Jan. 2010.

WHELAN, Terence Leonard; editorial consultant; Editor, Ideal Home Magazine, 1977–95; *b* 5 Dec. 1936; *s* of Thomas James and Gertrude Beatrice Whelan; *m* 1972, Margaret Elizabeth Bowen; one *d*, and two *s* from previous marriage. *Educ:* Oakfield Secondary School. NDD 1955; MSTD 1972. Studied Graphic Design at Beckenham College of Art, 1953–56. Art Editor, Publishers, Condé Nast, working on Vogue Pattern Book, Vogue South Africa and British Vogue, 1959–68; gained a number of Design and Art Direction awards during this period; Art Editor, 1968–74, Asst Editor/Art Director, 1974–77, Ideal Home magazine. FRSA 1993. Editor of the Year, Special Interest Section, British Soc. of Magazine Editors, 1988. *Publications:* writer and broadcaster on home improvements. *Died 16 Sept. 2006.*

WHELER, Sir Edward (Woodford), 14th Bt *cr* 1660, of City of Westminster; Company Secretary, Robert Lewis (St James's) Ltd, 1981–90; *b* 13 June 1920; *s* of Sir Trevor Wood Wheler, 13th Bt, and Margaret Idris (*d* 1987), *y d* of late Sir Ernest Birch, KCMG; *S* father, 1986; *m* 1945, Molly Ashworth (*d* 2000), *e d* of Thomas Lever, Devon; one *s* one *d*. *Educ:* Radley College. Joined Army (RA), 1940; commnd Royal Sussex Regt, 1941; attached 15 Punjab Regt, IA, 1941–45; BAOR, 1945–47. Oversea Audit Service, Uganda and Ghana, 1948–58; Automobile Association of East Africa, Kenya, 1958–70; Benson & Hedges Ltd, 1971–81, Director 1979–81. Liveryman, Co. of Pipe Makers and Tobacco Blenders, 1980; Freeman, City of London, 1980. *Heir: s* Trevor Woodford Wheler [*b* 11 April 1946; *m* 1974, Rosalie Margaret, *d* of late Ronald Thomas Stunt; two *s*]. *Died 22 June 2008.*

WHEWAY, Albert James; Director, Hogg Robinson Travel Ltd, since 1976; *b* 6 April 1922; *s* of Albert and Alice Wheway; *m* 1st, 1946, Joan Simpson; 2nd, 1984, Susannah Mary Gray (*née* Luesby). *Educ:* Kimberworth School, Rotherham. Cooper Bros (later Cooper Lybrand), 1946–53; S. G. Warburg, 1953–57; industry, 1957–63; Ionian Bank, 1963–70; internat. industry and commerce, 1970–; Chm., Hogg Robinson Group plc, 1983–87. *Recreations:* art collecting, music. *Address:* Bilancia, Cappella Alta, Lucca 55060, Italy. *T:* (583) 394473. *Died 17 Dec. 2007.*

WHISHAW, Sir Charles (Percival Law), Kt 1969; solicitor (retired); *b* 29 Oct. 1909; 2nd *s* of late Montague Law Whishaw and Erna Louise (*née* Spies); *m* 1936, Margaret Joan (*d* 1989), *e d* of late Col T. H. Hawkins, CMG, RMLI; one *s* two *d*. *Educ:* Charterhouse; Worcester College, Oxford. Called to the Bar, Inner Temple, 1932; Solicitor, 1938; Partner in Freshfields, 1943–74. Trustee, Calouste Gulbenkian Foundn, 1956–81. Member: Iron and Steel Holding and Realisation Agency, 1953–67; Council, Law Soc., 1967–76. Comdr, Order of Prince Henry (Portugal), 1981. *Address:* Crispins Nursing Home, 43a Waverley Lane, Farnham, Surrey GU9 8BH.
Died 15 Dec. 2006.

WHITE, Colin Saunders, FSA, FRHistS; Director, Royal Naval Museum, Portsmouth, since 2006; *b* 28 Aug. 1951; *s* of Philip Saunders White and Margaret Joyce White (*née* Gummer). *Educ:* Culford Sch., Bury St Edmunds; Southampton Univ. (BA Hons); King's Coll., London (MA). FRHistS 2005. Royal Naval Museum, Portsmouth: Asst Curator, 1975–82; Chief Curator, 1982–96; Dep. Dir and Hd, Mus. Services, 1996–2001; Dir, Trafalgar 200, Nat. Maritime Mus., 2001–06. Chm., Official Nelson Commemorations Cttee, 2001–06. FSA 2003. Hon. DLitt Portsmouth, 2004; Hon. MA Chichester, 2005. *Publications:* The End of the Sailing

Navy 1815–1870, 1981; The Heyday of Steam 1870–1910, 1983; The Nelson Companion, 1995, 2nd edn 2005; 1797: Nelson's Year of Destiny, 1998; The Nelson Encyclopaedia, 2002, 2nd edn 2005; Nelson: the new letters, 2005, 2nd edn 2006 (Dist. Book Award, Soc. for Mil. Hist. 2006); The Trafalgar Captains: their lives and memorials, 2005; Nelson the Admiral, 2005; articles in Mariners' Mirror, Jl Maritime Res., History Today, BBC History, Trafalgar Chronicle, Nelson Dispatch. *Recreations:* Church of England (passionate liberal catholic), amateur drama (Mem., Southsea Shakespeare Actors), historical novels, the Mediterranean, messing about in boats. *Address:* Royal Naval Museum, HM Naval Base, Portsmouth PO1 3NH. *T:* (023) 9272 7574; *e-mail:* colin.white@royalnavalmuseum.org. *Clubs:* Army and Navy, Naval. *Died 25 Dec. 2008.*

WHITE, (Edward) Martin (Everatt); *b* 22 Feb. 1938; *s* of Frank and Norah White; *m* 1969, Jean Catherine Armour; one *s* one *d*. *Educ:* Priory Boys' Grammar Sch., Shrewsbury; King's Coll., Cambridge (MA). Solicitor Asst Solicitor, Lancs County Council, 1962–65; Sen. Asst Solicitor, then Asst Clerk, later Principal Asst Clerk, Kent County Council, 1965–72; Dep. Chief Exec., Somerset County Council, 1972–74; Chief Executive: Winchester City Council, 1974–80; Bucks County Council, 1980–88; Nat. Assoc. of Citizens Advice Bureaux, 1988–90. CCMI. *Recreations:* gardening, walking, theatre, music, travel. *Address:* 1 School Lane, Itchen Abbas, Winchester SO21 1BE. *T:* (01962) 779617. *Died 26 Jan. 2008.*

WHITE, Sir Henry Arthur Dalrymple D.; *see* Dalrymple-White.

WHITE, James; Managing Director, Glasgow Car Collection Ltd, 1959–87; *b* 10 April 1922; *m* 1948, Mary Dempsey (*d* 2002); one *s* two *d*. *Educ:* Knightswood Secondary School. Served Eighth Army, War of 1939–45 (African and Italian Stars; Defence Medal). MP (Lab) Glasgow (Pollok), 1970–87. Mem. Commonwealth Parly Assoc. Delegns, Bangladesh, 1973, Nepal, 1981. *Address:* 23 Alder Road, Glasgow G43 2UU. *Died 19 Feb. 2009.*

WHITE, Hon. Sir John (Charles), Kt 1982; MBE (mil.) 1942; Judge of High Court of New Zealand, retired 1981, sat as retired Judge, 1982–84; *b* 1 Nov. 1911; *s* of Charles Gilbert White and Nora Addison Scott White; *m* 1st, 1943, Dora Eyre Wild (*d* 1982); one *s* three *d*; 2nd, 1987, Margaret Elspeth Maxwell Fletcher. *Educ:* Wellesley Coll., Wellington; John McGlashan Coll., Dunedin; Victoria University Coll., Wellington; Univ. of New Zealand (LLM Hons). Barrister and Solicitor of Supreme Court of New Zealand. Judge's Associate, 1937–38; served War, Middle East, Greece, Crete, N Africa, Italy, 1940–45, ADC to Gen. Freyberg, 2nd NZEF, ME, 1940–45 (final rank Major); formerly Dominion Vice-Pres., New Zealand Returned Services Assoc.; Private practice as barrister and solicitor, Wellington, 1945–66; Pres., Wellington Law Soc., Vice-Pres., NZ Law Soc., 1966; QC and Solicitor General of New Zealand, 1966; Judge of the Supreme Court (later High Court), 1970, retd 1981; Judge Advocate General of Defence Forces, 1966–87. Actg Chief Justice, Solomon Islands, 1984. Pres., Solomon Is Court of Appeal, 1985–87. Royal Comr, Inquiry into 1982 Fiji Gen. Election, 1983. Asst Editor, Sim's Practice & Procedure, 9th edn, 1955, and 10th edn 1966. *Publications:* letters and commentaries in mil. pubns and the press on hist. of NZ Forces in ME during World War II, and world peace through rule of law. *Recreations:* formerly Rugby, cricket, tennis, golf, bowls. *Address:* 23 Selwyn Terrace, Wellington 6001, New Zealand. *T:* (4) 4725502. *Clubs:* Wellington; Dunedin; Melbourne. *Died 27 Oct. 2007.*

WHITE, Martin; *see* White, E. M. E.

WHITE, Adm. Sir Peter, GBE 1977 (KBE 1976; CBE 1960; MBE 1944); Chief of Fleet Support, 1974–77; *b* 25 Jan. 1919; *s* of William White, Amersham, Bucks; *m* 1st,

1947, Audrey Eileen (*d* 1991), *d* of Ernest Wallin, Northampton; two *s*; 2nd, 2007, Joan, *d* of A. P. B. Davenport, Pointe-a-Pierre, Trinidad. *Educ:* Dover College. Secretary: to Chief of Staff, Home Fleet, 1942–43; to Flag Officer Comdg 4th Cruiser Sqdn, 1944–45; to Asst Chief of Naval Personnel, 1946–47; to Flag Officer, Destroyers, Mediterranean, 1948–49; to Controller of the Navy, 1949–53; to C-in-C Home Fleet and C-in-C Eastern Atlantic, 1954–55; Naval Asst to Chm. BJSM, Washington, and UK Rep. of Standing Group, NATO, 1956–59; Supply Officer, HMS Adamant, 1960–61; Dep. Dir of Service Conditions and Fleet Supply Duties, Admty, 1961–63; idc 1964; CO HMS Raleigh, 1965–66; Principal Staff Officer to Chief of Defence Staff, 1967–69; Dir-Gen. Fleet Services, 1969–71; Port Admiral, Rosyth, 1972–74. Consultant, Wilkinson Match Ltd, 1978–79; Associate Director: The Industrial Soc., 1980–88; BITC, 1988–96. Chm., Officers Pension Society, 1982–90. Mem. Foundn Cttee, Gordon Boys' Sch., 1979–89. *Died 22 May 2010.*

WHITE, Thomas Anthony B.; *see* Blanco White.

WHITEHEAD, Dr John Ernest Michael, FRCPath; Director of Public Health Laboratory Service, 1981–85; *b* 7 Aug. 1920; *s* of Dr Charles Ernest Whitehead and Bertha Whitehead; *m* 1946, Elizabeth Bacchus (*née* Cochran) (*d* 1996); one *s* one *d*. *Educ:* Merchant Taylors' Sch.; Gonville and Caius Coll., Cambridge (MA); St Thomas's Hosp. Med. Sch. (MB BChir, DipBact). Jun. House appts, St Thomas' Hosp., 1944–47; Lectr in Bacteriology, St Thomas's Hosp. Med. Sch., 1948–51; Travelling Fellowship, State Serum Inst., Copenhagen, 1949–50; Asst Bacteriologist, Central Public Health Laboratory, 1952–53; Dep. Dir, Public Health Lab., Sheffield, 1953–58; Dir, Public Health Lab., Coventry, 1958–75; Cons. Microbiologist, Coventry Hosps, 1958–75; Dep. Dir, Public Health Laboratory Service, 1975–81. Hon. Lecturer: Univ. of Sheffield, 1954–58; Univ. of Birmingham, 1962–75. Vice-Pres., RCPath, 1983–86; Member: Adv. Cttee on Dangerous Pathogens, 1981–85; Adv. Cttee on Irradiated and Novel Foods, 1982–86; Expert Adv. Gp on AIDS, 1985; Consultant Advr in Microbiol., DHSS, 1982–85; Specialist Advr to H of C Agric. Cttee, 1988–91, to H of C Social Services Cttee, 1989–90; Temporary Adviser and Chm., Working Gp on Safety Measures in Microbiology, WHO, 1976–82; Chm., Working Gp on Orgn and Admin of Public Health Laboratory Services, Council of Europe, 1977–79. *Publications:* chapters in The Pathological Basis of Medicine, ed R. C. Curran and D. G. Harnden, 1974; papers and reviews in med. microbiology in various med. and scientific jls. *Recreations:* house and garden visiting, modern languages. *Address:* Ashleigh Cottage, The Street, Frampton on Severn, Gloucester GL2 7ED. *T:* (01452) 741698. *Died 10 Aug. 2007.*

WHITEHEAD, Sir Rowland (John Rathbone), 5th Bt *cr* 1889; *b* 24 June 1930; *s* of Major Sir Philip Henry Rathbone Whitehead, 4th Bt, and 1st wife Gertrude, *d* of J. C. Palmer, West Virginia, USA; *S* father, 1953; *m* 1954, Marie-Louise, *d* of Arnold Christian Gausel, Stavanger, Norway; one *s* one *d*. *Educ:* Radley; Trinity Hall, Cambridge (BA). Late 2nd Lieut RA. Chm., First Media Syndicate Ltd. Chairman: Trustees, Rowland Hill Benevolent Fund, 1982–; Brogdale Trust Appeal, 1995–97; Trustee: Baronets' Trust, 1984– (founder Chm., 1984–89); Standing Council of the Baronetage, 1972–2002 (Chm., 1984–87, Vice-Pres., 2003–, Exec. Cttee); Brogdale Horticultural Trust, 1994–2002; Kelmscott House Trust, 1970–2002; Royal Aero Club Trust, 1998–; Brunel Engine House, 2004–. Vice Pres., English Music Fest., 2005–. Chm. and Trustee, Romanian Orthodox Church in London Trust, 2004–. Vice Chm., Tyndale Soc., 2001–; Pres., Rising Stars Foundn, Romania, 1998–. Hon. Mem., British Weights and Measures Assoc., 1998–. Pres., Inst. of Translation and Interpreting, 1996–2002 (Hon. Past Pres., 2002). Governor, Appleby Grammar Sch., 1964–. Churchwarden, St Mary Abchurch, City of London,

1996–. Freeman, City of London; Master, Co. of Fruiterers', 1995–96; Court, Guild of PR Practitioners, 2000– (Master, 2002–03). FRGS 2002. Comdr, Order of Merit (Romania), 2003. *Recreations:* poetry, rural indolence. *Heir: s* Philip Henry Rathbone Whitehead [*b* 13 Oct. 1957; *m* 1987, Emma (marr. diss. 2002), *d* of Captain A. M. D. Milne Home; two *s*. Late Welsh Guards]. *Address:* Sutton House, Chiswick Mall, W4 2PR. *T:* (020) 8994 2710; Walnut Tree Cottage, Fyfield, Lechlade, Glos GL7 3NT. *T:* (01367) 850267; *e-mail:* rowlandwhitehead@hotmail.com. *Club:* Arts. *Died 28 July 2007.*

WHITELAW, Prof. James Hunter, FRS 1996; FREng, FIMechE; Professor of Convective Heat Transfer, Imperial College, London, since 1974; *b* 28 Jan. 1936; *s* of James Whitelaw and Jean Ross Whitelaw (*née* Scott); *m* 1959, Elizabeth Shields; three *s*. *Educ:* Univ. of Glasgow (BSc 1957; PhD 1961); DSc London 1981. Res. Associate, Brown Univ., 1961–63; Lectr, Imperial Coll., 1963–69; Reader, Imperial Coll., 1969–74. Chair Prof. of Pollution and Combustion, Hong Kong Poly. Univ., 2000–04. Editor, Experiments in Fluids, 1983–99. FREng (FEng 1991); FCGI 1999. Foreign Associate, US Acad. of Engrg, 2000. DSc *hc*: Lisbon, 1980; Valencia, 1996; TCD, 1999; Nat. Technical Univ. of Athens, 2001. *Publications:* (jtly) Data and Formulae Handbook, 1967, 2nd edn 1976; (jtly) Principles and Practice of Laser-Doppler Anemometry, 1976, 2nd edn 1981; (jtly) Engineering Calculation Methods for Turbulent Flow, 1981; ed. 30 vols proc., and published over 380 papers in learned jls, incl. Jl of Fluid Mechanics, Experiments in Fluids, proc. of learned socs. *Recreations:* gardening, music. *Address:* 149a Coombe Lane West, Kingston-upon-Thames KT2 7DH. *T:* (020) 8942 1836. *Died 16 Aug. 2006.*

WHITESIDE, Prof. Derek Thomas, PhD; FBA 1975; University Professor of History of Mathematics and Exact Sciences, Cambridge, 1987–99, then Emeritus; *b* 23 July 1932; *s* of Ernest Whiteside and Edith (*née* Watts); *m* 1962, Ruth Isabel Robinson (*d* 1997); one *s* one *d*. *Educ:* Blackpool Grammar Sch.; Bristol Univ. (BA); Cambridge Univ. (PhD). Leverhulme Research Fellow, 1959–61; DSIR Research Fellow, 1961–63; Research Asst, 1963–72, Asst Dir of Research, 1972–76, University Reader in History of Mathematics, 1976–87, Univ. of Cambridge. Editor, The Mathematical Papers of Isaac Newton (8 vols), 1967–81. Hon. DLitt Lancaster, 1987. Médaille Koyré, Académie Internat. d'Histoire des Sciences, 1968; Sarton Medal, Amer. History of Sci. Soc., 1977. *Publications:* Patterns of Mathematical Thought in the later Seventeenth Century, 1961; (ed) The Preliminary Manuscripts for Isaac Newton's 1687 Principia: 1684–1685 (in facsimile), 1989; articles in Brit. Jl Hist. Science, Jl for Hist. of Astronomy, Physis, etc; *Festschrift:* The Investigation of Difficult Things, 1992. *Recreation:* looking into space creatively. *Address:* Centre for Mathematical Sciences, Wilberforce Road, Cambridge CB3 0WB. *Died 22 April 2008.*

WHITLEY, Elizabeth Young, (Mrs H. C. Whitley); social worker and journalist; *b* 28 Dec. 1915; *d* of Robert Thom and Mary Muir Wilson; *m* 1939, Henry Charles Whitley (Very Rev. Dr H. C. Whitley, CVO; *d* 1976); two *s* two *d* (and one *s* decd). *Educ:* Laurelbank School, Glasgow; Glasgow University (MA 1936). Courses: in Italian at Perugia Univ., 1935, in Social Science at London School of Economics and Glasgow School of Social Science, 1938–39. Ran Girls' Clubs in Govan and Plantation, Glasgow, and Young Mothers' Clubs in Partick and Port Glasgow; Vice-Chm. Scottish Association of Girls' Clubs and Mixed Clubs, 1957–61, and Chm. of Advisory Cttee, 1958–59. Broadcast regular programme with BBC (Scottish Home Service), 1953. Member: Faversham Committee on AID, 1958–60; Pilkington Committee on Broadcasting, 1960–62. Columnist, Scottish Daily Express. Adopted as Parly candidate for SNP by West Perth and Kinross, 1968. *Publications:* Plain Mr Knox, 1960; The Two Kingdoms:

the story of the Scottish covenanters, 1977; descriptive and centenary articles for Scottish papers, particularly Glasgow Herald and Scotland's Magazine. *Recreations:* listening to Radio 4 and Radio Scotland, gardening. *Address:* The Glebe, Southwick, by Dumfries DG2 8AR. *T:* (01387) 780276. *Died 11 Sept. 2010.*

WHITLEY, His Honour John Reginald; a Circuit Judge, 1986–96; Resident Judge, Portsmouth Combined Court Centre, 1988–96; *b* 22 March 1926; *o s* of late Reginald Whitley and of Marjorie Whitley (*née* Orton); *m* 1966, Susan Helen Kennaway; one *d*. *Educ:* Sherborne Sch.; Corpus Christi Coll., Cambridge. Served War, Army, Egypt, Palestine, 1944–48; commissioned, KRRC, 1945. Called to the Bar, Gray's Inn, 1953; Western Circuit, 1953; a Recorder, 1978–86. *Recreation:* golf. *Address:* Kingurod, Friday's Hill, Kingsley Green, near Haslemere, Surrey GU27 3LL. *Died 17 June 2009.*

WHITSEY, Fred, VMH; Gardening Correspondent, Daily Telegraph, 1971–2006; *b* 18 July 1919; *m* 1947, Patricia Searle. *Educ:* outside school hours, and continuously ever since. Popular Gardening; Assistant Editor, 1948–64, Associate Editor, 1964–67, Editor, 1967–82. Gardening correspondent, Sunday Telegraph, 1961–71. Vice-Pres., RHS, 1996–. Gold Veitch Meml Medal, RHS, 1979; VMH 1986; Lifetime Achievement Award, Garden Writers' Guild, 1994. *Publications:* Sunday Telegraph Gardening Book, 1966; Fred Whitsey's Garden Calendar, 1985; Garden for All Seasons, 1986; The Garden at Hidcote, 2007; contribs to Country Life and The Garden. *Recreations:* gardening, music. *Address:* Avens Mead, 20 Oast Road, Oxted, Surrey RH8 9DU. *Died 15 Aug. 2009.*

WHITTINGTON, Prof. Harry Blackmore, FRS 1971; Woodwardian Professor of Geology, Cambridge University, 1966–83; *b* 24 March 1916; *s* of Harry Whittington and Edith M. (*née* Blackmore); *m* 1940, Dorothy E. Arnold (*d* 1997); no *c*. *Educ:* Handsworth Gram. Sch.; Birmingham Univ. Commonwealth Fund Fellow, Yale Univ., 1938–40; Lectr in Geology, Judson Coll., Rangoon, 1940–42; Prof. of Geography, Ginling Coll., Chengtu, W China, 1943–45; Lectr in Geology, Birmingham Univ., 1945–49; Harvard Univ.: Vis. Lectr, 1949–50; Assoc. Prof. of Geology, 1950–58; Prof. of Geology, 1958–66. Trustee: British Museum (Nat. History), 1980–89; Uppingham Sch., 1983–91. Hon. Fellow, Geol Soc. of America, 1983. Hon. AM, Harvard Univ., 1950. Medal, Paleontol Soc., USA, 1983; Lyell Medal, 1986, Wollaston Medal, 2001, Geological Soc.; Mary Clark Thompson Medal, US Nat. Acad. of Scis, 1990; Lapworth Medal, Palaeontol Assoc., 2000; Medal, Geol Assoc. of Canada, 2000; Internat. Prize for Biology, Japan, 2001. *Publications:* The Burgess Shale, 1985; Trilobites, 1992; articles in Jl of Paleontology, Bulletin Geol. Soc. of Amer., Quarterly Jl Geol. Soc. London, Phil. Trans. Royal Soc., etc. *Club:* Geological. *Died 20 June 2010.*

WHITWELL, Stephen John, CMG 1969; MC; HM Diplomatic Service, retired; *b* 30 July 1920; *s* of Arthur Percy Whitwell and Marion Whitwell (*née* Greenwood). *Educ:* Stowe; Christ Church, Oxford. Coldstream Guards, 1941–47; joined HM Foreign Service (later Diplomatic Service), 1947; served: Tehran, 1947; FO, 1949; Belgrade, 1952; New Delhi, 1954; FO, 1958; Seoul, 1961. Pol Advr to C-in-C Middle East, Aden, 1964; Counsellor, Belgrade, 1965; Ambassador to Somalia, 1968–70; Head of East-West Contacts Dept, FCO, 1970–71. *Recreations:* reading, painting, looking at buildings. *Club:* Travellers. *Died 6 Oct. 2010.*

WHYTE, John Stuart, CBE 1976; MSc(Eng); FREng, FIEE; Chairman, GPT (International) Ltd, 1988–90; *b* High Wycombe, 20 July 1923; *s* of late William W. Whyte and Ethel K. Whyte; *m* 1951, (Edna) Joan (Mary) (*née* Budd) (*d* 1995); one *s* one *d*. *Educ:* The John Lyon Sch., Harrow; Northampton Polytechnic, London Univ. BSc(Eng) (Hons), MSc(Eng). Post Office Radio

Laboratory, Castleton, Cardiff, 1949–57; PO Research Station, Dollis Hill: Sen. Exec. Engr, 1957–61; Asst Staff Engr, 1961–65. Asst Sec., HM Treasury, 1965–68; Dep. Dir of Engrg, PO, 1968–71; Dir, Operational Programming, PO, 1971–75; Dir of Purchasing and Supply, 1975–76, Sen. Dir of Develt, 1977–79, Dep. Man. Dir, 1979–81, PO Telecommunications; Engr-in-Chief, Man. Dir (major systems), and Mem. Main Bd, British Telecom, 1981–83; Dir, British Telecommunications Systems Ltd, 1979–83; Chm., Astronet Corp., 1984–85; Pres., 1984–85, Chm., 1985–86, Stromberg Carlson Corp; Chm., Plessey Telecommunications (Internat.) Ltd, 1983–85; Dep. Chm., Plessey Telecommunications and Office Systems Ltd, 1985–88. Manager, Royal Instn, 1971–74 (Vice-Pres., 1972, 1973, 1974), Mem. Cttee of Visitors, 1975–78 (Chm., 1977–78), Chm., Membership Cttee, 1975–77. Mem., Nat. Electronics Council, 1977–2000 (Mem. Exec Cttee, 1977–2000; Dep. Chm., 1980–2000); Mem. Council, EPA, 1977–83. President: Instn of PO Electrical Engrs, 1977–82; Instn of British Telecommunications Engrs, 1982–83 (Hon. Mem., 1984); Mem. Council, IEE, 1980–84 (Vice-Pres., 1981–84; Chm. Professional Bd, 1981–84). FREng (FEng 1980). Governor, Internat. Council for Computer Communication, 1985–91. Liveryman, Scientific Instrument Makers' Co. Freeman, City of London, 1979. Leader, British Hinku Expedn, 1979; Pres., Assoc. of British Members of Swiss Alpine Club, 1988–90. *Publications:* various articles and papers in professional telecommunications jls. *Recreations:* mountaineering, opera, foreign travel, genealogy. *Address:* Wild Hatch, Coleshill Lane, Winchmore Hill, Amersham, Bucks HP7 0NT. *T.* (01494) 722663. *Clubs:* Alpine; Cambridge University Alpine (Hon.). *Died 24 Feb. 2006.*

WICKINS, David Allen; Founder and Chairman, Southern Counties Car Auctions, later The British Car Auction Group, 1946–89; *b* 15 Feb. 1920; *s* of Samuel Wickins and Edith Hannah Robinson; *m* 1969, Karen Esther Young; three *d*, and one *s* two *d* from previos marriages. *Educ:* St George's College, Weybridge. Trained as chartered accountant with Deloitte & Co., attached to Johannesburg Consolidated Investment Co. and moved to S Africa, 1938, to work on audits for Rhodesian copper mines and sawmills. War of 1939–45: S African Naval Forces (18 months with Eastern Fleet); seconded to RN; served with UK Coastal Forces. Former Chairman: Attwoods plc; Group Lotus plc; Expedier Leisure plc. *Recreations:* tennis, golf, sailing. *Clubs:* St James's, Royal Thames Yacht; Sunningdale Golf. *Died 28 Jan. 2007.*

WICKRAMASINGHE, Prof. Sunitha Nimal, PhD, ScD; FRCP, FRCPath; FIBiol; Professor, and Head of Department of Haematology, Imperial College, University of London, 1979–2000, Professor Emeritus, since 2000; *b* 2 July 1941; *s* of Percival Herbert Wickramasinghe and Theresa Elizabeth Wickramasinghe; *m* 1968, Priyanthi Soummia Fernando; one *s* two *d*. *Educ:* Royal Coll., Colombo; Univ. of Ceylon (MB BS); PhD 1968, ScD 1984, Cantab. FRCPath 1986; FRCP 1991; FIBiol 1982. Gulbenkian Res. Student, Churchill Coll., Cambridge, 1966–68; John Lucas Walker Sen. Student, Univ. of Cambridge, 1968; Clin. Res. Fellow, Univ. of Leeds, 1969; Lectr, 1970–73, Sen. Lectr, 1973–78, Reader in Haematol., 1978–79, St Mary's Hosp. Med. Sch., Univ. of London; Dep. Dean, ICSM at St Mary's, 1995–97; Hon. Consultant Haematologist: St Mary's Hosp., London, 1979–2006; Oxford Radcliffe Hosps, 2000–05. Vis. Prof. in Haematol., Univ. of Oxford, 2000–. Guest Lectr, Univ. degli Studi di Ferrara, Italy, 1993–97. Hon. Fellow, Sri Lanka Coll. of Haematologists, 1999; E. H. Cooray Meml Orator, Coll. of Pathologists, Sri Lanka, 1995; Sri Lanka Med. Assoc. Orator, 2005. Guest Editor: Megaloblastic Anaemia, 1995; Haematological Aspects of Infection, 2000. *Publications:* Human Bone Marrow, 1975; (ed) Blood and Bone Marrow: systemic pathology, 3rd edn 1986; (with N. C. Hughes-Jones) Lecture Notes on Haematology,

5th edn 1991, 6th edn 1996, (with N. C. Hughes-Jones and C. Hatton) 7th edn 2004, 8th edn 2008; (ed with J. McCullough) Blood and Bone Marrow Pathology, 2003; contrib. papers on abnormal erythropoiesis, esp. on congenital dyserythropoietic anaemias. *Recreations:* photography, travel, biology. *Address:* 32 Braywick Road, Maidenhead, Berks SL6 1DA. *T:* (01628) 621665.
Died 28 June 2009.

WICKS, (Edward) Allan, CBE 1988; Organist, Canterbury Cathedral, 1961–88; *b* 6 June 1923; *s* of late Edward Kemble Wicks, priest, and Nancie (*née* Murgatroyd); *m* 1955, Elizabeth Kay Butcher; two *d*. *Educ:* Leatherhead; Christ Church, Oxford. Sub-organist, York Minster, 1947; Organist, Manchester Cathedral, 1954. MusDoc Lambeth, 1974; Hon. DMus Kent, 1985. *Address:* 27 Chequers Park, Wye, Ashford, Kent TN25 5BB. *T:* (01233) 813920. *Died 4 Feb. 2010.*

WIDDAS, Prof. Wilfred Faraday, MB, BS; BSc; PhD; DSc; Professor of Physiology in the University of London, and Head of the Department of Physiology, Bedford College, 1960–81, then Professor Emeritus; *b* 2 May 1916; *s* of late Percy Widdas, BSc, mining engineer, and Annie Maude (*née* Snowdon); *m* 1940, Gladys Green (*d* 1983); one *s* two *d*. *Educ:* Durham School; University of Durham College of Medicine and Royal Victoria Infirmary, Newcastle upon Tyne. MB, BS 1938; BSc 1947; PhD 1953; DSc 1958. Assistant in General Practice, 1938–39. Served in RAMC, 1939–47; Deputy Assistant Director-General Army Medical Services, War Office (Major), 1942–47. Research Fellow, St Mary's Hospital Medical School, 1947–49; Lecturer and Sen. Lecturer in Physiology, St Mary's Hospital Medical School, 1949–55; Senior Lecturer in Physiology, King's College, 1955–56; University Reader in Physiology at King's College, 1956–60. FRSocMed. Mem., Royal Institution of Gt Britain; Hon. Mem., Physiological Society. *Publications:* papers on membrane transporters for glucose, the red cell anion exchanger and bicarbonate permeability; other research papers. *Address:* Honeysuckle Farm, Jarvis Gate, Sutton St James, Lincs PE12 0EU. *Died 23 Oct. 2008.*

WIDDOWS, Air Commodore (Stanley) Charles, CB 1959; DFC 1941 (despatches); RAF retired; People's Deputy, States of Guernsey, 1973–79; *b* 4 Oct. 1909; *s* of P. L. Widdows, Southend, Bradfield, Berkshire; *m* 1939, Irene Ethel, *d* of S. H. Rawlings, Ugley, Essex; two *s*. *Educ:* St Bartholomew's School, Newbury; No 1 School of Technical Training, RAF, Halton; Royal Air Force College, Cranwell. Commissioned, 1931; Fighting Area, RAF, 1931–32; RAF Middle East, Sudan and Palestine, 1933–37; Aeroplane and Armament Experimental Estab., 1937–40; OC 29 (Fighter) Sqdn, 1940–41; OC RAF West Malling, 1941–42; Gp Capt., Night Ops, HQ 11 and 12 Gp, 1942; SASO, No 85 (Base Defence) Gp, 1943–44, for Operation Overlord; Gp Capt. Organisation, HQ, Allied Expeditionary Air Force, 1944; OC, RAF Wahn, Germany, 1944–46; RAF Directing Staff, Sen. Officers War Course, RNC, Greenwich, 1946–48; Fighter Command, 1948–54: SASO HQ No 12 Gp; Chief Instructor, Air Defence Wing, School of Land/Air Warfare; Sector Commander, Eastern Sector. Imperial Defence College, 1955; Director of Operations (Air Defence), Air Ministry, 1956–58. Bailiwick Rep., RAF Benevolent Fund, 1973–93. Vice-Pres., Guernsey Scout Assoc., 1990– (Chm., 1974–90). *Address:* Les Granges de Beauvoir, Rohais, St Peter Port, Guernsey GY1 1QT. *T:* (01481) 720219. *Died 8 Jan. 2010.*

WIGDOR, Lucien Simon, CEng, FRAeS; President, L. S. Wigdor Inc., New Hampshire, 1984; Managing Director, L. S. Wigdor Ltd, 1976; *b* Oct. 1919; *s* of William and Adèle Wigdor; *m* 1951, Marion Louise, *d* of Henry Risner; one *s* one *d*. *Educ:* Highgate Sch.; College of Aeronautical Engineering (Dip. 1939). CEng 1989; FRAeS 2001. Served War, RAF, early helicopter pilot, 1940–46 (Sqn Ldr; FAI Helicopter Aviators Cert. No 10); Operational Research, BEA: Research Engr, 1947–51; Manager, Industrial and Corporate

Develt, Boeing Vertol Corp., USA, 1951–55; Managing Dir, Tunnel Refineries Ltd, 1955–69, Vice-Chm., 1969–72; Corporate Consultant, The Boeing Company, 1960–72; Dep. Dir-Gen., CBI, 1972–76; Chief Exec., Leslie & Godwin (Holdings) Ltd, 1977–78, Dir 1977–81; Chm., Weir Pumps Ltd, 1978–81; Director: The Weir Group, 1978–81; Rothschild Investment Trust, 1977–82; Zambian Engineering Services Ltd, 1979–84; Rothschild Internat. Investments SA, 1981–82. Special Adviser on Internat. Affairs, Bayerische Hypotheken-SPTund Wechsel-SPTBank AG, 1981–83; Consultant: Lazard Bros, 1982–84; Manufacturing and Financial Services Industries (L. S. Wigdor Inc.), 1984. *Publications:* papers to Royal Aeronautical Soc., American Helicopter Soc. *Recreations:* ski-ing, experimental engineering. *Address:* Indian Point, Little Sunapee Road, PO Box 1035, New London, NH 03257, USA. *T:* (603) 5264456, *Fax:* (603) 5264963. *Club:* Royal Air Force. *Died 12 Aug. 2008.*

WIGMORE, His Honour James Arthur Joseph; a Circuit Judge, 1990–2001; *b* 7 Aug. 1928; *s* of Sqdn-Ldr Arthur J. O. Wigmore, MB, and Kathleen (*née* Jowett); *m* 1966, Diana (*d* 2004), *d* of Comdr H. J. Holemans, RN; three *d*. *Educ:* Downside Sch.; Royal Military Acad., Sandhurst; English Coll., Rome. BSc London; PhL, STL, Gregorian Univ., Rome. Served Royal Signals, 1946–52, commnd 1948. Lectured in Philosophy: Downside Abbey, 1960–63; Oscott Coll., 1963–66. Called to the Bar, Inner Temple, 1971; Dep. Coroner, Bristol, 1976–88; a Recorder, 1989. *Club:* Naval and Military.
Died 4 Dec. 2007.

WILCOCK, Prof. William Leslie; consultant in industrial instrumentation; Professor of Physics, University College of North Wales, Bangor, 1965–82, then Emeritus; *b* 7 July 1922; *m* Pamela; one *s* one *d*. *Educ:* Manchester Univ. (BSc, PhD). Instrument Dept, RAE, 1943–45. Asst Lectr in Physics, 1945–48, Lectr, 1950–56, Manchester Univ.; DSIR Res. Fellow, St Andrews Univ., 1948–50; Reader in Instrument Technol., 1956–61, in Applied Physics, 1961–65, Imperial Coll. of Science and Technology, London. Arnold O. Beckman Award, Instrument Soc. of Amer., 1977. Mem., SERC, 1981–85. *Publications:* (contrib.) Principles of Optics, 1959; Advances in Electronics and Electron Physics, vols 12–16 (ed jtly), 1960–61; numerous papers in scientific jls. *Address:* 3 Garth Court, Llandudno LL30 2HF.
Died 4 Oct. 2006.

WILD, Dr (John) Paul, AC 1986; CBE 1978; FRS 1970; FAA; FTSE; Chairman and Chief Executive, Commonwealth Scientific and Industrial Research Organization, 1978–85 (Associate Member of Executive, 1977; Chief, Division of Radiophysics, 1971); *b* 17 May 1923; *s* of late Alwyn Howard Wild and Bessie Delafield (*née* Arnold); *m* 1st, 1948, Elaine Poole Hull (*d* 1991); two *s* one *d*, 2nd, 1991, Margaret Lyndon. *Educ:* Whitgift Sch.; Peterhouse, Cambridge (ScD 1962; Hon. Fellow 1982). FAA 1962; FTSE (FTS 1978). Radar Officer in Royal Navy, 1943–47; joined Research Staff of Div. of Radiophysics, 1947, working on problems in radio astronomy, esp. of the sun, later also radio navigation (Interscan aircraft landing system). Dep. Chm., 1973–75, 1980–82, Chm., 1975–80, Anglo-Australian Telescope Bd; Mem. Bd, Interscan (Australia) Pty Ltd, 1978–84. For. Sec., Australian Acad. of Science, 1973–77. For. Hon. Mem., Amer. Acad. of Arts and Scis, 1961; For. Mem., Amer. Philos. Soc., 1962; Corresp. Mem., Royal Soc. of Scis, Liège, 1969. Hon. FIE(Aust), 1991; Hon. FRSA 1991. Hon. DSc: ANU, 1979; Newcastle (NSW), 1982. Edgeworth David Medal, 1958; Hendryk Arctowski Gold Medal, US Nat. Acad. of Scis, 1969; Balthasar van der Pol Gold Medal, Internat. Union of Radio Science, 1969; 1st Herschel Medal, RAS, 1974; Thomas Ranken Lyle Medal, Aust. Acad. of Science, 1975; Royal Medal, Royal Soc., 1980; Hale Medal, Amer. Astronomical Soc., 1980; ANZAAS Medal, 1984; Hartnett Medal, RSA, 1988; Centenary Medal, Australia, 2003. *Publications:* numerous research papers and reviews on radio astronomy in scientific jls. *Address:* (Dec.–March) 4/1 Grant Crescent, Griffith, ACT 2603, Australia; (April–Nov.) 800 Avon Road, Ann Arbor, MI 48104, USA.   *Died 10 May 2008.*

WILDE, Peter Appleton; HM Diplomatic Service, retired; *b* 5 April 1925; *m* 1950, Frances Elisabeth Candida Bayliss; two *s*. *Educ:* Chesterfield Grammar Sch.; St Edmund Hall, Oxford. Army (National Service), 1943–47; Temp. Asst Lectr, Southampton, 1950; FO, 1950; 3rd Sec., Bangkok, 1951–53; Vice-Consul, Zürich, 1953–54; FO, 1954–57; 2nd Sec., Baghdad, 1957–58; 1st Sec., UK Delegn to OEEC (later OECD), Paris, 1958–61; 1st Sec., Katmandu, 1961–64; FO (later FCO), 1964–69; Consul-Gen., Lourenço Marques, 1969–71; Dep. High Comr, Colombo, 1971–73. Mem., Llanfihangel Rhosycorn Community Council, 1974–83. Member: Management Cttee, Carmarthenshire Pest Control Soc. Ltd, 1974–82; Council, Royal Forestry Soc., 1977–86; Regional Adv. Cttee, Wales Conservancy, Forestry Commn, 1985–87 (Mem., Regional Adv. Cttee, S Wales Conservancy, 1983–85). *Recreation:* forestry. *Address:* Nantyperchyll, Gwernogle, Carmarthen SA32 7RR. *T:* (01267) 223181.
                                    Died 22 Sept. 2009.

WILFORD, Sir (Kenneth) Michael, GCMG 1980 (KCMG 1976 CMG 1967); HM Diplomatic Service, retired; *b* Wellington, New Zealand, 31 Jan. 1922; *yr s* of late George McLean Wilford and Dorothy Veronica (*née* Wilson); *m* 1944, Joan Mary, *d* of Captain E. F. B. Law, RN; three *d*. *Educ:* Wrekin College; Pembroke College, Cambridge. Served in Royal Engineers, 1940–46 (despatches). Entered HM Foreign (subseq. Diplomatic) Service, 1947; Third Sec., Berlin, 1947; Asst Private Secretary to Secretary of State, Foreign Office, 1949; Paris, 1952; Singapore, 1955; Asst Private Sec. to Sec. of State, Foreign Office, 1959; Private Sec. to the Lord Privy Seal, 1960; served Rabat, 1962; Counsellor (Office of British Chargé d'Affaires) also Consul-General, Peking, 1964–66; Visiting Fellow of All Souls, Oxford, 1966–67; Actg Pol Advr to Gov. of Hong Kong, 1967; Counsellor, Washington, 1967–69; Asst Under Sec. of State, FCO, 1969–73; Dep. Under Sec. of State, FCO, 1973–75; Ambassador to Japan, 1975–80. Director: Lloyds Bank Internat., 1982–85; Lloyds Merchant Bank Ltd, 1986–87; Adviser, Baring Internat. Investment Management, 1982–90. Chm., Royal Soc. for Asian Affairs, 1984–94 (Hon. Vice Pres., 1994–); Hon. Pres., Japan Assoc., 1981–2001. Pres., Old Wrekinian Assoc., 1995–. *Recreations:* golf, gardening. *Address:* Brook Cottage, Abbotts Ann, Andover, Hants SP11 7DS. *T:* (01264) 710509.   *Died 28 June 2006.*

WILKES, Prof. Eric, OBE (civil) 1974 (MBE (mil.) 1943); DL; FRCP, FRCGP, FRCPsych; Professor of Community Care and General Practice, Sheffield University, 1973–83, then Emeritus; *b* 12 Jan. 1920; *s* of George and Doris Wilkes; *m* 1953, Jessica Mary Grant; two *s* one *d*. *Educ:* Royal Grammar Sch., Newcastle upon Tyne; King's Coll., Cambridge (MA); St Thomas' Hosp., SE1 (MB, BChir). Lt-Col, Royal Signals, 1944. General Medical Practitioner, Derbyshire, 1954–73. High Sheriff of S Yorkshire, 1977–78. Med. Director, St Luke's Nursing Home, later St Luke's Hospice, Sheffield, 1971–86; Emeritus Consultant, Centre for Palliative and Continuing Care, Trent RHA, 1993. Chairman: Sheffield and Rotherham Assoc. for the Care and Resettlement of Offenders, 1976–83; Sheffield Council on Alcoholism, 1976–83; Prevention Cttee, Nat. Council on Alcoholism, 1980–83; Trinity Day Care Trust, 1979–83; Sheffield Victim Support Scheme, 1983–84; Mem., Nat. Cancer sub cttee, 1979–88; President: Inst. of Religion and Medicine, 1982–83; Thornhill House, Great Longstone, Derbyshire, 1992–2004; Co-Pres., St Luke's Hospice, Sheffield, 1986–; Hon. Vice-Pres., Nat. Hospice Council, 1992–2007; Trustee, Help the Hospices, 1984–95 (Vice-Chm., 1993–95; Co-Chm., 1984–93). DL Derbys, 1984. Hon. Fellow, Sheffield City Polytechnic, 1985. Hon. MD Sheffield, 1986.

Publications: The Dying Patient, 1982; Long-Term Prescribing, 1982; various chapters and papers, mainly on chronic and incurable illness. *Recreations:* gardening, walking, natural history. *Address:* Curbar View Farm, Calver, Hope Valley S32 3XR. *T:* (01433) 631291.
                                    Died 2 Nov. 2009.

WILKES, Sir Maurice (Vincent), Kt 2000; PhD; FRS 1956; FREng, FIET, FBCS; Professor of Computer Technology, 1965–80, then Emeritus, and Head of Computer Laboratory, 1970–80, University of Cambridge; Fellow of St John's College, Cambridge, since 1950; *b* 26 June 1913; *s* of late Vincent J. Wilkes, OBE; *m* 1947, Nina Twyman (*d* 2008); one *s* two *d*. *Educ:* King Edward's School, Stourbridge; St John's College, Cambridge (Mathematical Tripos (Wrangler); MA, PhD 1938). Research in physics at Cavendish Lab.; Univ. Demonstrator, 1937. Served War of 1939–45, Radar and Operational Research. Univ. Lectr and Acting Dir, 1945, Dir, 1946–70, Mathematical Laboratory, Univ. of Cambridge. Computer Engr, Digital Equipment Corp., USA, 1980–86; Mem. for Res. Strategy, Olivetti Res. Bd, 1986–96; Advr on Res. Strategy, Olivetti and Oracle Res. Lab., 1996–99; Staff Consultant, AT&T Laboratories, 1999–2002. Adjunct Prof. of Computer Sci. and Elect. Engrg, MIT, 1981–85. Member: Measurement and Control Section Committee, IEE, 1956–59; Council, IEE, 1973–76; First President British Computer Soc., 1957–60, Distinguished Fellow 1973. Mem. Council, IFIP, 1960–63; Chm. IEE E Anglia Sub-Centre, 1969–70; Turing Lectr Assoc. for Computing Machinery, 1967. Foreign Hon. Mem., Amer. Acad. of Arts and Sciences, 1974; Foreign Corresponding Member: Royal Spanish Acad. of Sciences, 1979; Royal Spanish Acad. of Engrg, 1999; Foreign Associate: US Nat. Acad. of Engrg, 1977; US Nat. Acad. of Scis, 1980. FREng (FEng 1976). Hon. DSc: Newcastle upon Tyne, 1972; Hull, 1974; Kent, 1975; City, 1975; Amsterdam, 1978; Munich, 1978; Bath, 1987; Pennsylvania, 1996; Hon. ScD Cantab, 1993; Hon. DTech Linköping, 1975. Harry Goode Award, Amer. Fedn of Inf. Processing Socs, 1968; Eckert-Mauchly Award, Assoc. for Computing Machinery and IEEE Computer Soc., 1980; McDowell Award, 1981, 60th Anniversary Award, 2007, IEEE Computer Soc.; Faraday Medal, IEE, 1981; Pender Award, Univ. of Pennsylvania, 1982; C & C Prize, Foundn for C & C Promotions, Tokyo, 1988; Italgas Prize for Computer Science, 1991; Kyoto Prize, Inamori Foundn, 1992; John von Neumann Medal, IEEE, 1997; Mountbatten Medal, Nat. Electronics Council, 1997. *Publications:* Oscillations of the Earth's Atmosphere, 1949; (joint) Preparations of Programs for an Electronic Digital Computer, Addison-Wesley (Cambridge, Mass), 1951, 2nd edn 1958; Automatic Digital Computers, 1956; A Short Introduction to Numerical Analysis, 1966; Time-sharing Computer System, 1968, 3rd edn 1975; (jtly) The Cambridge CAP Computer and its Operating System, 1979; Memoirs of a Computer Pioneer, 1985; Computing Perspectives, 1995; papers in scientific jls. *Address:* Computer Laboratory, University of Cambridge, William Gates Building, J. J. Thomson Avenue, Cambridge CB3 0FD. *T:* (01223) 763699. *Club:* Athenæum.   *Died 29 Nov. 2010.*

WILKINSON, Sir Philip (William), Kt 1988; FCIB; Director: National Westminster Bank PLC, 1979–90 (Deputy Chairman, 1987–90); HandelsBank NatWest, 1983–90 (Deputy Chairman, 1987–90); *b* 8 May 1927; *m* 1951, Eileen Patricia (*née* Malkin) (*d* 1991); one *s* two *d*. *Educ:* Leyton County High School. With Westminster Bank, later National Westminster Bank, 1943–90; Chief Executive, Lombard North Central Ltd, 1975; General Manager, Related Banking Services Division, 1978; Dir, 1979–90; Dep. Group Chief Executive, 1980; Group Chief Executive, 1983–87; Chm., NatWest Investment Bank, 1987–89; Director: Internat. Westminster Bank, 1982–90; NatWest Bank, USA, 1987–90. Director: BAe, 1987–91; Nat. Power, 1990–93. Former Mem., Bd of Banking Supervision, Bank of England; a Vice-Pres., Chartered Inst. of Bankers, 1989–. Dir, ENO,

1987–93. Mem. Council, 1990–2000, a Vice Pres., 2000–02, ICRF; Chm., Wishbone Trust, 1994–2003. Trustee, Baptist Building Fund, 1987–. Freeman, City of London, 1969. Hon. Fellow, British Orthopaedic Assoc., 2001. *Recreations:* theatre, golf, watching sport. *Address:* Pine Court, Whichert Close, Knotty Green, Beaconsfield, Bucks HP9 2TP. *Club:* Royal Automobile.
Died 23 Aug. 2007.

WILLAN, Edward Gervase, CMG 1964; HM Diplomatic Service, retired; Ambassador to Czechoslovakia, 1974–77; *b* 17 May 1917; *er s* of late Captain F. G. L. Willan, RNR; *m* 1944, Mary Bickley Joy (*d* 1992), *d* of late Lieut-Colonel H. A. Joy, IAOC. *Educ:* Radley; Pembroke Coll., Cambridge (Exhibitioner, MA). Indian Civil Service, 1939–47; 2nd Secretary (from 1948, 1st Secretary) on staff of UK High Commissioner, New Delhi, 1947–49; appointed to HM Diplomatic Service, 1948; Foreign Office, 1949–52; 1st Secretary, HM Embassy, The Hague, 1953–55; 1st Secretary, HM Legation, Bucharest, 1956–58 (Chargé d'Affaires, 1956, 1957 and 1958); Head of Communications Dept, FO, 1958–62; Political Adviser to Hong Kong Government, 1962–65; Head of Scientific Relations Dept, FO, 1966–68; Minister, Lagos, 1968–70; Ambassador at Rangoon, 1970–74. *Recreations:* walking, gardening. *Address:* Cherry Tree Cottage, Shappen Hill, Burley, Hants BH24 4AH. *Died 12 Feb. 2006.*

WILLCOCK, Prof. Malcolm Maurice; Professor of Latin, 1980–91, then Emeritus, and Vice-Provost, 1988–91, University College London; *b* 1 Oct. 1925; *s* of late Dr Maurice Excel Willcock and Evelyn Clarice Willcock (*née* Brooks); *m* 1957, Sheena Gourlay; four *d*. *Educ:* Fettes Coll.; Pembroke Coll., Cambridge (MA). Served Royal Air Force, 1944–47. Research Fellow, Pembroke Coll., Cambridge, 1951–52; Sidney Sussex College: Fellow, 1952–65; Sen. Tutor, 1962–65; University of Lancaster: first Professor of Classics, 1965–79; Principal, Bowland Coll., 1966–79; Pro-Vice-Chancellor, 1975–79. *Publications:* ed, Plautus, Casina, 1976; Companion to the Iliad, 1976; ed, Iliad of Homer, vol. 1 (Books I–XII) 1978, vol. 2 (Books XIII–XXIV) 1984; ed, Plautus, Pseudolus, 1987. *Recreation:* bridge. *Address:* 1 Lancaster Avenue, SE27. *T:* (020) 8761 5615.
Died 2 May 2006.

WILLEBRANDS, His Eminence Cardinal Johannes Gerardus Maria; President, Vatican Secretariat for Promoting Christian Unity, 1969–89, then President Emeritus; Archbishop of Utrecht and Primate of Holland, 1975–83; *b* Netherlands, 4 Sept. 1909. *Educ:* Warmond Seminary, Holland; Angelicum, Rome (Dr Phil.). Priest, 1934; Chaplain, Begijnhof Church, Amsterdam, 1937–40; Prof. of Philosophy, Warmond, 1940; Director, 1945; Pres., St Willibrord Assoc., 1946; organised Catholic Conf. on Ecumenical Questions, 1951; Sec., Vatican Secretariat for Promoting Christian Unity, 1960; Titular Bishop of Mauriana, 1964; Cardinal, 1969; Cardinal with the Title of St Sebastian, Martyr, 1975. Hon. Dr of Letters: St Louis Univ., 1968; St Olaf Coll., USA, 1976; St Thomas' Coll., St Paul's, Minn, 1979; Assumption Coll., Worcester, Mass, 1980; Hon. Dr of Theology: Catholic Univ. of Louvain, 1971; Leningrad Theological Acad., 1973; Catholic Univ., Lublin, Poland, 1985; Catholic Univ., München, 1987; St Michael's UC, Toronto, 1990; Hon. DD Oxon, 1987; Hon. DH Hellenic Coll./Holy Cross Orthodox Sch. of Theol., Brookline, Mass, 1989; Hon. LLD: Notre Dame Univ., 1970; Catholic Univ., Washington, 1974; Seton Hall Univ., NJ, 1987. *Publications:* Oecuménisme et Problèmes Actuels, 1969; Mandatum Unitatis: Beiträge zur Oekumene, 1989; Church and Jewish People, 1992; reports on the ecumenical situation and articles on inter-church relationships. *Address:* Pont. Collegio Olandese, Via Ercole Rosa 1, 00153 Rome, Italy. *Died 1 Aug. 2006.*

WILLETT, Prof. Frank, CBE 1985; FRSE 1979; Emeritus Professor and Hon. Senior Research Fellow, Hunterian Museum, University of Glasgow, since 1990; *b* 18 Aug. 1925; *s* of Thomas Willett and Frances (*née* Latham); *m* 1950, (Mary) Constance Hewitt; one *s* three *d*. *Educ:* Bolton Municipal Secondary Sch.; University Coll., Oxford. MA (Oxon); Dip. Anthropology (Oxon). War damage clerk, Inland Revenue, 1940; RAF Linguist, Japanese, 1943–44. Keeper, Dept of Ethnology and Gen. Archaeology, Manchester Museum, 1950–58; Hon. Surveyor of Antiquities, Nigerian Federal Govt, 1956–57, 1957–58; Archaeologist and Curator, Mus. of Ife Antiquities, Nigerian Fed. Govt, 1958–63; Supply Teacher, Bolton Educn Cttee, 1963–64; Leverhulme Research Fellow, 1964; Research Fellow, Nuffield Coll., Oxford, 1964–66; Prof. of Art History, African and Interdisciplinary Studies, Northwestern Univ., Evanston, Ill, USA, 1966–76; Dir and Titular Prof., Hunterian Mus. and Art Gall., Glasgow, 1976–90. Research Collaborator, Smithsonian Instn, 1992–2004. Vis. Fellow, Clare Hall, Cambridge, 1970–71. Curator, RSE, 1992–97. Hon. Corresp. Member, Manchester Literary and Philosophical Soc., 1958–. Leadership Award, Arts Council of the African Studies Assoc., 1995; Bicentenary Medal, RSE, 1997. *Publications:* Ife in the History of West African Sculpture, 1967, rev. edn, Ife: une Civilisation Africaine, 1971; African Art: An Introduction, 1971, new edn 2002; (with Ekpo Eyo) Treasures of Ancient Nigeria, 1980; The Art of Ife: a descriptive catalogue and database, 2004; articles in Encyc. Britannica, Man, Jl of Afr. Hist., Afr. Arts, Africa, Jl of Nigerian Historical Soc., Odu, SA Archaeol Bull., Archæometry; many conf. reports and chapters in several books. *Recreations:* relaxing, baiting architects. *Address:* Hunterian Museum, University of Glasgow, Glasgow G12 8QQ. *T:* (0141) 330 4221. *Club:* Royal Commonwealth Society. *Died 15 June 2006.*

WILLIAMS, Albert; General Secretary, Union of Construction, Allied Trades and Technicians, 1985–92; President, European Federation of Building and Woodworkers, 1988–92; *b* 12 Feb. 1927; *s* of William Arthur Williams and Phyllis Williams (*née* Barnes); *m* 1954, Edna Bradley; two *s*. *Educ:* Houldsworth School, Reddish; Manchester School of Building (1st and 2nd year Union of Lancs and Cheshire Insts Certs of Training). Apprentice bricklayer, Manchester City Corp., 1941; Armed Forces, 1944–48; bricklaying for various contractors; Member: Exec., Amalgamated Union of Building Trade Workers, 1958; Exec., Council of UCATT, 1971–92; Construction Ind. Trng Bd, 1979–92; Gen. Council, TUC, 1986–92; Dir, Bldg and Civil Engrg Holidays Scheme Management Ltd, 1979–92; Operatives' Side Sec., Nat. Jt Council for Building Industry, 1984–. Dir, Labour Train Contract Services, 1994–. Chm. of Trustees, Working Class Liby, Salford, 1971–. *Recreation:* poetry and work. *Address:* 3 Cornflower Lane, Shirley, Croydon, Surrey CR0 8XJ.
Died 28 Nov. 2007.

WILLIAMS, Prof. Sir Bruce (Rodda), KBE 1980; Professor of the University of Sydney, since 1967, Fellow of the Senate, 1994–98 and Vice-Chancellor and Principal, 1967–81; *b* 10 Jan. 1919; *s* of late Rev. W. J. Williams and Helen Baud; *m* 1942, Roma Olive Hotten (*d* 1991); five *d*. *Educ:* Wesley College; Queen's College, University of Melbourne (BA 1939). MA Adelaide 1942; MA(Econ) Manchester, 1963. FASSA 1968. Lecturer in Economics, University of Adelaide, 1939–46 and at Queen's University of Belfast, 1946–50; Professor of Economics, University College of North Staffordshire, 1950–59; Robert Otley Prof., 1959–63, and Stanley Jevons Prof., 1963–67, Univ. of Manchester; Dir, Technical Change Centre and Vis. Prof., Imperial Coll., London, 1981–86. Vis. Fellow, ANU, 1987, 1988, 1990, 1992–94. Secretary and Joint Director of Research, Science and Industry Committee, 1952–59. Member, National Board for Prices and Incomes, 1966–67; Econ. Adviser to Minister of Technology, 1966–67; Member: Central Advisory Council on Science and Technology, 1967; Australian Reserve Bank Board, 1969–81; Chairman: NSW State Cancer Council, 1967–81; Australian Vice Chancellors Cttee, 1972–74; Aust. Govt Cttee of Inquiry into Educn and Trng, 1976–79;

(Australian) Review of Discipline of Engrg, 1987–88; Dep. Chm., Parramatta Hosps Bd, 1979–81. President: Sydney Conservatorium of Music Foundn, 1994–98; Sydney Spring Fest. of New Music, 1999–2003; Chm., Internat. Piano Comp. of Australia, 1986–2004. Editor, The Sociological Review, 1953–59, and The Manchester Sch., 1959–67. President Economics Section of British Assoc., 1964. Hon. FIEAust 1989; CPEng 1989. Hon. DLitt: Keele, 1973; Sydney, 1982; Hon. DEcon Qld, 1980; Hon. LLD: Melbourne, 1981; Manchester, 1982; Hon. DSc Aston, 1982. Kirby Meml Award, IProdE, 1988. *Publications:* The Socialist Order and Freedom, 1942; (with C. F. Carter): Industry and Technical Progress, 1957, Investment in Innovation, 1958, and Science in Industry, 1959; Investment Behaviour, 1962; Investment Proposals and Decisions, 1965; Investment, Technology and Growth, 1967; (ed) Science and Technology in Economic Growth, 1973; Systems of Higher Education: Australia, 1978; Education, Training and Employment, 1979; Living with Technology, 1982; (ed) Knowns and Unknowns in Technical Change, 1985; Attitudes to New Technologies and Economic Growth, 1986; Review of the Discipline of Engineering, 1988; Academic Status and Leadership, 1990; University Responses to Research Selectivity, 1991; Higher Education and Employment, 1994; Liberal Education and Useful Knowledge, 2002; Making and Breaking Universities, 2005; Fortune's Favours, 2006. *Address:* 24 Mansfield Street, Glebe, NSW 2037, Australia; 31 Queen Anne's Gardens, Ealing, W5 5QD. *Club:* Athenæum.
Died 9 Aug. 2010.

WILLIAMS, David Beverley; QC 2003; a Recorder, since 2002; *b* 11 Feb. 1949; *s* of Daniel David Williams and late Gwyneth Williams (*née* Davies); *m* 1995, Christine Seaman; one *s*. *Educ:* Beaudesert Park; Cheltenham Coll.; Inns of Court Sch. of Law; City Univ. (LLM 1999). Called to the Bar, Middle Temple, 1972; in practice, specialising in criminal law, fraud, and money laundering. *Recreations:* field sports, gardening, theatre. *Address:* No 5 Chambers, Fountain Court, Birmingham B4 6DR. *Club:* National Liberal. *Died 2 Oct. 2010.*

WILLIAMS, Sir David (Glyndwr Tudor), Kt 1991; DL; Vice-Chancellor, Cambridge University, 1989–96; Fellow of Emmanuel College, Cambridge, since 1996; Chancellor (formerly President), Swansea University (formerly University of Wales, Swansea), since 2001; *b* 22 Oct. 1930; *s* of late Tudor Williams, OBE (Headmaster of Queen Elizabeth Grammar Sch., Carmarthen, 1929–55); and Anne Williams; *m* 1959, Sally Gillian Mary Cole; one *s* two *d. Educ:* Queen Elizabeth Grammar Sch., Carmarthen; Emmanuel Coll., Cambridge (MA, LLB, Hon. Fellow 1984). LLM Calif. Nat. Service, RAF, 1949–50. Called to the Bar, Lincoln's Inn, 1956, Hon. Bencher, 1985. Commonwealth Fund Fellow of Harkness Foundn, Berkeley and Harvard, 1956–58; Lecturer: Univ. of Nottingham, 1958–63; Univ. of Oxford, 1963–67 (Fellow of Keble Coll.); University of Cambridge: Fellow, 1967–80, Sen. Tutor and Tutor for Admissions, 1970–76, Emmanuel Coll.; Reader in Public Law, 1976–83; Rouse Ball Prof. of English Law, 1983–92; Pres., Wolfson Coll., 1980–92 (Hon. Fellow, 1993); Prof. of Law, 1996–98. Vis. Fellow, 1974, Dist. Anniv. Fellow, 1996, ANU, Canberra; Allen, Allen and Hemsley Vis. Fellow, Law Dept, Univ. of Sydney, 1985; George P. Smith Dist. Visiting Professor: Indiana Univ., 2000; Univ. of Hong Kong, 2007; Hon. Prof., Chinese Univ. of Hong Kong, 2006–. Lectures: Stevens, Cornell, 1984; Martland, Alberta and Calgary, 1988; Read, Dalhousie, 1989; Fuchs, Indiana, 1993; Laskin, Osgoode Hall, 1993; Samuel Gee, RCP, 1993; Morris of Borth-y-Gest, Bangor, 1993; Wynne Baxter Godfree, Sussex, 1994; Spencer Mason, Auckland, 1994; Harry Street, Manchester, 1999; Shann, Hong Kong, 2004; Austen Owen, Richmond, Va, 2006; Jamestown, Gray's Inn, 2006. Pres., Nat. Soc. for Clean Air, 1983–85; Chairman: Animal Procedures Cttee, 1987–90; RAC Adv. Gp on Cars and the Envmt, 1991–92. Member: Clean Air Council, 1971–79; Royal Commn on Environmental

Pollution, 1976–83; Commn on Energy and Environment, 1978–81; Council on Tribunals, 1972–8; Justice/All Souls Cttee on Administrative Law, 1978–88 Berrill Cttee of Investigation, SSRC, 1982–83; Marre Cttee on Future of Legal Profession, 1986–88; Sen. Salaries Review Body, 1998–2004; Univ. Comr, 1988–93. Pres., Cambridge Soc., 1997–2004. Mem., Amer. Law Inst., 1986; For. Hon. Mem., Amer. Acad. of Arts and Scis, 1994. Mem., Internat. Jury, Indira Gandhi Prize, 1992–2002. DL Cambs, 1995. Hon. Fellow: Keble Coll., Oxford, 1992; Pembroke Coll., Cambridge, 1993; Trinity Coll., Carmarthen, 1994; Hon. QC 1994. Hon. DLitt: William Jewell Coll., 1984; Loughborough Univ. of Technology, 1988; Davidson Coll., 1992; Hon. LLD: Hull, 1989; Sydney 1990; Nottingham, 1991; Liverpool, 1994; McGill, De Montfort, 1995; Duke, 1996; Cambridge, 1997; Victoria Univ. of Technol., Melbourne, 2003; Hon. DCL Western Ontario, 2008. *Publications:* Not in the Public Interest, 1965; Keeping the Peace, 1967; articles in legal jls. *Address:* Emmanuel College, Cambridge CB2 3AP. *T:* (01223) 334200. *Died 6 Sept. 2009.*

WILLIAMS, David Wakelin, (Lyn), MSc, PhD; CBiol, FIBiol; Director, Department of Agriculture and Fisheries for Scotland, Agricultural Scientific Services, 1963–73; *b* 2 Oct. 1913; *e s* of John Thomas Williams and Ethel (*née* Lock); *m* 1948, Margaret Mary Wills, BSc (*d* 1993), *d* of late Rev. R. H. Wills; one *s. Educ:* Rhondda Grammar School, Porth; University College, Cardiff. Demonstrator, Zoology Dept, Univ. Coll., Cardiff, 1937–38; Lectr in Zoology and Botany, Tech. Coll., Crumlin, Mon., 1938–39; research work on nematode physiology, etc. (MSc, PhD), 1937–41; biochemical work on enzymes (Industrial Estate, Treforest), 1942–43. Food Infestation Control Inspector (Min. of Food), Glasgow; Sen. Inspector, W Scotland, 1945; Scotland and N Ireland, 1946. Prin. Scientific Officer, Dept Agriculture for Scotland, 1948; Sen. Prin. Scientific Officer, 1961; Dep. Chief Scientific Officer (Director), 1963. Chairman, Potato Trials Advisory Cttee, 1963–; FIBiol 1966 (Council Mem. Scottish Br., 1966–69). MBIM, 1970–76. *Publications:* various papers, especially for the intelligent layman, on the environment, and on pest control and its side effects. *Recreations:* writing, music, Hi-Fi, photography, natural history. *Address:* 8 Hillview Road, Edinburgh EH12 8QN. *T:* (0131) 334 1108. *Died 13 Jan. 2009.*

WILLIAMS, Prof. Dudley Howard, PhD, ScD; FRS 1983; Professor of Biological Chemistry, University of Cambridge, 1996–2004, then Professor Emeritus; Fellow of Churchill College, Cambridge, since 1964; *b* 25 May 1937; *s* of Lawrence Williams and Evelyn (*née* Hudson); *m* 1963, Lorna Patricia Phyllis, *d* of Anthony and Lorna Bedford; two *s. Educ:* Grammar Sch., Pudsey, Yorks; Univ. of Leeds (state schol.; BSc, PhD); MA, ScD Cantab. Fulbright Schol., Post-doctoral Fellow and Research Associate, Stanford Univ., Calif, 1961–64; University of Cambridge: Sen. Asst in Research, 1964–66; Asst Dir of Research, 1966–74; Reader in Organic Chemistry, 1974–96. Visiting Professor: Univ. of California, Irvine, 1967, 1986, 1989 and 1997; Univ. of Cape Town, 1972; Univ. of Wisconsin, 1975; Univ. of Copenhagen, 1976; ANU, 1980; Lee Kuan Yew Dist. Visitor, Singapore, 2000. Lectures: Nuffield Vis., Sydney Univ., 1973; Arun Guthikonda Meml Award, Columbia Univ., 1985; Dist. Vis., Texas A & M Univ., 1986; Rohrer, Ohio State Univ., 1989; Foundn, Univ. of Auckland, 1991; Pacific Coast, 1991; Steel, Univ. of Queensland, 1994; Marvin Carmack Dist., Indiana Univ., 2001; Paul Ehrlich, France, 2001; James Sprague, Univ. of Wisconsin, 2002; Merck Res., RSC, 2002. Mem. Acad. Europaea. Meldola Medal, RIC, 1966; Corday-Morgan Medal, 1968; Tilden Medal and Lectr, 1983; Structural Chemistry Award, 1984, Bader Award, 1991, RSC; Leo Friend Award, ACS, 1996. *Publications:* Applications of NMR in Organic Chemistry, 1964; Spectroscopic Methods in Organic Chemistry, 1966, 6th edn 2008; Mass Spectrometry of Organic Compounds,

1967; Mass Spectrometry—Principles and Applications, 1981; papers in chemical and biochemical jls, incl. co-discovery of human hormone (1,25-dihydroxyvitamin D) responsible for calcium absorption, and chemistry and action of antibiotics vancomycin and teicoplanin. *Recreations:* music, gardening. *Address:* 7 Balsham Road, Fulbourn, Cambridge CB21 5BZ. *T:* (01223) 740971.
Died 3 Nov. 2010.

WILLIAMS, Rev. Harry Abbott; Community of the Resurrection, since 1969; *b* 10 May 1919; *s* of late Captain Harry Williams, RN, and Annie Williams. *Educ:* Cranleigh Sch.; Trinity Coll., Cambridge; Cuddesdon Coll., Oxford. BA 1941; MA 1945. Deacon, 1943; Priest, 1944. Curate of St Barnabas, Pimlico, 1943–45; Curate of All Saints, Margaret Street, 1945–48; Chaplain and Tutor of Westcott House, Cambridge, 1948–51; Fellow of Trinity Coll., Cambridge, 1951–69; Dean of Chapel, 1958–69, and Tutor, 1958–68; Exam. Chaplain to Bishop of London, 1948–69. Mem., Anglican delegation to Russian Orthodox Church, Moscow, 1956; Select Preacher, Univ. of Cambridge, 1950, 1958, 1975; Hulsean Preacher, 1962, 1975; Select Preacher, Univ. of Oxford, 1974. Licensed to officiate in Dio. of Ely, 1948–, Dio. of Wakefield, 1979–. *Publications:* Jesus and the Resurrection, 1951; God's Wisdom in Christ's Cross, 1960; The Four Last Things, 1960; The True Wilderness, 1965; True Resurrection, 1972; Poverty, Chastity and Obedience: the true virtues, 1975; Tensions, 1976; Becoming What I Am, 1977; The Joy of God, 1979; Some Day I'll Find You (autobiog.), 1982; contribs to: Soundings, 1962; Objections to Christian Belief, 1963; The God I Want, 1967. *Recreation:* idleness and religion. *Address:* House of the Resurrection, Mirfield, West Yorks WF14 0BN. *Died 30 Jan. 2006.*

WILLIAMS, John Brinley, OBE 1988; FCILT; Managing Director, Associated British Ports (formerly British Transport Docks Board), 1985–89 (Board Member, 1980–89; Joint Managing Director, 1982–85); *b* 18 Aug. 1927; *s* of late Leslie Williams and Alice Maud Williams; *m* 1951, Eileen (*née* Court) one *s* one *d. Educ:* Eveswell Sch., Newport. FCILT (FCIT 1979; FILT 1998). Asst Manager, Cardiff Docks, 1963–65; Commercial and Development Asst to Chief Docks Manager, South Wales Ports, 1965–67; Docks Manager: Cardiff and Penarth Docks, 1968–72; Hull Docks, 1972–75; Port Director: South Wales Ports, 1976–78; Southampton, 1978–82. *Recreations:* Rugby, open air pursuits. *Address:* 34 Marine Drive, Barry, S Glamorgan CF6 6QP. *T:* (01446) 737477. *Died 12 Nov. 2006.*

WILLIAMS, Sir (John) Kyffin, Kt 1999; OBE 1982; DL; RA 1974 (ARA 1970); *b* 9 May 1918; *s* of Henry Inglis Wynne Williams and Essyllt Mary Williams (*née* Williams). *Educ:* Shrewsbury Sch.; Slade Sch. of Art. Sen. Art Master, Highgate Sch., 1944–73. One-man shows: Leicester Galleries, 1951, 1953, 1956, 1960, 1966, 1970; Colnaghi Galleries, 1948, 1949, 1965, 1970; Thackeray Gall., biennially 1975–; Albany Gall., Cardiff, 1997. Retrospective exhibn, Nat. Mus. of Wales, Mostyn Art Gall., Llandudno and Glynn Vivian Art Gall., Swansea, 1987. Pres., Royal Cambrian Acad., 1969–76 and 1992–. Winston Churchill Fellow, 1968; Hon. Fellow: University Coll. of Swansea, 1989; UCNW, 1991; UCW, Aberystwyth, 1992. DL Gwynedd 1985. Hon. MA Wales, 1973; Hon. DLitt Wales, 1993. Medal, Hon. Soc. of Cymmrodorion, 1991. *Publications:* Across the Straits (autobiog.), 1973; A Wider Sky (autobiog.), 1991; Portraits, 1996; Boyo Ballads, 1996; The Land and the Sea, 1998; Drawings, 2001; Cutting Images, 2002. *Recreations:* the countryside, sport. *Address:* Pwllfanogl, Llanfairpwll, Gwynedd LL61 6PD. *T:* (01248) 714693.
Died 1 Sept. 2006.

WILLIAMS, Kevin Raymond; Chief Executive Officer, Postal and Logistics Consulting Worldwide, since 2004; *b* 14 May 1948; *s* of Kenneth Williams and Betty (*née* Haskell); *m* 1972, Shionagh Mary Gee; two *s* one *d. Educ:* St Bartholomew's Grammar Sch., Newbury; Exeter Univ. (BA Hons). Head Postmaster: Aldershot,

1982–85; Portsmouth, 1985–86; Dist Head Postmaster, City of London, 1986–88; Royal Mail: Dir, Employee Relns, 1988–90; Dir, Business Develt, 1990–92; Ops Dir, 1992–93; Man. Dir, Parcelforce, 1993–99; Gp Man. Dir, Distribution Services, The Post Office, subseq. Consignia, then Royal Mail Gp plc, 1999–2003; Man. Dir, Internat. Royal Mail Gp, 2002–03. Non-exec. Dir, Intone Gp., 2006–. Lt Col, Engr and Logistics Staff Corps, 1996–. Trustee: Help the Aged, 1998–; Golden Charter Trust Ltd, 2004–. Freeman, City of London, 1988. CMILT (MILog 1998); FRSA. *Recreations:* cricket, travel, gardening, European twinning movement, supporting Aldershot Town FC. *Club:* Headley Cricket.
Died 20 Feb. 2008.

WILLIAMS, Sir Kyffin; *see* Williams, Sir J. K.

WILLIAMS, Sir Leonard, KBE 1981; CB 1975; Director-General for Energy, Commission of the European Communities, 1976–81; *b* 19 Sept. 1919; *m* Anne Taylor Witherley; three *d. Educ:* St Olave's Grammar Sch.; King's Coll., London. Inland Revenue, 1938. War Service (RA), 1940–47. Ministry of Defence, 1948; NATO, 1951–54; Min. of Supply (later Aviation), 1954; Min. of Technology (later DTI), 1964; IDC 1966; Dep. Sec., 1973; Dept of Energy, 1974–76. *Address:* Blue Vines, Bramshott Vale, Liphook, Hants GU30 7PZ.
Died 1 Aug. 2006.

WILLIAMS, Leonard Edmund Henry, CBE 1981; DFC 1944; President, Nationwide Anglia Building Society, 1989–92 (Chairman, 1987–88); *b* 6 Dec. 1919; *s* of William Edmund Williams; *m* 1946, Marie Harries-Jones; four *s* one *d. Educ:* Acton County Grammar School. FCA, FCIB, IPFA. RAF, 1939–46. Acton Borough Council, 1935–39, Chief Internal Auditor 1946–49; Asst Accountant, Gas Council, 1949–53; Nationwide Building Society: Finance Officer, 1954–61; Dep. Gen. Man., 1961–67; Chief Exec., 1967–81; Dir 1975–87; Chm., 1982–87. Director: Y. J. Lovell (Hldgs) plc, 1982–89; Peachey Property Corp. plc, 1982–88; Dep. Chm., BUPA Ltd, 1988–90 (Governor, 1982–88); Mem., Housing Corp., 1976–82. Chm., Building Socs Assoc., 1979–81 (Dep. Chm., 1977–79); Pres., Metrop. Assoc. of Building Socs, 1989–92 (Chm., 1972–73). Pres., Chartered Building Socs Inst., 1969–70. Mem. Ct of Assts, Basketmakers' Co., 1992–2006. FRSA; CCMI. Hon. Life Mem., Internat. Union of Housing Finance Instns. *Publications:* Building Society Accounts, 1966. *Recreation:* reading. *Address:* The Romanys, 11 Albury Road, Burwood Park, Walton-on-Thames, Surrey KT12 5DY. *T:* (01932) 242758. *Clubs:* Royal Air Force, City Livery. *Died 9 June 2007.*

WILLIAMS, Lyn; *see* Williams, D. W.

WILLIAMS, Prof. Michael, FBA 1989; Professor of Geography, 1996–2002, Fellow of Oriel College, 1993–2002 (Vice Provost, 2000–02), then Emeritus, Distinguished Research Associate, since 2004, and Lecturer, St Anne's College, 1978–2002, University of Oxford; *b* 24 June 1935; *s* of Benjamin Williams and Ethel (*née* Marshell); *m* 1955, Eleanore Lerch; two *d. Educ:* Emmanuel Grammar Sch.; Dynevor Grammar Sch., Swansea; Swansea UC (BA 1956; PhD 1960; DLitt 1991); St Catharine's Coll., Cambridge (DipEd 1960). Deptl Demonstrator in Geography, Swansea, 1957–60; University of Adelaide: Lectr in Geog., 1960–66; Sen. Lectr, 1966–69; Reader, 1970–77; Oxford University: Lectr in Geog., 1978–89; Reader, 1990–96; Dir, MSc course, Envmtl Change Unit, 1994–98; Sir Walter Ralegh Fellow, Oriel Coll., 1993–2002. Visiting Professor: Univ. of Wisconsin-Madison, 1973 and 1994; Univ. of Chicago, 1989; UCLA, 1994; Vis. Lectr, UCL, 1966, 1973. Mem., State Commn on Uniform Regl Boundaries, SA, 1974–75; Chm., Histl Geog. Res. Gp, Inst. of British Geographers, 1983–86; Sec., Inst. of Aust. Geographers, 1969–72; Pres., SA Br., RGS, 1975–76 (Ed. of Procs, 1962–70). Mem. Council, British Acad., 1993–96 (Chm., Sect. N, Geog. and Social Anthropology, 1994–97). Editor: Trans of Inst. of British

Geographers, 1983-88; Progress in Human Geography, 1991-2001; Global Environmental Change, 1993-97. John Lewis Gold Medal, RGS, SA, 1979; Lit. Prize, Adelaide Fest. of Arts, 1976; Hidy Award, 1987, Weyerhaeuser Prize, 1990 and 2004, Forest Hist. Soc., Durham, NC (Hon. Fellow, 1990); Meridian Award, Assoc. of American Geog., 2004. *Publications:* South Australia from the Air, 1969; The Draining of the Somerset Levels, 1970, 2nd edn 2009; The Making of the South Australian Landscape, 1974; (ed jtly) Australian Space, Australian Time, 1975; The Changing Rural Landscape of South Australia, 1977, 2nd edn 1992; Americans and their Forests, 1989; (ed) Wetlands: a threatened landscape, 1991; (ed) Planet Management, 1992; (ed jtly) The Relations of History and Geography, 2002; Deforesting the Earth: prehistory to global crisis, 2003, 2nd edn 2006; (ed jtly) A Century of British Geography, 2003; To Leave a Good Earth: Carl O. Sauer, 2010; edited vols of essays; contribs to geogl and histl jls. *Recreations:* walking, music. *Address:* Westgates, Vernon Avenue, Harcourt Hill, Oxford OX2 9AU. *T:* (01865) 243725.   *Died 26 Oct. 2009.*

WILLIAMS, Paul Glyn; Chairman and Managing Director, Mount Charlotte Investments, 1966-77; *b* 14 Nov. 1922; *s* of late Samuel O. Williams and Esmée I. Williams (*née* Cail); *m* 1947, Barbara Joan Hardy (marr. diss. 1964); two *d*; *m* 1964, Gillian Foote, *e d* of late A. G. Howland Jackson, Elstead, Surrey, and of Mrs E. J. Foote and step *d* of late E. J. Foote; one *d*. *Educ:* Marlborough; Trinity Hall, Cambridge (MA; athletics ½ blue, Mem. LX Club, 1942). MP (C) Sunderland South, (C 1953-57, Ind. C 1957-58, C 1958-64). Chairman, Monday Club, 1964-69. Chm., Backer Electric Co., 1978-87. Director: First South African Cordage, 1947-54; Transair, 1955-62; Hodgkinson Partners Ltd, PR consultants, 1956-64; Minster Executive, 1977-83; Henry Sykes, 1980-83; consultant: P-E Internat. plc, 1983-91; Hogg Robinson Career Services, 1991-95. FInstD; FCMI. *Address:* Hill House, Stert, near Devizes, Wilts SN10 3JB. *T:* (01380) 721197.   *Died 10 Sept. 2008.*

WILLIAMS, Paul H.; *see* Hodder-Williams.

WILLIAMS, Richard Hall; Under Secretary, Agriculture Department, Welsh Office, Cardiff, 1981-86; Deputy Chairman, Local Government Boundary Commission for Wales, 1989-96; *b* 21 Oct. 1926; *s* of late Edward Hall Williams and Kitty Hall Williams; *m* 1949, Nia Wynn (*née* Jones); two *s* two *d*. *Educ:* Barry Grammar Sch., Glamorgan; University College of Wales, Aberystwyth (BScEcon Hons). Career within Welsh Office included service in Health and Economic Planning Groups before entering Agriculture Dept, 1978. Treasurer, Ministerial Bd, Presbyterian Church of Wales, 1986-95. Vice Chm., Age Concern Wales, 1990-93. Moderator, E Glam Presbytery (Welsh), Presbyterian Ch of Wales, 2000-01. *Recreation:* enjoying all things Welsh. *Address:* Argoed, 17 West Orchard Crescent, Llandaff, Cardiff CF5 1AR. *T:* (029) 2056 2472.   *Died 24 July 2008.*

WILLINK, Sir Charles (William), 2nd Bt *cr* 1957; *b* 10 Sept. 1929; *s* of Rt Hon. Sir Henry Urmston Willink, 1st Bt, MC, QC (*d* 1973), and Cynthia Frances (*d* 1959), *d* of H. Morley Fletcher, MD, FRCP; *S* father, 1973; *m* 1954, Elizabeth, *d* of Humfrey Andrewes, Highgate, London; one *s* one *d*. *Educ:* Eton College (scholar); Trinity College, Cambridge (scholar; MA, PhD). Assistant Master: Marlborough College, 1952-54; Eton College, 1954-85 (Housemaster, 1964-77). *Publications:* (ed) Euripides' Orestes, 1986; articles in Classical Quarterly. *Recreations:* bridge, field botany, music (bassoon). *Heir: s* Edward Daniel Willink, *b* 18 Feb. 1957. *Address:* 22 North Grove, Highgate, N6 4SL. *T:* (020) 8340 3996.
                                              Died 10 March 2009.

WILLIS, Maj.-Gen. John Brooker, CB 1981; Director General, Fighting Vehicles and Engineer Equipment, 1977-81; *b* 28 July 1926; *s* of late William Noel Willis and of Elaine Willis; *m* 1959, Yda Belinda Jane Firbank; two *s* two *d*. *Educ:* privately, until 1941; Redhill Technical

Coll. ptsc, jssc. Enlisted in Royal Navy (Fleet Air Arm) as Trainee Pilot; basic training in USA, 1944; transf. to Indian Army, attended Armoured OTS Ahmed Nagar, 1945; commnd 1947, joined 10th Royal Hussars; attended 13 Technical Staff Course, RMCS, 1958-60; Bt Lt-Col 1965, in comd 10th Hussars Aden and BAOR; GSO1 (Armour) DS RMCS, 1968-69; Col GS MGO Secretariat, MoD, 1969-71; Dep. Comdt, RAC Centre, 1971-74; Sen. Officers' War Course, Greenwich, 1974; Dir, Projects (Fighting Vehicles), 1974-77. *Recreations:* gardening, aviation.   *Died 1 Feb. 2010.*

WILLIS, Air Chief Marshal Sir John (Frederick), GBE 1997 (CBE 1988); KCB 1993 (CB 1991); Vice Chief of the Defence Staff, 1995-97; *b* 27 Oct. 1937; *s* of F. A. and K. E. Willis; *m* 1959, Merrill Thewliss; three *s* two *d*. *Educ:* Dulwich Coll.; RAF Coll., Cranwell. Entered RAF, 1955; commd, 1958; Pilot, 83/44/9/Sqdns (Vulcan), 1958-64; Flying Instr, 1964-67; Officer and Aircrew Selection Centre, 1967-69; Staff Coll., 1970; Chief Flying Instr, Vulcan OCU, Flt Comdr/Sqdn Comdr, 27 Sqdn, 1971-77; Policy Div., Air Force Dept, MoD, 1977-82; Stn Comdr, Akrotiri, Cyprus, 1982-84; Briefing Officer to CAS, 1984-85; SHAPE, 1985-88; ACDS (Policy and Nuclear), 1989-90; Dir Gen. of Trng, RAF, 1991-92; AOC-in-C, RAF Support Comd, 1992-94; COS, RAF Logistics Comd, 1994-95. FRAeS 1997. *Recreation:* making things. *Address:* c/o Lloyds TSB, Cox's and King's Branch, PO Box 1190, 7 Pall Mall, SW1Y 5NA. *Club:* Royal Air Force.   *Died 9 Jan. 2008.*

WILLISON, Lt-Gen. Sir David (John), KCB 1973; OBE 1958; MC 1945; Director General of Intelligence (Deputy Under-Secretary of State), Ministry of Defence, 1975-78; Chief Royal Engineer, 1977-82; *b* 25 Dec. 1919; *s* of Brig. A. C. Willison, DSO, MC; *m* 1st, 1941, Betty Vernon Bates (*d* 1989); one *s* two *d*; 2nd, 1994, Trisha Clitherow. *Educ:* Wellington; RMA Woolwich. 2/Lt RE, 1939; First Instructor, Bailey Bridge SME Ripon, 1942-43; OC 17 and 246 Field Cos, 1944-45; Staff Coll., Camberley 1945; Brigade Major, 1 Indian Inf. Brigade, Java, 1946; Malaya, 1947; WO, 1948-50; OC 16 Field Sqn, Egypt, 1950-52; SO, MGA, 1952-53; GHQ MELF, 1952-53; OC, RE Troops, Berlin, 1953-55; Directing Staff, Staff Coll., Camberley, 1955-58; AQMG (Ops), HQ British Forces Aden, 1958-60; CO, 38 Engr Regt, 1960-63; Col GS MI/DI4, MoD, 1963-66; idc 1966; BGS (Intell.), MoD, 1967-70; BGS (Intell. and Security)/ACOS, G2, HQ NORTHAG, 1970-71; Dir of Service Intelligence, MoD, 1971-72; Dep. Chief Defence Staff (Int.), 1972-75. Col Comdt RE, 1973-82. Chm., RE Widows Soc., 1987-91. Consultant on Internat. Affairs, Nat. Westminster Bank Gp, 1980-84; Consultant: County Natwest Investment Bank, 1985-91, Pareto Partners, 1991-95. Pres., Western Area, Hants, St John's Ambulance, 1987-94; Freeman, City of London, 1981. *Recreations:* sailing, shooting, fishing, gardening. *Clubs:* Naval and Military; Royal Lymington Yacht.
                                            Died 24 April 2009.

WILLMOTT, Prof. John Charles, CBE 1983; PhD; Professor of Physics, University of Manchester, 1964-89 (Director of the Physical Laboratories, 1967-89; a Pro-Vice-Chancellor, 1982-85; Adviser to Vice-Chancellor on Research Exploitation, 1988-93); *b* 1 April 1922; *s* of Arthur George Willmott and Annie Elizabeth Willmott; *m* 1952, Sheila Madeleine Dumbell (*d* 2003); two *s* one *d*. *Educ:* Bancroft's Sch., Woodford; Imperial Coll. of Science and Technol. (BSc, PhD). ARCS. Lectr in Physics, Liverpool Univ., 1948-58, Sen. Lectr, 1958-63, Reader, 1963-64. Member: SERC (formerly SRC), 1978-82; Science for Stability Cttee, NATO, 1981-97. *Publications:* Tables of Coefficients for the Analysis of Triple Angular Correlations of Gamma-rays from Aligned Nuclei, 1968; Atomic Physics, 1975; articles on nuclear structure in learned jls. *Address:* 37 Hall Moss Lane, Bramhall, Cheshire SK7 1RB. *T:* (0161) 439 4169.
                                              Died 15 June 2009.

WILLOUGHBY, Kenneth James; *b* 6 Nov. 1922; *y s* of late Frank Albert Willoughby and Florence Rose Willoughby (*née* Darbyshire); *m* 1943, Vera May Dickerson (*d* 2005); one *s* one *d. Educ:* Hackney Downs (Grocers') Sch.; Selwyn Coll., Cambridge. Tax Officer, Inland Revenue, 1939; Royal Engineers, UK, Egypt, Italy, Austria, Greece, 1941–47 (despatches, Captain); Asst Auditor, Exchequer and Audit Dept, 1947; Asst Prin., Min. of Civil Aviation, 1949; Asst Private Sec. to Minister of Civil Aviation, 1950; Private Sec. to Perm. Sec., 1951; Principal, Min. of Transport (and later, Civil Aviation), 1951; Sec., Air Transport Adv. Council, 1957–61; Asst Sec., Min. of Aviation, 1962; Under-Secretary: Min. of Technology, 1968–70; DTI, 1970–74. *Recreations:* music, reading, gardening. *Address:* 84 Douglas Avenue, Exmouth, Devon EX8 2HG. *T:* (01395) 271175.   *Died 24 Dec. 2007.*

WILLOUGHBY, Rt Rev. Noel Vincent; Bishop of Cashel and Ossory, 1980–97; *b* 15 Dec. 1926; *s* of George and Mary Jane Willoughby; *m* 1959, Valerie Moore, Dungannon, Tyrone; two *s* one *d. Educ:* Tate School, Wexford; Trinity Coll., Dublin (Scholar, Moderator and Gold Medallist in Philosophy). Deacon 1950, priest 1951, Armagh Cathedral; Curate: Drumglass Parish, 1950–53; St Catherine's, Dublin, 1953–55; Bray Parish, 1955–59; Rector: Delgany Parish, 1959–69; Glenageary Parish, 1969–80; Hon. Sec., General Synod, 1976–80; Treasurer, St Patrick's Cathedral, Dublin, 1976–80; Archdeacon of Dublin, 1979–80. *Recreations:* gardening, golf, tennis, fishing. *Address:* Dromingle, Belmont, Newtown, Wexford, Ireland. *T:* (53) 20008.   *Died 6 Feb. 2006.*

WILLOUGHBY, Roger James; Registrar of Members' Interests, House of Commons, 1994–2000; *b* 30 Sept. 1939; *s* of late Hugh Lloyd Willoughby and Gerd Willoughby; *m* 1970, Veronica, *d* of Frank and Elisabeth Lepper. *Educ:* Shrewsbury Sch.; Balliol Coll., Oxford (BA); Birkbeck Coll., London (DipTh 2005). A Clerk in the House of Commons, 1962–2000: Dep. Principal Clerk, 1975; Sec. to UK Delegn to European Parlt, 1976; Clerk of Home Affairs Cttee, 1979; Clerk of Supply, Public Bill Office, 1984; Clerk of Private Bills, H of C, 1988–97. *Recreations:* literature, cricket, walking in solitary places, bonfires. *Address:* 35 Defoe Avenue, Kew, Richmond, Surrey TW9 4DS. *T:* (020) 8876 1718.
                                       Died 4 May 2006.

WILMSHURST, Michael Joseph; HM Diplomatic Service, retired; *b* 14 Sept. 1934; *s* of Mr and Mrs E. J. Wilmshurst; *m* 1958, Mary Elizabeth Kemp; one *s* one *d. Educ:* Latymer Upper Sch.; Christ's Coll., Cambridge (BA 1959). Entered Foreign Service, 1953. 2nd Lieut, Royal Signals, 1953–55. Asst Private Sec. to Foreign Secretary, 1960–62; 2nd Sec., The Hague, 1962–65; 1st Sec. (Commercial), Bogotá, 1965–67; Western European Dept, FCO, 1968–70; 1st Sec. (Commercial), Cairo, 1970–73; Asst Head of Energy Dept, FCO, 1974–75; Asst Head of Energy and Arms Control and Disarmament Depts, 1975–77; Counsellor and Head of Joint Nuclear Unit, FCO, 1977–78; Consul, Guatemala City, 1978–81; Sabbatical, Stiftung Wissenschaft und Politik, Ebenhausen, 1982; UK Permanent Rep. to IAEA, UNIDO and UN, Vienna, 1982–87; seconded to IAEA, Vienna as Dir of External Relns, 1987; retd from HM Diplomatic Service, 1989, from IAEA, 1991. *Publications:* Nuclear Non-Proliferation: can the policies of the Eighties prove more successful than those of the Seventies?, 1982; (contrib.) The International Nuclear Non-Proliferation System: challenges and choices, 1984. *Recreations:* reading, bird-watching. *Address:* 7 East Street, Southwold, Suffolk IP18 6EH.   *Died 12 Oct. 2006.*

WILSON, 2nd Baron *cr* 1946, of Libya and of Stowlangtoft; **Patrick Maitland Wilson;** *b* 14 Sept. 1915; *s* of Field-Marshal 1st Baron Wilson, GCB, GBE, DSO, and Hester Mary (*d* 1979), *d* of Philip James Digby Wykeham, Tythrop House, Oxon; *S* father, 1964; *m* 1945, Violet Storeen (*d* 1990), *d* of late Major James Hamilton Douglas

Campbell, OBE. *Educ:* Eton; King's College, Cambridge. Served War of 1939–45 (despatches). *Heir:* none. *Address:* c/o Barclays Bank, Cambridge CB2 3PZ.
                                     Died 1 Feb. 2009 (ext).

WILSON, Austin Peter; Assistant Under Secretary of State, 1981–96; Member, Criminal Injuries Compensation Appeals Panel, 1997–2005; *b* 31 March 1938; *s* of Joseph and Irene Wilson; *m* 1962, Norma Louise, *y d* of D. R. Mill; one *s* two *d. Educ:* Leeds Grammar Sch.; St Edmund Hall, Oxford (BA). Entered Home Office, 1961; Private Secretary to Minister of State, 1964–66; Principal, 1966; Secretary, Dept'l Cttee on Death Certification and Coroners (Brodrick Cttee), 1968–71; Asst Sec., 1974, Prison Dept; seconded to N Ireland Office, 1977–80; Asst Under Secretary of State, Criminal Justice Dept, 1981; Hd of Community Progs and Equal Opportunities Dept, 1982–86, Equal Opportunities and Gen. Dept, 1986–87, Police Dept, 1987–88, Home Office; NI Office, 1988–92; Criminal Policy Dept, 1992–94, Fire and Emergency Planning Dept, 1994–96, Home Office. *Recreations:* theatre, reading, walking, travel. *Address:* 2 Stocks Hill Garth, Main Street, Menston, W Yorks LS29 6EG. *T:* (01943) 877691.   *Died 19 April 2006.*

WILSON, Sir Colin (Alexander) St John, Kt 1998; RA 1991 (ARA 1990); FRIBA; Professor of Architecture, Cambridge University, 1975–89, then Emeritus Professor; Fellow, Pembroke College, Cambridge, since 1977; architect (own private practice); *b* 14 March 1922; *yr s* of late Rt Rev. Henry A. Wilson, CBE, DD; *m* 1st, 1955, Muriel Lavender (marr. diss. 1971); 2nd, 1972, Mary Jane Long; one *s* one *d. Educ:* Felsted Sch.; Corpus Christi Coll., Cambridge, 1940–42 (MA; Hon. Fellow, 1998); Sch. of Architecture, London Univ., 1946–49 (Dip. Lond.). Served War, RNVR, 1942–46. Asst in Housing Div., Architects Dept, LCC, 1950–55; Lectr at Sch. of Architecture, Univ. of Cambridge, 1955–69; Fellow, Churchill Coll., Cambridge, 1962–71, Hon. Fellow 1998. Practised in assoc. with Sir Leslie Martin, 1956–64: on bldgs in Cambridge (Harvey Court, Gonville and Caius Coll.; Stone Building, Peterhouse); Univ. of Oxford, Law Library; Univ. of Leicester, Science Campus; Univ. of London, Royal Holloway Coll. In own practice, buildings included: Extension to Sch. of Architecture, Cambridge; Research Laboratory, Babraham; Extension to British Museum; Library for QMC, Univ. of London (SCONUL award for design excellence); Meml Library for Bishop Wilson Sch., Spring Field; The British Library, St Pancras; Pallant House Gall., Chichester (Architects' Jl/Bovis/RA Grand Award, 2000); various residences; Projects for Liverpool Civic and Social Centre, and Group Headquarters and Research Campus for Lucas Industries Ltd. Exhibitions: Venice Biennale, 1996; retrospective, RIBA, 1997, Bristol, and Glasgow, 1998; architecture of British Liby exhibition, tour, USA, 2000. Vis. Critic, 1960, 1964 and 1983, Bishop Vis. Prof., 2000, Yale Sch. of Architecture, USA; Bemis Prof. of Architecture, MIT, USA, 1970–72. Consultant, Chicago City Library. Member: Fitzwilliam Mus. Syndicate, 1985–89; Arts Council of GB, 1990–94 (Chair, Architecture Unit, 1992–94); Bd of Advisors, MAArch, Helsinki Univ. of Technology, Finland, 1994–. Trustee: Tate Gall., 1973–80; Nat. Gall., 1977–80; British Architectural Liby, 2001–. FRSA. DUniv Essex, 1998; Hon. LittD Cambridge, 1999; Hon. LLD Sheffield, 1999. Commander, Order of the Lion (Finland), 1992. *Publications:* Architectural Reflections, 1992; The Other Tradition of Modern Architecture, 1995; The Design and Construction of the British Library, 1998; The Artist at Work, 1999; articles in: The Observer; professional jls in UK, USA, France, Spain, Japan, Germany, Norway, Italy, Switzerland, Finland, etc. *Address:* 31A Grove End Road, NW8. *T:* (020) 7286 8306; (office) Colin St John Wilson & Associates, Clarendon Buildings, 27 Horsell Road, N5 1XL. *T:* (020) 7607 3084.   *Died 14 May 2007.*

WILSON, Lt-Col Eric Charles Twelves, VC 1940; b 2 Oct. 1912; s of late Rev. C. C. C. Wilson; m 1943, Ann (from whom he obtained a divorce, 1953), d of Major Humphrey Pleydell-Bouverie, MBE; one s (and one s decd); m 1953, Angela Joy, d of Lt-Col J. McK. Gordon, MC; one s. Educ: Marlborough; RMC, Sandhurst. Commissioned in East Surrey Regt, 1933; seconded to King's African Rifles, 1937; seconded to Somaliland Camel Corps, 1939; Long Range Desert Gp, 1941–42; Burma, 1944; seconded to N Rhodesia Regt, 1946; retd from Regular Army, 1949; Admin. Officer, HM Overseas Civil Service, Tanganyika, 1949–61; Dep. Warden, London House, 1962, Warden, 1966–77. Hon. Sec., Anglo-Somali Soc., 1972–77 and 1988–90. Publications: Stowell in the Blackmore Vale, 1986. Recreation: country life. T: (01963) 370264.
Died 23 Dec. 2008.

WILSON, Ven. Hewitt; see Wilson, Ven. J. H.

WILSON, Brig. James, CBE 1986; Director, Edinburgh Old Town Trust, 1987–90; Chief Executive, Livingston Development Corporation, 1977–87; b 12 March 1922; s of late Alexander Robertson Wilson and Elizabeth Wylie Wilson (née Murray); m 1949, Audrie Veronica, er d of late A. W. and O. V. Haines; three d. Educ: Irvine Royal Academy; Edinburgh Academy; Aberdeen Univ. Commissioned RA, 1941; served War with 71 (West Riding) Field Regt, N Africa and Italy, 1941–45; Instructor, Sch. of Artillery, India, 1945–47; Adjt, Sussex Yeo., 1948–49; active service in Malaya and ME, 1950–53; psc 1954; DAQMG, War Office, 1955–57; Instructor, Staff Coll., 1959–61; CO, 439 (Tyne) Light Air Defence Regt, 1964–67; AQMG, Northern Comd, 1967–68; Col GS SD, HQ BAOR, 1969–71; AMA and DCBAS, Washington, 1972–73; DQMG, HQ UKLF, 1974–77. Member: Executive Council, TCPA (Scotland), 1977–87; Edin. Univ. Careers Adv. Cttee, 1982–86; Scottish Cttee, Inst. of Dirs, 1983–86; Dir, Edinburgh Chamber of Commerce, 1979–82. Mem., Royal Artillery Council for Scotland, 1979–93; Chairman: W Lothian SSAFA, 1983–93; E Scotland SSAFA Cttee, 1986–93; RA Assoc. (Scotland), 1987–91 (Pres., 1991–94); Vice Pres. Tetbury Br., RBL, 1996–; Chm., Tetbury Civic Soc., 1999–2003. FCMI (FBIM 1980). Recreations: golf, gardening, bridge. Address: The Stables, The Green, Tetbury, Glos GL8 8DN. T: (01666) 503030. Clubs: Army and Navy; Hon. Co. of Edinburgh Golfers; Minchinhampton Golf.
Died 27 Aug. 2006.

WILSON, Dr James Maxwell Glover, FRCP, FRCPE, FFPH; Senior Principal Medical Officer, Department of Health and Social Security, 1972–76; b 31 Aug. 1913; s of late James Thomas Wilson and Mabel Salomons; m Lallie Methley; three s. Educ: King's College Choir Sch., Cambridge; Oundle Sch.; St John's Coll., Cambridge (MA, MB, BChir); University College Hosp., London. Clinical appts, London and Cambridge, 1937–39. Served War, RAMC (Major, 6th Airborne Div.), 1939–45. Hospital appts, London and Edinburgh, 1945–54; medical work on tea estates in India, 1954–57; Medical Staff, Min. of Health (later DHSS), concerned with the centrally financed research programme, 1957–76; Sen. Res. Fellow, Inf. Services Div., Common Services Agency, Scottish Health Service, 1976–81. Lectr (part-time), Public Health Dept, London Sch. of Hygiene and Tropical Med., 1968–72. Publications: (with G. Jungner) Principles and Practice of Screening for Disease (WHO), 1968; contribs to med. jls, mainly on screening for disease. Recreations: reading, conservation. Address: Millhill House, 77 Millhill, Musselburgh, Midlothian EH21 7RP. T: (0131) 665 5829.
Died 31 Dec. 2006.

WILSON, James Noel, OBE 1996; ChM; FRCS; Consultant Orthopædic Surgeon: Royal National Orthopædic Hospital, London (Surgeon i/c Accident Unit, RNOH Stanmore), 1955–84; National Hospitals for Nervous Diseases, Queen Square and Maida Vale, 1962–84; Teacher of Orthopædics, Institute of Orthopædics, University of London, retired; b Coventry,

25 Dec. 1919; s of Alexander Wilson and Isobel Barbara Wilson (née Fairweather); m 1945, Patricia Norah McCullough; two s two d. Educ: King Henry VIII Sch., Coventry; University of Birmingham. Peter Thompson Prize in Anatomy, 1940; Sen. Surgical Prize, 1942; Arthur Foxwell Prize in Clinical Medicine, 1943; MB, ChB 1943; MRCS, LRCP, 1943; FRCS 1948; ChM (Birmingham) 1949; House Surgeon, Birmingham General Hospital, 1943; Heaton Award as Best Resident for 1943. Service in RAMC, Nov. 1943–Oct. 1946, discharged as Captain; qualified as Parachutist and served with 1st Airborne Division. Resident surgical posts, Birmingham General Hospital and Coventry and Warwickshire Hospital, 1947–49; Resident Surgical Officer, Robert Jones and Agnes Hunt Orthopædic Hospital, Oswestry, 1949–52; Consultant Orthopædic Surgeon to Cardiff Royal Infirmary and Welsh Regional Hospital Board, 1952–55. Prof. of Orthopaedics, Addis Ababa Univ., 1989. Old Oswestrian Gold Medal Lectr, 1971; Watson-Jones Lectr, RCS, 1988; Duraiswami Meml Oration, Delhi Orthopaedic Assoc., 1989; Jackson Burrows Medal Lectr, Inst. of Orthopaedics, 1991. World Orthopaedic Concern: Pres., 1979–84; Chm., UK Region, 1984–90; Editor, News-Letter, 1988–2000. Vice-Chm., Impact (UK) Foundn, 1988–2000; Pres., Orthopaedic Section, RSocMed, 1982–83; former Mem. Brit. Editorial Bd, Jl of Bone and Joint Surgery; Sen. Fellow, and formerly Editorial Sec., British Orthopædic Assoc. (BOA Travelling Fellowship to USA, 1954); FRSocMed 1959, Hon. FRSocMed 1998. Life Mem., Bangladesh Orthopaedic Soc.; Hon. Mem., Egyptian Orthopaedic Assoc. Publications: (ed) Watson Jones Fractures and Joint Injuries, 6th edn 1982; former contributor, Butterworth's Operative Surgery; chapters and articles on orthopædic subjects to various books and journals. Recreations: golf, reluctant gardening, photography. Address: The Chequers, Waterdell, Watford, Herts WD25 0GP. T: (01923) 672364. Club: Royal Society of Medicine.
Died 2 March 2006.

WILSON, Ven. (John) Hewitt, CB 1977; Chaplain-in-Chief and Archdeacon, Royal Air Force, 1973–80; Archdeacon Emeritus, since 1980; Canon and Prebendary of Lincoln Cathedral, 1974–80; Canon Emeritus, since 1980; b 14 Feb. 1924; 2nd s of John Joseph and Marion Wilson; m 1951, Gertrude Elsie Joan Weir; three s two d. Educ: Kilkenny Coll., Kilkenny; Mountjoy Sch., Dublin; Trinity Coll., Dublin (BA 1946; MA 1956). Curate, St George's Church, Dublin, 1947–50; entered RAF, 1950: RAF Coll., Cranwell, 1950–52; Aden, 1952–55; RAF Wittering, 1955–57; RAF Cottesmore, 1957–58; RAF Germany, 1958–61; Staff Chaplain, Air Ministry, 1961–63; RAF Coll., Cranwell, 1963–66; Asst Chaplain-in-Chief: Far East Air Force, 1966–69; Strike command, 1969–73; Rector of The Heyfords with Rousham and Somerton, diocese of Oxford, 1981–93, QHC 1972–80. Liveryman, Coachmakers' and Coach-Harness Makers' Co., 1994– (Hon. Chaplain, 1977–2007, then Chaplain Emeritus). Recreations: Rugby football, golf, tennis, gardening, theatre. Address: Glencree, Philcote Street, Deddington, Banbury, Oxon OX15 0TB. T: (01869) 338903; e-mail: glencree@freecall-uk.co.uk. Club: Royal Air Force.
Died 29 June 2008.

WILSON, Dr John Murray, MBE 1964; Controller, Home Division, British Council, 1985–86; b 25 July 1926; s of Maurice John and Mary Ellen Wilson (née Murray); m 1957, Audrey Miriam Simmons; one s one d. Educ: Selwyn Avenue Junior, Highams Park; Bancroft's School, Essex; St John's College, Oxford (MA Botany 1952; DPhil 1957; prox. acc. Christopher Welch Scholarship 1951). Served RAF, 1945–48. British Council, 1955–86: Science Dept, 1955–58; Chile, 1958–62; Brazil, 1962–66; India, 1966–71; Dep. Rep./Sci. Officer, Italy, 1971–74; Sci. Officer, Germany, 1974–79; Dep. Rep., Germany, 1979–81; Dep. Controller, Home Div., 1981–85. Publications: (with J. L. Harley) papers in New Phytologist. Recreations: gardening, photography, messing about.
Died 28 Dec. 2007.

WILSON, Leslie William; JP; Director-General, Association of Special Libraries and Information Bureaux (Aslib), 1950–78, retired; *b* 26 Sept. 1918; *s* of Harry Wilson and Ada Jane Wilson; *m* 1942, Valerie Jones; one *s* two *d*. *Educ:* Cambridgeshire High Sch.; Trinity Hall, Cambridge (Open Scholar, MA Mod. Langs). Army Service, India, 1940–46. Foreign Editor, Times Educnl Supplement, 1946–50. Mem., Parly and Scientific Cttee, 1965–78. Hon. Fellow, Internat. Fedn for Documentation, 1978; Hon. Member: Inst. of Information Scientists, 1977; US Special Libraries Assoc., 1978; Aslib, 1978. Chm., Richmond Assoc. for Nat. Trust, 1997–2001. JP Middx, 1971. Dep. Grand Master, Masonic Province of Middx, 1989–93.
Died 7 Dec. 2007.

WILSON, Lynn Anthony; Deputy Chairman, Wilson Connolly Holdings PLC, 2001–03 (Chairman, 1982–2000); Director of 20 subsidiary companies; *b* 8 Dec. 1939; *s* of Connolly Thomas Wilson and Frances (*née* Chapman); *m* 1964, Judith Helen Mann; two *s*. *Educ:* Oakham Sch., Rutland. FCIOB. Wilson Builders (Northampton) Ltd, 1957; Man. Dir, Wilson (Connolly) Holdings, on flotation, 1966. Nat. Pres., House Builders Fedn, 1981. Pres., Old Oakhamian Club, 1988; Trustee, Oakham Sch., 1983–96. Pres., Northants CCC, 2000–05 (Chm., 1990–2000); Mem. Cttee, 1971–80; Treas., 1974–79; Patron, 2005–). Hon. Fellow, Univ. of Northampton, 2007. *Recreations:* cricket, golf, horseracing, shooting. *Address:* The Maltings, Tithe Farm, Moulton Road, Holcot, Northampton NN6 9SH. *Clubs:* East India, Turf, MCC; Northants CC.
Died 9 July 2008.

WILSON, Philip Alexander P.; *see* Poole-Wilson.

WILSON, Prof. Robert McLachlan, FBA 1977; Professor of Biblical Criticism, University of St Andrews, 1978–83; *b* 13 Feb. 1916; *er s* of Hugh McL. Wilson and Janet N. (*née* Struthers); *m* 1945, Enid Mary (*d* 2003), *d* of Rev. and Mrs F. J. Bomford, Bournemouth, Hants; two *s*. *Educ:* Greenock Acad.; Royal High Sch., Edinburgh; Univ. of Edinburgh (MA 1939, BD 1942); Univ. of Cambridge (PhD 1945). Minister of Rankin Church, Strathaven, Lanarkshire, 1946–54; Lectr in New Testament Language and Literature, St Mary's Coll., Univ. of St Andrews, 1954, Sen. Lectr, 1964, Prof., 1969–78. Vis. Prof., Vanderbilt Divinity Sch., Nashville, Tenn, 1964–65. Pres., Studiorum Novi Testamenti Societas, 1981–82. Hon. Mem., Soc. of Biblical Literature, 1972–. Associate Editor, New Testament Studies, 1967–77, Editor 1977–83; Mem., Internat. Cttee for publication of Nag Hammadi Codices, and Editorial Bd of Nag Hammadi Studies monograph series. Hon. DD Aberdeen, 1982. Burkitt Medal for Biblical Studies, British Academy, 1990. *Publications:* The Gnostic Problem, 1958; Studies in the Gospel of Thomas, 1960; The Gospel of Philip, 1962; Gnosis and the New Testament, 1968; (ed) English trans., Hennecke-Schneemelcher, NT Apocrypha: vol. 1, 1963 (3rd edn, completely revised, 1991); vol. 2, 1965 (3rd edn 1993); (ed) English trans., Haenchen, The Acts of the Apostles, 1971; (ed) English trans., Foerster, Gnosis: vol. 1, 1972; vol. 2, 1974; (ed and trans., jtly) Jung Codex treatises: De Resurrectione, 1963, Epistula Jacobi Apocrypha, 1968, Tractatus Tripartitus, pars I, 1973, partes II et III, 1975; (ed) Nag Hammadi and Gnosis, 1978; (ed) The Future of Coptology, 1978; (ed jtly) Text and Interpretation, 1979; (ed) English trans., Rudolph, Gnosis, 1983; Commentary on Hebrews, 1987; Commentary on Colossians and Philemon, 2005; articles in British, Amer. and continental jls. *Address:* 10 Murrayfield Road, St Andrews, Fife KY16 9NB. *T:* (01334) 474331. *Died 27 June 2010.*

WILSON, Ronald Marshall, CBE 1982; sole proprietor, Ronnie Wilson, Chartered Surveyors, since 1983; Chairman, Nightingale Secretariat PLC, 1985–92; *b* 6 March 1923; *s* of Marshall Lang Wilson and Margaret Wilson Wilson; *m* 1948, Marion Robertson Scobie (marr. diss. 1985); two *s*. *Educ:* Sedbergh; London Univ. (BSc Estate Management 1950). Served War of 1939–45;

North Irish Horse; Court Orderly Officer, Wüppertal War Crimes Trial, 1946. Partner, Bell-Ingram, Chartered Surveyors, 1957–83. Director: Central Farmers Ltd, 1972–86; Control Securities plc, 1986–92. Royal Institution of Chartered Surveyors: Mem. General Council, 1973–; President, 1979–80; Mem. Land Agency and Agricl Divisional Council, 1970–77 (Chm., 1974–75); Chm., Internat. Cttee, 1976–78. *Publications:* articles on technical and professional subjects, incl. Planning in the Countryside. *Recreations:* golf, fishing, shooting. *Club:* Farmers'. *Died 8 Feb. 2006.*

WILSON, William; DL; *b* 28 June 1913; *s* of Charles and Charlotte Wilson; *m* 1939, Bernice Wilson (*d* 1993); one *s*. *Educ:* Wheatley St Sch.; Cheylesmore Sch.; Coventry Jun. Technical Sch. Qual. as solicitor, 1939, retired 1999. Entered Army, 1941; served in N Africa, Italy and Greece; demobilised, 1946 (Sergeant). Contested (Lab) Warwick and Leamington, 1951, 1955, March 1957, 1959. MP (Lab) Coventry S, 1964–74, Coventry SE, 1974–83; Mem., Commons Select Cttee on Race Relations and Immigration, 1970–79. Mem., Warwicks CC, 1958–70 (Leader Labour Group), 1972–93. DL County of Warwick, 1967. *Recreations:* gardening, theatre, watching Association football, voluntary work in Warwickshire CC Record Office.
Died 18 Aug. 2010.

WILTSHAW, Eve, OBE 1992; MD; FRCP, FRCOG; Medical Director, Royal Marsden Hospital, 1986–94; *b* 23 Jan. 1927. *Educ:* Univ. of Wales Med. Sch. (MB BCh, MD). Jun. med. posts, 1951–52; jun. post in clin. haematol., Tufts Med. Sch., Boston, 1953–55; Inst. of Cancer Res., 1955–74; Consultant in Cancer Medicine, Royal Marsden Hosp., 1974–92. *Publications:* A History of the Royal Marsden Hospital, 1998.
Died 13 May 2008.

WINCKLER, Andrew Stuart; Chairman, UK Financial Services Regulatory Practice, Ernst & Young, 1998–2006; *b* 8 Jan. 1949; *s* of Aubrey Norman Toussaint Winckler and Pamela Elizabeth Essie (*née* Webb); *m* 1971, Marie Estelle Sigwart; three *s*. *Educ:* Bedford Modern Sch.; Christ's Coll., Cambridge (Open Exhibn; BA Hist. 1970; Dip Econ. 1975). MSI. HM Treasury, 1970–82, seconded to HM Diplomatic Service as First Sec. (Finance), British Embassy, Washington, 1978–81; Lloyds Bank, 1982–87: Syndicates Manager, Internat. Bank, 1982–85; Dir, Merchant Bank, 1985–87; Dir, Security Pacific Hoare Govett, 1987–90; Dep. Chm., European Capital Co., 1990–94; Exec. Dir, Head of Supervision, SIB, 1994–95; Chief Exec., SIB, 1996–97, FSA, 1997–98. Sen. Independent Dir, CrestCo Ltd, 1998–2002; Mem. Bd, Euroclear plc, 2003–06. Member: Bd, Housing Corp., 1998–2005; Jersey Financial Services Commn, 1998–2006; ESRC, 2003–06. Trustee, Kennedy Meml Trust, 1998–2003. Mem. Council, QMW, 2000–04. FRGS 1995. *Recreations:* reading, gardening, opera, bridge. *Address:* 61 Marsham Court, Marsham Street, SW1P 4JZ. *Club:* Oxford and Cambridge. *Died 15 Jan. 2007.*

WINDLESHAM, 3rd Baron *cr* 1937; David James George Hennessy, CVO 1981; PC 1973; DLitt; Bt 1927; Baron Hennessy (Life Peer), 1999; Principal, Brasenose College, Oxford, 1989–2002, Hon. Fellow 2002; Chairman, Trustees of the British Museum, 1986–96 (Trustee, 1981–96); *b* 28 Jan. 1932; *s* of 2nd Baron Windlesham; *S* father, 1962; *m* 1965, Prudence Glynn (*d* 1986); one *s* one *d*. *Educ:* Ampleforth; Trinity Coll., Oxford (MA; DLitt 1995; Hon. Fellow 1982). Chairman, Bow Group, 1959–60, 1962–63; Member, Westminster City Council, 1958–62. Minister of State, Home Office, 1970–72; Minister of State for Northern Ireland, 1972–73; Lord Privy Seal and Leader of the House of Lords, 1973–74. Mem., Cttee of Privy Counsellors on Ministerial Memoirs, 1975. Man. Dir, Grampian Television, 1967–70; Jt Man. Dir, 1974–75, Man. Dir, 1975–81, Chm., 1981, ATV Network; Director: The Observer, 1981–89; W. H. Smith Gp, plc, 1986–95. Vis. Fellow, All Souls Coll., Oxford, 1986;

Weinberg/Goldman Sachs Vis. Prof., 1997, and Vis. Prof., Public and Internat. Affairs, 2002–03; Princeton Univ. Chm., The Parole Bd for England and Wales, 1982–88. Pres., Victim Support, 1992–2001; Vice-Pres., Royal Television Soc., 1977–82; Jt Dep. Chm., Queen's Silver Jubilee Appeal, 1977; Dep. Chm., The Royal Jubilee Trusts, 1977–80; Chairman: Oxford Preservation Trust, 1979–89; Oxford Society, 1985–88; Mem., Museums and Galleries Commn, 1984–86. Ditchley Foundation: Governor and Mem., Council of Management, 1983–; Vice-Chm., 1987–; Trustee: Charities Aid Foundn, 1977–81; Community Service Volunteers, 1981–2000; Royal Collection Trust, 1993–2000; Chm., Butler Trust, 2004–06. Hon. Bencher, Inner Temple, 1999. Hon. FBA 2005. Hon. LLD London, 2002. Commendatore, Order of Merit, (Italian Republic), 2003. *Publications:* Communication and Political Power, 1966; Politics in Practice, 1975; Broadcasting in a Free Society, 1980; Responses to Crime, Vol. 1 1987, Vol. 2 1993, Vol. 3 1996, Vol. 4 2001; (with Richard Rampton) The Windlesham/Rampton Report on Death on the Rock, 1989; Politics, Punishment, and Populism, 1998. *Heir: s* Hon. James Hennessy [*b* 9 Nov. 1968; *m* 2004, Deborah Jane Wallace; one *s*]. *Address:* c/o House of Lords, SW1A 0PW.
Died 21 Dec. 2010.

WING, Prof. John Kenneth, CBE 1990; MD, PhD; DPM; FRCPsych; Director of Research Unit, Royal College of Psychiatrists, 1989–94; Professor of Social Psychiatry, Institute of Psychiatry and London School of Hygiene and Tropical Medicine, 1970–89, then Emeritus Professor, University of London; *b* 22 Oct. 1923; *m* 1950, Lorna Gladys Tolchard (OBE 1995); one *d*. *Educ:* Strand Sch.; University College London (MB, BS, MD, PhD). Served RNVR, 1942–46, Lieut (A). Dir, MRC Social Psychiatry Unit, 1965–89. Mem., MRC, 1985–89 (Chm., Neurosciences Bd, 1985–87; Chm., Health Services Res. Cttee, 1987–89). Hon. Consultant Psychiatrist, Maudsley and Bethlem Royal Hosp., 1960–89. Advr to H of C Social Services Cttee, 1984–85 and 1990. Founder FMedSci 1998. Hon MD Heidelberg, 1977. *Publications:* (ed) Early Childhood Autism, 1966, 2nd edn 1975 (trans. Italian 1970, German 1973); (with G. W. Brown) Institutionalism and Schizophrenia, 1970; (with J. E. Cooper and N. Sartorius) Description and Classification of Psychiatric Symptoms, 1974 (trans. German 1978, French 1980, Japanese 1981); Reasoning about Madness, 1978 (trans. Portuguese 1978, German 1982, Italian 1983); ed, Schizophrenia: towards a new synthesis, 1978; ed (with R. Olsen), Community Care for the Mentally Disabled, 1979; (with J. Leach) Helping Destitute Men, 1979; (ed jtly) What is a Case?, 1981; (ed jtly) Handbook of Psychiatric Rehabilitation, 1981; (with L. G. Wing) Psychoses of Uncertain Aetiology, vol. III of Cambridge Handbook of Psychiatry, 1982; (ed) Contributions to Health Services Planning and Research, 1989; (ed) Measurement for Mental Health, 1995; (jtly) Diagnosis and Clinical Measurement in Psychiatry, 1998; (with P. Lelliott) Progress on Health of the Nation Outcome Scales, 2000; Epidemiological Needs Assessment: severe mental illness, 2000. *Died 18 April 2010.*

WINGFIELD DIGBY, Very Rev. Richard Shuttlewort; Dean of Peterborough, 1966–80, Dean Emeritus since 1980; *b* 19 Aug. 1911; *s* of late Everard George Wingfield Digby and Dorothy (*née* Loughnan); *m* 1936, Rosamond Frances, *d* of late Col W. T. Digby, RE; two *s* one *d*. *Educ:* Nautical Coll., Pangbourne; Royal Navy; Christ's Coll., Cambridge (BA 1935; MA 1939); Westcott House, Cambridge. Ordained deacon 1936, priest 1937; Asst Curate of St Andrew's, Rugby, 1936–46. Chaplain to the Forces (4th Cl. Emergency Commn), 1940–45; POW, 1940–45. Vicar of All Saints, Newmarket, 1946–53; Rector of Bury, Lancs, 1953–66; Rural Dean of Bury, 1962–66. Pres. and Chm., Bury Trustee Savings Bank, 1953–66; Dep. Chm., Trustee Savings Bank Assoc., North-West Area, 1965–66. Hon. Canon of Manchester Cathedral, 1965; Hon. Chaplain to

Regt XX, The Lancs Fusiliers, 1965. Chm., C of E Council for Places of Worship, 1976–81. *Recreations:* walking, dry stone walling. *Died 29 Jan. 2007.*

WINKLER, Jan; Ambassador of the Czech Republic to the Court of St James's, since 2005; *b* 7 May 1957; *s* of Otto and Helena Winkler; *m* 1979, Jana Zajícová; one *s* two *d*. *Educ:* Charles Univ., Prague (JUD). Company lawyer, 1981–90; Registrar, Charles Univ., Prague, 1990–95; Ministry of Foreign Affairs: Hd, Policy Planning, 1995–97; Vice-Minister, 1997–99; Consultant: for Andersen Consulting, later Accenture, 1999–2002; for PricewaterhouseCoopers, 2002–03; Vice-Minister, Min. of Foreign Affairs, 2003–05. *Publications:* jointly: Obnova ideje university, 1993; Rethinking University, 1994; Uniqueness in Unity, 1995; The Future Development of CEFTA, 1996; The Pilsen Talks, 1997; contrib. many articles to Perspectives, Universidad Futura, Higher Education Mgt, International Politik, Europäische Rundschau, Mezinárodni Vztahy, Aula, etc. *Recreations:* reading, exhibitions, biking, ski-ing, roller blades. *Address:* (office) 26 Kensington Palace Gardens, W8 4QY. *T:* (020) 7243 7902, *Fax:* (020) 7727 9654; *e-mail:* jan_winkler@mzv.cz. *Clubs:* Athenæum, Travellers. *Died 16 Feb. 2009.*

WINSTANLEY, John, MC 1944; TD 1951; FRCS, FRCOphth; Hon. Consultant Ophthalmic Surgeon, St Thomas' Hospital, since 1983 (Ophthalmic Surgeon, 1960–83); *b* 11 May 1919; 3rd *s* of late Captain Bernard Joseph Winstanley and Grace Taunton; *m* 1959, Jane Frost; one *s* two *d*. *Educ:* Wellington Coll., Berks; St Thomas's Hosp. Med. Sch. (MB, BS 1951). FRCS 1957; FRCOphth (FCOphth 1988). Served 4th Bn Queen's Own Royal West Kent Regt, 1937–46 (despatches BEF, 1940). Resident med. appts, St Thomas' and Moorfields Eye Hosps, 1951–56; Chief Clin. Asst, Moorfields Eye Hosp., 1956–60; Sen. Registrar, St Thomas' Hosp., 1956–60; recog. teacher of ophthalmol., St Thomas' Hosp., 1960–83; Ophth. Surg., Lewisham and Greenwich Health Dists, 1959–70; Hon. Ophthalmic Surgeon: Royal Hosp., Chelsea, 1963–85; Queen Alexandra's Mil. Hosp., Millbank, 1966–72; Queen Elizabeth Mil. Hosp., Woolwich, 1972–83. Hon. Civilian Consultant in Ophthalmol. to MOD (Army), 1971–83. Examiner in Ophthalmology (DipOphth of Examining Bd of RCP and RCS, 1968–72; Mem. Court of Examiners, RCS, 1972–78). FRSocMed 1963 (Vice-Pres., Sect. of Ophth., 1979); Member: Ophthal. Soc. UK, 1958–88 (Hon. Sec. 1966–68, Vice-Pres. 1980–83); Faculty of Ophthalmologists, 1958–88, Mem. Council, 1973–85, Vice-Pres., 1979–85; Mem. Council, Medical Protection Soc., 1979–90. Liveryman, Soc. of Apothecaries, 1965 (Mem. Livery Cttee, 1982). *Publications:* chapter, Rose's Medical Ophthalmology, 1983; papers on ophthalmic topics and med. hist. in med. jls. *Recreations:* fishing, medical history. *Address:* The Old Post Office, 1 The Square, Brill, Aylesbury, Bucks HP18 9RP. *Clubs:* Army and Navy, Flyfishers'. *Died 4 Jan. 2008.*

WINSTON-FOX, Ruth, MBE 1996; JP; Co-Chairman, Women's National Commission, 1979–81 (Member, 1971); *b* 12 Sept. 1912; *d* of Major the Rev. Solomon Lipson, Hon. SCF, and Tilly Lipson (*née* Shandel); *m* 1st, 1938, Laurence Winston (*d* 1949); two *s* one *d*; 2nd, 1960, Goodwin Fox (*d* 1974). *Educ:* St Paul's Girls' Sch.; London Univ. BSc Household and Social Sci.; Home Office Child Care Cert. Mental Hosps Dept and Child Care Dept, LCC, 1936–39; Dep. Centre Organiser, WVS, Southgate, 1941–45; Southgate Borough Council: Member, 1945–65; Alderman, 1955–65; Mayor of Southgate, 1958–59; Dep. Mayor, 1959–61; Sen. Officer, Adoptions Consultant, Social Services Dept, Herts CC, 1949–77. Member: London Rent Assessment Panel and Tribunals, 1975–83; Review Cttee for Secure Accommodation, London Borough of Enfield, 1982; Bd of Deputies of British Jews, 1960– (Chm. Educn Cttee, 1974–80; voluntary nat. organiser, exhibn Jewish Way of Life, 1978, which visited 44 communities in Britain);

Vice-Pres., Internat. Council of Jewish Women, 1974–81 (Chairman: Status of Women Cttee, 1966–75; Inter-Affiliate Travel Cttee, 1975–81); Mem. Governing Body, World Jewish Congress, 1981–; Co-Chm., Jewish Community Exhibn Centre, 1984–. Founder, one of first Day Centres for the Elderly in GB, Ruth Winston House, Southgate Old People's Centre, opened by Princess Alexandra, 1961, and again, 1972; Vice-President: Southgate Old People's Welfare Cttee, 1974–; Southgate Horticultural Soc.; President: League of Jewish Women, 1969–72; First Women's Lodge, England, 1972–74; Enfield Relate (formerly Enfield Marriage Guidance Council), 1984–. JP Middx Area GLC, 1954. *Publications:* articles only. *Recreations:* five grandchildren, travel, voluntary service. *Address:* 4 Morton Crescent, Southgate, N14 7AH. *T:* (020) 8886 5056. *Clubs:* University Women's, Bnai Brith.   *Died 23 Nov. 2007.*

WISDOM, Sir Norman, Kt 2000; OBE 1995; actor/comedian; *b* 4 Feb. 1915; *m* 1947, Freda Simpson (marr. diss. 1969); one *s* one *d.* Starred regularly on stage and screen, from 1952. First film Trouble in Store, in 1953 (winning an Academy Award), from which starred in 19 major films in both England and America; two Broadway awards for stage musical, Walking Happy; numerous Royal Performances, both film and stage; major UK theatre tours, 1982–2004. Albums include The Musical World of Wisdom, Follow a Star, A World of Wisdom, Nobody's Fool. Freeman: Tirana, Albania, 1995; City of London, 1995. Lifetime Achievement Award for Comedy, British Comedy Awards, 1991; Roy Castle Trophy for Outstanding Services to Variety, Encore Mag. Awards, 2001. *Publications:* (with William Hall) Don't Laugh at Me, 1992; (with Bernard Bale) 'Cos I'm a Fool, 1996; (with William Hall) My Turn, 2002. *Recreation:* all sports. *Address:* c/o Johnny Mans, Johnny Mans Productions Ltd, PO Box 196, Hoddesdon, Herts EN10 7WG.   *Died 4 Oct. 2010.*

WISE, Derek; *see* Wise, R. D.

WISE, Prof. Douglass, OBE 1980; FRIBA; Principal, Douglass Wise & Partners, Architects, since 1959; Director, Institute of Advanced Architectural Studies, University of York, 1975–92; *b* 6 Nov. 1927; *s* of Horace Watson Wise and Doris Wise; *m* 1958, Yvonne Jeannine Czeiler (marr. diss. 1985); one *s* one *d. Educ:* King's Coll., Newcastle, Durham Univ. (BArch; DipTP). Lecturer in Architecture, 1959–65, Prof. of Architecture, 1965–69, Head of Dept of Architecture, 1969–75, Newcastle Univ. RIBA: Chm., Moderators, 1969–75; Chm., Examinations Cttee, 1969–75; Mem. Council, 1976–79; Chm., Heads of Schools Cttee, 1971–73; Mem. Bd of Management, North Eastern Housing Assoc., 1967–76 (Vice-Chm., 1974–76); Mem. Council, Newcastle Polytechnic, 1974–77; past Mem. Council, Senate and Court, Newcastle Univ.; Governor, Building Centre Trust, London, 1976–92; Chairman: NE Civic Trust, 1993–2002; Northern Regl Centre for the Built Envmt, 1994–98. Hon. LittD Sheffield, 1992. *Publications:* contribs to various technical jls on housing, continuing educn and architectural theory. *Recreations:* painting, natural history. *Address:* Welburn, Kirkwhelpington, Newcastle upon Tyne NE19 2SA. *T:* (01830) 540219.
                    Died 18 Oct. 2008.

WISE, Peter Anthony Surtees, MBE 1993; Director, Wise Consultancy Ltd; *b* 26 June 1934; *s* of late J. A. S. (Tony) Wise and Lenore Dugdale; *m* 1st, 1956, Elizabeth Muirhead Odhams (*d* 1995); two *s*; 2nd, 1998, Jill Fountain-Barber. *Educ:* Royal Naval College, Dartmouth. Served Royal Navy, 1948–56 (invalided). Marconi Instruments Ltd, 1956–60; Vickers Ltd, 1961–74; First Secretary, later Counsellor (Hong Kong Affairs), UK Mission, Geneva, 1974–78; Head of Commercial Div. (formerly Asst Comr (Commercial)), Hong Kong Govt Office, London, 1978–93; also Rep. for Commercial Relns with Austria and the Nordic Countries, 1980–93 (formerly non-resident Counsellor (HK Trade Affairs), Helsinki, Oslo, Stockholm, Vienna).

Address: Lennoxdale House, Goatacre Road, Medstead, Alton, Hants GU34 5PU. *T:* (01420) 562915. *Club:* Hong Kong (Hong Kong).   *Died 4 May 2007.*

WISE, (Reginald) Derek, CBE 1977; Partner, Wise & Mercer, Paris, 1983–96; avocat honoraire; *b* 29 July 1917; *s* of Reginald and Rita Wise; *m* 1957, Nancy Brenta Scialoya; two *s* one *d. Educ:* St Paul's Sch. Admitted solicitor, 1947. Served War of 1939–45, RA and Intell. Partner, Theodore Goddard, Paris, 1957–82. Legal Adviser, British Embassy, Paris, 1962–96. *Address:* 203 bis Boulevard St Germain, 75007 Paris, France. *T:* 142220794.   *Died 23 Feb. 2007.*

WISEMAN, Prof. Donald John, OBE 1943; DLit; FBA 1966; FSA; Professor of Assyriology in the University of London, 1961–82, Emeritus 1982; *b* 25 Oct. 1918; *s* of Air Cdre Percy John Wiseman, CBE, RAF; *m* 1948, Mary Catherine (*d* 2006), *d* of P. O. Ruoff; three *d. Educ:* Dulwich College; King's College, London. BA (London); AKC, McCaul Hebrew Prize, 1939; FKC 1982. Served War of 1939–45, in RAFVR. Ops, 11 Fighter Group, 1939–41; Chief Intelligence Officer, Mediterranean Allied Tactical Air Forces with Rank of Group Capt., 1942–45. Heap Exhibitioner in Oriental Languages, Wadham Coll., Oxford, 1945–47; MA 1949. Asst Keeper, Dept of Egyptian and Assyrian, later Western Asiatic, Antiquities, British Museum, 1948–61. Epigraphist on archæological excavations at Nimrud, Harran, Rimah; Jt Dir of British School of Archæology in Iraq, 1961–65, Chm. 1970–88, Vice-Pres., 1988–93, Pres., 1993–2001. Trustee, British Sch. of Archæology in Jerusalem, 1984–92. Pres., Soc. for Old Testament Studies, 1980; Chm., Tyndale House for Biblical Research, Cambridge, 1957–86. Corresp. Mem., German Archæological Inst., 1961. Editor, Journal IRAQ, 1953–78; Joint Editor, Reallexikon der Assyriologie, 1959–83. Bronze Star (USA), 1944. *Publications:* The Alalakh Tablets, 1953; Chronicles of Chaldaean Kings, 1956; Cuneiform Texts from Cappadocian Tablets in the British Museum, V, 1956; Cylinder-Seals of Western Asia, 1958; Vassal-Treaties of Esarhaddon, 1958; Illustrations from Biblical Archæology, 1958; Catalogue of Western Asiatic Seals in the British Museum, vol. I, 1963; Peoples of Old Testament Times, 1973; Archaeology and the Bible, 1979; Essays on the Patriarchal Narratives, 1980; Nebuchadrezzar and Babylon, 1985; I and II Kings (commentary), 1993; Nimrud Literary Texts, 1996; Memoirs, 2003; contrib. to journals. *Address:* Low Barn, 26 Downs Way, Tadworth, Surrey KT20 5DZ. *T:* (01737) 813536.   *Died 2 Feb. 2010.*

WISHART, Maureen; *see* Lehane, M.

WITTS, Canon Diana Katharine, OBE 2000; General Secretary, Church Mission Society, 1995–2000; *b* 14 May 1936; *d* of Maj.-Gen. Frederick Vavasour Broome Witts, CB, CBE, DSO, MC and Alice Mary Witts (*née* Wrigley). *Educ:* Bristol Univ. (BSc Physics). Hospital Physicist: Charing Cross Hosp., 1958–59; Royal Victoria Hosp., Montreal, 1959–61; Teacher of Maths and Physics: Parliament Hill Sch., 1961–63; Highlands Sch., Eldoret, Kenya, 1963–65; Mem., Lee Abbey Community, Devon, 1966; Teacher of Maths and Physics, Alliance Girls' High Sch., Kenya, 1966–70; Sen. Mistress, introducing co-educn, Gordonstoun Sch., 1970–75; educnl work with Maasai girls in Kenya, 1976–79; Tutor, Crowther Hall, Birmingham, 1980; CMS Rep. in E Africa, 1981–83; theol educn by extension, Zaïre, 1983–84; CMS Regl Sec. for W Africa, Sudan and Zaïre, 1985–95. Reader, Southwark Dio., 1991–; Lay Canon, Salisbury Cathedral, 1998–. Cross of St Augustine, 1994. *Publications:* Springs of Hope (autobiog.), 2005. *Recreation:* hill-walking. *Address:* 107 Gloucester Court, Kew Road, Richmond, Surrey TW9 3DZ.   *Died 19 March 2006.*

WIX, Ethel Rose; Special Commissioner of Income Tax, 1977–86; *b* 1 Nov. 1921; *d* of Michael Wix and Anna Wix (*née* Snyder). *Educ:* Henrietta Barnett Sch.;

Cheltenham Ladies' Coll.; University Coll. London (BA Hons 1942); Hull University Coll. (Cert Ed 1943). Special Operations Executive, 1944–45; lived in S Africa, 1948–54; work for S African Inst. of Race Relations, 1950–54; Africa Bureau, London, 1955–56; Solicitor of Supreme Court, 1960; Partner, Herbert Oppenheimer, Nathan & Vandyk, 1960–75; General Commissioner of Income Tax, 1976–78. Mem., Arbitrators Panel, The Securities and Futures Authy Consumer Arbitration Scheme, 1988–94. Member: Exec. Cttee, Jewish Mus., 1987–93 (Hon. Treas., 1987–89); Exec. Cttee, Inst. of Jewish Affairs, 1990–92; Liby Cttee, Oxford Centre for Postgrad. Hebrew Studies, 1990–94. Mem. Council: Richmond Fellowship, 1975–85; Trinity Hospice, Clapham, 1981–90; Cheltenham Ladies' Coll., 1983–93 (Vice-Chm., 1990–92); St Christopher's Hospice, 1985–95; Clifton Coll., 1987–91; Governor, Warwick Schs Foundn, 1988–90, and 1992–96 (Vice-Chm., 1994–96). *Publications:* papers on Cost of Living, 1951, and Industrial Feeding Facilities, 1953, for S African Inst of Race Relations; summary of Royal Commn Report on E Africa, 1956, for Africa Bureau. *Recreations:* reading, cooking, theatre. *Club:* Special Forces.
Died 3 April 2009.

WOHL, Maurice, CBE 1992; Founder, Maurice Wohl Charitable Foundation and Maurice Wohl Charitable Trust, since 1965; *b* London, 4 Jan. 1917; *s* of Max Wohl and Miriam Rachel Wohl; *m* 1966, Vivienne Susan Monica Horowitz (decd). *Educ:* Grocers' Co. Sch.; City of London Sch. Chm., United Real Property Trust, 1960–74. Pres., Jerusalem Great Synagogue, 1987–. Fellow: RPMS, 1991; ICSM, 1999; Presentation Fellow, KCL, 1992. Hon. FRCSE 2000, CompRCSE, 2006; Hon. Fellow: City of Jerusalem, 1998; UCL, 2000. Hon. PhD Bar-Ilan, 2001. Médaille de la Ville de Paris, 1988. *Recreations:* reading, walking, art collecting. *Address:* c/o Claridge's, Brook Street, Mayfair, W1K 4HR.
Died 28 June 2007.

WOLF, Prof. Peter Otto, FREng, FICE, FCIWEM; FRMetS; FASCE; consultant; Director, Pell Frischmann Consulting Engineers Ltd, 1993–2003; Professor and Head of Department of Civil Engineering, 1966–82, The City University, London, then Professor Emeritus; *b* 9 May 1918; *s* of Richard Wolf and Dora (*née* Bondy); *m* 1st, 1944, Jennie Robinson (marr. diss. 1977); two *s* one *d*; 2nd, 1977, Janet Elizabeth Robertson. *Educ:* University of London (BScEng). Assistant under agreement to C. E. Farren, Cons. Engr, 1941–44; Civilian Asst, a Dept of the War Office, 1944–45; Engineer (Chief Designer, Loch Sloy Project), under James Williamson, Cons. Engr, 1945–47; Engineer for Mullardoch Dam (Affric Project), John Cochrane & Sons Ltd, 1947–49; Imperial College of Science and Technology; Lectr in Fluid Mechanics and Hydraulic Engrg, 1949–55; Reader in Hydrology in Univ. of London, 1955–66. Private consultancy, London, 1950–. Chairman: Cttee on Flood Protection Res., MAFF, 1984–85; Standing Cttee on Natural Hazards, Hazards Forum, 1991–94 (Trustee, 1994–99, Dist. Mem., 1999–); Mem., UK Co-ordination Cttee, UN Internat. Decade of Natural Disaster Reduction, 1993–97. Visiting Professor: Stanford Univ., Calif, 1959–60, 1961–64; Cornell Univ., 1963. Mem. Ct, Brunel Univ., 1999–2002. Hon. Member: BHRA, 1984–; Amer. Inst. of Hydrology, 1985– (Jubilee Lectr, 2001); British Hydrol Soc., 1994– (Pres., 1987–89). Hon. DrIng Technological Univ. of Dresden, 1986. *Publications:* trans. and ed, Engineering Fluid Mechanics, by Charles Jaeger, 1956; papers in Proc. ICE, Jl IWE, UNESCO Reports, UNESCO Nature and Resources, Proc. Internat. Water Resources Assoc., etc. *Recreations:* classical music, reading, ski-ing, walking. *Address:* 69 Shepherds Hill, N6 5RE. *T:* and *Fax:* (020) 8340 6638. *Club:* Athenæum.
Died 6 Oct. 2007.

WOLFE, William Cuthbertson; Member, National Council, Scottish National Party, since 1991; *b* 22 Feb. 1924; *s* of late Major Tom Wolfe, TD, and Katie Cuthbertson; *m* 1st, 1953, Arna Mary (marr. diss. 1989), *d*

of late Dr Melville Dinwiddie, CBE, DSO, MC; two *s* two *d*; 2nd, 1993, Catherine Margaret, *d* of late James Parker, and *widow* of John McAteer. *Educ:* Bathgate Academy; George Watson's Coll., Edinburgh. CA. Army service, 1942–47, NW Europe and Far East; Air OP Pilot. Hon. Publications Treas., Saltire Society, 1953–60; Scout County Comr, West Lothian, 1960–64; Hon. Pres. (Rector), Students' Assoc., Heriot-Watt Univ., 1966–69. Contested (SNP): West Lothian, 1962, 1964, 1966, 1970, Feb. and Oct. 1974, 1979; North Edinburgh, Nov. 1973; Scottish National Party: Chm., 1969–79; Pres., 1980–82; Mem., NEC, 1998–2002. Treas., Scottish CND, 1982–85; Sec., Scottish Poetry Liby, 1985–91. Mem., Forestry Commn Nat. Cttee for Scotland, 1974–87. *Publications:* Scotland Lives, 1973. *Address:* 17 Limekilnburn Road, Quarter, Hamilton ML3 7XA. *T:* (01698) 281072.
Died 18 March 2010.

WOLFF, Prof. Otto Herbert, CBE 1985; MD, FRCP; Nuffield Professor of Child Health, University of London, 1965–85, then Emeritus Professor; Dean of the Institute of Child Health, 1982–85; *b* 10 Jan. 1920; *s* of Dr H. A. J. Wolff; *m* 1952, Dr Jill Freeborough (*d* 2002); one *s* one *d. Educ:* Peterhouse, Cambridge; University College Hospital, London. Lieut and Capt. RAMC, 1944–47. Resident Medical Officer, Registrar and Sen. Med. Registrar, Birmingham Children's Hospital, 1948–51; Lecturer, Sen. Lectr, Reader, Dept of Pædiatrics and Child Health, Univ. of Birmingham, 1951–64. Senator, London Univ.; Representative of London Univ. on GMC. Past Pres., British Pædiatric Assoc.; Member: Royal Society of Medicine; American Pædiatric Society; New York Academy of Sciences; Amer. Academy of Pediatrics; European Soc. for Paediatric Research; European Soc. for Paediatric Gastroenterology; Deutsche Akad. der Naturforscher Leopoldina. Corresp. Member: Société Française de Pédiatrie; Société Suisse de Pédiatrie; Osterreichische Gesellschaft für Kinderheilkunde; Società Italiana di Pediatria; Deutsche Gesellschaft für Kinderheilkunde; Fellow, Indian Acad. of Pediatrics. Chm. of Trustees, Child-to-Child Charity, 1989–93. Hon. FRCPCH 1996; Hon. FRSocMed 2009. Dawson Williams Meml Prize, BMA, 1984; Medal, Assoc. Française pour le Dépistage et la Prévention des Maladies Métaboliques et des Handicaps de l'Enfant, 1986; Harding Award, Action Res. for Crippled Child, 1987; James Spence Medal, BPA, 1988. *Publications:* chapter on Disturbances of Serum Lipoproteins in Endocrine and Genetic Diseases of Childhood (ed L. I. Gardner); chapter on Obesity in Recent Advances in Paediatrics (ed David Hull); articles in Lancet, British Medical Journal, Archives of Disease in Childhood, Quarterly Jl of Medicine, etc. *Recreation:* music. *Address:* 53 Danbury Street, N1 8LE. *T:* (020) 7226 0748.
Died 27 April 2010.

WOLFSON, Baron *cr* 1985 (Life Peer), of Marylebone in the City of Westminster; **Leonard Gordon Wolfson,** Kt 1977; Bt 1962; Chairman, since 1972, and Founder Trustee, since 1955, Wolfson Foundation; Chairman: Great Universal Stores, 1981–96 (Managing Director, 1962–81; Director, 1952); Burberrys Ltd, 1978–96; *b* London, 11 Nov. 1927; *s* of Sir Isaac Wolfson, 1st Bt, FRS (*d* 1991) and Lady (Edith) Wolfson (*d* 1981); *m* 1st, 1949, Ruth Sterling (marr. diss. 1991); four *d*; 2nd, 1991, Estelle (*née* Feldman), *widow* of Michael Jackson, FCA; one *step s* one *step d. Educ:* King's School, Worcester. President: Jewish Welfare Bd, 1972–82; Shaare Zedek UK, 2006–. Hon. Pres., British Technion Soc., 2006. Trustee, Imperial War Mus., 1988–94. Fellow: Royal Albert Hall, 2003; Birkbeck Coll., Univ. of London, 2006. Hon. Fellow: St Catherine's Coll., Oxford; Wolfson Coll., Cambridge; Wolfson Coll., Oxford; Worcester Coll., Oxford; UCL; LSHTM 1985; QMC 1985; Poly. of Central London, 1991; Imperial Coll., 1991; LSE, 1999; Somerville Coll., Oxford, 1999; Inst. of Educn, London Univ., 2001; RAM, 2003; Hon. Mem., Emmanuel Coll., Cambridge, 1996. Hon. Fellow: Israel Mus., 2001; Royal Instn, 2002; Ashmolean Mus., 2009. Hon. FRCP 1977; Hon. FRCS 1988; Hon. FBA 1986; Hon. FREng (Hon. FEng 1997); Hon. FRS 2005; Hon.

MRCSEd 1997, Companion, RCSE, 2006. Hon. DCL Oxon, 1972; Hon. LLD: Strathclyde, 1972; Dundee, 1979; Cantab, 1982; London, 1982; Hon. DSc: Hull, 1977; Wales, 1984; E Anglia, 1986; Sheffield, 2005; Cape Town, 2008; Imperial Coll. London, 2008; Durham, 2009; Hon. PhD: Tel Aviv, 1971; Hebrew Univ., 1978; Bar Ilan, 1983; Weizmann Inst., 1988; DUniv: Surrey, 1990; Glasgow, 1997; Hon. MD Birmingham, 1992; Dr *hc*: Technion, 1995; Edinburgh, 1996; Hon. DLitt Loughborough, 2003. Sir Winston Churchill Award, British Technion Soc., 1989; President's Award, Hebrew Univ., 2005. *Address:* 8 Queen Anne Street, W1G 9LD.
Died 20 May 2010 (Btcy ext).

WOLFSON, Sir Brian (Gordon), Kt 1990; Chairman, Kepner Tregoe Inc., USA, since 2000 (Director, since 1980); *b* 2 Aug. 1935; *s* of Gabriel and Eve Wolfson; *m* 1958, Helen, *d* of late Lewis Grodner; one *s* one *d*. *Educ:* Liverpool Coll.; Liverpool Univ. Joined Granada Group, 1961, Jt Man. Dir, 1967–70; Chairman: Anglo Nordic Holdings, 1976–87; Wembley Stadium Ltd, 1986–95; PST (Internat.) Ltd, 1997–2003; Fruit of the Loom Inc., Chicago, 2000–02; Dir, Charles Ede Ltd, London, 1971–. Chairman: Trng Commn, later Trng Agency, then Nat. Trng Task Force, 1988–92; Investors in People (UK), 1992–99. First non-North American World Pres., Young Presidents' Orgn, 1979–80; Mem., NEDC, 1989–92 (Chm., Cttee on leisure, 1986–92). University of Pennsylvania: Mem. Adv. Bd, Wharton Center for Internat. Management Studies, 1980–; Bd, Joseph H. Lauder Inst., 1983–. Governor: Liverpool Coll., 1990– (Chm., Audit Cttee, 2002–); Ashridge Management Coll., 1991– (Chm., Ashridge MBA Prog., 1988–93); NIESR, 1993–95. CCMI (FBIM 1969, CBIM 1970; Chm., 1986–88; Vice-Pres., 1988; Verulam Medal, 1995; Fellow, Inst BE. Hon. DBA Liverpool Poly., 1989; Hon. LLD Liverpool, 2002. *Recreations:* archaeological digs, making wildlife films. *Address:* Apartment 17, 35–37 Grosvenor Square, W1K 2HN.
Died 10 May 2007.

WOMERSLEY, (Denis) Keith, CBE 1974; HM Diplomatic Service, retired; *b* 21 March 1920; *s* of late Alfred Womersley, Bradford, Yorks, and late Agnes (*née* Keighley); *m* 1st, 1955, Eileen Georgina (*d* 1990), *d* of late George and Margaret Howe; 2nd, 1992, Gillian Anne, *widow* of Dr Gerard O'Donnell; three step *s* one step *d*. *Educ:* Christ's Hospital; Caius Coll., Cambridge (Hons, MA). Served War, HM Forces, 1940–46. Entered Foreign (later Diplomatic) Service, 1946; Foreign Office, 1948, Control Commn Germany, 1952; Vienna, 1955; Hong Kong, 1957, FO, 1960; Baghdad, 1962; FO, 1963; Aden, 1966; Beirut, 1967; FCO, 1969–71; Bonn, 1971–74; Counsellor, FCO, 1974–77. FRSA 1976. Gov., Christ's Hosp., 1991–. *Recreations:* violin-playing, Abbeyfield Soc. work. *Club:* Christ's Hospital (Horsham).
Died 28 Dec. 2010.

WOOD, Ven. Arnold; Warden, Community of the Epiphany, 1985–2000; Archdeacon of Cornwall and Canon Residentiary (Librarian), Truro Cathedral, 1981–88; Archdeacon and Canon Emeritus, 1988; *b* 24 Oct. 1918; *s* of Harry and Annie Wood; *m* 1945, Dorothy Charlotte Tapper (*d* 1998); two *d*. *Educ:* Holy Trinity School, Halifax; London Univ. (Dip. Economics); Clifton Theol Coll.; Open Univ. (Dip.Eur.Hum.). Commissioned, RASC, 1939–49. Legal Adviser and Man. Director, CMI Engineering Co. Ltd, 1949–63; ordained deacon 1965, priest 1966; Curate, Kirkheaton, W Yorks, 1965–67; Vicar, Mount Pellon, W Yorks, 1967–73; Rector of Lanreath and Vicar of Pelynt, 1973–81; Rural Dean, West Wivelshire, dio. Truro, 1976–81. Mem., General Synod, 1985–88. Gen. Comr of Income Tax, 1977–93. *Recreations:* walking, bowls, music. *Address:* 13 Groveville, Northedge Lane, Hipperholme, Halifax HX3 8LD. *T:* (01422) 207014. *Club:* Royal Commonwealth Society. *Died 27 April 2007.*

WOOD, Christopher Edward Russell; art historian, dealer and consultant; *b* 31 Oct. 1941; *s* of Russell Wood and Muriel Wood; *m* 1st, 1967 (marr. diss. 1995); two *s*

one *d*; 2nd, 2004, Rosemary Bingham. *Educ:* Sedbergh Sch.; St John's Coll., Cambridge (BA 1963). Dir, Christie's, 1969–76; Man. Dir, Christopher Wood Gall., 1977–; Dir, Mallett plc, 1988–95. Prof. of Art Hist., Southampton Inst. Antiques Roadshow, 1999–2004. *Publications:* The Dictionary of Victorian Painters, 2 vols, 1971, 6th edn 1999; Victorian Panorama: paintings of Victorian life, 1976; The Pre-Raphaelites, 1981; Olympian Dreamers, 1983; Tissot, 1986; (with Penelope Hobhouse) Painted Gardens: English watercolours 1850–1914, 1988; Paradise Lost: paintings of English country life and landscape 1850–1914, 1988; Victorian Painting in Oils and Watercolours, 1996; The Great Art Boom 1970–1997, 1997; Burne-Jones, 1998; Victorian Painting, 1999; Fairies in Victorian Art, 2000; William Powell Frith, RA: painter of modern life, 2006. *Recreations:* gardening, music, collecting. *Address:* 10 St James's Place, SW1A 1NP. *T:* (020) 7409 7081; *e-mail:* cwood@christopherwoodgallery.com. *Clubs:* Brooks's, Beefsteak, Chelsea Arts. *Died 6 Jan. 2009.*

WOOD, Joseph Neville, (Johnnie), CBE 1978; Director General, The General Council of British Shipping, 1975–78; *b* 25 Oct. 1916; *o s* of late Robert Hind Wood and Emily Wood, Durham; *m* 1st, 1944, Elizabeth May (*d* 1959); three *d*; 2nd, 1965, Josephine Samuel (*née* Dane) (*d* 1985); 3rd, 1986, Frances Howarth (*née* Skeer). *Educ:* Johnston School, Durham; London School of Economics. Entered Civil Service (Board of Trade), 1935; Ministry of War Transport, 1940; jssc 1950; Ministry of Transport: Asst Sec., 1951; Far East Representative, 1952–55; Under-Sec., 1961; Chief of Highway Administration, 1967–68. Joined Chamber of Shipping of the UK, 1968, Dep. Dir, 1970, Dir, 1972–78. Mem., Baltic Exchange, 1968–96; Director: Finance for Shipping Ltd, 1978–82; Ship Mortgage Finance Co. Ltd, 1978–83. Mem. Chichester DC, 1979–91. Vice Pres., Shipwrecked Fishermen and Mariners Royal Benevolent Soc., 1989–2001 (Dep. Chm., 1983–89). FCIT 1976. Freeman, City of London, 1978. Officer, Ordre de Mérite Maritime, 1950. *Recreation:* gardening. *Address:* Barbers Cottage, Heyshott, Midhurst, Sussex GU29 0DE. *T:* (01730) 814282. *Died 29 March 2010.*

WOOD, Rt Rev. Maurice Arthur Ponsonby, DSC 1944; RNR; an Hon. Assistant Bishop, Diocese of London, 1985–2002; *b* 26 Aug. 1916; *o s* of late Arthur Sheppard Wood and Jane Elspeth Dalzell Wood (*née* Piper); *m* 1st, 1947, Marjorie (*née* Pennell) (*d* 1954); two *s* one *d*; 2nd, 1955, M. Margaret (*née* Sandford), SRN, SCM; two *s* one *d*. *Educ:* Monkton Combe Sch.; Queens' Coll., Cambridge (MA); Ridley Hall, Cambridge. Deacon, 1940; priest, 1941; Curate, St Paul's, Portman Square, 1940–43. Royal Naval Chaplain, 1943–47 (continued as Chap. to Commando Assoc.); attached RM Commandos, 1944–46 (landed on D-Day, June 1944); Chaplain, RNR, 1971–. Rector, St Ebbe's, Oxford, 1947–52; Vicar and RD of Islington, and Pres. Islington Clerical Conf., 1952–61; Principal, Oak Hill Theological Coll., Southgate, N14, 1961–71; Prebendary of St Paul's Cathedral, 1969–71; Bishop of Norwich, 1971–85; introduced to House of Lords, 1975; Abbot of St Benet's, 1971–85; Resident Priest of Englefield, 1987–94; Hon. Asst Bishop, dio. of Oxford, 1989–95. Proctor in Convocation of Canterbury and Mem. House of Clergy and Gen. Synod of Church of England (formerly Church Assembly), 1954–85 (House of Bishops, 1971–85); Member: Archbishops' Council on Evangelism, 1972–85; Church Comrs' Houses Cttee, 1980–85; Lords and Commons Family and Child Protection Gp, 1980–. Chairman: Theological Colls Principals' Conf., 1970–71; Norfolk Water Safety Assoc., 1966–71; Norwich RSPCA, 1971–85; The Mansion Trust (India), 1984–2001; Order of Christian Unity, 1986–96 (Pres., 1996–); President: Hildenborough Hall Christian Conf. Centre, 1970–85; Christian Communications Council, 1997–; Vice-President: Crosslinks Soc.; Crusaders Movt; Boys' Brigade, 1986– (Chm., Anglican Council); Trustee: Mary Whitehouse Trust, 1986–90; Riding Lights Theatre Co., 1986–; Parly Christian Fellowship Trust, 1989–;

Council Member: Wycliffe Hall, Oxford, 1981–94; British Atlantic Council, 1985–88; Commonwealth Human Ecology Council, 1986–2001. Patron, Friends of St Catherine's Church, Ludham, 1994–. Governor: Monkton Combe Sch., Bath; Gresham's Sch., Holt, 1971–85; St Helen's Sch., Abingdon, 1989–; Visitor: Langley Sch., Norfolk, 1980–89; Luckley-Oakfield Sch., 1990–. Chaplain, Weavers' Co., 1986–93, Hon. Freeman, 1993. Mission work with Dr Billy Graham in Tokyo, Toronto, Virginia, Osaka, Boston, Amsterdam. Mem., House of Lords, 1975–85. *Publications:* Like a Mighty Army, 1956; Comfort in Sorrow, 1957; Your Suffering, 1959; Christian Stability, 1968; To Everyman's Door, 1968; Into the Way of Peace, 1982; This is our Faith, 1985; series of 12 booklets incl. How Can I Find God, 1954. *Recreations:* swimming, painting, (still) supporting Norwich City FC. *Address:* Abbot's Cottage, 12 Upper Street, Horning, Norwich, Norfolk NR12 8NE. *T:* (01692) 630908. *Club:* Royal Commonwealth Society. *Died 24 June 2007.*

WOOD, Rt Rev. Richard James; Hon. Assistant Bishop of York, 1985–99; *b* 25 Aug. 1920; *s* of Alexander and Irene Wood; *m* 1st, 1946, Elsa Magdalena de Beer (*d* 1969); one *s* one *d* (twins); 2nd, 1972, Cathleen Anne Roark; two *d*. *Educ:* Oldham Hulme Grammar School; Regent St Polytechnic; Wells Theological Coll. Electrical Officer, RAF, then with Ceylon Fire Insurance Assoc. Curate, St Mary's, Calne, 1952–55; Curate, St Mark's Cathedral, George, S Africa, 1955–58; Rector, Christ Church, Beaufort West, 1958–62; Vicar of St Andrew's, Riversdale, 1962–65; Chaplain, S African Defence Force, 1965–68; Asst, St Alban's, E London, 1968; Rector of St John's, Fort Beaufort, 1969–71; Rector of Keetmanshoop, Dio. Damaraland, 1971; Priest-in-Charge of Grace Church and St Michael's, Windhoek and Canon of St George's Cathedral, 1972; Vicar Gen. and Suffragan Bishop of Damaraland, 1973–75; expelled by S Africa, 1975; Hon. Asst Bishop of Damaraland, 1976–; Sec. to The Africa Bureau, 1977; Priest-in-Charge of St Mary, Lowgate, Hull, Chaplain to Hull Coll. of Higher Education and Hon. Asst Bishop of York, 1978–79; at St Mark's Theolog. Coll., Dar es Salaam, 1979–83; Interim Rector: St Matthew's, Wheeling, W Virginia, 1983–84; Trinity, Martinsburg, W Virginia, 1984–85. Hon. Life Mem., Hull Univ. Student Union. *Recreation:* general home interests. *Address:* 3 Plough Steep, Itchen Abbas, Winchester SO21 1BQ. *T:* (01962) 779400. *Died 9 Oct. 2008.*

WOOD, Sir Russell (Dillon), KCVO 1985 (CVO 1979; MVO 1975); VRD 1964; Lt-Comdr, RNR; Deputy Treasurer to the Queen, 1969–85; an Extra Gentleman Usher to the Queen, since 1986; *b* 16 May 1922; *s* of late William G. S. Wood, Whitstable, Kent, and Alice Wood; *m* 1948, Jean Violet Yelwa Davidson, *d* of late Alan S. Davidson, Lenham, Kent; one *s* three *d*. *Educ:* King's Sch., Canterbury. Fleet Air Arm Pilot, 1940–46 (despatches twice). Qual. as Chartered Accountant, 1951; financial management career with major public companies, 1951–68. *Recreations:* private flying, sailing, shooting. *Address:* Skylarks, Bakers Lane, Westleton, Saxmundham, Suffolk IP17 3AZ. *T:* (01728) 648595. *Clubs:* Naval and Military; Aldeburgh Yacht. *Died 15 Dec. 2008.*

WOOD, Terence Courtney, CMG 1989; HM Diplomatic Service, retired; Ambassador to Austria, 1992–96; *b* 6 Sept. 1936; *s* of Courtney and Alice Wood; *m* 1st, 1962, Kathleen Mary Jones (marr. diss. 1981); one *s* one *d*; 2nd, 1982, Diana Humphreys-Roberts. *Educ:* King Edward VI Sch., Chelmsford; Trinity Coll., Cambridge. BA Hons 1960. RA, 1955–57 (2nd Lieut). Information Officer, FBI (later CBI), 1963–67; entered HM Diplomatic Service, 1968; Foreign Office, 1968–69; 1st Sec., Rome, 1969–73; FCO, 1973–77; sowc, RNC, Greenwich, 1977; Counsellor (Economic and Commercial), New Delhi, 1977–81; Political Advr and Hd of Chancery, Brit. Mil. Govt, Berlin, 1981–84; Hd of S Asian Dept, FCO, 1984–86; Vis. Fellow, Center for

Internat. Affairs, Harvard Univ., 1986–87; Minister, Rome, 1987–92; Head, UK Delegn to Negotiations on Conventional Arms Control in Europe, Vienna, 1992–93. Gov., Bruton Sch. for Girls, 1999– (Chm. of Govs, 2002–08). Grosses Goldenes Ehrenzeichen: Styria, 1996; Carinthia, 1996. *Recreations:* music, painting. *Address:* Knapp Cottage, Charlton Horethorne, Sherborne, Dorset DT9 4PQ. *Club:* Travellers. *Died 3 June 2009.*

WOOD, Sir William (Alan), KCVO 1978; CB 1970; Second Crown Estate Commissioner, 1968–78; Ombudsman, Mirror Group Newspapers, 1985–89; Chairman, London and Quadrant Housing Trust, 1980–89; *b* 8 Dec. 1916; *m* 1st, 1943, Zoë (*d* 1985), *d* of Rev. Dr D. Frazer-Hurst; two *s* two *d*; 2nd, 1985, Mrs Mary Hall (*née* Cowper). *Educ:* Dulwich Coll.; Corpus Christi Coll., Cambridge (Scholar). Ministry of Home Affairs, N. Ireland, 1939. Lieut, RNVR, 1942–46. Ministry of Town and Country Planning, 1946; Minister's Private Secretary, 1951; Principal Regional Officer (West Midlands), Ministry of Housing and Local Government, 1954; Asst Secretary, 1956; Under-Secretary, 1964–68. Chm. Council, King Alfred Sch., 1966–78, Pres. 1978–2000. *Club:* Athenæum. *Died 28 June 2010.*

WOODS, Rev. Canon John Mawhinney; *b* 16 Dec. 1919; *s* of Robert and Sarah Hannah Woods. *Educ:* Edinburgh Theological College. Deacon 1958, for St Peter's, Kirkcaldy, Fife; priest, 1959; Rector of Walpole St Peter, Norfolk, 1960–75; Provost, St Andrew's Cathedral, Inverness, 1975–80; Rector of The Suttons with Tydd, 1980–85; Canon of Inverness, 1980–. *Address:* 24 Queen Street, King's Lynn, Norfolk PE30 1HT. *Died 4 June 2009.*

WOODS, Prof. Leslie Colin, DPhil, DSc; Professor of Mathematics (Theory of Plasma), University of Oxford, 1970–90, then Emeritus Professor; Fellow of Balliol College, Oxford, 1970–90, Emeritus Fellow, since 1991; *b* Reporoa, NZ, 6 Dec. 1922; *s* of Alexander Binnie Woodhead, Sandringham, NZ; *m* 1st, 1943, Gladys Elizabeth Bayley (marr. diss. 1977); three *d* (and two *d* decd); 2nd, 1977, Dr Helen Louise Troughton (marr. diss.); 3rd, 1990, Jacqueline Suzanne Griffiths (marr. diss.). *Educ:* Auckland Univ. Coll. (BE 194; DSc 1954); Merton Coll., Oxford (MA; DPhil 1950; DSc 1958). Fighter pilot, RNZAF, Pacific Area, 1942–45. Rhodes Schol., Merton Coll., Oxford, 1948–51; Scientist (NZ Scientific Defense Corps) with Aerodynamics Div., NPL Mddx, 1951–54; Senior Lectr in Applied Maths, Sydney Univ., 1954–56; Nuffield Research Prof. of Engineering, Univ. of New South Wales, 1956–60; Fellow and Tutor in Engrg Science, Balliol Coll., Oxford, 1960–70; Reader in Applied Maths, Oxford, 1964–70. Chm., Mathematical Inst., Oxford, 1984–89. Hon. DSc Auckland, 1983. *Publications:* The Theory of Subsonic Plane Flow, 1961; Introduction to Neutron Distribution Theory, 1964; The Thermodynamics of Fluid Systems, 1975; Principles of Magnetoplasma Dynamics, 1987; Kinetic Theory of Gases and Magnetoplasmas, 1993; Thermodynamic Inequalities in Gases and Magnetoplasmas, 1996; Against the Tide: an autobiographical account of a professional outsider, 2000; Physics of Plasmas, 2004; Theory of Tokamak Transport, 2006; many research papers in aerodynamics and plasma physics in Proc. Royal Soc., Physics of Fluids, etc. *Recreations:* music, philosophy. *Address:* Balliol College, Oxford OX1 3BJ. *Died 15 April 2007.*

WOODWARD, Hon. Sir (Albert) Edward, AC 2001; Kt 1982; OBE 1969; Chairman, Australian Banking Industry Ombudsman Council, 1997–2002; *b* 6 Aug. 1928; *s* of Lt-Gen. Sir Eric Winslow Woodward, KCMG, KCVO, CB, CBE, DSO, and Amy Freame Woodward (*née* Weller); *m* 1950, Lois Thorpe, AM; one *s* six *d*. *Educ:* Melbourne C of E Grammar Sch.; Melbourne Univ. (LLM). Practising barrister, 1953–72; QC 1965; Judge: Australian Industrial Court and Supreme Court of Australian Capital Territory, 1972–90; Federal Ct of

Australia, 1977–90. Chairman, Armed Services Pay Inquiry, 1972; Royal Commissioner: Aboriginal Land Rights, 1973–75; into Australian Meat Industry, 1981–82; into Tricontinental Gp Cos, 1991–92; President: Trade Practices Tribunal, 1974–76; Defence Force Discipline Appeal Tribunal, 1988–90; Director-General of Security, 1976–81. Chairman: Victorian Dried Fruits Bd, 1963–72; Nat. Stevedoring Industry Conf. and Stevedoring Industry Council, 1965–72; Australian Defence Force Academy Council, 1982–99; Schizophrenia Australia Foundn, 1985–97. Mem. Council, Melbourne Univ., 1973–76, 1986–2001, Chancellor, 1990–2001; Chm. Council, Camberwell Grammar Sch., 1983–87. Hon. LLD: New South Wales, 1986; Melbourne, 2001; Hon. DLitt Ballarat, 1998. *Address:* 1/81 Park Street, South Yarra, Vic 3141, Australia. *T:* (3) 98677477. *Died 15 April 2010.*

WOODWARD, Edward, OBE 1978; actor and singer, since 1946; *b* 1 June 1930; *s* of Edward Oliver Woodward and Violet Edith Woodward; *m* 1st, 1952, Venetia Mary Collett (marr. diss. 1986); two *s* one *d*; 2nd, 1987, Michele Dotrice; one *d*. *Educ:* Kingston Coll.; RADA. *Stage:* Castle Theatre, Farnham, 1946; appeared for some years in rep. cos throughout England and Scotland; first appearance on London stage, Where There's a Will, Garrick, 1955; Mercutio in Romeo and Juliet, and Laertes in Hamlet, Stratford, 1958; Rattle of a Simple Man, Garrick, 1962; Two Cities (musical), 1968; Cyrano in Cyrano de Bergerac, and Flamineo in The White Devil, Nat. Theatre Co., 1971; The Wolf, Apollo, 1973; Male of the Species, Piccadilly, 1975; On Approval, Theatre Royal Haymarket, 1976; The Dark Horse, Comedy, 1978; starred in and directed Beggar's Opera, 1980; Private Lives, Australia, 1980; The Assassin, Greenwich, 1982; Richard III, Ludlow Fest., 1982; The Dead Secret, Plymouth and Richmond, 1992; Gilbert, nat. tour 2003; Cemetery Club, nat. tour 2004; appeared in 3 prodns in NY (Rattle of a Simple Man, High Spirits, and Best Laid Plans); *films:* Becket, 1966; File on the Golden Goose, 1968; Hunted, 1973; Sitting Target, Young Winston, The Wicker Man, 1974; Stand Up Virgin Soldiers, 1977; Breaker Morant, 1980; The Appointment, 1981; Who Dares Wins, Forever Love, Merlin and the Sword, 1982; Champions, 1983; Christmas Carol, 1984; King David, Uncle Tom's Cabin, 1986; Mister Johnson, 1990; Deadly Advice, 1993; A Christmas Reunion, 1994; Gulliver's Travels, 1995; The Abduction Club, 2000; Hot Stuff, 2006; *television:* over 2000 prodns, inc. Callan (series and film, and in Wet Job, 1981); The Trial of Lady Chatterley, Blunt Instrument, 1980; Churchill: The Wilderness Years, 1981; The Equalizer (series), 1985–89; Codename Kyril, 1987; Hunted, 1988; The Man in the Brown Suit, 1988; Hands of a Murderer, or The Napoleon of Crime, 1990; Over My Dead Body (series), 1990; In Suspicious Circumstances (series), 1991–95; In My Defence, 1991; America at Risk (series), 1991–92; Harrison, 1994; Common as Muck (series), 1994, 1996; Cry of the City, 1995; The Woodward File, 1995; The House of Angelo, 1997; The New Professionals (series), 1998–99; Emma's Boy, 2000; Nikita (series), 2000; Night and Day, 2001; Messiah, 2001; Night Flight, 2002; Murder in Suburbia, 2003; 5 Days (mini series), 2006; Congregation of Ghosts, 2008; presenter, two national Nelson events, 2005; 12 long-playing records (singing), 3 records (poetry) and 14 talking book recordings. Over 20 national and internat. acting awards incl. BAFTA best actor award and an Emmy. *Recreations:* boating, geology. *Address:* c/o Janet Glass, Eric Glass Ltd, 25 Ladbroke Crescent, W11 1PS. *T:* (020) 7229 9500, *Fax:* (020) 7229 6220. *Clubs:* Garrick, Green Room. *Died 16 Nov. 2009.*

WOOLDRIDGE, Ian Edmund, OBE 1991; Sports Columnist, Daily Mail, since 1972; BBC Television documentary reporter and writer; *b* 14 Jan. 1932; *s* of late Edmund and Bertha Wooldridge; *m* 1st, 1957, Veronica Ann Churcher (marr. diss. 1979); three *s*; 2nd, 1980, Sarah Margaret Chappell Lourenço. *Educ:* Brockenhurst Grammar School. New Milton Advertiser, 1948; Bournemouth Times, 1953; News Chronicle, 1956; Sunday Dispatch, 1960; Daily Mail, 1961. Columnist of Year, 1975 and 1976; Sportswriter of Year, 1972, 1974, 1981, 1989, in British Press Awards; Sports Council Awards: Sportswriter of the Year, 1987, 1988, 1996; Sports Feature Writer of the Year, 1991, 1997. *Publications:* Cricket, Lovely Cricket, 1963; (with Mary Peters) Mary P, 1974; (with Colin Cowdrey) MCC: The Autobiography of a Cricketer, 1976; The Best of Wooldridge, 1978; Travelling Reserve, 1982; Sport in the Eighties, 1989. *Recreations:* travel, golf, Beethoven and dry Martinis. *Address:* 22 Gloucester Walk, W8 4HZ. *Club:* Reform. *Died 4 March 2007.*

WOOLHOUSE, Prof. John George, CBE 1988; Professor of Education and Industry, and Director of Centre for Education and Industry, University of Warwick, 1988–97, then Emeritus; *b* 17 June 1931; *s* of George Francis Woolhouse and Doris May Woolhouse (*née* Webber); *m* 1958, Ruth Carolyn Harrison; two *s* one *d*. *Educ:* Chichester High Sch. for Boys; Ardingly Coll; Brasenose Coll., Univ. of Oxford (MA). Rolls-Royce Ltd, 1954–72: Dir, Rolls-Royce and Associates, 1965–68; Co. Educn and Trng Officer, 1968–72; Asst Dir, Kingston Polytechnic and Dir, Kingston Regl Management Centre, 1972–78; Dir Atkins Planning, W. S. Atkins Gp Consultants, and Hd of Human Resources Develt, 1978–82; Dir, Technical and Vocational Educn Initiative, MSC, 1983–86; Dir of Educn Progs, MSC, 1986–87. Chm., Assoc. of Regional Management Centres, 1977–78. *Publications:* chapters in: The Training of Youth in Industry, 1966; The Management Development Handbook, 1973; Gower Handbook of Management, 1983; Reform of Post-16 Education and Training in England and Wales, 1993. *Recreations:* travel, music, boating, fishing. *Address:* Ivy Farmhouse, Ivy Farm Lane, Coventry CV4 7BW. *Club:* Royal Air Force. *Died 1 Feb. 2008.*

WOOLLAM, John Victor; barrister-at-law; *b* 14 Aug. 1927; *s* of Thomas Alfred and Edie Moss Woollam; *m* 1964, Lavinia Rosamond Ela (*d* 2005), *d* of S. R. E. Snow; two *s*. *Educ:* Liverpool Univ. Called to the Bar, Inner Temple. Contested (C) Scotland Div. of Liverpool, 1950; MP (C) W Derby Div. of Liverpool, Nov. 1954–Sept. 1964; Parliamentary Private Sec. to Minister of Labour, 1960–62. *Recreation:* philately. *Address:* Old Ruggs Cottage, The Street, Kilmington, Devon EX13 7RW. *T:* (01297) 33336. *Died 1 Feb. 2006.*

WOOLLCOMBE, Rt Rev. Kenneth John; an Assistant Bishop, Diocese of Worcester, since 1989; *b* 2 Jan. 1924; *s* of late Rev. E. P. Woollcombe, OBE, and Elsie Ockenden Woollcombe; *m* 1st, 1950, Gwendoline Rhona Vyvien Hodges (*d* 1976); three *d*; 2nd, 1980, Rev. Juliet Dearmer; one *d*. *Educ:* Haileybury Coll., Hertford; St John's Coll., Oxford; Westcott House, Cambridge. Sub-Lieut (E) RNVR, 1945. Curate, St James, Grimsby, 1951; Fellow, Chaplain and Tutor, St John's Coll., Oxford, 1953, Hon. Fellow, 1971; Professor of Dogmatic Theology, General Theological Seminary, New York, 1960; Principal of Episcopal Theological Coll., Edinburgh, 1963; Bishop of Oxford, 1971–78; Asst Bishop, Diocese of London, 1978–81; Canon Residentiary of St Paul's, 1981–89, Precentor 1982–89. Chm., SPCK, 1973–79; Mem., Central Cttee, World Council of Churches, 1975–83; Chm., Churches' Council for Covenanting, 1978–82; Co-Chm., English Anglican-RC Cttee, 1985–88; Judge in Court of Ecclesiastical Causes Reserved, 1984–89. Hon. Chaplain, 1978–87, Hon. Liveryman, 1986, Glass Sellers' Co. STD Univ. of the South, Sewanee, USA, 1963; Hon. DD Hartford, Conn, 1975. *Publications:* (contrib.) The Historic Episcopate, 1954; (jointly) Essays on Typology, 1957. *Address:* 19 Ashdale Avenue, Pershore, Worcs WR10 1PL. *Died 3 March 2008.*

WOOLLETT, Maj.-Gen. John Castle, CBE 1957 (OBE 1955); MC 1945; FICE; Planning Inspector, Department of the Environment, 1971–81; Member, Lord

Chancellor's Panel, 1982–87; *b* 5 Nov. 1915; *o s* of John Castle Woollett and Lily Bradley Woollett, Bredgar, Kent; *m* 1st, 1941, Joan Eileen Stranks (marr. diss., 1957); two *s* (and one *s* decd); 2nd, 1959, Helen Wendy Willis (decd); two step *s*. *Educ*: St Benedict's Sch.; RMA Woolwich; St John's Coll., Cambridge (MA). Joined RE, 1935; 23 Field Co., 1938–40 (BEF, 1939–40); 6 Commando, 1940–42; Major Comdg 16 Field Sqdn and 16 Assault Sqdn RE, 1942–45 (BLA, 1944–45); Student, Staff Coll., Camberley, 1946; DAAG and GSO2, Brit. Service Mission to Burma, 1947–50; Major Comdg 51 Port Sqdn RE, 1950; Instructor, Staff Coll., Camberley, 1950–53; Lt-Col Comdg 28 Field Engr Regt, 1954–55 (Korea); Bt Lt-Col 1955; Comdr Christmas Is, 1956–57; GSO1, Northern Army Gp, 1957–59; Col GS, US Army Staff Coll., Fort Leavenworth, 1959–61; DQMG (Movements), BAOR, 1962–64; Brig. Comdg Hants Sub District and Transportation Centre, RE, 1964–65; Sch. of Transport, 1965–66; Dep. Engr-in-Chief, 1966–67; Maj.-Gen., Chief Engineer, BAOR, 1967–70, retired. Col Comdt, RE, 1973–78. Pres., Instn of RE, 1974–79. *Clubs*: Army and Navy, Royal Cruising; Royal Lymington Yacht. *Died 30 May 2007.*

WOOLMER, Robert Andrew; Coach, Pakistan Cricket Team, since 2004; *b* India, 14 May 1948; *s* of late Clarence Shirley Woolmer and Stella Kathleen Woolmer (*née* Birks); *m* 1974, (Shirley) Gillian Hall; two *s*. *Educ*: Skinners' Sch. Cricketer: Kent CCC, 1968–84 (county cap, 1970); England, one day internat. début, 1972, 19 Test Matches, 1975–81; Avendale CC, Capetown, SA, 1981–89. Coach: Transvaal Cricket Union, 1970–71; Avendale CC, 1981–99; South African Cricket Team, 1994–99; Dir of Coaching, Warwicks CCC, 1991–94 and 2000–02; High Perf. Manager, ICC, 2002–04. Order clerk, ICI, 1966–68; teacher, Holmewood House Prep. Sch., 1968–71; Coach, Transvaal Cricket Union, 1970–71; Thwaites and Matthews Caterers, 1975–77; Proprietor, Bob Woolmer Sports, Tonbridge, Kent, 1977–84; sports admin, Herzlia High Sch., SA, 1985–87. *Publications*: Pirate and Rebel (autobiog.), 1984; Skilful Cricket, 1993; Woolmer on Cricket, 2000. *Died 18 March 2007.*

WOOZLEY, Prof. Anthony Douglas, MA; University Professor Emeritus of Philosophy and Law, University of Virginia, since 1983; *b* 14 Aug. 1912; *o s* of David Adams Woozley and Kathleen Lucy Moore; *m* 1st, 1937, Thelma Suffield (marr. diss. 1978), *e d* of late Frank Townshend, Worcester; one *d*; 2nd, 1995, Cora, *e d* of late Abraham Diamond, New York. *Educ*: Haileybury College; Queen's College, Oxford. Open Scholar, Queen's College, 1931–35; 1st Cl. Class. Hon. Mods, 1933; 1st Cl. Lit. Hum., 1935; John Locke Schol., 1935. Served War, 1940–46 (despatches); commissioned King's Dragoon Guards, 1941; served N Africa, Italy, Greece, Egypt, Syria, Palestine; Major. Fellow of All Souls College, 1935–37; Fellow and Praelector in Philosophy, Queen's Coll., 1937–54; Librarian, 1938–54; Tutor, Queen's College, 1946–54; University Lecturer in Philosophy, 1947–54; Senior Proctor, 1953–54; Prof. of Moral Philosophy, Univ. of St Andrews, 1954–67; University of Virginia: Prof. of Philosophy, 1966; Commonwealth Prof. of Philosophy, 1974–77; Commonwealth Prof. and Univ. Prof. of Philosophy and Law, 1977–83. Editor of The Philosophical Quarterly, 1957–62; Editor, Home University Library, 1962–68. Visiting Professor of Philosophy: Univ. of Rochester, USA, 1965; Univ. of Arizona, 1972. *Publications*: (ed) Thomas Reid's Essays on the Intellectual Powers of Man, 1941; Theory of Knowledge, 1949; (with R. C. Cross) Plato's Republic: a Philosophical Commentary, 1964; (ed) John Locke's Essay Concerning Human Understanding, 1964; Law and Obedience, 1979; articles and reviews in Mind, etc. *Address*: 655 Kearsarge Circle, Charlottesville, VA 22903, USA. *Died 6 April 2008.*

WORKMAN, Charles Joseph, TD 1966; Part-time Chairman: Industrial Tribunals for Scotland, 1986–92; Social Security Appeal Tribunals, 1986–94; Disability Appeal Tribunals, 1992–94; *b* 25 Aug. 1920; *s* of Hugh William O'Brien Workman and Annie Shields; *m* 1949, Margaret Jean Mason; one *s* two *d*. *Educ*: St Mungo's Acad., Glasgow; Univ. of Glasgow (MA 1950, LLB 1952). Admitted solicitor, 1952. Served War, 1939–45: France, Belgium, Holland, Germany; commnd Second Fife and Forfar Yeomanry, RAC, 1942; Captain, 1945; served Intell. Corps TA and TAVR, 1954–69; Bt Lt-Col 1969; Hon. Col, Intell. and Security Gp (V), 1977–86. Entered Office of Solicitor to Sec. of State for Scotland as Legal Asst, 1955; Sen. Legal Asst, 1961; Asst Solicitor, 1966; Dep. Solicitor to Sec. of State, 1976; Dir, Scottish Courts Administration, 1978–82; Senior Dep. Sec. (Legal Aid), Law Soc. of Scotland, 1982–86. Chm., Public Service and Commerce Gp, Law Soc. of Scotland, 1977–78. Founder Mem., Edinburgh Chamber Music Trust, 1977–2006. *Publications*: (contrib.) The Laws of Scotland: Stair Memorial Encyclopaedia, vol. 2, 1987. *Recreations*: walking, swimming, music. *Address*: Ravenswood, 6 Lower Broomieknowe, Lasswade, Midlothian EH18 1LW. *Club*: New (Edinburgh). *Died 28 Feb. 2009.*

WORSLEY, Giles Arthington, PhD; FSA, FRHistS; Architecture Critic, The Daily Telegraph, since 1998; *b* 22 March 1961, 2nd *s* of Sir (William) Marcus (John) Worsley, 5th Bt and late Hon. Bridget Assheton, *d* of 1st Baron Clitheroe, PC, KCVO; *m* 1996, Joanna Pitman; three *d*. *Educ*: Eton; New Coll., Oxford; Courtauld Inst., Univ. of London (PhD 1989). Country Life: architectural writer, 1985–88; Architectural Editor, 1989–94; Editor: Georgian Group Jl, 1991–94; Perspectives on Architecture, 1994–98. Sen. Res. Fellow, Inst. of Historical Res., 2002–. Member: Royal Fine Art Commn, 1994–99; Historic Buildings and Areas Adv. Cttee, English Heritage, 1995–98; Exec. Cttee, Save Britain's Heritage, 1985–; Exec. Cttee, Georgian Gp, 1990–; Somerset House Trust, 1997–; Bldg Cttee, Nat. Gall. Trustees, 1998–; Architectural Adv. Cttee, World Monuments Fund of England, 2001–; Design Review Cttee, CABE, 2005–. Trustee, Marc Fitch Fund, 2001–. FSA 1991; FRHistS 2002. Hon. FRIBA 2004. Prizes incl. Alexander Prize, RHistS, 1992. *Publications*: Architectural Drawings of the Regency Period, 1991; Classical Architecture in Britain: the heroic age, 1995; (ed) Brian Wragg, The Life and Works of John Carr, 2000; England's Lost Houses, 2002; The British Stable, 2004. *Recreations*: walking, reading, buildings. *Address*: The Daily Telegraph, 1 Canada Square, Canary Wharf, E14 5DT. *T*: (020) 8962 6371, *Fax*: (020) 8968 0693. *Died 17 Jan. 2006.*

WORTHINGTON, Prof. Brian Stewart, FRCR, FMedSci; FRS 1998; Professor of Diagnostic Radiology, University of Nottingham, 1981–98, then Professor Emeritus; *b* 9 June 1938; *s* of late Eric Worthington and Jessie Worthington (*née* Dibb); *m* 1961, Margaret Ann Mayne; two *s*. *Educ*: Hulme Grammar Sch., Oldham; Guy's Hosp., London (Ken Clifford Scholar; BSc Physiol. 1960; MB BS 1963). LRCP 1963; MRCS 1963; DMRD 1967; FRCR (Rohan Williams Medal) 1969; LIMA 1979; FInstP 1998. Registrar, London Hosp., 1965–70; Consultant Radiologist, Nottingham Hosps, 1970–71; Consultant Neuroradiologist, Nottingham Hosps and Derby Royal Infirmary, 1971–75; Reader, Dept of Radiology, Univ. of Nottingham, 1975–81. Kodak Vis. Prof., Univ. of Dublin, 1987; Visiting Professor: Univs of Turku and Helsinki, 1992; Univ. of Vancouver, 1994. Lectures: George Simon Meml, Nottingham, 1982; Malthé Meml, Oslo, 1983; Grout Meml, Sheffield, 1983; W. S. Moore Meml, London, 1996. Examiner: RCR, 1977–82; Coll. of Radiographers, 1977–87; Univ. of Liverpool, 1987–91. Pres., BIR, 1988–89. Member: Radiol Adv. Cttee, DHSS, 1987–90; MRC Molecular and Cellular Medicine Bd, 1996–2000. Fellow, Soc. of Magnetic Resonance in Medicine, 1997 (Mem. Bd of Trustees, 1987–90). Founder FMedSci 1998. Hon. Mem., Radiol Socs of Iceland, 1986, Finland, 1993, and N America, 2004. Mem., Radiological Visiting Club, 1974–. Gold Medal: Back Pain Assoc., 1985; Soc. of

Magnetic Resonance in Medicine, 1990; RCR, 1998; Barclay Medal, BIR, 1992; Trent Medal, NHS Exec., 1997; President's Prize and Medal, Nottingham Medico-Chirurgical Soc., 1999. *Publications:* (with G. Whitehouse) Techniques in Diagnostic Imaging, 1983, 3rd edn 1996; contrib. papers in learned jls on neuroradiology, magnetic resonance imaging and cognitive aspects of diagnostic radiology. *Recreations:* Icelandic language and culture, classical music, archaeology. *Address:* Cliff Cottage, Belper Road, Shirland, Alfreton, Derbys DE55 6AG. *T:* (01773) 834096. *Died 9 Dec. 2007.*

WRIGHT, Claud William, CB 1969; Deputy Secretary, Department of Education and Science, 1971–76; *b* 9 Jan. 1917; *s* of Horace Vipan Wright and Catherine Margaret Sales; *m* 1947, Alison Violet Readman (*d* 2003); one *s* four *d. Educ:* Charterhouse; Christ Church, Oxford (MA). Assistant Principal, War Office, 1939; Private, Essex Regiment, 1940; 2nd Lieut, KRRC, 1940; War Office, rising to GSO2, 1942–45; Principal, War Office, 1944; Min. of Defence: Principal, 1947; Asst Sec., 1951; Asst Under-Sec. of State, 1961–68; Dep. Under-Sec. of State, 1968–71. Chm., Cttee on Provincial Museums and Galleries, 1971–73. Research Fellow, Wolfson Coll., Oxford, 1977–83. President, Geologists Assoc., 1956–58. Lyell Fund, 1947, R. H. Worth Prize, 1958, Prestwick Medal, 1987, Geological Society of London; Foulerton Award, Geologists Association, 1955; Stamford Raffles Award, Zoological Society of London, 1965; Phillips Medal, Yorks Geol. Soc., 1976; Strimple Award, Paleontol Soc., USA, 1988; H. H. Bloomer Award for Zoology, Linnean Soc., 1998. Hon. Associate, British Museum (Nat. Hist.), 1973; fil.Dr *hc* Uppsala, 1979; Hon. DSc Hull, 1987. *Publications:* (with W. J. Arkell *et al*) vol. on Ammonites, 1957, 2nd edn 1996, (with W. K. Spencer) on Starfish, 1966, in Treatise on Invertebrate Palaeontology; (with J. S. H. Collins) British Cretaceous Crabs, 1972; (with W. J. Kennedy) Ammonites of the Middle Chalk, 1981; (with W. J. Kennedy) Ammonites of the Lower Chalk, pt I, 1984, pt II, 1987, pt III, 1990, pt IV, 1995, pt V, 1996; (with A. B. Smith) British Cretaceous Echinoidea, pt I, 1988, pt II, 1990, pt III, 1993, pt IV, 1996, pt V, 1999, pt VI, 2000, pt VII, 2004, pt VIII, 2009; papers in geological, palaeontological and archaeological journals. *Recreations:* palaeontology, natural history, gardening, archæology. *Address:* The Cotswold Home, Woodside Drive, Bradwell Village, Burford, Oxfordshire OX18 4XA. *T:* (01993) 824430. *Died 15 Feb. 2010.*

WRIGHT, Hannah Margaret, (Mrs E. G. Wright); *see* Cross, H. M.

WRIGHT, Joe Booth, CMG 1979; HM Diplomatic Service, retired; Ambassador to Ivory Coast, Upper Volta and Niger, 1975–78; *b* 24 Aug. 1920; *s* of Joe Booth Wright and Annie Elizabeth Wright; *m* 1st, 1945, Pat (*née* Beaumont); one *s* two *d*; 2nd, 1967, Patricia Maxine (*née* Nicholls). *Educ:* King Edward VI Grammar Sch., Retford; Univ. of London. BA Hons, French. GPO, 1939–47. Served War, HM Forces: RAOC, Intelligence Corps, 1941–46. Entered Foreign Office, 1947; FO, 1947–51; Vice-Consul, Jerusalem, 1951; Consul, Munich, 1952, and Basra, 1954; Dep. Consul, Tamsui, 1956; FO, 1959–64; Consul, Surabaya, 1964; Consul, Medan, 1965–67; First Sec. (Information), Nicosia, 1968; Head of Chancery and Consul, Tunis, 1968–71; Consul-General: Hanoi, 1971–72; Geneva, 1973–75. Mem., Inst. of Linguists and Translators' Guild, 1982–. FRSA 1987. *Publications:* Francophone Black Africa Since Independence, 1981; Zaire Since Independence, 1983; Paris As It Was, 1985; Who Was the Enemy?, 1993; Security and Cooperation in Europe: the view from the East, 1993; Enlarging the European Union: risks and benefits, 1998. *Recreations:* cricket, film-going, music, Chinese painting. *Address:* 29 Brittany Road, St Leonards-on-Sea, East Sussex TN38 0RB. *Died 11 Nov. 2008.*

WRIGHT, John Hurrell C.; *see* Collier-Wright.

WRIGHT, Sir (John) Oliver, GCMG 1981 (KCMG 1974; CMG 1964); GCVO 1978; DSC 1944; HM Diplomatic Service, retired; King of Arms, Most Distinguished Order of St Michael and St George, 1987–96; *b* 6 March 1921; *m* 1942, Lillian Marjory Osborne; three *s. Educ:* Solihull School; Christ's College, Cambridge (MA; Hon. Fellow 1981; pre-elected Master, May 1982, resigned July 1982). Served in RNVR, 1941–45. Joined HM Diplomatic Service, Nov. 1945; served: New York, 1946–47; Bucharest, 1948–50; Singapore, 1950–51; Foreign Office, 1952–54; Berlin, 1954–56; Pretoria, 1957–58. Imperial Defence College, 1959. Asst Private Sec. to Sec. of State for Foreign Affairs, 1960; Counsellor and Private Sec., 1963; Private Sec. to the Prime Minister, 1964–66 (to Rt Hon. Sir Alec Douglas-Home, and subseq. to Rt Hon. Harold Wilson); Ambassador to Denmark, 1966–69; seconded to Home Office as UK Rep. to NI Govt, Aug. 1969–March 1970; Chief Clerk, HM Diplomatic Service, 1970–72; Dep. Under-Sec. of State, FCO, 1972–75; Ambassador to Federal Republic of Germany, 1975–81; retired, later re-apptd, Ambassador to Washington, 1982–86. Director: Siemens Ltd, 1981–82; Amalgamated Metal Corp., April–July 1982; Savoy Hotel plc, 1987–94; Berkeley Hotel, 1994–96; General Technology Systems Inc., 1990–95; Enviromed plc, 1993–97. Distinguished Vis. Prof., Univ. of S Carolina, 1986–90; Clark Fellow, Cornell Univ., 1987; Lewin Vis. Prof., Washington Univ., St Louis, 1988. Pres., German Chamber of Industry and Commerce, London, 1989–92. Bd Mem., British Council, 1981–82, 1986–90. Trustee: British Museum, 1986–91; Internat. Shakespeare Globe Centre, 1986–2002; Chm., British Königswinter Conf. Steering Cttee, 1987–97; Co-Chm., Anglo-Irish Encounter, 1986–91. Gov., Reigate Grammar Sch., 1987–97 (Chm., 1990–97). Hon. DHL Univ. of Nebraska, 1983; Hon. DL Rockford Coll., Ill, 1985. Grand Cross, German Order of Merit, 1978. *Recreations:* theatre, gardening. *Address:* Burstow Hall, near Horley, Surrey RH6 9SR. *T:* (01293) 783494. *Club:* Travellers. *Died 1 Sept. 2009.*

WRIGHT, Prof. Margaret S.; *see* Scott Wright.

WRIGHT, Michael Thomas, FSA; writer and lecturer on architecture, fine arts and conservation; *b* 10 Dec. 1936; *o c* of Thomas Manning Wright and Hilda Evelyn Wright (*née* Whiting); *m* 1st, 1964, Jennifer Olga Angus (marr. diss. 1990), 2nd *d* of C. B. Angus, Singapore; two *s*; 2nd, 1990, Wendelina Elisabeth Pascall (*née* van Manen). *Educ:* Bristol Grammar Sch.; Gonville and Caius Coll., Cambridge (MA); Trinity Coll., Dublin. FSA 1998. Formerly: Financial Analyst, Ford Motor Co. Asst Sec., Town Planning Inst.; Editor, Town Planning Inst. Jl; Asst Editor, Country Life; Managing Editor, Journal of Royal Inst. of British Architects; Dep. Editor, Country Life; Publisher: Country Life, 1984–87 (Editor, 1973–84, Editor in Chief, 1980–84); Practical Woodworking, 1985–87; Television, 1985–87; Editor in Chief and Publisher, Antique Dealer and Collectors' Guide, 1982–87; Dir, Nat. Heritage Meml Fund, 1987–88; Editorial Consultant, Country Life Books, 1978–86. Vis. Lectr in British Architecture, Roger Williams Univ., USA, 1995–99. Member, Honourable Society of Gray's Inn. Churchwarden, St Michael's Parish Church, Highgate, 1974–79; Chm., Highgate Soc., 1985–87. Judge, RICS (formerly RICS/The Times) Conservation Awards, 1976–89, 1991–2001. Lectr, NADFAS, 1989–2005; Tutor, Dept of Continuing Educn, Univ. of Cambridge, 1999–, and UEA, 2003–. Chairman: Lutyens Trust, 1993–95 (Trustee, 1986–95); Friends of Bristol Art Gall., 1993–97; Member: DoE Working Party on Rural Settlements; Cttee, SPAB, 1987–96. FRSA 1980. JP Haringey, 1986–89. *Publications:* Explore Britain's Country Gardens, 1993; contrib. articles to: TPI Jl; RIBA Jl; Water Space; Country Life; Homes and Gardens. *Recreations:* music, tennis, walking; participation in local amenity society work. *Address:* Gorse Bank, 5 Heathlands, Southwold, Suffolk IP18 6RW. *T:* (01502) 725314. *Club:* Royal Over-Seas League. *Died 9 June 2006.*

WRIGHT, Sir Oliver; *see* Wright, Sir J. O.

WRIGHT, Robert Anthony Kent; QC 1973; *b* 7 Jan. 1922; *s* of Robert and Eva Wright; *m* 1956, Gillian Elizabeth Drummond Hancock. *Educ:* Hilton Coll., Natal, S Africa; St Paul's Sch., London; The Queen's Coll., Oxford (MA). Indian Army, 1942–46. Oxford, 1946–48. Called to Bar, Lincoln's Inn, 1949, Bencher 1979; retired from practice, 1999. Hon. Fellow, Univ. of Central England, 1991. *Recreations:* music, walking. *Address:* 18 Parkside Avenue, SW19 5ES. *T:* (020) 8946 5978; *e-mail:* robert.wright12@ btinternet.com. *Clubs:* National Liberal; Island Sailing (Cowes). *Died 3 Oct. 2009.*

WRIGHT, Stanley Harris; Under-Secretary, HM Treasury, 1970–72; Executive Director, Lazard Brothers & Co. Ltd, 1972–81; *b* 9 April 1930; *er s* of John Charles Wright and Doris Wright; *m* 1st, 1957, Angela Vivien Smith (marr. diss. 1973), one *s*; 2nd, 1973, Hon. Alison Elizabeth Franks (*d* 2000), *d* of Baron Franks, OM, GCMG, KCB, KCVO, CBE, FBA. *Educ:* Bolton Sch.; Merton Coll., Oxford (Postmaster); 1st cl. hons PPE. Nat. Service, Manchester Regt, 1948–49. Asst Principal, BoT, 1952–55; 2nd Sec., UK Delegn to OEEC, Paris, 1955–57; Principal, HM Treasury, 1958–64; 1st Sec. (Financial), British Embassy, Washington, 1964–66; Asst Sec., HM Treasury, 1966 68; Lazard Bros & Co. Ltd, 1969 and 1970 (Dir 1969). Exec. Chm., International Commercial Bank Plc, 1981–83; non-executive Director: Wilkinson Match Ltd, 1974–81; Scripto Inc., 1977–81; Law Land Co., 1979–81; Wolstenholme Rink, 1980–93 (Chm., 1982–91); Royal Trust Bank, 1984–88; Royal Trust Asset Management (UK Holdings) Ltd, 1987–88 (Chm.), James Ferguson Holdings Plc, 1987–88; Stadium Group plc, 1989–96; Partner, Price Waterhouse and Partners, 1985–88. Business consultant, 1989–93. Chm., British Bankers Assoc. Fiscal Cttee, 1974–80; Member: Layfield Cttee on Local Government Finance, 1974–76; Armstrong Cttee on Budgetary Reform, 1979–80; (and Dir of Studies), CBI Wkg Pty on Tax Reform, 1984–85; CS Commn Final Selection Bd, 1986–; Panel for Financial Services Tribunal, 1988–91. Mem. Council, 1977–89, Hon. Treas., 1987–89, Westfield Coll., Univ. of London; Mem. Council, 1989–2000, Treas., 1989–99, QMW. Hon. Fellow, Queen Mary, Univ. of London, 2002. *Publications:* Two Cheers for the Institutions, 1994; articles on financial and fiscal matters. *Recreation:* various. *Address:* 903 St John's, 79 Marsham Street, SW1P 4SB. *T:* (020) 7233 6543. *Clubs:* Reform, Capital, MCC. *Died 23 July 2008.*

WYETH, Andrew Newell; artist; landscape painter; *b* 12 July 1917; *s* of Newell and Carolyn Wyeth; *m* 1940, Betsy Merle James; two *s*. *Educ:* privately. First one man exhibn, William Macbeth Gall., NY, 1937; subsequent exhibitions include: Doll & Richards, Boston, 1938, 1940, 1942, 1944; Cornell Univ., 1938; Macbeth Gall., 1938, 1941, 1943, 1945; Art Inst. of Chicago, 1941; Museum of Modern Art, NYC, 1943; M. Knoedler & Co., NYC, 1953, 1958; Dunn Internat. Exhibn, London, 1963; MIT, Cambridge, 1966; The White House, Washington, 1970; Tokyo, 1974, 1979; Metropolitan Museum, NY, 1976; RA, 1980 (first by living American artist); Arnot Museum, Elmira, NY, 1985; Seibu-Pisa, Tokyo, 1986; Moscow, Leningrad, 1987; Nat. Gall. of Art, Corcoran Gall. of Art, Washington, 1987; Milan, 1987; Fitzwilliam Mus., Cambridge, 1988. Member: Nat. Inst. of Arts and Letters (Gold Medal, 1965); Amer. Acad. of Arts and Sciences; Amer. Acad. of Arts and Letters (Medal of Merit, 1947); Académie des Beaux-Arts, 1977; Hon. Mem., Soviet Acad. of the Arts, 1978; Hon. RA 1996. Presidential Medal of Freedom, 1963; Einstein Award, 1967; Congressional Medal, USA, 1988. Hon. AFD: Colby Coll., Maine, 1954; Harvard, 1955; Dickinson, 1958; Swarthmore, 1958; Nasson Coll., Maine, 1963; Temple Univ., 1963; Maryland, 1964; Delaware, 1964; Northwestern Univ., 1964; Hon. LHD Tufts, 1963. *Publications:* The Helga Paintings, 1987;

Andrew Wyeth: autobiography, 1995. *Address:* c/o Frank E. Fowler, PO Box 247, Lookout Mountain, TN 37350, USA. *Died 16 Jan. 2009.*

WYLLIE, William, MBE 2000; JP; Vice Lord-Lieutenant of Aberdeen, 2004–07; *b* 5 Feb. 1932; *s* of late William Riach and Alexandra Thomson Wyllie; *m* 1954, Mary Anne, (Nancy), Stott; three *d*. *Educ:* Robert Gordon's Coll., Aberdeen; Gordonstoun Sch., Elgin; North Coll. of Agriculture. W. Smith & Son Ltd, seedsmen, nurserymen and landscape gardeners, Aberdeen, 1950–85: Dir, 1961–85; Man. Dir, 1965–85; Dir, W. Smith & Son (Wholesale) Ltd, 1970–85. Presenter and Originator, The Grampian Garden (weekly live TV prog.), Grampian TV, 1962–80; occasional writer/radio broadcaster on gardening. Director: Spencers Paints, 1984–87 (Chm., 1986–87); Grampian Regl Transport, 1984–88; Mairs Coaches, 1985–88 (Chm., 1986–88); Hazlewood Consultants Ltd, 1985–90; Blenheim Travel, 1986–89; Chm., Thistle Street Properties, 1994–2000. Member: Aviation Cttee, British Chambers of Commerce, 1977–86 (Chm., 1983–86); BA Consumer Council, 1980–83; Scottish Mem., Air Transport Users Council, 1985–91 (Chm., Airports Sub-Cttee, 1987–91). Sec./Treas., NE Scotland Horticultural Trng Gp, 1970–92; Vice-Chm., Scotbloom, 1989–92. Dir, Aberdeen MMB, 1976–79; Member: Council, Aberdeen Chamber of Commerce, 1967–87 (Pres., 1974–76); Aberdeen Airport Consultative Cttee, 1976–86 (Chm., 1983–86); Cttee, Aberdeen & Grampian Tourist Bd, 1977–97; Valuation Appeal Cttee, Grampian, 1978–81. Robert Gordon University, Aberdeen: Gov., 1992–2001; Convenor of Estates and Bldgs, 1996–99; Special Advr to Principal on Estates, 2001–04. Mem. Cttee, Gordon Highlanders Mus., 2001–04; Chm. Adv. Cttee, Lord Provost's Charitable Trust, 2003–07. Dean of Guild, City of Aberdeen, 1981–98; Co-founder, Court, Deans of Guild in Scotland, 1988 (Lord Pres., 1990–91). JP, DL, Aberdeen, 1993. Hon. DBA Robert Gordon Univ., Aberdeen, 2000. *Recreations:* gardening, DIY, swimming daily, travel, reading, good food and wine. *Address:* 156 Kings Gate, Aberdeen AB15 6BR. *T:* (01224) 317811. *Clubs:* Royal Northern and University (Chm., 1982–83), City of Aberdeen Probus (Pres., 1999–2000) (Aberdeen). *Died 22 Aug. 2007.*

WYLLIE, William Robert Alexander, AM 1993; Chairman, Wyllie Group (formerly Asia Securities) Pty Ltd, since 1973; *b* 9 Oct. 1932; *s* of Robert Wyllie and Marion Margaret Rae (*née* McDonald); *m* 1959, Ann Helena Mary Lewis (*d* 1986); two *s* one *d*; *m* 1988, Rhonda Noreen (*née* McGrath); one *s* one *d*. *Educ:* Scarborough State Sch., Perth, W Australia; Perth Technical Coll. (qual. Automobile and Aeronautical Engrg). MIRTE. Sen. Exec./Br. Manager, Wearne Bros Ltd, Malaysia/Singapore, 1953–64; Man. Dir, Harpers Internat. Ltd, Hong Kong, 1964–73; Chm. and Chief Exec., China Engineers Holdings Ltd, Hong Kong, 1973–75; Deputy Chairman and Chief Executive: Hutchison Internat. Ltd, Hong Kong, 1975–Dec. 1977; Hutchison Whampoa Ltd, Hong Kong, Jan. 1978–June 1979 (Chm. and Chief Exec., 1979–80); Chm. and Chief Exec., Asia Securities Ltd, Hong Kong, 1971–90; Chm., Asia Securities International Ltd, 1987–90. *Recreations:* power boating, water skiing, Scuba diving, restoration of vintage cars, flying planes. *Address:* c/o Wyllie Group Pty Ltd, PO Box 7751, Cloisters Square, Perth, WA 6850, Australia. *Clubs:* Royal Aero, Royal Perth Yacht, Pearce Flying, Fremantle Sailing (Perth); Hong Kong, American, Shek O Country, Hong Kong Jockey, Royal Hong Kong Yacht (Hong Kong). *Died 13 March 2006.*

WYMER, Dr John James, FSA; FBA 1996; Director of English Rivers Palaeolithic Survey for English Heritage, 1991–99; *b* 5 March 1928; *s* of Bertram Osborn Wymer and Leah Wymer (*née* Vidal); *m* 1st, 1948, Pauline May (marr. diss. 1972); two *s* three *d*; 2nd, 1976, Eunice Mollie (*née* Spurling) (*d* 1999). *Educ:* Richmond and East Sheen County Sch.; Shoreditch Training Coll. FSA 1963. Archaeologist, Reading Museum, 1956–65; Res.

Associate, Univ. of Chicago and UEA, 1965–80; Field Officer: Essex Archaeol. Unit, 1981–82; Norfolk Archaeol. Unit, 1983–90; directed excavations at numerous sites, mainly of Palaeolithic or later prehistoric periods. Pres., Quaternary Res. Assoc., 1975–77; Vice-President: Suffolk Inst. of Archaeol. and History, 1985–; Norfolk and Norwich Archaeol. Soc., 1994–; Berkshire Archaeol. Soc., 1995–; former exec. mem., other learned socs. Hon. MA Durham 1969; Hon. DSc Reading 1993. Stopes Meml Medal, 1972; Grahame Clark Medal for Prehistoric Archaeology, British Acad., 2002. *Publications:* Lower Palaeolithic Archaeology in Britain, 1968; Gazetteer of Mesolithic Sites, 1977; The Palaeolithic Age, 1982; (with R. Singer) The Middle Stone Age at Klasies River Mouth in South Africa, 1982; The Palaeolithic Sites of East Anglia, 1985; (with R. Singer and B. G. Gladfelter) The Lower Palaeolithic Site at Hoxne, England, 1993; The Lower Palaeolithic Occupation of Britain, 1999. *Recreations:* travelling, reading, gardening, carpentry, drinking good beer in congenial company. *Address:* 17 Duke Street, Bildeston, Ipswich, Suffolk IP7 7EW. *T:* (01449) 741691.   *Died 10 Feb. 2006.*

Y

YATES, Alfred, CBE 1983; FBPsS; Director, National Foundation for Educational Research in England and Wales, 1972–83; *b* 17 Nov. 1917; *s* of William Oliver Yates and Frances Yates; *m* 1st, 1943, Joan Mary Lawrence-Fellows (*d* 1987); one *s* one *d*; 2nd, 1989, Elsie Roberts. *Educ:* Farnworth Grammar Sch.; Sheffield Univ. (BA); Oxford Univ. (MA); QUB (MEd). FBPsS 1957. Served War, Army, 1940–46: Captain, REME. Schoolmaster, Launceston Coll., Cornwall, 1939–40; Lectr, QUB, 1946–51; Sen. Res. Officer, NFER, 1951–59; Sen. Tutor, Dept of Educnl Studies, Oxford Univ., 1959–72. FCP 1981. *Publications:* Admission to Grammar Schools, 1957; Grouping in Education, 1966; An Introduction to Educational Measurement, 1968; The Role of Research in Educational Change, 1971; The Organisation of Schooling, 1971. *Recreations:* reading, theatre, watching Association football and cricket. *Address:* 12 Sharples Hall Fold, Sharples, Bolton BL1 7EH. *T:* (01204) 595642. *Died 8 May 2006.*

YATES, (Edith) Anne, (Mrs S. J. Yates), CBE 1972; *b* 21 Dec. 1912; *d* of William Blakeman and Frances Dorothea (*née* Thacker); *m* 1935, Stanley James Yates (*d* 1990); one *s* one *d* (and one *s* decd). *Educ:* Barrs' Hill Girls' Sch., Coventry. Nottinghamshire County Council: Mem., 1955–93; Alderman, 1966; Chm., 1968–74; Leader, Cons. Gp, 1991–92. Mem., BTEC Bd for Distribution, Hotel and Catering and Leisure Services, 1984–88. Chairman: E Midlands Tourist Bd, 1971–76; E Midlands Sports Council, 1972–77; Indep. Chm., Nat. Cttee on Recreation Management Trng, 1976–82 (Yates Report, 1984); Member: Sports Council, 1971–74; E Midlands Council of Sport and Recreation, 1977–82; MSC, 1974–76; E Midlands Regional MSC, 1977–82; English Tourist Bd, 1975–81; Nat. Water Council, 1973–79 (Chm., Water Training Cttee, 1973–79). Life Vice Pres., Inst. of Trading Standards Admin, 1965. Chm., Notts Internat. Rowing Regatta, 1987–90; Mem., Sports Aid Foundn, 1984–94; Chm., Sports Aid Foundn (E Midlands), 1990–94. *Recreations:* reading, music, theatre. *Died 18 Feb. 2006.*

YATES, Rt Rev. John; Bishop of Gloucester, 1975–91; an Hon. Assistant Bishop, Diocese of Winchester; *b* 17 April 1925; *s* of late Frank and Edith Ethel Yates; *m* 1st, 1954, Jean Kathleen Dover (*d* 1995); one *s* two *d*; 2nd, 1998, Rev. Mrs Beryl Kathleen Wensley (*d* 2006). *Educ:* Battersea Grammar School; Blackpool Grammar School; Jesus College, Cambridge (MA). RAFVR (Aircrew), 1943–47; University of Cambridge, 1947–49; Lincoln Theological College, 1949–51. Curate, Christ Church, Southgate, 1951–54; Tutor and Chaplain, Lincoln Theological College, 1954–59; Vicar, Bottesford-with-Ashby, 1959–65; Principal, Lichfield Theological College, 1966–72; Bishop Suffragan of Whitby, 1972–75; Head, Archbp of Canterbury's staff (with title of Bp at Lambeth), 1991–94. Chm., Gen. Synod Bd for Social Responsibility, 1987–91. Hon. DLitt CNAA, 1992. *Address:* 15 Abbotts Ann Road, Winchester, Hants SO22 6ND. *Died 26 Feb. 2008.*

YATES, William, PhD; The Administrator of Christmas Island, Indian Ocean, 1982–83; *b* 15 Sept. 1921; *er s* of late William Yates and of Mrs John T. Renshaw, Burrells, Appleby, Westmorland; *m* 1st, 1946, Hon. Rosemary (marr. diss. 1955), *yr d* of 1st Baron Elton; two *d* (one *s* decd); 2nd, 1957, Camilla, *d* of late E. W. D. Tennant, Orford House, Ugley, Bishop's Stortford; four *s*. *Educ:* Uppingham; Hertford Coll., Oxford (BA); Melbourne Univ. (PhD 2003). Served War, 1940–45, North Africa and Italy; Captain The Bays, 1945. Shropshire Yeomanry, 1956–67. Appointed Legal Officer to report on State lands in Department of Custodian's Office in Tripoli, Libya, 1951. MP (C) The Wrekin Division of Shropshire,

1955–66. Myron Taylor Lectures in International Affairs, Cornell Univ., USA, 1958 and 1966. MP (L) Holt, Vic, Aust. Commonwealth, 1975–80; Mem. Liberal Party Parly Cttee for Defence and Foreign Affairs, 1975–80; Mem., Cttee of Privileges, House of Representatives, 1977–80. Mem., Inst. of Internat. Affairs, Victoria. *Address:* The Old House, 16 Jarvis Creek Road, Old Tallangatta, Vic 3701, Australia. *Club:* Cavalry and Guards. *Died 18 April 2010.*

YELLOWLEES, Sir Henry, KCB 1975 (CB 1971); Chief Medical Officer, Department of Health and Social Security, Department of Education and Science and Home Office, 1973–83; *b* 16 April 1919; *s* of late Henry Yellowlees, OBE, psychiatrist, Bath; *m* 1st, 1948, Gwyneth, (Sally), Comber (*née* Maddox) (decd); one *s* two *d*; 2nd, 2001, Mary Porter (*née* McGowan). *Educ:* Stowe Sch.; University Coll., Oxford (MA, BM, BCh 1950). FRCP 1971 (MRCP 1966, LRCP 1950); FFCM 1972; FRCS 1983 (MRCS 1950); FRCPE 1993. Pilot, RAF, 1941–45. Resident Med. Officer, Mddx Hosp., London, 1951–54; Asst Senior Med. Officer, South West Regional Hosp. Bd, 1954–59; Dep. Sen. Admin. Med. Officer, North West Metropolitan Regional Hosp. Bd, 1959–63; Principal Med. Officer, Min. of Health, 1963–65 (seconded); Senior Principal Med. Officer, 1965–67 (established); Dep. Chief Med. Officer, 1967–72, 2nd Chief Med. Officer, 1972–73, Dept of Health and Social Security. Consultant, MoD, 1985; Occasional Consultant, European Reg., WHO, 1985–95. Chm., WHO Commn to investigate health care of Bulgarian citizens arriving in Turkey, 1989. Member: Medical Research Council, 1974–83; Gen. Medical Council, 1979–89; Health Services Supervisory Bd, 1983; Council, BMA, 1986–90; Council, British Nutrition Foundn, 1973–95. Hon. FRCP Glasgow, 1974; Hon. FRCPsych, 1977; FBIM, 1974–83; Vice-Pres., Mental After-Care Assoc.; Hon. Mem., Nat. Assoc. of Clinical Tutors. *Address:* 33 Lea Road, Harpenden, Herts AL5 4PQ. *Died 22 March 2006.*

YELTSIN, Boris Nikolayevich; President, Russian Federation, 1991–99, and Supreme Commander-in-Chief of the Armed Forces, 1992–99; *b* Sverdlovsk, 1 Feb. 1931; *m* Naina Iosifovna (*née* Grinyova); two *d*. *Educ:* Urals Polytechnic Inst. (Construction Engr Dip., 1955). Foreman, then chief of works, chief engr, head of construction admin, Yushgoistvoy trust, 1955–63; chief engr, dir, Sverdlovsk house building complex, 1963–68. Mem., CPSU, 1961–90: Sec., Sverdlovsk regl cttee, 1968–76; First Sec., Dist Central Cttee, Sverdlosk, 1976–85; Mem., Party Central Cttee, 1981; Sec., Central Cttee, 1985–86 (Hd, Construction Dept); First Sec., Moscow Party Cttee, 1985–87; Candidate Mem., Politburo, 1986–88; First Dep. Chm., State Cttee for Construction, 1987–89; Chm., Cttee for Construction and Architecture, 1989–90; Mem., Congress of People's Deputies, 1989–91. Chairman: Supreme Soviet, RSFSR, 1990–91; Russian Fedn, 1991–92; Commonwealth of Ind. States, 1993–99. *Publications:* Against the Grain (autobiog.), 1990; Three Days, 1992; The View from the Kremlin (memoirs), 1994; Midnight Diaries (memoirs), 2000. *Address:* c/o The Kremlin, Moscow, Russia. *Died 23 April 2007.*

YEO, Douglas; Director, Shell Research Ltd, Thornton Research Centre, 1980–85; *b* 13 June 1925; *s* of Sydney and Hylda Yeo; *m* 1947, Joan Elisabeth Chell; two *d*. *Educ:* Secondary Sch., St Austell; University Coll., Exeter (BSc London). Expedn on locust control, Kenya, 1945. HMOCS, 1948–63; Tropical Pesticides Research Inst., Uganda and Tanzania, 1948–61 (Scientific Officer, 1948–51, Sen. Scientific Officer, 1951–57, Prin. Scientific Officer, 1957–61). Internat. African Migratory Locust

Control Organisation, Mali: on secondment, 1958, 1960; Dir and Sec. Gen., 1961–63. Shell Research Ltd: Research Dir, Woodstock Agricultural Research Centre, 1963–69, Dir, 1969–76; Dir, Biosciences Lab., Sittingbourne, 1976–80. Mem. Council, RHBNC, London Univ., 1985–90. FSB. *Publications:* papers in Bulletin Ent. Res., Bull. WHO, Anti-Locust Bull., Qly Jl Royal Met. Soc., Jl Sci. Fd. Agric., Plant Protection Confs, etc. *Recreations:* sailing, hill walking, fishing. *Address:* Tremarne, Tremarne Close, Feock, Truro TR3 6SB. *Died 16 Oct. 2010.*

YEOMANS, Richard Millett, CEng, FIET; FIMechE; Chief Executive, Scottish Nuclear Ltd, 1989–91; *b* 19 July 1932; *s* of late Maj. Richard J. Yeomans and Lillian (*née* Spray); *m* 1957, Jennifer Margaret Wingfield Pert; three *s* one *d*. *Educ:* Durban, SA; Cornwall Tech. Coll. Student apprentice, CEGB, 1948. Lt, REME, 1953–55. CEGB power stations, 1955–67; South of Scotland Electricity Board: Dep. Manager, Longannet Power Stn, 1971–75; Manager, Inverkip Power Stn, 1975–77; Manager, Hunterston A&B Nuclear Power Stns, 1977–80; Generation Engineer (Nuclear), 1980–87; Chief Engineer, 1987–89. *Recreations:* sailing, golf, gardening. *Address:* Garden Cottage, Ashcraig, Skelmorlie, Ayrshire PA17 5HB. *T:* (01475) 520298. *Died 2 Feb. 2010.*

YEUNG, Kai-yin, GBS 2005; CBE 1993; JP; Vice-Chairman, Opera Hong Kong Ltd, 2004–06; Chief Executive Officer, Kowloon-Canton Railway Corporation, 2001–03 (Chairman and Chief Executive, 1996–2001); *b* 6 Jan. 1941; *s* of late K. F. Yeung and C. H. Lai; *m* 1964, Anna Lau (*d* 2007); one *s* one *d*. *Educ:* Univ. of Hong Kong (BA Hons 1962). Joined Hong Kong Civil Service, 1962: staff appts, Hong Kong Admin. Service, 1962–73; Directorate rank, 1973–93; various appts at Asst and Dep. Head of Dept level, in trade, econ. devel and public finance, 1973–84; Comr, Hong Kong Export Credit Insce Corp., 1984–86; Dir Gen. of Industry, 1986–89; Sec. for Educn and Manpower, 1989–91; Sec. for the Treasury, 1991–93; Sec. for Transport, 1993; Exec. Dir, Sino Land Co. Ltd, 1993–96. Dir, Hong Kong Community Chest, 1997–2003; Chm., Vocational Training Council, Hong Kong, 1998–2005. Mem., Long Term Housing Strategy Adv. Cttee, 1999–2003. Advr to govt of China on Hong Kong affairs, 1995–97. JP Hong Kong, 1976. *Recreations:* serious music, racing, golf. *Address:* Flat 11B, Tower 5, Beverly Villas, 16 La Salle Road, Kowloon, Hong Kong. *Clubs:* Hong Kong, Hong Kong Jockey (Voting Mem.). *Died 8 Feb. 2007.*

YOUNG, Rt Rev. David Nigel de Lorentz, CBE 2000; Bishop of Ripon, 1977–99; Honorary Assistant Bishop, Diocese of Bradford, since 2000; *b* 2 Sept. 1931; *s* of late Brig. K. de L. Young, CIE, MC and Ada Lilian Young (*née* Tollinton); *m* 1962, Rachel Melverley Lewis (*d* 1966); one *s* one *d*; *m* 1967, Jane Havill, *y d* of late L. H. and E. M. Collison; three *s*. *Educ:* Wellington Coll.; Balliol Coll., Oxford (MA 1st. cl. Maths). 2nd Lt RE, Sch. of Military Survey, 1950–51; Wycliffe Hall, Oxford (BD qualifying exam 1959). Res. mathematician, Plessey Co., 1955–56. Ordained deacon, 1959, priest, 1960; Curate: All Hallows, Allerton, 1959–62; St Mark's, St John's Wood, 1962–63; studied Sanskrit and Pali, SOAS, 1962–63; CMS Missionary, Sri Lanka, 1964–67; Director, Dept of Buddhist Studies, Theological Coll. of Lanka, 1965–67; Lecturer in Buddhist Studies, Manchester Univ., 1967–70; Vicar of Burwell, Cambridge, 1970–75; Lectr, Faculty of Divinity, Univ. of Cambridge, 1970–75; Archdeacon of Huntingdon, 1975–77; Vicar of Great with Little and Steeple Gidding, 1975–77; Rector of Hemingford Abbots, 1977; Hon. Canon of Ely Cathedral, 1975–77. Entered H of L, 1984. Mem., Doctrine Commn, 1978–81; Chairman: Partnership for World Mission, 1978–86; Governing Body, SPCK, 1979–88; Anglican Interfaith Consultants, 1981–91; Scargill Council, 1984–90; Leeds Educn 2000, 1990–99; C of E Bd of Educn, 1994–99; Standing Cttee, Nat. Soc., 1994–99; Govs, UC of Ripon and York St

John, 1995–97. *Publications:* contribs to Religious Studies. *Recreation:* writing. *Address:* Chapel House, Lawkland, Austwick, Lancaster LA2 8AT. *Died 10 Aug. 2008.*

YOUNG, George Bell, CBE 1976; Managing Director, East Kilbride Development Corporation, 1973–90 (and Stonehouse, 1973–77); *b* 17 June 1924; *s* of late George Bell Young and late Jemima Mackinlay; *m* 1946, Margaret Wylie Boyd (decd); one *s*; *m* 1979, Joyce Marguerite McAteer. *Educ:* Queens Park, Glasgow. MIEx 1958; FInstM 1984 (MInstM 1969). RNVR, 1942–45, Lieut (destroyers and mine-sweepers). Journalist and Feature Writer, Glasgow Herald, 1945–48; North of Scotland Hydro-Electric Board, 1948–52; Chief Exec. (London), Scottish Council (Development and Industry), 1952–68 (Founder Fellow, 1986); Gen. Man., E Kilbride Develt Corp., 1968–73. Pres., Lanarks Br., BIM, 1985; Chm., BIM Scotland, 1988–91. Mem. Council, Nat. Trust for Scotland, 1974–79; Dir, Royal Caledonian Schools, 1957–85; Chm., East Kilbride and District National Savings Cttee, 1968–78; Trustee, Strathclyde Scanner Campaign; Scottish Chm., British Heart Foundn, 1975–79 (Mem., East Kilbride Cttee, 1970–97; Pres., Scottish Appeal, 1980–97). Hon. Vice-Pres., East Kilbride Dist Sports Council, 1984. Chm., E Kilbride Cttee, Order of St John, 1972–88 (CStJ 1979). Mem., Amer. Inst. of Corporate Asset Managers, 1985. Member: Saints and Sinners Club of Scotland (Hon. Sec., 1982–89; Chm., 1990; Hon. Mem., 1998); Royal Glasgow Inst. of the Fine Arts; The Merchants House of Glasgow; Mem. Scotland Cttee, Nat. Children's Homes, 1980–88. FRSA 1968; CBIM 1988 (FBIM 1982). Freeman, East Kilbride, 1990. *Recreations:* reading, travel, watching the sunsets on the Firth of Clyde. *Address:* 40 Noddleburn Meadow, Largs, Ayrshire KA30 8UD. *Died 12 Jan. 2006.*

YOUNG, Hon. Sir Harold (William), KCMG 1983; Senator for South Australia, 1967–83, President of the Senate, 1981–83, retired; *b* 30 June 1923; *s* of Frederick James Garfield Young and Edith Mabel Scott; *m* 1952, Eileen Margaret Downing; two *s* two *d*. *Educ:* Prince Alfred Coll., Adelaide. Farmer and grazier prior to entering Parliament; former Vice Pres., United Farmers' and Graziers' Assoc. of SA; served on SA Wheat Res. Cttee, and Federal Exporters and Overseas Transport Shipping Freight Negotiating Cttee; Mem., Australian Wool Industry Council. Government Whip in the Senate, 1971–72; Opposition Whip, 1972–75; Shadow Spokesman on the Media, 1975; Chm., Govt Members' Cttee on National Resources, Energy and Trade, 1976–81; Senate: Temp. Chm. of Cttees, 1976–81; Chm., Select Cttee on Offshore Petroleum Resources, 1971 (Mem., 1968); Member: Industry and Trade Cttee, 1970–75; Estimates Cttee, 1970–81; Parlt Publications Cttee; Standing Orders Cttee; Broadcasting of Parlt Proceedings; Jt Foreign Affairs and Defence Cttee; Library Cttee; Jt Statutory Cttee on Public Works; Jt House Cttee; Jt Chm., New Parlt House Cttee, 1981–83 (Mem., 1976–83); Leader Delegn to S America and Africa. International Parliamentary Union: Leader, Delegn to Madrid and Sofia, 1976–77; to European Parlt, 1977; Mem., Internat. Exec., 1976–77. Order of Diplomatic Service Merit (Korea), 1982. *Address:* 1C Kingsley Avenue, Glenunga, SA 5064, Australia. *Died 21 Nov. 2006.*

YOUNG, John Allen, CBE 1975; Chairman, Young & Co.'s Brewery, since 1962 (Chief Executive, 1989–99); *b* 7 Aug. 1921; *e s* of late William Allen Young and of Joan Barrow Simonds; *m* 1951, Yvonne Lieutenant, Liège (*d* 2002); one *s* one *d*. *Educ:* Nautical Coll., Pangbourne; Corpus Christi Coll., Cambridge (BA Hons Econs). Served War, 1939–45: Lt-Comdr (A) RNVR; comd 888 Naval Air Sqdn (despatches). Runciman Ltd, 1947; Moor Line, 1949; Young & Co.'s Brewery, 1954–, Man. Dir, 1955–62. Chairman: Foster-Probyn Ltd; Cockburn & Campbell; RI Shipping Ltd. Gen. Comr of Taxes, 1965–91. President: London Carthorse Parade Soc., 1957–62; Shire Horse Soc., 1963–64 (Treas., 1962–73); Greater London Horse

Show, 1972–74; Battersea Scouts, 1974–86; London Harness Horse Parade Soc., 1992–. Chm. Bd of Governors, Nat. Hosps for Nervous Diseases, 1982–86 (Mem. Bd, 1972–86; Chm. Finance, 1974–82); Dep. Chm., Inst. of Neurology, 1982–86 (Chm., Jt Res. Adv. Cttee, 1973–82); Pres., Nat. Hosps Develt Foundn, 1993– (Chm., 1984–93); Vice Pres., Chalfont Centre for Epilepsy, 1995– (Governor, 1983–95); Mem. Bd of Management, Royal Hosp. and Home, Putney, 1990–95. Trustee: Licensed Trade Charities Trust, 1984–91; Clapham Junction Disaster Fund, 1989–. Freeman: City of London, 1986; Borough of Wandsworth, 1992. Hon. Fellow, UCH, 1999. Hon. Citizen, Valletta, Malta, 2002. *Recreations:* music, sailing. *Address:* Moonsbrook Cottage, Wisborough Green, West Sussex RH14 0EG. *Club:* Royal Yacht Squadron (Cowes). *Died 17 Sept. 2006.*

YOUNG, Hon. Sir John (McIntosh), AC 1989; KCMG 1975; Lieutenant-Governor of Victoria, Australia, 1974–95; Chief Justice, Supreme Court of Victoria, 1974–91; *b* Melbourne, 17 Dec. 1919; *s* of George David Young, Glasgow, and Kathleen Mildred Young, Melbourne; *m* 1951, Elisabeth Mary (decd), *yr d* of late Dr Edward Wing Twining, Manchester; one *s* two *d*. *Educ:* Geelong Grammar Sch.; Brasenose Coll., Oxford (MA; Hon. Fellow, 1991); Inner Temple; Univ. of Melbourne (LLB). Served War: Scots Guards, 1940–46 (Captain 1943); NW Europe (despatches), 1945. Admitted Victorian Bar, 1948; Associate to Mr Justice Dixon, High Court of Australia, 1948; practice as barrister, 1949–74; Hon. Sec., Victorian Bar Council, 1950–60; Lectr in Company Law, Univ. of Melbourne, 1957–61; Hon. Treas., Medico Legal Soc. of Vic., 1955–65 (Vice-Pres., 1966–68; Pres., 1968–69). QC (Vic) 1961; admitted Tasmanian Bar, 1964, QC 1964; NSW Bar, 1968, QC 1968; Consultant, Faculty of Law, Monash Univ., 1968–74. Mem., Bd of Examiners for Barristers and Solicitors, 1969–72; Pres., Victorian Council of Legal Educn and Victoria Law Foundn, 1974–91; Chm., Police Board of Vic, 1992–98. Pres., Scout Assoc. of Australia, 1986–89, 1996–97 (Vice-Pres., 1985; Pres., Victorian Br., 1974–87); Chief Scout of Australia, 1989–96; Pres., St John Council for Victoria, 1975–82; GCStJ 1991 (KStJ 1977); Chancellor, Order of St John in Australia, 1982–91. Hon. Colonel: 4th/19th Prince of Wales's Light Horse, 1978–97; Royal Victoria Regt, 1994–99; Rep. Hon. Col, RAAC, 1986–97; Hon. Air Cdre, No 21 (City of Melbourne) Sqn, RAAF, 1986–98. Mem. Council, Geelong GS, 1974. Hon. LLD: Monash, 1986; Melbourne, 1989. *Publications:* (co-author) Australian Company Law and Practice, 1965; articles in legal jls. *Recreation:* reading. *Address:* 2/18 Huntingtower Road, Armadale, Victoria 3143, Australia. *T:* (3) 98226259. *Clubs:* Melbourne, Australian (Melbourne). *Died 6 Oct. 2008.*

YOUNG, Priscilla Helen Ferguson, CBE 1982; Director, Central Council for Education and Training in Social Work, 1971–86; *b* 25 Nov. 1925; *d* of Fergus Ferguson Young and Helen Frances Graham (*née* Murphy). *Educ:* Kingsley Sch., Leamington Spa; Univ. of Edinburgh (MA). Social Worker: London Family Welfare Assoc., 1947–51; Somerset CC Children's Dept, 1951–53; Oxford City Children's Dept, 1953–58 (Dep. Children's Officer); Child and Family Services, Portland, Me, USA, 1958–61; Lectr/Sen. Lectr, Sch. of Social Work, Univ. of Leicester, 1961–71. Nat. Chairperson, Family Service Units, 1987–93. Hon. Fellow, Sheffield City Polytechnic, 1977. Hon. DLitt Ulster, 1987. *Died 8 Jan. 2006.*

YOUNG, Sir Richard (Dilworth), Kt 1970; BSc, FIMechE; Chairman, Boosey & Hawkes Ltd, 1979–84 (Deputy Chairman, 1978–79); Director: The Rugby Group PLC (formerly Rugby Portland Cement Co.), 1968–89; Commonwealth Finance Development Corp.

Ltd, 1968–86; *b* 9 April 1914; *s* of Philip Young and Constance Maria Lloyd; *m* 1951, Jean Barbara Paterson Lockwood, *d* of F. G. Lockwood; four *s*. *Educ:* Bromsgrove; Bristol Univ. Joined Weldless Steel Tube Co. Ltd, 1934; served with Tube Investments companies in engineering capacities until 1944; Man. Dir of Tubos Britanicos (Argentina) Ltda, 1945–50; Man. Dir of TI (Export) Ltd, 1950–53; Sales Dir of TI Aluminium Ltd, 1953–56; Asst to Chm. of Tube Investments Ltd, 1957–60; Dir, 1958; Asst Man. Dir, 1959; Man. Dir, 1961–64; Chairman: Park Gate Iron & Steel Co., 1959–64; Raleigh Industries Ltd, 1960–64; Alfred Herbert Ltd: Dep. Chm., 1965–66; Chm., 1966–74; Director: Ingersoll Milling Machine Co., USA, 1967–71; Ingersoll Engineers Inc., 1976–86; Retirement Securities Ltd, 1983–94. Member: Council BIM, 1960–65; Council, CBI, 1967–74; Council, IMechE, 1969–76; Adv. Cttee on Scientific Manpower, 1962–65; SSRC, 1973–75; Council, Warwick Univ., 1966–89; Central Adv. Council on Science and Technol., 1967–70; SRC Engineering Bd, 1974–76. Freeman, City of London, 1987. CCMI. Hon. DSc Warwick, 1987. *Club:* Athenæum. *Died 16 May 2008.*

YOUNG, Wayland Hilton; *see* Kennet, Baron.

YOUNG, Hon. William Lambert, CMG 1992; JP; High Commissioner for New Zealand in UK, 1982–85; concurrently Ambassador to Ireland and High Commissioner in Nigeria, 1982–85; *b* 13 Nov. 1913; *s* of James Young and Alice Gertrude Annie Young; *m* 1946, Isobel Joan Luke; one *s* four *d*. *Educ:* Wellington Coll. Commenced work, 1930; spent first 16 yrs with farm servicing co., interrupted by War Service, N Africa with Eighth Army, 1940–43; took over management of wholesale distributing co. handling imported and NZ manufactured goods; Gen. Man. of co. manufg and distributing radios, records, electronic equipment and owning 32 retail stores, 1956; purchased substantial interest in importing and distributing business, 1962. MP (National) Miramar, 1966–81; Minister of Works and Develt, 1975–81; introduced Women's Rights of Employment Bill, 1975; Pres., Assoc. of Former MPs of NZ, 1993–95. Formerly Chairman: National Roads Bd; National Water and Soil Authority; NZ Fishing Licensing Authority. Formerly Director: Johnsons Wax of NZ Ltd (subsid. of USA Co.); Howard Rotovator Co. Ltd; AA Mutual Insurance Co.; J. J. Niven Ltd; NZ Motor Bodies Ltd; Trustee, Wellington Savings Bank. Patron, Star Boating Club, 1997– (Pres., 1981–97); Mem. Council, NZ Amateur Rowing Assoc., 1984–87. Life Mem., AA of Wellington (Mem. Council, 1976–81). JP 1962. *Address:* 3/28 Oriental Terrace, Oriental Bay, Wellington 6006, New Zealand. *T:* (4) 8010030. *Club:* Wellington (Wellington, NZ). *Died 13 July 2009.*

YOUNGER, Maj.-Gen. Allan Elton, DSO 1944; OBE 1962; MA; Director-General, Royal United Services Institute for Defence Studies, 1976–78; *b* 4 May 1919; *s* of late Brig. Arthur Allan Shakespear Younger, DSO, and Marjorie Rhoda Younger (*née* Halliley); *m* 1942, Diana Lanyon; three *d*. *Educ:* Gresham's; RMA Woolwich; Christ's Coll., Cambridge. Commnd RE, 1939; France and Belgium, 1940; France, Holland and Germany, 1944–45; Burma, 1946–47; Malaya, 1948; Korea, 1950–51; RMA Sandhurst, 1954–57; Bt Lt–Col 1959; comd 36 Corps Engineer Regt in UK and Kenya, 1960–62; Instructor US Army Comd and Gen. Staff Coll., Fort Leavenworth, 1963–66; Programme Evaluation Gp, 1966–68; Chief Engr, Army Strategic Comd, 1968–69; COS, HQ Allied Forces Northern Europe, Oslo, 1970–72; Sen. Army Mem., Directing Staff, RCDS, 1972–75. Col Comdt, RE, 1974–79. Silver Star (US), 1951. *Publications:* Blowing Our Bridges, 2004; contribs to RUSI Jl, Military Review (USA). *Recreation:* gardening. *Died 5 July 2010.*

Z

ZARNECKI, Prof. Jerzy, (George), CBE 1970; MA, PhD; FSA; FBA 1968; Professor of History of Art, University of London, 1963–82, then Emeritus Professor (Reader, 1959–63); Deputy Director, Courtauld Institute of Art, 1961–74; *b* 12 Sept. 1915; *m* 1945, Anne Leslie Frith; one *s* one *d. Educ:* Cracow Univ. MA Cracow Univ., 1938; PhD Univ. of London, 1950. Junior Asst, Inst. of History of Art, Cracow Univ., 1936–39. Served War of 1939–45 as Lance-Corporal in Polish Army; in France, 1939–40 (Polish Cross of Valour (two bars) and Croix de Guerre (silver star), 1940); prisoner of war, 1940–42; interned in Spain, 1942–43; in Polish Army in UK, 1943–45. On staff of Courtauld Institute of Art, Univ. of London, 1945–82, Hon. Fellow, 1986. Slade Professor of Fine Art, Univ. of Oxford, 1960–61. Vice-President: Soc. of Antiquaries of London, 1968–72; British Soc. of Master Glass Painters, 1976–90; British Archaeol Assoc., 1979–; British Academy: Member: Corpus Vitrearum Medii Aevi Cttee, 1956–85; Publications Cttee, 1978–84; Corpus of Romanesque Sculpture in Britain and Ireland, 1988–; Chm., Corpus of Anglo-Saxon Sculpture Cttee, 1979–84. Member: Conservation Cttee, Council for Places of Worship, 1969–75; Royal Commn on Historical Monuments, 1971–84; Arts Sub-Cttee of UGC, 1972–77; Sub-Cttee for Higher Doctorates, CNAA, 1978–82; Chm., Working Cttee organizing Arts Council exhibition, English Romanesque Art 1066–1200, 1984. Mem., Inst. for Advanced Study, Princeton, 1966; Foreign Member: Polish Acad. of Learning, 1992; Polish Acad. of Scis, 1994. Hon. Mem., Royal Archaeol Inst., 1985. Hon. DLitt: Warwick, 1978; East Anglia, 1981; Hon. LittD Dublin, 1984. Gold Medal, Soc. of Antiquaries, 1986. Gold Medal of Merit (Poland), 1978. Order of Isabel la Católica (Spain), 1997. *Publications:* English Romanesque Sculpture 1066–1140, 1951; Later English Romanesque Sculpture 1140–1210, 1953; English Romanesque Lead Sculpture, 1957; Early Sculpture of Ely Cathedral, 1958; Gislebertus, sculpteur d'Autun, 1960 (English edn, 1961); Romanesque Sculpture at Lincoln Cathedral, 1964; La sculpture à Payerne, Lausanne, 1966; 1066 and Architectural Sculpture (Proceedings of Brit. Acad.), 1966; Romanik (Belser Stilgeschichte, VI), 1970 (English edn, Romanesque Art, 1971); The Monastic Achievement, 1972; (contrib.) Westminster Abbey, 1972; Art of the Medieval World, 1975 (trans. Chinese, 1991); Studies in Romanesque Sculpture, 1979; Romanesque Lincoln, 1988; Further Studies in Romanesque Sculpture, 1992; articles in archaeological journals. *Address:* 22 Essex Park, N3 1NE. *T:* (020) 8346 6497.
Died 8 Sept. 2008.

ZEHETMAYR, John Walter Lloyd, OBE 1991; VRD 1963; FICFor; Senior Officer for Wales and Conservator South Wales, Forestry Commission, 1966–81, retired; *b* 24 Dec. 1921; *s* of late Walter Zehetmayr and Gladys Zehetmayr; *m* 1945, Isabell (Betty) Neill-Kennedy; two *s* one *d. Educ:* St Paul's, Kensington; Keble Coll., Oxford (BA). Served RNVR, 1942–46 (despatches); then Lt Comdr RNR retired. Forestry Commission: Silviculturist, 1948–56; Chief Work Study Officer, 1956–64; Conservator West Scotland, 1964–66. Warden, Lavernock Point Nature Reserve, 1976–. Chm., Forestry Safety Council, 1986–92. Member: Prince of Wales' Cttee, 1970–89; Brecon Beacons Nat. Park Cttee, 1982–91. Vice-Pres., Glamorgan Wildlife Trust, 1992–97 and 2009–. Wales Volunteer of the Year Award, Wales Council for Voluntary Action, 2007. *Publications:* Experiments in Tree Planting on Peat, 1954; Afforestation of Upland Heaths, 1960; The Gwent Small Woods Project 1979–84, 1985; Forestry in Wales, 1985; The Effectiveness of Health and Safety Measures in Forestry, 1992. *Recreations:* conservation, butterfly recording, skiing (club coach on plastic, 1996–2008). *Address:* 2 Highfields, Bradford Place, Penarth, Vale of Glam CF64 1AF.
Died 3 July 2009.

ZIENKIEWICZ, Prof. Olgierd Cecil, CBE 1989; FRS 1979; FREng; Professor and Head of Civil Engineering Department, 1961–88, and Director, Institute for Numerical Methods in Engineering, 1976–88, University of Wales at Swansea, then Professor Emeritus; UNESCO Professor of Numerical Methods in Engineering, Universidad Politécnica de Cataluña, Barcelona; J. Walter Professor of Engineering, University of Texas, Austin, 1988–98; *b* Caterham, 18 May 1921; *s* of Casimir Zienkiewicz and Edith Violet (*née* Penny); *m* 1952, Helen Jean (*née* Fleming), Toronto; two *s* one *d. Educ:* Katowice, Poland; Imperial Coll., London (FIC 1993). BSc (Eng); ACGI; PhD; DIC; DSc (Eng); DipEng; FICE; FASCE; FREng (FEng 1979). Consulting engrg, 1945–49; Lectr, Univ. of Edinburgh, 1949–57; Prof. of Structural Mechanics, Northwestern Univ., 1957–61. Naval Sea Systems Comd Res. Prof., Monterey, Calif, 1979–80; Chalmers Jubilee Prof., Gothenburg, 1990, 1992. Hon. Founder Mem., GAMNI, France. Chairman: Cttee on Analysis and Design, Internat. Congress of Large Dams; Jt Computer Cttee, Instn of Civil Engineers. Mem. Council, ICE, 1972–75 (Chm., S Wales and Mon. Br.); Telford Premium, ICE, 1963–67. Pres., Internat. Assoc. Computational Mechanics, 1986–90. General Editor, Internat. Jl Numerical Methods in Engineering, 1968–98; Member Editorial Board: Internat. Jl Solids and Structures; Internat. Jl Earthquakes and Structural Mechanics; Internat. Jl Rock Mechanics, Numerical and Analytical Methods in Geomechanics. For. Associate, US Nat. Acad. of Engrg, 1981; Foreign Member: Polish Acad. of Sci., 1985; Chinese Acad. of Sci., 1998; Nat. Acad. of Sci., Italy, 1999. Hon. Prof., Dalian Inst. of Technology, China, 1987; Hon. Dr, Lisbon, 1972; Hon. DSc: NUI, 1975; Northwestern Univ., Illinois, 1984; Chalmers Univ. of Technology, Gothenburg, 1987; Univ. of Technol., Warsaw, 1989; Technical Univ., Krakow, 1989; Technical Univ., Budapest, 1992; Univ. of Hong Kong, 1992; Univ. of Padua, 1992; Aristotelian Univ. of Thessaloniki, 1993; Brunel Univ., 1993; Univ. of Wales, 1993; Ecole Normale Supérieure de Cachan, Paris, 1997; Technical Univ. of Madrid, 1998; Milan, 2001; Technical Univ., Lisbon, 2001; Silesian Univ., Poland, 2001; Hon. DTech: Norwegian Inst. of Technol., Trondheim, 1985; Technische Univ., Vienna, 1993; Hon. DSci Free Univ., Brussels, 1982; Hon. LLD Dundee, 1987; Hon. DEng Glasgow, 2007. FCGI 1979. James Clayton Fund Prizes, IMechE, 1967, 1973; James Alfred Ewing Medal, ICE, 1980; Newmark Medal, ASCE, 1980; Worcester Reed Warner Medal, ASME, 1980; Gauss Medal, Acad. of Science, Braunschweig, West Germany, 1987; Royal Medal, Royal Soc., 1990; Gold Medal, IStructE, 1992; Leonardo da Vinci Medal, FEANI, 1997; Timoshenko Medal, ASME, 1998; Prince Philip Gold Medal, RAEng, 2006. Chevalier, Ordre des Palmes Académiques (France), 1996. *Publications:* Stress Analysis, 1965; Rock Mechanics, 1968; Finite Element Method, 1967, (with R. L. Taylor) 4th edn 1989 to 6th edn 2006; Optimum Design of Structures, 1973; Finite Elements in Fluids, 1975; Numerical Methods in Offshore Engineering, 1977; Finite Elements and Approximation, 1983; numerous papers in Jl ICE, Jl Mech. Sci., Proc. Royal Soc., Internat. Jl of Num. Methods in Engrg, etc. *Recreation:* sailing. *Address:* 29 Somerset Road, Langland, Swansea SA3 4PG. *T:* (01792) 368776. *Club:* Rotary (Mumbles).
Died 2 Jan. 2009.